The SportingNews

BASEBALL REGISTER

2002 EDITION

Editors/Baseball Register
JEFF PAUR
DAVID WALTON

Contributing Editor/Baseball Register
JOHN DUXBURY

Copyright ©2002 by The Sporting News, a division of Vulcan Sports Media, Inc., 10176 Corporate Square Drive, Suite 200, St. Louis, MO 63132-2924. All rights reserved. Printed in the U.S.A.

No part of the *Baseball Register* may be reproduced or transmitted in any form or by any means, electronic or mechanical, including photocopy, recording or any information storage and retrieval system now known or to be invented, without permission in writing from the publisher, except by a reviewer who wishes to quote brief passages in connection with a review written for inclusion in a magazine, newspaper or broadcast.

THE SPORTING NEWS is a registered trademark of The Sporting News.

ISBN: 0-89204-672-4

10 9 8 7 6 5 4 3 2 1

CONTENTS

EXPLANATION OF FOOTNOTES AND ABBREVIATIONS

Note for statistical comparisons: Player strikes forced the cancellation of games in the 1972 season (10 days missed), the 1981 season (50 days missed), the 1994 season (52 days missed) and the 1995 season (18 games missed).

Positions are listed in descending order of games played; because of limited space, pinch-hitter and pinch-runner are listed in the regular-season section only if a player did not play a defensive position.

*   Led league. For fielding statistics, the player led the league at the position shown.

•   Tied for league lead. For fielding statistics, the player tied for the league lead at the position shown.

†   Led league, but number indicated is total figure for two or more positions. Actual league-leading figure for a position is mentioned in "Statistical Notes" section.

‡   Tied for league lead, but number indicated is total figure for two or more positions. Actual league-tying figure for a position is mentioned in "Statistical Notes" section.

§   Led or tied for league lead, but total figure is divided between two different teams. Actual league-leading or league-tying figure is mentioned in "Statistical Notes" section.

■   Indicates a player's movement from one major league organization to another major league organization or to an independent minor league organization.

. . .   Statistic unavailable, inapplicable, unofficial or mathematically impossible to calculate.

—   Manager statistic inapplicable.

LEAGUES: A.A., Am. Assoc.—American Association. **A.L.**—American. **App., Appal.**—Appalachian. **Ar., Ariz.**—Arizona. **Cal., Calif.**—California. **Car., Caro.**—Carolina. **CRL**—Cocoa Rookie. **DSL**—Dominican Summer. **East.**—Eastern. **Evan.**—Evangeline. **Fla. St., Florida St.**, **FSL**—Florida State. **GCL**—Gulf Coast. **GSL**—Gulf States. **In.-Am.**—Inter-American. **Int'l.**—International. **J.P., Jap. Pac., Jp. Pac.**—Japan Pacific. **Jp. Cen., Jp. Cn.**—Japan Central. **Mex.**—Mexican. **Mex. Cen.**—Mexican Center. **Mid., Midw.**—Midwest. **Miss.-O.V.**—Mississippi-Ohio Valley. **N.C. St.**—North Carolina State. **N.L.**—National. **North.**—Northern. **N'west**—Northwest. **NYP, NY-Penn**—New York-Pennsylvania. **Pac. Coast, PCL**—Pacific Coast. **Pio.**—Pioneer. **S. Atl., SAL**—South Atlantic. **Soph.**—Sophomore. **Sou., South.**—Southern. **Taiw.**—Taiwan. **Tex.**—Texas. **W. Car., W. Caro.**—Western Carolinas.

TEAMS: Aguas.—Aguascalientes. **Alb./Colon.**—Albany/Colonie. **Ariz.**—Arizona. **Ariz. D-backs**—Arizona League Diamondbacks. **Belling.**—Bellingham. **Birm.**—Birmingham. **Brevard Co.**—Brevard County. **Cant./Akr.**—Canton/Akron. **Ced. Rap.**—Cedar Rapids. **Cent. Ore.**—Central Oregon. **Central Vall.**—Central Valley. **Char., Charl.**—Charleston. **Chatt.**—Chattanooga. **Chiba Lot.**—Chiba Lotte. **Ciu. Juarez**—Ciudad Juarez. **Colo. Spr., Colo. Springs**—Colorado Springs. **Dall./Fort W.**—Dallas/Fort Worth. **Day. Beach.**—Daytona Beach. **Dm., Dom.**—Dominican. **Dom. B. Jays**—Dominican Blue Jays. **Elizabeth.**—Elizabethton. **Estadio Quis.**—Estadio Quisqueya. **Eve.**—Everett. **Fort Lauder.**—Fort Lauderdale. **Fukuoka**—Fukuoka Daiei. **GC**—Gulf Coast. **GC Astros-Or.**—Gulf Coast Astros-Orange. **GC Royals-Bl.**—Gulf Coast Royals-Blue. **GC Whi. Sox**—Gulf Coast White Sox. **Grays Har.**—Grays Harbor. **Greens.**—Greensboro. **Greenw.**—Greenwood. **Guana.**—Guanajuato. **H.P.-Thomas.**—High Point-Thomasville. **Hunting.**—Huntington. **Jacksonv.**—Jacksonville. **Johns. City**—Johnson City. **Kane Co.**—Kane County. **Lake Charl.**—Lake Charles. **Matt.**—Mattoon. **M.C., Mex. City**—Mexico City. **Med. Hat**—Medicine Hat. **Monc.**—Monclova. **Niag. F., Niag. Falls**—Niagara Falls. **Okla. City**—Oklahoma City. **Pan. City**—Panama City. **Phoe.**—Phoenix. **Pomp. Beach**—Pompano Beach. **Pres. Lions**—President Lions. **Prin. Will., Prin. William**—Prince William. **Ral./Dur.**—Raleigh/Durham. **Rancho Cuca.**—Rancho Cucamonga. **Rocky Mount.**—Rocky Mountain. **Salt.**—Saltillo. **San. Dom., San. Domingo**—Santo Domingo. **San Bern.**—San Bernardino. **San Fran.**—San Francisco. **Schen.**—Schenectady. **Scran./W.B.**—Scranton/Wilkes-Barre. **S.C.**—South Carolina. **S.F. de Mac.**—San Francisco de Macoris. **San Luis Pot.**—San Luis Potosi. **S. Oregon**—Southern Oregon. **Spartan.**—Spartanburg. **St. Cath., St. Cathar.**—St. Catharines. **St. Peters.**—St. Petersburg. **States.**—Statesville. **Stock.**—Stockton. **T.-C.**—Tri-Cities. **Vanc.**—Vancouver. **Vent. Co.**—Ventura County. **W. Mich.**—West Michigan. **Win.-Salem, Winst.-Salem**—Winston-Salem. **Wis. Rap., Wis. Rapids**—Wisconsin Rapids. **W.P. Beach**—West Palm Beach. **W.Va.**—West Virginia. **Yuc.**—Yucatan.

STATISTICS: A—assists. **AB**—at-bats. **Avg.**—average. **BB**—bases on balls. **CG**—complete games. **E**—errors. **ER**—earned runs. **ERA**—earned-run average. **G**—games. **GIDP**—grounded into double plays. **GS**—games started. **H**—hits. **HR**—home runs. **IP**—innings pitched. **L**—losses. **Pct.**—winning percentage. **PO**—putouts. **Pos.**—position. **R**—runs. **RBI**—runs batted in. **SB**—stolen bases. **ShO**—shutouts. **SO**—strikeouts. **Sv.**—saves. **W**—wins. **2B**—doubles. **3B**—triples.

A

ABAD, ANDY — OF/1B — MARLINS

PERSONAL: Born August 25, 1972, in Palm Beach, Fla. ... 6-1/185. ... Bats left, throws left. ... Full name: Fausto Andres Abad.
JUNIOR COLLEGE: Middle Georgia.
TRANSACTIONS/CAREER NOTES: Selected by Boston Red Sox organization in 16th round of free-agent draft (June 3, 1993). ... Granted free agency (October 15, 1999). ... Signed by Kintetsu Buffaloes of Japan Pacific League (2000). ... Signed by Oakland Athletics organization (November 15, 2000). ... Granted free agency (October 15, 2001). ... Signed by Florida Marlins organization (November 20, 2001).
STATISTICAL NOTES: Led Gulf Coast League outfielders with 116 total chances in 1996.

								BATTING								FIELDING		
Year	Team (League)	Pos.	G	AB	R	H	2B	3B	HR	RBI	Avg.	BB	SO	SB	PO	A	E	Avg.
1993—GC Red Sox (GCL)		OF-1B	59	230	24	57	9	2	1	28	.248	25	27	2	193	13	1	.995
1994—Sarasota (FSL)		OF-1B	111	354	39	102	20	0	2	35	.288	42	58	2	180	15	5	.975
1995—Trenton (East.)		OF	89	287	29	69	14	3	4	32	.240	36	58	5	143	9	2	.987
—Sarasota (FSL)		1B-OF	18	59	5	17	3	0	0	10	.288	6	13	4	90	6	2	.980
1996—Sarasota (FSL)		1B-OF-P	58	202	28	58	15	1	2	41	.287	37	28	10	298	23	5	.985
—Trenton (East.)		1B-OF	65	213	33	59	22	1	4	39	.277	33	41	5	368	20	1	.997
1997—Trenton (East.)		1B-OF	45	165	37	50	13	0	8	24	.303	33	27	2	200	15	3	.986
1998—Pawtucket (I.L.)		1B-OF	111	365	71	112	18	1	16	66	.307	68	70	10	726	66	5	.994
1999—Pawtucket (I.L.)		OF-1B	102	377	61	112	21	4	15	65	.297	68	70	10	726	66	5	.994
2000—Kintetsu (Jap. Pac.)■.			32	92	7	15	1	0	4	13	.163	9	17	0	...	...	...	...
—Kintetsu (Jp. West.) ..			61	233	35	72	12	1	8	48	.309	30	18	3	...	...	...	...
2001—Sacramento (PCL)■..		OF-1B	124	462	72	139	19	2	19	82	.301	58	67	4	213	8	6	.974
—Oakland (A.L.)		1B	1	1	0	0	0	0	0	0	.000	0	0	0	2	0	0	1.000
Major League totals (1 year)			1	1	0	0	0	0	0	0	.000	0	0	0	2	0	0	1.000

RECORD AS PITCHER

Year	League	W	L	Pct.	ERA	G	GS	CG	ShO	Sv.	IP	H	R	ER	BB	SO
1990—Sarasota (FSL)		0	0	...	0.00	1	0	0	0	0	$^2/_3$	0	0	0	0	0

ABBOTT, JEFF — OF

PERSONAL: Born August 17, 1972, in Atlanta. ... 6-2/200. ... Bats right, throws left. ... Full name: Jeffrey William Abbott.
HIGH SCHOOL: Dunwoody (Ga.).
COLLEGE: Kentucky.
TRANSACTIONS/CAREER NOTES: Selected by Chicago White Sox organization in 32nd round of free-agent draft (June 3, 1993); did not sign. ... Selected by White Sox organization in fourth round of free-agent draft (June 2, 1994). ... On Charlotte disabled list (May 30-June 28 and August 1-10, 1999). ... Traded by White Sox to Florida Marlins for OF Julio Ramirez (December 10, 2000). ... On Florida disabled list (March 29-June 12, 2001; included rehabilitation assignments to Brevard County (May 15-18), Portland (May 19-30) and Calgary (June 1-12). ... On Calgary disabled list (June 27-July 4, 2001). ... Granted free agency (December 21, 2001).

								BATTING								FIELDING		
Year	Team (League)	Pos.	G	AB	R	H	2B	3B	HR	RBI	Avg.	BB	SO	SB	PO	A	E	Avg.
1994—Sarasota (GCL)..........		OF	4	15	4	7	1	0	1	3	.467	4	0	2	4	0	0	1.000
—Hickory (S.Atl.)..........		OF	63	224	47	88	16	6	6	48	.393	38	33	2	106	0	2	.981
1995—Prince William (Caro.)		OF	70	264	41	92	16	0	4	47	.348	26	25	7	88	3	4	.958
—Birmingham (Sou.).......		OF	55	197	25	63	11	1	3	28	.320	19	20	1	55	1	2	.966
1996—Nashville (A.A.)........		OF-DH	113	440	64	143	27	1	14	60	.325	32	50	12	186	5	2	.990
1997—Nashville (A.A.)........		OF-DH	118	465	*88	152	35	3	11	63	.327	41	52	12	237	6	0	*1.000
—Chicago (A.L.)		OF-DH	19	38	8	10	1	0	1	2	.263	0	6	0	15	0	0	1.000
1998—Chicago (A.L.)		OF-DH	89	244	33	68	14	1	12	41	.279	9	28	3	132	0	4	.971
1999—Chicago (A.L.)		OF	17	57	5	9	0	0	2	6	.158	5	12	1	25	0	1	.962
—Charlotte (I.L.)		OF	67	277	42	88	24	1	9	37	.318	16	27	2	136	4	3	.979
2000—Chicago (A.L.)		OF-DH	80	215	31	59	15	1	3	29	.274	21	38	2	101	2	2	.981
2001—Brev. County (FSL)■.		OF	3	8	2	2	0	0	0	2	.250	1	1	0	3	0	0	1.000
—Portland (East.)		OF	7	26	4	12	1	0	2	6	.462	2	0	0	9	0	0	1.000
—Calgary (PCL)		OF	47	175	25	56	9	0	9	24	.320	6	33	1	72	2	2	.974
—Florida (N.L.)		OF	28	42	5	11	3	0	0	5	.262	3	7	0	26	0	1	.963
American League totals (4 years)			205	554	77	146	30	2	18	78	.264	35	84	6	273	2	7	.975
National League totals (1 year)			28	42	5	11	3	0	0	5	.262	3	7	0	26	0	1	.963
Major League totals (5 years)			233	596	82	157	33	2	18	83	.263	38	91	6	299	2	8	.974

DIVISION SERIES RECORD

								BATTING								FIELDING		
Year	Team (League)	Pos.	G	AB	R	H	2B	3B	HR	RBI	Avg.	BB	SO	SB	PO	A	E	Avg.
2000—Chicago (A.L.)		PH-OF	1	1	0	0	0	0	0	0	.000	0	0	0	1	0	0	1.000

ABBOTT, KURT — IF — TWINS

PERSONAL: Born June 2, 1969, in Zanesville, Ohio. ... 6-0/200. ... Bats right, throws right. ... Full name: Kurt Thomas Abbott.
HIGH SCHOOL: Dixie Hollins (St. Petersburg, Fla.).
JUNIOR COLLEGE: St. Petersburg (Fla.) Junior College.
TRANSACTIONS/CAREER NOTES: Selected by Oakland Athletics organization in 15th round of free-agent draft (June 5, 1989). ... On Modesto disabled list (May 26-June 6, 1991). ... Traded by A's to Florida Marlins for OF Kerwin Moore (December 20, 1993). ... On Florida disabled list (April 19-May 6, 1995); included rehabilitation assignment to Charlotte (April 30-May 6). ... On Florida disabled list (May 6-21, 1996); included rehabilitation assignment to Charlotte (May 16-20). ... Traded by Marlins to A's for P Eric Ludwick (December 19, 1997). ... On Oakland disabled list (March 22-April 16, 1998); included rehabilitation assignment to Edmonton (April 7-16). ... Traded by A's to Colorado Rockies for a

player to be named later and cash (June 9, 1998); A's acquired P Ara Petrosian to complete deal (June 16, 1998). ... On disabled list (May 23-June 7 and July 23-August 7, 1999). ... Granted free agency (November 1, 1999). ... Signed by New York Mets organization (January 26, 2000). ... On New York disabled list (July 3-27, 2000); included rehabilitation assignment to Norfolk (July 25-27). ... Granted free agency (November 3, 2000). ... Signed by Atlanta Braves organization (December 13, 2000). ... On Atlanta disabled list (April 14, 2001-remainder of season); included rehabilitation assignments to Greenville (May 18-21) and Richmond (June 22-28). ... Granted free agency (November 5, 2001). ... Signed as free agent by Minnesota Twins organization (January 14, 2002).

STATISTICAL NOTES: Led Arizona League shortstops with .922 fielding percentage in 1989. ... Led Southern League shortstops with 87 double plays in 1992. ... Career major league grand slams: 3.

Year	Team (League)	Pos.	G	AB	R	H	2B	3B	HR	RBI	Avg.	BB	SO	SB	PO	A	E	Avg.
1989—	Ariz. Athletics (Ariz.) ..	SS-2B-3B	36	155	27	42	5	3	0	25	.271	8	40	0	59	90	10	†.937
—S. Oregon (N'West)....		SS	5	10	2	1	0	0	0	1	.100	0	3	1	6	7	1	.929
1990—	Madison (Midw.)........	SS-2B-3B	104	362	38	84	18	0	0	28	.232	47	74	21	180	268	40	.918
1991—	Modesto (Calif.)	SS	58	216	36	55	8	2	3	25	.255	29	55	6	78	130	9	.959
—Huntsville (Sou.)		SS	53	182	18	46	6	1	0	11	.253	17	39	6	89	164	13	.951
1992—	Huntsville (Sou.)	SS	124	452	64	115	14	5	9	52	.254	31	75	16	196	342	29	*.949
—Tacoma (PCL)		SS	11	39	2	6	1	0	0	1	.154	4	9	1	21	32	4	.930
1993—	Tacoma (PCL)	SS-DH	133	480	75	153	36	11	12	79	.319	33	123	19	*210	367	30	.951
—Oakland (A.L.)		OF-SS-2B	20	61	11	15	1	0	3	9	.246	3	20	2	36	13	2	.961
1994—	Florida (N.L.)■	SS	101	345	41	86	17	3	9	33	.249	16	98	3	162	260	15	.966
1995—	Charlotte (I.L.)............	SS	5	18	3	5	0	0	1	3	.278	1	3	1	5	15	2	.909
—Florida (N.L.)		SS	120	420	60	107	18	7	17	60	.255	36	110	4	149	290	19	.959
1996—	Florida (N.L.)............	SS-3B-2B	109	320	37	81	18	7	8	33	.253	22	99	3	123	205	12	.965
—Charlotte (I.L.)............		SS-2B-3B	18	69	20	26	10	1	5	11	.377	7	18	2	31	60	2	.978
1997—	Florida (N.L.).............	2-O-S-3-DH	94	252	35	69	18	2	6	30	.274	14	68	3	126	136	8	.970
1998—	Edmonton (PCL)■	SS-DH	7	25	5	10	2	0	2	4	.400	6	8	0	9	13	4	.846
—Oakland (A.L.)		SS-OF-DH-3B	35	123	17	33	7	1	2	9	.268	10	34	2	46	70	11	.913
—Colorado (N.L.)■		O-2-S-3-DH	42	71	9	18	6	0	3	15	.254	2	19	0	32	24	1	.982
1999—	Colorado (N.L.)■	2B-1B-OF-SS	96	286	41	78	17	2	8	41	.273	16	69	3	188	151	4	.988
2000—	New York (N.L.)■	SS-2B-3B-OF	79	157	22	34	7	1	6	12	.217	14	51	1	74	105	7	.962
—Norfolk (I.L.)		SS	2	4	1	1	0	0	0	0	.250	0	0	0	1	2	0	1.000
2001—	Atlanta (N.L.)■	2B-SS	6	9	0	2	0	0	0	0	.222	0	3	1	2	8	0	1.000
—Greenville (Sou.)		2B	2	6	0	0	0	0	0	0	.000	1	1	0	6	7	0	1.000
—Richmond (I.L.)		2B-SS	4	14	0	3	1	0	0	0	.214	0	7	1	4	3	0	1.000
American League totals (2 years)			55	184	28	48	8	1	5	18	.261	13	54	4	82	83	13	.927
National League totals (8 years)			647	1860	245	475	101	22	57	224	.255	120	517	18	856	1179	66	.969
Major League totals (9 years)			702	2044	273	523	109	23	62	242	.256	133	571	22	938	1262	79	.965

DIVISION SERIES RECORD

Year	Team (League)	Pos.	G	AB	R	H	2B	3B	HR	RBI	Avg.	BB	SO	SB	PO	A	E	Avg.
1997—	Florida (N.L.).............	2B-PH	3	8	0	2	0	0	0	0	.250	0	0	0	3	6	0	1.000
2000—	New York (N.L.).........	SS	1	2	0	0	0	0	0	0	.000	0	1	0	0	0	0	...
Division series totals (2 years)			4	10	0	2	0	0	0	0	.200	0	1	0	3	6	0	1.000

CHAMPIONSHIP SERIES RECORD

Year	Team (League)	Pos.	G	AB	R	H	2B	3B	HR	RBI	Avg.	BB	SO	SB	PO	A	E	Avg.
1997—	Florida (N.L.).............	2B	2	8	0	3	1	0	0	0	.375	0	2	0	4	1	0	1.000
2000—	New York (N.L.).........	PR-SS	2	3	0	0	0	0	0	0	.000	0	2	0	1	0	1	.500
Championship series totals (2 years)			4	11	0	3	1	0	0	0	.273	0	4	0	5	1	1	.857

NOTES: Member of World Series championship team (1997).

WORLD SERIES RECORD

Year	Team (League)	Pos.	G	AB	R	H	2B	3B	HR	RBI	Avg.	BB	SO	SB	PO	A	E	Avg.
1997—	Florida (N.L.).............	DH-PH	3	3	0	0	0	0	0	0	.000	0	1	0	...	...	...	...
2000—	New York (N.L.).........	SS-PH	5	8	0	2	1	0	0	0	.250	1	3	0	3	5	0	1.000
World Series totals (2 years)			8	11	0	2	1	0	0	0	.182	1	4	0	3	5	0	1.000

ABBOTT, PAUL   P   MARINERS

PERSONAL: Born September 15, 1967, in Van Nuys, Calif. ... 6-3/195. ... Throws right, bats right. ... Full name: Paul David Abbott.

HIGH SCHOOL: Sunny Hills (Fullerton, Calif.).

TRANSACTIONS/CAREER NOTES: Selected by Minnesota Twins organization in third round of free-agent draft (June 3, 1985). ... On Minnesota disabled list (March 28-June 5 and August 14-September 1, 1992). ... Released by Twins (March 2, 1993). ... Signed by Cleveland Indians organization (March 27, 1993). ... On Canton/Akron disabled list (April 8-May 6, 1993). ... Granted free agency (October 15, 1993). ... Signed by Kansas City Royals organization (November 21, 1993). ... On disabled list (March 18-May 25 and June 16-30, 1994). ... Released by Royals (June 30, 1994). ... Signed by Chicago Cubs organization (March 17, 1995). ... Granted free agency (October 16, 1995). ... Signed by San Diego Padres organization (November 29, 1995). ... Granted free agency (October 15, 1996). ... Signed by Seattle Mariners organization (January 10, 1997). ... On Tacoma disabled list (May 23-July 14, 1997). ... On Orlando disabled list (April 2-August 21, 1998); included rehabilitation assignment to Arizona League Mariners (August 19-21). ... Released by Mariners (December 14, 1998). ... Re-signed by Mariners (January 21, 1999). ... On New Haven disabled list (April 9-June 12, 1999). ... On Seattle disabled list (April 1-28, 2001); included rehabilitation assignment to Tacoma (April 23-28).

STATISTICAL NOTES: Pitched 3-0 no-hit victory against Palm Springs (June 26, 1988, seven innings).

Year	League	W	L	Pct.	ERA	G	GS	CG	ShO	Sv.	IP	H	R	ER	BB	SO
1985—	Elizabethton (Appl.)............	1	5	.167	6.94	10	10	1	0	0	35	33	32	27	32	34
1986—	Kenosha (Midw.)................	6	10	.375	4.50	25	15	1	0	0	98	102	62	49	73	73
1987—	Kenosha (Midw.)................	13	6	.684	3.65	26	25	1	0	0	145 1/3	102	76	59	103	138
1988—	Visalia (Calif.)....................	11	9	.550	4.18	28	•28	4	2	0	172 1/3	141	95	80	*143	*205
1989—	Orlando (Sou.)	9	3	.750	4.37	17	17	1	0	0	90 2/3	71	48	44	48	102

Year	League	W	L	Pct.	ERA	G	GS	CG	ShO	Sv.	IP	H	R	ER	BB	SO
1990—	Portland (PCL)	5	14	.263	4.56	23	23	4	1	0	128 1/3	110	75	65	82	129
—	Minnesota (A.L.)	0	5	.000	5.97	7	7	0	0	0	34 2/3	37	24	23	28	25
1991—	Portland (PCL)	2	3	.400	3.89	8	8	1	1	0	44	36	19	19	28	40
—	Minnesota (A.L.)	3	1	.750	4.75	15	3	0	0	0	47 1/3	38	27	25	36	43
1992—	Portland (PCL)	4	1	.800	2.33	7	7	0	0	0	46 1/3	30	13	12	31	46
—	Minnesota (A.L.)	0	0	...	3.27	6	0	0	0	0	11	12	4	4	5	13
1993—	Canton/Akron (East.)■	4	5	.444	4.06	13	12	1	0	0	75 1/3	72	34	34	28	86
—	Cleveland (A.L.)	0	1	.000	6.38	5	5	0	0	0	18 1/3	19	15	13	11	7
—	Charlotte (I.L.)	0	1	.000	6.63	4	4	0	0	0	19	25	16	14	7	12
1994—	Omaha (A.A.)■	4	1	.800	4.87	15	10	0	0	0	57 1/3	57	32	31	45	48
1995—	Iowa (A.A.)■	7	7	.500	3.67	46	11	0	0	0	115 1/3	104	50	47	64	*127
1996—	Las Vegas (PCL)■	4	2	.667	4.18	28	0	0	0	7	28	27	14	13	12	37
1997—	Tacoma (PCL)■	8	4	.667	4.13	17	14	3	0	0	93 2/3	80	48	43	29	117
—	Arizona Mariners (Ariz.)	0	0	...	0.93	3	3	0	0	0	9 2/3	0	2	1	7	13
1998—	Arizona Mariners (Ariz.)	0	0	...	0.00	1	0	0	0	0	3	1	0	0	0	6
—	Tacoma (PCL)	1	0	1.000	1.20	3	3	0	0	0	15	9	2	2	5	20
—	Seattle (A.L.)	3	1	.750	4.01	4	4	0	0	0	24 2/3	24	11	11	10	22
1999—	Tacoma (PCL)	1	1	.500	6.43	2	2	0	0	0	14	21	11	10	4	10
—	Seattle (A.L.)	6	2	.750	3.10	25	7	0	0	0	72 2/3	50	31	25	32	68
2000—	Seattle (A.L.)	9	7	.563	4.22	35	27	0	0	0	179	164	89	84	80	100
2001—	Tacoma (PCL)	0	0	...	0.00	1	1	0	0	0	4	1	0	0	4	4
—	Seattle (A.L.)	17	4	.810	4.25	28	27	1	0	0	163	145	79	77	87	118
Major League totals (8 years)		38	21	.644	4.28	125	80	1	0	0	550 2/3	489	280	262	289	396

DIVISION SERIES RECORD

Year	League	W	L	Pct.	ERA	G	GS	CG	ShO	Sv.	IP	H	R	ER	BB	SO
2000—	Seattle (A.L.)	1	0	1.000	1.59	1	1	0	0	0	5 2/3	5	2	1	3	1
2001—	Seattle (A.L.)	0	0	...	24.00	1	0	0	0	0	3	9	8	8	5	3
Division series totals (2 years)		1	0	1.000	9.35	2	1	0	0	0	8 2/3	14	10	9	8	4

CHAMPIONSHIP SERIES RECORD

Year	League	W	L	Pct.	ERA	G	GS	CG	ShO	Sv.	IP	H	R	ER	BB	SO
2000—	Seattle (A.L.)	0	1	.000	5.40	1	1	0	0	0	5	3	3	3	3	3
2001—	Seattle (A.L.)	0	0	...	0.00	1	1	0	0	0	5	0	0	0	8	2
Champ. series totals (2 years)		0	1	.000	2.70	2	2	0	0	0	10	3	3	3	11	5

ABERNATHY, BRENT   2B   DEVIL RAYS

PERSONAL: Born September 23, 1977, in Atlanta, Ga. ... 6-1/185. ... Bats right, throws right. ... Full name: Michael Brent Abernathy.
HIGH SCHOOL: Lovett School (Atlanta, Ga.).
TRANSACTIONS/CAREER NOTES: Selected by Toronto Blue Jays organization in second round of free-agent draft (June 4, 1996); pick received as part of compensation from Florida Marlins for signing of Type B free agent OF Devon White. ... On Syracuse disabled list (June 21-28, 2000). ... Traded by Blue Jays with player to be named later to Tampa Bay Devil Rays for P Steve Trachsel and P Mark Guthrie (July 31, 2000). ... On Durham disabled list (April 15-May 2, 2001).
STATISTICAL NOTES: Led Southern League second basemen with 669 total chances in 1999.
MISCELLANEOUS: Member of 2000 U.S. Olympic baseball team.

							BATTING						FIELDING			
Year	Team (League)	Pos.	G	AB	R	H	2B	3B	HR	RBI	Avg.	BB	SO	SB	PO	A	E	Avg.
1997—	Hagerstown (S.Atl.)	2B	99	379	69	117	27	2	1	26	.309	30	32	22	178	258	12	.973
1998—	Dunedin (FSL)	2B	124	485	85	169	36	1	3	65	.348	44	38	35	240	338	16	.973
1999—	Knoxville (Sou.)	2B	136	*577	*108	*168	42	1	13	62	.291	55	47	34	*292	*361	16	.976
2000—	Syracuse (I.L.)	2B	92	358	47	106	21	2	4	35	.296	36	32	14	146	258	11	.973
—	Durham (I.L.)■	2B	27	91	14	24	6	0	1	15	.264	11	11	9	53	55	3	.973
2001—	Durham (I.L.)	2B	61	252	45	76	20	4	4	23	.302	16	23	11	107	179	9	.969
—	Tampa Bay (A.L.)	2B	79	304	43	82	17	1	5	33	.270	27	35	8	150	209	7	.981
Major League totals (1 year)			79	304	43	82	17	1	5	33	.270	27	35	8	150	209	7	.981

ABREU, BOBBY   OF   PHILLIES

PERSONAL: Born March 11, 1974, in Aragua, Venezuela. ... 6-0/197. ... Bats left, throws right. ... Full name: Bob Kelly Abreu. ... Name pronounced uh-BRAY-yew.
TRANSACTIONS/CAREER NOTES: Signed as non-drafted free agent by Houston Astros organization (August 21, 1990). ... On Houston disabled list (May 25-July 1, 1997); included rehabilitation assignments to Jackson (June 23-26) and New Orleans (June 27-July 1). ... Selected by Tampa Bay Devil Rays in first round (sixth pick overall) of expansion draft (November 18, 1997). ... Traded by Devil Rays to Philadelphia Phillies for SS Kevin Stocker (November 18, 1997).
STATISTICAL NOTES: Led Gulf Coast League outfielders with 11 assists in 1991. ... Led Texas League with .530 slugging percentage in 1994. ... Led Pacific Coast League outfielders with 18 assists in 1995. ... Led Pacific Coast League in caught stealing with 18 in 1996. ... Career major league grand slams: 2.

							BATTING						FIELDING			
Year	Team (League)	Pos.	G	AB	R	H	2B	3B	HR	RBI	Avg.	BB	SO	SB	PO	A	E	Avg.
1991—	GC Astros (GCL)	OF-SS	56	183	21	55	7	3	0	20	.301	17	27	10	70	†13	5	.943
1992—	Asheville (S.Atl.)	OF	135	480	81	140	21	4	8	48	.292	63	79	15	167	15	11	.943
1993—	Osceola (FSL)	OF	129	474	62	134	21	17	5	55	.283	51	90	10	179	18	8	.961
1994—	Jackson (Texas)	OF	118	400	61	121	25	9	16	73	.303	42	81	12	113	3	4	.967
1995—	Tucson (PCL)	OF-2B	114	415	72	126	24	*17	10	75	.304	67	120	16	207	†18	7	.970
1996—	Tucson (PCL)	OF-DH	132	484	86	138	14	*16	13	68	.285	83	111	24	202	15	7	.969
—	Houston (N.L.)	OF	15	22	1	5	1	0	0	1	.227	2	5	0	6	0	0	1.000
1997—	Houston (N.L.)	OF	59	188	22	47	10	2	3	26	.250	21	48	7	84	4	2	.978
—	Jackson (Texas)	OF	3	12	2	2	1	0	0	0	.167	1	5	0	1	0	0	1.000
—	New Orleans (A.A.)	OF	47	194	25	52	9	4	2	22	.268	21	49	7	99	4	1	.990

							BATTING								FIELDING		
Year Team (League)	Pos.	G	AB	R	H	2B	3B	HR	RBI	Avg.	BB	SO	SB	PO	A	E	Avg.
1998— Philadelphia (N.L.)■ ..	OF	151	497	68	155	29	6	17	74	.312	84	133	19	272	17	8	.973
1999— Philadelphia (N.L.)......	OF-DH	152	546	118	183	35	•11	20	93	.335	109	113	27	260	8	3	.989
2000— Philadelphia (N.L.)......	OF	154	576	103	182	42	10	25	79	.316	100	116	28	337	13	4	.989
2001— Philadelphia (N.L.)......	OF	•162	588	118	170	48	4	31	110	.289	106	137	36	308	11	8	.976
Major League totals (6 years)		693	2417	430	742	165	33	96	383	.307	422	550	117	1267	53	25	.981

DIVISION SERIES RECORD

							BATTING								FIELDING		
Year Team (League)	Pos.	G	AB	R	H	2B	3B	HR	RBI	Avg.	BB	SO	SB	PO	A	E	Avg.
1997— Houston (N.L.)	PH	3	3	0	1	0	0	0	0	.333	0	2	1	...	...	...	...

A

ABREU, WINSTON   P   PADRES

PERSONAL: Born April 5, 1977, in Cotui, Dominican Republic. ... 6-2/155. ... Throws right, bats right. ... Full name: Winston Leonardo Abreu.
HIGH SCHOOL: Cotiu (Dominican Republic).
TRANSACTIONS/CAREER NOTES: Signed as non-drafted free agent by Atlanta Braves organization (July 2, 1993). ... On disabled list (April 21, 1997-entire season). ... On Greenville disabled list (April 13-July 5, 2000). ... Traded by Braves to San Diego Padres (September 6, 2001), completing deal in which Padres traded P Rudy Seanez to Braves for a player to be named later (August 31, 2001).

Year League	W	L	Pct.	ERA	G	GS	CG	ShO	Sv.	IP	H	R	ER	BB	SO
1994— Gulf Coast Braves (GCL)	0	*8	.000	4.08	13	11	0	0	0	57 1/3	57	35	26	24	53
1995— Danville (Appl.)................	6	3	.667	2.31	13	13	1	0	0	74	54	29	19	13	90
1996— Macon (S.Atl.)..................	4	3	.571	3.00	12	12	0	0	0	60	51	29	20	25	60
1997—							Did not play.								
1998— Eugene (N'West)	0	4	.000	6.35	17	10	0	0	0	45 1/3	39	36	32	31	52
1999— Macon (S.Atl.)	7	2	.778	1.69	14	14	0	0	0	69 1/3	41	17	13	26	95
— Myrtle Beach (Caro.)	3	2	.600	3.28	13	12	0	0	0	68 2/3	53	26	25	41	76
2000— Greenville (Sou.)	0	1	.000	2.25	1	1	0	0	0	4	4	1	1	3	5
— Gulf Coast Braves (GCL)	0	0	...	3.00	2	2	0	0	0	3	2	1	1	2	2
— Macon (S.Atl.)	2	1	.667	1.88	11	1	0	0	3	28 2/3	11	6	6	6	48
— Richmond (I.L.)	0	1	.000	7.00	3	0	0	0	0	9	7	8	7	10	5
2001— Greenville (Sou.)	3	5	.375	4.64	34	7	0	0	0	73 2/3	56	40	38	45	93

ACEVEDO, JOSE   P   REDS

PERSONAL: Born December 18, 1977, in Santo Domingo, Dominican Republic. ... 6-0/185. ... Throws right, bats right. ... Full name: Jose Omar Acevedo. ... Cousin of Juan Marichal, pitcher with San Francisco Giants (1960-73), Boston Red Sox (1974) and Los Angeles Dodgers (1975).
TRANSACTIONS/CAREER NOTES: Signed as non-drafted free agent by Cincinnati Reds organization (December 7, 1996).

Year League	W	L	Pct.	ERA	G	GS	CG	ShO	Sv.	IP	H	R	ER	BB	SO
1997— Charleston, W.Va. (S.Atl.)...	3	3	.500	3.92	15	8	0	0	0	57 1/3	61	29	25	9	34
1998— Charleston, W.Va. (S.Atl.)...	9	9	.500	3.91	25	25	2	0	0	158 2/3	169	74	69	40	132
1999— Clinton (Midw.)	8	6	.571	3.77	24	24	1	1	0	133 2/3	119	65	56	43	136
2000— Dayton (Midw.)	11	5	.688	3.89	25	23	0	0	0	141	135	74	61	53	123
2001— Chattanooga (Sou.)	4	4	.500	3.69	16	11	0	0	0	78	68	34	32	25	82
— Cincinnati (N.L.)	5	7	.417	5.44	18	18	0	0	0	96	101	61	58	34	68
Major League totals (1 year)........	5	7	.417	5.44	18	18	0	0	0	96	101	61	58	34	68

ACEVEDO, JUAN   P   TIGERS

PERSONAL: Born May 5, 1970, in Juarez, Mexico. ... 6-2/243. ... Throws right, bats right. ... Full name: Juan Carlos Lara Acevedo. ... Name pronounced ah-sah-VAY-doh.
HIGH SCHOOL: Dundee-Crown (Carpentersville, Ill.).
JUNIOR COLLEGE: Parkland College (Ill.).
TRANSACTIONS/CAREER NOTES: Selected by Colorado Rockies organization in 14th round of free-agent draft (June 1, 1992). ... Traded by Rockies with P Arnold Gooch to New York Mets for P Bret Saberhagen and a player to be named later (July 31, 1995); Rockies acquired P David Swanson to complete deal (August 4, 1995). ... On New York disabled list (March 26-May 9, 1996); included rehabilitation assignment to Norfolk (April 10-May 9). ... Traded by Mets to St. Louis Cardinals for P Rigo Beltran (March 29, 1998). ... On St. Louis disabled list (July 18-August 16, 1998); included rehabilitation assignment to Memphis (August 6-16). ... Traded by Cardinals with two players to be named later to Milwaukee Brewers for 2B Fernando Vina (December 20, 1999); Brewers acquired P Matt Parker and C Eliezer Alfonzo to complete deal (June 13, 2000). ... On Milwaukee disabled list (April 7-30, 2000); included rehabilitation assignment to Indianapolis (April 25-29). ... Traded by Brewers with P Kane Davis and IF Jose Flores to Rockies for P Mark Leiter, P Mike DeJean and 2B/SS Elvis Pena (April 4, 2001). ... On Colorado disabled list (April 7-22 and April 29-May 24, 2001); included rehabilitation assignments to Colorado Springs (April 17-22 and May 17-24). ... Traded by Rockies to Florida Marlins for IF Josue Espada (August 6, 2001). ... Granted free agency (November 26, 2001). ... Signed by Detroit Tigers organization (December 20, 2001).
HONORS: Named Eastern League Pitcher of the Year (1994).
STATISTICAL NOTES: Tied for Eastern League lead with five balks in 1994. ... Tied for International League lead with four balks in 1997.

Year League	W	L	Pct.	ERA	G	GS	CG	ShO	Sv.	IP	H	R	ER	BB	SO
1992— Bend (N'West)...................	0	0	...	13.50	1	0	0	0	0	2	4	3	3	1	3
— Visalia (Calif.)	3	4	.429	5.43	12	12	1	0	0	64 2/3	75	46	39	33	37
1993— Central Valley (Calif.)..........	9	8	.529	4.40	27	20	1	0	0	118 2/3	119	68	58	58	107
1994— New Haven (East.)..............	*17	6	.739	*2.37	26	26	5	2	0	174 2/3	142	56	46	38	161
1995— Colorado (N.L.)	4	6	.400	6.44	17	11	0	0	0	65 2/3	82	53	47	20	40
— Colorado Springs (PCL)	1	1	.500	6.14	3	3	0	0	0	14 2/3	18	11	10	7	7
— Norfolk (I.L.)■...................	0	0	...	0.00	2	2	0	0	0	3	0	0	0	1	2
1996— Norfolk (I.L.)	4	6	.333	5.96	19	19	2	1	0	102 2/3	116	70	68	53	83
1997— Norfolk (I.L.)	6	6	.500	3.86	18	18	1	0	0	116 2/3	111	55	50	34	99
— New York (N.L.)	3	1	.750	3.59	25	2	0	0	0	47 2/3	52	24	19	22	33

Year League	W	L	Pct.	ERA	G	GS	CG	ShO	Sv.	IP	H	R	ER	BB	SO
1998— St. Louis (N.L.)■	8	3	.727	2.56	50	9	0	0	15	98 1/3	83	30	28	29	56
— Memphis (PCL).................	0	0	...	0.00	2	2	0	0	0	8 2/3	5	0	0	1	6
1999— St. Louis (N.L.)...............	6	8	.429	5.89	50	12	0	0	4	102 1/3	115	71	67	48	52
2000— Milwaukee (N.L.)■...........	3	7	.300	3.81	62	0	0	0	0	82 2/3	77	38	35	31	51
— Indianapolis (I.L.)	0	0	...	0.00	2	2	0	0	0	4	3	0	0	0	4
2001— Colorado (N.L.)■	0	2	.000	5.63	39	0	0	0	0	32	37	24	20	19	26
— Colorado Springs (PCL)	0	0	...	1.29	6	0	0	0	1	7	3	2	1	4	7
— Florida (N.L.)■..................	2	3	.400	2.54	20	0	0	0	0	28 1/3	31	11	8	16	21
Major League totals (6 years)	26	30	.464	4.41	263	34	0	0	19	457	477	251	224	185	279

ADAMS, TERRY — P — PHILLIES

PERSONAL: Born March 6, 1973, in Mobile, Ala. ... 6-3/215. ... Throws right, bats right. ... Full name: Terry Wayne Adams.
HIGH SCHOOL: Mary G. Montgomery (Semmes, Ala.).
TRANSACTIONS/CAREER NOTES: Selected by Chicago Cubs organization in fourth round of free-agent draft (June 3, 1991). ... On disabled list (June 21-September 21, 1993). ... On Chicago disabled list (March 26-May 8 and June 19-July 4, 1999); included rehabilitation assignments to West Tenn (April 30-May 4) and Iowa (May 6-8). ... Traded by Cubs with P Chad Ricketts and a player to be named later to Los Angeles Dodgers for P Ismael Valdes and 2B Eric Young (December 12, 1999); Dodgers acquired P Brian Stephenson to complete deal (December 16, 1999). ... Granted free agency (November 5, 2001). ... Signed by Philadelphia Phillies (January 15, 2002).

Year League	W	L	Pct.	ERA	G	GS	CG	ShO	Sv.	IP	H	R	ER	BB	SO
1991— Huntington (Appl.)	0	*9	.000	5.77	14	13	0	0	0	57 2/3	67	*56	37	62	52
1992— Peoria (Midw.)..................	7	12	.368	4.41	25	25	3	1	0	157	144	95	77	86	96
1993— Daytona (FSL)	3	5	.375	4.97	13	13	0	0	0	70 2/3	78	47	39	43	35
1994— Daytona (FSL)	9	10	.474	4.38	39	7	0	0	7	84 1/3	87	47	41	46	64
1995— Orlando (Sou.)	2	3	.400	1.43	37	0	0	0	19	37 2/3	23	9	6	16	26
— Iowa (A.A.)	0	0	...	0.00	7	0	0	0	5	6 1/3	3	0	0	2	10
— Chicago (N.L.)	1	1	.500	6.50	18	0	0	0	1	18	22	15	13	10	15
1996— Chicago (N.L.)	3	6	.333	2.94	69	0	0	0	4	101	84	36	33	49	78
1997— Chicago (N.L.)	2	9	.182	4.62	74	0	0	0	18	74	91	43	38	40	64
1998— Chicago (N.L.)	7	7	.500	4.33	63	0	0	0	1	72 2/3	72	39	35	41	73
— Iowa (PCL)	0	0	...	0.00	3	0	0	0	0	4	1	1	0	3	5
1999— West Tenn (Sou.)	0	0	...	16.88	2	1	0	0	0	2 2/3	5	6	5	2	2
— Chicago (N.L.)	6	3	.667	4.02	52	0	0	0	13	65	60	33	29	28	57
2000— Los Angeles (N.L.)■	6	9	.400	3.52	66	0	0	0	2	84 1/3	80	42	33	39	56
2001— Los Angeles (N.L.)	12	8	.600	4.33	43	22	0	0	0	166 1/3	172	84	80	54	141
Major League totals (7 years)	37	43	.463	4.04	385	22	0	0	39	581 1/3	581	292	261	261	484

AFFELDT, JEREMY — P — ROYALS

PERSONAL: Born June 5, 1979, in Phoenix, Ariz. ... 6-4/185. ... Throws left, bats left. ... Full name: Jeremy David Affeldt.
HIGH SCHOOL: Northwest Christian (Spokane, Wash.).
TRANSACTIONS/CAREER NOTES: Selected by Kansas City Royals organization in third round of free-agent draft (June 3, 1997).

Year League	W	L	Pct.	ERA	G	GS	CG	ShO	Sv.	IP	H	R	ER	BB	SO
1997— Gulf Coast Royals (GCL)	2	0	1.000	4.50	10	9	0	0	0	40	34	24	20	21	36
1998— Lansing (Midw.)	0	3	.000	9.53	6	3	0	0	0	17	27	21	18	12	8
— Gulf Coast Royals (GCL)	4	3	.571	2.89	12	9	0	0	0	56	50	24	18	24	67
1999— Charleston, S.C. (S.Atl.)	7	7	.500	3.83	27	27	2	1	0	143 1/3	140	78	61	80	111
2000— Wilmington (Caro.).............	5	15	.250	4.09	27	26	0	0	0	147 1/3	158	87	67	59	92
2001— Wichita (Texas)	10	6	.625	3.90	25	25	0	0	0	145 1/3	153	74	63	46	128

AGBAYANI, BENNY — OF — ROCKIES

PERSONAL: Born December 28, 1971, in Honolulu, Hawaii. ... 6-0/225. ... Bats right, throws right. ... Full name: Benny Peter Agbayani Jr.
HIGH SCHOOL: St. Louis (Honolulu, Hawaii).
COLLEGE: Oregon Tech, then Hawaii Pacific.
TRANSACTIONS/CAREER NOTES: Selected by California Angels organization in 25th round of free-agent draft (June 1, 1992); did not sign. ... Selected by New York Mets organization in 30th round of free-agent draft (June 3, 1993). ... On Norfolk disabled list (May 10-June 6, 1998). ... On New York disabled list (April 9-24 and September 18, 2001-remainder of season); included rehabilitation assignment to Norfolk (April 20-24). ... Traded by Mets to Colorado Rockies as part of three-way deal in which Mets traded P Glendon Rusch to Milwaukee Brewers, Rockies traded 1B/OF Ross Gload and P Craig House to Mets, Brewers traded P Jeff D'Amico, OF Jeromy Burnitz, IF Lou Collier, OF/1B Mark Sweeney and cash to Mets, Mets traded 1B/3B Todd Zeile, IF/OF Lenny Harris and cash to Rockies and Rockies traded OF Alex Ochoa to Brewers (January 21, 2002)
STATISTICAL NOTES: Tied for International League lead in caught stealing with 14 in 1997. ... Career major league grand slams: 1.

Year Team (League)	Pos.	G	AB	R	H	2B	3B	HR	RBI	Avg.	BB	SO	SB	PO	A	E	Avg.
1993— Pittsfield (NY-Penn)....	OF	51	167	26	42	6	3	2	22	.251	20	43	7	62	1	2	.969
1994— St. Lucie (FSL)	OF	119	411	72	115	13	5	5	63	.280	58	67	8	143	6	1	.993
1995— Binghamton (East.)	OF	88	295	38	81	11	2	1	26	.275	39	51	12	100	3	3	.972
— St. Lucie (FSL)	OF	44	155	24	48	9	3	2	29	.310	26	27	8	37	1	2	.950
1996— Binghamton (East.)	OF	21	53	7	9	1	0	2	8	.170	11	13	1	19	1	1	.952
— Norfolk (I.L.)	OF-1B	99	331	43	92	13	9	7	56	.278	30	57	14	172	8	2	.989
1997— Norfolk (I.L.)	OF	127	468	90	145	24	2	11	51	.310	67	106	29	207	12	5	.978
1998— Norfolk (I.L.)	OF-1B	90	322	43	91	20	5	11	53	.283	50	58	16	151	4	4	.975
— New York (N.L.)...........	OF	11	15	1	2	0	0	0	0	.133	1	5	0	6	0	0	1.000
1999— Norfolk (I.L.)	OF-1B-DH	28	101	21	36	8	1	8	32	.356	16	19	5	113	6	2	.983
— New York (N.L.)...........	OF-DH	101	276	42	79	18	3	14	42	.286	32	60	6	121	2	2	.984
2000— New York (N.L.).........	OF-DH	119	350	59	101	19	1	15	60	.289	54	68	5	155	3	4	.975
2001— New York (N.L.).........	OF	91	296	28	82	14	2	6	27	.277	36	73	4	123	1	6	.954
— Norfolk (I.L.)	OF	4	16	3	5	1	0	1	3	.313	1	0	1	5	0	0	1.000
Major League totals (4 years)		322	937	130	264	51	6	35	129	.282	123	206	15	405	6	12	.972

DIVISION SERIES RECORD

Year Team (League)	Pos.	G	AB	R	H	2B	3B	HR	RBI	Avg.	BB	SO	SB	PO	A	E	Avg.
1999— New York (N.L.).........	OF-PH	4	10	1	3	1	0	0	1	.300	0	3	0	5	0	0	1.000
2000— New York (N.L.).........	OF	4	15	1	5	1	0	1	1	.333	3	3	0	10	0	0	1.000
Division series totals (2 years)		8	25	2	8	2	0	1	2	.320	3	6	0	15	0	0	1.000

CHAMPIONSHIP SERIES RECORD

Year Team (League)	Pos.	G	AB	R	H	2B	3B	HR	RBI	Avg.	BB	SO	SB	PO	A	E	Avg.
1999— New York (N.L.).........	OF-PH	4	7	2	1	0	0	0	0	.143	4	2	1	4	0	0	1.000
2000— New York (N.L.).........	OF	5	17	0	6	2	0	0	3	.353	4	0	0	11	0	1	.917
Championship series totals (2 years)		9	24	2	7	2	0	0	3	.292	8	2	1	15	0	1	.938

WORLD SERIES RECORD

Year Team (League)	Pos.	G	AB	R	H	2B	3B	HR	RBI	Avg.	BB	SO	SB	PO	A	E	Avg.
2000— New York (N.L.).........	OF	5	18	2	5	2	0	0	2	.278	3	6	0	9	0	0	1.000

AINSWORTH, KURT   P   GIANTS

PERSONAL: Born September 9, 1978, in Baton Rouge, La. ... 6-3/190. ... Throws right, bats right. ... Full name: Kurt Harold Ainsworth.
HIGH SCHOOL: Catholic (Baton Rouge, La.).
COLLEGE: Louisiana State.
TRANSACTIONS/CAREER NOTES: Selected by San Francisco Giants organization in first round (24th pick overall) of free-agent draft (June 2, 1999).
MISCELLANEOUS: Member of 2000 Olympic baseball team.

Year League	W	L	Pct.	ERA	G	GS	CG	ShO	Sv.	IP	H	R	ER	BB	SO
1999— Salem-Kaizer (N'West)	3	3	.500	1.61	10	10	1	0	0	44²/₃	34	18	8	18	64
2000— Shreveport (Texas).............	10	9	.526	3.30	28	28	0	0	0	158	138	67	58	63	130
2001— Fresno (PCL).................	10	9	.526	5.07	27	26	0	0	0	149	139	91	84	54	157
— San Francisco (N.L.)	0	0	...	13.50	2	0	0	0	0	2	3	3	3	2	3
Major League totals (1 year)........	0	0	...	13.50	2	0	0	0	0	2	3	3	3	2	3

ALCANTARA, ISRAEL   1B/OF

PERSONAL: Born May 6, 1973, in Bani, Dominican Republic. ... 6-2/180. ... Bats right, throws right. ... Full name: Israel Crisostomo Alcantara.
TRANSACTIONS/CAREER NOTES: Signed as non-drafted free agent by Montreal Expos organization (July 2, 1990). ... On Harrisburg disabled list (June 24-August 16, 1996). ... Granted free agency (October 15, 1997). ... Signed by Tampa Bay Devil Rays organization (December 16, 1997). ... On Durham disabled list (April 9-May 9, 1998). ... Granted free agency (October 15, 1998). ... Signed by Boston Red Sox organization (December 14, 1998). ... Granted free agency (October 15, 1999). ... Re-signed by Red Sox organization (January 4, 2000). ... On Pawtucket disabled list (May 15-22, 2001). ... On Boston disabled list (August 14-September 1, 2000); included rehabilitation assignment to Pawtucket (August 19-September 1). ... Granted free agency (December 21, 2000). ... Re-signed by Red Sox organization (January 11, 2001). ... Granted free agency (December 21, 2001).
STATISTICAL NOTES: Led Gulf Coast League with four intentional bases on balls received in 1992. ... Led Midwest League third basemen with 371 total chances in 1993. ... Led International League with 270 total bases and .599 slugging percentage in 2001.

Year Team (League)	Pos.	G	AB	R	H	2B	3B	HR	RBI	Avg.	BB	SO	SB	PO	A	E	Avg.
1991— Dom. Expos (DSL)		68	239	42	68	9	2	•13	51	.285	32	41	8	...	...	...	...
1992— GC Expos (GCL)	3B-2B-SS	59	*224	29	62	14	2	3	37	.277	17	35	6	55	137	14	.932
1993— Burlington (Midw.)	3B	126	470	65	115	26	3	18	73	.245	20	125	6	*98	216	*57	.846
1994— W.P. Beach (FSL)........	3B	125	471	65	134	26	4	15	69	.285	26	130	9	97	199	*32	.902
1995— Harrisburg (East.)........	3B-DH	71	237	25	50	12	2	10	29	.211	21	81	1	48	118	20	.892
— W.P. Beach (FSL)........	3B-DH-OF	39	134	16	37	7	2	3	22	.276	9	35	3	34	58	9	.911
1996— Harrisburg (East.)........	3B-DH	62	218	26	46	5	0	8	19	.211	14	62	1	33	133	16	.912
— GC Expos (GCL)	3B-DH	7	30	4	9	2	0	2	10	.300	3	6	0	7	15	3	.880
— W.P. Beach (FSL)........	3B-DH	15	61	11	19	2	0	4	14	.311	3	13	0	11	24	4	.897
1997— Harrisburg (East.).......3B-1B-DH-OF		89	301	48	85	9	2	27	68	.282	29	84	4	254	80	19	.946
1998— St. Pete. (FSL)■........	3B-OF-DH	38	141	21	47	5	0	10	26	.333	21	29	1	35	44	8	.908
— Reading (East.)..........DH-1B-3B-OF		53	203	36	63	12	2	15	44	.310	17	37	0	152	23	7	.962
— Orlando (Sou.) DH-1B-OF-3B		15	55	8	13	4	0	3	18	.236	7	15	0	22	4	1	.963
1999— Trenton (East.)■........	OF-DH-1B	77	293	48	86	26	0	20	60	.294	27	78	4	185	10	2	.990
— Pawtucket (I.L.)........	OF-DH-1B	24	81	13	22	3	0	9	23	.272	9	29	0	62	2	0	1.000
2000— Pawtucket (I.L.)........	OF-1B	78	299	60	92	17	1	29	76	.308	25	84	2	121	7	8	.941
— Boston (A.L.)..............	DH-OF-1B	21	45	9	13	1	0	4	7	.289	3	7	0	17	0	1	.944
2001— Pawtucket (I.L.)........	OF-1B	119	451	80	134	26	1	*36	90	.297	57	107	9	188	9	5	.975
— Boston (A.L.)..............	OF-1B-DH	14	38	3	10	1	0	0	3	.263	1	13	1	25	3	2	.933
Major League totals (2 years)		35	83	12	23	2	0	4	10	.277	6	20	1	42	3	3	.938

ALDRIDGE, CORY   OF   BRAVES

PERSONAL: Born June 13, 1979, in San Angelo, Texas. ... 6-0/210. ... Bats left, throws right. ... Full name: Cory Coty Jerome Aldridge.
HIGH SCHOOL: Cooper (Abilene, Texas).
TRANSACTIONS/CAREER NOTES: Selected by Atlanta Braves organization in fourth round of free-agent draft (June 3, 1997). ... On disabled list (June 13-July 10, 2000).

Year Team (League)	Pos.	G	AB	R	H	2B	3B	BATTING HR	RBI	Avg.	BB	SO	SB	FIELDING PO	A	E	Avg.
1997— GC Braves (GCL)	OF	46	169	26	47	8	1	3	37	.278	14	37	1	21	0	1	.955
1998— Danville (Appl.)	OF	60	214	37	63	16	1	3	33	.294	29	48	16	64	0	3	.955
1999— Macon (S.Atl.)	OF	124	443	48	111	19	4	12	65	.251	33	123	9	176	4	7	.963
2000— Myrtle Beach (Caro.) ..	OF	109	401	51	100	18	5	15	64	.249	33	118	10	165	2	4	.977
2001— Greenville (Sou.)	OF	131	452	57	111	19	2	19	56	.246	48	139	12	208	7	8	.964
— Atlanta (N.L.)	OF	8	5	1	0	0	0	0	0	.000	0	4	0	2	0	0	1.000
Major League totals (1 year)		8	5	1	0	0	0	0	0	.000	0	4	0	2	0	0	1.000

ALFONSECA, ANTONIO — P — MARLINS

PERSONAL: Born April 16, 1972, in La Romana, Dominican Republic. ... 6-5/235. ... Throws right, bats right.

TRANSACTIONS/CAREER NOTES: Signed as non-drafted free agent by Montreal Expos organization (July 3, 1989). ... Selected by Edmonton, Florida Marlins organization from Expos organization in Rule 5 minor league draft (December 13, 1993). ... On disabled list (May 15-June 15, 1995). ... On disabled list (July 12-September 3, 1996). ... On disabled list (May 14-31, 1998).

HONORS: Named N.L. Fireman of the Year by THE SPORTING NEWS (2000).

MISCELLANEOUS: Holds Florida Marlins all-time record for most games pitched (274).

Year League	W	L	Pct.	ERA	G	GS	CG	ShO	Sv.	IP	H	R	ER	BB	SO
1990— Dominican Expos (DSL)	3	5	.375	3.60	13	13	1	0	0	60	60	29	24	32	19
1991— Gulf Coast Expos (GCL)	3	3	.500	3.88	11	10	0	0	0	51	46	33	22	25	38
1992— Gulf Coast Expos (GCL)	3	4	.429	3.68	12	10	1	1	0	66	65	31	27	35	62
1993— Jamestown (NY-Penn)	2	2	.500	6.15	15	4	0	0	1	33²/₃	31	26	23	22	29
1994— Kane County (Midw.)■.....	6	5	.545	4.07	32	9	0	0	0	86¹/₃	78	41	39	21	74
1995— Portland (East.)	9	3	.750	3.64	19	17	1	0	0	96¹/₃	81	43	39	42	75
1996— Charlotte (I.L.)	4	4	.500	5.53	14	13	0	0	1	71²/₃	86	47	44	22	41
1997— Charlotte (I.L.)	7	2	.778	4.32	46	0	0	0	7	58¹/₃	58	34	28	20	45
— Florida (N.L.)	1	3	.250	4.91	17	0	0	0	0	25²/₃	36	16	14	10	19
1998— Florida (N.L.)	4	6	.400	4.08	58	0	0	0	8	70²/₃	75	36	32	33	46
1999— Florida (N.L.)	4	5	.444	3.24	73	0	0	0	21	77²/₃	79	28	28	29	46
2000— Florida (N.L.)	5	6	.455	4.24	68	0	0	0	*45	70	82	35	33	24	47
2001— Florida (N.L.)	4	4	.500	3.06	58	0	0	0	28	61²/₃	68	24	21	15	40
Major League totals (5 years)	18	24	.429	3.77	274	0	0	0	102	305²/₃	340	139	128	111	198

DIVISION SERIES RECORD

Year League	W	L	Pct.	ERA	G	GS	CG	ShO	Sv.	IP	H	R	ER	BB	SO
1997— Florida (N.L.)							Did not play.								

CHAMPIONSHIP SERIES RECORD

Year League	W	L	Pct.	ERA	G	GS	CG	ShO	Sv.	IP	H	R	ER	BB	SO
1997— Florida (N.L.)							Did not play.								

NOTES: Member of World Series championship team (1997).

WORLD SERIES RECORD

Year League	W	L	Pct.	ERA	G	GS	CG	ShO	Sv.	IP	H	R	ER	BB	SO
1997— Florida (N.L.)	0	0	...	0.00	3	0	0	0	0	6¹/₃	6	0	0	1	5

ALFONZO, EDGARDO — 3B — METS

PERSONAL: Born November 8, 1973, in St. Teresa, Venezuela. ... 5-11/187. ... Bats right, throws right. ... Full name: Edgardo Antonio Alfonzo. ... Brother of Roberto Alfonzo, second baseman with New York Mets organization (1993-94).

HIGH SCHOOL: Cecilio Acosto (Venezuela).

TRANSACTIONS/CAREER NOTES: Signed as non-drafted free agent by New York Mets organization (February 19, 1991). ... On disabled list (August 11, 1995-remainder of season; and May 4-19, 1998). ... On New York disabled list (June 14-July 3, 2001); included rehabilitation assignment to Norfolk (June 30-July 3).

RECORDS: Shares major league single-game records for most runs scored—6 (August 30, 1999); and most double plays by third basemen—4 (May 14, 1997).

HONORS: Named second baseman on THE SPORTING NEWS N.L. All-Star team (1999). ... Named second baseman on THE SPORTING NEWS N.L. Silver Slugger team (1999).

STATISTICAL NOTES: Led New York-Pennsylvania League shortstops with 389 total chances and 39 double plays in 1992. ... Had 20-game hitting streak (June 10-July 10, 1997). ... Hit three home runs in one game (August 30, 1999). ... Collected six hits in one game (August 30, 1999). ... Had 15-game hitting streak (August 28-September 23, 2001). ... Career major league grand slams: 1.

Year Team (League)	Pos.	G	AB	R	H	2B	3B	BATTING HR	RBI	Avg.	BB	SO	SB	FIELDING PO	A	E	Avg.
1991— GC Mets (GCL)	2B-SS-3B	54	175	29	58	8	4	0	27	.331	34	12	6	99	108	9	.958
1992— St. Lucie (FSL)	2B	4	5	0	0	0	0	0	0	.000	0	0	0	1	3	0	1.000
— Pittsfield (NY-Penn)....	SS	74	*298	44	*106	13	5	1	44	*.356	18	31	7	*126	*237	*26	.933
1993— St. Lucie (FSL)	SS	128	494	75	145	18	3	11	86	.294	57	51	26	183	425	29	.954
1994— Binghamton (East.)	SS-2B-1B	127	498	89	146	34	2	15	75	.293	64	55	14	206	408	27	.958
1995— New York (N.L.)	3B-2B-SS	101	335	26	93	13	5	4	41	.278	12	37	1	81	171	7	.973
1996— New York (N.L.)	2B-3B-SS	123	368	36	96	15	2	4	40	.261	25	56	2	146	246	11	.973
1997— New York (N.L.)	3B-SS-2B	151	518	84	163	27	2	10	72	.315	63	56	11	98	290	12	.970
1998— New York (N.L.)	3B-SS	144	557	94	155	28	2	17	78	.278	65	77	8	117	248	9	.976
1999— New York (N.L.)	2B	158	628	123	191	41	1	27	108	.304	85	85	9	298	409	5	*.993
2000— New York (N.L.)	2B-DH	150	544	109	176	40	2	25	94	.324	95	70	3	316	362	10	.985
2001— New York (N.L.)	2B	124	457	64	111	22	0	17	49	.243	51	62	5	211	301	7	.987
— Norfolk (I.L.)	2B	2	8	0	0	0	0	0	0	.000	0	0	0	6	8	0	1.000
Major League totals (7 years)		951	3407	536	985	186	14	104	482	.289	396	443	39	1267	2027	61	.982

DIVISION SERIES RECORD

RECORDS: Shares N.L. single-series record for most runs scored—6 (1999). ... Shares single-game records for most home runs—2; most grand slams—1; and most runs batted in—5 (October 5, 1999). ... Shares single-inning record for most runs batted in—4 (October 5, 1999, ninth inning).

Year Team (League)	Pos.	G	AB	R	H	2B	3B	HR	RBI	Avg.	BB	SO	SB	PO	A	E	Avg.
1999— New York (N.L.)..........	2B	4	16	6	4	1	0	3	6	.250	3	2	0	5	11	0	1.000
2000— New York (N.L.)..........	2B	4	18	1	5	2	0	1	5	.278	1	2	0	6	7	0	1.000
Division series totals (2 years)		8	34	7	9	3	0	4	11	.265	4	4	0	11	18	0	1.000

CHAMPIONSHIP SERIES RECORD

Year Team (League)	Pos.	G	AB	R	H	2B	3B	HR	RBI	Avg.	BB	SO	SB	PO	A	E	Avg.
1999— New York (N.L.)..........	2B	6	27	2	6	4	0	0	1	.222	1	9	0	15	18	1	.971
2000— New York (N.L.)..........	2B	5	18	5	8	1	1	0	4	.444	4	1	0	3	10	0	1.000
Championship series totals (2 years)		11	45	7	14	5	1	0	5	.311	5	10	0	18	28	1	.979

WORLD SERIES RECORD

Year Team (League)	Pos.	G	AB	R	H	2B	3B	HR	RBI	Avg.	BB	SO	SB	PO	A	E	Avg.
2000— New York (N.L.)..........	2B	5	21	1	3	0	0	0	1	.143	1	5	0	7	19	0	1.000

ALL-STAR GAME RECORD

Year League	Pos.	AB	R	H	2B	3B	HR	RBI	Avg.	BB	SO	SB	PO	A	E	Avg.
2000— National.....................	2B	2	0	0	0	0	0	0	.000	0	1	0	0	1	0	1.000

ALICEA, LUIS   2B   ROYALS

PERSONAL: Born July 29, 1965, in Santurce, Puerto Rico. ... 5-9/176. ... Bats both, throws right. ... Full name: Luis Rene Alicea. ... Brother of Ed Alicea, minor league infielder with Atlanta Braves (1988-93), Colorado Rockies (1993) and New York Mets (1995). ... Name pronounced AH-la-SAY-uh.

HIGH SCHOOL: Liceo Castro (Rio Piedras, Puerto Rico).

COLLEGE: Florida State.

TRANSACTIONS/CAREER NOTES: Selected by St. Louis Cardinals organization in first round (23rd pick overall) of free-agent draft (June 2, 1986). ... On St. Petersburg disabled list (April 6-June 4, 1990). ... On Louisville disabled list (April 25-May 25, 1991). ... On St. Louis disabled list (June 1-July 6, 1992; included rehabilitation assignment to Louisville (July 2-6). ... Traded by Cardinals to Boston Red Sox for P Nate Minchey and OF Jeff McNeely (December 7, 1994). ... Claimed on waivers by Cardinals (March 19, 1996). ... Granted free agency (October 31, 1996). ... Signed by Anaheim Angels organization (January 20, 1997). ... Granted free agency (October 30, 1997). ... Signed by Texas Rangers (December 9, 1997). ... Granted free agency (October 28, 1999). ... Re-signed by Rangers (December 7, 1999). ... Granted free agency (October 31, 2000). ... Signed by Kansas City Royals (January 26, 2001). ... Granted free agency (November 5, 2001). ... Re-signed by Royals (December 7, 2001).

HONORS: Named second baseman on THE SPORTING NEWS college All-America team (1986).

STATISTICAL NOTES: Switch-hit home runs in one game (July 28, 1995). ... Led A.L. second basemen with 699 total chances and 103 double plays in 1995. ... Career major league grand slams: 1.

Year Team (League)	Pos.	G	AB	R	H	2B	3B	HR	RBI	Avg.	BB	SO	SB	PO	A	E	Avg.
1986—Erie (NY-Penn)	2B	47	163	40	46	6	1	3	18	.282	37	20	27	94	163	12	.955
— Arkansas (Texas).......	2B-SS	25	68	8	16	3	0	0	3	.235	5	11	0	39	63	4	.962
1987— Arkansas (Texas).......	2B	101	337	57	91	14	3	4	47	.270	49	28	13	184	251	11	*.975
— Louisville (A.A.).......	2B	29	105	18	32	10	2	2	20	.305	9	9	4	69	81	4	.974
1988— Louisville (A.A.).......	2B-SS-OF	49	191	21	53	11	6	1	21	.277	11	21	8	116	165	0	1.000
— St. Louis (N.L.).........	2B	93	297	20	63	10	4	1	24	.212	25	32	1	206	240	14	.970
1989— Louisville (A.A.).......	2B	124	412	53	102	20	3	8	48	.248	59	55	13	240	310	16	.972
1990— St. Petersburg (FSL) ..	2B	29	95	14	22	1	4	0	12	.232	20	14	9	20	23	0	1.000
— Arkansas (Texas).......	2B	14	49	11	14	3	1	0	4	.286	7	8	2	24	34	4	.935
— Louisville (A.A.).......	3B	25	92	10	32	6	3	0	10	.348	5	12	0	14	39	6	.898
1991— Louisville (A.A.).......	2B	31	112	26	44	6	3	4	16	.393	14	8	5	68	95	5	.970
— St. Louis (N.L.).........	2B-3B-SS	56	68	5	13	3	0	0	0	.191	8	19	0	19	23	0	1.000
1992— Louisville (A.A.).......	2B-SS	20	71	11	20	8	0	0	6	.282	16	6	0	44	52	4	.960
— St. Louis (N.L.).........	2B-SS	85	265	26	65	9	11	2	32	.245	27	40	2	136	233	7	.981
1993— St. Louis (N.L.).........	2B-OF-3B	115	362	50	101	19	3	3	46	.279	47	54	11	210	281	11	.978
1994— St. Louis (N.L.).........	2B-OF	88	205	32	57	12	5	5	29	.278	30	38	4	126	149	4	.986
1995— Boston (A.L.)■..........	2B	132	419	64	113	20	3	6	44	.270	63	61	13	254	429	16	.977
1996— St. Louis (N.L.)■........	2B	129	380	54	98	26	3	5	42	.258	52	78	11	241	288	*24	.957
1997— Anaheim (A.L.)■........	2B-3B-DH	128	388	59	98	16	7	5	37	.253	69	65	22	223	287	12	.977
1998— Texas (A.L.)■............	2-3-DH-O	101	259	51	71	15	3	6	33	.274	37	40	4	97	143	9	.964
1999— Texas (A.L.)..............	2B-3B-DH-OF	68	164	33	33	10	0	3	17	.201	28	32	2	66	100	5	.971
2000— Texas (A.L.)..............	2B-3B-DH-SS	139	540	85	159	25	8	6	63	.294	59	75	1	253	328	18	.970
2001— Kansas City (A.L.)■ ...	2B-DH-3B	113	387	44	106	16	4	4	32	.274	23	56	8	117	218	14	.960
American League totals (6 years)		681	2157	336	580	102	25	30	226	.269	279	329	50	1010	1505	74	.971
National League totals (6 years)		566	1577	187	397	79	26	16	173	.252	189	261	29	938	1214	60	.973
Major League totals (12 years)		1247	3734	523	977	181	51	46	399	.262	468	590	79	1948	2719	134	.972

DIVISION SERIES RECORD

Year Team (League)	Pos.	G	AB	R	H	2B	3B	HR	RBI	Avg.	BB	SO	SB	PO	A	E	Avg.
1995— Boston (A.L.).............	2B	3	10	1	6	1	0	1	1	.600	2	1	1	6	11	1	.944
1996— St. Louis (N.L.)..........	2B	3	11	1	2	2	0	0	0	.182	1	4	0	2	5	1	.875
1998— Texas (A.L.)..............	PH-DH	1	1	0	0	0	0	0	0	.000	0	0	0	...	...	...	...
1999— Texas (A.L.)..............						Did not play.											
Division series totals (3 years)		7	22	2	8	3	0	1	1	.364	3	6	1	8	16	2	.923

CHAMPIONSHIP SERIES RECORD

Year Team (League)	Pos.	G	AB	R	H	2B	3B	HR	RBI	Avg.	BB	SO	SB	PO	A	E	Avg.
1996— St. Louis (N.L.)..........	2B-PH	5	8	0	0	0	0	0	0	.000	2	1	0	5	7	1	.923

ALLEN, CHAD — OF

PERSONAL: Born February 6, 1975, in Dallas. ... 6-1/195. ... Bats right, throws right. ... Full name: John Chad Allen.
HIGH SCHOOL: Duncanville (Texas).
COLLEGE: Texas A&M.
TRANSACTIONS/CAREER NOTES: Selected by Cincinnati Reds organization in 38th round of free-agent draft (June 3, 1993); did not sign. ... Selected by Minnesota Twins organization in fourth round of free-agent draft (June 4, 1996). ... On Salt Lake disabled list (April 11-22, 2000). ... On Minnesota disabled list (June 4-19 and August 15, 2001-remainder of season). ... Granted free agency (October 24, 2001).
MISCELLANEOUS: Member of 1996 U.S. Olympic baseball team.

Year Team (League)	Pos.	G	AB	R	H	2B	3B	HR	RBI	Avg.	BB	SO	SB	PO	A	E	Avg.
1996—Fort Wayne (Midw.)....	OF	7	21	2	9	0	0	0	2	.429	3	2	1	4	1	0	1.000
1997—Fort Myers (FSL).......	OF	105	401	66	124	18	4	3	45	.309	40	51	27	206	10	5	.977
—New Britain (East.).....	OF	30	115	20	29	9	1	4	18	.252	9	21	2	35	1	1	.973
1998—New Britain (East.).....	OF	137	504	70	132	31	7	8	82	.262	51	78	21	185	11	4	.980
1999—Minnesota (A.L.)........	OF-DH	137	481	69	133	21	3	10	46	.277	37	89	14	267	9	7	.975
2000—Salt Lake (PCL).........	OF	96	389	71	121	21	5	9	67	.311	31	72	10	146	2	1	.993
—Minnesota (A.L.)........	OF	15	50	2	15	3	0	0	7	.300	3	14	0	26	2	0	1.000
2001—Minnesota (A.L.)........	OF-DH	57	175	20	46	13	2	4	20	.263	19	37	1	57	3	2	.968
—Edmonton (PCL)........	OF	6	22	4	8	2	0	1	1	.364	4	1	2	10	1	0	1.000
Major League totals (3 years)		209	706	91	194	37	5	14	73	.275	59	140	15	350	14	9	.976

ALLEN, LUKE — 3B — DODGERS

PERSONAL: Born August 4, 1978, in Covington, Ga. ... 6-2/208. ... Bats left, throws right. ... Full name: Lucas G. Allen.
HIGH SCHOOL: Newton County (Covington, Ga.).
TRANSACTIONS/CAREER NOTES: Signed as non-drafted free agent by Los Angeles Dodgers organization (August 4, 1996).

Year Team (League)	Pos.	G	AB	R	H	2B	3B	HR	RBI	Avg.	BB	SO	SB	PO	A	E	Avg.
1997—Great Falls (Pio.)........	3B-OF	67	258	50	89	12	6	7	40	.345	19	53	12	38	107	22	.868
1998—San Bern. (Calif.)........	OF	105	399	51	119	25	6	4	46	.298	30	93	18	190	8	6	.971
—San Antonio (Texas)...	OF	23	78	9	26	3	1	3	10	.333	6	16	1	42	3	4	.918
1999—San Antonio (Texas)...	3B	137	533	90	150	16	12	14	82	.281	44	102	14	80	222	53	.851
2000—San Antonio (Texas)...	1B-3B	90	339	55	90	15	5	7	60	.265	40	71	14	63	166	27	.895
2001—Jacksonville (Sou.).....	OF	125	486	74	141	32	6	16	73	.290	42	111	13	225	•15	7	.972
—Las Vegas (PCL)	OF	2	9	1	2	1	0	0	0	.222	0	0	0	1	1	1	.667

ALMANZA, ARMANDO — P — MARLINS

PERSONAL: Born October 26, 1972, in El Paso, Texas. ... 6-3/220. ... Throws left, bats left.
HIGH SCHOOL: Bel Air (El Paso, Texas).
JUNIOR COLLEGE: New Mexico Junior College.
TRANSACTIONS/CAREER NOTES: Selected by St. Louis Cardinals organization in 21st round of free-agent draft (June 3, 1993). ... On disabled list (April 8, 1994-entire season). ... On Memphis disabled list (July 10-21, 1998). ... Traded by Cardinals with P Braden Looper and SS Pablo Ozuna to Florida Marlins for SS Edgar Renteria (December 14, 1998). ... On Calgary disabled list (May 10-June 2, 1999).
STATISTICAL NOTES: Tied for Arizona League lead with 14 wild pitches in 1993.

Year League	W	L	Pct.	ERA	G	GS	CG	ShO	Sv.	IP	H	R	ER	BB	SO
1993—Arizona Cardinals (Ariz.)	4	1	.800	3.21	20	4	0	0	0	42	38	19	15	14	56
—Johnson City (Appl.)	1	1	.500	4.15	3	3	0	0	0	4 1/3	6	2	2	3	4
1994—Madison (Midw.)						Did not play.									
1995—Savannah (S.Atl.)	3	9	.250	3.92	20	20	0	0	0	108	108	62	47	40	72
1996—Peoria (Midw.)	8	6	.571	2.76	52	1	0	0	0	62	50	27	19	32	67
1997—Prince William (Caro.) ...	2	3	.400	1.67	•58	0	0	0	*36	64 2/3	38	18	12	32	83
1998—Arkansas (Texas)	4	1	.800	3.31	28	0	0	0	8	32 2/3	27	13	12	18	46
—Memphis (PCL)	3	1	.750	3.03	31	0	0	0	1	35 2/3	35	18	12	19	45
1999—Calgary (PCL)■................	2	2	.500	10.90	15	0	0	0	0	17 1/3	29	27	21	18	20
—Portland (East.)	0	1	.000	3.97	10	0	0	0	3	11 1/3	5	5	5	4	20
—Florida (N.L.)	0	1	.000	1.72	14	0	0	0	0	15 2/3	8	4	3	9	20
2000—Florida (N.L.)	4	2	.667	4.86	67	0	0	0	0	46 1/3	38	27	25	43	46
2001—Florida (N.L.)	2	2	.500	4.83	52	0	0	0	0	41	34	24	22	26	45
Major League totals (3 years)	6	5	.545	4.37	133	0	0	0	0	103	80	55	50	78	111

ALMANZAR, CARLOS — P

PERSONAL: Born November 6, 1973, in Santiago, Dominican Republic. ... 6-2/200. ... Throws right, bats right. ... Full name: Carlos Manuel Almanzar.
TRANSACTIONS/CAREER NOTES: Signed as non-drafted free agent by Toronto Blue Jays organization (December 10, 1990). ... On Knoxville disabled list (May 27-June 3, 1997). ... Traded by Blue Jays with P Woody Williams and OF Peter Tucci to San Diego Padres for P Joey Hamilton (December 13, 1998). ... On San Diego disabled list (April 24-May 27, 1999); included rehabilitation assignment to Las Vegas (May 22-27). ... Traded by Padres to New York Yankees for P David Lee (March 25, 2001). ... Granted free agency (October 15, 2001).

Year League	W	L	Pct.	ERA	G	GS	CG	ShO	Sv.	IP	H	R	ER	BB	SO
1991—Dom. Blue Jays (DSL).......	3	1	.750	2.83	6	6	1	0	0	35	36	17	11	11	20
1992—Dom. Blue Jays (DSL).......	10	0	1.000	2.01	13	11	2	1	1	67	45	26	15	31	60
1993—Dom. Blue Jays (DSL).......	5	2	.714	3.38	16	9	0	0	0	69 1/3	60	35	26	32	60
1994—Medicine Hat (Pio.)	7	4	.636	2.87	14	14	0	0	0	84 2/3	82	38	27	19	77
1995—Knoxville (Sou.).................	3	12	.200	3.99	35	19	0	0	2	126 1/3	144	77	56	32	93

Year	League	W	L	Pct.	ERA	G	GS	CG	ShO	Sv.	IP	H	R	ER	BB	SO
1996—Knoxville (Sou.)		7	8	.467	4.85	54	0	0	0	9	94 2/3	106	58	51	33	105
1997—Knoxville (Sou.)		1	1	.500	4.91	21	0	0	0	8	25 2/3	30	14	14	5	25
—Syracuse (I.L.)		5	1	.833	1.41	32	0	0	0	3	51	30	9	8	8	47
—Toronto (A.L.)		0	1	.000	2.70	4	0	0	0	0	3 1/3	1	1	1	1	4
1998—Toronto (A.L.)		2	2	.500	5.34	25	0	0	0	0	28 2/3	34	18	17	8	20
—Syracuse (I.L.)		3	6	.333	2.31	30	0	0	0	10	50 2/3	44	21	13	13	53
1999—San Diego (N.L.)■		0	0	...	7.47	28	0	0	0	0	37 1/3	48	32	31	15	30
—Las Vegas (PCL)		1	3	.250	9.53	11	3	0	0	0	22 2/3	32	25	24	8	18
2000—San Diego (N.L.)		4	5	.444	4.39	62	0	0	0	0	69 2/3	73	35	34	25	56
—Las Vegas (PCL)		0	0	...	4.50	4	0	0	0	0	6	9	4	3	0	7
2001—New York (A.L.)■		0	1	.000	3.38	10	0	0	0	0	10 2/3	14	4	4	2	6
—Columbus (I.L.)■		2	1	.667	2.43	35	0	0	0	18	33 1/3	36	10	9	6	26
A.L. totals (3 years)		2	4	.333	4.64	39	0	0	0	0	42 2/3	49	23	22	11	30
N.L. totals (2 years)		4	5	.444	5.47	90	0	0	0	0	107	121	67	65	40	86
Major League totals (5 years)		6	9	.400	5.23	129	0	0	0	0	149 2/3	170	90	87	51	116

ALMONTE, EDWIN — P — WHITE SOX

PERSONAL: Born December 17, 1976, in Santiago, Dominican Republic. ... 6-3/200. ... Throws right, bats right.
HIGH SCHOOL: Seward Park (New York, N.Y.).
COLLEGE: St. Francis (N.Y.).
TRANSACTIONS/CAREER NOTES: Selected by Chicago White Sox organization in 26th round of free-agent draft (June 2, 1998).

Year	League	W	L	Pct.	ERA	G	GS	CG	ShO	Sv.	IP	H	R	ER	BB	SO
1998—Arizona White Sox (Ariz.)		0	0	...	0.93	5	0	0	0	0	9 2/3	6	5	1	1	6
—Bristol (Appl.)		3	0	1.000	3.38	8	3	0	0	0	26 2/3	29	14	10	4	26
1999—Burlington (Midw.)		9	12	.429	3.03	37	5	2	0	5	115 2/3	107	48	39	28	85
2000—Winston-Salem (Caro.)		3	1	.750	3.16	33	7	0	0	2	77	66	32	27	20	73
—Birmingham (Sou.)		1	3	.250	4.54	7	6	0	0	0	39 2/3	45	22	20	9	21
2001—Birmingham (Sou.)		1	4	.200	1.49	54	0	0	0	*36	66 1/3	58	16	11	16	62

ALMONTE, ERICK — SS — YANKEES

PERSONAL: Born February 1, 1978, in Santo Domingo, Dominican Republic. ... 6-2/180. ... Bats right, throws right. ... Full name: Erick R. Almonte.
TRANSACTIONS/CAREER NOTES: Signed as non-drafted free agent by New York Yankees organization (February 12, 1996). ... On Norwich disabled list (June 14-26, 2001). ... On Columbus disabled list (July 23-August 4, 2001).
STATISTICAL NOTES: Led Gulf Coast League third basemen with 163 total chances in 1998. ... Led South Atlantic League in grounding into double plays with 17 in 1999.

Year	Team (League)	Pos.	G	AB	R	H	2B	3B	HR	RBI	Avg.	BB	SO	SB	PO	A	E	Avg.
1996—Dom. Yankees (DSL)		3B	58	216	37	61	7	0	8	36	.282	15	30	3	68	133	36	.848
1997—GC Yankees (GCL)		3B	52	180	32	51	4	4	3	31	.283	21	27	8	*53	92	18	.890
1998—Greensboro (S.Atl.)		SS	120	450	53	94	13	0	6	33	.209	29	121	6	176	307	47	.911
1999—Tampa (FSL)		SS	61	230	36	59	8	2	5	25	.257	18	49	3	88	217	20	.938
—GC Yankees (GCL)		SS	9	30	5	9	2	0	2	9	.300	3	10	1	4	23	2	.931
2000—Norwich (East.)		3B	131	454	56	123	18	4	15	77	.271	35	129	12	235	308	*33	.943
2001—Columbus (I.L.)		SS	97	345	55	99	19	3	12	55	.287	44	90	4	134	258	*27	.936
—Norwich (East.)		SS	3	12	2	3	0	0	0	0	.250	1	6	1	4	5	1	.900
—New York (A.L.)		SS-DH	8	4	0	2	1	0	0	0	.500	0	1	2	4	3	1	.875
Major League totals (1 year)			8	4	0	2	1	0	0	0	.500	0	1	2	4	3	1	.875

ALOMAR, ROBERTO — 2B — METS

PERSONAL: Born February 5, 1968, in Ponce, Puerto Rico. ... 6-0/185. ... Bats both, throws right. ... Full name: Roberto Velazquez Alomar. ... Son of Sandy Alomar Sr., major league infielder with six teams (1964-78) and coach, Chicago Cubs; and brother of Sandy Alomar Jr., catcher, Chicago White Sox.
TRANSACTIONS/CAREER NOTES: Signed as non-drafted free agent by San Diego Padres organization (February 16, 1985). ... Traded by Padres with OF Joe Carter to Toronto Blue Jays for 1B Fred McGriff and SS Tony Fernandez (December 5, 1990). ... On suspended list (May 23-24, 1995). ... Granted free agency (October 30, 1995). ... Signed by Baltimore Orioles (December 21, 1995). ... On suspended list (April 1-7, 1997). ... On disabled list (July 30-August 26, 1997; and July 19-August 4, 1998). ... Granted free agency (October 26, 1998). ... Signed by Cleveland Indians (December 1, 1998). ... Traded by Indians with P Mike Bacsik and OF Danny Peoples to New York Mets for OF Matt Lawton, OF Alex Escobar, P Jerrod Riggan and two players to be named later (December 11, 2001); Indians acquired P Billy Traber and 1B Earl Snyder to complete deal (December 13, 2001).
RECORDS: Holds A.L. career records for highest fielding percentage by second basemen—.987; and most consecutive errorless games by second baseman—104 (June 21, 1994 through July 3, 1995). ... Holds A.L. single-season records for fewest double plays by second baseman (150 or more games)—66 (1992); and most runs by switch-hitter—138 (1999). ... Shares A.L. single-season records for most games with switch-hit home runs—2 (1996); and fewest errors by second baseman (150 or more games)—5 (1992 and 2001).
HONORS: Won A.L. Gold Glove at second base (1991-96 and 1998-2001). ... Named second baseman on THE SPORTING NEWS A.L. All-Star team (1992, 1996, 1998, 1999 and 2000). ... Named second baseman on THE SPORTING NEWS A.L. Silver Slugger team (1992, 1996, 1999 and 2000).
STATISTICAL NOTES: Led South Atlantic League second basemen with 35 errors in 1985. ... Led Texas League shortstops with 167 putouts and 34 errors in 1987. ... Led N.L. with 17 sacrifice hits in 1989. ... Led N.L. second basemen with 17 errors in 1990. ... Switch-hit home runs in one game five times (May 10, 1991; May 3, 1995; July 25 and August 14, 1996; and July 16, 2001). ... Had 22-game hitting streak (May 12-June 8, 1996). ... Hit three home runs in one game (April 26, 1997). ... Led A.L. with 13 sacrifice flies in 1999. ... Had 17-game hitting streak (May 5-25, 2000). ... Had 18-game hitting streak (September 17-October 1, 2000). ... Had 15-game hitting streak (May 28-June 13, 2001). ... Career major league grand slams: 6.
MISCELLANEOUS: Holds Toronto Blue Jays all-time record for highest career batting average (.307).

Year Team (League)	Pos.	G	AB	R	H	2B	3B	HR	RBI	Avg.	BB	SO	SB	PO	A	E	Avg.
1985—Charl., S.C. (S.Atl.).....	2B-SS	*137	*546	89	160	14	3	0	54	.293	61	73	36	298	339	†36	.947
1986—Reno (Calif.)............	2B	90	356	53	123	16	4	4	49	.346	32	38	14	198	265	18	.963
1987—Wichita (Texas)	SS-2B	130	536	88	171	41	4	12	68	.319	49	74	43	†188	309	†36	.932
1988—Las Vegas (PCL)	2B	9	37	5	10	1	0	2	14	.270	1	4	3	22	29	1	.981
—San Diego (N.L.)	2B	143	545	84	145	24	6	9	41	.266	47	83	24	319	459	16	.980
1989—San Diego (N.L.)	2B	158	623	82	184	27	1	7	56	.295	53	76	42	341	472	*28	.967
1990—San Diego (N.L.)	2B-SS	147	586	80	168	27	5	6	60	.287	48	72	24	316	404	†19	.974
1991—Toronto (A.L.)■........	2B	161	637	88	188	41	11	9	69	.295	57	86	53	333	447	15	.981
1992—Toronto (A.L.)............	2B-DH	152	571	105	177	27	8	8	76	.310	87	52	49	287	378	5	.993
1993—Toronto (A.L.)............	2B	153	589	109	192	35	6	17	93	.326	80	67	55	254	439	14	.980
1994—Toronto (A.L.)............	2B	107	392	78	120	25	4	8	38	.306	51	41	19	176	275	4	.991
1995—Toronto (A.L.)............	2B	130	517	71	155	24	7	13	66	.300	47	45	30	*272	267	4	*.993
1996—Baltimore (A.L.)■......	2B-DH	153	588	132	193	43	4	22	94	.328	90	65	17	279	445	11	.985
1997—Baltimore (A.L.)........	2B-DH	112	412	64	137	23	2	14	60	.333	40	43	9	202	301	6	.988
1998—Baltimore (A.L.)........	2B-DH	147	588	86	166	36	1	14	56	.282	59	70	18	251	*449	11	.985
1999—Cleveland (A.L.)■......	2B-DH	159	563	*138	182	40	3	24	120	.323	99	96	37	270	466	6	*.992
2000—Cleveland (A.L.)........	2B	155	610	111	189	40	2	19	89	.310	64	82	39	293	*437	15	.980
2001—Cleveland (A.L.)........	2B	157	575	113	193	34	12	20	100	.336	80	71	30	268	423	5	.993
American League totals (11 years)		1586	6042	1095	1892	368	60	168	861	.313	754	718	356	2885	4327	96	.987
National League totals (3 years)		448	1754	246	497	78	12	22	157	.283	148	231	90	976	1335	63	.973
Major League totals (14 years)		2034	7796	1341	2389	446	72	190	1018	.306	902	949	446	3861	5662	159	.984

DIVISION SERIES RECORD

RECORDS: Shares single-series record for most doubles—4 (1999).

Year Team (League)	Pos.	G	AB	R	H	2B	3B	HR	RBI	Avg.	BB	SO	SB	PO	A	E	Avg.
1996—Baltimore (A.L.)........	2B	4	17	2	5	0	0	1	4	.294	2	3	0	10	6	0	1.000
1997—Baltimore (A.L.)........	2B-PH	4	10	1	3	2	0	0	2	.300	1	1	0	3	6	0	1.000
1999—Cleveland (A.L.)........	2B	5	19	4	7	4	0	0	3	.368	2	3	2	13	14	1	.964
2001—Cleveland (A.L.)........	2B	5	21	3	4	3	0	0	3	.190	2	5	0	9	9	0	1.000
Division series totals (4 years)		18	67	10	19	9	0	1	12	.284	7	12	2	35	35	1	.986

CHAMPIONSHIP SERIES RECORD

RECORDS: Shares career record for most times grounded into double play—5.
NOTES: Named Most Valuable Player (1992).

Year Team (League)	Pos.	G	AB	R	H	2B	3B	HR	RBI	Avg.	BB	SO	SB	PO	A	E	Avg.
1991—Toronto (A.L.)............	2B	5	19	3	9	0	0	0	4	.474	2	3	2	14	9	0	1.000
1992—Toronto (A.L.)............	2B	6	26	4	11	1	0	2	4	.423	2	1	5	16	15	0	1.000
1993—Toronto (A.L.)............	2B	6	24	3	7	1	0	0	4	.292	4	3	4	14	19	0	1.000
1996—Baltimore (A.L.)........	2B	5	23	2	5	2	0	1	1	.217	0	4	0	15	26	2	.953
1997—Baltimore (A.L.)........	2B	6	22	2	4	0	0	1	2	.182	7	3	0	10	17	2	.931
Championship series totals (5 years)		28	114	14	36	4	0	3	15	.316	15	14	11	69	86	4	.975

WORLD SERIES RECORD

RECORDS: Shares record for most at-bats in one inning—2 (October 20, 1993, eighth inning).
NOTES: Member of World Series championship team (1992 and 1993).

Year Team (League)	Pos.	G	AB	R	H	2B	3B	HR	RBI	Avg.	BB	SO	SB	PO	A	E	Avg.
1992—Toronto (A.L.)............	2B	6	24	3	5	1	0	0	0	.208	3	3	3	5	12	0	1.000
1993—Toronto (A.L.)............	2B	6	25	5	12	2	1	0	6	.480	2	3	4	9	21	2	.938
World Series totals (2 years)		12	49	8	17	3	1	0	6	.347	5	6	7	14	33	2	.959

ALL-STAR GAME RECORD

RECORDS: Shares single-game record for most stolen bases—2 (July 14, 1992).
NOTES: Named Most Valuable Player (1998).

Year League	Pos.	AB	R	H	2B	3B	HR	RBI	Avg.	BB	SO	SB	PO	A	E	Avg.
1990—National	2B	1	0	0	0	0	0	0	.000	0	0	0	1	2	0	1.000
1991—American	2B	4	0	0	0	0	0	0	.000	0	0	0	2	5	0	1.000
1992—American	2B	3	1	1	0	0	0	0	.333	0	0	2	0	1	0	1.000
1993—American	2B	3	1	1	0	0	1	1	.333	0	0	0	0	0	0	...
1994—American	2B	3	1	1	0	0	0	0	.333	0	0	1	0	0	0	...
1995—America	PR-2B	1	0	0	0	0	0	0	.000	0	0	1	0	0	0	...
1996—American	2B	3	0	1	0	0	0	0	.333	0	0	0	0	3	0	1.000
1997—American	2B	2	0	0	0	0	0	0	.000	0	0	0	1	5	0	1.000
1998—American	2B	4	2	3	0	0	1	1	.750	1	0	1	3	2	0	1.000
1999—American	2B	2	0	0	0	0	0	1	.000	0	1	0	2	2	1	.800
2000—American	2B	2	0	0	0	0	0	0	.000	0	0	0	3	1	0	1.000
2001—American	2B	2	0	0	0	0	0	0	.000	0	0	0	0	1	0	1.000
All-Star Game totals (12 years)		30	5	7	0	0	2	3	.233	1	1	5	12	22	1	.971

ALOMAR, SANDY   C   WHITE SOX

PERSONAL: Born June 18, 1966, in Salinas, Puerto Rico. ... 6-5/220. ... Bats right, throws right. ... Full name: Santos Velazquez Alomar Jr. ... Son of Sandy Alomar Sr., major league infielder with six teams (1964-78) and coach, Chicago Cubs; and brother of Roberto Alomar, second baseman, New York Mets.
HIGH SCHOOL: Luis Munoz Rivera (Salinas, Puerto Rico).
TRANSACTIONS/CAREER NOTES: Signed as non-drafted free agent by San Diego Padres organization (October 21, 1983). ... Traded by Padres with OF Chris James and 3B Carlos Baerga to Cleveland Indians for OF Joe Carter (December 6, 1989). ... On Cleveland disabled list (May 15-

June 17 and July 29, 1991-remainder of season); included rehabilitation assignments to Colorado Springs (June 8-17 and August 9-12). ... On disabled list (May 2-18, 1992). ... On suspended list (July 29-August 2, 1992). ... On Cleveland disabled list (May 1-August 7, 1993); included rehabilitation assignment to Charlotte, S.C. (July 22-August 7). ... On disabled list (April 24-May 11, 1994). ... On Cleveland disabled list (April 19-June 29, 1995); included rehabilitation assignment to Canton/Akron (June 22-29). ... On Cleveland disabled list (May 11-September 6, 1999); included rehabilitation assignment to Akron (July 5-19 and September 3-6) and Buffalo (August 10-27). ... On disabled list (April 19-May 8, 2000). ... Granted free agency (October 27, 2000). ... Signed by Chicago White Sox (December 18, 2000). ... On disabled list (August 8-September 18, 2001).

A

RECORDS: Shares major league single-game record for most doubles—4 (June 6, 1997).

HONORS: Named Minor League co-Player of the Year by THE SPORTING NEWS (1988). ... Named Pacific Coast League Player of the Year (1988 and 1989). ... Named Minor League Player of the Year by THE SPORTING NEWS (1989). ... Named A.L. Rookie Player of the Year by THE SPORTING NEWS (1990). ... Won A.L. Gold Glove at catcher (1990). ... Named A.L. Rookie of the Year by Baseball Writers' Association of America (1990).

STATISTICAL NOTES: Led Northwest League catchers with .985 fielding percentage and 421 putouts in 1984. ... Led Pacific Coast League catchers with 14 errors in 1988. ... Led Pacific Coast League catchers with 573 putouts in 1988 and 702 in 1989. ... Led Pacific Coast League catchers with 633 total chances in 1988 and 761 in 1989. ... Had 30-game hitting streak (May 25-July 6, 1997). ... Career major league grand slams: 2.

MISCELLANEOUS: Batted as switch hitter (1984-86).

Year Team (League)	Pos.	G	AB	R	H	2B	3B	HR	RBI	Avg.	BB	SO	SB	PO	A	E	Avg.
1984— Spokane (N'West)	C-1B	59	219	13	47	5	0	0	21	.215	13	20	3	†465	51	8	†.985
1985— Charl., S.C. (S.Atl.).....	C-OF	100	352	38	73	7	0	3	43	.207	31	30	3	779	75	18	.979
1986— Beaumont (Texas)	C	100	346	36	83	15	1	4	27	.240	15	35	2	505	60	*18	.969
1987— Wichita (Texas)	C	103	375	50	115	19	1	8	65	.307	21	37	1	*606	50	*15	.978
1988— Las Vegas (PCL)	C-OF	93	337	59	100	9	5	16	71	.297	28	35	1	†574	46	†14	.978
— San Diego (N.L.)	PH	1	1	0	0	0	0	0	0	.000	0	1	0	...	...	...	...
1989— Las Vegas (PCL)	C-OF	131	*523	88	160	33	8	13	101	.306	42	58	3	†706	47	12	.984
— San Diego (N.L.)	C	7	19	1	4	1	0	1	6	.211	3	3	0	33	1	0	1.000
1990— Cleveland (A.L.)■......	C	132	445	60	129	26	2	9	66	.290	25	46	4	686	46	*14	.981
1991— Cleveland (A.L.)..........	C-DH	51	184	10	40	9	0	1	7	.217	8	24	0	280	19	4	.987
— Colo. Springs (PCL) ...	C	12	35	5	14	2	0	1	10	.400	5	0	0	5	0	1	.833
1992— Cleveland (A.L.)..........	C-DH	89	299	22	75	16	0	2	26	.251	13	32	3	477	39	2	.996
1993— Cleveland (A.L.)..........	C	64	215	24	58	7	1	6	32	.270	11	28	3	342	25	6	.984
— Charlotte (I.L.)...........	C	12	44	8	16	5	0	1	8	.364	5	8	0	20	1	0	1.000
1994— Cleveland (A.L.)..........	C	80	292	44	84	15	1	14	43	.288	25	31	8	453	41	2	.996
1995— Canton/Akron (East.)..	C-DH	6	15	3	6	1	0	0	1	.400	1	1	0	23	0	1	.958
— Cleveland (A.L.)..........	C	66	203	32	61	6	0	10	35	.300	7	26	3	364	22	2	.995
1996— Cleveland (A.L.)..........	C-1B	127	418	53	110	23	0	11	50	.263	19	42	1	724	48	9	.988
1997— Cleveland (A.L.)..........	C-DH	125	451	63	146	37	0	21	83	.324	19	48	0	743	40	*12	.985
1998— Cleveland (A.L.)..........	C-DH	117	409	45	96	26	2	6	44	.235	18	45	0	712	42	6	.992
1999— Cleveland (A.L.)..........	C-DH	37	137	19	42	13	0	6	25	.307	4	23	0	257	10	7	.974
— Akron (East.)	DH-C	10	29	8	9	0	0	1	6	.310	3	2	1	12	1	1	.929
— Buffalo (I.L.).............	C	10	33	9	9	2	1	2	10	.273	6	3	0	35	0	3	.921
2000— Cleveland (A.L.)..........	C-DH	97	356	44	103	16	2	7	42	.289	16	41	2	661	42	8	.989
2001— Chicago (A.L.)■........	C	70	220	17	54	8	1	4	21	.245	12	17	1	367	19	4	.990
American League totals (12 years)		1055	3629	433	998	202	9	96	474	.275	177	403	25	6066	393	76	.988
National League totals (2 years)		8	20	1	4	1	0	1	6	.200	3	4	0	33	1	0	1.000
Major League totals (14 years)		1063	3649	434	1002	203	9	97	480	.275	180	407	25	6099	394	76	.988

DIVISION SERIES RECORD

Year Team (League)	Pos.	G	AB	R	H	2B	3B	HR	RBI	Avg.	BB	SO	SB	PO	A	E	Avg.
1995— Cleveland (A.L.)..........	C	3	11	1	2	1	0	0	1	.182	0	1	0	22	1	0	1.000
1996— Cleveland (A.L.)..........	C	4	16	0	2	0	0	0	3	.125	0	2	0	40	4	1	.978
1997— Cleveland (A.L.)..........	C	5	19	4	6	1	0	2	5	.316	0	2	0	28	1	1	.967
1998— Cleveland (A.L.)..........	C	4	13	2	3	3	0	0	2	.231	1	4	0	29	0	1	.967
1999— Cleveland (A.L.)..........	C	5	14	1	2	0	0	0	1	.143	2	6	0	33	1	1	.971
Division series totals (5 years)		21	73	8	15	5	0	2	12	.205	3	15	0	152	7	4	.975

CHAMPIONSHIP SERIES RECORD

Year Team (League)	Pos.	G	AB	R	H	2B	3B	HR	RBI	Avg.	BB	SO	SB	PO	A	E	Avg.
1995— Cleveland (A.L.)..........	C	5	15	0	4	1	1	0	1	.267	1	1	0	30	3	1	.971
1997— Cleveland (A.L.)..........	C	6	24	3	3	0	0	1	4	.125	1	3	0	49	1	0	1.000
1998— Cleveland (A.L.)..........	C	5	16	1	1	0	0	0	0	.063	0	2	0	29	1	2	.938
Championship series totals (3 years)		16	55	4	8	1	1	1	5	.145	2	6	0	108	5	3	.974

WORLD SERIES RECORD

Year Team (League)	Pos.	G	AB	R	H	2B	3B	HR	RBI	Avg.	BB	SO	SB	PO	A	E	Avg.
1995— Cleveland (A.L.)..........	C	5	15	0	3	2	0	0	1	.200	0	2	0	28	0	0	1.000
1997— Cleveland (A.L.)..........	C	7	30	5	11	1	0	2	10	.367	2	3	0	49	3	0	1.000
World Series totals (2 years)		12	45	5	14	3	0	2	11	.311	2	5	0	77	3	0	1.000

ALL-STAR GAME RECORD

NOTES: Named Most Valuable Player (1997).

Year League	Pos.	AB	R	H	2B	3B	HR	RBI	Avg.	BB	SO	SB	PO	A	E	Avg.
1990— American	C	3	1	2	0	0	0	0	.667	0	0	0	3	0	0	1.000
1991— American	C	2	0	0	0	0	0	0	.000	0	0	0	2	0	0	1.000
1992— American	C	3	0	1	0	0	0	0	.333	0	0	0	3	0	0	1.000
1996— American	PH-C	2	0	0	0	0	0	0	.000	0	0	0	1	0	0	1.000
1997— American	C	1	1	1	0	0	1	2	1.000	0	0	0	4	0	0	1.000
1998— American	C	1	0	1	0	0	0	1	1.000	0	0	0	5	0	0	1.000
All-Star Game totals (6 years)		12	2	5	0	0	1	3	.417	0	0	0	18	0	0	1.000

PERSONAL: Born July 3, 1966, in Atlanta. ... 6-3/195. ... Bats right, throws right. ... Full name: Moises Rojas Alou. ... Son of Felipe Alou, manager, Montreal Expos (1992-2001) and major league outfielder with six teams (1958-1974); nephew of Jesus Alou, major league outfielder with four teams (1963-75 and 1978-79); nephew of Matty Alou, major league outfielder with six teams (1960-74); and cousin of Mel Rojas, pitcher with five major league teams (1990-99). ... Name pronounced moy-SEZZ ah-LOO.

HIGH SCHOOL: C.E.E. (Santo Domingo, Dominican Republic).

JUNIOR COLLEGE: Canada College (Calif.).

TRANSACTIONS/CAREER NOTES: Selected by Pittsburgh Pirates organization in first round (second pick overall) of free-agent draft (January 14, 1986). ... Traded by Pirates to Montreal Expos (August 16, 1990), completing deal in which Expos traded P Zane Smith to Pirates for P Scott Ruskin, SS Willie Greene and a player to be named later (August 8, 1990). ... On Montreal disabled list (March 19, 1991-entire season; July 7-27, 1992; September 18, 1993-remainder of season; August 18-September 5 and September 11, 1995-remainder of season). ... On disabled list (July 8-23, 1996). ... On suspended list (August 23-27, 1996). ... Granted free agency (December 7, 1996). ... Signed by Florida Marlins (December 12, 1996). ... Traded by Marlins to Houston Astros for P Oscar Henriquez, P Manuel Barrios and a player to be named later (November 11, 1997); Marlins acquired P Mark Johnson to complete deal (December 16, 1997). ... On disabled list (April 3, 1999-entire season; April 27-May 14, 2000; and March 29-April 16, 2001). ... Granted free agency (November 5, 2001). ... Signed by Chicago Cubs (December 19, 2001).

HONORS: Named outfielder on The Sporting News N.L. All-Star team (1994 and 1998). ... Named outfielder on The Sporting News N.L. Silver Slugger team (1994 and 1998).

STATISTICAL NOTES: Led American Association outfielders with seven double plays in 1990. ... Led N.L. in grounding into double plays with 21 in 2000. ... Had 23-game hitting streak (June 22-July 18, 2001). ... Career major league grand slams: 2.

Year Team (League)	Pos.	G	AB	R	H	2B	3B	HR	RBI	Avg.	BB	SO	SB	PO	A	E	Avg.
1986— Watertown (NY-Penn)	OF	69	254	30	60	9	*8	6	35	.236	22	72	14	134	6	7	.952
1987— Macon (S.Atl.)	OF	4	8	1	1	0	0	0	0	.125	2	4	0	6	0	0	1.000
— Watertown (NY-Penn)	OF	39	117	20	25	6	2	4	8	.214	16	36	6	43	1	2	.957
1988— Augusta (S.Atl.)	OF	105	358	58	112	23	5	7	62	.313	51	84	24	220	10	9	.962
1989— Salem (Caro.)	OF	86	321	50	97	29	2	14	53	.302	35	69	12	166	12	10	.947
— Harrisburg (East.)	OF	54	205	36	60	5	2	3	19	.293	17	38	8	89	1	2	.978
1990— Harrisburg (East.)	OF	36	132	19	39	12	2	3	22	.295	16	21	7	93	2	1	.990
— Buffalo (A.A.)	OF	75	271	38	74	4	6	5	31	.273	30	43	9	169	10	8	.957
— Pittsburgh (N.L.)	OF	2	5	0	1	0	0	0	0	.200	0	0	0	3	0	0	1.000
— Indianapolis (A.A.)■	OF	15	55	6	12	1	0	0	6	.218	3	7	4	27	2	0	1.000
— Montreal (N.L.)	OF	14	15	4	3	0	1	0	0	.200	0	3	0	6	1	0	1.000
1991— Montreal (N.L.)						Did not play.											
1992— Montreal (N.L.)	OF	115	341	53	96	28	2	9	56	.282	25	46	16	170	6	4	.978
1993— Montreal (N.L.)	OF	136	482	70	138	29	6	18	85	.286	38	53	17	254	11	4	.985
1994— Montreal (N.L.)	OF	107	422	81	143	31	5	22	78	.339	42	63	7	201	4	3	.986
1995— Montreal (N.L.)	OF	93	344	48	94	22	0	14	58	.273	29	56	4	147	5	3	.981
1996— Montreal (N.L.)	OF	143	540	87	152	28	2	21	96	.281	49	83	9	259	8	3	.989
1997— Florida (N.L.)■	OF	150	538	88	157	29	5	23	115	.292	70	85	9	248	4	3	.988
1998— Houston (N.L.)■	OF-DH	159	584	104	182	34	5	38	124	.312	84	87	11	232	11	5	.980
1999— Houston (N.L.)						Did not play.											
2000— Houston (N.L.)	OF-DH	126	454	82	161	28	2	30	114	.355	52	45	3	191	5	6	.970
2001— Houston (N.L.)	OF-DH	136	513	79	170	31	1	27	108	.331	57	57	5	205	10	2	.991
Major League totals (10 years)		1181	4238	696	1297	260	29	202	834	.306	446	578	81	1916	65	33	.984

DIVISION SERIES RECORD

Year Team (League)	Pos.	G	AB	R	H	2B	3B	HR	RBI	Avg.	BB	SO	SB	PO	A	E	Avg.
1997— Florida (N.L.)	OF	3	14	1	3	1	0	0	1	.214	0	3	0	5	0	0	1.000
1998— Houston (N.L.)	OF	4	16	0	3	0	0	0	0	.188	0	2	0	4	0	0	1.000
2001— Houston (N.L.)	OF	3	12	0	2	1	0	0	1	.167	0	1	0	5	0	0	1.000
Division series totals (3 years)		10	42	1	8	2	0	0	2	.190	0	6	0	14	0	0	1.000

CHAMPIONSHIP SERIES RECORD

Year Team (League)	Pos.	G	AB	R	H	2B	3B	HR	RBI	Avg.	BB	SO	SB	PO	A	E	Avg.
1997— Florida (N.L.)	OF-PH	5	15	0	1	1	0	0	5	.067	1	3	0	3	0	0	1.000

WORLD SERIES RECORD

NOTES: Member of World Series championship team (1997).

Year Team (League)	Pos.	G	AB	R	H	2B	3B	HR	RBI	Avg.	BB	SO	SB	PO	A	E	Avg.
1997— Florida (N.L.)	OF	7	28	6	9	2	0	3	9	.321	3	6	1	11	0	0	1.000

ALL-STAR GAME RECORD

Year League	Pos.	AB	R	H	2B	3B	HR	RBI	Avg.	BB	SO	SB	PO	A	E	Avg.
1994— National	OF	1	0	1	1	0	0	1	1.000	0	0	0	0	0	0	...
1997— National	OF	2	0	1	0	0	0	0	.500	0	0	0	1	0	0	1.000
1998— National	OF	3	1	1	0	0	0	0	.333	0	2	0	0	0	0	...
2001— National	OF	1	0	0	0	0	0	0	.000	0	1	0	1	0	0	1.000
All-Star Game totals (4 years)		7	1	3	1	0	0	1	.429	0	3	0	2	0	0	1.000

ALVAREZ, WILSON — P — DEVIL RAYS

PERSONAL: Born March 24, 1970, in Maracaibo, Venezuela. ... 6-1/245. ... Throws left, bats left. ... Full name: Wilson Eduardo Alvarez.

TRANSACTIONS/CAREER NOTES: Signed as non-drafted free agent by Texas Rangers organization (September 23, 1986). ... Traded by Rangers with IF Scott Fletcher and OF Sammy Sosa to Chicago White Sox for OF Harold Baines and IF Fred Manrique (July 29, 1989). ...

Traded by White Sox with P Danny Darwin and P Roberto Hernandez to San Francisco Giants for SS Michael Caruso, OF Brian Manning, P Lorenzo Barcelo, P Keith Foulke, P Bobby Howry and P Ken Vining (July 31, 1997). ... Granted free agency (November 1, 1997). ... Signed by Tampa Bay Devil Rays (December 3, 1997). ... On Tampa Bay disabled list (May 21-July 6, 1998); included rehabilitation assignments to Gulf Coast Devil Rays (June 26-29), St. Petersburg (June 30-July 4) and Durham (July 5-6). ... On disabled list (April 12-29 and July 24-August 8, 1999). ... On Tampa Bay disabled list (March 25, 2000-entire season); included rehabilitation assignment to St. Petersburg (April 15). ... On Tampa Bay disabled list (March 23, 2001-entire season); included to rehabilitation assignments to Orlando (June 9-18 and July 29-August 13) and Durham (June 19-July 3 and August 14-27).

RECORDS: Shares major league single-inning record for most strikeouts—4 (July 21, 1997, seventh inning).

STATISTICAL NOTES: Tied for Gulf Coast League lead with six home runs allowed in 1987. ... Pitched 7-0 no-hit victory for Chicago against Baltimore (August 11, 1991).

Year League	W	L	Pct.	ERA	G	GS	CG	ShO	Sv.	IP	H	R	ER	BB	SO
1987—Gastonia (S.Atl.)	1	5	.167	6.47	8	6	0	0	0	32	39	24	23	23	19
—Gulf Coast Rangers (GCL)	2	5	.286	5.24	10	10	0	0	0	44²/₃	41	29	26	21	46
1988—Gastonia (S.Atl.)	4	11	.267	2.98	23	23	1	0	0	127	113	63	42	49	134
—Oklahoma City (A.A.)	1	1	.500	3.78	5	3	0	0	0	16²/₃	17	8	7	6	9
1989—Charlotte (FSL)	7	4	.636	2.11	13	13	3	2	0	81	68	29	19	21	51
—Tulsa (Texas)	2	2	.500	2.06	7	7	1	1	0	48	40	14	11	16	29
—Texas (A.L.)	0	1	.000	...	1	1	0	0	0	3	3	3	2	0	5
—Birmingham (Sou.)■	2	1	.667	3.03	6	6	0	0	0	35²/₃	32	12	12	16	18
1990—Birmingham (Sou.)	5	1	.833	4.27	7	7	1	0	0	46¹/₃	44	24	22	25	36
—Vancouver (PCL)	7	7	.500	6.00	17	15	1	0	0	75	91	54	50	51	35
1991—Birmingham (Sou.)	10	6	.625	1.83	23	23	3	2	0	152¹/₃	109	46	31	74	165
—Chicago (A.L.)	3	2	.600	3.51	10	9	2	1	0	56¹/₃	47	26	22	29	32
1992—Chicago (A.L.)	5	3	.625	5.20	34	9	0	0	1	100¹/₃	103	64	58	65	66
1993—Chicago (A.L.)	15	8	.652	2.95	31	31	1	1	0	207²/₃	168	78	68	*122	155
—Nashville (A.A.)	0	1	.000	2.84	1	1	0	0	0	6¹/₃	7	7	2	2	8
1994—Chicago (A.L.)	12	8	.600	3.45	24	24	2	1	0	161²/₃	147	72	62	62	108
1995—Chicago (A.L.)	8	11	.421	4.32	29	29	3	0	0	175	171	96	84	93	118
1996—Chicago (A.L.)	15	10	.600	4.22	35	35	0	0	0	217¹/₃	216	106	102	97	181
1997—Chicago (A.L.)	9	8	.529	3.03	22	22	2	1	0	145²/₃	126	61	49	55	110
—San Francisco (N.L.)■	4	3	.571	4.48	11	11	0	0	0	66¹/₃	54	36	33	36	69
1998—Tampa Bay (A.L.)■	6	14	.300	4.73	25	25	0	0	0	142²/₃	130	78	75	68	107
—GC Devil Rays (GCL)	0	0	...	0.00	1	1	0	0	0	3	2	0	0	1	4
—St. Petersburg (FSL)	0	1	.000	27.00	1	1	0	0	0	1²/₃	5	5	5	2	2
—Durham (I.L.)	0	0	...	3.86	1	1	0	0	0	4²/₃	4	2	2	2	6
1999—Tampa Bay (A.L.)	9	9	.500	4.22	28	28	1	0	0	160	159	92	75	79	128
2000—St. Petersburg (FSL)	0	0	...	0.00	1	1	0	0	0	4	0	0	0	0	2
2001—Orlando (Sou.)	1	3	.250	4.43	5	5	0	0	0	20¹/₃	24	10	10	6	18
—Durham (I.L.)	1	1	.500	3.00	4	4	0	0	0	18	20	8	6	6	16
A.L. totals (10 years)	82	74	.526	3.94	239	213	11	4	1	1366²/₃	1270	676	598	672	1005
N.L. totals (1 year)	4	3	.571	4.48	11	11	0	0	0	66¹/₃	54	36	33	36	69
Major League totals (10 years)	86	77	.528	3.96	250	224	11	4	1	1433	1324	712	631	708	1074

DIVISION SERIES RECORD

Year League	W	L	Pct.	ERA	G	GS	CG	ShO	Sv.	IP	H	R	ER	BB	SO
1997—San Francisco (N.L.)	0	1	.000	6.00	1	1	0	0	0	6	6	4	4	4	4

CHAMPIONSHIP SERIES RECORD

Year League	W	L	Pct.	ERA	G	GS	CG	ShO	Sv.	IP	H	R	ER	BB	SO
1993—Chicago (A.L.)	1	0	1.000	1.00	1	1	1	0	0	9	7	1	1	2	6

ALL-STAR GAME RECORD

Year League	W	L	Pct.	ERA	GS	CG	ShO	Sv.	IP	H	R	ER	BB	SO
1994—American	0	0	...	0.00	0	0	0	0	1	0	0	0	0	0

AMEZAGA, ALFREDO   SS/2B   ANGELS

PERSONAL: Born January 16, 1978, in Obregon, Mexico. ... 5-10/165. ... Bats right, throws right.
HIGH SCHOOL: Miami Senior (Miami).
JUNIOR COLLEGE: St. Petersburg (Fla.).
TRANSACTIONS/CAREER NOTES: Selected by Anaheim Angels organization in 13th round of free-agent draft (June 2, 1999). ... On Arkansas disabled list (April 21-May 4, 2001).
STATISTICAL NOTES: Tied for Texas League lead with 15 caught stealing in 2001.

								BATTING						FIELDING		
Year Team (League)	Pos.	G	AB	R	H	2B	3B	HR	RBI	Avg.	BB	SO	SB	PO	A	E	Avg.
1999—Butte (Pio.)	2B-SS	8	34	11	10	2	0	0	5	.294	5	5	6	15	18	0	1.000
—Boise (N'West)	2B-SS	48	205	52	66	6	4	2	29	.322	23	29	14	101	144	12	.953
2000—Lake Elsinore (Calif.)	2B-SS	108	420	90	117	13	4	4	44	.279	63	70	73	218	323	22	.961
2001—Arkansas (Texas)	SS	70	285	50	89	10	5	4	21	.312	22	55	24	132	214	13	.964
—Salt Lake (PCL)	SS	49	200	28	50	5	4	1	16	.250	14	45	9	91	137	11	.954

ANDERSON, BRADY   OF   INDIANS

PERSONAL: Born January 18, 1964, in Silver Spring, Md. ... 6-1/202. ... Bats left, throws left. ... Full name: Brady Kevin Anderson.
HIGH SCHOOL: Carlsbad (Calif.).
COLLEGE: UC Irvine.
TRANSACTIONS/CAREER NOTES: Selected by Boston Red Sox organization in 10th round of free-agent draft (June 3, 1985). ... Traded by Red Sox with P Curt Schilling to Baltimore Orioles for P Mike Boddicker (July 29, 1988). ... On Baltimore disabled list (June 8-July 20, 1990); included rehabilitation assignments to Hagerstown (July 5-12) and Frederick (July 13-17). ... On Baltimore disabled list (May 28-June 14, 1991 and June 23-July 8, 1993). ... Granted free agency (October 27, 1997). ... Re-signed by Orioles (December 7, 1997). ... On disabled list (April 20-May 8, 1998). ... Released by Orioles (November 16, 2001). ... Signed by Cleveland Indians (December 6, 2001).

RECORDS: Holds major league single-season record for most home runs leading off game—12 (1996). ... Shares major league single-inning record for most times hit by pitch—2 (May 23, 1999, first inning).

STATISTICAL NOTES: Led A.L. outfielders with six double plays in 1992. ... Led A.L. in being hit by pitch with 22 in 1996, 19 in 1997 and 24 in 1999. ... Career major league grand slams: 3.

MISCELLANEOUS: Holds Baltimore Orioles all-time record for stolen bases (307).

Year Team (League)	Pos.	G	AB	R	H	2B	3B	HR	RBI	Avg.	BB	SO	SB	PO	A	E	Avg.
1985—Elmira (NY-Penn)	OF	71	215	36	55	7	•6	5	21	.256	*67	32	13	119	5	3	.976
1986—Winter Haven (FSL)	OF	126	417	86	133	19	11	12	87	.319	*107	47	44	280	5	1	*.997
1987—New Britain (East.)	OF	52	170	30	50	4	3	6	35	.294	45	24	7	127	2	2	.985
—Pawtucket (I.L.)	OF	23	79	18	30	4	0	2	8	.380	16	8	2	48	1	0	1.000
1988—Boston (A.L.)	OF	41	148	14	34	5	3	0	12	.230	15	35	4	87	3	1	.989
—Pawtucket (I.L.)	OF	49	167	27	48	6	1	4	19	.287	26	33	8	115	4	2	.983
—Baltimore (A.L.)■	OF	53	177	17	35	8	1	1	9	.198	8	40	6	156	1	3	.981
1989—Baltimore (A.L.)	OF-DH	94	266	44	55	12	2	4	16	.207	43	45	16	191	3	3	.985
—Rochester (I.L.)	OF	21	70	14	14	1	2	1	8	.200	12	13	2	1	0	0	1.000
1990—Baltimore (A.L.)	OF-DH	89	234	24	54	5	2	3	24	.231	31	46	15	149	3	2	.987
—Hagerstown (East.)	OF	9	34	8	13	0	2	1	5	.382	5	5	2	8	1	0	1.000
—Frederick (Caro.)	OF	2	7	2	3	1	0	0	3	.429	1	1	0	1	0	0	1.000
1991—Baltimore (A.L.)	OF-DH	113	256	40	59	12	3	2	27	.230	38	44	12	150	3	3	.981
—Rochester (I.L.)	OF	7	26	5	10	3	0	0	2	.385	7	4	4	19	1	0	1.000
1992—Baltimore (A.L.)	OF	159	623	100	169	28	10	21	80	.271	98	98	53	382	10	8	.980
1993—Baltimore (A.L.)	OF-DH	142	560	87	147	36	8	13	66	.263	82	99	24	296	7	2	.993
1994—Baltimore (A.L.)	OF	111	453	78	119	25	5	12	48	.263	57	75	31	247	4	1	.996
1995—Baltimore (A.L.)	OF	143	554	108	145	33	10	16	64	.262	87	111	26	268	1	3	.989
1996—Baltimore (A.L.)	OF-DH	149	579	117	172	37	5	50	110	.297	76	106	21	341	10	3	.992
1997—Baltimore (A.L.)	OF-DH	151	590	97	170	39	7	18	73	.288	84	105	18	276	2	3	.989
1998—Baltimore (A.L.)	OF-DH	133	479	84	113	28	3	18	51	.236	75	78	21	269	1	4	.985
1999—Baltimore (A.L.)	OF-DH	150	564	109	159	28	5	24	81	.282	96	105	36	308	3	1	.997
2000—Baltimore (A.L.)	OF-DH	141	506	89	130	26	0	19	50	.257	92	103	16	301	1	1	.997
2001—Baltimore (A.L.)	OF-DH	131	430	50	87	12	3	8	45	.202	60	77	12	239	8	3	.988
Major League totals (14 years)		**1800**	**6419**	**1058**	**1648**	**334**	**67**	**209**	**756**	**.257**	**942**	**1167**	**311**	**3660**	**60**	**41**	**.989**

NOTES: Hit home run in first at-bat (October 1, 1996).

DIVISION SERIES RECORD

Year Team (League)	Pos.	G	AB	R	H	2B	3B	HR	RBI	Avg.	BB	SO	SB	PO	A	E	Avg.
1996—Baltimore (A.L.)	OF	4	17	3	5	0	0	2	4	.294	2	3	0	7	0	0	1.000
1997—Baltimore (A.L.)	OF	4	17	3	6	1	0	1	4	.353	1	4	1	6	0	0	1.000
Division series totals (2 years)		**8**	**34**	**6**	**11**	**1**	**0**	**3**	**8**	**.324**	**3**	**7**	**1**	**13**	**0**	**0**	**1.000**

CHAMPIONSHIP SERIES RECORD

Year Team (League)	Pos.	G	AB	R	H	2B	3B	HR	RBI	Avg.	BB	SO	SB	PO	A	E	Avg.
1996—Baltimore (A.L.)	OF	5	21	5	4	1	0	1	1	.190	3	5	0	8	0	0	1.000
1997—Baltimore (A.L.)	OF	6	25	5	9	2	0	2	3	.360	4	4	2	13	0	1	.929
Championship series totals (2 years)		**11**	**46**	**10**	**13**	**3**	**0**	**3**	**4**	**.283**	**7**	**9**	**2**	**21**	**0**	**1**	**.955**

ALL-STAR GAME RECORD

Year League	Pos.	AB	R	H	2B	3B	HR	RBI	Avg.	BB	SO	SB	PO	A	E	Avg.
1992—American	OF	3	0	0	0	0	0	0	.000	0	0	0	1	0	0	1.000
1996—American	OF	2	0	0	0	0	0	0	.000	0	0	0	0	0	0	...
1997—American	OF	4	0	2	1	0	0	0	.500	0	0	0	1	0	0	1.000
All-Star Game totals (3 years)		**9**	**0**	**2**	**1**	**0**	**0**	**0**	**.222**	**0**	**0**	**0**	**2**	**0**	**0**	**1.000**

ANDERSON, BRIAN   P   DIAMONDBACKS

PERSONAL: Born April 26, 1972, in Geneva, Ohio. ... 6-1/183. ... Throws left, bats both. ... Full name: Brian James Anderson.

HIGH SCHOOL: Geneva (Ohio).

COLLEGE: Wright State.

TRANSACTIONS/CAREER NOTES: Selected by California Angels organization in first round (third pick overall) of free-agent draft (June 3, 1993). ... On California disabled list (May 7-June 7, 1994); included rehabilitation assignment to Lake Elsinore (May 27-June 7). ... On California disabled list (May 6-June 20, 1995); included rehabilitation assignment to Lake Elsinore (June 4-20). ... Traded by Angels to Cleveland Indians for P Jason Grimsley and P Pep Harris (February 15, 1996). ... On Cleveland disabled list (July 5-August 12, 1997); included rehabilitation assignment to Buffalo (August 3-13). ... Selected by Arizona Diamondbacks in first round (second pick overall) of expansion draft (November 18, 1997). ... On Arizona disabled list (April 12-May 2 and June 3-July 1, 2001); included rehabilitation assignments to Tuscon (April 27-May 2 and June 26-27).

RECORDS: Shares major league single-inning record for most home runs allowed—4 (September 5, 1995, second inning). ... Shares N.L. single-inning record for most consecutive home runs allowed—3 (July 22, 2001).

HONORS: Named A.L. Rookie Pitcher of the Year by THE SPORTING NEWS (1994).

STATISTICAL NOTES: Tied for A.L. lead with five balks in 1994 and three in 1995. ... Tied for American Association lead with three balks in 1996. ... Led N.L. with six balks and tied for lead with 39 home runs allowed in 1998.

MISCELLANEOUS: Scored one run in three appearances as pinch runner (1998). ... Scored a run in only appearance as pinch runner (1999). ... Walked and grounded into fielder's choice in two appearances as pinch hitter and scored one run in two appearances as pinch runner (2000). ... Appeared in one game as pinch hitter (2001). ... Appeared in three games as pinch runner (2001).

Year League	W	L	Pct.	ERA	G	GS	CG	ShO	Sv.	IP	H	R	ER	BB	SO
1993— Midland (Texas)	0	1	.000	3.38	2	2	0	0	0	10²/₃	16	5	4	0	9
— Vancouver (PCL)	0	1	.000	12.38	2	2	0	0	0	8	13	12	11	6	2
— California (A.L.)	0	0	...	3.97	4	1	0	0	0	11¹/₃	11	5	5	2	4
1994— California (A.L.)	7	5	.583	5.22	18	18	0	0	0	101²/₃	120	63	59	27	47
— Lake Elsinore (Calif.)	0	1	.000	3.00	2	2	0	0	0	12	6	4	4	0	9
1995— California (A.L.)	6	8	.429	5.87	18	17	1	0	0	99²/₃	110	66	65	30	45
— Lake Elsinore (Calif.)	1	1	.500	1.93	3	3	0	0	0	14	10	3	3	1	13
1996— Buffalo (A.A.)■	11	5	.688	3.59	19	19	2	0	0	128	125	57	51	28	85
— Cleveland (A.L.)	3	1	.750	4.91	10	9	0	0	0	51¹/₃	58	29	28	14	21
1997— Buffalo (A.A.)	7	1	.875	3.05	15	15	1	1	0	85²/₃	78	33	29	15	60
— Cleveland (A.L.)	4	2	.667	4.69	8	8	0	0	0	48	55	28	25	11	22
1998— Arizona (N.L.)■	12	13	.480	4.33	32	32	2	1	0	208	221	109	100	24	95
1999— Arizona (N.L.)	8	2	.800	4.57	31	19	2	1	1	130	144	69	66	28	75
— Tucson (PCL)	0	1	.000	5.40	2	2	0	0	0	6²/₃	9	5	4	1	8
2000— Arizona (N.L.)	11	7	.611	4.05	33	32	2	0	0	213¹/₃	226	101	96	39	104
2001— Arizona (N.L.)	4	9	.308	5.20	29	22	1	0	0	133¹/₃	156	93	77	30	55
— Tucson (PCL)	1	0	1.000	1.50	2	2	0	0	0	12	7	2	2	2	8
A.L. totals (5 years)	20	16	.556	5.25	58	53	1	0	0	312	354	191	182	84	139
N.L. totals (4 years)	35	31	.530	4.46	125	105	7	2	1	684²/₃	747	372	339	121	329
Major League totals (9 years)	55	47	.539	4.70	183	158	8	2	1	996²/₃	1101	563	521	205	468

DIVISION SERIES RECORD

Year League	W	L	Pct.	ERA	G	GS	CG	ShO	Sv.	IP	H	R	ER	BB	SO
1999— Arizona (N.L.)	0	0	...	2.57	1	1	0	0	0	7	7	2	2	0	4
2001— Arizona (N.L.)	0	0	...	2.25	2	0	0	0	0	4	3	1	1	0	3
Division series totals (2 years)	0	0	...	2.45	3	1	0	0	0	11	10	3	3	0	7

CHAMPIONSHIP SERIES RECORD

Year League	W	L	Pct.	ERA	G	GS	CG	ShO	Sv.	IP	H	R	ER	BB	SO
1997— Cleveland (A.L.)	1	0	1.000	1.42	3	0	0	0	0	6¹/₃	1	1	1	3	7
2001— Arizona (N.L.)	1	0	1.000	2.70	1	0	0	0	0	3¹/₃	4	1	1	1	0
Champ. series totals (2 years)	2	0	1.000	1.86	4	0	0	0	0	9²/₃	5	2	2	4	7

WORLD SERIES RECORD

NOTES: Member of World Series championship team (2001).

Year League	W	L	Pct.	ERA	G	GS	CG	ShO	Sv.	IP	H	R	ER	BB	SO
1997— Cleveland (A.L.)	0	0	...	2.45	3	0	0	0	1	3²/₃	2	1	1	0	2
2001— Arizona (N.L.)	0	1	.000	3.38	1	1	0	0	0	5¹/₃	5	2	2	3	1
World Series totals (2 years)	0	1	.000	3.00	4	1	0	0	1	9	7	3	3	3	3

ANDERSON, GARRET   OF   ANGELS

PERSONAL: Born June 30, 1972, in Los Angeles. ... 6-3/220. ... Bats left, throws left. ... Full name: Garret Joseph Anderson.
HIGH SCHOOL: John F. Kennedy (Granada Hills, Calif.).
TRANSACTIONS/CAREER NOTES: Selected by California Angels organization in fourth round of free-agent draft (June 4, 1990). ... Angels franchise renamed Anaheim Angels for 1997 season.
HONORS: Named A.L. Rookie Player of the Year by THE SPORTING NEWS (1995).
STATISTICAL NOTES: Collected six hits in one game (September 27, 1996). ... Had 28-game hitting streak (June 28-July 31, 1998). ... Had 16-game hitting streak (July 6-25, 1999). ... Had 17-game hitting streak (August 30-September 17, 1999). ... Career major league grand slams: 5.

Year Team (League)	Pos.	G	AB	R	H	2B	3B	HR	RBI	Avg.	BB	SO	SB	PO	A	E	Avg.
1990— Arizona Angels (Ariz.)	OF	32	127	5	27	2	0	0	14	.213	2	24	3	53	2	2	.965
— Boise (N'West)	OF	25	83	11	21	3	1	1	8	.253	4	18	0	38	0	2	.950
1991— Quad City (Midw.)	OF	105	392	40	102	22	2	2	42	.260	20	89	5	158	7	10	.943
1992— Palm Springs (Calif.)	OF	81	322	46	104	15	2	1	62	.323	21	61	1	137	4	6	.959
— Midland (Texas)	OF	39	146	16	40	5	0	2	19	.274	9	30	2	62	6	1	.986
1993— Vancouver (PCL)	OF-1B	124	467	57	137	34	4	4	71	.293	31	95	3	198	13	2	.991
1994— Vancouver (PCL)	OF-DH-1B	123	505	75	162	42	6	12	102	.321	28	93	3	196	10	2	.990
— California (A.L.)	OF	5	13	0	5	0	0	0	1	.385	0	2	0	10	0	0	1.000
1995— California (A.L.)	OF-DH	106	374	50	120	19	1	16	69	.321	19	65	6	213	7	5	.978
— Vancouver (PCL)	OF-DH	14	61	9	19	7	0	0	12	.311	5	14	0	22	0	1	.957
1996— California (A.L.)	OF-DH	150	607	79	173	33	2	12	72	.285	27	84	7	316	5	7	.979
1997— Anaheim (A.L.)	OF-DH	154	624	76	189	36	3	8	92	.303	30	70	10	343	14	3	.992
1998— Anaheim (A.L.)	OF	156	622	62	183	41	7	15	79	.294	29	80	8	326	11	6	.983
1999— Anaheim (A.L.)	OF-DH	157	620	88	188	36	2	21	80	.303	34	81	3	*406	7	3	.993
2000— Anaheim (A.L.)	OF-DH-1B	159	647	92	185	40	3	35	117	.286	24	87	7	380	5	4	.990
2001— Anaheim (A.L.)	OF-DH	161	672	83	194	39	2	28	123	.289	27	100	13	313	9	2	.994
Major League totals (8 years)		1048	4179	530	1237	244	20	135	633	.296	190	569	54	2307	58	30	.987

ANDERSON, JIMMY   P   PIRATES

PERSONAL: Born January 22, 1976, in Portsmouth, Va. ... 6-1/215. ... Throws left, bats left. ... Full name: James Drew Anderson Jr.
HIGH SCHOOL: Western Branch (Chesapeake, Va.).
TRANSACTIONS/CAREER NOTES: Selected by Pittsburgh Pirates organization in ninth round of free-agent draft (June 2, 1994). ... On disabled list (July 5-12, 1998).
STATISTICAL NOTES: Tied for Pacific Coast League lead with four balks in 1997.

Year	League	W	L	Pct.	ERA	G	GS	CG	ShO	Sv.	IP	H	R	ER	BB	SO
1994—	Gulf Coast Pirates (GCL)	5	1	.833	1.60	10	10	0	0	0	56 1/3	35	21	10	27	66
1995—	Augusta (S.Atl.)	4	2	.667	1.53	14	14	0	0	0	76 2/3	51	15	13	31	75
—	Lynchburg (Caro.)	1	5	.167	4.13	10	9	0	0	0	52 1/3	56	29	24	21	32
1996—	Lynchburg (Caro.)	5	3	.625	1.93	11	11	1	1	0	65 1/3	51	25	14	21	56
—	Carolina (Sou.)	8	5	.615	3.34	17	16	0	0	0	97	92	40	36	44	79
1997—	Carolina (Sou.)	2	1	.667	1.46	4	4	0	0	0	24 2/3	16	6	4	9	23
—	Calgary (PCL)	7	6	.538	5.68	21	21	0	0	0	103	124	78	65	64	71
1998—	Nashville (PCL)	9	10	.474	5.02	35	17	0	0	0	123 2/3	144	87	69	72	63
1999—	Nashville (PCL)	11	2	*.846	3.84	21	21	1	0	0	133 2/3	153	67	57	41	93
—	Pittsburgh (N.L.)	2	1	.667	3.99	13	4	0	0	0	29 1/3	25	15	13	16	13
2000—	Nashville (PCL)	0	0	...	4.15	2	2	0	0	0	13	18	6	6	4	7
—	Pittsburgh (N.L.)	5	11	.313	5.25	27	26	1	0	0	144	169	94	84	58	73
—	Altoona (East.)	1	0	1.000	0.00	1	1	1	0	0	9	7	1	0	1	6
2001—	Pittsburgh (N.L.)	9	17	.346	5.10	34	34	1	0	0	206 1/3	232	123	117	83	89
Major League totals (3 years)		16	29	.356	5.07	74	64	2	0	0	379 2/3	426	232	214	157	175

ANDERSON, MARLON — 2B — PHILLIES

PERSONAL: Born January 6, 1974, in Montgomery, Ala. ... 5-11/198. ... Bats left, throws right. ... Full name: Marlon Ordell Anderson.
HIGH SCHOOL: Prattville (Ala.).
COLLEGE: South Alabama.
TRANSACTIONS/CAREER NOTES: Selected by Philadelphia Phillies organization in second round of free-agent draft (June 1, 1995); choice received from St. Louis Cardinals as part of compensation for Cardinals signing Type A free-agent P Danny Jackson.
STATISTICAL NOTES: Led New York-Pennsylvania League second basemen with 398 total chances and 67 double plays in 1995. ... Led Eastern League with 748 total chances in 1997. ... Hit home run in first major league at-bat (September 8, 1998). ... Led International League second basemen with 681 total chances in 1998. ... Led International League in intentional bases on balls received with 12 in 2000.

							BATTING								FIELDING		
Year	Team (League)	Pos.	G	AB	R	H	2B	3B	HR	RBI	Avg.	BB	SO	SB	PO	A	E	Avg.
1995—	Batavia (NY-Penn)	2B	74	*312	52	92	13	4	3	40	.295	15	20	22	*153	*231	14	*.965
1996—	Clearwater (FSL)	2B	60	257	37	70	10	3	2	22	.272	14	18	26	142	221	16	.958
—	Reading (East.)	2B	75	314	38	86	14	3	3	28	.274	26	44	17	166	239	18	.957
1997—	Reading (East.)	2B	137	*553	88	147	18	6	10	62	.266	42	77	27	*323	*396	*29	.961
1998—	Scranton/W.B. (I.L.) ...	2B	136	575	104	*176	32	*14	16	86	.306	28	77	24	262	391	28	.959
—	Philadelphia (N.L.).....	2B	17	43	4	14	3	0	1	4	.326	1	6	2	14	30	1	.978
1999—	Philadelphia (N.L.).....	2B	129	452	48	114	26	4	5	54	.252	24	61	13	234	284	11	.979
2000—	Scranton/W.B. (I.L.) ...	2B	103	397	57	121	18	8	8	53	.305	39	43	24	167	269	•14	.969
—	Philadelphia (N.L.).....	2B	41	162	10	37	8	1	1	15	.228	12	22	2	87	100	2	.989
2001—	Philadelphia (N.L.).....	2B	147	522	69	153	30	2	11	61	.293	35	74	8	270	387	12	.982
Major League totals (4 years)			334	1179	131	318	67	7	18	134	.270	72	163	25	605	801	26	.982

ANDERSON, MATT — P — TIGERS

PERSONAL: Born August 17, 1976, in Louisville, Ky. ... 6-4/200. ... Throws right, bats right. ... Full name: Matthew Jason Anderson.
HIGH SCHOOL: St. Xavier (Louisville, Ky.).
COLLEGE: Rice.
TRANSACTIONS/CAREER NOTES: Selected by Detroit Tigers organization in first round (first pick overall) of free-agent draft (June 3, 1997).

Year	League	W	L	Pct.	ERA	G	GS	CG	ShO	Sv.	IP	H	R	ER	BB	SO
1998—	Lakeland (FSL)	1	0	1.000	0.69	17	0	0	0	3	26	18	4	2	8	34
—	Jacksonville (Sou.)	1	0	1.000	0.60	13	0	0	0	10	15	7	1	1	5	11
—	Detroit (A.L.)	5	1	.833	3.27	42	0	0	0	0	44	38	16	16	31	44
1999—	Detroit (A.L.)	2	1	.667	5.68	37	0	0	0	0	38	33	27	24	35	32
—	Toledo (I.L.)	0	4	.000	6.39	24	4	0	0	5	38	32	27	27	31	35
2000—	Detroit (A.L.)	3	2	.600	4.72	69	0	0	0	1	74 1/3	61	44	39	45	71
2001—	Detroit (A.L.)	3	1	.750	4.82	62	0	0	0	22	56	56	33	30	18	52
Major League totals (4 years)		13	5	.722	4.62	210	0	0	0	23	212 1/3	188	120	109	129	199

ANDERSON, RYAN — P — MARINERS

PERSONAL: Born July 12, 1979, in Southfield, Mich. ... 6-10/225. ... Throws left, bats left. ... Full name: Ryan York Anderson.
HIGH SCHOOL: Divine Child (Dearborn, Mich.).
TRANSACTIONS/CAREER NOTES: Selected by Seattle Mariners organization in first round (19th pick overall) of free-agent draft (June 3, 1997). ... On disabled list (May 4-11 and July 20, 2000-remainder of season). ... On disabled list (April 5, 2001-entire season).

Year	League	W	L	Pct.	ERA	G	GS	CG	ShO	Sv.	IP	H	R	ER	BB	SO
1998—	Wisconsin (Midw.)	6	5	.545	3.23	22	22	0	0	0	111 1/3	86	47	40	67	152
1999—	New Haven (East.)	9	13	.409	4.50	24	24	0	0	0	134	131	77	67	86	*162
2000—	Tacoma (PCL)	5	8	.385	3.98	20	20	1	1	0	104	83	51	46	55	146
2001—	San Antonio (Texas)									Did not play.						

ANDERSON, WES — P — MARLINS

PERSONAL: Born September 10, 1979, in Pine Bluff, Ark. ... 6-4/175. ... Throws right, bats right. ... Full name: Wesley Patrick Anderson.
HIGH SCHOOL: Pine Bluff (Ark.).
TRANSACTIONS/CAREER NOTES: Selected by Florida Marlins organization in 14th round of free-agent draft (June 3, 1997). ... On Portland disabled list (May 20-June 22, 2000). ... On Brevard County disabled list (May 12-July 12 and July 14, 2001-remainder of season).

Year League	W	L	Pct.	ERA	G	GS	CG	ShO	Sv.	IP	H	R	ER	BB	SO
1998—Gulf Coast Marlins (GCL) ...	5	2	.714	*1.39	11	11	•1	•1	0	64²/₃	44	25	10	18	66
1999—Kane County (Midw.).........	9	5	.643	3.21	23	23	2	1	0	137¹/₃	111	55	49	51	134
2000—Brevard County (FSL)........	6	9	.400	3.42	22	21	0	0	0	115²/₃	108	55	44	66	91
2001—Brevard County (FSL)........	1	6	.143	5.63	8	8	0	0	0	32	48	26	20	21	17
—Gulf Coast Marlins (GCL) ...	0	1	.000	27.00	1	1	0	0	0	¹/₃	3	2	1	1	0

A

ANKIEL, RICK   P   CARDINALS

PERSONAL: Born July 19, 1979, in Fort Pierce, Fla. ... 6-1/210. ... Throws left, bats left. ... Full name: Richard Alexander Ankiel.
HIGH SCHOOL: Port St. Lucie (Fla.).
TRANSACTIONS/CAREER NOTES: Selected by St. Louis Cardinals organization in second round of free-agent draft (June 3, 1997).
HONORS: Named Carolina League Pitcher of the Year (1998). ... Named Minor League Player of the Year by THE SPORTING NEWS (1999). ... Named N.L. Rookie Pitcher of the Year by THE SPORTING NEWS (2000). ... Named Appalachian League Pitcher of the Year (2001).
MISCELLANEOUS: Appeared in one game as pinch runner (2000). ... Struck out three times in three appearances as pinch hitter (2000).

Year League	W	L	Pct.	ERA	G	GS	CG	ShO	Sv.	IP	H	R	ER	BB	SO
1998—Peoria (Midw.)...................	3	0	1.000	2.06	7	7	0	0	0	35	15	8	8	12	41
—Prince William (Caro.)........	9	6	.600	2.79	21	21	1	0	0	126	91	46	39	38	181
1999—Arkansas (Texas)................	6	0	1.000	0.91	8	8	1	•1	0	49¹/₃	25	6	5	16	75
—Memphis (PCL)...................	7	3	.700	3.16	16	16	0	0	0	88¹/₃	73	37	31	46	119
—St. Louis (N.L.)...................	0	1	.000	3.27	9	5	0	0	1	33	26	12	12	14	39
2000—St. Louis (N.L.).................	11	7	.611	3.50	31	30	0	0	0	175	137	80	68	90	194
2001—St. Louis (N.L.).................	1	2	.333	7.13	6	6	0	0	0	24	25	21	19	25	27
—Memphis (PCL)...................	0	2	.000	20.77	3	3	0	0	0	4¹/₃	3	10	10	17	4
—Johnson City (Appl.)	5	3	.625	1.33	14	•14	1	0	0	*87²/₃	42	20	13	18	*158
Major League totals (3 years).......	12	10	.545	3.84	46	41	0	0	1	232	188	113	99	129	260

DIVISION SERIES RECORD

Year League	W	L	Pct.	ERA	G	GS	CG	ShO	Sv.	IP	H	R	ER	BB	SO
2000—St. Louis (N.L.).................	0	0	...	13.50	1	1	0	0	0	2²/₃	4	4	4	6	3

CHAMPIONSHIP SERIES RECORD

RECORDS: Shares career record for most wild pitches—4. ... Shares single-inning record for most wild pitches—2 (October 12, 2000, first inning and October 16, 2000, seventh inning).

Year League	W	L	Pct.	ERA	G	GS	CG	ShO	Sv.	IP	H	R	ER	BB	SO
2000—St. Louis (N.L.).................	0	0	...	20.25	2	1	0	0	0	1¹/₃	1	3	3	5	2

RECORD AS POSITION PLAYER

Year Team (League)	Pos.	G	AB	R	H	2B	3B	HR	RBI	Avg.	BB	SO	SB	PO	A	E	Avg.
							BATTING								FIELDING		
2001—Johnson City (Appl.) ..	DH	41	105	21	30	7	0	10	35	.286	11	26	0	...	...	...	...

APPIER, KEVIN   P   ANGELS

PERSONAL: Born December 6, 1967, in Lancaster, Calif. ... 6-2/200. ... Throws right, bats right. ... Full name: Robert Kevin Appier. ... Name pronounced APE-ee-er.
HIGH SCHOOL: Antelope Valley (Lancaster, Calif.).
JUNIOR COLLEGE: Antelope Valley College (Calif.).
COLLEGE: Fresno State.
TRANSACTIONS/CAREER NOTES: Selected by Kansas City Royals organization in first round (ninth pick overall) of free-agent draft (June 2, 1987). ... On disabled list (July 26-August 12, 1995). ... On Kansas City disabled list (March 20-September 1, 1998); included rehabilitation assignments to Gulf Coast Royals (July 16-21), Lansing (July 22-26), Wichita (July 27-30) and Omaha (July 31-August 27). ... Traded by Royals to Oakland Athletics for P Blake Stein, P Jeff D'Amico, and P Brad Rigby (July 31, 1999). ... On disabled list (April 25-May 13, 2000). ... Granted free agency (October 31, 2000). ... Signed by New York Mets (December 11, 2000). ... Traded by Mets to Anaheim Angels for 1B Mo Vaughn (December 27, 2001).
RECORDS: Shares major league record for most strikeouts in one inning—4 (September 3, 1996, fourth inning).
HONORS: Named A.L. Rookie Pitcher of the Year by THE SPORTING NEWS (1990).
STATISTICAL NOTES: Pitched 4-0 one-hit, complete-game victory for Kansas City against Detroit (July 7, 1990). ... Pitched 1-0 one-hit, complete-game loss against Texas (July 27, 1993). ... Tied for A.L. lead with 14 wild pitches in 1997.
MISCELLANEOUS: Holds Kansas City Royals all-time record for strikeouts (1,451).

Year League	W	L	Pct.	ERA	G	GS	CG	ShO	Sv.	IP	H	R	ER	BB	SO
1987—Eugene (N'West)	5	2	.714	3.04	15	•15	0	0	0	77	81	43	26	29	72
1988—Baseball City (FSL)	10	9	.526	2.75	24	24	1	0	0	147¹/₃	134	58	45	39	112
—Memphis (Sou.)..................	2	0	1.000	1.83	3	3	0	0	0	19²/₃	11	5	4	7	18
1989—Omaha (A.A.).....................	8	8	.500	3.95	22	22	3	2	0	139	141	70	61	42	109
—Kansas City (A.L.)	1	4	.200	9.14	6	5	0	0	0	21²/₃	34	22	22	12	10
1990—Omaha (A.A.)	2	0	1.000	1.50	3	3	0	0	0	18	15	3	3	3	17
—Kansas City (A.L.)	12	8	.600	2.76	32	24	3	3	0	185²/₃	179	67	57	54	127
1991—Kansas City (A.L.)	13	10	.565	3.42	34	31	6	3	0	207²/₃	205	97	79	61	158
1992—Kansas City (A.L.)	15	8	.652	2.46	30	30	3	0	0	208¹/₃	167	59	57	68	150
1993—Kansas City (A.L.)	18	8	.692	*2.56	34	34	5	1	0	238²/₃	183	74	68	81	186
1994—Kansas City (A.L.)	7	6	.538	3.83	23	23	1	0	0	155	137	68	66	63	145
1995—Kansas City (A.L.)	15	10	.600	3.89	31	31	4	1	0	201¹/₃	163	90	87	80	185
1996—Kansas City (A.L.)	14	11	.560	3.62	32	32	5	1	0	211¹/₃	192	87	85	75	207
1997—Kansas City (A.L.)	9	13	.409	3.40	34	34	4	1	0	235²/₃	215	96	89	74	196
1998—Gulf Coast Royals (GCL)	0	1	.000	2.70	1	1	0	0	0	3¹/₃	3	3	1	1	2
—Lansing (Midw.)	0	0	...	2.25	1	1	0	0	0	4	4	1	1	0	5
—Wichita (Texas)	0	1	.000	6.00	1	1	0	0	0	6	8	4	4	2	1
—Omaha (PCL)	3	2	.600	7.03	6	6	0	0	0	32	41	25	25	12	22
—Kansas City (A.L.)	1	2	.333	7.80	3	3	0	0	0	15	21	13	13	5	9

A

Year	League	W	L	Pct.	ERA	G	GS	CG	ShO	Sv.	IP	H	R	ER	BB	SO
1999—	Kansas City (A.L.)	9	9	.500	4.87	22	22	1	0	0	140 1/3	153	81	76	51	78
	—Oakland (A.L.)■	7	5	.583	5.77	12	12	0	0	0	68 2/3	77	50	44	33	53
2000—	Oakland (A.L.)	15	11	.577	4.52	31	31	1	1	0	195 1/3	200	109	98	*102	129
2001—	New York (N.L.)■	11	10	.524	3.57	33	33	1	1	0	206 2/3	181	89	82	64	172
A.L. totals (12 years)		136	105	.564	3.63	324	312	33	11	0	2084 2/3	1926	913	841	759	1633
N.L. totals (1 year)		11	10	.524	3.57	33	33	1	1	0	206 2/3	181	89	82	64	172
Major League totals (13 years)		147	115	.561	3.63	357	345	34	12	0	2291 1/3	2107	1002	923	823	1805

DIVISION SERIES RECORD

Year	League	W	L	Pct.	ERA	G	GS	CG	ShO	Sv.	IP	H	R	ER	BB	SO
2000—	Oakland (A.L.)	0	1	.000	3.48	2	1	0	0	0	10 1/3	10	4	4	6	13

ALL-STAR GAME RECORD

Year	League	W	L	Pct.	ERA	GS	CG	ShO	Sv.	IP	H	R	ER	BB	SO
1995—	American	0	0	...	0.00	0	0	0	0	2	0	0	0	0	1

ARAMBOLES, RICARDO — P — REDS

PERSONAL: Born December 4, 1981, in Santo Domingo, Dominican Republic. ... 6-2/170. ... Throws right, bats right. ... Full name: Ricardo B. Aramboles.

TRANSACTIONS/CAREER NOTES: Signed as non-drafted free agent by Florida Marlins organization (July 2, 1996). ... Declared free agent by Major League Baseball (July 3, 1997). ... Signed by New York Yankees organization (February 26, 1998). ... On disabled list (April-June 1999). ... Traded by Yankees to Cincinnati Reds for P Mark Wohlers (June 30, 2001). ... On Dayton disabled list (July 31, 2001-remainder of season).

Year	League	W	L	Pct.	ERA	G	GS	CG	ShO	Sv.	IP	H	R	ER	BB	SO
1997—	Dominican Marlins (DSL)...	1	1	.500	1.71	8	2	0	0	0	21	15	7	4	7	14
1998—	GC Yankees (GCL)■	2	1	.667	2.92	10	9	0	0	0	40	33	14	13	13	44
	—Oneonta (NY-Penn)	1	0	1.000	1.50	1	1	0	0	0	6	4	2	1	1	8
1999—	Gulf Coast Yankees (GCL) ..	2	3	.400	3.89	9	7	0	0	0	34 2/3	35	18	15	14	42
	—Greensboro (S.Atl.)	1	2	.333	2.34	6	6	1	0	0	34 2/3	25	9	9	12	34
2000—	Greensboro (S.Atl.)	5	13	.278	4.31	25	25	2	0	0	137 2/3	150	81	66	47	150
2001—	Tampa (FSL)....................	7	2	.778	4.06	12	11	0	0	0	68 2/3	72	37	31	19	59
	—Columbus (I.L.)	1	3	.250	3.04	4	4	0	0	0	23 2/3	26	11	8	4	14
	—Chattanooga (Sou.)■	0	2	.000	8.00	2	1	0	0	0	9	12	8	8	0	5
	—Dayton (Midw.)	1	2	.333	3.66	4	4	0	0	0	19 2/3	23	8	8	4	9

ARIAS, ALEX — SS — MARINERS

PERSONAL: Born November 20, 1967, in New York. ... 6-3/202. ... Bats right, throws right. ... Full name: Alejandro Arias. ... Name pronounced air-REE-ahs.

HIGH SCHOOL: George Washington (New York).

TRANSACTIONS/CAREER NOTES: Selected by Chicago Cubs organization in third round of free-agent draft (June 2, 1987). ... Traded by Cubs with 3B Gary Scott to Florida Marlins for P Greg Hibbard (November 17, 1992). ... On disabled list (June 14-July 2, 1997). ... Released by Marlins (December 12, 1997). ... Signed by Philadelphia Phillies (December 26, 1997). ... Granted free agency (October 30, 2000). ... Signed by San Diego Padres (December 13, 2000). ... On disabled list (August 20-September 4, 2001). ... Traded by Padres for with C Ben Davis and P Wascar Serrano to Seattle Mariners for P Brett Tomko, C Tom Lampkin and SS Ramon Vazquez (December 11, 2001).

STATISTICAL NOTES: Led Midwest League shortstops with 655 total chances and 83 double plays in 1989. ... Led Southern League shortstops with 583 total chances and 81 double plays in 1991.

Year	Team (League)	Pos.	G	AB	R	H	2B	3B	HR	RBI	Avg.	BB	SO	SB	PO	A	E	Avg.
1987—	Wytheville (Appl.).......	SS-3B	61	233	41	69	7	0	0	24	.296	27	29	16	77	141	16	.932
1988—	Charl., W.Va. (S.Atl.) ..	SS-3B-2B	127	472	57	122	12	1	0	33	.258	54	44	41	184	396	32	.948
1989—	Peoria (Midw.)...........	SS	*136	506	74	140	10	*11	2	64	.277	49	67	31	*210	*408	37	.944
1990—	Charlotte (Sou.).........	SS	119	419	55	103	16	3	4	38	.246	42	53	12	171	284	*42	.915
1991—	Charlotte (Sou.).........	SS	134	488	69	134	26	0	4	47	.275	47	42	23	*203	*351	29	*.950
1992—	Iowa (A.A.)................	SS-2B	106	409	52	114	23	3	5	40	.279	44	27	14	183	290	14	.971
	—Chicago (N.L.)..........	SS	32	99	14	29	6	0	0	7	.293	11	13	0	43	74	4	.967
1993—	Florida (N.L.)■..........	2B-SS	96	249	27	67	5	1	2	20	.269	27	18	1	94	144	6	.975
1994—	Florida (N.L.)............	SS-3B	59	113	4	27	5	0	0	15	.239	9	19	0	37	51	2	.978
1995—	Florida (N.L.)............	SS-3B-2B	94	216	22	58	9	2	3	26	.269	22	20	1	57	127	9	.953
1996—	Florida (N.L.)............	3-S-1-2	100	224	27	62	11	2	3	26	.277	17	28	2	48	127	7	.962
1997—	Florida (N.L.)............	3B-SS	74	93	13	23	2	0	1	11	.247	12	12	0	26	38	2	.970
1998—	Philadelphia (N.L.)■...	SS-3B-2B	56	133	17	39	8	0	1	16	.293	13	18	2	43	88	2	.985
1999—	Philadelphia (N.L.)......	SS-3B-2B	118	347	43	105	20	1	4	48	.303	36	31	2	120	208	4	.988
2000—	Philadelphia (N.L.)......	SS-3B-2B	70	155	17	29	9	0	2	15	.187	16	28	1	45	98	5	.966
2001—	San Diego (N.L.)■ 3B-1B-2B-SS		70	137	19	31	9	0	2	12	.226	17	22	1	132	61	5	.975
Major League totals (10 years)			769	1766	203	470	84	6	18	196	.266	180	209	10	645	1016	46	.973

DIVISION SERIES RECORD

Year	Team (League)	Pos.	G	AB	R	H	2B	3B	HR	RBI	Avg.	BB	SO	SB	PO	A	E	Avg.
1997—	Florida (N.L.)	PH	1	1	0	1	0	0	0	1	1.000	0	0	0	...	...	...	...

CHAMPIONSHIP SERIES RECORD

Year	Team (League)	Pos.	G	AB	R	H	2B	3B	HR	RBI	Avg.	BB	SO	SB	PO	A	E	Avg.
1997—	Florida (N.L.)	3B-PH	3	1	0	1	0	0	0	0	1.000	0	0	0	0	0	0	...

WORLD SERIES RECORD

NOTES: Member of World Series championship team (1997).

Year	Team (League)	Pos.	G	AB	R	H	2B	3B	HR	RBI	Avg.	BB	SO	SB	PO	A	E	Avg.
1997—	Florida (N.L.)	3B-PR	2	1	1	0	0	0	0	0	.000	0	0	0	0	0	0	...

ARMAS, TONY   P   EXPOS

PERSONAL: Born April 29, 1978, in Puerto Piritu, Venezuela. ... 6-4/205. ... Throws right, bats right. ... Full name: Antonio Jose Armas Jr. ... Son of Tony Armas, outfielder with four major league teams (1976-89).

TRANSACTIONS/CAREER NOTES: Signed as non-drafted free agent by New York Yankees organization (August 16, 1994). ... Traded by Yankees with a player to be named later to Boston Red Sox for C Mike Stanley and SS Randy Brown (August 13, 1997); Red Sox acquired P Jim Mecir to complete deal (September 29, 1997). ... Traded by Red Sox to Montreal Expos (December 18, 1997), completing deal in which Red Sox traded P Carl Pavano and a player to be named later to Expos for P Pedro Martinez (November 18, 1997). ... On Montreal disabled list (April 1-28 and July 19-September 6, 2000); included rehabilitation assignments to Jupiter (April 22-28) and Ottawa (August 27-September 4).

Year League	W	L	Pct.	ERA	G	GS	CG	ShO	Sv.	IP	H	R	ER	BB	SO
1995—Gulf Coast Yankees (GCL)..	0	1	.000	0.64	5	4	0	0	0	14	12	9	1	6	13
1996—Oneonta (NY-Penn)	1	1	.500	5.74	3	3	0	0	0	15 2/3	14	12	10	11	14
—Gulf Coast Yankees (GCL)..	4	1	.800	3.15	8	7	0	0	1	45 2/3	41	18	16	13	45
1997—Greensboro (S.Atl.)	5	2	.714	1.05	9	9	2	1	0	51 2/3	36	13	6	13	64
—Tampa (FSL)	3	1	.750	3.33	9	9	0	0	0	46	43	23	17	16	26
—Sarasota (FSL)■	2	1	.667	6.62	3	3	0	0	0	17 2/3	18	13	13	12	9
1998—Jupiter (FSL)■	12	8	.600	2.88	27	27	1	1	0	153 1/3	140	63	49	59	136
1999—Harrisburg (East.)	9	7	.563	2.89	24	24	2	1	0	149 2/3	123	62	48	55	106
—Montreal (N.L.)	0	1	.000	1.50	1	1	0	0	0	6	8	4	1	2	2
2000—Jupiter (FSL)	0	0	...	0.00	1	1	0	0	0	4 2/3	4	0	0	0	8
—Ottawa (I.L.)	1	2	.333	3.79	4	4	0	0	0	19	22	11	8	4	12
—Montreal (N.L.)	7	9	.438	4.36	17	17	0	0	0	95	74	49	46	50	59
2001—Montreal (N.L.)	9	14	.391	4.03	34	34	0	0	0	196 2/3	180	101	88	91	176
Major League totals (3 years)	16	24	.400	4.08	52	52	0	0	0	297 2/3	262	154	135	143	237

ARROJO, ROLANDO   P   RED SOX

PERSONAL: Born July 18, 1968, in Havana, Cuba. ... 6-4/220. ... Throws right, bats right. ... Full name: Luis Rolando Arrojo.

TRANSACTIONS/CAREER NOTES: Signed as non-drafted free agent by Tampa Bay Devil Rays organization (April 21, 1997). ... On disabled list (September 21, 1998-remainder of season). ... On Tampa Bay disabled list (May 25-July 15, 1999); included rehabilitation assignment to St. Petersburg (July 2-15). ... Traded by Devil Rays with IF Aaron Ledesma to Colorado Rockies for 3B Vinny Castilla (December 13, 1999). ... On Colorado disabled list (April 21-May 6, 2000). ... Traded by Rockies with P Rick Croushore, 2B Mike Lansing and cash to Boston Red Sox for P Brian Rose, P John Wasdin, P Jeff Taglienti and 2B Jeff Frye (July 27, 2000). ... On Boston disabled list (August 13-September 2, 2001); included rehabilitation assignment to Sarasota (August 27-September 2).

HONORS: Named A.L. Rookie Pitcher of the Year by THE SPORTING NEWS (1998).

STATISTICAL NOTES: Led A.L. with 19 hit batsmen in 1998.

MISCELLANEOUS: Member of Cuban national baseball team (1986-96). ... Shares Tampa Bay Devil Rays all-time record for most shutouts (2).

Year League	W	L	Pct.	ERA	G	GS	CG	ShO	Sv.	IP	H	R	ER	BB	SO
1997—St. Petersburg (FSL)	5	6	.455	3.43	16	16	4	1	0	89 1/3	73	40	34	13	73
1998—Tampa Bay (A.L.)	14	12	.538	3.56	32	32	2	2	0	202	195	84	80	65	152
1999—Tampa Bay (A.L.)	7	12	.368	5.18	24	24	2	0	0	140 2/3	162	84	81	60	107
—St. Petersburg (FSL)	0	1	.000	4.50	2	2	0	0	0	10	11	6	5	1	10
2000—Colorado (N.L.)■	5	9	.357	6.04	19	19	0	0	0	101 1/3	120	77	68	46	80
—Boston (A.L.)■	5	2	.714	5.05	13	13	0	0	0	71 1/3	67	41	40	22	44
2001—Boston (A.L.)	5	4	.556	3.48	41	9	0	0	5	103 1/3	88	44	40	35	78
—Sarasota (FSL)	0	1	.000	6.00	2	2	0	0	0	3	4	2	2	1	5
A.L. totals (4 years)	31	30	.508	4.19	110	78	4	2	5	517 1/3	512	253	241	182	381
N.L. totals (1 year)	5	9	.357	6.04	19	19	0	0	0	101 1/3	120	77	68	46	80
Major League totals (4 years)	36	39	.480	4.50	129	97	4	2	5	618 2/3	632	330	309	228	461

ALL-STAR GAME RECORD

Year League	W	L	Pct.	ERA	GS	CG	ShO	Sv.	IP	H	R	ER	BB	SO
1998—American	0	0	...	0.00	0	0	0	0	1	2	0	0	0	1

ARROYO, BRONSON   P   PIRATES

PERSONAL: Born February 24, 1977, in Key West, Fla. ... 6-5/181. ... Throws right, bats right. ... Full name: Bronson Anthony Arroyo.

HIGH SCHOOL: Hernando (Fla.).

TRANSACTIONS/CAREER NOTES: Selected by Pittsburgh Pirates organization in third round of free-agent draft (June 1, 1995). ... On suspended list (May 29-June 1, 1996). ... On disabled list (May 18-June 7 and June 18-July 4, 1998).

MISCELLANEOUS: Appeared in one game as pinch runner and grounded out in only appearance as pinch hitter (2000).

Year League	W	L	Pct.	ERA	G	GS	CG	ShO	Sv.	IP	H	R	ER	BB	SO
1995—Gulf Coast Pirates (GCL)	5	4	.556	4.26	13	9	0	0	1	61 1/3	72	39	29	9	48
1996—Augusta (S.Atl.)	8	6	.571	3.52	26	26	0	0	0	135 2/3	123	64	53	36	107
1997—Lynchburg (Caro.)	•12	4	.750	3.31	24	24	3	1	0	160 1/3	154	69	59	33	121
1998—Carolina (Sou.)	9	8	.529	5.46	23	22	1	0	0	127	158	91	77	51	90
1999—Altoona (East.)	•15	4	.789	3.65	25	25	2	1	0	153	167	73	62	58	100
—Nashville (PCL)	0	2	.000	10.38	3	3	0	0	0	13	22	15	15	10	11
2000—Nashville (PCL)	8	2	.800	3.65	13	13	1	0	0	88 2/3	82	43	36	25	52
—Pittsburgh (N.L.)	2	6	.250	6.40	20	12	0	0	0	71 2/3	88	61	51	36	50
—Lynchburg (Caro.)	0	0	...	3.86	1	1	0	0	0	7	8	3	3	2	3
2001—Pittsburgh (N.L.)	5	7	.417	5.09	24	13	1	0	0	88 1/3	99	54	50	34	39
—Nashville (PCL)	6	2	.750	3.93	9	9	2	1	0	66 1/3	63	32	29	15	49
Major League totals (2 years)	7	13	.350	5.68	44	25	1	0	0	160	187	115	101	70	89

A

PERSONAL: Born July 11, 1967, in Kansas City, Mo. ... 6-1/202. ... Throws right, bats right. ... Full name: Andrew Jason Ashby.

HIGH SCHOOL: Park Hill (Kansas City, Mo.).

JUNIOR COLLEGE: Crowder College (Mo.).

TRANSACTIONS/CAREER NOTES: Signed as non-drafted free agent by Philadelphia Phillies organization (May 4, 1986). ... On Spartanburg disabled list (April 7-July 10, 1988). ... On Spartanburg disabled list (April 6-26, 1989). ... On Philadelphia disabled list (April 27-August 11, 1992); included rehabilitation assignments to Scranton/Wilkes-Barre (July 8-August 2 and August 6-10). ... Selected by Colorado Rockies in first round (25th pick overall) of expansion draft (November 17, 1992). ... Traded by Rockies to San Diego Padres (July 27, 1993), completing deal in which Padres traded P Bruce Hurst and P Greg W. Harris to Rockies for C Brad Ausmus, P Doug Bochtler and a player to be named later (July 26, 1993). ... On disabled list (June 6-22, June 29-July 15 and July 27-September 1, 1996; May 20-June 15, 1997; and June 7-24, 1999). ... Traded by Padres to Phillies for P Carlton Loewer, P Steve Montgomery and P Adam Eaton (November 10, 1999). ... On Philadelphia disabled list (June 12-27, 2000). ... Traded by Phillies to Atlanta Braves for P Bruce Chen and P Jimmy Osting (July 12, 2000). ... Granted free agency (November 1, 2000). ... Signed by Los Angeles Dodgers (December 6, 2000). ... On disabled list (April 16, 2001-remainder of season).

RECORDS: Shares major league record by striking out side on nine pitches (June 15, 1991, fourth inning).

MISCELLANEOUS: Had sacrifice hit in only appearance as pinch-hitter (1996). ... Appeared in one game as pinch runner (1997). ... Appeared in one game as pinch runner with Atlanta (2000). ... Appeared in one game as pinch runner (2001).

Year	League	W	L	Pct.	ERA	G	GS	CG	ShO	Sv.	IP	H	R	ER	BB	SO
1986—	Bend (N'West)	1	2	.333	4.95	16	6	0	0	2	60	56	40	33	34	45
1987—	Spartanburg (S.Atl.)	4	6	.400	5.60	13	13	1	0	0	64 1/3	73	45	40	38	52
—	Utica (NY-Penn)	3	7	.300	4.05	13	13	0	0	0	60	56	38	27	36	51
1988—	Spartanburg (S.Atl.)	1	1	.500	2.70	3	3	0	0	0	16 2/3	13	7	5	7	16
—	Batavia (NY-Penn)	3	1	.750	1.61	6	6	2	1	0	44 2/3	25	11	8	16	32
1989—	Spartanburg (S.Atl.)	5	9	.357	2.87	17	17	3	1	0	106 2/3	95	48	34	49	100
—	Clearwater (FSL)	1	4	.200	1.24	6	6	2	1	0	43 2/3	28	9	6	21	44
1990—	Reading (East.)	10	7	.588	3.42	23	23	4	1	0	139 2/3	134	65	53	48	94
1991—	Scranton/W.B. (I.L.)	11	11	.500	3.46	26	26	•6	•3	0	161 1/3	144	78	62	60	113
—	Philadelphia (N.L.)	1	5	.167	6.00	8	8	0	0	0	42	41	28	28	19	26
1992—	Philadelphia (N.L.)	1	3	.250	7.54	10	8	0	0	0	37	42	31	31	21	24
—	Scranton/W.B. (I.L.)	0	3	.000	3.00	7	7	1	0	0	33	23	13	11	14	18
1993—	Colorado (N.L.)■	0	4	.000	8.50	20	9	0	0	1	54	89	54	51	32	33
—	Colorado Springs (PCL)	4	2	.667	4.10	7	6	1	0	0	41 2/3	45	25	19	12	35
—	San Diego (N.L.)■	3	6	.333	5.48	12	12	0	0	0	69	79	46	42	24	44
1994—	San Diego (N.L.)	6	11	.353	3.40	24	24	4	0	0	164 1/3	145	75	62	43	121
1995—	San Diego (N.L.)	12	10	.545	2.94	31	•31	2	2	0	192 2/3	180	79	63	62	150
1996—	San Diego (N.L.)	9	5	.643	3.23	24	24	1	0	0	150 2/3	147	60	54	34	85
1997—	San Diego (N.L.)	9	11	.450	4.13	30	30	2	0	0	200 2/3	207	108	92	49	144
1998—	San Diego (N.L.)	17	9	.654	3.34	33	33	5	1	0	226 2/3	223	90	84	58	151
1999—	San Diego (N.L.)	14	10	.583	3.80	31	31	4	*3	0	206	204	95	87	54	132
2000—	Philadelphia (N.L.)■	4	7	.364	5.68	16	16	1	0	0	101 1/3	113	75	64	38	51
—	Atlanta (N.L.)■	8	6	.571	4.13	15	15	2	1	0	98	103	49	45	23	55
2001—	Los Angeles (N.L.)■	2	0	1.000	3.86	2	2	0	0	0	11 2/3	14	5	5	1	7
Major League totals (11 years)		86	87	.497	4.10	256	243	21	7	1	1554	1587	795	708	458	1023

DIVISION SERIES RECORD

Year	League	W	L	Pct.	ERA	G	GS	CG	ShO	Sv.	IP	H	R	ER	BB	SO
1996—	San Diego (N.L.)	0	0	...	6.75	1	1	0	0	0	5 1/3	7	4	4	1	5
1998—	San Diego (N.L.)	0	0	...	6.75	1	1	0	0	0	4	6	3	3	1	4
2000—	Atlanta (N.L.)	0	0	...	2.45	2	0	0	0	0	3 2/3	1	1	1	3	5
Division series totals (3 years)		0	0	...	5.54	4	2	0	0	0	13	14	8	8	5	14

CHAMPIONSHIP SERIES RECORD

Year	League	W	L	Pct.	ERA	G	GS	CG	ShO	Sv.	IP	H	R	ER	BB	SO
1998—	San Diego (N.L.)	0	0	...	2.08	2	2	0	0	0	13	14	3	3	2	5

WORLD SERIES RECORD

Year	League	W	L	Pct.	ERA	G	GS	CG	ShO	Sv.	IP	H	R	ER	BB	SO
1998—	San Diego (N.L.)	0	1	.000	13.50	1	1	0	0	0	2 2/3	10	7	4	1	1

ALL-STAR GAME RECORD

Year	League	W	L	Pct.	ERA	GS	CG	ShO	Sv.	IP	H	R	ER	BB	SO
1998—	National	0	0	...	9.00	0	0	0	0	1	1	1	1	1	0
1999—	National	0	0	...	0.00	0	0	0	0	1/3	0	0	0	0	0
All-Star Game totals (2 years)		0	0	...	6.75	0	0	0	0	1 1/3	1	1	1	1	0

ASTACIO, PEDRO P METS

PERSONAL: Born November 28, 1969, in Hato Mayor, Dominican Republic. ... 6-2/210. ... Throws right, bats right. ... Full name: Pedro Julio Astacio. ... Name pronounced ah-STA-see-oh.

HIGH SCHOOL: Pilar Rondon (Dominican Republic).

TRANSACTIONS/CAREER NOTES: Signed as non-drafted free agent by Los Angeles Dodgers organization (November 21, 1987). ... On Albuquerque disabled list (April 26-May 21, 1992). ... Traded by Dodgers to Colorado Rockies for 2B Eric Young (August 19, 1997). ... Traded by Rockies to Houston Astros for P Scott Elarton and a player to be named later (July 31, 2001). ... On Houston disabled list (August 29, 2001-remainder of season). ... Granted free agency (November 8, 2001). ... Signed by New York Mets (January 16, 2002).

STATISTICAL NOTES: Led N.L. with nine balks in 1993. ... Led N.L. with 17 hit batsmen and tied for lead with 39 home runs allowed in 1998. ... Led N.L. with 38 home runs allowed in 1999.

MISCELLANEOUS: Holds Colorado Rockies all-time record for most wins (53), strikeouts (749), innings pitched (827 1/3) and complete games (14). ... Struck out in both appearances as pinch hitter and appeared in one game as pinch runner (1999).

Year	League	W	L	Pct.	ERA	G	GS	CG	ShO	Sv.	IP	H	R	ER	BB	SO
1989— Gulf Coast Dodgers (GCL)..		7	3	.700	3.17	12	12	1	•1	0	76 2/3	77	30	27	12	52
1990— Vero Beach (FSL)		1	5	.167	6.32	8	8	0	0	0	47	54	39	33	23	41
— Yakima (N'West)		2	0	1.000	1.74	3	3	0	0	0	20 2/3	9	8	4	4	22
— Bakersfield (Calif.)		5	2	.714	2.77	10	7	1	0	0	52	46	22	16	15	34
1991— Vero Beach (FSL)		5	3	.625	1.67	9	9	3	1	0	59 1/3	44	19	11	8	45
— San Antonio (Texas)		4	11	.267	4.78	19	19	2	1	0	113	142	67	60	39	62
1992— Albuquerque (PCL)		6	6	.500	5.47	24	15	1	0	0	98 2/3	115	68	60	44	66
— Los Angeles (N.L.)		5	5	.500	1.98	11	11	4	4	0	82	80	23	18	20	43
1993— Los Angeles (N.L.)		14	9	.609	3.57	31	31	3	2	0	186 1/3	165	80	74	68	122
1994— Los Angeles (N.L.)		6	8	.429	4.29	23	23	3	1	0	149	142	77	71	47	108
1995— Los Angeles (N.L.)		7	8	.467	4.24	48	11	1	1	0	104	103	53	49	29	80
1996— Los Angeles (N.L.)		9	8	.529	3.44	35	32	0	0	0	211 2/3	207	86	81	67	130
1997— Los Angeles (N.L.)		7	9	.438	4.10	26	24	2	1	0	153 2/3	151	75	70	47	115
— Colorado (N.L.)■		5	1	.833	4.25	7	7	0	0	0	48 2/3	49	23	23	14	51
1998— Colorado (N.L.)		13	14	.481	6.23	35	34	0	0	0	209 1/3	245	*160	*145	74	170
1999— Colorado (N.L.)		17	11	.607	5.04	34	34	7	0	0	232	258	140	130	75	210
2000— Colorado (N.L.)		12	9	.571	5.27	32	32	3	0	0	196 1/3	217	119	115	77	193
2001— Colorado (N.L.)		6	13	.316	5.49	22	22	4	1	0	141	151	91	86	50	125
— Houston (N.L.)■		2	1	.667	3.14	4	4	0	0	0	28 2/3	30	10	10	4	19
Major League totals (10 years)		103	96	.518	4.50	308	265	27	10	0	1742 2/3	1798	937	872	572	1366

DIVISION SERIES RECORD

Year	League	W	L	Pct.	ERA	G	GS	CG	ShO	Sv.	IP	H	R	ER	BB	SO
1995— Los Angeles (N.L.)		0	0	...	0.00	3	0	0	0	0	3 1/3	1	0	0	0	5
1996— Los Angeles (N.L.)		0	0	...	0.00	1	0	0	0	0	1 2/3	0	0	0	0	1
Division series totals (2 years)		0	0	...	0.00	4	0	0	0	0	5	1	0	0	0	6

ATCHLEY, JUSTIN P REDS

PERSONAL: Born September 5, 1973, in Sedro Woolley, Wash. ... 6-3/215. ... Throws left, bats left. ... Full name: Justin Scott Atchley.
HIGH SCHOOL: Sedro Woolley (Wash.).
JUNIOR COLLEGE: Walla Walla (Wash.) Community College.
COLLEGE: Texas A&M.
TRANSACTIONS/CAREER NOTES: Selected by San Diego Padres organization in 15th round of free-agent draft (June 3, 1991); did not sign. ... Selected by Atlanta Braves organization in sixth round of free-agent draft (June 1, 1992); did not sign. ... Selected by Cincinnati Reds organization in 12th round of free-agent draft (June 1, 1995). ... On Indianapolis disabled list (April 2, 1998-enitre season; August 11-24, 1999). ... On Chattanooga disabled list (May 7-17, 1999). ... On Indianapolis disabled list (May 5-14, 2000). ... Released by Reds (January 9, 2001). ... Re-signed by Reds organization (January 22, 2001). ... On Louisville disabled list (April 16-May 9 and May 30-June 8, 2001). ... On Cincinnati disabled list (July 13, 2001-remainder of season); included rehabilitation assignment to Louisville (August 8-September 5).

Year	League	W	L	Pct.	ERA	G	GS	CG	ShO	Sv.	IP	H	R	ER	BB	SO
1995— Billings (Pio.)		*10	0	*1.000	3.51	13	13	0	0	0	77	91	33	30	20	65
1996— Charleston, W.Va. (S.Atl.)		3	3	.500	3.46	17	16	0	0	1	91	98	42	35	23	78
— Winston-Salem (Caro.)		3	3	.500	5.09	12	12	0	0	0	69	74	48	39	16	50
1997— Chattanooga (Sou.)		4	2	.667	4.70	13	13	1	0	0	67	75	45	35	14	48
1998— Indianapolis (I.L.)								Did not play.								
1999— Chattanooga (Sou.)		4	9	.308	3.42	17	17	0	0	0	97 1/3	114	48	37	22	70
— Indianapolis (I.L.)		2	1	.667	5.40	5	4	0	0	1	23 1/3	39	14	14	2	6
2000— Louisville (I.L.)		8	6	.571	5.89	30	19	0	0	1	122 1/3	168	83	80	26	69
2001— Cincinnati (N.L.)		0	0	...	6.10	15	0	0	0	0	10 1/3	12	7	7	5	8
— Louisville (I.L.)		1	0	1.000	0.64	15	0	0	0	2	14	14	1	1	3	15
Major League totals (1 year)		0	0	...	6.10	15	0	0	0	0	10 1/3	12	7	7	5	8

AURILIA, RICH SS GIANTS

PERSONAL: Born September 2, 1971, in Brooklyn, N.Y. ... 6-1/185. ... Bats right, throws right. ... Full name: Richard Santo Aurilia. ... Name pronounced uh-REEL-yuh.
HIGH SCHOOL: Xaverian (Brooklyn, N.Y.).
COLLEGE: St. John's.
TRANSACTIONS/CAREER NOTES: Selected by Texas Rangers organization in 24th round of free-agent draft (June 1, 1992). ... On disabled list (April 9-16, 1993). ... Traded by Rangers with IF/OF Desi Wilson to San Francisco Giants for P John Burkett (December 24, 1994). ... On San Francisco disabled list (September 24, 1996-remainder of season). ... On disabled list (July 4-20, 1998).
HONORS: Named shortstop on N.L. Silver Slugger team (2001). ... Named shortstop on THE SPORTING NEWS N.L. All-Star team (2001).
STATISTICAL NOTES: Led Texas League shortstops with 635 total chances and tied for lead with 82 double plays in 1994. ... Career major league grand slams: 1.

Year Team (League)	Pos.	G	AB	R	H	2B	3B	HR	RBI	Avg.	BB	SO	SB	PO	A	E	Avg.
1992— Butte (Pio.)	SS	59	202	37	68	11	3	3	30	.337	42	18	13	78	154	14	*.943
1993— Charlotte (FSL)	SS	122	440	80	136	16	5	5	56	.309	75	57	15	200	445	24	.964
1994— Tulsa (Texas)	SS	129	458	67	107	18	6	12	57	.234	53	74	10	*237	374	24	*.962
1995— Shreveport (Texas)■	SS	64	226	29	74	17	1	4	42	.327	27	26	10	122	237	14	.962
— Phoenix (PCL)	SS	71	258	42	72	12	0	5	34	.279	35	29	2	104	246	9	.975
— San Francisco (N.L.) ..	SS	9	19	4	9	3	0	2	4	.474	1	2	1	8	16	0	1.000
1996— Phoenix (PCL)	SS-2B	7	30	9	13	7	0	0	4	.433	2	3	1	10	25	1	.972
— San Francisco (N.L.) ..	SS-2B	105	318	27	76	7	1	3	26	.239	25	52	4	142	246	10	.975
1997— San Francisco (N.L.) ..	SS	46	102	16	28	8	0	5	19	.275	8	15	1	47	91	3	.979
— Phoenix (PCL)	SS	8	34	9	10	2	0	1	5	.294	5	4	2	14	22	0	1.000
1998— San Francisco (N.L.) ..	SS	122	413	54	110	27	2	9	49	.266	31	62	3	154	310	10	.979
1999— San Francisco (N.L.) ..	SS	152	558	68	157	23	1	22	80	.281	43	71	2	218	411	*28	.957
2000— San Francisco (N.L.) ..	SS	141	509	67	138	24	2	20	79	.271	54	90	1	218	403	21	.967
2001— San Francisco (N.L.) ..	SS	156	636	114	*206	37	5	37	97	.324	47	83	1	246	423	17	.975
Major League totals (7 years)		731	2555	350	724	129	11	98	354	.283	209	375	13	1033	1903	89	.971

DIVISION SERIES RECORD

					BATTING									FIELDING		
Year Team (League)	Pos.	G	AB	R	H	2B	3B	HR	RBI	Avg.	BB	SO	SB	PO	A	E	Avg.
2000—San Francisco (N.L.) ..	SS	4	15	0	2	1	0	0	0	.133	0	3	0	10	11	1	.955

ALL-STAR GAME RECORD

				BATTING								FIELDING		
Year League	Pos.	AB	R	H	2B	3B	HR	RBI	Avg.	BB	SO	SB	PO	A	E	Avg.
2001—National	SS	2	0	0	0	0	0	0	.000	0	0	0	1	3	0	1.000

AUSMUS, BRAD   C   ASTROS

PERSONAL: Born April 14, 1969, in New Haven, Conn. ... 5-11/195. ... Bats right, throws right. ... Full name: Bradley David Ausmus.
HIGH SCHOOL: Cheshire (Conn.).
COLLEGE: Dartmouth.
TRANSACTIONS/CAREER NOTES: Selected by New York Yankees organization in 47th round of free-agent draft (June 2, 1987). ... Selected by Colorado Rockies in third round (54th pick overall) of expansion draft (November 17, 1992). ... Traded by Rockies with P Doug Bochtler and a player to be named later to San Diego Padres for P Bruce Hurst and P Greg W. Harris (July 26, 1993); Padres acquired P Andy Ashby to complete deal (July 27, 1993). ... Traded by Padres with SS Andujar Cedeno and P Russ Spear to Detroit Tigers for C John Flaherty and SS Chris Gomez (June 18, 1996). ... On Detroit suspended list (September 4-5, 1996). ... Traded by Tigers with P Jose Lima, P C.J. Nitkowski, P Trever Miller and IF Daryle Ward to Houston Astros for OF Brian L. Hunter, IF Orlando Miller, P Doug Brocail, P Todd Jones and cash (December 10, 1996). ... Traded by Astros with P C.J. Nitkowski to Tigers for C Paul Bako, P Dean Crow, P Mark Persails, P Brian Powell, and 3B Carlos Villalobos (January 14, 1999). ... Traded by Tigers with P Doug Brocail and P Nelson Cruz to Astros for C Mitch Meluskey, P Chris Holt and OF Roger Cedeno (December 11, 2000).
RECORDS: Holds A.L. single-season record for fewest passed balls (150 or more games)—3 (2000).
HONORS: Won N.L. Gold Glove at catcher (2001).
STATISTICAL NOTES: Led Gulf Coast League catchers with 434 total chances in 1988. ... Led International League catchers with 666 putouts and 738 total chances in 1992. ... Led N.L. catchers with 683 putouts and 749 total chances in 1994. ... Led N.L. catchers with 14 double plays in 1995. ... Tied for N.L. lead in assists by catcher with 63 in 1995. ... Led A.L. catchers with 898 putouts, 68 assists and 974 total chances in 2000. ... Career major league grand slams: 1.

						BATTING								FIELDING		
Year Team (League)	Pos.	G	AB	R	H	2B	3B	HR	RBI	Avg.	BB	SO	SB	PO	A	E	Avg.
1988—Oneonta (NY-Penn)	C	2	4	0	1	0	0	0	0	.250	0	2	0	0	0	0	...
—Sarasota (FSL)	C	43	133	22	34	2	0	0	15	.256	11	25	5	*378	*47	9	.979
1989—Oneonta (NY-Penn)	C-3B	52	165	29	43	6	0	1	18	.261	22	28	6	401	43	7	.984
1990—Prince William (Caro.) ..	C	107	364	46	86	12	2	0	27	.236	32	73	2	662	84	5	*.993
1991—Prince William (Caro.) ..	C	63	230	28	70	14	3	2	30	.304	24	37	17	419	54	5	.990
—Albany/Colonie (East.) ..	C	67	229	36	61	9	2	1	29	.266	27	36	14	470	56	4	.992
1992—Albany/Colonie (East.) ..	C	5	18	0	3	0	1	0	1	.167	2	3	2	30	2	1	.970
—Columbus (I.L.)	C-OF	111	364	48	88	14	3	2	35	.242	40	56	19	†666	63	9	.988
1993—Colo. Springs (PCL)■	C-DH-OF	76	241	31	65	10	4	2	33	.270	27	41	10	393	57	6	.987
—San Diego (N.L.)■	C	49	160	18	41	8	1	5	12	.256	6	28	2	272	34	8	.975
1994—San Diego (N.L.)	C-1B	101	327	45	82	12	1	7	24	.251	30	63	5	†686	59	7	.991
1995—San Diego (N.L.)	C-1B	103	328	44	96	16	4	5	34	.293	31	56	16	656	†63	6	.992
1996—San Diego (N.L.)	C	50	149	16	27	4	0	1	13	.181	13	27	1	300	22	6	.982
—Detroit (A.L.)■..........	C	75	226	30	56	12	0	4	22	.248	26	45	3	452	35	4	.992
1997—Houston (N.L.)■	C	130	425	45	113	25	1	4	44	.266	38	78	14	807	73	7	.992
1998—Houston (N.L.)	C	128	412	62	111	10	4	6	45	.269	53	60	10	850	58	7	.992
1999—Detroit (A.L.)	C	127	458	62	126	25	6	9	54	.275	51	71	12	754	56	2	*.998
2000—Detroit (A.L.)	C-1B-2B-3B	150	523	75	139	25	3	7	51	.266	69	79	11	†900	†68	8	.992
2001—Houston (N.L.)■	C	128	422	45	98	23	4	5	34	.232	30	64	4	948	62	3	.997
American League totals (3 years)		352	1207	167	321	62	9	20	127	.266	146	195	26	2106	159	14	.994
National League totals (7 years)		689	2223	275	568	98	15	33	206	.256	201	376	52	4519	371	44	.991
Major League totals (9 years)		1041	3430	442	889	160	24	53	333	.259	347	571	78	6625	530	58	.992

DIVISION SERIES RECORD

						BATTING								FIELDING		
Year Team (League)	Pos.	G	AB	R	H	2B	3B	HR	RBI	Avg.	BB	SO	SB	PO	A	E	Avg.
1997—Houston (N.L.)	C	2	5	1	2	1	0	0	2	.400	0	1	0	13	0	0	1.000
1998—Houston (N.L.)	C	4	9	0	2	0	0	0	0	.222	0	4	0	28	1	0	1.000
2001—Houston (N.L.)	C-PH	3	8	1	2	0	0	1	2	.250	0	0	0	14	2	0	1.000
Division series totals (3 years)		9	22	2	6	1	0	1	4	.273	0	5	0	55	3	0	1.000

ALL-STAR GAME RECORD

				BATTING								FIELDING		
Year League	Pos.	AB	R	H	2B	3B	HR	RBI	Avg.	BB	SO	SB	PO	A	E	Avg.
1999—American	C	1	0	0	0	0	0	0	.000	0	0	0	2	1	0	1.000

AUSTIN, JEFF   P   ROYALS

PERSONAL: Born October 19, 1976, in San Bernardino, Calif. ... 6-0/185. ... Throws right, bats right. ... Full name: Jeffrey Wellington Austin.
HIGH SCHOOL: Kingwood (Texas).
COLLEGE: Stanford.
TRANSACTIONS/CAREER NOTES: Selected by Montreal Expos organization in 10th round of free-agent draft (June 1, 1995); did not sign. ... Selected by Kansas City Royals organization in first round (fourth pick overall) of free-agent draft (June 2, 1998).

Year League	W	L	Pct.	ERA	G	GS	CG	ShO	Sv.	IP	H	R	ER	BB	SO
1999—Wilmington (Caro.)............	7	2	.778	3.77	18	18	0	0	0	112 1/3	108	52	47	39	97
—Wichita (Texas)	3	1	.750	4.46	6	6	0	0	0	34 1/3	40	19	17	11	21
2000—Wichita (Texas)	2	2	.500	2.93	6	6	1	0	0	43	33	16	14	4	31
—Omaha (PCL)......................	7	9	.438	4.48	23	19	1	1	0	126 2/3	150	85	63	35	57
2001—Omaha (PCL)......................	3	7	.300	6.88	28	8	0	0	2	70 2/3	89	56	54	27	55
—Kansas City (A.L.)	0	0	...	5.54	21	0	0	0	0	26	27	17	16	14	27
Major League totals (1 year)........	0	0	...	5.54	21	0	0	0	0	26	27	17	16	14	27

AVEN, BRUCE — OF

PERSONAL: Born March 4, 1972, in Orange, Texas. ... 5-9/180. ... Bats right, throws right. ... Full name: David Bruce Aven.
HIGH SCHOOL: West Orange-Stark (Orange, Texas).
COLLEGE: Lamar.
TRANSACTIONS/CAREER NOTES: Selected by Cleveland Indians organization in 30th round of free-agent draft (June 2, 1994). ... On Buffalo disabled list (April 9-17, April 23-May 13 and May 27, 1998-remainder of season). ... Claimed on waivers by Florida Marlins (October 20, 1998). ... Traded by Marlins to Pittsburgh Pirates for OF Brant Brown (December 13, 1999). ... On Pittsburgh disabled list (June 30-July 18, 2000); included rehabilitation assignment to Nashville (July 14-18). ... Traded by Pirates to Los Angeles Dodgers for a player to be named later (August 6, 2000). ... Granted free agency (October 17, 2001).
STATISTICAL NOTES: Led Eastern League outfielders with 289 total chances in 1996. ... Tied for American Association lead in being hit by pitch with 11 in 1997. ... Career major league grand slams: 2.

Year	Team (League)	Pos.	G	AB	R	H	2B	3B	HR	RBI	Avg.	BB	SO	SB	PO	A	E	Avg.
1994—Watertown (NY-Penn)		OF	61	220	49	73	14	5	5	33	.332	20	45	12	88	6	1	.989
1995—Kinston (Caro.)		OF	130	479	70	125	23	5	23	69	.261	41	109	15	158	11	3	.983
1996—Canton/Akron (East.)		OF	131	481	91	143	31	4	23	79	.297	43	101	22	280	3	6	.979
—Buffalo (A.A.)		OF	3	9	5	6	0	0	1	2	.667	1	1	0	7	0	0	1.000
1997—Buffalo (A.A.)		OF-DH	121	432	69	124	27	3	17	77	.287	50	99	10	219	3	2	.991
—Cleveland (A.L.)		OF	13	19	4	4	1	0	0	2	.211	1	5	0	15	1	0	1.000
1998—Buffalo (I.L.)		DH	5	15	4	3	1	0	1	1	.200	6	5	3	0	0	0	...
1999—Florida (N.L.)■		OF-DH	137	381	57	110	19	2	12	70	.289	44	82	3	181	4	3	.984
2000—Pittsburgh (N.L.)■		OF	72	148	18	37	11	0	5	25	.250	5	31	2	49	0	1	.980
—Nashville (PCL)		OF	3	10	1	3	1	0	0	3	.300	1	3	0	6	0	0	1.000
—Albuquerque (PCL)■		OF	9	32	7	9	1	0	0	3	.281	6	6	0	11	1	0	1.000
—Los Angeles (N.L.)		OF	9	20	2	5	0	0	2	4	.250	3	8	0	12	0	0	1.000
2001—Las Vegas (PCL)		OF	86	292	43	76	17	0	8	32	.260	24	59	5	108	5	2	.983
—Los Angeles (N.L.)		OF	21	24	3	8	2	0	1	2	.333	0	5	0	5	0	0	1.000
American League totals (1 year)			13	19	4	4	1	0	0	2	.211	1	5	0	15	1	0	1.000
National League totals (3 years)			239	573	80	160	32	2	20	101	.279	52	126	5	247	4	4	.984
Major League totals (4 years)			252	592	84	164	33	2	20	103	.277	53	131	5	262	5	4	.985

AYBAR, MANNY — P

PERSONAL: Born November 28, 1969, in Bani, Dominican Republic. ... 6-1/177. ... Throws right, bats right. ... Full name: Manuel Antonio Aybar. ... Name pronounced I-bar.
TRANSACTIONS/CAREER NOTES: Signed as non-drafted free agent by St. Louis Cardinals organization (October 21, 1991). ... Traded by Cardinals with P Jose Jimenez, P Rick Croushore and IF Brent Butler to Colorado Rockies for P Darryl Kile, P Dave Veres and P Luther Hackman (November 16, 1999). ... Traded by Rockies to Cincinnati Reds for P Gabe White (April 7, 2000). ... On Cincinnati disabled list (July 2-24, 2000); included rehabilitation assignment to Louisville (July 8-23). ... Traded by Reds to Florida Marlins for P Jorge Cordova (July 26, 2000). ... Traded by Marlins to Chicago Cubs for P Oswaldo Mairena (March 30, 2001). ... Traded by Cubs with a player to be named later to Tampa Bay Devil Rays for 1B Fred McGriff (July 27, 2001); Devil Rays acquired SS Jason Smith to complete deal (August 5, 2001). ... Granted free agency (October 12, 2001).
MISCELLANEOUS: Appeared in two games as pinch runner (1999).

Year	League	W	L	Pct.	ERA	G	GS	CG	ShO	Sv.	IP	H	R	ER	BB	SO
1992—Dominican Cardinals (DSL)		1	0	1.000	0.00	55	0	0	0	0	3	1	0	0	3	1
1993—Dominican Cardinals (DSL)		4	4	.500	3.15	13	11	1	0	0	71 1/3	54	33	25	33	66
1994—Arizona Cardinals (Ariz.)		6	1	.857	2.12	13	13	1	0	0	72 1/3	69	25	17	9	79
1995—Savannah (S.Atl.)		3	8	.273	3.04	18	18	2	1	0	112 2/3	82	46	38	36	99
—St. Petersburg (FSL)		2	5	.286	3.35	9	9	0	0	0	48 1/3	42	27	18	16	43
1996—Arkansas (Texas)		8	6	.571	3.05	20	20	0	0	0	121	120	53	41	34	83
—Louisville (A.A.)		2	2	.500	3.23	5	5	0	0	0	30 2/3	26	12	11	7	25
1997—Louisville (A.A.)		5	8	.385	3.48	22	22	3	•2	0	137	131	60	53	45	114
—St. Louis (N.L.)		2	4	.333	4.24	12	12	0	0	0	68	66	33	32	29	41
1998—St. Louis (N.L.)		6	6	.500	5.98	20	14	0	0	0	81 1/3	90	58	54	42	57
—Memphis (PCL)		10	0	*1.000	2.60	13	13	0	0	0	83	62	24	24	17	63
1999—St. Louis (N.L.)		4	5	.444	5.47	65	1	0	0	3	97	104	67	59	36	74
2000—Colorado (N.L.)■		0	1	.000	16.20	1	0	0	0	0	1 2/3	5	3	3	0	0
—Cincinnati (N.L.)■		1	1	.500	4.83	32	0	0	0	0	50 1/3	51	31	27	22	31
—Louisville (I.L.)		0	2	.000	13.50	3	2	0	0	0	6 2/3	10	10	10	10	1
—Florida (N.L.)■		1	0	1.000	2.63	21	0	0	0	0	27 1/3	18	8	8	13	14
2001—Chicago (N.L.)■		2	1	.667	6.35	17	1	0	0	0	22 2/3	28	19	16	17	16
—Iowa (PCL)■		1	2	.333	5.02	8	7	1	1	0	43	42	26	24	16	32
—Durham (I.L.)■		1	3	.250	5.68	11	3	0	0	0	31 2/3	40	25	20	9	29
Major League totals (5 years)		16	18	.471	5.14	168	28	0	0	3	348 1/3	362	219	199	159	233

RECORD AS POSITION PLAYER

Year	Team (League)	Pos.	G	AB	R	H	2B	3B	HR	RBI	Avg.	BB	SO	SB	PO	A	E	Avg.
1992—Dom. Cardinals (DSL)		IF	55	153	18	31	5	0	1	11	.203	10	27	2	53	131	19	.906

BACSIK, MIKE — P — METS

PERSONAL: Born November 11, 1977, in Dallas. ... 6-3/190. ... Throws left, bats left. ... Full name: Michael J. Bacsik.
HIGH SCHOOL: Duncanville (Texas).
TRANSACTIONS/CAREER NOTES: Selected by Cleveland Indians organization in 18th round of free-agent draft (June 4, 1996). ... Traded by Indians with 2B Roberto Alomar and OF Danny Peoples to New York Mets for OF Matt Lawton, OF Alex Escobar, P Jerrod Riggan and two players to be named later (December 11, 2001); Indians acquired P Billy Traber and 1B Earl Snyder to complete deal (December 13, 2001).
STATISTICAL NOTES: Led Carolina League pitchers with 17 home runs allowed in 1998.

Year League	W	L	Pct.	ERA	G	GS	CG	ShO	Sv.	IP	H	R	ER	BB	SO
1996—Burlington (Appl.).............	4	2	.667	2.20	13	13	1	0	0	69²/₃	49	23	17	14	61
1997—Columbus (S.Atl.)..............	4	14	.222	5.44	28	28	0	0	0	139	163	94	84	47	100
1998—Kinston (Caro.)...............	10	9	.526	2.88	27	27	1	0	0	165²/₃	147	64	53	37	128
1999—Akron (East.)	11	11	.500	4.64	26	26	1	0	0	149¹/₃	164	84	77	47	84
2000—Kinston (Caro.)	3	6	.333	4.57	11	11	0	0	0	65	72	36	33	8	56
—Akron (East.)	7	1	.875	2.78	11	11	1	1	0	71¹/₃	61	23	22	15	44
—Buffalo (I.L.)	0	3	.000	5.59	5	5	0	0	0	29	31	20	18	7	9
2001—Buffalo (I.L.)	12	5	.706	3.26	21	20	2	0	0	121¹/₃	115	47	44	25	81
—Akron (East.)	1	1	.500	1.98	4	4	1	1	0	27¹/₃	21	7	6	3	19
—Cleveland (A.L.)	0	0	...	9.00	3	0	0	0	0	9	13	10	9	3	4
Major League totals (1 year)........	0	0	...	9.00	3	0	0	0	0	9	13	10	9	3	4

B

BAEZ, BENITO   P   MARLINS

PERSONAL: Born May 6, 1977, in Bonao, Dominican Republic. ... 6-0/160. ... Throws left, bats left.

TRANSACTIONS/CAREER NOTES: Signed as non-drafted free agent by Oakland Athletics organization (November 8, 1993). ... On disabled list (April 11-May 1, 2000). ... Granted free agency (October 15, 2000). ... Signed by Florida Marlins organization (January 4, 2001). ... On Calgary disabled list (June 30-July 8, 2001).

Year League	W	L	Pct.	ERA	G	GS	CG	ShO	Sv.	IP	H	R	ER	BB	SO
1994—Dominican Athletics (DSL).	8	5	.615	2.93	16	3	0	0	1	58¹/₃	44	34	19	30	44
1995—Arizona Athletics (Ariz.)......	5	1	.833	3.34	14	11	1	0	0	70	64	35	26	28	83
1996—West Michigan (Midw.)	8	4	.667	3.47	32	20	0	0	4	129²/₃	123	60	50	52	92
1997—Visalia (Calif.)	5	5	.500	3.54	16	15	1	0	0	96²/₃	83	40	38	28	87
—Huntsville (Sou.)	2	4	.333	9.14	15	7	0	0	0	42¹/₃	64	47	43	22	27
1998—Huntsville (Sou.)	3	8	.273	5.80	34	17	0	0	0	122²/₃	161	92	79	64	83
1999—Midland (Texas)	5	1	.833	5.47	37	0	0	0	3	54¹/₃	68	35	33	15	51
—Vancouver (PCL)	0	2	.000	3.50	11	0	0	0	1	18	18	7	7	7	19
2000—Midland (Texas).............	5	4	.556	4.89	37	0	0	0	0	53¹/₃	61	35	29	27	50
2001—Calgary (PCL)■.................	7	1	.875	3.03	49	0	0	0	1	59¹/₃	53	22	20	7	56
—Florida (N.L.)	0	0	...	13.50	8	0	0	0	0	9¹/₃	22	14	14	6	14
Major League totals (1 year)........	0	0	...	13.50	8	0	0	0	0	9¹/₃	22	14	14	6	14

BAEZ, DANYS   P   INDIANS

PERSONAL: Born September 10, 1977, in Pinar del Rio, Cuba. ... 6-3/225. ... Throws right, bats right.

TRANSACTIONS/CAREER NOTES: Signed as non-drafted free agent by Cleveland Indians organization (November 5, 1999). ... On Buffalo disabled list (June 19-July 4, 2000). ... On Buffalo disabled list (June 4-29, 2001).

Year League	W	L	Pct.	ERA	G	GS	CG	ShO	Sv.	IP	H	R	ER	BB	SO
2000—Kinston (Caro.)	2	2	.500	4.71	9	9	0	0	0	49²/₃	45	29	26	20	56
—Akron (East.)	4	9	.308	3.68	18	18	0	0	0	102²/₃	98	46	42	32	77
2001—Buffalo (I.L.)	2	0	1.000	3.20	16	0	0	0	3	25¹/₃	18	9	9	9	30
—Akron (East.)	0	0	...	0.00	1	0	0	0	0	2	1	0	0	0	2
—Cleveland (A.L.)	5	3	.625	2.50	43	0	0	0	0	50¹/₃	34	22	14	20	52
Major League totals (1 year)........	5	3	.625	2.50	43	0	0	0	0	50¹/₃	34	22	14	20	52

DIVISION SERIES RECORD

Year League	W	L	Pct.	ERA	G	GS	CG	ShO	Sv.	IP	H	R	ER	BB	SO
2001—Cleveland (A.L.).................	0	0	...	2.45	3	0	0	0	0	3²/₃	4	1	1	0	6

BAGWELL, JEFF   1B   ASTROS

PERSONAL: Born May 27, 1968, in Boston. ... 6-0/195. ... Bats right, throws right. ... Full name: Jeffrey Robert Bagwell.

HIGH SCHOOL: Xavier (Middletown, Conn.).

COLLEGE: Hartford.

TRANSACTIONS/CAREER NOTES: Selected by Boston Red Sox organization in fourth round of free-agent draft (June 5, 1989). ... Traded by Red Sox to Houston Astros for P Larry Andersen (August 31, 1990). ... On Houston disabled list (July 31-September 1, 1995); included rehabilitation assignment to Jackson (August 28-September 1). ... On disabled list (May 13-28, 1998).

RECORDS: Shares major league single-game records for most doubles—4 (June 14, 1996); and most bases on balls—6 (August 20, 1999, 16 innings). ... Shares major league single-inning record for most home runs—2 (June 24, 1994, sixth inning). ... Shares N.L. career record for most major league ballparks, one or more home runs (since 1900)—22.

HONORS: Named Eastern League Most Valuable Player (1990). ... Named N.L. Rookie Player of the Year by THE SPORTING NEWS (1991). ... Named N.L. Rookie of the Year by Baseball Writers' Association of America (1991). ... Named Major League Player of the Year by THE SPORTING News (1994). ... Named first baseman on THE SPORTING NEWS N.L. All-Star team (1994, 1996, 1997 and 1999). ... Won N.L. Gold Glove at first base (1994). ... Named first baseman on THE SPORTING NEWS N.L. Silver Slugger team (1994, 1997 and 1999). ... Named N.L. Most Valuable Player by Baseball Writers' Association of America (1994).

STATISTICAL NOTES: Led Eastern League with 220 total bases and 12 intentional bases on balls received in 1990. ... Led N.L. in being hit by pitch with 13 in 1991. ... Led N.L. with 13 sacrifice flies in 1992. ... Hit three home runs in one game (June 24, 1994; and April 21 and June 9, 1999). ... Led N.L. with .750 slugging percentage in 1994. ... Led N.L. first basemen with 120 assists in 1994. ... Tied for N.L. lead in errors by first basemen with nine and double plays by first basemen with 94 in 1994. ... Had 18-game hitting streak (August 2-20, 2000). ... Hit for the cycle (July 18, 2001). ... Career major league grand slams: 5.

MISCELLANEOUS: Holds Houston Astros all-time record for most home runs (349), runs batted in (1,223) and highest career batting average (.303).

Year	Team (League)	Pos.	G	AB	R	H	2B	3B	HR	RBI	Avg.	BB	SO	SB	PO	A	E	Avg.
1989—	GC Red Sox (GCL)	3B-2B	5	19	3	6	1	0	0	3	.316	3	0	0	2	12	2	.875
	— Winter Haven (FSL)....	3B-2B-1B	64	210	27	65	13	2	2	19	.310	22	25	1	53	109	12	.931
1990—	New Britain (East.)	3B	136	481	63	*160	•34	7	4	61	.333	73	57	5	93	267	34	.914
1991—	Houston (N.L.)■.......	1B	156	554	79	163	26	4	15	82	.294	75	116	7	1270	106	12	.991
1992—	Houston (N.L.)	1B	•162	586	87	160	34	6	18	96	.273	84	97	10	1334	133	7	.995
1993—	Houston (N.L.)	1B	142	535	76	171	37	4	20	88	.320	62	73	13	1200	113	9	.993
1994—	Houston (N.L.)	1B-OF	110	400	*104	147	32	2	39	*116	.368	65	65	15	923	†121	‡9	.991
1995—	Houston (N.L.)	1B	114	448	88	130	29	0	21	87	.290	79	102	12	1004	*129	7	.994
	— Jackson (Texas)	1B-DH	4	12	0	2	0	0	0	0	.167	3	2	0	24	6	0	1.000
1996—	Houston (N.L.)	1B	*162	568	111	179	*48	2	31	120	.315	135	114	21	1336	*136	*16	.989
1997—	Houston (N.L.)	1B-DH	•162	566	109	162	40	2	43	135	.286	127	122	31	1404	*137	11	.993
1998—	Houston (N.L.)	1B	147	540	124	164	33	1	34	111	.304	109	90	19	1239	128	7	.995
1999—	Houston (N.L.)	1B-DH	•162	562	*143	171	35	0	42	126	.304	*149	127	30	1336	106	8	.994
2000—	Houston (N.L.)	1B-DH	159	590	*152	183	37	1	47	132	.310	107	116	9	1264	116	9	.994
2001—	Houston (N.L.)	1B	161	600	126	173	43	4	39	130	.288	106	135	11	1291	143	12	.992
Major League totals (11 years)			1637	5949	1199	1803	394	26	349	1223	.303	1098	1157	178	13601	1368	107	.993

DIVISION SERIES RECORD

Year	Team (League)	Pos.	G	AB	R	H	2B	3B	HR	RBI	Avg.	BB	SO	SB	PO	A	E	Avg.
1997—	Houston (N.L.)	1B	3	12	0	1	0	0	0	0	.083	1	5	0	17	6	2	.920
1998—	Houston (N.L.)	1B	4	14	0	2	0	0	0	4	.143	1	6	0	31	4	0	1.000
1999—	Houston (N.L.)	1B	4	13	3	2	0	0	0	0	.154	5	4	0	36	3	0	1.000
2001—	Houston (N.L.)	1B	3	7	0	3	0	0	0	0	.429	5	1	0	21	2	0	1.000
Division series totals (4 years)			14	46	3	8	0	0	0	4	.174	12	16	0	105	15	2	.984

ALL-STAR GAME RECORD

Year	League	Pos.	AB	R	H	2B	3B	HR	RBI	Avg.	BB	SO	SB	PO	A	E	Avg.
1994—	National	PH-1B	4	1	2	0	0	0	0	.500	0	1	0	3	2	0	1.000
1996—	National	1B	2	0	0	0	0	0	0	.000	0	1	0	5	0	0	1.000
1997—	National	1B	3	0	0	0	0	0	0	.000	0	0	0	8	1	0	1.000
1999—	National	DH	3	0	1	0	0	0	0	.333	0	2	0	...	...	...	...
All-Star Game totals (4 years)			12	1	3	0	0	0	0	.250	0	4	0	16	3	0	1.000

BAILEY, CORY   P   ROYALS

PERSONAL: Born January 24, 1971, in Herrin, Ill. ... 6-1/210. ... Throws right, bats right. ... Full name: Phillip Cory Bailey.
HIGH SCHOOL: Marion (Ill.).
COLLEGE: Southeastern Illinois.
TRANSACTIONS/CAREER NOTES: Selected by Boston Red Sox organization in 15th round of free-agent draft (June 3, 1991). ... Traded by Red Sox with 3B Scott Cooper and a player to be named later to St. Louis Cardinals for P Rheal Cormier and OF Mark Whiten (April 8, 1995). ... Traded by Cardinals to Texas Rangers for P David Chavarria and a player to be named later (December 16, 1996). ... Traded by Rangers to San Francisco Giants for P Chad Hartvigson (July 29, 1997). ... On disabled list (August 14-September 1, 1999). ... Granted free agency (October 4, 1999). ... Signed by Pittsburgh Pirates organization (January 18, 2000). ... Granted free agency (October 18, 2000). ... Signed by Kansas City Royals organization (June 7, 2000).

Year	League	W	L	Pct.	ERA	G	GS	CG	ShO	Sv.	IP	H	R	ER	BB	SO
1991—	Gulf Coast Red Sox (GCL)..	0	0	...	0.00	1	0	0	0	1	2	2	1	0	1	1
	— Elmira (NY-Penn)	2	4	.333	1.85	28	0	0	0	*15	39	19	10	8	12	54
1992—	Lynchburg (Caro.)	5	7	.417	2.44	49	0	0	0	*23	66 1/3	43	20	18	30	87
1993—	Pawtucket (I.L.)..................	4	5	.444	2.88	52	0	0	0	20	65 2/3	48	21	21	31	59
	— Boston (A.L.)......................	0	1	.000	3.45	11	0	0	0	0	15 2/3	12	7	6	12	11
1994—	Pawtucket (I.L.)..................	4	3	.571	3.23	53	0	0	0	19	61 1/3	44	25	22	38	52
	— Boston (A.L.)......................	0	1	.000	12.46	5	0	0	0	0	4 1/3	10	6	6	3	4
1995—	Louisville (A.A.)■................	5	3	.625	4.55	55	0	0	0	*25	59 1/3	51	30	30	30	49
	— St. Louis (N.L.)..................	0	0	...	7.36	3	0	0	0	0	3 2/3	2	3	3	2	5
1996—	St. Louis (N.L.)	5	2	.714	3.00	51	0	0	0	0	57	57	21	19	30	38
	— Louisville (A.A.).................	2	4	.333	5.82	22	0	0	0	1	34	29	22	22	20	27
1997—	Oklahoma City (A.A.)■.......	3	4	.429	3.40	42	0	0	0	15	50 1/3	49	20	19	23	38
	— Phoenix (PCL)...................	4	0	1.000	1.56	13	0	0	0	3	17 1/3	16	4	3	6	14
	— San Francisco (N.L.)	0	0	.000	8.38	7	0	0	0	0	9 2/3	15	9	9	4	5
1998—	Fresno (PCL)	7	2	.778	2.47	57	0	0	0	10	94 2/3	79	31	26	18	76
	— San Francisco (N.L.)	0	0	...	2.70	5	0	0	0	0	3 1/3	2	1	1	1	2
1999—	Fresno (PCL)	2	1	.667	3.30	43	0	0	0	18	46 1/3	47	24	17	17	52
2000—	Nashville (PCL)■................	2	4	.333	3.47	55	0	0	0	12	72 2/3	76	32	28	35	62
2001—	Omaha (PCL)■....................	1	0	1.000	0.00	5	0	0	0	1	10	2	0	0	5	7
	— Kansas City (A.L.)	1	1	.500	3.48	53	0	0	0	0	67 1/3	57	28	26	33	61
A.L. totals (3 years)		1	3	.250	3.92	69	0	0	0	0	87 1/3	79	41	38	48	76
N.L. totals (4 years)		5	3	.625	3.91	66	0	0	0	0	73 2/3	76	34	32	37	50
Major League totals (7 years)		6	6	.500	3.91	135	0	0	0	0	161	155	75	70	85	126

BAINES, HAROLD   DH

PERSONAL: Born March 15, 1959, in St. Michaels, Md. ... 6-2/195. ... Bats left, throws left. ... Full name: Harold Dougleas Baines.
HIGH SCHOOL: St. Michaels (Easton, Md.).
TRANSACTIONS/CAREER NOTES: Selected by Chicago White Sox organization in first round (first pick overall) of free-agent draft (June 7, 1977). ... On disabled list (April 7-May 8, 1987). ... Traded by White Sox with IF Fred Manrique to Texas Rangers for SS Scott Fletcher, OF Sammy Sosa and P Wilson Alvarez (July 29, 1989). ... Traded by Rangers to Oakland Athletics for two players to be named later (August 29,

1990); Rangers acquired P Joe Bitker and P Scott Chiamparino to complete deal (September 4, 1990). ... Granted free agency (October 27, 1992); accepted arbitration. ... Traded by A's to Baltimore Orioles for P Bobby Chouinard and P Allen Plaster (January 14, 1993). ... On Baltimore disabled list (May 5-27, 1993); included rehabilitation assignment to Bowie (May 25-27). ... Granted free agency (November 1, 1993). ... Re-signed by Orioles (December 2, 1993). ... Granted free agency (October 20, 1994). ... Re-signed by Orioles (December 23, 1994). ... Granted free agency (November 6, 1995). ... Signed by White Sox (December 11, 1995). ... Granted free agency (November 18, 1996). ... Re-signed by White Sox (January 10, 1997). ... Traded by White Sox to Orioles for a player to be named later (July 29, 1997); White Sox acquired SS Juan Bautista to complete deal (August 18, 1997). ... Granted free agency (October 29, 1997). ... Re-signed by Orioles (December 19, 1997). ... On disabled list (July 11-August 4, 1998). ... Traded by Orioles to Cleveland Indians for P Juan Aracena and a player to be named later (August 27, 1999); Orioles acquired P Jimmy Hamilton to complete deal (August 31, 1999). ... Granted free agency (October 29, 1999). ... Signed by Orioles (December 9, 1999). ... Traded by Orioles with C Charles Johnson to White Sox for C Brook Fordyce, P Miguel Felix, P Juan Figueroa and P Jason Lakman (July 29, 2000). ... Granted free agency (November 3, 2000). ... Re-signed by White Sox organization (January 8, 2001). ... On Chicago disabled list (June 14-September 4, 2001); included rehabilitation assignment to Charlotte (September 2-4). ... Granted free agency (November 6, 2001).

RECORDS: Shares major league single-game record for most plate appearances—12 (May 8, finished May 9, 1984, 25 innings). ... Shares A.L. record for longest errorless game by outfielder—25 innings (May 8, finished May 9, 1984). ... Shares A.L. single-game record for most innings by outfielder—25 (May 8, finished May 9, 1984).

HONORS: Named outfielder on THE SPORTING NEWS A.L. All-Star team (1985). ... Named designated hitter on THE SPORTING NEWS A.L. All-Star team (1988-89). ... Named designated hitter on THE SPORTING NEWS A.L. Silver Slugger team (1989).

STATISTICAL NOTES: Tied for American Association lead in double plays by outfielder with four in 1979. ... Hit three home runs in one game (July 7, 1982; September 17, 1984 and May 7, 1991). ... Led A.L. with 22 game-winning RBIs in 1983. ... Led A.L. with .541 slugging percentage in 1984. ... Career major league grand slams: 13.

Year — Team (League)	Pos.	G	AB	R	H	2B	3B	HR	RBI	Avg.	BB	SO	SB	PO	A	E	Avg.
1977—Appleton (Midw.)	OF	69	222	37	58	11	2	5	29	.261	36	62	2	94	10	7	.937
1978—Knoxville (Sou.)	OF-1B	137	502	70	138	16	6	13	72	.275	43	91	3	291	22	13	.960
1979—Iowa (A.A.)	OF	125	466	87	139	25	8	22	87	.298	33	80	5	222	•16	11	.956
1980—Chicago (A.L.)	OF-DH	141	491	55	125	23	6	13	49	.255	19	65	2	229	6	9	.963
1981—Chicago (A.L.)	OF-DH	82	280	42	80	11	7	10	41	.286	12	41	6	120	10	2	.985
1982—Chicago (A.L.)	OF	161	608	89	165	29	8	25	105	.271	49	95	10	326	10	7	.980
1983—Chicago (A.L.)	OF	156	596	76	167	33	2	20	99	.280	49	85	7	312	10	9	.973
1984—Chicago (A.L.)	OF	147	569	72	173	28	10	29	94	.304	54	75	1	307	8	6	.981
1985—Chicago (A.L.)	OF-DH	160	640	86	198	29	3	22	113	.309	42	89	1	318	8	2	.994
1986—Chicago (A.L.)	OF-DH	145	570	72	169	29	2	21	88	.296	38	89	2	295	15	5	.984
1987—Chicago (A.L.)	DH-OF	132	505	59	148	26	4	20	93	.293	46	82	0	13	0	0	1.000
1988—Chicago (A.L.)	DH-OF	158	599	55	166	39	1	13	81	.277	67	109	0	14	1	2	.882
1989—Chicago (A.L.)	DH-OF	70	333	55	107	20	1	13	56	.321	60	52	0	52	0	1	.981
— Texas (A.L.)■	DH-OF	46	172	18	49	9	0	3	16	.285	13	27	0	2	0	1	.667
1990—Texas (A.L.)	DH	103	321	41	93	10	1	13	44	.290	47	63	0	...	...	...	...
— Oakland (A.L.)■	DH-OF	32	94	11	25	5	0	3	21	.266	20	17	0	5	0	1	.833
1991—Oakland (A.L.)	DH-OF	141	488	76	144	25	1	20	90	.295	72	67	0	11	1	1	.923
1992—Oakland (A.L.)	DH-OF	140	478	58	121	18	0	16	76	.253	59	61	1	27	0	1	.964
1993—Baltimore (A.L.)■	DH	118	416	64	130	22	0	20	78	.313	57	52	0	...	...	...	...
— Bowie (East.)	DH	2	6	0	0	0	0	0	0	.000	1	1	0	...	...	...	...
1994—Baltimore (A.L.)	DH	94	326	44	96	12	1	16	54	.294	30	49	0	...	...	...	...
1995—Baltimore (A.L.)	DH	127	385	60	115	19	1	24	63	.299	70	45	0	...	...	...	...
1996—Chicago (A.L.)	DH	143	495	80	154	29	0	22	95	.311	73	62	3	...	...	...	...
1997—Chicago (A.L.)	DH-OF	93	318	40	97	18	0	12	52	.305	41	47	0	0	0	0	...
— Baltimore (A.L.)■	DH	44	134	15	39	5	0	4	15	.291	14	15	0	...	...	...	...
1998—Baltimore (A.L.)	DH	104	293	40	88	17	0	9	57	.300	32	40	0	...	...	...	...
1999—Baltimore (A.L.)	DH	107	345	57	111	16	1	24	81	.322	43	38	1	...	...	...	...
— Cleveland (A.L.)■	DH	28	85	5	23	2	0	1	22	.271	11	10	0	...	...	...	...
2000—Baltimore (A.L.)■	DH	72	222	24	59	8	0	10	30	.266	29	39	0	...	...	...	...
— Chicago (A.L.)■	DH	24	61	2	13	5	0	1	9	.213	7	11	0	...	...	...	...
2001—Chicago (A.L.)	DH	32	84	3	11	1	0	0	6	.131	8	16	0	...	...	...	...
— Charlotte (I.L.)	DH	2	8	0	0	0	0	0	0	.000	0	1	0	...	...	...	...
Major League totals (22 years)		2800	9908	1299	2866	488	49	384	1628	.289	1062	1441	34	2031	69	47	.978

DIVISION SERIES RECORD

NOTES: Hit home run in first at-bat (October 2, 1997).

Year — Team (League)	Pos.	G	AB	R	H	2B	3B	HR	RBI	Avg.	BB	SO	SB	PO	A	E	Avg.
1997—Baltimore (A.L.)	DH-PH	2	5	2	2	0	0	1	1	.400	1	0	0	...	...	...	...
1999—Cleveland (A.L.)	DH	4	14	1	5	0	0	1	4	.357	2	1	0	...	...	...	...
2000—Chicago (A.L.)	PH-DH	2	4	1	1	1	0	0	0	.250	0	1	0	...	...	...	...
Division series totals (3 years)		8	23	4	8	1	0	2	5	.348	3	2	0	...	...	...	...

CHAMPIONSHIP SERIES RECORD

Year — Team (League)	Pos.	G	AB	R	H	2B	3B	HR	RBI	Avg.	BB	SO	SB	PO	A	E	Avg.
1983—Chicago (A.L.)	OF	4	16	0	2	0	0	0	0	.125	1	3	0	5	1	0	1.000
1990—Oakland (A.L.)	DH	4	14	2	5	1	0	0	3	.357	2	1	1	...	...	...	...
1992—Oakland (A.L.)	DH	6	25	6	11	2	0	1	4	.440	0	3	0	...	...	...	...
1997—Baltimore (A.L.)	DH	6	17	1	6	0	0	1	2	.353	2	1	0	...	...	...	...
Championship series totals (4 years)		20	72	9	24	3	0	2	9	.333	5	8	1	5	1	0	1.000

WORLD SERIES RECORD

Year — Team (League)	Pos.	G	AB	R	H	2B	3B	HR	RBI	Avg.	BB	SO	SB	PO	A	E	Avg.
1990—Oakland (A.L.)	DH-PH	3	7	1	1	0	0	1	2	.143	1	2	0	...	...	...	...

ALL-STAR GAME RECORD

Year	League	Pos.	AB	R	H	2B	3B	HR	RBI	Avg.	BB	SO	SB	PO	A	E	Avg.
1985—American		PH	1	0	1	0	0	0	0	1.000	0	0	0	...	...	...	...
1986—American		PH	1	0	0	0	0	0	0	.000	0	0	0	...	...	...	...
1987—American		PH	1	0	0	0	0	0	0	.000	0	0	0	...	...	...	...
1989—American		DH	3	1	1	0	0	0	1	.333	0	1	0	...	...	...	...
1991—American		PH-DH	1	0	0	0	0	0	1	.000	0	0	0	...	...	...	...
1999—American		PH-DH	1	0	1	0	0	0	0	1.000	0	0	0	...	...	...	...
All-Star Game totals (6 years)			8	1	3	0	0	0	2	.375	0	1	0	...	...	...	...

BAKO, PAUL   C   BRAVES

B

PERSONAL: Born June 20, 1972, in Lafayette, La. ... 6-2/205. ... Bats left, throws right. ... Full name: Gabor Paul Bako.
HIGH SCHOOL: Lafayette (La.).
COLLEGE: Southwestern Louisiana.
TRANSACTIONS/CAREER NOTES: Selected by Cincinnati Reds organization in fifth round of free-agent draft (June 3, 1993). ... Traded by Reds with P Donne Wall to Detroit Tigers for OF Melvin Nieves (November 11, 1997). ... Traded by Tigers with P Dean Crow, P Mark Persails, P Brian Powell and 3B Carlos Villalobos to Houston Astros for C Brad Ausmus and P C.J. Nitkowski (January 14, 1999). ... Traded by Astros to Florida Marlins for a player to be named to later (April 11, 2000); Astros acquired cash to complete deal (October 10, 2000). ... Claimed on waivers by Atlanta Braves (July 21, 2000).
STATISTICAL NOTES: Tied for Carolina League lead with 15 passed balls in 1995. ... Led Southern League catchers with 791 total chances in 1996. ... Tied for American Association lead in double plays with 10 and passed balls with nine by a catcher in 1997.

Year	Team (League)	Pos.	G	AB	R	H	2B	3B	HR	RBI	Avg.	BB	SO	SB	PO	A	E	Avg.
1993—Billings (Pio.)		C-1B	57	194	34	61	11	0	4	30	.314	22	37	5	323	45	6	.984
1994—Win.-Salem (Caro.)		C	90	289	29	59	9	1	3	26	.204	35	81	2	570	73	15	.977
1995—Win.-Salem (Caro.)		C	82	249	29	71	11	2	7	27	.285	42	66	3	478	49	6	.989
1996—Chattanooga (Sou.)		C	110	360	53	106	27	0	8	48	.294	48	93	1	*694	*84	13	.984
1997—Indianapolis (A.A.)......		C	104	321	34	78	14	1	8	43	.243	34	81	0	622	64	6	.991
1998—Toledo (I.L.)■..........		C	13	48	5	14	3	1	1	6	.292	1	13	0	75	5	1	.988
—Detroit (A.L.)		C	96	305	23	83	12	1	3	30	.272	23	82	1	493	45	6	.989
1999—New Orleans (PCL)■..		C	12	47	2	9	3	1	1	4	.191	1	11	0	58	4	1	.984
—Houston (N.L.)		C	73	215	16	55	14	1	2	17	.256	26	57	1	461	35	6	.988
2000—Houston (N.L.)		C	1	2	0	0	0	0	0	0	.000	0	1	0	2	1	0	1.000
—Florida (N.L.)■..........		C	56	161	10	39	6	1	0	14	.242	22	48	0	318	21	3	.991
—Atlanta (N.L.)■..........		C-1B	24	58	8	11	4	0	2	6	.190	5	15	0	118	9	1	.992
2001—Atlanta (N.L.).............		C	61	137	19	29	10	1	2	15	.212	20	34	1	319	29	3	.991
American League totals (1 year)			96	305	23	83	12	1	3	30	.272	23	82	1	493	45	6	.989
National League totals (3 years)			215	573	53	134	34	3	6	52	.234	73	155	2	1218	95	13	.990
Major League totals (4 years)			311	878	76	217	46	4	9	82	.247	96	237	3	1711	140	19	.990

DIVISION SERIES RECORD

Year	Team (League)	Pos.	G	AB	R	H	2B	3B	HR	RBI	Avg.	BB	SO	SB	PO	A	E	Avg.
2000—Atlanta (N.L.).............		C	2	1	0	0	0	0	0	0	.000	0	1	0	4	0	1	.800
2001—Atlanta (N.L.).............		C	3	7	1	2	1	0	1	3	.286	1	0	0	17	0	0	1.000
Division series totals (2 years)			5	8	1	2	1	0	1	3	.250	1	1	0	21	0	1	.955

CHAMPIONSHIP SERIES RECORD

Year	Team (League)	Pos.	G	AB	R	H	2B	3B	HR	RBI	Avg.	BB	SO	SB	PO	A	E	Avg.
2001—Atlanta (N.L.).............		C	3	3	0	0	0	0	0	0	.000	0	0	0	10	1	0	1.000

BALDWIN, JAMES   P

PERSONAL: Born July 15, 1971, in Southern Pines, N.C. ... 6-3/210. ... Throws right, bats right. ... Full name: James Baldwin Jr.
HIGH SCHOOL: Pinecrest (Southern Pines, N.C.).
TRANSACTIONS/CAREER NOTES: Selected by Chicago White Sox organization in fourth round of free-agent draft (June 4, 1990). ... On disabled list (August 3-19, 1994). ... On Chicago disabled list (March 23-April 21, 2001); included rehabilitation assignment to Charlotte (April 11-17). ... Traded by White Sox to Los Angeles Dodgers for P Onan Masaoka, P Gary Majewski and OF Jeff Barry (July 26, 2001). ... Granted free agency (November 5, 2001).
RECORDS: Shares A.L. single-game record for most hit batsmen (nine innings)—4 (August 17, 2000).
HONORS: Named A.L. Rookie Pitcher of the Year by THE SPORTING NEWS (1996).
STATISTICAL NOTES: Led American Association with 27 home runs allowed and tied for lead with three balks in 1995. ... Tied for A.L. lead with 14 wild pitches and three balks in 1997.

Year	League	W	L	Pct.	ERA	G	GS	CG	ShO	Sv.	IP	H	R	ER	BB	SO
1990—GC White Sox (GCL)		1	6	.143	4.10	9	7	0	0	0	$37\frac{1}{3}$	32	29	17	18	32
1991—GC White Sox (GCL)		3	1	.750	2.12	6	6	0	0	0	34	16	8	8	16	48
—Utica (NY-Penn)		1	4	.200	5.30	7	7	1	0	0	$37\frac{1}{3}$	40	26	22	27	23
1992—South Bend (Midw.)		9	5	.643	2.42	21	21	1	1	0	$137\frac{2}{3}$	118	53	37	45	137
—Sarasota (FSL)		1	2	.333	2.87	6	6	1	0	0	$37\frac{2}{3}$	31	13	12	7	39
1993—Birmingham (Sou.)............		8	5	.615	*2.25	17	17	•4	0	0	120	94	48	30	43	107
—Nashville (A.A.)		5	4	.556	2.61	10	10	1	0	0	69	43	21	20	36	61
1994—Nashville (A.A.)		12	6	.667	3.72	26	26	2	0	0	162	144	75	67	83	*156
1995—Chicago (A.L.)		0	1	.000	12.89	6	4	0	0	0	$14\frac{2}{3}$	32	22	21	9	10
—Nashville (A.A.)		5	9	.357	5.85	18	18	0	0	0	$95\frac{1}{3}$	120	76	62	44	89
1996—Nashville (A.A.)		1	1	.500	0.64	2	2	1	0	0	14	5	1	1	4	15
—Chicago (A.L.)		11	6	.647	4.42	28	28	0	0	0	169	168	88	83	57	127

Year League	W	L	Pct.	ERA	G	GS	CG	ShO	Sv.	IP	H	R	ER	BB	SO
1997—Chicago (A.L.)	12	•15	.444	5.26	32	32	1	0	0	200	205	128	117	83	140
1998—Chicago (A.L.)	13	6	.684	5.32	37	24	1	0	0	159	176	103	94	60	108
1999—Chicago (A.L.)	12	13	.480	5.10	35	33	1	0	0	199 1/3	219	119	113	81	123
2000—Chicago (A.L.)	14	7	.667	4.65	29	28	2	1	0	178	185	96	92	59	116
2001—Charlotte (I.L.)	1	0	1.000	5.25	2	2	0	0	0	12	12	7	7	2	11
—Chicago (A.L.)	7	5	.583	4.61	17	16	2	1	0	95 2/3	109	56	49	38	42
—Los Angeles (N.L.)■	3	6	.333	4.20	12	12	0	0	0	79 1/3	82	39	37	25	53
A.L. totals (7 years)	69	53	.566	5.04	184	165	7	2	0	1015 2/3	1094	612	569	387	666
N.L. totals (1 year)	3	6	.333	4.20	12	12	0	0	0	79 1/3	82	39	37	25	53
Major League totals (7 years)	72	59	.550	4.98	196	177	7	2	0	1095	1176	651	606	412	719

DIVISION SERIES RECORD

Year League	W	L	Pct.	ERA	G	GS	CG	ShO	Sv.	IP	H	R	ER	BB	SO
2000—Chicago (A.L.)	0	0	...	1.50	1	1	0	0	0	6	3	1	1	3	2

ALL-STAR GAME RECORD

Year League	W	L	Pct.	ERA	GS	CG	ShO	Sv.	IP	H	R	ER	BB	SO
2000—American	1	0	1.000	9.00	0	0	0	0	1	2	1	1	0	0

B

BALE, JOHN   P   ORIOLES

PERSONAL: Born May 22, 1974, in Cheverly, Md. ... 6-4/205. ... Throws left, bats left. ... Full name: John Robert Bale.
HIGH SCHOOL: Crestview (Fla.).
JUNIOR COLLEGE: Jefferson Davis Community College (Ala.).
COLLEGE: Southern Mississippi.
TRANSACTIONS/CAREER NOTES: Selected by St. Louis Cardinals organization in 12th round of free-agent draft (June 2, 1994); did not sign. ... Selected by Toronto Blue Jays organization in fifth round of free-agent draft (June 4, 1996). ... On Syracuse disabled list (May 4-19 and June 29-July 20, 2000). ... Traded by Blue Jays to Baltimore Orioles for C Jayson Werth (December 11, 2000). ... On Rochester disabled list (June 11-July 16, 2001).

Year League	W	L	Pct.	ERA	G	GS	CG	ShO	Sv.	IP	H	R	ER	BB	SO
1996—St. Catharines (NY-Penn)	3	2	.600	4.86	8	8	0	0	0	33 1/3	39	21	18	11	35
1997—Hagerstown (S.Atl.)	7	7	.500	4.30	25	25	0	0	0	140 1/3	130	83	67	63	155
1998—Dunedin (FSL)	4	5	.444	4.64	24	9	0	0	4	66	68	39	34	23	78
—Knoxville (Sou.)	0	0	...	6.75	3	0	0	0	0	1 1/3	1	1	1	0	0
1999—Knoxville (Sou.)	2	2	.500	3.75	33	4	0	0	1	62 1/3	64	32	26	16	91
—Syracuse (I.L.)	0	3	.000	3.97	6	4	0	0	0	22 2/3	16	14	10	10	10
—Toronto (A.L.)	0	0	...	13.50	1	0	0	0	0	2	2	3	3	2	4
2000—Syracuse (I.L.)	3	4	.429	3.19	21	12	0	0	0	79	68	35	28	41	70
—Toronto (A.L.)	0	0	...	14.73	2	0	0	0	0	3 2/3	5	7	6	3	6
2001—Rochester (I.L.)■	1	1	.500	2.05	9	7	0	0	0	30 2/3	31	8	7	5	41
—Baltimore (A.L.)	1	0	1.000	3.04	14	0	0	0	0	26 2/3	18	14	9	17	21
—Gulf Coast Orioles (GCL)	0	0	...	2.25	2	2	0	0	0	4	1	1	1	2	7
Major League totals (3 years)	1	0	1.000	5.01	17	0	0	0	0	32 1/3	25	24	18	22	31

BALFOUR, GRANT   P   TWINS

PERSONAL: Born December 30, 1977, in Sydney, Australia. ... 6-2/170. ... Throws right, bats right. ... Full name: Grant Robert Balfour.
HIGH SCHOOL: William Clarke College (Kellyville, New South Wales, Australia).
TRANSACTIONS/CAREER NOTES: Signed as non-drafted free agent by Minnesota Twins organization (January 19, 1997). ... On New Britain disabled list (April 6-26, 2001).

Year League	W	L	Pct.	ERA	G	GS	CG	ShO	Sv.	IP	H	R	ER	BB	SO
1997—Gulf Coast Twins (GCL)	2	4	.333	3.76	13	12	0	0	0	67	•73	31	28	20	43
1998—Elizabethton (Appl.)	*7	2	.778	3.36	13	13	0	0	0	77 2/3	70	36	29	27	75
1999—Quad City (Midw.)	8	5	.615	3.53	19	14	0	0	1	91 2/3	66	39	36	37	95
2000—Fort Myers (FSL)	8	5	.615	4.25	35	10	0	0	6	89	91	46	42	34	90
2001—New Britain (East.)	2	1	.667	1.08	35	0	0	0	13	50	26	6	6	22	72
—Minnesota (A.L.)	0	0	...	13.50	2	0	0	0	0	2 2/3	3	4	4	3	2
—Edmonton (PCL)	2	2	.500	5.51	11	0	0	0	0	16 1/3	18	11	10	10	17
Major League totals (1 year)	0	0	...	13.50	2	0	0	0	0	2 2/3	3	4	4	3	2

BANKS, WILLIE   P   RED SOX

PERSONAL: Born February 27, 1969, in Jersey City, N.J. ... 6-1/200. ... Throws right, bats right. ... Full name: Willie Anthony Banks.
HIGH SCHOOL: St. Anthony (Jersey City, N.J.).
TRANSACTIONS/CAREER NOTES: Selected by Minnesota Twins organization in first round (third pick overall) of free-agent draft (June 2, 1987). ... Traded by Twins to Chicago Cubs for P Dave Stevens and C Matt Walbeck (November 24, 1993). ... Traded by Cubs to Los Angeles Dodgers for P Dax Winslett (June 19, 1995). ... Claimed on waivers by Florida Marlins (August 10, 1995). ... Claimed on waivers by Philadelphia Phillies (October 4, 1995). ... Released by Phillies (March 8, 1996). ... Signed by New York Yankees organization (January 3, 1997). ... Traded by Yankees to Arizona Diamondbacks for P Scott Brow and P Joe Lisio (June 3, 1998). ... Granted free agency (December 21, 1998). ... Signed by Orix Blue Wave of Japan Pacific League (1999). ... Signed by New York Mets organization (July 12, 2000). ... Granted free agency (October 18, 2000). ... Signed by Toronto Blue Jays organization (April 2, 2001). ... Released by Blue Jays (August 15, 2001). ... Signed by Boston Red Sox organization (August 23, 2001).
STATISTICAL NOTES: Led Appalachian League with 28 wild pitches and tied for lead with three balks in 1987. ... Pitched 1-0 no-hit victory for Visalia against Palm Springs (May 24, 1989). ... Led California League with 22 wild pitches in 1989. ... Tied for Pacific Coast League lead with 14 wild pitches in 1991. ... Tied for A.L. lead with five balks in 1993.
MISCELLANEOUS: Appeared in two games as pinch runner and struck out in only appearance as pinch hitter with Florida (1995).

Year League	W	L	Pct.	ERA	G	GS	CG	ShO	Sv.	IP	H	R	ER	BB	SO
1987— Elizabethton (Appl.)	1	8	.111	6.99	13	13	0	0	0	65²/₃	73	*71	*51	*62	71
1988— Kenosha (Midw.)	10	10	.500	3.72	24	24	0	0	0	125²/₃	109	73	52	*107	113
1989— Visalia (Calif.)	12	9	.571	2.59	27	27	7	•4	0	174	122	70	50	85	*173
— Orlando (Sou.)	1	0	1.000	5.14	1	1	0	0	0	7	10	4	4	0	9
1990— Orlando (Sou.)	7	9	.438	3.93	28	28	1	0	0	162²/₃	161	93	71	98	114
1991— Portland (PCL)	9	8	.529	4.55	25	24	1	1	0	146¹/₃	156	81	74	76	63
— Minnesota (A.L.)	1	1	.500	5.71	5	3	0	0	0	17¹/₃	21	15	11	12	16
1992— Portland (PCL)	6	1	.857	1.92	11	11	2	1	0	75	62	20	16	34	41
— Minnesota (A.L.)	4	4	.500	5.70	16	12	0	0	0	71	80	46	45	37	37
1993— Minnesota (A.L.)	11	12	.478	4.04	31	30	0	0	0	171¹/₃	186	91	77	78	138
1994— Chicago (N.L.)■............	8	12	.400	5.40	23	23	1	1	0	138¹/₃	139	88	83	56	91
1995— Chicago (N.L.)	0	1	.000	15.43	10	0	0	0	0	11²/₃	27	23	20	12	9
— Los Angeles (N.L.)■.........	0	2	.000	4.03	6	6	0	0	0	29	36	21	13	16	23
— Florida (N.L.)■	2	3	.400	4.32	9	9	0	0	0	50	43	27	24	30	30
1996—										Out of organized baseball.					
1997— Columbus (I.L.)■............	14	5	.737	4.27	33	24	1	0	3	154	164	87	73	45	130
— New York (A.L.)	3	0	1.000	1.93	5	1	0	0	0	14	9	3	3	6	8
1998— New York (A.L.)	1	1	.500	10.05	9	0	0	0	0	14¹/₃	20	16	16	12	8
— Arizona (N.L.)■............	1	2	.333	3.09	33	0	0	0	1	43²/₃	34	21	15	25	32
1999— Orix (Jap.Pacific)■	3	3	.500	3.94	13	2	0	0	1	30	27	16	13	21	26
— Orix (Jap. Western)............	4	1	.800	3.20	10	6	0	0	0	39	36	15	14	23	35
2000— Surpass (Jap. Western)■ ..	0	5	.000	6.40	13	10	0	0	0	58	69	44	41	55	37
— Norfolk (I.L.)■	2	4	.333	5.08	9	9	0	0	0	51¹/₃	56	32	29	25	20
2001— Syracuse (I.L.)■	8	5	.615	3.25	24	23	0	0	0	146²/₃	151	63	53	53	121
— Pawtucket (I.L.)■	2	0	1.000	1.42	2	2	0	0	0	12²/₃	8	3	2	3	12
— Boston (A.L.)	0	0	...	0.84	5	0	0	0	0	10²/₃	5	4	1	4	10
A.L. totals (6 years)	20	18	.526	4.61	71	46	0	0	0	298²/₃	321	175	153	149	217
N.L. totals (3 years)	11	20	.355	5.12	81	38	1	1	1	272²/₃	279	180	155	139	185
Major League totals (8 years)	31	38	.449	4.85	152	84	1	1	1	571¹/₃	600	355	308	288	402

BARAJAS, ROD   C   DIAMONDBACKS

PERSONAL: Born September 5, 1975, in Ontario, Calif. ... 6-2/220. ... Bats right, throws right. ... Full name: Rodrigo Richard Barajas.
HIGH SCHOOL: Sante Fe Springs (Calif.).
JUNIOR COLLEGE: Cerritos.
TRANSACTIONS/CAREER NOTES: Signed as non-drafted free agent by Arizona Diamondbacks organization (January 23, 1996). ... Loaned by Diamondbacks to Visalia, Oakland Athletics organization (April 5-June 16, 1996).
STATISTICAL NOTES: Led Pioneer League catchers with .985 fielding percentage in 1996. ... Led Texas League catchers with 787 putouts, 95 assists, 14 errors and 896 total chances in 1999. ... Tied Pacific Coast League lead with 11 sacrifice flies in 2000. ... Led Pacific Coast League catchers with 69 assists in 2000. ... Tied for Pacific Coast League lead with 11 errors by catchers in 2000.

						BATTING								FIELDING		
Year Team (League)	Pos.	G	AB	R	H	2B	3B	HR	RBI	Avg.	BB	SO	SB	PO	A	E	Avg.
1996— Visalia (Calif.)■..........	C	27	74	6	12	3	0	0	8	.162	7	21	0	83	14	0	1.000
— Lethbridge (Pio.)■....	C-1B	51	175	47	59	9	3	10	50	.337	12	24	2	301	43	5	†.986
1997— High Desert (Calif.)....	C-1B	57	199	24	53	11	0	7	30	.266	8	41	0	374	38	3	.993
1998— High Desert (Calif.)....	C	113	442	67	134	26	0	23	81	.303	25	81	1	749	85	14	.983
1999— El Paso (Texas)..........	C-DH-1B	127	510	77	162	41	2	14	95	.318	24	73	2	†827	†97	†14	.985
— Arizona (N.L.)............	C	5	16	3	4	1	0	1	3	.250	1	1	0	30	1	0	1.000
2000— Tucson (PCL)	C-1B-3B	110	416	43	94	25	0	13	75	.226	14	65	4	623	80	‡14	.980
— Arizona (N.L.)............	C	5	13	1	3	0	0	1	3	.231	0	4	0	23	0	0	1.000
2001— Arizona (N.L.)............	C	51	106	9	17	3	0	3	9	.160	4	26	0	179	11	1	.995
— Tucson (PCL)	C-1B-3B	45	162	23	52	13	0	9	32	.321	9	23	3	275	21	3	.990
Major League totals (3 years)		61	135	13	24	4	0	5	15	.178	5	31	0	232	12	1	.996

DIVISION SERIES RECORD

						BATTING								FIELDING		
Year Team (League)	Pos.	G	AB	R	H	2B	3B	HR	RBI	Avg.	BB	SO	SB	PO	A	E	Avg.
2001— Arizona (N.L.)............	C	1	0	0	0	0	0	0	0	...	0	0	0	0	0	0	...

CHAMPIONSHIP SERIES RECORD

						BATTING								FIELDING		
Year Team (League)	Pos.	G	AB	R	H	2B	3B	HR	RBI	Avg.	BB	SO	SB	PO	A	E	Avg.
2001— Arizona (N.L.)............							Did not play.										

WORLD SERIES RECORD

NOTES: Member of World Series championship team (2001).

						BATTING								FIELDING		
Year Team (League)	Pos.	G	AB	R	H	2B	3B	HR	RBI	Avg.	BB	SO	SB	PO	A	E	Avg.
2001— Arizona (N.L.)............	C	2	5	1	2	0	0	1	1	.400	0	0	0	9	2	0	1.000

BARCELO, LORENZO   P   WHITE SOX

PERSONAL: Born August 10, 1977, in San Pedro de Macoris, Dominican Republic. ... 6-4/220. ... Throws right, bats right. ... Full name: Lorenzo A. Barcelo. ... Brother of Orger Barcelo, player in Atlanta Braves organization (1990).
HIGH SCHOOL: Sanatonio (San Pedro de Macoris, Dominican Republic).
TRANSACTIONS/CAREER NOTES: Signed as non-drafted free agent by San Francisco Giants organization (May 23, 1994). ... Traded by Giants with SS Mike Caruso, OF Brian Manning, P Keith Foulke, P Bob Howry and P Ken Vining by Giants to Chicago White Sox for P Wilson Alvarez, P Danny Darwin and P Roberto Hernandez (July 31, 1997). ... On Birmingham disabled list (April 2, 1998-entire season); included rehabilitation assignment to Arizona League White Sox (June 29-July 9). ... On Birmingham disabled list (April 8-August 13, 1999); included rehabilitation assignment to Burlington (August 11-13). ... On Chicago disabled list (June 4, 2001-remainder of season).
STATISTICAL NOTES: Led Midwest League with 19 home runs allowed in 1996.

B

Year League	W	L	Pct.	ERA	G	GS	CG	ShO	Sv.	IP	H	R	ER	BB	SO
1994—Dominican Giants (DSL)	0	0	...	4.32	22	0	0	0	0	41 2/3	45	37	20	28	25
1995—Bellingham (N'West)	3	2	.600	3.45	12	11	0	0	0	47	43	23	18	19	34
1996—Burlington (Midw.)	12	10	.545	3.54	26	26	1	0	0	152 2/3	138	70	60	46	139
1997—San Jose (Calif.)	5	4	.556	3.94	16	16	1	1	0	89	91	45	39	30	89
—Shreveport (Texas)	2	0	1.000	4.02	5	5	0	0	0	31 1/3	30	19	14	8	20
—Birmingham (Sou.)■	2	1	.667	4.86	6	6	0	0	0	33 1/3	36	20	18	9	29
1998—Arizona White Sox (Ariz.) ...	0	1	.000	1.50	3	3	0	0	0	6	6	1	1	0	9
1999—Arizona White Sox (Ariz.) ...	2	1	.667	1.69	9	9	0	0	0	42 2/3	36	14	8	6	57
—Burlington (Midw.)	1	0	1.000	3.60	1	1	0	0	0	5	3	2	2	0	6
—Birmingham (Sou.)	0	1	.000	3.60	4	4	0	0	0	20	14	8	8	6	14
2000—Charlotte (I.L.)	5	6	.455	4.26	17	17	0	0	0	99 1/3	114	53	47	17	62
—Chicago (A.L.)	4	2	.667	3.69	22	1	0	0	0	39	34	17	16	9	26
2001—Charlotte (I.L.)	1	0	1.000	5.40	2	0	0	0	0	5	6	3	3	1	5
—Chicago (A.L.)	1	0	1.000	4.71	17	0	0	0	0	21	24	13	11	8	15
Major League totals (2 years)	5	2	.714	4.05	39	1	0	0	0	60	58	30	27	17	41

DIVISION SERIES RECORD

Year League	W	L	Pct.	ERA	G	GS	CG	ShO	Sv.	IP	H	R	ER	BB	SO
2000—Chicago (A.L.)	0	0	...	0.00	1	0	0	0	0	1 2/3	0	0	0	1	0

BARKER, GLEN — OF

PERSONAL: Born May 10, 1971, in Albany, N.Y. ... 5-10/180. ... Bats right, throws right. ... Full name: Glen F. Barker.
HIGH SCHOOL: Albany (N.Y.).
COLLEGE: The College of St. Rose (N.Y.).
TRANSACTIONS/CAREER NOTES: Selected by Detroit Tigers organization in 11th round of free-agent draft (June 3, 1993). ... Selected by Houston Astros from Tigers organization in Rule 5 major league draft (December 14, 1998). ... On disabled list (August 24-September 8, 1999). ... On New Orleans disabled list (May 16-26, 2000). ... Granted free agency (December 21, 2001).
STATISTICAL NOTES: Led Southern League outfielders in total chances with 323 and seven double plays in 1998.

Year Team (League)	Pos.	G	AB	R	H	2B	3B	HR	RBI	Avg.	BB	SO	SB	PO	A	E	Avg.
1993—Niagara Falls (NY-P) ...	OF	72	253	49	55	11	4	5	23	.217	24	71	*37	148	3	1	*.993
1994—Fayetteville (S.Atl.)	OF	74	267	38	61	13	5	1	30	.228	33	79	41	144	6	3	.980
—Lakeland (FSL)	OF	28	104	10	19	5	1	2	6	.183	4	34	5	71	4	2	.974
1995—Jacksonville (Sou.)	OF	133	507	74	121	26	4	10	49	.239	33	*143	39	284	9	8	.973
1996—Jacksonville (Sou.)	OF	43	120	9	19	2	1	0	8	.158	8	36	6	91	2	2	.979
—Fayetteville (S.Atl.)	OF	37	132	23	38	1	0	1	9	.288	16	34	20	91	3	1	.989
—Toledo (I.L.)................	OF	24	80	13	20	2	1	0	2	.250	9	25	6	51	3	1	.982
1997—Toledo (I.L.)................	OF	21	47	9	9	1	0	1	3	.191	5	15	6	24	1	0	1.000
—Lakeland (FSL)	OF	13	57	9	18	4	0	1	11	.316	4	17	7	34	0	0	1.000
—Jacksonville (Sou.)........	OF	69	257	47	72	8	4	6	29	.280	29	72	17	154	6	2	.988
1998—Jacksonville (Sou.)........	OF	110	453	95	127	29	6	6	54	.280	57	120	31	*307	16	0	*1.000
1999—Houston (N.L.)■	OF-DH	81	73	23	21	2	0	1	11	.288	11	19	17	50	2	1	.981
2000—Houston (N.L.)	OF	84	67	18	15	2	1	2	6	.224	7	23	9	64	1	1	.985
—New Orleans (PCL).....	OF	26	107	15	29	5	0	2	10	.271	10	12	11	63	2	2	.970
2001—Houston (N.L.)	OF	70	24	12	2	0	0	0	1	.083	3	6	4	36	0	0	1.000
—New Orleans (PCL).....	OF	46	168	28	47	2	4	2	20	.280	12	45	7	91	6	2	.980
Major League totals (3 years)		235	164	53	38	4	1	3	18	.232	21	48	30	150	3	2	.987

DIVISION SERIES RECORD

Year Team (League)	Pos.	G	AB	R	H	2B	3B	HR	RBI	Avg.	BB	SO	SB	PO	A	E	Avg.
1999—Houston (N.L.)	OF-PR	2	3	1	0	0	0	0	0	.000	0	2	1	1	0	0	1.000

BARKETT, ANDY — 1B/OF

PERSONAL: Born September 5, 1974, in Miami. ... 6-1/205. ... Bats left, throws left. ... Full name: Andrew Jon Barkett.
HIGH SCHOOL: Killian (Miami, Fla.).
COLLEGE: North Carolina State.
TRANSACTIONS/CAREER NOTES: Signed by Butte Copper Kings, Pioneer League (June 17, 1995). ... Contract purchased by Texas Rangers organization from Butte (August 10, 1995). ... Released by Rangers (May 4, 2000). ... Signed by Atlanta Braves organization (May 5, 2000). ... Granted free agency (October 15, 2000). ... Signed by Pittsburgh Pirates organization (January 12, 2001). ... Granted free agency (October 15, 2001).
STATISTICAL NOTES: Led Texas League first basemen with 1,205 total chances in 1997.

Year Team (League)	Pos.	G	AB	R	H	2B	3B	HR	RBI	Avg.	BB	SO	SB	PO	A	E	Avg.
1995—Butte (Pio.)................	1B-3B	45	162	33	54	11	5	5	51	.333	33	39	1	407	39	4	.991
—Charl., S.C. (S.Atl.)■..	1B-OF	21	78	7	17	6	0	0	12	.218	10	27	0	135	11	2	.986
1996—Charlotte (FSL)	1B	115	392	57	112	22	3	6	54	.286	57	59	3	822	72	6	.993
1997—Tulsa (Texas)	1B	130	471	82	141	34	8	8	65	.299	63	86	1	*1114	*76	15	.988
1998—Tulsa (Texas)	1B	43	157	23	42	11	1	2	31	.268	27	22	0	370	23	2	.995
—Oklahoma (PCL)........	1B	80	255	38	80	17	5	4	36	.314	35	43	3	612	33	4	.994
1999—Oklahoma (PCL)........	1B	132	486	70	149	32	5	10	76	.307	44	71	7	*1003	87	6	*.995
2000—Oklahoma (PCL)........	1B	13	45	4	8	2	0	0	1	.178	2	6	0	85	7	1	.989
—Richmond (I.L.)■........	1B-OF	75	260	22	63	17	1	6	38	.242	16	37	4	417	29	4	.991
2001—Nashville (PCL)■	1B-OF	91	273	37	66	17	0	6	42	.242	37	46	2	571	44	8	.987
—Pittsburgh (N.L.)	OF-1B-DH	17	46	5	14	2	0	1	3	.304	4	7	1	50	4	0	1.000
Major League totals (1 year)		17	46	5	14	2	0	1	3	.304	4	7	1	50	4	0	1.000

BARNES, JOHN   OF   ROCKIES

PERSONAL: Born April 24, 1976, in San Diego. ... 6-2/205. ... Bats right, throws right. ... Full name: John Delbert Barnes.
HIGH SCHOOL: Granite Hills (El Cajon, Calif.).
JUNIOR COLLEGE: Grossmont College (Calif.).
TRANSACTIONS/CAREER NOTES: Selected by Boston Red Sox oraganization in fourth round of free-agent draft (June 4, 1996). ... Traded by Red Sox with P Joe Thomas and P Matt Kinney to Minnesota Twins for P Greg Swindell and 1B Orlando Merced (July 31, 1998). ... On New Britain disabled list (August 23-September 3, 1998). ... On Minnesota disabled list (March 23-June 11, 2001); included rehabilitation assignment to Edmonton (May 21-June 6). ... Claimed on waivers by Colorado Rockies (September 18, 2001).

Year Team (League)	Pos.	G	AB	R	H	2B	3B	HR	RBI	Avg.	BB	SO	SB	PO	A	E	Avg.
1996— GC Red Sox (GCL)	OF	30	101	9	28	4	0	1	17	.277	5	17	4	39	3	1	.977
1997— Michigan (Midw.)	OF	130	490	80	149	19	5	6	73	.304	65	42	19	213	8	6	.974
1998— Trenton (East.)	OF	100	380	53	104	18	0	14	36	.274	40	47	3	134	6	3	.979
— New Britain (East.)■	OF	20	71	9	19	4	1	0	6	.268	9	9	1	39	2	0	1.000
1999— New Britain (East.)	OF	129	452	62	119	21	1	13	58	.263	49	40	10	247	12	4	.985
2000— Salt Lake (PCL)	OF	119	441	107	161	37	6	13	87	.365	57	48	7	244	8	6	.977
— Minnesota (A.L.)	OF	11	37	5	13	4	0	0	2	.351	2	6	0	28	2	0	1.000
2001— Edmonton (PCL)	OF	81	311	42	91	21	2	8	42	.293	27	28	3	132	8	0	1.000
— Minnesota (A.L.)	OF	9	21	1	1	0	0	0	0	.048	1	3	0	16	1	2	.895
Major League totals (2 years)		20	58	6	14	4	0	0	2	.241	3	9	0	44	3	2	.959

BARNES, LARRY   1B   ANGELS

PERSONAL: Born July 23, 1974, in Bakersfield, Calif. ... 6-1/195. ... Bats left, throws left. ... Full name: Larry Richard Barnes Jr.
HIGH SCHOOL: Bakersfield (Calif.).
JUNIOR COLLEGE: Bakersfield (Calif.) College.
COLLEGE: Fresno State.
TRANSACTIONS/CAREER NOTES: Selected by Florida Marlins organization in 69th round of free-agent draft (June 3, 1993); did not sign. ... Signed as non-drafted free agent by California Angels organization (June 6, 1995). ... Angels franchise renamed Anaheim Angels for 1997 season. ... On disabled list (September 1, 1999-remainder of season). ... On disabled list (July 26-August 9, 2000). ... On Salt Lake disabled list (May 12-24, 2001).
HONORS: Named Midwest League Most Valuable Player (1996).
STATISTICAL NOTES: Led Arizona League first basemen with 520 total chances and 49 double plays in 1995. ... Led Midwest League with 282 total bases and .577 slugging percentage in 1996. ... Tied for Midwest League lead with 80 assists by first baseman in 1996. ... Led California League first basemen with .993 fielding percentage in 1997. ... Led Eastern League with 16 sacrifice flies and seven intentional bases on balls received in 1999.

Year Team (League)	Pos.	G	AB	R	H	2B	3B	HR	RBI	Avg.	BB	SO	SB	PO	A	E	Avg.
1995— Arizona Angels (Ariz.)	1B	•56	197	•42	61	8	3	3	•37	.310	27	42	12	*494	19	7	.987
1996— Cedar Rapids (Midw.)	1B-DH-OF-C	131	489	84	155	•36	5	*27	*112	.317	58	101	9	1062	‡81	11	.990
1997— Lake Elsinore (Calif.)	1B-DH	115	446	68	128	32	2	13	71	.287	43	84	3	1048	87	8	†.993
1998— Lake Elsinore (Calif.)	1B	51	183	32	45	11	2	7	33	.246	22	49	2	451	17	6	.987
— Midland (Texas)	1B-DH-OF	69	245	29	67	16	4	6	35	.273	28	54	4	534	37	7	.988
1999— Erie (East.)	1B-DH	130	497	73	142	25	9	20	100	.286	49	99	14	1047	87	9	.992
2000— Edmonton (PCL)	1B-OF	103	397	56	102	22	11	7	54	.257	48	81	3	779	51	3	.996
2001— Salt Lake (PCL)	1B-OF	100	404	78	117	21	8	18	73	.290	29	90	6	680	53	7	.991
— Anaheim (A.L.)	1B-OF	16	40	2	4	0	0	1	2	.100	1	9	0	86	7	0	1.000
Major League totals (1 year)		16	40	2	4	0	0	1	2	.100	1	9	0	86	7	0	1.000

BARRETT, MICHAEL   C   EXPOS

PERSONAL: Born October 22, 1976, in Atlanta. ... 6-2/200. ... Bats right, throws right. ... Full name: Michael Patrick Barrett.
HIGH SCHOOL: Pace Academy (Atlanta).
TRANSACTIONS/CAREER NOTES: Selected by Montreal Expos organization in first round (28th pick overall) of free-agent draft (June 1, 1995). ... On Montreal disabled list (June 24-July 11, 1999); included rehabilitation assignment to Ottawa (July 9-10).

Year Team (League)	Pos.	G	AB	R	H	2B	3B	HR	RBI	Avg.	BB	SO	SB	PO	A	E	Avg.
1995— GC Expos (GCL)	SS-3B	50	183	22	57	13	4	0	19	.311	15	19	7	65	143	25	.893
— Vermont (NY-Penn)	SS	3	10	0	1	0	0	0	1	.100	1	1	0	1	3	0	1.000
1996— Delmarva (S.Atl.)	C-DH-3B	129	474	57	113	29	4	4	62	.238	18	42	5	607	74	15	.978
1997— W.P. Beach (FSL)	C-DH	119	423	52	120	30	0	8	61	.284	36	49	7	629	78	13	.982
1998— Harrisburg (East.)	C-3B-DH	120	453	78	145	32	2	19	87	.320	27	43	7	517	113	12	.981
— Montreal (N.L.)	C-3B	8	23	3	7	2	0	1	2	.304	3	6	0	22	9	3	.912
1999— Montreal (N.L.)	3B-C-SS	126	433	53	127	32	3	8	52	.293	32	39	0	374	130	14	.973
— Ottawa (I.L.)	3B	2	7	1	3	0	0	0	2	.429	1	0	0	0	4	1	.800
2000— Montreal (N.L.)	3B-C	89	271	28	58	15	1	1	22	.214	23	35	0	186	95	15	.949
2001— Montreal (N.L.)	C	132	472	42	118	33	2	6	38	.250	25	54	2	880	50	7	.993
Major League totals (4 years)		355	1199	126	310	82	6	16	114	.259	83	134	2	1462	284	39	.978

BARTEE, KIMERA   OF

PERSONAL: Born July 21, 1972, in Omaha, Neb. ... 6-0/200. ... Bats right, throws right. ... Full name: Kimera Anotchi Bartee.
HIGH SCHOOL: Central (Omaha, Neb.).
COLLEGE: Creighton.

TRANSACTIONS/CAREER NOTES: Selected by Baltimore Orioles organization in 14th round of free-agent draft (June 3, 1993). ... On Bowie disabled list (June 8-August 8, 1995). ... Traded by Orioles to Minnesota Twins (September 18, 1995), completing deal in which Orioles acquired P Scott Erickson from Twins for P Scott Klingenbeck and a player to be named later (July 7, 1995). ... Selected by Orioles from Twins organization in Rule 5 major league draft (December 4, 1995). ... Claimed on waivers by Detroit Tigers (March 13, 1996). ... Traded by Tigers to Cincinnati Reds for a player to be named later or cash (December 12, 1999). ... On Louisville disabled list (July 27-August 3, 2000). ... Released by Reds (December 1, 2000). ... Signed by Anaheim Angels (December 11, 2000). ... On Anaheim disabled list (March 23-June 4, 2001); included rehabilitation assignment to Rancho Cucamonga (May 12-June 4). ... Traded by Angels to Colorado Rockies for IF Chone Figgins (July 13, 2001). ... Granted free agency (October 8, 2001).
STATISTICAL NOTES: Led Carolina League outfielders with 317 total chances in 1994. ... Tied for International League lead in total chances by outfielder with 341 in 1997.
MISCELLANEOUS: Batted as switch-hitter (1993-98).

Year Team (League)	Pos.	G	AB	R	H	2B	3B	HR	RBI	Avg.	BB	SO	SB	PO	A	E	Avg.
1993—Bluefield (Appl.)	OF	66	264	59	65	15	2	4	37	.246	44	66	*27	124	5	4	.970
1994—Frederick (Caro.)	OF	130	514	97	150	22	4	10	57	.292	56	117	44	*304	7	6	.981
1995—GC Orioles (GCL)	OF	5	21	5	5	0	0	1	3	.238	3	2	1	15	0	0	1.000
—Bowie (East.)	OF	53	218	45	62	9	1	3	19	.284	23	45	22	155	4	6	.964
—Rochester (I.L.)	OF	15	52	5	8	2	1	0	3	.154	0	16	0	37	2	0	1.000
1996—Detroit (A.L.)■	OF-DH	110	217	32	55	6	1	1	14	.253	17	77	20	217	1	2	.991
1997—Toledo (I.L.)	OF	136	501	67	109	13	7	3	33	.218	52	*154	*33	*336	4	1	.997
—Detroit (A.L.)	OF-DH	12	5	4	1	0	0	0	0	.200	2	2	3	3	0	0	1.000
1998—Detroit (A.L.)	OF-DH	57	98	20	19	5	1	3	15	.194	6	35	9	51	3	2	.964
—Toledo (I.L.)	OF-DH	51	215	24	53	10	0	2	13	.247	16	42	6	124	6	0	1.000
1999—Toledo (I.L.)	OF	104	416	64	119	13	8	12	43	.286	38	76	21	239	5	1	*.996
—Detroit (A.L.)	OF-DH	41	77	11	15	1	3	0	3	.195	9	20	3	67	0	1	.985
2000—Louisville (I.L.)■	OF	119	453	69	135	19	4	8	48	.298	48	64	28	263	3	2	.993
—Cincinnati (N.L.)	OF	11	4	2	0	0	0	0	0	.000	0	2	1	1	0	0	1.000
2001—Rancho Cuca.(Calif.)■	OF	7	30	3	8	2	0	0	1	.267	1	11	3	13	0	0	1.000
—Salt Lake (PCL)	OF	40	167	23	46	13	2	3	27	.275	19	26	5	88	4	1	.989
—Colorado (N.L.)■	OF	12	15	0	0	0	0	0	1	.000	2	5	0	8	0	1	.889
—Colo. Springs (PCL)	OF	24	78	14	15	2	0	5	15	.192	6	31	3	43	2	0	1.000
American League totals (4 years)		220	397	67	90	12	5	4	32	.227	34	134	35	338	4	5	.986
National League totals (2 years)		23	19	2	0	0	0	0	1	.000	2	7	1	9	0	1	.900
Major League totals (6 years)		243	416	69	90	12	5	4	33	.216	36	141	36	347	4	6	.983

BARTOSH, CLIFF   P   PADRES

PERSONAL: Born September 5, 1979, in West, Texas. ... 6-2/175. ... Throws left, bats left. ... Full name: Clifford Paul Bartosh.
HIGH SCHOOL: Duncanville (Texas).
TRANSACTIONS/CAREER NOTES: Selected by San Diego Padres organization in 29th round of free-agent draft (June 27, 1998).

Year League	W	L	Pct.	ERA	G	GS	CG	ShO	Sv.	IP	H	R	ER	BB	SO
1998—Arizona Padres (Ariz.)	3	2	.600	3.48	13	5	0	0	0	44	43	23	17	16	43
1999—Fort Wayne (Midw.)	5	12	.294	4.44	35	20	1	1	0	$129\frac{2}{3}$	136	76	64	49	100
2000—Fort Wayne (Midw.)	8	4	.667	3.04	50	4	0	0	1	77	50	40	26	44	94
2001—Lake Elsinore (Calif.)	6	2	.750	1.58	38	0	0	0	10	$45\frac{2}{3}$	42	17	8	12	66
—Mobile (Sou.)	1	2	.333	3.97	20	0	0	0	2	$22\frac{2}{3}$	20	12	10	13	20

BATISTA, MIGUEL   P   DIAMONDBACKS

PERSONAL: Born February 19, 1971, in Santo Domingo, Dominican Republic. ... 6-0/190. ... Throws right, bats right. ... Full name: Miguel Jerez Decartes Batista.
HIGH SCHOOL: Nuevo Horizondes (San Pedro de Macoris, Dominican Republic).
TRANSACTIONS/CAREER NOTES: Signed as non-drafted free agent by Montreal Expos organization (February 29, 1988). ... Selected by Pittsburgh Pirates from Expos organization in Rule 5 major league draft (December 9, 1991). ... Returned to Expos organization (April 23, 1992). ... On disabled list (April 14-30 and May 7, 1994-remainder of season). ... Released by Expos (November 18, 1994). ... Signed by Florida Marlins organization (December 9, 1994). ... Claimed on waivers by Chicago Cubs (December 17, 1996). ... Traded by Cubs to Expos for OF Henry Rodriguez (December 12, 1997). ... On Montreal disabled list (July 16-August 10, 1999); included rehabilitation assignment to Ottawa (July 30-August 8). ... Traded by Expos to Kansas City Royals for P Brad Rigby (April 25, 2000). ... Granted free agency (October 2, 2000). ... Signed by Arizona Diamondbacks organization (November 3, 2000).

Year League	W	L	Pct.	ERA	G	GS	CG	ShO	Sv.	IP	H	R	ER	BB	SO
1988—						Dominican Summer League statistics unavailable.									
1989—Dominican Expos (DSL)	1	7	.125	4.24	13	11	0	0	0	68	56	46	32	50	60
1990—Gulf Coast Expos (GCL)	4	3	.571	2.06	9	6	0	0	0	$39\frac{1}{3}$	33	16	9	17	21
—Rockford (Midw.)	0	1	.000	8.76	3	2	0	0	0	$12\frac{1}{3}$	16	13	12	5	7
1991—Rockford (Midw.)	11	5	.688	4.04	23	23	2	1	0	$133\frac{2}{3}$	126	74	60	57	90
1992—Pittsburgh (N.L.)■	0	0	...	9.00	1	0	0	0	0	2	4	2	2	3	1
—West Palm Beach (FSL)■	7	7	.500	3.79	24	24	1	0	0	$135\frac{1}{3}$	130	69	57	54	92
1993—Harrisburg (East.)	13	5	.722	4.34	26	26	0	0	0	141	139	79	68	86	91
1994—Harrisburg (East.)	0	1	.000	2.38	3	3	0	0	0	$11\frac{1}{3}$	8	3	3	9	5
1995—Charlotte (I.L.)■	6	12	.333	4.80	34	18	0	0	0	$116\frac{1}{3}$	118	79	62	60	58
1996—Charlotte (I.L.)	4	3	.571	5.38	47	2	0	0	4	77	93	57	46	39	56
—Florida (N.L.)	0	0	...	5.56	9	0	0	0	0	$11\frac{1}{3}$	9	8	7	7	6
1997—Iowa (A.A.)■	9	4	.692	4.20	31	14	2	•2	0	122	117	60	57	38	95
—Chicago (N.L.)	0	5	.000	5.70	11	6	0	0	0	$36\frac{1}{3}$	36	24	23	24	27
1998—Montreal (N.L.)■	3	5	.375	3.80	56	13	0	0	0	135	141	66	57	65	92
1999—Ottawa (I.L.)	0	1	.000	2.25	3	3	0	0	0	8	3	2	2	4	7
—Montreal (N.L.)	8	7	.533	4.88	39	17	2	1	1	$134\frac{2}{3}$	146	88	73	58	95

Year League	W	L	Pct.	ERA	G	GS	CG	ShO	Sv.	IP	H	R	ER	BB	SO
2000— Montreal (N.L.)	0	1	.000	14.04	4	0	0	0	0	8 1/3	19	14	13	3	7
— Kansas City (A.L.)■	2	6	.250	7.74	14	9	0	0	0	57	66	54	49	34	30
— Omaha (PCL)	2	2	.500	6.04	18	1	0	0	3	28 1/3	35	20	19	7	27
2001— Arizona (N.L.)■	11	8	.579	3.36	48	18	0	0	0	139 1/3	113	57	52	60	90
A.L. totals (1 year)	2	6	.250	7.74	14	9	0	0	0	57	66	54	49	34	30
N.L. totals (7 years)	22	26	.458	4.37	168	54	2	1	1	467	468	259	227	220	318
Major League totals (7 years)	24	32	.429	4.74	182	63	2	1	1	524	534	313	276	254	348

DIVISION SERIES RECORD

Year League	W	L	Pct.	ERA	G	GS	CG	ShO	Sv.	IP	H	R	ER	BB	SO
2001— Arizona (N.L.)	1	0	1.000	2.70	2	1	0	0	0	6 2/3	3	2	2	1	4

CHAMPIONSHIP SERIES RECORD

Year League	W	L	Pct.	ERA	G	GS	CG	ShO	Sv.	IP	H	R	ER	BB	SO
2001— Arizona (N.L.)	0	1	.000	5.14	2	1	0	0	0	7	5	4	4	2	3

WORLD SERIES RECORD

NOTES: Member of World Series championship team (2001).

Year League	W	L	Pct.	ERA	G	GS	CG	ShO	Sv.	IP	H	R	ER	BB	SO
2001— Arizona (N.L.)	0	0	...	0.00	2	1	0	0	0	8	5	0	0	5	6

B

BATISTA, TONY — 3B — ORIOLES

PERSONAL: Born December 9, 1973, in Puerto Plata, Dominican Republic. ... 6-0/205. ... Bats right, throws right. ... Full name: Leocadio Francisco Batista.

TRANSACTIONS/CAREER NOTES: Signed as non-drafted free agent by Oakland Athletics organization (February 8, 1991). ... On Tacoma disabled list (July 29, 1993-remainder of season). ... On Oakland disabled list (August 27-September 12, 1997); included rehabilitation assignment to Edmonton (September 11-12). ... Selected by Arizona Diamondbacks in first round (27th pick overall) of expansion draft (November 18, 1997). ... Traded by Diamondbacks with P John Frascatore to Toronto Blue Jays for P Dan Plesac (June 12, 1999). ... Claimed on waivers by Baltimore Orioles (June 25, 2001).

STATISTICAL NOTES: Led California League shortstops with .950 fielding percentage in 1994. ... Had 17-game hitting streak (July 30-August 16, 1999). ... Led A.L. third basemen with 35 double plays in 2000. ... Career major league grand slams: 4.

Year Team (League)	Pos.	G	AB	R	H	2B	3B	HR	RBI	Avg.	BB	SO	SB	PO	A	E	Avg.
1992— Ariz. Athletics (Ariz.)	2B-SS-OF	45	167	32	41	6	2	0	22	.246	15	29	1	67	124	8	.960
1993— Ariz. Athletics (Ariz.)	3B-2B-SS	24	104	21	34	6	2	2	17	.327	6	14	6	34	54	3	.967
— Tacoma (PCL)	OF	4	12	1	2	1	0	0	1	.167	1	4	0	6	9	0	1.000
1994— Modesto (Calif.)	SS-2B	119	466	91	131	26	3	17	68	.281	54	108	7	182	372	30	†.949
1995— Huntsville (Sou.)	SS-2B	120	419	55	107	23	1	16	61	.255	29	98	7	168	371	29	.949
1996— Edmonton (PCL)	SS	57	205	33	66	17	4	8	40	.322	15	30	2	75	213	8	.973
— Oakland (A.L.)	2-3-DH-S	74	238	38	71	10	2	6	25	.298	19	49	7	96	191	5	.983
1997— Oakland (A.L.)	S-3-DH-2	68	188	22	38	10	1	4	18	.202	14	31	2	96	174	8	.971
— Edmonton (PCL)	SS-DH	33	124	25	39	10	1	3	21	.315	17	18	2	40	78	6	.952
1998— Arizona (N.L.)■	2B-SS-3B	106	293	46	80	16	1	18	41	.273	18	52	1	123	205	6	.982
1999— Arizona (N.L.)	SS	44	144	16	37	5	0	5	21	.257	16	17	2	60	130	4	.979
— Toronto (A.L.)■	SS	98	375	61	107	25	1	26	79	.285	22	79	2	165	308	12	.975
2000— Toronto (A.L.)	3B	154	620	96	163	32	2	41	114	.263	35	121	5	120	318	17	.963
2001— Toronto (A.L.)	3B	72	271	29	56	11	1	13	45	.207	13	66	0	56	145	10	.953
— Baltimore (A.L.)■	DH-3B-SS	84	308	41	82	16	5	12	42	.266	19	47	5	51	116	6	.965
American League totals (5 years)		550	2000	287	517	104	12	102	323	.259	122	393	21	584	1252	58	.969
National League totals (2 years)		150	437	62	117	21	1	23	62	.268	34	69	3	183	335	10	.981
Major League totals (6 years)		700	2437	349	634	125	13	125	385	.260	156	462	24	767	1587	68	.972

ALL-STAR GAME RECORD

		BATTING											FIELDING			
Year League	Pos.	AB	R	H	2B	3B	HR	RBI	Avg.	BB	SO	SB	PO	A	E	Avg.
2000— American	PH-3B	1	0	0	0	0	0	0	.000	0	1	0	0	0	0	...

BAUER, RICK — P — ORIOLES

PERSONAL: Born January 10, 1977, in Garden Grove, Calif. ... 6-6/215. ... Throws right, bats right. ... Full name: Richard Edward Bauer.

HIGH SCHOOL: Centennial (Meridian, Idaho).

JUNIOR COLLEGE: Treasure Valley (Ore.).

TRANSACTIONS/CAREER NOTES: Selected by Baltimore Orioles organization in fifth round of free-agent draft (June 3, 1997).

Year League	W	L	Pct.	ERA	G	GS	CG	ShO	Sv.	IP	H	R	ER	BB	SO
1997— Bluefield (Appl.)	8	3	.727	2.86	13	13	0	0	0	72 1/3	58	31	23	20	67
— Delmarva (S.Atl.)	0	0	...	0.00	1	0	0	0	1	2	0	0	0	1	2
1998— Delmarva (S.Atl.)	5	8	.385	4.73	22	22	1	1	0	118	127	69	62	44	81
1999— Frederick (Caro.)	10	9	.526	4.56	26	26	•4	0	0	152	159	85	77	54	123
2000— Bowie (East.)	6	8	.429	5.30	26	23	1	0	1	129	154	89	76	39	87
— Frederick (Caro.)	1	0	1.000	5.21	3	3	0	0	0	19	20	13	11	6	15
2001— Bowie (East.)	2	6	.250	3.54	9	9	2	0	0	61	52	27	24	10	34
— Rochester (I.L.)	10	4	.714	3.89	19	18	1	1	0	113 1/3	119	63	49	28	89
— Baltimore (A.L.)	0	5	.000	4.64	6	6	0	0	0	33	35	22	17	9	16
Major League totals (1 year)	0	5	.000	4.64	6	6	0	0	0	33	35	22	17	9	16

PERSONAL: Born May 24, 1972, in Santo Domingo, Dominican Republic. ... 5-11/170. ... Bats right, throws right. ... Full name: Daniel Bautista. ... Stepson of Jesus de la Rosa, outfielder with Houston Astros (1974). ... Name pronounced bough-TEES-tuh.

TRANSACTIONS/CAREER NOTES: Signed as non-drafted free agent by Detroit Tigers organization (June 24, 1989). ... On disabled list (May 24-July 10, 1991). ... On Toledo disabled list (June 8-July 31, 1994). ... Traded by Tigers to Atlanta Braves for OF Anton French (May 31, 1996). ... On Atlanta disabled list (June 28, 1996-remainder of season). ... On Atlanta disabled list (March 23-April 23, 1997); included rehabilitation assignment to Richmond (April 18-23). ... On Atlanta disabled list (April 17-May 7 and August 25-September 17, 1998); included rehabilitation assignment to Greenville (May 5-7). ... Released by Braves (April 2, 1999). ... Signed by Florida Marlins organization (April 8, 1999). ... On Calgary disabled list (June 1-8, 1999). ... Traded by Marlins to Arizona Diamondbacks for IF Andy Fox (June 10, 2000). ... Granted free agency (November 8, 2001). ... Re-signed by Diamondbacks (December 18, 2001).

RECORDS: Shares major league single-game record for most strikeouts (nine-inning game)—5 (May 28, 1995).

STATISTICAL NOTES: Had 15-game hitting streak (August 13-September 1, 2000).

						BATTING								FIELDING		
Year	Team (League)	Pos.	G	AB	R	H	2B	3B	HR	RBI	Avg.	BB	SO	SB	PO	A	E	Avg.
1989—						Dominican Summer League statistics unavailable.										
1990—Bristol (Appl.)		OF	27	95	9	26	3	0	2	12	.274	8	21	2	43	2	0	1.000
1991—Fayetteville (S.Atl.)		OF	69	234	21	45	6	4	1	30	.192	21	65	7	137	6	4	.973
1992—Fayetteville (S.Atl.)		OF	121	453	59	122	22	0	5	52	.269	29	76	18	210	17	6	.974
1993—London (East.)		OF-DH	117	424	55	121	21	0	6	48	.285	32	69	28	256	13	3	.989
—Detroit (A.L.)		OF-DH	17	61	6	19	3	0	1	9	.311	1	10	3	38	2	0	1.000
1994—Detroit (A.L.)		OF-DH	31	99	12	23	4	1	4	15	.232	3	18	1	66	0	0	1.000
—Toledo (I.L.)		OF	27	98	7	25	7	0	2	14	.255	6	23	2	54	1	1	.982
1995—Detroit (A.L.)		OF	89	271	28	55	9	0	7	27	.203	12	68	4	164	3	2	.988
—Toledo (I.L.)		OF	18	58	6	14	3	0	0	4	.241	1	10	1	32	1	2	.943
1996—Detroit (A.L.)		OF-DH	25	64	12	16	2	0	2	8	.250	9	15	1	38	0	1	.974
—Atlanta (N.L.)■		OF	17	20	1	3	0	0	0	1	.150	2	5	0	10	0	0	1.000
1997—Richmond (I.L.)		OF-DH	46	170	28	48	10	3	2	28	.282	19	30	1	104	4	0	1.000
—Atlanta (N.L.)		OF	64	103	14	25	3	2	3	9	.243	5	24	2	59	1	1	.984
1998—Atlanta (N.L.)		OF-DH	82	144	17	36	11	0	3	17	.250	7	21	1	47	0	2	.959
—Greenville (Sou.)		OF	2	6	1	2	0	0	1	2	.333	1	1	0	6	0	0	1.000
1999—Calgary (PCL)■		OF-DH	38	135	25	43	8	1	8	28	.319	11	18	3	90	5	3	.969
—Florida (N.L.)		OF	70	205	32	59	10	1	5	24	.288	4	30	3	140	3	3	.979
2000—Florida (N.L.)		OF	44	89	9	17	4	0	4	12	.191	5	20	1	46	2	1	.980
—Arizona (N.L.)■		OF	87	262	45	83	16	7	7	47	.317	20	30	5	142	6	2	.987
2001—Arizona (N.L.)		OF	100	222	26	67	11	2	5	26	.302	14	31	3	102	4	0	1.000
American League totals (4 years)			162	495	58	113	18	1	14	59	.228	25	111	9	306	5	3	.990
National League totals (6 years)			464	1045	144	290	55	12	27	136	.278	57	161	15	546	16	9	.984
Major League totals (9 years)			626	1540	202	403	73	13	41	195	.262	82	272	24	852	21	12	.986

DIVISION SERIES RECORD

						BATTING							FIELDING		
Year	Team (League)	Pos.	G	AB	R	H	2B	3B	HR	RBI	Avg.	BB	SO	SB	PO	A	E	Avg.
1997—Atlanta (N.L.)		OF	3	3	0	1	0	0	0	2	.333	0	1	0	0	0	0	...
1998—Atlanta (N.L.)		OF	2	2	0	1	1	0	0	0	.500	0	0	0	2	0	0	1.000
2001—Arizona (N.L.)		PH-OF-PR	3	6	1	0	0	0	0	1	.000	0	1	0	2	0	0	1.000
Division series totals (3 years)			8	11	1	2	1	0	0	3	.182	0	2	0	4	0	0	1.000

CHAMPIONSHIP SERIES RECORD

						BATTING							FIELDING		
Year	Team (League)	Pos.	G	AB	R	H	2B	3B	HR	RBI	Avg.	BB	SO	SB	PO	A	E	Avg.
1997—Atlanta (N.L.)		OF	2	4	0	1	0	0	0	0	.250	0	0	0	4	0	0	1.000
1998—Atlanta (N.L.)		PR-OF	5	5	0	0	0	0	0	0	.000	0	1	0	2	0	1	.667
2001—Arizona (N.L.)		OF	2	4	1	1	0	0	0	1	.250	1	1	0	2	0	0	1.000
Championship series totals (3 years)			9	13	1	2	0	0	0	1	.154	1	2	0	8	0	1	.889

WORLD SERIES RECORD

NOTES: Member of World Series championship team (2001).

						BATTING							FIELDING		
Year	Team (League)	Pos.	G	AB	R	H	2B	3B	HR	RBI	Avg.	BB	SO	SB	PO	A	E	Avg.
2001—Arizona (N.L.)		OF-PH-DH	5	12	1	7	2	0	0	7	.583	1	1	0	9	1	0	1.000

PERSONAL: Born November 18, 1979, in Medford, Ore. ... 6-2/207. ... Throws right, bats right. ... Full name: Steven Scott Bechler.

HIGH SCHOOL: South Medford (Medford, Ore.).

TRANSACTIONS/CAREER NOTES: Selected by Baltimore Orioles organization in third round of free-agent draft (June 2, 1998).

STATISTICAL NOTES: Led Carolina League with 19 home runs allowed in 2000.

Year	League	W	L	Pct.	ERA	G	GS	CG	ShO	Sv.	IP	H	R	ER	BB	SO
1998—Gulf Coast Orioles (GCL)		2	4	.333	2.72	9	9	0	0	0	49²/₃	51	22	15	8	39
1999—Delmarva (S.Atl.)		8	12	.400	3.54	26	26	1	1	0	152¹/₃	137	69	60	58	139
2000—Frederick (Caro.)		8	12	.400	4.83	27	27	2	0	0	162	*179	*98	*87	57	137
2001—Frederick (Caro.)		5	2	.714	2.27	13	13	1	1	0	83¹/₃	73	24	21	22	71
—Rochester (I.L.)		1	1	.500	15.95	2	2	0	0	0	7¹/₃	14	14	13	5	6
—Bowie (East.)		3	5	.375	3.08	12	12	2	0	0	79	63	31	27	15	58

PERSONAL: Born August 3, 1968, in Burbank, Calif. ... 6-1/235. ... Throws right, bats right. ... Full name: Rodney Roy Beck.

HIGH SCHOOL: Grant (Van Nuys, Calif.).

TRANSACTIONS/CAREER NOTES: Selected by Oakland Athletics organization in 13th round of free-agent draft (June 2, 1986). ... Traded by A's to San Francisco Giants for P Charlie Corbell (March 23, 1988). ... On disabled list (April 6-30, 1994). ... Granted free agency (October 27, 1997). ... Signed by Chicago Cubs (January 15, 1998). ... On Chicago disabled list (May 17-July 21, 1999); included rehablitation assignment to Iowa (July 17-21). ... Traded by Cubs to Boston Red Sox for P Mark Guthrie and a player to named later (August 31, 1999); Cubs acquired 3B Cole Liniak to complete deal (September 1, 1999). ... On Boston disabled list (March 18-June 13 and July 3-22, 2000); included rehabilitation assignment to Pawtucket (June 2-13). ... Granted free agency (November 5, 2001).

MISCELLANEOUS: Holds San Francisco Giants franchise all-time record for most saves (199).

Year League	W	L	Pct.	ERA	G	GS	CG	ShO	Sv.	IP	H	R	ER	BB	SO
1986—Medford (N'West)	1	3	.250	5.23	13	6	0	0	1	32²/₃	47	25	19	11	21
1987—Medford (N'West)	5	8	.385	5.18	17	12	2	0	0	92	106	74	53	26	69
1988—Clinton (Midw.)■	12	7	.632	3.00	28	23	5	1	0	177	177	68	59	27	123
1989—San Jose (Calif.)	11	2	*.846	2.40	13	13	4	0	0	97¹/₃	91	29	26	26	88
—Shreveport (Texas)	7	3	.700	3.55	16	14	4	1	0	99	108	45	39	16	74
1990—Shreveport (Texas)	10	3	.769	2.23	14	14	2	1	0	93	85	26	23	17	71
—Phoenix (PCL)	4	7	.364	4.93	12	12	2	0	0	76²/₃	100	51	42	18	43
1991—Phoenix (PCL)	4	3	.571	2.02	23	5	3	0	6	71¹/₃	56	18	16	13	35
—San Francisco (N.L.)	1	1	.500	3.78	31	0	0	0	1	52¹/₃	53	22	22	13	38
1992—San Francisco (N.L.)	3	3	.500	1.76	65	0	0	0	17	92	62	20	18	15	87
1993—San Francisco (N.L.)	3	1	.750	2.16	76	0	0	0	48	79¹/₃	57	20	19	13	86
1994—San Francisco (N.L.)	2	4	.333	2.77	48	0	0	0	28	48²/₃	49	17	15	13	39
1995—San Francisco (N.L.)	5	6	.455	4.45	60	0	0	0	33	58²/₃	60	31	29	21	42
1996—San Francisco (N.L.)	0	9	.000	3.34	63	0	0	0	35	62	56	23	23	10	48
1997—San Francisco (N.L.)	7	4	.636	3.47	73	0	0	0	37	70	67	31	27	8	53
1998—Chicago (N.L.)■	3	4	.429	3.02	*81	0	0	0	51	80¹/₃	86	33	27	20	81
1999—Chicago (N.L.)	2	4	.333	7.80	31	0	0	0	7	30	41	26	26	13	13
—Iowa (PCL)	0	0	...	0.00	2	0	0	0	0	2	1	0	0	0	2
—Boston (A.L.)■	0	1	.000	1.93	12	0	0	0	3	14	9	3	3	5	12
2000—Pawtucket (I.L.)	1	0	1.000	0.00	3	0	0	0	0	6	4	0	0	0	7
—Boston (A.L.)	3	0	1.000	3.10	34	0	0	0	0	40²/₃	34	15	14	12	35
2001—Boston (A.L.)	6	4	.600	3.90	68	0	0	0	6	80²/₃	77	42	35	28	63
A.L. totals (3 years)	9	5	.643	3.46	114	0	0	0	9	135¹/₃	120	60	52	45	110
N.L. totals (9 years)	26	36	.419	3.23	528	0	0	0	257	573¹/₃	531	223	206	126	487
Major League totals (11 years)	35	41	.461	3.28	642	0	0	0	266	708²/₃	651	283	258	171	597

DIVISION SERIES RECORD

Year League	W	L	Pct.	ERA	G	GS	CG	ShO	Sv.	IP	H	R	ER	BB	SO
1997—San Francisco (N.L.)	0	0	...	0.00	1	0	0	0	0	1¹/₃	1	0	0	0	1
1998—Chicago (N.L.)	0	0	...	16.20	1	0	0	0	0	1²/₃	5	3	3	2	1
1999—Boston (A.L.)	0	0	...	0.00	2	0	0	0	0	2	2	0	0	0	2
Division series totals (3 years)	0	0	...	5.40	4	0	0	0	0	5	8	3	3	2	4

CHAMPIONSHIP SERIES RECORD

Year League	W	L	Pct.	ERA	G	GS	CG	ShO	Sv.	IP	H	R	ER	BB	SO
1999—Boston (A.L.)	0	1	.000	27.00	2	0	0	0	0	²/₃	2	2	2	0	1

ALL-STAR GAME RECORD

Year League	W	L	Pct.	ERA	GS	CG	ShO	Sv.	IP	H	R	ER	BB	SO
1993—National	0	0	...	9.00	0	0	0	0	1	2	1	1	0	1
1994—National	0	0	...	0.00	0	0	0	0	1²/₃	1	0	0	0	1
1997—National							Did not play.							
All-Star Game totals (2 years)	0	0	...	3.38	0	0	0	0	2²/₃	3	1	1	0	2

BECKETT, JOSH   P   MARLINS

PERSONAL: Born May 15, 1980, in Spring, Texas. ... 6-4/190. ... Throws right, bats right. ... Full name: Joshua Patrick Beckett.
HIGH SCHOOL: Spring (Texas).
TRANSACTIONS/CAREER NOTES: Selected by Florida Marlins organization in first round (second pick overall) of free-agent draft (June 2, 1999). ... On Brevard County disabled list (April 17-May 30 and August 16-September 11, 2000).

Year League	W	L	Pct.	ERA	G	GS	CG	ShO	Sv.	IP	H	R	ER	BB	SO
2000—Kane County (Midw.)	2	3	.400	2.12	13	12	0	0	0	59¹/₃	45	18	14	15	61
2001—Brevard County (FSL)	6	0	1.000	1.23	13	12	0	0	0	65²/₃	32	13	9	15	101
—Portland (East.)	8	1	.889	1.82	13	13	0	0	0	74¹/₃	50	16	15	19	102
—Florida (N.L.)	2	2	.500	1.50	4	4	0	0	0	24	14	9	4	11	24
Major League totals (1 year)	2	2	.500	1.50	4	4	0	0	0	24	14	9	4	11	24

BEDARD, ERIK   P   ORIOLES

PERSONAL: Born March 6, 1979, in Naum, Ont. ... 6-1/180. ... Throws left, bats left. ... Full name: Erik Joseph Bedard.
JUNIOR COLLEGE: Norwalk Tech (Conn.).
TRANSACTIONS/CAREER NOTES: Selected by Baltimore Orioles organization in sixth round of free-agent draft (June 2, 1999). ... On Frederick disabled list (July 3-23, 2001).

Year League	W	L	Pct.	ERA	G	GS	CG	ShO	Sv.	IP	H	R	ER	BB	SO
1999—Gulf Coast Orioles (GCL)	2	1	.667	1.86	8	6	0	0	0	29	20	7	6	13	41
2000—Delmarva (S.Atl.)	9	4	.692	3.57	29	22	1	1	2	111	98	48	44	35	131
2001—Frederick (Caro.)	9	2	.818	2.15	17	17	0	0	0	96¹/₃	68	27	23	26	130
—Gulf Coast Orioles (GCL)	0	1	.000	3.00	2	2	0	0	0	6	4	2	2	3	7

BEIMEL, JOE   P   PIRATES

PERSONAL: Born April 19, 1977, in St. Mary's, Pa. ... 6-2/200. ... Throws left, bats left. ... Full name: Joseph Ronald Beimel.
HIGH SCHOOL: St. Mary's Area (St. Mary's, Pa.).

TRANSACTIONS/CAREER NOTES: Selected by Pittsburgh Pirates organization in 18th round of free-agent draft (June 3, 1998).

Year League	W	L	Pct.	ERA	G	GS	CG	ShO	Sv.	IP	H	R	ER	BB	SO
1998— Erie (NY-Penn)	1	4	.200	6.32	17	6	0	0	0	47	56	39	33	22	37
1999— Hickory (S.Atl.)	5	11	.313	4.43	29	22	0	0	0	130	146	81	64	43	102
2000— Lynchburg (Caro.)	10	6	.625	3.36	18	18	2	1	0	120²/₃	111	49	45	44	82
— Altoona (East.)	1	6	.143	4.16	10	10	1	0	0	62²/₃	72	38	29	21	28
2001— Pittsburgh (N.L.)	7	11	.389	5.23	42	15	0	0	0	115¹/₃	131	72	67	49	58
Major League totals (1 year)	7	11	.389	5.23	42	15	0	0	0	115¹/₃	131	72	67	49	58

BEIRNE, KEVIN   P   BLUE JAYS

PERSONAL: Born January 1, 1974, in Houston. ... 6-4/210. ... Throws right, bats left. ... Full name: Kevin P. Beirne. ... Son of Jim Beirne, wide receiver/tight end with Houston Oilers (1968-73, 1975 and 1976) and San Diego Chargers (1974).
HIGH SCHOOL: McCollough (The Woodlands, Texas).
COLLEGE: Texas A&M.
TRANSACTIONS/CAREER NOTES: Selected by Cincinnati Reds organization in 43rd round of free-agent draft (June 2, 1992); did not sign. ... Selected by Chicago White Sox organization in 11th round of free-agent draft (June 1, 1995). ... On Charlotte disabled list (May 6-14 and August 6, 1999-remainder of season). ... Traded by White Sox with P Mike Sirotka, OF Brian Simmons, P Mike Williams to Toronto Blue Jays for P David Wells and P Matt DeWitt (January 14, 2001). ... On Syracuse disabled list (April 26-July 27, 2001).

Year League	W	L	Pct.	ERA	G	GS	CG	ShO	Sv.	IP	H	R	ER	BB	SO
1995— GC White Sox (GCL)	0	0	...	2.45	2	0	0	0	2	3²/₃	2	2	1	1	3
— Bristol (Appl.)	1	0	1.000	0.00	9	0	0	0	2	9	4	0	0	4	12
— Hickory (S.Atl.)	0	0	...	4.50	3	0	0	0	1	4	7	2	2	0	4
1996— South Bend (Midw.)	4	11	.267	4.15	26	25	1	0	0	145¹/₃	153	85	67	60	110
1997— Winston-Salem (Caro.)	4	4	.500	3.05	13	13	1	0	0	82²/₃	66	38	28	28	75
— Birmingham (Sou.)	6	4	.600	4.92	13	12	0	0	0	75	76	51	41	41	49
1998— Birmingham (Sou.)	13	9	.591	3.44	26	26	2	1	0	167¹/₃	142	77	64	87	153
— Calgary (PCL)	0	0	...	4.50	2	2	0	0	0	8	12	5	4	4	6
1999— Charlotte (I.L.)	5	5	.500	5.42	20	20	0	0	0	113	134	75	68	36	63
2000— Charlotte (I.L.)	1	2	.333	3.51	7	7	0	0	0	33¹/₃	39	13	13	7	28
— Chicago (A.L.)	1	3	.250	6.70	29	1	0	0	0	49²/₃	50	41	37	20	41
2001— Toronto (A.L.)■	0	0	...	12.86	5	0	0	0	0	7	13	10	10	6	5
— Syracuse (I.L.)	1	1	.500	1.57	18	0	0	0	0	28²/₃	24	6	5	3	17
— Auburn (NY-Penn)	0	0	...	5.40	2	2	0	0	0	3¹/₃	6	2	2	1	2
Major League totals (2 years)	1	3	.250	7.46	34	1	0	0	0	56²/₃	63	51	47	26	46

BELITZ, TODD   P   ROCKIES

PERSONAL: Born October 23, 1975, in Des Moines, Iowa. ... 6-3/200. ... Throws left, bats left. ... Full name: Todd Stephen Belitz.
HIGH SCHOOL: Edison (Huntington Beach, Calif.).
COLLEGE: Washington State.
TRANSACTIONS/CAREER NOTES: Selected by Kansas City Royals organization in eighth round of free-agent draft (June 2, 1994); did not sign. ... Selected by Tampa Bay Devil Rays organization in fourth round of free-agent draft (June 3, 1997). ... Traded by Devil Rays with P Jim Mecir to Oakland Athletics for P Jesus Colome and a player to be named later (July 28, 2000). ... Traded by A's with OF Mario Encarnacion and 2B/SS Jose Ortiz to Colorado Rockies for OF Jermaine Dye (July 25, 2001).

Year League	W	L	Pct.	ERA	G	GS	CG	ShO	Sv.	IP	H	R	ER	BB	SO
1997— Hudson Valley (NY-Penn)	4	5	.444	3.53	15	15	0	0	0	74	65	41	29	18	78
1998— Charleston, S.C. (S.Atl.)	6	4	.600	2.42	21	21	0	0	0	130	99	44	35	48	123
— St. Petersburg (FSL)	2	2	.500	5.04	7	7	0	0	0	44²/₃	39	28	25	14	40
1999— Orlando (Sou.)	9	9	.500	5.77	28	•28	0	0	0	160²/₃	169	*114	*103	65	118
2000— Durham (I.L.)	1	1	.500	3.83	43	0	0	0	2	47	33	24	20	28	46
— Sacramento (PCL)■	0	0	.000	4.38	12	0	0	0	1	12¹/₃	12	6	6	5	10
— Oakland (A.L.)	0	0	...	2.70	5	0	0	0	0	3¹/₃	4	2	1	4	3
2001— Sacramento (PCL)	4	2	.667	5.13	38	0	0	0	0	52²/₃	52	38	30	16	54
— Colorado Springs (PCL)■	0	2	.000	9.82	14	0	0	0	2	11	19	15	12	3	8
— Colorado (N.L.)	1	1	.500	7.71	8	0	0	0	0	9¹/₃	9	8	8	3	5
A.L. totals (1 year)	0	0	...	2.70	5	0	0	0	0	3¹/₃	4	2	1	4	3
N.L. totals (1 year)	1	1	.500	7.71	8	0	0	0	0	9¹/₃	9	8	8	3	5
Major League totals (2 years)	1	1	.500	6.39	13	0	0	0	0	12²/₃	13	10	9	7	8

BELL, DAVID   3B

PERSONAL: Born September 14, 1972, in Cincinnati. ... 5-10/190. ... Bats right, throws right. ... Full name: David Michael Bell. ... Son of Buddy Bell, major league third baseman with four teams (1972-89) and manager, Colorado Rockies; brother of Mike Bell, third baseman with Cincinnati Reds (2000); and grandson of Gus Bell, major league outfielder with four teams (1950-64).
HIGH SCHOOL: Moeller (Cincinnati).
TRANSACTIONS/CAREER NOTES: Selected by Cleveland Indians organization in seventh round of free-agent draft (June 4, 1990). ... Traded by Indians with C Pepe McNeal and P Rick Heiserman to St. Louis Cardinals for P Ken Hill (July 27, 1995). ... On St. Louis disabled list (April 29-June 30, 1997); included rehabilitation assignments to Arkansas (June 10-19) and Louisville (June 20-26). ... Claimed on waivers by Indians (April 14, 1998). ... Traded by Indians to Seattle Mariners for 2B Joey Cora (August 31, 1998). ... Granted free agency (November 7, 2001).
STATISTICAL NOTES: Led South Atlantic League in grounding into double plays with 22 in 1991. ... Led South Atlantic League third basemen with 389 total chances in 1991. ... Led Eastern League third basemen with 32 double plays in 1993. ... Led International League third basemen with .950 fielding percentage in 1994. ... Led A.L. second baseman with 313 putouts and 118 double plays in 1999.

Year— Team (League)	Pos.	G	AB	R	H	2B	3B	HR	RBI	Avg.	BB	SO	SB	PO	A	E	Avg.
1990— GC Indians (GCL)	3B	30	111	18	29	5	1	0	13	.261	10	8	1	29	50	7	.919
— Burlington (Appl.).......	3B	12	42	4	7	1	1	0	2	.167	2	5	2	8	27	3	.921
1991— Columbus (S.Atl.)........	3B	136	491	47	113	24	1	5	63	.230	37	50	3	90	*268	31	.920
1992— Kinston (Caro.)...........	3B	123	464	52	117	17	2	6	47	.252	54	66	2	83	264	20	.946
1993— Canton/Akron (East.)..	3B-2B-SS	129	483	69	141	20	2	9	60	.292	43	54	3	117	283	21	.950
1994— Charlotte (I.L.).............	3B-SS-2B	134	481	66	141	17	4	18	88	.293	41	54	2	109	326	20	†.956
1995— Buffalo (A.A.)..............	3B-SS-2B	70	254	34	69	11	1	8	34	.272	22	37	0	46	172	11	.952
— Cleveland (A.L.)............	3B	2	2	0	0	0	0	0	0	.000	0	0	0	0	2	0	1.000
— Louisville (A.A.)■........	2B	18	76	9	21	3	1	1	9	.276	2	10	4	39	54	1	.989
— St. Louis (N.L.)...........	3B	39	144	13	36	7	2	2	19	.250	4	25	1	77	108	7	.964
1996— St. Louis (N.L.)...........	3B-2B-SS	62	145	12	31	6	0	1	9	.214	10	22	1	45	113	5	.969
— Louisville (A.A.)........	2B-3B-SS	42	136	9	24	5	1	0	7	.176	7	15	1	66	114	5	.973
1997— St. Louis (N.L.)...........	3B-2B-SS	66	142	9	30	7	2	1	12	.211	10	28	1	55	95	8	.949
— Arkansas (Texas)........	3B-2B	9	32	3	7	2	0	1	3	.219	2	2	1	3	15	1	.947
— Louisville (A.A.)........2B-3B-DH-SS		6	22	3	5	0	0	1	4	.227	0	6	0	6	10	1	.941
1998— St. Louis (N.L.)...........	3B-2B	4	9	0	2	1	0	0	0	.222	0	3	0	1	4	0	1.000
— Cleveland (A.L.)■........	2-3-1-S	107	340	37	89	21	2	10	41	.262	22	54	0	201	306	9	.983
— Seattle (A.L.)■........2B-1B-3B-OF		21	80	11	26	8	0	0	8	.325	5	8	0	61	46	1	.991
1999— Seattle (A.L.).............	2B-1B-SS	157	597	92	160	31	2	21	78	.268	58	90	7	†329	427	17	.978
2000— Seattle (A.L.)............3-2-1-DH-S		133	454	57	112	24	2	11	47	.247	42	66	2	139	253	15	.963
2001— Seattle (A.L.).............	3B-1B	135	470	62	122	28	0	15	64	.260	28	59	2	98	257	14	.962
American League totals (5 years)		**555**	**1943**	**259**	**509**	**112**	**6**	**57**	**238**	**.262**	**155**	**277**	**11**	**828**	**1291**	**56**	**.974**
National League totals (4 years)		**171**	**440**	**34**	**99**	**21**	**4**	**4**	**40**	**.225**	**24**	**78**	**3**	**178**	**320**	**20**	**.961**
Major League totals (7 years)		**726**	**2383**	**293**	**608**	**133**	**10**	**61**	**278**	**.255**	**179**	**355**	**14**	**1006**	**1611**	**76**	**.972**

DIVISION SERIES RECORD

Year— Team (League)	Pos.	G	AB	R	H	2B	3B	HR	RBI	Avg.	BB	SO	SB	PO	A	E	Avg.
2000— Seattle (A.L.)	3B	3	11	0	4	1	0	0	1	.364	2	2	0	2	4	0	1.000
2001— Seattle (A.L.)	3B	5	16	2	5	1	0	1	2	.313	1	6	0	1	7	0	1.000
Division series totals (2 years)		**8**	**27**	**2**	**9**	**2**	**0**	**1**	**3**	**.333**	**3**	**8**	**0**	**3**	**11**	**0**	**1.000**

CHAMPIONSHIP SERIES RECORD

Year— Team (League)	Pos.	G	AB	R	H	2B	3B	HR	RBI	Avg.	BB	SO	SB	PO	A	E	Avg.
2000— Seattle (A.L.)	3B	5	18	0	4	0	0	0	0	.222	0	0	0	5	9	0	1.000
2001— Seattle (A.L.)	3B	5	16	1	3	0	0	0	4	.188	0	3	0	0	12	1	.923
Championship series totals (2 years)		**10**	**34**	**1**	**7**	**0**	**0**	**0**	**4**	**.206**	**0**	**3**	**0**	**5**	**21**	**1**	**.963**

BELL, DEREK — OF — PIRATES

PERSONAL: Born December 11, 1968, in Tampa. ... 6-2/215. ... Bats right, throws right. ... Full name: Derek Nathaniel Bell.

HIGH SCHOOL: King (Tampa).

TRANSACTIONS/CAREER NOTES: Selected by Toronto Blue Jays organization in second round of free-agent draft (June 2, 1987). ... On Knoxville disabled list (July 30, 1988-remainder of season; June 13-21 and July 2-12, 1990). ... On Toronto disabled list (April 9-May 8, 1992); included rehabilitation assignment to Dunedin (April 27-May 4). ... Traded by Blue Jays with OF Stoney Briggs to San Diego Padres for OF Darrin Jackson (March 30, 1993). ... On suspended list (July 9-12, 1993 and July 9-17, 1994). ... Traded by Padres with OF Phil Plantier, P Pedro Martinez, P Doug Brocail, IF Craig Shipley and SS Ricky Gutierrez to Houston Astros for 3B Ken Caminiti, OF Steve Finley, SS Andujar Cedeno, 1B Robert Petagine, P Brian Williams and a player to be named later (December 28, 1994); Padres acquired P Sean Fesh to complete deal (May 1, 1995). ... On Houston disabled list (May 14-June 13, 1997); included rehabilitation assignment to New Orleans (June 6-13). ... On disabled list (August 17-September 1, 1999). ... Traded by Astros with P Mike Hampton to New York Mets for OF Roger Cedeno, P Octavio Dotel and P Kyle Kessel (December 23, 1999). ... Granted free agency (October 31, 2000). ... Signed by Pittsburgh Pirates (December 10, 2000). ... On Pittsburgh disabled list (May 18-June 15 and July 13, 2001-remainder of season); included rehabilitation assignments to Nashville (May 22-June 12 and August 26-September 4).

HONORS: Named International League Most Valuable Player (1991).

STATISTICAL NOTES: Led International League with 243 total bases in 1991. ... Led International League outfielders with seven double plays in 1991. ... Tied for N.L. lead with 10 sacrifice flies in 1998. ... Career major league grand slams: 1.

Year— Team (League)	Pos.	G	AB	R	H	2B	3B	HR	RBI	Avg.	BB	SO	SB	PO	A	E	Avg.
1987— St. Catharines (NY-P).	OF	74	273	46	72	11	3	10	42	.264	18	60	12	126	6	2	.985
1988— Knoxville (Sou.).........	OF	14	52	5	13	3	1	0	4	.250	1	14	2	18	2	2	.909
— Myrtle Beach (S.Atl.)..	OF	91	352	55	121	29	5	12	60	*.344	15	67	18	148	12	10	.941
1989— Knoxville (Sou.).........	OF	136	513	72	124	22	6	16	75	.242	26	92	15	216	12	9	.962
1990— Syracuse (I.L.)............	OF	109	402	57	105	13	5	7	56	.261	23	75	21	220	9	5	.979
1991— Syracuse (I.L.)............	OF	119	457	*89	*158	22	•12	13	*93	*.346	57	69	27	278	*15	*16	.948
— Toronto (A.L.)...........	OF	18	28	5	4	0	0	0	1	.143	6	5	3	16	0	2	.889
1992— Toronto (A.L.)...........	OF-DH	61	161	23	39	6	3	2	15	.242	15	34	7	105	4	0	1.000
— Dunedin (FSL)............	OF	7	25	7	6	2	0	0	4	.240	4	4	3	13	0	2	.867
1993— San Diego (N.L.)■....	OF-3B	150	542	73	142	19	1	21	72	.262	23	122	26	334	37	17	.956
1994— San Diego (N.L.)......	OF	108	434	54	135	20	0	14	54	.311	29	88	24	247	3	10	.962
1995— Houston (N.L.)■......	OF	112	452	63	151	21	2	8	86	.334	33	71	27	201	10	8	.963
1996— Houston (N.L.)	OF	158	627	84	165	40	3	17	113	.263	40	123	29	283	16	7	.977
1997— Houston (N.L.)	OF-DH	129	493	67	136	29	3	15	71	.276	40	94	15	226	5	8	.967
— New Orleans (A.A.).....	OF	5	13	0	2	0	0	0	1	.154	1	1	1	10	0	0	1.000
1998— Houston (N.L.)	OF	156	630	111	198	41	2	22	108	.314	51	126	13	281	8	8	.973
1999— Houston (N.L.)	OF	128	509	61	120	22	0	12	66	.236	50	129	18	192	4	3	.985
2000— New York (N.L.)■......	OF-P	144	546	87	145	31	1	18	69	.266	65	125	8	252	5	3	.988
2001— Pittsburgh (N.L.)■	OF	46	156	14	27	3	0	5	13	.173	25	38	0	78	3	1	.988
— Nashville (PCL)	OF	22	68	12	11	3	0	1	9	.162	9	19	0	15	0	1	.938
American League totals (2 years)		**79**	**189**	**28**	**43**	**6**	**3**	**2**	**16**	**.228**	**21**	**39**	**10**	**121**	**4**	**2**	**.984**
National League totals (9 years)		**1131**	**4389**	**614**	**1219**	**226**	**12**	**132**	**652**	**.278**	**356**	**916**	**160**	**2094**	**91**	**65**	**.971**
Major League totals (11 years)		**1210**	**4578**	**642**	**1262**	**232**	**15**	**134**	**668**	**.276**	**377**	**955**	**170**	**2215**	**95**	**67**	**.972**

DIVISION SERIES RECORD

Year Team (League)	Pos.	G	AB	R	H	2B	3B	HR	RBI	Avg.	BB	SO	SB	PO	A	E	Avg.
1997—Houston (N.L.)	OF	3	13	0	0	0	0	0	0	.000	0	3	0	3	0	0	1.000
1998—Houston (N.L.)	OF	4	16	1	2	0	0	1	1	.125	0	7	0	5	0	0	1.000
1999—Houston (N.L.)	OF-PH	2	3	0	1	0	0	0	0	.333	0	0	0	1	0	0	1.000
2000—New York (N.L.)	OF	1	1	0	0	0	0	0	0	.000	0	0	0	0	0	0	...
Division series totals (4 years)		10	33	1	3	0	0	1	1	.091	0	10	0	9	0	0	1.000

CHAMPIONSHIP SERIES RECORD

Year Team (League)	Pos.	G	AB	R	H	2B	3B	HR	RBI	Avg.	BB	SO	SB	PO	A	E	Avg.
1992—Toronto (A.L.)	PR-OF	2	0	1	0	0	0	0	0	...	1	0	0	1	0	0	1.000

WORLD SERIES RECORD

NOTES: Member of World Series championship team (1992).

Year Team (League)	Pos.	G	AB	R	H	2B	3B	HR	RBI	Avg.	BB	SO	SB	PO	A	E	Avg.
1992—Toronto (A.L.)	PH	2	1	1	0	0	0	0	0	.000	1	0	0	...	...	...	...

RECORD AS PITCHER

Year League	W	L	Pct.	ERA	G	GS	CG	ShO	Sv.	IP	H	R	ER	BB	SO
2000—New York (N.L.)	0	0	...	36.00	1	0	0	0	0	1	3	5	4	3	0

BELL, JAY   2B   DIAMONDBACKS

PERSONAL: Born December 11, 1965, in Eglin AFB, Fla. ... 6-0/184. ... Bats right, throws right. ... Full name: Jay Stuart Bell.

HIGH SCHOOL: Tate (Gonzalez, Fla.).

TRANSACTIONS/CAREER NOTES: Selected by Minnesota Twins organization in first round (eighth pick overall) of free-agent draft (June 4, 1984). ... Traded by Twins with P Curt Wardle, OF Jim Weaver and a player to be named later to Cleveland Indians for P Bert Blyleven (August 1, 1985); Indians acquired P Rich Yett to complete deal (September 17, 1985). ... Traded by Indians to Pittsburgh Pirates for SS Felix Fermin (March 25, 1989). ... Traded by Pirates with 1B/3B Jeff King to Kansas City Royals for 3B Joe Randa, P Jeff Granger, P Jeff Martin and P Jeff Wallace (December 13, 1996). ... Granted free agency (November 4, 1997). ... Signed by Arizona Diamondbacks (November 17, 1997).

HONORS: Named shortstop on THE SPORTING NEWS N.L. All-Star team (1993). ... Won N.L. Gold Glove at shortstop (1993). ... Named shortstop on THE SPORTING NEWS N.L. Silver Slugger team (1993).

STATISTICAL NOTES: Led Appalachian League shortstops with 352 total chances and 43 double plays in 1984. ... Led California League shortstops with 84 double plays in 1985. ... Hit home run in first major league at-bat on first pitch (September 29, 1986). ... Led Eastern League shortstops with 613 total chances in 1986. ... Led American Association shortstops with 198 putouts, 322 assists, 30 errors and 550 total chances in 1987. ... Led N.L. with 39 sacrifice hits in 1990 and 30 in 1991. ... Had 22-game hitting streak (August 24-September 17, 1992). ... Led N.L. shortstops with 741 total chances in 1990, 754 in 1991, 816 in 1992, 794 in 1993 and 547 in 1994. ... Led N.L. shortstops with 94 double plays in 1992. ... Led N.L. second basemen with 22 errors in 1999. ... Career major league grand slams: 6.

MISCELLANEOUS: Holds Arizona Diamondbacks all-time record for most runs (357).

Year Team (League)	Pos.	G	AB	R	H	2B	3B	HR	RBI	Avg.	BB	SO	SB	PO	A	E	Avg.
1984—Elizabethton (Appl.)	SS	66	245	43	54	12	1	6	30	.220	42	50	4	*109	*218	25	.929
1985—Visalia (Calif.)	SS	106	376	56	106	16	6	9	59	.282	41	73	10	176	330	53	.905
—Waterbury (East.)■...	SS	29	114	13	34	11	2	1	14	.298	9	16	3	41	79	6	.952
1986—Waterbury (East.)	SS	138	494	86	137	28	4	7	74	.277	87	65	10	197	*371	*45	.927
—Cleveland (A.L.)	2B-DH	5	14	3	5	2	0	1	4	.357	2	3	0	1	6	2	.778
1987—Buffalo (A.A.)	SS-2B	110	362	71	94	15	4	17	60	.260	70	84	6	†201	†325	†30	.946
—Cleveland (A.L.)	SS	38	125	14	27	9	1	2	13	.216	8	31	2	67	93	9	.947
1988—Cleveland (A.L.)	SS-DH	73	211	23	46	5	1	2	21	.218	21	53	4	103	170	10	.965
—Colo. Springs (PCL) ...	SS	49	181	35	50	12	2	7	24	.276	26	27	3	87	171	18	.935
1989—Pittsburgh (N.L.)■....	SS	78	271	33	70	13	3	2	27	.258	19	47	5	109	197	10	.968
—Buffalo (A.A.)	SS-3B	86	298	49	85	15	3	10	54	.285	38	55	12	110	223	16	.954
1990—Pittsburgh (N.L.)	SS	159	583	93	148	28	7	7	52	.254	65	109	10	*260	459	22	.970
1991—Pittsburgh (N.L.)	SS	157	608	96	164	32	8	16	67	.270	52	99	10	239	*491	*24	.968
1992—Pittsburgh (N.L.)	SS	159	632	87	167	36	6	9	55	.264	55	103	7	*268	*526	22	.973
1993—Pittsburgh (N.L.)	SS	154	604	102	187	32	9	9	51	.310	77	122	16	*256	*527	11	*.986
1994—Pittsburgh (N.L.)	SS	110	424	68	117	35	4	9	45	.276	49	82	2	152	*380	15	.973
1995—Pittsburgh (N.L.)	SS-3B	138	530	79	139	28	4	13	55	.262	55	110	2	206	415	14	.978
1996—Pittsburgh (N.L.)	SS	151	527	65	132	29	3	13	71	.250	54	108	6	215	*478	10	*.986
1997—Kansas City (A.L.)■...	SS-3B	153	573	89	167	28	3	21	92	.291	71	101	10	229	450	10	.985
1998—Arizona (N.L.)■..........	SS	155	549	79	138	29	5	20	67	.251	81	129	3	224	437	19	.972
1999—Arizona (N.L.)	2B-DH-SS	151	589	132	170	32	6	38	112	.289	82	132	7	320	340	†22	.968
2000—Arizona (N.L.)	2B-DH	149	565	87	151	30	6	18	68	.267	70	88	7	290	345	8	.988
2001—Arizona (N.L.)	2B-3B-DH	129	428	59	106	24	1	13	46	.248	65	79	0	175	224	7	.983
American League totals (4 years)		269	923	129	245	44	5	26	130	.265	102	188	16	400	719	31	.973
National League totals (12 years)		1690	6310	980	1689	348	62	167	716	.268	724	1208	75	2714	4819	184	.976
Major League totals (16 years)		1959	7233	1109	1934	392	67	193	846	.267	826	1396	91	3114	5538	215	.976

DIVISION SERIES RECORD

Year Team (League)	Pos.	G	AB	R	H	2B	3B	HR	RBI	Avg.	BB	SO	SB	PO	A	E	Avg.
1999—Arizona (N.L.)	2B	4	14	3	4	1	0	0	3	.286	1	0	0	8	11	1	.950
2001—Arizona (N.L.)	2B-PH	2	4	0	1	0	0	0	0	.250	0	1	0	3	2	0	1.000
Division series totals (2 years)		6	18	3	5	1	0	0	3	.278	1	1	0	11	13	1	.960

RECORDS: Shares single-series record for most singles—9 (1991).

Year	Team (League)	Pos.	G	AB	R	H	2B	3B	HR	RBI	Avg.	BB	SO	SB	PO	A	E	Avg.
1990—	Pittsburgh (N.L.)	SS	6	20	3	5	1	0	1	1	.250	4	3	0	4	22	1	.963
1991—	Pittsburgh (N.L.)	SS	7	29	2	12	2	0	1	1	.414	0	10	0	13	19	1	.970
1992—	Pittsburgh (N.L.)	SS	7	29	3	5	2	0	1	4	.172	3	4	0	6	8	1	.933
2001—	Arizona (N.L.)	2B	1	4	0	0	0	0	0	0	.000	0	0	0	1	3	0	1.000
Championship series totals (4 years)			21	82	8	22	5	0	3	6	.268	7	17	0	24	52	3	.962

WORLD SERIES RECORD

NOTES: Member of World Series championship team (2001).

Year	Team (League)	Pos.	G	AB	R	H	2B	3B	HR	RBI	Avg.	BB	SO	SB	PO	A	E	Avg.
2001—	Arizona (N.L.)	PH-2B	3	7	3	1	0	0	0	1	.143	0	2	0	7	1	0	1.000

ALL-STAR GAME RECORD

Year	League	Pos.	AB	R	H	2B	3B	HR	RBI	Avg.	BB	SO	SB	PO	A	E	Avg.
1993—	National	2B	1	0	0	0	0	0	0	.000	0	0	0	1	1	0	1.000
1999—	National	2B	1	0	0	0	0	0	0	.000	1	1	0	1	1	0	1.000
All-Star Game totals (2 years)			2	0	0	0	0	0	0	.000	1	1	0	2	2	0	1.000

B

BELL, ROB — P — RANGERS

PERSONAL: Born January 17, 1977, in Newburgh, N.Y. ... 6-5/225. ... Throws right, bats right. ... Full name: Robert Allen Bell.
HIGH SCHOOL: Marlboro (N.Y.) Central.
TRANSACTIONS/CAREER NOTES: Selected by Atlanta Braves organization in third round of free-agent draft (June 1, 1995). ... Traded by Braves with OF Michael Tucker and P Denny Neagle to Cincinnati Reds for 2B Bret Boone and P Mike Remlinger (November 10, 1998). ... On Chattanooga disabled list (April 20-July 20, 1999). ... Traded by Reds to Texas Rangers for OF Ruben Mateo and 3B Edwin Encarnacion (June 15, 2001).

Year	League	W	L	Pct.	ERA	G	GS	CG	ShO	Sv.	IP	H	R	ER	BB	SO
1995—	Gulf Coast Braves (GCL)	1	6	.143	6.88	10	8	0	0	0	34	38	29	26	14	33
1996—	Eugene (N'West)	5	6	.455	5.11	16	*16	0	0	0	81	89	49	46	29	74
1997—	Macon (S.Atl.)	•14	7	.667	3.68	27	27	1	0	0	146 2/3	144	72	60	41	140
1998—	Danville (Caro.)	7	9	.438	3.28	28	•28	2	0	0	*178 1/3	169	79	65	46	*197
1999—	Chattanooga (Sou.)■	3	6	.333	3.13	12	12	2	1	0	72	75	30	25	17	68
	— Gulf Coast Reds (GCL)	0	0	...	1.13	2	2	0	0	0	8	3	1	1	0	11
2000—	Cincinnati (N.L.)	7	8	.467	5.00	26	26	1	0	0	140 1/3	130	84	78	73	112
	— Louisville (I.L.)	4	0	1.000	3.73	6	6	0	0	0	41	35	18	17	13	47
2001—	Cincinnati (N.L.)	0	5	.000	5.48	9	9	0	0	0	44 1/3	46	28	27	17	33
	— Louisville (I.L.)	2	2	.500	3.33	5	4	0	0	0	27	32	10	10	4	26
	— Texas (A.L.)■	5	5	.500	7.18	18	18	0	0	0	105 1/3	130	87	84	47	64
A.L. totals (1 year)		5	5	.500	7.18	18	18	0	0	0	105 1/3	130	87	84	47	64
N.L. totals (2 years)		7	13	.350	5.12	35	35	1	0	0	184 2/3	176	112	105	90	145
Major League totals (2 years)		12	18	.400	5.87	53	53	1	0	0	290	306	199	189	137	209

BELLE, ALBERT — OF — ORIOLES

PERSONAL: Born August 25, 1966, in Shreveport, La. ... 6-2/225. ... Bats right, throws right. ... Full name: Albert Jojuan Belle. ... Formerly known as Joey Belle.
HIGH SCHOOL: Huntington (Shreveport, La.).
COLLEGE: Louisiana State.
TRANSACTIONS/CAREER NOTES: Selected by Cleveland Indians organization in second round of free-agent draft (June 2, 1987). ... On suspended list (July 12-18, 1991; August 4-8, 1992; June 4-7, 1993; August 1-7, 1994; and June 21-22, 1996). ... Granted free agency (October 28, 1996). ... Signed by Chicago White Sox (November 19, 1996). ... Granted free agency (October 27, 1998). ... Signed by Baltimore Orioles (December 1, 1998). ... On disabled list (March 9, 2001-entire season).
RECORDS: Shares major league records for fewest double plays by outfielder (150 or more games)—0 (1996 and 1997); and most home runs in two consecutive games—5 (September 18 [2] and 19 [3], 1995). ... Shares major league single-game record for most doubles—4 (August 29, 1989; and September 23, 1999). ... Shares A.L. single-season record for fewest errors by outfielder who led league in errors—8 (1998). ... Shares major league single-month records for most home runs—16 (July 1998); and—17 September 1995).
HONORS: Named outfielder on THE SPORTING NEWS A.L. All-Star team (1993-96 and 1998). ... Named outfielder on THE SPORTING NEWS A.L. Silver Slugger team (1993-96 and 1998). ... Named Major League Player of the Year by THE SPORTING NEWS (1995).
STATISTICAL NOTES: Hit three home runs in one game (September 4, 1992; September 19, 1995; and July 25, 1999). ... Led A.L. with 14 sacrifice flies in 1993. ... Led A.L. outfielders with seven double plays in 1993. ... Led A.L. in total bases with 294 in 1994 and 377 in 1995. ... Led A.L. with .690 slugging percentage in 1995. ... Led A.L. in grounding into double plays with 24 in 1995. ... Had 21-game hitting streak (April 27-May 21, 1996). ... Had 27-game hitting streak (May 3-June 1, 1997). ... Led A.L. in grounding into double plays with 26 in 1997. ... Led A.L. with 399 total bases, 15 sacrifice flies and .655 slugging percentage in 1998. ... Had 15-game hitting streak (September 1-17, 1999). ... Career major league grand slams: 13.

Year	Team (League)	Pos.	G	AB	R	H	2B	3B	HR	RBI	Avg.	BB	SO	SB	PO	A	E	Avg.
1987—	Kinston (Caro.)	OF	10	37	5	12	2	0	3	9	.324	8	16	0	5	0	0	1.000
1988—	Kinston (Caro.)	OF	41	153	21	46	16	0	8	39	.301	18	45	2	43	5	5	.906
	— Waterloo (Midw.)	OF	9	28	2	7	1	0	1	2	.250	1	9	0	11	1	0	1.000
1989—	Canton/Akron (East.)	OF	89	312	48	88	20	0	20	69	.282	32	82	8	136	4	3	.979
	— Cleveland (A.L.)	OF-DH	62	218	22	49	8	4	7	37	.225	12	55	2	92	3	2	.979
1990—	Cleveland (A.L.)	DH-OF	9	23	1	4	0	0	1	3	.174	1	6	0	0	0	0	...
	— Colo. Springs (PCL)	OF	24	96	16	33	3	1	5	19	.344	5	16	4	31	0	2	.939
	— Canton/Akron (East.)	DH	9	32	4	8	1	0	0	3	.250	3	7	0	...	...	...	...
1991—	Cleveland (A.L.)	OF-DH	123	461	60	130	31	2	28	95	.282	25	99	3	170	8	•9	.952
	— Colo. Springs (PCL)	OF	16	61	9	20	3	2	2	16	.328	2	8	1	19	1	1	.952

					BATTING									FIELDING		
Year Team (League)	Pos.	G	AB	R	H	2B	3B	HR	RBI	Avg.	BB	SO	SB	PO	A	E	Avg.
1992—Cleveland (A.L.).........	DH-OF	153	585	81	152	23	1	34	112	.260	52	128	8	94	1	3	.969
1993—Cleveland (A.L.).........	OF-DH	159	594	93	172	36	3	38	*129	.290	76	96	23	338	16	5	.986
1994—Cleveland (A.L.).........	OF-DH	106	412	90	147	35	2	36	101	.357	58	71	9	205	8	6	.973
1995—Cleveland (A.L.).........	OF-DH	143	546	•121	173	•52	1	*50	•126	.317	73	80	5	304	7	6	.981
1996—Cleveland (A.L.).........	OF-DH	158	602	124	187	38	3	48	*148	.311	99	87	11	309	11	10	.970
1997—Chicago (A.L.)■.........	OF-DH	161	634	90	174	45	1	30	116	.274	53	105	4	351	1	10	.972
1998—Chicago (A.L.).........	OF-DH	*163	609	113	200	48	2	49	152	.328	81	84	6	316	11	•8	.976
1999—Baltimore (A.L.)■......	OF-DH	161	610	108	181	36	1	37	117	.297	101	82	17	252	•17	4	.985
2000—Baltimore (A.L.).........	OF-DH	141	559	71	157	37	1	23	103	.281	52	68	0	211	8	3	.986
2001—Baltimore (A.L.).........						Did not play.											
Major League totals (12 years)		1539	5853	974	1726	389	21	381	1239	.295	683	961	88	2642	91	66	.976

DIVISION SERIES RECORD

					BATTING									FIELDING		
Year Team (League)	Pos.	G	AB	R	H	2B	3B	HR	RBI	Avg.	BB	SO	SB	PO	A	E	Avg.
1995—Cleveland (A.L.).........	OF	3	11	3	3	1	0	1	3	.273	4	3	0	7	0	1	.875
1996—Cleveland (A.L.).........	OF	4	15	2	3	0	0	2	6	.200	4	2	1	11	1	0	1.000
Division series totals (2 years)		7	26	5	6	1	0	3	9	.231	8	5	1	18	1	1	.950

CHAMPIONSHIP SERIES RECORD

					BATTING									FIELDING		
Year Team (League)	Pos.	G	AB	R	H	2B	3B	HR	RBI	Avg.	BB	SO	SB	PO	A	E	Avg.
1995—Cleveland (A.L.).........	OF	5	18	1	4	1	0	1	1	.222	3	5	0	4	0	2	.667

WORLD SERIES RECORD

					BATTING									FIELDING		
Year Team (League)	Pos.	G	AB	R	H	2B	3B	HR	RBI	Avg.	BB	SO	SB	PO	A	E	Avg.
1995—Cleveland (A.L.).........	OF	6	17	4	4	0	0	2	4	.235	7	5	0	10	0	1	.909

ALL-STAR GAME RECORD

				BATTING									FIELDING		
Year League	Pos.	AB	R	H	2B	3B	HR	RBI	Avg.	BB	SO	SB	PO	A	E	Avg.
1993— American..................	PH-DH	1	2	1	0	0	0	1	1.000	1	0	0	...	...	...	...
1994— American..................	OF	2	0	0	0	0	0	0	.000	0	0	0	1	0	0	1.000
1995— American..................	OF	3	0	0	0	0	0	0	.000	0	1	0	1	0	0	1.000
1996— American..................	OF	4	0	0	0	0	0	0	.000	0	3	0	1	0	0	1.000
1997— American..................						Did not play.										
All-Star Game totals (4 years)		10	2	1	0	0	0	1	.100	1	4	0	3	0	0	1.000

BELLHORN, MARK   3B   CUBS

PERSONAL: Born August 23, 1974, in Boston. ... 6-4/214. ... Bats both, throws right. ... Full name: Mark Christian Bellhorn.
HIGH SCHOOL: Oviedo (Fla.).
COLLEGE: Auburn.
TRANSACTIONS/CAREER NOTES: Selected by Oakland Athletics organization in second round of free agent draft (June 1, 1995). ... On Vancouver disabled list (April 8-July 29, 1999). ... On Sacramento disabled list (May 12-24, 2000). ... Traded by A's to Chicago Cubs for IF Adam Morrissey (November 2, 2001).
STATISTICAL NOTES: Tied for Arizona League lead with two intentional bases on balls received in 1999.

					BATTING									FIELDING		
Year Team (League)	Pos.	G	AB	R	H	2B	3B	HR	RBI	Avg.	BB	SO	SB	PO	A	E	Avg.
1995—Modesto (Calif.)........	SS	56	229	35	59	12	0	6	31	.258	27	52	5	94	172	21	.927
1996—Huntsville (Sou.).......	IF	131	468	84	117	24	5	10	71	.250	73	124	19	208	344	32	.945
1997—Edmonton (PCL) 2B-SS-3B-DH	70	241	54	79	18	3	11	46	.328	64	59	6	105	187	13	.957
—Oakland (A.L.) 3B-2B-DH-SS	68	224	33	51	9	1	6	19	.228	32	70	7	72	123	9	.956
1998—Edmonton (PCL) 3-2-DH-S-1	87	309	57	77	20	4	10	44	.249	62	90	6	95	205	11	.965
—Oakland (A.L.) 3B-DH-SS-2B	11	12	1	1	1	0	0	1	.083	3	4	2	3	7	0	1.000
1999—Ariz. Athletics (Ariz.) ..	2B-DH	12	43	11	10	3	0	0	5	.233	11	9	0	22	17	0	1.000
—Midland (Texas)...........	2B	17	57	12	17	3	0	2	8	.298	11	13	1	30	41	2	.973
2000—Sacramento (PCL)......3B-2B-SS-1B	43	436	*111	116	17	11	24	73	.266	*94	121	20	111	216	15	.956
—Oakland (A.L.) 2B-3B-SS	9	13	2	2	0	0	0	0	.154	2	6	0	0	5	0	1.000
2001—Sacramento (PCL)......OF-2B-SS-3B	43	156	30	42	6	0	12	36	.269	22	60	3	64	68	2	.985
—Oakland (A.L.) 2-3-S-D-O	38	74	11	10	1	2	1	4	.135	7	37	0	21	47	5	.932
Major League totals (4 years)		126	323	47	64	11	3	7	24	.198	44	117	9	96	182	14	.952

BELLIARD, RON   2B   BREWERS

PERSONAL: Born July 4, 1976, in Bronx, N.Y. ... 5-8/190. ... Bats right, throws right. ... Full name: Ronald Belliard. ... Name pronounced BELL-ee-ard.
HIGH SCHOOL: Central (Miami).
TRANSACTIONS/CAREER NOTES: Selected by Milwaukee Brewers organization in eighth round of free-agent draft (June 2, 1994). ... On disabled list (August 8-September 30, 2001).
STATISTICAL NOTES: Led Midwest League second basemen with 25 errors in 1995. ... Led Pacific Coast League second basemen with 229 putouts, 358 assists, 24 errors and 611 total chances and tied for league lead with 92 double plays in 1997. ... Led International League second basemen with 401 assists and 98 double plays in 1998. ... Led N.L. second basemen with 793 total chances and 130 double plays in 2000.

Year Team (League)	Pos.	G	AB	R	H	2B	3B	HR	RBI	Avg.	BB	SO	SB	PO	A	E	Avg.
1994—Ariz. Brewers (Ariz.)...	2B-3B-SS	39	143	32	42	7	3	0	27	.294	14	25	7	54	119	12	.935
1995—Beloit (Midw.)...	2B-3B	130	461	76	137	28	5	13	76	.297	36	67	16	221	346	†26	.956
1996—El Paso (Texas)...	2B-DH	109	416	73	116	20	8	3	57	.279	60	51	26	246	314	16	.972
1997—Tucson (PCL)...	2B-SS	118	443	80	125	35	4	4	55	.282	61	69	10	†233	†369	†26	.959
1998—Louisville (I.L.)...	2B-SS	133	507	*114	163	36	7	14	73	.321	69	77	33	231	†408	14	.979
—Milwaukee (N.L.)...	2B	8	5	1	1	0	0	0	0	.200	0	0	0	0	0	0	...
1999—Louisville (I.L.)...	2B	29	108	14	26	4	0	1	8	.241	14	13	12	51	66	3	.975
—Milwaukee (N.L.)...	2B-3B-SS	124	457	60	135	29	4	8	58	.295	64	59	4	250	333	13	.978
2000—Milwaukee (N.L.)...	2B	152	571	83	150	30	9	8	54	.263	82	84	7	*336	437	*19	.976
2001—Milwaukee (N.L.)...	2B	101	364	69	96	30	3	11	36	.264	35	65	5	213	290	5	.990
Major League totals (4 years)		385	1397	213	382	89	16	27	148	.273	181	208	16	799	1060	37	.980

BELLINGER, CLAY — OF/IF — B

PERSONAL: Born November 18, 1968, in Oneonta, N.Y. ... 6-3/215. ... Bats right, throws right. ... Full name: Clayton Daniel Bellinger.
HIGH SCHOOL: Oneonta (N.Y.).
COLLEGE: Rollins.
TRANSACTIONS/CAREER NOTES: Selected by San Francisco Giants organization in second round of free-agent draft (June 5, 1989). ... Granted free agency (October 16, 1995). ... Signed by Baltimore Orioles organization (November 22, 1995). ... Granted free agency (October 15, 1996). ... Signed by New York Yankees organization (November 4, 1996). ... Released by Yankees (January 17, 2002).

Year Team (League)	Pos.	G	AB	R	H	2B	3B	HR	RBI	Avg.	BB	SO	SB	PO	A	E	Avg.
1989—Everett (N'West)...	SS	51	185	29	37	8	1	4	16	.200	19	47	3	57	110	24	.874
1990—Clinton (Midw.)...	SS-3B	109	383	52	83	17	4	10	48	.217	27	102	13	144	229	29	.928
1991—San Jose (Calif.)...	SS	105	368	65	95	29	2	8	62	.258	53	88	13	157	297	32	.934
1992—Shreveport (Texas)...	SS	126	433	45	90	18	3	13	50	.208	36	82	7	183	346	*41	.928
1993—Phoenix (PCL)...	3B-SS-1B	122	407	50	104	20	3	6	49	.256	38	81	7	123	272	28	.934
1994—Phoenix (PCL)...	0-S-1-3-2-C	106	337	48	90	15	1	7	50	.267	18	56	6	248	140	8	.980
1995—Phoenix (PCL)...	S-3-0-2-1-C	97	277	34	76	16	1	2	32	.274	27	52	3	116	145	8	.970
1996—Rochester (I.L.)■...	SS-1B-2B	125	459	68	138	34	4	15	78	.301	33	90	8	445	228	22	.968
1997—Columbus (I.L.)■...	3-0-S-1-2	111	416	55	114	31	3	12	59	.274	34	74	10	187	137	15	.956
1998—Columbus (I.L.)...	1-S-3-2-0-C	115	397	35	89	20	2	9	40	.224	35	79	6	342	185	14	.974
1999—New York (A.L.)...	3-1-DH-0-2-S	32	45	12	9	2	0	1	2	.200	1	10	1	23	18	0	1.000
—Columbus (I.L.)...	3-S-0-2-1	40	141	19	33	10	1	2	14	.234	13	32	6	68	89	2	.987
2000—New York (A.L.)...	0-2-3-1-S	98	184	33	38	8	2	6	21	.207	17	48	5	127	87	5	.977
—Columbus (I.L.)...	1B-OF-SS-C	8	28	3	9	2	0	0	2	.321	2	5	1	38	3	1	.976
2001—New York (A.L.)...	0-3-1-S-D	51	81	12	13	1	1	5	12	.160	4	23	1	45	34	3	.963
—Columbus (I.L.)...	0-S-3-1-2	26	98	13	21	10	0	1	9	.214	5	22	3	33	40	3	.961
Major League totals (3 years)		181	310	57	60	11	3	12	35	.194	22	81	7	195	139	8	.977

DIVISION SERIES RECORD

Year Team (League)	Pos.	G	AB	R	H	2B	3B	HR	RBI	Avg.	BB	SO	SB	PO	A	E	Avg.
1999—New York (A.L.)...	PR-DH	1	0	0	0	0	0	0	0	...	0	0	0	...	...	...	...
2000—New York (A.L.)...	OF	2	1	0	1	1	0	0	1	1.000	0	0	0	0	0	0	...
2001—New York (A.L.)...	PR	1	0	0	0	0	0	0	0	...	0	0	0	...	...	...	...
Division series totals (3 years)		4	1	0	1	1	0	0	1	1.000	0	0	0	0	0	0	...

CHAMPIONSHIP SERIES RECORD

Year Team (League)	Pos.	G	AB	R	H	2B	3B	HR	RBI	Avg.	BB	SO	SB	PO	A	E	Avg.
1999—New York (A.L.)...	PH-SS-PR-DH	3	1	0	0	0	0	0	0	.000	0	1	0	0	1	0	1.000
2000—New York (A.L.)...	OF-PR	5	1	0	0	0	0	0	0	.000	0	1	0	1	0	0	1.000
2001—New York (A.L.)...	OF	1	1	0	0	0	0	0	0	.000	0	0	0	1	0	0	1.000
Championship series totals (3 years)		9	3	0	0	0	0	0	0	.000	0	2	0	2	1	0	1.000

WORLD SERIES RECORD

NOTES: Member of World Series championship team (1999 and 2000).

Year Team (League)	Pos.	G	AB	R	H	2B	3B	HR	RBI	Avg.	BB	SO	SB	PO	A	E	Avg.
1999—New York (A.L.)...					Did not play.												
2000—New York (A.L.)...	PR-OF	4	0	0	0	0	0	0	0	...	0	0	0	2	0	0	1.000
2001—New York (A.L.)...	PR-OF-PH	2	2	0	0	0	0	0	0	.000	0	2	0	1	0	0	1.000
World Series totals (2 years)		6	2	0	0	0	0	0	0	.000	0	2	0	3	0	0	1.000

RECORD AS PITCHER

Year League	W	L	Pct.	ERA	G	GS	CG	ShO	Sv.	IP	H	R	ER	BB	SO
1994—Phoenix (PCL)...	0	0	...	9.00	2	0	0	0	0	2	6	2	2	0	0
1998—Columbus (I.L.)...	0	0	...	0.00	1	0	0	0	0	1/3	1	0	0	1	0

BELTRAN, CARLOS — OF — ROYALS

PERSONAL: Born April 24, 1977, in Manati, Puerto Rico. ... 6-1/190. ... Bats both, throws right. ... Full name: Carlos Ivan Beltran.
HIGH SCHOOL: Fernando Callejas (Manati, Puerto Rico).
TRANSACTIONS/CAREER NOTES: Selected by Kansas City Royals organization in second round of free-agent draft (June 1, 1995). ... On Kansas City disabled list (July 4-September 4, 2000); included rehabilitation assignments to Gulf Coast Royals (August 21-24), Wilmington (August 25-30) and Omaha (August 31-September 4).
HONORS: Named A.L. Rookie Player of the Year by THE SPORTING NEWS (1999). ... Named A.L. Rookie of the Year by Baseball Writers' Association of America (1999).
STATISTICAL NOTES: Led A.L. outfielders with 423 total chances in 1999. ... Switch-hit home runs in one game (June 29, 2000). ... Career major league grand slams: 2.

Year	Team (League)	Pos.	G	AB	R	H	2B	3B	HR	RBI	Avg.	BB	SO	SB	PO	A	E	Avg.
1995—	GC Royals (GCL)	OF	52	180	29	50	9	0	0	23	.278	13	30	5	79	6	2	.977
1996—	Lansing (Midw.)	OF	11	42	3	6	2	0	0	0	.143	1	11	1	28	2	2	.938
—	Spokane (N'West)	OF	59	215	29	58	8	3	7	29	.270	31	65	10	99	6	7	.938
1997—	Wilmington (Caro.)	OF	120	419	57	96	15	4	11	46	.229	46	96	17	236	7	8	.968
1998—	Wilmington (Caro.)	OF	52	192	32	53	14	0	5	32	.276	25	39	11	109	4	2	.983
—	Wichita (Texas)	OF	47	182	50	64	13	3	14	44	.352	23	30	7	93	2	4	.960
—	Kansas City (A.L.)	OF	14	58	12	16	5	3	0	7	.276	3	12	3	44	0	1	.978
1999—	Kansas City (A.L.)	OF-DH	156	663	112	194	27	7	22	108	.293	46	123	27	395	16	*12	.972
2000—	Kansas City (A.L.)	OF-DH	98	372	49	92	15	4	7	44	.247	35	69	13	231	5	6	.975
—	GC Royals (GCL)	DH	1	4	3	2	1	0	1	1	.500	1	0	0	...	...	...	...
—	Wilmington (Caro.)	OF	3	13	2	4	0	1	2	6	.308	0	5	0	2	0	0	1.000
—	Omaha (PCL)	OF	5	18	4	6	1	0	2	2	.333	3	3	1	6	0	0	1.000
2001—	Kansas City (A.L.)	OF-DH	155	617	106	189	32	12	24	101	.306	52	120	31	404	14	5	.988
Major League totals (4 years)			423	1710	279	491	79	26	53	260	.287	136	324	74	1074	35	24	.979

BELTRE, ADRIAN   3B   DODGERS

PERSONAL: Born April 7, 1979, in Santo Domingo, Dominican Republic. ... 5-11/170. ... Bats right, throws right. ... Full name: Adrian Perez Beltre. ... Name pronounced bell-TREE.

HIGH SCHOOL: Liceo Maximo Gomez (Santo Domingo, Dominican Republic).

TRANSACTIONS/CAREER NOTES: Signed as non-drafted free agent by Los Angeles Dodgers (July 7, 1994). ... On San Bernardino disabled list (June 25-July 2, 1996). ... On Albuquerque disabled list (April 23-May 1 and May 12-19, 1998). ... On disabled list (May 28-June 17, 2000). ... On Los Angeles disabled list (March 23-May 12, 2001); included rehabilitation assignments to Vero Beach (May 6-9) and Las Vegas (May 10-12).

HONORS: Named Florida State League Most Valuable Player (1997).

STATISTICAL NOTES: Led Florida State League with .561 slugging percentage and 12 intentional bases on balls received in 1997. ... Led Florida State League third basemen with 26 double plays in 1997. ... Led N.L. third basemen with 116 putouts and 412 total chances in 2000. ... Had 17-game hitting streak (August 25-September 18, 2001). ... Career major league grand slams: 2.

Year	Team (League)	Pos.	G	AB	R	H	2B	3B	HR	RBI	Avg.	BB	SO	SB	PO	A	E	Avg.
1995—	Dom. Dodgers (DSL)	3B	62	218	56	67	15	3	8	40	.307	54	26	2	187	31	19	.920
1996—	Savannah (S.Atl.)	3B-2B	68	244	48	75	14	3	16	59	.307	35	46	4	55	143	19	.912
—	San Bern. (Calif.)	3B-DH	63	238	40	62	13	1	10	40	.261	19	44	3	32	110	7	.953
1997—	Vero Beach (FSL)	3B-OF	123	435	95	138	24	2	*26	*104	.317	67	66	25	83	231	37	.895
1998—	San Antonio (Texas)	3B-DH	64	246	49	79	21	2	13	56	.321	39	37	20	41	130	17	.910
—	Los Angeles (N.L.)	3B-SS	77	195	18	42	9	0	7	22	.215	14	37	3	32	131	13	.926
1999—	Los Angeles (N.L.)	3B	152	538	84	148	27	5	15	67	.275	61	105	18	121	274	•29	.932
2000—	Los Angeles (N.L.)	3B-SS	138	510	71	148	30	2	20	85	.290	56	80	12	†117	273	23	.944
2001—	Vero Beach (FSL)	3B	3	9	0	4	1	0	0	1	.444	2	1	0	4	0	1.000
—	Las Vegas (PCL)	3B	2	5	2	3	1	0	1	2	.600	2	0	0	2	3	1	.833
—	Los Angeles (N.L.)	3B-SS	126	475	59	126	22	4	13	60	.265	28	82	13	103	218	16	.953
Major League totals (4 years)			493	1718	232	464	88	11	55	234	.270	159	304	46	373	896	81	.940

BENARD, MARVIN   OF   GIANTS

PERSONAL: Born January 20, 1970, in Bluefields, Nicaragua. ... 5-9/185. ... Bats left, throws left. ... Full name: Marvin Larry Benard. ... Name pronounced buh-NARD.

HIGH SCHOOL: Bell (Bell Gardens, Calif.).

JUNIOR COLLEGE: Los Angeles Harbor College.

COLLEGE: Lewis-Clark State (Idaho).

TRANSACTIONS/CAREER NOTES: Selected by Philadelphia Phillies organization in 20th round of free-agent draft (June 4, 1990); did not sign. ... Selected by San Francisco Giants organization in 50th round of free-agent draft (June 1, 1992). ... On disabled list (April 17-28, 1993).

STATISTICAL NOTES: Tied for Texas League lead in grounding into double plays with 15 in 1994. ... Led Texas League outfielders with five double plays in 1994. ... Career major league grand slams: 1.

Year	Team (League)	Pos.	G	AB	R	H	2B	3B	HR	RBI	Avg.	BB	SO	SB	PO	A	E	Avg.
1992—	Everett (N'West)	OF	64	161	31	38	10	2	1	17	.236	24	39	17	90	8	3	.970
1993—	Clinton (Midw.)	OF	112	349	84	105	14	2	5	50	.301	56	66	42	179	10	5	.974
1994—	Shreveport (Texas)	OF	125	454	66	143	32	3	4	48	.315	31	58	24	259	17	*12	.958
1995—	Phoenix (PCL)	OF-DH	111	378	70	115	14	6	6	32	.304	50	66	10	183	5	8	.959
—	San Francisco (N.L.)	OF	13	34	5	13	2	0	1	4	.382	1	7	1	19	0	0	1.000
1996—	Phoenix (PCL)	OF	4	19	2	7	0	0	0	4	.368	2	2	1	9	0	0	1.000
—	San Francisco (N.L.)	OF	135	488	89	121	17	4	5	27	.248	59	84	25	309	7	5	.984
1997—	San Francisco (N.L.)	OF-DH	84	114	13	26	4	0	1	13	.228	13	29	3	27	2	1	.967
—	Phoenix (PCL)	OF	17	60	14	20	5	0	0	5	.333	11	9	4	26	2	1	.966
1998—	San Francisco (N.L.)	OF-DH	121	286	41	92	21	1	3	36	.322	34	39	11	109	1	2	.982
1999—	San Francisco (N.L.)	OF	149	562	100	163	36	5	16	64	.290	55	97	27	323	5	4	.988
2000—	San Francisco (N.L.)	OF	149	560	102	147	27	6	12	55	.263	63	97	22	323	11	1	.997
2001—	San Francisco (N.L.)	OF	129	392	70	104	19	2	15	44	.265	29	66	10	213	5	8	.965
Major League totals (7 years)			780	2436	420	666	126	18	53	243	.273	254	419	99	1323	31	21	.985

DIVISION SERIES RECORD

Year	Team (League)	Pos.	G	AB	R	H	2B	3B	HR	RBI	Avg.	BB	SO	SB	PO	A	E	Avg.
1997—	San Francisco (N.L.)	PH	2	2	0	0	0	0	0	0	.000	0	1	0	...	...	...	...
2000—	San Francisco (N.L.)	OF-PH	4	14	0	1	0	0	0	1	.071	1	7	0	12	0	0	1.000
Division series totals (2 years)			6	16	0	1	0	0	0	1	.063	1	8	0	12	0	0	1.000

PERSONAL: Born January 21, 1972, in Evansville, Ind. ... 6-5/235. ... Throws right, bats right. ... Full name: Alan Paul Benes. ... Brother of Andy Benes, pitcher, St. Louis Cardinals; and brother of Adam Benes, pitcher with Cardinals organization (1995-2000). ... Name pronounced BEN-es.
HIGH SCHOOL: Lake Forest (Ill.).
COLLEGE: Creighton.
TRANSACTIONS/CAREER NOTES: Selected by San Diego Padres organization in 49th round of free-agent draft (June 4, 1990); did not sign. ... Selected by St. Louis Cardinals organization in first round (16th pick overall) of free-agent draft (June 3, 1993). ... On Louisville disabled list (May 3-August 9, 1995). ... On disabled list (July 31, 1997-remainder of season; and March 22, 1998-entire season). ... On St. Louis disabled list (March 26-September 5, 1999); included rehabilitation assignments to Arkansas (August 5-10 and August 26-30), Potomac (August 11-15 and August 31-September 3) and Memphis (August 16-25 and September 4-5). ... Granted free agency (December 21, 2001). ... Signed by Chicago Cubs organization (January 16, 2002).
HONORS: Named N.L. Rookie Pitcher of the Year by THE SPORTING NEWS (1996).

Year	League	W	L	Pct.	ERA	G	GS	CG	ShO	Sv.	IP	H	R	ER	BB	SO
1993—	Glens Falls (NY-Penn)	0	4	.000	3.65	7	7	0	0	0	37	39	20	15	14	29
1994—	Savannah (S.Atl.)	2	0	1.000	1.48	4	4	0	0	0	24 1/3	21	5	4	7	24
	—St. Petersburg (FSL)	7	1	.875	1.61	11	11	0	0	0	78 1/3	55	18	14	15	69
	—Arkansas (Texas)	7	2	.778	2.98	13	13	1	0	0	87 2/3	58	38	29	26	75
	—Louisville (A.A.)	1	0	1.000	2.93	2	2	1	0	0	15 1/3	10	5	5	4	16
1995—	Louisville (A.A.)	4	2	.667	2.41	11	11	2	1	0	56	37	16	15	14	54
	—St. Louis (N.L.)	1	2	.333	8.44	3	3	0	0	0	16	24	15	15	4	20
1996—	St. Louis (N.L.)	13	10	.565	4.90	34	32	3	1	0	191	192	120	104	87	131
1997—	St. Louis (N.L.)	9	9	.500	2.89	23	23	2	0	0	161 2/3	128	60	52	68	160
1998—	St. Louis (N.L.)							Did not play.								
1999—	Arkansas (Texas)	0	0	...	6.23	2	2	0	0	0	4 1/3	6	3	3	1	0
	—Potomac (Caro.)	0	0	...	1.80	2	2	0	0	0	5	1	1	1	4	2
	—Memphis (PCL)	0	1	.000	3.18	3	3	0	0	0	5 2/3	8	3	2	2	3
	—St. Louis (N.L.)	0	0	...	0.00	2	2	0	0	0	2	2	0	0	0	2
2000—	Memphis (PCL)	1	2	.333	5.95	9	8	0	0	0	39 1/3	45	31	26	21	26
	—St. Louis (N.L.)	2	2	.500	5.67	30	0	0	0	0	46	54	33	29	23	26
2001—	Memphis (PCL)	7	6	.538	3.55	25	25	1	0	0	142	164	71	56	51	96
	—St. Louis (N.L.)	2	0	1.000	7.36	9	1	0	0	0	14 2/3	14	12	12	12	10
Major League totals (6 years)		27	23	.540	4.42	101	59	5	1	0	431 1/3	414	240	212	194	349

CHAMPIONSHIP SERIES RECORD

Year	League	W	L	Pct.	ERA	G	GS	CG	ShO	Sv.	IP	H	R	ER	BB	SO
1996—	St. Louis (N.L.)	0	1	.000	2.84	2	1	0	0	0	6 1/3	3	2	2	3	5

B

PERSONAL: Born August 20, 1967, in Evansville, Ind. ... 6-6/245. ... Throws right, bats right. ... Full name: Andrew Charles Benes. ... Brother of Alan Benes, pitcher, Chicago Cubs; and brother of Adam Benes, pitcher with Cardinals organization (1995-2000). ... Name pronounced BEN-ess.
HIGH SCHOOL: Central (Evansville, Ind.).
COLLEGE: Evansville.
TRANSACTIONS/CAREER NOTES: Selected by San Diego Padres organization in first round (first pick overall) of free-agent draft (June 1, 1988). ... On suspended list (September 28, 1993-remainder of season). ... Traded by Padres with a player to be named later to Seattle Mariners for P Ron Villone and OF Marc Newfield (July 31, 1995); Mariners acquired P Greg Keagle to complete deal (September 16, 1995). ... Granted free agency (October 31, 1995). ... Signed by St. Louis Cardinals organization (December 23, 1995). ... On St. Louis disabled list (March 23-April 28, 1997); included rehabilitation assignments to Prince William (April 11), Louisville (April 16) and Arkansas (April 22). ... Granted free agency (October 29, 1997). ... Signed by Arizona Diamondbacks (February 3, 1998). ... Granted free agency (October 29, 1999). ... Signed by Cardinals (January 7, 2000). ... On disabled list (August 15-September 3, 2000).
RECORDS: Holds major league single-season record for fewest hits allowed for leader in most hits allowed—230 (1992). ... Shares major league record for most home runs allowed in one inning—4 (July 23, 2000, second inning).
HONORS: Named N.L. Rookie Pitcher of the Year by THE SPORTING NEWS (1989). ... Named Texas League Pitcher of the Year (1989).
STATISTICAL NOTES: Tied for N.L. lead with five balks in 1990. ... Pitched 7-0 one-hit, complete-game victory against New York (July 3, 1994).
MISCELLANEOUS: Holds San Diego Padres all-time record for most strikeouts (1,036). ... Member of 1988 U.S. Olympic baseball team (1988). ... Made an out in only appearance as pinch hitter (1998).

Year	League	W	L	Pct.	ERA	G	GS	CG	ShO	Sv.	IP	H	R	ER	BB	SO
1989—	Wichita (Texas)	8	4	.667	2.16	16	16	5	*3	0	108 1/3	79	32	26	39	115
	—Las Vegas (PCL)	2	1	.667	8.10	5	5	0	0	0	26 2/3	41	29	24	12	29
	—San Diego (N.L.)	6	3	.667	3.51	10	10	0	0	0	66 2/3	51	28	26	31	66
1990—	San Diego (N.L.)	10	11	.476	3.60	32	31	2	0	0	192 1/3	177	87	77	69	140
1991—	San Diego (N.L.)	15	11	.577	3.03	33	33	4	1	0	223	194	76	75	59	167
1992—	San Diego (N.L.)	13	14	.481	3.35	34	34	2	2	0	231 1/3	*230	90	86	61	169
1993—	San Diego (N.L.)	15	15	.500	3.78	34	34	4	2	0	230 2/3	200	111	97	86	179
1994—	San Diego (N.L.)	6	*14	.300	3.86	25	25	2	2	0	172 1/3	155	82	74	51	*189
1995—	San Diego (N.L.)	4	7	.364	4.17	19	19	1	1	0	118 2/3	121	65	55	45	126
	—Seattle (A.L.)■	7	2	.778	5.86	12	12	0	0	0	63	72	42	41	33	45
1996—	St. Louis (N.L.)■	18	10	.643	3.83	36	34	3	1	1	230 1/3	215	107	98	77	160
1997—	Prince William (Caro.)	0	0	...	0.00	1	1	0	0	0	5	3	1	0	1	9
	—Louisville (A.A.)	0	0	...	1.80	1	1	0	0	0	5	3	1	1	1	5
	—Arkansas (Texas)	1	0	1.000	1.29	1	1	0	0	0	7	2	1	1	2	6
	—St. Louis (N.L.)	10	7	.588	3.10	26	26	0	0	0	177	149	64	61	61	175
1998—	Arizona (N.L.)■	14	13	.519	3.97	34	34	1	0	0	231 1/3	221	111	102	74	164
1999—	Arizona (N.L.)	13	12	.520	4.81	33	32	0	0	0	198 1/3	216	117	106	82	141
2000—	St. Louis (N.L.)■	12	9	.571	4.88	30	27	1	0	0	166	174	95	90	68	137
2001—	St. Louis (N.L.)	7	7	.500	7.38	27	19	0	0	0	107 1/3	122	92	88	61	78
A.L. totals (1 year)		7	2	.778	5.86	12	12	0	0	0	63	72	42	41	33	45
N.L. totals (13 years)		143	133	.518	3.97	373	358	20	9	1	2345 1/3	2225	1125	1035	825	1891
Major League totals (13 years)		150	135	.526	4.02	385	370	20	9	1	2408 1/3	2297	1167	1076	858	1936

DIVISION SERIES RECORD

Year League	W	L	Pct.	ERA	G	GS	CG	ShO	Sv.	IP	H	R	ER	BB	SO
1995— Seattle (A.L.)	0	0	...	5.40	2	2	0	0	0	11 2/3	10	7	7	9	8
1996— St. Louis (N.L.)	0	0	...	5.14	1	1	0	0	0	7	6	4	4	1	9
2000— St. Louis (N.L.)							Did not play.								
2001— St. Louis (N.L.)							Did not play.								
Division series totals (2 years)	0	0	...	5.30	3	3	0	0	0	18 2/3	16	11	11	10	17

CHAMPIONSHIP SERIES RECORD

RECORDS: Shares N.L. single-series record for most hits allowed—19 (1996).

Year League	W	L	Pct.	ERA	G	GS	CG	ShO	Sv.	IP	H	R	ER	BB	SO
1995— Seattle (A.L.)	0	1	.000	23.14	1	1	0	0	0	2 1/3	6	6	6	2	3
1996— St. Louis (N.L.)	0	0	...	5.28	3	2	0	0	0	15 1/3	19	9	9	3	9
2000— St. Louis (N.L.)	1	0	1.000	2.25	1	1	0	0	0	8	6	2	2	3	5
Champ. series totals (3 years)	1	1	.500	5.96	5	4	0	0	0	25 2/3	31	17	17	8	17

ALL-STAR GAME RECORD

Year League	W	L	Pct.	ERA	GS	CG	ShO	Sv.	IP	H	R	ER	BB	SO
1993— National	0	0	...	4.50	0	0	0	0	2	2	1	1	0	2

B

BENITEZ, ARMANDO   P   METS

PERSONAL: Born November 3, 1972, in Ramon Santana, Dominican Republic. ... 6-4/229. ... Throws right, bats right.

TRANSACTIONS/CAREER NOTES: Signed as non-drafted free agent by Baltimore Orioles organization (April 1, 1990). ... On Baltimore disabled list (April 20-August 26, 1996); included rehabilitation assignments to Bowie (May 17-19) and Gulf Coast Orioles (August 13-26). ... On suspended list (May 20-28, 1998). ... Traded by Orioles to New York Mets for C Charles Johnson (December 1, 1998).

HONORS: Named N.L. co-Reliever of the Year by THE SPORTING NEWS (2001).

Year League	W	L	Pct.	ERA	G	GS	CG	ShO	Sv.	IP	H	R	ER	BB	SO
1990— Dominican (DSL)	3	1	.750	2.72	19	0	0	0	8	43	39	23	13	20	34
1991— Gulf Coast Orioles (GCL)	3	2	.600	2.72	14	3	0	0	0	36 1/3	35	16	11	11	33
1992— Bluefield (Appl.)	1	2	.333	4.31	25	0	0	0	5	31 1/3	35	31	15	23	37
1993— Albany (S.Atl.)	5	1	.833	1.52	40	0	0	0	14	53 1/3	31	10	9	19	83
— Frederick (Caro.)	3	0	1.000	0.66	12	0	0	0	4	13 2/3	7	1	1	4	29
1994— Bowie (East.)	8	4	.667	3.14	53	0	0	0	16	71 2/3	41	29	25	39	106
— Baltimore (A.L.)	0	0	...	0.90	3	0	0	0	0	10	8	1	1	4	14
1995— Baltimore (A.L.)	1	5	.167	5.66	44	0	0	0	2	47 2/3	37	33	30	37	56
— Rochester (I.L.)	2	2	.500	1.25	17	0	0	0	8	21 2/3	10	4	3	7	37
1996— Baltimore (A.L.)	1	0	1.000	3.77	18	0	0	0	4	14 1/3	7	6	6	6	20
— Bowie (East.)	0	0	...	4.50	4	4	0	0	0	6	7	3	3	0	8
— Gulf Coast Orioles (GCL)	1	0	1.000	0.00	1	0	0	0	0	2	1	0	0	0	5
— Rochester (I.L.)	0	0	...	2.25	2	0	0	0	0	4	3	1	1	1	5
1997— Baltimore (A.L.)	4	5	.444	2.45	71	0	0	0	9	73 1/3	49	22	20	43	106
1998— Baltimore (A.L.)	5	6	.455	3.82	71	0	0	0	22	68 1/3	48	29	29	39	87
1999— New York (N.L.)■	4	3	.571	1.85	77	0	0	0	22	78	40	17	16	41	128
2000— New York (N.L.)	4	4	.500	2.61	76	0	0	0	41	76	39	24	22	38	106
2001— New York (N.L.)	6	4	.600	3.77	73	0	0	0	43	76 1/3	59	32	32	40	93
A.L. totals (5 years)	11	16	.407	3.62	207	0	0	0	37	213 2/3	149	91	86	129	283
N.L. totals (3 years)	14	11	.560	2.74	226	0	0	0	106	230 1/3	138	73	70	119	327
Major League totals (8 years)	25	27	.481	3.16	433	0	0	0	143	444	287	164	156	248	610

DIVISION SERIES RECORD

Year League	W	L	Pct.	ERA	G	GS	CG	ShO	Sv.	IP	H	R	ER	BB	SO
1996— Baltimore (A.L.)	2	0	1.000	2.25	3	0	0	0	0	4	1	1	1	2	6
1997— Baltimore (A.L.)	0	0	...	3.00	3	0	0	0	0	3	3	1	1	2	4
1999— New York (N.L.)	0	0	...	0.00	2	0	0	0	0	2 1/3	2	0	0	1	2
2000— New York (N.L.)	1	0	1.000	6.00	2	0	0	0	0	3	4	2	2	1	3
Division series totals (4 years)	3	0	1.000	2.92	10	0	0	0	0	12 1/3	10	4	4	6	15

CHAMPIONSHIP SERIES RECORD

Year League	W	L	Pct.	ERA	G	GS	CG	ShO	Sv.	IP	H	R	ER	BB	SO
1996— Baltimore (A.L.)	0	0	...	7.71	3	0	0	0	1	2 1/3	3	2	2	4	2
1997— Baltimore (A.L.)	0	2	.000	12.00	4	0	0	0	0	3	3	4	4	4	6
1999— New York (N.L.)	0	0	...	1.35	5	0	0	0	1	6 2/3	3	1	1	2	9
2000— New York (N.L.)	0	0	...	0.00	3	0	0	0	1	3	3	2	0	2	2
Champ. series totals (4 years)	0	2	.000	4.20	15	0	0	0	3	15	12	9	7	12	19

WORLD SERIES RECORD

Year League	W	L	Pct.	ERA	G	GS	CG	ShO	Sv.	IP	H	R	ER	BB	SO
2000— New York (N.L.)	0	0	...	3.00	3	0	0	0	1	3	3	1	1	2	2

BENJAMIN, MIKE   IF   PIRATES

PERSONAL: Born November 22, 1965, in Euclid, Ohio. ... 6-0/175. ... Bats right, throws right. ... Full name: Michael Paul Benjamin.

HIGH SCHOOL: Bellflower (Calif.).

JUNIOR COLLEGE: Cerritos College (Calif.).

COLLEGE: Arizona State.

TRANSACTIONS/CAREER NOTES: Selected by Minnesota Twins organization in seventh round of free-agent draft (January 9, 1985); did not sign. ... Selected by San Francisco Giants organization in third round of free-agent draft (June 2, 1987). ... On San Francisco disabled list (March 31-June 5, 1992); included rehabilitation assignment to Phoenix (April 20-May 10). ... On San Francisco disabled list (July 8-August 6, 1993); included rehabilitation assignment to San Jose (August 4-6). ... Traded by Giants to Philadelphia Phillies for P Jeff Juden and OF/1B Tommy Eason (October 6, 1995). ... On Philadelphia disabled list (March 23-April 26 and July 20, 1996-remainder of season); included

– 48 –

rehabilitation assignments to Clearwater (April 8-17) and Scranton/Wilkes-Barre (April 21-26). ... Granted free agency (October 8, 1996). ... Signed by Boston Red Sox organization (January 31, 1997). ... Granted free agency (October 27, 1997). ... Re-signed by Red Sox (November 21, 1997). ... Granted free agency (October 26, 1998). ... Signed by Pittsburgh Pirates (November 17, 1998). ... On disabled list (July 24-August 11, 1999; and March 31, 2001-entire season).

RECORDS: Holds modern major league record for most hits in three consecutive games—14 (June 11 [4], 13 [4] and 14 [6], 1995).

STATISTICAL NOTES: Led Pacific Coast League shortstops with 626 total chances in 1990. ... Collected six hits in one game (June 14, 1995).

							BATTING								FIELDING		
Year Team (League)	Pos.	G	AB	R	H	2B	3B	HR	RBI	Avg.	BB	SO	SB	PO	A	E	Avg.
1987—Fresno (Calif.)	SS	64	212	25	51	6	4	6	24	.241	24	71	6	89	188	21	.930
1988—Shreveport (Texas)	SS	89	309	48	73	19	5	6	37	.236	22	63	14	134	248	11	.972
—Phoenix (PCL)	SS	37	106	13	18	4	1	0	6	.170	13	32	2	41	74	4	.966
1989—Phoenix (PCL)	SS-2B	113	363	44	94	17	6	3	36	.259	18	82	10	149	332	15	.970
—San Francisco (N.L.)	SS	14	6	6	1	0	0	0	0	.167	0	1	0	4	4	0	1.000
1990—Phoenix (PCL)	SS	118	419	61	105	21	7	5	39	.251	25	89	13	*216	*386	24	.962
—San Francisco (N.L.)	SS	22	56	7	12	3	1	2	3	.214	3	10	1	29	53	1	.988
1991—San Francisco (N.L.)	SS-3B	54	106	12	13	3	0	2	8	.123	7	26	3	64	123	3	.984
—Phoenix (PCL)	SS	64	226	34	46	13	2	6	31	.204	20	67	3	109	252	9	.976
1992—San Francisco (N.L.)	SS-3B	40	75	4	13	2	1	1	3	.173	4	15	1	34	71	1	.991
—Phoenix (PCL)	SS-2B	31	108	15	33	10	2	0	17	.306	3	18	4	51	92	2	.986
1993—San Francisco (N.L.)	SS-2B-3B	63	146	22	29	7	0	4	16	.199	9	23	0	74	133	5	.976
—San Jose (Calif.)	SS-2B	2	8	1	0	0	0	0	0	.000	1	0	0	1	5	0	1.000
1994—San Francisco (N.L.)	SS-2B-3B	38	62	9	16	5	1	1	9	.258	5	16	5	33	70	3	.972
1995—San Francisco (N.L.)	3B-SS-2B	68	186	19	41	6	0	3	12	.220	8	51	11	51	121	4	.977
1996—Clearwater (FSL)■	SS	8	23	3	4	1	0	0	0	.174	3	4	1	9	20	2	.935
—Scranton/W.B. (I.L.)	SS	4	13	2	5	2	0	0	4	.385	3	0	0	3	12	0	1.000
—Philadelphia (N.L.)	SS-2B	35	103	13	23	5	1	4	13	.223	12	21	3	38	87	6	.954
1997—Pawtucket (I.L.)■...SS-DH-3B-2B	33	105	12	26	4	1	4	12	.248	8	20	4	46	86	5	.964
—Boston (A.L.)...3-S-2-1-DH-P	49	116	12	27	9	1	0	7	.233	4	27	2	50	81	6	.956
1998—Boston (A.L.)...2-S-3-1-DH	124	349	46	95	23	0	4	39	.272	15	73	3	233	275	3	.994
1999—Pittsburgh (N.L.)■	SS-2B-3B	110	368	42	91	26	7	1	37	.247	20	90	10	162	334	8	.984
2000—Pittsburgh (N.L.)...3B-SS-2B-1B	93	233	28	63	18	2	2	19	.270	12	45	5	104	206	4	.987
2001—Pittsburgh (N.L.)						Did not play.											
American League totals (2 years)		173	465	58	122	32	1	4	46	.262	19	100	5	283	356	9	.986
National League totals (10 years)		537	1341	162	302	75	13	20	120	.225	80	298	39	593	1202	35	.981
Major League totals (12 years)		710	1806	220	424	107	14	24	166	.235	99	398	44	876	1558	44	.982

DIVISION SERIES RECORD

							BATTING								FIELDING		
Year Team (League)	Pos.	G	AB	R	H	2B	3B	HR	RBI	Avg.	BB	SO	SB	PO	A	E	Avg.
1998—Boston (A.L.)	2B-1B	4	11	1	1	0	0	0	0	.091	1	3	0	13	9	0	1.000

RECORD AS PITCHER

Year League	W	L	Pct.	ERA	G	GS	CG	ShO	Sv.	IP	H	R	ER	BB	SO
1997—Boston (A.L.)	0	0	...	0.00	1	0	0	0	0	1	0	0	0	0	0
Major League totals (1 year)	0	0	...	0.00	1	0	0	0	0	1	0	0	0	0	0

BENNETT, GARY   C   ROCKIES

PERSONAL: Born April 17, 1972, in Waukegan, Ill. ... 6-0/208. ... Bats right, throws right. ... Full name: Gary David Bennett Jr.

HIGH SCHOOL: Waukegan East (Ill.).

TRANSACTIONS/CAREER NOTES: Selected by Philadelphia Phillies organization in 11th round of free-agent draft (June 4, 1990). ... On Clearwater disabled list (September 5-15, 1993). ... Granted free agency (October 8, 1996). ... Signed by Boston Red Sox organization (February 10, 1997). ... Granted free agency (October 15, 1997). ... Signed by Phillies organization (December 27, 1997). ... On Scranton/Wilkes-Barre disabled list (June 23-July 4, 2000). ... Traded by Phillies to New York Mets for C Todd Pratt (July 23, 2001). ... Traded by Mets to Colorado Rockies for a player to be named later (August 24, 2001); Mets acquired OF Ender Chavez to complete deal (December 27, 2001).

STATISTICAL NOTES: Led Eastern League with 22 passed balls in 1994. ... Led Eastern League catchers with 13 double plays in 1995.

							BATTING								FIELDING		
Year Team (League)	Pos.	G	AB	R	H	2B	3B	HR	RBI	Avg.	BB	SO	SB	PO	A	E	Avg.
1990—Martinsville (Appl.)	C	16	52	3	14	2	1	0	10	.269	4	15	0	80	3	3	.965
1991—Martinsville (Appl.)	C	41	136	15	32	7	0	1	16	.235	17	26	0	291	34	2	.994
1992—Batavia (NY-Penn)	C	47	146	22	30	2	0	1	12	.205	15	27	2	292	42	2	*.994
1993—Spartanburg (S.Atl.)	C	42	126	18	32	4	1	0	15	.254	12	22	0	199	35	2	.992
—Clearwater (FSL)	C	17	55	5	18	0	0	1	6	.327	3	10	0	70	12	0	1.000
1994—Clearwater (FSL)	C	19	55	6	13	3	0	0	10	.236	8	6	0	101	10	1	.991
—Reading (East.)	C	63	208	13	48	9	0	3	22	.231	14	26	0	376	64	2	.995
1995—Reading (East.)	C-DH	86	271	27	64	11	0	4	40	.236	22	36	0	551	65	4	.994
—Scranton/W.B. (I.L.)	C	7	20	1	3	0	0	0	1	.150	2	2	0	38	4	0	1.000
—Philadelphia (N.L.)	PH	1	1	0	0	0	0	0	0	.000	0	1	0	...	...	...	...
1996—Scranton/W.B. (I.L.)	C	91	286	37	71	15	1	8	37	.248	24	43	1	517	61	7	.988
—Philadelphia (N.L.)	C	6	16	0	4	0	0	0	1	.250	2	6	0	35	5	0	1.000
1997—Pawtucket (I.L.)■	C-1B	71	224	16	48	7	1	4	22	.214	18	39	1	528	36	8	.986
1998—Scranton/W.B. (I.L.)	C-DH-1B	86	282	33	72	18	0	10	40	.255	25	41	0	425	35	1	.998
—Philadelphia (N.L.)	C	9	31	4	9	0	0	0	3	.290	5	5	0	50	2	0	1.000
1999—Philadelphia (N.L.)	C	36	88	7	24	4	0	1	21	.273	4	11	0	129	6	4	.971
2000—Scranton/W.B. (I.L.)	C	92	317	47	97	24	0	12	52	.306	40	44	1	483	34	2	*.996
—Philadelphia (N.L.)	C	31	74	8	18	5	0	2	5	.243	13	15	0	173	11	1	.995
2001—Philadelphia (N.L.)	C	26	75	8	16	3	1	1	6	.213	9	19	0	151	5	2	.987
—New York (N.L.)■	PH	1	1	0	1	0	0	0	0	1.000	0	0	0	...	...	...	...
—Norfolk (I.L.)	C-3B	20	67	7	20	5	0	2	14	.299	4	12	0	94	5	0	1.000
—Colorado (N.L.)■	C	19	55	7	15	3	0	1	4	.273	3	5	0	96	4	0	1.000
Major League totals (6 years)		129	341	34	87	15	1	5	40	.255	36	62	0	634	33	7	.990

BENOIT, JOAQUIN — P — RANGERS

PERSONAL: Born July 26, 1979, in Santiago, Dominican Republic. ... 6-3/205. ... Throws right, bats right. ... Full name: Joaquin Antonio Benoit.

TRANSACTIONS/CAREER NOTES: Signed as non-drafted free agent by Texas Rangers organization (May 20, 1996). ... On disabled list (May 2-June 21, 2000).

Year League	W	L	Pct.	ERA	G	GS	CG	ShO	Sv.	IP	H	R	ER	BB	SO
1996— Dominican Rangers (DSL) .	6	5	.545	2.28	14	13	2	1	0	75	63	26	19	23	63
1997— Gulf Coast Rangers (GCL)..	3	3	.500	2.05	10	10	1	0	0	44	40	14	10	11	38
1998— Savannah (S.Atl.)	4	3	.571	3.83	15	1	0	0	0	80	79	41	34	18	68
1999— Charlotte (FSL)	7	4	.636	5.31	22	22	0	0	0	105	117	67	62	50	83
2000— Tulsa (Texas)	4	4	.500	3.83	16	16	0	0	0	82 1/3	73	40	35	30	72
2001— Tulsa (Texas)	1	0	1.000	3.32	4	4	0	0	0	21 2/3	23	8	8	6	23
— Oklahoma (PCL).................	9	5	.643	4.19	24	24	1	1	0	131	113	63	61	73	142
— Texas (A.L.).......................	0	0	...	10.80	1	1	0	0	0	5	8	6	6	3	4
Major League totals (1 year)........	**0**	**0**	**...**	**10.80**	**1**	**1**	**0**	**0**	**0**	**5**	**8**	**6**	**6**	**3**	**4**

BENSON, KRIS — P — PIRATES

PERSONAL: Born November 7, 1974, in Superior, Wis. ... 6-4/195. ... Throws right, bats right. ... Full name: Kristen James Benson.
HIGH SCHOOL: Spayberry (Marietta, Ga.).
COLLEGE: Clemson.
TRANSACTIONS/CAREER NOTES: Selected by Pittsburgh Pirates organization in first round (first pick overall) of free-agent draft (June 2, 1996). ... On disabled list (March 31, 2001-entire season).
MISCELLANEOUS: Member of 1996 U.S. Olympic baseball team.

Year League	W	L	Pct.	ERA	G	GS	CG	ShO	Sv.	IP	H	R	ER	BB	SO
1997— Lynchburg (Caro.)	5	2	.714	2.58	10	10	0	0	0	59 1/3	49	20	17	13	72
— Carolina (Sou.)..................	3	5	.375	4.98	14	14	0	0	0	68 2/3	81	49	38	32	66
1998— Nashville (PCL)	8	10	.444	5.37	28	28	1	1	0	156	162	102	93	50	129
1999— Pittsburgh (N.L.)	11	14	.440	4.07	31	31	2	0	0	196 2/3	184	105	89	83	139
2000— Pittsburgh (N.L.)	10	12	.455	3.85	32	32	2	1	0	217 2/3	206	104	93	86	184
2001— Pittsburgh (N.L.)								Did not play.							
Major League totals (2 years).......	**21**	**26**	**.447**	**3.95**	**63**	**63**	**4**	**1**	**0**	**414 1/3**	**390**	**209**	**182**	**169**	**323**

BERE, JASON — P — CUBS

PERSONAL: Born May 26, 1971, in Cambridge, Mass. ... 6-3/215. ... Throws right, bats right. ... Full name: Jason Phillip Bere. ... Name pronounced burr-AY.
HIGH SCHOOL: Wilmington (Mass.).
JUNIOR COLLEGE: Middlesex Community College (Mass.).
TRANSACTIONS/CAREER NOTES: Selected by Chicago White Sox organization in 36th round of free-agent draft (June 4, 1990). ... On Chicago disabled list (August 5-20, 1995); included rehabilitation assignment to South Bend (August 13-18). ... On Chicago disabled list (April 22-September 3 and September 14, 1996-remainder of season); included rehabilitation assignments to Nashville (May 14-19 and August 27-28), Gulf Coast White Sox (August 5-10), Hickory (August 10-16) and Birmingham (August 16-27). ... On Chicago disabled list (March 31-August 19, 1997); included rehabilitation assignments to Gulf Coast White Sox (July 2-7), Hickory (July 12), Birmingham (July 17-22) and Nashville (July 29-August 14). ... Released by White Sox (July 16, 1998). ... Signed by Cincinnati Reds organization (July 21, 1998). ... On Cincinnati disabled list (June 16-August 4, 1999); included rehabilitation assignment to Indianapolis (July 11-August 4). ... Released by Reds (August 4, 1999). ... Signed by Milwaukee Brewers organization (August 12, 1999). ... Granted free agency (November 1, 1999). ... Re-signed by Brewers (November 19, 1999). ... Traded by Brewers with P Bob Wickman and P Steve Woodard to Cleveland Indians for 1B/OF Richie Sexson, P Paul Rigdon, P Kane Davis and a player to be named later (July 28, 2000); Brewers acquired 2B Marcos Scutaro to complete deal (August 30, 2000). ... Granted free agency (October 31, 2000). ... Signed by Chicago Cubs (December 18, 2000).

Year League	W	L	Pct.	ERA	G	GS	CG	ShO	Sv.	IP	H	R	ER	BB	SO
1990— GC White Sox (GCL)	0	4	.000	2.37	16	2	0	0	1	38	26	19	10	19	41
1991— South Bend (Midw.)	9	12	.429	2.87	27	27	2	1	0	163	116	66	52	*100	158
1992— Sarasota (FSL)	7	2	.778	2.41	18	18	1	1	0	116	84	35	31	34	106
— Birmingham (Sou.)............	4	4	.500	3.00	8	8	4	2	0	54	44	22	18	20	45
— Vancouver (PCL)	0	0	...	0.00	1	0	0	0	0	1	2	0	0	0	2
1993— Nashville (A.A.)	5	1	.833	2.37	8	8	0	0	0	49 1/3	36	19	13	25	52
— Chicago (A.L.)	12	5	.706	3.47	24	24	1	0	0	142 2/3	109	60	55	81	129
1994— Chicago (A.L.)	12	2	*.857	3.81	24	24	0	0	0	141 2/3	119	65	60	80	127
1995— Chicago (A.L.)	8	•15	.348	7.19	27	27	1	0	0	137 2/3	151	120	110	106	110
— Nashville (A.A.)	1	0	1.000	3.38	1	1	0	0	0	5 1/3	6	2	2	2	7
1996— Chicago (A.L.)	0	1	.000	10.26	5	5	0	0	0	16 2/3	26	19	19	18	19
— Nashville (A.A.)	0	0	...	1.42	3	3	0	0	0	12 2/3	9	2	2	4	15
— GC White Sox (GCL)	0	1	.000	6.00	1	1	0	0	0	3	3	2	2	1	3
— Hickory (S.Atl.)	1	0	1.000	0.00	1	1	0	0	0	5	5	0	0	0	5
— Birmingham (Sou.)............	0	0	...	4.15	1	1	0	0	0	4 1/3	4	2	2	4	5
1997— GC White Sox (GCL)	0	0	...	0.00	2	2	0	0	0	5	2	0	0	0	5
— Hickory (S.Atl.)	0	0	...	6.00	1	1	0	0	0	3	4	2	2	2	2
— Birmingham (Sou.)............	0	1	.000	7.71	2	2	0	0	0	7	8	7	6	7	7
— Nashville (A.A.)	1	1	.500	5.59	4	4	0	0	0	19 1/3	23	13	12	7	13
— Chicago (A.L.)	4	2	.667	4.71	6	6	0	0	0	28 2/3	20	15	15	17	21
1998— Chicago (A.L.) ■.............	3	7	.300	6.45	18	15	0	0	0	83 2/3	98	71	60	58	53
— Cincinnati (N.L.)■.............	3	2	.600	4.12	9	7	0	0	0	43 2/3	39	20	20	20	31
1999— Cincinnati (N.L.)	3	0	1.000	6.85	12	10	0	0	0	43 1/3	56	37	33	40	28
— Indianapolis (I.L.).............	0	2	.000	10.19	5	4	0	0	0	17 2/3	25	20	20	19	8
— Louisville (I.L.)■.............	2	1	.667	2.08	5	5	0	0	0	26	21	8	6	8	27
— Milwaukee (N.L.)................	2	0	1.000	4.63	5	4	0	0	0	23 1/3	23	15	12	10	19

Year	League	W	L	Pct.	ERA	G	GS	CG	ShO	Sv.	IP	H	R	ER	BB	SO
2000—	Milwaukee (N.L.)	6	7	.462	4.93	20	20	0	0	0	115	115	66	63	63	98
	—Cleveland (A.L.)■	6	3	.667	6.63	11	11	0	0	0	54 1/3	65	41	40	26	44
2001—	Chicago (N.L.)■	11	11	.500	4.31	32	32	2	0	0	188	171	99	90	77	175
A.L. totals (7 years)		45	35	.563	5.34	115	112	2	0	0	605 1/3	588	391	359	386	503
N.L. totals (4 years)		25	20	.556	4.75	78	73	2	0	0	413 1/3	404	237	218	210	351
Major League totals (9 years)		70	55	.560	5.10	193	185	4	0	0	1018 2/3	992	628	577	596	854

CHAMPIONSHIP SERIES RECORD

Year	League	W	L	Pct.	ERA	G	GS	CG	ShO	Sv.	IP	H	R	ER	BB	SO
1993—	Chicago (A.L.)	0	0	...	11.57	1	1	0	0	0	2 1/3	5	3	3	2	3

ALL-STAR GAME RECORD

Year	League	W	L	Pct.	ERA	GS	CG	ShO	Sv.	IP	H	R	ER	BB	SO
1994—	American	0	1	.000	...	0	0	0	0	2	1	1	0	0

BERG, DAVID   IF   BLUE JAYS

PERSONAL: Born September 3, 1970, in Roseville, Calif. ... 5-11/196. ... Bats right, throws right. ... Full name: David Scott Berg.
HIGH SCHOOL: Roseville (Calif.).
JUNIOR COLLEGE: Sacramento City College.
COLLEGE: Miami (Fla.).
TRANSACTIONS/CAREER NOTES: Selected by California Angels organization in 32nd round of free-agent draft (June 4, 1990); did not sign. ... Selected by Florida Marlins organization in 38th round of free-agent draft (June 3, 1993). ... On Florida disabled list (April 2-25, 2000); included rehabilitation assignment to Brevard County (April 22-25). ... Granted free agency (December 21, 2001). ... Signed by Toronto Blue Jays organization (January 13, 2002).
STATISTICAL NOTES: Led New York-Penn League third basemen with 158 assists in 1993. ... Led Midwest League third basemen with .948 fielding percentage in 1994.

						BATTING							FIELDING		
Year	Team (League)	Pos.	G	AB	R	H	2B	3B	HR	RBI	Avg.	BB	SO	SB	PO	A	E	Avg.
1993—	Elmira (NY-Penn)	3B-2B-OF	75	281	37	74	13	1	4	28	.263	34	37	7	55	†193	20	.925
1994—	Kane County (Midw.)..	3B-2B	121	437	80	117	27	8	9	53	.268	54	80	8	73	236	17	†.948
1995—	Brevard County (FSL).	SS-3B-2B	114	382	71	114	18	1	3	39	.298	68	61	9	157	348	26	.951
1996—	Portland (East.)	SS-3B	109	414	64	125	28	5	9	73	.302	42	60	17	143	358	26	.951
1997—	Charlotte (I.L.)	SS-2B-3B	117	424	76	125	26	6	9	47	.295	55	71	16	136	324	22	.954
1998—	Florida (N.L.)	2B-3B-SS	81	182	18	57	11	0	2	21	.313	26	46	3	90	130	7	.969
1999—	Florida (N.L.)	S-2-3-O	109	304	42	87	18	1	3	25	.286	27	59	2	103	195	8	.974
2000—	Brevard County (FSL).	2B-3B-SS	3	11	2	3	0	0	0	2	.273	1	3	0	6	7	0	1.000
	—Florida (N.L.)	SS-3B-2B	82	210	23	53	14	1	1	21	.252	25	46	3	71	142	8	.964
2001—	Florida (N.L.)	2B-SS-3B	82	215	26	52	12	1	4	16	.242	14	39	0	66	130	8	.961
Major League totals (4 years)			354	911	109	249	55	3	10	83	.273	92	190	8	330	597	31	.968

BERGER, BRANDON   OF   ROYALS

PERSONAL: Born February 21, 1975, in Covington, Ky. ... 5-11/205. ... Bats right, throws right. ... Full name: Brandon Charles Berger.
HIGH SCHOOL: Beechwood (Fort Mitchell, Ky.).
COLLEGE: Eastern Kentucky.
TRANSACTIONS/CAREER NOTES: Selected by Kansas City Royals organization in 14th round of free-agent draft (June 4, 1996).
STATISTICAL NOTES: Led Texas League with .648 slugging percentage in 2001.

						BATTING							FIELDING		
Year	Team (League)	Pos.	G	AB	R	H	2B	3B	HR	RBI	Avg.	BB	SO	SB	PO	A	E	Avg.
1996—	Spokane (N'West)	OF	71	283	46	87	12	1	13	58	.307	31	64	17	106	*10	4	.967
1997—	Lansing (Midw.)	OF	107	393	64	115	22	6	12	73	.293	42	79	13	136	7	3	.979
1998—	Wilmington (Caro.)	OF-P	110	338	53	75	18	3	8	50	.222	53	94	13	139	4	2	.986
1999—	Wilmington (Caro.)	OF	119	450	73	132	27	4	16	73	.293	45	93	29	130	2	5	.964
2000—	Wichita (Texas)	OF	27	86	9	14	2	0	3	8	.163	7	27	6	21	3	0	1.000
	—Wilmington (Caro.)	OF	102	379	63	108	18	4	15	71	.285	40	71	12	169	7	3	.983
2001—	Wichita (Texas)	OF	120	454	98	140	28	3	*40	118	.308	43	91	14	131	4	4	.971
	—Kansas City (A.L.)	OF-DH	6	16	4	5	1	1	2	2	.313	2	2	0	7	0	0	1.000
Major League totals (1 year)			6	16	4	5	1	1	2	2	.313	2	2	0	7	0	0	1.000

RECORD AS PITCHER

Year	League	W	L	Pct.	ERA	G	GS	CG	ShO	Sv.	IP	H	R	ER	BB	SO
1998—	Wilmington (Caro.)	0	0	...	13.50	1	0	0	0	0	2	3	3	3	4	0

BERGERON, PETER   OF   EXPOS

PERSONAL: Born November 9, 1977, in Greenfield, Mass. ... 6-0/185. ... Bats left, throws right. ... Full name: Peter Francis Bergeron.
HIGH SCHOOL: Greenfield (Mass.).
TRANSACTIONS/CAREER NOTES: Selected by Los Angeles Dodgers organization in fourth round of free-agent draft (June 4, 1996). ... Traded by Dodgers with 2B Wilton Guerrero, P Ted Lilly and 1B Jonathan Tucker to Montreal Expos for P Carlos Perez, SS Mark Grudzielanek and OF Hiram Bocachica (July 31, 1998).
STATISTICAL NOTES: Led Texas League outfielders with five double plays in 1998. ... Had 19-game hitting streak (July 1-23, 2001).

Year Team (League)	Pos.	G	AB	R	H	2B	3B	HR	RBI	Avg.	BB	SO	SB	PO	A	E	Avg.
1996—Yakima (N'West)	OF	61	232	36	59	5	3	5	21	.254	28	59	13	99	3	1	*.990
1997—Savannah (S.Atl.)	OF	131	492	89	138	18	5	5	36	.280	67	110	32	240	8	4	.984
—San Bern. (Calif.)	OF	2	8	1	2	0	0	0	1	.250	0	2	2	5	1	0	1.000
1998—San Antonio (Texas) ...	OF	109	416	81	132	17	8	8	54	.317	61	69	33	228	17	2	*.992
—Harrisburg (East.)■ ...	OF	34	134	22	33	8	4	0	9	.246	17	26	8	67	5	0	1.000
1999—Harrisburg (East.)	OF-DH	42	162	29	53	14	2	4	18	.327	24	29	9	72	1	1	.986
—Ottawa (I.L.)	OF-DH	58	194	36	61	12	3	3	20	.314	23	40	14	64	8	2	.973
—Montreal (N.L.)	OF	16	45	12	11	2	0	0	1	.244	9	5	0	27	2	1	.967
2000—Montreal (N.L.)	OF	148	518	80	127	25	7	5	31	.245	58	100	11	303	*16	5	.985
2001—Montreal (N.L.)	OF	102	375	53	79	11	4	3	16	.211	28	87	10	220	6	1	.996
—Ottawa (I.L.)	OF	52	206	29	49	5	3	0	8	.238	20	42	15	110	3	2	.983
Major League totals (3 years)		266	938	145	217	38	11	8	48	.231	95	192	21	550	24	7	.988

B

BERKMAN, LANCE   OF   ASTROS

PERSONAL: Born February 10, 1976, in Waco, Texas. ... 6-1/205. ... Bats both, throws left. ... Full name: William Lance Berkman.
HIGH SCHOOL: Canyon (New Braunfels, Texas).
COLLEGE: Rice.
TRANSACTIONS/CAREER NOTES: Selected by Houston Astros organization in first round (16th pick overall) of free-agent draft (June 3, 1997). ... On New Orleans disabled list (April 13-May 14, 1999).
RECORDS: Holds major league single-season record for most doubles by switch-hitter—55 (2001); and most extra-base hits by switch-hitter—94 (2001).
HONORS: Named first baseman on THE SPORTING NEWS college All-America first team (1997).
STATISTICAL NOTES: Led Texas League with 10 intentional bases on balls in 1998. ... Had 21-game hitting streak (June 17-July 8, 2001). ... Career major league grand slams: 1.

Year Team (League)	Pos.	G	AB	R	H	2B	3B	HR	RBI	Avg.	BB	SO	SB	PO	A	E	Avg.
1997—Kissimmee (FSL)	OF-DH	53	184	31	54	10	0	12	35	.293	37	38	2	70	2	0	1.000
1998—Jackson (Texas)	OF-DH	122	425	82	130	34	0	24	89	.306	85	82	6	183	9	4	.980
—New Orleans (PCL).....	OF	17	59	14	16	4	0	6	13	.271	12	16	0	30	0	0	1.000
1999—New Orleans (PCL)	OF-1B-DH	64	226	42	73	20	0	8	49	.323	39	47	7	135	6	4	.972
—Houston (N.L.)	OF-1B	34	93	10	22	2	0	4	15	.237	12	21	5	43	0	2	.956
2000—New Orleans (PCL).....	OF-1B	31	112	18	37	4	2	6	27	.330	31	20	4	103	7	2	.982
—Houston (N.L.)	OF-1B	114	353	76	105	28	1	21	67	.297	56	73	6	176	7	6	.968
2001—Houston (N.L.)	OF	156	577	110	191	*55	5	34	126	.331	92	121	7	306	6	6	.981
Major League totals (3 years)		304	1023	196	318	85	6	59	208	.311	160	215	18	525	13	14	.975

DIVISION SERIES RECORD

Year Team (League)	Pos.	G	AB	R	H	2B	3B	HR	RBI	Avg.	BB	SO	SB	PO	A	E	Avg.
2001—Houston (N.L.)	OF	3	12	0	2	0	0	0	0	.167	0	4	0	6	0	0	1.000

ALL-STAR GAME RECORD

Year League	Pos.	AB	R	H	2B	3B	HR	RBI	Avg.	BB	SO	SB	PO	A	E	Avg.
2001—National	OF	2	0	1	0	0	0	0	.500	0	0	0	2	0	0	1.000

BERNERO, ADAM   P   TIGERS

PERSONAL: Born November 28, 1976, in San Jose, Calif. ... 6-4/205. ... Throws right, bats right. ... Full name: Adam G. Bernero.
HIGH SCHOOL: John F. Kennedy (Sacramento, Calif.).
COLLEGE: Armstrong Atlantic State (Ga.).
TRANSACTIONS/CAREER NOTES: Signed as non-drafted free agent by Detroit Tigers organization (May 21, 1999). ... On Jacksonville disabled list (April 10-28, 2000). ... On Toledo disabled list (June 18-July 4, 2001).
STATISTICAL NOTES: Tied for International League lead with five balks in 2001.

Year League	W	L	Pct.	ERA	G	GS	CG	ShO	Sv.	IP	H	R	ER	BB	SO
1999—West Michigan (Midw.)	8	4	.667	2.54	15	15	2	1	0	$95^2/_3$	75	36	27	23	80
2000—Jacksonville (Sou.)............	2	5	.286	2.79	10	10	0	0	0	$61^1/_3$	54	26	19	24	46
—Toledo (I.L.).....	3	1	.750	2.47	7	7	1	1	0	$47^1/_3$	34	16	13	10	37
—Detroit (A.L.)....................	0	1	.000	4.19	12	4	0	0	0	$34^1/_3$	33	18	16	13	20
2001—Toledo (I.L.).....................	6	11	.353	5.13	26	25	1	0	0	$140^1/_3$	172	90	80	54	99
—Detroit (A.L.)....................	0	0	...	7.30	5	0	0	0	0	$12^1/_3$	13	13	10	4	8
Major League totals (2 years)	0	1	.000	5.01	17	4	0	0	0	$46^2/_3$	46	31	26	17	28

BERROA, ANGEL   SS   ROYALS

PERSONAL: Born January 27, 1980, in Santo Domingo, Dominican Republic. ... 6-0/175. ... Bats right, throws right. ... Full name: Angel Maria Berroa.
TRANSACTIONS/CAREER NOTES: Signed as non-drafted free agent by Oakland Athletics organization (August 14, 1997). ... Traded by Athletics with C A.J. Hinch and cash to Kansas City Royals as part of three-way deal in which Royals received P Roberto Hernandez from Tampa Devil Rays, A's received P Cory Lidle from Devil Rays and OF Johnny Damon, IF Mark Ellis and player to be named from Royals and Devil Rays received OF Ben Grieve and a player to be named or cash from A's (January 8, 2001).
STATISTICAL NOTES: Led California League shortstops with 593 total chances in 2000.

Year Team (League)	Pos.	G	AB	R	H	2B	3B	HR	RBI	Avg.	BB	SO	SB	PO	A	E	Avg.
1998—Dom. Athletics (DSL) .		58	196	51	48	7	4	8	37	.245	25	37	4	...	...	...	...
1999—Ariz. Athletics (Ariz.) ..SS-2B-3B-OF		46	169	42	49	11	4	2	24	.290	16	26	11	86	137	18	.925
—Midland (Texas)..........	SS	4	17	3	1	1	0	0	1	.059	0	2	0	10	6	2	.889
2000—Visalia (Calif.)	SS	129	429	61	119	25	6	10	63	.277	30	70	11	•195	344	*54	.909
2001—Wilmington (Caro.)■.	SS	51	199	43	63	18	4	6	25	.317	9	41	10	89	149	17	.933
—Wichita (Texas)	SS	80	304	63	90	20	4	8	42	.296	17	55	15	148	213	13	.965
—Kansas City (A.L.)	SS	15	53	8	16	2	0	0	4	.302	3	10	2	21	40	3	.953
Major League totals (1 year)		15	53	8	16	2	0	0	4	.302	3	10	2	21	40	3	.953

BETEMIT, WILSON   SS   BRAVES

PERSONAL: Born November 2, 1981, in Santo Domingo, Dominican Republic. ... 6-2/155. ... Bats both, throws right.
TRANSACTIONS/CAREER NOTES: Signed as non-drafted free agent by Atlanta Braves organization (July 28, 1996).
STATISTICAL NOTES: Led Appalachian League shortstops with 326 total chances in 1999.

Year Team (League)	Pos.	G	AB	R	H	2B	3B	HR	RBI	Avg.	BB	SO	SB	PO	A	E	Avg.
1997—GC Braves (GCL)	SS	32	113	12	24	6	1	0	15	.212	9	32	0	48	71	*20	.856
1998—GC Braves (GCL)	SS	51	173	23	38	8	4	5	16	.220	20	49	6	63	135	20	.908
1999—Danville (Appl.)...........	SS	67	259	39	83	18	2	5	53	.320	27	63	6	*92	201	33	.899
2000—Jamestown (NY-P)	SS	69	269	54	89	15	2	5	37	.331	30	37	3	111	183	•29	.910
2001—Myrtle Beach (Caro.) ..	SS	84	318	38	88	20	1	7	43	.277	23	71	8	130	257	23	.944
—Greenville (Sou.)	SS	47	183	22	65	14	0	5	19	.355	12	36	6	56	132	9	.954
—Atlanta (N.L.)...............	SS	8	3	1	0	0	0	0	0	.000	2	3	1	0	0	0	...
Major League totals (1 year)		8	3	1	0	0	0	0	0	.000	2	3	1	0	0	0	...

BEVIS, P. J.   P   DIAMONDBACKS

PERSONAL: Born July 28, 1980, in Brisbane, Australia. ... 6-3/180. ... Throws right, bats right. ... Full name: Peter Jon Bevis.
HIGH SCHOOL: Cavendish Road State (Queensland, Australia).
TRANSACTIONS/CAREER NOTES: Signed as non-drafted free agent by Arizona Diamondbacks organization (May 21, 1998).

Year League	W	L	Pct.	ERA	G	GS	CG	ShO	Sv.	IP	H	R	ER	BB	SO
1998—Ariz. Diamondbacks (Ariz.).	3	3	.500	5.96	14	9	0	0	0	45 1/3	55	39	30	10	48
1999—Missoula (Pio.).................	6	2	.750	4.62	15	15	0	0	0	85 2/3	83	51	44	30	69
2000—Missoula (Pio.).................	3	6	.333	3.33	14	14	0	0	0	83 2/3	92	50	31	22	63
2001—El Paso (Texas).................	0	0	...	2.16	14	0	0	0	6	16 2/3	11	4	4	6	19
—Yakima (N'West)..................	1	1	.500	0.64	12	0	0	0	8	14	9	1	1	7	22

BICHETTE, DANTE   OF

PERSONAL: Born November 18, 1963, in West Palm Beach, Fla. ... 6-2/235. ... Bats right, throws right. ... Full name: Alphonse Dante Bichette. ... Name pronounced bih-SHETT.
HIGH SCHOOL: Jupiter (Fla.).
JUNIOR COLLEGE: Palm Beach Community College (Fla.).
TRANSACTIONS/CAREER NOTES: Selected by California Angels organization in 17th round of free-agent draft (June 4, 1984). ... Traded by Angels to Milwaukee Brewers for DH Dave Parker (March 14, 1991). ... Traded by Brewers to Colorado Rockies for OF Kevin Reimer (November 17, 1992). ... Traded by Rockies with cash to Cincinnati Reds for OF Jeffrey Hammonds and P Stan Belinda (October 30, 1999). ... Traded by Reds to Boston Red Sox for P Chris Reitsma and P John Curtice (August 31, 2000). ... Granted free agency (November 5, 2001).
HONORS: Named outfielder on The Sporting News N.L. All-Star team (1995). ... Named outfielder on The Sporting News N.L. Silver Slugger team (1995).
STATISTICAL NOTES: Led A.L. outfielders with seven double plays in 1991. ... Led N.L. outfielders with four double plays in 1994. ... Led N.L. with .620 slugging percentage and 359 total bases in 1995. ... Had 23-game hitting streak (May 22-June 18, 1995). ... Tied for N.L. lead with 10 sacrifice flies in 1996. ... Hit for the cycle (June 10, 1998). ... Tied for N.L. lead with six double plays by outfielder in 1998. ... Tied for N.L. lead with 10 sacrifice flies in 1999. ... Had 17-game hitting streak (June 30-July 23, 2000). ... Career major league grand slams: 9.
MISCELLANEOUS: Holds Colorado Rockies all-time records for most hits (1,278), doubles (270) and runs batted in (826).

Year Team (League)	Pos.	G	AB	R	H	2B	3B	HR	RBI	Avg.	BB	SO	SB	PO	A	E	Avg.
1984—Salem (N'West)	OF-1B-3B	64	250	27	58	9	2	4	30	.232	6	53	6	224	24	11	.958
1985—Quad Cities (Midw.)....	1B-OF-C	137	547	58	145	28	4	11	78	.265	25	89	25	300	21	15	.955
1986—Palm Springs (Calif.)..	OF-3B	68	290	39	79	15	0	10	73	.272	21	53	2	78	68	11	.930
—Midland (Texas)..........	OF-3B	62	243	43	69	16	2	12	36	.284	18	50	3	131	30	11	.936
1987—Edmonton (PCL)	OF-3B	92	360	54	108	20	3	13	50	.300	26	68	3	169	21	9	.955
1988—Edmonton (PCL)	OF	132	509	64	136	29	•10	14	81	.267	25	78	7	218	*22	*15	.941
—California (A.L.)	OF	21	46	1	12	2	0	0	8	.261	0	7	0	44	2	1	.979
1989—California (A.L.)	OF-DH	48	138	13	29	7	0	3	15	.210	6	24	3	95	6	1	.990
—Edmonton (PCL)	OF	61	226	39	55	11	2	11	40	.243	24	39	4	92	9	1	.990
1990—California (A.L.)	OF	109	349	40	89	15	1	15	53	.255	16	79	5	183	12	7	.965
1991—Milwaukee (A.L.)■.....	OF-3B	134	445	53	106	18	3	15	59	.238	22	107	14	270	14	7	.976
1992—Milwaukee (A.L.)	OF-DH	112	387	37	111	27	2	5	41	.287	16	74	18	188	6	2	.990
1993—Colorado (N.L.)■	OF	141	538	93	167	43	5	21	89	.310	28	99	14	308	14	9	.973
1994—Colorado (N.L.)	OF	*116	*484	74	147	33	2	27	95	.304	19	70	21	211	10	2	.991
1995—Colorado (N.L.)	OF	139	579	102	•197	38	2	*40	*128	.340	22	96	13	208	9	3	.986
1996—Colorado (N.L.)	OF	159	633	114	198	39	3	31	141	.313	45	105	31	255	5	9	.967
1997—Colorado (N.L.)	OF-DH	151	561	81	173	31	2	26	118	.308	30	90	6	225	4	3	.987
1998—Colorado (N.L.)	OF-DH	161	662	97	*219	48	2	22	122	.331	28	76	14	289	14	11	.965
1999—Colorado (N.L.)	OF-DH	151	593	104	177	38	2	34	133	.298	54	84	6	238	17	13	.951

Year	Team (League)	Pos.	G	AB	R	H	2B	3B	HR	RBI	Avg.	BB	SO	SB	PO	A	E	Avg.
2000—Cincinnati (N.L.)■......		OF	125	461	67	136	27	2	16	76	.295	41	69	5	235	11	8	.969
—Boston (A.L.)■.........		DH	30	114	13	33	5	0	7	14	.289	8	22	0	...	...	...	...
2001—Boston (A.L.)............		OF-DH	107	391	45	112	30	1	12	49	.286	20	76	2	80	4	4	.955
American League totals (7 years)			561	1870	202	492	104	7	57	239	.263	88	389	42	860	44	22	.976
National League totals (8 years)			1143	4511	732	1414	297	20	217	902	.313	267	689	110	1969	84	58	.973
Major League totals (14 years)			1704	6381	934	1906	401	27	274	1141	.299	355	1078	152	2829	128	80	.974

DIVISION SERIES RECORD

RECORDS: Shares N.L. single-series record for most runs scored—6 (1995).

Year	Team (League)	Pos.	G	AB	R	H	2B	3B	HR	RBI	Avg.	BB	SO	SB	PO	A	E	Avg.
1995—Colorado (N.L.)		OF	4	17	6	10	3	0	1	3	.588	1	3	0	9	0	0	1.000

ALL-STAR GAME RECORD

Year	League	Pos.	AB	R	H	2B	3B	HR	RBI	Avg.	BB	SO	SB	PO	A	E	Avg.
1994—National................	PH	1	0	1	0	0	0	0	1.000	0	0	0	...	...		
1995—National................	OF	1	0	0	0	0	0	0	.000	0	1	0	2	0	0	1.000
1996—National................	OF	3	1	1	1	0	0	0	.333	0	1	0	0	0	0	...
1998—National................	OF	2	0	0	0	0	0	0	.000	0	1	0	1	0	0	1.000
All-Star Game totals (4 years)		7	1	2	1	0	0	0	.286	0	3	0	3	0	0	1.000

BIDDLE, ROCKY   P   WHITE SOX

PERSONAL: Born May 21, 1976, in Las Vegas, Nev. ... 6-3/230. ... Throws right, bats right. ... Full name: Lee F. Biddle.
HIGH SCHOOL: Temple City (Calif.).
COLLEGE: Long Beach State.
TRANSACTIONS/CAREER NOTES: Selected by Chicago White Sox organization in supplemental round ("sandwich" pick between first and second round, 51st pick overall) of free-agent draft (June 3, 1997); pick received as compensation for failure to sign 1996 first-round pick P Bobby Seay. ... On disabled list (April 9, 1999-entire season). ... On disabled list (September 21, 2001-remainder of season).

Year	League	W	L	Pct.	ERA	G	GS	CG	ShO	Sv.	IP	H	R	ER	BB	SO
1997—Hickory (S.Atl.)...................	0	1	.000	4.64	13	0	0	0	1	21 1/3	22	18	11	10	25
1998—Winston-Salem (Caro.).......	4	5	.444	4.57	16	16	0	0	0	82 2/3	92	55	42	45	72
—Arizona White Sox (Ariz.) ...	1	0	1.000	3.94	5	2	0	0	0	16	15	9	7	8	18
1999—Winston-Salem (Caro.).......							Did not play.								
2000—Birmingham (Sou.).............	11	6	.647	3.08	23	23	2	2	0	146 1/3	138	63	50	54	118
—Chicago (A.L.)	1	2	.333	8.34	4	4	0	0	0	22 2/3	31	25	21	8	7
2001—Chicago (A.L.)	7	8	.467	5.39	30	21	0	0	0	128 2/3	137	87	77	52	85
Major League totals (2 years).......	8	10	.444	5.83	34	25	0	0	0	151 1/3	168	112	98	60	92

BIERBRODT, NICK   P   DEVIL RAYS

PERSONAL: Born May 16, 1978, in Tarzana, Calif. ... 6-5/185. ... Throws left, bats left. ... Full name: Nicholas Raymond Bierbrodt.
HIGH SCHOOL: Millikan (Long Beach, Calif.).
TRANSACTIONS/CAREER NOTES: Selected by Arizona Diamondbacks organization in first round (30th pick overall) of free-agent draft (June 4, 1996). ... On Tucson disabled list (May 4-July 8 and July 23-28, 2000). ... On Arizona disabled list (March 23-April 19, 2001); included rehabilitation assignment to El Paso (May 1-19). ... Traded by Diamondbacks with OF Jason Conti to Tampa Bay Devil Rays for P Albie Lopez and C Mike Difelice (July 25, 2001).
MISCELLANEOUS: Appeared in one game as pinch runner (2001).

Year	League	W	L	Pct.	ERA	G	GS	CG	ShO	Sv.	IP	H	R	ER	BB	SO
1996—Ariz. Diamondbacks (Ariz.).	1	1	.500	1.66	8	8	0	0	0	38	25	9	7	13	46
—Lethbridge (Pio.)	2	0	1.000	0.50	3	3	0	0	0	18	12	4	1	5	23
1997—South Bend (Midw.)...........	2	4	.333	4.04	15	15	0	0	0	75 2/3	77	43	34	37	64
1998—High Desert (Calif.)...........	8	7	.533	3.40	24	23	1	0	0	129 2/3	122	66	49	64	88
1999—El Paso (Texas)..................	5	6	.455	4.62	14	14	2	•1	0	76	78	45	39	37	55
—Tucson (PCL)	1	4	.200	7.27	11	11	0	0	0	43 1/3	57	42	35	30	43
2000—Tucson (PCL)	2	1	.667	4.82	4	3	0	0	0	18 2/3	13	10	10	14	11
—Ariz. Diamondbacks (Ariz.).	0	0	...	4.50	4	3	0	0	0	8	4	4	4	5	10
—El Paso (Texas)	1	3	.250	7.13	7	7	0	0	0	35 1/3	37	30	28	24	36
2001—El Paso (Texas)	2	1	.667	1.37	4	4	0	0	0	19 2/3	13	3	3	6	18
—Tucson (PCL)	4	1	.800	2.18	7	6	0	0	0	45 1/3	48	15	11	9	56
—Arizona (N.L.)	2	2	.500	8.22	5	5	0	0	0	23	29	21	21	12	17
—Tampa Bay (A.L.)■.............	3	4	.429	4.55	11	11	0	0	0	61 1/3	71	38	31	27	56
A.L. totals (1 year)......................	3	4	.429	4.55	11	11	0	0	0	61 1/3	71	38	31	27	56
N.L. totals (1 year)......................	2	2	.500	8.22	5	5	0	0	0	23	29	21	21	12	17
Major League totals (1 year)........	5	6	.455	5.55	16	16	0	0	0	84 1/3	100	59	52	39	73

BIGBIE, LARRY   OF   ORIOLES

PERSONAL: Born November 4, 1977, in Hobart, Ind. ... 6-4/190. ... Bats left, throws left. ... Full name: Larry R. Bigbie.
HIGH SCHOOL: Hobart (Ind.).
COLLEGE: Ball State.
TRANSACTIONS/CAREER NOTES: Selected by Baltimore Orioles organization in first round (21st pick overall) of free-agent draft (June 2, 1999); pick received from Texas Rangers as part of compensation for Type A free agent 1B Rafael Palmeiro. ... On Frederick disabled list (April 22-29, 2000). ... On Bowie disabled list (July 28, 2000-remainder of season).

Year Team (League)	Pos.	G	AB	R	H	2B	3B	HR	RBI	Avg.	BB	SO	SB	PO	A	E	Avg.
1999— Bluefield (Appl.)	OF	8	30	3	8	0	0	0	4	.267	3	8	1	7	1	0	1.000
—Delmarva (S.Atl.)	OF	43	165	18	46	7	3	2	27	.279	29	42	3	54	3	3	.950
2000— Frederick (Caro.)	OF	55	201	33	59	11	0	2	28	.294	23	34	7	111	5	3	.975
— Bowie (East.)	OF	31	112	11	27	6	0	0	5	.241	11	28	3	63	2	0	1.000
2001— Bowie (East.)	OF	71	262	41	77	13	3	8	33	.294	40	54	10	136	4	4	.972
— Rochester (I.L.)	OF	10	42	5	13	4	0	1	2	.310	3	8	1	20	2	0	1.000
— Baltimore (A.L.)	OF	47	131	15	30	6	0	2	11	.229	17	42	4	71	2	0	1.000
Major League totals (1 year)		47	131	15	30	6	0	2	11	.229	17	42	4	71	2	0	1.000

BIGGIO, CRAIG — 2B — ASTROS

B

PERSONAL: Born December 14, 1965, in Smithtown, N.Y. ... 5-11/180. ... Bats right, throws right. ... Full name: Craig Alan Biggio. ... Name pronounced BEE-jee-oh.

HIGH SCHOOL: Kings Park (N.Y.).

COLLEGE: Seton Hall.

TRANSACTIONS/CAREER NOTES: Selected by Houston Astros organization in first round (22nd pick overall) of free-agent draft (June 2, 1987). ... Granted free agency (October 31, 1995). ... Re-signed by Astros (December 14, 1995). ... On disabled list (August 2, 2000-remainder of season).

RECORDS: Shares N.L. record for most years leading league in games by second baseman—8.

HONORS: Named catcher on THE SPORTING NEWS college All-America team (1987). ... Named catcher on THE SPORTING NEWS N.L. Silver Slugger team (1989). ... Named second baseman on THE SPORTING NEWS N.L. All-Star team (1994-95, 1997-98 and 2001). ... Won N.L. Gold Glove at second base (1994-97). ... Named second baseman on THE SPORTING NEWS N.L. Silver Slugger team (1994-95 and 1997-98).

STATISTICAL NOTES: Led N.L. catchers with 889 putouts, 963 total chances and 13 passed balls in 1991. ... Led N.L. in being hit by pitch with 22 in 1995, 27 in 1996, 34 in 1997 and 28 in 2001. ... Led N.L. second basemen in total chances with 728 in 1995, 811 in 1996 and 863 in 1997. ... Led N.L. second basemen with 359 putouts, 430 assists, 801 total chances and 117 double plays in 1999. ... Had 16-game hitting streak (April 5-26, 2000). ... Had 18-game hitting streak (May 29-June 18, 2001). ... Career major league grand slams: 2.

MISCELLANEOUS: Holds Houston Astros all-time record for most runs (1,305), hits (2,149) and doubles (437).

Year Team (League)	Pos.	G	AB	R	H	2B	3B	HR	RBI	Avg.	BB	SO	SB	PO	A	E	Avg.
1987— Asheville (S.Atl.)........	C-OF	64	216	59	81	17	2	9	49	.375	39	33	31	378	46	2	.995
1988— Tucson (PCL)	C-OF	77	281	60	90	21	4	3	41	.320	40	39	19	318	33	6	.983
— Houston (N.L.)	C	50	123	14	26	6	1	3	5	.211	7	29	6	292	28	3	.991
1989— Houston (N.L.)	C-OF	134	443	64	114	21	2	13	60	.257	49	64	21	742	56	9	.989
1990— Houston (N.L.)	C-OF	150	555	53	153	24	2	4	42	.276	53	79	25	657	60	13	.982
1991— Houston (N.L.)	C-2B-OF	149	546	79	161	23	4	4	46	.295	53	71	19	†894	73	11	.989
1992— Houston (N.L.)	2B	•162	613	96	170	32	3	6	39	.277	94	95	38	*344	413	12	.984
1993— Houston (N.L.)	2B	155	610	98	175	41	5	21	64	.287	77	93	15	306	*447	14	.982
1994— Houston (N.L.)	2B	114	437	88	139	*44	5	6	56	.318	62	58	*39	•225	*338	7	.988
1995— Houston (N.L.)	2B	141	553	*123	167	30	2	22	77	.302	80	85	33	299	*419	10	.986
1996— Houston (N.L.)	2B	•162	605	113	174	24	4	15	75	.288	75	72	25	*361	*440	10	.988
1997— Houston (N.L.)	2B-DH	•162	619	*146	191	37	8	22	81	.309	84	107	47	*341	*504	18	.979
1998— Houston (N.L.)	2B-DH	160	646	123	210	*51	2	20	88	.325	64	113	50	318	431	15	.980
1999— Houston (N.L.)	2B-OF-DH	160	639	123	188	*56	0	16	73	.294	88	107	28	†365	†431	12	.985
2000— Houston (N.L.)	2B	101	377	67	101	13	5	8	35	.268	61	73	12	181	280	6	.987
2001— Houston (N.L.)	2B-DH	155	617	118	180	35	3	20	70	.292	66	100	7	280	389	11	.984
Major League totals (14 years)		1955	7383	1305	2149	437	46	180	811	.291	913	1146	365	5605	4309	151	.985

DIVISION SERIES RECORD

Year Team (League)	Pos.	G	AB	R	H	2B	3B	HR	RBI	Avg.	BB	SO	SB	PO	A	E	Avg.
1997— Houston (N.L.)	2B	3	12	0	1	0	0	0	0	.083	1	0	0	4	8	1	.923
1998— Houston (N.L.)	2B	4	11	3	2	1	0	0	1	.182	4	4	0	9	10	1	.950
1999— Houston (N.L.)	2B	4	19	1	2	0	0	0	0	.105	1	5	0	14	10	0	1.000
2001— Houston (N.L.)	2B	3	12	0	2	0	0	0	0	.167	0	1	0	6	7	0	1.000
Division series totals (4 years)		14	54	4	7	1	0	0	1	.130	6	10	0	33	35	2	.971

ALL-STAR GAME RECORD

Year League	Pos.	AB	R	H	2B	3B	HR	RBI	Avg.	BB	SO	SB	PO	A	E	Avg.
1991— National	C	1	0	0	0	0	0	0	.000	0	0	0	2	0	1	.667
1992— National	2B	2	0	0	0	0	0	0	.000	0	0	0	0	2	0	1.000
1994— National	2B	1	1	0	0	0	0	0	.000	0	0	0	2	1	0	1.000
1995— National	2B	2	1	1	0	0	1	1	.500	0	0	0	2	1	0	1.000
1996— National	2B	3	0	0	0	0	0	1	.000	0	1	0	1	1	0	1.000
1997— National	2B	3	0	0	0	0	0	0	.000	0	1	0	0	4	0	1.000
1998— National	2B	3	0	0	0	0	0	0	.000	0	3	0	2	4	0	1.000
All-Star Game totals (7 years)		15	2	1	0	0	1	2	.067	0	5	0	9	13	1	.957

BLAIR, WILLIE — P

PERSONAL: Born December 18, 1965, in Paintsville, Ky. ... 6-1/185. ... Throws right, bats right. ... Full name: William Allen Blair.

HIGH SCHOOL: Johnson Central (Paintsville, Ky.).

COLLEGE: Morehead State.

TRANSACTIONS/CAREER NOTES: Selected by Toronto Blue Jays organization in 11th round of free-agent draft (June 2, 1986). ... Traded by Blue Jays to Cleveland Indians for P Alex Sanchez (November 6, 1990). ... Traded by Indians with C Eddie Taubensee to Houston Astros for OF Kenny Lofton and IF Dave Rohde (December 10, 1991). ... Selected by Colorado Rockies in first round (21st pick overall) of expansion draft (November 17, 1992). ... Granted free agency (December 20, 1994). ... Signed by San Diego Padres organization (April 10, 1995).

Granted free agency (December 21, 1995). ... Re-signed by Padres (December 27, 1995). ... Traded by Padres with C Brian Johnson to Detroit Tigers for P Joey Eischen and P Cam Smith (December 17, 1996). ... On Detroit disabled list (May 5-June 3, 1997); included rehabilitation assignment to West Michigan (May 23-June 3). ... Granted free agency (October 27, 1997). ... Signed by Arizona Diamondbacks (December 6, 1997). ... Traded by Diamondbacks with C Jorge Fabregas and a player to be named later to New York Mets for OF Bernard Gilkey, P Nelson Figueroa and cash (July 31, 1998); Mets received cash to complete deal (September 3, 1998). ... Traded by Mets to Tigers for 3B Joe Randa (December 4, 1998). ... Granted free agency (November 3, 2000). ... Signed by Indians organization (February 8, 2001). ... Released by Indians (March 31, 2001). ... Re-signed by Indians organization (April 10, 2001). ... Released by Indians (June 14, 2001). ... Signed by Tigers (June 15, 2001). ... Granted free agency (October 22, 2001).

STATISTICAL NOTES: Combined with starter Pat Hentgen and Enrique Burgos in 2-1 no-hit victory for Dunedin against Osceola (May 10, 1988).

Year	League	W	L	Pct.	ERA	G	GS	CG	ShO	Sv.	IP	H	R	ER	BB	SO
1986—	St. Catharines (NY-Penn) ...	5	0	1.000	1.68	21	0	0	0	*12	53²/₃	32	10	10	20	55
1987—	Dunedin (FSL)..................	2	9	.182	4.43	50	0	0	0	13	85¹/₃	99	51	42	29	72
1988—	Dunedin (FSL)..................	2	0	1.000	2.70	4	0	0	0	0	6²/₃	5	2	2	4	5
—	Knoxville (Sou.).............	5	5	.500	3.62	34	9	0	0	3	102	94	49	41	35	76
1989—	Syracuse (I.L.)...............	5	6	.455	3.97	19	17	3	1	0	106²/₃	94	55	47	38	76
1990—	Toronto (A.L.)................	3	5	.375	4.06	27	6	0	0	0	68²/₃	66	33	31	28	43
—	Syracuse (I.L.)...............	0	2	.000	4.74	3	3	1	0	0	19	20	13	10	8	6
1991—	Colorado Springs (PCL)■..	9	6	.600	4.99	26	15	0	0	4	113²/₃	130	74	63	30	57
—	Cleveland (A.L.).............	2	3	.400	6.75	11	5	0	0	0	36	58	27	27	10	13
1992—	Tucson (PCL)■..............	4	4	.500	2.39	21	2	1	0	2	52²/₃	50	20	14	12	35
—	Houston (N.L.)...............	5	7	.417	4.00	29	8	0	0	0	78²/₃	74	47	35	25	48
1993—	Colorado (N.L.)■...........	6	10	.375	4.75	46	18	1	0	0	146	184	90	77	42	84
1994—	Colorado (N.L.).............	0	5	.000	5.79	47	1	0	0	3	77²/₃	98	57	50	39	68
1995—	San Diego (N.L.)■.........	7	5	.583	4.34	40	12	0	0	0	114	112	60	55	45	83
1996—	San Diego (N.L.)...........	2	6	.250	4.60	60	0	0	0	1	88	80	52	45	29	67
1997—	Detroit (A.L.)■...............	16	8	.667	4.17	29	27	2	0	0	175	186	85	81	46	90
—	West Michigan (Midw.) ...	0	0	...	0.00	1	1	0	0	0	5	1	0	0	0	7
—	Toledo (I.L.)..................	0	0	...	0.00	1	1	0	0	0	7	1	1	0	2	4
1998—	Arizona (N.L.)■..............	4	15	.211	5.34	23	23	0	0	0	146²/₃	165	91	87	51	71
—	New York (N.L.)■............	1	1	.500	3.14	11	2	0	0	0	28²/₃	23	10	10	10	21
1999—	Detroit (A.L.)■...............	3	11	.214	6.85	39	16	0	0	0	134	169	107	102	44	82
2000—	Detroit (A.L.)................	10	6	.625	4.88	47	17	0	0	0	156²/₃	185	89	85	35	74
2001—	Buffalo (I.L.)■...............	4	3	.571	2.75	11	10	1	0	0	72	72	30	22	7	50
—	Detroit (A.L.)■...............	1	4	.200	10.50	9	4	0	0	0	24	38	30	28	11	15
A.L. totals (6 years)	....	35	37	.486	5.36	162	75	2	0	0	594¹/₃	702	371	354	174	317
N.L. totals (6 years)	....	25	49	.338	4.75	256	64	1	0	4	679²/₃	736	407	359	241	442
Major League totals (12 years)	.....	60	86	.411	5.04	418	139	3	0	4	1274	1438	778	713	415	759

DIVISION SERIES RECORD

Year	League	W	L	Pct.	ERA	G	GS	CG	ShO	Sv.	IP	H	R	ER	BB	SO
1996—	San Diego (N.L.)	0	0	...	0.00	1	0	0	0	0	2	1	0	0	2	3

BLAKE, CASEY   3B   TWINS

PERSONAL: Born August 23, 1973, in Des Moines, Iowa. ... 6-2/200. ... Bats right, throws right. ... Full name: William Casey Blake.
HIGH SCHOOL: Indianola (Iowa).
COLLEGE: Wichita State.
TRANSACTIONS/CAREER NOTES: Selected by Philadelphia Phillies organization in 11th round of free-agent draft (June 1, 1992); did not sign. ... Selected by New York Yankees organization in 45th round of free-agent draft (June 1, 1995); did not sign. ... Selected by Toronto Blue Jays organization in seventh round of free-agent draft (June 4, 1996). ... Claimed on waivers by Minnesota Twins (May 23, 2000). ... On Salt Lake disabled list (June 28-July 7, 2000). ... Claimed on waivers by Baltimore Orioles (September 21, 2001). ... Claimed on waivers by Twins (October 12, 2001).
STATISTICAL NOTES: Led Florida State League third basemen with 98 putouts and 39 errors in 1997. ... Led International League third basemen with .967 fielding percentage in 1999. ... Tied for International League lead with 94 putouts by third basemen in 1999.

							BATTING								FIELDING		
Year	Team (League)	Pos.	G	AB	R	H	2B	3B	HR	RBI	Avg.	BB	SO	SB	PO	A	E	Avg.
1996—	Hagerstown (S.Atl.)....	3B-1B-OF	48	172	29	43	13	1	2	18	.250	11	40	5	33	83	12	.906
1997—	Dunedin (FSL)...........	3B-SS	129	449	56	107	21	0	7	39	.238	48	91	19	†98	235	†39	.895
1998—	Dunedin (FSL)...........	3B	88	340	62	119	28	3	11	65	*.350	30	81	9	64	183	16	.939
—	Knoxville (Sou.).........	3B	45	172	41	64	15	4	7	38	.372	22	25	10	27	89	11	.913
1999—	Syracuse (I.L.)...........	3B-DH-SS	110	387	69	95	16	2	22	75	.245	61	82	9	‡94	169	10	†.963
—	Toronto (A.L.)............	3B	14	39	6	10	2	0	1	1	.256	2	7	0	12	23	0	1.000
—	St. Catharines (NY-P).	3B	1	3	0	2	0	0	0	0	.667	1	0	0	1	3	0	1.000
2000—	Syracuse (I.L.)...........	3B-SS	30	106	10	23	6	1	2	7	.217	8	23	0	24	42	2	.971
—	Salt Lake (PCL)■......	3B-SS-1B	80	293	59	93	22	2	12	52	.317	39	59	7	49	150	14	.934
—	Minnesota (A.L.)	3B-DH-1B	7	16	1	3	2	0	0	1	.188	3	7	0	7	5	0	1.000
2001—	Edmonton (PCL).........	3-1-2-S-O	94	375	64	116	24	6	10	49	.309	34	66	14	93	175	11	.961
—	Minnesota (A.L.)........	3B-DH-1B	13	22	1	7	1	0	0	2	.318	3	8	1	16	5	1	.955
—	Baltimore (A.L.)■.......	1B-DH	6	15	2	2	0	0	1	2	.133	1	4	2	29	0	1	.967
Major League totals (3 years)			40	92	10	22	5	0	2	6	.239	9	26	3	64	33	2	.980

BLANCO, HENRY   C   BREWERS

PERSONAL: Born August 29, 1971, in Caracas, Venezuela. ... 5-11/224. ... Bats right, throws right. ... Full name: Henry Ramon Blanco.
HIGH SCHOOL: Antonio Jose de Sucre (Venezuela).
TRANSACTIONS/CAREER NOTES: Signed as non-drafted free agent by Los Angeles Dodgers organization (November 12, 1989). ... On disabled list (June 16-25, 1993). ... On Los Angeles disabled list (March 22-July 29, 1998); included rehabilitation assignment to San Bernardino (May 19-27). ... Granted free agency (October 15, 1998). ... Signed by Colorado Rockies organization (December 18, 1998). ... Traded by Rockies with P Jamey Wright to Milwaukee Brewers as part of three-way deal in which Rockies received 3B Jeff Cirillo, P Scott Karl and cash from

Brewers, Oakland Athletics received P Justin Miller and cash from Rockies and Brewers received P Jimmy Haynes from A's (December 13, 1999). ... On Milwaukee disabled list (April 14-May 2, 2000); included rehabilitation assignment to Indianapolis (April 30-May 2).

STATISTICAL NOTES: Led Pioneer League third basemen with .947 fielding percentage and 10 double plays in 1991. ... Led California League third basemen with 345 total chances and 34 double plays in 1992. ... Led Texas League third basemen with .944 fielding percentage, 92 putouts and 270 total chances in 1993. ... Led Texas League catchers with 13 errors and 17 passed balls in 1996. ... Led Pacific Coast League catchers with 64 assists and 11 double plays in 1997. ... Career major league grand slams: 1.

							BATTING								FIELDING		
Year Team (League)	Pos.	G	AB	R	H	2B	3B	HR	RBI	Avg.	BB	SO	SB	PO	A	E	Avg.
1990— GC Dodgers (GCL)	3B	60	178	23	39	8	0	1	19	.219	26	41	7	*48	129	11	.941
1991— Vero Beach (FSL)	3B-SS	5	7	0	1	0	0	0	0	.143	2	0	0	6	4	0	1.000
— Great Falls (Pio.)	3B-1B	62	216	35	55	7	1	5	28	.255	27	39	3	93	99	8	†.960
1992— Bakersfield (Calif.)	3B	124	401	42	94	21	2	5	52	.234	51	91	10	*95	*236	14	*.959
1993— San Antonio (Texas)	3B-1B-SS	117	374	33	73	19	1	10	42	.195	29	80	3	†150	169	16	†.952
1994— San Antonio (Texas)	3B-1B-P	*132	405	36	93	23	2	6	38	.230	53	67	6	77	178	21	.924
1995— San Antonio (Texas)	3B-C	88	302	37	77	18	4	12	48	.255	29	52	1	81	210	11	.964
— Albuquerque (PCL)	3B-1B-OF	29	97	11	22	4	1	2	13	.227	10	23	0	115	47	2	.988
1996— San Antonio (Texas)	C-3B	92	307	39	82	14	1	5	40	.267	28	38	2	532	65	†13	.979
— Albuquerque (PCL)	C	2	6	1	1	0	0	0	0	.167	0	3	0	11	1	0	1.000
1997— Albuquerque (PCL)	C-1B-DH-OF	91	294	38	92	20	1	6	47	.313	37	63	7	607	†68	3	.996
— Los Angeles (N.L.)	1B-3B	3	5	1	2	0	0	1	1	.400	0	1	0	5	0	0	1.000
1998— San Bern. (Calif.)	C-DH	7	19	5	6	1	0	2	3	.316	4	6	1	17	3	0	1.000
— Albuquerque (PCL)	C-DH	48	134	19	36	11	0	4	23	.269	22	27	2	243	20	4	.985
1999— Colo. Springs (PCL)■	C	15	57	8	19	4	0	3	12	.333	1	12	0	87	12	1	.990
— Colorado (N.L.)	C-OF	88	263	30	61	12	3	6	28	.232	34	38	1	562	58	5	.992
2000— Milwaukee (N.L.)■	C	93	284	29	67	24	0	7	31	.236	36	60	0	506	58	5	.991
— Indianapolis (I.L.)	DH	1	3	1	1	1	0	0	0	.333	1	0	0	...	...	...	...
2001— Milwaukee (N.L.)	C	104	314	33	66	18	3	6	31	.210	34	72	3	645	68	6	.992
Major League totals (4 years)		288	866	93	196	54	6	20	91	.226	104	171	4	1718	184	16	.992

RECORD AS PITCHER

Year League	W	L	Pct.	ERA	G	GS	CG	ShO	Sv.	IP	H	R	ER	BB	SO
1994— San Antonio (Texas)	0	0	...	9.00	1	0	0	0	0	1	3	1	1	0	1

BLANK, MATT P EXPOS

PERSONAL: Born April 5, 1976, in Texarkana, Texas. ... 6-2/195. ... Throws left, bats left. ... Full name: Clarence Matt Blank.
HIGH SCHOOL: James W. Martin (Arlington, Texas).
COLLEGE: Texas A&M.
TRANSACTIONS/CAREER NOTES: Selected by New York Yankees organization in 37th round of free-agent draft (June 2, 1994); did not sign. ... Selected by Florida Marlins organization in 40th round of free-agent draft (June 3, 1995); did not sign. ... Selected by Montreal Expos organization in 11th round of free-agent draft (June 3, 1997). ... On disabled list (May 19, 2000-remainder of season). ... On Ottawa disabled list (July 15-September 6, 2001).

Year League	W	L	Pct.	ERA	G	GS	CG	ShO	Sv.	IP	H	R	ER	BB	SO
1997— Vermont (NY-Penn)	6	4	.600	*1.69	16	15	2	0	0	95²/₃	74	26	18	14	84
1998— Cape Fear (S.Atl.)	9	2	.818	2.61	21	21	2	2	0	134²/₃	121	45	39	24	114
— Jupiter (FSL)	5	1	.833	2.34	8	6	0	0	0	42¹/₃	33	14	11	10	26
1999— Jupiter (FSL)	9	5	.643	2.40	14	14	3	1	0	90	64	26	24	19	66
— Harrisburg (East.)	6	3	.667	3.92	15	14	0	0	0	85	94	41	37	26	42
2000— Montreal (N.L.)	0	1	.000	5.14	13	0	0	0	0	14	12	8	8	5	4
2001— Ottawa (I.L.)	6	7	.462	5.18	14	14	1	0	0	81²/₃	89	52	47	30	58
— Montreal (N.L.)	2	2	.500	5.16	5	4	0	0	0	22²/₃	23	14	13	13	11
Major League totals (2 years)	2	3	.400	5.15	18	4	0	0	0	36²/₃	35	22	21	18	15

BLOOMQUIST, WILLIAM SS/2B MARINERS

PERSONAL: Born November 27, 1977, in Bremerton, Wash. ... 5-11/185. ... Bats right, throws right. ... Full name: William Willie Bloomquist.
HIGH SCHOOL: South Kitsap (Port Orchard, Wash.).
COLLEGE: Arizona State.
TRANSACTIONS/CAREER NOTES: Selected by Seattle Mariners organization in eighth round of free-agent draft (June 4, 1996); did not sign. ... Selected by Mariners organization in third round of free-agent draft (June 2, 1999). ... On Lancaster disabled list (August 6, 2000-remainder of season).

							BATTING								FIELDING		
Year Team (League)	Pos.	G	AB	R	H	2B	3B	HR	RBI	Avg.	BB	SO	SB	PO	A	E	Avg.
1999— Everett (N'West)	2B-OF	42	178	35	51	10	3	2	27	.287	22	25	17	65	79	7	.954
2000— Lancaster (Calif.)	2B-SS	64	256	63	97	19	6	2	51	.379	37	27	22	118	176	12	.961
— Tacoma (PCL)	2B	51	191	17	43	5	1	1	23	.225	7	28	5	105	123	3	.987
2001— San Antonio (Texas)	SS-2B	123	491	59	125	23	2	0	28	.255	28	55	34	185	372	24	.959

BLUM, GEOFF 3B/OF EXPOS

PERSONAL: Born April 26, 1973, in Redwood City, Calif. ... 6-3/195. ... Bats both, throws right. ... Full name: Geoffery Edward Blum.
HIGH SCHOOL: Chino (Calif.).
COLLEGE: California.
TRANSACTIONS/CAREER NOTES: Selected by Montreal Expos organization in seventh round of free-agent draft (June 2, 1994). ... On Ottawa disabled list (May 21-June 15, 1999).
STATISTICAL NOTES: Switch-hit home runs in one game (July 5, 2001).

Year	Team (League)	Pos.	G	AB	R	H	2B	3B	HR	RBI	Avg.	BB	SO	SB	PO	A	E	Avg.
1994—	Vermont (NY-Penn)....	SS	63	241	48	83	15	1	3	38	.344	33	21	5	87	185	15	.948
1995—	W.P. Beach (FSL).......	2B-SS-3B	125	457	54	120	20	2	1	62	.263	34	61	6	166	298	18	.963
1996—	Harrisburg (East.)........	2-S-1-O	120	396	47	95	22	2	1	41	.240	59	51	6	259	281	9	.984
1997—	Ottawa (I.L.)..............	2B-SS-3B	118	407	59	101	21	2	3	35	.248	52	73	14	223	305	17	.969
1998—	Ottawa (I.L.).............	2B	8	23	1	4	0	0	0	1	.174	3	6	0	18	12	0	1.000
	—GC Expos (GCL)	2B	5	18	0	3	1	1	0	1	.167	1	4	0	4	12	0	1.000
	—Jupiter (FSL)	2B-3B-SS	17	58	13	16	6	0	0	5	.276	13	14	1	31	51	2	.976
	—Harrisburg (East.).......	SS-3B-2B-1B	39	139	25	43	12	3	6	21	.309	17	24	2	48	94	2	.986
1999—	Ottawa (I.L.)........	S-1-2-3-DH	77	268	43	71	14	1	10	37	.265	37	39	6	154	179	12	.965
	—Montreal (N.L.).......	SS-2B	45	133	21	32	7	2	8	18	.241	17	25	1	47	84	10	.929
2000—	Montreal (N.L.)..........	3B-SS-2B-1B	124	343	40	97	20	2	11	45	.283	26	60	1	122	210	9	.974
2001—	Montreal (N.L.).......	3-0-2-1-S	148	453	57	107	25	0	9	50	.236	43	94	9	215	180	8	.980
Major League totals (3 years)			317	929	118	236	52	4	28	113	.254	86	179	11	384	474	27	.969

BOCACHICA, HIRAM — 2B — DODGERS

PERSONAL: Born March 4, 1976, in Ponce, Puerto Rico. ... 5-11/165. ... Bats right, throws right. ... Full name: Hiram Colon Bocachica.
HIGH SCHOOL: Rexville (Bayamon, Puerto Rico).
TRANSACTIONS/CAREER NOTES: Selected by Montreal Expos organization in first round (21st pick overall) of free-agent draft (June 2, 1994). ... On West Palm Beach disabled list (May 16-July 12, 1996). ... On Harrisburg suspended list (June 15-18, 1997). ... On Harrisburg disabled list (June 18-25, 1997). ... Traded by Expos with P Carlos Perez and SS Mark Grudzielanek to Los Angeles Dodgers for 2B Wilton Guerrero, P Ted Lilly, OF Peter Bergeron and 1B Jonathan Tucker (July 31, 1998). ... On San Antonio suspended list (August 16-19, 1999). ... On Albuquerque disabled list (May 23-June 2, 2000). ... On disabled list (July 9-26, 2001).
STATISTICAL NOTES: Led South Atlantic League shortstops with 58 errors in 1995. ... Led Texas League in being hit by pitch with 13 in 1999. ... Tied for Texas League lead with 77 double plays by second basemen in 1999. ... Led Pacific Coast League second basemen with 99 double plays in 2000. ... Tied for Pacific Coast League lead with nine sacrifice hits in 2000.

Year	Team (League)	Pos.	G	AB	R	H	2B	3B	HR	RBI	Avg.	BB	SO	SB	PO	A	E	Avg.
1994—	GC Expos (GCL)	SS	43	168	31	47	9	0	5	16	.280	15	42	11	72	126	*23	.896
1995—	Albany (S.Atl.)	SS-2B	96	380	65	108	20	10	2	30	.284	52	78	47	165	265	†58	.881
1996—	W.P. Beach (FSL)........	DH-SS	71	267	50	90	17	5	2	26	.337	34	47	21	37	83	24	.833
	—GC Expos (GCL)	DH	9	32	11	8	3	0	0	2	.250	5	3	2	...	...	...	...
1997—	Harrisburg (East.)........	SS-2B-DH	119	443	82	123	19	3	11	35	.278	41	98	29	135	186	32	.909
1998—	Harrisburg (East.)........	OF-DH	80	296	39	78	18	4	4	27	.264	21	61	20	171	4	10	.946
	—Ottawa (I.L.)	OF	12	41	5	8	3	1	0	5	.195	6	14	2	23	1	0	1.000
	—Albuquerque (PCL)■..	OF	26	101	16	24	7	1	4	16	.238	13	24	5	80	2	2	.976
1999—	San Antonio (Texas)...	2B-DH	123	477	84	139	22	10	11	60	.291	60	71	30	227	313	*31	.946
2000—	Albuquerque (PCL).......	2B	124	482	99	155	38	4	23	84	.322	40	100	10	273	326	*23	.963
	—Los Angeles (N.L.)	2B	8	10	2	3	0	0	0	0	.300	0	2	0	3	9	0	1.000
2001—	Los Angeles (N.L.)	2B-OF-3B	75	133	15	31	11	1	2	9	.233	9	33	4	32	47	7	.919
Major League totals (2 years)			83	143	17	34	11	1	2	9	.238	9	35	4	35	56	7	.929

BOEHRINGER, BRIAN — P

PERSONAL: Born January 8, 1970, in St. Louis. ... 6-2/190. ... Throws right, bats both. ... Full name: Brian Edward Boehringer. ... Name pronounced BO-ring-er.
HIGH SCHOOL: Northwest (House Springs, Mo.).
JUNIOR COLLEGE: St. Louis Community College at Meramec.
COLLEGE: UNLV.
TRANSACTIONS/CAREER NOTES: Selected by Houston Astros organization in 10th round of free-agent draft (June 4, 1990); did not sign. ... Selected by Chicago White Sox organization in fourth round of free-agent draft (June 3, 1991). ... On Utica disabled list (June 29-August 25, 1991). ... On disabled list (June 24-August 25, 1992). ... Traded by White Sox to New York Yankees for P Paul Assenmacher (March 21, 1994). ... On New York disabled list (May 27-August 19, 1997); included rehabilitation assignments to Gulf Coast Yankees (August 10-12) and Tampa (August 13-19). ... Selected by Tampa Bay Devil Rays in second round (30th pick overall) of expansion draft (November 18, 1997). ... Traded by Devil Rays with SS Andy Sheets to San Diego Padres for C John Flaherty (November 18, 1997). ... On disabled list (August 14, 1999-remainder of season). ... On San Diego disabled list (April 21-May 24 and July 4, 2000-remainder of season); included rehabilitation assignment to Rancho Cucamonga (May 17-24). ... Granted free agency (October 25, 2000). ... Signed by Yankees organization (December 14, 2000). ... Traded by Yankees to San Francisco Giants for C Bobby Estalella and P Joe Smith (July 5, 2001). ... Granted free agency (December 21, 2001).
STATISTICAL NOTES: Tied for Eastern League lead with five balks in 1994. ... Led International League with 11 hit batsmen in 1996.

Year	League	W	L	Pct.	ERA	G	GS	CG	ShO	Sv.	IP	H	R	ER	BB	SO
1991—	GC White Sox (GCL)	1	1	.500	6.57	5	1	0	0	0	$12\frac{1}{3}$	14	9	9	5	10
	—Utica (NY-Penn)	1	1	.500	2.37	4	4	0	0	0	19	14	8	5	8	19
1992—	South Bend (Midw.)	6	7	.462	4.38	15	15	2	0	0	$86\frac{1}{3}$	87	52	42	40	59
1993—	Sarasota (FSL)	10	4	.714	2.80	18	17	3	0	0	119	103	47	37	51	92
	—Birmingham (Sou.)	2	1	.667	3.54	7	7	1	0	0	$40\frac{2}{3}$	41	20	16	14	29
1994—	Albany/Colonie (East.)■	10	11	.476	3.62	27	27	5	1	0	$171\frac{2}{3}$	165	85	69	57	145
1995—	New York (A.L.)	0	3	.000	13.75	7	3	0	0	0	$17\frac{2}{3}$	24	27	27	22	10
	—Columbus (I.L.)	8	6	.571	2.77	17	17	3	0	0	104	101	39	32	31	58
1996—	Columbus (I.L.)	11	7	.611	4.00	25	25	3	1	0	153	155	79	68	56	132
	—New York (A.L.)	2	4	.333	5.44	15	3	0	0	0	$46\frac{1}{3}$	46	28	28	21	37
1997—	New York (A.L.)	3	2	.600	2.63	34	0	0	0	0	48	39	16	14	32	53
	—Gulf Coast Yankees (GCL)	0	0	...	0.00	1	1	0	0	0	2	1	0	0	0	2
	—Tampa (FSL)	0	1	.000	5.00	3	3	0	0	0	9	9	5	5	5	8
1998—	San Diego (N.L.)■	5	2	.714	4.36	56	1	0	0	0	$76\frac{1}{3}$	75	38	37	45	67
1999—	San Diego (N.L.)	6	5	.545	3.24	33	11	0	0	0	$94\frac{1}{3}$	97	38	34	35	64
2000—	San Diego (N.L.)	0	3	.000	5.74	7	3	0	0	0	$15\frac{2}{3}$	18	15	10	10	9

Year	League	W	L	Pct.	ERA	G	GS	CG	ShO	Sv.	IP	H	R	ER	BB	SO
— Rancho Cuca. (Calif.)		0	2	.000	5.40	4	2	0	0	0	5	8	3	3	1	5
2001— New York (A.L.)■..............		0	1	.000	3.12	22	0	0	0	1	34 2/3	35	15	12	12	33
— San Francisco (N.L.)■		0	3	.000	4.19	29	0	0	0	1	34 1/3	32	20	16	17	27
A.L. totals (4 years)		5	10	.333	4.97	78	6	0	0	1	146 2/3	144	86	81	87	133
N.L. totals (4 years)		11	13	.458	3.96	125	15	0	0	1	220 2/3	222	111	97	107	167
Major League totals (7 years)		16	23	.410	4.36	203	21	0	0	2	367 1/3	366	197	178	194	300

DIVISION SERIES RECORD

Year	League	W	L	Pct.	ERA	G	GS	CG	ShO	Sv.	IP	H	R	ER	BB	SO
1996— New York (A.L.)..................		1	0	1.000	6.75	2	0	0	0	0	1 1/3	3	2	1	2	0
1997— New York (A.L.)..................		0	0	...	0.00	1	0	0	0	0	1 2/3	1	0	0	1	2
1998— San Diego (N.L.)							Did not play.									
Division series totals (2 years)		1	0	1.000	3.00	3	0	0	0	0	3	4	2	1	3	2

CHAMPIONSHIP SERIES RECORD

Year	League	W	L	Pct.	ERA	G	GS	CG	ShO	Sv.	IP	H	R	ER	BB	SO
1998— San Diego (N.L.)		0	0	...	0.00	3	0	0	0	0	3	3	0	0	1	1

WORLD SERIES RECORD

NOTES: Member of World Series championship team (1996).

Year	League	W	L	Pct.	ERA	G	GS	CG	ShO	Sv.	IP	H	R	ER	BB	SO
1996— New York (A.L.)..................		0	0	...	5.40	2	0	0	0	0	5	5	5	3	0	5
1998— San Diego (N.L.)		0	0	...	9.00	2	0	0	0	0	2	4	2	2	2	3
World Series totals (2 years)		0	0	...	6.43	4	0	0	0	0	7	9	7	5	2	8

BOGAR, TIM   IF

PERSONAL: Born October 28, 1966, in Indianapolis. ... 6-2/198. ... Bats right, throws right. ... Full name: Timothy Paul Bogar.
HIGH SCHOOL: Buffalo Grove (Ill.).
COLLEGE: Eastern Illinois.
TRANSACTIONS/CAREER NOTES: Selected by New York Mets organization in eighth round of free-agent draft (June 2, 1987). ... On disabled list (June 14, 1990-remainder of season). ... On disabled list (August 16-September 1, 1993). ... On New York disabled list (May 6-June 9, 1994); included rehabilitation assignment to Norfolk (June 4-9). ... Traded by Mets to Houston Astros for IF Luis Lopez (March 31, 1997). ... On disabled list (September 5, 1997-remainder of season). ... Granted free agency (October 23, 1998). ... Re-signed by Astros (December 7, 1998). ... Granted free agency (October 30, 2000). ... Signed by Los Angeles Dodgers organization (January 17, 2001). ... On Los Angeles disabled list (April 4-May 28, June 14-30 and July 2, 2001-remainder of season); included rehabilitation assignments to Las Vegas (April 21-27 and August 25-September 4). ... Granted free agency (November 12, 2001).
MISCELLANEOUS: Played all nine positions in one game for Tidewater (September 4, 1991).

Year	Team (League)	Pos.	G	AB	R	H	2B	3B	HR	RBI	Avg.	BB	SO	SB	PO	A	E	Avg.
							BATTING								FIELDING			
1987— Little Falls (NY-Penn) .		SS-2B	58	205	31	48	9	0	0	23	.234	18	39	2	79	194	24	.919
1988— Columbia (S.Atl.).........		2B-SS	45	142	19	40	4	2	3	21	.282	22	29	5	89	120	8	.963
— St. Lucie (FSL)		2B-SS-3B	76	236	34	65	7	1	2	30	.275	34	57	9	141	214	19	.949
1989— Jackson (Texas)		SS	112	406	44	108	13	5	4	45	.266	41	57	8	185	351	29	.949
1990— Tidewater (I.L.)............		SS	33	117	10	19	2	0	0	4	.162	8	22	1	57	89	10	.936
1991— Williamsport (East.) ...3B-2B-1B-SS			63	243	33	61	12	2	2	25	.251	20	44	13	100	137	8	.967
— Tidewater (I.L.).......S-2-3-C-1-O-P			65	218	23	56	11	0	1	23	.257	20	35	1	111	183	11	.964
1992— Tidewater (I.L.)............		2-S-3-P-1	129	481	54	134	32	1	5	38	.279	14	65	7	211	327	15	.973
1993— New York (N.L.)............		SS-3B-2B	78	205	19	50	13	0	3	25	.244	14	29	0	105	217	9	.973
1994— New York (N.L.)...........		3-1-S-2-0	50	52	5	8	0	0	2	5	.154	4	11	1	77	38	1	.991
— Norfolk (I.L.)		3B-2B	5	19	0	2	0	0	0	1	.105	1	4	0	5	11	0	1.000
1995— New York (N.L.)...........		S-3-1-2-0	78	145	17	42	7	0	1	21	.290	9	25	1	82	100	6	.968
1996— New York (N.L.)........1B-3B-SS-2B			91	89	17	19	4	0	0	6	.213	8	20	1	104	61	1	.994
1997— Houston (N.L.)■...........		SS-3B-1B	97	241	30	60	14	4	4	30	.249	24	42	4	110	229	6	.983
1998— Houston (N.L.)........SS-2B-3B-DH			79	156	12	24	4	1	1	8	.154	9	36	2	63	147	3	.986
1999— Houston (N.L.)		SS-3B-2B	107	309	44	74	16	2	4	31	.239	38	52	3	130	277	9	.978
2000— Houston (N.L.) SS-P-2B-3B			110	304	32	63	9	2	7	33	.207	35	56	1	121	245	12	.968
2001— Los Angeles (N.L.)■ ..		1B-SS-3B	12	15	4	5	2	0	2	2	.333	2	1	0	10	2	0	1.000
— Las Vegas (PCL)		SS-3B	16	52	8	13	5	0	0	4	.250	3	11	0	28	37	3	.956
Major League totals (9 years)			702	1516	180	345	69	9	24	161	.228	143	272	13	802	1316	47	.978

DIVISION SERIES RECORD

Year	Team (League)	Pos.	G	AB	R	H	2B	3B	HR	RBI	Avg.	BB	SO	SB	PO	A	E	Avg.
							BATTING								FIELDING			
1999— Houston (N.L.)		PH-SS	2	4	0	3	1	0	0	1	.750	1	0	0	4	4	0	1.000

RECORD AS PITCHER

Year	League	W	L	Pct.	ERA	G	GS	CG	ShO	Sv.	IP	H	R	ER	BB	SO
1991— Tidewater (I.L.)..................		0	0	...	27.00	1	0	0	0	0	1/3	0	1	1	0	1
1992— Tidewater (I.L.)..................		0	0	...	12.00	3	0	0	0	0	3	4	4	4	3	1
2000— Houston (N.L.)		0	0	...	4.50	2	0	0	0	0	2	2	1	1	1	1

BOHANON, BRIAN   P   REDS

PERSONAL: Born August 1, 1968, in Denton, Texas. ... 6-2/240. ... Throws left, bats left. ... Full name: Brian Edward Bohanon Jr.
HIGH SCHOOL: North Shore (Houston).
TRANSACTIONS/CAREER NOTES: Selected by Texas Rangers organization in first round (19th pick overall) of free-agent draft (June 2, 1987). ... On disabled list (April 17, 1988-remainder of season). ... On Charlotte disabled list (April 7-May 2, 1989). ... On Texas disabled list (April 7-July 1, 1991); included rehabilitation assignments to Charlotte (June 1-10), Tulsa (June 10-23) and Oklahoma City (June 23-30). ... On Texas disabled list (April 28-May 13, 1992). ... On Texas disabled list (June 9-30, 1993); included rehabilitation assignment to Oklahoma City (June 21-30).

... Granted free agency (December 23, 1994). ... Signed by Detroit Tigers organization (March 6, 1995). ... Released by Tigers (October 13, 1995). ... Signed by Toronto Blue Jays organization (February 20, 1996). ... Granted free agency (October 3, 1996). ... Signed by New York Mets organization (December 18, 1996). ... Traded by Mets to Los Angeles Dodgers for P Greg McMichael and cash (July 10, 1998). ... Granted free agency (October 27, 1998). ... Signed by Colorado Rockies (November 9, 1998). ... On Colorado disabled list (May 8-26 and June 28-July 13 and August 19, 2001-remainder of season); included rehabilitation assignment to Colorado Springs (May 21-26). ... Granted free agency (November 5, 2001). ... Signed by Cincinnati Reds organization (January 11, 2002).

MISCELLANEOUS: Shares Colorado Rockies all-time record for most shutouts (2). ... Singled and struck out once in two appearances as pinch hitter (1997). ... Grounded out in only appearance as pinch hitter (1999). ... Grounded out in only appearance as pinch hitter (2000). ... Appeared in one game as pinch hitter (2001).

Year	League	W	L	Pct.	ERA	G	GS	CG	ShO	Sv.	IP	H	R	ER	BB	SO
1987—	Gulf Coast Rangers (GCL)..	0	2	.000	4.71	5	4	0	0	0	21	15	13	11	5	21
1988—	Charlotte (FSL).................	0	1	.000	5.40	2	2	0	0	0	6²/₃	6	4	4	5	9
1989—	Charlotte (FSL).................	0	3	.000	1.81	11	7	0	0	1	54²/₃	40	16	11	20	33
—	Tulsa (Texas)	5	0	1.000	2.20	11	11	1	1	0	73²/₃	59	20	18	27	44
1990—	Texas (A.L.)	0	3	.000	6.62	11	6	0	0	0	34	40	30	25	18	15
—	Oklahoma City (A.A.).........	1	2	.333	3.66	14	4	0	0	1	32	35	16	13	8	22
1991—	Charlotte (FSL)	1	0	1.000	3.86	2	2	0	0	0	11²/₃	6	5	5	4	7
—	Tulsa (Texas)	0	1	.000	2.31	2	2	0	0	0	11²/₃	9	8	3	11	6
—	Oklahoma City (A.A.).........	0	4	.000	2.91	7	7	0	0	0	46¹/₃	49	19	15	15	37
—	Texas (A.L.)	4	3	.571	4.84	11	11	1	0	0	61¹/₃	66	35	33	23	34
1992—	Oklahoma City (A.A.).........	4	2	.667	2.73	9	9	3	0	0	56	53	21	17	15	24
—	Texas (A.L.)	1	1	.500	6.31	18	7	0	0	0	45²/₃	57	38	32	25	29
—	Tulsa (Texas)	2	1	.667	1.27	6	6	1	0	0	28¹/₃	25	7	4	9	25
1993—	Texas (A.L.)	4	4	.500	4.76	36	8	0	0	0	92²/₃	107	54	49	46	45
—	Oklahoma City (A.A.)	0	1	.000	6.43	2	2	0	0	0	7	7	6	5	3	7
1994—	Oklahoma City (A.A.)	5	10	.333	4.12	15	15	2	1	0	98¹/₃	106	56	45	33	68
—	Texas (A.L.)	2	2	.500	7.23	11	5	0	0	0	37¹/₃	51	31	30	8	26
1995—	Detroit (A.L.)■..................	1	1	.500	5.54	52	10	0	0	1	105²/₃	121	68	65	41	63
1996—	Toronto (A.L.)■.................	0	1	.000	7.77	20	0	0	0	1	22	27	19	19	19	17
—	Syracuse (I.L.)	4	3	.571	3.86	31	0	0	0	0	58¹/₃	56	29	25	17	38
1997—	Norfolk (I.L.)■..................	9	3	.750	2.63	15	14	4	2	0	96	88	37	28	32	84
—	New York (N.L.)	6	4	.600	3.82	19	14	0	0	0	94¹/₃	95	49	40	34	66
1998—	New York (N.L.);................	2	4	.333	3.15	25	4	0	0	0	54¹/₃	47	21	19	21	39
—	Los Angeles (N.L.)■..........	5	7	.417	2.40	14	14	2	0	0	97¹/₃	74	35	26	36	72
1999—	Colorado (N.L.)■..............	12	12	.500	6.20	33	33	3	1	0	197¹/₃	236	146	136	92	120
2000—	Colorado (N.L.)	12	10	.545	4.68	34	26	2	1	0	177	181	101	92	79	98
2001—	Colorado (N.L.)	5	8	.385	7.14	20	19	0	0	0	97	127	79	77	47	47
—	Colorado Springs (PCL)	0	0	...	1.80	1	1	0	0	0	5	8	1	1	1	2
A.L. totals (7 years)		12	15	.444	5.71	159	47	1	0	2	398²/₃	469	275	253	180	229
N.L. totals (5 years)		42	45	.483	4.89	145	110	7	2	0	717¹/₃	760	431	390	309	442
Major League totals (12 years)		54	60	.474	5.19	304	157	8	2	2	1116	1229	706	643	489	671

BONDS, BARRY   OF   GIANTS

PERSONAL: Born July 24, 1964, in Riverside, Calif. ... 6-2/210. ... Bats left, throws left. ... Full name: Barry Lamar Bonds. ... Son of Bobby Bonds, outfielder with eight major league teams (1968-81); and coach with Cleveland Indians (1984-87) and San Francisco Giants (1993-96). **HIGH SCHOOL:** Serra (San Mateo, Calif.).

COLLEGE: Arizona State.

TRANSACTIONS/CAREER NOTES: Selected by San Francisco Giants organization in second round of free-agent draft (June 7, 1982); did not sign. ... Selected by Pittsburgh Pirates organization in first round (sixth pick overall) of free-agent draft (June 3, 1985). ... On disabled list (June 15-July 4, 1992). ... Granted free agency (October 26, 1992). ... Signed by Giants (December 8, 1992). ... On suspended list (August 14-16, 1998). ... On disabled list (April 18-June 9, 1999). ... Granted free agency (November 5, 2001). ... Re-signed by Giants (January 14, 2002).

RECORDS: Holds N.L. career record for highest slugging percentage—.585; most home runs by lefthanded batter—567; most consecutive years leading league in bases on balls—4 (1994-97); and most years leading in bases on balls—7 (1992, 1994-97, and 2000-01). ... Holds major league career record for most intentional bases on balls—355. ... Shares major league record for most seasons and consecutive seasons leading league in intentional bases on balls received—7 (1992-98). ... Shares major league single-season record for fewest assists by outfielder who led league in assists—14 (1990). ... Shares major league record for fewest double plays by outfielder (150 or more games)—0 (1997 and 1998); most consecutive home runs—4 (May 19 [2] and 20 [2], 2001); most home runs in three consecutive games—6 (May 18, 19 [3], 20 [2], 2001 and May 19 [3], 20 [2], 21, 2001); and most home runs in five consecutive games—8 (May 17, 18, 19 [3], 20 [2], 21, 2001 and May 18, 19 [3], 20 [2], 21, 22, 2001). ... Shares N.L. single-season records for most consecutive times reached base safely—15 (August 31 [1], September 1 [5], 2 [4], 4 [5], 1998 [5 singles, 2 doubles, 2 home runs, 6 bases on balls]; fewest assists by outfielder (150 or more games)—2 (1993 and 1998); and most extra base hits—102 (2001). ... Holds N.L. single-season record for most home runs in six consecutive games—9 (May 17, 18, 19 [3], 20 [2], 21, 22, 2001). ... Holds major league single-season records for most home runs—73 (2001); most home runs by outfielder—71 (2001); highest slugging percentage—.863 (2001); fewest singles in season (150 or more games)—49 (2001); most bases on balls—177 (2001); and extra bases on long hits—255 (2001). ... Holds major league single-month record for most home runs—17 (May 2001).

HONORS: Named outfielder on THE SPORTING NEWS college All-America team (1985). ... Named Major League Player of the Year by THE SPORTING NEWS (1990 and 2001). ... Named N.L. Player of the Year by THE SPORTING NEWS (1990 and 1991). ... Named outfielder on THE SPORTING NEWS N.L. All-Star team (1990-94, 1996-97 and 2000-01). ... Won N.L. Gold Glove as outfielder (1990-94 and 1996-98). ... Named outfielder on THE SPORTING NEWS N.L. Silver Slugger team (1990-94, 1996, 1997 and 2000). ... Named N.L. Most Valuable Player by Baseball Writers' Association of America (1990, 1992-93 and 2001). ... Named outfielder on N.L. Silver Slugger team (2001).

STATISTICAL NOTES: Led N.L. with .565 slugging percentage in 1990, .624 in 1992, .677 in 1993 and .863 in 2001. ... Led N.L. with 32 intentional bases on balls received in 1992, 43 in 1993, 18 in 1994, 22 in 1995, 30 in 1996, 34 in 1997 and 29 in 1998. ... Led N.L. with .410 on-base percentage in 1991, .456 in 1992, .458 in 1993, .431 in 1995 and .515 in 2001. ... Led N.L. with 365 total bases in 1993. ... Hit three home runs in one game (August 2, 1994; May 19, 2001; and September 9, 2001). ... Tied N.L. outfielders for lead in double plays with four in 2000. ... Had 15-game hitting streak (May 11-27, 2001). ... Career major league grand slams: 10.

Year Team (League)	Pos.	G	AB	R	H	2B	3B	HR	RBI	Avg.	BB	SO	SB	PO	A	E	Avg.
								BATTING							FIELDING		
1985— Prince William (Caro.)	OF	71	254	49	76	16	4	13	37	.299	37	52	15	202	4	5	.976
1986— Hawaii (PCL)	OF	44	148	30	46	7	2	7	37	.311	33	31	16	109	4	2	.983
— Pittsburgh (N.L.)	OF	113	413	72	92	26	3	16	48	.223	65	102	36	280	9	5	.983
1987— Pittsburgh (N.L.)	OF	150	551	99	144	34	9	25	59	.261	54	88	32	330	15	5	.986
1988— Pittsburgh (N.L.)	OF	144	538	97	152	30	5	24	58	.283	72	82	17	292	5	6	.980
1989— Pittsburgh (N.L.)	OF	159	580	96	144	34	6	19	58	.248	93	93	32	365	14	6	.984
1990— Pittsburgh (N.L.)	OF	151	519	104	156	32	3	33	114	.301	93	83	52	338	•14	6	.983
1991— Pittsburgh (N.L.)	OF	153	510	95	149	28	5	25	116	.292	107	73	43	321	13	3	.991
1992— Pittsburgh (N.L.)	OF	140	473	*109	147	36	5	34	103	.311	*127	69	39	310	4	3	.991
1993— San Fran. (N.L.)■	OF	159	539	129	181	38	4	*46	*123	.336	126	79	29	310	7	5	.984
1994— San Francisco (N.L.)	OF	112	391	89	122	18	1	37	81	.312	*74	43	29	198	10	3	.986
1995— San Francisco (N.L.)	OF	•144	506	109	149	30	7	33	104	.294	*120	83	31	279	12	6	.980
1996— San Francisco (S.C.)	OF	158	517	122	159	27	3	42	129	.308	*151	76	40	286	10	6	.980
1997— San Francisco (N.L.)	OF	159	532	123	155	26	5	40	101	.291	*145	87	37	289	10	5	.984
1998— San Francisco (N.L.)	OF	156	552	120	167	44	7	37	122	.303	130	92	28	301	2	5	.984
1999— San Francisco (N.L.)	OF-DH	102	355	91	93	20	2	34	83	.262	73	62	15	177	4	3	.984
2000— San Francisco (N.L.)	OF	143	480	129	147	28	4	49	106	.306	*117	77	11	255	8	3	.989
2001— San Francisco (N.L.)	OF-DH	153	476	129	156	32	2	*73	137	.328	*177	93	13	246	8	6	.977
Major League totals (16 years)		2296	7932	1713	2313	483	71	567	1542	.292	1724	1282	484	4577	145	76	.984

DIVISION SERIES RECORD

Year Team (League)	Pos.	G	AB	R	H	2B	3B	HR	RBI	Avg.	BB	SO	SB	PO	A	E	Avg.
								BATTING							FIELDING		
1997— San Francisco (N.L.)	OF	3	12	0	3	2	0	0	2	.250	0	3	1	6	0	0	1.000
2000— San Francisco (N.L.)	OF	4	17	2	3	1	1	0	1	.176	3	4	1	10	0	0	1.000
Division series totals (2 years)		7	29	2	6	3	1	0	3	.207	3	7	2	16	0	0	1.000

CHAMPIONSHIP SERIES RECORD

RECORDS: Shares single-inning record for most hits—2 (October 13, 1992, second inning).

Year Team (League)	Pos.	G	AB	R	H	2B	3B	HR	RBI	Avg.	BB	SO	SB	PO	A	E	Avg.
								BATTING							FIELDING		
1990— Pittsburgh (N.L.)	OF	6	18	4	3	0	0	1	1	.167	6	5	2	13	0	0	1.000
1991— Pittsburgh (N.L.)	OF	7	27	1	4	1	0	0	0	.148	2	4	3	14 •·	1	1	.938
1992— Pittsburgh (N.L.)	OF	7	23	5	6	1	0	1	2	.261	6	4	1	17	0	0	1.000
Championship series totals (3 years)		20	68	10	13	2	0	1	3	.191	14	13	6	44	1	1	.978

ALL-STAR GAME RECORD

Year League	Pos.	AB	R	H	2B	3B	HR	RBI	Avg.	BB	SO	SB	PO	A	E	Avg.
							BATTING							FIELDING		
1990— National	OF	1	0	0	0	0	0	0	.000	1	0	0	2	0	0	1.000
1992— National	OF	3	1	1	1	0	0	0	.333	0	0	0	2	0	0	1.000
1993— National	OF	3	2	2	2	0	0	0	.667	0	0	0	1	0	0	1.000
1994— National	OF	3	0	0	0	0	0	1	.000	0	2	0	1	0	0	1.000
1995— National	OF	3	0	0	0	0	0	0	.000	0	1	0	0	0	0	...
1996— National	OF	3	0	1	0	0	0	0	.333	0	0	0	2	0	0	1.000
1997— National	OF	2	0	0	0	0	0	0	.000	1	1	0	2	0	0	1.000
1998— National	OF	2	1	1	0	0	1	0	.500	1	0	0	1	0	0	1.000
2000— National						Selected, did not play—injured.										
2001— National	OF	2	0	0	0	0	0	0	.000	0	1	0	0	0	0	...
All-Star Game totals (9 years)		22	4	5	3	0	1	4	.227	3	5	1	11	0	0	1.000

BONES, RICKY P

PERSONAL: Born April 7, 1969, in Salinas, Puerto Rico. ... 6-0/202. ... Throws right, bats right. ... Full name: Ricardo Bones. ... Name pronounced Bone-ess.

HIGH SCHOOL: Guayama (Puerto Rico).

TRANSACTIONS/CAREER NOTES: Signed as non-drafted free agent by San Diego Padres organization (May 13, 1986). ... Traded by Padres with SS Jose Valentin and OF Matt Mieske to Milwaukee Brewers for 3B Gary Sheffield and P Geoff Kellogg (March 27, 1992). ... Traded by Brewers with a player to be named later to New York Yankees as compensation for injured status of OF/IF Pat Listach (August 29, 1996); Yankees acquired IF Gabby Martinez to complete deal (November 5, 1996). ... Granted free agency (October 25, 1996). ... Signed by Cincinnati Reds (December 10, 1996). ... Released by Reds (May 6, 1997). ... Signed by Brewers organization (May 12, 1997). ... Traded by Brewers to Kansas City Royals organization for cash (June 26, 1997). ... Granted free agency (November 5, 1997). ... Signed by Minnesota Twins organization (January 6, 1998). ... Released by Twins (May 22, 1998). ... Signed by Royals organization (May 26, 1998). ... Granted free agency (October 29, 1998). ... Signed by Baltimore Orioles (December 21, 1998). ... On Baltimore disabled list (July 2-17, 1999). ... Released by Orioles (August 20, 1999). ... Signed by Florida Marlins organization (December 22, 1999). ... On disabled list (May 6-21, 2000). ... Granted free agency (November 1, 2000). ... Re-signed by Marlins (November 9, 2000). ... Granted free agency (November 5, 2001).

STATISTICAL NOTES: Led Texas League with 22 home runs allowed in 1989.

MISCELLANEOUS: Appeared in one game as outfielder with no chances (1993). ... Appeared in one game as pinch runner with Kansas City (1997). ... Scored a run in only appearance as pinch runner (1999).

Year League	W	L	Pct.	ERA	G	GS	CG	ShO	Sv.	IP	H	R	ER	BB	SO
1986— Spokane (N'West)	1	3	.250	5.59	18	9	0	0	0	58	63	44	36	29	46
1987— Charleston, S.C. (S.Atl.)	12	6	.706	3.65	26	26	4	1	0	170 1/3	*183	81	69	45	130
1988— Riverside (Calif.)	15	6	.714	3.64	25	25	5	2	0	175 1/3	162	80	71	64	129
1989— Wichita (Texas)	10	9	.526	5.74	24	24	2	0	0	136 1/3	162	103	87	47	88
1990— Wichita (Texas)	6	4	.600	3.48	21	21	2	1	0	137	138	66	53	45	96
— Las Vegas (PCL)	2	1	.667	3.47	5	5	0	0	0	36 1/3	45	17	14	10	25
1991— Las Vegas (PCL)	8	6	.571	4.22	23	23	1	0	0	136 1/3	155	90	64	43	95
— San Diego (N.L.)	4	6	.400	4.83	11	11	0	0	0	54	57	33	29	18	31
1992— Milwaukee (A.L.)■	9	10	.474	4.57	31	28	0	0	0	163 1/3	169	90	83	48	65

Year League	W	L	Pct.	ERA	G	GS	CG	ShO	Sv.	IP	H	R	ER	BB	SO
1993— Milwaukee (A.L.)	11	11	.500	4.86	32	31	3	0	0	203 2/3	222	122	110	63	63
1994— Milwaukee (A.L.)	10	9	.526	3.43	24	24	4	1	0	170 2/3	166	76	65	45	57
1995— Milwaukee (A.L.)	10	12	.455	4.63	32	31	3	0	0	200 1/3	218	108	103	83	77
1996— Milwaukee (A.L.)	7	14	.333	5.83	32	23	0	0	0	145	170	104	94	62	59
— New York (A.L.)■	0	0	...	14.14	4	1	0	0	0	7	14	11	11	6	4
1997— Cincinnati (N.L.)■	0	1	.000	10.19	9	2	0	0	0	17 2/3	31	22	20	11	8
— Tucson (PCL)■	5	0	1.000	2.79	8	7	0	0	0	42	40	18	13	8	22
1998— Kansas City (A.L.)■	4	7	.364	5.97	21	11	1	0	0	78 1/3	102	59	52	25	36
— Salt Lake (PCL)■	5	1	.833	3.42	8	8	0	0	0	47 1/3	41	20	18	19	41
— Omaha (PCL)■	1	2	.333	8.59	3	3	0	0	0	14 2/3	19	16	14	10	8
— Kansas City (A.L.)	2	2	.500	3.04	32	0	0	0	1	53 1/3	49	18	18	24	38
1999— Baltimore (A.L.)■	0	3	.000	5.98	30	2	0	0	0	43 2/3	59	29	29	19	26
2000— Florida (N.L.)■	2	3	.400	4.54	56	0	0	0	0	77 1/3	94	43	39	27	59
2001— Florida (N.L.)	4	4	.500	5.06	61	0	0	0	0	64	71	39	36	33	41
A.L. totals (8 years)	53	68	.438	4.77	238	151	11	1	1	1065 1/3	1169	617	565	375	425
N.L. totals (4 years)	10	14	.417	5.24	137	13	0	0	0	213	253	137	124	89	139
Major League totals (11 years)	63	82	.434	4.85	375	164	11	1	1	1278 1/3	1422	754	689	464	564

ALL-STAR GAME RECORD

Year League	W	L	Pct.	ERA	GS	CG	ShO	Sv.	IP	H	R	ER	BB	SO
1994— American					Did not play.									

BONG, JUNG — P — BRAVES

PERSONAL: Born July 15, 1980, in Seoul, South Korea. ... 6-3/175. ... Throws left, bats left. ... Full name: Jung Keun Bong.
TRANSACTIONS/CAREER NOTES: Signed as non-drafted free agent by Atlanta Braves organization (November 6, 1997).

Year League	W	L	Pct.	ERA	G	GS	CG	ShO	Sv.	IP	H	R	ER	BB	SO
1998— Gulf Coast Braves (GCL)	1	1	.500	1.49	11	10	0	0	0	48 1/3	31	9	8	14	56
1999— Macon (S.Atl.)	6	5	.545	3.98	26	20	0	0	1	108 2/3	111	61	48	50	100
2000— Macon (S.Atl.)	7	7	.500	4.23	20	19	0	0	0	112 2/3	119	65	53	45	90
— Myrtle Beach (Caro.)	3	1	.750	2.18	7	6	0	0	0	41 1/3	33	14	10	7	37
2001— Myrtle Beach (Caro.)	13	9	.591	3.00	28	•28	0	0	0	168	151	67	56	47	145

BONILLA, BOBBY — OF

PERSONAL: Born February 23, 1963, in New York. ... 6-3/240. ... Bats both, throws right. ... Full name: Roberto Martin Antonio Bonilla. ... Name pronounced bo-NEE-yah.
HIGH SCHOOL: Lehman (Bronx, N.Y.).
COLLEGE: New York Technical College.
TRANSACTIONS/CAREER NOTES: Signed as non-drafted free agent by Pittsburgh Pirates organization (July 11, 1981). ... On Pittsburgh disabled list (March 25-July 19, 1985). ... Selected by Chicago White Sox from Pirates organization in Rule 5 major league draft (December 10, 1985). ... Traded by White Sox to Pittsburgh Pirates for P Jose DeLeon (July 23, 1986). ... Granted free agency (October 28, 1991). ... Signed by New York Mets (December 2, 1991). ... On suspended list (July 27-28, 1992). ... On disabled list (August 3-19, 1992). ... Traded by Mets with a player to be named later to Baltimore Orioles for OF Alex Ochoa and OF Damon Buford (July 28, 1995); Orioles acquired P Jimmy Williams to complete deal (August 17, 1995). ... Granted free agency (November 18, 1996). ... Signed by Florida Marlins (November 22, 1996). ... On Florida disabled list (March 22-April 12, 1998). ... Traded by Marlins with OF Gary Sheffield, C Charles Johnson, OF Jim Eisenreich and P Manuel Barrios to Los Angeles Dodgers for C Mike Piazza and 3B Todd Zeile (May 15, 1998). ... On Los Angeles disabled list (June 18-July 3 and July 15-August 5, 1998). ... Traded by Dodgers to Mets for P Mel Rojas (November 11, 1998). ... On New York disabled list (May 11-31 and July 3-September 1, 1999); included rehabilitation assignment to Norfolk (August 27-September 1). ... Released by Mets (January 3, 2000). ... Signed by Atlanta Braves organization (January 28, 2000). ... Granted free agency (October 31, 2000). ... Signed by St. Louis Cardinals (January 5, 2001). ... On disabled list (March 25-April 9, 2001). ... On suspended list (June 4-5, 2001). ... Granted free agency (November 5, 2001).
RECORDS: Holds N.L. career record for most home runs by switch-hitter—247. ... Shares major league record for most doubles in one inning—2 (July 21, 1995, eighth inning). ... Shares A.L. single-season record for most sacrifice flies—17 (1996).
HONORS: Named third baseman on THE SPORTING NEWS N.L. All-Star team (1988). ... Named third baseman on THE SPORTING NEWS N.L. Silver Slugger team (1988). ... Named outfielder on THE SPORTING NEWS N.L. All-Star team (1990 and 1991). ... Named outfielder on THE SPORTING NEWS N.L. Silver Slugger team (1990 and 1991).
STATISTICAL NOTES: Led Eastern League outfielders with 15 errors in 1984. ... Switch-hit home runs in one game six times (July 3, 1987; April 6, 1988; April 23 and June 10, 1993; May 4, 1994; and May 12, 1995). ... Led N.L. third basemen with 489 total chances in 1988. ... Led N.L. third basemen with 35 errors in 1989. ... Led N.L. third basemen with 31 double plays in 1989. ... Led N.L. with 15 sacrifice flies in 1990. ... Had 20-game hitting streak (September 10-October 1, 1995). ... Led A.L. with 17 sacrifice flies in 1996. ... Career major league grand slams: 9.

Year Team (League)	Pos.	G	AB	R	H	2B	3B	HR	RBI	Avg.	BB	SO	SB	PO	A	E	Avg.
1981— GC Pirates (GCL)	1B-C-3B	22	69	6	15	5	0	0	7	.217	7	17	2	124	23	5	.967
1982— GC Pirates (GCL)	1B	47	167	20	38	3	0	5	26	.228	11	20	2	318	36	*14	.962
1983— Alexandria (Caro.)	OF-1B	•136	504	88	129	19	7	11	59	.256	78	105	28	259	12	15	.948
1984— Nashua (East.)	OF-1B	136	484	74	128	19	5	11	71	.264	49	89	15	312	8	†15	.955
1985— Prince William (Caro.)	1B-3B	39	130	15	34	4	1	3	11	.262	16	29	1	180	9	2	.990
1986— Chicago (A.L.)■	OF-1B	75	234	27	63	10	2	2	26	.269	33	49	4	361	22	2	.995
— Pittsburgh (N.L.)■	OF-1B-3B	63	192	28	46	6	2	1	17	.240	29	39	4	90	16	3	.972
1987— Pittsburgh (N.L.)	3B-OF-1B	141	466	58	140	33	3	15	77	.300	39	64	3	142	139	16	.946
1988— Pittsburgh (N.L.)	3B	159	584	87	160	32	7	24	100	.274	85	82	3	121	*336	*32	.935
1989— Pittsburgh (N.L.)	3B-1B-OF	•163	616	96	173	37	10	24	86	.281	76	93	8	190	334	†35	.937
1990— Pittsburgh (N.L.)	OF-3B-1B	160	625	112	175	39	7	32	120	.280	45	103	4	315	35	15	.959
1991— Pittsburgh (N.L.)	OF-3B-1B	157	577	102	174	*44	6	18	100	.302	90	67	2	247	144	15	.963
1992— New York (N.L.)■	OF-1B	128	438	62	109	23	0	19	70	.249	66	73	4	277	9	4	.986
1993— New York (N.L.)	OF-3B-1B	139	502	81	133	21	3	34	87	.265	72	96	3	238	112	17	.954
1994— New York (N.L.)	3B	108	403	60	117	24	1	20	67	.290	55	101	1	78	215	*18	.942

Year Team (League)	Pos.	G	AB	R	H	2B	3B	HR	RBI	Avg.	BB	SO	SB	PO	A	E	Avg.
1995— New York (N.L.)..........	3B-OF-1B	80	317	49	103	25	4	18	53	.325	31	48	0	164	80	14	.946
— Baltimore (A.L.)■....	OF-3B	61	237	47	79	12	4	10	46	.333	23	31	0	80	48	5	.962
1996— Baltimore (A.L.).........OF-DH-1B-3B		159	595	107	171	27	5	28	116	.287	75	85	1	214	12	6	.974
1997— Florida (N.L.)■....	3B-DH-1B	153	562	77	167	39	3	17	96	.297	73	94	6	107	225	22	.938
1998— Florida (N.L.)....	3B	28	97	11	27	5	0	4	15	.278	12	22	0	18	41	5	.922
— Los Angeles (N.L.)■..	3B-OF	72	236	28	56	6	1	7	30	.237	29	37	1	56	84	13	.915
1999— New York (N.L.)■......	OF-1B-DH	60	119	12	19	5	0	4	18	.160	19	16	0	59	4	2	.969
— Norfolk (I.L.)......	DH	3	13	1	3	0	0	0	1	.231	0	1	0	0	0	0	...
2000— Atlanta (N.L.)■..........	OF-DH-3B	114	239	23	61	13	3	5	28	.255	37	51	0	51	1	4	.929
2001— St. Louis (N.L.)■........	3B-OF-DH-P	93	174	17	37	7	0	5	21	.213	23	53	1	239	11	2	.992
American League totals (3 years)		295	1066	181	313	49	11	40	188	.294	131	165	5	655	82	13	.983
National League totals (15 years)		1818	6147	903	1697	359	50	247	985	.276	781	1039	40	2392	1786	217	.951
Major League totals (16 years)		2113	7213	1084	2010	408	61	287	1173	.279	912	1204	45	3047	1868	230	.955

DIVISION SERIES RECORD

Year Team (League)	Pos.	G	AB	R	H	2B	3B	HR	RBI	Avg.	BB	SO	SB	PO	A	E	Avg.
1996— Baltimore (A.L.).........	OF	4	15	4	3	0	0	2	5	.200	4	6	0	9	0	1	.900
1997— Florida (N.L.).........	3B	3	12	1	4	0	0	1	3	.333	2	1	0	3	5	0	1.000
1999— New York (N.L.).........	PH	2	1	1	0	0	0	0	0	.000	1	0	0	...	...	...	...
2000— Atlanta (N.L.).............	PH-OF	3	2	0	0	0	0	0	0	.000	2	0	0	0	0	0	...
2001— St. Louis (N.L.).........								Did not play.									
Division series totals (4 years)		12	30	6	7	0	0	3	8	.233	9	7	0	12	5	1	.944

CHAMPIONSHIP SERIES RECORD
RECORDS: Shares single-game record for most strikeouts—4 (October 10, 1996).

Year Team (League)	Pos.	G	AB	R	H	2B	3B	HR	RBI	Avg.	BB	SO	SB	PO	A	E	Avg.
1990— Pittsburgh (N.L.)	OF-3B	6	21	0	4	1	0	0	1	.190	3	1	0	4	5	1	.900
1991— Pittsburgh (N.L.)	OF	7	23	2	7	2	0	0	1	.304	6	2	0	12	1	0	1.000
1996— Baltimore (A.L.).........	OF	5	20	1	1	0	0	1	2	.050	1	4	0	11	0	0	1.000
1997— Florida (N.L.).........	3B	6	23	3	6	1	0	0	4	.261	1	6	0	5	13	0	1.000
1999— New York (N.L.).........	PH	3	3	0	1	0	0	0	0	.333	0	2	0	...	...	...	...
Championship series totals (5 years)		27	90	6	19	4	0	1	8	.211	11	15	0	32	19	1	.981

WORLD SERIES RECORD
NOTES: Member of World Series championship team (1997).

Year Team (League)	Pos.	G	AB	R	H	2B	3B	HR	RBI	Avg.	BB	SO	SB	PO	A	E	Avg.
1997— Florida (N.L.)	3B	7	29	5	6	1	0	1	3	.207	3	5	0	3	20	2	.920

ALL-STAR GAME RECORD

Year League	Pos.	AB	R	H	2B	3B	HR	RBI	Avg.	BB	SO	SB	PO	A	E	Avg.
1988— National....................	3B	4	0	0	0	0	0	0	.000	0	0	0	0	2	0	1.000
1989— National....................	PH-DH	2	0	2	0	0	0	0	1.000	0	0	0	...	...	...	...
1990— National....................	1B	1	0	0	0	0	0	0	.000	0	0	0	1	0	0	1.000
1991— National....................	DH	4	0	2	0	0	0	1	.500	0	1	0	...	...	...	...
1993— National....................	OF	1	0	1	0	0	0	0	1.000	0	0	0	2	0	0	1.000
1995— National....................	3B	1	0	0	0	0	0	0	.000	0	1	0	0	0	0	...
All-Star Game totals (6 years)		13	0	5	0	0	0	1	.385	0	2	0	3	2	0	1.000

RECORD AS PITCHER

Year League	W	L	Pct.	ERA	G	GS	CG	ShO	Sv.	IP	H	R	ER	BB	SO
2001—St. Louis (N.L.)	0	0	...	18.00	1	0	0	0	0	1	3	2	2	1	0

BOOKER, CHRIS   P   REDS

PERSONAL: Born December 9, 1976, in Monroeville, Ala. ... 6-3/230. ... Throws right, bats right. ... Full name: Christopher Scott Booker.
HIGH SCHOOL: Monroe County (Monroeville, Ala.).
TRANSACTIONS/CAREER NOTES: Selected by Chicago Cubs organization in 20th round of free-agent draft (June 1, 1995). ... Traded by Cubs with P Ben Shafer to Cincinnati Reds for OF Michael Tucker (July 20, 2001).
STATISTICAL NOTES: Led Southern League with 61 games pitched in 2001.

Year League	W	L	Pct.	ERA	G	GS	CG	ShO	Sv.	IP	H	R	ER	BB	SO
1995— Gulf Coast Cubs (GCL).......	3	2	.600	2.76	13	7	0	0	1	42 1/3	36	22	13	16	43
1996— Daytona (FSL)	0	0	...	0.00	1	1	0	0	0	2 1/3	1	1	0	3	2
— Williamsport (NY-Penn)	4	6	.400	5.31	14	14	0	0	0	61	57	51	36	51	52
1997— Williamsport (NY-Penn)	1	5	.167	3.35	24	3	0	0	0	45 2/3	39	20	17	25	60
1998— Rockford (Midw.)............	1	2	.333	3.38	44	1	0	0	4	64	47	32	24	53	78
1999— Daytona (FSL)	2	5	.286	3.95	42	0	0	0	6	73	72	45	32	37	68
2000— Daytona (FSL)	0	2	.000	2.28	31	0	0	0	10	27 2/3	25	12	7	14	34
— West Tenn (Sou.)	1	0	1.000	3.68	12	0	0	0	0	14 2/3	10	8	6	12	21
2001— West Tenn (Sou.)	2	6	.250	4.33	45	0	0	0	1	52	39	29	25	36	76
— Chattanooga (Sou.)■........	2	0	1.000	3.94	§16	0	0	0	1	16	13	7	7	11	25

BOONE, AARON   3B   REDS

PERSONAL: Born March 9, 1973, in La Mesa, Calif. ... 6-2/200. ... Bats right, throws right. ... Full name: Aaron John Boone. ... Son of Bob Boone, manager, Cincinnati Reds; and catcher with three major league teams (1972-90); brother of Bret Boone, second baseman, Seattle Mariners; grandson of Ray Boone, major league infielder with six teams (1948-60); and nephew of Rodney Boone, minor league catcher/outfielder (1972-75).

HIGH SCHOOL: Villa Park (Calif.).

COLLEGE: Southern California.

TRANSACTIONS/CAREER NOTES: Selected by California Angels organization in 43rd round of free-agent draft (June 3, 1991); did not sign. ... Selected by Cincinnati Reds organization in third round of free-agent draft (June 2, 1994). ... On disabled list (July 10, 2000-remainder of season). ... On Cincinnati disabled list (May 15-June 15, August 15-September 1 and September 24, 2001-remainder of season); included rehabilitation assignment to Louisville (June 14-15).

STATISTICAL NOTES: Led Pioneer League third basemen with 46 putouts, 156 assists, 220 total chances and 13 double plays in 1994. ... Led Southern League third basemen with 101 putouts, 347 total chances and 28 double plays in 1996. ... Led American Association third basemen with 76 putouts, 241 assists, 336 total chances and 27 double plays in 1997. ... Career major league grand slams: 1.

Year—Team (League)	Pos.	G	AB	R	H	2B	3B	HR	RBI	Avg.	BB	SO	SB	PO	A	E	Avg.
								BATTING							FIELDING		
1994—Billings (Pio.)	3B-1B	67	256	48	70	15	5	7	55	.273	36	35	6	†60	†158	18	.924
1995—Chattanooga (Sou.)....	3B	23	66	6	15	3	0	0	3	.227	5	12	2	14	28	6	.875
—Win.-Salem (Caro.)	3B	108	395	61	103	19	1	14	50	.261	43	77	11	59	*272	21	*.940
1996—Chattanooga (Sou.)	3B-SS-DH	136	*548	86	158	*44	7	17	95	.288	38	77	21	†123	257	22	.945
1997—Indianapolis (A.A.)......	3B-SS-2B	131	476	79	138	30	4	22	75	.290	40	81	12	†112	†269	24	.941
—Cincinnati (N.L.)	3B	16	49	5	12	1	0	0	5	.245	2	5	1	11	22	3	.917
1998—Cincinnati (N.L.)	3B-2B-SS	58	181	24	51	13	2	2	28	.282	15	36	6	37	97	8	.944
—Indianapolis (I.L.).......	3B-2B-SS	87	332	56	80	18	1	7	38	.241	31	71	17	72	243	19	.943
1999—Cincinnati (N.L.)	3B-SS	139	472	56	132	26	5	14	72	.280	30	79	17	87	258	15	.958
—Indianapolis (I.L.).......	3B-2B-SS	11	41	6	14	2	1	0	7	.341	3	4	2	11	29	3	.930
2000—Cincinnati (N.L.)	3B-SS	84	291	44	83	18	0	12	43	.285	24	52	6	63	157	6	.965
2001—Cincinnati (N.L.)	3B	103	381	54	112	26	2	14	62	.294	29	71	6	72	207	19	.936
—Louisville (I.L.)	3B	1	4	0	1	0	0	0	0	.250	0	0	0	1	2	0	1.000
Major League totals (5 years)		400	1374	183	390	84	9	42	210	.284	100	243	36	270	741	53	.950

BOONE, BRET   2B   MARINERS

PERSONAL: Born April 6, 1969, in El Cajon, Calif. ... 5-10/180. ... Bats right, throws right. ... Full name: Bret Robert Boone. ... Son of Bob Boone, manager, Cincinnati Reds; and catcher with three major league teams (1972-90); brother of Aaron Boone, third baseman, Cincinnati Reds; grandson of Ray Boone, major league infielder with six teams (1948-60); and nephew of Rodney Boone, minor league catcher/outfielder (1972-75).

HIGH SCHOOL: El Dorado (Yorba Linda, Calif.).

COLLEGE: Southern California.

TRANSACTIONS/CAREER NOTES: Selected by Minnesota Twins organization in 28th round of free-agent draft (June 2, 1987); did not sign. ... Selected by Seattle Mariners organization in fifth round of free-agent draft (June 4, 1990). ... Traded by Mariners with P Erik Hanson to Cincinnati Reds for P Bobby Ayala and C Dan Wilson (November 2, 1993). ... On disabled list (April 1-16, 1996). ... Traded by Reds with P Mike Remlinger to Atlanta Braves for P Denny Neagle, OF Michael Tucker and P Rob Bell (November 10, 1998). ... Traded by Braves with OF/1B Ryan Klesko and P Jason Shiell to San Diego Padres for 2B Quilvio Veras, 1B Wally Joyner and OF Reggie Sanders (December 22, 1999). ... On disabled list (August 27, 2000-remainder of season). ... Granted free agency (October 31, 2000). ... Signed by Mariners (December 22, 2000). ... Granted free agency (November 5, 2001). ... Re-signed by Mariners (January 16, 2002).

RECORDS: Holds major league single-season record for highest fielding percentage by second baseman (100 or more games)—.997 (1997). ... Holds A.L. single-season record for most home runs by second baseman—36 (2001).

HONORS: Won N.L. Gold Glove at second base (1998). ... Named second baseman on A.L. Silver Slugger team (2001). ... Named second baseman on THE SPORTING NEWS A.L. All-Star team (2001).

STATISTICAL NOTES: Tied for Southern League lead in grounding into double plays with 21 in 1991. ... Led Southern League second basemen with 288 putouts in 1991. ... Led Pacific Coast League second basemen with 90 double plays in 1992. ... Led N.L. second basemen with 106 double plays in 1995. ... Hit three home runs in one game (September 20, 1998; and June 23, 2000). ... Career major league grand slams: 2.

Year—Team (League)	Pos.	G	AB	R	H	2B	3B	HR	RBI	Avg.	BB	SO	SB	PO	A	E	Avg.
								BATTING							FIELDING		
1990—Peninsula (Caro.)	2B	74	255	42	68	13	2	8	38	.267	47	57	5	154	216	19	.951
1991—Jacksonville (Sou.).....	2B-3B	•139	475	64	121	18	1	19	75	.255	72	123	9	†300	369	21	.970
1992—Calgary (PCL)............	2B-SS	118	439	73	138	26	5	13	73	.314	60	88	17	268	366	10	.984
—Seattle (A.L.)...........	2B-3B	33	129	15	25	4	0	4	15	.194	4	34	1	72	96	6	.966
1993—Calgary (PCL)............	2B	71	274	48	91	18	3	8	56	.332	28	58	3	146	180	8	.976
—Seattle (A.L.)...........	2B-DH	76	271	31	68	12	2	12	38	.251	17	52	2	140	177	3	.991
1994—Cincinnati (N.L.)■.......	2B-3B	108	381	59	122	25	2	12	68	.320	24	74	3	191	269	12	.975
1995—Cincinnati (N.L.)	2B	138	513	63	137	34	2	15	68	.267	41	84	5	*311	362	4	*.994
1996—Cincinnati (N.L.)	2B	142	520	56	121	21	3	12	69	.233	31	100	3	315	381	6	*.991
1997—Cincinnati (N.L.)	2B	139	443	40	99	25	1	7	46	.223	45	101	5	271	334	2	*.997
—Indianapolis (A.A.)......	2B	3	7	1	2	1	0	0	1	.286	2	2	1	6	10	0	1.000
1998—Cincinnati (N.L.)	2B	157	583	76	155	38	1	24	95	.266	48	104	6	329	416	9	.988
1999—Atlanta (N.L.)■..........	2B	152	608	102	153	38	1	20	63	.252	47	112	14	270	424	13	.982
2000—San Diego (N.L.)■	2B	127	463	61	116	18	2	19	74	.251	50	97	8	292	334	15	.977
2001—Seattle (A.L.)■..........	2B-DH	158	623	118	206	37	3	37	*141	.331	40	110	5	286	409	10	.986
American League totals (3 years)		267	1023	164	299	53	5	53	194	.292	61	196	8	498	682	19	.984
National League totals (7 years)		963	3511	457	903	199	12	109	483	.257	286	672	44	1979	2520	61	.987
Major League totals (10 years)		1230	4534	621	1202	252	17	162	677	.265	347	868	52	2477	3202	80	.986

DIVISION SERIES RECORD

RECORDS: Shares N.L. single-game record for most at-bats—6 (October 8, 1999).

Year—Team (League)	Pos.	G	AB	R	H	2B	3B	HR	RBI	Avg.	BB	SO	SB	PO	A	E	Avg.
								BATTING							FIELDING		
1995—Cincinnati (N.L.)	2B	3	10	4	3	1	0	1	1	.300	1	3	1	7	5	0	1.000
1999—Atlanta (N.L.)............	2B	4	19	3	9	1	0	0	1	.474	0	4	1	11	15	0	1.000
2001—Seattle (A.L.)	2B	5	21	1	2	0	0	0	0	.095	1	11	1	12	12	1	.960
Division series totals (3 years)		12	50	8	14	2	0	1	2	.280	2	18	3	30	32	1	.984

RECORDS: Shares A.L. single-game record for most runs batted in—5 (October 20, 2001).

Year Team (League)	Pos.	G	AB	R	H	2B	3B	HR	RBI	Avg.	BB	SO	SB	PO	A	E	Avg.
							BATTING								FIELDING		
1995— Cincinnati (N.L.)	2B	4	14	1	3	0	0	0	0	.214	1	2	0	9	13	0	1.000
1999— Atlanta (N.L.)	2B	6	22	2	4	1	0	0	1	.182	1	7	2	5	14	0	1.000
2001— Seattle (A.L.)	2B	5	19	2	6	0	0	2	6	.316	2	2	0	9	13	0	1.000
Championship series totals (3 years)		15	55	5	13	1	0	2	7	.236	4	11	2	23	40	0	1.000

WORLD SERIES RECORD

Year Team (League)	Pos.	G	AB	R	H	2B	3B	HR	RBI	Avg.	BB	SO	SB	PO	A	E	Avg.
							BATTING								FIELDING		
1999— Atlanta (N.L.)	2B-PH	4	13	1	7	4	0	0	3	.538	1	3	0	4	9	0	1.000

ALL-STAR GAME RECORD

Year League	Pos.	AB	R	H	2B	3B	HR	RBI	Avg.	BB	SO	SB	PO	A	E	Avg.
							BATTING							FIELDING		
1998— National....................							Did not play.									
2001— American..................	2B	2	0	0	0	0	0	0	.000	0	0	0	1	0	0	1.000

B

BORBON, PEDRO   P   BLUE JAYS

PERSONAL: Born November 15, 1967, in Mao, Dominican Republic. ... 6-1/224. ... Throws left, bats left. ... Full name: Pedro Felix Borbon Jr. ... Son of Pedro Borbon, pitcher with four major league teams (1969-80). ... Name pronounced bor-BONE.

HIGH SCHOOL: DeWitt Clinton (Sioux, N.J.).

JUNIOR COLLEGE: Ranger (Texas) Junior College.

TRANSACTIONS/CAREER NOTES: Selected by Milwaukee Brewers organization in 35th round of free-agent draft (June 3, 1985); did not sign. ... Selected by Los Angeles Dodgers organization in secondary phase of free-agent draft (January 14, 1986); did not sign. ... Signed as non-drafted free agent by Chicago White Sox organization (June 4, 1988). ... Released by White Sox (April 1, 1989). ... Signed by Atlanta Braves organization (August 25, 1989). ... On Atlanta disabled list (April 8-26 and August 23, 1996-remainder of season); included rehabilitation assignment to Greenville (April 23-26). ... On disabled list (March 30, 1997-entire season). ... On Atlanta disabled list (March 29, 1998-entire season); included rehabilitation assignments to Macon (June 4-7), Greenville (June 9-July 5 and July 9-14) and Richmond (July 16-August 31 and September 1-8). ... Granted free agency (October 1, 1998). ... Signed by Dodgers organization (December 30, 1998). ... Traded by Dodgers with OF Raul Mondesi to Toronto Blue Jays for OF Shawn Green and 2B Jorge Nunez (November 8, 1999).

STATISTICAL NOTES: Led Gulf Coast League with 14 balks in 1988.

Year League	W	L	Pct.	ERA	G	GS	CG	ShO	Sv.	IP	H	R	ER	BB	SO
1988— GC White Sox (GCL)	5	3	.625	2.41	16	11	1	1	1	74^2/₃	52	28	20	17	67
1989—							Did not play.								
1990— Burlington (Midw.)/■.........	11	3	.786	1.47	14	14	6	2	0	97^2/₃	73	25	16	23	76
— Durham (Caro.)	4	5	.444	5.43	11	11	0	0	0	61^1/₃	73	40	37	16	37
1991— Durham (Caro.)	4	3	.571	2.27	37	6	1	0	5	91	85	40	23	35	79
— Greenville (Sou.)	0	1	.000	2.79	4	4	0	0	0	29	23	12	9	10	22
1992— Greenville (Sou.)	8	2	.800	3.06	39	10	0	0	3	94	73	36	32	42	79
— Atlanta (N.L.)	0	1	.000	6.75	2	0	0	0	0	1^1/₃	2	1	1	1	1
1993— Richmond (I.L.)..................	5	5	.500	4.23	52	0	0	0	1	76^2/₃	71	40	36	42	95
— Atlanta (N.L.)	0	0	...	21.60	3	0	0	0	0	1^2/₃	3	4	4	3	2
1994— Richmond (I.L.)..................	3	4	.429	2.79	59	0	0	0	4	80^2/₃	66	29	25	41	82
1995— Atlanta (N.L.)	2	2	.500	3.09	41	0	0	0	2	32	29	12	11	17	33
1996— Atlanta (N.L.)	3	0	1.000	2.75	43	0	0	0	1	36	26	12	11	7	31
— Greenville (Sou.)	0	0	...	0.00	1	0	0	0	0	1	0	0	0	0	0
1997— Atlanta (N.L.)							Did not play.								
1998— Macon (S.Atl.)	0	0	...	9.00	3	0	0	0	0	3	4	3	3	1	3
— Greenville (Sou.)	0	2	.000	4.74	16	0	0	0	0	19	21	14	10	14	10
— Richmond (I.L.)..................	0	1	.000	5.70	20	0	0	0	0	23^2/₃	29	17	15	8	15
1999— Los Angeles (N.L.)/■.........	4	3	.571	4.09	70	0	0	0	1	50^2/₃	39	23	23	29	33
2000— Toronto (A.L.)/■...............	1	1	.500	6.48	59	0	0	0	1	41^2/₃	45	37	30	38	29
2001— Toronto (A.L.)....................	2	4	.333	3.71	71	0	0	0	0	53^1/₃	48	24	22	12	45
A.L. totals (2 years)	3	5	.375	4.93	130	0	0	0	1	95	93	61	52	50	74
N.L. totals (5 years)	9	6	.600	3.70	159	0	0	0	4	121^2/₃	99	52	50	57	100
Major League totals (7 years)	12	11	.522	4.24	289	0	0	0	5	216^2/₃	192	113	102	107	174

DIVISION SERIES RECORD

Year League	W	L	Pct.	ERA	G	GS	CG	ShO	Sv.	IP	H	R	ER	BB	SO
1995— Atlanta (N.L.)	0	0	...	0.00	1	0	0	0	0	1	1	0	0	0	3

CHAMPIONSHIP SERIES RECORD

Year League	W	L	Pct.	ERA	G	GS	CG	ShO	Sv.	IP	H	R	ER	BB	SO
1995— Atlanta (N.L.)							Did not play.								

WORLD SERIES RECORD

NOTES: Member of World Series championship team (1995).

Year League	W	L	Pct.	ERA	G	GS	CG	ShO	Sv.	IP	H	R	ER	BB	SO
1995— Atlanta (N.L.)	0	0	...	0.00	1	0	0	0	1	1	0	0	0	0	2

BORDERS, PAT   C

PERSONAL: Born May 14, 1963, in Columbus, Ohio. ... 6-2/200. ... Bats right, throws right. ... Full name: Patrick Lance Borders. ... Brother of Todd Borders, minor league catcher (1988).

HIGH SCHOOL: Lake Wales (Fla.).

TRANSACTIONS/CAREER NOTES: Selected by Toronto Blue Jays organization in sixth round of free-agent draft (June 7, 1982). ... On Toronto disabled list (July 5-August 19, 1988); included rehabilitation assignment to Syracuse (July 30-August 19). ... Granted free agency (October 21, 1994).

... Signed by Kansas City Royals (April 10, 1995). ... Traded by Royals to Houston Astros for a player to be named later (August 12, 1995); Royals acquired P Rick Huisman to complete deal (August 17, 1995). ... On Houston suspended list (September 8-14, 1995). ... Granted free agency (November 6, 1995). ... Signed by St. Louis Cardinals organization (January 10, 1996). ... Traded by Cardinals to California Angels for P Ben VanRyn (June 15, 1996). ... Traded by Angels to Chicago White Sox for P Robert Ellis (July 27, 1996). ... Granted free agency (November 8, 1996). ... Signed by Cleveland Indians organization (December 13, 1996). ... Granted free agency (November 7, 1997). ... Re-signed by Indians organization (December 17, 1997). ... Granted free agency (November 3, 1998). ... Re-signed by Indians organization (February 26, 1999). ... Released by Indians (August 30, 1999). ... Signed by Blue Jays (August 31, 1999). ... Granted free agency (November 11, 1999). ... Signed by Tampa Bay Devil Rays (January 27, 2000). ... Contract sold by Devil Rays to Seattle Mariners organization (August 27, 2001). ... Granted free agency (November 7, 2001).

STATISTICAL NOTES: Tied for Southern League lead with 16 passed balls in 1987. ... Led A.L. catchers with 880 total chances in 1992 and 962 in 1993. ... Led A.L. with nine passed balls in 1994. ... Career major league grand slams: 1.

MISCELLANEOUS: Member of 2000 U.S. Olympic baseball team.

						BATTING									FIELDING		
Year Team (League)	Pos.	G	AB	R	H	2B	3B	HR	RBI	Avg.	BB	SO	SB	PO	A	E	Avg.
1982—Medicine Hat (Pio.)	3B	61	217	30	66	12	2	5	33	.304	24	52	1	23	96	*25	.826
1983—Florence (S.Atl.)	3B	131	457	62	125	31	4	5	54	.274	46	116	4	70	233	*41	.881
1984—Florence (S.Atl.)	1B-3B-OF	131	467	69	129	32	5	12	85	.276	56	109	3	650	77	25	.967
1985—Kinston (Caro.)	1B	127	460	43	120	16	1	10	60	.261	45	116	6	854	42	*20	.978
1986—Florence (S.Atl.)	C-OF	16	40	8	15	7	0	3	9	.375	2	9	0	22	1	0	1.000
—Knoxville (Sou.)	C-1B	12	34	3	12	1	0	2	5	.353	1	6	0	45	5	3	.943
—Kinston (Caro.)	C-1B-OF	49	174	24	57	10	0	6	26	.328	10	42	0	211	26	7	.971
1987—Dunedin (FSL)	1B	3	11	0	4	0	0	0	1	.364	0	3	0	21	1	0	1.000
—Knoxville (Sou.)	C-3B	94	349	44	102	14	1	11	51	.292	20	56	2	432	49	12	.976
1988—Toronto (A.L.) C-DH-2B-3B		56	154	15	42	6	3	5	21	.273	3	24	0	205	19	7	.970
—Syracuse (I.L.)	C	35	120	11	29	8	0	3	14	.242	16	22	0	202	17	2	.991
1989—Toronto (A.L.)	C-DH	94	241	22	62	11	1	3	29	.257	11	45	2	261	27	6	.980
1990—Toronto (A.L.)	C-DH	125	346	36	99	24	2	15	49	.286	18	57	0	515	46	4	.993
1991—Toronto (A.L.)	C	105	291	22	71	17	0	5	36	.244	11	45	0	505	48	4	.993
1992—Toronto (A.L.)	C	138	480	47	116	26	2	13	53	.242	33	75	1	784	*88	8	.991
1993—Toronto (A.L.)	C	138	488	38	124	30	0	9	55	.254	20	66	2	869	*80	*13	.986
1994—Toronto (A.L.)	C	85	295	24	73	13	1	3	26	.247	15	50	1	583	*60	8	.988
1995—Kansas City (A.L.)■ ...	C-DH	52	143	14	33	8	1	4	13	.231	7	22	0	182	18	0	1.000
—Houston (N.L.)■	C	11	35	1	4	0	0	0	0	.114	2	7	0	70	5	1	.987
1996—St. Louis (N.L.)■	C-1B	26	69	3	22	3	0	0	4	.319	1	14	0	117	9	3	.977
—California (A.L.)■	C	19	57	6	13	3	0	2	8	.228	3	11	0	111	14	2	.984
—Chicago (A.L.)■	C-DH	31	94	6	26	1	0	3	6	.277	5	18	0	144	16	3	.982
1997—Cleveland (A.L.)■	C	54	159	17	47	7	1	4	15	.296	9	27	0	312	19	0	1.000
1998—Cleveland (A.L.)	C-3B	54	160	12	38	6	0	0	6	.238	10	40	0	283	20	8	.974
1999—Buffalo (I.L.)	C-DH	55	198	17	47	7	0	5	23	.237	12	31	0	316	25	5	.986
—Cleveland (A.L.)	C	8	20	2	6	0	1	0	3	.300	0	3	0	32	1	2	.943
—Toronto (A.L.)	DH-C	6	14	1	3	0	0	1	3	.214	1	2	0	7	2	0	1.000
2000—Durham (I.L.)■	C-1B	96	348	44	95	16	0	12	55	.273	20	66	7	520	63	3	.995
2001—Durham (I.L.)	C-1B	87	313	26	74	15	1	2	28	.236	16	61	3	325	31	4	.989
—Tacoma (PCL)■	C	3	11	2	3	0	0	1	2	.273	1	1	0	20	4	0	1.000
—Seattle (A.L.)	C	5	6	1	3	0	0	0	0	.500	0	1	0	10	2	1	.923
American League totals (13 years)		969	2948	263	756	152	12	67	323	.256	146	486	6	4803	460	66	.988
National League totals (2 years)		37	104	4	26	3	0	0	4	.250	3	21	0	187	14	4	.980
Major League totals (13 years)		1006	3052	267	782	155	12	67	327	.256	149	507	6	4990	474	70	.987

CHAMPIONSHIP SERIES RECORD

						BATTING									FIELDING		
Year Team (League)	Pos.	G	AB	R	H	2B	3B	HR	RBI	Avg.	BB	SO	SB	PO	A	E	Avg.
1989—Toronto (A.L.)	PH-C	1	1	0	1	0	0	1	1.000	0	0	0	1	0	0	1.000
1991—Toronto (A.L.)	C	5	19	0	5	1	0	0	2	.263	0	0	0	38	4	2	.955
1992—Toronto (A.L.)	C	6	22	3	7	0	0	1	3	.318	1	1	0	38	3	1	.976
1993—Toronto (A.L.)	C	6	24	1	6	1	0	0	3	.250	0	6	1	41	4	0	1.000
Championship series totals (4 years)		18	66	4	19	2	0	1	9	.288	1	7	1	118	11	3	.977

WORLD SERIES RECORD

NOTES: Named Most Valuable Player (1992). ... Member of World Series championship team (1992 and 1993).

						BATTING									FIELDING		
Year Team (League)	Pos.	G	AB	R	H	2B	3B	HR	RBI	Avg.	BB	SO	SB	PO	A	E	Avg.
1992—Toronto (A.L.)............	C	6	20	2	9	3	0	1	3	.450	2	1	0	48	5	1	.981
1993—Toronto (A.L.)............	C	6	23	2	7	0	0	0	1	.304	2	1	0	50	2	1	.981
World Series totals (2 years)		12	43	4	16	3	0	1	4	.372	4	2	0	98	7	2	.981

BORDICK, MIKE   SS   ORIOLES

PERSONAL: Born July 21, 1965, in Marquette, Mich. ... 5-11/175. ... Bats right, throws right. ... Full name: Michael Todd Bordick.

HIGH SCHOOL: Hampden (Maine) Academy.

COLLEGE: Maine.

TRANSACTIONS/CAREER NOTES: Signed as non-drafted free agent by Oakland Athletics organization (July 10, 1986). ... On Tacoma disabled list (April 14-May 13, 1991). ... On Oakland disabled list (May 8-27, 1995); included rehabilitation assignment to Modesto (May 23-26). ... Granted free agency (December 7, 1996). ... Signed by Baltimore Orioles (December 13, 1996). ... Traded by Orioles to New York Mets for OF Melvin Mora, 3B Mike Kinkade, P Lesli Brea and P Pat Gorman (July 28, 2000). ... Granted free agency (October 27, 2000). ... Signed by Orioles (December 20, 2000). ... On Baltimore disabled list (June 14, 2001-remainder of season); included rehabilitation assignments to Bowie (August 2-3) and Delmarva (August 4-10).

STATISTICAL NOTES: Led Pacific Coast League shortstops with .972 fielding percentage and 82 double plays in 1990. ... Led A.L. shortstops with 280 putouts and tied for lead with 108 double plays in 1993. ... Led A.L. with 15 sacrifice hits in 1998. ... Led A.L. shortstops with 797 total chances and 132 double plays in 1999. ... Career major league grand slams: 1.

Year Team (League)	Pos.	G	AB	R	H	2B	3B	HR	RBI	Avg.	BB	SO	SB	PO	A	E	Avg.
										BATTING					**FIELDING**		
1986— Medford (N'West)	SS	46	187	30	48	3	1	0	19	.257	40	21	6	68	143	18	.921
1987— Modesto (Calif.)	SS	133	497	73	133	17	0	3	75	.268	87	92	8	216	305	17	*.968
1988— Huntsville (Sou.)	2B-SS-3B	132	481	48	130	13	2	0	28	.270	87	50	7	260	406	24	.965
1989— Tacoma (PCL)	2B-SS-3B	136	487	55	117	17	1	1	43	.240	58	51	4	261	431	33	.954
1990— Oakland (A.L.)	3B-SS-2B	25	14	0	1	0	0	0	0	.071	1	4	0	9	8	0	1.000
— Tacoma (PCL)	SS-2B	111	348	49	79	16	1	2	30	.227	46	40	3	210	366	16	†.973
1991— Tacoma (PCL)	SS	26	81	15	22	4	1	2	14	.272	17	10	0	35	79	3	.974
— Oakland (A.L.)	SS-2B-3B	90	235	21	56	5	1	0	21	.238	14	37	3	146	213	11	.970
1992— Oakland (A.L.)	2B-SS	154	504	62	151	19	4	3	48	.300	40	59	12	311	449	16	.979
1993— Oakland (A.L.)	SS-2B	159	546	60	136	21	2	3	48	.249	60	58	10	†285	420	13	.982
1994— Oakland (A.L.)	SS-2B	114	391	38	99	18	4	2	37	.253	38	44	7	187	320	14	.973
1995— Oakland (A.L.)	SS-DH	126	428	46	113	13	0	8	44	.264	35	48	11	*245	338	10	.983
— Modesto (Calif.)	SS	1	2	0	0	0	0	0	0	.000	0	0	0	2	1	0	1.000
1996— Oakland (A.L.)	SS	155	525	46	126	18	4	5	54	.240	52	59	5	265	*476	16	.979
1997— Baltimore (A.L.)■........	SS	153	509	55	120	19	1	7	46	.236	33	66	0	224	424	13	.980
1998— Baltimore (A.L.)	SS	151	465	59	121	29	1	13	51	.260	39	65	6	236	*446	7	.990
1999— Baltimore (A.L.)	SS	160	631	93	175	35	7	10	77	.277	54	102	14	277	*511	9	*.989
2000— Baltimore (A.L.)	SS	100	391	70	116	22	1	16	59	.297	34	71	6	161	258	9	.979
— New York (N.L.)■........	SS	56	192	18	50	8	0	4	21	.260	15	28	3	71	140	7	.968
2001— Baltimore (A.L.).........	SS	58	229	32	57	13	0	7	30	.249	17	36	9	107	146	6	.977
— Bowie (East.).............	DH	1	4	0	1	0	0	0	0	.250	0	1	0	...	...	...	...
— Delmarva (S.Atl.)........	SS	3	8	0	0	0	0	0	0	.000	2	1	0	0	0	0	...
American League totals (12 years)		1445	4868	582	1271	212	25	74	515	.261	417	649	83	2453	4009	124	.981
National League totals (1 year)		56	192	18	50	8	0	4	21	.260	15	28	3	71	140	7	.968
Major League totals (12 years)		1501	5060	600	1321	220	25	78	536	.261	432	677	86	2524	4149	131	.981

DIVISION SERIES RECORD

Year Team (League)	Pos.	G	AB	R	H	2B	3B	HR	RBI	Avg.	BB	SO	SB	PO	A	E	Avg.
										BATTING					**FIELDING**		
1997— Baltimore (A.L.)..........	SS	4	10	4	4	1	0	0	4	.400	4	2	0	4	15	0	1.000
2000— New York (N.L.)..........	SS	4	12	3	2	0	0	0	0	.167	3	4	0	7	10	0	1.000
Division series totals (2 years)		8	22	7	6	1	0	0	4	.273	7	6	0	11	25	0	1.000

CHAMPIONSHIP SERIES RECORD

Year Team (League)	Pos.	G	AB	R	H	2B	3B	HR	RBI	Avg.	BB	SO	SB	PO	A	E	Avg.
										BATTING					**FIELDING**		
1990— Oakland (A.L.)............							Did not play.										
1992— Oakland (A.L.)	SS-2B	6	19	1	1	0	0	0	0	.053	1	2	1	15	14	0	1.000
1997— Baltimore (A.L.)..........	SS	6	19	0	3	1	0	0	2	.158	0	6	0	5	14	0	1.000
2000— New York (N.L.)..........	SS	5	13	2	1	0	0	0	0	.077	3	1	0	10	11	0	1.000
Championship series totals (3 years)		17	51	3	5	1	0	0	2	.098	4	9	1	30	39	0	1.000

WORLD SERIES RECORD

Year Team (League)	Pos.	G	AB	R	H	2B	3B	HR	RBI	Avg.	BB	SO	SB	PO	A	E	Avg.
										BATTING					**FIELDING**		
1990— Oakland (A.L.)	SS-PR	3	0	0	0	0	0	0	0	...	0	0	0	0	2	0	1.000
2000— New York (N.L.)..........	SS	4	8	0	1	0	0	0	0	.125	0	3	0	4	7	1	.917
World Series totals (2 years)		7	8	0	1	0	0	0	0	.125	0	3	0	4	9	1	.929

ALL-STAR GAME RECORD

Year League	Pos.	AB	R	H	2B	3B	HR	RBI	Avg.	BB	SO	SB	PO	A	E	Avg.
									BATTING					**FIELDING**		
2000— American...................	PH	1	0	0	0	0	0	0	.000	0	0	0	...	...	...	...

BORKOWSKI, DAVE   P   TIGERS

PERSONAL: Born February 7, 1977, in Detroit. ... 6-1/200. ... Throws right, bats right. ... Full name: David Richard Borkowski.
HIGH SCHOOL: Sterling Heights (Mich.).
TRANSACTIONS/CAREER NOTES: Selected by Detroit Tigers organization in 11th round of free-agent draft (June 1, 1995). ... On Toledo disabled list (May 30-August 28, 2000). ... On Detroit disabled list (July 7, 2001-remainder of season). ... Released by Tigers (November 5, 2001). ... Re-signed by Tigers organization (November 7, 2001).
STATISTICAL NOTES: Pitched 6-0 no-hit victory against Kane County (April 20, 1997). ... Led Southern League with 25 home runs allowed in 1998.

Year League	W	L	Pct.	ERA	G	GS	CG	ShO	Sv.	IP	H	R	ER	BB	SO
1995— Gulf Coast Tigers (GCL)	3	2	.600	2.96	10	10	1	0	0	51 2/3	45	24	17	8	36
— Lakeland (FSL)	1	0	1.000	0.00	1	1	0	0	0	5	2	0	0	1	3
1996— Fayetteville (S.Atl.)	10	10	.500	3.33	27	27	5	0	0	178 1/3	158	85	66	54	117
1997— West Michigan (Midw.)	•15	3	•.833	3.46	25	25	4	2	0	164	143	79	63	31	104
1998— Jacksonville (Sou.).............	*16	7	.696	4.63	28	28	3	1	0	178 2/3	204	99	92	54	97
1999— Toledo (I.L.)	6	8	.429	3.50	19	19	3	0	0	126	119	59	49	43	94
— Detroit (A.L.)	2	6	.250	6.10	17	12	0	0	0	76 2/3	86	58	52	40	50
2000— Toledo (I.L.)	3	1	.750	4.40	8	8	0	0	0	47	44	27	23	14	29
— Detroit (A.L.)	0	1	.000	21.94	2	1	0	0	0	5 1/3	11	13	13	7	1
— Gulf Coast Tigers (GCL)	0	0	...	2.25	3	3	0	0	0	8	7	3	2	0	6
— Lakeland (FSL)	0	1	.000	8.59	2	2	0	0	0	7 1/3	11	7	7	4	5
2001— Toledo (I.L.)	1	2	.333	3.54	18	0	0	0	1	28	22	14	11	9	22
— Detroit (A.L.)	0	2	.000	6.37	15	0	0	0	0	29 2/3	30	21	21	15	30
Major League totals (3 years).......	2	9	.182	6.93	34	13	0	0	0	111 2/3	127	92	86	62	81

BORLAND, TOBY — P — MARLINS

PERSONAL: Born May 29, 1969, in Ruston, La. ... 6-6/193. ... Throws right, bats right. ... Full name: Toby Shawn Borland.
HIGH SCHOOL: Quitman (La.).
TRANSACTIONS/CAREER NOTES: Selected by Philadelphia Phillies organization in 27th round of free-agent draft (June 2, 1987). ... On Philadelphia disabled list (June 14-July 8, 1995); included rehabilitation assignment to Scranton/Wilkes-Barre (June 22-July 8). ... Traded by Phillies with P Ricardo Jordan to New York Mets for 1B Rico Brogna (November 27, 1996). ... Traded by Mets to Boston Red Sox for P Rick Trlicek (May 12, 1997). ... Granted free agency (October 15, 1997). ... Signed by Cincinnati Reds organization (November 27, 1997). ... Released by Reds (March 5, 1998). ... Signed by Philadelphia Phillies organization (March 6, 1998). ... Released by Phillies (July 6, 1998). ... Signed by Florida Marlins organization (July 14, 1998). ... Granted free agency (October 15, 1998). ... Signed by Anaheim Angels (November 23, 1998). ... On Edmonton disabled list (June 1, 1999-remainder of season). ... Granted free agency (October 15, 1999). ... On Edmonton disabled list (April 7-July 25, 2000). ... Granted free agency (October 18, 2000). ... Re-signed by Angels organization (November 27, 2000). ... On Salt Lake disabled list (August 29, 2001-remainder of season). ... Granted free agency (October 8, 2001). ... Signed by Florida Marlins organization (November 20, 2001).
STATISTICAL NOTES: Tied for Eastern League lead with three balks in 1991. ... Pitched one inning, combining with starter Craig Holman (two innings), Gregory Brown (two innings) and Ricky Bottalico (two innings) in seven-inning 2-0 no-hit victory for Reading against New Britain (September 4, 1993, first game).

Year League	W	L	Pct.	ERA	G	GS	CG	ShO	Sv.	IP	H	R	ER	BB	SO
1988—Martinsville (Appl.)	2	3	.400	4.04	34	0	0	0	*12	49	42	26	22	29	43
1989—Spartanburg (S.Atl.)	4	5	.444	2.97	47	0	0	0	9	66 2/3	62	29	22	35	48
1990—Clearwater (FSL)	1	2	.333	2.26	44	0	0	0	5	59 2/3	44	21	15	35	44
—Reading (East.)	4	1	.800	1.44	14	0	0	0	0	25	16	6	4	11	26
1991—Reading (East.)	8	3	.727	2.70	*59	0	0	0	•24	76 1/3	68	31	23	56	72
1992—Scranton/W.B. (I.L.)	0	1	.000	7.24	27	0	0	0	1	27 1/3	25	23	22	26	25
—Reading (East.)	2	4	.333	3.43	32	0	0	0	5	42	39	23	16	32	45
1993—Reading (East.)	2	2	.500	2.52	44	0	0	0	13	53 2/3	38	17	15	20	74
—Scranton/W.B. (I.L.)	2	4	.333	5.76	26	0	0	0	1	29 2/3	31	20	19	20	20
1994—Scranton/W.B. (I.L.)	4	1	.800	1.68	27	1	0	0	4	53 2/3	36	12	10	21	61
—Philadelphia (N.L.)	1	0	1.000	2.36	24	0	0	0	1	34 1/3	31	10	9	14	26
1995—Philadelphia (N.L.)	1	3	.250	3.77	50	0	0	0	6	74	81	37	31	37	59
—Scranton/W.B. (I.L.)	0	0	...	0.00	8	0	0	0	1	11 1/3	5	0	0	6	15
1996—Philadelphia (N.L.)	7	3	.700	4.07	69	0	0	0	1	90 2/3	83	51	41	43	76
1997—New York (N.L.)	0	1	.000	6.07	13	0	0	0	1	13 1/3	11	9	9	14	7
—Boston (A.L.)	0	0	...	13.50	3	0	0	0	0	3 1/3	6	5	5	7	1
—Pawtucket (I.L.)	2	0	1.000	3.99	28	2	0	0	2	47 1/3	50	22	21	25	46
1998—Reading (East.)	1	3	.250	9.64	8	0	0	0	3	9 1/3	18	12	10	5	13
—Scranton/W.B. (I.L.)	0	2	.000	5.68	13	0	0	0	5	12 2/3	14	8	8	3	15
—Philadelphia (N.L.)	0	0	...	5.00	6	0	0	0	1	9	8	5	5	5	9
—Charlotte (I.L.)	3	0	1.000	2.70	19	0	0	0	1	36 2/3	33	12	11	21	26
1999—Edmonton (PCL)	2	1	.667	7.00	21	0	0	0	0	27	31	24	21	23	34
2000—Erie (East.)	1	3	.250	4.50	9	1	0	0	1	12	12	8	6	7	12
2001—Salt Lake (PCL)	7	3	.700	2.30	45	1	0	0	3	74 1/3	53	25	19	29	92
—Anaheim (A.L.)	0	1	.000	10.80	2	0	0	0	0	3 1/3	8	5	4	1	0
A.L. totals (2 years)	0	1	.000	12.15	5	0	0	0	0	6 2/3	14	10	9	8	1
N.L. totals (5 years)	9	7	.563	3.86	162	0	0	0	8	221 1/3	214	112	95	113	177
Major League totals (6 years)	9	8	.529	4.11	167	0	0	0	8	228	228	122	104	121	178

BOROWSKI, JOE — P

PERSONAL: Born May 4, 1971, in Bayonne, N.J. ... 6-2/225. ... Throws right, bats right. ... Full name: Joseph Thomas Borowski.
HIGH SCHOOL: Marist (Bayonne, N.J.).
COLLEGE: Rutgers.
TRANSACTIONS/CAREER NOTES: Selected by Chicago White Sox organization in 32nd round of free-agent draft (June 5, 1989). ... Traded by White Sox organization to Baltimore Orioles organization for IF Pete Rose Jr. (March 21, 1991). ... Traded by Orioles with P Rachaad Stewart to Atlanta Braves for P Kent Mercker (December 17, 1995). ... Claimed on waivers by New York Yankees (September 15, 1997). ... On New York disabled list (August 24-September 8, 1998). ... Claimed on waivers by Milwaukee Brewers (December 4, 1998). ... Granted free agency (October 15, 1999). ... Signed by Cincinnati Reds organization (November 9, 1999). ... Released by Reds (April 14, 2000). ... Signed by Newark, Atlantic League (2000). ... Signed by Monterrey, Mexican League (2000). ... Signed by Chicago Cubs organization (December 11, 2000). ... Granted free agency (October 10, 2001).

Year League	W	L	Pct.	ERA	G	GS	CG	ShO	Sv.	IP	H	R	ER	BB	SO
1990—GC White Sox (GCL)	2	•8	.200	5.58	12	11	0	0	0	61 1/3	74	*47	*38	25	67
1991—Kane County (Midw.)	7	2	.778	2.56	49	0	0	0	13	81	60	26	23	43	76
1992—Frederick (Caro.)	5	6	.455	3.70	48	0	0	0	10	80 1/3	71	40	33	50	85
1993—Frederick (Caro.)	1	1	.500	3.61	42	2	0	0	11	62 1/3	61	30	25	37	70
—Bowie (East.)	3	0	1.000	0.00	9	0	0	0	0	17 2/3	11	0	0	11	17
1994—Bowie (East.)	3	4	.429	1.91	49	0	0	0	14	66	52	14	14	28	73
1995—Rochester (I.L.)	1	3	.250	4.04	28	0	0	0	6	35 2/3	32	16	16	18	32
—Bowie (East.)	2	2	.500	3.92	16	0	0	0	7	20 2/3	16	9	9	7	32
—Baltimore (A.L.)	0	0	...	1.23	6	0	0	0	0	7 1/3	5	1	1	4	3
1996—Richmond (I.L.)	1	5	.167	3.71	34	0	0	0	7	53 1/3	42	25	22	30	40
—Atlanta (N.L.)	2	4	.333	4.85	22	0	0	0	0	26	33	15	14	13	15
1997—Atlanta (N.L.)	2	2	.500	3.75	20	0	0	0	0	24	27	11	10	16	6
—Richmond (I.L.)	1	2	.333	3.58	21	0	0	0	2	37 2/3	32	16	15	19	34
—New York (A.L.)	0	1	.000	9.00	1	0	0	0	0	2	2	2	2	4	2
1998—Columbus (I.L.)	3	3	.500	2.93	45	0	0	0	4	73 2/3	66	25	24	39	67
—New York (A.L.)	1	0	1.000	6.52	8	0	0	0	0	9 2/3	11	7	7	4	7
1999—Louisville (I.L.)	6	2	.750	5.46	58	0	0	0	4	89	94	59	54	44	70
2000—Newark (Atl.)	6	3	.667	5.50	28	0	0	0	0	37 2/3	44	23	23	17	39
—Monterrey (Mex.)	4	2	.667	3.19	12	5	0	0	0	42 1/3	31	15	15	18	44
2001—Iowa (PCL)	8	7	.533	2.62	39	12	1	1	1	110	87	35	32	26	131
—Chicago (N.L.)	0	1	.000	32.40	1	1	0	0	0	1 2/3	6	6	6	3	1
A.L. totals (3 years)	1	1	.500	4.74	15	0	0	0	0	19	18	10	10	12	12
N.L. totals (3 years)	4	7	.364	5.23	43	1	0	0	0	51 2/3	66	32	30	32	22
Major League totals (5 years)	5	8	.385	5.09	58	1	0	0	0	70 2/3	84	42	40	44	34

PERSONAL: Born August 26, 1969, in New Britain, Conn. ... 6-1/215. ... Throws right, bats left. ... Full name: Richard Paul Bottalico. ... Name pronounced ba-TAL-eh-koh.
HIGH SCHOOL: South Catholic (Hartford, Conn.).
COLLEGE: Florida Southern, then Central Connecticut State.
TRANSACTIONS/CAREER NOTES: Signed as non-drafted free agent by Philadelphia Phillies organization (July 21, 1991). ... On Philadelphia disabled list (April 24-July 1, 1998); included rehabilitation assignment to Scranton/Wilkes-Barre (June 6-July 1). ... On suspended list (August 25-28, 1998). ... Traded by Phillies with P Garrett Stephenson to St. Louis Cardinals for OF Ron Gant, P Jeff Brantley and P Cliff Politte (November 19, 1998). ... Granted free agency (December 21, 1999). ... Signed by Kansas City Royals (January 27, 2000). ... Granted free agency (November 4, 2000). ... Signed by Phillies (December 15, 2000). ... On Philadelphia disabled list (June 29-July 20, 2001); included rehabilitation assignment to Reading (July 13-20). ... Granted free agency (November 5, 2001). ... Re-signed by Phillies (January 8, 2002).
STATISTICAL NOTES: Pitched two innings, combining with starter Craig Holman (two innings), Gregory Brown (two innings) and Toby Borland (one inning) in seven-inning, 2-0 no-hit victory for Reading against New Britain (September 4, 1993, first game).

Year League	W	L	Pct.	ERA	G	GS	CG	ShO	Sv.	IP	H	R	ER	BB	SO
1991—Martinsville (Appl.)	3	2	.600	4.09	7	6	2	•1	0	33	32	20	15	13	38
—Spartanburg (S.Atl.)	2	0	1.000	0.00	2	2	0	0	0	15	4	0	0	2	11
1992—Spartanburg (S.Atl.)	5	10	.333	2.41	42	11	1	0	13	119²/₃	94	41	32	56	118
1993—Clearwater (FSL)	1	0	1.000	2.75	13	0	0	0	4	19²/₃	19	6	6	5	19
—Reading (East.)	3	3	.500	2.25	49	0	0	0	20	72	63	22	18	26	65
1994—Scranton/W.B. (I.L.)	3	1	.750	8.87	19	0	0	0	3	22¹/₃	32	27	22	22	22
—Reading (East.)	2	2	.500	2.53	38	0	0	0	22	42²/₃	29	13	12	10	51
—Philadelphia (N.L.)	0	0	...	0.00	3	0	0	0	0	3	3	0	0	1	3
1995—Philadelphia (N.L.)	5	3	.625	2.46	62	0	0	0	1	87²/₃	50	25	24	42	87
1996—Philadelphia (N.L.)	4	5	.444	3.19	61	0	0	0	34	67²/₃	47	24	24	23	74
1997—Philadelphia (N.L.)	2	5	.286	3.65	69	0	0	0	34	74	68	31	30	42	89
1998—Philadelphia (N.L.)	1	5	.167	6.44	39	0	0	0	6	43¹/₃	54	31	31	25	27
—Scranton/W.B. (I.L.)	0	1	.000	2.92	10	5	0	0	1	12¹/₃	8	4	4	9	4
1999—St. Louis (N.L.)■	3	7	.300	4.91	68	0	0	0	20	73¹/₃	83	45	40	49	66
2000—Kansas City (A.L.)■	9	6	.600	4.83	62	0	0	0	16	72²/₃	65	40	39	41	56
2001—Philadelphia (N.L.)■	3	4	.429	3.90	66	0	0	0	3	67	58	31	29	25	57
—Reading (East.)	0	1	.000	1.80	3	3	0	0	0	5	3	2	1	1	5
A.L. totals (1 year)	9	6	.600	4.83	62	0	0	0	16	72²/₃	65	40	39	41	56
N.L. totals (7 years)	18	29	.383	3.85	368	0	0	0	98	416	363	187	178	207	403
Major League totals (8 years)	27	35	.435	4.00	430	0	0	0	114	488²/₃	428	227	217	248	459

ALL-STAR GAME RECORD

Year League	W	L	Pct.	ERA	GS	CG	ShO	Sv.	IP	H	R	ER	BB	SO
1996—National	0	0	...	0.00	0	0	0	0	1	0	0	0	0	1

PERSONAL: Born November 14, 1968, in Portland, Ore. ... 6-3/240. ... Throws right, bats right. ... Full name: Kent Dennis Bottenfield. ... Twin brother of Keven Bottenfield, minor league catcher/infielder (1986-87).
HIGH SCHOOL: James Madison (Portland, Ore.).
TRANSACTIONS/CAREER NOTES: Selected by Montreal Expos organization in fourth round of free-agent draft (June 2, 1986). ... Traded by Expos to Colorado Rockies for P Butch Henry (July 16, 1993). ... On Colorado disabled list (March 25-May 9, 1994); included rehabilitation assignment to Colorado Springs (April 10-May 9). ... Granted free agency (June 27, 1994). ... Signed by San Francisco Giants organization (June 29, 1994). ... Released by Giants (November 8, 1994). ... Signed by Detroit Tigers organization (April 3, 1995). ... Granted free agency (October 16, 1995). ... Signed by Chicago Cubs organization (March 9, 1996). ... Granted free agency (December 21, 1997). ... Signed by St. Louis Cardinals (January 8, 1998). ... Traded by Cardinals with 2B/SS Adam Kennedy to Anaheim Angels for OF Jim Edmonds (March 23, 2000). ... On Anaheim disabled list (June 8-24, 2000). ... Traded by Angels to Philadelphia Phillies for OF Ron Gant (July 30, 2000). ... Granted free agency (October 30, 2000). ... Signed by Houston Astros (January 3, 2001). ... On Houston disabled list (June 10, 2001-remainder of season); included rehabilitation assignment to Round Rock (August 13-14). ... Granted free agency (November 7, 2001).

Year League	W	L	Pct.	ERA	G	GS	CG	ShO	Sv.	IP	H	R	ER	BB	SO
1986—Gulf Coast Expos (GCL)	5	6	.455	3.27	13	13	2	0	0	74¹/₃	73	•42	27	30	41
1987—Burlington (Midw.)	9	13	.409	4.53	27	27	6	3	0	161	175	98	81	42	103
1988—West Palm Beach (FSL)	10	8	.556	3.33	27	27	9	4	0	181	165	80	67	47	120
1989—Jacksonville (Sou.)	3	*17	.150	5.26	25	25	1	0	0	138²/₃	137	101	81	73	91
1990—Jacksonville (Sou.)	12	10	.545	3.41	29	28	2	1	0	169	158	72	64	67	121
1991—Indianapolis (A.A.)	8	15	.348	4.06	29	27	•5	2	0	166¹/₃	155	97	75	61	108
1992—Indianapolis (A.A.)	•12	8	.600	3.43	25	23	3	1	0	152¹/₃	139	64	58	58	111
—Montreal (N.L.)	1	2	.333	2.23	10	4	0	0	1	32¹/₃	26	9	8	11	14
1993—Montreal (N.L.)	2	5	.286	4.12	23	11	0	0	0	83	93	49	38	33	33
—Colorado (N.L.)■	3	5	.375	6.10	14	14	1	0	0	76²/₃	86	53	52	38	30
1994—Colorado Springs (PCL)	1	2	.333	4.94	5	4	1	0	0	31	35	19	17	11	17
—Colorado (N.L.)	3	1	.750	5.84	15	1	0	0	1	24²/₃	28	16	16	10	15
—Phoenix (PCL)■	2	1	.667	2.57	8	5	1	1	0	35	30	13	10	11	11
—San Francisco (N.L.)	0	0	...	10.80	1	0	0	0	0	1²/₃	5	2	2	0	0
1995—Toledo (I.L.)■	5	11	.313	4.54	27	19	2	1	1	136²/₃	148	80	69	55	68
1996—Iowa (A.A.)■	1	2	.333	2.19	28	0	0	0	18	24²/₃	19	9	6	8	14
—Chicago (N.L.)	3	5	.375	2.63	48	0	0	0	1	61²/₃	59	25	18	19	33
1997—Chicago (N.L.)	2	3	.400	3.86	64	0	0	0	2	84	82	39	36	35	74
1998—St. Louis (N.L.)■	4	6	.400	4.44	44	17	0	0	4	133²/₃	128	72	66	57	98
1999—St. Louis (N.L.)	18	7	.720	3.97	31	31	0	0	0	190¹/₃	197	91	84	89	124
2000—Anaheim (A.L.)■	7	8	.467	5.71	21	21	0	0	0	127²/₃	144	82	81	56	75
—Philadelphia (N.L.)■	1	2	.333	4.50	8	8	1	1	0	44	41	24	22	21	31
2001—Houston (N.L.)■	2	5	.286	6.40	13	9	0	0	1	52	61	44	37	16	39
—Round Rock (Texas)	0	1	.000	20.25	1	1	0	0	0	2²/₃	4	6	6	3	3
A.L. totals (1 year)	7	8	.467	5.71	21	21	0	0	0	127²/₃	144	82	81	56	75
N.L. totals (9 years)	39	41	.488	4.35	271	95	2	1	10	784	806	424	379	329	491
Major League totals (9 years)	46	49	.484	4.54	292	116	2	1	10	911²/₃	950	506	460	385	566

ALL-STAR GAME RECORD

Year League	W	L	Pct.	ERA	GS	CG	ShO	Sv.	IP	H	R	ER	BB	SO
1999—National	0	0	...	18.00	0	0	0	0	1	1	2	2	1	2

BOWLES, BRIAN   P   BLUE JAYS

PERSONAL: Born August 18, 1976, in Harbor City, Calif. ... 6-5/220. ... Throws right, bats right.
HIGH SCHOOL: Peninsula (Manhattan Beach, Calif.).
COLLEGE: UC-Santa Barbara.
TRANSACTIONS/CAREER NOTES: Selected by Toronto Blue Jays organization in 50th round of free-agent draft (June 2, 1994).

Year League	W	L	Pct.	ERA	G	GS	CG	ShO	Sv.	IP	H	R	ER	BB	SO
1995— Gulf Coast Blue Jays (GCL)	0	1	.000	2.40	8	0	0	0	0	15	18	12	4	3	11
1996— Medicine Hat (Pio.)	2	2	.500	6.35	24	0	0	0	1	39²/₃	53	35	28	21	29
1997— Hagerstown (S.Atl.)...........	1	0	1.000	6.97	4	0	0	0	0	10¹/₃	14	10	8	5	9
— Dunedin (FSL)....................	0	2	.000	7.53	7	1	0	0	0	14¹/₃	20	14	12	7	9
— St. Catharines (NY-Penn)...	5	8	.385	5.03	16	16	0	0	0	78²/₃	76	53	44	35	64
1998— Dunedin (FSL)...................	1	2	.333	3.33	9	2	1	0	0	27	32	13	10	16	17
— Hagerstown (S.Atl.)...........	2	4	.333	4.52	31	4	0	0	0	67²/₃	80	41	34	18	48
1999— Hagerstown (S.Atl.)...........	6	2	.750	3.97	48	1	0	0	3	79¹/₃	73	41	35	39	80
2000— Tennessee (Sou.)	4	4	.500	2.98	49	0	0	0	0	81²/₃	64	31	27	36	72
2001— Syracuse (I.L.)..................	3	5	.375	2.91	*66	0	0	0	6	77¹/₃	56	30	25	44	81
— Toronto (A.L.)...................	0	0	...	0.00	2	0	0	0	0	3²/₃	4	0	0	1	4
Major League totals (1 year)........	**0**	**0**	**...**	**0.00**	**2**	**0**	**0**	**0**	**0**	**3²/₃**	**4**	**0**	**0**	**1**	**4**

BRADFORD, CHAD   P   ATHLETICS

PERSONAL: Born September 14, 1974, in Jackson, Miss. ... 6-5/205. ... Throws right, bats right. ... Full name: Chadwick Lee Bradford.
HIGH SCHOOL: Byram (Jackson, Miss.).
JUNIOR COLLEGE: Hinds Community College (Miss.).
COLLEGE: Southern Mississippi.
TRANSACTIONS/CAREER NOTES: Selected by Chicago White Sox organization in 13th round of free-agent draft (June 4, 1996). ... On Charlotte disabled list (June 28-July 5, 2000). ... Traded by White Sox to Oakland Athletics for a player to be named later (December 7, 2000); White Sox acquired C Miguel Olivo to complete deal (December 13, 2000).

Year League	W	L	Pct.	ERA	G	GS	CG	ShO	Sv.	IP	H	R	ER	BB	SO
1996— Hickory (S.Atl.).................	0	2	.000	0.90	28	0	0	0	18	30	21	7	3	7	27
1997— Winston-Salem (Caro.).......	3	7	.300	3.95	46	0	0	0	15	54²/₃	51	30	24	25	43
1998— Birmingham (Sou.)...........	1	1	.500	2.60	10	0	0	0	1	17¹/₃	13	6	5	8	14
— Calgary (PCL)..................	4	1	.800	1.94	29	0	0	0	0	51	50	12	11	11	27
— Chicago (A.L.)...................	2	1	.667	3.23	29	0	0	0	1	30²/₃	27	16	11	7	11
1999— Charlotte (I.L.).................	9	3	.750	1.94	47	0	0	0	5	74¹/₃	63	19	16	15	56
— Chicago (A.L.)...................	0	0	...	19.64	3	0	0	0	0	3²/₃	9	8	8	5	0
2000— Charlotte (I.L.).................	2	4	.333	1.51	55	0	0	0	10	53²/₃	38	18	9	12	42
— Chicago (A.L.)...................	1	0	1.000	1.98	12	0	0	0	0	13²/₃	13	4	3	1	9
2001— Sacramento (PCL)■...........	0	0	...	0.38	12	0	0	0	2	23²/₃	15	2	1	2	24
— Oakland (A.L.)	2	1	.667	2.70	35	0	0	0	1	36²/₃	41	12	11	6	34
Major League totals (4 years).......	**5**	**2**	**.714**	**3.51**	**79**	**0**	**0**	**0**	**2**	**84²/₃**	**90**	**40**	**33**	**19**	**54**

DIVISION SERIES RECORD

Year League	W	L	Pct.	ERA	G	GS	CG	ShO	Sv.	IP	H	R	ER	BB	SO
2000— Chicago (A.L.)	0	0	...	0.00	1	0	0	0	0	²/₃	2	0	0	0	0
2001— Oakland (A.L.)	0	0	...	0.00	1	0	0	0	0	1	0	0	0	0	1
Division series totals (2 years)	**0**	**0**	**...**	**0.00**	**2**	**0**	**0**	**0**	**0**	**1²/₃**	**2**	**0**	**0**	**0**	**1**

BRADLEY, MILTON   OF   INDIANS

PERSONAL: Born April 15, 1978, in Harbor City, Fla. ... 6-0/170. ... Bats both, throws right. ... Full name: Milton Obelle Bradley.
HIGH SCHOOL: Polytechnic (Long Beach, Calif.).
TRANSACTIONS/CAREER NOTES: Selected by Montreal Expos organization in second round of free-agent draft (June 4, 1996). ... On disabled list (June 14-25, 1999). ... Traded by Expos to Cleveland Indians for P Zach Day (July 31, 2001).

Year Team (League)	Pos.	G	AB	R	H	2B	3B	HR	RBI	Avg.	BB	SO	SB	PO	A	E	Avg.
1996— GC Expos (GCL)	OF	32	112	18	27	7	1	4	12	.241	13	15	7	54	2	3	.949
1997— Vermont (NY-Penn)....	OF	50	200	29	60	7	5	3	30	.300	17	34	7	113	3	4	.967
— GC Expos (GCL)	OF	9	25	6	5	2	0	1	2	.200	4	4	2	15	0	1	.938
1998— Cape Fear (S.Atl.)	OF	75	281	54	85	21	4	6	50	.302	23	57	13	87	5	3	.968
— Jupiter (FSL)	OF	67	261	55	75	14	1	5	34	.287	30	42	17	138	8	1	.993
1999— Harrisburg (East.)........	OF-DH	87	346	62	114	22	5	12	50	.329	33	61	14	166	3	5	.971
2000— Ottawa (I.L.)	OF	88	342	58	104	20	1	6	29	.304	45	56	10	216	7	3	.987
— Montreal (N.L.).............	OF	42	154	20	34	8	1	2	15	.221	14	32	2	88	6	2	.979
2001— Montreal (N.L.)...........	OF	67	220	19	49	16	3	1	19	.223	19	62	7	155	5	2	.988
— Ottawa (I.L.)	OF	35	136	21	37	7	2	2	13	.272	23	30	14	80	4	3	.966
— Buffalo (I.L.)■..............	OF	30	114	18	29	3	0	5	15	.254	19	31	9	57	3	0	1.000
— Cleveland (A.L.)..........	OF-DH	10	18	3	4	1	0	0	0	.222	2	3	1	12	1	1	.929
American League totals (1 year)		**10**	**18**	**3**	**4**	**1**	**0**	**0**	**0**	**.222**	**2**	**3**	**1**	**12**	**1**	**1**	**.929**
National League totals (2 years)		**109**	**374**	**39**	**83**	**24**	**4**	**3**	**34**	**.222**	**33**	**94**	**9**	**243**	**11**	**4**	**.984**
Major League totals (2 years)		**119**	**392**	**42**	**87**	**25**	**4**	**3**	**34**	**.222**	**35**	**97**	**10**	**255**	**12**	**5**	**.982**

BRAGG, DARREN   OF   METS

PERSONAL: Born September 7, 1969, in Waterbury, Conn. ... 5-9/180. ... Bats left, throws right. ... Full name: Darren William Bragg.
HIGH SCHOOL: Taft (Watertown, Conn.).
COLLEGE: Georgia Tech.

TRANSACTIONS/CAREER NOTES: Selected by Seattle Mariners organization in 22nd round of free-agent draft (June 30, 1991). ... Traded by Mariners to Boston Red Sox for P Jamie Moyer (July 30, 1996). ... Granted free agency (December 21, 1998). ... Signed by St. Louis Cardinals (January 12, 1999). ... On disabled list (August 3, 1999-remainder of season). ... Released by Cardinals (December 16, 1999). ... Signed by Colorado Rockies (February 1, 2000). ... Released by Rockies (July 24, 2000). ... Signed by New York Mets organization (January 9, 2001). ... Claimed on waivers by New York Yankees (June 12, 2001). ... Granted free agency (October 9, 2001). ... Signed by Mets organization (January 15, 2002).

STATISTICAL NOTES: Led Carolina League in caught stealing with 19 in 1992. ... Led Pacific Coast League outfielders with 344 total chances and five double plays in 1994. ... Career major league grand slams: 2.

Year Team (League)	Pos.	G	AB	R	H	2B	3B	HR	RBI	Avg.	BB	SO	SB	PO	A	E	Avg.
1991— Peninsula (Caro.)	OF-2B	69	237	42	53	14	0	3	29	.224	66	72	21	167	9	4	.978
1992— Peninsula (Caro.)	OF	135	428	*83	117	29	5	9	58	.273	*105	76	44	262	11	4	.986
1993— Jacksonville (Sou.)	OF-P	131	451	74	119	26	3	11	46	.264	81	82	19	306	14	10	.970
1994— Calgary (PCL)	OF	126	500	112	175	33	6	17	85	.350	68	72	28	317	20	7	.980
— Seattle (A.L.)	DH-OF	8	19	4	3	1	0	0	2	.158	2	5	0	1	0	0	1.000
1995— Seattle (A.L.)	OF-DH	52	145	20	34	5	1	3	12	.234	18	37	9	83	7	1	.989
— Tacoma (PCL)	OF-DH	53	212	24	65	13	4	4	31	.307	23	39	10	115	7	4	.968
1996— Seattle (A.L.)	OF	69	195	36	53	12	1	7	25	.272	33	35	8	118	7	1	.992
— Tacoma (PCL)	OF	20	71	17	20	8	0	3	8	.282	14	14	1	32	2	0	1.000
— Boston (A.L.)■	OF	58	222	38	56	14	1	3	22	.252	36	39	6	136	5	2	.986
1997— Boston (A.L.)	OF-3B	153	513	65	132	35	2	9	57	.257	61	102	10	364	11	5	.987
1998— Boston (A.L.)	OF-DH	129	409	51	114	29	3	8	57	.279	42	99	5	218	6	1	*.996
1999— St. Louis (N.L.)■	OF	93	273	38	71	12	1	6	26	.260	44	67	3	155	7	3	.982
2000— Colorado (N.L.)■	OF	71	149	16	33	7	1	3	21	.221	17	41	4	53	0	0	1.000
2001— Norfolk (I.L.)■	OF	32	99	22	33	4	0	4	7	.333	23	22	5	41	2	0	1.000
— New York (N.L.)	OF	18	57	4	15	6	0	0	5	.263	4	23	3	21	1	0	1.000
— New York (A.L.)■	OF	5	4	1	1	1	0	0	0	.250	0	1	0	2	0	0	1.000
— Columbus (I.L.)	OF	53	199	30	58	11	2	7	21	.291	27	51	3	52	4	0	1.000
American League totals (6 years)		474	1507	215	393	97	8	30	175	.261	192	318	38	922	36	10	.990
National League totals (3 years)		182	479	58	119	25	2	9	52	.248	65	131	10	229	8	3	.988
Major League totals (8 years)		656	1986	273	512	122	10	39	227	.258	257	449	48	1151	44	13	.989

DIVISION SERIES RECORD

Year Team (League)	Pos.	G	AB	R	H	2B	3B	HR	RBI	Avg.	BB	SO	SB	PO	A	E	Avg.
1998— Boston (A.L.)	OF	3	12	0	1	0	0	0	0	.083	0	5	0	4	0	0	1.000

RECORD AS PITCHER

Year League	W	L	Pct.	ERA	G	GS	CG	ShO	Sv.	IP	H	R	ER	BB	SO
1993— Jacksonville (Sou.)	0	0	...	9.00	1	0	0	0	0	1	3	1	1	0	0

BRANSON, JEFF   IF

PERSONAL: Born January 26, 1967, in Waynesboro, Miss. ... 6-0/180. ... Bats left, throws right. ... Full name: Jeffery Glenn Branson.

HIGH SCHOOL: Southern Choctaw (Silas, Ala.).

COLLEGE: Livingston (Ala.) University.

TRANSACTIONS/CAREER NOTES: Selected by Cincinnati Reds organization in second round of free-agent draft (June 1, 1988). ... Traded by Reds with P John Smiley to Cleveland Indians for P Danny Graves, P Jim Crowell, P Scott Winchester and IF Damian Jackson (July 31, 1997). ... On Cleveland disabled list (August 2-September 1, 1998); included rehabilitation assignment to Buffalo (August 21-September 1). ... Granted free agency (October 23, 1998). ... Signed by Reds organization (November 17, 1998). ... Granted free agency (October 15, 1999). ... Signed by Los Angeles Dodgers organization (December 27, 1999). ... Granted free agency (October 16, 2000). ... Re-signed by Dodgers organization (December 18, 2000). ... Granted free agency (October 17, 2001).

STATISTICAL NOTES: Led International League shortstops with .974 fielding percentage and 81 double plays in 1999.

MISCELLANEOUS: Member of 1988 U.S. Olympic baseball team.

Year Team (League)	Pos.	G	AB	R	H	2B	3B	HR	RBI	Avg.	BB	SO	SB	PO	A	E	Avg.
1989— Cedar Rapids (Midw.)	SS	127	469	70	132	28	1	10	68	.281	41	90	5	172	394	33	.945
1990— Cedar Rapids (Midw.)	SS	62	239	37	60	13	4	6	24	.251	24	44	11	96	152	7	.973
— Chattanooga (Sou.)	2B-SS	63	233	19	49	9	1	2	29	.210	13	48	3	122	151	13	.955
1991— Chattanooga (Sou.)	SS-2B	88	304	35	80	13	3	2	28	.263	31	51	3	126	212	12	.966
— Nashville (A.A.)	SS-2B-OF	43	145	10	35	4	1	0	11	.241	8	31	5	61	93	8	.951
1992— Nashville (A.A.)	SS-2B-3B-OF	36	123	18	40	6	3	4	12	.325	9	19	0	59	76	5	.964
— Cincinnati (N.L.)	2B-3B-SS	72	115	12	34	7	1	0	15	.296	5	16	0	46	63	7	.940
1993— Cincinnati (N.L.)	SS-2B-3B-1B	125	381	40	92	15	1	3	22	.241	19	73	4	185	260	11	.976
1994— Cincinnati (N.L.)	2B-3B-SS-1B	58	109	18	31	4	1	6	16	.284	5	16	0	39	52	1	.989
1995— Cincinnati (N.L.)	3B-SS-2B-1B	122	331	43	86	18	2	12	45	.260	44	69	2	84	245	9	.973
1996— Cincinnati (N.L.)	3B-SS-2B	129	311	34	76	16	4	9	37	.244	31	67	2	97	201	14	.955
1997— Indianapolis (A.A.)	SS-3B	15	57	7	12	3	0	1	4	.211	6	10	0	18	32	1	.980
— Cincinnati (N.L.)	3B-2B-SS	65	98	9	15	3	1	1	5	.153	7	23	1	35	56	4	.958
— Cleveland (A.L.)■	2B-3B-SS-DH	29	72	5	19	4	0	2	7	.264	7	17	0	23	60	1	.988
1998— Cleveland (A.L.)	2B-3B-1B-SS	63	100	6	20	4	1	1	9	.200	3	21	0	49	55	5	.954
— Buffalo (I.L.)	3B-2B	12	46	5	12	4	1	0	2	.261	5	9	0	20	29	0	1.000
1999— Indianapolis (I.L.)■	S-3-2-D-1	124	430	57	109	18	2	7	56	.253	46	86	2	182	360	15	†.973
2000— Albuquerque (PCL)■	3B-SS-1B	108	332	45	96	23	2	5	41	.289	27	71	6	86	227	8	.975
— Los Angeles (N.L.)	SS-2B-3B	18	17	3	4	1	0	0	0	.235	1	6	0	8	13	1	.955
2001— Las Vegas (PCL)	2B-SS-3B	96	289	28	79	18	0	4	20	.273	26	71	3	145	218	9	.976
— Los Angeles (N.L.)	2B-SS-3B	13	21	3	6	0	0	0	0	.286	0	4	0	7	10	1	.944
American League totals (2 years)		92	172	11	39	8	1	3	16	.227	10	38	0	72	115	6	.969
National League totals (8 years)		602	1383	162	344	64	10	31	140	.249	112	274	9	501	900	48	.967
Major League totals (9 years)		694	1555	173	383	72	11	34	156	.246	122	312	9	573	1015	54	.967

DIVISION SERIES RECORD

Year Team (League)	Pos.	G	AB	R	H	2B	3B	HR	RBI	Avg.	BB	SO	SB	PO	A	E	Avg.
						— BATTING —									— FIELDING —		
1995— Cincinnati (N.L.)........	3B	3	7	0	2	1	0	0	2	.286	2	0	0	1	8	0	1.000
1998— Cleveland (A.L.)								Did not play.									

CHAMPIONSHIP SERIES RECORD

Year Team (League)	Pos.	G	AB	R	H	2B	3B	HR	RBI	Avg.	BB	SO	SB	PO	A	E	Avg.
						— BATTING —									— FIELDING —		
1995— Cincinnati (N.L.)........	3B-PH	4	9	2	1	1	0	0	0	.111	0	2	1	1	3	0	1.000
1997— Cleveland (A.L.).........	DH	1	2	0	0	0	0	0	0	.000	0	2	0	...	...	...	...
1998— Cleveland (A.L.).........	PH	1	1	0	0	0	0	0	0	.000	0	0	0	...	...	...	...
Championship series totals (3 years)		6	12	2	1	1	0	0	0	.083	0	4	1	1	3	0	1.000

WORLD SERIES RECORD

Year Team (League)	Pos.	G	AB	R	H	2B	3B	HR	RBI	Avg.	BB	SO	SB	PO	A	E	Avg.
						— BATTING —									— FIELDING —		
1997— Cleveland (A.L.).........	PH	1	1	0	0	0	0	0	0	.000	0	1	0	...	...	...	...

BRANTLEY, JEFF P

PERSONAL: Born September 5, 1963, in Florence, Ala. ... 5-10/197. ... Throws right, bats right. ... Full name: Jeffrey Hoke Brantley.

HIGH SCHOOL: W.A. Berry (Florence, Ala.).

COLLEGE: Mississippi State.

TRANSACTIONS/CAREER NOTES: Selected by Montreal Expos organization in 13th round of free-agent draft (June 4, 1984); did not sign. ... Selected by San Francisco Giants organization in sixth round of free-agent draft (June 3, 1985). ... Granted free agency (December 20, 1993). ... Signed by Cincinnati Reds (January 4, 1994). ... Granted free agency (October 17, 1994). ... Re-signed by Reds (October 28, 1994). ... On disabled list (March 19-April 6, 1996). ... On disabled list (March 27-April 15 and May 20, 1997-remainder of season). ... Traded by Reds to St. Louis Cardinals for 1B Dmitri Young (November 10, 1997). ... On St. Louis disabled list (March 23-April 9, 1998); included rehabilitation assignment to Arkansas (April 5-9). ... Traded by Cardinals with OF Ron Gant and P Cliff Politte to Philadelphia Phillies for P Ricky Bottalico and P Garrett Stephenson (November 19, 1998). ... On disabled list (April 29-May 16 and May 24, 1999-remainder of season). ... Granted free agency (November 1, 1999). ... Re-signed by Phillies (December 7, 1999). ... On Philadelphia disabled list (March 25-May 4, 2000); included rehabilitation assignments to Clearwater (April 6-15) and Scranton (April 16-23 and May 2-4). ... Granted free agency (October 31, 2000). ... Signed by Texas Rangers organization (January 12, 2001). ... Released by Rangers (May 29, 2001).

STATISTICAL NOTES: Tied for Pacific Coast League lead with 11 hit batsmen in 1987.

MISCELLANEOUS: Appeared in one game as pinch runner with San Francisco (1989).

Year League	W	L	Pct.	ERA	G	GS	CG	ShO	Sv.	IP	H	R	ER	BB	SO
1985— Fresno (Calif.)...................	8	2	.800	3.33	14	13	3	0	0	94 2/3	83	39	35	37	85
1986— Shreveport (Texas)...........	8	10	.444	3.48	26	26	•8	3	0	165 2/3	139	78	64	68	125
1987— Shreveport (Texas)...........	0	1	.000	3.09	2	2	0	0	0	11 2/3	12	7	4	4	7
— Phoenix (PCL)................	6	11	.353	4.65	29	28	2	0	0	170 1/3	187	110	88	82	111
1988— Phoenix (PCL)................	9	5	.643	4.33	27	19	1	0	0	122 2/3	130	65	59	39	83
— San Francisco (N.L.).......	0	1	.000	5.66	9	1	0	0	1	20 2/3	22	13	13	6	11
1989— San Francisco (N.L.).......	7	1	.875	4.07	59	1	0	0	0	97 1/3	101	50	44	37	69
— Phoenix (PCL)................	1	1	.500	1.26	7	0	0	0	3	14 1/3	6	2	2	6	20
1990— San Francisco (N.L.).......	5	3	.625	1.56	55	0	0	0	19	86 2/3	77	18	15	33	61
1991— San Francisco (N.L.).......	5	2	.714	2.45	67	0	0	0	15	95 1/3	78	27	26	52	81
1992— San Francisco (N.L.).......	7	7	.500	2.95	56	4	0	0	7	91 2/3	67	32	30	45	86
1993— San Francisco (N.L.).......	5	6	.455	4.28	53	12	0	0	0	113 2/3	112	60	54	46	76
1994— Cincinnati (N.L.)■............	6	6	.500	2.48	50	0	0	0	15	65 1/3	46	20	18	28	63
1995— Cincinnati (N.L.).............	3	2	.600	2.82	56	0	0	0	28	70 1/3	53	22	22	20	62
1996— Cincinnati (N.L.).............	1	2	.333	2.41	66	0	0	0	•44	71	54	21	19	28	76
1997— Cincinnati (N.L.).............	1	1	.500	3.86	13	0	0	0	1	11 2/3	9	5	5	7	16
1998— Arkansas (Texas)■..........	0	0	...	0.00	2	0	0	0	0	1 2/3	0	0	0	1	3
— St. Louis (N.L.)...............	0	5	.000	4.44	48	0	0	0	14	50 2/3	40	26	25	18	48
1999— Philadelphia (N.L.)■........	1	2	.333	5.19	10	0	0	0	5	8 2/3	5	6	5	8	11
2000— Philadelphia (N.L.).........	2	7	.222	5.86	55	0	0	0	23	55 1/3	64	36	36	29	57
— Clearwater (FSL).............	2	0	1.000	3.00	5	1	0	0	0	6	5	2	2	3	5
— Scranton/W.B. (I.L.)........	0	0	...	3.60	5	1	0	0	0	5	3	2	2	1	4
2001— Texas (A.L.)■.................	0	1	.000	5.14	18	0	0	0	0	21	26	12	12	9	11
A.L. totals (1 year)	0	1	.000	5.14	18	0	0	0	0	21	26	12	12	9	11
N.L. totals (13 years)	43	45	.489	3.35	597	18	0	0	172	838 1/3	728	336	312	357	717
Major League totals (14 years)	43	46	.483	3.39	615	18	0	0	172	859 1/3	754	348	324	366	728

DIVISION SERIES RECORD

Year League	W	L	Pct.	ERA	G	GS	CG	ShO	Sv.	IP	H	R	ER	BB	SO
1995— Cincinnati (N.L.)..................	0	0	...	6.00	3	0	0	0	1	3	5	2	2	0	2

CHAMPIONSHIP SERIES RECORD

Year League	W	L	Pct.	ERA	G	GS	CG	ShO	Sv.	IP	H	R	ER	BB	SO
1989— San Francisco (N.L.)	0	0	...	0.00	3	0	0	0	0	5	1	0	0	2	3
1995— Cincinnati (N.L.).	0	0	...	0.00	2	0	0	0	0	2 2/3	0	0	0	2	1
Champ. series totals (2 years)	0	0	...	0.00	5	0	0	0	0	7 2/3	1	0	0	4	4

WORLD SERIES RECORD

Year League	W	L	Pct.	ERA	G	GS	CG	ShO	Sv.	IP	H	R	ER	BB	SO
1989— San Francisco (N.L.)	0	0	...	4.15	3	0	0	0	0	4 1/3	5	2	2	3	1

ALL-STAR GAME RECORD

Year League	W	L	Pct.	ERA	GS	CG	ShO	Sv.	IP	H	R	ER	BB	SO
1990— National	0	1	.000	54.00	0	0	0	0	1/3	2	2	2	0	0

BRANYAN, RUSSELL · 3B · INDIANS

PERSONAL: Born December 19, 1975, in Warner Robins, Ga. ... 6-3/195. ... Bats left, throws right. ... Full name: Russell Oles Branyan.
HIGH SCHOOL: Stratford Academy (Warner Robins, Ga.).
TRANSACTIONS/CAREER NOTES: Selected by Cleveland Indians organization in seventh round of free-agent draft (June 2, 1994). ... On Akron disabled list (April 23-May 11 and May 16-August 15, 1998).
HONORS: Named Appalachian League Most Valuable Player (1996).
STATISTICAL NOTES: Led South Atlantic League with .575 slugging percentage in 1996. ... Led South Atlantic League third basemen with 24 double plays in 1996. ... Career major league grand slams: 2.

| | | | | | | | BATTING | | | | | | | | FIELDING | | |
Year Team (League)	Pos.	G	AB	R	H	2B	3B	HR	RBI	Avg.	BB	SO	SB	PO	A	E	Avg.
1994— Burlington (Appl.).......	3B	55	171	21	36	10	0	5	13	.211	25	64	4	32	88	21	.851
1995— Columbus (S.Atl.).......	3B	76	277	46	71	8	6	19	55	.256	27	120	1	34	120	26	.856
1996— Columbus (S.Atl.).......	3B-DH	130	482	102	129	20	4	*40	*106	.268	62	166	7	82	256	44	.885
1997— Kinston (Caro.)...........	3B-DH	83	297	59	86	26	2	27	75	.290	52	94	3	64	118	21	.897
— Akron (East.)...........	3B-DH	41	137	26	32	4	0	12	30	.234	28	56	0	31	98	11	.921
1998— Akron (East.)...........	3B-DH	43	163	35	48	11	3	16	46	.294	35	58	1	24	72	7	.932
— Cleveland (A.L.)..........	3B	1	4	0	0	0	0	0	0	.000	0	2	0	0	1	0	1.000
1999— Buffalo (I.L.)...........	3B-DH	109	395	51	82	11	1	30	67	.208	52	*187	8	63	205	23	.921
— Cleveland (A.L.)..........	3B-DH	11	38	4	8	2	0	1	6	.211	3	19	0	6	18	1	.960
2000— Buffalo (I.L.)...........	3B-OF	64	229	46	56	9	2	21	60	.245	28	93	1	75	70	9	.942
— Cleveland (A.L.).........	OF-DH-3B	67	193	32	46	7	2	16	38	.238	22	76	0	59	3	3	.954
2001— Cleveland (A.L.).......	3B-OF-DH	113	315	48	73	16	2	20	54	.232	38	132	1	78	111	14	.931
Major League totals (4 years)		192	550	84	127	25	4	37	98	.231	63	229	1	143	133	18	.939

DIVISION SERIES RECORD

| | | | | | | | BATTING | | | | | | | | FIELDING | | |
Year Team (League)	Pos.	G	AB	R	H	2B	3B	HR	RBI	Avg.	BB	SO	SB	PO	A	E	Avg.
2001— Cleveland (A.L.).........	OF-PH	2	3	1	1	0	0	0	0	.333	0	1	0	0	0	0	...

BREA, LESLIE · P · ORIOLES

PERSONAL: Born October 12, 1978, in San Pedro de Macoris, Dominican Republic. ... 5-11/170. ... Throws right, bats right. ... Full name: Leslie Guillermo Brea.
HIGH SCHOOL: Santo Domingo (San Pedro de Macoris, Dominican Republic).
TRANSACTIONS/CAREER NOTES: Signed as non-drafted free agent by Seattle Mariners organization (January 20, 1996). ... Traded by Mariners to New York Mets for OF Butch Huskey (December 14, 1998). ... Traded by Mets with OF Melvin Mora, 3B Mike Kinkade and P Pat Gorman to Baltimore Orioles for SS Mike Bordick (July 28, 2000).

Year League	W	L	Pct.	ERA	G	GS	CG	ShO	Sv.	IP	H	R	ER	BB	SO
1996— Arizona Mariners (Ariz.).....	1	0	1.000	5.06	7	0	0	0	0	10 2/3	7	10	6	6	12
1997— Lancaster (Calif.)............	0	0	...	13.50	1	0	0	0	0	2	5	5	3	1	1
— Everett (N'West)............	2	4	.333	7.99	23	0	0	0	3	32 2/3	34	29	29	29	49
1998— Wisconsin (Midw.)............	3	4	.429	2.76	49	0	0	0	12	58 2/3	47	26	18	40	86
1999— St. Lucie (FSL)■..............	1	7	.125	3.73	32	18	0	0	3	120 2/3	95	64	50	68	136
2000— Norfolk (I.L.).................	0	0	...	0.00	1	1	0	0	0	5	4	2	0	4	4
— Binghamton (East.)............	5	8	.385	4.24	19	18	0	0	0	93 1/3	85	53	44	61	86
— Bowie (East.)■.................	1	1	.500	4.26	2	2	0	0	0	12 2/3	12	6	6	9	3
— Baltimore (A.L.)................	0	1	.000	11.00	6	1	0	0	0	9	12	11	11	10	5
— Rochester (I.L.)................	1	2	.333	6.05	4	4	0	0	0	19 1/3	27	18	13	8	13
2001— Rochester (I.L.)................	2	6	.250	3.83	63	0	0	0	1	82 1/3	80	44	35	35	98
— Baltimore (A.L.)................	0	0	...	18.00	2	0	0	0	0	2	6	4	4	3	0
Major League totals (2 years).......	0	1	.000	12.27	8	1	0	0	0	11	18	15	15	13	5

BREWER, JACE · SS · DEVIL RAYS

PERSONAL: Born August 6, 1979, in Washington, Okla. ... 6-0/170. ... Bats right, throws right. ... Full name: Jace A. Brewer.
HIGH SCHOOL: Washington (Okla.).
COLLEGE: Baylor.
TRANSACTIONS/CAREER NOTES: Selected by Montreal Expos organization in 43rd round of free-agent draft (June 2, 1998). ... Selected by Tampa Bay Devil Rays organization in fifth round of free-agent draft (June 5, 2000). ... On disabled list (May 2-25, 2001).

| | | | | | | | BATTING | | | | | | | | FIELDING | | |
Year Team (League)	Pos.	G	AB	R	H	2B	3B	HR	RBI	Avg.	BB	SO	SB	PO	A	E	Avg.
2000— Charl., S.C. (S.Atl.).....	SS-2B	37	137	10	30	7	2	0	15	.219	6	28	3	38	91	9	.935
2001— Charl., S.C. (S.Atl.).....	SS	108	414	50	90	12	4	3	35	.217	18	74	6	142	286	29	.937

BRIDGES, DONNIE · P · EXPOS

PERSONAL: Born December 10, 1978, in Hattiesburg, Miss. ... 6-4/195. ... Throws right, bats right. ... Full name: Donald Wayne Bridges.
HIGH SCHOOL: Oak Grove (Hattiesburg, Miss.).
TRANSACTIONS/CAREER NOTES: Selected by Montreal Expos organization in first round (23rd pick overall) of free-agent draft (June 3, 1997). ... On Ottawa disabled list (May 17-July 23, 2001).

Year League	W	L	Pct.	ERA	G	GS	CG	ShO	Sv.	IP	H	R	ER	BB	SO
1997— Gulf Coast Expos (GCL).....	0	2	.000	6.30	5	2	0	0	0	10	14	9	7	5	6
1998— Vermont (NY-Penn).............	5	6	.455	4.90	13	13	0	0	0	68	71	42	37	37	43
1999— Cape Fear (S.Atl.).............	6	1	.857	2.28	8	8	1	0	0	47 1/3	37	12	12	17	44
— Jupiter (FSL).....................	4	6	.400	4.09	18	18	1	1	0	99	116	53	45	36	63

Year League	W	L	Pct.	ERA	G	GS	CG	ShO	Sv.	IP	H	R	ER	BB	SO
2000—Jupiter (FSL)	5	5	.500	3.19	11	11	0	0	0	73 1/3	58	29	26	20	66
—Harrisburg (East.)	11	7	.611	2.39	19	19	6	4	0	128	104	39	34	49	84
2001—Ottawa (I.L.)	3	5	.375	7.48	13	13	0	0	0	55 1/3	60	50	46	43	49
—GC Expos	0	1	.000	8.44	2	2	0	0	0	5 1/3	2	6	5	5	9
—Harrisburg (East.)	1	2	.333	3.24	3	3	0	0	0	16 2/3	14	10	6	13	14
—Jupiter (FSL)	0	1	.000	6.75	1	1	0	0	0	4	7	6	3	3	2

BROCAIL, DOUG   P   ASTROS

PERSONAL: Born May 16, 1967, in Clearfield, Pa. ... 6-5/235. ... Throws right, bats left. ... Full name: Douglas Keith Brocail.
HIGH SCHOOL: Lamar (Colo.).
JUNIOR COLLEGE: Lamar (Colo.) Community College.
TRANSACTIONS/CAREER NOTES: Selected by San Diego Padres organization in first round (12th pick overall) of free-agent draft (January 14, 1986). ... On Las Vegas disabled list (May 5-12, 1993). ... On San Diego disabled list (April 2-June 28, 1994); included rehabilitation assignments to Wichita (May 26-June 3) and Las Vegas (June 3-23). ... Traded by Padres with OF Phil Plantier, OF Derek Bell, P Pedro Martinez, IF Craig Shipley and SS Ricky Gutierrez to Houston Astros for 3B Ken Caminiti, OF Steve Finley, SS Andujar Cedeno, 1B Robert Petagine, P Brian Williams and a player to be named later (December 28, 1994); Padres acquired P Sean Fesh to complete deal (May 1, 1995). ... On Houston disabled list (May 11-August 15, 1996); included rehabilitation assignments to Jackson (May 27-June 4) and Tucson (July 29-August 15). ... Traded by Astros with OF Brian L. Hunter, IF Orlando Miller, P Todd Jones and cash to Detroit Tigers for C Brad Ausmus, P Jose Lima, P C.J. Nitkowski, P Trever Miller and IF Daryle Ward (December 10, 1996). ... On suspended list (June 10-13, 1998). ... On disabled list (August 9-24, 1998). ... On suspended list (April 28-May 1, 2000). ... On disabled list (August 14-September 1 and September 29, 2000-remainder of season). ... Traded by Tigers with C Brad Ausmus and P Nelson Cruz to Astros for C Mitch Meluskey, P Chris Holt and OF Roger Cedeno (December 11, 2000). ... On Houston disabled list (March 31, 2001-entire season); included rehabilitation assignments to New Orleans (April 3-5) and Round Rock (April 9-16). ... Granted free agency (November 8, 2001). ... Re-signed by Astros organization (December 7, 2001).
MISCELLANEOUS: Appeared in six games as pinch runner with San Diego (1993). ... Appeared in two games as pinch runner with San Diego (1994). ... Appeared in one game as pinch runner with Houston (1995). ... Appeared in two games as pinch runner with Houston (1996).

Year League	W	L	Pct.	ERA	G	GS	CG	ShO	Sv.	IP	H	R	ER	BB	SO
1986—Spokane (N'West)	5	4	.556	3.81	16	•15	0	0	0	85	85	52	36	53	77
1987—Charleston, S.C. (S.Atl.)	2	6	.250	4.09	19	18	0	0	0	92 1/3	94	51	42	28	68
1988—Charleston, S.C. (S.Atl.)	8	6	.571	2.69	22	13	5	0	2	107	107	40	32	25	107
1989—Wichita (Texas)	5	9	.357	5.21	23	22	1	1	0	134 2/3	158	88	78	50	95
1990—Wichita (Texas)	2	2	.500	4.33	12	9	0	0	0	52	53	30	25	24	27
1991—Wichita (Texas)	10	7	.588	3.87	34	16	3	•3	6	146 1/3	147	77	63	43	108
1992—Las Vegas (PCL)	10	10	.500	3.97	29	25	4	0	0	172 1/3	187	82	76	63	103
—San Diego (N.L.)	0	0	...	6.43	3	3	0	0	0	14	17	10	10	5	15
1993—Las Vegas (PCL)	4	2	.667	3.68	10	8	0	0	1	51 1/3	51	26	21	14	32
—San Diego (N.L.)	4	13	.235	4.56	24	24	0	0	0	128 1/3	143	75	65	42	70
1994—Wichita (Texas)	0	0	...	0.00	2	0	0	0	0	4	3	1	0	1	2
—Las Vegas (PCL)	0	0	...	7.11	7	3	0	0	0	12 2/3	21	12	10	2	8
—San Diego (N.L.)	0	0	...	5.82	12	0	0	0	0	17	21	13	11	5	11
1995—Houston (N.L.)■	6	4	.600	4.19	36	7	0	0	1	77 1/3	87	40	36	22	39
—Tucson (PCL)	1	0	1.000	3.86	3	3	0	0	0	16 1/3	18	9	7	4	16
1996—Houston (N.L.)	1	5	.167	4.58	23	4	0	0	0	53	58	31	27	23	34
—Jackson (Texas)	0	0	...	0.00	2	2	0	0	0	4	1	0	0	1	5
—Tucson (PCL)	0	1	.000	7.36	5	1	0	0	0	7 1/3	12	6	6	1	4
1997—Detroit (A.L.)■	3	4	.429	3.23	61	4	0	0	2	78	74	31	28	36	60
1998—Detroit (A.L.)	5	2	.714	2.73	60	0	0	0	0	62 2/3	47	23	19	18	55
1999—Detroit (A.L.)	4	4	.500	2.52	70	0	0	0	2	82	60	23	23	25	78
2000—Detroit (A.L.)	5	4	.556	4.09	49	0	0	0	0	50 2/3	57	25	23	14	41
2001—New Orleans (PCL)■	0	0	...	0.00	2	0	0	0	0	2 1/3	2	0	0	1	2
—Round Rock (Texas)	0	0	...	0.00	1	1	0	0	0	1	0	0	0	0	1
A.L. totals (4 years)	17	14	.548	3.06	240	4	0	0	4	273 1/3	238	102	93	93	234
N.L. totals (5 years)	11	22	.333	4.63	98	38	0	0	1	289 2/3	326	169	149	97	169
Major League totals (9 years)	28	36	.438	3.87	338	42	0	0	5	563	564	271	242	190	403

BROCK, CHRIS   P   ORIOLES

PERSONAL: Born February 5, 1970, in Orlando. ... 6-0/185. ... Throws right, bats right. ... Full name: Terrence Christopher Brock.
HIGH SCHOOL: Lyman (Longwood, Fla.).
COLLEGE: Florida State.
TRANSACTIONS/CAREER NOTES: Selected by Atlanta Braves organization in 12th round of free-agent draft (June 1, 1992). ... On disabled list (July 26, 1995-remainder of season). ... Granted free agency (October 15, 1997). ... Signed by San Francisco Giants organization (December 20, 1997). ... On disabled list (July 24, 1999-remainder of season). ... Traded by Giants to Philadelphia Phillies for C Bobby Estalella (December 12, 1999). ... Traded by Phillies to Baltimore Orioles for P John Wasdin (December 13, 2001).

Year League	W	L	Pct.	ERA	G	GS	CG	ShO	Sv.	IP	H	R	ER	BB	SO
1992—Idaho Falls (Pio.)	6	4	.600	2.31	15	15	1	0	0	78	61	27	20	48	72
1993—Macon (S.Atl.)	7	5	.583	2.70	14	14	1	0	0	80	61	37	24	33	92
—Durham (Caro.)	5	2	.714	2.51	12	12	1	0	0	79	63	28	22	35	67
1994—Greenville (Sou.)	7	6	.538	3.74	25	23	2	2	0	137 1/3	128	68	57	47	94
1995—Richmond (I.L.)	2	8	.200	5.40	22	9	0	0	0	60	68	37	36	27	43
1996—Richmond (I.L.)	10	11	.476	4.67	26	25	3	0	0	150 1/3	137	95	78	61	112
1997—Richmond (I.L.)	10	6	.625	3.34	20	19	0	0	0	118 2/3	97	50	44	51	83
—Atlanta (N.L.)	0	0	...	5.58	7	6	0	0	0	30 2/3	34	23	19	19	16
1998—Fresno (PCL)■	11	3	.786	3.29	17	17	2	0	0	115	111	47	42	33	112
—San Francisco (N.L.)	0	0	...	3.90	13	0	0	0	0	27 2/3	31	13	12	7	19
1999—San Francisco (N.L.)	6	8	.429	5.48	19	19	0	0	0	106 2/3	124	69	65	41	76
2000—Philadelphia (N.L.)■	7	8	.467	4.34	63	5	0	0	1	93 1/3	85	48	45	41	69
2001—Philadelphia (N.L.)	3	0	1.000	4.13	24	0	0	0	0	32 2/3	35	16	15	15	26
—Scranton/W.B. (I.L.)	6	2	.750	3.55	13	13	2	0	0	78 2/3	75	31	31	16	56
Major League totals (5 years)	16	16	.500	4.82	126	30	0	0	1	291	309	169	156	123	206

BROGNA, RICO   1B

PERSONAL: Born April 18, 1970, in Turners Falls, Mass. ... 6-2/203. ... Bats left, throws left. ... Full name: Rico Joseph Brogna. ... Name pronounced BRONE-yah.
HIGH SCHOOL: Watertown (Conn.).
TRANSACTIONS/CAREER NOTES: Selected by Detroit Tigers organization in first round (26th pick overall) of free-agent draft (June 1, 1988). ... On Toledo disabled list (May 25-June 2, 1991). ... Traded by Tigers to New York Mets for 1B Alan Zinter (March 31, 1994). ... On disabled list (June 20, 1996-remainder of season). ... Traded by Mets to Philadelphia Phillies for P Ricardo Jordan and P Toby Borland (November 27, 1996). ... On Philadelphia disabled list (May 11-July 20, 2000); included rehabilitation assignment to Clearwater (July 12-20). ... Claimed on waivers by Boston Red Sox (August 3, 2000). ... Granted free agency (November 1, 2000). ... Signed by Atlanta Braves (December 13, 2000). ... Announced retirement (July 17, 2001).
STATISTICAL NOTES: Led Eastern League first basemen with 1,261 total chances and 117 double plays in 1990. ... Tied for N.L. lead with 10 sacrifice flies in 1998. ... Career major league grand slams: 3.

Year Team (League)	Pos.	G	AB	R	H	2B	3B	HR	RBI	Avg.	BB	SO	SB	PO	A	E	Avg.
1988— Bristol (Appl.)	1B-OF	60	209	37	53	11	2	7	33	.254	25	42	3	319	26	6	.983
1989— Lakeland (FSL)	1B	128	459	47	108	20	7	5	51	.235	38	82	2	1098	83	13	.989
1990— London (East.)	1B	137	488	70	128	21	3	*21	•77	.262	50	100	1	*1155	*93	13	.990
1991— Toledo (I.L.)	1B	41	132	13	29	6	1	2	13	.220	4	26	2	311	37	5	.986
— London (East.)	1B-OF	77	293	40	80	13	1	13	51	.273	25	59	0	368	46	6	.986
1992— Toledo (I.L.)	1B	121	387	45	101	19	4	10	58	.261	31	85	1	896	76	9	.991
— Detroit (A.L.)	1B-DH	9	26	3	5	1	0	1	3	.192	3	5	0	48	6	1	.982
1993— Toledo (I.L.)	1B-DH	129	483	55	132	30	3	11	59	.273	31	94	7	937	97	8	.992
1994— Norfolk (I.L.)■	1B	67	258	33	63	14	5	12	37	.244	15	62	1	583	47	3	.995
— New York (N.L.)	1B	39	131	16	46	11	2	7	20	.351	6	29	1	307	28	1	.997
1995— New York (N.L.)	1B	134	495	72	143	27	2	22	76	.289	39	111	0	1111	93	3	*.998
1996— New York (N.L.)	1B	55	188	18	48	10	1	7	30	.255	19	50	0	440	31	2	.996
1997— Philadelphia (N.L.)■	1B	148	543	68	137	36	1	20	81	.252	33	116	12	1053	119	7	.994
1998— Philadelphia (N.L.)	1B	153	565	77	150	36	3	20	104	.265	49	125	7	1238	141	5	.996
1999— Philadelphia (N.L.)	1B	157	619	90	172	29	4	24	102	.278	54	132	8	1240	123	7	.995
2000— Philadelphia (N.L.)	1B	38	129	12	32	14	0	1	13	.248	7	28	1	248	17	1	.996
— Clearwater (FSL)	1B	7	32	2	7	1	0	0	2	.219	1	4	0	72	6	0	1.000
— Boston (A.L.)■	1B-DH	43	56	8	11	3	0	1	8	.196	3	13	0	165	9	3	.983
2001— Atlanta (N.L.)■	1B	72	206	15	51	9	0	3	21	.248	14	46	3	431	42	3	.994
American League totals (2 years)		52	82	11	16	4	0	2	11	.195	6	18	0	213	15	4	.983
National League totals (8 years)		796	2876	368	779	172	13	104	447	.271	221	637	32	6068	594	29	.996
Major League totals (9 years)		848	2958	379	795	176	13	106	458	.269	227	655	32	6281	609	33	.995

BROHAWN, TROY   P   DIAMONDBACKS

PERSONAL: Born January 14, 1973, in Cambridge, Md. ... 6-1/190. ... Throws left, bats left. ... Full name: Michael Troy Brohawn.
HIGH SCHOOL: Cambridge South Dorchester (Cambridge, Md.).
COLLEGE: Nebraska.
TRANSACTIONS/CAREER NOTES: Selected by San Francisco Giants organization in fourth round of free-agent draft (June 2, 1994). ... Traded by Giants to Arizona Diamondbacks (December 21, 1998), completing deal in which Diamondbacks traded P Felix Rodriguez to Giants for future considerations (December 8, 1998). ... On Tucson disabled list (April 24-August 30, 1999). ... On Arizona disabled list (August 31, 1999-remainder of season). ... On Tucson disabled list (April 6-July 31, 2000).

Year League	W	L	Pct.	ERA	G	GS	CG	ShO	Sv.	IP	H	R	ER	BB	SO
1994— San Jose (Calif.)	0	2	.000	7.02	4	4	0	0	0	$16\frac{2}{3}$	27	15	13	5	13
1995— San Jose (Calif.)	7	3	.700	1.65	11	10	0	0	0	$65\frac{1}{3}$	45	14	12	20	57
1996— Shreveport (Texas)	9	10	.474	4.60	28	28	0	0	0	$156\frac{2}{3}$	163	99	80	49	82
1997— Shreveport (Texas)	13	5	.722	*2.56	26	26	1	•1	0	169	148	57	48	64	98
1998— Fresno (PCL)	10	8	.556	5.25	30	19	0	0	0	$121\frac{2}{3}$	144	75	71	36	87
1999— Tucson (PCL)■	1	0	1.000	3.29	3	2	0	0	0	$13\frac{2}{3}$	22	8	5	3	12
2000— Tucson (PCL)	0	0	...	3.78	11	1	0	0	0	$16\frac{2}{3}$	18	7	7	5	16
— Ariz. Diamondbacks (Ariz.)	0	0	...	0.00	3	0	0	0	0	4	5	1	0	1	6
2001— Tucson (PCL)	0	0	...	0.00	2	0	0	0	0	$3\frac{1}{3}$	1	0	0	1	4
— Arizona (N.L.)	2	3	.400	4.93	59	0	0	0	1	$49\frac{1}{3}$	55	27	27	23	30
Major League totals (1 year)	2	3	.400	4.93	59	0	0	0	1	$49\frac{1}{3}$	55	27	27	23	30

DIVISION SERIES RECORD

Year League	W	L	Pct.	ERA	G	GS	CG	ShO	Sv.	IP	H	R	ER	BB	SO
2001— Arizona (N.L.)					Did not play.										

CHAMPIONSHIP SERIES RECORD

Year League	W	L	Pct.	ERA	G	GS	CG	ShO	Sv.	IP	H	R	ER	BB	SO
2001— Arizona (N.L.)					Did not play.										

WORLD SERIES RECORD

NOTES: Member of World Series championship team (2001).

Year League	W	L	Pct.	ERA	G	GS	CG	ShO	Sv.	IP	H	R	ER	BB	SO
2001— Arizona (N.L.)	0	0	...	0.00	1	0	0	0	0	1	1	0	0	0	1

BROSIUS, SCOTT   3B

PERSONAL: Born August 15, 1966, in Hillsboro, Ore. ... 6-1/202. ... Bats right, throws right. ... Full name: Scott David Brosius. ... Name pronounced BRO-shus.
HIGH SCHOOL: Rex Putnam (Milwaukie, Ore.).
COLLEGE: Linfield College (Ore.).

TRANSACTIONS/CAREER NOTES: Selected by Oakland Athletics organization in 20th round of free-agent draft (June 2, 1987). … On Tacoma disabled list (April 17-May 29, 1991). … On Oakland disabled list (April 18-May 12, 1992); included rehabilitation assignment to Tacoma (May 6-12). … On Oakland disabled list (July 13-August 3, 1992); included rehabilitation assignment to Tacoma (July 27-August 3). … On Tacoma disabled list (July 28-August 5, 1993). … On disabled list (June 8-26, 1994). … On Oakland disabled list (May 5-June 25, 1996); included rehabilitation assignment to Edmonton (June 22-25). … On Oakland disabled list (August 7-29, 1997); included rehabilitation assignment to Modesto (August 27-29). … Traded by A's to New York Yankees (November 18, 1997), completing deal in which Yankees traded P Kenny Rogers and cash to A's for a player to be named later (November 7, 1997). … Granted free agency (October 27, 1998). … Re-signed by Yankees (November 10, 1998). … On New York disabled list (April 14-29, 1999); included rehabilitation assignment to Tampa (April 27). … On New York disabled list (April 5-25, 2000); included rehabilitation assignment to Tampa (April 22-25). … On disabled list (August 2-September 7, 2001). … Granted free agency (November 5, 2001). … Announced retirement (November 27, 2001).

RECORDS: Shares major league record for most double plays by third basemen—4 (July 6, 2001).

HONORS: Named third baseman on THE SPORTING NEWS A.L. All-Star team (1998). … Won A.L. Gold Glove at third base (1999).

STATISTICAL NOTES: Led Northwest League with seven sacrifice flies in 1987. … Led Southern League with 274 total bases in 1990. … Tied for Pacific Coast League lead in double plays by third baseman with 24 in 1992. … Career major league grand slams: 3.

Year	Team (League)	Pos.	G	AB	R	H	2B	3B	HR	RBI	Avg.	BB	SO	SB	PO	A	E	Avg.
1987—Medford (N'West)		3-S-2-1-P	65	255	34	73	18	1	3	49	.286	26	36	5	123	148	38	.877
1988—Madison (Midw.)		S-3-0-1	132	504	82	153	28	2	9	58	.304	56	67	13	151	305	61	.882
1989—Huntsville (Sou.)		2-3-S-1	128	461	68	125	22	2	7	60	.271	58	62	4	225	316	34	.941
1990—Huntsville (Sou.)		SS-2B-3B	•142	547	94	*162	*39	2	23	88	.296	81	81	12	253	419	41	.942
—Tacoma (PCL)		2B	3	7	2	1	0	1	0	0	.143	1	3	0	3	5	0	1.000
1991—Tacoma (PCL)		3B-SS-2B	65	245	28	70	16	3	8	31	.286	18	29	4	49	168	14	.939
—Oakland (A.L.)		2B-OF-3B-DH	36	68	9	16	5	0	2	4	.235	3	11	3	31	16	0	1.000
1992—Oakland (A.L.)		O-3-1-DH-S	38	87	13	19	2	0	4	13	.218	3	13	3	68	15	1	.988
—Tacoma (PCL)		3B-OF	63	236	29	56	13	0	9	31	.237	23	44	8	50	167	10	.956
1993—Oakland (A.L.)		O-1-3-S-DH	70	213	26	53	10	1	6	25	.249	14	37	6	173	29	2	.990
—Tacoma (PCL)		3-0-2-1-S	56	209	38	62	13	2	8	41	.297	21	50	8	101	109	13	.942
1994—Oakland (A.L.)		3B-OF-1B	96	324	31	77	14	1	14	49	.238	24	57	2	82	157	13	.948
1995—Oakland (A.L.)		3-0-1-2-S-D	123	389	69	102	19	2	17	46	.262	41	67	4	208	121	15	.956
1996—Oakland (A.L.)		3B-1B-OF	114	428	73	130	25	0	22	71	.304	59	85	7	128	234	10	.973
—Edmonton (PCL)		3B	3	8	5	5	1	0	0	0	.625	3	1	0	0	4	2	.667
1997—Oakland (A.L.)		3B-SS-OF	129	479	59	97	20	1	11	41	.203	34	102	9	142	246	10	.975
—Modesto (Calif.)		3B	2	3	1	1	0	0	0	1	.333	1	0	0	1	1	1	.667
1998—New York (A.L.)■		3B-1B-OF	152	530	86	159	34	0	19	98	.300	52	97	11	114	294	22	.949
1999—New York (A.L.)		3B-DH	133	473	64	117	26	1	17	71	.247	39	74	9	87	239	13	*.962
—Tampa (FSL)		3B	1	3	0	1	0	0	0	0	.333	0	0	0	2	0	0	1.000
2000—New York (A.L.)		3-1-0-D	135	470	57	108	20	0	16	64	.230	45	73	0	104	231	11	.968
—Tampa (FSL)		3B	2	4	0	1	0	0	0	0	.250	0	1	0	2	2	0	1.000
2001—New York (A.L.)		3B-OF	120	428	57	123	25	2	13	49	.287	34	83	3	82	238	22	.936
Major League totals (11 years)			1146	3889	544	1001	200	8	141	531	.257	348	699	57	1219	1820	119	.962

DIVISION SERIES RECORD

Year	Team (League)	Pos.	G	AB	R	H	2B	3B	HR	RBI	Avg.	BB	SO	SB	PO	A	E	Avg.
1998—New York (A.L.)		3B	3	10	1	4	0	0	1	3	.400	0	3	0	2	6	0	1.000
1999—New York (A.L.)		3B	3	10	0	1	1	0	0	1	.100	0	0	0	2	3	0	1.000
2000—New York (A.L.)		3B	5	17	0	3	1	0	0	1	.176	1	4	0	5	8	0	1.000
2001—New York (A.L.)		3B	5	17	0	1	0	0	0	1	.059	0	3	0	5	10	3	.833
Division series totals (4 years)			16	54	1	9	2	0	1	6	.167	1	10	0	14	27	3	.932

CHAMPIONSHIP SERIES RECORD

Year	Team (League)	Pos.	G	AB	R	H	2B	3B	HR	RBI	Avg.	BB	SO	SB	PO	A	E	Avg.
1998—New York (A.L.)		3B	6	20	2	6	1	0	1	6	.300	4	4	0	4	10	1	.933
1999—New York (A.L.)		3B	5	18	3	4	0	1	2	3	.222	1	4	0	5	4	0	1.000
2000—New York (A.L.)		3B	6	18	2	4	0	0	0	2	.222	2	3	0	4	7	1	.917
2001—New York (A.L.)		3B	5	16	3	2	1	0	0	2	.188	0	6	0	5	9	0	1.000
Championship series totals (4 years)			22	72	10	16	2	1	3	11	.236	7	17	0	18	30	2	.960

WORLD SERIES RECORD

RECORDS: Shares record for most home runs in two consecutive innings—2 (October 20, 1998, seventh and eighth innings). … Shares single-inning record for most at-bats—2 (October 17, 1998, seventh inning).

NOTES: Named Most Valuable Player (1998). … Member of World Series championship team (1998, 1999 and 2000).

Year	Team (League)	Pos.	G	AB	R	H	2B	3B	HR	RBI	Avg.	BB	SO	SB	PO	A	E	Avg.
1998—New York (A.L.)		3B	4	17	3	8	0	0	2	6	.471	0	4	0	3	6	0	1.000
1999—New York (A.L.)		3B	4	16	2	6	1	0	0	1	.375	0	5	0	8	7	0	1.000
2000—New York (A.L.)		3B	5	13	2	4	0	0	1	3	.308	2	2	0	1	9	0	1.000
2001—New York (A.L.)		3B	7	24	1	4	2	0	1	3	.167	0	8	0	5	15	1	.952
World Series totals (4 years)			20	70	8	22	3	0	4	13	.314	2	19	0	17	37	1	.982

ALL-STAR GAME RECORD

Year	League	Pos.	AB	R	H	2B	3B	HR	RBI	Avg.	BB	SO	SB	PO	A	E	Avg.
1998—American		3B	2	1	1	0	0	0	0	.500	0	1	1	0	0	1	.000

RECORD AS PITCHER

Year	League	W	L	Pct.	ERA	G	GS	CG	ShO	Sv.	IP	H	R	ER	BB	SO
1987—Medford (N'West)		0	0	...	0.00	1	0	0	0	0	2	0	0	0	0	1

BROUSSARD, BEN   OF   REDS

PERSONAL: Born September 24, 1976, in Beaumont, Texas. ... 6-2/220. ... Bats left, throws left. ... Full name: Benjamin Isaac Broussard.
COLLEGE: McNeese State.
TRANSACTIONS/CAREER NOTES: Selected by Cincinnati Reds organization in second round of free-agent draft (June 2, 1999). ... On disabled list (May 10-June 26, 2000). ... On Chattanooga disabled list (May 22-29, 2001).
STATISTICAL NOTES: Led Southern League with .592 slugging percentage in 2001.

														FIELDING		
Year Team (League)	Pos.	G	AB	R	H	2B	3B	HR	RBI	Avg.	BB	SO	SB	PO	A	E	Avg.
1999— Billings (Pio.)	OF-1B	38	145	39	59	11	2	14	48	.407	34	30	1	122	8	5	.963
—Clinton (Midw.)	1B-OF	5	20	8	11	4	1	2	6	.550	3	4	0	25	0	2	.926
—Chattanooga (Sou.)	OF-1B	35	127	26	27	5	0	8	21	.213	11	41	1	139	10	2	.987
2000— Chattanooga (Sou.)	OF-1B	87	286	64	73	8	4	14	51	.255	72	78	15	214	15	10	.958
2001— Mudville (Calif.)..........	1B	30	102	14	25	5	0	5	21	.245	16	31	0	238	18	2	.992
—Chattanooga (Sou.) ...	1B-OF	100	353	81	113	27	0	23	69	.320	61	69	10	740	55	8	.990

BROWER, JIM   P   REDS

PERSONAL: Born December 29, 1972, in Edina, Minn. ... 6-2/205. ... Throws right, bats right. ... Full name: James Robert Brower.
HIGH SCHOOL: Minnetonka (Minn.).
COLLEGE: Minnesota.
TRANSACTIONS/CAREER NOTES: Selected by Texas Rangers organization in sixth round of free-agent draft (June 2, 1994). ... Released by Rangers (April 15, 1998). ... Signed by Cleveland Indians organization (April 18, 1998). ... Granted free agency (October 16, 1998). ... Re-signed by Indians organization (January 4, 1999). ... Traded by Indians with P Robert Pugmire to Cincinnati Reds for C Eddie Taubensee (November 16, 2000).
MISCELLANEOUS: Appeared in two games as pinch runner (2001).

Year League	W	L	Pct.	ERA	G	GS	CG	ShO	Sv.	IP	H	R	ER	BB	SO
1994— Hudson Valley (NY-Penn)...	2	1	.667	3.20	4	4	1	0	0	19²/₃	14	10	7	6	15
—Charleston, S.C. (S.Atl.) ...	7	3	.700	1.72	12	12	3	2	0	78²/₃	52	18	15	26	84
1995— Charlotte (FSL).................	7	10	.412	3.89	27	27	2	1	0	173²/₃	170	93	75	62	110
1996— Charlotte (FSL).................	9	8	.529	3.79	23	21	2	0	0	145	148	67	61	40	86
—Tulsa (Texas)	3	2	.600	3.78	5	5	1	1	0	33¹/₃	35	16	14	10	16
1997— Tulsa (Texas)	5	12	.294	5.21	23	23	1	0	0	140	156	99	81	42	103
—Oklahoma City (A.A.).........	2	1	.667	7.23	4	3	0	0	0	18²/₃	30	17	15	8	7
1998— Akron (East.)■................	13	5	.722	3.01	23	23	2	2	0	155²/₃	142	60	52	38	91
1999— Buffalo (I.L.).....................	11	11	.500	4.72	27	27	0	0	0	160	164	101	84	59	76
—Cleveland (A.L.)...............	3	1	.750	4.56	9	2	0	0	0	25²/₃	27	13	13	10	18
2000— Buffalo (I.L.).....................	9	4	.692	3.11	16	15	1	0	0	101¹/₃	99	41	35	24	68
—Cleveland (A.L.)...............	2	3	.400	6.24	17	11	0	0	0	62	80	45	43	31	32
2001— Louisville (I.L.)■............	1	0	1.000	4.09	2	2	0	0	0	11	12	5	5	2	11
—Cincinnati (N.L.)...............	7	10	.412	3.97	46	10	0	0	1	129¹/₃	119	65	57	60	94
A.L. totals (2 years)	5	4	.556	5.75	26	13	0	0	0	87²/₃	107	58	56	41	50
N.L. totals (1 year)	7	10	.412	3.97	46	10	0	0	1	129¹/₃	119	65	57	60	94
Major League totals (3 years)	12	14	.462	4.69	72	23	0	0	1	217	226	123	113	101	144

BROWN, ADRIAN   OF   PIRATES

PERSONAL: Born February 7, 1974, in McComb, Miss. ... 6-0/185. ... Bats both, throws right. ... Full name: Adrian Demond Brown.
HIGH SCHOOL: McComb (Miss.).
TRANSACTIONS/CAREER NOTES: Selected by Pittsburgh Pirates organization in 48th round of free-agent draft (June 1, 1992). ... Loaned by Pirates organization to Lethbridge of Pioneer League (June 11-September 19, 1993). ... On Pittsburgh disabled list (June 13-July 4 and July 6-August 7, 2000); included rehabilitation assignments to Altoona (July 2-4) and Nashville (July 30-August 7). ... On Pittsburgh disabled list (April 17, 2001-remainder of season); included rehabilitation assignments to Altoona (May 7-15), Lynchburg (August 28-September 2) and Williamsport (September 3-13).

														FIELDING		
Year Team (League)	Pos.	G	AB	R	H	2B	3B	HR	RBI	Avg.	BB	SO	SB	PO	A	E	Avg.
1992— GC Pirates (GCL)........	OF-1B	39	121	11	31	2	0	0	12	.256	0	12	8	60	4	1	.985
1993— Lethbridge (Pio.)........	OF	69	282	47	75	12	*9	3	27	.266	17	34	22	119	4	1	*.992
1994— Augusta (S.Atl.).........	OF	79	308	41	80	17	1	1	18	.260	14	38	19	121	6	2	.984
1995— Lynchburg (Caro.)......	OF	54	215	30	52	5	2	1	14	.242	12	20	11	110	6	2	.983
—Augusta (S.Atl.)..........	OF	76	287	64	86	15	4	4	31	.300	33	23	25	124	8	7	.950
1996— Lynchburg (Caro.)......	OF	52	215	39	69	9	3	4	25	.321	14	24	18	99	4	2	.981
—Carolina (Sou.)..........	OF	84	341	48	101	11	3	3	25	.296	25	40	27	185	5	2	.990
1997— Carolina (Sou.)..........	OF	37	145	29	44	4	4	2	15	.303	18	12	9	63	2	3	.956
—Pittsburgh (N.L.)........	OF	48	147	17	28	6	0	1	10	.190	13	18	8	74	3	1	.987
—Calgary (PCL)............	OF	62	248	53	79	10	1	1	19	.319	27	38	20	130	3	1	.993
1998— Nashville (PCL)........	OF	85	311	58	90	12	5	3	27	.289	28	38	25	204	7	5	.977
—Pittsburgh (N.L.)........	OF	41	152	20	43	4	1	0	5	.283	9	18	4	83	3	2	.977
1999— Pittsburgh (N.L.)........	OF	116	226	34	61	5	2	4	17	.270	33	39	5	111	3	4	.966
—Nashville (PCL)........	OF	17	56	10	18	3	1	0	4	.321	11	8	6	31	0	1	.969
2000— Pittsburgh (N.L.)........	OF	104	308	64	97	18	3	4	28	.315	29	34	13	154	7	4	.976
—Altoona (East.)	OF	2	5	1	0	0	0	0	0	.000	3	1	0	3	1	0	1.000
—Nashville (PCL)........	OF	8	26	3	6	1	0	0	2	.231	2	4	3	11	1	0	1.000
2001— Pittsburgh (N.L.)........	OF	8	31	3	6	0	0	1	2	.194	3	3	2	18	0	0	1.000
—Altoona (East.)	DH	7	30	7	10	1	1	0	1	.333	1	7	1	...	...	...	...
—Lynchburg (Caro.)......	DH	4	18	2	6	0	0	1	1	.333	1	3	2	...	...	...	...
—Williamsport (NY-P) ...	DH	4	18	4	6	0	1	0	4	.333	1	2	2	...	...	...	...
Major League totals (5 years)		317	864	138	235	33	6	10	62	.272	87	112	32	440	16	11	.976

B

BROWN, DEE   OF   ROYALS

PERSONAL: Born March 27, 1978, in Bronx, N.Y. ... 6-0/215. ... Bats left, throws right. ... Full name: Dermal Bram Brown.
HIGH SCHOOL: Marlboro (N.Y.) Central.
TRANSACTIONS/CAREER NOTES: Selected by Kansas City Royals organization in first round (14th pick overall) of free-agent draft (June 2, 1996). ... On Kansas City disabled list (June 17-July 27, 2001); included rehabilitation assignment to Omaha (July 12-27).
HONORS: Named Northwest League Most Valuable Player in 1997.
STATISTICAL NOTES: Led Northwest League with 168 total bases and .564 slugging percentage in 1997. ... Tied for Carolina League lead with five intentional bases on balls received in 1998. ... Tied for Carolina League lead with six intentional bases on balls received in 1999.

Year Team (League)	Pos.	G	AB	R	H	2B	3B	HR	RBI	Avg.	BB	SO	SB	PO	A	E	Avg.
1996—GC Royals (GCL)	DH	7	20	1	1	1	0	0	1	.050	0	6	0	...	...	...	...
1997—Spokane (N'West)	OF	73	298	67	97	20	6	13	*73	.326	38	65	17	80	2	7	.921
1998—Wilmington (Caro.)	OF	128	442	64	114	30	2	10	58	.258	53	115	26	124	5	13	.908
—Kansas City (A.L.)	DH-OF	5	3	2	0	0	0	0	0	.000	0	1	0	1	0	0	1.000
1999—Wilmington (Caro.)	OF-DH	61	221	49	68	10	2	13	46	.308	44	56	20	91	4	2	.979
—Wichita (Texas)	OF	65	235	58	83	14	3	12	56	.353	35	41	10	110	4	5	.958
—Kansas City (A.L.)	OF-DH	12	25	1	2	0	0	0	0	.080	2	7	0	12	1	1	.929
2000—Omaha (PCL)	OF	125	479	76	129	25	6	23	70	.269	37	112	20	193	6	7	.966
—Kansas City (A.L.)	OF	15	25	4	4	1	0	0	4	.160	3	9	0	12	0	1	1.000
2001—Kansas City (A.L.)	OF-DH	106	380	39	93	19	0	7	40	.245	22	81	5	159	3	2	.988
—Omaha (PCL)	OF	10	37	5	11	0	0	2	6	.297	3	5	0	16	3	1	.950
Major League totals (4 years)		138	433	46	99	20	0	7	44	.229	27	98	5	184	4	3	.984

BROWN, EMIL   OF

PERSONAL: Born December 29, 1974, in Chicago. ... 6-2/193. ... Bats right, throws right. ... Full name: Emil Quincy Brown. ... Name pronounced E-meal.
HIGH SCHOOL: Harlan (Chicago).
JUNIOR COLLEGE: Indian River Community College (Fla.).
TRANSACTIONS/CAREER NOTES: Selected by Oakland Athletics organization in sixth round of free-agent draft (June 2, 1994). ... On Modesto disabled list (April 10-July 1, 1996). ... On Modesto suspended list (August 29-September 2, 1996). ... Selected by Pittsburgh Pirates organization from A's organization in Rule 5 major league draft (December 9, 1996). ... On Nashville disabled list (April 24-May 2, 1999). ... On Pittsburgh disabled list (June 19-July 4, 2000); included rehabilitation assignment to Nashville (June 30-July 4). ... Traded by Pirates to San Diego Padres for P Shawn Camp and OF Shawn Garrett (July 10, 2001). ... Granted free agency (October 15, 2001).
STATISTICAL NOTES: Led Midwest League outfielders with four double plays in 1995.

Year Team (League)	Pos.	G	AB	R	H	2B	3B	HR	RBI	Avg.	BB	SO	SB	PO	A	E	Avg.
1994—Ariz. Athletics (Ariz.)	OF	32	86	13	19	1	1	3	12	.221	13	12	5	43	3	1	.979
1995—W. Michigan (Midw.)	OF	124	459	63	115	17	3	3	67	.251	52	77	35	165	12	8	.957
1996—Modesto (Calif.)	OF	57	211	50	64	10	1	10	47	.303	32	51	13	97	5	4	.962
—Scottsdale (Ariz.)	OF	4	15	5	4	3	0	0	2	.267	3	2	1	3	1	0	1.000
1997—Pittsburgh (N.L.)■	OF	66	95	16	17	2	1	2	6	.179	10	32	5	53	2	3	.948
1998—Carolina (Sou.)	OF-DH	123	466	89	154	31	2	14	67	.330	50	71	24	199	10	6	.972
—Pittsburgh (N.L.)	OF	13	39	2	10	1	0	0	3	.256	1	11	0	21	2	0	1.000
1999—Nashville (PCL)	OF-DH	110	430	97	132	20	5	18	60	.307	35	80	16	173	10	*10	.948
—Pittsburgh (N.L.)	OF	6	14	0	2	1	0	0	0	.143	0	3	0	8	0	0	1.000
2000—Nashville (PCL)	OF	70	237	44	74	20	1	5	25	.312	40	44	26	127	9	3	.978
—Pittsburgh (N.L.)	OF	50	119	13	26	5	0	3	16	.218	11	34	3	54	3	0	1.000
2001—Pittsburgh (N.L.)	OF	61	123	18	25	4	1	3	13	.203	15	42	10	79	4	1	.988
—San Diego (N.L.)■	OF	13	14	3	1	0	0	0	0	.071	1	7	2	9	0	0	1.000
—Portland (PCL)	OF	22	78	10	25	8	2	3	8	.321	6	17	3	39	2	0	1.000
Major League totals (5 years)		209	404	52	81	13	2	8	38	.200	38	129	20	224	11	4	.983

BROWN, KEVIN   P   DODGERS

PERSONAL: Born March 14, 1965, in McIntyre, Ga. ... 6-4/200. ... Throws right, bats right. ... Full name: James Kevin Brown.
HIGH SCHOOL: Wilkinson County (Irwinton, Ga.).
COLLEGE: Georgia Tech.
TRANSACTIONS/CAREER NOTES: Selected by Texas Rangers organization in first round (fourth pick overall) of free-agent draft (June 2, 1986). ... On disabled list (August 14-29, 1990 and March 27-April 11, 1993). ... Granted free agency (October 15, 1994). ... Signed by Baltimore Orioles (April 9, 1995). ... On disabled list (June 23-July 17, 1995). ... Granted free agency (November 3, 1995). ... Signed by Florida Marlins (December 22, 1995). ... On disabled list (May 13-28, 1996). ... Traded by Marlins to San Diego Padres for P Rafael Medina, P Steve Hoff and 1B Derrek Lee (December 15, 1997). ... Granted free agency (October 26, 1998). ... Signed by Los Angeles Dodgers (December 12, 1998). ... On disabled list (April 9-25, 2000; March 24-April 10, May 30-June 24 and July 16-August 28, 2001).
RECORDS: Holds modern N.L. single-season record for most putouts by pitcher—41 (2000).
HONORS: Named righthanded pitcher on THE SPORTING NEWS college All-America team (1986). ... Named N.L. Pitcher of the Year by THE SPORTING NEWS (1998). ... Named righthanded pitcher on THE SPORTING NEWS N.L. All-Star team (1998).
STATISTICAL NOTES: Tied for A.L. lead with 13 hit batsmen in 1991. ... Tied for N.L. lead with 16 hit batsmen in 1996. ... Pitched 9-0 no-hit victory against San Francisco (June 10, 1997). ... Pitched 5-1 one-hit, complete-game victory against Los Angeles (July 16, 1997). ... Led N.L. with 14 hit batsmen in 1997. ... Pitched 4-0 one-hit, complete-game victory against Milwaukee (August 16, 1998).
MISCELLANEOUS: Made an out in only appearance as pinch hitter (1990). ... Appeared in one game as pinch runner (1993). ... Appeared in two games as pinch runner (1996). ... Holds Florida Marlins all-time records for most shutouts (5), complete games (11) and lowest earned-run average (2.30).

Year League	W	L	Pct.	ERA	G	GS	CG	ShO	Sv.	IP	H	R	ER	BB	SO
1986— Gulf Coast Rangers (GCL)..	0	0	...	6.00	3	0	0	0	0	6	7	4	4	2	1
— Tulsa (Texas)	0	0	...	4.50	3	2	0	0	0	10	9	7	5	5	10
— Texas (A.L.)	1	0	1.000	3.60	1	1	0	0	0	5	6	2	2	0	4
1987— Tulsa (Texas)	1	4	.200	7.29	8	8	0	0	0	42	53	36	34	18	26
— Oklahoma City (A.A.).........	0	5	.000	10.73	5	5	0	0	0	24 1/3	32	32	29	17	9
— Charlotte (FSL).................	0	2	.000	2.72	6	6	1	0	0	36 1/3	33	14	11	17	21
1988— Tulsa (Texas)	12	10	.545	3.51	26	26	5	0	0	174 1/3	174	94	68	61	118
— Texas (A.L.)	1	1	.500	4.24	4	4	1	0	0	23 1/3	33	15	11	8	12
1989— Texas (A.L.)	12	9	.571	3.35	28	28	7	0	0	191	167	81	71	70	104
1990— Texas (A.L.)	12	10	.545	3.60	26	26	6	2	0	180	175	84	72	60	88
1991— Texas (A.L.)	9	12	.429	4.40	33	33	0	0	0	210 2/3	233	116	103	90	96
1992— Texas (A.L.)	•21	11	.656	3.32	35	35	11	1	0	*265 2/3	*262	117	98	76	173
1993— Texas (A.L.)	15	12	.556	3.59	34	34	12	3	0	233	228	105	93	74	142
1994— Texas (A.L.)	7	9	.438	4.82	26	•25	3	0	0	170	*218	109	91	50	123
1995— Baltimore (A.L.)■.............	10	9	.526	3.60	26	26	3	1	0	172 1/3	155	73	69	48	117
1996— Florida (N.L.)■................	17	11	.607	*1.89	32	32	5	*3	0	233	187	60	49	33	159
1997— Florida (N.L.)	16	8	.667	2.69	33	33	6	2	0	237 1/3	214	77	71	66	205
1998— San Diego (N.L.)■	18	7	.720	2.38	36	•35	7	3	0	257	225	77	68	49	257
1999— Los Angeles (N.L.)■	18	9	.667	3.00	35	•35	5	1	0	252 1/3	210	99	84	59	221
2000— Los Angeles (N.L.)	13	6	.684	*2.58	33	33	5	1	0	230	181	76	66	47	216
2001— Los Angeles (N.L.)	10	4	.714	2.65	20	19	1	0	0	115 2/3	94	41	34	38	104
A.L. totals (9 years)	88	73	.547	3.78	213	212	43	7	0	1451	1477	702	610	476	859
N.L. totals (6 years)	92	45	.672	2.53	189	187	29	10	0	1325 1/3	1111	430	372	292	1162
Major League totals (15 years).....	180	118	.604	3.18	402	399	72	17	0	2776 1/3	2588	1132	982	768	2021

DIVISION SERIES RECORD

RECORDS: Holds career record for most hit batsmen—3.

Year League	W	L	Pct.	ERA	G	GS	CG	ShO	Sv.	IP	H	R	ER	BB	SO
1997— Florida (N.L.)	0	0	...	1.29	1	1	0	0	0	7	4	1	1	0	5
1998— San Diego (N.L.)	1	0	1.000	0.61	2	2	0	0	0	14 2/3	5	1	1	7	21
Division series totals (2 years)	1	0	1.000	0.83	3	3	0	0	0	21 2/3	9	2	2	7	26

CHAMPIONSHIP SERIES RECORD

RECORDS: Shares single-game record for most hits allowed—11 (October 14, 1997).

Year League	W	L	Pct.	ERA	G	GS	CG	ShO	Sv.	IP	H	R	ER	BB	SO
1997— Florida (N.L.)	2	0	1.000	4.20	2	2	1	0	0	15	16	7	7	5	11
1998— San Diego (N.L.)	1	1	.500	2.61	2	1	1	1	0	10 1/3	5	3	3	4	12
Champ. series totals (2 years)	3	1	.750	3.55	4	3	2	1	0	25 1/3	21	10	10	9	23

WORLD SERIES RECORD

NOTES: Member of World Series championship team (1997).

Year League	W	L	Pct.	ERA	G	GS	CG	ShO	Sv.	IP	H	R	ER	BB	SO
1997— Florida (N.L.)	0	2	.000	8.18	2	2	0	0	0	11	15	10	10	5	6
1998— San Diego (N.L.)	0	1	.000	4.40	2	2	0	0	0	14 1/3	14	7	7	6	13
World Series totals (2 years)	0	3	.000	6.04	4	4	0	0	0	25 1/3	29	17	17	11	19

ALL-STAR GAME RECORD

Year League	W	L	Pct.	ERA	GS	CG	ShO	Sv.	IP	H	R	ER	BB	SO
1992— American	1	0	1.000	0.00	1	0	0	0	1	0	0	0	0	1
1996— National	0	0	...	0.00	0	0	0	0	1	0	0	0	0	0
1997— National	0	0	...	0.00	0	0	0	0	1	1	0	0	0	1
1998— National	0	0	...	0.00	0	0	0	0	2/3	0	0	0	0	1
2000— National	0	0	...	9.00	0	0	0	0	1	1	1	1	3	0
All-Star Game totals (5 years)	1	0	1.000	1.93	1	0	0	0	4 2/3	2	1	1	3	2

BROWN, KEVIN   C   DEVIL RAYS

PERSONAL: Born April 21, 1973, in Valparaiso, Ind. ... 6-2/224. ... Bats right, throws right. ... Full name: Kevin Lee Brown.
HIGH SCHOOL: Pike Central (Petersburg, Ind.).
COLLEGE: Southern Indiana.
TRANSACTIONS/CAREER NOTES: Selected by Texas Rangers organization in second round of free-agent draft (June 2, 1994). ... Traded by Rangers to Toronto Blue Jays for P Tim Crabtree (March 14, 1998). ... On Toronto disabled list (June 13-30, 1998); included rehabilitation assignment to Syracuse (June 28-30). ... On Syracuse disabled list (April 25-May 5, 2000). ... Traded by Blue Jays to Milwaukee Brewers for OF Alvin Morrow (July 25, 2000). ... Granted free agency (October 10, 2001). ... Signed by Tampa Bay Devil Rays organization (January 24, 2002).
STATISTICAL NOTES: Led American Association catchers with .991 fielding percentage and tied for the league lead in double plays with 10 in 1997.

Year Team (League)	Pos.	G	AB	R	H	2B	3B	HR	RBI	Avg.	BB	SO	SB	PO	A	E	Avg.
1994— Hudson Valley (NY-P).	C	68	233	33	57	*19	1	6	32	.245	23	•86	0	316	34	7	.980
1995— Charlotte (FSL)..........	C-1B	107	355	48	94	25	1	11	57	.265	50	96	2	535	60	9	.985
— Oklahoma City (A.A.)..	C	3	10	1	4	1	0	0	0	.400	2	4	0	6	0	2	.750
1996— Tulsa (Texas)	C-DH-1B	128	460	77	121	27	1	26	86	.263	73	*150	0	594	69	13	.981
— Texas (A.L.)	C-DH	3	4	1	0	0	0	0	1	.000	2	2	0	11	1	0	1.000
1997— Oklahoma City (A.A.)..	C-1B-DH	116	403	56	97	18	2	19	50	.241	38	111	2	640	62	5	†.993
— Texas (A.L.)	C	4	5	1	2	0	0	1	1	.400	0	0	0	9	0	1	.900
1998— Toronto (A.L.)■............	C	52	110	17	29	7	1	2	15	.264	9	31	0	261	19	2	.993
— Syracuse (I.L.)..........	C	2	8	2	5	2	0	0	0	.625	0	2	0	7	1	0	1.000
1999— Syracuse (I.L.)..........	C-DH	88	295	39	76	18	2	13	51	.258	21	79	0	575	42	*13	.979
— Toronto (A.L.)..........	C	2	9	1	4	2	0	0	1	.444	0	3	0	10	1	0	1.000
2000— Syracuse (I.L.)..........	C	51	179	26	60	15	1	7	29	.335	8	46	0	280	32	3	.990
— Indianapolis (I.L.)■....	C	23	82	5	20	5	0	1	6	.244	6	24	0	129	14	0	1.000

Year Team (League)	Pos.	G	AB	R	H	2B	3B	HR	RBI	Avg.	BB	SO	SB	PO	A	E	Avg.
—Milwaukee (N.L.)........	C	5	17	3	4	3	0	0	1	.235	1	5	0	20	2	1	.957
2001—Indianapolis (I.L.).......	C	82	290	19	67	16	1	9	34	.231	18	110	0	439	45	4	.992
—Milwaukee (N.L.)........	C	17	43	7	9	0	1	4	12	.209	2	18	0	68	6	0	1.000
American League totals (4 years)		61	128	20	35	9	1	3	18	.273	11	36	0	291	21	3	.990
National League totals (2 years)		22	60	10	13	3	1	4	13	.217	3	23	0	88	8	1	.990
Major League totals (6 years)		83	188	30	48	12	2	7	31	.255	14	59	0	379	29	4	.990

B

BROWN, ROOSEVELT — OF — CUBS

PERSONAL: Born August 3, 1975, in Vicksburg, Miss. ... 5-11/195. ... Bats left, throws right. ... Full name: Roosevelt Lawayne Brown. ... Cousin of Ellis Burks, designated hitter/outfielder, Cleveland Indians; cousin of Michael Carter, outfielder in Cubs organization.
HIGH SCHOOL: Vicksburg (Miss.).
TRANSACTIONS/CAREER NOTES: Selected by Atlanta Braves organization in 20th round of free-agent draft (June 3, 1993). ... Traded by Braves to Florida Marlins for 3B Terry Pendleton (August 13, 1996). ... Selected by Chicago Cubs organization from Marlins organization in Rule 5 minor league draft (December 15, 1997).
STATISTICAL NOTES: Career major league grand slams: 1.

Year Team (League)	Pos.	G	AB	R	H	2B	3B	HR	RBI	Avg.	BB	SO	SB	PO	A	E	Avg.
1993—GC Braves (GCL).......	OF	26	80	4	9	1	2	0	5	.113	2	9	2	18	4	4	.846
1994—Idaho Falls (Pio.).......	OF	48	160	28	53	8	1	3	22	.331	17	15	8	63	3	1	.985
1995—Eugene (N'West)........	OF	57	165	28	51	14	4	7	32	.309	13	30	6	45	3	8	.857
1996—Macon (S.Atl.)...........	OF	113	413	61	115	27	0	19	64	.278	33	60	21	154	6	•12	.930
—Kane Co. (Midw.)■....	OF	11	40	1	6	2	0	0	3	.150	1	10	0	13	1	1	.933
1997—Kane County (Midw.)..	OF	61	211	29	50	7	1	4	30	.237	22	52	5	75	5	6	.930
—Brevard County (FSL).	OF	33	114	8	28	7	1	1	12	.246	7	31	0	44	5	1	.980
1998—Daytona (FSL)■.......	OF	68	244	49	84	15	5	9	43	.344	23	46	3	106	4	2	.982
—West Tenn (Sou.).......	OF	42	160	20	42	11	0	6	24	.263	13	30	3	61	4	3	.956
—Iowa (PCL)...............	DH	1	3	0	1	1	0	0	2	.333	0	0	0	...	...	...	...
1999—West Tenn (Sou.).......	OF	34	125	12	37	12	0	3	12	.296	14	29	6	52	5	1	.983
—Chicago (N.L.)..........	OF	33	64	6	14	6	1	1	10	.219	2	14	1	20	1	1	.955
—Iowa (PCL)...............	OF-DH	74	268	50	96	25	2	22	79	.358	19	54	3	107	11	5	.959
2000—Chicago (N.L.).........	OF	45	91	11	32	8	0	3	14	.352	4	22	0	38	1	0	1.000
—Iowa (PCL)...............	OF	100	363	67	112	32	0	12	55	.309	37	60	10	159	6	10	.943
2001—Chicago (N.L.).........	OF-DH	39	83	13	22	6	1	4	22	.265	7	12	0	20	0	1	.952
—Iowa (PCL)...............	OF	88	364	68	126	34	1	22	77	.346	14	67	3	127	7	4	.971
Major League totals (3 years)		117	238	30	68	20	2	8	46	.286	13	48	1	78	2	2	.976

BRUMBAUGH, CLIFF — OF/IF — ROCKIES

PERSONAL: Born April 21, 1974, in Wilmington, Del. ... 6-2/205. ... Bats right, throws right. ... Full name: Clifford Michael Brumbaugh.
COLLEGE: Delaware.
TRANSACTIONS/CAREER NOTES: Selected by Texas Rangers organization in 13th round of free-agent draft (June 1, 1995). ... Claimed on waivers by Colorado Rockies (June 14, 2001). ... Granted free agency (December 21, 2001). ... Re-signed by Rockies organization (January 15, 2002).
HONORS: Named New York-Pennsylvania League Most Valuable Player (1995).
STATISTICAL NOTES: Led New York-Pennsylvania League with .437 on-base percentage in 1995. ... Led Florida State League third baseman with 271 assists, .958 fielding percentage and 380 total chances in 1997. ... Led Texas League first baseman with .990 fielding percentage in 1998.

Year Team (League)	Pos.	G	AB	R	H	2B	3B	HR	RBI	Avg.	BB	SO	SB	PO	A	E	Avg.
1995—Hudson Valley (NY-P.)	3B-1B	74	282	44	*101	19	4	2	45	*.358	39	51	15	60	149	19	.917
1996—Charl., S.C. (S.Atl.).....	3B-1B	132	458	70	111	23	7	6	45	.242	72	103	20	481	194	28	.960
1997—Charlotte (FSL)...........	3-1-2-S-C	139	522	78	136	27	4	15	70	.261	47	99	13	96	280	16	.959
1998—Tulsa (Texas).............	1B-3B-OF	132	483	65	125	34	1	15	76	.259	54	77	1	881	109	13	.987
1999—Tulsa (Texas) OF-1B-2B-3B	135	513	94	144	35	3	25	89	.281	71	88	18	346	21	6	.984
—Oklahoma (PCL)........	OF-1B	4	12	1	3	0	0		1	.250	0	2	0	3	2	1	1.000
2000—Tulsa (Texas).............	OF-3B	7	27	5	6	1	0	2	3	.222	9	10	1	6	7	1	.929
—Oklahoma (PCL)........	OF-1B-3B	127	454	81	126	28	4	10	56	.278	85	72	9	507	76	5	.991
2001—Oklahoma (PCL)..........	OF-1B	54	202	38	62	11	3	8	42	.307	33	41	3	154	9	3	.982
—Texas (A.L.)................	OF	7	10	1	0	0	0	0	0	.000	1	5	0	6	0	0	1.000
—Colo. Springs (PCL)■OF-3B-1B-2B	53	208	31	69	18	1	3	39	.332	34	52	5	88	38	9	.933
—Colorado (N.L.)............	OF	14	36	5	10	2	0	1	4	.278	2	9	0	15	0	0	1.000
American League totals (1 year)		7	10	1	0	0	0	0	0	.000	1	5	0	6	0	0	1.000
National League totals (1 year)		14	36	5	10	2	0	1	4	.278	2	9	0	15	0	0	1.000
Major League totals (1 year)		21	46	6	10	2	0	1	4	.217	3	14	0	21	0	0	1.000

BUCHANAN, BRIAN — OF — TWINS

PERSONAL: Born July 21, 1973, in Miami. ... 6-4/230. ... Bats right, throws right. ... Full name: Brian James Buchanan.
HIGH SCHOOL: Fairfax (Va.).
COLLEGE: Virginia.
TRANSACTIONS/CAREER NOTES: Selected by New York Yankees organization in first round (24th pick overall) of free-agent draft (June 2, 1994). ... On disabled list (April 29, 1995-remainder of season). ... Traded by Yankees with P Eric Milton, P Danny Mota, SS Cristian Guzman and cash to Minnesota Twins for 2B Chuck Knoblauch (February 6, 1998). ... On disabled list (July 18-27 and July 29-August 9, 1999). ... On disabled list (June 29-July 14, 2001).
STATISTICAL NOTES: Tied for Pacific Coast League lead with three double plays by outfielder in 1998. ... Tied Pacific Coast League lead with 11 sacrifice flies in 2000.

Year Team (League)	Pos.	G	AB	R	H	2B	3B	HR	RBI	Avg.	BB	SO	SB	PO	A	E	Avg.
1994— Oneonta (NY-Penn)	OF	50	177	28	40	9	2	4	26	.226	24	53	5	87	2	0	1.000
1995— Greensboro (S.Atl.)	OF	23	96	19	29	3	0	3	12	.302	9	17	7	31	1	1	.970
1996— Tampa (FSL)	OF	131	526	65	137	22	4	10	58	.260	37	108	23	178	11	6	.969
1997— Norwich (East.)	OF	116	470	75	145	25	2	10	69	.309	32	85	11	192	11	8	.962
— Columbus (I.L.)	OF	18	61	8	17	1	0	4	7	.279	4	11	2	17	1	1	.947
1998— Salt Lake (PCL)■	OF	133	500	74	139	29	3	17	82	.278	36	90	14	244	6	8	.969
1999— Salt Lake (PCL)	OF-DH	107	391	67	116	24	1	10	60	.297	28	85	11	184	9	4	.980
2000— Salt Lake (PCL)	OF-1B	95	364	82	108	20	1	27	103	.297	41	75	5	184	11	4	.980
— Minnesota (A.L.)	OF-DH	30	82	10	19	3	0	1	8	.232	8	22	0	34	1	0	1.000
2001— Minnesota (A.L.)	OF-DH	69	197	28	54	12	0	10	32	.274	19	58	1	70	1	2	.973
Major League totals (2 years)		99	279	38	73	15	0	11	40	.262	27	80	1	104	2	2	.981

BUCK, JOHN   C   ASTROS

PERSONAL: Born July 7, 1980, in Kemmerer, Wyo. ... 6-3/210. ... Bats right, throws right. ... Full name: Johnathan R. Buck.
HIGH SCHOOL: Taylorsville (Utah).
TRANSACTIONS/CAREER NOTES: Selected by Houston Astros organization in seventh round of free-agent draft (June 2, 1998).
STATISTICAL NOTES: Led New York-Pennsylvania League catchers with 617 total chances and tied for lead in double plays in 1999. ... Led Midwest League catchers with 844 total chances and 11 double plays in 2000. ... Led South Atlantic League catchers with 1,130 total chances in 2001.

Year Team (League)	Pos.	G	AB	R	H	2B	3B	HR	RBI	Avg.	BB	SO	SB	PO	A	E	Avg.
1998— GC Astros (GCL)	C	36	126	24	36	9	0	3	15	.286	13	22	2	209	21	4	.983
1999— Auburn (NY-Penn)	C	63	233	36	57	17	0	3	29	.245	25	48	7	*549	*52	*16	.974
— Michigan (Midw.)	C	4	10	1	1	1	0	0	0	.100	2	3	0	28	3	0	1.000
2000— Michigan (Midw.)	C	109	390	57	110	33	0	10	71	.282	55	81	2	*748	81	•15	.982
2001— Lexington (S.Atl.)	C	122	443	72	122	24	1	22	73	.275	37	84	4	*1006	*118	6	*.995

BUDDIE, MIKE   P   BREWERS

PERSONAL: Born December 12, 1970, in Berea, Ohio. :.. 6-3/219. ... Throws right, bats right. ... Full name: Michael Joseph Buddie.
HIGH SCHOOL: St. Ignatius (Cleveland).
COLLEGE: Wake Forest.
TRANSACTIONS/CAREER NOTES: Selected by New York Yankees organization in fourth round of free-agent draft (June 1, 1992). ... Released by Yankees (June 9, 2000). ... Signed by Milwaukee Brewers organization (June 12, 2000). ... On Milwaukee disabled list (July 8-27, 2001).

Year League	W	L	Pct.	ERA	G	GS	CG	ShO	Sv.	IP	H	R	ER	BB	SO
1992— Oneonta (NY-Penn)	1	4	.200	3.88	13	13	1	0	0	67 1/3	69	36	29	34	87
1993— Greensboro (S.Atl.)	13	10	.565	4.87	27	26	0	0	0	155 1/3	138	104	84	89	143
1994— Tampa (FSL)	12	5	.706	4.01	25	24	2	0	0	150 1/3	143	75	67	66	113
1995— Norwich (East.) ■	10	*12	.455	4.81	29	27	2	0	1	149 2/3	155	*102	80	81	106
1996— Norwich (East.)	7	12	.368	4.45	29	26	4	0	0	159 2/3	176	101	79	71	103
1997— Norwich (East.)	0	0	...	0.00	1	0	0	0	0	1	0	0	0	0	3
— Columbus (I.L.)	6	6	.500	2.64	53	0	0	0	13	75	85	24	22	25	67
1998— New York (A.L.)	4	1	.800	5.62	24	2	0	0	0	41 2/3	46	29	26	13	20
— Columbus (I.L.)	5	0	1.000	2.74	26	0	0	0	4	42 2/3	35	15	13	15	30
1999— Columbus (I.L.)	9	2	.818	2.86	49	2	0	0	0	78 2/3	80	30	25	22	68
— New York (A.L.)	0	0	...	4.50	2	0	0	0	0	2	3	1	1	0	1
2000— Columbus (I.L.)	1	3	.250	7.50	6	6	0	0	0	30	34	30	25	20	16
— Indianapolis (I.L.)■	7	2	.778	2.62	30	0	0	0	2	58 1/3	40	20	17	29	39
— Milwaukee (N.L.)	0	0	...	4.50	5	0	0	0	0	6	8	3	3	1	5
2001— Indianapolis (I.L.)	4	1	.800	2.31	27	0	0	0	3	46 2/3	36	13	12	25	31
— Milwaukee (N.L.)	0	1	.000	3.89	31	0	0	0	2	41 2/3	34	20	18	17	22
A.L. totals (2 years)	4	1	.800	5.56	26	2	0	0	0	43 2/3	49	30	27	13	21
N.L. totals (2 years)	0	1	.000	3.97	36	0	0	0	2	47 2/3	42	23	21	18	27
Major League totals (4 years)	4	2	.667	4.73	62	2	0	0	2	91 1/3	91	53	48	31	48

BUEHRLE, MARK   P   WHITE SOX

PERSONAL: Born March 23, 1979, in St. Charles, Mo. ... 6-2/200. ... Throws left, bats left. ... Full name: Mark A. Buehrle.
HIGH SCHOOL: Francis Howell North (St. Charles, Mo.).
JUNIOR COLLEGE: Jefferson College (Mo.).
TRANSACTIONS/CAREER NOTES: Selected by Chicago White Sox organization in 38th round of free-agent draft (June 2, 1998).
HONORS: Named Southern League Most Outstanding Pitcher (2000).
STATISTICAL NOTES: Pitched 4-0 one-hit, complete-game victory against Tampa Bay (August 3, 2001).

Year League	W	L	Pct.	ERA	G	GS	CG	ShO	Sv.	IP	H	R	ER	BB	SO
1999— Burlington (Midw.)	7	4	.636	4.10	20	14	1	1	3	98 2/3	105	49	45	16	91
2000— Birmingham (Sou.)	8	4	.667	2.28	16	16	1	1	0	118 2/3	95	37	30	17	68
— Chicago (A.L.)	4	1	.800	4.21	28	3	0	0	0	51 1/3	55	27	24	19	37
2001— Chicago (A.L.)	16	8	.667	3.29	32	32	4	2	0	221 1/3	188	89	81	48	126
Major League totals (2 years)	20	9	.690	3.47	60	35	4	2	0	272 2/3	243	116	105	67	163

DIVISION SERIES RECORD

Year League	W	L	Pct.	ERA	G	GS	CG	ShO	Sv.	IP	H	R	ER	BB	SO
2000— Chicago (A.L.)	0	0	...	0.00	1	0	0	0	0	1/3	2	0	0	0	1

PERSONAL: Born June 12, 1970, in Baltimore. ... 5-10/180. ... Bats right, throws right. ... Full name: Damon Jackson Buford. ... Son of Don Buford, outfielder with Chicago White Sox (1963-67) and Baltimore Orioles (1968); and brother of Don Buford Jr., minor league infielder (1987-89).

HIGH SCHOOL: Birmingham (Calif.).

COLLEGE: Southern California.

TRANSACTIONS/CAREER NOTES: Selected by Baltimore Orioles organization in 10th round of free-agent draft (June 4, 1990). ... Traded by Orioles with OF Alex Ochoa to New York Mets for 3B/OF Bobby Bonilla and a player to be named later (July 28, 1995); Orioles acquired P Jimmy Williams to complete deal (August 17, 1995). ... Traded by Mets to Texas Rangers for OF Terrell Lowery (January 25, 1996). ... Traded by Rangers with C Jim Leyritz to Boston Red Sox for P Aaron Sele, P Mark Brandenburg and C Bill Haselman (November 6, 1997). ... On disabled list (May 18-June 3 and August 27-September 11, 1998; and August 5-23, 1999). ... Traded by Red Sox to Chicago Cubs for IF Manny Alexander (December 11, 1999). ... Released by Cubs (May 16, 2001). ... Signed by Orioles organization (June 8, 2001). ... On Rochester disabled list (July 21-31, 2001). ... Released by Orioles (August 9, 2001). ... Signed by Cincinnati Reds organization (August 18, 2001). ... Granted free agency (October 15, 2001).

STATISTICAL NOTES: Led Eastern League outfielders with 279 total chances in 1992. ... Led International League outfielders with 347 total chances in 1994. ... Career major league grand slams: 3.

Year	Team (League)	Pos.	G	AB	R	H	2B	3B	HR	RBI	Avg.	BB	SO	SB	PO	A	E	Avg.
1990—	Wausau (Midw.)	OF	41	160	31	48	7	2	1	14	.300	21	32	15	89	2	2	.978
1991—	Frederick (Caro.)	OF	133	505	71	138	25	6	8	54	.273	51	92	50	293	7	5	.984
1992—	Hagerstown (East.)	OF	101	373	53	89	17	3	1	30	.239	42	62	41	*264	13	2	.993
—	Rochester (I.L.)	OF	45	155	29	44	10	2	1	12	.284	14	23	23	100	1	3	.971
1993—	Rochester (I.L.)	OF	27	116	24	33	6	1	1	4	.284	7	16	10	73	3	3	.962
—	Baltimore (A.L.)	OF-DH	53	79	18	18	5	0	2	9	.228	9	19	2	61	2	1	.984
1994—	Baltimore (A.L.)	DH-OF	4	2	2	1	0	0	0	0	.500	0	1	0	0	0	0	...
—	Rochester (I.L.)	OF-DH	111	452	*89	122	21	4	16	66	.270	35	81	31	*339	4	4	.988
1995—	Baltimore (A.L.)	OF	24	32	6	2	0	0	0	2	.063	6	7	3	40	0	0	1.000
—	Rochester (I.L.)	OF	46	188	40	58	12	3	4	18	.309	17	26	17	115	2	2	.983
—	New York (N.L.)■	OF	44	136	24	32	5	0	4	12	.235	19	28	7	67	2	2	.972
1996—	Texas (A.L.)■	OF-DH	90	145	30	41	9	0	6	20	.283	15	34	8	93	3	0	1.000
1997—	Texas (A.L.)■	OF-DH	122	366	49	82	18	0	8	39	.224	30	83	18	282	7	3	.990
1998—	Boston (A.L.)■	O-DH-2-3	86	216	37	61	14	4	10	42	.282	22	43	5	134	4	0	1.000
1999—	Boston (A.L.)	OF-DH	91	297	39	72	15	2	6	38	.242	21	74	9	189	6	3	.985
2000—	Chicago (N.L.)■	OF	150	464	64	124	18	3	15	48	.251	47	118	4	336	4	5	.986
2001—	Chicago (N.L.)	OF	35	85	11	15	2	0	3	8	.176	4	23	0	53	0	0	1.000
—	Rochester (I.L.)■	OF	39	149	20	38	10	0	4	12	.255	22	26	3	86	0	0	1.000
—	Louisville (I.L.)	OF	13	54	14	20	5	1	3	14	.370	10	17	0	22	1	1	.958
American League totals (7 years)			470	1137	181	277	61	6	32	150	.244	103	261	45	799	22	7	.992
National League totals (3 years)			229	716	99	171	25	3	22	68	.239	70	169	11	456	6	7	.985
Major League totals (9 years)			699	1853	280	448	86	9	54	218	.242	173	430	56	1255	28	14	.989

DIVISION SERIES RECORD

Year	Team (League)	Pos.	G	AB	R	H	2B	3B	HR	RBI	Avg.	BB	SO	SB	PO	A	E	Avg.
1996—	Texas (A.L.)	PR	2	0	0	0	0	0	0	0	...	0	0	0	...	...	...	...
1998—	Boston (A.L.)	PR-OF-PH-DH	3	1	2	0	0	0	0	0	.000	0	0	0	1	0	0	1.000
1999—	Boston (A.L.)	OF	1	3	0	0	0	0	0	0	.000	0	1	0	3	0	0	1.000
Division series totals (3 years)			6	4	2	0	0	0	0	0	.000	0	1	0	4	0	0	1.000

CHAMPIONSHIP SERIES RECORD

Year	Team (League)	Pos.	G	AB	R	H	2B	3B	HR	RBI	Avg.	BB	SO	SB	PO	A	E	Avg.
1999—	Boston (A.L.)	PR-OF-PH	4	5	1	2	0	0	0	0	.400	0	2	1	4	0	0	1.000

PERSONAL: Born August 13, 1964, in Louisville, Ky. ... 6-3/210. ... Bats right, throws right. ... Full name: Jay Campbell Buhner. ... Brother of Shawn Buhner, former infielder in Mariners organization. ... Name pronounced BYOO-ner.

HIGH SCHOOL: Clear Creek (League City, Texas).

JUNIOR COLLEGE: McLennan Community College (Texas).

TRANSACTIONS/CAREER NOTES: Selected by Atlanta Braves organization in ninth round of free-agent draft (June 6, 1983); did not sign. ... Selected by Pittsburgh Pirates organization in secondary phase of free-agent draft (January 17, 1984). ... Traded by Pirates organization with IF Dale Berra and P Alfonso Pulido to New York Yankees for OF Steve Kemp, IF Tim Foli and cash (December 20, 1984). ... On disabled list (April 11-July 28, 1986). ... Traded by Yankees with P Rich Balabon and a player to be named later to Seattle Mariners for DH Ken Phelps (July 21, 1988); Mariners acquired P Troy Evers to complete deal (October 12, 1988). ... On Seattle disabled list (June 29-August 19, 1989); included rehabilitation assignment to Calgary (August 16-19). ... On Seattle disabled list (March 31-June 1, 1990); included rehabilitation assignment to Calgary (May 18-June 1). ... On Seattle disabled list (June 17-August 23, 1990). ... Granted free agency (October 28, 1994). ... Re-signed by Mariners (December 21, 1994). ... On disabled list (June 6-22, 1995). ... On Seattle disabled list (April 7-June 11 and September 8, 1998-remainder of season); included rehabilitation assignment to Tacoma (June 9-11). ... On disabled list (May 19-July 15, 1999). ... On suspended list (August 25-28, 1999). ... Granted free agency (November 11, 1999). ... Re-signed by Mariners (December 6, 1999). ... On disabled list (August 17-September 1, 2000). ... Granted free agency (November 10, 2000). ... Re-signed by Mariners (December 7, 2000). ... On Seattle disabled list (March 31-September 1, 2001); included rehabilitation assignments to Tacoma (August 13-18) and Everett (August 19-September 1). ... Granted free agency (November 5, 2001). ... Announced retirement (December 18, 2001).

RECORDS: Shares major league records for most strikeouts in two consecutive nine-inning games—8 (August 23-24, 1990); and most strikeouts in three consecutive nine-inning games—10 (August 23-25, 1990).

HONORS: Won A.L. Gold Glove as outfielder (1996).

STATISTICAL NOTES: Tied for International League lead in double plays by outfielder with six in 1987. ... Hit for the cycle (June 23, 1993). ... Career major league grand slams: 10.

Year Team (League)	Pos.	G	AB	R	H	2B	3B	HR	RBI	Avg.	BB	SO	SB	PO	A	E	Avg.
						BATTING									**FIELDING**		
1984— Watertown (NY-Penn)	OF	65	229	43	74	16	3	9	•58	.323	42	58	3	106	8	1	.991
1985— Fort Laud. (FSL)■......	OF	117	409	65	121	18	10	11	76	.296	65	76	6	235	12	7	.972
1986— Fort Lauderdale (FSL)	OF	36	139	24	42	9	1	*7	31	.302	15	30	1	84	7	3	.968
1987— Columbus (I.L.).........	OF	134	502	83	140	23	1	*31	85	.279	55	124	4	275	*20	6	.980
— New York (A.L.).........	OF	7	22	0	5	2	0	0	1	.227	1	6	0	11	1	0	1.000
1988— Columbus (I.L.).........	OF	38	129	26	33	5	0	8	18	.256	19	33	1	83	3	1	.989
— New York (A.L.).........	OF	25	69	8	13	0	0	3	13	.188	3	25	0	52	2	2	.964
— Seattle (A.L.)■..........	OF	60	192	28	43	13	1	10	25	.224	25	68	1	134	7	1	.993
1989— Calgary (PCL)............	OF	56	196	43	61	12	1	11	45	.311	44	56	4	97	8	2	.981
— Seattle (A.L.)............	OF	58	204	27	56	15	1	9	33	.275	19	55	1	106	6	4	.966
1990— Calgary (PCL)............	OF	13	34	6	7	1	0	2	5	.206	7	11	0	14	1	0	1.000
— Seattle (A.L.)............	OF-DH	51	163	16	45	12	0	7	33	.276	17	50	2	55	1	2	.966
1991— Seattle (A.L.)............	OF	137	406	64	99	14	4	27	77	.244	53	117	0	244	15	5	.981
1992— Seattle (A.L.)............	OF	152	543	69	132	16	3	25	79	.243	71	146	0	314	14	2	.994
1993— Seattle (A.L.)............	OF-DH	158	563	91	153	28	3	27	98	.272	100	144	2	263	8	6	.978
1994— Seattle (A.L.)............	OF-DH	101	358	74	100	23	4	21	68	.279	66	63	0	178	11	2	.990
1995— Seattle (A.L.)............	OF-DH	126	470	86	123	23	0	40	121	.262	60	120	0	180	5	2	.989
1996— Seattle (A.L.)............	OF-DH	150	564	107	153	29	0	44	138	.271	84	*159	0	251	9	3	.989
1997— Seattle (A.L.)............	OF-DH	157	540	104	131	18	2	40	109	.243	119	*175	0	295	5	1	*.997
1998— Seattle (A.L.)............	OF-DH	72	244	33	59	7	1	15	45	.242	38	71	0	127	5	2	.985
— Tacoma (PCL)	DH-OF	2	4	2	2	2	0	0	2	.500	2	2	0	0	0	0	...
1999— Seattle (A.L.)............	OF-1B	87	266	37	59	11	0	14	38	.222	69	100	0	136	7	1	.993
2000— Seattle (A.L.)............	OF-DH	112	364	50	92	20	0	26	82	.253	59	98	0	176	4	0	1.000
2001— Tacoma (PCL)	OF	11	34	5	8	0	0	3	9	.235	5	13	0	10	0	0	1.000
— Everett (N'West)........	OF	3	10	3	6	1	0	2	3	.600	1	2	0	0	0	0	...
— Seattle (A.L.)............	OF-DH	19	45	4	10	2	0	2	5	.222	8	9	0	15	0	0	1.000
Major League totals (15 years)		1472	5013	798	1273	233	19	310	965	.254	792	1406	6	2537	100	33	.988

DIVISION SERIES RECORD

Year Team (League)	Pos.	G	AB	R	H	2B	3B	HR	RBI	Avg.	BB	SO	SB	PO	A	E	Avg.
						BATTING									**FIELDING**		
1995— Seattle (A.L.)	OF	5	24	2	11	1	0	1	3	.458	2	4	0	11	1	0	1.000
1997— Seattle (A.L.)	OF	4	13	2	3	0	0	2	2	.231	3	6	0	5	1	0	1.000
2000— Seattle (A.L.)	OF	2	5	1	1	0	0	1	1	.200	2	0	0	4	0	0	1.000
2001— Seattle (A.L.)	OF	2	3	0	0	0	0	0	0	.000	2	1	0	4	1	1	.833
Division series totals (4 years)		13	45	5	15	1	0	4	6	.333	9	11	0	24	3	1	.964

CHAMPIONSHIP SERIES RECORD

RECORDS: Shares A.L. single-series record for most strikeouts—8 (1995).

Year Team (League)	Pos.	G	AB	R	H	2B	3B	HR	RBI	Avg.	BB	SO	SB	PO	A	E	Avg.
						BATTING									**FIELDING**		
1995— Seattle (A.L.)	OF	6	23	5	7	2	0	3	5	.304	2	8	0	15	0	1	.938
2000— Seattle (A.L.)	OF-PH	4	11	0	2	0	0	0	0	.182	1	6	0	4	0	0	1.000
2001— Seattle (A.L.)	OF-PH	3	6	2	2	0	0	1	1	.333	1	3	0	3	0	0	1.000
Championship series totals (3 years)		13	40	7	11	2	0	4	6	.275	4	17	0	22	0	1	.957

ALL-STAR GAME RECORD

Year League	Pos.	AB	R	H	2B	3B	HR	RBI	Avg.	BB	SO	SB	PO	A	E	Avg.
					BATTING									**FIELDING**		
1996— American	OF	2	0	0	0	0	0	0	.000	0	0	0	1	0	0	1.000

BURBA, DAVE   P   RANGERS

PERSONAL: Born July 7, 1966, in Dayton, Ohio. ... 6-4/240. ... Throws right, bats right. ... Full name: David Allen Burba. ... Nephew of Ray Hathaway, pitcher with Brooklyn Dodgers (1945).

HIGH SCHOOL: Kenton Ridge (Springfield, Ohio).

COLLEGE: Ohio State.

TRANSACTIONS/CAREER NOTES: Selected by Seattle Mariners organization in second round of free-agent draft (June 2, 1987). ... Traded by Mariners with P Bill Swift and P Mike Jackson to San Francisco Giants for OF Kevin Mitchell and P Mike Remlinger (December 11, 1991). ... Traded by Giants with OF Darren Lewis and P Mark Portugal to Cincinnati Reds for OF Deion Sanders, P John Roper, P Ricky Pickett, P Scott Service and IF Dave McCarty (July 21, 1995). ... On disabled list (August 7-27, 1997). ... Traded by Reds to Cleveland Indians for 1B Sean Casey (March 30, 1998). ... Granted free agency (November 6, 2001). ... Signed by Texas Rangers (Decemer 19, 2001).

RECORDS: Shares major league record for most home runs allowed in one inning—4 (June 29, 2001, fourth inning).

Year League	W	L	Pct.	ERA	G	GS	CG	ShO	Sv.	IP	H	R	ER	BB	SO
1987— Bellingham (N'West)	3	1	.750	1.93	5	5	0	0	0	23 1/3	20	10	5	3	24
— Salinas (Calif.)	1	6	.143	4.61	9	9	0	0	0	54 2/3	53	31	28	29	46
1988— San Bernardino (Calif.).......	5	7	.417	2.68	20	20	0	0	0	114	106	41	34	54	102
1989— Williamsport (East.)	11	7	.611	3.16	25	25	5	1	0	156 2/3	138	69	55	55	89
1990— Calgary (PCL)	10	6	.625	4.67	31	18	1	0	2	113 2/3	124	64	59	45	47
— Seattle (A.L.)	0	0	...	4.50	6	0	0	0	0	8	8	6	4	2	4
1991— Calgary (PCL)	6	4	.600	3.53	23	9	0	0	4	71 1/3	82	35	28	27	42
— Seattle (A.L.)	2	2	.500	3.68	22	2	0	0	1	36 2/3	34	16	15	14	16
1992— San Francisco (N.L.)■	2	7	.222	4.97	23	11	0	0	0	70 2/3	80	43	39	31	47
— Phoenix (PCL)	5	5	.500	4.72	13	13	0	0	0	74 1/3	86	40	39	24	44
1993— San Francisco (N.L.)	10	3	.769	4.25	54	5	0	0	0	95 1/3	95	49	45	37	88
1994— San Francisco (N.L.)	3	6	.333	4.38	57	0	0	0	0	74	59	39	36	45	84
1995— San Francisco (N.L.)	4	2	.667	4.98	37	0	0	0	0	43 1/3	38	26	24	25	46
— Cincinnati (N.L.)■.............	6	2	.750	3.27	15	9	1	1	0	63 1/3	52	24	23	26	50
1996— Cincinnati (N.L.)■.............	11	13	.458	3.83	34	33	0	0	0	195	179	96	83	97	148
1997— Cincinnati (N.L.)...............	11	10	.524	4.72	30	27	2	0	0	160	157	88	84	73	131

Year League	W	L	Pct.	ERA	G	GS	CG	ShO	Sv.	IP	H	R	ER	BB	SO
1998—Cleveland (A.L.)■	15	10	.600	4.11	32	31	0	0	0	203 2/3	210	100	93	69	132
1999—Cleveland (A.L.)	15	9	.625	4.25	34	34	1	0	0	220	211	113	104	96	174
2000—Cleveland (A.L.)	16	6	.727	4.47	32	32	0	0	0	191 1/3	199	99	95	91	180
2001—Cleveland (A.L.)	10	10	.500	6.21	32	27	1	0	0	150 2/3	188	112	104	54	118
A.L. totals (6 years)	58	37	.611	4.61	158	126	2	0	1	810 1/3	850	446	415	326	624
N.L. totals (6 years)	47	43	.522	4.28	250	85	3	1	0	701 2/3	660	365	334	334	594
Major League totals (12 years)	105	80	.568	4.46	408	211	5	1	1	1512	1510	811	749	660	1218

DIVISION SERIES RECORD

Year League	W	L	Pct.	ERA	G	GS	CG	ShO	Sv.	IP	H	R	ER	BB	SO
1995—Cincinnati (N.L.)	1	0	1.000	0.00	1	0	0	0	0	1	2	0	0	1	0
1998—Cleveland (A.L.)	1	0	1.000	5.06	1	0	0	0	0	5 1/3	4	3	3	2	4
1999—Cleveland (A.L.)	0	0	...	5.00	1	1	0	0	0	4	1	0	0	1	0
2001—Cleveland (A.L.)	0	0	...	0.00	1	0	0	0	0	1	0	0	0	0	1
Division series totals (4 years)	2	0	1.000	2.38	4	1	0	0	0	11 1/3	7	3	3	4	5

CHAMPIONSHIP SERIES RECORD

Year League	W	L	Pct.	ERA	G	GS	CG	ShO	Sv.	IP	H	R	ER	BB	SO
1995—Cincinnati (N.L.)	0	0	...	0.00	2	0	0	0	0	3 2/3	3	0	0	4	0
1998—Cleveland (A.L.)	1	0	1.000	3.00	3	0	0	0	0	6	3	4	2	5	8
Champ. series totals (2 years)	1	0	1.000	1.86	5	0	0	0	0	9 2/3	6	4	2	9	8

BURKE, JAMIE — C/IF — ANGELS

PERSONAL: Born September 24, 1971, in Roseburg, Ore. ... 6-0/195. ... Bats right, throws right. ... Full name: James Eugene Burke.
HIGH SCHOOL: Roseburg (Ore.).
COLLEGE: Oregon State.
TRANSACTIONS/CAREER NOTES: Selected by California Angels organization in ninth round of free-agent draft (June 3, 1993).

Year Team (League)	Pos.	G	AB	R	H	2B	3B	HR	RBI	Avg.	BB	SO	SB	PO	A	E	Avg.
1993—Boise (N'West)	3B	66	226	32	68	11	1	1	30	.301	39	28	2	34	90	18	.873
1994—Cedar Rapids (Midw.)	1B-3B	127	469	57	124	24	1	1	47	.264	40	64	6	620	168	22	.973
1995—Lake Elsinore (Calif.)	3B-1B	106	365	47	100	15	6	2	56	.274	32	53	6	220	191	22	.949
1996—Midland (Texas)	3B-OF-C-1B	45	144	24	46	8	2	2	16	.319	20	22	1	117	33	5	.968
—Vancouver (PCL)	3B-OF-C	41	156	12	39	5	0	1	14	.250	7	18	2	45	55	5	.952
1997—Midland (Texas)	3B-C-OF-1B	116	428	77	141	44	3	6	72	.329	40	46	2	363	228	27	.956
—Vancouver (PCL)	C-3B	8	27	4	8	1	0	0	3	.296	3	2	0	28	8	3	.923
1998—Vancouver (PCL)	C-3B-1B	61	162	16	35	6	0	2	14	.216	13	25	0	278	48	5	.985
—Midland (Texas)	3B	12	41	7	10	1	0	0	4	.244	7	4	0	4	16	3	.870
1999—Edmonton (PCL)	3B-C-1B-2B-P	46	149	29	50	9	0	3	16	.336	23	18	0	54	60	5	.958
2000—Edmonton (PCL)	3B-C-2B	75	263	25	63	12	0	0	17	.240	19	42	1	151	143	6	.980
2001—Salt Lake (PCL)	C-3B-1B-OF	61	215	25	47	10	3	0	27	.219	19	28	1	344	53	5	.988
—Anaheim (A.L.)	C-1B-DH	9	5	1	1	0	0	0	0	.200	0	2	0	12	1	0	1.000
Major League totals (1 year)		9	5	1	1	0	0	0	0	.200	0	2	0	12	1	0	1.000

RECORD AS PITCHER

Year League	W	L	Pct.	ERA	G	GS	CG	ShO	Sv.	IP	H	R	ER	BB	SO
1999—Edmonton (PCL)	1	0	1.000	0.00	1	0	0	0	0	3	1	0	0	1	3

BURKETT, JOHN — P — RED SOX

PERSONAL: Born November 28, 1964, in New Brighton, Pa. ... 6-3/215. ... Throws right, bats right. ... Full name: John David Burkett. ... Name pronounced bur-KETT.
HIGH SCHOOL: Beaver (Pa.).
TRANSACTIONS/CAREER NOTES: Selected by San Francisco Giants organization in sixth round of free-agent draft (June 6, 1983). ... Traded by Giants to Texas Rangers for IF Rich Aurilia and OF Desi Wilson (December 22, 1994). ... Granted free agency (April 7, 1995). ... Signed by Florida Marlins (April 9, 1995). ... Traded by Marlins to Texas Rangers for P Ryan Dempster and a player to be named later (August 8, 1996); Marlins acquired P Rick Helling to complete deal (September 3, 1996). ... On Texas disabled list (August 6-31, 1997); included rehabilitation assignment to Oklahoma City (August 26). ... On Texas disabled list (April 21-May 9, 1999); included rehabilitation assignment to Tulsa (May 1-9). ... Granted free agency (November 1, 1999). ... Signed by Tampa Bay Devil Rays organization (January 17, 2000). ... Released by Devil Rays (March 29, 2000). ... Signed by Atlanta Braves (April 2, 2000). ... Granted free agency (October 31, 2000). ... Re-signed by Braves (December 20, 2000). ... Granted free agency (November 6, 2001). ... Signed by Boston Red Sox (December 19, 2001).
STATISTICAL NOTES: Led N.L. 10 hit batsmen in 1991.
MISCELLANEOUS: Had sacrifice hit in only appearance as pinch hitter (1995).

Year League	W	L	Pct.	ERA	G	GS	CG	ShO	Sv.	IP	H	R	ER	BB	SO
1983—Great Falls (Pio.)	2	6	.250	6.26	13	9	0	0	0	50 1/3	73	44	35	30	38
1984—Clinton (Midw.)	7	6	.538	4.33	20	20	2	0	0	126 2/3	128	81	61	38	83
1985—Fresno (Calif.)	7	4	.636	2.87	20	20	1	1	0	109 2/3	98	43	35	46	72
1986—Fresno (Calif.)	0	3	.000	5.47	4	4	0	0	0	24 2/3	34	19	15	8	14
—Shreveport (Texas)	10	6	.625	2.66	22	21	4	2	0	128 2/3	99	46	38	42	73
1987—Shreveport (Texas)	•14	8	.636	3.34	27	27	6	1	0	*177 2/3	181	75	66	53	126
—San Francisco (N.L.)	0	0	...	4.50	3	0	0	0	0	6	7	4	3	3	5
1988—Phoenix (PCL)	5	11	.313	5.21	21	21	0	0	0	114	141	79	66	49	74
—Shreveport (Texas)	5	1	.833	2.13	7	7	2	1	0	50 2/3	33	15	12	18	34
1989—Phoenix (PCL)	10	11	.476	5.05	28	•28	2	1	0	167 2/3	197	111	94	59	105
1990—Phoenix (PCL)	2	1	.667	2.74	3	3	2	1	0	23	18	8	7	3	9
—San Francisco (N.L.)	14	7	.667	3.79	33	32	2	0	1	204	201	92	86	61	118
1991—San Francisco (N.L.)	12	11	.522	4.18	36	34	3	1	0	206 2/3	223	103	96	60	131
1992—San Francisco (N.L.)	13	9	.591	3.84	32	32	3	0	0	189 2/3	194	96	81	45	107

B

Year League	W	L	Pct.	ERA	G	GS	CG	ShO	Sv.	IP	H	R	ER	BB	SO
1993—San Francisco (N.L.)	•22	7	.759	3.65	34	34	2	1	0	231²/₃	224	100	94	40	145
1994—San Francisco (N.L.)	6	8	.429	3.62	25	25	0	0	0	159¹/₃	176	72	64	36	85
1995—Florida (N.L.)■	14	14	.500	4.30	30	30	4	0	0	188¹/₃	208	95	90	57	126
1996—Florida (N.L.)	6	10	.375	4.32	24	24	1	0	0	154	154	84	74	42	108
— Texas (A.L.)■	5	2	.714	4.06	10	10	1	1	0	68²/₃	75	33	31	16	47
1997—Texas (A.L.)	9	12	.429	4.56	30	30	2	0	0	189¹/₃	240	106	96	30	139
— Oklahoma City (A.A.)	1	0	1.000	3.60	1	1	0	0	0	5	6	2	2	2	3
1998—Texas (A.L.)	9	13	.409	5.68	32	32	0	0	0	195	230	131	*123	46	131
1999—Texas (A.L.)	9	8	.529	5.62	30	25	0	0	0	147¹/₃	184	95	92	46	96
— Tulsa (Texas)	0	1	.000	2.70	2	2	0	0	0	6²/₃	7	5	2	3	3
2000—Atlanta (N.L.)■	10	6	.625	4.89	31	22	0	0	0	134¹/₃	162	79	73	51	110
2001—Atlanta (N.L.)	12	12	.500	3.04	34	34	1	1	0	219¹/₃	187	83	74	70	187
A.L. totals (4 years)	32	35	.478	5.13	102	97	3	1	0	600¹/₃	729	365	342	138	413
N.L. totals (10 years)	109	84	.565	3.91	282	267	16	4	1	1693¹/₃	1736	808	735	465	1122
Major League totals (13 years)	141	119	.542	4.23	384	364	19	5	1	2293²/₃	2465	1173	1077	603	1535

DIVISION SERIES RECORD

Year League	W	L	Pct.	ERA	G	GS	CG	ShO	Sv.	IP	H	R	ER	BB	SO
1996—Texas (A.L.)	1	0	1.000	2.00	1	1	1	0	0	9	10	2	2	1	7
1998—Texas (A.L.)							Did not play.								
1999—Texas (A.L.)							Did not play.								
2000—Atlanta (N.L.)	0	0	...	6.75	1	0	0	0	0	1¹/₃	1	1	1	0	0
2001—Atlanta (N.L.)	1	0	1.000	2.84	1	1	0	0	0	6¹/₃	6	2	2	2	4
Division series totals (3 years)	2	0	1.000	2.70	3	2	1	0	0	16²/₃	17	5	5	3	11

CHAMPIONSHIP SERIES RECORD

Year League	W	L	Pct.	ERA	G	GS	CG	ShO	Sv.	IP	H	R	ER	BB	SO
2001—Atlanta (N.L.)	0	1	.000	8.31	1	1	0	0	0	4¹/₃	7	5	4	2	2

ALL-STAR GAME RECORD

Year League	W	L	Pct.	ERA	GS	CG	ShO	Sv.	IP	H	R	ER	BB	SO
1993—National	0	1	.000	40.50	0	0	0	0	²/₃	4	3	3	0	1
2001—National	0	0	...	0.00	0	0	0	0	1	0	0	0	0	1
All-Star Game totals (2 years)	0	1	.000	16.20	0	0	0	0	1²/₃	4	3	3	0	2

BURKHART, MORGAN — 1B

PERSONAL: Born January 29, 1972, in St. Louis. ... 5-11/225. ... Bats both, throws left.
HIGH SCHOOL: Hazelwood West (Hazelwood, Mo.).
COLLEGE: Texas State, then Central Missouri State.
TRANSACTIONS/CAREER NOTES: Signed by Richmond, Frontier League (1995). ... Contract sold by Richmond to Boston Red Sox organization (October 21, 1998). ... Released by Red Sox (October 9, 2001).
HONORS: Named Frontier League Most Valuable Player (1996, 1997 and 1998).

						BATTING								FIELDING			
Year Team (League)	Pos.	G	AB	R	H	2B	3B	HR	RBI	Avg.	BB	SO	SB	PO	A	E	Avg.
1995—Richmond (Fron.).......	1B	70	282	58	*93	*28	1	9	*70	.330	41	24	16	...	...	...	...
1996—Richmond (Fron.).......	1B	74	266	60	95	*27	1	17	64	.357	49	24	22	...	...	...	...
1997—Richmond (Fron.).......	1B	80	285	*76	92	22	0	*24	74	.323	73	47	8	...	...	...	...
1998—Richmond (Fron.).......	1B	80	280	*97	113	16	1	*36	*98	*.404	85	38	13	...	...	...	...
1999—Sarasota (FSL)■	1B	69	245	56	89	18	0	*23	67	.363	37	33	5	488	32	4	.992
— Trenton (East.)	1B	66	239	40	55	14	1	12	41	.230	31	43	3	215	7	3	.987
2000—Pawtucket (I.L.)	1B-OF	105	353	59	90	17	1	23	77	.255	69	89	0	508	46	4	.993
— Boston (A.L.)	DH-1B	25	73	16	21	3	0	4	18	.288	17	25	0	26	1	1	.964
2001—Pawtucket (I.L.)	1B-OF	120	412	64	111	19	1	25	62	.269	68	113	1	790	58	7	.992
— Boston (A.L.)	DH-1B	11	33	3	6	1	0	1	4	.182	1	11	0	29	2	0	1.000
Major League totals (2 years)		36	106	19	27	4	0	5	22	.255	18	36	0	55	3	1	.983

BURKS, ELLIS — DH/OF — INDIANS

PERSONAL: Born September 11, 1964, in Vicksburg, Miss. ... 6-2/205. ... Bats right, throws right. ... Full name: Ellis Rena Burks. ... Cousin of Roosevelt Brown, outfielder, Chicago Cubs.
HIGH SCHOOL: Everman (Texas).
JUNIOR COLLEGE: Ranger (Texas) Junior College.
TRANSACTIONS/CAREER NOTES: Selected by Boston Red Sox organization in first round (20th pick overall) of free-agent draft (January 11, 1983). ... On disabled list (March 26-April 12, 1988). ... On Boston disabled list (June 15-August 1, 1989); included rehabilitation assignment to Pawtucket (July 26-August 1). ... On disabled list (June 25, 1992-remainder of season). ... Granted free agency (December 19, 1992). ... Signed by Chicago White Sox (January 4, 1993). ... Granted free agency (October 27, 1993). ... Signed by Colorado Rockies (November 30, 1993). ... On Colorado disabled list (May 18-July 31, 1994); included rehabilitation assignment to Colorado Springs (July 18-20). ... On Colorado disabled list (April 17-May 5, 1995); included rehabilitation assignment to Colorado Springs (April 25-May 5). ... On disabled list (June 28-July 29, 1997). ... Traded by Rockies to San Francisco Giants for OF Darryl Hamilton, P James Stoops and a player to be named later (July 31, 1998); Rockies acquired P Jason Brester to complete deal (August 17, 1998). ... Granted free agency (November 2, 1998). ... Re-signed by Giants (November 13, 1998). ... On disabled list (June 9-26, 1999; and May 9-24, 2000). ... Granted free agency (October 30, 2000). ... Signed by Cleveland Indians (November 19, 2000). ... On disabled list (July 16-August 1, 2001).
RECORDS: Shares major league single-inning record for most home runs—2 (August 27, 1990, fourth inning). ... Shares major league career record for most major league ballparks, one or more home runs (since 1900)—39.
HONORS: Named outfielder on THE SPORTING NEWS A.L. All-Star team (1990). ... Named outfielder on THE SPORTING NEWS A.L. Silver Slugger team (1990). ... Won A.L. Gold Glove as outfielder (1990). ... Named outfielder on THE SPORTING NEWS N.L. All-Star team (1996). ... Named outfielder on THE SPORTING NEWS N.L. Silver Slugger team (1996).

STATISTICAL NOTES: Tied for Florida State League lead in double plays by outfielder with six in 1984. ... Led N.L. with 392 total bases and .639 slugging percentage in 1996. ... Hit three home runs in one game (June 19, 2001). ... Career major league grand slams: 10.

Year	Team (League)	Pos.	G	AB	R	H	2B	3B	HR	RBI	Avg.	BB	SO	SB	PO	A	E	Avg.
1983—Elmira (NY-Penn)		OF	53	174	30	42	9	0	2	23	.241	17	43	9	89	5	2	.979
1984—Winter Haven (FSL)		OF	112	375	52	96	15	4	6	43	.256	42	68	29	196	12	5	.977
1985—New Britain (East.)		OF	133	476	66	121	25	7	10	61	.254	42	85	17	306	9	8	.975
1986—New Britain (East.)		OF	124	462	70	126	20	3	14	55	.273	44	75	31	318	5	5	.985
1987—Pawtucket (I.L.)		OF	11	40	11	9	3	1	3	6	.225	7	7	1	25	0	0	1.000
—Boston (A.L.)		OF-DH	133	558	94	152	30	2	20	59	.272	41	98	27	320	15	4	.988
1988—Boston (A.L.)		OF-DH	144	540	93	159	37	5	18	92	.294	62	89	25	370	9	9	.977
1989—Boston (A.L.)		OF-DH	97	399	73	121	19	6	12	61	.303	36	52	21	245	7	6	.977
—Pawtucket (I.L.)		OF	5	21	4	3	1	0	0	0	.143	2	3	0	16	0	0	1.000
1990—Boston (A.L.)		OF-DH	152	588	89	174	33	8	21	89	.296	48	82	9	324	7	2	.994
1991—Boston (A.L.)		OF-DH	130	474	56	119	33	3	14	56	.251	39	81	6	283	2	2	.993
1992—Boston (A.L.)		OF-DH	66	235	35	60	8	3	8	30	.255	25	48	5	120	3	2	.984
1993—Chicago (A.L.)■		OF	146	499	75	137	24	4	17	74	.275	60	97	6	313	6	6	.982
1994—Colorado (N.L.)■		OF	42	149	33	48	8	3	13	24	.322	16	39	3	79	2	3	.964
—Colo. Springs (PCL)		OF	2	8	4	4	1	0	1	2	.500	2	1	0	5	0	0	1.000
1995—Colo. Springs (PCL)		OF-DH	8	29	9	9	2	1	2	6	.310	4	8	0	16	0	0	1.000
—Colorado (N.L.)		OF	103	278	41	74	10	6	14	49	.266	39	72	7	158	3	5	.970
1996—Colorado (N.L.)		OF	156	613	*142	211	45	8	40	128	.344	61	114	32	279	6	5	.983
1997—Colorado (N.L.)		OF	119	424	91	123	19	2	32	82	.290	47	75	7	207	6	4	.982
1998—Colorado (N.L.)		OF	100	357	54	102	22	5	16	54	.286	39	80	3	187	5	5	.975
—San Fran. (N.L.)■		OF	42	147	22	45	6	1	5	22	.306	19	31	8	89	1	1	.989
1999—San Francisco (N.L.)		OF-DH	120	390	73	110	19	0	31	96	.282	69	86	7	210	3	2	.991
2000—San Francisco (N.L.)		OF-DH	122	393	74	135	21	5	24	96	.344	56	49	5	215	4	4	.982
2001—Cleveland (A.L.)■		DH-OF	124	439	83	123	29	1	28	74	.280	62	85	5	25	2	0	1.000
American League totals (8 years)			992	3732	598	1045	213	32	138	535	.280	373	632	104	2000	51	31	.985
National League totals (7 years)			804	2751	530	848	150	30	175	551	.308	346	546	72	1424	30	29	.980
Major League totals (15 years)			1796	6483	1128	1893	363	62	313	1086	.292	719	1178	176	3424	81	60	.983

DIVISION SERIES RECORD

Year	Team (League)	Pos.	G	AB	R	H	2B	3B	HR	RBI	Avg.	BB	SO	SB	PO	A	E	Avg.
1995—Colorado (N.L.)		OF	2	6	1	2	1	0	0	2	.333	0	1	0	4	0	1	.800
2000—San Francisco (N.L.)		OF	4	13	2	3	1	0	1	4	.231	4	2	0	12	0	0	1.000
2001—Cleveland (A.L.)		DH	5	19	4	6	1	0	1	1	.316	1	3	0	...	...	...	...
Division series totals (3 years)			11	38	7	11	3	0	2	7	.289	5	6	0	16	0	1	.941

CHAMPIONSHIP SERIES RECORD

Year	Team (League)	Pos.	G	AB	R	H	2B	3B	HR	RBI	Avg.	BB	SO	SB	PO	A	E	Avg.
1988—Boston (A.L.)		OF	4	17	2	4	1	0	0	1	.235	0	3	0	10	0	0	1.000
1990—Boston (A.L.)		OF	4	15	1	4	2	0	0	0	.267	1	1	1	9	1	0	1.000
1993—Chicago (A.L.)		OF	6	23	4	7	1	0	1	3	.304	3	5	0	15	0	0	1.000
Championship series totals (3 years)			14	55	7	15	4	0	1	4	.273	4	9	1	34	1	0	1.000

ALL-STAR GAME RECORD

NOTES: Named to A.L. All-Star team for 1990 game; replaced by Brook Jacoby due to injury.

Year	League	Pos.	AB	R	H	2B	3B	HR	RBI	Avg.	BB	SO	SB	PO	A	E	Avg.
1990—American						Selected, did not play—injured.											
1996—National		OF	2	0	1	0	1	0	0	.500	0	1	0	1	0	0	1.000

BURNETT, A.J.　　　　　　P　　　　　　MARLINS

PERSONAL: Born January 3, 1977, in North Little Rock, Ark. ... 6-5/205. ... Throws right, bats right. ... Full name: Allen James Burnett.

HIGH SCHOOL: Central Arkansas Christian (North Little Rock, Ark.).

TRANSACTIONS/CAREER NOTES: Selected by New York Mets organization in eighth round of free-agent draft (June 1, 1995). ... Traded by Mets with P Jesus Sanchez and OF Robert Stratton to Florida Marlins for P Al Leiter and 2B Ralph Milliard (February 6, 1998). ... On Florida disabled list (March 17-July 20, 2000); included rehabilitation assignments to Brevard County (July 4-14) and Calgary (July 15-20). ... On Florida disabled list (March 23-May 7, 2001); included rehabilitation assignment to Brevard County (April 24-May 1).

STATISTICAL NOTES: Tied for Appalachian League lead in wild pitches with 16 in 1996. ... Pitched 3-0 no-hit victory against San Diego (May 12, 2001).

Year	League	W	L	Pct.	ERA	G	GS	CG	ShO	Sv.	IP	H	R	ER	BB	SO
1995—Gulf Coast Mets (GCL)	2	3	.400	4.28	9	8	1	0	0	33 2/3	27	16	16	23	26
1996—Kingsport (Appl.)	4	0	1.000	3.88	12	12	0	0	0	58	31	26	25	*54	68
1997—Gulf Coast Mets (GCL)	0	1	.000	3.18	3	2	0	0	0	11 1/3	8	8	4	8	15
—Pittsfield (NY-Penn)	3	1	.750	4.70	20	9	0	0	0	44	28	26	23	35	48
1998—Kane County (Midw.)■	10	4	.714	1.97	20	20	0	0	0	119	74	27	26	45	186
1999—Portland (East.)	6	12	.333	5.52	26	23	0	0	0	120 2/3	132	91	74	71	121
—Florida (N.L.)	4	2	.667	3.48	7	7	0	0	0	41 1/3	37	23	16	25	33
2000—Calgary (PCL)	0	0	...	0.00	1	1	0	0	0	6	0	0	0	3	6
—Brevard County (FSL)	0	0	...	3.68	2	2	0	0	0	7 1/3	4	3	3	6	6
—Florida (N.L.)	3	7	.300	4.79	13	13	0	0	0	82 2/3	80	46	44	44	57
2001—Brevard County (FSL)	0	0	...	1.93	2	2	0	0	0	9 1/3	4	2	2	4	10
—Florida (N.L.)	11	12	.478	4.05	27	27	2	1	0	173 1/3	145	82	78	83	128
Major League totals (3 years)	18	21	.462	4.18	47	47	2	1	0	297 1/3	262	151	138	152	218

PERSONAL: Born April 15, 1969, in Westminster, Calif. ... 6-0/213. ... Bats left, throws right. ... Full name: Jeromy Neal Burnitz.
HIGH SCHOOL: Conroe (Texas).
COLLEGE: Oklahoma State.
TRANSACTIONS/CAREER NOTES: Selected by Milwaukee Brewers organization in 24th round of free-agent draft (June 2, 1987); did not sign. ... Selected by New York Mets organization in first round (17th pick overall) of free-agent draft (June 4, 1990). ... On disabled list (August 23-September 18, 1992). ... On Norfolk suspended list (August 11-13, 1994). ... Traded by Mets with P Joe Roa to Cleveland Indians for P Paul Byrd, P Jerry DiPoto, P Dave Mlicki and a player to be named later (November 18, 1994); Mets acquired 2B Jesus Azuaje to complete deal (December 6, 1994). ... Traded by Indians to Milwaukee Brewers for 3B/1B Kevin Seitzer (August 31, 1996). ... On disabled list (July 18-August 20, 1999). ... Traded by Brewers to Mets as part of three-way deal in which Mets traded P Glendon Rusch to Brewers, Colorado Rockies traded 1B/OF Ross Gload and P Craig House to Mets, Brewers traded P Jeff D'Amico, IF Lou Collier, OF/1B Mark Sweeney and cash to Mets, Mets traded 1B/3B Todd Zeile, OF Benny Agbayani, IF/OF Lenny Harris and cash to Rockies and Rockies traded OF Alex Ochoa to Brewers (January 21, 2002).
RECORDS: Shares A.L. record for most home runs by pinch-hitter in consecutive at-bats—2 (August 2 and 3, 1997).
STATISTICAL NOTES: Led New York-Pennsylvania League with .444 on-base percentage and tied for lead with six intentional bases on balls received in 1990. ... Led American Association with .503 slugging percentage in 1995. ... Led American Association with eight intentional bases on balls received in 1995. ... Hit three home runs in one game (May 10, 2001 and September 25, 2001). ... Career major league grand slams: 6.

Year	Team (League)	Pos.	G	AB	R	H	2B	3B	HR	RBI	Avg.	BB	SO	SB	PO	A	E	Avg.
									BATTING						FIELDING			
1990—	Pittsfield (NY-Penn)....	OF	51	173	37	52	6	5	6	22	.301	45	39	12	79	2	0	1.000
	—St. Lucie (FSL)	OF	11	32	6	5	1	0	0	3	.156	7	12	1	18	1	0	1.000
1991—	Williamsport (East.) ...	OF	135	457	80	103	16	•10	*31	•85	.225	*104	127	31	237	13	•11	.958
1992—	Tidewater (I.L.)	OF	121	445	56	108	21	3	8	40	.243	33	84	30	222	11	8	.967
1993—	Norfolk (I.L.)	OF	65	255	33	58	15	3	8	44	.227	25	53	10	133	9	1	.993
	—New York (N.L.).........	OF	86	263	49	64	10	6	13	38	.243	38	66	3	165	6	4	.977
1994—	New York (N.L.).........	OF	45	143	26	34	4	0	3	15	.238	23	45	1	63	1	2	.970
	—Norfolk (I.L.)	OF-DH	85	314	58	75	15	5	14	49	.239	49	82	18	170	13	4	.979
1995—	Buffalo (A.A.)■........	OF	128	443	72	126	26	7	19	•85	.284	50	83	13	241	12	5	.981
	—Cleveland (A.L.)........	OF-DH	9	7	4	4	1	0	0	0	.571	0	0	0	10	0	0	1.000
1996—	Cleveland (A.L.)........	OF-DH	71	128	30	36	10	0	7	26	.281	25	31	2	44	0	0	1.000
	—Milwaukee (A.L.)■....	OF	23	72	8	17	4	0	2	14	.236	8	16	2	38	1	1	.975
1997—	Milwaukee (A.L.)	OF	153	494	85	139	37	8	27	85	.281	75	111	20	256	13	7	.975
1998—	Milwaukee (N.L.)	OF	161	609	92	160	28	1	38	125	.263	70	158	7	306	10	9	.972
1999—	Milwaukee (N.L.)	OF-DH	130	467	87	126	33	2	33	103	.270	91	124	7	262	8	5	.982
2000—	Milwaukee (N.L.)	OF-DH	161	564	91	131	29	2	31	98	.232	99	121	6	317	12	7	.979
2001—	Milwaukee (N.L.)	OF	154	562	104	141	32	4	34	100	.251	80	150	2	295	13	6	.981
	American League totals (3 years)		256	701	127	196	52	8	36	125	.280	108	158	24	348	14	8	.978
	National League totals (6 years)		737	2608	449	656	136	15	152	479	.252	401	664	24	1408	50	33	.978
	Major League totals (9 years)		993	3309	576	852	188	23	188	604	.257	509	822	48	1756	64	41	.978

ALL-STAR GAME RECORD

Year	League	Pos.	AB	R	H	2B	3B	HR	RBI	Avg.	BB	SO	SB	PO	A	E	Avg.
						BATTING									FIELDING		
1999—	National	OF	2	1	1	1	0	0	0	.500	0	0	0	0	0	0	...

BURNSIDE, ADRIAN   P   PIRATES

PERSONAL: Born March 15, 1977, in Alice Springs, Australia. ... 6-3/168. ... Throws left, bats right. ... Full name: Adrian Mark Burnside.
TRANSACTIONS/CAREER NOTES: Signed as non-drafted free agent by Los Angeles Dodgers organization (July 12, 1995). ... On disabled list (April 22-May 7, 1999). ... Selected by Cincinnati Reds from Dodgers organization in Rule 5 major league draft (December 13, 1999). ... Returned to Dodgers organization (March 14, 2000). ... On disabled list (June 4-17 and July 17-September 11, 2000). ... On Jacksonville disabled list (April 5-May 19, 2001). ... Traded by Dodgers with P Mike Fetters to Pittsburgh Pirates for P Terry Mulholland (July 31, 2001).

Year	League	W	L	Pct.	ERA	G	GS	CG	ShO	Sv.	IP	H	R	ER	BB	SO
1996—	Great Falls (Pio.)	1	3	.250	6.80	14	5	0	0	0	41	44	35	31	38	33
1997—	Yakima (N'West)	6	3	.667	4.93	15	13	0	0	0	65²/₃	67	53	36	49	66
1998—	San Bernardino (Calif.).......	1	10	.091	7.81	21	12	0	0	0	78¹/₃	97	79	68	48	65
	—Yakima (N'West)	1	4	.200	4.05	8	6	0	0	0	33¹/₃	27	21	15	30	34
1999—	San Bernardino (Calif.).......	10	9	.526	4.17	26	22	0	0	0	131²/₃	124	69	61	55	129
2000—	San Antonio (Texas)	6	5	.545	2.90	17	17	0	0	0	93	73	40	30	55	82
2001—	Jacksonville (Sou.).............	4	3	.571	2.66	13	12	0	0	0	67²/₃	44	21	20	30	67
	—Altoona (East.)■.............	0	2	.000	3.62	6	6	0	0	0	32¹/₃	28	15	13	14	32

BURRELL, PAT   OF   PHILLIES

PERSONAL: Born October 10, 1976, in Eureka Springs, Ark. ... 6-4/225. ... Bats right, throws right. ... Name pronounced BURL.
HIGH SCHOOL: Bellarmine Prep (San Jose, Calif.).
COLLEGE: Miami (Fla.).
TRANSACTIONS/CAREER NOTES: Selected by Boston Red Sox organization in 43rd round of free-agent draft (June 1, 1995); did not sign. ... Selected by Philadelphia Phillies organization in first round (first pick overall) of free-agent draft (June 2, 1998).
STATISTICAL NOTES: Career major league grand slams: 3.

Year	Team (League)	Pos.	G	AB	R	H	2B	3B	HR	RBI	Avg.	BB	SO	SB	PO	A	E	Avg.
									BATTING						FIELDING			
1998—	Clearwater (FSL)	1B	37	132	29	40	7	1	7	30	.303	27	22	2	202	13	1	.995
1999—	Reading (East.)...........	1B-OF-DH	117	417	84	139	28	6	28	90	.333	79	103	3	715	56	12	.985
	—Scranton/W.B. (I.L.) ..	1B-OF	10	33	4	5	0	0	1	4	.152	4	8	0	62	1	0	1.000
2000—	Scranton/W.B. (I.L.) ..	OF-1B	40	143	31	42	15	1	4	25	.294	32	36	1	135	16	2	.987
	—Philadelphia (N.L.)......	1B-OF-DH	111	408	57	106	27	1	18	79	.260	63	139	0	533	28	8	.986
2001—	Philadelphia (N.L.)......	OF-DH	155	539	70	139	29	2	27	89	.258	70	162	2	226	18	7	.972
	Major League totals (2 years)		266	947	127	245	56	3	45	168	.259	133	301	2	759	46	15	.982

BUSH, HOMER   2B   BLUE JAYS

PERSONAL: Born November 12, 1972, in East St. Louis, Ill. ... 5-10/208. ... Bats right, throws right. ... Full name: Homer Giles Bush.
HIGH SCHOOL: East St. Louis (Ill.).
COLLEGE: Southern Illinois-Edwardsville.
TRANSACTIONS/CAREER NOTES: Selected by San Diego Padres organization in seventh round of free-agent draft (June 3, 1991). ... On Rancho Cucamonga disabled list (April 27-May 4 and May 9-26, 1994). ... On disabled list (May 20, 1996-remainder of season). ... Traded by Padres with rights to P Hideki Irabu, OF Gordon Amerson and player to be named later to New York Yankees for OF Ruben Rivera, P Rafael Medina and cash (April 22, 1997); Yankees acquired OF Vernon Maxwell to complete deal (June 9, 1997). ... Traded by Yankees with P David Wells and P Graeme Lloyd to Toronto Blue Jays for P Roger Clemens (February 18, 1999). ... On Toronto disabled list (April 11-May 14, 1999); included rehabilitation assignment to Dunedin (May 9-14). ... On disabled list (May 22-June 6 and July 31, 2000-remainder of season). ... On Toronto disabled list (April 5-May 18 and June 26-August 1, 2001); included rehabilitation assignments to Dunedin (May 7-18) and Syracuse (July 28-August 1).

| | | | | | | | — BATTING — | | | | | | | | — FIELDING — | | |
Year Team (League)	Pos.	G	AB	R	H	2B	3B	HR	RBI	Avg.	BB	SO	SB	PO	A	E	Avg.
1991—Arizona Padres (Ariz.)	3B	32	127	16	41	3	2	0	16	.323	4	33	11	25	60	10	.895
1992—Charl., S.C. (S.Atl.)	2B	108	367	37	86	10	5	0	18	.234	13	85	14	199	287	*34	.935
1993—Waterloo (Midw.)	2B	130	472	63	*152	19	3	5	51	.322	19	87	39	215	289	38	.930
1994—Rancho Cuca. (Calif.)	2B	39	161	37	54	10	3	0	16	.335	9	29	9	69	102	7	.961
—Wichita (Texas)	2B	59	245	35	73	11	4	3	14	.298	10	39	20	101	135	8	.967
1995—Memphis (Sou.)	2B-DH	108	432	53	121	12	5	5	37	.280	15	83	34	235	268	16	.969
1996—Las Vegas (PCL)	2B-DH	32	116	24	42	11	1	2	3	.362	3	33	3	67	88	5	.969
1997—Las Vegas (PCL)	2B-DH	38	155	25	43	10	1	3	14	.277	7	40	5	73	103	4	.978
—Columbus (I.L.)■	2B	74	275	36	68	10	3	2	26	.247	25	56	12	153	253	9	.978
—New York (A.L.)	2B-DH	10	11	2	4	0	0	0	3	.364	0	0	0	8	13	2	.913
1998—New York (A.L.)	2-DH-3-S	45	71	17	27	3	0	1	5	.380	5	19	6	38	38	2	.974
1999—Toronto (A.L.)■	2B-SS	128	485	69	155	26	4	5	55	.320	21	82	32	246	404	16	.976
—Dunedin (FSL)	2B-DH	4	14	3	5	2	0	0	0	.357	1	1	1	7	7	0	1.000
2000—Toronto (A.L.)	2B	76	297	38	64	8	0	1	18	.215	18	60	9	165	246	6	.986
2001—Toronto (A.L.)	2B	78	271	32	83	11	1	3	27	.306	8	50	13	153	254	4	.990
—Dunedin (FSL)	2B	4	17	4	6	0	0	0	2	.353	2	3	1	3	9	0	1.000
—Syracuse (I.L.)	2B	9	32	11	8	2	0	0	3	.250	3	6	0	13	23	0	1.000
Major League totals (5 years)		337	1135	158	333	48	5	10	108	.293	52	211	60	610	955	30	.981

DIVISION SERIES RECORD

| | | | | | | | — BATTING — | | | | | | | | — FIELDING — | | |
Year Team (League)	Pos.	G	AB	R	H	2B	3B	HR	RBI	Avg.	BB	SO	SB	PO	A	E	Avg.
1998—New York (A.L.)	PR-DH	1	0	0	0	0	0	0	0	...	0	0	1	...	...	...	...

CHAMPIONSHIP SERIES RECORD

| | | | | | | | — BATTING — | | | | | | | | — FIELDING — | | |
Year Team (League)	Pos.	G	AB	R	H	2B	3B	HR	RBI	Avg.	BB	SO	SB	PO	A	E	Avg.
1998—New York (A.L.)	PR-DH	2	0	1	0	0	0	0	0	...	0	0	1	...	...	...	...

WORLD SERIES RECORD

NOTES: Member of World Series championship team (1998).

| | | | | | | | — BATTING — | | | | | | | | — FIELDING — | | |
Year Team (League)	Pos.	G	AB	R	H	2B	3B	HR	RBI	Avg.	BB	SO	SB	PO	A	E	Avg.
1998—New York (A.L.)	PR-DH	2	0	0	0	0	0	0	0	...	0	0	0	...	...	...	...

BUTLER, BRENT   2B/SS   ROCKIES

PERSONAL: Born February 11, 1978, in Laurinburg, N.C. ... 6-0/180. ... Bats right, throws right. ... Full name: Justin Brent Butler.
HIGH SCHOOL: Scotland County (Laurinburg, N.C.).
TRANSACTIONS/CAREER NOTES: Selected by St. Louis Cardinals organization in third round of free-agent draft (June 2, 1996). ... On disabled list (June 21-June 28, 1998). ... Traded by Cardinals with P Jose Jimenez, P Manny Aybar and P Rick Croushore to Colorado Rockies for P Darryl Kile, P Dave Veres and P Luther Hackman (November 16, 1999). ... On Colorado Springs disabled list (August 29-September 12, 2000).

| | | | | | | | — BATTING — | | | | | | | | — FIELDING — | | |
Year Team (League)	Pos.	G	AB	R	H	2B	3B	HR	RBI	Avg.	BB	SO	SB	PO	A	E	Avg.
1996—Johnson City (Appl.)	SS	62	248	45	*85	21	1	8	50	.343	25	29	8	81	127	12	*.945
1997—Peoria (Midw.)	SS	129	480	81	147	37	2	15	71	.306	63	69	6	*220	345	35	.942
1998—Prince William (Caro.)	S-3-DH-2	126	475	63	136	27	2	11	76	.286	39	74	3	152	349	29	.945
1999—Arkansas (Texas)	SS-3B-2B	•139	528	68	142	21	1	13	54	.269	26	47	0	183	333	17	.968
2000—Colo. Springs (PCL)■	2B-SS	122	438	73	128	35	1	8	54	.292	44	46	1	222	311	16	.971
2001—Colo. Springs (PCL)	2B-SS-3B	65	272	51	91	20	3	7	38	.335	15	26	4	112	160	5	.982
—Colorado (N.L.)	2B-SS-3B	53	119	17	29	7	1	1	14	.244	7	7	1	53	68	5	.960
Major League totals (1 year)		53	119	17	29	7	1	1	14	.244	7	7	1	53	68	5	.960

BYRD, PAUL   P   ROYALS

PERSONAL: Born December 3, 1970, in Louisville, Ky. ... 6-1/184. ... Throws right, bats right. ... Full name: Paul Gregory Byrd.
HIGH SCHOOL: St. Xavier (Louisville, Ky.).
COLLEGE: Louisiana State.
TRANSACTIONS/CAREER NOTES: Selected by Cincinnati Reds organization in 13th round of free-agent draft (June 1, 1988); did not sign. ... Selected by Cleveland Indians organization in fourth round of free-agent draft (June 3, 1991). ... On disabled list (August 12, 1992-remainder of season). ... On disabled list (May 23-July 24, 1993). ... Traded by Indians organization with P Dave Mlicki, P Jerry DiPoto and a player to be named later to New York Mets organization for OF Jeromy Burnitz and P Joe Roa (November 18, 1994); Mets acquired 2B Jesus Azuaje to

complete deal (December 6, 1994). ... On Norfolk disabled list (June 1-19, 1995). ... On New York disabled list (March 22-June 9, 1996); included rehabilitation assignment to Norfolk (May 27-June 9). ... Traded by Mets with a player to be named later to Atlanta Braves for P Greg McMichael (November 25, 1996); Braves acquired P Andy Zwirchitz to complete deal (May 25, 1997). ... On Richmond disabled list (June 3-July 2, 1998). ... Claimed on waivers by Philadelphia Phillies (August 14, 1998). ... On Philadelphia disabled list (July 27, 2000-remainder of season). ... Granted free agency (October 12, 2000). ... Re-signed by Phillies organization (January 29, 2001). ... Traded by Phillies to Kansas City Royals for P Jose Santiago (June 5, 2001). ... On Kansas City disabled list (September 22, 2001-remainder of season). ... Granted free agency (December 21, 2001). ... Re-signed by Royals (January 10, 2002).

STATISTICAL NOTES: Led Carolina League with seven balks in 1991. ... Led N.L. with 17 hit batsmen in 1999. ... Tied for N.L. lead in errors by a pitcher with six in 1999.

MISCELLANEOUS: Appeared in one game as pinch runner (2001).

Year League	W	L	Pct.	ERA	G	GS	CG	ShO	Sv.	IP	H	R	ER	BB	SO
1991—Kinston (Caro.)	4	3	.571	3.16	14	11	0	0	0	62 2/3	40	27	22	36	62
1992—Canton/Akron (East.)	14	6	.700	3.01	24	24	4	0	0	152 1/3	122	68	51	75	118
1993—Charlotte (I.L.)	7	4	.636	3.89	14	14	1	1	0	81	80	43	35	30	54
—Canton/Akron (East.)	0	0	...	3.60	2	1	0	0	0	10	7	4	4	3	8
1994—Canton/Akron (East.)	5	9	.357	3.81	21	20	4	1	0	139 1/3	135	70	59	52	106
—Charlotte (I.L.)	2	2	.500	3.93	9	4	0	0	1	36 2/3	33	19	16	11	15
1995—Norfolk (I.L.)■	3	5	.375	2.79	22	10	1	0	6	87	71	29	27	21	61
—New York (N.L.)	2	0	1.000	2.05	17	0	0	0	0	22	18	6	5	7	26
1996—New York (N.L.)	1	2	.333	4.24	38	0	0	0	0	46 2/3	48	22	22	21	31
—Norfolk (I.L.)	2	0	1.000	3.52	5	0	0	0	1	7 2/3	4	3	3	4	8
1997—Atlanta (N.L.)■	4	4	.500	5.26	31	4	0	0	0	53	47	34	31	28	37
—Richmond (I.L.)	2	1	.667	3.18	3	3	0	0	0	17	14	6	6	1	14
1998—Richmond (I.L.)	5	5	.500	3.69	17	17	2	0	0	102 1/3	92	44	42	36	84
—Atlanta (N.L.)	0	0	...	13.50	1	0	0	0	0	2	4	3	3	1	1
—Philadelphia (N.L.)■	5	2	.714	2.29	8	8	2	1	0	55	41	16	14	17	38
1999—Philadelphia (N.L.)	15	11	.577	4.60	32	32	1	0	0	199 2/3	205	119	102	70	106
2000—Philadelphia (N.L.)	2	9	.182	6.51	17	15	0	0	0	83	89	67	60	35	53
—Scranton/W.B. (I.L.)	2	0	1.000	1.73	3	3	2	0	0	26	20	6	5	6	10
2001—Clearwater (FSL)	0	3	.000	3.42	4	4	0	0	0	23 2/3	24	10	9	5	17
—Scranton/W.B. (I.L.)	1	3	.250	3.65	5	5	0	0	0	37	34	18	15	7	35
—Philadelphia (N.L.)	0	1	.000	8.10	3	1	0	0	0	10	10	9	9	4	3
—Kansas City (A.L.)■	6	6	.500	4.05	16	15	1	0	0	93 1/3	110	45	42	22	49
A.L. totals (1 year)	6	6	.500	4.05	16	15	1	0	0	93 1/3	110	45	42	22	49
N.L. totals (7 years)	29	29	.500	4.70	147	60	3	1	0	471 1/3	462	276	246	183	295
Major League totals (7 years)	35	35	.500	4.59	163	75	4	1	0	564 2/3	572	321	288	205	344

ALL-STAR GAME RECORD

Year League	W	L	Pct.	ERA	GS	CG	ShO	Sv.	IP	H	R	ER	BB	SO
1999—National							Selected, did not play.							

BYRNES, ERIC   OF   ATHLETICS

PERSONAL: Born February 16, 1976, in Redwood City, Calif. ... 6-2/205. ... Bats right, throws right. ... Full name: Eric James Byrnes.
HIGH SCHOOL: St. Francis (Mountain View, Calif.).
COLLEGE: UCLA.
TRANSACTIONS/CAREER NOTES: Selected by Oakland Athletics organization in eighth round of free-agent draft (June 2, 1998).
STATISTICAL NOTES: Led Pacific Coast League outfielders with five double plays in 2001.

Year Team (League)	Pos.	G	AB	R	H	2B	3B	HR	RBI	Avg.	BB	SO	SB	PO	A	E	Avg.
1998—S. Oregon (N'West)	OF	42	169	36	53	10	2	7	31	.314	16	16	6	67	2	1	.986
—Visalia (Calif.)	OF	29	108	26	46	9	2	4	21	.426	18	15	11	56	4	3	.952
1999—Modesto (Calif.)	OF	96	365	86	123	28	1	6	66	.337	58	37	28	133	10	6	.960
—Midland (Texas)	OF	43	164	25	39	14	0	1	22	.238	17	32	6	59	1	5	.923
2000—Midland (Texas)	OF	67	259	49	78	25	2	5	37	.301	43	38	21	114	5	2	.983
—Sacramento (PCL)	OF	67	243	55	81	23	1	9	47	.333	31	30	12	94	3	2	.980
—Oakland (A.L.)	OF-DH	10	10	5	3	0	0	0	0	.300	0	1	2	4	0	0	1.000
2001—Sacramento (PCL)	OF	100	415	81	120	23	2	20	51	.289	33	66	25	175	6	5	.973
—Oakland (A.L.)	OF-DH	19	38	9	9	1	0	3	5	.237	4	6	1	14	0	1	.933
Major League totals (2 years)		29	48	14	12	1	0	3	5	.250	4	7	3	18	0	1	.947

DIVISION SERIES RECORD

Year Team (League)	Pos.	G	AB	R	H	2B	3B	HR	RBI	Avg.	BB	SO	SB	PO	A	E	Avg.
2001—Oakland (A.L.)	PH	2	2	0	0	0	0	0	0	.000	0	2	0	...	...	...	...

CABRERA, JOLBERT   IF/OF   INDIANS

PERSONAL: Born December 8, 1972, in Cartagena, Colombia. ... 6-0/177. ... Bats right, throws right. ... Full name: Jolbert Alexis Cabrera. ... Brother of Orlando Cabrera, shortstop, Montreal Expos.
HIGH SCHOOL: Confenalco (Cartagena, Colombia).
TRANSACTIONS/CAREER NOTES: Signed as non-drafted free agent by Montreal Expos organization (July 3, 1990). ... Loaned by Expos organization to San Bernardino, California League (July 27-September 1, 1994). ... Granted free agency (October 17, 1997). ... Signed by Cleveland Indians organization (January 19, 1998).
STATISTICAL NOTES: Tied for International League lead in caught stealing with 15 in 1998.

Year	Team (League)	Pos.	G	AB	R	H	2B	3B	HR	RBI	Avg.	BB	SO	SB	PO	A	E	Avg.
1990—	Dom. Expos (DSL)	SS	29	115	31	36	3	2	0	12	.313	14	10	14	...	...	...	...
1991—	Sumter (S.Atl.)	SS	101	324	33	66	4	0	1	20	.204	19	62	10	141	256	28	.934
1992—	Albany (S.Atl.)	SS	118	377	44	86	9	2	0	23	.228	34	77	22	169	277	35	.927
1993—	Burlington (Midw.)	SS	128	507	62	129	24	2	0	38	.254	39	93	31	•173	300	*36	.929
1994—	W.P. Beach (FSL)	SS	83	266	32	54	4	0	0	13	.203	14	48	7	136	228	26	.933
	—San Bern. (Calif.)■...	SS	30	109	14	27	5	1	0	11	.248	14	24	2	51	82	7	.950
	—Harrisburg (East.)■...	SS	3	2	0	0	0	0	0	0	.000	0	1	0	0	1	0	1.000
1995—	W.P. Beach (FSL)	SS-2B-3B	103	357	62	102	23	2	1	25	.286	38	61	19	148	294	29	.938
	—Harrisburg (East.)......	SS	9	35	4	10	2	0	0	1	.286	1	3	3	11	18	2	.935
1996—	Harrisburg (East.)	SS-OF-3B	107	354	40	85	18	2	3	29	.240	23	63	10	179	306	25	.951
1997—	Harrisburg (East.)	2B-SS-OF	48	171	28	43	9	0	2	11	.251	28	28	5	98	76	9	.951
	—Ottawa (I.L.)	3B-2B-SS-OF	68	191	28	54	10	4	0	12	.283	11	31	15	51	127	7	.962
1998—	Cleveland (A.L.)■.......	SS	1	2	0	0	0	0	0	0	.000	0	1	0	2	2	0	1.000
	—Buffalo (I.L.)	SS-OF-2B	129	494	94	157	24	1	10	45	.318	68	71	25	235	352	27	.956
1999—	Cleveland (A.L.)	OF-2B-DH	30	37	6	7	1	0	0	0	.189	1	8	3	26	4	1	.968
	—Buffalo (I.L.) OF-SS-2B-3B		71	279	44	74	13	4	0	27	.265	26	43	20	153	82	6	.975
2000—	Buffalo (I.L.)	OF-SS-2B	20	74	18	25	6	1	3	11	.338	5	8	2	44	25	0	1.000
	—Cleveland (A.L.)	O-2-S-D	100	175	27	44	3	1	2	15	.251	8	15	6	109	39	1	.993
2001—	Cleveland (A.L.)	O-2-3-S-D	141	287	50	75	16	3	1	38	.261	16	41	10	130	89	6	.973
Major League totals (4 years)			272	501	83	126	20	4	3	53	.251	25	65	19	267	134	8	.980

DIVISION SERIES RECORD

Year	Team (League)	Pos.	G	AB	R	H	2B	3B	HR	RBI	Avg.	BB	SO	SB	PO	A	E	Avg.
2001—	Cleveland (A.L.)	OF-PH	2	1	1	1	0	0	0	1	1.000	0	0	0	0	0	0	...

CABRERA, JOSE   P   BRAVES

PERSONAL: Born March 24, 1972, in Santiago, Dominican Republic. ... 6-0/180. ... Throws right, bats right. ... Full name: Jose Alberto Cabrera.

TRANSACTIONS/CAREER NOTES: Signed as non-drafted free agent by Cleveland Indians organization (October 12, 1990). ... On disabled list (May 11-28, 1993). ... On disabled list (April 25-May 24, 1995). ... Loaned by Indians organization to Bakersfield, California League (April 4-May 9, 1996). ... On Buffalo disabled list (April 4-13 and 17-25, 1997). ... Traded by Indians to Houston Astros for P Alvin Morman (May 10, 1997). ... On Houston disabled list (April 5, 1998-remainder of season); included rehabilitation assignment to New Orleans (July 4-20). ... Claimed on waivers by Atlanta Braves (April 12, 2001).

Year	League	W	L	Pct.	ERA	G	GS	CG	ShO	Sv.	IP	H	R	ER	BB	SO
1991—	Dominican Indians (DSL)...	6	4	.600	3.07	16	12	1	0	0	73 1/3	64	32	25	17	40
1992—	Burlington (Appl.)	•8	3	.727	1.75	13	13	1	0	0	92 1/3	74	27	18	18	79
1993—	Columbus (S.Atl.)	11	6	.647	2.67	26	26	1	0	0	155 1/3	122	54	46	53	105
1994—	Kinston (Caro.)	4	13	.235	4.44	24	24	0	0	0	133 2/3	134	84	66	43	110
1995—	Canton/Akron (East.)	1	1	.500	1.02	4	3	0	0	0	17 2/3	7	2	2	8	19
1996—	Bakersfield (Calif.)■........	2	2	.500	3.95	7	7	0	0	0	41	40	25	18	21	52
	—Kinston (Caro.)■...........	1	1	.500	1.00	4	3	0	0	0	18	7	2	2	8	19
	—Canton/Akron (East.)	4	3	.571	5.63	15	7	0	0	0	62 1/3	78	45	39	17	40
1997—	Buffalo (A.A.)	3	0	1.000	1.20	5	0	0	0	0	15	8	2	2	7	11
	—New Orleans (A.A.)■......	2	2	.500	2.54	31	0	0	0	0	46	31	13	13	13	48
	—Houston (N.L.)	0	0	...	1.17	12	0	0	0	0	15 1/3	6	2	2	6	18
1998—	Houston (N.L.)	0	0	...	8.31	3	0	0	0	0	4 1/3	7	4	4	1	1
	—New Orleans (PCL)........	0	0	...	5.40	5	0	0	0	1	5	2	3	3	1	6
1999—	New Orleans (PCL).........	3	1	.750	2.82	31	0	0	0	7	51	34	18	16	12	41
	—Houston (N.L.)	4	0	1.000	2.15	26	0	0	0	0	29 1/3	21	7	7	9	28
2000—	New Orleans (PCL).........	2	3	.400	5.92	52	0	0	0	2	59 1/3	74	40	39	17	41
	—New Orleans (PCL)........	0	1	...	2.93	12	0	0	0	4	15 1/3	15	6	5	5	12
2001—	Atlanta (N.L.)■...............	7	4	.636	2.88	55	0	0	0	2	59 1/3	52	24	19	25	43
Major League totals (5 years)		13	7	.650	3.81	148	0	0	0	4	167 2/3	160	77	71	58	131

DIVISION SERIES RECORD

Year	League	W	L	Pct.	ERA	G	GS	CG	ShO	Sv.	IP	H	R	ER	BB	SO
1999—	Houston (N.L.)	0	0	...	0.00	1	0	0	0	0	2	2	0	0	0	6

CABRERA, ORLANDO   SS   EXPOS

PERSONAL: Born November 2, 1974, in Cartagena, Columbia. ... 5-10/175. ... Bats right, throws right. ... Full name: Orlando Luis Cabrera. ... Brother of Jolbert Cabrera, infielder/outfielder, Cleveland Indians.

TRANSACTIONS/CAREER NOTES: Signed as non-drafted free agent by Montreal Expos organization (June 1, 1993). ... On disabled list (August 9, 1999-remainder of season). ... On Montreal disabled list (July 15-August 15, 2000); included rehabilitation assignment to Ottawa (August 12-15).

HONORS: Won N.L. Gold Glove at shortstop (2001).

Year	Team (League)	Pos.	G	AB	R	H	2B	3B	HR	RBI	Avg.	BB	SO	SB	PO	A	E	Avg.
1993—	Dom. Expos (DSL)	IF	38	122	24	42	6	1	1	17	.344	18	11	14	86	76	3	.982
1994—	GC Expos (GCL)	2B-SS-OF	22	73	13	23	4	1	0	11	.315	5	8	6	22	42	4	.941
1995—	Vermont (NY-Penn)	2B-SS	65	248	37	70	12	5	3	33	.282	16	28	15	135	189	17	.950
1996—	Delmarva (S.Atl.)	SS-2B	134	512	86	129	28	4	14	65	.252	54	63	51	205	344	27	.953
1997—	W.P. Beach (FSL)........	SS-DH-2B	69	279	56	77	19	2	5	26	.276	27	33	32	92	162	20	.927
	—Harrisburg (East.)........	SS-2B	35	133	34	41	13	2	5	20	.308	15	18	7	57	83	5	.966
	—Ottawa (I.L.)	SS-2B	31	122	17	32	5	2	2	14	.262	7	16	8	45	94	3	.979
	—Montreal (N.L.)...........	SS-2B	16	18	4	4	0	0	0	2	.222	1	3	1	11	15	1	.963
1998—	Ottawa (I.L.)	SS-2B	66	272	31	63	9	4	0	26	.232	28	27	19	122	190	12	.963

Year	Team (League)	Pos.	G	AB	R	H	2B	3B	HR	RBI	Avg.	BB	SO	SB	PO	A	E	Avg.
	— Montreal (N.L.)..........	SS-2B	79	261	44	73	16	5	3	22	.280	18	27	6	122	196	7	.978
1999—	Montreal (N.L.)..........	SS	104	382	48	97	23	5	8	39	.254	18	38	2	186	289	10	.979
2000—	Montreal (N.L.)..........	SS-2B	125	422	47	100	25	1	13	55	.237	25	28	4	167	338	10	.981
	— Ottawa (I.L.)...............	SS	2	6	1	4	0	0	0	0	.667	1	0	1	3	7	0	1.000
2001—	Montreal (N.L.)..........	SS	*162	626	64	173	41	6	14	96	.276	43	54	19	246	514	11	.986
Major League totals (5 years)			486	1709	207	447	105	17	38	214	.262	105	150	32	732	1352	39	.982

CACERES, WILMY SS/2B DEVIL RAYS

PERSONAL: Born October 2, 1978, in Santo Domingo, Dominican Republic. ... 6-0/165. ... Bats both, throws right. ... Full name: Wilmy Antonio Caceres.

TRANSACTIONS/CAREER NOTES: Signed as non-drafted free agent by Cincinnati Reds organization (December 5, 1996). ... Traded by Reds to Anaheim Angels for P Seth Etherton (December 10, 2000). ... On disabled list (May 1-8 and July 26-August 10, 2001). ... Traded by Angels to Tampa Bay Devil Rays for P Mickey Callaway (December 17, 2001).

Year	Team (League)	Pos.	G	AB	R	H	2B	3B	HR	RBI	Avg.	BB	SO	SB	PO	A	E	Avg.
1997—	Billings (Pio.)	2B-SS	15	38	10	10	2	0	0	9	.263	2	3	1	22	30	6	.897
1998—	Charl., W.Va. (S.Atl.) ..	SS	103	394	48	102	12	7	0	27	.259	18	62	24	167	303	39	.923
	— Burlington (Midw.).....	SS	35	150	23	44	8	0	1	14	.293	4	24	7	40	92	9	.936
1999—	Clinton (Midw.)	SS	117	476	77	124	18	5	1	30	.261	30	65	52	179	340	*42	.925
	— GC Reds (GCL)...........	2B-SS	2	9	2	3	0	0	0	0	.333	0	1	0	3	4	0	1.000
2000—	Chattanooga (Sou.)....	SS-2B	130	534	69	143	23	4	2	33	.268	37	71	36	256	454	27	.963
2001—	Salt Lake (PCL)■	SS-2B	87	325	38	81	5	4	0	21	.249	12	45	12	158	248	16	.962

CAIRO, MIGUEL 2B/OF CARDINALS

PERSONAL: Born May 4, 1974, in Anaco, Venezuela. ... 6-1/200. ... Bats right, throws right. ... Full name: Miguel Jesus Cairo. ... Name pronounced KI-ro.

HIGH SCHOOL: Escuela Anaco (Anaco, Venezuela).

TRANSACTIONS/CAREER NOTES: Signed as non-drafted free agent by Los Angeles Dodgers organization (September 20, 1990). ... Traded by Dodgers with 3B Willis Otanez to Seattle Mariners for 3B Mike Blowers (November 29, 1995). ... Traded by Mariners with P Bill Risley to Toronto Blue Jays for P Edwin Hurtado and P Paul Menhart (December 18, 1995). ... Traded by Blue Jays to Chicago Cubs for P Jason Stevenson (November 20, 1996). ... Selected by Tampa Bay Devil Rays in first round (eighth pick overall) of expansion draft (November 18, 1997). ... On Tampa Bay disabled list (April 24-May 17 and July 26-August 11, 1999); included rehabilitation assignments to Orlando (May 14-17) and St. Petersburg (August 7-11). ... Released by Devil Rays (November 27, 2000). ... Signed by Oakland Athletics organization (January 7, 2001). ... Traded by A's to Chicago Cubs for 3B/1B Eric Hinske (March 28, 2001). ... Claimed on waivers by St. Louis Cardinals (August 10, 2001).

STATISTICAL NOTES: Led California League in caught stealing with 23 in 1994. ... Led International League second basemen with 64 double plays in 1996. ... Tied for American Association lead in caught stealing with 15 in 1997.

MISCELLANEOUS: Holds Tampa Bay Devil Rays all-time record for most stolen bases (69).

Year	Team (League)	Pos.	G	AB	R	H	2B	3B	HR	RBI	Avg.	BB	SO	SB	PO	A	E	Avg.
1991—	Dom. Dodgers (DSL) .	IF	57	203	16	45	5	1	0	17	.222	0	17	8	...	...	...	...
1992—	Vero Beach (FSL)	2B-3B	36	125	7	28	0	0	0	7	.224	11	12	5	69	76	10	.935
	— GC Dodgers (GCL)	SS-3B	21	76	10	23	5	2	0	9	.303	2	6	1	26	56	4	.953
1993—	Vero Beach (FSL)	2B-SS	90	346	50	109	10	1	1	23	.315	28	22	23	172	244	18	.959
1994—	Bakersfield (Calif.)	2B-SS	133	533	76	155	23	4	2	48	.291	34	37	44	268	376	28	.958
1995—	San Antonio (Texas)...	2B-SS-DH	107	435	53	121	20	1	1	41	.278	26	31	33	210	316	23	.958
1996—	Syracuse (I.L.)■	2B-3B-SS	120	465	71	129	14	4	3	48	.277	26	44	27	193	295	23	.955
	— Toronto (A.L.)..........	2B	9	27	5	6	2	0	0	1	.222	2	9	0	22	18	0	1.000
1997—	Iowa (A.A.)	2B-SS	135	*569	82	159	35	4	5	46	.279	24	54	*40	248	386	20	.969
	— Chicago (N.L.)..........	2B-SS	16	29	7	7	1	0	0	1	.241	2	3	0	16	18	0	1.000
1998—	Tampa Bay (A.L.)■.....	2B-DH	150	515	49	138	26	5	5	46	.268	24	44	19	278	429	16	.978
1999—	Tampa Bay (A.L.)	2B-DH	120	465	61	137	15	5	3	36	.295	24	46	22	251	377	9	.986
	— Orlando (Sou.)	2B	3	13	1	5	2	0	0	1	.385	0	1	0	2	7	0	1.000
	— St. Petersburg (FSL) ..	2B	3	13	2	5	0	0	0	0	.385	1	2	1	8	15	1	.958
2000—	Tampa Bay (A.L.)	2B-DH	119	375	49	98	18	2	1	34	.261	29	34	28	218	302	9	.983
2001—	Iowa (PCL)■	2B-SS-3B	34	123	22	37	7	1	3	14	.301	8	11	3	58	74	3	.978
	— Chicago (N.L.)..........	2B-SS	66	123	20	35	3	1	2	9	.285	16	21	2	25	52	7	.917
	— St. Louis (N.L.)■	O-2-3-1-S	27	33	5	11	5	0	1	7	.333	2	2	0	9	4	1	.929
American League totals (4 years)			398	1382	164	379	61	12	9	117	.274	79	133	69	769	1126	34	.982
National League totals (2 years)			109	185	32	53	9	1	3	17	.286	20	26	2	50	74	8	.939
Major League totals (6 years)			507	1567	196	432	70	13	12	134	.276	99	159	71	819	1200	42	.980

DIVISION SERIES RECORD

Year	Team (League)	Pos.	G	AB	R	H	2B	3B	HR	RBI	Avg.	BB	SO	SB	PO	A	E	Avg.
2001—	St. Louis (N.L.)..........	PH-OF	3	5	0	1	0	0	0	0	.200	0	1	1	1	0	0	1.000

CALLAWAY, MICKEY P ANGELS

PERSONAL: Born May 13, 1975, in Memphis, Tenn. ... 6-2/196. ... Throws right, bats right. ... Full name: Michael Christopher Callaway.
HIGH SCHOOL: Germantown (Tenn.).
COLLEGE: Mississippi.

TRANSACTIONS/CAREER NOTES: Selected by Tampa Bay Devil Rays organization in seventh round of free-agent draft (June 4, 1996). ... Loaned to Seattle Mariners organization (April 2-July 21, 1998). ... On Tampa Bay disabled list (June 19-July 6, 1999). ... On disabled list (May 22-June 5, 2000). ... Traded by Devil Rays to Anaheim Angels for SS/2B Wilmy Caceres (December 17, 2001).
STATISTICAL NOTES: Tied for Florida State League lead with seven balks in 1997.
MISCELLANEOUS: Appeared in one game as pinch runner (1999).

Year	League	W	L	Pct.	ERA	G	GS	CG	ShO	Sv.	IP	H	R	ER	BB	SO
1996—	Butte (Pio.)	6	2	.750	3.71	16	11	0	0	0	63	70	37	26	25	57
1997—	St. Petersburg (FSL)	11	7	.611	3.22	28	•28	3	0	0	170²/₃	162	74	61	39	109
1998—	Orlando (Sou.)■	5	6	.455	4.42	18	17	0	0	0	89²/₃	103	56	44	44	57
—	Durham (I.L.)■	5	3	.625	4.53	9	8	0	0	0	47²/₃	49	27	24	17	19
1999—	Orlando (Sou.)	1	1	.500	4.50	2	2	0	0	0	10	15	6	5	2	7
—	Durham (I.L.)	7	1	.875	4.20	15	15	0	0	0	81¹/₃	86	45	38	28	56
—	Tampa Bay (A.L.)	1	2	.333	7.45	5	4	0	0	0	19¹/₃	30	20	16	14	11
2000—	Durham (I.L.)	11	6	.647	5.29	26	20	0	0	0	117¹/₃	151	88	69	50	64
2001—	Durham (I.L.)	11	7	.611	3.07	29	21	2	1	0	129	131	50	44	24	81
—	Tampa Bay (A.L.)	0	0	...	7.20	2	0	0	0	0	5	3	4	4	2	2
Major League totals (2 years)		1	2	.333	7.40	7	4	0	0	0	24¹/₃	33	24	20	16	13

C

PERSONAL: Born January 8, 1973, in La Grange, Ga. ... 6-2/190. ... Bats right, throws right. ... Full name: Michael Terrance Cameron.
HIGH SCHOOL: La Grange (Ga.).
TRANSACTIONS/CAREER NOTES: Selected by Chicago White Sox organization in 18th round of free-agent draft (June 3, 1991). ... Traded by White Sox to Cincinnati Reds for 1B/3B Paul Konerko (November 11, 1998). ... Traded by Reds with P Brett Tomko, IF Antonio Perez and P Jake Meyer to Seattle Mariners for OF Ken Griffey Jr. (February 10, 2000).
HONORS: Won A.L. Gold Glove as outfielder (2001).
STATISTICAL NOTES: Tied for Carolina League lead in double plays by outfielder with four in 1994. ... Led Southern League with .600 slugging percentage and tied for lead in caught stealing with 15 in 1996. ... Led Southern League outfielders with 264 total chances in 1996. ... Career major league grand slams: 2.

							BATTING						FIELDING		
Year	Team (League)	Pos.	G	AB	R	H	2B	3B	HR	RBI	Avg.	BB	SO	SB	PO	A	E	Avg.

Year	Team (League)	Pos.	G	AB	R	H	2B	3B	HR	RBI	Avg.	BB	SO	SB	PO	A	E	Avg.
1991—	GC White Sox (GCL)	OF	44	136	20	30	3	0	0	11	.221	17	29	13	55	3	3	.951
1992—	Utica (NY-Penn)	OF	26	87	15	24	1	4	2	12	.276	11	26	3	60	3	0	1.000
—	South Bend (Midw.)	OF	35	114	19	26	8	1	1	9	.228	10	37	2	67	0	3	.957
1993—	South Bend (Midw.)	OF	122	411	52	98	14	5	0	30	.238	27	101	19	248	13	4	.985
1994—	Prince William (Caro.)	OF	131	468	86	116	15	*17	6	48	.248	60	101	22	275	10	6	.979
1995—	Birmingham (Sou.)	OF	107	350	64	87	20	5	11	60	.249	54	104	21	250	7	4	.985
—	Chicago (A.L.)	OF	28	38	4	7	2	0	1	2	.184	3	15	0	33	1	0	1.000
1996—	Birmingham (Sou.)	OF-DH	123	473	*120	142	34	12	28	77	.300	71	117	*39	*249	8	7	.973
—	Chicago (A.L.)	OF-DH	11	11	1	1	0	0	0	0	.091	1	3	0	7	0	0	1.000
1997—	Nashville (A.A.)	OF-DH	30	120	21	33	7	3	6	17	.275	18	31	4	63	3	1	.985
—	Chicago (A.L.)	OF-DH	116	379	63	98	18	3	14	55	.259	55	105	23	334	5	5	.985
1998—	Chicago (A.L.)	OF	141	396	53	83	16	5	8	43	.210	37	101	27	313	6	4	.988
1999—	Cincinnati (N.L.)■	OF	146	542	93	139	34	9	21	66	.256	80	145	38	372	7	8	.979
2000—	Seattle (A.L.)■	OF	155	543	96	145	28	4	19	78	.267	78	133	24	399	5	6	.985
2001—	Seattle (A.L.)	OF-DH	150	540	99	144	30	5	25	110	.267	69	155	34	410	8	6	.986
American League totals (6 years)			601	1907	316	478	94	17	67	288	.251	243	512	108	1496	25	21	.986
National League totals (1 year)			146	542	93	139	34	9	21	66	.256	80	145	38	372	7	8	.979
Major League totals (7 years)			747	2449	409	617	128	26	88	354	.252	323	657	146	1868	32	29	.985

DIVISION SERIES RECORD

							BATTING						FIELDING		
Year	Team (League)	Pos.	G	AB	R	H	2B	3B	HR	RBI	Avg.	BB	SO	SB	PO	A	E	Avg.
2000—	Seattle (A.L.)	OF	3	12	2	3	0	0	0	2	.250	0	0	1	12	0	0	1.000
2001—	Seattle (A.L.)	OF	5	18	2	4	3	0	1	3	.222	2	7	0	11	0	0	1.000
Division series totals (2 years)			8	30	4	7	3	0	1	5	.233	2	7	1	23	0	0	1.000

CHAMPIONSHIP SERIES RECORD

							BATTING						FIELDING		
Year	Team (League)	Pos.	G	AB	R	H	2B	3B	HR	RBI	Avg.	BB	SO	SB	PO	A	E	Avg.
2000—	Seattle (A.L.)	OF	6	18	3	2	0	0	0	1	.111	2	7	1	16	0	0	1.000
2001—	Seattle (A.L.)	OF	5	17	3	3	2	0	0	0	.176	4	4	0	13	0	0	1.000
Championship series totals (2 years)			11	35	6	5	2	0	0	1	.143	6	11	1	29	0	0	1.000

ALL-STAR GAME RECORD

						BATTING						FIELDING		
Year	League	Pos.	AB	R	H	2B	3B	HR	RBI	Avg.	BB	SO	SB	PO	A	E	Avg.
2001—	American	OF	3	0	1	1	0	0	0	.333	0	1	0	1	0	0	1.000

PERSONAL: Born April 21, 1963, in Hanford, Calif. ... 6-0/200. ... Bats both, throws right. ... Full name: Kenneth Gene Caminiti. ... Name pronounced CAM-uh-NET-ee.
HIGH SCHOOL: Leigh (San Jose, Calif.).
COLLEGE: San Jose State.
TRANSACTIONS/CAREER NOTES: Selected by Houston Astros organization in third round of free-agent draft (June 4, 1984). ... On disabled list (April 19-May 11, 1992). ... Traded by Astros with OF Steve Finley, SS Andujar Cedeno, 1B Robert Petagine, P Brian Williams and a player to be named later to San Diego Padres for OF Phil Plantier, OF Derek Bell, P Pedro Martinez, P Doug Brocail, IF Craig Shipley and SS Ricky Gutierrez (December 28, 1994); Padres acquired P Sean Fesh to complete deal (May 1, 1995). ... On disabled list (May 12-27, 1997; and May 2-23, 1998).

... Granted free agency (October 23, 1998). ... Signed by Astros (November 17, 1998). ... On Houston disabled list (May 22-August 16, 1999); included rehabilitation assignment to New Orleans (August 9-16). ... On disabled list (June 16, 2000-remainder of season). ... Granted free agency (October 30, 2000). ... Signed by Texas Rangers (December 10, 2000). ... On Texas disabled list (June 17-July 2, 2001). ... Released by Rangers (July 2, 2001). ... Signed by Atlanta Braves (July 5, 2001). ... Granted free agency (November 6, 2001).

RECORDS: Holds major league record for most consecutive games with switch-hit home runs—2 (September 16-17, 1995). ... Holds major league single-season record for most games with switch-hit home runs—4 (1996). ... Shares major league single-season record for most runs batted in by switch hitter—130 (1996). ... Holds N.L. career record for most games with switch-hit home runs—10. ... Holds N.L. record for most home runs by switch hitter in two consecutive seasons—66 (1995-96 and 1996-97).

HONORS: Named third baseman on THE SPORTING NEWS college All-America team (1984). ... Won N.L. Gold Glove at third base (1995-97). ... Named third baseman on THE SPORTING NEWS N.L. All-Star team (1996). ... Named third baseman on THE SPORTING NEWS N.L. Silver Slugger team (1996). ... Named N.L. Most Valuable Player by Baseball Writers' Association of America (1996).

STATISTICAL NOTES: Led Southern League third basemen with 34 double plays in 1986. ... Led Pacific Coast League third basemen with 382 total chances and 25 double plays in 1988. ... Switch-hit home runs in one game ten times (July 3, 1994; September 16, September 17 and September 19, 1995; August 1, August 21, August 28 and September 11, 1996; July 12, 1998; and August 20, 1999). ... Led N.L. third basemen with 424 total chances and 28 double plays in 1995. ... Tied for N.L. lead with 10 sacrifice flies in 1996. ... Hit three home runs in one game (July 12, 1998). ... Career major league grand slams: 6.

Year Team (League)	Pos.	G	AB	R	H	2B	3B	HR	RBI	Avg.	BB	SO	SB	PO	A	E	Avg.
1985— Osceola (FSL)............	3B	126	468	83	133	26	9	4	73	.284	51	54	14	53	193	20	.925
1986— Columbus (Sou.)........	3B	137	513	82	154	29	3	12	81	.300	56	79	5	105	*299	33	.924
1987— Columbus (Sou.)........	3B	95	375	66	122	25	2	15	69	.325	25	58	11	55	205	21	.925
— Houston (N.L.).........	3B	63	203	10	50	7	1	3	23	.246	12	44	0	50	98	8	.949
1988— Tucson (PCL)	3B	109	416	54	113	24	7	5	66	.272	29	54	13	*105	*250	27	.929
— Houston (N.L.)	3B	30	83	5	15	2	0	1	7	.181	5	18	0	12	43	3	.948
1989— Houston (N.L.)...........	3B	161	585	71	149	31	3	10	72	.255	51	93	4	126	335	22	.954
1990— Houston (N.L.)...........	3B	153	541	52	131	20	2	4	51	.242	48	97	9	118	243	21	.945
1991— Houston (N.L.)...........	3B	152	574	65	145	30	3	13	80	.253	46	85	4	129	293	23	.948
1992— Houston (N.L.)...........	3B	135	506	68	149	31	2	13	62	.294	44	68	10	102	210	11	.966
1993— Houston (N.L.)...........	3B	143	543	75	142	31	0	13	75	.262	49	88	8	123	264	24	.942
1994— Houston (N.L.)...........	3B	111	406	63	115	28	2	18	75	.283	43	71	4	79	200	9	.969
1995— San Diego (N.L.)■......	3B	143	526	74	159	33	0	26	94	.302	69	94	12	102	*295	*27	.936
1996— San Diego (N.L.)	3B	146	546	109	178	37	2	40	130	.326	78	99	11	103	310	20	.954
1997— San Diego (N.L.)	3B	137	486	92	141	28	0	26	90	.290	80	118	11	90	291	24	.941
1998— San Diego (N.L.)	3B	131	452	87	114	29	0	29	82	.252	71	108	6	77	207	*21	.931
1999— Houston (N.L.)■........	3B	78	273	45	78	11	1	13	56	.286	46	58	6	52	139	14	.932
— New Orleans (PCL)...	3B	6	20	6	7	4	0	0	3	.350	2	1	0	2	5	3	.700
2000— Houston (N.L.)	3B	59	208	42	63	13	0	15	45	.303	42	37	3	37	81	11	.915
2001— Texas (A.L.)■............	3B	54	185	24	43	8	1	9	25	.232	22	41	0	42	99	9	.940
— Atlanta (N.L.)■............	1B-3B-DH	64	171	12	38	9	0	6	16	.222	21	44	0	249	33	8	.972
American League totals (1 year)		54	185	24	43	8	1	9	25	.232	22	41	0	42	99	9	.940
National League totals (15 years)		1706	6103	870	1667	340	16	230	958	.273	705	1122	88	1449	3042	246	.948
Major League totals (15 years)		1760	6288	894	1710	348	17	239	983	.272	727	1163	88	1491	3141	255	.948

DIVISION SERIES RECORD

RECORDS: Shares N.L. career record for most home runs—6. ... Shares single-game record for most home runs—2 (October 5, 1996). ... Shares N.L. single-game record for most at-bats—6 (October 8, 1999).

Year Team (League)	Pos.	G	AB	R	H	2B	3B	HR	RBI	Avg.	BB	SO	SB	PO	A	E	Avg.
1996— San Diego (N.L.)	3B	3	10	3	3	0	0	3	3	.300	3	5	0	5	3	.625
1998— San Diego (N.L.)	3B	4	14	2	2	0	0	0	0	.143	1	3	0	2	5	1	.875
1999— Houston (N.L.)	3B	4	17	3	8	0	0	3	8	.471	2	1	0	1	10	0	1.000
2001— Atlanta (N.L.)	PH	2	2	0	0	0	0	0	0	.000	0	1	0	...	...	...	...
Division series totals (4 years)		13	43	8	13	0	0	6	11	.302	6	10	0	3	20	4	.852

CHAMPIONSHIP SERIES RECORD

RECORDS: Shares single-game record for most bases on balls received—4 (October 8, 1998).

Year Team (League)	Pos.	G	AB	R	H	2B	3B	HR	RBI	Avg.	BB	SO	SB	PO	A	E	Avg.
1998— San Diego (N.L.)	3B	6	22	3	6	0	0	2	4	.273	5	4	0	5	10	0	1.000
2001— Atlanta (N.L.)..............						Did not play.											

WORLD SERIES RECORD

Year Team (League)	Pos.	G	AB	R	H	2B	3B	HR	RBI	Avg.	BB	SO	SB	PO	A	E	Avg.
1998— San Diego (N.L.)	3B	4	14	1	2	1	0	0	1	.143	2	7	0	2	2	2	.667

ALL-STAR GAME RECORD

Year League	Pos.	AB	R	H	2B	3B	HR	RBI	Avg.	BB	SO	SB	PO	A	E	Avg.
1994— National....................	3B	1	0	0	0	0	0	0	.000	0	0	0	0	0	0	...
1996— National....................	3B	2	1	1	0	0	1	1	.500	0	1	0	0	0	1	.000
1997— National....................	3B	2	0	0	0	0	0	0	.000	0	0	0	0	0	0	...
All-Star Game totals (3 years)		5	1	1	0	0	1	1	.200	0	1	0	0	0	1	.000

CAMMACK, ERIC   P   METS

PERSONAL: Born August 14, 1975, in Nederland, Texas. ... 6-1/180. ... Throws right, bats right. ... Full name: Eric Wade Cammack.
HIGH SCHOOL: Nederland (Texas).
COLLEGE: Lamar.
TRANSACTIONS/CAREER NOTES: Selected by New York Mets organization in 13th round of free-agent draft (June 3, 1997). ... On disabled list (March 20, 2001-entire season).

Year League	W	L	Pct.	ERA	G	GS	CG	ShO	Sv.	IP	H	R	ER	BB	SO
1997—Pittsfield (NY-Penn)...........	0	1	.000	0.86	23	0	0	0	8	31 1/3	9	4	3	14	32
1998—Capital City (S.Atl.)............	4	0	1.000	2.81	25	0	0	0	8	32	17	13	10	13	49
— St. Lucie (FSL)...................	3	2	.600	2.02	29	0	0	0	11	35 2/3	22	12	8	14	53
1999— Binghamton (East.)	4	2	.667	2.38	45	0	0	0	15	56 2/3	28	17	15	38	83
— Norfolk (I.L.)	0	0	...	3.12	9	0	0	0	4	8 2/3	7	3	3	1	17
2000— Norfolk (I.L.)	6	2	.750	1.70	47	0	0	0	9	63 2/3	38	14	12	31	67
— New York (N.L.)..................	0	0	...	6.30	8	0	0	0	0	10	7	7	7	10	9
2001—New York (N.L.).................								Did not play.							
Major League totals (1 year)........	0	0	...	6.30	8	0	0	0	0	10	7	7	7	10	9

CANIZARO, JAY — 2B — TWINS

PERSONAL: Born July 4, 1973, in Orange, Texas. ... 5-9/178. ... Bats right, throws right. ... Full name: Jason Kyle Canizaro.
HIGH SCHOOL: West Orange-Stark (Orange, Texas).
JUNIOR COLLEGE: Blinn College (Texas).
COLLEGE: Oklahoma State.
TRANSACTIONS/CAREER NOTES: Selected by San Francisco Giants organization in fourth round of free-agent draft (June 3, 1993). ... On Fresno disabled list (July 10-August 15, 1999). ... Released by Giants (April 3, 2000). ... Signed by Minnesota Twins organization (April 4, 2000). ... On disabled list (March 24, 2001-entire season).
STATISTICAL NOTES: Led Arizona League second basemen with 33 double plays in 1993. ... Led Texas League second basemen with 19 errors in 1995. ... Career major league grand slams: 2.

							BATTING							FIELDING		
Year Team (League)	Pos.	G	AB	R	H	2B	3B	HR	RBI	Avg.	BB	SO	SB	PO	A	E	Avg.
1993— Arizona Giants (Ariz.) .	2B-SS	49	180	34	47	10	•6	3	*41	.261	22	40	12	102	106	10	.954
1994— San Jose (Calif.)	2-S-3-O	126	464	77	117	16	2	15	69	.252	46	98	12	262	362	30	.954
1995— Shreveport (Texas)......	2B-SS	126	440	83	129	25	7	12	60	.293	58	98	16	254	333	†23	.962
1996— Phoenix (PCL)	2-S-3-DH	102	363	50	95	21	2	7	46	.262	46	77	14	194	308	14	.973
— San Francisco (N.L.) ..	2B-SS	43	120	11	24	4	1	2	8	.200	9	38	0	64	91	6	.963
1997— Phoenix (PCL)	2B-3B	23	81	12	16	7	0	2	12	.198	9	24	2	32	46	2	.975
— Shreveport (Texas)......	2-S-3-DH	50	176	36	45	9	0	11	38	.256	26	44	2	80	124	6	.971
1998— Shreveport (Texas)......	2B	83	281	47	63	7	1	12	32	.224	53	46	5	145	255	10	.976
— Fresno (PCL).............	2-DH-O-S	45	106	23	24	6	2	6	14	.226	17	23	0	49	64	2	.983
1999— Fresno (PCL)	2B-SS-3B	105	364	76	102	20	2	26	78	.280	49	79	16	184	268	15	.968
— San Francisco (N.L.) ..	2B	12	18	5	8	2	0	1	9	.444	1	2	1	2	5	0	1.000
2000— Salt Lake (PCL)■	2B-SS-3B	27	101	21	36	9	2	6	32	.356	17	17	4	42	89	7	.949
— Minnesota (A.L.)	2B-DH	102	346	43	93	21	1	7	40	.269	24	57	4	120	199	6	.982
2001— Minnesota (A.L.)								Did not play.								
American League totals (1 year)		102	346	43	93	21	1	7	40	.269	24	57	4	120	199	6	.982
National League totals (2 years)		55	138	16	32	6	1	3	17	.232	10	40	1	66	96	6	.964
Major League totals (3 years)		157	484	59	125	27	2	10	57	.258	34	97	5	186	295	12	.976

CANSECO, JOSE — DH/OF

PERSONAL: Born July 2, 1964, in Havana, Cuba. ... 6-4/240. ... Bats right, throws right. ... Full name: Jose Canseco Jr. ... Identical twin brother of Ozzie Canseco, outfielder with Oakland Athletics (1990) and St. Louis Cardinals (1992). ... Name pronounced can-SAY-co.
HIGH SCHOOL: Miami Coral Park Senior.
TRANSACTIONS/CAREER NOTES: Selected by Oakland Athletics organization in 15th round of free-agent draft (June 7, 1982). ... On Huntsville disabled list (May 14-June 3, 1985). ... On Oakland disabled list (March 23-July 13, 1989); included rehabilitation assignments to Huntsville (May 6 and June 28-July 13). ... On disabled list (June 8-23, 1990 and July 1-16, 1992). ... Traded by A's to Texas Rangers for OF Ruben Sierra, P Jeff Russell, P Bobby Witt and cash (August 31, 1992). ... On disabled list (June 24, 1993-remainder of season). ... Traded by Rangers to Boston Red Sox for OF Otis Nixon and 3B Luis Ortiz (December 9, 1994). ... On disabled list (May 15-June 20, 1995); included rehabilitation assignment to Pawtucket (June 18-20). ... Granted free agency (October 30, 1995). ... Re-signed by Red Sox (December 6, 1995). ... On Boston disabled list (April 24-May 9 and July 26-September 17, 1996); included rehabilitation assignment to Pawtucket (May 7-9). ... Traded by Red Sox to A's for P John Wasdin and cash (January 27, 1997). ... On disabled list (August 1-20 and August 27, 1997-remainder of season). ... Granted free agency (October 31, 1997). ... Signed by Toronto Blue Jays (February 4, 1998). ... Granted free agency (October 22, 1998). ... Signed by Tampa Bay Devil Rays (December 11, 1998). ... On disabled list (July 10-August 20, 1999). ... On Tampa Bay disabled list (May 25-July 18, 2000). ... Claimed on waivers by New York Yankees (August 7, 2000). ... Granted free agency (November 10, 2000). ... Signed by Anaheim Angels organization (January 16, 2001). ... Released by Angels (March 28, 2001). ... Signed by Newark, Atlantic League (April 19, 2001). ... Signed by Chicago White Sox organization (June 20, 2001). ... Granted free agency (November 5, 2001).
RECORDS: Shares major league record for most strikeouts in two consecutive games—8 (July 14 [3] and 16 [5], 1997). ... Shares major league single-game record for most strikeouts (nine-inning game)—5 (July 16, 1997). ... Shares major league record for most consecutive bases on balls received—7 (August 4-5, 1992).
HONORS: Named Minor League Player of the Year by THE SPORTING NEWS (1985). ... Named Southern League Most Valuable Player (1985). ... Named A.L. Rookie Player of the Year by THE SPORTING NEWS (1986). ... Named A.L. Rookie of the Year by Baseball Writers' Association of America (1986). ... Named A.L. Player of the Year by THE SPORTING NEWS (1988). ... Named outfielder on THE SPORTING NEWS A.L. All-Star team (1988 and 1990-91). ... Named outfielder on THE SPORTING NEWS A.L. Silver Slugger team (1988 and 1990-91). ... Named A.L. Most Valuable Player by Baseball Writers' Association of America (1988). ... Named designated hitter on THE SPORTING NEWS A.L. Silver Slugger team (1998).
STATISTICAL NOTES: Led California League outfielders with eight double plays in 1984. ... Hit three home runs in one game (July 3, 1988 and June 13, 1994). ... Led A.L. with .569 slugging percentage in 1988. ... Led A.L. in grounding into double plays with 20 in 1994. ... Career major league grand slams: 6.

							BATTING							FIELDING		
Year Team (League)	Pos.	G	AB	R	H	2B	3B	HR	RBI	Avg.	BB	SO	SB	PO	A	E	Avg.
1982—Miami (FSL)	3B	6	9	0	1	0	0	0	0	.111	1	3	0	3	1	1	.800
— Idaho Falls (Pio.).........	3B-OF	28	57	13	15	3	0	2	7	.263	9	13	3	6	17	3	.885
1983— Madison (Midw.)........	OF	34	88	8	14	4	0	3	10	.159	10	36	2	23	2	1	.962
— Medford (N'West)	OF	59	197	34	53	15	2	11	40	.269	30	*78	6	46	5	5	.911
1984— Modesto (Calif.)	OF	116	410	61	113	21	2	15	73	.276	74	127	10	216	17	9	.963

Year Team (League)	Pos.	G	AB	R	H	2B	3B	HR	RBI	Avg.	BB	SO	SB	PO	A	E	Avg.
1985—Huntsville (Sou.)	OF	58	211	47	67	10	2	25	80	.318	30	55	6	117	9	7	.947
—Tacoma (PCL)	OF	60	233	41	81	16	1	11	47	.348	40	66	5	81	7	2	.978
—Oakland (A.L.)	OF	29	96	16	29	3	0	5	13	.302	4	31	1	56	2	3	.951
1986—Oakland (A.L.)	OF-DH	157	600	85	144	29	1	33	117	.240	65	175	15	319	4	•14	.958
1987—Oakland (A.L.)	OF-DH	159	630	81	162	35	3	31	113	.257	50	157	15	263	12	7	.975
1988—Oakland (A.L.)	OF-DH	158	610	120	187	34	0	*42	*124	.307	78	128	40	304	11	7	.978
1989—Huntsville (Sou.)	OF	9	29	2	6	0	0	0	3	.207	5	11	1	9	0	1	1.000
—Oakland (A.L.)	OF-DH	65	227	40	61	9	1	17	57	.269	23	69	6	119	5	3	.976
1990—Oakland (A.L.)	OF-DH	131	481	83	132	14	2	37	101	.274	72	158	19	182	7	1	.995
1991—Oakland (A.L.)	OF-DH	154	572	115	152	32	1	•44	122	.266	78	152	26	245	5	•9	.965
1992—Oakland (A.L.)	OF-DH	97	366	66	90	11	0	22	72	.246	48	104	5	163	5	2	.988
—Texas (A.L.)■	OF-DH	22	73	8	17	4	0	4	15	.233	15	24	1	32	0	1	.970
1993—Texas (A.L.)	OF-DH-P	60	231	30	59	14	1	10	46	.255	16	62	6	94	4	3	.970
1994—Texas (A.L.)	DH	111	429	88	121	19	2	31	90	.282	69	114	15	...	...	...	...
1995—Boston (A.L.)■	DH-OF	102	396	64	121	25	1	24	81	.306	42	93	4	1	0	0	1.000
—Pawtucket (I.L.)	DH	2	6	1	1	0	0	0	1	.167	1	5	0	...	...	...	...
1996—Boston (A.L.)	DH-OF	96	360	68	104	22	1	28	82	.289	63	82	3	17	1	0	1.000
—Pawtucket (I.L.)	DH	2	5	0	1	0	0	0	0	.200	0	3	0	...	...	...	...
1997—Boston (A.L.)■	DH-OF	108	388	56	91	19	0	23	74	.235	51	122	8	74	2	5	.938
1998—Toronto (A.L.)■	DH-OF	151	583	98	138	26	0	46	107	.237	65	*159	29	117	4	5	.960
1999—Tampa Bay (A.L.)■	DH-OF	113	430	75	120	18	1	34	95	.279	58	135	3	7	1	0	1.000
2000—Tampa Bay (A.L.)	DH	61	218	31	56	15	0	9	30	.257	41	65	2	...	...	...	...
—New York (A.L.)■	DH-OF	37	111	16	27	3	0	6	19	.243	23	37	0	9	0	2	.818
2001—Newark (Atl.)■	DH	41	134	30	38	9	0	7	27	.284	40	39	10	...	...	...	...
—Chicago (A.L.)■	DH-OF	76	256	46	66	8	0	16	49	.258	45	75	2	1	0	0	1.000
Major League totals (17 years)		1887	7057	1186	1877	340	14	462	1407	.266	906	1942	200	2003	63	62	.971

DIVISION SERIES RECORD

Year Team (League)	Pos.	G	AB	R	H	2B	3B	HR	RBI	Avg.	BB	SO	SB	PO	A	E	Avg.
1995—Boston (A.L.)	DH-OF	3	13	0	0	0	0	0	0	.000	2	2	0	4	0	0	1.000
2000—New York (A.L.)							Did not play.										

CHAMPIONSHIP SERIES RECORD

Year Team (League)	Pos.	G	AB	R	H	2B	3B	HR	RBI	Avg.	BB	SO	SB	PO	A	E	Avg.
1988—Oakland (A.L.)	OF	4	16	4	5	1	0	3	4	.313	1	2	1	6	0	0	1.000
1989—Oakland (A.L.)	OF-PH	5	17	1	5	0	0	1	3	.294	3	7	0	6	1	1	.875
1990—Oakland (A.L.)	OF	4	11	3	2	0	0	0	1	.182	5	5	2	14	0	0	1.000
2000—New York (A.L.)							Did not play.										
Championship series totals (3 years)		13	44	8	12	1	0	4	8	.273	9	14	3	26	1	1	.964

WORLD SERIES RECORD

RECORDS: Shares single-game record for most grand slams—1 (October 15, 1988). ... Shares single-inning record for most runs batted in—4 (October 15, 1988, second inning).

NOTES: Hit home run in first at-bat (October 15, 1988). ... Member of World Series championship team (1989 and 2000).

Year Team (League)	Pos.	G	AB	R	H	2B	3B	HR	RBI	Avg.	BB	SO	SB	PO	A	E	Avg.
1988—Oakland (A.L.)	OF	5	19	1	1	0	0	1	5	.053	2	4	1	8	0	0	1.000
1989—Oakland (A.L.)	OF	4	14	5	5	0	0	1	3	.357	4	3	1	6	0	0	1.000
1990—Oakland (A.L.)	OF-PH-DH	4	12	1	1	0	0	1	2	.083	2	3	0	4	0	0	1.000
2000—New York (A.L.)	PH	1	1	0	0	0	0	0	0	.000	0	1	0	...	...	...	...
World Series totals (4 years)		14	46	7	7	0	0	3	10	.152	8	11	2	18	0	0	1.000

ALL-STAR GAME RECORD

Year League	Pos.	AB	R	H	2B	3B	HR	RBI	Avg.	BB	SO	SB	PO	A	E	Avg.
1986—American							Did not play.									
1988—American	OF	4	0	0	0	0	0	0	.000	0	1	0	3	0	0	1.000
1989—American						Selected, did not play—injured.										
1990—American	OF	4	0	0	0	0	0	0	.000	1	1	1	1	0	0	1.000
1992—American						Selected, did not play—injured.										
1999—American						Selected, did not play—injured.										
All-Star Game totals (2 years)		8	0	0	0	0	0	0	.000	1	2	1	4	0	0	1.000

RECORD AS PITCHER

Year League	W	L	Pct.	ERA	G	GS	CG	ShO	Sv.	IP	H	R	ER	BB	SO
1993—Texas (A.L.)	0	0	...	27.00	1	0	0	0	0	1	2	3	3	3	0

CARDONA, JAVIER   C   TIGERS

PERSONAL: Born September 15, 1975, in Santurce, Puerto Rico. ... 6-1/185. ... Bats right, throws right. ... Full name: Javier Peterson Cardona.

HIGH SCHOOL: Jose Alegria (Barrio Maguayo, Puerto Rico).

JUNIOR COLLEGE: Lake Land Community College (Ill.).

TRANSACTIONS/CAREER NOTES: Selected by Detroit Tigers organization in 19th round of free-agent draft (June 3, 1993); did not sign. ... Selected by Tigers organization in 23rd round of free-agent draft (June 4, 1994).

STATISTICAL NOTES: Led Southern League with .569 slugging percentage in 1999.

Year Team (League)	Pos.	G	AB	R	H	2B	3B	HR	RBI	Avg.	BB	SO	SB	PO	A	E	Avg.
							BATTING								FIELDING		
1994—Jamestown (NY-P)	C	19	46	6	12	2	0	0	5	.261	7	9	0	89	17	4	.964
1995—Fayetteville (S.Atl.)	C	51	165	18	34	8	0	3	19	.206	13	30	1	339	48	4	.990
1996—Fayetteville (S.Atl.)	C	97	348	42	98	21	0	4	28	.282	28	53	1	677	112	15	.981
1997—Lakeland (FSL)	C	85	284	28	82	15	0	7	38	.289	25	51	1	498	75	12	.979
1998—Jacksonville (Sou.)	C	46	163	31	54	16	1	4	40	.331	15	29	0	208	33	6	.976
—Toledo (I.L.)	C	47	162	12	31	4	0	5	16	.191	9	32	0	262	31	5	.983
1999—Jacksonville (Sou.)	C	108	418	84	129	31	0	*26	92	.309	46	69	4	565	58	11	.983
2000—Toledo (I.L.)	C	56	218	29	60	10	0	11	43	.275	15	33	0	317	25	5	.986
—Detroit (A.L.)	C	26	40	1	7	1	0	1	2	.175	0	9	0	66	7	2	.973
2001—Detroit (A.L.)	C-DH	46	96	10	25	8	0	1	10	.260	2	12	0	132	15	3	.980
Major League totals (2 years)		72	136	11	32	9	0	2	12	.235	2	21	0	198	22	5	.978

CARPENTER, CHRIS — P — BLUE JAYS

PERSONAL: Born April 27, 1975, in Exeter, N.H. ... 6-6/225. ... Throws right, bats right. ... Full name: Christopher John Carpenter.
HIGH SCHOOL: Trinity (Manchester, N.H.).
TRANSACTIONS/CAREER NOTES: Selected by Toronto Blue Jays organization in first round (15th pick overall) of free-agent draft (June 3, 1993). ... On Toronto disabled list (June 3-28, 1999); included rehabilitation assignment to St. Catharines (June 23-28).

Year League	W	L	Pct.	ERA	G	GS	CG	ShO	Sv.	IP	H	R	ER	BB	SO
1994—Medicine Hat (Pio.)	6	3	.667	2.76	15	15	0	0	0	84 2/3	76	40	26	39	80
1995—Dunedin (FSL)	3	5	.375	2.17	15	15	0	0	0	99 1/3	83	29	24	50	56
—Knoxville (Sou.)	3	7	.300	5.18	12	12	0	0	0	64 1/3	71	47	37	31	53
1996—Knoxville (Sou.)	7	9	.438	3.94	28	28	1	0	0	171 1/3	161	94	75	91	150
1997—Syracuse (I.L.)	4	9	.308	4.50	19	19	3	2	0	120	113	64	60	53	97
—Toronto (A.L.)	3	7	.300	5.09	14	13	1	1	0	81 1/3	108	55	46	37	55
1998—Toronto (A.L.)	12	7	.632	4.37	33	24	1	1	0	175	177	97	85	61	136
1999—Toronto (A.L.)	9	8	.529	4.38	24	24	4	1	0	150	177	81	73	48	106
—St. Catharines (NY-Penn)	0	0	...	4.50	1	1	0	0	0	4	5	2	2	1	6
2000—Toronto (A.L.)	10	12	.455	6.26	34	27	2	0	0	175 1/3	204	*130	*122	83	113
2001—Toronto (A.L.)	11	11	.500	4.09	34	34	3	2	0	215 2/3	229	112	98	75	157
Major League totals (5 years)	45	45	.500	4.79	139	122	11	5	0	797 1/3	895	475	424	304	567

CARRARA, GIOVANNI — P — DODGERS

PERSONAL: Born March 4, 1968, in Edo Anzuategni, Venezuela. ... 6-2/210. ... Throws right, bats right. ... Full name: Giovanni Jiminez Carrara.
TRANSACTIONS/CAREER NOTES: Signed as non-drafted free agent by Toronto Blue Jays organization (January 23, 1990). ... Claimed on waivers by Cincinnati Reds (July 3, 1996). ... Granted free agency (October 15, 1996). ... Signed by Baltimore Orioles organization (November 12, 1996). ... Released by Orioles (May 14, 1997). ... Signed by Reds organization (May 17, 1997). ... Granted free agency (September 11, 1997). ... Played for Seibu Lions of Japan Pacific League (1998). ... Signed by Reds organization (December 23, 1998). ... Granted free agency (October 15, 1998). ... Signed by Colorado Rockies organization (December 1, 1999). ... On Colorado Springs disabled list (May 29-June 21, 2000). ... On Colorado disabled list (August 3-September 4, 2000); included rehabilitation assignment to Colorado Springs (August 29-September 4). ... Granted free agency (October 4, 2000). ... Signed by Los Angeles Dodgers organization (January 4, 2001).

Year League	W	L	Pct.	ERA	G	GS	CG	ShO	Sv.	IP	H	R	ER	BB	SO
1990—Dominican Dodgers (DSL)	8	2	.800	2.62	15	14	4	0	0	86	88	31	25	28	55
1991—St. Catharines (NY-Penn)	5	2	.714	1.71	15	13	2	•2	0	89 2/3	66	26	17	21	83
1992—Dunedin (FSL)	0	1	.000	4.63	5	4	0	0	0	23 1/3	22	13	12	11	16
—Myrtle Beach (S.Atl.)	11	7	.611	3.14	22	16	1	0	0	100 1/3	86	40	35	36	100
1993—Dunedin (FSL)	6	11	.353	3.45	27	24	1	0	0	140 2/3	136	69	54	59	108
1994—Knoxville (Sou.)	13	7	.650	3.89	26	26	1	0	0	164 1/3	158	85	71	59	96
1995—Syracuse (I.L.)	7	7	.500	3.96	21	21	0	0	0	131 2/3	116	72	58	56	81
—Toronto (A.L.)	2	4	.333	7.21	12	7	1	0	0	48 2/3	64	46	39	25	27
1996—Syracuse (I.L.)	4	4	.500	3.58	9	6	1	0	0	37 2/3	37	16	15	12	28
—Toronto (A.L.)	0	1	.000	11.40	11	0	0	0	0	15	23	19	19	12	10
—Indianapolis (A.A.)■	4	0	1.000	0.76	9	6	1	1	1	47 2/3	25	6	4	9	45
—Cincinnati (N.L.)	1	0	1.000	5.87	8	5	0	0	0	23	31	17	15	13	13
1997—Rochester (I.L.)■	4	2	.667	4.44	8	8	0	0	0	46 2/3	45	23	23	16	48
—Indianapolis (A.A.)■	12	5	.706	3.51	19	18	2	0	0	120 2/3	111	50	47	51	105
—Cincinnati (N.L.)	0	1	.000	7.84	2	2	0	0	0	10 1/3	14	9	9	6	5
1998—Seibu (Jap. Pac.)■	1	2	.333	1.11	33	0	0	0	1	73	68	44	40	40	50
1999—Indianapolis (I.L.)■	12	7	.632	•3.47	39	21	2	1	0	158	144	68	61	58	114
2000—Colorado Springs (PCL)■	7	2	.778	3.26	18	15	0	0	0	96 2/3	89	39	35	30	89
—Colorado (N.L.)	0	1	.000	12.82	8	0	0	0	0	13 1/3	21	19	19	11	15
2001—Las Vegas (PCL)■	1	2	.333	3.10	6	6	0	0	0	29	27	10	10	9	35
—Los Angeles (N.L.)	6	1	.857	3.16	47	3	0	0	0	85 1/3	73	30	30	24	70
A.L. totals (2 years)	2	5	.286	8.20	23	7	1	0	0	63 2/3	87	65	58	37	37
N.L. totals (4 years)	7	3	.700	4.98	65	10	0	0	0	132	139	75	73	54	103
Major League totals (5 years)	9	8	.529	6.03	88	17	1	0	0	195 2/3	226	140	131	91	140

CARRASCO, HECTOR — P — RANGERS

PERSONAL: Born October 22, 1969, in San Pedro de Macoris, Dominican Republic. ... 6-2/220. ... Throws right, bats right. ... Full name: Hector Pacheco Pipo Carrasco. ... Name pronounced kuh-ROSS-ko.
HIGH SCHOOL: Liceo Mattias Mella (San Pedro de Macoris, Dominican Republic).
TRANSACTIONS/CAREER NOTES: Signed as non-drafted free agent by New York Mets organization (March 20, 1988). ... Released by Mets (January 6, 1992). ... Signed by Houston Astros organization (January 21, 1992). ... Traded by Astros with P Brian Griffiths to Florida Marlins for P Tom Edens (November 17, 1992). ... Traded by Marlins to Cincinnati Reds (September 10, 1993), completing deal in which Reds traded

P Chris Hammond to Marlins for 3B Gary Scott and a player to be named later (March 27, 1993). ... On disabled list (May 12-June 1, 1994). ... Traded by Reds with P Scott Service to Kansas City Royals for OF Jon Nunnally and IF/OF Chris Stynes (July 15, 1997). ... Selected by Arizona Diamondbacks in second round (49th pick overall) of expansion draft (November 18, 1997). ... Claimed on waivers by Minnesota Twins (April 3, 1998). ... On Minnesota disabled list (April 3-June 25, 1999); included rehabilitation assignments to Fort Myers (June 16-17) and Salt Lake (June 18-25). ... Traded by Twins to Boston Red Sox for OF Lew Ford (September 10, 2000). ... Granted free agency (November 1, 2000). ... Signed by Toronto Blue Jays organization (January 9, 2001). ... Released by Blue Jays (March 28, 2001). ... Signed by Twins organization (March 31, 2001). ... Granted free agency (October 19, 2001). ... Signed by Texas Rangers organization (January 19, 2002).

Year League	W	L	Pct.	ERA	G	GS	CG	ShO	Sv.	IP	H	R	ER	BB	SO
1988— Gulf Coast Mets (GCL)	0	2	.000	4.17	14	2	0	0	0	36²/₃	37	29	17	13	21
1989— Kingsport (Appl.)	1	6	.143	5.74	12	10	0	0	0	53¹/₃	69	49	34	34	55
1990— Kingsport (Appl.)	0	0	...	4.05	3	1	0	0	0	6²/₃	8	3	3	1	5
1991— Pittsfield (NY-Penn)	0	1	.000	5.40	12	1	0	0	1	23¹/₃	25	17	14	21	20
1992— Asheville (S.Atl.)■	5	5	.500	2.99	49	0	0	0	8	78¹/₃	66	30	26	47	67
1993— Kane County (Midw.)■	6	12	.333	4.11	28	*28	0	0	0	149	153	90	68	76	127
1994— Cincinnati (N.L.)■	5	6	.455	2.24	45	0	0	0	6	56¹/₃	42	17	14	30	41
1995— Cincinnati (N.L.)	2	7	.222	4.12	64	0	0	0	5	87¹/₃	86	45	40	46	64
1996— Cincinnati (N.L.)	4	3	.571	3.75	56	0	0	0	0	74¹/₃	58	37	31	45	59
— Indianapolis (A.A.)	0	1	.000	2.14	13	2	0	0	0	21	18	7	5	13	17
1997— Indianapolis (A.A.)	0	0	...	6.23	3	0	0	0	1	4¹/₃	5	3	3	3	4
— Cincinnati (N.L.)	1	2	.333	3.68	38	0	0	0	0	51¹/₃	51	25	21	25	46
— Kansas City (A.L.)■	1	6	.143	5.45	28	0	0	0	0	34²/₃	29	21	21	16	30
1998— Minnesota (A.L.)■	4	2	.667	4.38	63	0	0	0	1	61²/₃	75	30	30	31	46
1999— Fort Myers (FSL)	0	0	...	4.50	1	1	0	0	0	2	2	1	1	1	1
— Salt Lake (PCL)	1	0	1.000	0.00	3	0	0	0	1	4¹/₃	3	0	0	1	3
— Minnesota (A.L.)	2	3	.400	4.96	39	0	0	0	1	49	48	29	27	18	35
2000— Minnesota (A.L.)	4	3	.571	4.25	61	0	0	0	1	72	75	38	34	33	57
— Boston (A.L.)■	1	1	.500	9.45	8	1	0	0	0	6²/₃	15	8	7	5	7
2001— Minnesota (A.L.)■	4	3	.571	4.64	56	0	0	0	1	73²/₃	77	40	38	30	70
A.L. totals (5 years)	16	18	.471	4.75	255	1	0	0	4	297²/₃	319	166	157	133	245
N.L. totals (4 years)	12	18	.400	3.54	203	0	0	0	11	269¹/₃	237	124	106	146	210
Major League totals (8 years)	28	36	.438	4.17	458	1	0	0	15	567	556	290	263	279	455

CHAMPIONSHIP SERIES RECORD

Year League	W	L	Pct.	ERA	G	GS	CG	ShO	Sv.	IP	H	R	ER	BB	SO
1995— Cincinnati (N.L.)	0	0	...	0.00	1	0	0	0	0	1¹/₃	1	0	0	0	3

CASANOVA, RAUL　　　　C　　　　BREWERS

PERSONAL: Born August 23, 1972, in Humacao, Puerto Rico. ... 6-0/221. ... Bats both, throws right.
HIGH SCHOOL: Ponce (Puerto Rico).
TRANSACTIONS/CAREER NOTES: Selected by New York Mets organization in eighth round of free-agent draft (June 4, 1990). ... Traded by Mets to San Diego Padres (December 7, 1992), completing deal in which Padres traded SS Tony Fernandez to Mets for P Wally Whitehurst, OF D.J. Dozier and a player to be named later (October 26, 1992). ... Traded by Padres with P Richie Lewis and OF Melvin Nieves to Detroit Tigers for P Sean Bergman, P Cade Gaspar and OF Todd Steverson (March 22, 1996). ... On Toledo disabled list (May 3-14, 1996). ... On Detroit disabled list (June 19-August 13, 1996); included rehabilitation assignments to Jacksonville (July 31-August 9) and Toledo (August 9-13). ... On Detroit disabled list (April 25-May 28 and July 21, 1998-remainder of season); included rehabilitation assignments to Toledo (May 8-27 and July 30-August 3). ... On Detroit disabled list (March 31-July 12, 1999); included rehabilitation assignments to the Gulf Coast Tigers (June 24-28), Lakeland (June 29-July 4) and Toledo (July 5-July 12). ... Granted free agency (October 15, 1999). ... Signed by Colorado Rockies organization (December 15, 1999). ... Released by Rockies (March 24, 2000). ... Signed by Milwaukee Brewers organization (March 25, 2000). ... On disabled list (August 11, 2001-remainder of season).
STATISTICAL NOTES: Switch-hit home runs in one game (June 6, 1996). ... Career major league grand slams: 2.

						BATTING								FIELDING		
Year Team (League)	Pos.	G	AB	R	H	2B	3B	HR	RBI	Avg.	BB	SO	SB	PO	A	E	Avg.
1990— GC Mets (GCL)	C	23	65	4	5	0	0	0	1	.077	4	16	0	141	20	8	.953
1991— GC Mets (GCL)	C	32	111	19	27	4	2	0	9	.243	12	22	3	211	24	5	.979
— Kingsport (Appl.)	C	5	18	0	1	0	0	0	0	.056	1	10	0	35	4	1	.975
1992— Columbia (S.Atl.)	C	5	18	2	3	0	0	0	1	.167	1	4	0	29	1	0	1.000
— Kingsport (Appl.)	C	42	137	25	37	9	1	4	27	.270	26	25	3	286	34	6	.982
1993— Waterloo (Midw.)■	C-3B	76	227	32	58	12	0	6	30	.256	21	46	0	361	50	10	.976
1994— Rancho Cuca. (Calif.)	C	123	471	83	*160	27	2	23	120	*.340	43	97	1	593	55	14	.979
1995— Memphis (Sou.)	C-DH	89	306	42	83	18	0	12	44	.271	25	51	4	531	55	*12	.980
1996— Toledo (I.L.)■	C-DH	49	161	23	44	11	0	8	28	.273	20	24	0	234	15	2	.992
— Detroit (A.L.)	C-DH	25	85	6	16	1	0	4	9	.188	6	18	0	123	12	3	.978
— Jacksonville (Sou.)	DH-C	8	30	5	10	2	0	4	9	.333	2	7	0	21	1	0	1.000
1997— Toledo (I.L.)	C	12	41	1	8	0	0	1	3	.195	3	8	0	77	8	2	.977
— Detroit (A.L.)	C-DH	101	304	27	74	10	1	5	24	.243	26	48	1	543	38	9	.985
1998— Detroit (A.L.)	C	16	42	4	6	2	0	1	3	.143	5	10	0	81	6	3	.967
— Toledo (I.L.)	C-DH	50	171	17	44	8	0	7	26	.257	22	28	0	295	35	9	.973
1999— GC Tigers (GCL)	C	2	5	1	4	0	0	1	1	.800	0	0	0	7	0	0	1.000
— Lakeland (FSL)	C-DH	4	12	3	6	2	0	1	6	.500	0	1	0	14	2	0	1.000
— Toledo (I.L.)	C-DH	44	160	21	33	9	0	6	23	.206	7	28	0	173	21	3	.985
2000— Indianapolis (I.L.)■	C	20	73	10	21	2	0	5	12	.288	7	10	0	120	15	2	.985
— Milwaukee (N.L.)	C-DH	86	231	20	57	13	3	6	36	.247	26	48	1	358	28	4	.990
2001— Milwaukee (N.L.)	C-DH	71	192	21	50	10	0	11	33	.260	12	29	0	305	25	3	.991
American League totals (3 years)		142	431	37	96	13	1	10	36	.223	37	76	1	747	56	15	.982
National League totals (2 years)		157	423	41	107	23	3	17	69	.253	38	77	1	663	53	7	.990
Major League totals (5 years)		299	854	78	203	36	4	27	105	.238	75	153	2	1410	109	22	.986

CASEY, SEAN — 1B — REDS

PERSONAL: Born July 2, 1974, in Willingsboro, N.J. ... 6-4/225. ... Bats left, throws right. ... Full name: Sean Thomas Casey.
HIGH SCHOOL: Upper St. Clair (Pittsburgh).
COLLEGE: Richmond.
TRANSACTIONS/CAREER NOTES: Selected by Cleveland Indians organization in second round of free-agent draft (June 1, 1995). ... On disabled list (July 23-September 23, 1996). ... On Akron disabled list (April 4-June 8, 1997). ... Traded by Indians to Cincinnati Reds for P Dave Burba (March 30, 1998). ... On Cincinnati disabled list (April 2-May 5, 1998; included rehabilitation assignment to Indianapolis (April 30-May 5). ... On disabled list (April 2-19, 2000).
RECORDS: Shares major league single-game record for most times reached base (nine-inning game)—7 (May 19, 1999).
STATISTICAL NOTES: Led Carolina League with .544 slugging percentage in 1996. ... Had 21-game hitting streak (July 4-30, 2000).

Year Team (League)	Pos.	G	AB	R	H	2B	3B	HR	RBI	Avg.	BB	SO	SB	PO	A	E	Avg.
1995—Watertown (NY-Penn)	1B	55	207	26	68	18	0	2	37	.329	18	21	3	510	24	8	.985
1996—Kinston (Caro.)	1B-DH	92	344	62	114	31	3	12	57	*.331	36	47	1	632	15	6	.991
1997—Akron (East.)	1B-DH	62	241	38	93	19	1	10	66	.386	23	34	0	405	22	5	.988
—Buffalo (A.A.)	DH-1B	20	72	12	26	7	0	5	18	.361	9	11	0	17	1	0	1.000
—Cleveland (A.L.)	DH-1B	6	10	1	2	0	0	0	1	.200	1	2	0	2	0	0	1.000
1998—Cincinnati (N.L.)■	1B	96	302	44	82	21	1	7	52	.272	43	45	1	643	36	4	.994
—Indianapolis (I.L.)	1B-DH	27	95	14	31	8	1	1	13	.326	14	10	0	205	10	2	.991
1999—Cincinnati (N.L.)	1B-DH	151	594	103	197	42	3	25	99	.332	61	88	0	1189	55	6	.995
2000—Cincinnati (N.L.)	1B	133	480	69	151	33	2	20	85	.315	52	80	1	1064	60	6	.995
2001—Cincinnati (N.L.)■	1B-DH	145	533	69	165	40	0	13	89	.310	43	63	3	1146	62	7	.994
American League totals (1 year)		6	10	1	2	0	0	0	1	.200	1	2	0	2	0	0	1.000
National League totals (4 years)		525	1909	285	595	136	6	65	325	.312	199	276	5	4042	213	23	.995
Major League totals (5 years)		531	1919	286	597	136	6	65	326	.311	200	278	5	4044	213	23	.995

ALL-STAR GAME RECORD

Year League	Pos.	AB	R	H	2B	3B	HR	RBI	Avg.	BB	SO	SB	PO	A	E	Avg.
1999—National	1B	1	0	0	0	0	0	0	.000	0	0	0	4	0	0	1.000
2001—National	PH	1	0	0	0	0	0	0	.000	0	1	0	...	...	...	...
All-Star Game totals (2 years)		2	0	0	0	0	0	0	.000	0	1	0	4	0	0	1.000

CASTILLA, VINNY — 3B — BRAVES

PERSONAL: Born July 4, 1967, in Oaxaca, Mexico. ... 6-1/205. ... Bats right, throws right. ... Full name: Vinicio Soria Castilla. ... Name pronounced kass-TEE-uh.
HIGH SCHOOL: Instituto Carlos Gracida (Oaxaca, Mexico).
COLLEGE: Benito Suarez.
TRANSACTIONS/CAREER NOTES: Signed as non-drafted free agent by Saltillo of Mexican League (1987). ... Contract sold by Saltillo to Atlanta Braves organization (March 19, 1990). ... Selected by Colorado Rockies in second round (40th pick overall) of expansion draft (November 17, 1992). ... On disabled list (May 20-June 4, 1993). ... Traded by Rockies to Tampa Bay Devil Rays for P Rolando Arrojo and IF Aaron Ledesma (December 13, 1999). ... On Tampa Bay disabled list (March 25-April 11, June 14-July 3 and July 30-September 4, 2000); included rehabilitation assignment to Durham (July 1-3). ... Released by Devil Rays (May 10, 2001). ... Signed by Houston Astros (May 15, 2001). ... Granted free agency (November 6, 2001). ... Signed by Braves (December 11, 2001).
RECORDS: Holds major league single-month record for most home runs—2 (March 2001).
HONORS: Named third baseman on THE SPORTING NEWS N.L. All-Star team (1995 and 1997-98). ... Named third baseman on THE SPORTING NEWS N.L. Silver Slugger team (1995 and 1997-98).
STATISTICAL NOTES: Led International League shortstops with 550 total chances and 72 double plays in 1992. ... Led N.L. third basemen with 506 total chances and 43 double plays in 1996. ... Had 22-game hitting streak (August 9-September 1, 1997). ... Led N.L. third basemen with 41 double plays in 1997. ... Hit three home runs in one game (June 5, 1999 and July 28, 2001). ... Career major league grand slams: 3.

Year Team (League)	Pos.	G	AB	R	H	2B	3B	HR	RBI	Avg.	BB	SO	SB	PO	A	E	Avg.
1987—Saltillo (Mex.)	3B	13	27	0	5	2	0	0	1	.185	0	5	0	10	31	1	.976
1988—Salt.-Monc. (Mex.)■	SS	50	124	22	30	2	2	5	18	.242	8	29	1	53	105	13	.924
1989—Saltillo (Mex.)■	SS-3B	128	462	70	142	25	13	10	58	.307	33	70	11	224	427	34	.950
1990—Sumter (S.Atl.)■	SS	93	339	47	91	15	2	9	53	.268	28	54	2	139	320	23	.952
—Greenville (Sou.)	SS	46	170	20	40	5	1	4	16	.235	13	23	4	71	167	7	.971
1991—Greenville (Sou.)	SS	66	259	34	70	17	3	7	44	.270	9	35	1	86	221	11	.965
—Richmond (I.L.)	SS	67	240	25	54	7	4	7	36	.225	14	32	1	93	208	12	.962
—Atlanta (N.L.)	SS	12	5	1	1	0	0	0	0	.200	0	2	0	6	6	0	1.000
1992—Richmond (I.L.)	SS	127	449	49	113	29	1	7	44	.252	21	68	1	162	357	*31	.944
—Atlanta (N.L.)	SS-3B	9	16	1	4	1	0	0	1	.250	1	4	0	2	12	1	.933
1993—Colorado (N.L.)■	SS	105	337	36	86	9	7	9	30	.255	13	45	2	141	282	11	.975
1994—Colorado (N.L.)	SS-2B-3B-1B	52	130	16	43	11	1	3	18	.331	7	23	2	67	78	2	.986
—Colo. Springs (PCL)	3B-2B-SS	22	78	13	19	6	1	1	11	.244	7	11	0	20	60	3	.964
1995—Colorado (N.L.)	3B-SS	139	527	82	163	34	2	32	90	.309	30	87	2	86	264	15	.959
1996—Colorado (N.L.)	3B	160	629	97	191	34	0	40	113	.304	35	88	7	97	*389	20	.960
1997—Colorado (N.L.)	3B	159	612	94	186	25	2	40	113	.304	44	108	2	112	*323	21	.954
1998—Colorado (N.L.)	3B-SS	*162	645	108	206	28	4	46	144	.319	40	89	5	110	316	13	.970
1999—Colorado (N.L.)	3B	158	615	83	169	24	1	33	102	.275	53	75	2	96	298	19	.954
2000—Tampa Bay (A.L.)■	3B	85	331	22	73	9	1	6	42	.221	14	41	0	50	185	8	.967
—Durham (I.L.)	3B	2	8	1	3	1	0	1	3	.375	1	0	0	0	2	0	1.000
2001—Tampa Bay (A.L.)	3B	24	93	7	20	6	0	2	9	.215	3	22	0	26	45	5	.934
—Houston (N.L.)	3B-SS	122	445	62	120	28	1	23	82	.270	32	86	1	83	231	12	.963
American League totals (2 years)		109	424	29	93	15	1	8	51	.219	17	63	1	76	230	13	.959
National League totals (10 years)		1078	3961	580	1169	194	18	226	693	.295	255	607	23	800	2199	114	.963
Major League totals (11 years)		1187	4385	609	1262	209	19	234	744	.288	272	670	24	876	2429	127	.963

DIVISION SERIES RECORD

					BATTING									FIELDING			
Year	Team (League)	Pos.	G	AB	R	H	2B	3B	HR	RBI	Avg.	BB	SO	SB	PO	A	E	Avg.
1995— Colorado (N.L.)		3B	4	15	3	7	1	0	3	6	.467	0	1	0	3	13	1	.941
2001— Houston (N.L.)		3B	3	11	1	3	0	0	1	1	.273	0	3	0	5	7	0	1.000
Division series totals (2 years)			7	26	4	10	1	0	4	7	.385	0	4	0	8	20	1	.966

ALL-STAR GAME RECORD

					BATTING									FIELDING		
Year	League	Pos.	AB	R	H	2B	3B	HR	RBI	Avg.	BB	SO	SB	PO	A	E	Avg.
1995— National	3B	2	0	0	0	0	0	0	.000	0	1	0	0	0	0	...
1998— National	3B	2	0	0	0	0	0	0	.000	0	0	0	2	0	1.000
All-Star Game totals (2 years)		4	0	0	0	0	0	0	.000	0	1	0	0	2	0	1.000

CASTILLO, ALBERTO   C   YANKEES

PERSONAL: Born February 10, 1970, in San Juan de la Maguana, Dominican Republic. ... 6-0/200. ... Bats right, throws right. ... Full name: Alberto Terrero Castillo.
HIGH SCHOOL: Mercedes Maria Mateo (Dominican Republic).
TRANSACTIONS/CAREER NOTES: Signed as non-drafted free agent by New York Mets organization (April 15, 1987). ... On disabled list (July 3, 1992-remainder of season; and June 1-July 13, 1994). ... On suspended list (August 27-29, 1994). ... Granted free agency (October 15, 1998). ... Signed by Philadelphia Phillies organization (November 5, 1998). ... Selected by St. Louis Cardinals from Phillies organization in Rule 5 major league draft (December 14, 1998). ... Traded by Cardinals with P Lance Painter and P Matt DeWitt to Toronto Blue Jays for P Pat Hentgen and P Paul Spoljaric (November 11, 1999). ... Released by Blue Jays (December 12, 2001). ... Signed by New York Yankees organization (December 21, 2001).
STATISTICAL NOTES: Led International League catchers with 827 total chances and nine double plays in 1996.

					BATTING									FIELDING		
Year	Team (League)	Pos.	G	AB	R	H	2B	3B	HR	RBI	Avg.	BB	SO	SB	PO	A	E	Avg.
1987— Kingsport (Appl.)........	C	7	9	1	1	0	0	0	0	.111	5	3	1	21	4	0	1.000
1988— GC Mets (GCL)..........	C	22	68	7	18	4	0	0	10	.265	4	4	2	126	13	1	.993
— Kingsport (Appl.)........	C	24	75	7	22	3	0	1	14	.293	15	14	0	161	18	5	.973
1989— Kingsport (Appl.)........	C-1B	27	74	15	19	4	0	3	12	.257	11	14	2	140	19	1	.994
— Pittsfield (NY-Penn)....	C	34	123	13	29	8	0	1	13	.236	7	26	2	186	26	2	.991
1990— Columbia (S.Atl.)........	C	30	103	8	24	4	3	1	14	.233	10	21	1	187	22	5	.977
— Pittsfield (NY-Penn)....	C-OF-1B	58	187	19	41	8	1	4	24	.219	26	35	3	378	61	9	.980
— St. Lucie (FSL)	C	3	11	4	4	0	0	1	3	.364	1	1	0	16	2	0	1.000
1991— Columbia (S.Atl.)........	C	90	267	35	74	20	3	3	47	.277	43	44	6	*734	86	15	.982
1992— St. Lucie (FSL)	C	60	162	11	33	6	0	3	17	.204	16	37	0	317	40	12	.967
1993— St. Lucie (FSL)	C	105	333	37	86	21	0	5	42	.258	28	46	0	*604	80	12	.983
1994— Binghamton (East.)	C-1B	90	315	33	78	14	0	7	42	.248	41	46	1	643	54	6	.991
1995— Norfolk (I.L.)	C-DH	69	217	23	58	13	1	4	31	.267	26	32	2	469	44	7	.987
— New York (N.L.).........	C	13	29	2	3	0	0	0	0	.103	3	9	1	66	9	2	.974
1996— New York (N.L.)	C	6	11	1	4	0	0	0	0	.364	0	4	0	23	0	1	1.000
— Norfolk (I.L.)	C	113	341	34	71	12	1	11	39	.208	39	67	2	*747	*72	8	.990
1997— New York (N.L.)	C	35	59	3	12	1	0	0	7	.203	9	16	0	142	8	2	.987
— Norfolk (I.L.)	C-OF	34	83	4	18	1	0	1	8	.217	17	16	1	197	16	7	.968
1998— New York (N.L.)	C-DH	38	83	13	17	4	0	2	7	.205	9	17	0	193	15	2	.990
— Norfolk (I.L.)	C-OF	21	49	4	9	2	0	1	6	.184	11	12	0	110	6	1	.991
1999— St. Louis (N.L.)■......	C	93	255	21	67	8	0	4	31	.263	24	48	0	514	38	5	.991
2000— Toronto (A.L.)■..........	C	66	185	14	39	7	0	1	16	.211	21	36	0	372	31	3	.993
2001— Toronto (A.L.)...........	C	66	131	9	26	4	0	1	4	.198	7	30	1	324	25	4	.989
American League totals (2 years)		132	316	23	65	11	0	2	20	.206	28	66	1	696	56	7	.991
National League totals (5 years)		185	437	40	103	13	0	6	45	.236	45	94	1	938	70	11	.989
Major League totals (7 years)		317	753	63	168	24	0	8	65	.223	73	160	2	1634	126	18	.990

CASTILLO, CARLOS   P

PERSONAL: Born April 21, 1975, in Boston. ... 6-2/250. ... Throws right, bats right.
HIGH SCHOOL: Southwest (Miami).
TRANSACTIONS/CAREER NOTES: Selected by Chicago White Sox organization in third round of free-agent draft (June 2, 1994). ... Released by White Sox (March 29, 2000). ... Signed by Florida Marlins organization (April 5, 2000). ... Released by Marlins (June 18, 2000). ... Signed by Boston Red Sox organization (June 26, 2000). ... On Pawtucket disabled list (July 24-August 3, 2000). ... Granted free agency (October 18, 2000). ... Re-signed by Red Sox organization (October 27, 2000). ... Released by Red Sox (September 26, 2001).
STATISTICAL NOTES: Tied for A.L. lead with three balks in 1998. ... Tied for International League lead with 28 home runs allowed in 1999.

Year	League	W	L	Pct.	ERA	G	GS	CG	ShO	Sv.	IP	H	R	ER	BB	SO
1994— GC White Sox (GCL)	4	3	.571	2.59	12	12	0	0	0	59	53	20	17	10	57
— Hickory (S.Atl.)..................	2	0	1.000	0.00	3	1	0	0	0	12	3	0	0	2	17
1995— Hickory (S.Atl.)..................	5	6	.455	3.73	14	12	2	0	1	79²/₃	85	42	33	18	67
1996— South Bend (Midw.)	9	9	.500	4.05	20	19	•5	0	0	133¹/₃	131	74	60	29	128
— Prince William (Caro.)........	2	4	.333	3.95	6	6	•4	0	0	43¹/₃	45	22	19	4	30
1997— Chicago (A.L.)	2	1	.667	4.48	37	2	0	0	0	66¹/₃	68	35	33	33	43
— Nashville (A.A.)	0	0	...	1.50	4	0	0	0	3	6	4	1	1	0	4
1998— Chicago (A.L.)	6	4	.600	5.11	54	2	0	0	0	100¹/₃	94	61	57	35	64
— Calgary (PCL)...................	1	1	.500	9.00	2	2	0	0	0	8	12	8	8	4	4
1999— Charlotte (I.L.)...................	9	6	.600	5.15	20	20	*5	0	0	136¹/₃	150	88	78	30	105
— Chicago (A.L.)	2	2	.500	5.71	18	2	0	0	0	41	45	26	26	14	23
2000— Calgary (PCL)■...............	1	7	.125	7.15	13	10	0	0	1	61²/₃	94	59	49	16	37
— Pawtucket (I.L.)■..............	2	3	.400	4.66	16	4	0	0	0	48¹/₃	42	26	25	8	27
— Gulf Coast Red Sox (GCL)..	1	0	1.000	2.35	2	1	0	0	0	7²/₃	11	8	2	5	5
2001— Pawtucket (I.L.).................	9	11	.450	3.41	28	21	*5	1	0	163²/₃	179	78	62	24	114
— Boston (A.L.)...................	0	0	...	6.00	2	0	0	0	0	3	3	2	2	0	0
Major League totals (4 years)	10	7	.588	5.04	111	6	0	0	1	210²/₃	210	124	118	82	130

PERSONAL: Born April 1, 1969, in El Paso, Texas. ... 6-1/200. ... Throws right, bats right. ... Full name: Frank Anthony Castillo.
HIGH SCHOOL: Eastwood (El Paso, Texas).
TRANSACTIONS/CAREER NOTES: Selected by Chicago Cubs organization in sixth round of free-agent draft (June 2, 1987). ... On disabled list (April 1-July 23, 1988). ... On Iowa disabled list (April 12-June 6, 1991). ... On Chicago disabled list (August 11-27, 1991). ... On suspended list (September 20-24, 1993). ... On Chicago disabled list (March 20-May 12, 1994); included rehabilitation assignments to Daytona (April 24), Orlando (April 25-May 2) and Iowa (May 2-10). ... On Iowa disabled list (June 21-July 1, 1994). ... Traded by Cubs to Colorado Rockies for P Matt Pool (July 15, 1997). ... Granted free agency (October 30, 1997). ... Signed by Detroit Tigers (December 11, 1997). ... On Detroit disabled list (March 24-April 28, 1998); included rehabilitation assignment to Lakeland (April 18-28). ... Granted free agency (October 27, 1998). ... Signed by Arizona Diamondbacks organization (January 12, 1999). ... Released by Diamondbacks (March 27, 1999). ... Signed by Pittsburgh Pirates organization (April 20, 1999). ... Granted free agency (October 15, 1999). ... Signed by Toronto Blue Jays organization (December 21, 1999). ... On disabled list (August 14-September 16, 2000). ... Granted free agency (October 31, 2000). ... Signed by Boston Red Sox (December 7, 2000). ... On Boston disabled list (June 29-August 8, 2001); included rehabilitation assignment to Pawtucket (July 28-August 7).
HONORS: Named Appalachian League Player of the Year (1987).
STATISTICAL NOTES: Pitched 4-0 no-hit victory against Huntsville (July 13, 1990, first game). ... Pitched 7-0 one-hit, complete-game victory against St. Louis (September 25, 1995).

Year League	W	L	Pct.	ERA	G	GS	CG	ShO	Sv.	IP	H	R	ER	BB	SO
1987—Wytheville (Appl.)	*10	1	*.909	2.29	12	12	•5	0	0	90 1/3	86	31	23	21	83
—Geneva (NY-Penn)	1	0	1.000	0.00	1	1	0	0	0	6	3	1	0	1	6
1988—Peoria (Midw.)	6	1	.857	0.71	9	8	2	2	0	51	25	5	4	10	58
1989—Winston-Salem (Caro.)	9	6	.600	2.51	18	18	8	1	0	129 1/3	118	42	36	24	114
—Charlotte (Sou.)	3	4	.429	3.84	10	10	4	0	0	68	73	35	29	12	43
1990—Charlotte (Sou.)	6	6	.500	3.88	18	18	4	1	0	111 1/3	113	54	48	27	112
1991—Iowa (A.A.)	3	1	.750	2.52	4	4	1	1	0	25	20	7	7	7	20
—Chicago (N.L.)	6	7	.462	4.35	18	18	0	0	0	111 2/3	107	56	54	33	73
1992—Chicago (N.L.)	10	11	.476	3.46	33	33	0	0	0	205 1/3	179	91	79	63	135
1993—Chicago (N.L.)	5	8	.385	4.84	29	25	2	0	0	141 1/3	162	83	76	39	84
1994—Daytona (FSL)	0	1	.000	4.50	1	1	0	0	0	4	7	3	2	0	1
—Orlando (Sou.)	1	0	1.000	1.29	1	1	0	0	0	7	4	2	1	1	2
—Iowa (A.A.)	4	2	.667	3.27	11	11	0	0	0	66	57	30	24	10	64
—Chicago (N.L.)	2	1	.667	4.30	4	4	1	0	0	23	25	13	11	5	19
1995—Chicago (N.L.)	11	10	.524	3.21	29	29	2	2	0	188	179	75	67	52	135
1996—Chicago (N.L.)	7	•16	.304	5.28	33	33	1	1	0	182 1/3	209	112	107	46	139
1997—Chicago (N.L.)	6	9	.400	5.42	20	19	0	0	0	98	113	64	59	44	67
—Colorado (N.L.)■	6	3	.667	5.42	14	14	0	0	0	86 1/3	107	57	52	25	59
1998—Lakeland (FSL)■	1	0	1.000	0.00	1	1	0	0	0	5	2	0	0	0	4
—Detroit (A.L.)	3	9	.250	6.83	27	19	0	0	1	116	150	91	88	44	81
1999—Nashville (PCL)■	7	5	.583	4.68	19	19	0	0	0	119 1/3	139	72	62	32	90
2000—Toronto (A.L.)■	10	5	.667	3.59	25	24	0	0	0	138	112	58	55	56	104
2001—Boston (A.L.)■	10	9	.526	4.21	26	26	0	0	0	136 2/3	138	72	64	35	89
—Pawtucket (I.L.)	0	0	...	0.00	2	2	0	0	0	7 2/3	7	1	0	0	3
A.L. totals (3 years)	23	23	.500	4.77	78	69	0	0	1	390 2/3	400	221	207	135	274
N.L. totals (7 years)	53	65	.449	4.39	180	175	10	3	0	1036	1081	551	505	307	711
Major League totals (10 years)	76	88	.463	4.49	258	244	10	3	1	1426 2/3	1481	772	712	442	985

PERSONAL: Born September 12, 1975, in San Pedro de Macoris, Dominican Republic. ... 5-11/196. ... Bats both, throws right. ... Full name: Luis Antonio Donato Castillo.
HIGH SCHOOL: Colegio San Benito Abad (San Pedro de Macoris, Dominican Republic).
TRANSACTIONS/CAREER NOTES: Signed as non-drafted free agent by Florida Marlins organization (August 19, 1992). ... On disabled list (July 20-September 11, 1995). ... On Florida disabled list (May 7-22, 1997). ... On Florida disabled list (April 16-May 5, 2000); included rehabilitation assignment to Calgary (April 28-May 5).
RECORDS: Holds N.L. single-season record for fewest errors for leader by second baseman—13 (2001).
STATISTICAL NOTES: Tied for Gulf Coast League lead in caught stealing with 12 in 1994. ... Led Gulf Coast League second basemen with 142 putouts, 318 total chances, 40 double plays and .972 fielding percentage in 1994. ... Led Eastern League in caught stealing with 28 in 1996. ... Led Eastern League second basemen with 557 total chances and 87 double plays in 1996. ... Tied for International League lead in caught stealing with 15 in 1998. ... Had 22-game hitting streak (August 9-September 3, 1999). ... Had 19-game hitting streak (July 3-28, 2000). ... Led N.L. in caught stealing with 22 in 2000.
MISCELLANEOUS: Holds Florida Marlins all-time records for most stolen bases (181).

Year Team (League)	Pos.	G	AB	R	H	2B	3B	HR	RBI	Avg.	BB	SO	SB	PO	A	E	Avg.
1993—Dom. Marlins (DSL)	IF	69	266	48	75	7	1	4	31	.282	36	22	21	151	180	20	.943
1994—GC Marlins (GCL)	2B-SS	57	216	49	57	8	0	0	16	.264	37	36	†144	170	9	†.972	
1995—Kane County (Midw.)	2B	89	340	71	111	4	4	0	23	.326	55	50	41	193	241	17	.962
1996—Portland (East.)	2B	109	420	83	133	15	7	1	35	.317	66	68	*51	217	*326	14	*.975
—Florida (N.L.)	2B	41	164	26	43	2	1	1	8	.262	14	46	17	99	118	3	.986
1997—Florida (N.L.)	2B	75	263	27	63	8	0	0	8	.240	27	53	16	129	177	9	.971
—Charlotte (I.L.)	2B	37	130	25	46	5	0	0	5	.354	16	22	8	66	97	5	.970
1998—Charlotte (I.L.)	2B	100	381	74	109	11	2	0	15	.286	75	68	41	232	281	16	.970
—Florida (N.L.)	2B	44	153	21	31	3	2	1	10	.203	22	33	3	117	113	7	.970
1999—Florida (N.L.)	2B	128	487	76	147	23	4	0	28	.302	67	85	50	257	343	15	.976
2000—Florida (N.L.)	2B	136	539	101	180	17	3	2	17	.334	78	86	*62	282	365	11	.983
—Calgary (PCL)	2B	4	13	4	4	1	1	0	0	.308	4	2	1	7	10	1	.944
2001—Florida (N.L.)	2B	134	537	76	141	16	10	2	45	.263	67	90	33	260	387	*13	.980
Major League totals (6 years)		558	2143	327	605	69	20	6	116	.282	275	393	181	1144	1503	58	.979

CASTRO, JUAN — IF — REDS

PERSONAL: Born June 20, 1972, in Los Mochis, Mexico. ... 5-10/187. ... Bats right, throws right. ... Full name: Juan Gabriel Castro.
HIGH SCHOOL: CBTIS 43 (Los Mochis, Mexico).
TRANSACTIONS/CAREER NOTES: Signed as non-drafted free agent by Los Angeles Dodgers organization (June 13, 1991). ... On Los Angeles disabled list (June 5-August 1, 1997). ... Traded by Dodgers to Cincinnati Reds for a player to be named later and cash (April 1, 2000); Dodgers acquired P Kenny Lutz to complete deal (June 8, 2000).
STATISTICAL NOTES: Tied for Texas League lead in double plays by shortstop with 82 in 1994.

							BATTING								FIELDING		
Year Team (League)	Pos.	G	AB	R	H	2B	3B	HR	RBI	Avg.	BB	SO	SB	PO	A	E	Avg.
1991— Great Falls (Pio.)	SS-2B	60	217	36	60	4	2	1	27	.276	33	31	7	90	155	21	.921
1992— Bakersfield (Calif.)	SS	113	446	56	116	15	4	4	42	.260	37	64	14	180	309	38	.928
1993— San Antonio (Texas)....	SS-2B	118	424	55	117	23	8	7	41	.276	30	40	12	169	314	28	.945
1994— San Antonio (Texas)......	SS	123	445	55	128	25	4	4	44	.288	31	66	4	187	377	29	.951
1995— Albuquerque (PCL).....	SS-2B	104	341	51	91	18	4	3	43	.267	20	42	4	152	344	14	.973
— Los Angeles (N.L.)	3B-SS	11	4	0	1	0	0	0	0	.250	1	1	0	3	7	0	1.000
1996— Albuquerque (PCL).....	3B-SS-2B	17	56	12	21	4	2	1	8	.375	6	7	1	17	33	2	.962
— Los Angeles (N.L.)	S-3-2-O	70	132	16	26	5	3	0	5	.197	10	27	1	54	84	3	.979
1997— Albuquerque (PCL).....	SS-2B	27	101	11	31	5	2	2	11	.307	4	20	1	33	83	9	.928
— Los Angeles (N.L.)	SS-2B-3B	40	75	3	11	3	1	0	4	.147	7	20	0	36	65	1	.990
1998— Los Angeles (N.L.)	SS-2B-3B	89	220	25	43	7	0	2	14	.195	15	37	0	95	182	10	.965
1999— Albuquerque (PCL).....	S-3-2-DH	116	423	52	116	25	4	7	51	.274	34	70	2	126	286	19	.956
— Los Angeles (N.L.)	2B-SS	2	1	0	0	0	0	0	0	.000	0	1	0	1	4	0	1.000
2000— Louisville (I.L.)■........	SS-2B-3B	19	60	9	19	5	1	2	10	.317	12	12	0	28	58	4	.956
— Cincinnati (N.L.)	SS-2B-3B	82	224	20	54	12	2	4	23	.241	14	33	0	102	165	2	.993
2001— Cincinnati (N.L.) SS-2B-3B-1B		96	242	27	54	10	0	3	13	.223	13	50	0	96	163	8	.970
Major League totals (7 years)		390	898	91	189	37	6	9	59	.210	60	169	1	387	670	24	.978

DIVISION SERIES RECORD

							BATTING								FIELDING		
Year Team (League)	Pos.	G	AB	R	H	2B	3B	HR	RBI	Avg.	BB	SO	SB	PO	A	E	Avg.
1996— Los Angeles (N.L.)	2B	2	5	0	1	1	0	0	1	.200	1	1	0	4	3	0	1.000

CASTRO, RAMON — C — MARLINS

PERSONAL: Born March 1, 1976, in Vega Baja, Puerto Rico. ... 6-3/225. ... Bats right, throws right. ... Full name: Ramon Abraham Castro.
HIGH SCHOOL: Lino P. Rivera (Vega Baja, Puerto Rico).
TRANSACTIONS/CAREER NOTES: Selected by Houston Astros organization in first round (17th pick overall) of free-agent draft (June 2, 1994). ... On Jackson disabled list (April 27-May 15, 1998). ... Traded by Astros to Florida Marlins for P Jay Powell and C Scott Makarewicz (July 6, 1998). ... On Calgary disabled list (April 20-May 5, 2000).

							BATTING								FIELDING		
Year Team (League)	Pos.	G	AB	R	H	2B	3B	HR	RBI	Avg.	BB	SO	SB	PO	A	E	Avg.
1994— GC Astros (GCL)	C	37	123	17	34	7	0	3	14	.276	17	14	5	210	24	4	.983
1995— Kissimmee (FSL)	C	36	120	6	25	5	0	0	8	.208	6	21	0	184	18	7	.967
— Auburn (NY-Penn)......	C	63	224	40	67	17	0	9	49	.299	24	27	0	297	46	2	.994
1996— Quad City (Midw.)	C	96	314	38	78	15	0	7	43	.248	31	61	2	660	82	10	.987
1997— Kissimmee (FSL)	C	115	410	53	115	22	1	8	65	.280	53	73	1	630	88	6	*.992
1998— Jackson (Texas)	C	48	168	27	43	6	0	8	25	.256	13	31	0	329	40	10	.974
— Portland (East.)■......	C	31	88	9	22	3	0	3	11	.250	8	21	0	82	5	5	.946
1999— Calgary (PCL)	C-DH	97	349	43	90	22	0	15	61	.258	24	64	0	552	67	7	.989
— Florida (N.L.)	C	24	67	4	12	4	0	2	4	.179	10	14	0	105	17	1	.992
2000— Calgary (PCL)	C	67	218	44	73	22	0	14	45	.335	16	38	0	360	32	4	.990
— Florida (N.L.)	C	50	138	10	33	4	0	2	14	.239	16	36	0	274	24	6	.980
2001— Florida (N.L.)	C	7	11	0	2	0	0	0	1	.182	1	1	0	10	1	0	1.000
— Calgary (PCL)	C	108	390	81	131	33	0	27	90	.336	38	74	1	589	45	7	.989
Major League totals (3 years)		81	216	14	47	8	0	4	19	.218	27	51	0	389	42	7	.984

CASTRO, NELSON — SS — GIANTS

PERSONAL: Born June 4, 1976, in Monte Cristi, Dominican Republic. ... 5-10/190. ... Bats right, throws right. ... Full name: Nelson Daniel Castro Reynoso.
TRANSACTIONS/CAREER NOTES: Signed as non-drafted free agent by California Angels organization (January 14, 1994). ... Angels franchise renamed Anaheim Angels for 1997 season. ... Claimed on waivers by San Francisco Giants (October 13, 1999).
STATISTICAL NOTES: Led Arizona League shortstops with 297 total chances and 32 double plays in 1996. ... Led Northwest League shortstops with 323 total chances in 1997. ... Led California League shortstops with 591 total chances and 71 double plays in 1998. ... Led California League shortstops with 603 total chances and 74 double plays in 1999. ... Led Texas League shortstops with 612 total chances in 2001.

							BATTING								FIELDING		
Year Team (League)	Pos.	G	AB	R	H	2B	3B	HR	RBI	Avg.	BB	SO	SB	PO	A	E	Avg.
1994— Dom. Angels (DSL)	SS	59	205	44	52	6	1	1	33	.254	38	28	15	109	186	45	.868
1995— Arizona Angels (Ariz.).	SS	55	190	34	37	1	2	0	22	.195	27	50	15	*106	*173	18	.939
1996— Boise (N'West)	PH	1	1	0	0	0	0	0	0	.000	0	0	0	...	...	...	...
— Arizona Angels (Ariz.).	SS	53	222	31	38	4	3	3	14	.171	32	42	25	75	164	14	.945
1997— Boise (N'West)	SS	69	293	74	86	16	1	7	37	.294	38	53	26	80	218	25	*.923
1998— Lake Elsinore (Calif.)..	SS	131	470	73	110	16	7	4	41	.234	40	101	16	•185	*372	34	.942
1999— Lake Elsinore (Calif.)..	SS	125	444	68	111	16	12	1	50	.250	36	75	*53	210	*370	23	*.962
2000— Bakersfield (Calif.)■...	SS	53	218	38	62	14	3	5	41	.284	20	40	27	97	145	12	.953
— Fresno (PCL)	SS	67	244	27	62	7	2	5	20	.254	14	51	10	78	201	23	.924
2001— Fresno (PCL)	2B-SS	6	23	3	3	1	0	0	1	.130	1	5	0	10	21	1	.969
— Shreveport (Texas)	SS	122	479	76	142	27	6	11	60	.296	42	122	*38	*207	*373	*32	.948

C

CATALANOTTO, FRANK — OF/IF — RANGERS

PERSONAL: Born April 27, 1974, in Smithtown, N.Y. ... 6-0/195. ... Bats left, throws right. ... Full name: Frank John Catalanotto.
HIGH SCHOOL: Smithtown (N.Y.) East.
COLLEGE: C.W. Post (Brookville, N.Y.).
TRANSACTIONS/CAREER NOTES: Selected by Detroit Tigers organization in 10th round of free-agent draft (June 1, 1992). ... Selected by Oakland Athletics from Tigers organization in Rule 5 major league draft (December 9, 1996). ... Returned to Tigers organization (March 21, 1997). ... On Toledo disabled list (June 18-25, 1998). ... Traded by Tigers with P Justin Thompson, P Francisco Cordero, OF Gabe Kapler, C Bill Haselman and P Alan Webb to Texas Rangers for OF Juan Gonzalez, P Danny Patterson and C Gregg Zaun (November 2, 1999). ... On Texas disabled list (April 22-May 15, 2000); included rehabilitation assignment to Oklahoma (May 12-15).
STATISTICAL NOTES: Led Southern League second basemen with 681 total chances and 98 double plays in 1995. ... Led Southern League second basemen with 689 total chances and 99 double plays in 1996. ... Led International League second basemen with .984 fielding percentage in 1997. ... Career major league grand slams: 1.

| | | | | | | | | BATTING | | | | | | FIELDING | | |
Year	Team (League)	Pos.	G	AB	R	H	2B	3B	HR	RBI	Avg.	BB	SO	SB	PO	A	E	Avg.
1992—	Bristol (Appl.)............	2B	21	50	6	10	2	0	0	4	.200	8	8	0	8	6	2	.875
1993—	Bristol (Appl.)............	2B	55	199	37	61	9	5	3	22	.307	15	19	3	96	128	10	.957
1994—	Fayetteville (S.Atl.).....	2B	119	458	72	149	24	8	3	56	.325	37	54	4	244	304	15	.973
1995—	Jacksonville (Sou.)......	2B	134	491	66	111	19	5	8	48	.226	49	56	13	252	*411	18	*.974
1996—	Jacksonville (Sou.)......	2B	132	497	105	148	34	6	17	67	.298	74	69	15	246	*421	•22	.968
1997—	Toledo (I.L.)................	2-3-O-DH	134	500	75	150	32	3	16	68	.300	47	80	12	168	351	18	†.966
—	Detroit (A.L.).............	2B-DH	13	26	2	8	2	0	0	3	.308	3	7	0	7	9	0	1.000
1998—	Detroit (A.L.).............	2-DH-1-3	89	213	23	60	13	2	6	25	.282	12	39	3	162	51	3	.986
—	Toledo (I.L.)................	1B-2B-DH	28	105	20	35	6	3	4	28	.333	14	21	0	131	43	2	.989
1999—	Detroit (A.L.).............	1-2-3-DH	100	286	41	79	19	0	11	35	.276	15	49	3	252	98	5	.986
2000—	Texas (A.L.)■...........	2-DH-1-O	103	282	55	82	13	2	10	42	.291	33	36	6	169	110	9	.969
—	Oklahoma (PCL)........	OF-2B	3	11	2	3	0	0	0	1	.273	0	4	0	1	0	0	1.000
2001—	Texas (A.L.)...............O-2-3-1-DH		133	463	77	153	31	5	11	54	.330	39	55	15	217	44	4	.985
Major League totals (5 years)			438	1270	198	382	78	9	38	159	.301	102	186	27	807	312	21	.982

CEDENO, JOVANNY — P — RANGERS

PERSONAL: Born October 25, 1979, in La Romana, Domincan Republic. ... 6-0/160. ... Throws right, bats right. ... Full name: Jovanny R. Cedeno.
TRANSACTIONS/CAREER NOTES: Signed as non-drafted free agent by Texas Rangers organization (February 2, 1997). ... On disabled list (September 1, 2000-remainder of season). ... On disabled list (April 22, 2001-remainder of season).

Year	League	W	L	Pct.	ERA	G	GS	CG	ShO	Sv.	IP	H	R	ER	BB	SO
1997—	Dominican Rangers (DSL) .	10	2	.833	2.56	14	14	1	0	0	84 1/3	70	29	24	23	73
1998—	Dominican Rangers (DSL) .	1	0	1.000	1.42	5	2	0	0	1	19	14	5	3	5	22
1999—	Gulf Coast Rangers (GCL)..	3	0	1.000	0.33	6	6	1	•1	0	27 1/3	13	3	1	4	32
—	Charlotte (FSL)................	1	0	1.000	5.40	1	1	0	0	0	5	7	3	3	1	5
2000—	Savannah (S.Atl.)	11	4	.733	2.42	24	22	0	0	0	130 1/3	95	40	35	53	153
2001—	Charlotte (FSL)................	0	0	...	1.86	3	3	0	0	0	9 2/3	3	2	2	5	12

CEDENO, ROGER — OF — METS

PERSONAL: Born August 16, 1974, in Valencia, Venezuela. ... 6-1/205. ... Bats both, throws right. ... Full name: Roger Leandro Cedeno.
TRANSACTIONS/CAREER NOTES: Signed as non-drafted free agent by Los Angeles Dodgers organization (March 28, 1991). ... On disabled list (June 27-July 14, 1994). ... On Los Angeles disabled list (March 25-April 17 and August 25, 1997-remainder of season); included rehabilitation assignment to Albuquerque (April 17-21). ... On Los Angeles disabled list (March 22-April 24, 1998); included rehabilitation assignment to Vero Beach (April 16-24). ... Traded by Dodgers with C Charles Johnson to New York Mets for C Todd Hundley and P Arnold Gooch (December 1, 1998). ... Traded by Mets with P Octavio Dotel and P Kyle Kessel to Houston Astros for P Mike Hampton and OF Derek Bell (December 23, 1999). ... On Houston disabled list (May 26-August 18, 2000); included rehabilitation assignment to New Orleans (August 10-18). ... Traded by Astros with P Mitch Meluskey and P Chris Holt to Detroit Tigers for C Brad Ausmus, P Doug Brocail and P Nelson Cruz (December 11, 2000). ... Granted free agency (November 5, 2001). ... Signed by Mets (December 13, 2001).
STATISTICAL NOTES: Tied for Pioneer League lead with three intentional bases on balls received in 1992. ... Led Texas League in caught stealing with 20 in 1993. ... Led Pacific Coast League in caught stealing with 18 in 1995. ... Led A.L. in caught stealing with 15 in 2001.

| | | | | | | | | BATTING | | | | | | FIELDING | | |
Year	Team (League)	Pos.	G	AB	R	H	2B	3B	HR	RBI	Avg.	BB	SO	SB	PO	A	E	Avg.
1991—	Dom. Dodgers (DSL) .	OF	58	209	25	50	1	1	0	7	.239	0	0	26	...	...	...	...
1992—	Great Falls (Pio.)	OF	69	256	60	81	6	5	2	27	.316	51	53	*40	113	6	8	.937
1993—	San Antonio (Texas)...	OF	122	465	70	134	12	8	4	30	.288	45	90	28	213	6	9	.961
—	Albuquerque (PCL).....	OF	6	18	1	4	1	1	0	4	.222	3	3	0	12	0	1	.923
1994—	Albuquerque (PCL).....	OF	104	383	84	123	18	5	4	49	.321	51	57	30	194	7	8	.962
1995—	Albuquerque (PCL).....	OF-DH	99	367	67	112	19	9	2	44	.305	53	56	23	189	3	3	.985
—	Los Angeles (N.L.)	OF	40	42	4	10	2	0	0	3	.238	3	10	1	43	0	1	.977
1996—	Los Angeles (N.L.)	OF	86	211	26	52	11	1	2	18	.246	24	47	5	117	2	2	.983
—	Albuquerque (PCL).....	OF	33	125	16	28	2	3	1	10	.224	15	22	6	71	2	0	1.000
1997—	Los Angeles (N.L.)	OF	80	194	31	53	10	2	3	17	.273	25	44	9	148	1	1	.987
—	Albuquerque (PCL).....	OF	29	113	21	40	4	4	2	9	.354	22	16	5	53	1	2	.964
1998—	Vero Beach (FSL)	OF	6	21	5	9	0	1	1	6	.429	5	5	1	14	0	1	.933
—	Los Angeles (N.L.)	OF	105	240	33	58	11	4	0	17	.242	27	57	8	86	4	2	.978
1999—	New York (N.L.)■	OF-2B	155	453	90	142	23	4	4	36	.313	60	100	66	256	9	3	.989
2000—	Houston (N.L.)■........	OF	74	259	54	73	2	5	6	26	.282	43	47	25	135	1	3	.978
—	New Orleans (PCL).....	OF	6	20	2	7	0	1	0	3	.350	2	5	1	6	0	0	1.000
2001—	Detroit (A.L.)■..........	OF-DH	131	523	79	153	14	11	6	48	.293	36	83	55	236	5	12	.953
American League totals (1 year)			131	523	79	153	14	11	6	48	.293	36	83	55	236	5	12	.953
National League totals (6 years)			540	1399	238	388	59	13	17	117	.277	182	305	114	785	17	13	.984
Major League totals (7 years)			671	1922	317	541	73	24	23	165	.281	218	388	169	1021	22	25	.977

						BATTING								FIELDING		
Year Team (League)	Pos.	G	AB	R	H	2B	3B	HR	RBI	Avg.	BB	SO	SB	PO	A	E	Avg.
1999— New York (N.L.).........	OF-PH	4	7	1	2	0	0	0	2	.286	1	1	1	4	0	0	1.000

CHAMPIONSHIP SERIES RECORD

						BATTING								FIELDING		
Year Team (League)	Pos.	G	AB	R	H	2B	3B	HR	RBI	Avg.	BB	SO	SB	PO	A	E	Avg.
1999— New York (N.L.).........	OF-PR	5	12	2	6	1	0	0	1	.500	0	1	2	12	0	0	1.000

CHACON, SHAWN   P   ROCKIES

PERSONAL: Born December 23, 1977, in Anchorage, Alaska. ... 6-3/212. ... Throws right, bats right. ... Full name: Shawn A. Chacon.
HIGH SCHOOL: Greeley (Colo.) Central.
TRANSACTIONS/CAREER NOTES: Selected by Colorado Rockies organization in third round of free-agent draft (June 4, 1996).

Year League	W	L	Pct.	ERA	G	GS	CG	ShO	Sv.	IP	H	R	ER	BB	SO
1996— Arizona Rockies (Ariz.).......	1	2	.333	*1.60	11	11	1	0	0	56 1/3	46	17	10	15	64
— Portland (N'West)	0	2	.000	6.86	4	4	0	0	0	19 2/3	24	18	15	9	17
1997— Asheville (S.Atl.)...............	11	7	.611	3.89	28	27	1	0	0	162	155	80	70	63	149
1998— Salem (Caro.)....................	0	4	.000	5.30	12	12	0	0	0	56	53	35	33	31	54
1999— Salem (Caro.)....................	5	5	.500	4.13	12	12	0	0	0	72	69	44	33	34	66
2000— Carolina (Sou.).................	10	10	.500	3.16	27	*27	4	*3	0	173 2/3	151	71	61	*85	*172
2001— Colorado Springs (PCL)	2	0	1.000	2.25	4	4	0	0	0	24	18	6	6	7	28
— Colorado (N.L.)...................	6	10	.375	5.06	27	27	0	0	0	160	157	96	90	87	134
Major League totals (1 year)........	**6**	**10**	**.375**	**5.06**	**27**	**27**	**0**	**0**	**0**	**160**	**157**	**96**	**90**	**87**	**134**

CHARLTON, NORM   P   MARINERS

PERSONAL: Born January 6, 1963, in Fort Polk, La. ... 6-3/205. ... Throws left, bats both. ... Full name: Norman Wood Charlton III.
HIGH SCHOOL: James Madison (San Antonio).
COLLEGE: Rice.
TRANSACTIONS/CAREER NOTES: Selected by Montreal Expos organization in supplemental round ("sandwich pick" between first and second round, 28th pick overall) of free-agent draft (June 4, 1984); pick received as compensation for San Francisco Giants signing Type B free-agent 2B Manny Trillo. ... Traded by Expos with a player to be named later to Cincinnati Reds for IF Wayne Krenchicki (March 31, 1986); Reds acquired 2B Tim Barker to complete deal (April 2, 1986). ... On Cincinnati disabled list (April 6-June 26, 1987); included rehabilitation assignment to Nashville (June 9-26). ... On disabled list (May 26-June 11 and June 17-July 19, 1991). ... On suspended list (September 29 and October 4-6, 1991). ... Traded by Reds to Seattle Mariners for OF Kevin Mitchell (November 17, 1992). ... On suspended list (July 9-16, 1993). ... On disabled list (July 21-August 5 and August 8, 1993-remainder of season). ... Granted free agency (November 18, 1993). ... Signed by Philadelphia Phillies organization (February 3, 1994). ... On disabled list (March 31, 1994-entire season). ... Granted free agency (October 28, 1994). ... Re-signed by Phillies organization (December 22, 1994). ... Released by Phillies (July 10, 1995). ... Signed by Mariners (July 14, 1995). ... Granted free agency (November 7, 1997). ... Signed by Baltimore Orioles organization (December 15, 1997). ... Released by Orioles (July 28, 1998). ... Signed by Atlanta Braves organization (August 5, 1998). ... Granted free agency (October 27, 1998). ... Signed by Tampa Bay Devil Rays organization (January 20, 1999). ... On Durham disabled list (April 8-17, 1999). ... Granted free agency (November 2, 1999). ... Re-signed by Devil Rays organization (January 7, 2000). ... Released by Devil Rays (March 31, 2000). ... Signed by Reds organization (April 9, 2000). ... Released by Reds (April 28, 2000). ... Signed by Mariners organization (December 19, 2000). ... On Seattle disabled list (May 31-June 15 and June 23-July 26, 2001); included rehabilitation assignment to Tacoma (July 22-26). ... Granted free agency (November 5, 2001). ... Re-signed by Mariners (December 12, 2001).
STATISTICAL NOTES: Led American Association with 13 wild pitches in 1988.
MISCELLANEOUS: Appeared in one game as pinch runner (1990). ... Appeared in two games as pinch runner (1991).

Year League	W	L	Pct.	ERA	G	GS	CG	ShO	Sv.	IP	H	R	ER	BB	SO
1984— West Palm Beach (FSL)	1	4	.200	4.58	8	8	0	0	0	39 1/3	51	27	20	22	27
1985— West Palm Beach (FSL)	7	10	.412	4.57	24	23	5	2	0	128	135	79	65	79	71
1986— Vermont (East.)■.............	10	6	.625	2.83	22	22	6	1	0	136 2/3	109	55	43	74	96
1987— Nashville (A.A.)	2	8	.200	4.30	18	17	3	1	0	98 1/3	97	57	47	44	74
1988— Nashville (A.A.)	11	10	.524	3.02	27	27	8	1	0	182	149	69	61	56	*161
— Cincinnati (N.L.)	4	5	.444	3.96	10	10	0	0	0	61 1/3	60	27	27	20	39
1989— Cincinnati (N.L.)	8	3	.727	2.93	69	0	0	0	0	95 1/3	67	38	31	40	98
1990— Cincinnati (N.L.)	12	9	.571	2.74	56	16	1	1	2	154 1/3	131	53	47	70	117
1991— Cincinnati (N.L.)	3	5	.375	2.91	39	11	0	0	1	108 1/3	92	37	35	34	77
1992— Cincinnati (N.L.)	4	2	.667	2.99	64	0	0	0	26	81 1/3	79	39	27	26	90
1993— Seattle (A.L.)■...............	1	3	.250	2.34	34	0	0	0	18	34 2/3	22	12	9	17	48
1994— Philadelphia (N.L.)■							Did not play.								
1995— Philadelphia (N.L.).............	2	5	.286	7.36	25	0	0	0	0	22	23	19	18	15	12
— Seattle (A.L.)■...............	2	1	.667	1.51	30	0	0	0	14	47 2/3	23	12	8	16	58
1996— Seattle (A.L.)	4	7	.364	4.04	70	0	0	0	20	75 2/3	68	37	34	38	73
1997— Seattle (A.L.)	3	8	.273	7.27	71	0	0	0	14	69 1/3	89	59	56	47	55
1998— Baltimore (A.L.)■.............	2	1	.667	6.94	36	0	0	0	0	35	46	27	27	25	41
— Richmond (I.L.)■.............	0	0	...	0.00	2	0	0	0	0	2	2	0	0	0	1
— Atlanta (N.L.)...............	0	0	...	1.38	13	0	0	0	1	13	7	2	2	8	6
1999— Durham (I.L.)■...............	3	2	.600	3.69	18	0	0	0	1	31 2/3	27	13	13	10	29
— Tampa Bay (A.L.).............	2	3	.400	4.44	42	0	0	0	0	50 2/3	49	29	25	36	45
2000— Louisville (I.L.)■.............	0	0	...	0.00	4	0	0	0	0	2 2/3	0	0	0	2	5
— Cincinnati (N.L.).............	0	0	...	27.00	2	0	0	0	0	3	6	9	9	6	1
2001— Seattle (A.L.)■.................	4	2	.667	3.02	44	0	0	0	1	47 2/3	36	19	16	11	48
— Tacoma (PCL)	0	1	.000	3.00	4	2	0	0	0	6	4	2	2	2	9
A.L. totals (7 years)	**18**	**25**	**.419**	**4.37**	**327**	**0**	**0**	**0**	**67**	**360 2/3**	**333**	**195**	**175**	**190**	**368**
N.L. totals (8 years)	**33**	**29**	**.532**	**3.27**	**278**	**37**	**1**	**1**	**30**	**538 2/3**	**465**	**224**	**196**	**219**	**440**
Major League totals (13 years)	**51**	**54**	**.486**	**3.71**	**605**	**37**	**1**	**1**	**97**	**899 1/3**	**798**	**419**	**371**	**409**	**808**

DIVISION SERIES RECORD

Year League	W	L	Pct.	ERA	G	GS	CG	ShO	Sv.	IP	H	R	ER	BB	SO
1995—Seattle (A.L.)	1	0	1.000	2.45	4	0	0	0	1	7 1/3	4	2	2	3	9
1997—Seattle (A.L.)	0	0	...	0.00	2	0	0	0	0	2 1/3	2	0	0	0	1
2001—Seattle (A.L.)	0	0	...	0.00	1	0	0	0	0	1 2/3	0	0	0	0	2
Division series totals (3 years)	**1**	**0**	**1.000**	**1.59**	**7**	**0**	**0**	**0**	**1**	**11 1/3**	**6**	**2**	**2**	**3**	**12**

CHAMPIONSHIP SERIES RECORD

Year League	W	L	Pct.	ERA	G	GS	CG	ShO	Sv.	IP	H	R	ER	BB	SO
1990—Cincinnati (N.L.)	1	1	.500	1.80	4	0	0	0	0	5	4	2	1	3	3
1995—Seattle (A.L.)	1	0	1.000	0.00	3	0	0	0	1	6	1	0	0	1	5
2001—Seattle (A.L.)	0	0	...	0.00	2	0	0	0	0	1 2/3	1	0	0	2	2
Champ. series totals (3 years)	**2**	**1**	**.667**	**0.71**	**9**	**0**	**0**	**0**	**1**	**12 2/3**	**6**	**2**	**1**	**6**	**10**

WORLD SERIES RECORD

NOTES: Member of World Series championship team (1990).

Year League	W	L	Pct.	ERA	G	GS	CG	ShO	Sv.	IP	H	R	ER	BB	SO
1990—Cincinnati (N.L.)	0	0	...	0.00	1	0	0	0	0	1	1	0	0	0	0

ALL-STAR GAME RECORD

Year League	W	L	Pct.	ERA	GS	CG	ShO	Sv.	IP	H	R	ER	BB	SO
1992—National	0	0	...	0.00	0	0	0	0	1	0	0	0	0	1

CHAVEZ, ENDY   OF   TIGERS

PERSONAL: Born February 7, 1978, in Valencia, Venezuela. ... 6-0/150. ... Bats left, throws left. ... Full name: Endy DeJesus Chavez.
HIGH SCHOOL: Liceo Bataila Carabobo (Venezuela).
TRANSACTIONS/CAREER NOTES: Signed as non-drafted free agent by New York Mets organization (April 29, 1996). ... Selected by Kansas City Royals from Mets organization in Rule 5 major league draft (December 11, 2000). ... Returned to Mets organization (March 30, 2001). ... Traded by Mets to Royals for OF Michael Curry (March 30, 2001). ... Claimed on waivers by Detroit Tigers (December 20, 2001).

Year Team (League)	Pos.	G	AB	R	H	2B	3B	HR	RBI	Avg.	BB	SO	SB	PO	A	E	Avg.
1996—Dom. Mets (DSL)	OF	48	164	42	58	11	1	7	29	.354	22	16	3	77	1	3	.963
1997—GC Mets (GCL)	OF	33	119	26	33	6	3	0	15	.277	20	10	1	50	8	2	.967
—Kingsport (Appl.)	OF	19	73	16	22	4	0	0	4	.301	13	10	5	43	2	2	.957
1998—Kingsport (Appl.)	OF	33	114	26	33	8	4	0	16	.289	17	17	10	29	3	2	.941
1999—Columbia (S.Atl.)	OF	73	253	40	64	8	1	0	15	.253	34	36	20	140	8	5	.967
—St. Lucie (FSL)	OF	45	183	33	57	8	3	2	18	.311	22	22	9	95	3	2	.980
2000—St. Lucie (FSL)	OF	111	433	84	129	20	2	1	43	.298	47	48	38	228	15	5	.980
2001—Wichita (Texas)■	OF	43	168	27	50	6	1	1	13	.298	16	13	11	95	4	1	.990
—Kansas City (A.L.)	OF	29	77	4	16	2	0	0	5	.208	3	8	0	40	2	0	1.000
—Omaha (PCL)	OF	23	104	16	35	6	0	0	4	.337	0	13	4	38	2	0	1.000
Major League totals (1 year)	****	**29**	**77**	**4**	**16**	**2**	**0**	**0**	**5**	**.208**	**3**	**8**	**0**	**40**	**2**	**0**	**1.000**

CHAVEZ, ERIC   3B   ATHLETICS

PERSONAL: Born December 7, 1977, in Los Angeles. ... 6-0/204. ... Bats left, throws right. ... Full name: Eric Cesar Chavez.
HIGH SCHOOL: Mount Carmel (San Diego).
TRANSACTIONS/CAREER NOTES: Selected by Oakland Athletics organization in first round (10th pick overall) of free-agent draft (June 2, 1996). ... On Oakland disabled list (August 21-September 19, 1999); included rehabilitation assignment to Vancouver (September 14-19).
HONORS: Won A.L. Gold Glove at third base (2001).
STATISTICAL NOTES: Had 15-game hitting streak (May 27-June 18, 2000). ... Hit for the cycle (June 21, 2000). ... Career major league grand slams: 3.

Year Team (League)	Pos.	G	AB	R	H	2B	3B	HR	RBI	Avg.	BB	SO	SB	PO	A	E	Avg.
1997—Visalia (Calif.)	3B-DH	134	520	67	141	30	3	18	100	.271	37	91	13	84	268	*32	.917
1998—Huntsville (Sou.)	3B-DH	88	335	66	110	27	1	22	86	.328	42	61	12	54	146	14	.935
—Edmonton (PCL)	3B-DH	47	194	38	63	18	0	11	40	.325	12	32	2	34	66	7	.935
—Oakland (A.L.)	3B	16	45	6	14	4	1	0	6	.311	3	5	1	11	21	0	1.000
1999—Oakland (A.L.)	3B-DH-SS	115	356	47	88	21	2	13	50	.247	46	56	1	69	155	9	.961
2000—Oakland (A.L.)	3B-SS-DH	153	501	89	139	23	4	26	86	.277	62	94	2	92	256	18	.951
2001—Oakland (A.L.)	3-1-S-DH	151	552	91	159	43	0	32	114	.288	41	99	8	100	321	12	.972
Major League totals (4 years)	****	**435**	**1454**	**233**	**400**	**91**	**7**	**71**	**256**	**.275**	**152**	**254**	**12**	**272**	**753**	**39**	**.963**

DIVISION SERIES RECORD

Year Team (League)	Pos.	G	AB	R	H	2B	3B	HR	RBI	Avg.	BB	SO	SB	PO	A	E	Avg.
2000—Oakland (A.L.)	3B	5	21	4	7	3	0	0	4	.333	0	5	0	4	8	0	1.000
2001—Oakland (A.L.)	3B	5	21	0	3	1	0	0	0	.143	0	5	0	4	11	1	.938
Division series totals (2 years)	****	**10**	**42**	**4**	**10**	**4**	**0**	**0**	**4**	**.238**	**0**	**10**	**0**	**8**	**19**	**1**	**.964**

CHAVEZ, RAUL   C   ASTROS

PERSONAL: Born March 18, 1973, in Valencia, Venezuela. ... 5-11/210. ... Bats right, throws right. ... Full name: Raul Alexander Chavez.
TRANSACTIONS/CAREER NOTES: Signed as non-drafted free agent by Houston Astros organization (January 10, 1990). ... Traded by Astros with P Dave Veres to Montreal Expos for 3B Sean Berry (December 20, 1995). ... Traded by Expos to Seattle Mariners for OF Robert Perez (May 8, 1998). ... Granted free agency (October 15, 1999). ... Signed by Astros organization (January 5, 2000). ... On disabled list (August 10-19, 2001).

STATISTICAL NOTES:
Tied for International League lead in double plays by catcher with nine in 1997. ... Led Pacific Coast League catchers with 12 double plays in 1998. ... Led Pacific Coast League catchers with 74 assists in 1999. ... Tied for Pacific Coast League lead in assists by catcher with 62 and double plays with 10 in 2001.

									BATTING						FIELDING		
Year Team (League)	Pos.	G	AB	R	H	2B	3B	HR	RBI	Avg.	BB	SO	SB	PO	A	E	Avg.
1990— GC Astros (GCL)	SS-2B-3B	48	155	23	50	8	1	0	23	.323	7	12	5	67	119	9	.954
1991— Burlington (Midw.)	SS-3B	114	420	54	108	17	0	3	41	.257	25	65	1	144	293	41	.914
1992— Asheville (S.Atl.)	C	95	348	37	99	22	1	2	40	.284	16	39	1	456	77	13	.976
1993— Osceola (FSL)	C	58	197	13	45	5	1	0	16	.228	8	19	1	303	62	5	.986
1994— Jackson (Texas)	C	89	251	17	55	7	0	1	22	.219	17	41	1	*563	64	9	.986
1995— Tucson (PCL)	C	32	103	14	27	5	0	0	10	.262	8	13	0	203	39	5	.980
— Jackson (Texas)	C	58	188	16	54	8	0	4	25	.287	8	17	0	316	52	5	.987
1996— Ottawa (I.L.)■	C	60	198	15	49	10	0	2	24	.247	11	31	0	363	50	4	.990
— Montreal (N.L.)	C	4	5	1	1	0	0	0	0	.200	1	1	1	14	0	0	1.000
1997— Ottawa (I.L.)	C	92	310	31	76	17	0	4	46	.245	18	42	1	593	*77	*15	.978
— Montreal (N.L.)	C	13	26	0	7	0	0	0	2	.269	0	5	1	47	8	0	1.000
1998— Ottawa (I.L.)	C	11	31	2	7	0	0	0	1	.226	5	5	0	71	15	0	1.000
— Tacoma (PCL)■	C	76	233	27	52	6	0	4	34	.223	22	41	1	523	*70	6	.990
— Seattle (A.L.)	C	1	1	0	0	0	0	0	0	.000	0	0	0	3	0	0	1.000
1999— Tacoma (PCL)	C-1-2-3-S	102	354	39	95	20	1	3	40	.268	28	63	1	669	†82	10	.987
2000— New Orleans (PCL)■.	C	99	303	31	74	13	0	2	36	.244	34	44	3	571	52	8	.987
— Houston (N.L.)	C	14	43	3	11	2	0	1	5	.256	3	6	0	67	6	1	.986
2001— New Orleans (PCL)	C-1B-3B	85	278	38	84	17	0	8	40	.302	19	34	1	533	†65	5	.992
American League totals (1 year)		1	1	0	0	0	0	0	0	.000	0	0	0	3	0	0	1.000
National League totals (3 years)		31	74	4	19	2	0	1	7	.257	4	12	2	128	14	1	.993
Major League totals (4 years)		32	75	4	19	2	0	1	7	.253	4	12	2	131	14	1	.993

CHEN, BRUCE P METS

PERSONAL: Born June 19, 1977, in Panama City, Panama. ... 6-2/210. ... Throws left, bats left. ... Full name: Bruce Kastulo Chen.
HIGH SCHOOL: Instituto Panamericano (Panama).
TRANSACTIONS/CAREER NOTES: Signed as non-drafted free agent by Atlanta Braves organization (July 1, 1993). ... Traded by Braves with P Jimmy Osting to Philadelphia Phillies for P Andy Ashby (July 12, 2000). ... Traded by Phillies with P Adam Walker to New York Mets for P Turk Wendell and P Dennis Cook (July 27, 2001).
HONORS: Named Southern League Most Outstanding Pitcher (1998).
STATISTICAL NOTES: Led South Atlantic League with 19 home runs allowed in 1997.

Year League	W	L	Pct.	ERA	G	GS	CG	ShO	Sv.	IP	H	R	ER	BB	SO
1994— Gulf Coast Braves (GCL)	1	4	.200	3.80	9	7	0	0	1	42 2/3	42	21	18	3	26
1995— Danville (Appl.)	4	4	.500	3.97	14	13	1	0	0	70 1/3	78	42	31	19	56
1996— Eugene (N'West)	4	1	.800	2.27	11	8	0	0	0	35 2/3	23	13	9	14	55
1997— Macon (S.Atl.)	12	7	.632	3.51	28	28	1	1	0	146 1/3	120	67	57	44	*182
1998— Greenville (Sou.)	13	7	.650	3.29	24	23	1	0	0	139 1/3	106	57	51	48	164
— Richmond (I.L.)	2	1	.667	1.88	4	4	0	0	0	24	17	5	5	19	29
— Atlanta (N.L.)	2	0	1.000	3.98	4	4	0	0	0	20 1/3	23	9	9	9	17
1999— Richmond (I.L.)	6	3	.667	3.81	14	14	0	0	0	78	73	36	33	26	90
— Atlanta (N.L.)	2	2	.500	5.47	16	7	0	0	0	51	38	32	31	27	45
2000— Atlanta (N.L.)	4	0	1.000	2.50	22	0	0	0	0	39 2/3	35	15	11	19	32
— Richmond (I.L.)	1	0	1.000	0.00	1	1	0	0	0	6	5	0	0	1	6
— Philadelphia (N.L.)■	3	4	.429	3.63	15	15	0	0	0	94 1/3	81	39	38	27	80
2001— Philadelphia (N.L.)	4	5	.444	5.00	16	16	0	0	0	86 1/3	90	53	48	31	79
— Reading (East.)	1	0	1.000	0.00	1	1	0	0	0	6	3	0	0	0	7
— Scranton/W.B. (I.L.)	1	0	1.000	3.86	3	3	0	0	0	18 2/3	14	8	8	5	14
— New York (N.L.)■	3	2	.600	4.68	11	11	0	0	0	59 2/3	56	37	31	28	47
Major League totals (4 years)	18	13	.581	4.30	84	53	0	0	0	351 1/3	323	185	168	141	300

DIVISION SERIES RECORD

Year League	W	L	Pct.	ERA	G	GS	CG	ShO	Sv.	IP	H	R	ER	BB	SO
1999— Atlanta (N.L.)							Did not play.								

CHAMPIONSHIP SERIES RECORD

Year League	W	L	Pct.	ERA	G	GS	CG	ShO	Sv.	IP	H	R	ER	BB	SO
1999— Atlanta (N.L.)							Did not play.								

WORLD SERIES RECORD

Year League	W	L	Pct.	ERA	G	GS	CG	ShO	Sv.	IP	H	R	ER	BB	SO
1999— Atlanta (N.L.)							Did not play.								

CHEN, CHIN-FENG OF DODGERS

PERSONAL: Born October 28, 1977, in Tainan City, Taiwan. ... 6-1/189. ... Bats right, throws right.
TRANSACTIONS/CAREER NOTES: Signed as non-drafted free agent by Los Angeles Dodgers organization (January 5, 1999).
HONORS: Named California League Most Valuable Player (1999).

									BATTING						FIELDING		
Year Team (League)	Pos.	G	AB	R	H	2B	3B	HR	RBI	Avg.	BB	SO	SB	PO	A	E	Avg.
1999— San Bern. (Calif.)	OF	131	510	98	161	22	10	31	•123	.316	75	129	31	195	7	6	.971
2000— San Antonio (Texas)	OF	133	516	66	143	27	3	6	67	.277	61	131	23	239	11	3	.988
2001— Vero Beach (FSL)	OF	62	235	38	63	15	3	5	41	.268	28	56	2	19	3	0	1.000
— Jacksonville (Sou.)	OF	66	224	47	70	16	2	17	50	.313	41	65	5	80	5	3	.966

CHIASSON, SCOTT — P — CUBS

PERSONAL: Born August 14, 1977, in Norwich, Conn. ... 6-2/185. ... Throws right, bats right. ... Full name: Scott Christopher Chiasson.
HIGH SCHOOL: Norwich Free Academy (Conn.).
COLLEGE: Eastern Connecticut College.
TRANSACTIONS/CAREER NOTES: Selected by Kansas City Royals organization in fifth round of free-agent draft (June 2, 1998). ... Traded by Royals to Oakland Athletics (June 10, 1999), completing deal in which A's sent P Jay Witasick to Royals for a player to be named later and cash (March 30, 1999). ... Selected by Chicago Cubs from A's organization in Rule 5 major league draft (December 11, 2000).

Year League	W	L	Pct.	ERA	G	GS	CG	ShO	Sv.	IP	H	R	ER	BB	SO
1998— Gulf Coast Royals (GCL)	2	0	1.000	4.88	13	0	0	0	1	24	24	17	13	11	26
1999— S. Oregon (N'West)■	2	2	.500	5.22	15	13	0	0	0	69	80	52	40	39	51
2000— Visalia (Calif.)	11	4	.733	3.06	31	23	0	0	2	156	146	66	53	57	150
2001— West Tenn (Sou.)■	3	4	.429	1.76	52	0	0	0	24	61 1/3	43	15	12	20	62
— Iowa (PCL)..........................	0	0	...	2.25	11	0	0	0	10	12	11	3	3	0	14
— Chicago (N.L.)...................	1	1	.500	2.70	6	0	0	0	0	6 2/3	5	2	2	2	6
Major League totals (1 year)........	1	1	.500	2.70	6	0	0	0	0	6 2/3	5	2	2	2	6

CHILDERS, MATT — P — BREWERS

PERSONAL: Born December 3, 1978, in Douglas, Ga. ... 6-5/195. ... Throws right, bats right. ... Full name: Matthew Wilkie Childers.
HIGH SCHOOL: Westside (Augusta, Ga.).
TRANSACTIONS/CAREER NOTES: Selected by Milwaukee Brewers organization in ninth round of free-agent draft (June 3, 1997).

Year League	W	L	Pct.	ERA	G	GS	CG	ShO	Sv.	IP	H	R	ER	BB	SO
1997— Helena (Pio.)	1	4	.200	6.20	14	10	0	0	1	61	81	49	42	24	19
1998— Helena (Pio.)	1	0	1.000	0.64	2	2	1	1	0	14	9	1	1	4	4
— Beloit (Midw.).....................	3	7	.300	5.10	14	14	3	0	0	67	89	55	38	20	49
1999— Beloit (Midw.)..................	3	10	.231	5.94	20	19	0	0	0	100	129	72	66	30	32
2000— Beloit (Midw.)..................	8	2	.800	2.71	12	12	1	1	0	73	64	33	22	17	47
— Mudville (Calif.)	3	9	.250	4.75	15	15	0	0	0	85 1/3	103	59	45	32	43
2001— High Desert (Calif.)...........	6	11	.353	6.44	20	20	0	0	0	117 1/3	155	95	84	29	76
— Huntsville (Sou.)	2	2	.500	3.43	7	7	0	0	0	39 1/3	41	19	15	12	21

CHOATE, RANDY — P — YANKEES

PERSONAL: Born September 5, 1975, in San Antonio. ... 6-3/180. ... Throws left, bats left. ... Full name: Randy Doyle Choate.
HIGH SCHOOL: Winston Churchill (San Antonio).
COLLEGE: Florida State.
TRANSACTIONS/CAREER NOTES: Selected by New York Yankees organization in fifth round of free-agent draft (June 3, 1997).

Year League	W	L	Pct.	ERA	G	GS	CG	ShO	Sv.	IP	H	R	ER	BB	SO
1997— Oneonta (NY-Penn)	5	1	.833	1.73	10	10	0	0	0	62 1/3	49	12	12	12	61
1998— Tampa (FSL)	1	8	.111	5.27	13	13	0	0	0	70	83	57	41	22	55
— Greensboro (S.Atl.)	1	5	.167	3.00	8	8	1	0	0	39	46	21	13	7	32
1999— Tampa (FSL)	2	2	.500	4.50	47	0	0	0	1	50	51	25	25	24	62
2000— Columbus (I.L.)	2	0	1.000	2.04	33	0	0	0	1	35 1/3	34	8	8	14	37
— New York (A.L.)■................	0	1	.000	4.76	22	0	0	0	0	17	14	10	9	8	12
2001— New York (A.L.)...............	3	1	.750	3.35	37	0	0	0	0	48 1/3	34	21	18	27	35
— Columbus (I.L.).................	1	1	.500	2.08	4	0	0	0	0	4 1/3	7	1	1	3	4
Major League totals (2 years).......	3	2	.600	3.72	59	0	0	0	0	65 1/3	48	31	27	35	47

DIVISION SERIES RECORD

Year League	W	L	Pct.	ERA	G	GS	CG	ShO	Sv.	IP	H	R	ER	BB	SO
2000— New York (A.L.)................	0	0	...	6.75	1	0	0	0	0	1 1/3	0	1	1	1	1
2001— New York (A.L.)................								Did not play.							

CHAMPIONSHIP SERIES RECORD

Year League	W	L	Pct.	ERA	G	GS	CG	ShO	Sv.	IP	H	R	ER	BB	SO
2000— New York (A.L.)................	0	0	...	0.00	1	0	0	0	0	1/3	0	0	0	0	1
2001— New York (A.L.)................								Did not play.							

WORLD SERIES RECORD

NOTES: Member of World Series championship team (2000).

Year League	W	L	Pct.	ERA	G	GS	CG	ShO	Sv.	IP	H	R	ER	BB	SO
2000— New York (A.L.)................								Did not play.							
2001— New York (A.L.)................	0	0	...	2.45	2	0	0	0	0	3 2/3	7	4	1	1	2

CHOI, HEE SEOP — 1B — CUBS

PERSONAL: Born March 16, 1979, in Chun-Nam, Korea. ... 6-5/235. ... Bats left, throws left.
HIGH SCHOOL: Kwang-Ju Jae (Kwang-Ju, Korea).
COLLEGE: Korea University.
TRANSACTIONS/CAREER NOTES: Signed as non-drafted free agent by Chicago Cubs organization (March 8, 1999). ... On disabled list (May 24-June 17 and June 25-August 3, 2001).

Year Team (League)	Pos.	G	AB	R	H	2B	3B	HR	RBI	Avg.	BB	SO	SB	PO	A	E	Avg.
1999— Lansing (Midw.)..........	1B	79	290	71	93	18	6	18	70	.321	50	68	2	694	50	18	.976
2000— Daytona (FSL)	1B	96	345	60	102	25	6	15	70	.296	37	78	4	722	52	4	.995
— West Tenn (Sou.)	1B	36	122	25	37	9	0	10	25	.303	25	38	3	285	14	1	.997
2001— Iowa (PCL)	1B	77	266	38	61	11	0	13	45	.229	34	67	5	518	39	3	.995

CHOUINARD, BOBBY   P

PERSONAL: Born May 1, 1972, in Manilla, The Phillipines. ... 6-1/190. ... Throws right, bats right. ... Full name: Robert William Chouinard.
HIGH SCHOOL: Forest Grove (Ore.).
TRANSACTIONS/CAREER NOTES: Selected by Baltimore Orioles organization in fifth round of free-agent draft (June 4, 1990). ... Traded by Orioles with P Allen Plaster to Oakland Athletics for OF Harold Baines (January 14, 1993). ... Granted free agency (October 15, 1997). ... Signed by Milwaukee Brewers organization (October 31, 1997). ... Claimed on waivers by Arizona Diamondbacks (June 1, 1998). ... On Arizona disabled list (August 22-September 8, 1998); included rehabilitation assignment to Tucson (September 6-8). ... On Tucson disabled list (June 20-28, 1999). ... Released by Diamondbacks (February 2, 2000). ... Signed by Colorado Rockies (June 17, 2000). ... On Colorado disabled list (March 30-May 1 and September 19, 2001-remainder of season); included rehabilitation assignment to Colorado Springs (April 17-May 1). ... On Colorado Springs disabled list (July 13-20, 2001). ... Granted free agency (October 17, 2001).

Year League	W	L	Pct.	ERA	G	GS	CG	ShO	Sv.	IP	H	R	ER	BB	SO
1990— Bluefield (Appl.)	2	5	.286	3.70	10	10	2	1	0	56	61	34	23	14	30
1991— Kane County (Midw.)..........	2	4	.333	4.64	6	6	0	0	0	33	45	24	17	5	17
— Bluefield (Appl.)	5	1	.833	3.48	6	6	0	0	0	33²/₃	44	19	13	11	31
1992— Kane County (Midw.)..........	10	14	.417	*2.08	26	26	*9	*2	0	181²/₃	151	60	42	38	112
1993— Modesto (Calif.)■	8	10	.444	4.26	24	24	1	0	0	145²/₃	154	75	69	56	82
1994— Modesto (Calif.)	12	5	.706	2.59	29	20	0	0	3	145²/₃	147	53	42	32	74
1995— Huntsville (Sou.)	14	8	.636	3.62	29	*29	1	1	0	166²/₃	155	81	67	50	106
1996— Edmonton (PCL)	10	2	.833	2.77	15	15	0	0	0	84¹/₃	70	32	26	24	45
— Oakland (A.L.)	4	2	.667	6.10	13	11	0	0	0	59	75	41	40	32	32
1997— Edmonton (PCL)	6	6	.500	6.03	25	21	1	0	0	100	129	80	67	26	58
1998— Louisville (I.L.)■	2	1	.667	4.93	7	7	0	0	0	42	52	31	23	15	33
— Milwaukee (N.L.)	0	0	...	3.00	1	0	0	0	0	3	5	1	1	0	1
— Tucson (PCL)■	0	0	...	4.26	4	0	0	0	1	6¹/₃	6	3	3	0	6
— Arizona (N.L.)	0	2	.000	4.23	26	2	0	0	0	38¹/₃	41	23	18	11	26
1999— Tucson (PCL)	4	1	.800	4.06	12	9	0	0	0	62	70	33	28	13	63
— Arizona (N.L.)	5	2	.714	2.68	32	0	0	0	1	40¹/₃	31	16	12	12	23
2000— Colorado Springs (PCL)■ ..	0	0	...	3.63	9	0	0	0	1	17¹/₃	18	10	7	3	12
— Colorado (N.L.)	2	2	.500	3.86	31	0	0	0	0	32²/₃	35	17	14	9	23
2001— Colorado Springs (PCL)	3	1	.750	3.66	39	0	0	0	1	39¹/₃	44	19	16	13	47
— Colorado (N.L.)	0	0	...	8.22	8	0	0	0	0	7²/₃	10	7	7	1	5
A.L. totals (1 year)	4	2	.667	6.10	13	11	0	0	0	59	75	41	40	32	32
N.L. totals (4 years)	7	6	.538	3.84	98	2	0	0	1	122	122	64	52	33	78
Major League totals (5 years).......	11	8	.579	4.57	111	13	0	0	1	181	197	105	92	65	110

DIVISION SERIES RECORD

Year League	W	L	Pct.	ERA	G	GS	CG	ShO	Sv.	IP	H	R	ER	BB	SO
1999— Arizona (N.L.)	0	0	...	4.50	2	0	0	0	0	2	3	1	1	0	1

CHRISTENSEN, BEN   P   CUBS

PERSONAL: Born February 7, 1978, in Waterloo, Iowa. ... 6-4/205. ... Throws right, bats right. ... Full name: Benjamin Jay Christensen.
HIGH SCHOOL: Goddard (Kan.).
COLLEGE: Wichita State.
TRANSACTIONS/CAREER NOTES: Selected by Chicago Cubs organization in first round (26th pick overall) of free-agent draft (June 2, 1999). ... On disabled list (April 26, 2001-remainder of season).

Year League	W	L	Pct.	ERA	G	GS	CG	ShO	Sv.	IP	H	R	ER	BB	SO
1999— Arizona Cubs (Ariz.)	0	1	.000	3.00	3	3	0	0	0	9	8	3	3	5	10
— Eugene (N'West)	0	2	.000	5.91	5	5	0	0	0	21¹/₃	21	14	14	14	21
— Daytona (FSL)	1	3	.250	6.35	4	4	0	0	0	22²/₃	25	16	16	11	18
2000— Daytona (FSL)	4	2	.667	2.10	10	10	1	0	0	64¹/₃	43	18	15	15	63
— West Tenn (Sou.)	3	1	.750	2.76	7	7	0	0	0	42¹/₃	36	18	13	15	42
2001— West Tenn (Sou.)	2	1	.667	6.48	3	3	0	0	0	16²/₃	20	12	12	9	9

CHRISTENSEN, McKAY   OF   DODGERS

PERSONAL: Born August 14, 1975, in Upland, Calif. ... 5-11/180. ... Bats left, throws left. ... Full name: McKay A. Christensen.
HIGH SCHOOL: Clovis West (Fresno, Calif.).
TRANSACTIONS/CAREER NOTES: Selected by California Angels organization in first round (sixth pick overall) of free-agent draft (June 2, 1994). ... Traded by Angels with P Andrew Lorraine, P Bill Simas and P John Snyder to Chicago White Sox for P Jim Abbott and P Tim Fortugno (July 27, 1995). ... On disabled list (April 10-28 and June 2-17, 1998). ... On Birmingham disabled list (July 13-August 1, 1999). ... On Charlotte disabled list (August 2-26, 2000). ... Traded by White Sox to Los Angeles Dodgers for P Wade Parrish (July 13, 2001).
STATISTICAL NOTES: Tied for Carolina League lead with three double plays by outfielder in 1998.

Year Team (League)	Pos.	G	AB	R	H	2B	3B	HR	RBI	Avg.	BB	SO	SB	PO	A	E	Avg.
1996— GC White Sox (GCL) ..	OF	35	133	17	35	7	5	1	16	.263	10	23	10	54	2	1	.982
— Hickory (S.Atl.)...........	OF	6	11	0	0	0	0	0	0	.000	1	4	0	4	0	0	1.000
1997— Hickory (S.Atl.)	OF	127	503	95	141	12	*12	5	47	.280	52	81	28	*280	5	9	.969
1998— Win.-Salem (Caro.)	OF	95	361	69	103	17	6	4	32	.285	53	54	20	199	6	4	.981
1999— Chicago (A.L.)	OF	28	53	10	12	1	0	1	6	.226	4	7	2	50	0	3	.943
— Birmingham (Sou.).....	OF	75	293	53	85	8	6	3	28	.290	31	46	18	190	2	2	.990
— Charlotte (I.L.)	OF	1	4	0	1	0	0	0	0	.250	0	0	1	2	0	0	1.000
2000— Chicago (A.L.)	OF	32	19	4	2	0	0	0	1	.105	2	6	1	20	1	0	1.000
— Charlotte (I.L.)...........	OF	90	337	49	89	13	2	6	29	.264	32	51	28	184	3	7	.964
2001— Charlotte (I.L.)	OF	69	273	53	75	15	6	7	25	.275	30	52	17	147	4	3	.981
— Chicago (A.L.)	OF	7	4	0	1	0	0	0	0	.250	0	2	0	2	0	0	1.000
— Las Vegas (PCL)■	OF	16	57	8	14	2	1	1	3	.246	5	11	3	32	1	2	.943
— Los Angeles (N.L.)	OF	28	49	7	16	2	0	1	7	.327	3	10	3	22	0	2	.917
American League totals (3 years)		67	76	14	15	1	0	1	7	.197	6	15	3	72	1	3	.961
National League totals (1 year)		28	49	7	16	2	0	1	7	.327	3	10	3	22	0	2	.917
Major League totals (3 years)		95	125	21	31	3	0	2	14	.248	9	25	6	94	1	5	.950

DIVISION SERIES RECORD

Year	Team (League)	Pos.	G	AB	R	H	2B	3B	HR	RBI	Avg.	BB	SO	SB	PO	A	E	Avg.
								BATTING								FIELDING		
2000— Chicago (A.L.)		OF	1	0	0	0	0	0	0	0	...	0	0	0	0	0	0	...

CHRISTENSON, RYAN — OF — BREWERS

PERSONAL: Born March 28, 1974, in Redlands, Calif. ... 6-0/210. ... Bats right, throws right. ... Full name: Ryan Alan Christenson.
HIGH SCHOOL: Apple Valley (Calif.).
COLLEGE: Pepperdine.
TRANSACTIONS/CAREER NOTES: Selected by Oakland Athletics organization in 10th round of free-agent draft (June 1, 1995). ... On Sacramento disabled list (May 20-June 9, 2001). ... Traded by A's to Arizona Diamondbacks for OF Rob Ryan (June 19, 2001). ... Selected by Milwaukee Brewers from Diamondbacks organization in Rule 5 major league draft (December 13, 2001).

Year Team (League)	Pos.	G	AB	R	H	2B	3B	HR	RBI	Avg.	BB	SO	SB	PO	A	E	Avg.
								BATTING								FIELDING		
1995— S. Oregon (N'West)....	OF	49	158	14	30	4	1	1	16	.190	22	33	5	84	3	2	.978
1996— S. Oregon (N'West)....	OF	36	136	31	39	11	0	5	21	.287	19	21	8	78	5	4	.954
— West Mich. (Midw.)....	OF-3B	33	122	21	38	2	2	2	18	.311	13	22	2	64	1	3	.956
1997— Visalia (Calif.)........	OF	83	308	69	90	18	8	13	54	.292	70	72	20	164	4	3	.982
— Huntsville (Sou.)........	OF	29	120	39	44	9	3	2	18	.367	24	23	5	81	1	1	.988
— Edmonton (PCL)........	OF	16	49	12	14	2	2	2	5	.286	11	11	2	42	1	0	1.000
1998— Edmonton (PCL)........	OF	22	88	17	23	6	1	1	7	.261	15	24	4	56	2	0	1.000
— Oakland (A.L.)........	OF	117	370	56	95	22	2	5	40	.257	36	106	5	284	7	5	.983
1999— Oakland (A.L.)........	OF-DH	106	268	41	56	12	1	4	24	.209	38	58	7	213	3	7	.969
— Vancouver (PCL)........	OF	33	128	30	44	8	1	1	16	.344	22	21	7	88	1	2	.978
2000— Oakland (A.L.)........	OF	121	129	31	32	2	2	4	18	.248	19	33	1	95	2	5	.951
2001— Oakland (A.L.)........	OF-DH	7	4	1	0	0	0	0	0	.000	0	1	0	1	0	0	1.000
— Sacramento (PCL)......	OF	19	70	7	12	4	0	1	3	.171	4	13	2	30	1	0	1.000
— Arizona (N.L.)■..........	OF	19	4	3	1	1	0	0	1	.250	1	1	1	1	0	0	1.000
— Tucson (PCL)...........	OF	57	215	32	62	17	0	6	27	.288	23	43	5	130	2	7	.950
American League totals (4 years)		351	771	129	183	36	5	13	82	.237	93	198	13	593	12	17	.973
National League totals (1 year)		19	4	3	1	1	0	0	1	.250	1	1	1	1	0	0	1.000
Major League totals (4 years)		370	775	132	184	37	5	13	83	.237	94	199	14	594	12	17	.973

DIVISION SERIES RECORD

Year Team (League)	Pos.	G	AB	R	H	2B	3B	HR	RBI	Avg.	BB	SO	SB	PO	A	E	Avg.
								BATTING								FIELDING		
2000— Oakland (A.L.)	OF-PR	2	2	0	1	0	0	0	1	.500	0	1	0	2	0	0	1.000

CHRISTIANSEN, JASON — P — GIANTS

PERSONAL: Born September 21, 1969, in Omaha, Neb. ... 6-5/241. ... Throws left, bats right. ... Full name: Jason Samuel Christiansen.
HIGH SCHOOL: Elkhorn (Neb.).
JUNIOR COLLEGE: Iowa Western College.
COLLEGE: Cameron (Okla.).
TRANSACTIONS/CAREER NOTES: Signed as non-drafted free agent by Pittsburgh Pirates organization (July 5, 1991). ... On Calgary disabled list (August 12-September 5, 1996). ... On Pittsburgh disabled list (March 31-June 19, 1997). ... On Pittsburgh disabled list (July 29-August 21 and August 24-September 23, 1999); included rehabilitation assignments to Altoona (May 22-28) and Nashville (August 16-21). ... Traded by Pirates to St. Louis Cardinals for SS Jack Wilson (July 30, 2000). ... On St. Louis disabled list (March 23-May 7, 2001); included rehabilitation assignment to Memphis (April 17-May 7). ... Traded by Cardinals to San Francisco Giants for P Kevin Joseph and a player to be named later or cash (July 31, 2001). ... Granted free agency (November 6, 2001). ... Re-signed by Giants (December 5, 2001).

Year League	W	L	Pct.	ERA	G	GS	CG	ShO	Sv.	IP	H	R	ER	BB	SO
1991— Gulf Coast Pirates (GCL)....	1	0	1.000	0.00	6	0	0	0	1	8	4	0	0	1	8
— Welland (NY-Penn)............	0	1	.000	2.53	8	1	0	0	0	21 1/3	15	9	6	12	17
1992— Augusta (S.Atl.)................	1	0	1.000	1.80	10	0	0	0	2	20	12	4	4	8	21
— Salem (Caro.)................	3	1	.750	3.24	10	0	0	0	2	50	47	20	18	22	59
1993— Salem (Caro.)................	1	1	.500	3.15	57	0	0	0	4	71 1/3	48	30	25	24	70
— Carolina (Sou.)............	0	0	...	0.00	2	0	0	0	0	2 2/3	3	0	0	1	2
1994— Carolina (Sou.)............	2	1	.667	2.09	28	0	0	0	2	38 2/3	30	10	9	14	43
— Buffalo (A.A.)............	3	1	.750	2.41	33	0	0	0	0	33 2/3	19	9	9	16	39
1995— Pittsburgh (N.L.)	1	3	.250	4.15	63	0	0	0	0	56 1/3	49	28	26	34	53
1996— Calgary (PCL)	1	0	1.000	3.27	2	2	0	0	0	11	9	4	4	1	10
— Pittsburgh (N.L.)	3	3	.500	6.70	33	0	0	0	0	44 1/3	56	34	33	19	38
1997— Pittsburgh (N.L.)	3	0	1.000	2.94	39	0	0	0	0	33 2/3	37	11	11	17	37
— Carolina (Sou.)	0	1	.000	4.20	8	1	0	0	1	15	17	7	7	5	25
1998— Pittsburgh (N.L.)	3	3	.500	2.51	60	0	0	0	6	64 2/3	51	22	18	27	71
1999— Pittsburgh (N.L.)	2	3	.400	4.06	39	0	0	0	3	37 2/3	26	17	17	22	35
— Altoona (East.)	0	0	...	0.00	2	1	0	0	0	3	1	0	0	1	2
— Nashville (PCL)	0	0	...	0.00	2	0	0	0	0	2	0	0	0	0	1
2000— Pittsburgh (N.L.)	2	8	.200	4.97	44	0	0	0	1	38	28	22	21	25	41
— St. Louis (N.L.)■	1	0	1.000	5.40	21	0	0	0	0	10	13	7	6	2	12
2001— Memphis (PCL)	0	0	...	2.25	7	1	0	0	0	8	9	2	2	0	9
— St. Louis (N.L.)	1	1	.500	4.66	30	0	0	0	3	19 1/3	15	10	10	10	19
— San Francisco (N.L.)■	1	0	1.000	1.59	25	0	0	0	0	17	14	3	3	5	12
Major League totals (7 years).......	17	21	.447	4.07	354	0	0	0	13	321	289	154	145	161	318

DIVISION SERIES RECORD

Year League	W	L	Pct.	ERA	G	GS	CG	ShO	Sv.	IP	H	R	ER	BB	SO
2000— St. Louis (N.L.)................	0	0	...	0.00	1	0	0	0	0	1/3	0	0	0	0	0

CHAMPIONSHIP SERIES RECORD

Year League	W	L	Pct.	ERA	G	GS	CG	ShO	Sv.	IP	H	R	ER	BB	SO
2000— St. Louis (N.L.)................	0	0	...	0.00	2	0	0	0	0	2	0	0	0	0	1

PERSONAL: Born March 31, 1975, in Oneonta, N.Y. ... 6-0/195. ... Throws left, bats left. ... Full name: Timothy A. Christman.

HIGH SCHOOL: Oneonta (N.Y.).

COLLEGE: Siena.

TRANSACTIONS/CAREER NOTES: Selected by Colorado Rockies organization in 11th round of free-agent draft (June 4, 1996). ... On disabled list (April 10, 1998-entire season). ... On Salem disabled list (April 8-23, 1999). ... On disabled list (May 5-September 12, 2000). ... On Colorado Springs disabled list (May 24-July 5, 2001).

Year League	W	L	Pct.	ERA	G	GS	CG	ShO	Sv.	IP	H	R	ER	BB	SO
1996— Portland (N'West)	1	2	.333	4.28	21	0	0	0	2	40	30	23	19	23	56
1997— Asheville (S.Atl.)	7	3	.700	3.41	29	0	0	0	3	63⅓	55	32	24	18	87
1998—							Did not play.								
1999— Salem (Caro.)	1	2	.333	2.42	38	0	0	0	2	48⅓	38	18	13	12	64
2000— Carolina (Sou.)	0	0	...	2.53	8	0	0	0	0	10⅔	6	3	3	7	13
2001— Colorado Springs (PCL)	2	5	.286	6.30	38	0	0	0	2	40	52	31	28	21	42
— Colorado (N.L.)	0	0	...	4.50	1	0	0	0	0	2	1	1	1	0	2
Major League totals (1 year)	0	0	...	4.50	1	0	0	0	0	2	1	1	1	0	2

PERSONAL: Born December 17, 1978, in Humacao, Puerto Rico. ... 6-1/170. ... Bats both, throws right.

HIGH SCHOOL: Mech-Tech (Caguas, Puerto Rico).

TRANSACTIONS/CAREER NOTES: Selected by Arizona Diamondbacks organization in 36th round of free-agent draft (June 3, 1997). ... On Tucson disabled list (April 30-May 8, 2001).

STATISTICAL NOTES: Led Pacific Coast League with 20 sacrifice hits in 2001. ... Led Pacific Coast League shortstops with 30 errors in 2001.

							BATTING								FIELDING			
Year Team (League)	Pos.	G	AB	R	H	2B	3B	HR	RBI	Avg.	BB	SO	SB	PO	A	E	Avg.
1997— Ariz. D'backs (Ariz.)	SS	43	152	23	30	6	1	0	20	.197	21	32	1	85	118	15	.931
— Lethbridge (Pio.)	SS	1	3	0	1	0	0	0	0	.333	0	1	0	3	3	1	.857
1998— Lethbridge (Pio.)	SS	67	258	41	68	11	4	3	34	.264	20	32	8	107	209	27	.921
1999— High Desert (Calif.)	SS	128	499	78	153	25	4	3	64	.307	19	65	15	223	308	28	.950
2000— El Paso (Texas)	SS	125	522	83	157	30	6	4	59	.301	29	56	9	219	387	32	.950
2001— Tucson (PCL)	SS-2B	107	425	53	124	24	3	3	35	.292	15	48	9	165	305	†32	.936
— Arizona (N.L.)	SS	8	7	0	2	0	1	0	0	.286	0	0	0	2	6	0	1.000
Major League totals (1 year)		8	7	0	2	0	1	0	0	.286	0	0	0	2	6	0	1.000

PERSONAL: Born September 23, 1969, in Pasadena, Calif. ... 6-1/195. ... Bats right, throws right. ... Full name: Jeffrey Howard Cirillo.

HIGH SCHOOL: Providence (Burbank, Calif.).

COLLEGE: Southern California.

TRANSACTIONS/CAREER NOTES: Selected by Chicago Cubs organization in 37th round of free-agent draft (June 2, 1987); did not sign. ... Selected by Milwaukee Brewers organization in 11th round of free-agent draft (June 3, 1991). ... On New Orleans disabled list (July 22-August 6, 1993). ... Traded by Brewers with P Scott Karl and cash to Colorado Rockies as part of three-way deal in which Brewers received P Jamey Wright and C Henry Blanco from Rockies, Oakland Athletics received P Justin Miller and cash from Rockies and Brewers received P Jimmy Haynes from A's (December 13, 1999). ... On Colorado disabled list (April 27-May 13, 2001); included rehabilitation assignment to Colorado Springs (May 12-13). ... Traded by Rockies to Seattle Mariners for P Jose Paniagua, P Dennis Stark and P Brian Fuentes (December 15, 2001).

RECORDS: Holds N.L. single-season record for most consecutive errorless games by third baseman—85 (June 20 through October 7, 2001); and most consecutive chances accepted without an error by third baseman—85 (June 20 through October 7, 2001). ... Shares N.L. single-season record for most double plays by third baseman—45 (1998).

STATISTICAL NOTES: Led Pioneer League in grounding into double plays with 11 in 1991. ... Led Pioneer League third basemen with 60 putouts, 104 assists and 179 total chances in 1991. ... Tied for Midwest League lead with six intentional bases on balls received in 1992. ... Led A.L. third basemen with 18 errors in 1996. ... Led A.L. third basemen with 463 total chances and 29 double plays in 1997. ... Led N.L. in grounding into double plays with 26 in 1998. ... Led N.L. third basemen with 340 assists and 45 double plays in 1998. ... Led N.L. third basemen in double plays with 35 in 1999 and 41 in 2000. ... Had 15-game hitting streak (April 21-May 9, 2000). ... Hit three home runs in one game (June 28, 2000). ... Career major league grand slams: 1.

MISCELLANEOUS: Holds Milwaukee Brewers all-time record for highest career batting average (.307).

							BATTING								FIELDING			
Year Team (League)	Pos.	G	AB	R	H	2B	3B	HR	RBI	Avg.	BB	SO	SB	PO	A	E	Avg.
1991— Helena (Pio.)	3B-OF	•70	286	60	100	16	2	10	51	.350	31	28	3	†71	†104	15	.921
1992— Stockton (Calif.)	3B	7	27	2	6	1	0	0	5	.222	2	0	0	7	10	0	1.000
— Beloit (Midw.)	3B-2B	126	444	65	135	27	3	9	71	.304	84	85	21	115	309	26	.942
1993— El Paso (Texas)	2B-3B	67	249	53	85	16	2	9	41	.341	26	37	2	83	142	9	.962
— New Orleans (A.A.)	3-2-S-DH	58	215	31	63	13	2	3	32	.293	29	33	2	46	145	5	.974
1994— New Orleans (A.A.)	3-2-DH-S	61	236	45	73	18	2	10	46	.309	28	39	4	67	139	8	.963
— Milwaukee (A.L.)	3B-2B	39	126	17	30	9	0	3	12	.238	11	16	0	23	60	3	.965
1995— Milwaukee (A.L.)	3-2-1-S	125	328	57	91	19	4	9	39	.277	47	42	7	113	230	15	.958
1996— Milwaukee (A.L.)	3-DH-1-2	158	566	101	184	46	5	15	83	.325	58	69	4	112	242	†18	.952
1997— Milwaukee (A.L.)	3B-DH	154	580	74	167	46	2	10	82	.288	60	74	4	•126	*320	17	.963
1998— Milwaukee (N.L.)	3B-1B	156	604	97	194	31	1	14	68	.321	79	88	10	149	†353	11	.979
1999— Milwaukee (N.L.)	3B	157	607	98	198	35	1	15	88	.326	75	83	7	*124	312	15	.967
2000— Colorado (N.L.)■	3B	157	598	111	195	53	2	11	115	.326	67	72	3	92	*304	15	.963
2001— Colorado (N.L.)	3B	138	528	72	165	26	4	17	83	.313	43	63	12	78	308	7	.982
— Colo. Springs (PCL)	3B	1	4	2	3	1	0	0	3	.750	1	0	0	1	2	0	1.000
American League totals (4 years)		476	1600	249	472	120	11	37	216	.295	176	201	15	374	852	53	.959
National League totals (4 years)		608	2337	378	752	145	8	57	354	.322	264	306	32	443	1276	48	.973
Major League totals (8 years)		1084	3937	627	1224	265	19	94	570	.311	440	507	47	817	2128	101	.967

Year League	Pos.	AB	R	H	2B	3B	HR	RBI	Avg.	BB	SO	SB	PO	A	E	Avg.
1997—American	3B	1	0	0	0	0	0	0	.000	0	1	0	0	0	0	
2000—National	3B	1	0	0	0	0	0	0	.000	0	0	0	2	1	0	1.000
All-Star Game totals (2 years)		2	0	0	0	0	0	0	.000	0	1	0	2	1	0	1.000

CLAPP, STUBBY 2B/OF CARDINALS

PERSONAL: Born February 24, 1973, in Windsor, Ont. ... 5-8/175. ... Bats both, throws right. ... Full name: Richard Keith Clapp.
HIGH SCHOOL: Riverside (Windsor, Ont.).
JUNIOR COLLEGE: Paris (Texas).
COLLEGE: Texas Tech.
TRANSACTIONS/CAREER NOTES: Selected by St. Louis Cardinals organization in 36th round of free-agent draft (June 4, 1996).
STATISTICAL NOTES: Led Texas League second baseman with 332 putouts, 436 assists, .978 fielding percentage, 785 total chances and 113 double plays in 1998. ... Led Pacific Coast League second baseman with 284 putouts, 341 assists, 640 total chances and 89 double plays in 2000. ... Tied second basemen for Pacific Coast League lead with 236 assists in 2001.

Year Team (League)	Pos.	G	AB	R	H	2B	3B	HR	RBI	Avg.	BB	SO	SB	PO	A	E	Avg.
1996—Johnson City (Appl.) ..	2B-3B	29	94	25	21	3	2	1	15	.223	26	15	9	45	70	3	.975
1997—Prince William (Caro.)	2B-OF	78	267	51	85	21	6	4	46	.318	52	41	9	117	107	8	.966
1998—Arkansas (Texas)........	2B-OF-3B	139	514	113	143	30	9	12	57	.278	86	100	18	*333	*438	17	.978
1999—Memphis (PCL).........2B-OF-3B-SS		110	393	72	102	26	2	14	62	.260	53	96	7	172	177	8	.978
2000—Memphis (PCL)..........	2B-3B	129	505	89	138	28	8	1	52	.273	80	88	10	†284	†341	15	.977
2001—Memphis (PCL)..........	2B-OF	86	299	48	91	14	7	5	33	.304	43	46	8	186	†237	10	.977
—St. Louis (N.L.)...........	2B-OF	23	25	0	5	2	0	0	1	.200	1	7	0	4	6	0	1.000
Major League totals (1 year)		23	25	0	5	2	0	0	1	.200	1	7	0	4	6	0	1.000

CLARK, BRADY OF REDS

PERSONAL: Born April 18, 1973, in Portland, Ore. ... 6-2/195. ... Bats right, throws right. ... Full name: Brady William Clark.
HIGH SCHOOL: Sunset (Beaverton, Ore.).
COLLEGE: San Diego State.
TRANSACTIONS/CAREER NOTES: Signed as non-drafted free agent by Cincinnati Reds organization (January 13, 1996). ... Released by Reds (April 10, 1996). ... Re-signed by Reds organization (February 15, 1997).
HONORS: Named Southern League Most Valuable Player (1999).
STATISTICAL NOTES: Led Midwest League outfielders with 278 total chances in 1997. ... Led Southern League with 261 total bases in 1999. ... Tied for International League lead with nine sacrifice flies in 2000. ... Tied for International League outfielders lead with 314 total chances and four double plays in 2000.

Year Team (League)	Pos.	G	AB	R	H	2B	3B	HR	RBI	Avg.	BB	SO	SB	PO	A	E	Avg.
1997—Burlington (Midw.)	OF	126	459	108	149	29	7	11	63	.325	76	71	31	*265	9	4	.986
1998—Chattanooga (Sou.)	OF	64	222	41	60	13	1	2	16	.270	31	34	12	149	3	1	.993
1999—Chattanooga (Sou.)	OF-3B	*138	506	103	165	37	4	17	75	.326	89	58	25	255	10	5	.981
2000—Louisville (I.L.)	OF	132	487	90	148	*41	6	16	79	.304	72	51	12	*298	10	6	.981
—Cincinnati (N.L.)	OF	11	11	1	3	1	0	0	2	.273	0	2	0	6	0	0	1.000
2001—Louisville (I.L.)	OF	49	167	24	44	5	1	2	18	.263	18	17	6	105	1	2	.981
—Cincinnati (N.L.)	OF-DH	89	129	22	34	3	0	6	18	.264	22	16	4	52	0	1	.981
Major League totals (2 years)		100	140	23	37	4	0	6	20	.264	22	18	4	58	0	1	.983

CLARK, JERMAINE 2B MARINERS

PERSONAL: Born September 29, 1976, in Berkeley, Calif. ... 5-10/175. ... Bats left, throws right. ... Full name: Jermaine Marcel Clark.
HIGH SCHOOL: Will C. Wood (Vavaville, Calif.).
COLLEGE: University of San Francisco.
TRANSACTIONS/CAREER NOTES: Selected by Seattle Mariners organzation in fifth round of free-agent draft (June 3, 1997). ... Selected by Detroit Tigers from Mariners organization in Rule 5 major-league draft (December 11, 2000). ... Returned to Mariners (April 19, 2001). ... On Tacoma disabled list (June 5-17, 2001).
STATISTICAL NOTES: Led California League second baseman with 599 total chances and 92 double plays in 1999.

Year Team (League)	Pos.	G	AB	R	H	2B	3B	HR	RBI	Avg.	BB	SO	SB	PO	A	E	Avg.
1997—Everett (N'West)	2B-3B	59	199	42	67	13	2	3	29	.337	34	31	22	81	119	9	.957
1998—Wisconsin (Midw.)	2B-OF	123	448	81	145	24	*13	6	55	.324	57	64	40	173	285	14	.970
1999—Lancaster (Calif.)	2B	126	502	*112	158	27	8	6	61	.315	58	80	33	*243	*346	10	.983
2000—New Haven (East.)......	2B	133	447	80	131	23	9	2	44	.293	87	69	38	232	329	13	.977
2001—Detroit (A.L.)■..........	PR	3	0	1	0	0	0	0	0	...	0	0	0	...	...	...	...
—Tacoma (PCL)■	2B	74	216	35	54	7	3	1	26	.250	27	39	13	118	173	6	.980
Major League totals (1 year)		3	0	1	0	0	0	0	0	...	0	0	0	...	...	...	...

CLARK, TONY 1B/DH RED SOX

PERSONAL: Born June 15, 1972, in Newton, Kan. ... 6-7/245. ... Bats both, throws right. ... Full name: Anthony Christopher Clark.
HIGH SCHOOL: Valhalla (El Cajon, Calif.), then Christian (El Cajon, Calif.).
COLLEGE: Arizona (did not play baseball), then San Diego State.

TRANSACTIONS/CAREER NOTES: Selected by Detroit Tigers organization in first round (second pick overall) of free-agent draft (June 4, 1990). ... On Niagara Falls temporarily inactive list (June 17, 1991-remainder of season and August 17, 1992-remainder of season). ... On disabled list (August 24, 1993-remainder of season). ... On Detroit disabled list (May 26-June 10, 1999); included rehabilitation assignment to Toledo (June 8-10). ... On Detroit disabled list (May 13-June 12, July 15-September 1 and September 19, 2000-remainder of season); included rehabilitation assignments to Toledo (June 9-12 and August 28-September 1). ... Claimed on waivers by Boston Red Sox (November 20, 2001).

RECORDS: Holds A.L. single-season record for most games with switch-hit home runs—3 (1998).

STATISTICAL NOTES: Switch-hit home runs in one game six times (April 5, 1997; June 17, July 26 and August 1, 1998; and July 18 and July 25, 1999). ... Led A.L. first basemen with 1,533 total chances in 1997. ... Had 19-game hitting streak (July 10-August 1, 1999). ... Career major league grand slams: 2.

Year Team (League)	Pos.	G	AB	R	H	2B	3B	HR	RBI	Avg.	BB	SO	SB	PO	A	E	Avg.
1990— Bristol (Appl.)............	OF	25	73	2	12	2	0	1	8	.164	6	28	0	23	3	0	1.000
1991— Niagara Falls (NY-P)...								Did not play.									
1992— Niagara Falls (NY-P)	OF	27	85	12	26	9	0	5	17	.306	9	34	1	18	1	0	1.000
1993— Lakeland (FSL)	OF	36	117	14	31	4	1	1	22	.265	18	32	0	34	0	2	.944
1994— Trenton (East.)	DH-1B	107	394	50	110	25	0	21	86	.279	40	113	0	505	48	•13	.977
—Toledo (I.L.)...............	1B-DH	25	92	10	24	4	0	2	13	.261	12	25	2	144	12	0	1.000
1995— Toledo (I.L.)...............	1B-DH	110	405	50	98	17	2	14	63	.242	52	*129	0	615	51	*13	.981
—Detroit (A.L.)..............	1B	27	101	10	24	5	1	3	11	.238	8	30	0	253	18	4	.985
1996— Toledo (I.L.)...............	1B-DH	55	194	42	58	7	1	14	36	.299	31	58	1	400	28	3	.993
—Detroit (A.L.)..............	1B-DH	100	376	56	94	14	0	27	72	.250	29	127	0	766	54	6	.993
1997— Detroit (A.L.)..............	1B-DH	159	580	105	160	28	3	32	117	.276	93	144	1	*1423	100	10	.993
1998— Detroit (A.L.)..............	1B-DH	157	602	84	175	37	0	34	103	.291	63	128	3	1265	102	13	.991
1999— Detroit (A.L.)..............	1B-DH	143	536	74	150	29	0	31	99	.280	64	133	2	1126	85	10	.992
—Toledo (I.L.)...............	1B	1	3	0	0	0	0	0	0	.000	1	1	0	10	1	0	1.000
2000— Detroit (A.L.)..............	1B-DH	60	208	32	57	14	0	13	37	.274	24	51	0	488	45	4	.993
—Toledo (I.L.)...............	1B	6	22	1	2	1	0	1	2	.091	1	1	0	40	3	0	1.000
2001— Detroit (A.L.)..............	1B-DH	126	428	67	123	29	3	16	75	.287	62	108	0	647	48	3	.996
Major League totals (7 years)		772	2831	428	783	156	7	156	514	.277	343	721	6	5968	452	50	.992

ALL-STAR GAME RECORD

Year League	Pos.	AB	R	H	2B	3B	HR	RBI	Avg.	BB	SO	SB	PO	A	E	Avg.
2001— American	PH-DH	1	0	0	0	0	0	0	.000	0	1	0	...	...	...	...

CLAUSSEN, BRANDON — P — YANKEES

PERSONAL: Born May 1, 1979, in Rapid City, S.D. ... 6-2/175. ... Throws left, bats left. ... Full name: Brandon A. Claussen.
HIGH SCHOOL: Goddard (Roswell, N.M.).
JUNIOR COLLEGE: Howard (Texas).
TRANSACTIONS/CAREER NOTES: Selected by New York Yankees oranization in 34th round of free-agent draft (June 2, 1998).

Year League	W	L	Pct.	ERA	G	GS	CG	ShO	Sv.	IP	H	R	ER	BB	SO
1999— Gulf Coast Yankees (GCL)..	0	1	.000	3.18	2	2	0	0	0	11 1/3	7	4	4	2	16
—Staten Island (NY-Penn).....	6	4	.600	3.38	12	12	1	0	0	72	70	30	27	12	89
—Greensboro (S.Atl.)	0	1	.000	10.50	1	1	0	0	0	6	8	7	7	2	5
2000— Greensboro (S.Atl.)	8	5	.615	4.05	17	17	1	0	0	97 2/3	91	49	44	44	98
—Tampa (FSL)......................	2	5	.286	3.10	9	9	1	1	0	52 1/3	49	24	18	17	44
2001— Tampa (FSL)......................	5	2	.714	2.73	8	8	0	0	0	56	47	21	17	13	69
—Norwich (East.)	9	2	.818	2.13	21	21	1	1	0	131	101	42	31	55	151

CLAYTON, ROYCE — SS — WHITE SOX

PERSONAL: Born January 2, 1970, in Burbank, Calif. ... 6-0/183. ... Bats right, throws right. ... Full name: Royce Spencer Clayton.
HIGH SCHOOL: St. Bernard (Playa del Ray, Calif.).
TRANSACTIONS/CAREER NOTES: Selected by San Francisco Giants organization in first round (15th pick overall) of free-agent draft (June 1, 1988); pick received as compensation for Cincinnati Reds signing Type B free-agent OF Eddie Milner. ... Traded by Giants with a player to be named later to St. Louis Cardinals for P Allen Watson, P Rich DeLucia and P Doug Creek (December 14, 1995); Cardinals acquired 2B Chris Wimmer to complete deal (January 16, 1996). ... On St. Louis disabled list (June 24-July 9, 1998). ... Traded by Cardinals with P Todd Stottlemyre to Texas Rangers for P Darren Oliver, 3B Fernando Tatis and a player to be named later (July 31, 1998); Cardinals acquired OF Mark Little to complete deal (August 9, 1998). ... Granted free agency (October 23, 1998). ... Re-signed by Rangers (December 2, 1998). ... On Texas disabled list (May 1-21, 1999); included rehabilitation assignment to Oklahoma (May 18-21). ... Traded by Rangers to Chicago White Sox for P Aaron Myette and P Brian Schmack (December 14, 2000).
STATISTICAL NOTES: Led Texas League shortstops with 80 double plays in 1991. ... Led N.L. shortstops with 103 double plays in 1993. ... Led N.L. shortstops with 654 total chances in 1995. ... Career major league grand slams: 1.

Year Team (League)	Pos.	G	AB	R	H	2B	3B	HR	RBI	Avg.	BB	SO	SB	PO	A	E	Avg.
1988— Everett (N'West)	SS	60	212	35	55	4	0	3	29	.259	27	54	10	75	166	35	.873
1989— Clinton (Midw.)	SS	104	385	39	91	13	3	0	24	.236	39	101	28	182	332	31	.943
—San Jose (Calif.)........	SS	28	92	5	11	2	0	0	4	.120	13	27	10	53	71	8	.939
1990— San Jose (Calif.)........	SS	123	460	80	123	15	10	7	71	.267	68	98	33	*202	358	37	.938
1991— Shreveport (Texas)	SS	126	485	84	136	22	8	5	68	.280	61	104	36	174	379	29	.950
—San Francisco (N.L.) ..	SS	9	26	0	3	1	0	0	2	.115	1	6	0	16	6	3	.880
1992— San Francisco (N.L.) ..	SS-3B	98	321	31	72	7	4	4	24	.224	26	63	8	142	257	11	.973
—Phoenix (PCL)...........	SS	48	192	30	46	6	2	3	18	.240	17	25	15	81	150	7	.971
1993— San Francisco (N.L.) ..	SS	153	549	54	155	21	5	6	70	.282	38	91	11	251	449	27	.963
1994— San Francisco (N.L.) ..	SS	108	385	38	91	14	6	3	30	.236	30	74	23	177	330	14	.973
1995— San Francisco (N.L.) ..	SS	138	509	56	124	29	3	5	58	.244	38	109	24	*223	•411	20	.969
1996— St. Louis (N.L.)■	SS	129	491	64	136	20	4	6	35	.277	33	89	33	171	347	15	.972

C

Year Team (League)	Pos.	G	AB	R	H	2B	3B	HR	RBI	Avg.	BB	SO	SB	PO	A	E	Avg.
1997—St. Louis (N.L.)..........	SS	154	576	75	153	39	5	9	61	.266	33	109	30	228	*452	19	.973
1998—St. Louis (N.L.)..........	SS	90	355	59	83	19	1	4	29	.234	40	51	19	140	286	13	.970
—Texas (A.L.)■.............	SS	52	186	30	53	12	1	5	24	.285	13	32	5	88	152	7	.972
1999—Texas (A.L.)..............	SS	133	465	69	134	21	5	14	52	.288	39	100	8	204	406	*25	.961
—Oklahoma (PCL)............	SS	2	7	1	1	0	0	0	1	.143	3	3	0	4	7	0	1.000
2000—Texas (A.L.)...............	SS	148	513	70	124	21	5	14	54	.242	42	92	11	*265	411	16	.977
2001—Chicago (A.L.)■........	SS	135	433	62	114	21	4	9	60	.263	33	72	10	196	367	7	.988
American League totals (4 years)		468	1597	231	425	75	15	42	190	.266	127	296	34	753	1336	55	.974
National League totals (8 years)		879	3212	377	817	150	28	37	309	.254	239	592	148	1348	2538	122	.970
Major League totals (11 years)		1347	4809	608	1242	225	43	79	499	.258	366	888	182	2101	3874	177	.971

DIVISION SERIES RECORD

Year Team (League)	Pos.	G	AB	R	H	2B	3B	HR	RBI	Avg.	BB	SO	SB	PO	A	E	Avg.
1996—St. Louis (N.L.)..........	SS	2	6	1	2	0	0	0	0	.333	3	1	0	4	5	0	1.000
1998—Texas (A.L.)...............	SS	3	9	0	2	0	0	0	0	.222	0	4	0	5	8	1	.929
1999—Texas (A.L.)...............	SS	3	10	0	0	0	0	0	0	.000	0	1	0	4	10	0	1.000
Division series totals (3 years)		8	25	1	4	0	0	0	0	.160	3	6	0	13	23	1	.973

CHAMPIONSHIP SERIES RECORD

Year Team (League)	Pos.	G	AB	R	H	2B	3B	HR	RBI	Avg.	BB	SO	SB	PO	A	E	Avg.
1996—St. Louis (N.L.)..........	SS	5	20	4	7	0	0	0	1	.350	1	4	1	5	16	2	.913

ALL-STAR GAME RECORD

Year League	Pos.	AB	R	H	2B	3B	HR	RBI	Avg.	BB	SO	SB	PO	A	E	Avg.
1997—National.....................	SS	1	0	0	0	0	0	0	.000	0	1	0	0	1	0	1.000

CLEMENS, ROGER　　　P　　　YANKEES

PERSONAL: Born August 4, 1962, in Dayton, Ohio. ... 6-4/238. ... Throws right, bats right. ... Full name: William Roger Clemens.

HIGH SCHOOL: Spring Woods (Houston).

JUNIOR COLLEGE: San Jacinto (North) College (Texas).

COLLEGE: Texas.

TRANSACTIONS/CAREER NOTES: Selected by New York Mets organization in 12th round of free-agent draft (June 8, 1981); did not sign. ... Selected by Boston Red Sox organization in first round (19th pick overall) of free-agent draft (June 6, 1983). ... On disabled list (July 8-August 3 and August 21, 1985-remainder of season). ... On suspended list (April 26-May 3, 1991). ... On Boston disabled list (June 19-July 16, 1993); included rehabilitation assignment to Pawtucket (July 11-16). ... On Boston disabled list (April 16-June 2, 1995); included rehabilitation assignments to Sarasota (May 25-28) and Pawtucket (May 28-June 2). ... Granted free agency (November 5, 1996). ... Signed by Toronto Blue Jays (December 13, 1996). ... Traded by Blue Jays to New York Yankees for P David Wells, P Graeme Lloyd and 2B Homer Bush (February 18, 1999). ... On disabled list (April 28-May 21, 1999; and June 15-July 2, 2000).

RECORDS: Holds A.L. record for most consecutive seasons with 100 or more strikeouts—16 (1986-2001). ... Shares major league single-game record for most strikeouts (nine-inning game)—20 (April 29, 1986 and September 18, 1996). ... Shares major league record for most putouts by pitcher in one inning—3 (June 27, 1992, sixth inning). ... Holds A.L. record for most consecutive games won—20 (June 3, 1998-June 1, 1999). ... Shares A.L. records for most consecutive seasons with 200 or more strikeouts—7 (1986-92); most seasons with 200 or more strikeouts—11. ... Shares A.L. single-game record for most consecutive strikeouts—8 (April 29, 1986). ... Holds A.L. career record for most strikeouts—3,717; and most consecutive starting assignments—532 (July 26, 1984-present). ... Shares A.L. single-season record for most consecutive games won—16 (May 26-September 19, 2001).

HONORS: Named Major League Player of the Year by THE SPORTING NEWS (1986). ... Named A.L. Pitcher of the Year by THE SPORTING NEWS (1986, 1991, 1997, 1998 and 2001). ... Named righthanded pitcher on THE SPORTING NEWS A.L. All-Star team (1986-87, 1991, 1997 and 2001). ... Named A.L. Most Valuable Player by Baseball Writers' Association of America (1986). ... Named A.L. Cy Young Award winner by Baseball Writers' Association of America (1986, 1987, 1991, 1997, 1998 and 2001).

STATISTICAL NOTES: Struck out 15 batters in one game (August 21, 1984; July 9, 1988; August 15 and September 21, 1998). ... Struck out 20 batters in one game (April 29, 1986 and September 18, 1996). ... Struck out 16 batters in one game (May 9 and July 15, 1988 and July 12, 1997). ... Pitched 6-0 one-hit, complete-game victory against Cleveland (September 10, 1988). ... Led A.L. with 14 hit batsmen in 1995. ... Struck out 18 batters in one game (August 25, 1998). ... Tied for A.L. lead with 14 wild pitches in 2001.

MISCELLANEOUS: Singled in only appearance as pinch hitter (1996).

Year League	W	L	Pct.	ERA	G	GS	CG	ShO	Sv.	IP	H	R	ER	BB	SO
1983—Winter Haven (FSL)............	3	1	.750	1.24	4	4	3	1	0	29	22	4	4	0	36
—New Britain (East.)	4	1	.800	1.38	7	7	1	1	0	52	31	8	8	12	59
1984—Pawtucket (I.L.)..............	2	3	.400	1.93	7	6	3	1	0	46²/₃	39	12	10	14	50
—Boston (A.L.)..................	9	4	.692	4.32	21	20	5	1	0	133¹/₃	146	67	64	29	126
1985—Boston (A.L.)..................	7	5	.583	3.29	15	15	3	1	0	98¹/₃	83	38	36	37	74
1986—Boston (A.L.)■■............	*24	4	*.857	*2.48	33	33	10	1	0	254	179	77	70	67	238
1987—Boston (A.L.)...................	●20	9	.690	2.97	36	36	*18	*7	0	281²/₃	248	100	93	83	256
1988—Boston (A.L.)...................	18	12	.600	2.93	35	35	●14	*8	0	264	217	93	86	62	*291
1989—Boston (A.L.)...................	17	11	.607	3.13	35	35	8	3	0	253¹/₃	215	101	88	93	230
1990—Boston (A.L.)...................	21	6	.778	*1.93	31	31	7	●4	0	228¹/₃	193	59	49	54	209
1991—Boston (A.L.)...................	18	10	.643	*2.62	35	●35	13	*4	0	*271¹/₃	219	93	79	65	*241
1992—Boston (A.L.)...................	18	11	.621	*2.41	32	32	11	*5	0	246²/₃	203	80	66	62	208
1993—Boston (A.L.)...................	11	14	.440	4.46	29	29	2	1	0	191²/₃	175	99	95	67	160
—Pawtucket (I.L.)...............	0	0	...	0.00	1	1	0	0	0	3²/₃	1	0	0	4	8
1994—Boston (A.L.)...................	9	7	.563	2.85	24	24	3	1	0	170²/₃	124	62	54	71	168
1995—Sarasota (FSL)	0	0	...	0.00	1	1	0	0	0	4	0	0	0	2	7
—Pawtucket (I.L.)...............	0	0	...	0.00	1	1	0	0	0	5	1	0	0	3	5
—Boston (A.L.)..................	10	5	.667	4.18	23	23	0	0	0	140	141	70	65	60	132
1996—Boston (A.L.)...................	10	13	.435	3.63	34	34	6	2	0	242²/₃	216	106	98	106	*257
1997—Toronto (A.L.)■■..........	*21	7	.750	*2.05	34	34	●9	●3	0	●264	204	65	60	68	*292

– 112 –

Year League	W	L	Pct.	ERA	G	GS	CG	ShO	Sv.	IP	H	R	ER	BB	SO
1998—Toronto (A.L.)	•20	6	.769	*2.65	33	33	5	3	0	234 2/3	169	78	69	88	*271
1999—New York (A.L.)■	14	10	.583	4.60	30	30	1	1	0	187 2/3	185	101	96	90	163
2000—New York (A.L.)	13	8	.619	3.70	32	32	1	0	0	204 1/3	184	96	84	84	188
2001—New York (A.L.)	20	3	.870	3.51	33	33	0	0	0	220 1/3	205	94	86	72	213
Major League totals (18 years)	280	145	.659	3.10	545	544	116	45	0	3887	3306	1479	1338	1258	3717

DIVISION SERIES RECORD

RECORDS: Shares A.L. career record for most losses—3.

Year League	W	L	Pct.	ERA	G	GS	CG	ShO	Sv.	IP	H	R	ER	BB	SO
1995—Boston (A.L.)	0	0	...	3.86	1	1	0	0	0	7	5	3	3	1	5
1999—New York (A.L.)	1	0	1.000	0.00	1	1	0	0	0	7	3	0	0	2	2
2000—New York (A.L.)	0	2	.000	8.18	2	2	0	0	0	11	13	10	10	8	10
2001—New York (A.L.)	0	1	.000	5.40	2	2	0	0	0	8 1/3	9	5	5	4	6
Division series totals (4 years)	1	3	.250	4.86	6	6	0	0	0	33 1/3	30	18	18	15	23

CHAMPIONSHIP SERIES RECORD

RECORDS: Holds A.L. career record for most strikeouts—53. ... Holds single-series record for most hits allowed—22 (1986). ... Shares single-series record for most earned runs allowed—11 (1986). ... Shares single-game records for most earned runs allowed—7 (October 7, 1986); and most consecutive strikeouts—4 (October 6, 1988). ... Holds A.L. single-series record for most innings pitched—22 2/3 (1986). ... Shares A.L. single-game record for most runs allowed—8 (October 7, 1986). ... Holds single-game record for fewest hits allowed—1 (October 14, 2000).

Year League	W	L	Pct.	ERA	G	GS	CG	ShO	Sv.	IP	H	R	ER	BB	SO
1986—Boston (A.L.)	1	1	.500	4.37	3	3	0	0	0	22 2/3	22	12	11	7	17
1988—Boston (A.L.)	0	0	...	3.86	1	1	0	0	0	7	6	3	3	0	8
1990—Boston (A.L.)	0	1	.000	3.52	2	2	0	0	0	7 2/3	7	3	3	5	4
1999—New York (A.L.)	0	1	.000	22.50	1	1	0	0	0	2	6	5	5	2	2
2000—New York (A.L.)	1	0	1.000	0.00	1	1	1	1	0	9	1	0	0	2	15
2001—New York (A.L.)	0	0	...	0.00	1	1	0	0	0	5	1	0	0	4	7
Champ. series totals (6 years)	2	3	.400	3.71	9	9	1	1	0	53 1/3	43	23	22	20	53

WORLD SERIES RECORD

NOTES: Member of World Series championship team (1999 and 2000).

Year League	W	L	Pct.	ERA	G	GS	CG	ShO	Sv.	IP	H	R	ER	BB	SO
1986—Boston (A.L.)	0	0	...	3.18	2	2	0	0	0	11 1/3	9	5	4	6	11
1999—New York (A.L.)	1	0	1.000	1.17	1	1	0	0	0	7 2/3	4	1	1	2	4
2000—New York (A.L.)	1	0	1.000	0.00	1	1	0	0	0	8	2	0	0	0	9
2001—New York (A.L.)	1	0	1.000	1.35	2	2	0	0	0	13 1/3	10	2	2	4	19
World Series totals (4 years)	3	0	1.000	1.56	6	6	0	0	0	40 1/3	25	8	7	12	43

ALL-STAR GAME RECORD

NOTES: Named Most Valuable Player (1986).

Year League	W	L	Pct.	ERA	GS	CG	ShO	Sv.	IP	H	R	ER	BB	SO
1986—American	1	0	1.000	0.00	1	0	0	0	3	0	0	0	0	2
1988—American	0	0	...	0.00	0	0	0	0	1	0	0	0	0	1
1990—American							Did not play.							
1991—American	0	0	...	9.00	0	0	0	0	1	1	1	1	0	0
1992—American	0	0	...	0.00	0	0	0	0	1	2	0	0	0	0
1997—American	0	0	...	0.00	0	0	0	0	1	1	0	0	0	0
1998—American	0	0	...	18.00	0	0	0	0	1	2	2	2	1	1
2001—American	0	0	...	0.00	1	0	0	0	2	0	0	0	0	1
All-Star Game totals (7 years)	1	0	1.000	2.70	2	0	0	0	10	6	3	3	1	5

CLEMENT, MATT　　　　P　　　　MARLINS

PERSONAL: Born August 12, 1974, in McCandless Township, Pa. ... 6-3/195. ... Throws right, bats right. ... Full name: Matthew Paul Clement.
HIGH SCHOOL: Butler (Pa.).
TRANSACTIONS/CAREER NOTES: Selected by San Diego Padres organization in third round of free-agent draft (June 3, 1993). ... Traded by Padres with OF Eric Owens and P Omar Ortiz to Florida Marlins for OF Mark Kotsay and OF Cesar Crespo (March 28, 2001).
RECORDS: Shares major league single-season record for most grand slams allowed—4 (2000).
STATISTICAL NOTES: Led Pioneer League with 19 wild pitches in 1995. ... Led Pacific Coast League with 30 hit batsmen in 1998. ... Led N.L. with 23 wild pitches in 2000 and 15 in 2001.
MISCELLANEOUS: Appeared one game as pinch hitter (2001).

Year League	W	L	Pct.	ERA	G	GS	CG	ShO	Sv.	IP	H	R	ER	BB	SO
1994—Peoria (Ariz.)	•8	5	.615	4.43	13	13	0	0	0	67	65	38	33	17	76
—Spokane (N'West)	1	1	.500	6.14	2	2	0	0	0	7 1/3	8	7	5	11	4
1995—Rancho Cuca. (Calif.)	3	4	.429	4.24	12	12	0	0	0	57 1/3	61	37	27	49	33
—Idaho Falls (Pio.)	6	3	.667	4.33	14	14	0	0	0	81	61	53	39	42	65
1996—Clinton (Midw.)	8	3	.727	2.80	16	16	1	•1	0	96 1/3	66	31	30	52	109
—Rancho Cuca. (Calif.)	4	5	.444	5.59	11	11	0	0	0	56 1/3	61	40	35	26	75
1997—Rancho Cuca. (Calif.)	6	3	.667	1.60	14	14	2	1	0	101	74	30	18	31	109
—Mobile (Sou.)	6	5	.545	2.56	13	13	1	1	0	88	83	37	25	32	92
1998—Las Vegas (PCL)	10	9	.526	3.98	27	27	1	0	0	171 2/3	157	94	76	85	*160
—San Diego (N.L.)	2	0	1.000	4.61	4	2	0	0	0	13 2/3	15	8	7	7	13
1999—San Diego (N.L.)	10	12	.455	4.48	31	31	0	0	0	180 2/3	190	106	90	86	135
2000—San Diego (N.L.)	13	17	.433	5.14	34	34	0	0	0	205	194	131	117	*125	170
2001—Florida (N.L.)■	9	10	.474	5.05	31	31	0	0	0	169 1/3	172	102	95	85	134
Major League totals (4 years)	34	39	.466	4.89	100	98	0	0	0	568 2/3	571	347	309	303	452

PERSONAL: Born September 24, 1977, in Santo Domingo, Dominican Republic. ... 6-1/185. ... Throws right, bats right. ... Full name: Pasqual Reynoso Coco.

TRANSACTIONS/CAREER NOTES: Signed as non-drafted free agent by Toronto Blue Jays organization (August 10, 1994).

STATISTICAL NOTES: Pitched 3-1 no-hit loss for St. Catharines against Jamestown (August 16, 1998). ... Led Southern League with 17 hit batsmen in 2000. ... Tied for Southern League lead with three balks in 2000.

Year	League	W	L	Pct.	ERA	G	GS	CG	ShO	Sv.	IP	H	R	ER	BB	SO
1995—	Dom. Blue Jays (DSL)	7	1	.875	2.78	11	11	0	0	0	58 1/3	51	30	18	36	38
1996—	Dom. Blue Jays (DSL)	7	2	.778	2.99	17	16	2	0	0	96 1/3	77	46	32	53	92
1997—	St. Catharines (NY-Penn)	1	4	.200	4.89	10	8	0	0	0	46	48	32	25	16	44
1998—	St. Catharines (NY-Penn)	3	7	.300	3.20	15	15	1	0	0	81 2/3	62	52	29	32	84
1999—	Hagerstown (S.Atl.)	11	1	*.917	2.21	14	14	0	0	0	97 2/3	67	29	24	25	83
—	Dunedin (FSL)	4	6	.400	5.28	13	13	2	0	0	75	79	52	44	33	44
2000—	Tennessee (Sou.)	12	7	.632	3.76	27	26	2	0	0	167 2/3	154	83	70	68	142
—	Toronto (A.L.)	0	0	...	9.00	1	1	0	0	0	4	5	4	4	5	2
2001—	Tennessee (Sou.)	0	1	.000	3.94	3	3	0	0	0	16	13	7	7	5	13
—	Syracuse (I.L.)	8	6	.571	4.66	22	22	0	0	0	121 2/3	128	67	63	50	82
—	Toronto (A.L.)	1	0	1.000	4.40	7	1	0	0	0	14 1/3	12	8	7	6	9
Major League totals (2 years)		1	0	1.000	5.40	8	2	0	0	0	18 1/3	17	12	11	11	11

C

PERSONAL: Born May 16, 1977, in Curacao, Netherlands Antilles. ... 6-1/192. ... Bats left, throws right. ... Full name: Ivanon Angelino Coffie.

TRANSACTIONS/CAREER NOTES: Signed as non-drafted free agent by Baltimore Orioles organization (July 28, 1995). ... Traded by Orioles to Chicago Cubs for a player to be named later (November 16, 2001). ... On Rochester disabled list (April 28-July 17, 2001).

STATISTICAL NOTES: Led Gulf Coast League shortstops with .941 fielding percentage in 1996.

Year	Team (League)	Pos.	G	AB	R	H	2B	3B	HR	RBI	Avg.	BB	SO	SB	PO	A	E	Avg.
1996—	GC Orioles (GCL)	SS-3B	56	193	29	42	8	4	0	20	.218	23	26	6	81	175	16	†.941
1997—	Delmarva (S.Atl.)	SS-3B	90	305	41	84	14	5	3	48	.275	23	45	19	126	203	19	.945
1998—	Frederick (Caro.)	3B-SS	130	473	62	121	19	2	16	75	.256	48	109	17	126	216	25	.932
1999—	Bowie (East.)	3B-SS	57	195	21	36	9	3	3	23	.185	20	46	2	39	90	8	.942
—	Frederick (Caro.)	3B-SS-DH	73	276	35	78	18	4	11	53	.283	28	62	7	51	139	20	.905
2000—	Bowie (East.)	SS-3B	87	341	49	91	21	3	9	44	.267	36	53	1	98	199	19	.940
—	Baltimore (A.L.)	3B-SS-DH	23	60	6	13	4	1	0	6	.217	5	11	1	13	32	1	.978
—	Rochester (I.L.)	SS-3B	21	78	4	17	2	1	0	10	.218	2	21	0	19	45	3	.955
2001—	Rochester (I.L.)	3B-1B	56	206	33	55	10	1	8	35	.267	15	47	3	106	34	1	.933
—	GC Orioles (GCL)	DH	6	18	2	5	1	0	1	2	.278	2	5	0	...	...	...	...
Major League totals (1 year)			23	60	6	13	4	1	0	6	.217	5	11	1	13	32	1	.978

PERSONAL: Born December 21, 1976, in Chicago. ... 6-2/205. ... Throws left, bats left. ... Full name: Anthony Michael Cogan.

HIGH SCHOOL: Highland Park (Ill.).

COLLEGE: Stanford.

TRANSACTIONS/CAREER NOTES: Selected by Kansas City Royals organization in 12th round of free-agent draft (June 2, 1999).

Year	League	W	L	Pct.	ERA	G	GS	CG	ShO	Sv.	IP	H	R	ER	BB	SO
1999—	Spokane (N'West)	1	3	.250	1.36	27	0	0	0	4	39 2/3	26	10	6	14	37
2000—	Wilmington (Caro.)	2	4	.333	4.35	16	3	0	0	1	39 1/3	39	22	19	18	31
—	Charleston, W.Va. (S.Atl.)	6	2	.750	1.83	13	13	0	0	0	78 2/3	65	19	16	14	51
—	Wichita (Texas)	1	1	.500	11.57	2	0	0	0	0	2 1/3	6	4	3	2	1
2001—	Kansas City (A.L.)	0	4	.000	5.84	39	0	0	0	0	24 2/3	32	17	16	13	17
—	Wichita (Texas)	1	1	.500	2.08	8	0	0	0	1	17 1/3	13	6	4	4	12
—	Omaha (PCL)	1	1	.500	2.79	9	0	0	0	2	9 2/3	14	3	3	3	8
Major League totals (1 year)		0	4	.000	5.84	39	0	0	0	0	24 2/3	32	17	16	13	17

PERSONAL: Born October 30, 1976, in Covina, Calif. ... 6-4/205. ... Throws right, bats right. ... Full name: David Raymond Coggin.

HIGH SCHOOL: Upland (Calif.).

TRANSACTIONS/CAREER NOTES: Selected by Philadelphia Phillies organization in supplemental round ("sandwich pick" between first and second round, 30th pick overall) of free-agent draft (June 1, 1995). ... On disabled list (April 20-May 25, 1998; May 14-June 4 and June 26, 1999-remainder of season). ... On Scranton/Wilkes-Barre disabled list (June 5-15, 2001).

STATISTICAL NOTES: Led Florida State League with 24 wild pitches in 1997.

Year	League	W	L	Pct.	ERA	G	GS	CG	ShO	Sv.	IP	H	R	ER	BB	SO
1995—	Martinsville (Appl.)	5	3	.625	3.00	11	11	0	0	0	48	45	25	16	31	37
1996—	Piedmont (S.Atl.)	9	12	.429	4.31	28	•28	3	3	0	169 1/3	156	87	*81	46	129
1997—	Clearwater (FSL)	11	8	.579	4.70	27	27	3	•2	0	155	160	96	81	86	110
1998—	Reading (East.)	4	8	.333	4.14	20	20	0	0	0	108 2/3	106	58	50	62	65
1999—	Reading (East.)	2	5	.286	7.50	9	9	0	0	0	42	55	37	35	20	21
2000—	Clearwater (FSL)	2	2	.500	2.67	6	5	0	0	0	33 2/3	25	11	10	13	26
—	Reading (East.)	3	2	.400	4.93	7	7	0	0	0	42	49	24	23	13	30
—	Scranton/W.B. (I.L.)	3	2	.600	4.34	9	9	0	0	0	45 2/3	35	27	22	33	27
—	Philadelphia (N.L.)	2	0	1.000	5.33	5	5	0	0	0	27	35	20	16	12	17
2001—	Scranton/W.B. (I.L.)	5	5	.500	3.05	15	15	0	0	0	97 1/3	93	36	33	31	53
—	Philadelphia (N.L.)	6	7	.462	4.17	17	17	0	0	0	95	99	46	44	39	62
Major League totals (2 years)		8	7	.533	4.43	22	22	0	0	0	122	134	66	60	51	79

PERSONAL: Born October 22, 1976, in Teaneck, N.J. ... 6-1/185. ... Bats right, throws right. ... Full name: Michael Gus Colangelo.
HIGH SCHOOL: C.D. Hylton (Woodbridge, Va.).
COLLEGE: George Mason.
TRANSACTIONS/CAREER NOTES: Selected by Anaheim Angels organization in 21st round of free-agent draft (June 3, 1997). ... On Anaheim disabled list (June 14, 1999-remainder of season). ... On disabled list (March 20, 2000-entire season). ... Claimed on waivers by Arizona Diamondbacks (October 5, 2000). ... Claimed on waivers by San Diego Padres (October 17, 2000). ... Granted free agency (October 18, 2001). ... Signed by Oakland Athletics (November 15, 2001).

							BATTING								FIELDING		
Year Team (League)	Pos.	G	AB	R	H	2B	3B	HR	RBI	Avg.	BB	SO	SB	PO	A	E	Avg.
1998— Cedar Rapids (Midw.)	OF	22	83	13	23	8	0	4	8	.277	12	16	5	14	0	1	.933
— Lake Elsinore (Calif.) ..	OF	36	145	33	55	11	3	5	21	.379	13	24	2	78	3	0	1.000
1999— Erie (East.)	OF-DH	28	109	24	37	10	3	1	13	.339	14	22	3	35	3	2	.950
— Edmonton (PCL)	OF	26	105	13	38	7	1	0	9	.362	13	18	2	29	3	2	.941
— Anaheim (A.L.)	OF	1	2	0	1	0	0	0	0	.500	1	0	0	1	1	0	1.000
2000— Anaheim (A.L.)...........							Did not play.										
2001— Mobile (Sou.)■■	OF	9	34	5	9	0	1	1	4	.265	4	8	0	7	3	1	.909
— Portland (PCL)	OF	61	180	27	47	11	1	3	22	.261	31	44	5	99	6	1	.991
— San Diego (N.L.)	OF	50	91	10	22	3	3	2	8	.242	8	30	0	45	1	1	.979
American League totals (1 year)		1	2	0	1	0	0	0	0	.500	1	0	0	1	1	0	1.000
National League totals (1 year)		50	91	10	22	3	3	2	8	.242	8	30	0	45	1	1	.979
Major League totals (2 years)		51	93	10	23	3	3	2	8	.247	9	30	0	46	2	1	.980

C

PERSONAL: Born July 26, 1969, in Fontana, Calif. ... 6-0/205. ... Bats right, throws right. ... Full name: Gregory Joseph Colbrunn.
HIGH SCHOOL: Fontana (Calif.).
TRANSACTIONS/CAREER NOTES: Selected by Montreal Expos organization in sixth round of free-agent draft (June 2, 1987). ... On disabled list (April 10, 1991-entire season). ... On Indianapolis disabled list (April 9-May 5, 1992). ... On Montreal disabled list (August 2-18, 1992); included rehabilitation assignment to Indianapolis (August 13-18). ... On Montreal disabled list (April 5-21, 1993); included rehabilitation assignment to West Palm Beach (April 9-20). ... On Montreal disabled list (July 12, 1993-remainder of season); included rehabilitation assignment to Ottawa (July 27-August 2). ... Claimed on waivers by Florida Marlins (October 7, 1993). ... On Florida disabled list (April 9-May 27, and July 15-30, 1994); included rehabilitation assignments to Brevard County (May 12-18 and July 28-30) and Edmonton (May 18-27). ... On disabled list (July 24-August 8, 1996). ... Granted free agency (December 20, 1996). ... Signed by Minnesota Twins organization (January 24, 1997). ... Traded by Twins to Atlanta Braves for a player to be named later (August 14, 1997); Twins acquired OF Marc Lewis to complete deal (October 1, 1997). ... Granted free agency (October 23, 1997). ... Signed by Colorado Rockies organization (December 23, 1997). ... Traded by Rockies to Braves for P David Cortes, P Mike Porzio and a player to be named later (July 30, 1998); Rockies acquired P Anthony Briggs to complete deal (September 9, 1998). ... Granted free agency (October 23, 1998). ... Signed by Arizona Diamondbacks (November 17, 1998). ... On Arizona disabled list (June 6-25 and June 27-August 17, 2001); included rehabilitation assignment to Tucson (August 10-17).
STATISTICAL NOTES: Had 21-game hitting streak (May 31-June 23, 1996). ... Career major league grand slams: 2.

							BATTING								FIELDING		
Year Team (League)	Pos.	G	AB	R	H	2B	3B	HR	RBI	Avg.	BB	SO	SB	PO	A	E	Avg.
1988— Rockford (Midw.).......	C	115	417	55	111	18	2	7	46	.266	22	60	5	595	81	15	.978
1989— W.P. Beach (FSL).......	C	59	228	20	54	8	0	0	25	.237	6	29	3	376	49	5	.988
— Jacksonville (Sou.).....	C	55	178	21	49	11	1	3	18	.275	13	33	0	304	34	4	.988
1990— Jacksonville (Sou.).....	C	125	458	57	138	29	1	13	76	.301	38	78	1	698	58	15	.981
1991—							Did not play.										
1992— Indianapolis (A.A.)......	1B	57	216	32	66	19	1	11	48	.306	7	41	1	441	27	4	.992
— Montreal (N.L.)...........	1B	52	168	12	45	8	0	2	18	.268	6	34	3	363	29	3	.992
1993— W.P. Beach (FSL).......	1B	8	31	6	12	2	1	1	5	.387	4	1	0	74	5	1	.988
— Montreal (N.L.)...........	1B	70	153	15	39	9	0	4	23	.255	6	33	4	372	27	2	.995
— Ottawa (I.L.)...............	1B	6	22	4	6	1	0	0	8	.273	1	2	1	50	1	0	1.000
1994— Florida (N.L.)■..........	1B	47	155	17	47	10	0	6	31	.303	9	27	1	304	26	4	.988
— Brevard County (FSL).	DH-1B	7	11	3	6	2	0	1	2	.545	1	0	0	16	1	1	.944
— Edmonton (PCL)	1B-DH	7	17	2	4	0	0	1	2	.235	0	1	0	28	1	1	.967
1995— Florida (N.L.).............	1B	138	528	70	146	22	1	23	89	.277	22	69	11	1066	90	5	.996
1996— Florida (N.L.).............	1B	141	511	60	146	26	2	16	69	.286	25	76	4	1169	101	6	.995
1997— Minnesota (A.L.)■.......	1B-DH	70	217	24	61	14	0	5	26	.281	8	38	1	475	35	6	.988
— Atlanta (N.L.).............	1B-DH	28	54	3	15	3	0	2	9	.278	2	11	0	54	6	1	.984
1998— Colorado (N.L.)■...1B-OF-DH-C		62	122	12	38	8	2	2	13	.311	8	23	1	222	21	2	.992
— Atlanta (N.L.).............	1B-OF	28	44	6	13	3	0	1	10	.295	2	11	1	57	4	0	1.000
1999— Arizona (N.L.)■.........	1B-DH-3B	67	135	20	44	5	3	5	24	.326	12	23	1	203	19	1	.996
2000— Arizona (N.L.).............	1B-DH-3B	116	329	48	103	22	1	15	57	.313	43	45	0	649	52	8	.989
2001— Arizona (N.L.).............	1B-3B	59	97	12	28	8	0	4	18	.289	9	14	0	73	17	3	.968
— Tucson (PCL)	1B	5	13	1	5	1	0	0	4	.385	2	0	0	24	3	0	1.000
American League totals (1 year)		70	217	24	61	14	0	5	26	.281	8	38	1	475	35	6	.988
National League totals (10 years)		808	2296	275	664	124	9	80	361	.289	144	366	28	4532	392	35	.993
Major League totals (10 years)		878	2513	299	725	138	9	85	387	.288	152	404	29	5007	427	41	.993

DIVISION SERIES RECORD

RECORDS: Shares N.L. career record for most pinch hits—3.

							BATTING								FIELDING		
Year Team (League)	Pos.	G	AB	R	H	2B	3B	HR	RBI	Avg.	BB	SO	SB	PO	A	E	Avg.
1997— Atlanta (N.L.).............	PH	1	1	0	1	0	0	0	2	1.000	0	0	0	...	...	...	...
1998— Atlanta (N.L.).............	PH	2	2	0	0	0	0	0	0	.000	0	0	0	...	...	...	...
1999— Arizona (N.L.).............	1B	2	5	1	2	1	0	1	2	.400	2	2	0	17	0	0	1.000
2001— Arizona (N.L.).............	PH-1B	4	6	0	2	0	0	0	1	.333	1	0	0	11	0	0	1.000
Division series totals (4 years)		9	14	1	5	1	0	1	5	.357	3	2	0	28	0	0	1.000

CHAMPIONSHIP SERIES RECORD

Year	Team (League)	Pos.	G	AB	R	H	2B	3B	HR	RBI	Avg.	BB	SO	SB	PO	A	E	Avg.
1997—Atlanta (N.L.).............	PH	3	3	0	2	0	0	0	0	.667	0	0	0	...	...	...	...
1998—Atlanta (N.L.).............	PH	6	6	0	2	0	0	0	0	.333	0	2	0	...	...	...	...
2001—Arizona (N.L.)............	PH	1	1	0	0	0	0	0	0	.000	0	0	0	...	...	...	...
Championship series totals (3 years)		10	10	0	4	0	0	0	0	.400	0	2	0	...	...	...	

WORLD SERIES RECORD

RECORDS: Shares single-inning record for most runs—2 (November 3, 2001, third inning).

NOTES: Member of World Series championship team (2001).

Year	Team (League)	Pos.	G	AB	R	H	2B	3B	HR	RBI	Avg.	BB	SO	SB	PO	A	E	Avg.
2001—Arizona (N.L.)............	1B	1	5	2	2	0	0	0	1	.400	1	1	0	5	0	0	1.000

COLEMAN, MICHAEL — OF — RED SOX

PERSONAL: Born August 16, 1975, in Nashville, Tenn. ... 5-11/215. ... Bats right, throws right. ... Full name: Michael D. Coleman.

HIGH SCHOOL: Stratford (Nashville, Tenn.).

TRANSACTIONS/CAREER NOTES: Selected by Boston Red Sox organization in 18th round of free-agent draft (June 2, 1994). ... On Pawtucket disabled list (May 9-June 11, 1998; and April 8-27 and July 3-10, 1999). ... On Pawtucket disabled list (April 29-June 27, 2000). ... On Boston disabled list (June 27, 2000-remainder of season). ... Traded by Red Sox with IF Donnie Sadler to Cincinnati Reds for IF Chris Stynes (November 16, 2000). ... Traded by Reds with 3B Drew Henson to New York Yankees for OF Wily Pena (March 21, 2001). ... On Columbus disabled list (July 18, 2001-remainder of season). ... Granted free agency (October 15, 2001). ... Signed by Red Sox organization (November 21, 2001).

Year	Team (League)	Pos.	G	AB	R	H	2B	3B	HR	RBI	Avg.	BB	SO	SB	PO	A	E	Avg.
1994—GC Red Sox (GCL)	OF	25	95	15	26	6	1	3	15	.274	10	20	5	32	0	0	1.000
—Utica (NY-Penn)	OF	23	65	16	11	2	0	1	3	.169	14	21	11	35	2	2	.949
1995—Michigan (Midw.)........	OF	112	422	70	113	16	2	11	61	.268	40	93	29	251	5	5	.981
1996—Sarasota (FSL)	OF	110	407	54	100	20	5	1	36	.246	38	86	24	261	9	2	*.993
1997—Trenton (East.)	OF-DH	102	385	56	116	17	8	14	58	.301	41	89	20	259	6	5	.981
—Pawtucket (I.L.)	OF	28	113	27	36	9	2	7	19	.319	12	27	4	53	2	4	.932
—Boston (A.L.).............	OF	8	24	2	4	1	0	0	2	.167	0	11	1	16	0	1	.941
1998—Pawtucket (I.L.).........	OF-DH	93	340	47	86	13	0	14	37	.253	27	92	12	173	9	4	.978
1999—Pawtucket (I.L.).........	OF-DH	115	467	95	125	29	2	30	74	.268	51	128	14	299	2	6	.980
—Boston (A.L.).............	OF	2	5	1	1	0	0	0	0	.200	1	0	0	0	0	0	...
2000—Pawtucket (I.L.)........	OF	18	66	11	17	5	1	6	15	.258	3	23	3	26	1	1	.964
2001—New York (A.L.)■......	OF-DH	12	38	5	8	0	0	1	7	.211	0	15	0	8	0	0	1.000
—Columbus (I.L.)	OF	29	101	16	24	3	3	4	17	.238	13	35	3	48	2	4	.926
Major League totals (3 years)		22	67	8	13	1	0	1	9	.194	1	26	1	24	0	1	.960

COLLIER, LOU — IF — METS

PERSONAL: Born August 21, 1973, in Chicago. ... 5-10/182. ... Bats right, throws right. ... Full name: Louis Keith Collier.

HIGH SCHOOL: Vocational (Chicago).

JUNIOR COLLEGE: Kishwaukee Junior College (Ill.), then Triton Community College (Ill.).

TRANSACTIONS/CAREER NOTES: Selected by Pittsburgh Pirates organization in 31st round of free-agent draft (June 1, 1992). ... On Pittsburgh disabled list (May 22-June 7, 1998; included rehabilitation assignment to Lynchburg (June 3-7). ... Claimed on waivers by Milwaukee Brewers (December 18, 1998). ... On Indianapolis disabled list (April 27-July 7, 2000). ... Traded by Brewers to New York Mets as part of three-way deal in which Mets traded P Glendon Rusch to Brewers, Colorado Rockies traded 1B/OF Ross Gload and P Craig House to Mets, Brewers traded P Jeff D'Amico, OF Jeromy Burnitz, OF/1B Mark Sweeney and cash to Mets, Mets traded 1B/3B Todd Zeile, OF Benny Agbayani, IF/OF Lenny Harris and cash to Rockies and Rockies traded OF Alex Ochoa to Brewers (January 21, 2002).

Year	Team (League)	Pos.	G	AB	R	H	2B	3B	HR	RBI	Avg.	BB	SO	SB	PO	A	E	Avg.
1993—Welland (NY-Penn).....	SS	50	201	35	61	6	2	1	19	.303	12	31	8	74	138	27	.887
1994—Augusta (S.Atl.).........	SS	85	318	48	89	17	4	7	40	.280	25	53	32	106	262	34	.915
—Salem (Caro.).............	SS	43	158	25	42	4	1	6	16	.266	15	29	5	65	129	11	.946
1995—Lynchburg (Caro.)......	SS	114	399	68	110	19	3	4	38	.276	51	60	31	156	361	35	.937
1996—Carolina (Sou.)..........	SS-DH	119	443	76	124	20	3	3	49	.280	48	73	29	189	310	30	.943
1997—Calgary (PCL)............	SS-2B-DH	112	397	65	131	31	5	1	48	.330	37	47	12	187	315	34	.937
—Pittsburgh (N.L.).........	SS	18	37	3	5	0	0	0	3	.135	1	11	1	9	36	0	1.000
1998—Pittsburgh (N.L.).......	SS	110	334	30	82	13	6	2	34	.246	31	70	2	148	287	18	.960
—Lynchburg (Caro.)........	SS	5	18	4	3	2	0	0	0	.167	2	0	2	5	16	4	.840
1999—Milwaukee (N.L.)■....SS-OF-3B-2B		74	135	18	35	9	0	2	21	.259	14	32	3	42	56	5	.951
—Louisville (I.L.) 3B-SS-OF		27	91	25	35	10	0	4	11	.385	15	14	6	17	59	3	.962
2000—Indianapolis (I.L.)....... OF-2B-3B		17	56	7	14	4	1	0	12	.250	11	9	2	31	11	3	.933
—Huntsville (Sou.) 3B-OF-2B-SS		50	172	29	46	4	2	2	29	.267	30	44	7	35	69	8	.929
—Milwaukee (N.L.)........	OF-3B	14	32	9	7	1	0	1	2	.219	6	4	0	16	2	0	1.000
2001—Indianapolis (I.L.)........	3B-2B-3B	86	312	48	90	17	2	14	36	.288	24	64	9	184	60	6	.976
—Milwaukee (N.L.)........	OF-3B-DH	50	127	19	32	8	1	2	14	.252	17	30	5	48	25	4	.948
Major League totals (5 years)		266	665	79	161	31	7	7	74	.242	69	147	11	263	406	27	.961

COLOME, JESUS — P — DEVIL RAYS

PERSONAL: Born June 2, 1980, in San Pedro de Macoris, Dominican Republic. ... 6-4/170. ... Throws right, bats right. ... Full name: Jesus Colome De La Cruz.

TRANSACTIONS/CAREER NOTES: Signed as non-drafted free agent by Oakland Athletics organization (September 29, 1996). ... Traded by A's with player to be named to Tampa Bay Devil Rays for P Jim Mecir and P Todd Belitz (July 28, 2000). ... On Durham disabled list (April 5-May 20, 2001).

Year League	W	L	Pct.	ERA	G	GS	CG	ShO	Sv.	IP	H	R	ER	BB	SO
1997—Dominican Athletics (DSL).	9	3	.750	2.70	18	7	3	0	0	90	73	33	27	22	55
1998—Arizona Athletics (Ariz.)......	2	5	.286	3.18	12	11	0	0	0	56^2/$_3$	47	27	20	16	62
1999—Modesto (Calif.)	8	4	.667	3.36	31	22	0	0	1	128^2/$_3$	125	63	48	60	127
2000—Midland (Texas)..................	9	4	.692	3.59	20	20	0	0	0	110^1/$_3$	99	62	44	50	95
—Orlando (Sou.)■...............	1	2	.333	6.75	3	3	0	0	0	14^2/$_3$	18	12	11	7	9
2001—Durham (I.L.)	0	3	.000	6.23	13	0	0	0	0	17^1/$_3$	22	13	12	6	18
—Tampa Bay (A.L.)................	2	3	.400	3.33	30	0	0	0	0	48^2/$_3$	37	22	18	25	31
Major League totals (1 year)........	2	3	.400	3.33	30	0	0	0	0	48^2/$_3$	37	22	18	25	31

COLON, BARTOLO   P   INDIANS

PERSONAL: Born May 24, 1975, in Altamira, Dominican Republic. ... 6-0/230. ... Throws right, bats right.

TRANSACTIONS/CAREER NOTES: Signed as non-drafted free agent by Cleveland Indians organization (June 26, 1993). ... On Canton/Akron disabled list (May 30-July 24, 1996). ... On Cleveland disabled list (April 16-May 12, 2000); included rehabilitation assignment to Buffalo (May 7-12). ... On suspended list (July 28-August 2, 2001).

HONORS: Named Carolina League Pitcher of the Year (1995).

STATISTICAL NOTES: Pitched 4-0 no-hit victory against New Orleans (June 20, 1997). ... Pitched 2-0 one-hit, complete-game victory against New York Yankees (September 18, 2000).

Year League	W	L	Pct.	ERA	G	GS	CG	ShO	Sv.	IP	H	R	ER	BB	SO
1993—Santiago (DSL)...................	6	1	.857	2.59	11	10	2	1	1	66	44	24	19	33	48
1994—Burlington (Appl.)...............	7	4	.636	3.14	12	12	0	0	0	66	46	32	23	44	84
1995—Kinston (Caro.).................	13	3	*.813	1.96	21	21	0	0	0	128^2/$_3$	91	31	28	39	*152
1996—Canton/Akron (East.)..........	2	2	.500	1.74	13	12	0	0	0	62	44	17	12	25	56
—Buffalo (A.A.)......................	0	0	...	6.00	8	0	0	0	0	15	16	10	10	8	19
1997—Cleveland (A.L.).................	4	7	.364	5.65	19	17	1	0	0	94	107	66	59	45	66
—Buffalo (A.A.)......................	7	1	.875	2.22	10	10	1	1	0	56^2/$_3$	45	15	14	23	54
1998—Cleveland (A.L.).................	14	9	.609	3.71	31	31	6	2	0	204	205	91	84	79	158
1999—Cleveland (A.L.).................	18	5	.783	3.95	32	32	1	1	0	205	185	97	90	76	161
2000—Cleveland (A.L.).................	15	8	.652	3.88	30	30	2	1	0	188	163	86	81	98	212
—Buffalo (I.L.)......................	1	0	1.000	1.80	1	1	0	0	0	5	6	1	1	0	4
2001—Cleveland (A.L.).................	14	12	.538	4.09	34	34	1	0	0	222^1/$_3$	220	106	101	90	201
Major League totals (5 years).......	65	41	.613	4.09	146	144	11	4	0	913^1/$_3$	880	446	415	388	798

DIVISION SERIES RECORD

Year League	W	L	Pct.	ERA	G	GS	CG	ShO	Sv.	IP	H	R	ER	BB	SO
1997—Cleveland (A.L.).................							Did not play.								
1998—Cleveland (A.L.).................	0	0	...	1.59	1	1	0	0	0	5^2/$_3$	5	1	1	4	3
1999—Cleveland (A.L.).................	0	1	.000	9.00	2	2	0	0	0	9	11	9	9	4	12
2001—Cleveland (A.L.).................	1	1	.500	1.84	2	2	0	0	0	14^2/$_3$	12	3	3	6	13
Division series totals (3 years)	1	2	.333	3.99	5	5	0	0	0	29^1/$_3$	28	13	13	14	28

CHAMPIONSHIP SERIES RECORD

Year League	W	L	Pct.	ERA	G	GS	CG	ShO	Sv.	IP	H	R	ER	BB	SO
1997—Cleveland (A.L.).................							Did not play.								
1998—Cleveland (A.L.).................	1	0	1.000	1.00	1	1	0	0	0	9	4	1	1	4	3

WORLD SERIES RECORD

Year League	W	L	Pct.	ERA	G	GS	CG	ShO	Sv.	IP	H	R	ER	BB	SO
1997—Cleveland (A.L.).................							Did not play.								

ALL-STAR GAME RECORD

Year League	W	L	Pct.	ERA	GS	CG	ShO	Sv.	IP	H	R	ER	BB	SO
1998—American	1	0	1.000	27.00	0	0	0	0	1	2	3	3	1	1

CONE, DAVID   P

PERSONAL: Born January 2, 1963, in Kansas City, Mo. ... 6-1/200. ... Throws right, bats left. ... Full name: David Brian Cone.

HIGH SCHOOL: Rockhurst (Kansas City, Mo.).

TRANSACTIONS/CAREER NOTES: Selected by Kansas City Royals organization in third round of free-agent draft (June 8, 1981). ... On disabled list (April 8, 1983-entire season). ... Traded by Royals with C Chris Jelic to New York Mets for C Ed Hearn, P Rick Anderson and P Mauro Gozzo (March 27, 1987). ... On New York disabled list (May 28-August 14, 1987); included rehabilitation assignment to Tidewater (July 30-August 14). ... Traded by Mets to Toronto Blue Jays for IF Jeff Kent and a player to be named later (August 27, 1992); Mets acquired OF Ryan Thompson to complete deal (September 1, 1992). ... Granted free agency (October 30, 1992). ... Signed by Royals (December 8, 1992). ... Traded by Royals to Blue Jays for P David Sinnes, IF Chris Stynes and IF Tony Medrano (April 6, 1995). ... Traded by Blue Jays to New York Yankees for P Marty Janzen, P Jason Jarvis and P Mike Gordon (July 28, 1995). ... Granted free agency (November 3, 1995). ... Re-signed by Yankees (December 21, 1995). ... On New York disabled list (May 3-September 2, 1996); included rehabilitation assignment to Norwich (August 21-September 1). ... On disabled list (August 18-September 20, 1997). ... Granted free agency (November 5, 1998). ... Re-signed by Yankees (November 11, 1998). ... Granted free agency (November 3, 1999). ... Re-signed by Yankees (December 6, 1999). ... Granted free agency (November 7, 2000). ... Signed by Boston Red Sox (January 11, 2001). ... On Boston disabled list (March 21-May 14, 2001); included rehabilitation assignment to Sarasota (May 12-14). ... Granted free agency (November 6, 2001).

RECORDS: Shares major league record for striking out side on nine pitches (August 30, 1991, seventh inning).

HONORS: Named righthanded pitcher on THE SPORTING NEWS A.L. All-Star team (1994). ... Named A.L. Cy Young Award winner by Baseball Writers' Association of America (1994).

STATISTICAL NOTES: Led Southern League with 27 wild pitches in 1984. ... Pitched 6-0 one-hit, complete-game victory against San Diego (August 29, 1988). ... Tied for N.L. lead with 10 balks in 1988. ... Pitched 1-0 one-hit, complete-game victory against St. Louis (September 20, 1991). ... Struck out 19 batters in one game (October 6, 1991). ... Pitched 4-0 one-hit, complete-game victory against California (May 22, 1994).

... Led A.L. with 229 $\frac{1}{3}$ innings pitched in 1995. ... Struck out 16 batters in one game (June 23, 1997). ... Tied for A.L. lead with 14 wild pitches in 1997. ... Pitched 6-0 perfect game against Montreal (July 18, 1999).
MISCELLANEOUS: Singled in only appearance as pinch hitter (1990).

Year League	W	L	Pct.	ERA	G	GS	CG	ShO	Sv.	IP	H	R	ER	BB	SO
1981—GC Royals-Blue (GCL)	6	4	.600	2.55	14	12	0	0	0	67	52	24	19	33	45
1982—Charleston, S.C. (S.Atl.)	9	2	.818	2.06	16	16	1	1	0	104 $\frac{2}{3}$	84	38	24	47	87
—Fort Myers (FSL)	7	1	.875	2.12	10	9	6	1	0	72 $\frac{1}{3}$	56	21	17	25	57
1983—Jacksonville (Sou.)							Did not play.								
1984—Memphis (Sou.)	8	12	.400	4.28	29	29	9	1	0	178 $\frac{2}{3}$	162	103	85	114	110
1985—Omaha (A.A.)	9	15	.375	4.65	28	27	5	1	0	158 $\frac{2}{3}$	157	90	82	*93	115
1986—Omaha (A.A.)	8	4	.667	2.79	39	2	2	0	14	71	60	23	22	25	63
—Kansas City (A.L.)	0	0	...	5.56	11	0	0	0	0	22 $\frac{2}{3}$	29	14	14	13	21
1987—New York (N.L.)■	5	6	.455	3.71	21	13	1	0	1	99 $\frac{1}{3}$	87	46	41	44	68
—Tidewater (I.L.)	0	1	.000	5.73	3	3	0	0	0	11	10	8	7	6	7
1988—New York (N.L.)	20	3	*.870	2.22	35	28	8	4	0	231 $\frac{1}{3}$	178	67	57	80	213
1989—New York (N.L.)	14	8	.636	3.52	34	33	7	2	0	219 $\frac{2}{3}$	183	92	86	74	190
1990—New York (N.L.)	14	10	.583	3.23	31	30	6	2	0	211 $\frac{2}{3}$	177	84	76	65	*233
1991—New York (N.L.)	14	14	.500	3.29	34	34	5	2	0	232 $\frac{2}{3}$	204	95	85	73	*241
1992—New York (N.L.)	13	7	.650	2.88	27	27	7	•5	0	196 $\frac{2}{3}$	162	75	63	*82	214
—Toronto (A.L.)■	4	3	.571	2.55	8	7	0	0	0	53	39	16	15	29	47
1993—Kansas City (A.L.)■	11	14	.440	3.33	34	34	6	1	0	254	205	102	94	114	191
1994—Kansas City (A.L.)	16	5	.762	2.94	23	23	4	3	0	171 $\frac{2}{3}$	130	60	56	54	132
1995—Toronto (A.L.)■	9	6	.600	3.38	17	17	5	2	0	130 $\frac{1}{3}$	113	53	49	41	102
—New York (A.L.)■	9	2	.818	3.82	13	13	1	0	0	§99	82	42	42	47	89
1996—New York (A.L.)	7	2	.778	2.88	11	11	1	0	0	72	50	25	23	34	71
—Norwich (East.)	0	0	...	0.90	2	2	0	0	0	10	9	3	1	1	13
1997—New York (A.L.)	12	6	.667	2.82	29	29	1	0	0	195	155	67	61	86	222
1998—New York (A.L.)	•20	7	.741	3.55	31	31	3	0	0	207 $\frac{2}{3}$	186	89	82	59	209
1999—New York (A.L.)	12	9	.571	3.44	31	31	1	1	0	193 $\frac{1}{3}$	164	84	74	90	177
2000—New York (A.L.)	4	14	.222	6.91	30	29	0	0	0	155	192	124	119	82	120
2001—Sarasota (FSL)■	0	0	...	0.00	1	1	0	0	0	4	2	0	0	0	6
—Boston (A.L.)	9	7	.563	4.31	25	25	0	0	0	135 $\frac{2}{3}$	148	74	65	57	115
A.L. totals (11 years)	113	75	.601	3.70	263	250	22	7	0	1689 $\frac{1}{3}$	1493	750	694	706	1496
N.L. totals (6 years)	80	48	.625	3.08	182	165	34	15	1	1191 $\frac{1}{3}$	991	459	408	418	1159
Major League totals (16 years)	193	123	.611	3.44	445	415	56	22	1	2880 $\frac{2}{3}$	2484	1209	1102	1124	2655

DIVISION SERIES RECORD

Year League	W	L	Pct.	ERA	G	GS	CG	ShO	Sv.	IP	H	R	ER	BB	SO
1995—New York (A.L.)	1	0	1.000	4.60	2	2	0	0	0	15 $\frac{2}{3}$	15	8	8	9	14
1996—New York (A.L.)	0	1	.000	9.00	1	1	0	0	0	6	8	6	6	2	8
1997—New York (A.L.)	0	0	...	16.20	1	1	0	0	0	3 $\frac{1}{3}$	7	6	6	2	2
1998—New York (A.L.)	1	0	1.000	0.00	1	1	0	0	0	5 $\frac{2}{3}$	2	0	0	1	6
1999—New York (A.L.)							Did not play.								
Division series totals (4 years)	2	1	.667	5.87	5	5	0	0	0	30 $\frac{2}{3}$	32	20	20	14	30

CHAMPIONSHIP SERIES RECORD

Year League	W	L	Pct.	ERA	G	GS	CG	ShO	Sv.	IP	H	R	ER	BB	SO
1988—New York (N.L.)	1	1	.500	4.50	3	2	1	0	0	12	10	6	6	5	9
1992—Toronto (A.L.)	1	1	.500	3.00	2	2	0	0	0	12	11	7	4	5	9
1996—New York (A.L.)	0	0	...	3.00	1	1	0	0	0	6	5	2	2	5	5
1998—New York (A.L.)	1	0	1.000	4.15	2	2	0	0	0	13	12	6	6	6	13
1999—New York (A.L.)	1	0	1.000	2.57	1	1	0	0	0	7	7	2	2	3	9
2000—New York (A.L.)	0	0	...	0.00	1	0	0	0	0	1	0	0	0	3	0
Champ. series totals (6 years)	4	2	.667	3.53	10	8	1	0	0	51	45	23	20	24	45

WORLD SERIES RECORD

NOTES: Member of World Series championship team (1992, 1996, 1998, 1999 and 2000).

Year League	W	L	Pct.	ERA	G	GS	CG	ShO	Sv.	IP	H	R	ER	BB	SO
1992—Toronto (A.L.)	0	0	...	3.48	2	2	0	0	0	10 $\frac{1}{3}$	9	5	4	8	8
1996—New York (A.L.)	1	0	1.000	1.50	1	1	0	0	0	6	4	1	1	4	3
1998—New York (A.L.)	0	0	...	3.00	1	1	0	0	0	6	2	3	2	3	4
1999—New York (A.L.)	1	0	1.000	0.00	1	1	0	0	0	7	1	0	0	5	4
2000—New York (A.L.)	0	0	...	0.00	1	0	0	0	0	$\frac{1}{3}$	0	0	0	0	0
World Series totals (5 years)	2	0	1.000	2.12	6	5	0	0	0	29 $\frac{2}{3}$	16	9	7	20	19

ALL-STAR GAME RECORD

Year League	W	L	Pct.	ERA	GS	CG	ShO	Sv.	IP	H	R	ER	BB	SO
1988—National	0	0	...	0.00	0	0	0	0	1	0	0	0	0	1
1992—National	0	0	...	0.00	0	0	0	0	1	0	0	0	0	1
1994—American	0	0	...	13.50	0	0	0	0	2	4	3	3	0	3
1997—American	0	0	...	0.00	0	0	0	0	1	0	0	0	2	0
1999—American	0	0	...	4.50	0	0	0	0	2	4	1	1	1	3
All-Star Game totals (5 years)	0	0	...	5.14	0	0	0	0	7	8	4	4	3	8

C

CONINE, JEFF — 1B/OF — ORIOLES

PERSONAL: Born June 27, 1966, in Tacoma, Wash. ... 6-1/220. ... Bats right, throws right. ... Full name: Jeffrey Guy Conine.
HIGH SCHOOL: Eisenhower (Rialto, Calif.).
COLLEGE: UCLA.
TRANSACTIONS/CAREER NOTES: Selected by Kansas City Royals organization in 58th round of free-agent draft (June 2, 1987). ... On disabled list (June 28, 1991-remainder of season). ... Selected by Florida Marlins in first round (22nd pick overall) of expansion draft (November 17, 1992). ... Traded by Marlins to Royals for P Blaine Mull (November 20, 1997). ... On Kansas City disabled list (March 25-May 5 and July

27-August 19, 1998); included rehabilitation assignment to Omaha (August 17-19). ... Traded by Royals to Baltimore Orioles for P Chris Fussell (April 2, 1999). ... Granted free agency (November 5, 1999). ... Re-signed by Orioles (December 15, 1999).

RECORDS: Shares major league rookie-season record for most games—162 (1993).

HONORS: Named Southern League Most Valuable Player (1990).

STATISTICAL NOTES: Led Southern League first basemen with 1,164 putouts, 95 assists, 22 errors, 1,281 total chances and 108 double plays in 1990. ... Led N.L. with 12 sacrifice flies in 1995. ... Career major league grand slams: 5.

MISCELLANEOUS: Holds Florida Marlins all-time records for most hits (737) and runs batted in (422).

| | | | | | | | BATTING | | | | | | | | FIELDING | | |
Year Team (League)	Pos.	G	AB	R	H	2B	3B	HR	RBI	Avg.	BB	SO	SB	PO	A	E	Avg.
1988—Baseball City (FSL).....	1B-3B	118	415	63	113	23	9	10	59	.272	46	77	26	661	51	22	.970
1989—Baseball City (FSL).....	1B	113	425	68	116	12	7	14	60	.273	40	91	32	830	65	18	.980
1990—Memphis (Sou.).........	1B-3B	137	487	89	156	37	8	15	95	.320	94	88	21	†1164	†95	†22	.983
—Kansas City (A.L.).....	1B	9	20	3	5	2	0	0	2	.250	2	5	0	39	4	1	.977
1991—Omaha (A.A.)............	1B-OF	51	171	23	44	9	1	3	15	.257	26	39	0	392	41	7	.984
1992—Omaha (A.A.)............	1B-OF	110	397	69	120	24	5	20	72	.302	54	67	4	845	60	6	.993
—Kansas City (A.L.).....	OF-1B	28	91	10	23	5	2	0	9	.253	8	23	0	75	3	0	1.000
1993—Florida (N.L.)■..........	OF-1B	*162	595	75	174	24	3	12	79	.292	52	135	2	403	25	2	.995
1994—Florida (N.L.)...........	OF-1B	115	451	60	144	27	6	18	82	.319	40	92	1	408	24	6	.986
1995—Florida (N.L.)...........	OF-1B	133	483	72	146	26	2	25	105	.302	66	94	2	292	18	6	.981
1996—Florida (N.L.)...........	OF-1B	157	597	84	175	32	2	26	95	.293	62	121	1	478	48	8	.985
1997—Florida (N.L.)...........	1B-OF	151	405	46	98	13	1	17	61	.242	57	89	2	897	104	8	.992
1998—Kansas City (A.L.)■...	OF-1B-DH	93	309	30	79	26	0	8	43	.256	26	68	3	235	7	1	.996
—Omaha (PCL)........	DH-OF	2	9	0	0	0	0	0	0	.000	0	3	0	2	0	0	1.000
1999—Baltimore (A.L.)■.......	1-DH-O-3	139	444	54	129	31	1	13	75	.291	30	40	0	848	53	7	.992
2000—Baltimore (A.L.).........	3-1-DH-O	119	409	53	116	20	2	13	46	.284	36	53	4	363	108	15	.969
2001—Baltimore (A.L.).........	1B-OF-3B-DH	139	524	75	163	23	2	14	97	.311	64	75	12	746	71	4	.995
American League totals (6 years)		527	1797	225	515	107	7	48	272	.287	166	264	19	2306	246	28	.989
National League totals (5 years)		718	2531	337	737	122	14	98	422	.291	277	531	8	2478	219	30	.989
Major League totals (11 years)		1245	4328	562	1252	229	21	146	694	.289	443	795	27	4784	465	58	.989

DIVISION SERIES RECORD

| | | | | | | | BATTING | | | | | | | | FIELDING | | |
Year Team (League)	Pos.	G	AB	R	H	2B	3B	HR	RBI	Avg.	BB	SO	SB	PO	A	E	Avg.
1997—Florida (N.L.)..............	1B	3	11	3	4	1	0	0	0	.364	1	0	0	24	3	1	.964

CHAMPIONSHIP SERIES RECORD

| | | | | | | | BATTING | | | | | | | | FIELDING | | |
Year Team (League)	Pos.	G	AB	R	H	2B	3B	HR	RBI	Avg.	BB	SO	SB	PO	A	E	Avg.
1997—Florida (N.L.)..............	1B	6	18	1	2	0	0	0	1	.111	1	4	0	34	5	0	1.000

NOTES: Member of World Series championship team (1997).

WORLD SERIES RECORD

| | | | | | | | BATTING | | | | | | | | FIELDING | | |
Year Team (League)	Pos.	G	AB	R	H	2B	3B	HR	RBI	Avg.	BB	SO	SB	PO	A	E	Avg.
1997—Florida (N.L.)..............	1B-PH	6	13	1	3	0	0	0	2	.231	0	0	0	30	2	0	1.000

NOTES: Hit home run in first at-bat (July 11, 1995). ... Named Most Valuable Player (1995).

ALL-STAR GAME RECORD

| | | | | | | BATTING | | | | | | | FIELDING | | |
Year League	Pos.	AB	R	H	2B	3B	HR	RBI	Avg.	BB	SO	SB	PO	A	E	Avg.
1994—National.....................							Did not play.									
1995—National....................	PH	1	1	1	0	0	1	1	1.000	0	0	0	...	...	...	...

CONTI, JASON — OF — DEVIL RAYS

PERSONAL: Born January 27, 1975, in Pittsburgh. ... 5-11/180. ... Bats left, throws right. ... Full name: Stanley Jason Conti.

HIGH SCHOOL: Seneca Valley (Harmony, Pa.).

COLLEGE: Pittsburgh.

TRANSACTIONS/CAREER NOTES: Selected by Arizona Diamondbacks organization in 32nd round of free-agent draft (June 4, 1996). ... Loaned by Diamondbacks to Tulsa, Texas Rangers organization (April 1-September 14, 1998). ... Traded by Diamondbacks with P Nick Bierbrodt to Tampa Bay Devil Rays for P Albie Lopez and C Mike Difelice (July 25, 2001).

STATISTICAL NOTES: Tied for Midwest League lead in double plays by outfielder with six in 1997. ... Led Pacific Coast League outfielders with 303 total chances in 1999.

| | | | | | | | BATTING | | | | | | | | FIELDING | | |
Year Team (League)	Pos.	G	AB	R	H	2B	3B	HR	RBI	Avg.	BB	SO	SB	PO	A	E	Avg.
1996—Lethbridge (Pio.)........	OF	63	226	63	83	15	1	4	49	.367	30	29	30	80	5	4	.955
1997—South Bend (Midw.)...	OF	117	458	78	142	22	10	3	43	.310	45	99	30	240	13	5	.981
—High Desert (Calif.).....	OF	14	59	15	21	5	1	2	8	.356	10	12	1	27	2	5	.853
1998—Tulsa (Texas)■..........	OF	130	530	*125	167	31	12	15	67	.315	63	96	19	183	*20	5	.976
1999—Tucson (PCL)■.........	OF	133	520	100	151	23	8	9	57	.290	55	89	22	278	17	8	.974
2000—Tucson (PCL)..........	OF	93	383	75	117	20	5	11	57	.305	23	57	11	186	6	10	.950
—Arizona (N.L.)............	OF	47	91	11	21	4	3	1	15	.231	7	30	3	53	4	1	.983
2001—Tucson (PCL)	OF	92	362	68	120	23	6	9	52	.331	33	54	2	205	5	2	.991
—Arizona (N.L.)............	OF	5	4	1	1	0	0	0	0	.250	1	2	0	0	0	0	...
—Durham (I.L.)■.........	OF	38	157	24	48	12	0	5	18	.306	9	31	3	71	7	1	.987
Major League totals (2 years)		52	95	12	22	4	3	1	15	.232	8	32	3	53	4	1	.983

COOK, AARON　　　　　P　　　　　ROCKIES

PERSONAL: Born February 8, 1979, in Fort Campbell, Ky. ... 6-3/175. ... Throws right, bats right. ... Full name: Aaron Lane Cook.
HIGH SCHOOL: Hamilton (Ohio).
TRANSACTIONS/CAREER NOTES: Selected by Colorado Rockies organization in second round of free-agent draft (June 3, 1997).

Year	League	W	L	Pct.	ERA	G	GS	CG	ShO	Sv.	IP	H	R	ER	BB	SO
1997—	Arizona Rockies (Ariz.)	1	3	.250	3.13	9	8	0	0	0	46	48	27	16	17	35
1998—	Portland (N'West)	5	8	.385	4.88	15	15	•1	0	0	79 1/3	87	50	43	39	38
1999—	Asheville (S.Atl.)	4	12	.250	6.44	25	25	2	0	0	121 2/3	157	•99	87	42	73
2000—	Asheville (S.Atl.)	10	7	.588	2.96	21	21	4	•2	0	142 2/3	130	54	47	23	118
—	Salem (Caro.)	1	6	.143	5.44	7	7	1	0	0	43	52	33	26	12	37
2001—	Salem (Caro.)	11	11	.500	3.08	27	27	0	0	0	155	157	73	53	38	122

COOK, DENNIS　　　　　P　　　　　ANGELS

PERSONAL: Born October 4, 1962, in Lamarque, Texas. ... 6-3/190. ... Throws left, bats left. ... Full name: Dennis Bryan Cook.
HIGH SCHOOL: Dickinson (Texas).
JUNIOR COLLEGE: Angelina College (Texas).
COLLEGE: Texas.
TRANSACTIONS/CAREER NOTES: Selected by San Diego Padres organization in sixth round of free-agent draft (January 11, 1983); did not sign. ... Selected by San Francisco Giants organization in 18th round of free-agent draft (June 3, 1985). ... Traded by Giants with P Terry Mulholland and 3B Charlie Hayes to Philadelphia Phillies for P Steve Bedrosian and a player to be named later (June, 18, 1989); Giants acquired IF Rick Parker to complete deal (August 7, 1989). ... Traded by Phillies to Los Angeles Dodgers for C Darrin Fletcher (September 13, 1990). ... Traded by Dodgers with P Mike Christopher to Cleveland Indians for P Rudy Seanez (December 10, 1991). ... Granted free agency (October 15, 1993). ... Signed by Chicago White Sox organization (January 5, 1994). ... Claimed on waivers by Indians (October 17, 1994). ... Traded by Indians to Texas Rangers for SS Guillermo Mercedes (June 22, 1995). ... Granted free agency (October 29, 1996). ... Signed by Florida Marlins (December 10, 1996). ... On suspended list (July 4-5, 1997). ... Traded by Marlins to New York Mets for OF Fletcher Bates and P Scott Comer (December 18, 1997). ... Granted free agency (October 23, 1998). ... Re-signed by Mets (November 18, 1998). ... Traded by Mets with P Turk Wendell to Phillies for P Bruce Chen and P Adam Walker (July 27, 2001). ... On Philadelphia disabled list (July 30-August 14, 2001); included rehabilitation assignment to Scranton (August 13-14). ... Granted free agency (November 5, 2001). ... Signed by Anaheim Angels (December 19, 2001).
HONORS: Named Texas League Pitcher of the Year (1987).
STATISTICAL NOTES: Led A.L. with five balks in 1992.
MISCELLANEOUS: Appeared in one game as pinch runner with Philadelphia (1989). ... Singled once and scored once in five games as pinch hitter and appeared in one game as pinch runner with Philadelphia (1990). ... Appeared in one game as pinch runner (1997). ... Singled twice, scored once and had an RBI in two games as pinch hitter (1997).

Year	League	W	L	Pct.	ERA	G	GS	CG	ShO	Sv.	IP	H	R	ER	BB	SO
1985—	Clinton (Midw.)	5	4	.556	3.36	13	13	1	0	0	83	73	35	31	27	40
1986—	Fresno (Calif.)	12	7	.632	3.97	27	25	2	1	1	170	141	92	75	100	*173
1987—	Shreveport (Texas)	9	2	.818	2.13	16	16	1	1	0	105 2/3	94	32	25	20	98
—	Phoenix (PCL)	2	5	.286	5.23	12	11	1	0	0	62	72	45	36	26	24
1988—	Phoenix (PCL)	11	9	.550	3.88	26	25	5	1	0	141 1/3	138	73	61	51	110
—	San Francisco (N.L.)	2	1	.667	2.86	4	4	1	1	0	22	9	8	7	11	13
1989—	Phoenix (PCL)	7	4	.636	3.12	12	12	3	1	0	78	73	29	27	19	85
—	San Francisco (N.L.)	1	0	1.000	1.80	2	2	1	0	0	15	13	3	3	5	9
—	Philadelphia (N.L.)■	6	8	.429	3.99	21	16	1	1	0	106	97	56	47	33	58
1990—	Philadelphia (N.L.)	8	3	.727	3.56	42	13	2	1	1	141 2/3	132	61	56	54	58
—	Los Angeles (N.L.)■	1	1	.500	7.53	5	3	0	0	0	14 1/3	23	13	12	2	6
1991—	Albuquerque (PCL)	7	3	.700	3.63	14	14	1	0	0	91 2/3	73	46	37	32	84
—	Los Angeles (N.L.)	1	0	1.000	0.51	20	1	0	0	0	17 2/3	12	3	1	7	8
—	San Antonio (Texas)	1	3	.250	2.49	7	7	1	0	0	50 2/3	43	20	14	10	45
1992—	Cleveland (A.L.)■	5	7	.417	3.82	32	25	1	0	0	158	156	79	67	50	96
1993—	Cleveland (A.L.)	5	5	.500	5.67	25	6	0	0	0	54	62	36	34	16	34
—	Charlotte (I.L.)	3	2	.600	5.06	12	6	0	0	0	42 2/3	46	26	24	6	40
1994—	Chicago (A.L.)■	3	1	.750	3.55	38	0	0	0	0	33	29	17	13	14	26
1995—	Cleveland (A.L.)■	0	0	...	6.39	11	0	0	0	0	12 2/3	16	9	9	10	13
—	Texas (A.L.)■	0	2	.000	4.00	35	1	0	0	2	45	47	23	20	16	40
1996—	Texas (A.L.)	5	2	.714	4.09	60	0	0	0	0	70 1/3	53	34	32	35	64
1997—	Florida (N.L.)■	1	2	.333	3.90	59	0	0	0	0	62 1/3	64	28	27	28	63
1998—	New York (N.L.)■	8	4	.667	2.38	73	0	0	0	1	68	60	21	18	27	79
1999—	New York (N.L.)	10	5	.667	3.86	71	0	0	0	3	63	50	27	27	27	68
2000—	New York (N.L.)	6	3	.667	5.34	68	0	0	0	2	59	63	35	35	31	53
2001—	New York (N.L.)	1	1	.500	4.25	43	0	0	0	0	36	28	18	17	10	34
—	Philadelphia (N.L.)■	0	0	...	5.59	19	0	0	0	0	9 2/3	15	6	6	4	4
—	Scranton/W.B. (I.L.)	0	0	...	9.00	1	1	0	0	0	1	1	1	1	2	1
A.L. totals (5 years)		18	17	.514	4.22	201	32	1	0	2	373	363	198	175	141	273
N.L. totals (9 years)		45	28	.616	3.75	427	39	5	3	7	614 2/3	566	279	256	239	453
Major League totals (14 years)		63	45	.583	3.93	628	71	6	3	9	987 2/3	929	477	431	380	726

DIVISION SERIES RECORD

Year	League	W	L	Pct.	ERA	G	GS	CG	ShO	Sv.	IP	H	R	ER	BB	SO
1996—	Texas (A.L.)	0	0	...	0.00	2	0	0	0	0	1 1/3	0	0	0	1	0
1997—	Florida (N.L.)	1	0	1.000	0.00	2	0	0	0	0	3	0	0	0	1	3
1999—	New York (N.L.)	0	0	...	0.00	1	0	0	0	0	1 2/3	1	0	0	1	1
2000—	New York (N.L.)	0	0	...	0.00	2	0	0	0	0	1 1/3	0	0	0	2	1
Division series totals (4 years)		1	0	1.000	0.00	7	0	0	0	0	7 1/3	1	0	0	5	5

CHAMPIONSHIP SERIES RECORD

Year	League	W	L	Pct.	ERA	G	GS	CG	ShO	Sv.	IP	H	R	ER	BB	SO
1997—	Florida (N.L.)	0	0	...	0.00	2	0	0	0	0	2 1/3	0	0	0	0	2
1999—	New York (N.L.)	0	0	...	0.00	3	0	0	0	0	1 1/3	1	0	0	2	1
2000—	New York (N.L.)	0	0	...	0.00	1	0	0	0	0	1	1	0	0	0	2
Champ. series totals (3 years)		0	0	...	0.00	6	0	0	0	0	4 2/3	2	0	0	2	5

WORLD SERIES RECORD

NOTES: Member of World Series championship team (1997).

Year	League	W	L	Pct.	ERA	G	GS	CG	ShO	Sv.	IP	H	R	ER	BB	SO
1997—	Florida (N.L.)	1	0	1.000	0.00	3	0	0	0	0	$3\frac{2}{3}$	1	0	0	1	5
2000—	New York (N.L.)	0	0	...	0.00	3	0	0	0	0	$\frac{2}{3}$	1	0	0	3	1
World Series totals (2 years)		**1**	**0**	**1.000**	**0.00**	**6**	**0**	**0**	**0**	**0**	**$4\frac{1}{3}$**	**2**	**0**	**0**	**4**	**6**

COOLBAUGH, MIKE   3B   CARDINALS

PERSONAL: Born June 5, 1972, in Binghamton, N.Y. ... 6-1/185. ... Bats right, throws right. ... Full name: Michael Robert Coolbaugh. ... Brother of Scott Coolbaugh, third baseman with Texas Rangers (1989-1990), San Diego Padres (1991) and St. Louis Cardinals (1994).

HIGH SCHOOL: Theodore Roosevelt (San Antonio).

TRANSACTIONS/CAREER NOTES: Selected by Toronto Blue Jays organization in 16th round of free-agent draft (June 4, 1990). ... On disabled list (June 23-August 21, 1993). ... Selected by Texas Rangers organization from Blue Jays organization in Rule 5 minor league draft (December 4, 1996). ... Granted free agency (October 18, 1996). ... Signed by Oakland Athletics organization (November 4, 1996). ... Granted free agency (October 17, 1997). ... Signed by Colorado Rockies organization prior to 1998 season. ... On Colorado Springs disabled list (April 18-May 5 and July 23-31, 1998). ... Granted free agency (October 16, 1998). ... Signed by New York Yankees (November 17, 1998). ... Granted free agency (October 15, 1999). ... Re-signed by Yankees organization (October 22, 1999). ... Granted free agency (October 18, 2000). ... Signed by Milwaukee Brewers organization (July 23, 2001). ... Granted free agency (October 15, 2001). ... Signed by St. Louis Cardinals organization (November 21, 2001).

STATISTICAL NOTES: Led Southern League with 303 total bases in 1997. ... Led Southern League third basemen with .943 fielding percentage, 94 putouts, 302 assists, 420 total chances and 35 double plays in 1997.

							BATTING							FIELDING			
Year	Team (League)	Pos.	G	AB	R	H	2B	3B	HR	RBI	Avg.	BB	SO	SB	PO	A	E	Avg.
1990—	Medicine Hat (Pio.)	SS-2B-3B	58	211	21	40	9	0	2	16	.190	13	47	3	77	136	33	.866
1991—	St. Catharines (NY-P)	.1B-2B-3B-OF	71	256	28	59	13	2	3	25	.230	17	40	4	461	75	12	.978
1992—	St. Catharines (NY-P)	3B-OF	15	49	3	14	1	1	0	2	.286	3	12	0	16	16	4	.889
1993—	Hagerstown (S.Atl.)	.2B-3B-1B-OF	112	389	58	95	23	1	16	62	.244	32	94	4	213	173	17	.958
1994—	Dunedin (FSL)	3-S-OF-1-2	122	456	53	120	33	3	16	66	.263	28	94	3	85	293	22	.945
1995—	Knoxville (Sou.)	3-1-2-0	•142	500	71	120	32	2	9	56	.240	37	110	7	159	296	25	.948
1996—	Charlotte (FSL)■	S-1-3-0-P	124	449	76	129	33	4	15	75	.287	42	80	8	366	180	22	.961
	Tulsa (Texas)	2B-1B	7	23	6	8	3	0	2	9	.348	2	3	1	31	23	0	1.000
1997—	Huntsville (Sou.)	3B-SS-2B	*139	*559	100	172	37	2	•30	*132	.308	52	105	8	†106	†330	26	†.944
1998—	Colo. Springs (PCL)■	3B-1B-2B-OF	108	386	62	107	35	2	16	75	.277	32	93	0	187	186	26	.935
1999—	Columbus (I.L.)■	3B-OF-1B-DH	114	391	65	108	31	2	15	66	.276	38	112	5	188	111	21	.934
2000—	Columbus (I.L.)	S-2-OF-3-1	117	387	63	105	28	0	23	61	.271	67	96	6	233	246	17	.966
2001—	Indianapolis (I.L.)■	3B-SS	94	347	49	93	24	3	10	50	.268	39	92	3	99	241	14	.960
	Milwaukee (N.L.)	3B-SS	39	70	10	14	6	0	2	7	.200	5	16	0	13	28	1	.976
Major League totals (1 year)			39	70	10	14	6	0	2	7	.200	5	16	0	13	28	1	.976

RECORD AS PITCHER

Year	League	W	L	Pct.	ERA	G	GS	CG	ShO	Sv.	IP	H	R	ER	BB	SO
1986—	Charlotte (FSL)	0	0	...	36.00	1	0	0	0	0	1	5	4	4	0	2

COOMER, RON   1B

PERSONAL: Born November 18, 1966, in Chicago. ... 5-11/206. ... Bats right, throws right. ... Full name: Ronald Bryan Coomer.

HIGH SCHOOL: Lockport (Ill.).

JUNIOR COLLEGE: Taft (Calif.) Junior College.

TRANSACTIONS/CAREER NOTES: Selected by Oakland Athletics organization in 14th round of free-agent draft (June 2, 1987). ... Released by A's (August 1, 1990). ... Signed by Chicago White Sox organization (March 18, 1991). ... On disabled list (June 5-19, 1992). ... On Birmingham disabled list (June 12-21, 1993). ... Traded by White Sox to Los Angeles Dodgers for P Isidro Martinez (December 27, 1993). ... Traded by Dodgers with P Greg Hansell, P Jose Parra and a player to be named later to Minnesota Twins for P Kevin Tapani and P Mark Guthrie (July 31, 1995); Twins acquired OF Chris Latham to complete deal (October 30, 1995). ... Granted free agency (December 21, 2000). ... Signed by Chicago Cubs (January 10, 2001). ... On Chicago disabled list (April 3-25, 2001); included rehabilitation assignment to Iowa (April 21-25). ... Granted free agency (November 7, 2001).

STATISTICAL NOTES: Led Southern League with eight sacrifice flies and tied for lead in grounding into double plays with 21 in 1991. ... Led Southern League third basemen with 94 putouts, 396 total chances, 24 double plays and tied for lead with 26 errors in 1991. ... Led Pacific Coast League with 293 total bases in 1994. ... Led Pacific Coast League third basemen with .952 fielding percentage, 399 total chances and 299 assists in 1994. ... Tied for A.L. lead in grounding into double plays with 22 in 1998. ... Career major league grand slams: 1.

							BATTING							FIELDING			
Year	Team (League)	Pos.	G	AB	R	H	2B	3B	HR	RBI	Avg.	BB	SO	SB	PO	A	E	Avg.
1987—	Medford (N'West)	3B-1B	45	168	23	58	10	2	1	26	.345	19	22	1	54	78	11	.923
1988—	Modesto (Calif.)	3B-1B	131	495	67	138	23	2	17	85	.279	60	88	2	78	105	16	.920
1989—	Madison (Midw.)	3B-1B	61	216	28	69	15	0	4	28	.319	30	34	0	67	64	6	.956
1990—	Huntsville (Sou.)	2B-1B-3B	66	194	22	43	7	0	3	27	.222	21	40	3	200	100	11	.965
1991—	Birmingham (Sou.)■	3B-1B	137	505	*81	129	27	5	13	76	.255	59	78	0	†113	278	‡26	.938
1992—	Vancouver (PCL)	3B	86	262	29	62	10	0	9	40	.237	16	36	3	49	115	13	.927
1993—	Birmingham (Sou.)	3B-1B	69	262	44	85	18	0	13	50	.324	15	43	1	43	106	11	.931
	Nashville (A.A.)	3B	59	211	34	66	14	0	13	51	.313	10	29	1	30	107	16	.895
1994—	Albuquerque (PCL)■	3B-DH-2B	127	535	89	181	34	6	22	*123	.338	26	62	4	81	†299	19	†.952
1995—	Albuquerque (PCL)	3B-1B-DH	85	323	54	104	23	2	16	76	.322	18	28	5	335	93	9	.979
	Minnesota (A.L.)■	1-3-DH-O	37	101	15	26	3	1	5	19	.257	9	11	0	138	32	2	.988
1996—	Minnesota (A.L.)	1-O-3-DH	95	233	34	69	12	1	12	41	.296	17	24	3	275	42	4	.988
1997—	Minnesota (A.L.)	3-1-DH-O	140	523	63	156	30	2	13	85	.298	22	91	4	123	223	11	.969
1998—	Minnesota (A.L.)	3-1-DH-O	137	529	54	146	22	1	15	72	.276	18	72	2	428	150	6	.990
1999—	Minnesota (A.L.)	1-3-DH-O	127	467	53	123	25	1	16	65	.263	30	69	2	542	148	6	.991
2000—	Minnesota (A.L.)	1B-DH-3B	140	544	64	147	29	1	16	82	.270	36	50	2	1023	82	5	.995

Year	Team (League)	Pos.	G	AB	R	H	2B	3B	HR	RBI	Avg.	BB	SO	SB	PO	A	E	Avg.
2001—Chicago (N.L.)■		3B-1B-DH	111	349	25	91	19	1	8	53	.261	29	70	0	179	114	7	.977
—Iowa (PCL)		1B-3B	4	12	0	4	0	0	0	0	.333	1	3	0	10	4	0	1.000
American League totals (6 years)			676	2397	283	667	121	7	77	364	.278	132	317	13	2529	677	34	.990
National League totals (1 year)			111	349	25	91	19	1	8	53	.261	29	70	0	179	114	7	.977
Major League totals (7 years)			787	2746	308	758	140	8	85	417	.276	161	387	13	2708	791	41	.988

(Header spanning: BATTING covers AB–SB; FIELDING covers PO–Avg.)

ALL-STAR GAME RECORD

Year	League	Pos.	AB	R	H	2B	3B	HR	RBI	Avg.	BB	SO	SB	PO	A	E	Avg.
1999—American		1B	1	0	0	0	0	0	0	.000	0	1	0	4	0	0	1.000

(Header spanning: BATTING covers AB–SB; FIELDING covers PO–Avg.)

COOPER, BRIAN — P — BLUE JAYS

PERSONAL: Born October 22, 1976, in North Hollywood, Calif. ... 6-1/185. ... Throws right, bats right. ... Full name: Brian John Cooper.
HIGH SCHOOL: Glendora (Calif.).
COLLEGE: Southern California.
TRANSACTIONS/CAREER NOTES: Selected by California Angels organization in fourth round of free-agent draft (June 1, 1995). ... Angels franchise renamed Anaheim Angels for 1997 season. ... On Salt Lake disabled list (June 24-July 2, 2001). ... Traded by Angels to Toronto Blue Jays for DH/1B Brad Fullmer (January 17, 2002).
STATISTICAL NOTES: Led Texas League with 35 home runs allowed in 1998.

Year	League	W	L	Pct.	ERA	G	GS	CG	ShO	Sv.	IP	H	R	ER	BB	SO
1995—Boise (N'West)		3	2	.600	3.92	13	11	0	0	1	62	60	31	27	22	66
1996—Lake Elsinore (Calif.)		7	9	.438	4.21	26	23	1	1	0	162 1/3	177	100	76	39	155
1997—Lake Elsinore (Calif.)		7	3	.700	3.54	17	17	1	0	0	117	111	56	46	27	104
1998—Midland (Texas)		8	10	.444	7.13	32	24	5	0	1	161 2/3	*215	*138	*128	59	*141
1999—Erie (East.)		10	5	.667	3.30	22	22	*6	0	0	158	146	61	58	29	143
—Edmonton (PCL)		2	1	.667	3.77	5	5	0	0	0	31	30	17	13	10	32
—Anaheim (A.L.)		1	1	.500	4.88	5	5	0	0	0	27 2/3	23	15	15	18	15
2000—Edmonton (PCL)		3	7	.300	7.23	11	11	1	1	0	61	87	51	49	18	37
—Anaheim (A.L.)		4	8	.333	5.90	15	15	1	1	0	87	105	66	57	35	36
—Lake Elsinore (Calif.)		0	0	...	0.00	1	1	0	0	0	7	4	1	0	2	3
2001—Salt Lake (PCL)		12	8	.600	4.63	28	28	1	0	0	173	181	98	89	58	109
—Anaheim (A.L.)		0	1	.000	2.63	7	1	0	0	0	13 2/3	10	5	4	4	7
Major League totals (3 years)		5	10	.333	5.33	27	21	1	1	0	128 1/3	138	86	76	57	58

COPPINGER, ROCKY — P — ATHLETICS

PERSONAL: Born March 19, 1974, in El Paso, Texas. ... 6-5/250. ... Throws right, bats right. ... Full name: John Thomas Coppinger. ... Name pronounced COP-in-jer.
HIGH SCHOOL: Coronado (El Paso, Texas).
JUNIOR COLLEGE: Hills Junior College (Hillsboro, Texas).
TRANSACTIONS/CAREER NOTES: Selected by Baltimore Orioles in 17th round of free-agent draft (June 3, 1993). ... On Baltimore disabled list (March 31-April 15 and May 10, 1997-remainder of season); included rehabilitation assignments to Rochester (May 14-22), Gulf Coast Orioles (July 1-12) and Bowie (July 17-27). ... On Bowie disabled list (April 10-May 24, 1998). ... Traded by Orioles to Milwaukee Brewers for a player to be named later (July 17, 1999); Orioles acquired P Al Reyes to complete deal (July 21, 1999). ... On disabled list (March 28, 2000-entire season). ... Granted free agency (October 27, 2000). ... Re-signed by Brewers organization (October 30, 2000). ... On Indianapolis disabled list (April 5-May 8, 2001). ... Granted free agency (October 15, 2001). ... Signed by Oakland Athletics organization (November 7, 2001).

Year	League	W	L	Pct.	ERA	G	GS	CG	ShO	Sv.	IP	H	R	ER	BB	SO
1994—Bluefield (Appl.)		4	3	.571	2.45	14	13	0	0	0	73 1/3	51	24	20	40	88
1995—Frederick (Caro.)		7	1	.875	1.57	11	11	2	1	0	68 2/3	46	16	12	24	91
—Bowie (East.)		6	2	.750	2.69	13	13	2	2	0	83 2/3	58	33	25	43	62
—Rochester (I.L.)		3	0	1.000	1.04	5	5	0	0	0	34 2/3	23	5	4	17	19
1996—Rochester (I.L.)		6	4	.600	4.19	12	12	0	0	0	73	65	36	34	39	81
—Baltimore (A.L.)		10	6	.625	5.18	23	22	0	0	0	125	126	76	72	60	104
1997—Baltimore (A.L.)		1	1	.500	6.30	5	4	0	0	0	20	21	14	14	16	22
—Rochester (I.L.)		1	2	.333	5.52	3	3	0	0	0	14 2/3	16	10	9	11	9
—Gulf Coast Orioles (GCL)		0	0	...	1.80	3	3	0	0	0	10	7	3	2	0	13
—Bowie (East.)		1	1	.500	4.80	3	3	0	0	0	15	15	9	8	3	15
1998—Bowie (East.)■		2	2	.500	4.35	7	6	0	0	0	31	26	18	15	11	30
—Rochester (I.L.)		8	3	.727	3.50	14	13	1	0	0	87 1/3	80	38	34	43	64
—Baltimore (A.L.)		0	0	...	5.17	6	1	0	0	0	15 2/3	16	9	9	7	13
1999—Rochester (I.L.)		2	2	.500	3.66	5	5	0	0	0	32	28	13	13	12	37
—Baltimore (A.L.)		0	1	.000	8.31	11	2	0	0	0	21 2/3	25	21	20	19	17
—Milwaukee (N.L.)■		5	3	.625	3.68	29	0	0	0	0	36 2/3	35	16	15	23	39
2000—Milwaukee (N.L.)								Did not play.								
2001—Huntsville (Sou.)		2	0	1.000	2.12	16	0	0	0	4	29 2/3	28	9	7	11	24
—Indianapolis (I.L.)		6	1	.857	1.88	15	5	0	0	0	48	25	10	10	20	42
—Milwaukee (N.L.)		1	0	1.000	6.75	8	3	0	0	0	22 2/3	24	17	17	15	15
A.L. totals (4 years)		11	8	.579	5.68	45	29	0	0	0	182 1/3	188	120	115	102	156
N.L. totals (2 years)		6	3	.667	4.85	37	3	0	0	0	59 1/3	59	33	32	38	54
Major League totals (5 years)		17	11	.607	5.47	82	32	0	0	0	241 2/3	247	153	147	140	210

DIVISION SERIES RECORD

Year	League	W	L	Pct.	ERA	G	GS	CG	ShO	Sv.	IP	H	R	ER	BB	SO
1996—Baltimore (A.L.)								Did not play.								

CHAMPIONSHIP SERIES RECORD

Year	League	W	L	Pct.	ERA	G	GS	CG	ShO	Sv.	IP	H	R	ER	BB	SO
1996—Baltimore (A.L.)		0	1	.000	8.44	1	1	0	0	0	5 1/3	6	5	5	1	3

CORA, ALEX   SS   DODGERS

PERSONAL: Born October 18, 1975, in Caguas, Puerto Rico. ... 6-0/180. ... Bats left, throws right. ... Full name: Jose Alexander Cora. ... Brother of Joey Cora, second baseman with four major league teams (1987-98).
HIGH SCHOOL: Bautista (Caguas, Puerto Rico).
COLLEGE: Miami (Fla.).
TRANSACTIONS/CAREER NOTES: Selected by Los Angeles Dodgers organization in third round of free-agent draft (June 4, 1996). ... On Los Angeles disabled list (March 25-June 27, 1999); included rehabilitation assignment to Albuquerque (June 8-27).
STATISTICAL NOTES: Led Texas League shortstops with 629 total chances and 88 double plays in 1997.

							BATTING								FIELDING		
Year — Team (League)	Pos.	G	AB	R	H	2B	3B	HR	RBI	Avg.	BB	SO	SB	PO	A	E	Avg.
1996— Vero Beach (FSL)	SS-OF	61	214	26	55	5	4	0	26	.257	12	36	5	86	164	16	.940
1997— San Antonio (Texas)...	SS	127	448	52	105	20	4	3	48	.234	25	60	12	*197	*412	20	*.968
1998— Albuquerque (PCL).....	SS-2B	81	299	42	79	17	5	5	45	.264	15	38	10	126	270	18	.957
— Los Angeles (N.L.).....	SS-2B	29	33	1	4	0	1	0	0	.121	2	8	0	26	29	2	.965
1999— Albuquerque (PCL).....	SS-DH-2B	80	302	51	93	11	7	4	37	.308	12	37	9	134	234	12	.968
— Los Angeles (N.L.).....	SS-2B	11	30	2	5	1	0	0	3	.167	0	4	0	13	20	2	.943
2000— Albuquerque (PCL).....	SS	30	110	18	41	8	3	0	20	.373	7	10	5	74	90	7	.959
— Los Angeles (N.L.).....	SS-2B	109	353	39	84	18	6	4	32	.238	26	53	4	163	273	12	.973
2001— Los Angeles (N.L.).....	SS-2B	134	405	38	88	18	3	4	29	.217	31	58	0	179	329	20	.962
Major League totals (4 years)		283	821	80	181	37	10	8	64	.220	59	123	4	381	651	36	.966

CORDERO, FRANCISCO   P   RANGERS   C

PERSONAL: Born August 11, 1977, in Santo Domingo, Dominican Republic. ... 6-2/200. ... Throws right, bats right. ... Full name: Francisco Javier Cordero.
HIGH SCHOOL: Colegio Luz de Arroyo Hondo (Dominican Republic).
TRANSACTIONS/CAREER NOTES: Signed as non-drafted free agent by Detroit Tigers organization (June 18, 1994). ... On Jamestown disabled list (June 28, 1996-remainder of season). ... On Jacksonville disabled list (May 22-June 18 and June 26, 1998-remainder of season). ... Traded by Tigers with P Justin Thompson, OF Gabe Kapler, C Bill Haselman, 2B Frank Catalanotto and P Alan Webb to Texas Rangers for OF Juan Gonzalez, P Danny Patterson and C Gregg Zaun (November 2, 1999). ... On Texas disabled list (March 23-June 19 and June 26, 2001-remainder of season); included rehabilitation assignment to Oklahoma (May 21-June 19).
HONORS: Named Southern League Most Outstanding Pitcher (1999).

Year — League	W	L	Pct.	ERA	G	GS	CG	ShO	Sv.	IP	H	R	ER	BB	SO
1994— Dominican Tigers (DSL).....	4	3	.571	3.90	12	12	0	0	0	60	65	47	26	27	36
1995— Fayetteville (S.Atl.)	0	3	.000	6.30	4	4	0	0	0	20	26	16	14	12	19
— Jamestown (NY-Penn)	4	7	.364	5.22	15	14	0	0	0	88	96	62	51	37	54
1996— Fayetteville (S.Atl.)	0	0	...	2.57	2	1	0	0	0	7	2	2	2	6	7
— Jamestown (NY-Penn)	0	0	...	0.82	2	2	0	0	0	11	5	1	1	2	10
1997— West Michigan (Midw.).......	6	1	.857	0.99	50	0	0	0	*35	54 1/3	36	13	6	15	67
1998— Jacksonville (Sou.)............	1	1	.500	4.86	17	0	0	0	8	16 2/3	19	12	9	9	18
— Lakeland (FSL)	0	0	...	0.00	1	0	0	0	0	16 2/3	1	0	0	0	0
1999— Jacksonville (Sou.)............	4	1	.800	1.38	47	0	0	0	*27	52 1/3	35	9	8	22	58
— Detroit (A.L.)	2	2	.500	3.32	20	0	0	0	0	19	19	7	7	18	19
2000— Texas (A.L.)■..................	1	2	.333	5.35	56	0	0	0	0	77 1/3	87	51	46	48	49
— Oklahoma (PCL).................	0	0	...	4.15	3	0	0	0	1	4 1/3	7	3	2	3	5
2001— Oklahoma (PCL)................	0	1	.000	0.59	12	0	0	0	6	15 1/3	8	2	1	3	20
— Texas (A.L.)	0	1	.000	3.86	3	0	0	0	0	2 1/3	3	1	1	2	1
Major League totals (3 years)	3	5	.375	4.93	79	0	0	0	0	98 2/3	109	59	54	68	69

CORDERO, WIL   OF   INDIANS

PERSONAL: Born October 3, 1971, in Mayaguez, Puerto Rico. ... 6-2/200. ... Bats right, throws right. ... Full name: Wilfredo Nieva Cordero. ... Name pronounced cor-DARE-oh.
HIGH SCHOOL: Centro de Servicios Education de Mayaguez (Puerto Rico).
TRANSACTIONS/CAREER NOTES: Signed as non-drafted free agent by Montreal Expos organization (May 24, 1988). ... On Indianapolis disabled list (August 1, 1991-remainder of season; and May 12-June 11 and July 7-20, 1992). ... Traded by Expos with P Bryan Eversgerd to Boston Red Sox for P Rheal Cormier, 1B Ryan McGuire and P Shayne Bennett (January 10, 1996). ... On Boston disabled list (May 21-August 12, 1996; included rehabilitation assignments to Gulf Coast Red Sox (July 23-27) and Pawtucket (July 27-August 6). ... Released by Red Sox (September 28, 1997). ... Signed by Chicago White Sox (March 23, 1998). ... Granted free agency (November 3, 1998). ... Signed by Cleveland Indians (February 3, 1999). ... On Cleveland disabled list (June 9-September 8, 1999); included rehabilitation assignment to Akron (September 3-8). ... Granted free agency (October 29, 1999). ... Signed by Pittsburgh Pirates (December 14, 1999). ... Traded by Pirates to Indians for OF Alex Ramirez and IF Enrique Wilson (July 28, 2000). ... On suspended list (September 19-23, 2000). ... On disabled list (June 11-26, 2001).
HONORS: Named shortstop on THE SPORTING NEWS N.L. Silver Slugger team (1994).
STATISTICAL NOTES: Had 15-game hitting streak (April 29-May 23, 2000). ... Career major league grand slams: 2.

							BATTING								FIELDING		
Year — Team (League)	Pos.	G	AB	R	H	2B	3B	HR	RBI	Avg.	BB	SO	SB	PO	A	E	Avg.
1988— Jamestown (NY-P)......	SS	52	190	18	49	3	0	2	22	.258	15	44	3	82	159	31	.886
1989— W.P. Beach (FSL)........	SS	78	289	37	80	12	2	6	29	.277	33	58	2	121	224	29	.922
— Jacksonville (Sou.)........	SS	39	121	9	26	6	1	3	17	.215	12	33	1	62	93	7	.957
1990— Jacksonville (Sou.)......	SS	131	444	63	104	18	4	7	40	.234	56	122	9	179	349	41	.928
1991— Indianapolis (A.A.)......	SS	98	360	48	94	16	4	11	52	.261	26	89	9	157	287	27	.943
1992— Indianapolis (A.A.)......	SS	52	204	32	64	11	1	6	27	.314	24	54	6	75	146	12	.948
— Montreal (N.L.)............	SS-2B	45	126	17	38	4	1	2	8	.302	9	31	0	51	92	8	.947
1993— Montreal (N.L.)..........	SS-3B	138	475	56	118	32	2	10	58	.248	34	60	12	163	373	36	.937
1994— Montreal (N.L.)..........	SS	110	415	65	122	30	3	15	63	.294	41	62	16	124	316	22	.952
1995— Montreal (N.L.)..........	SS-OF	131	514	64	147	35	2	10	49	.286	36	88	9	168	281	22	.953

– 123 –

							BATTING							FIELDING			
Year	Team (League)	Pos.	G	AB	R	H	2B	3B	HR	RBI	Avg.	BB	SO	SB	PO	A	E	Avg.
1996—Boston (A.L.)■........	2B-DH-1B	59	198	29	57	14	0	3	37	.288	11	31	2	82	110	10	.950
—GC Red Sox (GCL)	DH-2B	3	10	1	3	0	0	1	3	.300	0	2	0	1	1	0	1.000
—Pawtucket (I.L.)	2B-DH	4	10	2	3	1	0	1	2	.300	2	3	0	2	6	0	1.000
1997—Boston (A.L.).............	OF-DH-2B	140	570	82	160	26	3	18	72	.281	31	122	1	248	11	2	.992
1998—Birmingham (Sou.)■ .	1B-DH	11	35	6	10	2	0	2	11	.286	7	3	0	81	9	1	.989
—Chicago (A.L.)	1B-OF	96	341	58	91	18	2	13	49	.267	22	66	2	713	66	7	.991
1999—Cleveland (A.L.)■......	OF-DH	54	194	35	58	15	0	8	32	.299	15	37	2	51	0	1	.981
—Akron (East.)	OF-DH	3	11	2	4	2	0	0	0	.364	0	3	0	0	0	0	...
2000—Pittsburgh (N.L.)■	OF-DH	89	348	46	98	24	3	16	51	.282	25	58	1	110	3	2	.983
—Cleveland (A.L.)■......	OF	38	148	18	39	11	2	0	17	.264	7	18	0	79	2	0	1.000
2001—Cleveland (A.L.)	OF-1B-DH	89	268	30	67	11	1	4	21	.250	22	50	0	225	11	2	.992
American League totals (6 years)		476	1719	252	472	95	8	46	228	.275	108	324	7	1398	200	22	.986
National League totals (5 years)		513	1878	248	523	125	11	53	229	.278	145	299	38	616	1065	90	.949
Major League totals (10 years)		989	3597	500	995	220	19	99	457	.277	253	623	45	2014	1265	112	.967

DIVISION SERIES RECORD

							BATTING							FIELDING			
Year	Team (League)	Pos.	G	AB	R	H	2B	3B	HR	RBI	Avg.	BB	SO	SB	PO	A	E	Avg.
1999—Cleveland (A.L.)	PH-DH-OF	3	9	3	5	0	0	1	2	.556	1	2	0	3	0	0	1.000
2001—Cleveland (A.L.)	PH-OF	1	1	0	0	0	0	0	0	.000	0	0	0	1	0	0	1.000
Division series totals (2 years)		4	10	3	5	0	0	1	2	.500	1	2	0	4	0	0	1.000

ALL-STAR GAME RECORD

						BATTING							FIELDING			
Year	League	Pos.	AB	R	H	2B	3B	HR	RBI	Avg.	BB	SO	SB	PO	A	E	Avg.
1994—National	SS	2	0	0	0	0	0	0	0	.000	0	0	0	1	1	0	1.000

CORDOVA, MARTY — OF — ORIOLES

PERSONAL: Born July 10, 1969, in Las Vegas. ... 6-0/206. ... Bats right, throws right. ... Full name: Martin Keevin Cordova.
HIGH SCHOOL: Bishop Gorman (Las Vegas).
JUNIOR COLLEGE: Orange Coast College (Calif.).
COLLEGE: UNLV.
TRANSACTIONS/CAREER NOTES: Selected by San Diego Padres organization in eighth round of free-agent draft (June 2, 1987); did not sign. ... Selected by Minnesota Twins organization in 10th round of free-agent draft (June 5, 1989). ... On Visalia disabled list (April 12-May 20, 1991). ... On Salt Lake disabled list (April 17-May 11, 1994). ... On Minnesota disabled list (April 11-May 26, 1997); included rehabilitation assignment to Salt Lake (May 20-26). ... On disabled list (April 27-May 12, 1998). ... Granted free agency (October 7, 1999). ... Signed by Boston Red Sox organization (January 19, 2000). ... Released by Red Sox (March 26, 2000). ... Signed by Toronto Blue Jays organization (March 27, 2000). ... Granted free agency (October 4, 2000). ... Signed by Cleveland Indians organization (December 20, 2000). ... Granted free agency (November 5, 2001). ... Signed by Baltimore Orioles (December 6, 2001).
HONORS: Named California League Most Valuable Player (1992). ... Named A.L. Rookie of the Year by Baseball Writers' Association of America (1995).
STATISTICAL NOTES: Led California League with 302 total bases and .589 slugging percentage and tied for lead in grounding into double plays with 20 in 1992. ... Had 23-game hitting streak (June 5-29, 1996). ... Had 22-game hitting streak (April 22-May 18, 2001). ... Career major league grand slams: 1.

							BATTING							FIELDING			
Year	Team (League)	Pos.	G	AB	R	H	2B	3B	HR	RBI	Avg.	BB	SO	SB	PO	A	E	Avg.
1989—Elizabethton (Appl.)....	OF-3B	38	148	32	42	2	3	8	29	.284	14	29	2	6	9	4	.789
1990—Kenosha (Midw.)........	OF	81	269	35	58	7	5	7	25	.216	28	73	6	87	5	5	.948
1991—Visalia (Calif.)	OF	71	189	31	40	6	1	7	19	.212	17	46	2	58	2	5	.923
1992—Visalia (Calif.)	OF	134	513	103	175	31	6	*28	*131	.341	76	99	13	173	10	3	.984
1993—Nashville (Sou.)..........	OF	138	508	83	127	30	5	19	77	.250	64	*153	10	209	7	2	*.991
1994—Salt Lake (PCL)	OF-DH	103	385	69	138	25	4	19	66	.358	39	63	17	187	13	8	.962
1995—Minnesota (A.L.)	OF	137	512	81	142	27	4	24	84	.277	52	111	20	345	12	5	.986
1996—Minnesota (A.L.)	OF	145	569	97	176	46	1	16	111	.309	53	96	11	328	9	3	.991
1997—Minnesota (A.L.)	OF-DH	103	378	44	93	18	4	15	51	.246	30	92	5	217	12	2	.991
—Salt Lake (PCL)	DH-OF	6	24	5	9	4	0	1	4	.375	2	3	1	3	0	1	.750
1998—Minnesota (A.L.)	OF-DH	119	438	52	111	20	2	10	69	.253	50	103	3	257	5	6	.978
1999—Minnesota (A.L.)	OF	124	425	62	121	28	3	14	70	.285	48	96	13	38	0	3	.927
2000—Toronto (A.L.)■..........	OF-DH	62	200	23	49	7	0	4	18	.245	18	35	2	55	1	1	.982
2001—Cleveland (A.L.)■.......	OF-DH	122	409	61	123	20	2	20	69	.301	23	81	0	200	8	2	.990
Major League totals (7 years)		812	2931	420	815	166	16	103	472	.278	274	614	55	1440	47	22	.985

DIVISION SERIES RECORD

							BATTING							FIELDING			
Year	Team (League)	Pos.	G	AB	R	H	2B	3B	HR	RBI	Avg.	BB	SO	SB	PO	A	E	Avg.
2001—Cleveland (A.L.)	OF	4	12	0	3	0	0	0	1	.250	0	5	0	5	0	0	1.000

COREY, MARK — P — METS

PERSONAL: Born November 16, 1974, in Coudersport, Pa. ... 6-3/210. ... Throws right, bats right. ... Full name: Mark Franklin Corey.
HIGH SCHOOL: Austin Area (Austin, Pa.).
COLLEGE: Edinboro.
TRANSACTIONS/CAREER NOTES: Selected by Cincinnati Reds organization in fourth round of free-agent draft (June 1, 1995). ... On disabled list (June 12, 1996-entire season). ... Traded by Reds to New York Mets for IF Ralph Millard (February 4, 1999).

Year	League	W	L	Pct.	ERA	G	GS	CG	ShO	Sv.	IP	H	R	ER	BB	SO
1995—	Princeton (Appl.)	1	1	.500	3.68	4	3	0	0	0	14²/₃	12	7	6	6	8
1996—						Did not play.										
1997—	Charleston, W.Va. (S.Atl.)	8	13	.381	4.57	26	26	1	0	0	136	169	87	69	42	97
1998—	Burlington (Midw.)	12	6	.667	2.44	20	20	•6	•2	0	140	125	55	38	36	109
—	Chattanooga (Sou.)	0	4	.000	8.20	6	6	0	0	0	26¹/₃	32	25	24	16	6
—	Indianapolis (I.L.)	0	1	.000	4.50	1	1	1	0	0	6	4	3	3	3	2
1999—	Binghamton (East.)■	7	13	.350	5.40	29	27	0	0	0	155	175	108	93	64	111
2000—	Binghamton (East.)	0	0	...	1.05	14	2	0	0	0	25²/₃	15	5	3	11	19
—	Norfolk (I.L.)	3	7	.300	6.79	20	11	0	0	1	63²/₃	80	52	48	29	43
2001—	Binghamton (East.)	1	2	.333	1.80	25	0	0	0	17	35	23	10	7	12	50
—	Norfolk (I.L.)	8	2	.800	1.47	28	0	0	0	10	36²/₃	24	7	6	22	42
—	New York (N.L.)	0	0	...	3.86	2	0	0	0	0	2¹/₃	3	1	1	2	1
Major League totals (1 year)		0	0	...	3.86	2	0	0	0	0	2¹/₃	3	1	1	2	1

CORMIER, RHEAL — P — PHILLIES

PERSONAL: Born April 23, 1967, in Moncton, New Brunswick. ... 5-10/187. ... Throws left, bats left. ... Full name: Rheal Paul Cormier. ... Name pronounced ree-AL COR-mee-AY.
HIGH SCHOOL: Polyvalente Louis J. Robichaud.
JUNIOR COLLEGE: Community College of Rhode Island.
TRANSACTIONS/CAREER NOTES: Selected by St. Louis Cardinals organization in sixth round of free-agent draft (June 6, 1988). ... On Louisville disabled list (April 10-29, 1991). ... On disabled list (August 12-September 7, 1993). ... On St. Louis disabled list (April 28-May 13 and May 21-August 3, 1994); included rehabilitation assignments to Arkansas (July 7-18) and Louisville (July 18-30). ... Traded by Cardinals with OF Mark Whiten to Boston Red Sox for 3B Scott Cooper, P Cory Bailey and a player to be named later (April 8, 1995). ... Traded by Red Sox with 1B Ryan McGuire and P Shayne Bennett to Montreal Expos for SS Wil Cordero and P Bryan Eversgerd (Jaury 10, 1996). ... On disabled list (August 26-September 10, 1996). ... Granted free agency (October 30, 1997). ... Signed by Cleveland Indians organization (December 18, 1997). ... On Buffalo disabled list (April 9-June 2, 1998). ... On Akron disabled list (June 18, 1998-remainder of season). ... Granted free agency (October 15, 1998). ... Signed by Red Sox organization (January 5, 1999). ... On suspended list (May 7-10, 1999). ... Granted free agency (November 1, 2000). ... Signed by Philadelphia Phillies (November 29, 2000). ... On Philadelphia disabled list (August 10-29, 2001); included rehabilitation assignment to Reading (August 27-29).
MISCELLANEOUS: Member of 1988 Canadian Olympic baseball team.

Year	League	W	L	Pct.	ERA	G	GS	CG	ShO	Sv.	IP	H	R	ER	BB	SO
1989—	St. Petersburg (FSL)	12	7	.632	2.23	26	26	4	1	0	169²/₃	141	63	42	33	122
1990—	Arkansas (Texas)	5	•12	.294	5.04	22	21	3	1	0	121¹/₃	133	81	68	30	102
—	Louisville (A.A.)	1	1	.500	2.25	4	4	0	0	0	24	18	8	6	3	9
1991—	Louisville (A.A.)	7	9	.438	4.23	21	21	3	*3	0	127²/₃	140	64	60	31	74
—	St. Louis (N.L.)	4	5	.444	4.12	11	10	2	0	0	67²/₃	74	35	31	8	38
1992—	Louisville (A.A.)	0	1	.000	6.75	1	1	0	0	0	4	8	4	3	0	1
—	St. Louis (N.L.)	10	10	.500	3.68	31	30	3	0	0	186	194	83	76	33	117
1993—	St. Louis (N.L.)	7	6	.538	4.33	38	21	1	0	0	145¹/₃	163	80	70	27	75
1994—	St. Louis (N.L.)	3	2	.600	5.45	7	7	0	0	0	39²/₃	40	24	24	7	26
—	Arkansas (Texas)	1	0	1.000	1.93	2	2	0	0	0	9¹/₃	9	2	2	0	11
—	Louisville (A.A.)	1	2	.333	4.50	3	3	1	0	0	22	21	11	11	8	13
1995—	Boston (A.L.)■	7	5	.583	4.07	48	12	0	0	0	115	131	60	52	31	69
1996—	Montreal (N.L.)■	7	10	.412	4.17	33	27	1	1	0	159²/₃	165	80	74	41	100
1997—	Montreal (N.L.)	0	1	.000	33.75	1	1	0	0	0	1¹/₃	4	5	5	1	0
1998—	Akron (East.)■	0	0	...	6.52	3	3	0	0	0	9²/₃	15	7	7	2	6
1999—	Boston (A.L.)■	2	0	1.000	3.69	60	0	0	0	0	63¹/₃	61	34	26	18	39
2000—	Boston (A.L.)	3	3	.500	4.61	64	0	0	0	0	68¹/₃	74	40	35	17	43
2001—	Philadelphia (N.L.)■	5	6	.455	4.21	60	0	0	0	1	51¹/₃	49	26	24	17	37
—	Reading (East.)	0	0	...	0.00	1	1	0	0	0	2	0	0	0	1	2
A.L. totals (3 years)		12	8	.600	4.12	172	12	0	0	0	246²/₃	266	134	113	66	151
N.L. totals (7 years)		36	40	.474	4.20	181	96	7	1	1	651	689	333	304	134	393
Major League totals (10 years)		48	48	.500	4.18	353	108	7	1	1	897²/₃	955	467	417	200	544

DIVISION SERIES RECORD

Year	League	W	L	Pct.	ERA	G	GS	CG	ShO	Sv.	IP	H	R	ER	BB	SO
1995—	Boston (A.L.)	0	0	...	13.50	2	0	0	0	0	²/₃	2	1	1	1	2
1999—	Boston (A.L.)	0	0	...	0.00	2	0	0	0	0	4	2	0	0	1	4
Division series totals (2 years)		0	0	...	1.93	4	0	0	0	0	4²/₃	4	1	1	2	6

CHAMPIONSHIP SERIES RECORD

Year	League	W	L	Pct.	ERA	G	GS	CG	ShO	Sv.	IP	H	R	ER	BB	SO
1999—	Boston (A.L.)	0	0	...	0.00	4	0	0	0	0	3²/₃	3	0	0	3	4

CORNEJO, NATE — P — TIGERS

PERSONAL: Born September 24, 1979, in Wellington, Kan. ... 6-5/200. ... Throws right, bats right. ... Full name: Nathan J. Cornejo.
HIGH SCHOOL: Wellington (Kan.).
TRANSACTIONS/CAREER NOTES: Selected by Detroit Tigers organization in supplemental round ("sandwich pick" between first and second round, 34th pick overall) of free-agent draft (June 2, 1998); pick received as part of compensation for Arizona Diamondbacks signing Type A free-agent P Willie Blair.

Year	League	W	L	Pct.	ERA	G	GS	CG	ShO	Sv.	IP	H	R	ER	BB	SO
1998—	Gulf Coast Tigers (GCL)	1	0	1.000	1.26	5	0	0	0	1	14¹/₃	12	2	2	2	9
1999—	West Michigan (Midw.)	9	11	.450	3.71	28	•28	4	1	0	174²/₃	173	87	72	67	125
2000—	Lakeland (FSL)	5	5	.500	3.04	12	12	1	0	0	77	67	37	26	31	60
—	Jacksonville (Sou.)	5	7	.417	4.61	16	16	0	0	0	91²/₃	91	52	47	43	60
2001—	Erie (East.)	12	3	.800	2.68	19	19	3	1	0	124¹/₃	107	47	37	41	105
—	Toledo (I.L.)	4	0	1.000	2.12	4	4	0	0	0	29²/₃	24	8	7	7	22
—	Detroit (A.L.)	4	4	.500	7.38	10	10	0	0	0	42²/₃	63	38	35	28	22
Major League totals (1 year)		4	4	.500	7.38	10	10	0	0	0	42²/₃	63	38	35	28	22

PERSONAL: Born February 7, 1979, in San Luis Rio Colorado, Mexico. ... 6-0/175. ... Bats right, throws right. ... Full name: Humberto Figueroa Cota.

HIGH SCHOOL: Preparatoria Abierta.

TRANSACTIONS/CAREER NOTES: Signed as non-drafted free agent by Atlanta Braves organization (December 22, 1995). ... Loaned by Braves organization to Mexico City Tigers, Mexican League (June 23-September 23, 1996); did not play. ... Released by Braves (January 27, 1997). ... Signed by Tampa Bay Devil Rays organization (May 22, 1997). ... Traded by Devil Rays with C Joe Oliver to Pittsburgh Pirates for OF Jose Guillen and P Jeff Sparks (July 23, 1999). ... On Nashville disabled list (April 18-26, 2001).

STATISTICAL NOTES: Tied for Gulf Coast League lead in double plays by catcher with four in 1997. ... Led Eastern League catchers with 15 passed balls in 2000.

							BATTING							FIELDING		
Year — Team (League)	Pos.	G	AB	R	H	2B	3B	HR	RBI	Avg.	BB	SO	SB	PO	A	E	Avg.
1996—M.C. Tigres (Mex.)							Did not play.										
1997—Hudson Val. (NY-P)■..	C	3	9	0	2	0	0	0	2	.222	0	1	0	29	0	0	1.000
— GC Devil Rays (GCL)..	C	44	133	14	32	6	1	2	20	.241	17	27	3	294	26	5	.985
1998—Princeton (Appl.)	C	67	245	48	76	13	4	15	61	.310	32	59	4	*382	48	•12	.973
1999—Charl., S.C. (S.Atl.).....	C-1B	85	336	42	94	21	1	9	61	.280	20	51	1	443	61	7	.986
— Hickory (S.Atl.)■........	C	37	133	28	36	11	2	2	20	.271	21	20	3	235	22	2	.992
2000—Altoona (East.)	C-1B	112	429	49	112	20	1	8	44	.261	21	80	6	572	51	*17	.973
2001—Nashville (PCL)	C	111	377	61	112	22	2	14	72	.297	25	74	7	523	27	8	.986
— Pittsburgh (N.L.)	C	7	9	0	2	0	0	0	1	.222	0	5	0	11	0	0	1.000
Major League totals (1 year)		7	9	0	2	0	0	0	1	.222	0	5	0	11	0	0	1.000

PERSONAL: Born August 21, 1970, in South Bend, Ind. ... 6-0/175. ... Bats left, throws right. ... Full name: Craig John Counsell. ... Son of John Counsell, outfielder in Minnesota Twins organization (1964-68).

HIGH SCHOOL: Whitefish Bay (Milwaukee).

COLLEGE: Notre Dame.

TRANSACTIONS/CAREER NOTES: Selected by Colorado Rockies organization in 11th round of free-agent draft (June 1, 1992). ... On disabled list (April 7-May 13, July 30-August 6 and August 7-27, 1994). ... On disabled list (May 1-July 15 and July 18-September 3, 1996). ... Traded by Rockies to Florida Marlins for P Mark Hutton (July 27, 1997). ... On disabled list (August 4, 1998-remainder of season). ... Traded by Marlins to Los Angeles Dodgers for a player to be named later (June 15, 1999); Marlins acquired P Ryan Moskau to complete deal (July 15, 1999). ... Released by Dodgers (March 15, 2000). ... Signed by Arizona Diamondbacks organization (March 20, 2000).

STATISTICAL NOTES: Led California League shortstops with 621 total chances in 1993. ... Led Pacific Coast League shortstops with 598 total chances and 86 double plays in 1995. ... Career major league grand slams: 2.

							BATTING							FIELDING		
Year — Team (League)	Pos.	G	AB	R	H	2B	3B	HR	RBI	Avg.	BB	SO	SB	PO	A	E	Avg.
1992—Bend (N'West)	2B-SS	18	61	11	15	6	1	0	8	.246	9	10	1	23	36	2	.967
1993—Central Valley (Calif.)..	SS	131	471	79	132	26	3	5	59	.280	95	68	14	*233	353	35	.944
1994—New Haven (East.)......	SS-2B	83	300	47	84	20	1	5	37	.280	37	32	4	122	242	27	.931
1995—Colo. Springs (PCL) ...	SS	118	399	60	112	22	6	5	53	.281	34	47	10	182	386	30	.950
— Colorado (N.L.)	SS	3	1	0	0	0	0	0	0	.000	1	0	0	1	1	0	1.000
1996—Colo. Springs (PCL) ...	2B-3B-SS	25	75	17	18	3	0	2	10	.240	24	7	4	35	64	4	.961
1997—Colo. Springs (PCL) ...	2B-SS	96	376	77	126	31	6	5	63	.335	45	38	12	213	260	9	.981
— Florida (N.L.)■...........	PR	1	0	0	0	0	0	0	0	...	0	0	0	...	...	...	...
— Florida (N.L.)	2B	51	164	20	49	9	2	1	16	.299	18	17	1	124	149	3	.989
1998—Florida (N.L.)	2B	107	335	43	84	19	5	4	40	.251	51	47	3	237	299	5	.991
1999—Florida (N.L.)	2B	37	66	4	10	1	0	0	2	.152	5	10	0	20	29	1	.980
— Los Angeles (N.L.)■..	2B-SS	50	108	20	28	6	0	0	9	.259	9	14	1	54	86	1	.993
2000—Tucson (PCL)............	2B-3B-SS	50	198	45	69	14	3	3	27	.348	22	20	4	77	133	4	.981
— Arizona (N.L.)	2B-3B-SS	67	152	23	48	8	1	2	11	.316	20	18	3	38	95	6	.957
2001—Arizona (N.L.)...........SS-2B-3B-1B	141	458	76	126	22	3	4	38	.275	61	76	6	193	316	8	.985
Major League totals (6 years)		457	1284	186	345	65	11	11	116	.269	165	182	14	667	975	24	.986

DIVISION SERIES RECORD

							BATTING							FIELDING		
Year — Team (League)	Pos.	G	AB	R	H	2B	3B	HR	RBI	Avg.	BB	SO	SB	PO	A	E	Avg.
1997—Florida (N.L.)	2B	3	5	0	2	1	0	0	1	.400	1	0	0	5	2	1	.875
2001—Arizona (N.L.)	2B-PH	5	16	2	3	0	0	1	3	.188	2	2	0	8	11	0	1.000
Division series totals (2 years)		8	21	2	5	1	0	1	4	.238	3	2	0	13	13	1	.963

CHAMPIONSHIP SERIES RECORD

RECORDS: Shares N.L. single-game record for most at-bats—6 (October 20, 2001).

NOTES: Named Most Valuable Player (2001).

							BATTING							FIELDING		
Year — Team (League)	Pos.	G	AB	R	H	2B	3B	HR	RBI	Avg.	BB	SO	SB	PO	A	E	Avg.
1997—Florida (N.L.)	2B-PH	5	14	0	6	0	0	0	2	.429	3	3	0	7	9	1	.941
2001—Arizona (N.L.)	2B-SS	5	21	5	8	3	0	0	4	.381	0	3	1	8	11	0	1.000
Championship series totals (2 years)		10	35	5	14	3	0	0	6	.400	3	6	1	15	20	1	.972

WORLD SERIES RECORD

NOTES: Member of World Series championship team (1997 and 2001).

							BATTING							FIELDING		
Year — Team (League)	Pos.	G	AB	R	H	2B	3B	HR	RBI	Avg.	BB	SO	SB	PO	A	E	Avg.
1997—Florida (N.L.)	2B	7	22	4	4	1	0	0	2	.182	6	5	1	18	15	1	.971
2001—Arizona (N.L.)	2B	6	24	1	2	0	0	1	1	.083	0	7	0	11	16	0	1.000
World Series totals (2 years)		13	46	5	6	1	0	1	3	.130	6	12	1	29	31	1	.984

COX, STEVE 1B DEVIL RAYS

PERSONAL: Born October 31, 1974, in Delano, Calif. ... 6-4/222. ... Bats left, throws left. ... Full name: Charles Steven Cox.
HIGH SCHOOL: Monache (Porterville, Calif.).
TRANSACTIONS/CAREER NOTES: Selected by Oakland Athletics organization in fifth round of free-agent draft (June 1, 1992). ... On disabled list (July 23, 1993-remainder of season). ... Selected by Tampa Bay Devil Rays in second round (46th pick overall) of expansion draft (November 18, 1997). ... On disabled list (April 12-26, 1998). ... On Tampa Bay disabled list (August 6-23, 2001); included rehabilitation assignment to Orlando (August 19-23).
HONORS: Named International League Most Valuable Player (1999).
STATISTICAL NOTES: Led California League with 10 sacrifice flies in 1995. ... Tied for Pacific Coast League lead with nine sacrifice flies in 1997. ... Led International League first basemen with 1,079 total chances in 1998. ... Led International League with 314 total bases, a .588 slugging percentage and 11 intentional bases on balls received in 1999. ... Led International League first basemen with 1,203 total chances and 121 double plays in 1999. ... Career major league grand slams: 1.

Year — Team (League)	Pos.	G	AB	R	H	2B	3B	HR	RBI	Avg.	BB	SO	SB	PO	A	E	Avg.
								BATTING						FIELDING			
1992— Scottsdale (Ariz.)........	1B	52	184	30	43	4	1	1	35	.234	27	51	2	407	28	11	.975
1993— S. Oregon (N'West)	1B	15	57	10	18	4	1	2	16	.316	5	15	0	104	11	2	.983
1994— W. Michigan (Midw.)...	1B-OF	99	311	37	75	19	2	6	32	.241	41	95	2	727	49	10	.987
1995— Modesto (Calif.)	1B	132	483	95	144	29	3	*30	*110	.298	84	88	5	991	77	17	.984
1996— Huntsville (Sou.)	1B-DH	104	381	59	107	21	1	12	61	.281	51	65	2	909	72	15	.985
1997— Edmonton (PCL)........	1B-DH	131	467	84	128	34	1	15	93	.274	*88	90	1	1043	70	*10	.991
1998— Durham (I.L.)■..........	1B-OF-DH	119	430	64	109	23	2	13	67	.253	56	100	3	*1011	62	7	.994
1999— Durham (I.L.)............	1B-DH	134	534	*107	*182	*49	4	25	*127	.341	67	74	3	*1125	73	5	.996
— Tampa Bay (A.L.)........	1B-OF	6	19	0	4	1	0	0	0	.211	0	2	0	20	1	0	1.000
2000— Tampa Bay (A.L.)........	OF-1B-DH	116	318	44	90	19	1	11	35	.283	46	47	1	267	13	8	.972
2001— Tampa Bay (A.L.)........	1B-OF-DH	108	342	37	88	22	0	12	51	.257	24	75	2	580	49	1	.998
— Orlando (Sou.)	1B	4	14	2	3	1	0	1	3	.214	2	1	0	24	1	1	.962
Major League totals (3 years)		230	679	81	182	42	1	23	86	.268	70	124	3	867	63	9	.990

CRABTREE, TIM P

PERSONAL: Born October 13, 1969, in Jackson, Mich. ... 6-4/220. ... Throws right, bats right. ... Full name: Timothy Lyle Crabtree.
HIGH SCHOOL: Grass Lake (Mich.).
COLLEGE: Michigan State.
TRANSACTIONS/CAREER NOTES: Selected by Toronto Blue Jays organization in second round of free-agent draft (June 1, 1992). ... On disabled list (August 16-September 6, 1996). ... On Toronto disabled list (June 4-August 3, 1997); included rehabilitation assignments to St. Catherines (July 22-24) and Syracuse (July 27-August 4). ... Traded by Blue Jays to Texas Rangers for C Kevin Brown (March 14, 1998). ... On Texas disabled list (April 15-May 8 and July 1, 2001-remainder of season); included rehabilitation assignment to Tulsa (May 4-8). ... Granted free agency (November 6, 2001).

Year — League	W	L	Pct.	ERA	G	GS	CG	ShO	Sv.	IP	H	R	ER	BB	SO
1992— St. Catharines (NY-Penn) ...	6	3	.667	1.57	12	12	2	0	0	69	45	19	12	22	47
— Knoxville (Sou.)..................	0	2	.000	0.95	3	3	1	0	0	19	14	8	2	4	13
1993— Knoxville (Sou.)..................	9	14	.391	4.08	27	27	2	2	0	158²/₃	178	93	72	59	67
1994— Syracuse (I.L.)..................	2	6	.250	4.17	51	9	0	0	2	108	125	58	50	49	58
1995— Syracuse (I.L.)..................	0	2	.000	5.40	26	0	0	0	5	31²/₃	38	25	19	12	22
— Toronto (A.L.)..................	0	2	.000	3.09	31	0	0	0	0	32	30	16	11	13	21
1996— Toronto (A.L.)..................	5	3	.625	2.54	53	0	0	0	1	67¹/₃	59	26	19	22	57
1997— Toronto (A.L.)..................	3	3	.500	7.08	37	0	0	0	2	40²/₃	65	32	32	17	26
— St. Catharines (NY-Penn) ...	0	0	...	3.00	2	1	0	0	0	3	3	2	1	0	3
— Syracuse (I.L.)..................	0	0	...	9.82	3	0	0	0	1	3²/₃	7	4	4	1	3
1998— Texas (A.L.)■..................	6	1	.857	3.59	64	0	0	0	0	85¹/₃	86	40	34	35	60
1999— Texas (A.L.)..................	5	1	.833	3.46	68	0	0	0	0	65	71	26	25	18	54
2000— Texas (A.L.)..................	2	7	.222	5.15	68	0	0	0	2	80¹/₃	86	52	46	31	54
2001— Texas (A.L.)..................	0	5	.000	6.56	21	0	0	0	4	23¹/₃	37	18	17	14	16
— Tulsa (Texas)	0	1	.000	3.00	2	2	0	0	0	3	3	1	1	1	0
Major League totals (7 years)	21	22	.488	4.20	342	0	0	0	9	394	434	210	184	150	288

DIVISION SERIES RECORD

Year — League	W	L	Pct.	ERA	G	GS	CG	ShO	Sv.	IP	H	R	ER	BB	SO
1998— Texas (A.L.).....................	0	0	...	0.00	2	0	0	0	0	4	1	0	0	0	2
1999— Texas (A.L.).....................	0	0	...	5.40	2	0	0	0	0	1²/₃	1	2	1	1	1
Division series totals (2 years)	0	0	...	1.59	4	0	0	0	0	5²/₃	2	2	1	1	3

CRAWFORD, PAXTON P RED SOX

PERSONAL: Born August 4, 1977, in Little Rock, Ark. ... 6-3/205. ... Throws right, bats right. ... Full name: Paxton Keith Crawford.
HIGH SCHOOL: Carlsbad (N.M.).
TRANSACTIONS/CAREER NOTES: Selected by Boston Red Sox organization in ninth round of free-agent draft (June 1, 1995). ... On Pawtucket disabled list (July 20-August 19, 2000). ... On Pawtucket disabled list (June 18, 2001-remainder of season).
STATISTICAL NOTES: Pitched 3-0 no-hit victory for Pawtucket against Ottawa (July 18, 2000; first game).

Year — League	W	L	Pct.	ERA	G	GS	CG	ShO	Sv.	IP	H	R	ER	BB	SO
1995— Gulf Coast Red Sox (GCL) ..	2	4	.333	2.74	12	7	1	0	2	46	38	17	14	12	44
1996— Michigan (Midw.)..............	6	11	.353	3.58	22	22	1	0	0	128¹/₃	120	62	51	42	105
1997— Sarasota (FSL)	4	8	.333	4.55	12	11	2	1	0	65¹/₃	69	42	33	27	56
1998— Trenton (East.)	6	5	.545	4.17	22	20	1	0	0	108	104	53	50	39	82
1999— Trenton (East.)	7	8	.467	4.08	28	•28	1	1	0	163¹/₃	151	81	74	59	111
2000— Trenton (East.)	2	3	.400	3.10	9	9	0	0	0	52¹/₃	50	20	18	6	54
— Pawtucket (I.L.)..................	7	4	.636	4.55	12	11	1	1	0	61¹/₃	47	32	31	22	47
— Boston (A.L.).....................	2	1	.667	3.41	7	4	0	0	0	29	25	15	11	13	17
2001— Boston (A.L.)..................	3	0	1.000	4.75	8	7	0	0	0	36	40	19	19	13	25
— Pawtucket (I.L.)..................	1	3	.250	5.52	6	6	1	0	0	29¹/₃	43	19	18	7	15
Major League totals (2 years)	5	1	.833	4.15	15	11	0	0	0	65	65	34	30	26	42

CREDE, JOE   3B   WHITE SOX

PERSONAL: Born April 26, 1978, in Jefferson City, Mo. ... 6-3/195. ... Bats right, throws right. ... Full name: Joseph Crede.
HIGH SCHOOL: Fatima (Westphalia, Mo.).
TRANSACTIONS/CAREER NOTES: Selected by Chicago White Sox organization in fifth round of free-agent draft (June 2, 1996). ... On disabled list (July 2, 1999-remainder of season).
HONORS: Named Carolina League Most Valuable Player (1998). ... Named Southern League Most Valuable Player (2000).
STATISTICAL NOTES: Led Gulf Coast League third basemen with 175 total chances in 1996. ... Led Carolina League with 253 total bases and 11 sacrifice flies in 1998. ... Led Carolina League third basemen with 420 total chances in 1998. ... Led Southern League with 261 total bases in 2000. ... Led Southern League in grounding into double plays with 18 in 2000. ... Led Southern League third basemen with 328 total chances in 2000.

Year	Team (League)	Pos.	G	AB	R	H	2B	3B	HR	RBI	Avg.	BB	SO	SB	PO	A	E	Avg.
											BATTING					FIELDING		
1996—	GC White Sox (GCL) ..	3B	56	221	30	66	17	1	4	32	.299	9	41	1	*42	*108	*25	.857
1997—	Hickory (S.Atl.)...........	3B	113	402	45	109	25	0	5	62	.271	24	83	3	84	232	33	.905
1998—	Win.-Salem (Caro.) ...	3B	*137	492	•92	155	32	3	20	*88	*.315	53	98	9	*100	*290	*30	.929
1999—	Birmingham (Sou.)......	3B	74	291	37	73	14	1	4	42	.251	22	47	2	68	133	20	.910
2000—	Birmingham (Sou.)......	3B	138	533	84	*163	35	0	21	94	.306	56	111	3	91	218	19	.942
—	Chicago (A.L.)...........	3B-DH	7	14	2	5	1	0	0	3	.357	0	3	0	5	9	1	.933
2001—	Charlotte (I.L.)...........	3B	124	463	67	128	34	1	17	65	.276	46	88	2	93	258	20	.946
—	Chicago (A.L.)...........	3B	17	50	1	11	1	1	0	7	.220	3	11	1	17	18	0	1.000
Major League totals (2 years)			24	64	3	16	2	1	0	10	.250	3	14	1	22	27	1	.980

C   CREEK, DOUG   P   DEVIL RAYS

PERSONAL: Born March 1, 1969, in Winchester, Va. ... 6-0/200. ... Throws left, bats left. ... Full name: Paul Douglas Creek.
HIGH SCHOOL: Martinsburg (W.Va.).
COLLEGE: Georgia Tech.
TRANSACTIONS/CAREER NOTES: Selected by California Angels organization in fifth round of free-agent draft (June 4, 1990); did not sign. ... Selected by St. Louis Cardinals organization in seventh round of free-agent draft (June 3, 1991). ... On Arkansas disabled list (April 10-May 21, 1992; July 25-August 1, 1993; and June 25-July 10, 1994). ... Traded by Cardinals with P Allen Watson and P Rich DeLucia to San Francisco Giants for SS Royce Clayton and a player to be named later (December 14, 1995); Cardinals acquired 2B Chris Wimmer to complete deal (January 16, 1996). ... Contract purchased by Chicago White Sox from Giants organization (November 7, 1997). ... Contract sold by White Sox to Hanshin Tigers of Japan Central League (December 4, 1997). ... Signed by Chicago Cubs organization (January 29, 1999). ... Released by Cubs (September 13, 1999). ... Signed by Tampa Bay Devil Rays organization (February 1, 2000). ... On Durham disabled list (April 6-25, 2000).
STATISTICAL NOTES: Tied for Pacific Coast League lead with 12 hit batsmen in 1999.

Year	League	W	L	Pct.	ERA	G	GS	CG	ShO	Sv.	IP	H	R	ER	BB	SO
1991—	Hamilton (NY-Penn)	3	2	.600	5.12	7	6	0	0	0	38²/₃	39	22	22	18	45
—	Savannah (S.Atl.)	2	1	.667	4.45	5	5	0	0	0	28¹/₃	24	14	14	17	32
1992—	Springfield (Midw.)	4	1	.800	2.58	6	6	0	0	0	38¹/₃	32	11	11	13	43
—	St. Petersburg (FSL)	5	4	.556	2.82	13	13	0	0	0	73¹/₃	57	31	23	37	63
1993—	Louisville (A.A.)................	0	0	...	3.21	2	2	0	0	0	14	10	5	5	9	9
—	Arkansas (Texas)............	11	10	.524	4.02	25	25	1	1	0	147²/₃	142	75	66	48	128
1994—	Louisville (A.A.)..............	1	4	.200	8.54	7	7	0	0	0	26¹/₃	37	26	25	23	16
—	Arkansas (Texas)............	3	10	.231	4.40	17	17	1	0	0	92	96	54	45	36	65
1995—	Louisville (A.A.)...............	3	2	.600	3.23	26	0	0	0	0	30²/₃	20	12	11	21	50
—	Arkansas (Texas)............	4	2	.667	2.88	26	0	0	0	1	34¹/₃	24	12	11	16	50
—	St. Louis (N.L.)................	0	0	...	0.00	6	0	0	0	0	6²/₃	2	0	0	3	10
1996—	San Francisco (N.L.)■	0	2	.000	6.52	63	0	0	0	0	48¹/₃	45	41	35	32	38
1997—	Phoenix (PCL)..............	8	6	.571	4.93	25	23	2	1	0	129²/₃	140	76	71	66	*137
—	San Francisco (N.L.)	1	2	.333	6.75	3	3	0	0	0	13¹/₃	12	12	10	14	14
1998—	Hanshin (Jap. Cen.)■	0	4	.000	3.14	7	6	0	0	0	28²/₃	23	21	18	25	24
—	Hanshin (Jap. Wes.)........	9	1	.900	2.16	17	16	2	...	0	100	77	28	24	52	101
1999—	Iowa (PCL)■................	7	3	.700	3.79	25	20	0	0	1	130²/₃	116	66	55	62	140
—	Chicago (N.L.).............	0	0	...	10.50	3	0	0	0	0	6	6	7	7	8	6
2000—	Durham (I.L.)...............	0	0	...	1.96	10	1	0	0	0	18¹/₃	10	5	4	14	22
—	Tampa Bay (A.L.)...........	1	3	.250	4.60	45	0	0	0	1	60²/₃	49	33	31	39	73
2001—	Tampa Bay (A.L.)...........	2	5	.286	4.31	66	0	0	0	0	62²/₃	51	34	30	49	66
A.L. totals (2 years)		3	8	.273	4.45	111	0	0	0	1	123¹/₃	100	67	61	88	139
N.L. totals (4 years)		1	4	.200	6.30	75	3	0	0	0	74¹/₃	65	60	52	57	68
Major League totals (6 years).......		4	12	.250	5.15	186	3	0	0	1	197²/₃	165	127	113	145	207

CRESPO, CESAR   OF/IF   PADRES

PERSONAL: Born May 23, 1979, in Rio Piedras, Puerto Rico. ... 5-11/170. ... Bats both, throws right. ... Full name: Cesar Antonio Crespo. ... Brother of Felipe Crespo, infielder/outfielder, Philadelphia Phillies.
HIGH SCHOOL: Notre Dame (Caguas, Puerto Rico).
TRANSACTIONS/CAREER NOTES: Selected by New York Mets organization in third round of free-agent draft (June 3, 1997). ... Traded by Mets to Florida Marlins (September 12, 1998), completing deal in which Marlins traded OF Robert Stratton to Mets for a player to be named later (March 20, 1998). ... On disabled list (May 19-31, 1999). ... Traded by Marlins to San Diego Padres for OF Eric Owens, P Matt Clement and P Omar Ortiz (March 28, 2001). ... On Portland disabled list (May 11-21, 2001).
STATISTICAL NOTES: Tied for Eastern League lead in assists by outfielder with nine in 2000.

Year	Team (League)	Pos.	G	AB	R	H	2B	3B	HR	RBI	Avg.	BB	SO	SB	PO	A	E	Avg.
											BATTING					FIELDING		
1998—	Capital City (S.Atl.)	2B-SS	116	428	61	108	18	4	6	48	.252	44	114	47	224	271	27	.948
1999—	Brev. County (FSL)■..	2B	115	427	63	122	17	2	6	40	.286	62	86	22	227	274	24	.954
2000—	Portland (East.)...........	OF-2B-SS	134	482	96	124	21	6	9	60	.257	77	118	41	288	‡51	15	.958
2001—	Portland (PCL)■.........2B-OF-SS-3B	78	273	46	71	18	3	8	29	.260	39	66	23	129	158	4	.986
—	San Diego (N.L.) 2B-OF-3B-SS	55	153	27	32	6	0	4	12	.209	25	50	6	93	69	4	.976
Major League totals (1 year)			55	153	27	32	6	0	4	12	.209	25	50	6	93	69	4	.976

CRESPO, FELIPE   IF/OF   PHILLIES

PERSONAL: Born March 5, 1973, in Rio Piedras, Puerto Rico. ... 5-11/200. ... Bats both, throws right. ... Full name: Felipe Javier Clauso Crespo. ... Brother of Cesar Crespo, outfielder/infielder, San Diego Padres.
HIGH SCHOOL: Notre Dame (Caguas, Puerto Rico).
TRANSACTIONS/CAREER NOTES: Selected by Toronto Blue Jays organization in third round of free-agent draft (June 4, 1990). ... On disabled list (May 26-July 2, 1995). ... On Toronto disabled list (April 1-24, 1996); included rehabilitation assignment to Dunedin (April 12-24). ... Released by Blue Jays (March 17, 1999). ... Signed by San Francisco Giants organization (April 27, 1999). ... Granted free agency (October 15, 1999). ... Re-signed by Giants organization (October 29, 1999). ... On San Francisco disabled list (April 26-May 27, 2001); included rehabilitation assignment to Fresno (May 24-27). ... Traded by Giants to Philadelphia Phillies for P Wayne Gomes (July 27, 2001).
STATISTICAL NOTES: Led Southern League third basemen with 127 putouts and 42 errors in 1994. ... Led Pacific Coast League with a .616 slugging percentage and a .447 on-base percentage in 1999.

| | | | | | | | | BATTING | | | | | | | | FIELDING | | |
Year	Team (League)	Pos.	G	AB	R	H	2B	3B	HR	RBI	Avg.	BB	SO	SB	PO	A	E	Avg.
1991—	Medicine Hat (Pio.)	2B	49	184	40	57	11	4	4	31	.310	25	31	6	*97	133	*23	.909
1992—	Myrtle Beach (S.Atl.)..	2B-3B	81	263	43	74	14	3	1	29	.281	58	38	7	161	149	22	.934
1993—	Dunedin (FSL)	2B	96	345	51	103	16	8	6	39	.299	47	40	18	198	269	25	.949
1994—	Knoxville (Sou.).........	3B-2B	129	502	74	135	30	4	8	49	.269	57	95	20	†127	270	†42	.904
1995—	Syracuse (I.L.)............	2B-DH	88	347	56	102	20	5	13	41	.294	41	56	12	160	220	*25	.938
1996—	Dunedin (FSL)	2B	9	34	3	11	1	0	2	6	.324	2	3	1	18	18	2	.947
—	Toronto (A.L.)............	2B-3B-1B	22	49	6	9	4	0	0	4	.184	12	13	1	34	38	1	.986
—	Syracuse (I.L.)............	2-0-3-1	98	355	53	100	25	4	8	58	.282	56	39	10	220	143	19	.950
1997—	Toronto (A.L.)............	3B-DH-2B	12	28	3	8	0	1	1	5	.286	2	4	0	9	9	1	.947
—	Syracuse (I.L.)...........O-2-1-DH-3		80	290	53	75	12	0	12	26	.259	46	38	7	247	103	12	.967
1998—	Toronto (A.L.).............O-2-DH-3-1		66	130	11	34	8	1	1	15	.262	15	27	4	67	17	4	.955
1999—	Fresno (PCL)■	IF-OF-DH	112	385	98	128	27	5	24	84	.332	78	73	17	620	77	13	.982
2000—	San Fran. (N.L.)■.......	O-1-2-DH	89	131	17	38	6	1	4	29	.290	10	23	3	57	4	1	.984
2001—	San Francisco (N.L.) ..1B-2B-OF-DH		40	66	8	13	1	0	4	10	.197	7	26	1	105	6	4	.965
—	Fresno (PCL)	1B-2B-OF	3	8	2	3	1	0	1	1	.375	0	3	0	6	4	0	1.000
—	Philadelphia (N.L.)■....	OF-1B-2B	33	41	1	7	3	1	0	5	.171	4	8	0	29	1	0	1.000
American League totals (3 years)			100	207	20	51	12	2	2	24	.246	29	44	5	110	64	6	.967
National League totals (2 years)			162	238	26	58	10	2	8	44	.244	21	57	4	191	11	5	.976
Major League totals (5 years)			262	445	46	109	22	4	10	68	.245	50	101	9	301	75	11	.972

DIVISION SERIES RECORD

| | | | | | | | | BATTING | | | | | | | | FIELDING | | |
Year	Team (League)	Pos.	G	AB	R	H	2B	3B	HR	RBI	Avg.	BB	SO	SB	PO	A	E	Avg.
2000—	San Francisco (N.L.) ..	PH	4	4	0	1	0	0	0	0	.250	0	0	0	...	...	...	...

CRESSEND, JACK   P   TWINS

PERSONAL: Born May 13, 1975, in New Orleans. ... 6-1/185. ... Throws right, bats right. ... Full name: John Baptiste Cressend III.
HIGH SCHOOL: Mandeville (La.).
COLLEGE: Tulane.
TRANSACTIONS/CAREER NOTES: Signed as non-drafted free agent by Boston Red Sox organization (July 24, 1996). ... Claimed on waivers by Minnesota Twins (April 22, 1999).

Year	League	W	L	Pct.	ERA	G	GS	CG	ShO	Sv.	IP	H	R	ER	BB	SO
1996—	Lowell (NY-Penn)	3	2	.600	2.36	9	8	0	0	0	45 2/3	37	15	12	17	57
1997—	Sarasota (FSL)	8	11	.421	3.80	28	25	2	1	0	165 2/3	163	98	70	56	149
1998—	Trenton (East.)	10	11	.476	4.34	29	•29	1	1	0	149 1/3	168	86	72	55	130
1999—	Trenton (East.)	1	0	1.000	7.20	3	3	0	0	0	15	19	12	12	7	11
—	New Britain (East.)■	7	10	.412	4.34	25	24	2	*2	0	145	152	79	70	50	125
2000—	Salt Lake (PCL)	4	4	.500	3.44	54	1	0	0	8	86 1/3	87	40	33	39	87
—	Minnesota (A.L.)	0	0	...	5.27	11	0	0	0	0	13 2/3	20	8	8	6	6
2001—	Edmonton (PCL)	2	2	.500	3.50	12	0	0	0	1	18	19	12	7	7	9
—	Minnesota (A.L.)	3	2	.600	3.67	44	0	0	0	0	56 1/3	50	24	23	16	40
Major League totals (2 years).......		3	2	.600	3.99	55	0	0	0	0	70	70	32	31	22	46

CROMER, D.T.   1B

PERSONAL: Born March 19, 1971, in Lake City, S.C. ... 6-2/220. ... Bats left, throws left. ... Full name: David Thomas Cromer. ... Son of Roy Cromer, former scout with St. Louis Cardinals and minor league pitcher/second baseman (1960-63); brother of Brandon Cromer, minor league shortstop (1992-2000); brother of Tripp Cromer, infielder, Houston Astros; and brother of Burke Cromer, pitcher, Atlanta Braves organization (1992-93).
HIGH SCHOOL: Lexington (S.C.).
COLLEGE: South Carolina.
TRANSACTIONS/CAREER NOTES: Selected by Oakland Athletics organization in 11th round of free-agent draft (June 1, 1992). ... Granted free agency (October 15, 1998). ... Signed by Cincinnati Reds organization (December 15, 1998). ... Granted free agency (October 18, 2001).
HONORS: Named California League Most Valuable Player (1996).
STATISTICAL NOTES: Led California League with 316 total bases and .626 slugging percentage in 1996. ... Led Southern League first basemen with 1,167 putouts, 18 errors, 1,285 total chances and 129 double plays in 1997. ... Led Pacific Coast League first basemen with 1,015 putouts, 89 assists, 1,117 total chances and 113 double plays in 1998.

Year Team (League)	Pos.	G	AB	R	H	2B	3B	HR	RBI	Avg.	BB	SO	SB	PO	A	E	Avg.
1992—S. Oregon (N'West)....	OF	50	168	17	35	7	0	4	26	.208	13	34	4	61	6	5	.931
1993—Madison (Midw.)........	OF-1B-DH	98	321	37	84	20	4	4	41	.262	22	72	8	233	8	7	.972
1994—W. Michigan (Midw.)..	OF-1B	102	349	50	89	20	5	10	58	.255	33	76	11	328	28	10	.973
1995—Modesto (Calif.)	OF-1B	108	378	59	98	18	5	14	52	.259	36	66	5	160	16	8	.957
1996—Modesto (Calif.)	1B-OF-DH	124	505	100	166	40	10	30	130	.329	32	67	20	549	67	14	.978
1997—Huntsville (Sou.)	1B-DH-OF	134	545	100	*176	*40	6	15	121	.323	60	102	12	†1169	101	†18	.986
1998—Edmonton (PCL)	1B-DH-OF	125	504	75	148	30	3	16	85	.294	32	93	12	†1018	†89	15	.987
1999—Indianapolis (I.L.)■...	OF-1B-DH	136	535	83	166	37	4	30	107	.310	44	98	4	507	38	9	.984
2000—Cincinnati (N.L.)........	1B	35	47	7	16	4	0	2	8	.340	1	14	0	50	3	2	.964
—Louisville (I.L.)	1B-OF	106	415	58	112	26	3	14	67	.270	33	84	6	461	49	10	.981
2001—Louisville (I.L.)	1B	62	242	35	69	12	2	11	49	.285	15	48	4	398	34	5	.989
—Cincinnati (N.L.)	1B-DH	50	57	7	16	3	0	5	12	.281	3	19	0	32	4	1	.973
Major League totals (2 years)		85	104	14	32	7	0	7	20	.308	4	33	0	82	7	3	.967

CRUZ, DEIVI — SS

PERSONAL: Born November 6, 1975, in Nizao de Bani, Dominican Republic. ... 6-0/184. ... Bats right, throws right. ... Full name: Deivi Garcia Cruz.

HIGH SCHOOL: Liceo Aliro Paulino Nizao (Dominican Republic).

TRANSACTIONS/CAREER NOTES: Signed as non-drafted free agent by San Francisco Giants organization (April 23, 1993). ... Selected by Los Angeles Dodgers from Giants organization in Rule 5 major league draft (December 9, 1996). ... Traded by Dodgers with OF Juan Hernaiz to Detroit Tigers for 2B Jeff Berblinger (December 9, 1996). ... On Detroit disabled list (March 20-April 27, 1998); included rehabilitation assignments to Lakeland (April 21-23) and Toledo (April 24-27). ... On Detroit disabled list (June 8-July 18, 2001); included rehabilitation assignment to Erie (July 14-18). ... Granted free agency (December 21, 2001).

STATISTICAL NOTES: Led Northwest League third basemen with 47 putouts and .941 fielding percentage in 1995. ... Led Midwest League shortstops with 427 assists and .980 fielding percentage in 1996. ... Career major league grand slams: 1.

Year Team (League)	Pos.	G	AB	R	H	2B	3B	HR	RBI	Avg.	BB	SO	SB	PO	A	E	Avg.
1993—Arizona Giants (Ariz.) .	3B-SS-1B	28	82	8	28	3	0	0	15	.341	4	5	3	17	52	2	.972
1994—Arizona Giants (Ariz.) .	SS-3B	18	53	10	16	8	0	0	5	.302	5	3	0	11	37	1	.980
1995—Burlington (Midw.) ..	2B-3B-SS	16	58	2	8	1	0	1	9	.138	4	7	1	20	42	2	.969
—Bellingham (N'West) ..	3B-2B	62	223	32	66	17	0	3	28	.296	19	21	6	†55	124	10	†.947
1996—Burlington (Midw.) ..	SS-3B	127	517	72	152	27	2	9	64	.294	35	49	12	159	†444	13	†.979
1997—Detroit (A.L.)	SS	147	436	35	105	26	0	2	40	.241	14	55	3	192	420	13	.979
1998—Lakeland (FSL)	SS	2	9	0	0	0	0	0	1	.000	0	1	0	1	2	0	1.000
—Toledo (I.L.).................	SS	2	9	1	1	1	0	0	2	.111	2	3	0	2	7	0	1.000
—Detroit (A.L.)	SS	135	454	52	118	22	3	5	45	.260	13	55	3	196	445	11	.983
1999—Detroit (A.L.)	SS	155	518	64	147	35	0	13	58	.284	12	57	1	230	453	12	.983
2000—Detroit (A.L.)	SS	156	583	68	176	46	5	10	82	.302	13	43	1	222	482	13	.982
2001—Detroit (A.L.)	SS-3B	110	414	39	106	28	1	7	52	.256	17	46	4	162	299	17	.964
—Erie (East.)	SS-3B	4	12	2	5	1	0	1	3	.417	0	0	1	4	9	1	.929
Major League totals (5 years)		703	2405	258	652	157	9	37	277	.271	69	256	12	1002	2099	66	.979

CRUZ, JACOB — OF — TIGERS

PERSONAL: Born January 28, 1973, in Oxnard, Calif. ... 6-0/215. ... Bats left, throws left.

HIGH SCHOOL: Channel Islands (Oxnard, Calif.).

COLLEGE: Arizona State.

TRANSACTIONS/CAREER NOTES: Selected by California Angels organization in 45th round of free-agent draft (June 3, 1991); did not sign. ... Selected by San Francisco Giants organization in supplemental round ("sandwich pick" between first and second round; 32nd pick overall) of free-agent draft (June 2, 1994); pick received as part of compensation for Texas Rangers signing Type A free agent 1B Will Clark. ... Traded by Giants with P Steve Reed to Cleveland Indians for P Jose Mesa, IF Shawon Dunston and P Alvin Morman (July 24, 1998). ... On Cleveland disabled list (March 30-April 29 and August 3, 1999-remainder of season); included rehabilitation assignment to Buffalo (April 18-29). ... On disabled list (April 30, 2000-remainder of season). ... Traded by Indians to Colorado Rockies for C Josh Bard and OF Jody Gerut (June 2, 2001). ... On Colorado disabled list (July 17-August 17, 2001); included rehabilitation assignment to Colorado Springs (July 30-August 13). ... Released by Rockies (November 30, 2001). ... Signed by Detroit Tigers organization (December 21, 2001).

STATISTICAL NOTES: Led Pacific Coast League with 11 sacrifice flies in 1996. ... Led Pacific Coast League with .434 on-base percentage and tied for league lead with nine intentional bases on balls in 1997.

Year Team (League)	Pos.	G	AB	R	H	2B	3B	HR	RBI	Avg.	BB	SO	SB	PO	A	E	Avg.
1994—San Jose (Calif.)........	OF	31	118	14	29	7	0	0	12	.246	9	22	0	42	2	2	.957
1995—Shreveport (Texas)........	OF	127	458	88	136	33	1	13	77	.297	57	72	9	235	16	1	*.996
1996—Phoenix (PCL)...........	OF-DH	121	435	60	124	26	4	7	75	.285	62	77	5	249	11	3	.989
—San Francisco (N.L.) ...	OF	33	77	10	18	3	0	3	10	.234	12	24	0	41	1	1	.977
1997—Phoenix (PCL)...........	OF-DH	127	493	90	178	*45	3	12	95	*.361	64	64	18	239	*16	8	.970
—San Francisco (N.L.) ..	OF	16	25	3	4	1	0	0	3	.160	3	4	0	12	2	1	.933
1998—Fresno (PCL)...........	OF-DH	89	342	60	102	17	3	18	62	.298	46	57	12	152	5	6	.963
—San Francisco (N.L.) ..	PH	3	3	0	0	0	0	0	0	.000	0	2	0	0	0	0	
—Buffalo (I.L.)■...........	OF	43	169	32	56	8	2	13	36	.331	13	26	2	70	5	4	.949
—Cleveland (A.L.)...........	PH	1	1	0	0	0	0	0	0	.000	0	1	0	0	0	0	
1999—Buffalo (I.L.)...........	OF-DH	54	202	29	55	7	2	7	31	.272	21	39	4	77	5	4	.953
—Cleveland (A.L.)...........	OF-DH	32	88	14	29	5	1	3	17	.330	5	13	0	48	0	0	1.000
2000—Cleveland (A.L.)........	OF-DH	11	29	3	7	3	0	0	5	.241	5	4	1	16	1	0	1.000
2001—Cleveland (A.L.)........	OF	28	68	12	15	4	0	3	11	.221	5	23	0	40	0	1	.976
—Colorado (N.L.)■	OF	44	76	7	16	1	0	1	7	.211	10	27	0	26	1	2	.931
—Colo. Springs (PCL) ...	OF	20	86	18	28	5	2	6	25	.326	1	23	1	39	5	0	1.000
American League totals (4 years)		72	186	29	51	12	1	6	33	.274	15	41	1	104	1	1	.991
National League totals (4 years)		96	181	20	38	5	0	4	20	.210	25	57	0	79	4	4	.954
Major League totals (6 years)		168	367	49	89	17	1	10	53	.243	40	98	1	183	5	5	.974

CRUZ, JOSE   OF   BLUE JAYS

PERSONAL: Born April 19, 1974, in Arroyo, Puerto Rico. ... 6-0/200. ... Bats both, throws right. ... Full name: Jose Cruz Jr. ... Son of Jose Cruz Sr., outfielder with St. Louis Cardinals (1970-1974), Houston Astros (1975-1987) and New York Yankees (1988); and coach, Houston Astros; nephew of Hector Cruz, outfielder/third baseman with four major league teams (1973, 1975-82); and nephew of Tommy Cruz, outfielder with St. Louis Cardinals (1973), Chicago White Sox (1977) and Nippon Ham Fighters of Japan League (1980-85).
HIGH SCHOOL: Bellaire (Houston).
COLLEGE: Rice.
TRANSACTIONS/CAREER NOTES: Selected by Atlanta Braves organization in 15th round of free-agent draft (June 1, 1992); did not sign. ... Selected by Seattle Mariners organization in first round (third pick overall) of free-agent draft (June 1, 1995). ... Traded by Mariners to Toronto Blue Jays for P Mike Timlin and P Paul Spoljaric (July 31, 1997). ... On Toronto disabled list (June 24-July 9, 1999); included rehabilitation assignment to Syracuse (July 5-9). ... On disabled list (May 6-21, 2001).
RECORDS: Shares A.L. single-month record for most home runs—4 (October 2001).
STATISTICAL NOTES: Switch-hit home runs in one game (August 24, 1997). ... Had 18-game hitting streak (August 5-24, 1998). ... Led A.L. outfielders with 417 total chances in 2000. ... Had 19-game hitting streak (April 4-27, 2001). ... Career major league grand slams: 1.

								BATTING							FIELDING		
Year	Team (League)	Pos.	G	AB	R	H	2B	3B	HR	RBI	Avg.	BB	SO	SB	PO	A	E	Avg.
1995—Everett (N'West)	OF	3	11	6	5	0	0	0	2	.455	3	3	1	7	0	0	1.000
—Riverside (Calif.)	OF	35	144	34	37	7	1	7	29	.257	24	50	3	70	4	3	.961
1996—Lancaster (Calif.)	OF-DH	53	203	38	66	17	1	6	43	.325	39	33	7	62	7	1	.986
—Port City (Sou.)	OF-DH	47	181	39	51	10	2	3	31	.282	27	38	5	90	6	1	.990
—Tacoma (PCL)	OF	22	76	15	18	1	2	6	15	.237	18	12	1	36	4	0	1.000
1997—Tacoma (PCL)	OF-DH	50	190	33	51	16	2	6	30	.268	34	44	3	70	3	0	1.000
—Seattle (A.L.)	OF	49	183	28	49	12	1	12	34	.268	13	45	1	83	1	3	.966
—Toronto (A.L.)■	OF	55	212	31	49	7	0	14	34	.231	28	72	6	98	3	2	.981
1998—Toronto (A.L.)	OF	105	352	55	89	14	3	11	42	.253	57	99	11	247	7	4	.984
—Syracuse (I.L.)	OF	40	141	29	42	14	1	7	23	.298	32	32	8	99	7	1	.991
1999—Toronto (A.L.)	OF	106	349	63	84	19	3	14	45	.241	64	91	14	277	8	3	.990
—Syracuse (I.L.)	OF-DH	31	103	17	19	3	1	3	14	.184	28	20	5	75	2	0	1.000
2000—Toronto (A.L.)	OF	•162	603	91	146	32	5	31	76	.242	71	129	15	*405	9	3	.993
2001—Toronto (A.L.)	OF-DH	146	577	92	158	38	4	34	88	.274	45	138	32	286	5	3	.990
Major League totals (5 years)		623	2276	360	575	122	16	116	319	.253	278	574	79	1396	33	18	.988

CRUZ, JUAN   P   CUBS

PERSONAL: Born October 15, 1978, in Bonao, Dominican Republic. ... 6-2/155. ... Throws right, bats right. ... Full name: Juan Carlos Cruz.
TRANSACTIONS/CAREER NOTES: Signed as non-drafted free agent by Chicago Cubs organization (July 4, 1997).
STATISTICAL NOTES: Led Southern League with 16 hit batsmen in 2001.
MISCELLANEOUS: Appeared in three games as pinch runner (2001).

Year	League	W	L	Pct.	ERA	G	GS	CG	ShO	Sv.	IP	H	R	ER	BB	SO
1998—Arizona Cubs (Ariz.)	2	4	.333	6.10	12	6	0	0	0	41 1/3	61	48	28	14	36
1999—Eugene (N'West)	5	6	.455	5.94	15	15	0	0	0	80 1/3	97	59	53	33	65
2000—Lansing (Midw.)	5	5	.500	3.28	17	17	2	1	0	96	75	50	35	60	106
—Daytona (FSL)	3	0	1.000	3.25	8	7	1	0	0	44 1/3	30	22	16	18	54
2001—West Tenn (Sou.)	9	6	.600	4.01	23	23	0	0	0	121 1/3	107	56	54	60	137
—Chicago (N.L.)	3	1	.750	3.22	8	8	0	0	0	44 2/3	40	16	16	17	39
Major League totals (1 year)	3	1	.750	3.22	8	8	0	0	0	44 2/3	40	16	16	17	39

CRUZ, NELSON   P   ASTROS

PERSONAL: Born September 13, 1972, in Puerta Plata, Dominican Republic. ... 6-1/185. ... Throws right, bats right. ... Cousin of Jose Roman, pitcher with Cleveland Indians (1984-86).
HIGH SCHOOL: Liceo Jose Castellanos (Puerto Plata, Dominican Republic).
TRANSACTIONS/CAREER NOTES: Signed as non-drafted free agent by Montreal Expos organization (July 5, 1989). ... Released by Expos (March 27, 1992). ... Signed by Chicago White Sox organization (December 10, 1994). ... Granted free agency (October 15, 1998). ... Signed by Detroit Tigers (November 19, 1998). ... On Toledo disabled list (May 7-24, 2000). ... Traded by Tigers with C Brad Ausmus and P Doug Brocail to Houston Astros for C Mitch Meluskey, P Chris Holt and OF Roger Cedeno (December 11, 2000).

Year	League	W	L	Pct.	ERA	G	GS	CG	ShO	Sv.	IP	H	R	ER	BB	SO
1990—Dominican Expos (DSL)	9	2	.818	2.62	16	16	0	0	0	103	105	49	30	42	83
1991—Gulf Coast Expos (GCL)	2	4	.333	2.40	12	8	1	•1	0	48 2/3	40	18	13	19	34
1992—							Out of organized baseball.									
1993—							Out of organized baseball.									
1994—							Out of organized baseball.									
1995—Bristol (Appl.)■	0	0	...	9.00	1	0	0	0	0	1	2	1	1	0	0
—Hickory (S.Atl.)	2	7	.222	2.70	44	0	0	0	9	66 2/3	65	31	20	15	68
—Prince William (Caro.)	2	1	.667	0.47	9	0	0	0	1	19 1/3	12	1	1	6	15
1996—Birmingham (Sou.)	6	6	.500	3.20	37	18	2	1	1	149	150	65	53	41	142
1997—Nashville (A.A.)	11	7	.611	5.11	21	20	1	0	0	123 1/3	139	75	70	31	93
—Chicago (A.L.)	0	2	.000	6.49	19	0	0	0	0	26 1/3	29	19	19	9	23
1998—Calgary (PCL)	10	6	.625	5.33	35	18	2	1	0	126 2/3	159	85	75	40	101
1999—Toledo (I.L.)■	7	1	.875	2.73	10	10	4	•2	0	62 2/3	47	20	19	21	41
—Detroit (A.L.)	2	5	.286	5.67	29	6	0	0	0	66 2/3	74	44	42	23	46
2000—Toledo (I.L.)	2	4	.333	4.82	11	10	0	0	0	52 1/3	54	37	28	17	39
—Detroit (A.L.)	5	2	.714	3.07	27	0	0	0	0	41	39	14	14	13	34
2001—Houston (N.L.)■	3	3	.500	4.15	66	0	0	0	2	82 1/3	72	41	38	24	75
A.L. totals (3 years)	7	9	.438	5.04	75	6	0	0	0	134	142	77	75	45	103
N.L. totals (1 year)	3	3	.500	4.15	66	0	0	0	2	82 1/3	72	41	38	24	75
Major League totals (4 years)	10	12	.455	4.70	141	6	0	0	2	216 1/3	214	118	113	69	178

DIVISION SERIES RECORD

Year	League	W	L	Pct.	ERA	G	GS	CG	ShO	Sv.	IP	H	R	ER	BB	SO
2001—Houston (N.L.)	0	0	...	0.00	2	0	0	0	0	2 2/3	1	0	0	1	1

CUBILLAN, DARWIN   P   EXPOS

PERSONAL: Born November 15, 1974, in Bobure, Venezuela. ... 6-2/170. ... Throws right, bats right. ... Full name: Darwin Harrikson Salom Cubillan.

TRANSACTIONS/CAREER NOTES: Signed as non-drafted free agent by New York Yankees organization (June 28, 1993). ... On disabled list (April 4, 1996-entire season). ... Granted free agency (October 15, 1999). ... Signed by Toronto Blue Jays organization (November 12, 1999). ... Traded by Blue Jays with 2B/SS Mike Young to Texas Rangers for P Esteban Loaiza (July 19, 2000). ... Traded by Rangers to Montreal Expos for P Mike Johnson (May 8, 2001).

Year League	W	L	Pct.	ERA	G	GS	CG	ShO	Sv.	IP	H	R	ER	BB	SO
1993—Dominican Yankees (DSL)..	0	2	.000	9.45	4	2	0	0	0	6²/₃	8	9	7	14	3
1994—Gulf Coast Yankees (GCL)..	4	2	.667	2.35	13	8	1	1	0	57¹/₃	45	16	15	16	48
—Greensboro (S.Atl.)	0	0	...	18.00	1	0	0	0	0	2	6	5	4	2	1
1995—Greensboro (S.Atl.)	5	5	.500	3.62	22	14	1	1	0	97	86	50	39	38	78
1996—							Did not play.								
1997—Gulf Coast Yankees (GCL)..	0	0	...	0.00	1	1	0	0	0	1²/₃	1	0	0	1	2
1998—Tampa (FSL)..................	9	2	.818	4.71	45	1	0	0	1	65	79	45	34	36	70
1999—Tampa (FSL)..................	7	4	.636	2.51	55	0	0	0	3	75¹/₃	57	27	21	32	76
2000—Syracuse (I.L.)■..............	3	1	.750	0.55	24	0	0	0	6	32²/₃	14	2	2	13	41
—Toronto (A.L.)..................	1	0	1.000	8.04	7	0	0	0	0	15²/₃	20	14	14	11	14
—Oklahoma (PCL)■..............	0	0	...	1.08	8	0	0	0	2	16²/₃	9	2	2	4	12
—Texas (A.L.).....................	0	0	...	10.70	13	0	0	0	0	17²/₃	32	22	21	14	13
2001—Oklahoma (PCL)...............	1	1	.500	10.38	9	0	0	0	2	13	20	16	15	12	8
—Ottawa (I.L.)■.................	2	2	.500	5.28	17	4	0	0	2	30²/₃	31	22	18	15	29
—Montreal (N.L.).................	0	0	...	4.10	29	0	0	0	0	26¹/₃	31	13	12	12	19
A.L. totals (1 year)	1	0	1.000	9.45	20	0	0	0	0	33¹/₃	52	36	35	25	27
N.L. totals (1 year)	0	0	...	4.10	29	0	0	0	0	26¹/₃	31	13	12	12	19
Major League totals (2 years).......	1	0	1.000	7.09	49	0	0	0	0	59²/₃	83	49	47	37	46

CUDDYER, MIKE   3B   TWINS

PERSONAL: Born March 27, 1979, in Norfolk, Va. ... 6-2/200. ... Bats right, throws right. ... Full name: Michael Brent Cuddyer.
HIGH SCHOOL: Great Bridge (Chesapeake, Va.).

TRANSACTIONS/CAREER NOTES: Selected by Minnesota Twins organization in first round (ninth pick overall) of free-agent draft (June 3, 1997).

STATISTICAL NOTES: Led Midwest League shortstops with 61 errors and 654 total chances in 1998. ... Led Florida State League in grounding into double plays with 20 in 1999. ... Tied for Florida State League lead in double plays by third baseman with 25 in 1999.

						BATTING								FIELDING		
Year Team (League)	Pos.	G	AB	R	H	2B	3B	HR	RBI	Avg.	BB	SO	SB	PO	A	E	Avg.
1998—Fort Wayne (Midw.).....	SS-2B	129	497	82	137	37	7	12	81	.276	61	107	16	201	393	†61	.907
1999—Fort Myers (FSL)........	3B	130	466	87	139	24	4	16	82	.298	•76	91	14	81	245	28	.921
2000—New Britain (East.)......	3B	138	490	72	129	30	8	6	61	.263	55	93	5	84	231	*34	.903
2001—New Britain (East.)	3B-1B-OF	141	509	95	153	36	3	30	87	.301	75	106	5	535	199	28	.963
—Minnesota (A.L.)	1B-3B-DH	8	18	1	4	2	0	0	1	.222	2	6	1	37	2	1	.975
Major League totals (1 year)		8	18	1	4	2	0	0	1	.222	2	6	1	37	2	1	.975

CUMMINGS, MIDRE   OF

PERSONAL: Born October 14, 1971, in St. Croix, Virgin Islands. ... 6-0/195. ... Bats left, throws right. ... Full name: Midre Almeric Cummings.
HIGH SCHOOL: Miami Edison Senior.

TRANSACTIONS/CAREER NOTES: Selected by Minnesota Twins organization in supplemental round ("sandwich pick" between first and second round, 29th pick overall) of free-agent draft (June 4, 1990); pick received as part of compensation for Boston Red Sox signing Type A free-agent P Jeff Reardon. ... Traded by Twins with P Denny Neagle to Pittsburgh Pirates for P John Smiley (March 17, 1992). ... On Buffalo disabled list (April 21-June 6, 1994). ... On Calgary disabled list (June 17-July 1, 1995). ... Claimed on waivers by Philadelphia Phillies (July 8, 1997). ... Released by Phillies (February 24, 1998). ... Signed by Cincinnati Reds organization (February 27, 1998). ... Claimed on waivers by Boston Red Sox (March 19, 1998). ... On disabled list (July 29-September 7, 1998). ... Released by Red Sox (March 30, 1999). ... Signed by Twins organization (May 14, 1999). ... Traded by Twins to Red Sox for IF Hector De Los Santos (August 31, 2000). ... Granted free agency (October 13, 2000). ... Signed by Arizona Diamondbacks (December 15, 2000). ... On Tucson disabled list (July 24-August 15, 2001). ... Granted free agency (December 21, 2001).
MISCELLANEOUS: Batted as switch-hitter (1990-92).

						BATTING								FIELDING		
Year Team (League)	Pos.	G	AB	R	H	2B	3B	HR	RBI	Avg.	BB	SO	SB	PO	A	E	Avg.
1990—GC Twins (GCL).........	OF	47	177	28	56	3	4	5	28	.316	13	32	14	73	2	6	.926
1991—Kenosha (Midw.)........	OF	106	382	59	123	20	4	4	54	*.322	22	66	28	166	6	•13	.930
1992—Salem (Caro.)■..........	OF	113	420	55	128	20	5	14	75	.305	35	67	23	151	10	6	.964
1993—Carolina (Sou.).........	OF	63	237	33	70	17	2	6	26	.295	14	23	5	99	7	4	.964
—Buffalo (A.A.)..............	OF	60	232	36	64	12	1	9	21	.276	22	45	5	90	1	2	.978
—Pittsburgh (N.L.)	OF	13	36	5	4	1	0	0	3	.111	4	9	0	21	0	0	1.000
1994—Buffalo (A.A.)..........	OF	49	183	23	57	12	4	2	22	.311	13	26	5	117	2	0	1.000
—Pittsburgh (N.L.)	OF	24	86	11	21	4	0	1	12	.244	4	18	0	49	1	2	.962
1995—Pittsburgh (N.L.)	OF	59	152	13	37	7	1	2	15	.243	13	30	1	79	2	1	.988
—Calgary (PCL)............	OF	45	159	19	44	9	1	1	16	.277	6	27	1	96	4	6	.943
1996—Calgary (PCL)............	OF-DH	97	368	60	112	24	3	8	55	.304	21	60	6	176	9	5	.974
—Pittsburgh (N.L.)	OF	24	85	11	19	3	1	3	7	.224	0	16	0	49	0	1	.980
1997—Pittsburgh (N.L.)	OF	52	106	11	20	6	2	3	8	.189	8	26	0	37	1	0	1.000
—Philadelphia (N.L.)■ ..	OF	63	208	24	63	16	4	1	23	.303	23	30	2	113	1	1	.991
1998—Boston (A.L.)■..........	DH-OF	67	120	20	34	8	0	5	15	.283	17	19	3	16	0	1	.941

					BATTING								FIELDING			
Year Team (League)	Pos.	G	AB	R	H	2B	3B	HR	RBI	Avg.	BB	SO	SB	PO	A	E	Avg.
1999— New Britain (East.)■ ..	OF	24	93	28	35	7	0	2	15	.376	17	14	3	50	2	0	1.000
— Salt Lake (PCL)	OF-DH	69	261	50	84	19	4	13	68	.322	23	43	4	101	3	5	.954
— Minnesota (A.L.)	OF-DH	16	38	1	10	0	0	1	9	.263	3	7	2	5	0	0	1.000
2000— Minnesota (A.L.)	OF-DH	77	181	28	50	10	0	4	22	.276	11	25	0	58	4	0	1.000
— Boston (A.L.)■..........	OF-DH	21	25	1	7	0	0	0	2	.280	6	3	0	7	0	0	1.000
2001— Arizona (N.L.)■........	OF	20	20	1	6	1	0	0	1	.300	0	4	0	4	0	0	1.000
— Tucson (PCL)	OF-1B	77	263	38	87	23	9	5	38	.331	24	49	2	123	6	2	.985
American League totals (3 years)		181	364	50	101	18	0	10	48	.277	37	54	5	86	4	1	.989
National League totals (6 years)		255	693	76	170	38	8	10	69	.245	52	133	3	352	5	5	.986
Major League totals (9 years)		436	1057	126	271	56	8	20	117	.256	89	187	8	438	9	6	.987

DIVISION SERIES RECORD

					BATTING								FIELDING			
Year Team (League)	Pos.	G	AB	R	H	2B	3B	HR	RBI	Avg.	BB	SO	SB	PO	A	E	Avg.
1998— Boston (A.L.)............	PH	3	3	0	0	0	0	0	0	.000	0	0	0	...	...	...	...
2001— Arizona (N.L.)...........	PR	2	0	1	0	0	0	0	0	...	0	0	0	...	...	...	...
Division series totals (2 years)		5	3	1	0	0	0	0	0	.000	0	0	0	...	...	...	...

CHAMPIONSHIP SERIES RECORD

					BATTING								FIELDING			
Year Team (League)	Pos.	G	AB	R	H	2B	3B	HR	RBI	Avg.	BB	SO	SB	PO	A	E	Avg.
2001— Arizona (N.L.)...........	PH	1	1	0	0	0	0	0	0	.000	0	0	0	...	...	...	...

WORLD SERIES RECORD

NOTES: Member of World Series championship team (2001).

					BATTING								FIELDING			
Year Team (League)	Pos.	G	AB	R	H	2B	3B	HR	RBI	Avg.	BB	SO	SB	PO	A	E	Avg.
2001— Arizona (N.L.)...........	PR-DH	2	0	2	0	0	0	0	0	...	0	0	0	...	...	...	...

CUNNANE, WILL   P

PERSONAL: Born April 24, 1974, in Suffern, N.Y. ... 6-2/200. ... Throws right, bats right. ... Full name: William Joseph Cunnane.
HIGH SCHOOL: Clarkstown North (New City, N.Y.).
TRANSACTIONS/CAREER NOTES: Signed as non-drafted free agent by Florida Marlins organization (August 18, 1992). ... On Portland disabled list (August 7-23, 1996). ... Selected by San Diego Padres from Marlins organization in Rule 5 major league draft (December 9, 1996). ... On San Diego disabled list (March 29-June 21, 1998); included rehabilitation assignment to Las Vegas (June 9-21). ... Traded by Padres to Milwaukee Brewers for OF Chad Green (December 20, 2000), completing deal in which Brewers traded SS Santiago Perez and a player to be named later or cash to San Deigo Padres for P Brandon Kolb (December 1, 2000). ... Granted free agency (October 8, 2001).
MISCELLANEOUS: Appeared in one game as pinch runner (1997). ... Appeared in one game as pinch runner (2001).

Year League	W	L	Pct.	ERA	G	GS	CG	ShO	Sv.	IP	H	R	ER	BB	SO
1993— Gulf Coast Marlins (GCL) ...	3	3	.500	2.70	16	9	0	0	2	66 2/3	75	32	20	8	64
1994— Kane County (Midw.)..........	11	3	.786	*1.43	32	16	5	*4	1	138 2/3	110	27	22	23	106
1995— Portland (East.)	9	2	*.818	3.67	21	21	1	1	0	117 2/3	120	48	48	34	83
1996— Portland (East.)	10	12	.455	3.74	25	25	4	0	0	151 2/3	156	73	63	30	101
1997— San Diego (N.L.)■	6	3	.667	5.81	54	8	0	0	0	91 1/3	114	69	59	49	79
1998— Las Vegas (PCL)	1	2	.333	5.25	33	0	0	0	4	36	45	26	21	19	30
— San Diego (N.L.)	0	0	...	6.00	3	0	0	0	0	3	4	2	2	1	1
1999— Las Vegas (PCL)	2	1	.667	0.98	28	0	0	0	11	36 2/3	30	5	4	16	54
— San Diego (N.L.)	2	1	.667	5.23	24	0	0	0	0	31	34	19	18	12	22
2000— San Diego (N.L.)	1	1	.500	4.23	27	3	0	0	0	38 1/3	35	21	18	21	34
— Las Vegas (PCL)	7	4	.636	3.98	17	17	1	1	0	97 1/3	96	46	43	26	97
2001— Milwaukee (N.L.)■.............	0	3	.000	5.40	31	1	0	0	0	51 2/3	66	34	31	22	37
— Indianapolis (I.L.)...............	0	1	.000	3.86	7	3	0	0	1	23 1/3	25	10	10	6	25
Major League totals (5 years).......	9	8	.529	5.35	139	12	0	0	0	215 1/3	253	145	128	105	173

CURTIS, CHAD   OF

PERSONAL: Born November 6, 1968, in Marion, Ind. ... 5-10/185. ... Bats right, throws right. ... Full name: Chad David Curtis.
HIGH SCHOOL: Benson (Ariz.) Union.
JUNIOR COLLEGE: Yavapai College (Ariz.), then Cochise County Community College (Ariz.).
COLLEGE: Grand Canyon (Ariz.).
TRANSACTIONS/CAREER NOTES: Selected by California Angels organization in 45th round of free-agent draft (June 5, 1989). ... On disabled list (June 5-20, 1991). ... On suspended list (June 8-12, 1993). ... Traded by Angels to Detroit Tigers for OF/3B Tony Phillips (April 12, 1995). ... Traded by Tigers to Los Angeles Dodgers for P Joey Eischen and P John Cummings (July 31, 1996). ... Granted free agency (October 15, 1996). ... Signed by Cleveland Indians (December 18, 1996). ... On Cleveland disabled list (May 14-June 9, 1997). ... Traded by Indians to New York Yankees for P David Weathers (June 9, 1997). ... On New York disabled list (June 9-11, 1997). ... Traded by Yankees to Texas Rangers for P Brandon Knight and P Sam Marsonek (December 13, 1999). ... On Texas disabled list (May 3-August 9, 2001); included rehabilitation assignments to Oklahoma (June 3-8) and Tulsa (July 30-August 9). ... Granted free agency (November 5, 2001).
STATISTICAL NOTES: Led Midwest League with 223 total bases in 1990. ... Tied for A.L. lead in caught stealing with 24 in 1993. ... Led A.L. outfielders with 448 total chances and tied for lead with nine errors in 1993. ... Led A.L. outfielders with 345 total chances in 1994. ... Career major league grand slams: 1.

Year	Team (League)	Pos.	G	AB	R	H	2B	3B	HR	RBI	Avg.	BB	SO	SB	PO	A	E	Avg.
								BATTING								FIELDING		
1989—	Arizona Angels (Ariz.).	2B-OF	32	122	30	37	4	4	3	20	.303	14	20	17	62	58	6	.952
—	Quad City (Midw.)	OF	23	78	7	19	3	0	2	11	.244	6	17	7	34	1	1	.972
1990—	Quad City (Midw.)	2B-OF	135	*492	87	*151	28	1	14	65	.307	57	76	64	216	221	26	.944
1991—	Edmonton (PCL)	3B-2B-OF	115	431	81	136	28	7	9	61	.316	51	56	46	124	220	25	.932
1992—	California (A.L.)	OF-DH	139	441	59	114	16	2	10	46	.259	51	71	43	250	*16	6	.978
1993—	California (A.L.)	OF-2B	152	583	94	166	25	3	6	59	.285	70	89	48	426	13	‡9	.980
1994—	California (A.L.)	OF	114	453	67	116	23	4	11	50	.256	37	69	25	*332	9	4	.988
1995—	Detroit (A.L.)■	OF	144	586	96	157	29	3	21	67	.268	70	93	27	362	5	3	.992
1996—	Detroit (A.L.)	OF	104	400	65	105	20	1	10	37	.263	53	73	16	243	6	9	.965
—	Los Angeles (N.L.)■	OF	43	104	20	22	5	0	2	9	.212	17	15	2	62	2	1	.985
1997—	Cleveland (A.L.)■	OF	22	29	8	6	1	0	3	5	.207	7	10	0	20	0	0	1.000
—	Akron (East.)	OF	4	18	5	7	1	0	3	6	.389	0	3	0	5	2	0	1.000
—	New York (A.L.)■	OF	93	320	51	93	21	1	12	50	.291	36	49	12	168	6	4	.978
1998—	New York (A.L.)	OF-DH	151	456	79	111	21	1	10	56	.243	75	80	21	306	8	5	.984
1999—	New York (A.L.)	OF	96	195	37	51	6	0	5	24	.262	43	35	8	98	2	1	.990
2000—	Texas (A.L.)■	OF-DH	108	335	48	91	25	1	8	48	.272	37	71	3	135	4	5	.965
2001—	Texas (A.L.)	OF-DH	38	115	24	29	3	0	3	10	.252	14	21	7	80	2	1	.988
—	Oklahoma (PCL)	DH	4	14	3	4	0	0	1	1	.286	2	2	0	...	...	...	...
—	Tulsa (Texas)	OF	6	22	3	4	0	0	1	2	.182	5	6	1	11	0	1	.917
American League totals (10 years)			1161	3913	628	1039	190	16	99	452	.266	493	661	210	2420	71	47	.981
National League totals (1 year)			43	104	20	22	5	0	2	9	.212	17	15	2	62	2	1	.985
Major League totals (10 years)			1204	4017	648	1061	195	16	101	461	.264	510	676	212	2482	73	48	.982

DIVISION SERIES RECORD

Year	Team (League)	Pos.	G	AB	R	H	2B	3B	HR	RBI	Avg.	BB	SO	SB	PO	A	E	Avg.
								BATTING								FIELDING		
1996—	Los Angeles (N.L.)	OF	1	2	0	0	0	0	0	0	.000	1	1	0	2	0	0	1.000
1997—	New York (A.L.)	OF-PR	4	6	0	1	0	0	0	0	.167	3	1	0	4	0	0	1.000
1998—	New York (A.L.)	OF	3	3	1	2	1	0	0	0	.667	1	1	1	3	0	0	1.000
1999—	New York (A.L.)	OF-PR	3	3	1	0	0	0	0	0	.000	0	0	0	0	0	0	...
Division series totals (4 years)			11	14	2	3	1	0	0	0	.214	5	3	1	9	0	0	1.000

CHAMPIONSHIP SERIES RECORD

Year	Team (League)	Pos.	G	AB	R	H	2B	3B	HR	RBI	Avg.	BB	SO	SB	PO	A	E	Avg.
								BATTING								FIELDING		
1998—	New York (A.L.)	OF	2	4	0	0	0	0	0	0	.000	1	2	0	1	0	0	1.000
1999—	New York (A.L.)	OF-PR-DH	3	6	1	0	0	0	0	0	.000	0	2	1	0	0	0	...
Championship series totals (2 years)			5	10	1	0	0	0	0	0	.000	1	4	1	1	0	0	1.000

WORLD SERIES RECORD

NOTES: Member of World Series championship team (1998 and 1999).

Year	Team (League)	Pos.	G	AB	R	H	2B	3B	HR	RBI	Avg.	BB	SO	SB	PO	A	E	Avg.
								BATTING								FIELDING		
1998—	New York (A.L.)								Did not play.									
1999—	New York (A.L.)	PR-OF-PH	3	6	3	2	0	0	2	2	.333	0	0	0	5	0	0	1.000

CUST, JACK — OF — ROCKIES

PERSONAL: Born January 16, 1979, in Flemington, N.J. ... 6-1/205. ... Bats left, throws right. ... Full name: John Joseph Cust.
HIGH SCHOOL: Immaculata (Somerville, N.J.).
TRANSACTIONS/CAREER NOTES: Selected by Arizona Diamondbacks organization in first round (30th pick overall) of free-agent draft (June 3, 1997). ... Traded by Diamondbacks with C J.D. Closser to Colorado Rockies for P Mike Myers (January 7, 2002).

Year	Team (League)	Pos.	G	AB	R	H	2B	3B	HR	RBI	Avg.	BB	SO	SB	PO	A	E	Avg.
								BATTING								FIELDING		
1997—	Ariz. D'backs (Ariz.)	OF	35	121	26	37	11	1	3	33	.306	31	39	2	46	0	5	.902
1998—	South Bend (Midw.)	OF	16	62	5	15	3	0	0	4	.242	5	20	0	150	9	4	.975
—	Lethbridge (Pio.)	OF	73	223	75	77	20	2	11	56	.345	86	71	15	82	2	0	1.000
1999—	High Desert (Calif.)	OF	125	455	107	152	42	3	32	112	.334	96	145	1	136	5	12	.922
2000—	El Paso (Texas)	OF	129	447	100	131	32	6	20	75	.293	117	150	12	176	10	11	.944
2001—	Tucson (PCL)	OF	135	442	81	123	24	2	27	79	.278	102	160	6	195	6	*11	.948
—	Arizona (N.L.)	OF	3	2	0	1	0	0	0	0	.500	1	0	0	0	0	0	...
Major League totals (1 year)			3	2	0	1	0	0	0	0	.500	1	0	0	0	0	0	...

CYR, ERIC — P — PADRES

PERSONAL: Born February 11, 1979, in Montreal. ... 6-4/200. ... Throws right, bats left.
HIGH SCHOOL: Polyvalente Edouard Montpetit (Montreal).
JUNIOR COLLEGE: Seminole (Okla.).
TRANSACTIONS/CAREER NOTES: Selected by San Diego Padres organization in 30th round of free-agent draft (June 2, 1998). ... On Fort Wayne disabled list (May 8-August 25, 2000).

Year	League	W	L	Pct.	ERA	G	GS	CG	ShO	Sv.	IP	H	R	ER	BB	SO
1999—	Arizona Padres (Ariz.)	2	1	.667	3.26	11	5	0	0	0	38²/₃	34	19	14	15	39
—	Idaho Falls (Pio.)	1	0	1.000	1.80	1	1	0	0	0	5	5	1	1	1	3
2000—	Fort Wayne (Midw.)	2	2	.500	4.68	9	6	0	0	0	32²/₃	28	18	17	15	31
—	Arizona Padres (Ariz.)	0	0	...	3.00	2	1	0	0	0	3	4	1	1	2	4
2001—	Lake Elsinore (Calif.)	7	4	.636	1.61	21	16	0	0	0	100²/₃	68	28	18	24	131

PERSONAL: Born March 1, 1972, in Maracaibo, Venezuela. ... 6-3/195. ... Throws left, bats left. ... Full name: Omar Jose Cordaro Daal.

HIGH SCHOOL: Valencia (Venezuela) Superior.

TRANSACTIONS/CAREER NOTES: Signed as non-drafted free agent by Los Angeles Dodgers organization (August 24, 1990). ... Traded by Dodgers to Montreal Expos for P Rick Clelland (December 14, 1995). ... Claimed on waivers by Toronto Blue Jays (July 25, 1997). ... Selected by Arizona Diamondbacks in second round (31st pick overall) of expansion draft (November 18, 1997). ... On Arizona disabled list (June 22-July 11, 1998); included rehabilitation assignment to Tucson (July 9-11). ... Traded by Diamondbacks with OF Travis Lee, P Vicente Padilla and P Nelson Figueroa to Philadelphia Phillies for P Curt Schilling (July 26, 2000). ... Traded by Phillies to Los Angeles Dodgers for P Eric Junge and P Jesus Cordero (November 9, 2001).

STATISTICAL NOTES: Led N.L. with 19 losses in 2000. ... Tied for N.L. lead with three balks in 2001.

Year League	W	L	Pct.	ERA	G	GS	CG	ShO	Sv.	IP	H	R	ER	BB	SO
1990—Dominican Dodgers (DSL).	3	6	.333	1.18	17	13	6	0	2	91 2/3	61	29	12	29	91
1991—Dominican Dodgers (DSL).	7	2	.778	1.16	13	13	0	0	0	93	30	17	12	32	81
1992—Albuquerque (PCL)........	0	2	.000	7.84	12	0	0	0	0	10 1/3	14	9	9	11	9
—San Antonio (Texas).........	2	6	.250	5.02	35	5	0	0	5	57 1/3	60	39	32	33	52
1993—Albuquerque (PCL)........	1	1	.500	3.38	6	0	0	0	0	5 1/3	5	2	2	3	2
—Los Angeles (N.L.)	2	3	.400	5.09	47	0	0	0	0	35 1/3	36	20	20	21	19
1994—Albuquerque (PCL)........	4	2	.667	5.19	11	5	0	0	1	34 2/3	38	20	20	16	28
—Los Angeles (N.L.)	0	0	...	3.29	24	0	0	0	0	13 2/3	12	5	5	5	9
1995—Albuquerque (PCL)........	2	3	.400	4.05	17	9	0	0	0	53 1/3	56	28	24	26	46
—Los Angeles (N.L.)	4	0	1.000	7.20	28	0	0	0	0	20	29	16	16	15	11
1996—Montreal (N.L.)■...........	4	5	.444	4.02	64	6	0	0	0	87 1/3	74	40	39	37	82
1997—Montreal (N.L.).............	1	2	.333	9.79	33	0	0	0	1	30 1/3	48	35	33	15	16
—Ottawa (I.L.)	0	1	.000	5.63	2	2	0	0	0	8	10	6	5	1	9
—Toronto (A.L.)■.................	1	1	.500	4.00	9	3	0	0	0	27	34	13	12	6	28
1998—Arizona (N.L.)■.............	8	12	.400	2.88	33	23	3	1	0	162 2/3	146	60	52	51	132
—Tucson (PCL)	0	0	...	3.00	1	1	0	0	0	3	3	2	1	1	4
1999—Arizona (N.L.)..............	16	9	.640	3.65	32	32	2	1	0	214 2/3	188	92	87	79	148
2000—Arizona (N.L.)..............	2	10	.167	7.22	20	16	0	0	0	96	127	88	77	42	45
—Philadelphia (N.L.)■	2	§9	.182	4.69	12	12	0	0	0	71	81	40	37	30	51
2001—Philadelphia (N.L.)........	13	7	.650	4.46	32	32	0	0	0	185 2/3	199	100	92	56	107
A.L. totals (1 year)	1	1	.500	4.00	9	3	0	0	0	27	34	13	12	6	28
N.L. totals (9 years)	52	57	.477	4.50	325	121	5	2	1	916 2/3	940	496	458	351	620
Major League totals (9 years).......	53	58	.477	4.48	334	124	5	2	1	943 2/3	974	509	470	357	648

DIVISION SERIES RECORD

Year League	W	L	Pct.	ERA	G	GS	CG	ShO	Sv.	IP	H	R	ER	BB	SO
1999—Arizona (N.L.)...............	0	1	.000	6.75	1	1	0	0	0	4	6	3	3	3	4

DALESANDRO, MARK   C/3B

PERSONAL: Born May 14, 1968, in Chicago. ... 6-0/195. ... Bats right, throws right. ... Full name: Mark Anthony Dalesandro. ... Name pronounced DEE-uh-SAN-droh.

HIGH SCHOOL: St. Ignatius College Prep School (Chicago).

COLLEGE: Illinois.

TRANSACTIONS/CAREER NOTES: Selected by California Angels organization in 18th round of free-agent draft (June 4, 1990). ... Released by Angels (February 6, 1996). ... Signed by New York Yankees organization (February 12, 1996). ... Released by Yankees (April 4, 1996). ... Re-signed by Yankees organization (May 3, 1996). ... Granted free agency (October 15, 1996). ... Signed by Chicago Cubs organization (December 23, 1996). ... On Iowa disabled list (April 27-May 4, 1997). ... Granted free agency (October 17, 1997). ... Signed by Toronto Blue Jays organization (December 2, 1997). ... On Syracuse disabled list (July 22, 1999-remainder of season). ... On Syracuse disabled list (April 6-25, 2000). ... Released by Blue Jays (April 28, 2000). ... Signed by Milwaukee Brewers organization (April 28, 2000). ... On Indianapolis disabled list (May 19-28, 2000). ... Released by Brewers (July 26, 2000). ... Signed by Chicago Cubs organization (August 8, 2000). ... Granted free agency (October 18, 2000). ... Signed by Chicago White Sox organization (November 15, 2000). ... Granted free agency (October 15, 2001).

STATISTICAL NOTES: Tied for California League lead in grounding into double plays with 20 in 1992.

Year Team (League)	Pos.	G	AB	R	H	2B	3B	HR	RBI	Avg.	BB	SO	SB	PO	A	E	Avg.
1990—Boise (N'West)	OF-3B-1B	55	224	35	75	10	2	6	44	.335	18	42	6	37	23	6	.909
1991—Quad City (Midw.)	3B-1B	125	487	63	133	17	8	5	69	.273	34	58	1	198	186	25	.939
1992—Palm Springs (Calif.)..	1B-3B	126	492	72	146	30	3	7	92	.297	33	50	6	594	114	15	.979
1993—Palm Springs (Calif.)..	C-1B	46	176	22	43	5	3	1	25	.244	15	20	3	271	42	7	.978
—Midland (Texas).........	3B-C-1B	57	235	33	69	9	0	2	36	.294	8	30	1	137	60	12	.943
—Vancouver (PCL)	3B	26	107	16	32	8	1	2	15	.299	6	13	1	19	59	7	.918
1994—Vancouver (PCL)	3-C-1-O	51	199	29	63	9	1	1	31	.317	7	19	1	153	71	11	.953
—California (A.L.).........	C-3B-OF	19	25	5	5	1	0	1	2	.200	2	4	0	19	5	1	.960
1995—California (A.L.).........	C-OF	11	10	1	1	1	0	0	0	.100	0	2	0	11	0	0	1.000
—Vancouver (PCL)	O-3-DH-C-1	34	123	16	41	13	1	1	18	.333	6	12	2	56	8	2	.970
1996—Columbus (I.L.)■.......	3-C-O-2	78	255	34	72	29	4	2	38	.282	17	31	2	128	75	10	.953
1997—Iowa (A.A.)■..............	C-3-1-O	115	405	48	106	14	0	8	48	.262	33	51	0	467	90	4	.993
1998—Toronto (A.L.)■.........C-3B-1B-OF	32	67	8	20	5	0	2	14	.299	1	6	0	76	9	2	.977
—Syracuse (I.L.)...........	3B-C-OF	45	164	25	44	9	1	10	30	.268	12	20	1	60	16	3	.962
1999—Toronto (A.L.)............	C-DH-3B	16	27	3	5	0	0	0	1	.185	0	2	1	22	3	0	1.000
—Syracuse (I.L.)..........	OF-C-3B	20	71	9	16	2	0	0	5	.225	1	7	1	32	5	0	1.000
2000—Syracuse (I.L.)	C	3	3	1	1	0	0	1	1	.333	0	1	0	6	0	1	.857
—Indianapolis (I.L.)■....	C-1-O-3-2	37	95	10	17	1	0	1	7	.179	3	10	0	158	13	3	.983
—Iowa (PCL)■..............	C-1B-3B	15	49	5	19	3	1	0	8	.388	1	4	0	79	6	3	.966
2001—Charlotte (I.L.)■.........	C-1B-2B	75	262	16	68	18	0	4	23	.260	6	24	0	455	40	2	.996
—Chicago (A.L.)	C	1	0	0	0	0	0	0	0	...	0	0	0	0	0	0	...
Major League totals (5 years)		79	129	17	31	7	0	3	17	.240	3	14	1	128	17	3	.980

PERSONAL: Born December 27, 1975, in St. Petersburg, Fla. ... 6-7/250. ... Throws right, bats right. ... Full name: Jeffrey Charles D'Amico.
HIGH SCHOOL: Northeast (St. Petersburg, Fla.).
TRANSACTIONS/CAREER NOTES: Selected by Milwaukee Brewers organization in first round (23rd pick overall) of free-agent draft (June 3, 1993). ... On disabled list (June 24, 1994-entire season). ... On Milwaukee disabled list (July 28-September 2, 1997; and January 14, 1998-entire season). ... On Milwaukee disabled list (March 29-September 25, 1999); included rehabilitation assignments to Beloit (July 6-15), Huntsville (July 16-21) and Louisville (August 12-25). ... On Milwaukee disabled list (June 6-30, 2000). ... On Milwaukee disabled list (April 23-September 1, 2001); included rehabilitation assignments to Beloit (June 6-11 and August 29-31) and Huntsville (June 12). ... Traded by Brewers to New York Mets as part of three-way deal in which Mets traded P Glendon Rusch to Brewers, Colorado Rockies traded 1B/OF Ross Gload and P Craig House to Mets, Brewers traded OF Jeromy Burnitz, IF Lou Collier, OF/1B Mark Sweeney and cash to Mets, Mets traded 1B/3B Todd Zeile, OF Benny Agbayani, IF/OF Lenny Harris and cash to Rockies and Rockies traded OF Alex Ochoa to Brewers (January 21, 2002).

Year League	W	L	Pct.	ERA	G	GS	CG	ShO	Sv.	IP	H	R	ER	BB	SO
1994—Arizona Brewers (Ariz.)							Did not play.								
1995—Beloit (Midw.).................	13	3	*.813	2.39	21	20	3	1	0	132	102	40	35	31	119
1996—El Paso (Texas).................	5	4	.556	3.19	13	13	3	0	0	96	89	42	34	13	76
—Milwaukee (A.L.).............	6	6	.500	5.44	17	17	0	0	0	86	88	53	52	31	53
1997—Milwaukee (A.L.).............	9	7	.563	4.71	23	23	1	1	0	135²/₃	139	81	71	43	94
—Beloit (Midw.).................	0	0	...	0.00	1	1	0	0	0	3	0	0	0	1	7
1998—Milwaukee (A.L.).............							Did not play.								
1999—Beloit (Midw.).................	1	0	1.000	0.00	2	2	0	0	0	8	7	0	0	1	6
—Huntsville (Sou.).............	0	0	...	36.00	1	1	0	0	0	2	6	8	8	1	2
—Louisville (I.L.).............	0	0	...	13.50	1	1	0	0	0	3¹/₃	6	5	5	2	1
—Milwaukee (N.L.).............	0	0	...	0.00	1	0	0	0	0	1	1	0	0	0	1
2000—Indianapolis (I.L.)............	1	1	.500	3.16	6	6	0	0	0	31¹/₃	25	11	11	11	20
—Milwaukee (N.L.).............	12	7	.632	2.66	23	23	1	1	0	162¹/₃	143	55	48	46	101
2001—Milwaukee (N.L.).............	2	4	.333	6.08	10	10	0	0	0	47¹/₃	60	42	32	16	32
—Beloit (Midw.).................	0	0	...	5.40	2	2	0	0	0	8¹/₃	11	6	5	1	6
—Huntsville (Sou.).............	1	0	1.000	2.57	1	1	0	0	0	7	3	2	2	2	5
A.L. totals (2 years)	15	13	.536	4.99	40	40	1	1	0	221²/₃	227	134	123	74	147
N.L. totals (3 years)	14	11	.560	3.42	34	33	1	1	0	210²/₃	204	97	80	62	134
Major League totals (5 years)	29	24	.547	4.23	74	73	2	2	0	432¹/₃	431	231	203	136	281

D

PERSONAL: Born November 5, 1973, in Fort Riley, Kan. ... 6-2/190. ... Bats left, throws left. ... Full name: Johnny David Damon.
HIGH SCHOOL: Dr. Phillips (Orlando).
TRANSACTIONS/CAREER NOTES: Selected by Kansas City Royals organization in supplemental round ("sandwich pick" between first and second round, 35th pick overall) of free-agent draft (June 1, 1992); pick received as part of compensation for San Diego Padres signing Type A free-agent IF Kurt Stillwell. ... On suspended list (September 5-7, 1997). ... Traded by Royals with IF Mark Ellis and a player to be named later to Oakland Athletics as part of three-way deal in which Royals received P Roberto Hernandez from Tampa Bay Devil Rays, A's received P Cory Lidle from Devil Rays, Royals received C A.J. Hinch, IF Ángel Berroa and cash from A's and Devil Rays received OF Ben Grieve and a player to be named later or cash from A's (January 8, 2001). ... Granted free agency (November 5, 2001). ... Signed by Boston Red Sox (December 21, 2001).
RECORDS: Shares major league single-game record for most doubles—4 (July 18, 2000). ... Shares A.L. record for most hits in four consecutive games—15 (July 18-21, 2000).
HONORS: Named Texas League Player of the Year (1995).
STATISTICAL NOTES: Led Gulf Coast League with 109 total bases in 1992. ... Led Midwest League outfielders with five double plays in 1993. ... Led Texas League with .434 on-base percentage in 1995. ... Led Texas League with .534 slugging percentage in 1995. ... Led Texas League with 13 intentional bases on balls received in 1995. ... Had 16-game hitting streak (April 27-May 12, 1999). ... Had 16-game hitting streak (August 5-21, 2000). ... Career major league grand slams: 3.

Year Team (League)	Pos.	G	AB	R	H	2B	3B	HR	RBI	Avg.	BB	SO	SB	PO	A	E	Avg.
1992—GC Royals (GCL)	OF	50	192	*58	67	12	*9	4	24	*.349	31	21	33	77	7	1	.988
—Baseball City (FSL)	OF	1	1	0	0	0	0	0	0	.000	0	0	0	0	0	0	...
1993—Rockford (Midw.)	OF	127	511	82	148	25	*13	5	50	.290	52	83	59	240	14	6	.977
1994—Wilmington (Caro.)........	OF	119	472	96	149	25	13	6	75	.316	62	55	44	273	9	3	.989
1995—Wichita (Texas)	OF	111	423	83	145	15	9	16	54	.343	67	35	26	296	11	5	.984
—Kansas City (A.L.)	OF	47	188	32	53	11	5	3	23	.282	12	22	7	110	0	1	.991
1996—Kansas City (A.L.)	OF-DH	145	517	61	140	22	5	6	50	.271	31	64	25	350	6	3	.983
1997—Kansas City (A.L.)	OF-DH	146	472	70	130	12	8	8	48	.275	42	70	16	322	5	4	.988
1998—Kansas City (A.L.)	OF	161	642	104	178	30	10	18	66	.277	58	84	26	372	10	4	.990
1999—Kansas City (A.L.)	OF-DH	145	583	101	179	39	9	14	77	.307	67	50	36	301	8	4	.987
2000—Kansas City (A.L.)	OF-DH	159	655	*136	214	42	10	16	88	.327	65	60	*46	334	6	5	.986
2001—Oakland (A.L.)■	OF	155	644	108	165	34	4	9	49	.256	61	70	27	345	4	3	.991
Major League totals (7 years)		958	3701	612	1059	190	51	74	401	.286	336	420	183	2134	38	27	.988

DIVISION SERIES RECORD

Year Team (League)	Pos.	G	AB	R	H	2B	3B	HR	RBI	Avg.	BB	SO	SB	PO	A	E	Avg.
2001—Oakland (A.L.)	OF	5	22	3	9	2	1	0	0	.409	1	1	2	10	0	0	1.000

PERSONAL: Born November 13, 1970, in Los Angeles. ... 5-10/165. ... Throws left, bats left. ... Full name: Victor Anthony Darensbourg.
HIGH SCHOOL: Westchester (Los Angeles).
COLLEGE: Lewis and Clark (Ore.).
TRANSACTIONS/CAREER NOTES: Signed as non-drafted free agent by Florida Marlins organization (June 11, 1992). ... On disabled list entire 1995 season. ... On Portland disabled list (April 4-15, 1996). ... On disabled list (April 25-June 21 and July 29-September 6, 1997). ... On disabled list (August 20-September 17, 2001).
MISCELLANEOUS: Appeared in one game as pinch runner (2001).

Year League	W	L	Pct.	ERA	G	GS	CG	ShO	Sv.	IP	H	R	ER	BB	SO
1992—Gulf Coast Marlins (GCL) ...	2	1	.667	0.64	8	4	0	0	2	42	28	5	3	11	37
1993—Kane County (Midw.).........	9	1	.900	2.14	46	0	0	0	16	71 1/3	58	17	17	28	89
—High Desert (Calif.).........	0	0	...	0.00	1	0	0	0	0	1	0	0	0	0	1
1994—Portland (East.).................	10	7	.588	3.81	35	21	1	1	4	149	146	76	63	60	103
1995—Florida (N.L.)						Did not play.									
1995—						Did not play.									
1996—Brevard County (FSL)........	0	0	...	0.00	2	0	0	0	0	3	1	0	0	1	5
—Charlotte (I.L.).................	1	5	.167	3.69	47	0	0	0	7	63 1/3	61	30	26	32	66
1997—Charlotte (I.L.)	4	2	.667	4.38	27	0	0	0	7	24 2/3	22	12	12	15	21
1998—Florida (N.L.)...................	0	7	.000	3.68	59	0	0	0	1	71	52	29	29	30	74
1999—Florida (N.L.)...................	0	1	.000	8.83	56	0	0	0	0	34 2/3	50	36	34	21	16
—Calgary (PCL)...................	0	0	...	4.63	9	0	0	0	1	11 2/3	13	6	6	0	12
2000—Florida (N.L.)...................	5	3	.625	4.06	56	0	0	0	0	62	61	32	28	28	59
2001—Florida (N.L.)...................	1	2	.333	4.25	58	0	0	0	1	48 2/3	52	24	23	10	33
Major League totals (4 years).......	6	13	.316	4.74	229	0	0	0	2	216 1/3	215	121	114	89	182

DARR, MIKE   OF   PADRES

PERSONAL: Born March 21, 1976, in Corona, Calif. ... 6-3/205. ... Bats left, throws right. ... Full name: Michael Curtis Darr.
HIGH SCHOOL: Corona (Calif.).
TRANSACTIONS/CAREER NOTES: Selected by Detroit Tigers organization in second round of free-agent draft (June 2, 1994). ... On disabled list (April 4-May 28, 1996). ... Traded by Tigers with P Mike Skrmetta to San Diego Padres for 2B Jody Reed (March 22, 1997). ... On Las Vegas disabled list (April 25-May 7, 1999). ... On San Diego disabled list (May 2-23, 2001); included rehabilitation assignment to Mobile (May 21-23).

Year Team (League)	Pos.	G	AB	R	H	2B	3B	HR	RBI	Avg.	BB	SO	SB	PO	A	E	Avg.
									BATTING						FIELDING		
1994—Bristol (Appl.).............	OF	44	149	23	41	6	0	1	18	.275	23	22	4	59	4	4	.940
1995—Fayetteville (S.Atl.)	OF	112	395	58	114	21	2	5	66	.289	58	88	5	123	15	9	.939
1996—Lakeland (FSL)............	OF	85	311	26	77	14	7	0	38	.248	28	64	7	128	8	3	.978
1997—Rancho Cuca. (Calif.)■	OF	134	521	104	179	32	11	15	94	.344	57	90	23	176	12	8	.959
1998—Mobile (Sou.)	OF	132	523	105	162	41	4	6	90	.310	62	79	28	261	13	6	.979
1999—Las Vegas (PCL)	OF-DH	100	383	57	114	34	0	10	62	.298	50	103	10	172	11	2	.989
—San Diego (N.L.)	OF	25	48	6	13	1	0	2	3	.271	5	18	2	28	0	0	1.000
2000—Las Vegas (PCL)	OF	91	366	79	126	23	5	9	65	.344	44	55	13	205	6	5	.977
—San Diego (N.L.)	OF	58	205	21	55	14	4	1	30	.268	23	45	9	124	7	0	1.000
2001—San Diego (N.L.)	OF	105	289	36	80	13	1	2	34	.277	39	72	6	183	6	2	.990
—Mobile (Sou.)	OF	2	5	1	1	0	0	0	0	.200	2	4	0	2	0	0	1.000
Major League totals (3 years)		188	542	63	148	28	5	5	67	.273	67	135	17	335	13	2	.994

DAUBACH, BRIAN   1B/DH   RED SOX

PERSONAL: Born February 11, 1972, in Belleville, Ill. ... 6-1/201. ... Bats left, throws right. ... Full name: Brian Michael Daubach.
HIGH SCHOOL: Belleville (Ill.) West.
TRANSACTIONS/CAREER NOTES: Selected by New York Mets organization in 17th round of free-agent draft (June 4, 1990). ... Granted free agency (October 15, 1996). ... Signed by Florida Marlins organization (November 7, 1996). ... Granted free agency (October 17, 1997). ... Re-signed by Marlins organization (January 6, 1998). ... Released by Marlins (November 19, 1998). ... Signed by Boston Red Sox organization (December 18, 1998). ... On Boston disabled list (August 15-September 2, 2001); included rehabilitation assignments to Pawtucket (August 29-30) and Lowell (August 31-September 1).
STATISTICAL NOTES: Tied for Appalachian League lead in intentional bases on balls received with five in 1991. ... Led Appalachian League first basemen with 623 total chances and 41 double plays in 1991. ... Tied for Florida State League lead in double plays by first basemen with 127 in 1994. ... Led Eastern League first basemen with 111 double plays and .992 fielding percentage and tied for lead with 98 assists in 1995. ... Led Eastern League first basemen with 115 assists in 1996. ... Led International League with 10 sacrifice flies in 1997. ... Led International League with 315 total bases, .634 slugging percentage and nine intentional bases on balls received and tied for lead in being hit by pitch with 15 in 1998. ... Career major league grand slams: 1.

Year Team (League)	Pos.	G	AB	R	H	2B	3B	HR	RBI	Avg.	BB	SO	SB	PO	A	E	Avg.
									BATTING						FIELDING		
1990—GC Mets (GCL)...........	1B	45	152	26	41	8	4	1	19	.270	22	41	2	274	16	7	.976
—Charlotte (I.L.)............	OF-1B	140	497	102	157	45	4	35	124	.316	80	114	9	262	28	3	.990
1991—Kingsport (Appl.)........	1B	65	218	30	53	9	1	7	42	.243	33	64	1	*562	*52	9	.986
1992—Pittsfield (NY-Penn).....	1B	72	260	26	63	15	2	2	40	.242	30	61	4	609	•44	12	.982
1993—Capital City (S.Atl.)......	1B-OF	102	379	50	106	19	3	7	72	.280	52	84	6	393	43	5	.989
1994—St. Lucie (FSL)...........	1B	129	450	52	123	30	2	6	74	.273	58	120	14	1172	*115	12	.991
1995—Binghamton (East.)	1B-3B	135	469	61	115	25	2	10	72	.245	51	104	6	1137	‡98	10	†.992
—Norfolk (I.L.)	1B	2	7	0	0	0	0	0	0	.000	1	0	0	21	3	0	1.000
1996—Binghamton (East.)	1B-3B	122	436	80	129	24	1	22	72	.296	74	103	7	1108	†115	11	.991
—Norfolk (I.L.)	1B	17	54	7	11	2	0	0	6	.204	6	14	1	72	3	0	1.000
1997—Charlotte (I.L.)■.........	1B	136	461	66	128	40	2	21	93	.278	65	126	4	870	62	8	.991
1998—Charlotte (I.L.)...........	OF-1B	140	497	102	157	*45	4	*35	*124	.316	80	114	9	362	28	3	.992
—Florida (N.L.)	1B	10	15	0	3	1	0	0	3	.200	1	5	0	23	1	0	1.000
1999—Boston (A.L.)■..........	1-DH-O-3	110	381	61	112	33	3	21	73	.294	36	92	0	420	35	8	.983
—Pawtucket (I.L.).........	1B-OF	9	31	4	9	2	0	1	6	.290	6	8	0	31	2	1	.971
2000—Boston (A.L.)...........	1-DH-O-3	142	495	55	123	32	2	21	76	.248	44	130	1	662	52	3	.996
2001—Boston (A.L.)...........	1B-OF	122	407	54	107	28	3	22	71	.263	53	108	1	861	75	11	.988
—Pawtucket (I.L.).........	DH	1	4	0	1	0	0	0	0	.250	0	2	0	...	...	...	...
—Lowell (NY-Penn)	1B	1	2	0	0	0	0	0	0	.000	1	1	0	4	0	0	1.000
American League totals (3 years)		374	1283	170	342	93	8	64	220	.267	133	330	2	1943	162	22	.990
National League totals (1 year)		10	15	0	3	1	0	0	3	.200	1	5	0	23	1	0	1.000
Major League totals (4 years)		384	1298	170	345	94	8	64	223	.266	134	335	2	1966	163	22	.990

D

DIVISION SERIES RECORD

RECORDS: Holds single-game record for most at-bats with no hits—6 (October 10, 1999). ... Shares single-game record for most at-bats (nine-inning game)—6 (October 10, 1999).

Year Team (League)	Pos.	G	AB	R	H	2B	3B	HR	RBI	Avg.	BB	SO	SB	PO	A	E	Avg.
										BATTING					FIELDING		
1999— Boston (A.L.)	DH-PH-1B	4	16	3	4	2	0	1	3	.250	0	7	0	1	0	0	1.000

CHAMPIONSHIP SERIES RECORD

Year Team (League)	Pos.	G	AB	R	H	2B	3B	HR	RBI	Avg.	BB	SO	SB	PO	A	E	Avg.
										BATTING					FIELDING		
1999— Boston (A.L.)	DH-1B-PH	5	17	2	3	1	0	1	3	.176	1	4	0	0	0	0	...

DaVANON, JEFF — OF — ANGELS

PERSONAL: Born December 8, 1973, in San Diego. ... 6-0/185. ... Bats both, throws right. ... Full name: Jeffrey Graham DaVanon. ... Son of Jerry DaVanon, infielder with five major league teams (1969-77).
HIGH SCHOOL: Bellaire (Texas).
COLLEGE: San Diego State.
TRANSACTIONS/CAREER NOTES: Selected by Oakland Athletics organization in 26th round of free-agent draft (June 1, 1995). ... Traded by Athletics with P Elvin Nina and OF Nathan Haynes to Anaheim Angels for P Omar Olivares and 2B Randy Velarde (July 29, 1999). ... On disabled list (March 20, 2000-entire season). ... On Salt Lake disabled list (April 14-21, 2001).

Year Team (League)	Pos.	G	AB	R	H	2B	3B	HR	RBI	Avg.	BB	SO	SB	PO	A	E	Avg.
										BATTING					FIELDING		
1995— S. Oregon (N'West)	OF	57	167	29	42	6	2	1	17	.251	34	49	6	47	4	8	.864
1996— W. Michigan (Midw.)	OF-1B-2B	89	289	43	70	13	4	2	33	.242	49	66	5	72	9	2	.976
1997— Visalia (Calif.)	OF	119	408	70	104	17	3	6	38	.255	81	101	23	166	*17	10	.948
1998— Modesto (Calif.)	OF	84	301	66	101	17	4	5	60	.336	59	69	33	112	7	13	.902
1999— Midland (Texas)	OF-DH	100	374	87	128	29	11	11	60	.342	53	68	18	162	8	7	.960
—Edmonton (PCL)■	OF-DH	34	132	35	43	8	3	6	19	.326	20	27	11	74	6	0	1.000
—Anaheim (A.L.)	OF-DH	7	20	4	4	0	1	1	4	.200	2	7	0	5	0	0	1.000
2000— Anaheim (A.L.)							Did not play.										
2001— Salt Lake (PCL)	OF	69	256	46	80	19	8	10	48	.313	32	57	8	123	5	1	.992
—Anaheim (A.L.)	OF-DH	40	88	7	17	2	1	5	9	.193	11	29	1	45	3	1	.980
Major League totals (2 years)		47	108	11	21	2	2	6	13	.194	13	36	1	50	3	1	.981

DAVENPORT, JOE — P — EXPOS

PERSONAL: Born March 24, 1976, in Chicago. ... 6-5/225. ... Throws right, bats right. ... Full name: Joseph Jonathan Davenport.
HIGH SCHOOL: Santee (Santee, Calif.).
TRANSACTIONS/CAREER NOTES: Selected by Toronto Blue Jays organization in 13th round of free-agent draft (June 2, 1994). ... Selected by Chicago White Sox organization from Blue Jays organization in Rule 5 minor league draft (December 15, 1997). ... Granted free agency (October 18, 2000). ... Signed by Colorado Rockies organization (November 8, 2000). ... On Colorado Springs disabled list (August 3-10, 2001). ... Granted free agency (October 15, 2001). ... Signed by Montreal Expos organization (January 11, 2002).
STATISTICAL NOTES: Tied for International League lead with 11 hit batsmen in 2000.

Year League	W	L	Pct.	ERA	G	GS	CG	ShO	Sv.	IP	H	R	ER	BB	SO
1994— Gulf Coast Blue Jays (GCL)	0	0	...	3.27	7	1	0	0	0	11	12	5	4	7	2
1995— Hagerstown (S.Atl.)	0	1	.000	6.11	13	0	0	0	0	17 2/3	22	19	12	13	13
—Gulf Coast Blue Jays (GCL)	2	3	.400	5.66	15	10	1	0	1	55 2/3	67	47	35	30	29
1996— St. Catharines (NY-Penn)	2	4	.333	5.13	20	8	0	0	0	66 2/3	71	44	38	23	43
1997— Hagerstown (S.Atl.)	4	6	.400	3.68	37	0	0	0	10	51 1/3	43	26	21	24	43
1998— Winston-Salem (Caro.)■	2	0	1.000	1.38	20	0	0	0	2	26	25	9	4	4	26
—Birmingham (Sou.)	3	2	.600	7.22	26	0	0	0	1	38 2/3	54	36	31	30	22
1999— Birmingham (Sou.)	3	5	.375	3.10	40	0	0	0	10	49 1/3	43	26	17	19	24
—Chicago (A.L.)	0	0	...	0.00	3	0	0	0	0	1 2/3	1	0	0	2	0
—Charlotte (I.L.)	0	0	...	8.00	6	0	0	0	0	9	13	8	8	1	6
2000— Charlotte (I.L.)	1	4	.200	4.58	59	0	0	0	9	70 2/3	74	41	36	27	42
2001— Colorado Springs (PCL)■	2	2	.500	8.47	31	0	0	0	0	34	62	38	32	15	23
—Colorado (N.L.)	0	0	...	3.48	7	0	0	0	0	10 1/3	8	7	4	7	8
A.L. totals (1 year)	0	0	...	0.00	3	0	0	0	0	1 2/3	1	0	0	2	0
N.L. totals (1 year)	0	0	...	3.48	7	0	0	0	0	10 1/3	8	7	4	7	8
Major League totals (2 years)	0	0	...	3.00	10	0	0	0	0	12	9	7	4	9	8

DAVEY, TOM — P — PADRES

PERSONAL: Born September 11, 1973, in Garden City, Mich. ... 6-7/230. ... Throws right, bats right. ... Full name: Thomas Joseph Davey.
HIGH SCHOOL: Plymouth Salem (Canton, Mich.).
JUNIOR COLLEGE: Henry Ford Community College (Mich.).
TRANSACTIONS/CAREER NOTES: Selected by Toronto Blue Jays organization in fifth round of free-agent draft (June 2, 1994). ... Selected by Baltimore Orioles from Blue Jays organization in Rule 5 major league draft (December 9, 1996). ... Returned to Blue Jays organization (March 20, 1997). ... Traded by Blue Jays with P Steve Sinclair to Seattle Mariners for 1B David Segui (July 28, 1999). ... Traded by Mariners with OF/3B John Mabry to San Diego Padres for OF Al Martin (July 31, 2000). ... On disabled list (July 28, 2001-remainder of season).

Year League	W	L	Pct.	ERA	G	GS	CG	ShO	Sv.	IP	H	R	ER	BB	SO
1994— Medicine Hat (Pio.)	2	•8	.200	5.12	14	14	0	0	0	65	76	59	37	*59	35
1995— St. Catharines (NY-Penn)	4	3	.571	3.32	7	7	0	0	0	38	27	19	14	21	29
—Hagerstown (S.Atl.)	4	1	.800	3.38	8	8	0	0	0	37 1/3	29	23	14	31	25
1996— Hagerstown (S.Atl.)	10	9	.526	3.87	26	26	2	1	0	155 2/3	132	76	67	91	98

Year League	W	L	Pct.	ERA	G	GS	CG	ShO	Sv.	IP	H	R	ER	BB	SO
1997— Dunedin (FSL)	1	3	.250	4.31	7	6	0	0	0	39²/₃	44	21	19	15	36
— Knoxville (Sou.)	6	7	.462	5.83	20	16	0	0	0	92²/₃	108	65	60	50	72
1998— Knoxville (Sou.)	5	3	.625	3.87	48	9	0	0	16	76²/₃	70	35	33	52	78
1999— Toronto (A.L.)	1	1	.500	4.70	29	0	0	0	1	44	40	28	23	26	42
— Syracuse (I.L.)	1	2	.333	3.48	6	6	0	0	0	33²/₃	30	15	13	19	20
— Seattle (A.L.)■	1	0	1.000	4.71	16	0	0	0	0	21	22	13	11	14	17
2000— Tacoma (PCL)	8	6	.571	4.61	28	12	0	0	2	93²/₃	104	59	48	37	77
— Las Vegas (PCL)■	1	2	.333	4.02	13	0	0	0	0	15²/₃	27	13	7	7	17
— San Diego (N.L.)	2	1	.667	0.71	11	0	0	0	0	12²/₃	12	1	1	2	6
2001— San Diego (N.L.)	2	4	.333	4.50	39	0	0	0	0	38	41	22	19	17	37
A.L. totals (1 year)	2	1	.667	4.71	45	0	0	0	1	65	62	41	34	40	59
N.L. totals (2 years)	4	5	.444	3.55	50	0	0	0	0	50²/₃	53	23	20	19	43
Major League totals (3 years)	6	6	.500	4.20	95	0	0	0	1	115²/₃	115	64	54	59	102

DAVIS, BEN C MARINERS

PERSONAL: Born March 10, 1977, in Chester, Pa. ... 6-4/215. ... Bats both, throws right. ... Full name: Matthew Benjamin Davis.
HIGH SCHOOL: Malvern (Pa.) Prep.
TRANSACTIONS/CAREER NOTES: Selected by San Diego Padres organization in first round (second pick overall) of free-agent draft (June 3, 1995). ... On San Diego disabled list (August 13-September 1, 2000). ... Traded by Padres with P Wascar Serrano and SS Alex Arias to Seattle Mariners for P Brett Tomko, C Tom Lampkin and SS Ramon Vazquez (December 11, 2001).
STATISTICAL NOTES: Led Pioneer League catchers with 412 total chances in 1995. ... Led California League catchers with 992 putouts and 1,109 total chances in 1997. ... Led Southern League catchers with 1,002 total chances in 1998. ... Career major league grand slams: 1.

Year Team (League)	Pos.	G	AB	R	H	2B	3B	HR	RBI	Avg.	BB	SO	SB	PO	A	E	Avg.
										BATTING					FIELDING		
1995— Idaho Falls (Pio.)	C	52	197	36	55	8	3	5	46	.279	17	36	0	*362	44	6	.985
1996— Rancho Cuca. (Calif.)	C-DH	98	353	35	71	10	1	6	41	.201	31	89	1	642	51	9	.987
1997— Rancho Cuca. (Calif.)	C-DH-1B	122	474	67	132	30	1	17	76	.278	28	107	3	†993	103	14	.987
1998— Mobile (Sou.)	C-DH	116	433	65	124	29	2	14	75	.286	42	60	4	*920	76	6	.994
— San Diego (N.L.)	C	1	1	0	0	0	0	0	0	.000	0	0	0	2	0	0	1.000
1999— Las Vegas (PCL)	C	58	201	27	62	18	1	5	44	.308	24	41	4	454	32	4	.992
— San Diego (N.L.)	C	76	266	29	65	14	1	5	30	.244	25	70	2	471	29	7	.986
2000— Las Vegas (PCL)	C	59	221	38	58	16	1	7	40	.262	38	43	5	441	37	7	.986
— San Diego (N.L.)	C-DH	43	130	12	29	6	0	3	14	.223	14	35	1	236	17	1	.996
2001— San Diego (N.L.)	C-1B	138	448	56	107	20	0	11	57	.239	66	112	1	854	61	9	.990
Major League totals (4 years)		258	845	97	201	40	1	19	101	.238	105	217	7	1563	107	17	.990

DAVIS, DOUG P RANGERS

PERSONAL: Born September 21, 1975, in Sacramento. ... 6-3/190. ... Throws left, bats right. ... Full name: Douglas P. Davis.
HIGH SCHOOL: Northgate (Walnut Creek, Calif.).
JUNIOR COLLEGE: City College of San Francisco.
TRANSACTIONS/CAREER NOTES: Selected by Texas Rangers organization in 10th round of free-agent draft (June 4, 1996).

Year League	W	L	Pct.	ERA	G	GS	CG	ShO	Sv.	IP	H	R	ER	BB	SO
1996— Gulf Coast Rangers (GCL)	3	1	.750	1.90	8	7	0	0	0	42²/₃	28	13	9	26	49
1997— Gulf Coast Rangers (GCL)	3	1	.750	1.71	4	4	0	0	0	21	14	5	4	15	27
— Charlotte (FSL)	5	3	.625	3.10	9	8	1	0	0	49¹/₃	29	19	17	33	52
1998— Charlotte (FSL)	11	7	.611	3.24	27	27	1	1	0	155¹/₃	129	69	56	74	*173
1999— Tulsa (Texas)	4	4	.500	2.42	12	12	1	0	0	74¹/₃	65	26	20	25	79
— Oklahoma (PCL)	7	0	1.000	3.00	13	11	0	0	0	78	77	27	26	31	74
— Texas (A.L.)	0	0	...	33.75	2	0	0	0	0	2²/₃	12	10	10	0	3
2000— Texas (A.L.)	7	6	.538	5.38	30	13	1	0	0	98²/₃	109	61	59	58	66
— Oklahoma (PCL)	8	3	.727	2.84	12	12	2	0	0	69²/₃	62	32	22	34	53
2001— Texas (A.L.)	11	10	.524	4.45	30	30	1	0	0	186	220	103	92	69	115
— Oklahoma (PCL)	2	0	1.000	2.87	2	2	0	0	0	15²/₃	10	5	5	4	14
Major League totals (3 years)	18	16	.529	5.04	62	43	2	0	0	287¹/₃	341	174	161	127	184

DAVIS, ERIC OF

PERSONAL: Born May 29, 1962, in Los Angeles. ... 6-3/200. ... Bats right, throws right. ... Full name: Eric Keith Davis.
HIGH SCHOOL: Fremont (Los Angeles).
TRANSACTIONS/CAREER NOTES: Selected by Cincinnati Reds organization in eighth round of free-agent draft (June 3, 1980). ... On Cincinnati disabled list (August 16-September 1, 1984; May 3-18, 1989; April 25-May 19, 1990; June 12-27 and July 31-August 26, 1991). ... Traded by Reds with P Kip Gross to Los Angeles Dodgers for P Tim Belcher and P John Wetteland (November 27, 1991). ... On disabled list (May 23-June 19 and August 2-25, 1992). ... Granted free agency (November 3, 1992). ... Re-signed by Dodgers (December 1, 1992). ... Traded by Dodgers to Detroit Tigers for a player to be named later (August 31, 1993); Dodgers acquired P John DeSilva to complete deal (September 7, 1993). ... Granted free agency (October 28, 1993). ... Re-signed by Tigers (November 1, 1993). ... On disabled list (May 23-July 19 and July 27, 1994-remainder of season). ... Granted free agency (October 20, 1994). ... On retired list (October 20, 1994-January 2, 1996). ... Signed by Reds organization (January 2, 1996). ... On disabled list (May 26-June 10, 1996). ... Granted free agency (October 28, 1996). ... Signed by Baltimore Orioles (December 19, 1996). ... On disabled list (May 26-September 15, 1997). ... Granted free agency (October 27, 1998). ... Signed by St. Louis Cardinals (November 19, 1998). ... On disabled list (June 28, 1999-remainder of season). ... Granted free agency (November 2, 2000). ... Signed by San Francisco Giants (January 11, 2001). ... On disabled list (May 27-June 15, 2001). ... Granted free agency (November 6, 2001).
RECORDS: Shares major league records for most grand slams in two consecutive games—2 (May 4 and 5, 1996); and most strikeouts in two consecutive games—9 (April 24 [4] and 25 [5], 1987, 21 innings). ... Shares major league single-month record for most grand slams—3 (May 1987). ... Shares major league record for most grand slams in two consecutive games—2 (August 13 and 14, 1991).

HONORS: Named outfielder on THE SPORTING NEWS N.L. All-Star team (1987 and 1989). ... Named outfielder on THE SPORTING NEWS N.L. Silver Slugger team (1987 and 1989). ... Won N.L. Gold Glove as outfielder (1987-89). ... Named N.L. Comeback Player of the Year by THE SPORTING NEWS (1996).

STATISTICAL NOTES: Hit three home runs in one game (September 10, 1986; and May 3, 1987). ... Led N.L. outfielders with 394 total chances in 1987. ... Led N.L. with 21 game-winning RBIs in 1988. ... Hit for the cycle (June 2, 1989). ... Had 30-game hitting streak (July 12-August 15, 1998). ... Career major league grand slams: 11.

Year Team (League)	Pos.	G	AB	R	H	2B	3B	HR	RBI	Avg.	BB	SO	SB	PO	A	E	Avg.
1980—Eugene (N'West)	SS-2B-OF	33	73	12	16	1	0	1	11	.219	14	26	10	29	36	11	.855
1981—Eugene (N'West)	OF	62	214	*67	69	10	4	11	39	.322	57	59	*40	94	11	4	.963
1982—Cedar Rapids (Midw.)	OF	111	434	80	120	20	5	15	56	.276	51	103	53	239	9	9	.965
1983—Waterbury (East.)	OF	89	293	56	85	13	1	15	43	.290	65	75	39	214	8	2	.991
—Indianapolis (A.A.)	OF	19	77	18	23	4	0	7	19	.299	8	22	9	61	1	1	.984
1984—Wichita (A.A.)	OF	52	194	42	61	9	5	14	34	.314	25	55	27	110	5	5	.958
—Cincinnati (N.L.)	OF	57	174	33	39	10	1	10	30	.224	24	48	10	125	4	1	.992
1985—Cincinnati (N.L.)	OF	56	122	26	30	3	3	8	18	.246	7	39	16	75	3	1	.987
—Denver (A.A.)	OF	64	206	48	57	10	2	15	38	.277	29	67	35	94	5	3	.971
1986—Cincinnati (N.L.)	OF	132	415	97	115	15	3	27	71	.277	68	100	80	274	2	7	.975
1987—Cincinnati (N.L.)	OF	129	474	120	139	23	4	37	100	.293	84	134	50	*380	10	4	.990
1988—Cincinnati (N.L.)	OF	135	472	81	129	18	3	26	93	.273	65	124	35	300	2	6	.981
1989—Cincinnati (N.L.)	OF	131	462	74	130	14	2	34	101	.281	68	116	21	298	2	5	.984
1990—Cincinnati (N.L.)	OF	127	453	84	118	26	2	24	86	.260	60	100	21	257	11	2	.993
1991—Cincinnati (N.L.)	OF	89	285	39	67	10	0	11	33	.235	48	92	14	190	5	3	.985
1992—Los Angeles (N.L.)■	OF	76	267	21	61	8	1	5	32	.228	36	71	19	123	0	5	.961
1993—Los Angeles (N.L.)	OF	108	376	57	88	17	0	14	53	.234	41	88	33	221	7	2	.991
—Detroit (A.L.)■	OF-DH	23	75	14	19	1	1	6	15	.253	14	18	2	52	0	1	.981
1994—Detroit (A.L.)	OF	37	120	19	22	4	0	3	13	.183	18	45	5	85	1	1	.989
1995—							Did not play—retired.										
1996—Cincinnati (N.L.)■	OF-1B	129	415	81	119	20	0	26	83	.287	70	121	23	279	3	3	.989
1997—Baltimore (A.L.)■	OF-DH	42	158	29	48	11	0	8	25	.304	14	47	6	39	0	1	.975
1998—Baltimore (A.L.)	OF-DH	131	452	81	148	29	1	28	89	.327	44	108	7	119	4	1	.992
1999—St. Louis (N.L.)■	OF-DH	58	191	27	49	9	2	5	30	.257	30	49	5	93	4	0	1.000
2000—St. Louis (N.L.)	OF-DH	92	254	38	77	14	0	6	40	.303	36	60	1	120	1	4	.968
2001—San Fran. (N.L.)■	OF-DH	74	156	17	32	7	3	4	22	.205	13	38	1	74	1	3	.962
American League totals (4 years)		233	805	143	237	45	2	45	142	.294	90	218	20	295	5	4	.987
National League totals (14 years)		1393	4516	795	1193	194	24	237	792	.264	650	1180	329	2809	55	46	.984
Major League totals (17 years)		1626	5321	938	1430	239	26	282	934	.269	740	1398	349	3104	60	50	.984

DIVISION SERIES RECORD

Year Team (League)	Pos.	G	AB	R	H	2B	3B	HR	RBI	Avg.	BB	SO	SB	PO	A	E	Avg.
1997—Baltimore (A.L.)	OF	3	9	0	2	0	0	0	2	.222	0	5	0	1	0	0	1.000
2000—St. Louis (N.L.)	OF-PH	2	4	0	0	0	0	0	1	.000	0	2	0	0	0	0	...
Division series totals (2 years)		5	13	0	2	0	0	0	3	.154	0	7	0	1	0	0	1.000

CHAMPIONSHIP SERIES RECORD

Year Team (League)	Pos.	G	AB	R	H	2B	3B	HR	RBI	Avg.	BB	SO	SB	PO	A	E	Avg.
1990—Cincinnati (N.L.)	OF	6	23	2	4	1	0	0	2	.174	1	9	0	12	1	0	1.000
1997—Baltimore (A.L.)	OF-DH	6	13	1	2	0	0	1	1	.154	1	3	0	3	0	0	1.000
2000—St. Louis (N.L.)	OF-PH	4	10	1	2	1	0	0	1	.200	0	2	0	5	0	0	1.000
Championship series totals (3 years)		16	46	4	8	2	0	1	4	.174	2	14	0	20	1	0	1.000

NOTES: Hit home run in first at-bat (October 16, 1990). ... Member of World Series championship team (1990).

WORLD SERIES RECORD

Year Team (League)	Pos.	G	AB	R	H	2B	3B	HR	RBI	Avg.	BB	SO	SB	PO	A	E	Avg.
1990—Cincinnati (N.L.)	OF	4	14	3	4	0	0	1	5	.286	0	0	0	4	0	0	1.000

ALL-STAR GAME RECORD

Year League	Pos.	AB	R	H	2B	3B	HR	RBI	Avg.	BB	SO	SB	PO	A	E	Avg.
1987—National	OF	3	0	0	0	0	0	0	.000	0	1	0	1	0	0	1.000
1989—National	OF	2	0	0	0	0	0	0	.000	1	0	1	1	0	0	1.000
All-Star Game totals (2 years)		5	0	0	0	0	0	0	.000	1	1	1	2	0	0	1.000

DAVIS, J.J.　　　　OF　　　　PIRATES

PERSONAL: Born October 25, 1978, in Glendora, Calif. ... 6-4/250. ... Bats right, throws right. ... Full name: Jerry C. Davis.
HIGH SCHOOL: Baldwin Park (Calif.).
TRANSACTIONS/CAREER NOTES: Selected by Pittsburgh Pirates organization in first round (eighth pick overall) of free-agent draft (June 3, 1997). ... On Altoona disabled list (June 22-August 23, 2001).

Year Team (League)	Pos.	G	AB	R	H	2B	3B	HR	RBI	Avg.	BB	SO	SB	PO	A	E	Avg.
1997—GC Pirates (GCL)	OF	45	165	19	42	10	2	1	18	.255	14	44	0	42	1	0	1.000
—Erie (NY-Penn)	DH	4	13	1	1	0	0	0	0	.077	0	4	0	...	...	...	...
1998—Augusta (S.Atl.)	OF	30	106	11	21	6	0	4	11	.198	3	24	1	35	1	3	.923
—Erie (NY-Penn)	OF	52	196	25	53	12	2	8	39	.270	20	54	4	95	1	7	.932
1999—Hickory (S.Atl.)	OF	86	317	58	84	26	1	19	65	.265	44	99	2	73	3	4	.950
2000—Lynchburg (Caro.)	OF	130	485	77	118	36	4	20	80	.243	52	171	9	214	7	18	.925
2001—Altoona (East.)	OF	67	228	21	57	13	3	4	26	.250	21	79	2	110	1	0	1.000
—GC Pirates (GCL)	OF	4	17	3	8	1	0	2	6	.471	1	2	0	2	0	1	.667

DAVIS, KANE   P   ROCKIES

PERSONAL: Born June 25, 1975, in Ripley, W.Va. ... 6-3/194. ... Throws right, bats right. ... Full name: Kane Thomas Davis.
HIGH SCHOOL: Spencer (W.Va.).
TRANSACTIONS/CAREER NOTES: Selected by Pittsburgh Pirates organization in 13th round of free-agent draft (June 3, 1993). ... On Pittsburgh disabled list (March 22-May 1, 1998). ... On Carolina disabled list (May 17-June 6, 1998). ... On Nashville disabled list (August 25-September 2, 1999). ... Granted free agency (October 15, 1999). ... Signed by Cleveland Indians organization (December 22, 1999). ... On Buffalo disabled list (April 7-24, 2000). ... Traded by Indians with P Paul Rigdon, 1B/OF Richie Sexson and a player to be named later to Milwaukee Brewers for P Bob Wickman, P Steve Woodard and P Jason Bere (July 28, 2000). ... Brewers acquired 2B Marcos Scutaro to complete deal (August 30, 2000). ... Traded by Brewers with P Juan Acevedo and IF Jose Flores to Colorado Rockies for P Mark Leiter, P Mike DeJean and 2B/SS Elvis Pena (April 4, 2001). ... On Colorado disabled list (July 8-August 6, 2001); included rehabilitation assignment to Colorado Springs (July 27-August 6).

Year League	W	L	Pct.	ERA	G	GS	CG	ShO	Sv.	IP	H	R	ER	BB	SO
1993— Gulf Coast Pirates (GCL)	0	4	.000	7.07	11	4	0	0	0	28	34	30	22	19	24
1994— Welland (NY-Penn)	5	5	.500	2.65	15	•15	0	0	0	98 1/3	90	36	29	32	74
1995— Augusta (S.Atl.)	12	6	.667	3.75	26	25	1	0	0	139 1/3	136	73	58	43	78
1996— Lynchburg (Caro.)	11	9	.550	4.29	26	26	3	1	0	157 1/3	160	84	75	56	116
1997— Carolina (Sou.)	0	3	.000	3.77	6	6	0	0	0	28 2/3	22	17	12	16	23
1998— Augusta (S.Atl.)	0	0	...	6.00	2	2	0	0	0	9	8	6	6	3	6
— Carolina (Sou.)	1	11	.083	9.24	18	16	0	0	0	74	102	84	76	38	39
1999— Altoona (East.)	4	6	.400	3.78	16	16	0	0	0	95 1/3	97	51	40	41	53
— Nashville (PCL)	3	2	.600	6.75	12	9	0	0	0	49 1/3	65	38	37	17	31
2000— Akron (East.)■	0	1	.000	2.70	5	5	0	0	0	20	17	7	6	5	13
— Buffalo (I.L.)	2	0	1.000	4.20	6	4	0	0	0	30	30	16	14	12	19
— Cleveland (A.L.)	0	3	.000	14.73	5	2	0	0	0	11	20	21	18	8	2
— Milwaukee (N.L.)■	0	0	...	6.75	3	0	0	0	0	4	7	3	3	5	2
— Indianapolis (I.L.)	1	1	.500	3.54	4	4	0	0	0	20 1/3	19	8	8	7	12
2001— Colorado (N.L.)■	2	4	.333	4.35	57	0	0	0	0	68 1/3	66	36	33	32	47
— Colorado Springs (PCL)	0	0	...	3.60	4	0	0	0	0	5	5	2	2	3	7
A.L. totals (1 year)	0	3	.000	14.73	5	2	0	0	0	11	20	21	18	8	2
N.L. totals (2 years)	2	4	.333	4.48	60	0	0	0	0	72 1/3	73	39	36	37	49
Major League totals (2 years)	2	7	.222	5.83	65	2	0	0	0	83 1/3	93	60	54	45	51

DAVIS, LANCE   P   REDS

PERSONAL: Born September 1, 1976, in Winter Haven, Fla. ... 6-0/170. ... Throws right, bats left. ... Full name: Johnny Lance Davis.
HIGH SCHOOL: Lake Gibson (Lakeland, Fla.).
TRANSACTIONS/CAREER NOTES: Selected by Cincinnati Reds organization in 16th round of free-agent draft (June 1, 1995).
MISCELLANEOUS: Appeared in one game as pinch runner (2001).

Year League	W	L	Pct.	ERA	G	GS	CG	ShO	Sv.	IP	H	R	ER	BB	SO
1995— Princeton (Appl.)	3	7	.300	3.88	15	9	0	0	0	58	77	39	25	25	43
1996— Charleston, W.Va. (S.Atl.)...	1	0	1.000	2.45	4	0	0	0	0	3 2/3	4	1	1	2	5
— Billings (Pio.)	2	3	.400	6.70	16	5	0	0	0	45 2/3	59	41	34	33	43
— Princeton (Appl.)	2	0	1.000	1.20	2	2	1	1	0	15	6	4	2	3	19
1997— Burlington (Midw.)	4	6	.400	6.59	30	13	0	0	0	97	121	78	71	55	51
1998— Burlington (Midw.)	4	2	.667	1.99	25	4	0	0	0	54 1/3	35	17	12	29	38
1999— Rockford (Midw.)	7	5	.583	3.82	22	20	1	0	0	127 1/3	135	62	54	49	95
2000— Chattanooga (Sou.)	7	5	.583	2.18	25	16	1	1	0	115 2/3	96	41	28	52	98
— Louisville (I.L.)	1	0	1.000	3.38	5	5	0	0	0	32	32	19	12	8	14
2001— Louisville (I.L.)	7	2	.778	3.05	13	13	1	1	0	79 2/3	81	31	27	15	47
— Cincinnati (N.L.)	8	4	.667	4.74	20	20	1	0	0	106 1/3	124	60	56	34	53
Major League totals (1 year)	8	4	.667	4.74	20	20	1	0	0	106 1/3	124	60	56	34	53

DAVIS, RUSS   3B

PERSONAL: Born September 13, 1969, in Birmingham, Ala. ... 6-0/195. ... Bats right, throws right. ... Full name: Russell Stewart Davis.
HIGH SCHOOL: Hueytown (Ala.).
JUNIOR COLLEGE: Shelton State Junior College (Ala.).
TRANSACTIONS/CAREER NOTES: Selected by New York Yankees organization in 29th round of free-agent draft (June 1, 1988). ... On disabled list (July 13-August 1, 1993). ... On Columbus disabled list (April 7-15 and August 26, 1994-remainder of season). ... Traded by Yankees with P Sterling Hitchcock to Seattle Mariners for 1B Tino Martinez, P Jeff Nelson and P Jim Mecir (December 7, 1995). ... On disabled list (June 8, 1996-remainder of season; and August 25-September 26, 1997). ... Granted free agency (December 21, 1999). ... Signed by San Francisco Giants organization (January 24, 2000). ... On suspended list (April 25-27, 2001). ... Released by Giants (June 21, 2001).
HONORS: Named Eastern League Most Valuable Player (1992).
STATISTICAL NOTES: Tied for New York-Pennsylvania League lead with 11 double plays by third baseman in 1989. ... Led Carolina League third basemen with 336 total chances and 18 double plays in 1990. ... Tied for Eastern League lead with .917 fielding percentage, 83 putouts, 205 assists, 26 errors and 314 total chances by third basemen in 1991. ... Led Eastern League with 237 total bases and .483 slugging percentage in 1992. ... Led International League third basemen with 25 errors in 1993. ... Led A.L. third basemen with 32 errors in 1998. ... Career major league grand slams: 1.

						BATTING								FIELDING		
Year Team (League)	Pos.	G	AB	R	H	2B	3B	HR	RBI	Avg.	BB	SO	SB	PO	A	E	Avg.
1988— GC Yankees (GCL)	2B-3B	58	213	33	49	11	3	2	30	.230	16	39	6	64	105	15	.918
1989— Fort Lauderdale (FSL)	3B-2B	48	147	8	27	5	1	2	22	.184	11	38	3	32	72	17	.860
— Oneonta (NY-Penn)	3B	65	236	33	68	7	5	7	42	.288	19	44	3	27	87	17	.870
1990— Prince William (Caro.)	3B	137	510	55	127	*37	3	16	71	.249	37	136	3	*68	*244	24	.929
1991— Albany/Colonie (East.)	3B-2B	135	473	57	103	23	3	8	58	.218	50	102	3	‡83	‡206	‡26	‡.917
1992— Albany/Colonie (East.)	3B	132	491	77	140	23	4	22	71	.285	49	93	3	78	185	23	.920
1993— Columbus (I.L.)	3B-SS	113	424	63	108	24	1	26	83	.255	40	118	1	85	245	†26	.927

Year Team (League)	Pos.	G	AB	R	H	2B	3B	HR	RBI	Avg.	BB	SO	SB	PO	A	E	Avg.
1994—Columbus (I.L.)	3B-DH-1B	117	416	76	115	30	2	25	69	.276	62	93	3	86	250	23	.936
—New York (A.L.)	3B	4	14	0	2	0	0	0	1	.143	0	4	0	2	6	0	1.000
1995—Columbus (I.L.)	3B-1B	20	76	12	19	4	1	2	15	.250	17	23	0	17	31	7	.873
—New York (A.L.)	3B-DH-1B	40	98	14	27	5	2	2	12	.276	10	26	0	16	45	2	.968
1996—Seattle (A.L.)■	3B	51	167	24	39	9	0	5	18	.234	17	50	2	31	67	7	.933
1997—Seattle (A.L.)	3B-DH	119	420	57	114	29	1	20	63	.271	27	100	6	56	219	18	.939
1998—Seattle (A.L.)	3B-OF	141	502	68	130	30	1	20	82	.259	34	134	4	56	254	†34	.901
1999—Seattle (A.L.)	3B-SS	124	432	55	106	17	1	21	59	.245	32	111	3	71	207	12	.959
2000—San Fran. (N.L.)■	3B-1B-DH	80	180	27	47	5	0	9	24	.261	9	29	0	37	43	6	.930
2001—San Francisco (N.L.)	3B-DH	53	167	16	43	13	1	7	17	.257	17	49	1	20	61	10	.890
American League totals (6 years)		479	1633	218	418	90	5	68	235	.256	120	425	15	232	798	73	.934
National League totals (2 years)		133	347	43	90	18	1	16	41	.259	26	78	1	57	104	16	.910
Major League totals (8 years)		612	1980	261	508	108	6	84	276	.257	146	503	16	289	902	89	.930

DIVISION SERIES RECORD

Year Team (League)	Pos.	G	AB	R	H	2B	3B	HR	RBI	Avg.	BB	SO	SB	PO	A	E	Avg.
1995—New York (A.L.)	3B	2	5	0	1	0	0	0	0	.200	0	2	0	0	1	0	1.000
2000—San Francisco (N.L.)	PH	2	2	0	0	0	0	0	0	.000	0	1	0	...	...	...	...
Division series totals (2 years)		4	7	0	1	0	0	0	0	.143	0	3	0	0	1	0	1.000

DAWKINS, GOOKIE   SS   REDS

PERSONAL: Born May 12, 1979, in Newberry, S.C. ... 6-1/180. ... Bats right, throws right. ... Full name: Travis Sentell Dawkins.
HIGH SCHOOL: Newberry (S.C.).
TRANSACTIONS/CAREER NOTES: Selected by Cincinnati Reds organization in second round of free-agent draft (June 3, 1997). ... On Louisville disabled list (August 1-8, 2000). ... On disabled list (April 5-12 and April 28-May 9, 2001).
STATISTICAL NOTES: Led Pioneer League shortstops with 368 total chances in 1997.
MISCELLANEOUS: Member of 2000 U.S. Olympic baseball team.

Year Team (League)	Pos.	G	AB	R	H	2B	3B	HR	RBI	Avg.	BB	SO	SB	PO	A	E	Avg.
1997—Billings (Pio.)	SS	70	253	47	61	5	0	4	37	.241	30	38	16	*118	*216	34	.908
1998—Burlington (Midw.)	SS	102	367	52	97	7	6	1	30	.264	37	60	37	149	298	36	.925
1999—Rockford (Midw.)	SS	76	305	56	83	10	6	8	32	.272	35	38	38	120	206	17	.950
—Chattanooga (Sou.)	SS	32	129	24	47	7	0	2	13	.364	14	17	15	52	89	3	.979
—Cincinnati (N.L.)	SS	7	7	1	1	0	0	0	0	.143	0	4	0	2	4	0	1.000
2000—Cincinnati (N.L.)	SS	14	41	5	9	2	0	0	3	.220	2	7	0	21	34	2	.965
—Chattanooga (Sou.)	SS-2B	95	368	54	85	20	6	6	31	.231	40	71	22	185	290	19	.962
2001—Chattanooga (Sou.)	SS	104	394	59	89	16	3	8	40	.226	32	88	14	166	261	16	*.964
Major League totals (2 years)		21	48	6	10	2	0	0	3	.208	2	11	0	23	38	2	.968

DAY, ZACH   P   EXPOS

PERSONAL: Born June 15, 1978, in Cincinnati. ... 6-4/185. ... Throws right, bats right. ... Full name: Stephen Zachary Day.
HIGH SCHOOL: La Salle (Cincinnati).
TRANSACTIONS/CAREER NOTES: Selected by New York Yankees organization in fifth round of free-agent draft (June 4, 1996). ... Traded by Yankees to Cleveland Indians with P Jake Westbrook (July 24, 2000), completing deal in which Indians traded OF David Justice to Yankees for OF Ricky Ledee and two players to be named later (June 29, 2000). ... Traded by Indians to Montreal Expos for OF Milton Bradley (July 31, 2001).

Year League	W	L	Pct.	ERA	G	GS	CG	ShO	Sv.	IP	H	R	ER	BB	SO
1996—Gulf Coast Yankees (GCL)	5	2	.714	5.61	7	5	0	0	0	33 2/3	41	26	21	3	23
1997—Oneonta (NY-Penn)	7	2	.778	2.15	14	14	0	0	0	92	82	26	22	23	92
1998—Tampa (FSL)	5	8	.385	5.49	18	17	0	0	0	100	142	89	61	32	69
—Greensboro (S.Atl.)	1	2	.333	2.75	7	6	1	0	0	36	35	22	11	6	37
1999—Gulf Coast Yankees (GCL)	1	1	.500	3.78	5	4	0	0	0	16 2/3	20	10	7	4	17
—Greensboro (S.Atl.)	0	1	.000	2.25	2	2	0	0	0	8	14	11	2	1	4
2000—Greensboro (S.Atl.)	9	3	.750	1.90	13	13	1	1	0	85 1/3	72	29	18	31	101
—Tampa (FSL)■	2	4	.333	4.19	7	7	0	0	0	34 1/3	33	22	16	15	36
—Akron (East.)■■	4	2	.667	3.52	8	8	0	0	0	46	38	20	18	21	43
2001—Akron (East.)	9	10	.474	3.10	22	22	2	0	0	136 2/3	123	57	47	45	94
—Buffalo (I.L.)	1	0	1.000	1.50	1	1	0	0	0	6	3	1	1	1	2
—Ottawa (I.L.)■	2	2	.500	7.43	6	5	0	0	0	26 2/3	38	23	22	8	15

DE LA ROSA, JORGE   P   RED SOX

PERSONAL: Born November 5, 1981, in Monterey, Mexico. ... 6-1/190. ... Throws left, bats left. ... Full name: Jorge Alberto De La Rosa.
TRANSACTIONS/CAREER NOTES: Signed as non-drafted free agent by Arizona Diamondbacks organization (March 20, 1998). ... Released by Diamondbacks (2000). ... Signed by Monterrey, Mexican League (2000). ... Contract purchased by Boston Red Sox organization from Monterrey (March 15, 2001).

Year League	W	L	Pct.	ERA	G	GS	CG	ShO	Sv.	IP	H	R	ER	BB	SO
1998—Dom. D'backs (DSL)	1	0	1.000	4.50	13	0	0	0	1	14	8	7	7	8	21
1999—Ariz. Diamondbacks (Ariz.)	0	0	...	3.21	8	0	0	0	2	14	12	5	5	3	17
—High Desert (Calif.)	0	0	...	0.00	2	0	0	0	3	1	0	0	2	3	
—Missoula (Pio.)	0	1	.000	7.98	13	0	0	0	2	14 2/3	22	17	13	9	14
2000—Monterrey (Mex.)■	3	2	.600	6.28	37	0	0	0	1	38 2/3	38	27	27	32	50
2001—Sarasota (FSL)	0	1	.000	1.21	12	0	0	0	2	29 2/3	13	7	4	12	27
—Trenton (East.)	1	3	.250	5.84	29	0	0	0	0	37	56	35	24	20	27

DE LA ROSA, TOMAS   SS   EXPOS

PERSONAL: Born January 28, 1978, in La Victoria, Dominican Republic. ... 5-10/165. ... Bats right, throws right. ... Full name: Tomas Agramonte De La Rosa.
HIGH SCHOOL: Licey Padre Garcia (La Victoria, Dominican Republic).
TRANSACTIONS/CAREER NOTES: Signed as non-drafted free agent by Montreal Expos organization (July 12, 1995).
STATISTICAL NOTES: Led Gulf Coast League shortstops with 301 total chances in 1996. ... Led Eastern League shortstops with 83 double plays in 1999. ... Led International League shortstops with 578 total chances in 2001.

| | | | | | | BATTING | | | | | | | | FIELDING | | | |
Year Team (League)	Pos.	G	AB	R	H	2B	3B	HR	RBI	Avg.	BB	SO	SB	PO	A	E	Avg.
1996— GC Expos (GCL)	SS	54	187	35	47	7	1	0	21	.251	22	25	8	86	*189	26	.914
—Vermont (NY-Penn)....	SS	3	8	1	2	0	0	0	1	.250	0	3	0	1	4	1	.833
1997—W.P. Beach (FSL).......	SS	4	9	1	2	0	0	0	0	.222	2	3	2	5	6	1	.917
—Vermont (NY-Penn)...	SS	69	271	46	72	14	6	2	40	.266	32	47	19	85	201	21	.932
1998— Jupiter (FSL)	SS	117	390	56	98	22	1	3	43	.251	37	61	27	*208	382	30	.952
1999—Harrisburg (East.).......	SS	135	467	70	122	22	3	6	43	.261	42	64	28	219	381	34	.946
2000— Ottawa (I.L.)	SS	103	340	27	69	10	1	1	36	.203	31	43	10	156	270	16	.964
— Montreal (N.L.)..........	SS-DH	32	66	7	19	3	1	2	9	.288	7	11	2	39	58	2	.980
2001— Ottawa (I.L.)	SS	121	420	56	100	24	0	7	30	.238	40	63	12	*190	368	20	.965
— Montreal (N.L.)............	PH	1	1	0	0	0	0	0	0	.000	0	0	0	...	...	...	...
Major League totals (2 years)		33	67	7	19	3	1	2	9	.284	7	11	2	39	58	2	.980

DE LOS SANTOS, VALERIO   P   BREWERS

PERSONAL: Born October 6, 1975, in Las Matas, Dominican Republic. ... 6-2/206. ... Throws left, bats left. ... Full name: Valerio Lorenzo De Los Santos.
TRANSACTIONS/CAREER NOTES: Signed as non-drafted free agent by Milwaukee Brewers organization (January 26, 1993). ... On El Paso disabled list (April 27-May 4, 1998). ... On Milwaukee disabled list (April 29-September 23, 1999). ... On disabled list (April 4, 2001-remainder of season).
STATISTICAL NOTES: Tied for Arizona League lead with two intentional bases on balls issued in 1995.

Year League	W	L	Pct.	ERA	G	GS	CG	ShO	Sv.	IP	H	R	ER	BB	SO
1993—Dominican Brewers (DSL)..	1	7	.125	6.50	19	6	1	0	0	63 2/3	91	57	46	37	39
1994—Dominican Brewers (DSL)..	7	6	.538	3.69	17	•16	1	1	0	90 1/3	90	52	37	35	50
1995—Arizona Brewers (Ariz.) ..	4	6	.400	2.20	14	12	0	0	0	82	*81	34	20	12	57
1996—Beloit (Midw.)..................	10	8	.556	3.55	33	23	•5	•1	0	164 2/3	164	83	65	59	137
1997—El Paso (Texas).................	6	10	.375	5.75	26	16	1	0	2	114 1/3	146	83	73	38	61
1998—El Paso (Texas).................	6	2	.750	3.91	42	4	0	0	10	66 2/3	81	34	29	25	62
—Milwaukee (N.L.)..............	0	0	...	2.91	21	0	0	0	0	21 2/3	11	7	7	2	18
—Louisville (I.L.)...............	0	0	...	3.60	5	0	0	0	0	5	4	2	2	0	0
1999—Milwaukee (N.L.).............	0	1	.000	6.48	7	0	0	0	0	8 1/3	12	6	6	7	5
2000—Milwaukee (N.L.).............	2	3	.400	5.13	66	2	0	0	0	73 2/3	72	43	42	33	70
2001—Milwaukee (N.L.).............	0	0	...	9.00	1	0	0	0	0	1	1	1	1	1	1
Major League totals (4 years).......	2	4	.333	4.82	87	2	0	0	0	104 2/3	96	57	56	43	94

DeHAAN, KORY   OF   PADRES

PERSONAL: Born July 16, 1976, in Pella, Iowa. ... 6-2/187. ... Bats left, throws right. ... Full name: Korwin Jay DeHaan.
HIGH SCHOOL: Pella (Iowa) Christian.
COLLEGE: Morningside College (Iowa).
TRANSACTIONS/CAREER NOTES: Selected by Pittsburgh Pirates organization in seventh round of free-agent draft (June 3, 1997). ... Selected by San Diego Padres from Pirates organization in Rule 5 major league draft (December 13, 1999). ... On San Diego disabled list (April 1-24, 2000); included rehabilitation assignments to Rancho Cucamonga (April 11-15) and Las Vegas (April 16-24).

| | | | | | | BATTING | | | | | | | | FIELDING | | | |
Year Team (League)	Pos.	G	AB	R	H	2B	3B	HR	RBI	Avg.	BB	SO	SB	PO	A	E	Avg.
1997—Erie (NY-Penn)	OF	58	205	43	49	8	6	1	18	.239	38	43	14	105	0	1	.991
1998—Augusta (S.Atl.).........	OF	132	475	85	149	*39	8	8	75	.314	69	114	33	244	7	4	.984
1999—Lynchburg (Caro.)......	OF	78	295	55	96	19	5	7	42	.325	36	63	32	164	2	4	.976
—Altoona (East.)...........	OF	47	190	26	51	13	2	3	24	.268	11	46	14	88	1	1	.989
2000—Rancho Cuca. (Calif.)■	OF	4	14	2	3	1	0	1	1	.214	1	4	0	4	0	0	1.000
—Las Vegas (PCL).........	OF	10	41	7	12	4	0	0	3	.293	2	11	3	37	0	0	1.000
—San Diego (N.L.).........	OF-DH	90	103	19	21	7	0	2	13	.204	5	39	4	50	3	0	1.000
2001—Portland (PCL)	OF	87	304	35	77	9	5	7	28	.253	20	71	12	198	9	2	.990
—Mobile (Sou.)	OF	42	159	29	47	8	2	4	23	.296	22	27	12	80	3	1	.988
Major League totals (1 year)		90	103	19	21	7	0	2	13	.204	5	39	4	50	3	0	1.000

DeJEAN, MIKE   P   BREWERS

PERSONAL: Born September 28, 1970, in Baton Rouge, La. ... 6-2/212. ... Throws right, bats right. ... Full name: Michael Dwain DeJean.
HIGH SCHOOL: Walker (La.).
JUNIOR COLLEGE: Mississippi Delta Community College.
COLLEGE: Livingston (La.).
TRANSACTIONS/CAREER NOTES: Selected by New York Yankees organization in 24th round of free-agent draft (June 1, 1992). ... On disabled list (June 4-July 21 and July 26, 1993-remainder of season). ... Traded by Yankees with a player to be named later to Colorado Rockies for C Joe Girardi (November 20, 1995); Rockies acquired P Steve Shoemaker to complete deal (December 6, 1995). ... On Colorado disabled list (July 18-August 8, 1997); included rehabilitation assignment to New Haven (July 30-August 8). ... On disabled list (September 2, 1998-remainder of season). ... On Colorado disabled list (August 14-September 1, 1999); included rehabilitation assignment to Colorado Springs

(August 30-September 1). ... On Colorado disabled list (March 29-April 28 and July 25-August 15, 2000); included rehabilitation assignment to Colorado Springs (April 6-28 and August 10-13). ... Traded by Rockies with P Mark Leiter and 2B/SS Elvis Pena to Milwaukee Brewers for P Juan Acevedo, P Kane Davis and IF Jose Flores (April 4, 2001).

Year	League	W	L	Pct.	ERA	G	GS	CG	ShO	Sv.	IP	H	R	ER	BB	SO
1992—Oneonta (NY-Penn)		0	0	...	0.44	20	0	0	0	16	20 2/3	12	3	1	3	20
1993—Greensboro (S.Atl.)		2	3	.400	5.00	20	0	0	0	9	18	22	12	10	8	16
1994—Tampa (FSL)		0	2	.000	2.38	34	0	0	0	16	34	39	15	9	13	22
—Albany (East.)		0	2	.000	4.38	16	0	0	0	4	24 2/3	22	14	12	15	13
1995—Norwich (East.)		5	5	.500	2.99	59	0	0	0	20	78 1/3	58	29	26	34	57
1996—Colorado Springs (PCL)■		0	2	.000	5.13	30	0	0	0	1	40 1/3	52	24	23	21	31
—New Haven (East.)		0	0	...	3.22	16	0	0	0	11	22 1/3	20	9	8	8	12
1997—Colorado Springs (PCL)		0	1	.000	5.40	10	0	0	0	4	10	17	6	6	7	9
—Colorado (N.L.)		5	0	1.000	3.99	55	0	0	0	2	67 2/3	74	34	30	24	38
—New Haven (East.)		0	1	.000	6.00	2	0	0	0	0	3	3	2	2	2	2
1998—Colorado (N.L.)		3	1	.750	3.03	59	1	0	0	2	74 1/3	78	29	25	24	27
1999—Colorado (N.L.)		2	4	.333	8.41	56	0	0	0	0	61	83	61	57	32	31
—Colorado Springs (PCL)		0	0	...	0.00	1	0	0	0	0	1	1	0	0	0	0
2000—Colorado Springs (PCL)		1	1	.500	2.51	12	0	0	0	5	14 1/3	15	4	4	4	12
—Colorado (N.L.)		4	4	.500	4.89	54	0	0	0	0	53 1/3	54	31	29	30	34
2001—Milwaukee (N.L.)■		4	2	.667	2.77	75	0	0	0	2	84 1/3	75	31	26	39	68
Major League totals (5 years)		18	11	.621	4.41	299	1	0	0	6	340 2/3	364	186	167	149	198

PERSONAL: Born June 25, 1972, in Aguadilla, Puerto Rico. ... 6-3/230. ... Bats left, throws right. ... Full name: Carlos Juan Delgado.

HIGH SCHOOL: Jose de Diego (Aguadilla, Puerto Rico).

TRANSACTIONS/CAREER NOTES: Signed as non-drafted free agent by Toronto Blue Jays organization (October 9, 1988). ... On Toronto disabled list (March 15-April 24, 1998); included rehabilitation assignments to Dunedin (April 17-19) and Syracuse (April 20-24).

HONORS: Named Florida State League Most Valuable Player (1992). ... Named Southern League Most Valuable Player (1993). ... Named first baseman on THE SPORTING NEWS A.L. Silver Slugger team (1999 and 2000). ... Named Major League Player of the Year by THE SPORTING NEWS (2000). ... Named first baseman on THE SPORTING NEWS A.L. All-Star team (2000).

STATISTICAL NOTES: Led New York-Pennsylvania League catchers with 540 total chances and six double plays in 1990. ... Led South Atlantic League with 29 passed balls in 1991. ... Led Florida State League with 281 total bases, .579 slugging percentage, .402 on-base percentage and 11 intentional bases on balls received in 1992. ... Led Florida State League catchers with 784 total chances in 1992. ... Led Southern League with .524 slugging percentage, .430 on-base percentage and 18 intentional bases on balls received in 1993. ... Led Southern League catchers with 800 total chances in 1993. ... Led International League with .610 slugging percentage in 1995. ... Led International League with seven intentional bases on balls received in 1995. ... Had 19-game hitting streak (May 21-June 9, 1998). ... Hit three home runs in one game (August 4, 1998; August 6, 1999; April 4, 2001; and April 20, 2001). ... Led A.L. first baseman with 134 double plays in 1999. ... Had 22-game hitting streak (June 4-29, 2000). ... Led A.L. first baseman with 1,511 total chances and 157 double plays in 2000. ... Led A.L. with 378 total bases in 2000. ... Tied for A.L. lead in being hit by pitch with 15 in 2000. ... Career major league grand slams: 7.

MISCELLANEOUS: Holds Toronto Blue Jays all-time record for most home runs (229).

Year	Team (League)	Pos.	G	AB	R	H	2B	3B	HR	RBI	Avg.	BB	SO	SB	PO	A	E	Avg.
1989—St. Catharines (NY-P)		C	31	89	9	16	5	0	0	11	.180	23	39	0	63	13	2	.974
1990—St. Catharines (NY-P)		C	67	228	30	64	13	0	6	39	.281	35	65	2	*471	*62	7	.987
1991—Myrtle Beach (S.Atl.)		C	132	441	72	126	18	2	18	70	.286	75	97	9	679	*100	19	.976
—Syracuse (I.L.)		C	1	3	0	0	0	0	0	0	.000	0	2	0	5	0	0	1.000
1992—Dunedin (FSL)		C	133	485	83	*157	•30	2	*30	*100	.324	59	91	2	*684	89	11	.986
1993—Knoxville (Sou.)		C	140	468	91	142	28	0	*25	*102	.303	*102	98	10	*683	*103	*14	.983
—Toronto (A.L.)		DH-C	2	1	0	0	0	0	0	0	.000	1	0	0	2	0	0	1.000
1994—Toronto (A.L.)		OF-C	43	130	17	28	2	0	9	24	.215	25	46	1	56	2	2	.967
—Syracuse (I.L.)		DH-C-1B	85	307	52	98	11	0	19	58	.319	42	58	1	235	25	7	.974
1995—Toronto (A.L.)		OF-DH-1B	37	91	7	15	3	0	3	11	.165	6	26	0	54	2	0	1.000
—Syracuse (I.L.)		1B-OF	91	333	59	106	23	4	22	74	.318	45	78	0	724	49	4	.995
1996—Toronto (A.L.)		DH-1B	138	488	68	132	28	2	25	92	.270	58	139	0	221	13	4	.983
1997—Toronto (A.L.)		1B-DH	153	519	79	136	42	3	30	91	.262	64	133	0	962	67	12	.988
1998—Dunedin (FSL)		DH-1B	4	16	4	5	1	0	2	7	.313	2	4	0	13	0	0	1.000
—Syracuse (I.L.)		1B	2	7	4	4	2	0	1	6	.571	2	0	0	22	2	0	1.000
—Toronto (A.L.)		1B-DH	142	530	94	155	43	1	38	115	.292	73	139	3	1165	87	10	.992
1999—Toronto (A.L.)		1B-DH	152	573	113	156	39	0	44	134	.272	86	141	1	*1306	84	*14	.990
2000—Toronto (A.L.)		1B	•162	569	115	196	*57	1	41	137	.344	123	104	0	*1416	82	13	.991
2001—Toronto (A.L.)		1B	•162	574	102	160	31	1	39	102	.279	111	136	3	1518	103	9	.994
Major League totals (9 years)			991	3475	595	978	245	8	229	706	.281	547	864	8	6700	440	64	.991

ALL-STAR GAME RECORD

Year	League	Pos.	AB	R	H	2B	3B	HR	RBI	Avg.	BB	SO	SB	PO	A	E	Avg.
2000—American		1B	1	0	1	1	0	0	0	1.000	0	0	0	4	0	0	1.000

PERSONAL: Born July 15, 1975, in San Cristobal, Dominican Republic. ... 5-11/165. ... Bats both, throws right. ... Full name: Wilson Duran Delgado.

TRANSACTIONS/CAREER NOTES: Signed as non-drafted free agent by Seattle Mariners organization (October 29, 1992). ... Traded by Mariners with P Shawn Estes to San Francisco Giants for P Salomon Torres (May 21, 1995). ... Traded by Giants to New York Yankees for SS Juan Melo (March 23, 2000). ... Traded by Yankees to Kansas City Royals for SS Nick Ortiz (August 11, 2000). ... Granted free agency (October 9, 2001).

STATISTICAL NOTES: Led Pacific Coast League shortstops with 197 putouts, 547 total chances and 86 double plays in 1997.

Year Team (League)	Pos.	G	AB	R	H	2B	3B	HR	RBI	Avg.	BB	SO	SB	PO	A	E	Avg.
1993— Dom. Mariners (DSL).	IF	60	171	19	50	8	0	0	26	.292	34	25	5	96	148	16	.938
1994— Ariz. Mariners (Ariz.)..	SS-2B	39	149	30	56	5	4	0	10	*.376	15	24	13	58	114	10	.945
1995— Wis. Rapids (Midw.)...	SS	19	70	13	17	3	0	0	7	.243	3	15	3	29	65	6	.940
— Burlington (Midw.)■..	SS	93	365	52	113	20	3	5	37	.310	32	57	9	127	285	19	.956
1996— San Jose (Calif.).........	SS	121	462	59	124	19	6	2	54	.268	48	89	8	192	343	24	.957
— Phoenix (PCL)	SS	12	43	1	6	0	1	0	1	.140	3	7	0	30	47	2	.975
— San Francisco (N.L.) ..	SS	6	22	3	8	0	0	0	2	.364	1	5	1	12	12	1	.960
1997— San Francisco (N.L.) ..	2B-SS	8	7	1	1	0	0	0	0	.143	0	2	0	2	3	0	1.000
— Phoenix (PCL)	SS-2B	119	416	47	120	22	4	9	59	.288	24	70	9	†208	347	18	.969
1998— Fresno (PCL).............	SS	127	512	87	142	22	2	12	63	.277	52	92	9	205	373	23	.962
— San Francisco (N.L.) ..	SS	10	12	1	2	1	0	0	1	.167	1	3	0	3	6	0	1.000
1999— Fresno (PCL)	SS-2B	57	213	28	64	10	3	1	33	.300	18	35	4	86	166	15	.944
— San Francisco (N.L.) ..	SS-2B	35	71	7	18	2	1	0	3	.254	5	9	1	39	42	5	.942
2000— New York (A.L.)■...	2B-SS-3B	31	45	6	11	1	0	1	4	.244	5	9	1	23	37	3	.952
— Kansas City (A.L.)■...	2B-SS-3B	33	83	15	22	1	0	0	7	.265	6	17	1	38	97	1	.993
2001— Omaha (PCL)..............	2B-3B-SS	76	255	24	63	11	2	4	30	.247	16	43	8	118	168	11	.963
— Kansas City (A.L.)	SS-3B-2B	14	25	1	3	0	0	0	1	.120	3	10	0	4	21	0	1.000
American League totals (2 years)		78	153	22	36	2	0	1	12	.235	14	36	2	65	155	4	.982
National League totals (4 years)		59	112	12	29	4	1	0	6	.259	7	19	2	56	63	6	.952
Major League totals (6 years)		137	265	34	65	6	1	1	18	.245	21	55	4	121	218	10	.971

DELLAERO, JASON   SS   WHITE SOX

PERSONAL: Born December 17, 1976, in Mount Kisco, N.Y. ... 6-2/195. ... Bats both, throws right. ... Full name: Jason Christopher Dellaero.
HIGH SCHOOL: Brewster (N.Y.).
COLLEGE: South Florida.
TRANSACTIONS/CAREER NOTES: Selected by New York Mets organization in 17th round of free-agent draft (June 2, 1994); did not sign. ... Selected by Chicago White Sox organization in first round (15th pick overall) of free-agent draft (June 3, 1997).

Year Team (League)	Pos.	G	AB	R	H	2B	3B	HR	RBI	Avg.	BB	SO	SB	PO	A	E	Avg.
1997— GC White Sox (GCL) ..	SS	5	15	1	3	2	0	0	1	.200	1	2	0	5	6	2	.846
— Hickory (S.Atl.)...........	SS	55	191	37	53	10	3	6	29	.277	17	49	3	79	150	14	.942
1998— Win.-Salem (Caro.)	SS	121	428	45	89	23	3	10	49	.208	25	147	12	183	306	*46	.914
1999— Win.-Salem (Caro.)	SS	54	184	22	41	13	0	2	19	.223	18	59	9	89	170	19	.932
— Birmingham (Sou.).....	SS	81	272	40	73	13	3	10	44	.268	14	76	6	138	227	20	.948
— Chicago (A.L.)............	SS	11	33	1	3	0	0	0	2	.091	1	13	0	16	28	4	.917
2000— Birmingham (Sou.).....	SS	122	438	36	81	18	1	7	42	.185	20	142	9	201	347	25	.956
2001— Charlotte (I.L.)...........	SS	115	377	32	67	10	0	11	28	.178	17	113	4	157	299	15	*.968
Major League totals (1 year)		11	33	1	3	0	0	0	2	.091	1	13	0	16	28	4	.917

DELLUCCI, DAVID   OF   DIAMONDBACKS

PERSONAL: Born October 31, 1973, in Baton Rouge, La. ... 5-11/198. ... Bats left, throws left. ... Full name: David Michael Dellucci. ... Name pronounced duh-LOO-chee.
HIGH SCHOOL: Catholic (Baton Rouge, La.).
COLLEGE: Mississippi.
TRANSACTIONS/CAREER NOTES: Selected by Baltimore Orioles organization in 10th round of free agent draft (June 1, 1995). ... Selected by Arizona Diamondbacks in second round (45th pick overall) of expansion draft (November 18, 1997). ... On disabled list (July 25, 1999-remainder of season). ... On Tucson disabled list (May 8-July 26, 2000).
STATISTICAL NOTES: Career major league grand slams: 1.

Year Team (League)	Pos.	G	AB	R	H	2B	3B	HR	RBI	Avg.	BB	SO	SB	PO	A	E	Avg.
1995— Frederick (Caro.)	OF	28	96	16	27	3	0	1	10	.281	12	10	1	26	2	1	.966
— Bluefield (Appl.)..........	OF	20	69	11	23	5	1	2	12	.333	6	7	3	11	0	2	.846
1996— Frederick (Caro.)	OF	59	185	33	60	11	1	4	28	.324	38	34	5	100	4	3	.972
— Bowie (East.).............	OF	66	251	27	73	14	1	2	33	.291	28	56	2	134	5	3	.979
1997— Bowie (East.).............	OF-DH	107	385	71	126	29	3	20	55	.327	58	69	11	162	2	1	.994
— Baltimore (A.L.)..........	OF-DH	17	27	3	6	1	0	1	3	.222	4	7	0	20	1	0	1.000
1998— Tucson (PCL)■...........	OF	17	72	17	22	4	3	1	11	.306	5	8	4	38	0	0	1.000
— Arizona (N.L.)............	OF	124	416	43	108	19	*12	5	51	.260	33	103	3	230	3	3	.987
1999— Arizona (N.L.)............	OF-DH	63	109	27	43	7	1	1	15	.394	11	24	2	37	1	0	1.000
2000— Arizona (N.L.)............	OF	34	50	2	15	3	0	0	2	.300	4	9	0	15	0	0	1.000
— Tucson (PCL)	OF	33	122	16	28	6	3	3	17	.230	13	15	4	55	1	2	.966
— Ariz. D'backs (Ariz.)....	OF	2	6	0	2	1	0	0	2	.333	0	1	0	0	0	0	...
— South Bend (Midw.) ...	OF	2	5	3	1	1	0	0	1	.200	2	0	0	1	0	0	1.000
2001— Arizona (N.L.)............	OF	115	217	28	60	10	2	10	40	.276	22	52	2	90	0	1	.989
American League totals (1 year)		17	27	3	6	1	0	1	3	.222	4	7	0	20	1	0	1.000
National League totals (4 years)		336	792	100	226	39	15	16	108	.285	70	188	7	372	4	4	.989
Major League totals (5 years)		353	819	103	232	40	15	17	111	.283	74	195	7	392	5	4	.990

DIVISION SERIES RECORD

Year Team (League)	Pos.	G	AB	R	H	2B	3B	HR	RBI	Avg.	BB	SO	SB	PO	A	E	Avg.
2001— Arizona (N.L.)............	PH	2	0	0	0	0	0	0	0	...	0	0	0	...	...	...	...

Year	Team (League)	Pos.	G	AB	R	H	2B	3B	HR	RBI	Avg.	BB	SO	SB	PO	A	E	Avg.
						BATTING										FIELDING		
2001—	Arizona (N.L.)............	PH	2	2	1	1	0	0	0	0	.500	0	0	0	...	...	...	...

WORLD SERIES RECORD

NOTES: Member of World Series championship team (2001).

Year	Team (League)	Pos.	G	AB	R	H	2B	3B	HR	RBI	Avg.	BB	SO	SB	PO	A	E	Avg.
						BATTING										FIELDING		
2001—	Arizona (N.L.)............	PR-OF	2	2	0	1	0	0	0	0	.500	0	0	0	1	0	0	1.000

DEMPSTER, RYAN — P — MARLINS

PERSONAL: Born May 3, 1977, in Sechelt, B.C. ... 6-1/201. ... Throws right, bats right. ... Full name: Ryan Scott Dempster.

HIGH SCHOOL: Elphinstone (Gibsons, B.C.).

TRANSACTIONS/CAREER NOTES: Selected by Texas Rangers organization in third round of free-agent draft (June 1, 1995). ... Traded by Rangers with a player to be named later to Florida Marlins for P John Burkett (August 8, 1996); Marlins acquired P Rick Helling to complete deal (September 3, 1996).

STATISTICAL NOTES: Pitched 3-0 one-hit, complete-game victory against New York Mets (May 7, 2000).

MISCELLANEOUS: Holds Florida Marlins all-time record for most strikeouts (541). ... Shares Florida Marlins all-time record for most wins (37). ... Appeared in one game as pinch runner (1999).

Year	League	W	L	Pct.	ERA	G	GS	CG	ShO	Sv.	IP	H	R	ER	BB	SO
1995—	Gulf Coast Rangers (GCL)..	3	1	.750	2.36	8	6	1	0	0	34 1/3	34	21	9	17	37
	—Hudson Valley (NY-Penn)...	1	0	1.000	3.18	1	1	0	0	0	5 2/3	7	2	2	1	6
1996—	Charleston, S.C. (S.Atl.).....	7	11	.389	3.30	23	23	2	0	0	144 1/3	120	71	53	58	141
	—Kane County (Midw.)■......	2	1	.667	2.73	4	4	1	1	0	26 1/3	18	10	8	18	16
1997—	Brevard County (FSL).........	10	9	.526	4.90	28	26	2	1	0	165 1/3	190	100	*90	46	131
1998—	Portland (East.).................	4	3	.571	3.22	7	7	0	0	0	44 2/3	34	20	16	15	33
	—Florida (N.L.)..................	1	5	.167	7.08	14	11	0	0	0	54 2/3	72	47	43	38	35
	—Charlotte (I.L.).................	3	1	.750	3.27	5	5	1	0	0	33	33	14	12	12	24
1999—	Calgary (PCL)..................	1	1	.500	4.99	5	5	0	0	0	30 2/3	30	17	17	10	29
	—Florida (N.L.)..................	7	8	.467	4.71	25	25	0	0	0	147	146	77	77	93	126
2000—	Florida (N.L.)..................	14	10	.583	3.66	33	33	2	1	0	226 1/3	210	102	92	97	209
2001—	Florida (N.L.)..................	15	12	.556	4.94	34	34	2	1	0	211 1/3	218	123	116	*112	171
Major League totals (4 years).......		37	35	.514	4.62	106	103	4	2	0	639 1/3	646	349	328	340	541

ALL-STAR GAME RECORD

Year	League	W	L	Pct.	ERA	GS	CG	ShO	Sv.	IP	H	R	ER	BB	SO
2000—	National............................							Did not play.							

DePAULA, SEAN — P — INDIANS

PERSONAL: Born November 7, 1973, in Newton, Mass. ... 6-4/215. ... Throws right, bats right. ... Full name: Sean Michael DePaula.

HIGH SCHOOL: Pinkerton Academy (Derry, N.H.), then Cushing Academy (Ashburnham, Mass.).

COLLEGE: Wake Forest.

TRANSACTIONS/CAREER NOTES: Selected by Boston Red Sox organization in eighth round of free-agent draft (June 3, 1993); did not sign. ... Selected by Cleveland Indians organization in ninth round of free-agent draft (June 4, 1996). ... On Cleveland disabled list (May 28-July 9 and September 8, 2000-remainder of season); included rehabilitation assignment to Akron (June 24-July 9). ... On Buffalo disabled list (August 2-September 6, 2000). ... On disabled list (April 23, 2001-remainder of season).

Year	League	W	L	Pct.	ERA	G	GS	CG	ShO	Sv.	IP	H	R	ER	BB	SO
1996—	Burlington (Appl.)..............	4	2	.667	3.82	23	0	0	0	1	35 1/3	31	16	15	13	42
	—Watertown (NY-Penn)	0	0	...	0.00	1	0	0	0	0	2	0	0	0	0	5
1997—	Columbus (S.Atl.)..............	4	5	.444	5.20	29	1	0	0	0	71	71	56	41	43	75
	—Watertown (NY-Penn)	1	1	.500	2.84	9	0	0	0	0	19	21	6	6	8	17
1998—	Kinston (Caro.).................	3	2	.600	2.36	28	1	0	0	1	49 2/3	50	20	13	18	59
	—Akron (East.)	1	1	.500	4.76	8	1	0	0	0	17	16	10	9	15	17
1999—	Kinston (Caro.).................	4	2	.667	2.28	23	0	0	0	7	51 1/3	36	17	13	17	75
	—Akron (East.)	1	0	1.000	3.54	14	0	0	0	1	28	20	11	11	17	31
	—Buffalo (I.L.)	0	0	...	0.00	5	0	0	0	2	5	0	0	0	3	7
	—Cleveland (A.L.)	0	0	...	4.63	11	0	0	0	0	11 2/3	8	6	6	3	18
2000—	Buffalo (I.L.)	1	0	1.000	5.54	9	0	0	0	1	13	16	10	8	7	11
	—Cleveland (A.L.)	0	0	...	5.94	13	0	0	0	0	16 2/3	20	11	11	14	16
	—Akron (East.)	0	0	...	1.80	4	0	0	0	0	5	1	1	1	2	4
2001—	Buffalo (I.L.)	1	0	1.000	1.04	6	0	0	0	1	8 2/3	2	1	1	4	6
Major League totals (2 years).......		0	0	...	5.40	24	0	0	0	0	28 1/3	28	17	17	17	34

DIVISION SERIES RECORD

Year	League	W	L	Pct.	ERA	G	GS	CG	ShO	Sv.	IP	H	R	ER	BB	SO
1999—	Cleveland (A.L.).................	0	0	...	1.80	3	0	0	0	0	5	2	1	1	3	5

DeROSA, MARK — SS — BRAVES

PERSONAL: Born February 2, 1975, in Passaic, N.J. ... 6-1/195. ... Bats right, throws right. ... Full name: Mark Thomas DeRosa.

HIGH SCHOOL: Bergen Catholic (Oradell, N.J.).

COLLEGE: Pennsylvania.

TRANSACTIONS/CAREER NOTES: Selected by Atlanta Braves organization in seventh round of free-agent draft (June 4, 1996).

STATISTICAL NOTES: Led Northwest League in grounding into double plays with 10 in 1996.

Year Team (League)	Pos.	G	AB	R	H	2B	3B	HR	RBI	Avg.	BB	SO	SB	PO	A	E	Avg.
										BATTING						FIELDING	
1996— Eugene (N'West)	SS	70	255	43	66	13	1	2	28	.259	38	48	3	82	196	24	.921
1997— Durham (Caro.)	SS	92	346	51	93	11	3	8	37	.269	25	73	6	136	245	21	.948
1998— Greenville (Sou.)	SS	125	461	67	123	26	2	8	49	.267	60	57	7	195	338	20	*.964
—Atlanta (N.L.)	SS	5	3	2	1	0	0	0	0	.333	0	1	0	1	1	0	1.000
1999— Richmond (I.L.)	SS-DH	105	364	41	99	16	2	1	40	.272	21	49	7	139	249	20	.951
—Atlanta (N.L.)	SS	7	8	0	0	0	0	0	0	.000	0	2	0	2	2	0	1.000
2000— Richmond (I.L.)	SS-2B-3B	101	370	62	108	22	3	3	35	.292	38	36	13	146	287	19	.958
—Atlanta (N.L.)	SS	22	13	9	4	1	0	0	3	.308	2	1	0	6	7	0	1.000
2001— Richmond (I.L.)	SS-3B-2B	49	186	31	55	18	0	2	17	.296	17	22	7	62	116	4	.978
—Atlanta (N.L.)	S-2-D-3-O	66	164	27	47	8	0	3	20	.287	12	19	2	59	137	7	.966
Major League totals (4 years)		100	188	38	52	9	0	3	23	.277	14	23	2	68	147	7	.968

DIVISION SERIES RECORD

Year Team (League)	Pos.	G	AB	R	H	2B	3B	HR	RBI	Avg.	BB	SO	SB	PO	A	E	Avg.
2001— Atlanta (N.L.)	SS	1	1	0	1	0	0	0	0	1.000	0	0	0	0	1	0	1.000

CHAMPIONSHIP SERIES RECORD

Year Team (League)	Pos.	G	AB	R	H	2B	3B	HR	RBI	Avg.	BB	SO	SB	PO	A	E	Avg.
2001— Atlanta (N.L.)	PH-SS	4	4	0	0	0	0	0	0	.000	0	0	0	0	1	0	1.000

DeSHIELDS, DELINO   2B/OF   CUBS

PERSONAL: Born January 15, 1969, in Seaford, Del. ... 6-1/175. ... Bats left, throws right. ... Full name: Delino Lamont DeShields. ... Name pronounced duh-LINE-oh.

HIGH SCHOOL: Seaford (Del.).

COLLEGE: Villanova.

TRANSACTIONS/CAREER NOTES: Selected by Montreal Expos organization in first round (12th pick overall) of free-agent draft (June 2, 1987). ... On disabled list (June 16-July 12, 1990 and August 12-September 11, 1993). ... Traded by Expos to Los Angeles Dodgers for P Pedro J. Martinez (November 19, 1993). ... On disabled list (May 26-June 20, 1994). ... Granted free agency (October 29, 1996). ... Signed by St. Louis Cardinals (November 20, 1996). ... On St. Louis disabled list (July 5-August 10, 1998); included rehabilitation assignment to Arkansas (August 5-10). ... Granted free agency (October 23, 1998). ... Signed by Baltimore Orioles (December 7, 1998). ... On Baltimore disabled list (March 25-April 11, June 21-July 23 and October 1, 1999-remainder of season); included rehabilitation assignments to Bowie (April 9-11 and July 20-22), Delmarva (July 15-16) and Frederick (July 17-19). ... Released by Orioles (July 2, 2001). ... Signed by Chicago Cubs (July 7, 2001). ... Granted free agency (November 5, 2001). ... Re-signed by Cubs (December 6, 2001).

RECORDS: Shares modern N.L. record for most hits in first major league game—4 (April 9, 1990). ... Shares major league single-game record for most strikeouts (nine-inning game)—5 (September 17, 1991, second game).

STATISTICAL NOTES: Led Gulf Coast League shortstops with 22 errors in 1987. ... Had 21-game hitting streak (June 28-July 21, 1993). ... Had 18-game hitting streak (May 30-June 20, 1998). ... Career major league grand slams: 1.

Year Team (League)	Pos.	G	AB	R	H	2B	3B	HR	RBI	Avg.	BB	SO	SB	PO	A	E	Avg.
1987— GC Expos (GCL)	SS-3B	31	111	17	24	5	2	1	4	.216	21	30	16	47	90	†22	.862
—Jamestown (NY-P)	SS	34	96	16	21	1	2	1	5	.219	24	28	14	25	57	21	.796
1988— Rockford (Midw.)	SS	129	460	97	116	26	6	12	46	.252	95	110	59	173	344	42	.925
1989— Jacksonville (Sou.)	SS	93	307	55	83	10	6	3	35	.270	76	80	37	127	218	34	.910
—Indianapolis (A.A.)	SS	47	181	29	47	8	4	2	14	.260	16	53	16	73	101	13	.930
1990— Montreal (N.L.)	2B	129	499	69	144	28	6	4	45	.289	66	96	42	236	371	12	.981
1991— Montreal (N.L.)	2B	151	563	83	134	15	4	10	51	.238	95	*151	56	285	405	*27	.962
1992— Montreal (N.L.)	2B	135	530	82	155	19	8	7	56	.292	54	108	46	251	360	15	.976
1993— Montreal (N.L.)	2B	123	481	75	142	17	7	2	29	.295	72	64	43	243	381	11	.983
1994— Los Angeles (N.L.)■..	2B-SS	89	320	51	80	11	3	2	33	.250	54	53	27	156	282	7	.984
1995— Los Angeles (N.L.)	2B	127	425	66	109	18	3	8	37	.256	63	83	39	204	330	•11	.980
1996— Los Angeles (N.L.)	2B	154	581	75	130	12	8	5	41	.224	53	124	48	274	400	17	.975
1997— St. Louis (N.L.)■	2B	150	572	92	169	26	*14	11	58	.295	55	72	55	272	398	19	.972
1998— St. Louis (N.L.)	2B-1B	117	420	74	122	21	8	7	44	.290	56	61	26	247	273	9	.983
—Arkansas (Texas)	2B-DH	4	13	1	2	0	0	0	0	.154	2	6	0	6	5	0	1.000
1999— Bowie (East.)■	2B-DH	4	15	2	4	1	0	0	0	.267	3	2	0	5	5	0	1.000
—Baltimore (A.L.)	2B	96	330	46	87	11	2	6	34	.264	37	52	11	178	249	10	.977
—Delmarva (S.Atl.)	2B	2	7	1	2	0	0	1	2	.286	1	1	0	4	5	0	1.000
—Frederick (Caro.)	2B	2	8	1	1	0	0	1	2	.125	1	0	1	5	5	0	1.000
2000— Baltimore (A.L.)	2B-OF-DH	151	561	84	166	43	5	10	86	.296	69	82	37	247	257	13	.975
2001— Baltimore (A.L.)	OF-DH	58	188	29	37	8	2	3	21	.197	31	42	11	87	2	3	.967
—Chicago (N.L.)■	OF-2B-3B-1B	68	163	26	45	9	3	2	16	.276	28	35	12	69	26	3	.969
American League totals (3 years)		305	1079	159	290	62	9	19	141	.269	137	176	59	512	508	26	.975
National League totals (10 years)		1243	4554	693	1230	176	64	58	410	.270	596	847	394	2237	3226	131	.977
Major League totals (12 years)		1548	5633	852	1520	238	73	77	551	.270	733	1023	453	2749	3734	157	.976

DIVISION SERIES RECORD

Year Team (League)	Pos.	G	AB	R	H	2B	3B	HR	RBI	Avg.	BB	SO	SB	PO	A	E	Avg.
1995— Los Angeles (N.L.)	2B	3	12	1	3	0	0	0	0	.250	1	3	0	8	7	0	1.000
1996— Los Angeles (N.L.)	2B	2	4	0	0	0	0	0	0	.000	0	1	0	3	2	0	1.000
Division series totals (2 years)		5	16	1	3	0	0	0	0	.188	1	4	0	11	9	0	1.000

DESSENS, ELMER — P — REDS

PERSONAL: Born January 13, 1972, in Hermosillo, Mexico. ... 6-0/187. ... Throws right, bats right. ... Full name: Elmer Dessens Jusaino. ... Name pronounced DAH-cenz.

HIGH SCHOOL: Carrera Technica (Hermosillo, Mexico).

TRANSACTIONS/CAREER NOTES: Signed as non-drafted free agent by Pittsburgh Pirates organization (January 27, 1993). ... Loaned by Pirates organization to Mexico City Red Devils, Mexican League for 1993 and 1994 seasons; returned to Pirates organization for 1995 season. ... Loaned by Pirates organization to Red Devils (May 7, 1996). ... Returned to Pirates organization (June 21, 1996). ... On Pittsburgh disabled list (July 31-September 10, 1996); included rehabilitation assignment to Carolina (August 16-September 10). ... Loaned by Pirates to Red Devils (March 27-September 5, 1997). ... On Pittsburgh disabled list (April 8-24, 1998); included rehabilitation assignment to Nashville (April 21-24). ... Released by Pirates (March 31, 1999). ... Played for Yomiuri Giants of Japan Central League (1999). ... Signed by Cincinnati Reds (December 15, 1999).

MISCELLANEOUS: Appeared in one game as pinch hitter (2001).

Year	League	W	L	Pct.	ERA	G	GS	CG	ShO	Sv.	IP	H	R	ER	BB	SO
1993—	M.C. Red Devils (Mex.)	3	1	.750	2.35	14	0	0	0	2	30²/₃	31	8	8	5	16
1994—	M.C. Red Devils (Mex.)	11	4	.733	2.04	37	15	4	1	3	127²/₃	121	37	29	32	51
1995—	Carolina (Sou.)■	*15	8	.652	*2.49	27	27	1	0	0	152	170	62	42	21	68
1996—	Calgary (PCL)	2	2	.500	3.15	6	6	0	0	0	34¹/₃	40	14	12	15	15
—	M.C. Red Devils (Mex.)■	7	0	1.000	1.26	7	7	1	0	0	50	44	12	7	10	17
—	Pittsburgh (N.L.)■	0	2	.000	8.28	15	3	0	0	0	25	40	23	23	4	13
—	Carolina (Sou.)	0	1	.000	5.40	5	1	0	0	0	11²/₃	15	8	7	4	7
1997—	M.C. Red Devils (Mex.)■	•16	5	.762	3.56	26	25	3	1	0	159¹/₃	156	73	63	51	61
—	Pittsburgh (N.L.)■	0	0	...	0.00	3	0	0	0	0	3¹/₃	2	0	0	0	2
1998—	Pittsburgh (N.L.)	2	6	.250	5.67	43	5	0	0	0	74²/₃	90	50	47	25	43
—	Nashville (PCL)	3	1	.750	3.30	6	5	0	0	0	30	32	12	11	6	13
1999—	Yomiuri (Jap. Cen.)■	0	1	.000	3.86	8	0	0	0	0	16¹/₃	24	7	7	4	6
—	Yomiuri (Jap. East.)	4	3	.571	2.09	15	14	2	...	0	95	67	26	22	24	58
2000—	Louisville (I.L.)■	2	0	1.000	3.18	4	4	0	0	0	22²/₃	24	10	8	7	14
—	Cincinnati (N.L.)	11	5	.688	4.28	40	16	1	0	1	147¹/₃	170	73	70	43	85
2001—	Cincinnati (N.L.)	10	14	.417	4.48	34	34	1	1	0	205	221	103	102	56	128
Major League totals (5 years)		23	27	.460	4.78	135	58	2	1	1	455¹/₃	523	249	242	128	271

DeWITT, MATT — P — BLUE JAYS

PERSONAL: Born September 4, 1977, in San Bernardino, Calif. ... 6-3/210. ... Throws right, bats right. ... Full name: Matthew Brian DeWitt.

HIGH SCHOOL: Valley (Las Vegas).

TRANSACTIONS/CAREER NOTES: Selected by St. Louis Cardinals organization in 10th round of free-agent draft (June 1, 1995). ... Traded by Cardinals with P Lance Painter and C Alberto Castillo to Toronto Blue Jays for P Pat Hentgen and P Paul Spoljaric (November 11, 1999). ... On Toronto disabled list (August 23, 2000-remainder of season). ... Traded by Blue Jays with P David Wells to Chicago White Sox for P Mike Sirotka, P Kevin Beirne, OF Brian Simmons and P Mike Williams (January 14, 2001). ... Traded by White Sox to Blue Jays for P Mike Williams (March 20, 2001).

STATISTICAL NOTES: Led Appalachian League pitchers with 17 home runs allowed in 1996.

Year	League	W	L	Pct.	ERA	G	GS	CG	ShO	Sv.	IP	H	R	ER	BB	SO
1995—	Johnson City (Appl.)	2	6	.250	7.04	13	12	0	0	0	62²/₃	84	56	*49	32	45
1996—	Johnson City (Appl.)	5	5	.500	5.42	14	*14	0	0	0	*79²/₃	66	53	48	26	58
1997—	Peoria (Midw.)	9	9	.500	4.09	27	•27	1	0	0	158¹/₃	152	84	72	57	121
1998—	Prince William (Caro.)	6	9	.400	3.64	24	24	1	0	0	148¹/₃	132	65	60	18	118
1999—	Arkansas (Texas)	9	8	.529	4.43	26	26	0	0	0	148¹/₃	153	87	73	59	107
2000—	Syracuse (I.L.)■	4	5	.444	4.87	31	7	0	0	15	64²/₃	78	42	35	25	41
—	Toronto (A.L.)	1	0	1.000	8.56	8	0	0	0	0	13²/₃	20	13	13	9	6
2001—	Syracuse (I.L.)	3	2	.600	2.78	53	0	0	0	*27	58¹/₃	45	20	18	17	44
—	Toronto (A.L.)	0	2	.000	3.79	16	0	0	0	0	19	22	8	8	10	13
Major League totals (2 years)		1	2	.333	5.79	24	0	0	0	0	32²/₃	42	21	21	19	19

DIAZ, EINAR — C — INDIANS

PERSONAL: Born December 28, 1972, in Chiniqui, Panama. ... 5-10/185. ... Bats right, throws right. ... Full name: Einar Antonio Diaz.

TRANSACTIONS/CAREER NOTES: Signed as non-drafted free agent by Cleveland Indians organization (October 5, 1990).

STATISTICAL NOTES: Led Appalachian League third basemen with 125 assists and .959 fielding percentage in 1992. ... Led Appalachian League catchers with 54 assists and nine errors in 1993. ... Led South Atlantic League in grounding into double plays with 18 in 1994. ... Led South Atlantic League catchers with 966 total chances, 845 putouts, 112 assists and tied for lead with eight double plays in 1994. ... Led Carolina League catchers with 107 assists and .992 fielding percentage in 1995. ... Led Eastern League catchers with 15 errors in 1996. ... Led American Association catchers with 18 errors in 1997. ... Led International League catchers with 873 total chances in 1998.

Year	Team (League)	Pos.	G	AB	R	H	2B	3B	HR	RBI	Avg.	BB	SO	SB	PO	A	E	Avg.
1991—	Dom. Indians (DSL)	...	62	239	35	67	6	3	1	29	.280	14	5	10	...	...	...	...
1992—	Burlington (Appl.)	3B-SS	52	178	19	37	3	0	1	14	.208	20	9	2	27	†137	7	†.959
1993—	Burlington (Appl.)	C-3B	60	231	40	69	15	3	5	33	.299	8	7	7	315	†55	†10	.974
—	Columbus (S.Atl.)	C	1	5	0	0	0	0	0	0	.000	0	1	0	3	1	0	1.000
1994—	Columbus (S.Atl.)	C-3B	120	491	67	137	23	2	16	71	.279	17	34	4	†848	†134	9	.991
1995—	Kinston (Caro.)	C-3B-DH	104	373	46	98	21	0	6	43	.263	12	29	3	676	†111	7	†.991
1996—	Canton/Akron (East.)	C-3B	104	395	47	111	26	2	3	35	.281	12	22	3	765	88	†15	.983
—	Cleveland (A.L.)	C	4	1	0	0	0	0	0	0	.000	0	0	0	4	0	0	1.000
1997—	Buffalo (A.A.)	C-3B	109	336	40	86	18	2	3	31	.256	18	34	2	653	67	†19	.974
—	Cleveland (A.L.)	C	5	7	1	1	1	0	0	1	.143	0	2	0	18	3	1	.955
1998—	Cleveland (A.L.)	C	17	48	8	11	1	0	2	9	.229	3	2	0	101	9	3	.973
—	Buffalo (I.L.)	C	115	415	62	130	21	3	8	63	.313	21	33	3	*791	*70	*12	.986
1999—	Cleveland (A.L.)	C	119	392	43	110	21	1	3	32	.281	23	41	11	751	81	10	.988
2000—	Cleveland (A.L.)	C-3B	75	250	29	68	14	2	4	25	.272	11	29	4	579	48	4	.994
2001—	Cleveland (A.L.)	C-2B	134	437	54	121	34	1	4	56	.277	17	44	1	959	94	8	.992
Major League totals (6 years)			354	1135	135	311	71	4	13	123	.274	54	118	16	2412	235	26	.990

Year	Team (League)	Pos.	G	AB	R	H	2B	3B	HR	RBI	Avg.	BB	SO	SB	PO	A	E	Avg.
1998—	Cleveland (A.L.)							Did not play.										
1999—	Cleveland (A.L.)	C-PH	2	1	0	0	0	0	0	0	.000	0	0	0	3	0	0	1.000
2001—	Cleveland (A.L.)	C	5	16	3	5	0	0	0	2	.313	2	1	0	51	4	1	.982
	Division series totals (2 years)		7	17	3	5	0	0	0	2	.294	2	1	0	54	4	1	.983

CHAMPIONSHIP SERIES RECORD

Year	Team (League)	Pos.	G	AB	R	H	2B	3B	HR	RBI	Avg.	BB	SO	SB	PO	A	E	Avg.
1998—	Cleveland (A.L.)	C	4	4	0	0	0	0	0	0	.000	0	1	0	13	3	0	1.000

DIAZ, FELIX   P   GIANTS

PERSONAL: Born July 27, 1981, in Las Mata de Farfan, Dominican Republic. ... 6-1/180. ... Throws right, bats right.
TRANSACTIONS/CAREER NOTES: Signed as non-drafted free agent by San Francisco Giants organization (March 20, 1998). ... On disabled list (May 26-June 9, June 16-July 15 and July 16-August 23, 2001).

Year	League	W	L	Pct.	ERA	G	GS	CG	ShO	Sv.	IP	H	R	ER	BB	SO
1998—	Dominican Giants (DSL)	0	4	.000	7.55	14	5	0	0	0	39 1/3	52	44	33	26	34
1999—	Dominican Giants (DSL)	0	0	...	0.75	3	3	0	0	0	12	6	2	1	7	19
2000—	Arizona Giants (Ariz.)	3	4	.429	4.16	11	11	0	0	0	62 2/3	56	35	29	16	58
—	Salem-Kaizer (N'West)	0	1	.000	8.10	3	0	0	0	0	3 1/3	6	6	3	1	2
2001—	Hagerstown (S.Atl.)	1	4	.200	3.66	15	12	0	0	0	51 2/3	49	27	21	16	56

DIAZ, JUAN   1B   RED SOX

PERSONAL: Born February 19, 1976, in San Jose de las Lajas, Cuba. ... 6-2/228. ... Bats right, throws right. ... Full name: Juan C. Diaz.
TRANSACTIONS/CAREER NOTES: Signed as non-drafted free agent by Los Angeles Dodgers organization (May 19, 1996). ... Contract voided by Major League Baseball (June 25, 1999). ... Signed by Boston Red Sox organization (March 4, 2000). ... On disabled list (April 5-June 3, 2001).

Year	Team (League)	Pos.	G	AB	R	H	2B	3B	HR	RBI	Avg.	BB	SO	SB	PO	A	E	Avg.
1996—	Dom. Dodgers (DSL)	1B	13	47	15	17	7	0	4	16	.362	11	13	1				
1997—	Savannah (S.Atl.)	1B	127	460	63	106	24	2	25	83	.230	48	155	2	608	23	15	.977
—	Vero Beach (FSL)	1B	2	7	2	3	0	0	1	3	.429	0	4	0	8	1	0	1.000
1998—	Vero Beach (FSL)	1B	67	250	33	73	12	1	17	51	.292	21	52	1	484	23	7	.986
—	San Antonio (Texas)	1B	56	188	26	50	13	0	13	30	.266	15	45	0	377	18	15	.963
1999—	San Antonio (Texas)	1B	66	254	42	77	21	1	9	52	.303	26	77	0	377	18	15	.963
2000—	Sarasota (FSL)■	1B	14	51	7	14	2	1	4	12	.275	4	15	0	112	8	1	.992
—	Trenton (East.)	1B	50	198	36	62	14	1	17	53	.313	10	56	0	275	17	8	.973
—	Pawtucket (I.L.)	1B	13	43	11	12	0	0	7	17	.279	6	9	1	94	4	2	.980
2001—	Pawtucket (I.L.)	1B	74	279	45	75	17	1	20	51	.269	17	85	0	307	11	•10	.970

DICKEY, R.A.   P   RANGERS

PERSONAL: Born October 29, 1974, in Nashville, Tenn. ... 6-3/205. ... Throws right, bats right. ... Full name: Robert Alan Dickey.
HIGH SCHOOL: Montgomery Bell Academy (Nashville, Tenn.).
COLLEGE: Tennessee.
TRANSACTIONS/CAREER NOTES: Selected by Detroit Tigers organization in 10th round of free-agent draft (June 3, 1993); did not sign. ... Selected by Texas Rangers organization in first round (18th pick overall) of free-agent draft (June 4, 1996). ... On disabled list (May 11, 1997-remainder of season).
MISCELLANEOUS: Member of 1996 U.S. Olympic baseball team.

Year	League	W	L	Pct.	ERA	G	GS	CG	ShO	Sv.	IP	H	R	ER	BB	SO
1997—	Charlotte (FSL)	1	4	.200	6.94	8	6	0	0	0	35	51	32	27	12	32
1998—	Charlotte (FSL)	1	5	.167	3.30	57	0	0	0	*38	60	58	31	22	22	53
1999—	Tulsa (Texas)	6	7	.462	4.55	35	11	0	0	10	95	105	60	48	40	59
—	Oklahoma (PCL)	2	2	.500	4.37	6	2	0	0	0	22 2/3	23	12	11	7	17
2000—	Oklahoma (PCL)	8	9	.471	4.49	30	23	2	0	1	158 1/3	167	83	79	65	85
2001—	Oklahoma (PCL)	11	7	.611	3.75	24	24	3	0	0	163	164	77	68	45	120
—	Texas (A.L.)	0	1	.000	6.75	4	0	0	0	0	12	13	9	9	7	4
	Major League totals (1 year)	0	1	.000	6.75	4	0	0	0	0	12	13	9	9	7	4

DIFELICE, MIKE   C   CARDINALS

PERSONAL: Born May 28, 1969, in Philadelphia. ... 6-2/205. ... Bats right, throws right. ... Full name: Michael William Difelice. ... Name pronounced DEE-fah-lease.
HIGH SCHOOL: Bearden (Knoxville, Tenn.).
COLLEGE: Tennessee.
TRANSACTIONS/CAREER NOTES: Selected by St. Louis Cardinals organization in 11th round of free-agent draft (June 3, 1991). ... Selected by Tampa Bay Devil Rays in first round (20th pick overall) of expansion draft (November 18, 1997). ... Traded by Devil Rays with P Albie Lopez to Arizona Diamondbacks for OF Jason Conti and P Nick Bierbrodt (July 25, 2001). ... Released by Diamondbacks (September 4, 2001). ... Signed by Cardinals (November 20, 2001).
RECORDS: Shares major league single-season record for fewest double plays by catcher for leader—8 (1998).
STATISTICAL NOTES: Tied for N.L. lead in passed balls with 12 in 1997. ... Tied for A.L. lead in double plays by catcher with eight in 1998.

Year	Team (League)	Pos.	G	AB	R	H	2B	3B	HR	RBI	Avg.	BB	SO	SB	PO	A	E	Avg.
1991—	Hamilton (NY-Penn) ...	C	43	157	10	33	5	0	4	15	.210	9	40	1	297	40	9	.974
1992—	Hamilton (NY-Penn) ...	C-1B	18	58	11	20	3	0	2	9	.345	4	7	2	135	19	5	.969
—	St. Petersburg (FSL) ..	C	17	53	0	12	3	0	0	4	.226	3	11	0	73	11	2	.977
1993—	Springfield (Midw.)	C	8	20	5	7	1	0	0	3	.350	2	3	0	52	9	0	1.000
—	St. Petersburg (FSL) ..	C	30	97	5	22	2	0	0	8	.227	11	13	1	165	23	7	.964
1994—	Arkansas (Texas).......	C	71	200	19	50	11	2	2	15	.250	12	48	0	419	40	6	.987
1995—	Arkansas (Texas).......	C	62	176	14	47	10	1	1	24	.267	23	29	0	327	48	6	.984
—	Louisville (A.A.)...........	C	21	63	8	17	4	0	0	3	.270	5	11	1	111	10	2	.984
1996—	Louisville (A.A.)...........	C	79	246	25	70	13	0	9	33	.285	20	43	0	455	48	8	.984
—	St. Louis (N.L.).............	C	4	7	0	2	1	0	0	2	.286	0	1	0	15	1	0	1.000
1997—	Arkansas (Texas).......	C	1	3	0	1	1	0	0	0	.333	1	0	0	6	2	0	1.000
—	St. Louis (N.L.).............	C-1B	93	260	16	62	10	1	4	30	.238	19	61	1	587	64	6	.991
—	Louisville (A.A.)...........	C	1	4	1	1	0	0	1	1	.250	0	1	0	3	1	0	1.000
1998—	Tampa Bay (A.L.)■....	C	84	248	17	57	12	3	3	23	.230	15	56	0	483	52	4	.993
1999—	Tampa Bay (A.L.).......	C	51	179	21	55	11	0	6	27	.307	8	23	0	344	28	5	.987
2000—	Tampa Bay (A.L.).......	C	60	204	23	49	13	1	6	19	.240	12	40	0	351	35	8	.980
2001—	Tampa Bay (A.L.).......	C	48	149	13	31	5	1	2	9	.208	8	39	1	293	29	6	.982
—	Arizona (N.L.)■...........	C	12	21	1	1	0	0	0	1	.048	0	10	0	53	3	1	.982
—	Tucson (PCL)	C-1B	7	26	6	9	0	0	1	2	.346	3	6	0	47	0	3	.940
American League totals (4 years)			243	780	74	192	41	5	17	78	.246	43	158	1	1471	144	23	.986
National League totals (3 years)			109	288	17	65	11	1	4	33	.226	19	72	1	655	68	7	.990
Major League totals (6 years)			352	1068	91	257	52	6	21	111	.241	62	230	2	2126	212	30	.987

DINGMAN, CRAIG — P — REDS

PERSONAL: Born March 12, 1974, in Wichita, Kan. ... 6-4/215. ... Throws right, bats right. ... Full name: Craig Allen Dingman.
HIGH SCHOOL: North (Wichita, Kan.).
JUNIOR COLLEGE: Hutchinson (Kan.) Community College.
TRANSACTIONS/CAREER NOTES: Selected by New York Yankees organization in 36th round of free-agent draft (June 3, 1993). ... On disabled list (June 19, 1995-entire season). ... Traded by Yankees to Colorado Rockies for a player to be named later (March 31, 2001). ... On Colorado disabled list (April 9-24, 2001); included rehabilitation assignment to Colorado Springs (April 16-24). ... Granted free agency (October 15, 2001). ... Signed by Cincinnati Reds organization (December 21, 2001).

Year	League	W	L	Pct.	ERA	G	GS	CG	ShO	Sv.	IP	H	R	ER	BB	SO
1994—	Gulf Coast Yankees (GCL)..	0	5	.000	3.38	17	1	0	0	1	32	27	17	12	10	51
1995—								Did not play.								
1996—	Oneonta (NY-Penn)	0	0	.000	2.04	20	0	0	0	9	35 1/3	17	11	8	9	52
1997—	Greensboro (S.Atl.)	2	0	1.000	1.91	30	0	0	0	19	33	19	7	7	12	41
—	Tampa (FSL)	0	4	.000	5.24	19	0	0	0	6	22 1/3	15	14	13	14	26
1998—	Tampa (FSL)	5	4	.556	2.93	50	0	0	0	7	70 2/3	48	29	23	39	95
1999—	Norwich (East.)	8	6	.571	1.57	55	0	0	0	9	74 1/3	56	16	13	12	90
2000—	Columbus (I.L.)	6	1	.857	3.05	47	2	0	0	1	73 2/3	60	31	25	20	65
—	New York (A.L.)	0	0	...	6.55	10	0	0	0	0	11	18	8	8	3	8
2001—	Colorado Springs (PCL)■..	3	5	.375	3.75	46	0	0	0	7	48	57	28	20	9	55
—	Colorado (N.L.)	0	0	...	13.50	7	0	0	0	1	7 1/3	11	11	11	3	2
A.L. totals (1 year)		0	0	...	6.55	10	0	0	0	0	11	18	8	8	3	8
N.L. totals (1 year)		0	0	...	13.50	7	0	0	0	1	7 1/3	11	11	11	3	2
Major League totals (2 years)		0	0	...	9.33	17	0	0	0	1	18 1/3	29	19	19	6	10

DONNELLY, BRENDAN — P — ANGELS

PERSONAL: Born July 4, 1971, in Washington, D.C. ... 6-3/200. ... Throws right, bats right. ... Full name: Brendan Kevin Donnelly.
HIGH SCHOOL: Sandia (Albuquerque, N.M.).
JUNIOR COLLEGE: Mesa (Colo.).
TRANSACTIONS/CAREER NOTES: Selected by Chicago White Sox organization in 27th round of free-agent draft (June 1, 1992). ... Released by White Sox (April 16, 1993). ... Signed by Chicago Cubs organization (June 16, 1993). ... Released by Cubs (March 29, 1994). ... Signed by Ohio Valley, Frontier League (July 1994). ... Signed by Cincinnati Reds organization (March 4, 1995). ... Granted free agency (October 16, 1998). ... Signed by Reds organization (March 15, 1999). ... Released by Reds (April 3, 1999). ... Signed by Nashua, Atlantic League (May 1999). ... Sold by Nashua to Tampa Bay Devil Rays organization (May 15, 1999). ... Released by Devil Rays (August 12, 1999). ... Signed by Pittsburgh Pirates organization (August 18, 1999). ... Released by Pirates (August 25, 1999). ... Signed by Toronto Blue Jays organization (August 26, 1999). ... Released by Blue Jays (July 28, 2000). ... Signed by Cubs organization (August 10, 2000). ... Granted free agency (October 15, 2000). ... Signed by Anaheim Angels organization (January 9, 2001).

Year	League	W	L	Pct.	ERA	G	GS	CG	ShO	Sv.	IP	H	R	ER	BB	SO
1992—	GC White Sox (GCL)	0	3	.000	3.67	9	7	0	0	1	41 2/3	41	25	17	21	31
1993—	Geneva (NY-Penn)■..........	4	0	1.000	6.28	21	3	0	0	1	43	39	34	30	29	29
1994—	Ohio Valley (Fron.)■	1	1	.500	2.57	10	0	0	0	0	14	13	5	4	4	20
1995—	Charleston, W.Va. (S.Atl.)■	1	1	.500	1.19	24	0	0	0	12	30 1/3	14	4	4	7	33
—	Winston-Salem (Caro.).......	1	2	.333	1.02	23	0	0	0	2	35 1/3	20	6	4	14	32
—	Indianapolis (A.A.).............	1	1	.500	23.63	3	0	0	0	0	2 2/3	7	8	7	2	1
1996—	Chattanooga (Sou.)	1	2	.333	5.52	22	0	0	0	0	29 1/3	27	21	18	17	22
1997—	Chattanooga (Sou.)	6	4	.600	3.27	62	0	0	0	6	82 2/3	71	43	30	37	64
1998—	Chattanooga (Sou.)	2	5	.286	2.98	38	0	0	0	13	45 1/3	43	16	15	24	47
—	Indianapolis (I.L.)...............	4	1	.800	2.65	19	1	0	0	0	37 1/3	29	16	11	16	39
1999—	Nashua (Atl.)■	0	0	...	3.00	3	0	0	0	0	3	1	1	1	3	4
—	Durham (I.L.)■	5	5	.500	3.05	37	1	0	0	2	62	53	23	21	18	61
—	Altoona (East.)■	0	0	...	7.71	2	0	0	0	1	2 1/3	4	2	2	2	2
—	Syracuse (I.L.)■	0	1	.000	2.89	5	0	0	0	0	9 1/3	8	4	3	4	9
2000—	Syracuse (I.L.)	4	6	.400	5.48	37	0	0	0	0	42 2/3	47	34	26	27	34
—	Iowa (PCL)■	0	3	.000	7.56	9	0	0	0	1	16 2/3	25	19	14	6	14
2001—	Arkansas (Texas)■............	4	1	.800	2.48	27	0	0	0	12	29	21	8	8	13	37
—	Salt Lake (PCL)	5	1	.833	2.40	29	0	0	0	1	41 1/3	38	11	11	8	50

PERSONAL: Born April 21, 1966, in Los Angeles. ... 6-0/185. ... Bats left, throws right. ... Full name: Chris Barton Donnels. ... Name pronounced DON-uls.

HIGH SCHOOL: South Torrance (Calif.).

COLLEGE: Loyola Marymount.

TRANSACTIONS/CAREER NOTES: Selected by New York Mets organization in first round (24th pick overall) of free-agent draft (June 2, 1987). ... On Tidewater disabled list (June 20-28, 1991). ... Selected by Florida Marlins in third round (67th pick overall) of expansion draft (November 17, 1992). ... Claimed on waivers by Houston Astros (December 18, 1992). ... On Houston disabled list (April 23-May 12, 1995); included rehabilitation assignment to Jackson (May 8-12). ... Traded by Astros to Boston Red Sox for a player to be named later (June 10, 1995). ... Released by Red Sox (October 26, 1995). ... Signed by Kintetsu Buffaloes, Japan Pacific League (1996). ... Signed by Red Sox (December 20, 1996). ... Released by Red Sox (March 26, 1997). ... Played with Orix Blue Wave of Japan Pacific League (1997-99). ... Signed by Los Angeles Dodgers organization (February 8, 2000). ... On Los Angeles disabled list (August 2-September 1, 2000); included rehabilitation assignment to Albuquerque (August 12-31). ... On Los Angeles disabled list (May 19-June 4, 2001); included rehabilitation assignment to Las Vegas (May 31-June 4). ... Granted free agency (October 16, 2001). ... Signed by Arizona Diamondbacks organization (January 11, 2002).

HONORS: Named Florida State League Most Valuable Player (1989).

STATISTICAL NOTES: Led Florida State League with .510 slugging percentage and 15 intentional bases on balls received in 1989. ... Led Florida State League third basemen with 93 putouts, 202 assists and 320 total chances in 1989. ... Led Texas League third basemen with 79 putouts, 242 assists, 31 errors, 352 total chances and 24 double plays in 1990. ... Led Pacific Coast League with .660 slugging percentage in 2000.

Year — Team (League)	Pos.	G	AB	R	H	2B	3B	HR	RBI	Avg.	BB	SO	SB	PO	A	E	Avg.
1987— Kingsport (Appl.)	3B	26	86	18	26	4	0	3	16	.302	17	17	4	16	44	6	.909
— Columbia (S.Atl.)	3B	41	136	20	35	7	0	2	17	.257	24	27	3	32	86	10	.922
1988— St. Lucie (FSL)	3B	65	198	25	43	14	2	3	22	.217	32	53	4	40	116	15	.912
— Columbia (S.Atl.)	3B	42	133	19	32	6	0	2	13	.241	30	25	5	29	84	7	.942
1989— St. Lucie (FSL)	3B	117	386	70	121	23	1	17	*78	.313	83	65	18	†242	†209	28	.942
1990— Jackson (Texas)	3B-1B-2B	130	419	66	114	24	0	12	63	.272	*111	81	11	†95	†244	†32	.914
1991— Tidewater (I.L.)	3B-2B	84	287	45	87	19	2	8	56	.303	62	56	1	88	189	14	.952
— New York (N.L.)	1B-3B	37	89	7	20	2	0	0	5	.225	14	19	1	131	34	2	.988
1992— Tidewater (I.L.)	3B-2B	81	279	35	84	15	3	5	32	.301	58	45	12	160	156	16	.952
— New York (N.L.)	3B-2B	45	121	8	21	4	0	0	6	.174	17	25	1	34	77	5	.957
1993— Houston (N.L.)■	3B-1B-2B	88	179	18	46	14	2	2	24	.257	19	33	2	169	54	8	.965
1994— Houston (N.L.)	3B-1B-2B	54	86	12	23	5	0	3	5	.267	13	18	1	42	28	0	1.000
1995— Jackson (Texas)	3B	4	12	1	2	1	0	0	1	.167	4	4	0	6	7	1	.929
— Houston (N.L.)	3B	19	30	4	9	0	0	0	2	.300	3	6	0	3	7	2	.833
— Boston (A.L.)■	3B-1B-2B	40	91	13	23	2	2	2	11	.253	9	18	0	54	41	4	.960
— Pawtucket (I.L.)	3B-DH	4	15	1	6	0	0	1	4	.400	1	3	0	2	3	1	.833
1996— Kintetsu (Jap. Pac.)■.		108	324	50	91	20	2	20	53	.281	54	86	3	...	...	...	...
1997— Orix (Jap. Pac.)■		112	384	55	116	25	1	17	67	.302	84	80	0	...	...	...	...
1998— Orix (Jap. Pac.)		44	140	17	37	9	0	5	22	.264	23	44	1	...	...	...	...
— Orix (Jap. Wes.)		8	20	4	10	4	0	1	4	.500	7	2	0	...	...	...	...
1999— Orix (Jap. Wes.)		36	90	10	22	5	0	2	13	.244	14	15	0	...	...	...	...
2000— Albuquerque (PCL)■.	1B-3B-2B-C	105	332	79	109	27	1	27	84	.328	66	52	6	513	79	9	.985
— Los Angeles (N.L.)	OF-1B-3B-2B	27	34	8	10	3	0	4	9	.294	6	7	0	29	1	1	.968
2001— Los Angeles (N.L.)	3B-1B-P	66	88	8	15	2	0	3	8	.170	12	25	0	46	22	3	.958
— Las Vegas (PCL)	1B-3B	39	137	17	32	5	0	7	25	.234	21	24	0	204	20	2	.991
American League totals (1 year)		40	91	13	23	2	2	2	11	.253	9	18	0	54	41	4	.960
National League totals (7 years)		336	627	65	144	30	2	12	50	.230	84	133	5	454	223	21	.970
Major League totals (7 years)		376	718	78	167	32	4	14	70	.233	93	151	5	508	264	25	.969

RECORD AS PITCHER

Year — League	W	L	Pct.	ERA	G	GS	CG	ShO	Sv.	IP	H	R	ER	BB	SO
2001— Los Angeles (N.L.)	0	0	...	0.00	1	0	0	0	0	⅓	0	0	0	0	0

PERSONAL: Born August 12, 1978, in New London, Conn. ... 6-1/175. ... Bats right, throws right. ... Full name: Todd William Donovan.

HIGH SCHOOL: East Lyme (Conn.).

COLLEGE: Siena.

TRANSACTIONS/CAREER NOTES: Selected by San Diego Padres organization in eighth round of free-agent draft (June 2, 1999). ... On disabled list (July 14, 2000-remainder of season). ... On disabled list (April 19-May 21 and May 25-September 1, 2001).

Year — Team (League)	Pos.	G	AB	R	H	2B	3B	HR	RBI	Avg.	BB	SO	SB	PO	A	E	Avg.
1999— Idaho Falls (Pio.)	OF	53	198	57	59	11	3	1	22	.298	25	39	40	81	6	2	.978
2000— Fort Wayne (Midw.)	OF	53	204	39	58	12	4	0	23	.284	25	45	18	101	4	1	.991
2001— Lake Elsinore (Calif.)	OF	41	168	37	51	7	0	1	12	.304	19	25	23	73	2	3	.962

PERSONAL: Born November 25, 1975, in Santo Domingo, Dominican Republic. ... 6-0/175. ... Throws right, bats right. ... Full name: Octavio Eduardo Dotel. ... Brother of Angel Dotel, third baseman in Los Angeles Dodgers organization (1991-93).

HIGH SCHOOL: Liceo Eansino Afuera (Dominican Republic).

TRANSACTIONS/CAREER NOTES: Signed as non-drafted free agent by New York Mets organization (March 20, 1993). ... On disabled list (July 18-August 16, 1996). ... On Binghamton disabled list (June 3-24, 1997). ... On Norfolk disabled list (May 7-17, 1999). ... Traded by Mets with OF Roger Cedeno and P Kyle Kessel to Houston Astros for P Mike Hampton and OF Derek Bell (December 23, 1999).

Year League	W	L	Pct.	ERA	G	GS	CG	ShO	Sv.	IP	H	R	ER	BB	SO
1993— Dominican Mets (DSL)	6	2	.750	4.10	...	11	0	0	0	59 1/3	46	30	27	38	48
1994— Dominican Mets (DSL)	5	0	1.000	4.32	15	14	1	0	0	81 1/3	84	53	39	31	95
1995— Gulf Coast Mets (GCL)	•7	4	.636	2.18	13	12	2	0	0	*74 1/3	48	23	18	17	*86
— St. Lucie (FSL)	1	0	1.000	5.63	3	0	0	0	0	8	10	5	5	4	9
1996— Columbia (S.Atl.)	11	3	.786	3.59	22	19	0	0	0	115 1/3	89	49	46	49	142
1997— St. Lucie (FSL)	5	2	.714	2.52	9	8	1	1	0	50	44	18	14	23	39
— Binghamton (East.)	3	4	.429	5.98	12	12	0	0	0	55 2/3	66	50	37	38	40
— Gulf Coast Mets (GCL)	0	0	...	0.96	3	2	0	0	1	9 1/3	9	1	1	2	7
1998— Binghamton (East.)	4	2	.667	1.97	10	10	2	1	0	68 2/3	41	19	15	24	82
— Norfolk (I.L.)	8	6	.571	3.45	17	16	1	0	0	99	82	47	38	43	118
1999— Norfolk (I.L.)	5	2	.714	3.84	13	13	1	0	0	70 1/3	52	33	30	34	90
— New York (N.L.)	8	3	.727	5.38	19	14	0	0	0	85 1/3	69	52	51	49	85
2000— Houston (N.L.)■	3	7	.300	5.40	50	16	0	0	16	125	127	80	75	61	142
2001— Houston (N.L.)	7	5	.583	2.66	61	4	0	0	2	105	79	35	31	47	145
Major League totals (3 years)	18	15	.545	4.48	130	34	0	0	18	315 1/3	275	167	157	157	372

DIVISION SERIES RECORD

Year League	W	L	Pct.	ERA	G	GS	CG	ShO	Sv.	IP	H	R	ER	BB	SO
1999— New York (N.L.)	0	0	...	54.00	1	0	0	0	0	1/3	1	2	2	2	0
2001— Houston (N.L.)	0	0	...	5.40	2	0	0	0	0	3 1/3	5	2	2	0	5
Division series totals (2 years)	0	0	...	9.82	3	0	0	0	0	3 2/3	6	4	4	2	5

CHAMPIONSHIP SERIES RECORD

Year League	W	L	Pct.	ERA	G	GS	CG	ShO	Sv.	IP	H	R	ER	BB	SO
1999— New York (N.L.)	1	0	1.000	3.00	1	0	0	0	0	3	4	1	1	2	5

DOUGLASS, SEAN P ORIOLES

PERSONAL: Born April 28, 1979, in Lancaster, Calif. ... 6-6/200. ... Throws right, bats right. ... Full name: Sean R. Douglass.
HIGH SCHOOL: Antelope Valley (Lancaster, Calif.).
TRANSACTIONS/CAREER NOTES: Selected by Baltimore Orioles organization in second round of free-agent draft (June 3, 1997).

Year League	W	L	Pct.	ERA	G	GS	CG	ShO	Sv.	IP	H	R	ER	BB	SO
1997— Gulf Coast Orioles (GCL)	1	3	.250	6.11	9	1	0	0	0	17 2/3	20	14	12	9	10
1998— Bluefield (Appl.)	2	2	.500	3.23	10	0	0	0	0	53	45	20	19	14	62
1999— Frederick (Caro.)	5	6	.455	3.32	16	16	1	0	0	97 2/3	101	48	36	58	161
2000— Bowie (East.)	9	8	.529	4.02	27	27	2	0	0	159	174	88	71	34	105
2001— Rochester (I.L.)	8	9	.471	3.49	27	27	0	0	0	162 1/3	160	79	63	61	156
— Baltimore (A.L.)	2	1	.667	5.31	4	4	0	0	0	20 1/3	21	12	12	11	17
Major League totals (1 year)	2	1	.667	5.31	4	4	0	0	0	20 1/3	21	12	12	11	17

DOWNS, SCOTT P EXPOS

PERSONAL: Born March 17, 1976, in Louisville, Ky. ... 6-2/190. ... Throws left, bats left. ... Full name: Scott Jeremy Downs.
HIGH SCHOOL: Pleasure Ridge Park (Louisville, Ky.).
COLLEGE: Kentucky.
TRANSACTIONS/CAREER NOTES: Selected by Chicago Cubs organization in third round of free-agent draft (June 3, 1997). ... Traded by Cubs to Minnesota Twins (November 3, 1998), completing deal in which Twins traded P Mike Morgan to Cubs for cash and a player to be named later (August 25, 1998). ... Traded by Twins with P Rick Aguilera to Cubs for P Kyle Lohse and P Jason Ryan (May 21, 1999). ... Traded by Cubs to Montreal Expos for OF Rondell White (July 31, 2000). ... On Montreal disabled list (August 9, 2000-remainder of season). ... On disabled list (March 23, 2001-entire season).

Year League	W	L	Pct.	ERA	G	GS	CG	ShO	Sv.	IP	H	R	ER	BB	SO
1997— Williamsport (NY-Penn)	0	2	.000	2.74	5	5	0	0	0	23	15	11	7	7	28
— Rockford (Midw.)	3	0	1.000	1.25	5	5	0	0	0	36	17	5	5	8	43
1998— Daytona (FSL)	8	9	.471	3.90	27	27	2	0	0	161 2/3	179	83	70	55	117
1999— New Britain (East.)■	0	0	...	8.69	6	3	0	0	0	19 2/3	33	21	19	10	22
— Fort Myers (FSL)	0	1	.000	0.00	2	2	0	0	0	9 2/3	7	3	0	6	9
— Daytona (FSL)■	5	0	1.000	1.88	7	7	1	1	0	48	41	12	10	11	41
— West Tenn (Sou.)	8	1	.889	1.35	13	12	1	0	0	80	56	13	12	28	101
2000— Chicago (N.L.)	4	3	.571	5.17	18	18	0	0	0	94	117	59	54	37	63
— Montreal (N.L.)■	0	0	...	9.00	1	1	0	0	0	3	5	3	3	3	0
2001— Montreal (N.L.)							Did not play.								
Major League totals (1 year)	4	3	.571	5.29	19	19	0	0	0	97	122	62	57	40	63

DRANSFELDT, KELLY SS RANGERS

PERSONAL: Born April 16, 1975, in Joliet, Ill. ... 6-2/195. ... Bats right, throws right. ... Full name: Kelly Daniel Dransfeldt.
HIGH SCHOOL: Morris (Ill.).
COLLEGE: Michigan.
TRANSACTIONS/CAREER NOTES: Selected by Texas Rangers organization in fourth round of free-agent draft (June 4, 1996). ... On Oklahoma disabled list (June 29-July 7, 1999).
STATISTICAL NOTES: Led New York-Pennsylvania League shortstops with 391 total chances and 45 double plays in 1996. ... Led Florida State League shortstops with 227 putouts and 85 double plays in 1997. ... Led Pacific Coast League shortstops with 86 double plays in 2000. ... Led Pacific Coast League shortstops with 105 double plays and 692 total chances in 2001.

Year	Team (League)	Pos.	G	AB	R	H	2B	3B	HR	RBI	Avg.	BB	SO	SB	PO	A	E	Avg.
							BATTING									FIELDING		
1996—Hudson Valley (NY-P).	SS	75	284	42	67	17	1	7	29	.236	27	76	13	*117	*253	*21	.946
1997—Charlotte (FSL)..........	SS-3B	135	466	64	106	20	7	6	58	.227	42	115	25	†227	369	36	.943
1998—Charlotte (FSL)..........	SS	67	245	46	79	17	0	18	76	.322	29	67	7	100	205	19	.941
—Tulsa (Texas)	SS	58	226	43	57	15	4	9	36	.252	18	79	8	81	184	14	.950
1999—Oklahoma (PCL).........	SS-2B-DH	102	359	55	85	21	2	10	44	.237	24	108	6	162	297	19	.960
—Texas (A.L.)	SS	16	53	3	10	1	0	1	5	.189	3	12	0	31	54	3	.966
2000—Oklahoma (PCL).........	SS	117	441	60	109	22	3	8	42	.247	38	123	10	208	345	22	.962
—Texas (A.L.)	SS-2B	16	26	2	3	2	0	0	2	.115	1	14	0	13	29	0	1.000
2001—Oklahoma (PCL).........	SS	*143	*551	76	138	29	5	9	63	.250	50	116	12	*268	*400	24	.965
—Texas (A.L.)	SS-3B	4	3	0	0	0	0	0	0	.000	0	0	0	0	4	0	1.000
Major League totals (3 years)		36	82	5	13	3	0	1	7	.159	4	26	0	44	87	3	.978

DREIFORT, DARREN — P — DODGERS

PERSONAL: Born May 3, 1972, in Wichita, Kan. ... 6-2/211. ... Throws right, bats right. ... Full name: Darren John Dreifort. ... Name pronounced DRY-fert.

HIGH SCHOOL: Wichita (Kan.) Heights.

COLLEGE: Wichita State.

TRANSACTIONS/CAREER NOTES: Selected by New York Mets organization in 11th round of free-agent draft (June 4, 1990); did not sign. ... Selected by Los Angeles Dodgers organization in first round (second pick overall) of free-agent draft (June 3, 1993). ... On San Antonio disabled list (July 7-28, 1994). ... On Albuquerque disabled list (August 27, 1994-remainder of season). ... On disabled list (April 23, 1995-entire season). ... On Los Angeles disabled list (March 25-May 16, 1996); included rehabilitation assignment to Albuquerque (April 18-May 15). ... On Los Angeles disabled list (May 12-June 17, 1997); included rehabilitation assignment to Albuquerque (June 11-17). ... Granted free agency (October 30, 2000). ... Re-signed by Dodgers (December 11, 2000). ... On disabled list (June 30, 2001-remainder of season).

HONORS: Named righthanded pitcher on THE SPORTING NEWS college All-America team (1992-93). ... Named Golden Spikes Award winner by USA Baseball (1993).

STATISTICAL NOTES: Tied for N.L. lead with four balks in 1999.

MISCELLANEOUS: Member of 1992 U.S. Olympic baseball team. ... Singled with an RBI in one game as pinch hitter with Los Angeles (1994). ... Made an out in only appearance as pinch hitter with Los Angeles (1996). ... Received a base on balls in only appearance as pinch hitter (1998).

Year	League	W	L	Pct.	ERA	G	GS	CG	ShO	Sv.	IP	H	R	ER	BB	SO
1994—Los Angeles (N.L.)		0	5	.000	6.21	27	0	0	0	6	29	45	21	20	15	22
—San Antonio (Texas)..........		3	1	.750	2.80	8	8	0	0	0	35 1/3	36	14	11	13	32
—Albuquerque (PCL).............		1	0	1.000	5.68	1	1	0	0	0	6 1/3	8	4	4	3	3
1995—Los Angeles (N.L.)								Did not play.								
1996—Albuquerque (PCL).............		5	6	.455	4.17	18	18	0	0	0	86 1/3	88	49	40	52	75
—Los Angeles (N.L.)		1	4	.200	4.94	19	0	0	0	0	23 2/3	23	13	13	12	24
1997—Los Angeles (N.L.)		5	2	.714	2.86	48	0	0	0	4	63	45	21	20	34	63
—Albuquerque (PCL).............		0	0	...	1.59	2	2	0	0	0	5 2/3	2	1	1	1	3
1998—Los Angeles (N.L.)		8	12	.400	4.00	32	26	1	1	0	180	171	84	80	57	168
1999—Los Angeles (N.L.)		13	13	.500	4.79	30	29	1	1	0	178 2/3	177	105	95	76	140
2000—Los Angeles (N.L.)		12	9	.571	4.16	32	32	1	1	0	192 2/3	175	105	89	87	164
2001—Los Angeles (N.L.)		4	7	.364	5.13	16	16	0	0	0	94 2/3	89	62	54	47	91
Major League totals (7 years).......		43	52	.453	4.38	204	103	3	3	10	761 2/3	725	411	371	328	672

DIVISION SERIES RECORD

Year	League	W	L	Pct.	ERA	G	GS	CG	ShO	Sv.	IP	H	R	ER	BB	SO
1996—Los Angeles (N.L.)		0	0	...	0.00	1	0	0	0	0	2/3	0	0	0	0	0

DRESE, RYAN — P — INDIANS

PERSONAL: Born April 5, 1976, in San Francisco. ... 6-3/220. ... Throws right, bats right. ... Full name: Ryan T. Drese.

HIGH SCHOOL: Bishop O'Dowd (Oakland).

COLLEGE: California.

TRANSACTIONS/CAREER NOTES: Selected by Oakland Athletics organization in fifth round of free-agent draft (June 2, 1994); did not sign. ... Selected by Cleveland Indians organization in fifth round of free-agent draft (June 2, 1998). ... On disabled list (April 10-June 20, 2000).

Year	League	W	L	Pct.	ERA	G	GS	CG	ShO	Sv.	IP	H	R	ER	BB	SO
1998—Watertown (NY-Penn)		2	5	.286	4.07	9	9	0	0	0	42	40	21	19	14	40
1999—Kinston (Caro.)...................		5	4	.556	4.93	15	15	1	0	0	69 1/3	46	47	38	52	81
—Mahoning Valley (NY-P)....		0	2	.000	2.65	5	5	0	0	0	17	8	6	5	7	26
—Columbia (S.Atl.)................		2	2	.000	4.50	2	2	0	0	0	12	9	6	6	4	15
2000—Kinston (Caro.)...................		0	1	.000	3.86	1	1	0	0	0	2 1/3	2	1	1	1	4
2001—Akron (East.).....................		5	7	.417	3.35	14	13	1	1	0	86	64	34	32	29	73
—Buffalo (I.L.)......................		5	1	.833	4.01	11	10	0	0	0	60 2/3	60	28	27	17	52
—Cleveland (A.L.).................		1	2	.333	3.44	9	4	0	0	0	36 2/3	32	15	14	15	24
Major League totals (1 year)........		1	2	.333	3.44	9	4	0	0	0	36 2/3	32	15	14	15	24

DREW, J.D. — OF — CARDINALS

PERSONAL: Born November 20, 1975, in Valdosta, Ga. ... 6-1/195. ... Bats left, throws right. ... Full name: David Jonathan Drew. ... Brother of Tim Drew, pitcher, Cleveland Indians.

HIGH SCHOOL: Lowndes County (Hahira, Ga.).

COLLEGE: Florida State.

TRANSACTIONS/CAREER NOTES: Selected by San Francisco Giants organization in 20th round of free-agent draft (June 2, 1994); did not sign. ... Selected by Philadelphia Phillies organization in first round (second pick overall) of free-agent draft (June 3, 1997); did not sign. ... Selected by St. Louis Cardinals organization in first round (fifth pick overall) of free-agent draft (June 2, 1998). ... On Arkansas disabled list

(July 21-August 6, 1998). ... On St. Louis disabled list (May 16-June 17, 1999); included rehabilitation assignment to Memphis (May 28-June 17). ... On disabled list (July 8-27, 2000). ... On St. Louis disabled list (June 18-July 31, 2001); included rehabilitation assignment to Peoria (July 26-31).

HONORS: Named Golden Spikes Award winner by USA Baseball (1997). ... Named college Player of the Year by THE SPORTING NEWS (1997). ... Named outfielder on THE SPORTING NEWS college All-America team (1997).

STATISTICAL NOTES: Led N.L. outfielders with six double plays in 1999. ... Career major league grand slams: 1.

Year Team (League)	Pos.	G	AB	R	H	2B	3B	HR	RBI	Avg.	BB	SO	SB	PO	A	E	Avg.
1997— St. Paul (Nor.)	OF	44	170	51	58	6	1	18	50	.341	30	40	5	...	...	...	...
1998— St. Paul (Nor.)	OF	30	114	27	44	11	2	9	33	.386	21	32	8	...	...	...	...
— Arkansas (Texas)■.....	OF	19	67	18	22	3	1	5	11	.328	13	15	2	46	2	1	.980
— Memphis (PCL)..........	OF	26	79	15	25	8	1	2	13	.316	22	18	1	54	3	2	.966
— St. Louis (N.L.)............	OF	14	36	9	15	3	1	5	13	.417	4	10	0	19	1	0	1.000
1999— St. Louis (N.L.)............	OF	104	368	72	89	16	6	13	39	.242	50	77	19	235	9	7	.972
— Memphis (PCL)...........	OF	25	87	11	26	5	1	2	15	.299	8	20	6	44	2	0	1.000
2000— St. Louis (N.L.)............	OF	135	407	73	120	17	2	18	57	.295	67	99	17	248	6	9	.966
2001— St. Louis (N.L.)............	OF	109	375	80	121	18	5	27	73	.323	57	75	13	209	7	6	.973
— Peoria (Midw.)............	OF	3	11	3	6	2	0	0	0	.545	1	0	0	4	0	0	1.000
Major League totals (4 years)		362	1186	234	345	54	14	63	182	.291	178	261	49	711	23	22	.971

DIVISION SERIES RECORD

Year Team (League)	Pos.	G	AB	R	H	2B	3B	HR	RBI	Avg.	BB	SO	SB	PO	A	E	Avg.
2000— St. Louis (N.L.)...........	OF	2	6	1	1	0	0	0	0	.167	2	1	2	2	0	0	1.000
2001— St. Louis (N.L.)...........	OF	5	13	1	2	0	0	1	2	.154	3	1	0	12	0	0	1.000
Division series totals (2 years)		7	19	2	3	0	0	1	2	.158	5	2	2	14	0	0	1.000

CHAMPIONSHIP SERIES RECORD

Year Team (League)	Pos.	G	AB	R	H	2B	3B	HR	RBI	Avg.	BB	SO	SB	PO	A	E	Avg.
2000— St. Louis (N.L.)..........	OF-PH	5	12	2	4	1	0	0	1	.333	0	3	0	7	0	0	1.000

DREW, TIM   P   INDIANS

D

PERSONAL: Born August 31, 1978, in Valdosta, Ga. ... 6-1/195. ... Throws right, bats right. ... Full name: Timothy Andrew Drew. ... Brother of J.D. Drew, outfielder, St. Louis Cardinals.

HIGH SCHOOL: Lowndes County (Hahira, Ga.).

TRANSACTIONS/CAREER NOTES: Selected by Cleveland Indians organization in first round (28th pick overall) of free-agent draft (June 3, 1997). ... On Buffalo disabled list (June 18-26, 2001).

Year League	W	L	Pct.	ERA	G	GS	CG	ShO	Sv.	IP	H	R	ER	BB	SO
1997— Burlington (Appl.)...............	0	1	.000	6.17	4	4	0	0	0	11 2/3	16	15	8	4	14
— Watertown (NY-Penn)	0	0	...	1.93	1	1	0	0	0	4 2/3	4	1	1	3	9
1998— Columbus (S.Atl.)...............	4	3	.571	3.79	13	13	0	0	0	71 1/3	68	43	30	26	64
— Kinston (Caro.)..................	3	8	.273	5.20	15	15	0	0	0	90	105	58	52	31	67
1999— Kinston (Caro.)..................	*13	5	*.722	3.73	28	*28	2	0	0	169	154	79	70	60	125
2000— Akron (East.)....................	3	2	.600	2.42	9	9	0	0	0	52	41	19	14	15	22
— Cleveland (A.L.).................	1	0	1.000	10.00	3	3	0	0	0	9	17	12	10	8	5
— Buffalo (I.L.)....................	7	8	.467	5.87	16	16	2	0	0	95	122	69	62	31	53
2001— Cleveland (A.L.).................	0	2	.000	7.97	8	6	0	0	0	35	51	39	31	16	15
— Buffalo (I.L.)....................	8	6	.571	3.92	18	18	1	1	0	108	115	54	47	27	75
Major League totals (2 years).......	1	2	.333	8.39	11	9	0	0	0	44	68	51	41	24	20

DUCEY, ROB   OF

PERSONAL: Born May 24, 1965, in Toronto. ... 6-2/183. ... Bats left, throws right. ... Full name: Robert Thomas Ducey.

HIGH SCHOOL: Glenview Park (Toronto).

JUNIOR COLLEGE: Seminole Community College (Fla.).

TRANSACTIONS/CAREER NOTES: Signed as non-drafted free agent by Toronto Blue Jays organization (May 16, 1984). ... On Toronto disabled list (June 9-September 2, 1989); included rehabilitation assignments to Syracuse (July 5-14 and August 24-September 2). ... Traded by Blue Jays with C Greg Myers to California Angels for P Mark Eichhorn (July 30, 1992). ... Released by Angels (November 19, 1992). ... Signed by Texas Rangers organization (December 18, 1992). ... On Oklahoma City disabled list (April 21-May 16, 1993). ... Contract purchased by Nippon Ham Fighters of Japan Pacific League from Rangers (October 14, 1994). ... Signed by Seattle Mariners organization (January 22, 1997). ... On Seattle disabled list (August 3-21, 1997). ... On disabled list (March 27-April 20, 1998). ... Granted free agency (December 21, 1998). ... Signed by Philadelphia Phillies (December 22, 1998). ... Traded by Phillies to Blue Jays for a player to be named later (July 26, 2000); Phillies acquired P John Sneed to complete deal (July 31, 2000). ... Traded by Blue Jays to Phillies (August 7, 2000), completing deal in which Phillies traded 2B Mickey Morandini to Blue Jays for a player to be named later (August 6, 2000). ... On Philadelphia disabled list (April 1-16, 2001); included rehabilitation assignment to Scranton/Wilkes-Barre (April 11-16). ... Released by Phillies (June 7, 2001). ... Signed by Montreal Expos (June 12, 2001). ... On Montreal disabled list (July 23, 2001-remainder of season). ... Granted free agency (November 6, 2001).

STATISTICAL NOTES: Tied for Southern League lead in double plays by outfielder with six in 1986. ... Tied for International League lead in double plays by outfielder with four in 1990.

Year Team (League)	Pos.	G	AB	R	H	2B	3B	HR	RBI	Avg.	BB	SO	SB	PO	A	E	Avg.
1984— Medicine Hat (Pio.)	OF-1B	63	235	49	71	10	3	12	49	.302	41	61	13	185	11	6	.970
1985— Florence (S.Atl.)	OF-1B	134	529	78	133	22	2	13	86	.251	49	103	12	228	8	9	.963
1986— Ventura (Calif.)	OF-1B	47	178	36	60	11	3	12	38	.337	21	24	17	97	3	2	.980
— Knoxville (Sou.)............	OF	88	344	49	106	22	3	11	58	.308	29	59	7	186	10	6	.970
1987— Syracuse (I.L.)...........	OF	100	359	62	102	14	•10	10	60	.284	61	89	8	171	13	6	.968
— Toronto (A.L.).............	OF-DH	34	48	12	9	1	0	1	6	.188	8	10	2	31	0	0	1.000
1988— Syracuse (I.L.)...........	OF	90	317	40	81	14	4	7	42	.256	43	81	7	233	6	4	.984
— Toronto (A.L.).............	OF-DH	27	54	15	17	4	1	0	6	.315	5	7	1	35	1	0	1.000

Year Team (League)	Pos.	G	AB	R	H	2B	3B	HR	RBI	Avg.	BB	SO	SB	PO	A	E	Avg.
										BATTING						**FIELDING**	
1989— Toronto (A.L.)............	OF-DH	41	76	5	16	4	0	0	7	.211	9	25	2	56	3	0	1.000
— Syracuse (I.L.)............	OF	10	29	0	3	0	1	0	3	.103	10	13	0	14	0	1	.933
1990— Syracuse (I.L.)............	OF	127	438	53	117	32	7	7	47	.267	60	87	13	262	13	13	.955
— Toronto (A.L.)............	OF	19	53	7	16	5	0	0	7	.302	7	15	1	37	0	0	1.000
1991— Syracuse (I.L.)............	OF	72	266	53	78	10	3	8	40	.293	51	58	5	120	1	0	1.000
— Toronto (A.L.)............	OF-DH	39	68	8	16	2	2	1	4	.235	6	26	2	32	1	4	.892
1992— Toronto (A.L.)............	OF-DH	23	21	3	1	1	0	0	0	.048	0	10	0	11	0	0	1.000
— California (A.L.)■......	OF-DH	31	59	4	14	3	0	0	2	.237	5	12	2	32	2	2	.944
1993— Okla. City (A.A.)■......	OF	105	389	68	118	17	•10	17	56	.303	46	97	17	244	8	7	.973
— Texas (A.L.)	OF	27	85	15	24	6	3	2	9	.282	10	17	2	51	1	0	1.000
1994— Oklahoma City (A.A.)..	OF	115	403	69	108	27	9	17	65	.268	75	91	9	221	9	4	.983
— Texas (A.L.)	OF	11	29	1	5	1	0	0	1	.172	2	1	0	15	0	2	.882
1995— Nippon (Jap. Pac.)■...		117	425	61	106	19	4	25	61	.249	54	103	7	...	...	...	...
1996— Nippon (Jap. Pac.)		120	427	68	105	17	5	26	59	.246	86	90	3	...	...	...	...
1997— Tacoma (PCL)............	OF	23	74	8	24	8	0	0	11	.324	8	15	0	44	3	3	.940
— Seattle (A.L.).............	OF	76	143	25	41	15	2	5	10	.287	6	31	3	66	3	1	.986
1998— Seattle (A.L.).............	OF	97	217	30	52	18	2	5	23	.240	23	61	4	127	4	4	.970
1999— Philadelphia (N.L.)■ ..	OF-DH	104	188	29	49	10	2	8	33	.261	38	57	2	89	1	0	1.000
2000— Philadelphia (N.L.)......	OF-DH	112	152	24	30	4	1	6	25	.197	29	47	1	44	1	3	.938
— Toronto (A.L.)............	OF	5	13	2	2	1	0	0	1	.154	2	2	0	8	0	1	.889
2001— Scranton/W.B. (I.L.)■	OF	4	20	3	6	1	0	1	5	.300	2	6	0	4	0	0	1.000
— Philadelphia (N.L.)......	OF	30	27	4	6	1	0	1	4	.222	6	11	0	5	0	0	1.000
— Montreal (N.L.)■........	OF-DH	27	46	6	11	2	0	2	8	.239	10	14	0	23	1	0	1.000
American League totals (11 years)		430	866	127	213	61	10	14	76	.246	83	217	19	501	15	14	.974
National League totals (3 years)		273	413	63	96	17	3	17	70	.232	83	129	3	161	3	3	.982
Major League totals (13 years)		703	1279	190	309	78	13	31	146	.242	166	346	22	662	18	17	.976

DIVISION SERIES RECORD

Year Team (League)	Pos.	G	AB	R	H	2B	3B	HR	RBI	Avg.	BB	SO	SB	PO	A	E	Avg.
										BATTING						**FIELDING**	
1997— Seattle (A.L.)	PH-OF	2	4	0	2	0	0	0	1	.500	0	0	0	0	0	0	...

CHAMPIONSHIP SERIES RECORD

Year Team (League)	Pos.	G	AB	R	H	2B	3B	HR	RBI	Avg.	BB	SO	SB	PO	A	E	Avg.
										BATTING						**FIELDING**	
1989— Toronto (A.L.)								Did not play.									
1991— Toronto (A.L.)............	PR-OF	1	1	0	0	0	0	0	0	.000	0	0	0	0	0	0	...

DUCHSCHERER, JUSTIN   P   RANGERS

PERSONAL: Born November 19, 1977, in Aberdeen, S.D. ... 6-3/165. ... Throws right, bats right. ... Full name: Justin Craig Duchscherer.
HIGH SCHOOL: Coronado (Lubbock, Texas).
TRANSACTIONS/CAREER NOTES: Selected by Boston Red Sox organization in eighth round of free-agent draft (June 4, 1996). ... Traded by Red Sox to Texas Rangers for C Doug Mirabelli (June 12, 2001).

Year League	W	L	Pct.	ERA	G	GS	CG	ShO	Sv.	IP	H	R	ER	BB	SO
1996— Gulf Coast Red Sox (GCL)..	0	2	.000	3.13	13	8	0	0	1	54²/₃	52	26	19	14	45
1997— Gulf Coast Red Sox (GCL)..	2	3	.400	1.81	10	8	0	0	0	44²/₃	34	18	9	17	59
— Michigan (Midw.)	1	1	.500	5.63	4	4	0	0	0	24	26	17	15	10	19
1998— Michigan (Midw.)	7	12	.368	4.79	30	26	0	0	0	142²/₃	166	87	76	47	106
1999— Augusta (S.Atl.)	4	0	1.000	0.22	6	6	0	0	0	41	21	1	1	8	39
— Sarasota (FSL)	7	7	.500	4.49	20	18	0	0	0	112¹/₃	101	62	56	30	105
2000— Trenton (East.)	7	9	.438	3.39	24	24	2	2	0	143¹/₃	134	59	54	35	126
2001— Trenton (East.)	6	3	.667	2.44	12	12	1	1	0	73²/₃	49	25	20	14	69
— Tulsa (Texas)■	4	0	1.000	2.08	6	6	1	0	0	43¹/₃	39	14	10	10	55
— Texas (A.L.)	1	1	.500	12.27	5	2	0	0	0	14²/₃	24	20	20	4	11
— Oklahoma (PCL)	3	3	.500	2.84	7	7	1	1	0	50²/₃	48	20	16	10	52
Major League totals (1 year)........	1	1	.500	12.27	5	2	0	0	0	14²/₃	24	20	20	4	11

DUCKWORTH, BRANDON   P   PHILLIES

PERSONAL: Born January 23, 1976, in Salt Lake City. ... 6-2/185. ... Throws right, bats both. ... Full name: Brandon J. Duckworth.
HIGH SCHOOL: Kearns (Utah).
JUNIOR COLLEGE: Southern Idaho.
COLLEGE: Cal State-Fullerton.
TRANSACTIONS/CAREER NOTES: Selected by Toronto Blue Jays organization in 30th round of free-agent draft (June 1, 1995); did not sign. ... Selected by Arizona Diamondbacks organization in 61st round of free-agent draft (June 4, 1996); did not sign. ... Signed by Philadelphia Phillies organization as non-drafted free agent (August 13, 1997).
HONORS: Named International League Most Valuable Pitcher (2001).

Year League	W	L	Pct.	ERA	G	GS	CG	ShO	Sv.	IP	H	R	ER	BB	SO
1998— Piedmont (S.Atl.).................	9	8	.529	2.80	21	21	•5	•3	0	147²/₃	116	58	46	24	119
— Clearwater (FSL)	6	2	.750	3.74	9	9	1	1	0	53	64	25	22	22	46
1999— Clearwater (FSL)	11	5	.688	4.84	27	17	0	0	1	132	164	84	71	40	101
2000— Reading (East.)	13	7	.650	3.16	27	27	1	0	0	165	145	70	58	52	•178
2001— Scranton/W.B. (I.L.)	*13	2	*.867	2.63	22	20	2	1	0	147	122	46	43	36	150
— Philadelphia (N.L.)............	3	2	.600	3.52	11	11	0	0	0	69	57	29	27	29	40
Major League totals (1 year)........	3	2	.600	3.52	11	11	0	0	0	69	57	29	27	29	40

DUNCAN, COURTNEY P CUBS

PERSONAL: Born October 9, 1974, in Mobile, Ala. ... 6-0/180. ... Throws right, bats left. ... Full name: Courtney Demond Duncan.
HIGH SCHOOL: Daphne (Ala.).
COLLEGE: Grambling State.
TRANSACTIONS/CAREER NOTES: Selected by Chicago Cubs organization in 20th round of free-agent draft (June 2, 1996). ... On West Tenn disabled list (June 10-24, 1999). ... On Chicago disabled list (June 29-July 16 and July 20-September 1, 2001); included rehabilitation assignment to Iowa (August 14-September 1).

Year	League	W	L	Pct.	ERA	G	GS	CG	ShO	Sv.	IP	H	R	ER	BB	SO
1996—Williamsport (NY-Penn)		*11	1	*.917	2.19	15	•15	1	0	0	90 1/3	58	28	22	34	91
1997—Daytona (FSL)		8	4	.667	*1.63	19	19	1	0	0	121 2/3	90	35	22	35	120
—Orlando (Sou.)		2	2	.500	3.40	8	8	0	0	0	45	37	28	17	29	45
1998—West Tenn (Sou.)		7	9	.438	4.26	29	•29	0	0	0	162 2/3	141	89	77	*108	157
1999—West Tenn (Sou.)		1	7	.125	7.13	11	8	0	0	0	41 2/3	44	42	33	42	42
—Daytona (FSL)		4	5	.444	5.54	15	11	1	1	1	65	70	60	40	34	48
2000—West Tenn (Sou.)		5	4	.556	3.07	61	0	0	0	25	73 1/3	57	32	25	33	72
2001—Chicago (N.L.)		3	3	.500	5.06	36	0	0	0	0	42 2/3	42	24	24	25	49
—Iowa (PCL)		1	0	1.000	3.24	7	0	0	0	0	8 1/3	7	3	3	5	15
Major League totals (1 year)		**3**	**3**	**.500**	**5.06**	**36**	**0**	**0**	**0**	**0**	**42 2/3**	**42**	**24**	**24**	**25**	**49**

DUNN, ADAM OF REDS

PERSONAL: Born November 9, 1979, in Houston. ... 6-6/235. ... Bats left, throws right. ... Full name: Adam Troy Dunn.
HIGH SCHOOL: New Caney (Texas).
COLLEGE: Texas.
TRANSACTIONS/CAREER NOTES: Selected by Cincinnati Reds organization in second round of free-agent draft (June 2, 1998). ... On Clinton disabled list (June 8-25, 2000).
STATISTICAL NOTES: Led Midwest League with .428 on-base percentage in 2000.

Year	Team (League)	Pos.	G	AB	R	H	2B	3B	HR	RBI	Avg.	BB	SO	SB	PO	A	E	Avg.
								BATTING								FIELDING		
1998—Billings (Pio.)		OF	34	125	26	36	3	1	4	13	.288	22	33	4	35	2	6	.860
1999—Rockford (Midw.)		OF	93	313	62	96	16	2	11	44	.307	46	64	21	85	5	8	.918
2000—Dayton (Midw.)		OF	122	420	101	118	29	1	16	79	.281	100	101	24	197	10	9	.958
2001—Chattanooga (Sou.)		OF	39	140	30	48	9	0	12	31	.343	24	31	6	65	8	3	.961
—Louisville (I.L.)		OF	55	210	44	69	13	0	20	53	.329	38	51	5	93	10	5	.954
—Cincinnati (N.L.)		OF	66	244	54	64	18	1	19	43	.262	38	74	4	136	3	2	.986
Major League totals (1 year)			**66**	**244**	**54**	**64**	**18**	**1**	**19**	**43**	**.262**	**38**	**74**	**4**	**136**	**3**	**2**	**.986**

DUNSTON, SHAWON OF/IF GIANTS

PERSONAL: Born March 21, 1963, in Brooklyn, N.Y. ... 6-1/180. ... Bats right, throws right. ... Full name: Shawon Donnell Dunston.
HIGH SCHOOL: Thomas Jefferson (Brooklyn, N.Y.).
TRANSACTIONS/CAREER NOTES: Selected by Chicago Cubs organization in first round (first pick overall) of free-agent draft (June 7, 1982). ... On disabled list (May 31-June 10, 1983). ... On Chicago disabled list (June 16-August 21, 1987); included rehabilitation assignment to Iowa (August 14-21). ... On disabled list (May 5, 1992-remainder of season and March 27-September 1, 1993). ... On suspended list (September 8-12, 1995). ... Granted free agency (October 31, 1995). ... Signed by San Francisco Giants (January 9, 1996). ... On disabled list (April 24-May 13 and August 5-October 1, 1996). ... Granted free agency (November 18, 1996). ... Signed by Cubs (December 7, 1996). ... On Chicago disabled list (June 9-24, 1997). ... Traded by Cubs to Pittsburgh Pirates for a player to be named later (August 31, 1997). ... Granted free agency (October 28, 1997). ... Signed by Cleveland Indians (February 16, 1998). ... Traded by Indians with P Jose Mesa and P Alvin Morman to Giants for P Steve Reed and OF Jacob Cruz (July 23, 1998). ... Granted free agency (October 23, 1998). ... Signed by St. Louis Cardinals (February 16, 1999). ... On suspended list (June 17-20, 1999). ... On St. Louis disabled list (June 23-July 9, 1999). ... Traded by Cardinals to New York Mets for IF Craig Paquette (July 31, 1999). ... Granted free agency (October 29, 1999). ... Signed by Cardinals organization (February 3, 2000). ... Granted free agency (October 27, 2000). ... Signed by Giants (December 8, 2000). ... On disabled list (August 4-19, 2001).
RECORDS: Shares modern major league single-game record for most triples—3 (July 28, 1990).
HONORS: Named shortstop on The Sporting News N.L. All-Star team (1989).
STATISTICAL NOTES: Led N.L. shortstops with 817 total chances and tied for lead in double plays with 96 in 1986. ... Career major league grand slams: 5.

Year	Team (League)	Pos.	G	AB	R	H	2B	3B	HR	RBI	Avg.	BB	SO	SB	PO	A	E	Avg.
								BATTING								FIELDING		
1982—GC Cubs (GCL)		SS-3B	53	190	27	61	11	0	2	28	.321	11	22	32	61	129	24	.888
1983—Quad Cities (Midw.)		SS	117	455	65	141	17	8	4	62	.310	7	51	58	172	326	47	.914
1984—Midland (Texas)		SS	73	298	44	98	13	3	3	34	.329	11	38	11	164	203	32	.920
—Iowa (A.A.)		SS	61	210	25	49	11	1	7	27	.233	4	40	9	90	165	26	.907
1985—Chicago (N.L.)		SS	74	250	40	65	12	4	4	18	.260	19	42	11	144	248	17	.958
—Iowa (A.A.)		SS	73	272	24	73	9	6	2	28	.268	5	48	17	138	176	12	.963
1986—Chicago (N.L.)		SS	150	581	66	145	37	6	17	68	.250	21	114	13	*320	*465	*32	.961
1987—Chicago (N.L.)		SS	95	346	40	85	18	3	5	22	.246	10	68	12	160	271	14	.969
—Iowa (A.A.)		SS	5	19	1	8	1	0	0	2	.421	0	3	1	6	12	1	.947
1988—Chicago (N.L.)		SS	155	575	69	143	23	6	9	56	.249	16	108	30	*257	455	20	.973
1989—Chicago (N.L.)		SS	138	471	52	131	20	6	9	60	.278	30	86	19	213	379	17	.972
1990—Chicago (N.L.)		SS	146	545	73	143	22	8	17	66	.262	15	87	25	255	392	20	.970
1991—Chicago (N.L.)		SS	142	492	59	128	22	7	12	50	.260	23	64	21	*261	383	21	.968
1992—Chicago (N.L.)		SS	18	73	8	23	3	1	0	2	.315	3	13	2	28	42	1	.986
1993—Chicago (N.L.)		SS	7	10	3	4	2	0	0	2	.400	0	1	0	5	0	0	1.000
1994—Chicago (N.L.)		SS	88	331	38	92	19	0	11	35	.278	16	48	3	121	218	12	.966
1995—Chicago (N.L.)		SS	127	477	58	141	30	6	14	69	.296	10	75	10	187	336	17	.969
1996—San Fran. (N.L.)■		SS	82	287	27	86	12	2	5	25	.300	13	40	8	116	217	15	.957

Year	Team (League)	Pos.	G	AB	R	H	2B	3B	HR	RBI	Avg.	BB	SO	SB	PO	A	E	Avg.
1997—	Chicago (N.L.)■........	SS-OF	114	419	57	119	18	4	9	41	.284	8	64	29	179	227	12	.971
—Pittsburgh (N.L.)■	SS	18	71	14	28	4	1	5	16	.394	0	11	3	28	55	3	.965
1998—Cleveland (A.L.)■.....	2-S-O-DH	62	156	26	37	11	3	3	12	.237	6	18	9	63	76	4	.972
—San Fran. (N.L.)■........	SS-OF-2B	36	51	10	9	2	0	3	8	.176	0	10	0	20	5	2	.926
1999—St. Louis (N.L.)■ O-1-S-3-DH		62	150	23	46	5	2	5	25	.307	2	23	6	78	23	2	.981
—New York (N.L.)■	OF-3B	42	93	12	32	6	1	0	16	.344	0	16	4	44	2	1	.979
2000—St. Louis (N.L.)■ O-S-1-3-DH		98	216	28	54	11	2	12	43	.250	6	47	3	110	10	2	.984
2001—San Fran. (N.L.)■.......	OF-1B-DH	88	186	26	52	10	3	9	25	.280	2	32	3	80	4	3	.966
American League totals (1 year)		62	156	26	37	11	3	3	12	.237	6	18	9	63	76	4	.972
National League totals (17 years)		1680	5624	703	1526	276	59	146	647	.271	194	949	202	2606	3732	211	.968
Major League totals (17 years)		1742	5780	729	1563	287	62	149	659	.270	200	967	211	2669	3808	215	.968

DIVISION SERIES RECORD

Year	Team (League)	Pos.	G	AB	R	H	2B	3B	HR	RBI	Avg.	BB	SO	SB	PO	A	E	Avg.
1999—New York (N.L.)..........	OF-PH-PR	4	6	0	1	0	0	0	0	.167	0	1	0	7	0	0	1.000
2000—St. Louis (N.L.)...........	PH	1	1	0	1	0	0	0	0	1.000	0	0	0	...	...	...	...
Division series totals (2 years)		5	7	0	2	0	0	0	0	.286	0	1	0	7	0	0	1.000

CHAMPIONSHIP SERIES RECORD

Year	Team (League)	Pos.	G	AB	R	H	2B	3B	HR	RBI	Avg.	BB	SO	SB	PO	A	E	Avg.
1989—Chicago (N.L.)............	SS	5	19	2	6	0	0	0	0	.316	1	1	1	10	14	1	.960
1999—New York (N.L.)...........	PH-OF	5	7	2	1	0	0	0	0	.143	0	2	1	0	0	0	...
2000—St. Louis (N.L.)...........	PH-OF	4	6	1	2	1	0	0	0	.333	0	0	0	1	0	0	1.000
Championship series totals (3 years)		14	32	5	9	1	0	0	0	.281	1	3	2	11	14	1	.962

ALL-STAR GAME RECORD

Year	League	Pos.	AB	R	H	2B	3B	HR	RBI	Avg.	BB	SO	SB	PO	A	E	Avg.
1988—National....................								Did not play.									
1990—National....................	SS	2	0	0	0	0	0	0	.000	0	0	0	0	0	0	...

DUNWOODY, TODD   OF   INDIANS

D

PERSONAL: Born April 11, 1975, in Lafayette, Ind. ... 6-1/205. ... Bats left, throws left. ... Full name: Todd Franklin Dunwoody.
HIGH SCHOOL: West Lafayette (Ind.) Harrison.
TRANSACTIONS/CAREER NOTES: Selected by Florida Marlins organization in seventh round of free-agent draft (June 3, 1993). ... On Charlotte disabled list (April 11-18, 1998). ... Traded by Marlins to Kansas City Royals for IF Sean McNally (December 15, 1999). ... On Kansas City disabled list (March 24-June 3, 2000); included rehabilitation assignments to Omaha (May 13-20 and June 1-3). ... Granted free agency (December 21, 2000). ... Signed by Chicago Cubs organization (January 9, 2001). ... Granted free agency (October 15, 2001). ... Signed by Cleveland Indians organization (November 6, 2001).
STATISTICAL NOTES: Tied for Midwest League lead in intentional bases on balls received with seven in 1995. ... Led Eastern League with 267 total bases in 1996.

Year	Team (League)	Pos.	G	AB	R	H	2B	3B	HR	RBI	Avg.	BB	SO	SB	PO	A	E	Avg.
1993—GC Marlins (GCL).......	OF	31	109	13	21	2	2	0	7	.193	7	28	5	45	1	1	.979
1994—GC Marlins (GCL).......	OF	46	169	32	44	6	6	1	25	.260	21	28	11	91	1	1	.989
—Kane County (Midw.)..	OF	15	45	7	5	0	0	1	1	.111	5	17	1	21	2	0	1.000
1995—Kane County (Midw.)..	OF	132	494	89	140	20	8	14	89	.283	52	105	39	284	6	5	.983
1996—Portland (East.)........	OF	138	*552	88	153	30	6	24	93	.277	45	*149	24	254	2	1	*.996
1997—Charlotte (I.L.)...........	OF-DH	107	401	74	105	16	7	23	62	.262	39	129	25	231	5	2	.992
—Florida (N.L.)............	OF	19	50	7	13	2	2	2	7	.260	7	21	2	26	0	2	.929
1998—Charlotte (I.L.)...........	OF	28	102	20	31	6	3	6	22	.304	12	28	4	76	2	1	.987
—Florida (N.L.)............	OF	116	434	53	109	27	7	5	28	.251	21	113	5	273	9	3	.989
1999—Florida (N.L.)............	OF	64	186	20	41	6	3	2	20	.220	12	41	3	102	3	2	.981
—Calgary (PCL)...........	OF-DH	65	246	35	67	16	7	9	36	.272	10	56	7	159	10	4	.977
2000—Omaha (PCL)■	OF	9	31	5	10	1	0	1	5	.323	4	8	1	11	0	0	1.000
—Kansas City (A.L.) ...	OF-DH	61	178	12	37	9	0	1	23	.208	8	42	3	81	0	2	.976
2001—Iowa (PCL)............	OF	75	251	31	71	18	3	8	32	.283	17	75	6	107	7	3	.974
—Chicago (N.L.)...........	OF	33	61	6	13	4	0	1	3	.213	3	14	0	35	1	1	.973
American League totals (1 year)		61	178	12	37	9	0	1	23	.208	8	42	3	81	0	2	.976
National League totals (4 years)		232	731	86	176	39	12	10	58	.241	43	189	10	436	13	8	.982
Major League totals (5 years)		293	909	98	213	48	12	11	81	.234	51	231	13	517	13	10	.981

DURAZO, ERUBIEL   1B   DIAMONDBACKS

PERSONAL: Born January 23, 1974, in Hermosillo, Mexico. ... 6-3/225. ... Bats left, throws left. ... Full name: Erubiel Durazo Cardenas.
HIGH SCHOOL: Amphitheater (Tucson, Ariz.).
JUNIOR COLLEGE: Pima Community College (Ariz.).
TRANSACTIONS/CAREER NOTES: Signed by Monterrey, Mexican League (1997). ... Contract sold by Monterrey to Arizona Diamondbacks organization (December 16, 1998). ... On Arizona disabled list (May 30-June 24, June 27-July 13 and August 20, 2000-remainder of season); included rehabilitation assignments to Tuscon (June 20-24 and July 8-9) and Arizona League Diamondbacks (July 9-13). ... On Arizona disabled list (August 15-September 1, 2001); included rehabilitation assignment to Tucson (August 28-September 1).

Year	Team (League)	Pos.	G	AB	R	H	2B	3B	HR	RBI	Avg.	BB	SO	SB	PO	A	E	Avg.
1997—Monterrey (Mex.)		1B-OF	110	358	47	101	21	10	8	61	.282	52	43	3	480	48	3	.994
1998—Monterrey (Mex.)		OF-1B	119	420	84	147	32	2	19	98	.350	99	71	4	219	15	0	1.000
1999—El Paso (Texas)■		1B	64	226	53	91	18	3	14	55	.403	44	37	2	523	36	10	.982
—Tucson (PCL)		1B	30	118	27	48	7	0	10	28	.407	14	18	1	241	20	1	.996
—Arizona (N.L.)		1B	52	155	31	51	4	2	11	30	.329	26	43	1	324	20	0	1.000
2000—Arizona (N.L.)		1B	67	196	35	52	11	0	8	33	.265	34	43	1	422	23	5	.989
—Tucson (PCL)		1B	13	43	9	18	6	0	3	10	.419	6	7	0	61	5	3	.957
—Ariz. D'backs (Ariz.)		1B	2	5	2	3	0	0	1	2	.600	1	0	0	6	2	0	1.000
2001—Arizona (N.L.)		1B-DH-OF	92	175	34	47	11	0	12	38	.269	28	49	0	252	18	2	.993
—Tucson (PCL)		1B	3	11	3	3	0	0	1	1	.273	1	3	0	18	2	0	1.000
Major League totals (3 years)			211	526	100	150	26	2	31	101	.285	88	135	2	998	61	7	.993

DIVISION SERIES RECORD

Year	Team (League)	Pos.	G	AB	R	H	2B	3B	HR	RBI	Avg.	BB	SO	SB	PO	A	E	Avg.
1999—Arizona (N.L.)		1B	2	7	1	1	0	0	1	1	.143	1	0	0	15	1	0	1.000
2001—Arizona (N.L.)		PH	1	1	0	0	0	0	0	0	.000	0	0	0	...	...	...	...
Division series totals (2 years)			3	8	1	1	0	0	1	1	.125	1	0	0	15	1	0	1.000

CHAMPIONSHIP SERIES RECORD

Year	Team (League)	Pos.	G	AB	R	H	2B	3B	HR	RBI	Avg.	BB	SO	SB	PO	A	E	Avg.
2001—Arizona (N.L.)		PH-1B	2	3	1	1	0	0	1	2	.333	0	1	0	2	0	0	1.000

WORLD SERIES RECORD

NOTES: Member of World Series championship team (2001).

Year	Team (League)	Pos.	G	AB	R	H	2B	3B	HR	RBI	Avg.	BB	SO	SB	PO	A	E	Avg.
2001—Arizona (N.L.)		DH-PH	4	11	0	4	1	0	0	1	.364	3	4	0	...	...	...	...

DURBIN, CHAD P ROYALS

PERSONAL: Born December 3, 1977, in Spring Valley, Ill. ... 6-2/200. ... Throws right, bats right. ... Full name: Chad Griffin Durbin.
HIGH SCHOOL: Woodlawn (Shreveport, La.).
TRANSACTIONS/CAREER NOTES: Selected by Kansas City Royals organization in third round of free-agent draft (June 4, 1996).

Year	League	W	L	Pct.	ERA	G	GS	CG	ShO	Sv.	IP	H	R	ER	BB	SO
1996—Gulf Coast Royals (GCL)		3	2	.600	4.26	11	8	1	1	0	44 1/3	34	22	21	25	43
1997—Lansing (Midw.)		5	8	.385	4.79	26	26	0	0	0	144 2/3	157	85	77	53	116
1998—Wilmington (Caro.)		10	7	.588	2.93	26	26	0	0	0	147 2/3	126	57	48	59	162
1999—Wichita (Texas)		8	10	.444	4.64	28	27	1	•1	0	157	154	88	81	49	122
—Kansas City (A.L.)		0	0	...	0.00	1	0	0	0	0	2 1/3	1	0	0	1	3
2000—Kansas City (A.L.)		2	5	.286	8.21	16	16	0	0	0	72 1/3	91	71	66	43	37
—Omaha (PCL)		4	4	.500	4.46	12	12	0	0	0	72 2/3	75	37	36	22	53
2001—Kansas City (A.L.)		9	16	.360	4.93	29	29	2	0	0	179	201	109	98	58	95
—Omaha (PCL)		2	2	.500	3.33	5	5	0	0	0	27	22	11	10	6	35
Major League totals (3 years)		11	21	.344	5.82	46	45	2	0	0	253 2/3	293	180	164	102	135

DURHAM, RAY 2B WHITE SOX

PERSONAL: Born November 30, 1971, in Charlotte. ... 5-8/180. ... Bats both, throws right.
HIGH SCHOOL: Harding (Charlotte).
TRANSACTIONS/CAREER NOTES: Selected by Chicago White Sox organization in fifth round of free-agent draft (June 4, 1990). ... On Utica suspended list (April 1-May 22, 1992). ... On Sarasota disabled list (June 16-July 9, 1992).
RECORDS: Holds major league single-season record for fewest putouts by second baseman (150 or more games)—236 (1996).
STATISTICAL NOTES: Led Southern League in caught stealing with 25 in 1993. ... Led Southern League second basemen with 541 total chances in 1993. ... Led American Association with 261 total bases in 1994. ... Led American Association second basemen with 702 total chances and 92 double plays in 1994. ... Led A.L. second basemen with 738 total chances and 128 double plays in 1998. ... Led A.L. second basemen with 126 double plays in 2000. ... Career major league grand slams: 3.

Year	Team (League)	Pos.	G	AB	R	H	2B	3B	HR	RBI	Avg.	BB	SO	SB	PO	A	E	Avg.
1990—GC White Sox (GCL)		2B-SS	35	116	18	32	3	3	0	13	.276	15	36	23	61	85	15	.907
1991—Utica (NY-Penn)		2B	39	142	29	36	2	7	0	17	.254	25	44	12	54	101	12	.928
—GC White Sox (GCL)		2B	6	23	3	7	1	0	0	4	.304	3	5	5	18	15	0	1.000
1992—Sarasota (FSL)		2B	57	202	37	55	6	3	0	7	.272	32	36	28	66	107	10	.945
—GC White Sox (GCL)		2B	5	13	3	7	2	0	0	2	.538	3	1	1	4	3	0	1.000
1993—Birmingham (Sou.)		2B	137	528	83	143	22	*10	3	37	.271	42	100	39	227	284	*30	.945
1994—Nashville (A.A.)		2B	133	527	89	156	33	•12	16	66	.296	46	91	34	*254	*429	*19	*.973
1995—Chicago (A.L.)		2B-DH	125	471	68	121	27	6	7	51	.257	31	83	18	245	298	15	.973
1996—Chicago (A.L.)		2B-DH	156	557	79	153	33	5	10	65	.275	58	95	30	236	423	11	.984
1997—Chicago (A.L.)		2B-DH	155	634	106	172	27	5	11	53	.271	61	96	33	270	395	*18	.974
1998—Chicago (A.L.)		2B	158	635	126	181	35	8	19	67	.285	73	105	36	282	438	18	.976
1999—Chicago (A.L.)		2B-DH	153	612	109	181	30	8	13	60	.296	73	105	34	305	412	19	.974
2000—Chicago (A.L.)		2B	151	614	121	172	35	9	17	75	.280	75	105	25	299	419	15	.980
2001—Chicago (A.L.)		2B-DH	152	611	104	163	42	10	20	65	.267	64	110	23	280	446	10	.986
Major League totals (7 years)			1050	4134	713	1143	229	51	97	436	.276	435	699	199	1917	2831	106	.978

DIVISION SERIES RECORD

							BATTING									FIELDING		
Year	Team (League)	Pos.	G	AB	R	H	2B	3B	HR	RBI	Avg.	BB	SO	SB	PO	A	E	Avg.
2000— Chicago (A.L.)		2B	3	10	2	2	1	0	1	1	.200	3	3	0	10	6	0	1.000

ALL-STAR GAME RECORD

						BATTING									FIELDING		
Year	League	Pos.	AB	R	H	2B	3B	HR	RBI	Avg.	BB	SO	SB	PO	A	E	Avg.
1998— American		2B	1	1	1	0	0	0	1	1.000	0	0	0	0	0		...
2000— American		2B	2	1	1	0	0	0	0	.500	0	0	0	1	3	0	1.000
All-Star Game totals (2 years)			3	2	2	0	0	0	1	.667	0	0	0	1	3	0	1.000

DUVALL, MIKE   P   TWINS

PERSONAL: Born October 11, 1974, in Warrenton, Va. ... 6-0/200. ... Throws left, bats right. ... Full name: Michael Alan Duvall.
HIGH SCHOOL: Fauquier (Warrenton, Va.).
JUNIOR COLLEGE: Potomac State College (W.Va.).
TRANSACTIONS/CAREER NOTES: Selected by Florida Marlins organization in 19th round of free-agent draft (June 1, 1995). ... Selected by Tampa Bay Devil Rays in second round (32nd pick overall) of expansion draft (November 18, 1997). ... On Durham disabled list (April 9-May 13, 1998). ... On Tampa Bay disabled list (June 9-July 6, 1999). ... On Durham disabled list (April 6-20 and August 19-September 1, 2000). ... Released by Devil Rays (March 22, 2001). ... Signed by Minnesota Twins organization (September 19, 2001).

Year	League	W	L	Pct.	ERA	G	GS	CG	ShO	Sv.	IP	H	R	ER	BB	SO
1995— Gulf Coast Marlins (GCL) ...		5	0	1.000	2.22	16	1	0	0	1	28 1/3	15	8	7	12	34
1996— Kane County (Midw.)..........		4	1	.800	2.06	41	0	0	0	8	48	43	20	11	21	46
1997— Brevard County (FSL)........		1	0	1.000	0.73	11	0	0	0	6	12 1/3	7	1	1	3	9
— Portland (East.)		4	6	.400	1.84	45	0	0	0	18	68 1/3	63	20	14	20	49
1998— St. Petersburg (FSL)■......		0	0	...	2.70	2	0	0	0	0	3 1/3	4	1	1	2	3
— Durham (I.L.)		5	3	.625	3.22	32	9	1	0	0	72 2/3	74	31	26	32	55
— Tampa Bay (A.L.)...............		0	0	...	6.75	3	0	0	0	0	4	4	3	3	2	1
1999— Tampa Bay (A.L.)............		1	1	.500	4.05	40	0	0	0	0	40	46	21	18	27	18
— Durham (I.L.)		2	2	.500	5.40	19	1	0	0	2	30	32	20	18	12	27
2000— Durham (I.L.)		6	2	.750	4.59	30	8	0	0	0	80 1/3	85	47	41	44	49
— Tampa Bay (A.L.)...............		0	0	...	7.71	2	0	0	0	0	2 1/3	5	2	2	1	0
2001— Edmonton (PCL)..........		2	2	.500	4.45	55	0	0	0	3	62 2/3	73	32	31	21	63
— Minnesota (A.L.)...............		0	0	...	7.71	8	0	0	0	0	4 2/3	7	4	4	2	4
Major League totals (4 years).......		1	1	.500	4.76	53	0	0	0	0	51	62	30	27	32	23

DYE, JERMAINE   OF   ATHLETICS

PERSONAL: Born January 28, 1974, in Vacaville, Calif. ... 6-5/220. ... Bats right, throws right. ... Full name: Jermaine Trevell Dye.
HIGH SCHOOL: Will C. Wood (Vacaville, Calif.).
JUNIOR COLLEGE: Cosumnes River (Calif.) College.
TRANSACTIONS/CAREER NOTES: Selected by Atlanta Braves organization in 17th round of free-agent draft (June 3, 1993). ... On disabled list (July 13-August 9, 1995). ... Traded by Braves with P Jamie Walker to Kansas City Royals for OF Michael Tucker and IF Keith Lockhart (March 27, 1997). ... On Kansas City disabled list (April 17-May 3, 1997; included rehabilitation assignment to Omaha (May 1-3). ... On Kansas City disabled list (July 10-August 13, 1997); included rehabilitation assignment to Omaha (July 27-August 13). ... On Kansas City disabled list (March 23-May 8 and September 1, 1998-remainder of season); included rehabilitation assignment to Omaha (April 21-May 8). ... Traded by Royals to Colorado Rockies for SS Neifi Perez (July 25, 2001). ... Traded by Rockies to Oakland Athletics for OF Mario Encarnacion, 2B/SS Jose Ortiz and P Todd Belitz (July 25, 2001).
HONORS: Won A.L. Gold Glove as outfielder (2000).
STATISTICAL NOTES: Led South Atlantic League outfielders with six double plays in 1994. ... Led A.L. outfielders with six double plays in 1999. ... Had 16-game hitting streak (August 25-September 18, 2001). ... Career major league grand slams: 3.
MISCELLANEOUS: Hit home run in first major league at-bat (May 17, 1996).

							BATTING									FIELDING		
Year	Team (League)	Pos.	G	AB	R	H	2B	3B	HR	RBI	Avg.	BB	SO	SB	PO	A	E	Avg.
1993— GC Braves (GCL)........		OF-3B	31	124	17	43	14	0	0	27	.347	5	13	5	46	9	3	.948
— Danville (Appl.)..........		OF	25	94	6	26	6	1	2	12	.277	8	10	19	51	1	2	.963
1994— Macon (S.Atl.).........		OF	135	506	73	151	*41	1	15	98	.298	33	82	19	263	*22	9	.969
1995— Greenville (Sou.)		OF	104	403	50	115	26	4	15	71	.285	27	74	4	234	*22	5	.981
1996— Richmond (I.L.)........		OF	36	142	25	33	7	1	6	19	.232	5	25	3	83	2	4	.955
— Atlanta (N.L.)...........		OF	98	292	32	82	16	0	12	37	.281	8	67	1	150	2	8	.950
1997— Kansas City (A.L.)■...		OF	75	263	26	62	14	0	7	22	.236	17	51	2	164	7	6	.966
— Omaha (A.A.)...........		OF-DH	39	144	21	44	6	0	10	25	.306	9	25	0	41	2	0	1.000
1998— Omaha (PCL)...........		OF-1B-DH	41	157	29	47	6	0	12	35	.299	19	29	7	119	4	1	.992
— Kansas City (A.L.)		OF	60	214	24	50	5	1	5	23	.234	11	46	2	152	4	2	.987
1999— Kansas City (A.L.)		OF-DH	158	608	96	179	44	8	27	119	.294	58	119	2	362	•17	6	.984
2000— Kansas City (A.L.)		OF-DH	157	601	107	193	41	2	33	118	.321	69	99	0	277	11	7	.976
2001— Kansas City (A.L.)		OF-DH	97	367	50	100	14	0	13	47	.272	30	68	7	178	5	3	.984
— Oakland (A.L.)■........		OF	61	232	41	69	17	1	13	59	.297	27	44	2	93	8	3	.971
American League totals (5 years)			608	2285	344	653	135	12	98	388	.286	212	427	15	1226	52	27	.979
National League totals (1 year)			98	292	32	82	16	0	12	37	.281	8	67	1	150	2	8	.950
Major League totals (6 years)			706	2577	376	735	151	12	110	425	.285	220	494	16	1376	54	35	.976

DIVISION SERIES RECORD

							BATTING									FIELDING		
Year	Team (League)	Pos.	G	AB	R	H	2B	3B	HR	RBI	Avg.	BB	SO	SB	PO	A	E	Avg.
1996— Atlanta (N.L.).............		OF	3	11	1	2	0	0	1	1	.182	0	6	1	11	1	0	1.000
2001— Oakland (A.L.)		OF	4	13	0	3	2	0	0	0	.231	2	2	0	5	0	0	1.000
Division series totals (2 years)			7	24	1	5	2	0	1	1	.208	2	8	1	16	1	0	1.000

RECORDS: Shares N.L. single-game record for most at-bats—6 (October 14, 1996).

						BATTING									FIELDING			
Year	Team (League)	Pos.	G	AB	R	H	2B	3B	HR	RBI	Avg.	BB	SO	SB	PO	A	E	Avg.
1996—Atlanta (N.L.)..............		OF	7	28	2	6	1	0	0	4	.214	1	7	0	14	0	0	1.000

WORLD SERIES RECORD

						BATTING									FIELDING			
Year	Team (League)	Pos.	G	AB	R	H	2B	3B	HR	RBI	Avg.	BB	SO	SB	PO	A	E	Avg.
1996—Atlanta (N.L.)..............		OF	5	17	0	2	0	0	0	1	.118	1	1	0	15	0	1	.938

ALL-STAR GAME RECORD

				BATTING									FIELDING			
Year	League	Pos.	AB	R	H	2B	3B	HR	RBI	Avg.	BB	SO	SB	PO	A	E	Avg.
2000—American..................		OF	2	1	0	0	0	0	0	.000	1	1	0	1	0	0	1.000

EASLEY, DAMION   2B   TIGERS

PERSONAL: Born November 11, 1969, in New York. ... 5-11/185. ... Bats right, throws right. ... Full name: Jacinto Damion Easley.
HIGH SCHOOL: Lakewood (Calif.).
JUNIOR COLLEGE: Long Beach (Calif.) City College.
COLLEGE: Long Beach State.
TRANSACTIONS/CAREER NOTES: Selected by California Angels organization in 30th round of free-agent draft (June 1, 1988). ... On disabled list (June 19-July 4 and July 28, 1993-remainder of season; and May 30-June 17, 1994). ... On California disabled list (April 1-May 10, 1996); included rehabilitation assignment to Vancouver (April 30-May 10). ... Traded by Angels to Detroit Tigers for P Greg Gohr (July 31, 1996). ... On Detroit disabled list (April 10-25 and May 9-June 2, 2000); included rehabilitation assignments to Toledo (April 24-25 and May 29-June 2).
RECORDS: Holds major league single-season record for fewest putouts by second baseman for leader—285 (1998). ... Shares major league single-game record for most times hit by pitch—3 (May 31, 1999).
HONORS: Named second baseman on THE SPORTING NEWS A.L. Silver Slugger team (1998).
STATISTICAL NOTES: Led A.L. second basemen with 285 putouts and .985 fielding percentage in 1998. ... Had 19-game hitting streaks (May 10-30 and July 3-23, 1998). ... Hit for the cycle (June 8, 2001). ... Collected six hits in one game (August 8, 2001). ... Career major league grand slams: 1.

						BATTING									FIELDING			
Year	Team (League)	Pos.	G	AB	R	H	2B	3B	HR	RBI	Avg.	BB	SO	SB	PO	A	E	Avg.
1989—Bend (N'West)..........	2B	36	131	34	39	5	1	4	21	.298	25	21	9	49	89	22	.863
1990—Quad City (Midw.)	SS	103	365	59	100	19	3	10	56	.274	41	60	25	136	206	41	.893
1991—Midland (Texas)........	SS	127	452	73	115	24	5	6	57	.254	58	67	23	186	388	*47	.924
1992—Edmonton (PCL)	SS-3B	108	429	61	124	18	3	3	44	.289	31	44	26	152	342	30	.943
—California (A.L.).........	3B-SS	47	151	14	39	5	0	1	12	.258	8	26	9	30	102	5	.964
1993—California (A.L.).........	2B-3B-DH	73	230	33	72	13	2	2	22	.313	28	35	6	111	157	6	.978
1994—California (A.L.).........	3B-2B	88	316	41	68	16	1	6	30	.215	29	48	4	122	179	7	.977
1995—California (A.L.).........	2B-SS	114	357	35	77	14	2	4	35	.216	32	47	5	186	276	10	.979
1996—Vancouver (PCL)	SS-2B-3B	12	48	13	15	2	1	2	8	.313	9	6	4	20	26	2	.958
—Midland (Texas)........	3B-SS	4	14	1	6	2	0	0	2	.429	0	0	1	5	12	1	.944
—California (A.L.)........S-2-3-DH-O	28	45	4	7	1	0	2	7	.156	6	12	0	23	39	3	.954
—Detroit (A.L.)■.........	2-S-3-DH	21	67	10	23	1	0	2	10	.343	4	13	3	22	47	3	.958
1997—Detroit (A.L.)	2B-SS-DH	151	527	97	139	37	3	22	72	.264	68	102	28	244	405	12	.982
1998—Detroit (A.L.)	2B-SS-DH	153	594	84	161	38	2	27	100	.271	39	112	15	†312	480	12	†.985
1999—Detroit (A.L.)	2B-SS	151	549	83	146	30	1	20	65	.266	51	124	11	318	445	8	.990
2000—Detroit (A.L.)	2B	126	464	76	120	27	2	14	58	.259	55	79	13	198	411	6	*.990
—Toledo (I.L.)...............	2B	4	13	3	3	1	0	1	4	.231	4	2	0	5	9	0	1.000
2001—Detroit (A.L.)	2B	154	585	77	146	27	7	11	65	.250	52	90	10	279	496	14	.982
Major League totals (10 years)		1106	3885	554	998	209	20	111	476	.257	372	688	104	1845	3037	86	.983

ALL-STAR GAME RECORD

				BATTING									FIELDING			
Year	League	Pos.	AB	R	H	2B	3B	HR	RBI	Avg.	BB	SO	SB	PO	A	E	Avg.
1998—American..................	PH	1	1	1	0	0	0	0	1.000	0	0	0	0	0	0	...

EATON, ADAM   P   PADRES

PERSONAL: Born November 23, 1977, in Seattle. ... 6-2/190. ... Throws right, bats right. ... Full name: Adam Thomas Eaton.
HIGH SCHOOL: Snohomish (Wash.).
TRANSACTIONS/CAREER NOTES: Selected by Philadelphia Phillies organization in first round (11th pick overall) of free-agent draft (June 4, 1996). ... Traded by Phillies with P Carlton Loewer and P Steve Montgomery to San Diego Padres for P Andy Ashby (November 10, 1999). ... On disabled list (July 6, 2001-remainder of season).
STATISTICAL NOTES: Pitched 1-0 no-hit loss for Reading against Norwich (June 22, 1999).
MISCELLANEOUS: Appeared in one game as pinch runner (2000). ... Appeared in five games as pinch runner (2001). ... Appeared in one game as pinch hitter (2001).

Year	League	W	L	Pct.	ERA	G	GS	CG	ShO	Sv.	IP	H	R	ER	BB	SO
1997—Piedmont (S.Atl.).............	5	6	.455	4.16	14	14	0	0	0	71 1/3	81	38	33	30	57
1998—Clearwater (FSL)	9	8	.529	4.44	24	23	1	0	0	131 2/3	152	68	65	47	89
1999—Clearwater (FSL)	5	5	.500	3.91	13	13	0	0	0	69	81	39	30	24	50
—Reading (East.).............	5	4	.556	2.92	12	12	2	0	0	77	60	30	25	28	67
—Scranton/W.B. (I.L.)	1	1	.500	3.00	3	3	0	0	0	21	17	10	7	6	10
2000—Mobile (Sou.)■..............	4	1	.800	2.68	10	10	1	1	0	57	47	20	17	18	58
—San Diego (N.L.)	7	4	.636	4.13	22	22	0	0	0	135	134	63	62	61	90
2001—San Diego (N.L.)	8	5	.615	4.32	17	17	2	0	0	116 2/3	108	61	56	40	109
Major League totals (2 years).......	15	9	.625	4.22	39	39	2	0	0	251 2/3	242	124	118	101	199

EBERWEIN, KEVIN — 3B — PADRES

PERSONAL: Born March 30, 1977, in Tacoma, Wash. ... 6-4/200. ... Bats right, throws right. ... Full name: Kevin M. Eberwein.
HIGH SCHOOL: Green Valley (Henderson, Nev.).
COLLEGE: UNLV.
TRANSACTIONS/CAREER NOTES: Selected by San Diego Padres organization in fifth round of free-agent draft (June 2, 1998). ... On Mobile disabled list (July 6-14 and August 28-September 13, 2000). ... On Portland disabled list (April 5-27, May 29-June 7 and June 22-September 6, 2001).

Year Team (League)	Pos.	G	AB	R	H	2B	3B	HR	RBI	Avg.	BB	SO	SB	PO	A	E	Avg.
1998— Clinton (Midw.)	3B-1B	65	247	42	73	20	3	10	38	.296	26	66	4	42	115	17	.902
1999— Rancho Cuca. (Calif.) .	3B-1B-SS	110	417	69	108	30	4	18	69	.259	42	139	7	84	192	18	.939
— Mobile (Sou.)	3B	10	35	5	6	1	0	1	2	.171	3	16	0	3	19	1	.957
2000— Mobile (Sou.)	1B-3B	100	372	57	98	16	2	18	71	.263	45	77	2	776	50	7	.992
2001— Portland (PCL)	1B-3B	27	94	16	25	8	1	3	11	.266	10	22	0	121	26	3	.980
— Lake Elsinore (Calif.) ..	3B	9	30	6	10	4	0	2	4	.333	6	6	0	5	7	2	.857

ECHEVARRIA, ANGEL — OF

PERSONAL: Born May 25, 1971, in Bridgeport, Conn. ... 6-3/230. ... Bats right, throws right. ... Full name: Angel Santos Echevarria.
HIGH SCHOOL: Bassick (Bridgeport, Conn.).
COLLEGE: Rutgers.
TRANSACTIONS/CAREER NOTES: Selected by Colorado Rockies organization in 17th round of free-agent draft (June 1, 1992). ... On Colorado disabled list (April 29-June 4 and July 29-August 16, 1997). ... Claimed on waivers by Milwaukee Brewers (July 19, 2000). ... Granted free agency (October 9, 2001).

Year Team (League)	Pos.	G	AB	R	H	2B	3B	HR	RBI	Avg.	BB	SO	SB	PO	A	E	Avg.
1992— Bend (N'West)............	OF	57	205	24	46	4	1	5	30	.224	19	54	8	65	7	0	1.000
1993— Central Valley (Calif.)..	OF	104	358	45	97	16	2	6	52	.271	44	74	6	141	8	6	.961
1994— Central Valley (Calif.)..	OF	50	192	25	58	8	1	6	35	.302	9	25	2	52	3	1	.982
— New Haven (East.)......	OF	58	205	25	52	6	0	6	32	.254	15	46	2	91	5	2	.980
1995— New Haven (East.)......	OF	124	453	78	136	30	1	21	*100	.300	56	93	8	202	*20	5	.978
1996— Colo. Springs (PCL) ...	OF-DH	110	415	67	140	19	2	16	74	.337	38	81	4	168	8	4	.978
— Colorado (N.L.)	OF	26	21	2	6	0	0	0	6	.286	2	5	0	1	0	0	1.000
1997— Colo. Springs (PCL) ...	OF-DH-1B	77	295	59	95	24	0	13	80	.322	28	47	6	135	9	1	.993
— Colorado (N.L.)	OF	15	20	4	5	2	0	0	0	.250	2	5	0	4	1	0	1.000
1998— Colo. Springs (PCL) ...	1B-OF-DH	85	301	50	98	21	2	15	60	.326	14	47	0	408	28	7	.984
— Colorado (N.L.)	1B-OF	19	29	7	11	3	0	1	9	.379	2	3	0	23	2	0	1.000
1999— Colorado (N.L.)	OF-1B	102	191	28	56	7	0	11	35	.293	17	34	1	122	7	1	.992
2000— Colo. Springs (PCL) ...	OF-1B	74	284	46	95	23	2	7	50	.335	26	44	1	196	13	4	.981
— Colorado (N.L.)	1B-OF	10	9	0	1	0	0	0	2	.111	0	2	0	3	0	0	1.000
— Milwaukee (N.L.)■......	1B-OF	31	42	3	9	2	0	1	4	.214	7	9	0	29	4	0	1.000
2001— Milwaukee (N.L.)........	OF-1B-DH	75	133	12	34	11	0	5	13	.256	8	29	0	74	2	2	.974
Major League totals (6 years)		278	445	56	122	25	0	18	69	.274	38	87	1	256	16	3	.989

ECKSTEIN, DAVID — 2B — ANGELS

PERSONAL: Born January 20, 1975, in Sanford, Fla. ... 5-8/165. ... Bats right, throws right. ... Full name: David Mark Eckstein.
HIGH SCHOOL: Seminole (Sanford, Fla.).
COLLEGE: Florida.
TRANSACTIONS/CAREER NOTES: Selected by Boston Red Sox organization in 19th round of free-agent draft (June 3, 1997). ... Claimed on waivers by Anaheim Angels (August 16, 2000).
STATISTICAL NOTES: Tied for New York-Pennsylvania League lead in sacrifice hits with eight in 1997. ... Led Florida State League in being hit by pitch with 22 in 1998. ... Led Florida State League second basemen in fielding percentage with .989 in 1998. ... Tied for Eastern League lead with 87 double plays by second baseman in 1999. ... Led International League in being hit by pitch with 20 in 2000. ... Led International League with .992 fielding percentage in 2000. ... Led A.L. with 16 sacrifice hits in 2001. ... Led A.L. in being hit by pitch with 21 in 2001.

Year Team (League)	Pos.	G	AB	R	H	2B	3B	HR	RBI	Avg.	BB	SO	SB	PO	A	E	Avg.
1997— Lowell (NY-Penn)	2B	68	249	43	75	11	4	4	39	.301	33	29	21	139	166	9	*.971
1998— Sarasota (FSL)	2B-SS	135	503	99	154	29	4	3	58	.306	87	51	45	214	368	8	†.986
1999— Trenton (East.)	2B-DH	131	483	109	151	22	5	6	52	.313	89	48	32	232	359	9	*.985
2000— Pawtucket (I.L.)	2B-SS	119	422	77	104	20	0	1	31	.246	60	45	11	183	324	4	†.992
— Edmonton (PCL)■......	2B	15	52	17	18	8	0	3	8	.346	9	1	5	27	28	0	1.000
2001— Anaheim (A.L.)	SS-2B-DH	153	582	82	166	26	2	4	41	.285	43	60	29	199	366	18	.969
Major League totals (1 year)		153	582	82	166	26	2	4	41	.285	43	60	29	199	366	18	.969

EDMONDS, JIM — OF — CARDINALS

PERSONAL: Born June 27, 1970, in Fullerton, Calif. ... 6-1/212. ... Bats left, throws left. ... Full name: James Patrick Edmonds. ... Name pronounced ED-muns.
HIGH SCHOOL: Diamond Bar (Calif.).
TRANSACTIONS/CAREER NOTES: Selected by California Angels organization in seventh round of free-agent draft (June 1, 1988). ... On disabled list (June 19-September 2, 1989; April 10-May 7 and May 23, 1991-remainder of season). ... On Vancouver disabled list (June 29-July 19, 1993). ... On California disabled list (May 26-June 10 and June 12-July 18, 1996); included rehabilitation assignment to Lake Elsinore (July 13-18). ... Angels franchise renamed Anaheim Angels for 1997 season. ... On disabled list (August 1-16, 1997). ... On Anaheim disabled list (March 30-August 2, 1999): included rehabilitation assignment to Lake Elsinore (July 26-August 2). ... Traded by Angels to St. Louis Cardinals for 2B/SS Adam Kennedy and P Kent Bottenfield (March 23, 2000).

E

RECORDS: Holds N.L. single-season record for most strikeouts by lefthander—167 (2000).
HONORS: Named outfielder on The Sporting News A.L. All-Star team (1995). ... Won A.L. Gold Glove as outfielder (1997-98). ... Won N.L. Gold Glove as outfielder (2000-01).
STATISTICAL NOTES: Had 23-game hitting streak (June 4-29, 1995). ... Career major league grand slams: 3.

Year Team (League)	Pos.	G	AB	R	H	2B	3B	HR	RBI	Avg.	BB	SO	SB	PO	A	E	Avg.
1988—Bend (N'West)	OF	35	122	23	27	4	0	0	13	.221	20	44	4	59	1	1	.984
1989—Quad City (Midw.)	OF	31	92	11	24	4	0	1	4	.261	7	34	1	47	2	3	.942
1990—Palm Springs (Calif.)	OF	91	314	36	92	18	6	3	56	.293	27	75	5	199	9	10	.954
1991—Palm Springs (Calif.)	OF-1B-P	60	187	28	55	15	1	2	27	.294	40	57	2	97	6	0	1.000
1992—Midland (Texas)	OF	70	246	42	77	15	2	8	32	.313	41	83	3	139	6	5	.967
—Edmonton (PCL)	OF	50	194	37	58	15	2	6	36	.299	14	55	3	79	5	1	.988
1993—Vancouver (PCL)	OF	95	356	59	112	28	4	9	74	.315	41	81	6	167	4	3	.983
—California (A.L.)	OF	18	61	5	15	4	1	0	4	.246	2	16	0	47	4	1	.981
1994—California (A.L.)	OF-1B	94	289	35	79	13	1	5	37	.273	30	72	4	301	20	3	.991
1995—California (A.L.)	OF	141	558	120	162	30	4	33	107	.290	51	130	1	401	8	1	.998
1996—California (A.L.)	OF-DH	114	431	73	131	28	3	27	66	.304	46	101	4	280	6	1	.997
—Lake Elsinore (Calif.)	OF-DH	5	15	4	6	2	0	1	4	.400	1	1	0	5	0	1	1.000
1997—Anaheim (A.L.)	OF-1B-DH	133	502	82	146	27	0	26	80	.291	60	80	5	395	16	5	.988
1998—Anaheim (A.L.)	OF	154	599	115	184	42	1	25	91	.307	57	114	7	392	10	5	.988
1999—Lake Elsinore (Calif.)	DH	5	19	4	8	2	0	0	3	.421	4	2	2	0	0	0	...
—Junior (A.L.)	OF-DH-1B	55	204	34	51	17	2	5	23	.250	28	45	5	138	5	1	.993
2000—St. Louis (N.L.)■	OF-1B	152	525	129	155	25	0	42	108	.295	103	167	10	392	14	4	.990
2001—St. Louis (N.L.)	OF-1B	150	500	95	152	38	1	30	110	.304	93	136	5	325	14	6	.983
American League totals (7 years)		709	2644	464	768	161	12	121	408	.290	274	558	26	1954	69	17	.992
National League totals (2 years)		302	1025	224	307	63	1	72	218	.300	196	303	15	717	28	10	.987
Major League totals (9 years)		1011	3669	688	1075	224	13	193	626	.293	470	861	41	2671	97	27	.990

DIVISION SERIES RECORD

RECORDS: Holds N.L. career record for most doubles—5. ... Shares N.L. career record for most extra-base hits—9.

Year Team (League)	Pos.	G	AB	R	H	2B	3B	HR	RBI	Avg.	BB	SO	SB	PO	A	E	Avg.
2000—St. Louis (N.L.)	OF	3	14	5	8	4	0	2	7	.571	1	2	1	7	0	0	1.000
2001—St. Louis (N.L.)	OF	5	17	3	4	1	0	2	3	.235	3	6	0	10	1	0	1.000
Division series totals (2 years)		8	31	8	12	5	0	4	10	.387	4	8	1	17	1	0	1.000

CHAMPIONSHIP SERIES RECORD

Year Team (League)	Pos.	G	AB	R	H	2B	3B	HR	RBI	Avg.	BB	SO	SB	PO	A	E	Avg.
2000—St. Louis (N.L.)	OF	5	22	1	5	1	0	1	5	.227	1	9	0	13	1	1	.933

ALL-STAR GAME RECORD

Year League	Pos.	AB	R	H	2B	3B	HR	RBI	Avg.	BB	SO	SB	PO	A	E	Avg.
1995—American	PH-OF	1	0	0	0	0	0	0	.000	0	1	0	0	0	0	...
2000—National	OF	2	0	1	0	0	0	0	.500	0	0	0	3	0	0	1.000
All-Star Game totals (2 years)		3	0	1	0	0	0	0	.333	0	1	0	3	0	0	1.000

RECORD AS PITCHER

Year League	W	L	Pct.	ERA	G	GS	CG	ShO	Sv.	IP	H	R	ER	BB	SO
1991—Palm Springs (Calif.)	0	0	...	0.00	1	0	0	0	0	2	1	0	0	3	2

EISCHEN, JOEY   P

PERSONAL: Born May 25, 1970, in West Covina, Calif. ... 6-1/200. ... Throws left, bats left. ... Full name: Joseph Raymond Eischen. ... Name pronounced EYE-shen.
HIGH SCHOOL: West Covina (Calif.).
JUNIOR COLLEGE: Pasadena (Calif.) City College.
TRANSACTIONS/CAREER NOTES: Selected by Chicago White Sox organization in fifth round of free-agent draft (June 1, 1988); did not sign. ... Selected by Texas Rangers organization in fourth round of free-agent draft (June 5, 1989). ... Traded by Rangers with P Jonathan Hurst and a player to be named later to Montreal Expos for P Oil Can Boyd (July 21, 1991); Expos acquired P Travis Buckley to complete deal (September 1, 1991). ... Traded by Expos with OF Roberto Kelly to Los Angeles Dodgers for OF Henry Rodriguez and IF Jeff Treadway (May 23, 1995). ... Traded by Dodgers with P John Cummings to Detroit Tigers for OF Chad Curtis (July 31, 1996). ... Traded by Tigers with P Cam Smith to San Diego Padres for C Brian Johnson and P Willie Blair (December 17, 1996). ... Traded by Padres to Cincinnati Reds for a player to be named later (March 16, 1997); Padres acquired IF Ray Brown to complete deal (March 19, 1997). ... On Cincinnati disabled list (March 25-April 26 and April 29-July 18, 1997); included rehabilitation assignment to Indianapolis (April 13-26). ... Granted free agency (December 21, 1997). ... Signed by New York Yankees organization (February 3, 1998). ... Released by Yankees (March 11, 1998). ... Signed by Reds (March 19, 1998). ... Released by Reds (March 12, 1999). ... Signed by Arizona Diamondbacks organization (March 18, 1999). ... Released by Diamondbacks (July 1, 1999). ... Signed by Adirondack, Northern League (July 1999). ... Signed by Cleveland Indians organization (December 23, 1999). ... Released by Indians (April 29, 2000). ... Signed by Expos organization (July 12, 2000). ... Granted free agency (October 12, 2001).
HONORS: Named Eastern League Pitcher of the Year (1993).
STATISTICAL NOTES: Led Pioneer League with 11 balks in 1989. ... Led Florida State League with 86 runs allowed in 1991. ... Pitched 5-0 no-hit victory against Vero Beach (June 16, 1992, first game).

Year League	W	L	Pct.	ERA	G	GS	CG	ShO	Sv.	IP	H	R	ER	BB	SO
1989—Butte (Pio.)	3	7	.300	5.30	12	12	0	0	0	52 2/3	50	45	31	38	57
1990—Gastonia (S.Atl.)	3	7	.300	2.70	17	14	0	0	0	73 1/3	51	36	22	40	69
1991—Charlotte (FSL)	4	10	.286	3.41	18	18	1	0	0	108 1/3	99	59	41	55	80
—West Palm Beach (FSL)■	4	2	.667	5.17	8	8	1	0	0	38 1/3	35	§27	22	24	26
1992—West Palm Beach (FSL)	9	8	.529	3.08	27	26	3	2	0	169 2/3	128	68	58	*83	167
1993—Harrisburg (East.)	*14	4	*.778	3.62	20	20	0	0	0	119 1/3	122	62	48	60	110
—Ottawa (I.L.)	2	2	.500	3.54	6	6	0	0	0	40 2/3	34	18	16	15	29

Year	League	W	L	Pct.	ERA	G	GS	CG	ShO	Sv.	IP	H	R	ER	BB	SO
1994— Ottawa (I.L.)		2	6	.250	4.94	48	2	0	0	2	62	54	38	34	40	57
— Montreal (N.L.)		0	0	...	54.00	1	0	0	0	0	$^2/_3$	4	4	4	0	1
1995— Ottawa (I.L.)		2	1	.667	1.72	11	0	0	0	0	$15^2/_3$	9	4	3	8	13
— Los Angeles (N.L.)■		0	0	...	3.10	17	0	0	0	0	$20^1/_3$	19	9	7	11	15
— Albuquerque (PCL)		3	0	1.000	0.00	13	0	0	0	2	$16^1/_3$	8	0	0	3	14
1996— Los Angeles (N.L.)		0	1	.000	4.78	28	0	0	0	0	$43^1/_3$	48	25	23	20	36
— Detroit (A.L.)■		1	1	.500	3.24	24	0	0	0	0	25	27	11	9	14	15
1997— Cincinnati (N.L.)■		0	0	...	6.75	1	0	0	0	0	$1^1/_3$	2	2	1	1	2
— Indianapolis (A.A.)		1	0	1.000	1.27	26	5	0	0	2	$42^2/_3$	41	7	6	13	26
1998— Indianapolis (I.L.)		2	5	.286	4.54	61	0	0	0	2	$73^1/_3$	73	42	37	29	60
1999— Tucson (PCL)■		1	3	.250	9.07	27	1	0	0	1	$41^2/_3$	63	47	42	26	36
— Adirondack (Nor.)■		4	2	.667	3.75	7	7	1	0	0	48	52	22	20	11	49
2000— Buffalo (I.L.)■		0	0	...	40.50	1	0	0	0	0	$^2/_3$	4	3	3	0	0
— Ottawa (I.L.)■		0	4	.000	3.64	10	9	0	0	0	$59^1/_3$	55	31	24	22	34
2001— Ottawa (I.L.)		2	3	.400	2.24	34	1	0	0	7	$52^1/_3$	42	16	13	11	54
— Montreal (N.L.)		0	1	.000	4.85	24	0	0	0	0	$29^2/_3$	29	17	16	16	19
A.L. totals (1 year)		1	1	.500	3.24	24	0	0	0	0	25	27	11	9	14	15
N.L. totals (5 years)		0	2	.000	4.81	71	0	0	0	0	$95^1/_3$	102	57	51	48	73
Major League totals (5 years)		1	3	.250	4.49	95	0	0	0	0	$120^1/_3$	129	68	60	62	88

ELARTON, SCOTT   P   ROCKIES

PERSONAL: Born February 23, 1976, in Lamar, Colo. ... 6-7/240. ... Throws right, bats right. ... Full name: Vincent Scott Elarton.
HIGH SCHOOL: Lamar (Colo.).
TRANSACTIONS/CAREER NOTES: Selected by Houston Astros organization in first round (25th pick overall) of free-agent draft (June 2, 1994). ... On Houston disabled list (March 29-April 23, 2000); included rehabilitation assignments to New Orleans (April 6-11) and Round Rock (April 18). ... On Houston disabled list (July 17-31, 2001). ... Traded by Astros with a player to be named later to Colorado Rockies for P Pedro Astacio (July 31, 2001). ... On Colorado disabled list (July 31-September 4, 2001); included rehabilitation assignment to Colorado Springs (August 29-September 4).
STATISTICAL NOTES: Tied for Florida State League lead with 13 home runs allowed in 1996.
MISCELLANEOUS: Appeared in one game as outfielder with no chances (1999).

Year	League	W	L	Pct.	ERA	G	GS	CG	ShO	Sv.	IP	H	R	ER	BB	SO
1994— Gulf Coast Astros (GCL).....		4	0	1.000	0.00	5	5	0	0	0	28	9	0	0	5	28
— Quad City (Midw.)		4	1	.800	3.29	9	9	0	0	0	$54^2/_3$	42	23	20	18	42
1995— Quad City (Midw.)		13	7	.650	4.45	26	26	0	0	0	$149^2/_3$	149	86	74	71	112
1996— Kissimmee (FSL)		12	7	.632	2.92	27	27	3	1	0	$172^1/_3$	154	67	56	54	130
1997— Jackson (Texas)		7	4	.636	3.24	20	20	2	0	0	$133^1/_3$	103	57	48	47	141
— New Orleans (A.A.)		4	4	.500	5.33	9	9	0	0	0	54	51	36	32	17	50
1998— New Orleans (PCL)		9	4	.692	4.01	14	14	2	1	0	92	71	42	41	41	100
— Houston (N.L.)		2	1	.667	3.32	28	2	0	0	2	57	40	21	21	20	56
1999— Houston (N.L.)		9	5	.643	3.48	42	15	0	0	1	124	111	55	48	43	121
2000— New Orleans (PCL)		1	0	1.000	0.75	2	2	0	0	0	12	3	1	1	4	12
— Round Rock (Texas)		1	0	1.000	2.84	1	1	0	0	0	$6^1/_3$	7	2	2	0	7
— Houston (N.L.)		17	7	.708	4.81	30	30	2	0	0	$192^2/_3$	198	117	103	84	131
2001— Houston (N.L.)		4	8	.333	7.14	20	20	0	0	0	$109^2/_3$	126	88	87	49	76
— Colorado Springs (PCL)■..		0	1	.000	7.04	2	2	0	0	0	$7^2/_3$	14	6	6	0	8
— Colorado (N.L.)		0	2	.000	6.65	4	4	0	0	0	23	20	17	17	10	11
Major League totals (4 years)		32	23	.582	4.91	124	71	2	0	3	$506^1/_3$	495	298	276	206	395

DIVISION SERIES RECORD

Year	League	W	L	Pct.	ERA	G	GS	CG	ShO	Sv.	IP	H	R	ER	BB	SO
1998— Houston (N.L.)		0	1	.000	4.50	1	0	0	0	0	2	1	1	1	1	3
1999— Houston (N.L.)		0	0	...	3.86	2	0	0	0	0	$2^1/_3$	4	1	1	1	3
Division series totals (2 years)		0	1	.000	4.15	3	0	0	0	0	$4^1/_3$	5	2	2	2	6

ELDRED, CAL   P

PERSONAL: Born November 24, 1967, in Cedar Rapids, Iowa. ... 6-4/237. ... Throws right, bats right. ... Full name: Calvin John Eldred.
HIGH SCHOOL: Urbana (Iowa) Community.
COLLEGE: Iowa.
TRANSACTIONS/CAREER NOTES: Selected by Milwaukee Brewers organization in first round (17th pick overall) of free-agent draft (June 5, 1989). ... On disabled list (May 15, 1995-remainder of season). ... On Milwaukee disabled list (March 29-July 14, 1996); included rehabilitation assignment to New Orleans (June 10-July 9). ... On disabled list (July 26, 1998-remainder of season). ... On Milwaukee disabled list (March 29-April 20 and July 2-August 15, 1999); included rehabilitation assignments to Huntsville (April 8-17) and Louisville (April 18-20 and July 31-August 15). ... Traded by Brewers with SS Jose Valentin to Chicago White Sox for P Jaime Navarro and P John Snyder (January 12, 2000). ... On Chicago disabled list (July 15-September 27, 2000); included rehabilitation assignment to Charlotte (August 29-September 22). ... Granted free agency (November 8, 2000). ... Re-signed by White Sox (December 7, 2000). ... On disabled list (April 12, 2001-remainder of season). ... Granted free agency (November 7, 2001).
RECORDS: Shares N.L. single-inning record for most consecutive home runs allowed—3 (August 22, 1999, first inning).
HONORS: Named A.L. Rookie Pitcher of the Year by THE SPORTING NEWS (1992).
STATISTICAL NOTES: Led American Association with 12 hit batsmen in 1991.
MISCELLANEOUS: Appeared in one game as pinch runner (1998). ... Scored one run in three appearances as pinch runner (1999).

Year	League	W	L	Pct.	ERA	G	GS	CG	ShO	Sv.	IP	H	R	ER	BB	SO
1989— Beloit (Midw.)		2	1	.667	2.30	5	5	0	0	0	$31^1/_3$	23	10	8	11	32
1990— Stockton (Calif.)		4	2	.667	1.62	7	7	3	1	0	50	31	12	9	19	75
— El Paso (Texas).................		5	4	.556	4.49	19	19	0	0	0	$110^1/_3$	126	61	55	47	93
1991— Denver (A.A.)...................		13	9	.591	3.75	29	*29	3	1	0	*185	161	82	77	84	*168
— Milwaukee (A.L.)		2	0	1.000	4.50	3	3	0	0	0	16	20	9	8	6	10

E

Year League	W	L	Pct.	ERA	G	GS	CG	ShO	Sv.	IP	H	R	ER	BB	SO
1992—Denver (A.A.)	10	6	.625	3.00	19	19	4	1	0	141	122	49	47	42	99
—Milwaukee (A.L.)	11	2	.846	1.79	14	14	2	1	0	100 1/3	76	21	20	23	62
1993—Milwaukee (A.L.)	16	16	.500	4.01	36	•36	8	1	0	*258	232	120	115	91	180
1994—Milwaukee (A.L.)	11	11	.500	4.68	25	•25	6	0	0	179	158	96	93	84	98
1995—Milwaukee (A.L.)	1	1	.500	3.42	4	4	0	0	0	23 2/3	24	10	9	10	18
1996—New Orleans (A.A.)	2	2	.500	3.34	6	6	0	0	0	32 1/3	24	12	12	17	30
—Milwaukee (A.L.)	4	4	.500	4.46	15	15	0	0	0	84 2/3	82	43	42	38	50
1997—Milwaukee (A.L.)	13	•15	.464	4.99	34	34	1	1	0	202	207	118	112	89	122
1998—Milwaukee (A.L.)	4	8	.333	4.80	23	23	0	0	0	133	157	82	71	61	86
1999—Huntsville (Sou.)	0	1	.000	7.50	2	2	1	0	0	12	13	10	10	3	10
—Louisville (I.L.)	0	1	.000	5.30	4	4	0	0	0	18 2/3	19	12	11	10	21
—Milwaukee (N.L.)	2	8	.200	7.79	20	15	0	0	0	82	101	75	71	46	60
2000—Chicago (A.L.)■	10	2	.833	4.58	20	20	2	1	0	112	103	61	57	59	97
—Charlotte (I.L.)	0	1	.000	7.20	2	2	0	0	0	5	4	4	4	0	1
2001—Chicago (A.L.)	0	1	.000	13.50	2	2	0	0	0	6	12	9	9	3	6
A.L. totals (9 years)	68	52	.567	4.26	153	153	19	4	0	981 2/3	914	487	465	403	643
N.L. totals (2 years)	6	16	.273	5.94	43	38	0	0	0	215	258	157	142	107	146
Major League totals (11 years)	74	68	.521	4.57	196	191	19	4	0	1196 2/3	1172	644	607	510	789

ELLIS, MARK — SS/2B — ATHLETICS

PERSONAL: Born June 6, 1977, in Rapid City, S.D. ... 5-11/180. ... Bats right, throws right. ... Full name: Mark William Ellis.
HIGH SCHOOL: Stevens (Rapid City, S.D.).
COLLEGE: Florida.
TRANSACTIONS/CAREER NOTES: Selected by Kansas City Royals organization in ninth round of free-agent draft (June 2, 1999). ... Traded by Royals with OF Johnny Damon and player to be named later to Oakland Athletics as part of three-way deal in which Royals received P Roberto Hernandez from Tampa Bay Devil Rays, A's received P Cory Lidle from Devil Rays, Royals received C A.J. Hinch, IF Angel Berroa and cash from A's and Devil Rays received OF Ben Grieve and player to be named later or cash from A's (January 8, 2001).
STATISTICAL NOTES: Led Northwest League shortstops with 384 total chances in 1999. ... Led Carolina League with .404 on-base percentage in 2000. ... Led Carolina League shortstops with 219 putouts, 31 errors and 78 double plays in 2000.

							BATTING							FIELDING		
Year Team (League)	Pos.	G	AB	R	H	2B	3B	HR	RBI	Avg.	BB	SO	SB	PO	A	E	Avg.
1999—Spokane (N'West)	SS	71	281	67	92	14	0	7	47	.327	47	40	21	*138	230	16	*.958
2000—Wilmington (Caro.)	SS-2B	132	484	83	*146	27	4	6	62	.302	78	72	25	†224	421	†31	.954
—Wichita (Texas)	2B	7	22	4	7	1	0	0	4	.318	5	5	1	15	15	0	1.000
2001—Sacramento (PCL)■	SS	132	472	71	129	38	0	10	53	.273	54	78	21	199	382	19	.968

ELLIS, ROBERT — P

E

PERSONAL: Born December 15, 1970, in Baton Rouge, La. ... 6-5/220. ... Throws right, bats right. ... Full name: Robert Randolph Ellis.
HIGH SCHOOL: Belaire (Baton Rouge, La.).
JUNIOR COLLEGE: Panola Junior College (Texas).
COLLEGE: Northwestern State (La.).
TRANSACTIONS/CAREER NOTES: Selected by Chicago White Sox organization in third round of free-agent draft (June 4, 1990). ... On South Bend disabled list (May 20-July 1, 1992). ... On disabled list (July 25, 1994-remainder of season and May 17, 1995-remainder of season). ... Traded by White Sox to California Angels for C Pat Borders (July 27, 1996). ... Angels franchise renamed Anaheim Angels for 1997 season. ... Granted free agency (October 15, 1997). ... Signed by Detroit Tigers organization (November 10, 1997). ... Released by Tigers (March 3, 1998). ... Signed by Milwaukee Brewers organization (March 4, 1998). ... On Louisville disabled list (March 23-30, 1998). ... Granted free agency (October 16, 1998). ... Signed by Houston Astros organization (January 15, 1999). ... Granted free agency (October 15, 1999). ... Signed by Toronto Blue Jays organization (January 6, 2000). ... Released by Blue Jays (May 23, 2000). ... Signed by Monterrey, Mexican League (June 2000). ... Signed by Arizona Diamondbacks organization (October 10, 2000). ... On Arizona disabled list (July 23-September 25, 2001); included rehabilitation assignment to Tucson (August 4-16). ... Granted free agency (December 21, 2001).

Year League	W	L	Pct.	ERA	G	GS	CG	ShO	Sv.	IP	H	R	ER	BB	SO
1991—Utica (NY-Penn)	3	•9	.250	4.62	15	15	1	1	0	87 2/3	86	*66	45	61	66
1992—South Bend (Midw.)	6	5	.545	2.34	18	18	1	1	0	123	90	46	32	35	97
—GC White Sox (GCL)	1	0	1.000	10.80	1	1	0	0	0	5	10	6	6	1	4
1993—Sarasota (FSL)	7	8	.467	2.51	15	15	*8	2	0	104	81	37	29	31	79
—Birmingham (Sou.)	6	3	.667	3.10	12	12	2	1	0	81 1/3	68	33	28	21	77
1994—Nashville (A.A.)	4	10	.286	6.09	19	19	1	0	0	105	126	77	71	55	76
1995—Nashville (A.A.)	1	1	.500	2.18	4	4	0	0	0	20 2/3	16	7	5	10	9
1996—Nashville (A.A.)	3	8	.273	6.01	19	13	1	0	0	70 1/3	78	49	47	45	35
—Birmingham (Sou.)	0	1	.000	11.05	2	2	0	0	0	7 1/3	6	9	9	8	8
—Vancouver (PCL)■	2	3	.400	3.25	7	7	1	0	0	44 1/3	30	19	16	28	29
—California (A.L.)	0	0	...	0.00	3	0	0	0	0	5	0	0	0	4	5
1997—Vancouver (PCL)■	9	10	.474	5.92	29	23	3	0	0	149	185	108	98	83	70
1998—Louisville (I.L.)■	10	10	.500	5.63	30	28	0	0	0	150 1/3	171	103	94	78	79
1999—New Orleans (PCL)■	7	12	.368	5.43	27	27	1	0	0	155 2/3	176	106	94	51	105
2000—Syracuse (I.L.)■	1	1	.500	4.50	16	0	0	0	2	18	17	10	9	15	18
—Monterrey (Mex.)■	8	5	.615	3.51	15	14	3	0	0	92 1/3	78	39	36	32	70
2001—Tucson (PCL)■	1	1	.500	3.08	5	5	0	0	0	26 1/3	25	12	9	5	13
—Arizona (N.L.)	6	5	.545	5.77	19	17	0	0	0	92	106	61	59	34	41
A.L. totals (1 year)	0	0	...	0.00	3	0	0	0	0	5	0	0	0	4	5
N.L. totals (1 year)	6	5	.545	5.77	19	17	0	0	0	92	106	61	59	34	41
Major League totals (2 years)	6	5	.545	5.47	22	17	0	0	0	97	106	61	59	38	46

PERSONAL: Born January 23, 1970, in Vancouver, Wash. ... 6-2/190. ... Throws left, bats left. ... Full name: Alan Duane Embree.

HIGH SCHOOL: Prairie (Vancouver, Wash.).

TRANSACTIONS/CAREER NOTES: Selected by Cleveland Indians organization in fifth round of free-agent draft (June 5, 1989). ... On Cleveland disabled list (April 1-June 2 and June 2, 1993-remainder of season); included rehabilitation assignment to Canton/Akron (June 2-15). ... On Cleveland disabled list (August 1-September 7, 1996); included rehabilitation assignment to Buffalo (August 6-September 4). ... Traded by Indians with OF Kenny Lofton to Atlanta Braves for OF Marquis Grissom and OF Dave Justice (March 25, 1997). ... Traded by Braves to Arizona Diamondbacks for P Russ Springer (June 23, 1998). ... Traded by Diamondbacks to San Francisco Giants for OF Dante Powell (November 10, 1998). ... On San Francisco disabled list (May 23-June 12, 2001); included rehabilitation assignment to Fresno (May 28-June 12). ... Traded by Giants to Chicago White Sox for P Derek Hasselhoff (June 29, 2001). ... Granted free agency (November 6, 2001). ... Signed by San Diego Padres (December 27, 2001).

RECORDS: Shares major league record for most home runs allowed in one inning—4 (May 20, 2001, seventh inning).

Year League	W	L	Pct.	ERA	G	GS	CG	ShO	Sv.	IP	H	R	ER	BB	SO
1990— Burlington (Appl.)	4	4	.500	2.64	15	•15	0	0	0	81 2/3	87	36	24	30	58
1991— Columbus (S.Atl.)	10	8	.556	3.59	27	26	3	1	0	155 1/3	126	80	62	77	137
1992— Kinston (Caro.)	10	5	.667	3.30	15	15	1	0	0	101	89	48	37	32	115
— Canton/Akron (East.)	7	2	.778	2.28	12	12	0	0	0	79	61	24	20	28	56
— Cleveland (A.L.)	0	2	.000	7.00	4	4	0	0	0	18	19	14	14	8	12
1993— Canton/Akron (East.)	0	0	...	3.38	1	1	0	0	0	5 1/3	3	2	2	3	4
1994— Canton/Akron (East.)	9	•16	.360	5.50	30	27	2	1	0	157	183	106	96	64	81
1995— Buffalo (A.A.)	3	4	.429	0.89	30	0	0	0	5	40 2/3	31	10	4	19	56
— Cleveland (A.L.)	3	2	.600	5.11	23	0	0	0	1	24 2/3	23	16	14	16	23
1996— Cleveland (A.L.)	1	1	.500	6.39	24	0	0	0	0	31	30	26	22	21	33
— Buffalo (A.A.)	4	1	.800	3.93	20	0	0	0	5	34 1/3	26	16	15	14	46
1997— Atlanta (N.L.)■	3	1	.750	2.54	66	0	0	0	0	46	36	13	13	20	45
1998— Atlanta (N.L.)	1	0	1.000	4.34	20	0	0	0	0	18 2/3	23	14	9	10	19
— Arizona (N.L.)■	3	2	.600	4.11	35	0	0	0	1	35	33	18	16	13	24
1999— San Francisco (N.L.)■	3	2	.600	3.38	68	0	0	0	0	58 2/3	42	22	22	26	53
2000— San Francisco (N.L.)	3	5	.375	4.95	63	0	0	0	2	60	62	34	33	25	49
2001— San Francisco (N.L.)	0	2	.000	11.25	22	0	0	0	0	20	34	26	25	10	25
— Fresno (PCL)	1	0	1.000	1.13	7	0	0	0	1	8	5	3	1	1	6
— Chicago (A.L.)■	1	2	.333	5.03	39	0	0	0	0	34	31	21	19	7	34
A.L. totals (4 years)	5	7	.417	5.77	90	4	0	0	1	107 2/3	103	77	69	52	102
N.L. totals (5 years)	13	12	.520	4.46	274	0	0	0	3	238 1/3	230	127	118	104	215
Major League totals (8 years)	18	19	.486	4.86	364	4	0	0	4	346	333	204	187	156	317

DIVISION SERIES RECORD

Year League	W	L	Pct.	ERA	G	GS	CG	ShO	Sv.	IP	H	R	ER	BB	SO
1996— Cleveland (A.L.)	0	0	...	9.00	3	0	0	0	0	1	0	1	1	0	1
2000— San Francisco (N.L.)	0	0	...	0.00	2	0	0	0	0	1 2/3	0	0	0	0	0
Division series totals (2 years)	0	0	...	3.38	5	0	0	0	0	2 2/3	0	1	1	0	1

CHAMPIONSHIP SERIES RECORD

Year League	W	L	Pct.	ERA	G	GS	CG	ShO	Sv.	IP	H	R	ER	BB	SO
1995— Cleveland (A.L.)	0	0	...	0.00	1	0	0	0	0	1/3	0	0	0	0	0
1997— Atlanta (N.L.)	0	0	...	0.00	1	0	0	0	0	1	0	0	0	1	1
Champ. series totals (2 years)	0	0	...	0.00	2	0	0	0	0	1 1/3	0	0	0	1	2

WORLD SERIES RECORD

Year League	W	L	Pct.	ERA	G	GS	CG	ShO	Sv.	IP	H	R	ER	BB	SO
1995— Cleveland (A.L.)	0	0	...	2.70	4	0	0	0	0	3 1/3	2	1	1	2	2

E

PERSONAL: Born March 8, 1976, in Las Matas de Faran, Dominican Republic. ... 6-3/187. ... Bats right, throws right. ... Full name: Juan DeDios Encarnacion. ... Name pronounced en-car-nah-CION.

HIGH SCHOOL: Liceo Mercedes Maria Mateo (Las Matas de Faran, Dominican Republic).

TRANSACTIONS/CAREER NOTES: Signed as non-drafted free agent by Detroit Tigers organization (December 27, 1992). ... On Detroit disabled list (March 20-April 29, 1998); included rehabilitation assignment to Lakeland (April 24-29). ... On suspended list (May 27-29, 2000). ... Traded by Tigers with P Luis Pineda to Cincinnati Reds for OF Dmitri Young (December 11, 2001).

STATISTICAL NOTES: Tied for Florida State League lead in double plays by outfielder with four in 1996. ... Led Southern League in being hit by pitch with 19 in 1997. ... Tied for International League lead in double plays by outfielder with three in 1998. ... Had 19-game hitting streak (April 16-May 7, 2000). ... Career major league grand slams: 1.

Year Team (League)	Pos.	G	AB	R	H	2B	3B	HR	RBI	Avg.	BB	SO	SB	PO	A	E	Avg.
1993— Dom. Tigers (DSL)	OF	72	251	36	63	13	4	13	49	.251	15	65	6	110	13	17	.879
1994— Bristol (Appl.)	OF	54	197	16	49	7	1	4	31	.249	13	54	9	83	*9	3	.968
— Fayetteville (S.Atl.)	OF	24	83	6	16	1	1	1	4	.193	8	36	1	22	1	2	.920
— Lakeland (FSL)	OF	3	6	1	2	0	0	0	0	.333	0	3	0	0	0	0	...
1995— Fayetteville (S.Atl.)	OF	124	457	62	129	31	7	16	72	.282	30	113	30	143	10	7	.956
1996— Lakeland (FSL)	OF	131	499	54	120	31	2	15	58	.240	24	104	11	233	12	6	.976
1997— Jacksonville (Sou.)	OF	131	493	91	159	31	4	26	90	.323	43	86	17	208	12	3	.987
— Detroit (A.L.)	OF	11	33	3	7	1	1	1	5	.212	3	12	3	22	0	0	1.000
1998— Lakeland (FSL)	OF	4	16	4	4	0	1	0	4	.250	2	4	4	7	1	0	1.000
— Toledo (I.L.)	OF	92	356	55	102	17	3	8	41	.287	29	85	24	168	10	5	.973
— Detroit (A.L.)	OF-DH	40	164	30	54	9	4	7	21	.329	7	31	7	60	4	1	.985
1999— Detroit (A.L.)	OF	132	509	62	130	30	6	19	74	.255	14	113	33	264	10	9	.968
2000— Detroit (A.L.)	OF	141	547	75	158	25	6	14	72	.289	29	90	16	363	3	5	.987
2001— Detroit (A.L.)	OF-DH	120	417	52	101	19	7	12	52	.242	25	93	9	247	5	6	.977
Major League totals (5 years)		444	1670	222	450	84	24	53	224	.269	78	339	68	956	22	21	.979

ENCARNACION, MARIO — OF — ROCKIES

PERSONAL: Born September 24, 1977, in Bani, Dominican Republic. ... 6-2/205. ... Bats right, throws right. ... Full name: Mario Gonzalez Encarnacion.

TRANSACTIONS/CAREER NOTES: Signed as non-drafted free agent by Oakland Athletics organization (July 11, 1994). ... On Sacramento disabled list (May 25-July 7, 2000). ... On Sacramento disabled list (April 5-July 5, 2001). ... Traded by A's with 2B/SS Jose Ortiz and P Todd Belitz to Colorado Rockies for OF Jermaine Dye (July 25, 2001). ... On Colorado Springs disabled list (August 10-21, 2001).

Year — Team (League)	Pos.	G	AB	R	H	2B	3B	HR	RBI	Avg.	BB	SO	SB	PO	A	E	Avg.
1995—Dom. Athletics (DSL) .	OF	64	229	56	79	11	5	8	44	.345	40	36	17	112	9	7	.945
1996—W. Michigan (Midw.)..	OF	118	401	55	92	14	3	7	43	.229	49	131	23	192	13	11	.949
1997—Modesto (Calif.)	OF	111	364	70	108	17	9	18	78	.297	42	121	14	145	7	12	.927
1998—Huntsville (Sou.)	OF	110	357	70	97	15	2	15	61	.272	60	123	11	181	8	6	.969
1999—Midland (Texas).........	OF-DH	94	353	69	109	21	4	18	71	.309	47	86	9	126	6	9	.936
—Vancouver (PCL)	OF-DH	39	145	18	35	5	0	3	17	.241	6	44	5	91	6	4	.960
2000—Sacramento (PCL)......	OF	81	301	51	81	16	3	13	61	.269	36	95	15	165	10	5	.972
—Modesto (Calif.)	OF	5	15	1	3	0	0	0	1	.200	1	4	0	11	2	0	1.000
2001—Sacramento (PCL).....	OF	51	186	29	53	8	2	12	33	.285	17	61	4	66	5	4	.947
—Colo. Springs (PCL)■	OF	16	45	8	17	5	0	2	10	.378	4	8	0	22	1	0	1.000
—Colorado (N.L.)	OF	20	62	3	14	1	0	0	3	.226	5	14	2	35	1	0	1.000
Major League totals (1 year)		20	62	3	14	1	0	0	3	.226	5	14	2	35	1	0	1.000

ENNIS, JOHN — P — BRAVES

PERSONAL: Born October 17, 1979, in Montrose, Colo. ... 6-5/220. ... Throws right, bats right. ... Full name: John Wayne Ennis.
HIGH SCHOOL: Monroe (Panorama City, Calif.).
TRANSACTIONS/CAREER NOTES: Selected by Atlanta Braves organization in 14th round of free-agent draft (June 2, 1998). ... On disabled list (May 15-30, 2001).

Year — League	W	L	Pct.	ERA	G	GS	CG	ShO	Sv.	IP	H	R	ER	BB	SO
1998—Gulf Coast Braves (GCL)	0	3	.000	4.62	8	2	0	0	0	25 1/3	30	16	13	6	18
1999—Danville (Appl.)..................	4	3	.571	5.07	13	13	13	0	0	65 2/3	71	46	37	21	60
2000—Macon (S.Atl.)	7	4	.636	2.55	18	16	0	0	0	98 2/3	77	37	28	25	105
2001—Myrtle Beach (Caro.)	6	8	.429	3.58	25	25	1	0	0	138 1/3	111	63	55	45	144

ENSBERG, MORGAN — 3B — ASTROS

PERSONAL: Born August 26, 1975, in Redondo Beach, Calif. ... 6-2/210. ... Bats right, throws right. ... Full name: Morgan P. Ensberg.
HIGH SCHOOL: Redondo Union (Redondo Beach, Calif.).
COLLEGE: Southern California.
TRANSACTIONS/CAREER NOTES: Selected by Houston Astros organization in ninth round of free-agent draft (June 2, 1998). ... On disabled list (June 22-August 10, 2001).
STATISTICAL NOTES: Led New York-Pennsylvania League third basemen with .926 fielding percentage in 1998. ... Led Texas League with 415 total chances in 2000.

Year — Team (League)	Pos.	G	AB	R	H	2B	3B	HR	RBI	Avg.	BB	SO	SB	PO	A	E	Avg.
1998—Auburn (NY-Penn)......	3B-SS	59	196	39	45	10	1	5	31	.230	46	51	15	39	101	11	†.927
1999—Kissimmee (FSL)........	3B-SS-1B	123	427	72	102	25	2	15	69	.239	68	90	17	73	243	35	.900
2000—Round Rock (Texas)...	3B	137	483	95	145	34	0	28	90	.300	92	107	9	•84	*307	24	*.942
—Houston (N.L.).........	3B	4	7	0	2	0	0	0	0	.286	0	1	0	1	1	1	.667
2001—New Orleans (PCL).....	3B-SS	87	316	65	98	20	0	23	61	.310	45	60	6	50	172	17	.929
Major League totals (1 year)		4	7	0	2	0	0	0	0	.286	0	1	0	1	1	1	.667

ERDOS, TODD — P

PERSONAL: Born November 21, 1973, in Washington, Pa. ... 6-1/204. ... Throws right, bats right. ... Full name: Todd Michael Erdos. ... Name pronounced er-DOHS.
HIGH SCHOOL: Meadville (Pa.).
TRANSACTIONS/CAREER NOTES: Selected by San Diego Padres organization in ninth round of free-agent draft (June 1, 1992). ... On disabled list (June 4, 1994-entire season). ... Selected by Arizona Diamondbacks in second round (41st pick overall) of expansion draft (November 18, 1997). ... Traded by Diamondbacks with P Marty Janzen to New York Yankees for IF Andy Fox (March 8, 1998). ... On Columbus disabled list (July 24, 1998-remainder of season). ... Claimed on waivers by Padres (July 12, 2000). ... Granted free agency (October 15, 2000). ... Signed by Boston Red Sox organization (January 29, 2001). ... Granted free agency (December 21, 2001).
STATISTICAL NOTES: Led Northwest League with 13 home runs allowed in 1993.

Year — League	W	L	Pct.	ERA	G	GS	CG	ShO	Sv.	IP	H	R	ER	BB	SO
1992—Arizona Padres (Ariz.)	3	4	.429	2.65	12	9	1	0	0	57 2/3	36	28	17	18	61
—Spokane (N'West)	1	0	1.000	0.69	2	2	0	0	0	13	9	2	1	5	11
1993—Spokane (N'West)	5	6	.455	3.19	16	15	0	0	0	90 1/3	73	39	32	•53	64
—Waterloo (Midw.)	1	9	.100	8.31	11	11	0	0	0	47 2/3	64	51	44	31	27
1994—Arizona Padres (Ariz.)							Did not play.								
1995—Idaho Falls (Pio.)................	5	3	.625	3.48	32	0	0	0	0	41 1/3	34	19	16	30	48
1996—Rancho Cuca. (Calif.)	3	3	.500	3.74	55	0	0	0	17	67 1/3	63	33	28	37	82
1997—Mobile (Sou.)	1	4	.200	3.36	55	0	0	0	27	59	45	22	22	22	49
—San Diego (N.L.)	2	0	1.000	5.27	11	0	0	0	0	13 2/3	17	9	8	4	13
1998—Columbus (I.L.)■..............	3	2	.600	4.62	39	0	0	0	16	48 2/3	52	27	25	20	50
—New York (A.L.).................	0	0	...	9.00	2	0	0	0	0	2	5	2	2	1	0

E

Year League	W	L	Pct.	ERA	G	GS	CG	ShO	Sv.	IP	H	R	ER	BB	SO
1999— Columbus (I.L.)	3	2	.600	6.56	27	8	0	0	0	59	70	47	43	25	53
—New York (A.L.)	0	0	...	3.86	4	0	0	0	0	7	5	4	3	4	4
2000—New York (A.L.)	0	0	...	5.04	14	0	0	0	1	25	31	14	14	11	18
—San Diego (N.L.)■	0	0	...	6.67	22	0	0	0	1	$29^{2}/_{3}$	32	24	22	17	16
2001—Pawtucket (I.L.)■	5	1	.833	3.06	49	0	0	0	7	$67^{2}/_{3}$	59	25	23	24	54
—Boston (A.L.)	0	0	...	4.96	10	0	0	0	0	$16^{1}/_{3}$	15	9	9	8	7
A.L. totals (4 years)	0	0	...	5.01	30	0	0	0	1	$50^{1}/_{3}$	56	29	28	24	29
N.L. totals (2 years)	2	0	1.000	6.23	33	0	0	0	1	$43^{1}/_{3}$	49	33	30	21	29
Major League totals (5 years)	2	0	1.000	5.57	63	0	0	0	2	$93^{2}/_{3}$	105	62	58	45	58

ERICKSON, SCOTT   P   ORIOLES

PERSONAL: Born February 2, 1968, in Long Beach, Calif. ... 6-4/230. ... Throws right, bats right. ... Full name: Scott Gavin Erickson.
HIGH SCHOOL: Homestead (Cupertino, Calif.).
JUNIOR COLLEGE: San Jose City College.
COLLEGE: Arizona.
TRANSACTIONS/CAREER NOTES: Selected by New York Mets organization in 36th round of free-agent draft (June 2, 1986); did not sign. ... Selected by Houston Astros organization in 34th round of free-agent draft (June 2, 1987); did not sign. ... Selected by Toronto Blue Jays organization in 44th round of free-agent draft (June 1, 1988); did not sign. ... Selected by Minnesota Twins organization in fourth round of free-agent draft (June 5, 1989). ... On disabled list (June 30-July 15, 1991; April 3-18, 1993 and May 15-31, 1994). ... Traded by Twins to Baltimore Orioles for P Scott Klingenbeck and a player to be named later (July 7, 1995); Twins acquired OF Kimera Bartee to complete deal (September 18, 1995). ... On Baltimore disabled list (March 28-May 4 and July 7, 2000-remainder of season); included rehabilitation assignments to Frederick (April 25) and Bowie (April 30). ... On disabled list (April 1, 2001-entire season).
STATISTICAL NOTES: Pitched 5-0 one-hit, complete-game victory against Boston (July 24, 1992, first game). ... Pitched 6-0 no-hit victory against Milwaukee (April 27, 1994). ... Tied for A.L. lead with nine hit batsmen in 1994.
MISCELLANEOUS: Appeared in one game as pinch runner (2000).

Year League	W	L	Pct.	ERA	G	GS	CG	ShO	Sv.	IP	H	R	ER	BB	SO
1989— Visalia (Calif.)	3	4	.429	2.97	12	12	2	0	0	$78^{2}/_{3}$	79	29	26	22	59
1990— Orlando (Sou.)	8	3	.727	3.03	15	15	3	1	0	101	75	38	34	24	69
—Minnesota (A.L.)	8	4	.667	2.87	19	17	1	0	0	113	108	49	36	51	53
1991— Minnesota (A.L.)	•20	8	.714	3.18	32	32	5	3	0	204	189	80	72	71	108
1992— Minnesota (A.L.)	13	12	.520	3.40	32	32	5	3	0	212	197	86	80	83	101
1993— Minnesota (A.L.)	8	*19	.296	5.19	34	34	1	0	0	$218^{2}/_{3}$	*266	*138	126	71	116
1994— Minnesota (A.L.)	8	11	.421	5.44	23	23	2	1	0	144	173	95	87	59	104
1995— Minnesota (A.L.)	4	6	.400	5.95	15	15	0	0	0	$87^{2}/_{3}$	102	61	58	32	45
—Baltimore (A.L.)■	9	4	.692	3.89	17	16	7	2	0	$108^{2}/_{3}$	111	47	47	35	61
1996— Baltimore (A.L.)	13	12	.520	5.02	34	34	6	0	0	$222^{1}/_{3}$	262	137	124	66	100
1997— Baltimore (A.L.)	16	7	.696	3.69	34	33	3	2	0	$221^{2}/_{3}$	218	100	91	61	131
1998— Baltimore (A.L.)	16	13	.552	4.01	36	*36	*11	2	0	*$251^{1}/_{3}$	*284	125	112	69	186
1999— Baltimore (A.L.)	15	12	.556	4.81	34	34	6	*3	0	$230^{1}/_{3}$	244	127	123	*99	106
2000— Frederick (Caro.)	0	0	...	2.70	1	1	0	0	0	$6^{2}/_{3}$	3	2	2	1	5
—Bowie (East.)	0	0	...	0.00	1	1	0	0	0	7	4	0	0	0	5
—Baltimore (A.L.)	5	8	.385	7.87	16	16	1	0	0	$92^{2}/_{3}$	127	81	81	48	41
2001— Baltimore (A.L.)								Did not play.							
Major League totals (11 years)	135	116	.538	4.43	326	322	48	16	0	$2106^{1}/_{3}$	2281	1126	1037	745	1152

DIVISION SERIES RECORD

Year League	W	L	Pct.	ERA	G	GS	CG	ShO	Sv.	IP	H	R	ER	BB	SO
1996— Baltimore (A.L.)	0	0	...	4.05	1	1	0	0	0	$6^{2}/_{3}$	6	3	3	2	6
1997— Baltimore (A.L.)	1	0	1.000	4.05	1	1	0	0	0	$6^{2}/_{3}$	7	3	3	2	6
Division series totals (2 years)	1	0	1.000	4.05	2	2	0	0	0	$13^{1}/_{3}$	13	6	6	4	12

CHAMPIONSHIP SERIES RECORD

RECORDS: Shares A.L. record for most runs allowed in one inning—6 (October 13, 1996, third inning). ... Holds record for most home runs allowed in one inning—3 (October 13, 1996, third inning).

Year League	W	L	Pct.	ERA	G	GS	CG	ShO	Sv.	IP	H	R	ER	BB	SO
1991— Minnesota (A.L.)	0	0	...	4.50	1	1	0	0	0	4	3	2	2	5	2
1996— Baltimore (A.L.)	0	1	.000	2.38	2	2	0	0	0	$11^{1}/_{3}$	14	9	3	4	8
1997— Baltimore (A.L.)	1	0	1.000	4.26	2	2	0	0	0	$12^{2}/_{3}$	15	7	6	1	6
Champ. series totals (3 years)	1	1	.500	3.54	5	5	0	0	0	28	32	18	11	10	16

WORLD SERIES RECORD

NOTES: Member of World Series championship team (1991).

Year League	W	L	Pct.	ERA	G	GS	CG	ShO	Sv.	IP	H	R	ER	BB	SO
1991— Minnesota (A.L.)	0	0	...	5.06	2	2	0	0	0	$10^{2}/_{3}$	10	7	6	4	5

ERSTAD, DARIN   OF   ANGELS

PERSONAL: Born June 4, 1974, in Jamestown, N.D. ... 6-2/212. ... Bats left, throws left. ... Full name: Darin Charles Erstad.
HIGH SCHOOL: Jamestown (N.D.).
COLLEGE: Nebraska.
TRANSACTIONS/CAREER NOTES: Selected by New York Mets organization in 13th round of free-agent draft (June 1, 1992); did not sign. ... Selected by California Angels organization in first round (first pick overall) of free-agent draft (June 1, 1995). ... Angels franchise renamed Anaheim Angels for 1997 season. ... On disabled list (August 4-19, 1998; and August 11-26, 1999).
HONORS: Won A.L. Gold Glove as outfielder (2000). ... Named outfielder on The Sporting News A.L. All-Star team (2000). ... Named outfielder on The Sporting News A.L. Silver Slugger team (2000).
STATISTICAL NOTES: Had 15-game hitting streak (April 1-18, 1998). ... Had 15-game hitting streak (May 19-June 5, 2001). ... Career major league grand slams: 1.

Year— Team (League)	Pos.	G	AB	R	H	2B	3B	HR	RBI	Avg.	BB	SO	SB	PO	A	E	Avg.
1995— Arizona Angels (Ariz.)	OF	4	18	2	10	1	0	0	1	.556	1	1	1	3	0	0	1.000
— Lake Elsinore (Calif.)	OF	25	113	24	41	7	2	5	24	.363	6	22	3	65	2	1	.985
1996— Vancouver (PCL)	OF-1B	85	351	63	107	22	5	6	41	.305	44	53	11	184	10	1	.995
— California (A.L.)	OF	57	208	34	59	5	1	4	20	.284	17	29	3	121	2	3	.976
1997— Anaheim (A.L.)	1B-DH-OF	139	539	99	161	34	4	16	77	.299	51	86	23	1003	64	11	.990
1998— Anaheim (A.L.)	OF-1B-DH	133	537	84	159	39	3	19	82	.296	43	77	20	580	43	3	.995
1999— Anaheim (A.L.)	1B-OF-DH	142	585	84	148	22	5	13	53	.253	47	101	13	854	48	1	.999
2000— Anaheim (A.L.)	OF-DH-1B	157	*676	121	*240	39	6	25	100	.355	64	82	28	355	9	3	.992
2001— Anaheim (A.L.)	OF-1B-DH	157	631	89	163	35	1	9	53	.258	62	113	24	462	17	1	.998
Major League totals (6 years)		785	3176	511	930	174	20	86	395	.293	284	488	111	3375	183	22	.994

ALL-STAR GAME RECORD

Year League	Pos.	AB	R	H	2B	3B	HR	RBI	Avg.	BB	SO	SB	PO	A	E	Avg.
1998— American	OF	2	1	0	0	0	0	0	.000	0	0	0	3	0	0	1.000
2000— American	OF	2	0	0	0	0	0	1	.000	0	0	0	0	0	0	...
All-Star Game totals (2 years)		4	1	0	0	0	0	1	.000	0	0	0	3	0	0	1.000

ESCOBAR, ALEX   OF   INDIANS

PERSONAL: Born September 6, 1978, in Valencia, Venezuela. ... 6-1/180. ... Bats right, throws right. ... Full name: Alexander Jose Escobar.
HIGH SCHOOL: El Santuario (Valencia, Venezuela).
TRANSACTIONS/CAREER NOTES: Signed as non-drafted free agent by New York Mets organization (July 1, 1995). ... On St. Lucie disabled list (April 14-June 21 and July 8, 1999-remainder of season). ... Traded by Mets with OF Matt Lawton, P Jerrod Riggan and two players to be named later to Cleveland Indians for 2B Roberto Alomar, P Mike Bacsik and OF Danny Peoples (December 11, 2001); Indians acquired P Billy Traber and 1B Earl Snyder to complete deal (December 13, 2001).

Year— Team (League)	Pos.	G	AB	R	H	2B	3B	HR	RBI	Avg.	BB	SO	SB	PO	A	E	Avg.
1996— GC Mets (GCL)	OF-SS	24	75	15	27	4	0	0	10	.360	4	9	0	42	2	3	.936
1997— Little Falls (NY-Penn)	OF	10	36	6	7	3	0	0	3	.194	3	8	1	19	0	2	.905
— GC Mets (GCL)	OF	26	73	12	18	4	1	1	11	.247	10	17	0	26	2	1	.966
1998— Capital City (S.Atl.)	OF	112	416	90	129	23	5	27	91	.310	54	133	49	186	5	12	.941
1999— GC Mets (GCL)	OF	2	8	1	3	2	0	0	1	.375	1	2	0	1	0	0	1.000
— St. Lucie (FSL)	OF	1	3	1	2	0	0	1	3	.667	1	1	1	2	0	0	1.000
2000— Binghamton (East.)	OF	122	437	79	126	25	7	16	67	.288	57	114	24	276	10	5	.983
2001— Norfolk (I.L.)	OF	111	397	55	106	21	4	12	52	.267	35	146	18	242	8	5	.980
— New York (N.L.)	OF	18	50	3	10	1	0	3	8	.200	3	19	1	26	3	2	.935
Major League totals (1 year)		18	50	3	10	1	0	3	8	.200	3	19	1	26	3	2	.935

ESCOBAR, KELVIM   P   BLUE JAYS

PERSONAL: Born April 11, 1976, in La Guaria, Venezuela. ... 6-1/210. ... Throws right, bats right. ... Full name: Kelvim Jose Bolivar Escobar.
TRANSACTIONS/CAREER NOTES: Signed as non-drafted free agent by Toronto Blue Jays organization (July 9, 1992). ... On Toronto disabled list (April 16-May 6, 1998); included rehabilitation assignment to Syracuse (May 2-6).
STATISTICAL NOTES: Pitched 2-0 no-hit victory against Ogden (July 20, 1995, first game).

Year League	W	L	Pct.	ERA	G	GS	CG	ShO	Sv.	IP	H	R	ER	BB	SO
1993— Dom. Blue Jays (DSL)	2	1	.667	4.13	8	7	0	0	0	32 2/3	34	17	15	25	31
1994— GC Blue Jays (GCL)	4	4	.500	2.35	11	10	1	0	1	65	56	23	17	18	64
1995— Dom. Blue Jays (DSL)	0	1	.000	1.72	3	2	0	0	0	15 2/3	14	3	3	5	20
— Medicine Hat (Pio.)	3	3	.500	5.71	14	14	1	•1	0	69 1/3	66	47	44	33	75
1996— Dunedin (FSL)	9	5	.643	2.69	18	18	1	0	0	110 1/3	101	44	33	33	113
— Knoxville (Sou.)	3	4	.429	5.33	10	10	0	0	0	54	61	36	32	24	44
1997— Knoxville (Sou.)	2	1	.667	3.70	5	5	1	0	0	24 1/3	20	13	10	16	31
— Dunedin (FSL)	0	1	.000	3.75	3	2	0	0	0	12	16	9	5	3	16
— Toronto (A.L.)	3	2	.600	2.90	27	0	0	0	14	31	28	12	10	19	36
1998— Toronto (A.L.)	7	3	.700	3.73	22	10	0	0	0	79 2/3	72	37	33	35	72
— Syracuse (I.L.)	2	2	.500	3.77	13	10	0	0	1	59 2/3	51	26	25	24	64
1999— Toronto (A.L.)	14	11	.560	5.69	33	30	1	0	0	174	203	118	110	81	129
2000— Toronto (A.L.)	10	15	.400	5.35	43	24	3	1	2	180	186	118	107	85	142
2001— Toronto (A.L.)	6	8	.429	3.50	59	11	1	1	0	126	93	51	49	52	121
Major League totals (5 years)	40	39	.506	4.71	184	75	5	2	16	590 2/3	582	336	309	272	500

ESPINOSA, DAVID   SS   REDS

PERSONAL: Born December 16, 1981, in Miami, Fla. ... 6-1/170. ... Bats both, throws right.
TRANSACTIONS/CAREER NOTES: Selected by Cincinnati Reds organization in first round (23rd pick overall) of free-agent draft (June 5, 2000).

Year— Team (League)	Pos.	G	AB	R	H	2B	3B	HR	RBI	Avg.	BB	SO	SB	PO	A	E	Avg.
2001— Dayton (Midw.)	SS	122	493	88	129	29	8	7	37	.262	55	120	15	161	319	*48	.909

ESSLINGER, CAM   P   ROCKIES

PERSONAL: Born December 28, 1976, in Vineland, N.J. ... 5-11/170. ... Throws right, bats right. ... Full name: Cameron Scott Esslinger.
HIGH SCHOOL: Millville (N.J.).
COLLEGE: Seton Hall.
TRANSACTIONS/CAREER NOTES: Selected by Colorado Rockies organization in 16th round of free-agent draft (June 2, 1999). ... On disabled list (July 31-August 13 and August 30, 2001-remainder of season).

Year League	W	L	Pct.	ERA	G	GS	CG	ShO	Sv.	IP	H	R	ER	BB	SO
1999— Portland (N'West)	6	3	.667	3.83	14	14	0	0	0	80	76	37	34	35	68
2000— Asheville (S.Atl.)	4	2	.667	3.06	47	2	0	0	24	64 2/3	55	23	22	23	84
2001— Carolina (Sou.)	1	1	.500	4.93	40	0	0	0	16	42	32	26	23	31	51

ESTALELLA, BOBBY   C   YANKEES

PERSONAL: Born August 23, 1974, in Hialeah, Fla. ... 6-1/205. ... Bats right, throws right. ... Full name: Robert M. Estalella. ... Grandson of Bobby Estalella, outfielder with Washington Senators (1935-36, 1939 and 1942), St. Louis Browns (1941), and Philadelphia Athletics (1943-45 and 1949).

HIGH SCHOOL: Cooper City (Fla.).

JUNIOR COLLEGE: Miami-Dade (South) Community College.

TRANSACTIONS/CAREER NOTES: Selected by Philadelphia Phillies organization in 23rd round of free-agent draft (June 1, 1992). ... On Philadelphia disabled list (March 27-April 29, 1999); included rehabilitation assignments to Clearwater (April 9-17) and to Scranton/Wilkes-Barre (April 19-29). ... Traded by Phillies to San Francisco Giants for P Chris Brock (December 12, 1999). ... Traded by Giants with P Joe Smith to New York Yankees for P Brian Boehringer (July 5, 2001).

STATISTICAL NOTES: Tied for South Atlantic League lead in double plays by catcher with eight in 1994. ... Led Florida State League catchers with 864 total chances in 1995. ... Led International League with 928 total chances and tied for league lead in double plays by catcher with nine in 1997. ... Hit three home runs in one game (September 4, 1997). ... Led International League catchers with 10 double plays in 1999. ... Led N.L. catchers with 14 double plays in 2000. ... Career major league grand slams: 2.

							BATTING							FIELDING			
Year Team (League)	Pos.	G	AB	R	H	2B	3B	HR	RBI	Avg.	BB	SO	SB	PO	A	E	Avg.
1993—Martinsville (Appl.).....	C	35	122	14	36	11	0	3	19	.295	14	24	0	210	25	6	.975
—Clearwater (FSL)	C	11	35	4	8	0	0	0	4	.229	2	3	0	47	8	0	1.000
1994—Spartanburg (S.Atl.) ...	C	86	299	34	65	19	1	9	41	.217	31	85	0	592	87	10	.985
—Clearwater (FSL)	C	13	46	3	12	1	0	2	9	.261	3	17	0	92	5	1	.990
1995—Clearwater (FSL)	C	117	404	61	105	24	1	15	58	.260	56	76	0	*771	82	11	.987
—Reading (East.)..........	C	10	34	5	8	1	0	2	9	.235	4	7	0	60	9	1	.986
1996—Reading (East.)..........	C	111	365	48	89	14	2	23	72	.244	67	104	2	775	84	14	.984
—Scranton/W.B. (I.L.) ...	C	11	36	7	9	3	0	3	8	.250	5	10	0	55	6	2	.968
—Philadelphia (N.L.)......	C	7	17	5	6	0	0	2	4	.353	1	6	1	24	1	0	1.000
1997—Scranton/W.B. (I.L.) ...	C	123	433	63	101	32	0	16	65	.233	56	109	3	*844	71	13	.986
—Philadelphia (N.L.)......	C	13	29	9	10	1	0	4	9	.345	7	7	0	49	3	0	1.000
1998—Scranton/W.B. (I.L.) ...	C	76	242	49	68	14	1	17	49	.281	66	49	0	469	25	5	.990
—Philadelphia (N.L.)......	C	47	165	16	31	6	1	8	20	.188	13	49	0	321	12	4	.988
1999—Clearwater (FSL)	C-DH	8	26	3	11	3	0	1	8	.423	3	3	0	37	4	1	.976
—Scranton/W.B. (I.L.) ...	C	110	386	58	89	23	2	15	62	.231	55	100	4	652	43	5	.993
—Philadelphia (N.L.)......	C	9	18	2	3	0	0	0	1	.167	4	7	0	38	2	1	.976
2000—San Fran. (N.L.)■......	C	106	299	45	70	22	3	14	53	.234	57	92	3	654	49	5	.993
2001—San Francisco (N.L.) ..	C	29	93	11	19	5	1	3	10	.204	11	28	0	185	14	0	1.000
—Fresno (PCL)	1B-C	6	22	3	7	1	0	1	4	.318	1	9	0	17	1	0	1.000
—Columbus (I.L.)■.......	C-1B	48	171	26	44	10	1	10	38	.257	21	45	0	267	19	2	.993
—New York (A.L.)...........	C	3	4	1	0	0	0	0	0	.000	1	2	0	14	1	0	1.000
American League totals (1 year)		3	4	1	0	0	0	0	0	.000	1	2	0	14	1	0	1.000
National League totals (6 years)		211	621	88	139	34	5	31	97	.224	93	189	4	1271	81	10	.993
Major League totals (6 years)		214	625	89	139	34	5	31	97	.222	94	191	4	1285	82	10	.993

DIVISION SERIES RECORD

							BATTING							FIELDING			
Year Team (League)	Pos.	G	AB	R	H	2B	3B	HR	RBI	Avg.	BB	SO	SB	PO	A	E	Avg.
2000—San Francisco (N.L.) ..	C	4	12	1	1	0	0	0	1	.083	0	2	0	25	2	0	1.000

ESTES, SHAWN   P   METS

PERSONAL: Born February 18, 1973, in San Francisco. ... 6-2/195. ... Throws left, bats right. ... Full name: Aaron Shawn Estes. ... Name pronounced EST-us.

HIGH SCHOOL: Douglas (Minden, Nev.).

TRANSACTIONS/CAREER NOTES: Selected by Seattle Mariners organization in first round (11th pick overall) of free-agent draft (June 3, 1991). ... On disabled list (August 19, 1993-remainder of season). ... On Appleton disabled list (April 8-July 19 and July 25-August 15, 1994). ... Traded by Mariners with IF Wilson Delgado to San Francisco Giants for P Salomon Torres (May 21, 1995). ... On disabled list (March 23-April 6, 1997). ... On San Francisco disabled list (July 11-September 4, 1998); included rehabilitation assignments to Bakersfield (August 26-29) and Fresno (August 30-September 4). ... On San Francisco disabled list (March 29-April 17, 2000); included rehabilitation assignments to Fresno (April 7-12) and San Jose (April 13-17). ... On disabled list (May 9-24 and August 23, 2001-remainder of season). ... Traded by Giants to New York Mets for OF Tsuyoshi Shinjo and SS Desi Relaford (December 16, 2001).

STATISTICAL NOTES: Tied for N.L. lead with 15 wild pitches in 1999. ... Career major league grand slams: 1.

MISCELLANEOUS: Appeared in four games as pinch runner with San Francisco (1996). ... Appeared in four games as pinch runner (1997). ... Scored two runs in two games as pinch runner with San Francisco (1998). ... Struck out in both appearances as pinch hitter and scored two runs in eight appearances as pinch runner (1999). ... Appeared in two games as pinch runner (2000).

Year League	W	L	Pct.	ERA	G	GS	CG	ShO	Sv.	IP	H	R	ER	BB	SO
1991—Bellingham (N'West)	1	3	.250	6.88	9	9	0	0	0	34	27	33	26	55	35
1992—Bellingham (N'West)	3	3	.500	4.32	15	15	0	0	0	77	84	55	37	45	77
1993—Appleton (Midw.)...............	5	9	.357	7.24	19	18	0	0	0	83 1/3	108	85	67	52	65
1994—Appleton (Midw.)...............	0	2	.000	4.58	5	4	0	0	0	19 2/3	19	13	10	17	28
—Arizona Mariners (Ariz.)	0	3	.000	3.15	5	5	0	0	0	20	16	9	7	6	31
1995—Wisconsin Rapids (Midw.).	0	0	...	0.90	2	2	0	0	0	10	5	1	1	5	11
—Burlington (Midw.)■.........	0	0	...	4.11	4	4	0	0	0	15 1/3	13	8	7	12	22
—San Jose (Calif.).............	5	2	.714	2.17	9	8	0	0	0	49 2/3	32	13	12	17	61
—Shreveport (Texas)............	2	0	1.000	2.01	4	4	0	0	0	22 1/3	14	5	5	10	18
—San Francisco (N.L.)	0	3	.000	6.75	3	3	0	0	0	17 1/3	16	14	13	5	14
1996—Phoenix (PCL)..................	9	3	.750	3.43	18	18	0	0	0	110 1/3	92	43	42	38	95
—San Francisco (N.L.)	3	5	.375	3.60	11	11	0	0	0	70	63	30	28	39	60
1997—San Francisco (N.L.)	19	5	.792	3.18	32	32	3	2	0	201	162	80	71	*100	181
1998—San Francisco (N.L.)	7	12	.368	5.06	25	25	1	1	0	149 1/3	150	89	84	80	136
—Bakersfield (Calif.)...........	0	0	...	0.00	1	1	0	0	0	4 1/3	3	0	0	1	5
—Fresno (PCL).....................	1	0	1.000	1.80	1	1	0	0	0	5	3	1	1	3	6

E

Year League	W	L	Pct.	ERA	G	GS	CG	ShO	Sv.	IP	H	R	ER	BB	SO
1999—San Francisco (N.L.)	11	11	.500	4.92	32	32	1	1	0	203	209	121	111	112	159
2000—Fresno (PCL)	0	1	.000	9.00	1	1	0	0	0	3	5	9	3	2	2
—San Jose (Calif.)	1	0	1.000	0.00	1	1	0	0	0	7	2	0	0	1	11
—San Francisco (N.L.)	15	6	.714	4.26	30	30	4	2	0	190 1/3	194	99	90	108	136
2001—San Francisco (N.L.)	9	8	.529	4.02	27	27	0	0	0	159	151	78	71	77	109
Major League totals (7 years)......	64	50	.561	4.25	160	160	9	6	0	990	945	511	468	521	795

DIVISION SERIES RECORD

Year League	W	L	Pct.	ERA	G	GS	CG	ShO	Sv.	IP	H	R	ER	BB	SO
1997—San Francisco (N.L.)	0	0	...	15.00	1	1	0	0	0	3	5	5	5	4	3
2000—San Francisco (N.L.)	0	0	...	6.00	1	1	0	0	0	3	3	2	2	3	3
Division series totals (2 years)	0	0	...	10.50	2	2	0	0	0	6	8	7	7	7	6

ALL-STAR GAME RECORD

Year League	W	L	Pct.	ERA	GS	CG	ShO	Sv.	IP	H	R	ER	BB	SO
1997—National	0	1	.000	18.00	0	0	0	0	1	1	2	2	1	1

ESTRADA, HORACIO — P

PERSONAL: Born October 19, 1975, in San Joaquin, Venezuela. ... 6-0/192. ... Throws left, bats left. ... Full name: Horacio Jimenez Estrada.
HIGH SCHOOL: Domingo Segado (San Joaquin, Venezuela).
TRANSACTIONS/CAREER NOTES: Signed as non-drafted free agent by Milwaukee Brewers organization (July 3, 1992). ... On Louisville disabled list (May 28, 1998-remainder of season; and June 9-19, 1999). ... Claimed on waivers by Florida Marlins (March 27, 2001). ... Claimed on waivers by Colorado Rockies (March 30, 2001). ... On Colorado disabled list (April 16-July 15, 2001); included rehabilitation assignments to Colorado Springs (April 26-May 9, June 12-July 8 and July 12-14). ... Granted free agency (October 15, 2001).

Year League	W	L	Pct.	ERA	G	GS	CG	ShO	Sv.	IP	H	R	ER	BB	SO
1993—Dominican Brewers (DSL)..	1	2	.333	4.41	22	3	0	0	0	51	39	33	25	37	60
1994—Dominican Brewers (DSL)..	3	4	.429	2.67	26	2	0	0	7	60 2/3	41	27	18	46	52
1995—Arizona Brewers (Ariz.)	0	1	.000	3.71	8	1	0	0	2	17	13	9	7	8	21
—Helena (Pio.)	1	2	.333	5.40	13	0	0	0	0	30	27	21	18	24	30
1996—Beloit (Midw.).................	2	1	.667	1.23	17	0	0	0	1	29 1/3	21	8	4	11	34
—Stockton (Calif.)	1	3	.250	4.59	29	0	0	0	3	51	43	29	26	21	62
1997—El Paso (Texas).................	8	10	.444	4.74	29	23	1	0	0	153 2/3	174	93	81	70	127
1998—El Paso (Texas).................	5	0	1.000	4.53	8	8	0	0	0	49 2/3	50	27	25	21	37
—Louisville (I.L.)	0	0	...	3.00	2	2	0	0	0	12	10	4	4	5	4
1999—Louisville (I.L.)	6	6	.500	5.67	25	24	1	0	0	131 2/3	128	87	83	65	112
—Milwaukee (N.L.)...............	0	0	...	7.36	4	0	0	0	0	7 1/3	10	6	6	4	5
2000—Indianapolis (I.L.)...............	*14	4	.778	3.33	25	25	3	•2	0	159 1/3	149	63	59	45	103
—Milwaukee (N.L.)...............	3	0	1.000	6.29	7	4	0	0	0	24 1/3	30	18	17	20	13
2001—Colorado (N.L.)■..............	1	1	.500	14.54	4	0	0	0	0	4 1/3	8	7	7	1	4
—Colo. Springs (PCL)	8	4	.667	4.73	16	16	0	0	0	91 1/3	102	51	48	20	77
Major League totals (3 years).......	4	1	.800	7.50	15	4	0	0	0	36	48	31	30	25	22

ESTRADA, JOHNNY — C — PHILLIES

PERSONAL: Born June 27, 1976, in Hayward, Calif. ... 5-11/210. ... Bats both, throws right. ... Full name: Johnny P. Estrada III.
HIGH SCHOOL: Roosevelt (Fresno, Calif.).
JUNIOR COLLEGE: Fresno City, then Sequoias.
TRANSACTIONS/CAREER NOTES: Selected by Houston Astros organization in 71st round of free-agent draft (June 2, 1994); did not sign. ... Selected by Phiadelphia Phillies organization in 17th round of free-agent draft (June 3, 1997).
STATISTICAL NOTES: Led New York-Pennsylvania League catchers with 391 putouts, 434 total chances and 1.000 fielding percentage in 1997. ... Tied for South Atlantic League lead in double plays by catcher with six in 1998.

Year Team (League)	Pos.	G	AB	R	H	2B	3B	HR	RBI	Avg.	BB	SO	SB	PO	A	E	Avg.
1997—Batavia (NY-Penn)......	C-1B	58	223	28	70	17	2	6	43	.314	9	15	0	†403	44	0	†1.000
1998—Piedmont (S.Atl.)........	C	77	303	33	94	14	2	7	44	.310	6	19	0	523	63	6	.990
—Clearwater (FSL)	C	37	117	8	26	8	0	0	13	.222	5	7	0	200	32	5	.979
1999—Clearwater (FSL)	C	98	346	35	96	15	0	9	52	.277	14	26	1	417	54	5	.989
2000—Reading (East.)...........	C	95	356	42	105	18	0	12	42	.295	10	20	1	603	64	7	.990
2001—Scranton/W.B. (I.L.) ...	C	32	131	13	38	13	0	0	16	.290	5	6	0	246	19	0	1.000
—Philadelphia (N.L.)......	C	89	298	26	68	15	0	8	37	.228	16	32	0	543	30	4	.993
Major League totals (1 year)		89	298	26	68	15	0	8	37	.228	16	32	0	543	30	4	.993

ETHERTON, SETH — P — REDS

PERSONAL: Born October 17, 1976, in Laguna Beach, Calif. ... 6-1/200. ... Throws right, bats right. ... Full name: Seth Michael Etherton.
HIGH SCHOOL: Dana Hills (Dana Point, Calif.).
COLLEGE: Southern California.
TRANSACTIONS/CAREER NOTES: Selected by St. Louis Cardinals organization in ninth-round of free-agent draft (June 3, 1997); did not sign. ... Selected by Anaheim Angels organization in first round (18th pick overall) of free-agent draft (June 2, 1998). ... On Anaheim disabled list (August 5, 2000-remainder of season) ... Traded by Angels to Cincinnati Reds for SS Wilmy Caceres (December 10, 2000). ... On disabled list (March 22, 2001-entire season).

Year League	W	L	Pct.	ERA	G	GS	CG	ShO	Sv.	IP	H	R	ER	BB	SO
1998—Midland (Texas)..................	1	5	.167	6.14	9	7	1	0	0	48 1/3	57	36	33	12	35
1999—Erie (East.)	10	10	.500	3.27	24	24	4	1	0	167 2/3	153	72	61	43	153
—Edmonton (PCL)	0	2	.000	5.48	4	4	0	0	0	21 1/3	25	13	13	6	19
2000—Edmonton (PCL)	3	0	.600	4.01	9	9	0	0	0	58 1/3	60	30	26	19	50
—Anaheim (A.L.).................	5	1	.833	5.52	11	11	0	0	0	60 1/3	68	38	37	22	32
2001—Cincinnati (N.L.)■.............							Did not play.								
Major League totals (1 year)........	5	1	.833	5.52	11	11	0	0	0	60 1/3	68	38	37	22	32

EUSEBIO, TONY   C

PERSONAL: Born April 27, 1967, in San Jose de Los Llames, Dominican Republic. ... 6-2/210. ... Bats right, throws right. ... Full name: Raul Antonio Eusebio. ... Name pronounced you-SAY-bee-o.

HIGH SCHOOL: San Rafael (Dominican Republic).

TRANSACTIONS/CAREER NOTES: Signed as non-drafted free agent by Houston Astros organization (May 30, 1985). ... On disabled list (August 5, 1990-remainder of season; April 16-23, 1992; and August 24, 1993-remainder of season). ... On Houston disabled list (May 8-June 17 and June 22-August 7, 1996); included rehabilitation assignments to Tucson (June 10-17 and July 29-August 7). ... On disabled list (July 30-August 15, 1999). ... Granted free agency (October 28, 1999). ... Re-signed by Astros (December 2, 1999). ... Granted free agency (November 5, 2001).

STATISTICAL NOTES: Tied for Southern League lead in double plays by catcher with eight in 1989. ... Led Texas League catchers with .9963 fielding percentage and 12 double plays in 1992. ... Had 24-game hitting streak (July 9-August 28, 2000). ... Career major league grand slams: 2.

Year	Team (League)	Pos.	G	AB	R	H	2B	3B	HR	RBI	Avg.	BB	SO	SB	PO	A	E	Avg.
1985—	....						Dominican Summer League statistics unavailable.											
	—GC Astros (GCL)	C	1	1	0	0	0	0	0	0	.000	0	0	0	4	0	0	1.000
1986—	....						Dominican Summer League statistics unavailable.											
1987—	GC Astros (GCL)	C-1B	42	125	26	26	1	2	1	15	.208	18	19	8	204	24	4	.983
1988—	Osceola (FSL)...........	C-OF	118	392	45	96	6	3	0	40	.245	40	69	19	611	66	8	.988
1989—	Columbus (Sou.).......	C	65	203	20	38	6	1	0	18	.187	38	47	7	355	46	7	.983
	—Osceola (FSL)...........	C	52	175	22	50	6	3	0	30	.286	19	27	5	290	40	5	.985
1990—	Columbus (Sou.).......	C	92	318	36	90	18	0	4	37	.283	21	80	6	558	69	4	*.994
1991—	Jackson (Texas)	C	66	222	27	58	8	3	2	31	.261	25	54	3	424	48	7	.985
	—Tucson (PCL)	C	5	20	5	8	1	0	0	2	.400	3	3	1	40	1	0	1.000
	—Houston (N.L.)	C	10	19	4	2	1	0	0	0	.105	6	8	0	49	4	1	.981
1992—	Jackson (Texas)	C	94	339	33	104	9	3	5	44	.307	25	58	1	493	51	2	*.996
1993—	Tucson (PCL)	C	78	281	39	91	20	1	1	43	.324	22	40	1	450	46	3	.994
1994—	Houston (N.L.)	C	55	159	18	47	9	1	5	30	.296	8	33	0	263	24	2	.993
1995—	Houston (N.L.)	C	113	368	46	110	21	1	6	58	.299	31	59	0	645	49	5	.993
1996—	Houston (N.L.)	C	58	152	15	41	7	2	1	19	.270	18	20	0	255	24	1	.996
	—Tucson (PCL)	C	15	53	8	22	4	0	0	14	.415	2	7	0	45	1	0	1.000
1997—	Houston (N.L.)	C	60	164	12	45	2	0	1	18	.274	19	27	0	297	16	4	.987
1998—	Houston (N.L.)	C	66	182	13	46	6	1	1	36	.253	18	31	1	352	19	3	.992
1999—	Houston (N.L.)	C	103	323	31	88	15	0	4	33	.272	40	67	0	652	37	4	.994
2000—	Houston (N.L.)	C	74	218	24	61	18	0	7	33	.280	25	45	0	411	17	5	.988
2001—	Houston (N.L.)	C	59	154	16	39	8	0	5	14	.253	17	34	0	300	22	3	.991
Major League totals (9 years)			598	1739	179	479	87	5	30	241	.275	182	324	1	3224	212	28	.992

DIVISION SERIES RECORD

Year	Team (League)	Pos.	G	AB	R	H	2B	3B	HR	RBI	Avg.	BB	SO	SB	PO	A	E	Avg.
1997—	Houston (N.L.)	C	1	3	1	2	0	0	0	0	.667	0	1	1	6	1	0	1.000
1998—	Houston (N.L.)	C	1	3	0	1	1	0	0	0	.333	0	2	0	6	0	0	1.000
1999—	Houston (N.L.)	C	4	15	2	4	0	0	1	3	.267	1	2	0	34	3	1	.974
2001—	Houston (N.L.)	C	1	3	1	2	1	0	0	0	.667	0	0	0	4	1	0	1.000
Division series totals (4 years)			7	24	4	9	2	0	1	3	.375	1	5	1	50	5	1	.982

EVERETT, ADAM   SS   ASTROS

PERSONAL: Born February 2, 1977, in Austell, Ga. ... 6-0/156. ... Bats right, throws right.

HIGH SCHOOL: Harrison (Kennesaw, Ga.).

COLLEGE: North Carolina State, then South Carolina.

TRANSACTIONS/CAREER NOTES: Selected by Boston Red Sox organization in first round (12th pick overall) of free-agent draft (June 2, 1998). ... Traded by Red Sox with P Greg Miller to Houston Astros for OF Carl Everett (December 14, 1999).

MISCELLANEOUS: Member of 2000 U.S. Olympic baseball team.

Year	Team (League)	Pos.	G	AB	R	H	2B	3B	HR	RBI	Avg.	BB	SO	SB	PO	A	E	Avg.
1998—	Lowell (NY-Penn)	SS	21	71	11	21	6	2	0	9	.296	11	13	2	34	67	9	.918
1999—	Trenton (East.)	SS	98	338	56	89	11	0	10	44	.263	41	64	21	150	273	18	.959
2000—	New Orleans (PCL)■..	SS	126	453	82	111	25	2	5	37	.245	75	100	13	172	*410	25	.959
2001—	New Orleans (PCL).....	SS	114	441	69	110	20	8	5	40	.249	39	74	24	189	329	24	.956
	—Houston (N.L.)	SS	9	3	1	0	0	0	0	0	.000	0	1	1	2	2	2	.667
Major League totals (1 year)			9	3	1	0	0	0	0	0	.000	0	1	1	2	2	2	.667

EVERETT, CARL   OF   RANGERS

PERSONAL: Born June 3, 1971, in Tampa. ... 6-0/215. ... Bats both, throws right. ... Full name: Carl Edward Everett.

HIGH SCHOOL: Hillsborough (Tampa).

TRANSACTIONS/CAREER NOTES: Selected by New York Yankees organization in first round (10th pick overall) of free-agent draft (June 4, 1990). ... On Fort Lauderdale disabled list (July 7-August 15, 1992). ... Selected by Florida Marlins in second round (27th pick overall) of expansion draft (November 17, 1992). ... On High Desert disabled list (April 8-13, 1993). ... On Florida disabled list (July 23-August 10, 1994). ... On Edmonton suspended list (August 29, 1994-remainder of season). ... Traded by Marlins to New York Mets for 2B Quilvio Veras (November 29, 1994). ... On disabled list (April 12-27, 1996). ... Traded by Mets to Houston Astros for P John Hudek (December 22, 1997). ... On disabled list (July 16-August 6, 1999). ... Traded by Astros to Boston Red Sox for SS Adam Everett and P Greg Miller (December 14, 1999). ... On suspended list (July 24-August 5, 2000). ... On suspended list (March 29-30, 2001). ... On Boston disabled list (June 22-July 28, 2001); included rehabilitation assignments to Sarasota (July 21-24) and Gulf Coast Red Sox (July 25-28). ... Traded by Red Sox to Texas Rangers for P Darren Oliver (December 13, 2001).

STATISTICAL NOTES: Led South Atlantic League in being hit by pitch with 23 in 1991. ... Switch-hit home runs in one game five times (April 20, 1997, first game; April 24, 1998; August 7, 1999; April 11 and August 29, 2000). ... Career major league grand slams: 7.

Year	Team (League)	Pos.	G	AB	R	H	2B	3B	HR	RBI	Avg.	BB	SO	SB	PO	A	E	Avg.
1990—	GC Yankees (GCL)......	OF	48	185	28	48	8	5	1	14	.259	15	38	15	64	5	5	.932
1991—	Greensboro (S.Atl.)....	OF	123	468	96	127	18	0	4	40	.271	57	122	28	250	14	7	.974
1992—	Fort Lauderdale (FSL)	OF	46	183	30	42	8	2	2	9	.230	12	40	11	111	5	3	.975
	— Prince William (Caro.)	OF	6	22	7	7	0	0	4	9	.318	5	7	1	12	1	0	1.000
1993—	High Desert (Calif.)■ .	OF	59	253	48	73	12	6	10	52	.289	22	73	24	124	6	2	.985
	— Florida (N.L.)............	OF	11	19	0	2	0	0	0	0	.105	1	9	1	6	0	1	.857
	— Edmonton (PCL)	OF-DH	35	136	28	42	13	4	6	16	.309	19	45	12	69	12	2	.976
1994—	Edmonton (PCL)	OF-DH	78	321	63	108	17	2	11	47	.336	19	65	16	167	11	2	.989
	— Florida (N.L.)............	OF	16	51	7	11	1	0	2	6	.216	3	15	4	28	2	0	1.000
1995—	New York (N.L.)■.......	OF	79	289	48	75	13	1	12	54	.260	39	67	2	148	9	3	.981
	— Norfolk (I.L.)	OF-DH-SS	67	260	52	78	16	4	6	35	.300	20	47	12	133	7	0	1.000
1996—	New York (N.L.).........	OF	101	192	29	46	8	1	1	16	.240	21	53	6	96	4	7	.935
1997—	New York (N.L.).........	OF	142	443	58	110	28	3	14	57	.248	32	102	17	226	8	7	.971
1998—	Houston (N.L.)■	OF	133	467	72	138	34	4	15	76	.296	44	102	14	296	12	4	.987
1999—	Houston (N.L.)..........	OF-DH	123	464	86	151	33	3	25	108	.325	50	94	27	256	11	6	.978
2000—	Boston (A.L.)■..........	OF-DH	137	496	82	149	32	4	34	108	.300	52	113	11	276	11	6	.980
2001—	Boston (A.L.).............	OF-DH	102	409	61	105	24	4	14	58	.257	27	104	9	185	4	5	.974
	— Sarasota (FSL)	DH	2	7	0	3	0	0	0	0	.429	2	0	0	..	..	...	...
	— GC Red Sox (GCL)	OF	3	10	2	2	0	0	2	2	.200	1	3	0	5	0	0	1.000
American League totals (2 years)			239	905	143	254	56	8	48	166	.281	79	217	20	461	15	11	.977
National League totals (7 years)			605	1925	300	533	117	12	69	317	.277	190	442	71	1056	46	28	.975
Major League totals (9 years)			844	2830	443	787	173	20	117	483	.278	269	659	91	1517	61	39	.976

DIVISION SERIES RECORD

Year	Team (League)	Pos.	G	AB	R	H	2B	3B	HR	RBI	Avg.	BB	SO	SB	PO	A	E	Avg.
1998—	Houston (N.L.)	OF-PH	4	13	1	2	0	0	0	0	.154	0	4	0	8	0	0	1.000
1999—	Houston (N.L.)	OF	4	15	2	2	0	0	0	1	.133	2	8	1	8	0	0	1.000
Division series totals (2 years)			8	28	3	4	0	0	0	1	.143	2	12	1	16	0	0	1.000

ALL-STAR GAME RECORD

Year	League	Pos.	AB	R	H	2B	3B	HR	RBI	Avg.	BB	SO	SB	PO	A	E	Avg.
2000—	American...................	OF	2	0	0	0	0	0	1	.000	1	0	0	1	0	0	1.000

EYRE, SCOTT　　　　　P　　　　　BLUE JAYS

PERSONAL: Born May 30, 1972, in Inglewood, Calif. ... 6-1/200. ... Throws left, bats left. ... Full name: Scott Alan Eyre.
HIGH SCHOOL: Cyprus (Magna, Utah).
JUNIOR COLLEGE: College of Southern Idaho.
TRANSACTIONS/CAREER NOTES: Selected by Texas Rangers organization in ninth round of free-agent draft (June 3, 1991). ... Traded by Rangers to Chicago White Sox for SS Esteban Beltre (March 28, 1994). ... On disabled list (April 8-27, 1994). ... On Prince William disabled list (April 6-September 7, 1995). ... On Charlotte disabled list (June 2-13, 1999). ... On Chicago disabled list (August 31-September 26, 1999); included rehabilitation assignment to Charlotte (September 8-26). ... Traded by White Sox to Toronto Blue Jays for P Gary Glover (November 7, 2000).
HONORS: Named Southern League Most Outstanding Pitcher (1997).

Year	League	W	L	Pct.	ERA	G	GS	CG	ShO	Sv.	IP	H	R	ER	BB	SO
1992—	Butte (Pio.)........................	7	3	.700	2.90	15	14	2	1	0	80 2/3	71	30	26	39	94
1993—	Charleston, S.C. (S.Atl.)	11	7	.611	3.45	26	26	0	0	0	143 2/3	115	74	55	59	154
1994—	South Bend (Midw.)■........	8	4	.667	3.47	19	18	2	0	0	111 2/3	108	56	43	37	111
1995—	GC White Sox (GCL)	0	2	.000	2.30	9	9	0	0	0	27 1/3	16	7	7	12	40
1996—	Birmingham (Sou.).............	12	7	.632	4.38	27	27	0	0	0	158 1/3	170	90	77	79	137
1997—	Birmingham (Sou.).............	•13	5	.722	3.84	22	22	0	0	0	126 2/3	110	61	54	55	127
	— Chicago (A.L.)..................	4	4	.500	5.04	11	11	0	0	0	60 2/3	62	36	34	31	36
1998—	Chicago (A.L.)....................	3	8	.273	5.38	33	17	0	0	0	107	114	78	64	64	73
1999—	Charlotte (I.L.)...................	6	4	.600	3.82	12	11	0	0	0	68 1/3	75	32	29	23	63
	— Chicago (A.L.)..................	1	1	.500	7.56	21	0	0	0	0	25	38	22	21	15	17
2000—	Chicago (A.L.)....................	1	1	.500	6.63	13	1	0	0	0	19	29	15	14	12	16
	— Charlotte (I.L.).................	3	2	.600	3.00	47	0	0	0	12	48	33	18	16	20	46
2001—	Syracuse (I.L.)■	4	6	.400	3.18	62	2	0	0	0	79 1/3	67	30	28	26	96
	— Toronto (A.L.)..................	1	2	.333	3.45	17	0	0	0	2	15 2/3	15	6	6	7	16
Major League totals (5 years)......		10	16	.385	5.50	95	29	0	0	2	227 1/3	258	157	139	129	158

FABREGAS, JORGE　　　　　C　　　　　ANGELS

PERSONAL: Born March 13, 1970, in Miami. ... 6-3/215. ... Bats left, throws right. ... Name pronounced FAB-ruh-gas.
HIGH SCHOOL: Christopher Columbus (Miami).
COLLEGE: Miami (Fla.).
TRANSACTIONS/CAREER NOTES: Selected by Cleveland Indians organization in 11th round of free-agent draft (June 1, 1988); did not sign. ... Selected by California Angels organization in supplemental round ("sandwich pick" between first and second round, 34th pick overall) of free-agent draft (June 3, 1991); pick received as part of compensation for Minnesota Twins signing Type A free-agent OF/DH Chili Davis. ... On disabled list (April 12-May 4 and July 28-September 5, 1992). ... Angels franchise renamed Anaheim Angels for 1997 season. ... Traded by Angels with P Chuck McElroy to Chicago White Sox for OF Tony Phillips and C Chad Kreuter (May 18, 1997). ... Selected by Arizona Diamondbacks in first round (seventh pick overall) of expansion draft (November 18, 1997). ... On Arizona disabled list (May 31-June 30, 1998); included rehabilitation assignment to Tucson (June 22-30). ... Traded by Diamondbacks with P Willie Blair and cash considerations to

New York Mets for OF Bernard Gilkey, P Nelson Figueroa and cash (July 31, 1998). ... Traded by Mets to Florida Marlins for P Oscar Henriquez (November 20, 1998). ... Released by Marlins (August 26, 1999). ... Signed by Atlanta Braves (August 31, 1999). ... Released by Braves (November 5, 1999). ... Signed by Kansas City Royals organization (January 12, 2000). ... On Kansas City disabled list (July 19-September 1, 2000); included rehabilitation assignment to Omaha (July 31-August 9 and August 24-September 1). ... Granted free agency (November 1, 2000). ... Signed by Angels (November 20, 2000). ... On disabled list (May 6-22, 2001). ... Granted free agency (November 5, 2001). ... Re-signed by Angels (November 19, 2001).

STATISTICAL NOTES: Led Texas League with 17 passed balls in 1993. ... Career major league grand slams: 1.

Year Team (League)	Pos.	G	AB	R	H	2B	3B	HR	RBI	Avg.	BB	SO	SB	PO	A	E	Avg.
1992— Palm Springs (Calif.)..	C	70	258	35	73	13	0	0	40	.283	30	27	0	436	63	*17	.967
1993— Midland (Texas)	C	113	409	63	118	26	3	6	56	.289	31	60	1	620	99	•11	.985
— Vancouver (PCL)	C	4	13	1	3	1	0	0	1	.231	1	3	0	30	3	0	1.000
1994— Vancouver (PCL)	C-DH	66	211	17	47	6	1	1	24	.223	12	25	1	365	41	4	.990
— California (A.L.)	C	43	127	12	36	3	0	0	16	.283	7	18	2	217	16	3	.987
1995— California (A.L.)	C	73	227	24	56	10	0	1	22	.247	17	28	0	391	36	6	.986
— Vancouver (PCL)	C	21	73	9	18	3	0	4	10	.247	9	12	0	112	12	4	.969
1996— California (A.L.)	C-DH	90	254	18	73	6	0	2	26	.287	17	27	0	502	46	6	.989
— Vancouver (PCL)	DH-C-1B	10	37	4	11	3	0	0	5	.297	4	4	0	27	2	0	1.000
1997— Anaheim (A.L.)	C	21	38	2	3	1	0	0	3	.079	3	3	0	81	5	1	.989
— Chicago (A.L.)	C-1B	100	322	31	90	10	1	7	48	.280	11	43	1	520	46	7	.988
1998— Arizona (N.L.)■	C	50	151	8	30	4	0	1	15	.199	13	26	0	228	30	1	.996
— Tucson (PCL)	C-DH	6	20	2	5	1	0	0	3	.250	3	1	0	28	3	0	1.000
— New York (N.L.)■	C	20	32	3	6	0	0	1	5	.188	1	6	0	62	6	2	.971
1999— Florida (N.L.)■	C	82	223	20	46	10	2	3	21	.206	26	27	0	404	52	5	.989
— Atlanta (N.L.)■	C-1B	6	8	0	0	0	0	0	0	.000	0	0	0	21	1	0	1.000
2000— Omaha (PCL)■	C-1B	37	129	8	32	5	1	1	18	.248	12	9	1	183	20	3	.985
— Kansas City (A.L.)	C-DH	43	142	13	40	4	0	3	17	.282	8	11	1	219	21	2	.992
2001— Anaheim (A.L.)■	C	53	148	9	33	4	2	2	16	.223	3	15	0	267	23	3	.990
American League totals (6 years)		423	1258	109	331	38	3	15	148	.263	66	145	4	2197	193	28	.988
National League totals (2 years)		158	414	31	82	14	2	5	41	.198	40	59	0	715	89	8	.990
Major League totals (8 years)		581	1672	140	413	52	5	20	189	.247	106	204	4	2912	282	36	.989

DIVISION SERIES RECORD

Year Team (League)	Pos.	G	AB	R	H	2B	3B	HR	RBI	Avg.	BB	SO	SB	PO	A	E	Avg.
1999— Atlanta (N.L.)								Did not play.									

CHAMPIONSHIP SERIES RECORD

Year Team (League)	Pos.	G	AB	R	H	2B	3B	HR	RBI	Avg.	BB	SO	SB	PO	A	E	Avg.
1999— Atlanta (N.L.)	PH	2	2	0	0	0	0	0	0	.000	0	1	0	...	...	...	...

WORLD SERIES RECORD

Year Team (League)	Pos.	G	AB	R	H	2B	3B	HR	RBI	Avg.	BB	SO	SB	PO	A	E	Avg.
1999— Atlanta (N.L.)	PH	1	1	0	0	0	0	0	0	.000	0	1	0	...	...	...	...

FARNSWORTH, KYLE — P — CUBS

PERSONAL: Born April 14, 1976, in Wichita, Kan. ... 6-4/215. ... Throws right, bats right. ... Full name: Kyle Lynn Farnsworth.
HIGH SCHOOL: Milton (Alpharetta, Ga.).
JUNIOR COLLEGE: Abraham Baldwin Agricultural College (Ga.).
TRANSACTIONS/CAREER NOTES: Selected by Chicago Cubs organization in 47th round of free-agent draft (June 2, 1994).
RECORDS: Shares N.L. single-inning record for most consecutive home runs allowed—3 (April 6, 2000, third inning).

Year League	W	L	Pct.	ERA	G	GS	CG	ShO	Sv.	IP	H	R	ER	BB	SO
1995— Gulf Coast Cubs (GCL)	3	2	.600	0.87	16	0	0	0	1	31	22	8	3	11	18
1996— Rockford (Midw.)	9	6	.600	3.70	20	20	1	0	0	112	122	62	46	35	82
1997— Daytona (FSL)	10	10	.500	4.09	27	27	2	0	0	156 1/3	178	91	71	47	105
1998— West Tenn (Sou.)	8	2	.800	2.77	13	13	0	0	0	81 1/3	70	32	25	21	73
— Iowa (PCL)	5	9	.357	6.93	18	18	0	0	0	102 2/3	129	88	79	36	79
1999— Iowa (PCL)	2	2	.500	3.20	6	6	0	0	0	39 1/3	38	16	14	9	29
— Chicago (N.L.)	5	9	.357	5.05	27	21	1	1	0	130	140	80	73	52	70
2000— Chicago (N.L.)	2	9	.182	6.43	46	5	0	0	1	77	90	58	55	50	74
— Iowa (PCL)	0	2	.000	3.20	22	0	0	0	9	25 1/3	24	10	9	18	22
2001— Chicago (N.L.)	4	6	.400	2.74	76	0	0	0	2	82	65	26	25	29	107
Major League totals (3 years)	11	24	.314	4.76	149	26	1	1	3	289	295	164	153	131	251

F

FASANO, SAL — C

PERSONAL: Born August 10, 1971, in Chicago. ... 6-2/230. ... Bats right, throws right. ... Full name: Salvatore Frank Fasano.
HIGH SCHOOL: Hoffman Estates (Ill.).
COLLEGE: Evansville.
TRANSACTIONS/CAREER NOTES: Selected by Kansas City Royals organization in 37th round of free-agent draft (June 3, 1993). ... On Kansas City disabled list (April 20-May 9 and August 30, 1998-remainder of season); included rehabilitation assignment to Omaha (May 5-9). ... On Omaha disabled list (August 1-26, 1999). ... Traded by Royals to Oakland Athletics for cash (March 30, 2000). ... Contract purchased by Royals from A's (May 22, 2001). ... Traded by Royals with P Mac Suzuki to Colorado Rockies for C Brent Mayne (June 24, 2001). ... Granted free agency (December 21, 2001).
STATISTICAL NOTES: Led Northwest League catchers with seven double plays in 1993. ... Led Pacific Coast League in being hit by pitch with 26 in 1999. ... Tied for Pacific Coast League lead with 12 errors by catcher in 1999. ... Career major league grand slams: 1.

Year	Team (League)	Pos.	G	AB	R	H	2B	3B	HR	RBI	Avg.	BB	SO	SB	PO	A	E	Avg.
1993—	Eugene (N'West)	C	49	176	25	47	11	1	10	36	.267	19	49	4	276	38	1	.997
1994—	Rockford (Midw.)	C-1B	97	345	61	97	16	1	25	81	.281	33	66	8	527	86	12	.981
	—Wilmington (Caro.).....	C-1B	23	90	15	29	7	0	7	32	.322	13	24	0	80	9	4	.957
1995—	Wilmington (Caro.).....	C-1B	23	88	12	20	2	1	2	7	.227	5	16	0	132	12	0	1.000
	—Wichita (Texas)	C-1B	87	317	60	92	19	2	20	66	.290	27	61	3	589	64	14	.979
1996—	Kansas City (A.L.)	C	51	143	20	29	2	0	6	19	.203	14	25	1	291	14	5	.984
	—Omaha (A.A.).............	C-1B-3B	29	104	12	24	4	0	4	15	.231	6	21	0	198	21	4	.982
1997—	Omaha (A.A.).............	C-DH	49	152	17	25	7	0	4	14	.164	12	53	0	296	34	4	.988
	—Kansas City (A.L.)	C-DH	13	38	4	8	2	0	1	1	.211	1	12	0	53	3	1	.982
	—Wichita (Texas)	C-1B	40	131	27	31	5	0	13	27	.237	20	35	0	232	21	4	.984
1998—	Kansas City (A.L.)	C-1B-DH	74	216	21	49	10	0	8	31	.227	10	56	1	437	25	2	.996
	—Omaha (PCL).............	C	4	14	1	3	1	0	1	2	.214	1	4	0	26	1	0	1.000
1999—	Omaha (PCL).............	C-DH-1B	88	280	63	77	15	0	21	49	.275	42	69	4	582	51	‡12	.981
	—Kansas City (A.L.)	C	23	60	11	14	2	0	5	16	.233	7	17	0	143	8	0	1.000
2000—	Oakland (A.L.)■........	C	52	126	21	27	6	0	7	19	.214	14	47	0	231	22	5	.981
2001—	Oakland (A.L.)	C-DH	11	21	2	1	0	0	0	0	.048	1	12	0	37	3	2	.952
	—Kansas City (A.L.)■...	C	3	1	0	0	0	0	0	0	.000	0	0	0	2	0	0	1.000
	—Omaha (PCL).............	C-1B	13	46	6	11	1	0	2	7	.239	4	11	0	72	12	3	.966
	—Colo. Springs (PCL)■	C	26	82	16	25	4	0	7	23	.305	9	26	0	167	15	3	.984
	—Colorado (N.L.)	C	25	63	10	16	5	0	3	9	.254	4	19	0	153	14	3	.982
American League totals (6 years)			227	605	79	128	22	0	27	86	.212	47	169	2	1194	75	15	.988
National League totals (1 year)			25	63	10	16	5	0	3	9	.254	4	19	0	153	14	3	.982
Major League totals (6 years)			252	668	89	144	27	0	30	95	.216	51	188	2	1347	89	18	.988

DIVISION SERIES RECORD

Year	Team (League)	Pos.	G	AB	R	H	2B	3B	HR	RBI	Avg.	BB	SO	SB	PO	A	E	Avg.
2000—	Oakland (A.L.)	C	1	0	0	0	0	0	0	0	...	0	0	0	1	0	0	1.000

FASSERO, JEFF   P   CUBS

PERSONAL: Born January 5, 1963, in Springfield, Ill. ... 6-1/195. ... Throws left, bats left. ... Full name: Jeffrey Joseph Fassero. ... Name pronounced fuh-SAIR-oh.

HIGH SCHOOL: Griffin (Springfield, Ill.).

JUNIOR COLLEGE: Lincoln Land Community College (Ill.).

COLLEGE: Mississippi.

TRANSACTIONS/CAREER NOTES: Selected by St. Louis Cardinals organization in 22nd round of free-agent draft (June 4, 1984). ... Selected by Chicago White Sox organization from Cardinals organization in Rule 5 minor league draft (December 5, 1989). ... Released by White Sox (April 3, 1990). ... Signed by Cleveland Indians organization (April 9, 1990). ... Granted free agency (October 15, 1990). ... Signed by Montreal Expos organization (January 3, 1991). ... On disabled list (July 24-August 11, 1994). ... Traded by Expos with P Alex Pacheco to Seattle Mariners for C Chris Widger, P Trey Moore and P Matt Wagner (October 29, 1996). ... On disabled list (March 22-April 12, 1998). ... Traded by Mariners to Texas Rangers for a player to named later (August 27, 1999); Mariners acquired OF Adrian Myers to complete deal (September 22, 1999). ... Granted free agency (October 28, 1999). ... Signed by Boston Red Sox (December 22, 1999). ... On disabled list (June 19-July 5, 2000). ... Granted free agency (November 1, 2000). ... Signed by Chicago Cubs (December 8, 2000).

STATISTICAL NOTES: Pitched 5-0 no-hit victory for Arkansas against Jackson (June 12, 1989).

Year	League	W	L	Pct.	ERA	G	GS	CG	ShO	Sv.	IP	H	R	ER	BB	SO
1984—	Johnson City (Appl.)	4	7	.364	4.59	13	11	2	0	1	66²/₃	65	42	34	39	59
1985—	Springfield (Midw.)	4	8	.333	4.01	29	15	1	0	1	119	125	78	53	45	65
1986—	St. Petersburg (FSL)	13	7	.650	2.45	26	•26	6	1	0	*176	156	63	48	56	112
1987—	Arkansas (Texas).............	10	7	.588	4.10	28	27	2	1	0	151¹/₃	168	90	69	67	118
1988—	Arkansas (Texas).............	5	5	.500	3.58	70	1	0	0	17	78	97	48	31	41	72
1989—	Louisville (A.A.).................	3	10	.231	5.22	22	19	0	0	0	112	136	79	65	47	73
	—Arkansas (Texas).............	4	1	.800	1.64	6	6	2	1	0	44	32	11	8	12	38
1990—	Canton/Akron (East.)■......	5	4	.556	2.80	*61	0	0	0	6	64¹/₃	66	24	20	24	61
1991—	Indianapolis (A.A.)■.......	3	0	1.000	1.47	18	0	0	0	4	18¹/₃	11	3	3	7	12
	—Montreal (N.L.).................	2	5	.286	2.44	51	0	0	0	8	55¹/₃	39	17	15	17	42
1992—	Montreal (N.L.).................	8	7	.533	2.84	70	0	0	0	1	85²/₃	81	35	27	34	63
1993—	Montreal (N.L.).................	12	5	.706	2.29	56	15	1	0	1	149²/₃	119	50	38	54	140
1994—	Montreal (N.L.).................	8	6	.571	2.99	21	21	1	0	0	138²/₃	119	54	46	40	119
1995—	Montreal (N.L.).................	13	14	.481	4.33	30	30	1	0	0	189	207	102	91	74	164
1996—	Montreal (N.L.).................	15	11	.577	3.30	34	34	5	1	0	231²/₃	217	95	85	55	222
1997—	Seattle (A.L.)■.................	16	9	.640	3.61	35	•35	2	1	0	234¹/₃	226	108	94	84	189
1998—	Seattle (A.L.).................	13	12	.520	3.97	32	32	7	0	0	224²/₃	223	115	99	66	176
1999—	Seattle (A.L.).................	4	14	.222	7.38	30	24	0	0	0	139	188	123	114	73	101
	—Texas (A.L.)■.................	1	0	1.000	5.71	7	3	0	0	0	17¹/₃	20	12	11	10	13
2000—	Boston (A.L.)■.................	8	8	.500	4.78	38	23	0	0	0	130	153	72	69	50	97
2001—	Chicago (N.L.)■.................	4	4	.500	3.42	82	0	0	0	12	73²/₃	66	31	28	23	79
A.L. totals (4 years)		42	43	.494	4.67	142	117	9	1	0	745¹/₃	810	430	387	283	576
N.L. totals (7 years)		62	52	.544	3.22	344	100	8	1	22	923²/₃	848	384	330	297	829
Major League totals (11 years)		104	95	.523	3.87	486	217	17	2	22	1669	1658	814	717	580	1405

DIVISION SERIES RECORD

Year	League	W	L	Pct.	ERA	G	GS	CG	ShO	Sv.	IP	H	R	ER	BB	SO
1997—	Seattle (A.L.)	1	0	1.000	1.13	1	1	0	0	0	8	3	1	1	4	3
1999—	Texas (A.L.)	0	0	...	9.00	1	0	0	0	0	1	2	1	1	1	1
Division series totals (2 years)		1	0	1.000	2.00	2	1	0	0	0	9	5	2	2	5	4

FEBLES, CARLOS — 2B — ROYALS

PERSONAL: Born May 24, 1976, in El Seybo, Dominican Republic. ... 5-11/185. ... Bats right, throws right. ... Full name: Carlos Manuel Febles.
HIGH SCHOOL: Sagrado Corazon de Jesus (Dominican Republic).
TRANSACTIONS/CAREER NOTES: Signed as non-drafted free agent by Kansas City Royals (November 2, 1993). ... On disabled list (August 24-September 17, 1999). ... On Kansas City disabled list (June 5-July 18 and August 14-September 2, 2000); included rehabilitation assignments to Gulf Coast Royals (June 29-30), Wichita (July 1-4) and Omaha (July 10-18). ... On Kansas City disabled list (April 20-June 8, 2001); included rehabilitation assignment to Omaha (June 4-8).
STATISTICAL NOTES: Led Gulf Coast League second basemen with 230 total chances and 39 double plays in 1995. ... Led Carolina League with 590 total chances and 85 double plays in 1997. ... Led Texas League with .441 on-base percentage in 1998. ... Had 15-game hitting streak (April 6-21, 2000).

Year Team (League)	Pos.	G	AB	R	H	2B	3B	HR	RBI	Avg.	BB	SO	SB	PO	A	E	Avg.
1994—Dom. Royals (DSL)....	2B	56	184	38	61	9	3	2	37	.332	38	27	12	113	113	16	.934
1995—GC Royals (GCL).......	2B	54	188	40	53	13	5	3	20	.282	26	30	16	*117	101	12	.948
1996—Lansing (Midw.)........	2B-SS	102	363	84	107	23	5	5	43	.295	66	64	30	206	292	19	.963
1997—Wilmington (Caro.).....	2B	122	438	78	104	27	6	3	29	.237	51	95	49	212	*355	*23	.961
1998—Wichita (Texas).........	2B	126	432	110	141	28	9	14	52	.326	80	70	*51	248	334	19	.968
— Kansas City (A.L.).....	2B	11	25	5	10	1	2	0	2	.400	4	7	2	16	18	0	1.000
1999—Kansas City (A.L.).....	2B	123	453	71	116	22	9	10	53	.256	47	91	20	272	375	14	.979
2000—Kansas City (A.L.).....	2B	100	339	59	87	12	1	2	29	.257	36	48	17	165	285	10	.978
— GC Royals (GCL).......	2B	1	3	0	1	1	0	0	0	.333	1	0	1	0	1	0	1.000
— Wichita (Texas)........	2B	4	15	2	2	0	0	0	1	.133	2	4	2	5	13	0	1.000
— Omaha (PCL).............	2B	11	42	6	9	4	0	1	5	.214	7	10	3	27	31	1	.983
2001—Kansas City (A.L.).....	2B	79	292	45	69	9	2	8	25	.236	22	58	5	128	224	7	.981
— Omaha (PCL).............	2B	25	98	23	33	7	1	2	9	.337	9	14	6	45	66	0	1.000
Major League totals (4 years)		313	1109	180	282	44	14	20	109	.254	109	204	44	581	902	31	.980

FELIZ, PEDRO — 3B — GIANTS

PERSONAL: Born April 27, 1977, in Azua, Dominican Republic. ... 6-1/195. ... Bats right, throws right.
HIGH SCHOOL: Augustine de Chequer (Dominican Republic).
TRANSACTIONS/CAREER NOTES: Signed as non-drafted free agent by San Francisco Giants organization (February 7, 1994).
STATISTICAL NOTES: Led California League third basemen with 457 total chances and 39 double plays in 1997. ... Led Texas League third basemen with 31 double plays in 1998. ... Led Texas League in grounding into double plays with 18 in 1999. ... Led Texas League third baseman with 407 total chances in 1999. ... Led Pacific Coast League third basemen with 287 assists, 24 errors and 394 total chances in 2000.

Year Team (League)	Pos.	G	AB	R	H	2B	3B	HR	RBI	Avg.	BB	SO	SB	PO	A	E	Avg.
1994—Arizona Giants (Ariz.) .	3B	38	119	7	23	0	0	0	3	.193	2	20	2	19	82	5	.953
1995—Bellingham (N'West)..	3B-1B	43	113	14	31	2	1	0	16	.274	7	33	1	30	37	2	.971
1996—Burlington (Midw.).....	3B-1B	93	321	36	85	12	2	5	36	.265	18	65	5	66	186	17	.937
1997—Bakersfield (Calif.)......	3B	135	515	59	140	25	4	14	56	.272	23	90	5	*112	*322	23	*.950
1998—Shreveport (Texas).....	3B	100	364	39	96	23	2	12	50	.264	9	62	0	*71	204	22	*.926
— Fresno (PCL).............	3B	3	7	1	3	1	0	1	3	.429	1	0	0	2	0	0	1.000
1999—Shreveport (Texas).....	3B	131	491	52	124	24	6	13	77	.253	19	90	4	76	*304	27	.934
2000—Fresno (PCL).............	3B-SS	128	503	85	150	34	2	33	105	.298	30	94	1	84	†288	†24	.939
— San Francisco (N.L.) ..	3B	8	7	1	2	0	0	0	0	.286	0	1	0	0	0	0	...
2001—San Francisco (N.L.) ..	3B-DH	94	220	23	50	9	1	7	22	.227	10	50	2	40	79	12	.908
Major League totals (2 years)		102	227	24	52	9	1	7	22	.229	10	51	2	40	79	12	.908

FERNANDEZ, JARED — P — REDS

PERSONAL: Born February 2, 1972, in Salt Lake City, Utah. ... 6-1/225. ... Throws right, bats right. ... Full name: Jared Wade Fernandez.
HIGH SCHOOL: Kearns (Utah).
JUNIOR COLLEGE: Eastern Utah.
COLLEGE: Fresno State.
TRANSACTIONS/CAREER NOTES: Signed as non-drafted free agent by Boston Red Sox organization (June 23, 1994). ... On disabled list (July 30, 2000-remainder of season). ... Granted free agency (October 15, 2000). ... Signed by Cincinnati Reds organization (December 15, 2000).
STATISTICAL NOTES: Led Eastern League pitchers with nine sacrifice flies allowed in 1996. ... Led International League pitchers with 20 wild pitches in 2001.

Year League	W	L	Pct.	ERA	G	GS	CG	ShO	Sv.	IP	H	R	ER	BB	SO
1994—Utica (NY-Penn)	1	1	.500	3.60	21	1	0	0	4	30	43	18	12	8	24
1995—Utica (NY-Penn)	3	2	.600	1.89	5	5	1	0	0	38	30	11	8	9	23
— Trenton (East.)	5	4	.556	3.90	11	10	1	0	0	67	64	32	29	28	40
1996—Trenton (East.)	9	9	.500	5.08	30	*29	3	0	0	179	185	•115	*101	83	94
1997—Trenton (East.)	4	6	.400	5.41	21	16	1	0	0	121 1/3	138	90	73	66	73
— Pawtucket (I.L.)	0	5	.000	5.79	11	11	0	0	0	60 2/3	76	45	39	28	33
1998—Trenton (East.)	3	7	.300	5.25	36	7	0	0	1	118 1/3	132	80	69	51	70
— Pawtucket (I.L.)	1	1	.500	4.74	5	4	0	0	0	24 2/3	26	16	13	7	15
1999—Trenton (East.)	3	0	1.000	3.38	7	0	0	0	1	18 2/3	18	9	7	8	10
— Pawtucket (I.L.)	12	9	.571	4.25	27	20	3	0	0	163	172	88	77	39	76
2000—Pawtucket (I.L.)	10	4	.714	3.02	31	9	2	0	4	113 1/3	103	51	38	36	65
2001—Louisville (I.L.)■..............	10	5	.526	4.13	33	28	4	1	0	*196 1/3	*218	105	90	54	118
— Cincinnati (N.L.)	0	1	.000	4.38	5	2	0	0	0	12 1/3	13	9	6	6	5
Major League totals (1 year).........	0	1	.000	4.38	5	2	0	0	0	12 1/3	13	9	6	6	5

F

FERNANDEZ, JOSE — 3B

PERSONAL: Born November 2, 1974, in La Vega, Dominican Republic. ... 6-3/220. ... Bats left, throws right. ... Full name: Jose Mayobanex Fernandez.

HIGH SCHOOL: Instituto Evangelico (Santo Domingo, Dominican Republic).

COLLEGE: Universidad Madre y Maestra (Santiago, Dominican Republic).

TRANSACTIONS/CAREER NOTES: Signed as non-drafted free agent by Montreal Expos organization (March 2, 1993). ... On Ottawa disabled list (September 1, 1998-remainder of season). ... Released by Expos (December 13, 1999). ... Signed by Milwaukee Brewers organization (January 3, 2000). ... Granted free agency (October 18, 2000). ... Signed by Anaheim Angels (January 10, 2001). ... On Salt Lake disabled list (May 11-18, 2001). ... Claimed on waivers by Chicago Cubs (October 10, 2001). ... Released by Cubs (October 26, 2001).

STATISTICAL NOTES: Tied for International League lead with 94 putouts by third baseman in 1999. ... Led International League third basemen with 31 errors in 1999. ... Led International League third basemen with .955 fielding percentage and 97 putouts in 2000. ... Led Pacific Coast League with .421 on-base percentage in 2001. ... Led Pacific Coast League third basemen with 320 total chances and 234 assists in 2001.

Year Team (League)	Pos.	G	AB	R	H	2B	3B	HR	RBI	Avg.	BB	SO	SB	PO	A	E	Avg.
1993—Dom. Expos (DSL)	IF	65	251	40	80	8	1	10	49	.319	32	23	2	103	223	25	.929
1994—GC Expos (GCL)	3B-1B	45	172	27	40	8	0	5	23	.233	14	35	11	87	77	9	.948
—Ottawa (I.L.)	3B-1B	21	60	8	16	4	1	0	4	.267	5	14	3	35	18	5	.914
1995—Vermont (NY-Penn)	3B	66	270	38	74	6	7	4	41	.274	13	51	29	48	157	21	.907
1996—Delmarva (S.Atl.)........	3B	126	421	72	115	23	6	12	70	.273	50	76	23	*102	239	35	.907
1997—Harrisburg (East.).......	3B-1B	29	96	10	22	3	1	4	11	.229	11	28	2	41	31	6	.923
—W.P. Beach (FSL)........	3B-1B	97	350	49	108	21	3	9	58	.309	37	76	22	89	193	15	.949
1998—Harrisburg (East.).......	3B-1B	104	369	59	109	27	1	17	58	.295	36	73	16	119	167	22	.929
1999—Ottawa (I.L.)	3-1-DH-2	124	465	73	126	30	2	14	68	.271	31	136	14	‡185	229	†31	.930
—Montreal (N.L.)............	3B	8	24	0	5	2	0	0	1	.208	1	7	0	7	9	2	.889
2000—Indianapolis (I.L.)■....	3B-1B-2B	133	468	70	134	37	4	11	68	.286	49	93	10	123	228	18	.951
2001—Salt Lake (PCL)■....	3B-1B-OF	122	452	99	153	37	1	30	*114	.338	55	91	9	77	†234	15	.954
—Anaheim (A.L.)	DH-1B-3B	13	25	1	2	1	0	0	0	.080	2	10	0	0	0	1	.000
American League totals (1 year)		13	25	1	2	1	0	0	0	.080	2	10	0	0	0	1	.000
National League totals (1 year)		8	24	0	5	2	0	0	1	.208	1	7	0	7	9	2	.889
Major League totals (2 years)		21	49	1	7	3	0	0	1	.143	3	17	0	7	9	3	.842

FERNANDEZ, OSVALDO — P

PERSONAL: Born November 4, 1968, in Holguin, Cuba. ... 6-2/193. ... Throws right, bats right.

HIGH SCHOOL: Universidad de Holguin (Holguin, Cuba).

TRANSACTIONS/CAREER NOTES: Signed as non-drafted free agent by San Francisco Giants organization (January 16, 1996). ... On San Francisco disabled list (May 20-June 19 and June 26-September 28, 1997); included rehabilitation assignment to Phoenix (June 11-20). ... On disabled list (March 22, 1998-entire season). ... Granted free agency (December 21, 1998). ... Re-signed by Giants organization (January 4, 1999). ... On Fresno disabled list (April 8-August 1, 1999). ... On San Jose disabled list (August 25, 1999-remainder of season). ... Granted free agency (October 15, 1999). ... Signed by Cincinnati Reds organization (February 15, 2000). ... On Cincinnati disabled list (July 7-September 1, 2000); included rehabilitation assignment to Louisville (August 5-September 1). ... Granted free agency (October 8, 2001).

MISCELLANEOUS: Appeared in three games as pinch runner (1996). ... Appeared in one game as pinch runner with San Francisco (1997).

Year League	W	L	Pct.	ERA	G	GS	CG	ShO	Sv.	IP	H	R	ER	BB	SO
1996—San Francisco (N.L.)	7	13	.350	4.61	30	28	2	0	0	$171\frac{2}{3}$	193	95	88	57	106
1997—San Francisco (N.L.)	3	4	.429	4.95	11	11	0	0	0	$56\frac{1}{3}$	74	39	31	15	31
—Phoenix (PCL)...................	0	0	...	3.00	2	2	0	0	0	12	10	5	4	3	4
1998—San Francisco (N.L.)							Did not play.								
1999—San Jose (Calif.)	0	1	.000	6.00	4	4	0	0	0	9	6	6	6	2	5
2000—Chattanooga (Sou.)■....	0	0	...	12.71	1	1	0	0	0	$5\frac{2}{3}$	11	9	8	3	1
—Louisville (I.L.).................	6	1	.857	4.13	10	10	0	0	0	$56\frac{2}{3}$	57	27	26	19	44
—Cincinnati (N.L.).............	4	3	.571	3.62	15	14	1	0	0	$79\frac{2}{3}$	69	33	32	31	36
2001—Cincinnati (N.L.).............	5	6	.455	6.92	20	14	0	0	0	$79\frac{1}{3}$	103	62	61	33	35
—Louisville (I.L.).................	3	2	.600	3.86	9	9	0	0	0	$53\frac{2}{3}$	54	26	23	12	31
Major League totals (4 years).......	19	26	.422	4.93	76	67	3	0	0	387	439	229	212	136	208

FERNANDEZ, TONY — 3B/DH

PERSONAL: Born June 30, 1962, in San Pedro de Macoris, Dominican Republic. ... 6-2/195. ... Bats both, throws right. ... Full name: Octavio Antonio Castro Fernandez.

HIGH SCHOOL: Gasto Fernando de Ligne (San Pedro de Macoris, Dominican Republic).

TRANSACTIONS/CAREER NOTES: Signed as non-drafted free agent by Toronto Blue Jays organization (April 24, 1979). ... On Syracuse disabled list (August 10-27, 1981). ... On disabled list (April 8-May 2, 1989). ... Traded by Blue Jays with 1B Fred McGriff to San Diego Padres for OF Joe Carter and 2B Roberto Alomar (December 5, 1990). ... Traded by Padres to New York Mets for P Wally Whitehurst, OF D.J. Dozier and a player to be named later (October 26, 1992); Padres acquired C Raul Casanova from Mets to complete deal (December 7, 1992). ... Traded by Mets to Blue Jays for OF Darrin Jackson (June 11, 1993). ... Granted free agency (November 3, 1993). ... Signed by Cincinnati Reds organization (March 8, 1994). ... Granted free agency (October 13, 1994). ... Signed by New York Yankees (December 15, 1994). ... On disabled list (May 21-June 8, 1995). ... On disabled list (March 24, 1996-remainder of season). ... Granted free agency (November 18, 1996). ... Signed by Cleveland Indians (December 28, 1996). ... Granted free agency (October 30, 1997). ... Signed by Blue Jays (December 8, 1997). ... Granted free agency (November 5, 1999). ... Signed by Seibu Lions of Japan Pacific League (February 7, 2000). ... Signed by Milwaukee Brewers organization (February 8, 2001). ... Released by Brewers (May 29, 2001). ... Signed by Blue Jays organization (June 8, 2001). ... Granted free agency (November 5, 2001).

RECORDS: Shares major league record for most times caught stealing in one inning—2 (June 26, 1992, fifth inning). ... Holds A.L. single-season record for most games by shortstop—163 (1986). ... Shares A.L. single-season record for most games by switch hitter—163 (1986).

HONORS: Named shortstop on THE SPORTING NEWS A.L. All-Star team (1986). ... Won A.L. Gold Glove at shortstop (1986-89).

STATISTICAL NOTES: Led International League shortstops with 87 double plays in 1983. ... Led A.L. shortstops with 791 total chances in 1985 and 786 in 1990. ... Led N.L. third basemen with .991 fielding percentage in 1994. ... Hit for the cycle (September 3, 1995, 10 innings). ... Career major league grand slams: 3.

MISCELLANEOUS: Holds Toronto Blue Jays all-time record for most hits (1,583), doubles (291) and triples (72).

Year Team (League)	Pos.	G	AB	R	H	2B	3B	HR	RBI	Avg.	BB	SO	SB	PO	A	E	Avg.
1980— Kinston (Caro.)	SS	62	187	28	52	6	2	0	12	.278	28	17	7	93	205	28	.914
1981— Kinston (Caro.)	SS	75	280	57	89	10	6	1	13	.318	49	20	15	121	227	19	.948
— Syracuse (I.L.)	SS	31	115	13	32	6	2	1	9	.278	7	15	9	69	80	3	.980
1982— Syracuse (I.L.)	SS	134	523	78	158	21	6	4	56	.302	42	31	22	*246	364	23	*.964
1983— Syracuse (I.L.)	SS	117	437	65	131	18	6	5	38	.300	57	27	35	*211	361	26	.957
— Toronto (A.L.)	SS-DH	15	34	5	9	1	1	0	2	.265	2	2	0	16	17	0	1.000
1984— Syracuse (I.L.)	SS	26	94	12	24	1	0	0	6	.255	13	9	1	46	72	5	.959
— Toronto (A.L.)	SS-3B-DH	88	233	29	63	5	3	3	19	.270	17	15	5	119	195	9	.972
1985— Toronto (A.L.)	SS	161	564	71	163	31	10	2	51	.289	43	41	13	283	*478	30	.962
1986— Toronto (A.L.)	SS	*163	*687	91	213	33	9	10	65	.310	27	52	25	*294	445	13	*.983
1987— Toronto (A.L.)	SS	146	578	90	186	29	8	5	67	.322	51	48	32	*270	396	14	.979
1988— Toronto (A.L.)	SS	154	648	76	186	41	4	5	70	.287	45	65	15	247	470	14	.981
1989— Toronto (A.L.)	SS	140	573	64	147	25	9	11	64	.257	29	51	22	260	475	6	*.992
1990— Toronto (A.L.)	SS	161	635	84	175	27	*17	4	66	.276	71	70	26	*297	*480	9	.989
1991— San Diego (N.L.)■	SS	145	558	81	152	27	5	4	38	.272	55	74	23	247	440	20	.972
1992— San Diego (N.L.)■	SS	155	622	84	171	32	4	4	37	.275	56	62	20	240	405	11	.983
1993— New York (N.L.)■	SS	48	173	20	39	5	2	1	14	.225	25	19	6	83	150	6	.975
— Toronto (A.L.)■	SS	94	353	45	108	18	9	4	50	.306	31	26	15	196	260	7	.985
1994— Cincinnati (N.L.)■	3B-SS-2B	104	366	50	102	18	6	8	50	.279	44	40	12	67	195	4	†.985
1995— New York (N.L.)■	SS-2B	108	384	57	94	20	2	5	45	.245	42	40	6	148	283	10	.977
1996— New York (A.L.)							Did not play.										
1997— Cleveland (A.L.)■	2B-SS-DH	120	409	55	117	21	1	11	44	.286	22	47	6	219	322	11	.980
1998— Cleveland (A.L.)■	2B-3B-DH	138	486	71	156	36	2	9	72	.321	45	53	13	160	296	13	.972
1999— Cleveland (A.L.)■	3B-DH-2B	142	485	73	159	41	0	6	75	.328	77	62	6	65	212	18	.939
2000— Seibu (Jap. Pac.)■	...	370	64	121	24	1	11	74	.327	...	...	2	...	...	...	...	
2001— Milwaukee (N.L.)■	3B	28	64	6	18	0	0	1	3	.281	7	9	1	3	25	1	.966
— Toronto (A.L.)■	DH	48	59	5	18	4	0	1	12	.305	1	8	0	...	...	...	...
American League totals (14 years)		1678	6128	816	1794	332	75	76	702	.293	503	580	184	2574	4329	154	.978
National League totals (5 years)		480	1783	241	482	82	17	18	142	.270	187	204	62	640	1215	42	.978
Major League totals (17 years)		2158	7911	1057	2276	414	92	94	844	.288	690	784	246	3214	5544	196	.978

DIVISION SERIES RECORD

Year Team (League)	Pos.	G	AB	R	H	2B	3B	HR	RBI	Avg.	BB	SO	SB	PO	A	E	Avg.
1995— New York (A.L.)	SS	5	21	0	5	2	0	0	0	.238	2	2	0	9	15	0	1.000
1997— Cleveland (A.L.)	2B-PH	4	11	0	2	1	0	0	4	.182	0	0	0	8	9	0	1.000
Division series totals (2 years)		9	32	0	7	3	0	0	4	.219	2	2	0	17	24	0	1.000

CHAMPIONSHIP SERIES RECORD

Year Team (League)	Pos.	G	AB	R	H	2B	3B	HR	RBI	Avg.	BB	SO	SB	PO	A	E	Avg.
1985— Toronto (A.L.)	SS	7	24	2	8	2	0	0	2	.333	1	2	0	11	15	2	.929
1989— Toronto (A.L.)	SS	5	20	6	7	3	0	0	1	.350	1	2	5	9	15	0	1.000
1993— Toronto (A.L.)	SS	6	22	1	7	0	0	0	1	.318	2	4	0	12	8	0	1.000
1997— Cleveland (A.L.)	2B-PH	5	14	1	5	1	0	1	2	.357	1	2	0	9	10	1	.950
Championship series totals (4 years)		23	80	10	27	6	0	1	6	.338	5	10	5	41	48	3	.967

WORLD SERIES RECORD

NOTES: Member of World Series championship team (1993).

Year Team (League)	Pos.	G	AB	R	H	2B	3B	HR	RBI	Avg.	BB	SO	SB	PO	A	E	Avg.
1993— Toronto (A.L.)	SS	6	21	2	7	1	0	0	9	.333	3	3	0	11	8	0	1.000
1997— Cleveland (A.L.)	2B-PH	5	17	1	8	1	0	0	4	.471	0	1	0	9	14	2	.920
World Series totals (2 years)		11	38	3	15	2	0	0	13	.395	3	4	2	20	22	2	.955

ALL-STAR GAME RECORD

Year League	Pos.	AB	R	H	2B	3B	HR	RBI	Avg.	BB	SO	SB	PO	A	E	Avg.
1986— American	SS	0	0	0	0	0	0		...	0	0	0	0	0	0	...
1987— American	SS	2	0	0	0	0	0	0	.000	0	0	0	1	3	0	1.000
1989— American	PR-SS	1	0	0	0	0	0	0	.000	0	0	0	2	2	0	1.000
1992— National	SS	2	1	1	0	0	0	0	.500	0	0	0	3	0	0	1.000
1999— American	3B	2	0	0	0	0	0	0	.000	0	1	0	0	2	0	1.000
All-Star Game totals (5 years)		7	1	1	0	0	0	0	.143	0	1	0	6	7	0	1.000

FETTERS, MIKE   P   PIRATES

PERSONAL: Born December 19, 1964, in Van Nuys, Calif. ... 6-4/226. ... Throws right, bats right. ... Full name: Michael Lee Fetters.
HIGH SCHOOL: Iolani (Honolulu, Hawaii).
COLLEGE: Pepperdine.
TRANSACTIONS/CAREER NOTES: Selected by Los Angeles Dodgers organization in 22nd round of free-agent draft (June 6, 1983); did not sign. ... Selected by California Angels organization in supplemental round ("sandwich pick" between first and second round, 27th pick overall) of free-agent draft (June 2, 1986); pick received as compensation for Baltimore Orioles signing Type A free-agent OF/IF Juan Beniquez. ... Traded by Angels with P Glenn Carter to Milwaukee Brewers for P Chuck Crim (December 10, 1991). ... On disabled list (May 3-19, 1992 and May 25-June 9, 1995). ... On Milwaukee disabled list (April 4-May 5, 1997); included rehabilitation assignment to Tucson (April 30-May 5). ... Traded by Brewers with P Ben McDonald and P Ron Villone to Cleveland Indians for OF Marquis Grissom and P Jeff Juden (December 8, 1997). ... Traded by Indians to Oakland Athletics for P Steve Karsay (December 8, 1997). ... On Oakland disabled list (April 6-26, 1998). ... Traded by A's to Anaheim Angels for a player to be named later and cash (August 10, 1998). ... Granted free agency (October 26, 1998). ... Signed by Baltimore Orioles organization (February 4, 1999). ... On Baltimore disabled list (June 7-September 1, 1999); included rehabilitation assignment to Rochester (August 23-31). ... Granted free agency (November 1, 1999). ... Signed by Dodgers organization (December 15, 1999). ... On disabled list (May 4-26, 2000). ... On suspended list (July 21-22, 2000). ... On Los Angeles disabled list (June 20-July 5, 2001). ... Traded by Dodgers with P Adrian Burnside to Pittsburgh Pirates for P Terry Mulholland (July 31, 2001).

Year League	W	L	Pct.	ERA	G	GS	CG	ShO	Sv.	IP	H	R	ER	BB	SO
1986—Salem (N'West)	4	2	.667	3.38	12	12	1	0	0	72	60	39	27	51	72
1987—Palm Springs (Calif.)	9	7	.563	3.57	19	19	2	0	0	116	106	62	46	73	105
1988—Midland (Texas)	8	8	.500	5.92	20	20	2	0	0	114	116	78	75	67	101
—Edmonton (PCL)	2	0	1.000	1.93	2	2	1	0	0	14	8	3	3	10	11
1989—Edmonton (PCL)	12	8	.600	3.80	26	26	•6	2	0	168	160	80	71	72	*144
—California (A.L.)	0	0	...	8.10	1	0	0	0	0	3 1/3	5	4	3	1	4
1990—Edmonton (PCL)	1	1	.500	0.99	5	5	1	1	0	27 1/3	22	9	3	13	26
—California (A.L.)	1	1	.500	4.12	26	2	0	0	1	67 2/3	77	33	31	20	35
1991—Edmonton (PCL)	2	7	.222	4.87	11	11	1	0	0	61	65	39	33	26	43
—California (A.L.)	2	5	.286	4.84	19	4	0	0	0	44 2/3	53	29	24	28	24
1992—Milwaukee (A.L.)■	5	1	.833	1.87	50	0	0	0	2	62 2/3	38	15	13	24	43
1993—Milwaukee (A.L.)	3	3	.500	3.34	45	0	0	0	0	59 1/3	59	29	22	22	23
1994—Milwaukee (A.L.)	1	4	.200	2.54	42	0	0	0	17	46	41	16	13	27	31
1995—Milwaukee (A.L.)	0	3	.000	3.38	40	0	0	0	22	34 2/3	40	16	13	20	33
1996—Milwaukee (A.L.)	3	5	.500	3.38	61	0	0	0	32	61 1/3	65	28	23	26	53
1997—Milwaukee (A.L.)	1	5	.167	3.45	51	0	0	0	6	70 1/3	62	30	27	33	62
—Tucson (PCL)	0	0	...	10.80	2	0	0	0	0	1 2/3	1	2	2	1	0
1998—Oakland (A.L.)■	1	6	.143	3.99	48	0	0	0	5	47 1/3	48	26	21	21	34
—Anaheim (A.L.)■	1	2	.333	5.56	12	0	0	0	0	11 1/3	14	8	7	4	9
1999—Baltimore (A.L.)■	1	0	1.000	5.81	27	0	0	0	0	31	35	23	20	22	22
—Rochester (I.L.)	0	0	...	0.00	4	0	0	0	0	3 2/3	0	0	0	2	6
2000—Los Angeles (N.L.)■	6	2	.750	3.24	51	0	0	0	5	50	35	18	18	25	40
2001—Los Angeles (N.L.)	2	1	.667	6.07	34	0	0	0	1	29 2/3	33	23	20	13	26
—Pittsburgh (N.L.)■	1	1	.500	4.58	20	0	0	0	8	17 2/3	16	9	9	13	11
A.L. totals (11 years)	19	33	.365	3.62	422	6	0	0	85	539 2/3	537	257	217	248	373
N.L. totals (2 years)	9	4	.692	4.35	105	0	0	0	14	97 1/3	84	50	47	51	77
Major League totals (13 years)	28	37	.431	3.73	527	6	0	0	99	637	621	307	264	299	450

FICK, ROBERT   C/1B   TIGERS

PERSONAL: Born March 15, 1974, in Torrance, Calif. ... 6-1/189. ... Bats left, throws right. ... Full name: Robert Charles John Fick. ... Brother of Chris Fick, former outfielder/first baseman in St. Louis Cardinals and Arizona Diamondbacks organizations; and brother of Chuck Fick, St. Louis Cardinals scout and former catcher in Montreal Expos and Oakland Athletics organization.
HIGH SCHOOL: Newbury Park (Calif.).
JUNIOR COLLEGE: Ventura (Calif.) College.
COLLEGE: Cal State-Northridge.
TRANSACTIONS/CAREER NOTES: Selected by Oakland Athletics organization in 45th round of free-agent draft (June 1, 1992); did not sign. ... Selected by Detroit Tigers organization in 43rd round of free-agent draft (June 1, 1995); did not sign. ... Selected by Tigers organization in fifth round of free-agent draft (June 4, 1996). ... On Detroit disabled list (March 31-September 7, 1999); included rehabilitation assignments to Gulf Coast Tigers (August 18-20), West Michigan (August 21-23) and Toledo (August 24-September 6). ... On suspended list (May 23-26, 2000). ... On Detroit disabled list (July 6-September 1, 2000); included rehabilitation assignment to Toledo (August 13-September 1). ... On suspended list (September 22-27, 2001).
HONORS: Named Midwest League Most Valuable Player (1996).
STATISTICAL NOTES: Led Midwest League with 262 total bases and .566 slugging percentage in 1997. ... Career major league grand slams: 1.

Year Team (League)	Pos.	G	AB	R	H	2B	3B	HR	RBI	Avg.	BB	SO	SB	PO	A	E	Avg.
1996—Jamestown (NY-P)	C	43	133	18	33	6	0	1	14	.248	12	25	3	155	13	3	.982
1997—W. Michigan (Midw.)	1B-C-3B	122	463	100	*158	*50	3	16	90	*.341	75	74	13	1043	68	12	.989
1998—Jacksonville (Sou.)	C-1B-OF	130	515	101	164	•47	6	18	114	.318	71	83	8	540	45	9	.985
—Detroit (A.L.)	C-DH-1B	7	22	6	8	1	0	3	7	.364	2	7	1	27	1	1	.966
1999—GC Tigers (GCL)	DH-C-1B	3	9	2	3	1	0	0	2	.333	2	0	1	13	5	0	1.000
—W. Michigan (Midw.)	DH-C-1B	3	11	2	3	0	0	0	0	.273	2	0	1	18	3	2	.913
—Toledo (I.L.)	1B-C-DH-3B	14	48	11	15	0	1	2	8	.313	8	5	1	77	8	5	.944
—Detroit (A.L.)	DH-C	15	41	6	9	0	0	3	10	.220	7	6	1	24	1	0	1.000
2000—Detroit (A.L.)	1B-C-DH	66	163	18	41	7	2	3	22	.252	22	39	2	272	21	5	.983
—Toledo (I.L.)	1B	17	68	5	10	5	0	1	7	.147	6	13	1	53	4	0	1.000
2001—Detroit (A.L.)	C-1B-OF-DH	124	401	62	109	21	2	19	61	.272	39	62	0	596	39	7	.989
Major League totals (4 years)		212	627	92	167	29	4	28	100	.266	70	114	4	919	62	13	.987

FIGUEROA, LUIS   SS/2B   METS

PERSONAL: Born February 16, 1974, in Bayamon, Puerto Rico. ... 5-9/150. ... Bats both, throws right. ... Full name: Luis R. Figueroa.
HIGH SCHOOL: Berkshire (Homestead, Fla.).
TRANSACTIONS/CAREER NOTES: Signed as non-drafted free agent by Pittsburgh Pirates organization (March 31, 1997). ... Claimed on waivers by New York Mets (August 15, 2001).
STATISTICAL NOTES: Led Eastern League shortstops with 222 putouts and 641 total chances in 1999.

Year Team (League)	Pos.	G	AB	R	H	2B	3B	HR	RBI	Avg.	BB	SO	SB	PO	A	E	Avg.
1997—Augusta (S.Atl.)	SS-2B	71	248	38	56	8	0	0	21	.226	35	29	22	107	196	19	.941
—Lynchburg (Caro.)	2B	26	89	12	25	5	0	0	2	.281	7	6	1	46	58	1	.990
1998—Carolina (Sou.)	SS-2B	117	350	54	87	9	3	0	24	.249	71	46	6	200	359	27	.954
1999—Altoona (East.)	SS-2B	131	418	61	110	15	5	3	50	.263	52	44	9	†222	396	28	.957
2000—Altoona (East.)	SS	94	342	45	97	10	4	1	28	.284	37	32	14	166	307	26	.948
—Nashville (PCL)	SS-2B-3B	23	64	6	16	1	0	3	8	.250	1	8	2	23	31	5	.915
2001—Nashville (PCL)	SS-2B-3B	92	347	45	104	11	1	4	29	.300	31	26	8	157	303	19	.960
—Pittsburgh (N.L.)	2B	4	2	0	0	0	0	0	0	.000	0	0	0	1	4	0	1.000
—Norfolk (I.L.)■	SS-2B	17	58	7	15	3	1	1	5	.259	5	6	2	26	52	2	.975
Major League totals (1 year)		4	2	0	0	0	0	0	0	.000	0	0	0	1	4	0	1.000

F

FIGUEROA, NELSON   P   PHILLIES

PERSONAL: Born May 18, 1974, in Brooklyn, N.Y. ... 6-1/155. ... Throws right, bats both. ... Full name: Nelson Walter Figueroa Jr.
HIGH SCHOOL: Abraham Lincoln (Brooklyn, N.Y.).
COLLEGE: Brandeis (Mass.).
TRANSACTIONS/CAREER NOTES: Selected by New York Mets organization in 30th round of free-agent draft (June 1, 1995). ... Traded by Mets with OF Bernard Gilkey and cash to Arizona Diamondbacks for P Willie Blair, C Jorge Fabregas and cash considerations (July 31, 1998). ... On Tucson disabled list (June 12-23 and July 6-30, 1999). ... Traded by Diamondbacks with OF Travis Lee, P Omar Daal and P Vicente Padilla to Philadelphia Phillies for P Curt Schilling (July 26, 2000).
HONORS: Named South Atlantic League Most Outstanding Pitcher (1996).

Year	League	W	L	Pct.	ERA	G	GS	CG	ShO	Sv.	IP	H	R	ER	BB	SO
1995—	Kingsport (Appl.)	7	3	.700	3.07	12	12	2	*2	0	76 1/3	57	31	26	22	79
1996—	Columbia (S.Atl.)	14	7	.667	*2.04	26	25	*8	*4	0	*185 1/3	119	55	42	58	*200
1997—	Binghamton (East.)	5	11	.313	4.34	33	22	0	0	0	143	137	76	69	68	116
1998—	Binghamton (East.)	12	3	.800	4.66	21	21	3	2	0	123 2/3	133	73	64	44	116
—	Tucson (PCL)■	2	2	.500	3.70	7	7	0	0	0	41 1/3	46	22	17	16	29
1999—	Tucson (PCL)	11	6	.647	3.94	24	21	1	1	0	128	128	59	56	41	106
—	Ariz. Diamondbacks (Ariz.)	0	1	.000	0.00	1	1	0	0	0	3	3	1	0	0	2
2000—	Tucson (PCL)	9	4	.692	2.81	17	16	1	0	0	112	101	41	35	28	78
—	Arizona (N.L.)	0	1	.000	7.47	3	3	0	0	0	15 2/3	17	13	13	5	7
—	Scranton/W.B. (I.L.)■	4	3	.571	3.78	8	8	1	0	0	50	50	28	21	11	35
2001—	Scranton/W.B. (I.L.)	4	2	.667	2.47	13	12	3	0	0	87 1/3	74	33	24	18	74
—	Philadelphia (N.L.)	4	5	.444	3.94	19	13	0	0	0	89	95	40	39	37	61
Major League totals (2 years)		**4**	**6**	**.400**	**4.47**	**22**	**16**	**0**	**0**	**0**	**104 2/3**	**112**	**53**	**52**	**42**	**68**

FIKAC, JEREMY   P   PADRES

PERSONAL: Born April 8, 1975, in Shine, Texas. ... 6-2/185. ... Throws right, bats right. ... Full name: Jeremy Joseph Fikac.
HIGH SCHOOL: Somerville (Texas).
COLLEGE: Southwest Texas State.
TRANSACTIONS/CAREER NOTES: Selected by San Diego Padres organization in 19th round of free-agent draft (June 2, 1998).

Year	League	W	L	Pct.	ERA	G	GS	CG	ShO	Sv.	IP	H	R	ER	BB	SO
1998—	Idaho Falls (Pio.)	2	0	1.000	2.25	12	0	0	0	1	20	11	6	5	8	19
1999—	Rancho Cuca. (Calif.)	8	3	.727	5.08	40	6	0	0	0	85	94	50	48	43	75
2000—	Rancho Cuca. (Calif.)	5	3	.625	1.80	61	0	0	0	20	75	46	19	15	24	101
2001—	Mobile (Sou.)	6	0	1.000	1.97	53	0	0	0	18	68 2/3	54	16	15	20	75
—	Portland (PCL)	0	0	...	3.00	1	0	0	0	0	3	3	1	1	0	3
—	San Diego (N.L.)	2	0	1.000	1.37	23	0	0	0	0	26 1/3	15	6	4	5	19
Major League totals (1 year)		**2**	**0**	**1.000**	**1.37**	**23**	**0**	**0**	**0**	**0**	**26 1/3**	**15**	**6**	**4**	**5**	**19**

FILE, BOB   P   BLUE JAYS

PERSONAL: Born January 28, 1977, in Philadelphia. ... 6-4/210. ... Throws right, bats right. ... Full name: Robert Michael File.
HIGH SCHOOL: Father Judge (Philadelphia).
COLLEGE: Philadelphia College of Textiles and Science.
TRANSACTIONS/CAREER NOTES: Selected by Toronto Blue Jays organization in 19th round of free-agent draft (June 2, 1998).

Year	League	W	L	Pct.	ERA	G	GS	CG	ShO	Sv.	IP	H	R	ER	BB	SO
1998—	Medicine Hat (Pio.)	2	1	.667	1.41	28	0	0	0	•16	32	24	7	5	5	28
1999—	Dunedin (FSL)	4	1	.800	1.70	47	0	0	0	26	53	30	13	10	14	48
2000—	Tennessee (Sou.)	4	3	.571	3.12	36	0	0	0	20	34 2/3	29	20	12	13	40
—	Syracuse (I.L.)	2	0	1.000	0.93	20	0	0	0	8	19 1/3	14	2	2	2	10
2001—	Tennessee (Sou.)	0	0	...	3.00	3	0	0	0	1	3	3	1	1	0	2
—	Toronto (A.L.)	5	3	.625	3.27	60	0	0	0	0	74 1/3	57	28	27	29	38
—	Syracuse (I.L.)	0	0	...	0.00	2	0	0	0	0	4	1	0	0	0	3
Major League totals (1 year)		**5**	**3**	**.625**	**3.27**	**60**	**0**	**0**	**0**	**0**	**74 1/3**	**57**	**28**	**27**	**29**	**38**

FINLEY, CHUCK   P   INDIANS

PERSONAL: Born November 26, 1962, in Monroe, La. ... 6-6/225. ... Throws left, bats left. ... Full name: Charles Edward Finley.
HIGH SCHOOL: West Monroe (La.).
COLLEGE: Northeast Louisiana.
TRANSACTIONS/CAREER NOTES: Selected by California Angels organization in 15th round of free-agent draft (June 4, 1984); did not sign. ... Selected by Angels organization in secondary phase of free-agent draft (January 9, 1985). ... On disabled list (August 22-September 15, 1989; and April 6-22, 1992). ... Granted free agency (November 7, 1995). ... Re-signed by Angels (January 4, 1996). ... Angels franchise renamed Anaheim Angels for 1997 season. ... On Anaheim disabled list (March 23-April 15 and August 20, 1997-remainder of season); included rehabilitation assignment to Lake Elsinore (April 5-10). ... Granted free agency (November 2, 1999). ... Signed by Cleveland Indians (December 16, 1999). ... On Cleveland disabled list (May 29-June 20 and June 26-August 9, 2001); included rehabilitation assignments to Akron (July 15 and August 1-9).
RECORDS: Shares major league single-inning record for most strikeouts—4 (May 12, 1999, third inning; August 15, 1999, first inning; and April 16, 2000, third inning).
HONORS: Named lefthanded pitcher on THE SPORTING NEWS A.L. All-Star team (1989-90).
STATISTICAL NOTES: Pitched 5-0 one-hit, complete-game victory against Boston (May 26, 1989). ... Struck out 15 batters in one game (June 24, 1989; and May 23, 1995). ... Led A.L. with 17 wild pitches in 1996 and 15 wild pitches in 1999.
MISCELLANEOUS: Holds Anaheim Angels all-time records for most wins (165), innings pitched (2,675) and games pitched (436).

F

Year	League	W	L	Pct.	ERA	G	GS	CG	ShO	Sv.	IP	H	R	ER	BB	SO
1985—	Salem (N'West)	3	1	.750	4.66	18	0	0	0	5	29	34	21	15	10	32
1986—	Quad Cities (Midw.)...........	1	0	1.000	0.00	10	0	0	0	6	12	4	0	0	3	16
	— California (A.L.).............	3	1	.750	3.30	25	0	0	0	0	46 1/3	40	17	17	23	37
1987—	California (A.L.).............	2	7	.222	4.67	35	3	0	0	0	90 2/3	102	54	47	43	63
1988—	California (A.L.).............	9	15	.375	4.17	31	31	2	0	0	194 1/3	191	95	90	82	111
1989—	California (A.L.).............	16	9	.640	2.57	29	29	9	1	0	199 2/3	171	64	57	82	156
1990—	California (A.L.).............	18	9	.667	2.40	32	32	7	2	0	236	210	77	63	81	177
1991—	California (A.L.).............	18	9	.667	3.80	34	34	4	2	0	227 1/3	205	102	96	101	171
1992—	California (A.L.).............	7	12	.368	3.96	31	31	4	1	0	204 1/3	212	99	90	98	124
1993—	California (A.L.).............	16	14	.533	3.15	35	35	*13	2	0	251 1/3	243	108	88	82	187
1994—	California (A.L.).............	10	10	.500	4.32	25	•25	7	2	0	*183 1/3	178	95	88	71	148
1995—	California (A.L.).............	15	12	.556	4.21	32	32	2	1	0	203	192	106	95	93	195
1996—	California (A.L.).............	15	16	.484	4.16	35	35	4	1	0	238	241	124	110	94	215
1997—	Lake Elsinore (Calif.)	0	0	...	2.00	2	2	0	0	0	9	5	3	2	4	12
	— Anaheim (A.L.)	13	6	.684	4.23	25	25	3	1	0	164	152	79	77	65	155
1998—	Anaheim (A.L.)	11	9	.550	3.39	34	34	1	1	0	223 1/3	210	97	84	109	212
1999—	Anaheim (A.L.)	12	11	.522	4.43	33	33	1	0	0	213 1/3	197	117	105	94	200
2000—	Cleveland (A.L.)■	16	11	.593	4.17	34	34	3	0	0	218	211	108	101	101	189
2001—	Cleveland (A.L.).............	8	7	.533	5.54	22	22	1	0	0	113 2/3	131	78	70	35	96
	— Akron (East.)	1	1	.500	0.82	2	2	0	0	0	11	7	3	1	2	11
Major League totals (16 years)		**189**	**158**	**.545**	**3.83**	**492**	**435**	**61**	**14**	**0**	**3006 2/3**	**2886**	**1420**	**1278**	**1254**	**2436**

DIVISION SERIES RECORD

Year	League	W	L	Pct.	ERA	G	GS	CG	ShO	Sv.	IP	H	R	ER	BB	SO
2001—	Cleveland (A.L.).................	0	2	.000	7.56	2	2	0	0	0	8 1/3	9	7	7	6	10

CHAMPIONSHIP SERIES RECORD

Year	League	W	L	Pct.	ERA	G	GS	CG	ShO	Sv.	IP	H	R	ER	BB	SO
1986—	California (A.L.)	0	0	...	0.00	3	0	0	0	0	2	1	0	0	0	1

ALL-STAR GAME RECORD

Year	League	W	L	Pct.	ERA	GS	CG	ShO	Sv.	IP	H	R	ER	BB	SO
1989—	American						Did not play.								
1990—	American	0	0	...	0.00	0	0	0	0	1	0	0	0	1	1
1995—	American						Did not play.								
1996—	American	0	0	...	4.50	0	0	0	0	2	3	1	1	0	4
2000—	American						Did not play.								
All-Star Game totals (2 years)		**0**	**0**	**...**	**3.00**	**0**	**0**	**0**	**0**	**3**	**3**	**1**	**1**	**1**	**5**

FINLEY, STEVE   OF   DIAMONDBACKS

PERSONAL: Born March 12, 1965, in Union City, Tenn. ... 6-2/180. ... Bats left, throws left. ... Full name: Steven Allen Finley.
HIGH SCHOOL: Paducah (Ky.) Tilghman.
COLLEGE: Southern Illinois.
TRANSACTIONS/CAREER NOTES: Selected by Atlanta Braves organization in 11th round of free-agent draft (June 2, 1986); did not sign. ... Selected by Baltimore Orioles organization in 13th round of free-agent draft (June 2, 1987). ... On Baltimore disabled list (April 4-22, 1989). ... On Baltimore disabled list (July 29-September 1, 1989); included rehabilitation assignment to Hagerstown (August 21-23). ... Traded by Orioles with P Pete Harnisch and P Curt Schilling to Houston Astros for 1B Glenn Davis (January 10, 1991). ... On disabled list (April 25-May 14, 1993). ... On Houston disabled list (June 13-July 3, 1994); included rehabilitation assignment to Jackson (June 28-July 3). ... Traded by Astros with 3B Ken Caminiti, SS Andujar Cedeno, 1B Roberto Petagine, P Brian Williams and a player to be named later to San Diego Padres for OF Phil Plantier, OF Derek Bell, P Pedro Martinez, P Doug Brocail, IF Craig Shipley and SS Ricky Gutierrez (December 28, 1994); Padres acquired P Sean Fesh to complete deal (May 1, 1995). ... On San Diego disabled list (April 20-May 6, 1997); included rehabilitation assignment to Rancho Cucamonga (April 25-May 6). ... Granted free agency (October 26, 1998). ... Signed by Arizona Diamondbacks (December 18, 1998).
RECORDS: Shares major league single-season record for fewest double plays by outfielder (150 or more games)—0 (1999).
HONORS: Won N.L. Gold Glove as outfielder (1995, 1996, 1999 and 2000).
STATISTICAL NOTES: Led International League outfielders with 315 total chances in 1988. ... Had 21-game hitting streak (June 20-July 14, 1996). ... Hit three home runs in one game (May 19 and June 23, 1997; and September 8, 1999). ... Tied for N.L. lead with six double plays by outfielder in 1998. ... Career major league grand slams: 8.

						BATTING								FIELDING			
Year	Team (League)	Pos.	G	AB	R	H	2B	3B	HR	RBI	Avg.	BB	SO	SB	PO	A	E	Avg.
1987—	Newark (NY-Penn)......	OF	54	222	40	65	13	2	3	33	.293	22	24	26	122	7	4	.970
	— Hagerstown (Caro.)....	OF	15	65	9	22	3	2	1	5	.338	1	6	7	32	5	0	1.000
1988—	Hagerstown (Caro.)....	OF	8	28	2	6	2	0	0	3	.214	4	3	4	17	0	0	1.000
	— Charlotte (Sou.).........	OF	10	40	7	12	4	2	1	6	.300	4	3	2	14	0	0	1.000
	— Rochester (I.L.).........	OF	120	456	61	*143	19	7	5	54	*.314	28	55	20	*289	14	*12	.962
1989—	Baltimore (A.L.).........	OF-DH	81	217	35	54	5	2	2	25	.249	15	30	17	144	1	2	.986
	— Rochester (I.L.).........	OF	7	25	2	4	0	0	0	2	.160	1	5	3	17	2	0	1.000
	— Hagerstown (East.).....	OF	11	48	11	20	3	1	0	7	.417	4	3	4	35	2	3	.925
1990—	Baltimore (A.L.).........	OF-DH	142	464	46	119	16	4	3	37	.256	32	53	22	298	4	7	.977
1991—	Houston (N.L.)■.....	OF	159	596	84	170	28	10	8	54	.285	42	65	34	323	13	5	.985
1992—	Houston (N.L.).........	OF	•162	607	84	177	29	13	5	55	.292	58	63	44	417	8	3	.993
1993—	Houston (N.L.).........	OF	142	545	69	145	15	*13	8	44	.266	28	65	19	329	12	4	.988
1994—	Houston (N.L.).........	OF	94	373	64	103	16	5	11	33	.276	28	52	13	214	9	4	.982
	— Jackson (Texas)	OF-DH	5	13	3	4	0	0	0	0	.308	4	0	1	6	0	0	1.000
1995—	San Diego (N.L.)■.....	OF	139	562	104	167	23	8	10	44	.297	59	62	36	291	8	7	.977
1996—	San Diego (N.L.).........	OF	161	655	126	195	45	9	30	95	.298	56	87	22	385	7	7	.982
1997—	San Diego (N.L.)........	OF	143	560	101	146	26	5	28	92	.261	43	92	15	338	10	4	.989
	— Rancho Cuca. (Calif.) .	DH-OF	4	14	3	4	0	0	2	3	.286	3	2	1	0	0	0	...
	— Mobile (Sou.)	DH	1	4	1	2	0	0	1	2	.500	1	2	0	...	...	...	...
1998—	San Diego (N.L.)	OF	159	619	92	154	40	6	14	67	.249	45	103	12	351	12	7	.981

Year	Team (League)	Pos.	G	AB	R	H	2B	3B	HR	RBI	Avg.	BB	SO	SB	PO	A	E	Avg.
1999—Arizona (N.L.)■	OF-DH	156	590	100	156	32	10	34	103	.264	63	94	8	397	5	2	.995
2000—Arizona (N.L.)	OF-DH	152	539	100	151	27	5	35	96	.280	65	87	12	342	10	3	.992
2001—Arizona (N.L.)	OF-P	140	495	66	136	27	4	14	73	.275	47	67	11	300	6	2	.994
American League totals (2 years)		223	681	81	173	21	6	5	62	.254	47	83	39	442	5	9	.980
National League totals (11 years)		1607	6141	990	1700	308	88	197	756	.277	534	837	226	3687	100	48	.987
Major League totals (13 years)		1830	6822	1071	1873	329	94	202	818	.275	581	920	265	4129	105	57	.987

DIVISION SERIES RECORD

RECORDS: Shares N.L. single-game record for most runs batted in—5 (October 6, 1999).

Year	Team (League)	Pos.	G	AB	R	H	2B	3B	HR	RBI	Avg.	BB	SO	SB	PO	A	E	Avg.
1996—San Diego (N.L.)	OF	3	12	0	1	0	0	0	1	.083	0	4	1	10	0	0	1.000
1998—San Diego (N.L.)	OF-PR	4	10	2	1	1	0	0	1	.100	1	4	0	6	0	0	1.000
1999—Arizona (N.L.)	OF	4	13	0	5	1	0	0	5	.385	3	1	0	10	0	0	1.000
2001—Arizona (N.L.)	OF	5	19	1	8	1	0	0	2	.421	0	2	0	11	0	0	1.000
Division series totals (4 years)		16	54	3	15	3	0	0	9	.278	4	11	1	37	0	0	1.000

CHAMPIONSHIP SERIES RECORD

Year	Team (League)	Pos.	G	AB	R	H	2B	3B	HR	RBI	Avg.	BB	SO	SB	PO	A	E	Avg.
1998—San Diego (N.L.)	OF	6	21	3	7	1	0	0	2	.333	6	2	1	15	0	0	1.000
2001—Arizona (N.L.)	OF	5	14	1	4	1	0	0	4	.286	3	1	1	12	0	0	1.000
Championship series totals (2 years)		11	35	4	11	2	0	0	6	.314	9	3	2	27	0	0	1.000

WORLD SERIES RECORD

NOTES: Member of World Series championship team (2001).

Year	Team (League)	Pos.	G	AB	R	H	2B	3B	HR	RBI	Avg.	BB	SO	SB	PO	A	E	Avg.
1998—San Diego (N.L.)	OF	3	12	0	1	1	0	0	0	.083	0	2	1	9	1	0	1.000
2001—Arizona (N.L.)	OF-PH	7	19	5	7	0	0	1	2	.368	4	5	0	16	0	0	1.000
World Series totals (2 years)		10	31	5	8	1	0	1	2	.258	4	7	1	25	1	0	1.000

ALL-STAR GAME RECORD

Year	League	Pos.	AB	R	H	2B	3B	HR	RBI	Avg.	BB	SO	SB	PO	A	E	Avg.
1997—National	OF	1	0	0	0	0	0	0	.000	0	1	0	1	0	0	1.000
2000—National	OF	1	0	1	0	0	0	1	1.000	0	0	0	0	0	0	...
All-Star Game totals (2 years)		2	0	1	0	0	0	1	.500	0	1	0	1	0	0	1.000

RECORD AS PITCHER

Year	League	W	L	Pct.	ERA	G	GS	CG	ShO	Sv.	IP	H	R	ER	BB	SO
2001—Arizona (N.L.)	0	0	...	0.00	1	0	0	0	0	1	0	0	0	1	0

FIORE, TONY   P   TWINS

PERSONAL: Born October 12, 1971, in Oak Park, Ill. ... 6-4/210. ... Throws right, bats right. ... Full name: Anthony James Fiore.
HIGH SCHOOL: Holy Cross (River Grove, Ill.).
JUNIOR COLLEGE: Triton College (Ill.).
TRANSACTIONS/CAREER NOTES: Selected by Philadelphia Phillies organization in 28th round of free-agent draft (June 1, 1992). ... On disabled list (April 2-20, 1995). ... Granted free agency (October 15, 1998). ... Re-signed by Phillies organization (November 28, 1998). ... Released by Phillies (May 19, 1999). ... Signed by Minnesota Twins organization (June 3, 1999). ... Granted free agency (October 15, 1999). ... Signed by Tampa Bay Devil Rays organization (January 14, 2000). ... On suspended list (September 22-24, 2000). ... Released by Devil Rays (May 25, 2001). ... Signed by Twins organization (May 30, 2001).

Year	League	W	L	Pct.	ERA	G	GS	CG	ShO	Sv.	IP	H	R	ER	BB	SO
1992—Martinsville (Appl.)	2	3	.400	4.18	17	2	0	0	0	32 1/3	32	20	15	31	30
1993—Batavia (NY-Penn)	2	•8	.200	3.05	16	•16	1	0	0	97 1/3	82	51	33	40	55
1994—Spartanburg (S.Atl.)	12	13	.480	4.10	28	•28	*9	1	0	166 2/3	162	94	76	77	113
1995—Clearwater (FSL)	6	2	.750	3.71	24	10	0	0	0	70 1/3	70	41	29	44	45
1996—Clearwater (FSL)	8	4	.667	3.16	22	22	3	1	0	128	102	61	45	56	80
—Reading (East.)	1	2	.333	4.35	5	5	0	0	0	31	32	21	15	18	19
1997—Reading (East.)	8	3	.727	3.01	17	16	0	0	0	104 2/3	89	47	35	40	64
—Scranton/W.B. (I.L.)	3	5	.375	3.86	9	9	1	0	0	60 2/3	60	34	26	26	56
1998—Scranton/W.B. (I.L.)	4	7	.364	4.47	41	7	0	0	1	95	92	53	47	52	71
1999—Scranton/W.B. (I.L.)	0	0	...	6.64	13	0	0	0	0	20 1/3	28	19	15	15	13
—Salt Lake (PCL)■	2	1	.667	3.47	40	0	0	0	19	46 2/3	45	21	18	26	38
2000—Durham (I.L.)■	8	5	.615	2.28	53	1	0	0	8	75	62	22	19	38	39
—Tampa Bay (A.L.)	1	1	.500	8.40	11	0	0	0	0	15	21	16	14	9	8
2001—Durham (I.L.)	1	0	1.000	0.00	15	0	0	0	3	20 1/3	7	0	0	8	11
—Tampa Bay (A.L.)	0	0	...	5.40	3	0	0	0	0	3 1/3	4	2	2	1	3
—Edmonton (PCL)■	5	0	1.000	3.68	32	6	0	0	1	80 2/3	85	35	33	25	58
—Minnesota (A.L.)	0	1	.000	5.68	4	0	0	0	0	6 1/3	5	4	4	2	5
Major League totals (2 years)	1	2	.333	7.30	18	0	0	0	0	24 2/3	30	22	20	12	16

F

FLAHERTY, JOHN   C   DEVIL RAYS

PERSONAL: Born October 21, 1967, in New York. ... 6-1/200. ... Bats right, throws right. ... Full name: John Timothy Flaherty.
HIGH SCHOOL: St. Joseph's Regional (Montvale, N.J.).
COLLEGE: George Washington.
TRANSACTIONS/CAREER NOTES: Selected by Boston Red Sox organization in 25th round of free-agent draft (June 1, 1988). ... Traded by Red Sox to Detroit Tigers for C Rich Rowland (April 1, 1994). ... Traded by Tigers with SS Chris Gomez to San Diego Padres for C Brad

Ausmus, SS Andujar Cedeno and P Russ Spear (June 18, 1996). ... Traded by Padres to Tampa Bay Devil Rays for P Brian Boehringer and IF Andy Sheets (November 18, 1997). ... On Tampa Bay disabled list (May 26-June 20, 1998); included rehabilitation assignment to Durham (June 14-20).

STATISTICAL NOTES: Tied for Florida State League lead with 19 passed balls in 1989. ... Had 27-game hitting streak (June 21-July 27, 1996). ... Career major league grand slams: 1.

Year Team (League)	Pos.	G	AB	R	H	2B	3B	HR	RBI	Avg.	BB	SO	SB	PO	A	E	Avg.
1988—Elmira (NY-Penn)	C	46	162	17	38	3	0	3	16	.235	12	23	2	235	39	7	.975
1989—Winter Haven (FSL)	C-1B	95	334	31	87	14	2	4	28	.260	20	44	1	369	60	9	.979
1990—Pawtucket (I.L.)	C-3B	99	317	35	72	18	0	4	32	.227	24	43	1	509	59	10	.983
—Lynchburg (Caro.)	C	1	4	0	0	0	0	0	1	1.000	0	1	0	3	2	0	1.000
1991—New Britain (East.)	C	67	225	27	65	9	0	3	18	.289	31	22	0	337	46	9	.977
—Pawtucket (I.L.)	C	45	156	18	29	7	0	3	13	.186	15	14	0	270	18	•9	.970
1992—Boston (A.L.)	C	35	66	3	13	2	0	0	2	.197	3	7	0	102	7	2	.982
—Pawtucket (I.L.)	C	31	104	11	26	3	0	0	7	.250	5	8	0	158	17	4	.978
1993—Pawtucket (I.L.)	C	105	365	29	99	22	0	6	35	.271	26	41	0	626	78	10	.986
—Boston (A.L.)	C	13	25	3	3	2	0	0	2	.120	2	6	0	35	9	0	1.000
1994—Toledo (I.L.)■	C-DH	44	151	20	39	10	2	7	17	.258	6	21	3	286	24	2	.994
—Detroit (A.L.)	C-DH	34	40	2	6	1	0	0	4	.150	1	11	0	78	9	0	1.000
1995—Detroit (A.L.)	C	112	354	39	86	22	1	11	40	.243	18	47	0	569	33	*11	.982
1996—Detroit (A.L.)	C	47	152	18	38	12	0	4	23	.250	8	25	1	243	13	5	.981
—San Diego (N.L.)■	C	72	264	22	80	12	0	9	41	.303	9	36	2	471	29	5	.990
1997—San Diego (N.L.)	C	129	439	38	120	21	1	9	46	.273	33	62	4	753	65	11	.987
1998—Tampa Bay (A.L.)■	C	91	304	21	63	11	0	3	24	.207	22	46	0	542	45	4	.993
—Durham (I.L.)	DH-C	6	23	1	3	1	0	0	2	.130	1	5	0	23	4	0	1.000
1999—Tampa Bay (A.L.)	C-DH	117	446	53	124	19	0	14	71	.278	19	64	0	726	*87	6	.993
2000—Tampa Bay (A.L.)	C	109	394	36	103	15	0	10	39	.261	20	57	0	611	51	5	.993
2001—Tampa Bay (A.L.)	C	78	248	20	59	17	1	4	29	.238	10	33	1	458	28	7	.986
American League totals (9 years)		636	2029	195	495	101	2	46	234	.244	103	296	2	3364	282	40	.989
National League totals (2 years)		201	703	60	200	33	1	18	87	.284	42	98	6	1224	94	16	.988
Major League totals (10 years)		837	2732	255	695	134	3	64	321	.254	145	394	8	4588	376	56	.989

DIVISION SERIES RECORD

Year Team (League)	Pos.	G	AB	R	H	2B	3B	HR	RBI	Avg.	BB	SO	SB	PO	A	E	Avg.
1996—San Diego (N.L.)	C	2	4	0	0	0	0	0	0	.000	0	1	0	9	0	0	1.000

FLETCHER, DARRIN — C — BLUE JAYS

PERSONAL: Born October 3, 1966, in Elmhurst, Ill. ... 6-2/205. ... Bats left, throws right. ... Full name: Darrin Glen Fletcher. ... Son of Tom Fletcher, pitcher with Detroit Tigers (1962); and grandson of Glen Fletcher, pitcher in Philadelphia Phillies organization (1938-48).
HIGH SCHOOL: Oakwood (Ill.).
COLLEGE: Illinois.
TRANSACTIONS/CAREER NOTES: Selected by Los Angeles Dodgers organization in sixth round of free-agent draft (June 2, 1987). ... Traded by Dodgers to Philadelphia Phillies for P Dennis Cook (September 13, 1990). ... Traded by Phillies with cash to Montreal Expos for P Barry Jones (December 9, 1991). ... On Montreal disabled list (May 12-June 15, 1992); included rehabilitation assignment to Indianapolis (May 31-June 14). ... On disabled list (June 18-July 3, 1997). ... Granted free agency (October 27, 1997). ... Signed by Toronto Blue Jays (November 26, 1997). ... On disabled list (May 30-June 14, 1998). ... On Toronto disabled list (May 1-June 1, 1999); included rehabilitation assignment to Syracuse (May 24-27). ... On disabled list (June 11-July 4, 2000).
STATISTICAL NOTES: Tied for Texas League lead in double plays by catcher with nine in 1988. ... Led Pacific Coast League catchers with 787 total chances in 1990. ... Led N.L. with 12 sacrifice flies in 1994. ... Hit three home runs in one game (August 27, 2000). ... Career major league grand slams: 6.

Year Team (League)	Pos.	G	AB	R	H	2B	3B	HR	RBI	Avg.	BB	SO	SB	PO	A	E	Avg.
1987—Vero Beach (FSL)	C	43	124	13	33	7	0	0	15	.266	22	12	0	212	35	3	.988
1988—San Antonio (Texas)	C	89	279	19	58	8	0	1	20	.208	17	42	2	529	64	5	*.992
1989—Albuquerque (PCL)	C	100	315	34	86	16	1	5	44	.273	30	38	1	632	63	9	.987
—Los Angeles (N.L.)	C	5	8	1	4	0	0	1	2	.500	1	0	0	16	1	0	1.000
1990—Albuquerque (PCL)	C	105	350	58	102	23	1	13	65	.291	40	37	1	*715	64	8	.990
—Los Angeles (N.L.)	C	2	1	0	0	0	0	0	0	.000	0	1	0	0	0	0	...
—Philadelphia (N.L.)■	C	9	22	3	3	1	0	0	1	.136	1	5	0	30	3	0	1.000
1991—Scranton/W.B. (I.L.)	C-1B	90	306	39	87	13	1	8	50	.284	23	29	1	491	44	5	.991
—Philadelphia (N.L.)	C	46	136	5	31	8	0	1	12	.228	5	15	0	242	22	2	.992
1992—Montreal (N.L.)■	C	83	222	13	54	10	2	2	26	.243	14	28	0	360	33	2	.995
—Indianapolis (A.A.)	C	13	51	2	13	2	0	1	9	.255	2	10	0	65	7	1	.986
1993—Montreal (N.L.)	C	133	396	33	101	20	1	9	60	.255	34	40	0	620	41	8	.988
1994—Montreal (N.L.)	C	94	285	28	74	18	1	10	57	.260	25	23	0	479	20	2	.996
1995—Montreal (N.L.)	C	110	350	42	100	21	1	11	45	.286	32	23	0	613	44	4	.994
1996—Montreal (N.L.)	C	127	394	41	105	22	0	12	57	.266	27	42	0	721	30	6	.992
1997—Montreal (N.L.)	C	96	310	39	86	20	1	17	55	.277	17	35	1	606	26	4	.994
1998—Toronto (A.L.)■	C-DH	124	407	37	115	23	1	9	52	.283	25	39	0	832	51	8	.991
1999—Toronto (A.L.)	C	115	412	48	120	26	0	18	80	.291	26	47	0	638	42	2	.997
—Syracuse (I.L.)	C-DH	4	15	0	4	0	0	0	0	.267	1	1	0	18	5	0	1.000
2000—Toronto (A.L.)	C	122	416	43	133	19	1	20	58	.320	20	45	1	621	39	4	.994
2001—Toronto (A.L.)	C-DH	134	416	36	94	20	0	11	56	.226	24	43	0	720	41	4	.995
American League totals (4 years)		495	1651	164	462	88	2	58	246	.280	95	174	1	2811	173	18	.994
National League totals (9 years)		705	2124	205	558	120	6	63	315	.263	156	212	1	3687	220	28	.993
Major League totals (13 years)		1200	3775	369	1020	208	8	121	561	.270	251	386	2	6498	393	46	.993

ALL-STAR GAME RECORD

Year League	Pos.	AB	R	H	2B	3B	HR	RBI	Avg.	BB	SO	SB	PO	A	E	Avg.
1994—National	C	0	0	0	0	0	0	0	...	0	0	0	3	0	0	1.000

F

FLORIE, BRYCE   P

PERSONAL: Born May 21, 1970, in Charleston, S.C. ... 5-11/192. ... Throws right, bats right. ... Full name: Bryce Bettencourt Florie.
HIGH SCHOOL: Hanahan (Charleston, S.C.).
COLLEGE: Trident Technical College (S.C.).
TRANSACTIONS/CAREER NOTES: Selected by San Diego Padres organization in fifth round of free-agent draft (June 1, 1988). ... Traded by Padres with P Ron Villone and OF Marc Newfield to Milwaukee Brewers for OF Greg Vaughn and a player to be named later (July 31, 1996); Padres acquired OF Gerald Parent to complete deal (September 16, 1996). ... On disabled list (August 31-September 8, 1997). ... Traded by Brewers with a player to be named later to Detroit Tigers for P Mike Myers, P Rick Greene and SS Santiago Perez (November 20, 1997). ... On Detroit disabled list (June 23-July 20, 1998); included rehabilitation assignment to Toledo (July 14-20). ... On Detroit disabled list (March 31-May 6, 1999); included rehabilitation assignment to Lakeland (May 1-6). ... Traded by Tigers to Boston Red Sox for P Mike Maroth (July 31, 1999). ... On Boston disabled list (April 9-June 19 and September 10, 2000-remainder of season); included rehabilitation assignments to Sarasota (June 8-12) and Trenton (June 13-19). ... On Boston disabled list (March 31-June 27, 2001); included rehabilitation assignments to Sarasota (May 24-June 4) and Trenton (June 5-22). ... Released by Red Sox (July 30, 2001). ... Signed by Detroit Tigers organization (August 2, 2001). ... Granted free agency (October 15, 2001).
STATISTICAL NOTES: Led Texas League with 25 wild pitches in 1993.

Year	League	W	L	Pct.	ERA	G	GS	CG	ShO	Sv.	IP	H	R	ER	BB	SO
1988—	Arizona Padres (Ariz.)	4	5	.444	7.98	11	6	0	0	0	38 1/3	52	44	34	22	29
1989—	Spokane (N'West)	4	5	.444	7.08	14	14	0	0	0	61	79	•66	48	40	50
—	Charleston, S.C. (S.Atl.)	1	7	.125	6.95	12	12	0	0	0	44	54	47	34	42	22
1990—	Waterloo (Midw.)	4	5	.444	4.39	14	14	1	0	0	65 2/3	60	37	32	37	38
1991—	Waterloo (Midw.)	7	6	.538	3.92	23	23	2	0	0	133	119	66	58	79	90
1992—	High Desert (Calif.)	9	7	.563	4.12	26	24	0	0	0	137 2/3	99	79	63	*114	106
—	Charleston, S.C. (S.Atl.)	0	1	.000	1.80	1	1	0	0	0	5	5	3	1	0	5
1993—	Wichita (Texas)	11	8	.579	3.96	27	•27	0	0	0	154 2/3	128	80	68	*100	133
1994—	Las Vegas (PCL)	2	5	.286	5.15	50	0	0	0	1	71 2/3	76	47	41	47	67
—	San Diego (N.L.)	0	0	...	0.96	9	0	0	0	0	9 1/3	8	1	1	3	8
1995—	San Diego (N.L.)	2	2	.500	3.01	47	0	0	0	1	68 2/3	49	30	23	38	68
1996—	San Diego (N.L.)	2	2	.500	4.01	39	0	0	0	0	49 1/3	45	24	22	27	51
—	Milwaukee (A.L.)■	0	1	.000	6.63	15	0	0	0	0	19	20	16	14	13	12
1997—	Milwaukee (A.L.)	4	4	.500	4.32	32	8	0	0	0	75	74	43	36	42	53
1998—	Detroit (A.L.)■	8	9	.471	4.80	42	16	0	0	0	133	141	80	71	59	97
—	Toledo (I.L.)	0	0	...	0.00	1	1	0	0	0	4	0	0	0	0	3
1999—	Lakeland (FSL)	0	0	...	0.00	1	1	0	0	0	3	0	0	0	0	7
—	Detroit (A.L.)	2	1	.667	4.56	27	3	0	0	0	51 1/3	61	31	26	20	40
—	Boston (A.L.)■	2	0	1.000	4.80	14	2	0	0	0	30	33	19	16	15	25
2000—	Boston (A.L.)	0	4	.000	4.56	29	0	0	0	1	49 1/3	57	30	25	19	34
—	Sarasota (FSL)	0	0	...	0.00	1	1	0	0	0	3	3	1	0	1	2
—	Trenton (East.)	0	0	...	0.00	3	1	0	0	0	5	2	0	0	2	11
2001—	Sarasota (FSL)	0	0	...	0.00	2	0	0	0	0	4 2/3	3	0	0	5	7
—	Trenton (East.)	0	1	.000	1.64	6	1	0	0	2	11	5	4	2	6	17
—	Boston (A.L.)	0	1	.000	11.42	7	0	0	0	0	8 2/3	12	11	11	7	7
—	Toledo (I.L.)■	2	1	.667	6.17	10	0	0	0	0	16 2/3	14	8	8	13	10
A.L. totals (6 years)■		16	20	.444	4.89	166	29	0	0	1	366 1/3	398	230	199	175	268
N.L. totals (3 years)		4	4	.500	3.25	95	0	0	0	1	127 1/3	102	55	46	68	127
Major League totals (8 years)		20	24	.455	4.47	261	29	0	0	2	493 2/3	500	285	245	243	395

DIVISION SERIES RECORD

Year	League	W	L	Pct.	ERA	G	GS	CG	ShO	Sv.	IP	H	R	ER	BB	SO
1999—	Boston (A.L.)							Did not play.								

CHAMPIONSHIP SERIES RECORD

Year	League	W	L	Pct.	ERA	G	GS	CG	ShO	Sv.	IP	H	R	ER	BB	SO
1999—	Boston (A.L.)							Did not play.								

FLOYD, CLIFF   OF   MARLINS   F

PERSONAL: Born December 5, 1972, in Chicago. ... 6-4/240. ... Bats left, throws right. ... Full name: Cornelius Clifford Floyd.
HIGH SCHOOL: Thornwood (South Holland, Ill.).
TRANSACTIONS/CAREER NOTES: Selected by Montreal Expos organization in first round (14th pick overall) of free-agent draft (June 3, 1991). ... On disabled list (May 16-September 11, 1995). ... Traded by Expos to Florida Marlins for OF Joe Orsulak and P Dustin Hermanson (March 26, 1997). ... On Florida disabled list (May 9-24 and June 21-September 1, 1997); included rehabilitation assignment to Charlotte (July 20-September 1). ... On Florida disabled list (March 30-April 27 and June 20-September 7, 1999); included rehabilitation assigment to Calgary (August 28-September 7). ... On disabled list (July 29-August 29, 2000).
HONORS: Named Minor League Player of the Year by THE SPORTING NEWS (1993). ... Named Eastern League Most Valuable Player (1993).
STATISTICAL NOTES: Led South Atlantic League with 261 total bases and nine intentional bases on balls received in 1992. ... Led Eastern League with .600 slugging percentage and 12 intentional bases on balls received in 1993. ... Had 18-game hitting streak (June 5-24, 2001). ... Career major league grand slams: 2.
MISCELLANEOUS: Holds Florida Marlins all-time records for most doubles (147) and highest career batting average (.295).

Year	Team (League)	Pos.	G	AB	R	H	2B	3B	HR	RBI	Avg.	BB	SO	SB	PO	A	E	Avg.
1991—	GC Expos (GCL)	1B	56	214	35	56	9	3	6	30	.262	19	37	13	451	27	*15	.970
1992—	Albany (S.Atl.)	OF-1B	134	516	83	157	24	*16	16	*97	.304	45	75	32	423	29	17	.964
—	W.P. Beach (FSL)	OF	1	4	0	0	0	0	0	1	.000	0	1	0	2	0	0	1.000
1993—	Harrisburg (East.)	1B-OF	101	380	82	125	17	4	•26	*101	.329	54	71	31	564	27	19	.969
—	Ottawa (I.L.)	1B	32	125	12	30	2	2	2	18	.240	16	34	2	272	23	5	.983
—	Montreal (N.L.)	1B	10	31	3	7	0	0	1	2	.226	0	9	0	79	4	0	1.000
1994—	Montreal (N.L.)	1B-OF	100	334	43	94	19	4	4	41	.281	24	63	10	565	42	6	.990
1995—	Montreal (N.L.)	OF-1B	29	69	6	9	1	0	1	8	.130	7	22	3	146	12	3	.981
1996—	Ottawa (I.L.)	OF-DH-3B	20	76	7	23	3	1	1	8	.303	7	20	2	38	1	2	.951
—	Montreal (N.L.)	OF-1B	117	227	29	55	15	4	6	26	.242	30	52	7	109	2	5	.957

Year Team (League)	Pos.	G	AB	R	H	2B	3B	HR	RBI	Avg.	BB	SO	SB	PO	A	E	Avg.
1997—Florida (N.L.)■	OF-1B	61	137	23	32	9	1	6	19	.234	24	33	6	96	5	3	.971
—Charlotte (I.L.)	OF-1B	39	131	27	48	10	0	9	33	.366	10	29	7	79	5	1	.988
1998—Florida (N.L.)	OF-DH	153	588	85	166	45	3	22	90	.282	47	112	27	251	10	7	.974
1999—Florida (N.L.)	OF-DH	69	251	37	76	19	1	11	49	.303	30	47	5	115	4	6	.952
—Calgary (PCL)	OF	9	31	6	12	1	0	3	8	.387	2	8	0	8	0	0	1.000
2000—Florida (N.L.)	OF-DH	121	420	75	126	30	0	22	91	.300	50	82	24	168	7	9	.951
2001—Florida (N.L.)	OF-DH	149	555	123	176	44	4	31	103	.317	59	101	18	269	8	8	.972
Major League totals (9 years)		809	2612	424	741	182	17	104	429	.284	271	521	100	1798	94	47	.976

DIVISION SERIES RECORD

Year Team (League)	Pos.	G	AB	R	H	2B	3B	HR	RBI	Avg.	BB	SO	SB	PO	A	E	Avg.
1997—Florida (N.L.)								Did not play.									

CHAMPIONSHIP SERIES RECORD

Year Team (League)	Pos.	G	AB	R	H	2B	3B	HR	RBI	Avg.	BB	SO	SB	PO	A	E	Avg.
1997—Florida (N.L.)								Did not play.									

WORLD SERIES RECORD

NOTES: Member of World Series championship team (1997).

Year Team (League)	Pos.	G	AB	R	H	2B	3B	HR	RBI	Avg.	BB	SO	SB	PO	A	E	Avg.
1997—Florida (N.L.)	PH-DH	4	2	1	0	0	0	0	0	.000	1	1	0	...	...	...	...

ALL-STAR GAME RECORD

Year League	Pos.	AB	R	H	2B	3B	HR	RBI	Avg.	BB	SO	SB	PO	A	E	Avg.
2001—National	PH-DH	2	0	0	0	0	0	0	.000	0	0	0	...	...	...	...

FOGG, JOSH   P   PIRATES

PERSONAL: Born December 13, 1976, in Lynn, Mass. ... 6-2/205. ... Throws right, bats right. ... Full name: Joshua Smith Fogg.
HIGH SCHOOL: Cadinal Gibbons (Fort Lauderdale, Fla.).
COLLEGE: Florida.
TRANSACTIONS/CAREER NOTES: Selected by Chicago White Sox organization in third round of free-agent draft (June 2, 1998). ... Traded by White Sox with P Kip Wells and P Sean Lowe to Pittsburgh Pirates for P Todd Ritchie and C Lee Evans (December 13, 2001).

Year League	W	L	Pct.	ERA	G	GS	CG	ShO	Sv.	IP	H	R	ER	BB	SO
1998—Arizona White Sox (Ariz.)	1	0	1.000	0.00	2	0	0	0	0	4	0	0	0	1	5
—Hickory (S.Atl.)	1	3	.250	2.18	8	8	0	0	0	41 1/3	36	17	10	13	29
—Winston-Salem (Caro.)	0	1	.000	0.00	1	0	0	0	0	1	2	2	0	0	2
1999—Winston-Salem (Caro.)	10	5	.667	2.96	17	17	1	1	0	103 1/3	93	44	34	33	109
—Birmingham (Sou.)	3	2	.600	5.89	10	10	0	0	0	55	66	37	36	18	40
2000—Birmingham (Sou.)	11	7	.611	2.57	27	27	2	0	0	192 1/3	190	68	55	44	136
2001—Charlotte (I.L.)	4	7	.364	4.79	40	16	0	0	4	114 2/3	129	68	61	30	89
—Chicago (A.L.)	0	0	...	2.03	11	0	0	0	0	13 1/3	10	3	3	3	17
Major League totals (1 year)	0	0	...	2.03	11	0	0	0	0	13 1/3	10	3	3	3	17

FORBES, P.J.   2B

PERSONAL: Born September 22, 1967, in Pittsburg, Kan. ... 5-10/160. ... Bats right, throws right. ... Full name: Patrick Joseph Forbes.
HIGH SCHOOL: St. Mary's Colgan (Pittsburg, Kan.).
COLLEGE: Wichita State.
TRANSACTIONS/CAREER NOTES: Selected by California Angels organization in 20th round of free-agent draft (June 4, 1990). ... On Vancouver disabled list (July 15-August 18, 1994). ... Granted free agency (October 15, 1996). ... Signed by Rochester, Baltimore Orioles organization (January 14, 1997). ... Granted free agency (October 15, 1997). ... Re-signed by Orioles (December 12, 1997). ... Released by Orioles (November 25, 1998). ... Signed by Texas Rangers organization (January 3, 1999). ... On Oklahoma disabled list (May 20-27, 1999). ... Granted free agency (October 15, 1999). ... Signed by Philadelphia Phillies organization (November 2, 1999). ... On disabled list (July 6-15, 2000). ... Granted free agency (October 18, 2000). ... Re-signed by Phillies organization (November 15, 2000). ... Granted free agency (October 15, 2001).
STATISTICAL NOTES: Led Northwest League with eight sacrifice hits in 1990. ... Led Midwest League with 24 sacrifice hits in 1992. ... Led Texas League second basemen with 251 assists, 74 double plays and .970 fielding percentage in 1993. ... Led Pacific Coast League second basemen with .986 fielding percentage in 1995. ... Led Pacific Coast League second basemen with .986 fielding percentage in 1996.

Year Team (League)	Pos.	G	AB	R	H	2B	3B	HR	RBI	Avg.	BB	SO	SB	PO	A	E	Avg.
1990—Boise (N'West)	2B	43	169	29	42	9	1	0	20	.249	23	22	11	93	109	8	.962
1991—Palm Springs (Calif.)	2B-OF-1B-SS	94	349	45	93	14	2	2	26	.266	36	44	18	220	281	17	.967
1992—Quad City (Midw.)	2B-3B	105	376	53	106	16	5	2	46	.282	44	51	15	145	269	12	.972
1993—Midland (Texas)	2B-1B	126	498	*90	159	23	2	15	64	.319	26	50	6	†260	372	19	†.971
—Vancouver (PCL)	2B	5	16	1	4	2	0	0	3	.250	0	3	0	15	13	0	1.000
1994—Arizona Angels (Ariz.)	2B	2	6	1	0	0	0	0	0	.000	0	1	0	2	5	0	1.000
—Vancouver (PCL)	2B-SS-3B	90	318	39	91	21	2	1	40	.286	22	42	4	187	233	11	.974
1995—Vancouver (PCL)	2B-SS	109	369	47	101	22	3	1	52	.274	21	46	4	190	271	6	†.987
1996—Vancouver (PCL)	2B-3B-SS-OF	117	409	58	112	24	2	0	46	.274	42	44	4	235	308	9	.984
1997—Rochester (I.L.)■	2-3-S-DH-OF	116	434	67	118	22	1	8	54	.272	35	42	15	150	237	12	.970
1998—Rochester (I.L.)	2B-SS-3B-DH	116	460	74	135	37	3	6	52	.293	36	54	10	207	305	7	.987
—Baltimore (A.L.)	2B-3B-SS	9	10	0	1	0	0	0	2	.100	0	0	0	6	9	0	1.000

Year Team (League)	Pos.	G	AB	R	H	2B	3B	HR	RBI	Avg.	BB	SO	SB	PO	A	E	Avg.
1999— Oklahoma (PCL)■......2B-SS-DH-3B		22	67	4	7	1	0	0	2	.104	5	12	0	33	56	2	.978
— Rochester (I.L.)■......3-2-S-OF-DH		88	349	49	92	16	1	0	19	.264	26	40	5	140	212	7	.981
2000— Scranton/W.B. (I.L.)■ OF-3B-2B-SS		99	334	51	92	22	1	2	32	.275	30	29	7	126	60	1	.995
2001— Scranton/W.B. (I.L.) ...2B-SS-OF-3B		133	514	79	157	29	2	5	61	.305	48	72	5	250	343	8	.987
— Philadelphia (N.L.)......	2B	3	7	1	2	0	0	0	1	.286	0	2	0	2	2	0	1.000
American League totals (1 year)		9	10	0	1	0	0	0	2	.100	0	0	0	6	9	0	1.000
National League totals (1 year)		3	7	1	2	0	0	0	1	.286	0	2	0	2	2	0	1.000
Major League totals (2 years)		12	17	1	3	0	0	0	3	.176	0	2	0	8	11	0	1.000

FORDYCE, BROOK — C — ORIOLES

PERSONAL: Born May 7, 1970, in New London, Conn. ... 6-0/190. ... Bats right, throws right. ... Full name: Brook Alexander Fordyce. ... Name pronounced FOR-dice.
HIGH SCHOOL: St. Bernard (Uncasville, Conn.).
TRANSACTIONS/CAREER NOTES: Selected by New York Mets organization in third round of free-agent draft (June 5, 1989). ... On disabled list (June 19-July 2 and July 18-August 30, 1994). ... On suspended list (August 30-September 1, 1994). ... Claimed on waivers by Cleveland Indians (May 15, 1995). ... Granted free agency (October 16, 1995). ... Signed by Cincinnati Reds organization (December 7, 1995). ... On disabled list (July 16-August 5, 1997); included rehabilitation assignment to Indianapolis (July 21-August 5). ... On Cincinnati disabled list (July 13-August 12, 1998); included rehabilitation assignment to Indianapolis (August 4-12). ... Traded by Reds to Chicago White Sox for P Jake Meyer (March 25, 1999). ... On Chicago disabled list (March 25-May 23, 2000); included rehabilitation assignment to Charlotte (May 5-23). ... Traded by White Sox with P Miguel Felix, P Juan Figueroa and P Jason Lakman to Baltimore Orioles for C Charles Johnson and DH Harold Baines (July 29, 2000).
STATISTICAL NOTES: Led Appalachian League catchers with .991 fielding percentage in 1989. ... Led South Atlantic League in slugging percentage with .478 and tied for lead in grounding into double plays with 18 in 1990. ... Led South Atlantic League with 30 passed balls in 1990. ... Led Eastern League catchers with 795 total chances in 1992. ... Led International League catchers with 810 total chances and tied for lead in double plays by catcher with 11 in 1993. ... Tied for International League lead in double plays by catcher with nine in 1996.

Year Team (League)	Pos.	G	AB	R	H	2B	3B	HR	RBI	Avg.	BB	SO	SB	PO	A	E	Avg.
1989— Kingsport (Appl.)........	C-OF-3B	69	226	45	74	15	0	9	38	.327	30	26	10	311	28	4	†.988
1990— Columbia (S.Atl.)........	C	104	372	45	117	29	1	10	54	.315	39	42	4	574	63	15	.977
1991— St. Lucie (FSL)	C	115	406	42	97	19	3	7	55	.239	37	50	4	630	87	13	.982
1992— Binghamton (East.)	C	118	425	59	118	30	0	11	61	.278	37	78	1	*713	*79	3	*.996
1993— Norfolk (I.L.)	C	116	409	33	106	21	2	2	41	.259	26	62	2	*735	67	8	.990
1994— Norfolk (I.L.)	C-DH	66	229	26	60	13	3	3	32	.262	19	26	1	330	33	7	.981
1995— New York (N.L.).........	PH-PR	4	2	1	1	1	0	0	0	.500	1	0	0	...	...	...	...
— Buffalo (A.A.)■.......	C-OF-DH	58	176	18	44	13	0	0	9	.250	14	20	1	306	18	3	.991
1996— Indianapolis (A.A.)■ ..	C-DH-1B	107	374	48	103	20	3	16	64	.275	25	56	2	620	49	4	†.994
— Cincinnati (N.L.).......	C	4	7	0	2	1	0	0	1	.286	3	1	0	18	0	0	1.000
1997— Cincinnati (N.L.).......	C-DH	47	96	7	20	5	0	1	8	.208	8	15	2	162	12	3	.983
— Indianapolis (A.A.).....	C-DH	12	47	7	11	2	0	2	6	.234	5	6	1	73	8	0	1.000
1998— Cincinnati (N.L.).......	C	57	146	8	37	9	0	3	14	.253	11	28	0	288	20	7	.978
— Indianapolis (I.L.).......	C	6	24	4	6	1	0	2	3	.250	1	2	0	28	4	0	1.000
1999— Chicago (A.L.)■........	C	105	333	36	99	25	1	9	49	.297	21	48	2	561	30	8	.987
2000— Charlotte (I.L.)...........	C	17	67	9	16	5	0	2	12	.239	8	13	0	76	3	0	1.000
— Chicago (A.L.)........	C	40	125	18	34	7	1	5	21	.272	6	23	0	251	13	0	1.000
— Baltimore (A.L.)■.......	C	53	177	23	57	11	0	9	28	.322	11	27	0	313	20	4	.988
2001— Baltimore (A.L.).........	C	95	292	30	61	18	0	5	19	.209	21	56	1	541	30	10	.983
American League totals (3 years)		293	927	107	251	61	2	28	117	.271	59	154	3	1666	93	22	.988
National League totals (4 years)		112	251	16	60	16	0	4	23	.239	23	44	2	468	32	10	.980
Major League totals (7 years)		405	1178	123	311	77	2	32	140	.264	82	198	5	2134	125	32	.986

FOSSUM, CASEY — P — RED SOX

F

PERSONAL: Born January 9, 1978, in Cherry Hill, N.J. ... 6-1/160. ... Throws left, bats both. ... Full name: Casey Paul Fossum.
HIGH SCHOOL: Midway (Waco, Texas).
COLLEGE: Texas A&M.
TRANSACTIONS/CAREER NOTES: Selected by Arizona Diamondbacks organization in sixth round of free-agent draft (June 4, 1996); did not sign. ... Selected by Boston Red Sox organization as "sandwich pick" between first and second round of free-agent draft (June 2, 1999); pick received as part of compensation for Arizona Diamondbacks signing Type A free agent P Greg Swindell.

Year League	W	L	Pct.	ERA	G	GS	CG	ShO	Sv.	IP	H	R	ER	BB	SO
1999— Lowell (NY-Penn)	0	1	.000	1.26	5	5	0	0	0	14 1/3	6	2	2	5	16
2000— Sarasota (FSL)	9	10	.474	3.44	27	27	3	*3	0	149 1/3	147	71	57	36	143
2001— Trenton (East.)	3	7	.300	2.83	20	20	0	0	0	117 2/3	102	47	37	28	130
— Boston (A.L.)....................	3	2	.600	4.87	13	7	0	0	0	44 1/3	44	26	24	20	26
Major League totals (1 year)........	3	2	.600	4.87	13	7	0	0	0	44 1/3	44	26	24	20	26

FOSTER, JOHN — P — BRAVES

PERSONAL: Born May 17, 1978, in Stockton, Calif. ... 6-0/200. ... Throws left, bats left. ... Full name: John N. Foster.
COLLEGE: Lewis-Clark State (Idaho).
TRANSACTIONS/CAREER NOTES: Selected by Atlanta Braves organization in 25th round of free-agent draft (June 2, 1999).
STATISTICAL NOTES: Tied for Southern League lead with 11 sacrifice hits allowed and seven intentional bases on balls allowed in 2001.

Year League	W	L	Pct.	ERA	G	GS	CG	ShO	Sv.	IP	H	R	ER	BB	SO
1999— Danville (Appl.).................	4	1	.800	1.38	18	0	0	0	1	39	28	10	6	6	36
2000— Myrtle Beach (Caro.)	2	1	.667	1.85	38	0	0	0	3	48 2/3	48	13	10	14	46
2001— Greenville (Sou.)	8	7	.533	3.01	50	0	0	0	7	68 2/3	71	30	23	33	63

FOSTER, KEVIN   P

PERSONAL: Born January 13, 1969, in Evanston, Ill. ... 6-1/175. ... Throws right, bats right. ... Full name: Kevin Christopher Foster.
HIGH SCHOOL: Evanston (Ill.) Township.
COLLEGE: Kishwaukee College (Ill.).
TRANSACTIONS/CAREER NOTES: Selected by Montreal Expos organization in 29th round of free-agent draft (June 2, 1987). ... On Albany (Ga.) suspended list (April 9-May 6, 1992). ... Traded by Expos with P Dave Wainhouse to Seattle Mariners for IF Frank Bolick and a player to be named later (November 20, 1992); Expos acquired C Miah Bradbury to complete deal (December 8, 1992). ... Traded by Mariners to Philadelphia Phillies for P Bob Ayrault (June 12, 1993). ... Traded by Phillies to Chicago Cubs for P Shawn Boskie (April 12, 1994). ... On disabled list (August 17-September 1, 1997). ... On Chicago disabled list (March 22-June 9, 1998); included rehabilitation assignments to Daytona (May 23-27), West Tenn (May 28-June 3) and Iowa (June 4-9). ... Granted free agency (October 6, 1998). ... Signed by Cincinnati Reds organization (November 17, 1998). ... Contract voided by Major League Baseball (December 18, 1998). ... Signed by Milwaukee Brewers organization (February 7, 2000). ... Released by Brewers (March 21, 2000). ... Signed by Boston Red Sox organization (April 5, 2000). ... On Pawtucket disabled list (April 6-May 21, 2000). ... Granted free agency (October 18, 2000). ... Signed by Texas Rangers organization (December 13, 2000). ... Released by Rangers (August 27, 2001).
STATISTICAL NOTES: Led N.L. with 32 home runs allowed in 1995.
MISCELLANEOUS: Played infield (1988-89). ... Appeared in three games as pinch runner (1995). ... Appeared in two games as pinch runner for Chicago (1996). ... Struck out three times and had a sacrifice hit in four appearances as pinch hitter (1997).

Year	League	W	L	Pct.	ERA	G	GS	CG	ShO	Sv.	IP	H	R	ER	BB	SO
1990—	Gulf Coast Expos (GCL)	2	0	1.000	5.06	4	0	0	0	0	10²/₃	9	6	6	6	11
	— Gate City (Pio.)	1	7	.125	4.58	10	10	0	0	0	55	43	42	28	34	52
1991—	Sumter (S.Atl.)	10	4	.714	2.74	34	11	1	1	1	102	62	36	31	68	111
1992—	West Palm Beach (FSL)	7	2	.778	1.95	16	11	0	0	0	69¹/₃	45	19	15	31	66
1993—	Jacksonville (Sou.)■	4	4	.500	3.97	12	12	1	1	0	65²/₃	53	32	29	29	72
	— Scranton/W.B. (I.L.)■	1	1	.500	3.93	17	9	1	0	0	71	63	32	31	29	59
	— Philadelphia (N.L.)	0	1	.000	14.85	2	1	0	0	0	6²/₃	13	11	11	7	6
1994—	Reading (East.)	0	1	.000	6.00	1	1	0	0	0	6	7	4	4	1	3
	— Orlando (Sou.)■	1	0	1.000	0.95	3	3	1	1	0	19	8	2	2	2	21
	— Iowa (A.A.)	3	1	.750	4.28	6	6	1	0	0	33²/₃	28	17	16	14	35
	— Chicago (N.L.)	3	4	.429	2.89	13	13	0	0	0	81	70	31	26	35	75
1995—	Chicago (N.L.)	12	11	.522	4.51	30	28	0	0	0	167³/₃	149	90	84	65	146
1996—	Chicago (N.L.)	7	6	.538	6.21	17	16	1	0	0	87	98	63	60	35	53
	— Iowa (A.A.)	7	6	.538	4.30	18	18	3	1	0	115	106	56	55	46	87
1997—	Chicago (N.L.)	10	7	.588	4.61	26	25	1	0	0	146¹/₃	141	79	75	66	118
1998—	Daytona (FSL)	0	0	...	10.13	3	0	0	0	0	2²/₃	2	7	3	7	3
	— West Tenn (Sou.)	1	0	1.000	2.25	2	0	0	0	0	4	5	1	1	1	5
	— Iowa (PCL)	5	6	.455	6.85	17	11	1	1	0	67	74	52	51	38	75
	— Chicago (N.L.)	0	0	...	16.20	3	0	0	0	0	3¹/₃	8	6	6	2	3
1999—								Did not play.								
2000—	Trenton (East.)■	4	3	.571	4.21	11	11	1	0	0	62	49	30	29	30	52
	— Pawtucket (I.L.)	2	4	.333	4.02	9	9	0	0	0	47	39	23	21	27	50
2001—	Oklahoma (PCL)■	3	1	.750	2.80	16	3	0	0	0	54²/₃	33	18	17	22	65
	— Texas (A.L.)	0	1	.000	6.62	9	0	0	0	0	17²/₃	21	14	13	10	16
A.L. totals (1 year)		0	1	.000	6.62	9	0	0	0	0	17²/₃	21	14	13	10	16
N.L. totals (6 years)		32	29	.525	4.79	91	83	2	0	0	492	479	280	262	210	401
Major League totals (7 years)		32	30	.516	4.86	100	83	2	0	0	509²/₃	500	294	275	220	417

RECORD AS POSITION PLAYER

Year	Team (League)	Pos.	G	AB	R	H	2B	3B	HR	RBI	Avg.	BB	SO	SB	PO	A	E	Avg.
							BATTING									FIELDING		
1988—	GC Expos (GCL)	3B-2B-SS	49	164	21	42	10	1	2	21	.256	21	33	16	38	92	18	.878
	— W.P. Beach (FSL)	3B	4	10	0	2	0	0	1	1	.200	0	0	0	1	3	2	.667
1989—	Rockford (Midw.)	3B-2B	44	117	9	19	3	2	1	15	.162	18	44	1	29	70	12	.892
1990—	W.P. Beach (FSL)	3B	3	6	0	1	0	1	0	2	.167	1	1	0	2	1	0	1.000

F

FOSTER, KRIS   P   ORIOLES

PERSONAL: Born June 30, 1974, in Riverdale, N.J. ... 6-1/200. ... Throws right, bats right. ... Full name: John Kristian Foster.
HIGH SCHOOL: Riverdale (Fort Myers, Fla.).
JUNIOR COLLEGE: Edison Community College (Fla.).
TRANSACTIONS/CAREER NOTES: Selected by Montreal Expos organization in 39th round of free-agent draft (June 1, 1992). ... Traded by Expos to Los Angeles Dodgers for SS Rafael Bournigal (June 10, 1995). ... On Albuquerque disabled list (April 8-20, 1999). ... Granted free agency (October 15, 1999). ... Re-signed by Dodgers (October 22, 1999). ... On Los Angeles disabled list (March 28, 2000-entire season); included rehabilitation assignment to San Bernardino (July 9-September 3). ... On Las Vegas disabled list (June 30-July 24, 2001). ... Traded by Dodgers with C Geronimo Gil to Baltimore Orioles for P Mike Trombley (July 31, 2001).

Year	League	W	L	Pct.	ERA	G	GS	CG	ShO	Sv.	IP	H	R	ER	BB	SO
1993—	Gulf Coast Expos (GCL)	1	6	.143	3.43	17	3	0	0	1	44²/₃	44	26	17	16	30
1994—	Gulf Coast Expos (GCL)	4	2	.667	1.55	18	5	0	0	4	52¹/₃	34	21	9	32	65
1995—	Yakima (N'West)■	2	3	.400	2.89	15	10	0	0	3	56	38	27	18	38	55
1996—	San Bernardino (Calif.)	3	5	.375	3.86	30	8	0	0	2	81²/₃	66	46	35	54	78
1997—	Vero Beach (FSL)	6	3	.667	5.32	17	17	2	0	0	89²/₃	97	69	53	44	77
1998—	Vero Beach (FSL)	3	5	.375	6.79	24	6	0	0	1	53	59	45	40	27	52
1999—	Vero Beach (FSL)	1	1	.500	1.76	8	0	0	0	0	15¹/₃	10	5	3	2	15
	— San Antonio (Texas)	0	2	.000	3.59	33	0	0	0	4	52²/₃	43	24	21	26	53
2000—	San Bernardino (Calif.)	0	0	...	0.77	10	1	0	0	2	11²/₃	7	2	1	1	19
2001—	Jacksonville (Sou.)	3	0	1.000	1.00	17	0	0	0	7	18	6	2	2	2	29
	— Las Vegas (PCL)	0	1	.000	3.86	21	0	0	0	12	21	25	13	9	4	17
	— Rochester (I.L.)■	0	1	.000	5.40	9	0	0	0	6	10	11	8	6	6	11
	— Baltimore (A.L.)	0	0	...	2.70	7	0	0	0	0	10	9	4	3	8	8
Major League totals (1 year)		0	0	...	2.70	7	0	0	0	0	10	9	4	3	8	8

FOULKE, KEITH P WHITE SOX

PERSONAL: Born October 19, 1972, in San Diego. ... 6-0/200. ... Throws right, bats right. ... Full name: Keith Charles Foulke.
HIGH SCHOOL: Hargrove (Huffman, Texas).
JUNIOR COLLEGE: Galveston (Texas) College.
COLLEGE: Lewis-Clark State (Idaho).
TRANSACTIONS/CAREER NOTES: Selected by San Francisco Giants organization in ninth round of free-agent draft (June 2, 1994). ... Traded by Giants with SS Mike Caruso, OF Brian Manning, P Lorenzo Barcelo, P Bobby Howry and P Ken Vining to Chicago White Sox for P Wilson Alvarez, P Danny Darwin and P Roberto Hernandez (July 31, 1997). ... On disabled list (August 28, 1998-remainder of season). ... On suspended list (May 5-7, 2000).

Year League	W	L	Pct.	ERA	G	GS	CG	ShO	Sv.	IP	H	R	ER	BB	SO
1994— Everett (N'West)	2	0	1.000	0.93	4	4	0	0	0	19 1/3	17	4	2	3	22
1995— San Jose (Calif.)	13	6	.684	3.50	28	26	2	1	0	177 1/3	166	85	69	32	168
1996— Shreveport (Texas)	12	7	.632	*2.76	27	27	4	2	0	*182 2/3	149	61	56	35	129
1997— Phoenix (PCL)	5	4	.556	4.50	12	12	0	0	0	76	79	38	38	15	54
— San Francisco (N.L.)	1	5	.167	8.26	11	8	0	0	0	44 2/3	60	41	41	18	33
— Nashville (A.A.)■	0	0	...	5.79	1	1	0	0	0	4 2/3	8	3	3	0	4
— Chicago (A.L.)	3	0	1.000	3.45	16	0	0	0	3	28 2/3	28	11	11	5	21
1998— Chicago (A.L.)	3	2	.600	4.13	54	0	0	0	1	65 1/3	51	31	30	20	57
1999— Chicago (A.L.)	3	3	.500	2.22	67	0	0	0	9	105 1/3	72	28	26	21	123
2000— Chicago (A.L.)	3	1	.750	2.97	72	0	0	0	34	88	66	31	29	22	91
2001— Chicago (A.L.)	4	9	.308	2.33	72	0	0	0	42	81	57	21	21	22	75
A.L. totals (5 years)	16	15	.516	2.86	281	0	0	0	89	368 1/3	274	122	117	90	367
N.L. totals (1 year)	1	5	.167	8.26	11	8	0	0	0	44 2/3	60	41	41	18	33
Major League totals (5 years)	17	20	.459	3.44	292	8	0	0	89	413	334	163	158	108	400

DIVISION SERIES RECORD

Year League	W	L	Pct.	ERA	G	GS	CG	ShO	Sv.	IP	H	R	ER	BB	SO
2000— Chicago (A.L.)	0	1	.000	11.57	2	0	0	0	0	2 1/3	4	3	3	2	2

FOX, ANDY IF MARLINS

PERSONAL: Born January 12, 1971, in Sacramento. ... 6-4/202. ... Bats left, throws right. ... Full name: Andrew Junipero Fox.
HIGH SCHOOL: Christian Brothers (Sacramento).
TRANSACTIONS/CAREER NOTES: Selected by New York Yankees organization in second round of free-agent draft (June 5, 1989). ... On disabled list (June 11-21, 1991; April 9-22, 1992 and June 10-August 1, 1993). ... On Columbus disabled list (August 5-19, 1997). ... Traded by Yankees to Arizona Diamondbacks for P Marty Janzen and P Todd Erdos (March 8, 1998). ... On disabled list (August 28-September 11, 1999). ... On Arizona disabled list (March 23-April 17, 2000); included rehabilitation assignments to El Paso (April 10-14) and Tucson (April 15-17). ... Traded by Diamondbacks to Florida Marlins for OF Danny Bautista (June 9, 2000). ... On Florida disabled list (April 11-July 12, 2001); included rehabilitation assignments to Calgary (June 5-15 and July 2-9).
STATISTICAL NOTES: Led Carolina League third basemen with 96 putouts in 1992. ... Led Eastern League third basemen with 30 errors in 1994. ... Led International League third basemen with 22 double plays in 1995.

Year Team (League)	Pos.	G	AB	R	H	2B	3B	HR	RBI	Avg.	BB	SO	SB	PO	A	E	Avg.
1989— GC Yankees (GCL)	3B	40	141	26	35	9	2	3	25	.248	31	29	6	37	78	10	.920
1990— Greensboro (S.Atl.)	3B	134	455	68	99	19	4	9	55	.218	92	132	26	93	238	*45	.880
1991— Prince William (Caro.)	3B	126	417	60	96	22	2	10	46	.230	81	104	15	85	247	*29	.920
1992— Prince William (Caro.)	3B-SS	125	473	75	113	18	3	7	42	.239	54	81	28	†97	304	27	.937
1993— Albany/Colonie (East.)	3B	65	236	44	65	16	1	3	24	.275	32	54	12	59	150	19	.917
1994— Albany/Colonie (East.)	3B-SS-2B	121	472	75	105	20	3	11	43	.222	62	102	22	110	261	†34	.916
1995— Norwich (East.)	SS	44	175	23	36	3	5	5	17	.206	19	36	8	77	127	9	.958
— Columbus (I.L.)	3B-SS-OF-2B	82	302	61	105	16	6	9	37	.348	43	41	22	84	211	9	.970
1996— New York (A.L.)	2-3-S-DH-O	113	189	26	37	4	0	3	13	.196	20	28	11	96	158	12	.955
1997— Columbus (I.L.)	3-2-S-O-DH	95	318	66	87	11	4	6	33	.274	54	64	28	111	218	14	.959
— New York (A.L.)	3-2-DH-S-O	22	31	13	7	1	0	0	1	.226	7	9	2	19	30	1	.980
1998— Arizona (N.L.)■	2-0-3-1	139	502	67	139	21	6	9	44	.277	43	97	14	307	175	8	.984
1999— Arizona (N.L.)	SS-3B	99	274	34	70	12	2	6	33	.255	33	61	4	100	196	14	.955
2000— El Paso (Texas)	3B-SS-OF	4	15	3	6	2	0	0	4	.400	2	2	1	2	3	2	.714
— Tucson (PCL)	2B-3B-SS	3	13	1	3	0	1	0	3	.231	0	1	0	5	6	1	.917
— Arizona (N.L.)	3B-OF-1B	31	86	10	18	4	0	1	10	.209	4	16	2	21	29	2	.962
— Florida (N.L.)■	SS-OF-3B-2B	69	164	19	40	4	2	3	10	.244	18	37	8	51	115	11	.938
2001— Florida (N.L.)	SS-3B-2B-OF	54	81	8	15	0	1	3	7	.185	15	17	1	25	41	3	.957
— Calgary (PCL)	2-S-O-1-3	11	42	10	18	2	1	2	8	.429	3	2	1	19	15	1	.971
American League totals (2 years)		135	220	39	44	5	0	3	14	.200	27	37	13	115	188	13	.959
National League totals (4 years)		392	1107	138	282	41	11	22	104	.255	113	228	29	504	556	38	.965
Major League totals (6 years)		527	1327	177	326	46	11	25	118	.246	140	265	42	619	744	51	.964

DIVISION SERIES RECORD

Year Team (League)	Pos.	G	AB	R	H	2B	3B	HR	RBI	Avg.	BB	SO	SB	PO	A	E	Avg.
1996— New York (A.L.)	DH-PR	2	0	0	0	0	0	0	0	...	0	0	0	...	...	...	...
1997— New York (A.L.)	2B-PR	2	0	0	0	0	0	0	0	...	0	0	0	0	0	0	...
1999— Arizona (N.L.)	SS	1	3	0	0	0	0	0	0	.000	0	1	0	1	2	1	.750
Division series totals (3 years)		5	3	0	0	0	0	0	0	.000	0	1	0	1	2	1	.750

CHAMPIONSHIP SERIES RECORD

Year Team (League)	Pos.	G	AB	R	H	2B	3B	HR	RBI	Avg.	BB	SO	SB	PO	A	E	Avg.
1996— New York (A.L.)	DH-PR	2	0	0	0	0	0	0	0	...	0	0	0	...	...	...	...

WORLD SERIES RECORD

NOTES: Member of World Series championship team (1996).

Year Team (League)	Pos.	G	AB	R	H	2B	3B	HR	RBI	Avg.	BB	SO	SB	PO	A	E	Avg.
1996— New York (A.L.)	2B-PR-3B	4	0	1	0	0	0	0	0	...	0	0	0	1	0	0	1.000

F

PERSONAL: Born September 3, 1970, in Coronado, Calif. ... 6-3/190. ... Throws right, bats right. ... Full name: Chad Douglas Fox.
HIGH SCHOOL: Westfield (Houston).
JUNIOR COLLEGE: Blinn College (Texas).
COLLEGE: Tarleton State (Texas).
TRANSACTIONS/CAREER NOTES: Selected by Cincinnati Reds organization in 23rd round of free-agent draft (June 1, 1992). ... Traded by Reds with a player to be named later to Atlanta Braves for OF Mike Kelly (January 9, 1996); Braves acquired P Ray King to complete deal (June 11, 1996). ... On disabled list (July 16-September 3, 1996). ... Traded by Braves to Milwaukee Brewers for OF Gerald Williams (December 11, 1997). ... On Milwaukee disabled list (May 11-June 30, 1998); included rehabilitation assignment to Beloit (June 25-July 1). ... On disabled list (April 21, 1999-remainder of season; and March 28, 2000-entire season).
STATISTICAL NOTES: Led Carolina League with 20 wild pitches in 1994.

Year	League	W	L	Pct.	ERA	G	GS	CG	ShO	Sv.	IP	H	R	ER	BB	SO
1992—	Princeton (Appl.)	4	2	.667	4.74	15	8	0	0	0	49 1/3	55	43	26	34	37
1993—	Charleston, W.Va. (S.Atl.)	9	12	.429	5.37	27	26	0	0	0	135 2/3	138	100	81	97	81
1994—	Winston-Salem (Caro.)	12	5	.706	3.86	25	25	1	0	0	156 1/3	121	77	67	*94	137
1995—	Chattanooga (Sou.)	4	5	.444	5.06	20	17	0	0	0	80	76	49	45	52	56
1996—	Richmond (I.L.)■	3	10	.231	4.72	18	18	1	0	0	93 1/3	91	57	49	49	87
1997—	Richmond (I.L.)	1	0	1.000	3.70	13	0	0	0	0	24 1/3	24	10	10	14	25
—	Atlanta (N.L.)	0	1	.000	3.29	30	0	0	0	0	27 1/3	24	12	10	16	28
1998—	Milwaukee (N.L.)■	1	4	.200	3.95	49	0	0	0	0	57	56	27	25	20	64
—	Beloit (Midw.)	0	1	.000	4.50	2	1	0	0	0	2	1	1	1	0	3
1999—	Milwaukee (N.L.)	0	0	...	10.80	6	0	0	0	0	6 2/3	11	8	8	4	12
2000—	Milwaukee (N.L.)								Did not play.							
2001—	Indianapolis (I.L.)	3	0	1.000	1.50	4	0	0	0	0	6	4	1	1	3	8
—	Milwaukee (N.L.)	5	2	.714	1.89	65	0	0	0	2	66 2/3	44	16	14	36	80
Major League totals (4 years)		6	7	.462	3.25	150	0	0	0	2	157 2/3	135	63	57	76	184

PERSONAL: Born September 17, 1960, in Brooklyn, N.Y. ... 5-10/185. ... Throws left, bats left. ... Full name: John Anthony Franco.
HIGH SCHOOL: Lafayette (Brooklyn, N.Y.).
COLLEGE: St. John's.
TRANSACTIONS/CAREER NOTES: Selected by Los Angeles Dodgers organization in fifth round of free-agent draft (June 8, 1981). ... Traded by Dodgers with P Brett Wise to Cincinnati Reds for IF Rafael Landestoy (May 9, 1983). ... Traded by Reds with OF Don Brown to New York Mets for P Randy Myers and P Kip Gross (December 6, 1989). ... On disabled list (June 30-August 1 and August 26, 1992-remainder of season; April 17-May 7 and August 3-26, 1993). ... Granted free agency (October 18, 1994). ... Re-signed by Mets (April 5, 1995). ... On New York disabled list (July 3-September 4, 1999); included rehabilitation assignment to Binghamton (September 3-4). ... Granted free agency (October 31, 2000). ... Re-signed by Mets (November 25, 2000).
RECORDS: Holds N.L. career record for most saves—422.
HONORS: Named N.L. Fireman of the Year by The Sporting News (1988, 1990 and 1994).
MISCELLANEOUS: Holds Cincinnati Reds all-time record for most saves (148). ... Holds New York Mets all-time records for most saves (274) and games pitched (605).

Year	League	W	L	Pct.	ERA	G	GS	CG	ShO	Sv.	IP	H	R	ER	BB	SO
1981—	Vero Beach (FSL)	7	4	.636	3.53	13	11	3	0	0	79	78	41	31	41	60
1982—	Albuquerque (PCL)	1	2	.333	7.24	5	5	0	0	0	27 1/3	41	22	22	15	24
—	San Antonio (Texas)	10	5	.667	4.96	17	17	3	0	0	105 1/3	137	70	58	46	76
1983—	Albuquerque (PCL)	0	0	...	5.40	11	0	0	0	0	15	10	11	9	11	8
—	Indianapolis (A.A.)■	6	10	.375	4.85	23	18	2	0	2	115	148	69	62	42	54
1984—	Wichita (A.A.)	1	0	1.000	5.79	6	0	0	0	0	9 1/3	8	6	6	4	11
—	Cincinnati (N.L.)	6	2	.750	2.61	54	0	0	0	4	79 1/3	74	28	23	36	55
1985—	Cincinnati (N.L.)	12	3	.800	2.18	67	0	0	0	12	99	83	27	24	40	61
1986—	Cincinnati (N.L.)	6	6	.500	2.94	74	0	0	0	29	101	90	40	33	44	84
1987—	Cincinnati (N.L.)	8	5	.615	2.52	68	0	0	0	32	82	76	26	23	27	61
1988—	Cincinnati (N.L.)	6	6	.500	1.57	70	0	0	0	*39	86	60	18	15	27	46
1989—	Cincinnati (N.L.)	4	8	.333	3.12	60	0	0	0	32	80 2/3	77	35	28	36	60
1990—	New York (N.L.)■	5	3	.625	2.53	55	0	0	0	*33	67 2/3	66	22	19	21	56
1991—	New York (N.L.)	5	9	.357	2.93	52	0	0	0	30	55 1/3	61	27	18	18	45
1992—	New York (N.L.)	6	2	.750	1.64	31	0	0	0	15	33	24	6	6	11	20
1993—	New York (N.L.)	4	3	.571	5.20	35	0	0	0	10	36 1/3	46	24	21	19	29
1994—	New York (N.L.)	1	4	.200	2.70	47	0	0	0	*30	50	47	20	15	19	42
1995—	New York (N.L.)	5	3	.625	2.44	48	0	0	0	29	51 2/3	48	17	14	17	41
1996—	New York (N.L.)	4	3	.571	1.83	51	0	0	0	28	54	54	15	11	21	48
1997—	New York (N.L.)	5	3	.625	2.55	59	0	0	0	36	60	49	18	17	20	53
1998—	New York (N.L.)	0	8	.000	3.62	61	0	0	0	38	64 2/3	66	28	26	29	59
1999—	New York (N.L.)	0	2	.000	2.88	46	0	0	0	19	40 2/3	40	14	13	19	41
—	Binghamton (East.)	0	0	...	0.00	1	1	0	0	0	1 1/3	0	0	0	0	1
2000—	New York (N.L.)	5	4	.556	3.40	62	0	0	0	4	55 1/3	46	24	21	26	56
2001—	New York (N.L.)	6	2	.750	4.05	58	0	0	0	2	53 1/3	55	25	24	19	50
Major League totals (18 years)		88	76	.537	2.75	998	0	0	0	422	1150 1/3	1062	414	351	449	907

DIVISION SERIES RECORD

Year	League	W	L	Pct.	ERA	G	GS	CG	ShO	Sv.	IP	H	R	ER	BB	SO
1999—	New York (N.L.)	1	0	1.000	0.00	3	0	0	0	0	3 2/3	1	0	0	0	2
2000—	New York (N.L.)	0	0	...	0.00	2	0	0	0	1	2 2/3	1	0	0	0	2
Division series totals (2 years)		1	0	1.000	0.00	5	0	0	0	1	5 2/3	2	0	0	0	4

CHAMPIONSHIP SERIES RECORD

Year	League	W	L	Pct.	ERA	G	GS	CG	ShO	Sv.	IP	H	R	ER	BB	SO
1999—	New York (N.L.)■	0	0	...	3.38	3	0	0	0	0	2 2/3	3	1	1	1	3
2000—	New York (N.L.)	0	0	...	6.75	3	0	0	0	0	2 2/3	3	2	2	2	2
Champ. series totals (2 years)		0	0	...	5.06	6	0	0	0	0	5 1/3	6	3	3	3	5

F

WORLD SERIES RECORD

Year	League	W	L	Pct.	ERA	G	GS	CG	ShO	Sv.	IP	H	R	ER	BB	SO
2000—	New York (N.L.)..................	1	0	1.000	0.00	4	0	0	0	0	3 1/3	3	0	0	0	1

ALL-STAR GAME RECORD

Year	League	W	L	Pct.	ERA	GS	CG	ShO	Sv.	IP	H	R	ER	BB	SO
1986—	National.............................				Did not play.										
1987—	National.............................	0	0	...	0.00	0	0	0	0	2/3	0	0	0	0	0
1989—	National.............................				Did not play.										
1990—	National.............................	0	0	...	0.00	0	0	0	0	1	0	0	0	0	0
1991—	National.............................				Did not play.										
All-Star Game totals (2 years)		0	0	...	0.00	0	0	0	0	1 2/3	0	0	0	0	0

FRANCO, JULIO — 1B/DH — BRAVES

PERSONAL: Born August 23, 1961, in San Pedro de Macoris, Dominican Republic. ... 6-1/200. ... Bats right, throws right. ... Full name: Julio Cesar Franco.

HIGH SCHOOL: Divine Providence (San Pedro de Macoris, Dominican Republic).

TRANSACTIONS/CAREER NOTES: Signed as non-drafted free agent by Philadelphia Phillies organization (June 23, 1978). ... Traded by Phillies with 2B Manny Trillo, OF George Vukovich, P Jay Baller and C Jerry Willard to Cleveland Indians for OF Von Hayes (December 9, 1982). ... On disabled list (July 13-August 8, 1987). ... Traded by Indians to Texas Rangers for 1B Pete O'Brien, OF Oddibe McDowell and 2B Jerry Browne (December 6, 1988). ... On disabled list (March 28-April 19, May 4-June 1 and July 9, 1992-remainder of season). ... Granted free agency (October 27, 1993). ... Signed by Chicago White Sox (December 15, 1993). ... Granted free agency (October 21, 1994). ... Signed by Chiba Lotte Marines of Japan Pacific League (December 28, 1994). ... Signed by Indians (December 7, 1995). ... On disabled list (July 7-25 and August 4-30, 1996). ... Released by Indians (August 13, 1997). ... Signed by Milwaukee Brewers (August 13, 1997). ... Granted free agency (October 28, 1997). ... Played for Chiba Lotte Marines of Japan Pacific League (1998). ... Signed by Tampa Bay Devil Rays organization (February 19, 1999). ... Loaned by Devil Rays organization to Mexico City Tigres, Mexican League (March 29-September 18, 1999). ... Granted free agency (October 13, 1999). ... Contract purchased by Atlanta Braves organization from Mexico City, Mexican League (August 31, 2001). ... Granted free agency (November 5, 2001). ... Re-signed by Braves organization (December 17, 2001).

HONORS: Named Carolina League Most Valuable Player (1980). ... Named second baseman on THE SPORTING NEWS A.L. Silver Slugger team (1988-91). ... Named second baseman on THE SPORTING NEWS A.L. All-Star team (1989-91). ... Named designated hitter on THE SPORTING NEWS A.L. Silver Slugger team (1994).

STATISTICAL NOTES: Led Northwest League with 153 total bases in 1979. ... Led Northwest League shortstops with 390 total chances and 45 double plays in 1979. ... Led Carolina League shortstops with 73 double plays in 1980. ... Led American Association shortstops with 42 errors in 1982. ... Led A.L. shortstops with 35 errors in 1985. ... Led A.L. in grounding into double plays with 28 in 1986 and 27 in 1989. ... Had 21-game hitting streak (May 11-June 3, 1988). ... Had 22-game hitting streak (July 3-27, 1988). ... Led Mexican League with .656 slugging percentage and .541 on-base percentage in 1999. ... Led Mexican League with 276 total bases, .497 on-base percentage and .678 slugging percentage in 2001. ... Career major league grand slams: 6.

								BATTING						FIELDING		
Year	Team (League)	Pos.	G	AB	R	H	2B	3B	HR	RBI	Avg.	BB	SO	SB	PO	A	E	Avg.
1978—	Butte (Pio.).............	SS	47	141	34	43	5	2	3	28	.305	17	30	4	37	52	25	.781
1979—	C. Oregon (N'West)....	SS	•71	299	57	*98	15	5	•10	45	.328	24	59	22	103	*256	31	.921
1980—	Peninsula (Caro.)	SS	•140	*555	105	178	25	6	11	*99	.321	33	66	44	179	*412	42	.934
1981—	Reading (East.)............	SS	*139	*532	70	160	17	3	8	74	.301	52	60	27	246	437	30	.958
1982—	Oklahoma City (A.A.)..	SS-3B	120	463	80	139	19	5	21	66	.300	39	56	33	211	350	†42	.930
	— Philadelphia (N.L.)......	SS-3B	16	29	3	8	1	0	0	3	.276	2	4	0	8	25	0	1.000
1983—	Cleveland (A.L.)■.......	SS	149	560	68	153	24	8	8	80	.273	27	50	32	247	438	28	.961
1984—	Cleveland (A.L.)..........	SS-DH	160	*658	82	188	22	5	3	79	.286	43	68	19	280	481	*36	.955
1985—	Cleveland (A.L.)..	SS-2B-DH	160	636	97	183	33	4	6	90	.288	54	74	13	252	437	†36	.950
1986—	Cleveland (A.L.)........	SS-2B-DH	149	599	80	183	30	5	10	74	.306	32	66	10	248	413	19	.972
1987—	Cleveland (A.L.)..	SS-2B-DH	128	495	86	158	24	3	8	52	.319	57	56	32	175	313	18	.964
1988—	Cleveland (A.L.)..........	2B-DH	152	613	88	186	23	6	10	54	.303	56	72	25	310	434	14	.982
1989—	Texas (A.L.)■..............	2B-DH	150	548	80	173	31	5	13	92	.316	66	69	21	256	386	13	.980
1990—	Texas (A.L.)	2B-DH	157	582	96	172	27	1	11	69	.296	82	83	31	310	444	•19	.975
1991—	Texas (A.L.)	2B	146	589	108	201	27	3	15	78	*.341	65	78	36	294	372	14	.979
1992—	Texas (A.L.)	DH-2B-OF	35	107	19	25	7	0	2	8	.234	15	17	1	21	17	3	.927
1993—	Texas (A.L.)	DH	144	532	85	154	31	3	14	84	.289	62	95	9	...	...	...	...
1994—	Chicago (A.L.)■	DH-1B	112	433	72	138	19	2	20	98	.319	62	75	8	88	7	3	.969
1995—	Chiba Lot. (Jp. Cn.)■..	1B	127	474	60	145	25	3	10	58	.306	...	...	11	...	...	...	...
1996—	Cleveland (A.L.)..........	1B-DH	112	432	72	139	20	1	14	76	.322	61	82	8	852	77	9	.990
1997—	Cleveland (A.L.)..	DH-2B-1B	78	289	46	82	13	1	3	25	.284	38	75	8	70	107	3	.983
	— Milwaukee (A.L.)■.......	DH-1B	42	141	22	34	3	0	4	19	.241	31	41	7	108	11	1	.992
1998—	Chiba Lot. (Jp. Cn.)■..		131	487	78	141	27	2	18	77	.290	...	...	7	...	...	...	...
1999—	Tigres (Mex.)■.........	1B	93	326	90	138	22	6	14	77	*.423	80	44	9	253	23	2	.993
	— Tampa Bay (A.L.)■.....	1B	1	1	0	0	0	0	0	0	.000	0	1	0	2	0	0	1.000
2000—	....						Played in Korea.										
2001—	Tigres (Mex.)■.........	1B-DH-OF	110	407	90	*178	34	5	18	90	*.437	50	56	15	489	57	5	.991
	— Atlanta (N.L.)...........	1B	25	90	13	27	4	0	3	11	.300	10	20	0	181	16	1	.995
American League totals (15 years)			1875	7215	1101	2169	334	47	141	978	.301	751	1002	260	3513	3937	216	.972
National League totals (2 years)			41	119	16	35	5	0	3	14	.294	12	24	0	189	41	1	.996
Major League totals (17 years)			1916	7334	1117	2204	339	47	144	992	.301	763	1026	260	3702	3978	217	.973

DIVISION SERIES RECORD

								BATTING						FIELDING		
Year	Team (League)	Pos.	G	AB	R	H	2B	3B	HR	RBI	Avg.	BB	SO	SB	PO	A	E	Avg.
1996—	Cleveland (A.L.)..........	1B-DH	4	15	1	2	0	0	0	1	.133	1	6	0	18	1	0	1.000
2001—	Atlanta (N.L.).............	1B	3	13	3	4	0	0	1	1	.308	0	1	0	24	2	0	1.000
Division series totals (2 years)			7	28	4	6	0	0	1	2	.214	1	7	0	42	3	0	1.000

F

Year	Team (League)	Pos.	G	AB	R	H	2B	3B	HR	RBI	Avg.	BB	SO	SB	PO	A	E	Avg.
									BATTING							FIELDING		
2001—Atlanta (N.L.).............		1B	5	23	2	6	0	0	1	2	.261	0	2	0	40	7	0	1.000

NOTES: Named Most Valuable Player (1990).

ALL-STAR GAME RECORD

Year	League	Pos.	AB	R	H	2B	3B	HR	RBI	Avg.	BB	SO	SB	PO	A	E	Avg.
								BATTING							FIELDING		
1989— American..................		2B	3	0	1	0	0	0	0	.333	0	0	0	1	1	0	1.000
1990— American..................		PH-2B	3	0	1	1	0	0	2	.333	0	0	0	1	0	0	1.000
1991— American..................								Did not play.									
All-Star Game totals (2 years)			6	0	2	1	0	0	2	.333	0	0	0	2	1	0	1.000

FRANK, MIKE — OF — YANKEES

PERSONAL: Born January 14, 1975, in Pomona, Calif. ... 6-2/195. ... Bats left, throws left. ... Full name: Stephen Michael Frank.
HIGH SCHOOL: Escondido (Calif.).
COLLEGE: Santa Clara.
TRANSACTIONS/CAREER NOTES: Selected by Cincinnati Reds organization in seventh round of free-agent draft (June 3, 1997). ... On Cincinnati disabled list (July 27-August 25, 1998). ... Traded by Reds with P Denny Neagle to New York Yankees for 3B Drew Henson, OF Jackson Melian, P Brian Reith and P Ed Yarnall (July 12, 2000). ... On disabled list (September 2, 2001-remainder of season).
STATISTICAL NOTES: Tied for Pioneer League lead in intentional bases on balls received with five in 1997.

Year	Team (League)	Pos.	G	AB	R	H	2B	3B	HR	RBI	Avg.	BB	SO	SB	PO	A	E	Avg.
									BATTING							FIELDING		
1997—Billings (Pio.)		OF	69	266	62	100	22	6	10	62	.376	35	24	18	•118	*11	4	.970
1998—Chattanooga (Sou.)		OF	58	231	43	75	12	4	12	43	.325	19	28	5	127	3	2	.985
— Indianapolis (I.L.)......		OF	22	88	8	30	4	0	0	13	.341	7	9	1	44	2	1	.979
— Cincinnati (N.L.)........		OF	28	89	14	20	6	0	0	7	.225	7	12	0	60	1	0	1.000
1999—Indianapolis (I.L.)........		OF-DH	121	433	73	128	36	7	9	62	.296	36	55	10	220	10	1	.996
2000—Louisville (I.L.)		OF	62	197	30	54	16	2	6	28	.274	20	26	8	106	4	0	1.000
—Chattanooga (Sou.)		OF	8	30	6	8	1	2	0	5	.267	1	1	0	9	0	0	1.000
—Columbus (I.L.)■........		OF	45	138	19	33	5	3	2	12	.239	16	13	5	90	4	0	1.000
2001—Columbus (I.L.)........		OF	106	356	45	90	20	2	10	53	.253	41	52	11	165	6	2	.988
Major League totals (1 year)			28	89	14	20	6	0	0	7	.225	7	12	0	60	1	0	1.000

FRANKLIN, RYAN — P — MARINERS

PERSONAL: Born March 5, 1973, in Fort Smith, Ark. ... 6-3/165. ... Throws right, bats right. ... Full name: Ryan Ray Franklin.
HIGH SCHOOL: Spiro (Okla.).
JUNIOR COLLEGE: Seminole (Okla.) State College.
TRANSACTIONS/CAREER NOTES: Selected by Toronto Blue Jays organization in 25th round of free-agent draft (June 3, 1991); did not sign. ... Selected by Seattle Mariners organization in 23rd round of free-agent draft (June 1, 1992).
STATISTICAL NOTES: Led Southern League with 16 hit batsmen in 1996. ... Pitched 6-0 no-hit victory against Carolina (April 21, 1997, first game). ... Led Pacific Coast League with 28 home runs allowed in 2000.
MISCELLANEOUS: Member of 2000 U.S. Olympic baseball team.

Year	League	W	L	Pct.	ERA	G	GS	CG	ShO	Sv.	IP	H	R	ER	BB	SO
1993—Bellingham (N'West)		5	3	.625	2.92	15	14	1	1	0	74	72	38	24	27	55
1994—Appleton (Midw.)...............		9	6	.600	3.13	18	18	5	1	0	118	105	60	41	23	102
— Riverside (Calif.)............		4	2	.667	3.06	8	8	1	1	0	61²/₃	61	26	21	8	35
— Calgary (PCL)...............		0	0	...	7.94	1	1	0	0	0	5²/₃	9	6	5	1	2
1995—Port City (Sou.).............		6	10	.375	4.32	31	20	1	1	0	146	153	84	70	43	102
1996—Port City (Sou.).............		6	12	.333	4.01	28	27	2	0	0	182	186	99	81	37	127
1997—Memphis (Sou.).............		4	2	.667	3.03	11	8	2	•2	0	59¹/₃	45	22	20	14	49
—Tacoma (PCL)		5	5	.500	4.18	14	14	0	0	0	90¹/₃	97	48	42	24	59
1998—Tacoma (PCL)		5	6	.455	4.51	34	16	1	0	1	127²/₃	148	75	64	32	90
1999—Tacoma (PCL)		6	9	.400	4.71	29	19	2	1	2	135²/₃	142	81	71	33	94
— Seattle (A.L.)		0	0	...	4.76	6	0	0	0	0	11¹/₃	10	6	6	8	6
2000—Tacoma (PCL)		11	5	.688	3.90	31	22	4	0	0	164	147	85	71	35	142
2001—Seattle (A.L.)		5	1	.833	3.56	38	0	0	0	0	78¹/₃	76	32	31	24	60
—Tacoma (PCL)		0	0	...	0.00	1	0	0	0	0	3²/₃	2	0	0	0	3
Major League totals (2 years).......		5	1	.833	3.71	44	0	0	0	0	89²/₃	86	38	37	32	66

FRANKLIN, WAYNE — P — ASTROS

PERSONAL: Born March 9, 1974, in Wilmington, Del. ... 6-2/195. ... Throws left, bats left. ... Full name: Gary Wayne Franklin Jr.
HIGH SCHOOL: Northeast (Md.).
COLLEGE: Maryland-Baltimore County.
TRANSACTIONS/CAREER NOTES: Selected by Los Angeles Dodgers organization in 36th round of free-agent draft (June 4, 1996). ... Selected by Houston Astros organization from Dodgers organization in Rule 5 minor league draft (December 14, 1998).

Year	League	W	L	Pct.	ERA	G	GS	CG	ShO	Sv.	IP	H	R	ER	BB	SO
1996—Yakima (N'West)		1	0	1.000	2.52	20	0	0	0	1	25	32	10	7	12	22
1997—Savannah (S.Atl.)		5	3	.625	3.18	28	7	1	0	2	82	79	41	29	35	58
—San Bernardino (Calif.).......		0	0	...	0.00	1	0	0	0	0	2	2	0	0	0	1
1998—Vero Beach (FSL).............		9	3	.750	3.53	48	0	0	0	10	86²/₃	81	43	34	26	78
1999—Kissimmee (FSL)■...........		3	0	1.000	1.53	12	0	0	0	1	17²/₃	11	4	3	6	22
—Jackson (Texas)		3	1	.750	1.61	46	0	0	0	20	50¹/₃	31	11	9	16	40
2000—New Orleans (PCL)............		3	3	.500	3.63	48	0	0	0	4	44²/₃	51	29	18	19	37
—Houston (N.L.)		0	0	...	5.48	25	0	0	0	0	21¹/₃	24	14	13	12	21
2001—Houston (N.L.)		0	0	...	6.75	11	0	0	0	0	12	17	9	9	9	9
—New Orleans (PCL)............		2	1	.667	3.81	41	0	0	0	0	49²/₃	47	28	21	18	51
Major League totals (2 years)......		0	0	...	5.94	36	0	0	0	0	33¹/₃	41	23	22	21	30

FRASCATORE, JOHN   P   METS

PERSONAL: Born February 4, 1970, in Queens, N.Y. ... 6-1/223. ... Throws right, bats right. ... Full name: John Vincent Frascatore. ... Name pronounced FRASS-kuh-TOR-ee.
HIGH SCHOOL: Oceanside (N.Y.).
COLLEGE: C.W. Post (N.Y.).
TRANSACTIONS/CAREER NOTES: Selected by St. Louis Cardinals organization in 24th round of free-agent draft (June 3, 1991). ... Traded by Cardinals to Arizona Diamondbacks for P Clint Sodowsky (March 30, 1999). ... Traded by Diamondbacks with SS Tony Batista to Toronto Blue Jays for P Dan Plesac (June 12, 1999). ... Released by Blue Jays (July 31, 2001). ... Signed by New York Mets organization (December 28, 2001).
RECORDS: Shares N.L. single-inning record for most consecutive home runs allowed—3 (August 26, 1998, ninth inning).

Year League	W	L	Pct.	ERA	G	GS	CG	ShO	Sv.	IP	H	R	ER	BB	SO
1991—Hamilton (NY-Penn)	2	7	.222	9.20	30	1	0	0	1	30⅓	44	38	31	22	18
1992—Savannah (S.Atl.)	5	7	.417	3.84	50	0	0	0	23	58⅔	49	32	25	29	56
1993—Springfield (Midw.)	7	12	.368	3.78	27	26	2	1	0	157⅓	157	84	66	33	126
1994—Arkansas (Texas)	7	3	.700	3.10	12	12	4	1	0	78⅓	76	37	27	15	63
—Louisville (A.A.)	8	3	.727	3.39	13	12	2	1	0	85	82	34	32	33	58
—St. Louis (N.L.)	0	1	.000	16.20	1	1	0	0	0	3⅓	7	6	6	2	2
1995—Louisville (A.A.)	2	8	.200	3.95	28	10	1	0	5	82	89	54	36	34	55
—St. Louis (N.L.)	1	1	.500	4.41	14	4	0	0	0	32⅔	39	19	16	16	21
1996—Louisville (A.A.)	6	*13	.316	5.18	36	21	3	0	0	156⅓	180	•106	90	42	95
1997—St. Louis (N.L.)	5	2	.714	2.47	59	0	0	0	0	80	74	25	22	33	58
1998—St. Louis (N.L.)	3	4	.429	4.14	69	0	0	0	0	95⅔	95	48	44	36	49
1999—Arizona (N.L.)■	1	4	.200	4.09	26	0	0	0	0	33	31	16	15	12	15
—Toronto (A.L.)■	7	1	.875	3.41	33	0	0	0	1	37	42	16	14	9	22
2000—Toronto (A.L.)	2	4	.333	5.42	60	0	0	0	0	73	87	51	44	33	30
2001—Syracuse (I.L.)	1	4	.200	4.14	37	0	0	0	2	37	47	20	17	9	18
—Toronto (A.L.)	1	0	1.000	2.20	12	0	0	0	0	16⅓	16	4	4	4	9
A.L. totals (3 years)	10	5	.667	4.42	105	0	0	0	1	126⅓	145	71	62	46	61
N.L. totals (5 years)	10	12	.455	3.79	169	5	0	0	0	244⅔	246	114	103	99	145
Major League totals (7 years)	20	17	.541	4.00	274	5	0	0	1	371	391	185	165	145	206

FREDERICK, KEVIN   P   TWINS

PERSONAL: Born November 4, 1976, in Evanston, Ill. ... 6-1/210. ... Throws left, bats right. ... Full name: Kevin Albert Francis Frederick.
HIGH SCHOOL: Adlai E. Stevenson (Lincolnshire, Ill.).
COLLEGE: Creighton.
TRANSACTIONS/CAREER NOTES: Selected by Minnesota Twins organization in 34th round of free-agent draft (June 2, 1998). ... On disabled list (July 6-August 19, 1999).

Year League	W	L	Pct.	ERA	G	GS	CG	ShO	Sv.	IP	H	R	ER	BB	SO
1998—Elizabethton (Appl.)	1	4	.200	4.25	17	0	0	0	1	29⅔	28	21	14	10	46
1999—Gulf Coast Twins (GCL)	0	0	—	15.43	2	0	0	0	0	2⅓	6	5	4	1	3
2000—Quad City (Midw.)	5	0	1.000	2.35	27	0	0	0	4	46	34	17	12	23	51
—Fort Myers (FSL)	2	1	.667	2.70	19	0	0	0	3	30	20	11	9	14	37
2001—Fort Myers (FSL)	2	0	1.000	1.00	9	0	0	0	1	18	9	2	2	3	19
—New Britain (East.)	6	2	.750	1.63	44	0	0	0	7	82⅔	56	17	15	28	109

FREEL, RYAN   OF   DEVIL RAYS

F

PERSONAL: Born March 8, 1976, in Jacksonville. ... 5-10/185. ... Bats right, throws right. ... Full name: Ryan Paul Freel.
HIGH SCHOOL: Englewood (Jacksonville).
JUNIOR COLLEGE: Tallahassee (Fla.) Community College.
TRANSACTIONS/CAREER NOTES: Selected by St. Louis Cardinals organization in 14th round of free-agent draft (June 2, 1994); did not sign. ... Selected by Toronto Blue Jays organization in 10th round of free-agent draft (June 1, 1995). ... On Dunedin disabled list (July 2-18 and July 23-30, 1997). ... On Syracuse disabled list (May 10, 1999-remainder of season). ... On Tennessee disabled list (April 10-May 3 and May 10-21, 2000). ... Granted free agency (October 19, 2001). ... Signed by Tampa Bay Devil Rays organization (January 24, 2002).

Year Team (League)	Pos.	G	AB	R	H	2B	3B	HR	RBI	Avg.	BB	SO	SB	PO	A	E	Avg.
1995—St. Catharines (NY-P)	2B	65	243	30	68	10	5	3	29	.280	22	49	12	118	181	*19	.940
1996—Knoxville (Sou.)	OF-SS-2B	66	252	47	72	17	3	4	36	.286	33	32	18	127	35	3	.982
—Dunedin (FSL)	2B-3B	104	381	64	97	23	3	4	41	.255	33	76	19	193	276	20	.959
1997—Knoxville (Sou.)	SS	33	94	18	19	1	1	0	4	.202	19	13	5	44	92	13	.913
—Dunedin (FSL)	SS-OF-2B-3B	61	181	42	51	8	2	3	17	.282	46	28	24	88	93	18	.910
1998—Knoxville (Sou.)	OF-2B-SS	66	252	47	72	17	3	4	36	.286	33	32	18	127	35	3	.982
—Syracuse (I.L.)	OF-2B	37	118	19	27	4	0	2	12	.229	26	16	9	57	19	3	.962
1999—Knoxville (Sou.)	OF	11	46	9	13	5	1	1	9	.283	8	4	4	23	1	0	1.000
—Syracuse (I.L.)	OF-SS-DH	20	77	15	23	3	2	1	11	.299	8	13	10	39	2	1	.976
2000—Tennessee (Sou.)	OF-2B	12	44	11	13	3	1	0	8	.295	8	6	2	25	7	0	1.000
—Dunedin (FSL)	OF	4	18	7	9	1	0	3	6	.500	0	1	0	3	0	0	1.000
—Syracuse (I.L.)	2B-OF-3B-SS	80	283	62	81	14	5	10	30	.286	35	44	30	101	99	9	.957
2001—Toronto (A.L.)	2B-OF	9	22	1	6	1	0	0	3	.273	1	4	2	11	20	1	.969
—Syracuse (I.L.)	OF-2B-3B-SS	85	319	60	83	21	3	5	33	.260	42	42	22	145	68	9	.959
Major League totals (1 year)		9	22	1	6	1	0	0	3	.273	1	4	2	11	20	1	.969

FRESE, NATE SS CUBS

PERSONAL: Born July 10, 1977, in Cedar Rapids, Iowa. ... 6-3/200. ... Bats right, throws right. ... Full name: Nathan Robert Frese. ... Great-great nephew of Hal Trosky, first basemen with Cleveland Indians (1933-41) and Chicago White Sox (1944, 1946); and cousin of Hal Trosky Jr., pitcher for Chicago White Sox (1958). ... Name pronounced FREEZE.

HIGH SCHOOL: Benton Community (Van Horne, Iowa).

COLLEGE: Iowa.

TRANSACTIONS/CAREER NOTES: Selected by Chicago Cubs organization in 10th round of free-agent draft (June 2, 1998). ... On disabled list (July 1, 2001-remainder of season).

						BATTING								FIELDING			
Year Team (League)	Pos.	G	AB	R	H	2B	3B	HR	RBI	Avg.	BB	SO	SB	PO	A	E	Avg.
1998—Williamsport (NY-P) ...	SS	54	174	28	38	8	0	2	18	.218	16	38	5	88	163	11	.958
1999—Lansing (Midw.)	SS	107	373	68	99	27	4	4	49	.265	58	67	10	176	371	21	.963
2000—Daytona (FSL)	SS	117	425	70	126	24	5	7	52	.296	64	84	10	139	364	13	*.975
2001—West Tenn (Sou.)	SS	72	233	25	42	5	1	4	19	.180	38	62	0	97	178	1	.996

FRYE, JEFF 2B

PERSONAL: Born August 31, 1966, in Oakland. ... 5-9/160. ... Bats right, throws right. ... Full name: Jeffrey Dustin Frye.

HIGH SCHOOL: Panama (Okla.).

JUNIOR COLLEGE: Carl Albert (Poteau, Okla.).

COLLEGE: Southeastern State (Okla.).

TRANSACTIONS/CAREER NOTES: Selected by Texas Rangers organization in 30th round of free-agent draft (June 1, 1988). ... On Texas disabled list (March 27, 1993-entire season; June 9-24, 1994; and June 3-18 and June 21-July 6, 1995). ... Granted free agency (December 21, 1995). ... Re-signed by Rangers organization (March 25, 1996). ... Released by Rangers organization (June 5, 1996). ... Signed by Boston Red Sox (June 5, 1996). ... On disabled list (March 13, 1998-entire season). ... On Boston disabled list (June 16-September 1, 1999); included rehabilitation assignments to Gulf Coast Red Sox (July 31-August 9) and Pawtucket (August 10-18). ... Traded by Red Sox with P Brian Rose, P John Wasdin and P Jeff Taglienti to Colorado Rockies for P Rolando Arrojo, P Rick Croushore, 2B Mike Lansing and cash (July 27, 2000). ... Granted free agency (October 30, 2000). ... Signed by Toronto Blue Jays (December 11, 2000). ... On Toronto disabled list (March 23-April 9, 2001); included rehabilitation assignment to Dunedin (April 5-9). ... Granted free agency (November 5, 2001).

STATISTICAL NOTES: Led Pioneer League second basemen with 44 double plays in 1988. ... Tied for American Association lead in being hit by pitch with 11 in 1992. ... Hit for the cycle (August 17, 2001).

						BATTING								FIELDING			
Year Team (League)	Pos.	G	AB	R	H	2B	3B	HR	RBI	Avg.	BB	SO	SB	PO	A	E	Avg.
1988—Butte (Pio.)..................	2B	54	185	47	53	7	1	0	14	.286	35	25	16	96	149	7	.972
1989—Gastonia (S.Atl.).........	2B	125	464	85	145	26	3	1	40	*.313	72	53	33	242	340	14	*.977
1990—Charlotte (FSL)...........	2B	131	503	77	137	16	7	0	50	.272	80	66	29	252	350	13	*.979
1991—Tulsa (Texas)..............	2B	131	503	92	152	32	11	4	41	.302	71	60	15	262	322	*26	.957
1992—Oklahoma City (A.A.)..	2B	87	337	64	101	26	2	2	28	.300	51	39	11	212	248	7	.985
—Texas (A.L.)................	2B	67	199	24	51	9	1	1	12	.256	16	27	1	120	196	7	.978
1993—Texas (A.L.)..............					Did not play.												
1994—Oklahoma City (A.A.)..	2B	17	68	7	19	3	0	1	5	.279	6	7	2	28	44	1	.986
—Texas (A.L.).......	2B-DH-3B	57	205	37	67	20	3	0	18	.327	29	23	6	90	136	4	.983
1995—Texas (A.L.)..............	2B	90	313	38	87	15	2	4	29	.278	24	45	3	173	248	11	.975
1996—Oklahoma City (A.A.)..2B-SS-OF-3B		49	181	25	43	10	0	1	18	.238	24	21	10	94	148	8	.968
—Boston (A.L.)■.......	2-0-S-DH	105	419	74	120	27	2	4	41	.286	54	57	18	211	317	9	.983
1997—Boston (A.L.)...........	IF-OF-DH	127	404	56	126	36	2	3	51	.312	27	44	19	227	264	12	.976
1998—Boston (A.L.)					Did not play.												
1999—Boston (A.L.)...........2B-3B-DH-SS		41	114	14	32	3	0	1	12	.281	14	11	2	52	71	4	.969
—GC Red Sox (GCL)	2B-DH	6	20	4	8	1	0	0	1	.400	2	2	0	3	12	0	1.000
—Pawtucket (I.L.)	2B	3	9	0	3	0	0	0	2	.333	2	1	0	1	11	0	1.000
2000—Boston (A.L.)...........2B-OF-DH-3B		69	239	35	69	13	0	1	13	.289	28	38	1	116	124	2	.992
—Colorado (N.L.)■........	2B-3B	37	87	14	31	6	0	0	3	.356	8	16	4	37	60	1	.990
2001—Dunedin (FSL)■........	2B	4	12	4	6	0	0	0	1	.500	2	1	1	6	6	0	1.000
—Toronto (A.L.)...........2B-3B-SS-OF		74	175	24	43	6	1	2	15	.246	12	18	2	90	146	1	.996
American League totals (8 years)		630	2068	302	595	129	11	16	191	.288	204	263	52	1079	1502	50	.981
National League totals (1 year)		37	87	14	31	6	0	0	3	.356	8	16	4	37	60	1	.990
Major League totals (8 years)		667	2155	316	626	135	11	16	194	.290	212	279	56	1116	1562	51	.981

FRYMAN, TRAVIS 3B INDIANS

PERSONAL: Born March 25, 1969, in Lexington, Ky. ... 6-1/195. ... Bats right, throws right. ... Full name: David Travis Fryman.

HIGH SCHOOL: Tate (Gonzalez, Fla.).

TRANSACTIONS/CAREER NOTES: Selected by Detroit Tigers organization in supplemental round ("sandwich pick" between first and second round, 30th pick overall) of free-agent draft (June 2, 1987); pick received as compensation for Philadelphia Phillies signing Type A free-agent C Lance Parrish. ... Traded by Tigers to Arizona Diamondbacks for 3B Joe Randa, P Matt Drews and 3B Gabe Alvarez (November 18, 1997). ... Traded by Diamondbacks with P Tom Martin and cash to Cleveland Indians for 3B Matt Williams (December 1, 1997). ... On Cleveland disabled list (June 6-25 and July 4-September 2, 1999); included rehabilitation assignments to Akron (August 24-30) and Buffalo (August 31-September 2). ... On Cleveland disabled list (March 23-June 2, 2001); included rehabilitation assignments to Buffalo (April 5-7) and Akron (May 14-June 2).

RECORDS: Holds A.L. single-season record for fewest putouts by third baseman (150 or more games)—79 (2000).

HONORS: Named shortstop on THE SPORTING NEWS A.L. All-Star team (1992). ... Named shortstop on THE SPORTING NEWS A.L. Silver Slugger team (1992). ... Named third baseman on THE SPORTING NEWS A.L. All-Star team (1993 and 2000). ... Won A.L. Gold Glove as third baseman (2000).

STATISTICAL NOTES: Led Appalachian League shortstops with 313 total chances in 1987. ... Hit for the cycle (July 28, 1993). ... Tied for A.L. lead with 13 sacrifice flies in 1994. ... Led A.L. third basemen with 313 total chances in 1994 and 458 in 1995. ... Led A.L. third basemen with 38 double plays in 1995. ... Led A.L. third basemen with 271 assists and .979 fielding percentage in 1996. ... Led A.L. third basemen with .978 fielding percentage in 2000. ... Career major league grand slams: 5.

						BATTING									FIELDING			
Year Team (League)	Pos.	G	AB	R	H	2B	3B	HR	RBI	Avg.	BB	SO	SB	PO	A	E	Avg.
1987—Bristol (Appl.)............	SS	67	248	25	58	9	0	2	20	.234	22	39	6	*103	187	•23	.927
1988—Fayetteville (S.Atl.)	SS-2B	123	411	44	96	17	4	0	47	.234	24	83	16	174	390	32	.946
1989—London (East.)	SS	118	426	52	113	*30	1	9	56	.265	19	78	5	192	346	*27	.952
1990—Toledo (I.L.)...............	SS	87	327	38	84	22	2	10	53	.257	17	59	4	128	277	26	.940
—Detroit (A.L.)	3B-SS-DH	66	232	32	69	11	1	9	27	.297	17	51	3	47	145	14	.932
1991—Detroit (A.L.)..............	3B-SS	149	557	65	144	36	3	21	91	.259	40	149	12	153	354	23	.957
1992—Detroit (A.L.)..............	SS-3B	161	*659	87	175	31	4	20	96	.266	45	144	8	220	489	22	.970
1993—Detroit (A.L.)	SS-3B-DH	151	607	98	182	37	5	22	97	.300	77	128	9	169	382	23	.960
1994—Detroit (A.L.)..............	3B	114	*464	66	122	34	5	18	85	.263	45	*128	2	78	*221	14	.955
1995—Detroit (A.L.)..............	3B	144	567	79	156	21	5	15	81	.275	63	100	4	107	*337	14	.969
1996—Detroit (A.L.)..............	3B-SS	157	616	90	165	32	3	22	100	.268	57	118	4	149	†354	10	†.981
1997—Detroit (A.L.)..............	3B	154	595	90	163	27	3	22	102	.274	46	113	16	•126	312	10	*.978
1998—Cleveland (A.L.)■....	3B-SS-DH	146	557	74	160	33	2	28	96	.287	44	125	10	101	242	13	.963
1999—Cleveland (A.L.).........	3B	85	322	45	82	16	2	10	48	.255	25	57	2	41	146	6	.969
—Akron (East.)............	DH-3B	4	12	4	3	0	0	1	4	.250	2	4	0	0	2	0	1.000
—Buffalo (I.L.).............	3B-DH	3	11	1	2	0	0	1	2	.182	0	3	0	0	3	1	.750
2000—Cleveland (A.L.).........	3B-DH-1B	155	574	93	184	38	4	22	106	.321	73	111	1	83	276	8	†.978
2001—Buffalo (I.L.)..............	3B	8	27	9	13	1	0	2	8	.481	5	6	1	7	11	0	1.000
—Akron (East.)............	DH	6	25	3	9	2	0	1	3	.360	2	5	0	...	...	...	...
—Cleveland (A.L.).........	3B-DH-SS	98	334	34	88	15	0	3	38	.263	30	63	1	66	139	12	.945
Major League totals (12 years)		1580	6084	853	1690	331	37	212	967	.278	562	1287	72	1340	3397	169	.966

DIVISION SERIES RECORD

						BATTING									FIELDING			
Year Team (League)	Pos.	G	AB	R	H	2B	3B	HR	RBI	Avg.	BB	SO	SB	PO	A	E	Avg.
1998—Cleveland (A.L.).........	3B	4	13	1	2	1	0	0	0	.154	3	4	1	5	8	0	1.000
1999—Cleveland (A.L.).........	3B	5	15	2	4	0	0	1	4	.267	3	2	1	0	10	0	1.000
2001—Cleveland (A.L.).........	3B	5	17	4	3	1	0	0	2	.176	2	7	0	2	8	0	1.000
Division series totals (3 years)		14	45	7	9	2	0	1	6	.200	8	13	2	7	26	0	1.000

CHAMPIONSHIP SERIES RECORD

						BATTING									FIELDING			
Year Team (League)	Pos.	G	AB	R	H	2B	3B	HR	RBI	Avg.	BB	SO	SB	PO	A	E	Avg.
1998—Cleveland (A.L.).........	3B	6	23	2	4	0	0	0	0	.174	1	5	1	1	7	1	.889

ALL-STAR GAME RECORD

					BATTING									FIELDING			
Year League	Pos.	AB	R	H	2B	3B	HR	RBI	Avg.	BB	SO	SB	PO	A	E	Avg.
1992—American	SS	1	1	1	0	0	0	1	1.000	1	0	0	0	3	0	1.000
1993—American	SS	1	0	0	0	0	0	0	.000	0	0	0	1	1	0	1.000
1994—American	PH	1	0	0	0	0	0	0	.000	0	0	0	...	...	...	...
1996—American	PH-3B	1	0	0	0	0	0	0	.000	0	1	0	0	1	0	1.000
2000—American	3B	2	1	1	0	0	0	0	.500	0	1	0	0	0		...
All-Star Game totals (5 years)		6	2	2	0	0	0	1	.333	1	2	0	1	5	0	1.000

FUENTES, BRIAN   P   ROCKIES

PERSONAL: Born August 9, 1975, in Merced, Calif. ... 6-4/220. ... Throws left, bats left. ... Full name: Brian Christopher Fuentes.
HIGH SCHOOL: Merced (Calif.).
JUNIOR COLLEGE: Merced (Calif.) Junior College.
TRANSACTIONS/CAREER NOTES: Selected by Seattle Mariners organization in 25th round of free-agent draft (June 1, 1995). ... On disabled list (April 2-20, 1998). ... On disabled list (June 9-August 22, 1999). ... On Tacoma disabled list (August 26, 2001-remainder of season). ... Traded by Mariners with P Jose Paniagua and P Dennis Stark to Colorado Rockies for 3B Jeff Cirillo (December 15, 2001).
STATISTICAL NOTES: Tied for Eastern League lead with 14 wild pitches in 2000.

Year League	W	L	Pct.	ERA	G	GS	CG	ShO	Sv.	IP	H	R	ER	BB	SO
1996—Everett (N'West)	0	1	.000	4.39	13	2	0	0	0	26²/₃	23	14	13	13	26
1997—Wisconsin (Midw.)	6	7	.462	3.56	22	22	0	0	0	118²/₃	84	52	47	59	153
1998—Lancaster (Calif.)	7	7	.500	4.17	24	22	0	0	0	118²/₃	121	73	55	81	137
1999—New Haven (East.)	3	3	.500	4.95	15	14	0	0	0	60	53	36	33	46	66
2000—New Haven (East.)	7	12	.368	4.51	26	26	1	0	0	139²/₃	127	80	70	70	152
2001—Tacoma (PCL)	3	2	.600	2.94	35	0	0	0	6	52	35	19	17	25	70
—Seattle (A.L.)	1	1	.500	4.63	10	0	0	0	0	11²/₃	6	6	6	6	10
Major League totals (1 year)........	1	1	.500	4.63	10	0	0	0	0	11²/₃	6	6	6	6	10

FULLMER, BRAD   DH/1B   ANGELS

PERSONAL: Born January 17, 1975, in Chatsworth, Calif. ... 6-0/215. ... Bats left, throws right. ... Full name: Bradley Ryan Fullmer.
HIGH SCHOOL: Montclair Prep (Van Nuys, Calif.).
TRANSACTIONS/CAREER NOTES: Selected by Montreal Expos organization in second round of free-agent draft (June 3, 1993). ... On disabled list (June 20, 1994-entire season). ... Traded by Expos to Toronto Blue Jays as part of three-way deal in which Blue Jays sent 1B/DH David Segui and cash to Texas Rangers and Rangers sent 1B Lee Stevens to Expos (March 16, 2000). ... Traded by Blue Jays to Anaheim Angels for P Brian Cooper (January 17, 2002).
STATISTICAL NOTES: Hit home run in first major league at-bat (September 2, 1997). ... Had 16-game hitting streak (August 7-22, 1999). ... Career major league grand slams: 4.

Year	Team (League)	Pos.	G	AB	R	H	2B	3B	HR	RBI	Avg.	BB	SO	SB	PO	A	E	Avg.
1994—	....								Did not play.									
1995—	Albany (S.Atl.)	3B-1B	123	468	69	•151	38	4	8	67	.323	36	33	10	269	66	30	.918
1996—	W.P. Beach (FSL)	OF-1B	102	380	52	115	29	1	5	63	.303	32	43	4	197	10	7	.967
—	Harrisburg (East.)	OF-1B	24	98	11	27	4	1	4	14	.276	3	8	0	43	1	2	.957
1997—	Harrisburg (East.)	1B-OF-DH	94	357	60	111	24	2	19	62	.311	30	25	6	538	41	6	.990
—	Ottawa (I.L.)	1B-DH-OF	24	91	13	27	7	0	3	17	.297	3	10	1	173	12	1	.995
—	Montreal (N.L.)	1B-OF	19	40	4	12	2	0	3	8	.300	2	7	0	50	7	2	.966
1998—	Montreal (N.L.)	1B	140	505	58	138	44	2	13	73	.273	39	70	6	1070	79	*17	.985
1999—	Montreal (N.L.)	1B	100	347	38	96	34	2	9	47	.277	22	35	2	700	41	7	.991
—	Ottawa (I.L.)	1B-DH	39	142	31	45	9	0	11	32	.317	12	16	2	187	13	2	.990
2000—	Toronto (A.L.)■	DH-1B	133	482	76	142	29	1	32	104	.295	30	68	3	2	1	0	1.000
2001—	Toronto (A.L.)	DH-1B	146	522	71	143	31	2	18	83	.274	38	88	5	12	1	0	1.000
	American League totals (2 years)		279	1004	147	285	60	3	50	187	.284	68	156	8	14	2	0	1.000
	National League totals (3 years)		259	892	100	246	80	4	25	128	.276	63	112	8	1820	127	26	.987
	Major League totals (5 years)		538	1896	247	531	140	7	75	315	.280	131	268	16	1834	129	26	.987

FULTZ, AARON — P — GIANTS

PERSONAL: Born September 4, 1973, in Memphis, Tenn. ... 6-0/196. ... Throws left, bats left. ... Full name: Richard Aaron Fultz.
HIGH SCHOOL: Munford (Tenn.).
JUNIOR COLLEGE: North Florida Junior College.
TRANSACTIONS/CAREER NOTES: Selected by San Francisco Giants organization in sixth round of free-agent draft (June 1, 1992). ... Traded by Giants with SS Andres Duncan and P Greg Brummett to Minnesota Twins for P Jim Deshaies (August 28, 1993). ... Released by Twins (April 1, 1996). ... Signed by Giants organization (April 4, 1996). ... Granted free agency (October 16, 1998). ... Re-signed by Giants organization (October 23, 1998).

Year	League	W	L	Pct.	ERA	G	GS	CG	ShO	Sv.	IP	H	R	ER	BB	SO
1992—	Arizona Giants (Ariz.)	3	2	.600	2.13	14	•14	0	0	0	67²/₃	51	24	16	33	72
1993—	Clinton (Midw.)	14	8	.636	3.41	26	25	2	1	0	148	132	63	56	64	143
—	Fort Wayne (Midw.)■	0	0	...	9.00	1	1	0	0	0	4	10	4	4	0	3
1994—	Fort Myers (FSL)	9	10	.474	4.33	28	28	3	0	0	168¹/₃	193	95	*81	60	132
1995—	New Britain (East.)	0	2	.000	6.60	3	3	0	0	0	15	11	12	11	9	12
—	Fort Myers (FSL)	3	6	.333	3.25	21	21	2	2	0	122	115	52	44	41	127
1996—	San Jose (Calif.)■	9	5	.643	3.96	36	12	0	0	1	104²/₃	101	52	46	54	103
1997—	Shreveport (Texas)	6	3	.667	2.83	49	0	0	0	1	70	65	30	22	19	60
1998—	Shreveport (Texas)	5	7	.417	3.77	54	0	0	0	15	62	58	40	26	29	61
—	Fresno (PCL)	0	0	...	5.06	10	0	0	0	0	16	22	10	9	2	13
1999—	Fresno (PCL)	9	8	.529	4.98	37	20	1	0	0	137¹/₃	141	87	76	51	151
2000—	San Francisco (N.L.)	5	2	.714	4.67	58	0	0	0	1	69¹/₃	67	38	36	28	62
2001—	San Francisco (N.L.)	3	1	.750	4.56	66	0	0	0	1	71	70	40	36	21	67
	Major League totals (2 years)	8	3	.727	4.62	124	0	0	0	2	140¹/₃	137	78	72	49	129

DIVISION SERIES RECORD

Year	League	W	L	Pct.	ERA	G	GS	CG	ShO	Sv.	IP	H	R	ER	BB	SO
2000—	San Francisco (N.L.)	0	1	.000	6.75	1	0	0	0	0	1¹/₃	3	1	1	0	0

FURCAL, RAFAEL — SS/2B — BRAVES

PERSONAL: Born August 24, 1980, in Loma De Cabrera, Dominican Republic. ... 5-10/165. ... Bats both, throws right. ... Full name: Rafael Antoni Furcal.
HIGH SCHOOL: Jose Cabrera (Loma De Cabrera, Dominican Republic).
TRANSACTIONS/CAREER NOTES: Signed as non-drafted free agent by Atlanta Braves organization (November 9, 1996). ... On Atlanta disabled list (June 13-29, 2000). ... On disabled list (July 7, 2001-remainder of season).
HONORS: Named N.L. Rookie Player of the Year by The Sporting News (2000). ... Named N.L. Rookie of the Year by Baseball Writers' Association of America (2000).
STATISTICAL NOTES: Led Gulf Coast League second basemen with 122 putouts and 257 total chances in 1997. ... Led Appalachian League in caught stealing with 15 in 1998. ... Led Appalachian League second basemen with 395 total chances and 51 double plays in 1998. ... Led South Atlantic League in on-base percentage with .417 in 1999.

Year	Team (League)	Pos.	G	AB	R	H	2B	3B	HR	RBI	Avg.	BB	SO	SB	PO	A	E	Avg.
1997—	GC Braves (GCL)	2B-OF	50	190	31	49	5	4	1	9	.258	20	21	15	†122	125	10	.961
1998—	Danville (Appl.)	2B	66	268	56	88	15	4	0	23	.328	36	29	*60	*183	198	14	.965
1999—	Macon (S.Atl.)	SS	83	335	73	113	15	1	1	29	*.337	41	36	*73	117	192	30	.912
—	Myrtle Beach (Caro.)	SS	43	184	32	54	9	3	0	12	.293	14	42	23	48	109	4	.975
2000—	Greenville (Sou.)	SS	3	10	1	2	0	0	1	3	.200	1	0	0	8	1	1	.889
—	Atlanta (N.L.)	SS-2B	131	455	87	134	20	4	4	37	.295	73	80	40	192	362	24	.958
2001—	Atlanta (N.L.)	SS	79	324	39	89	19	0	4	30	.275	24	56	22	126	224	11	.970
	Major League totals (2 years)		210	779	126	223	39	4	8	67	.286	97	136	62	318	586	35	.963

DIVISION SERIES RECORD

Year	Team (League)	Pos.	G	AB	R	H	2B	3B	HR	RBI	Avg.	BB	SO	SB	PO	A	E	Avg.
2000—	Atlanta (N.L.)	2B-SS	3	11	2	1	0	0	0	0	.091	3	0	1	3	11	1	.933

FYHRIE, MICHAEL — P — ATHLETICS

PERSONAL: Born December 9, 1969, in Westminster, Calif. ... 6-2/203. ... Throws right, bats right. ... Full name: Michael Edwin Fyhrie. ... Name pronounced Feery.

HIGH SCHOOL: Ocean View (Huntington Beach, Calif.).

COLLEGE: UCLA.

TRANSACTIONS/CAREER NOTES: Selected by Kansas City Royals organization in 12th round of free-agent draft (June 3, 1991). ... Traded by Royals to New York Mets for a player to be named later (March 23, 1996). ... Contract sold by Mets to Chiba Lotte of Japan Pacific League (November 25, 1996). ... Re-signed by Mets organization (December 6, 1997). ... On disabled list (August 2, 1998-remainder of season). ... Granted free agency (October 15, 1998). ... Signed by Anaheim Angels organization (November 18, 1998). ... On Anaheim disabled list (August 12-September 4, 2000). ... Traded by Angels with a player to be named later to Chicago Cubs for SS/2B Jose Nieves (March 25, 2001). ... On Chicago disabled list (May 2-July 14, 2001); included rehabilitation assignments to Arizona League Cubs (July 2-7) and Iowa (July 7-14). ... Traded by Cubs to Oakland Athletics for OF Michael Wenner (September 4, 2001).

HONORS: Named International League Most Valuable Pitcher in 1996.

Year League	W	L	Pct.	ERA	G	GS	CG	ShO	Sv.	IP	H	R	ER	BB	SO
1991— Eugene (N'West)	2	1	.667	2.52	21	0	0	0	5	39 1/3	42	17	11	19	45
1992— Baseball City (FSL)	7	13	.350	2.50	26	26	0	0	0	162	148	65	45	37	92
1993— Wilmington (Caro.)	3	2	.600	3.68	5	5	0	0	0	29 1/3	32	15	12	8	19
— Memphis (Sou.)	11	4	.733	3.56	22	22	3	0	0	131 1/3	143	59	52	59	59
1994— Omaha (A.A.)	6	5	.545	5.72	18	16	0	0	0	85	100	57	54	33	37
— Memphis (Sou.)	2	5	.286	3.22	11	11	0	0	0	67	67	29	24	17	38
1995— Wichita (Texas)	3	2	.600	3.04	17	9	0	0	1	74	76	31	25	23	41
— Omaha (A.A.)	3	4	.429	4.45	14	11	0	0	0	60 2/3	71	34	30	14	39
1996— Norfolk (I.L.)■	*15	6	.714	3.04	27	27	2	•2	0	169	150	61	57	33	103
— New York (N.L.)	0	1	.000	15.43	2	0	0	0	0	2 1/3	4	4	4	3	0
1997— Chiba Lotte (Jap. Cen.)■	3	4	.429	5.86	8	8	0	0	0	43	54	29	28	15	15
— Chiba (Jap. East.)	4	2	.667	3.09	15	11	1	...	1	70	77	25	24	24	33
1998— Norfolk (I.L.)■	3	7	.300	6.64	24	17	0	0	0	100 1/3	115	83	74	45	60
1999— Edmonton (PCL)■	9	5	.643	3.47	19	18	0	0	0	114	90	47	44	40	113
— Anaheim (A.L.)	0	4	.000	5.05	16	7	0	0	0	51 2/3	61	32	29	21	26
2000— Anaheim (A.L.)	0	0	...	2.39	32	0	0	0	0	52 2/3	54	14	14	15	43
— Edmonton (PCL)	2	1	.667	2.30	9	0	0	0	1	15 2/3	6	4	4	12	9
2001— Chicago (N.L.)■	0	2	.000	4.20	15	0	0	0	0	15	16	7	7	7	6
— Arizona Cubs (Ariz.)	0	0	...	0.00	2	2	0	0	0	2	1	0	0	0	4
— Iowa (PCL)	1	0	1.000	4.80	13	0	0	0	2	15	14	8	8	8	15
— Oakland (A.L.)■	0	0	...	0.00	3	0	0	0	0	5	2	0	0	1	5
A.L. totals (3 years)	0	4	.000	3.54	51	7	0	0	0	109 1/3	117	46	43	37	74
N.L. totals (2 years)	0	3	.000	5.71	17	0	0	0	0	17 1/3	20	11	11	10	6
Major League totals (4 years)	0	7	.000	3.84	68	7	0	0	0	126 2/3	137	57	54	47	80

GAGNE, ERIC — P — DODGERS

PERSONAL: Born January 7, 1976, in Montreal. ... 6-2/195. ... Throws right, bats right. ... Full name: Eric Serge Gagne. ... Name pronounced GAHN-yay.

HIGH SCHOOL: Polyvalente Edouard Montpetit (Montreal).

TRANSACTIONS/CAREER NOTES: Signed as non-drafted free agent by Los Angeles Dodgers organization (July 26, 1995). ... On disabled list entire 1997 season. ... On San Antonio suspended list (April 26-29, 1999).

HONORS: Named Texas League Pitcher of the Year (1999).

Year League	W	L	Pct.	ERA	G	GS	CG	ShO	Sv.	IP	H	R	ER	BB	SO
1996— Savannah (S.Atl.)	7	6	.538	3.28	23	21	1	1	0	115 1/3	94	48	42	43	131
1997—					Did not play.										
1998— Vero Beach (FSL)	9	7	.563	3.74	25	25	3	1	0	139 2/3	118	69	58	48	144
1999— San Antonio (Texas)	12	4	.750	*2.63	26	26	0	0	0	167 2/3	122	55	49	64	*185
— Los Angeles (N.L.)	1	1	.500	2.10	5	5	0	0	0	30	18	8	7	15	30
2000— Albuquerque (PCL)	5	1	.833	3.88	9	9	0	0	0	55 2/3	56	30	24	15	59
— Los Angeles (N.L.)	4	6	.400	5.15	20	19	0	0	0	101 1/3	106	62	58	60	79
2001— Los Angeles (N.L.)	6	7	.462	4.75	33	24	0	0	0	151 2/3	144	90	80	46	130
— Las Vegas (PCL)	3	0	1.000	1.52	4	4	0	0	0	23 2/3	15	4	4	8	31
Major League totals (3 years)	11	14	.440	4.61	58	48	0	0	0	283	268	160	145	121	239

GALARRAGA, ANDRES — 1B

PERSONAL: Born June 18, 1961, in Caracas, Venezuela. ... 6-3/235. ... Bats right, throws right. ... Full name: Andres Jose Galarraga. ... Name pronounced GAHL-ah-RAH-guh.

HIGH SCHOOL: Enrique Felmi (Caracas, Venezuela).

TRANSACTIONS/CAREER NOTES: Signed as non-drafted free agent by Montreal Expos organization (January 19, 1979). ... On disabled list (July 10-August 19 and August 20-September 4, 1986; and May 26-July 4, 1991). ... Traded by Expos to St. Louis Cardinals for P Ken Hill (November 25, 1991). ... On St. Louis disabled list (April 8-May 22, 1992); included rehabilitation assignment to Louisville (May 13-22). ... Granted free agency (October 27, 1992). ... Signed by Colorado Rockies (November 16, 1992). ... On disabled list (May 10-27 and July 25-August 21, 1993). ... Granted free agency (October 25, 1993). ... Re-signed by Rockies (December 6, 1993). ... On disabled list (July 29, 1994-remainder of season). ... On suspended list (August 3-5, 1997). ... Granted free agency (October 27, 1997). ... Signed by Atlanta Braves (November 20, 1997). ... On suspended list (September 2-5, 1998). ... On Atlanta disabled list (April 3, 1999-entire season). ... On suspended list (September 7-10, 2000). ... Granted free agency (October 30, 2000). ... Signed by Texas Rangers (December 8, 2000). ... Traded by Rangers to San Francisco Giants for P Erasma Ramirez, IF Chris Magruder and P Todd Ozias (July 24, 2001). ... Granted free agency (November 7, 2001).

RECORDS: Shares major league single-inning record for most times hit by pitch—2 (July 12, 1996, seventh inning).

HONORS: Named Southern League Most Valuable Player (1984). ... Named first baseman on THE SPORTING NEWS N.L. Silver Slugger team (1988 and 1996). ... Won N.L. Gold Glove at first base (1989-90). ... Named N.L. Comeback Player of the Year by THE SPORTING NEWS (1993 and 2000).

STATISTICAL NOTES: Led Southern League with 271 total bases, .508 slugging percentage and 10 intentional bases on balls received and tied for lead in being hit by pitch with nine in 1984. ... Led Southern League first basemen with 1,428 total chances and 130 double plays in 1984. ... Led N.L. in being hit by pitch with 10 in 1987 and tied for lead with 13 in 1989. ... Led N.L. with 329 total bases in 1988. ... Hit three home runs in one game (June 25, 1995). ... Collected six hits in one game (July 3, 1995). ... Led N.L. first basemen with 1,432 total chances and 129 double plays in 1995. ... Led N.L. first basemen with 1,528 putouts, 1,658 total chances and 154 double plays in 1996. ... Led N.L. first basemen with 1,590 total chances and 176 double plays in 1997. ... Had 15-game hitting streak (April 23-May 8, 1998). ... Career major league grand slams: 10.

Year	Team (League)	Pos.	G	AB	R	H	2B	3B	HR	RBI	Avg.	BB	SO	SB	PO	A	E	Avg.
1979	W.P. Beach (FSL)	1B	7	23	3	3	0	0	0	1	.130	2	11	0	2	1	0	1.000
—	Calgary (Pio.)	1B-3B-C	42	112	14	24	3	1	4	16	.214	9	42	1	187	21	5	.977
1980	Calgary (Pio.)	1B-3B-C-OF	59	190	27	50	11	4	4	22	.263	7	55	3	287	52	21	.942
1981	Jamestown (NY-P)	C-1B-OF-3B	47	154	24	40	5	4	6	26	.260	15	44	0	154	15	0	1.000
1982	W.P. Beach (FSL)	1B-OF	105	338	39	95	20	2	14	51	.281	34	77	2	462	36	9	.982
1983	W.P. Beach (FSL)	1B-OF-3B	104	401	55	116	18	3	10	66	.289	33	68	7	861	77	13	.986
1984	Jacksonville (Sou.)	1B	143	533	81	154	28	4	27	87	.289	59	122	2	*1302	*110	16	.989
1985	Indianapolis (A.A.)	1B-OF	121	439	*75	118	15	8	25	87	.269	45	103	3	930	63	14	.986
—	Montreal (N.L.)	1B	24	75	9	14	1	0	2	4	.187	3	18	1	173	22	1	.995
1986	Montreal (N.L.)	1B	105	321	39	87	13	0	10	42	.271	30	79	6	805	40	4	.995
1987	Montreal (N.L.)	1B	147	551	72	168	40	3	13	90	.305	41	127	7	*1300	103	10	.993
1988	Montreal (N.L.)	1B	157	609	99	*184	*42	8	29	92	.302	39	*153	13	1464	103	15	.991
1989	Montreal (N.L.)	1B	152	572	76	147	30	1	23	85	.257	48	*158	12	1335	91	11	.992
1990	Montreal (N.L.)	1B	155	579	65	148	29	0	20	87	.256	40	*169	10	1300	94	10	.993
1991	Montreal (N.L.)	1B	107	375	34	82	13	2	9	33	.219	23	86	5	887	80	9	.991
1992	St. Louis (N.L.)■	1B	95	325	38	79	14	2	10	39	.243	11	69	5	777	62	8	.991
—	Louisville (A.A.)	1B	11	34	3	6	0	1	2	3	.176	0	8	1	61	7	2	.971
1993	Colorado (N.L.)■	1B	120	470	71	174	35	4	22	98	*.370	24	73	2	1018	103	11	.990
1994	Colorado (N.L.)	1B	103	417	77	133	21	0	31	85	.319	19	93	8	953	65	8	.992
1995	Colorado (N.L.)	1B	143	554	89	155	29	3	31	106	.280	32	*146	12	*1299	120	*13	.991
1996	Colorado (N.L.)	1B-3B	159	626	119	190	39	3	*47	*150	.304	40	157	18	†1528	116	14	.992
1997	Colorado (N.L.)	1B	154	600	120	191	31	3	41	*140	.318	54	141	15	*1458	117	*15	.991
1998	Atlanta (N.L.)■	1B-DH	153	555	103	169	27	1	44	121	.305	63	146	7	1218	81	11	.992
1999	Atlanta (N.L.)					Did not play.												
2000	Atlanta (N.L.)	1B-DH	141	494	67	149	25	1	28	100	.302	36	126	3	1105	61	14	.988
2001	Texas (A.L.)■	DH-1B	72	243	33	57	16	0	10	34	.235	18	68	1	195	16	1	.995
—	San Fran. (N.L.)■	1B	49	156	17	45	12	1	7	35	.288	13	49	0	288	13	5	.984
American League totals (1 year)			72	243	33	57	16	0	10	34	.235	18	68	1	195	16	1	.995
National League totals (16 years)			1964	7279	1095	2115	401	32	367	1307	.291	516	1790	124	16908	1271	159	.991
Major League totals (16 years)			2036	7522	1128	2172	417	32	377	1341	.289	534	1858	125	17103	1287	160	.991

DIVISION SERIES RECORD

Year	Team (League)	Pos.	G	AB	R	H	2B	3B	HR	RBI	Avg.	BB	SO	SB	PO	A	E	Avg.
1995	Colorado (N.L.)	1B	4	18	1	5	1	0	0	2	.278	0	6	0	41	2	0	1.000
1998	Atlanta (N.L.)	1B	3	12	1	3	0	0	0	0	.250	1	3	0	5	0	0	1.000
2000	Atlanta (N.L.)	1B	3	10	1	2	1	0	0	1	.200	2	4	0	26	1	0	1.000
Division series totals (3 years)			10	40	3	10	2	0	0	3	.250	3	13	0	72	3	0	1.000

CHAMPIONSHIP SERIES RECORD

RECORDS: Shares single-inning record for most runs batted in—4 (October 11, 1998, seventh inning).

Year	Team (League)	Pos.	G	AB	R	H	2B	3B	HR	RBI	Avg.	BB	SO	SB	PO	A	E	Avg.
1998	Atlanta (N.L.)	1B	6	21	1	2	0	0	1	4	.095	6	6	0	63	11	4	.949

ALL-STAR GAME RECORD

Year	League	Pos.	AB	R	H	2B	3B	HR	RBI	Avg.	BB	SO	SB	PO	A	E	Avg.
1988	National	1B	2	0	0	0	0	0	0	.000	0	1	0	6	0	0	1.000
1993	National	1B	1	0	0	0	0	0	0	.000	0	0	0	0	0	0	...
1997	National	PH-DH	1	0	0	0	0	0	0	.000	0	1	0	0	0	0	...
1998	National	1B	2	0	0	0	0	0	0	.000	0	0	0	7	0	0	1.000
2000	National	1B	2	0	1	0	0	0	0	.500	0	0	0	4	0	0	1.000
All-Star Game totals (5 years)			8	0	1	0	0	0	0	.125	0	2	0	17	0	0	1.000

GANDARILLAS, GUS   P   BREWERS

PERSONAL: Born July 19, 1971, in Coral Gables, Fla. ... 6-0/190. ... Throws right, bats right. ... Full name: Gustavo Gandarillas. ... Name pronounced gan-dar-REE-yas.

HIGH SCHOOL: Hialeah (Fla.)-Miami Lakes.

JUNIOR COLLEGE: Miami-Dade (South) Community College.

COLLEGE: Miami (Fla.).

TRANSACTIONS/CAREER NOTES: Selected by Minnesota Twins organization in third round of free-agent draft (June 1, 1992). ... On Salt Lake disabled list (April 4-August 10, 1996). ... Granted free agency (October 15, 1998). ... Signed by Pittsburgh Pirates organization (February 2, 1999). ... Released by Pirates (April 5, 1999). ... Signed by Twins organization (April 6, 1999). ... On disabled list (September 13, 2000-remainder of season). ... Granted free agency (October 18, 2000). ... Signed by Boston Red Sox organization (January 29, 2001). ... Released by Red Sox (May 16, 2001). ... Signed by Milwaukee Brewers organization (May 26, 2001). ... Granted free agency (October 15, 2001). ... Re-signed by Brewers organization (November 20, 2001).

Year	League	W	L	Pct.	ERA	G	GS	CG	ShO	Sv.	IP	H	R	ER	BB	SO
1992—	Elizabethton (Appl.)	1	2	.333	3.00	*29	0	0	0	•13	36	24	14	12	10	34
1993—	Fort Wayne (Midw.)	5	5	.500	3.26	52	0	0	0	25	66 1/3	66	37	24	22	59
1994—	Fort Myers (FSL)	4	1	.800	0.77	37	0	0	0	20	46 2/3	37	7	4	13	39
—	Nashville (Sou.)	2	2	.500	3.16	28	0	0	0	8	37	34	13	13	10	29
1995—	Salt Lake (PCL)	2	3	.400	6.44	22	0	0	0	2	29 1/3	34	23	21	19	17
—	New Britain (East.)	2	4	.333	6.12	25	0	0	0	7	32 1/3	38	26	22	16	25
1996—	Gulf Coast Twins (GCL)	0	0	...	1.00	3	1	0	0	2	9	10	3	1	3	14
—	Fort Myers (FSL)	0	0	...	9.00	4	0	0	0	1	6	9	7	6	8	3
1997—	New Britain (East.)	2	4	.333	4.70	17	7	1	0	0	61 1/3	67	34	32	15	29
—	Salt Lake (PCL)	1	0	1.000	3.18	11	2	0	0	2	22 2/3	22	8	8	6	13
1998—	Salt Lake (PCL)	4	5	.444	5.27	53	1	0	0	4	70	88	47	41	24	42
1999—	New Britain (East.)	1	3	.250	8.63	18	0	0	0	1	32 1/3	38	32	31	21	26
—	Salt Lake (PCL)	2	2	.500	4.55	42	0	0	0	2	61 1/3	73	37	31	20	47
2000—	Salt Lake (PCL)	9	4	.692	4.30	63	1	0	0	7	90	105	50	43	33	75
2001—	Pawtucket (I.L.)■	2	1	.667	4.30	12	0	0	0	1	14 2/3	19	9	7	10	7
—	Indianapolis (I.L.)■	2	2	.500	2.70	28	5	0	0	1	66 2/3	62	30	20	13	52
—	Milwaukee (N.L.)	0	0	...	5.49	16	0	0	0	0	19 2/3	25	13	12	10	7
Major League totals (1 year)		0	0	...	5.49	16	0	0	0	0	19 2/3	25	13	12	10	7

GANT, RON — OF — PADRES

PERSONAL: Born March 2, 1965, in Victoria, Texas. ... 6-0/196. ... Bats right, throws right. ... Full name: Ronald Edwin Gant.

HIGH SCHOOL: Victoria (Texas).

TRANSACTIONS/CAREER NOTES: Selected by Atlanta Braves organization in fourth round of free-agent draft (June 6, 1983). ... On suspended list (July 31, 1991). ... Released by Braves (March 15, 1994). ... Signed by Cincinnati Reds (June 21, 1994). ... On disabled list (June 21, 1994-remainder of season). ... On suspended list (September 11-15, 1995). ... Granted free agency (October 30, 1995). ... Signed by St. Louis Cardinals (December 23, 1995). ... On disabled list (May 11-June 14, 1996). ... On disabled list (June 21-July 11, 1998). ... Traded by Cardinals with P Jeff Brantley and P Cliff Politte to Philadelphia Phillies for P Ricky Bottalico and P Garrett Stephenson (November 19, 1998). ... Traded by Phillies to Anaheim Angels for P Kent Bottenfield (July 30, 2000). ... Granted free agency (October 30, 2000). ... Signed by Colorado Rockies (December 10, 2000). ... Traded by Rockies to Oakland Athletics for OF Robin Jennings (July 3, 2001). ... Granted free agency (November 5, 2001). ... Signed by San Diego Padres organization (January 18, 2002).

HONORS: Named outfielder on THE SPORTING NEWS N.L. All-Star team (1991). ... Named outfielder on THE SPORTING NEWS N.L. Silver Slugger team (1991). ... Named N.L. Comeback Player of the Year by THE SPORTING NEWS (1995).

STATISTICAL NOTES: Led Carolina League with 271 total bases in 1986. ... Led Southern League second basemen with 783 total chances and 108 double plays in 1987. ... Led N.L. second basemen with 26 errors in 1988. ... Career major league grand slams: 4.

							BATTING								FIELDING		
Year	Team (League)	Pos.	G	AB	R	H	2B	3B	HR	RBI	Avg.	BB	SO	SB	PO	A	E	Avg.
1983—	GC Braves (GCL)	SS	56	193	32	45	2	2	1	14	.233	41	34	4	68	134	22	.902
1984—	Anderson (S.Atl.)	2B	105	359	44	85	14	6	3	38	.237	29	65	13	248	263	31	.943
1985—	Sumter (S.Atl.)	2B-SS-OF	102	305	46	78	14	4	7	37	.256	33	59	19	160	200	10	.973
1986—	Durham (Caro.)	2B	137	512	108	142	31	10	*26	102	.277	78	85	35	240	384	26	.960
1987—	Greenville (Sou.)	2B	140	527	78	130	27	3	14	82	.247	59	91	24	*328	*434	21	*.973
—	Atlanta (N.L.)	2B	21	83	9	22	4	0	2	9	.265	1	11	4	45	59	3	.972
1988—	Richmond (I.L.)	2B	12	45	3	14	2	2	0	4	.311	2	10	1	22	23	5	.900
—	Atlanta (N.L.)	2B-3B	146	563	85	146	28	8	19	60	.259	46	118	19	316	417	†31	.959
1989—	Atlanta (N.L.)	3B-OF	75	260	26	46	8	3	9	25	.177	20	63	9	70	103	17	.911
—	Sumter (S.Atl.)	OF	12	39	13	15	4	1	1	5	.385	11	3	4	19	1	2	.909
—	Richmond (I.L.)	OF-3B	63	225	42	59	13	2	11	27	.262	29	42	6	111	14	5	.962
1990—	Atlanta (N.L.)	OF	152	575	107	174	34	3	32	84	.303	50	86	33	357	7	8	.978
1991—	Atlanta (N.L.)	OF	154	561	101	141	35	3	32	105	.251	71	104	34	338	7	6	.983
1992—	Atlanta (N.L.)	OF	153	544	74	141	22	6	17	80	.259	45	101	32	277	5	4	.986
1993—	Atlanta (N.L.)	OF	157	606	113	166	27	4	36	117	.274	67	117	26	271	5	*11	.962
1994—	Cincinnati (N.L.)■							Did not play.										
1995—	Cincinnati (N.L.)	OF	119	410	79	113	19	4	29	88	.276	74	108	23	191	7	3	.985
1996—	St. Louis (N.L.)■	OF	122	419	74	103	14	2	30	82	.246	73	98	13	216	4	5	.978
1997—	St. Louis (N.L.)	OF-DH	139	502	68	115	21	4	17	62	.229	58	162	14	247	4	6	.977
1998—	St. Louis (N.L.)	OF	121	383	60	92	17	1	26	67	.240	51	92	8	162	4	5	.971
1999—	Philadelphia (N.L.) ■	OF-DH	138	516	107	134	27	5	17	77	.260	85	112	13	260	7	2	.993
2000—	Philadelphia (N.L.)	OF	89	343	54	87	16	2	20	38	.254	36	73	5	175	4	6	.968
—	Anaheim (A.L.)■	OF-DH	34	82	15	19	3	1	6	16	.232	20	18	1	42	1	1	.977
2001—	Colorado (N.L.)■	OF	59	171	31	44	8	2	8	22	.257	24	56	3	81	2	3	.965
—	Oakland (A.L.)■	DH-OF	34	81	15	21	5	1	2	13	.259	11	24	2	4	0	0	1.000
American League totals (2 years)			68	163	30	40	8	2	8	29	.245	31	42	3	46	1	1	.979
National League totals (14 years)			1645	5936	988	1524	280	47	294	916	.257	701	1301	236	3006	635	110	.971
Major League totals (14 years)			1713	6099	1018	1564	288	49	302	945	.256	732	1343	239	3052	636	111	.971

DIVISION SERIES RECORD

							BATTING								FIELDING		
Year	Team (League)	Pos.	G	AB	R	H	2B	3B	HR	RBI	Avg.	BB	SO	SB	PO	A	E	Avg.
1995—	Cincinnati (N.L.)	OF	3	13	3	3	0	0	1	2	.231	0	3	0	8	1	0	1.000
1996—	St. Louis (N.L.)	OF	3	10	3	4	1	0	1	4	.400	2	0	2	5	0	0	1.000
2001—	Oakland (A.L.)	PH-DH-OF	4	11	1	2	0	0	1	1	.182	0	3	0	3	0	0	1.000
Division series totals (3 years)			10	34	7	9	1	0	3	7	.265	2	6	2	16	1	0	1.000

CHAMPIONSHIP SERIES RECORD

RECORDS: Shares single-game record for most grand slams—1 (October 7, 1992). ... Shares single-inning records for most runs batted in—4 (October 7, 1992, fifth inning); and most stolen bases—2 (October 10, 1991, third inning). ... Holds N.L. career record for most strikeouts—26. ... Holds N.L. single-series record for most stolen bases—7 (1991). ... Shares N.L. single-game record for most stolen bases—3 (October 10, 1991).

G

Year	Team (League)	Pos.	G	AB	R	H	2B	3B	HR	RBI	Avg.	BB	SO	SB	PO	A	E	Avg.
1991—Atlanta (N.L.)..............		OF	7	27	4	7	1	0	1	3	.259	2	4	7	15	2	0	1.000
1992—Atlanta (N.L.)..............		OF	7	22	5	4	0	0	2	6	.182	4	4	1	16	0	0	1.000
1993—Atlanta (N.L.)..............		OF	6	27	4	5	3	0	0	3	.185	2	9	0	10	1	1	.917
1995—Cincinnati (N.L.)........		OF	4	16	1	3	0	0	0	1	.188	0	3	0	9	0	0	1.000
1996—St. Louis (N.L.)..........		OF	7	25	3	6	1	0	2	4	.240	2	6	0	12	0	0	1.000
Championship series totals (5 years)			31	117	17	25	5	0	5	17	.214	10	26	8	62	3	1	.985

WORLD SERIES RECORD

Year	Team (League)	Pos.	G	AB	R	H	2B	3B	HR	RBI	Avg.	BB	SO	SB	PO	A	E	Avg.
1991—Atlanta (N.L.)..............		OF	7	30	3	8	0	1	0	4	.267	2	3	1	19	0	0	1.000
1992—Atlanta (N.L.)..............		OF-PR-PH	4	8	2	1	1	0	0	0	.125	1	2	2	3	1	0	1.000
World Series totals (2 years)			11	38	5	9	1	1	0	4	.237	3	5	3	22	1	0	1.000

ALL-STAR GAME RECORD

Year	League	Pos.	AB	R	H	2B	3B	HR	RBI	Avg.	BB	SO	SB	PO	A	E	Avg.
1992—National	PH-OF	2	0	0	0	0	0	0	.000	0	0	0	1	0	0	1.000
1995—National	DH	2	0	0	0	0	0	0	.000	0	1	0	...	...	...	...
All-Star Game totals (2 years)		4	0	0	0	0	0	0	.000	0	1	0	1	0	0	1.000

GARCES, RICH   P   RED SOX

PERSONAL: Born May 18, 1971, in Maracay, Venezuela. ... 6-0/215. ... Throws right, bats right. ... Full name: Richard Aron Garces Jr. ... Name pronounced gar-SESS.

HIGH SCHOOL: Jose Felix Rivas (Maracay, Venezuela).

COLLEGE: Venezuela Universidad.

TRANSACTIONS/CAREER NOTES: Signed as non-drafted free agent by Minnesota Twins organization (December 29, 1987). ... On Portland suspended list (May 17-September 16, 1991). ... On Portland disabled list (July 28, 1991-remainder of season). ... Granted free agency (October 15, 1994). ... Signed by Chicago Cubs organization (January 30, 1995). ... Claimed on waivers by Florida Marlins (August 9, 1995). ... Granted free agency (October 16, 1995). ... Signed by Boston Red Sox (April 25, 1996). ... On Boston disabled list (July 25-August 20 and August 24, 1996-remainder of season); included rehabilitation assignment to Pawtucket (August 9-20). ... On Boston disabled list (March 27-April 27 and June 2-23, 1997); included rehabilitation assignments to Pawtucket (April 18-21, April 25-27 and June 12-23). ... On Boston disabled list (April 11-May 7, July 1-17 and August 3, 1998-remainder of season); included rehabilitation assignments to Pawtucket (April 21-May 7 and August 30-September 3) and Gulf Coast Red Sox (August 12-29). ... Released by Red Sox (November 23, 1998). ... Re-signed by Red Sox organization (January 26, 1999). ... On Pawtucket disabled list (April 8-22 and May 15-31, 1999). ... On Boston disabled list (June 26-July 12, 2001); included rehabilitation assignment to Lowell (July 8-12).

Year	League	W	L	Pct.	ERA	G	GS	CG	ShO	Sv.	IP	H	R	ER	BB	SO
1988—Elizabethton (Appl.)		5	4	.556	2.29	17	3	1	0	5	59	51	22	15	27	69
1989—Kenosha (Midw.)		9	10	.474	3.41	24	24	4	1	0	142 2/3	117	70	54	62	84
1990—Visalia (Calif.)		2	2	.500	1.81	47	0	0	0	*28	54 2/3	33	14	11	16	75
— Orlando (Sou.)		2	1	.667	2.08	15	0	0	0	8	17 1/3	17	4	4	14	22
— Minnesota (A.L.)		0	0	...	1.59	5	0	0	0	2	5 2/3	4	2	1	4	1
1991—Portland (PCL)		0	1	.000	4.85	10	0	0	0	0	13	10	7	7	8	13
— Orlando (Sou.)		2	1	.667	3.31	10	0	0	0	0	16 1/3	12	6	6	14	17
1992—Orlando (Sou.)		3	3	.500	4.54	58	0	0	0	13	73 1/3	76	46	37	39	72
1993—Portland (PCL)		1	3	.250	8.33	35	7	0	0	4	54	70	55	50	64	48
— Minnesota (A.L.)		0	0	...	0.00	3	0	0	0	0	4	4	2	0	2	3
1994—Nashville (Sou.)		4	5	.444	3.72	40	1	0	0	3	77 1/3	70	40	32	31	76
1995—Iowa (A.A.) ■		0	2	.000	2.86	23	0	0	0	7	28 1/3	25	10	9	8	36
— Chicago (N.L.)		0	0	...	3.27	7	0	0	0	0	11	11	6	4	3	6
— Florida (N.L.) ■		0	2	.000	5.40	11	0	0	0	0	13 1/3	14	9	8	8	16
1996—Pawtucket (I.L.) ■		4	0	1.000	2.30	10	0	0	0	0	15 2/3	10	4	4	5	13
— Boston (A.L.)		3	2	.600	4.91	37	0	0	0	0	44	42	26	24	33	55
1997—Boston (A.L.)		0	1	.000	4.61	12	0	0	0	0	13 2/3	14	9	7	9	12
— Pawtucket (I.L.)		2	1	.667	1.45	26	0	0	0	5	31	24	5	5	13	42
1998—Boston (A.L.)		1	1	.500	3.33	30	0	0	0	1	46	36	19	17	27	34
— Pawtucket (I.L.)		0	1	.000	5.40	7	0	0	0	3	8 1/3	6	5	5	2	10
— Gulf Coast Red Sox (GCL)..		0	0	...	3.27	7	7	0	0	0	11	11	4	4	0	8
1999—Pawtucket (I.L.)		1	0	1.000	3.25	21	0	0	0	7	27 2/3	24	11	10	10	24
— Boston (A.L.)		5	1	.833	1.55	30	0	0	0	2	40 2/3	25	9	7	18	33
2000—Boston (A.L.)		8	1	.889	3.25	64	0	0	0	1	74 2/3	64	28	27	23	69
2001—Boston (A.L.)		6	1	.857	3.90	62	0	0	0	1	67	55	32	29	25	51
— Lowell (NY-Penn)		0	0	...	0.00	2	2	0	0	0	2	1	0	0	0	1
A.L. totals (8 years)		23	7	.767	3.41	243	0	0	0	7	295 2/3	244	127	112	141	258
N.L. totals (1 year)		0	2	.000	4.44	18	0	0	0	0	24 1/3	25	15	12	11	22
Major League totals (9 years)		23	9	.719	3.49	261	0	0	0	7	320	269	142	124	152	280

DIVISION SERIES RECORD

Year	League	W	L	Pct.	ERA	G	GS	CG	ShO	Sv.	IP	H	R	ER	BB	SO
1999—Boston (A.L.)		1	0	1.000	3.86	2	0	0	0	0	2 1/3	2	1	1	3	2

CHAMPIONSHIP SERIES RECORD

Year	League	W	L	Pct.	ERA	G	GS	CG	ShO	Sv.	IP	H	R	ER	BB	SO
1999—Boston (A.L.)		0	0	...	12.00	2	0	0	0	0	3	3	5	4	1	2

GARCIA, CARLOS   P   DODGERS

PERSONAL: Born September 23, 1978, in Guaymas, Mexico. ... 6-3/232. ... Throws right, bats right.

TRANSACTIONS/CAREER NOTES: Signed as non-drafted free agent by Los Angeles Dodgers organization (July 14, 1996). ... Loaned by Dodgers organization to Mexico City Red Devils, Mexican League (March 18-October 28, 1998; and June 18-September 20, 1999). ... On disabled list (April 5, 2001-entire season).

HONORS: Named California League Pitcher of the Year (2000).

Year League	W	L	Pct.	ERA	G	GS	CG	ShO	Sv.	IP	H	R	ER	BB	SO
1997—Dominican Dodgers (DSL).	8	1	.889	1.70	12	12	0	0	0	69	57	17	13	19	58
1998—M.C. Red Devils (Mex.)■..	2	1	.667	5.74	17	0	0	0	0	31 1/3	37	21	20	15	11
1999—M.C. Red Devils (Mex.)......	12	4	.750	4.05	25	25	2	1	0	153 1/3	170	78	69	78	58
2000—San Bernardino (Calif.)■....	14	7	.667	2.57	27	27	2	1	0	*182	162	61	52	49	106
2001—Jacksonville (Sou.)............							Did not play.								

PERSONAL: Born October 6, 1976, in Caracas, Venezuela. ... 6-4/235. ... Throws right, bats right. ... Full name: Freddy Antonio Garcia.

TRANSACTIONS/CAREER NOTES: Signed as non-drafted free agent by Houston Astros organization (October 21, 1993). ... Traded by Astros with SS Carlos Guillen and a player to be named later to Seattle Mariners for P Randy Johnson (July 31, 1998); Mariners acquired P John Halama to complete deal (October 1, 1998). ... On Seattle disabled list (April 22-July 7, 2000); included rehabilitation assignments to Tacoma (June 15-20) and Everett (June 21-July 7).

STATISTICAL NOTES: Tied for A.L. lead with three balks in 1999.

MISCELLANEOUS: Struck out in only appearance as pinch hitter (1999).

Year League	W	L	Pct.	ERA	G	GS	CG	ShO	Sv.	IP	H	R	ER	BB	SO
1994—Dominican Astros (DSL).....	4	6	.400	5.29	16	15	0	0	0	85	80	61	50	38	68
1995—Gulf Coast Astros (GCL).....	6	3	.667	4.47	11	11	0	0	0	58 1/3	60	32	29	14	58
1996—Quad City (Midw.)	5	4	.556	3.12	13	13	0	0	0	60 2/3	57	27	21	27	50
1997—Kissimmee (FSL)...............	10	8	.556	2.56	27	27	5	•2	0	179	165	63	51	49	131
1998—Jackson (Texas)	6	7	.462	3.24	19	19	2	0	0	119 1/3	94	48	43	58	115
—New Orleans (PCL).............	1	0	1.000	3.14	2	2	0	0	0	14 1/3	14	5	5	1	13
—Tacoma (PCL)■.................	3	1	.750	3.86	5	5	0	0	0	32 2/3	30	14	14	13	30
1999—Seattle (A.L.)	17	8	.680	4.07	33	33	2	1	0	201 1/3	205	96	91	90	170
2000—Seattle (A.L.)	9	5	.643	3.91	21	20	0	0	0	124 1/3	112	62	54	64	79
—Tacoma (PCL)	1	0	1.000	2.57	1	1	0	0	0	7	5	2	2	2	11
—Everett (N'West)................	0	0	...	4.50	2	2	0	0	0	10	11	5	5	2	15
2001—Seattle (A.L.)	18	6	.750	*3.05	34	34	4	3	0	*238 2/3	199	88	81	69	163
Major League totals (3 years)	44	19	.698	3.60	88	87	6	4	0	564 1/3	516	246	226	223	412

DIVISION SERIES RECORD

Year League	W	L	Pct.	ERA	G	GS	CG	ShO	Sv.	IP	H	R	ER	BB	SO
2000—Seattle (A.L.)	0	0	...	10.80	1	1	0	0	0	3 1/3	6	4	4	3	2
2001—Seattle (A.L.)	1	1	.500	3.86	2	2	0	0	0	11 2/3	13	6	5	3	13
Division series totals (2 years)	1	1	.500	5.40	3	3	0	0	0	15	19	10	9	6	15

CHAMPIONSHIP SERIES RECORD

Year League	W	L	Pct.	ERA	G	GS	CG	ShO	Sv.	IP	H	R	ER	BB	SO
2000—Seattle (A.L.)	2	0	1.000	1.54	2	2	0	0	0	11 2/3	10	2	2	4	11
2001—Seattle (A.L.)	0	1	.000	3.68	1	1	0	0	0	7 1/3	7	3	3	4	6
Champ. series totals (2 years)	2	1	.667	2.37	3	3	0	0	0	19	17	5	5	8	17

ALL-STAR GAME RECORD

Year League	W	L	Pct.	ERA	GS	CG	ShO	Sv.	IP	H	R	ER	BB	SO
2001—American	1	0	1.000	0.00	0	0	0	0	1	0	0	0	0	0

PERSONAL: Born September 24, 1973, in Corpus Christi, Texas. ... 5-10/171. ... Bats right, throws right. ... Full name: Jesus Jesse Garcia Jr.

HIGH SCHOOL: Robstown (Texas).

JUNIOR COLLEGE: Lee College (Texas).

TRANSACTIONS/CAREER NOTES: Selected by Baltimore Orioles organization in 26th round of free-agent draft (June 3, 1993). ... On disabled list (June 19, 1994-remainder of season). ... Granted free agency (December 21, 1998). ... Re-signed by Orioles organization (December 21, 1998). ... On Rochester disabled list (May 25-July 18, 1999). ... Traded by Orioles for Atlanta Braves for IF Steve Sisco (December 18, 2000).

STATISTICAL NOTES: Led California League with 20 sacrifice hits in 1996. ... Led California League second basemen with 263 putouts, 409 assists, .968 fielding percentage, 694 total chances and 81 double plays in 1996; tied for lead in errors with 22. ... Led Eastern League with 24 sacrifice hits in 1997. ... Led Eastern League second basemen with .985 fielding percentage in 1997. ... Tied for International League lead with 16 sacrifice hits in 2000. ... Tied for International League lead with 21 sacrifice hits in 2001.

Year Team (League)	Pos.	G	AB	R	H	2B	3B	HR	RBI	Avg.	BB	SO	SB	PO	A	E	Avg.
1993—GC Orioles (GCL)........	2B-SS-3B	48	156	20	37	4	0	0	16	.237	21	32	14	61	136	14	.934
1994—Bluefield (Appl.)..........							Did not play.										
1995—Frederick (Caro.)	2B	124	365	52	82	11	3	3	27	.225	49	75	5	283	275	28	.952
1996—High Desert (Calif.)......	2B-SS	137	459	94	122	21	5	10	66	.266	57	81	25	†263	†409	‡22	†.968
1997—Bowie (East.)..............	2B-SS-3B	*141	437	52	103	18	1	5	42	.236	38	71	7	290	377	13	†.981
1998—Bowie (East.)..............	2B-SS-OF	86	258	46	73	13	1	2	20	.283	34	37	12	133	196	9	.973
—Rochester (I.L.)..........	2B	44	160	20	47	6	4	0	18	.294	7	22	7	102	145	8	.969
1999—Baltimore (A.L.)..........SS-2B-3B-DH	17	29	6	6	0	0	2	2	.207	2	3	0	16	22	0	1.000
—Rochester (I.L.)..........	SS-2B	62	220	25	56	10	2	2	23	.255	11	21	9	95	156	15	.944
2000—Baltimore (A.L.)..........	2B-SS	14	17	2	1	0	0	0	0	.059	2	2	0	9	22	0	1.000
—Rochester (I.L.)..........	SS-2B-3B	106	372	44	90	12	2	1	23	.242	27	60	9	164	299	18	.963
2001—Richmond (I.L.)■........	SS-2B-3B	105	375	50	100	22	3	2	22	.267	22	54	18	147	276	20	.955
—Atlanta (N.L.).............	2B-SS	22	5	3	1	0	0	0	0	.200	0	1	0	6	3	0	1.000
American League totals (2 years)		31	46	8	7	0	0	2	2	.152	4	5	0	25	44	0	1.000
National League totals (1 year)		22	5	3	1	0	0	0	0	.200	0	1	0	6	3	0	1.000
Major League totals (3 years)		53	51	11	8	0	0	2	2	.157	4	6	0	28	47	0	1.000

G

PERSONAL: Born April 29, 1978, in San Gabriel, Calif. ... 6-3/195. ... Throws right, bats right. ... Full name: Jose Antonio Garcia.
HIGH SCHOOL: Baldwin Park (Calif.).
TRANSACTIONS/CAREER NOTES: Selected by Milwaukee Brewers organization in second round of free-agent draft (June 4, 1996). ... On disabled list (April 8, 1999-entire season; April 14-May 19 and July 7-23, 2000; and July 31, 2001-remainder of season).

Year League	W	L	Pct.	ERA	G	GS	CG	ShO	Sv.	IP	H	R	ER	BB	SO
1996—Helena (Pio.)	0	0	...	16.20	2	0	0	0	0	1 2/3	1	3	3	3	2
1997—Beloit (Midw.)	6	11	.353	4.00	27	26	2	0	0	155 1/3	145	89	69	70	126
1998—Stockton (Calif.)	11	12	.478	3.67	28	•28	1	0	0	*169 1/3	147	89	69	*91	167
1999—Huntsville (Sou.)							Did not play.								
2000—Huntsville (Sou.)	4	8	.333	3.76	19	18	0	0	0	103	107	52	43	54	78
2001—Huntsville (Sou.)	6	5	.545	3.73	21	21	1	0	0	111	99	52	46	49	84

PERSONAL: Born October 29, 1975, in Ciudad Obregon, Mexico. ... 6-0/172. ... Bats left, throws left. ... Full name: Gustavo Garcia.
HIGH SCHOOL: Preparatoria Abierta (Ciudad Obregon, Mexico).
TRANSACTIONS/CAREER NOTES: Signed as non-drafted free agent by Los Angeles Dodgers organization (July 16, 1992). ... On Los Angeles disabled list (September 1, 1997-remainder of season). ... Selected by Arizona Diamondbacks in first round (ninth pick overall) of expansion draft (November 18, 1997). ... Traded by Diamondbacks to Detroit Tigers for OF Luis Gonzalez (December 28, 1998). ... Traded by Tigers to Baltimore Orioles for future considerations (June 12, 2000). ... On suspended list (September 1-4, 2000). ... Released by Orioles (October 17, 2000). ... Signed by Cleveland Indians organization (December 22, 2000).
HONORS: Named Minor League Player of the Year by THE SPORTING NEWS (1995).
STATISTICAL NOTES: Led Pacific Coast League with 257 total bases in 1995. ... Career major league grand slams: 1.

Year Team (League)	Pos.	G	AB	R	H	2B	3B	HR	RBI	Avg.	BB	SO	SB	PO	A	E	Avg.
1993—Bakersfield (Calif.)	OF	123	460	61	111	20	9	19	54	.241	37	109	5	193	12	*13	.940
1994—Vero Beach (FSL)	OF	121	452	72	120	28	10	*21	84	.265	37	112	8	229	12	5	.980
1995—Albuquerque (PCL)	OF-DH	124	474	88	151	26	10	20	•91	.319	38	102	12	185	7	*14	.932
—Los Angeles (N.L.)	OF	13	20	1	4	0	0	0	0	.200	0	4	0	5	2	0	1.000
1996—Albuquerque (PCL)	OF-DH	84	327	54	97	17	10	13	58	.297	29	67	6	148	4	13	.921
—San Antonio (Texas)	OF	35	129	21	32	6	1	5	22	.248	9	38	1	60	6	2	.971
—Los Angeles (N.L.)	OF	1	1	0	0	0	0	0	0	.000	0	1	0	0	0	0	...
1997—Albuquerque (PCL)	OF-DH	71	262	53	80	17	6	20	66	.305	23	70	11	97	3	5	.952
—Los Angeles (N.L.)	OF	15	39	5	5	0	0	1	8	.128	6	14	0	13	0	0	1.000
1998—Arizona (N.L.)■	OF	113	333	39	74	10	8	9	43	.222	18	78	5	191	6	5	.975
—Tucson (PCL)	OF	27	106	21	33	4	2	10	27	.311	15	24	5	67	1	3	.958
1999—Detroit (A.L.)■	OF-DH	96	288	38	69	10	3	14	32	.240	20	67	2	152	7	7	.958
2000—Detroit (A.L.)	OF-DH	8	17	1	3	0	0	0	0	.176	0	4	0	8	0	0	1.000
—Toledo (I.L.)	OF	40	155	31	46	6	2	15	38	.297	11	32	2	82	5	4	.956
—Rochester (I.L.)■	OF	76	270	38	75	17	1	13	54	.278	34	70	3	121	4	3	.977
—Baltimore (A.L.)	DH-OF	8	16	0	0	0	0	0	0	.000	0	6	0	2	0	0	1.000
2001—Buffalo (I.L.)■	OF-1B	125	462	73	122	16	4	31	85	.264	44	106	4	240	11	7	.973
—Cleveland (A.L.)	OF-1B	20	45	8	14	3	0	5	9	.311	3	13	0	18	4	2	.917
American League totals (3 years)		132	366	47	86	13	3	19	41	.235	23	90	2	180	11	9	.955
National League totals (4 years)		142	393	45	83	10	8	10	51	.211	24	97	5	209	8	5	.977
Major League totals (7 years)		274	759	92	169	23	11	29	92	.223	47	187	7	389	19	14	.967

PERSONAL: Born November 5, 1978, in Guadalajara, Mexico. ... 6-4/185. ... Bats right, throws right. ... Full name: Luis Alfonso Garcia.
TRANSACTIONS/CAREER NOTES: Signed as non-drafted free agent by Boston Red Sox organization (March 14, 1996). ... Loaned by Red Sox organization to Mexico, Arizona League (April 30-September 20, 1999). ... Traded by Red Sox with OF Rick Asadoorian and 1B Dustin Brisson to St. Louis Cardinals for P Dustin Hermanson (December 15, 2001).

Year Team (League)	Pos.	G	AB	R	H	2B	3B	HR	RBI	Avg.	BB	SO	SB	PO	A	E	Avg.
1998—Dom. Red Sox (DSL)	1B	54	189	31	40	6	2	8	32	.212	27	33	3	...	...	...	...
1999—Mexico (Ariz.)■	OF-1B	50	188	35	62	9	6	13	40	.330	22	31	1	183	8	6	.970
2000—Augusta (S.Atl.)■	1B	128	493	72	128	27	5	20	77	.260	51	112	8	941	52	15	.985
2001—Sarasota (FSL)	1B-OF-3B	65	267	38	81	14	1	12	44	.303	18	61	2	477	31	9	.983
—Trenton (East.)	1B	63	229	35	71	14	1	14	45	.310	28	68	0	446	32	5	.990

RECORD AS PITCHER

Year League	W	L	Pct.	ERA	G	GS	CG	ShO	Sv.	IP	H	R	ER	BB	SO
1996—Dominican Red Sox (DSL)	2	0	1.000	3.75	14	0	0	0	0	24	13	12	10	23	17
1997—Gulf Coast Red Sox (GCL)	1	2	.333	2.87	8	1	0	0	1	15 2/3	12	10	5	10	18

PERSONAL: Born July 23, 1973, in Whittier, Calif. ... 6-0/180. ... Bats right, throws right. ... Full name: Anthony Nomar Garciaparra. ... Brother of Michael Garciaparra, shortstop, Seattle Mariners organization.
HIGH SCHOOL: St. John Bosco (Bellflower, Calif.).
COLLEGE: Georgia Tech.

G

TRANSACTIONS/CAREER NOTES: Selected by Milwaukee Brewers organization in fifth round of free-agent draft (June 3, 1991); did not sign. ... Selected by Boston Red Sox organization in first round (12th pick overall) of free-agent draft (June 2, 1994). ... On Pawtucket disabled list (April 4-15 and April 19-July 11, 1996). ... On disabled list (May 9-28, 1998; and May 12-27, 2000). ... On Boston disabled list (March 21-July 29 and August 27, 2001-remainder of season); included rehabilitation assignment to Pawtucket (July 24-29).

RECORDS: Shares major league single-game record for most grand slams—2 (May 10, 1999). ... Holds A.L. rookie-season record for most consecutive games batted safely—30 (1997).

HONORS: Named A.L. Rookie Player of the Year by The Sporting News (1997). ... Named shortstop on The Sporting News A.L. All-Star team (1997 and 1999). ... Named shortstop on The Sporting News A.L. Silver Slugger team (1997). ... Named A.L. Rookie of the Year by Baseball Writers' Association of America (1997).

STATISTICAL NOTES: Led Eastern League shortstops with 624 total chances in 1995. ... Had 30-game hitting streak (July 26-August 29, 1997). ... Led A.L. shortstops in total chances with 720 and double plays with 113 in 1997. ... Had 16-game hitting streak (April 2-19, 1998). ... Had 24-game hitting streak (June 7-July 3, 1998). ... Had 16-game hitting streak (April 26-May 14, 1999). ... Hit three home runs in one game (May 10, 1999). ... Had 17-game hitting streak (June 13-July 2, 1999). ... Had 20-game hitting streak (September 10-29, 2000). ... Led A.L. with 20 intentional bases on balls received in 2000. ... Career major league grand slams: 3.

MISCELLANEOUS: Member of 1992 U.S. Olympic baseball team.

Year Team (League)	Pos.	G	AB	R	H	2B	3B	HR	RBI	Avg.	BB	SO	SB	PO	A	E	Avg.
1994— Sarasota (FSL)	SS	28	105	20	31	8	1	1	16	.295	10	6	5	42	72	3	.974
1995— Trenton (East.)	SS	125	513	77	137	20	8	8	47	.267	50	42	35	205	*396	23	.963
1996— Pawtucket (I.L.)	SS	43	172	40	59	15	2	16	46	.343	14	21	3	63	120	5	.973
— GC Red Sox (GCL)	SS	5	14	4	4	2	1	0	5	.286	1	0	0	7	12	1	.950
— Boston (A.L.)	SS-DH-2B	24	87	11	21	2	3	4	16	.241	4	14	5	37	51	1	.989
1997— Boston (A.L.)	SS	153	*684	122	*209	44	*11	30	98	.306	35	92	22	*249	450	21	.971
1998— Boston (A.L.)	SS	143	604	111	195	37	8	35	122	.323	33	62	12	228	402	25	.962
1999— Boston (A.L.)	SS	135	532	103	190	42	4	27	104	*.357	51	39	14	232	357	17	.972
2000— Boston (A.L.)	SS-DH	140	529	104	197	51	3	21	96	*.372	61	50	5	201	402	18	.971
2001— Pawtucket (I.L.)	SS	4	16	3	7	2	0	1	4	.438	1	2	0	4	12	1	.941
— Boston (A.L.)	SS	21	83	13	24	3	0	4	8	.289	7	9	0	34	56	3	.968
Major League totals (6 years)		616	2519	464	836	179	29	121	444	.332	191	266	58	981	1718	85	.969

DIVISION SERIES RECORD

Year Team (League)	Pos.	G	AB	R	H	2B	3B	HR	RBI	Avg.	BB	SO	SB	PO	A	E	Avg.
1998— Boston (A.L.)	SS	4	15	4	5	1	0	3	11	.333	2	0	0	3	7	0	1.000
1999— Boston (A.L.)	SS	4	12	6	5	2	0	2	4	.417	3	3	0	5	11	0	1.000
Division series totals (2 years)		8	27	10	10	3	0	5	15	.370	5	3	0	8	18	0	1.000

CHAMPIONSHIP SERIES RECORD

Year Team (League)	Pos.	G	AB	R	H	2B	3B	HR	RBI	Avg.	BB	SO	SB	PO	A	E	Avg.
1999— Boston (A.L.)	SS	5	20	2	8	2	0	2	5	.400	2	2	1	7	13	4	.833

ALL-STAR GAME RECORD

Year League	Pos.	AB	R	H	2B	3B	HR	RBI	Avg.	BB	SO	SB	PO	A	E	Avg.
1997— American	SS	1	0	0	0	0	0	0	.000	0	0	0	1	0	0	1.000
1999— American	SS	2	0	0	0	0	0	0	.000	0	0	0	0	0	0	...
2000— American	SS	2	1	1	0	0	0	0	.500	0	0	0	2	2	2	.667
All-Star Game totals (3 years)		5	1	1	0	0	0	0	.200	0	0	0	3	2	2	.714

GARDNER, MARK — P

PERSONAL: Born March 1, 1962, in Los Angeles. ... 6-1/220. ... Throws right, bats right. ... Full name: Mark Allan Gardner.

HIGH SCHOOL: Clovis (Calif.).

JUNIOR COLLEGE: Fresno (Calif.) City College.

COLLEGE: Fresno State.

TRANSACTIONS/CAREER NOTES: Selected by California Angels organization in sixth round of free-agent draft (January 11, 1983); did not sign. ... Selected by Cleveland Indians organization in 17th round of free-agent draft (June 4, 1984); did not sign. ... Selected by Montreal Expos organization in eighth round of free-agent draft (June 3, 1985). ... On disabled list (September 20, 1990-remainder of season). ... On Montreal disabled list (April 2-May 14, 1991; included rehabilitation assignment to Indianapolis (April 11-May 8). ... Traded by Expos with P Doug Piatt to Kansas City Royals for C Tim Spehr and P Jeff Shaw (December 9, 1992). ... On Kansas City disabled list (July 7-August 21, 1993; included rehabilitation assignment to Omaha (July 28-August 26). ... Released by Royals (December 8, 1993). ... Signed by Florida Marlins organization (January 6, 1994). ... On Florida disabled list (June 8-26, 1994; included rehabilitation assignment to Brevard County (June 18-22). ... Granted free agency (February 17, 1995). ... Re-signed by Marlins (April 7, 1995). ... Granted free agency (October 16, 1995). ... Re-signed by Marlins organization (December 8, 1995) ... Granted free agency (March 28, 1996). ... Signed by San Francisco Giants (March 29, 1996). ... On San Francisco disabled list (July 3-21, 1996; included rehabilitation assignment to San Jose (July 17-21). ... Granted free agency (October 23, 1998). ... Re-signed by Giants (November 9, 1998). ... On San Francisco disabled list (April 17-May 9, 1999; included rehabilitation assignment to San Jose (April 28-May 9). ... Granted free agency (October 31, 2000). ... Re-signed by Giants (December 7, 2000). ... On San Francisco disabled list (July 7-September 1, 2001; included rehabilitation assignment to Fresno (August 25-September 1). ... Granted free agency (November 8, 2001).

RECORDS: Shares major league single-inning record for most hit batsmen—3 (August 15, 1992, first inning).

HONORS: Named American Association Pitcher of the Year (1989).

STATISTICAL NOTES: Led N.L. with nine hit batsmen in 1990. ... Pitched nine hitless innings against Los Angeles Dodgers, but gave up two hits in 10th inning and lost, 1-0, when reliever Jeff Fassero gave up game-winning hit in 10th (July 26, 1991).

MISCELLANEOUS: Struck out once in two appearances as pinch hitter for Montreal (1991). ... Had two sacrifice hits in three appearances as pinch hitter for San Francisco (1996).

G

Year	League	W	L	Pct.	ERA	G	GS	CG	ShO	Sv.	IP	H	R	ER	BB	SO
1985—	Jamestown (NY-Penn)	0	0	...	2.77	3	3	0	0	0	13	9	4	4	4	16
—	West Palm Beach (FSL)	5	4	.556	2.37	10	9	4	0	0	60 2/3	54	24	16	18	44
1986—	Jacksonville (Sou.)............	10	11	.476	3.84	29	28	3	1	0	168 2/3	144	88	72	90	140
1987—	Indianapolis (A.A.).............	3	3	.500	5.67	9	9	0	0	0	46	48	32	29	28	41
—	Jacksonville (Sou.)............	4	6	.400	4.19	17	17	1	0	0	101	101	50	47	42	78
1988—	Jacksonville (Sou.)............	6	3	.667	1.60	15	15	4	2	0	112 1/3	72	24	20	36	130
—	Indianapolis (A.A.).............	4	2	.667	2.77	13	13	3	1	0	84 1/3	65	30	26	32	71
1989—	Indianapolis (A.A.).............	12	4	*.750	2.37	24	23	4	2	0	163 1/3	122	51	43	59	*175
—	Montreal (N.L.)...................	0	3	.000	5.13	7	4	0	0	0	26 1/3	26	16	15	11	21
1990—	Montreal (N.L.)...................	7	9	.438	3.42	27	26	3	3	0	152 2/3	129	62	58	61	135
1991—	Indianapolis (A.A.).............	2	0	1.000	3.48	6	6	0	0	0	31	26	13	12	16	38
—	Montreal (N.L.)...................	9	11	.450	3.85	27	27	0	0	0	168 1/3	139	78	72	75	107
1992—	Montreal (N.L.)...................	12	10	.545	4.36	33	30	0	0	0	179 2/3	179	91	87	60	132
1993—	Kansas City (A.L.)■	4	6	.400	6.19	17	16	0	0	0	91 2/3	92	65	63	36	54
—	Omaha (A.A.).....................	4	2	.667	2.79	8	8	1	0	0	48 1/3	34	17	15	19	41
1994—	Florida (N.L.)■	4	4	.500	4.87	20	14	0	0	0	92 1/3	97	53	50	30	57
—	Edmonton (PCL)	1	0	1.000	0.00	1	1	0	0	0	6	4	0	0	1	11
—	Brevard County (FSL)........	1	0	1.000	0.00	1	1	0	0	0	5	1	0	0	1	3
1995—	Florida (N.L.).....................	5	5	.500	4.49	39	11	1	1	1	102 1/3	109	60	51	43	87
1996—	San Francisco (N.L.)■	12	7	.632	4.42	30	28	4	1	0	179 1/3	200	105	88	57	145
—	San Jose (Calif.)	0	0	...	3.18	1	1	0	0	0	5 2/3	4	2	2	0	7
1997—	San Francisco (N.L.)	12	9	.571	4.29	30	30	2	1	0	180 1/3	188	92	86	57	136
1998—	San Francisco (N.L.)	13	6	.684	4.33	33	33	4	2	0	212	203	106	102	65	151
1999—	San Francisco (N.L.)	5	11	.313	6.47	29	21	1	0	0	139	142	103	100	57	86
—	San Jose (Calif.)...............	1	0	1.000	4.50	2	2	0	0	0	10	10	5	5	3	13
2000—	San Francisco (N.L.)	11	7	.611	4.05	30	20	0	0	0	149	155	72	67	42	92
2001—	San Francisco (N.L.)	5	5	.500	5.40	23	15	0	0	0	91 2/3	93	57	55	34	53
—	Fresno (PCL)	0	1	.000	6.00	3	3	0	0	0	6	10	4	4	1	7
A.L. totals (1 year)		4	6	.400	6.19	17	16	0	0	0	91 2/3	92	65	63	36	54
N.L. totals (12 years)		95	87	.522	4.47	328	259	15	8	1	1673	1660	895	831	592	1202
Major League totals (13 years)		99	93	.516	4.56	345	275	15	8	1	1764 2/3	1752	960	894	628	1256

DIVISION SERIES RECORD

Year	League	W	L	Pct.	ERA	G	GS	CG	ShO	Sv.	IP	H	R	ER	BB	SO
2000—	San Francisco (N.L.)	0	1	.000	8.31	1	1	0	0	0	4 1/3	4	4	4	2	5

GARLAND, JON — P — WHITE SOX

PERSONAL: Born September 27, 1979, in Valencia, Calif. ... 6-6/205. ... Throws right, bats right. ... Full name: Jon Steven Garland.
HIGH SCHOOL: John F. Kennedy (Granada Hills, Calif.).
TRANSACTIONS/CAREER NOTES: Selected by Chicago Cubs organization in first round (10th pick overall) of free-agent draft (June 3, 1997). ... Traded by Cubs to Chicago White Sox for P Matt Karchner (July 29, 1998). ... On Chicago disabled list (August 19-September 3, 2000); included rehabilitation assignment to Birmingham (August 30-September 3).
HONORS: Named International League Most Valuable Pitcher (2000).

Year	League	W	L	Pct.	ERA	G	GS	CG	ShO	Sv.	IP	H	R	ER	BB	SO
1997—	Arizona Cubs (Ariz.)	3	2	.600	2.70	10	7	0	0	0	40	37	14	12	10	39
1998—	Rockford (Midw.)	4	7	.364	5.03	19	19	1	0	0	107 1/3	124	69	60	45	70
—	Hickory (S.Atl.)■...............	1	4	.200	5.40	5	5	0	0	0	26 2/3	36	20	16	13	19
1999—	Winston-Salem (Caro.)	5	7	.417	3.33	19	19	2	1	0	119	109	57	44	39	84
—	Birmingham (Sou.)............	3	1	.750	4.38	7	7	0	0	0	39	39	22	19	18	27
2000—	Charlotte (I.L.)	9	2	.818	2.26	16	16	2	1	0	103 2/3	99	28	26	32	63
—	Chicago (A.L.)..................	4	8	.333	6.46	15	13	0	0	0	69 2/3	82	55	50	40	42
—	Birmingham (Sou.)............	0	0	...	0.00	1	1	0	0	0	6	4	0	0	1	10
2001—	Charlotte (I.L.)	0	3	.000	2.73	5	5	1	0	0	33	31	10	10	11	26
—	Chicago (A.L.)..................	6	7	.462	3.69	35	16	0	0	1	117	123	59	48	55	61
Major League totals (2 years)		10	15	.400	4.72	50	29	0	0	1	186 2/3	205	114	98	95	103

GEORGE, CHRIS — P — ROYALS

PERSONAL: Born September 16, 1979, in Houston. ... 6-2/200. ... Throws left, bats left. ... Full name: Christopher Coleman George.
HIGH SCHOOL: Klein (Texas).
TRANSACTIONS/CAREER NOTES: Selected by Kansas City Royals organization as "sandwich pick" between first and second round of free-agent draft (June 2, 1998); pick received as part of compensation for Arizona Diamondbacks signing Type A free agent IF Jay Bell.
MISCELLANEOUS: Member of 2000 U.S. Olympic baseball team.

Year	League	W	L	Pct.	ERA	G	GS	CG	ShO	Sv.	IP	H	R	ER	BB	SO
1998—	Gulf Coast Royals (GCL)	0	1	.000	2.87	5	4	0	0	0	15 2/3	14	9	5	4	10
1999—	Wilmington (Caro.)............	9	7	.563	3.60	27	27	0	0	0	145	142	65	58	53	142
2000—	Wichita (Texas)	8	5	.615	3.14	18	18	0	0	0	97 1/3	92	41	34	51	80
—	Omaha (PCL)	3	2	.600	4.84	8	8	0	0	0	44 2/3	47	29	24	20	27
2001—	Omaha (PCL).....................	11	3	.786	3.53	20	20	0	0	0	117 1/3	103	54	46	51	84
—	Kansas City (A.L.)	4	8	.333	5.59	13	13	1	0	0	74	83	48	46	18	32
Major League totals (1 year)		4	8	.333	5.59	13	13	1	0	0	74	83	48	46	18	32

GERMAN, ESTEBAN — 2B — ATHLETICS

PERSONAL: Born December 26, 1978, in Haina, Dominican Republic. ... 5-9/165. ... Bats right, throws right. ... Full name: Esteban German Guridi.
TRANSACTIONS/CAREER NOTES: Signed as non-drafted free agent by Oakland Athletics organization (July 4, 1996).
STATISTICAL NOTES: Led Arizona League second basemen with 216 total chances in 1998. ... Led California League second basemen with 21 errors in 2000.

G

Year Team (League)	Pos.	G	AB	R	H	2B	3B	HR	RBI	Avg.	BB	SO	SB	PO	A	E	Avg.
1997—Dom. Athletics (DSL).		69	249	69	79	17	1	2	29	.317	73	30	58	...	...	...	...
1998—Dom. Athletics (DSL).		10	32	9	10	1	1	0	4	.313	7	2	1	...	...	...	...
—Ariz. Athletics (Ariz.)..	2B	•55	202	*52	62	3	*10	2	28	.307	33	43	*40	*87	*116	*13	.940
1999—Modesto (Calif.)	2B	128	501	107	156	16	12	4	52	.311	*102	128	40	201	321	*38	.932
2000—Midland (Texas).........	2B	24	75	13	16	1	0	1	6	.213	18	21	5	33	64	5	.951
—Visalia (Calif.)	2B-SS	109	428	82	113	14	10	2	35	.264	61	86	*78	228	275	†25	.953
2001—Midland (Texas)..........	2B	92	335	79	95	20	3	6	30	.284	63	66	31	170	242	16	.963
—Sacramento (PCL)......	2B	38	150	40	56	8	0	4	14	.373	18	20	17	78	97	7	.962

GERMAN, FRANKLYN   P   ATHLETICS

PERSONAL: Born January 20, 1980, in San Cristobal, Dominican Republic. ... 6-4/170. ... Throws right, bats right. ... Full name: Franklyn Miguel German Made.

TRANSACTIONS/CAREER NOTES: Signed as non-drafted free agent by Oakland Athletics organization (July 2, 1996).

Year League	W	L	Pct.	ERA	G	GS	CG	ShO	Sv.	IP	H	R	ER	BB	SO
1997—Dominican Athletics (DSL).	8	3	.727	2.33	13	13	5	...	0	89	66	33	23	31	80
1998—Arizona Athletics (Ariz.)......	2	1	.667	6.13	14	12	0	0	0	54 1/3	69	43	37	18	48
1999—Southern Oregon (N'West).	3	5	.375	5.99	15	15	0	0	0	73 2/3	89	52	49	45	58
2000—Modesto (Calif.)	5	5	.500	5.50	17	14	0	0	0	72	88	55	44	37	52
—Vancouver (N'West)	1	0	1.000	1.77	9	2	0	0	0	20 1/3	13	4	4	10	20
2001—Visalia (Calif.)	2	4	.333	3.98	53	0	0	0	19	63 1/3	67	34	28	31	93

GIAMBI, JASON   1B   YANKEES

PERSONAL: Born January 8, 1971, in West Covina, Calif. ... 6-3/235. ... Bats left, throws right. ... Full name: Jason Gilbert Giambi. ... Brother of Jeremy Giambi, first baseman/outfielder, Oakland Athletics. ... Name pronounced GEE-om-bee.

HIGH SCHOOL: South Hills (West Covina, Calif.).

COLLEGE: Long Beach State.

TRANSACTIONS/CAREER NOTES: Selected by Milwaukee Brewers organization in 43rd round of free-agent draft (June 5, 1989); did not sign. ... Selected by Oakland Athletics organization in second round of free-agent draft (June 1, 1992). ... On disabled list (July 27-August 28, 1993). ... On Huntsville disabled list (April 7-14, 1994). ... Granted free agency (November 5, 2001). ... Signed by New York Yankees (December 13, 2001).

HONORS: Named A.L. Most Valuable Player by Baseball Writers' Association of America (2000). ... Named first baseman on A.L. Silver Slugger team (2001).

STATISTICAL NOTES: Had 25-game hitting streak (May 12-June 23, 1997). ... Had 17-game hitting streak (July 16-August 2, 1998). ... Had 16-game hitting streak (September 5-24, 1998). ... Had 18-game hitting streak (July 23-August 10, 1999). ... Led A.L. with .476 on-base percentage in 2000 and .477 in 2001. ... Led A.L. with .660 slugging percentage in 2001. ... Career major league grand slams: 8.

MISCELLANEOUS: Member of 1992 U.S. Olympic baseball team. ... Holds Oakland Athletics all-time record for highest career batting average (.308).

Year Team (League)	Pos.	G	AB	R	H	2B	3B	HR	RBI	Avg.	BB	SO	SB	PO	A	E	Avg.
1992—S. Oregon (N'West)	3B	13	41	9	13	3	0	3	13	.317	9	6	1	5	20	1	.962
1993—Modesto (Calif.)	3B	89	313	72	91	16	2	12	60	.291	73	47	2	49	145	19	.911
1994—Huntsville (Sou.)	3B-1B	56	193	31	43	9	0	6	30	.223	27	31	0	111	77	11	.945
—Tacoma (PCL)	3B-SS	52	176	28	56	20	0	4	38	.318	25	32	1	39	110	8	.949
1995—Edmonton (PCL)	3B-DH-1B	55	190	34	65	26	1	3	41	.342	34	26	0	38	98	9	.938
—Oakland (A.L.)	3B-1B-DH	54	176	27	45	7	0	6	25	.256	28	31	2	194	55	4	.984
1996—Oakland (A.L.)	1-0-3-DH	140	536	84	156	40	1	20	79	.291	51	95	0	478	117	11	.982
1997—Oakland (A.L.)	OF-1B-DH	142	519	66	152	41	2	20	81	.293	55	89	0	501	44	7	.987
1998—Oakland (A.L.)	1B-DH	153	562	92	166	28	0	27	110	.295	81	102	2	1255	73	*14	.990
1999—Oakland (A.L.)	1B-DH-3B	158	575	115	181	36	1	33	123	.315	105	106	1	1251	45	7	.995
2000—Oakland (A.L.)	1B-DH	152	510	108	170	29	1	43	137	.333	*137	96	2	1161	59	6	.995
2001—Oakland (A.L.)	1B-DH	154	520	109	178	*47	2	38	120	.342	*129	83	2	1224	76	11	.992
Major League totals (7 years)		953	3398	601	1048	228	7	187	675	.308	586	602	9	6064	469	60	.991

DIVISION SERIES RECORD

Year Team (League)	Pos.	G	AB	R	H	2B	3B	HR	RBI	Avg.	BB	SO	SB	PO	A	E	Avg.
2000—Oakland (A.L.)	1B	5	14	2	4	0	0	0	1	.286	7	2	1	40	0	1	.976
2001—Oakland (A.L.)	1B	5	17	2	6	0	0	1	4	.353	4	2	0	53	2	1	.982
Division series totals (2 years)		10	31	4	10	0	0	1	5	.323	11	4	1	93	2	2	.979

ALL-STAR GAME RECORD

Year League	Pos.	AB	R	H	2B	3B	HR	RBI	Avg.	BB	SO	SB	PO	A	E	Avg.
2000—American	1B	2	0	0	0	0	0	0	.000	1	2	0	2	0	0	1.000
2001—American	PR-1B	1	1	0	0	0	0	0	.000	0	0	0	1	0	0	1.000
All-Star Game totals (2 years)		3	1	0	0	0	0	0	.000	1	2	0	3	0	0	1.000

G

GIAMBI, JEREMY   1B/OF   ATHLETICS

PERSONAL: Born September 30, 1974, in San Jose, Calif. ... 6-0/200. ... Bats left, throws left. ... Full name: Jeremy Dean Giambi. ... Brother of Jason Giambi, first baseman, New York Yankees.

HIGH SCHOOL: South Hills (West Covina, Calif.).

COLLEGE: Cal State-Fullerton.

TRANSACTIONS/CAREER NOTES: Selected by Kansas City Royals organization in sixth round of free-agent draft (June 4, 1996). ... On Omaha disabled list (July 12-August 2, 1998). ... On Kansas City disabled list (March 27-May 15, 1999); included rehabilitation assignment to Omaha (April 28-May 15). ... Traded by Royals to Oakland Athletics for P Brett Laxton (February 18, 2000). ... On Oakland disabled list (August 22-September 8, 2000); included rehabilitation assignment to Sacramento (September 6-8). ... On Oakland disabled list (May 16-June 9, 2001); included rehabilitation assignment to Sacramento (May 25-June 9).

HONORS: Led Northwest League with .440 on-base percentage in 1996. ... Led Pacific Coast League with .469 on-base percentage in 1998.

STATISTICAL NOTES: Career major league grand slams: 1.

Year Team (League)	Pos.	G	AB	R	H	2B	3B	HR	RBI	Avg.	BB	SO	SB	PO	A	E	Avg.
1996— Spokane (N'West)	OF	67	231	•58	63	17	0	6	39	.273	*61	32	22	97	3	*11	.901
1997— Lansing (Midw.)	OF	31	116	33	39	11	1	5	21	.336	23	16	5	30	2	0	1.000
— Wichita (Texas)	OF-1B	74	268	50	86	15	1	11	52	.321	44	47	4	117	2	3	.975
1998— Omaha (PCL)	OF-1B	96	325	68	121	21	2	20	66	*.372	57	64	8	113	8	3	.976
— Kansas City (A.L.)	OF-DH	18	58	6	13	4	0	2	8	.224	11	9	0	14	1	0	1.000
1999— Kansas City (A.L.)	DH-1B-OF	90	288	34	82	13	1	3	34	.285	40	67	0	213	8	2	.991
— Omaha (PCL)	OF-1B-DH	35	127	31	44	5	1	12	28	.346	31	30	1	156	9	2	.988
2000— Oakland (A.L.)■	OF-DH-1B	104	260	42	66	10	2	10	50	.254	32	61	0	136	8	3	.980
— Sacramento (PCL)	OF-1B	8	31	8	11	2	0	2	8	.355	8	7	1	23	1	1	.960
2001— Oakland (A.L.)	DH-OF-1B	124	371	64	105	26	0	12	57	.283	63	83	0	123	3	5	.962
— Sacramento (PCL)	OF	9	27	1	9	1	0	0	1	.333	1	6	0	7	0	0	1.000
Major League totals (4 years)		336	977	146	266	53	3	27	149	.272	146	220	0	486	20	10	.981

DIVISION SERIES RECORD

Year Team (League)	Pos.	G	AB	R	H	2B	3B	HR	RBI	Avg.	BB	SO	SB	PO	A	E	Avg.
2000— Oakland (A.L.)	DH-OF-PH	4	9	1	3	0	0	0	1	.333	2	2	0	1	0	0	1.000
2001— Oakland (A.L.)	DH-PH	5	13	0	4	1	0	0	2	.308	1	0	1	...	...	...	...
Division series totals (2 years)		9	22	1	7	1	0	0	3	.318	3	2	1	1	0	0	1.000

GIBBONS, JAY   OF/1B   ORIOLES

PERSONAL: Born March 2, 1977, in Rochester, Mich. ... 6-0/200. ... Bats left, throws left. ... Full name: Jay Jonathon Gibbons.
HIGH SCHOOL: Mayfair (Lakewood, Calif.).
COLLEGE: UCLA.
TRANSACTIONS/CAREER NOTES: Selected by Toronto Blue Jays organization in 14th round of free-agent draft (June 4, 1998). ... Selected by Baltimore Orioles from Blue Jays organization in Rule 5 major league draft (December 11, 2000). ... On disabled list (August 5, 2001-remainder of season).
HONORS: Named Pioneer League Most Valuable Player (1998).
STATISTICAL NOTES: Led Pioneer League with 203 total bases, nine sacrifice flies and .700 slugging percentage in 1998.

Year Team (League)	Pos.	G	AB	R	H	2B	3B	HR	RBI	Avg.	BB	SO	SB	PO	A	E	Avg.
1998— Medicine Hat (Pio.)	1B	73	290	66	*115	*29	1	*19	*98	*.397	37	25	2	334	15	6	.983
1999— Hagerstown (S.Atl.)	1B-OF	71	292	53	89	20	2	16	69	.305	32	56	3	224	12	6	.975
— Dunedin (FSL)	1B	60	212	34	66	14	0	9	39	.311	25	38	2	527	33	5	.991
2000— Tennessee (Sou.)	1B-OF	132	474	85	152	38	1	19	75	.321	61	67	3	831	37	8	.991
2001— Baltimore (A.L.)■	OF-DH-1B	73	225	27	53	10	0	15	36	.236	17	39	0	98	4	0	1.000
Major League totals (1 year)		73	225	27	53	10	0	15	36	.236	17	39	0	98	4	0	1.000

GIL, BENJI   SS   ANGELS

PERSONAL: Born October 6, 1972, in Tijuana, Mexico. ... 6-2/190. ... Bats right, throws right. ... Full name: Romas Benjamin Gil.
HIGH SCHOOL: Castle Park (Chula Vista, Calif.).
TRANSACTIONS/CAREER NOTES: Selected by Texas Rangers organization in first round (19th pick overall) of free-agent draft (June 3, 1991). ... On Texas disabled list (March 22-May 22, 1996); included rehabilitation assigments to Charlotte (May 2-17) and Oklahoma City (May 17-21). ... Traded by Rangers to Chicago White Sox for P Al Levine and P Larry Thomas (December 19, 1997). ... On disabled list (August 12-20, 1998). ... Selected by Florida Marlins organization from White Sox organization in Rule 5 minor league draft (December 15, 1998). ... Granted free agency (October 15, 1999). ... Signed by Anaheim Angels organization (February 1, 2000).
STATISTICAL NOTES: Led American Association shortstops with 660 total chances and 85 double plays in 1994. ... Career major league grand slams: 1.

Year Team (League)	Pos.	G	AB	R	H	2B	3B	HR	RBI	Avg.	BB	SO	SB	PO	A	E	Avg.
1991— Butte (Pio.)	SS	32	129	25	37	4	3	2	15	.287	14	36	9	61	88	14	.914
1992— Gastonia (S.Atl.)	SS	132	482	75	132	21	1	9	55	.274	50	106	26	226	384	45	.931
1993— Texas (A.L.)	SS	22	57	3	7	0	0	0	2	.123	5	22	1	27	76	5	.954
— Tulsa (Texas)	SS	101	342	45	94	9	1	17	59	.275	35	89	20	159	285	19	.959
1994— Oklahoma City (A.A.)	SS	*139	487	62	121	20	6	10	55	.248	33	120	14	*222	*401	*37	.944
1995— Texas (A.L.)	SS	130	415	36	91	20	3	9	46	.219	26	147	2	226	409	17	.974
1996— Charlotte (FSL)	SS-DH	11	31	2	8	6	0	1	7	.258	3	7	0	6	21	2	.931
— Oklahoma City (A.A.)	SS	84	292	32	65	15	1	6	28	.223	21	90	4	121	267	21	.949
— Texas (A.L.)	SS	5	5	0	2	0	0	0	1	.400	1	1	0	5	7	1	.923
1997— Texas (A.L.)	SS-DH	110	317	35	71	13	2	5	31	.224	17	96	1	163	328	19	.963
1998— Calgary (PCL)■	SS-DH-OF	128	460	80	114	24	5	14	69	.248	41	90	11	161	319	30	.941
1999— Calgary (PCL)	SS-OF	116	412	74	115	29	1	17	64	.279	27	101	17	183	304	29	.944
2000— Anaheim (A.L.)■	S-2-DH-1	110	301	28	72	14	1	6	23	.239	30	59	10	164	280	18	.961
2001— Anaheim (A.L.)	S-2-1-D-O	104	260	33	77	15	4	8	39	.296	14	57	3	177	171	14	.961
Major League totals (6 years)		481	1355	135	320	62	10	28	142	.236	93	382	17	762	1271	74	.965

PERSONAL: Born August 7, 1975, in Oxaca, Mexico. ... 6-2/195. ... Bats right, throws right.

TRANSACTIONS/CAREER NOTES: Signed by Mexico City Red Devils, Mexican League (1993). ... Contract sold by Mexico City to Los Angeles Dodgers organization (February 15, 1996). ... Traded by Dodgers with P Kris Foster to Baltimore Orioles for P Mike Trombley (July 31, 2001).

STATISTICAL NOTES: Led Texas League catchers with 10 double plays in 2000.

									BATTING					FIELDING		
Year	Team (League)	Pos.	G	AB	R	H	2B	3B	HR	RBI	Avg.	BB	SO	SB	PO	A	E	Avg.
1993— M.C. Red Devils (Mex.)			1	1	0	0	0	0	0	0	.000	0	1	0	...	...	...	...
1995— M.C. Red Devils (Mex.)		OF	4	7	1	2	0	0	0	0	.286	0	1	0	2	1	0	1.000
1996— Savannah (S.Atl.)■		C	79	276	29	67	13	1	7	38	.243	8	69	0	514	56	10	.983
1997— Vero Beach (FSL)		C	66	213	30	53	13	1	6	24	.249	15	41	3	457	58	13	.975
1998— San Antonio (Texas)		C-OF-1B	75	241	27	70	17	3	6	29	.290	15	43	2	278	31	9	.972
1999— San Antonio (Texas) ...C-OF-1B-3B			106	343	47	97	26	1	15	59	.283	49	58	2	568	56	9	.986
2000— San Antonio (Texas) ...C-OF-1B-3B			100	352	42	100	19	1	11	58	.284	33	65	3	581	60	8	.988
— Albuquerque (PCL).....		C-OF-3B	15	50	9	19	5	0	2	22	.380	5	8	0	62	9	3	.959
2001— Las Vegas (PCL)		C-1B-SS	82	281	40	83	15	0	9	40	.295	16	56	0	584	50	3	.995
— Rochester (I.L.)■.......		C	23	82	7	22	6	1	2	14	.268	0	23	0	185	22	3	.986
— Baltimore (A.L.).........		C	17	58	3	17	2	0	0	6	.293	5	7	0	121	10	2	.985
Major League totals (1 year)			17	58	3	17	2	0	0	6	.293	5	7	0	121	10	2	.985

GILES, BRIAN   OF   PIRATES

PERSONAL: Born January 20, 1971, in El Cajon, Calif. ... 5-10/200. ... Bats left, throws left. ... Full name: Brian Stephen Giles. ... Brother of Marcus Giles, second baseman, Atlanta Braves. ... Name pronounced JYLES.

HIGH SCHOOL: Granite Hills (El Cajon, Calif.).

TRANSACTIONS/CAREER NOTES: Selected by Cleveland Indians organization in 17th round of free-agent draft (June 5, 1989). ... On Canton/Akron disabled list (May 15-July 7, 1992). ... On Cleveland disabled list (June 1-July 7, 1998); included rehabilitation assignment to Buffalo (June 23-July 7). ... Traded by Indians to Pittsburgh Pirates for P Ricardo Rincon (November 18, 1998).

STATISTICAL NOTES: Led International League with 10 intentional bases on balls received in 1994. ... Led International League outfielders with five double plays in 1994. ... Career major league grand slams: 4.

									BATTING					FIELDING		
Year	Team (League)	Pos.	G	AB	R	H	2B	3B	HR	RBI	Avg.	BB	SO	SB	PO	A	E	Avg.
1989— Burlington (Appl.).......		OF	36	129	18	40	7	0	0	20	.310	11	19	6	52	3	1	.982
1990— Watertown (NY-Penn)		OF	70	246	44	71	15	2	1	23	.289	48	23	11	108	8	1	.991
1991— Kinston (Caro.)...........		OF	125	394	71	122	14	0	4	47	.310	68	70	19	187	10	5	.975
1992— Canton/Akron (East.)..		OF	23	74	6	16	4	0	0	3	.216	10	10	3	45	0	0	1.000
— Kinston (Caro.)...........		OF	42	140	28	37	5	1	3	18	.264	30	21	3	74	3	1	.987
1993— Canton/Akron (East.)..		OF	123	425	64	139	17	6	6	64	.327	57	43	18	186	3	5	.974
1994— Charlotte (I.L.)...........		OF	128	434	74	136	18	3	16	58	.313	55	61	8	242	12	4	.984
1995— Buffalo (A.A.)............		OF-DH	123	413	67	128	18	•8	15	67	.310	54	40	7	248	4	5	.981
— Cleveland (A.L.).........		OF-DH	6	9	6	5	0	0	1	3	.556	0	1	0	2	1	0	1.000
1996— Buffalo (A.A.)............		OF	83	318	65	100	17	6	20	64	.314	42	29	1	132	5	2	.986
— Cleveland (A.L.).........		DH-OF	51	121	26	43	14	1	5	27	.355	19	13	3	26	0	0	1.000
1997— Cleveland (A.L.).........		OF-DH	130	377	62	101	15	3	17	61	.268	63	50	13	201	7	6	.972
1998— Cleveland (A.L.).........		OF-DH	112	350	56	94	19	0	16	66	.269	73	75	10	213	7	5	.978
— Buffalo (I.L.).............		OF-DH	13	46	5	11	2	0	2	7	.239	6	8	0	18	0	1	.947
1999— Pittsburgh (N.L.)■		OF-DH	141	521	109	164	33	3	39	115	.315	95	80	6	294	8	3	.990
2000— Pittsburgh (N.L.)		OF	156	559	111	176	37	7	35	123	.315	114	69	6	316	14	6	.982
2001— Pittsburgh (N.L.)		OF	160	576	116	178	37	7	37	95	.309	90	67	13	307	7	10	.969
American League totals (4 years)			299	857	150	243	48	4	39	157	.284	155	139	26	442	15	11	.976
National League totals (3 years)			457	1656	336	518	107	17	111	333	.313	299	216	25	917	29	19	.980
Major League totals (7 years)			756	2513	486	761	155	21	150	490	.303	454	355	51	1359	44	30	.979

DIVISION SERIES RECORD

									BATTING					FIELDING		
Year	Team (League)	Pos.	G	AB	R	H	2B	3B	HR	RBI	Avg.	BB	SO	SB	PO	A	E	Avg.
1996— Cleveland (A.L.)..........		PH	1	1	0	0	0	0	0	0	.000	0	1	0	...	...	...	...
1997— Cleveland (A.L.)..........		OF	3	7	0	1	0	0	0	0	.143	0	1	0	4	1	0	1.000
1998— Cleveland (A.L.)..........		OF-DH	3	10	1	2	1	0	0	0	.200	1	4	0	4	0	0	1.000
Division series totals (3 years)			7	18	1	3	1	0	0	0	.167	1	6	0	8	1	0	1.000

CHAMPIONSHIP SERIES RECORD

									BATTING					FIELDING		
Year	Team (League)	Pos.	G	AB	R	H	2B	3B	HR	RBI	Avg.	BB	SO	SB	PO	A	E	Avg.
1997— Cleveland (A.L.)..........		OF	6	16	1	3	3	0	0	0	.188	2	6	0	9	0	0	1.000
1998— Cleveland (A.L.)..........		OF-PH	4	12	0	1	0	0	0	0	.083	1	3	0	7	0	1	.875
Championship series totals (2 years)			10	28	1	4	3	0	0	0	.143	3	9	0	16	0	1	.941

WORLD SERIES RECORD

									BATTING					FIELDING		
Year	Team (League)	Pos.	G	AB	R	H	2B	3B	HR	RBI	Avg.	BB	SO	SB	PO	A	E	Avg.
1997— Cleveland (A.L.)..........		PH-OF	5	4	1	2	1	0	0	2	.500	4	1	0	2	0	0	1.000

ALL-STAR GAME RECORD

							BATTING					FIELDING		
Year	League	Pos.	AB	R	H	2B	3B	HR	RBI	Avg.	BB	SO	SB	PO	A	E	Avg.
2000— National		OF	2	0	0	0	0	0	0	.000	0	0	0	0	0	0	...
2001— National		PH	1	0	0	0	0	0	0	.000	0	0	0	...	...	...	...
All-Star Game totals (2 years)			3	0	0	0	0	0	0	.000	0	0	0	0	0	0	...

G

GILES, MARCUS   2B   BRAVES

PERSONAL: Born May 18, 1978, in San Diego, Calif. ... 5-8/180. ... Bats right, throws right. ... Full name: Marcus William Giles. ... Brother of Brian Giles, outfielder, Pittsburgh Pirates. ... Name pronounced JYLES.
HIGH SCHOOL: Granite Hills (Calif.).
JUNIOR COLLEGE: Grossmont (Calif.).
TRANSACTIONS/CAREER NOTES: Selected by Atlanta Braves organization in 53rd round of free-agent draft (June 4, 1996).
HONORS: Named South Atlantic League Most Valuable Player (1998). ... Named Carolina League Most Valuable Player (1999).
STATISTICAL NOTES: Led South Atlantic League with 321 total bases and .636 slugging percentage in 1998. ... Led Southern League second basemen with 655 total chances and 70 double plays in 2000. ... Career major league grand slams: 1.

							BATTING							FIELDING		
Year Team (League)	Pos.	G	AB	R	H	2B	3B	HR	RBI	Avg.	BB	SO	SB	PO	A	E	Avg.
1997— Danville (Appl.)..........	2B	55	207	53	72	13	3	8	45	.348	32	47	5	86	92	7	.962
1998— Macon (S.Atl.)............	2B	135	505	*111	166	38	3	*37	*108	.329	*85	103	12	229	294	25	.954
1999— Myrtle Beach (Caro.)..	2B	126	497	80	*162	*40	7	13	73	*.326	54	89	9	222	291	8	*.985
2000— Greenville (Sou.)........	2B	132	458	73	133	28	2	17	62	.290	72	71	25	*304	*333	18	*.973
2001— Richmond (I.L.).........2B-SS-3B-OF		67	252	48	84	19	1	6	44	.333	22	48	13	138	169	8	.975
— Atlanta (N.L.)............	2B	68	244	36	64	10	2	9	31	.262	28	37	2	104	166	6	.978
Major League totals (1 year)		68	244	36	64	10	2	9	31	.262	28	37	2	104	166	6	.978

DIVISION SERIES RECORD

							BATTING							FIELDING		
Year Team (League)	Pos.	G	AB	R	H	2B	3B	HR	RBI	Avg.	BB	SO	SB	PO	A	E	Avg.
2001— Atlanta (N.L.)............	2B	3	12	2	3	1	0	0	1	.250	0	3	0	6	10	0	1.000

CHAMPIONSHIP SERIES RECORD

							BATTING							FIELDING		
Year Team (League)	Pos.	G	AB	R	H	2B	3B	HR	RBI	Avg.	BB	SO	SB	PO	A	E	Avg.
2001— Atlanta (N.L.)............	2B	5	20	4	4	1	0	1	1	.200	3	4	0	10	12	2	.917

GILKEY, BERNARD   OF

PERSONAL: Born September 24, 1966, in St. Louis. ... 6-0/198. ... Bats right, throws right. ... Full name: Otis Bernard Gilkey.
HIGH SCHOOL: University City (Mo.).
TRANSACTIONS/CAREER NOTES: Signed as non-drafted free agent by St. Louis Cardinals organization (August 22, 1984). ... On disabled list (April 10-25, 1986 and May 29, 1987-remainder of season). ... On St. Louis disabled list (June 14-July 11, 1991 and May 29-May 14, 1993). ... On suspended list (July 8-9, 1994). ... Granted free agency (April 7, 1995). ... Re-signed by Cardinals (April 8, 1995). ... On St. Louis disabled list (June 28-July 17, 1995); included rehabilitation assignment to Louisville (July 15-17). ... Traded by Cardinals to New York Mets for P Eric Ludwick, P Erik Hiljus and OF Yudith Ozorio (January 22, 1996). ... On New York disabled list (April 27-May 12, 1998). ... Traded by Mets with P Nelson Figueroa and cash to Arizona Diamondbacks for P Willie Blair, C Jorge Fabregas and a player to be named later (July 31, 1998). ... Released by Diamondbacks (June 27, 2000). ... Signed by Boston Red Sox (July 4, 2000). ... Granted free agency (November 1, 2000). ... Signed by Cardinals organization (January 5, 2001). ... Released by Cardinals (April 3, 2001). ... Signed by Atlanta Braves organization (April 12, 2001). ... On Atlanta disabled list (June 29-July 17, 2001). ... Granted free agency (November 9, 2001).
STATISTICAL NOTES: Led New York-Pennsylvania League outfielders with 185 total chances in 1985. ... Led Texas League in caught stealing with 22 in 1989. ... Led American Association in caught stealing with 33 in 1990. ... Led N.L. outfielders with 19 assists in 1993. ... Tied for N.L. lead in double plays by outfielder with four in 1995. ... Tied for N.L. lead with 12 sacrifice flies in 1997.

							BATTING							FIELDING		
Year Team (League)	Pos.	G	AB	R	H	2B	3B	HR	RBI	Avg.	BB	SO	SB	PO	A	E	Avg.
1985— Erie (NY-Penn)	OF	•77	*294	57	60	9	1	7	27	.204	55	57	34	*164	*13	*8	.957
1986— Savannah (S.Atl.)	OF	105	374	64	88	15	4	6	36	.235	84	57	32	220	7	5	.978
1987— Springfield (Midw.)	OF	46	162	30	37	5	0	0	9	.228	39	28	18	79	5	4	.955
1988— Springfield (Midw.)	OF	125	491	84	120	18	7	6	36	.244	65	54	54	165	10	6	.967
1989— Arkansas (Texas)........	OF	131	500	*104	139	25	3	6	57	.278	70	54	*53	236	*22	9	.966
1990— Louisville (A.A.)	OF	132	499	83	147	26	8	3	46	.295	*75	49	45	236	18	•11	.958
— St. Louis (N.L.)..........	OF	18	64	11	19	5	2	1	3	.297	8	5	6	47	2	2	.961
1991— St. Louis (N.L.)..........	OF	81	268	28	58	7	2	5	20	.216	39	33	14	164	6	1	.994
— Louisville (A.A.)	OF	11	41	5	6	2	0	0	2	.146	6	10	1	33	1	0	1.000
1992— St. Louis (N.L.)..........	OF	131	384	56	116	19	4	7	43	.302	39	52	18	217	9	5	.978
1993— St. Louis (N.L.)..........	OF-1B	137	557	99	170	40	5	16	70	.305	56	66	15	251	†20	8	.971
1994— St. Louis (N.L.)..........	OF	105	380	52	96	22	1	6	45	.253	39	65	15	168	9	3	.983
1995— St. Louis (N.L.)..........	OF	121	480	73	143	33	4	17	69	.298	42	70	12	206	10	3	.986
— Louisville (A.A.)	OF	2	6	3	2	1	0	1	1	.333	1	0	0	2	0	0	1.000
1996— New York (N.L.)■.......	OF	153	571	108	181	44	3	30	117	.317	73	125	17	309	*18	6	.982
1997— New York (N.L.)..........	OF-DH	145	518	85	129	31	1	18	78	.249	70	111	7	251	*17	3	.989
1998— New York (N.L.)..........	OF	82	264	33	60	15	0	4	28	.227	32	66	5	121	9	1	.992
— Arizona (N.L.)■..........	OF	29	101	8	25	0	0	1	5	.248	11	14	4	49	3	1	.981
1999— Arizona (N.L.)..........	OF	94	204	28	60	16	1	8	39	.294	29	42	2	90	3	3	.969
2000— Arizona (N.L.)..........	OF	38	73	6	8	1	0	2	6	.110	7	16	0	29	1	0	1.000
— Boston (A.L.)■..........	OF-DH	36	91	11	21	5	1	1	9	.231	10	12	0	36	1	0	1.000
2001— Richmond (I.L.)■.......	OF	13	48	5	13	3	0	0	2	.271	4	8	0	18	1	0	1.000
— Atlanta (N.L.)............	OF-DH	69	106	8	29	6	0	2	14	.274	11	31	0	40	0	0	1.000
American League totals (1 year)		36	91	11	21	5	1	1	9	.231	10	12	0	36	1	0	1.000
National League totals (12 years)		1203	3970	595	1094	239	23	117	537	.276	456	696	115	1942	107	36	.983
Major League totals (12 years)		1239	4061	606	1115	244	24	118	546	.275	466	708	115	1978	108	36	.983

DIVISION SERIES RECORD

							BATTING							FIELDING		
Year Team (League)	Pos.	G	AB	R	H	2B	3B	HR	RBI	Avg.	BB	SO	SB	PO	A	E	Avg.
1999— Arizona (N.L.)............	OF	2	6	0	0	0	0	0	0	.000	0	0	0	5	0	0	1.000
2001— Atlanta (N.L.)								Did not play.									

CHAMPIONSHIP SERIES RECORD

							BATTING							FIELDING		
Year Team (League)	Pos.	G	AB	R	H	2B	3B	HR	RBI	Avg.	BB	SO	SB	PO	A	E	Avg.
2001— Atlanta (N.L.)	OF-PH	3	5	0	1	0	0	0	0	.200	2	1	0	1	0	0	1.000

G

PERSONAL: Born May 5, 1976, in Norwalk, Conn. ... 5-10/190. ... Bats right, throws right. ... Full name: Keith Michael Ginter.
HIGH SCHOOL: Fullerton Union (Fullerton, Calif.).
JUNIOR COLLEGE: Cypress (Calif.) College.
COLLEGE: Texas Tech.
TRANSACTIONS/CAREER NOTES: Selected by Houston Astros organization in 10th round of free-agent draft (June 2, 1998).
HONORS: Named Texas League Most Valuable Player (2000).
STATISTICAL NOTES: Led Texas League with .457 on-base percentage and in being hit by pitch with 24 in 2000. ... Tied second basemen for Pacific Coast League lead with 236 assists in 2001.

						BATTING								FIELDING		
Year Team (League)	Pos.	G	AB	R	H	2B	3B	HR	RBI	Avg.	BB	SO	SB	PO	A	E	Avg.
1998— Auburn (NY-Penn)......	2B	71	241	•55	76	22	1	8	41	.315	*60	68	10	93	178	8	*.971
1999— Kissimmee (FSL).......	2B	103	376	66	99	15	4	13	46	.263	61	90	9	209	281	21	.959
—Jackson (Texas)	2B	9	34	9	13	1	0	1	6	.382	4	6	0	19	24	2	.956
2000— Round Rock (Texas)...	2B	125	462	108	154	30	3	26	92	.333	82	127	24	255	*338	17	.972
—Houston (N.L.)...........	2B	5	8	3	2	0	0	1	3	.250	1	3	0	4	5	0	1.000
2001— New Orleans (PCL)...	2B-OF-3B	132	457	76	123	31	5	16	70	.269	61	147	8	215	‡245	12	.975
—Houston (N.L.)..........	PH	1	1	0	0	0	0	0	0	.000	0	0	0	...	...	...	...
Major League totals (2 years)		6	9	3	2	0	0	1	3	.222	1	3	0	4	5	0	1.000

PERSONAL: Born December 24, 1977, in Lexington, Ky. ... 6-1/215. ... Throws right, bats right. ... Full name: Matthew Shane Ginter.
HIGH SCHOOL: George Rogers Clark (Winchester, Ky.).
COLLEGE: Mississippi State.
TRANSACTIONS/CAREER NOTES: Selected by New York Yankees organization in 17th round of free-agent draft (June 4, 1996); did not sign. ... Selected by Chicago White Sox organization in first round (22nd pick overall) of free-agent draft (June 2, 1999); pick received from New York Mets as compensation for signing Type A free agent 3B Robin Ventura.

Year League	W	L	Pct.	ERA	G	GS	CG	ShO	Sv.	IP	H	R	ER	BB	SO
1999— Ariz. White Sox (Ariz.)...	1	0	1.000	3.24	3	0	0	0	1	8 1/3	5	4	3	3	10
—Burlington (Midw.).............	4	2	.667	4.05	9	9	0	0	0	40	38	20	18	19	29
2000— Birmingham (Sou.).............	11	8	.579	2.25	27	26	0	0	0	179 2/3	153	72	45	60	126
—Chicago (A.L.)...................	1	0	1.000	13.50	7	0	0	0	0	9 1/3	18	14	14	7	6
2001— Charlotte (I.L.).................	2	3	.400	2.59	22	10	0	0	0	76 1/3	62	26	22	24	67
—Chicago (A.L.)...................	1	0	1.000	5.22	20	0	0	0	0	39 2/3	34	23	23	14	24
Major League totals (2 years).......	2	0	1.000	6.80	27	0	0	0	0	49	52	37	37	21	30

PERSONAL: Born December 16, 1972, in Orange, Calif. ... 6-2/180. ... Bats right, throws right. ... Full name: Charles Wells Gipson Jr.
HIGH SCHOOL: Loara (Anaheim, Calif.).
JUNIOR COLLEGE: Cypress (Calif.) College.
TRANSACTIONS/CAREER NOTES: Selected by Seattle Mariners organization in 63rd round of free-agent draft (June 3, 1991). ... On disabled list (May 4-19, 1993). ... On Seattle disabled list (July 11-September 1, 1999); included rehabilitation assignments to New Haven (August 14-21) and Everett (August 22-September 1).
STATISTICAL NOTES: Led Midwest League in being hit by pitch with 27 in 1993. ... Tied for Southern League lead in caught stealing with 15 in 1996.

						BATTING								FIELDING		
Year Team (League)	Pos.	G	AB	R	H	2B	3B	HR	RBI	Avg.	BB	SO	SB	PO	A	E	Avg.
1992— Ariz. Mariners (Ariz.)..	SS	39	124	30	29	2	0	0	14	.234	13	19	11	49	114	•23	.876
1993— Appleton (Midw.).......	2B-OF-SS	109	348	53	89	13	1	0	20	.256	61	76	21	192	201	28	.933
1994— Riverside (Calif.).......	OF	128	481	*102	141	12	3	1	41	.293	76	67	34	293	14	9	.972
1995— Port City (Sou.).........	OF-2B	112	391	36	87	11	2	0	29	.223	30	66	10	235	19	6	.977
1996— Port City (Sou.).........	OF-SS	119	407	54	109	12	3	1	30	.268	41	62	15	210	162	15	.961
1997— Memphis (Sou.)........	SS-3B-2B-OF	88	320	56	79	9	4	1	28	.247	34	71	31	143	211	23	.939
—Tacoma (PCL)	3B-OF-2B-SS	11	35	5	11	2	0	0	5	.314	4	3	0	15	16	3	.912
1998— Seattle (A.L.)	OF-3B-DH	44	51	11	12	1	0	0	2	.235	5	9	2	40	5	2	.957
—Tacoma (PCL)	OF-SS-2B-3B	75	278	39	67	16	2	0	11	.241	27	50	14	142	88	11	.954
1999— Seattle (A.L.)	O-3-DH-2-S	55	80	16	18	5	2	0	9	.225	6	13	3	35	52	3	.967
—Tacoma (PCL)	S-O-3-2-DH	47	174	26	52	6	3	0	21	.299	14	24	18	76	65	9	.940
—New Haven (East.).......	2-DH-3-S-O	5	18	2	0	0	0	0	0	.000	3	2	1	10	7	1	.944
—Everett (N'West)	SS	1	2	0	1	0	1	0	1	.500	2	0	1	0	4	0	1.000
2000— Seattle (A.L.)	OF-3B-SS-DH	59	29	7	9	1	1	0	3	.310	4	9	2	23	12	0	1.000
—Tacoma (PCL)	OF-3B-SS-2B	75	214	27	53	6	6	1	22	.248	31	38	16	119	80	6	.971
2001— Seattle (A.L.)	O-D-3-S-2	94	64	16	14	2	2	0	5	.219	4	20	1	51	18	2	.972
Major League totals (4 years)		252	224	50	53	9	5	0	19	.237	19	51	8	149	87	7	.971

DIVISION SERIES RECORD

						BATTING								FIELDING		
Year Team (League)	Pos.	G	AB	R	H	2B	3B	HR	RBI	Avg.	BB	SO	SB	PO	A	E	Avg.
2000—Seattle (A.L.)..............							Did not play.									
2001—Seattle (A.L.)..............	PH	1	1	0	0	0	0	0	0	.000	0	0	0	...	...	...	...

CHAMPIONSHIP SERIES RECORD

						BATTING								FIELDING		
Year Team (League)	Pos.	G	AB	R	H	2B	3B	HR	RBI	Avg.	BB	SO	SB	PO	A	E	Avg.
2000— Seattle (A.L.)	OF	2	0	0	0	0	0	0	0	...	0	0	0	0	0	0	...
2001— Seattle (A.L.)	PR-DH-OF	2	1	1	0	0	0	0	0	.000	0	0	0	0	0	0	...
Championship series totals (2 years)		4	1	1	0	0	0	0	0	.000	0	0	0	0	0	0	...

G

PERSONAL: Born October 14, 1964, in Peoria, Ill. ... 5-11/200. ... Bats right, throws right. ... Full name: Joseph Elliott Girardi. ... Name pronounced jeh-RAR-dee.

HIGH SCHOOL: Spalding Institute (Peoria, Ill.).

COLLEGE: Northwestern.

TRANSACTIONS/CAREER NOTES: Selected by Chicago Cubs organization in fifth round of free-agent draft (June 2, 1986). ... On disabled list (August 27, 1986-remainder of season; and August 7, 1988-remainder of season). ... On Chicago disabled list (April 17-August 6, 1991); included rehabilitation assignment to Iowa (July 23-August 6). ... Selected by Colorado Rockies in first round (19th pick overall) of expansion draft (November 17, 1992). ... On Colorado disabled list (June 5-August 11, 1993); included rehabilitation assignment to Colorado Springs (August 1-11). ... On disabled list (July 11-26, 1994). ... Traded by Rockies to New York Yankees for P Mike DeJean and a player to be named later (November 20, 1995); Rockies acquired P Steve Shoemaker to complete deal (December 6, 1995). ... Granted free agency (November 5, 1996). ... Re-signed by Yankees (December 3, 1996). ... Granted free agency (November 5, 1999). ... Signed by Cubs (December 15, 1999).

STATISTICAL NOTES: Led Carolina League catchers with 661 total chances and tied for lead with 17 passed balls in 1987. ... Led Eastern League catchers with .992 fielding percentage, 448 putouts, 76 assists and 528 total chances and tied for lead with five double plays in 1988. ... Tied for N.L. lead with 16 passed balls in 1990.

Year Team (League)	Pos.	G	AB	R	H	2B	3B	HR	RBI	Avg.	BB	SO	SB	PO	A	E	Avg.
1986—Peoria (Midw.)............	C	68	230	36	71	13	1	3	28	.309	17	36	6	405	34	5	.989
1987—Win.-Salem (Caro.)	C	99	364	51	102	9	8	8	46	.280	33	64	9	*569	*74	18	.973
1988—Pittsfield (East.)........	C-OF	104	357	44	97	14	1	7	41	.272	29	51	7	†460	†76	6	†.989
1989—Chicago (N.L.)............	C	59	157	15	39	10	0	1	14	.248	11	26	2	332	28	7	.981
—Iowa (A.A.)................	C	32	110	12	27	4	2	2	11	.245	5	19	3	172	21	1	.995
1990—Chicago (N.L.)............	C	133	419	36	113	24	2	1	38	.270	17	50	8	653	61	11	.985
1991—Chicago (N.L.)............	C	21	47	3	9	2	0	0	6	.191	6	6	0	95	11	3	.972
—Iowa (A.A.)................	C	12	36	3	8	1	0	0	4	.222	4	8	2	62	5	3	.957
1992—Chicago (N.L.)............	C	91	270	19	73	3	1	1	12	.270	19	38	0	369	51	4	.991
1993—Colorado (N.L.)■.........	C	86	310	35	90	14	5	3	31	.290	24	41	6	478	46	6	.989
—Colo. Springs (PCL) ...	C	8	31	6	15	1	1	1	6	.484	0	3	1	40	3	1	.977
1994—Colorado (N.L.)...........	C	93	330	47	91	9	4	4	34	.276	21	48	3	549	56	5	.992
1995—Colorado (N.L.)...........	C	125	462	63	121	17	2	8	55	.262	29	76	3	730	60	10	.988
1996—New York (A.L.)■.......	C-DH	124	422	55	124	22	3	2	45	.294	30	55	13	803	46	3	.996
1997—New York (A.L.).........	C	112	398	38	105	23	1	1	50	.264	26	53	2	829	55	5	.994
1998—New York (A.L.).........	C	78	254	31	70	11	4	3	31	.276	14	38	2	541	38	3	.995
1999—New York (A.L.).........	C	65	209	23	50	16	1	2	27	.239	10	26	3	452	34	8	.984
2000—Chicago (N.L.)■.........	C	106	363	47	101	15	1	6	40	.278	32	61	1	706	43	5	.993
2001—Chicago (N.L.)...........	C	78	229	22	58	10	1	3	25	.253	21	50	0	504	33	0	1.000
American League totals (4 years)		379	1283	147	349	72	9	8	153	.272	80	172	20	2625	173	19	.993
National League totals (9 years)		792	2587	287	695	104	16	27	255	.269	180	396	23	4416	389	51	.989
Major League totals (13 years)		1171	3870	434	1044	176	25	35	408	.270	260	568	43	7041	562	70	.991

DIVISION SERIES RECORD

Year Team (League)	Pos.	G	AB	R	H	2B	3B	HR	RBI	Avg.	BB	SO	SB	PO	A	E	Avg.
1995—Colorado (N.L.)	C	4	16	0	2	0	0	0	0	.125	0	2	0	25	3	1	.966
1996—New York (A.L.)..........	C-PR	4	9	1	2	0	0	0	0	.222	4	1	0	28	1	1	.967
1997—New York (A.L.)..........	C	5	15	2	2	0	0	0	0	.133	1	3	0	21	2	0	1.000
1998—New York (A.L.)..........	C	2	7	0	3	0	0	0	0	.429	0	1	0	19	1	0	1.000
1999—New York (A.L.)..........	C	2	6	0	0	0	0	0	0	.000	0	1	0	12	0	0	1.000
Division series totals (5 years)		17	53	3	9	0	0	0	0	.170	5	8	0	105	7	2	.982

CHAMPIONSHIP SERIES RECORD

Year Team (League)	Pos.	G	AB	R	H	2B	3B	HR	RBI	Avg.	BB	SO	SB	PO	A	E	Avg.
1989—Chicago (N.L.)............	C	4	10	1	1	0	0	0	0	.100	1	2	0	20	0	0	1.000
1996—New York (A.L.).........	C-PH	4	12	1	3	0	1	0	0	.250	1	3	0	22	0	0	1.000
1998—New York (A.L.).........	C	3	8	2	2	0	0	0	0	.250	1	0	0	22	1	0	1.000
1999—New York (A.L.).........	C	3	8	0	2	0	0	0	0	.250	0	2	0	20	1	0	1.000
Championship series totals (4 years)		14	38	4	8	0	1	0	0	.211	3	7	0	84	2	0	1.000

WORLD SERIES RECORD

NOTES: Member of World Series championship team (1996, 1998 and 1999).

Year Team (League)	Pos.	G	AB	R	H	2B	3B	HR	RBI	Avg.	BB	SO	SB	PO	A	E	Avg.
1996—New York (A.L.).........	C	4	10	1	2	0	1	0	1	.200	1	2	0	23	4	0	1.000
1998—New York (A.L.).........	C	2	6	0	0	0	0	0	0	.000	0	2	0	9	2	0	1.000
1999—New York (A.L.).........	C	2	7	1	2	0	0	0	0	.286	0	1	0	9	2	0	1.000
World Series totals (3 years)		8	23	2	4	0	1	0	1	.174	1	5	0	41	8	0	1.000

ALL-STAR GAME RECORD

Year League	Pos.	AB	R	H	2B	3B	HR	RBI	Avg.	BB	SO	SB	PO	A	E	Avg.
2000—National.....................							Did not play.										

G

PERSONAL: Born August 25, 1970, in Hackensack, N.J. ... 6-2/172. ... Bats right, throws right. ... Full name: Douglas Metunwa Glanville.

HIGH SCHOOL: Teaneck (N.J.).

COLLEGE: Pennsylvania.

TRANSACTIONS/CAREER NOTES: Selected by Chicago Cubs organization in first round (12th pick overall) of free-agent draft (June 3, 1991). ... Traded by Cubs to Philadelphia Phillies for 2B Mickey Morandini (December 23, 1997).
STATISTICAL NOTES: Led Carolina League outfielders with 312 total chances in 1992. ... Led Southern League in caught stealing with 20 in 1994. ... Led Southern League outfielders with 339 total chances in 1994. ... Had 18-game hitting streak (May 1-20, 1998). ... Had 17-game hitting streak (May 30-June 17, 1998). ... Tied N.L. outfielders for lead in double plays with four in 2000. ... Had 15-game hitting streaks (May 3-19, 2001 and May 27-June 12, 2001).

						BATTING							FIELDING			
Year — Team (League)	Pos.	G	AB	R	H	2B	3B	HR	RBI	Avg.	BB	SO	SB	PO	A	E	Avg.
1991— Geneva (NY-Penn)......	OF	36	152	29	46	8	0	2	12	.303	11	25	17	77	4	0	1.000
1992— Win.-Salem (Caro.)	OF	120	485	72	125	18	4	4	36	.258	40	78	32	*293	12	7	.978
1993— Daytona (FSL)	OF	61	239	47	70	10	1	2	21	.293	28	24	18	123	11	7	.950
— Orlando (Sou.)	OF	73	296	42	78	14	4	9	40	.264	12	41	15	168	8	5	.972
1994— Orlando (Sou.)	OF	130	483	53	127	22	2	5	52	.263	24	49	26	*322	14	3	.991
1995— Iowa (A.A.)	OF-DH	112	419	48	113	16	2	4	37	.270	16	64	13	209	9	4	.982
1996— Iowa (A.A.)	OF-DH	90	373	53	115	23	3	3	34	.308	12	35	15	217	6	3	.987
— Chicago (N.L.)	OF	49	83	10	20	5	1	1	10	.241	3	11	2	35	1	1	.973
1997— Chicago (N.L.)	OF	146	474	79	142	22	5	4	35	.300	24	46	19	247	12	3	.989
1998— Philadelphia (N.L.)■ ..	OF	158	*678	106	189	28	7	8	49	.279	42	89	23	360	14	2	.995
1999— Philadelphia (N.L.).....	OF	150	628	101	204	38	6	11	73	.325	48	82	34	385	13	8	.980
2000— Philadelphia (N.L.).....	OF	154	637	89	175	27	6	8	52	.275	31	76	31	380	9	4	.990
2001— Philadelphia (N.L.).....	OF	153	634	74	166	24	3	14	55	.262	19	91	28	413	8	4	.991
Major League totals (6 years)		810	3134	459	896	144	28	46	274	.286	167	395	137	1820	57	22	.988

GLAUS, TROY — 3B — ANGELS

PERSONAL: Born August 3, 1976, in Tarzana, Calif. ... 6-5/229. ... Bats right, throws right. ... Full name: Troy Edward Glaus. ... Name pronounced GLOSS.
HIGH SCHOOL: Carlsbad (Calif.).
COLLEGE: UCLA.
TRANSACTIONS/CAREER NOTES: Selected by San Diego Padres organization in second round of free-agent draft (June 2, 1994); did not sign. ... Selected by Anaheim Angels organization in first round (third pick overall) of free-agent draft (June 3, 1997).
RECORDS: Hold A.L. single-season record for most home runs by third baseman—46 (2000).
HONORS: Named third baseman on The Sporting News A.L. Silver Slugger team (2000). ... Named third baseman on A.L. Silver Slugger team (2001). ... Named third baseman on The Sporting News A.L. All-Star team (2001).
STATISTICAL NOTES: Led A.L. third basemen with 349 assists and 493 total chances in 2000. ... Tied for A.L. lead with 33 errors in 2000. ... Career major league grand slams: 1.
MISCELLANEOUS: Member of 1996 U.S. Olympic baseball team.

						BATTING							FIELDING			
Year — Team (League)	Pos.	G	AB	R	H	2B	3B	HR	RBI	Avg.	BB	SO	SB	PO	A	E	Avg.
1998— Midland (Texas)..........	3B	50	188	51	58	11	2	19	51	.309	39	41	4	34	101	11	.925
— Vancouver (PCL)........	3B	59	219	33	67	16	0	16	42	.306	21	55	3	46	131	13	.932
— Anaheim (A.L.)	3B	48	165	19	36	9	0	1	23	.218	15	51	1	27	85	7	.941
1999— Anaheim (A.L.)	3B-DH	154	551	85	132	29	0	29	79	.240	71	143	5	114	277	19	.954
2000— Anaheim (A.L.)	3B-SS-DH	159	563	120	160	37	1	*47	102	.284	112	163	14	112	†353	‡33	.934
2001— Anaheim (A.L.)	3B-SS-DH	161	588	100	147	38	2	41	108	.250	107	158	10	103	287	19	.954
Major League totals (4 years)		522	1867	324	475	113	3	118	312	.254	305	515	30	356	1002	78	.946

ALL-STAR GAME RECORD

					BATTING							FIELDING			
Year — League	Pos.	AB	R	H	2B	3B	HR	RBI	Avg.	BB	SO	SB	PO	A	E	Avg.
2000— American	3B	1	0	0	0	0	0	0	.000	0	0	0	2	0	0	1.000
2001— American	3B	1	0	0	0	0	0	0	.000	0	0	0	0	2	0	1.000
All-Star Game totals (2 years)		2	0	0	0	0	0	0	.000	0	0	0	2	2	0	1.000

GLAVINE, TOM — P — BRAVES

PERSONAL: Born March 25, 1966, in Concord, Mass. ... 6-0/185. ... Throws left, bats left. ... Full name: Thomas Michael Glavine. ... Brother of Mike Glavine, first baseman, Cleveland Indians organization (1995-98) and Atlanta Braves organization (1999-2001). ... Name pronounced GLAV-in.
HIGH SCHOOL: Billerica (Mass.).
TRANSACTIONS/CAREER NOTES: Selected by Atlanta Braves organization in second round of free-agent draft (June 4, 1984).
HONORS: Named N.L. Pitcher of the Year by The Sporting News (1991 and 2000). ... Named lefthanded pitcher on The Sporting News N.L. All-Star team (1991-92, 1998 and 2000). ... Named pitcher on The Sporting News N.L. Silver Slugger team (1991, 1995, 1996 and 1998). ... Named N.L. Cy Young Award winner by Baseball Writers' Association of America (1991 and 1998).
STATISTICAL NOTES: Led Gulf Coast League with 12 wild pitches in 1984. ... Led N.L. pitchers with 59 assists in 1999. ... Tied for N.L. lead in double plays by a pitcher with six in 1999. ... Tied for N.L. lead with 17 sacrifice hits in 2001.
MISCELLANEOUS: Selected by Los Angeles Kings in fourth round (69th pick overall) of NHL entry draft (June 9, 1984). ... Appeared in eight games as pinch runner (1988). ... Appeared in one game as pinch runner (1989). ... Appeared in one game as pinch runner (1990). ... Received a base on balls and scored once in one game as pinch hitter and appeared in one game as pinch runner (1991). ... Singled and struck out in two appearances as pinch hitter (1992). ... Struck out in only appearance as pinch hitter (1994). ... Singled and struck out in three appearances as pinch hitter (1996). ... Had a sacrifice hit in only appearance as pinch hitter (1999). ... Grounded out twice in two appearances as pinch hitter (2000).

Year — League	W	L	Pct.	ERA	G	GS	CG	ShO	Sv.	IP	H	R	ER	BB	SO
1984— Gulf Coast Braves (GCL)	2	3	.400	3.34	8	7	0	0	0	32 1/3	29	17	12	13	34
1985— Sumter (S.Atl.)	9	6	.600	*2.35	26	26	2	1	0	168 2/3	114	58	44	73	174
1986— Greenville (Sou.)	11	6	.647	3.41	22	22	2	1	0	145 1/3	129	62	55	70	114
— Richmond (I.L.).................	1	5	.167	5.63	7	7	1	1	0	40	40	29	25	27	12

G

Year League	W	L	Pct.	ERA	G	GS	CG	ShO	Sv.	IP	H	R	ER	BB	SO
1987— Richmond (I.L.)	6	12	.333	3.35	22	22	4	1	0	150⅓	142	70	56	56	91
— Atlanta (N.L.)	2	4	.333	5.54	9	9	0	0	0	50⅓	55	34	31	33	20
1988— Atlanta (N.L.)	7	*17	.292	4.56	34	34	1	0	0	195⅓	201	111	99	63	84
1989— Atlanta (N.L.)	14	8	.636	3.68	29	29	6	4	0	186	172	88	76	40	90
1990— Atlanta (N.L.)	10	12	.455	4.28	33	33	1	0	0	214⅓	232	111	102	78	129
1991— Atlanta (N.L.)	•20	11	.645	2.55	34	34	•9	1	0	246⅔	201	83	70	69	192
1992— Atlanta (N.L.)	•20	8	.714	2.76	33	33	7	•5	0	225	197	81	69	70	129
1993— Atlanta (N.L.)	•22	6	.786	3.20	36	•36	4	2	0	239⅓	236	91	85	90	120
1994— Atlanta (N.L.)	13	9	.591	3.97	25	25	2	0	0	165⅓	173	76	73	70	140
1995— Atlanta (N.L.)	16	7	.696	3.08	29	29	3	1	0	198⅔	182	76	68	66	127
1996— Atlanta (N.L.)	15	10	.600	2.98	36	*36	1	0	0	235⅓	222	91	78	85	181
1997— Atlanta (N.L.)	14	7	.667	2.96	33	33	5	2	0	240	197	86	79	79	152
1998— Atlanta (N.L.)	*20	6	.769	2.47	33	33	4	3	0	229⅓	202	67	63	74	157
1999— Atlanta (N.L.)	14	11	.560	4.12	35	•35	2	0	0	234	*259	115	107	83	138
2000— Atlanta (N.L.)	*21	9	.700	3.40	35	•35	4	2	0	241	222	101	91	65	152
2001— Atlanta (N.L.)	16	7	.696	3.57	35	•35	1	1	0	219⅓	213	92	87	97	116
Major League totals (15 years)	224	132	.629	3.40	469	469	50	21	0	3120	2964	1303	1178	1062	1927

DIVISION SERIES RECORD

RECORDS: Holds N.L. career record for most bases on balls allowed—16.

Year League	W	L	Pct.	ERA	G	GS	CG	ShO	Sv.	IP	H	R	ER	BB	SO
1995— Atlanta (N.L.)	0	0	...	2.57	1	1	0	0	0	7	5	3	2	1	3
1996— Atlanta (N.L.)	1	0	1.000	1.35	1	1	0	0	0	6⅔	5	1	1	3	7
1997— Atlanta (N.L.)	1	0	1.000	4.50	1	1	0	0	0	6	5	3	3	5	4
1998— Atlanta (N.L.)	0	0	...	1.29	1	1	0	0	0	7	3	1	1	1	8
1999— Atlanta (N.L.)	0	0	...	3.00	1	1	0	0	0	6	5	2	2	3	6
2000— Atlanta (N.L.)	0	1	.000	27.00	1	1	0	0	0	2⅓	6	7	7	1	2
2001— Atlanta (N.L.)	1	0	1.000	0.00	1	1	0	0	0	8	6	0	0	2	3
Division series totals (7 years)	3	1	.750	3.35	7	7	0	0	0	43	35	17	16	16	33

CHAMPIONSHIP SERIES RECORD

RECORDS: Holds career records for most losses—9; games started—15; hits allowed—91; and bases on balls allowed—37. ... Shares N.L. career record for home runs allowed—8; and hit batsmen—5. ... Holds single-inning records for most runs allowed—8 (October 13, 1992, second inning); and most earned runs allowed—7 (October 13, 1992, second inning). ... Shares single-game record for most earned runs allowed—7 (October 13, 1992 and October 14, 1997). ... Shares single-inning record for most hits allowed—6 (October 13, 1992, second inning).

NOTES: Received a base on balls in only appearance as pinch hitter (1998).

Year League	W	L	Pct.	ERA	G	GS	CG	ShO	Sv.	IP	H	R	ER	BB	SO
1991— Atlanta (N.L.)	0	2	.000	3.21	2	2	0	0	0	14	12	5	5	6	11
1992— Atlanta (N.L.)	0	2	.000	12.27	2	2	0	0	0	7⅓	13	11	10	3	2
1993— Atlanta (N.L.)	1	0	1.000	2.57	1	1	0	0	0	7	6	2	2	0	5
1995— Atlanta (N.L.)	0	0	...	1.29	1	1	0	0	0	7	7	1	1	2	5
1996— Atlanta (N.L.)	1	1	.500	2.08	2	2	0	0	0	13	10	3	3	0	9
1997— Atlanta (N.L.)	1	1	.500	5.40	2	2	0	0	0	13⅓	13	8	8	11	9
1998— Atlanta (N.L.)	0	2	.000	2.31	2	2	0	0	0	11⅔	13	6	3	9	8
1999— Atlanta (N.L.)	1	0	1.000	0.00	1	1	0	0	0	7	7	0	0	1	8
2001— Atlanta (N.L.)	1	1	.500	1.50	2	2	0	0	0	12	10	4	2	5	5
Champ. series totals (9 years)	5	9	.357	3.31	15	15	0	0	0	92⅓	91	40	34	37	62

WORLD SERIES RECORD

RECORDS: Shares single-inning records for most bases on balls allowed—4 (October 24, 1991, sixth inning); and most consecutive bases on balls allowed—3 (October 24, 1991, sixth inning).

NOTES: Named Most Valuable Player (1995). ... Member of World Series championship team (1995).

Year League	W	L	Pct.	ERA	G	GS	CG	ShO	Sv.	IP	H	R	ER	BB	SO
1991— Atlanta (N.L.)	1	1	.500	2.70	2	2	1	0	0	13⅓	8	6	4	7	8
1992— Atlanta (N.L.)	1	1	.500	1.59	2	2	2	0	0	17	10	3	3	4	8
1995— Atlanta (N.L.)	2	0	1.000	1.29	2	2	0	0	0	14	4	2	2	6	11
1996— Atlanta (N.L.)	0	1	.000	1.29	1	1	0	0	0	7	4	2	1	3	8
1999— Atlanta (N.L.)	0	0	...	5.14	1	1	0	0	0	7	7	5	4	0	3
World Series totals (5 years)	4	3	.571	2.16	8	8	3	0	0	58⅓	33	18	14	20	38

ALL-STAR GAME RECORD

RECORDS: Holds single-game record for most hits allowed—9 (July 14, 1992). ... Holds single-inning record for most hits allowed—7 (July 14, 1992, first inning).

Year League	W	L	Pct.	ERA	GS	CG	ShO	Sv.	IP	H	R	ER	BB	SO
1991— National	0	0	...	0.00	1	0	0	0	2	1	0	0	1	3
1992— National	0	1	.000	27.00	1	0	0	0	1⅔	9	5	5	0	2
1993— National						Did not play.								
1996— National	0	0	...	0.00	0	0	0	0	1	0	0	0	0	1
1997— National						Did not play.								
1998— National	0	0	...	27.00	0	0	0	0	1⅓	5	4	4	3	0
2000— National	0	0	...	0.00	0	0	0	0	1	0	0	0	0	1
All-Star Game totals (5 years)	0	1	.000	11.57	2	0	0	0	7	15	9	9	4	7

G

GLOAD, ROSS — 1B/OF — METS

PERSONAL: Born April 5, 1976, in Brooklyn, N.Y. ... 6-0/185. ... Bats left, throws left. ... Full name: Ross Peter Gload.
HIGH SCHOOL: East Hampton (N.Y.).
COLLEGE: South Florida.

TRANSACTIONS/CAREER NOTES: Selected by Florida Marlins organization in 13th round of free-agent draft (June 3, 1997). ... Traded by Marlins with P David Noyce to Chicago Cubs for OF Henry Rodriguez (July 31, 2000). ... Claimed on waivers by Colorado Rockies (September 12, 2001). ... Traded by Rockies to New York Mets as part of three-way deal in which Mets traded P Glendon Rusch to Milwaukee Brewers, Rockies traded P Craig House to Mets, Brewers traded P Jeff D'Amico, OF Jeromy Burnitz, IF Lou Collier, OF/1B Mark Sweeney and cash to Mets, Mets traded 1B/3B Todd Zeile, OF Benny Agbayani, IF/OF Lenny Harris and cash to Rockies and Rockies traded OF Alex Ochoa to Brewers (January 21, 2002).

STATISTICAL NOTES: Led New York Pennsylvania League first basemen with 599 total chances in 1997. ... Led Midwest League with seven intentional bases on balls received in 1998.

| | | | | | | | | BATTING | | | | | | FIELDING | | |
Year Team (League)	Pos.	G	AB	R	H	2B	3B	HR	RBI	Avg.	BB	SO	SB	PO	A	E	Avg.
1997—Utica (NY-Penn)	1B	68	245	28	64	15	2	3	43	.261	28	57	1	*546	37	*16	.973
1998—Kane County (Midw.)..	1B	132	501	77	157	*41	3	12	92	.313	58	84	7	1160	69	14	.989
1999—Brevard County (FSL).	1B	133	490	80	146	26	3	10	74	.298	53	76	3	1200	83	9	.993
2000—Portland (East.)	OF-1B	100	401	60	114	28	4	16	65	.284	29	53	4	462	30	7	.986
—Iowa (PCL)■	OF	28	104	24	42	10	2	14	39	.404	9	13	1	42	2	4	.917
—Chicago (N.L.)	OF-1B	18	31	4	6	0	1	1	3	.194	3	10	0	15	0	0	1.000
2001—Iowa (PCL)	1B-OF	133	475	70	141	32	*10	15	93	.297	35	88	9	457	41	3	.994
Major League totals (1 year)		18	31	4	6	0	1	1	3	.194	3	10	0	15	0	0	1.000

GLOVER, GARY — P — WHITE SOX

PERSONAL: Born December 3, 1976, in Cleveland. ... 6-5/205. ... Throws right, bats right. ... Full name: John Gary Glover II.
HIGH SCHOOL: Deland (Fla.).
TRANSACTIONS/CAREER NOTES: Selected by Toronto Blue Jays organization in 15th round of free-agent draft (June 2, 1994). ... On disabled list (August 10-September 8, 1994). ... Traded by Blue Jays to Chicago White Sox for P Scott Eyre (November 7, 2000).

Year League	W	L	Pct.	ERA	G	GS	CG	ShO	Sv.	IP	H	R	ER	BB	SO
1994—Gulf Coast Blue Jays (GCL)	0	0	...	47.25	2	0	0	0	0	1 1/3	4	8	7	4	2
1995—Gulf Coast Blue Jays (GCL)	3	7	.300	4.91	12	10	2	0	0	62 1/3	62	48	34	26	46
1996—Medicine Hat (Pio.)	3	*12	.200	7.75	15	•15	*2	0	0	83 2/3	*119	*94	*72	29	54
1997—Hagerstown (S.Atl.)...........	6	*17	.261	3.73	28	28	3	0	0	173 2/3	165	94	72	58	155
1998—Knoxville (Sou.).............	0	5	.000	6.75	8	8	0	0	0	37 1/3	41	36	28	28	14
—Dunedin (FSL)	7	6	.538	4.28	19	18	0	0	0	109 1/3	117	66	52	36	88
1999—Knoxville (Sou.).............	8	2	.800	3.56	13	13	1	0	0	86	70	39	34	27	77
—Syracuse (I.L.)...................	4	6	.400	5.19	14	14	0	0	0	76 1/3	93	50	44	35	57
—Toronto (A.L.)...................	0	0	...	0.00	1	0	0	0	0	1	0	0	0	1	0
2000—Syracuse (I.L.)...............	9	9	.500	5.02	27	27	1	0	0	166 2/3	181	104	93	62	119
2001—Charlotte (I.L.)■...	2	1	.667	1.88	6	6	1	1	0	38 1/3	21	8	8	5	29
—Chicago (A.L.)................	5	5	.500	4.93	46	11	0	0	0	100 1/3	98	61	55	32	63
Major League totals (2 years)	5	5	.500	4.88	47	11	0	0	0	101 1/3	98	61	55	33	63

GLYNN, RYAN — P — BREWERS

PERSONAL: Born November 1, 1974, in Portsmouth, Va. ... 6-3/195. ... Throws right, bats right. ... Full name: Ryan David Glynn.
HIGH SCHOOL: Churchland (Portsmouth, Va.).
COLLEGE: Virginia Military Institute.
TRANSACTIONS/CAREER NOTES: Selected by Texas Rangers organization in fourth round of free-agent draft (June 1, 1995). ... On Texas disabled list (July 2-17 and August 15-29, 2000); included rehabilitation assignment to Oklahoma (August 24-29). ... On Texas disabled list (June 1-July 1, 2001); included rehabilitation assignment to Oklahoma (June 22-July 1). ... Granted free agency (October 15, 2001). ... Signed by Milwaukee Brewers organization (January 11, 2002).

Year League	W	L	Pct.	ERA	G	GS	CG	ShO	Sv.	IP	H	R	ER	BB	SO
1995—Hudson Valley (NY-Penn)...	3	3	.500	4.70	9	8	0	0	0	44	56	27	23	16	21
1996—Charleston, S.C. (S.Atl.)	8	7	.533	4.54	19	19	2	1	0	121	118	70	61	59	72
1997—Charlotte (FSL).................	8	7	.533	4.97	23	22	5	1	1	134	148	81	74	44	96
—Tulsa (Texas)	1	1	.500	3.38	3	3	0	0	0	21 1/3	21	9	8	10	18
1998—Tulsa (Texas)	9	6	.600	3.44	26	24	4	1	0	157	140	66	60	64	111
1999—Oklahoma (PCL)................	6	2	.750	3.39	16	16	2	1	0	90 1/3	81	46	34	36	55
—Texas (A.L.)	2	4	.333	7.24	13	10	0	0	0	54 2/3	71	46	44	35	39
2000—Oklahoma (PCL)................	4	2	.667	3.55	15	14	2	2	0	83 2/3	72	36	33	33	66
—Texas (A.L.)	5	7	.417	5.58	16	16	0	0	0	88 2/3	107	65	55	41	33
2001—Texas (A.L.)	1	5	.167	7.04	12	9	0	0	0	46	59	38	36	26	15
—Oklahoma (PCL)................	2	6	.250	6.49	13	13	1	0	0	79	87	62	57	41	52
Major League totals (3 years)	8	16	.333	6.42	41	35	0	0	0	189 1/3	237	149	135	102	87

GOETZ, GEOFF — P — MARLINS

G

PERSONAL: Born March 3, 1979, in Pompton Plains, N.J. ... 5-11/165. ... Throws left, bats left. ... Full name: Geoffrey Bryan Goetz.
HIGH SCHOOL: Jesuit (Tampa, Fla.).
TRANSACTIONS/CAREER NOTES: Selected by New York Mets organization in first round (sixth pick overall) of free agent draft (June 3, 1997). ... Traded by Mets to Florida Marlins (July 3, 1998), completing deal in which Marlins traded C Mike Piazza to Mets for OF Preston Wilson, P Ed Yarnall and a player to be named later (May 22, 1998). ... On disabled list (June 2-August 10, 2001).

Year League	W	L	Pct.	ERA	G	GS	CG	ShO	Sv.	IP	H	R	ER	BB	SO
1997—Gulf Coast Marlins (GCL) ...	0	2	.000	2.73	8	6	0	0	1	26 1/3	23	11	8	18	28
1998—Columbia (S.Atl.).............	5	4	.556	3.96	15	15	0	0	0	77 1/3	68	45	34	37	68
—Kane County (Midw.)...........	1	4	.200	4.64	9	9	0	0	0	42 2/3	44	22	22	24	36
1999—Kane County (Midw.)........	5	3	.625	4.26	16	12	0	0	0	50 2/3	52	28	24	24	43
2000—Brevard County (FSL)........	6	2	.750	1.75	27	0	0	0	5	67	43	19	13	36	61
—Portland (East.)	1	2	.333	5.96	17	0	0	0	1	22 2/3	27	15	15	11	21
2001—Portland (East.)	2	2	.500	1.53	25	0	0	0	0	29 1/3	22	10	5	12	24

GOMES, WAYNE — P

PERSONAL: Born January 15, 1973, in Hampton, Va. ... 6-2/227. ... Throws right, bats right. ... Full name: Wayne Maurice Gomes.
HIGH SCHOOL: Phoebus (Hampton, Va.).
COLLEGE: Old Dominion.
TRANSACTIONS/CAREER NOTES: Selected by Philadelphia Phillies organization in first round (fourth pick overall) of free-agent draft (June 3, 1993). ... On disabled list (May 12-June 23, 1995). ... On Philadelphia disabled list (July 7-August 8, 2000); included rehabilitation assignment to Scranton/Wilkes-Barre (August 1-8). ... On Philadelphia disabled list (May 30-June 19, 2001); included rehabilitation assignment to Lakewood (June 16-19). ... Traded by Phillies to San Francisco Giants for IF/OF Felipe Crespo (July 27, 2001). ... On San Francisco disabled list (August 19-September 3, 2001). ... Released by Giants (November 28, 2001).
STATISTICAL NOTES: Led Florida State League with 27 wild pitches in 1994. ... Tied for Eastern League lead with six balks in 1995.

Year League	W	L	Pct.	ERA	G	GS	CG	ShO	Sv.	IP	H	R	ER	BB	SO
1993—Batavia (NY-Penn)	1	0	1.000	1.23	5	0	0	0	0	7 1/3	1	1	1	8	11
—Clearwater (FSL)	0	0	...	1.17	9	0	0	0	4	7 2/3	4	1	1	9	13
1994—Clearwater (FSL)	6	8	.429	4.74	23	21	1	1	0	104 1/3	85	63	55	82	102
1995—Reading (East.)	7	4	.636	3.96	22	22	1	1	0	104 2/3	89	54	46	70	102
1996—Reading (East.)	0	4	.000	4.48	*67	0	0	0	24	64 1/3	53	35	32	48	79
1997—Scranton/W.B. (I.L.)	3	1	.750	2.37	26	0	0	0	7	38	31	11	10	24	36
—Philadelphia (N.L.)	5	1	.833	5.27	37	0	0	0	0	42 2/3	45	26	25	24	24
1998—Philadelphia (N.L.)	9	6	.600	4.24	71	0	0	0	1	93 1/3	94	48	44	35	86
1999—Philadelphia (N.L.)	5	5	.500	4.26	73	0	0	0	19	74	70	38	35	56	58
2000—Philadelphia (N.L.)	4	6	.400	4.40	65	0	0	0	7	73 2/3	72	41	36	35	49
—Scranton/W.B. (I.L.)	0	0	...	2.25	3	0	0	0	0	4	3	1	1	1	1
2001—Philadelphia (N.L.)	4	3	.571	4.31	42	0	0	0	1	48	51	23	23	22	35
—Lakewood (S.Atl.)	0	0	...	3.00	2	2	0	0	0	3	2	1	1	3	3
—San Francisco (N.L.)■	2	0	1.000	8.40	13	0	0	0	0	15	21	14	14	7	17
Major League totals (5 years)	29	21	.580	4.60	301	0	0	0	28	346 2/3	353	190	177	179	269

GOMEZ, ALEXIS — OF — ROYALS

PERSONAL: Born August 6, 1980, in Loma de Cabrera, Dominican Republic. ... 6-2/160. ... Bats left, throws left. ... Full name: Alexis De Jesus Gomez.
HIGH SCHOOL: Liceo General Jose Cabrera (Loma de Cabrera, Dominican Republic).
TRANSACTIONS/CAREER NOTES: Signed as non-drafted free agent by Kansas City Royals organization (February 21, 1997).
STATISTICAL NOTES: Led Gulf Coast League outfielders with 140 total chances in 1999.

Year Team (League)	Pos.	G	AB	R	H	2B	3B	HR	RBI	Avg.	BB	SO	SB	PO	A	E	Avg.
1997—Dom. Royals (DSL)		64	248	51	87	12	9	0	42	.351	33	52	9	...	...	...	...
1998—Dom. Royals (DSL)		67	233	51	66	11	3	1	34	.283	50	46	17	...	...	...	...
1999—GC Royals (GCL)	OF	56	214	44	59	12	1	5	31	.276	32	48	13	*131	7	2	.986
2000—Wilmington (Caro.)	OF	121	461	63	117	13	4	1	33	.254	45	121	21	261	3	14	.950
2001—Wilmington (Caro.)	OF	48	169	29	51	8	2	1	9	.302	11	43	7	108	3	5	.957
—Wichita (Texas)	OF	83	342	55	96	15	6	4	34	.281	27	70	16	203	1	6	.971

GOMEZ, CHRIS — SS — DEVIL RAYS

PERSONAL: Born June 16, 1971, in Los Angeles. ... 6-1/195. ... Bats right, throws right. ... Full name: Christopher Cory Gomez.
HIGH SCHOOL: Lakewood (Calif.).
COLLEGE: Loyola Marymount, then Long Beach State.
TRANSACTIONS/CAREER NOTES: Selected by California Angels organization in 37th round of free-agent draft (June 5, 1989); did not sign. ... Selected by Detroit Tigers organization in third round of free-agent draft (June 1, 1992). ... Traded by Tigers with C John Flaherty to San Diego Padres for C Brad Ausmus, SS Andujar Cedeno and P Russ Spear (June 18, 1996). ... On San Diego disabled list (June 2-July 31, 1999); included rehabilitation assignment to Las Vegas (July 15-30). ... On disabled list (June 22, 2000-remainder of season). ... Released by Padres (June 22, 2001). ... Signed by Tampa Bay Devil Rays organization (June 27, 2001). ... Granted free agency (November 5, 2001). ... Re-signed by Devil Rays (December 7, 2001).

Year Team (League)	Pos.	G	AB	R	H	2B	3B	HR	RBI	Avg.	BB	SO	SB	PO	A	E	Avg.
1992—London (East.)	SS	64	220	20	59	13	2	1	19	.268	20	34	1	100	174	14	.951
1993—Toledo (I.L.)	SS	87	277	29	68	12	2	0	20	.245	23	37	6	133	261	16	.961
—Detroit (A.L.)	SS-2B-DH	46	128	11	32	7	1	0	11	.250	9	17	2	69	118	5	.974
1994—Detroit (A.L.)	SS-2B	84	296	32	76	19	0	8	53	.257	33	64	5	140	210	8	.978
1995—Detroit (A.L.)	SS-2B-DH	123	431	49	96	20	2	11	50	.223	41	96	4	210	361	15	.974
1996—Detroit (A.L.)	SS	48	128	21	31	5	0	1	16	.242	18	20	1	77	114	6	.970
—San Diego (N.L.)■	SS	89	328	32	86	16	1	3	29	.262	39	64	2	124	261	13	.967
1997—San Diego (N.L.)	SS	150	522	62	132	19	2	5	54	.253	53	114	5	226	433	15	.978
1998—San Diego (N.L.)	SS	145	449	55	120	32	3	4	39	.267	51	87	1	180	397	12	*.980
1999—San Diego (N.L.)	SS	76	234	20	59	8	1	1	15	.252	27	49	1	101	195	12	.961
—Las Vegas (PCL)	SS	10	27	3	9	1	0	0	4	.333	2	6	0	8	20	2	.933
2000—San Diego (N.L.)	SS-2B	33	54	4	12	0	0	0	3	.222	7	5	0	27	43	5	.933
2001—San Diego (N.L.)	SS-2B	40	112	6	21	3	0	0	7	.188	9	14	1	40	69	6	.948
—Portland (PCL)	SS-2B	11	40	5	12	3	0	1	5	.300	2	4	1	13	34	2	.959
—Durham (I.L.)■	SS	23	93	16	28	5	1	4	17	.301	11	5	1	23	65	2	.968
—Tampa Bay (A.L.)	SS	58	189	31	57	16	0	8	36	.302	8	24	3	80	131	7	.968
American League totals (5 years)		359	1172	144	292	67	3	28	166	.249	109	221	15	576	934	41	.974
National League totals (6 years)		533	1699	179	430	78	7	13	147	.253	186	333	10	698	1398	63	.971
Major League totals (9 years)		892	2871	323	722	145	10	41	313	.251	295	554	25	1274	2332	104	.972

G

DIVISION SERIES RECORD

Year Team (League)	Pos.	G	AB	R	H	2B	3B	HR	RBI	Avg.	BB	SO	SB	PO	A	E	Avg.
1996—San Diego (N.L.)	SS	3	12	0	2	0	0	0	1	.167	0	4	0	8	5	0	1.000
1998—San Diego (N.L.)	SS	4	11	1	3	0	0	0	0	.273	4	1	0	6	9	1	.938
Division series totals (2 years)		7	23	1	5	0	0	0	1	.217	4	5	0	14	14	1	.966

CHAMPIONSHIP SERIES RECORD

Year Team (League)	Pos.	G	AB	R	H	2B	3B	HR	RBI	Avg.	BB	SO	SB	PO	A	E	Avg.
1998—San Diego (N.L.)	SS	6	20	2	3	1	0	0	0	.150	2	5	0	5	14	1	.950

WORLD SERIES RECORD

Year Team (League)	Pos.	G	AB	R	H	2B	3B	HR	RBI	Avg.	BB	SO	SB	PO	A	E	Avg.
1998—San Diego (N.L.)	SS	4	11	2	4	0	1	0	0	.364	1	1	0	5	9	0	1.000

GOMEZ, LUIS OF DIAMONDBACKS

PERSONAL: Born May 18, 1980, in Barahona, Dominican Republic. ... 6-2/185. ... Bats both, throws right. ... Full name: Luis Enrique Terrero Gomez.
HIGH SCHOOL: Barney Morgan (Barahona, Dominican Republic).
TRANSACTIONS/CAREER NOTES: Signed as non-drafted free agent by Arizona Diamondbacks organization (October 15, 1997). ... On South Bend disabled list (May 8-June 15, 2001).
STATISTICAL NOTES: Led Pioneer League outfielders with 152 total chances in 1999.

Year Team (League)	Pos.	G	AB	R	H	2B	3B	HR	RBI	Avg.	BB	SO	SB	PO	A	E	Avg.
1998—Dom. D'backs (DSL) ..		56	169	19	39	7	1	2	15	.231	13	44	9	...	...	...	...
1999—Missoula (Pio.).........	OF	71	272	*74	78	13	7	8	40	.287	32	*91	27	*129	12	*11	.928
2000—High Desert (Calif.).....	OF	19	79	10	15	3	1	0	1	.190	3	16	5	46	2	3	.941
—Missoula (Pio.)...........	OF	68	276	48	72	10	0	8	44	.261	10	75	23	80	14	5	.949
2001—El Paso (Texas)..........	OF	34	147	29	44	13	3	3	8	.299	4	45	9	78	4	5	.943
—Yakima (N'West)	OF	11	41	7	13	2	1	0	0	.317	2	8	0	17	0	0	1.000
—Lancaster (Calif.)........	OF	19	71	16	32	9	1	4	11	.451	1	14	5	33	1	1	.971

GONZALEZ, ALEX SS CUBS

PERSONAL: Born April 8, 1973, in Miami. ... 6-0/195. ... Bats right, throws right. ... Full name: Alexander Scott Gonzalez.
HIGH SCHOOL: Miami Killian.
TRANSACTIONS/CAREER NOTES: Selected by Toronto Blue Jays organization in 14th round of free-agent draft (June 3, 1991). ... On Toronto disabled list (April 29-May 27, 1994); included rehabilitation assignment to Syracuse (May 14-27). ... On disabled list (August 13-September 14, 1997; and May 17, 1999-remainder of season). ... On Toronto disabled list (July 7-22, 2000); included rehabilitation assignment to Syracuse (July 21). ... Granted free agency (October 30, 2000). ... Re-signed by Blue Jays (December 10, 2000). ... Traded by Blue Jays to Chicago Cubs for P Felix Heredia and a player to be named later (December 10, 2001); Blue Jays acquired IF James Deschaine to complete deal (December 13, 2001).
RECORDS: Shares major league single-game record for most strikeouts—6 (September 9, 1998, 13 innings). ... Shares A.L. record for most assists by shortstop (nine-inning game)—13 (April 26, 1996).
STATISTICAL NOTES: Led Gulf Coast League shortstops with 247 total chances in 1991. ... Led South Atlantic League shortstops with 702 total chances in 1992. ... Led Southern League with 253 total bases in 1993. ... Led Southern League shortstops with 682 total chances and 92 double plays in 1993. ... Led International League shortstops with 542 total chances in 1994. ... Led A.L. shortstops with 765 total chances and 122 double plays in 1996. ... Had 15-game hitting streak (August 2-18, 2000). ... Led A.L. with 16 sacrifice hits in 2000.

Year Team (League)	Pos.	G	AB	R	H	2B	3B	HR	RBI	Avg.	BB	SO	SB	PO	A	E	Avg.
1991—GC Blue Jays (GCL)....	SS	53	191	29	40	5	4	0	10	.209	12	41	7	66	*160	21	.915
1992—Myrtle Beach (S.Atl.)..	SS	134	535	83	145	22	9	10	62	.271	38	119	26	*248	*406	48	.932
1993—Knoxville (S.Atl.)	SS	*142	561	*93	162	29	7	16	69	.289	39	110	38	*224	*428	30	*.956
1994—Toronto (A.L.).............	SS	15	53	7	8	3	1	0	1	.151	4	17	3	18	49	6	.918
—Syracuse (I.L.).............	SS-DH	110	437	69	124	22	4	12	57	.284	53	92	23	*163	*348	*31	.943
1995—Toronto (A.L.).............	SS-3B-DH	111	367	51	89	19	4	10	42	.243	44	114	4	164	227	19	.954
1996—Toronto (A.L.).............	SS	147	527	64	124	30	5	14	64	.235	45	127	16	279	465	21	.973
1997—Toronto (A.L.).............	SS	126	426	46	102	23	2	12	35	.239	34	94	15	209	341	8	*.986
1998—Toronto (A.L.).............	SS	158	568	70	136	28	1	13	51	.239	28	121	21	259	427	17	.976
1999—Toronto (A.L.).............	SS-DH	38	154	22	45	13	0	2	12	.292	16	23	4	69	132	4	.980
2000—Toronto (A.L.).............	SS	141	527	68	133	31	2	15	69	.252	43	113	4	213	407	16	.975
—Syracuse (I.L.).............	SS	1	5	0	0	0	0	0	0	.000	0	2	0	2	3	0	1.000
2001—Toronto (A.L.).............	SS	154	636	79	161	25	5	17	76	.253	43	149	18	249	509	10	.987
Major League totals (8 years)		890	3258	407	798	172	20	83	350	.245	257	758	85	1460	2557	101	.975

GONZALEZ, ALEX SS MARLINS

PERSONAL: Born February 15, 1977, in Cagua, Venezuela. ... 6-0/170. ... Bats right, throws right. ... Full name: Alexander Gonzalez.
HIGH SCHOOL: Liceo Ramon Bastidas (Venezuela).
TRANSACTIONS/CAREER NOTES: Signed as non-drafted free agent by Florida Marlins organization (April 18, 1994). ... On Kane County disabled list (April 5-August 17, 1996). ... On Portland disabled list (September 7, 1996-remainder of season). ... On Florida disabled list (July 28-September 1, 2000); included rehabilitation assignment to Brevard County (August 26-31).

G

Year	Team (League)	Pos.	G	AB	R	H	2B	3B	HR	RBI	Avg.	BB	SO	SB	PO	A	E	Avg.
1994—	Dom. Marlins (DSL)...	SS	54	239	30	54	7	3	3	31	.226	15	36	4	140	222	34	.914
1995—	GC Marlins (GCL).......	SS	53	187	30	55	7	4	2	30	.294	19	27	11	65	168	17	.932
	— Brevard County (FSL).	SS	17	59	6	12	2	1	0	8	.203	1	14	1	26	51	8	.906
1996—	Portland (East.).........	SS	11	34	4	8	0	1	0	1	.235	2	10	0	17	38	7	.887
	— Kane County (Midw.)..	SS	4	10	2	2	0	0	0	0	.200	2	4	0	2	10	0	1.000
	— GC Marlins (GCL)......	SS	10	41	6	16	3	0	0	6	.390	2	4	1	14	30	5	.898
1997—	Portland (East.)..........	SS	133	449	69	114	16	4	19	65	.254	27	83	4	192	423	*37	.943
1998—	Charlotte (I.L.)...........	SS	108	422	71	117	20	10	10	51	.277	28	80	4	161	322	20	.960
	— Florida (N.L.).............	SS	25	86	11	13	2	0	3	7	.151	9	30	0	29	58	2	.978
1999—	Florida (N.L.).............	SS	136	560	81	155	28	8	14	59	.277	15	113	3	237	339	27	.955
2000—	Florida (N.L.).............	SS	109	385	35	77	17	4	7	42	.200	13	77	7	139	288	19	.957
	— Brevard County (FSL).	SS	4	17	1	2	0	0	0	2	.118	1	3	1	8	11	0	1.000
2001—	Florida (N.L.).............	SS-C	145	515	57	129	36	1	9	48	.250	30	107	2	220	396	26	.960
Major League totals (4 years)			415	1546	184	374	83	13	33	156	.242	67	327	12	625	1081	74	.958

ALL-STAR GAME RECORD

Year	League	Pos.	AB	R	H	2B	3B	HR	RBI	Avg.	BB	SO	SB	PO	A	E	Avg.
1999—	National....................	PH-SS	1	0	0	0	0	0	0	0	.000	0	0	0	1	0	0	1.000

GONZALEZ, DICKY   P   METS

PERSONAL: Born October 21, 1978, in Bayamon, Puerto Rico. ... 5-11/170. ... Throws right, bats right. ... Full name: Dicky Angel Gonzalez.
HIGH SCHOOL: Puig (Puerto Rico).
TRANSACTIONS/CAREER NOTES: Selected by New York Mets organization in 16th round of free-agent draft (June 4, 1996).

Year	League	W	L	Pct.	ERA	G	GS	CG	ShO	Sv.	IP	H	R	ER	BB	SO
1996—	Gulf Coast Mets (GCL).......	4	2	.667	2.66	11	8	2	1	0	47 1/3	50	19	14	3	51
	— Little Falls (NY-Penn).....	1	0	1.000	1.80	1	1	0	0	0	5	4	2	1	0	7
1997—	Capital City (S.Atl.)..........	1	4	.200	4.94	10	7	1	0	0	47 1/3	50	28	26	15	49
	— Little Falls (NY-Penn).....	3	6	.333	4.36	12	12	1	0	0	66	70	38	32	10	76
1998—	St. Lucie (FSL)	2	1	.667	3.09	8	8	0	0	0	46 2/3	46	22	16	13	23
	— Capital City (S.Atl.).......	10	3	.769	3.31	18	18	1	0	0	111 1/3	104	57	41	14	107
1999—	St. Lucie (FSL)	14	9	.609	2.83	25	25	3	0	0	168 2/3	156	66	53	30	143
	— Norfolk (I.L.)	0	1	.000	2.70	1	1	0	0	0	6 2/3	5	2	2	1	3
2000—	Binghamton (East.)	13	5	.722	3.84	26	25	2	1	0	147 2/3	130	75	63	36	138
2001—	Norfolk (I.L.)	6	5	.545	3.09	17	16	2	*2	0	96	96	35	33	20	70
	— New York (N.L.).............	3	2	.600	4.88	16	7	0	0	0	59	72	33	32	17	31
Major League totals (1 year)........		3	2	.600	4.88	16	7	0	0	0	59	72	33	32	17	31

GONZALEZ, JUAN   OF   RANGERS

PERSONAL: Born October 16, 1969, in Vega Baja, Puerto Rico. ... 6-3/220. ... Bats right, throws right. ... Full name: Juan Alberto Vazquez Gonzalez.
HIGH SCHOOL: Vega Baja (Puerto Rico).
TRANSACTIONS/CAREER NOTES: Signed as non-drafted free agent by Texas Rangers organization (May 30, 1986). ... On disabled list (April 27-June 17, 1988; March 30-April 26, 1991; April 16-June 1 and July 27-August 16, 1995; May 8-June 1, 1996; and March 24-May 2, 1997). ... Traded by Rangers with P Danny Patterson and C Gregg Zaun to Detroit Tigers for P Justin Thompson, P Francisco Cordero, OF Gabe Kapler, C Bill Haselman, 2B Frank Catalanotto and P Alan Webb (November 2, 1999). ... On disabled list (July 8-26, 2000). ... Granted free agency (November 1, 2000). ... Signed by Cleveland Indians (January 9, 2001). ... Granted free agency (November 5, 2001). ... Signed by Rangers (January 8, 2002).
RECORDS: Shares major league single-game record for most sacrifice flies—3 (July 3, 1999). ... Holds A.L. single-season record for most major league ballparks, one or more home runs—16 (1999).
HONORS: Named American Association Most Valuable Player (1990). ... Named outfielder on THE SPORTING NEWS A.L. Silver Slugger team (1992-93 and 1996-98). ... Named outfielder on THE SPORTING NEWS A.L. All-Star team (1993, 1996, 1998 and 2001). ... Named A.L. Most Valuable Player by Baseball Writers' Association of America (1996 and 1998). ... Named outfielder on A.L. Silver Slugger team (2001).
STATISTICAL NOTES: Led Texas League with 254 total bases in 1989. ... Led American Association with 252 total bases in 1990. ... Hit three home runs in one game (June 7, 1992; August 28, 1993; and September 24, 1999). ... Led A.L. with .632 slugging percentage in 1993. ... Had 21-game hitting streaks (June 25-July 19 and August 8-31, 1996). ... Had 20-game hitting streak (August 20-September 9, 1998). ... Had 15-game hitting streak (August 29-September 19, 2001). ... Led A.L. with 16 sacrifice flies in 2001. ... Career major league grand slams: 8.
MISCELLANEOUS: Holds Texas Rangers all-time records for most runs (791), hits (1,421), home runs (340) and runs batted in (1,075).

Year	Team (League)	Pos.	G	AB	R	H	2B	3B	HR	RBI	Avg.	BB	SO	SB	PO	A	E	Avg.
1986—	GC Rangers (GCL)......	OF	60	*233	24	56	4	1	0	36	.240	21	57	7	89	6	•6	.941
1987—	Gastonia (S.Atl.)........	OF	127	509	69	135	21	2	14	74	.265	30	92	9	234	10	12	.953
1988—	Charlotte (FSL)	OF	77	277	25	71	14	3	8	43	.256	25	64	5	139	5	4	.973
1989—	Tulsa (Texas)	OF	133	502	73	147	30	7	21	85	.293	31	98	1	292	15	9	.972
	— Texas (A.L.)	OF	24	60	6	9	3	0	1	7	.150	6	17	0	53	0	2	.964
1990—	Oklahoma City (A.A.)..	OF	128	496	78	128	29	4	*29	*101	.258	32	109	2	220	7	8	.966
	— Texas (A.L.)	OF-DH	25	90	11	26	7	1	4	12	.289	2	18	0	33	0	0	1.000
1991—	Texas (A.L.)	OF-DH	142	545	78	144	34	1	27	102	.264	42	118	4	310	6	6	.981
1992—	Texas (A.L.)	OF-DH	155	584	77	152	24	2	*43	109	.260	35	143	0	379	9	10	.975
1993—	Texas (A.L.)	OF-DH	140	536	105	166	33	1	*46	118	.310	37	99	4	265	5	4	.985
1994—	Texas (A.L.)	OF	107	422	57	116	18	4	19	85	.275	30	66	6	223	9	2	.991
1995—	Texas (A.L.)	DH-OF	90	352	57	104	20	2	27	82	.295	17	66	0	6	1	0	1.000
1996—	Texas (A.L.)	OF-DH	134	541	89	170	33	2	47	144	.314	45	82	2	163	6	2	.988
1997—	Texas (A.L.)	DH-OF	133	533	87	158	24	3	42	131	.296	33	107	0	128	6	4	.971
1998—	Texas (A.L.)	OF-DH	154	606	110	193	*50	2	45	*157	.318	46	126	2	213	8	4	.982
1999—	Texas (A.L.) ■............	OF-DH	144	562	114	183	36	1	39	128	.326	51	105	3	223	7	4	.983
2000—	Detroit (A.L.) ■...........	OF-DH	115	461	69	133	30	2	22	67	.289	32	84	1	118	2	1	.992
2001—	Cleveland (A.L.) ■.......	OF-DH	140	532	97	173	34	1	35	140	.325	41	94	1	214	10	3	.987
Major League totals (13 years)			1503	5824	957	1727	346	22	397	1282	.297	417	1125	23	2328	69	42	.983

G

RECORDS: Shares A.L. career record for most home runs—8. ... Shares single-series record for most home runs—5 (1996). ... Shares single-game record for most home runs—2 (October 2, 1996). ... Shares single-game record for most at-bats (nine-inning game)—6 (October 13, 2001).

NOTES: Shares postseason single-series record for most home runs—5 (1996).

Year Team (League)	Pos.	G	AB	R	H	2B	3B	HR	RBI	Avg.	BB	SO	SB	PO	A	E	Avg.
1996— Texas (A.L.)	OF	4	16	5	7	0	0	5	9	.438	4	2	0	8	0	0	1.000
1998— Texas (A.L.)	OF	3	12	1	1	1	0	0	0	.083	0	3	0	8	0	0	1.000
1999— Texas (A.L.)	OF	3	11	1	2	0	0	1	1	.182	1	3	0	5	0	0	1.000
2001— Cleveland (A.L.)	OF	5	23	4	8	3	0	2	5	.348	0	7	0	4	1	0	1.000
Division series totals (4 years)		15	62	11	18	4	0	8	15	.290	5	15	0	25	1	0	1.000

ALL-STAR GAME RECORD

Year League	Pos.	AB	R	H	2B	3B	HR	RBI	Avg.	BB	SO	SB	PO	A	E	Avg.
1993— American	OF	1	0	0	0	0	0	0	.000	1	1	0	1	0	0	1.000
1998— American	OF	3	0	0	0	0	0	1	.000	0	1	0	0	0	0	...
2001— American	OF	1	0	0	0	0	0	0	.000	0	0	0	1	0	0	1.000
All-Star Game totals (3 years)		5	0	0	0	0	0	1	.000	1	2	0	2	0	0	1.000

GONZALEZ, LUIS   OF   DIAMONDBACKS

PERSONAL: Born September 2, 1967, in Tampa. ... 6-2/190. ... Bats left, throws right. ... Full name: Luis Emilio Gonzalez.

HIGH SCHOOL: Jefferson (Tampa).

COLLEGE: South Alabama.

TRANSACTIONS/CAREER NOTES: Selected by Houston Astros organization in fourth round of free-agent draft (June 1, 1988). ... On disabled list (May 26-July 5, 1989 and August 29-September 13, 1991). ... On Houston disabled list (July 21-August 5, 1992). ... Traded by Astros with C Scott Servais to Chicago Cubs for C Rick Wilkins (June 28, 1995). ... Granted free agency (December 7, 1996). ... Signed by Astros (December 19, 1996). ... Granted free agency (October 28, 1997). ... Signed by Detroit Tigers (December 9, 1997). ... Traded by Tigers to Arizona Diamondbacks for OF Karim Garcia (December 28, 1998).

RECORDS: Shares major league single-month record for most home runs—13 (April 2001). ... Shares major league single-season record for highest fielding percentage by outfielder (150 or more games)—1.000 (2001); and fewest errors by outfielder—0 (2001). ... Shares N.L. single-season record for most consecutive errorless games by outfielder—161 (April 3 through October 7, 2001).

HONORS: Named outfielder on N.L. Silver Slugger team (2001). ... Named outfielder on THE SPORTING NEWS N.L. All-Star team (2001).

STATISTICAL NOTES: Tied for Southern League lead with 12 sacrifice flies and nine intentional bases on balls received in 1990. ... Led N.L. with 10 sacrifice flies in 1993. ... Had 23-game hitting streak (May 26-June 20, 1997). ... Had 30-game hitting streak (April 11-May 18, 1999). ... Had 16-game hitting streak (August 16-September 1, 1999). ... Hit for the cycle (July 5, 2000). ... Hit three home runs in one game (June 8, 2001). ... Career major league grand slams: 3.

MISCELLANEOUS: Holds Arizona Diamondbacks all-time record for most hits (596), doubles (128), home runs (114), runs batted in (367) and highest career batting average (.324).

Year Team (League)	Pos.	G	AB	R	H	2B	3B	HR	RBI	Avg.	BB	SO	SB	PO	A	E	Avg.
1988— Asheville (S.Atl.)	3B	31	115	13	29	7	1	2	14	.252	12	17	2	19	62	6	.931
— Auburn (NY-Penn)	3B-SS-1B	39	157	32	49	10	3	5	27	.312	12	19	2	37	83	13	.902
1989— Osceola (FSL)	DH	86	287	46	82	16	7	6	38	.286	37	49	2	...	...	...	...
1990— Columbus (Sou.)	1B-3B	138	495	86	131	30	6	•24	89	.265	54	100	27	1039	88	23	.980
— Houston (N.L.)	3B-1B	12	21	1	4	2	0	0	0	.190	2	5	0	22	10	0	1.000
1991— Houston (N.L.)	OF	137	473	51	120	28	9	13	69	.254	40	101	10	294	6	5	.984
1992— Houston (N.L.)	OF	122	387	40	94	19	3	10	55	.243	24	52	7	261	5	2	.993
— Tucson (PCL)	OF	13	44	11	19	4	2	1	9	.432	5	7	4	26	0	1	.963
1993— Houston (N.L.)	OF	154	540	82	162	34	3	15	72	.300	47	83	20	347	10	8	.978
1994— Houston (N.L.)	OF	112	392	57	107	29	4	8	67	.273	49	57	15	228	5	2	.991
1995— Houston (N.L.)	OF	56	209	35	54	10	4	6	35	.258	18	30	1	94	2	2	.980
— Chicago (N.L.)■	OF	77	262	34	76	19	4	7	34	.290	39	33	5	172	5	4	.978
1996— Chicago (N.L.)	OF-1B	146	483	70	131	30	4	15	79	.271	61	49	9	244	7	3	.988
1997— Houston (N.L.)■	OF-1B	152	550	78	142	31	2	10	68	.258	71	67	10	266	10	5	.982
1998— Detroit (A.L.)■	OF-DH	154	547	84	146	35	5	23	71	.267	57	62	12	232	8	3	.988
1999— Arizona (N.L.)■	OF-DH	153	614	112	*206	45	4	26	111	.336	66	63	9	271	10	5	.983
2000— Arizona (N.L.)	OF	•162	618	106	192	47	2	31	114	.311	78	85	2	293	4	3	.990
2001— Arizona (N.L.)	OF	•162	609	128	198	36	7	57	142	.325	100	83	1	280	8	0	1.000
American League totals (1 year)		154	547	84	146	35	5	23	71	.267	57	62	12	232	8	3	.988
National League totals (11 years)		1445	5158	794	1486	330	46	198	846	.288	595	708	89	2772	82	39	.987
Major League totals (12 years)		1599	5705	878	1632	365	51	221	917	.286	652	770	101	3004	90	42	.987

DIVISION SERIES RECORD

Year Team (League)	Pos.	G	AB	R	H	2B	3B	HR	RBI	Avg.	BB	SO	SB	PO	A	E	Avg.
1997— Houston (N.L.)	OF	3	12	0	4	0	0	0	0	.333	0	1	0	13	1	1	.933
1999— Arizona (N.L.)	OF	4	10	3	2	1	0	1	2	.200	5	1	0	6	0	0	1.000
2001— Arizona (N.L.)	OF	5	19	1	5	0	0	1	1	.263	2	4	0	3	0	0	1.000
Division series totals (3 years)		12	41	4	11	1	0	2	3	.268	7	6	0	22	1	1	.958

CHAMPIONSHIP SERIES RECORD

Year Team (League)	Pos.	G	AB	R	H	2B	3B	HR	RBI	Avg.	BB	SO	SB	PO	A	E	Avg.
2001— Arizona (N.L.)	OF	5	19	4	4	0	0	1	4	.211	3	3	0	7	0	0	1.000

G

NOTES: Member of World Series championship team (2001).

							BATTING									FIELDING		
Year	Team (League)	Pos.	G	AB	R	H	2B	3B	HR	RBI	Avg.	BB	SO	SB	PO	A	E	Avg.
2001—	Arizona (N.L.)............	OF	7	27	4	7	2	0	1	5	.259	1	11	0	11	0	0	1.000

ALL-STAR GAME RECORD

							BATTING							FIELDING		
Year	League	Pos.	AB	R	H	2B	3B	HR	RBI	Avg.	BB	SO	SB	PO	A	E	Avg.
1999—	National....................	OF	2	0	1	1	0	0	0	.500	0	0	0	0	0		...
2001—	National....................	OF	2	0	1	0	0	0	0	.500	0	0	0	0	0		...
All-Star Game totals (2 years)			4	0	2	1	0	0	0	.500	0	0	0	0	0		...

GONZALEZ, RAUL — OF — REDS

PERSONAL: Born December 27, 1973, in Santurce, Puerto Rico. ... 5-9/190. ... Bats right, throws right. ... Full name: Victor Raul Gonzalez.
HIGH SCHOOL: Gilberto Concepcion (Carolina, Puerto Rico).
TRANSACTIONS/CAREER NOTES: Selected by Kansas City Royals organization in 17th round free-agent draft (June 4, 1990). ... On disabled list (April 28-September 19, 1996). ... Granted free agency (October 17, 1997). ... Re-signed by Royals organization (November 27, 1997). ... Granted free agency (October 16, 1998). ... Signed by Boston Red Sox organization (November 18, 1998). ... Granted free agency (October 15, 1999). ... Signed by Chicago Cubs organization (November 18, 1999). ... On Iowa disabled list (July 8-26 and August 2-September 5, 2000). ... Granted free agency (October 18, 2000). ... Signed by Cincinnati Reds organization (December 21, 2000).

							BATTING								FIELDING		
Year	Team (League)	Pos.	G	AB	R	H	2B	3B	HR	RBI	Avg.	BB	SO	SB	PO	A	E	Avg.
1991—	GC Royals (GCL)........	OF	47	160	24	47	5	3	0	17	.294	19	21	3	62	2	4	.941
1992—	Appleton (Midw.)........	OF	119	449	82	115	32	1	9	51	.256	57	58	13	248	10	5	.981
1993—	Wilmington (Caro.).....	OF	127	461	59	124	30	3	11	55	.269	54	58	13	227	19	8	.969
1994—	Wilmington (Caro.).....	OF	115	414	60	108	19	8	9	51	.261	45	50	0	154	5	10	.941
1995—	Wichita (Texas)	OF	22	79	14	23	3	2	2	11	.291	8	13	4	38	6	2	.957
—	Wilmington (Caro.).....	OF	86	308	36	90	19	3	11	49	.292	14	34	6	137	5	5	.966
1996—	Wichita (Texas)	OF	23	84	17	24	5	1	1	9	.286	5	12	1	30	1	1	.969
1997—	Wichita (Texas)	OF	129	452	66	129	30	4	13	74	.285	36	52	12	167	9	*14	.926
1998—	Wichita (Texas)	OF	118	455	84	148	31	1	17	86	.325	58	53	12	191	11	9	.957
1999—	Trenton (East.)■	OF	127	505	80	*169	33	4	18	103	.335	51	71	12	268	4	2	.993
2000—	Iowa (PCL)■.............	OF	69	241	35	64	13	1	4	33	.266	21	20	5	110	4	3	.974
—	Chicago (N.L.)...........	OF	3	2	0	0	0	0	0	0	.000	0	2	0	0	0		...
2001—	Louisville (I.L.).........	OF	*142	539	*90	*161	*39	1	11	66	.299	64	70	6	313	7	9	.973
—	Cincinnati (N.L.)........	OF	11	14	0	3	0	0	0	0	.214	1	3	0	4	0	0	1.000
Major League totals (2 years)			14	16	0	3	0	0	0	0	.188	1	5	0	4	0	0	1.000

GONZALEZ, WIKI — C — PADRES

PERSONAL: Born May 17, 1974, in Aragua, Venezuela. ... 5-11/203. ... Bats right, throws right. ... Full name: Wiklenman Vicente Gonzalez.
TRANSACTIONS/CAREER NOTES: Signed as non-drafted free agent by Pittsburgh Pirates organization (February 12, 1992). ... Selected by San Diego Padres organization from Pirates organization in Rule 5 minor league draft (December 9, 1996). ... Granted free agency (October 16, 1998). ... Re-signed by Padres organization (October 23, 1998). ... On Mobile disabled list (May 24-June 6, 1999). ... On San Diego disabled list (June 3-July 3, 2001); included rehabilitation assignment to Lake Elsinore (June 28-July 3).

							BATTING								FIELDING		
Year	Team (League)	Pos.	G	AB	R	H	2B	3B	HR	RBI	Avg.	BB	SO	SB	PO	A	E	Avg.
1992—	Dom. Pirates (DSL)....	C	63	190	20	48	6	1	3	33	.253	22	12	4	244	42	9	.969
1993—	Dom. Pirates (DSL)....	C-IF	69	244	47	73	10	3	7	47	.299	40	15	24	506	48	8	.986
1994—	GC Pirates (GCL).......	C-1B	41	143	25	48	8	2	4	26	.336	13	13	2	259	37	12	.961
1995—	Augusta (S.Atl.).........	C	84	278	41	67	17	0	3	36	.241	26	32	5	345	43	6	.985
1996—	Augusta (S.Atl.).........	C	118	419	52	106	21	3	4	62	.253	58	41	4	810	115	*23	.976
1997—	Rancho Cuca. (Calif.)■	C	33	110	18	33	9	1	5	26	.300	7	25	1	117	17	2	.985
—	Mobile (Sou.)...........	C	47	143	15	39	7	1	4	25	.273	10	12	1	250	24	3	.989
1998—	Rancho Cuca. (Calif.) .	C	75	292	51	84	24	2	10	59	.288	26	54	0	346	56	3	.993
—	Mobile (Sou.)...........	C	22	67	20	26	9	0	4	26	.388	14	4	0	65	7	0	1.000
1999—	Mobile (Sou.)	C-DH	61	225	38	76	16	2	10	49	.338	29	28	0	329	43	7	.982
—	Las Vegas (PCL)	C-DH	24	92	13	25	6	0	6	12	.272	5	10	0	175	10	3	.984
—	San Diego (N.L.)	C	30	83	7	21	2	1	3	12	.253	1	8	0	109	15	1	.992
2000—	San Diego (N.L.)	C	95	284	25	66	15	1	5	30	.232	30	31	1	525	42	5	.991
2001—	San Diego (N.L.)	C-DH	64	160	16	44	6	0	8	27	.275	11	28	2	246	21	3	.989
—	Lake Elsinore (Calif.) ..	C	4	13	1	2	0	0	1	.154	2	4	0	32	4	1	.973
Major League totals (3 years)			189	527	48	131	23	2	16	69	.249	42	67	3	880	78	9	.991

GOODWIN, TOM — OF — DODGERS

PERSONAL: Born July 27, 1968, in Fresno, Calif. ... 6-1/175. ... Bats left, throws right. ... Full name: Thomas Jones Goodwin.
HIGH SCHOOL: Central (Fresno, Calif.).
COLLEGE: Fresno State.
TRANSACTIONS/CAREER NOTES: Selected by Pittsburgh Pirates organization in sixth round of free-agent draft (June 2, 1986); did not sign. ... Selected by Los Angeles Dodgers organization in first round (22nd pick overall) of free-agent draft (June 5, 1989). ... Claimed on waivers by Kansas City Royals (January 6, 1994). ... Traded by Royals to Texas Rangers for 3B Dean Palmer (July 25, 1997). ... On Texas disabled list (June 11-27 and June 28-August 6, 1999); included rehabilitation assignment to Charlotte (August 2-6). ... Granted free agency (October 28, 1999). ... Signed by Colorado Rockies (December 9, 1999). ... Traded by Rockies with cash to Dodgers for OF Todd Hollandsworth, OF Kevin Gibbs and P Randey Dorame (July 31, 2000). ... On Los Angeles disabled list (July 21-August 9, 2001); included rehabilitation assignment to Wilmington (August 7-9).
HONORS: Named outfielder on THE SPORTING NEWS college All-America team (1989).

G

STATISTICAL NOTES: Tied for Pacific Coast League lead in caught stealing with 23 in 1991. ... Led American Association in caught stealing with 20 in 1994. ... Led A.L. in sacrifice hits with 14 in 1995 and 21 in 1996. ... Led A.L. in caught stealing with 22 in 1996 and 20 in 1998. ... Career major league grand slams: 2.

MISCELLANEOUS: Member of 1988 U.S. Olympic baseball team.

							BATTING								FIELDING		
Year Team (League)	Pos.	G	AB	R	H	2B	3B	HR	RBI	Avg.	BB	SO	SB	PO	A	E	Avg.
1989— Great Falls (Pio.)	OF	63	240	*55	74	12	3	2	33	.308	28	30	*60	67	3	1	.986
1990— San Antonio (Texas)...	OF	102	428	76	119	15	4	0	28	.278	38	72	*60	264	7	3	*.989
—Bakersfield (Calif.)......	OF	32	134	24	39	6	2	0	13	.291	11	22	22	55	2	0	1.000
1991— Albuquerque (PCL)	OF	132	509	84	139	19	4	1	45	.273	59	83	48	284	6	3	.990
—Los Angeles (N.L.)	OF	16	7	3	1	0	0	0	0	.143	0	0	1	8	0	0	1.000
1992— Albuquerque (PCL).....	OF	82	319	48	96	10	4	2	28	.301	37	47	27	184	5	1	.995
—Los Angeles (N.L.)	OF	57	73	15	17	1	1	0	3	.233	6	10	7	43	0	0	1.000
1993— Los Angeles (N.L.)	OF	30	17	6	5	1	0	0	1	.294	1	4	1	8	0	0	1.000
—Albuquerque (PCL).....	OF	85	289	48	75	5	5	1	28	.260	30	51	21	145	1	2	.986
1994— Kansas City (A.L.)■...	DH-OF	2	2	0	0	0	0	0	0	.000	0	1	0	1	0	0	1.000
—Omaha (A.A.)...............	OF	113	429	67	132	17	7	2	34	.308	23	60	*50	276	3	2	.993
1995— Kansas City (A.L.)	OF-DH	133	480	72	138	16	3	4	28	.288	38	72	50	292	6	3	.990
1996— Kansas City (A.L.)	OF-DH	143	524	80	148	14	4	1	35	.282	39	79	66	303	7	5	.984
1997— Kansas City (A.L.)	OF	97	367	51	100	13	4	2	22	.272	19	51	34	232	3	1	.996
—Texas (A.L.)■............	OF	53	207	39	49	13	2	0	17	.237	25	37	16	138	3	2	.986
1998— Texas (A.L.).............	OF-DH	154	520	102	151	13	3	2	33	.290	73	90	38	370	5	3	.992
1999— Texas (A.L.).............	OF	109	405	63	105	12	6	3	33	.259	40	61	39	258	4	3	.989
—Charlotte (FSL)..........	OF	3	11	2	4	1	0	0	0	.364	1	4	0	8	0	0	1.000
2000— Colorado (N.L.)■......	OF	91	317	65	86	8	8	5	47	.271	50	76	39	208	3	3	.986
—Los Angeles (N.L.)■..	OF	56	211	29	53	3	1	1	11	.251	18	41	16	138	2	0	1.000
2001— Los Angeles (N.L.)	OF	105	286	51	66	8	5	4	22	.231	23	58	22	153	1	1	.994
—Wilmington (S.Atl.)	OF	2	5	2	2	0	1	0	1	.400	1	0	0	3	0	0	1.000
American League totals (6 years)		691	2505	407	691	81	22	12	168	.276	234	391	243	1594	28	17	.990
National League totals (5 years)		355	911	169	228	21	15	10	84	.250	98	189	86	558	6	4	.993
Major League totals (11 years)		1046	3416	576	919	102	37	22	252	.269	332	580	329	2152	34	21	.990

DIVISION SERIES RECORD

							BATTING								FIELDING		
Year Team (League)	Pos.	G	AB	R	H	2B	3B	HR	RBI	Avg.	BB	SO	SB	PO	A	E	Avg.
1998— Texas (A.L.)................	OF	2	4	0	1	0	0	0	0	.250	0	1	0	1	0	0	1.000
1999— Texas (A.L.)................	OF	3	7	0	1	0	0	0	0	.143	0	1	0	6	0	0	1.000
Division series totals (2 years)		5	11	0	2	0	0	0	0	.182	0	2	0	7	0	0	1.000

GORDON, TOM   P   CUBS

PERSONAL: Born November 18, 1967, in Sebring, Fla. ... 5-9/190. ... Throws right, bats right. ... Full name: Thomas Gordon.

HIGH SCHOOL: Avon Park (Fla.).

TRANSACTIONS/CAREER NOTES: Selected by Kansas City Royals organization in sixth round of free-agent draft (June 2, 1986). ... On disabled list (August 12-September 1, 1992; and May 8-24, 1995). ... Granted free agency (October 30, 1995). ... Signed by Boston Red Sox (December 21, 1995). ... On Boston disabled list (April 18-May 10 and June 12-September 27, 1999); included rehabilitation assignments to Trenton (September 11-13) and Augusta (September 14-25). ... On disabled list (April 2, 2000-entire season). ... Granted free agency (November 1, 2000). ... Signed by Chicago Cubs (December 14, 2000). ... On Chicago disabled list (March 23-May 1, 2001); included rehabilitation assignments to Daytona (April 23-27) and Iowa (April 28-May 1).

HONORS: Named A.L. Rookie Pitcher of the Year by The Sporting News (1989). ... Named A.L. Fireman of the Year by The Sporting News (1998).

STATISTICAL NOTES: Tied for Northwest League lead with four balks in 1987.

MISCELLANEOUS: Appeared in one game as pinch runner (1991). ... Appeared in one game as pinch runner (1995).

Year League	W	L	Pct.	ERA	G	GS	CG	ShO	Sv.	IP	H	R	ER	BB	SO
1986— Gulf Coast Royals (GCL)	3	1	.750	1.02	9	7	2	1	0	44	31	12	5	23	47
—Omaha (A.A.)................	0	0	...	47.25	1	0	0	0	0	1 1/3	6	7	7	2	3
1987— Eugene (N'West)	•9	0	•1.000	2.86	15	13	0	0	1	72 1/3	48	33	23	47	91
—Fort Myers (FSL)............	1	0	1.000	2.63	3	3	0	0	0	13 2/3	5	4	4	17	11
1988— Appleton (Midw.)...............	7	5	.583	2.06	17	17	5	1	0	118	69	30	27	43	*172
—Memphis (Sou.)...............	6	0	1.000	0.38	6	6	2	2	0	47 1/3	16	3	2	17	62
—Omaha (A.A.)................	3	0	1.000	1.33	3	3	0	0	0	20 1/3	11	3	3	15	29
—Kansas City (A.L.)	0	2	.000	5.17	5	2	0	0	0	15 2/3	16	9	9	7	18
1989— Kansas City (A.L.)	17	9	.654	3.64	49	16	1	1	1	163	122	67	66	86	153
1990— Kansas City (A.L.)	12	11	.522	3.73	32	32	6	1	0	195 1/3	192	99	81	99	175
1991— Kansas City (A.L.)	9	14	.391	3.87	45	14	1	1	1	158	129	76	68	87	167
1992— Kansas City (A.L.)	6	10	.375	4.59	40	11	0	0	0	117 2/3	116	67	60	55	98
1993— Kansas City (A.L.)	12	6	.667	3.58	48	14	2	0	1	155 2/3	125	65	62	77	143
1994— Kansas City (A.L.)	11	7	.611	4.35	24	24	0	0	0	155 1/3	136	79	75	87	126
1995— Kansas City (A.L.)	12	12	.500	4.43	31	31	2	0	0	189	204	110	93	89	119
1996— Boston (A.L.)■.................	12	9	.571	5.59	34	34	4	1	0	215 2/3	249	143	*134	105	171
1997— Boston (A.L.).................	6	10	.375	3.74	42	25	2	1	11	182 2/3	155	85	76	78	159
1998— Boston (A.L.).................	7	4	.636	2.72	73	0	0	0	*46	79 1/3	55	24	24	25	78
1999— Boston (A.L.).................	0	2	.000	5.60	21	0	0	0	11	17 2/3	17	11	11	12	24
2000— Boston (A.L.).................							Did not play.								
2001— Daytona (FSL)■...............	0	0	...	0.00	2	2	0	0	0	2	0	0	0	0	3
—Iowa (PCL)	0	0	...	0.00	2	0	0	0	0	2	1	0	0	1	2
—Chicago (N.L.)	1	2	.333	3.38	47	0	0	0	27	45 1/3	32	18	17	16	67
A.L. totals (12 years)	104	96	.520	4.15	444	203	18	4	71	1645	1516	835	759	807	1431
N.L. totals (1 year)	1	2	.333	3.38	47	0	0	0	27	45 1/3	32	18	17	16	67
Major League totals (13 years)	105	98	.517	4.13	491	203	18	4	98	1690 1/3	1548	853	776	823	1498

G

DIVISION SERIES RECORD

Year	League	W	L	Pct.	ERA	G	GS	CG	ShO	Sv.	IP	H	R	ER	BB	SO
1998—Boston (A.L.)		0	1	.000	9.00	2	0	0	0	0	3	4	3	3	4	1
1999—Boston (A.L.)		0	0	...	4.50	2	0	0	0	0	2	1	1	1	1	3
Division series totals (2 years)		0	1	.000	7.20	4	0	0	0	0	5	5	4	4	5	4

CHAMPIONSHIP SERIES RECORD

Year	League	W	L	Pct.	ERA	G	GS	CG	ShO	Sv.	IP	H	R	ER	BB	SO
1999—Boston (A.L.)		0	0	...	13.50	3	0	0	0	0	2	3	3	3	1	3

ALL-STAR GAME RECORD

Year	League	W	L	Pct.	ERA	GS	CG	ShO	Sv.	IP	H	R	ER	BB	SO
1998—American		0	0	...	18.00	0	0	0	0	1	3	2	2	1	0

GRABOW, JOHN — P — PIRATES

PERSONAL: Born November 4, 1978, in Arcadia, Calif. ... 6-2/190. ... Throws left, bats left. ... Full name: John William Grabow.
HIGH SCHOOL: San Gabriel (Calif.).
TRANSACTIONS/CAREER NOTES: Selected by Pittsburgh Pirates organization in third round of free-agent draft (June 3, 1997). ... On disabled list (June 20-July 6, 2000). ... On Altoona disabled list (May 20-June 25 and July 17-26, 2001).

Year	League	W	L	Pct.	ERA	G	GS	CG	ShO	Sv.	IP	H	R	ER	BB	SO
1997—Gulf Coast Pirates (GCL)	2	•7	.222	4.57	11	8	0	0	0	45 1/3	57	32	23	14	28	
1998—Augusta (S.Atl.)	6	3	.667	5.78	17	16	0	0	0	71 2/3	84	59	46	34	67	
1999—Hickory (S.Atl.)	9	10	.474	3.80	26	26	0	0	0	156 1/3	152	82	66	32	164	
2000—Altoona (East.)	8	7	.533	4.33	24	24	1	0	0	145 1/3	145	81	70	65	109	
2001—Altoona (East.)	2	5	.286	3.38	10	10	0	0	0	50 2/3	30	23	19	39	42	
—Gulf Coast Pirates (GCL)	0	1	.000	3.75	6	6	0	0	0	12	11	6	5	4	9	
—Lynchburg (Caro.)	1	3	.250	6.38	7	7	0	0	0	36 2/3	42	30	26	26	35	

GRABOWSKI, JASON — 3B — ATHLETICS

PERSONAL: Born May 24, 1976, in New Haven, Conn. ... 6-3/200. ... Bats left, throws right. ... Full name: Jason William Grabowski.
HIGH SCHOOL: The Morgan School (Clinton, Conn.).
COLLEGE: Connecticut.
TRANSACTIONS/CAREER NOTES: Selected by New York Yankees organization in 17th round of free-agent draft (June 2, 1994); did not sign. ... Selected by Texas Rangers organization in second round of free-agent draft (June 3, 1997). ... Signed by Seattle Mariners organization (February 6, 2001). ... On disabled list (June 22-July 2, 2001). ... Selected by Oakland Athletics from Mariners organization in Rule 5 major league draft (December 13, 2001).

Year	Team (League)	Pos.	G	AB	R	H	2B	3B	HR	RBI	Avg.	BB	SO	SB	PO	A	E	Avg.
1997—Pulaski (Appl.)	C	50	174	36	51	14	0	4	24	.293	40	32	6	386	40	8	.982	
1998—Savannah (S.Atl.)	C-1B	104	352	63	95	13	6	14	52	.270	57	93	16	573	50	6	.990	
1999—Charlotte (FSL)	3B-1B	123	434	68	136	31	6	12	87	.313	65	66	13	100	199	27	.917	
—Tulsa (Texas)	DH	2	6	1	1	0	0	0	0	.167	2	2	0	...	...	...	...	
2000—Tulsa (Texas)	3B	135	493	93	135	33	5	19	90	.274	88	106	8	•84	270	*40	.898	
2001—Tacoma (PCL)■	3B-OF-1B-SS	114	394	60	117	32	3	9	58	.297	61	94	7	215	125	21	.942	

GRACE, MARK — 1B — DIAMONDBACKS

PERSONAL: Born June 28, 1964, in Winston-Salem, N.C. ... 6-2/200. ... Bats left, throws left. ... Full name: Mark Eugene Grace.
HIGH SCHOOL: Tustin (Calif.).
JUNIOR COLLEGE: Saddleback Community College (Calif.).
COLLEGE: San Diego State.
TRANSACTIONS/CAREER NOTES: Selected by Minnesota Twins organization in 15th round of free-agent draft (January 17, 1984); did not sign. ... Selected by Chicago Cubs organization in 24th round of free-agent draft (June 3, 1985). ... On disabled list (June 5-23, 1989). ... Granted free agency (October 15, 1994). ... Re-signed by Cubs (April 7, 1995). ... Granted free agency (November 3, 1995). ... Re-signed by Cubs (December 19, 1995). ... On disabled list (June 11-28, 1996; April 4-19, 1997; and May 11-31, 2000). ... Granted free agency (October 30, 2000). ... Signed by Arizona Diamondbacks (December 8, 2000).
RECORDS: Holds major league single-season record for fewest double plays by first baseman (150 or more games)—82 (1998). ... Shares major league record for most assists by first baseman in one inning—3 (May 23, 1990, fourth inning). ... Holds N.L. single-season record for most assists by first baseman—180 (1990).
HONORS: Named Eastern League Most Valuable Player (1987). ... Named N.L. Rookie Player of the Year by THE SPORTING NEWS (1988). ... Won N.L. Gold Glove at first base (1992-93 and 1995-96).
STATISTICAL NOTES: Led Midwest League first basemen with 103 double plays in 1986. ... Led Eastern League with .545 slugging percentage in 1987. ... Led N.L. first basemen with 1,695 total chances in 1991, 1,725 in 1992 and 1,573 in 1993. ... Tied for N.L. lead in grounding into double plays with 25 in 1993. ... Led N.L. first basemen with 134 double plays in 1993. ... Hit for the cycle (May 9, 1993). ... Tied for N.L. lead with 10 sacrifice flies in 1999. ... Had 18-game hitting streak (May 18-June 10, 2001). ... Career major league grand slams: 3.

Year	Team (League)	Pos.	G	AB	R	H	2B	3B	HR	RBI	Avg.	BB	SO	SB	PO	A	E	Avg.
1986—Peoria (Midw.)	1B-OF	126	465	81	159	30	4	15	95	*.342	60	28	6	1050	69	13	.989	
1987—Pittsfield (East.)	1B	123	453	81	151	29	8	17	*101	.333	48	24	5	1054	*96	6	*.995	
1988—Iowa (A.A.)	1B	21	67	11	17	4	0	0	14	.254	13	4	1	189	20	1	.995	
—Chicago (N.L.)	1B	134	486	65	144	23	4	7	57	.296	60	43	3	1182	87	•17	.987	
1989—Chicago (N.L.)	1B	142	510	74	160	28	3	13	79	.314	80	42	14	1324	126	6	.996	
1990—Chicago (N.L.)	1B	157	589	72	182	32	1	9	82	.309	59	54	15	1324	*180	12	.992	
1991—Chicago (N.L.)	1B	160	*619	87	169	28	5	8	58	.273	70	53	3	*1520	*167	8	.995	
1992—Chicago (N.L.)	1B	158	603	72	185	37	5	9	79	.307	72	36	6	*1580	*141	4	.998	
1993—Chicago (N.L.)	1B	155	594	86	193	39	4	14	98	.325	71	32	8	*1456	112	5	.997	
1994—Chicago (N.L.)	1B	106	403	55	120	23	3	6	44	.298	48	41	0	925	78	7	.993	
1995—Chicago (N.L.)	1B	143	552	97	180	*51	3	16	92	.326	65	46	6	1211	114	7	.995	
1996—Chicago (N.L.)	1B	142	547	88	181	39	1	9	75	.331	62	41	2	1259	107	4	.997	

G

Year Team (League)	Pos.	G	AB	R	H	2B	3B	HR	RBI	Avg.	BB	SO	SB	PO	A	E	Avg.
1997— Chicago (N.L.)............	1B	151	555	87	177	32	5	13	78	.319	88	45	2	1202	120	6	.995
1998— Chicago (N.L.)............	1B	158	595	92	184	39	3	17	89	.309	93	56	4	1279	122	8	.994
1999— Chicago (N.L.)............	1B	161	593	107	183	44	5	16	91	.309	83	44	3	1335	93	8	.994
2000— Chicago (N.L.)............	1B	143	510	75	143	41	1	11	82	.280	95	28	1	1098	103	4	*.997
2001— Arizona (N.L.)■..........	1B	145	476	66	142	31	2	15	78	.298	67	36	1	995	62	5	.995
Major League totals (14 years)		2055	7632	1123	2343	487	45	163	1082	.307	1013	597	68	17596	1612	101	.995

DIVISION SERIES RECORD

Year Team (League)	Pos.	G	AB	R	H	2B	3B	HR	RBI	Avg.	BB	SO	SB	PO	A	E	Avg.
1998— Chicago (N.L.)............	1B	3	12	0	1	0	0	0	1	.083	0	2	0	20	2	0	1.000
2001— Arizona (N.L.)............	1B	4	14	0	3	1	0	0	0	.214	2	3	0	32	2	0	1.000
Division series totals (2 years)		7	26	0	4	1	0	0	1	.154	2	5	0	52	4	0	1.000

CHAMPIONSHIP SERIES RECORD

NOTES: Hit home run in first at-bat (October 4, 1989).

Year Team (League)	Pos.	G	AB	R	H	2B	3B	HR	RBI	Avg.	BB	SO	SB	PO	A	E	Avg.
1989— Chicago (N.L.)............	1B	5	17	3	11	3	1	1	8	.647	4	1	1	44	3	0	1.000
2001— Arizona (N.L.)............	1B	5	16	1	6	0	0	0	1	.375	2	1	0	43	4	0	1.000
Championship series totals (2 years)		10	33	4	17	3	1	1	9	.515	6	2	1	87	7	0	1.000

WORLD SERIES RECORD

NOTES: Member of World Series championship team (2001).

Year Team (League)	Pos.	G	AB	R	H	2B	3B	HR	RBI	Avg.	BB	SO	SB	PO	A	E	Avg.
2001— Arizona (N.L.)............	1B	6	19	1	5	1	0	1	3	.263	4	1	0	53	2	1	.982

ALL-STAR GAME RECORD

Year League	Pos.	AB	R	H	2B	3B	HR	RBI	Avg.	BB	SO	SB	PO	A	E	Avg.
1993— National	DH	3	0	0	0	0	0	0	.000	0	0	0	...	...	...	...
1995— National	1B	0	0	0	0	0	0	0	...	0	0	0	1	0	0	1.000
1997— National	1B	1	0	0	0	0	0	0	.000	0	0	0	1	0	0	1.000
All-Star Game totals (3 years)		4	0	0	0	0	0	0	.000	0	0	0	2	0	0	1.000

GRAFFANINO, TONY   SS/2B   WHITE SOX

PERSONAL: Born June 6, 1972, in Amityville, N.Y. ... 6-1/195. ... Bats right, throws right. ... Full name: Anthony Joseph Graffanino. ... Name pronounced GRAF-uh-NEE-noh.

HIGH SCHOOL: East Islip (Islip Terrace, N.Y.).

TRANSACTIONS/CAREER NOTES: Selected by Atlanta Braves organization in 10th round of free-agent draft (June 4, 1990). ... On disabled list (July 3, 1995-remainder of season). ... Released by Braves (April 2, 1999). ... Signed by Tampa Bay Devil Rays organization (April 9, 1999). ... Traded by Devil Rays to Chicago White Sox for P Tanyon Sturtze (May 31, 2000).

STATISTICAL NOTES: Led Pioneer League shortstops with 41 double plays in 1991. ... Led Carolina League second basemen with .968 fielding percentage in 1993. ... Led International League second basemen with 441 total chances in 1996. ... Career major league grand slams: 1.

Year Team (League)	Pos.	G	AB	R	H	2B	3B	HR	RBI	Avg.	BB	SO	SB	PO	A	E	Avg.
1990— Pulaski (Appl.)............	SS	42	131	23	27	5	1	0	11	.206	26	17	6	60	105	24	.873
1991— Idaho Falls (Pio.)........	SS	66	274	53	95	16	4	4	56	.347	27	37	19	112	187	*29	.912
1992— Macon (S.Atl.)............	2B	112	400	50	96	15	5	10	31	.240	50	84	9	178	239	17	.961
1993— Durham (Caro.)..........	2B-DH-SS	123	459	78	126	30	5	15	69	.275	45	78	24	186	263	15	†.968
1994— Greenville (Sou.)........	2B-DH	124	440	66	132	28	3	7	52	.300	50	53	29	254	326	14	.976
1995— Richmond (I.L.)..........	2B	50	179	20	34	6	0	4	17	.190	15	49	2	102	127	4	.983
1996— Richmond (I.L.)..........	2B	96	353	57	100	29	2	7	33	.283	34	72	11	*215	216	10	.977
— Atlanta (N.L.)............	2B	22	46	7	8	1	1	0	2	.174	4	13	0	24	39	2	.969
1997— Atlanta (N.L.)............	2B-3B-SS-1B	104	186	33	48	9	1	8	20	.258	26	46	6	90	180	5	.982
1998— Atlanta (N.L.)............	2B-SS-3B	105	289	32	61	14	1	5	22	.211	24	68	1	139	227	11	.971
1999— Durham (I.L.)■..........	2B-DH-3B	87	345	66	108	25	6	9	58	.313	37	46	16	182	233	1	.998
— Tampa Bay (A.L.).......	2B-SS-DH-3B	39	130	20	41	9	4	2	19	.315	9	22	3	66	114	5	.973
2000— Tampa Bay (A.L.).......	2B-3B-SS	13	20	8	6	1	0	0	1	.300	1	2	0	14	19	0	1.000
— Durham (I.L.)............	SS-2B-1B-3B	10	35	9	10	3	0	2	6	.286	7	8	2	13	27	0	1.000
— Chicago (A.L.)■..........	SS-2B-3B-DH	57	148	25	40	5	1	2	16	.270	21	25	7	61	122	6	.968
2001— Chicago (A.L.) 3-2-S-O-D-1		74	145	23	44	9	0	2	15	.303	16	29	4	56	99	7	.957
American League totals (3 years)		183	443	76	131	24	5	6	51	.296	47	78	14	197	354	18	.968
National League totals (3 years)		231	521	72	117	24	3	13	44	.225	54	127	7	253	446	18	.975
Major League totals (6 years)		414	964	148	248	48	8	19	95	.257	101	205	21	450	800	36	.972

DIVISION SERIES RECORD

Year Team (League)	Pos.	G	AB	R	H	2B	3B	HR	RBI	Avg.	BB	SO	SB	PO	A	E	Avg.
1997— Atlanta (N.L.)............	2B	3	3	0	0	0	0	0	0	.000	2	1	0	1	6	0	1.000
1998— Atlanta (N.L.)............	PH	1	0	0	0	0	0	0	0	...	0	0	0	...	...	...	...
2000— Chicago (A.L.)	PR-3B	1	0	0	0	0	0	0	0	...	0	0	0	0	1	0	1.000
Division series totals (3 years)		5	3	0	0	0	0	0	0	.000	2	1	0	1	7	0	1.000

CHAMPIONSHIP SERIES RECORD

Year Team (League)	Pos.	G	AB	R	H	2B	3B	HR	RBI	Avg.	BB	SO	SB	PO	A	E	Avg.
1997— Atlanta (N.L.)............	2B	3	8	1	2	1	0	0	0	.250	0	3	0	4	2	0	1.000
1998— Atlanta (N.L.)............	PH-2B	4	3	2	1	1	0	0	1	.333	2	1	0	2	5	0	1.000
Championship series totals (2 years)		7	11	3	3	2	0	0	1	.273	2	4	0	6	7	0	1.000

G

GRAMAN, ALEX | P | YANKEES

PERSONAL: Born November 17, 1977, in Huntingburg, Ind. ... 6-4/200. ... Throws left, bats left. ... Full name: Alex J. Graman.
HIGH SCHOOL: Southridge (Huntingburg, Ind.).
COLLEGE: Indiana State.
TRANSACTIONS/CAREER NOTES: Selected by New York Yankees organization in third round of free-agent draft (June 2, 1999).

Year	League	W	L	Pct.	ERA	G	GS	CG	ShO	Sv.	IP	H	R	ER	BB	SO
1999—	Staten Island (NY-Penn).....	6	3	.667	2.99	14	14	0	0	0	81 1/3	74	30	27	16	85
2000—	Tampa (FSL).....................	8	9	.471	3.65	28	•28	3	1	0	143	120	64	58	58	111
—	Norwich (East.)	0	1	.000	11.81	1	1	0	0	0	5 1/3	6	7	7	4	3
2001—	Norwich (East.)	12	9	.571	3.52	28	28	1	0	0	166 1/3	174	83	65	60	138

GRAVES, DANNY | P | REDS

PERSONAL: Born August 7, 1973, in Saigon, Vietnam. ... 5-11/185. ... Throws right, bats right. ... Full name: Daniel Peter Graves.
HIGH SCHOOL: Brandon (Fla.).
COLLEGE: Miami (Fla.).
TRANSACTIONS/CAREER NOTES: Selected by Cleveland Indians organization in fourth round of free-agent draft (June 2, 1994). ... Traded by Indians with P Jim Crowell, P Scott Winchester and IF Damian Jackson to Cincinnati Reds for P John Smiley and IF Jeff Branson (July 31, 1997).

Year	League	W	L	Pct.	ERA	G	GS	CG	ShO	Sv.	IP	H	R	ER	BB	SO
1995—	Kinston (Caro.)..................	3	1	.750	0.82	38	0	0	0	21	44	30	11	4	12	46
—	Canton/Akron (East.)..........	1	0	1.000	0.00	17	0	0	0	10	23 1/3	10	1	0	2	11
—	Buffalo (A.A.)	0	0	...	3.00	3	0	0	0	0	3	5	4	1	1	2
1996—	Buffalo (A.A.)....................	4	3	.571	1.48	43	0	0	0	19	79	57	14	13	24	46
—	Cleveland (A.L.).................	2	0	1.000	4.55	15	0	0	0	0	29 2/3	29	18	15	10	22
1997—	Buffalo (A.A.)....................	2	3	.400	4.19	19	3	0	0	2	43	45	21	20	11	21
—	Cleveland (A.L.).................	0	0	...	4.76	5	0	0	0	0	11 1/3	15	8	6	9	4
—	Indianapolis (A.A.)■..........	1	0	1.000	3.09	11	0	0	0	5	11 2/3	7	4	4	5	5
—	Cincinnati (N.L.)	0	0	...	6.14	10	0	0	0	0	14 2/3	26	14	10	11	7
1998—	Indianapolis (I.L.)	1	0	1.000	1.93	13	0	0	0	0	14	15	3	3	3	11
—	Cincinnati (N.L.)	2	1	.667	3.32	62	0	0	0	8	81 1/3	76	31	30	28	44
1999—	Cincinnati (N.L.)...............	8	7	.533	3.08	75	0	0	0	27	111	90	42	38	49	69
2000—	Cincinnati (N.L.)...............	10	5	.667	2.56	66	0	0	0	30	91 1/3	81	31	26	42	53
2001—	Cincinnati (N.L.)...............	6	5	.545	4.15	66	0	0	0	32	80 1/3	83	41	37	18	49
A.L. totals (2 years)		2	0	1.000	4.61	20	0	0	0	0	41	44	26	21	19	26
N.L. totals (5 years)		26	18	.591	3.35	279	0	0	0	97	378 2/3	356	159	141	148	222
Major League totals (6 years).......		28	18	.609	3.47	299	0	0	0	97	419 2/3	400	185	162	167	248

ALL-STAR GAME RECORD

Year	League	W	L	Pct.	ERA	GS	CG	ShO	Sv.	IP	H	R	ER	BB	SO
2000—	National	0	0	...	0.00	0	0	0	0	1	1	0	0	0	1

GREBECK, CRAIG | IF |

PERSONAL: Born December 29, 1964, in Johnstown, Pa. ... 5-7/155. ... Bats right, throws right. ... Full name: Craig Allen Grebeck. ... Brother of Brian Grebeck, infielder with California Angels and Houston Astros organizations (1990-97). ... Name pronounced GRAY-bek.
HIGH SCHOOL: Lakewood (Calif.).
COLLEGE: Cal State Dominguez Hills.
TRANSACTIONS/CAREER NOTES: Signed as non-drafted free agent by Chicago White Sox organization (August 13, 1986). ... On disabled list (August 9, 1992-remainder of season). ... On Chicago disabled list (May 21-June 30, 1994); included rehabilitation assignment at Nashville (June 23-30). ... Granted free agency (December 21, 1995). ... Signed by Florida Marlins organization (December 22, 1995). ... On disabled list (July 4-August 13, 1996). ... Granted free agency (October 31, 1996). ... Signed by Anaheim Angels (December 6, 1996). ... Granted free agency (October 9, 1997). ... Signed by Toronto Blue Jays organization (November 27, 1997). ... On Toronto disabled list (April 20-May 5, 1998). ... Granted free agency (October 23, 1998). ... Re-signed by Blue Jays (October 27, 1998). ... On Toronto disabled list (April 11-May 14 and August 5, 1999-remainder of season); included rehabilitation assignment to Syracuse (May 10-14). ... Granted free agency (November 1, 2000). ... Signed by Boston Red Sox organization (January 19, 2001). ... On disabled list (May 2-18, 2001 and June 3, 2001-remainder of season). ... Released by Red Sox (October 9, 2001).
STATISTICAL NOTES: Led Southern League in grounding into double plays with 15 in 1989. ... Career major league grand slams: 1.

Year	Team (League)	Pos.	G	AB	R	H	2B	3B	HR	RBI	Avg.	BB	SO	SB	PO	A	E	Avg.
1987—	Peninsula (Caro.)	SS-3B	104	378	63	106	22	3	15	67	.280	37	62	3	137	278	16	.963
1988—	Birmingham (Sou.)......	2B	133	450	57	126	21	1	9	53	.280	65	72	5	238	368	19	.970
1989—	Birmingham (Sou.)......	SS-3B-2B	•143	•533	85	*153	25	4	5	80	.287	63	77	14	234	364	28	.955
1990—	Chicago (A.L.)	3B-SS-2B	59	119	7	20	3	1	1	9	.168	8	24	0	36	98	3	.978
—	Vancouver (PCL)	SS-3B-2B	12	41	8	8	0	0	1	3	.195	6	7	1	28	26	1	.982
1991—	Chicago (A.L.)	3B-2B-SS	107	224	37	63	16	3	6	31	.281	38	40	1	104	183	10	.966
1992—	Chicago (A.L.)	SS-3B-OF	88	287	24	77	21	2	3	35	.268	30	34	0	112	283	8	.980
1993—	Chicago (A.L.)	SS-2B-3B	72	190	25	43	5	0	1	12	.226	26	26	1	91	185	5	.982
1994—	Chicago (A.L.)	2B-SS-3B	35	97	17	30	5	0	0	5	.309	12	5	0	44	65	2	.982
—	Nashville (A.A.)	SS	5	15	3	6	2	0	0	4	.400	1	2	0	5	12	1	.944
1995—	Chicago (A.L.)	SS-3B-2B	53	154	19	40	12	0	1	18	.260	21	23	0	76	127	7	.967
1996—	Florida (N.L.)■.........	2B-SS-3B	50	95	8	20	1	0	1	9	.211	4	14	0	67	66	2	.985
1997—	Anaheim (A.L.)■......	2-S-3-O-DH	63	126	12	34	9	0	1	6	.270	18	11	0	68	88	2	.987
1998—	Toronto (A.L.)■........	2B-SS-3B	102	301	33	77	17	2	2	27	.256	29	42	2	151	269	11	.974
—	Syracuse (I.L.)..........	2B	1	3	0	1	0	0	0	0	.333	0	0	0	2	6	0	1.000
1999—	Toronto (A.L.)............	2B-DH-SS-3B	34	113	18	41	7	0	0	10	.363	15	13	0	42	45	5	.946
—	Syracuse (I.L.)...........	2B-SS	4	16	3	4	1	0	1	2	.250	1	1	0	9	10	2	.905

G

Year	Team (League)	Pos.	G	AB	R	H	2B	3B	HR	RBI	Avg.	BB	SO	SB	PO	A	E	Avg.
2000— Toronto (A.L.)	2B-SS	66	241	38	71	19	0	3	23	.295	25	33	0	110	193	9	.971
2001— Boston (A.L.)■	SS	23	41	1	2	1	0	0	2	.049	2	9	0	16	32	0	1.000
American League totals (11 years)		702	1893	231	498	115	8	18	178	.263	224	260	4	850	1568	62	.975
National League totals (1 year)		50	95	8	20	1	0	1	9	.211	4	14	0	67	66	2	.985
Major League totals (12 years)		752	1988	239	518	116	8	19	187	.261	228	274	4	917	1634	64	.976

CHAMPIONSHIP SERIES RECORD

Year	Team (League)	Pos.	G	AB	R	H	2B	3B	HR	RBI	Avg.	BB	SO	SB	PO	A	E	Avg.
1993— Chicago (A.L.)	PH-3B	1	1	0	1	0	0	0	0	1.000	0	0	0	0	0	0	...

GREEN, NICK 2B/SS BRAVES

PERSONAL: Born September 10, 1978, in Pensacola, Fla. ... 6-0/180. ... Bats right, throws right. ... Full name: Nicholas A. Green.
HIGH SCHOOL: Duluth (Ga.).
JUNIOR COLLEGE: DeKalb (Ga.).
TRANSACTIONS/CAREER NOTES: Selected by Atlanta Braves organization in 32nd round of free-agent draft (June 2, 1998). ... On Myrtle Beach disabled list (July 16, 2001-remainder of season).

Year	Team (League)	Pos.	G	AB	R	H	2B	3B	HR	RBI	Avg.	BB	SO	SB	PO	A	E	Avg.
1999— Jamestown (NY-P)	2B	73	273	52	81	15	0	11	41	.297	26	66	14	141	174	15	.955
— Macon (S.Atl.)	2B	3	10	1	2	0	0	1	3	.200	0	4	1	2	1	0	1.000
2000— Macon (S.Atl.)	SS-2B	91	339	47	83	19	4	11	43	.245	22	75	10	141	247	37	.913
— Myrtle Beach (Caro.)	SS-2B	27	91	13	22	6	0	1	6	.242	10	23	3	33	40	9	.890
2001— Myrtle Beach (Caro.)	2B-SS	80	297	49	79	18	1	10	42	.266	32	70	9	107	192	13	.958
— Richmond (I.L.)	2B	2	5	0	1	0	0	0	1	.200	0	3	0	4	1	1	.833

GREEN, SHAWN OF DODGERS

PERSONAL: Born November 10, 1972, in Des Plaines, Ill. ... 6-4/200. ... Bats left, throws left. ... Full name: Shawn David Green.
HIGH SCHOOL: Tustin (Calif.).
TRANSACTIONS/CAREER NOTES: Selected by Toronto Blue Jays organization in first round (16th pick overall) of free-agent draft (June 3, 1991); pick received as compensation for San Francisco Giants signing Type A free-agent P Bud Black. ... On disabled list (June 30-July 23, 1992). ... On Knoxville disabled list (June 11-July 24, 1993). ... Traded by Blue Jays with 2B Jorge Nunez to Los Angeles Dodgers for OF Raul Mondesi and P Pedro Borbon (November 8, 1999).
RECORDS: Shares major league single-season record for fewest double plays by outfielder (150 or more games)—0 (2001).
HONORS: Won A.L. Gold Glove as outfielder (1999). ... Named outfielder on THE SPORTING NEWS A.L. All-Star team (1999). ... Named outfielder on THE SPORTING NEWS A.L. Silver Slugger team (1999).
STATISTICAL NOTES: Tied for Florida State League lead with eight sacrifice flies in 1992. ... Had 28-game hitting streak (June 29-July 31, 1999). ... Led A.L. with 361 total bases in 1999. ... Hit three home runs in one game (August 15, 2001). ... Career major league grand slams: 5.

Year	Team (League)	Pos.	G	AB	R	H	2B	3B	HR	RBI	Avg.	BB	SO	SB	PO	A	E	Avg.
1992— Dunedin (FSL)	OF	114	417	44	114	21	3	1	49	.273	28	66	22	182	3	5	.974
1993— Knoxville (Sou.)	OF	99	360	40	102	14	2	4	34	.283	26	72	4	172	3	8	.956
— Toronto (A.L.)	OF-DH	3	6	0	0	0	0	0	0	.000	0	1	0	1	0	0	1.000
1994— Syracuse (I.L.)	OF-DH	109	433	82	149	27	3	13	61	*.344	40	54	19	220	5	1	*.996
— Toronto (A.L.)	OF	14	33	1	3	1	0	0	1	.091	1	8	1	12	2	0	1.000
1995— Toronto (A.L.)	OF	121	379	52	109	31	4	15	54	.288	20	68	1	207	9	6	.973
1996— Toronto (A.L.)	OF-DH	132	422	52	118	32	3	11	45	.280	33	75	5	254	10	2	.992
1997— Toronto (A.L.)	OF-DH	135	429	57	123	22	4	16	53	.287	36	99	14	173	6	3	.984
1998— Toronto (A.L.)	OF	158	630	106	175	33	4	35	100	.278	50	142	35	311	14	7	.979
1999— Toronto (A.L.)	OF	153	614	134	190	*45	0	42	123	.309	66	117	20	340	5	1	.997
2000— Los Angeles (N.L.)■	OF	•162	610	98	164	44	4	24	99	.269	90	121	24	280	9	6	.980
2001— Los Angeles (N.L.)	OF-1B	161	619	121	184	31	4	49	125	.297	72	107	20	317	6	6	.982
American League totals (7 years)		716	2513	402	718	164	15	119	376	.286	206	510	76	1298	46	19	.986
National League totals (2 years)		323	1229	219	348	75	8	73	224	.283	162	228	44	597	17	12	.981
Major League totals (9 years)		1039	3742	621	1066	239	23	192	600	.285	368	738	120	1895	63	31	.984

ALL-STAR GAME RECORD

Year	League	Pos.	AB	R	H	2B	3B	HR	RBI	Avg.	BB	SO	SB	PO	A	E	Avg.
1999— American	OF	1	0	1	0	0	0	0	1.000	0	0	0	0	0	0	...

GREEN, STEVE P ANGELS

PERSONAL: Born January 26, 1978, in Greenfield Park, Que. ... 6-2/195. ... Throws right, bats right.
HIGH SCHOOL: Polyvalente Edouard Montpetit (Montreal).
JUNIOR COLLEGE: Fort Scott (Kan.) Community College.
TRANSACTIONS/CAREER NOTES: Selected by Anaheim Angels organization in 10th round of free-agent draft (June 3, 1997). ... On Edmonton disabled list (July 16-28 and August 21-September 29, 2000). ... On Salt Lake disabled list (June 2, 2001-remainder of season).

Year	League	W	L	Pct.	ERA	G	GS	CG	ShO	Sv.	IP	H	R	ER	BB	SO
1998— Cedar Rapids (Midw.)	2	6	.250	4.54	18	10	1	0	0	83 1/3	86	49	42	25	61
1999— Lake Elsinore (Calif.)	7	6	.538	3.95	19	19	4	*4	0	120 2/3	130	70	53	37	91
— Erie (East.)	3	1	.750	3.32	6	6	1	0	0	40 2/3	34	25	15	19	32
2000— Erie (East.)	7	4	.636	3.40	13	13	0	0	0	79 1/3	71	34	30	34	66
— Edmonton (PCL)	0	4	.000	7.29	8	8	0	0	0	42	55	35	34	27	24
2001— Anaheim (A.L.)	0	0	...	3.00	1	1	0	0	0	6	4	2	2	6	4
— Salt Lake (PCL)	6	2	.750	3.66	10	10	1	0	0	59	59	30	24	13	40
Major League totals (1 year)	0	0	...	3.00	1	1	0	0	0	6	4	2	2	6	4

G

PERSONAL: Born May 8, 1971, in Augusta, Ga. ... 5-10/208. ... Bats right, throws right. ... Full name: Todd Anthony Greene.
HIGH SCHOOL: Evans (Ga.).
COLLEGE: Georgia Southern.
TRANSACTIONS/CAREER NOTES: Selected by Atlanta Braves organization in 27th round of free-agent draft (June 5, 1989); did not sign. ... Selected by California Angels organization in 12th round of free-agent draft (June 3, 1993). ... On Vancouver disabled list (April 11-May 25, 1996). ... Angels franchise renamed Anaheim Angels for 1997 season. ... On Anaheim disabled list (August 20, 1997-remainder of season). ... On Anaheim disabled list (March 19-August 5, 1998); included rehabilitation assignments to Lake Elsinore (April 14-May 16, May 21 and May 27-31) and Vancouver (May 17-20, May 22-26, June 1-2 and July 17-August 5). ... On suspended list (May 13-16, 1999). ... Released by Angels (March 29, 2000). ... Signed by Toronto Blue Jays organization (April 10, 2000). ... On Toronto disabled list (June 7-23, 2000); included rehabilitation assignment to Dunedin (June 20-22). ... Released by Blue Jays (March 28, 2001). ... Signed by New York Yankees organization (April 5, 2001).
HONORS: Named California League Most Valuable Player (1994).
STATISTICAL NOTES: Led California League with 306 total bases, 12 intentional bases on balls received and .584 slugging percentage in 1994. ... Led California League catchers with 15 errors, 13 double plays and 44 passed balls in 1994. ... Career major league grand slams: 1.

									BATTING							FIELDING			
Year	Team (League)	Pos.	G	AB	R	H	2B	3B	HR	RBI	Avg.	BB	SO	SB	PO	A	E	Avg.	
1993—Boise (N'West)		OF	•76	*305	55	82	15	3	*15	*71	.269	34	44	4	136	4	3	.979	
1994—Lake Elsinore (Calif.)		C-OF-1B	133	524	98	158	*39	2	*35	*124	.302	64	96	10	624	90	†15	.979	
1995—Midland (Texas)		C-DH-1B	82	318	59	104	19	1	26	57	.327	17	55	3	314	44	3	.992	
—Vancouver (PCL)		C-DH	43	168	28	42	3	1	14	35	.250	11	36	1	175	17	1	.995	
1996—Vancouver (PCL)		C-DH	60	223	27	68	18	0	5	33	.305	16	36	0	219	37	3	.988	
—California (A.L.)		C-DH	29	79	9	15	1	0	2	9	.190	4	11	2	119	19	0	1.000	
1997—Anaheim (A.L.)		C-DH	34	124	24	36	6	0	9	24	.290	7	25	2	153	7	0	1.000	
—Vancouver (PCL)		C-DH-1B-OF	64	260	51	92	22	0	25	75	.354	20	31	5	331	43	3	.992	
1998—Lake Elsinore (Calif.)		DH-1B	12	44	9	10	2	0	1	6	.227	4	7	1	9	1	2	.833	
—Vancouver (PCL)		DH-1B-C-OF	30	108	16	30	12	0	7	20	.278	12	17	1	97	7	1	.990	
—Anaheim (A.L.)		OF-DH-1B	29	71	3	18	4	0	1	7	.254	2	20	0	28	1	0	1.000	
1999—Anaheim (A.L.)		DH-OF-C	97	321	36	78	20	0	14	42	.243	12	63	1	91	8	2	.980	
—Edmonton (PCL)		OF-DH	19	74	10	18	6	0	5	14	.243	0	12	0	23	0	0	1.000	
2000—Syracuse (I.L.)■		OF-C	24	91	14	27	3	0	7	14	.297	6	16	1	31	1	1	.970	
—Toronto (A.L.)		DH-C-OF	34	85	11	20	2	0	5	10	.235	5	18	0	2	0	0	1.000	
—Dunedin (FSL)		OF	5	20	2	4	1	0	1	4	.200	2	4	0	4	0	0	1.000	
2001—Columbus (I.L.)■		C-DH	34	131	16	33	8	0	6	17	.252	4	19	3	204	15	4	.982	
—New York (A.L.)		C-DH	35	96	9	20	4	0	1	11	.208	3	21	0	187	14	0	1.000	
Major League totals (6 years)			258	776	92	187	37	0	32	103	.241	33	158	5	580	49	2	.997	

DIVISION SERIES RECORD

									BATTING							FIELDING			
Year	Team (League)	Pos.	G	AB	R	H	2B	3B	HR	RBI	Avg.	BB	SO	SB	PO	A	E	Avg.	
2001—New York (A.L.)									Did not play.										

CHAMPIONSHIP SERIES RECORD

									BATTING							FIELDING			
Year	Team (League)	Pos.	G	AB	R	H	2B	3B	HR	RBI	Avg.	BB	SO	SB	PO	A	E	Avg.	
2001—New York (A.L.)		C	1	1	0	0	0	0	0	0	.000	0	0	0	1	0	0	1.000	

WORLD SERIES RECORD

									BATTING							FIELDING			
Year	Team (League)	Pos.	G	AB	R	H	2B	3B	HR	RBI	Avg.	BB	SO	SB	PO	A	E	Avg.	
2001—New York (A.L.)		C	2	2	1	1	1	0	0	0	.500	0	0	0	4	0	0	1.000	

GREER, RUSTY   OF   RANGERS

PERSONAL: Born January 21, 1969, in Fort Rucker, Ala. ... 6-0/195. ... Bats left, throws left. ... Full name: Thurman Clyde Greer III.
HIGH SCHOOL: Albertville (Ala.).
COLLEGE: Montevallo (Ala.).
TRANSACTIONS/CAREER NOTES: Selected by Texas Rangers organization in 10th round of free-agent draft (June 4, 1990). ... On disabled list (July 31-August 22, 1992). ... On Texas disabled list (April 15-May 27, 2000); included rehabilitation assignment to Tulsa (May 15-27). ... On Texas disabled list (June 12, 2001-remainder of season); included rehabilitation assignment to Tulsa (July 18-23).
RECORDS: Shares major league record for fewest double plays by outfielder (150 or more games)—0 (1997 and 1998).
STATISTICAL NOTES: Led Florida State League with .395 on-base percentage in 1991. ... Career major league grand slams: 6.

									BATTING							FIELDING			
Year	Team (League)	Pos.	G	AB	R	H	2B	3B	HR	RBI	Avg.	BB	SO	SB	PO	A	E	Avg.	
1990—Butte (Pio.)		OF	62	226	48	78	12	6	10	50	.345	41	23	9	84	5	*8	.918	
1991—Charlotte (FSL)		OF-1B	111	388	52	114	25	1	5	48	.294	66	48	12	213	15	7	.970	
—Tulsa (Texas)		OF	20	64	12	19	3	2	3	12	.297	17	6	2	34	0	0	1.000	
1992—Tulsa (Texas)		1B-OF	106	359	47	96	22	4	5	37	.267	60	63	2	814	50	11	.987	
1993—Tulsa (Texas)		1B	129	474	76	138	25	6	15	59	.291	53	79	10	1055	93	8	.993	
—Oklahoma City (A.A.)		1B	8	27	6	6	2	0	1	4	.222	6	7	0	16	0	0	1.000	
1994—Oklahoma City (A.A.)		OF-DH-1B	31	111	18	35	12	1	3	13	.315	18	24	1	52	3	3	.948	
—Texas (A.L.)		OF-1B	80	277	36	87	16	1	10	46	.314	46	46	0	216	4	6	.973	
1995—Texas (A.L.)		OF-1B	131	417	58	113	21	2	13	61	.271	55	66	3	240	6	6	.976	
1996—Texas (A.L.)		OF-DH-1B	139	542	96	180	41	6	18	100	.332	62	86	9	304	6	5	.984	
1997—Texas (A.L.)		OF-DH	157	601	112	193	42	3	26	87	.321	83	87	9	318	9	*12	.965	
1998—Texas (A.L.)		OF	155	598	107	183	31	5	16	108	.306	80	93	2	304	6	3	.990	
1999—Texas (A.L.)		OF-DH	147	556	107	167	41	3	20	101	.300	96	67	2	286	3	5	.983	
2000—Texas (A.L.)		OF-DH	105	394	65	117	34	3	8	65	.297	51	61	4	194	3	3	.985	
—Tulsa (Texas)		OF	2	7	0	1	0	0	0	1	.143	1	3	0	2	1	0	1.000	
2001—Texas (A.L.)		OF-DH	62	245	38	67	23	0	7	29	.273	27	32	1	124	2	5	.962	
—Tulsa (Texas)		DH	1	3	1	0	0	0	0	0	.000	1	1	0	...	...	...	...	
Major League totals (8 years)			976	3630	619	1107	249	23	118	597	.305	500	538	30	1986	42	45	.978	

DIVISION SERIES RECORD

					BATTING										FIELDING		
Year	Team (League)	Pos.	G	AB	R	H	2B	3B	HR	RBI	Avg.	BB	SO	SB	PO	A	E	Avg.
1996—Texas (A.L.)................		OF	4	16	2	2	0	0	0	0	.125	3	3	0	12	0	0	1.000
1998—Texas (A.L.)................		OF	3	11	0	1	0	0	0	0	.091	1	2	0	4	1	0	1.000
1999—Texas (A.L.)................		OF	3	9	0	1	0	0	0	0	.111	3	1	0	9	0	0	1.000
Division series totals (3 years)			10	36	2	4	0	0	0	0	.111	7	6	0	25	1	0	1.000

GRIEVE, BEN — OF — DEVIL RAYS

PERSONAL: Born May 4, 1976, in Arlington, Texas. ... 6-4/230. ... Bats left, throws right. ... Full name: Benjamin Grieve. ... Son of Tom Grieve, outfielder with four major league teams (1970-79); first father/son combination to be selected in first round of free-agent draft.

HIGH SCHOOL: James W. Martin (Arlington, Texas).

TRANSACTIONS/CAREER NOTES: Selected by Oakland Athletics organization in first round (second pick overall) of free-agent draft (June 2, 1994). ... Traded by A's with a player to be named later or cash to Tampa Bay Devil Rays as part of three-way deal in which Kansas City Royals received P Roberto Hernandez from Devil Rays, A's received P Cory Lidle from Devil Rays, A's received OF Johnny Damon, IF Mark Ellis and a player to be named later from Royals and Royals received C A.J. Hinch, IF Angel Berroa and cash from A's (January 8, 2001).

RECORDS: Shares major league record for fewest double plays by outfielder (150 or more games)—0 (1998).

HONORS: Named Minor League Player of the Year by THE SPORTING NEWS (1997). ... Named Southern League Most Valuable Player (1997). ... Named A.L. Rookie Player of the Year by THE SPORTING NEWS (1998). ... Named A.L. Rookie of the Year by Baseball Writers' Association of America (1998).

STATISTICAL NOTES: Tied for Northwest League lead with seven intentional bases on balls received in 1994. ... Led Southern League with .455 on-base percentage in 1997. ... Led A.L. in grounding into double plays with 32 in 2000. ... Career major league grand slams: 5.

					BATTING										FIELDING		
Year	Team (League)	Pos.	G	AB	R	H	2B	3B	HR	RBI	Avg.	BB	SO	SB	PO	A	E	Avg.
1994—S. Oregon (N'West)....		OF	72	252	44	83	13	0	7	50	.329	51	48	2	133	8	6	.959
1995—W. Michigan (Midw.)..		OF	102	371	53	97	16	1	4	62	.261	60	75	11	125	6	8	.942
—Modesto (Calif.)		OF	28	107	17	28	5	0	2	14	.262	14	15	2	37	2	2	.951
1996—Modesto (Calif.)		OF-DH	72	281	61	100	20	1	11	51	.356	38	52	8	104	5	5	.956
—Huntsville (Sou.)		OF-DH	63	232	34	55	8	1	8	32	.237	35	53	0	79	2	4	.953
1997—Huntsville (Sou.)		OF-DH	100	372	100	122	29	2	24	108	.328	81	75	5	193	6	•8	.961
—Edmonton (PCL)		OF	27	108	27	46	11	1	7	28	.426	12	16	0	51	2	2	.964
—Oakland (A.L.)		OF	24	93	12	29	6	0	3	24	.312	13	25	0	39	1	0	1.000
1998—Oakland (A.L.)		OF-DH	155	583	94	168	41	2	18	89	.288	85	123	2	262	7	2	.993
1999—Oakland (A.L.)		OF-DH	148	486	80	129	21	0	28	86	.265	63	108	4	232	6	3	.988
2000—Oakland (A.L.)		OF-DH	158	594	92	166	40	1	27	104	.279	73	130	3	237	6	3	.988
2001—Tampa Bay (A.L.)■.....		OF-DH	154	542	72	143	30	2	11	72	.264	87	159	7	240	4	4	.984
Major League totals (5 years)			639	2298	350	635	138	5	87	375	.276	321	545	16	1010	24	12	.989

DIVISION SERIES RECORD

					BATTING										FIELDING		
Year	Team (League)	Pos.	G	AB	R	H	2B	3B	HR	RBI	Avg.	BB	SO	SB	PO	A	E	Avg.
2000—Oakland (A.L.)		OF	5	17	1	2	0	0	2	.118	3	7	0	7	0	0	1.000

ALL-STAR GAME RECORD

				BATTING								FIELDING		
Year	League	Pos.	AB	R	H	2B	3B	HR	RBI	Avg.	BB	SO	SB	PO	A	E	Avg.
1998—American		PH	0	0	0	0	0	0	0	...	1	0	0	...	...	...	...

GRIFFEY, KEN — OF — REDS

PERSONAL: Born November 21, 1969, in Donora, Pa. ... 6-3/205. ... Bats left, throws left. ... Full name: George Kenneth Griffey Jr. ... Son of Ken Griffey Sr., coach, Cincinnati Reds, and major league outfielder with four teams (1973-91); and brother of Craig Griffey, outfielder in Seattle Mariners and Cincinnati Reds organizations (1991-97).

HIGH SCHOOL: Moeller (Cincinnati).

TRANSACTIONS/CAREER NOTES: Selected by Seattle Mariners organization in first round (first pick overall) of free-agent draft (June 2, 1987). ... On San Bernardino disabled list (June 9-August 15, 1988). ... On disabled list (July 24-August 20, 1989; June 9-25, 1992; and June 20-July 13, 1996). ... On Seattle disabled list (May 27-August 15, 1995); included rehabilitation assignment to Tacoma (August 13-15). ... Traded by Mariners to Cincinnati Reds for P Brett Tomko, OF Mike Cameron, IF Antonio Perez and P Jake Meyer (February 10, 2000). ... On disabled list (April 29-June 15, 2001).

RECORDS: Shares major league record for most consecutive games with one or more home runs—8 (July 20 through July 28, 1993). ... Holds A.L. single-season record for most major league ballparks, one or more home runs—16 (1998). ... Shares A.L. career record for most major league ballparks, one or more home runs (since 1900)—24. ... Shares major league single-month record for most home runs—13 (April 1997).

HONORS: Won A.L. Gold Glove as outfielder (1990-99). ... Named outfielder on THE SPORTING NEWS A.L. All-Star team (1991, 1993-94 and 1996-99). ... Named outfielder on THE SPORTING NEWS A.L. Silver Slugger team (1991, 1993-94 and 1996-99). ... Named Major League Player of the Year by THE SPORTING NEWS (1997). ... Named A.L. Most Valuable Player by Baseball Writers' Association of America (1997).

STATISTICAL NOTES: Led A.L. outfielders with six double plays in 1989. ... Led A.L. with 359 total bases in 1993 and 393 in 1997. ... Hit three home runs in one game (May 24, 1996 and April 25, 1997). ... Led A.L. with 23 intentional bases on balls received in 1997. ... Led A.L. in slugging percentage with .646 in 1997. ... Led A.L. outfielders with 409 putouts and 425 total chances in 1998. ... Had 16-game hitting streak (May 10-28, 1999). ... Tied for A.L. lead with 17 intentional bases on balls received in 1999. ... Career major league grand slams: 14.

MISCELLANEOUS: Holds Seattle Mariners franchise all-time record for most runs (1,063), home runs (398) and runs batted in (1,152).

					BATTING										FIELDING		
Year	Team (League)	Pos.	G	AB	R	H	2B	3B	HR	RBI	Avg.	BB	SO	SB	PO	A	E	Avg.
1987—Bellingham (N'West) ..		OF	54	182	43	57	9	1	14	40	.313	44	42	13	117	4	1	*.992
1988—San Bern. (Calif.)........		OF	58	219	50	74	13	3	11	42	.338	34	39	32	145	3	2	.987
—Vermont (East.)..........		OF	17	61	10	17	5	1	2	10	.279	5	12	4	40	2	1	.977
1989—Seattle (A.L.)		OF-DH	127	455	61	120	23	0	16	61	.264	44	83	16	302	12	•10	.969

G

Year Team (League)	Pos.	G	AB	R	H	2B	3B	HR	RBI	Avg.	BB	SO	SB	PO	A	E	Avg.
						BATTING									FIELDING		
1990—Seattle (A.L.)	OF	155	597	91	179	28	7	22	80	.300	63	81	16	330	8	7	.980
1991—Seattle (A.L.)	OF-DH	154	548	76	179	42	1	22	100	.327	71	82	18	360	15	4	.989
1992—Seattle (A.L.)	OF-DH	142	565	83	174	39	4	27	103	.308	44	67	10	359	8	1	.997
1993—Seattle (A.L.)	OF-DH-1B	156	582	113	180	38	3	45	109	.309	96	91	17	317	8	3	.991
1994—Seattle (A.L.)	OF-DH	111	433	94	140	24	4	*40	90	.323	56	73	11	225	12	4	.983
1995—Seattle (A.L.)	OF-DH	72	260	52	67	7	0	17	42	.258	52	53	4	190	5	2	.990
—Tacoma (PCL)	DH	1	3	0	0	0	0	0	0	.000	0	1	0	...	...	...	...
1996—Seattle (A.L.)	OF-DH	140	545	125	165	26	2	49	140	.303	78	104	16	375	10	4	.990
1997—Seattle (A.L.)	OF-DH	157	608	*125	185	34	3	*56	*147	.304	76	121	15	388	9	6	.985
1998—Seattle (A.L.)	OF-DH-1B	161	633	120	180	33	3	*56	146	.284	76	121	20	†409	11	5	.988
1999—Seattle (A.L.)	OF-DH	160	606	123	173	26	3	*48	134	.285	91	108	24	387	10	9	.978
2000—Cincinnati (N.L.)■	OF	145	520	100	141	22	3	40	118	.271	94	117	6	375	9	5	.987
2001—Cincinnati (N.L.)	OF-DH	111	364	57	104	20	2	22	65	.286	44	72	2	195	1	3	.985
American League totals (11 years)		1535	5832	1063	1742	320	30	398	1152	.299	747	984	167	3642	108	55	.986
National League totals (2 years)		256	884	157	245	42	5	62	183	.277	138	189	8	570	10	8	.986
Major League totals (13 years)		1791	6716	1220	1987	362	35	460	1335	.296	885	1173	175	4212	118	63	.986

DIVISION SERIES RECORD

RECORDS: Holds single-series record for most runs scored—9 (1995). ... Shares single-game record for most home runs—2 (October 3, 1995). ... Shares single-series record for most home runs—5 (1996).

NOTES: Shares postseason single-series record for most home runs—5 (1995).

Year Team (League)	Pos.	G	AB	R	H	2B	3B	HR	RBI	Avg.	BB	SO	SB	PO	A	E	Avg.
						BATTING									FIELDING		
1995—Seattle (A.L.)	OF	5	23	9	9	0	0	5	7	.391	2	4	1	15	1	0	1.000
1997—Seattle (A.L.)	OF	4	15	0	2	0	0	0	2	.133	1	3	2	12	1	0	1.000
Division series totals (2 years)		9	38	9	11	0	0	5	9	.289	3	7	3	27	2	0	1.000

CHAMPIONSHIP SERIES RECORD

Year Team (League)	Pos.	G	AB	R	H	2B	3B	HR	RBI	Avg.	BB	SO	SB	PO	A	E	Avg.
						BATTING									FIELDING		
1995—Seattle (A.L.)	OF	6	21	2	7	2	0	1	2	.333	4	4	2	13	0	1	.929

ALL-STAR GAME RECORD

NOTES: Named Most Valuable Player (1992).

Year League	Pos.	AB	R	H	2B	3B	HR	RBI	Avg.	BB	SO	SB	PO	A	E	Avg.
					BATTING									FIELDING		
1990—American	OF	2	0	0	0	0	0	0	.000	1	0	0	2	0	0	1.000
1991—American	OF	3	0	2	0	0	0	0	.667	0	0	0	2	0	0	1.000
1992—American	OF	3	2	3	1	0	1	2	1.000	0	0	0	1	0	0	1.000
1993—American	OF	3	1	1	0	0	0	1	.333	0	1	0	2	0	0	1.000
1994—American	OF	3	0	2	1	0	0	1	.667	0	0	0	2	0	0	1.000
1995—American							Selected, did not play—injured.									
1996—American							Selected, did not play—injured.									
1997—American	OF	4	0	0	0	0	0	0	.000	0	2	0	0	0		...
1998—American	OF	3	1	2	0	0	0	1	.667	1	0	1	0	0	1	.000
1999—American	OF	2	0	0	0	0	0	0	.000	0	1	0	0	0	0	...
2000—National							Selected, did not play—injured.									
All-Star Game totals (8 years)		23	4	10	2	0	1	5	.435	2	4	1	9	0	1	.900

GRILLI, JASON   P   MARLINS

PERSONAL: Born November 11, 1976, in Royal Oak, Mich. ... 6-4/185. ... Throws right, bats right. ... Full name: Jason Michael Grilli. ... Son of Steve Grilli, pitcher with Detroit Tigers (1975-77) and Toronto Blue Jays (1979).

HIGH SCHOOL: C.W. Baker (Baldwinsville, N.Y.).

COLLEGE: Seton Hall.

TRANSACTIONS/CAREER NOTES: Selected by San Francisco Giants organization in first round (fourth pick overall) of free-agent draft (June 3, 1997). ... Traded by Giants with P Nathan Bump to Florida Marlins for P Livan Hernandez (July 24, 1999). ... On Calgary disabled list (May 23-September 5, 2000). ... On Calgary disabled list (May 17-July 18, 2001).

Year League	W	L	Pct.	ERA	G	GS	CG	ShO	Sv.	IP	H	R	ER	BB	SO
1998—Shreveport (Texas)	7	10	.412	3.79	21	21	3	0	0	123 1/3	113	60	52	37	100
—Fresno (PCL)	2	3	.400	5.14	8	8	0	0	0	42	49	30	24	18	37
1999—Fresno (PCL)	7	5	.583	5.54	19	19	1	0	0	100 2/3	124	69	62	39	76
—Calgary (PCL)■	1	5	.167	7.68	8	8	0	0	0	41	56	48	35	23	27
2000—Calgary (PCL)	1	4	.200	7.19	8	8	0	0	0	41 1/3	58	37	33	23	21
—Florida (N.L.)	1	0	1.000	5.40	1	1	0	0	0	6 2/3	11	4	4	2	3
2001—Florida (N.L.)	2	2	.500	6.07	6	5	0	0	0	26 2/3	30	18	18	11	17
—Calgary (PCL)	1	2	.333	4.02	8	8	0	0	0	47	46	26	21	20	35
—Gulf Coast Marlins (GCL)	0	0	...	0.00	2	2	0	0	0	4	2	0	0	0	6
—Brevard County (FSL)	2	0	1.000	1.98	3	3	0	0	0	13 2/3	12	4	3	5	14
—Portland (East.)	0	1	.000	2.25	1	1	0	0	0	4	3	1	1	0	3
Major League totals (2 years)	3	2	.600	5.94	7	6	0	0	0	33 1/3	41	22	22	13	20

GRIMSLEY, JASON   P   ROYALS

PERSONAL: Born August 7, 1967, in Cleveland, Texas. ... 6-3/205. ... Throws right, bats right. ... Full name: Jason Alan Grimsley.

HIGH SCHOOL: Tarkington (Cleveland, Texas).

TRANSACTIONS/CAREER NOTES: Selected by Philadelphia Phillies organization in 10th round of free-agent draft (June 3, 1985). ... On Clearwater disabled list (April 8-May 10, 1988). ... On Philadelphia disabled list (June 6-August 22, 1991); included rehabilitation assignments to Scranton/Wilkes-Barre (June 15-30 and August 7-21). ... Traded by Phillies to Houston Astros for P Curt Schilling (April 2, 1992). ... On disabled list (May 14-June 14, 1992). ... Released by Astros (March 30, 1993). ... Signed by Cleveland Indians organization (April 7, 1993). ... On Charlotte disabled list (April 15-26, 1993). ... Traded by Indians with P Pep Harris to California Angels for P Brian Anderson (February 15, 1996). ... Granted free agency (October 8, 1996). ... Signed by Detroit Tigers organization (January 17, 1997). ... Released by Tigers (March 20, 1997). ... Signed by Milwaukee Brewers (April 3, 1997). ... Traded by Brewers to Kansas City Royals for P Jamie Brewington (July 29, 1997). ... Granted free agency (October 15, 1997). ... Signed by Indians organization (January 8, 1998). ... Granted free agency (October 15, 1998). ... Signed by New York Yankees organization (January 26, 1999). ... On suspended list (August 11-15, 1999). ... Released by Yankees (November 20, 2000). ... Signed by Royals (January 19, 2001).

STATISTICAL NOTES: Led New York-Pennsylvania League with 11 hit batsmen and 18 wild pitches in 1986. ... Pitched 3-0 no-hit victory for Reading against Harrisburg (May 3, 1989, first game). ... Led International League with 18 wild pitches in 1990. ... Tied for A.L. lead with 13 hit batsmen in 1996. ... Led Pacific Coast League with 20 wild pitches in 1997.

MISCELLANEOUS: Appeared in one game as pinch runner with Philadelphia (1990).

Year League	W	L	Pct.	ERA	G	GS	CG	ShO	Sv.	IP	H	R	ER	BB	SO
1985— Bend (N'West)	0	1	.000	13.50	6	1	0	0	0	11 1/3	12	21	17	25	10
1986— Utica (NY-Penn)	1	•10	.091	6.40	14	14	3	0	0	64 2/3	63	61	46	*77	46
1987— Spartanburg (S.Atl.)	7	4	.636	3.16	23	9	3	0	0	88 1/3	59	48	31	54	98
1988— Clearwater (FSL)	4	7	.364	3.73	16	15	2	0	0	101 1/3	80	48	42	37	90
— Reading (East.)	1	3	.250	7.17	5	4	0	0	0	21 1/3	20	19	17	13	14
1989— Reading (East.)	11	8	.579	2.98	26	26	8	2	0	172	121	65	57	*109	134
— Philadelphia (N.L.)	1	3	.250	5.89	4	4	0	0	0	18 1/3	19	13	12	19	7
1990— Scranton/W.B. (I.L.)	8	5	.615	3.93	22	22	0	0	0	128 1/3	111	68	56	78	99
— Philadelphia (N.L.)	3	2	.600	3.30	11	11	0	0	0	57 1/3	47	21	21	43	41
1991— Philadelphia (N.L.)	1	7	.125	4.87	12	12	0	0	0	61	54	34	33	41	42
— Scranton/W.B. (I.L.)	2	3	.400	4.35	9	9	0	0	0	51 2/3	48	28	25	37	43
1992— Tucson (PCL)■	8	7	.533	5.05	26	20	0	0	0	124 2/3	152	79	70	55	90
1993— Charlotte (I.L.)■■	6	6	.500	3.39	28	19	3	1	0	135 1/3	138	64	51	49	102
— Cleveland (A.L.)	3	4	.429	5.31	10	6	0	0	0	42 1/3	52	26	25	20	27
1994— Charlotte (I.L.)	7	0	1.000	3.42	10	10	2	0	0	71	58	36	27	17	60
— Cleveland (A.L.)	5	2	.714	4.57	14	13	1	0	0	82 2/3	91	47	42	34	59
1995— Cleveland (A.L.)	0	0	...	6.09	15	2	0	0	1	34	37	24	23	32	25
— Buffalo (A.A.)	5	3	.625	2.91	10	10	2	0	0	68	61	26	22	19	40
1996— Vancouver (PCL)■	2	0	1.000	1.20	2	2	1	0	0	15	8	2	2	3	11
— California (A.L.)	5	7	.417	6.84	35	20	2	1	0	130 1/3	150	110	99	74	82
1997— Tucson (PCL)■	5	10	.333	5.70	36	10	0	0	4	85 1/3	96	70	54	43	65
— Omaha (A.A.)■	1	5	.167	6.68	7	6	0	0	0	31	36	26	23	29	22
1998— Buffalo (I.L.)■	6	3	.667	3.76	52	0	0	0	0	88 2/3	76	40	37	57	68
1999— New York (A.L.)	7	2	.778	3.60	55	0	0	0	1	75	66	39	30	40	49
2000— New York (A.L.)	3	2	.600	5.04	63	4	0	0	1	96 1/3	100	58	54	42	53
2001— Kansas City (A.L.)■	1	5	.167	3.02	73	0	0	0	0	80 1/3	71	32	27	28	61
A.L. totals (7 years)	24	22	.522	4.99	265	45	3	1	3	541	567	336	300	270	356
N.L. totals (3 years)	5	12	.294	4.35	27	27	0	0	0	136 2/3	120	68	66	103	90
Major League totals (10 years)	29	34	.460	4.86	292	72	3	1	3	677 2/3	687	404	366	373	446

DIVISION SERIES RECORD

Year League	W	L	Pct.	ERA	G	GS	CG	ShO	Sv.	IP	H	R	ER	BB	SO
1999— New York (A.L.)						Did not play.									
2000— New York (A.L.)						Did not play.									

CHAMPIONSHIP SERIES RECORD

Year League	W	L	Pct.	ERA	G	GS	CG	ShO	Sv.	IP	H	R	ER	BB	SO
1999— New York (A.L.)						Did not play.									
2000— New York (A.L.)	0	0	...	0.00	2	0	0	0	0	1	2	0	0	3	1

WORLD SERIES RECORD

NOTES: Member of World Series championship team (1999 and 2000).

Year League	W	L	Pct.	ERA	G	GS	CG	ShO	Sv.	IP	H	R	ER	BB	SO
1999— New York (A.L.)	0	0	...	0.00	1	0	0	0	0	2 1/3	2	0	0	2	0
2000— New York (A.L.)						Did not play.									

GRISSOM, MARQUIS   OF   DODGERS

G

PERSONAL: Born April 17, 1967, in Atlanta. ... 5-11/190. ... Bats right, throws right. ... Full name: Marquis Deon Grissom. ... Brother of Antonio Grissom, outfielder in Philadelphia Phillies (1990-91) and Montreal Expos organizations (1992-94). ... Name pronounced mar-KEESE.

HIGH SCHOOL: Lakeshore (College Park, Ga.).

COLLEGE: Florida A&M.

TRANSACTIONS/CAREER NOTES: Selected by Montreal Expos organization in third round of free-agent draft (June 1, 1988). ... On Montreal disabled list (May 29-June 30, 1990); included rehabilitation assignment to Indianapolis (June 25-30). ... Traded by Expos to Atlanta Braves for OF Roberto Kelly, OF Tony Tarasco and P Esteban Yan (April 6, 1995). ... Traded by Braves with OF Dave Justice to Cleveland Indians for OF Kenny Lofton and P Alan Embree (March 25, 1997). ... On disabled list (April 22-May 5, 1997). ... Traded by Indians with P Jeff Juden to Milwaukee Brewers for P Ben McDonald, P Mike Fetters and P Ron Villone (December 8, 1997). ... Traded by Brewers with a player to be named later to Los Angeles Dodgers for OF Devon White (February 25, 2001); Dodgers acquired P Rudy Lugo to complete deal (June 1, 2001). ... On suspended list (July 18-24, 2001).

HONORS: Won N.L. Gold Glove as outfielder (1993-96).

STATISTICAL NOTES: Led New York-Pennsylvania League with 146 total bases in 1988. ... Led N.L. outfielders with 333 total chances in 1994. ... Had 28-game hitting streak (July 25-August 24, 1996). ... Career major league grand slams: 3.

						BATTING								FIELDING		
Year Team (League)	Pos.	G	AB	R	H	2B	3B	HR	RBI	Avg.	BB	SO	SB	PO	A	E	Avg.
1988— Jamestown (NY-P)	OF	74	*291	*69	94	14	7	8	39	.323	35	39	23	123	•11	3	.978
1989— Jacksonville (Sou.)	OF	78	278	43	83	15	4	3	31	.299	24	31	24	141	7	3	.980
— Indianapolis (A.A.)	OF	49	187	28	52	10	4	2	21	.278	14	23	16	106	5	0	1.000
— Montreal (N.L.)	OF	26	74	16	19	2	0	1	2	.257	12	21	1	32	1	2	.943
1990— Montreal (N.L.)	OF	98	288	42	74	14	2	3	29	.257	27	40	22	165	5	2	.988
— Indianapolis (A.A.)	OF	5	22	3	4	0	0	2	3	.182	0	5	1	16	0	0	1.000

Year—Team (League)	Pos.	G	AB	R	H	2B	3B	HR	RBI	Avg.	BB	SO	SB	PO	A	E	Avg.
1991—Montreal (N.L.)..........	OF	148	558	73	149	23	9	6	39	.267	34	89	*76	350	•15	6	.984
1992—Montreal (N.L.)..........	OF	159	*653	99	180	39	6	14	66	.276	42	81	*78	401	7	7	.983
1993—Montreal (N.L.)..........	OF	157	630	104	188	27	2	19	95	.298	52	76	53	416	8	7	.984
1994—Montreal (N.L.)..........	OF	110	475	96	137	25	4	11	45	.288	41	66	36	*321	7	5	.985
1995—Atlanta (N.L.)■.........	OF	139	551	80	142	23	3	12	42	.258	47	61	29	309	9	2	.994
1996—Atlanta (N.L.)..........	OF	158	671	106	207	32	10	23	74	.308	41	73	28	338	10	1	.997
1997—Cleveland (A.L.)■.......	OF	144	558	74	146	27	6	12	66	.262	43	89	22	356	7	3	.992
1998—Milwaukee (N.L.)■.....	OF	142	542	57	147	28	1	10	60	.271	24	78	13	317	8	3	.991
1999—Milwaukee (N.L.).......	OF	154	603	92	161	27	1	20	83	.267	49	109	24	374	1	5	.987
2000—Milwaukee (N.L.).......	OF	146	595	67	145	18	2	14	62	.244	39	99	20	352	3	3	.992
2001—Los Angeles (N.L.)■..	OF-DH	135	448	56	99	17	1	21	60	.221	16	107	7	227	6	0	1.000
American League totals (1 year)		144	558	74	146	27	6	12	66	.262	43	89	22	356	7	3	.992
National League totals (12 years)		1572	6088	888	1648	275	41	154	657	.271	424	900	387	3602	80	43	.988
Major League totals (13 years)		1716	6646	962	1794	302	47	166	723	.270	467	989	409	3958	87	46	.989

DIVISION SERIES RECORD

RECORDS: Holds single-game record for most hits—5 (October 7, 1995). ... Holds N.L. single-series record for most hits—11 (1995). ... Shares single-game records for most at-bats (nine-inning game)—6 (October 4, 1995); and most home runs—2 (October 4, 1995). ... Shares career record for most triples—1.

Year—Team (League)	Pos.	G	AB	R	H	2B	3B	HR	RBI	Avg.	BB	SO	SB	PO	A	E	Avg.
1995—Atlanta (N.L.).............	OF	4	21	5	11	2	0	3	4	.524	0	3	2	9	0	0	1.000
1996—Atlanta (N.L.).............	OF	3	12	2	1	0	0	0	0	.083	1	2	1	4	0	1	.800
1997—Cleveland (A.L.).........	OF	5	17	3	4	0	1	0	0	.235	1	2	0	14	0	0	1.000
Division series totals (3 years)		12	50	10	16	2	1	3	4	.320	2	7	3	27	0	1	.964

CHAMPIONSHIP SERIES RECORD

RECORDS: Holds single-series record for most at-bats—35 (1996). ... Shares single-game record for most strikeouts—4 (October 11 [12 innings] and 15 [11 innings], 1997). ... Shares N.L. single-game record for most at-bats—6 (October 14 and 17, 1996).
NOTES: Named A.L. Championship Series Most Valuable Player (1997).

Year—Team (League)	Pos.	G	AB	R	H	2B	3B	HR	RBI	Avg.	BB	SO	SB	PO	A	E	Avg.
1995—Atlanta (N.L.).............	OF	4	19	2	5	0	1	0	0	.263	1	4	0	8	0	1	.889
1996—Atlanta (N.L.).............	OF	7	35	7	10	1	0	1	3	.286	0	8	2	17	0	1	.944
1997—Cleveland (A.L.)..........	OF	6	23	2	6	0	0	1	4	.261	1	9	3	13	1	0	1.000
Championship series totals (3 years)		17	77	11	21	1	1	2	7	.273	2	21	5	38	1	2	.951

WORLD SERIES RECORD

NOTES: Member of World Series championship team (1995).

Year—Team (League)	Pos.	G	AB	R	H	2B	3B	HR	RBI	Avg.	BB	SO	SB	PO	A	E	Avg.
1995—Atlanta (N.L.).............	OF	6	25	3	9	1	0	0	1	.360	1	3	3	13	0	0	1.000
1996—Atlanta (N.L.).............	OF	6	27	4	12	2	1	0	5	.444	1	2	1	7	0	1	.875
1997—Cleveland (A.L.)..........	OF	7	25	5	9	1	0	0	2	.360	4	4	0	19	0	1	.950
World Series totals (3 years)		19	77	12	30	4	1	0	8	.390	6	9	4	39	0	2	.951

ALL-STAR GAME RECORD

Year League	Pos.	AB	R	H	2B	3B	HR	RBI	Avg.	BB	SO	SB	PO	A	E	Avg.
1993—National	OF	3	0	0	0	0	0	0	.000	0	1	0	1	0	0	1.000
1994—National	OF	1	1	1	0	0	1	1	1.000	1	0	0	2	1	0	1.000
All-Star Game totals (2 years)		4	1	1	0	0	1	1	.250	1	1	0	3	1	0	1.000

GROOM, BUDDY — P — ORIOLES

PERSONAL: Born July 10, 1965, in Dallas. ... 6-2/207. ... Throws left, bats left. ... Full name: Wedsel Gary Groom Jr.
HIGH SCHOOL: Red Oak (Texas).
COLLEGE: Mary Hardin-Baylor (Texas).
TRANSACTIONS/CAREER NOTES: Selected by Chicago White Sox organization in 12th round of free-agent draft (June 2, 1987). ... Selected by Detroit Tigers organization from White Sox organization in Rule 5 minor league draft (December 3, 1990). ... Traded by Tigers to Florida Marlins for a player to be named later (August 7, 1995); Tigers acquired P Mike Myers to complete deal (August 9, 1995). ... Granted free agency (October 16, 1995). ... Signed by Oakland Athletics organization (November 27, 1995). ... Granted free agency (November 1, 1999). ... Signed by Baltimore Orioles (December 21, 1999).

Year—League	W	L	Pct.	ERA	G	GS	CG	ShO	Sv.	IP	H	R	ER	BB	SO
1987—GC White Sox (GCL)	1	0	1.000	0.75	4	1	0	0	1	12	12	1	1	2	8
—Daytona Beach (FSL).........	7	2	.778	3.59	11	10	2	0	0	67²/₃	60	30	27	33	29
1988—Tampa (FSL).........	13	10	.565	2.54	27	27	8	0	0	*195	181	69	55	51	118
1989—Birmingham (Sou.).........	13	8	.619	4.52	26	26	3	1	0	167¹/₃	172	101	84	78	94
1990—Birmingham (Sou.).........	6	8	.429	5.07	20	20	0	0	0	115¹/₃	135	81	65	48	66
1991—Toledo (I.L.)■.........	2	5	.286	4.32	24	6	0	0	1	75	75	39	36	25	49
—London (East.)	7	1	.875	3.48	11	7	0	0	0	51²/₃	51	20	20	12	39
1992—Toledo (I.L.).........	7	7	.500	2.80	16	16	1	0	0	109¹/₃	102	41	34	23	71
—Detroit (A.L.)	0	5	.000	5.82	12	7	0	0	1	38²/₃	48	28	25	22	15
1993—Toledo (I.L.).........	9	3	.750	2.74	16	15	0	0	0	102	98	34	31	30	78
—Detroit (A.L.)	0	2	.000	6.14	19	3	0	0	0	36²/₃	48	25	25	13	15
1994—Toledo (I.L.).........	0	0	...	2.25	5	0	0	0	0	4	2	1	1	0	6
—Detroit (A.L.)	0	1	.000	3.94	40	0	0	0	1	32	31	14	14	13	21
1995—Detroit (A.L.).........	1	3	.250	7.52	23	4	0	0	1	40²/₃	55	35	34	26	23
—Toledo (I.L.)	2	3	.400	1.91	6	5	1	0	0	33	31	14	7	4	24
—Florida (N.L.)■.........	1	2	.333	7.20	14	0	0	0	0	15	26	12	12	6	12

Year	League	W	L	Pct.	ERA	G	GS	CG	ShO	Sv.	IP	H	R	ER	BB	SO
1996—Oakland (A.L.)■		5	0	1.000	3.84	72	1	0	0	2	77 1/3	85	37	33	34	57
1997—Oakland (A.L.)		2	2	.500	5.15	78	0	0	0	3	64 2/3	75	38	37	24	45
1998—Oakland (A.L.)		3	1	.750	4.24	75	0	0	0	0	57 1/3	62	30	27	20	36
1999—Oakland (A.L.)		3	2	.600	5.09	•76	0	0	0	0	46	48	29	26	18	32
2000—Baltimore (A.L.)■		6	3	.667	4.85	70	0	0	0	4	59 1/3	63	37	32	21	44
2001—Baltimore (A.L.)		1	4	.200	3.55	70	0	0	0	11	66	64	28	26	9	54
A.L. totals (10 years)		21	23	.477	4.84	535	15	0	0	23	518 2/3	579	301	279	200	348
N.L. totals (1 year)		1	2	.333	7.20	14	0	0	0	0	15	26	12	12	6	12
Major League totals (10 years)		22	25	.468	4.91	549	15	0	0	23	533 2/3	605	313	291	206	360

GRUDZIELANEK, MARK — 2B — DODGERS

PERSONAL: Born June 30, 1970, in Milwaukee. ... 6-1/185. ... Bats right, throws right. ... Full name: Mark James Grudzielanek. ... Name pronounced gress-UH-lawn-ick.
HIGH SCHOOL: J.M. Hanks (El Paso, Texas).
JUNIOR COLLEGE: Trinidad (Colo.) State Junior College.
COLLEGE: Oklahoma State.
TRANSACTIONS/CAREER NOTES: Selected by New York Mets organization in 17th round of free-agent draft (June 5, 1989); did not sign. ... Selected by Montreal Expos organization in 11th round of free-agent draft (June 3, 1991). ... On disabled list (July 13-August 9, 1993 and May 12-19, 1994). ... Traded by Expos with P Carlos Perez and OF Hiram Bocachica to Los Angeles Dodgers for 2B Wilton Guerrero, P Ted Lilly, OF Peter Bergeron and 1B Jonathan Tucker (July 31, 1998). ... On Los Angeles disabled list (June 12-July 6, 1999); included rehabilitation assignment to San Bernadino (July 2-6). ... On disabled list (June 12-28, 2001).
RECORDS: Holds major league single-season record for fewest chances accepted by shortstop who led league in chances accepted—683 (1997). ... Shares major league single-season record for fewest putouts by shortstop (150 or more games)—180 (1996).
HONORS: Named Eastern League Most Valuable Player (1994).
STATISTICAL NOTES: Led Eastern League shortstops with .959 fielding percentage in 1994. ... Led N.L. shortstops with 715 total chances and 99 double plays in 1997. ... Led N.L. shortstops with 33 errors in 1998. ... Career major league grand slams: 1.

Year	Team (League)	Pos.	G	AB	R	H	2B	3B	HR	RBI	Avg.	BB	SO	SB	PO	A	E	Avg.
1991—Jamestown (NY-P)	SS	72	275	44	72	9	3	2	32	.262	18	43	14	112	206	23	.933
1992—Rockford (Midw.)	SS	128	496	64	122	12	5	5	54	.246	22	59	25	173	290	41	.919
1993—W.P. Beach (FSL)	2B-SS-OF-3B	86	300	41	80	11	6	1	34	.267	14	42	17	105	135	13	.949
1994—Harrisburg (East.)	SS-3B	122	488	92	157	•37	3	11	66	.322	43	66	32	178	344	23	†.958
1995—Montreal (N.L.)	SS-3B-2B	78	269	27	66	12	2	1	20	.245	14	47	8	94	198	10	.967
—Ottawa (I.L.)	SS	49	181	26	54	9	1	1	22	.298	10	17	12	58	156	14	.939
1996—Montreal (N.L.)	SS	153	657	99	201	34	4	6	49	.306	26	83	33	180	453	27	.959
1997—Montreal (N.L.)	SS	156	*649	76	177	*54	3	4	51	.273	23	76	25	237	446	*32	.955
1998—Montreal (N.L.)	SS	105	396	51	109	15	1	8	41	.275	21	50	11	152	283	23	.950
—Los Angeles (N.L.)■	SS	51	193	11	51	6	0	2	21	.264	5	23	7	78	172	§10	.962
1999—Los Angeles (N.L.)	SS	123	488	72	159	23	5	7	46	.326	31	65	6	171	306	13	.973
—San Bern. (Calif.)	SS	4	16	2	4	0	0	0	0	.250	0	1	0	1	11	0	1.000
2000—Los Angeles (N.L.)	2B-SS	148	617	101	172	35	6	7	49	.279	45	81	12	288	416	17	.976
2001—Los Angeles (N.L.)	2B	133	539	83	146	21	3	13	55	.271	28	83	4	245	359	10	.984
Major League totals (7 years)		947	3808	520	1081	200	24	48	332	.284	193	508	106	1445	2633	142	.966

ALL-STAR GAME RECORD

Year	League	Pos.	AB	R	H	2B	3B	HR	RBI	Avg.	BB	SO	SB	PO	A	E	Avg.
1996—National	3B	1	0	0	0	0	0	0	.000	0	0	0	0	0	0	...

GRYBOSKI, KEVIN — P — BRAVES

PERSONAL: Born November 15, 1973, in Wilkes-Barre, Pa. ... 6-5/220. ... Throws right, bats right. ... Full name: Kevin John Gryboski.
COLLEGE: Wilkes.
TRANSACTIONS/CAREER NOTES: Selected by Seattle Mariners organization in 16th round of free-agent draft (June 1, 1995). ... On disabled list (May 11-June 14 and July 31-August 12, 1997). ... On Lancaster disabled list (May 3-10, 1998). ... On Tacoma disabled list (July 24-31, 2000). ... Traded by Mariners to Atlanta Braves for P Elvis Perez (January 18, 2002).

Year	League	W	L	Pct.	ERA	G	GS	CG	ShO	Sv.	IP	H	R	ER	BB	SO
1995—Everett (N'West)	1	5	.167	3.50	25	0	0	0	2	36	27	18	14	18	25
1996—Wisconsin (Midw.)	10	5	.667	4.74	32	21	3	0	1	138 2/3	146	90	73	62	100
1997—Lancaster (Calif.)	0	7	.000	9.89	21	15	0	0	0	67 1/3	113	82	74	26	41
1998—Lancaster (Calif.)	5	5	.500	2.65	3	0	0	0	8	85	75	35	25	31	73
—Orlando (Sou.)	0	0	...	9.00	2	0	0	0	0	5	8	5	5	1	4
1999—New Haven (East.)	2	5	.286	2.89	47	0	0	0	10	62 1/3	67	27	20	20	41
2000—New Haven (East.)	2	2	.500	2.50	16	0	0	0	9	18	15	5	5	8	20
—Tacoma (PCL)	2	2	.500	4.83	31	0	0	0	2	41	45	23	22	23	35
2001—Tacoma (PCL)	2	5	.286	3.90	58	0	0	0	22	60	64	29	26	19	50

GUARDADO, EDDIE — P — TWINS

PERSONAL: Born October 2, 1970, in Stockton, Calif. ... 6-0/194. ... Throws left, bats right. ... Full name: Edward Adrian Guardado. ... Name pronounced gwar-DAH-doh.
HIGH SCHOOL: Franklin (Stockton, Calif.).
JUNIOR COLLEGE: San Joaquin Delta College (Calif.).
TRANSACTIONS/CAREER NOTES: Selected by Minnesota Twins organization in 21st round of free-agent draft (June 4, 1990). ... On Minnesota disabled list (May 22-June 28, 1999); included rehabilitation assignment to New Britain (June 22-28). ... On disabled list (June 5-20, 2001).
STATISTICAL NOTES: Pitched 5-0 no-hit victory against Pulaski (August 26, 1991).

Year League	W	L	Pct.	ERA	G	GS	CG	ShO	Sv.	IP	H	R	ER	BB	SO
1991—Elizabethton (Appl.)	8	4	.667	1.86	14	13	3	•1	0	92	67	30	19	31	*106
1992—Kenosha (Midw.)	5	10	.333	4.37	18	18	2	1	0	101	106	57	49	30	103
—Visalia (Calif.)	7	0	1.000	1.64	7	7	1	1	0	49 1/3	47	13	9	10	39
1993—Nashville (Sou.)	4	0	1.000	1.24	10	10	2	2	0	65 1/3	53	10	9	10	57
—Minnesota (A.L.)	3	8	.273	6.18	19	16	0	0	0	94 2/3	123	68	65	36	46
1994—Salt Lake (PCL)	12	7	.632	4.83	24	24	2	0	0	151	171	90	81	51	87
—Minnesota (A.L.)	0	2	.000	8.47	4	4	0	0	0	17	26	16	16	4	8
1995—Minnesota (A.L.)	4	9	.308	5.12	51	5	0	0	2	91 1/3	99	54	52	45	71
1996—Minnesota (A.L.)	6	5	.545	5.25	•83	0	0	0	4	73 2/3	61	45	43	33	74
1997—Minnesota (A.L.)	0	4	.000	3.91	69	0	0	0	1	46	45	23	20	17	54
1998—Minnesota (A.L.)	3	1	.750	4.52	79	0	0	0	0	65 2/3	66	34	33	28	53
1999—Minnesota (A.L.)	2	5	.286	4.50	63	0	0	0	2	48	37	24	24	25	50
—New Britain (East.)	0	0	...	1.93	3	0	0	0	0	4 2/3	3	1	1	0	5
2000—Minnesota (A.L.)	7	4	.636	3.94	70	0	0	0	9	61 2/3	55	27	27	25	52
2001—Minnesota (A.L.)	7	1	.875	3.51	67	0	0	0	12	66 2/3	47	27	26	23	67
Major League totals (9 years)	32	39	.451	4.88	505	25	0	0	30	564 2/3	559	318	306	236	475

GUERRERO, VLADIMIR — OF — EXPOS

PERSONAL: Born February 9, 1976, in Nizao Bani, Dominican Republic. ... 6-3/205. ... Bats right, throws right. ... Full name: Vladimir Alvino Guerrero. ... Brother of Wilton Guerrero, outfielder/second baseman, Cincinnati Reds.

TRANSACTIONS/CAREER NOTES: Signed as non-drafted free agent by Montreal Expos organization (March 1, 1993). ... On Montreal disabled list (March 30-May 2, June 5-21 and July 12-27, 1997); included rehabilitation assignment to West Palm Beach (April 29-May 2).

HONORS: Named Eastern League Most Valuable Player (1996). ... Named Minor League Player of the Year by THE SPORTING NEWS (1996). ... Named outfielder on THE SPORTING NEWS N.L. All-Star team (1999 and 2000). ... Named outfielder on THE SPORTING NEWS N.L. Silver Slugger team (1999 and 2000).

STATISTICAL NOTES: Led Eastern League with .438 on-base percentage and 13 intentional bases on balls received in 1996. ... Had 31-game hitting streak (July 27-August 26, 1999). ... Led N.L. with 23 intentional bases on balls received in 2000. ... Led N.L. in grounding into double plays with 24 in 2001. ... Career major league grand slams: 1.

MISCELLANEOUS: Holds Montreal Expos all-time record for highest career batting average (.319).

Year Team (League)	Pos.	G	AB	R	H	2B	3B	HR	RBI	Avg.	BB	SO	SB	PO	A	E	Avg.
1993—Dom. Expos (DSL)	OF-IF-P	34	105	19	35	4	0	1	14	.333	8	13	4	75	7	5	.943
1994—Dom. Expos (DSL)	OF	25	92	34	39	11	0	12	35	.424	21	6	5	38	6	2	.957
—GC Expos (GCL)	OF	37	137	24	43	13	3	5	25	.314	11	18	0	64	9	1	.986
1995—Albany (S.Atl.)	OF	110	421	77	140	21	10	16	63	*.333	30	45	12	207	15	11	.953
1996—W.P. Beach (FSL)	OF	20	80	16	29	8	0	5	18	.363	3	10	2	28	5	3	.917
—Harrisburg (East.)	OF	118	417	84	150	32	8	19	78	*.360	51	42	17	184	13	8	.961
—Montreal (N.L.)	OF	9	27	2	5	0	0	1	1	.185	0	3	0	11	0	0	1.000
1997—W.P. Beach (FSL)	OF	3	10	0	4	2	0	0	2	.400	1	0	1	4	1	0	1.000
—Montreal (N.L.)	OF	90	325	44	98	22	2	11	40	.302	19	39	3	148	10	*12	.951
1998—Montreal (N.L.)	OF	159	623	108	202	37	7	38	109	.324	42	95	11	323	9	*17	.951
1999—Montreal (N.L.)	OF	160	610	102	193	37	5	42	131	.316	55	62	14	332	15	*19	.948
2000—Montreal (N.L.)	OF-DH	154	571	101	197	28	11	44	123	.345	58	74	9	299	12	•10	.969
2001—Montreal (N.L.)	OF	159	599	107	184	45	4	34	108	.307	60	88	37	320	14	12	.965
Major League totals (6 years)		731	2755	464	879	169	29	170	512	.319	234	361	74	1433	60	70	.955

ALL-STAR GAME RECORD

Year League	Pos.	AB	R	H	2B	3B	HR	RBI	Avg.	BB	SO	SB	PO	A	E	Avg.
1999—National	OF	1	0	0	0	0	0	0	.000	0	0	0	1	0	0	1.000
2000—National	OF	2	0	1	0	0	0	0	.500	0	0	0	1	0	0	1.000
2001—National	PH-OF	1	0	0	0	0	0	0	.000	0	0	0	1	0	0	1.000
All-Star Game totals (3 years)		4	0	1	0	0	0	0	.250	0	0	0	3	0	0	1.000

RECORD AS PITCHER

Year League	W	L	Pct.	ERA	G	GS	CG	ShO	Sv.	IP	H	R	ER	BB	SO
1993—Dominican Expos (DSL)	0	0	...	2.25	3	0	0	0	0	8	10	3	2	4	6

GUERRERO, WILTON — OF/2B — REDS

G

PERSONAL: Born October 24, 1974, in Don Gregorio, Dominican Republic. ... 6-0/175. ... Bats both, throws right. ... Full name: Wilton Alvaro Guerrero. ... Brother of Vladimir Guerrero, outfielder, Montreal Expos.

HIGH SCHOOL: Escuela Primaria Don Gregorio (Dominican Republic).

TRANSACTIONS/CAREER NOTES: Signed as non-drafted free agent by Los Angeles Dodgers organization (October 8, 1991). ... On Albuquerque disabled list (June 26-July 5 and July 26-August 23, 1996). ... On suspended list (June 2-9, 1997). ... Traded by Dodgers with P Ted Lilly, OF Peter Bergeron and 1B Jonathan Tucker to Montreal Expos for P Carlos Perez, SS Mark Grudzielanek and OF Hiram Bocachica (July 31, 1998). ... Granted free agency (December 21, 2000). ... Signed by Cincinnati Reds (January 9, 2001). ... On Louisville disabled list (May 14-21, 2001).

STATISTICAL NOTES: Led Florida State League in caught stealing with 20 in 1994. ... Led Texas League in caught stealing with 22 in 1995. ... Career major league grand slams: 1.

Year Team (League)	Pos.	G	AB	R	H	2B	3B	HR	RBI	Avg.	BB	SO	SB	PO	A	E	Avg.
1992—Dom. Dodgers (DSL)	SS	61	225	52	87	7	4	0	38	.387	34	21	15	104	215	21	.938
1993—Great Falls (Pio.)	SS	66	256	44	76	5	1	0	21	.297	24	33	20	76	184	21	.925
—Dom. Dodgers (DSL)	SS	8	31	6	11	0	1	0	4	.355	4	3	2	15	18	1	.971
1994—Vero Beach (FSL)	SS	110	402	55	118	11	4	1	32	.294	29	71	23	111	292	17	.960
1995—San Antonio (Texas)	SS	95	382	53	133	13	6	0	26	*.348	26	63	21	121	263	19	.953
—Albuquerque (PCL)	SS-OF	14	49	10	16	1	1	0	2	.327	1	7	2	13	39	9	.852
1996—Albuquerque (PCL)	2B-SS	98	425	79	146	17	12	2	38	.344	26	48	26	183	306	19	.963
—Los Angeles (N.L.)	OF	5	2	1	0	0	0	0	0	.000	0	2	0	0	0	0	...

Year Team (League)	Pos.	G	AB	R	H	2B	3B	HR	RBI	Avg.	BB	SO	SB	PO	A	E	Avg.
1997— Los Angeles (N.L.)	2B-SS	111	357	39	104	10	9	4	32	.291	8	52	6	148	231	4	.990
—Albuquerque (PCL)....	SS-2B	10	45	9	18	0	1	0	5	.400	2	3	3	16	38	5	.915
1998— Los Angeles (N.L.)	2B-SS-OF	64	180	21	51	4	3	0	7	.283	4	33	5	71	91	7	.959
—Albuquerque (PCL)....	2B-OF-DH	30	121	15	36	3	2	1	10	.298	9	12	11	55	49	1	.990
—Montreal (N.L.)■........	2B	52	222	29	63	10	6	2	20	.284	10	30	3	103	130	6	.975
1999— Montreal (N.L.)........	2B-OF-DH	132	315	42	92	15	7	2	31	.292	13	38	7	86	98	12	.939
2000— Montreal (N.L.)........	OF-DH-2B	127	288	30	77	7	2	2	23	.267	19	41	8	115	4	4	.967
2001— Cincinnati (N.L.)■ S-2-O-3-DH		60	142	16	48	5	1	1	8	.338	3	17	5	50	59	5	.956
—Louisville (I.L.)	2B-SS-OF	54	227	23	69	14	2	0	28	.304	12	30	12	98	111	8	.963
Major League totals (6 years)		551	1506	178	435	51	28	11	121	.289	57	213	34	573	613	38	.969

GUERRIER, MATT — P — WHITE SOX

PERSONAL: Born August 2, 1978, in Cleveland. ... 6-3/185. ... Throws right, bats right. ... Full name: Matthew Olson Guerrier.
HIGH SCHOOL: Shaker Heights (Ohio).
COLLEGE: Kent State.
TRANSACTIONS/CAREER NOTES: Selected by Kansas City Royals organization in 33rd round of free-agent draft (June 4, 1996); did not sign. ... Selected by Chicago White Sox organization in 10th round of free-agent draft (June 2, 1999).

Year League	W	L	Pct.	ERA	G	GS	CG	ShO	Sv.	IP	H	R	ER	BB	SO
1999— Bristol (Appl.)...................	5	0	1.000	1.05	21	0	0	0	10	25 2/3	18	9	3	14	37
—Winston-Salem (Caro.).......	0	0	...	5.40	4	0	0	0	2	3 1/3	3	2	2	0	5
2000— Winston-Salem (Caro.).......	0	3	.000	1.30	30	0	0	0	19	34 2/3	25	13	5	12	35
—Birmingham (Sou.).............	3	1	.750	2.70	23	0	0	0	7	23 1/3	17	9	7	12	19
2001— Birmingham (Sou.).............	11	3	.786	3.10	15	15	1	1	0	98 2/3	85	42	34	32	75
—Charlotte (I.L.).................	7	1	.875	3.54	12	12	3	0	0	81 1/3	75	33	32	18	43

GUILLEN, CARLOS — SS — MARINERS

PERSONAL: Born September 30, 1975, in Maracay, Venezuela. ... 6-1/180. ... Bats both, throws right. ... Full name: Carlos Alfonso Guillen.
TRANSACTIONS/CAREER NOTES: Signed as non-drafted free agent by Houston Astros organization (September 19, 1992). ... On disabled list (June 1, 1994-entire season). ... On disabled list (May 2, 1996-remainder of season). ... Traded by Astros with P Freddy Garcia and a player to be named later to Seattle Mariners for P Randy Johnson (July 31, 1998); Mariners acquired P John Halama to complete deal (October 1, 1998). ... On disabled list (April 7, 1999-remainder of season). ... On Seattle disabled list (April 13-28, 2000); included rehabilitation assignment to Tacoma (April 22-28).
STATISTICAL NOTES: Career major league grand slams: 1.

Year Team (League)	Pos.	G	AB	R	H	2B	3B	HR	RBI	Avg.	BB	SO	SB	PO	A	E	Avg.
1993— Dom. Astros (DSL).....	IF	18	56	12	14	4	2	0	8	.250	8	12	0	37	6	2	.956
1994—								Did not play.									
1995— GC Astros (GCL)		30	105	17	31	4	2	2	15	.295	9	17	17	...	...	...	...
1996— Quad City (Midw.)	SS	29	112	23	37	7	1	3	17	.330	16	25	13	47	71	9	.929
1997— Jackson (Texas)	SS-DH	115	390	47	99	16	1	10	39	.254	38	78	6	169	313	35	.932
—New Orleans (A.A.).....	SS	3	13	3	4	1	0	0	0	.308	0	4	0	5	6	0	1.000
1998— New Orleans (PCL).....	SS	100	374	67	109	18	4	12	51	.291	31	61	3	145	287	26	.943
—Tacoma (PCL)■........	2B	24	92	8	21	1	1	1	4	.228	9	17	1	49	63	2	.982
—Seattle (A.L.)	2B	10	39	9	13	1	1	0	5	.333	3	9	2	15	29	0	1.000
1999— Seattle (A.L.)	SS-2B	5	19	2	3	0	0	1	3	.158	1	6	0	12	15	1	.964
2000— Seattle (A.L.)	3B-SS	90	288	45	74	15	2	7	42	.257	28	53	1	85	160	21	.921
—Tacoma (PCL)	3B-SS	24	87	19	26	4	1	2	11	.299	12	17	4	27	48	6	.926
2001— Seattle (A.L.)	SS-DH	140	456	72	118	21	4	5	53	.259	53	89	4	187	313	10	.980
Major League totals (4 years)		245	802	128	208	37	7	13	103	.259	85	157	7	299	517	32	.962

DIVISION SERIES RECORD

Year Team (League)	Pos.	G	AB	R	H	2B	3B	HR	RBI	Avg.	BB	SO	SB	PO	A	E	Avg.
2000— Seattle (A.L.)	PH	1	1	0	1	0	0	0	1	1.000	0	0	0	...	...	...	...
2001— Seattle (A.L.)								Did not play.									

CHAMPIONSHIP SERIES RECORD

Year Team (League)	Pos.	G	AB	R	H	2B	3B	HR	RBI	Avg.	BB	SO	SB	PO	A	E	Avg.
2000— Seattle (A.L.)	3B	2	5	1	1	0	0	1	2	.200	2	2	0	1	3	0	1.000
2001— Seattle (A.L.)	SS-PH	3	8	1	2	0	0	0	0	.250	0	1	0	5	6	0	1.000
Championship series totals (2 years)		5	13	2	3	0	0	1	2	.231	2	3	0	6	9	0	1.000

GUILLEN, JOSE — OF — DIAMONDBACKS

PERSONAL: Born May 17, 1976, in San Cristobal, Dominican Republic. ... 5-11/195. ... Bats right, throws right. ... Full name: Jose Manuel Guillen.
TRANSACTIONS/CAREER NOTES: Signed as non-drafted free agent by Pittsburgh Pirates organization (August 19, 1992). ... Traded by Pirates with P Jeff Sparks to Tampa Bay Devil Rays for C Joe Oliver and C Humberto Cota (July 23, 1999). ... On Durham disabled list (July 23-30, 1999). ... On Tampa Bay disabled list (March 28-April 12, 2000). ... On Tampa Bay disabled list (May 17-June 24 and June 25-July 30, 2001); included rehabilitation assignments to Durham (June 10-24 and July 14-30). ... On Durham disabled list (August 7-24, 2001). ... Released by Devil Rays (November 27, 2001). ... Signed by Arizona Diamondbacks (December 12, 2001).
RECORDS: Shares major league single-inning record for most doubles—2 (May 16, 1999, fourth inning; and May 28, 2000, eighth inning).
HONORS: Named Carolina League Most Valuable Player (1996).
STATISTICAL NOTES: Led Carolina League with 263 total bases and grounding into double plays with 16 in 1996. ... Led Carolina League outfielders with six double plays in 1996. ... Career major league grand slams: 2.

G

Year Team (League)	Pos.	G	AB	R	H	2B	3B	HR	RBI	Avg.	BB	SO	SB	PO	A	E	Avg.
1993—Dom. Pirates (DSL)....	OF	63	234	39	53	3	4	11	41	.226	21	55	10	112	12	7	.947
1994—GC Pirates (GCL).......	OF	30	110	17	29	4	1	4	11	.264	7	15	2	59	5	2	.970
1995—Erie (NY-Penn)..........	OF	66	258	41	81	17	1	*12	46	.314	10	44	1	107	10	13	.900
—Augusta (S.Atl.).......	OF	10	34	6	8	1	1	2	6	.235	2	9	0	5	0	0	1.000
1996—Lynchburg (Caro.)......	OF-DH	136	*528	78	*170	30	0	*21	94	.322	20	73	24	224	16	*13	.949
1997—Pittsburgh (N.L.).......	OF	143	498	58	133	20	5	14	70	.267	17	88	1	226	9	9	.963
1998—Pittsburgh (N.L.).......	OF	153	573	60	153	38	2	14	84	.267	21	100	3	283	16	10	.968
1999—Pittsburgh (N.L.).......	OF	40	120	18	32	6	0	1	18	.267	10	21	1	58	1	3	.952
—Nashville (PCL).........	OF-DH	35	132	28	44	10	0	5	22	.333	8	21	0	57	5	4	.939
—Durham (I.L.)■.........	OF	9	34	8	13	1	0	3	12	.382	7	7	0	19	1	0	1.000
—Tampa Bay (A.L.)........	OF	47	168	24	41	10	0	2	13	.244	10	36	0	80	5	3	.966
2000—Durham (I.L.)...........	OF	19	78	20	33	8	2	9	31	.423	8	11	0	29	2	3	.912
—Tampa Bay (A.L.)........	OF	105	316	40	80	16	5	10	41	.253	18	65	3	169	7	4	.978
2001—Tampa Bay (A.L.).......	OF-DH	41	135	14	37	5	0	3	11	.274	6	26	2	86	7	3	.969
—Durham (I.L.)...........	OF	33	119	18	35	9	0	7	29	.294	3	28	0	49	5	1	.982
American League totals (3 years)		193	619	78	158	31	5	15	65	.255	34	127	5	335	19	10	.973
National League totals (3 years)		336	1191	136	318	64	7	29	172	.267	48	209	5	567	26	22	.964
Major League totals (5 years)		529	1810	214	476	95	12	44	237	.263	82	336	10	902	45	32	.967

GULAN, MIKE — 3B

PERSONAL: Born December 18, 1970, in Steubenville, Ohio. ... 6-1/192. ... Bats right, throws right. ... Full name: Michael Watts Gulan. ... Name pronounced GOO-len.

HIGH SCHOOL: Catholic Central (Steubenville, Ohio).

COLLEGE: Kent State.

TRANSACTIONS/CAREER NOTES: Selected by St. Louis Cardinals organization in second round of free-agent draft (June 1, 1992). ... On disabled list (April 27-May 12, 1994). ... On disabled list (April 4-8, 1996). ... Released by Cardinals (April 2, 1998). ... Signed by Florida Marlins organization (May 21, 1998). ... On disabled list (July 5-August 11, 1998). ... On disabled list (April 27-June 12, 1999). ... Granted free agency (October 15, 1999). ... Re-signed by Marlins organization (November 11, 1999). ... Granted free agency (October 18, 2000). ... Re-signed by Marlins organization (January 17, 2001). ... Released by Marlins (October 24, 2001).

STATISTICAL NOTES: Led American Association third basemen with 24 errors in 1996. ... Led American Association third basemen with .948 fielding percentage in 1997.

Year Team (League)	Pos.	G	AB	R	H	2B	3B	HR	RBI	Avg.	BB	SO	SB	PO	A	E	Avg.
1992—Hamilton (NY-Penn) ...	3B-1B	62	242	33	66	8	4	7	36	.273	23	53	12	51	113	11	.937
1993—Springfield (Midw.)	3B	132	455	81	118	28	4	23	76	.259	34	135	8	78	*255	28	.922
1994—St. Petersburg (FSL) ..	3B	120	466	39	113	30	2	8	56	.242	26	108	2	86	218	26	.921
1995—Arkansas (Texas)........	3B	64	242	47	76	16	3	12	48	.314	11	52	4	33	150	14	.929
—Louisville (A.A.).........	3B-DH	58	195	21	46	10	4	5	27	.236	10	53	2	38	90	7	.948
1996—Louisville (A.A.)........	3B-DH-1B	123	419	47	107	27	4	17	55	.255	26	119	7	67	240	†24	.927
1997—Louisville (A.A.)......	3B-DH-1B-OF	116	412	50	110	20	6	14	61	.267	28	121	5	78	221	16	*.949
—St. Louis (N.L.).........	3B	5	9	2	0	0	0	0	1	.000	1	5	0	1	1	0	1.000
1998—Portland (East.)■......	3B-DH-OF	46	160	24	49	16	2	5	23	.306	10	40	3	16	43	7	.894
1999—Calgary (PCL)...........	3B-DH-OF	84	286	41	79	23	2	13	51	.276	10	82	2	45	121	8	.954
2000—Calgary (PCL)...........	3B-OF-SS	119	426	66	135	40	2	17	74	.317	27	94	5	125	122	12	.954
2001—Calgary (PCL)...........	3B	124	485	78	157	44	2	22	92	.324	35	145	2	62	196	*18	.935
—Florida (N.L.)...........	3B	6	6	1	0	0	0	0	0	.000	2	2	0	2	2	0	1.000
Major League totals (2 years)		11	15	3	0	0	0	0	1	.000	3	7	0	3	3	0	1.000

GUTHRIE, MARK — P — METS

PERSONAL: Born September 22, 1965, in Buffalo. ... 6-4/215. ... Throws left, bats right. ... Full name: Mark Andrew Guthrie.

HIGH SCHOOL: Venice (Fla.).

COLLEGE: Louisiana State.

TRANSACTIONS/CAREER NOTES: Selected by St. Louis Cardinals organization in fourth round of free-agent draft (June 2, 1986); did not sign. ... Selected by Minnesota Twins organization in seventh round of free-agent draft (June 2, 1987). ... On disabled list (May 29, 1993-remainder of season). ... Traded by Twins with P Kevin Tapani to Los Angeles Dodgers for 1B/3B Ron Coomer, P Greg Hansell, P Jose Parra and a player to be named later (July 31, 1995); Twins acquired OF Chris Latham to complete deal (October 30, 1995). ... Granted free agency (October 29, 1996). ... Re-signed by Dodgers (November 6, 1996). ... Granted free agency (October 26, 1998). ... Signed by Boston Red Sox (December 19, 1998). ... On Boston disabled list (July 5-24, 1999); included rehabilitation assignment to Pawtucket (July 22-23). ... Traded by Red Sox with a player to named later to Chicago Cubs for P Rod Beck (August 31, 1999); Cubs acquired 3B Cole Liniak to complete deal (September 1, 1999). ... Traded by Cubs to Tampa Bay Devil Rays for OF Dave Martinez (May 12, 2000). ... Traded by Devil Rays with P Steve Trachsel to Toronto Blue Jays for 2B Brent Abernathy and a player to be named later (July 31, 2000). ... Granted free agency (October 31, 2000). ... Signed by Oakland Athletics (January 5, 2001). ... Traded by A's with P Tyler Yates to New York Mets for OF David Justice (December 14, 2001).

MISCELLANEOUS: Appeared in one game as pinch runner (1991).

Year League	W	L	Pct.	ERA	G	GS	CG	ShO	Sv.	IP	H	R	ER	BB	SO
1987—Visalia (Calif.)....................	2	1	.667	4.50	4	1	0	0	0	12	10	7	6	5	9
1988—Visalia (Calif.)..................	12	9	.571	3.31	25	25	4	1	0	171 1/3	169	81	63	86	182
1989—Orlando (Sou.)..................	8	3	.727	1.97	14	14	0	0	0	96	75	32	21	38	103
—Portland (PCL)..................	3	4	.429	3.65	7	7	1	0	0	44 1/3	45	21	18	16	35
—Minnesota (A.L.)..................	2	4	.333	4.55	13	8	0	0	0	57 1/3	66	32	29	21	38
1990—Minnesota (A.L.).................	7	9	.438	3.79	24	21	3	1	0	144 2/3	154	65	61	39	101
—Portland (PCL)..................	1	3	.250	2.98	9	8	1	0	0	42 1/3	47	19	14	12	39
1991—Minnesota (A.L.).................	7	5	.583	4.32	41	12	0	0	2	98	116	52	47	41	72
1992—Minnesota (A.L.).................	2	3	.400	2.88	54	0	0	0	5	75	59	27	24	23	76
1993—Minnesota (A.L.).................	2	1	.667	4.71	22	0	0	0	0	21	20	11	11	16	15
1994—Minnesota (A.L.).................	4	2	.667	6.14	50	0	0	0	1	51 1/3	65	43	35	18	38

G

Year League	W	L	Pct.	ERA	G	GS	CG	ShO	Sv.	IP	H	R	ER	BB	SO
1995— Minnesota (A.L.)	5	3	.625	4.46	36	0	0	0	0	42 1/3	47	22	21	16	48
—Los Angeles (N.L.)■	0	2	.000	3.66	24	0	0	0	0	19 2/3	19	11	8	9	19
1996— Los Angeles (N.L.)	2	3	.400	2.22	66	0	0	0	1	73	65	21	18	22	56
1997— Los Angeles (N.L.)	1	4	.200	5.32	62	0	0	0	1	69 1/3	71	44	41	30	42
1998— Los Angeles (N.L.)	2	1	.667	3.50	53	0	0	0	0	54	56	26	21	24	45
1999— Boston (A.L.)■	1	1	.500	5.83	46	0	0	0	2	46 1/3	50	32	30	20	36
—Pawtucket (I.L.)..............	0	0	...	0.00	1	1	0	0	0	1	0	0	0	0	1
—Chicago (N.L.)■	0	2	.000	3.65	11	0	0	0	0	12 1/3	7	6	5	4	9
2000— Chicago (N.L.)	2	3	.400	4.82	19	0	0	0	0	18 2/3	17	11	10	10	17
—Tampa Bay (A.L.)■	1	1	.500	4.50	34	0	0	0	0	32	33	18	16	18	26
—Toronto (A.L.)■	0	2	.000	4.79	23	0	0	0	0	20 2/3	20	12	11	9	20
2001— Oakland (A.L.)■	6	2	.750	4.47	54	0	0	0	1	52 1/3	49	29	26	20	52
A.L. totals (10 years)	37	33	.529	4.37	397	43	3	1	11	641	679	343	311	241	522
N.L. totals (6 years)	7	15	.318	3.75	235	0	0	0	2	247	235	119	103	99	188
Major League totals (13 years)	44	48	.478	4.20	632	43	3	1	13	888	914	462	414	340	710

DIVISION SERIES RECORD

Year League	W	L	Pct.	ERA	G	GS	CG	ShO	Sv.	IP	H	R	ER	BB	SO
1995— Los Angeles (N.L.)	0	0	...	6.75	3	0	0	0	0	1 1/3	2	1	1	1	1
1996— Los Angeles (N.L.)	0	0	...	0.00	1	0	0	0	0	1/3	0	0	0	1	1
2001— Oakland (A.L.)	0	0	...	0.00	2	0	0	0	0	3	0	0	0	0	2
Division series totals (3 years)	0	0	...	1.93	6	0	0	0	0	4 2/3	2	1	1	2	4

CHAMPIONSHIP SERIES RECORD

Year League	W	L	Pct.	ERA	G	GS	CG	ShO	Sv.	IP	H	R	ER	BB	SO
1991— Minnesota (A.L.)	1	0	1.000	0.00	2	0	0	0	0	2 2/3	0	0	0	0	0

WORLD SERIES RECORD

NOTES: Member of World Series championship team (1991).

Year League	W	L	Pct.	ERA	G	GS	CG	ShO	Sv.	IP	H	R	ER	BB	SO
1991— Minnesota (A.L.)	0	1	.000	2.25	4	0	0	0	0	4	3	1	1	4	3

GUTIERREZ, RICKY   2B   INDIANS

PERSONAL: Born May 23, 1970, in Miami. ... 6-1/195. ... Bats right, throws right. ... Full name: Ricardo Gutierrez.

HIGH SCHOOL: American (Hialeah, Fla.).

TRANSACTIONS/CAREER NOTES: Selected by Baltimore Orioles organization in supplemental round ("sandwich pick" between first and second round, 28th pick overall) of free-agent draft (June 1, 1988); pick received as compensation for Orioles failing to sign 1987 No. 1 pick P Brad DuVall. ... Traded by Orioles to San Diego Padres (September 4, 1992), completing deal in which Padres traded P Craig Lefferts to Orioles for P Erik Schullstrom and a player to be named later (August 31, 1992). ... Traded by Padres with OF Phil Plantier, OF Derek Bell, P Pedro Martinez, P Doug Brocail and IF Craig Shipley to Houston Astros for 3B Ken Caminiti, OF Steve Finley, SS Andujar Cedeno, 1B Robert Petagine, P Brian Williams and a player to be named later (December 28, 1994); Padres acquired P Sean Fesh to complete deal (May 1, 1995). ... On Houston disabled list (March 31-May 6, 1997); included rehabilitation assignment to New Orleans (April 29-May 6). ... On Houston disabled list (April 28-June 7 and July 10-August 9, 1999); included rehabilitation assignments to Jackson (June 3-7) and New Orleans (August 5-9). ... Granted free agency (October 28, 1999). ... Signed by Chicago Cubs (December 20, 1999). ... On Chicago disabled list (May 25-June 23, 2000); included rehabilitation assignment to Daytona (June 19-23). ... Granted free agency (November 5, 2001). ... Signed by Cleveland Indians (December 17, 2001).

STATISTICAL NOTES: Led Appalachian League shortstops with 309 total chances in 1988. ... Led N.L. with 16 sacrifice bunts in 2000. ... Tied for N.L. lead with 17 sacrifice hits in 2001. ... Career major league grand slams: 1.

							BATTING								FIELDING		
Year Team (League)	Pos.	G	AB	R	H	2B	3B	HR	RBI	Avg.	BB	SO	SB	PO	A	E	Avg.
1988—Bluefield (Appl.)	SS	62	208	35	51	8	2	2	19	.245	44	40	5	*100	175	34	.890
1989—Frederick (Caro.)	SS	127	456	48	106	16	2	3	41	.232	39	89	15	190	372	34	*.943
1990—Frederick (Caro.)	SS	112	425	54	117	16	4	1	46	.275	38	59	12	192	286	26	.948
—Hagerstown (East.).....	SS	20	64	4	15	0	1	0	6	.234	3	8	2	31	36	4	.944
1991—Hagerstown (East.).....	SS	84	292	47	69	6	4	0	30	.236	57	52	11	158	196	22	.941
—Rochester (I.L.)	SS-3B	49	157	23	48	5	3	0	15	.306	24	27	4	61	129	8	.960
1992—Rochester (I.L.)	2B-SS	125	431	54	109	9	3	0	41	.253	53	77	14	251	283	15	.973
—Las Vegas (PCL)■	SS	3	6	0	1	0	0	0	1	.167	1	3	0	1	8	0	1.000
1993—Las Vegas (PCL)	2B-SS	5	24	4	10	4	0	0	4	.417	0	4	4	11	14	2	.926
—San Diego (N.L.) SS-2B-OF-3B	133	438	76	110	10	5	5	26	.251	50	97	4	194	305	14	.973
1994—San Diego (N.L.)	SS-2B	90	275	27	66	11	2	1	28	.240	32	54	2	93	202	22	.931
1995—Houston (N.L.)■	SS-3B	52	156	22	43	6	0	0	12	.276	10	33	5	64	108	8	.956
—Tucson (PCL)	SS-DH	64	236	46	71	12	4	1	26	.301	28	28	9	91	167	6	.977
1996—Houston (N.L.)	SS-3B-2B	89	218	28	62	8	1	1	15	.284	23	42	6	86	149	12	.951
1997—New Orleans (A.A.)	SS	7	27	2	5	1	0	0	4	.185	2	4	0	12	21	1	.971
—Houston (N.L.)	SS-3B-2B	102	303	33	79	14	4	3	34	.261	21	50	5	104	191	8	.974
1998—Houston (N.L.)	SS	141	491	55	128	24	3	2	46	.261	54	84	13	215	404	15	.976
1999—Houston (N.L.)	SS-3B	85	268	33	70	7	5	1	25	.261	37	45	2	102	203	9	.971
—Jackson (Texas)	SS-DH	4	12	4	4	1	0	0	1	.333	4	3	0	2	5	0	1.000
—New Orleans (PCL).....	SS	4	14	0	3	0	0	0	1	.214	2	3	0	10	11	3	.875
2000—Chicago (N.L.)■	SS	125	449	73	124	19	2	11	56	.276	66	58	8	190	290	7	*.986
—Daytona (FSL)	SS	4	10	0	4	1	0	0	1	.400	2	2	1	2	6	3	.727
2001—Chicago (N.L.)	SS	147	528	76	153	23	3	10	66	.290	40	56	4	173	360	16	.971
Major League totals (9 years)		964	3126	423	835	122	25	34	308	.267	333	519	49	1221	2212	111	.969

DIVISION SERIES RECORD

							BATTING								FIELDING		
Year Team (League)	Pos.	G	AB	R	H	2B	3B	HR	RBI	Avg.	BB	SO	SB	PO	A	E	Avg.
1997—Houston (N.L.)	SS	3	8	0	1	0	0	0	0	.125	2	1	0	5	5	0	1.000
1998—Houston (N.L.)	SS	4	10	1	3	0	0	0	0	.300	3	7	1	7	13	0	1.000
1999—Houston (N.L.)	SS	3	10	0	0	0	0	0	0	.000	2	5	0	4	16	1	.952
Division series totals (3 years)		10	28	1	4	0	0	0	0	.143	7	13	1	16	34	1	.980

G

GUZMAN, CRISTIAN   SS   TWINS

PERSONAL: Born March 21, 1978, in Santo Domingo, Dominican Republic. ... 6-0/195. ... Bats both, throws right. ... Full name: Cristian Antonio Guzman.

TRANSACTIONS/CAREER NOTES: Signed as non-drafted free agent by New York Yankees organization (August 24, 1994). ... Traded by Yankees with P Eric Milton, P Danny Mota, OF Brian Buchanan and cash to Minnesota Twins for 2B Chuck Knoblauch (February 6, 1998). ... On disabled list (May 27-June 11, 1999). ... On suspended list (September 10-13, 1999). ... On Minnesota disabled list (July 13-August 17, 2001); included rehabilitation assignment to Gulf Coast Twins (August 13-17).

RECORDS: Shares major league record for fewest errors for leader by shortstop—21 (2001).

STATISTICAL NOTES: Led South Atlantic League shortstops with 68 double plays in 1997. ... Led Eastern League with 17 sacrifice hits in 1998. ... Led Eastern League shortstops with 95 double plays in 1998. ... Had 17-game hitting streak (June 8-26, 2001). ... Career major league grand slams: 1.

Year Team (League)	Pos.	G	AB	R	H	2B	3B	HR	RBI	Avg.	BB	SO	SB	PO	A	E	Avg.
1995—Dom. Yankees (DSL)..	SS	46	160	24	43	6	5	3	20	.269	12	23	11	159	29	13	.935
1996—GC Yankees (GCL)......	SS	42	170	37	50	8	2	1	21	.294	10	31	7	55	106	20	.890
1997—Tampa (FSL)............	SS	4	14	4	4	0	0	0	1	.286	1	1	0	6	10	2	.889
—Greensboro (S.Atl.)......	SS	124	495	68	135	21	4	4	52	.273	17	105	23	173	364	37	.936
1998—New Britain (East.)■..	SS	•140	566	68	157	29	5	1	40	.277	21	111	23	211	*426	*32	.952
1999—Minnesota (A.L.).......	SS	131	420	47	95	12	3	1	26	.226	22	90	9	196	363	24	.959
2000—Minnesota (A.L.).......	SS-DH	156	631	89	156	25	*20	8	54	.247	46	101	28	228	413	22	.967
2001—Minnesota (A.L.).......	SS	118	493	80	149	28	*14	1	51	.302	21	78	25	165	327	*21	.959
—GC Twins (GCL).........	SS	5	16	4	4	0	1	0	0	.250	2	4	0	4	3	0	1.000
Major League totals (3 years)		405	1544	216	400	65	37	19	131	.259	89	269	62	589	1103	67	.962

ALL-STAR GAME RECORD

Year League	Pos.	AB	R	H	2B	3B	HR	RBI	Avg.	BB	SO	SB	PO	A	E	Avg.
2001—American..................	PH-SS	1	0	0	0	0	0	0	.000	0	1	0	0	0	0	...

GUZMAN, EDWARDS   3B/C   GIANTS

PERSONAL: Born September 11, 1976, in Bayamon, Puerto Rico. ... 5-11/205. ... Bats left, throws right.

HIGH SCHOOL: Emilio Delgado (Corozal, Puerto Rico).

TRANSACTIONS/CAREER NOTES: Selected by San Francisco Giants organization in 50th round of free-agent draft (June 1, 1995). ... On Fresno disabled list (June 12-23, 1999).

Year Team (League)	Pos.	G	AB	R	H	2B	3B	HR	RBI	Avg.	BB	SO	SB	PO	A	E	Avg.
1996—San Jose (Calif.)........	3B-OF	106	367	41	99	19	5	1	40	.270	39	60	3	69	213	25	.919
1997—Shreveport (Texas).....	3B	118	380	52	108	15	4	3	42	.284	33	57	3	73	199	19	.935
1998—Fresno (PCL)............	3B-C	102	325	50	99	17	0	9	48	.305	24	47	1	80	131	14	.938
1999—Fresno (PCL)............	3B-C-1B-DH	90	358	48	98	13	0	7	48	.274	17	50	6	282	129	26	.941
—San Francisco (N.L.)...	3B-C	14	15	0	0	0	0	0	0	.000	0	4	0	3	7	0	1.000
2000—Fresno (PCL)............	2-C-3-0-1	115	421	52	118	24	1	6	52	.280	17	43	1	318	144	18	.963
2001—Fresno (PCL)............	OF-3B-1B-2B	18	72	13	26	3	2	0	11	.361	4	3	0	89	31	0	1.000
—San Francisco (N.L.)..	C-1-3-2-0	61	115	8	28	6	0	3	7	.243	5	16	0	127	19	3	.980
Major League totals (2 years)		75	130	8	28	6	0	3	7	.215	5	20	0	130	26	3	.981

GUZMAN, ELPIDIO   OF   ANGELS

PERSONAL: Born February 24, 1979, in Santo Domingo, Dominican Republic. ... 6-0/165. ... Bats left, throws left.

HIGH SCHOOL: Carl Morgan (Santo Domingo, Dominican Republic).

TRANSACTIONS/CAREER NOTES: Signed as non-drafted free agent by California Angels organization (October 15, 1995). ... Angels franchise renamed Anaheim Angels for 1997 season.

STATISTICAL NOTES: Led Pioneer League outfielders with 147 total chances in 1998. ... Led California League with 11 sacrifice flies in 2000.

Year Team (League)	Pos.	G	AB	R	H	2B	3B	HR	RBI	Avg.	BB	SO	SB	PO	A	E	Avg.
1996—Dom. Angels (DSL)	OF	42	116	11	27	6	0	0	13	.233	19	17	11	76	2	6	.929
1997—Butte (Pio.)..............	OF	17	43	12	13	2	1	3	13	.302	5	5	3	21	2	1	.958
1998—Butte (Pio.)..............	OF	69	299	70	99	16	5	9	61	.331	24	44	40	*136	6	5	.966
1999—Cedar Rapids (Midw.)	OF	130	526	74	144	26	13	4	48	.274	41	84	52	256	9	13	.953
2000—Lake Elsinore (Calif.)..	OF	135	532	96	150	20	*16	9	72	.282	61	116	53	297	15	*14	.957
2001—Arkansas (Texas)........	OF	117	459	58	112	21	8	7	46	.244	17	89	18	231	10	4	.984

GUZMAN, GERALDO   P

PERSONAL: Born November 28, 1973, in Teoares, Dominican Republic. ... 6-2/180. ... Throws right, bats right.

TRANSACTIONS/CAREER NOTES: Signed as non-drafted free agent by Montreal Expos organization (September 27, 1989). ... Released by Expos (October 14, 1991). ... Out of organized baseball (1992-98). ... Played with China Trust, Taiwan (1999). ... Signed by Arizona Diamondbacks organization (November 12, 1999). ... On Tucson disabled list (August 10-September 13, 2001). ... On Arizona disabled list (September 26, 2001-remainder of season). ... Released by Diamondbacks (November 16, 2001).

Year League	W	L	Pct.	ERA	G	GS	CG	ShO	Sv.	IP	H	R	ER	BB	SO
1990—Dominican Expos (DSL).....	2	1	.667	2.98	8	7	0	0	0	45 1/3	45	22	15	10	16
1991—Dominican Expos (DSL).....	5	5	.500	3.00	15	15	3	1	0	75	72	40	25	26	38
1999—China Trust (Taiwan)■	0	0	...	2.08	9	...	...	...	1	13	15	...	...	3	6
2000—Tucson (PCL)■	4	1	.800	1.42	6	6	1	1	0	38	23	7	6	10	44
—Arizona (N.L.).................	5	4	.556	5.37	13	10	0	0	0	60 1/3	66	36	36	22	52
—El Paso (Texas)...............	3	3	.500	3.75	17	7	0	0	3	50 1/3	47	23	21	22	53
2001—Tucson (PCL)...............	3	6	.333	4.85	20	14	0	0	0	94 2/3	92	56	51	30	85
—Arizona (N.L.).................	0	0	...	2.89	4	0	0	0	0	9 1/3	7	4	3	3	4
Major League totals (2 years).......	5	4	.556	5.04	17	10	0	0	0	69 2/3	73	40	39	25	56

G

GUZMAN, WILSON   P   PIRATES

PERSONAL: Born July 14, 1977, in Palo Verde, Dominican Republic. ... 5-9/200. ... Throws left, bats left. ... Full name: Wilson Camilo Guzman.
TRANSACTIONS/CAREER NOTES: Signed as non-drafted free agent by Pittsburgh Pirates organization (November 17, 1994). ... On disabled list (April 5, 2001-entire season).

Year League	W	L	Pct.	ERA	G	GS	CG	ShO	Sv.	IP	H	R	ER	BB	SO
1995—Dominican Pirates (DSL)....	5	0	1.000	1.47	16	6	1	0	4	55	52	17	9	17	48
1996—Dominican Pirates (DSL)....	1	6	.143	4.22	14	11	1	0	1	59 2/3	61	33	28	21	56
1997—Gulf Coast Pirates (GCL)....	4	1	.800	2.90	9	8	0	0	0	40 1/3	43	15	13	8	48
—Erie (NY-Penn)	1	2	.333	5.06	5	5	0	0	0	26 2/3	26	20	15	6	25
1998—Augusta (S.Atl.).................	6	3	.667	2.57	42	0	0	0	4	70	55	24	20	24	73
—Lynchburg (Caro.)	0	1	.000	13.50	3	0	0	0	0	2 2/3	4	4	4	5	2
1999—Lynchburg (Caro.)	1	2	.333	3.44	35	0	0	0	2	65 1/3	70	35	25	12	78
2000—Lynchburg (Caro.)	4	3	.571	2.88	10	10	0	0	0	59 1/3	65	28	19	19	58
—Altoona (East.)	10	4	.714	2.97	18	18	3	1	0	178 2/3	164	77	59	64	135
2001—Altoona (East.)						Did not play.									

GWYNN, TONY   OF

PERSONAL: Born May 9, 1960, in Los Angeles. ... 5-11/225. ... Bats left, throws left. ... Full name: Anthony Keith Gwynn. ... Brother of Chris Gwynn, outfielder with Los Angeles Dodgers (1987-91 and 1994-95), Kansas City Royals (1992-93) and San Diego Padres (1996).
HIGH SCHOOL: Long Beach (Calif.) Polytechnic.
COLLEGE: San Diego State.
TRANSACTIONS/CAREER NOTES: Selected by San Diego Padres organization in third round of free-agent draft (June 8, 1981). ... On San Diego disabled list (August 26-September 10, 1982). ... On San Diego disabled list (March 26-June 21, 1983; included rehabilitation to Las Vegas (May 31-June 20). ... On disabled list (May 8-29, 1988; July 2-August 6, 1996; and August 13-September 1, 1998). ... On disabled list (May 22-June 12 and June 20-July 19, 1999; April 29-May 15 and June 24, 2000-remainder of season). ... Granted free agency (October 31, 2000). ... Re-signed by Padres (December 7, 2000). ... On disabled list (April 21-May 8 and May 10-July 3, 2001). ... Granted free agency (November 5, 2001). ... Announced retirement effective at end of season (June 28, 2001).
RECORDS: Holds N.L. career records for most years leading league in singles—7 (1984, 1986, 1987, 1989, 1994, 1995 and 1997). ... Holds N.L. single-season record for lowest batting average by leader—.313 (1988). ... Shares N.L. career records for most consecutive years batting .300 or over (50 or more games) since 1900—18; most years batting .300 or over (50 or more games)—18; and most years leading league in hits—7. ... Shares N.L. single-season record for most times collecting five or more hits in one game—4 (1993). ... Shares N.L. career record for most years leading league in batting average—8.
HONORS: Named Northwest League Most Valuable Player (1981). ... Named outfielder on THE SPORTING NEWS N.L. All-Star team (1984, 1986-87, 1989, 1994 and 1997). ... Named outfielder on THE SPORTING NEWS N.L. Silver Slugger team (1984, 1986-87, 1989, 1994-95 and 1997). ... Won N.L. Gold Glove as outfielder (1986-87 and 1989-91).
STATISTICAL NOTES: Had 25-game hitting streak (August 21-September 18, 1983). ... Led N.L. with .410 on-base percentage in 1984. ... Led N.L. outfielders with 360 total chances in 1986. ... Collected six hits in one game (August 4, 1993, 12 innings). ... Led N.L. in grounding into double plays with 20 in 1994. ... Had 20-game hitting streak (May 20-June 10, 1997). ... Tied for N.L. lead with 12 sacrifice flies in 1997. ... Had 16-game hitting streak (September 5-21, 1999). ... Career major league grand slams: 3.
MISCELLANEOUS: Holds San Diego Padres all-time records for most runs (1,383), hits (3,141), doubles (543), triples (85), runs batted in (1,138), stolen bases (319) and highest career batting average (.338). ... Selected by San Diego Clippers in 10th round (210th pick overall) of 1981 NBA draft (June 9, 1981).

Year Team (League)	Pos.	G	AB	R	H	2B	3B	HR	RBI	Avg.	BB	SO	SB	PO	A	E	Avg.
1981—Walla Walla (N'West)..	OF	42	178	46	59	12	1	12	37	*.331	23	21	17	76	2	3	.963
—Amarillo (Texas)	OF	23	91	22	42	8	2	4	19	.462	5	7	5	41	1	0	1.000
1982—Hawaii (PCL)	OF	93	366	65	120	23	2	5	46	.328	18	18	14	208	11	4	.982
—San Diego (N.L.)	OF	54	190	33	55	12	2	1	17	.289	14	16	8	110	1	1	.991
1983—Las Vegas (PCL)	OF	17	73	15	25	6	0	0	7	.342	6	5	3	23	2	3	.893
—San Diego (N.L.)	OF	86	304	34	94	12	2	1	37	.309	23	21	7	163	9	1	.994
1984—San Diego (N.L.)	OF	158	606	88	*213	21	10	5	71	*.351	59	23	33	345	11	4	.989
1985—San Diego (N.L.)	OF	154	622	90	197	29	5	6	46	.317	45	33	14	337	14	4	.989
1986—San Diego (N.L.)	OF	*160	*642	•107	*211	33	7	14	59	.329	52	35	37	*337	19	4	.989
1987—San Diego (N.L.)	OF	157	589	119	*218	36	13	7	54	*.370	82	35	56	298	13	6	.981
1988—San Diego (N.L.)	OF	133	521	64	163	22	5	7	70	*.313	51	40	26	264	8	5	.982
1989—San Diego (N.L.)	OF	158	604	82	*203	27	7	4	62	*.336	56	30	40	353	13	6	.984
1990—San Diego (N.L.)	OF	141	573	79	177	29	10	4	72	.309	44	23	17	327	11	5	.985
1991—San Diego (N.L.)	OF	134	530	69	168	27	11	4	62	.317	34	19	8	291	8	3	.990
1992—San Diego (N.L.)	OF	128	520	77	165	27	3	6	41	.317	46	16	3	270	9	5	.982
1993—San Diego (N.L.)	OF	122	489	70	175	41	3	7	59	.358	36	19	14	244	8	5	.981
1994—San Diego (N.L.)	OF	110	419	79	*165	35	1	12	64	*.394	48	19	5	191	6	3	.985
1995—San Diego (N.L.)	OF	135	535	82	•197	33	1	9	90	*.368	35	15	17	245	8	2	.992
1996—San Diego (N.L.)	OF	116	451	67	159	27	2	3	50	*.353	39	17	11	182	2	2	.989
1997—San Diego (N.L.)	OF-DH	149	592	97	*220	49	2	17	119	*.372	43	28	12	218	8	4	.983
1998—San Diego (N.L.)	OF-DH	127	461	65	148	35	0	16	69	.321	35	18	3	142	5	1	.993
1999—San Diego (N.L.)	OF-DH	111	411	59	139	27	0	10	62	.338	29	14	7	147	4	1	.993
2000—San Diego (N.L.)	OF-DH	36	127	17	41	12	0	1	17	.323	9	4	0	31	1	0	1.000
2001—San Diego (N.L.)	OF-DH	71	102	5	33	9	1	1	17	.324	10	9	1	17	2	0	1.000
Major League totals (20 years)		2440	9288	1383	3141	543	85	135	1138	.338	790	434	319	4512	160	62	.987

DIVISION SERIES RECORD

Year Team (League)	Pos.	G	AB	R	H	2B	3B	HR	RBI	Avg.	BB	SO	SB	PO	A	E	Avg.
1996—San Diego (N.L.)	OF	3	13	0	4	1	0	0	1	.308	0	2	1	2	0	0	1.000
1998—San Diego (N.L.)	OF	4	15	1	3	2	0	0	2	.200	0	2	0	4	1	0	1.000
Division series totals (2 years)		7	28	1	7	3	0	0	3	.250	0	4	1	6	1	0	1.000

G

CHAMPIONSHIP SERIES RECORD

Year Team (League)	Pos.	G	AB	R	H	2B	3B	HR	RBI	Avg.	BB	SO	SB	PO	A	E	Avg.
1984—San Diego (N.L.)	OF	5	19	6	7	3	0	0	3	.368	1	2	0	9	0	0	1.000
1998—San Diego (N.L.)	OF	6	26	1	6	1	0	0	2	.231	1	2	0	5	0	0	1.000
Championship series totals (2 years)		11	45	7	13	4	0	0	5	.289	2	4	0	14	0	0	1.000

WORLD SERIES RECORD

Year Team (League)	Pos.	G	AB	R	H	2B	3B	HR	RBI	Avg.	BB	SO	SB	PO	A	E	Avg.
1984—San Diego (N.L.)	OF	5	19	1	5	0	0	0	0	.263	3	2	1	12	1	1	.929
1998—San Diego (N.L.)	OF	4	16	2	8	0	0	1	3	.500	1	0	0	6	0	0	1.000
World Series totals (2 years)		9	35	3	13	0	0	1	3	.371	4	2	1	18	1	1	.950

ALL-STAR GAME RECORD

RECORDS: Shares single-game record for most at-bats in nine-inning game—5 (July 12, 1994).
NOTES: Named to All-Star team for 1996 game; replaced by Henry Rodriguez due to injury.

Year League	Pos.	AB	R	H	2B	3B	HR	RBI	Avg.	BB	SO	SB	PO	A	E	Avg.
1984—National	OF	3	0	1	0	0	0	0	.333	0	0	0	0	0	0	...
1985—National	OF	1	0	0	0	0	0	0	.000	0	0	0	1	0	0	1.000
1986—National	OF	3	0	0	0	0	0	0	.000	0	0	0	1	0	0	1.000
1987—National	PH	1	0	0	0	0	0	0	.000	0	0	0	...	...	...	...
1989—National	OF	2	1	1	0	0	0	0	.500	1	1	1	2	0	0	1.000
1990—National	PH	0	0	0	0	0	0	0	...	1	0	0	...	...	...	...
1991—National	OF	4	1	2	0	0	0	0	.500	0	0	0	6	0	0	1.000
1992—National	OF	2	0	0	0	0	0	0	.000	1	0	0	0	2	0	1.000
1993—National	OF	1	0	0	0	0	0	0	.000	0	0	0	0	0	0	...
1994—National	OF	5	2	2	1	0	0	2	.400	0	0	0	2	0	0	1.000
1995—National	OF	2	0	0	0	0	0	0	.000	0	0	0	1	0	0	1.000
1996—National							Selected, did not play—injured.										
1997—National	DH	3	0	0	0	0	0	0	.000	0	0	0	...	...	...	...
1998—National	OF	2	0	1	0	0	0	2	.500	0	0	0	0	0	0	...
1999—National							Selected, did not play—injured.										
All-Star Game totals (13 years)		29	4	7	1	0	0	4	.241	3	1	1	13	2	0	1.000

HACKMAN, LUTHER — P — CARDINALS

PERSONAL: Born October 10, 1974, in Columbus, Miss. ... 6-4/195. ... Throws right, bats right. ... Full name: Luther Gean Hackman.
HIGH SCHOOL: Columbus (Miss.).
TRANSACTIONS/CAREER NOTES: Selected by Colorado Rockies organization in sixth round of free-agent draft (June 2, 1994). ... On disabled list (June 1-July 10, 1996). ... Traded by Rockies with P Darryl Kile and P Dave Veres to St. Louis Cardinals for P Jose Jimenez, P Manny Aybar, P Rick Croushore and SS Brent Butler (November 16, 1999). ... On Memphis disabled list (June 3-July 4, 2000). ... On St. Louis disabled list (March 23-May 9, 2001); included rehabilitation assignment to New Haven (May 1-9).
STATISTICAL NOTES: Led South Atlantic League in balks with seven in 1995.

Year League	W	L	Pct.	ERA	G	GS	CG	ShO	Sv.	IP	H	R	ER	BB	SO
1994—Arizona Rockies (Ariz.).......	1	3	.250	2.10	12	12	0	0	0	55 2/3	50	21	13	16	63
1995—Asheville (S.Atl.)........	11	11	.500	4.64	28	28	2	0	0	165	162	*95	*85	65	108
1996—Salem (Caro.)..................	5	7	.417	4.24	21	21	1	0	0	110 1/3	93	60	52	69	83
1997—New Haven (East.).............	0	6	.000	7.82	10	10	0	0	0	50 2/3	58	49	44	34	34
—Salem (Caro.).................	1	4	.200	5.80	15	15	2	0	0	80 2/3	99	60	52	37	59
1998—New Haven (East.).............	3	12	.200	5.44	28	23	1	0	0	139	169	•102	84	54	90
1999—Carolina (Sou.)...............	4	3	.571	4.04	11	10	0	0	0	62 1/3	53	33	28	28	50
—Colo. Springs (PCL).........	7	6	.538	3.74	15	15	1	1	0	101	106	49	42	44	88
—Colorado (N.L.)................	1	2	.333	10.69	5	3	0	0	0	16	26	19	19	12	10
2000—Memphis (PCL)■...............	8	9	.471	4.74	21	21	0	0	0	119 2/3	134	71	63	36	66
—St. Louis (N.L.)...............	0	0	...	10.13	1	0	0	0	0	2 2/3	4	3	3	4	0
2001—New Haven (East.).............	0	0	...	2.25	3	1	0	0	0	4	2	2	1	1	5
—Memphis (PCL).................	0	2	.000	2.78	16	0	0	0	0	22 2/3	21	7	7	1	12
—St. Louis (N.L.)...............	1	2	.333	4.29	35	0	0	0	1	35 2/3	28	18	17	14	24
Major League totals (3 years).......	2	4	.333	6.46	41	3	0	0	1	54 1/3	58	40	39	30	34

HAFNER, TRAVIS — 1B — RANGERS

PERSONAL: Born June 3, 1977, in Jamestown, N.D. ... 6-3/215. ... Bats left, throws left. ... Full name: Travis Lee Hafner.
HIGH SCHOOL: Bowdon-Hurdsfield-Sykeston (Bowdon, N.D.).
JUNIOR COLLEGE: Cowley County Community College (Kan.).
TRANSACTIONS/CAREER NOTES: Selected by Texas Rangers organization in 31st round of free-agent draft (June 4, 1996). ... On disabled list (August 6-22, 2000). ... On disabled list (April 5-May 11, 2001).
STATISTICAL NOTES: Led South Atlantic League with .546 slugging percentage in 1999. ... Led Florida State League with .447 on-base percentage in 2000.

Year Team (League)	Pos.	G	AB	R	H	2B	3B	HR	RBI	Avg.	BB	SO	SB	PO	A	E	Avg.
1997—GC Rangers (GCL).......	1B-OF	55	189	38	54	14	0	5	24	.286	24	45	7	315	24	3	.991
1998—Savannah (S.Atl.)	1B-3B-OF	123	405	62	96	15	4	16	84	.237	68	139	7	542	57	12	.980
1999—Savannah (S.Atl.)	1B-3B	134	480	94	140	30	4	•28	*111	.292	67	151	5	881	62	15	.984
2000—Charlotte (FSL)...........	1B-3B	122	436	90	151	34	1	22	109	.346	67	86	0	514	58	13	.978
2001—Tulsa (Texas)	1B	88	323	59	91	25	0	20	74	.282	59	82	3	672	40	5	.993

G
H

HAIRSTON, JERRY — 2B/SS — ORIOLES

PERSONAL: Born May 29, 1976, in Des Moines, Iowa. ... 5-10/175. ... Bats right, throws right. ... Full name: Jerry W. Hairston Jr. ... Grandson of Sam Hairston, catcher with Chicago White Sox (1951) and Cincinnati and Indianapolis of Negro American League (1945-49); son of Jerry Hairston, outfielder with Chicago White Sox (1973-77 and 1981-89) and Pittsburgh Pirates (1977); nephew of John Hairston, catcher/outfielder with Chicago Cubs (1969); and nephew of Sam Hairston Jr., former minor league player in Chicago White Sox organization (1966 and 1969).
HIGH SCHOOL: Naperville (Ill.) North.
COLLEGE: Southern Illinois-Carbondale.
TRANSACTIONS/CAREER NOTES: Selected by Baltimore Orioles organization in 11th round of free-agent draft (June 3, 1997). ... On Rochester disabled list (May 16-July 4, 2000).
STATISTICAL NOTES: Tied for Appalachian League lead in caught stealing with nine in 1997.

							BATTING								FIELDING		
Year Team (League)	Pos.	G	AB	R	H	2B	3B	HR	RBI	Avg.	BB	SO	SB	PO	A	E	Avg.
1997— Bluefield (Appl.)	SS	59	221	44	73	13	4	2	36	.330	21	29	13	84	174	14	*.949
1998— Frederick (Caro.)	SS-2B	80	293	56	83	22	3	5	33	.283	28	32	13	116	281	24	.943
— Bowie (East.)	2B-SS	55	221	42	72	12	3	5	37	.326	20	25	6	109	135	5	.980
— Baltimore (A.L.)	2B	6	7	2	0	0	0	0	0	.000	0	1	0	4	2	2	.750
1999— Rochester (I.L.)	2B-SS	107	413	65	120	24	5	7	48	.291	30	50	19	206	277	16	.968
— Baltimore (A.L.)	2B	50	175	26	47	12	1	4	17	.269	11	24	9	115	154	0	1.000
2000— Baltimore (A.L.)	2B	49	180	27	46	5	0	5	19	.256	21	22	8	101	156	5	.981
— Rochester (I.L.)	2B-SS	58	201	43	59	15	1	4	21	.294	29	32	6	136	149	11	.963
— GC Orioles (GCL)	2B	4	10	3	3	2	0	0	3	.300	3	2	4	5	5	0	1.000
— Frederick (Caro.)	2B	2	8	1	3	2	0	0	1	.375	1	0	0	2	7	0	1.000
2001— Baltimore (A.L.)	2B	159	532	63	124	25	5	8	47	.233	44	73	29	326	458	19	.976
Major League totals (4 years)		264	894	118	217	42	6	17	83	.243	76	120	46	546	770	26	.981

HALAMA, JOHN — P — MARINERS

PERSONAL: Born February 22, 1972, in Brooklyn, N.Y. ... 6-5/210. ... Throws left, bats left. ... Full name: John Thadeuz Halama. ... Name pronounced ha-LA-ma.
HIGH SCHOOL: Bishop Ford (Brooklyn, N.Y.).
COLLEGE: St. Francis (N.Y.).
TRANSACTIONS/CAREER NOTES: Selected by Houston Astros organization in 23rd round of free-agent draft (June 3, 1994). ... On New Orleans disabled list (July 2-August 6, 1998). ... Traded by Astros to Seattle Mariners (October 1, 1998), completing deal in which Mariners traded P Randy Johnson to Astros for SS Carlos Guillen, P Freddy Garcia and a player to be named later (July 31, 1998).

Year League	W	L	Pct.	ERA	G	GS	CG	ShO	Sv.	IP	H	R	ER	BB	SO
1994— Auburn (NY-Penn)	4	1	.800	1.29	6	3	0	0	1	28	18	5	4	5	27
— Quad City (Midw.)	3	4	.429	4.56	9	9	1	1	0	51 1/3	63	31	26	18	37
1995— Quad City (Midw.)	1	2	.333	2.02	55	0	0	0	2	62 1/3	48	16	14	22	56
1996— Jackson (Texas)	9	10	.474	3.21	27	27	0	0	0	162 2/3	151	77	58	59	110
1997— New Orleans (A.A.)	13	3	*.813	*2.58	26	24	1	0	0	171	150	57	49	32	126
1998— Houston (N.L.)	1	1	.500	5.85	6	6	0	0	0	32 1/3	37	21	21	13	21
— New Orleans (PCL)	12	3	.800	3.20	17	17	4	1	0	121	118	48	43	16	86
1999— Seattle (A.L.)■	11	10	.524	4.22	38	24	1	1	0	179	193	88	84	56	105
2000— Seattle (A.L.)	14	9	.609	5.08	30	30	1	1	0	166 2/3	206	108	94	56	87
2001— Seattle (A.L.)	10	7	.588	4.73	31	17	0	0	0	110 1/3	132	69	58	26	50
— Tacoma (PCL)	2	0	1.000	0.47	3	3	1	1	0	19	9	2	1	0	22
A.L. totals (3 years)	35	26	.574	4.66	99	71	2	2	0	456	531	265	236	138	242
N.L. totals (1 year)	1	1	.500	5.85	6	6	0	0	0	32 1/3	37	21	21	13	21
Major League totals (4 years)	36	27	.571	4.74	105	77	2	2	0	488 1/3	568	286	257	151	263

DIVISION SERIES RECORD

Year League	W	L	Pct.	ERA	G	GS	CG	ShO	Sv.	IP	H	R	ER	BB	SO
2000— Seattle (A.L.)							Did not play.								
2001— Seattle (A.L.)	0	0	...	0.00	2	0	0	0	0	3	3	0	0	0	3

CHAMPIONSHIP SERIES RECORD

Year League	W	L	Pct.	ERA	G	GS	CG	ShO	Sv.	IP	H	R	ER	BB	SO
2000— Seattle (A.L.)	0	0	...	2.89	2	2	0	0	0	9 1/3	10	3	3	5	3
2001— Seattle (A.L.)	0	0	...	13.50	2	0	0	0	0	2	3	3	3	0	0
Champ. series totals (2 years)	0	0	...	4.76	4	2	0	0	0	11 1/3	13	6	6	5	3

HALL, TOBY — C — DEVIL RAYS

PERSONAL: Born October 21, 1975, in Tacoma, Wash. ... 6-3/205. ... Bats right, throws right. ... Full name: Toby Jason Hall.
HIGH SCHOOL: El Dorado (Placentia, Calif.).
COLLEGE: UNLV.
TRANSACTIONS/CAREER NOTES: Selected by Tampa Bay Devil Rays organization in ninth round of free-agent draft (June 3, 1997).
HONORS: Named International League Most Valuable Player (2001).

							BATTING								FIELDING		
Year Team (League)	Pos.	G	AB	R	H	2B	3B	HR	RBI	Avg.	BB	SO	SB	PO	A	E	Avg.
1997— Hudson Valley (NY-P.)	C	55	200	25	50	3	0	1	27	.250	13	33	0	243	21	3	.989
1998— Charl. S.C. (S.Atl.)	C	105	377	59	121	25	1	6	50	.321	39	32	3	749	84	18	.979
1999— Orlando (Sou.)	C	46	173	20	44	7	0	9	34	.254	4	10	1	261	27	4	.986
— St. Petersburg (FSL)	C	56	212	24	63	13	1	4	36	.297	17	9	0	173	27	4	.980
2000— Orlando (Sou.)	C	68	271	37	93	14	0	9	50	.343	17	24	3	395	33	7	.984
— Durham (I.L.)	C	47	184	21	56	15	0	7	35	.304	3	19	0	249	22	2	.993
— Tampa Bay (A.L.)	C	4	12	1	2	0	0	1	1	.167	1	0	0	19	2	0	1.000
2001— Orlando (Sou.)	C	94	373	59	125	28	1	19	72	.335	29	22	1	408	43	6	.987
— Tampa Bay (A.L.)	C	49	188	28	56	16	0	4	30	.298	4	16	2	328	20	5	.986
Major League totals (2 years)		53	200	29	58	16	0	5	31	.290	5	16	2	347	22	5	.987

H

PERSONAL: Born May 14, 1977, in Denver. ... 6-6/230. ... Throws right, bats right. ... Full name: Harry Leroy Halladay III.
HIGH SCHOOL: Arvada (Colo.) West.
TRANSACTIONS/CAREER NOTES: Selected by Toronto Blue Jays organization in first round (17th pick overall) of free-agent draft (June 1, 1995). ... On Syracuse disabled list (May 15-June 17, 1998). ... On Tennessee disabled list (May 16-23, 2001).
STATISTICAL NOTES: Pitched 2-1 one-hit, complete-game victory against Detroit (September 27, 1998).

Year	League	W	L	Pct.	ERA	G	GS	CG	ShO	Sv.	IP	H	R	ER	BB	SO
1995—	Gulf Coast Blue Jays (GCL)	3	5	.375	3.40	10	8	0	0	0	50 1/3	35	25	19	16	48
1996—	Dunedin (FSL)	15	7	.682	2.73	27	27	2	•2	0	164 2/3	158	75	50	46	109
1997—	Knoxville (Sou.)	2	3	.400	5.40	7	7	0	0	0	36 2/3	46	26	22	11	30
—	Syracuse (I.L.)	7	10	.412	4.58	22	22	2	2	0	125 2/3	132	74	64	53	64
1998—	Syracuse (I.L.)	9	5	.643	3.79	21	21	1	1	0	116 1/3	107	52	49	53	71
—	Toronto (A.L.)	1	0	1.000	1.93	2	2	1	0	0	14	9	4	3	2	13
1999—	Toronto (A.L.)	8	7	.533	3.92	36	18	1	1	1	149 1/3	156	76	65	79	82
2000—	Toronto (A.L.)	4	7	.364	10.64	19	13	0	0	0	67 2/3	107	80	80	42	44
—	Syracuse (I.L.)	2	3	.400	5.50	11	11	3	0	0	73 2/3	85	46	45	21	38
2001—	Dunedin (FSL)	0	1	.000	3.97	13	0	0	0	2	22 2/3	28	12	10	3	15
—	Tennessee (Sou.)	2	1	.667	2.12	5	5	3	0	0	34	25	9	8	6	29
—	Syracuse (I.L.)	1	0	1.000	3.21	2	2	0	0	0	14	12	5	5	0	13
—	Toronto (A.L.)	5	3	.625	3.16	17	16	1	1	0	105 1/3	97	41	37	25	96
Major League totals (4 years)		**18**	**17**	**.514**	**4.95**	**74**	**49**	**3**	**2**	**1**	**336 1/3**	**369**	**208**	**185**	**148**	**235**

PERSONAL: Born November 8, 1969, in La Plata, Md. ... 6-0/180. ... Bats right, throws right. ... Full name: Shane David Halter.
HIGH SCHOOL: Hooks (Texas).
JUNIOR COLLEGE: Seminole (Okla.) Junior College.
COLLEGE: Texas.
TRANSACTIONS/CAREER NOTES: Selected by Cincinnati Reds organization in 16th round of free-agent draft (June 4, 1990); did not sign. ... Selected by Kansas City Royals organization in fifth round of free-agent draft (June 3, 1991). ... Loaned by Royals organization to Charlotte, Florida Marlins organization (April 11-May 7, 1996). ... Traded by Royals to New York Mets for OF Jonathan Guzman (March 23, 1999). ... Claimed on waivers by Detroit Tigers (March 13, 2000).
STATISTICAL NOTES: Led Midwest League shortstops with 64 double plays in 1992. ... Led American Association with 19 sacrifice hits in 1995. ... Led International League with 17 sacrifice hits and in caught stealing with 18 in 1999. ... Career major league grand slams: 1.

Year	Team (League)	Pos.	G	AB	R	H	2B	3B	HR	RBI	Avg.	BB	SO	SB	PO	A	E	Avg.
1991—	Eugene (N'West)	SS	64	236	41	55	9	1	1	18	.233	49	60	12	*118	154	21	.928
1992—	Appleton (Midw.)	SS	80	313	50	83	22	3	3	33	.265	41	54	21	150	227	16	.959
—	Baseball City (FSL)	SS	44	117	11	28	1	0	1	14	.239	24	31	5	70	115	6	.969
1993—	Wilmington (Caro.)	SS	54	211	44	63	8	5	5	32	.299	27	55	5	84	146	15	.939
—	Memphis (Sou.)	SS	81	306	50	79	7	0	4	20	.258	30	74	4	142	229	16	.959
1994—	Memphis (Sou.)	SS	129	494	61	111	23	1	6	35	.225	39	102	10	177	369	29	.950
1995—	Omaha (A.A.)	SS-2B	124	392	42	90	19	3	8	39	.230	40	97	2	225	355	19	.968
1996—	Omaha (A.A.)	O-3-S-2-P	93	299	43	77	24	0	3	33	.258	31	49	7	130	75	13	.940
—	Charlotte (I.L.)	O-2-DH-3-1	16	41	3	12	1	0	0	4	.293	2	8	0	15	10	1	.962
1997—	Omaha (A.A.)	3B-OF-2B-SS	14	49	10	13	1	1	2	9	.265	6	10	0	22	14	2	.947
—	Kansas City (A.L.)	O-2-3-S-DH	74	123	16	34	5	1	2	10	.276	10	28	4	63	40	1	.990
1998—	Kansas City (A.L.)	S-O-3-2-P-1	86	204	17	45	12	0	2	13	.221	12	38	2	91	177	10	.964
—	Omaha (PCL)	S-1-2-3-O	22	97	15	30	6	1	1	13	.309	6	15	4	64	46	3	.973
1999—	Norfolk (I.L.)■	S-O-2-3-C	127	474	77	130	22	3	6	35	.274	60	90	19	187	239	20	.955
—	New York (N.L.)	OF-SS	7	0	0	0	0	0	0	0	...	0	0	0	0	0	0	...
2000—	Detroit (A.L.)■	IF-OF-C-P	105	238	26	62	12	2	3	27	.261	14	49	5	245	125	8	.979
2001—	Detroit (A.L.)	3-S-1-D	136	450	53	128	32	7	12	65	.284	37	100	3	223	326	26	.955
American League totals (4 years)			401	1015	112	269	61	10	19	115	.265	73	215	14	622	668	45	.966
National League totals (1 year)			7	0	0	0	0	0	0	0	...	0	0	0	0	0	0	...
Major League totals (5 years)			408	1015	112	269	61	10	19	115	.265	73	215	14	622	668	45	.966

RECORD AS PITCHER

Year	League	W	L	Pct.	ERA	G	GS	CG	ShO	Sv.	IP	H	R	ER	BB	SO
1996—	Omaha (A.A.)	0	0	...	9.00	1	0	0	0	0	1	2	1	1	1	0
1998—	Kansas City (A.L.)	0	0	...	0.00	1	0	0	0	0	1	1	0	0	0	0
2000—	Detroit (A.L.)	0	0	...		1	0	0	0	0	0	0	0	0	0	0
Major League totals (2 years)		0	0	...	0.00	2	0	0	0	0	1	1	0	0	1	0

PERSONAL: Born December 3, 1964, in Baton Rouge, La. ... 6-1/192. ... Bats left, throws right. ... Full name: Darryl Quinn Hamilton.
HIGH SCHOOL: University (Baton Rouge, La.).
COLLEGE: Nicholls State (La.).
TRANSACTIONS/CAREER NOTES: Selected by Milwaukee Brewers organization in 11th round of free-agent draft (June 2, 1986). ... On disabled list (May 22-June 15, 1991; May 6-24, 1992; May 2-17, 1993; May 11-26 and June 10, 1994-remainder of season). ... Granted free agency (November 1, 1995). ... Signed by Texas Rangers (December 14, 1995). ... Granted free agency (November 18, 1996). ... Signed by San Francisco Giants (January 10, 1997). ... On San Francisco disabled list (April 18-May 8, 1997); included rehabilitation assignment to Phoenix (May 5-8). ... Traded by Giants with P James Stoops and a player to be named later to Colorado Rockies for OF Ellis Burks (July 31, 1998); Rockies acquired P Jason Brester to complete deal (August 17, 1998). ... Granted free agency (October 23, 1998). ... Re-signed by Rockies (November 9, 1998). ... Traded by Rockies with P Chuck McElroy to New York Mets for OF Brian McRae, P Rigo Beltran and OF Thomas Johnson (July 31, 1999). ... On New York disabled list (April 7-August 10, 2000); included rehabilitation assignments to St. Lucie

H

(June 28-29) and Norfolk (July 29-August 9). ... On New York disabled list (April 27-May 15, 2001). ... Released by Mets (July 11, 2001). ... Signed by Rockies organization (July 18, 2001). ... Released by Rockies (July 25, 2001).
RECORDS: Holds major league career record for highest fielding average by outfielder (1,000 or more games)—.995. ... Shares major league record for most times faced pitcher as batsman, nine-inning game—8 (August 28, 1992).
STATISTICAL NOTES: Led California League with nine intentional bases on balls received in 1987. ... Led N.L. outfielders with .997 fielding percentage in 1998. ... Led N.L. outfielders with 1.000 fielding percentage in 1999. ... Career major league grand slams: 3.

							BATTING							FIELDING		
Year Team (League)	Pos.	G	AB	R	H	2B	3B	HR	RBI	Avg.	BB	SO	SB	PO	A	E	Avg.
1986— Helena (Pio.)	OF	65	248	*72	•97	12	•6	0	35	*.391	51	18	34	132	9	0	*1.000
1987— Stockton (Calif.)	OF	125	494	102	162	17	6	8	61	.328	74	59	42	221	8	1	*.996
1988— Denver (A.A.).............	OF	72	277	55	90	11	4	0	32	.325	39	28	28	160	2	2	.988
— Milwaukee (A.L.)	OF-DH	44	103	14	19	4	0	1	11	.184	12	9	7	75	1	0	1.000
1989— Denver (A.A.).............	OF	129	497	72	142	24	4	2	40	.286	42	58	20	263	11	0	*1.000
1990— Milwaukee (A.L.)	OF-DH	89	156	27	46	5	0	1	18	.295	9	12	10	120	1	1	.992
1991— Milwaukee (A.L.)	OF	122	405	64	126	15	6	1	57	.311	33	38	16	234	3	1	.996
1992— Milwaukee (A.L.)	OF	128	470	67	140	19	7	5	62	.298	45	42	41	279	10	0	*1.000
1993— Milwaukee (A.L.)	OF-DH	135	520	74	161	21	1	9	48	.310	45	62	21	340	10	3	.992
1994— Milwaukee (A.L.)	OF-DH	36	141	23	37	10	1	1	13	.262	15	17	3	60	2	0	1.000
1995— Milwaukee (A.L.)	OF-DH	112	398	54	108	20	6	5	44	.271	47	35	11	262	4	3	.989
1996— Texas (A.L.)■............	OF	148	627	94	184	29	4	6	51	.293	54	66	15	387	2	0	•1.000
1997— San Fran. (N.L.)■.......	OF	125	460	78	124	23	3	5	43	.270	61	61	15	243	1	5	.980
— Phoenix (PCL)	OF	3	14	1	4	1	0	1	2	.286	0	2	0	6	0	0	1.000
1998— San Francisco (N.L.) ..	OF	97	367	65	108	19	2	1	26	.294	59	53	9	194	4	0	1.000
— Colorado (N.L.)■.........	OF	51	194	30	65	9	1	5	25	.335	23	20	4	103	1	1	§.990
1999— Colorado (N.L.)	OF	91	337	63	102	11	3	4	24	.303	38	21	4	205	1	0	§1.000
— New York (N.L.)■	OF	55	168	19	57	8	1	5	21	.339	19	18	2	100	2	0	§1.000
2000— New York (N.L.)..........	OF	43	105	20	29	4	1	1	6	.276	14	20	2	41	1	0	1.000
— St. Lucie (FSL)	OF	1	3	0	1	0	0	0	0	.333	1	0	0	0	0	0	...
— Norfolk (I.L.)	OF	10	40	3	9	0	0	1	4	.225	6	5	0	18	1	0	1.000
2001— New York (N.L.)..........	OF	52	126	15	27	7	1	1	5	.214	19	20	3	66	2	0	1.000
— Colo. Springs (PCL)■	OF	4	13	0	2	0	0	0	0	.154	2	2	0	7	1	0	1.000
American League totals (8 years)		814	2820	417	821	123	25	29	304	.291	260	281	124	1757	33	8	.996
National League totals (5 years)		514	1757	290	512	81	12	22	150	.291	233	213	39	952	12	6	.994
Major League totals (13 years)		1328	4577	707	1333	204	37	51	454	.291	493	494	163	2709	45	14	.995

DIVISION SERIES RECORD

							BATTING							FIELDING		
Year Team (League)	Pos.	G	AB	R	H	2B	3B	HR	RBI	Avg.	BB	SO	SB	PO	A	E	Avg.
1996— Texas (A.L.)	OF	4	19	0	3	0	0	0	0	.158	0	2	0	16	1	0	1.000
1997— San Francisco (N.L.) ..	OF	2	5	1	0	0	0	0	0	.000	0	1	0	3	0	0	1.000
1999— New York (N.L.)...........	OF-PH	4	8	0	1	0	0	0	2	.125	2	0	0	9	0	0	1.000
2000— New York (N.L.)...........	OF-PH	3	4	1	2	1	0	0	0	.500	1	1	0	0	0	0	...
Division series totals (4 years)		13	36	2	6	1	0	0	2	.167	3	4	0	28	1	0	1.000

CHAMPIONSHIP SERIES RECORD

							BATTING							FIELDING		
Year Team (League)	Pos.	G	AB	R	H	2B	3B	HR	RBI	Avg.	BB	SO	SB	PO	A	E	Avg.
1999— New York (N.L.)...........	OF	5	17	0	6	1	0	0	2	.353	0	4	0	8	0	0	1.000
2000— New York (N.L.)..........	PH	3	2	0	0	0	0	0	0	.000	0	0	0	...	...	...	...
Championship series totals (2 years)		8	19	0	6	1	0	0	2	.316	0	4	0	8	0	0	1.000

WORLD SERIES RECORD

							BATTING							FIELDING		
Year Team (League)	Pos.	G	AB	R	H	2B	3B	HR	RBI	Avg.	BB	SO	SB	PO	A	E	Avg.
2000— New York (N.L.)..........	PH	4	3	0	0	0	0	0	0	.000	0	2	0	...	...	...	...

HAMILTON, JOEY — P — REDS

PERSONAL: Born September 9, 1970, in Statesboro, Ga. ... 6-4/240. ... Throws right, bats right. ... Full name: Johns Joseph Hamilton.
HIGH SCHOOL: Statesboro (Ga.).
COLLEGE: Georgia Southern.
TRANSACTIONS/CAREER NOTES: Selected by Baltimore Orioles organization in 28th round of free-agent draft (June 1, 1988); did not sign. ... Selected by San Diego Padres organization in first round (eighth pick overall) of free-agent draft (June 3, 1991). ... On Rancho Cucamonga disabled list (April 5-20, 1993). ... On disabled list (April 24-May 17, 1997). ... Traded by Padres to Toronto Blue Jays for P Woody Williams, P Carlos Almanzar and OF Peter Tucci (December 13, 1998). ... On Toronto disabled list (April 14-May 24, 1999); included rehabilitation assignment to Syracuse (May 10-24). ... On Toronto disabled list (March 21-August 19, 2000); included rehabilitation assignment to Syracuse (July 17-August 15). ... Released by Blue Jays (August 3, 2001). ... Signed by Cincinnati Reds organization (August 17, 2001). ... Granted free agency (November 5, 2001). ... Re-signed by Reds organization (January 7, 2002).
HONORS: Named righthanded pitcher on THE SPORTING NEWS college All-America second team (1990).
MISCELLANEOUS: Made an out in only appearance as pinch hitter (1998).

Year League	W	L	Pct.	ERA	G	GS	CG	ShO	Sv.	IP	H	R	ER	BB	SO
1992— Charleston, S.C. (S.Atl.)	2	2	.500	3.38	7	7	0	0	0	34 2/3	37	24	13	4	35
— High Desert (Calif.).............	4	3	.571	2.74	9	8	0	0	0	49 1/3	46	20	15	18	43
— Wichita (Texas)	3	0	1.000	2.86	6	6	0	0	0	34 2/3	33	12	11	11	26
1993— Rancho Cuca. (Calif.)	1	0	1.000	2.86	2	2	0	0	0	11	11	5	5	2	6
— Wichita (Texas)	4	9	.308	3.97	15	15	0	0	0	90 2/3	101	55	40	36	50
— Las Vegas (PCL)	3	2	.600	4.40	8	8	0	0	0	47	49	25	23	22	33
1994— Las Vegas (PCL)	3	5	.375	2.73	9	9	1	1	0	59 1/3	69	25	18	22	32
— San Diego (N.L.)	9	6	.600	2.98	16	16	1	1	0	108 2/3	98	40	36	29	61
1995— San Diego (N.L.)	6	9	.400	3.08	31	30	2	2	0	204 1/3	189	89	70	56	123
1996— San Diego (N.L.)	15	9	.625	4.17	34	33	3	1	0	211 2/3	206	100	98	83	184

Year League	W	L	Pct.	ERA	G	GS	CG	ShO	Sv.	IP	H	R	ER	BB	SO
1997— San Diego (N.L.)	12	7	.632	4.25	31	29	1	0	0	192²/₃	199	100	91	69	124
1998— San Diego (N.L.)	13	13	.500	4.27	34	34	0	0	0	217¹/₃	220	113	103	*106	147
1999— Toronto (A.L.)■...............	7	8	.467	6.52	22	18	0	0	0	98	118	73	71	39	56
— Syracuse (I.L.)	0	1	.000	5.11	3	3	0	0	0	12¹/₃	15	8	7	5	9
2000— Syracuse (I.L.)	3	2	.600	3.66	6	6	1	0	0	39¹/₃	41	18	16	12	17
— Toronto (A.L.)	2	1	.667	3.55	6	6	0	0	0	33	28	13	13	12	15
2001— Toronto (A.L.)	5	8	.385	5.89	22	22	0	0	0	122¹/₃	170	88	80	38	82
— Louisville (I.L.)■.....	1	0	1.000	5.40	1	1	0	0	0	5	4	3	3	1	1
— Cincinnati (N.L.)	1	2	.333	6.23	4	4	0	0	0	17¹/₃	23	12	12	6	10
A.L. totals (3 years)	14	17	.452	5.83	50	46	0	0	0	253¹/₃	316	174	164	89	153
N.L. totals (6 years)	56	46	.549	3.88	150	146	7	4	0	952	935	454	410	349	649
Major League totals (8 years)	70	63	.526	4.29	200	192	7	4	0	1205¹/₃	1251	628	574	438	802

DIVISION SERIES RECORD

Year League	W	L	Pct.	ERA	G	GS	CG	ShO	Sv.	IP	H	R	ER	BB	SO
1996— San Diego (N.L.)	0	1	.000	4.50	1	1	0	0	0	6	5	3	3	0	6
1998— San Diego (N.L.)	0	0	...	0.00	2	0	0	0	0	3¹/₃	1	0	0	2	3
Division series totals (2 years)	0	1	.000	2.89	3	1	0	0	0	9¹/₃	6	3	3	2	9

CHAMPIONSHIP SERIES RECORD

Year League	W	L	Pct.	ERA	G	GS	CG	ShO	Sv.	IP	H	R	ER	BB	SO
1998— San Diego (N.L.)	0	1	.000	4.91	2	1	0	0	0	7¹/₃	7	4	4	3	6

WORLD SERIES RECORD

Year League	W	L	Pct.	ERA	G	GS	CG	ShO	Sv.	IP	H	R	ER	BB	SO
1998— San Diego (N.L.)	0	0	...	0.00	1	0	0	0	0	1	0	0	0	1	1

HAMMONDS, JEFFREY   OF   BREWERS

PERSONAL: Born March 5, 1971, in Scotch Plains, N.J. ... 6-0/200. ... Bats right, throws right. ... Full name: Jeffrey Bryan Hammonds. ... Brother of Reggie Hammonds, outfielder with Pittsburgh Pirates organization (1984-86).

HIGH SCHOOL: Scotch Plains (N.J.)-Fanwood.

COLLEGE: Stanford.

TRANSACTIONS/CAREER NOTES: Selected by Toronto Blue Jays organization in ninth round of free-agent draft (June 5, 1989); did not sign. ... Selected by Baltimore Orioles organization in first round (fourth pick overall) of free-agent draft (June 1, 1992). ... On Rochester disabled list (May 17-28, 1993). ... On Baltimore disabled list (August 8-September 1 and September 28, 1993-remainder of season); included rehabilitation assignment to Bowie (August 28-September 1). ... On Baltimore disabled list (May 4-June 16, 1994; July 18-September 3, 1995; and August 17-September 22, 1996). ... On Baltimore disabled list (June 3-July 11, 1998); included rehabilitation assignment to Bowie (July 9-11). ... Traded by Orioles to Cincinnati Reds for 3B/OF Willie Greene (August 10, 1998). ... Traded by Reds with P Stan Belinda to Colorado Rockies for OF Dante Bichette and cash (October 30, 1999). ... On disabled list (April 4-22, 2000). ... Granted free agency (October 27, 2000). ... Signed by Milwaukee Brewers (December 22, 2000). ... On Milwaukee disabled list (June 7, 2001-remainder of season); included rehabilitation assignment to Arizona League Brewers (July 15-18).

HONORS: Named outfielder on The Sporting News college All-America team (1990 and 1992).

STATISTICAL NOTES: Hit three home runs in one game (May 19, 1999). ... Had 18-game hitting streak (May 29-June 21, 2000). ... Career major league grand slams: 2.

MISCELLANEOUS: Member of 1992 U.S. Olympic baseball team.

Year Team (League)	Pos.	G	AB	R	H	2B	3B	HR	RBI	Avg.	BB	SO	SB	PO	A	E	Avg.
1992— Hagerstown (East.)					Did not play.												
1993— Bowie (East.)	OF	24	92	13	26	3	0	3	10	.283	9	18	4	48	2	0	1.000
— Rochester (I.L.)	OF	36	151	25	47	9	1	5	23	.311	5	27	6	72	1	0	1.000
— Baltimore (A.L.)	OF-DH	33	105	10	32	8	0	3	19	.305	2	16	4	47	2	2	.961
1994— Baltimore (A.L.)	OF	68	250	45	74	18	2	8	31	.296	17	39	5	147	5	6	.962
1995— Baltimore (A.L.)	OF-DH	57	178	18	43	9	1	4	23	.242	9	30	4	88	1	1	.989
— Bowie (East.)	OF-DH	9	31	7	12	3	1	1	11	.387	10	7	3	12	0	1	.923
1996— Baltimore (A.L.)	OF-DH	71	248	38	56	10	1	9	27	.226	23	53	3	145	3	3	.980
— Rochester (I.L.)	OF-DH	34	125	24	34	4	2	3	19	.272	19	19	3	75	1	1	.987
1997— Baltimore (A.L.)	OF-DH	118	397	71	105	19	3	21	55	.264	32	73	15	240	4	5	.980
1998— Baltimore (A.L.)	OF-DH	63	171	36	46	12	1	6	28	.269	26	38	7	94	2	2	.980
— Bowie (East.)	OF	3	6	4	2	0	0	0	0	.333	2	2	3	3	0	0	1.000
— Cincinnati (N.L.)■.....	OF	26	86	14	26	4	1	0	11	.302	13	18	1	64	3	1	.985
1999— Cincinnati (N.L.)	OF	123	262	43	73	13	0	17	41	.279	27	64	3	157	5	0	1.000
2000— Colorado (N.L.)■.....	OF	122	454	94	152	24	2	20	106	.335	44	83	14	207	8	2	.991
2001— Milwaukee (N.L.)■.....	OF	49	174	20	43	11	1	6	21	.247	14	42	5	106	2	2	.982
— Ariz. Brewers (Ariz.) ...	OF	1	3	0	1	0	0	0	0	.333	0	0	0	0	0	0	...
American League totals (6 years)		410	1349	218	356	76	8	51	183	.264	109	249	38	761	17	19	.976
National League totals (4 years)		320	976	171	294	52	4	43	179	.301	98	207	23	534	18	5	.991
Major League totals (9 years)		730	2325	389	650	128	12	94	362	.280	207	456	61	1295	35	24	.982

DIVISION SERIES RECORD

Year Team (League)	Pos.	G	AB	R	H	2B	3B	HR	RBI	Avg.	BB	SO	SB	PO	A	E	Avg.
1997— Baltimore (A.L.)	OF-PR	4	10	3	1	1	0	0	2	.100	2	2	1	8	1	0	1.000

CHAMPIONSHIP SERIES RECORD

Year Team (League)	Pos.	G	AB	R	H	2B	3B	HR	RBI	Avg.	BB	SO	SB	PO	A	E	Avg.
1997— Baltimore (A.L.)	PH-OF-PR	5	3	0	0	0	0	0	0	.000	1	2	1	2	0	0	1.000

ALL-STAR GAME RECORD

Year League	Pos.	AB	R	H	2B	3B	HR	RBI	Avg.	BB	SO	SB	PO	A	E	Avg.
2000— National	PH	1	0	0	0	0	0	0	.000	0	0	0	...	...	...	...

H

PERSONAL: Born September 9, 1972, in Brooksville, Fla. ... 5-10/180. ... Throws left, bats right. ... Full name: Michael William Hampton.
HIGH SCHOOL: Crystal River (Fla.).
TRANSACTIONS/CAREER NOTES: Selected by Seattle Mariners organization in sixth round of free-agent draft (June 4, 1990). ... Traded by Mariners with OF Mike Felder to Houston Astros for OF Eric Anthony (December 10, 1993). ... On disabled list (May 15-June 13, 1995; June 16-July 4, 1998). ... Traded by Astros with OF Derek Bell to New York Mets for OF Roger Cedeno, P Octavio Dotel and P Kyle Kessel (December 23, 1999). ... Granted free agency (November 4, 2000). ... Signed by Colorado Rockies (December 9, 2000). ... On suspended list (October 3-8, 2001).
RECORDS: Shares N.L. single-season record for most home runs by pitcher—7 (2001).
HONORS: Named N.L. Pitcher of the Year by The Sporting News (1999). ... Named lefthanded pitcher on The Sporting News N.L. All-Star team (1999). ... Named pitcher on The Sporting News N.L. Silver Slugger team (1999 and 2000). ... Named pitcher on N.L. Silver Slugger team (2001).
STATISTICAL NOTES: Led Arizona League with 10 wild pitches in 1990. ... Pitched 6-0 no-hit victory for San Bernardino against Visalia (May 31, 1991).
MISCELLANEOUS: Appeared in two games as pinch runner (1996). ... Scored run in only appearance as pinch runner (2000). ... Struck out in only appearance as pinch hitter (2000). ... Appeared in eight games as pinch runner (2001). ... Appeared in three games as pinch hitter (2001).

Year	League	W	L	Pct.	ERA	G	GS	CG	ShO	Sv.	IP	H	R	ER	BB	SO
1990—	Arizona Mariners (Ariz.)	•7	2	.778	2.66	14	•13	0	0	0	64 1/3	52	32	19	40	59
1991—	San Bernardino (Calif.)	1	7	.125	5.25	18	15	1	1	0	73 2/3	71	58	43	47	57
	—Bellingham (N'West)	5	2	.714	1.58	9	9	0	0	0	57	32	15	10	26	65
1992—	San Bernardino (Calif.)	13	8	.619	3.12	25	25	6	•2	0	170	163	75	59	66	132
	—Jacksonville (Sou.)	0	1	.000	4.35	2	2	1	0	0	10 1/3	13	5	5	1	6
1993—	Seattle (A.L.)	1	3	.250	9.53	13	3	0	0	1	17	28	20	18	17	8
	—Jacksonville (Sou.)	6	4	.600	3.71	15	14	1	0	0	87 1/3	71	43	36	33	84
1994—	Houston (N.L.)■	2	1	.667	3.70	44	0	0	0	0	41 1/3	46	19	17	16	24
1995—	Houston (N.L.)	9	8	.529	3.35	24	24	0	0	0	150 2/3	141	73	56	49	115
1996—	Houston (N.L.)	10	10	.500	3.59	27	27	2	1	0	160 1/3	175	79	64	49	101
1997—	Houston (N.L.)	15	10	.600	3.83	34	34	7	2	0	223	217	105	95	77	139
1998—	Houston (N.L.)	11	7	.611	3.36	32	32	1	1	0	211 2/3	227	92	79	81	137
1999—	Houston (N.L.)	*22	4	*.846	2.90	34	34	3	2	0	239	206	86	77	101	177
2000—	New York (N.L.)■	15	10	.600	3.14	33	33	3	1	0	217 2/3	194	89	76	99	151
2001—	Colorado (N.L.)■	14	13	.519	5.41	32	32	2	1	0	203	236	138	122	85	122
A.L. totals (1 year)		1	3	.250	9.53	13	3	0	0	1	17	28	20	18	17	8
N.L. totals (8 years)		98	63	.609	3.65	260	216	18	8	0	1446 2/3	1442	681	586	557	966
Major League totals (9 years)		99	66	.600	3.71	273	219	18	8	1	1463 2/3	1470	701	604	574	974

DIVISION SERIES RECORD

Year	League	W	L	Pct.	ERA	G	GS	CG	ShO	Sv.	IP	H	R	ER	BB	SO
1997—	Houston (N.L.)	0	1	.000	11.57	1	1	0	0	0	4 2/3	2	6	6	8	2
1998—	Houston (N.L.)	0	0	...	1.50	1	1	0	0	0	6	2	1	1	1	2
1999—	Houston (N.L.)	0	0	...	3.86	1	1	0	0	0	7	6	3	3	1	9
2000—	New York (N.L.)	0	1	.000	8.44	1	1	0	0	0	5 1/3	6	5	5	3	2
Division series totals (4 years)		0	2	.000	5.87	4	4	0	0	0	23	16	15	15	13	15

CHAMPIONSHIP SERIES RECORD

NOTES: Named Most Valuable Player (2000).

Year	League	W	L	Pct.	ERA	G	GS	CG	ShO	Sv.	IP	H	R	ER	BB	SO
2000—	New York (N.L.)	2	0	1.000	0.00	2	2	1	1	0	16	9	0	0	4	12

WORLD SERIES RECORD

Year	League	W	L	Pct.	ERA	G	GS	CG	ShO	Sv.	IP	H	R	ER	BB	SO
2000—	New York (N.L.)	0	1	.000	6.00	1	1	0	0	0	6	8	4	4	5	4

ALL-STAR GAME RECORD

Year	League	W	L	Pct.	ERA	GS	CG	ShO	Sv.	IP	H	R	ER	BB	SO
1999—	National	0	0	...	0.00	0	0	0	0	2/3	0	0	0	0	0
2001—	National	0	0	...	0.00	0	0	0	0	1	1	1	0	0	0
All-Star Game totals (2 years)		0	0	...	0.00	0	0	0	0	1 2/3	1	1	0	0	0

PERSONAL: Born November 24, 1968, in Long Beach, Calif. ... 6-0/195. ... Bats left, throws right. ... Full name: David Andrew Hansen.
HIGH SCHOOL: Rowland (Long Beach, Calif.).
TRANSACTIONS/CAREER NOTES: Selected by Los Angeles Dodgers organization in second round of free-agent draft (June 2, 1986). ... On disabled list (May 9-28, 1994). ... Granted free agency (November 27, 1996). ... Signed by Chicago Cubs organization (January 22, 1997). ... Granted free agency (October 27, 1997). ... Signed by Hanshin Tigers of Japan Central League (November 7, 1997). ... Signed by Dodgers (January 11, 1999). ... On Los Angeles disabled list (March 23-April 26, 2001); included rehabilitation assignment to Vero Beach (April 21-27).
RECORDS: Shares major league single-season record for most home runs by pinch-hitter—7 (2000).
STATISTICAL NOTES: Led California League third basemen with 45 errors in 1987. ... Led Florida State League with 210 total bases and tied for lead with nine sacrifice flies in 1988. ... Led Florida State League third basemen with 383 total chances and 24 double plays in 1988. ... Led Pacific Coast League third basemen with .926 fielding percentage, 254 assists, 349 total chances and 25 double plays in 1990. ... Career major league grand slams: 1.

Year	Team (League)	Pos.	G	AB	R	H	2B	3B	HR	RBI	Avg.	BB	SO	SB	PO	A	E	Avg.
1986—	Great Falls (Pio.)	OF-3B-C-2B	61	204	39	61	7	3	1	36	.299	27	28	9	54	10	7	.901
1987—	Bakersfield (Calif.)	3B-OF	132	432	68	113	22	1	3	38	.262	65	61	4	79	198	†45	.860
1988—	Vero Beach (FSL)	3B	135	512	68	*149	•28	6	7	*81	.291	56	46	2	*102	*263	18	*.953
1989—	San Antonio (Texas)	3B	121	464	72	138	21	4	6	52	.297	50	44	3	*92	208	16	*.949
	—Albuquerque (PCL)	3B	6	30	6	8	1	0	2	10	.267	2	3	0	3	8	3	.786

Year Team (League)	Pos.	G	AB	R	H	2B	3B	HR	RBI	BATTING Avg.	BB	SO	SB	PO	A	FIELDING E	Avg.
1990—Albuquerque (PCL).....	3B-OF-SS	135	487	90	154	20	3	11	92	.316	*90	54	9	71	†255	26	†.926
—Los Angeles (N.L.).....	3B	5	7	0	1	0	0	0	1	.143	0	0	0	0	1	1	.500
1991—Albuquerque (PCL).....	3B-SS	68	254	42	77	11	1	5	40	.303	49	33	4	43	125	6	.966
—Los Angeles (N.L.).....	3B-SS	53	56	3	15	4	0	1	5	.268	2	12	1	5	19	0	1.000
1992—Los Angeles (N.L.).....	3B	132	341	30	73	11	0	6	22	.214	34	49	0	61	183	8	*.968
1993—Los Angeles (N.L.).....	3B	84	105	13	38	3	0	4	30	.362	21	13	0	11	27	3	.927
1994—Los Angeles (N.L.).....	3B	40	44	3	15	3	0	0	5	.341	5	5	0	6	1	1	.857
1995—Los Angeles (N.L.).....	3B	100	181	19	52	10	0	1	14	.287	28	28	0	27	70	7	.933
1996—Los Angeles (N.L.).....	3B-1B	80	104	7	23	1	0	0	6	.221	11	22	0	60	23	1	.988
1997—Chicago (N.L.)■.....	3B-1B-2B	90	151	19	47	8	2	3	21	.311	31	32	1	45	47	7	.929
1998—Hanshin (Jap. Cen.)■	3B	121	400	42	101	13	1	11	55	.253	42	89	0	...	...	...	...
1999—Los Angeles (N.L.)■..	1-3-DH-O	100	107	14	27	8	1	2	17	.252	26	20	0	58	17	3	.962
2000—Los Angeles (N.L.).....	1-3-DH-O	102	121	18	35	6	2	8	26	.289	26	32	0	51	22	2	.973
2001—Vero Beach (FSL).......	3B	3	9	1	0	0	0	0	0	.000	1	2	0	2	1	0	1.000
—Los Angeles (N.L.).....	1B-3B-SS-DH	92	140	13	33	10	0	2	20	.236	32	29	0	173	46	6	.973
Major League totals (11 years)		878	1357	139	359	64	5	27	167	.265	216	242	2	491	461	39	.961

DIVISION SERIES RECORD

Year Team (League)	Pos.	G	AB	R	H	2B	3B	HR	RBI	BATTING Avg.	BB	SO	SB	PO	A	FIELDING E	Avg.
1995—Los Angeles (N.L.).....	PH	3	3	0	2	0	0	0	0	.667	0	0	0	...	...	...	...
1996—Los Angeles (N.L.).....	PH-3B	2	2	0	0	0	0	0	0	.000	0	0	0	1	0	0	1.000
Division series totals (2 years)		5	5	0	2	0	0	0	0	.400	0	0	0	1	0	0	1.000

HARNISCH, PETE   P

PERSONAL: Born September 23, 1966, in Huntington, N.Y. ... 6-0/228. ... Throws right, bats right. ... Full name: Peter Thomas Harnisch.
HIGH SCHOOL: Commack (N.Y.).
COLLEGE: Fordham.
TRANSACTIONS/CAREER NOTES: Selected by Baltimore Orioles organization in supplemental round ("sandwich pick" between first and second round, 27th pick overall) of free-agent draft (June 2, 1987); pick received as compensation for Cleveland Indians signing Type A free-agent C Rick Dempsey. ... Traded by Orioles with P Curt Schilling and OF Steve Finley to Houston Astros for 1B Glenn Davis (January 10, 1991). ... On suspended list (July 7-9, 1992). ... On Houston disabled list (May 23-June 30, 1994); included rehabilitation assignment to Tucson (June 25-26). ... Traded by Astros to New York Mets for two players to be named later (November 28, 1994); Astros acquired P Andy Beckerman (December 6, 1994) and P Juan Castillo (April 12, 1995) to complete deal. ... Granted free agency (December 23, 1994). ... Re-signed by Mets (April 7, 1995). ... On disabled list (August 2, 1995-remainder of season). ... On New York disabled list (March 26-April 14, 1996); included rehabilitation assignment to St. Lucie (March 30-April 14). ... On New York suspended list (May 22-31, 1996). ... On New York disabled list (April 2-August 5, 1997); included rehabilitation assignments to Gulf Coast Mets (July 7-10), St. Lucie (July 11-19) and Norfolk (July 20-August 5). ... Traded by Mets to Milwaukee Brewers for OF Donny Moore (August 31, 1997). ... Granted free agency (October 27, 1997). ... Signed by Cincinnati Reds (January 21, 1998). ... On Cincinnati disabled list (May 5-June 29, 2000); included rehabilitation assignment to Louisville (June 25-29). ... On Cincinnati disabled list (May 8, 2001-remainder of season); included rehabilitation assignment to Louisville (June 9-14). ... Granted free agency (November 5, 2001).
RECORDS: Shares major league record for striking out side on nine pitches (September 6, 1991, seventh inning). ... Shares N.L. record for most consecutive home runs allowed in one inning—4 (July 23, 1996, first inning).
STATISTICAL NOTES: Pitched 4-0 one-hit, complete-game victory against Chicago (July 10, 1993). ... Pitched 3-0 one-hit, complete-game victory against San Diego (September 17, 1993).
MISCELLANEOUS: Appeared in one game as pinch runner with Houston (1994). ... Appeared in one game as pinch runner with New York (1996). ... Appeared in two games as pinch runner (2000). ... Appeared in one game as pinch runner (2001).

Year League	W	L	Pct.	ERA	G	GS	CG	ShO	Sv.	IP	H	R	ER	BB	SO
1987—Bluefield (Appl.)	3	1	.750	2.56	9	9	0	0	0	52 2/3	38	19	15	26	64
—Hagerstown (Caro.)	1	2	.333	2.25	4	4	0	0	0	20	17	7	5	14	18
1988—Charlotte (Sou.)	7	6	.538	2.58	20	20	4	2	0	132 1/3	113	55	38	52	141
—Rochester (I.L.)	4	1	.800	2.16	7	7	3	2	0	58 1/3	44	16	14	14	43
—Baltimore (A.L.)	0	2	.000	5.54	2	2	0	0	0	13	13	8	8	9	10
1989—Baltimore (A.L.)	5	9	.357	4.62	18	17	2	0	0	103 1/3	97	55	53	64	70
—Rochester (I.L.)	5	5	.500	2.58	12	12	3	1	0	87 1/3	60	27	25	35	59
1990—Baltimore (A.L.)	11	11	.500	4.34	31	31	3	0	0	188 2/3	189	96	91	86	122
1991—Houston (N.L.)■	12	9	.571	2.70	33	33	4	2	0	216 2/3	169	71	65	83	172
1992—Houston (N.L.)	9	10	.474	3.70	34	34	0	0	0	206 2/3	182	92	85	64	164
1993—Houston (N.L.)	16	9	.640	2.98	33	33	5	*4	0	217 2/3	171	84	72	79	185
1994—Houston (N.L.)	8	5	.615	5.40	17	17	1	0	0	95	100	59	57	39	62
—Tucson (PCL)	0	0	...	0.00	1	1	0	0	0	5	2	0	0	1	1
1995—New York (N.L.)■	2	8	.200	3.68	18	18	0	0	0	110	111	55	45	24	82
1996—St. Lucie (FSL)	1	0	1.000	2.77	2	2	0	0	0	13	11	4	4	0	12
—New York (N.L.)	8	12	.400	4.21	31	31	2	1	0	194 2/3	195	103	91	61	114
1997—Gulf Coast Mets (GCL)	0	0	...	12.00	1	1	0	0	0	3	7	4	4	0	4
—St. Lucie (FSL)	1	0	1.000	3.00	2	2	0	0	0	12	5	5	4	4	7
—Norfolk (I.L.)	1	1	.500	5.40	3	3	0	0	0	16 2/3	16	12	10	10	16
—New York (N.L.)	0	1	.000	8.06	6	5	0	0	0	25 2/3	35	24	23	11	12
—Milwaukee (A.L.)■	1	1	.500	5.14	4	3	0	0	0	14	13	9	8	12	10
1998—Cincinnati (N.L.)■	14	7	.667	3.14	32	32	2	1	0	209	176	79	73	64	157
1999—Cincinnati (N.L.)	16	10	.615	3.68	33	33	2	2	0	198 1/3	190	86	81	57	120
2000—Cincinnati (N.L.)	8	6	.571	4.74	22	22	3	1	0	131	133	76	69	46	71
—Louisville (I.L.)	0	0	...	3.18	1	1	0	0	0	5 2/3	6	6	2	0	6
2001—Cincinnati (N.L.)	1	3	.250	6.37	7	7	0	0	0	35 1/3	48	29	25	17	17
—Louisville (I.L.)	0	1	.000	54.00	1	1	0	0	0	1/3	3	3	2	0	0
A.L. totals (4 years)	17	23	.425	4.51	55	53	5	0	0	319	312	168	160	171	212
N.L. totals (11 years)	94	80	.540	3.76	266	265	19	11	0	1640	1510	758	686	545	1156
Major League totals (14 years)	111	103	.519	3.89	321	318	24	11	0	1959	1822	926	846	716	1368

ALL-STAR GAME RECORD

Year League	W	L	Pct.	ERA	GS	CG	ShO	Sv.	IP	H	R	ER	BB	SO
1991—National	0	0	...	0.00	0	0	0	0	1	2	0	0	0	1

H

HARPER, TRAVIS   P   DEVIL RAYS

PERSONAL: Born May 21, 1976, in Harrisonburg, Va. ... 6-4/195. ... Throws right, bats left. ... Full name: Travis Boyd Harper.
HIGH SCHOOL: Circleville (W. Va.).
COLLEGE: James Madison.
TRANSACTIONS/CAREER NOTES: Selected by New York Mets organization in 14th round of free-agent draft (June 2, 1994); did not sign. ... Selected by Boston Red Sox organization in third round of free-agent draft (June 3, 1997). ... Contract with Red Sox voided due to pre-existing injury (October 29, 1997). ... Signed by Tampa Bay Devil Rays organization (June 29, 1998).

Year League	W	L	Pct.	ERA	G	GS	CG	ShO	Sv.	IP	H	R	ER	BB	SO
1998— Hudson Valley (NY-Penn)	6	2	.750	1.92	13	10	0	0	0	56 1/3	38	14	12	20	81
1999— St. Petersburg (FSL)	5	4	.556	3.43	14	14	0	0	0	81 1/3	82	36	31	23	79
— Orlando (Sou.)	6	3	.667	5.38	14	14	1	1	0	72	73	45	43	26	68
2000— Orlando (Sou.)	3	1	.750	2.63	9	9	0	0	0	51 1/3	49	19	15	11	33
— Durham (I.L.)	7	4	.636	4.24	17	17	0	0	0	104	98	53	49	26	48
— Tampa Bay (A.L.)	1	2	.333	4.78	6	5	1	1	0	32	30	17	17	15	14
2001— Tampa Bay (A.L.)	0	2	.000	7.71	2	2	0	0	0	7	15	11	6	3	2
— Durham (I.L.)	12	6	.667	3.70	25	25	1	1	0	155 2/3	140	70	64	38	115
Major League totals (2 years)	1	4	.200	5.31	8	7	1	1	0	39	45	28	23	18	16

HARRIS, LENNY   IF/OF   ROCKIES

PERSONAL: Born October 28, 1964, in Miami. ... 5-10/220. ... Bats left, throws right. ... Full name: Leonard Anthony Harris.
HIGH SCHOOL: Jackson (Miami).
JUNIOR COLLEGE: Miami-Dade (North) Community College.
TRANSACTIONS/CAREER NOTES: Selected by Cincinnati Reds organization in fifth round of free-agent draft (June 6, 1983). ... Loaned by Reds organization to Glens Falls, Detroit Tigers organization (May 6-28, 1988). ... Traded by Reds with OF Kal Daniels to Los Angeles Dodgers for P Tim Leary and SS Mariano Duncan (July 18, 1989). ... Granted free agency (October 8, 1993). ... Signed by Reds (December 1, 1993). ... Granted free agency (October 31, 1996). ... Re-signed by Reds (November 13, 1996). ... Traded by Reds to New York Mets for P John Hudek (July 3, 1998). ... Granted free agency (October 27, 1998). ... Signed by Colorado Rockies (November 9, 1998). ... Traded by Rockies to Arizona Diamondbacks for IF Belvani Martinez (August 31, 1999). ... Traded by Diamondbacks to Mets for P Bill Pulsipher (June 2, 2000). ... Traded by Mets to Rockies as part of three-way deal in which Mets traded P Glendon Rusch to Milwaukee Brewers, Rockies traded 1B/OF Ross Gload and P Craig House to Mets, Brewers traded P Jeff D'Amico, OF Jeromy Burnitz, IF Lou Collier, OF/1B Mark Sweeney and cash to Mets, Mets traded 1B/3B Todd Zeile, OF Benny Agbayani and cash to Rockies and Rockies traded OF Alex Ochoa to Brewers (January 21, 2002).
RECORDS: Holds major league career record for most pinch hits—151. ... Holds major league single-season records for most games by pinch hitter—95 and at bats by pinch hitter—83 (2001).
STATISTICAL NOTES: Led Florida State League third basemen with 34 double plays in 1985. ... Led Eastern League third basemen with 116 putouts, 28 errors and 360 total chances in 1986. ... Led American Association in caught stealing with 22 in 1988. ... Led American Association second basemen with 23 errors in 1988. ... Career major league grand slams: 3.

						BATTING								FIELDING		
Year Team (League)	Pos.	G	AB	R	H	2B	3B	HR	RBI	Avg.	BB	SO	SB	PO	A	E	Avg.
1983— Billings (Pio.)	3B	56	224	37	63	8	1	1	26	.281	13	35	7	34	95	22	.854
1984— Cedar Rapids (Midw.)	3B	132	468	52	115	15	3	6	53	.246	42	59	31	111	204	*34	.903
1985— Tampa (FSL)	3B	132	499	66	129	11	8	3	51	.259	37	57	15	89	*277	*35	.913
1986— Vermont (East.)	3B-SS	119	450	68	114	17	2	10	52	.253	29	38	36	†119	220	†28	.924
1987— Nashville (A.A.)	SS-3B	120	403	45	100	12	3	2	31	.248	27	43	30	124	210	34	.908
1988— Nashville (A.A.)■	2B-SS-3B	107	422	46	117	20	2	0	35	.277	22	36	*45	203	247	†25	.947
— Glens Falls (East.)■	2B	17	65	9	22	5	1	1	7	.338	9	6	6	40	49	5	.947
— Cincinnati (N.L.)■	3B-2B	16	43	7	16	1	0	0	8	.372	5	4	4	14	33	1	.979
1989— Cincinnati (N.L.)	2B-SS-3B	61	188	17	42	4	0	2	11	.223	9	20	10	92	134	13	.946
— Nashville (A.A.)	2B	8	34	6	9	2	0	3	6	.265	0	5	0	23	20	0	1.000
— Los Angeles (N.L.)■ .OF-2B-3B-SS	54	147	19	37	6	1	1	15	.252	11	13	4	55	34	2	.978
1990— Los Angeles (N.L.) .3B-2B-OF-SS	137	431	61	131	16	4	2	29	.304	29	31	15	140	205	11	.969
1991— Los Angeles (N.L.) .3B-2B-SS-OF	145	429	59	123	16	1	3	38	.287	37	32	12	125	250	20	.949
1992— Los Angeles (N.L.) .2B-3B-OF-SS	135	347	28	94	11	0	0	30	.271	24	24	19	199	248	27	.943
1993— Los Angeles (N.L.) .3B-OF-2B	107	160	20	38	6	1	2	11	.238	15	15	3	61	99	3	.982
1994— Cincinnati (N.L.)■ .3B-1B-OF-2B	66	100	13	31	3	1	0	14	.310	5	13	7	27	29	6	.903
1995— Cincinnati (N.L.) .3B-1B-OF-2B	101	197	32	41	8	3	2	16	.208	14	20	10	147	68	4	.982
1996— Cincinnati (N.L.) .OF-2B-3B-1B	125	302	33	86	17	2	5	32	.285	21	31	14	199	66	6	.978
1997— Cincinnati (N.L.) .OF-2B-3B-1B	120	238	32	65	13	1	3	28	.273	18	18	4	120	57	3	.983
1998— Cincinnati (N.L.)	OF-DH-P	57	122	12	36	8	0	0	10	.295	8	9	1	37	2	3	.929
— New York (N.L.)■	OF-3B-2B-1B	75	168	18	39	7	0	6	17	.232	9	12	5	84	14	2	.980
1999— Colorado (N.L.)■	2-O-DH-3	91	158	15	47	12	0	0	13	.297	6	6	1	60	53	9	.926
— Arizona (N.L.)■	3B-OF	19	29	2	11	1	0	1	7	.379	0	1	1	6	5	0	1.000
2000— Arizona (N.L.)	OF	36	85	9	16	1	1	1	13	.188	3	5	5	11	29	4	.909
— New York (N.L.)■	IF-OF-DH	76	138	22	42	6	3	3	13	.304	17	17	8	67	36	11	.904
2001— New York (N.L.)	3-O-1-DH-2	110	135	12	30	5	1	0	9	.222	8	9	3	42	8	3	.943
Major League totals (14 years)		1531	3417	411	925	141	19	31	314	.271	239	280	126	1486	1370	128	.957

DIVISION SERIES RECORD

						BATTING								FIELDING		
Year Team (League)	Pos.	G	AB	R	H	2B	3B	HR	RBI	Avg.	BB	SO	SB	PO	A	E	Avg.
1999— Arizona (N.L.)	PH-3B	2	2	0	0	0	0	0	0	.000	0	0	0	0	0	0	...
2000— New York (N.L.)	PH	2	2	1	0	0	0	0	0	.000	0	0	1	...	...	...	...
Division series totals (2 years)		4	4	1	0	0	0	0	0	.000	0	0	1	0	0	0	...

CHAMPIONSHIP SERIES RECORD

						BATTING								FIELDING		
Year Team (League)	Pos.	G	AB	R	H	2B	3B	HR	RBI	Avg.	BB	SO	SB	PO	A	E	Avg.
1995— Cincinnati (N.L.)	PH	3	2	0	2	0	0	0	1	1.000	0	0	1	...	...	...	...
2000— New York (N.L.)	PH	2	1	0	0	0	0	0	0	.000	0	1	0	...	...	...	...
Championship series totals (2 years)		5	3	0	2	0	0	0	1	.667	0	1	1	...	...	...	...

H

WORLD SERIES RECORD

					BATTING										FIELDING		
Year	Team (League)	Pos.	G	AB	R	H	2B	3B	HR	RBI	Avg.	BB	SO	SB	PO	A	E	Avg.
2000— New York (N.L.)..........	DH-PH	3	4	1	0	0	0	0	0	.000	1	1	0	...	...	...	...

RECORD AS PITCHER

Year	League	W	L	Pct.	ERA	G	GS	CG	ShO	Sv.	IP	H	R	ER	BB	SO
1998— Cincinnati (N.L.)		0	0	...	0.00	1	0	0	0	0	1	0	0	0	0	1

HARRIS, WILLIE — 2B/OF — ORIOLES

PERSONAL: Born June 22, 1978, in Cairo, Ga. ... 5-9/175. ... Bats left, throws right. ... Full name: William Charles Harris. ... Nephew of Ernest Riles, infielder with Milwaukee Brewers, San Francisco Giants, Oakland Athletics, Houston Astros and Boston Red Sox (1985-1993).
HIGH SCHOOL: Cairo (Ga.).
JUNIOR COLLEGE: Middle Georgia.
COLLEGE: Kennesaw State.
TRANSACTIONS/CAREER NOTES: Selected by Pittsburgh Pirates organization in 28th round of free-agent draft (June 4, 1996); did not sign. ... Selected by Baltimore Orioles organization in 24th round of free-agent draft (June 2, 1999).

					BATTING										FIELDING		
Year	Team (League)	Pos.	G	AB	R	H	2B	3B	HR	RBI	Avg.	BB	SO	SB	PO	A	E	Avg.
1999— Bluefield (Appl.)	2B	5	22	3	6	1	0	0	3	.273	4	2	1	15	13	1	.966
— Delmarva (S.Atl.)........	2B-OF	66	272	42	72	13	3	2	32	.265	20	41	11	128	176	11	.965
2000— Delmarva (S.Atl.)........	2B-OF-SS	133	474	106	130	27	10	6	60	.274	89	89	38	260	313	19	.968
2001— Bowie (East.).............	2B-OF	133	525	83	160	27	4	9	49	.305	46	71	54	313	220	14	.974
— Baltimore (A.L.).........	OF	9	24	3	3	1	0	0	0	.125	0	7	0	16	1	0	1.000
Major League totals (1 year)		9	24	3	3	1	0	0	0	.125	0	7	0	16	1	0	1.000

HART, JASON — 1B — RANGERS

PERSONAL: Born September 5, 1977, in Walnut Creek, Calif. ... 6-3/225. ... Bats right, throws right. ... Full name: Jason Wyatt Hart.
HIGH SCHOOL: Fair Grove (Mo.).
COLLEGE: Southwest Missouri.
TRANSACTIONS/CAREER NOTES: Selected by Oakland Athletics organization in fifth round of free-agent draft (June 2, 1998). ... Traded by A's with P Mario Ramos, C Gerald Laird and OF Ryan Ludwick to Texas Rangers for 1B Carlos Pena and P Mike Venafro (January 14, 2002).
HONORS: Named Northwest League Most Valuable Player (1998).
STATISTICAL NOTES: Led Northwest League with 157 total bases and eight sacrifice flies in 1998. ... Led Northwest League first basemen with 622 putouts, 12 errors, 679 total chances and 45 double plays in 1998. ... Led California League first basemen with 1,237 total chances in 1999. ... Led Texas League with 318 total bases in 2000. ... Led Texas League first basemen with 1,261 total chances and 117 double plays in 2000. ... Led Pacific Coast League first basemen with 1,208 total chances in 2001.

					BATTING										FIELDING		
Year	Team (League)	Pos.	G	AB	R	H	2B	3B	HR	RBI	Avg.	BB	SO	SB	PO	A	E	Avg.
1998— S. Oregon (N'West)....	1B-3B	•75	295	58	76	19	1	*20	69	.258	36	67	0	*622	45	*12	.982
1999— Modesto (Calif.)	1B	135	*550	96	168	*48	2	19	•123	.305	56	105	2	*1148	76	13	.989
2000— Midland (Texas).........	1B	135	*546	98	*178	44	3	30	*121	.326	67	112	4	*1184	66	11	*.991
— Sacramento (PCL)......	1B	5	18	4	5	1	0	1	4	.278	3	7	0	33	2	0	1.000
2001— Sacramento (PCL)......	1B	134	494	71	122	26	1	19	75	.247	57	102	3	*1130	62	•15	.988

HARVEY, KEN — 1B — ROYALS

PERSONAL: Born March 1, 1978, in Los Angeles. ... 6-2/240. ... Bats right, throws right. ... Full name: Kenneth Eugene Harvey.
HIGH SCHOOL: Beverly Hills (Calif.).
COLLEGE: Nebraska.
TRANSACTIONS/CAREER NOTES: Selected by Kansas City Royals organization in fifth round of free-agent draft (June 2, 1999).
STATISTICAL NOTES: Led Northwest League with .598 slugging percentage and .477 on-base percentage and tied for league lead in intentional bases on balls received with four in 1999. ... Tied for Texas League lead with eight sacrifice flies in 2001.

					BATTING										FIELDING		
Year	Team (League)	Pos.	G	AB	R	H	2B	3B	HR	RBI	Avg.	BB	SO	SB	PO	A	E	Avg.
1999— Spokane (N'West)	1B	56	204	49	81	17	0	8	41	*.397	23	30	7	289	22	5	.984
2000— Wilmington (Caro.).....	1B	46	164	20	55	10	0	4	25	.335	14	29	0	162	8	3	.983
2001— Wilmington (Caro.).....	1B	35	137	22	52	9	1	6	27	.380	13	21	3	166	18	3	.984
— Wichita (Texas)	1B-OF	79	314	54	106	20	3	9	63	.338	18	60	3	442	34	5	.990
— Kansas City (A.L.)	1B-DH	4	12	1	3	1	0	0	2	.250	0	4	0	11	1	0	1.000
Major League totals (1 year)		4	12	1	3	1	0	0	2	.250	0	4	0	11	1	0	1.000

HARVILLE, CHAD — P — ATHLETICS

PERSONAL: Born September 16, 1976, in Selmer, Tenn. ... 5-9/180. ... Throws right, bats right. ... Full name: Chad Ashley Harville.
HIGH SCHOOL: Hardin County (Savannah, Tenn.).
COLLEGE: Memphis.
TRANSACTIONS/CAREER NOTES: Selected by Oakland Athletics organization in second round of free-agent draft (June 3, 1997). ... On Oakland disabled list (March 31-June 9, 2001); included rehabilitation assignments to Visalia (June 3-5) and Modesto (June 5-9).

Year	League	W	L	Pct.	ERA	G	GS	CG	ShO	Sv.	IP	H	R	ER	BB	SO
1997— Southern Oregon (N'West)	1	0	1.000	0.00	3	0	0	0	0	5	3	0	0	3	6
— Visalia (Calif.)..................	0	0	...	5.79	14	0	0	0	0	18 2/3	25	14	12	13	24
1998— Visalia (Calif.)	4	3	.571	3.00	24	7	0	0	4	69	59	25	23	31	76
— Huntsville (Sou.)	0	0	...	2.45	12	0	0	0	8	14 2/3	6	4	4	13	24
1999— Midland (Texas)................	2	0	1.000	2.01	17	0	0	0	7	22 1/3	13	6	5	9	35
— Vancouver (PCL)	1	0	1.000	1.75	22	0	0	0	11	25 2/3	24	5	5	11	36
— Oakland (A.L.)	0	2	.000	6.91	15	0	0	0	0	14 1/3	18	11	11	10	15

H

Year	League	W	L	Pct.	ERA	G	GS	CG	ShO	Sv.	IP	H	R	ER	BB	SO
2000— Sacramento (PCL).............		5	3	.625	4.50	53	0	0	0	9	64	53	35	32	35	77
2001— Visalia (Calif.)...................		0	0	...	0.00	1	1	0	0	0	3	3	0	0	0	3
— Modesto (Calif.)...............		0	0	...	3.00	2	1	0	0	0	3	2	2	1	0	3
— Sacramento (PCL).............		5	2	.714	3.98	33	0	0	0	8	40 2/3	35	20	18	12	55
— Oakland (A.L.)..................		0	0	...	0.00	3	0	0	0	0	3	2	0	0	0	2
Major League totals (2 years).......		0	2	.000	5.71	18	0	0	0	0	17 1/3	20	11	11	10	17

HASEGAWA, SHIGETOSHI — P — MARINERS

PERSONAL: Born August 1, 1968, in Kobe, Japan ... 5-11/178. ... Throws right, bats right. ... Name pronounced SHE-geh-TOE-she HAH-seh-GAH-wah.

COLLEGE: Ritsumeikan University (Kyoto, Japan).

TRANSACTIONS/CAREER NOTES: Played for Orix Blue Wave of Japan Pacific League (1991-96). ... Signed as non-drafted free agent by Anaheim Angels (January 9, 1997). ... On Anaheim disabled list (May 20-June 29, 2001); included rehabilitation assignment to Rancho Cucamonga (June 25-29). ... Granted free agency (December 21, 2001). ... Signed by Seattle Mariners (January 11, 2002).

Year	League	W	L	Pct.	ERA	G	GS	CG	ShO	Sv.	IP	H	R	ER	BB	SO
1991— Orix (Jap. Pac.)		12	9	.571	3.55	28	25	11	3	1	185	184	76	73	50	111
1992— Orix (Jap. Pac.)		6	8	.429	3.27	24	19	4	0	1	143 1/3	138	60	52	51	86
1993— Orix (Jap. Pac.)		12	6	.667	2.71	23	22	9	3	0	159 2/3	146	61	48	48	86
1994— Orix (Jap. Pac.)		11	9	.550	3.11	25	22	8	3	1	156 1/3	169	61	54	46	86
1995— Orix (Jap. Pac.)		12	7	.632	2.89	24	23	9	4	0	171	167	62	55	51	91
1996— Orix (Jap. Pac.)		4	6	.400	5.34	18	16	2	0	1	87 2/3	109	66	52	40	55
1997— Anaheim (A.L.)■...............		3	7	.300	3.93	50	7	0	0	0	116 2/3	118	60	51	46	83
1998— Anaheim (A.L.)		8	3	.727	3.14	61	0	0	0	5	97 1/3	86	37	34	32	73
1999— Anaheim (A.L.)		4	6	.400	4.91	64	1	0	0	2	77	80	45	42	34	44
2000— Anaheim (A.L.)		10	6	.625	3.57	66	0	0	0	9	95 2/3	100	43	38	38	59
2001— Anaheim (A.L.)		5	6	.455	4.04	46	0	0	0	0	55 2/3	52	28	25	20	41
— Rancho Cuca. (Calif.)		0	0	...	0.00	2	2	0	0	0	2	3	1	0	0	1
Major League totals (5 years).......		30	28	.517	3.87	287	8	0	0	16	442 1/3	436	213	190	170	300

HASELMAN, BILL — C — RANGERS

PERSONAL: Born May 25, 1966, in Long Branch, N.J. ... 6-3/225. ... Bats right, throws right. ... Full name: William Joseph Haselman.

HIGH SCHOOL: Saratoga (Calif.).

COLLEGE: UCLA.

TRANSACTIONS/CAREER NOTES: Selected by Texas Rangers organization in first round (23rd pick overall) of free-agent draft (June 2, 1987); pick received as compensation for New York Yankees signing Type A free-agent OF Gary Ward. ... On Oklahoma City disabled list (March 28-May 4, 1992). ... Claimed on waivers by Seattle Mariners (May 29, 1992). ... On suspended list (July 22-25, 1993). ... Granted free agency (October 15, 1994). ... Signed by Boston Red Sox (November 7, 1994). ... On Boston disabled list (June 30-August 8, 1997); included rehabilitation assignment to Gulf Coast Red Sox (July 29-August 1) and Trenton (August 1-8). ... Traded by Red Sox with P Aaron Sele and P Mark Brandenburg to Rangers for C Jim Leyritz and OF Damon Buford (November 6, 1997). ... Granted free agency (October 23, 1998). ... Signed by Detroit Tigers (December 14, 1998). ... Traded by Tigers with P Justin Thompson, OF Gabe Kapler, 2B Frank Catalanotto and P Alan Webb to Rangers for OF Juan Gonzalez, P Danny Patterson and C Gregg Zaun (November 2, 1999). ... On Texas disabled list (March 31-June 22, 2001); included rehabilitation assignment to Oklahoma (June 13-22).

RECORDS: Holds major league record for most chances accepted in consecutive nine-inning games—37 (April 29 and 30, 1996). ... Shares A.L. single-game record for most chances accepted by catcher (nine-inning game)—20 (September 18, 1996).

STATISTICAL NOTES: Led Texas League with 12 passed balls in 1989. ... Led Texas League catchers with 676 putouts, 90 assists, 20 errors, 786 total chances and 20 passed balls in 1990. ... Led American Association catchers with 673 putouts and 751 total chances in 1991. ... Tied for A.L. lead in passed balls with 17 in 1997. ... Career major league grand slams: 1.

Year	Team (League)	Pos.	G	AB	R	H	2B	3B	HR	RBI	Avg.	BB	SO	SB	PO	A	E	Avg.
							BATTING									FIELDING		
1987— Gastonia (S.Atl.).........		C	61	235	35	72	13	1	8	33	.306	19	46	1	26	2	2	.933
1988— Charlotte (FSL)..........		C	122	453	56	111	17	2	10	54	.245	45	99	6	249	30	6	.979
1989— Tulsa (Texas)		C	107	352	38	95	17	2	7	36	.270	40	88	5	508	63	9	.984
1990— Tulsa (Texas) C-1B-OF-3B			120	430	68	137	39	2	18	80	.319	43	96	3	†722	†93	†20	.976
— Texas (A.L.)...................		DH-C	7	13	0	2	0	0	0	3	.154	1	5	0	8	0	0	1.000
1991— Oklahoma City (A.A.)..C-OF-1B-3B			126	442	57	113	22	2	9	60	.256	61	89	10	†706	71	11	.986
1992— Oklahoma City (A.A.)..		OF-C	17	58	8	14	5	0	1	9	.241	13	12	1	45	7	3	.945
— Calgary (PCL)■..........		C-OF	88	302	49	77	14	2	19	53	.255	41	89	3	227	23	6	.977
— Seattle (A.L.).............		C-OF	8	19	1	5	0	0	0	0	.263	0	7	0	19	2	0	1.000
1993— Seattle (A.L.)		C-DH-OF	58	137	21	35	8	0	5	16	.255	12	19	2	236	17	2	.992
1994— Seattle (A.L.)		C-DH-OF	38	83	11	16	7	1	1	8	.193	3	11	1	157	6	3	.982
— Calgary (PCL).............		C-DH-1B	44	163	44	54	10	0	15	46	.331	30	33	1	219	16	5	.979
1995— Boston (A.L.)■.........C-DH-1B-3B			64	152	22	37	6	1	5	23	.243	17	30	0	259	16	3	.989
1996— Boston (A.L.).............		C-DH-1B	77	237	33	65	13	1	8	34	.274	19	52	4	507	33	3	.994
1997— Boston (A.L.).............		C	67	212	22	50	15	0	6	26	.236	15	44	0	373	40	7	.983
— GC Red Sox (GCL)		DH	4	16	2	2	0	0	0	1	.125	0	1	1	0	0	0	...
— Trenton (East.)		C-DH	7	26	3	6	1	0	2	3	.231	2	2	0	30	2	0	1.000
1998— Texas (A.L.)■		C-DH	40	105	11	33	6	0	6	17	.314	3	17	0	176	8	1	.995
1999— Detroit (A.L.)■		C-DH	48	143	13	39	8	0	4	14	.273	10	26	2	231	13	1	.996
2000— Texas (A.L.)■.............		C	62	193	23	53	18	0	6	26	.275	15	36	0	336	20	4	.989
2001— Oklahoma (PCL)........		C	8	28	2	4	0	0	0	1	.143	1	10	0	22	0	1	.957
— Texas (A.L.)		C	47	130	12	37	6	0	3	25	.285	8	27	0	234	13	0	1.000
Major League totals (11 years)			516	1424	169	372	87	3	44	192	.261	103	274	9	2536	168	24	.991

DIVISION SERIES RECORD

Year	Team (League)	Pos.	G	AB	R	H	2B	3B	HR	RBI	Avg.	BB	SO	SB	PO	A	E	Avg.
							BATTING									FIELDING		
1995— Boston (A.L.).............		C	1	2	0	0	0	0	0	0	.000	0	0	0	6	0	0	1.000

H

PERSONAL: Born December 14, 1969, in Salem, Ore. ... 6-1/205. ... Bats left, throws right. ... Full name: Scott Allen Hatteberg. ... Name pronounced HAT-ee-berg.

HIGH SCHOOL: Eisenhower (Yakima, Wash.).

COLLEGE: Washington State.

TRANSACTIONS/CAREER NOTES: Selected by Philadelphia Phillies organization in 12th round of free-agent draft (June 1, 1988); did not sign. ... Selected by Boston Red Sox organization in supplemental round ("sandwich pick" between first and second round, 43rd pick overall) of free-agent draft (June 3, 1991); pick received as part of compensation for Kansas City signing Type A free-agent P Mike Boddicker. ... On disabled list (July 27-August 3, 1992). ... On Boston disabled list (April 15-May 7 and May 17-August 16, 1999); included rehabilitation assignments to Pawtucket (May 4-7 and August 3-13), Gulf Coast Red Sox (July 24-31) and Sarasota (August 1-2). ... Traded by Red Sox to Colorado Rockies for 2B Pokey Reese (December 19, 2001). ... Granted free agency (December 21, 2001). ... Signed by Oakland Athletics (December 30, 2001).

STATISTICAL NOTES: Tied for A.L. lead in double plays by catcher with 13 and passed balls with 17 in 1997. ... Career major league grand slams: 2.

							BATTING							FIELDING		
Year Team (League)	Pos.	G	AB	R	H	2B	3B	HR	RBI	Avg.	BB	SO	SB	PO	A	E	Avg.
1991— Winter Haven (FSL)....	C	56	191	21	53	7	3	1	25	.277	22	22	1	261	35	5	.983
— Lynchburg (Caro.)......	C	8	25	4	5	1	0	0	2	.200	7	6	0	35	2	0	1.000
1992— New Britain (East.).....	C	103	297	28	69	13	2	1	30	.232	41	49	1	473	44	11	.979
1993— New Britain (East.).....	C	68	227	35	63	10	2	7	28	.278	42	38	1	410	45	10	.978
— Pawtucket (I.L.).........	C	18	53	6	10	0	0	1	2	.189	6	12	0	131	4	5	.964
1994— New Britain (East.)......	C	20	68	6	18	4	1	1	9	.265	7	9	0	125	14	1	.993
— Pawtucket (I.L.).......	C	78	238	26	56	14	0	7	19	.235	32	49	2	467	36	7	.986
1995— Pawtucket (I.L.)............	C-DH	85	251	36	68	15	1	7	27	.271	40	39	2	446	45	•8	.984
— Boston (A.L.).............	C	2	2	1	1	0	0	0	0	.500	0	0	0	4	0	0	1.000
1996— Pawtucket (I.L.)............	C-DH	90	287	52	77	16	0	12	49	.268	58	66	1	566	42	6	.990
— Boston (A.L.).............	C	10	11	3	2	1	0	0	0	.182	3	2	0	32	2	0	1.000
1997— Boston (A.L.).............	C-DH	114	350	46	97	23	1	10	44	.277	40	70	0	574	46	11	.983
1998— Boston (A.L.).............	C	112	359	46	99	23	1	12	43	.276	43	58	0	664	61	5	.993
1999— Boston (A.L.).............	C-DH	30	80	12	22	5	0	1	11	.275	18	14	0	128	14	1	.993
— Pawtucket (I.L.).........	C-DH	10	34	3	6	2	0	0	4	.176	4	6	0	47	4	0	1.000
— GC Red Sox (GCL)	C-DH	6	15	4	6	2	0	1	6	.400	7	1	0	37	4	0	1.000
— Sarasota (FSL)	C	1	1	0	1	0	0	0	1	1.000	0	0	0	3	1	0	1.000
2000— Boston (A.L.).............	C-DH-3B	92	230	21	61	15	0	8	36	.265	38	39	0	297	16	6	.981
2001— Boston (A.L.).............	C-DH	94	278	34	68	19	0	3	25	.245	33	26	1	491	29	4	.992
Major League totals (7 years)		454	1310	163	350	86	2	34	159	.267	175	209	1	2190	168	27	.989

DIVISION SERIES RECORD

							BATTING							FIELDING		
Year Team (League)	Pos.	G	AB	R	H	2B	3B	HR	RBI	Avg.	BB	SO	SB	PO	A	E	Avg.
1998— Boston (A.L.).............	C	3	9	0	1	0	0	0	0	.111	3	1	0	20	0	0	1.000
1999— Boston (A.L.).............	C	1	1	1	1	0	0	0	1	1.000	0	0	0	2	0	0	1.000
Division series totals (2 years)		4	10	1	2	0	0	0	1	.200	3	1	0	22	0	0	1.000

CHAMPIONSHIP SERIES RECORD

							BATTING							FIELDING		
Year Team (League)	Pos.	G	AB	R	H	2B	3B	HR	RBI	Avg.	BB	SO	SB	PO	A	E	Avg.
1999— Boston (A.L.).............	PH-C	3	1	0	0	0	0	0	0	.000	0	1	0	0	0	0	...

HAWKINS, LaTROY   P   TWINS

PERSONAL: Born December 21, 1972, in Gary, Ind. ... 6-5/204. ... Throws right, bats right.

HIGH SCHOOL: West Side (Gary, Ind.).

TRANSACTIONS/CAREER NOTES: Selected by Minnesota Twins organization in seventh round of free-agent draft (June 3, 1991).

STATISTICAL NOTES: Tied for A.L. lead with three balks in 1997.

Year League	W	L	Pct.	ERA	G	GS	CG	ShO	Sv.	IP	H	R	ER	BB	SO
1991— Gulf Coast Twins (GCL)......	4	3	.571	4.75	11	11	0	0	0	55	62	34	29	26	47
1992— Gulf Coast Twins (GCL)......	3	2	.600	3.22	6	6	1	0	0	36 1/3	36	19	13	10	35
— Elizabethton (Appl.)...........	0	1	.000	3.38	5	5	1	0	0	26 2/3	21	12	10	11	36
1993— Fort Wayne (Midw.)...........	•15	5	.750	*2.06	26	23	4	•3	0	157 1/3	110	53	36	41	*179
1994— Fort Myers (FSL).............	4	0	1.000	2.33	6	6	1	1	0	38 2/3	32	10	10	6	36
— Nashville (Sou.).................	9	2	•.818	2.33	11	11	1	0	0	73 1/3	50	23	19	28	53
— Salt Lake (PCL).................	5	4	.556	4.08	12	12	1	0	0	81 2/3	92	42	37	33	37
1995— Minnesota (A.L.)	2	3	.400	8.67	6	6	0	0	0	27	39	29	26	12	9
— Salt Lake (PCL)	9	7	.563	3.55	22	22	4	1	0	144 1/3	150	63	57	40	74
1996— Minnesota (A.L.)	1	1	.500	8.20	7	6	0	0	0	26 1/3	42	24	24	9	24
— Salt Lake (PCL)	9	8	.529	3.92	20	20	4	1	0	137 2/3	138	66	60	31	99
1997— Salt Lake (PCL)	9	4	.692	5.45	14	13	2	1	0	76	100	53	46	16	53
— Minnesota (A.L.)	6	12	.333	5.84	20	20	0	0	0	103 1/3	134	71	67	47	58
1998— Minnesota (A.L.)	7	14	.333	5.25	33	33	0	0	0	190 1/3	227	126	111	61	105
1999— Minnesota (A.L.)	10	14	.417	6.66	33	33	1	0	0	174 1/3	238	*136	*129	60	103
2000— Minnesota (A.L.)	2	5	.286	3.39	66	0	0	0	14	87 2/3	85	34	33	32	59
2001— Minnesota (A.L.)	1	5	.167	5.96	62	0	0	0	28	51 1/3	59	34	34	39	36
Major League totals (7 years)......	29	54	.349	5.78	227	98	0	0	42	660 1/3	824	454	424	260	394

HAYES, CHARLIE   3B/1B

PERSONAL: Born May 29, 1965, in Hattiesburg, Miss. ... 6-0/215. ... Bats right, throws right. ... Full name: Charles Dewayne Hayes.

HIGH SCHOOL: Forrest County Agricultural (Brooklyn, Miss.).

H

TRANSACTIONS/CAREER NOTES: Selected by San Francisco Giants organization in fourth round of free-agent draft (June 6, 1983). ... On disabled list (July 20, 1983-remainder of season). ... Traded by Giants with P Dennis Cook and P Terry Mulholland to Philadelphia Phillies for P Steve Bedrosian and a player to be named later (June 18, 1989); Giants acquired IF Rick Parker to complete deal (August 7, 1989). ... Traded by Phillies to New York Yankees (February 19, 1992), completing deal in which Yankees traded P Darrin Chapin to Phillies for a player to be named later (January 8, 1992). ... Selected by Colorado Rockies in first round (third pick overall) of expansion draft (November 17, 1992). ... On suspended list (August 10-13, 1993). ... Granted free agency (December 23, 1994). ... Signed by Phillies (April 6, 1995). ... Granted free agency (November 2, 1995). ... Signed by Pittsburgh Pirates (December 28, 1995). ... Traded by Pirates to Yankees for a player to be named later (August 30, 1996); Pirates acquired P Chris Corn to complete deal (August 31, 1996). ... Traded by Yankees with cash to Giants for OF Chris Singleton and P Alberto Castillo (November 11, 1997). ... On suspended list (July 28-30, 1998). ... On suspended list (April 20-24, 1999). ... On disabled list (July 2-21, 1999). ... Granted free agency (November 1, 1999). ... Signed by New York Mets organization (January 19, 2000). ... Released by Mets (March 20, 2000). ... Signed by Milwaukee Brewers organization (March 22, 2000). ... Granted free agency (October 31, 2000). ... Signed by Houston Astros organization (January 2, 2001). ... On disabled list (May 3-17, 2001). ... On suspended list (June 29-July 1, 2001). ... Released by Astros (July 9, 2001).

STATISTICAL NOTES: Led Texas League third basemen with 27 double plays in 1986. ... Led Texas League third basemen with 334 total chances in 1987. ... Led Pacific Coast League in grounding into double plays with 19 in 1988. ... Led N.L. third basemen with 324 assists and tied for lead with 465 total chances in 1990. ... Tied for A.L. lead in double plays by third baseman with 29 in 1992. ... Tied for N.L. lead in grounding into double plays with 25 in 1993. ... Led N.L. in grounding into double plays with 23 in 1995. ... Career major league grand slams: 3.

Year Team (League)	Pos.	G	AB	R	H	2B	3B	HR	RBI	Avg.	BB	SO	SB	PO	A	E	Avg.
1983— Great Falls (Pio.)	3B-OF	34	111	9	29	4	2	0	9	.261	7	26	1	13	32	9	.833
1984— Clinton (Midw.)	3B	116	392	41	96	17	2	2	51	.245	34	110	4	68	216	28	.910
1985— Fresno (Calif.)............	3B	131	467	73	132	17	2	4	68	.283	56	95	7	*100	233	18	*.949
1986— Shreveport (Texas)	3B	121	434	52	107	23	2	5	45	.247	28	83	1	89	*259	25	.933
1987— Shreveport (Texas)	3B	128	487	66	148	33	3	14	75	.304	26	76	5	*100	*212	22	*.934
1988— Phoenix (PCL)	OF-3B	131	492	71	151	26	4	7	71	.307	34	91	4	206	100	23	.930
— San Francisco (N.L.) ..	OF-3B	7	11	0	1	0	0	0	0	.091	0	3	0	5	0	0	1.000
1989— Phoenix (PCL)	3-0-1-S-2	61	229	25	65	15	1	7	27	.284	15	48	5	76	76	8	.950
— San Francisco (N.L.) ..	3B	3	5	0	1	0	0	0	0	.200	0	1	0	2	1	0	1.000
— Scranton/W.B. (I.L.)■	3B	7	27	4	11	3	1	1	3	.407	0	3	0	8	8	0	1.000
— Philadelphia (N.L.)........	3B	84	299	26	77	15	1	8	43	.258	11	49	3	49	173	22	.910
1990— Philadelphia (N.L.)......	3B-1B-2B	152	561	56	145	20	0	10	57	.258	28	91	4	151	†329	20	.960
1991— Philadelphia (N.L.)......	3B-SS	142	460	34	106	23	1	12	53	.230	16	75	3	88	240	15	.956
1992— New York (A.L.)■........	3B-1B	142	509	52	131	19	2	18	66	.257	28	100	3	125	249	13	.966
1993— Colorado (N.L.)■	3B-SS	157	573	89	175	*45	2	25	98	.305	43	82	11	123	292	20	.954
1994— Colorado (N.L.)	3B	113	423	46	122	23	4	10	50	.288	36	71	3	72	216	17	.944
1995— Philadelphia (N.L.)■.....	3B	141	529	58	146	30	3	11	85	.276	50	88	5	•104	264	14	.963
1996— Pittsburgh (N.L.)■	3B	128	459	51	114	21	2	10	62	.248	36	78	6	66	275	18	.950
— New York (A.L.)■......	3B	20	67	7	19	3	0	2	13	.284	1	12	0	14	30	0	1.000
1997— New York (A.L.)■......	3B-2B	100	353	39	91	16	0	11	53	.258	40	66	3	67	169	13	.948
1998— San Fran. (N.L.)■......	3B-1B-DH	111	329	39	94	8	0	12	62	.286	34	61	2	369	101	3	.994
1999— San Francisco (N.L.) ..3B-1B-DH-OF		95	264	33	54	9	1	6	48	.205	33	41	3	130	91	7	.969
2000— Milwaukee (N.L.)■.....	3B-1B-DH	121	370	46	93	17	0	9	46	.251	57	84	1	438	119	7	.988
2001— Houston (N.L.)■........	3B-1B-DH	31	50	4	10	2	0	0	4	.200	7	16	0	14	12	0	1.000
American League totals (3 years)		262	929	98	241	38	2	31	132	.259	69	178	6	206	448	26	.962
National League totals (12 years)		1285	4333	482	1138	213	14	113	608	.263	351	740	41	1611	2113	143	.963
Major League totals (14 years)		1547	5262	580	1379	251	16	144	740	.262	420	918	47	1817	2561	169	.963

DIVISION SERIES RECORD

Year Team (League)	Pos.	G	AB	R	H	2B	3B	HR	RBI	Avg.	BB	SO	SB	PO	A	E	Avg.
1996— New York (A.L.)..........	3B-DH	3	5	0	1	0	0	0	1	.200	0	0	0	1	3	0	1.000
1997— New York (A.L.)..........	3B-2B	5	15	0	5	0	0	0	1	.333	0	2	0	3	9	3	.800
Division series totals (2 years)		8	20	0	6	0	0	0	2	.300	0	2	0	4	12	3	.842

CHAMPIONSHIP SERIES RECORD

Year Team (League)	Pos.	G	AB	R	H	2B	3B	HR	RBI	Avg.	BB	SO	SB	PO	A	E	Avg.
1996— New York (A.L.)..........	PH-3B-DH	4	7	0	1	0	0	0	0	.143	2	2	0	0	3	0	1.000

WORLD SERIES RECORD

NOTES: Member of World Series championship team (1996).

Year Team (League)	Pos.	G	AB	R	H	2B	3B	HR	RBI	Avg.	BB	SO	SB	PO	A	E	Avg.
1996— New York (A.L.)..........	3B-PH-1B	4	16	2	3	0	0	0	1	.188	1	5	0	3	6	0	1.000

HAYNES, JIMMY   P   REDS

PERSONAL: Born September 5, 1972, in La Grange, Ga. ... 6-4/214. ... Throws right, bats right. ... Full name: Jimmy Wayne Haynes.

HIGH SCHOOL: Troup (La Grange, Ga.).

TRANSACTIONS/CAREER NOTES: Selected by Baltimore Orioles organization in seventh round of free-agent draft (June 3, 1991). ... Traded by Orioles with a player to be named later to Oakland Athletics for OF Geronimo Berroa (June 27, 1997); A's acquired P Mark Seaver to complete deal (September 2, 1997). ... Traded by A's to Milwaukee Brewers as part of three-way deal in which A's received P Justin Miller and cash from Colorado Rockies, Brewers received P Jamey Wright and C Henry Blanco from Rockies and Rockies received 3B Jeff Cirillo, P Scott Karl and cash from Brewers (December 13, 1999). ... On disabled list (August 24-September 26, 2001). ... Granted free agency (December 21, 2001). ... Signed by Cincinnati Reds organization (January 11, 2002).

RECORDS: Shares N.L. single-inning record for most consecutive home runs allowed—3 (July 12, 2001, third inning).

MISCELLANEOUS: Appeared in one game as pinch runner (2001).

H

Year	League	W	L	Pct.	ERA	G	GS	CG	ShO	Sv.	IP	H	R	ER	BB	SO
1991—Gulf Coast Orioles (GCL)....		3	2	.600	1.60	14	8	1	0	2	62	44	27	11	21	67
1992—Kane County (Midw.)........		7	11	.389	2.56	24	24	4	0	0	144	131	66	41	45	141
1993—Frederick (Caro.)		12	8	.600	3.03	27	27	2	1	0	172 1/3	139	73	58	61	174
1994—Bowie (East.)		13	8	.619	2.90	25	25	5	1	0	173 2/3	154	67	56	46	*177
—Rochester (I.L.)		1	0	1.000	6.75	3	3	0	0	0	13 1/3	20	12	10	6	14
1995—Rochester (I.L.)...............		•12	8	.600	3.29	26	25	3	1	0	167	162	77	61	49	*140
—Baltimore (A.L.)		2	1	.667	2.25	4	3	0	0	0	24	11	6	6	12	22
1996—Baltimore (A.L.)...............		3	6	.333	8.29	26	11	0	0	1	89	122	84	82	58	65
—Rochester (I.L.)		1	1	.500	5.65	5	5	0	0	0	28 2/3	31	19	18	18	24
1997—Baltimore (A.L.)...............		5	4	.556	3.44	16	16	2	1	0	102	89	49	39	55	113
—Edmonton (PCL)■		0	2	.000	4.85	5	5	0	0	0	29 2/3	36	22	16	11	24
—Oakland (A.L.)		3	6	.333	4.42	13	13	0	0	0	73 1/3	74	38	36	40	65
1998—Oakland (A.L.)		11	9	.550	5.09	33	33	1	1	0	194 1/3	229	124	110	88	134
1999—Oakland (A.L.)		7	12	.368	6.34	30	25	0	0	0	142	158	112	100	80	93
2000—Milwaukee (N.L.)■...........		12	13	.480	5.33	33	33	0	0	0	199 1/3	228	128	118	100	88
2001—Milwaukee (N.L.)		8	17	.320	4.85	31	29	0	0	0	172 2/3	182	98	93	78	112
A.L. totals (5 years)		26	34	.433	5.75	106	85	1	1	1	522 2/3	594	364	334	278	379
N.L. totals (2 years)		20	30	.400	5.10	64	62	0	0	0	372	410	226	211	178	200
Major League totals (7 years)		46	64	.418	5.48	170	147	1	1	1	894 2/3	1004	590	545	456	579

HAYNES, NATHAN — OF — ANGELS

PERSONAL: Born September 7, 1979, in Oakland. ... 5-9/170. ... Bats left, throws left. ... Full name: Nathan Raymond Quinn Haynes.
HIGH SCHOOL: Pinole Valley (Pinole, Calif.).
TRANSACTIONS/CAREER NOTES: Selected by Oakland Athletics organization in supplemental round ("sandwich pick" between first and second round, 32nd pick overall) of free-agent draft (June 3, 1997); pick received as part of compensation for Baltimore Orioles signing service-time free agent SS Mike Bordick. ... Traded by A's with OF Jeff DaVanon and P Elvin Nina to Anaheim Angels for P Omar Olivares and 2B Randy Velarde (July 29, 1999). ... On Erie disabled list (June 4-13, 2000). ... On disabled list (April 30-June 22, 2001).
STATISTICAL NOTES: Tied for Texas League lead with 15 caught stealing in 2001.

							BATTING								FIELDING		
Year	Team (League)	Pos.	G	AB	R	H	2B	3B	HR	RBI	Avg.	BB	SO	SB	PO	A	E	Avg.
1997—Ariz. Athletics (Ariz.) ..		OF	17	54	8	15	1	0	0	6	.278	7	9	5	21	0	1	.955
—S. Oregon (N'West)		OF	24	82	18	23	1	1	0	9	.280	26	21	19	32	0	1	.970
1998—Modesto (Calif.)		OF	125	507	89	128	13	7	1	41	.252	54	139	42	211	5	•14	.939
1999—Visalia (Calif.)		OF	35	145	28	45	7	1	1	14	.310	17	27	12	65	5	2	.972
—Lake Elsin. (Calif.)■ ...		OF	26	110	19	36	5	5	1	15	.327	12	19	10	59	0	2	.967
—Erie (East.)		OF	5	19	3	3	1	0	0	0	.158	5	5	0	5	1	0	1.000
2000—Erie (East.)		OF	118	457	56	116	16	4	6	43	.254	33	107	37	244	7	9	.965
2001—Arkansas (Texas)........		OF	79	316	49	98	11	5	5	23	.310	32	65	33	190	3	3	.985

HEAVERLO, JEFF — P — MARINERS

PERSONAL: Born January 13, 1978, in Palo Alto, Calif. ... 6-1/215. ... Throws right, bats right. ... Full name: Jeffrey Edward Allen Heaverlo.
HIGH SCHOOL: Ephrata (Wash.).
COLLEGE: Washington.
TRANSACTIONS/CAREER NOTES: Selected by Detroit Tigers organization in 13th round of free-agent draft (June 4, 1996); did not sign. ... Selected by Seattle Mariners organization in supplemental round ("sandwich pick" between first and second round, 33rd pick overall) of free-agent draft (June 2, 1999); pick received as part of compensation for Baltimore Orioles signing Type A free agent P Mike Timlin.

Year	League	W	L	Pct.	ERA	G	GS	CG	ShO	Sv.	IP	H	R	ER	BB	SO
1999—Everett (N'West)		1	0	1.000	2.08	3	0	0	0	0	8 2/3	5	5	2	2	9
—Wisconsin (Midw.)...........		1	0	1.000	2.55	3	3	1	1	0	17 2/3	15	6	5	7	24
2000—Lancaster (Calif.)...............		14	6	.700	4.22	27	27	0	0	0	155 2/3	170	84	73	52	159
—Tacoma (PCL)		0	1	.000	4.85	2	2	0	0	0	13	14	7	7	6	4
2001—San Antonio (Texas)		11	6	.647	3.12	27	27	*4	*4	0	178 2/3	164	75	62	40	*173

HELLING, RICK — P — DIAMONDBACKS

PERSONAL: Born December 15, 1970, in Devils Lake, N.D. ... 6-3/220. ... Throws right, bats right. ... Full name: Ricky Allen Helling.
HIGH SCHOOL: Lakota (Fargo, N.D.), then Shanley (N.D.).
JUNIOR COLLEGE: Kishwaukee College (Ill.).
COLLEGE: North Dakota, then Stanford.
TRANSACTIONS/CAREER NOTES: Selected by New York Mets organization in 50th round of free-agent draft (June 4, 1990); did not sign. ... Selected by Texas Rangers organization in first round (22nd pick overall) of free-agent draft (June 1, 1992). ... Traded by Rangers to Florida Marlins (September 3, 1996), completing deal in which Marlins traded P John Burkett to Rangers for P Ryan Dempster and a player to be named later (August 8, 1996). ... Traded by Marlins to Rangers for P Ed Vosberg (August 12, 1997). ... Granted free agency (December 21, 2001). ... Signed by Arizona Diamondbacks (January 20, 2002).
STATISTICAL NOTES: Pitched 4-0 no-hit victory against Nashville (August 13, 1996). ... Led A.L. with 41 home runs allowed in 1999 and 38 in 2001.
MISCELLANEOUS: Member of 1992 U.S. Olympic baseball team.

Year	League	W	L	Pct.	ERA	G	GS	CG	ShO	Sv.	IP	H	R	ER	BB	SO
1992—Charlotte (FSL)..................		1	1	.500	2.29	3	3	0	0	0	19 2/3	13	5	5	4	20
1993—Tulsa (Texas)		12	8	.600	3.60	26	26	2	•2	0	177 1/3	150	76	71	46	*188
—Oklahoma City (A.A.).........		1	1	.500	1.64	2	2	1	0	0	11	5	3	2	3	17
1994—Texas (A.L.)		3	2	.600	5.88	9	9	1	1	0	52	62	34	34	18	25
—Oklahoma City (A.A.)........		4	12	.250	5.78	20	20	2	0	0	132 1/3	153	93	85	43	85
1995—Texas (A.L.)		0	2	.000	6.57	3	3	0	0	0	12 1/3	17	11	9	8	5
—Oklahoma City (A.A.).........		4	8	.333	5.33	20	20	3	0	0	109 2/3	132	73	65	41	80

H

Year League	W	L	Pct.	ERA	G	GS	CG	ShO	Sv.	IP	H	R	ER	BB	SO
1996— Oklahoma City (A.A.)	12	4	.750	2.96	23	22	2	1	0	140	124	54	46	38	157
— Texas (A.L.)	1	2	.333	7.52	6	2	0	0	0	20 1/3	23	17	17	9	16
— Florida (N.L.)■	2	1	.667	1.95	5	4	0	0	0	27 2/3	14	6	6	7	26
1997— Florida (N.L.)	2	6	.250	4.38	31	8	0	0	0	76	61	38	37	48	53
— Texas (A.L.)■	3	3	.500	4.58	10	8	0	0	0	55	47	29	28	21	46
1998— Texas (A.L.)	•20	7	.741	4.41	33	33	4	2	0	216 1/3	209	109	106	78	164
1999— Texas (A.L.)	13	11	.542	4.84	35	*35	3	0	0	219 1/3	228	127	118	85	131
2000— Texas (A.L.)	16	13	.552	4.48	35	•35	0	0	0	217	212	122	108	99	146
2001— Texas (A.L.)	12	11	.522	5.17	34	34	2	1	0	215 2/3	*256	*134	*124	63	154
A.L. totals (8 years)	68	51	.571	4.86	165	159	10	4	0	1008	1054	583	544	381	687
N.L. totals (2 years)	4	7	.364	3.73	36	12	0	0	0	103 2/3	75	44	43	55	79
Major League totals (8 years)	72	58	.554	4.75	201	171	10	4	0	1111 2/3	1129	627	587	436	766

DIVISION SERIES RECORD

Year League	W	L	Pct.	ERA	G	GS	CG	ShO	Sv.	IP	H	R	ER	BB	SO
1998— Texas (A.L.)	0	1	.000	4.50	1	1	0	0	0	6	8	3	3	1	9
1999— Texas (A.L.)	0	1	.000	2.84	1	1	0	0	0	6 1/3	5	2	2	1	8
Division series totals (2 years)	0	2	.000	3.65	2	2	0	0	0	12 1/3	13	5	5	2	17

HELMS, WES — 3B — BRAVES

PERSONAL: Born May 12, 1976, in Gastonia, N.C. ... 6-4/230. ... Bats right, throws right. ... Full name: Wesley Ray Helms.
HIGH SCHOOL: Ashbrook (Gastonia, N.C.).
TRANSACTIONS/CAREER NOTES: Selected by Atlanta Braves organization in 10th round of free-agent draft (June 2, 1994). ... On Atlanta disabled list (April 3-July 15 and September 5, 1999-remainder of season); included rehabilitation assignment to Gulf Coast Braves (June 22-July 11). ... On Greenville disabled list (August 15-September 4, 1999).
STATISTICAL NOTES: Led South Atlantic League third basemen with 400 total chances and 25 double plays in 1995. ... Led International League third basemen with 24 double plays in 1998. ... Led International League third basemen with 341 total chances and 28 double plays in 2000.

					BATTING								FIELDING		
Year Team (League)	Pos.	G	AB	R	H	2B	3B	HR	RBI	Avg.	BB	SO	SB	PO	A	E	Avg.
1994— GC Braves (GCL)	3B	56	184	22	49	15	1	4	29	.266	22	36	6	•47	93	20	.875
1995— Macon (S.Atl.)	3B	136	*539	89	149	32	1	11	85	.276	50	107	2	91	*269	40	.900
1996— Durham (Caro.)	3B	67	258	40	83	19	2	13	54	.322	12	51	1	40	133	15	.920
— Greenville (Sou.)	3B	64	231	24	59	13	2	4	22	.255	13	48	2	50	96	12	.924
1997— Richmond (I.L.)	3B	32	110	11	21	4	0	3	15	.191	10	34	1	18	65	9	.902
— Greenville (Sou.)	3B	86	314	50	93	14	1	11	44	.296	33	50	3	60	147	11	.950
1998— Richmond (I.L.)	3B-DH	125	451	56	124	27	1	13	75	.275	35	103	6	75	220	15	.952
— Atlanta (N.L.)	3B	7	13	2	4	1	0	1	2	.308	0	4	0	1	2	1	.750
1999— GC Braves (GCL)	DH-1B	9	33	1	15	2	0	0	10	.455	5	4	0	27	0	0	1.000
— Greenville (Sou.)	1B	30	113	15	34	6	0	8	26	.301	7	34	1	226	18	4	.984
2000— Richmond (I.L.)	3B	136	539	74	155	27	7	20	88	.288	27	92	0	96	222	23	.933
— Atlanta (N.L.)	3B	6	5	0	1	0	0	0	0	.200	0	2	0	1	4	1	.833
2001— Atlanta (N.L.)	1B-3B-OF	100	216	28	48	10	3	10	36	.222	21	56	1	439	41	4	.992
Major League totals (3 years)		113	234	30	53	11	3	11	38	.226	21	62	1	441	47	6	.988

HELTON, TODD — 1B — ROCKIES

PERSONAL: Born August 20, 1973, in Knoxville, Tenn. ... 6-2/206. ... Bats left, throws left. ... Full name: Todd Lynn Helton.
HIGH SCHOOL: Knoxville (Tenn.) Central.
COLLEGE: Tennessee.
TRANSACTIONS/CAREER NOTES: Selected by San Diego Padres organization in second round of free-agent draft (June 1, 1992); did not sign. ... Selected by Colorado Rockies organization in first round (eighth pick overall) of free-agent draft (June 3, 1995). ... On New Haven disabled list (June 15-24, 1996).
HONORS: Named N.L. Rookie Player of the Year by THE SPORTING NEWS (1998). ... Named first baseman on THE SPORTING NEWS N.L. All-Star team (2000 and 2001). ... Named first baseman on THE SPORTING NEWS N.L. Silver Slugger team (2000). ... Named first baseman on N.L. Silver Slugger team (2001). ... Won N.L. Gold Glove at first base (2001).
STATISTICAL NOTES: Led N.L. first basemen in double plays with 156 in 1998, 152 in 1999 and 143 in 2000.. ... Hit for the cycle (June 19, 1999). ... Led N.L. first basemen with 1,482 total chances in 2000. ... Hit three home runs in one game (May 1, 2000). ... Led N.L. with 405 total bases, .463 on base percentage and .698 slugging percentage in 2000. ... Career major league grand slams: 1.

					BATTING								FIELDING		
Year Team (League)	Pos.	G	AB	R	H	2B	3B	HR	RBI	Avg.	BB	SO	SB	PO	A	E	Avg.
1995— Asheville (S.Atl.)	1B-DH	54	201	24	51	11	1	1	15	.254	25	32	1	388	21	4	.990
1996— New Haven (East.)	1B-DH	93	319	46	106	24	2	7	51	.332	51	37	2	788	61	5	.994
— Colo. Springs (PCL)	1B-OF	21	71	13	25	4	1	2	13	.352	11	12	0	144	17	2	.988
1997— Colo. Springs (PCL) ...	1B-OF-DH	99	392	87	138	31	2	16	88	.352	61	68	3	622	64	9	.987
— Colorado (N.L.)	OF-1B	35	93	13	26	2	1	5	11	.280	8	11	0	84	12	0	1.000
1998— Colorado (N.L.)	1B	152	530	78	167	37	1	25	97	.315	53	54	3	1164	*146	7	.995
1999— Colorado (N.L.)	1B	159	578	114	185	39	5	35	113	.320	68	77	7	1243	103	9	.993
2000— Colorado (N.L.)	1B	160	580	138	*216	*59	2	42	*147	*.372	103	61	5	*1328	*148	7	.995
2001— Colorado (N.L.)	1B	159	587	132	197	54	2	49	146	.336	98	104	7	1302	120	2	.999
Major League totals (5 years)		665	2368	475	791	191	11	156	514	.334	330	307	22	5121	529	25	.996

ALL-STAR GAME RECORD

				BATTING								FIELDING		
Year League	Pos.	AB	R	H	2B	3B	HR	RBI	Avg.	BB	SO	SB	PO	A	E	Avg.
2000— National	PR-1B	2	0	0	0	0	0	0	.000	0	0	0	5	0	0	1.000
2001— National	1B	2	0	0	0	0	0	0	.000	0	1	0	3	0	0	1.000
All-Star Game totals (2 years)		4	0	0	0	0	0	0	.000	0	1	0	8	0	0	1.000

H

PERSONAL: Born December 25, 1958, in Chicago. ... 5-10/190. ... Bats right, throws left. ... Full name: Rickey Henley Henderson.

HIGH SCHOOL: Technical (Oakland).

TRANSACTIONS/CAREER NOTES: Selected by Oakland Athletics organization in fourth round of free-agent draft (June 8, 1976). ... Traded by A's with P Bert Bradley and cash to New York Yankees for OF Stan Javier, P Jay Howell, P Jose Rijo, P Eric Plunk and P Tim Birtsas (December 5, 1984). ... On New York disabled list (March 30-April 22, 1985); included rehabilitation assignment to Fort Lauderdale (April 19-22). ... On disabled list (June 5-29 and July 26-September 1, 1987). ... Traded by Yankees to A's for P Greg Cadaret, P Eric Plunk and OF Luis Polonia (June 21, 1989). ... Granted free agency (November 13, 1989). ... Re-signed by A's (November 28, 1989). ... On disabled list (April 12-27, 1991; May 28-June 17 and June 30-July 16, 1992). ... Traded by A's to Toronto Blue Jays for P Steve Karsay and a player to be named later (July 31, 1993); A's acquired OF Jose Herrera to complete deal (August 6, 1993). ... Granted free agency (October 29, 1993). ... Signed by A's (December 17, 1993). ... On disabled list (May 11-27, 1994). ... Granted free agency (October 30, 1995). ... Signed by San Diego Padres (December 29, 1995). ... On San Diago disabled list (May 9-24, 1997). ... Traded by Padres to Anaheim Angels for P Ryan Hancock, P Stevenson Agosto and a player to be named later (August 13, 1997); Padres acquired 3B George Arias to complete deal (August 19, 1997). ... Granted free agency (October 27, 1997). ... Signed by A's (January 22, 1998). ... Granted free agency (October 26, 1998). ... Signed by New York Mets (December 16, 1998). ... On disabled list (May 3-22, 1999). ... Released by Mets (May 13, 2000). ... Signed by Seattle Mariners (May 19, 2000). ... Granted free agency (November 3, 2000). ... Signed by Padres organization (March 19, 2001). ... Granted free agency (November 5, 2001).

RECORDS: Holds major league career records for most stolen bases—1,395; most bases on balls—2,141; most times caught stealing—333; most runs—2,248; and most home runs leading off game—79. ... Holds major league single-season records for most stolen bases—130 (1982); and most times caught stealing—42 (1982). ... Holds major league record for most seasons leading league in stolen bases—12; and most years with 50 or more stolen bases—13. ... Holds A.L. career records for most stolen bases—1,262; most home runs leading off game—72; and most times caught stealing—291. ... Holds A.L. record for most consecutive years with 50 or more stolen bases—7 (1980-86). ... Shares A.L. single-season record for fewest times caught stealing (50 or more stolen bases)—8 (1993). ... Shares A.L. record for most stolen bases in two consecutive games—7 (July 3 [4], 15 innings, and 4 [3], 1983).

HONORS: Named outfielder on THE SPORTING NEWS A.L. All-Star team (1981, 1985 and 1990). ... Named outfielder on THE SPORTING NEWS A.L. Silver Slugger team (1981, 1985 and 1990). ... Won A.L. Gold Glove as outfielder (1981). ... Won THE SPORTING NEWS Silver Shoe Award (1982). ... Won THE SPORTING NEWS Golden Shoe Award (1983). ... Named A.L. Most Valuable Player by Baseball Writers' Association of America (1990). ... Named N.L. Comeback Player of the Year by THE SPORTING NEWS (1999).

STATISTICAL NOTES: Led California League in caught stealing with 22 in 1977. ... Led Eastern League in caught stealing with 28 in 1978. ... Led Eastern League outfielders with four double plays in 1978. ... Led A.L. in caught stealing with 26 in 1980, 22 in 1981, 42 in 1982, 19 in 1983 and tied for lead with 18 in 1986. ... Led A.L. outfielders with 341 total chances in 1981. ... Tied for A.L. lead in double plays by outfielder with five in 1988. ... Led A.L. with 77 stolen bases and 126 bases on balls in 1989. ... Tied for A.L. lead with 113 runs scored in 1989. ... Led A.L. with .439 on-base percentage in 1990. ... Career major league grand slams: 3.

MISCELLANEOUS: Holds Oakland Athletics franchise all-time records for most runs (1,270) and most stolen bases (867). ... Holds New York Yankees all-time record for most stolen bases (326).

Year Team (League)	Pos.	G	AB	R	H	2B	3B	HR	RBI	Avg.	BB	SO	SB	PO	A	E	Avg.
1976—Boise (N'West)	OF	46	140	34	47	13	2	3	23	.336	33	32	29	99	3	*12	.895
1977—Modesto (Calif.)	OF	134	481	120	166	18	4	11	69	.345	104	67	*95	278	15	*20	.936
1978—Jersey City (East.)	OF	133	455	81	141	14	4	0	34	.310	83	67	*81	305	*15	7	.979
1979—Ogden (PCL)	OF	71	259	66	80	11	8	3	26	.309	53	41	44	149	6	6	.963
—Oakland (A.L.)	OF	89	351	49	96	13	3	1	26	.274	34	39	33	215	5	6	.973
1980—Oakland (A.L.)	OF-DH	158	591	111	179	22	4	9	53	.303	117	54	*100	407	15	7	.984
1981—Oakland (A.L.)	OF	108	423	*89	*135	18	7	6	35	.319	64	68	*56	*327	7	7	.979
1982—Oakland (A.L.)	OF-DH	149	536	119	143	24	4	10	51	.267	*116	94	*130	379	2	9	.977
1983—Oakland (A.L.)	OF-DH	145	513	105	150	25	7	9	48	.292	*103	80	*108	349	9	3	.992
1984—Oakland (A.L.)	OF	142	502	113	147	27	4	16	58	.293	86	81	*66	341	7	11	.969
1985—Fort Laud. (FSL)■	OF	3	6	5	1	0	1	0	3	.167	5	2	1	6	0	0	1.000
—New York (A.L.)	OF-DH	143	547	*146	172	28	5	24	72	.314	99	65	*80	439	7	9	.980
1986—New York (A.L.)	OF-DH	153	608	*130	160	31	5	28	74	.263	89	81	*87	426	4	6	.986
1987—New York (A.L.)	OF-DH	95	358	78	104	17	3	17	37	.291	80	52	41	189	3	4	.980
1988—New York (A.L.)	OF-DH	140	554	118	169	30	2	6	50	.305	82	54	*93	320	7	12	.965
1989—New York (A.L.)	OF	65	235	41	58	13	1	3	22	.247	56	29	25	144	3	1	.993
—Oakland (A.L.)■	OF-DH	85	306	§72	90	13	2	9	35	.294	§70	39	§52	191	3	3	.985
1990—Oakland (A.L.)	OF-DH	136	489	*119	159	33	3	28	61	.325	97	60	*65	289	5	5	.983
1991—Oakland (A.L.)	OF-DH	134	470	105	126	17	1	18	57	.268	98	73	*58	249	10	8	.970
1992—Oakland (A.L.)	OF-DH	117	396	77	112	18	3	15	46	.283	95	56	48	231	9	4	.984
1993—Oakland (A.L.)	OF-DH	90	318	77	104	19	1	17	47	.327	85	46	31	182	5	5	.974
—Toronto (A.L.)■	OF	44	163	37	35	3	1	4	12	.215	35	19	22	76	1	2	.975
1994—Oakland (A.L.)	OF-DH	87	296	66	77	13	0	6	20	.260	72	45	22	166	4	4	.977
1995—Oakland (A.L.)	OF-DH	112	407	67	122	31	1	9	54	.300	72	66	32	162	5	2	.988
1996—San Diego (N.L.)■	OF	148	465	110	112	17	2	9	29	.241	125	90	37	228	3	6	.975
1997—San Diego (N.L.)	OF-DH	88	288	63	79	11	0	6	27	.274	71	62	29	160	4	7	.959
—Anaheim (A.L.)■	DH-OF	32	115	21	21	3	0	2	7	.183	26	23	16	26	0	0	1.000
1998—Oakland (A.L.)	OF	152	542	101	128	16	1	14	57	.236	*118	114	*66	327	3	4	.988
1999—New York (N.L.)	OF-DH	121	438	89	138	30	0	12	42	.315	82	82	37	168	0	2	1.000
2000—New York (N.L.)	OF	31	96	17	21	1	0	0	2	.219	25	20	5	35	0	2	.946
—Seattle (A.L.)■	OF-DH	92	324	58	77	13	2	4	30	.238	63	55	31	181	0	3	.984
2001—San Diego (N.L.)■	OF-DH	123	379	70	86	17	3	8	42	.227	81	84	25	158	5	3	.982
American League totals (20 years)		2468	9044	1899	2564	427	60	255	952	.284	1757	1293	1262	5616	114	115	.980
National League totals (5 years)		511	1666	349	436	76	5	35	142	.262	384	338	133	749	12	20	.974
Major League totals (23 years)		2979	10710	2248	3000	503	65	290	1094	.280	2141	1631	1395	6365	126	135	.980

DIVISION SERIES RECORD

RECORDS: Shares career record for most stolen bases—9.

Year Team (League)	Pos.	G	AB	R	H	2B	3B	HR	RBI	Avg.	BB	SO	SB	PO	A	E	Avg.
1981—Oakland (A.L.)	OF	3	11	3	2	0	0	0	0	.182	2	0	2	8	0	0	1.000
1996—San Diego (N.L.)	OF	3	12	2	4	0	0	1	1	.333	2	3	0	4	0	0	1.000
1999—New York (N.L.)	OF	4	15	5	6	0	0	0	1	.400	3	1	6	7	1	0	1.000
2000—Seattle (A.L.)	OF-PR	3	5	3	2	0	0	0	0	.400	1	0	1	2	0	0	1.000
Division series totals (4 years)		13	43	13	14	0	0	1	2	.326	8	4	9	21	1	0	1.000

H

CHAMPIONSHIP SERIES RECORD

RECORDS: Holds career records for most stolen bases—17. ... Holds single-series record for most stolen bases—8 (1989). ... Holds single-game record for most stolen bases—4 (October 4, 1989). ... Shares career record for most doubles—7. ... Shares single inning records for most at-bats in—2; most hits in—2; most singles in—2 (October 6, 1990, ninth inning); and most stolen bases in—2 (October 4, 1989, fourth and seventh innings). ... Shares single-series record for most runs—8 (1989). ... Shares A.L. single-game record for most at-bats—6 (October 5, 1993).

NOTES: Named Most Valuable Player (1989).

Year Team (League)	Pos.	G	AB	R	H	2B	3B	HR	RBI	Avg.	BB	SO	SB	PO	A	E	Avg.
1981— Oakland (A.L.)	OF	3	11	0	4	2	1	0	1	.364	1	2	2	6	0	1	.857
1989— Oakland (A.L.)	OF	5	15	8	6	1	1	2	5	.400	7	0	8	13	0	1	.929
1990— Oakland (A.L.)	OF	4	17	1	5	0	0	0	3	.294	1	2	2	10	0	0	1.000
1992— Oakland (A.L.)	OF	6	23	5	6	0	0	0	1	.261	4	4	2	15	0	3	.833
1993— Toronto (A.L.)	OF	6	25	4	3	2	0	0	0	.120	4	5	2	9	0	1	.900
1999— New York (N.L.)	OF	6	23	2	4	1	0	0	1	.174	0	5	1	7	2	1	.900
2000— Seattle (A.L.)	OF	3	9	2	2	1	0	0	1	.222	2	2	0	2	0	0	1.000
Championship series totals (7 years)		33	123	22	30	7	2	2	12	.244	19	20	17	62	2	7	.901

WORLD SERIES RECORD

RECORDS: Shares single-game record for most at-bats—6 (October 28, 1989).

NOTES: Member of World Series championship team (1989 and 1993).

Year Team (League)	Pos.	G	AB	R	H	2B	3B	HR	RBI	Avg.	BB	SO	SB	PO	A	E	Avg.
1989— Oakland (A.L.)	OF	4	19	4	9	1	2	1	3	.474	2	2	3	9	0	0	1.000
1990— Oakland (A.L.)	OF	4	15	2	5	2	0	1	1	.333	3	4	3	12	1	0	1.000
1993— Toronto (A.L.)	OF	6	22	6	5	2	0	0	2	.227	5	2	1	8	0	0	1.000
World Series totals (3 years)		14	56	12	19	5	2	2	6	.339	10	8	7	29	1	0	1.000

ALL-STAR GAME RECORD

RECORDS: Shares single-game record for most singles—3 (July 13, 1982).

Year League	Pos.	AB	R	H	2B	3B	HR	RBI	Avg.	BB	SO	SB	PO	A	E	Avg.
1980— American	OF	1	0	0	0	0	0	0	.000	0	1	0	0	0	0	...
1982— American	OF	4	1	3	0	0	0	0	.750	0	0	1	3	0	1	.750
1983— American	OF	1	0	0	0	0	0	1	.000	0	0	0	0	0	0	...
1984— American	OF	2	0	0	0	0	0	0	.000	0	0	0	0	0	0	...
1985— American	OF	3	1	1	0	0	0	0	.333	0	1	1	1	0	0	1.000
1986— American	OF	3	0	0	0	0	0	0	.000	0	1	0	2	0	0	1.000
1987— American	OF	3	0	1	0	0	0	0	.333	0	0	0	0	0	0	...
1988— American	OF	2	0	1	0	0	0	0	.500	1	0	0	1	0	0	1.000
1990— American	OF	3	0	0	0	0	0	0	.000	0	1	0	2	0	0	1.000
1991— American	OF	2	1	1	0	0	0	0	.500	0	0	0	0	0	0	...
All-Star Game totals (10 years)		24	3	7	0	0	0	1	.292	1	4	2	9	0	1	.900

HENRY, DOUG　　　　　P　　　　　ROYALS

PERSONAL: Born December 10, 1963, in Sacramento. ... 6-4/205. ... Throws right, bats right. ... Full name: Richard Douglas Henry.

HIGH SCHOOL: Tennyson (Hayward, Calif.).

COLLEGE: Arizona State.

TRANSACTIONS/CAREER NOTES: Selected by New York Mets organization in 16th round of free-agent draft (June 7, 1982); did not sign. ... Selected by Milwaukee Brewers organization in eighth round of free-agent draft (June 3, 1985). ... On El Paso disabled list (April 5-June 5 and June 18-August 9, 1989). ... On Milwaukee disabled list (March 25-April 26, 1994); included rehabilitation assignments to El Paso (April 8-22) and New Orleans (April 22-26). ... Traded by Brewers to New York Mets for two players to be named later (November 30, 1994); Brewers acquired C Javier Gonzales (December 6, 1994) and IF Fernando Vina (December 22, 1994) to complete deal. ... Released by Mets (November 25, 1996). ... Signed by San Francisco Giants (January 8, 1997). ... Granted free agency (October 27, 1997). ... Signed by Houston Astros (November 26, 1997). ... On Houston disabled list (May 10-July 15, 1999); included rehabilitation assignments to New Orleans (July 4-12) and Jackson (July 13-15). ... Granted free agency (November 1, 1999). ... Re-signed by Astros (December 3, 1999). ... Traded by Astros to San Francisco Giants for P Scott Linebrink (July 30, 2000). ... Granted free agency (October 31, 2000). ... Signed by Kansas City Royals (December 11, 2000).

STATISTICAL NOTES: Combined with Michael Ignasiak in 6-3 no-hit victory for Stockton against San Jose (April 15, 1990, first game).

Year League	W	L	Pct.	ERA	G	GS	CG	ShO	Sv.	IP	H	R	ER	BB	SO
1986— Beloit (Midw.)...................	7	8	.467	4.65	27	24	4	1	1	143 1/3	153	95	74	56	115
1987— Beloit (Midw.)...................	8	9	.471	4.88	31	15	1	0	2	132 2/3	145	83	72	51	106
1988— Stockton (Calif.)................	7	1	.875	1.78	23	1	1	0	7	70 2/3	46	19	14	31	71
— El Paso (Texas)..................	4	0	1.000	3.15	14	3	3	1	0	45 2/3	33	16	16	19	50
1989— Stockton (Calif.)................	0	1	.000	0.00	4	3	0	0	0	11	9	4	0	3	9
— El Paso (Texas)..................	0	0	...	13.50	1	1	0	0	0	2	3	3	3	3	2
1990— Stockton (Calif.)................	1	0	1.000	1.13	4	0	0	0	1	8	4	1	1	3	13
— El Paso (Texas)..................	1	0	1.000	2.93	15	0	0	0	9	30 2/3	31	13	10	11	25
— Denver (A.A.)...................	2	3	.400	4.44	27	0	0	0	8	50 2/3	46	26	25	27	54
1991— Denver (A.A.)...................	3	2	.600	2.18	32	0	0	0	14	57 2/3	47	16	14	20	47
— Milwaukee (A.L.)...............	2	1	.667	1.00	32	0	0	0	15	36	16	4	4	14	28
1992— Milwaukee (A.L.)...............	1	4	.200	4.02	68	0	0	0	29	65	64	34	29	24	52
1993— Milwaukee (A.L.)...............	4	4	.500	5.56	54	0	0	0	17	55	67	37	34	25	38
1994— El Paso (Texas).................	1	0	1.000	5.40	6	0	0	0	3	8 1/3	7	5	5	2	10
— New Orleans (A.A.)...........	1	0	1.000	1.84	10	0	0	0	3	14 2/3	5	3	3	10	10
— Milwaukee (A.L.)...............	2	3	.400	4.60	25	0	0	0	0	31 1/3	32	17	16	23	20
1995— New York (N.L.)■	3	6	.333	2.96	51	0	0	0	4	67	48	23	22	25	62
1996— New York (N.L.).................	2	8	.200	4.68	58	0	0	0	9	75	82	48	39	36	58
1997— San Francisco (N.L.)■	4	5	.444	4.71	75	0	0	0	3	70 2/3	70	45	37	41	69

H

Year League	W	L	Pct.	ERA	G	GS	CG	ShO	Sv.	IP	H	R	ER	BB	SO
1998—Houston (N.L.)■	8	2	.800	3.04	59	0	0	0	2	71	55	25	24	35	59
1999—Houston (N.L.)	2	3	.400	4.65	35	0	0	0	2	40 2/3	45	24	21	24	36
—New Orleans (PCL)	0	0	...	4.50	3	3	0	0	0	4	4	2	2	3	3
—Jackson (Texas)	0	1	.000	4.50	2	1	0	0	0	2	2	1	1	1	3
2000—Houston (N.L.)	1	3	.250	4.42	45	0	0	0	1	53	39	26	26	28	46
—San Francisco (N.L.)■	3	1	.750	2.49	27	0	0	0	0	25 1/3	18	10	7	21	16
2001—Kansas City (A.L.)■	2	2	.500	6.07	53	0	0	0	0	75 2/3	75	53	51	45	57
A.L. totals (5 years)	11	14	.440	4.59	232	0	0	0	61	263	254	145	134	131	195
N.L. totals (6 years)	23	28	.451	3.93	350	0	0	0	21	402 2/3	357	201	176	210	346
Major League totals (11 years)	34	42	.447	4.19	582	0	0	0	82	665 2/3	611	346	310	341	541

DIVISION SERIES RECORD

Year League	W	L	Pct.	ERA	G	GS	CG	ShO	Sv.	IP	H	R	ER	BB	SO
1997—San Francisco (N.L.)	0	0	...	0.00	1	0	0	0	0	2	1	0	0	3	2
1998—Houston (N.L.)	0	0	...	5.40	2	0	0	0	0	1 2/3	2	1	1	0	1
1999—Houston (N.L.)	0	0	...	0.00	2	0	0	0	0	3 2/3	1	0	0	3	2
2000—San Francisco (N.L.)	0	0	...	2.25	3	0	0	0	0	4	1	1	1	3	1
Division series totals (4 years)	0	0	...	1.59	8	0	0	0	0	11 1/3	5	2	2	9	6

HENTGEN, PAT   P   ORIOLES

PERSONAL: Born November 13, 1968, in Detroit. ... 6-2/195. ... Throws right, bats right. ... Full name: Patrick George Hentgen.
HIGH SCHOOL: Fraser (Mich.).
TRANSACTIONS/CAREER NOTES: Selected by Toronto Blue Jays organization in fifth round of free-agent draft (June 2, 1986). ... On Toronto disabled list (August 13-September 29, 1992); included rehabilitation assignment to Syracuse (September 1-8). ... Traded by Blue Jays with P Paul Spoljaric to St. Louis Cardinals for P Lance Painter, C Alberto Castillo and P Matt DeWitt (November 11, 1999). ... Granted free agency (October 31, 2000). ... Signed by Baltimore Orioles (December 19, 2000). ... On disabled list (May 17, 2001-remainder of season).
HONORS: Named A.L. Pitcher of the Year by THE SPORTING NEWS (1996). ... Named righthanded pitcher on THE SPORTING NEWS A.L. All-Star team (1996). ... Named A.L. Cy Young Award winner by Baseball Writers' Association of America (1996).
STATISTICAL NOTES: Combined with relievers Willie Blair and Enrique Burgos in 2-1 no-hit victory against Osceola (May 10, 1988).

Year League	W	L	Pct.	ERA	G	GS	CG	ShO	Sv.	IP	H	R	ER	BB	SO
1986—St. Catharines (NY-Penn)	0	4	.000	4.50	13	11	0	0	1	40	38	27	20	30	30
1987—Myrtle Beach (S.Atl.)	11	5	.688	2.35	32	*31	2	2	0	*188	145	62	49	60	131
1988—Dunedin (FSL)	3	12	.200	3.45	31	*30	0	0	0	151 1/3	139	80	58	65	125
1989—Dunedin (FSL)	9	8	.529	2.68	29	28	0	0	0	151 1/3	123	53	45	71	148
1990—Knoxville (Sou.)	9	5	.643	3.05	28	26	0	0	0	153 1/3	121	57	52	68	142
1991—Syracuse (I.L.)	8	9	.471	4.47	31	*28	1	0	0	171	146	91	85	*90	*155
—Toronto (A.L.)	0	0	...	2.45	3	1	0	0	0	7 1/3	5	2	2	3	3
1992—Toronto (A.L.)	5	2	.714	5.36	28	2	0	0	0	50 1/3	49	30	30	32	39
—Syracuse (I.L.)	1	2	.333	2.66	4	4	0	0	0	20 1/3	15	6	6	8	17
1993—Toronto (A.L.)	19	9	.679	3.87	34	32	3	0	0	216 1/3	215	103	93	74	122
1994—Toronto (A.L.)	13	8	.619	3.40	24	24	6	3	0	174 2/3	158	74	66	59	147
1995—Toronto (A.L.)	10	14	.417	5.11	30	30	2	0	0	200 2/3	*236	*129	*114	90	135
1996—Toronto (A.L.)	20	10	.667	3.22	35	35	*10	•3	0	*265 2/3	238	105	95	94	177
1997—Toronto (A.L.)	15	10	.600	3.68	35	•35	•9	•3	0	•264	253	116	108	71	160
1998—Toronto (A.L.)	12	11	.522	5.17	29	29	0	0	0	177 2/3	208	109	102	69	94
1999—Toronto (A.L.)	11	12	.478	4.79	34	34	1	0	0	199	225	115	106	65	118
2000—St. Louis (N.L.)■	15	12	.556	4.72	33	33	1	1	0	194 1/3	202	107	102	89	118
2001—Baltimore (A.L.)■	2	3	.400	3.47	9	9	1	0	0	62 1/3	51	25	24	19	33
A.L. totals (10 years)	107	79	.575	4.12	261	231	32	9	0	1618	1638	808	740	576	1028
N.L. totals (1 year)	15	12	.556	4.72	33	33	1	1	0	194 1/3	202	107	102	89	118
Major League totals (11 years)	122	91	.573	4.18	294	264	33	10	0	1812 1/3	1840	915	842	665	1146

DIVISION SERIES RECORD

Year League	W	L	Pct.	ERA	G	GS	CG	ShO	Sv.	IP	H	R	ER	BB	SO
2000—St. Louis (N.L.)							Did not play.								

CHAMPIONSHIP SERIES RECORD

Year League	W	L	Pct.	ERA	G	GS	CG	ShO	Sv.	IP	H	R	ER	BB	SO
1993—Toronto (A.L.)	0	1	.000	18.00	1	1	0	0	0	3	9	6	6	2	3
2000—St. Louis (N.L.)	0	1	.000	14.73	1	1	0	0	0	3 2/3	7	6	6	5	2
Champ. series totals (2 years)	0	2	.000	16.20	2	2	0	0	0	6 2/3	16	12	12	7	5

WORLD SERIES RECORD

NOTES: Member of World Series championship team (1993).

Year League	W	L	Pct.	ERA	G	GS	CG	ShO	Sv.	IP	H	R	ER	BB	SO
1993—Toronto (A.L.)	1	0	1.000	1.50	1	1	0	0	0	6	5	1	1	3	6

ALL-STAR GAME RECORD

Year League	W	L	Pct.	ERA	GS	CG	ShO	Sv.	IP	H	R	ER	BB	SO
1993—American						Did not play.								
1994—American	0	0	...	0.00	0	0	0	0	1	1	0	0	0	0
1997—American	0	0	...	0.00	0	0	0	0	1	0	0	0	0	0
All-Star Game totals (2 years)	0	0	...	0.00	0	0	0	0	2	1	0	0	0	0

H HEREDIA, FELIX   P   BLUE JAYS

PERSONAL: Born June 18, 1976, in Barahona, Dominican Republic. ... 6-0/180. ... Throws left, bats left. ... Full name: Felix Perez Heredia. ... Name pronounced heh-RAY-dee-ah.
HIGH SCHOOL: Escuela Dominical (Barahona, Dominican Republic).

TRANSACTIONS/CAREER NOTES: Signed as non-drafted free agent by Florida Marlins organization (November 22, 1992). ... Traded by Marlins with P Steve Hoff to Chicago Cubs for 3B Kevin Orie, P Todd Noel and P Justin Speier (July 31, 1998). ... On disabled list (August 21-September 5 and September 18-October 3, 2001). ... Traded by Cubs with a player to be named later to Toronto Blue Jays for SS Alex Gonzalez (December 10, 2001); Blue Jays acquired IF James Deschaine to complete deal (December 13, 2001).

Year League	W	L	Pct.	ERA	G	GS	CG	ShO	Sv.	IP	H	R	ER	BB	SO
1993— Gulf Coast Marlins (GCL) ...	5	1	.833	2.47	12	•12	0	0	0	62	50	18	17	11	53
1994— Kane County (Midw.).........	4	5	.444	5.69	24	8	1	0	3	68	86	55	43	14	65
1995— Brevard County (FSL)........	6	4	.600	3.57	34	8	0	0	1	95²/₃	101	52	38	36	76
1996— Portland (East.).................	8	1	.889	1.50	55	0	0	0	5	60	48	11	10	15	42
— Florida (N.L.).................	1	1	.500	4.32	21	0	0	0	0	16²/₃	21	8	8	10	10
1997— Florida (N.L.)....................	5	3	.625	4.29	56	0	0	0	0	56²/₃	53	30	27	30	54
1998— Florida (N.L.)....................	0	3	.000	5.49	41	2	0	0	2	41	38	30	25	32	38
— Chicago (N.L.)■............	3	0	1.000	4.08	30	0	0	0	0	17²/₃	19	9	8	6	16
1999— Chicago (N.L.)	3	1	.750	4.85	69	0	0	0	1	52	56	35	28	25	50
2000— Chicago (N.L.)	7	3	.700	4.76	74	0	0	0	2	58²/₃	46	31	31	33	52
2001— Chicago (N.L.)	2	2	.500	6.17	48	0	0	0	0	35	45	27	24	16	28
Major League totals (6 years)	21	13	.618	4.89	339	2	0	0	5	277²/₃	278	170	151	152	248

DIVISION SERIES RECORD

Year League	W	L	Pct.	ERA	G	GS	CG	ShO	Sv.	IP	H	R	ER	BB	SO
1997— Florida (N.L.)						Did not play.									
1998— Chicago (N.L.)	0	0	...	54.00	1	0	0	0	0	¹/₃	0	2	2	2	0

CHAMPIONSHIP SERIES RECORD

Year League	W	L	Pct.	ERA	G	GS	CG	ShO	Sv.	IP	H	R	ER	BB	SO
1997— Florida (N.L.)	0	0	...	5.40	2	0	0	0	0	3¹/₃	3	2	2	2	4

WORLD SERIES RECORD

NOTES: Member of World Series championship team (1997).

Year League	W	L	Pct.	ERA	G	GS	CG	ShO	Sv.	IP	H	R	ER	BB	SO
1997— Florida (N.L.).....................	0	0	...	0.00	4	0	0	0	0	5¹/₃	2	0	0	1	5

HEREDIA, GIL   P

PERSONAL: Born October 26, 1965, in Nogales, Ariz. ... 6-1/221. ... Throws right, bats right. ... Full name: Gilbert Heredia. ... Name pronounced err-AY-dee-uh.

HIGH SCHOOL: Nogales (Ariz.).

JUNIOR COLLEGE: Pima Community College (Ariz.).

COLLEGE: Arizona.

TRANSACTIONS/CAREER NOTES: Selected by Pittsburgh Pirates organization in first round (16th pick overall) of free-agent draft (January 17, 1984); did not sign. ... Selected by Baltimore Orioles organization in sixth round of free-agent draft (January 9, 1985); did not sign. ... Selected by San Francisco Giants organization in ninth round of free-agent draft (June 2, 1987). ... Loaned by Giants organization to San Luis Potosi of Mexican League (1989). ... Claimed on waivers by Montreal Expos (August 18, 1992). ... Granted free agency (December 21, 1995). ... Signed by Texas Rangers organization (January 5, 1996). ... Released by Rangers (November 13, 1996). ... Signed by Expos organization (January 13, 1997). ... Traded by Expos to Chicago Cubs for 2B Saul Bustos and OF David Jefferson (June 23, 1997). ... Granted free agency (October 15, 1997). ... Signed by Oakland Athletics organization (December 16, 1997). ... Granted free agency (November 5, 2001).

Year League	W	L	Pct.	ERA	G	GS	CG	ShO	Sv.	IP	H	R	ER	BB	SO
1987— Everett (N'West).................	2	0	1.000	3.60	3	3	1	0	0	20	24	8	8	1	14
— Fresno (Calif.).................	5	3	.625	2.90	11	11	5	2	0	80²/₃	62	28	26	23	60
1988— San Jose (Calif.)................	13	12	.520	3.49	27	27	9	0	0	*206¹/₃	•216	107	80	46	121
1989— Shreveport (Texas)	1	0	1.000	2.55	7	2	1	0	0	24²/₃	28	10	7	4	8
— San Luis Potosi (Mex.)■....	14	9	.609	2.99	24	24	15	3	0	180²/₃	183	73	60	35	125
1990— Phoenix (PCL)...................	9	7	.563	4.10	29	19	0	0	1	147	159	81	67	37	75
1991— Phoenix (PCL)	9	11	.450	*2.82	33	15	•5	1	1	140¹/₃	155	60	44	28	75
— San Francisco (N.L.)	0	2	.000	3.82	7	4	0	0	0	33	27	14	14	7	13
1992— Phoenix (PCL)	5	5	.500	2.01	22	7	1	1	1	80²/₃	83	30	18	13	37
— San Francisco (N.L.)	2	3	.400	5.40	13	4	0	0	0	30	32	20	18	16	15
— Indianapolis (A.A.)■	2	0	1.000	1.02	3	3	0	0	0	17²/₃	18	2	2	3	10
— Montreal (N.L.)	0	0	...	1.84	7	1	0	0	0	14²/₃	12	3	3	4	7
1993— Ottawa (I.L.)	8	4	.667	2.98	16	16	1	0	0	102²/₃	97	46	34	26	66
— Montreal (N.L.)	4	2	.667	3.92	20	9	1	0	2	57¹/₃	66	28	25	14	40
1994— Montreal (N.L.)	6	3	.667	3.46	39	3	0	0	0	75¹/₃	85	34	29	13	62
1995— Montreal (N.L.)	5	6	.455	4.31	40	18	0	0	1	119	137	60	57	21	74
1996— Texas (A.L.)■	2	5	.286	5.89	44	0	0	0	1	73¹/₃	91	50	48	14	43
— Oklahoma City (A.A.).........	0	0	...	1.86	6	0	0	0	0	9²/₃	11	3	2	0	4
1997— Ottawa (I.L.)■	0	4	.000	4.70	28	0	0	0	0	44	50	29	23	9	41
— Iowa (A.A.)■	4	2	.667	3.86	31	1	0	0	1	46²/₃	54	22	20	9	30
1998— Edmonton (PCL)■	10	8	.556	3.67	29	19	*6	1	1	144²/₃	154	69	59	18	99
— Oakland (A.L.)	3	3	.500	2.74	8	6	0	0	0	42²/₃	43	14	13	3	27
1999— Oakland (A.L.)	13	8	.619	4.81	33	33	1	0	0	200¹/₃	228	119	107	34	117
2000— Oakland (A.L.)	15	11	.577	4.12	32	32	2	0	0	198²/₃	214	106	91	66	101
2001— Oakland (A.L.)	7	8	.467	5.58	24	18	0	0	0	109²/₃	144	75	68	29	48
A.L. totals (5 years)	40	35	.533	4.71	141	89	3	0	1	624²/₃	720	364	327	146	336
N.L. totals (5 years)	17	16	.515	3.99	126	39	1	0	3	329¹/₃	359	159	146	75	211
Major League totals (10 years)	57	51	.528	4.46	267	128	4	0	4	954	1079	523	473	221	547

DIVISION SERIES RECORD

Year League	W	L	Pct.	ERA	G	GS	CG	ShO	Sv.	IP	H	R	ER	BB	SO
2000— Oakland (A.L.)	1	1	.500	12.79	2	2	0	0	0	6¹/₃	11	9	9	3	3

H

HERGES, MATT — P — DODGERS

PERSONAL: Born April 1, 1970, in Champaign, Ill. ... 6-0/200. ... Throws right, bats left. ... Full name: Matthew Tyler Herges.
HIGH SCHOOL: Centennial (Champaign, Ill.).
COLLEGE: Illinois State.
TRANSACTIONS/CAREER NOTES: Signed as non-drafted free agent by Los Angeles Dodgers organization (June 13, 1992). ... Granted free agency (October 15, 1998). ... Re-signed by Dodgers organization (January 1, 1999).

Year League	W	L	Pct.	ERA	G	GS	CG	ShO	Sv.	IP	H	R	ER	BB	SO
1992—Yakima (N'West)	2	3	.400	3.22	27	0	0	0	9	44 2/3	33	21	16	24	57
1993—Bakersfield (Calif.)	2	6	.250	3.69	51	0	0	0	2	90 1/3	70	49	37	56	84
1994—Vero Beach (FSL)	8	9	.471	3.32	48	3	1	0	3	111	115	45	41	33	61
1995—San Antonio (Texas)	0	3	.000	4.88	19	0	0	0	8	27 2/3	34	16	15	16	18
—San Bernardino (Calif.)	5	2	.714	3.66	22	2	0	0	1	51 2/3	58	29	21	15	35
1996—San Antonio (Texas)	3	2	.600	2.71	30	6	0	0	3	83	83	38	25	28	45
—Albuquerque (PCL)	4	1	.800	2.60	10	4	2	1	0	34 2/3	33	11	10	14	15
1997—Albuquerque (PCL)	0	8	.000	8.89	31	12	0	0	0	85	120	92	84	46	61
—San Antonio (Texas)	0	1	.000	8.80	4	3	0	0	0	15 1/3	22	15	15	10	12
1998—Albuquerque (PCL)	3	5	.375	5.71	34	8	0	0	0	88 1/3	115	64	56	37	75
—San Antonio (Texas)	0	0	...	0.00	3	0	0	0	0	6	3	0	0	2	3
1999—Albuquerque (PCL)	8	3	.727	4.73	21	21	2	0	0	131 1/3	135	82	69	47	88
—Los Angeles (N.L.)	0	2	.000	4.07	17	0	0	0	0	24 1/3	24	13	11	8	18
2000—Los Angeles (N.L.)	11	3	.786	3.17	59	4	0	0	1	110 2/3	100	43	39	40	75
2001—Los Angeles (N.L.)	9	8	.529	3.44	75	0	0	0	1	99 1/3	97	39	38	46	76
Major League totals (3 years)	20	13	.606	3.38	151	4	0	0	2	234 1/3	221	95	88	94	169

HERMANSEN, CHAD — OF — PIRATES

PERSONAL: Born September 10, 1977, in Salt Lake City. ... 6-2/185. ... Bats right, throws right. ... Full name: Chad B. Hermansen.
HIGH SCHOOL: Green Valley (Henderson, Nev.).
TRANSACTIONS/CAREER NOTES: Selected by Pittsburgh Pirates organization in first round (10th pick overall) of free-agent draft (June 1, 1995).
STATISTICAL NOTES: Tied for Southern League lead in errors by outfielder with eight in 1997.

						BATTING								FIELDING		
Year Team (League)	Pos.	G	AB	R	H	2B	3B	HR	RBI	Avg.	BB	SO	SB	PO	A	E	Avg.
1995—GC Pirates (GCL)	SS	24	92	14	28	10	1	3	17	.304	9	19	0	20	56	10	.884
—GC Pirates (GCL)	SS	24	92	14	28	10	1	3	17	.304	9	19	0	20	56	10	.884
—Erie (NY-Penn)	SS	44	165	30	45	8	3	6	25	.273	18	39	4	52	104	30	.839
1996—Augusta (S.Atl.)	SS-DH	62	226	41	57	11	3	14	41	.252	38	65	11	71	135	25	.892
—Lynchburg (Caro.)	SS-DH	66	251	40	69	11	3	10	46	.275	29	56	5	75	168	28	.897
1997—Carolina (Sou.)	OF-S-2-DH	129	487	87	134	31	4	20	70	.275	69	*136	18	194	125	†39	.891
1998—Nashville (PCL)	OF-2B	126	458	81	118	26	5	28	78	.258	50	152	21	208	21	14	.942
1999—Nashville (PCL)	OF-DH	125	496	89	134	27	3	32	97	.270	35	119	19	258	9	3	.989
—Pittsburgh (N.L.)	OF	19	60	5	14	3	0	1	1	.233	7	19	2	29	0	0	1.000
2000—Pittsburgh (N.L.)	OF	33	108	12	20	4	1	2	8	.185	6	37	0	44	2	1	.979
—Nashville (PCL)	OF	78	294	47	66	12	1	11	38	.224	25	89	16	156	2	4	.975
2001—Nashville (PCL)	OF	123	447	75	110	22	6	17	64	.246	41	154	22	237	8	4	.984
—Pittsburgh (N.L.)	OF	22	55	5	9	1	0	2	5	.164	1	18	0	30	1	0	1.000
Major League totals (3 years)		74	223	22	43	8	1	5	14	.193	14	74	2	103	3	1	.991

HERMANSON, DUSTIN — P — RED SOX

PERSONAL: Born December 21, 1972, in Springfield, Ohio. ... 6-2/200. ... Throws right, bats right. ... Full name: Dustin Michael Hermanson.
HIGH SCHOOL: Kenton Ridge (Springfield, Ohio).
COLLEGE: Kent.
TRANSACTIONS/CAREER NOTES: Selected by Pittsburgh Pirates organization in 39th round of free-agent draft (June 3, 1991); did not sign. ... Selected by San Diego Padres organization in first round (third pick overall) of free-agent draft (June 2, 1994). ... Traded by Padres to Florida Marlins for 2B Quilvio Veras (November 21, 1996). ... Traded by Marlins with OF Joe Orsulak to Montreal Expos for OF/1B Cliff Floyd (March 26, 1997). ... On disabled list (May 15-30, 1998). ... Traded by Expos with P Steve Kline to St. Louis Cardinals for 3B Fernando Tatis and P Britt Reames (December 14, 2000). ... Traded by Cardinals to Boston Red Sox for OF Rick Asadoorian, 1B Luis Garcia and 1B Dustin Brisson (December 15, 2001).
STATISTICAL NOTES: Hit home run in first major league at-bat (April 16, 1997).
MISCELLANEOUS: Appeared in one game as pinch runner (2001).

Year League	W	L	Pct.	ERA	G	GS	CG	ShO	Sv.	IP	H	R	ER	BB	SO
1994—Wichita (Texas)	1	0	1.000	0.43	16	0	0	0	8	21	13	1	1	6	30
—Las Vegas (PCL)	0	0	...	6.14	7	0	0	0	3	7 1/3	6	5	5	5	6
1995—Las Vegas (PCL)	0	1	.000	3.50	31	0	0	0	11	36	35	23	14	29	42
—San Diego (N.L.)	3	1	.750	6.82	26	0	0	0	0	31 2/3	35	26	24	22	19
1996—Las Vegas (PCL)	1	4	.200	3.13	42	0	0	0	21	46	41	20	16	27	54
—San Diego (N.L.)	1	0	1.000	8.56	8	0	0	0	0	13 2/3	18	15	13	4	11
1997—Montreal (N.L.)■	8	8	.500	3.69	32	28	1	1	0	158 1/3	134	68	65	66	136
1998—Montreal (N.L.)	14	11	.560	3.13	32	30	1	0	0	187	163	80	65	56	154
1999—Montreal (N.L.)	9	14	.391	4.20	34	34	0	0	0	216 1/3	225	110	101	69	145
2000—Montreal (N.L.)	12	14	.462	4.77	38	30	2	1	4	198	226	128	105	75	94
2001—St. Louis (N.L.)■	14	13	.519	4.45	33	33	0	0	0	192 1/3	195	106	95	73	123
Major League totals (7 years)	61	61	.500	4.22	203	155	4	2	4	997 1/3	996	533	468	365	682

DIVISION SERIES RECORD

Year League	W	L	Pct.	ERA	G	GS	CG	ShO	Sv.	IP	H	R	ER	BB	SO
2001—St. Louis (N.L.)	0	0	...	0.00	1	0	0	0	0	3	0	0	0	0	0

H

HERNANDEZ, ADRIAN   P   YANKEES

PERSONAL: Born March 25, 1975, in Ciudad Havana, Cuba. ... 6-1/185. ... Throws right, bats right.
TRANSACTIONS/CAREER NOTES: Signed as non-drafted free agent by New York Yankees organization (June 2, 2000). ... On Columbus disabled list (August 1, 2000-remainder of season). ... On Columbus disabled list (June 1-10 and July 4-21, 2001).
STATISTICAL NOTES: Tied for International League lead with five balks in 2001.

Year League	W	L	Pct.	ERA	G	GS	CG	ShO	Sv.	IP	H	R	ER	BB	SO
2000— Tampa (FSL)......................	1	0	1.000	1.35	1	1	0	0	0	6 2/3	3	1	1	1	13
— Norwich (East.).................	5	1	.833	4.04	6	6	1	0	0	35 2/3	34	17	16	18	44
— Columbus (I.L.)...............	2	1	.667	4.40	5	5	2	1	0	30 2/3	24	18	15	18	29
2001— Columbus (I.L.)...............	8	7	.533	5.51	21	21	0	0	0	117 2/3	116	75	72	60	97
— New York (A.L.).................	0	3	.000	3.68	6	3	0	0	0	22	15	10	9	10	10
Major League totals (1 year)........	**0**	**3**	**.000**	**3.68**	**6**	**3**	**0**	**0**	**0**	**22**	**15**	**10**	**9**	**10**	**10**

HERNANDEZ, ALEX   OF   REDS

PERSONAL: Born May 28, 1977, in San Juan, Puerto Rico. ... 6-4/190. ... Bats left, throws left. ... Full name: Alexander Vargas Hernandez.
TRANSACTIONS/CAREER NOTES: Selected by Pittsburgh Pirates organization in fourth round of free-agent draft (June 1, 1995). ... On Pittsburgh disabled list (March 31-June 1, 2001); included rehabilitation assignment to Nashville (May 11-June 1). ... Granted free agency (October 15, 2001). ... Signed by Cincinnati Reds organization (December 21, 2001).

Year Team (League)	Pos.	G	AB	R	H	2B	3B	HR	RBI	Avg.	BB	SO	SB	PO	A	E	Avg.
1995— GC Pirates (GCL)........	OF-1B	49	186	24	50	5	3	1	17	.269	17	33	4	148	7	5	.969
1996— Erie (NY-Penn)	OF-1B	61	225	38	65	13	4	4	30	.289	20	47	7	305	19	7	.979
1997— Lynchburg (Caro.)	OF	131	520	75	151	37	4	5	68	.290	27	140	13	212	*15	9	.962
1998— Carolina (Sou.)	OF	115	452	62	117	22	7	8	48	.259	41	81	11	217	15	11	.955
1999— Altoona (East.)	OF-DH-1B	126	475	76	122	26	3	15	63	.257	54	110	11	249	15	5	.981
2000— Altoona (East.)	1B-OF	50	199	28	67	16	1	4	34	.337	13	42	1	140	7	2	.987
— Nashville (PCL)	OF-1B	76	276	29	76	17	2	8	37	.275	11	60	6	436	26	4	.991
— Pittsburgh (N.L.)	1B-OF	20	60	4	12	3	0	1	5	.200	0	13	1	127	4	1	.992
2001— Nashville (PCL)	1B-OF	88	342	45	101	16	1	8	36	.295	13	65	3	474	22	9	.982
— Pittsburgh (N.L.)	OF-1B	7	11	0	1	0	0	0	0	.091	0	2	0	7	1	0	1.000
Major League totals (2 years)		**27**	**71**	**4**	**13**	**3**	**0**	**1**	**5**	**.183**	**0**	**15**	**1**	**134**	**5**	**1**	**.993**

HERNANDEZ, CARLOS   P   ASTROS

PERSONAL: Born April 22, 1980, in Guacara, Venezuela. ... 5-10/145. ... Throws left, bats left.
TRANSACTIONS/CAREER NOTES: Signed as non-drafted free agent by Houston Astros organization (April 23, 1997).
STATISTICAL NOTES: Pitched 2-0 no-hit victory for Michigan against West Michigan (May 28, 2000; second game).

Year League	W	L	Pct.	ERA	G	GS	CG	ShO	Sv.	IP	H	R	ER	BB	SO
1997— VSL Astros (VSL)..............	5	1	.833	2.54	22	0	0	0	3	46	47	20	13	21	53
1998— Dominican Astros (DSL)	2	0	1.000	1.46	17	0	0	0	9	24 2/3	16	4	4	12	33
1999— Martinsville (Appl.)............	5	1	.833	1.79	13	9	0	0	0	55 1/3	36	21	11	23	82
2000— Michigan (Midw.).............	6	6	.500	3.82	22	22	2	1	0	110 2/3	92	57	47	63	115
2001— Round Rock (Texas)..........	12	3	.800	3.69	24	23	0	0	0	139	115	60	57	69	167
— Houston (N.L.)	1	0	1.000	1.02	3	3	0	0	0	17 2/3	11	2	2	7	17
Major League totals (1 year)........	**1**	**0**	**1.000**	**1.02**	**3**	**3**	**0**	**0**	**0**	**17 2/3**	**11**	**2**	**2**	**7**	**17**

HERNANDEZ, JOSE   SS   BREWERS

PERSONAL: Born July 14, 1969, in Vega Alta, Puerto Rico. ... 6-1/186. ... Bats right, throws right. ... Full name: Jose Antonio Hernandez.
HIGH SCHOOL: Maestro Ladi (Vega Alta, Puerto Rico).
COLLEGE: Interamerican (Puerto Rico).
TRANSACTIONS/CAREER NOTES: Signed as non-drafted free agent by Texas Rangers organization (January 13, 1987). ... Claimed on waivers by Cleveland Indians (April 3, 1992). ... Traded by Indians to Chicago Cubs for P Heathcliff Slocumb (June 1, 1993). ... Traded by Cubs with P Terry Mulholland to Atlanta Braves for P Micah Bowie, P Ruben Quevado and a player to be named later (July 31, 1999); Cubs acquired P Joey Nation to complete deal (August 24, 1999). ... Granted free agency (November 5, 1999). ... Signed by Milwaukee Brewers (December 16, 1999). ... On Milwaukee disabled list (August 10-September 1, 2000); included rehabilitation assignment to Indianapolis (August 29-31).
STATISTICAL NOTES: Led Gulf Coast League third basemen with .950 fielding percentage, 47 putouts and 11 double plays in 1988. ... Led Florida State League shortstops with .959 fielding percentage in 1990. ... Led Eastern League shortstops with 586 total chances in 1992. ... Career major league grand slams: 4.

Year Team (League)	Pos.	G	AB	R	H	2B	3B	HR	RBI	Avg.	BB	SO	SB	PO	A	E	Avg.
1987— GC Rangers (GCL)......	SS	24	52	5	9	1	1	0	2	.173	9	25	2	30	38	5	.932
1988— GC Rangers (GCL)......	3-2-S-1-O	55	162	19	26	7	1	1	13	.160	12	36	4	†68	115	8	†.958
1989— Gastonia (S.Atl.).........	3B-SS-2B-OF	91	215	35	47	7	6	1	16	.219	33	67	9	101	169	17	.941
1990— Charlotte (FSL)...........	SS-OF	121	388	43	99	14	7	1	44	.255	50	122	11	192	372	25	†.958
1991— Tulsa (Texas)	SS	91	301	36	72	17	4	1	20	.239	26	75	4	151	300	15	*.968
— Oklahoma City (A.A.) ..	SS	14	46	6	14	1	1	1	3	.304	4	10	0	32	43	3	.962
— Texas (A.L.)	SS-3B	45	98	8	18	2	1	0	4	.184	3	31	0	49	111	4	.976
1992— Cant./Akron (East.)∎..	SS	130	404	56	103	16	4	3	46	.255	37	108	7	*226	320	*40	.932
— Cleveland (A.L.)	SS	3	4	0	0	0	0	0	0	.000	0	2	0	3	3	1	.857
1993— Canton/Akron (East.)..	SS-3B	45	150	19	30	6	0	2	17	.200	10	39	9	75	135	7	.968
— Orlando (Sou.)∎	SS	71	263	42	80	8	3	8	33	.304	20	60	8	136	205	14	.961
— Iowa (A.A.)	SS	6	24	3	6	1	0	0	3	.250	0	2	0	14	26	1	.976
1994— Chicago (N.L.)	3B-SS-2B-OF	56	132	18	32	2	3	1	9	.242	8	29	2	46	86	4	.971

H

Year Team (League)	Pos.	G	AB	R	H	2B	3B	HR	RBI	Avg.	BB	SO	SB	PO	A	E	Avg.
						BATTING									FIELDING		
1995—Chicago (N.L.)	SS-2B-3B	93	245	37	60	11	4	13	40	.245	13	69	1	113	189	9	.971
1996—Chicago (N.L.)	SS-3B-2B-OF	131	331	52	80	14	1	10	41	.242	24	97	4	148	248	20	.952
1997—Chicago (N.L.)	IF-OF-DH	121	183	33	50	8	5	7	26	.273	14	42	2	79	91	8	.955
1998—Chicago (N.L.)	3-OF-S-1-2	149	488	76	124	23	7	23	75	.254	40	140	4	193	226	13	.970
1999—Chicago (N.L.)	SS-OF-1B	99	342	57	93	12	2	15	43	.272	40	101	7	140	249	11	.973
—Atlanta (N.L.)■	SS-1B-OF	48	166	22	42	8	0	4	19	.253	12	44	4	54	114	6	.966
2000—Milwaukee (N.L.)■	3B-SS-OF	124	446	51	109	22	1	11	59	.244	41	125	3	141	258	19	.955
—Indianapolis (I.L.)	3B	2	9	2	3	0	0	2	3	.333	1	3	0	0	2	0	1.000
2001—Milwaukee (N.L.)	SS-OF	152	542	67	135	26	2	25	78	.249	39	*185	5	206	427	18	.972
American League totals (2 years)		48	102	8	18	2	1	0	4	.176	3	33	0	52	114	5	.971
National League totals (8 years)		973	2875	413	725	126	25	109	390	.252	231	832	32	1120	1888	108	.965
Major League totals (10 years)		1021	2977	421	743	128	26	109	394	.250	234	865	32	1172	2002	113	.966

DIVISION SERIES RECORD

Year Team (League)	Pos.	G	AB	R	H	2B	3B	HR	RBI	Avg.	BB	SO	SB	PO	A	E	Avg.
						BATTING									FIELDING		
1998—Chicago (N.L.)	SS	2	7	1	2	0	0	0	0	.286	0	2	0	5	1	2	.750
1999—Atlanta (N.L.)	SS	4	11	1	1	0	0	0	0	.091	1	3	1	6	9	1	.938
Division series totals (2 years)		6	18	2	3	0	0	0	0	.167	1	5	1	11	10	3	.875

CHAMPIONSHIP SERIES RECORD

Year Team (League)	Pos.	G	AB	R	H	2B	3B	HR	RBI	Avg.	BB	SO	SB	PO	A	E	Avg.
						BATTING									FIELDING		
1999—Atlanta (N.L.)	PH	2	2	0	1	0	0	0	2	.500	0	1	0	...	...	...	...

WORLD SERIES RECORD

Year Team (League)	Pos.	G	AB	R	H	2B	3B	HR	RBI	Avg.	BB	SO	SB	PO	A	E	Avg.
						BATTING									FIELDING		
1999—Atlanta (N.L.)	PH-SS-DH	2	5	0	1	1	0	0	2	.200	0	2	1	1	0	0	1.000

HERNANDEZ, LIVAN   P   GIANTS

PERSONAL: Born February 20, 1975, in Villa Clara, Cuba. ... 6-2/222. ... Throws right, bats right. ... Full name: Eisler Hernandez. ... Half-brother of Orlando Hernandez, pitcher, New York Yankees. ... Name pronounced lee-VAHN.

TRANSACTIONS/CAREER NOTES: Signed as non-drafted free agent by Florida Marlins orgaization (January 13, 1996). ... Traded by Marlins to San Francisco Giants for P Jason Grilli and P Nathan Bump (July 24, 1999).

STATISTICAL NOTES: Led International League with four balks in 1996.

MISCELLANEOUS: Member of Cuban national baseball team (1994-95). ... Struck out once in two appearances as pinch hitter (1998). ... Struck out in only appearance as pinch hitter with Giants (1999). ... Struck out in only appearance as pinch hitter (2000). ... Appeared one game as pinch hitter (2001).

Year League	W	L	Pct.	ERA	G	GS	CG	ShO	Sv.	IP	H	R	ER	BB	SO
1996—Charlotte (I.L.)	2	4	.333	5.14	10	10	0	0	0	49	61	32	28	34	45
—Florida (N.L.)	0	0	...	0.00	1	0	0	0	0	3	3	0	0	2	2
1997—Portland (East.)	0	0	...	2.25	1	1	0	0	0	4	2	1	1	7	2
—Charlotte (I.L.)	5	3	.625	3.98	14	14	0	0	0	81 1/3	76	39	36	38	58
—Florida (N.L.)	9	3	.750	3.18	17	17	0	0	0	96 1/3	81	39	34	38	72
1998—Florida (N.L.)	10	12	.455	4.72	33	33	9	0	0	234 1/3	*265	133	123	104	162
1999—Florida (N.L.)	5	9	.357	4.76	20	20	2	0	0	136	161	78	72	55	97
—San Francisco (N.L.)■	3	3	.500	4.38	10	10	0	0	0	63 2/3	66	32	31	21	47
2000—San Francisco (N.L.)	17	11	.607	3.75	33	33	5	2	0	240	*254	114	100	73	165
2001—San Francisco (N.L.)	13	15	.464	5.24	34	34	2	0	0	226 2/3	*266	*143	*132	85	138
Major League totals (6 years)	57	53	.518	4.43	148	147	18	2	0	1000	1096	539	492	378	683

DIVISION SERIES RECORD

Year League	W	L	Pct.	ERA	G	GS	CG	ShO	Sv.	IP	H	R	ER	BB	SO
1997—Florida (N.L.)	0	0	...	2.25	1	0	0	0	0	4	3	1	1	0	3
2000—San Francisco (N.L.)	1	0	1.000	1.17	1	1	0	0	0	7 2/3	5	1	1	5	5
Division series totals (2 years)	1	0	1.000	1.54	2	1	0	0	0	11 2/3	8	2	2	5	8

CHAMPIONSHIP SERIES RECORD

NOTES: Named N.L. Championship Series Most Valuable Player (1997).

Year League	W	L	Pct.	ERA	G	GS	CG	ShO	Sv.	IP	H	R	ER	BB	SO
1997—Florida (N.L.)	2	0	1.000	0.84	1	1	0	0	0	10 2/3	5	1	1	2	16

WORLD SERIES RECORD

NOTES: Named Most Valuable Player (1997). ... Member of World Series championship team (1997).

Year League	W	L	Pct.	ERA	G	GS	CG	ShO	Sv.	IP	H	R	ER	BB	SO
1997—Florida (N.L.)	2	0	1.000	5.27	2	2	0	0	0	13 2/3	15	9	8	10	7

HERNANDEZ, ORLANDO   P   YANKEES

PERSONAL: Born October 11, 1965, in Villa Clara, Cuba. ... 6-2/220. ... Throws right, bats right. ... Full name: Orlando P. Hernandez. ... Nickname: El Duque. ... Half-brother of Livan Hernandez, pitcher, San Francisco Giants.

TRANSACTIONS/CAREER NOTES: Signed as non-drafted free agent by New York Yankees (March 23, 1998). ... On New York disabled list (July 18-August 6, 2000); included rehabilitation assignment to Tampa (August 1-3). ... On New York disabled list (June 1-August 21, 2001); included rehabilitation assignments to Tampa (August 6-16) and Staten Island (August 17-20).

MISCELLANEOUS: Member of Cuban national baseball team.

H

Year League	W	L	Pct.	ERA	G	GS	CG	ShO	Sv.	IP	H	R	ER	BB	SO
1998— Tampa (FSL)	1	1	.500	1.00	2	2	0	0	0	9	3	2	1	3	15
— Columbus (I.L.)	6	0	1.000	3.83	7	7	0	0	0	42 1/3	41	19	18	17	59
— New York (A.L.)	12	4	.750	3.13	21	21	3	1	0	141	113	53	49	52	131
1999— New York (A.L.)	17	9	.654	4.12	33	33	2	1	0	214 1/3	187	108	98	87	157
2000— New York (A.L.)	12	13	.480	4.51	29	29	3	0	0	195 2/3	186	104	98	51	141
— Tampa (FSL)	0	0	...	0.00	1	0	0	0	0	4	1	0	0	1	5
2001— New York (A.L.)	4	7	.364	4.85	17	16	0	0	0	94 2/3	90	51	51	42	77
— Tampa (FSL)	0	0	...	0.00	2	2	0	0	0	7	6	2	0	1	8
— Staten Island (NY-Penn)	1	0	1.000	0.00	1	1	0	0	0	6	2	0	0	1	11
Major League totals (4 years)	45	33	.577	4.13	100	99	8	2	0	645 2/3	576	316	296	232	506

DIVISION SERIES RECORD

Year League	W	L	Pct.	ERA	G	GS	CG	ShO	Sv.	IP	H	R	ER	BB	SO
1998— New York (A.L.)							Did not play.								
1999— New York (A.L.)	1	0	1.000	0.00	1	1	0	0	0	8	2	0	0	6	4
2000— New York (A.L.)	1	0	1.000	2.45	2	1	0	0	0	7 1/3	5	2	2	5	5
2001— New York (A.L.)	1	0	1.000	3.18	1	1	0	0	0	5 2/3	8	2	2	2	5
Division series totals (3 years)	3	0	1.000	1.71	4	3	0	0	0	21	15	4	4	13	14

CHAMPIONSHIP SERIES RECORD

NOTES: Named A.L. Championship Series Most Valuable Player (1999).

Year League	W	L	Pct.	ERA	G	GS	CG	ShO	Sv.	IP	H	R	ER	BB	SO
1998— New York (A.L.)	1	0	1.000	0.00	1	1	0	0	0	7	3	0	0	2	6
1999— New York (A.L.)	1	0	1.000	1.80	2	2	0	0	0	15	12	4	3	6	13
2000— New York (A.L.)	2	0	1.000	4.20	2	2	0	0	0	15	13	7	7	8	14
2001— New York (A.L.)	0	1	.000	7.20	1	1	0	0	0	5	5	5	4	5	7
Champ. series totals (4 years)	4	1	.800	3.00	6	6	0	0	0	42	33	16	14	21	40

WORLD SERIES RECORD

NOTES: Member of World Series championship team (1998, 1999 and 2000).

Year League	W	L	Pct.	ERA	G	GS	CG	ShO	Sv.	IP	H	R	ER	BB	SO
1998— New York (A.L.)	1	0	1.000	1.29	1	1	0	0	0	7	6	1	1	3	7
1999— New York (A.L.)	1	0	1.000	1.29	1	1	0	0	0	7	1	1	1	2	10
2000— New York (A.L.)	0	1	.000	4.91	1	1	0	0	0	7 1/3	9	4	4	3	12
2001— New York (A.L.)	0	0	...	1.42	1	1	0	0	0	6 1/3	4	1	1	4	5
World Series totals (4 years)	2	1	.667	2.28	4	4	0	0	0	27 2/3	20	7	7	12	34

HERNANDEZ, RAMON — C — ATHLETICS

PERSONAL: Born May 20, 1976, in Caracas, Venezuela. ... 6-0/227. ... Bats right, throws right. ... Full name: Ramon Jose Marin Hernandez.
TRANSACTIONS/CAREER NOTES: Signed as non-drafted free agent by Oakland Athletics organization (February 18, 1994). ... On Oakland disabled list (July 26-August 27, 1999); included rehabilitation assignment to Vancouver (August 13-27).
HONORS: Named Arizona League Most Valuable Player (1995).
STATISTICAL NOTES: Led Arizona League in slugging percentage with .594, on-base percentage with .510 and being hit by pitch with eight in 1992. ... Led Arizona League catchers with a .982 fielding percentage in 1995. ... Led Midwest League catchers with 877 putouts and 981 totals chances and tied for lead with 20 errors in 1996. ... Led California League with .427 on-base percentage in 1997. ... Led California League catchers with 16 errors in 1997. ... Led Southern League in being hit by pitch with 19 in 1998. ... Career major league grand slams: 1.

Year Team (League)	Pos.	G	AB	R	H	2B	3B	HR	RBI	Avg.	BB	SO	SB	PO	A	E	Avg.
1994— Dom. Athletics (DSL)	C	42	134	24	33	2	0	2	18	.246	18	10	1	182	28	2	.991
1995— Ariz. Athletics (Ariz.)	C-1B-3B	48	143	37	52	9	6	4	•37	*.364	•39	16	6	358	61	12	†.972
1996— W. Michigan (Midw.)	C-DH-1B	123	447	62	114	26	2	12	68	.255	69	62	2	†917	85	‡20	.980
1997— Visalia (Calif.)	C-DH-1B	86	332	57	120	21	2	15	85	*.361	35	47	2	577	80	†16	.976
— Huntsville (Sou.)	C-DH-1B-3B	44	161	27	31	3	0	4	24	.193	18	23	0	274	27	1	.997
1998— Huntsville (Sou.)	DH-C-1B	127	479	83	142	24	1	15	98	.296	57	61	4	524	42	11	.981
1999— Vancouver (PCL)	C-DH-3B-1B	77	291	38	76	11	3	13	55	.261	23	37	1	339	40	5	.987
— Oakland (A.L.)	C	40	136	13	38	7	0	3	21	.279	18	11	1	274	19	6	.980
2000— Oakland (A.L.)	C	143	419	52	101	19	0	14	62	.241	38	64	1	764	43	*13	.984
2001— Oakland (A.L.)	C-1B	136	453	55	115	25	0	15	60	.254	37	68	1	911	70	12	.988
Major League totals (3 years)		319	1008	120	254	51	0	32	143	.252	93	143	3	1949	132	31	.985

DIVISION SERIES RECORD

Year Team (League)	Pos.	G	AB	R	H	2B	3B	HR	RBI	Avg.	BB	SO	SB	PO	A	E	Avg.
2000— Oakland (A.L.)	C	5	16	3	6	2	0	0	3	.375	0	3	0	34	3	1	.974
2001— Oakland (A.L.)	C-PH	5	10	0	0	0	0	0	0	.000	1	4	0	17	2	0	1.000
Division series totals (2 years)		10	26	3	6	2	0	0	3	.231	1	7	0	51	5	1	.982

HERNANDEZ, ROBERTO — P — ROYALS

PERSONAL: Born November 11, 1964, in Santurce, Puerto Rico. ... 6-4/250. ... Throws right, bats right. ... Full name: Roberto Manuel Hernandez.
HIGH SCHOOL: New Hampton (N.H.) Prep.
COLLEGE: South Carolina-Aiken.
TRANSACTIONS/CAREER NOTES: Selected by California Angels organization in first round (16th pick overall) of free-agent draft (June 2, 1986); pick received as compensation for Baltimore Orioles signing Type A free-agent OF/IF Juan Beniquez. ... On disabled list (May 6-21 and June 4-August 14, 1987). ... Traded by Angels with OF Mark Doran to Chicago White Sox organization for OF Mark Davis (August 2, 1989). ... On Vancouver disabled list (May 17-August 10, 1991). ... Traded by White Sox with P Wilson Alvarez and P Danny Darwin to San Francisco Giants for SS Mike Caruso, OF Brian Manning, P Lorenzo Barcelo, P Keith Foulke, P Bobby Howry and P Ken Vining (July 31, 1997). ...

H

Granted free agency (October 30, 1997). ... Signed by Tampa Bay Devil Rays (November 18, 1997). ... Traded by Devil Rays to Kansas City Royals as part of three-way deal in which Devil Rays received OF Ben Grieve and a player to be named later or cash from the Oakland A's, A's received P Cory Lidle from Devil Rays, A's received OF Johnny Damon, IF Mark Ellis and a player to be named later from Royals and Royals received C A.J. Hinch, IF Angel Berroa and cash from A's (January 8, 2001).

MISCELLANEOUS: Holds Tampa Bay Devil Rays all-time record for most saves (101).

Year League	W	L	Pct.	ERA	G	GS	CG	ShO	Sv.	IP	H	R	ER	BB	SO
1986—Salem (N'West)	2	2	.500	4.58	10	10	0	0	0	55	57	37	28	42	38
1987—Quad City (Midw.)	2	3	.400	6.86	7	6	0	0	1	21	24	21	16	12	21
1988—Quad City (Midw.)	9	10	.474	3.17	24	24	6	1	0	164²/₃	157	70	58	48	114
— Midland (Texas)	0	2	.000	6.57	3	3	0	0	0	12¹/₃	16	13	9	8	7
1989—Midland (Texas)	2	7	.222	6.89	12	12	0	0	0	64	94	57	49	30	42
— Palm Springs (Calif.)	1	4	.200	4.64	7	7	0	0	0	42²/₃	49	27	22	16	33
— South Bend (Midw.)■	1	1	.500	3.33	4	4	0	0	0	24¹/₃	19	9	9	7	17
1990—Birmingham (Sou.)	8	5	.615	3.67	17	17	1	0	0	108	103	57	44	43	62
— Vancouver (PCL)	3	5	.375	2.84	11	11	3	1	0	79¹/₃	73	33	25	26	49
1991—Birmingham (Sou.)	2	1	.667	1.99	4	4	0	0	0	22²/₃	11	5	5	6	25
— Vancouver (PCL)	4	1	.800	3.22	7	7	0	0	0	44²/₃	41	17	16	23	40
— GC White Sox (GCL)	0	0	...	0.00	1	1	0	0	0	6	2	0	0	0	7
— Chicago (A.L.)	1	0	1.000	7.80	9	3	0	0	0	15	18	15	13	7	6
1992—Chicago (A.L.)	7	3	.700	1.65	43	0	0	0	12	71	45	15	13	20	68
— Vancouver (PCL)	3	3	.500	2.61	9	0	0	0	2	20²/₃	13	9	6	11	23
1993—Chicago (A.L.)	3	4	.429	2.29	70	0	0	0	38	78²/₃	66	21	20	20	71
1994—Chicago (A.L.)	4	4	.500	4.91	45	0	0	0	14	47²/₃	44	29	26	19	50
1995—Chicago (A.L.)	3	7	.300	3.92	60	0	0	0	32	59²/₃	63	30	26	28	84
1996—Chicago (A.L.)	6	5	.545	1.91	72	0	0	0	38	84²/₃	65	21	18	38	85
1997—Chicago (A.L.)	5	1	.833	2.44	46	0	0	0	27	48	38	15	13	24	47
— San Francisco (N.L.)■	5	2	.714	2.48	28	0	0	0	4	32²/₃	29	9	9	14	35
1998—Tampa Bay (A.L.)■	2	6	.250	4.04	67	0	0	0	26	71¹/₃	55	33	32	41	55
1999—Tampa Bay (A.L.)	2	3	.400	3.07	72	0	0	0	43	73¹/₃	68	27	25	33	69
2000—Tampa Bay (A.L.)	4	7	.364	3.19	68	0	0	0	32	73¹/₃	76	33	26	23	61
2001—Kansas City (A.L.)■	5	6	.455	4.12	63	0	0	0	28	67²/₃	69	34	31	26	46
A.L. totals (11 years)	42	46	.477	3.17	615	3	0	0	290	690¹/₃	607	273	243	279	642
N.L. totals (1 year)	5	2	.714	2.48	28	0	0	0	4	32²/₃	29	9	9	14	35
Major League totals (11 years)	47	48	.495	3.14	643	3	0	0	294	723	636	282	252	293	677

DIVISION SERIES RECORD

Year League	W	L	Pct.	ERA	G	GS	CG	ShO	Sv.	IP	H	R	ER	BB	SO
1997—San Francisco (N.L.)	0	1	.000	20.25	3	0	0	0	0	1¹/₃	5	3	3	3	1

CHAMPIONSHIP SERIES RECORD

Year League	W	L	Pct.	ERA	G	GS	CG	ShO	Sv.	IP	H	R	ER	BB	SO
1993—Chicago (A.L.)	0	0	...	0.00	4	0	0	0	1	4	4	0	0	0	1

ALL-STAR GAME RECORD

Year League	W	L	Pct.	ERA	GS	CG	ShO	Sv.	IP	H	R	ER	BB	SO
1996—American	0	0	...	0.00	0	0	0	0	1	1	0	0	0	0
1999—American	0	0	...	0.00	0	0	0	0	1	0	0	0	0	0
All-Star Game totals (2 years)	0	0	...	0.00	0	0	0	0	2	1	0	0	0	0

HERNDON, HARRY   P   PADRES

PERSONAL: Born September 11, 1978, in Liberal, Kan. ... 6-1/190. ... Throws right, bats right. ... Full name: Francis Herndon Jr.
HIGH SCHOOL: Moffat County (Craig, Colo.).
TRANSACTIONS/CAREER NOTES: Selected by San Diego Padres organization in ninth round of free-agent draft (June 3, 1997).

Year League	W	L	Pct.	ERA	G	GS	CG	ShO	Sv.	IP	H	R	ER	BB	SO
1997—Arizona Padres (Ariz.)	3	2	.600	4.42	14	•14	0	0	0	*77¹/₃	*80	51	38	32	65
— Idaho Falls (Pio.)	0	0	...	0.00	1	1	0	0	0	5	5	0	0	1	3
1998—Clinton (Midw.)	10	8	.556	2.99	21	21	3	1	0	132¹/₃	119	59	44	34	101
— Rancho Cuca. (Calif.)	3	2	.600	3.40	6	6	0	0	0	39²/₃	37	18	15	13	29
1999—Mobile (Sou.)	10	9	.526	4.69	26	26	2	•2	0	163	172	96	85	52	87
2000—Las Vegas (PCL)	10	11	.476	5.13	26	26	3	0	0	135	151	90	77	65	75
2001—Portland (PCL)	9	5	.643	4.58	21	21	0	0	0	116	132	72	59	39	47
— San Diego (N.L.)	2	6	.250	6.33	12	8	0	0	0	42²/₃	55	34	30	25	14
Major League totals (1 year)	2	6	.250	6.33	12	8	0	0	0	42²/₃	55	34	30	25	14

HERRERA, ALEX   P   INDIANS

PERSONAL: Born November 5, 1979, in Maracaibo, Venezuela. ... 5-11/175. ... Throws left, bats left. ... Full name: Alexander J. Herrera.
TRANSACTIONS/CAREER NOTES: Signed as non-drafted free agent by Cleveland Indians organization (July 4, 1997).

Year League	W	L	Pct.	ERA	G	GS	CG	ShO	Sv.	IP	H	R	ER	BB	SO
1998—Guacara 1 (VSL)	7	4	.636	2.30	18	11	0	0	3	74¹/₃	70	34	19	17	68
1999—San Felipe (VSL)	3	2	.600	1.28	16	9	0	0	5	56¹/₃	42	19	8	20	74
2000—Columbus (S.Atl.)	4	3	.571	3.43	20	0	0	0	0	42	41	25	16	21	41
— Kinston (Caro.)	0	1	.000	2.32	17	0	0	0	1	31	28	11	8	19	40
— Akron (East.)	0	0	...	0.00	2	0	0	0	0	1¹/₃	2	1	0	1	1
2001—Kinston (Caro.)	4	0	1.000	0.60	28	0	0	0	3	59²/₃	36	6	4	18	83
— Akron (East.)	3	0	1.000	2.83	15	0	0	0	2	28²/₃	24	9	9	9	22

H

HIATT, PHIL   3B   DODGERS

PERSONAL: Born May 1, 1969, in Pensacola, Fla. ... 6-3/200. ... Bats right, throws right. ... Full name: Philip Farrell Hiatt.
HIGH SCHOOL: Catholic (Pensacola, Fla.).
JUNIOR COLLEGE: Jefferson Davis Community College (Brewton, Ala.).
COLLEGE: Louisiana Tech.
TRANSACTIONS/CAREER NOTES: Selected by Kansas City Royals organization in eighth round of free-agent draft (June 4, 1990). ... On Omaha disabled list (April 15-May 2, 1994). ... On Kansas City disabled list (May 5-20, 1995). ... Traded by Royals to Detroit Tigers (September 14, 1995), completing deal in which Royals acquired 1B/OF Juan Samuel for a player to be named later (September 8, 1995). ... Released by Tigers (November 8, 1996). ... Signed with Hanshin Tigers of Japan Central League (November 14, 1996). ... Signed by Cleveland Indians organization (April 28, 1998). ... Granted free agency (October 15, 1998). ... Signed by Cincinnati Reds organization (December 15, 1998). ... On Indianapolis disabled list (April 8-June 8, 1999). ... Granted free agency (October 15, 1999). ... Signed by Colorado Rockies organization (December 1, 1999). ... Granted free agency (October 18, 2000). ... Signed by Los Angeles Dodgers organization (January 4, 2001).
HONORS: Named International League Most Valuable Player (1996). ... Named Pacific Coast League Most Valuable Player (2001).
STATISTICAL NOTES: Led Northwest League third basemen with 145 assists, 200 total chances and 18 double plays in 1990. ... Led International League with 304 total bases in 1996. ... Led International League third basemen with 456 total chances and 39 double plays in 1996. ... Led Pacific Coast League with 303 in 2000. ... Led Pacific Coast League with 315 total bases and .722 slugging percentage in 2001.

							BATTING								FIELDING		
Year Team (League)	Pos.	G	AB	R	H	2B	3B	HR	RBI	Avg.	BB	SO	SB	PO	A	E	Avg.
1990—Eugene (N'West)	3B-SS	73	289	33	85	18	5	2	44	.294	17	70	15	41	†151	16	.923
1991—Baseball City (FSL)	3B	81	315	41	94	21	6	5	33	.298	22	70	28	65	146	12	.946
—Memphis (Sou.)	3B	56	206	29	47	7	1	6	33	.228	9	63	6	36	112	13	.919
1992—Memphis (Sou.)	3B-OF-1B	129	487	71	119	20	5	27	83	.244	25	157	5	139	150	20	.935
—Omaha (A.A.)	3B	5	14	3	3	0	0	2	4	.214	2	3	1	2	13	1	.938
1993—Kansas City (A.L.)	3B-DH	81	238	30	52	12	1	7	36	.218	16	82	6	45	114	16	.909
—Omaha (A.A.)	3B	12	51	8	12	2	0	3	10	.235	4	20	0	11	24	2	.946
1994—Omaha (A.A.)	OF	6	22	2	4	1	0	1	2	.182	0	4	1	7	1	0	1.000
—Memphis (Sou.)	OF	108	400	57	120	26	4	17	66	.300	40	116	12	218	*18	6	.975
1995—Kansas City (A.L.)	OF-DH	52	113	11	23	6	0	4	12	.204	9	37	1	63	4	3	.957
—Omaha (A.A.)	OF	20	76	7	12	5	0	2	8	.158	2	25	0	37	1	1	.974
1996—Toledo (I.L.)■	3B-DH	*142	*555	*99	145	27	3	*42	*119	.261	50	*180	17	85	*345	*26	.943
—Detroit (A.L.)	3B-OF-DH	7	21	3	4	0	1	0	1	.190	2	11	0	3	8	0	1.000
1998—Buffalo (I.L.)■	1B-DH-OF-3B	119	453	81	112	19	0	31	74	.247	41	146	4	601	57	8	.988
1999—Indianapolis (I.L.)■	1B-3B-OF-DH	78	311	46	74	11	0	18	54	.238	30	103	0	361	68	2	.995
2000—Colo. Springs (PCL)■	1B-OF-3B	136	507	106	157	36	1	*36	*109	.310	63	*149	14	1031	83	13	.988
2001—Las Vegas (PCL)■	3B-1B	113	436	*107	144	29	5	*44	99	.330	52	109	6	172	172	18	.950
—Los Angeles (N.L.)	3B-1B	30	50	6	12	3	0	2	6	.240	3	19	0	29	8	1	.974
American League totals (3 years)		140	372	44	79	18	2	11	49	.212	27	130	7	111	126	19	.926
National League totals (1 year)		30	50	6	12	3	0	2	6	.240	3	19	0	29	8	1	.974
Major League totals (4 years)		170	422	50	91	21	2	13	55	.216	30	149	7	140	134	20	.932

HIDALGO, RICHARD   OF   ASTROS

PERSONAL: Born July 2, 1975, in Caracas, Venezuela. ... 6-3/190. ... Bats right, throws right. ... Full name: Richard Jose Hidalgo.
TRANSACTIONS/CAREER NOTES: Signed as non-drafted free agent by Houston Astros organization (July 2, 1991). ... On Houston disabled list (May 30-July 21, 1998); included rehabilitation assignment to New Orleans (July 11-21). ... On disabled list (August 9, 1999-remainder of season).
RECORDS: Shares major league single-game record for most times hit by pitch—3 (April 19, 2000).
STATISTICAL NOTES: Led Texas League in grounding into double plays with 24 in 1996. ... Led Texas League outfielders with six double plays in 1996. ... Had 15-game hitting streak (August 28-September 13, 2000). ... Career major league grand slams: 1.

							BATTING								FIELDING		
Year Team (League)	Pos.	G	AB	R	H	2B	3B	HR	RBI	Avg.	BB	SO	SB	PO	A	E	Avg.
1992—GC Astros (GCL)	OF	51	184	20	57	7	3	1	27	.310	13	27	14	67	6	0	1.000
1993—Asheville (S.Atl.)	OF	111	403	49	109	23	3	10	55	.270	30	76	21	197	*30	6	.974
1994—Quad City (Midw.)	OF	124	476	68	139	*47	6	12	76	.292	23	80	12	202	*23	11	.953
1995—Jackson (Texas)	OF	133	489	59	130	28	6	14	59	.266	32	76	8	238	14	5	.981
1996—Jackson (Texas)	OF-DH	130	513	66	151	34	2	14	78	.294	29	55	11	302	14	6	.981
1997—New Orleans (A.A.)	OF-DH	134	526	74	147	*37	5	11	78	.279	35	57	6	261	*15	9	.968
—Houston (N.L.)	OF	19	62	8	19	5	0	2	6	.306	4	18	1	28	0	0	1.000
1998—Houston (N.L.)	OF	74	211	31	64	15	0	7	35	.303	17	37	3	131	3	3	.978
—New Orleans (PCL)	OF	10	24	0	4	2	0	0	1	.167	3	2	0	17	0	0	1.000
1999—Houston (N.L.)	OF	108	383	49	87	25	2	15	56	.227	56	73	8	214	15	2	.991
2000—Houston (N.L.)	OF	153	558	118	175	42	3	44	122	.314	56	110	13	425	7	7	.984
2001—Houston (N.L.)	OF	146	512	70	141	29	3	19	80	.275	54	107	3	332	11	3	.991
Major League totals (5 years)		500	1726	276	486	116	8	87	299	.282	187	345	28	1130	36	15	.987

DIVISION SERIES RECORD

							BATTING								FIELDING		
Year Team (League)	Pos.	G	AB	R	H	2B	3B	HR	RBI	Avg.	BB	SO	SB	PO	A	E	Avg.
1997—Houston (N.L.)	OF	2	5	1	0	0	0	0	0	.000	1	2	0	5	0	0	1.000
1998—Houston (N.L.)	OF	1	4	0	1	0	0	0	0	.250	0	1	0	1	0	0	1.000
1999—Houston (N.L.)						Did not play.											
2001—Houston (N.L.)	OF	3	8	1	1	0	0	0	0	.125	3	2	0	6	0	0	1.000
Division series totals (3 years)		6	17	2	2	0	0	0	0	.118	4	5	0	12	0	0	1.000

HIGGINSON, BOBBY   OF   TIGERS

PERSONAL: Born August 18, 1970, in Philadelphia. ... 5-11/195. ... Bats left, throws right. ... Full name: Robert Leigh Higginson.
HIGH SCHOOL: Frankford (Philadelphia).
COLLEGE: Temple.

TRANSACTIONS/CAREER NOTES: Selected by Detroit Tigers organization in 12th round of free-agent draft (June 1, 1992). ... On Detroit disabled list (May 11-June 7, 1996); included rehabilitation assignment to Toledo (June 4-7). ... On disabled list (June 15-26, 1997). ... On suspended list (September 26, 1997). ... On disabled list (July 24-August 24, 1999). ... On suspended list (May 10-16, 2000). ... On disabled list (May 20-June 5, 2001).

RECORDS: Shares major league record for most consecutive home runs—4 (June 30 [3], July 1 [1], 1997).

STATISTICAL NOTES: Hit three home runs in one game (June 30, 1997; and June 24, 2000). ... Tied for A.L. lead in double plays by outfielder with five in 1997. ... Career major league grand slams: 4.

Year Team (League)	Pos.	G	AB	R	H	2B	3B	HR	RBI	Avg.	BB	SO	SB	PO	A	E	Avg.
1992— Niagara Falls (NY-P) ...	OF	70	232	35	68	17	4	2	37	.293	33	47	12	109	5	2	.983
1993— Lakeland (FSL)	OF	61	223	42	67	11	7	3	25	.300	40	31	8	88	7	2	.979
— London (East.)	OF	63	224	25	69	15	4	4	35	.308	19	37	3	100	11	2	.982
1994— Toledo (I.L.)...............	OF	137	476	81	131	28	3	23	67	.275	46	99	16	282	10	8	.973
1995— Detroit (A.L.)	OF-DH	131	410	61	92	17	5	14	43	.224	62	107	6	247	*13	4	.985
1996— Detroit (A.L.)	OF-DH	130	440	75	141	35	0	26	81	.320	65	66	6	227	9	9	.963
— Toledo (I.L.)...............	OF	3	13	4	4	0	1	0	1	.308	3	0	0	3	0	0	1.000
1997— Detroit (A.L.)	OF-DH	146	546	94	163	30	5	27	101	.299	70	85	12	287	*20	9	.972
1998— Detroit (A.L.)	OF-DH	157	612	92	174	37	4	25	85	.284	63	101	3	303	18	6	.982
1999— Detroit (A.L.)	OF-DH	107	377	51	90	18	0	12	46	.239	64	66	4	175	2	3	.983
2000— Detroit (A.L.)	OF-DH	154	597	104	179	44	4	30	102	.300	74	99	15	307	*19	7	.979
2001— Detroit (A.L.)	OF-DH	147	541	84	150	28	6	17	71	.277	80	65	20	321	10	8	.976
Major League totals (7 years)		972	3523	561	989	209	24	151	529	.281	478	589	66	1867	91	46	.977

HILJUS, ERIK   P   ATHLETICS

PERSONAL: Born December 25, 1972, in Panorama City, Calif. ... 6-5/230. ... Throws right, bats right. ... Full name: Erik Kristian Hiljus.

HIGH SCHOOL: Canyon (Anaheim).

TRANSACTIONS/CAREER NOTES: Selected by New York Mets organization in fourth round of free-agent draft (June 3, 1991). ... Traded by Mets with P Eric Ludwick and OF Yudith Ozono to St. Louis Cardinals for OF Bernard Gilkey (January 23, 1996). ... On disabled list (April 4-July 14, 1996). ... On disabled list (April 3-August 20, 1997). ... Released by Cardinals (August 20, 1997). ... Signed by Detroit Tigers organization (March 9, 1998). ... On Toledo disabled list (April 8-19, 1999). ... Released by Tigers (November 27, 2000). ... Signed by Oakland Athletics organization (December 6, 2000).

RECORDS: Shares major league single-inning record for most strikeouts—4 (June 30, 2001).

STATISTICAL NOTES: Tied for Florida State League lead with eight balks in 1994.

Year League	W	L	Pct.	ERA	G	GS	CG	ShO	Sv.	IP	H	R	ER	BB	SO
1991— Gulf Coast Mets (GCL)	2	3	.400	4.26	9	9	1	•1	0	38	31	27	18	37	38
1992— Little Falls (NY-Penn)	3	6	.333	5.09	12	11	0	0	0	70²/₃	66	49	40	40	63
1993— Capital City (S.Atl.)............	7	10	.412	4.32	27	27	1	0	0	145²/₃	114	76	70	*111	157
1994— St. Lucie (FSL).................	11	10	.524	3.98	26	26	3	1	0	160²/₃	159	85	71	*90	140
1995— St. Lucie (FSL)	8	4	.667	2.99	17	17	0	0	0	111¹/₃	85	46	37	50	98
— Binghamton (East.)	2	4	.333	5.86	10	10	0	0	0	55¹/₃	60	38	36	32	40
1996— Arkansas (Texas)■.............	3	5	.375	6.11	10	10	0	0	0	45²/₃	62	37	31	30	21
1997—							Did not play.								
1998— Jacksonville (Sou.)■.........	2	3	.400	3.70	42	0	0	0	2	65²/₃	49	31	27	35	85
1999— Lakeland (FSL)	0	0	...	2.25	3	0	0	0	0	4	4	1	1	0	9
— Jacksonville (Sou.).........	1	0	1.000	1.04	10	0	0	0	0	17¹/₃	5	4	2	5	28
— Toledo (I.L.)....................	2	3	.400	4.40	33	0	0	0	5	59¹/₃	49	31	29	16	73
— Detroit (A.L.)	0	0	...	5.19	6	0	0	0	0	8²/₃	7	5	5	5	1
2000— Toledo (I.L.).....................	5	3	.625	3.44	46	0	0	0	2	70²/₃	67	33	27	20	81
— Detroit (A.L.)	0	0	...	7.36	3	0	0	0	0	3²/₃	5	3	3	1	2
2001— Sacramento (PCL)■...........	8	5	.615	3.63	15	15	3	1	0	101²/₃	79	46	41	26	108
— Oakland (A.L.)..............	5	0	1.000	3.41	16	11	0	0	0	66	70	29	25	21	67
Major League totals (3 years)	5	0	1.000	3.79	25	11	0	0	0	78¹/₃	82	37	33	27	70

DIVISION SERIES RECORD

Year League	W	L	Pct.	ERA	G	GS	CG	ShO	Sv.	IP	H	R	ER	BB	SO
2001— Oakland (A.L.)	0	0	...	27.00	1	0	0	0	0	¹/₃	0	1	1	2	0

HILL, GLENALLEN   OF

PERSONAL: Born March 22, 1965, in Santa Cruz, Calif. ... 6-3/230. ... Bats right, throws right.

HIGH SCHOOL: Santa Cruz (Calif.).

TRANSACTIONS/CAREER NOTES: Selected by Toronto Blue Jays organization in ninth round of free-agent draft (June 6, 1983). ... On disabled list (July 6-21, 1990). ... Traded by Blue Jays with P Denis Boucher, OF Mark Whiten and a player to be named later to Cleveland Indians for P Tom Candiotti and OF Turner Ward (June 27, 1991); Indians acquired cash to complete deal (October 15, 1991). ... On Cleveland disabled list (September 8, 1991-remainder of season). ... On Cleveland disabled list (April 23-May 22, 1992); included rehabilitation assignment to Canton/Akron (May 18-22). ... Traded by Indians to Chicago Cubs for OF Candy Maldonado (August 19, 1993). ... Granted free agency (October 27, 1993). ... Re-signed by Cubs (November 24, 1993). ... Granted free agency (April 7, 1995). ... Signed by San Francisco Giants (April 9, 1995). ... On San Francisco disabled list (May 27-August 5, 1996); included rehabilitation assignment to Phoenix (July 29-August 5). ... Granted free agency (October 29, 1997). ... Signed by Seattle Mariners organization (January 8, 1998). ... Claimed on waivers by Cubs (July 6, 1998). ... Granted free agency (October 23, 1998). ... Re-signed by Cubs (December 7, 1998). ... On disabled list (May 8-23, 1999; and March 23-April 7, 2000). ... Traded by Cubs to New York Yankees for P Ben Ford and P Ozwaldo Mairena (July 21, 2000). ... Traded by Yankees to Anaheim Angels for OF Darren Blakely (March 28, 2001). ... On Anaheim disabled list (April 21-May 29, 2001); included rehabilitation assignment to Rancho Cucamonga (May 26-29). ... Released by Angels (June 1, 2001).

STATISTICAL NOTES: Led Southern League with 287 total bases and tied for lead with 13 sacrifice flies in 1986. ... Led International League with 279 total bases and .578 slugging percentage in 1989. ... Career major league grand slams: 5.

H

Year	Team (League)	Pos.	G	AB	R	H	2B	3B	HR	RBI	Avg.	BB	SO	SB	PO	A	E	Avg.
1983—	Medicine Hat (Pio.)	OF	46	133	34	63	3	4	6	27	.474	17	49	4	63	3	6	.917
1984—	Florence (S.Atl.)	OF	129	440	75	105	19	5	16	64	.239	63	*150	30	281	9	16	.948
1985—	Kinston (Caro.)..........	OF	131	466	57	98	13	0	20	56	.210	57	*211	42	234	12	13	.950
1986—	Knoxville (Sou.)..........	OF	*141	*570	87	159	23	6	*31	96	.279	43	*153	18	230	9	*21	.919
1987—	Syracuse (I.L.).............	OF	*137	536	65	126	25	6	16	77	.235	25	*152	22	176	10	10	.949
1988—	Syracuse (I.L.).............	OF	51	172	21	40	7	0	4	19	.233	15	59	7	101	2	1	.990
—	Knoxville (Sou.)..........	OF	79	269	37	71	13	2	12	38	.264	28	75	10	130	6	5	.965
1989—	Syracuse (I.L.).............	OF	125	483	*86	*155	31	*15	*21	72	.321	34	107	21	242	3	*7	.972
—	Toronto (A.L.).............	OF-DH	19	52	4	15	0	0	1	7	.288	3	12	2	27	0	1	.964
1990—	Toronto (A.L.).............	OF-DH	84	260	47	60	11	3	12	32	.231	18	62	8	115	4	2	.983
1991—	Toronto (A.L.).............	DH-OF	35	99	14	25	5	2	3	11	.253	7	24	2	29	0	1	.967
—	Cleveland (A.L.)■......	OF-DH	37	122	15	32	3	0	5	14	.262	16	30	4	89	0	2	.978
1992—	Cleveland (A.L.)........	OF-DH	102	369	38	89	16	1	18	49	.241	20	73	9	126	5	6	.956
—	Canton/Akron (East.)..	OF	3	9	1	1	1	0	0	1	.111	3	4	0	4	0	1	.800
1993—	Cleveland (A.L.)........	OF-DH	66	174	19	39	7	2	5	25	.224	11	50	7	62	1	4	.940
—	Chicago (N.L.)■........	OF	31	87	14	30	7	0	10	22	.345	6	21	1	42	2	2	.957
1994—	Chicago (N.L.)	OF	89	269	48	80	12	1	10	38	.297	29	57	19	149	0	2	.987
1995—	San Fran. (N.L.)■......	OF	132	497	71	131	29	4	24	86	.264	39	98	25	226	10	10	.959
1996—	San Francisco (N.L.) ..	OF	98	379	56	106	26	0	19	67	.280	33	95	6	160	6	7	.960
—	Phoenix (PCL)	OF	5	17	4	6	1	0	2	2	.353	0	3	1	8	0	0	1.000
1997—	San Francisco (N.L.) ..	OF-DH	128	398	47	104	28	4	11	64	.261	19	87	7	158	2	9	.947
1998—	Seattle (A.L.)■.........	OF	74	259	37	75	20	2	12	33	.290	14	45	1	107	2	4	.965
—	Chicago (N.L.)■........	OF	48	131	26	46	5	0	8	23	.351	14	34	0	59	3	1	.984
1999—	Chicago (N.L.)...........	OF-DH	99	253	43	76	9	1	20	55	.300	22	61	5	81	3	4	.955
2000—	Chicago (N.L.)...........	OF-DH	64	168	23	44	4	1	11	29	.262	10	43	0	39	3	2	.955
—	New York (A.L.)........	DH-OF	40	132	22	44	5	0	16	29	.333	9	33	0	19	0	0	1.000
2001—	Anaheim (A.L.)■.......	DH	16	66	4	9	0	0	1	2	.136	0	20	0	...	...	...	...
—	Rancho Cuca. (Calif.)	DH	3	12	1	2	1	0	1	3	.167	0	5	0	...	...	...	...
American League totals (8 years)			473	1533	200	388	67	10	73	202	.253	98	349	33	574	12	20	.967
National League totals (8 years)			689	2182	328	617	120	11	113	384	.283	172	496	63	914	29	37	.962
Major League totals (13 years)			1162	3715	528	1005	187	21	186	586	.271	270	845	96	1488	41	57	.964

DIVISION SERIES RECORD

Year	Team (League)	Pos.	G	AB	R	H	2B	3B	HR	RBI	Avg.	BB	SO	SB	PO	A	E	Avg.
1997—	San Francisco (N.L.) ..	OF-PH	3	7	0	0	0	0	0	0	.000	2	2	0	2	0	0	1.000
1998—	Chicago (N.L.)	OF	1	3	0	1	0	0	0	0	.333	1	2	1	3	0	0	1.000
2000—	New York (A.L.)	PH-DH	4	12	1	1	0	0	0	2	.083	1	5	0	...	...	...	...
Division series totals (3 years)			8	22	1	2	0	0	0	2	.091	4	9	1	5	0	0	1.000

CHAMPIONSHIP SERIES RECORD

Year	Team (League)	Pos.	G	AB	R	H	2B	3B	HR	RBI	Avg.	BB	SO	SB	PO	A	E	Avg.
2000—	New York (A.L.)	PH	2	2	0	0	0	0	0	0	.000	0	2	0	...	...	...	...

WORLD SERIES RECORD

NOTES: Member of World Series championship team (2000).

Year	Team (League)	Pos.	G	AB	R	H	2B	3B	HR	RBI	Avg.	BB	SO	SB	PO	A	E	Avg.
2000—	New York (A.L.)	PH-OF	3	3	0	0	0	0	0	0	.000	0	0	0	0	0	0	...

HILL, KEN   P

PERSONAL: Born December 14, 1965, in Lynn, Mass. ... 6-2/215. ... Throws right, bats right. ... Full name: Kenneth Wade Hill.

HIGH SCHOOL: Classical (Lynn, Mass.).

COLLEGE: North Adams (Mass.) State.

TRANSACTIONS/CAREER NOTES: Signed as non-drafted free agent by Detroit Tigers organization (February 14, 1985). ... Traded by Tigers with a player to be named later to St. Louis Cardinals for C Mike Heath (August 10, 1986); Cardinals acquired 1B Mike Laga to complete deal (September 2, 1986). ... On St. Louis disabled list (March 26-May 9, 1988). ... On St. Louis disabled list (August 11-September 1, 1991); included rehabilitation assignment to Louisville (August 29-30). ... Traded by Cardinals to Montreal Expos for 1B Andres Galarraga (November 25, 1991). ... On Montreal disabled list (June 26-July 17, 1993); included rehabilitation assignment to Ottawa (July 12-15). ... Traded by Expos to Cardinals for P Brian Eversgerd, P Kirk Bullinger and OF Darond Stovall (April 5, 1995). ... Traded by Cardinals to Cleveland Indians for 3B/2B David Bell, P Rick Heiserman and C Pepe McNeal (July 27, 1995). ... Granted free agency (November 1, 1995). ... Signed by Texas Rangers (December 22, 1995). ... Traded by Rangers to Anaheim Angels for C Jim Leyritz and a player to be named later (July 29, 1997); Rangers acquired IF Rob Sasser to complete deal (October 31, 1997). ... On disabled list (May 1-24, 1997); included rehabilitation assignment to Tulsa (May 20-24). ... Granted free agency (November 7, 1997). ... Re-signed by Angels (November 15, 1997). ... On Anaheim disabled list (June 11-August 28, 1998); included rehabilitation assignments to Cedar Rapids (August 9-17) and Lake Elsinore (August 18-24). ... On disabled list (July 1-19 and August 15-September 1, 1999). ... On Anaheim disabled list (May 10-June 28, 2000); included rehabilitation assignments to Lake Elsinore (June 10-15) and Edmonton (June 16-22). ... Released by Angels (August 7, 2000). ... Signed by Chicago White Sox organization (August 18, 2000). ... Released by White Sox (August 29, 2000). ... Signed by Tampa Bay Devil Rays organization (February 8, 2001). ... Released by Devil Rays (April 19, 2001). ... Signed by Cincinnati Reds organization (May 18, 2001). ... Released by Reds (June 18, 2001). ... Signed by Boston Red Sox organization (July 19, 2001). ... Granted free agency (October 15, 2001).

RECORDS: Shares N.L. single-season record for fewest games lost by pitcher who led league in games lost—15 (1989).

STATISTICAL NOTES: Pitched 6-0 one-hit, complete-game victory against New York (June 8, 1992). ... Led N.L. with 16 sacrifice hits in 1994. ... Pitched 11-0 one-hit, complete-game victory against Detroit (May 3, 1996). ... Led A.L. with four balks in 1996. ... Led A.L. with 95 bases on balls in 1997.

MISCELLANEOUS: Made an out in only appearance as pinch hitter with Montreal (1993). ... Had sacrifice hit in only appearance as pinch hitter (1994).

H

Year League	W	L	Pct.	ERA	G	GS	CG	ShO	Sv.	IP	H	R	ER	BB	SO
1985—Gastonia (S.Atl.)	3	6	.333	4.96	15	12	0	0	0	69	60	51	38	57	48
1986—Gastonia (S.Atl.)	9	5	.643	2.79	22	16	1	0	0	122²/₃	95	51	38	80	86
—Glens Falls (East.)	0	1	.000	5.14	1	1	0	0	0	7	4	4	4	6	4
—Arkansas (Texas)■	1	2	.333	4.50	3	3	1	0	0	18	18	10	9	7	9
1987—Arkansas (Texas)	3	5	.375	5.20	18	8	0	0	2	53²/₃	60	33	31	30	48
—St. Petersburg (FSL)	1	3	.250	4.17	18	4	0	0	2	41	38	19	19	17	32
1988—St. Louis (N.L.)	0	1	.000	5.14	4	1	0	0	0	14	16	9	8	6	6
—Arkansas (Texas)	9	9	.500	4.92	22	22	3	1	0	115¹/₃	129	76	63	50	107
1989—Louisville (A.A.)	0	2	.000	3.50	3	3	0	0	0	18	13	8	7	10	18
—St. Louis (N.L.)	7	•15	.318	3.80	33	33	2	1	0	196²/₃	186	92	83	*99	112
1990—St. Louis (N.L.)	5	6	.455	5.49	17	14	1	0	0	78²/₃	79	49	48	33	58
—Louisville (A.A.)	6	1	.857	1.79	12	12	2	1	0	85¹/₃	47	20	17	27	104
1991—St. Louis (N.L.)	11	10	.524	3.57	30	30	0	0	0	181¹/₃	147	76	72	67	121
—Louisville (A.A.)	0	0	...	0.00	1	1	0	0	0	1	0	0	0	0	2
1992—Montreal (N.L.)■	16	9	.640	2.68	33	33	3	3	0	218	187	76	65	75	150
1993—Montreal (N.L.)	9	7	.563	3.23	28	28	2	0	0	183²/₃	163	84	66	74	90
—Ottawa (I.L.)	0	0	...	0.00	1	1	0	0	0	4	1	0	0	1	0
1994—Montreal (N.L.)	•16	5	.762	3.32	23	23	2	1	0	154²/₃	145	61	57	44	85
1995—St. Louis (N.L.)■	6	7	.462	5.06	18	18	0	0	0	110¹/₃	125	71	62	45	50
—Cleveland (A.L.)■	4	1	.800	3.98	12	11	1	0	0	74²/₃	77	36	33	32	48
1996—Texas (A.L.)	16	10	.615	3.63	35	35	7	•3	0	250²/₃	250	110	101	95	170
1997—Texas (A.L.)	5	8	.385	5.19	19	19	0	0	0	111	129	69	64	56	68
—Tulsa (Texas)	0	0	...	0.00	1	1	0	0	0	5	2	0	0	1	3
—Anaheim (A.L.)■	4	4	.500	3.65	12	12	1	0	0	79	65	34	32	§39	38
1998—Anaheim (A.L.)	9	6	.600	4.98	19	19	0	0	0	103	123	60	57	47	57
—Cedar Rapids (Midw.)	0	0	...	1.23	2	2	0	0	0	7¹/₃	7	1	1	1	6
—Lake Elsinore (Calif.)	0	0	...	6.75	1	1	0	0	0	4	5	4	3	5	2
1999—Anaheim (A.L.)	4	11	.267	4.77	26	22	0	0	0	128¹/₃	129	72	68	76	76
2000—Anaheim (A.L.)	5	7	.417	6.52	16	16	0	0	0	78²/₃	102	59	57	53	50
—Lake Elsinore (Calif.)	0	0	...	0.00	1	1	0	0	0	4	5	2	0	1	3
—Edmonton (PCL)	0	0	...	6.52	2	2	0	0	0	9²/₃	14	8	7	8	5
—Charlotte (I.L.)■	0	0	...	4.50	1	1	0	0	0	4	6	2	2	0	7
—Chicago (A.L.)	0	1	.000	24.00	2	1	0	0	0	3	5	8	8	6	0
2001—Tampa Bay (A.L.)■	0	1	.000	12.27	5	0	0	0	0	7¹/₃	10	11	10	5	2
—Louisville (I.L.)■	2	1	.667	4.60	6	6	0	0	0	31¹/₃	33	19	16	12	16
—Pawtucket (I.L.)■	2	1	.667	6.54	8	8	0	0	0	31²/₃	42	27	23	11	17
A.L. totals (7 years)	47	49	.490	4.63	146	135	9	3	0	835²/₃	890	459	430	409	509
N.L. totals (8 years)	70	60	.538	3.65	186	180	10	5	0	1137¹/₃	1048	518	461	443	672
Major League totals (14 years)	117	109	.518	4.06	332	315	19	8	0	1973	1938	977	891	852	1181

DIVISION SERIES RECORD

Year League	W	L	Pct.	ERA	G	GS	CG	ShO	Sv.	IP	H	R	ER	BB	SO
1995—Cleveland (A.L.)	1	0	1.000	0.00	1	0	0	0	0	1¹/₃	1	0	0	0	2
1996—Texas (A.L.)	0	0	...	4.50	1	1	0	0	0	6	5	3	3	3	1
Division series totals (2 years)	1	0	1.000	3.68	2	1	0	0	0	7¹/₃	6	3	3	3	3

CHAMPIONSHIP SERIES RECORD

Year League	W	L	Pct.	ERA	G	GS	CG	ShO	Sv.	IP	H	R	ER	BB	SO
1995—Cleveland (A.L.)	1	0	1.000	0.00	1	1	0	0	0	7	5	0	0	3	6

WORLD SERIES RECORD

Year League	W	L	Pct.	ERA	G	GS	CG	ShO	Sv.	IP	H	R	ER	BB	SO
1995—Cleveland (A.L.)	0	1	.000	4.26	2	1	0	0	0	6¹/₃	7	3	3	4	1

ALL-STAR GAME RECORD

Year League	W	L	Pct.	ERA	GS	CG	ShO	Sv.	IP	H	R	ER	BB	SO
1994—National	0	0	...	0.00	0	0	0	0	2	0	0	0	1	0

HILLENBRAND, SHEA   3B   RED SOX

PERSONAL: Born July 27, 1975, in Mesa, Ariz. ... 6-1/200. ... Bats right, throws right. ... Full name: Shea Matthew Hillenbrand.
HIGH SCHOOL: Mountain View (Mesa, Ariz.).
JUNIOR COLLEGE: Mesa (Ariz.) Community College.
TRANSACTIONS/CAREER NOTES: Selected by Boston Red Sox organization in 10th round of free-agent draft (June 4, 1996). ... On Trenton disabled list (July 5-August 31, 1999). ... On Boston disabled list (August 31, 1999-remainder of season). ... Granted free agency (December 21, 1999). ... Re-signed by Red Sox organization (January 29, 2000).
STATISTICAL NOTES: Led New York-Penn League first beasmen with 17 errors in 1996. ... Led Midwest League with 272 total bases and .546 slugging percentage in 1998. ... Led Midwest League with 20 passed balls in 1998. ... Led Eastern League with seven double plays by catchers in 1999.

Year—Team (League)	Pos.	G	AB	R	H	2B	3B	HR	RBI	Avg.	BB	SO	SB	PO	A	E	Avg.
1996—Lowell (NY-Penn)	1B-SS-3B	72	279	33	88	18	2	2	38	.315	18	32	4	440	57	†33	.938
1997—Michigan (Midw.)	1B-3B	64	224	28	65	13	3	3	39	.290	9	20	1	137	16	8	.950
—Sarasota (FSL)	1B-3B	57	220	25	65	12	0	2	28	.295	7	29	9	198	53	20	.926
1998—Michigan (Midw.)	C-1B-3B	129	498	80	174	33	4	19	93	.349	19	49	13	700	64	14	.982
1999—Trenton (East.)	C-DH	69	282	41	73	15	0	7	36	.259	14	27	6	337	41	5	.987
2000—Trenton (East.)	1B-3B	135	529	77	*171	35	3	11	79	.323	19	39	3	594	95	15	.979
2001—Boston (A.L.)	3B-1B-DH	139	468	52	123	20	2	12	49	.263	13	61	3	138	203	18	.950
Major League totals (1 year)		139	468	52	123	20	2	12	49	.263	13	61	3	138	203	18	.950

H

HINCH, A.J.   C   ROYALS

PERSONAL: Born May 15, 1974, in Waverly, Iowa. ... 6-1/207. ... Bats right, throws right. ... Full name: Andrew Jay Hinch.
HIGH SCHOOL: Midwest City (Okla.).
COLLEGE: Stanford.
TRANSACTIONS/CAREER NOTES: Selected by Chicago White Sox organization in second round of free-agent draft (June 2, 1992); did not sign. ... Selected by Minnesota Twins organization in third round of free-agent draft (June 1, 1995); did not sign. ... Selected by Oakland Athletics organization in third round of free-agent draft (June 4, 1996). ... On Modesto suspended list (June 7-9, 1997). ... Traded by A's with IF Angel Berroa and cash to Kansas City Royals as part of three-way deal in which Royals received P Roberto Hernandez from Tampa Bay Devil Rays, A's received P Cory Lidle from Devil Rays, A's received OF Johnny Damon, IF Mark Ellis and a player to be named later from Royals and Devil Rays received OF Ben Grieve and a player to be named later or cash from A's (January 8, 2001).
RECORDS: Shares major league single-season record for fewest double plays by catcher for leader—8 (1998).
STATISTICAL NOTES: Led California League catchers with .996 fielding percentage in 1997. ... Tied for A.L. lead in double plays by catcher with eight in 1998. ... Led Pacific Coast League catchers with .994 fielding percentage in 2000. ... Career major league grand slams: 1.
MISCELLANEOUS: Member of 1996 U.S. Olympic baseball team.

								BATTING							FIELDING		
Year Team (League)	Pos.	G	AB	R	H	2B	3B	HR	RBI	Avg.	BB	SO	SB	PO	A	E	Avg.
1997— Modesto (Calif.)	C-DH-1B	95	333	70	103	25	3	20	73	.309	42	68	8	622	66	3	†.996
—Edmonton (PCL)	C-DH-OF	39	125	23	47	7	0	4	24	.376	20	13	2	201	7	3	.986
1998— Oakland (A.L.)	C	120	337	34	78	10	0	9	35	.231	30	89	3	602	47	•9	.986
1999— Oakland (A.L.)	C	76	205	26	44	4	1	7	24	.215	11	41	6	368	26	5	.987
—Vancouver (PCL)	C-DH	15	61	9	23	3	0	2	7	.377	3	12	1	83	3	1	.989
2000— Sacramento (PCL)......	C-1B	109	417	65	111	23	2	6	47	.266	45	67	5	586	47	4	.994
—Oakland (A.L.)	C-DH	6	8	1	2	0	0	0	0	.250	1	1	0	9	0	1	.900
2001— Kansas City (A.L.)■....	C-DH	45	121	10	19	3	0	6	15	.157	8	26	1	220	14	3	.987
—Omaha (PCL)..............	C-OF	45	168	28	54	14	0	10	33	.321	11	33	1	188	6	1	.995
Major League totals (4 years)		247	671	71	143	17	1	22	74	.213	50	157	10	1199	87	18	.986

HINCHLIFFE, BRETT   P

PERSONAL: Born July 21, 1974, in Detroit. ... 6-5/190. ... Throws right, bats right.
HIGH SCHOOL: Bishop Gallagher (Harper Woods, Mich.).
TRANSACTIONS/CAREER NOTES: Selected by Seattle Mariners organization in 16th round of free-agent draft (June 1, 1992). ... On suspended list (April 21-25, 1999). ... Released by Mariners (January 3, 2000). ... Signed by Anaheim Angels organization (January 19, 2000). ... On suspended by Angels with IF Keith Luuloa to Chicago Cubs for OF Chris Hatcher, P Mike Heathcott and SS Brett King (July 28, 2000). ... Granted free agency (October 18, 2000). ... Signed by New York Mets organization (December 5, 2000). ... On Norfolk disabled list (May 9-June 3, June 27-July 6 and August 1, 2001-remainder of season). ... Granted free agency (October 15, 2001).
STATISTICAL NOTES: Pitched 12-0 no-hit victory against Cedar Rapids (June 28, 1994).

Year League	W	L	Pct.	ERA	G	GS	CG	ShO	Sv.	IP	H	R	ER	BB	SO
1992— Arizona Mariners (Ariz.)	5	4	.556	2.31	*24	0	0	0	3	35	42	17	9	9	26
1993— Arizona Mariners (Ariz.)	0	4	.000	5.08	10	9	0	0	0	44 1/3	55	32	25	5	29
1994— Appleton (Midw.)...............	11	7	.611	3.21	27	27	3	1	0	173 2/3	140	79	62	50	160
1995— Riverside (Calif.)...............	3	8	.273	6.61	15	15	0	0	0	77 2/3	110	69	57	35	68
1996— Lancaster (Calif.)...............	11	10	.524	4.24	27	26	0	0	0	163 1/3	179	105	77	64	146
1997— Memphis (Sou.)	10	10	.500	4.45	24	24	*5	1	0	145 2/3	159	81	72	45	107
1998— Lancaster (Calif.)	1	1	.500	1.59	3	3	0	0	0	17	8	5	3	5	26
—Tacoma (PCL)	10	8	.556	4.00	25	25	2	1	0	159 2/3	132	80	71	*88	100
1999— Seattle (A.L.)	0	4	.000	8.80	11	4	0	0	0	30 2/3	41	31	30	21	14
—Tacoma (PCL)	9	7	.563	5.15	21	21	3	0	0	131	141	78	75	44	107
2000— Edmonton (PCL)■	2	3	.400	3.80	27	3	0	0	2	64	63	29	27	24	30
—Anaheim (A.L.)	0	0	...	5.40	2	0	0	0	0	1 2/3	1	1	1	1	0
—Iowa (PCL)■	2	0	1.000	2.81	7	4	1	0	0	32	32	10	10	8	22
2001— Norfolk (I.L.)■	3	2	.600	3.02	11	10	0	0	0	59 2/3	67	30	20	17	46
—New York (N.L.)	0	1	.000	36.00	1	1	0	0	0	2	9	8	8	1	2
A.L. totals (2 years)	0	4	.000	8.63	13	4	0	0	0	32 1/3	42	32	31	22	14
N.L. totals (1 year)....................	0	1	.000	36.00	1	1	0	0	0	2	9	8	8	1	2
Major League totals (3 years).......	0	5	.000	10.22	14	5	0	0	0	34 1/3	51	40	39	23	16

HINSKE, ERIC   3B   BLUE JAYS

PERSONAL: Born August 5, 1977, in Neenah, Wisc. ... 6-2/225. ... Bats left, throws right. ... Full name: Eric Scott Hinske. ... Name pronounced hin-SKEE.
HIGH SCHOOL: Menasha (Wisc.).
COLLEGE: Arkansas.
TRANSACTIONS/CAREER NOTES: Selected by Chicago Cubs organization in 17th round of free-agent draft (June 2, 1998). ... Traded by Cubs to Oakland Athletics for 2B Miguel Cairo (March 28, 2001). ... On disabled list (May 1-12, 2001). ... Traded by A's with P Justin Miller to Toronto Blue Jays for P Billy Koch (December 7, 2001).
STATISTICAL NOTES: Led New York-Pennsylvania League first basemen with 51 double plays and 612 total chances in 1998.

								BATTING							FIELDING		
Year Team (League)	Pos.	G	AB	R	H	2B	3B	HR	RBI	Avg.	BB	SO	SB	PO	A	E	Avg.
1998— Williamsport (NY-P) ...	1B	68	248	46	74	20	0	9	57	.298	35	61	19	*561	*49	2	*.997
—Rockford (Midw.)	1B	6	20	8	9	4	0	1	4	.450	5	6	1	15	0	0	1.000
1999— Daytona (FSL)	3B-1B-OF	130	445	76	132	28	6	19	79	.297	62	90	16	458	140	22	.965
—Iowa (PCL)	1B-3B	4	15	3	4	0	1	1	2	.267	1	4	0	17	3	1	.952
2000— West Tenn (Sou.)	3B-1B-OF	131	436	76	113	21	9	20	73	.259	78	133	14	112	194	28	.916
2001— Sacramento (PCL)■...	3B-2B	121	436	71	123	27	1	25	79	.282	54	113	20	73	197	17	.941

H

PERSONAL: Born April 29, 1971, in Fayetteville, N.C. ... 6-0/205. ... Throws left, bats left. ... Full name: Sterling Alex Hitchcock.
HIGH SCHOOL: Armwood (Seffner, Fla.).
TRANSACTIONS/CAREER NOTES: Selected by New York Yankees organization in ninth round of free-agent draft (June 5, 1989). ... On disabled list (June 26-August 14, 1991). ... On Columbus disabled list (May 23-July 21, 1993). ... Traded by Yankees with 3B Russ Davis to Seattle Mariners for 1B Tino Martinez, P Jeff Nelson and P Jim Mecir (December 7, 1995). ... Traded by Mariners to San Diego Padres for P Scott Sanders (December 6, 1996). ... On disabled list (June 6-July 3, 1997; and May 27, 2000-remainder of season). ... On San Diego disabled list (March 27-July 4, 2001); included rehabilitation assignments to Lake Elsinore (April 5-27 and June 14-18) and Portland (June 19-July 4). ... Traded by Padres to Yankees for P Brett Jodie and OF Darren Blakely (July 30, 2001). ... Granted free agency (November 6, 2001). ... Resigned by Yankees (December 18, 2001).
STATISTICAL NOTES: Pitched 1-0 no-hit victory against Sumter (July 16, 1990). ... Struck out 15 batters in one game (August 29, 1998). ... Tied for N.L. lead with 15 wild pitches in 1999.

Year League	W	L	Pct.	ERA	G	GS	CG	ShO	Sv.	IP	H	R	ER	BB	SO
1989—Gulf Coast Yankees (GCL)..	*9	1	.900	1.64	13	•13	0	0	0	76 2/3	48	16	14	27	*98
1990—Greensboro (S.Atl.)	12	12	.500	2.91	27	27	6	*5	0	173 1/3	122	68	56	60	*171
1991—Prince William (Caro.)	7	7	.500	2.64	19	19	2	0	0	119 1/3	111	49	35	26	101
1992—Albany/Colonie (East.)	6	9	.400	2.58	24	24	2	0	0	146 2/3	116	51	42	42	*155
—New York (A.L.)	0	2	.000	8.31	3	3	0	0	0	13	23	12	12	6	6
1993—Columbus (I.L.)	3	5	.375	4.81	16	16	0	0	0	76 2/3	80	43	41	28	85
—New York (A.L.)	1	2	.333	4.65	6	6	0	0	0	31	32	18	16	14	26
1994—New York (A.L.)	4	1	.800	4.20	23	5	1	0	2	49 1/3	48	24	23	29	37
—Columbus (I.L.)	3	4	.429	4.32	10	9	1	0	0	50	53	30	24	18	47
—Albany/Colonie (East.)	1	0	1.000	1.80	1	1	0	0	0	5	4	1	1	0	7
1995—New York (A.L.)	11	10	.524	4.70	27	27	4	1	0	168 1/3	155	91	88	63	121
1996—Seattle (A.L.)■	13	9	.591	5.35	35	35	0	0	0	196 2/3	245	131	117	73	132
1997—San Diego (N.L.)■	10	11	.476	5.20	32	28	1	0	0	161	172	102	93	55	106
1998—San Diego (N.L.)	9	7	.563	3.93	39	27	2	1	1	176 1/3	169	83	77	48	158
1999—San Diego (N.L.)	12	14	.462	4.11	33	33	1	0	0	205 2/3	202	99	94	76	194
2000—San Diego (N.L.)	1	6	.143	4.93	11	11	0	0	0	65 2/3	69	38	36	26	61
2001—Lake Elsinore (Calif.)	0	2	.000	4.10	6	6	0	0	0	26 1/3	33	18	12	1	31
—Portland (PCL)	2	0	1.000	3.71	3	3	0	0	0	17	20	7	7	2	11
—San Diego (N.L.)	2	1	.667	3.32	3	3	0	0	0	19	22	9	7	3	15
—New York (A.L.)■	4	4	.500	6.49	10	9	1	0	0	51 1/3	67	37	37	18	28
A.L. totals (6 years)	33	28	.541	5.17	104	85	6	1	2	509 2/3	570	313	293	208	350
N.L. totals (5 years)	34	39	.466	4.40	118	102	4	1	1	627 2/3	634	331	307	208	534
Major League totals (10 years)	67	67	.500	4.75	222	187	10	2	3	1137 1/3	1204	644	600	416	884

DIVISION SERIES RECORD

Year League	W	L	Pct.	ERA	G	GS	CG	ShO	Sv.	IP	H	R	ER	BB	SO
1995—New York (A.L.)	0	0	...	5.40	2	0	0	0	0	1 2/3	2	2	1	2	1
1998—San Diego (N.L.)	1	0	1.000	1.50	1	1	0	0	0	6	3	1	1	0	11
2001—New York (A.L.)	0	0	...	6.00	1	0	0	0	0	3	5	2	2	0	2
Division series totals (3 years)	1	0	1.000	3.38	4	1	0	0	0	10 2/3	10	5	4	2	14

CHAMPIONSHIP SERIES RECORD

RECORDS: Shares single-inning record for most wild pitches—2 (October 14, 1998, second inning).
NOTES: Named N.L. Championship Series Most Valuable Player (1998).

Year League	W	L	Pct.	ERA	G	GS	CG	ShO	Sv.	IP	H	R	ER	BB	SO
1998—San Diego (N.L.)	2	0	1.000	0.90	2	2	0	0	0	10	5	1	1	8	14
2001—New York (A.L.)							Did not play.								

WORLD SERIES RECORD

Year League	W	L	Pct.	ERA	G	GS	CG	ShO	Sv.	IP	H	R	ER	BB	SO
1998—San Diego (N.L.)	0	0	...	1.50	1	1	0	0	0	6	7	2	1	1	7
2001—New York (A.L.)	1	0	1.000	0.00	2	0	0	0	0	4	1	0	0	0	6
World Series totals (2 years)	1	0	1.000	0.90	3	1	0	0	0	10	8	2	1	1	13

PERSONAL: Born April 2, 1970, in Torrance, Calif. ... 5-10/183. ... Bats both, throws right. ... Full name: Dennis Lee Hocking.
HIGH SCHOOL: West Torrance (Calif.).
COLLEGE: El Camino College (Calif.).
TRANSACTIONS/CAREER NOTES: Selected by Minnesota Twins organization in 52nd round of free-agent draft (June 5, 1989). ... On Nashville disabled list (April 8-29, 1993). ... On Minnesota disabled list (March 22-April 30, May 30-June 29 and July 31-September 8, 1996); included rehabilitation assignments to Salt Lake (April 4-30, June 21-29 and August 24-September 8).
STATISTICAL NOTES: Led California League shortstops with 721 total chances in 1992. ... Led Pacific Coast League shortstops with .966 fielding percentage and 390 assists in 1995. ... Career major league grand slams: 1.

Year Team (League)	Pos.	G	AB	R	H	2B	3B	HR	RBI	Avg.	BB	SO	SB	PO	A	E	Avg.
1990—Elizabethton (Appl.)	SS-2B-3B	54	201	45	59	6	2	6	30	.294	40	26	14	77	179	20	.928
1991—Kenosha (Midw.)	SS	125	432	72	110	17	8	2	36	.255	77	69	22	193	308	42	.923
1992—Visalia (Calif.)	SS	135	*550	117	*182	34	9	7	81	.331	72	77	38	214	*469	38	.947
1993—Nashville (Sou.)	SS-DH-2B	107	409	54	109	9	4	8	50	.267	34	66	15	144	300	30	.937
—Minnesota (A.L.)	SS-2B	15	36	7	5	1	0	0	0	.139	6	8	1	19	23	1	.977
1994—Salt Lake (PCL)	SS	112	394	61	110	14	6	5	57	.279	28	57	13	143	342	26	.949
—Minnesota (A.L.)	SS	11	31	3	10	3	0	0	2	.323	0	4	2	11	27	0	1.000
1995—Salt Lake (PCL)	SS-DH-2B	117	397	51	112	24	2	8	75	.282	25	41	12	173	†393	20	†.966
—Minnesota (A.L.)	SS	9	25	4	5	0	2	0	3	.200	2	2	1	13	20	1	.971
1996—Minnesota (A.L.)	O-S-2-DH-1	49	127	16	25	6	0	1	10	.197	8	24	3	67	9	1	.987
—Salt Lake (PCL)	S-O-DH-1-2-3	37	130	18	36	6	2	3	22	.277	10	17	2	51	69	3	.976
1997—Minnesota (A.L.)	IF-OF-DH	115	253	28	65	12	4	2	25	.257	18	51	3	124	146	4	.985

H

Year	Team (League)	Pos.	G	AB	R	H	2B	3B	HR	RBI	Avg.	BB	SO	SB	PO	A	E	Avg.
1998—Minnesota (A.L.)		IF-OF-DH	110	198	32	40	6	1	3	15	.202	16	44	2	118	102	4	.982
1999—Minnesota (A.L.)		S-2-O-3-1	136	386	47	103	18	2	7	41	.267	22	54	11	193	190	3	.992
2000—Minnesota (A.L.)		OF-IF-DH	134	373	52	111	24	4	4	47	.298	48	77	7	183	143	5	.985
2001—Minnesota (A.L.)		S-2-1-D-3	112	327	34	82	16	2	3	25	.251	29	67	6	163	150	5	.984
Major League totals (9 years)			691	1756	223	446	86	15	20	168	.254	149	331	36	891	810	24	.986

HODGES, SCOTT　　　　　3B　　　　　EXPOS

PERSONAL: Born December 26, 1978, in Louisville, Ky. ... 6-0/185. ... Bats left, throws right. ... Full name: Scott Allen Hodges.
HIGH SCHOOL: Henry Clay (Lexington, Ky.).
TRANSACTIONS/CAREER NOTES: Selected by Montreal Expos organization in supplemental round ("sandwich pick" between first and second round, 38th pick overall) of free-agent draft (June 3, 1977); pick received as part of compensation for Florida Marlins signing service-time free agent Moises Alou. ... On disabled list (July 23-September 6, 2001).
STATISTICAL NOTES: Led South Atlantic League third basemen with 26 double plays in 1999.

Year	Team (League)	Pos.	G	AB	R	H	2B	3B	HR	RBI	Avg.	BB	SO	SB	PO	A	E	Avg.
1997—GC Expos (GCL)		3B-1B-OF	57	196	26	46	13	2	2	23	.235	23	47	2	178	79	10	.963
1998—Vermont (NY-Penn)		3B	67	266	35	74	13	3	3	35	.278	11	59	8	22	82	14	.881
1999—Cape Fear (S.Atl.)		3B	127	449	62	116	31	2	8	59	.258	45	105	8	*105	225	24	.932
2000—Jupiter (FSL)		1B-3B	111	422	75	129	32	1	14	83	.306	49	66	8	80	247	24	.932
—Harrisburg (East.)		3B	6	17	2	3	0	0	1	5	.176	2	4	1	3	3	0	1.000
2001—Harrisburg (East.)		3B	85	305	30	84	11	2	5	32	.275	25	56	3	54	137	17	.918

HOFFMAN, TREVOR　　　　　P　　　　　PADRES

PERSONAL: Born October 13, 1967, in Bellflower, Calif. ... 6-0/205. ... Throws right, bats right. ... Full name: Trevor William Hoffman. ... Brother of Glenn Hoffman, assistant coach, Los Angeles Dodgers; and infielder with Boston Red Sox (1980-87), Los Angeles Dodgers (1987) and California Angels (1989).
HIGH SCHOOL: Savanna (Anaheim).
JUNIOR COLLEGE: Cypress (Calif.) College.
COLLEGE: Arizona.
TRANSACTIONS/CAREER NOTES: Selected by Cincinnati Reds organization in 11th round of free-agent draft (June 5, 1989). ... Selected by Florida Marlins in first round (eighth pick overall) of expansion draft (November 17, 1992). ... Traded by Marlins with P Jose Martinez and P Andres Berumen to San Diego Padres for 3B Gary Sheffield and P Rich Rodriguez (June 24, 1993).
RECORDS: Shares N.L. single-season record for most saves—53 (1998).
HONORS: Named N.L. Fireman of the Year by THE SPORTING NEWS (1996 and 1998).
STATISTICAL NOTES: Tied for N.L. lead with 13 intentional bases on balls issued in 1993.
MISCELLANEOUS: Holds San Diego Padres all-time record for most games pitched (543), saves (312) and lowest career earned-run average (2.76).

Year	League	W	L	Pct.	ERA	G	GS	CG	ShO	Sv.	IP	H	R	ER	BB	SO
1991—Cedar Rapids (Midw.)		1	1	.500	1.87	27	0	0	0	12	33 2/3	22	8	7	13	52
—Chattanooga (Sou.)		1	0	1.000	1.93	14	0	0	0	8	14	10	4	3	7	23
1992—Chattanooga (Sou.)		3	0	1.000	1.52	6	6	0	0	0	29 2/3	22	6	5	11	31
—Nashville (A.A.)		4	6	.400	4.27	42	5	0	0	6	65 1/3	57	32	31	32	63
1993—Florida (N.L.)■		2	2	.500	3.28	28	0	0	0	2	35 2/3	24	13	13	19	26
—San Diego (N.L.)■		2	4	.333	4.31	39	0	0	0	3	54 1/3	56	30	26	20	53
1994—San Diego (N.L.)		4	4	.500	2.57	47	0	0	0	20	56	39	16	16	20	68
1995—San Diego (N.L.)		7	4	.636	3.88	55	0	0	0	31	53 1/3	48	25	23	14	52
1996—San Diego (N.L.)		9	5	.643	2.25	70	0	0	0	42	88	50	23	22	31	111
1997—San Diego (N.L.)		6	4	.600	2.66	70	0	0	0	37	81 1/3	59	25	24	24	111
1998—San Diego (N.L.)		4	2	.667	1.48	66	0	0	0	*53	73	41	12	12	21	86
1999—San Diego (N.L.)		2	3	.400	2.14	64	0	0	0	40	67 1/3	48	23	16	15	73
2000—San Diego (N.L.)		4	7	.364	2.99	70	0	0	0	43	72 1/3	61	29	24	11	85
2001—San Diego (N.L.)		3	4	.429	3.43	62	0	0	0	43	60 1/3	48	25	23	21	63
Major League totals (9 years)		43	39	.524	2.79	571	0	0	0	314	641 2/3	474	221	199	196	728

DIVISION SERIES RECORD

Year	League	W	L	Pct.	ERA	G	GS	CG	ShO	Sv.	IP	H	R	ER	BB	SO
1996—San Diego (N.L.)		0	1	.000	10.80	2	0	0	0	0	1 2/3	3	2	2	1	2
1998—San Diego (N.L.)		0	0	...	0.00	4	0	0	0	2	3	3	1	0	1	4
Division series totals (2 years)		0	1	.000	3.86	6	0	0	0	2	4 2/3	6	3	2	2	6

CHAMPIONSHIP SERIES RECORD

Year	League	W	L	Pct.	ERA	G	GS	CG	ShO	Sv.	IP	H	R	ER	BB	SO
1998—San Diego (N.L.)		1	0	1.000	2.08	3	0	0	0	1	4 1/3	2	1	1	2	7

WORLD SERIES RECORD

Year	League	W	L	Pct.	ERA	G	GS	CG	ShO	Sv.	IP	H	R	ER	BB	SO
1998—San Diego (N.L.)		0	1	.000	9.00	1	0	0	0	0	2	2	2	2	1	0

ALL-STAR GAME RECORD

Year	League	W	L	Pct.	ERA	GS	CG	ShO	Sv.	IP	H	R	ER	BB	SO
1998—National		0	0	...	9.00	0	0	0	0	1	1	1	1	0	1
1999—National		0	0	...	0.00	0	0	0	0	1/3	0	0	0	1	1
2000—National		0	0	...	27.00	0	0	0	0	1	3	3	3	0	2
All-Star Game totals (3 years)		0	0	...	15.43	0	0	0	0	2 1/3	4	4	4	0	4

RECORD AS POSITION PLAYER

Year	Team (League)	Pos.	G	AB	R	H	2B	3B	HR	RBI	Avg.	BB	SO	SB	PO	A	E	Avg.
1989—Billings (Pio.)		SS	61	201	22	50	5	0	1	20	.249	19	40	1	*116	140	•25	.911
1990—Charl., W.Va. (S.Atl.)		SS-3B	103	278	41	59	10	1	2	23	.212	38	53	3	114	209	30	.915

H

PERSONAL: Born April 20, 1973, in Dayton, Ohio. ... 6-2/215. ... Bats left, throws left. ... Full name: Todd Mathew Hollandsworth.
HIGH SCHOOL: Newport (Bellevue, Wash.).
TRANSACTIONS/CAREER NOTES: Selected by Los Angeles Dodgers organization in third round of free-agent draft (June 3, 1991); pick received as part of compensation for Kansas City Royals signing Type B free-agent OF/DH Kirk Gibson. ... On Los Angeles disabled list (May 3-July 7 and August 9-September 12, 1995); included rehabilitation assignments to San Bernardino (June 6-7) and Albuquerque (June 27-July 7). ... On Los Angeles disabled list (August 2-16 and August 17-September 6, 1997); included rehabilitation assignment to San Bernardino (August 15-17). ... On disabled list (June 5, 1998-remainder of season). ... On Los Angeles disabled list (April 3-23 and June 4-19, 1999); included rehabilitation assignments to San Bernardino (April 20-23 and June 18-19). ... Traded by Dodgers with OF Kevin Gibbs and P Randey Dorame to Colorado Rockies for OF Tom Goodwin and cash (July 31, 2000). ... Granted free agency (October 27, 2000). ... Re-signed by Rockies (November 16, 2000). ... On disabled list (May 12, 2001-remainder of season).
HONORS: Named N.L. Rookie of the Year by Baseball Writers' Association of America (1996).
STATISTICAL NOTES: Had 16-game hitting streak (April 14-May 3, 2001). ... Hit three home runs in one game (April 15, 2001). ... Career major league grand slams: 1.

Year Team (League)	Pos.	G	AB	R	H	2B	3B	HR	RBI	Avg.	BB	SO	SB	PO	A	E	Avg.
1991—Yakima (N'West)	OF	56	203	34	48	5	1	8	33	.236	27	57	11	106	1	7	.939
1992—Bakersfield (Calif.)......	OF	119	430	70	111	23	5	13	58	.258	50	113	27	230	8	6	.975
1993—San Antonio (Texas)...	OF	126	474	57	119	24	9	17	63	.251	29	101	24	246	13	12	.956
1994—Albuquerque (PCL).....	OF	132	505	80	144	31	5	19	91	.285	46	96	15	237	5	13	.949
1995—Los Angeles (N.L.)	OF	41	103	16	24	2	0	5	13	.233	10	29	2	60	1	4	.938
—San Bern. (Calif.)........	OF	1	2	0	1	0	0	0	0	.500	0	1	0	0	0	0	...
—Albuquerque (PCL)......	OF	10	38	9	9	2	0	2	4	.237	6	8	1	19	3	0	1.000
1996—Los Angeles (N.L.)	OF	149	478	64	139	26	4	12	59	.291	41	93	21	217	7	5	.978
1997—Los Angeles (N.L.)	OF	106	296	39	73	20	2	4	31	.247	17	60	5	185	2	3	.984
—Albuquerque (PCL)......	OF	13	56	13	24	4	3	1	14	.429	4	4	2	32	1	0	1.000
—San Bern. (Calif.)........	OF	2	8	1	2	0	1	0	2	.250	1	2	0	2	1	0	1.000
1998—Los Angeles (N.L.)	OF	55	175	23	47	6	4	3	20	.269	9	42	4	87	1	4	.957
1999—San Bern. (Calif.)........	OF	4	13	3	5	2	0	0	3	.385	2	4	0	3	1	0	1.000
—Los Angeles (N.L.)	OF-1B	92	261	39	74	12	2	9	32	.284	24	61	5	211	11	3	.987
2000—Los Angeles (N.L.)	OF	81	261	42	61	12	0	8	24	.234	30	61	11	143	6	2	.987
—Colorado (N.L.)■	OF	56	167	39	54	8	0	11	23	.323	11	38	7	74	6	1	.988
2001—Colorado (N.L.)	OF	33	117	21	43	15	1	6	19	.368	8	20	7	51	2	1	.981
Major League totals (7 years)		613	1858	283	515	101	13	58	221	.277	150	404	60	1028	36	23	.979

DIVISION SERIES RECORD

Year Team (League)	Pos.	G	AB	R	H	2B	3B	HR	RBI	Avg.	BB	SO	SB	PO	A	E	Avg.
1995—Los Angeles (N.L.)	OF-PH	2	2	0	0	0	0	0	0	.000	0	0	0	0	0	0	...
1996—Los Angeles (N.L.)	OF	3	12	1	4	3	0	0	1	.333	0	3	0	4	0	0	1.000
Division series totals (2 years)		5	14	1	4	3	0	0	1	.286	0	3	0	4	0	0	1.000

PERSONAL: Born January 1, 1980, in Stillwater, Okla. ... 6-4/235. ... Bats right, throws right. ... Full name: Matthew Thomas Holliday.
HIGH SCHOOL: Stillwater (Okla.).
TRANSACTIONS/CAREER NOTES: Selected by Colorado Rockies organization in seventh round of free-agent draft (June 2, 1998).

Year Team (League)	Pos.	G	AB	R	H	2B	3B	HR	RBI	Avg.	BB	SO	SB	PO	A	E	Avg.
1998—Ariz. Rockies (Ariz.)....	3B	32	117	20	40	4	1	5	23	.342	15	21	2	11	46	10	.851
1999—Asheville (S.Atl.).........	3B	121	444	76	117	28	0	16	64	.264	53	116	10	57	192	•37	.871
2000—Salem (Caro.)............	3B	123	460	64	126	28	2	7	72	.274	43	74	11	55	213	32	.893
2001—Salem (Caro.)............	OF-DH	72	255	36	70	16	1	11	52	.275	33	42	11	33	2	0	1.000

PERSONAL: Born May 25, 1966, in Orchard Park, NY. ... 6-1/232. ... Bats both, throws right. ... Full name: David Michael Hollins.
HIGH SCHOOL: Orchard Park (N.Y.).
COLLEGE: South Carolina.
TRANSACTIONS/CAREER NOTES: Selected by San Diego Padres organization in sixth round of free-agent draft (June 2, 1987). ... Selected by Philadelphia Phillies from Padres organization in Rule 5 major league draft (December 4, 1989). ... On Philadelphia disabled list (August 16-September 6, 1991); included rehabilitation assignment to Scranton/Wilkes-Barre (September 2-5). ... On suspended list (September 29-October 3, 1992). ... On disabled list (June 11-28, 1993). ... On Philadelphia disabled list (May 23-July 23 and July 25, 1994-remainder of season); included rehabilitation assignment to Scranton/Wilkes-Barre (July 16-23). ... On Philadelphia disabled list (June 12-27, 1995). ... Traded by Phillies to Boston Red Sox for OF Mark Whiten (July 24, 1995). ... On Boston disabled list (August 9, 1995-remainder of season). ... Granted free agency (December 21, 1995). ... Signed by Minnesota Twins (December 23, 1995). ... Traded by Twins to Seattle Mariners for a player to be named later (August 29, 1996); Twins acquired 1B David Arias to complete deal (September 13, 1996). ... Granted free agency (October 31, 1996). ... Signed by Anaheim Angels (November 20, 1996). ... On disabled list (August 10, 1998-remainder of season). ... Traded by Angels with cash to Toronto Blue Jays for SS Tomas Perez (March 30, 1999). ... On Toronto disabled list (April 18-May 21, 1999); included rehabilitation assignment to Syracuse (May 10-13). ... Released by Blue Jays (June 21, 1999). ... Signed by Chicago White Sox organization (July 1, 1999). ... Granted free agency (October 15, 1999). ... Signed by Tampa Bay Devil Rays organization (January 14, 2000). ... On Durham disabled list (April 24-May 21, 2000). ... Released by Devils Rays (May 21, 2000). ... Signed by Baltimore Orioles organization (July 13, 2000). ... Released by Orioles (August 3, 2000). ... Signed by Cleveland Indians organization (August 3, 2000). ... On Buffalo disabled list (August 20-September 10, 2000). ... Granted free agency (October 18, 2000). ... Re-signed by Indians organization (December 20, 2000). ... On Buffalo disabled list (April 30-May 13, 2001). ... Granted free agency (October 8, 2001).
STATISTICAL NOTES: Led Northwest League with seven intentional bases on balls received in 1987. ... Led Northwest League third basemen with 241 total chances in 1987. ... Led Texas League with 10 sacrifice flies in 1989. ... Led N.L. in being hit by pitch with 19 in 1992. ... Led A.L. third basemen with 29 errors in 1997. ... Tied for International League lead with eight intentional bases on balls received in 2001. ... Career major league grand slams: 3.

H

Year Team (League)	Pos.	G	AB	R	H	2B	3B	HR	RBI	Avg.	BB	SO	SB	PO	A	E	Avg.
1987— Spokane (N'West)	3B	75	278	52	86	14	4	2	44	.309	53	36	20	*59	*167	15	*.938
1988— Riverside (Calif.).........	3B-1B-SS	139	516	90	157	32	1	9	92	.304	82	67	13	102	248	29	.923
1989— Wichita (Texas)...........	3B	131	459	69	126	29	4	9	79	.275	63	88	8	77	209	25	.920
1990— Philadelphia (N.L.)■ ..	3B-1B	72	114	14	21	0	0	5	15	.184	10	28	0	27	37	4	.941
1991— Philadelphia (N.L.).......	3B-1B	56	151	18	45	10	2	6	21	.298	17	26	1	67	62	8	.942
— Scranton/W.B. (I.L.) ...	3B-1B	72	229	37	61	11	6	8	35	.266	43	43	4	67	105	10	.945
1992— Philadelphia (N.L.).......	3B-1B	156	586	104	158	28	4	27	93	.270	76	110	9	120	253	18	.954
1993— Philadelphia (N.L.).......	3B	143	543	104	148	30	4	18	93	.273	85	109	2	73	215	27	.914
1994— Philadelphia (N.L.).......	3B-OF	44	162	28	36	7	1	4	26	.222	23	32	1	39	48	11	.888
— Scranton/W.B. (I.L.)	OF	6	19	6	4	0	0	1	3	.211	5	4	0	12	1	2	.867
1995— Philadelphia (N.L.).......	1B	65	205	46	47	12	2	7	25	.229	53	38	1	532	30	7	.988
— Boston (A.L.)■............	DH-OF	5	13	2	2	0	0	0	1	.154	4	7	0	3	0	0	1.000
1996— Minnesota (A.L.)■.....	3B-DH-SS	121	422	71	102	26	0	13	53	.242	71	102	6	81	206	15	.950
— Seattle (A.L.)■............	3B-1B	28	94	17	33	3	0	3	25	.351	13	15	0	21	53	3	.961
1997— Anaheim (A.L.)■.........	3B-1B	149	572	101	165	29	2	16	85	.288	62	124	16	208	249	†29	.940
1998— Anaheim (A.L.)..........	3B-1B-DH	101	363	60	88	16	2	11	39	.242	44	69	11	107	150	17	.938
1999— Toronto (A.L.)■..........	DH	27	99	12	22	5	0	2	6	.222	5	22	0	...	...	...	...
— Syracuse (I.L.).............	DH	4	15	2	3	1	0	0	1	.200	1	5	0	...	...	...	...
— Charlotte (I.L.)■..........	3B-1B-DH	63	199	49	63	18	0	8	33	.317	33	37	5	92	58	10	.938
2000— Durham (I.L.)■...........	1B	11	27	4	5	2	0	1	3	.185	10	6	1	15	2	0	1.000
— Rochester (I.L.)■.........	3B	20	70	8	19	2	0	0	8	.271	9	12	1	11	18	2	.935
— Buffalo (I.L.)■.............	3B	5	13	0	1	1	0	0	2	.077	2	6	0	2	8	2	.833
2001— Buffalo (I.L.).............	1B-OF-3B	89	316	50	86	25	2	16	67	.272	45	79	0	136	12	3	.980
— Cleveland (A.L.)..........	DH	2	5	0	1	0	0	0	0	.200	1	2	0	...	...	...	...
American League totals (6 years)		433	1568	263	413	79	4	45	209	.263	200	341	33	420	658	64	.944
National League totals (6 years)		536	1761	314	455	87	13	67	273	.258	264	343	14	858	645	75	.952
Major League totals (11 years)		969	3329	577	868	166	17	112	482	.261	464	684	47	1278	1303	139	.949

CHAMPIONSHIP SERIES RECORD

Year Team (League)	Pos.	G	AB	R	H	2B	3B	HR	RBI	Avg.	BB	SO	SB	PO	A	E	Avg.
1993— Philadelphia (N.L.)......	3B	6	20	2	4	1	0	2	4	.200	5	4	1	5	4	0	1.000

WORLD SERIES RECORD

Year Team (League)	Pos.	G	AB	R	H	2B	3B	HR	RBI	Avg.	BB	SO	SB	PO	A	E	Avg.
1993— Philadelphia (N.L.)......	3B	6	23	5	6	1	0	0	2	.261	6	5	0	9	9	0	1.000

ALL-STAR GAME RECORD

Year League	Pos.	AB	R	H	2B	3B	HR	RBI	Avg.	BB	SO	SB	PO	A	E	Avg.
1993— National	3B	1	0	1	1	0	0	0	1.000	0	0	0	1	0	0	1.000

HOLT, CHRIS — P — ROCKIES

PERSONAL: Born September 18, 1971, in Dallas. ... 6-4/205. ... Throws right, bats right. ... Full name: Christopher Michael Holt.
HIGH SCHOOL: Skyline (Dallas).
JUNIOR COLLEGE: Navarro College (Texas).
TRANSACTIONS/CAREER NOTES: Selected by Houston Astros organization in third round of free-agent draft (June 1, 1992). ... On Houston disabled list (March 30, 1998-entire season); included rehabilitation assignment to Kissimmee (April 25-26). ... Traded by Astros with C Mitch Meluskey and OF Roger Cedeno to Detroit Tigers for C Brad Ausmus, P Doug Brocail and P Nelson Cruz (December 11, 2000). ... Released by Tigers (November 20, 2001). ... Signed by Colorado Rockies organization (January 15, 2002).
STATISTICAL NOTES: Pitched 7-0 one-hit, complete-game victory against Milwaukee (April 28, 2000).

Year League	W	L	Pct.	ERA	G	GS	CG	ShO	Sv.	IP	H	R	ER	BB	SO
1992— Auburn (NY-Penn).............	2	5	.286	4.45	14	14	0	0	0	83	75	48	41	24	81
1993— Quad City (Midw.)	11	10	.524	2.27	26	26	*10	•3	0	*186 1/3	162	70	47	54	176
1994— Jackson (Texas)	10	9	.526	3.45	26	25	5	•2	0	167	169	78	64	22	111
1995— Jackson (Texas)	2	2	.500	1.67	5	5	1	1	0	32 1/3	27	8	6	5	24
— Tucson (PCL)	5	8	.385	4.10	20	19	0	0	0	118 2/3	155	65	54	32	69
1996— Tucson (PCL)	9	6	.600	3.62	28	27	4	1	0	*186 1/3	208	87	75	38	137
— Houston (N.L.)	0	1	.000	5.79	4	0	0	0	0	4 2/3	5	3	3	3	0
1997— Houston (N.L.)	8	12	.400	3.52	33	32	0	0	0	209 2/3	211	98	82	61	109
1998— Kissimmee (FSL)	0	1	.000	9.00	1	1	0	0	0	4	6	4	4	1	1
1999— Houston (N.L.)	5	13	.278	4.66	32	26	0	0	1	164	193	92	85	57	115
2000— Houston (N.L.)	8	16	.333	5.35	34	32	3	1	0	207	247	131	123	75	136
2001— Detroit (A.L.)■................	7	9	.438	5.77	30	22	1	0	0	151 1/3	197	102	97	57	80
A.L. totals (1 year)	7	9	.438	5.77	30	22	1	0	0	151 1/3	197	102	97	57	80
N.L. totals (4 years)	21	42	.333	4.51	103	90	3	1	1	585 1/3	656	324	293	196	346
Major League totals (5 years)	28	51	.354	4.76	133	112	4	1	1	736 2/3	853	426	390	253	426

DIVISION SERIES RECORD

Year League	W	L	Pct.	ERA	G	GS	CG	ShO	Sv.	IP	H	R	ER	BB	SO
1999— Houston (N.L.)	0	0	...	...	1	0	0	0	0	0	3	3	3	0	0

HOLTZ, MIKE — P — ATHLETICS

PERSONAL: Born October 10, 1972, in Arlington, Va. ... 5-9/188. ... Throws left, bats left. ... Full name: Michael James Holtz.
HIGH SCHOOL: Central Cambria (Ebensburg, Pa.).
COLLEGE: Clemson.

TRANSACTIONS/CAREER NOTES: Selected by California Angels organization in 17th round of free-agent draft (June 2, 1994). ... Angels franchise renamed Anaheim Angels for 1997 season. ... On suspended list (June 18-20, 1998). ... On Anaheim disabled list (August 25-September 10, 1999). ... On Anaheim disabled list (May 11-30, 2001); included rehabilitation assignment to Rancho Cucamonga (May 26-30). ... Granted free agency (December 21, 2001). ... Signed by Oakland Athletics (January 2, 2002).

Year	League	W	L	Pct.	ERA	G	GS	CG	ShO	Sv.	IP	H	R	ER	BB	SO
1994— Boise (N'West)		0	0	...	0.51	22	0	0	0	11	35	22	4	2	11	59
1995— Lake Elsinore (Calif.)		4	4	.500	2.29	*56	0	0	0	3	82²/₃	70	26	21	23	101
1996— Midland (Texas)		1	2	.333	4.17	33	0	0	0	2	41	52	34	19	9	41
— California (A.L.)		3	3	.500	2.45	30	0	0	0	0	29¹/₃	21	11	8	19	31
1997— Anaheim (A.L.)		3	4	.429	3.32	66	0	0	0	2	43¹/₃	38	21	16	15	40
1998— Anaheim (A.L.)		2	2	.500	4.75	53	0	0	0	1	30¹/₃	38	16	16	15	29
— Vancouver (PCL)		0	0	...	1.74	10	0	0	0	2	10¹/₃	10	4	2	6	18
1999— Anaheim (A.L.)		2	3	.400	8.06	28	0	0	0	0	22¹/₃	26	20	20	15	17
— Edmonton (PCL)		2	1	.667	2.30	20	0	0	0	1	27¹/₃	20	7	7	11	39
2000— Edmonton (PCL)		0	1	.000	10.80	6	0	0	0	0	5	5	6	6	1	1
— Anaheim (A.L.)		3	3	.500	5.05	61	0	0	0	0	41	37	26	23	18	40
2001— Anaheim (A.L.)		1	2	.333	4.86	63	0	0	0	0	37	40	24	20	15	38
— Rancho Cuca. (Calif.)		0	0	...	9.00	2	2	0	0	0	2	3	2	2	1	3
Major League totals (6 years)		14	17	.452	4.56	301	0	0	0	3	203¹/₃	200	118	103	97	195

HOOVER, PAUL — C/IF — DEVIL RAYS

PERSONAL: Born April 14, 1976, in Columbus, Ohio. ... 6-1/210. ... Bats right, throws right. ... Full name: Paul Chester Hoover.
HIGH SCHOOL: Steubenville (Ohio).
COLLEGE: Kent State.
TRANSACTIONS/CAREER NOTES: Selected by Houston Astros organization in 64th round of free-agent draft (June 2, 1994); did not sign. ... Selected by Tampa Bay Devil Rays organization in 23rd round of free-agent draft (June 3, 1997).
STATISTICAL NOTES: Led Appalachian League shortstops with 343 total chances and 35 double plays in 1997.

							BATTING							FIELDING		
Year	Team (League)	Pos.	G	AB	R	H	2B	3B	HR	RBI	Avg.	BB	SO	SB	PO	A	E	Avg.
1997— Princeton (Appl.)		SS	66	251	55	76	16	4	4	37	.303	20	37	7	*111	*199	•33	.904
1998— Charl., S.C. (S.Atl.)	C-3B-SS-1B		40	124	24	36	10	1	3	19	.290	22	29	2	203	48	8	.969
— Hudson Valley (NY-P.)		C-3B	73	269	51	76	20	1	4	37	.283	39	44	26	447	50	5	.990
1999— St. Petersburg (FSL)	C-1B-3B		118	408	66	111	13	6	8	54	.272	54	81	23	569	75	5	.992
2000— Orlando (Sou.)	C-3-0-S-1-2		106	360	54	90	20	4	3	44	.250	67	66	9	302	141	18	.961
— Durham (I.L.)		C-3B-OF	4	10	0	3	0	0	0	0	.300	1	0	5	1	10	2	0	1.000
2001— Durham (I.L.)	C-3-0-1-S-2		89	293	37	63	18	4	3	21	.215	11	66	5	410	61	6	.987
— Tampa Bay (A.L.)		C	3	4	1	1	0	0	0	0	.250	0	1	0	2	1	0	1.000
Major League totals (1 year)			3	4	1	1	0	0	0	0	.250	0	1	0	2	1	0	1.000

HOUSE, CRAIG — P — METS

PERSONAL: Born July 8, 1977, in Nash AFB, Okinawa, Japan. ... 6-2/210. ... Throws right, bats right. ... Full name: Craig Michael House.
HIGH SCHOOL: Christian Brothers (Memphis, Tenn.).
COLLEGE: Memphis.
TRANSACTIONS/CAREER NOTES: Selected by Colorado Rockies organization in 12th round of free-agent draft (June 2, 1999). ... On disabled list (June 20-July 8, 2001). ... Traded by Rockies to New York Mets as part of three-way deal in which Mets traded P Glendon Rusch to Milwaukee Brewers, Rockies traded 1B/OF Ross Gload to Mets, Brewers traded P Jeff D'Amico, OF Jeromy Burnitz, IF Lou Collier, OF/1B Mark Sweeney and cash to Mets, Mets traded 1B/3B Todd Zeile, OF Benny Agbayani, IF/OF Lenny Harris and cash to Rockies and Rockies traded OF Alex Ochoa to Brewers (January 21, 2002).

Year	League	W	L	Pct.	ERA	G	GS	CG	ShO	Sv.	IP	H	R	ER	BB	SO
1999— Portland (N'West)		2	1	.667	2.08	26	0	0	0	11	34²/₃	28	14	8	14	58
2000— Salem (Caro.)		2	0	1.000	2.25	13	0	0	0	8	16	7	4	4	10	24
— Carolina (Sou.)		0	2	.000	3.80	18	0	0	0	9	21¹/₃	14	11	9	15	28
— Colo. Springs (PCL)		0	0	...	3.24	8	0	0	0	4	8¹/₃	6	4	3	2	8
— Colorado (N.L.)		1	1	.500	7.24	16	0	0	0	0	13²/₃	13	11	11	17	8
2001— Colo. Springs (PCL)		2	2	.500	4.45	54	0	0	0	6	58²/₃	50	32	29	31	62
Major League totals (1 year)		1	1	.500	7.24	16	0	0	0	0	13²/₃	13	11	11	17	8

HOUSE, J.R. — C — PIRATES

PERSONAL: Born November 11, 1979, in Charleston, W.Va. ... 6-1/202. ... Bats right, throws right. ... Full name: James Rodger House.
HIGH SCHOOL: Seabreeze (Daytona Beach, Fla.).
TRANSACTIONS/CAREER NOTES: Selected by Pittsburgh Pirates organization in fifth round of free-agent draft (June 2, 1999). ... On disabled list (April 24-May 1 and May 8-22, 2001).
HONORS: Shared South Atlantic League Most Valuable Player (2000).

							BATTING							FIELDING		
Year	Team (League)	Pos.	G	AB	R	H	2B	3B	HR	RBI	Avg.	BB	SO	SB	PO	A	E	Avg.
1999— GC Pirates (GCL)		1B-C-3B	33	113	13	37	9	3	5	23	.327	11	23	1	210	26	3	.987
— Williamsport (NY-P.)		C-1B	26	100	11	30	6	0	1	13	.300	9	21	0	180	14	3	.985
2000— Hickory (S.Atl.)		C-1B	110	420	78	146	29	1	23	90	.348	46	91	1	734	60	8	.990
2001— Altoona (East.)		C-1B	112	426	51	110	25	1	11	56	.258	37	103	1	690	64	7	.991

HOUSTON, TYLER — 3B — BREWERS

PERSONAL: Born January 17, 1971, in Long Beach, Calif. ... 6-1/218. ... Bats left, throws right. ... Full name: Tyler Sam Houston.
HIGH SCHOOL: Valley (Las Vegas).

TRANSACTIONS/CAREER NOTES: Selected by Atlanta Braves organization in first round (second pick overall) of free-agent draft (June 5, 1989). ... On Greenville disabled list (June 25-July 5, 1993). ... Traded by Braves to Chicago Cubs for P Ismael Villegas (June 27, 1996). ... On Chicago disabled list (May 3-19, 1997); included rehabilitation assignment to Iowa (May 14-19, 1997). ... On Chicago disabled list (June 11-July 11, 1997); included rehabilitation assignment to Rockford (July 9-11). ... On suspended list (September 16, 1997). ... On disabled list (May 26-June 24, 1998). ... Traded by Cubs to Cleveland Indians for P Richard Negrette (August 31, 1999). ... Granted free agency (December 21, 1999). ... Signed by Milwaukee Brewers (January 17, 2000). ... On disabled list (May 19-June 2, 2000). ... On Milwaukee disabled list (July 14-September 1 and September 8, 2001-remainder of season); included rehabilitation assignment to Beloit (August 29-September 1).
STATISTICAL NOTES: Led Pioneer League with 14 passed balls in 1989. ... Hit three home runs in one game (July 9, 2000). ... Career major league grand slams: 1.

Year Team (League)	Pos.	G	AB	R	H	2B	3B	HR	RBI	Avg.	BB	SO	SB	PO	A	E	Avg.
					BATTING									FIELDING			
1989— Idaho Falls (Pio.)	C	50	176	30	43	11	0	4	24	.244	25	41	4	148	15	5	.970
1990— Sumter (S.Atl.)	C	117	442	58	93	14	3	13	56	.210	49	101	6	498	55	*18	.968
1991— Macon (S.Atl.)	C	107	351	41	81	16	3	8	47	.231	39	70	10	591	75	10	.985
1992— Durham (Caro.)	C-3B-1B	117	402	39	91	17	1	7	38	.226	20	89	5	493	65	15	.974
1993— Greenville (Sou.)	C-OF	84	262	27	73	14	1	5	33	.279	13	50	5	410	34	9	.980
— Richmond (I.L.)	C-DH	13	36	4	5	1	1	1	3	.139	1	8	0	69	2	3	.959
1994— Richmond (I.L.)	1B-C-DH-OF	97	312	33	76	15	2	4	33	.244	16	44	3	619	54	7	.990
1995— Richmond (I.L.)	1B-C-O-3-DH	103	349	41	89	10	3	12	42	.255	18	62	3	579	69	11	.983
1996— Atlanta (N.L.)	1B-OF	33	27	3	6	2	1	1	8	.222	1	9	0	16	1	0	1.000
— Chicago (N.L.)■	C-3B-2B-1B	46	115	18	39	7	0	2	19	.339	8	18	3	139	25	3	.982
1997— Chicago (N.L.)	C-3-1-2-S	72	196	15	51	10	0	2	28	.260	9	35	1	280	37	5	.984
— Iowa (A.A.)	3B-DH-C	6	23	0	5	2	0	0	4	.217	0	2	0	6	9	2	.882
— Rockford (Midw.)	C-3B	2	6	1	3	1	0	0	1	.500	0	0	0	5	0	0	1.000
1998— Chicago (N.L.)	C-3B-1B	95	255	26	65	7	1	9	33	.255	13	53	2	451	36	5	.990
1999— Chicago (N.L.)	3B-C-1B-OF	100	249	26	58	9	1	9	27	.233	28	67	1	109	89	17	.921
— Cleveland (A.L.)■	3B-C	13	27	2	4	1	0	1	3	.148	3	11	0	7	11	0	1.000
2000— Milwaukee (N.L.)■	1B-3B-C	101	284	30	71	15	0	18	43	.250	17	72	2	399	80	13	.974
2001— Milwaukee (N.L.)	3B-1B	75	235	36	68	7	0	12	38	.289	18	62	0	42	99	10	.934
— Beloit (Midw.)	3B	1	3	0	0	0	0	0	0	.000	0	1	0	0	1	1	.500
American League totals (1 year)		13	27	2	4	1	0	1	3	.148	3	11	0	7	11	0	1.000
National League totals (6 years)		522	1361	154	358	57	3	53	196	.263	94	316	9	1436	367	53	.971
Major League totals (6 years)		535	1388	156	362	58	3	54	199	.261	97	327	9	1443	378	53	.972

DIVISION SERIES RECORD

Year Team (League)	Pos.	G	AB	R	H	2B	3B	HR	RBI	Avg.	BB	SO	SB	PO	A	E	Avg.
					BATTING									FIELDING			
1998— Chicago (N.L.)	C	3	6	1	1	0	0	1	1	.167	0	3	0	13	0	0	1.000
1999— Cleveland (A.L.)					Did not play.												

HOWARD, BEN   P   PADRES

PERSONAL: Born January 15, 1979, in Danville, Ill. ... 6-2/190. ... Throws right, bats right. ... Full name: Benjamin Richard Howard.
HIGH SCHOOL: Jackson-Central Merry (Jackson, Tenn.).
TRANSACTIONS/CAREER NOTES: Selected by San Diego Padres organization in second round of free-agent draft (June 3, 1997).
STATISTICAL NOTES: Tied for Arizona League lead in wild pitches with 19 in 1997. ... Led Pioneer League with 17 wild pitches and six balks in 1998.

Year League	W	L	Pct.	ERA	G	GS	CG	ShO	Sv.	IP	H	R	ER	BB	SO
1997— Arizona Padres (Ariz.)	1	4	.200	7.45	13	12	0	0	0	54 1/3	54	53	*45	*63	59
1998— Idaho Falls (Pio.)	4	5	.444	6.03	15	15	0	0	0	68 2/3	67	61	46	*87	79
1999— Fort Wayne (Midw.)	6	10	.375	4.73	28	28	0	0	0	144 2/3	123	100	76	*110	131
2000— Rancho Cuca. (Calif.)	5	11	.313	6.37	32	19	0	0	0	107 1/3	88	87	76	*111	150
2001— Lake Elsinore (Calif.)	8	2	.800	2.83	18	18	0	0	0	101 2/3	86	37	32	32	107
— Mobile (Sou.)	2	0	1.000	2.40	7	5	0	0	0	30	17	9	8	15	29

HOWRY, BOBBY   P   WHITE SOX

PERSONAL: Born August 4, 1973, in Phoenix. ... 6-5/215. ... Throws right, bats left. ... Full name: Bobby Dean Howry.
HIGH SCHOOL: Deer Valley (Phoenix).
JUNIOR COLLEGE: Yavapai College (Ariz.).
COLLEGE: McNeese State.
TRANSACTIONS/CAREER NOTES: Selected by San Francisco Giants organization in fifth round of free-agent draft (June 2, 1994). ... Traded by Giants with SS Mike Caruso, OF Brian Manning, P Keith Foulke, P Lorenzo Barcelo and P Ken Vining to Chicago White Sox for P Wilson Alvarez, P Danny Darwin and P Roberto Hernandez (July 31, 1997). ... On suspended list (April 28-May 30, 2000).

Year League	W	L	Pct.	ERA	G	GS	CG	ShO	Sv.	IP	H	R	ER	BB	SO
1994— Everett (N'West)	0	4	.000	4.74	5	5	0	0	0	19	29	15	10	10	16
— Clinton (Midw.)	1	3	.250	4.20	9	8	0	0	0	49 1/3	61	29	23	16	22
1995— San Jose (Calif.)	12	10	.545	3.54	27	25	1	0	0	165 1/3	171	79	65	54	107
1996— Shreveport (Texas)	12	10	.545	4.65	27	27	0	0	0	156 2/3	163	90	81	56	57
1997— Shreveport (Texas)	6	3	.667	4.91	48	0	0	0	*22	55	58	35	30	21	43
— Birmingham (Sou.)■	0	0	...	2.84	12	0	0	0	0	12 2/3	16	4	4	3	3
1998— Calgary (PCL)	1	2	.333	3.41	23	0	0	0	5	31 2/3	25	12	12	10	22
— Chicago (A.L.)	0	3	.000	3.15	44	0	0	0	9	54 1/3	37	20	19	19	51
1999— Chicago (A.L.)	5	3	.625	3.59	69	0	0	0	28	67 2/3	58	34	27	38	80
2000— Chicago (A.L.)	2	4	.333	3.17	65	0	0	0	7	71	54	26	25	29	60
2001— Chicago (A.L.)	4	5	.444	4.69	69	0	0	0	5	78 2/3	85	41	41	30	64
Major League totals (4 years)	11	15	.423	3.71	247	0	0	0	49	271 2/3	234	121	112	116	255

DIVISION SERIES RECORD

Year League	W	L	Pct.	ERA	G	GS	CG	ShO	Sv.	IP	H	R	ER	BB	SO
2000— Chicago (A.L.)	0	0	...	3.38	2	0	0	0	0	2 2/3	2	1	1	2	4

H

PERSONAL: Born February 16, 1971, in Lynchburg, Va. ... 6-1/205. ... Bats right, throws right. ... Full name: Michael Wayne Hubbard.
HIGH SCHOOL: Amherst (Va.) County.
COLLEGE: James Madison.
TRANSACTIONS/CAREER NOTES: Selected by Chicago Cubs organization in eighth round of free-agent draft (June 1, 1992). ... Claimed on waivers by Montreal Expos (March 30, 1998). ... Granted free agency (September 29, 1998). ... Signed by Texas Rangers organization (December 2, 1998). ... Granted free agency (October 15, 1999). ... Signed by Cincinnati Reds organization (December 16, 1999). ... On Louisville disabled list (April 19-28, 2000). ... Released by Reds (May 8, 2000). ... Signed by Atlanta Braves organization (May 10, 2000). ... Granted free agency (October 17, 2000). ... Signed by Rangers organization (November 6, 2000). ... On Texas disabled list (June 14, 2001-remainder of season). ... Granted free agency (October 11, 2001). ... Signed by Baltimore Orioles (November 2, 2001).
STATISTICAL NOTES: Led Pacific Coast League catchers with a .994 fielding percentage in 1999.

| | | | | | | | | | BATTING | | | | | | FIELDING | | | |
Year Team (League)	Pos.	G	AB	R	H	2B	3B	HR	RBI	Avg.	BB	SO	SB	PO	A	E	Avg.
1992—Geneva (NY-Penn)	C	50	183	25	44	4	4	3	25	.240	7	29	6	325	27	5	.986
1993—Daytona (FSL)	C-2B	68	245	25	72	10	3	1	20	.294	18	41	10	354	66	9	.979
1994—Orlando (Sou.)	C-3B-1B	104	357	52	102	13	3	11	39	.286	29	58	7	498	78	12	.980
1995—Iowa (A.A.)	C-DH-3B	75	254	28	66	6	3	5	23	.260	26	60	6	447	34	9	.982
—Chicago (N.L.)	C	15	23	2	4	0	0	0	1	.174	2	2	0	33	0	1	.971
1996—Iowa (A.A.)	C-3B-DH-OF	67	232	38	68	12	0	7	33	.293	10	56	2	372	27	5	.988
—Chicago (N.L.)	C	21	38	1	4	0	0	1	4	.105	0	15	0	53	3	0	1.000
1997—Iowa (A.A.)	C-DH-OF	50	186	24	52	15	1	6	26	.280	11	23	2	310	22	2	.994
—Chicago (N.L.)	C-3B	29	64	4	13	0	0	1	2	.203	2	21	0	120	8	1	.992
1998—Montreal (N.L.)■	C-2B	32	55	3	8	1	0	1	3	.145	0	17	0	83	4	0	1.000
—Ottawa (I.L.)	C	20	70	9	16	5	0	0	8	.229	3	13	0	121	8	1	.992
1999—Oklahoma (PCL)■	C-DH-1B-OF	110	392	48	111	19	0	9	49	.283	25	70	4	682	47	4	†.995
2000—Louisville (I.L.)■	C	8	8	1	3	1	0	0	0	.375	1	4	0	14	0	0	1.000
—Richmond (I.L.)■	C-1B	70	224	33	66	8	1	6	31	.295	22	24	4	349	20	5	.987
—Atlanta (N.L.)	C	2	1	0	0	0	0	0	0	.000	0	1	0	3	0	0	1.000
2001—Oklahoma (PCL)■	C-1B	35	129	22	40	8	1	6	23	.310	11	20	0	279	16	4	.987
—Texas (A.L.)	C	5	11	1	3	1	0	1	1	.273	0	4	0	15	2	0	1.000
American League totals (1 year)		5	11	1	3	1	0	1	1	.273	0	4	0	15	2	0	1.000
National League totals (5 years)		99	181	10	29	1	0	3	10	.160	4	56	0	292	15	2	.994
Major League totals (6 years)		104	192	11	32	2	0	4	11	.167	4	60	0	307	17	2	.994

HUBBARD, TRENIDAD　　　　　　　**OF**

PERSONAL: Born May 11, 1966, in Chicago. ... 5-9/203. ... Bats right, throws right. ... Full name: Trenidad Aviel Hubbard. ... Cousin of Joe Cribbs, running back with Buffalo Bills (1980-83 and 1985).
HIGH SCHOOL: South Shore (Chicago).
COLLEGE: Southern (La.).
TRANSACTIONS/CAREER NOTES: Selected by Houston Astros organization in 12th round of free-agent draft (June 2, 1986). ... Granted free agency (October 15, 1992). ... Signed by Colorado Rockies organization (October 30, 1992). ... On disabled list (June 15-24, 1993). ... Granted free agency (October 15, 1993). ... Re-signed by Rockies organization (December 3, 1993). ... Granted free agency (October 15, 1994). ... Re-signed by Rockies organization (November 14, 1994). ... Claimed on waivers by San Francisco Giants (August 21, 1996). ... On San Francisco disabled list (September 13, 1996-remainder of season). ... Traded by Giants to Cleveland Indians for P Joe Roa (December 16, 1996), completing deal in which Indians traded IF Jeff Kent, IF Jose Vizcaino, P Julian Tavarez and a player to be named later to Giants for 3B Matt Williams and a player to be named later (November 13, 1996). ... Granted free agency (October 8, 1997). ... Signed by Los Angeles Dodgers (December 3, 1997). ... On Los Angeles disabled list (May 14-June 22, 1998); included rehabilitation assignment to Albuquerque (June 9-22). ... Granted free agency (January 19, 2000). ... Signed by Atlanta Braves organization (January 20, 2000). ... Traded by Braves with P Luis Rivera and C Fernando Rivera to Baltimore Orioles for OF B.J. Surhoff and P Gabe Molina (July 31, 2000). ... Released by Orioles (October 5, 2000). ... Signed by Toronto Blue Jays organization (December 21, 2000). ... Released by Blue Jays (March 17, 2001). ... Signed by Kansas City Royals organization (March 23, 2001). ... Released by Royals (May 23, 2001). ... Signed by Chicago Cubs organization (July 4, 2001). ... Released by Cubs (September 10, 2001).
STATISTICAL NOTES: Led Texas League second basemen with 296 putouts, 653 total chances and 81 double plays in 1991. ... Tied for Pacific Coast League lead in caught stealing with 18 in 1993. ... Led Pacific Coast League with .416 on-base percentage in 1995. ... Led American Association with .401 on-base percentage in 1997. ... Tied for Pacific Coast League lead in caught stealing with 10 in 2001.
MISCELLANEOUS: Batted lefthanded on occasion though not a switch hitter (1986-91).

| | | | | | | | | | BATTING | | | | | | FIELDING | | | |
Year Team (League)	Pos.	G	AB	R	H	2B	3B	HR	RBI	Avg.	BB	SO	SB	PO	A	E	Avg.
1986—Auburn (NY-Penn)	2B-OF	70	242	42	75	12	1	1	32	.310	28	42	35	131	110	18	.931
1987—Asheville (S.Atl.)	2-O-C-3-P	101	284	39	67	8	1	1	35	.236	28	42	28	124	108	14	.943
1988—Osceola (FSL)	2-C-O-3-1	130	446	68	116	15	11	3	65	.260	61	72	44	261	150	12	.972
1989—Columbus (Sou.)	2B-C-OF-3B	104	348	55	92	7	8	3	37	.264	43	53	28	321	122	15	.967
—Tucson (PCL)	OF-3B-C	21	50	3	11	2	0	0	2	.220	1	10	3	20	9	1	.967
1990—Columbus (Sou.)	2B-OF-C-3B	95	335	39	84	14	4	4	35	.251	32	51	17	216	116	11	.968
—Tucson (PCL)	2B-3B-C	12	27	5	6	2	2	0	2	.222	3	6	1	20	22	3	.933
1991—Jackson (Texas)	2B-OF-1B-P	126	455	78	135	21	3	2	41	.297	65	81	39	†299	338	21	.968
—Tucson (PCL)	2B	2	4	0	0	0	0	0	0	.000	0	0	1	1	2	0	1.000
1992—Tucson (PCL)	2B-3B	115	420	69	130	16	4	2	33	.310	45	68	34	238	353	18	.970
1993—Colo. Springs (PCL)■	O-2-3-DH-S	117	439	83	138	24	8	7	56	.314	47	57	33	208	29	6	.975
1994—Colo. Springs (PCL)	OF	79	320	78	116	22	5	4	38	.363	44	40	28	183	5	7	.964
—Colorado (N.L.)	OF	18	25	3	7	1	1	1	3	.280	3	4	0	4	0	0	1.000
1995—Colo. Springs (PCL)	OF	123	480	*102	163	29	7	12	66	.340	61	59	*37	285	11	6	.980
—Colorado (N.L.)	OF	24	58	13	18	4	0	3	9	.310	8	6	2	16	1	0	1.000
1996—Colorado (N.L.)	OF	45	60	12	13	5	1	1	12	.217	9	22	2	32	0	0	1.000
—Colo. Springs (PCL)	OF-2B-3B-C	50	188	41	59	15	5	6	16	.314	28	14	6	89	55	4	.973
—San Fran. (N.L.)■	OF	10	29	3	6	0	1	1	2	.207	2	5	0	19	1	0	1.000
1997—Buffalo (A.A.)■	OF-3B-DH	103	375	71	117	22	1	16	60	.312	57	52	26	236	26	2	.992
—Cleveland (A.L.)	OF	7	12	3	3	1	0	0	0	.250	1	3	2	3	0	0	1.000

H

Year Team (League)	Pos.	G	AB	R	H	2B	3B	HR	RBI	Avg.	BB	SO	SB	PO	A	E	Avg.
1998— Los Angeles (N.L.)■ ..	OF-3B	94	208	29	62	9	1	7	18	.298	18	46	9	110	3	1	.991
—Albuquerque (PCL).....	OF-DH	11	30	6	9	0	0	3	5	.300	5	5	2	13	1	0	1.000
1999— Albuquerque (PCL)	OF-DH	32	123	24	41	8	2	5	24	.333	16	27	16	72	2	2	.974
—Los Angeles (N.L.)	OF-C-2B	82	105	23	33	5	0	1	13	.314	13	24	4	50	1	1	.981
2000— Atlanta (N.L.)■.....	OF	60	81	15	15	2	1	1	6	.185	11	20	2	39	1	0	1.000
—Baltimore (A.L.)■.......	OF-DH	31	27	3	5	0	1	0	6	.185	0	3	2	12	1	1	.929
2001— Omaha (PCL)■	OF	49	175	35	50	9	1	10	28	.286	30	34	8	99	4	0	1.000
—Kansas City (A.L.)	OF	5	12	2	3	0	1	0	0	.250	0	2	0	2	0	0	1.000
—Iowa (PCL)■	OF-3B	49	171	38	54	11	3	6	31	.316	37	27	17	79	9	1	.989
American League totals (3 years)		43	51	8	11	1	2	0	0	.216	1	8	4	17	1	1	.947
National League totals (6 years)		333	566	98	154	26	5	15	63	.272	64	127	19	270	7	2	.993
Major League totals (8 years)		376	617	106	165	27	7	15	63	.267	65	135	23	287	8	3	.990

DIVISION SERIES RECORD

Year Team (League)	Pos.	G	AB	R	H	2B	3B	HR	RBI	Avg.	BB	SO	SB	PO	A	E	Avg.
1995— Colorado (N.L.)	PH	3	2	0	0	0	0	0	0	.000	0	0	0	...	...	...	...

RECORD AS PITCHER

Year League	W	L	Pct.	ERA	G	GS	CG	ShO	Sv.	IP	H	R	ER	BB	SO
1987— Asheville (S.Atl.).................	0	0	...	0.00	1	0	0	0	0	1	1	0	0	1	0
1991— Jackson (Texas)	0	0	...	0.00	1	0	0	0	0	1	0	0	0	2	0

HUCKABY, KEN — C

PERSONAL: Born January 27, 1971, in San Leandro, Calif. ... 6-1/205. ... Bats right, throws right. ... Full name: Kenneth Paul Huckaby.
HIGH SCHOOL: Manteca (Calif.).
JUNIOR COLLEGE: San Joaquin Delta (Calif.).
TRANSACTIONS/CAREER NOTES: Selected by Los Angeles Dodgers organization in second round of free-agent draft (June 3, 1991). ... On disabled list (May 26-June 5 and July 2-21, 1992). ... On San Antonio disabled list (May 4-13, 1994). ... Granted free agency (October 15, 1997). ... Signed by Seattle Mariners organization (December 3, 1997). ... On Tacoma disabled list (April 7-May 3, 1998). ... Released by Mariners (June 13, 1998). ... Signed by New York Yankees organization (June 28, 1998). ... Granted free agency (October 16, 1998). ... Signed by Arizona Diamondbacks organization (January 22, 1999). ... Granted free agency (October 15, 1999). ... Re-signed by Diamondbacks organization (November 15, 1999). ... Granted free agency (October 18, 2000). ... Re-signed by Diamondbacks organization (November 2, 2000). ... Released by Diamondbacks (October 29, 2001).
STATISTICAL NOTES: Led Florida State League catchers with 14 double plays in 1993. ... Led Pacific Coast League catchers with 592 total chances in 1995. ... Led Pacific Coast League catchers with 11 double plays in 1996. ... Led Pacific Coast League catchers with 695 putouts and 756 total chances in 1999.

Year Team (League)	Pos.	G	AB	R	H	2B	3B	HR	RBI	Avg.	BB	SO	SB	PO	A	E	Avg.
1991— Great Falls (Pio.)	C	57	213	39	55	16	0	3	37	.258	17	38	3	456	48	*12	.977
1992— Vero Beach (FSL)	C	73	261	14	63	9	0	0	21	.241	7	42	1	442	56	9	.982
1993— San Antonio (Texas) ...	C	28	82	4	18	1	0	0	5	.220	2	7	0	149	29	4	.978
—Vero Beach (FSL)	C	79	281	22	75	14	1	4	41	.267	11	35	2	481	*99	12	.980
1994— San Antonio (Texas) ...	C	11	41	3	11	1	0	1	9	.268	1	1	1	73	8	6	.931
—Bakersfield (Calif.)	C	77	270	29	81	18	1	2	30	.300	10	37	2	591	93	10	.986
1995— Albuquerque (PCL)	C-1B	89	278	30	90	16	2	1	40	.324	12	26	3	518	61	16	.973
1996— Albuquerque (PCL)	C	103	287	37	79	16	2	3	41	.275	17	35	0	557	63	6	.990
1997— Albuquerque (PCL).....	C-DH	69	201	14	40	5	1	0	18	.199	9	36	1	359	25	10	.975
1998— Tacoma (PCL)■	C-1B	16	49	4	11	2	0	0	1	.224	5	6	0	91	4	0	1.000
—Columbus (I.L.)■.......	C	36	101	13	21	3	1	1	10	.208	11	14	0	201	21	5	.978
1999— Tucson (PCL)■ C-3B-DH-1B	107	355	44	107	20	1	2	42	.301	13	33	0	†706	55	10	.987
2000— Tucson (PCL) C-3B-OF-1B	76	243	31	67	11	1	4	33	.276	10	30	2	382	51	8	.982
2001— El Paso (Texas)	1B-C	30	104	14	36	4	0	2	14	.346	3	16	0	206	23	4	.983
—Tucson (PCL) C-1B-3B-2B	78	262	31	76	15	1	2	34	.290	7	62	1	432	57	14	.972
—Arizona (N.L.)	C	1	1	0	0	0	0	0	0	.000	0	1	0	5	0	0	1.000
Major League totals (1 year)		1	1	0	0	0	0	0	0	.000	0	1	0	5	0	0	1.000

HUDSON, LUKE — P — REDS

PERSONAL: Born May 2, 1977, in Fountain Valley, Calif. ... 6-3/195. ... Throws right, bats right. ... Full name: Luke Stephen Hudson.
HIGH SCHOOL: Fountain Valley (Calif.).
COLLEGE: Tennessee.
TRANSACTIONS/CAREER NOTES: Selected by Colorado Rockies organization in fourth round of free-agent draft (June 2, 1998). ... On Carolina disabled list (July 7-August 19, 2000). ... Traded by Rockies with P Gabe White to Cincinnati Reds for 2B Pokey Reese and P Dennys Reyes (December 18, 2001).
STATISTICAL NOTES: Led Southern League with 18 wild pitches in 2001.

Year League	W	L	Pct.	ERA	G	GS	CG	ShO	Sv.	IP	H	R	ER	BB	SO
1998— Portland (N'West)	3	6	.333	4.74	15	15	0	0	0	79²/₃	68	46	42	51	82
1999— Asheville (S.Atl.)................	6	5	.545	4.30	21	20	1	0	0	88	89	47	42	24	96
2000— Salem (Caro.)	5	8	.385	3.27	19	19	2	2	0	110	101	47	40	34	80
2001— Carolina (Sou.)	7	12	.368	4.20	29	•28	1	0	0	165	159	90	77	68	145

HUDSON, TIM — P — ATHLETICS

PERSONAL: Born July 14, 1975, in Columbus, Ga. ... 6-0/160. ... Throws right, bats right. ... Full name: Timothy Adam Hudson.
HIGH SCHOOL: Glenwood (Phenix City, Ala.).
COLLEGE: Auburn.

TRANSACTIONS/CAREER NOTES: Selected by Oakland Athletics organization in sixth-round of free-agent draft (June 3, 1997).
HONORS: Named A.L. Rookie Pitcher of the Year by THE SPORTING NEWS (1999).
STATISTICAL NOTES: Pitched 3-0 one-hit, complete-game victory against Chicago White Sox (August 28, 2000).
MISCELLANEOUS: Appeared in three games as pinch runner (1999). ... Appeared in one game as pinch runner (2000). ... Appeared in one game as pinch runner (2001).

Year League	W	L	Pct.	ERA	G	GS	CG	ShO	Sv.	IP	H	R	ER	BB	SO
1997—Southern Oregon (N'West).	3	1	.750	2.51	8	4	0	0	0	28²/₃	12	8	8	15	37
1998—Modesto (Calif.)	4	0	1.000	1.67	8	5	0	0	0	37²/₃	19	10	7	18	48
—Huntsville (Sou.)	10	9	.526	4.54	22	22	2	0	0	134²/₃	136	84	68	71	104
1999—Midland (Texas)	3	0	1.000	0.50	3	3	0	0	0	18	9	1	1	3	18
—Vancouver (PCL)	4	0	1.000	2.20	8	8	0	0	0	49	38	16	12	21	61
—Oakland (A.L.)	11	2	.846	3.23	21	21	1	0	0	136¹/₃	121	56	49	62	132
2000—Oakland (A.L.)	•20	6	*.769	4.14	32	32	2	2	0	202¹/₃	169	100	93	82	169
2001—Oakland (A.L.)	18	9	.667	3.37	35	•35	3	0	0	235	216	100	88	71	181
Major League totals (3 years)	49	17	.742	3.61	88	88	6	2	0	573²/₃	506	256	230	215	482

DIVISION SERIES RECORD

Year League	W	L	Pct.	ERA	G	GS	CG	ShO	Sv.	IP	H	R	ER	BB	SO
2000—Oakland (A.L.)	0	1	.000	3.38	1	1	1	0	0	8	6	4	3	4	5
2001—Oakland (A.L.)	1	0	1.000	0.93	2	1	0	0	0	9²/₃	8	1	1	1	5
Division series totals (2 years)	1	1	.500	2.04	3	2	1	0	0	17²/₃	14	5	4	5	10

ALL-STAR GAME RECORD

Year League	W	L	Pct.	ERA	GS	CG	ShO	Sv.	IP	H	R	ER	BB	SO
2000—American	0	0	...	0.00	0	0	0	0	1	0	0	0	0	1

HUFF, AUBREY — 3B — DEVIL RAYS

PERSONAL: Born December 20, 1976, in Marion, Ohio. ... 6-4/221. ... Bats left, throws right. ... Full name: Aubrey L. Huff.
HIGH SCHOOL: Brewer (Fort Worth, Texas).
JUNIOR COLLEGE: Vernon Regional (Texas).
COLLEGE: Miami (Fla.).
TRANSACTIONS/CAREER NOTES: Selected by Tampa Bay Devil Rays organization in fifth round of free-agent draft (June 2, 1998).
STATISTICAL NOTES: Led Southern League third baseman with 395 total chances in 1999.

						BATTING								FIELDING		
Year Team (League)	Pos.	G	AB	R	H	2B	3B	HR	RBI	Avg.	BB	SO	SB	PO	A	E	Avg.
1998—Charl., S.C. (S.Atl.)	3B	69	265	38	85	19	1	13	54	.321	24	40	3	47	133	8	.957
1999—Orlando (Sou.)	3B	133	491	85	148	40	3	22	78	.301	64	77	2	93	273	29	.927
2000—Durham (I.L.)	3B-1B	108	408	73	129	36	3	20	76	.316	51	72	2	60	166	21	.915
—Tampa Bay (A.L.)	3B	39	122	12	35	7	0	4	14	.287	5	18	0	24	53	5	.939
2001—Durham (I.L.)	3B	17	66	14	19	6	0	3	10	.288	5	7	0	18	34	4	.929
—Tampa Bay (A.L.)	3B-DH-1B	111	411	42	102	25	1	8	45	.248	23	72	1	170	141	20	.940
Major League totals (2 years)		150	533	54	137	32	1	12	59	.257	28	90	1	194	194	25	.939

HUGHES, TRAVIS — P — RANGERS

PERSONAL: Born May 25, 1978, in Newton, Kan. ... 6-5/215. ... Throws right, bats right. ... Full name: Travis W. Hughes.
HIGH SCHOOL: Elwood (Neb.).
JUNIOR COLLEGE: Cowly County (Kan.).
TRANSACTIONS/CAREER NOTES: Selected by Texas Rangers organization in 19th round of free-agent draft (June 3, 1997).

Year League	W	L	Pct.	ERA	G	GS	CG	ShO	Sv.	IP	H	R	ER	BB	SO
1998—Pulaski (Appl.)	2	6	.250	3.89	22	3	0	0	2	41²/₃	30	25	18	25	48
1999—Savannah (S.Atl.)	11	7	.611	2.81	30	23	1	0	2	157	127	60	49	54	150
2000—Charlotte (FSL)	9	9	.500	4.42	39	14	1	0	9	126¹/₃	122	76	62	54	96
2001—Tulsa (Texas)	5	7	.417	4.64	47	5	0	0	8	87¹/₃	91	52	45	45	86

HUNDLEY, TODD — C — CUBS

PERSONAL: Born May 27, 1969, in Martinsville, Va. ... 5-11/199. ... Bats both, throws right. ... Full name: Todd Randolph Hundley. ... Son of Randy Hundley, catcher with four major league teams (1964-77).
HIGH SCHOOL: William Fremd (Palatine, Ill.).
COLLEGE: William Rainey Harper College (Ill.).
TRANSACTIONS/CAREER NOTES: Selected by New York Mets organization in second round of free-agent draft (June 2, 1987); pick received as compensation for Baltimore Orioles signing Type B free-agent 3B/1B Ray Knight. ... On Tidewater disabled list (June 29-July 6, 1991). ... On disabled list (July 23, 1995-remainder of season). ... On New York disabled list (March 21-July 11 and August 28-September 12, 1998); included rehabilitation assignments to St. Lucie (June 24-July 6 and July 9), Gulf Coast Mets (July 7-8) and Norfolk (July 10-11 and August 31-September 8). ... Traded by Mets with P Arnold Gooch to Los Angeles Dodgers for C Charles Johnson and OF Roger Cedeno (December 1, 1998). ... On suspended list (July 22-24, 1999). ... On Los Angeles disabled list (May 31-June 26 and July 9-27, 2000); included rehabilitation assignment to Albuquerque (June 23-26). ... Granted free agency (October 27, 2000). ... Signed by Chicago Cubs (December 13, 2000). ... On Chicago disabled list (June 19-July 26, 2001); included rehabilitation assignment to West Tenn (June 29-July 2) and Iowa (July 7-25).
RECORDS: Holds major league single-season record for most home runs by catcher—41 (1996). ... Holds N.L. single-season record for most strikeouts by switch hitter—146 (1996).
STATISTICAL NOTES: Led South Atlantic League in intentional bases on balls received with 10 and in grounding into double plays with 20 in 1989. ... Led South Atlantic League catchers with 826 putouts and 930 total chances in 1989. ... Tied for International League lead in errors by catcher with nine and double plays with 12 in 1991. ... Switch-hit home runs in one game five times (June 18, 1994; May 18; June 10, 1996; May 5 and July 20, 1997). ... Career major league grand slams: 7.

H

						BATTING									FIELDING			
Year—Team (League)	Pos.	G	AB	R	H	2B	3B	HR	RBI	Avg.	BB	SO	SB	PO	A	E	Avg.
1987—Little Falls (NY-Penn) .	C	34	103	12	15	4	0	1	10	.146	12	27	0	181	25	7	.967
1988—Little Falls (NY-Penn) .	C	52	176	23	33	8	0	2	18	.188	16	31	1	345	54	8	.980
—St. Lucie (FSL)	C	1	1	0	0	0	0	0	0	.000	2	1	0	4	0	1	.800
1989—Columbia (S.Atl.)	C-OF	125	439	67	118	23	4	11	66	.269	54	67	6	†829	91	13	.986
1990—Jackson (Texas)	C-3B	81	279	27	74	12	2	1	35	.265	34	44	5	474	63	9	.984
—New York (N.L.).........	C	36	67	8	14	6	0	0	2	.209	6	18	0	162	8	2	.988
1991—Tidewater (I.L.)..........	C-1B	125	454	62	124	24	4	14	66	.273	51	95	1	585	63	‡9	.986
—New York (N.L.)..........	C	21	60	5	8	0	1	1	7	.133	6	14	0	85	11	0	1.000
1992—New York (N.L.).........	C	123	358	32	75	17	0	7	32	.209	19	76	3	700	48	3	.996
1993—New York (N.L.).........	C	130	417	40	95	17	2	11	53	.228	23	62	1	592	63	8	.988
1994—New York (N.L.).........	C	91	291	45	69	10	1	16	42	.237	25	73	2	448	28	5	.990
1995—New York (N.L.).........	C	90	275	39	77	11	0	15	51	.280	42	64	1	488	29	7	.987
1996—New York (N.L.).........	C	153	540	85	140	32	1	41	112	.259	79	146	1	911	72	8	.992
1997—New York (N.L.).........	C-DH	132	417	78	114	21	2	30	86	.273	83	116	2	678	54	10	.987
1998—St. Lucie (FSL)	OF-DH	12	42	4	9	2	0	1	6	.214	12	8	0	17	1	2	.900
—GC Mets (GCL)..........	OF	1	2	0	0	0	0	0	0	.000	2	1	0	2	0	0	1.000
—Norfolk (I.L.)............	OF-DH-C	10	30	9	13	1	0	4	15	.433	14	10	0	22	2	1	.960
—New York (N.L.).........	OF-C	53	124	8	20	4	0	3	12	.161	16	55	1	60	4	5	.928
1999—Los Angeles (N.L.)■ ..	C	115	376	49	78	14	0	24	55	.207	44	113	3	681	51	*16	.979
2000—Los Angeles (N.L.)	C-DH	90	299	49	85	16	0	24	70	.284	45	69	0	554	38	*13	.979
—Albuquerque (PCL).....	C	3	9	2	5	0	0	1	5	.556	1	0	0	15	0	0	1.000
2001—Chicago (N.L.)■........	C	79	246	23	46	10	0	12	31	.187	25	89	0	547	25	4	.993
—West Tenn (Sou.)	C	4	12	1	4	2	0	0	1	.333	1	3	0	7	1	0	1.000
—Iowa (PCL)	C	15	51	7	10	1	0	3	8	.196	4	23	0	51	5	0	1.000
Major League totals (12 years)		1113	3470	461	821	158	7	184	553	.237	413	895	14	5906	431	81	.987

ALL-STAR GAME RECORD

				BATTING									FIELDING		
Year—League	Pos.	AB	R	H	2B	3B	HR	RBI	Avg.	BB	SO	SB	PO	A	E	Avg.
1996—National	C	1	0	0	0	0	0	0	.000	0	0	0	1	0	0	1.000
1997—National......................							Did not play.									

HUNTER, BRIAN　　　　　OF　　　　　ASTROS

PERSONAL: Born March 5, 1971, in Portland, Ore. ... 6-3/180. ... Bats right, throws right. ... Full name: Brian Lee Hunter.

HIGH SCHOOL: Fort Vancouver (Vancouver, Wash.).

TRANSACTIONS/CAREER NOTES: Selected by Houston Astros organization in second round of free-agent draft (June 5, 1989); pick received as part of compensation for Texas Rangers signing Type A free-agent P Nolan Ryan. ... On Houston disabled list (July 5-23, 1995); included rehabilitation assignment to Jackson (July 21-23). ... On Houston disabled list (June 29-July 27, 1996); included rehabilitation assignment to Tucson (July 23-27). ... Traded by Astros with IF Orlando Miller, P Doug Brocail, P Todd Jones and cash to Detroit Tigers for C Brad Ausmus, P Jose Lima, P C.J. Nitkowski, P Trever Miller and IF Daryle Ward (December 10, 1996). ... Traded by Tigers to Seattle Mariners for two players to be named later (April 29, 1999); Tigers acquired P Andrew Vanhekken (June 27, 1999) and OF Jerry Amador (August 26, 1999) to complete deal. ... On Seattle disabled list (July 12-27, 1999). ... Released by Mariners (March 27, 2000). ... Signed by Colorado Rockies (March 31, 2000). ... Traded by Rockies from Cincinnati Reds for P Robert Averette (August 6, 2000). ... On suspended list (August 14-17, 2000). ... Released by Reds (November 27, 2000). ... Signed by Philadelphia Phillies (January 10, 2001). ... On Philadelphia disabled list (April 4-22, 2001); included rehabilitation assignment to Scranton/Wilkes-Barre (April 20-22). ... Granted free agency (November 5, 2001). ... Signed by Astros (December 3, 2001).

RECORDS: Holds major league record for most at-bats with no hits in doubleheader (more than 18 innings)—13 (June 20, 1998, 26 innings). ... Shares major league single season record for fewest double plays by outfielder (150 or more games)—0 (1997).

STATISTICAL NOTES: Led A.L. in caught stealing with 18 in 1997. ... Led A.L. outfielders with 420 total chances in 1997. ... Led A.L. with 44 stolen bases in 1999. ... Career major league grand slams: 1.

						BATTING									FIELDING		
Year—Team (League)	Pos.	G	AB	R	H	2B	3B	HR	RBI	Avg.	BB	SO	SB	PO	A	E	Avg.
1989—GC Astros (GCL)	OF	51	206	15	35	2	0	0	13	.170	7	42	12	95	4	2	.980
1990—Asheville (S.Atl.).........	OF	127	444	84	111	14	6	0	16	.250	60	72	45	219	13	11	.955
1991—Osceola (FSL).............	OF	118	392	51	94	15	3	1	30	.240	45	75	32	250	7	9	.966
1992—Osceola (FSL).............	OF	131	489	62	146	18	9	1	62	.299	31	76	39	295	10	9	.971
1993—Jackson (Texas)	OF-DH	133	523	84	154	22	5	10	52	.294	34	85	*35	276	9	*14	.953
1994—Tucson (PCL)	OF-DH	128	513	*113	*191	28	9	10	51	*.372	52	52	*49	244	14	5	.981
—Houston (N.L.)	OF	6	24	2	6	1	0	0	0	.250	1	6	2	14	1	1	.938
1995—Tucson (PCL)	OF	38	155	28	51	5	1	1	16	.329	17	13	11	91	1	0	1.000
—Houston (N.L.)	OF	78	321	52	97	14	5	2	28	.302	21	52	24	182	8	9	.955
—Jackson (Texas)	OF	2	6	1	3	0	0	0	0	.500	1	0	0	5	0	0	1.000
1996—Houston (N.L.)	OF	132	526	74	145	27	2	5	35	.276	17	92	35	279	11	•12	.960
—Tucson (PCL)	OF	3	14	3	5	0	1	0	1	.357	0	2	3	8	0	0	1.000
1997—Detroit (A.L.)■	OF	•162	658	112	177	29	7	4	45	.269	66	121	*74	*408	8	4	.990
1998—Detroit (A.L.)	OF	142	595	67	151	29	3	4	36	.254	36	94	42	386	11	5	.988
1999—Detroit (A.L.)	OF	18	55	8	13	2	1	0	0	.236	5	11	0	49	1	0	1.000
—Seattle (A.L.)■	OF	121	484	71	112	11	5	4	34	.231	32	80	§44	252	14	4	.985
2000—Colorado (N.L.)■	OF	72	200	36	55	4	1	1	13	.275	21	31	15	103	3	2	.981
—Cincinnati (N.L.)■	OF	32	40	11	9	1	0	0	1	.225	6	9	5	30	4	1	.971
2001—Philadelphia (N.L.)■ ...	OF-DH	83	145	22	40	6	0	2	16	.276	16	25	14	69	3	0	1.000
—Scranton/W.B. (I.L.) ...	OF	2	9	1	1	0	0	0	0	.111	1	3	0	5	0	1	.833
American League totals (3 years)		443	1792	258	453	71	16	12	115	.253	139	306	160	1095	34	13	.989
National League totals (5 years)		403	1256	197	352	53	8	10	93	.280	82	215	95	677	30	25	.966
Major League totals (8 years)		846	3048	455	805	124	24	22	208	.264	221	521	255	1772	64	38	.980

H

PERSONAL: Born July 18, 1975, in Pine Bluff, Ark. ... 6-2/205. ... Bats right, throws right. ... Full name: Torii Kedar Hunter. ... Name pronounced TORE-ee.

HIGH SCHOOL: Pine Bluff (Ark.).

TRANSACTIONS/CAREER NOTES: Selected by Minnesota Twins organization in first round (20th pick overall) of free-agent draft (June 3, 1993); pick recieved as part of compensation for Cincinnati Reds signing Type A free-agent P John Smiley. ... On New Britain disabled list (April 4-May 10, 1996). ... On Salt Lake disabled list (July 28-August 11, 1998). ... On disabled list (April 6-21, 2001).

HONORS: Won A.L. Gold Glove as outfielder (2001).

STATISTICAL NOTES: Led Florida State League outfielders with seven double plays in 1995. ... Tied for Eastern League lead for double plays by an outfielder with four in 1997. ... Career major league grand slams: 2.

Year Team (League)	Pos.	G	AB	R	H	2B	3B	HR	RBI	Avg.	BB	SO	SB	PO	A	E	Avg.
1993—GC Twins (GCL)	OF	28	100	6	19	3	0	0	8	.190	4	23	4	50	1	•6	.895
1994—Fort Wayne (Midw.)	OF	91	335	57	98	17	1	10	50	.293	25	80	8	224	12	7	.971
1995—Fort Myers (FSL)	OF	113	391	64	96	15	2	7	36	.246	38	77	7	242	15	7	.973
1996—New Britain (East.)	OF	99	342	49	90	20	3	7	33	.263	28	60	7	207	11	4	.982
—Fort Myers (FSL)	OF	4	16	1	3	0	0	0	1	.188	2	5	1	9	0	0	1.000
1997—New Britain (East.)	OF-DH	127	471	57	109	22	2	8	56	.231	47	94	8	252	7	7	.974
—Minnesota (A.L.)	PR	1	0	0	0	0	0	0	0	...	0	0	0	...	...	...	...
1998—New Britain (East.)	OF	82	308	42	87	24	3	6	32	.282	19	64	11	168	8	2	.989
—Minnesota (A.L.)	OF	6	17	0	4	1	0	0	2	.235	2	6	0	8	0	0	1.000
—Salt Lake (PCL)	OF-DH	26	92	15	31	7	0	4	20	.337	1	13	2	55	1	2	.966
1999—Minnesota (A.L.)	OF	135	384	52	98	17	2	9	35	.255	26	72	10	284	7	1	.997
2000—Minnesota (A.L.)	OF	99	336	44	94	14	7	5	44	.280	18	68	4	270	12	3	.989
2001—Minnesota (A.L.)	OF	148	564	82	147	32	5	27	92	.261	29	125	9	460	14	4	.992
Major League totals (5 years)		389	1301	178	343	64	14	41	173	.264	75	271	23	1022	33	8	.992

PERSONAL: Born February 21, 1977, in Del Mar, Calif. ... 6-5/230. ... Throws right, bats right. ... Full name: Chad Martin Hutchinson. ... Son of Lloyd Hutchinson, outfielder in Philadelphia Phillies organization (1969-72).

HIGH SCHOOL: Torrey Pines (Encinitas, Calif.).

COLLEGE: Stanford.

TRANSACTIONS/CAREER NOTES: Selected by Atlanta Braves organization in first round (26th overall) of free-agent draft (June 1, 1995); did not sign. ... Selected by St. Louis Cardinals organization in second round of free-agent draft (June 2, 1998). ... On Arkansas disabled list (June 12-August 24, 2000). ... On Memphis disabled list (August 10-17, 2001).

STATISTICAL NOTES: Led Texas League with 20 wild pitches in 1999. ... Led Pacific Coast League with 17 wild pitches in 2001.

Year League	W	L	Pct.	ERA	G	GS	CG	ShO	Sv.	IP	H	R	ER	BB	SO
1998—New Jersey (NY-Penn)	0	1	.000	3.52	3	3	0	0	0	15 1/3	15	7	6	4	20
—Prince William (Caro.)	2	0	1.000	2.79	5	5	0	0	0	29	20	12	9	11	31
1999—Arkansas (Texas)	7	11	.389	4.72	25	25	0	0	0	141	127	79	74	*85	150
—Memphis (PCL)	2	0	1.000	2.19	2	2	0	0	0	12 1/3	4	3	3	8	16
2000—Memphis (PCL)	0	1	.000	25.92	5	4	0	0	0	8 1/3	10	24	24	27	9
—Arkansas (Texas)	2	3	.400	3.38	11	11	1	1	0	48	40	21	18	27	54
2001—St. Louis (N.L.)	0	0	...	24.75	3	0	0	0	0	4	9	11	11	6	2
—Memphis (PCL)	4	9	.308	7.92	27	20	0	0	0	97 2/3	99	91	86	*104	111
Major League totals (1 year)	0	0	...	24.75	3	0	0	0	0	4	9	11	11	6	2

PERSONAL: Born December 6, 1971, in San Jose, Calif. ... 6-2/220. ... Bats right, throws right. ... Full name: Adam Davis Hyzdu. ... Name pronounced HIZE-doo.

HIGH SCHOOL: Moeller (Cincinnati).

COLLEGE: Xavier.

TRANSACTIONS/CAREER NOTES: Selected by San Francisco Giants organization in first round (15th pick overall) of free-agent draft (June 4, 1990); pick received as compensation for Houston Astros signing Type B free-agent IF Ken Oberkfell. ... Selected by Cincinnati Reds from Giants organization in Rule 5 major league draft (December 13, 1993). ... Released by Reds (March 23, 1996). ... Signed by Boston Red Sox organization (April 26, 1996). ... Signed by Arizona Diamondbacks organization (January 2, 1998). ... On disabled list (June 30-August 23, 1998). ... Granted free agency (October 15, 1998). ... Signed by Pittsburgh Pirates organization (May 10, 1999). ... Granted free agency (October 15, 1999). ... Re-signed by Pirates organization (October 30, 1999). ... Granted free agency (October 18, 2000). ... Re-signed by Pirates organization (October 24, 2000).

HONORS: Named Eastern League Most Valuable Player (2000).

STATISTICAL NOTES: Led Eastern League with .618 slugging percentage in 1996. ... Led Eastern League with 285 total bases in 2000. ... Tied for Eastern League lead with seven intentional bases on balls received in 2000.

Year Team (League)	Pos.	G	AB	R	H	2B	3B	HR	RBI	Avg.	BB	SO	SB	PO	A	E	Avg.
1990—Everett (N'West)	OF	69	253	31	62	16	1	6	34	.245	28	78	2	128	2	5	.963
1991—Clinton (Midw.)	OF	124	410	47	96	13	5	5	50	.234	64	131	4	185	8	9	.955
1992—San Jose (Calif.)	OF	128	457	60	127	25	5	9	60	.278	55	134	10	193	8	5	.976
1993—San Jose (Calif.)	OF	44	165	35	48	11	3	13	38	.291	29	53	1	72	5	3	.963
—Shreveport (Texas)	OF	86	302	30	61	17	0	6	25	.202	20	82	0	136	8	4	.973
1994—Chattanooga (Sou.)■	OF-DH-1B	38	133	17	35	10	0	3	9	.263	8	21	0	70	4	4	.949
—Indianapolis (A.A.)	OF	12	25	3	3	2	0	0	3	.120	1	5	0	10	1	1	.917
—Win.-Salem (Caro.)	OF-DH	55	210	30	58	11	1	15	39	.276	18	33	1	67	2	4	.945
1995—Chattanooga (Sou.)	OF	102	312	55	82	14	1	13	48	.263	45	56	3	182	4	1	*.995
1996—Trenton (East.)■	OF-DH-C	109	374	71	126	24	3	25	80	.337	56	75	1	135	9	3	.980

H

Year Team (League)	Pos.	G	AB	R	H	2B	3B	HR	RBI	Avg.	BB	SO	SB	PO	A	E	Avg.
1997—Pawtucket (I.L.).........	OF-DH	119	413	77	114	21	1	23	84	.276	72	113	10	170	10	4	.978
1998—Tucson (PCL)■........	OF-DH-P	34	100	21	34	7	1	4	14	.340	15	23	0	38	0	1	.974
1999—Pawtucket (I.L.)■......	OF-DH	12	35	4	8	0	0	1	6	.229	4	13	0	10	0	0	1.000
—Altoona (East.)■.......OF-1B-3B-DH		91	345	64	109	26	2	24	78	.316	40	62	8	275	27	11	.965
—Nashville (PCL)	OF	14	44	6	11	1	0	5	13	.250	4	11	0	26	1	0	1.000
2000—Altoona (East.)	OF-1B	*142	514	•96	149	39	2	*31	*106	.290	94	102	3	269	9	1	.996
—Pittsburgh (N.L.)	OF	12	18	2	7	2	0	1	4	.389	0	4	0	5	0	0	1.000
2001—Nashville (PCL)	OF-1B-3B	69	261	38	76	17	2	11	39	.291	17	68	1	169	4	1	.994
—Pittsburgh (N.L.)	OF-1B	51	72	7	15	1	0	5	9	.208	4	18	0	42	2	0	1.000
Major League totals (2 years)		63	90	9	22	3	0	6	13	.244	4	22	0	47	2	0	1.000

RECORD AS PITCHER

Year League	W	L	Pct.	ERA	G	GS	CG	ShO	Sv.	IP	H	R	ER	BB	SO
1998—Tucson (PCL)	0	0	...	0.00	1	0	0	0	0	1	0	0	0	0	1

IBANEZ, RAUL — OF — ROYALS

PERSONAL: Born June 2, 1972, in Manhattan, N.Y. ... 6-2/200. ... Bats left, throws right. ... Full name: Raul Javier Ibanez.
HIGH SCHOOL: Sunset (Miami).
JUNIOR COLLEGE: Miami-Dade (South) Community College.
TRANSACTIONS/CAREER NOTES: Selected by Seattle Mariners organization in 36th round of free-agent draft (June 1, 1992). ... On disabled list (June 4-July 16, 1994). ... On Seattle disabled list (March 30-June 29, 1998); included rehabilitation assignment to Tacoma (May 30-June 28). ... On Tacoma disabled list (July 7-14, 1998). ... On Seattle disabled list (May 18-June 3, 1999); included rehabilitation assignment to Tacoma (May 26-June 3). ... On Seattle disabled list (August 7-22, 2000); included rehabilitation assignment to Tacoma (August 11-22). ... Granted free agency (December 21, 2000). ... Signed by Kansas City Royals organization (January 22, 2001).
STATISTICAL NOTES: Led California League with .612 slugging percentage in 1995. ... Led California League with 25 passed balls in 1995. ... Career major league grand slams: 1.

Year Team (League)	Pos.	G	AB	R	H	2B	3B	HR	RBI	Avg.	BB	SO	SB	PO	A	E	Avg.
1992—Ariz. Mariners (Ariz.)..	1B-C-OF	33	120	25	37	8	2	1	16	.308	9	18	1	51	3	4	.931
1993—Appleton (Midw.)........	1B-C-OF	52	157	26	43	9	0	5	21	.274	24	31	0	98	2	2	.980
—Bellingham (N'West) ..	C	43	134	16	38	5	2	0	15	.284	21	23	0	137	15	1	.993
1994—Appleton (Midw.)........	C-1B-OF	91	327	55	102	30	3	7	59	.312	32	37	10	304	28	10	.971
1995—Riverside (Calif.)........	C-1B	95	361	59	120	23	9	20	108	.332	41	49	4	465	54	12	.977
1996—Tacoma (PCL)	OF-1B-DH	111	405	59	115	20	3	11	47	.284	44	56	7	201	12	11	.951
—Port City (Sou.).........OF-DH-C-1B		19	76	12	28	8	1	1	13	.368	8	7	3	36	2	4	.905
—Seattle (A.L.)	DH	4	5	0	0	0	0	0	0	.000	0	1	0	0	0	0	...
1997—Tacoma (PCL)	OF	111	438	84	133	30	5	15	84	.304	32	75	7	192	12	5	.976
—Seattle (A.L.)	OF-DH	11	26	3	4	0	1	1	4	.154	0	6	0	9	0	0	1.000
1998—Tacoma (PCL)	OF-DH	52	190	24	41	8	1	6	25	.216	24	47	1	78	2	1	.988
—Seattle (A.L.)	OF-1B-DH	37	98	12	25	7	1	2	12	.255	5	22	0	105	7	1	.991
1999—Seattle (A.L.) OF-1B-DH-C		87	209	23	54	7	0	9	27	.258	17	32	5	234	8	3	.988
—Tacoma (PCL)	OF-DH-1B	8	31	6	11	1	0	3	5	.355	1	7	1	13	0	0	1.000
2000—Seattle (A.L.)	OF-DH-1B	92	140	21	32	8	0	2	15	.229	14	25	2	99	1	2	.980
—Tacoma (PCL)	OF	10	40	3	10	4	0	0	6	.250	1	3	0	9	0	0	1.000
2001—Kansas City (A.L.)■...OF-DH-1B-3B		104	279	44	78	11	5	13	54	.280	32	51	0	114	11	5	.962
—Omaha (PCL).............	OF-SS	8	27	3	4	1	0	2	5	.148	1	10	0	6	0	1	.857
Major League totals (6 years)		335	757	103	193	33	7	27	112	.255	68	137	7	561	27	11	.982

DIVISION SERIES RECORD

Year Team (League)	Pos.	G	AB	R	H	2B	3B	HR	RBI	Avg.	BB	SO	SB	PO	A	E	Avg.
2000—Seattle (A.L.)	PR-OF	3	8	2	3	0	0	0	0	.375	0	0	0	4	0	0	1.000

CHAMPIONSHIP SERIES RECORD

Year Team (League)	Pos.	G	AB	R	H	2B	3B	HR	RBI	Avg.	BB	SO	SB	PO	A	E	Avg.
2000—Seattle (A.L.)	OF-PH	6	9	0	0	0	0	0	0	.000	0	2	0	6	0	0	1.000

INGE, BRANDON — C — TIGERS

PERSONAL: Born May 19, 1977, in Lynchburg, Va. ... 5-11/185. ... Bats both, throws right. ... Full name: Charles Brandon Inge.
HIGH SCHOOL: Brookville (Lynchburg, Va.).
COLLEGE: Virginia Commonwealth.
TRANSACTIONS/CAREER NOTES: Selected by Detroit Tigers organization in second round of free-agent draft (June 2, 1998). ... On Detroit disabled list (June 25-August 6, 2001); included rehabilitation assignments to Gulf Coast Tigers (July 25-29), West Michigan (July 30-August 2) and Toledo (August 3-6).
STATISTICAL NOTES: Led Southern League catchers with .990 fielding percentage in 2000.

Year Team (League)	Pos.	G	AB	R	H	2B	3B	HR	RBI	Avg.	BB	SO	SB	PO	A	E	Avg.
1998—Jamestown (NY-P)	C	51	191	24	44	10	1	8	29	.230	17	53	8	263	40	6	.981
1999—W. Michigan (Midw.)..	C	100	352	54	86	25	2	9	46	.244	39	87	15	703	*114	8	.990
2000—Jacksonville (Sou.).....	C-OF	78	298	39	77	25	1	6	53	.258	26	73	10	438	73	5	†.990
—Toledo (I.L.)...............	C	55	190	24	42	9	3	5	20	.221	15	51	2	308	37	3	.991
2001—Detroit (A.L.)	C	79	189	13	34	11	0	0	15	.180	9	41	1	330	40	4	.989
—GC Tigers (GCL)	C	3	10	1	1	0	0	1	2	.100	2	2	0	12	0	0	1.000
—W. Michigan (Midw.)..	C	4	16	3	3	1	0	0	2	.188	2	5	0	12	0	0	1.000
—Toledo (I.L.)...............	C	27	90	11	26	11	1	2	15	.289	7	24	1	160	20	2	.989
Major League totals (1 year)		79	189	13	34	11	0	0	15	.180	9	41	1	330	40	4	.989

PERSONAL: Born May 5, 1969, in Hyogo, Japan. ... 6-4/240. ... Throws right, bats right.

HIGH SCHOOL: Jinsei.

TRANSACTIONS/CAREER NOTES: Rights acquired by San Diego Padres from Chiba Lotte Marines of Japan Pacific League (January 13, 1997). ... Rights traded by Padres with 2B Homer Bush, OF Gordon Amerson and a player to be named later to New York Yankees for OF Ruben Rivera, P Rafael Medina and cash (April 22, 1997); Padres traded OF Vernon Maxwell to Yankees to complete deal (June 9, 1997). ... Signed by Yankees (May 29, 1997). ... Traded by Yankees to Montreal Expos for P Jake Westbrook and two players to be named (December 22, 1999); Yankees acquired P Ted Lilly (March 17, 2000) and P Christian Parker (March 22, 2000) to complete deal. ... On Montreal disabled list (May 27-July 26 and July 28, 2000-remainder of season); included rehabilitation assignments to Jupiter (July 8-18) and Ottawa (July 19-20). ... On Montreal disabled list (March 23-May 31, 2001 and June 14-September 6, 2001); included rehabilitation assignments to Jupiter (April 26-May 31) and Ottawa (August 22-30). ... Released by Expos (September 6, 2001). ... Signed by Texas Rangers organization (December 27, 2001).

STATISTICAL NOTES: Tied for A.L. lead with three balks in 1997.

Year	League	W	L	Pct.	ERA	G	GS	CG	ShO	Sv.	IP	H	R	ER	BB	SO
1988—	Lotte Orions (Jap. East.)	2	5	.286	3.89	14	6	...	...	1	39 1/3	30	19	17	15	21
1989—	Lotte Orions (Jap. East.)	0	2	.000	3.53	33	2	...	...	9	51	37	20	20	27	50
1990—	Lotte Orions (Jap. East.)	8	5	.615	3.78	34	7	...	...	0	123 2/3	110	56	52	72	102
1991—	Lotte Orions (Jap. East.)	3	8	.273	6.88	24	14	...	...	0	100 2/3	110	78	77	70	78
1992—	Chiba Lotte (Jap. Pac.)■....	0	5	.000	3.86	28	4	...	...	0	77	38	33	33	37	55
1993—	Chiba Lotte (Jap. Pac.).....	8	7	.533	3.10	32	8	...	...	1	142 1/3	125	59	49	58	160
1994—	Chiba Lotte (Jap. Pac.)......	*15	10	.600	3.04	27	20	...	...	0	207 1/3	170	77	70	94	*239
1995—	Chiba Lotte (Jap. Pac.)....	11	11	.500	*2.53	28	18	...	...	0	203	158	70	57	72	*239
1996—	Chiba Lotte (Jap. Pac.)....	12	6	.667	*2.40	23	20	3	...	0	157 1/3	108	57	42	59	167
1997—	Tampa (FSL)■............	1	0	1.000	0.00	2	2	0	0	0	9	4	0	0	0	12
	— Norwich (East.)	1	1	.500	4.50	2	2	0	0	0	10	13	5	5	0	9
	— Columbus (I.L.)	2	0	1.000	1.67	4	4	1	1	0	27	19	7	5	5	28
	— New York (A.L.)	5	4	.556	7.09	13	9	0	0	0	53 1/3	69	47	42	20	56
1998—	New York (A.L.)	13	9	.591	4.06	29	28	2	1	0	173	148	79	78	76	126
1999—	New York (A.L.)	11	7	.611	4.84	32	27	2	1	0	169 1/3	180	98	91	46	133
2000—	Montreal (N.L.)■	2	5	.286	7.24	11	11	0	0	0	54 2/3	77	45	44	14	42
	— Jupiter (FSL)	1	0	1.000	1.04	2	2	0	0	0	8 2/3	7	1	1	1	9
	— Ottawa (I.L.)	0	1	.000	3.18	1	1	0	0	0	5 2/3	5	2	2	2	6
2001—	Jupiter (FSL)	0	0	...	3.00	3	3	0	0	0	9	5	3	3	4	9
	— Montreal (N.L.)	0	2	.000	4.86	3	3	0	0	0	16 2/3	22	9	9	3	18
	— Ottawa (I.L.)	1	2	.333	4.43	4	4	0	0	0	22 1/3	22	12	11	6	21
A.L. totals (3 years)		29	20	.592	4.80	74	64	4	2	0	395 2/3	397	224	211	142	315
N.L. totals (2 years)		2	7	.222	6.69	14	14	0	0	0	71 1/3	99	54	53	17	60
Major League totals (5 years)		31	27	.534	5.09	88	78	4	2	0	467	496	278	264	159	375

DIVISION SERIES RECORD

Year	League	W	L	Pct.	ERA	G	GS	CG	ShO	Sv.	IP	H	R	ER	BB	SO
1998—	New York (A.L.)				Did not play.											
1999—	New York (A.L.)				Did not play.											

CHAMPIONSHIP SERIES RECORD

Year	League	W	L	Pct.	ERA	G	GS	CG	ShO	Sv.	IP	H	R	ER	BB	SO
1998—	New York (A.L.)				Did not play.											
1999—	New York (A.L.)	0	0	...	13.50	1	0	0	0	0	4 2/3	13	8	7	0	3

WORLD SERIES RECORD

NOTES: Member of World Series championship team (1998 and 1999).

Year	League	W	L	Pct.	ERA	G	GS	CG	ShO	Sv.	IP	H	R	ER	BB	SO
1998—	New York (A.L.)				Did not play.											
1999—	New York (A.L.)				Did not play.											

PERSONAL: Born September 7, 1972, in Brighton, Ill. ... 6-3/210. ... Throws right, bats right. ... Full name: Jason Derik Isringhausen. ... Name pronounced IS-ring-how-zin.

HIGH SCHOOL: Southwestern (Brighton, Ill.).

JUNIOR COLLEGE: Lewis & Clark Community College (Ill.).

TRANSACTIONS/CAREER NOTES: Selected by New York Mets organization in 44th round of free-agent draft (June 3, 1991). ... On disabled list (August 13-September 1, 1996). ... On disabled list (March 24-August 27, 1997); included rehabilitation assignments to Norfolk (April 6-11 and August 22-27), Gulf Coast Mets (August 6-11) and St. Lucie (August 11-22). ... On disabled list (March 21, 1998-entire season). ... Traded by Mets with P Greg McMichael to Oakland Athletics for P Billy Taylor (July 31, 1999). ... Granted free agency (November 5, 2001). ... Signed by St. Louis Cardinals (December 11, 2001).

HONORS: Named International League Most Valuable Pitcher (1995).

Year	League	W	L	Pct.	ERA	G	GS	CG	ShO	Sv.	IP	H	R	ER	BB	SO
1992—	Gulf Coast Mets (GCL)	2	4	.333	4.34	6	6	0	0	0	29	26	19	14	17	25
	— Kingsport (Appl.)............	4	1	.800	3.25	7	6	1	1	0	36	32	22	13	12	24
1993—	Pittsfield (NY-Penn)..........	7	4	.636	3.29	15	15	2	0	0	90 1/3	68	45	33	28	*104
1994—	St. Lucie (FSL)	6	4	.600	2.23	14	14	•6	•3	0	101	76	31	25	27	59
	— Binghamton (East.)	5	4	.556	3.02	14	14	2	0	0	92 1/3	78	35	31	23	69
1995—	Binghamton (East.)	2	1	.667	2.85	6	6	1	0	0	41	26	15	13	12	59
	— Norfolk (I.L.)	9	1	*.900	1.55	12	12	3	*3	0	87	64	17	15	24	75
	— New York (N.L.)	9	2	.818	2.81	14	14	1	0	0	93	88	29	29	31	55
1996—	New York (N.L.)	6	14	.300	4.77	27	27	2	1	0	171 2/3	190	103	91	73	114
1997—	Norfolk (I.L.)	0	2	.000	4.05	3	3	0	0	0	20	20	10	9	8	17
	— Gulf Coast Mets (GCL)	1	0	1.000	1.93	1	0	0	0	0	4 2/3	2	1	1	1	7
	— St. Lucie (FSL)	1	0	1.000	0.00	2	2	0	0	0	12	8	1	0	5	15
	— New York (N.L.)	2	2	.500	7.58	6	6	0	0	0	29 2/3	40	27	25	22	25

Year League	W	L	Pct.	ERA	G	GS	CG	ShO	Sv.	IP	H	R	ER	BB	SO
1998— New York (N.L.).................						Did not play.									
1999— Norfolk (I.L.)	3	1	.750	2.29	12	8	0	0	0	51	33	18	13	20	51
— New York (N.L.)..............	1	3	.250	6.41	13	5	0	0	1	39 1/3	43	29	28	22	31
— Oakland (A.L.)■................	0	1	.000	2.13	20	0	0	0	8	25 1/3	21	6	6	12	20
2000— Oakland (A.L.)	6	4	.600	3.78	66	0	0	0	33	69	67	34	29	32	57
2001— Oakland (A.L.)	4	3	.571	2.65	65	0	0	0	34	71 1/3	54	24	21	23	74
A.L. totals (3 years)	10	8	.556	3.04	151	0	0	0	75	165 2/3	142	64	56	67	151
N.L. totals (4 years)	18	21	.462	4.67	60	52	3	1	1	333 2/3	361	188	173	148	225
Major League totals (6 years).......	28	29	.491	4.13	211	52	3	1	76	499 1/3	503	252	229	215	376

DIVISION SERIES RECORD

Year League	W	L	Pct.	ERA	G	GS	CG	ShO	Sv.	IP	H	R	ER	BB	SO
2000— Oakland (A.L.)	0	0	...	0.00	2	0	0	0	1	2	1	0	0	0	3
2001— Oakland (A.L.)	0	0	...	0.00	2	0	0	0	2	1	1	0	0	1	3
Division series totals (2 years)	0	0	...	0.00	4	0	0	0	3	3	2	0	0	1	6

ALL-STAR GAME RECORD

Year League	W	L	Pct.	ERA	GS	CG	ShO	Sv.	IP	H	R	ER	BB	SO
2000— American	0	0	...	9.00	0	0	0	0	1	2	1	1	1	0

IZTURIS, CESAR — 2B/SS — DODGERS

PERSONAL: Born February 10, 1980, in Lara, Venezuela. ... 5-9/175. ... Bats both, throws right. ... Full name: Cesar D. Izturis.

TRANSACTIONS/CAREER NOTES: Signed as non-drafted free agent by Toronto Blue Jays organization (July 11, 1996). ... Traded by Blue Jays with P Paul Quantrill to Los Angeles Dodgers for P Luke Prokopec and P Chad Ricketts (December 13, 2001).

STATISTICAL NOTES: Led South Atlantic League shortstops with 183 assists and .951 fielding percentage in 1998. ... Led International League shortstops with 638 total chances and 87 double plays in 2000.

						BATTING								FIELDING		
Year Team (League)	Pos.	G	AB	R	H	2B	3B	HR	RBI	Avg.	BB	SO	SB	PO	A	E	Avg.
1997— St. Catharines (NY-P) .	2B-SS	70	231	32	44	3	0	1	11	.190	15	27	6	115	194	16	.951
1998— Hagerstown (S.Atl.).....	SS-2B-3B	130	413	56	108	13	1	1	38	.262	20	43	20	‡190	379	29	‡.952
1999— Dunedin (FSL)	SS-2B-3B	131	536	77	165	28	12	3	77	.308	22	58	32	224	437	21	.969
2000— Syracuse (I.L.)............	SS	132	435	54	95	16	5	0	27	.218	20	44	21	*231	395	12	*.981
2001— Syracuse (I.L.)............	SS-2B	87	342	32	100	16	3	2	35	.292	10	22	24	154	251	16	.962
— Toronto (A.L.)	2B-SS	46	134	19	36	6	2	2	9	.269	2	15	8	73	121	3	.985
Major League totals (1 year)		46	134	19	36	6	2	2	9	.269	2	15	8	73	121	3	.985

JACKSON, DAMIAN — SS — PADRES

PERSONAL: Born August 6, 1973, in Los Angeles. ... 5-11/185. ... Bats right, throws right. ... Full name: Damian Jacques Jackson.

HIGH SCHOOL: Ygnacio Valley (Concord, Calif.).

JUNIOR COLLEGE: Laney (Calif.).

TRANSACTIONS/CAREER NOTES: Selected by Cleveland Indians organization in 44th round of free-agent draft (June 3, 1991). ... Traded by Indians with P Danny Graves, P Jim Crowell and P Scott Winchester to Cincinnati Reds for P John Smiley and IF Jeff Branson (July 31, 1997). ... Traded by Reds with OF Reggie Sanders and P Josh Harris to San Diego Padres for OF Greg Vaughn and OF/1B Mark Sweeney (February 2, 1999). ... On San Diego disabled list (May 13-June 22, 2001); included rehabilitation assignment to Portland (June 18-21).

STATISTICAL NOTES: Led Appalachian League shortstops with 342 total chances and 45 double plays in 1992. ... Led Eastern League shortstops with 241 putouts, 446 assists, 54 errors, 741 total chances and 85 double plays in 1994. ... Led Eastern League in caught stealing with 22 in 1995. ... Tied for Eastern League lead in double plays by shortstop with 80 in 1995. ... Led American Association shortstops with 635 total chances and 84 double plays in 1996. ... Led International League shortstops with 227 putouts, 434 assists, 44 errors, 705 total chances and 101 double plays in 1998. ... Career major league grand slams: 2.

						BATTING								FIELDING		
Year Team (League)	Pos.	G	AB	R	H	2B	3B	HR	RBI	Avg.	BB	SO	SB	PO	A	E	Avg.
1992— Burlington (Appl.).......	SS	62	226	32	56	12	1	0	23	.248	32	31	29	*102	*217	23	*.933
1993— Columbus (S.Atl.).......	SS	108	350	70	94	19	3	6	45	.269	41	61	26	191	324	52	.908
1994— Canton/Akron (East.)..	SS-OF	138	531	85	143	29	5	5	60	.269	60	121	37	†241	†446	†54	.927
1995— Canton/Akron (East.)..	SS	131	484	67	120	20	2	3	34	.248	65	103	40	*220	337	*36	.939
1996— Buffalo (A.A.)............	SS	133	452	77	116	15	1	12	49	.257	48	78	24	*203	*403	29	.954
— Cleveland (A.L.)..........	SS	5	10	2	3	2	0	0	1	.300	1	4	0	3	13	0	1.000
1997— Buffalo (A.A.).............	SS-2B-OF	73	266	51	78	12	0	4	13	.293	37	45	20	128	246	23	.942
— Cleveland (A.L.)..........	SS-2B	8	9	2	1	0	0	0	0	.111	0	1	1	7	7	0	1.000
— Indianapolis (A.A.)■..	2B-SS	19	71	12	19	6	1	0	7	.268	10	17	4	36	55	5	.948
— Cincinnati (N.L.)	SS-2B	12	27	6	6	2	1	1	2	.222	4	7	1	12	21	1	.971
1998— Indianapolis (I.L.)........	SS-OF	131	517	102	135	36	10	6	49	.261	62	125	25	†230	†435	†44	.938
— Cincinnati (N.L.)	SS-OF	13	38	4	12	5	0	0	7	.316	6	4	2	20	21	1	.976
1999— San Diego (N.L.)■	SS-2B-OF	133	388	56	87	20	2	9	39	.224	53	105	34	174	303	26	.948
2000— San Diego (N.L.)	SS-2B-OF	138	470	68	120	27	6	6	37	.255	62	108	28	234	362	25	.960
2001— San Diego (N.L.)	2B-SS-OF	122	440	67	106	21	6	4	38	.241	44	128	23	245	329	8	.986
— Portland (PCL)	SS	3	10	4	3	3	0	0	0	.300	3	1	0	3	11	0	1.000
American League totals (2 years)		13	19	4	4	2	0	0	1	.211	1	5	1	10	20	0	1.000
National League totals (5 years)		418	1363	201	331	75	15	20	123	.243	169	352	88	685	1036	61	.966
Major League totals (6 years)		431	1382	205	335	77	15	20	124	.242	170	357	89	695	1056	61	.966

PERSONAL: Born December 22, 1964, in Houston. ... 6-2/225. ... Throws right, bats right. ... Full name: Michael Ray Jackson.
HIGH SCHOOL: Forest Brook (Houston).
JUNIOR COLLEGE: Hill Junior College (Texas).
TRANSACTIONS/CAREER NOTES: Selected by Philadelphia Phillies organization in 29th round of free-agent draft (June 6, 1983); did not sign. ... Selected by Phillies organization in secondary phase of free-agent draft (January 17, 1984). ... On Philadelphia disabled list (August 6-21, 1987). ... Traded by Phillies with OF Glenn Wilson and OF Dave Brundage to Seattle Mariners for OF Phil Bradley and P Tim Fortugno (December 9, 1987). ... Traded by Mariners with P Bill Swift and P Dave Burba to San Francisco Giants for OF Kevin Mitchell and P Mike Remlinger (December 11, 1991). ... On disabled list (July 24-August 9, 1993; June 17-July 2 and July 7, 1994-remainder of season). ... Granted free agency (October 17, 1994). ... Signed by Cincinnati Reds (April 8, 1995). ... On Cincinnati disabled list (April 20-June 5, 1995); included rehabilitation assignments to Chattanooga (May 21-30) and Indianapolis (May 30-June 5). ... Granted free agency (November 3, 1995). ... Signed by Mariners (February 2, 1996). ... Granted free agency (October 30, 1996). ... Signed by Cleveland Indians (December 12, 1996). ... Granted free agency (October 28, 1999). ... Signed by Phillies (December 7, 1999). ... On disabled list (March 31, 2000-entire season). ... Granted free agency (October 14, 2000). ... Signed by Houston Astros (December 14, 2000). ... Granted free agency (November 5, 2001). ... Signed by Minnesota Twins organization (January 23, 2002).
STATISTICAL NOTES: Led Carolina League with seven balks in 1985. ... Tied for N.L. lead with eight balks in 1987. ... Tied for A.L. lead with three balks in 1998.
MISCELLANEOUS: Holds Seattle Mariners all-time record for most games pitched (335).

Year League	W	L	Pct.	ERA	G	GS	CG	ShO	Sv.	IP	H	R	ER	BB	SO
1984— Spartanburg (S.Atl.)	7	2	.778	2.68	14	0	0	0	0	80²/₃	53	35	24	50	77
1985— Peninsula (Caro.)	7	9	.438	4.60	31	18	0	0	1	125¹/₃	127	71	64	53	96
1986— Reading (East.)..................	2	3	.400	1.66	30	0	0	0	6	43¹/₃	25	9	8	22	42
— Portland (PCL)............	3	1	.750	3.18	17	0	0	0	3	22²/₃	18	8	8	13	23
— Philadelphia (N.L.).............	0	0	...	3.38	9	0	0	0	0	13¹/₃	12	5	5	4	3
1987— Philadelphia (N.L.).............	3	10	.231	4.20	55	7	0	0	1	109¹/₃	88	55	51	56	93
— Maine (I.L.)................	1	0	1.000	0.82	2	2	0	0	0	11	9	2	1	5	13
1988— Seattle (A.L.)■............	6	5	.545	2.63	62	0	0	0	4	99¹/₃	74	37	29	43	76
1989— Seattle (A.L.)............	4	6	.400	3.17	65	0	0	0	7	99¹/₃	81	43	35	54	94
1990— Seattle (A.L.)............	5	7	.417	4.54	63	0	0	0	3	77¹/₃	64	42	39	44	69
1991— Seattle (A.L.)............	7	7	.500	3.25	72	0	0	0	14	88²/₃	64	35	32	34	74
1992— San Francisco (N.L.)■........	6	6	.500	3.73	67	0	0	0	2	82	76	35	34	33	80
1993— San Francisco (N.L.)	6	6	.500	3.03	*81	0	0	0	1	77¹/₃	58	28	26	24	70
1994— San Francisco (N.L.)	3	2	.600	1.49	36	0	0	0	4	42¹/₃	23	8	7	11	51
1995— Chattanooga (Sou.)■..........	0	0	0.00	3	2	0	0	0	3	2	0	0	0	2
— Indianapolis (A.A.)..........	0	0	...	0.00	2	1	0	0	0	2	0	0	0	0	1
— Cincinnati (N.L.)............	6	1	.857	2.39	40	0	0	0	2	49	38	13	13	19	41
1996— Seattle (A.L.)■............	1	1	.500	3.63	73	0	0	0	6	72	61	32	29	24	70
1997— Cleveland (A.L.)■............	2	5	.286	3.24	71	0	0	0	15	75	59	33	27	29	74
1998— Cleveland (A.L.).............	1	1	.500	1.55	69	0	0	0	40	64	43	11	11	13	55
1999— Cleveland (A.L.).............	3	4	.429	4.06	72	0	0	0	39	68²/₃	60	32	31	26	55
2000— Philadelphia (N.L.)■						Did not play.									
2001— Houston (N.L.)■	5	3	.625	4.70	67	0	0	0	4	69	68	36	36	22	46
A.L. totals (8 years)	29	36	.446	3.25	547	0	0	0	128	644¹/₃	506	265	233	267	567
N.L. totals (7 years)	29	28	.509	3.50	355	7	0	0	14	442¹/₃	363	180	172	169	384
Major League totals (15 years)	58	64	.475	3.35	902	7	0	0	142	1086²/₃	869	445	405	436	951

DIVISION SERIES RECORD

NOTES: Shares A.L. single-series record for most saves—3.

Year League	W	L	Pct.	ERA	G	GS	CG	ShO	Sv.	IP	H	R	ER	BB	SO
1995— Cincinnati (N.L.)	0	0	...	0.00	3	0	0	0	0	3²/₃	4	0	0	0	1
1997— Cleveland (A.L.)................	1	0	1.000	0.00	4	0	0	0	0	4¹/₃	3	0	0	1	5
1998— Cleveland (A.L.)................	0	0	...	4.50	3	0	0	0	3	4	3	2	2	1	1
1999— Cleveland (A.L.)................	0	0	...	4.50	2	0	0	0	0	2	2	1	1	1	1
2001— Houston (N.L.)	0	1	.000	27.00	2	0	0	0	0	²/₃	3	3	2	0	1
Division series totals (5 years)	1	1	.500	3.07	14	0	0	0	3	14²/₃	15	6	5	3	9

CHAMPIONSHIP SERIES RECORD

Year League	W	L	Pct.	ERA	G	GS	CG	ShO	Sv.	IP	H	R	ER	BB	SO
1995— Cincinnati (N.L.)	0	1	.000	23.14	3	0	0	0	0	2¹/₃	5	6	6	4	1
1997— Cleveland (A.L.)................	0	0	...	0.00	5	0	0	0	0	4¹/₃	1	0	0	1	7
1998— Cleveland (A.L.)................	0	0	...	0.00	1	0	0	0	1	1	0	0	0	0	2
Champ. series totals (3 years)	0	1	.000	7.04	9	0	0	0	1	7²/₃	6	6	6	5	10

WORLD SERIES RECORD

Year League	W	L	Pct.	ERA	G	GS	CG	ShO	Sv.	IP	H	R	ER	BB	SO
1997— Cleveland (A.L.)................	0	0	...	1.93	4	0	0	0	0	4²/₃	5	1	1	3	4

PERSONAL: Born November 11, 1971, in Orlando, Fla. ... 6-3/185. ... Bats left, throws left. ... Full name: Ryan De Witte Jackson.
HIGH SCHOOL: Cardinal Mooney (Sarasota, Fla.).
COLLEGE: Duke.
TRANSACTIONS/CAREER NOTES: Selected by Florida Marlins organization in seventh round of free-agent draft (June 2, 1994). ... On Kane County disabled list (April 5-August 1, 1996). ... On Portland disabled list (August 1-26, 1996). ... Claimed on waivers by Seattle Mariners

(April 2, 1999). ... Released by Mariners (December 21, 1999). ... Signed by Tampa Bay Devil Rays organization (January 14, 2000). ... Granted free agency (October 18, 2000). ... Signed by Detroit Tigers organization (January 18, 2001). ... Granted free agency (October 15, 2001).

STATISTICAL NOTES: Tied for Midwest League lead with seven intentional bases on balls received in 1995. ... Led International League first basemen with 1,303 total chances and 112 double plays in 2000. ... Career major league grand slams: 1.

Year Team (League)	Pos.	G	AB	R	H	2B	3B	HR	RBI	Avg.	BB	SO	SB	PO	A	E	Avg.
1994— Elmira (NY-Penn)	OF-1B	72	276	46	80	18	1	6	41	.290	22	40	4	176	15	7	.965
1995— Kane County (Midw.)..	OF-1B	132	471	78	138	*39	6	10	82	.293	67	74	13	571	32	7	.989
1996— Brevard County (FSL).	1B	6	26	4	8	2	0	1	4	.308	1	7	1	28	2	2	.938
— GC Marlins (GCL)	1B-OF	8	26	5	9	0	0	0	7	.346	1	3	2	35	3	0	1.000
1997— Portland (East.)	OF-1B	134	491	87	153	28	4	26	98	.312	51	85	2	227	9	5	.979
1998— Florida (N.L.)	1B-OF-DH	111	260	26	65	15	1	5	31	.250	20	73	1	341	21	10	.973
— Charlotte (I.L.)	1B-OF	13	50	5	19	4	0	2	11	.380	4	14	2	57	6	0	1.000
1999— Tacoma (PCL)■	1B-DH-OF	105	409	57	126	25	2	8	62	.308	36	64	12	714	56	9	.988
— Seattle (A.L.)	1B-OF	32	68	4	16	3	0	0	10	.235	6	19	3	167	11	2	.989
2000— Durham (I.L.)■	1B	139	502	69	156	38	2	18	85	.311	50	112	6	*1195	*96	12	.991
2001— Detroit (A.L.)■	1B-OF-DH	79	118	19	25	4	2	2	11	.212	5	26	3	159	12	2	.988
— Toledo (I.L.)	OF-1B	9	35	2	10	1	0	1	9	.286	5	6	0	21	0	1	.955
American League totals (2 years)		111	186	23	41	7	2	2	21	.220	11	45	6	326	23	4	.989
National League totals (1 year)		111	260	26	65	15	1	5	31	.250	20	73	1	341	21	10	.973
Major League totals (3 years)		222	446	49	106	22	3	7	52	.238	31	118	7	667	44	14	.981

JACQUEZ, TOM — P — WHITE SOX

PERSONAL: Born December 29, 1975, in Stockton, Calif. ... 6-2/195. ... Throws left, bats left. ... Full name: Thomas Patrick Jacquez.
HIGH SCHOOL: Lincoln (Stockton, Calif.).
COLLEGE: UCLA.
TRANSACTIONS/CAREER NOTES: Selected by Philadelphia Phillies organization in sixth round of free-agent draft (June 3, 1997). ... On disabled list (May 3-17, 2001). ... Claimed on waivers by Chicago White Sox (January 17, 2002).

Year League	W	L	Pct.	ERA	G	GS	CG	ShO	Sv.	IP	H	R	ER	BB	SO
1997— Batavia (NY-Penn)	2	1	.667	2.42	4	4	0	0	0	22 1/3	20	6	6	2	20
— Piedmont (S.Atl.)	2	4	.333	4.63	8	8	0	0	0	44 2/3	45	29	23	13	26
1998— Clearwater (FSL)	9	11	.450	4.30	29	•28	2	1	0	169 2/3	*215	102	81	31	108
1999— Reading (East.)	6	5	.545	5.28	38	14	0	0	1	122 2/3	149	84	72	32	68
— Scranton/W.B. (I.L.)	0	1	.000	2.45	3	0	0	0	0	3 2/3	4	1	1	0	4
2000— Reading (East.)	0	3	.000	2.96	13	0	0	0	3	27 1/3	26	11	9	9	21
— Scranton/W.B. (I.L.)	5	1	.833	1.98	35	1	0	0	1	54 2/3	53	15	12	20	34
— Philadelphia (N.L.)	0	0	...	11.05	9	0	0	0	1	7 1/3	10	9	9	3	6
2001— Scranton/W.B. (I.L.)	10	6	.625	3.13	33	9	1	0	0	109 1/3	100	43	38	29	86
Major League totals (1 year)	0	0	...	11.05	9	0	0	0	1	7 1/3	10	9	9	3	6

JAHA, JOHN — DH/1B

PERSONAL: Born May 27, 1966, in Portland, Ore. ... 6-1/217. ... Bats right, throws right. ... Full name: John Emil Jaha. ... Name pronounced JAH-ha.
HIGH SCHOOL: David Douglas (Portland, Ore.).
TRANSACTIONS/CAREER NOTES: Selected by Milwaukee Brewers organization in 14th round of free-agent draft (June 4, 1984). ... On disabled list (April 6-August 1, 1990 and May 21-June 6, 1995). ... On Milwaukee disabled list (June 24-July 27, 1995); included rehabilitation assignments to Beloit (July 16-20) and New Orleans (July 20-27). ... On disabled list (June 3, 1997-remainder of season). ... On Milwaukee disabled list (April 23-June 7 and August 16-September 1, 1998); included rehabilitation assignment to Beloit (June 4-8). ... Granted free agency (October 26, 1998). ... Signed by Oakland Athletics organization (February 17, 1999). ... On Oakland disabled list (April 24-June 3 and July 9, 2000-remainder of season); included rehabilitation assignment to Sacramento (May 28-31) and Modesto (June 1-3). ... On Oakland disabled list (March 31-May 9 and May 16-June 18, 2001); included rehabilitation assignments to Sacramento (April 5-11, April 21-May 9 and June 11-18). ... Announced retirement (June 30, 2001).
RECORDS: Shares major league single-game record for most strikeouts (nine-inning game)—5 (April 20, 2000).
HONORS: Named Texas League Most Valuable Player (1991). ... Named A.L. Comeback Player of the Year by THE SPORTING NEWS (1999).
STATISTICAL NOTES: Led Northwest League with 144 total bases and tied for lead with four intentional bases on balls received in 1986. ... Led California League with 13 sacrifice flies in 1989. ... Led Texas League with 301 total bases, .619 slugging percentage and .438 on-base percentage in 1991. ... Led Texas League first basemen with 81 assists in 1991. ... Career major league grand slams: 7.

Year Team (League)	Pos.	G	AB	R	H	2B	3B	HR	RBI	Avg.	BB	SO	SB	PO	A	E	Avg.
1985— Helena (Pio.)	3B	24	68	13	18	3	0	2	14	.265	14	23	4	9	32	1	.976
1986— Tri-Cities (N'West)	1B-3B	•73	258	65	82	13	2	*15	67	.318	*70	75	9	352	101	18	.962
1987— Beloit (Midw.)	3B-1B-SS	122	376	68	101	22	0	7	47	.269	102	86	10	493	113	18	.971
1988— Stockton (Calif.)	1B	99	302	58	77	14	6	8	54	.255	69	85	10	793	60	5	*.994
1989— Stockton (Calif.)	1B-3B	140	479	83	140	26	5	25	91	.292	*112	115	8	1081	62	8	.993
1990— Stockton (Calif.)	DH	26	84	12	22	5	0	4	19	.262	18	25	0	...	...	...	...
1991— El Paso (Texas)	1B-3B	130	486	*121	167	38	3	*30	*134	.344	78	101	12	883	†87	10	.990
1992— Denver (A.A.)	1B	79	274	61	88	18	2	18	69	.321	50	60	6	654	50	7	.990
— Milwaukee (A.L.)	1B-DH-OF	47	133	17	30	3	1	2	10	.226	12	30	10	286	22	0	1.000
1993— Milwaukee (A.L.)	1B-3B-2B	153	515	78	136	21	0	19	70	.264	51	109	13	1187	128	10	.992
1994— Milwaukee (A.L.)	1B-DH	84	291	45	70	14	0	12	39	.241	32	75	3	660	47	8	.989
— New Orleans (A.A.)	1B-DH	18	62	8	25	7	1	2	16	.403	12	8	2	122	14	1	.993
1995— Milwaukee (A.L.)	1B-DH	88	316	59	99	20	2	20	65	.313	36	66	2	649	60	2	.997
— Beloit (Midw.)	DH	1	4	1	0	0	0	0	0	.000	0	1	0	0	0	0	...
— New Orleans (A.A.)	DH-1B	3	10	2	4	1	0	1	3	.400	2	1	0	9	2	0	1.000

Year	Team (League)	Pos.	G	AB	R	H	2B	3B	HR	RBI	Avg.	BB	SO	SB	PO	A	E	Avg.
										BATTING						FIELDING		
1996— Milwaukee (A.L.)	1B-DH	148	543	108	163	28	1	34	118	.300	85	118	3	676	58	6	.992
1997— Milwaukee (A.L.)	1B-DH	46	162	25	40	7	0	11	26	.247	25	40	1	220	14	2	.992
1998— Milwaukee (N.L.)	1B-DH	73	216	29	45	6	1	7	38	.208	49	66	1	441	23	3	.994
— Beloit (Midw.)	DH	2	4	1	0	0	0	0	0	.000	2	2	0	...	...	...	...
1999— Oakland (A.L.)■	DH-1B	142	457	93	126	23	0	35	111	.276	101	129	2	42	4	0	1.000
2000— Oakland (A.L.)	DH	33	97	14	17	1	0	1	5	.175	33	38	1	...	...	...	...
— Sacramento (PCL).....	DH	3	9	0	4	1	0	0	2	.444	4	2	0	...	...	...	...
— Modesto (Calif.)	DH	1	2	1	0	0	0	0	0	.000	2	1	0	...	...	...	...
2001— Sacramento (PCL).....	DH	23	84	9	16	5	0	4	11	.190	11	32	0	...	...	...	...
— Oakland (A.L.)	DH	12	45	2	4	3	0	0	8	.089	6	15	0	...	...	...	...
American League totals (9 years)		753	2559	441	685	120	4	134	452	.268	381	620	35	3720	333	28	.993
National League totals (1 year)		73	216	29	45	6	1	7	38	.208	49	66	1	441	23	3	.994
Major League totals (10 years)		826	2775	470	730	126	5	141	490	.263	430	686	36	4161	356	31	.993

ALL-STAR GAME RECORD

Year	League	Pos.	AB	R	H	2B	3B	HR	RBI	Avg.	BB	SO	SB	PO	A	E	Avg.
							BATTING								FIELDING		
1999— American	PH-DH	1	0	0	0	0	0	0	.000	0	1	0	...	...	...	...

JAMES, DELVIN   P   DEVIL RAYS

PERSONAL: Born January 3, 1978, in Nacogdoches, Texas. ... 6-4/222. ... Throws right, bats right. ... Full name: Delvin Dewayne James.
HIGH SCHOOL: Nacogdoches (Texas).
TRANSACTIONS/CAREER NOTES: Selected by Tampa Bay Devil Rays organization in 14th round of free-agent draft (June 4, 1996).

Year	League	W	L	Pct.	ERA	G	GS	CG	ShO	Sv.	IP	H	R	ER	BB	SO
1996— GC Devil Rays (GCL)	2	8	.200	8.87	11	11	1	0	0	47²/₃	64	52	47	21	40
1997— Princeton (Appl.)	4	4	.500	4.94	20	5	0	0	0	58¹/₃	71	57	32	24	46
1998— St. Petersburg (FSL)	0	0	...	10.80	1	0	0	0	0	1²/₃	2	2	2	0	0
— Charleston, S.C. (S.Atl.)	2	0	1.000	5.40	7	0	0	0	0	8¹/₃	12	5	5	2	8
— Hudson Valley (NY-Penn)....	7	4	.636	2.98	15	15	0	0	0	81²/₃	71	39	27	32	64
1999— Charleston, S.C. (S.Atl.)	8	8	.500	3.64	25	25	1	0	0	158¹/₃	142	76	64	33	106
— St. Petersburg (FSL)	3	0	1.000	3.18	3	2	0	0	0	17	18	6	6	4	6
2000— St. Petersburg (FSL)	7	9	.438	4.26	22	22	3	1	0	137¹/₃	142	74	65	27	74
— Orlando (Sou.)	1	3	.250	2.92	6	6	1	0	0	37	31	15	12	7	26
2001— Orlando (Sou.)	2	0	1.000	1.65	7	7	0	0	0	43²/₃	25	8	8	9	31
— Durham (I.L.)	3	7	.300	4.80	31	9	1	0	0	84¹/₃	99	51	45	27	51

JAMES, MIKE   P

PERSONAL: Born August 15, 1967, in Fort Walton Beach, Fla. ... 6-3/180. ... Throws right, bats right. ... Full name: Michael Elmo James.
HIGH SCHOOL: Fort Walton Beach (Fla.).
JUNIOR COLLEGE: Lurleen B. Wallace State Junior College (Ala.).
TRANSACTIONS/CAREER NOTES: Selected by Los Angeles Dodgers organization in 43rd round of free-agent draft (June 2, 1987). ... On Albuquerque disabled list (July 12-August 26, 1992). ... On Vero Beach disabled list (July 2-9, 1993). ... Traded by Dodgers to California Angels for OF Reggie Williams (October 26, 1993). ... On California disabled list (May 11-June 1, 1995); included rehabilitation assignment to Lake Elsinore (May 25-June 1). ... Angels franchise renamed Anaheim Angels for 1997 season. ... On disabled list (July 3-27, 1997 and May 5, 1998-remainder of season). ... On Anaheim disabled list (March 24-September 7, 1999); included rehabilitation assignment to Lake Elsinore (July 31-September 3). ... Released by Angels (September 7, 1999). ... Signed by St. Louis Cardinals organization (October 15, 1999). ... On St. Louis disabled list (May 26-June 20, 2000); included rehabilitation assignment to Memphis (June 18-20). ... On St. Louis disabled list (July 7-September 1, 2001); included rehabilitation assignment to Memphis (August 8-September 1). ... Granted free agency (November 5, 2001).
MISCELLANEOUS: Scored run in only appearance as pinch runner (2000).

Year	League	W	L	Pct.	ERA	G	GS	CG	ShO	Sv.	IP	H	R	ER	BB	SO
1988— Great Falls (Pio.)	7	1	*.875	3.76	14	12	0	0	0	67	61	36	28	41	59
1989— Bakersfield (Calif.)	11	8	.579	3.78	27	27	1	1	0	159²/₃	144	82	67	78	127
1990— San Antonio (Texas)..........	11	4	.733	3.32	26	26	3	0	0	157	144	73	58	78	97
1991— Albuquerque (PCL)............	1	3	.250	6.60	13	8	0	0	0	45	51	36	33	30	39
— San Antonio (Texas)...........	9	5	.643	4.53	15	15	2	1	0	89¹/₃	88	54	45	51	74
1992— Albuquerque (PCL)............	2	1	.667	5.59	18	6	0	0	1	46²/₃	55	35	29	22	33
— San Antonio (Texas)...........	2	1	.667	2.67	8	8	0	0	0	54	39	16	16	20	52
1993— Albuquerque (PCL)............	1	0	1.000	7.47	16	0	0	0	2	31¹/₃	38	28	26	19	32
— Vero Beach (FSL)	2	3	.400	4.92	30	1	0	0	5	60¹/₃	54	37	33	33	60
1994— Vancouver (PCL)■............	5	3	.625	5.22	37	10	0	0	8	91¹/₃	101	56	53	34	66
1995— California (A.L.)	3	0	1.000	3.88	46	0	0	0	0	55²/₃	49	27	24	26	36
— Lake Elsinore (Calif.)	0	0	...	9.53	5	1	0	0	0	5²/₃	9	6	6	3	8
1996— California (A.L.)	5	5	.500	2.67	69	0	0	0	1	81	62	27	24	42	65
1997— Anaheim (A.L.)	5	5	.500	4.31	58	0	0	0	7	62²/₃	69	32	30	28	57
1998— Anaheim (A.L.)	0	0	...	1.93	11	0	0	0	0	14	10	3	3	7	12
1999— Lake Elsinore (Calif.)	0	0	...	5.79	3	3	0	0	0	9¹/₃	12	6	6	0	6
— Edmonton (PCL)	1	2	.333	8.64	8	1	0	0	0	8¹/₃	16	14	8	2	3
2000— Memphis (PCL)■.............	2	1	.667	0.93	8	0	0	0	1	9²/₃	6	3	1	4	8
— St. Louis (N.L.).................	2	2	.500	3.16	51	0	0	0	2	51¹/₃	40	22	18	24	41
2001— St. Louis (N.L.).................	1	2	.333	5.21	40	0	0	0	0	38	43	24	22	17	26
— Memphis (PCL).................	0	2	.000	4.00	10	0	0	0	0	9	10	6	4	4	9
A.L. totals (4 years)	13	10	.565	3.42	184	0	0	0	9	213¹/₃	190	89	81	103	170
N.L. totals (2 years)	3	4	.429	4.03	91	0	0	0	2	89¹/₃	83	46	40	41	67
Major League totals (6 years)	16	14	.533	3.60	275	0	0	0	11	302²/₃	273	135	121	144	237

Year League	W	L	Pct.	ERA	G	GS	CG	ShO	Sv.	IP	H	R	ER	BB	SO
2000— St. Louis (N.L.)...................	1	0	1.000	0.00	2	0	0	0	0	4 1/3	1	0	0	1	1

CHAMPIONSHIP SERIES RECORD

Year League	W	L	Pct.	ERA	G	GS	CG	ShO	Sv.	IP	H	R	ER	BB	SO
2000— St. Louis (N.L.)...................	0	0	...	15.43	4	0	0	0	0	2 1/3	5	4	4	1	0

JAMISON, RYAN   P   ASTROS

PERSONAL: Born January 5, 1978, in Rockford, Ill. ... 6-3/185. ... Throws right, bats right. ... Full name: Ryan Franklin Jamison.
HIGH SCHOOL: El Cajon (Calif.).
COLLEGE: Missouri.
TRANSACTIONS/CAREER NOTES: Selected by Houston Astros organization in 17th round of free-agent draft (June 2, 1999). ... On Lexington disabled list (May 5-June 4, 2001). ... On Round Rock disabled list (July 23-August 16, 2001).

Year League	W	L	Pct.	ERA	G	GS	CG	ShO	Sv.	IP	H	R	ER	BB	SO
1999— Auburn (NY-Penn).............	5	3	.625	4.11	15	15	0	0	0	87 2/3	83	45	40	36	83
2000— Michigan (Midw.)	8	3	.727	2.10	41	7	0	0	7	98 2/3	66	32	23	38	95
2001— Round Rock (Texas)..........	5	2	.714	3.50	10	9	0	0	0	46 1/3	49	25	18	23	32
— Lexington (S.Atl.)	4	2	.667	2.28	9	8	0	0	0	55 1/3	40	17	14	9	63

JARVIS, KEVIN   P   PADRES

PERSONAL: Born August 1, 1969, in Lexington, Ky. ... 6-2/200. ... Throws right, bats left. ... Full name: Kevin Thomas Jarvis.
HIGH SCHOOL: Tates Creek (Lexington, Ky.).
COLLEGE: Wake Forest.
TRANSACTIONS/CAREER NOTES: Selected by Cincinnati Reds organization in 21st round of free-agent draft (June 3, 1991). ... Claimed on waivers by Detroit Tigers (May 2, 1997). ... Claimed on waivers by Minnesota Twins (May 9, 1997). ... Claimed on waivers by Tigers (June 17, 1997). ... On Detroit disabled list (June 25-July 14, 1997); included rehabilitation assignment to Toledo (July 4-14). ... Released by Tigers (December 12, 1997). ... Signed by Chunichi Dragons of the Japan Central League (January 23, 1998). ... Signed by Reds organization (August 27, 1998). ... Released by Reds (September 9, 1998). ... Signed by Oakland Athletics organization (January 4, 1999). ... On Oakland disabled list (April 19-June 4, 1999); included rehabilitation assignment to Modesto (May 28-June 4). ... Granted free agency (October 8, 1999). ... Signed by Colorado Rockies organization (December 1, 1999). ... On Colorado disabled list (July 28-September 1, 2000); included rehabilitation assignment to Colorado Springs (August 12-September 1). ... Granted free agency (December 21, 2000). ... Signed by San Diego Padres (January 5, 2001).
RECORDS: Shares N.L. single-inning record for most consecutive home runs allowed—3 (August 3, 2001).
STATISTICAL NOTES: Tied for N.L. lead with 37 home runs allowed in 2001.
MISCELLANEOUS: Appeared in one game as pinch runner (2000). ... Appeared in two games as pinch hitter (2001).

Year League	W	L	Pct.	ERA	G	GS	CG	ShO	Sv.	IP	H	R	ER	BB	SO
1991— Princeton (Appl.)...............	5	6	.455	2.42	13	13	4	•1	0	85 2/3	73	34	23	29	79
1992— Cedar Rapids (Midw.)	0	0	...	0.00	1	0	0	0	0	1	1	0	0	0	0
— Charleston, W.Va. (S.Atl.)...	6	8	.429	3.11	28	18	2	1	0	133	123	59	46	37	131
1993— Winston-Salem (Caro.).......	8	7	.533	3.41	21	20	2	1	0	145	133	68	55	48	101
— Chattanooga (Sou.)...........	3	1	.750	1.69	7	3	2	0	0	37 1/3	26	7	7	11	18
1994— Cincinnati (N.L.)................	1	1	.500	7.13	6	3	0	0	0	17 2/3	22	14	14	5	10
— Indianapolis (A.A.).............	10	2	•.833	3.54	21	20	2	0	0	132 1/3	136	55	52	34	90
1995— Indianapolis (A.A.).............	4	2	.667	4.45	10	10	2	1	0	60 2/3	62	33	30	18	37
— Cincinnati (N.L.)	3	4	.429	5.70	19	11	1	1	0	79	91	56	50	32	33
1996— Indianapolis (A.A.).............	4	3	.571	5.06	8	8	0	0	0	42 2/3	45	27	24	12	32
— Cincinnati (N.L.)	8	9	.471	5.98	24	20	2	1	0	120 1/3	152	93	80	43	63
1997— Cincinnati (N.L.)	0	1	.000	10.13	9	0	0	0	1	13 1/3	21	16	15	7	12
— Toledo (I.L.)■..................	0	1	.000	6.75	2	2	0	0	0	8	7	6	6	4	5
— Minnesota (A.L.)■	0	0	...	12.46	6	2	0	0	0	13	23	18	18	8	9
— Detroit (A.L.)■..................	0	3	.000	5.40	17	3	0	0	0	41 2/3	55	28	25	14	27
1998— Chunichi (Jap. Cen.)■........	1	2	.333	4.41	4	3	0	0	0	16 1/3	18	8	8	5	7
— Indianapolis (I.L.)■............	1	0	1.000	9.00	2	2	0	0	0	7	10	7	7	1	5
1999— Vancouver (PCL)■.............	10	2	.833	3.41	17	16	2	1	0	103	110	47	39	26	64
— Oakland (A.L.)	0	1	.000	11.57	4	1	0	0	0	14	28	19	18	6	11
— Modesto (Calif.)	0	0	...	1.29	2	2	0	0	0	7	4	1	1	1	10
2000— Colorado Springs (PCL)■..	3	2	.600	0.69	7	7	0	0	0	39	18	6	3	13	18
— Colorado (N.L.)	3	4	.429	5.95	24	19	0	0	0	115	138	83	76	33	60
2001— San Diego (N.L.)■	12	11	.522	4.79	32	32	1	1	0	193 1/3	189	107	103	49	133
A.L. totals (2 years)	0	4	.000	8.00	27	6	0	0	0	68 2/3	106	65	61	28	47
N.L. totals (6 years)	27	30	.474	5.65	114	85	4	3	1	538 1/3	613	369	338	169	311
Major League totals (7 years)	27	34	.443	5.91	141	91	4	3	1	607 1/3	719	434	399	197	358

JAVIER, STAN   OF

PERSONAL: Born January 9, 1964, in San Francisco de Macoris, Dominican Republic. ... 6-0/200. ... Bats both, throws right. ... Full name: Stanley Julian Javier. ... Son of Julian Javier, infielder with St. Louis Cardinals (1960-71) and Cincinnati Reds (1972). ... Name pronounced HA-vee-AIR.
HIGH SCHOOL: La Altagracia (San Francisco de Macoris, Dominican Republic).

TRANSACTIONS/CAREER NOTES: Signed as non-drafted free agent by St. Louis Cardinals organization (March 26, 1981). ... Traded by Cardinals with SS Bobby Meacham to New York Yankees for OF Bob Helsom, P Marty Mason and P Steve Fincher (December 14, 1982). ... Traded by Yankees with P Jay Howell, P Jose Rijo, P Eric Plunk and P Tim Birtsas to Oakland Athletics for OF Rickey Henderson, P Bert Bradley and cash (December 5, 1984). ... On Oakland disabled list (August 3-September 1, 1987); included rehabilitation assignment to Tacoma (August 20-September 1). ... On disabled list (August 18-September 2, 1988; and July 7-24, 1989). ... Traded by A's to Los Angeles Dodgers for 2B Willie Randolph (May 13, 1990). ... Traded by Dodgers to Philadelphia Phillies for P Steve Searcy and a player to be named later (July 2, 1992); Dodgers acquired IF Julio Peguero to complete deal (July 28, 1992). ... Granted free agency (October 27, 1992). ... Signed by California Angels organization (January 15, 1993). ... Granted free agency (October 29, 1993). ... Signed by A's (December 7, 1993). ... Granted free agency (November 2, 1995). ... Signed by San Francisco Giants (December 8, 1995). ... On San Francisco disabled list (April 13-29 and July 17, 1996-remainder of season); included rehabilitation assignment to San Jose (April 26-29). ... On restricted list (April 13-18, 1997). ... Granted free agency (October 28, 1997). ... Re-signed by Giants (November 26, 1997). ... Traded by Giants to Houtson Astros for P Joe Messman (August 31, 1999). ... Granted free agency (October 28, 1999). ... Signed by Seattle Mariners (December 20, 1999). ... On disabled list (July 3-20, 2001). ... Granted free agency (November 5, 2001).

STATISTICAL NOTES: Led A.L. outfielders with 1.000 fielding percentage in 1995.

Year	Team (League)	Pos.	G	AB	R	H	2B	3B	HR	RBI	Avg.	BB	SO	SB	PO	A	E	Avg.
1981—	Johnson City (Appl.) ..	OF	53	144	30	36	5	4	3	19	.250	40	33	2	53	2	3	.948
1982—	Johnson City (Appl.) ..	OF	57	185	45	51	3	•4	8	36	.276	42	55	11	94	8	4	.962
1983—	Greensboro (S.Atl.)■ .	OF	129	489	109	152	*34	6	12	77	.311	75	95	33	250	10	15	.945
1984—	New York (A.L.)..........	OF	7	7	1	1	0	0	0	0	.143	0	1	0	3	0	0	1.000
—	Nashville (Sou.)..........	OF	76	262	40	76	17	4	7	38	.290	39	57	17	202	4	7	.967
—	Columbus (I.L.)	OF	32	99	12	22	3	1	0	7	.222	12	26	1	77	4	2	.976
1985—	Huntsville (Sou.)■	OF	140	486	105	138	22	8	9	64	.284	*112	92	61	363	8	7	.981
1986—	Tacoma (PCL)	OF-1B	69	248	50	81	16	2	4	51	.327	47	46	18	172	9	6	.968
—	Oakland (A.L.)	OF-DH	59	114	13	23	8	0	0	8	.202	16	27	8	118	1	0	1.000
1987—	Oakland (A.L.)	OF-1B-DH	81	151	22	28	3	1	2	9	.185	19	33	3	149	5	3	.981
—	Tacoma (PCL)	OF-1B	15	51	6	11	2	0	0	2	.216	4	12	3	26	0	2	.929
1988—	Oakland (A.L.)	OF-1B-DH	125	397	49	102	13	3	2	35	.257	32	63	20	274	7	5	.983
1989—	Oakland (A.L.)	OF-2B-1B	112	310	42	77	12	3	1	28	.248	31	45	12	221	8	2	.991
1990—	Oakland (A.L.)	OF-DH	19	33	4	8	0	2	0	3	.242	3	6	0	19	0	0	1.000
—	Los Angeles (N.L.)■..	OF	104	276	56	84	9	4	3	24	.304	37	44	15	204	2	0	1.000
1991—	Los Angeles (N.L.)	OF-1B	121	176	21	36	5	3	1	11	.205	16	36	7	90	4	3	.969
1992—	Los Angeles (N.L.)	OF	56	58	6	11	3	0	1	5	.190	6	11	1	17	0	0	1.000
—	Philadelphia (N.L.)■..	OF	74	276	36	72	14	1	0	24	.261	31	43	17	212	7	3	.986
1993—	California (A.L.)■......OF-1B-2B-DH	92	237	33	69	10	4	3	28	.291	27	33	12	167	4	4	.977
1994—	Oakland (A.L.)■........	OF-1B-3B	109	419	75	114	23	0	10	44	.272	49	76	24	274	4	4	.986
1995—	Oakland (A.L.)	OF-3B	130	442	81	123	20	2	8	56	.278	49	63	36	332	3	0	†1.000
1996—	San Fran. (N.L.)■......	OF	71	274	44	74	25	0	2	22	.270	25	51	14	180	2	3	.984
—	San Jose (Calif.)........	OF-DH	3	5	1	2	0	0	0	1	.400	1	1	0	1	0	0	1.000
1997—	San Francisco (N.L.) ..	OF-1B	142	440	69	126	16	4	8	50	.286	56	70	25	279	2	7	.976
1998—	San Francisco (N.L.) ..	OF	135	417	63	121	13	5	4	49	.290	65	63	21	217	0	3	.986
1999—	San Francisco (N.L.) ..	OF-DH	112	333	49	92	15	1	3	30	.276	29	55	13	158	4	4	.976
—	Houston (N.L.)■	OF	20	64	12	21	4	1	0	4	.328	9	8	3	31	1	0	1.000
2000—	Seattle (A.L.)■..........	OF-DH-1B	105	342	61	94	18	5	5	40	.275	42	64	4	161	7	1	.994
2001—	Seattle (A.L.)	OF-1B-DH	89	281	44	82	14	1	4	33	.292	36	47	11	165	4	1	.994
American League totals (11 years)			928	2733	425	721	121	21	35	284	.264	304	458	130	1883	43	20	.990
National League totals (7 years)			835	2314	356	637	104	19	22	219	.275	274	381	116	1388	22	23	.984
Major League totals (17 years)			1763	5047	781	1358	225	40	57	503	.269	578	839	246	3271	65	43	.987

DIVISION SERIES RECORD

Year	Team (League)	Pos.	G	AB	R	H	2B	3B	HR	RBI	Avg.	BB	SO	SB	PO	A	E	Avg.
1997—	San Francisco (N.L.) ..	OF	3	12	2	5	1	0	0	1	.417	0	2	1	11	0	0	1.000
1999—	Houston (N.L.)	PH-OF	4	11	1	3	0	0	0	0	.273	1	1	0	4	0	0	1.000
2000—	Seattle (A.L.)	PH-OF	3	6	0	1	0	0	0	1	.167	0	3	0	4	0	0	1.000
2001—	Seattle (A.L.)	OF	4	8	2	2	1	0	0	0	.250	2	1	0	6	0	0	1.000
Division series totals (4 years)			14	37	5	11	2	0	0	2	.297	3	7	1	25	0	0	1.000

CHAMPIONSHIP SERIES RECORD

Year	Team (League)	Pos.	G	AB	R	H	2B	3B	HR	RBI	Avg.	BB	SO	SB	PO	A	E	Avg.
1988—	Oakland (A.L.)	OF-PR	2	4	0	2	0	0	0	1	.500	1	0	0	5	0	0	1.000
1989—	Oakland (A.L.)	OF	1	2	0	0	0	0	0	0	.000	0	1	0	1	0	0	1.000
2000—	Seattle (A.L.)	OF-PH	4	14	0	1	0	0	0	1	.071	0	4	0	4	0	0	1.000
2001—	Seattle (A.L.)	PH-OF	5	14	2	3	0	0	1	2	.214	1	3	1	9	0	0	1.000
Championship series totals (4 years)			12	34	2	6	0	0	1	4	.176	2	8	1	19	0	0	1.000

WORLD SERIES RECORD

NOTES: Member of World Series championship team (1989).

Year	Team (League)	Pos.	G	AB	R	H	2B	3B	HR	RBI	Avg.	BB	SO	SB	PO	A	E	Avg.
1988—	Oakland (A.L.)	PR-OF	3	4	0	2	0	0	0	2	.500	0	1	0	1	0	0	1.000
1989—	Oakland (A.L.)	OF	1	0	0	0	0	0	0	0	...	0	0	0	0	0	0	...
World Series totals (2 years)			4	4	0	2	0	0	0	2	.500	0	1	0	1	0	0	1.000

JENKINS, GEOFF   OF   BREWERS

PERSONAL: Born July 21, 1974, in Olympia, Wash. ... 6-1/206. ... Bats left, throws right. ... Full name: Geoffrey Scott Jenkins.
HIGH SCHOOL: Cordova Senior (Rancho Cordova, Calif.).
COLLEGE: Southern California.
TRANSACTIONS/CAREER NOTES: Selected by Milwaukee Brewers organization in first round (ninth pick overall) of free-agent draft (June 1, 1995). ... On El Paso disabled list (May 8-July 23, 1996). ... On disabled list (July 4-August 11, 1997). ... On disabled list (May 7-29, 2000). ... On Milwaukee disabled list (May 2-19 and July 29-August 28, 2001); included rehabilitation assignment to Beloit (August 27-28).
STATISTICAL NOTES: Hit three home runs in one game (April 28, 2001).

								BATTING						FIELDING		
Year	Team (League)	Pos.	G	AB	R	H	2B	3B	HR	RBI	Avg.	BB	SO	SB	PO	A	E	Avg.
1995— Helena (Pio.)	OF	7	28	2	9	0	1	0	9	.321	3	11	0	15	1	0	1.000
— Stockton (Calif.)	OF	13	47	13	12	2	0	3	12	.255	10	12	2	14	3	2	.895
— El Paso (Texas)	OF	22	79	12	22	4	2	1	13	.278	8	23	3	41	1	7	.857
1996— El Paso (Texas)	DH	22	77	17	22	5	4	1	11	.286	12	21	1	...	...	...	...
— Stockton (Calif.)	DH-OF	37	138	27	48	8	4	3	25	.348	20	32	3	2	0	0	1.000
1997— Tucson (PCL)	OF-SS	93	347	44	82	24	3	10	56	.236	33	87	0	115	7	5	.961
1998— Louisville (I.L.)	OF	55	215	38	71	10	4	7	52	.330	14	39	1	90	3	2	.979
— Milwaukee (N.L.)	OF	84	262	33	60	12	1	9	28	.229	20	61	1	115	6	4	.968
1999— Milwaukee (N.L.)	OF	135	447	70	140	43	3	21	82	.313	35	87	5	250	14	7	.974
2000— Milwaukee (N.L.)	OF	135	512	100	155	36	4	34	94	.303	33	135	11	263	12	7	.975
2001— Milwaukee (N.L.)	OF	105	397	60	105	21	1	20	63	.264	36	120	4	210	8	3	.986
— Beloit (Midw.)	OF	1	3	1	1	1	0	0	1	.333	1	1	0	0	0	0	...
Major League totals (4 years)		459	1618	263	460	112	9	84	267	.284	124	403	21	838	40	21	.977

JENNINGS, JASON   P   ROCKIES

PERSONAL: Born July 17, 1978, in Dallas. ... 6-2/245. ... Throws right, bats right. ... Full name: Jason Ryan Jennings. ... Son of Jim Jennings, member of Texas Rangers organization.
HIGH SCHOOL: Dr. Ralph H. Poteet (Mesquite, Texas).
COLLEGE: Baylor.
TRANSACTIONS/CAREER NOTES: Selected by Colorado Rockies organization in first round (16th pick overall) of free-agent draft (June 2, 1999).

Year	League	W	L	Pct.	ERA	G	GS	CG	ShO	Sv.	IP	H	R	ER	BB	SO
1999— Portland (N'West)	1	0	1.000	1.00	2	2	0	0	0	9	5	1	1	2	11
— Asheville (S.Atl.)	2	2	.500	3.70	12	12	0	0	0	58 1/3	55	27	24	8	69
2000— Salem (Caro.)	7	10	.412	3.47	22	22	3	1	0	150 1/3	136	66	58	42	133
— Carolina (Sou.)	1	3	.250	3.44	6	6	0	0	0	36 2/3	32	19	14	11	33
2001— Carolina (Sou.)	2	0	1.000	2.88	4	4	0	0	0	25	25	9	8	8	24
— Colorado Springs (PCL)	7	8	.467	4.72	22	22	4	0	0	131 2/3	145	80	69	41	110
— Colorado (N.L.)	4	1	.800	4.58	7	7	1	1	0	39 1/3	42	21	20	19	26
Major League totals (1 year)	4	1	.800	4.58	7	7	1	1	0	39 1/3	42	21	20	19	26

JENNINGS, ROBIN   OF   REDS

PERSONAL: Born April 11, 1972, in Republic of Singapore. ... 6-2/210. ... Bats left, throws left. ... Full name: Robin Christopher Jennings.
HIGH SCHOOL: Annandale (Va.).
JUNIOR COLLEGE: Manatee Community College (Fla.).
TRANSACTIONS/CAREER NOTES: Selected by Baltimore Orioles organization in 30th round of free-agent draft (June 4, 1990); did not sign. ... Selected by Chicago Cubs organization in 33rd round of free-agent draft (June 3, 1991). ... On Iowa disabled list (May 31-June 11 and August 10-20, 1996). ... On Chicago disabled list (March 22-June 8, 1998); included rehabilitation assignments to West Tenn (June 1-3) and Iowa (June 4-8). ... On Chicago disabled list (April 1-June 21, 1999); included rehabilitation assignments to West Tenn (May 25-June 8) and Iowa (June 9-21). ... Granted free agency (October 15, 1999). ... Signed by Minnesota Twins organization (November 30, 1999). ... Released by Twins (July 25, 2000). ... Signed by Cincinnati Reds organization (July 28, 2000). ... Released by Reds (September 6, 2000). ... Signed by Oakland Athletics organization (December 21, 2000). ... Traded by A's to Colorado Rockies for OF Ron Gant (July 3, 2001). ... Traded by Rockies with 2B Todd Walker to Cincinnati Reds for OF Alex Ochoa (July 19, 2001).
STATISTICAL NOTES: Tied for New York-Pennsylvania League lead in double plays by outfielder with two in 1992. ... Led Midwest League outfielders with 20 assists in 1993. ... Career major league grand slams: 1.

								BATTING						FIELDING		
Year	Team (League)	Pos.	G	AB	R	H	2B	3B	HR	RBI	Avg.	BB	SO	SB	PO	A	E	Avg.
1992— Geneva (NY-Penn)	OF	72	275	39	82	12	2	7	47	.298	20	43	10	96	*9	4	.963
1993— Peoria (Midw.)	OF-1B	132	474	64	146	29	5	3	65	.308	46	73	11	219	†31	7	.973
1994— Daytona (FSL)	OF	128	476	54	133	24	5	8	60	.279	45	54	2	165	8	8	.956
1995— Orlando (Sou.)	OF	132	490	71	145	27	7	17	79	.296	44	61	7	242	15	10	.963
1996— Iowa (A.A.)	OF-DH	86	331	53	94	15	6	18	56	.284	32	53	2	156	5	3	.982
— Chicago (N.L.)	OF	31	58	7	13	5	0	0	4	.224	3	9	1	19	2	0	1.000
1997— Iowa (A.A.)	OF-DH	126	464	67	128	25	5	20	71	.276	56	73	5	197	10	3	.986
— Chicago (N.L.)	OF	9	18	1	3	1	0	0	2	.167	0	2	0	5	0	0	1.000
1998— West Tenn (Sou.)	OF	2	6	0	0	0	0	0	0	.000	0	2	0	1	0	0	1.000
— Iowa (PCL)	OF-1B	81	298	57	74	23	2	16	62	.248	33	49	4	129	5	5	.964
1999— West Tenn (Sou.)	OF	13	53	11	17	3	0	5	17	.321	5	7	1	18	1	0	1.000
— Iowa (PCL)	OF-DH-1B	67	259	47	80	20	5	9	43	.309	25	34	6	126	7	3	.978
— Chicago (N.L.)	PH	5	5	0	1	0	0	0	0	.200	0	2	0	...	...	...	...

Year	Team (League)	Pos.	G	AB	R	H	2B	3B	HR	RBI	Avg.	BB	SO	SB	PO	A	E	Avg.
2000—Salt Lake (PCL)■		OF-1B	91	345	70	107	33	6	11	61	.310	35	45	4	158	10	4	.977
—Louisville (I.L.)■		OF	32	122	18	46	14	1	5	27	.377	9	15	0	48	5	3	.946
2001—Oakland (A.L.)■		OF-1B-DH	20	52	4	13	3	0	0	4	.250	2	6	0	48	4	0	1.000
—Sacramento (PCL)		OF-1B	38	144	26	44	11	3	5	26	.306	9	26	5	45	2	3	.940
—Colo. Springs (PCL)■		OF-1B	11	39	8	11	1	0	2	5	.282	1	10	1	31	2	1	.971
—Colorado (N.L.)		OF	1	3	0	0	0	0	0	0	.000	0	1	0	0	0	1	.000
—Cincinnati (N.L.)■		OF-1B	27	77	10	22	5	2	3	14	.286	5	11	0	74	8	3	.965
—Louisville (I.L.)		OF	28	113	18	34	6	0	8	15	.301	9	22	2	36	4	2	.952
American League totals (1 year)			20	52	4	13	3	0	0	4	.250	2	6	0	48	4	0	1.000
National League totals (4 years)			73	161	18	39	11	2	3	20	.242	8	25	1	98	10	4	.964
Major League totals (4 years)			93	213	22	52	14	2	3	24	.244	10	31	1	146	14	4	.976

JENSEN, MARCUS — C — BREWERS

PERSONAL: Born December 14, 1972, in Oakland. ... 6-4/204. ... Bats both, throws right. ... Full name: Marcus C. Jensen.

HIGH SCHOOL: Skyline (Oakland).

TRANSACTIONS/CAREER NOTES: Selected by San Francisco Giants organization in supplemental round ("sandwich pick" between first and second round, 33rd pick overall) of free-agent draft (June 4, 1990); pick received as part of compensation for San Diego Padres signing Type A free-agent P Craig Lefferts. ... On disabled list (June 1-14, 1993). ... Traded by Giants to Detroit Tigers for C Brian Johnson (July 16, 1997). ... Granted free agency (July 22, 1997). ... Re-signed by Tigers (July 26, 1997). ... Released by Tigers (March 25, 1998). ... Signed by Milwaukee Brewers organization (April 5, 1998). ... On Louisville disabled list (April 9-21, 1998). ... Released by Brewers (September 29, 1998). ... Signed by St. Louis Cardinals organization (January 13, 1999). ... Granted free agency (October 15, 1999). ... Signed by Minnesota Twins organization (January 4, 2000). ... Granted free agency (October 2, 2000). ... Signed by Boston Red Sox organization (May 2, 2001). ... Claimed on waivers by Texas Rangers (June 15, 2001). ... Granted free agency (October 11, 2001). ... Signed by Brewers organization (January 18, 2002).

STATISTICAL NOTES: Tied for Arizona League lead with three intentional bases on balls received in 1991. ... Led California League catchers with 722 total chances in 1994. ... Led Texas League catchers with 546 total chances in 1995.

MISCELLANEOUS: Member of 2000 U.S. Olympic baseball team.

Year	Team (League)	Pos.	G	AB	R	H	2B	3B	HR	RBI	Avg.	BB	SO	SB	PO	A	E	Avg.
1990—Everett (N'West)		C	51	171	21	29	3	0	2	12	.170	24	60	0	191	27	3	.986
1991—Arizona Giants (Ariz.) .		C-1B	48	155	28	44	8	3	2	30	.284	34	22	4	226	29	7	.973
1992—Clinton (Midw.)		C-1B	86	264	35	62	14	0	4	33	.235	54	87	4	493	68	10	.982
1993—Clinton (Midw.)		C	104	324	53	85	24	2	11	56	.262	66	98	1	641	73	7	.990
1994—San Jose (Calif.)		C-DH	118	418	56	101	18	0	7	47	.242	61	100	1	*627	86	9	.988
1995—Shreveport (Texas)		C-DH	95	321	55	91	22	8	4	45	.283	41	68	0	*471	70	5	.991
1996—Phoenix (PCL)		C-DH	120	405	41	107	22	4	5	53	.264	44	95	1	568	65	8	.988
—San Francisco (N.L.) ..		C	9	19	4	4	1	0	0	4	.211	8	7	0	37	5	2	.955
1997—San Francisco (N.L.) ..		C	30	74	5	11	2	0	1	3	.149	7	23	0	106	10	2	.983
—Toledo (I.L.)■		C-DH	24	80	5	14	5	0	0	9	.175	9	25	0	149	6	1	.994
—Detroit (A.L.)		C	8	11	1	2	0	0	0	1	.182	1	5	0	26	1	1	.964
1998—Louisville (I.L.)■		C-1B	74	230	29	52	13	0	10	33	.226	33	64	0	444	34	3	.994
—Milwaukee (N.L.)		C	2	2	0	0	0	0	0	0	.000	0	2	0	1	0	0	1.000
1999—Memphis (PCL)■		C-DH	72	237	38	69	19	4	8	44	.291	30	59	0	380	32	2	.995
—St. Louis (N.L.)		C	16	34	5	8	5	0	1	1	.235	6	12	0	71	9	1	.988
2000—Minnesota (A.L.)■		C-DH	52	139	16	29	7	1	3	14	.209	24	36	0	261	13	2	.993
—Salt Lake (PCL)		C	15	55	10	16	4	0	1	12	.291	11	10	0	71	4	2	.974
2001—Pawtucket (I.L.)■		C	27	102	11	24	7	2	4	12	.235	6	27	0	146	11	1	.994
—Boston (A.L.)		C	1	4	0	1	0	0	0	0	.250	0	1	0	12	1	0	1.000
—Texas (A.L.)■		C	11	25	0	4	1	0	0	2	.160	0	9	0	35	3	0	1.000
—Oklahoma (PCL)		C	53	188	42	56	10	1	8	25	.298	46	46	0	375	18	0	1.000
American League totals (3 years)			72	179	17	36	8	1	3	17	.201	25	51	0	334	18	3	.992
National League totals (4 years)			57	129	14	23	8	0	2	8	.178	21	44	0	215	24	5	.980
Major League totals (6 years)			129	308	31	59	16	1	5	25	.192	46	95	0	549	42	8	.987

JENSEN, RYAN — P — GIANTS

PERSONAL: Born September 17, 1975, in Salt Lake City. ... 6-0/205. ... Throws right, bats right. ... Full name: Larry Ryan Jensen.

HIGH SCHOOL: Cottonwood (Salt Lake City).

COLLEGE: Southern Utah.

TRANSACTIONS/CAREER NOTES: Selected by San Francisco Giants organization in eighth round of free-agent draft (June 4, 1996). ... On disabled list (June 21-30, 1999).

STATISTICAL NOTES: Tied for Northwest League lead in home runs allowed with 10 in 1997.

Year	League	W	L	Pct.	ERA	G	GS	CG	ShO	Sv.	IP	H	R	ER	BB	SO
1996—Bellingham (N'West)		2	4	.333	4.98	13	11	0	0	0	47	35	30	26	38	31
1997—Bakersfield (Calif.)		0	0	...	13.50	1	1	0	0	0	1 1/3	3	2	2	0	2
—Salem-Kaizer (N'West)		7	3	.700	5.15	16	•16	0	0	0	80 1/3	87	55	46	32	67
1998—Bakersfield (Calif.)		11	12	.478	3.37	29	27	0	0	0	168 1/3	162	89	63	61	164
—Fresno (PCL)		0	0	...	4.76	2	1	0	0	0	5 2/3	4	5	3	4	6
1999—Fresno (PCL)		11	10	.524	5.12	27	27	0	0	0	156 1/3	160	96	89	68	150
2000—Fresno (PCL)		5	8	.385	5.79	26	26	1	0	0	135 1/3	167	106	87	63	114

Year	League	W	L	Pct.	ERA	G	GS	CG	ShO	Sv.	IP	H	R	ER	BB	SO
2001—Fresno (PCL)		11	2	.846	3.48	20	17	1	1	0	106	97	43	41	34	95
— San Francisco (N.L.)		1	2	.333	4.25	10	7	0	0	0	42⅓	44	21	20	25	26
Major League totals (1 year)		1	2	.333	4.25	10	7	0	0	0	42⅓	44	21	20	25	26

JETER, DEREK · SS · YANKEES

PERSONAL: Born June 26, 1974, in Pequannock, N.J. ... 6-3/195. ... Bats right, throws right. ... Full name: Derek Sanderson Jeter.

HIGH SCHOOL: Central (Kalamazoo, Mich.).

COLLEGE: Michigan.

TRANSACTIONS/CAREER NOTES: Selected by New York Yankees organization in first round (sixth pick overall) of free-agent draft (June 1, 1992). ... On New York disabled list (June 3-19, 1998); included rehabilitation assignment to Columbus (June 18-19). ... On New York disabled list (May 12-27, 2000); included rehabilitation assignment to Tampa (May 26-27). ... On disabled list (March 23-April 7, 2001).

RECORDS: Shares major league single-season record for most games with at least one hit—135 (1999). ... Shares A.L. single-season record for fewest putouts by shortstop (150 or more games)—212 (2001). ... Holds A.L. single-season record for fewest assists by shortstop (150 or more games)—343 (2001); and fewest chances accepted by shortstop (150 or more games)—555 (2001).

HONORS: Named Minor League Player of the Year by THE SPORTING NEWS (1994). ... Named A.L. Rookie Player of the Year by THE SPORTING NEWS (1996). ... Named A.L. Rookie of the Year by Baseball Writers' Association of America (1996).

STATISTICAL NOTES: Had 15-game hitting streak (May 2-20, 1998). ... Had 16-game hitting streak (May 4-22, 1999).

								BATTING							FIELDING			
Year	Team (League)	Pos.	G	AB	R	H	2B	3B	HR	RBI	Avg.	BB	SO	SB	PO	A	E	Avg.
1992—GC Yankees (GCL)		SS	47	173	19	35	10	0	3	25	.202	19	36	2	67	132	12	.943
—Greensboro (S.Atl.)		SS	11	37	4	9	0	0	1	4	.243	7	16	0	14	25	9	.813
1993—Greensboro (S.Atl.)		SS	128	515	85	152	14	11	5	71	.295	56	95	18	158	292	56	.889
1994—Tampa (FSL)		SS	69	292	61	96	13	8	0	39	.329	23	30	28	93	204	12	.961
—Albany/Colonie (East.)		SS	34	122	17	46	7	2	2	13	.377	15	16	12	42	105	6	.961
—Columbus (I.L.)		SS	35	126	25	44	7	1	3	16	.349	20	15	10	54	93	7	.955
1995—Columbus (I.L.)		SS	123	486	*96	154	27	9	2	45	.317	61	56	20	189	394	*29	.953
—New York (A.L.)		SS	15	48	5	12	4	1	0	7	.250	3	11	0	17	34	2	.962
1996—New York (A.L.)		SS	157	582	104	183	25	6	10	78	.314	48	102	14	244	444	22	.969
1997—New York (A.L.)		SS	159	654	116	190	31	7	10	70	.291	74	125	23	243	*457	18	.975
1998—New York (A.L.)		SS	149	626	*127	203	25	8	19	84	.324	57	119	30	223	393	9	.986
—Columbus (I.L.)		SS	1	5	2	2	2	0	0	0	.400	0	2	0	4	3	1	.875
1999—New York (A.L.)		SS	158	627	134	*219	37	9	24	102	.349	91	116	19	230	391	14	.978
2000—New York (A.L.)		SS	148	593	119	201	31	4	15	73	.339	68	99	22	237	349	24	.961
—Tampa (FSL)		SS	1	3	2	2	1	0	0	0	.667	0	0	0	1	3	0	1.000
2001—New York (A.L.)		SS	150	614	110	191	35	3	21	74	.311	56	99	27	212	343	15	.974
Major League totals (7 years)			936	3744	715	1199	188	38	99	488	.320	397	671	135	1406	2411	104	.973

DIVISION SERIES RECORD

RECORDS: Shares A.L. career record for hits—32.

								BATTING							FIELDING			
Year	Team (League)	Pos.	G	AB	R	H	2B	3B	HR	RBI	Avg.	BB	SO	SB	PO	A	E	Avg.
1996—New York (A.L.)		SS	4	17	2	7	1	0	0	1	.412	0	2	0	8	10	1	.947
1997—New York (A.L.)		SS	5	21	6	7	1	0	2	2	.333	3	5	1	12	15	0	1.000
1998—New York (A.L.)		SS	3	9	0	1	0	0	0	0	.111	2	2	0	4	5	0	1.000
1999—New York (A.L.)		SS	3	11	3	5	1	1	0	0	.455	2	3	0	3	10	0	1.000
2000—New York (A.L.)		SS	5	19	1	4	0	0	0	2	.211	2	3	0	6	15	0	1.000
2001—New York (A.L.)		SS	5	18	2	8	1	0	0	1	.444	1	0	0	9	10	0	1.000
Division series totals (6 years)			25	95	14	32	4	1	2	6	.337	10	15	1	42	65	1	.991

CHAMPIONSHIP SERIES RECORD

								BATTING							FIELDING			
Year	Team (League)	Pos.	G	AB	R	H	2B	3B	HR	RBI	Avg.	BB	SO	SB	PO	A	E	Avg.
1996—New York (A.L.)		SS	5	24	5	10	2	0	1	1	.417	0	5	2	6	13	0	1.000
1998—New York (A.L.)		SS	6	25	3	5	1	1	0	2	.200	2	5	3	9	13	0	1.000
1999—New York (A.L.)		SS	5	20	3	7	1	0	1	3	.350	2	3	0	10	10	2	.909
2000—New York (A.L.)		SS	6	22	6	7	0	0	2	5	.318	6	7	1	9	16	0	1.000
2001—New York (A.L.)		SS	5	17	0	2	0	0	0	2	.118	2	2	0	6	9	0	1.000
Championship series totals (5 years)			27	108	17	31	4	1	4	13	.287	12	22	6	40	61	2	.981

WORLD SERIES RECORD

NOTES: Named Most Valuable Player (2000). ... Member of World Series championship team (1996, 1998, 1999 and 2000).

								BATTING							FIELDING			
Year	Team (League)	Pos.	G	AB	R	H	2B	3B	HR	RBI	Avg.	BB	SO	SB	PO	A	E	Avg.
1996—New York (A.L.)		SS	6	20	5	5	0	0	0	1	.250	4	6	1	15	22	2	.949
1998—New York (A.L.)		SS	4	17	4	6	0	0	0	1	.353	3	3	0	7	8	0	1.000
1999—New York (A.L.)		SS	4	17	4	6	1	0	0	1	.353	1	3	3	6	15	0	1.000
2000—New York (A.L.)		SS	5	22	6	9	2	1	2	2	.409	3	8	0	5	15	0	1.000
2001—New York (A.L.)		SS	7	27	3	4	0	0	1	1	.148	0	6	0	7	17	0	1.000
World Series totals (5 years)			26	103	22	30	3	1	3	6	.291	11	26	4	40	77	2	.983

NOTES: Named Most Valuable Player (2000).

							BATTING							FIELDING		
Year	League	Pos.	AB	R	H	2B	3B	HR	RBI	Avg.	BB	SO	SB	PO	A	E	Avg.
1998— American	SS	1	0	0	0	0	0	0	.000	0	1	0	2	0	0	1.000
1999— American	SS	1	0	0	0	0	0	0	.000	0	1	0	1	0	0	1.000
2000— American	SS	3	1	3	1	0	0	2	1.000	0	0	0	0	1	0	1.000
2001— American	SS	1	1	1	0	0	1	1	1.000	0	0	0	0	0	0	...
All-Star Game totals (4 years)		6	2	4	1	0	1	3	.667	0	2	0	1	3	0	1.000

JIMENEZ, D'ANGELO — SS — PADRES

PERSONAL: Born December 21, 1977, in Santo Domingo, Dominican Republic. ... 6-0/194. ... Bats both, throws right.
TRANSACTIONS/CAREER NOTES: Signed as non-drafted free agent by New York Yankees organization (August 1, 1994). ... On Columbus disabled list (August 6-19, 1999). ... On New York disabled list (March 23-August 24, 2000); included rehabilitation assignments to Gulf Coast Yankees (July 26-31), Tampa (August 1-14) and Columbus (August 15-24). ... Traded by Yankees to San Diego Padres for P Jay Witasick (June 23, 2001).
STATISTICAL NOTES: Led Gulf Coast League shortstops with 289 total chances and 31 double plays in 1995. ... Led South Atlantic League shortstops with 640 total chances in 1996. ... Led International League shortstops with 188 putouts in 1999.

								BATTING							FIELDING		
Year	Team (League)	Pos.	G	AB	R	H	2B	3B	HR	RBI	Avg.	BB	SO	SB	PO	A	E	Avg.
1995— GC Yankees (GCL)	SS	57	214	41	60	14	*8	2	28	.280	23	31	6	*95	*173	21	.927
1996— Greensboro (S.Atl.)	SS	138	*537	68	131	25	5	6	48	.244	56	113	15	190	*400	*50	.922
1997— Columbus (A.A.)	SS	2	7	1	1	0	0	0	1	.143	0	1	0	2	8	2	.833
— Tampa (FSL)	SS	94	352	52	99	14	6	6	48	.281	50	50	8	147	283	21	.953
1998— Norwich (East.)	SS	40	152	21	41	6	2	2	21	.270	25	26	5	62	119	12	.938
— Columbus (I.L.)	SS-2B	91	344	55	88	19	4	8	51	.256	46	67	6	150	302	26	.946
1999— Columbus (I.L.)	SS-3B-2B	126	526	97	172	32	5	15	88	.327	59	75	26	†202	372	26	.957
— New York (A.L.)	3B-2B	7	20	3	8	2	0	0	4	.400	3	4	0	3	9	0	1.000
2000— GC Yankees (GCL)	2B-SS	4	10	2	1	0	0	0	0	.100	5	1	0	7	11	2	.900
— Tampa (FSL)	SS-2B	12	41	8	8	1	1	1	2	.195	8	7	0	19	30	7	.875
— Columbus (I.L.)	2B-3B-SS	21	73	11	17	3	1	1	5	.233	7	12	2	33	34	4	.944
2001— Columbus (I.L.)	2B-SS-3B	56	214	33	56	11	1	5	19	.262	24	31	5	84	109	7	.965
— San Diego (N.L.)■	SS	86	308	45	85	19	0	3	33	.276	39	68	2	130	255	21	.948
American League totals (1 year)		7	20	3	8	2	0	0	4	.400	3	4	0	3	9	0	1.000
National League totals (1 year)		86	308	45	85	19	0	3	33	.276	39	68	2	130	255	21	.948
Major League totals (2 years)		93	328	48	93	21	0	3	37	.284	42	72	2	133	264	21	.950

JIMENEZ, JOSE — P — ROCKIES

PERSONAL: Born July 7, 1973, in San Pedro de Macoris, Dominican Republic. ... 6-3/228. ... Throws right, bats right. ... Name pronounced he-MEN-ez.
TRANSACTIONS/CAREER NOTES: Signed as non-drafted free agent by St. Louis Cardinals organization (October 21, 1991). ... Traded by Cardinals with P Manny Aybar, P Rick Croushore and SS Brent Butler to Colorado Rockies for P Darryl Kile, P Dave Veres and P Luther Hackman (November 16, 1999). ... On disabled list (July 8-23 and August 20-September 17, 2001).
HONORS: Named Texas League Pitcher of the Year (1998).
STATISTICAL NOTES: Pitched 6-0 no-hit victory for Arkansas against Shreveport (August 27, 1998). ... Pitched 1-0 no-hit victory against Arizona (June 25, 1999).
MISCELLANEOUS: Scored one run in two appearances as pinch runner (1999).

Year	League	W	L	Pct.	ERA	G	GS	CG	ShO	Sv.	IP	H	R	ER	BB	SO
1992— Dominican Cardinals (DSL)	3	2	.600	6.10	18	2	0	0	0	48 2/3	68	43	33	23	21
1993— Dominican Cardinals (DSL)	3	5	.375	3.51	12	12	0	0	0	56 1/3	61	47	22	35	30
1994— Dominican Cardinals (DSL)	3	9	.250	2.77	19	9	0	0	3	68 1/3	54	43	21	30	54
1995— Johnson City (Appl.)	5	7	.417	3.49	14	•14	1	1	0	*90 1/3	81	48	35	25	85
1996— Peoria (Midw.)	12	9	.571	2.92	28	27	3	1	0	172 1/3	158	75	56	53	129
1997— Prince William (Caro.)	9	7	.563	3.09	24	24	2	0	0	145 2/3	128	73	50	42	81
1998— Arkansas (Texas)	*15	6	.714	3.11	26	26	1	•1	0	*179 2/3	156	71	62	68	88
— St. Louis (N.L.)	3	0	1.000	2.95	4	3	0	0	0	21 1/3	22	8	7	8	12
1999— St. Louis (N.L.)	5	14	.263	5.85	29	28	2	2	0	163	173	114	106	71	113
— Memphis (PCL)	2	2	.500	3.04	4	4	0	0	0	26 2/3	30	10	9	9	18
2000— Colorado (N.L.)■	5	2	.714	3.18	72	0	0	0	24	70 2/3	63	27	25	28	44
2001— Colorado (N.L.)	6	1	.857	4.09	56	0	0	0	17	55	56	27	25	22	37
Major League totals (4 years)	19	17	.528	4.73	161	31	2	2	41	310	314	176	163	129	206

JODIE, BRETT — P — YANKEES

PERSONAL: Born March 25, 1977, in Columbia, S.C. ... 6-4/210. ... Throws right, bats right. ... Full name: Brett Paul Jodie.
HIGH SCHOOL: Lexington (S.C.).
COLLEGE: South Carolina.
TRANSACTIONS/CAREER NOTES: Selected by New York Yankees organization in sixth round of free-agent draft (June 2, 1998). ... Traded by Yankees with OF Darren Blakely to San Diego Padres for P Sterling Hitchcock (July 30, 2001). ... Claimed on waivers by Yankees (January 4, 2002).

Year	League	W	L	Pct.	ERA	G	GS	CG	ShO	Sv.	IP	H	R	ER	BB	SO
1998— Oneonta (NY-Penn)	7	6	.538	2.59	15	15	1	•1	0	94	87	40	27	21	73
1999— Greensboro (S.Atl.)	9	6	.600	3.81	25	20	2	0	1	120 1/3	125	59	51	18	106
2000— Tampa (FSL)	11	4	.733	2.57	25	18	3	1	0	143 2/3	134	53	41	29	122
— Norwich (East.)	2	1	.667	3.15	3	3	1	1	0	20	16	8	7	5	9

Year	League	W	L	Pct.	ERA	G	GS	CG	ShO	Sv.	IP	H	R	ER	BB	SO
2001—Norwich (East.)		2	0	1.000	0.64	2	2	0	0	0	14	10	1	1	2	14
—Columbus (I.L.)		10	4	.714	3.01	19	19	2	1	0	119 2/3	123	46	40	25	59
—New York (A.L.)		0	1	.000	27.00	1	1	0	0	0	2	7	6	6	1	0
—Portland (PCL)■		2	1	.667	4.75	5	5	0	0	0	30 1/3	33	16	16	8	19
—San Diego (N.L.)		0	1	.000	4.63	7	2	0	0	0	23 1/3	19	12	12	12	13
A.L. totals (1 year)		0	1	.000	27.00	1	1	0	0	0	2	7	6	6	1	0
N.L. totals (1 year)		0	1	.000	4.63	7	2	0	0	0	23 1/3	19	12	12	12	13
Major League totals (1 year)		0	2	.000	6.39	8	3	0	0	0	25 1/3	26	18	18	13	13

JOHNSON, ADAM — P — TWINS

PERSONAL: Born July 12, 1979, in San Jose, Calif. ... 6-2/210. ... Throws right, bats right. ... Full name: Adam Bryant Johnson.
HIGH SCHOOL: Torrey Pines (Del Mar, Calif.).
COLLEGE: California State-Fullerton.
TRANSACTIONS/CAREER NOTES: Selected by Minnesota Twins organization in first round (second pick overall) of free-agent draft (June 5, 2000).

Year	League	W	L	Pct.	ERA	G	GS	CG	ShO	Sv.	IP	H	R	ER	BB	SO
2000—Fort Myers (FSL)		5	4	.556	2.47	13	12	1	1	0	69 1/3	45	21	19	20	92
2001—New Britain (East.)		5	6	.455	3.82	18	18	0	0	0	113	105	53	48	39	110
—Minnesota (A.L.)		1	2	.333	8.28	7	4	0	0	0	25	32	25	23	13	17
—Edmonton (PCL)		1	1	.500	5.70	4	4	0	0	0	23 2/3	19	15	15	10	25
Major League totals (1 year)		1	2	.333	8.28	7	4	0	0	0	25	32	25	23	13	17

JOHNSON, BRIAN — C

PERSONAL: Born January 8, 1968, in Oakland. ... 6-2/210. ... Bats right, throws right. ... Full name: Brian David Johnson.
HIGH SCHOOL: Skyline (Oakland).
COLLEGE: Stanford.
TRANSACTIONS/CAREER NOTES: Selected by Montreal Expos organization in 36th round of free-agent draft (June 2, 1986); did not sign. ... Selected by New York Yankees organization in 16th round of free-agent draft (June 5, 1989). ... Selected by San Diego Padres organization from Yankees organization in Rule 5 minor league draft (December 9, 1991). ... On disabled list (April 22-May 16, 1992). ... Traded by Padres with P Willie Blair to Detroit Tigers for P Joey Eischen and P Cam Smith (December 17, 1996). ... Traded by Tigers to San Francisco Giants for C Marcus Jensen (July 16, 1997). ... On San Francisco disabled list (May 4-21 and July 22-August 7, 1998); included rehabilitation assignment to Fresno (July 31-August 7). ... Granted free agency (December 21, 1998). ... Signed by Cincinnati Reds (January 11, 1999). ... On Cincinnati disabled list (June 14-August 1, 1999); included rehabilitation assignment to Indianapolis (July 23-30). ... Released by Reds (October 11, 1999). ... Signed by Kansas City Royals (December 14, 1999). ... Released by Royals (June 30, 2000). ... Signed by St. Louis Cardinals organization (July 11, 2000). ... Released by Cardinals (August 4, 2000). ... Signed by Yankees organization (August 8, 2000). ... Granted free agency (October 18, 2000). ... Signed by Los Angeles Dodgers organization (December 21, 2000). ... On Las Vegas disabled list (June 10-August 25, 2001). ... Granted free agency (October 16, 2001).
STATISTICAL NOTES: Led South Atlantic League catchers with 752 putouts and 844 total chances in 1990. ... Led Florida State League catchers with 654 putouts in 1991. ... Career major league grand slams: 3.

Year	Team (League)	Pos.	G	AB	R	H	2B	3B	HR	RBI	Avg.	BB	SO	SB	PO	A	E	Avg.
1989—GC Yankees (GCL)		C	17	61	7	22	1	1	0	8	.361	4	5	0	84	14	1	.990
1990—Greensboro (S.Atl.)	C-3B-1B	137	496	58	118	15	0	7	51	.238	57	65	4	†773	91	13	.985
1991—Albany/Colonie (East.)	C-1B	2	8	0	0	0	0	0	0	.000	0	2	0	10	2	0	1.000
—Fort Lauderdale (FSL)	C-1B-3B	113	394	35	94	19	0	1	44	.239	34	67	4	†738	65	13	.984
1992—Wichita (Texas)■	C-3B	75	245	30	71	20	0	3	26	.290	22	32	3	472	40	3	.994
1993—Las Vegas (PCL)	C-3B-DH-OF	115	416	58	141	35	6	10	71	.339	41	53	0	513	67	9	.985
1994—San Diego (N.L.)	C-1B	36	93	7	23	4	1	3	16	.247	5	21	0	185	15	0	1.000
—Las Vegas (PCL)	C-DH	15	51	6	11	1	0	2	9	.216	8	6	0	61	5	0	1.000
1995—San Diego (N.L.)	C-1B	68	207	20	52	9	0	3	29	.251	11	39	0	403	32	4	.991
1996—San Diego (N.L.)	C-1B-3B	82	243	18	66	13	1	8	35	.272	4	36	0	456	21	5	.990
1997—Detroit (A.L.)■	C-DH	45	139	13	33	6	1	2	18	.237	5	19	1	217	9	3	.987
—Toledo (I.L.)	C-DH	7	21	0	3	2	0	0	1	.143	0	2	0	38	4	0	1.000
—San Fran. (N.L.)■	C-1B	56	179	19	50	7	2	11	27	.279	14	26	0	352	24	2	.995
1998—San Francisco (N.L.)	C-OF	99	308	34	73	8	1	13	34	.237	28	67	0	591	33	4	.994
—Fresno (PCL)	OF	5	19	4	6	1	0	2	3	.316	1	5	0	10	0	0	1.000
1999—Cincinnati (N.L.)■	C	45	117	12	27	7	0	5	18	.231	9	31	0	201	11	1	.995
—Indianapolis (I.L.)	C	6	19	2	4	3	0	0	4	.211	1	3	0	22	2	0	1.000
2000—Kansas City (A.L.)■	C	37	125	9	26	6	0	4	18	.208	4	28	0	221	12	2	.991
—Memphis (PCL)■	C	15	48	6	12	6	0	2	7	.250	4	10	0	78	5	2	.976
—Columbus (I.L.)■	C	18	68	12	13	5	0	1	6	.191	8	9	0	139	8	1	.993
2001—Las Vegas (PCL)■	C-1B	48	166	21	50	12	0	6	31	.301	11	39	0	346	19	3	.992
—Los Angeles (N.L.)	C	3	4	0	1	0	0	0	1	.250	0	1	0	3	0	0	1.000
—GC Dodgers (GCL)	C	5	18	4	8	0	0	2	3	.444	2	0	0	29	1	0	1.000
American League totals (2 years)		82	264	22	59	12	1	6	36	.223	9	47	1	438	21	5	.989
National League totals (7 years)		389	1151	110	292	48	5	43	160	.254	71	221	0	2191	136	16	.993
Major League totals (8 years)		471	1415	132	351	60	6	49	196	.248	80	268	1	2629	157	21	.993

DIVISION SERIES RECORD

Year	Team (League)	Pos.	G	AB	R	H	2B	3B	HR	RBI	Avg.	BB	SO	SB	PO	A	E	Avg.
1996—San Diego (N.L.)		C	2	8	2	3	1	0	0	0	.375	0	1	0	15	3	0	1.000
1997—San Francisco (N.L.)		C	3	10	2	1	0	0	1	1	.100	1	4	0	18	0	0	1.000
Division series totals (2 years)			5	18	4	4	1	0	1	1	.222	1	5	0	33	3	0	1.000

PERSONAL: Born July 20, 1971, in Fort Pierce, Fla. ... 6-2/220. ... Bats right, throws right. ... Full name: Charles Edward Johnson Jr. ... Nephew of Fred McGriff, first baseman, Chicago Cubs.

HIGH SCHOOL: Westwood (Fort Pierce, Fla.).

COLLEGE: Miami (Fla.).

TRANSACTIONS/CAREER NOTES: Selected by Montreal Expos organization in first round (10th pick overall) of free-agent draft (June 5, 1989); did not sign. ... Selected by Florida Marlins organization in first round (28th pick overall) of free-agent draft (June 1, 1992). ... On Florida disabled list (August 9-September 1, 1995); included rehabilitation assignment to Portland (August 30-September 1). ... On disabled list (July 28-September 1, 1996). ... Traded by Marlins with OF Gary Sheffield, 3B Bobby Bonilla, OF Jim Eisenreich and P Manuel Barrios to Los Angeles Dodgers for C Mike Piazza and 3B Todd Zeile (May 15, 1998). ... Traded by Dodgers with OF Roger Cedeno to New York Mets for C Todd Hundley and P Arnold Gooch; then traded by Mets to Baltimore Orioles for P Armando Benitez (December 1, 1998). ... Traded by Orioles with DH Harold Baines to Chicago White Sox for C Brook Fordyce, P Miguel Felix, P Juan Figueroa and P Jason Lakman (July 29, 2000). ... Granted free agency (October 30, 2000). ... Signed by Marlins (December 18, 2000).

RECORDS: Holds major league career records for most consecutive errorless games by catcher—159 (June 24, 1996-September 28, 1997); and most consecutive chances accepted by catcher without an error—1,294 (June 23, 1996-September 28, 1997). ... Holds major league single-season records for most consecutive errorless games by catcher—123 (April 1 through September 28, 1997); and most chances accepted without an error by catcher—973 (April 1 through September 28, 1997). ... Shares major league single-season records for highest fielding average by catcher (100 or more games)—1.000 (1997); and fewest errors (100 or more games)—0 (1997).

HONORS: Named catcher on THE SPORTING NEWS college All-America team (1992). ... Won N.L. Gold Glove at catcher (1995-98).

STATISTICAL NOTES: Led Midwest League with 230 total bases in 1993. ... Led Midwest League catchers with 1,004 total chances in 1993. ... Led N.L. catchers with 12 double plays in 1996. ... Led A.L. catchers with 14 double plays in 1999. ... Career major league grand slams: 1.

MISCELLANEOUS: Member of 1992 U.S. Olympic baseball team.

Year	Team (League)	Pos.	G	AB	R	H	2B	3B	HR	RBI	Avg.	BB	SO	SB	PO	A	E	Avg.
1993—	Kane County (Midw.)..	C	•135	488	74	134	29	5	19	*94	.275	62	111	9	*852	*140	12	.988
1994—	Portland (East.)	C-DH	132	443	64	117	29	1	*28	80	.264	*74	97	4	713	*84	7	.991
—	Florida (N.L.)	C	4	11	5	5	1	0	1	4	.455	1	4	0	18	2	0	1.000
1995—	Florida (N.L.)	C	97	315	40	79	15	1	11	39	.251	46	71	0	641	•63	6	.992
—	Portland (East.)	C	2	7	0	0	0	0	0	0	.000	1	3	0	21	2	1	.958
1996—	Florida (N.L.)	C	120	386	34	84	13	1	13	37	.218	40	91	1	751	70	4	*.995
1997—	Florida (N.L.)	C	124	416	43	104	26	1	19	63	.250	60	109	0	901	73	0	*1.000
1998—	Florida (N.L.)	C	31	113	13	25	5	0	7	23	.221	16	30	0	193	10	2	.990
—	Los Angeles (N.L.)■..	C	102	346	31	75	13	0	12	35	.217	29	99	0	715	50	6	.992
1999—	Baltimore (A.L.)■......	C	135	426	58	107	19	1	16	54	.251	55	107	0	770	66	5	.994
2000—	Baltimore (A.L.)	C-DH	84	286	52	84	16	0	21	55	.294	32	69	2	498	30	3	.994
—	Chicago (A.L.)■......	C	44	135	24	44	8	0	10	36	.326	20	37	0	224	12	3	.987
2001—	Florida (N.L.)■.........	C	128	451	51	117	32	0	18	75	.259	38	133	0	846	62	4	.996
American League totals (2 years)			263	847	134	235	43	1	47	145	.277	107	213	2	1492	108	11	.993
National League totals (6 years)			606	2038	217	489	105	3	81	276	.240	230	537	1	4065	330	22	.995
Major League totals (8 years)			869	2885	351	724	148	4	128	421	.251	337	750	3	5557	438	33	.995

DIVISION SERIES RECORD

Year	Team (League)	Pos.	G	AB	R	H	2B	3B	HR	RBI	Avg.	BB	SO	SB	PO	A	E	Avg.
1997—	Florida (N.L.)	C	3	8	5	2	1	0	1	2	.250	3	2	0	21	3	0	1.000
2000—	Chicago (A.L.)	C	3	9	0	3	0	0	0	0	.333	1	1	0	13	2	0	1.000
Division series totals (2 years)			6	17	5	5	1	0	1	2	.294	4	3	0	34	5	0	1.000

CHAMPIONSHIP SERIES RECORD

Year	Team (League)	Pos.	G	AB	R	H	2B	3B	HR	RBI	Avg.	BB	SO	SB	PO	A	E	Avg.
1997—	Florida (N.L.)	C	6	17	1	2	2	0	0	5	.118	3	8	0	52	3	2	.965

WORLD SERIES RECORD

NOTES: Member of World Series championship team (1997).

Year	Team (League)	Pos.	G	AB	R	H	2B	3B	HR	RBI	Avg.	BB	SO	SB	PO	A	E	Avg.
1997—	Florida (N.L.)	C	7	28	4	10	0	0	1	3	.357	1	6	0	49	2	0	1.000

ALL-STAR GAME RECORD

Year	League	Pos.	AB	R	H	2B	3B	HR	RBI	Avg.	BB	SO	SB	PO	A	E	Avg.
1997—	National	C	1	0	0	0	0	0	0	.000	0	1	0	2	0	0	1.000
2001—	National	C	1	0	0	0	0	0	0	.000	0	0	0	3	0	0	1.000
All-Star Game totals (2 years)			2	0	0	0	0	0	0	.000	0	1	0	5	0	0	1.000

JOHNSON, JASON   P   ORIOLES

PERSONAL: Born October 27, 1973, in Santa Barbara, Calif. ... 6-6/235. ... Throws right, bats right. ... Full name: Jason Michael Johnson.

HIGH SCHOOL: Conner (Hebron, Ky.).

TRANSACTIONS/CAREER NOTES: Signed as non-drafted free agent by Pittsburgh Pirates organization (July 21, 1992). ... Selected by Tampa Bay Devil Rays in first round (14th pick overall) of expansion draft (November 18, 1997). ... On Tampa Bay disabled list (July 4, 1998-remainder of season). ... Traded by Devil Rays to Baltimore Orioles for OF Danny Clyburn and a player to be named later (March 29, 1999); Devil Rays acquired SS Bolivar Voquez to complete deal (April 22, 1999).

Year	League	W	L	Pct.	ERA	G	GS	CG	ShO	Sv.	IP	H	R	ER	BB	SO
1992— Gulf Coast Pirates (GCL)....		2	0	1.000	3.68	5	0	0	0	0	7⅓	6	3	3	6	3
1993— Gulf Coast Pirates (GCL)....		1	4	.200	2.33	9	9	0	0	0	54	48	22	14	14	39
— Welland (NY-Penn)............		1	5	.167	4.63	6	6	1	0	0	35	33	24	18	9	19
1994— Augusta (S.Atl.).............		2	12	.143	4.03	20	19	1	0	0	102⅔	119	67	46	32	69
1995— Augusta (S.Atl.).............		3	5	.375	4.36	11	11	1	0	0	53⅔	57	32	26	17	42
— Lynchburg (Caro.)............		1	2	.333	2.05	5	4	0	0	0	22	23	6	5	5	9
1996— Lynchburg (Caro.)............		1	4	.200	6.50	15	5	0	0	0	44⅓	56	37	32	12	27
— Augusta (S.Atl.).............		4	4	.500	3.11	14	14	1	1	0	84	82	40	29	25	83
1997— Lynchburg (Caro.)............		8	4	.667	3.71	17	17	0	0	0	99⅓	98	43	41	30	92
— Carolina (Sou.).............		3	3	.500	4.08	9	9	1	0	0	57⅓	56	31	26	16	63
— Pittsburgh (N.L.).............		0	0	...	6.00	3	0	0	0	0	6	10	4	4	1	3
1998— Durham (I.L.)■............		1	0	1.000	2.92	2	2	0	0	0	12⅓	6	4	4	2	14
— Tampa Bay (A.L.)............		2	5	.286	5.70	13	13	0	0	0	60	74	38	38	27	36
1999— Rochester (I.L.)■............		4	2	.667	3.65	8	8	0	0	0	44⅓	35	19	18	27	47
— Baltimore (A.L.).............		8	7	.533	5.46	22	21	0	0	0	115⅓	120	74	70	55	71
2000— Rochester (I.L.).............		3	1	.750	1.47	8	8	1	1	0	55	32	12	9	21	56
— Baltimore (A.L.).............		1	10	.091	7.02	25	13	0	0	0	107⅔	119	95	84	61	79
2001— Baltimore (A.L.).............		10	12	.455	4.09	32	32	2	0	0	196	194	109	89	77	114
A.L. totals (4 years)		21	34	.382	5.28	92	79	2	0	0	479	507	316	281	220	300
N.L. totals (1 year)		0	0	...	6.00	3	0	0	0	0	6	10	4	4	1	3
Major League totals (5 years)		21	34	.382	5.29	95	79	2	0	0	485	517	320	285	221	303

JOHNSON, JONATHAN   P

PERSONAL: Born July 16, 1974, in La Grange, Ga. ... 6-0/180. ... Throws right, bats right. ... Full name: Jonathan Kent Johnson.
HIGH SCHOOL: Forest (Ocala, Fla.).
COLLEGE: Florida State.
TRANSACTIONS/CAREER NOTES: Selected by Texas Rangers organization in first round (seventh pick overall) of free-agent draft (June 1, 1995). ... On Oklahoma disabled list (May 1-17, 1998; and May 13-July 5, 1999). ... Traded by Rangers to Arizona Diamondback for cash considerations (April 27, 2001). ... On Tucson disabled list (July 21, 2001-remainder of season). ... Granted free agency (October 15, 2001).

Year	League	W	L	Pct.	ERA	G	GS	CG	ShO	Sv.	IP	H	R	ER	BB	SO
1995— Charlotte (FSL).................		1	5	.167	2.70	8	7	1	0	0	43⅓	34	14	13	16	25
1996— Tulsa (Texas)................		*13	10	.565	3.56	26	25	*6	0	0	174⅓	176	86	69	41	97
— Oklahoma City (A.A.).........		1	0	1.000	0.00	1	1	1	1	0	9	2	0	0	1	6
1997— Oklahoma City (A.A.).........		1	8	.111	7.29	13	12	1	0	1	58	83	54	47	29	33
— Tulsa (Texas)................		5	4	.556	3.52	10	10	4	0	0	71⅔	70	35	28	15	47
1998— Oklahoma (PCL).................		6	6	.500	4.90	19	18	1	0	1	112	109	66	61	32	94
— Charlotte (FSL).................		0	2	.000	4.63	3	3	0	0	0	11⅔	10	6	6	4	11
— Texas (A.L.)................		0	0	...	8.31	1	1	0	0	0	4⅓	5	4	4	5	3
1999— Oklahoma (PCL).................		8	4	.667	6.25	21	8	0	0	2	67⅔	91	53	47	23	38
— Gulf Coast Rangers (GCL)..		0	0	...	1.80	1	1	0	0	0	5	3	1	1	0	5
— Tulsa (Texas)................		0	0	...	9.53	1	1	0	0	0	5⅔	12	6	6	0	4
— Texas (A.L.)................		0	0	...	15.00	1	0	0	0	0	3	9	5	5	2	3
2000— Oklahoma (PCL).................		4	7	.364	5.08	36	2	0	0	5	56⅔	55	38	32	26	63
— Texas (A.L.)................		1	1	.500	6.21	15	0	0	0	0	29	34	23	20	19	23
2001— Texas (A.L.)................		0	0	...	9.58	5	0	0	0	0	10⅓	13	11	11	7	11
— Tucson (PCL)■...............		4	4	.500	5.25	15	12	0	0	0	73⅔	63	48	43	42	51
Major League totals (4 years)		1	1	.500	7.71	22	1	0	0	0	46⅔	61	43	40	33	40

JOHNSON, MARK   1B   METS

PERSONAL: Born October 17, 1967, in Worcester, Mass. ... 6-4/230. ... Bats left, throws left. ... Full name: Mark Patrick Johnson.
HIGH SCHOOL: Holy Name (Worcester, Mass.).
COLLEGE: Dartmouth.
TRANSACTIONS/CAREER NOTES: Selected by Pittsburgh Pirates organization in 42nd round of free-agent draft (June 5, 1989); did not sign. ... Selected by Pirates organization in 20th round of free-agent draft (June 4, 1990). ... On Calgary disabled list (August 26-September 8, 1995). ... Claimed on waivers by Cincinnati Reds (August 29, 1997). ... Traded by Reds to Anaheim Angels for a player to be named later (September 11, 1998). ... Released by Angels (December 22, 1998). ... Signed by Hanshin Tigers of Japan Central League (December 22, 1998). ... Signed by New York Mets organization (February 22, 2000). ... Granted free agency (October 18, 2000). ... Re-signed by Mets (May 29, 2001). ... Granted free agency (October 15, 2001). ... Re-signed by Mets organization (December 19, 2001).
HONORS: Named Southern League Most Valuable Player (1994).
STATISTICAL NOTES: Led Southern League with 11 intentional bases on balls received in 1994. ... Career major league grand slams: 1.

Year	Team (League)	Pos.	G	AB	R	H	2B	3B	HR	RBI	Avg.	BB	SO	SB	PO	A	E	Avg.
1990— Welland (NY-Penn).....	1B	5	8	2	4	1	0	0	2	.500	2	0	0	2	1	0	1.000
— Augusta (S.Atl.)..........	1B	43	144	12	36	7	0	0	19	.250	24	18	4	240	18	5	.981
1991— Augusta (S.Atl.)..........	1B	49	139	23	36	7	4	2	25	.259	29	1	15	319	33	9	.975
— Salem (Caro.)...........	1B-OF-3B	37	103	12	26	2	0	2	13	.252	18	25	0	32	28	3	.952
1992— Carolina (Sou.)..........	1B	122	383	40	89	16	1	7	45	.232	55	94	16	610	41	8	.988
1993— Carolina (Sou.)..........	1B-OF	125	399	48	93	18	4	14	52	.233	66	93	6	500	40	4	.993
1994— Carolina (Sou.)..........	1B-OF	111	388	69	107	20	2	*23	85	.276	67	89	6	570	52	6	.990
1995— Pittsburgh (N.L.)........	1B	79	221	32	46	6	1	13	28	.208	37	66	5	527	36	8	.986
— Calgary (PCL)...........	1B	9	23	7	7	4	0	2	8	.304	6	4	1	65	5	2	.972
1996— Pittsburgh (N.L.)........	1B-OF	127	343	55	94	24	0	13	47	.274	44	64	6	778	73	6	.993
1997— Pittsburgh (N.L.)........	1B-DH	78	219	30	47	10	0	4	29	.215	43	78	1	542	44	5	.992
— Calgary (PCL)...........	1B-DH-OF	34	115	28	39	11	1	6	16	.339	22	28	4	183	25	0	1.000
— Indianapolis (A.A.)■ ..	1B	3	4	0	0	0	0	0	0	.000	2	2	0	17	2	0	1.000

Year	Team (League)	Pos.	G	AB	R	H	2B	3B	HR	RBI	Avg.	BB	SO	SB	PO	A	E	Avg.
						BATTING										**FIELDING**		
1998— Indianapolis (I.L.)	1B-OF-DH	116	357	65	107	33	1	22	75	.300	68	82	2	443	37	5	.990
— Anaheim (A.L.)■	1B-DH	10	14	1	1	0	0	0	0	.071	0	6	0	13	1	0	1.000
1999— Hanshin (Jap. Cen.)■	IF	125	438	52	95	23	1	20	66	.217	53	78	1	...	...	...	...
2000— Norfolk (I.L.)■	1B-OF	94	315	49	85	21	1	17	60	.270	67	54	14	368	33	3	.993
— New York (N.L.)	1B-DH-OF	21	22	2	4	0	0	1	6	.182	5	9	0	10	1	0	1.000
2001— Norfolk (I.L.)	1B-OF	42	152	27	48	15	0	8	25	.316	22	20	2	380	32	1	.998
— New York (N.L.)	1B-OF-DH	71	118	17	30	6	1	6	23	.254	16	31	0	111	7	1	.992
American League totals (1 year)		10	14	1	1	0	0	0	0	.071	0	6	0	13	1	0	1.000
National League totals (5 years)		376	923	136	221	46	2	37	133	.239	145	248	12	1968	161	20	.991
Major League totals (6 years)		386	937	137	222	46	2	37	133	.237	145	254	12	1981	162	20	.991

JOHNSON, MARK   C   WHITE SOX

PERSONAL: Born September 12, 1975, in Wheatridge, Colo. ... 6-0/185. ... Bats left, throws right. ... Full name: Mark Landon Johnson.
HIGH SCHOOL: Warner Robins (Ga.).
TRANSACTIONS/CAREER NOTES: Selected by Chicago White Sox organization in first round (26th pick overall) of free-agent draft (June 2, 1994).
STATISTICAL NOTES: Led Carolina League with .420 on-base percentage in 1997. ... Led Carolina League catchers with 1000 total chances and tied for league lead with eight double plays in 1997. ... Led Southern League with .443 on-base percentage in 1998.

Year	Team (League)	Pos.	G	AB	R	H	2B	3B	HR	RBI	Avg.	BB	SO	SB	PO	A	E	Avg.
						BATTING										**FIELDING**		
1994— GC White Sox (GCL)	C	32	87	10	21	5	0	0	14	.241	14	15	1	182	22	3	.986
1995— Hickory (S.Atl.)	C	107	319	31	58	9	0	2	17	.182	59	52	3	681	67	11	.986
1996— South Bend (Midw.)	C	67	214	29	55	14	3	2	27	.257	39	25	3	408	37	9	.980
— Prince William (Caro.)	C	18	58	9	14	3	0	0	3	.241	13	6	0	112	8	1	.992
1997— Win.-Salem (Caro.)	C	120	375	59	95	27	4	4	46	.253	*106	85	4	*899	90	11	*.989
1998— Birmingham (Sou.)	C-1B	117	382	68	108	17	3	9	59	.283	*105	72	0	723	65	8	.990
— Chicago (A.L.)	C	7	23	2	2	0	2	0	1	.087	1	8	0	36	2	0	1.000
1999— Chicago (A.L.)	C-DH	73	207	27	47	11	0	4	16	.227	36	58	3	413	33	3	.993
2000— Chicago (A.L.)	C-DH	75	213	29	48	11	0	3	23	.225	27	40	3	466	27	4	.992
2001— Charlotte (I.L.)	C-1B	55	196	24	53	5	2	4	24	.270	29	34	2	413	24	4	.991
— Chicago (A.L.)	C	61	173	21	43	6	1	5	18	.249	23	31	2	326	31	3	.992
Major League totals (4 years)		216	616	79	140	28	3	12	58	.227	87	137	8	1241	93	10	.993

JOHNSON, MIKE   P

PERSONAL: Born October 3, 1975, in Edmonton. ... 6-2/170. ... Throws right, bats left. ... Full name: Michael Keith Johnson.
HIGH SCHOOL: Salisbury Composite (Edmonton).
TRANSACTIONS/CAREER NOTES: Selected by Toronto Blue Jays organization in 17th round of free-agent draft (June 3, 1993). ... Selected by San Francisco Giants from Blue Jays in Rule 5 major league draft (December 9, 1996). ... Traded by Giants to Baltimore Orioles for cash considerations (December 9, 1996). ... Traded by Orioles to Montreal Expos for a player to be named later (July 31, 1997); Orioles acquired P Everett Stull to complete deal (October 31, 1997). ... Traded by Expos to Texas Rangers for P Darwin Cubillan (May 8, 2001). ... Granted free agency (October 15, 2001).
STATISTICAL NOTES: Led International League pitchers with six errors in 1999.

Year	League	W	L	Pct.	ERA	G	GS	CG	ShO	Sv.	IP	H	R	ER	BB	SO
1993— Gulf Coast Blue Jays (GCL)	0	2	.000	4.87	16	1	0	0	1	44 1/3	51	40	24	22	31
1994— Medicine Hat (Pio.)	1	3	.250	4.46	9	9	0	0	0	36 1/3	48	31	18	22	8
1995— Gulf Coast Blue Jays (GCL)	0	2	.000	7.20	3	3	0	0	0	15	20	15	12	8	13
— Medicine Hat (Pio.)	4	1	.800	3.86	19	0	0	0	3	49	46	26	21	25	32
1996— Hagerstown (S.Atl.)	11	8	.579	3.15	29	23	5	3	0	162 2/3	157	74	57	39	155
1997— Baltimore (A.L.)■	0	1	.000	7.94	14	5	0	0	2	39 2/3	52	36	35	16	29
— Montreal (N.L.)■	2	5	.286	5.94	11	11	0	0	0	50	54	34	33	21	28
1998— Harrisburg (East.)	3	2	.600	6.95	7	7	0	0	0	33 2/3	35	27	26	10	38
— Ottawa (I.L.)	4	9	.308	4.29	18	18	1	0	0	109	105	63	52	38	88
— Montreal (N.L.)	0	2	.000	14.73	2	2	0	0	0	7 1/3	16	12	12	2	4
1999— Ottawa (I.L.)	6	12	.333	5.38	28	27	0	0	0	147 1/3	174	105	88	63	120
— Montreal (N.L.)	0	0	...	8.64	3	1	0	0	0	8 1/3	12	8	8	7	6
2000— Ottawa (I.L.)	2	0	1.000	2.10	5	5	0	0	0	30	14	8	7	14	27
— Montreal (N.L.)	5	6	.455	6.39	41	13	0	0	0	101 1/3	107	73	72	53	70
2001— Montreal (N.L.)■	0	0	...	4.76	10	0	0	0	0	11 1/3	13	6	6	4	10
— Ottawa (I.L.)	2	0	1.000	4.50	2	0	0	0	0	10	7	5	5	3	8
— Oklahoma (PCL)■	3	5	.375	4.58	23	8	1	0	2	88 1/3	101	48	45	22	67
A.L. totals (1 year)	0	1	.000	7.94	14	5	0	0	2	39 2/3	52	36	35	16	29
N.L. totals (5 years)	7	13	.350	6.61	67	27	0	0	0	178 1/3	202	133	131	87	118
Major League totals (5 years)	7	14	.333	6.85	81	32	0	0	2	218	254	169	166	103	147

JOHNSON, NICK   1B   YANKEES

PERSONAL: Born September 19, 1978, in Sacramento. ... 6-3/224. ... Bats left, throws left. ... Full name: Nicholas Robert Johnson. ... Nephew of Larry Bowa, manager, Philadelphia Phillies and shortstop with Phillies (1970-81) and Chicago Cubs (1982-85).
HIGH SCHOOL: McClatchy (Sacramento).
TRANSACTIONS/CAREER NOTES: Selected by New York Yankees organization in third round of free-agent draft (June 4, 1996). ... On disabled list (April 2, 2000-entire season). ... On Columbus disabled list (May 18-June 3, 2001).
STATISTICAL NOTES: Led Gulf Coast League with .422 on-base percentage in 1996. ... Led South Atlantic League first basemen with 99 double plays in 1997. ... Led Florida State League with .466 on-base percentage in 1998. ... Led Eastern League with a .525 on-base percentage and in being hit by pitch with 37 in 1999. ... Led International League with .401 on-base percentage and in being hit by pitch with 14 in 2001.

Year Team (League)	Pos.	G	AB	R	H	2B	3B	HR	RBI	Avg.	BB	SO	SB	PO	A	E	Avg.
1996— GC Yankees (GCL)......	1B	47	157	31	45	11	1	2	33	.287	30	35	0	314	19	3	.991
1997— Greensboro (S.Atl.)	1B	127	433	77	118	23	1	16	75	.273	76	99	16	*1176	59	16	.987
1998— Tampa (FSL)............	1B	92	303	69	96	14	1	17	58	.317	68	76	1	785	58	12	.986
1999— Norwich (East.)	1B	132	420	*114	145	33	5	14	87	*.345	*123	88	8	1070	85	*20	.983
2000— New York (A.L.)								Did not play.									
2001— Columbus (I.L.)..........	1B	110	359	68	92	20	0	18	49	.256	81	105	9	856	63	•10	.989
— New York (A.L.)..........	1B-DH	23	67	6	13	2	0	2	8	.194	7	15	0	90	5	0	1.000
Major League totals (1 year)		23	67	6	13	2	0	2	8	.194	7	15	0	90	5	0	1.000

JOHNSON, RANDY — P — DIAMONDBACKS

PERSONAL: Born September 10, 1963, in Walnut Grove, Calif. ... 6-10/230. ... Throws left, bats right. ... Full name: Randall David Johnson.
HIGH SCHOOL: Livermore (Calif.).
COLLEGE: Southern California.
TRANSACTIONS/CAREER NOTES: Selected by Atlanta Braves organization in third round of free-agent draft (June 7, 1982); did not sign. ... Selected by Montreal Expos organization in second round of free-agent draft (June 3, 1985). ... Traded by Expos with P Brian Holman and P Gene Harris to Seattle Mariners for P Mark Langston and a player to be named later (May 25, 1989); Expos acquired P Mike Campbell to complete deal (July 31, 1989). ... On disabled list (June 11-27, 1992). ... On Seattle disabled list (May 15-August 6 and August 27, 1996-remainder of season); included rehabilitation assignment to Everett (August 3-6). ... On suspended list (April 24-27, 1998). ... Traded by Mariners to Houston Astros for SS Carlos Guillen, P Freddy Garcia and a player to be named later (July 31, 1998); Mariners acquired P John Halama to complete deal (October 1, 1998). ... Granted free agency (October 28, 1998). ... Signed by Arizona Diamondbacks (December 10, 1998).
RECORDS: Shares major league single-game record for most strikeouts by lefthander—19 (June 24 and August 8, 1997). ... Holds N.L. single-season record for most games with 10 or more strikeouts—23 (1999). ... Shares A.L. record for most strikeouts in two consecutive games—32 (August 8 [19] and 15 [13], 1997, 17 innings). ... Shares N.L. record for most strikeouts in three consecutive games—43 (June 25 [14] and 30 [17] and July 5 [12], 1999; April 28 [12], May 3 [11] and 8 [20], 2001; May 3 [11], 8 [20] and 13 [12], 2001); and most years with 300 or more strikeouts—3 (1999-2001). ... Shares N.L. single-game record for most strikeouts (extra-inning game)—20 (May 8, 2001). ... Holds N.L. single-game record for most strikeouts by relief pitcher—16 (July 18, 2001).
HONORS: Named A.L. Pitcher of the Year by THE SPORTING NEWS (1995). ... Named lefthanded pitcher on THE SPORTING NEWS A.L. All-Star team (1995 and 1997). ... Named A.L. Cy Young Award winner by Baseball Writers' Association of America (1995). ... Named N.L. Cy Young Award winner by Baseball Writers' Association of America (1999, 2000 and 2001). ... Named lefthanded pitcher on THE SPORTING NEWS N.L. All-Star team (2001).
STATISTICAL NOTES: Led American Association with 20 balks in 1988. ... Pitched 2-0 no-hit victory against Detroit (June 2, 1990). ... Pitched 4-0 one-hit, complete-game victory against Oakland (August 14, 1991). ... Struck out 15 batters in one game (September 16, 1992; June 14 and September 16, 1993; June 4 and August 11, 1994; June 24 and September 23, 1995; May 28 and June 8, 1997; April 10, May 24 and July 11, 1998; and April 10, 1999). ... Struck out 18 batters in one game (September 27, 1992). ... Led A.L. with 18 hit batsmen in 1992 and 16 in 1993. ... Pitched 7-0 one-hit, complete-game victory against Oakland (May 16, 1993). ... Struck out 16 batters in one game (July 15, 1995; July 18, 1997; August 28, 1998; July 18, 2001; August 23, 2001; and Septmeber 27, 2001). ... Struck out 19 batters in one game (June 24 and August 8, 1997). ... Pitched 3-0 one-hit, complete-game victory against Minnesota (July 16, 1998). ... Struck out 17 batters in one game (June 30, 1999). ... Struck out 20 batters in one game (May 8, 2001).
MISCELLANEOUS: Holds Seattle Mariners franchise all-time records for most wins (130), lowest earned-run average (3.42), most innings pitched (1,838 $^1/_3$), most strikeouts (2,162) and most shutouts (19). ... Appeared in one game as outfielder with no chances (1993). ... Shares Arizona Diamondbacks all-time record for most shutouts (2). ... Holds Arizona Diamondbacks all-time records for most wins (57), strikeouts (1,083), innings pitched (770), complete games (23), shutouts (7) and lowest earned-run average (2.54).

Year League	W	L	Pct.	ERA	G	GS	CG	ShO	Sv.	IP	H	R	ER	BB	SO
1985— Jamestown (NY-Penn)	0	3	.000	5.93	8	8	0	0	0	27$^1/_3$	29	22	18	24	21
1986— West Palm Beach (FSL)	8	7	.533	3.16	26	•26	2	1	0	119$^2/_3$	89	49	42	*94	133
1987— Jacksonville (Sou.).............	11	8	.579	3.73	25	24	0	0	0	140	100	63	58	128	*163
1988— Indianapolis (A.A.).............	8	7	.533	3.26	20	19	0	0	0	113$^1/_3$	85	52	41	72	111
— Montreal (N.L.)..................	3	0	1.000	2.42	4	4	1	0	0	26	23	8	7	7	25
1989— Montreal (N.L.)................	0	4	.000	6.67	7	6	0	0	0	29$^2/_3$	29	25	22	26	26
— Indianapolis (A.A.).............	1	1	.500	2.00	3	3	0	0	0	18	13	5	4	9	17
— Seattle (A.L.)■..................	7	9	.438	4.40	22	22	2	0	0	131	118	75	64	70	104
1990— Seattle (A.L.)................	14	11	.560	3.65	33	33	5	2	0	219$^2/_3$	174	103	89	*120	194
1991— Seattle (A.L.)................	13	10	.565	3.98	33	33	2	1	0	201$^1/_3$	151	96	89	*152	228
1992— Seattle (A.L.)................	12	14	.462	3.77	31	31	6	2	0	210$^1/_3$	154	104	88	*144	*241
1993— Seattle (A.L.)................	19	8	.704	3.24	35	34	10	3	1	255$^1/_3$	185	97	92	99	*308
1994— Seattle (A.L.)................	13	6	.684	3.19	23	23	*9	*4	0	172	132	65	61	72	*204
1995— Seattle (A.L.)................	18	2	*.900	*2.48	30	30	6	3	0	214$^1/_3$	159	65	59	65	*294
1996— Seattle (A.L.)................	5	0	1.000	3.67	14	8	0	0	1	61$^1/_3$	48	27	25	25	85
— Everett (N'West).............	0	0	...	0.00	1	1	0	0	0	2	0	0	0	0	5
1997— Seattle (A.L.)................	20	4	*.833	2.28	30	29	5	2	0	213	147	60	54	77	291
1998— Seattle (A.L.)................	9	10	.474	4.33	23	23	6	2	0	160	146	90	77	60	213
— Houston (N.L.)■.............	10	1	.909	1.28	11	11	4	4	0	84$^1/_3$	57	12	12	26	116
1999— Arizona (N.L.)■...............	17	9	.654	*2.48	35	•35	*12	2	0	*271$^2/_3$	207	86	75	70	*364
2000— Arizona (N.L.)...............	19	7	*.731	2.64	35	•35	•8	•3	0	248$^2/_3$	202	89	73	76	*347
2001— Arizona (N.L.)...............	21	6	.778	*2.49	35	34	3	2	0	249$^2/_3$	181	74	69	71	*372
A.L. totals (10 years)	130	74	.637	3.42	274	266	51	19	2	1838$^1/_3$	1414	782	698	884	2162
N.L. totals (6 years)	70	27	.722	2.55	127	125	28	11	0	910	699	294	258	276	1250
Major League totals (14 years)	200	101	.664	3.13	401	391	79	30	2	2748$^1/_3$	2113	1076	956	1160	3412

DIVISION SERIES RECORD

RECORDS: Holds career records for most losses—6; bases on balls allowed—19; and strikeouts—69. ... Holds single-game record for most strikeouts—13 (October 5, 1997). ... Holds A.L. career record for most strikeouts—32.

Year League	W	L	Pct.	ERA	G	GS	CG	ShO	Sv.	IP	H	R	ER	BB	SO
1995— Seattle (A.L.)	2	0	1.000	2.70	2	1	0	0	0	10	5	3	3	6	16
1997— Seattle (A.L.)	0	2	.000	5.54	2	2	1	0	0	13	14	8	8	6	16
1998— Houston (N.L.)	0	2	.000	1.93	2	2	0	0	0	14	12	4	3	2	17
1999— Arizona (N.L.)	0	1	.000	7.56	1	1	0	0	0	8$^1/_3$	8	7	7	3	11
2001— Arizona (N.L.)	0	1	.000	3.38	1	1	0	0	0	8	6	3	3	2	9
Division series totals (5 years)	2	6	.250	4.05	8	7	1	0	0	53$^1/_3$	45	25	24	19	69

CHAMPIONSHIP SERIES RECORD

Year League	W	L	Pct.	ERA	G	GS	CG	ShO	Sv.	IP	H	R	ER	BB	SO
1995— Seattle (A.L.)	0	1	.000	2.35	2	2	0	0	0	15⅓	12	6	4	2	13
2001— Arizona (N.L.)	2	0	1.000	1.13	2	2	1	1	0	16	10	2	2	3	19
Champ. series totals (2 years)	2	1	.667	1.72	4	4	1	1	0	31⅓	22	8	6	5	32

WORLD SERIES RECORD

RECORDS: Shares single-series record for most games won—3 (2001).
NOTES: Named co-Most Valuable Player (2001). ... Member of World Series championship team (2001).

Year League	W	L	Pct.	ERA	G	GS	CG	ShO	Sv.	IP	H	R	ER	BB	SO
2001— Arizona (N.L.)	3	0	1.000	1.04	3	2	1	1	0	17⅓	9	2	2	3	19

ALL-STAR GAME RECORD

Year League	W	L	Pct.	ERA	GS	CG	ShO	Sv.	IP	H	R	ER	BB	SO
1990— American					Did not play.									
1993— American	0	0	...	0.00	0	0	0	0	2	0	0	0	0	1
1994— American	0	0	...	9.00	0	0	0	0	1	2	1	1	0	0
1995— American	0	0	...	0.00	1	0	0	0	2	0	0	0	1	3
1997— American	0	0	...	0.00	1	0	0	0	2	0	0	0	1	2
1999— National	0	0	...	0.00	0	0	0	0	1	0	0	0	0	1
2000— National	0	0	...	0.00	1	0	0	0	1	1	0	0	0	1
2001— National	0	0	...	0.00	1	0	0	0	2	1	0	0	0	3
All-Star Game totals (7 years)	0	0	...	0.82	4	0	0	0	11	4	1	1	2	11

JOHNSON, RUSS   IF   DEVIL RAYS

PERSONAL: Born February 22, 1973, in Baton Rouge, La. ... 5-10/180. ... Bats right, throws right. ... Full name: William Russell Johnson.
HIGH SCHOOL: Denham Springs (La.).
COLLEGE: Louisiana State.
TRANSACTIONS/CAREER NOTES: Selected by Houston Astros organization in supplemental round ("sandwich pick" between first and second round, 30th pick overall) of free-agent draft (June 2, 1994); pick received as part of compensation for San Francisco Giants signing Type A free-agent P Mark Portugal. ... Traded by Astros to Tampa Bay Devil Rays for P Marc Valdes (May 27, 2000). ... On Tampa Bay disabled list (May 16-31, 2001); included rehabilitation assignment to Orlando (May 28-31).
STATISTICAL NOTES: Led Texas League shortstops with 664 total chances and 87 double plays in 1996. ... Led Pacific Coast League third basemen with .962 fielding percentage in 1998.

							— BATTING —							— FIELDING —		
Year Team (League)	Pos.	G	AB	R	H	2B	3B	HR	RBI	Avg.	BB	SO	SB	PO	A	E	Avg.
1995— Jackson (Texas)	SS	132	475	65	118	16	2	9	53	.248	50	60	10	182	383	13	*.978
1996— Jackson (Texas)	SS	132	496	86	154	24	5	15	74	.310	56	50	9	•219	411	34	.949
1997— New Orleans (A.A.).....	3B-SS-DH	122	445	72	123	16	6	4	49	.276	66	78	7	86	269	21	.944
—Houston (N.L.)	3B-2B	21	60	7	18	1	0	2	9	.300	6	14	1	13	24	1	.974
1998— New Orleans (PCL).....	3-2-S-DH	122	453	*95	140	28	2	7	52	.309	*90	64	11	76	235	11	†.966
—Houston (N.L.)	3B-2B	8	13	2	3	1	0	0	0	.231	1	5	1	3	9	0	1.000
1999— New Orleans (PCL).....	2B-SS-OF	22	77	17	27	6	0	1	12	.351	16	13	1	32	60	3	.968
—Houston (N.L.)	3B-2B-SS	83	156	24	44	10	0	5	23	.282	20	31	2	33	88	7	.945
2000— Houston (N.L.)	SS-3B-2B	26	45	4	8	0	0	3	.178	2	10	1	11	14	1	.962
—Tampa Bay (A.L.)■....	3B-2B-SS	74	185	28	47	8	0	2	17	.254	15	30	4	45	143	5	.974
2001— Tampa Bay (A.L.).......3B-2B-SS-DH	85	248	32	73	19	2	4	33	.294	34	57	2	84	136	7	.969
—Orlando (Sou.)	2B	1	3	0	2	0	0	0	0	.667	1	0	0	3	6	2	.818
American League totals (2 years)		159	433	60	120	27	2	6	50	.277	59	87	6	129	279	12	.971
National League totals (4 years)		138	274	37	73	12	0	7	35	.266	29	60	5	60	135	9	.956
Major League totals (5 years)		297	707	97	193	39	2	13	85	.273	88	147	11	189	414	21	.966

DIVISION SERIES RECORD

							— BATTING —							— FIELDING —		
Year Team (League)	Pos.	G	AB	R	H	2B	3B	HR	RBI	Avg.	BB	SO	SB	PO	A	E	Avg.
1997— Houston (N.L.)	PH	1	1	0	0	0	0	0	0	.000	0	1	0	...	...	...	...
1999— Houston (N.L.)	PH	2	1	0	1	1	0	0	0	1.000	1	0	0	...	...	...	...
Division series totals (2 years)		3	2	0	1	1	0	0	0	.500	1	1	0	...	...	...	...

JONES, ANDRUW   OF   BRAVES

PERSONAL: Born April 23, 1977, in Willemstad, Curacao. ... 6-1/210. ... Bats right, throws right. ... Full name: Andruw Rudolf Jones.
HIGH SCHOOL: St. Paulus (Willemstad, Curacao).
TRANSACTIONS/CAREER NOTES: Signed as non-drafted free agent by Atlanta Braves organization (July 1, 1993).
RECORDS: Holds N.L. single-season record for fewest singles (150 or more games)—55 (1997).
HONORS: Named South Atlantic League Most Valuable Player (1995). ... Won N.L. Gold Glove as outfielder (1998-2001).
STATISTICAL NOTES: Led South Atlantic League with nine sacrifice flies in 1995. ... Led South Atlantic League outfielders with 346 total chances in 1995. ... Led N.L. outfielders with 435 total chances and tied for lead with six double plays in 1998. ... Led N.L. outfielders in total chances with 515 in 1999 and 449 in 2000. ... Career major league grand slams: 1.

							— BATTING —							— FIELDING —		
Year Team (League)	Pos.	G	AB	R	H	2B	3B	HR	RBI	Avg.	BB	SO	SB	PO	A	E	Avg.
1994— GC Braves (GCL)........	OF	27	95	22	21	5	1	2	10	.221	16	19	5	90	0	3	.968
—Danville (Appl.)..........	OF	36	143	20	48	9	2	1	16	.336	9	25	16	81	3	2	.977
1995— Macon (S.Atl.)	OF	•139	537	*104	149	41	5	25	100	.277	70	122	*56	*332	10	4	.988
1996— Durham (Caro.)	OF	66	243	65	76	14	3	17	43	.313	42	54	16	174	9	7	.963
—Greenville (Sou.)	OF	38	157	39	58	10	1	12	37	.369	17	34	12	129	7	1	.993
—Richmond (I.L.)	OF	12	45	11	17	3	1	5	12	.378	1	9	2	34	1	1	.972
—Atlanta (N.L.)..............	OF	31	106	11	23	7	1	5	13	.217	7	29	3	73	4	2	.975

Year Team (League)	Pos.	G	AB	R	H	2B	3B	HR	RBI	Avg.	BB	SO	SB	PO	A	E	Avg.
1997—Atlanta (N.L.)..............	OF	153	399	60	92	18	1	18	70	.231	56	107	20	287	14	7	.977
1998—Atlanta (N.L.)..............	OF	159	582	89	158	33	8	31	90	.271	40	129	27	*413	•20	2	.995
1999—Atlanta (N.L.)..............	OF	•162	592	97	163	35	5	26	84	.275	76	103	24	*492	13	10	.981
2000—Atlanta (N.L.)..............	OF	161	*656	122	199	36	6	36	104	.303	59	100	21	*438	9	2	.996
2001—Atlanta (N.L.)..............	OF	161	625	104	157	25	2	34	104	.251	56	142	11	461	10	6	.987
Major League totals (6 years)		827	2960	483	792	154	23	150	465	.268	294	610	106	2164	70	29	.987

DIVISION SERIES RECORD

Year Team (League)	Pos.	G	AB	R	H	2B	3B	HR	RBI	Avg.	BB	SO	SB	PO	A	E	Avg.
1996—Atlanta (N.L.)..............	OF-PR	3	0	0	0	0	0	0	0	...	1	0	0	2	0	0	1.000
1997—Atlanta (N.L.)..............	OF	3	5	1	0	0	0	0	1	.000	1	1	0	10	0	0	1.000
1998—Atlanta (N.L.)..............	OF	3	9	2	0	0	0	0	1	.000	3	2	2	8	0	0	1.000
1999—Atlanta (N.L.)..............	OF	4	18	1	4	1	0	0	2	.222	1	3	0	12	0	0	1.000
2000—Atlanta (N.L.)..............	OF	3	9	3	1	0	0	1	1	.111	4	1	0	8	0	0	1.000
2001—Atlanta (N.L.)..............	OF	3	12	2	6	0	0	1	1	.500	0	3	0	7	0	0	1.000
Division series totals (6 years)		19	53	9	11	1	0	2	6	.208	10	10	2	47	0	0	1.000

CHAMPIONSHIP SERIES RECORD

Year Team (League)	Pos.	G	AB	R	H	2B	3B	HR	RBI	Avg.	BB	SO	SB	PO	A	E	Avg.
1996—Atlanta (N.L.)..............	OF-PR-PH	5	9	3	2	0	0	1	3	.222	3	2	0	5	0	0	1.000
1997—Atlanta (N.L.)..............	OF-PH	5	9	0	4	0	0	0	1	.444	1	1	0	12	1	0	1.000
1998—Atlanta (N.L.)..............	OF	6	22	3	6	0	0	1	2	.273	1	4	1	15	0	0	1.000
1999—Atlanta (N.L.)..............	OF	6	23	5	5	0	0	1	1	.217	4	3	0	17	0	0	1.000
2001—Atlanta (N.L.)..............	OF	5	17	4	3	0	0	1	1	.176	1	5	0	13	0	0	1.000
Championship series totals (5 years)		27	80	15	20	0	0	3	8	.250	10	15	1	62	1	0	1.000

WORLD SERIES RECORD

RECORDS: Shares record for most home runs in two consecutive innings—2 (October 20, 1996, second and third innings). ... Shares single-inning record for most putouts by outfielder—3 (October 24, 1999, seventh inning).

NOTES: Hit home runs in first two at-bats (October 20, 1996, second and third innings).

Year Team (League)	Pos.	G	AB	R	H	2B	3B	HR	RBI	Avg.	BB	SO	SB	PO	A	E	Avg.
1996—Atlanta (N.L.)..............	OF	6	20	4	8	1	0	2	6	.400	3	6	1	7	1	0	1.000
1999—Atlanta (N.L.)..............	OF	4	13	1	1	0	0	0	0	.077	1	3	0	10	0	0	1.000
World Series totals (2 years)		10	33	5	9	1	0	2	6	.273	4	9	1	17	1	0	1.000

ALL-STAR GAME RECORD

Year League	Pos.	AB	R	H	2B	3B	HR	RBI	Avg.	BB	SO	SB	PO	A	E	Avg.
2000—National	OF	2	0	1	0	0	0	1	.500	0	1	0	2	0	0	1.000

JONES, BOBBY   P   PADRES

PERSONAL: Born February 10, 1970, in Fresno, Calif. ... 6-4/225. ... Throws right, bats right. ... Full name: Robert Joseph Jones.

HIGH SCHOOL: Fresno (Calif.).

COLLEGE: Fresno State.

TRANSACTIONS/CAREER NOTES: Selected by New York Mets organization in supplemental round ("sandwich pick" between first and second round, 36th pick overall) of free-agent draft (June 3, 1991); pick received as part of compensation for Los Angeles Dodgers signing Type A free-agent OF Darryl Strawberry. ... On New York disabled list (May 24-September 10, 1999); included rehabilitation assignments to Binghamton (August 7-17 and September 5-10) and Norfolk (August 18-25). ... On New York disabled list (April 17-May 18, 2000); included rehabilitation assignment to Norfolk (May 7-18). ... Granted free agency (November 4, 2000). ... Signed by San Diego Padres (February 15, 2001).

HONORS: Named Eastern League Pitcher of the Year (1992).

STATISTICAL NOTES: Led International League with 11 hit batsmen in 1993. ... Led N.L. with 18 sacrifice hits in 1995. ... Tied for N.L. lead with 37 home runs allowed in 2001.

Year League	W	L	Pct.	ERA	G	GS	CG	ShO	Sv.	IP	H	R	ER	BB	SO
1991—Columbia (S.Atl.)	3	1	.750	1.85	5	5	0	0	0	24 1/3	20	5	5	3	35
1992—Binghamton (East.)	12	4	.750	*1.88	24	24	4	*4	0	158	118	40	33	43	143
1993—Norfolk (I.L.)	12	10	.545	3.63	24	24	6	*3	0	166	149	72	67	32	126
—New York (N.L.)	2	4	.333	3.65	9	9	0	0	0	61 2/3	61	35	25	22	35
1994—New York (N.L.)	12	7	.632	3.15	24	24	1	1	0	160	157	75	56	56	80
1995—New York (N.L.)	10	10	.500	4.19	30	30	3	1	0	195 2/3	209	107	91	53	127
1996—New York (N.L.)	12	8	.600	4.42	31	31	3	1	0	195 2/3	219	102	96	46	116
1997—New York (N.L.)	15	9	.625	3.63	30	30	2	1	0	193 1/3	177	88	78	63	125
1998—New York (N.L.)	9	9	.500	4.05	30	30	0	0	0	195 1/3	192	94	88	53	115
1999—New York (N.L.)	3	3	.500	5.61	12	9	0	0	0	59 1/3	69	37	37	11	31
—Binghamton (East.)	1	2	.333	3.86	3	3	0	0	0	11 2/3	11	5	5	5	12
—Norfolk (I.L.)	2	0	1.000	2.45	2	2	0	0	0	11	11	3	3	3	8
2000—New York (N.L.)	11	6	.647	5.06	27	27	1	0	0	154 2/3	171	90	87	49	85
—Norfolk (I.L.)	2	0	1.000	5.32	4	4	0	0	0	23 2/3	31	14	14	4	19
2001—San Diego (N.L.)■	8	*19	.296	5.12	33	33	1	0	0	195	250	137	111	38	113
Major League totals (9 years)	82	75	.522	4.27	226	223	11	4	0	1410 2/3	1505	765	669	391	827

DIVISION SERIES RECORD

RECORDS: Shares career record for most shutouts—1.

Year League	W	L	Pct.	ERA	G	GS	CG	ShO	Sv.	IP	H	R	ER	BB	SO
1999—New York (N.L.)					Did not play.										
2000—New York (N.L.)	1	0	1.000	0.00	1	1	1	1	0	9	1	0	0	2	5

CHAMPIONSHIP SERIES RECORD

Year League	W	L	Pct.	ERA	G	GS	CG	ShO	Sv.	IP	H	R	ER	BB	SO
1999— New York (N.L.)..................							Did not play.								
2000— New York (N.L.)..................	0	0	...	13.50	1	1	0	0	0	4	6	6	6	0	2

WORLD SERIES RECORD

Year League	W	L	Pct.	ERA	G	GS	CG	ShO	Sv.	IP	H	R	ER	BB	SO
2000— New York (N.L.)..................	0	1	.000	5.40	1	1	0	0	0	5	4	3	3	3	3

ALL-STAR GAME RECORD

Year League	W	L	Pct.	ERA	GS	CG	ShO	Sv.	IP	H	R	ER	BB	SO
1997— National.............................	0	0	...	0.00	0	0	0	0	1	1	0	0	0	2

JONES, CHIPPER   OF   BRAVES

PERSONAL: Born April 24, 1972, in De Land, Fla. ... 6-4/210. ... Bats both, throws right. ... Full name: Larry Wayne Jones Jr.

HIGH SCHOOL: The Bolles School (Jacksonville).

TRANSACTIONS/CAREER NOTES: Selected by Atlanta Braves organization in first round (first pick overall) of free-agent draft (June 4, 1990). ... On disabled list (March 20, 1994-entire season; and March 22-April 6, 1996).

RECORDS: Holds major league single-season records for fewest putouts by third baseman (150 or more games)—77 (1997); and fewest chances accepted by third baseman (150 or more games)—318. ... Shares major league single-season record for fewest double plays by third baseman (150 or more games)—10 (1999). ... Holds N.L. record for most home runs by switch hitter in two consecutive seasons—81 (1999-2000). ... Holds N.L. single-season records for most home runs by switch hitter—45 (1999); most home runs hit at home by switch hitter—25 (1999); highest slugging average by switch hitter—.633 (1999); most bases on balls by switch-hitter—126 (1999); fewest putouts by third baseman (150 or more games)—77 (1997); fewest assists by third baseman (150 or more games)—238 (1999); and fewest chances by third baseman (150 or more games)—318 (1997).

HONORS: Named N.L. Rookie Player of the Year by THE SPORTING NEWS (1995). ... Named N.L. Most Valuable Player by Baseball Writers' Association of America (1999). ... Named third baseman on THE SPORTING NEWS N.L. All-Star team (1999 and 2000-01). ... Named third baseman on THE SPORTING NEWS N.L. Silver Slugger team (1999 and 2000).

STATISTICAL NOTES: Led South Atlantic League with 10 sacrifice flies in 1991. ... Led South Atlantic League shortstops with 692 total chances and 71 double plays in 1991. ... Led International League with 268 total bases in 1993. ... Led International League shortstops with 619 total chances in 1993. ... Switch-hit home runs in one game five times (May 1, August 1 and September 21, 1999; and May 14 and July 5, 2000). ... Had 19-game hitting streak (June 1-21, 2000). ... Career major league grand slams: 6.

Year Team (League)	Pos.	G	AB	R	H	2B	3B	HR	RBI	Avg.	BB	SO	SB	PO	A	E	Avg.
1990— GC Braves (GCL)........	SS	44	140	20	32	1	1	1	18	.229	14	25	5	64	140	18	.919
1991— Macon (S.Atl.)...........	SS	136	473	*104	154	24	11	15	98	.326	69	70	40	*217	*419	56	.919
1992— Durham (Caro.).........	SS	70	264	43	73	22	1	4	31	.277	31	34	10	106	200	14	.956
— Greenville (Sou.)	SS	67	266	43	92	17	11	9	42	.346	11	32	14	92	218	18	.945
1993— Richmond (I.L.).........	SS	139	536	*97	*174	31	*12	13	89	.325	57	70	23	195	381	*43	.931
— Atlanta (N.L.).............	SS	8	3	2	2	1	0	0	0	.667	1	1	0	1	1	0	1.000
1994— Atlanta (N.L.)								Did not play.									
1995— Atlanta (N.L.).............	3B-OF	140	524	87	139	22	3	23	86	.265	73	99	8	103	255	25	.935
1996— Atlanta (N.L.)..........	3B-SS-OF	157	598	114	185	32	5	30	110	.309	87	88	14	103	288	17	.958
1997— Atlanta (N.L.).............	3B-OF	157	597	100	176	41	3	21	111	.295	76	88	20	83	241	15	.956
1998— Atlanta (N.L.).............	3B	160	601	123	188	29	5	34	107	.313	96	93	16	105	290	12	.971
1999— Atlanta (N.L.).............	3B-SS	157	567	116	181	41	1	45	110	.319	126	94	25	88	239	17	.951
2000— Atlanta (N.L.).............	3B-SS	156	579	118	180	38	1	36	111	.311	95	64	14	96	305	25	.941
2001— Atlanta (N.L.).............	3B-OF-DH	159	572	113	189	33	5	38	102	.330	98	82	9	91	233	18	.947
Major League totals (8 years)		1094	4041	773	1240	237	23	227	737	.307	652	609	106	670	1852	129	.951

DIVISION SERIES RECORD

RECORDS: Holds N.L. career records for most games—23; at-bats—79; runs—17; hits—26; total bases—47; bases on balls—21; strikeouts—18 and highest slugging average (50 or more at-bats)—.595. ... Shares N.L. career record for most home runs—6; extra-base hits—9; and runs batted in—16. ... Shares single-game record for most home runs—2 (October 3, 1995).

Year Team (League)	Pos.	G	AB	R	H	2B	3B	HR	RBI	Avg.	BB	SO	SB	PO	A	E	Avg.
1995— Atlanta (N.L.).............	3B	4	18	4	7	2	0	2	4	.389	2	2	0	3	4	0	1.000
1996— Atlanta (N.L.).............	3B	3	9	2	2	0	0	1	2	.222	3	4	1	1	3	0	1.000
1997— Atlanta (N.L.).............	3B	3	8	3	4	0	0	1	2	.500	3	2	1	2	3	1	.833
1998— Atlanta (N.L.).............	3B	3	10	2	2	0	0	0	1	.200	4	3	0	2	2	0	1.000
1999— Atlanta (N.L.).............	3B	4	13	2	3	0	0	0	1	.231	5	2	0	3	4	1	.875
2000— Atlanta (N.L.).............	3B	3	12	2	4	1	0	0	1	.333	1	4	0	3	5	2	.800
2001— Atlanta (N.L.).............	3B	3	9	2	4	0	0	2	5	.444	3	1	0	0	5	0	1.000
Division series totals (7 years)		23	79	17	26	3	0	6	16	.329	21	18	2	14	26	4	.909

CHAMPIONSHIP SERIES RECORD

RECORDS: Holds N.L. career record for most runs scored—20; and bases on balls received—24. ... Shares N.L. career record for most doubles—7. ... Shares N.L. single-series record for most singles—9 (1996). ... Shares single-game record for most singles—4 (October 9, 1996).

Year Team (League)	Pos.	G	AB	R	H	2B	3B	HR	RBI	Avg.	BB	SO	SB	PO	A	E	Avg.
1995— Atlanta (N.L.).............	3B	4	16	3	7	0	0	1	3	.438	3	1	1	4	13	0	1.000
1996— Atlanta (N.L.).............	3B	7	25	6	11	2	0	1	4	.440	3	1	1	5	7	1	.923
1997— Atlanta (N.L.).............	3B	6	24	5	7	1	0	2	4	.292	2	3	0	1	8	0	1.000
1998— Atlanta (N.L.).............	3B	6	24	2	5	1	0	0	1	.208	4	5	0	1	12	0	1.000
1999— Atlanta (N.L.).............	3B	6	19	3	5	2	0	0	1	.263	9	7	3	5	8	2	.867
2001— Atlanta (N.L.).............	3B	5	19	1	5	1	0	0	2	.263	3	6	0	2	10	1	.923
Championship series totals (6 years)		34	127	20	40	7	0	3	15	.315	24	23	5	18	58	4	.950

WORLD SERIES RECORD

NOTES: Member of World Series championship team (1995).

					BATTING									FIELDING			
Year Team (League)	Pos.	G	AB	R	H	2B	3B	HR	RBI	Avg.	BB	SO	SB	PO	A	E	Avg.
1995— Atlanta (N.L.).............	3B	6	21	3	6	3	0	0	1	.286	4	3	0	6	12	1	.947
1996— Atlanta (N.L.).............	3B-SS	6	21	3	6	3	0	0	3	.286	4	2	1	5	6	0	1.000
1999— Atlanta (N.L.).............	3B	4	13	2	3	0	0	1	2	.231	4	2	0	1	5	0	1.000
World Series totals (3 years)		16	55	8	15	6	0	1	6	.273	12	7	1	12	23	1	.972

ALL-STAR GAME RECORD

				BATTING									FIELDING			
Year League	Pos.	AB	R	H	2B	3B	HR	RBI	Avg.	BB	SO	SB	PO	A	E	Avg.
1996— National	3B	2	1	1	0	0	0	0	.500	0	0	0	1	1	0	1.000
1997— National	3B	1	0	0	0	0	0	0	.000	0	0	0	0	1	0	1.000
1998— National	3B	2	1	0	0	0	0	0	.000	1	0	0	0	0	0	...
2000— National	3B	3	1	3	0	0	1	1	1.000	0	0	0	1	0	0	1.000
2001— National	3B	2	0	0	0	0	0	0	.000	0	0	0	0	1	0	1.000
All-Star Game totals (5 years)		10	3	4	0	0	1	1	.400	1	0	0	2	3	0	1.000

JONES, JACQUE — OF — TWINS

PERSONAL: Born April 25, 1975, in San Diego. ... 5-10/176. ... Bats left, throws left. ... Full name: Jacque Dewayne Jones.
HIGH SCHOOL: San Diego High.
COLLEGE: Southern California.
TRANSACTIONS/CAREER NOTES: Selected by Minnesota Twins organization in second round of free-agent draft (June 2, 1996).
STATISTICAL NOTES: Career major league grand slams: 1.
MISCELLANEOUS: Member of 1996 U.S. Olympic baseball team.

						BATTING								FIELDING			
Year Team (League)	Pos.	G	AB	R	H	2B	3B	HR	RBI	Avg.	BB	SO	SB	PO	A	E	Avg.
1996— Fort Myers (FSL)	OF	1	3	0	2	1	0	0	1	.667	0	0	0	0	0	0	...
1997— Fort Myers (FSL)	OF	131	539	84	*160	33	6	15	82	.297	33	110	24	313	8	7	.979
1998— New Britain (East.)	OF-DH	134	518	78	155	39	3	21	85	.299	37	134	18	288	12	10	.968
1999— Salt Lake (PCL)	OF	52	198	32	59	13	2	4	26	.298	9	36	9	150	2	2	.987
— Minnesota (A.L.)	OF	95	322	54	93	24	2	9	44	.289	17	63	3	231	9	5	.980
2000— Minnesota (A.L.)	OF	154	523	66	149	26	5	19	76	.285	26	111	7	334	9	2	.994
2001— Minnesota (A.L.)	OF-DH	149	475	57	131	25	0	14	49	.276	39	92	12	278	8	5	.983
Major League totals (3 years)		398	1320	177	373	75	7	42	169	.283	82	266	22	843	26	12	.986

JONES, TERRY — OF

PERSONAL: Born February 15, 1971, in Birmingham, Ala. ... 5-10/160. ... Bats both, throws right. ... Full name: Terry Lee Jones.
HIGH SCHOOL: Pinson Valley (Pinson, Ala.).
JUNIOR COLLEGE: Wallace State Community College (Ala.).
COLLEGE: North Alabama.
TRANSACTIONS/CAREER NOTES: Selected by Colorado Rockies organization in 40th round of free-agent draft (June 3, 1993). ... Traded by Rockies with a player to be named later to Montreal Expos for P Dave Veres and a player to be named later (December 10, 1997). ... On Ottawa disabled list (April 21-May 7, 1999). ... Granted free agency (October 4, 1999). ... Signed by Los Angeles Dodgers organization (October 28, 1999). ... Traded by Dodgers to New York Yankees for a player to be named later (January 6, 2000). ... Claimed on waivers by Expos (March 31, 2000). ... On disabled list (July 18-August 4, 2000). ... On Montreal disabled list (March 28-May 31 and June 11-September 1, 2001); included rehabilitation assignments to Jupiter (May 22-24 and August 7-13) and Ottawa (May 25-31 and August 14-26). ... Granted free agency (October 12, 2001).
STATISTICAL NOTES: Led California League outfielders with 342 total chances and tied for lead with four double plays in 1994. ... Led Pacific Coast League outfielders with 311 total chances in 1996.

						BATTING								FIELDING			
Year Team (League)	Pos.	G	AB	R	H	2B	3B	HR	RBI	Avg.	BB	SO	SB	PO	A	E	Avg.
1993— Bend (N'West)	OF	33	138	21	40	5	4	0	18	.290	12	19	16	57	7	1	.985
— Central Valley (Calif.)..	OF	21	73	16	21	1	0	0	7	.288	10	15	5	36	2	1	.974
1994— Central Valley (Calif.)..	OF	129	*536	94	157	20	1	2	34	.293	42	85	44	*312	*16	14	.959
1995— New Haven (East.).......	OF	124	472	78	127	12	1	1	26	.269	39	104	*51	264	18	•10	.966
1996— Colo. Springs (PCL) ...	OF	128	497	75	143	7	4	0	33	.288	37	80	26	281	14	*16	.949
— Colorado (N.L.)	OF	12	10	6	3	0	0	0	1	.300	0	3	0	5	0	0	1.000
1997— Colo. Springs (PCL) ...	OF	92	363	70	98	14	4	1	25	.270	25	49	*36	139	11	1	.993
1998— Ottawa (I.L.)■	OF	81	278	36	66	3	4	0	21	.237	32	48	35	193	5	4	.980
— Montreal (N.L.)..........	OF	60	212	30	46	7	2	1	15	.217	21	46	16	161	4	2	.988
1999— Ottawa (I.L.)	OF-DH	88	332	49	87	17	2	0	23	.262	24	66	30	172	9	3	.984
— Montreal (N.L.)..........	OF	17	63	4	17	1	1	0	3	.270	3	14	1	47	2	0	1.000
2000— Montreal (N.L.)..........	OF	108	168	30	42	8	2	0	13	.250	10	32	7	95	4	3	.971
2001— Jupiter (FSL)	OF	7	25	4	4	1	0	0	1	.160	1	3	0	8	0	0	1.000
— Ottawa (I.L.)	OF	17	68	6	20	2	0	0	5	.294	3	13	2	20	5	0	1.000
— Montreal (N.L.)..........	OF	30	77	8	20	5	0	0	2	.260	2	11	3	41	2	1	.977
Major League totals (5 years)		227	530	78	128	21	5	1	34	.242	36	106	27	349	12	6	.984

JONES, TODD — P — ROCKIES

PERSONAL: Born April 24, 1968, in Marietta, Ga. ... 6-3/230. ... Throws right, bats right. ... Full name: Todd Barton Jones.
HIGH SCHOOL: Osborne (Ga.).
COLLEGE: Jacksonville (Ala.) State.
TRANSACTIONS/CAREER NOTES: Selected by New York Mets organization in 41st round of free-agent draft (June 2, 1986); did not sign. ... Selected by Houston Astros organization in supplemental round ("sandwich pick" between first and second round, 27th pick overall) of free-

agent draft (June 5, 1989); pick received as part of compensation for Texas Rangers signing Type A free-agent P Nolan Ryan. ... On suspended list (September 14-16, 1993). ... On Houston disabled list (July 19-August 12 and August 18-September 12, 1996); included rehabilitation assignment to Tucson (August 9-12). ... Traded by Astros with OF Brian Hunter, IF Orlando Miller, P Doug Brocail and cash to Detroit Tigers for C Brad Ausmus, P Jose Lima, P C.J. Nitkowski, P Trever Miller and IF Daryle Ward (December 10, 1996). ... Traded by Tigers to Minnesota Twins for P Mark Redman (July 28, 2001). ... Granted free agency (November 5, 2001). ... Signed by Colorado Rockies (January 11, 2002).

HONORS: Named A.L. Fireman of the Year by THE SPORTING NEWS (2000).

Year League	W	L	Pct.	ERA	G	GS	CG	ShO	Sv.	IP	H	R	ER	BB	SO
1989—Auburn (NY-Penn)	2	3	.400	5.44	11	9	1	0	0	49²/₃	47	39	30	42	71
1990—Osceola (FSL)	12	10	.545	3.51	27	•27	1	0	0	151¹/₃	124	81	59	*109	106
1991—Osceola (FSL)	4	4	.500	4.35	14	14	0	0	0	72¹/₃	69	38	35	35	51
—Jackson (Texas)	4	3	.571	4.88	10	10	0	0	0	55¹/₃	51	37	30	39	37
1992—Jackson (Texas)	3	7	.300	3.14	*61	0	0	0	25	66	52	28	23	44	60
—Tucson (PCL)	0	1	.000	4.50	3	0	0	0	0	4	1	2	2	10	4
1993—Tucson (PCL)	4	2	.667	4.44	41	0	0	0	12	48²/₃	49	26	24	31	45
—Houston (N.L.)	1	2	.333	3.13	27	0	0	0	2	37¹/₃	28	14	13	15	25
1994—Houston (N.L.)	5	2	.714	2.72	48	0	0	0	5	72²/₃	52	23	22	26	63
1995—Houston (N.L.)	6	5	.545	3.07	68	0	0	0	15	99²/₃	89	38	34	52	96
1996—Houston (N.L.)	6	3	.667	4.40	51	0	0	0	17	57¹/₃	61	30	28	32	44
—Tucson (PCL)	0	0	...	0.00	1	0	0	0	0	2	1	1	0	2	0
1997—Detroit (A.L.)■	5	4	.556	3.09	68	0	0	0	31	70	60	29	24	35	70
1998—Detroit (A.L.)	1	4	.200	4.97	65	0	0	0	28	63¹/₃	58	38	35	36	57
1999—Detroit (A.L.)	4	4	.500	3.80	65	0	0	0	30	66¹/₃	64	30	28	35	64
2000—Detroit (A.L.)	2	4	.333	3.52	67	0	0	0	•42	64	67	28	25	25	67
2001—Detroit (A.L.)	4	5	.444	4.62	45	0	0	0	11	48²/₃	60	31	25	22	39
—Minnesota (A.L.)■	1	0	1.000	3.26	24	0	0	0	2	19¹/₃	27	8	7	7	15
A.L. totals (5 years)	17	21	.447	3.91	334	0	0	0	144	331²/₃	336	164	144	160	312
N.L. totals (4 years)	18	12	.600	3.27	194	0	0	0	39	267	230	105	97	125	228
Major League totals (9 years)	35	33	.515	3.62	528	0	0	0	183	598²/₃	566	269	241	285	540

ALL-STAR GAME RECORD

Year League	W	L	Pct.	ERA	GS	CG	ShO	Sv.	IP	H	R	ER	BB	SO
2000—American	0	0	...	0.00	0	0	0	0	1	0	0	0	0	1

JORDAN, BRIAN — OF — DODGERS

PERSONAL: Born March 29, 1967, in Baltimore. ... 6-1/205. ... Bats right, throws right. ... Full name: Brian O'Neal Jordan.
HIGH SCHOOL: Milford (Baltimore).
COLLEGE: Richmond.
TRANSACTIONS/CAREER NOTES: Selected by Cleveland Indians organization in 20th round of free-agent draft (June 3, 1985); did not sign. ... Selected by St. Louis Cardinals organization in supplemental round ("sandwich pick" between first and second round, 30th pick overall) of free-agent draft (June 1, 1988); pick received as part of compensation for New York Yankees signing Type A free-agent 1B/OF Jack Clark. ... On disabled list (May 1-8 and June 3-10, 1991). ... On temporarily inactive list (July 3, 1991-remainder of season). ... On St. Louis disabled list (May 23-June 22, 1992); included rehabilitation assignment to Louisville (June 10-22). ... On Louisville disabled list (June 7-14, 1993). ... On disabled list (July 10, 1994-remainder of season; and March 31-April 15, 1996). ... On St. Louis disabled list (May 6-June 13, June 26-August 10 and August 25, 1997-remainder of season); included rehabilitation assignment to Louisville (June 5-13). ... Granted free agency (October 22, 1998). ... Signed by Atlanta Braves (November 23, 1998). ... On disabled list (April 4-19, 2000). ... Traded by Braves with P Odalis Perez and P Andy Brown to Los Angeles Dodgers for OF Gary Sheffield (January 15, 2002).
STATISTICAL NOTES: Tied for N.L. lead with six double plays by outfielder in 1998. ... Career major league grand slams: 4.

Year Team (League)	Pos.	G	AB	R	H	2B	3B	HR	RBI	Avg.	BB	SO	SB	PO	A	E	Avg.
1988—Hamilton (NY-Penn)	OF	19	71	12	22	3	1	4	12	.310	6	15	3	32	1	1	.971
1989—St. Petersburg (FSL)	OF	11	43	7	15	4	1	2	11	.349	0	8	0	22	2	0	1.000
1990—Arkansas (Texas)	OF	16	50	4	8	1	0	0	0	.160	0	11	0	28	0	2	.933
—St. Petersburg (FSL)	OF	9	30	3	5	0	1	0	1	.167	2	11	0	23	0	0	1.000
1991—Louisville (A.A.)	OF	61	212	35	56	11	4	4	24	.264	17	41	10	144	3	2	.987
1992—Louisville (A.A.)	OF	43	155	23	45	3	1	4	16	.290	8	21	13	89	3	1	.989
—St. Louis (N.L.)	OF	55	193	17	40	9	4	5	22	.207	10	48	7	101	4	1	.991
1993—St. Louis (N.L.)	OF	67	223	33	69	10	6	10	44	.309	12	35	6	140	4	4	.973
—Louisville (A.A.)	OF	38	144	24	54	13	2	5	35	.375	16	17	9	75	2	0	1.000
1994—St. Louis (N.L.)	OF-1B	53	178	14	46	8	2	5	15	.258	16	40	4	105	6	1	.991
1995—St. Louis (N.L.)	OF	131	490	83	145	20	4	22	81	.296	22	79	24	267	4	1	.996
1996—St. Louis (N.L.)	OF-1B	140	513	82	159	36	1	17	104	.310	29	84	22	310	9	2	.994
1997—St. Louis (N.L.)	OF	47	145	17	34	5	0	0	10	.234	10	21	6	82	2	0	1.000
—Louisville (A.A.)	OF-DH	6	20	1	3	0	0	0	2	.150	1	2	0	6	0	0	1.000
1998—St. Louis (N.L.)	OF-DH-3B	150	564	100	178	34	7	25	91	.316	40	66	17	284	12	9	.970
1999—Atlanta (N.L.)■	OF	153	576	100	163	28	4	23	115	.283	51	81	13	295	9	3	.990
2000—Atlanta (N.L.)	OF	133	489	71	129	26	0	17	77	.264	38	80	10	287	7	3	.990
2001—Atlanta (N.L.)	OF-DH	148	560	82	165	32	3	25	97	.295	31	88	3	321	11	3	.991
Major League totals (10 years)		1077	3931	599	1128	208	31	149	656	.287	259	622	112	2192	68	27	.988

DIVISION SERIES RECORD

RECORDS: Holds N.L. career record for highest batting average (50 or more at-bats)—.353. ... Shares N.L. career record for most runs batted in—16. ... Shares N.L. single-game record for most runs batted in—5 (October 8, 1999). ... Shares single-inning record for most at-bats—2 (October 9, 1999, sixth inning).

Year Team (League)	Pos.	G	AB	R	H	2B	3B	HR	RBI	Avg.	BB	SO	SB	PO	A	E	Avg.
1996—St. Louis (N.L.)	OF	3	12	4	4	0	0	1	3	.333	1	3	1	5	0	0	1.000
1999—Atlanta (N.L.)	OF	4	17	2	8	1	0	1	7	.471	1	2	0	12	1	0	1.000
2000—Atlanta (N.L.)	OF	3	11	1	4	1	0	0	4	.364	1	1	0	6	0	0	1.000
2001—Atlanta (N.L.)	OF	3	11	1	2	0	0	1	2	.182	0	5	0	10	0	0	1.000
Division series totals (4 years)		13	51	8	18	2	0	3	16	.353	3	11	1	33	1	0	1.000

CHAMPIONSHIP SERIES RECORD

									BATTING					FIELDING			
Year Team (League)	Pos.	G	AB	R	H	2B	3B	HR	RBI	Avg.	BB	SO	SB	PO	A	E	Avg.
1996—St. Louis (N.L.)...........	OF	7	25	3	6	1	1	1	2	.240	2	3	0	13	0	0	1.000
1999— Atlanta (N.L.)..............	OF	6	25	3	5	0	0	2	5	.200	3	5	0	17	0	0	1.000
2001— Atlanta (N.L.)..............	OF	5	21	1	4	2	0	0	3	.190	0	6	0	19	0	0	1.000
Championship series totals (3 years)		18	71	7	15	3	1	3	10	.211	5	14	0	49	0	0	1.000

WORLD SERIES RECORD

									BATTING					FIELDING			
Year Team (League)	Pos.	G	AB	R	H	2B	3B	HR	RBI	Avg.	BB	SO	SB	PO	A	E	Avg.
1999— Atlanta (N.L.)..............	OF	4	13	1	1	0	0	0	1	.077	4	2	0	8	0	1	.889

ALL-STAR GAME RECORD

							BATTING					FIELDING			
Year League	Pos.	AB	R	H	2B	3B	HR	RBI	Avg.	BB	SO	SB	PO	A	E	Avg.
1999— National	OF	1	0	1	0	0	0	0	1.000	1	0	0	0	0	0	...

RECORD AS FOOTBALL PLAYER

TRANSACTIONS/CAREER NOTES: Selected by Buffalo Bills in seventh round (173rd pick overall) of 1989 NFL draft. ... Signed by Bills (July 17, 1989). ... Claimed on waivers by Atlanta Falcons (September 5, 1989). ... On injured reserve with ankle injury (September 9-October 22, 1989). ... On developmental squad (October 23-December 2, 1989). ... Granted free agency (February 1, 1992).

PRO STATISTICS: 1989—Recovered two fumbles. 1990—Recovered one fumble. 1991—Credited with two safeties and recovered one fumble.

MISCELLANEOUS: Played safety. ... Named alternate for 1992 Pro Bowl.

		INTERCEPTIONS				SACKS	PUNT RETURNS				KICKOFF RETURNS				TOTAL		
Year Team	G	No.	Yds.	Avg.	TD	No.	No.	Yds.	Avg.	TD	No.	Yds.	Avg.	TD	TD	Pts.	Fum.
1989— Atlanta NFL................	4	0	0	...	0	0.0	4	34	8.5	0	3	27	9.0	0	0	0	1
1990— Atlanta NFL................	16	3	14	4.7	0	0.0	2	19	9.5	0	0	0	...	0	0	0	0
1991— Atlanta NFL................	16	2	3	1.5	0	4.0	14	116	8.3	0	5	100	20.0	0	0	4	0
Pro totals (3 years)	36	5	17	3.4	0	4.0	20	169	8.5	0	8	127	15.9	0	0	4	1

JORDAN, KEVIN   IF

PERSONAL: Born October 9, 1969, in San Francisco. ... 6-1/201. ... Bats right, throws right. ... Full name: Kevin Wayne Jordan.

HIGH SCHOOL: Lowell (San Francisco).

JUNIOR COLLEGE: Canada College (Calif.).

COLLEGE: Nebraska.

TRANSACTIONS/CAREER NOTES: Selected by Los Angeles Dodgers organization in 10th round of free-agent draft (June 5, 1989); did not sign. ... Selected by New York Yankees organization in 20th round of free-agent draft (June 4, 1990). ... Traded by Yankees with P Bobby Munoz and P Ryan Karp to Philadelphia Phillies for P Terry Mulholland and a player to be named later (February 9, 1994); Yankees acquired P Jeff Patterson to complete deal (November 8, 1994). ... On disabled list (May 1-June 20, 1994; and June 17, 1996-remainder of season). ... Granted free agency (December 21, 2000).

STATISTICAL NOTES: Led Eastern League with 234 total bases in 1993. ... Led Eastern League second basemen with 93 double plays in 1993. ... Career major league grand slams: 1.

									BATTING					FIELDING			
Year Team (League)	Pos.	G	AB	R	H	2B	3B	HR	RBI	Avg.	BB	SO	SB	PO	A	E	Avg.
1990— Oneonta (NY-Penn)	2B	73	276	· 47	92	13	•7	4	54	.333	23	31	19	131	158	8	.973
1991— Fort Lauderdale (FSL)	2B-1B	121	448	61	122	25	5	4	53	.272	37	66	14	182	306	16	.968
1992— Prince William (Caro.)	2B-3B	112	438	67	136	29	8	8	63	.311	27	54	6	192	288	20	.960
1993— Albany/Colonie (East.)	2B	135	513	87	145	*33	4	16	87	.283	41	53	8	261	359	21	.967
1994— Scranton/W.B. (I.L.)■	2B-3B-DH	81	314	44	91	22	1	12	57	.290	29	28	0	160	237	16	.961
1995— Scranton/W.B. (I.L.) ..	2B-DH	106	410	61	127	29	4	5	60	.310	28	36	3	217	279	12	.976
— Philadelphia (N.L.)......	2B-3B	24	54	6	10	1	0	2	6	.185	2	9	0	29	35	1	.985
1996— Philadelphia (N.L.)......	1B-2B-3B	43	131	15	37	10	0	3	12	.282	5	20	2	243	27	0	1.000
1997— Scranton/W.B. (I.L.) ..	3B-2B-1B	7	30	5	9	2	2	0	2	.300	2	6	2	23	18	1	.976
— Philadelphia (N.L.)......1B-3B-2B-DH		84	177	19	47	8	0	6	30	.266	3	26	0	157	31	6	.969
1998— Philadelphia (N.L.)......	1-2-DH-3	112	250	23	69	13	0	2	27	.276	8	30	0	195	77	4	.986
1999— Philadelphia (N.L.)......	3B-2B-1B	120	347	36	99	17	3	4	51	.285	24	34	0	151	164	10	.969
2000— Philadelphia (N.L.)......	2B-3B-1B	109	337	30	74	16	2	5	36	.220	17	41	0	147	163	7	.978
2001— Philadelphia (N.L.)......	1B-2B-3B	68	113	9	27	5	0	1	13	.239	14	21	0	70	37	5	.955
Major League totals (7 years)		560	1409	138	363	70	5	23	175	.258	73	181	2	992	534	33	.979

JOSEPH, KEVIN   P   CARDINALS

PERSONAL: Born August 1, 1976, in Camp Hill, Pa. ... 6-4/200. ... Throws right, bats right. ... Full name: Kevin John Joseph.

HIGH SCHOOL: Trinity Christian (Addison, Texas).

COLLEGE: Rice.

TRANSACTIONS/CAREER NOTES: Selected by San Francisco Giants organization in sixth round of free-agent draft (June 3, 1997). ... On Shreveport disabled list (May 11-June 9, 2000). ... Traded by Giants with a player to be named later or cash to St. Louis Cardinals for P Jason Christiansen (July 31, 2001).

Year League	W	L	Pct.	ERA	G	GS	CG	ShO	Sv.	IP	H	R	ER	BB	SO
1997— Salem-Kaizer (N'West)	3	5	.375	5.40	17	6	0	0	1	45	44	35	27	26	45
1998— Bakersfield (Calif.).............	0	4	.000	8.14	6	6	0	0	0	21	35	26	19	20	17
— Salem-Kaizer (N'West)	1	1	.500	4.36	23	0	0	0	0	43 1/3	36	25	21	27	37
1999— San Jose (Calif.).............	1	2	.333	2.35	20	0	0	0	2	30 2/3	17	9	8	13	30
— Shreveport (Texas).............	0	2	.000	1.42	7	0	0	0	0	12 2/3	8	4	2	5	16
2000— Shreveport (Texas).............	3	11	.214	5.17	27	16	0	0	1	102 2/3	116	60	59	48	71
2001— Shreveport (Texas).............	2	1	.667	2.43	24	0	0	0	1	33 1/3	31	9	9	13	27
— San Jose (Calif.).............	0	0		3.38	9	0	0	0	3	13 1/3	12	6	5	1	15
— Fresno (PCL).....................	0	1	.000	7.56	5	0	0	0	0	8 1/3	9	7	7	4	2
— Memphis (PCL)■...............	0	2	.000	6.75	12	0	0	0	0	12	8	9	9	11	6

PERSONAL: Born June 16, 1962, in Atlanta. ... 6-2/200. ... Bats left, throws left. ... Full name: Wallace Keith Joyner.
HIGH SCHOOL: Redan (Stone Mountain, Ga.).
COLLEGE: Brigham Young.
TRANSACTIONS/CAREER NOTES: Selected by California Angels organization in third round of free-agent draft (June 6, 1983); pick received as compensation for New York Yankees signing free-agent DH Don Baylor. ... On disabled list (July 12, 1990-remainder of season). ... Granted free agency (October 28, 1991). ... Signed by Kansas City Royals (December 9, 1991). ... On disabled list (June 26-July 14, 1994). ... Traded by Royals with P Aaron Dorlarque to San Diego Padres for 2B/OF Bip Roberts and P Bryan Wolff (December 21, 1995). ... On San Diego disabled list (June 3-July 11, 1996); included rehabilitation assignment to Rancho Cucamonga (July 7-11). ... On San Diego disabled list (April 28-May 13, 1997); included rehabilitation assignment to Las Vegas (May 8-12). ... On San Diego disabled list (May 17-June 25, 1999); included rehabilitation assignment to Las Vegas (June 18-25). ... Traded by Padres with 2B Quilvio Veras and OF Reggie Sanders to Atlanta Braves for OF/1B Ryan Klesko, 2B Bret Boone and P Jason Shiell (December 22, 1999). ... Granted free agency (October 30, 2000). ... Signed by Angels organization (January 25, 2001). ... Released by Angels (June 16, 2001). ... Announced retirement (June 16, 2001).
RECORDS: Shares major league record for most home runs in month of October—4 (1987).
STATISTICAL NOTES: Tied for Eastern League lead with eight intentional bases on balls received in 1984. ... Led Pacific Coast League first basemen with 1,229 total chances and 121 double plays in 1985. ... Led A.L. with 12 sacrifice flies in 1986. ... Hit three home runs in one game (October 3, 1987). ... Led A.L. first basemen with 1,520 total chances in 1988 and 1,441 in 1991. ... Led A.L. first basemen with 148 double plays in 1988 and 138 in 1992. ... Career major league grand slams: 6.

Year Team (League)	Pos.	G	AB	R	H	2B	3B	HR	RBI	Avg.	BB	SO	SB	PO	A	E	Avg.
1983—Peoria (Midw.)	1B	54	192	25	63	16	2	3	33	.328	19	25	1	480	45	6	.989
1984—Waterbury (East.)	1B-OF	134	467	81	148	24	7	12	72	.317	67	60	0	906	86	9	.991
1985—Edmonton (PCL)	1B	126	477	68	135	29	5	12	73	.283	60	64	2	*1107	*107	*15	.988
1986—California (A.L.)	1B	154	593	82	172	27	3	22	100	.290	57	58	5	1222	139	15	.989
1987—California (A.L.)	1B	149	564	100	161	33	1	34	117	.285	72	64	8	1276	92	10	.993
1988—California (A.L.)	1B	158	597	81	176	31	2	13	85	.295	55	51	8	*1369	*143	8	.995
1989—California (A.L.)	1B	159	593	78	167	30	2	16	79	.282	46	58	3	*1487	99	4	*.997
1990—California (A.L.)	1B	83	310	35	83	15	0	8	41	.268	41	34	2	727	62	4	.995
1991—California (A.L.)	1B	143	551	79	166	34	3	21	96	.301	52	66	2	*1335	98	8	.994
1992—Kansas City (A.L.)■■	1B-DH	149	572	66	154	36	2	9	66	.269	55	50	11	1236	137	10	.993
1993—Kansas City (A.L.)	1B	141	497	83	145	36	3	15	65	.292	66	67	5	1116	145	7	.994
1994—Kansas City (A.L.)	1B-DH	97	363	52	113	20	3	8	57	.311	47	43	3	777	64	8	.991
1995—Kansas City (A.L.)	1B-DH	131	465	69	144	28	0	12	83	.310	69	65	3	1111	118	3	*.998
1996—San Diego (N.L.)■	1B	121	433	59	120	29	1	8	65	.277	69	71	5	1059	89	3	*.997
—Rancho Cuca.(Calif.)	1B	3	10	1	3	1	0	0	2	.300	1	1	0	14	2	0	1.000
1997—San Diego (N.L.)	1B	135	455	59	149	29	2	13	83	.327	51	51	3	1027	89	4	*.996
—Las Vegas (PCL)	1B	3	8	1	2	0	0	0	1	.250	0	1	0	16	1	0	1.000
1998—San Diego (N.L.)	1B	131	439	58	131	30	1	12	80	.298	51	44	1	985	81	7	.993
1999—San Diego (N.L.)	1B-DH	110	323	34	80	14	2	5	43	.248	58	54	0	731	66	4	.995
—Las Vegas (PCL)	1B	6	17	4	4	0	0	0	2	.235	3	2	0	38	2	0	1.000
2000—Atlanta (N.L.)■	1B	119	224	24	63	12	0	5	32	.281	31	31	0	353	30	3	.992
2001—Anaheim (A.L.)■	1B-DH	53	148	14	36	5	1	3	14	.243	13	18	1	270	18	1	.997
American League totals (11 years)		1417	5253	739	1517	295	20	161	803	.289	573	574	51	11926	1115	78	.994
National League totals (5 years)		616	1874	234	543	114	6	43	303	.290	260	251	9	4155	355	21	.995
Major League totals (16 years)		2033	7127	973	2060	409	26	204	1106	.289	833	825	60	16081	1470	99	.994

DIVISION SERIES RECORD

Year Team (League)	Pos.	G	AB	R	H	2B	3B	HR	RBI	Avg.	BB	SO	SB	PO	A	E	Avg.
1996—San Diego (N.L.)	1B	3	9	0	1	0	0	0	0	.111	0	2	0	12	2	0	1.000
1998—San Diego (N.L.)	1B	4	6	1	1	0	0	1	2	.167	1	2	0	19	1	1	.952
2000—Atlanta (N.L.)	PH	3	3	0	1	1	0	0	0	.333	0	0	0	...	...	...	...
Division series totals (3 years)		10	18	1	3	1	0	1	2	.167	1	4	0	31	3	1	.971

CHAMPIONSHIP SERIES RECORD

Year Team (League)	Pos.	G	AB	R	H	2B	3B	HR	RBI	Avg.	BB	SO	SB	PO	A	E	Avg.
1986—California (A.L.)	1B	3	11	3	5	2	0	1	2	.455	2	0	0	24	1	0	1.000
1998—San Diego (N.L.)	1B	6	16	3	5	0	0	0	2	.313	4	3	0	45	6	0	1.000
Championship series totals (2 years)		9	27	6	10	2	0	1	4	.370	6	3	0	69	7	0	1.000

WORLD SERIES RECORD

Year Team (League)	Pos.	G	AB	R	H	2B	3B	HR	RBI	Avg.	BB	SO	SB	PO	A	E	Avg.
1998—San Diego (N.L.)	1B	3	8	0	0	0	0	0	0	.000	3	1	0	22	0	0	1.000

ALL-STAR GAME RECORD

Year League	Pos.	AB	R	H	2B	3B	HR	RBI	Avg.	BB	SO	SB	PO	A	E	Avg.
1986—American	1B	1	0	0	0	0	0	0	.000	0	0	0	3	1	0	1.000

PERSONAL: Born June 30, 1975, in San Diego. ... 6-1/217. ... Throws right, bats right. ... Full name: Michael Galen Judd.
HIGH SCHOOL: Helix (Calif.).
JUNIOR COLLEGE: Grossmont College (San Diego).
TRANSACTIONS/CAREER NOTES: Selected by New York Yankees organization in ninth round of free-agent draft (June 1, 1995). ... Traded by Yankees to Los Angeles Dodgers for P Billy Brewer (June 22, 1996). ... On Albuquerque disabled list (May 3-16, 2000). ... Traded by Dodgers to Tampa Bay Devil Rays for a player to be named later (March 28, 2001). ... On Tampa Bay disabled list (May 10-25, 2001). ... Claimed on waivers by Texas Rangers (May 29, 2001). ... On Oklahoma disabled list (July 10-18 and August 9, 2001-remainder of season). ... Granted free agency (October 15, 2001). ... Signed by Cincinnati Reds organization (December 21, 2001).

Year League	W	L	Pct.	ERA	G	GS	CG	ShO	Sv.	IP	H	R	ER	BB	SO
1995— Gulf Coast Yankees (GCL)..	1	1	.500	1.11	21	0	0	0	8	32 1/3	18	5	4	6	30
— Greensboro (S.Atl.)	0	0	...	0.00	1	0	0	0	0	2 2/3	2	0	0	0	1
1996— Greensboro (S.Atl.)	2	2	.500	3.81	29	0	0	0	10	28 1/3	22	14	12	8	36
— Savannah (S.Atl.)■	4	2	.667	2.44	15	8	1	0	3	55 1/3	40	21	15	15	62
1997— Vero Beach (FSL)	6	5	.545	3.53	14	14	1	0	0	86 2/3	67	37	34	39	104
— San Antonio (Texas)	4	2	.667	2.73	12	12	0	0	0	79	69	27	24	33	65
— Los Angeles (N.L.)	0	0	...	0.00	1	0	0	0	0	2 2/3	4	0	0	0	4
1998— Albuquerque (PCL)	5	7	.417	4.56	17	17	3	1	0	94 2/3	98	62	48	44	77
— Los Angeles (N.L.)	0	0	...	15.09	7	0	0	0	0	11 1/3	19	19	19	9	14
1999— Albuquerque (PCL)	8	7	.533	6.67	21	21	1	0	0	110 2/3	132	90	82	47	122
— Los Angeles (N.L.)	3	1	.750	5.46	7	4	0	0	0	28	30	17	17	12	22
2000— Albuquerque (PCL)	7	6	.538	4.51	24	23	1	0	0	141 2/3	153	86	71	62	92
— Los Angeles (N.L.)	0	1	.000	15.75	1	1	0	0	0	4	4	7	7	3	5
2001— Tampa Bay (A.L.)■	1	0	1.000	4.05	8	2	0	0	0	20	19	14	9	10	11
— Texas (A.L.)■	0	1	.000	8.00	4	1	0	0	0	9	15	10	8	5	5
— Oklahoma (PCL)	0	1	.000	10.13	2	0	0	0	0	2 2/3	6	3	3	2	3
A.L. totals (1 year)	1	1	.500	5.28	12	3	0	0	0	29	34	24	17	15	16
N.L. totals (4 years)	3	2	.600	8.41	16	5	0	0	0	46	57	43	43	24	45
Major League totals (5 years)	4	3	.571	7.20	28	8	0	0	0	75	91	67	60	39	61

J

JULIO, JORGE   P   ORIOLES

PERSONAL: Born March 3, 1979, in Caracas, Venezuela. ... 6-1/190. ... Throws right, bats right. ... Full name: Jorge Dandys Julio.

HIGH SCHOOL: Fundacion Bolivariana (Caracas, Venezuela).

TRANSACTIONS/CAREER NOTES: Signed as non-drafted free agent by Montreal Expos organization (February 14, 1996). ... Traded by Expos to Baltimore Orioles for 3B Ryan Minor (December 22, 2000).

Year League	W	L	Pct.	ERA	G	GS	CG	ShO	Sv.	IP	H	R	ER	BB	SO
1996— Dominican Expos (DSL)	1	1	.500	6.06	10	0	0	0	0	16 1/3	13	12	11	11	21
1997— Gulf Coast Expos (GCL)	5	6	.455	3.58	15	8	0	0	1	55 1/3	57	25	22	21	42
— West Palm Beach (FSL)	0	0	...	...	1	0	0	0	0	2	2	1	1	0	0
1998— Vermont (NY-Penn)	3	1	.750	2.57	7	7	0	0	0	42	30	12	12	15	52
— Cape Fear (S.Atl.)	2	2	.500	5.68	6	6	0	0	0	31 2/3	33	20	20	12	20
1999— Jupiter (FSL)	4	8	.333	3.92	23	22	0	0	0	114 2/3	116	62	50	34	80
2000— Jupiter (FSL)	2	10	.167	5.90	21	15	0	0	1	79 1/3	93	60	52	35	67
2001— Rochester (I.L.)■	1	2	.333	3.74	34	0	0	0	12	43 1/3	39	27	18	19	48
— Bowie (East.)	0	0	...	0.73	12	0	0	0	7	12 1/3	5	1	1	2	14
— Baltimore (A.L.)	1	1	.500	3.80	18	0	0	0	0	21 1/3	25	13	9	9	22
Major League totals (1 year)	1	1	.500	3.80	18	0	0	0	0	21 1/3	25	13	9	9	22

JUSTICE, DAVID   OF/DH   ATHLETICS

PERSONAL: Born April 14, 1966, in Cincinnati. ... 6-3/200. ... Bats left, throws left. ... Full name: David Christopher Justice.

HIGH SCHOOL: Covington (Ky.) Latin.

COLLEGE: Thomas More College (Ky.).

TRANSACTIONS/CAREER NOTES: Selected by Atlanta Braves organization in fourth round of free-agent draft (June 3, 1985). ... On Atlanta disabled list (June 27-August 20, 1991); included rehabilitation assignment to Macon (August 16-20). ... On disabled list (April 12-27, 1992; June 2-17, 1995 and May 16, 1996-remainder of season). ... Traded by Braves with OF Marquis Grissom to Cleveland Indians for OF Kenny Lofton and P Alan Embree (March 25, 1997). ... On disabled list (June 24-July 10, 1997). ... Traded by Indians to New York Yankees for OF Ricky Ledee and two players to be named later (June 29, 2000); Indians acquired P Jake Westbrook and P Zach Day to complete deal (July 25, 2000). ... On New York disabled list (June 15-30 and July 2-August 2, 2001); included rehabilitation assignment to Norwich (July 31-August 2). ... Traded by Yankees to New York Mets for 3B Robin Ventura (December 7, 2001). ... Traded by Mets to Oakland Athletics for P Mark Guthrie and P Tyler Yates (December 14, 2001).

RECORDS: Holds major league single-season record for fewest errors by outfielder who led league in errors—8 (1992).

HONORS: Named N.L. Rookie Player of the Year by THE SPORTING NEWS (1990). ... Named N.L. Rookie of the Year by Baseball Writers' Association of America (1990). ... Named outfielder on THE SPORTING NEWS N.L. All-Star team (1993). ... Named outfielder on THE SPORTING NEWS N.L. Silver Slugger team (1993). ... Named outfielder on THE SPORTING NEWS A.L. Silver Slugger team (1997). ... Named A.L. Comeback Player of the Year by THE SPORTING NEWS (1997). ... Named outfielder on THE SPORTING NEWS A.L. All-Star team (1997).

STATISTICAL NOTES: Tied for Appalachian League lead with five sacrifice flies in 1985. ... Career major league grand slams: 5.

Year Team (League)	Pos.	G	AB	R	H	2B	3B	HR	RBI	Avg.	BB	SO	SB	PO	A	E	Avg.
1985— Pulaski (Appl.).............	OF	66	204	39	50	8	0	•10	46	.245	40	30	0	86	2	4	.957
1986— Sumter (S.Atl.)	OF	61	220	48	66	16	0	10	61	.300	48	28	10	124	7	4	.970
— Durham (Caro.)	OF-1B	67	229	47	64	9	1	12	44	.279	46	24	2	163	5	1	.994
1987— Greenville (Sou.)	OF	93	348	38	79	12	4	6	40	.227	53	48	3	199	4	8	.962
1988— Richmond (I.L.)	OF	70	227	27	46	9	1	8	28	.203	39	55	4	136	5	4	.972
— Greenville (Sou.)	OF	58	198	34	55	13	1	9	37	.278	37	41	6	100	3	5	.954
1989— Richmond (I.L.)	OF-1B	115	391	47	102	24	3	12	58	.261	59	66	12	220	15	6	.975
— Atlanta (N.L.)	OF	16	51	7	12	3	0	1	3	.235	3	9	2	24	0	0	1.000
1990— Richmond (I.L.)	OF-1B	12	45	7	16	5	1	2	7	.356	7	6	0	23	4	2	.931
— Atlanta (N.L.)	1B-OF	127	439	76	124	23	2	28	78	.282	64	92	11	604	42	14	.979
1991— Atlanta (N.L.)	OF	109	396	67	109	25	1	21	87	.275	65	81	8	204	9	7	.968
— Macon (S.Atl.)	OF	3	10	2	2	0	0	2	5	.200	2	1	0	1	0	0	1.000
1992— Atlanta (N.L.)	OF	144	484	78	124	19	5	21	72	.256	79	85	2	313	8	*8	.976
1993— Atlanta (N.L.)	OF	157	585	90	158	15	4	40	120	.270	78	90	3	323	9	5	.985
1994— Atlanta (N.L.)	OF	104	352	61	110	16	2	19	59	.313	69	45	2	192	6	*11	.947
1995— Atlanta (N.L.)	OF	120	411	73	104	17	2	24	78	.253	73	68	4	233	8	4	.984
1996— Atlanta (N.L.)	OF	40	140	23	45	9	0	6	25	.321	21	22	1	88	3	0	1.000
1997— Cleveland (A.L.)■.......	OF-DH	139	495	84	163	31	1	33	101	.329	80	79	3	120	3	2	.984

Year	Team (League)	Pos.	G	AB	R	H	2B	3B	HR	RBI	Avg.	BB	SO	SB	PO	A	E	Avg.
								BATTING								FIELDING		
1998—Cleveland (A.L.).........	DH-OF	146	540	94	151	39	2	21	88	.280	76	98	9	37	0	0	1.000
1999—Cleveland (A.L.).........	OF-DH	133	429	75	123	18	0	21	88	.287	94	90	1	161	7	4	.977
2000—Cleveland (A.L.).........	OF-DH	68	249	46	66	14	1	21	58	.265	38	49	1	84	2	2	.977
—New York (A.L.)■......	OF-DH	78	275	43	84	17	0	20	60	.305	39	42	1	127	6	2	.985
2001—New York (A.L.).........	DH-OF	111	381	58	92	16	1	18	51	.241	54	83	1	49	4	1	.981
—Norwich (East.).........	DH	2	8	0	0	0	0	0	0	.000	0	1	0	...	...	...	...
American League totals (5 years)		675	2369	400	679	135	5	134	446	.287	381	441	16	578	22	11	.982
National League totals (8 years)		817	2858	475	786	127	16	160	522	.275	452	492	33	1981	85	49	.977
Major League totals (13 years)		1492	5227	875	1465	262	21	294	968	.280	833	933	49	2559	107	60	.978

DIVISION SERIES RECORD

RECORDS: Shares single-series record for most doubles—4 (1998).

Year	Team (League)	Pos.	G	AB	R	H	2B	3B	HR	RBI	Avg.	BB	SO	SB	PO	A	E	Avg.
								BATTING								FIELDING		
1995—Atlanta (N.L.)............	OF	4	13	2	3	0	0	0	0	.231	5	2	0	6	0	1	.857
1997—Cleveland (A.L.).........	DH	5	19	3	5	2	0	1	2	.263	2	3	0	...	...	...	...
1998—Cleveland (A.L.).........	DH-OF	4	16	2	5	4	0	1	6	.313	0	1	0	5	1	0	1.000
1999—Cleveland (A.L.).........	OF	3	8	0	0	0	0	0	1	.000	2	2	0	7	2	0	1.000
2000—New York (A.L.).........	OF	5	18	2	4	0	0	1	1	.222	3	4	0	10	0	0	1.000
2001—New York (A.L.).........	OF-DH-PH	4	13	3	3	0	1	1	1	.231	2	5	0	4	0	0	1.000
Division series totals (6 years)		25	87	12	20	6	1	4	11	.230	14	17	0	32	3	1	.972

CHAMPIONSHIP SERIES RECORD

RECORDS: Holds career record for most games—46; runs—24; runs batted in—27; bases on balls received—24; and at-bats—166. ... Shares career record for most doubles—7; and times grounded into double play—5.

NOTES: Named Most Valuable Player (2000).

Year	Team (League)	Pos.	G	AB	R	H	2B	3B	HR	RBI	Avg.	BB	SO	SB	PO	A	E	Avg.
								BATTING								FIELDING		
1991—Atlanta (N.L.).............	OF	7	25	4	5	1	0	1	2	.200	3	7	0	17	0	1	.944
1992—Atlanta (N.L.).............	OF	7	25	5	7	1	0	2	6	.280	6	2	0	19	3	0	1.000
1993—Atlanta (N.L.).............	OF	6	21	2	3	1	0	0	4	.143	3	3	0	14	0	1	.933
1995—Atlanta (N.L.).............	OF	3	11	1	3	0	0	0	1	.273	2	1	0	4	0	0	1.000
1997—Cleveland (A.L.).........	DH	6	21	3	7	1	0	0	3	.333	2	4	0	...	...	...	...
1998—Cleveland (A.L.).........	OF-DH-PH	6	19	2	3	0	0	1	2	.158	3	3	0	3	0	0	1.000
2000—New York (A.L.).........	OF	6	26	4	6	2	0	2	8	.231	2	7	0	9	0	0	1.000
2001—New York (A.L.).........	DH	5	18	3	5	1	0	0	4	.278	3	1	0	...	...	...	...
Championship series totals (8 years)		46	166	24	39	7	0	6	27	.235	24	28	0	66	3	2	.972

WORLD SERIES RECORD

RECORDS: Shares record for most consecutive strikeouts in one series—5 (October 30 [2] and 31 [3], 2001).

NOTES: Member of World Series championship team (1995 and 2000).

Year	Team (League)	Pos.	G	AB	R	H	2B	3B	HR	RBI	Avg.	BB	SO	SB	PO	A	E	Avg.
								BATTING								FIELDING		
1991—Atlanta (N.L.).............	OF	7	27	5	7	0	0	2	6	.259	5	5	2	21	1	1	.957
1992—Atlanta (N.L.).............	OF	6	19	4	3	0	0	1	3	.158	6	5	1	15	0	1	.938
1995—Atlanta (N.L.).............	OF	6	20	3	5	1	0	1	5	.250	5	1	0	16	0	0	1.000
1997—Cleveland (A.L.).........	OF-DH	7	27	4	5	0	0	0	4	.185	6	8	0	9	0	0	1.000
2000—New York (A.L.).........	OF	5	19	1	3	2	0	0	3	.158	3	2	0	8	1	0	1.000
2001—New York (A.L.).........	OF-PH-DH	5	12	0	2	0	0	0	0	.167	1	9	0	1	0	1	.500
World Series totals (6 years)		36	124	17	25	3	0	4	21	.202	26	30	3	70	2	3	.960

ALL-STAR GAME RECORD

Year	League	Pos.	AB	R	H	2B	3B	HR	RBI	Avg.	BB	SO	SB	PO	A	E	Avg.
						BATTING									FIELDING		
1993—National....................	OF	3	0	1	0	0	0	0	.333	0	0	0	1	0	1	.500
1994—National....................	OF	2	0	0	0	0	0	0	.000	0	0	0	1	0	0	1.000
1997—American..................						Selected, did not play—injured.											
All-Star Game totals (2 years)		5	0	1	0	0	0	0	.200	0	0	0	2	0	1	.667

KALINOWSKI, JOSH — P — ROCKIES

PERSONAL: Born December 12, 1976, in Pasco, Wash. ... 6-2/190. ... Throws left, bats left. ... Full name: Joshua David Kalinowski.

HIGH SCHOOL: Natrona County (Casper, Wyoming).

JUNIOR COLLEGE: Indian Hills Community College (Iowa).

TRANSACTIONS/CAREER NOTES: Selected by Colorado Rockies organization in 37th round of free-agent draft (June 1, 1995); did not sign. ... Selected by Rockies organization in 33rd round of free-agent draft (June 4, 1996). ... On disabled list (May 2-9, 1999). ... On Carolina disabled list (April 28-June 9 and June 16-August 31, 2000). ... On Colorado disabled list (September 1, 2000-remainder of season). ... On disabled list (May 7-June 6, 2001).

HONORS: Named Carolina League Pitcher of the Year (1999).

STATISTICAL NOTES: Pitches 5-0 no-hit victory for Asheville against Charleston, S.C. (August 26, 1998). ... Led Carolina League pitchers with 34 assists in 1999.

Year	League	W	L	Pct.	ERA	G	GS	CG	ShO	Sv.	IP	H	R	ER	BB	SO
1997—Portland (N'West).............	0	1	.000	2.41	6	6	0	0	0	18 2/3	15	6	5	10	27
1998—Asheville (S.Atl.)................	12	10	.545	3.92	28	28	3	1	0	172 1/3	159	93	75	65	*215
1999—Salem (Caro.)....................	11	6	.647	*2.11	27	27	1	0	0	162 1/3	119	47	38	71	*176
2000—Carolina (Sou.).................	1	3	.250	6.23	6	6	0	0	0	26	30	22	18	12	27
2001—Carolina (Sou.).................	7	8	.467	4.06	25	25	0	0	0	137 1/3	151	76	62	65	116

J

K

KALITA, TIM   P   TIGERS

PERSONAL: Born November 21, 1978, in Evanston, Ill. ... 6-2/220. ... Throws left, bats right. ... Full name: Timothy Ryan Kalita.
HIGH SCHOOL: Oak Park (Ill.).
COLLEGE: Notre Dame.
TRANSACTIONS/CAREER NOTES: Selected by Detroit Tigers organization in seventh round of free-agent draft (June 2, 1999).
STATISTICAL NOTES: Tied for Eastern League lead with 25 home runs allowed in 2001.

Year League	W	L	Pct.	ERA	G	GS	CG	ShO	Sv.	IP	H	R	ER	BB	SO
1999—Oneonta (NY-Penn)	0	0	...	0.00	3	3	0	0	0	12 1/3	3	1	0	5	15
—West Michigan (Midw.)	4	1	.800	4.18	9	9	0	0	0	47 1/3	46	26	22	27	35
2000—Lakeland (FSL)	7	12	.368	4.57	27	25	1	0	0	149 2/3	146	93	76	73	107
2001—Erie (East.)	15	9	.625	3.83	30	29	5	0	0	200	190	•98	85	49	147

KANE, KYLE   P   WHITE SOX

PERSONAL: Born February 4, 1976, in Temecula, Calif. ... 6-3/215. ... Throws right, bats left. ... Full name: Kyle J. Kane.
HIGH SCHOOL: Linfield Christian (Temecula, Calif.).
JUNIOR COLLEGE: Saddleback (Calif.).
COLLEGE: Nevada.
TRANSACTIONS/CAREER NOTES: Selected by Minnesota Twins organization in 10th round of free-agent draft (June 1, 1995); did not sign. ... Selected by Chicago White Sox organization in supplemental round ("sandwich pick" between first and second round, 33rd pick overall) of free-agent draft (June 3, 1997); pick received as part of compensation for Florida Marlins signing Type A free agent P Alex Fernandez. ... On disabled list (April 2-June 17, 1998). ... On Birmingham disabled list (July 27-August 16, 2001).

Year League	W	L	Pct.	ERA	G	GS	CG	ShO	Sv.	IP	H	R	ER	BB	SO
1998—Bristol (Appl.)	1	0	1.000	5.32	13	0	0	0	0	23 2/3	34	21	14	8	17
1999—Bristol (Appl.)	2	0	1.000	2.57	5	5	0	0	0	28	19	8	8	11	23
—Burlington (Midw.)	1	0	1.000	13.50	12	0	0	0	1	18	28	29	27	12	17
2000—Winston-Salem (Caro.)	1	2	.333	5.86	32	0	0	0	0	50 2/3	57	39	33	31	47
2001—Winston-Salem (Caro.)	1	0	1.000	2.08	14	0	0	0	1	21 2/3	10	5	5	8	32
—Charlotte (I.L.)	0	0	...	6.00	1	1	0	0	0	3	4	2	2	1	0
—Birmingham (Sou.)	2	1	.667	1.85	26	0	0	0	3	34	20	9	7	6	43

K

KAPLER, GABE   OF   RANGERS

PERSONAL: Born August 31, 1975, in Hollywood, Calif. ... 6-2/208. ... Bats right, throws right. ... Full name: Gabriel Stefan Kapler.
HIGH SCHOOL: Taft (Woodland Hills, Calif.).
JUNIOR COLLEGE: Moorpark (Calif.) College.
TRANSACTIONS/CAREER NOTES: Selected by Detroit Tigers organization in 57th round of free-agent draft (June 1, 1995). ... Traded by Tigers with P Justin Thompson, P Francisco Cordero, C Bill Haselman, 2B Frank Catalanotto and P Alan Webb to Texas Rangers for OF Juan Gonzalez, P Danny Patterson and C Gregg Zaun (November 2, 1999). ... On Texas disabled list (May 4-June 9, 2000); included rehabilitation assignments to Oklahoma (May 20-24) and Tulsa (June 5-9). ... On Texas disabled list (March 23-April 22, 2001); included rehabilitation assignment to Tulsa (April 17-22).
HONORS: Named Minor League Player of the Year by THE SPORTING NEWS (1998). ... Named Southern League Most Valuable Player (1998).
STATISTICAL NOTES: Led South Atlantic League with 280 total bases in 1996. ... Led Florida State League with 262 total bases in 1997. ... Led Southern League with 319 total bases and 11 sacrifice flies in 1998. ... Had 28-game hitting streak (July 17-August 15, 2000). ... Career major league grand slams: 1.

Year Team (League)	Pos.	G	AB	R	H	2B	3B	HR	RBI	Avg.	BB	SO	SB	PO	A	E	Avg.
1995—Jamestown (NY-P)	OF	63	236	38	68	19	4	4	34	.288	23	37	1	103	9	9	.926
1996—Fayetteville (S.Atl.)	OF-3B	138	524	81	*157	*45	0	26	99	.300	62	73	14	195	14	7	.968
1997—Lakeland (FSL)	OF	137	519	87	153	*40	6	19	87	.295	54	68	8	252	14	6	.978
1998—Jacksonville (Sou.)	OF-1B	•139	547	*113	*176	•47	6	*28	*146	.322	66	93	6	294	12	5	.984
—Detroit (A.L.)	OF-DH	7	25	3	5	0	1	0	0	.200	1	4	2	9	0	0	1.000
1999—Detroit (A.L.)	OF-DH	130	416	60	102	22	4	18	49	.245	42	74	11	302	4	6	.981
—Toledo (I.L.)	OF	14	54	11	17	6	2	3	14	.315	9	10	0	33	0	0	1.000
2000—Texas (A.L.)■	OF	116	444	59	134	32	1	14	66	.302	42	57	8	307	5	•10	.969
—Oklahoma (PCL)	OF	3	9	3	3	0	0	0	0	.333	3	2	0	1	1	0	1.000
—Tulsa (Texas)	OF	3	12	3	7	0	0	1	4	.583	1	2	0	6	0	0	1.000
2001—Tulsa (Texas)	OF	5	15	2	5	1	0	0	0	.333	6	1	0	2	0	0	1.000
—Texas (A.L.)	OF-DH	134	483	77	129	29	1	17	72	.267	61	70	23	344	8	1	.997
Major League totals (4 years)		387	1368	199	370	83	7	49	187	.270	146	205	44	962	17	17	.983

KARNUTH, JASON   P   CARDINALS

PERSONAL: Born May 15, 1976, in LaGrange, Ill. ... 6-2/190. ... Throws right, bats right. ... Full name: Jason A. Karnuth.
HIGH SCHOOL: Glenbard South (Glen Ellyn, Ill.).
COLLEGE: Illinois State.
TRANSACTIONS/CAREER NOTES: Selected by St. Louis Cardinals organization in eighth round of free-agent draft (June 3, 1997).

Year League	W	L	Pct.	ERA	G	GS	CG	ShO	Sv.	IP	H	R	ER	BB	SO
1997—New Jersey (NY-Penn)	4	1	.800	1.86	7	7	0	0	0	38 2/3	33	8	8	9	23
—Peoria (Midw.)	0	3	.000	6.65	4	4	0	0	0	23	29	19	17	7	12
1998—Prince William (Caro.)	8	1	.889	1.67	16	15	2	2	0	108	86	26	20	14	53
1999—Arkansas (Texas)	7	11	.389	5.22	26	26	2	0	0	160 1/3	175	105	93	55	71
2000—Arkansas (Texas)	2	3	.400	3.75	8	8	1	0	0	50 1/3	59	30	21	14	31
—Memphis (PCL)	5	4	.556	4.04	16	13	0	0	0	78	89	47	35	27	28
2001—Memphis (PCL)	4	4	.500	4.28	55	0	0	0	3	73 2/3	82	37	35	24	42
—St. Louis (N.L.)	0	0	...	1.80	4	0	0	0	0	5	6	1	1	4	1
Major League totals (1 year)	0	0	...	1.80	4	0	0	0	0	5	6	1	1	4	1

PERSONAL: Born November 4, 1967, in Hackensack, N.J. ... 6-4/226. ... Bats right, throws right. ... Full name: Eric Peter Karros. ... Name pronounced CARE-ose.

HIGH SCHOOL: Patrick Henry (San Diego).

COLLEGE: UCLA.

TRANSACTIONS/CAREER NOTES: Selected by Los Angeles Dodgers organization in sixth round of free-agent draft (June 1, 1988). ... On Los Angeles disabled list (March 29-April 24, 1998); included rehabilitation assignment to San Bernardino (April 19-25). ... On disabled list (May 22-June 15, 2001).

RECORDS: Shares major league single-inning record for most home runs—2 (August 22, 2000, sixth inning).

HONORS: Named N.L. Rookie Player of the Year by THE SPORTING NEWS (1992). ... Named N.L. Rookie of the Year by Baseball Writers' Association of America (1992). ... Named first baseman on THE SPORTING NEWS N.L. All-Star team (1995). ... Named first baseman on THE SPORTING NEWS N.L. Silver Slugger team (1995).

STATISTICAL NOTES: Tied for Pioneer League lead in errors by first baseman with 14 in 1988. ... Led California League first basemen with 1,232 putouts, 110 assists and 1,358 total chances in 1989. ... Led Texas League with 282 total bases in 1990. ... Led Texas League first basemen with 1,337 total chances and 129 double plays in 1990. ... Led Pacific Coast League with 269 total bases in 1991. ... Tied for Pacific Coast League lead with eight intentional bases on balls received in 1991. ... Led Pacific Coast League first basemen with 1,095 putouts, 109 assists and 1,215 total chances in 1991. ... Led N.L. in grounding into double plays with 27 in 1996. ... Career major league grand slams: 2.

							BATTING							FIELDING		
Year Team (League)	Pos.	G	AB	R	H	2B	3B	HR	RBI	Avg.	BB	SO	SB	PO	A	E	Avg.
1988—Great Falls (Pio.)	1B-3B	66	268	68	98	12	1	12	55	.366	32	35	8	516	31	‡19	.966
1989—Bakersfield (Calif.)	1B-3B	*142	545	86	*165	*40	1	15	86	.303	63	99	18	†1238	†113	19	.986
1990—San Antonio (Texas)	1B	•131	509	91	*179	*45	2	18	78	*.352	57	79	8	*1223	*106	8	*.994
1991—Albuquerque (PCL)	1B-3B	132	488	88	154	33	8	22	101	.316	58	80	3	†1095	†109	11	.991
—Los Angeles (N.L.)	1B	14	14	0	1	1	0	0	1	.071	1	6	0	33	2	0	1.000
1992—Los Angeles (N.L.)	1B	149	545	63	140	30	1	20	88	.257	37	103	2	1211	126	9	.993
1993—Los Angeles (N.L.)	1B	158	619	74	153	27	2	23	80	.247	34	82	0	1335	*147	12	.992
1994—Los Angeles (N.L.)	1B	111	406	51	108	21	1	14	46	.266	29	53	2	896	118	•9	.991
1995—Los Angeles (N.L.)	1B	143	551	83	164	29	3	32	105	.298	61	115	4	1234	109	7	.995
1996—Los Angeles (N.L.)	1B	154	608	84	158	29	0	34	111	.260	53	121	8	1314	121	15	.990
1997—Los Angeles (N.L.)	1B	•162	628	86	167	28	0	31	104	.266	61	116	15	1317	121	11	.992
1998—San Bern. (Calif.)	1B	4	15	3	4	1	0	0	1	.267	0	2	0	32	2	0	1.000
—Los Angeles (N.L.)	1B-DH	139	507	59	150	20	1	23	87	.296	47	93	7	1150	110	12	.991
1999—Los Angeles (N.L.)	1B	153	578	74	176	40	0	34	112	.304	53	119	8	1291	*126	13	.991
2000—Los Angeles (N.L.)	1B-DH	155	584	84	146	29	0	31	106	.250	63	122	4	1296	138	7	.995
2001—Los Angeles (N.L.)	1B	121	438	42	103	22	0	15	63	.235	41	101	3	963	71	4	.996
Major League totals (11 years)		1459	5478	700	1466	276	9	257	903	.268	480	1031	53	12040	1189	99	.993

DIVISION SERIES RECORD

RECORDS: Shares single-game record for most home runs—2 (October 4, 1995).

							BATTING							FIELDING		
Year Team (League)	Pos.	G	AB	R	H	2B	3B	HR	RBI	Avg.	BB	SO	SB	PO	A	E	Avg.
1995—Los Angeles (N.L.)	1B	3	12	3	6	1	0	2	4	.500	1	0	0	14	0	0	1.000
1996—Los Angeles (N.L.)	1B	3	9	0	0	0	0	0	0	.000	2	3	0	28	2	0	1.000
Division series totals (2 years)		6	21	3	6	1	0	2	4	.286	3	3	0	42	2	0	1.000

PERSONAL: Born March 24, 1972, in Flushing, N.Y. ... 6-3/215. ... Throws right, bats right. ... Full name: Stefan Andrew Karsay. ... Name pronounced CAR-say.

HIGH SCHOOL: Christ the King (Queens, N.Y.).

TRANSACTIONS/CAREER NOTES: Selected by Toronto Blue Jays organization in first round (22nd pick overall) of free-agent draft (June 4, 1990). ... On Knoxville disabled list (July 3-16, 1993). ... Traded by Blue Jays with a player to be named later to Oakland Athletics for OF Rickey Henderson (July 31, 1993); A's acquired OF Jose Herrera to complete deal (August 6, 1993). ... On disabled list (April 26, 1994-remainder of season; April 24, 1995-entire season; and August 6, 1997-remainder of season). ... Traded by A's to Cleveland Indians for P Mike Fetters (December 8, 1997). ... On Buffalo disabled list (May 14-25 and June 12-July 15, 1998). ... On disabled list (July 2-26 and August 25-September 22, 1999). ... Traded by Indians with P Steve Reed to Atlanta Braves for P John Rocker and 3B Troy Cameron (June 22, 2001). ... Granted free agency (November 5, 2001). ... Signed by New York Yankees (December 7, 2001).

MISCELLANEOUS: Appeared in one game as pinch runner (1997).

Year League	W	L	Pct.	ERA	G	GS	CG	ShO	Sv.	IP	H	R	ER	BB	SO
1990—St. Catharines (NY-Penn)	1	1	.500	0.79	5	5	0	0	0	22²/₃	11	4	2	12	25
1991—Myrtle Beach (S.Atl.)	4	9	.308	3.58	20	20	1	0	0	110²/₃	96	58	44	48	100
1992—Dunedin (FSL)	6	3	.667	2.73	16	16	3	2	0	85²/₃	76	32	26	29	87
1993—Knoxville (Sou.)	8	4	.667	3.38	19	18	1	0	0	104	98	42	39	32	100
—Huntsville (Sou.)■	0	0	...	5.14	2	2	0	0	0	14	13	8	8	3	22
—Oakland (A.L.)	3	3	.500	4.04	8	8	0	0	0	49	49	23	22	16	33
1994—Oakland (A.L.)	1	1	.500	2.57	4	4	1	0	0	28	26	8	8	8	15
1995—Oakland (A.L.)							Did not play.								
1996—Modesto (Calif.)	0	1	.000	2.65	14	14	0	0	0	34	35	16	10	1	31
1997—Oakland (A.L.)	3	12	.200	5.77	24	24	0	0	0	132²/₃	166	92	85	47	92
1998—Buffalo (I.L.)■	6	4	.600	3.76	16	14	0	0	0	79	89	39	33	15	63
—Cleveland (A.L.)	0	2	.000	5.92	11	1	0	0	0	24¹/₃	31	16	16	6	13
1999—Cleveland (A.L.)	10	2	.833	2.97	50	3	0	0	1	78²/₃	71	29	26	30	68
2000—Cleveland (A.L.)	5	9	.357	3.76	72	0	0	0	20	76²/₃	79	33	32	25	66
2001—Cleveland (A.L.)	0	1	.000	1.25	31	0	0	0	1	43¹/₃	29	6	6	8	44
—Atlanta (N.L.)■	3	4	.429	3.43	43	0	0	0	7	44²/₃	44	21	17	17	39
A.L. totals (7 years)	22	30	.423	4.06	200	40	1	0	22	432²/₃	451	207	195	140	331
N.L. totals (1 year)	3	4	.429	3.43	43	0	0	0	7	44²/₃	44	21	17	17	39
Major League totals (7 years)	25	34	.424	4.00	243	40	1	0	29	477¹/₃	495	228	212	157	370

DIVISION SERIES RECORD

Year League	W	L	Pct.	ERA	G	GS	CG	ShO	Sv.	IP	H	R	ER	BB	SO
1999—Cleveland (A.L.)...............	0	0	...	9.00	2	0	0	0	0	3	5	3	3	1	3
2001—Atlanta (N.L.)...................	0	0	...	0.00	1	0	0	0	0	1	0	0	0	0	1
Division series totals (2 years)	0	0	...	6.75	3	0	0	0	0	4	5	3	3	1	4

CHAMPIONSHIP SERIES RECORD

Year League	W	L	Pct.	ERA	G	GS	CG	ShO	Sv.	IP	H	R	ER	BB	SO
2001—Atlanta (N.L.).....................	0	0	...	2.08	4	0	0	0	0	4 1/3	3	1	1	1	6

KAYE, JUSTIN   P   MARINERS

PERSONAL: Born June 9, 1976, in Fort Lauderdale, Fla. ... 6-4/185. ... Throws right, bats right. ... Full name: Justin Malcolm Kaye.
HIGH SCHOOL: Bishop Gorman (Las Vegas, Nev.).
TRANSACTIONS/CAREER NOTES: Selected by Seattle Mariners organization in 19th round of free-agent draft (June 1, 1995).

Year League	W	L	Pct.	ERA	G	GS	CG	ShO	Sv.	IP	H	R	ER	BB	SO
1995—Arizona Mariners (Ariz.)	0	1	.000	10.71	12	0	0	0	0	19 1/3	33	28	23	19	13
1996—Arizona Mariners (Ariz.)	1	0	1.000	3.62	20	0	0	0	3	32 1/3	34	23	13	19	36
1997—Wisconsin (Midw.)	8	12	.400	7.30	26	26	0	0	0	127	129	113	103	104	115
1998—Wisconsin (Midw.)	6	2	.750	1.71	28	0	0	0	9	47 1/3	25	11	9	30	79
—Lancaster (Calif.).................	1	2	.333	6.82	16	0	0	0	0	30 1/3	37	24	23	13	34
1999—Lancaster (Calif.)	3	5	.375	5.75	53	0	0	0	14	61	68	42	39	40	66
2000—New Haven (East.).............	2	5	.286	2.67	50	0	0	0	8	84 1/3	80	32	25	36	109
2001—Tacoma (PCL)	3	2	.600	2.92	56	0	0	0	4	77	51	27	25	46	107

KEARNS, AUSTIN   OF   REDS

PERSONAL: Born May 20, 1980, in Lexington, Ky. ... 6-3/220. ... Bats right, throws right. ... Full name: Austin Ryan Kearns.
HIGH SCHOOL: Lafayette (Lexington, Ky.).
TRANSACTIONS/CAREER NOTES: Selected by Cincinnati Reds organization in first round (seventh pick overall) of free-agent draft (June 2, 1998). ... On Chattanooga disabled list (May 27-August 13, 2001).
STATISTICAL NOTES: Led Midwest League with 270 total bases in 2000. ... Tied for Midwest League lead in double plays by outfielder with five in 2000.

Year Team (League)	Pos.	G	AB	R	H	2B	3B	HR	RBI	Avg.	BB	SO	SB	PO	A	E	Avg.
1998—Billings (Pio.)	OF	30	108	17	34	9	0	1	14	.315	23	22	1	32	6	4	.905
1999—Rockford (Midw.)	OF	124	426	72	110	36	5	13	48	.258	50	120	21	185	14	13	.939
2000—Dayton (Midw.)	OF	*136	484	*110	148	37	2	*27	•104	.306	90	93	18	231	*23	12	.955
2001—Chattanooga (Sou.)	OF	59	205	30	55	11	2	6	36	.268	26	43	7	92	2	2	.979
—GC Reds (GCL)..........	OF	6	17	2	3	2	0	0	4	.176	2	7	0	4	0	0	1.000

KEISLER, RANDY   P   YANKEES

PERSONAL: Born February 24, 1976, in Richards, Texas. ... 6-3/190. ... Throws left, bats left. ... Full name: Randy Dean Keisler.
HIGH SCHOOL: Navasota (Texas), then Palmer (Texas).
JUNIOR COLLEGE: Navarro College (Texas).
COLLEGE: Louisiana State.
TRANSACTIONS/CAREER NOTES: Selected by Cleveland Indians organization in 40th round of free-agent draft (June 1, 1995); did not sign. ... Selected by Indians organization in 57th round of free-agent draft (June 4, 1996); did not sign. ... Selected by New York Yankees organization in second round of free-agent draft (June 2, 1998).

Year League	W	L	Pct.	ERA	G	GS	CG	ShO	Sv.	IP	H	R	ER	BB	SO
1998—Oneonta (NY-Penn)	1	1	.500	7.45	6	2	0	0	1	9 2/3	14	10	8	7	11
1999—Greensboro (S.Atl.)	1	1	.500	2.38	4	4	0	0	0	22 2/3	12	6	6	10	42
—Tampa (FSL).................	10	3	.769	3.30	15	15	1	0	0	90	67	43	33	40	77
—Norwich (East.)	3	4	.429	4.57	8	8	0	0	0	43 1/3	45	24	22	17	33
2000—Norwich (East.)	6	2	.750	2.60	11	11	1	0	0	72 2/3	63	29	21	34	70
—Columbus (I.L.)	8	3	.727	3.02	17	17	1	1	0	113 1/3	104	44	38	42	86
—New York (A.L.).............	1	0	1.000	11.81	4	1	0	0	0	10 2/3	16	14	14	8	6
2001—Columbus (I.L.)	5	7	.417	5.18	18	18	3	1	0	97 1/3	111	67	56	39	88
—New York (A.L.).............	1	2	.333	6.22	10	10	0	0	0	50 2/3	52	36	35	34	36
Major League totals (2 years)	2	2	.500	7.19	14	11	0	0	0	61 1/3	68	50	49	42	42

KELLER, KRIS   P   TIGERS

PERSONAL: Born March 1, 1978, in Williamsport, Pa. ... 6-2/225. ... Throws right, bats right. ... Full name: Kristopher Shane Keller.
HIGH SCHOOL: Fletcher (Neptune Beach, Fla.).
TRANSACTIONS/CAREER NOTES: Selected by Detroit Tigers organization in fourth round of free-agent draft (June 4, 1996).

Year League	W	L	Pct.	ERA	G	GS	CG	ShO	Sv.	IP	H	R	ER	BB	SO
1996—Gulf Coast Tigers (GCL)	1	1	.500	2.38	8	6	0	0	0	34	23	12	9	21	23
1997—Jamestown (NY-Penn)	0	2	.000	8.67	16	0	0	0	0	27	37	33	26	20	18
1998—Jamestown (NY-Penn)	1	3	.250	3.27	27	0	0	0	8	33	29	12	12	16	41
1999—West Michigan (Midw.)	5	3	.625	2.92	49	0	0	0	8	77	63	28	25	36	87
2000—Jacksonville (Sou.).............	2	3	.400	2.91	62	0	0	0	*26	68	58	24	22	44	60
2001—Toledo (I.L.)....................	5	2	.714	4.48	52	0	0	0	4	68 1/3	64	42	34	38	60

KELLY, KENNY — OF — MARINERS

PERSONAL: Born January 26, 1979, in Plant City, Fla. ... 6-2/180. ... Bats right, throws right. ... Full name: Kenneth Alphonso Kelly.
HIGH SCHOOL: Tampa Catholic.
COLLEGE: Miami (Fla.).
TRANSACTIONS/CAREER NOTES: Selected by Tampa Bay Devil Rays organization in second round of free-agent draft (June 3, 1997). ... Traded by Devil Rays to Seattle Mariners for cash considerations (April 4, 2001). ... On disabled list (June 3-10, 2001).
STATISTICAL NOTES: Led Southern League with 21 caught stealing in 2000. ... Tied outfielders for Texas League lead with three double plays in 2001.

							BATTING								FIELDING		
Year Team (League)	Pos.	G	AB	R	H	2B	3B	HR	RBI	Avg.	BB	SO	SB	PO	A	E	Avg.
1997— GC Devil Rays (GCL)..	OF	27	99	21	21	2	1	2	7	.212	11	24	6	43	3	2	.958
1998— Charl., S.C. (S.Atl.).....	OF	54	218	46	61	7	5	3	17	.280	19	52	19	122	10	5	.964
1999— St. Petersburg (FSL)..	OF	51	206	39	57	10	4	3	21	.277	18	46	14	121	9	4	.970
2000— Orlando (Sou.)	OF	124	489	73	123	17	8	3	29	.252	59	119	31	286	9	8	.974
— Tampa Bay (A.L.)........	DH	2	1	0	0	0	0	0	0	.000	0	0	0	...	...	...	...
2001— San Antonio (Texas)■	OF	121	478	72	125	20	5	11	46	.262	45	111	18	252	6	5	.981
Major League totals (1 year)		2	1	0	0	0	0	0	0	.000	0	0	0	...	...	...	...

KELTON, DAVE — 3B — CUBS

PERSONAL: Born December 17, 1979, in Dothan, Ala. ... 6-3/205. ... Bats right, throws right. ... Full name: David Wayne Kelton.
HIGH SCHOOL: Troup County (La Grange, Ga.).
TRANSACTIONS/CAREER NOTES: Selected by Chicago Cubs organization in second round of free-agent draft (June 2, 1998). ... On disabled list (June 16, 2001-remainder of season).
STATISTICAL NOTES: Led Arizona League third basemen with 138 total chances and nine double plays in 1998.

							BATTING								FIELDING		
Year Team (League)	Pos.	G	AB	R	H	2B	3B	HR	RBI	Avg.	BB	SO	SB	PO	A	E	Avg.
1998— Arizona Cubs (Ariz.) ...	3B	50	181	39	48	7	5	•6	29	.265	23	58	16	29	•94	15	.891
1999— Lansing (Midw.).........	3B	124	509	75	137	17	4	13	68	.269	39	121	22	59	207	32	.893
2000— Daytona (FSL)	3B	132	523	75	140	30	7	18	84	.268	38	120	7	49	176	26	.896
2001— West Tenn (Sou.)	3B	58	224	33	70	9	4	12	45	.313	24	55	1	26	87	15	.883

KENDALL, JASON — C — PIRATES

PERSONAL: Born June 26, 1974, in San Diego. ... 6-0/195. ... Bats right, throws right. ... Full name: Jason Daniel Kendall. ... Son of Fred Kendall, coach, Colorado Rockies; and catcher/first baseman with three major league teams (1969-80).
HIGH SCHOOL: Torrance (Calif.).
TRANSACTIONS/CAREER NOTES: Selected by Pittsburgh Pirates organization in first round (23rd pick overall) of free-agent draft (June 1, 1992). ... On suspended list (July 21-23, 1998). ... On disabled list (July 5, 1999-remainder of season). ... On suspended list (September 19-20, 2001).
HONORS: Named Southern League Most Valuable Player (1995). ... Named N.L. Rookie Player of the Year by THE SPORTING NEWS (1996).
STATISTICAL NOTES: Led Gulf Coast League with 13 passed balls in 1992. ... Led Southern League with .414 on-base percentage in 1995. ... Led Southern League catchers with 754 total chances in 1995. ... Led N.L. catchers with 20 double plays in 1997. ... Led N.L. in being hit by pitch with 31 in 1998. ... Led N.L. catchers in total chances with 1,082 in 1998 and 1,081 in 2000. ... Had 16-game hitting streak (May 20-June 7, 1999). ... Led N.L. catchers with 13 double plays in 1999. ... Led N.L. catchers with 11 passed balls in 2000. ... Hit for the cycle (May 19, 2000).

							BATTING								FIELDING		
Year Team (League)	Pos.	G	AB	R	H	2B	3B	HR	RBI	Avg.	BB	SO	SB	PO	A	E	Avg.
1992— GC Pirates (GCL).......	C	33	111	7	29	2	0	0	10	.261	8	9	2	182	36	5	.978
1993— Augusta (S.Atl.).........	C	102	366	43	101	17	4	1	40	.276	22	30	8	472	65	20	.964
1994— Salem (Caro.)	C	101	371	68	118	19	2	7	66	.318	47	21	14	409	33	9	.980
— Carolina (Sou.)..........	C	13	47	6	11	2	0	0	6	.234	2	3	0	54	9	2	.969
1995— Carolina (Sou.)..........	C	117	429	87	140	26	1	8	71	.326	56	22	10	*692	54	8	.989
1996— Pittsburgh (N.L.)........	C	130	414	54	124	23	5	3	42	.300	35	30	5	797	71	*18	.980
1997— Pittsburgh (N.L.)........	C	144	486	71	143	36	4	8	49	.294	49	53	18	952	*103	11	.990
1998— Pittsburgh (N.L.)........	C	149	535	95	175	36	3	12	75	.327	51	51	26	*1015	58	9	.992
1999— Pittsburgh (N.L.)........	C	78	280	61	93	20	3	8	41	.332	38	32	22	505	48	7	.988
2000— Pittsburgh (N.L.)........	C	152	579	112	185	33	6	14	58	.320	79	79	22	*990	*81	10	.991
2001— Pittsburgh (N.L.)........	C-OF	157	606	84	161	22	2	10	53	.266	44	48	13	786	53	17	.980
Major League totals (6 years)		810	2900	477	881	170	23	55	318	.304	296	293	106	5045	414	72	.987

ALL-STAR GAME RECORD

							BATTING								FIELDING		
Year League	Pos.	AB	R	H	2B	3B	HR	RBI	Avg.	BB	SO	SB	PO	A	E	Avg.
1996— National.....................	C	0	0	0	0	0	0	0	...	0	0	0	0	0	0	...
1998— National.....................	PH	1	0	1	0	0	0	0	1.000	0	0	0	...	...	...	...
2000— National.....................	C	2	0	0	0	0	0	0	.000	0	1	0	3	1	0	1.000
All-Star Game totals (3 years)		3	0	1	0	0	0	0	.333	0	1	0	3	1	0	1.000

KENNEDY, ADAM — 2B — ANGELS

PERSONAL: Born January 10, 1976, in Riverside, Calif. ... 6-1/180. ... Bats left, throws right. ... Full name: Adam Thomas Kennedy.
HIGH SCHOOL: J.W. North (Riverside, Calif.).
COLLEGE: Cal State-Northridge.

TRANSACTIONS/CAREER NOTES: Selected by St. Louis Cardinals organization in first round (20th pick overall) of free-agent draft (June 3, 1997). ... On Memphis disabled list (June 9-19, 1999). ... Traded by Cardinals with P Kent Bottenfield to Anaheim Angels for OF Jim Edmonds (March 23, 2000). ... On Anaheim disabled list (March 23-April 13, 2001); included rehabilitation assignment to Rancho Cucamonga (April 9-13).

STATISTICAL NOTES: Led A.L. second basemen with 781 total chances in 2000. ... Career major league grand slams: 1.

							BATTING									FIELDING		
Year Team (League)	Pos.	G	AB	R	H	2B	3B	HR	RBI	Avg.	BB	SO	SB	PO	A	E	Avg.
1997— New Jersey (NY-P)	SS	29	114	20	39	6	3	0	19	.342	13	10	9	41	96	7	.951
— Prince William (Caro.)	SS	35	154	24	48	9	3	1	27	.312	6	17	4	63	92	10	.939
1998— Prince William (Caro.)	2B-SS	17	69	9	18	6	0	0	7	.261	5	12	5	26	49	5	.938
— Arkansas (Texas)........	SS-2B	52	205	35	57	11	2	6	24	.278	8	21	6	91	143	15	.940
— Memphis (PCL)........	SS-2B	74	305	36	93	22	7	4	41	.305	12	42	15	128	225	10	.972
1999— Memphis (PCL) 2-S-O-3-DH		91	367	69	120	22	4	10	63	.327	29	36	20	160	206	18	.953
— St. Louis (N.L.)..........	2B	33	102	12	26	10	1	1	16	.255	3	8	0	68	64	4	.971
2000— Anaheim (A.L.)■.......	2B	156	598	82	159	33	11	9	72	.266	28	73	22	*337	425	*19	.976
2001— Rancho Cuca. (Calif.) .	2B	3	8	3	3	2	0	0	1	.375	2	1	3	2	7	0	1.000
— Anaheim (A.L.)..........	2B-DH	137	478	48	129	25	3	6	40	.270	27	71	12	236	376	10	.984
American League totals (2 years)		293	1076	130	288	58	14	15	112	.268	55	144	34	573	801	29	.979
National League totals (1 year)		33	102	12	26	10	1	1	16	.255	3	8	0	68	64	4	.971
Major League totals (3 years)		326	1178	142	314	68	15	16	128	.267	58	152	34	641	865	33	.979

KENNEDY, JOE — P — DEVIL RAYS

K

PERSONAL: Born May 24, 1979, in La Mesa, Calif. ... 6-4/225. ... Throws left, bats right. ... Full name: Joseph Darley Kennedy.
HIGH SCHOOL: El Cajon Valley (El Cajon, Calif.).
JUNIOR COLLEGE: Grossmont (Calif.).
TRANSACTIONS/CAREER NOTES: Selected by Tampa Bay Devil Rays organization in eighth round of free-agent draft (June 2, 1998).

Year League	W	L	Pct.	ERA	G	GS	CG	ShO	Sv.	IP	H	R	ER	BB	SO
1998—Princeton (Appl.)................	6	4	.600	3.74	13	13	0	0	0	67 1/3	66	37	28	26	44
1999—Hudson Valley (NY-Penn)...	6	5	.545	2.65	16	*16	1	1	0	*95	78	33	28	26	*101
2000—Charleston, S.C. (S.Atl.).....	11	6	.647	3.30	22	22	3	•2	0	136 1/3	122	59	50	29	142
2001—Orlando (Sou.)	4	0	1.000	0.19	7	7	0	0	0	47	29	3	1	3	52
— Durham (I.L.)	2	0	1.000	2.42	4	4	0	0	0	26	22	8	7	9	23
— Tampa Bay (A.L.)...............	7	8	.467	4.44	20	20	0	0	0	117 2/3	122	63	58	34	78
Major League totals (1 year)........	7	8	.467	4.44	20	20	0	0	0	117 2/3	122	63	58	34	78

KENT, JEFF — 2B — GIANTS

PERSONAL: Born March 7, 1968, in Bellflower, Calif. ... 6-1/205. ... Bats right, throws right. ... Full name: Jeffrey Franklin Kent.
HIGH SCHOOL: Edison (Huntington Beach, Calif.).
COLLEGE: California.
TRANSACTIONS/CAREER NOTES: Selected by Toronto Blue Jays organization in 20th round of free-agent draft (June 5, 1989). ... Traded by Blue Jays with a player to be named later to New York Mets for P David Cone (August 27, 1992); Mets acquired OF Ryan Thompson to complete deal (September 1, 1992). ... On disabled list (July 6-21, 1995). ... Traded by New York Mets with IF Jose Vizcaino to Cleveland Indians for 2B Carlos Baerga and IF Alvaro Espinoza (July 29, 1996). ... Traded by Indians with IF Jose Vizcaino, P Julian Tavarez and a player to be named later to San Francisco Giants for 3B Matt Williams and a player to be named later (November 13, 1996); Indians traded P Joe Roa to Giants for OF Trenidad Hubbard to complete deal (December 16, 1996). ... On suspended list (August 22-25, 1997). ... On disabled list (June 10-July 10, 1998; and August 3-21, 1999).
RECORDS: Shares major league single-inning record for most doubles—2 (May 10, 2001, sixth inning).
HONORS: Named second baseman on THE SPORTING NEWS N.L. All-Star team (2000). ... Named second baseman on THE SPORTING NEWS N.L. Silver Slugger team (2000). ... Named N.L. Most Valuable Player by Baseball Writers' Association of America (2000). ... Named second baseman on N.L. Silver Slugger team (2001).
STATISTICAL NOTES: Led Florida State League second basemen with 680 total chances and 83 double plays in 1990. ... Led Southern League second basemen with 673 total chances and 96 double plays in 1991. ... Led N.L. second basemen in errors with 18 in 1993 and 20 in 1998. ... Tied for N.L. lead with 10 sacrifice flies in 1998. ... Hit for the cycle (May 3, 1999). ... Led N.L. with 13 sacrifice flies in 2001. ... Career major league grand slams: 9.

							BATTING									FIELDING		
Year Team (League)	Pos.	G	AB	R	H	2B	3B	HR	RBI	Avg.	BB	SO	SB	PO	A	E	Avg.
1989—St. Catharines (NY-P) .	SS-3B	73	268	34	60	14	1	*13	37	.224	33	81	5	103	178	29	.906
1990—Dunedin (FSL)...........	2B	132	447	72	124	32	2	16	60	.277	53	98	17	*261	*404	15	.978
1991—Knoxville (Sou.)...........	2B	•139	445	68	114	*34	1	2	61	.256	80	104	25	249	*395	*29	.957
1992—Toronto (A.L.).............	3B-2B-1B	65	192	36	46	13	1	8	35	.240	20	47	2	62	112	11	.941
—New York (N.L.)■......	2B-SS-3B	37	113	16	27	8	1	3	15	.239	7	29	0	62	93	3	.981
1993—New York (N.L.).........	2B-3B-SS	140	496	65	134	24	0	21	80	.270	30	88	4	261	341	†22	.965
1994—New York (N.L.)..........	2B	107	415	53	121	24	5	14	68	.292	23	84	1	222	337	•14	.976
1995—New York (N.L.)..........	2B	125	472	65	131	22	3	20	65	.278	29	89	3	245	336	10	.984
1996—New York (N.L.)..........	3B	89	335	45	97	20	1	9	39	.290	21	56	4	75	184	21	.925
—Cleveland (A.L.)■......1B-2B-3B-DH		39	102	16	27	7	0	3	16	.265	10	22	2	125	46	1	.994
1997—San Fran. (N.L.)■.......	2B-1B	155	580	90	145	38	2	29	121	.250	48	133	11	405	429	16	.981
1998—San Francisco (N.L.) ..	2B-1B	137	526	94	156	37	3	31	128	.297	48	110	9	279	404	†20	.972
1999—San Francisco (N.L.) ..	2B-1B	138	511	86	148	40	2	23	101	.290	61	112	13	286	326	10	.984
2000—San Francisco (N.L.) ..	2B-1B	159	587	114	196	41	7	33	125	.334	90	107	12	375	394	12	.985
2001—San Francisco (N.L.) ..	2B-1B	159	607	84	181	49	6	22	106	.298	65	96	7	462	404	11	.987
American League totals (2 years)		104	294	52	73	20	1	11	51	.248	30	69	4	187	158	12	.966
National League totals (10 years)		1246	4642	712	1336	303	30	205	848	.288	422	904	64	2672	3266	139	.977
Major League totals (10 years)		1350	4936	764	1409	323	31	216	899	.285	452	973	68	2859	3424	151	.977

DIVISION SERIES RECORD

RECORDS: Shares single-game record for most home runs—2 (October 3, 1997).

Year	Team (League)	Pos.	G	AB	R	H	2B	3B	HR	RBI	Avg.	BB	SO	SB	PO	A	E	Avg.
1996—Cleveland (A.L.)	2B-1B-PR-3B	4	8	2	1	1	0	0	0	.125	0	0	0	3	3	0	1.000
1997—San Francisco (N.L.)	2B-1B	3	10	2	3	0	0	2	2	.300	2	1	0	19	7	0	1.000
2000—San Francisco (N.L.)	2B-1B	4	16	3	6	1	0	0	1	.375	1	3	1	9	13	0	1.000
Division series totals (3 years)		11	34	7	10	2	0	2	3	.294	3	4	1	31	23	0	1.000

ALL-STAR GAME RECORD

Year	League	Pos.	AB	R	H	2B	3B	HR	RBI	Avg.	BB	SO	SB	PO	A	E	Avg.
1999—National	2B	1	0	0	0	0	0	0	.000	1	0	0	1	2	0	1.000
2000—National	2B	2	0	0	0	0	0	0	.000	0	0	0	0	0	0	...
2001—National	2B	2	1	1	1	0	0	0	.500	0	0	0	0	4	1	.800
All-Star Game totals (3 years)		5	1	1	1	0	0	0	.200	1	0	0	1	6	1	.875

KIELTY, BOBBY   OF   TWINS

PERSONAL: Born August 5, 1976, in Fontana, Calif. ... 6-1/215. ... Bats both, throws right. ... Full name: Robert Michael Kielty.
HIGH SCHOOL: Canyon Springs (Moreno Valley, Calif.).
JUNIOR COLLEGE: Riverside.
COLLEGE: Southern California, then Mississippi.
TRANSACTIONS/CAREER NOTES: Signed as non-drafted free agent by Minnesota Twins organization (February 16, 1999). ... On disabled list (May 21-June 24 and August 25-September 3, 1999). ... On Edmonton disabled list (May 4-18, 2001).

Year	Team (League)	Pos.	G	AB	R	H	2B	3B	HR	RBI	Avg.	BB	SO	SB	PO	A	E	Avg.
1999—Quad City (Midw.)	OF	69	245	52	72	13	1	13	43	.294	43	56	12	125	4	3	.977
2000—New Britain (East.)	OF	129	451	79	118	30	3	14	65	.262	98	109	6	243	6	3	.988
—Salt Lake (PCL)	OF	9	33	8	8	4	0	0	2	.242	7	10	0	22	0	1	.957
2001—Edmonton (PCL)	OF	94	341	58	98	25	2	12	50	.287	53	76	5	221	11	2	.991
—Minnesota (A.L.)	OF-DH	37	104	8	26	8	0	2	14	.250	8	25	3	63	2	3	.956
Major League totals (1 year)		37	104	8	26	8	0	2	14	.250	8	25	3	63	2	3	.956

KIESCHNICK, BROOKS   OF

PERSONAL: Born June 6, 1972, in Robstown, Texas. ... 6-4/230. ... Bats left, throws right. ... Full name: Michael Brooks Kieschnick. ... Name pronounced KEY-shnik.
HIGH SCHOOL: Mary Carroll (Corpus Christi, Texas).
COLLEGE: Texas.
TRANSACTIONS/CAREER NOTES: Selected by Chicago Cubs organization in first round (10th pick overall) of free-agent draft (June 3, 1993). ... Selected by Tampa Bay Devil Rays in third round (64th pick overall) of expansion draft (November 18, 1997). ... On Durham disabled list (April 16-August 2, 1998). ... Loaned by Devil Rays organization to Edmonton, Anaheim Angels organization (May 24-September 20, 1999). ... Granted free agency (October 15, 1999). ... Signed by Cincinnati Reds organization (November 16, 1999). ... Granted free agency (October 3, 2000). ... Signed by Colorado Rockies organization (December 1, 2000). ... On Colorado disabled list (May 13-28, 2001); included rehabilitation assignment to Colorado Springs (May 19-28). ... Granted free agency (October 8, 2001).
STATISTICAL NOTES: Led American Association with 250 total bases in 1995.

Year	Team (League)	Pos.	G	AB	R	H	2B	3B	HR	RBI	Avg.	BB	SO	SB	PO	A	E	Avg.
1993—GC Cubs (GCL)	OF	3	9	0	2	1	0	0	0	.222	0	1	0	3	1	0	1.000
—Daytona (FSL)	OF	6	22	1	4	2	0	0	2	.182	1	4	0	9	1	0	1.000
—Orlando (Sou.)	OF	25	91	12	31	8	0	2	10	.341	7	19	1	22	1	3	.885
1994—Orlando (Sou.)	OF-1B-3B	126	468	57	132	25	3	14	55	.282	33	78	3	259	14	6	.978
1995—Iowa (A.A.)	OF-DH-1B	138	505	61	*149	30	1	*23	73	.295	58	91	2	179	15	2	.990
1996—Chicago (N.L.)	OF	25	29	6	10	2	0	1	6	.345	3	8	0	5	0	1	.833
—Iowa (A.A.)	1B-OF-DH	117	441	47	114	20	1	18	64	.259	37	108	0	498	28	8	.985
1997—Iowa (A.A.)	1B-OF-DH-3B	97	360	57	93	21	0	21	66	.258	36	89	0	562	54	8	.987
—Chicago (N.L.)	OF	39	90	9	18	2	0	4	12	.200	12	21	1	39	1	2	.952
1998—Durham (I.L.)	OF-1B	7	23	4	3	1	0	1	2	.130	4	8	0	21	0	1	.955
—St. Petersburg (FSL)	OF-DH	28	105	15	26	6	0	5	18	.248	11	18	0	24	0	3	.889
—GC Devil Rays (GCL)	DH-1B	4	12	4	6	1	0	2	8	.500	1	0	0	11	0	0	1.000
1999—Durham (I.L.)	DH-OF-P	23	75	6	15	5	0	1	5	.200	5	14	0	15	0	0	1.000
—Edmonton (PCL)	DH-1B-OF-3B	77	296	54	93	20	3	23	73	.314	19	60	0	246	26	5	.982
2000—Louisville (I.L.)	OF-1B	113	440	68	122	35	0	25	90	.277	38	107	2	444	35	5	.990
—Cincinnati (N.L.)	1B	12	10	0	0	0	0	0	0	.000	1	5	0	1	0	0	1.000
2001—Colo. Springs (PCL)	OF-1B	71	252	44	74	9	3	13	45	.294	24	72	3	105	4	2	.982
—Colorado (N.L.)	OF-1B	35	42	5	10	2	1	3	9	.238	3	13	0	10	0	2	.833
Major League totals (4 years)		113	173	20	38	6	1	8	27	.220	19	47	1	55	1	5	.918

RECORD AS PITCHER

Year	League	W	L	Pct.	ERA	G	GS	CG	ShO	Sv.	IP	H	R	ER	BB	SO
1999—Durham (I.L.)	0	0	...	0.00	1	0	0	0	0	2	1	1	0	1	1

KILE, DARRYL   P   CARDINALS

PERSONAL: Born December 2, 1968, in Garden Grove, Calif. ... 6-5/212. ... Throws right, bats right. ... Full name: Darryl Andrew Kile.
HIGH SCHOOL: Norco Senior (Calif.).
JUNIOR COLLEGE: Chaffey College (Calif.).
TRANSACTIONS/CAREER NOTES: Selected by Houston Astros organization in 30th round of free-agent draft (June 2, 1987). ... On Tucson disabled list (June 25-July 5, 1992). ... Granted free agency (October 28, 1997). ... Signed by Colorado Rockies (December 4, 1997). ... Traded by Rockies with P Dave Veres and P Luther Hackman to St. Louis Cardinals for P Jose Jimenez, P Manny Aybar, P Rick Croushore and SS Brent Butler (November 16, 1999).

RECORDS: Shares modern N.L. record for most hit batsmen (nine-inning game)—4 (June 2, 1996).
STATISTICAL NOTES: Led N.L. with 15 hit batsmen in 1993. ... Pitched 7-1 no-hit victory against New York (September 8, 1993). ... Tied for N.L. lead with 10 wild pitches in 1994. ... Tied for N.L. lead with 16 hit batsmen in 1996.
MISCELLANEOUS: Appeared in two games as pinch runner (1996). ... Had one sacrifice hit in two appearances as pinch hitter and appeared in one game as pinch runner (1998).

Year League	W	L	Pct.	ERA	G	GS	CG	ShO	Sv.	IP	H	R	ER	BB	SO
1988— Gulf Coast Astros (GCL).....	5	3	.625	3.17	12	12	0	0	0	59²/₃	48	34	21	33	54
1989— Columbus (Sou.)	11	6	.647	2.58	20	20	6	•2	0	125²/₃	74	47	36	68	108
—Tucson (PCL)	2	1	.667	5.96	6	6	1	1	0	25²/₃	33	20	17	13	18
1990— Tucson (PCL)	5	10	.333	6.64	26	23	1	0	0	123¹/₃	147	97	91	68	77
1991— Houston (N.L.)	7	11	.389	3.69	37	22	0	0	0	153²/₃	144	81	63	84	100
1992— Houston (N.L.)	5	10	.333	3.95	22	22	2	0	0	125¹/₃	124	61	55	63	90
—Tucson (PCL)	4	1	.800	3.99	9	9	0	0	0	56¹/₃	50	31	25	32	43
1993— Houston (N.L.)	15	8	.652	3.51	32	26	4	2	0	171²/₃	152	73	67	69	141
1994— Houston (N.L.)	9	6	.600	4.57	24	24	0	0	0	147²/₃	153	84	75	*82	105
1995— Houston (N.L.)	4	12	.250	4.96	25	21	0	0	0	127	114	81	70	73	113
—Tucson (PCL)	2	1	.667	8.51	4	4	0	0	0	24¹/₃	29	23	23	12	15
1996— Houston (N.L.)	12	11	.522	4.19	35	33	4	0	0	219	233	113	102	97	219
1997— Houston (N.L.)	19	7	.731	2.57	34	34	6	4	0	255²/₃	208	87	73	94	205
1998— Colorado (N.L.)■	13	*17	.433	5.20	36	•35	4	1	0	230¹/₃	257	141	133	96	158
1999— Colorado (N.L.)	8	13	.381	6.61	32	32	1	0	0	190²/₃	225	*150	*140	109	116
2000— St. Louis (N.L.)■	20	9	.690	3.91	34	34	5	1	0	232¹/₃	215	109	101	58	192
2001— St. Louis (N.L.)	16	11	.593	3.09	34	34	2	1	0	227¹/₃	228	83	78	65	179
Major League totals (11 years).....	**128**	**115**	**.527**	**4.14**	**345**	**317**	**28**	**9**	**0**	**2080²/₃**	**2053**	**1063**	**957**	**890**	**1618**

DIVISION SERIES RECORD

Year League	W	L	Pct.	ERA	G	GS	CG	ShO	Sv.	IP	H	R	ER	BB	SO
1997— Houston (N.L.)	0	1	.000	2.57	1	1	0	0	0	7	2	2	2	2	4
2000— St. Louis (N.L.)	1	0	1.000	2.57	1	1	0	0	0	7	4	2	2	2	6
2001— St. Louis (N.L.)	0	0	...	3.00	1	1	0	0	0	6	3	2	2	5	5
Division series totals (3 years)	**1**	**1**	**.500**	**2.70**	**3**	**3**	**0**	**0**	**0**	**20**	**9**	**6**	**6**	**9**	**15**

CHAMPIONSHIP SERIES RECORD

RECORDS: Shares single-game record for most earned runs allowed—7 (October 15, 2000).

Year League	W	L	Pct.	ERA	G	GS	CG	ShO	Sv.	IP	H	R	ER	BB	SO
2000— St. Louis (N.L.)	0	2	.000	9.00	2	2	0	0	0	10	13	10	10	5	3

ALL-STAR GAME RECORD

Year League	W	L	Pct.	ERA	GS	CG	ShO	Sv.	IP	H	R	ER	BB	SO
1993— National						Did not play.								
1997— National						Did not play.								
2000— National	0	0	...	0.00	0	0	0	0	2	2	0	0	0	0

KIM, BYUNG-HYUN — P — DIAMONDBACKS

PERSONAL: Born January 21, 1979, in Kwangsan-ku Songjunsdon, Korea. ... 5-11/176. ... Throws right, bats right.
HIGH SCHOOL: Kwang-ju (Korea).
TRANSACTIONS/CAREER NOTES: Signed as non-drafted free agent by Arizona Diamondbacks organization (February 19, 1999). ... On Arizona disabled list (July 28-September 7, 2000).
MISCELLANEOUS: Member of Korean National Team (1997-98).

Year League	W	L	Pct.	ERA	G	GS	CG	ShO	Sv.	IP	H	R	ER	BB	SO
1999— El Paso (Texas)	2	0	1.000	2.11	10	0	0	0	0	21¹/₃	6	5	5	9	32
—Tucson (PCL)	4	0	1.000	2.40	11	3	0	0	1	30	21	9	8	15	40
—Arizona (N.L.)	1	2	.333	4.61	25	0	0	0	1	27¹/₃	20	15	14	20	31
—Ariz. Diamondbacks (Ariz.)	0	0	...	0.00	1	1	0	0	0	2	1	0	0	1	2
2000— Arizona (N.L.)	6	6	.500	4.46	61	1	0	0	14	70²/₃	52	39	35	46	111
—Tucson (PCL)	0	0	...	0.00	2	2	0	0	0	8¹/₃	1	0	0	4	13
2001— Arizona (N.L.)	5	6	.455	2.94	78	0	0	0	19	98	58	32	32	44	113
Major League totals (3 years)	**12**	**14**	**.462**	**3.72**	**164**	**1**	**0**	**0**	**34**	**196**	**130**	**86**	**81**	**110**	**255**

DIVISION SERIES RECORD

Year League	W	L	Pct.	ERA	G	GS	CG	ShO	Sv.	IP	H	R	ER	BB	SO
2001— Arizona (N.L.)	0	0	...	0.00	1	0	0	0	1	1¹/₃	1	0	0	2	1

CHAMPIONSHIP SERIES RECORD

Year League	W	L	Pct.	ERA	G	GS	CG	ShO	Sv.	IP	H	R	ER	BB	SO
2001— Arizona (N.L.)	0	0	...	0.00	3	0	0	0	2	5	0	0	0	1	3

WORLD SERIES RECORD

NOTES: Member of World Series championship team (2001).

Year League	W	L	Pct.	ERA	G	GS	CG	ShO	Sv.	IP	H	R	ER	BB	SO
2001— Arizona (N.L.)	0	1	.000	13.50	2	0	0	0	0	3¹/₃	6	5	5	1	6

KIM, SUN-WOO — P — RED SOX

PERSONAL: Born September 4, 1977, in Inchon, Korea. ... 6-2/180. ... Throws right, bats right.
COLLEGE: Korea University.
TRANSACTIONS/CAREER NOTES: Signed as non-drafted free agent by Boston Red Sox organization (November 21, 1997).

Year League	W	L	Pct.	ERA	G	GS	CG	ShO	Sv.	IP	H	R	ER	BB	SO
1998— Sarasota (FSL)	12	8	.600	4.82	26	24	•5	0	0	153	159	88	82	40	132
1999— Trenton (East.)	9	8	.529	4.89	26	26	1	1	0	149	160	86	81	44	130
2000— Pawtucket (I.L.)	11	7	.611	6.03	26	25	0	0	0	134¹/₃	170	98	90	42	116
2001— Pawtucket (I.L.)	6	7	.462	5.36	19	14	0	0	0	89	93	55	53	27	79
—Boston (A.L.)	0	2	.000	5.83	20	2	0	0	0	41²/₃	54	27	27	21	27
Major League totals (1 year)	**0**	**2**	**.000**	**5.83**	**20**	**2**	**0**	**0**	**0**	**41²/₃**	**54**	**27**	**27**	**21**	**27**

PERSONAL: Born January 15, 1974, in Chicago. ... 6-1/240. ... Throws left, bats left. ... Full name: Raymond Keith King.
HIGH SCHOOL: Ripley (Tenn.).
COLLEGE: Lambuth (Tenn.).
TRANSACTIONS/CAREER NOTES: Selected by Cincinnati Red organization in eighth round of free-agent draft (June 1, 1995). ... Loaned by Reds organization to Macon, Atlanta Braves organization (March 22-June 11, 1996). ... Traded by Reds to Braves (June 11, 1996), completing deal in which Braves traded OF Mike Kelly to Reds for P Chad Fox and a player to be named later (January 9, 1996). ... Traded by Braves to Chicago Cubs for P Jon Ratliff (January 20, 1998). ... Traded by Cubs to Milwaukee Brewers for P Doug Johnston (April 14, 2000).

Year League	W	L	Pct.	ERA	G	GS	CG	ShO	Sv.	IP	H	R	ER	BB	SO
1995— Billings (Pio.)	3	0	1.000	1.67	28	0	0	0	5	43	31	11	8	15	43
1996— Macon (S.Atl.)■..............	3	5	.375	2.80	18	10	1	0	0	70²/₃	63	34	22	20	63
— Durham (Caro.)	3	6	.333	4.46	14	14	2	0	0	82²/₃	104	54	41	15	52
1997— Greenville (Sou.)	5	5	.500	6.85	12	9	0	0	0	65²/₃	85	53	50	24	42
— Durham (Caro.)	6	9	.400	5.40	24	6	0	0	3	71²/₃	89	54	43	26	60
1998— West Tenn (Sou.)■	1	2	.333	2.43	25	0	0	0	3	29²/₃	23	9	8	10	26
— Iowa (PCL)	1	3	.250	5.01	37	0	0	0	2	32¹/₃	36	20	18	15	26
1999— Iowa (PCL)	4	4	.500	1.88	37	0	0	0	2	43	31	11	9	22	41
— Chicago (N.L.)	0	0	...	5.91	10	0	0	0	0	10²/₃	11	8	7	10	5
2000— Iowa (PCL)	1	0	1.000	0.00	1	0	0	0	0	1¹/₃	1	0	0	0	1
— Indianapolis (I.L.)■.........	0	3	.000	3.51	29	0	0	0	1	25²/₃	26	15	10	12	20
— Milwaukee (N.L.)	3	2	.600	1.26	36	0	0	0	0	28²/₃	18	7	4	10	19
2001— Milwaukee (N.L.)	0	4	.000	3.60	82	0	0	0	1	55	49	22	22	25	49
Major League totals (3 years)	**3**	**6**	**.333**	**3.15**	**128**	**0**	**0**	**0**	**1**	**94¹/₃**	**78**	**37**	**33**	**45**	**73**

PERSONAL: Born August 20, 1976, in Oranjestad, Aruba. ... 6-3/194. ... Bats both, throws right. ... Full name: Eugene Humphrey Kingsale.
HIGH SCHOOL: John F. Kennedy Technical School (Oranjestad, Aruba).
TRANSACTIONS/CAREER NOTES: Signed as non-drafted free agent by Baltimore Orioles organization (June 19, 1993). ... On Frederick disabled list (May 29-August 31, 1996). ... On Bowie disabled list (April 8-August 8, 1997). ... On Baltimore disabled list (March 29-August 27, 2000); included rehabilitation assignments Gulf Coast Orioles (August 8-18), Frederick (August 19-25) and Bowie (August 26-27). ... Claimed on waivers by Seattle Mariners (July 10, 2001).
STATISTICAL NOTES: Tied for Gulf Coast League lead in double plays by outfielder with two in 1994.

Year Team (League)	Pos.	G	AB	R	H	2B	3B	HR	RBI	Avg.	BB	SO	SB	PO	A	E	Avg.
1994— GC Orioles (GCL)........	OF-2B	50	168	26	52	2	3	0	9	.310	18	24	15	100	2	3	.971
1995— Bluefield (Appl.)	OF	47	171	45	54	11	2	0	16	.316	27	31	20	95	3	*11	.899
1996— Frederick (Caro.)	OF	49	166	26	45	6	4	0	9	.271	19	32	23	100	1	4	.962
— Baltimore (A.L.)........	OF	3	0	0	0	0	0	0	0	...	0	0	0	2	0	0	1.000
1997— Bowie (East.)............	OF	13	46	8	19	6	0	0	4	.413	5	4	5	23	0	1	.958
— GC Orioles (GCL).......	OF	6	17	2	5	0	0	0	0	.294	2	2	1	16	0	1	.941
1998— Bowie (East.)............	OF	111	427	69	112	11	5	1	34	.262	48	79	29	279	9	6	.980
— Rochester (I.L.)........	OF-DH	18	55	3	12	1	1	0	2	.218	4	8	3	38	2	0	1.000
— Baltimore (A.L.)........	OF-DH	11	2	1	0	0	0	0	0	.000	0	1	0	2	0	0	1.000
1999— Bowie (East.)............	OF	67	268	43	63	11	4	3	23	.235	33	46	13	173	2	4	.978
— Rochester (I.L.)........	OF	48	191	31	59	9	0	2	20	.309	13	23	10	118	1	3	.975
— Baltimore (A.L.)........	OF-DH	28	85	9	21	2	0	0	7	.247	5	13	1	48	1	1	.980
2000— GC Orioles (GCL)........	OF	5	16	7	5	0	0	0	4	.313	4	0	2	2	0	0	1.000
— Frederick (Caro.)	OF	6	25	8	11	3	0	1	3	.440	1	6	2	12	0	0	1.000
— Bowie (East.)............	OF	3	11	5	4	2	0	1	5	.364	3	0	1	3	0	0	1.000
— Rochester (I.L.)........	OF	2	10	2	4	1	0	0	1	.400	0	0	1	11	1	0	1.000
— Baltimore (A.L.)........	OF-DH	26	88	13	21	2	1	0	9	.239	2	14	1	60	2	3	.954
2001— Rochester (I.L.)........	OF	64	244	31	49	12	2	0	15	.201	26	44	16	134	2	5	.965
— Baltimore (A.L.)........	OF	3	4	0	0	0	0	0	0	.000	0	2	1	1	0	0	1.000
— Tacoma (PCL)■	OF	51	215	30	63	14	4	3	24	.293	8	25	12	115	5	3	.976
— Seattle (A.L.)	OF	10	15	4	5	0	0	1	1	.333	2	2	2	12	0	0	1.000
Major League totals (5 years)		**81**	**194**	**27**	**47**	**4**	**1**	**0**	**17**	**.242**	**9**	**32**	**5**	**125**	**3**	**4**	**.970**

PERSONAL: Born May 6, 1973, in Livonia, Mich. ... 6-1/210. ... Bats right, throws right. ... Full name: Michael A. Kinkade.
HIGH SCHOOL: Tigard (Ore.).
COLLEGE: Washington State.
TRANSACTIONS/CAREER NOTES: Selected by Milwaukee Brewers organization in ninth round of free-agent draft (June 1, 1995). ... On Louisville disabled list (April 20-May 14, 1998). ... Traded by Brewers to New York Mets for P Bill Pulsipher (July 31, 1998). ... Traded by Mets with OF Melvin Mora, P Leslie Brea and P Pat Gorman to Baltimore Orioles for SS Mike Bordick (July 28, 2000). ... On disabled list (August 24-September 18 and October 3, 2001-remainder of season).
HONORS: Named Texas League Player of the Year (1997).
STATISTICAL NOTES: Led Midwest league in being hit by pitch with 32 in 1996. ... Led Texas League with .455 on-base percentage and tied for league lead with 275 total bases in 1997. ... Led Texas League third basemen with 288 total chances in 1997. ... Led Eastern League with .434 on-base percentage and .561 slugging percentage in 2000.
MISCELLANEOUS: Member of 2000 U.S. Olympic baseball team.

Year Team (League)	Pos.	G	AB	R	H	2B	3B	HR	RBI	Avg.	BB	SO	SB	PO	A	E	Avg.
1995—Helena (Pio.)	3B-1B-C	69	266	76	94	19	1	4	39	.353	43	38	26	291	79	10	.974
1996—Beloit (Midw.)..........	3B-C-1B	•135	499	*104	151	33	4	15	100	.303	47	69	23	148	310	39	.922
1997—El Paso (Texas)..........	3B-DH	125	468	•112	*180	35	12	12	*109	*.385	52	66	17	*79	249	*60	.845
1998—Louisville (I.L.)	3B-1B-DH	80	291	57	90	24	6	7	46	.309	36	52	10	183	120	15	.953
— Norfolk (I.L.)■............	3B-1B	30	125	12	35	5	0	1	18	.280	3	24	6	32	61	5	.949
— New York (N.L.)..........	3B	3	2	2	0	0	0	0	0	.000	0	0	0	0	0	0	...
1999— New York (N.L.)..........OF-3B-C-1B		28	46	3	9	2	1	2	6	.196	3	9	1	18	2	0	1.000
— Norfolk (I.L.) 3-C-1-O-DH		84	312	53	96	20	2	7	49	.308	21	31	7	209	88	10	.967
2000—Binghamton (East.)	C-3B-OF	90	317	66	116	24	3	10	67	.366	35	39	18	516	80	9	.985
— New York (N.L.)..........	OF	2	2	0	0	0	0	0	0	.000	0	1	0	0	0	0	...
— Bowie (East.)■............	C-3B	8	27	4	7	1	0	3	5	.259	3	7	0	29	3	0	1.000
— Rochester (I.L.)	C-1B-3B	15	55	10	20	5	0	1	10	.364	11	11	0	70	11	4	.953
— Baltimore (A.L.)	DH-1B	3	7	0	3	1	0	0	1	.429	0	0	0	1	0	0	1.000
2001—Baltimore (A.L.)..........O-3-DH-1-C		61	160	19	44	5	0	4	16	.275	14	31	2	72	13	2	.977
American League totals (2 years)		64	167	19	47	6	0	4	17	.281	14	31	2	73	13	2	.977
National League totals (3 years)		33	50	5	9	2	1	2	6	.180	3	10	1	18	2	0	1.000
Major League totals (4 years)		97	217	24	56	8	1	6	23	.258	17	41	3	91	15	2	.981

DIVISION SERIES RECORD

Year Team (League)	Pos.	G	AB	R	H	2B	3B	HR	RBI	Avg.	BB	SO	SB	PO	A	E	Avg.
1999— New York (N.L.)								Did not play.									

CHAMPIONSHIP SERIES RECORD

Year Team (League)	Pos.	G	AB	R	H	2B	3B	HR	RBI	Avg.	BB	SO	SB	PO	A	E	Avg.
1999— New York (N.L.)								Did not play.									

K

KINNEY, MATT — P — TWINS

PERSONAL: Born December 16, 1976, in Bangor, Maine. ... 6-5/220. ... Throws right, bats right. ... Full name: Matthew John Kinney.
HIGH SCHOOL: Bangor (Maine).
TRANSACTIONS/CAREER NOTES: Selected by Boston Red Sox organization in sixth round of free-agent draft (June 1, 1995). ... Traded by Red Sox with P Joe Thomas and OF John Barnes to Minnesota Twins for P Greg Swindell and 1B Orlando Merced (July 31, 1998). ... On New Britain disabled list (June 7-August 16, 1999). ... On disabled list (April 23-May 3, 2001).
STATISTICAL NOTES: Led Florida State League with 93 bases on balls and 25 wild pitches in 1998.

Year League	W	L	Pct.	ERA	G	GS	CG	ShO	Sv.	IP	H	R	ER	BB	SO
1995—Gulf Coast Red Sox (GCL)..	1	3	.250	2.93	8	2	0	0	2	27²/₃	29	13	9	10	11
1996—Lowell (NY-Penn)...........	3	9	.250	2.68	15	•15	0	0	0	87¹/₃	68	51	26	44	72
1997—Michigan (Midw.)	8	5	.615	3.53	22	22	2	1	0	117¹/₃	93	59	46	78	123
1998—Sarasota (FSL)	9	6	.600	4.01	22	20	2	1	1	121¹/₃	109	70	54	*75	96
— Fort Myers (FSL)■.............	3	2	.600	3.13	7	7	0	0	0	37¹/₃	31	18	13	§18	39
1999—New Britain (East.)	4	7	.364	7.12	14	13	0	0	0	60²/₃	69	54	48	36	50
— Gulf Coast Twins (GCL).......	0	1	.000	4.76	3	3	0	0	0	5²/₃	6	4	3	3	8
2000—New Britain (East.)	6	1	.857	2.71	15	15	0	0	0	86¹/₃	74	31	26	35	93
— Salt Lake (PCL)	5	2	.714	4.25	9	9	0	0	0	55	42	26	26	26	59
— Minnesota (A.L.)	2	2	.500	5.10	8	8	0	0	0	42¹/₃	41	26	24	25	24
2001—Edmonton (PCL)	6	11	.353	5.07	29	•29	2	0	0	161²/₃	178	101	91	74	146
Major League totals (1 year)........	2	2	.500	5.10	8	8	0	0	0	42¹/₃	41	26	24	25	24

KLESKO, RYAN — 1B — PADRES

PERSONAL: Born June 12, 1971, in Westminster, Calif. ... 6-3/220. ... Bats left, throws left. ... Full name: Ryan Anthony Klesko.
HIGH SCHOOL: Westminster (Calif.).
TRANSACTIONS/CAREER NOTES: Selected by Atlanta Braves organization in fifth round of free-agent draft (June 5, 1989). ... On Atlanta disabled list (May 3-18, 1995); included rehabilitation assignment to Greenville (May 13-17). ... Traded by Braves with 2B Bret Boone and P Jason Shiell to San Diego Padres for 2B Quilvio Veras, 1B Wally Joyner and OF Reggie Sanders (December 22, 1999).
HONORS: Named Southern League Most Valuable Player (1991).
STATISTICAL NOTES: Career major league grand slams: 7.

Year Team (League)	Pos.	G	AB	R	H	2B	3B	HR	RBI	Avg.	BB	SO	SB	PO	A	E	Avg.
1989—GC Braves (GCL)	DH	17	57	14	23	5	4	1	16	.404	6	6	4	...	...	...	...
— Sumter (S.Atl.)	1B	25	90	17	26	6	0	1	12	.289	11	14	1	173	11	4	.979
1990—Sumter (S.Atl.)	1B	63	231	41	85	15	1	10	38	.368	31	30	13	575	43	14	.978
— Durham (Caro.)	1B	77	292	40	80	16	1	7	47	.274	32	53	10	490	34	13	.976
1991—Greenville (Sou.)	1B	126	419	64	122	22	3	14	67	.291	75	60	14	1043	57	*17	.985
1992—Richmond (I.L.)	1B	123	418	63	105	22	2	17	59	.251	41	72	3	947	51	*11	.989
— Atlanta (N.L.)	1B	13	14	0	0	0	0	0	1	.000	0	5	0	25	0	0	1.000
1993—Richmond (I.L.)	1B-OF	98	343	59	94	14	2	22	74	.274	47	69	4	587	45	12	.981
— Atlanta (N.L.)	1B-OF	22	17	3	6	1	0	2	5	.353	3	4	0	8	0	0	1.000
1994—Atlanta (N.L.)	OF-1B	92	245	42	68	13	3	17	47	.278	26	48	1	89	3	7	.929
1995—Atlanta (N.L.)	OF-1B	107	329	48	102	25	2	23	70	.310	47	72	5	131	4	8	.944
— Greenville (Sou.)	DH-OF	4	13	1	3	0	0	1	4	.231	2	1	0	2	0	0	1.000
1996—Atlanta (N.L.)	OF-1B	153	528	90	149	21	4	34	93	.282	68	129	6	204	8	5	.977
1997—Atlanta (N.L.)	OF-1B	143	467	67	122	23	6	24	84	.261	48	130	4	245	6	6	.977
1998—Atlanta (N.L.)	OF-1B	129	427	69	117	29	1	18	70	.274	56	66	5	195	13	2	.990
1999—Atlanta (N.L.)	1B-OF-DH	133	404	55	120	28	2	21	80	.297	53	69	5	554	32	6	.990
2000—San Diego (N.L.)■	1B-OF	145	494	88	140	33	2	26	92	.283	91	81	23	1031	90	9	.992
2001—San Diego (N.L.)	1B	146	538	105	154	34	6	30	113	.286	88	89	23	1135	84	11	.991
Major League totals (10 years)		1083	3463	567	978	207	26	195	655	.282	480	693	72	3617	240	54	.986

DIVISION SERIES RECORD

RECORDS: Shares career record for most grand slams—1 (September 30, 1998). ... Shares single-inning record for most runs batted in—4 (September 30, 1998).

Year Team (League)	Pos.	G	AB	R	H	2B	3B	HR	RBI	Avg.	BB	SO	SB	PO	A	E	Avg.
1995— Atlanta (N.L.).............	OF	4	15	5	7	1	0	0	1	.467	0	3	0	3	0	0	1.000
1996— Atlanta (N.L.).............	OF	3	8	1	1	0	0	1	1	.125	3	4	1	2	0	1	.667
1997— Atlanta (N.L.).............	OF	3	8	2	2	1	0	1	1	.250	0	2	0	3	0	1	.750
1998— Atlanta (N.L.).............	OF	3	11	1	3	0	0	1	4	.273	0	3	0	5	0	0	1.000
1999— Atlanta (N.L.).............	1B-PH	4	12	3	4	0	0	0	1	.333	1	4	0	22	2	0	1.000
Division series totals (5 years)		17	54	12	17	2	0	3	8	.315	4	16	1	35	2	2	.949

CHAMPIONSHIP SERIES RECORD

Year Team (League)	Pos.	G	AB	R	H	2B	3B	HR	RBI	Avg.	BB	SO	SB	PO	A	E	Avg.
1995— Atlanta (N.L.).............	OF-PH	4	7	0	0	0	0	0	0	.000	3	4	0	1	0	0	1.000
1996— Atlanta (N.L.).............	OF	6	16	1	4	0	0	1	3	.250	2	6	0	13	0	0	1.000
1997— Atlanta (N.L.).............	OF	5	17	2	4	0	0	2	4	.235	2	3	0	5	0	0	1.000
1998— Atlanta (N.L.).............	OF-PH	5	12	2	1	0	0	0	1	.083	6	3	0	3	0	1	.750
1999— Atlanta (N.L.).............	1B-PH	4	8	1	1	0	0	1	1	.125	2	1	0	27	2	2	.935
Championship series totals (5 years)		24	60	6	10	0	0	4	9	.167	15	17	0	49	2	3	.944

WORLD SERIES RECORD

NOTES: Member of World Series championship team (1995).

Year Team (League)	Pos.	G	AB	R	H	2B	3B	HR	RBI	Avg.	BB	SO	SB	PO	A	E	Avg.
1995— Atlanta (N.L.).............	OF-DH	6	16	4	5	0	0	3	4	.313	3	4	0	1	0	0	1.000
1996— Atlanta (N.L.)..........DH-OF-1B-PH	5	10	2	1	0	0	0	1	.100	2	4	0	1	0	1	.500
1999— Atlanta (N.L.).............	1B-PH	4	12	0	2	0	0	0	0	.167	0	1	0	21	0	0	1.000
World Series totals (3 years)		15	38	6	8	0	0	3	5	.211	5	9	0	23	0	1	.958

ALL-STAR GAME RECORD

Year League	Pos.	AB	R	H	2B	3B	HR	RBI	Avg.	BB	SO	SB	PO	A	E	Avg.
2001— National......................	1B	1	0	0	0	0	0	1	.000	0	1	0	7	0	0	1.000

K

KLINE, STEVE — P — CARDINALS

PERSONAL: Born August 22, 1972, in Sunbury, Pa. ... 6-1/215. ... Throws left, bats both. ... Full name: Steven James Kline.
HIGH SCHOOL: Lewisburg (Pa.).
COLLEGE: West Virginia.
TRANSACTIONS/CAREER NOTES: Selected by Cleveland Indians organization in eighth round of free-agent draft (June 3, 1993). ... On disabled list (May 23-August 5, 1995). ... On temporarily inactive list (April 5-20, 1996). ... Traded by Indians to Montreal Expos for P Jeff Juden (July 31, 1997). ... On disabled list (April 11-27, 1999). ... Traded by Expos with P Dustin Hermanson to St. Louis Cardinals for 3B Fernando Tatis and P Britt Reames (December 14, 2000).
RECORDS: Shares major league single-inning record for most strikeouts—4 (August 17, 2000, seventh inning).

Year League	W	L	Pct.	ERA	G	GS	CG	ShO	Sv.	IP	H	R	ER	BB	SO
1993— Burlington (Appl.)...............	1	1	.500	4.91	2	1	0	0	0	7 1/3	11	4	4	2	4
— Watertown (NY-Penn)	5	4	.556	3.19	13	13	2	1	0	79	77	36	28	12	45
1994— Columbus (S.Atl.)..............	*18	5	.783	3.01	28	•28	2	1	0	*185 2/3	175	67	62	36	*174
1995— Canton/Akron (East.).........	2	3	.400	2.42	14	14	0	0	0	89 1/3	86	34	24	30	45
1996— Canton/Akron (East.).........	8	12	.400	5.46	25	24	0	0	0	146 2/3	168	98	89	55	107
1997— Cleveland (A.L.)................	3	1	.750	5.81	20	1	0	0	0	26 1/3	42	19	17	13	17
— Buffalo (A.A.)................	3	3	.500	4.03	20	4	0	0	1	51 1/3	53	26	23	13	41
— Montreal (N.L.)■................	1	3	.250	6.15	26	0	0	0	0	26 1/3	31	18	18	10	20
1998— Ottawa (I.L.)................	0	0	...	0.00	2	0	0	0	0	2 2/3	1	0	0	0	1
— Montreal (N.L.)................	3	6	.333	2.76	78	0	0	0	1	71 2/3	62	25	22	41	76
1999— Montreal (N.L.)................	7	4	.636	3.75	*82	0	0	0	0	69 2/3	56	32	29	33	69
2000— Montreal (N.L.)................	1	5	.167	3.50	*83	0	0	0	14	82 1/3	88	36	32	27	64
2001— St. Louis (N.L.)■................	3	3	.500	1.80	*89	0	0	0	9	75	53	16	15	29	54
A.L. totals (1 year)	3	1	.750	5.81	20	1	0	0	0	26 1/3	42	19	17	13	17
N.L. totals (5 years)	15	21	.417	3.21	358	0	0	0	24	325	290	127	116	140	283
Major League totals (5 years)	18	22	.450	3.41	378	1	0	0	24	351 1/3	332	146	133	153	300

DIVISION SERIES RECORD

Year League	W	L	Pct.	ERA	G	GS	CG	ShO	Sv.	IP	H	R	ER	BB	SO
2001— St. Louis (N.L.)..................	0	1	.000	2.08	4	0	0	0	2	4 1/3	4	1	1	2	0

KNIGHT, BRANDON — P — YANKEES

PERSONAL: Born October 1, 1975, in Oxnard, Calif. ... 6-0/170. ... Throws right, bats left. ... Full name: Brandon Michael Knight.
HIGH SCHOOL: Buena (Ventura, Calif.).
JUNIOR COLLEGE: Ventura (Calif.) College.
TRANSACTIONS/CAREER NOTES: Selected by Texas Rangers organization in 14th round of free-agent draft (June 1, 1995). ... Traded by Rangers with P Sam Marsonek to New York Yankees for OF Chad Curtis (December 13, 1999). ... Selected by Minnesota Twins from Yankees organization in Rule 5 major league draft (December 11, 2000). ... Returned to Yankees organization (March 28, 2001). ... Released by Yankees (March 30, 2001). ... Re-signed by Yankees organization (April 1, 2001).

Year— League	W	L	Pct.	ERA	G	GS	CG	ShO	Sv.	IP	H	R	ER	BB	SO
1995—Gulf Coast Rangers (GCL)..	2	1	.667	5.25	3	2	0	0	0	12	12	7	7	6	11
—Charleston, S.C. (S.Atl.)	4	2	.667	3.13	9	9	0	0	0	54²/₃	37	22	19	21	52
1996— Charlotte (FSL)	4	10	.286	5.12	19	17	2	0	0	102	118	65	58	45	74
—Hudson Valley (NY-Penn)...	2	2	.500	4.42	9	9	0	0	0	53	59	29	26	21	52
1997— Charlotte (FSL)	7	4	.636	2.23	14	12	3	1	0	92²/₃	82	33	23	22	91
—Tulsa (Texas)	6	4	.600	4.50	14	14	2	•1	0	90	83	52	45	35	84
1998— Tulsa (Texas)	6	6	.500	5.11	14	14	0	0	0	86¹/₃	94	54	49	37	87
—Oklahoma City (PCL)........	0	7	.000	9.74	16	12	0	0	0	64²/₃	100	75	70	29	52
1999— Oklahoma (PCL).................	9	8	.529	4.91	27	26	*5	0	0	163	173	96	89	47	97
2000— Columbus (I.L.)■..............	10	12	.455	4.44	28	•28	*8	1	0	*184²/₃	172	105	91	61	*138
2001— Columbus (I.L.)	12	7	.632	3.66	25	25	3	0	0	162¹/₃	174	77	66	45	173
—New York (A.L.).................	0	0	...	10.13	4	0	0	0	0	10²/₃	18	12	12	3	7
Major League totals (1 year)........	0	0	...	10.13	4	0	0	0	0	10²/₃	18	12	12	3	7

KNOBLAUCH, CHUCK   OF   ROYALS

PERSONAL: Born July 7, 1968, in Houston. ... 5-9/175. ... Bats right, throws right. ... Full name: Edward Charles Knoblauch. ... Son of Ray Knoblauch, minor league pitcher (1947-56); and nephew of Ed Knoblauch, minor league outfielder (1938-42 and 1947-55). ... Name pronounced NOB-lock.

HIGH SCHOOL: Bellaire (Houston).

COLLEGE: Texas A&M.

TRANSACTIONS/CAREER NOTES: Selected by Philadelphia Phillies organization in 18th round of free-agent draft (June 2, 1986); did not sign. ... Selected by Minnesota Twins organization in first round (25th pick overall) of free-agent draft (June 5, 1989). ... Traded by Twins to New York Yankees for P Eric Milton, P Danny Mota, OF Brian Buchanan, SS Cristian Guzman and cash (February 6, 1998). ... On New York disabled list (August 3-September 1, 2000); included rehabilitation assignment to Tampa (August 25-September 1). ... Granted free agency (November 5, 2001). ... Signed by Kansas City Royals (December 18, 2001).

HONORS: Named A.L. Rookie Player of the Year by THE SPORTING NEWS (1991). ... Named A.L. Rookie of the Year by Baseball Writers' Association of America (1991). ... Named second baseman on THE SPORTING NEWS A.L. All-Star team (1994 and 1997). ... Named second baseman on THE SPORTING NEWS A.L. Silver Slugger team (1995 and 1997). ... Won A.L. Gold Glove at second base (1997).

STATISTICAL NOTES: Had 20-game hitting streak (September 2-25, 1991). ... Led A.L. second basemen with 424 assists, 101 double plays and 718 total chances in 1997. ... Led A.L. in being hit by pitch with 18 in 1998. ... Career major league grand slams: 3.

MISCELLANEOUS: Holds Minnesota Twins all-time record for most stolen bases (276).

							BATTING								FIELDING		
Year	Team (League)	Pos.	G	AB	R	H	2B	3B	HR	RBI	Avg.	BB	SO	SB	PO	A	E	Avg.
1989— Kenosha (Midw.)........		SS	51	196	29	56	13	1	2	19	.286	32	23	9	60	124	21	.898
—Visalia (Calif.)		SS	18	77	20	28	10	0	0	21	.364	6	11	4	23	52	10	.882
1990— Orlando (Sou.)		2B	118	432	74	125	23	6	2	53	.289	63	31	23	275	300	20	.966
1991— Minnesota (A.L.)........		2B	151	565	78	159	24	6	1	50	.281	59	40	25	249	460	18	.975
1992— Minnesota (A.L.)	2B-DH-SS	155	600	104	178	19	6	2	56	.297	88	60	34	306	415	6	.992
1993— Minnesota (A.L.)	2B-SS-OF	153	602	82	167	27	4	2	41	.277	65	44	29	302	431	9	.988
1994— Minnesota (A.L.)	2B-SS	109	445	85	139	*45	3	5	51	.312	41	56	35	191	285	3	.994
1995— Minnesota (A.L.)	2B-SS	136	538	107	179	34	8	11	63	.333	78	95	46	254	400	10	.985
1996— Minnesota (A.L.)	2B-DH	153	578	140	197	35	*14	13	72	.341	98	74	45	271	390	8	*.988
1997— Minnesota (A.L.)	2B-DH-SS	156	611	117	178	26	10	9	58	.291	84	84	62	285	†428	12	.983
1998— New York (A.L.)■........	2B-DH	150	603	117	160	25	4	17	64	.265	76	70	31	275	408	13	.981
1999— New York (A.L.).........	2B	150	603	120	176	36	4	18	68	.292	83	57	28	254	425	*26	.963
2000— New York (A.L.).........	2B-DH	102	400	75	113	22	2	5	26	.283	46	45	15	149	190	15	.958
—Tampa (FSL)..............	2B	1	1	0	0	0	0	0	0	.000	0	1	0	0	1	0	1.000
2001— New York (A.L.).........	OF-DH	137	521	66	130	20	3	9	44	.250	58	73	38	171	8	2	.989
Major League totals (11 years)		1552	6066	1091	1776	313	64	92	593	.293	776	698	388	2707	3840	122	.982

DIVISION SERIES RECORD

							BATTING								FIELDING		
Year	Team (League)	Pos.	G	AB	R	H	2B	3B	HR	RBI	Avg.	BB	SO	SB	PO	A	E	Avg.
1998— New York (A.L.).........	2B	3	11	0	1	0	0	0	0	.091	0	4	0	4	10	1	.933
1999— New York (A.L.).........	2B	3	12	1	2	0	0	0	0	.167	1	3	0	2	11	1	.929
2000— New York (A.L.).........	DH-PR	3	9	1	3	0	0	0	1	.333	0	2	1	...	...	...	...
2001— New York (A.L.).........	OF	5	22	1	6	1	0	0	1	.273	0	0	1	12	0	1	.923
Division series totals (4 years)		14	54	3	12	1	0	0	2	.222	1	9	2	18	21	3	.929

CHAMPIONSHIP SERIES RECORD

RECORDS: Shares A.L. career record for most doubles—7.

							BATTING								FIELDING		
Year	Team (League)	Pos.	G	AB	R	H	2B	3B	HR	RBI	Avg.	BB	SO	SB	PO	A	E	Avg.
1991— Minnesota (A.L.)	2B	5	20	5	7	2	0	0	3	.350	3	3	2	8	14	0	1.000
1998— New York (A.L.).........	2B	6	25	4	5	1	0	0	0	.200	4	2	0	9	17	0	1.000
1999— New York (A.L.).........	2B	5	18	3	6	1	0	0	1	.333	3	1	0	8	10	1	.947
2000— New York (A.L.).........	DH	6	23	3	6	2	0	0	2	.261	3	4	0	...	...	...	...
2001— New York (A.L.).........	OF	5	18	0	6	1	0	0	3	.333	2	3	1	13	0	0	1.000
Championship series totals (5 years)		27	104	15	30	7	0	0	9	.288	15	12	3	38	41	1	.988

WORLD SERIES RECORD

NOTES: Member of World Series championship team (1991, 1998, 1999 and 2000).

							BATTING								FIELDING		
Year	Team (League)	Pos.	G	AB	R	H	2B	3B	HR	RBI	Avg.	BB	SO	SB	PO	A	E	Avg.
1991— Minnesota (A.L.)	2B	7	26	3	8	1	0	0	2	.308	4	2	4	15	14	1	.967
1998— New York (A.L.).........	2B	4	16	3	6	0	0	1	3	.375	3	2	1	7	10	1	.944
1999— New York (A.L.).........	2B	4	16	5	5	1	0	1	3	.313	1	3	1	10	10	0	1.000
2000— New York (A.L.).........	DH-PR	4	10	1	1	0	0	0	1	.100	2	1	0	...	...	...	...
2001— New York (A.L.)..........OF-DH-PR-PH	6	18	1	1	0	0	0	0	.056	1	2	0	1	1	0	1.000
World Series totals (5 years)		25	86	13	21	2	0	2	9	.244	11	10	6	33	35	2	.971

K

ALL-STAR GAME RECORD

Year	League	Pos.	AB	R	H	2B	3B	HR	RBI	Avg.	BB	SO	SB	PO	A	E	Avg.
										BATTING					FIELDING		
1992—American		PH-2B	1	0	0	0	0	0	0	.000	1	0	0	0	0	0	...
1994—American		2B	3	1	0	0	0	0	0	.000	0	2	0	1	2	0	1.000
1996—American		2B	1	0	1	0	0	0	0	1.000	0	0	0	3	1	0	1.000
1997—American		2B	0	0	0	0	0	0	0	...	0	0	0	1	1	0	1.000
All-Star Game totals (4 years)			5	1	1	0	0	0	0	.200	1	2	0	5	4	0	1.000

KNORR, RANDY   C

PERSONAL: Born November 12, 1968, in San Gabriel, Calif. ... 6-2/215. ... Bats right, throws right. ... Full name: Randy Duane Knorr. ... Name pronounced NOR.

HIGH SCHOOL: Baldwin Park (Calif.).

TRANSACTIONS/CAREER NOTES: Selected by Toronto Blue Jays organization in 10th round of free-agent draft (June 2, 1986). ... On disabled list (June 24-July 4, 1986; and May 10, 1989-remainder of season). ... On Syracuse disabled list (May 11-23, 1992). ... On Toronto disabled list (August 20-September 30, 1992). ... On Toronto disabled list (July 1-August 11, 1995); included rehabilitation assignment to Syracuse (July 21-August 9). ... Traded by Blue Jays to Houston Astros for cash (May 17, 1996). ... Granted free agency (December 20, 1996). ... Re-signed by Astros organization (December 23, 1996). ... On Houston disabled list (August 29-September 6, 1997); included rehabilitation assignment to New Orleans (August 29-September 6). ... Granted free agency (October 14, 1997). ... Signed by Florida Marlins organization (December 22, 1997). ... On Charlotte disabled list (April 24-May 22, 1998). ... Granted free agency (September 29, 1998). ... Signed by Astros organization (January 21, 1999). ... Granted free agency (October 15, 1999). ... Signed by Pittsburgh Pirates organization (December 20, 1999). ... Released by Pirates (May 6, 2000). ... Signed by Texas Rangers organization (May 11, 2000). ... Granted free agency (October 14, 2000). ... Signed by Montreal Expos organization (November 17, 2000). ... Granted free agency (November 6, 2001).

STATISTICAL NOTES: Led South Atlantic League catchers with 960 total chances and 25 passed balls in 1988.

Year	Team (League)	Pos.	G	AB	R	H	2B	3B	HR	RBI	Avg.	BB	SO	SB	PO	A	E	Avg.
											BATTING					FIELDING		
1986—Medicine Hat (Pio.)		1B	55	215	21	58	13	0	4	52	.270	17	53	0	451	29	10	.980
1987—Myrtle Beach (S.Atl.)		C-1B-2B	46	129	17	34	4	0	6	21	.264	6	46	0	95	7	1	.990
—Medicine Hat (Pio.)		C	26	106	21	31	7	0	10	24	.292	5	26	0	70	5	4	.949
1988—Myrtle Beach (S.Atl.)		C	117	364	43	85	13	0	9	42	.234	41	91	0	*870	75	15	.984
1989—Dunedin (FSL)		C	33	122	13	32	6	0	6	23	.262	6	21	0	186	20	2	.990
1990—Knoxville (Sou.)		C	116	392	51	108	12	1	13	64	.276	31	83	0	599	72	15	.978
1991—Knoxville (Sou.)		C-1B	24	74	7	13	4	0	0	4	.176	10	18	2	136	16	2	.987
—Syracuse (I.L.)		C	91	342	29	89	20	0	5	44	.260	23	58	1	477	49	7	.987
—Toronto (A.L.)		C	3	1	0	0	0	0	0	0	.000	1	1	0	6	1	0	1.000
1992—Syracuse (I.L.)		C	61	228	27	62	13	1	11	27	.272	17	38	1	220	22	3	.988
—Toronto (A.L.)		C	8	19	1	5	0	0	1	2	.263	1	5	0	33	3	0	1.000
1993—Toronto (A.L.)		C	39	101	11	25	3	2	4	20	.248	9	29	0	168	20	0	1.000
1994—Toronto (A.L.)		C	40	124	20	30	2	0	7	19	.242	10	35	0	247	21	2	.993
1995—Toronto (A.L.)		C	45	132	18	28	8	0	3	16	.212	11	28	0	243	22	8	.971
—Syracuse (I.L.)		C-DH	18	67	6	18	5	1	1	6	.269	5	14	0	129	14	3	.979
1996—Syracuse (I.L.)		C-DH	12	36	1	10	5	0	0	5	.278	5	8	0	53	2	0	1.000
—Houston (N.L.)■		C	37	87	7	17	5	0	1	7	.195	5	18	0	204	14	0	1.000
1997—New Orleans (A.A.)		C	72	244	22	58	10	0	5	27	.238	22	38	0	502	54	9	.984
		C-1B	4	8	1	3	0	0	1	1	.375	0	2	0	19	3	0	1.000
1998—Charlotte (I.L.)■		C-DH	68	201	30	66	15	0	7	39	.328	34	41	1	349	25	9	.977
—Florida (N.L.)		C	15	49	4	10	4	1	2	11	.204	1	10	0	82	7	1	.989
1999—New Orleans (PCL)■		C-1B-DH-OF	77	270	33	95	22	1	11	41	.352	20	41	0	437	40	7	.986
—Houston (N.L.)		C	13	30	2	5	1	0	0	0	.167	1	8	0	54	3	0	1.000
2000—Nashville (PCL)■		C	13	40	3	6	1	0	1	4	.150	6	11	0	69	9	3	.963
—Oklahoma (PCL)■		C-1B	70	252	36	64	16	1	6	41	.254	22	50	0	368	34	4	.990
—Texas (A.L.)		C	15	34	5	10	2	0	2	2	.294	0	3	0	64	2	1	.985
2001—Montreal (N.L.)■		C	34	91	13	20	2	0	3	10	.220	8	22	0	168	5	2	.989
American League totals (6 years)			150	411	55	98	15	2	17	59	.238	32	101	0	761	69	11	.987
National League totals (5 years)			103	265	27	55	12	1	7	29	.208	15	60	0	527	32	3	.995
Major League totals (11 years)			253	676	82	153	27	3	24	88	.226	47	161	0	1288	101	14	.990

CHAMPIONSHIP SERIES RECORD

Year	Team (League)	Pos.	G	AB	R	H	2B	3B	HR	RBI	Avg.	BB	SO	SB	PO	A	E	Avg.
								BATTING								FIELDING		
1992—Toronto (A.L.)									Did not play.									
1993—Toronto (A.L.)									Did not play.									

WORLD SERIES RECORD

NOTES: Member of World Series championship team (1992 and 1993).

Year	Team (League)	Pos.	G	AB	R	H	2B	3B	HR	RBI	Avg.	BB	SO	SB	PO	A	E	Avg.
								BATTING								FIELDING		
1992—Toronto (A.L.)									Did not play.									
1993—Toronto (A.L.)		C	1	0	0	0	0	0	0	0	...	0	0	0	3	0	0	1.000

KNOTT, ERIC   P

PERSONAL: Born September 23, 1974, in Harvey, Ill. ... 6-0/190. ... Throws left, bats left. ... Full name: Eric James Knott.

HIGH SCHOOL: Sebring (Fla.).

COLLEGE: Stetson.

TRANSACTIONS/CAREER NOTES: Selected by Arizona Diamondbacks organization in 24th round of free-agent draft (June 4, 1996). ... On Tucson disabled list (May 23-June 12, 2000). ... Released by Diamondbacks (June 12, 2000). ... Signed by Chiba Lotte Marines of Japan Pacific League (2000). ... Signed by Diamondbacks (November 25, 2000). ... On Tucson disabled list (April 5-12, 2001). ... Granted free agency (December 21, 2001).

STATISTICAL NOTES: Tied for California League lead in home runs allowed with 16 in 1998.

Year	League	W	L	Pct.	ERA	G	GS	CG	ShO	Sv.	IP	H	R	ER	BB	SO
1997—	Lethbridge (Pio.)	0	4	.000	2.87	21	3	0	0	3	47	41	21	15	9	62
1998—	High Desert (Calif.)	12	7	.632	4.52	28	22	1	0	0	143 1/3	175	84	72	28	96
1999—	El Paso (Texas)	7	11	.389	4.57	27	27	*3	0	0	161 1/3	*198	95	82	42	83
2000—	Tucson (PCL)	3	2	.600	6.35	11	7	0	0	0	39 2/3	59	30	28	8	21
—	Chiba (Jp. East.)■	1	1	.500	4.09	5	5	0	0	0	22	22	12	10	6	17
—	Chiba Lotte (Jap. Cen.)	1	1	.500	11.02	5	5	0	0	0	16 1/3	22	20	20	12	6
2001—	El Paso (Texas)■	4	1	.800	3.12	17	0	0	0	0	26	29	13	9	8	20
—	Tucson (PCL)	6	2	.750	3.80	25	8	0	0	1	73 1/3	82	34	31	8	43
—	Arizona (N.L.)	0	1	.000	1.93	3	1	0	0	0	4 2/3	8	9	1	0	4
Major League totals (1 year)		0	1	.000	1.93	3	1	0	0	0	4 2/3	8	9	1	0	4

KNOTTS, GARY   P   MARLINS

PERSONAL: Born February 12, 1977, in Decatur, Ala. ... 6-4/200. ... Throws right, bats right. ... Full name: Gary E. Knotts.
HIGH SCHOOL: Brewer (Somerville, Ala.).
JUNIOR COLLEGE: Northwest Shoals Community College (Ala.).
TRANSACTIONS/CAREER NOTES: Selected by Florida Marlins organization in 11th round of free agent draft (June 1, 1995). ... Granted free agency (December 21, 1999). ... Re-signed by Marlins organization (December 22, 1999). ... On Calgary disabled list (August 21, 2001-remainder of season).

Year	League	W	L	Pct.	ERA	G	GS	CG	ShO	Sv.	IP	H	R	ER	BB	SO
1996—	Gulf Coast Marlins (GCL)	4	2	.667	2.04	12	9	1	1	0	57 1/3	35	16	13	17	48
1997—	Kane County (Midw.)	1	5	.167	13.05	7	7	0	0	0	20	33	34	29	17	19
—	Utica (NY-Penn)	3	5	.375	3.62	12	12	1	0	0	69 2/3	70	34	28	27	65
1998—	Kane County (Midw.)	8	8	.500	3.87	27	27	3	0	0	158 1/3	144	84	68	66	148
1999—	Brevard County (FSL)	9	6	.600	4.60	16	16	3	2	0	94	101	52	48	29	65
—	Portland (East.)	6	3	.667	3.75	12	12	1	1	0	81 2/3	79	39	34	33	63
2000—	Portland (East.)	9	8	.529	4.66	27	27	2	0	0	156 1/3	161	102	81	63	113
2001—	Calgary (PCL)	6	7	.462	5.46	21	21	1	1	0	118 2/3	136	77	72	43	104
—	Florida (N.L.)	0	1	.000	6.00	2	1	0	0	0	6	7	4	4	1	9
Major League totals (1 year)		0	1	.000	6.00	2	1	0	0	0	6	7	4	4	1	9

KOCH, BILLY   P   ATHLETICS

PERSONAL: Born December 14, 1974, in Rockville Center, N.Y. ... 6-3/215. ... Throws right, bats right. ... Full name: William Christopher Koch.
HIGH SCHOOL: West Babylon (N.Y.).
COLLEGE: Clemson.
TRANSACTIONS/CAREER NOTES: Selected by Toronto Blue Jays organization in first round (fourth pick overall) of free-agent draft (June 4, 1996). ... On disabled list (April 14, 1997-remainder of season). ... Traded by Blue Jays to Oakland Athletics for P Justin Miller and 3B Eric Hinske (December 7, 2001).
MISCELLANEOUS: Member of 1996 U.S. Olympic baseball team.

Year	League	W	L	Pct.	ERA	G	GS	CG	ShO	Sv.	IP	H	R	ER	BB	SO
1997—	Dunedin (FSL)	0	1	.000	2.49	3	3	0	0	0	21 2/3	27	10	6	3	20
1998—	Dunedin (FSL)	•14	7	.667	3.75	25	25	0	0	0	124 2/3	120	65	52	41	108
—	Syracuse (I.L.)	0	1	.000	14.29	2	2	0	0	0	5 2/3	9	9	9	5	9
1999—	Syracuse (I.L.)	3	0	1.000	3.86	5	5	0	0	0	25 2/3	27	11	11	10	22
—	Toronto (A.L.)	0	5	.000	3.39	56	0	0	0	31	63 2/3	55	26	24	30	57
2000—	Toronto (A.L.)	9	3	.750	2.63	68	0	0	0	33	78 2/3	78	28	23	18	60
2001—	Toronto (A.L.)	2	5	.286	4.80	69	0	0	0	36	69 1/3	69	39	37	33	55
Major League totals (3 years)		11	13	.458	3.57	193	0	0	0	100	211 2/3	202	93	84	81	172

KOHLMEIER, RYAN   P   WHITE SOX

PERSONAL: Born June 25, 1977, in Salina, Kan. ... 6-2/195. ... Throws right, bats right. ... Full name: Ryan Lyle Kohlmeier.
HIGH SCHOOL: Chase County (Cottonwood Falls, Kan.).
JUNIOR COLLEGE: Butler County Community College (Kan.).
TRANSACTIONS/CAREER NOTES: Selected by Baltimore Orioles organization in 14th round of free-agent draft (June 14, 1996). ... Claimed on waivers by Chicago White Sox (November 19, 2001).

Year	League	W	L	Pct.	ERA	G	GS	CG	ShO	Sv.	IP	H	R	ER	BB	SO
1997—	Delmarva (S.Atl.)	2	2	.500	2.65	50	0	0	0	*24	74 2/3	48	22	22	17	99
—	Bowie (East.)	0	0	...	0.00	2	0	0	0	1	2 2/3	0	0	0	2	5
1998—	Bowie (East.)	4	4	.500	6.12	42	0	0	0	7	50	52	37	34	16	56
—	Frederick (Caro.)	1	2	.333	7.45	9	0	0	0	5	9 2/3	10	9	8	3	15
1999—	Bowie (East.)	3	7	.300	3.16	55	0	0	0	23	62 2/3	44	23	22	29	78
2000—	Rochester (I.L.)	1	4	.200	2.51	37	0	0	0	10	46 2/3	33	14	13	16	49
—	Baltimore (A.L.)	0	1	.000	2.39	25	0	0	0	13	26 1/3	30	9	7	15	17
2001—	Baltimore (A.L.)	1	2	.333	7.30	34	1	0	0	6	40 2/3	48	33	33	19	29
—	Rochester (I.L.)	1	4	.200	2.36	14	7	0	0	4	42	36	15	11	8	28
Major League totals (2 years)		1	3	.250	5.37	59	1	0	0	19	67	78	42	40	34	46

KOLB, BRANDON   P   REDS

PERSONAL: Born November 20, 1973, in Oakland. ... 6-1/190. ... Throws right, bats right. ... Full name: Brandon Charles Kolb.
HIGH SCHOOL: Danville (Calif.).
COLLEGE: Texas Tech.
TRANSACTIONS/CAREER NOTES: Selected by San Diego Padres organization in fourth round of free-agent draft (June 1, 1995). ... On Las Vegas disabled list (July 27-August 20, 1999). ... Traded by Padres to Milwaukee Brewers for SS Santiago Perez and a player to be named later or cash (December 1, 2000); Brewers traded OF Chad Green to Padres for P Wil Cunnane to complete deal (December 20, 2000). ... Granted free agency (October 15, 2001). ... Signed by Cincinnati Reds organization (December 21, 2001).

Year	League	W	L	Pct.	ERA	G	GS	CG	ShO	Sv.	IP	H	R	ER	BB	SO
1995—	Idaho Falls (Pio.)................	2	3	.400	7.04	9	8	0	0	0	38 1/3	42	33	30	29	21
—	Arizona Padres (Ariz.)	1	1	.500	1.17	4	4	1	•1	0	23	13	10	3	13	21
1996—	Clinton (Midw.)................	*16	9	.640	3.42	27	27	3	0	0	181 1/3	170	84	69	76	138
1997—	Rancho Cuca. (Calif.)	3	2	.600	3.00	10	10	0	0	0	63	60	29	21	22	49
1998—	Mobile (Sou.)	4	3	.571	4.50	21	6	0	0	1	62	46	33	31	40	58
—	Rancho Cuca. (Calif.)	0	2	.000	3.05	4	4	0	0	0	20 2/3	14	8	7	18	16
1999—	Mobile (Sou.)	0	2	.000	0.79	7	0	0	0	2	11 1/3	8	4	1	4	14
—	Las Vegas (PCL)	2	1	.667	3.94	42	0	0	0	4	61 2/3	72	36	27	29	63
2000—	Las Vegas (PCL)	3	3	.500	4.47	47	0	0	0	16	56 1/3	53	35	28	21	59
—	San Diego (N.L.)	0	1	.000	4.50	11	0	0	0	0	14	16	8	7	11	12
2001—	Milwaukee (N.L.)■................	0	0	...	13.03	10	0	0	0	0	9 2/3	16	16	14	8	8
—	Indianapolis (I.L.)................	3	5	.375	4.28	40	0	0	0	14	54 2/3	49	28	26	22	57
Major League totals (2 years)		0	1	.000	7.99	21	0	0	0	0	23 2/3	32	24	21	19	20

KOLB, DANNY — P — RANGERS

PERSONAL: Born March 29, 1975, in Sterling, Ill. ... 6-4/215. ... Throws right, bats right. ... Full name: Daniel Lee Kolb. ... Cousin of Gary Kolb, outfielder with four major league teams (1960-69).

HIGH SCHOOL: Walnut (Ill.).

JUNIOR COLLEGE: Sauk Valley Community College (Ill.).

COLLEGE: Illinois State.

TRANSACTIONS/CAREER NOTES: Selected by Minnesota Twins organization in 17th round of free-agent draft (June 3, 1993); did not sign. ... Selected by Texas Rangers organization in sixth round of free-agent draft (June 3, 1995). ... On Texas disabled list (October 3, 1999-remainder of season). ... On Texas disabled list (May 29, 2000-remainder of season). ... On Texas disabled list (March 23-July 11, 2001); included rehabilitation assignments to Charlotte (June 11-July 3) and Tulsa (July 4-10).

STATISTICAL NOTES: Pitched six-inning, 3-0 no-hit victory against Columbus (June 12, 1996). ... Tied for Appalachian League lead with 22 hit batsmen in 1996.

Year	League	W	L	Pct.	ERA	G	GS	CG	ShO	Sv.	IP	H	R	ER	BB	SO
1995—	Gulf Coast Rangers (GCL)..	1	7	.125	2.21	12	11	0	0	0	53	38	22	13	28	46
1996—	Charleston, S.C. (S.Atl.)	8	6	.571	2.57	20	20	4	2	0	126	80	50	36	60	127
—	Charlotte (FSL)................	2	2	.500	4.26	6	6	0	0	0	38	38	18	18	14	28
—	Tulsa (Texas)	1	0	1.000	0.77	2	2	0	0	0	11 2/3	5	1	1	8	7
1997—	Charlotte (FSL)................	4	10	.286	4.87	24	23	3	0	0	133	146	91	72	62	83
—	Tulsa (Texas)	0	2	.000	4.76	2	2	0	0	0	11 1/3	7	7	6	11	6
1998—	Tulsa (Texas)	12	11	.522	4.82	28	28	2	0	0	162 1/3	187	104	87	76	83
—	Oklahoma (PCL)	0	0	...	0.00	1	0	0	0	0	1	1	0	0	1	0
1999—	Tulsa (Texas)	1	2	.333	2.79	7	7	1	1	0	38 2/3	38	16	12	18	32
—	Oklahoma (PCL)	5	3	.625	5.10	11	8	0	0	0	60	74	35	34	27	21
—	Texas (A.L.)	2	1	.667	4.65	16	0	0	0	0	31	33	18	16	15	15
2000—	Oklahoma (PCL)	4	1	.800	0.98	13	0	0	0	4	18 1/3	11	6	2	8	18
—	Texas (A.L.)	0	0	...	67.50	1	0	0	0	0	2/3	5	5	5	2	0
2001—	Charlotte (FSL)................	1	2	.333	3.86	7	3	0	0	0	18 2/3	21	8	8	2	16
—	Tulsa (Texas)	1	0	1.000	0.00	1	0	0	0	0	2	0	0	0	1	0
—	Oklahoma (PCL)	0	1	.000	1.42	12	0	0	0	3	19	13	3	3	4	21
—	Texas (A.L.)	0	0	...	4.70	17	0	0	0	0	15 1/3	15	8	8	10	15
Major League totals (3 years)		2	1	.667	5.53	34	0	0	0	0	47	53	31	29	27	30

KOMIYAMA, SATORU — P — METS

PERSONAL: Born September 15, 1965, in Chiba, Japan. ... 6-2/195. ... Throws right, bats right.

TRANSACTIONS/CAREER NOTES: Played with Chiba Lotte Marines of Japan Pacific League (1990-99). ... Played with Yokohama BayStars of Japan Central League (2000 and 2001). ... Signed as non-drafted free agent by New York Mets organization (December 3, 2001).

Year	League	W	L	Pct.	ERA	G	GS	CG	ShO	Sv.	IP	H	R	ER	BB	SO
1990—	Chiba Lotte (Jap. Cen.)	6	10	.375	3.27	30	16	...	...	2	170 2/3	159	...	...	63	126
1991—	Chiba Lotte (Jap. Cen.)	10	16	.385	3.95	29	13	...	...	0	212	219	...	...	80	130
1992—	Chiba Lotte (Jap. Cen.)	8	15	.348	3.96	29	16	...	...	0	172 2/3	187	...	...	64	124
1993—	Chiba Lotte (Jap. Cen.)	12	14	.462	3.44	27	13	...	...	0	204 1/3	193	...	...	71	160
1994—	Chiba Lotte (Jap. Cen.)	3	9	.250	4.24	14	11	...	...	0	85	81	...	...	28	67
1995—	Chiba Lotte (Jap. Cen.)	11	4	.733	2.60	25	23	...	...	0	187	150	...	...	53	169
1996—	Chiba Lotte (Jap. Cen.)	8	13	.381	4.54	25	23	...	...	0	154 2/3	192	...	...	39	90
1997—	Chiba Lotte (Jap. Cen.)	11	9	.550	2.49	27	24	...	...	0	187 2/3	186	...	...	30	130
1998—	Chiba Lotte (Jap. Cen.)	11	12	.478	3.57	27	27	...	...	0	201 2/3	224	...	...	27	126
1999—	Chiba Lotte (Jap. Cen.)	7	10	.412	4.07	21	17	...	...	0	141 2/3	158	...	...	15	96
2000—	Yokohama (Jap. Cen.)■........	8	11	.421	3.96	26	19	...	...	0	161 2/3	166	...	...	37	108
2001—	Yokohama (Jap. Cen.)	12	9	.571	3.03	24	18	...	...	0	148 2/3	150	...	...	30	74

KONERKO, PAUL — 1B — WHITE SOX

PERSONAL: Born March 5, 1976, in Providence, R.I. ... 6-3/211. ... Bats right, throws right. ... Full name: Paul Henry Konerko.

HIGH SCHOOL: Chaparral (Scottsdale, Ariz.).

TRANSACTIONS/CAREER NOTES: Selected by Los Angeles Dodgers organization in first round (13th pick overall) of free-agent draft (June 2, 1994). ... Traded by Dodgers with P Dennis Reyes to Cincinnati Reds for P Jeff Shaw (July 4, 1998). ... Traded by Reds to Chicago White Sox for OF Mike Cameron (November 11, 1998).

HONORS: Named Pacific Coast League Most Valuable Player (1997).

STATISTICAL NOTES: Led Northwest League with seven sacrifice flies in 1994. ... Led Pacific Coast League with 300 total bases and .621 slugging percentage in 1997. ... Career major league grand slams: 3.

Year	Team (League)	Pos.	G	AB	R	H	2B	3B	HR	RBI	Avg.	BB	SO	SB	PO	A	E	Avg.
1994—Yakima (N'West)		C-DH	67	257	25	74	15	2	6	*58	.288	36	52	1	271	33	5	.984
1995—San Bern. (Calif.)		C-DH	118	448	7	124	21	1	19	77	.277	59	88	3	676	68	11	.985
1996—San Antonio (Texas)		1B-DH	133	470	78	141	23	2	29	86	.300	72	85	1	1114	92	14	.989
—Albuquerque (PCL)		1B	4	14	2	6	0	0	1	2	.429	1	2	0	30	0	0	1.000
1997—Albuquerque (PCL)		3-1-DH-2	130	483	97	156	31	1	*37	*127	.323	64	61	2	257	216	24	.952
—Los Angeles (N.L.)		1B-3B	6	7	0	1	0	0	0	0	.143	1	2	0	3	0	0	1.000
1998—Los Angeles (N.L.)		1B-3B-OF-DH	49	144	14	31	1	0	4	16	.215	10	30	0	187	30	2	.991
—Albuquerque (PCL)		OF-1B-3B	24	87	16	33	10	0	6	26	.379	11	12	0	61	3	3	.955
—Cincinnati (N.L.)■		3B-1B-OF	26	73	7	16	3	0	3	13	.219	6	10	0	48	24	0	1.000
—Indianapolis (I.L.)		3B	39	150	25	49	8	0	8	39	.327	19	18	1	21	68	4	.957
1999—Chicago (A.L.)■		1B-DH	142	513	71	151	31	4	24	81	.294	45	68	1	740	58	4	.995
2000—Chicago (A.L.)		1B-DH-3B	143	524	84	156	31	1	21	97	.298	47	72	1	1053	74	11	.990
2001—Chicago (A.L.)		1B-DH	156	582	92	164	35	0	32	99	.282	54	89	1	1276	90	8	.994
American League totals (3 years)			441	1619	247	471	97	5	77	277	.291	146	229	3	3069	222	23	.993
National League totals (2 years)			81	224	21	48	4	0	7	29	.214	17	42	0	238	54	2	.993
Major League totals (5 years)			522	1843	268	519	101	5	84	306	.282	163	271	3	3307	276	25	.993

DIVISION SERIES RECORD

Year	Team (League)	Pos.	G	AB	R	H	2B	3B	HR	RBI	Avg.	BB	SO	SB	PO	A	E	Avg.
2000—Chicago (A.L.)		1B-PH	3	9	1	0	0	0	0	0	.000	1	1	0	17	1	0	1.000

KOPLOVE, MIKE — P — DIAMONDBACKS

PERSONAL: Born August 30, 1976, in Philadelphia. ... 6-0/160. ... Throws right, bats right. ... Full name: Michael Paul Koplove.
HIGH SCHOOL: Chestnut Hill Academy (Philadelphia).
COLLEGE: Delaware.
TRANSACTIONS/CAREER NOTES: Selected by Arizona Diamondbacks organization in 29th round of free-agent draft (June 2, 1998). ... On El Paso disabled list (April 7-29, 2001).

Year	League	W	L	Pct.	ERA	G	GS	CG	ShO	Sv.	IP	H	R	ER	BB	SO
1998—Ariz. Diamondbacks (Ariz.)		0	0	...	9.00	2	0	0	0	0	4	4	4	4	2	5
—Lethbridge (Pio.)		1	2	.333	3.54	12	1	0	0	2	28	23	12	11	3	22
1999—South Bend (Midw.)		5	2	.714	2.04	45	45	0	0	7	84	70	23	19	29	98
2000—High Desert (Calif.)		2	0	1.000	1.42	20	0	0	0	8	25 1/3	14	4	4	10	31
—El Paso (Texas)		4	3	.571	4.46	35	0	0	0	6	40 1/3	38	28	20	19	47
2001—El Paso (Texas)		3	2	.600	2.66	34	0	0	0	6	44	44	18	13	19	43
—Tucson (PCL)		4	1	.800	2.82	17	0	0	0	9	22 1/3	17	7	7	10	22
—Arizona (N.L.)		0	1	.000	3.60	9	0	0	0	0	10	8	7	4	9	14
Major League totals (1 year)		0	1	.000	3.60	9	0	0	0	0	10	8	7	4	9	14

KOSKIE, COREY — 3B — TWINS

PERSONAL: Born June 28, 1973, in Anola, Man. ... 6-3/217. ... Bats left, throws right. ... Full name: Cordel Leonard Koskie.
HIGH SCHOOL: Springfield Collegiate (Oakbank, Man.).
JUNIOR COLLEGE: Des Moines (Iowa) Area Community College.
COLLEGE: Manitoba, then Kwantlen (B.C.).
TRANSACTIONS/CAREER NOTES: Selected by Minnesota Twins organization in 26th round of free-agent draft (June 2, 1994). ... On disabled list (May 10-28 and June 25-July 4, 1996).
STATISTICAL NOTES: Tied for Eastern League lead with 10 intentional bases on balls received in 1997. ... Career major league grand slams: 2.

Year	Team (League)	Pos.	G	AB	R	H	2B	3B	HR	RBI	Avg.	BB	SO	SB	PO	A	E	Avg.
1994—Elizabethton (Appl.)		3B	34	107	13	25	2	1	3	10	.234	18	27	0	23	84	8	.930
1995—Fort Wayne (Midw.)		3B	123	462	64	143	37	5	16	78	.310	38	79	2	80	244	36	.900
1996—Fort Myers (FSL)		3B	95	338	43	88	19	4	9	55	.260	40	76	1	62	176	19	.926
1997—New Britain (East.)		3B-DH	131	437	88	125	26	6	23	79	.286	90	106	9	72	234	22	.933
1998—Salt Lake (PCL)		3B-DH	135	505	91	152	32	5	26	105	.301	51	104	15	83	250	23	.935
—Minnesota (A.L.)		3B	11	29	2	4	0	0	1	2	.138	2	10	0	6	10	1	.941
1999—Minnesota (A.L.)		3B-OF-DH	117	342	42	106	21	0	11	58	.310	40	72	4	58	143	8	.962
2000—Minnesota (A.L.)		3B-DH	146	474	79	142	32	4	9	65	.300	77	104	5	96	241	12	.966
2001—Minnesota (A.L.)		3B-DH	153	562	100	155	37	2	26	103	.276	68	118	27	95	306	15	.964
Major League totals (4 years)			427	1407	223	407	90	6	47	228	.289	187	304	36	255	700	36	.964

KOTSAY, MARK — OF — PADRES

PERSONAL: Born December 2, 1975, in Whittier, Calif. ... 6-0/201. ... Bats left, throws left. ... Full name: Mark Steven Kotsay.
HIGH SCHOOL: Santa Fe Springs (Calif.).
COLLEGE: Cal State Fullerton.
TRANSACTIONS/CAREER NOTES: Selected by Florida Marlins organization in first round (ninth pick overall) of free-agent draft (June 4, 1996). ... Traded by Marlins with OF Cesar Crespo to San Diego Padres for OF Eric Owens, P Matt Clement and P Omar Ortiz (March 28, 2001). ... On disabled list (April 16-May 1, 2001).
HONORS: Named Golden Spikes Award winner by USA Baseball (1995). ... Named Most Outstanding Player of College World Series (1995).
STATISTICAL NOTES: Tied for Eastern League lead in double plays by outfielder with four in 1997. ... Tied for N.L. lead with 20 assists by outfielder in 1998. ... Led N.L. outfielders with 19 assists in 1999. ... Career major league grand slams: 2.
MISCELLANEOUS: Holds Florida Marlins all-time record for most triples (22). ... Member of 1996 U.S. Olympic baseball team.

Year	Team (League)	Pos.	G	AB	R	H	2B	3B	HR	RBI	Avg.	BB	SO	SB	PO	A	E	Avg.
1996—	Kane County (Midw.)..	OF	17	60	16	17	5	0	2	8	.283	16	8	3	37	2	0	1.000
1997—	Portland (East.)	OF-DH	114	438	*103	134	27	2	20	77	.306	75	65	17	230	12	2	*.992
	— Florida (N.L.)	OF	14	52	5	10	1	1	0	4	.192	4	7	3	31	2	0	1.000
1998—	Florida (N.L.)	OF-1B	154	578	72	161	25	7	11	68	.279	34	61	10	350	‡21	6	.984
1999—	Florida (N.L.)	OF-1B	148	495	57	134	23	9	8	50	.271	29	50	7	349	†27	5	.987
2000—	Florida (N.L.)	OF-1B	152	530	87	158	31	5	12	57	.298	42	46	19	289	14	3	.990
2001—	San Diego (N.L.)■..	OF	119	406	67	118	29	1	10	58	.291	48	58	13	277	4	4	.986
Major League totals (5 years)			587	2061	288	581	109	23	41	237	.282	157	222	52	1296	68	18	.987

KREUTER, CHAD — C — DODGERS

PERSONAL: Born August 26, 1964, in Greenbrae, Calif. ... 6-2/200. ... Bats both, throws right. ... Full name: Chad Michael Kreuter. ... Name pronounced CREW-ter.

HIGH SCHOOL: Redwood (Calif.).

COLLEGE: Pepperdine.

TRANSACTIONS/CAREER NOTES: Selected by Texas Rangers organization in fifth round of free-agent draft (June 3, 1985). ... Granted free agency (October 15, 1991). ... Signed by Detroit Tigers organization (January 2, 1992). ... Granted free agency (December 23, 1994). ... Signed by Seattle Mariners (April 8, 1995). ... On Seattle disabled list (June 19-July 6, 1995). ... On Tacoma disabled list (August 4-25, 1995). ... Granted free agency (October 16, 1995). ... Signed by Chicago White Sox organization (December 11, 1995). ... On disabled list (July 20, 1996-remainder of season). ... Granted free agency (October 14, 1996). ... Re-signed by White Sox organization (January 29, 1997). ... Traded by White Sox with OF Tony Phillips to Anaheim Angels for P Chuck McElroy and C Jorge Fabregas (May 18, 1997). ... Granted free agency (November 7, 1997). ... Signed by White Sox (December 10, 1997). ... Traded by White Sox to Angels for cash considerations (September 18, 1998). ... Granted free agency (October 26, 1998). ... Signed by Kansas City Royals (December 15, 1998). ... Granted free agency (October 29, 1999). ... Signed by Los Angeles Dodgers organization (January 20, 2000).

RECORDS: Shares major league single-game record for most sacrifice flies—3 (July 30, 1994). ... Shares major league record for most hits in one inning in first major league game—2 (September 14, 1988, fifth inning).

STATISTICAL NOTES: Led Carolina League catchers with 21 errors and 17 double plays and tied for lead with 113 assists in 1986. ... Tied for Texas League lead in double plays by catcher with nine in 1988. ... Led A.L. with 21 passed balls in 1989. ... Switch-hit home runs in one game (September 7, 1993). ... Career major league grand slams: 1.

MISCELLANEOUS: Batted righthanded only (1985 and 1990).

Year	Team (League)	Pos.	G	AB	R	H	2B	3B	HR	RBI	Avg.	BB	SO	SB	PO	A	E	Avg.
1985—	Burlington (Midw.)	C	69	199	25	53	9	0	4	26	.266	38	48	3	349	34	8	.980
1986—	Salem (Caro.)	C-OF-3B	125	387	55	85	21	2	6	49	.220	67	82	5	613	†115	†21	.972
1987—	Charlotte (FSL)	C-OF-3B	85	281	36	61	18	1	9	40	.217	31	32	1	380	54	8	.982
1988—	Tulsa (Texas)	C	108	358	46	95	24	6	3	51	.265	55	66	2	603	71	•13	.981
	— Texas (A.L.)	C	16	51	3	14	2	1	1	5	.275	7	13	0	93	8	1	.990
1989—	Texas (A.L.)	C	87	158	16	24	3	0	5	9	.152	27	40	0	453	26	4	.992
	— Oklahoma City (A.A.)..	C	26	87	10	22	3	0	0	6	.253	13	11	1	146	14	2	.988
1990—	Texas (A.L.)	C	22	22	2	1	1	0	0	2	.045	8	9	0	39	4	1	.977
	— Oklahoma City (A.A.)..	C	92	291	41	65	17	1	7	35	.223	52	80	0	559	64	10	.984
1991—	Texas (A.L.)	C	3	4	0	0	0	0	0	0	.000	0	1	0	5	0	0	1.000
	— Oklahoma City (A.A.)..	C	24	70	14	19	6	0	1	12	.271	18	16	2	146	23	7	.960
	— Tulsa (Texas)	C	42	128	23	30	5	1	2	10	.234	29	23	1	269	27	4	.987
1992—	Detroit (A.L.)■	C-DH	67	190	22	48	9	0	2	16	.253	20	38	0	271	22	5	.983
1993—	Detroit (A.L.)	C-DH-1B	119	374	59	107	23	3	15	51	.286	49	92	2	522	70	7	.988
1994—	Detroit (A.L.)	C-1B-OF	65	170	17	38	8	0	1	19	.224	28	36	0	280	22	4	.987
1995—	Seattle (A.L.)■	C	26	75	12	17	5	0	1	8	.227	5	22	0	151	12	4	.976
	— Tacoma (PCL)	C-DH	15	48	6	14	5	0	1	11	.292	8	11	0	70	10	1	.988
1996—	Chicago (A.L.)■	C-1B-DH	46	114	14	25	8	0	3	18	.219	13	29	0	182	12	2	.990
1997—	Chicago (A.L.)	C-1B	19	37	6	8	2	1	1	3	.216	8	9	0	59	4	2	.969
	— Anaheim (A.L.)■	C-DH	70	218	19	51	7	1	4	18	.234	21	57	0	431	29	3	.994
1998—	Chicago (A.L.)■	C	93	245	26	62	9	1	2	33	.253	32	45	1	424	35	7	.985
	— Anaheim (A.L.)■	C	3	7	1	1	1	0	0	0	.143	1	4	0	14	1	§2	.882
1999—	Kansas City (A.L.)■ ...	C-DH	107	324	31	73	15	0	5	35	.225	34	65	0	460	44	3	.994
2000—	Los Angeles (N.L.)■ ...	C	80	212	32	56	13	0	6	28	.264	54	48	1	483	35	3	.994
2001—	Los Angeles (N.L.)	C-DH	73	191	21	41	11	1	6	17	.215	41	52	0	486	29	0	1.000
American League totals (12 years)			743	1989	228	469	93	7	40	217	.236	253	460	3	3384	289	45	.988
National League totals (2 years)			153	403	53	97	24	1	12	45	.241	95	100	1	969	64	3	.997
Major League totals (14 years)			896	2392	281	566	117	8	52	262	.237	348	560	4	4353	353	48	.990

LACKEY, JOHN — P — ANGELS

PERSONAL: Born October 23, 1978, in Abilene, Texas. ... 6-6/205. ... Throws right, bats right. ... Full name: John Derran Lackey.

HIGH SCHOOL: Abilene (Texas).

JUNIOR COLLEGE: Grayson County (Texas).

TRANSACTIONS/CAREER NOTES: Selected by Anaheim Angels organization in second round of free-agent draft (June 2, 1999).

Year	League	W	L	Pct.	ERA	G	GS	CG	ShO	Sv.	IP	H	R	ER	BB	SO
1999—	Boise (N'West)	6	2	.750	4.98	15	15	1	0	0	81⅓	81	59	45	50	77
2000—	Cedar Rapids (Midw.)	3	2	.600	2.08	5	5	0	0	0	30⅓	20	7	7	5	21
	— Lake Elsinore (Calif.)	6	6	.500	3.40	15	15	2	•1	0	100⅔	94	56	38	42	74
	— Erie (East.)	6	1	.857	3.30	8	8	2	0	0	57⅓	58	23	21	9	43
2001—	Salt Lake (PCL)	3	4	.429	6.71	10	10	1	0	0	57⅔	75	44	43	16	42
	— Arkansas (Texas)...............	9	7	.563	3.46	18	18	3	2	0	127⅓	106	55	49	29	94

LAKER, TIM   C   INDIANS

PERSONAL: Born November 27, 1969, in Encino, Calif. ... 6-3/225. ... Bats right, throws right. ... Full name: Timothy John Laker.
HIGH SCHOOL: Simi Valley (Calif.).
JUNIOR COLLEGE: Oxnard (Calif.) College.
TRANSACTIONS/CAREER NOTES: Selected by Kansas City Royals organization in 49th round of free-agent draft (June 2, 1987); did not sign. ... Selected by Montreal Expos organization in sixth round of free-agent draft (June 1, 1988). ... On Ottawa disabled list (April 30-May 14, 1993). ... On disabled list (March 29, 1996-entire season). ... Claimed on waivers by Baltimore Orioles (March 25, 1997). ... On Rochester disabled list (June 5-16, 1997). ... Granted free agency (October 15, 1997). ... Signed by Tampa Bay Devil Rays (December 19, 1997). ... Released by Devil Rays (June 26, 1998). ... Signed by Pittsburgh Pirates organization (July 9, 1998). ... Released by Pirates (December 18, 1998). ... Signed by Los Angeles Dodgers organization (January 11, 1999). ... Traded by Dodgers to Pirates for a player to be named later (March 26, 1999). ... On Nashville suspended list (August 23-26, 1999). ... Granted free agency (October 14, 1999). ... Re-signed by Pirates organization (December 20, 1999). ... Granted free agency (October 18, 2000). ... Signed by Cleveland Indians organization (December 20, 2000).
STATISTICAL NOTES: Led New York-Pennsylvania League with 16 passed balls in 1989. ... Led Midwest League catchers with 125 assists, 18 errors and 944 total chances in 1990. ... Tied for International League lead in errors by catcher with 11 in 1993. ... Led International League with 20 passed balls in 1994. ... Tied for Pacific Coast League lead with 12 errors by catcher in 1999. ... Tied for Pacific Coast League lead with 11 errors by catchers in 2000.

							BATTING							FIELDING			
Year Team (League)	Pos.	G	AB	R	H	2B	3B	HR	RBI	Avg.	BB	SO	SB	PO	A	E	Avg.
1988—Jamestown (NY-P)	C-OF	47	152	14	34	9	0	0	17	.224	8	30	2	236	22	2	.992
1989—Rockford (Midw.)	C	14	48	4	11	1	1	0	4	.229	3	6	1	91	6	4	.960
—Jamestown (NY-P)	C	58	216	25	48	9	1	2	24	.222	16	40	8	437	61	8	.984
1990—Rockford (Midw.)	C-OF	120	425	46	94	18	3	7	57	.221	32	83	7	802	†125	†18	.981
—W.P. Beach (FSL)	C	2	3	0	0	0	0	0	0	.000	0	1	0	2	0	0	1.000
1991—Harrisburg (East.)	C	11	35	4	10	1	0	1	5	.286	2	5	0	67	4	3	.959
—W.P. Beach (FSL)	C	100	333	35	77	15	2	5	33	.231	22	51	10	560	87	*14	.979
1992—Harrisburg (East.)	C	117	409	55	99	19	3	15	68	.242	39	89	3	630	62	*14	.980
—Montreal (N.L.)	C	28	46	8	10	3	0	0	4	.217	2	14	1	102	8	1	.991
1993—Montreal (N.L.)	C	43	86	3	17	2	1	0	7	.198	2	16	2	136	18	2	.987
—Ottawa (I.L.)	C-1B	56	204	26	47	10	0	4	23	.230	21	41	3	341	37	‡11	.972
1994—Ottawa (I.L.)	C-DH	118	424	68	131	32	2	12	71	.309	47	96	11	643	*89	•11	.985
1995—Montreal (N.L.)	C	64	141	17	33	8	1	3	20	.234	14	38	0	265	22	7	.977
1996—Montreal (N.L.)						Did not play.											
1997—Rochester (I.L.)■	DH-C	79	290	45	75	11	1	11	37	.259	34	49	1	283	17	6	.980
—Baltimore (A.L.)	C	7	14	0	0	0	0	0	1	.000	2	9	0	28	0	1	.966
1998—Durham (I.L.)■	C-DH	40	134	36	32	7	0	11	26	.239	28	32	1	197	19	2	.991
—Tampa Bay (A.L.)	C-DH	3	5	1	1	0	0	0	0	.200	1	1	0	5	0	0	1.000
—Nashville (PCL)■	C-1B-DH	44	152	30	54	16	1	11	34	.355	21	26	1	277	26	4	.987
—Pittsburgh (N.L.)	1B-C	14	24	2	9	1	0	1	2	.375	1	3	0	35	1	0	1.000
1999—Nashville (PCL)	C-1B-DH-3B	112	405	48	109	29	3	12	65	.269	29	68	3	726	69	‡15	.981
—Pittsburgh (N.L.)	C	6	9	0	3	0	0	0	0	.333	0	2	0	9	0	0	1.000
2000—Nashville (PCL)	C-1B-3B	121	421	70	104	28	4	19	75	.247	54	73	5	660	75	†12	.984
2001—Buffalo (I.L.)■	C-1B	86	320	45	79	13	0	20	57	.247	28	53	2	581	42	6	.990
—Cleveland (A.L.)	C-P	16	33	5	6	0	0	1	5	.182	6	8	0	76	6	1	.988
American League totals (3 years)		26	52	6	7	0	0	1	6	.135	9	18	0	109	6	2	.983
National League totals (5 years)		155	306	30	72	14	2	4	33	.235	19	73	3	547	54	10	.984
Major League totals (7 years)		181	358	36	79	14	2	5	39	.221	28	91	3	656	60	12	.984

RECORD AS PITCHER

Year League	W	L	Pct.	ERA	G	GS	CG	ShO	Sv.	IP	H	R	ER	BB	SO
2001—Cleveland (A.L.)	0	0	.000	0.00	1	0	0	0	0	1	1	0	0	1	1

LAMB, MIKE   3B   RANGERS

PERSONAL: Born August 9, 1975, in West Covina, Calif. ... 6-1/195. ... Bats left, throws right. ... Full name: Michael Robert Lamb.
HIGH SCHOOL: Bishop Amat (La Puente, Calif.).
COLLEGE: Cal State Fullerton.
TRANSACTIONS/CAREER NOTES: Selected by Texas Rangers organization in seventh round of free-agent draft (June 3, 1997).
STATISTICAL NOTES: Led Florida State League third basemen with 98 putouts, 304 assists, 432 total chances, 19 double plays and .931 fielding percentage in 1998.

							BATTING							FIELDING			
Year Team (League)	Pos.	G	AB	R	H	2B	3B	HR	RBI	Avg.	BB	SO	SB	PO	A	E	Avg.
1997—Pulaski (Appl.)	3B	60	233	59	78	19	3	9	47	.335	31	18	7	38	118	25	.862
1998—Charlotte (FSL)	3B-1B	135	536	83	162	35	3	9	93	.302	45	63	18	†124	†305	31	†.933
1999—Tulsa (Texas)	3B-C	137	*544	98	*176	*51	5	21	100	.324	53	65	4	90	284	28	.930
—Oklahoma (PCL)	3B	2	2	0	1	0	0	0	0	.500	1	0	0	0	0	0	...
2000—Oklahoma (PCL)	3B	14	55	8	14	5	1	2	5	.255	5	6	2	12	17	7	.806
—Texas (A.L.)	3B-DH	138	493	65	137	25	2	6	47	.278	34	60	0	118	230	•33	.913
2001—Oklahoma (PCL)	3B	69	273	35	81	19	3	8	40	.297	13	31	0	39	109	15	.908
—Texas (A.L.)	3B	76	284	42	87	18	0	4	35	.306	14	27	2	52	139	18	.914
Major League totals (2 years)		214	777	107	224	43	2	10	82	.288	48	87	2	170	369	51	.914

LAMPKIN, TOM   C   PADRES

PERSONAL: Born March 4, 1964, in Cincinnati. ... 5-11/195. ... Bats left, throws right. ... Full name: Thomas Michael Lampkin.
HIGH SCHOOL: Blanchet (Seattle).
JUNIOR COLLEGE: Edmonds College (Wash.).
COLLEGE: Portland.
TRANSACTIONS/CAREER NOTES: Selected by Cleveland Indians organization in 11th round of free-agent draft (June 2, 1986). ... On disabled list (July 6, 1989-remainder of season). ... Traded by Indians to San Diego Padres for OF Alex Cole (July 11, 1990). ...

Traded by Padres to Milwaukee Brewers for cash (March 25, 1993). ... Granted free agency (December 20, 1993). ... Signed by San Francisco Giants organization (January 5, 1994). ... On San Francisco disabled list (March 31-April 24 and August 26, 1996-remainder of season); included rehabilitation assignment to San Jose (April 22-24). ... Traded by Giants to St. Louis Cardinals for a player to be named later or cash (December 19, 1996); Giants acquired P Rene Arocha to complete deal (February 12, 1997). ... Granted free agency (October 23, 1998). ... Signed by Seattle Mariners (December 14, 1998). ... On Seattle disabled list (March 25-April 13 and June 28, 2000-remainder of season); included rehabilitation assignment to Tacoma (April 8-13). ... Granted free agency (October 27, 2000). ... Re-signed by Mariners (December 22, 2000). ... Traded by Mariners with P Brett Tomko and SS Ramon Vazquez to San Diego Padres for C Ben Davis, P Wascar Serrano and SS Alex Arias (December 11, 2001).

STATISTICAL NOTES: Led Pacific Coast League catchers with 11 double plays in 1992. ... Led Pacific Coast League catchers with 595 putouts in 1994. ... Career major league grand slams: 1.

Year	Team (League)	Pos.	G	AB	R	H	2B	3B	HR	RBI	Avg.	BB	SO	SB	PO	A	E	Avg.
								BATTING								FIELDING		
1986—Batavia (NY-Penn)	C	63	190	24	49	5	1	1	20	.258	31	14	4	323	36	8	.978
1987—Waterloo (Midw.)	C	118	398	49	106	19	2	7	55	.266	34	41	5	689	*100	15	.981
1988—Williamsport (East.)	C	80	263	38	71	10	0	3	23	.270	25	20	1	431	60	9	.982
—Colo. Springs (PCL)	C	34	107	14	30	5	0	0	7	.280	9	2	0	171	28	5	.975
—Cleveland (A.L.)	C	4	4	0	0	0	0	0	0	.000	1	0	0	3	0	0	1.000
1989—Colo. Springs (PCL)	C	63	209	26	67	10	3	4	32	.321	10	18	4	305	21	8	.976
1990—Colo. Springs (PCL)	C-2B	69	199	32	44	7	5	1	18	.221	19	19	7	312	36	12	.967
—San Diego (N.L.)■	C	26	63	4	14	0	1	1	4	.222	4	9	0	91	10	3	.971
—Las Vegas (PCL)	C	1	2	0	1	0	0	0	0	.500	0	1	0	3	0	0	1.000
1991—San Diego (N.L.)	C	38	58	4	11	3	1	0	3	.190	3	9	0	49	5	0	1.000
—Las Vegas (PCL)	C-1B-OF	45	164	25	52	11	1	2	29	.317	10	19	2	211	26	6	.975
1992—Las Vegas (PCL)	C	108	340	45	104	17	4	3	48	.306	53	27	15	506	*64	12	.979
—San Diego (N.L.)	C-OF	9	17	3	4	0	0	0	0	.235	6	1	2	30	3	0	1.000
1993—New Orleans (A.A.)■	C-OF	25	80	18	26	5	0	2	10	.325	18	4	5	152	12	3	.982
—Milwaukee (A.L.)	C-OF-DH	73	162	22	32	8	0	4	25	.198	20	26	7	242	24	6	.978
1994—Phoenix (PCL)■	C-DH-OF	118	453	76	136	32	8	8	70	.300	42	49	8	†595	59	10	.985
1995—San Francisco (N.L.)	C-OF	65	76	8	21	2	0	1	9	.276	9	8	2	62	5	0	1.000
1996—San Jose (Calif.)	C	2	7	2	2	0	1	0	2	.286	1	2	0	10	1	0	1.000
—San Francisco (N.L.)	C	66	177	26	41	8	0	6	29	.232	20	22	1	342	27	3	.992
1997—St. Louis (N.L.)■	C	108	229	28	56	8	1	7	22	.245	28	30	2	413	37	5	.989
1998—St. Louis (N.L.)	C-OF-1B	93	216	25	50	12	1	6	28	.231	24	32	3	337	19	5	.986
1999—Seattle (A.L.)■	C-DH-OF	76	206	29	60	11	2	9	34	.291	13	32	1	292	27	5	.985
2000—Tacoma (PCL)	C	3	8	1	2	1	0	0	0	.250	3	2	0	12	2	0	1.000
—Seattle (A.L.)	C-DH	36	103	15	26	6	1	7	23	.252	9	17	0	138	13	2	.987
2001—Seattle (A.L.)	C-OF-DH	79	204	28	46	10	0	5	22	.225	18	41	1	375	23	2	.995
American League totals (5 years)		268	679	94	164	35	3	25	104	.242	61	116	9	1050	87	15	.987
National League totals (7 years)		405	836	98	197	33	4	21	95	.236	94	111	10	1324	106	16	.989
Major League totals (12 years)		673	1515	192	361	68	7	46	199	.238	155	227	19	2374	193	31	.988

DIVISION SERIES RECORD

Year	Team (League)	Pos.	G	AB	R	H	2B	3B	HR	RBI	Avg.	BB	SO	SB	PO	A	E	Avg.
								BATTING								FIELDING		
2001—Seattle (A.L.)	PH-C	2	2	0	0	0	0	0	0	.000	0	2	0	2	0	0	1.000

CHAMPIONSHIP SERIES RECORD

Year	Team (League)	Pos.	G	AB	R	H	2B	3B	HR	RBI	Avg.	BB	SO	SB	PO	A	E	Avg.
								BATTING								FIELDING		
2001—Seattle (A.L.)	C	2	4	0	1	0	0	0	0	.250	1	2	0	10	2	0	1.000

LANE, JASON   OF   ASTROS

PERSONAL: Born December 22, 1976, in Santa Rosa, Calif. ... 6-2/215. ... Bats right, throws left. ... Full name: Jason Dean Lane.
HIGH SCHOOL: Santa Rosa (Calif.).
JUNIOR COLLEGE: El Molino (Forestville, Calif.).
COLLEGE: Southern California.
TRANSACTIONS/CAREER NOTES: Selected by Houston Astros organization in sixth round of free-agent draft (June 2, 1999).
HONORS: Named Texas League Most Valuable Player (2001).
STATISTICAL NOTES: Led Midwest League with 13 sacrifice flies in 2000. ... Led Texas League with 320 total bases in 2001. ... Tied for Texas League lead with 11 intentional bases on balls received in 2001.

Year	Team (League)	Pos.	G	AB	R	H	2B	3B	HR	RBI	Avg.	BB	SO	SB	PO	A	E	Avg.
								BATTING								FIELDING		
1999—Auburn (NY-Penn)	1B-P	74	283	46	79	18	5	13	*59	.279	38	46	6	577	41	9	.986
2000—Michigan (Midw.)	OF-1B	133	511	98	153	38	0	23	•104	.299	62	91	20	338	18	5	.986
2001—Round Rock (Texas)	OF	137	526	*103	166	36	2	38	*124	.316	61	98	14	226	8	2	.992

RECORD AS PITCHER

Year	League	W	L	Pct.	ERA	G	GS	CG	ShO	Sv.	IP	H	R	ER	BB	SO
1999—Auburn (NY-Penn)		0	0	...	0.00	1	0	0	0	0	1	0	0	0	0	1

LANGERHANS, RYAN   OF   BRAVES

PERSONAL: Born February 20, 1980, in San Antonio, Texas. ... 6-3/195. ... Bats left, throws left. ... Full name: Ryan D. Langerhans.
HIGH SCHOOL: Round Rock (Texas).
TRANSACTIONS/CAREER NOTES: Selected by Atlanta Braves organization in third round of free-agent draft (June 2, 1998).

Year	Team (League)	Pos.	G	AB	R	H	2B	3B	HR	RBI	Avg.	BB	SO	SB	PO	A	E	Avg.
								BATTING								FIELDING		
1998—GC Braves (GCL)	OF	43	148	15	41	10	4	2	19	.277	19	38	2	74	3	2	.975
1999—Macon (S.Atl.)	OF	121	448	66	120	30	1	9	49	.268	52	99	19	193	17	5	.977
2000—Myrtle Beach (Caro.)	OF	116	392	55	83	14	7	6	37	.212	32	104	25	142	4	6	.961
2001—Myrtle Beach (Caro.)	OF	125	450	66	186	30	3	7	48	.413	55	104	22	230	12	7	.972

PERSONAL: Born June 5, 1967, in Los Angeles, Calif. ... 5-11/200. ... Bats left, throws left. ... Full name: Raymond Lewis Lankford. ... Nephew of Carl Nichols, catcher with Baltimore Orioles (1986-88) and Houston Astros (1989-91).
HIGH SCHOOL: Grace Davis (Modesto, Calif.).
JUNIOR COLLEGE: Modesto (Calif.) Junior College.
TRANSACTIONS/CAREER NOTES: Selected by Chicago Cubs organization in third round of free-agent draft (January 14, 1986); did not sign. ... Selected by St. Louis Cardinals organization in third round of free-agent draft (June 2, 1987). ... On disabled list (June 24-July 9, 1993). ... On St. Louis disabled list (March 27-April 22, 1997); included rehabilitation assignment to Prince William (April 14-22). ... On disabled list (March 26-April 24, 1999). ... Traded by Cardinals with cash to San Diego Padres for P Woody Williams (August 2, 2001).
RECORDS: Shares major league single-season record for fewest double plays by outfielder (150 or more games)—0 (1992).
HONORS: Named Texas League Most Valuable Player (1989).
STATISTICAL NOTES: Led Appalachian League outfielders with 155 total chances in 1987. ... Led Appalachian League in caught stealing with 11 in 1987. ... Led Midwest League with 242 total bases in 1988. ... Led Texas League outfielders with 387 total chances in 1989. ... Led American Association outfielders with 352 total chances in 1990. ... Tied for American Association lead with nine intentional bases on balls received in 1990. ... Hit for the cycle (September 15, 1991). ... Led N.L. in caught stealing with 24 in 1992. ... Career major league grand slams: 6.

							BATTING							FIELDING		
Year Team (League)	Pos.	G	AB	R	H	2B	3B	HR	RBI	Avg.	BB	SO	SB	PO	A	E	Avg.
1987— Johnson City (Appl.) ..	OF	66	253	45	78	17	4	3	32	.308	19	43	14	*143	7	5	.968
1988— Springfield (Midw.)	OF	135	532	90	151	26	*16	11	66	.284	60	92	33	284	5	7	.976
1989— Arkansas (Texas)........	OF	*134	498	98	*158	28	*12	11	98	.317	65	57	38	*367	9	11	.972
1990— Louisville (A.A.)..........	OF	132	473	61	123	25	8	10	72	.260	72	81	30	*333	8	•11	.969
— St. Louis (N.L.)............	OF	39	126	12	36	10	1	3	12	.286	13	27	8	92	1	1	.989
1991— St. Louis (N.L.)..........	OF	151	566	83	142	23	*15	9	69	.251	41	114	44	367	7	6	.984
1992— St. Louis (N.L.)..........	OF	153	598	87	175	40	6	20	86	.293	72	*147	42	*438	5	2	.996
1993— St. Louis (N.L.)..........	OF	127	407	64	97	17	3	7	45	.238	81	111	14	312	6	7	.978
1994— St. Louis (N.L.)..........	OF	109	416	89	111	25	5	19	57	.267	58	113	11	260	5	6	.978
1995— St. Louis (N.L.)..........	OF	132	483	81	134	35	2	25	82	.277	63	110	24	300	7	3	.990
1996— St. Louis (N.L.)..........	OF	149	545	100	150	36	8	21	86	.275	79	133	35	356	9	1	*.997
1997— Prince William (Caro.)	DH-OF	4	13	3	4	1	0	0	4	.308	4	5	1	6	0	0	1.000
— St. Louis (N.L.)............	OF	133	465	94	137	36	3	31	98	.295	95	125	21	293	4	9	.971
1998— St. Louis (N.L.)..........	OF-DH	154	533	94	156	37	1	31	105	.293	86	151	26	338	7	5	.986
1999— St. Louis (N.L.)..........	OF-DH	122	422	77	129	32	1	15	63	.306	49	110	14	214	6	3	.987
2000— St. Louis (N.L.)..........	OF-DH	128	392	73	99	16	3	26	65	.253	70	148	5	179	4	5	.973
2001— St. Louis (N.L.)..........	OF	91	264	38	62	18	3	15	39	.235	44	105	4	135	5	5	.966
— San Diego (N.L.)■	OF	40	125	20	36	10	1	4	19	.288	18	40	6	63	1	1	.985
Major League totals (12 years)		1528	5342	912	1464	335	52	226	826	.274	769	1434	254	3347	67	54	.984

DIVISION SERIES RECORD

							BATTING							FIELDING		
Year Team (League)	Pos.	G	AB	R	H	2B	3B	HR	RBI	Avg.	BB	SO	SB	PO	A	E	Avg.
1996— St. Louis (N.L.)..........	OF-PH	1	2	1	1	0	0	0	0	.500	1	0	0	4	0	0	1.000
2000— St. Louis (N.L.)..........	OF	3	10	2	2	1	0	0	3	.200	2	5	0	8	0	0	1.000
Division series totals (2 years)		4	12	3	3	1	0	0	3	.250	3	5	0	12	0	0	1.000

CHAMPIONSHIP SERIES RECORD

							BATTING							FIELDING		
Year Team (League)	Pos.	G	AB	R	H	2B	3B	HR	RBI	Avg.	BB	SO	SB	PO	A	E	Avg.
1996— St. Louis (N.L.)..........	OF-PH	5	13	1	0	0	0	0	1	.000	1	4	0	7	0	0	1.000
2000— St. Louis (N.L.)..........	PH-OF	5	12	1	4	1	0	0	1	.333	1	5	0	10	1	0	1.000
Championship series totals (2 years)		10	25	2	4	1	0	0	2	.160	2	9	0	17	1	0	1.000

ALL-STAR GAME RECORD

					BATTING						FIELDING		
Year League	Pos.	AB	R	H	2B	3B	HR	RBI	Avg.	BB	SO	SB	PO	A	E	Avg.
1997— National	OF	2	0	0	0	0	0	0	.000	1	1	0	0	0	0	...

PERSONAL: Born April 3, 1968, in Rawlins, Wyo. ... 6-0/195. ... Bats right, throws right. ... Full name: Michael Thomas Lansing.
HIGH SCHOOL: Natrona County (Casper, Wyo.).
COLLEGE: Wichita State.
TRANSACTIONS/CAREER NOTES: Selected by Baltimore Orioles organization in ninth round of free-agent draft (June 5, 1989); did not sign. ... Selected by Miami Miracle, independent, in sixth round of free-agent draft (June 4, 1990). ... On disabled list (April 29-May 9, 1991). ... Contract sold by Miami to Montreal Expos organization (September 18, 1991). ... On disabled list (May 31-June 15, 1995). ... Traded by Expos to Colorado Rockies for P Jake Westbrook, P John Nicholson and OF Mark Hamlin (November 18, 1997). ... On disabled list (May 21, 1999-remainder of season). ... Traded by Rockies with P Rolando Arrojo, P Rick Croushore and cash to Boston Red Sox for P Brian Rose, P John Wasdin, P Jeff Taglienti and 2B Jeff Frye (July 27, 2000). ... On disabled list (September 10, 2001-remainder of season). ... Granted free agency (November 13, 2001).
RECORDS: Shares major league single-inning record for most home runs—2 (May 7, 1997, sixth inning).
STATISTICAL NOTES: Led Eastern League shortstops with 76 double plays in 1992. ... Hit three home runs in one game (September 22, 1998). ... Hit for the cycle (June 18, 2000). ... Career major league grand slams: 2.

							BATTING							FIELDING		
Year Team (League)	Pos.	G	AB	R	H	2B	3B	HR	RBI	Avg.	BB	SO	SB	PO	A	E	Avg.
1990— Miami (FSL)	SS	61	207	20	50	5	2	2	11	.242	29	35	15	104	166	10	.964
1991— Miami (FSL)	SS-2B	104	384	54	110	20	7	6	55	.286	40	75	29	148	273	27	.940
1992— Harrisburg (East.)■ ...	SS	128	483	66	135	20	6	6	54	.280	52	64	46	189	*373	20	*.966
1993— Montreal (N.L.)..........	3B-SS-2B	141	491	64	141	29	1	3	45	.287	46	56	23	136	336	24	.952

Year	Team (League)	Pos.	G	AB	R	H	2B	3B	HR	RBI	Avg.	BB	SO	SB	PO	A	E	Avg.
1994—	Montreal (N.L.)..........	2B-3B-SS	106	394	44	105	21	2	5	35	.266	30	37	12	164	283	10	.978
1995—	Montreal (N.L.)..........	2B-SS	127	467	47	119	30	2	10	62	.255	28	65	27	306	373	6	.991
1996—	Montreal (N.L.)..........	2B-SS	159	641	99	183	40	2	11	53	.285	44	85	23	349	395	11	.985
1997—	Montreal (N.L.)..........	2B	144	572	86	161	45	2	20	70	.281	45	92	11	279	395	9	.987
1998—	Colorado (N.L.)■.......	2B-3B	153	584	73	161	39	2	12	66	.276	39	88	10	345	425	10	.987
1999—	Colorado (N.L.)..........	2B	35	145	24	45	9	0	4	15	.310	7	22	2	91	98	2	.990
2000—	Colorado (N.L.)..........	2B	90	365	62	94	14	6	11	47	.258	31	49	8	175	221	7	.983
—	Boston (A.L.)■...........	2B-3B	49	139	10	27	4	0	0	13	.194	7	26	0	73	106	0	1.000
2001—	Boston (A.L.)..............	SS-2B	106	352	45	88	23	0	8	34	.250	22	50	3	161	247	14	.967
American League totals (2 years)			155	491	55	115	27	0	8	47	.234	29	76	3	234	353	14	.977
National League totals (8 years)			955	3659	499	1009	227	17	76	393	.276	270	494	116	1845	2526	79	.982
Major League totals (9 years)			1110	4150	554	1124	254	17	84	440	.271	299	570	119	2079	2879	93	.982

LARKIN, BARRY   SS   REDS

PERSONAL: Born April 28, 1964, in Cincinnati. ... 6-0/185. ... Bats right, throws right. ... Full name: Barry Louis Larkin. ... Brother of Steve Larkin, outfielder/first baseman, Cincinnati Reds organization; and cousin of Nathan Davis, defensive tackle with Atlanta Falcons (1997) and Dallas Cowboys (1998-99).

HIGH SCHOOL: Moeller (Cincinnati).

COLLEGE: Michigan.

TRANSACTIONS/CAREER NOTES: Selected by Cincinnati Reds organization in second round of free-agent draft (June 7, 1982); did not sign. ... Selected by Reds organization in first round (fourth pick overall) of free-agent draft (June 3, 1985). ... On disabled list (April 13-May 2, 1987). ... On Cincinnati disabled list (July 11-September 1, 1989); included rehabilitation assignment to Nashville (August 27-September 1). ... On disabled list (May 18-June 4, 1991; April 19-May 8, 1992; and August 5, 1993-remainder of season). ... On disabled list (June 17-August 2 and September 1, 1997-remainder of season; March 12-April 7, 1998; April 22-May16, 2000; May 17-June 15 and June 29, 2001-remainder of season).

RECORDS: Holds major league single-season record for fewest putouts by shortstop for leader—230 (1996). ... Shares major league record for most home runs in two consecutive games—5 (June 27 [2] and 28 [3], 1991).

HONORS: Named shortstop on THE SPORTING NEWS college All-America team (1985). ... Named American Association Most Valuable Player (1986). ... Named shortstop on THE SPORTING NEWS N.L. All-Star team (1988-92, 1994-96, 1998 and 1999). ... Named shortstop on THE SPORTING NEWS N.L. Silver Slugger team (1988-92, 1995-96, 1998 and 1999). ... Won N.L. Gold Glove at shortstop (1994-96). ... Named N.L. Most Valuable Player by Baseball Writers' Association of America (1995).

STATISTICAL NOTES: Led American Association with .525 slugging percentage in 1986. ... Had 21-game hitting streak (September 10-October 2, 1988). ... Tied for N.L. lead in double plays by shortstop with 86 in 1990. ... Hit three home runs in one game (June 28, 1991). ... Had 16-game hitting streak (June 20-July 6, 1999). ... Career major league grand slams: 1.

MISCELLANEOUS: Member of 1984 U.S. Olympic baseball team.

Year	Team (League)	Pos.	G	AB	R	H	2B	3B	HR	RBI	Avg.	BB	SO	SB	PO	A	E	Avg.
1985—	Vermont (East.).........	SS	72	255	42	68	13	2	1	31	.267	23	21	12	110	166	17	.942
1986—	Denver (A.A.).............	SS-2B	103	413	67	136	31	10	10	51	.329	31	43	19	172	287	18	.962
—	Cincinnati (N.L.).......	SS-2B	41	159	27	45	4	3	3	19	.283	9	21	8	51	125	4	.978
1987—	Cincinnati (N.L.).......	SS	125	439	64	107	16	2	12	43	.244	36	52	21	168	358	19	.965
1988—	Cincinnati (N.L.).......	SS	151	588	91	174	32	5	12	56	.296	41	24	40	231	470	•29	.960
1989—	Cincinnati (N.L.).......	SS	97	325	47	111	14	4	4	36	.342	20	23	10	142	267	10	.976
—	Nashville (A.A.)	SS	2	5	2	5	1	0	0	0	1.000	0	0	0	1	3	0	1.000
1990—	Cincinnati (N.L.).......	SS	158	614	85	185	25	6	7	67	.301	49	49	30	254	*469	17	.977
1991—	Cincinnati (N.L.).......	SS	123	464	88	140	27	4	20	69	.302	55	64	24	226	372	15	.976
1992—	Cincinnati (N.L.).......	SS	140	533	76	162	32	6	12	78	.304	63	58	15	233	408	11	.983
1993—	Cincinnati (N.L.).......	SS	100	384	57	121	20	3	8	51	.315	51	33	14	159	281	16	.965
1994—	Cincinnati (N.L.).......	SS	110	427	78	119	23	5	9	52	.279	64	58	26	*178	312	10	.980
1995—	Cincinnati (N.L.).......	SS	131	496	98	158	29	6	15	66	.319	61	49	51	192	341	11	.980
1996—	Cincinnati (N.L.).......	SS	152	517	117	154	32	4	33	89	.298	96	52	36	*230	426	17	.975
1997—	Cincinnati (N.L.).......	SS-DH	73	224	34	71	17	3	4	20	.317	47	24	14	77	171	5	.980
1998—	Cincinnati (N.L.).......	SS	145	538	93	166	34	10	17	72	.309	79	69	26	207	361	12	.979
1999—	Cincinnati (N.L.).......	SS	161	583	108	171	30	4	12	75	.293	93	57	30	220	401	14	.978
2000—	Cincinnati (N.L.).......	SS-DH	102	396	71	124	26	5	11	41	.313	48	31	14	153	249	11	.973
2001—	Cincinnati (N.L.).......	SS	45	156	29	40	12	0	2	17	.256	27	25	3	65	108	9	.951
Major League totals (16 years)			1854	6843	1163	2048	373	70	181	851	.299	839	689	362	2786	5119	210	.974

DIVISION SERIES RECORD

Year	Team (League)	Pos.	G	AB	R	H	2B	3B	HR	RBI	Avg.	BB	SO	SB	PO	A	E	Avg.
1995—	Cincinnati (N.L.).........	SS	3	13	2	5	0	0	0	1	.385	1	2	4	3	8	0	1.000

CHAMPIONSHIP SERIES RECORD

Year	Team (League)	Pos.	G	AB	R	H	2B	3B	HR	RBI	Avg.	BB	SO	SB	PO	A	E	Avg.
1990—	Cincinnati (N.L.).........	SS	6	23	5	6	2	0	0	1	.261	3	1	3	21	15	1	.973
1995—	Cincinnati (N.L.).........	SS	4	18	1	7	2	1	0	0	.389	1	1	1	10	15	1	.962
Championship series totals (2 years)			10	41	6	13	4	1	0	1	.317	4	2	4	31	30	2	.968

WORLD SERIES RECORD

RECORDS: Shares single-inning record for most at-bats—2 (October 19, 1990, third inning).

NOTES: Member of World Series championship team (1990).

Year	Team (League)	Pos.	G	AB	R	H	2B	3B	HR	RBI	Avg.	BB	SO	SB	PO	A	E	Avg.
1990—	Cincinnati (N.L.)	SS	4	17	3	6	1	1	0	1	.353	2	0	0	1	14	0	1.000

Year	League	Pos.	AB	R	H	2B	3B	HR	RBI	Avg.	BB	SO	SB	PO	A	E	Avg.
1988—National		SS	2	0	0	0	0	0	0	.000	0	1	0	0	1	0	1.000
1989—National							Did not play.										
1990—National		PR-SS	0	0	0	0	0	0	0	...	0	0	1	1	2	0	1.000
1991—National		SS	1	0	0	0	0	0	0	.000	0	0	0	0	2	0	1.000
1993—National		SS	2	0	0	0	0	0	1	.000	0	1	0	2	1	0	1.000
1994—National							Selected, did not play—injured.										
1995—National		SS	3	0	0	0	0	0	0	.000	0	0	0	2	3	0	1.000
1996—National		SS	3	1	1	0	0	0	0	.333	0	0	0	0	2	0	1.000
1997—National							Selected, did not play—injured.										
1999—National		SS	3	0	1	0	0	0	1	.333	0	1	0	1	1	0	1.000
2000—National		SS	3	0	0	0	0	0	0	.000	0	0	0	0	2	1	.667
All-Star Game totals (8 years)			17	1	2	0	0	0	2	.118	0	3	1	6	14	1	.952

LARSON, BRANDON — 3B — REDS

PERSONAL: Born May 24, 1976, in San Angelo, Texas. ... 6-0/210. ... Bats right, throws right. ... Full name: Brandon John Larson.
HIGH SCHOOL: Holmes (San Antonio, Texas).
JUNIOR COLLEGE: Blinn College (Texas).
COLLEGE: Louisiana State.
TRANSACTIONS/CAREER NOTES: Selected by Pittsburgh Pirates organization in 46th round of free-agent draft (June 2, 1994); did not sign. ... Selected by Pittsburgh Pirates organization in 38th round of free-agent draft (June 1, 1995); did not sign. ... Selected by San Francisco Giants organization in 44th round of free-agent draft (June 4, 1996); did not sign. ... Selected by Cincinnati Reds organization in first round (14th pick overall) of free-agent draft (June 3, 1997). ... On Chattanooga disabled list (July 3-18, 1999).

Year	Team (League)	Pos.	G	AB	R	H	2B	3B	HR	RBI	Avg.	BB	SO	SB	PO	A	E	Avg.
1997—Chattanooga (Sou.)		SS	11	41	4	11	5	1	0	6	.268	1	10	0	19	22	5	.891
1998—Burlington (Midw.)		3B	18	68	5	15	3	0	2	9	.221	4	16	2	10	52	0	1.000
1999—Rockford (Midw.)		3B	69	250	38	75	18	1	13	52	.300	25	67	12	33	153	18	.912
—Chattanooga (Sou.)		3B	43	172	28	49	10	0	12	42	.285	10	51	4	22	93	15	.885
2000—Chattanooga (Sou.)		3B	111	427	61	116	26	0	20	64	.272	31	122	15	54	212	24	.917
—Louisville (I.L.)		3B	17	63	11	18	7	1	2	4	.286	4	16	0	6	46	4	.929
2001—Louisville (I.L.)		3B-SS-1B	115	424	61	108	22	2	14	55	.255	24	123	5	85	*287	20	.949
—Cincinnati (N.L.)		3B	14	33	2	4	2	0	0	1	.121	2	10	0	10	21	2	.939
Major League totals (1 year)			14	33	2	4	2	0	0	1	.121	2	10	0	10	21	2	.939

LaRUE, JASON — C — REDS

PERSONAL: Born March 19, 1974, in Houston. ... 5-11/200. ... Bats right, throws right. ... Full name: Michael Jason LaRue.
HIGH SCHOOL: Spring Valley (Spring Branch, Texas).
COLLEGE: Dallas Baptist.
TRANSACTIONS/CAREER NOTES: Selected by Cincinnati Reds organization in fifth round of free-agent draft (June 1, 1995). ... On disabled list (June 30-September 13, 1996).
STATISTICAL NOTES: Tied for Pioneer League lead in being hit by pitch with 12 in 1995. ... Led Pioneer League catchers with seven double plays in 1995. ... Led Southern League with .617 slugging percentage in 1998. ... Tied for Southern League lead with 21 passed balls in 1998. ... Career major league grand slams: 1.

Year	Team (League)	Pos.	G	AB	R	H	2B	3B	HR	RBI	Avg.	BB	SO	SB	PO	A	E	Avg.
1995—Billings (Pio.)		C	58	183	35	50	8	1	5	31	.273	16	28	3	346	46	8	.980
1996—Charl., W.Va. (S.Atl.)		C-1B	37	123	17	26	8	0	2	14	.211	11	28	3	234	48	6	.979
1997—Charl., W.Va. (S.Atl.)		C-1B-3B-OF	132	473	78	149	*50	3	8	81	.315	47	90	14	711	84	19	.977
1998—Chattanooga (Sou.)		C-3B-1B	105	386	71	141	39	8	14	82	*.365	40	60	4	546	90	10	.985
—Indianapolis (I.L.)		C	15	51	5	12	4	0	0	5	.235	4	8	0	83	11	0	1.000
1999—Indianapolis (I.L.)		C-DH	70	263	42	66	12	2	12	37	.251	15	52	0	384	45	7	.984
—Cincinnati (N.L.)		C	36	90	12	19	7	0	3	10	.211	11	32	4	179	15	2	.990
2000—Louisville (I.L.)		C	82	307	54	78	22	1	14	48	.254	22	52	3	445	57	8	.984
—Cincinnati (N.L.)		C	31	98	12	23	3	0	5	12	.235	5	19	0	190	22	2	.991
2001—Cincinnati (N.L.)		C-3B-OF-1B	121	364	39	86	21	2	12	43	.236	27	106	3	579	81	7	.990
Major League totals (3 years)			188	552	63	128	31	2	20	65	.232	43	157	7	948	118	11	.990

LATHAM, CHRIS — OF — BLUE JAYS

PERSONAL: Born May 26, 1973, in Coeur d'Alene, Idaho. ... 6-0/205. ... Bats both, throws right. ... Full name: Christopher Joseph Latham.
HIGH SCHOOL: Basic Technical (Las Vegas).
TRANSACTIONS/CAREER NOTES: Selected by Los Angeles Dodgers organization in 11th round of free-agent draft (June 3, 1991). ... Traded by Dodgers to Minnesota Twins (October 30, 1995), completing deal in which Twins traded P Mark Guthrie and P Kevin Tapani to Dodgers for 1B/3B Ron Coomer, P Greg Hansell, P Jose Parra and a player to be named later (July 31, 1995). ... On disabled list (August 30-September 9, 1996). ... Traded by Twins to Colorado Rockies for P Scott Randall (December 7, 1999). ... Granted free agency (October 18, 2000). ... Signed by Toronto Blue Jays organization (December 2, 2000).
STATISTICAL NOTES: Led Northwest League with 148 total bases and 20 caught stealing in 1994. ... Tied for Northwest League lead with seven intentional bases on balls received in 1994. ... Led Northwest League outfielders with 154 total chances in 1994. ... Led Pacific Coast League lead in caught stealing with 19 in 1997.

Year Team (League)	Pos.	G	AB	R	H	2B	3B	HR	RBI	Avg.	BB	SO	SB	PO	A	E	Avg.
1991—GC Dodgers (GCL)	2B	43	109	17	26	2	1	0	11	.239	16	45	14	47	63	10	.917
1992—Great Falls (Pio.)	2B	17	37	8	12	2	0	0	3	.324	8	8	1	17	24	6	.872
—GC Dodgers (GCL)	2B-SS-3B	14	48	4	11	2	0	0	2	.229	5	17	2	26	14	1	.976
1993—Yakima (N'West)	OF	54	192	46	50	2	*6	4	17	.260	39	53	25	83	5	6	.936
—Bakersfield (Calif.)	OF	6	27	1	5	1	0	0	3	.185	4	5	2	12	0	1	.923
1994—Bakersfield (Calif.)	OF	52	191	29	41	5	2	2	15	.215	28	49	28	88	4	7	.929
—Yakima (N'West)	OF	71	288	*69	*98	19	*8	5	32	*.340	55	66	33	*144	6	4	.974
1995—Vero Beach (FSL)	OF	71	259	53	74	13	4	6	39	.286	56	54	42	125	5	7	.949
—San Antonio (Texas) ...	OF	58	214	38	64	14	5	9	37	.299	33	59	11	135	2	4	.972
—Albuquerque (PCL)....	OF	5	18	2	3	0	1	0	3	.167	1	4	1	7	0	0	1.000
1996—Salt Lake (PCL)■.......	OF-DH	115	376	59	103	16	6	9	50	.274	36	91	26	235	9	9	.964
1997—Minnesota (A.L.)	OF	15	22	4	4	1	0	0	1	.182	0	8	0	11	0	1	.917
1998—Salt Lake (PCL)	OF-DH	97	377	81	122	21	4	11	51	.324	56	99	29	201	8	9	.959
—Minnesota (A.L.)	OF	34	94	14	15	1	0	1	5	.160	13	36	4	69	1	2	.972
1999—Minnesota (A.L.)	OF	14	22	1	2	0	0	0	3	.091	0	13	0	13	0	0	1.000
—Salt Lake (PCL)	OF	94	382	93	123	24	8	15	51	.322	54	95	18	262	9	6	.978
2000—Colo. Springs (PCL)■	3B	126	339	76	83	16	6	7	49	.245	71	105	29	228	6	7	.971
2001—Syracuse (I.L.)■.........	OF	79	288	57	80	20	9	13	54	.278	51	90	14	159	7	6	.965
—Toronto (A.L.).............	OF	43	73	12	20	3	1	2	10	.274	10	28	4	47	2	0	1.000
Major League totals (4 years)		106	211	31	41	5	1	3	19	.194	23	85	8	140	3	3	.979

LAWRENCE, BRIAN   P   PADRES

PERSONAL: Born May 14, 1976, in Fort Collins, Colo. ... 6-0/195. ... Throws right, bats right. ... Full name: Brian Michael Lawrence.
HIGH SCHOOL: Carthage (Texas).
COLLEGE: Northwestern State (La.).
TRANSACTIONS/CAREER NOTES: Selected by San Diego Padres organization in 17th round of free-agent draft (June 2, 1998).
STATISTICAL NOTES: Tied for California League lead with five balks in 1999.

Year League	W	L	Pct.	ERA	G	GS	CG	ShO	Sv.	IP	H	R	ER	BB	SO
1998—Idaho Falls (Pio.).............	3	0	1.000	2.45	4	4	2	•1	0	22	22	7	6	5	21
—Clinton (Midw.)	5	3	.625	2.80	12	12	2	0	0	80$^1/_3$	67	34	25	13	79
1999—Rancho Cuca. (Calif.)	12	8	.600	3.39	27	27	4	3	0	175$^1/_3$	178	72	66	30	166
2000—Mobile (Sou.)	7	6	.538	2.42	21	21	0	0	0	126$^2/_3$	99	40	34	28	119
—Las Vegas (PCL)	4	1	1.000	1.93	8	8	0	0	0	46$^2/_3$	48	13	10	7	46
2001—Portland (PCL)	1	3	.250	3.80	9	8	0	0	1	45	42	22	19	17	42
—San Diego (N.L.)	5	5	.500	3.45	27	15	1	0	0	114$^2/_3$	107	53	44	34	84
Major League totals (1 year)........	5	5	.500	3.45	27	15	1	0	0	114$^2/_3$	107	53	44	34	84

LAWRENCE, JOE   C   BLUE JAYS

PERSONAL: Born February 13, 1977, in Lake Charles, La. ... 6-2/190. ... Bats right, throws right. ... Full name: Joseph Dudley Lawrence.
HIGH SCHOOL: Barbe (Lake Charles, La.).
TRANSACTIONS/CAREER NOTES: Selected by Toronto Blue Jays organization in first round (16th pick overall) of free-agent draft (June 4, 1996); pick received as compensation for Baltimore Orioles signing Type A free-agent 2B Roberto Alomar. ... On disabled list (June 30, 1999-remainder of season). ... On disabled list (June 4-12, 2001).

Year Team (League)	Pos.	G	AB	R	H	2B	3B	HR	RBI	Avg.	BB	SO	SB	PO	A	E	Avg.
1996—St. Catharines (NY-P).	SS-3B	29	98	23	22	7	2	0	11	.224	14	17	1	31	67	11	.899
1997—Hagerstown (S.Atl.).....	SS	116	446	63	102	24	1	8	38	.229	49	107	10	134	278	33	.926
1998—Dunedin (FSL)	SS-3B	125	454	102	140	31	6	11	44	.308	*105	88	15	163	345	48	.914
1999—Knoxville (Sou.).........	3B-DH-SS	70	250	52	66	16	2	7	24	.264	56	48	7	30	114	14	.911
2000—Dunedin (FSL)	OF	101	375	69	113	32	1	13	67	.301	69	74	21	438	48	11	.978
—Tennessee (Sou.)	C	39	133	22	35	9	0	0	9	.263	30	27	7	207	19	5	.978
2001—Syracuse (I.L.)...........C-3B-1B-SS	93	318	27	70	11	4	1	26	.220	36	62	6	507	60	5	.991

LAWTON, MATT   OF   INDIANS

PERSONAL: Born November 3, 1971, in Gulfport, Miss. ... 5-10/186. ... Bats left, throws right. ... Full name: Matthew Lawton III. ... Brother of Marcus Lawton, outfielder with New York Yankees (1989).
HIGH SCHOOL: Harrison Central (Gulfport, Miss.).
JUNIOR COLLEGE: Gulf Coast Community College (Fla.).
TRANSACTIONS/CAREER NOTES: Selected by Minnesota Twins organization in 12th round of free-agent draft (June 3, 1991). ... On Minnesota disabled list (June 9-July 18, 1999); included rehabilitation assignments to Fort Myers (July 12-16) and Gulf Coast Twins (July 17-18). ... Traded by Twins to New York Mets for P Rick Reed (July 30, 2001). ... Traded by Mets with OF Alex Escobar, P Jerrod Riggan and two players to be named later to Cleveland Indians for 2B Roberto Alomar, P Mike Bacsik and OF Danny Peoples (December 11, 2001); Indians acquired P Billy Traber and 1B Earl Snyder to complete deal (December 13, 2001).
STATISTICAL NOTES: Led Florida State League with .407 on-base percentage in 1994. ... Had 16-game hitting streak (April 13-30, 2000). ... Career major league grand slams: 3.

Year Team (League)	Pos.	G	AB	R	H	2B	3B	HR	RBI	Avg.	BB	SO	SB	PO	A	E	Avg.
1992—GC Twins (GCL)..........	2B	53	173	39	45	8	3	2	26	.260	27	27	20	129	142	12	.958
1993—Fort Wayne (Midw.)......	OF	111	340	50	97	21	3	9	38	.285	65	42	23	65	6	3	.959
1994—Fort Myers (FSL)......	OF	122	446	79	134	30	1	7	51	.300	80	64	42	188	13	6	.971
1995—New Britain (East.)	OF-DH	114	412	75	111	19	5	13	54	.269	56	70	26	221	12	2	*.991
—Minnesota (A.L.)	OF-DH	21	60	11	19	4	1	1	12	.317	7	11	1	34	1	1	.972

Year	Team (League)	Pos.	G	AB	R	H	2B	3B	HR	RBI	Avg.	BB	SO	SB	PO	A	E	Avg.
1996—	Minnesota (A.L.)	OF-DH	79	252	34	65	7	1	6	42	.258	28	28	4	196	4	3	.985
	— Salt Lake (PCL)	OF-DH	53	212	40	63	16	1	7	33	.297	26	34	2	88	0	6	.936
1997—	Minnesota (A.L.)	OF	142	460	74	114	29	3	14	60	.248	76	81	7	278	9	7	.976
1998—	Minnesota (A.L.)	OF	152	557	91	155	36	6	21	77	.278	86	64	16	398	12	4	.990
1999—	Minnesota (A.L.)	OF-DH	118	406	58	105	18	0	7	54	.259	57	42	26	213	3	4	.982
	— Fort Myers (FSL)	OF	4	14	3	8	1	0	0	2	.571	3	1	1	8	0	0	1.000
	— GC Twins (GCL)	OF	1	4	0	1	0	0	0	1	.250	0	2	0	1	0	0	1.000
2000—	Minnesota (A.L.)	OF-DH	156	561	84	171	44	2	13	88	.305	91	63	23	278	4	5	.983
2001—	Minnesota (A.L.)	OF-DH	103	376	71	110	25	0	10	51	.293	63	46	19	193	2	4	.980
	— New York (N.L.)■	OF	48	183	24	45	11	1	3	13	.246	22	34	10	96	1	0	1.000
American League totals (7 years)			771	2672	423	739	163	13	72	384	.277	408	335	96	1590	35	28	.983
National League totals (1 year)			48	183	24	45	11	1	3	13	.246	22	34	10	96	1	0	1.000
Major League totals (7 years)			819	2855	447	784	174	14	75	397	.275	430	369	106	1686	36	28	.984

ALL-STAR GAME RECORD

Year	League	Pos.	AB	R	H	2B	3B	HR	RBI	Avg.	BB	SO	SB	PO	A	E	Avg.
2000—	American	OF	2	1	1	0	0	0	1	.500	0	0	1	0	0	0	...

LEACH, JAY   OF

PERSONAL: Born March 14, 1969, in San Francisco. ... 6-2/200. ... Bats left, throws left. ... Full name: Jalal Donnell Leach.
HIGH SCHOOL: San Marin (Novato, Calif.).
COLLEGE: Pepperdine.
TRANSACTIONS/CAREER NOTES: Selected by New York Yankees organization in seventh round of free-agent draft (June 4, 1990). ... Selected by Montreal Expos organization from Yankees organization in Rule 5 minor league draft (December 4, 1995). ... Granted free agency (October 15, 1996). ... Signed by Seattle Mariners organization (November 12, 1996). ... Granted free agency (October 15, 1997). ... Re-signed by Mariners (November 13, 1997). ... Traded with OF Scott Smith to San Francisco Giants for IF/OF David McCarty (January 30, 1998). ... Released by Giants (April 6, 1998). ... Re-signed by Giants organization (May 11, 1998). ... Granted free agency (October 15, 1998). ... Re-signed by Giants organization (January 15, 1999). ... Granted free agency (October 15, 1999). ... Signed by Philadelphia Phillies organization (November 8, 1999). ... Released by Phillies (June 28, 2000). ... Signed by Giants organization (July 3, 2000). ... Released by Giants (December 3, 2001).

Year	Team (League)	Pos.	G	AB	R	H	2B	3B	HR	RBI	Avg.	BB	SO	SB	PO	A	E	Avg.
1990—	Oneonta (NY-Penn)	OF	69	257	41	74	7	1	2	18	.288	37	52	33	107	4	3	.974
1991—	Fort Lauderdale (FSL)	OF	122	468	48	119	13	9	2	42	.254	44	122	28	253	9	5	.981
1992—	Prince William (Caro.)	OF	128	462	61	122	22	7	5	65	.264	47	114	18	249	9	7	.974
1993—	Albany/Colonie (East.)	OF	125	457	64	129	19	9	14	79	.282	47	113	15	210	9	9	.961
1994—	Columbus (I.L.)	OF-DH	132	444	56	116	18	9	6	56	.261	39	106	14	268	7	8	.972
1995—	Columbus (I.L.)	OF-DH	88	272	37	66	12	5	6	31	.243	22	60	11	97	2	6	.943
1996—	Harrisburg (East.)	OF-DH-1B	83	268	38	88	22	3	6	48	.328	21	55	3	123	3	3	.977
	— Ottawa (I.L.)	OF-DH	37	101	12	32	4	0	3	9	.317	8	17	0	27	1	0	1.000
1997—	Tacoma (PCL)	OF-DH	115	415	56	128	26	3	9	55	.308	32	74	6	205	8	5	.977
1998—	Shreveport (Texas)■ ..	OF-DH	72	253	43	87	17	2	10	45	.344	36	35	10	120	4	3	.976
	— Fresno (PCL)	OF-DH	35	130	23	46	8	2	9	26	.354	8	26	3	52	3	4	.932
1999—	Fresno (PCL)	OF-DH	116	371	58	109	19	5	15	75	.294	27	67	8	153	5	4	.975
2000—	Scranton/W.B. (I.L.)■ ..	OF	65	180	24	48	9	2	4	21	.267	19	34	4	83	2	1	.988
	— Fresno (PCL)■	OF	51	198	34	75	16	5	12	45	.379	18	28	8	80	2	2	.976
2001—	Fresno (PCL)	OF	130	467	68	133	30	3	16	70	.285	31	94	13	197	4	7	.966
	— San Francisco (N.L.) ..	OF	8	10	0	1	0	0	0	1	.100	2	3	0	1	0	0	1.000
Major League totals (1 year)			8	10	0	1	0	0	0	1	.100	2	3	0	1	0	0	1.000

LEBRON, FRANCIS   P   CUBS

PERSONAL: Born July 25, 1980, in Santo Domingo, Dominican Republic. ... 6-5/220. ... Throws right, bats right.
TRANSACTIONS/CAREER NOTES: Signed as non-drafted free agent by Chicago Cubs organization (November 15, 1996). ... On disabled list (June 9-July 24, 2001).

Year	League	W	L	Pct.	ERA	G	GS	CG	ShO	Sv.	IP	H	R	ER	BB	SO
1997—	Arizona Cubs (Ariz.)	0	1	.000	3.42	16	0	0	0	1	23²/₃	27	18	9	8	17
1998—	Arizona Cubs (Ariz.)	1	1	.500	5.55	12	5	0	0	0	35²/₃	49	23	22	14	26
1999—	Arizona Cubs (Ariz.)	0	1	.000	0.00	7	7	0	0	2	10²/₃	5	3	0	1	8
	— Eugene (N'West)	0	2	.000	8.36	16	0	0	0	0	28	41	32	26	14	28
2000—	Lansing (Midw.)	1	1	.500	9.68	16	0	0	0	0	17²/₃	24	22	19	19	16
	— Eugene (N'West)	2	2	.500	2.68	25	0	0	0	8	43²/₃	28	16	13	20	52
2001—	Daytona (FSL)	6	9	.400	5.00	21	18	0	0	0	95¹/₃	93	62	53	40	72

LeCROY, MATT   C   TWINS

PERSONAL: Born December 13, 1975, in Belton, S.C. ... 6-2/225. ... Bats right, throws right. ... Full name: Matthew Hanks LeCroy.
HIGH SCHOOL: Belton-Honea Path (S.C.).
COLLEGE: Clemson.
TRANSACTIONS/CAREER NOTES: Selected by Minnesota Twins organization in supplemental round ("sandwich pick" between first and second round, 50th pick overall) of free-agent draft (June 3, 1997); pick received as compensation for failure to sign 1996 first-round pick Travis Lee. ... On Salt Lake disabled list (September 10, 1999-remainder of season). ... On Edmonton disabled list (May 25-June 4 and June 5-23, 2001).
MISCELLANEOUS: Member of 1996 U.S. Olympic baseball team.

Year	Team (League)	Pos.	G	AB	R	H	2B	3B	HR	RBI	Avg.	BB	SO	SB	PO	A	E	Avg.
1998—Fort Wayne (Midw.)....		C	64	225	33	62	17	1	9	40	.276	34	45	0	344	35	1	.997
—Fort Myers (FSL)........		C	51	200	32	61	9	1	12	51	.305	21	35	2	309	28	3	.991
—Salt Lake (PCL).........		C	3	13	2	4	1	0	2	4	.308	0	7	0	6	0	0	1.000
1999—Fort Myers (FSL)........		C	89	333	54	93	20	1	20	69	.279	42	51	0	406	48	8	.983
—Salt Lake (PCL).........		C	29	119	23	36	4	1	10	30	.303	5	22	0	100	6	0	1.000
2000—Minnesota (A.L.).......		C-DH-1B	56	167	18	29	10	0	5	17	.174	17	38	0	330	16	4	.989
—New Britain (East.).....		C	54	195	33	55	12	1	10	38	.282	29	34	0	297	31	10	.970
—Salt Lake (PCL).........		C	16	65	15	20	5	0	5	15	.308	4	11	0	76	3	0	1.000
2001—Edmonton (PCL)........		C-1B	101	396	53	130	17	0	20	80	.328	36	95	0	227	14	5	.980
—Minnesota (A.L.)........		DH-C-1B	15	40	6	17	5	0	3	12	.425	0	8	0	10	1	0	1.000
Major League totals (2 years)			71	207	24	46	15	0	8	29	.222	17	46	0	340	17	4	.989

LEDEE, RICKY   OF

PERSONAL: Born November 22, 1973, in Ponce, Puerto Rico. ... 6-1/200. ... Bats left, throws left. ... Full name: Ricardo Alberto Ledee. ... Name pronounced le-DAY.

HIGH SCHOOL: Colonel Nuestra Sonora de Valvanera (Coano, Puerto Rico).

TRANSACTIONS/CAREER NOTES: Selected by New York Yankees organization in 16th round of free-agent draft (June 3, 1990). ... On Tampa disabled list (April 6-May 27, 1996). ... On Columbus disabled list (May 5-16 and May 22-August 4, 1997; and May 25-June 3, 1999). ... Traded by Yankees with two players to be named later to Cleveland Indians for OF David Justice (June 29, 2000); Indians acquired P Jake Westbrook and P Zach Day to complete deal (July 24, 2000). ... Traded by Indians to Texas Rangers for 1B/DH David Segui (July 28, 2000). ... On Texas disabled list (March 23-June 13, 2001); included rehabilitation assignment to Oklahoma (June 9-13). ... Granted free agency (December 21, 2001).

STATISTICAL NOTES: Career major league grand slams: 2.

Year	Team (League)	Pos.	G	AB	R	H	2B	3B	HR	RBI	Avg.	BB	SO	SB	PO	A	E	Avg.
1990—GC Yankees (GCL)......		OF	19	37	5	4	2	0	0	1	.108	6	18	2	18	1	0	1.000
1991—GC Yankees (GCL)......		OF	47	165	22	44	6	2	0	18	.267	22	40	3	79	6	6	.934
1992—GC Yankees (GCL)......		OF	52	179	25	41	9	2	2	23	.229	24	47	1	62	4	2	.971
1993—Oneonta (NY-Penn).....		OF	52	192	32	49	7	6	8	20	.255	25	46	7	91	6	3	.970
1994—Greensboro (S.Atl.)....		OF	134	484	87	121	23	9	22	71	.250	91	126	10	170	10	5	.973
1995—Greensboro (S.Atl.)....		OF	89	335	65	90	16	6	14	49	.269	51	66	10	160	7	3	.982
1996—Norwich (East.)		OF	39	137	27	50	11	1	8	37	.365	16	25	2	48	2	1	.980
—Columbus (I.L.)..........		OF	96	358	79	101	22	6	21	64	.282	44	95	6	97	3	5	.952
1997—Columbus (I.L.)..........		OF-DH	43	170	38	52	12	1	10	39	.306	21	49	4	56	0	2	.966
—GC Yankees (GCL)......		DH-OF	7	21	3	7	1	0	0	2	.333	2	4	0	1	0	0	1.000
1998—Columbus (I.L.)..........		OF-DH	96	360	70	102	21	1	19	41	.283	54	108	7	132	1	4	.971
—New York (A.L.).........		OF	42	79	13	19	5	2	1	12	.241	7	29	3	47	4	1	.981
1999—New York (A.L.).........		OF-DH	88	250	45	69	13	5	9	40	.276	28	73	4	143	3	9	.942
—Columbus (I.L.)..........		OF	30	115	18	29	7	1	4	15	.252	17	29	4	59	2	3	.953
2000—New York (A.L.).........		OF-DH	62	191	23	46	11	1	7	31	.241	26	39	7	94	1	2	.979
—Cleveland (A.L.)■......		OF	17	63	13	14	2	1	2	8	.222	8	9	0	39	1	0	1.000
—Texas (A.L.).............		OF	58	213	35	50	6	3	4	38	.235	25	50	6	128	0	3	.977
2001—Oklahoma (PCL).........		OF	4	16	4	8	1	0	1	3	.500	1	1	0	3	0	0	1.000
—Texas (A.L.)		OF	78	242	33	56	21	1	2	36	.231	23	58	3	137	1	3	.979
Major League totals (4 years)			345	1038	150	254	58	13	25	165	.245	117	258	23	588	10	18	.971

DIVISION SERIES RECORD

Year	Team (League)	Pos.	G	AB	R	H	2B	3B	HR	RBI	Avg.	BB	SO	SB	PO	A	E	Avg.
1998— New York (A.L.)									Did not play.									
1999—New York (A.L.).........		OF	3	11	1	3	2	0	0	2	.273	1	5	0	6	0	0	1.000

CHAMPIONSHIP SERIES RECORD

RECORDS: Shares single-game record for most grand slams—1 (October 17, 1999). ... Shares single-inning record for most runs batted in—4 (October 17, 1999, ninth inning).

Year	Team (League)	Pos.	G	AB	R	H	2B	3B	HR	RBI	Avg.	BB	SO	SB	PO	A	E	Avg.
1998—New York (A.L.)..........PH-OF-PR-DH			3	5	0	0	0	0	0	0	.000	0	0	0	3	0	0	1.000
1999—New York (A.L.)		OF-PH-DH	3	8	2	2	0	0	1	4	.250	1	4	0	3	0	1	.750
Championship series totals (2 years)			6	13	2	2	0	0	1	4	.154	1	4	0	6	0	1	.857

WORLD SERIES RECORD

NOTES: Member of World Series championship team (1998 and 1999).

Year	Team (League)	Pos.	G	AB	R	H	2B	3B	HR	RBI	Avg.	BB	SO	SB	PO	A	E	Avg.
1998—New York (A.L.).........		OF-PH	4	10	1	6	3	0	0	4	.600	2	1	0	8	0	0	1.000
1999—New York (A.L.)..........		OF	3	10	0	2	1	0	0	1	.200	1	4	0	1	0	0	1.000
World Series totals (2 years)			7	20	1	8	4	0	0	5	.400	3	5	0	9	0	0	1.000

LEE, CARLOS   OF   WHITE SOX

PERSONAL: Born June 20, 1976, in Aguadulce, Panama. ... 6-2/220. ... Bats right, throws right. ... Full name: Carlos Noriel Lee.

TRANSACTIONS/CAREER NOTES: Signed as non-drafted free agent by Chicago White Sox organization (February 8, 1994). ... On suspended list (April 28-May 1, 2000).

STATISTICAL NOTES: Led Appalachian League with 133 total bases and tied for league lead with three intentional bases on balls received in 1995. ... Led Appalachian League third basemen with 58 putouts and 10 double plays in 1995. ... Led South Atlantic League with 11 sacrifice flies in 1996. ... Led Carolina League with 282 total bases in 1997. ... Led Southern League in grounding into double plays with 32 in 1998. ... Hit home run in first major league at-bat (May 7, 1999). ... Had 15-game hitting streak (August 23-September 6, 1999). ... Career major league grand slams: 3.

							BATTING							FIELDING		
Year Team (League)	Pos.	G	AB	R	H	2B	3B	HR	RBI	Avg.	BB	SO	SB	PO	A	E	Avg.
1994— Sarasota (GCL)..........	3B	29	56	6	7	1	0	0	1	.125	4	8	0	18	29	2	.959
1995— Hickory (S.Atl.)..........	3B	63	218	18	54	9	1	4	30	.248	8	34	1	30	76	19	.848
— Bristol (Appl.)............	3B-1B	•67	*269	43	*93	17	1	7	45	.346	8	34	17	†84	107	18	.914
1996— Hickory (S.Atl.)..........	3B-1B	119	480	65	150	23	6	8	70	.313	23	50	18	149	235	32	.923
1997— Win.-Salem (Caro.)	3B-DH	*139	*546	81	*173	*50	4	17	82	.317	36	65	11	*93	233	34	.906
1998— Birmingham (Sou.)......	3B-DH	138	*549	77	166	33	2	15	106	.302	39	55	11	*99	223	*35	.902
1999— Charlotte (I.L.)............3B-OF-1B-DH		25	94	16	33	5	0	4	20	.351	8	14	2	56	22	4	.951
— Chicago (A.L.)	OF-DH-1B	127	492	66	144	32	2	16	84	.293	13	72	4	225	7	5	.979
2000— Chicago (A.L.)	OF-DH	152	572	107	172	29	2	24	92	.301	38	94	13	273	10	3	.990
2001— Chicago (A.L.)	OF-DH	150	558	75	150	33	3	24	84	.269	38	85	17	241	9	8	.969
Major League totals (3 years)		429	1622	248	466	94	7	64	260	.287	89	251	34	739	26	16	.980

DIVISION SERIES RECORD

							BATTING							FIELDING		
Year Team (League)	Pos.	G	AB	R	H	2B	3B	HR	RBI	Avg.	BB	SO	SB	PO	A	E	Avg.
2000— Chicago (A.L.)	OF	3	11	0	1	1	0	0	1	.091	0	2	0	6	0	0	1.000

LEE, DAVID   P   PADRES

PERSONAL: Born March 12, 1973, in Pittsburgh. ... 6-1/202. ... Throws right, bats right. ... Full name: David Emmer Lee.
HIGH SCHOOL: Langley (Pittsburgh).
JUNIOR COLLEGE: Community College of Allegheny County-North Campus (Pa.).
COLLEGE: Mercyhurst College (Pa.).
TRANSACTIONS/CAREER NOTES: Selected by Colorado Rockies organization in 23rd round of free-agent draft (June 1, 1995). ... On Colorado Springs disabled list (July 13-22, 2000). ... Traded by Rockies to New York Yankees for P Jay Tessmer and SS Seth Taylor (January 3, 2001). ... Traded by Yankees to San Diego Padres for P Carlos Almanzar (March 25, 2001). ... On San Diego disabled list (July 25-August 31, 2001); included rehabilitation assignment to Mobile (August 25-29).

Year League	W	L	Pct.	ERA	G	GS	CG	ShO	Sv.	IP	H	R	ER	BB	SO
1996— Portland (N'West)	5	1	.833	0.78	17	0	0	0	7	23	13	3	2	16	24
— Salem (Caro.)	0	2	.000	2.25	8	0	0	0	1	12	14	6	3	6	10
1997— Asheville (S.Atl.)...............	4	8	.333	4.08	51	0	0	0	22	53	61	30	24	23	59
1998— Salem (Caro.)	3	5	.375	3.77	54	0	0	0	25	57 1/3	57	26	24	15	54
1999— Carolina (Sou.)	0	0	...	1.04	16	0	0	0	10	17 1/3	8	3	2	3	16
— Colorado (N.L.)	3	2	.600	3.67	36	0	0	0	0	49	43	21	20	29	38
— Colorado Springs (PCL)	0	0	...	0.00	6	0	0	0	3	5 2/3	0	0	0	1	7
2000— Colorado (N.L.)	0	0	...	11.12	7	0	0	0	1	5 2/3	10	9	7	6	6
— Colorado Springs (PCL)	2	3	.400	5.96	47	0	0	0	12	48 1/3	50	38	32	28	44
2001— Portland (PCL)■............	1	0	1.000	0.75	9	0	0	0	1	12	5	1	1	5	14
— San Diego (N.L.)	1	0	1.000	3.70	41	0	0	0	1	48 2/3	52	20	20	27	42
— Mobile (Sou.)	0	0	...	0.00	2	0	0	0	0	2	2	0	0	0	3
Major League totals (3 years).......	4	2	.667	4.09	84	0	0	0	1	103 1/3	105	50	47	62	86

LEE, DERREK   1B   MARLINS

PERSONAL: Born September 6, 1975, in Sacramento. ... 6-5/242. ... Bats right, throws right. ... Full name: Derrek Leon Lee. ... Son of Leon Lee, infielder in St. Louis Cardinals organization (1969-71) and Lotte Orions (1978-82), Taiyo Whales (1983-85) and Yakult Swallows (1986-87) of Japan League; and nephew of Leron Lee, outfielder with four major league teams (1969-76) and Lotte Orions (1977-87) of Japan League.
HIGH SCHOOL: El Camino (Sacramento).
TRANSACTIONS/CAREER NOTES: Selected by San Diego Padres in first round (14th pick overall) of free-agent draft (June 1, 1993). ... Traded by Padres with P Rafael Medina and P Steve Hoff to Florida Marlins for P Kevin Brown (December 15, 1997).
RECORDS: Shares major league single-inning record for most assists by first baseman—3 (June 2, 1999, second inning).
HONORS: Named Southern League Most Valuable Player in 1996.
STATISTICAL NOTES: Led Southern League with 285 total bases in 1996. ... Led Southern League first basemen 1,121 putouts in 1996. ... Led Pacific Coast League first basemen with 1,189 total chances and 108 double plays in 1997. ... Career major league grand slams: 3.

							BATTING							FIELDING		
Year Team (League)	Pos.	G	AB	R	H	2B	3B	HR	RBI	Avg.	BB	SO	SB	PO	A	E	Avg.
1993— Arizona Padres (Ariz.)	1B	15	52	11	17	1	1	2	5	.327	6	7	4	115	14	2	.985
— Rancho Cuca. (Calif.) .	1B-DH	20	73	13	20	5	1	1	10	.274	10	20	0	115	6	5	.960
1994— Rancho Cuca. (Calif.) .	DH-1B	126	442	66	118	19	2	8	53	.267	42	95	18	289	27	4	.988
1995— Rancho Cuca. (Calif.) .	1B	128	502	82	151	25	2	23	95	.301	49	130	14	970	86	*18	.983
— Memphis (Sou.)	1B	2	9	0	1	0	0	0	1	.111	0	2	0	16	3	0	1.000
1996— Memphis (Sou.)	1B-DH-3B	134	500	98	140	39	2	34	*104	.280	65	*170	13	†1121	77	11	.991
1997— Las Vegas (PCL)	1B	125	472	86	153	29	2	13	64	.324	60	116	17	*1069	*111	9	*.992
— San Diego (N.L.)	1B	22	54	9	14	3	0	1	4	.259	9	24	0	131	13	0	1.000
1998— Florida (N.L.)■...........	1B	141	454	62	106	29	1	17	74	.233	47	120	5	950	114	8	.993
1999— Florida (N.L.).............	1B	70	218	21	45	9	1	5	20	.206	17	70	2	463	47	3	.994
— Calgary (PCL)............	1B-DH	89	339	60	96	20	1	19	73	.283	30	90	3	718	68	14	.983
2000— Florida (N.L.)	1B	158	477	70	134	18	3	28	70	.281	63	123	0	1101	102	8	.993
2001— Florida (N.L.)	1B	158	561	83	158	37	4	21	75	.282	50	126	4	1271	115	8	.994
Major League totals (5 years)		549	1764	245	457	96	9	72	243	.259	186	463	11	3916	391	27	.994

PERSONAL: Born May 26, 1975, in San Diego. ... 6-3/214. ... Bats left, throws left. ... Full name: Travis Reynolds Lee.
HIGH SCHOOL: Olympia (Wash.).
COLLEGE: San Diego State.
TRANSACTIONS/CAREER NOTES: Selected by Minnesota Twins organization in first round (second pick overall) of free-agent draft (June 4, 1996). ... Granted free agency (June 19, 1996). ... Signed by Arizona Diamondbacks organization (October 15, 1996). ... Loaned by Diamondbacks organization to Tucson, Milwaukee Brewers organization (June 5, 1997-remainder of season). ... On disabled list (July 25-August 9, 1998; and August 16-September 9, 1999). ... On Arizona disabled list (May 25-June 9, 2000); included rehabilitation assignment to El Paso (June 5-9). ... Traded by Diamondbacks with P Vicente Padilla, P Omar Daal and P Nelson Figueroa to Philadelphia Phillies for P Curt Schilling (July 26, 2000).
HONORS: Named Golden Spikes Award winner by USA Baseball (1996).
STATISTICAL NOTES: Led N.L. first basemen with .997 fielding percentage in 1999. ... Career major league grand slams: 3.
MISCELLANEOUS: Member of 1996 U.S. Olympic baseball team.

Year	Team (League)	Pos.	G	AB	R	H	2B	3B	HR	RBI	Avg.	BB	SO	SB	PO	A	E	Avg.
1997—	High Desert (Calif.).....	1B-DH	61	226	63	82	18	1	18	63	.363	47	36	5	553	67	1	.998
	—Tucson (PCL)■........	1B-DH-OF	59	227	42	68	16	2	14	46	.300	31	46	2	382	32	3	.993
1998—	Arizona (N.L.)■........	1B	146	562	71	151	20	2	22	72	.269	67	123	8	1269	100	3	.998
1999—	Arizona (N.L.)............	1B-OF	120	375	57	89	16	2	9	50	.237	58	50	17	805	62	3	†.997
2000—	Arizona (N.L.)............	OF-1B	72	224	34	52	13	0	8	40	.232	25	46	5	227	11	4	.983
	—El Paso (Texas).........	C	3	10	0	2	0	0	0	0	.200	2	1	0	15	1	0	1.000
	—Tucson (PCL)	1B-OF	7	30	4	11	4	0	0	3	.367	1	6	1	44	3	0	1.000
	—Philadelphia (N.L.)■ ..	1B-OF	56	180	19	43	11	1	1	14	.239	40	33	3	347	35	0	1.000
2001—	Philadelphia (N.L.).....	1B	157	555	75	143	34	2	20	90	.258	71	109	3	1332	75	6	.996
Major League totals (4 years)			551	1896	256	478	94	7	60	266	.252	261	361	36	3980	283	16	.996

PERSONAL: Born October 23, 1965, in Toms River, N.J. ... 6-3/220. ... Throws left, bats left. ... Full name: Alois Terry Leiter. ... Brother of Mark Leiter, pitcher with eight teams (1990-99 and 2001); and brother of Kurt Leiter, minor league pitcher (1982-84 and 1986). ... Name pronounced LIE-ter.
HIGH SCHOOL: Central Regional (Bayville, N.J.).
TRANSACTIONS/CAREER NOTES: Selected by New York Yankees organization in second round of free-agent draft (June 4, 1984). ... On New York disabled list (June 22-July 26, 1988); included rehabilitation assignment to Columbus (July 17-25). ... Traded by Yankees to Toronto Blue Jays for OF Jesse Barfield (April 30, 1989). ... On Toronto disabled list (May 11, 1989-remainder of season); included rehabilitation assignment to Dunedin (August 12-29). ... On Syracuse disabled list (May 20-June 13, 1990). ... On Toronto disabled list (April 27, 1991-remainder of season); included rehabilitation assignments to Dunedin (May 20-28 and July 19-August 7). ... On disabled list (April 24-May 9, 1993; and June 9-24, 1994). ... Granted free agency (November 6, 1995). ... Signed by Florida Marlins (December 14, 1995). ... On disabled list (May 1-20 and August 13-29, 1997). ... Traded by Marlins with 2B Ralph Milliard to New York Mets for P Jesus Sanchez, P A.J. Burnett and OF Robert Stratton (February 6, 1998). ... On disabled list (June 27-July 18, 1998; and April 21-May 18, 2001).
HONORS: Named lefthanded pitcher on THE SPORTING NEWS N.L. All-Star team (1996).
STATISTICAL NOTES: Tied for A.L. lead with five balks in 1994. ... Led A.L. with 14 wild pitches in 1995. ... Pitched 11-0 no-hit victory against Colorado (May 11, 1996). ... Struck out 15 batters in one game (August 1, 1999).

Year	League	W	L	Pct.	ERA	G	GS	CG	ShO	Sv.	IP	H	R	ER	BB	SO
1984—	Oneonta (NY-Penn)	3	2	.600	3.63	10	10	0	0	0	57	52	32	23	26	48
1985—	Oneonta (NY-Penn)	3	2	.600	2.37	6	6	2	0	0	38	27	14	10	25	34
	—Fort Lauderdale (FSL)	1	6	.143	6.48	17	17	1	0	0	82	87	70	59	57	44
1986—	Fort Lauderdale (FSL)	4	8	.333	4.05	22	21	1	1	0	117²/₃	96	64	53	90	101
1987—	Columbus (I.L.)...............	1	4	.200	6.17	5	5	0	0	0	23¹/₃	21	18	16	15	23
	—Albany/Colonie (East.).......	3	3	.500	3.35	15	14	2	0	0	78	64	34	29	37	71
	—New York (A.L.)...............	2	2	.500	6.35	4	4	0	0	0	22²/₃	24	16	16	15	28
1988—	New York (A.L.)...............	4	4	.500	3.92	14	14	0	0	0	57¹/₃	49	27	25	33	60
	—Columbus (I.L.)...............	0	2	.000	3.46	4	4	0	0	0	13	5	7	5	14	12
1989—	New York (A.L.)...............	1	2	.333	6.07	4	4	0	0	0	26²/₃	23	20	18	21	22
	—Toronto (A.L.)■...............	0	0	...	4.05	1	1	0	0	0	6²/₃	9	3	3	2	4
	—Dunedin (FSL)..............	0	2	.000	5.63	3	3	0	0	0	8	11	5	5	5	4
1990—	Dunedin (FSL)...............	0	0	...	2.63	6	6	0	0	0	24	18	8	7	12	14
	—Syracuse (I.L.)...............	3	8	.273	4.62	15	14	1	1	0	78	59	43	40	68	69
	—Toronto (A.L.)...............	0	0	...	0.00	4	0	0	0	0	6¹/₃	1	0	0	2	5
1991—	Toronto (A.L.)...............	0	0	...	27.00	3	0	0	0	0	1²/₃	3	5	5	5	1
	—Dunedin (FSL)..............	0	0	...	1.86	4	3	0	0	0	9²/₃	5	2	2	7	5
1992—	Syracuse (I.L.)...............	8	9	.471	3.86	27	27	2	0	0	163¹/₃	159	82	70	64	108
	—Toronto (A.L.)...............	0	0	...	9.00	1	0	0	0	0	1	1	1	1	2	0
1993—	Toronto (A.L.)...............	9	6	.600	4.11	34	12	1	1	2	105	93	52	48	56	66
1994—	Toronto (A.L.)...............	6	7	.462	5.08	20	20	1	0	0	111²/₃	125	68	63	65	100
1995—	Toronto (A.L.)...............	11	11	.500	3.64	28	28	2	1	0	183	162	80	74	*108	153
1996—	Florida (N.L.)■...............	16	12	.571	2.93	33	33	2	1	0	215¹/₃	153	74	70	*119	200
1997—	Florida (N.L.)...............	11	9	.550	4.34	27	27	0	0	0	151¹/₃	133	78	73	91	132
1998—	New York (N.L.)■...............	17	6	.739	2.47	28	28	4	2	0	193	151	55	53	71	174
1999—	New York (N.L.)...............	13	12	.520	4.23	32	32	1	1	0	213	209	107	100	93	162
2000—	New York (N.L.)...............	16	8	.667	3.20	31	31	2	1	0	208	176	84	74	76	200
2001—	New York (N.L.)...............	11	11	.500	3.31	29	29	0	0	0	187¹/₃	178	81	69	46	142
A.L. totals (9 years)		33	32	.508	4.36	113	83	4	2	2	522	490	272	253	309	439
N.L. totals (6 years)		84	58	.592	3.38	180	180	9	5	0	1168	1000	479	439	496	1010
Major League totals (15 years)		117	90	.565	3.69	293	263	13	7	2	1690	1490	751	692	805	1449

DIVISION SERIES RECORD

Year League	W	L	Pct.	ERA	G	GS	CG	ShO	Sv.	IP	H	R	ER	BB	SO
1997— Florida (N.L.)	0	0	...	9.00	1	1	0	0	0	4	7	4	4	3	3
1999— New York (N.L.)	0	0	...	3.52	1	1	0	0	0	7 2/3	3	3	3	3	4
2000— New York (N.L.)	0	0	...	2.25	1	1	0	0	0	8	5	2	2	3	6
Division series totals (3 years)	0	0	...	4.12	3	3	0	0	0	19 2/3	15	9	9	9	13

CHAMPIONSHIP SERIES RECORD

Year League	W	L	Pct.	ERA	G	GS	CG	ShO	Sv.	IP	H	R	ER	BB	SO
1993— Toronto (A.L.)	0	0	...	3.38	2	0	0	0	0	2 2/3	4	1	1	2	2
1997— Florida (N.L.)	0	1	.000	4.32	2	1	0	0	0	8 1/3	13	4	4	2	6
1999— New York (N.L.)	0	1	.000	6.43	2	2	0	0	0	7	5	6	5	4	5
2000— New York (N.L.)	0	0	...	3.86	1	1	0	0	0	7	8	3	3	0	9
Champ. series totals (4 years)	0	2	.000	4.68	7	4	0	0	0	25	30	14	13	8	22

WORLD SERIES RECORD

RECORDS: Shares single-inning record for most bases on balls allowed—4 (October 21, 1997, fourth inning).

NOTES: Member of World Series championship team (1993 and 1997).

Year League	W	L	Pct.	ERA	G	GS	CG	ShO	Sv.	IP	H	R	ER	BB	SO
1993— Toronto (A.L.)	1	0	1.000	7.71	3	0	0	0	0	7	12	6	6	2	5
1997— Florida (N.L.)	0	0	...	5.06	2	2	0	0	0	10 2/3	10	9	6	10	10
2000— New York (N.L.)	0	1	.000	2.87	2	2	0	0	0	15 2/3	12	6	5	6	16
World Series totals (3 years)	1	1	.500	4.59	7	4	0	0	0	33 1/3	34	21	17	18	31

ALL-STAR GAME RECORD

Year League	W	L	Pct.	ERA	G	GS	CG	ShO	Sv.	IP	H	R	ER	BB	SO
1996— National	0	0	...	0.00		0	0	0	0	1/3	0	0	0	0	0
2000— National	0	1	.000	9.00		0	0	0	0	1	2	2	1	1	1
All-Star Game totals (2 years)	0	1	.000	6.75		0	0	0	0	1 1/3	2	2	1	1	1

LEITER, MARK   P

PERSONAL: Born April 13, 1963, in Joliet, Ill. ... 6-3/220. ... Throws right, bats right. ... Full name: Mark Edward Leiter. ... Brother of Al Leiter, pitcher, New York Mets; and brother of Kurt Leiter, minor league pitcher (1982-84 and 1986). ... Name pronounced LIE-ter.

HIGH SCHOOL: Central Regional (Bayville, N.J.).

JUNIOR COLLEGE: Connors State College (Okla.).

COLLEGE: Ramapo College of New Jersey.

TRANSACTIONS/CAREER NOTES: Selected by Baltimore Orioles organization in fourth round of free-agent draft (January 11, 1983). ... On disabled list (April 10, 1986-entire season; April 10, 1987-entire season; and April 10-June 13, 1988). ... Released by Orioles (June 13, 1988). ... Signed by New York Yankees organization (September 29, 1988). ... Traded by Yankees to Detroit Tigers for IF Torey Lovullo (March 19, 1991). ... On Detroit disabled list (June 6-23, 1991; July 24-August 24, 1992; and August 4-September 1, 1993). ... Released by Tigers (March 15, 1994). ... Signed by California Angels (March 21, 1994). ... Granted free agency (December 23, 1994). ... Signed by Phoenix, San Francisco Giants organization (April 10, 1995). ... Traded by Giants to Montreal Expos for P Tim Scott and P Kirk Rueter (July 30, 1996). ... Granted free agency (November 5, 1996). ... Signed by Philadelphia Phillies (December 12, 1996). ... On disabled list (June 21-July 5, 1997). ... Traded by Phillies to Seattle Mariners for P Paul Spoljaric (November 9, 1998). ... On Seattle disabled list (March 26-April 28 and May 2, 1999-remainder of season); included rehabilitation assignment in Tacoma (April 14-17). ... Granted free agency (November 5, 1999). ... Signed by Pittsburgh Pirates organization (February 9, 2000). ... Released by Pirates (March 23, 2000). ... Signed by New York Mets organization (January 9, 2001). ... Traded by Mets to Colorado Rockies for P Brian Rose (March 26, 2001). ... Traded by Rockies with P Mike DeJean and 2B/SS Elvis Pena to Milwaukee Brewers for P Juan Acevedo, P Kane Davis and IF Jose Flores (April 4, 2001). ... On Milwaukee disabled list (May 11-September 1, 2001); included rehabilitation assignment to Beloit (August 29-31). ... Granted free agency (November 5, 2001).

STATISTICAL NOTES: Tied for A.L. lead with nine hit batsmen in 1994. ... Led N.L. with 17 hit batsmen in 1995 and tied for lead with 16 in 1996. ... Led N.L. with 37 home runs allowed in 1996.

Year League	W	L	Pct.	ERA	G	GS	CG	ShO	Sv.	IP	H	R	ER	BB	SO
1983— Bluefield (Appl.)	2	1	.667	2.70	6	6	2	0	0	36 2/3	33	17	11	13	35
— Hagerstown (Caro.)	1	5	.167	7.25	8	8	0	0	0	36	42	31	29	28	18
1984— Hagerstown (Caro.)	8	•13	.381	5.62	27	24	5	1	0	139 1/3	132	96	87	*108	105
1985— Hagerstown (Caro.)	2	8	.200	3.46	34	6	1	0	8	83 1/3	77	44	32	29	82
— Charlotte (Sou.)	0	1	.000	1.42	5	0	0	0	1	6 1/3	3	1	1	2	8
1986— Charlotte (Sou.)										Did not play.					
1987— Charlotte (Sou.)										Did not play.					
1988— Charlotte (Sou.)										Did not play.					
1989— Fort Lauderdale (FSL)■	2	2	.500	1.53	6	4	1	0	1	35 1/3	27	9	6	5	22
— Columbus (I.L.)	9	6	.600	5.00	22	12	0	0	0	90	102	50	50	34	70
1990— Columbus (I.L.)	9	4	.692	3.60	30	14	2	1	1	122 2/3	114	56	49	27	115
— New York (A.L.)	1	1	.500	6.84	8	3	0	0	0	26 1/3	33	20	20	9	21
1991— Toledo (I.L.)■	1	0	1.000	0.00	5	0	0	0	1	6 2/3	6	0	0	3	7
— Detroit (A.L.)	9	7	.563	4.21	38	15	1	0	1	134 2/3	125	66	63	50	103
1992— Detroit (A.L.)	8	5	.615	4.18	35	14	1	0	0	112	116	57	52	43	75
1993— Detroit (A.L.)	6	6	.500	4.72	27	13	1	0	0	106 2/3	111	61	56	44	70
1994— California (A.L.)■	4	7	.364	4.72	40	7	0	0	2	95 1/3	99	56	50	35	71
1995— San Francisco (N.L.)■	10	12	.455	3.82	30	29	7	1	0	195 2/3	185	91	83	55	129
1996— San Francisco (N.L.)	4	10	.286	5.19	23	22	1	0	0	135 1/3	151	93	78	50	118
— Montreal (N.L.)	4	2	.667	4.39	12	12	1	0	0	69 2/3	68	35	34	19	46
1997— Philadelphia (N.L.)■	10	*17	.370	5.67	31	31	3	0	0	182 2/3	216	*132	*115	64	148
1998— Philadelphia (N.L.)	7	5	.583	3.55	69	0	0	0	23	88 2/3	67	36	35	47	84
1999— Tacoma (PCL)■	0	0	...	4.50	1	1	0	0	0	2	2	1	1	0	3
— Seattle (A.L.)	0	0	...	6.75	2	0	0	0	0	1 1/3	2	1	1	0	1
2000—										Did not play.					
2001— Milwaukee (N.L.)■	2	1	.667	3.75	20	3	0	0	0	36	32	16	15	8	26
— Beloit (Midw.)	0	1	.000	2.45	1	0	0	0	0	3 2/3	4	1	1	0	4
A.L. totals (6 years)	28	26	.519	4.57	150	52	3	0	3	476 1/3	486	261	242	181	341
N.L. totals (5 years)	37	47	.440	4.58	185	97	12	1	23	708	719	403	360	243	551
Major League totals (11 years)	65	73	.471	4.57	335	149	15	1	26	1184 1/3	1205	664	602	424	892

LESKANIC, CURTIS   P   BREWERS

PERSONAL: Born April 2, 1968, in Homestead, Pa. ... 6-0/196. ... Throws right, bats right. ... Full name: Curtis John Leskanic. ... Name pronounced less-CAN-ik.

HIGH SCHOOL: Steel Valley (Munhall, Pa.).

COLLEGE: Louisiana State.

TRANSACTIONS/CAREER NOTES: Selected by Cleveland Indians organization in eighth round of free-agent draft (June 5, 1989). ... On disabled list (April 23-June 25, 1990). ... Traded by Indians with P Oscar Munoz to Minnesota Twins for 1B Paul Sorrento (March 28, 1992). ... Selected by Colorado Rockies in third round (66th pick overall) of expansion draft (November 17, 1992). ... Loaned by Rockies organization to Wichita, San Diego Padres organization (April 7-May 20, 1993). ... On Colorado disabled list (May 30-June 28, 1996); included rehabilitation assignment to Colorado Springs (June 22-27). ... On Colorado disabled list (March 23-April 12, 1997); included rehabilitation assignment to Salem (April 6-8). ... Traded by Rockies to Milwaukee Brewers for P Mike Myers (November 17, 1999). ... On disabled list (May 17-30, 2000).

MISCELLANEOUS: Had a sacrifice hit in only appearance as pinch hitter (1998). ... Holds Colorado Rockies all-time record for most games pitched (356).

Year League	W	L	Pct.	ERA	G	GS	CG	ShO	Sv.	IP	H	R	ER	BB	SO
1990— Kinston (Caro.)	6	5	.545	3.68	14	14	2	0	0	73 1/3	61	34	30	30	71
1991— Kinston (Caro.)	•15	8	.652	2.79	28	28	0	0	0	174 1/3	143	63	54	91	*163
1992— Orlando (Sou.)■	9	11	.450	4.30	26	23	3	0	0	152 2/3	158	84	73	64	126
— Portland (PCL)	1	2	.333	9.98	5	3	0	0	0	15 1/3	16	17	17	8	14
1993— Wichita (Texas)■	3	2	.600	3.45	7	7	0	0	0	44 1/3	37	20	17	17	42
— Colorado Springs (PCL)■..	4	3	.571	4.47	9	7	1	1	0	44 1/3	39	24	22	26	38
— Colorado (N.L.)	1	5	.167	5.37	18	8	0	0	0	57	59	40	34	27	30
1994— Colorado Springs (PCL)	5	7	.417	3.31	21	21	2	0	0	130 1/3	129	60	48	54	98
— Colorado (N.L.)	1	1	.500	5.64	8	3	0	0	0	22 1/3	27	14	14	10	17
1995— Colorado (N.L.)	6	3	.667	3.40	*76	0	0	0	10	98	83	38	37	33	107
1996— Colorado (N.L.)	7	5	.583	6.23	70	0	0	0	6	73 2/3	82	51	51	38	76
— Colorado Springs (PCL)	0	0	...	3.00	3	0	0	0	0	3	5	1	1	1	2
1997— Salem (Caro.)	0	0	...	3.86	2	1	0	0	0	2 1/3	5	2	1	1	3
— Colorado (N.L.)	4	0	1.000	5.55	55	0	0	0	2	58 1/3	59	36	36	24	53
— Colorado Springs (PCL)	0	0	...	3.79	10	3	0	0	2	19	11	9	8	18	20
1998— Colorado (N.L.)	6	4	.600	4.40	66	0	0	0	2	75 2/3	75	37	37	40	55
1999— Colorado (N.L.)	6	2	.750	5.08	63	0	0	0	0	85	87	54	48	49	77
2000— Milwaukee (N.L.)■	9	3	.750	2.56	73	0	0	0	12	77 1/3	58	23	22	51	75
2001— Milwaukee (N.L.)	2	6	.250	3.63	70	0	0	0	17	69 1/3	63	30	28	31	64
Major League totals (9 years)	42	29	.592	4.48	499	11	0	0	49	616 2/3	593	323	307	303	554

DIVISION SERIES RECORD

Year League	W	L	Pct.	ERA	G	GS	CG	ShO	Sv.	IP	H	R	ER	BB	SO
1995— Colorado (N.L.)	0	1	.000	6.00	3	0	0	0	0	3	3	2	2	0	4

LEVINE, AL   P   ANGELS

PERSONAL: Born May 22, 1968, in Park Ridge, Ill. ... 6-3/198. ... Throws right, bats right. ... Full name: Alan Brian Levine.

HIGH SCHOOL: Hoffman Estates (Ill.).

JUNIOR COLLEGE: Harper Junior College (Ill.).

COLLEGE: Southern Illinois-Carbondale.

TRANSACTIONS/CAREER NOTES: Selected by Chicago White Sox in 11th round of free-agent draft (June 3, 1991). ... Traded by White Sox with P Larry Thomas to Texas Rangers for SS Benji Gil (December 19, 1997). ... Claimed on waivers by Anaheim Angels (April 2, 1999). ... On Anaheim disabled list (July 31-August 19, 2000); included rehabilitation assignment to Erie (August 17).

Year League	W	L	Pct.	ERA	G	GS	CG	ShO	Sv.	IP	H	R	ER	BB	SO
1991— Utica (NY-Penn)	6	4	.600	3.18	16	12	2	1	1	85	75	45	30	26	83
1992— South Bend (Midw.)	9	5	.643	2.81	23	23	2	0	0	156 2/3	151	67	49	36	131
— Sarasota (FSL)	0	2	.000	4.02	3	2	0	0	0	15 2/3	17	11	7	5	11
1993— Sarasota (FSL)	11	8	.579	3.68	27	26	5	1	0	161 1/3	169	87	66	50	*129
1994— Birmingham (Sou.)	5	9	.357	3.31	18	18	1	0	0	114 1/3	117	50	42	44	94
— Nashville (A.A.)	0	2	.000	7.88	8	4	0	0	0	24	34	23	21	11	24
1995— Nashville (A.A.)	0	2	.000	5.14	3	3	0	0	0	14	20	10	8	7	14
— Birmingham (Sou.)	4	3	.571	2.34	43	1	0	0	7	73	61	22	19	25	68
1996— Nashville (A.A.)	4	5	.444	3.65	43	0	0	0	12	61 2/3	58	27	25	24	45
— Chicago (A.L.)	0	1	.000	5.40	16	0	0	0	0	18 1/3	22	14	11	7	12
1997— Chicago (A.L.)	2	2	.500	6.91	25	0	0	0	0	27 1/3	35	22	21	16	22
— Nashville (A.A.)	1	1	.500	7.13	26	0	0	0	0	35 1/3	58	32	28	11	29
1998— Oklahoma (PCL)■	1	3	.250	4.72	12	7	0	0	1	53 1/3	51	33	28	17	30
— Texas (A.L.)	0	1	.000	4.50	30	0	0	0	0	58	68	30	29	16	19
1999— Anaheim (A.L.)■	1	1	.500	3.39	50	1	0	0	0	85	76	40	32	29	37
2000— Anaheim (A.L.)	3	4	.429	3.87	51	5	0	0	2	95 1/3	98	44	41	49	42
— Erie (East.)	0	0	...	0.00	1	1	0	0	0	2	3	2	0	0	0
2001— Anaheim (A.L.)	8	10	.444	2.38	64	1	0	0	2	75 2/3	71	25	20	28	40
Major League totals (6 years)	14	19	.424	3.85	236	7	0	0	4	359 2/3	370	175	154	145	172

LEVIS, JESSE   C   REDS

PERSONAL: Born April 14, 1968, in Philadelphia. ... 5-9/200. ... Bats left, throws right.

HIGH SCHOOL: Northeast (Philadelphia).

COLLEGE: North Carolina.

TRANSACTIONS/CAREER NOTES: Selected by Philadelphia Phillies organization in 36th round of free-agent draft (June 2, 1986); did not sign. ... Selected by Cleveland Indians organization in fourth round of free-agent draft (June 5, 1989). ... Traded by Indians to Milwaukee Brewers for P Scott Nate and a player to be named later (April 4, 1996); Indians acquired P Jared Camp to complete deal (June 9, 1996). ...

On disabled list (May 8, 1998-remainder of season). ... Released by Brewers (September 29, 1998). ... Signed by Tampa Bay Devil Rays organization (December 18, 1998). ... On Durham disabled list (April 8-May 8, 1999). ... Released by Devil Rays (July 28, 1999). ... Signed by Indians (July 30, 1999). ... Granted free agency (October 4, 1999). ... Re-signed by Indians organization (January 13, 2000). ... On Buffalo disabled list (May 4-13, 2000). ... Granted free agency (October 18, 2000). ... Signed by Atlanta Braves organization (November 16, 2000). ... Released by Braves (August 3, 2001). ... Signed by Milwaukee Brewers organization (August 11, 2001). ... Granted free agency (October 15, 2001). ... Signed by Cincinnati Reds organization (December 21, 2001).

STATISTICAL NOTES: Led Eastern League catchers with 733 total chances in 1991.

							BATTING								FIELDING		
Year Team (League)	Pos.	G	AB	R	H	2B	3B	HR	RBI	Avg.	BB	SO	SB	PO	A	E	Avg.
1989— Burlington (Appl.).......	C	27	93	11	32	4	0	4	16	.344	10	7	1	189	27	2	.991
— Kinston (Caro.)........	C	27	87	11	26	6	0	2	11	.299	12	15	1	95	17	2	.982
— Colo. Springs (PCL) ...	PH	1	1	0	0	0	0	0	0	.000	0	0	0	...	...	...	...
1990— Kinston (Caro.)........	C	107	382	63	113	18	3	7	64	.296	64	42	4	517	63	5	.991
1991— Canton/Akron (East.)..	C	115	382	31	101	17	3	6	45	.264	40	36	2	*644	*77	12	.984
1992— Colo. Springs (PCL) ...	C	87	253	39	92	20	1	6	44	.364	37	25	1	375	47	4	.991
— Cleveland (A.L.).........	C-DH	28	43	2	12	4	0	1	3	.279	0	5	0	59	5	1	.985
1993— Charlotte (I.L.)..........	C	47	129	10	32	6	1	2	20	.248	15	12	0	266	22	4	.986
— Cleveland (A.L.).........	C	31	63	7	11	2	0	0	4	.175	2	10	0	109	7	1	.991
1994— Charlotte (I.L.)...........	C-DH	111	375	55	107	20	0	10	59	.285	55	39	2	452	34	4	.992
— Cleveland (A.L.).........	PH	1	1	0	0	0	0	0	0	1.000	0	0	0	...	...	...	...
1995— Buffalo (A.A.).............	C-DH	66	196	26	61	16	0	4	20	.311	32	11	0	338	20	2	.994
— Cleveland (A.L.).........	C	12	18	1	6	2	0	0	3	.333	1	0	0	33	5	0	1.000
1996— Milwaukee (A.L.)■..	C-DH	104	233	27	55	6	1	1	21	.236	38	15	0	373	26	1	*.998
1997— Milwaukee (A.L.)	C-DH	99	200	19	57	7	0	1	19	.285	24	17	1	296	19	2	.994
1998— Milwaukee (A.L.)	C	22	37	4	13	0	0	0	4	.351	7	6	1	83	2	0	1.000
1999— Durham (I.L.)■.........	C-DH	27	94	20	31	5	0	1	8	.330	15	9	0	142	9	0	1.000
— Orlando (Sou.)	C-DH	13	48	6	19	7	0	1	11	.396	6	4	0	52	4	1	.982
— Cleveland (A.L.)■.......	C	10	26	0	4	0	0	0	3	.154	1	6	0	53	3	0	1.000
2000— Buffalo (I.L.)..............	C	53	168	17	48	8	0	3	21	.286	17	12	0	286	20	1	.997
2001— Richmond (I.L.)■....	C	67	192	18	57	6	0	1	27	.297	24	15	2	398	43	2	.995
— Indianapolis (I.L.)■....	C	12	40	4	6	1	0	2	7	.150	2	6	0	81	8	0	1.000
— Milwaukee (N.L.)	C	12	33	6	8	2	0	0	3	.242	3	7	0	59	3	1	.984
American League totals (7 years)		285	584	56	146	21	1	3	53	.250	66	53	1	923	65	5	.995
National League totals (2 years)		34	70	10	21	2	0	0	7	.300	10	13	1	142	5	1	.993
Major League totals (9 years)		319	654	66	167	23	1	3	60	.255	76	66	2	1065	70	6	.995

LEVRAULT, ALLEN — P — BREWERS

PERSONAL: Born August 15, 1977, in Fall River, Mass. ... 6-3/230. ... Throws right, bats right. ... Full name: Allen Harry Levrault.
HIGH SCHOOL: Westport (Mass.).
JUNIOR COLLEGE: Community College of Rhode Island.
TRANSACTIONS/CAREER NOTES: Selected by Milwaukee Brewers organization in 13th round of free-agent draft (June 4, 1996). ... On Huntsville disabled list (June 20-July 10 and January 1-17, 1999). ... On Indianapolis disabled list (April 27-May 12 and September 12-19, 2000).
STATISTICAL NOTES: Led Midwest League with 12 balks in 1997.

Year League	W	L	Pct.	ERA	G	GS	CG	ShO	Sv.	IP	H	R	ER	BB	SO
1996— Helena (Pio.)	4	3	.571	5.32	18	11	0	0	1	71	70	43	42	22	68
1997— Beloit (Midw.)....................	3	10	.231	5.28	24	24	1	0	0	131 1/3	141	89	77	40	112
1998— Stockton (Calif.)	9	3	.750	2.87	16	15	*4	•1	0	97 1/3	76	33	31	27	86
— El Paso (Texas).................	1	5	.167	5.89	11	11	0	0	0	62 2/3	77	51	41	17	46
1999— Huntsville (Sou.)	9	2	*.818	3.43	16	16	2	1	0	99 2/3	77	44	38	33	82
— Louisville (I.L.)	1	3	.250	8.65	9	5	0	0	0	34 1/3	48	37	33	16	33
2000— Indianapolis (I.L.)..............	6	8	.429	4.24	21	18	1	0	0	108 1/3	98	55	51	46	78
— Milwaukee (N.L.)	0	1	.000	4.50	5	1	0	0	0	12	10	7	6	7	9
2001— Indianapolis (I.L.)..............	2	1	.667	2.64	5	5	0	0	0	30 2/3	22	9	9	8	30
— Milwaukee (N.L.)	6	10	.375	6.06	32	20	1	0	0	130 2/3	146	93	88	59	80
Major League totals (2 years)	6	11	.353	5.93	37	21	1	0	0	142 2/3	156	100	94	66	89

LEWIS, COLBY — P — RANGERS

PERSONAL: Born August 2, 1979, in Bakersfield, Calif. ... 6-4/215. ... Throws right, bats right. ... Full name: Colby P. Lewis.
HIGH SCHOOL: North (Bakersfield, Calif.).
JUNIOR COLLEGE: Bakersfield (Calif.).
TRANSACTIONS/CAREER NOTES: Selected by Texas Rangers organization in supplemental round ("sandwich pick" between first and second round, 38th pick overall) of free-agent draft (June 2, 1999); pick received as part of compensation for Arizona Diamondbacks signing Type A free agent P Todd Stottlemyre.
STATISTICAL NOTES: Led Texas League with 16 hit batsmen and 16 wild pitches in 2001.

Year League	W	L	Pct.	ERA	G	GS	CG	ShO	Sv.	IP	H	R	ER	BB	SO
1999— Pulaski (Appl.)....................	7	3	.700	1.95	14	11	1	1	0	64 2/3	46	24	14	27	84
2000— Charlotte (FSL)..................	11	10	.524	4.07	28	27	3	1	0	163 2/3	169	83	74	45	153
2001— Charlotte (FSL)..................	1	0	1.000	0.00	1	0	0	0	0	4 1/3	0	0	0	0	8
— Tulsa (Texas)	10	10	.500	4.50	25	25	1	0	0	156	150	85	78	62	162

LEWIS, DARREN — OF — CUBS

PERSONAL: Born August 28, 1967, in Berkeley, Calif. ... 6-0/190. ... Bats right, throws right. ... Full name: Darren Joel Lewis.
HIGH SCHOOL: Moreau (Hayward, Calif.).
JUNIOR COLLEGE: Chabot College (Calif.).
COLLEGE: California.

TRANSACTIONS/CAREER NOTES: Selected by Los Angeles Dodgers organization in sixth round of free-agent draft (January 14, 1986); did not sign. ... Selected by Toronto Blue Jays organization in 45th round of free-agent draft (June 2, 1987); did not sign. ... Selected by Oakland Athletics organization in 18th round of free-agent draft (June 1, 1988). ... Traded by A's with a player to be named later to San Francisco Giants for IF Ernest Riles (December 4, 1990); Giants acquired P Pedro Pena to complete deal (December 17, 1990). ... On disabled list (August 20-September 4, 1993). ... Traded by Giants with P Mark Portugal and P Dave Burba to Cincinnati Reds for OF Deion Sanders, P John Roper, P Ricky Pickett, P Scott Service and IF Dave McCarty (July 21, 1995). ... Released by Reds (December 1, 1995). ... Signed by Chicago White Sox (December 14, 1995). ... Traded by White Sox to Dodgers for a player to be named later (August 27, 1997); White Sox acquired IF Chad Fonville to complete deal (September 2, 1997). ... Granted free agency (October 27, 1997). ... Signed by Boston Red Sox (December 23, 1997). ... Granted free agency (November 3, 1998). ... Re-signed by Red Sox (November 5, 1998). ... On Boston disabled list (July 1-14, 2000); included rehabilitation assignment to Gulf Coast Red Sox (July 11-13). ... Granted free agency (November 5, 2001). ... Signed by Chicago Cubs (January 15, 2002).

RECORDS: Holds major league records for most consecutive errorless games by outfielder—392 (August 21, 1990-June 29, 1994); and most consecutive chances accepted without an error by outfielder—938 (August 21, 1990-June 29, 1994). ... Shares major league record for fewest double plays by outfielder (150 or more games)—0 (1998). ... Holds N.L. records for most consecutive errorless games by outfielder—369 (July 13, 1991-June 29, 1994); and most consecutive chances accepted without an error by outfielder—905 (July 13, 1991-June 29, 1994).

HONORS: Won N.L. Gold Glove as outfielder (1994).

STATISTICAL NOTES: Led California League outfielders with 324 total chances in 1989. ... Career major league grand slams: 1.

Year Team (League)	Pos.	G	AB	R	H	2B	3B	HR	RBI	Avg.	BB	SO	SB	PO	A	E	Avg.
1988— Ariz. Athletics (Ariz.) ..	OF	5	15	8	5	3	0	0	4	.333	6	5	4	15	1	0	1.000
— Madison (Midw.)........	OF-2B	60	199	38	49	4	1	0	11	.246	46	37	31	195	3	4	.980
1989— Modesto (Calif.)	OF	129	503	74	150	23	5	4	39	.298	59	84	27	*311	8	5	.985
— Huntsville (Sou.)	OF	9	31	7	10	1	1	1	7	.323	2	6	0	16	0	0	1.000
1990— Huntsville (Sou.)	OF	71	284	52	84	11	3	3	23	.296	36	28	21	186	6	0	1.000
— Tacoma (PCL)	OF	60	247	32	72	5	2	2	26	.291	16	35	16	132	9	2	.986
— Oakland (A.L.)	OF-DH	25	35	4	8	0	0	0	1	.229	7	4	2	33	0	0	1.000
1991— Phoenix (PCL)■........	OF	81	315	63	107	12	10	2	52	.340	41	36	32	243	5	2	.992
— San Francisco (N.L.) ..	OF	72	222	41	55	5	3	1	15	.248	36	30	13	159	2	0	1.000
1992— San Francisco (N.L.) ..	OF	100	320	38	74	8	1	1	18	.231	29	46	28	225	3	0	1.000
— Phoenix (PCL)	OF	42	158	22	36	5	2	0	6	.228	11	15	9	93	2	0	1.000
1993— San Francisco (N.L.) ..	OF	136	522	84	132	17	7	2	48	.253	30	40	46	344	4	0	•1.000
1994— San Francisco (N.L.) ..	OF	114	451	70	116	15	•9	4	29	.257	53	50	30	279	5	2	.993
1995— San Francisco (N.L.) ..	OF	74	309	47	78	10	3	1	16	.252	17	37	21	200	2	1	.995
— Cincinnati (N.L.)■.......	OF	58	163	19	40	3	0	0	8	.245	17	20	11	121	3	1	.992
1996— Chicago (A.L.)■........	OF	141	337	55	77	12	2	4	53	.228	45	40	21	287	0	3	.990
1997— Chicago (A.L.)	OF-DH	81	77	15	18	1	0	0	5	.234	11	14	11	90	1	0	1.000
— Los Angeles (N.L.)■...	OF	26	77	7	23	3	1	1	10	.299	6	17	3	49	1	1	.980
1998— Boston (A.L.)■..........	OF-DH	155	585	95	157	25	3	8	63	.268	70	94	29	382	6	3	.992
1999— Boston (A.L.)	OF-DH	135	470	63	113	14	6	2	40	.240	45	52	16	309	4	2	.994
2000— Boston (A.L.)	OF-DH	97	270	44	65	12	0	2	17	.241	22	34	10	152	5	3	.981
— GC Red Sox (GCL)	OF	2	6	0	1	0	0	0	1	.167	1	0	1	2	0	0	1.000
2001— Boston (A.L.)	OF-DH	82	164	18	46	9	1	1	12	.280	8	25	5	102	4	0	1.000
American League totals (7 years)		716	1938	294	484	73	12	17	191	.250	208	263	94	1355	20	11	.992
National League totals (6 years)		580	2064	306	518	61	24	10	144	.251	188	240	152	1377	20	5	.996
Major League totals (12 years)		1296	4002	600	1002	134	36	27	335	.250	396	503	246	2732	40	16	.994

DIVISION SERIES RECORD

Year Team (League)	Pos.	G	AB	R	H	2B	3B	HR	RBI	Avg.	BB	SO	SB	PO	A	E	Avg.
1995— Cincinnati (N.L.)	OF-PH	3	3	0	0	0	0	0	0	.000	0	1	0	3	0	0	1.000
1998— Boston (A.L.)	OF	4	14	4	5	2	0	0	0	.357	1	3	1	10	0	0	1.000
1999— Boston (A.L.)	OF	4	16	5	6	1	0	0	2	.375	0	2	1	7	0	0	1.000
Division series totals (3 years)		11	33	9	11	3	0	0	2	.333	1	6	2	20	0	0	1.000

CHAMPIONSHIP SERIES RECORD

Year Team (League)	Pos.	G	AB	R	H	2B	3B	HR	RBI	Avg.	BB	SO	SB	PO	A	E	Avg.
1995— Cincinnati (N.L.)	OF-PR	2	1	0	0	0	0	0	0	.000	0	0	0	2	0	0	1.000
1999— Boston (A.L.)	OF	5	17	2	2	1	0	0	1	.118	1	3	1	7	0	1	.875
Championship series totals (2 years)		7	18	2	2	1	0	0	1	.111	1	3	1	9	0	1	.900

LEWIS, DERRICK   P   BRAVES

PERSONAL: Born May 7, 1976, in Montgomery, Ala. ... 6-5/215. ... Throws right, bats right. ... Full name: Derrick Lamar Lewis.
HIGH SCHOOL: Sidney Lanier (Montgomery, Ala.).
JUNIOR COLLEGE: Central Alabama Community College.
COLLEGE: Florida A&M.
TRANSACTIONS/CAREER NOTES: Selected by Atlanta Braves organization in 20th round of free-agent draft (June 3, 1997). ... On disabled list (August 29-September 20, 1999). ... On disabled list (June 9-September 4, 2001).

Year League	W	L	Pct.	ERA	G	GS	CG	ShO	Sv.	IP	H	R	ER	BB	SO
1997— Danville (Appl.)...................	2	4	.333	6.34	16	9	0	0	0	49²/₃	59	48	35	31	46
1998— Macon (S.Atl.)..................	5	6	.455	3.81	23	23	0	0	0	113¹/₃	108	64	48	55	100
1999— Myrtle Beach (Caro.)	8	4	.667	2.40	24	23	0	0	0	131	100	44	35	*81	102
2000— Greenville (Sou.)	7	9	.438	3.30	27	•27	1	1	0	163²/₃	146	70	60	83	143
2001— Richmond (I.L.)	4	4	.500	4.45	12	12	0	0	0	60²/₃	50	34	30	37	50

LEWIS, MARK   3B/2B

PERSONAL: Born November 30, 1969, in Hamilton, Ohio. ... 6-1/195. ... Bats right, throws right. ... Full name: Mark David Lewis.
HIGH SCHOOL: Hamilton (Ohio).

| | | | | | | | | BATTING | | | | | | | | FIELDING | | |
Year	Team (League)	Pos.	G	AB	R	H	2B	3B	HR	RBI	Avg.	BB	SO	SB	PO	A	E	Avg.
1988—Burlington (Appl.).......	SS	61	227	39	60	13	1	7	43	.264	25	44	14	70	*177	23	.915
1989—Kinston (Caro.)..........	SS	93	349	50	94	16	3	1	32	.269	34	50	17	130	244	32	.921
—Canton/Akron (East.)..	SS	7	25	4	5	1	0	0	1	.200	1	3	0	15	28	2	.956
1990—Canton/Akron (East.)..	SS	102	390	55	106	19	3	10	60	.272	23	49	8	152	286	31	.934
—Colo. Springs (PCL)...	SS	34	124	16	38	8	1	1	21	.306	9	13	2	52	84	11	.925
1991—Colo. Springs (PCL)..	SS-2B-3B	46	179	29	50	10	3	2	31	.279	18	23	3	65	135	10	.952
—Cleveland (A.L.).........	2B-SS	84	314	29	83	15	1	0	30	.264	15	45	2	129	231	9	.976
1992—Cleveland (A.L.).........	SS-3B	122	413	44	109	21	0	5	30	.264	25	69	4	184	336	‡26	.952
1993—Charlotte (I.L.)..........	SS	126	507	93	144	30	4	17	67	.284	34	76	9	168	*403	23	.961
—Cleveland (A.L.).........	SS	14	52	6	13	2	0	1	5	.250	0	7	3	22	31	2	.964
1994—Cleveland (A.L.).........	SS-3B-2B	20	73	6	15	5	0	1	8	.205	2	13	1	17	40	6	.905
—Charlotte (I.L.)..........	SS	86	328	56	85	16	1	8	34	.259	35	48	2	117	199	12	.963
1995—Cincinnati (N.L.)■.......	3B-2B-SS	81	171	25	58	13	1	3	30	.339	21	33	0	19	107	4	.969
1996—Detroit (A.L.)■..........	2B-DH	145	545	69	147	30	3	11	55	.270	42	109	6	264	413	9	.987
1997—San Fran. (N.L.)■.......	3B-2B-DH	118	341	50	91	14	6	10	42	.267	23	62	3	74	157	14	.943
1998—Philadelphia (N.L.)■....	2B	142	518	52	129	21	2	9	54	.249	48	111	3	276	437	16	.978
1999—Cincinnati (N.L.)■.......	3B-2B	88	173	18	44	16	0	6	28	.254	7	24	0	21	55	6	.927
2000—Cincinnati (N.L.)■.......	3B	11	19	1	2	1	0	0	3	.105	1	3	0	2	8	1	.909
—Baltimore (A.L.)■........	3B-2B-SS-DH	71	163	19	44	17	0	2	21	.270	12	31	7	64	105	10	.944
2001—Buffalo (I.L.)■..........	3B-2B	48	184	22	55	10	1	4	29	.299	18	26	0	43	60	12	.896
—Cleveland (A.L.).........	3B-2B	6	13	1	1	0	0	0	0	.077	0	4	0	4	7	1	.917
American League totals (7 years)		462	1573	174	412	90	4	20	149	.262	96	278	23	684	1163	63	.967
National League totals (5 years)		440	1222	146	324	65	9	28	157	.265	100	233	6	392	764	41	.966
Major League totals (11 years)		902	2795	320	736	155	13	48	306	.263	196	511	29	1076	1927	104	.967

DIVISION SERIES RECORD

| | | | | | | | BATTING | | | | | | | | FIELDING | | |
Year	Team (League)	Pos.	G	AB	R	H	2B	3B	HR	RBI	Avg.	BB	SO	SB	PO	A	E	Avg.
1995—Cincinnati (N.L.)	3B-PH	2	2	2	1	0	0	1	5	.500	1	0	0	0	0	1	.000
1997—San Francisco (N.L.) ..	2B	1	5	0	3	0	0	1	1	.600	0	0	0	1	3	0	1.000
Division series totals (2 years)		3	7	2	4	0	0	1	6	.571	1	0	0	1	3	1	.800

CHAMPIONSHIP SERIES RECORD

| | | | | | | | BATTING | | | | | | | | FIELDING | | |
Year	Team (League)	Pos.	G	AB	R	H	2B	3B	HR	RBI	Avg.	BB	SO	SB	PO	A	E	Avg.
1995—Cincinnati (N.L.)	3B	2	4	0	1	0	0	0	0	.250	1	1	0	2	3	0	1.000

LIDGE, BRAD P ASTROS

PERSONAL: Born December 23, 1976, in Sacramento, Calif. ... 6-5/200. ... Throws right, bats right. ... Full name: Brad Thomas Lidge.
COLLEGE: Notre Dame.

Year	League	W	L	Pct.	ERA	G	GS	CG	ShO	Sv.	IP	H	R	ER	BB	SO
1998—Quad City (Midw.)		0	1	.000	3.27	4	4	0	0	0	11	10	5	4	5	6
1999—Kissimmee (FSL)...............		0	2	.000	3.38	6	6	0	0	0	21⅓	13	8	8	11	19
2000—Kissimmee (FSL)...............		2	1	.667	2.81	8	8	0	0	0	41⅔	28	14	13	15	46
2001—Round Rock (Texas)..........		2	0	1.000	1.73	5	5	0	0	0	26	21	5	5	7	42

LIDLE, CORY P ATHLETICS

PERSONAL: Born March 22, 1972, in Hollywood, Calif. ... 5-11/180. ... Throws right, bats right. ... Full name: Cory Fulton Lidle. ... Twin brother of Kevin Lidle, catcher, California Angels organization.
HIGH SCHOOL: South Hills (Covina, Calif.).

Year League	W	L	Pct.	ERA	G	GS	CG	ShO	Sv.	IP	H	R	ER	BB	SO
1991—Gulf Coast Twins (GCL)	1	1	.500	5.79	4	0	0	0	0	4 2/3	5	3	3	0	5
1992—Elizabethton (Appl.)	2	1	.667	3.71	19	2	0	0	6	43 2/3	40	29	18	21	32
1993—Pocatello (Pio.)■	•8	4	.667	4.13	17	16	3	0	1	106 2/3	104	59	49	54	91
1994—Stockton (Calif.)■	1	2	.333	4.43	25	1	0	0	4	42 2/3	60	32	21	13	38
—Beloit (Midw.)	3	4	.429	2.61	13	9	1	1	0	69	65	24	20	11	62
1995—El Paso (Texas)	5	4	.556	3.36	45	9	0	0	2	109 2/3	126	52	41	36	78
1996—Binghamton (East.)■	14	10	.583	3.31	27	27	•6	1	0	*190 1/3	186	78	70	49	141
1997—Norfolk (I.L.)	4	2	.667	3.64	7	7	1	0	0	42	46	20	17	10	34
—New York (N.L.)	7	2	.778	3.53	54	2	0	0	2	81 2/3	86	38	32	20	54
1998—High Desert (Calif.)■	0	0	...	0.00	1	1	0	0	0	2 2/3	2	1	0	2	6
—Tucson (PCL)	0	0	...	0.00	1	1	0	0	0	4 2/3	2	0	0	2	2
1999—St. Petersburg (FSL)■	0	0	...	0.00	2	2	0	0	0	5	2	0	0	2	0
—Durham (I.L.)	0	0	...	4.76	3	2	0	0	0	5 2/3	9	3	3	1	6
—Tampa Bay (A.L.)	1	0	1.000	7.20	5	1	0	0	0	5	8	4	4	2	4
2000—Durham (I.L.)	6	2	.750	2.52	9	9	0	0	0	50	52	15	14	8	44
—Tampa Bay (A.L.)	4	6	.400	5.03	31	11	0	0	0	96 2/3	114	61	54	29	62
2001—Sacramento (PCL)■	1	0	1.000	3.00	1	1	0	0	0	6	6	2	2	3	2
—Oakland (A.L.)	13	6	.684	3.59	29	29	1	0	0	188	170	84	75	47	118
A.L. totals (3 years)	18	12	.600	4.13	65	41	1	0	0	289 2/3	292	149	133	78	184
N.L. totals (1 year)	7	2	.778	3.53	54	2	0	0	2	81 2/3	86	38	32	20	54
Major League totals (4 years)	25	14	.641	4.00	119	43	1	0	2	371 1/3	378	187	165	98	238

DIVISION SERIES RECORD

Year League	W	L	Pct.	ERA	G	GS	CG	ShO	Sv.	IP	H	R	ER	BB	SO
2001—Oakland (A.L.)	0	1	.000	10.80	1	1	0	0	0	3 1/3	5	6	4	3	0

LIEBER, JON — P — CUBS

PERSONAL: Born April 2, 1970, in Council Bluffs, Iowa. ... 6-3/225. ... Throws right, bats left. ... Full name: Jonathan Ray Lieber. ... Name pronounced LEE-ber.

HIGH SCHOOL: Abraham Lincoln (Council Bluffs, Iowa.).

JUNIOR COLLEGE: Iowa Western Community College-Council Bluffs.

COLLEGE: South Alabama.

TRANSACTIONS/CAREER NOTES: Selected by Chicago Cubs organization in ninth round of free-agent draft (June 3, 1991); did not sign. ... Selected by Kansas City Royals organization in second round of free-agent draft (June 1, 1992); pick received as part of compensation for New York Yankees signing Type A free-agent OF Danny Tartabull. ... Traded by Royals with P Dan Miceli to Pittsburgh Pirates for P Stan Belinda (July 31, 1993). ... On disabled list (August 21-September 15, 1998). ... Traded by Pirates to Chicago Cubs for OF Brant Brown (December 14, 1998). ... On disabled list (April 21-May 8, 1999).

STATISTICAL NOTES: Pitched 3-0 one-hit, complete-game victory against Cincinnati (May 24, 2001).

MISCELLANEOUS: Walked in only appearance as pinch hitter (2000). ... Appeared in one game as pinch hitter (2001).

Year League	W	L	Pct.	ERA	G	GS	CG	ShO	Sv.	IP	H	R	ER	BB	SO
1992—Eugene (N'West)	3	0	1.000	1.16	5	5	0	0	0	31	26	6	4	2	23
—Baseball City (FSL)	3	3	.500	4.65	7	6	0	0	0	31	45	20	16	8	19
1993—Wilmington (Caro.)	9	3	.750	2.67	17	16	2	0	0	114 2/3	125	47	34	9	89
—Memphis (Sou.)	2	1	.667	6.86	4	4	0	0	0	21	32	16	16	6	17
—Carolina (Sou.)■	4	2	.667	3.97	6	6	0	0	0	34	39	15	15	10	28
1994—Carolina (Sou.)	2	0	1.000	1.29	3	3	1	1	0	21	13	4	3	2	21
—Buffalo (A.A.)	1	1	.500	1.69	3	3	0	0	0	21 1/3	16	4	4	1	21
—Pittsburgh (N.L.)	6	7	.462	3.73	17	17	1	0	0	108 2/3	116	62	45	25	71
1995—Pittsburgh (N.L.)	4	7	.364	6.32	21	12	0	0	0	72 2/3	103	56	51	14	45
—Calgary (PCL)	1	5	.167	7.01	14	14	0	0	0	77	122	69	60	19	34
1996—Pittsburgh (N.L.)	9	5	.643	3.99	51	15	0	0	1	142	156	70	63	28	94
1997—Pittsburgh (N.L.)	11	14	.440	4.49	33	32	1	0	0	188 1/3	193	102	94	51	160
1998—Pittsburgh (N.L.)	8	14	.364	4.11	29	28	2	0	1	171	182	93	78	40	138
1999—Chicago (N.L.)■	10	11	.476	4.07	31	31	3	1	0	203 1/3	226	107	92	46	186
2000—Chicago (N.L.)	12	11	.522	4.41	35	•35	6	1	0	*251	248	130	123	54	192
2001—Chicago (N.L.)	20	6	.769	3.80	34	34	5	1	0	232 1/3	226	104	98	41	148
Major League totals (8 years)	80	75	.516	4.23	251	204	18	3	2	1369 1/3	1450	724	644	299	1034

ALL-STAR GAME RECORD

RECORDS: Shares record for most home runs allowed in one inning—2 (July 10, 2001, sixth inning).

Year League	W	L	Pct.	ERA	GS	CG	ShO	Sv.	IP	H	R	ER	BB	SO
2001—National	0	0	...	18.00	0	0	0	0	1	3	2	2	0	1

LIEBERTHAL, MIKE — C — PHILLIES

PERSONAL: Born January 18, 1972, in Glendale, Calif. ... 6-0/190. ... Bats right, throws right. ... Full name: Michael Scott Lieberthal. ... Name pronounced LEE-ber-thal.

HIGH SCHOOL: Westlake (Westlake Village, Calif.).

TRANSACTIONS/CAREER NOTES: Selected by Philadelphia Phillies organization in first round (third pick overall) of free-agent draft (June 4, 1990). ... On Scranton/Wilkes-Barre disabled list (August 31, 1992-remainder of season). ... On disabled list (August 22, 1996-remainder of season; July 24-September 2, 1998; July 18-August 4 and September 11, 2000-remainder of season; and May 13, 2001-remainder of season).

HONORS: Won N.L. Gold Glove at catcher (1999).

STATISTICAL NOTES: Tied for N.L. lead with 12 passed balls in 1997. ... Tied for N.L. lead with 11 passed balls in 1999. ... Career major league grand slams: 2.

Year Team (League)	Pos.	G	AB	R	H	2B	3B	HR	RBI	Avg.	BB	SO	SB	PO	A	E	Avg.
1990—Martinsville (Appl.)	C	49	184	26	42	9	0	4	22	.228	11	40	2	421	*52	5	*.990
1991—Spartanburg (S.Atl.)	C	72	243	34	74	17	0	0	31	.305	23	25	1	565	68	10	.984
—Clearwater (FSL)	C	16	52	7	15	2	0	0	7	.288	3	12	0	128	9	1	.993
1992—Reading (East.)	C	86	309	30	88	16	1	2	37	.285	19	26	4	524	48	7	.988
—Scranton/W.B. (I.L.)	C	16	45	4	9	1	0	0	4	.200	2	5	0	86	6	1	.989
1993—Scranton/W.B. (I.L.)	C	112	382	35	100	17	0	7	40	.262	24	32	2	659	75	•11	.985
1994—Scranton/W.B. (I.L.)	C-DH	84	296	23	69	16	0	1	32	.233	21	29	1	472	50	9	.983
—Philadelphia (N.L.)	C	24	79	6	21	3	1	1	5	.266	3	5	0	122	4	4	.969
1995—Philadelphia (N.L.)	C	16	47	1	12	2	0	0	4	.255	5	5	0	95	10	1	.991
—Scranton/W.B. (I.L.)	C-DH-3B	85	278	44	78	20	2	6	42	.281	44	26	1	503	46	5	.991
1996—Philadelphia (N.L.)	C	50	166	21	42	8	0	7	23	.253	10	30	0	284	20	3	.990
1997—Philadelphia (N.L.)	C-DH	134	455	59	112	27	1	20	77	.246	44	76	3	934	73	12	.988
1998—Philadelphia (N.L.)	C	86	313	39	80	15	3	8	45	.256	17	44	2	607	41	8	.988
1999—Philadelphia (N.L.)	C	145	510	84	153	33	1	31	96	.300	44	86	0	881	*62	3	*.997
2000—Philadelphia (N.L.)	C	108	389	55	108	30	0	15	71	.278	40	53	2	724	40	5	.993
2001—Philadelphia (N.L.)	C	34	121	21	28	8	0	2	11	.231	12	21	0	243	9	2	.992
Major League totals (8 years)		597	2080	286	556	126	6	84	332	.267	175	320	7	3890	259	38	.991

ALL-STAR GAME RECORD

Year League	Pos.	AB	R	H	2B	3B	HR	RBI	Avg.	BB	SO	SB	PO	A	E	Avg.
1999—National	C	1	0	0	0	0	0	0	.000	0	0	0	1	0	0	1.000
2000—National	C	2	1	1	0	0	0	0	.500	0	0	0	4	0	0	1.000
All-Star Game totals (2 years)		3	1	1	0	0	0	0	.333	0	0	0	5	0	0	1.000

LIEFER, JEFF   OF/3B   WHITE SOX

PERSONAL: Born August 17, 1974, in Fontana, Calif. ... 6-3/195. ... Bats left, throws right. ... Full name: Jeffery David Liefer.
HIGH SCHOOL: Upland (Calif.).
COLLEGE: Long Beach State.
TRANSACTIONS/CAREER NOTES: Selected by Cleveland Indians organization in sixth round of free-agent draft (June 1, 1992); did not sign. ... Selected by Chicago White Sox organization in first round (25th pick overall) of free-agent draft (June 1, 1995). ... On Charlotte disabled list (August 30, 1999-remainder of season). ... On Chicago disabled list (March 25-April 17, 2000).

Year Team (League)	Pos.	G	AB	R	H	2B	3B	HR	RBI	Avg.	BB	SO	SB	PO	A	E	Avg.
1996—South Bend (Midw.)	DH-3B	74	277	60	90	14	0	15	58	.325	30	62	6	31	62	23	.802
—Prince William (Caro.)	DH	37	147	17	33	6	0	1	13	.224	11	27	0	...	...	...	...
1997—Birmingham (Sou.)	OF-DH	119	474	67	113	24	9	15	71	.238	38	115	2	166	2	•8	.955
1998—Birmingham (Sou.)	1B-DH-OF	127	471	84	137	33	6	21	89	.291	60	125	1	763	60	11	.987
—Calgary (PCL)	OF-DH-1B	8	31	3	8	3	0	1	10	.258	2	12	0	26	3	0	1.000
1999—Chicago (A.L.)	OF-1B-DH	45	113	8	28	7	1	0	14	.248	8	28	2	124	12	0	1.000
—Charlotte (I.L.)	1B-OF-3B	46	171	36	58	17	1	9	34	.339	21	26	2	226	24	3	.988
2000—Chicago (A.L.)	OF-1B	5	11	0	2	0	0	0	0	.182	0	4	0	8	1	1	.900
—Charlotte (I.L.)	1B-OF-3B	120	445	75	125	29	1	32	91	.281	53	107	2	580	80	9	.987
2001—Charlotte (I.L.)	1B-3B	32	119	23	34	7	0	6	21	.286	15	41	3	252	27	3	.989
—Chicago (A.L.)	OF-1B-3B-DH	83	254	36	65	13	0	18	39	.256	20	69	0	159	30	7	.964
Major League totals (3 years)		133	378	44	95	20	1	18	53	.251	28	101	2	291	43	8	.977

LIGTENBERG, KERRY   P   BRAVES

PERSONAL: Born May 11, 1971, in Rapid City, S.D. ... 6-2/215. ... Throws right, bats right. ... Full name: Kerry Dale Ligtenberg. ... Name pronounced Light-en-berg.
HIGH SCHOOL: Park (Cottage Grove, Minn.).
COLLEGE: Minnesota-Morris, then Minnesota.
TRANSACTIONS/CAREER NOTES: Signed by Minneapolis, North Central League (1994). ... Contract sold by Minneapolis to Seattle Mariners organization (March 28, 1995). ... Released by Mariners (April 2, 1995). ... Signed by Minneapolis, Prairie League (1995). ... Contract sold by Minneapolis to Atlanta Braves organization (January 27, 1996). ... On disabled list (April 3, 1999-entire season).

Year League	W	L	Pct.	ERA	G	GS	CG	ShO	Sv.	IP	H	R	ER	BB	SO
1994—Minneapolis (NCL)	5	5	.500	3.31	19	19	2	...	0	114 1/3	103	47	42	44	94
1995—Minneapolis (PRA)	11	2	.846	2.73	17	15	4	...	0	108 2/3	101	41	33	26	100
1996—Durham (Caro.)■	7	4	.636	2.41	49	0	0	0	20	59 2/3	58	20	16	16	76
1997—Greenville (Sou.)	3	1	.750	2.04	31	0	0	0	16	35 1/3	20	8	8	14	43
—Richmond (I.L.)	0	3	.000	4.32	14	0	0	0	1	25	21	13	12	2	35
—Atlanta (N.L.)	1	0	1.000	3.00	15	0	0	0	1	15	12	5	5	4	19
1998—Atlanta (N.L.)	3	2	.600	2.71	75	0	0	0	30	73	51	24	22	24	79
1999—Atlanta (N.L.)							Did not play.								
2000—Atlanta (N.L.)	2	3	.400	3.61	59	0	0	0	12	52 1/3	43	21	21	24	51
—Richmond (I.L.)	0	0	...	0.00	5	0	0	0	1	5 2/3	0	0	0	4	7
2001—Atlanta (N.L.)	3	3	.500	3.02	53	0	0	0	1	59 2/3	50	22	20	30	56
—Richmond (I.L.)	0	0	...	0.00	1	0	0	0	0	1	0	0	0	1	2
Major League totals (4 years)	9	8	.529	3.06	202	0	0	0	44	200	156	72	68	82	205

DIVISION SERIES RECORD

Year League	W	L	Pct.	ERA	G	GS	CG	ShO	Sv.	IP	H	R	ER	BB	SO
1998—Atlanta (N.L.)	0	0	...	0.00	3	0	0	0	0	3 1/3	1	0	0	4	3
2000—Atlanta (N.L.)	0	0	...	5.40	3	0	0	0	0	1 2/3	0	1	1	1	3
2001—Atlanta (N.L.)							Did not play.								
Division series totals (2 years)	0	0	...	1.80	6	0	0	0	0	5	1	1	1	5	6

CHAMPIONSHIP SERIES RECORD

Year League	W	L	Pct.	ERA	G	GS	CG	ShO	Sv.	IP	H	R	ER	BB	SO
1997—Atlanta (N.L.)	0	0	...	0.00	2	0	0	0	0	3	1	0	0	0	4
1998—Atlanta (N.L.)	0	1	.000	7.36	4	0	0	0	0	3 2/3	3	3	3	2	5
2001—Atlanta (N.L.)	0	0	...	0.00	2	0	0	0	0	3	0	0	0	1	2
Champ. series totals (3 years)	0	1	.000	2.79	8	0	0	0	0	9 2/3	4	3	3	3	11

PERSONAL: Born January 4, 1976, in Lameta, Calif. ... 6-0/185. ... Throws left, bats left. ... Full name: Theodore Roosevelt Lilly.
HIGH SCHOOL: Yosemite (Oakhurst, Calif.).
JUNIOR COLLEGE: Fresno (Calif.) City College.
TRANSACTIONS/CAREER NOTES: Selected by Los Angeles Dodgers in 23rd round of free-agent draft (June 4, 1996). ... Traded by Dodgers with 2B Wilton Guerrero, OF Peter Bergeron and 1B Jonathan Tucker to Montreal Expos for P Carlos Perez, SS Mark Grudzielanek and IF Hiram Bocachica (July 31, 1998). ... On Ottawa disabled list (June 21, 1999-remainder of season). ... Traded by Expos to New York Yankees (March 17, 2000), as part of deal in which Yankees traded P Hideki Irabu to Expos for P Jake Westbrook and two players to be named later (December 29, 1999); Yankees acquired P Christian Parker to complete deal (March 22, 2000). ... On New York disabled list (April 2-May 23, 2000); included rehabilitation assignments to Tampa (April 27-May 1) and Columbus (May 2-6 and May 20-23). ... On New York suspended list (August 11-17, 2001).
HONORS: Named California League Pitcher of the Year (1997).
STATISTICAL NOTES: Pitched 8-0 no-hit victory against Lake Elsinore (May 10, 1997). ... Tied for International League lead with four balks in 2000.

Year	League	W	L	Pct.	ERA	G	GS	CG	ShO	Sv.	IP	H	R	ER	BB	SO
1996—	Yakima (N'West)	4	0	1.000	0.84	13	8	0	0	0	53²/₃	25	9	5	14	75
1997—	San Bernardino (Calif.)	7	8	.467	*2.81	23	21	2	1	0	134²/₃	116	52	42	32	158
1998—	San Antonio (Texas)	8	4	.667	3.30	17	17	0	0	0	111²/₃	114	50	41	37	96
	—Albuquerque (PCL)	1	3	.250	4.94	5	5	0	0	0	31	39	20	17	9	25
	—Ottawa (I.L.)■	2	2	.500	4.85	7	7	0	0	0	39	45	28	21	19	49
1999—	Ottawa (I.L.)	8	5	.615	3.84	16	16	0	0	0	89	81	40	38	23	78
	—Montreal (N.L.)	0	1	.000	7.61	9	3	0	0	0	23²/₃	30	20	20	9	28
2000—	Tampa (FSL)■	0	0	...	1.35	1	1	0	0	0	6²/₃	5	3	1	1	6
	—Columbus (I.L.)	8	11	.421	4.19	22	22	3	1	0	137¹/₃	157	77	64	48	127
	—New York (A.L.)	0	0	...	5.63	7	0	0	0	0	8	8	6	5	5	11
2001—	Columbus (I.L.)	0	0	...	2.84	5	5	0	0	0	25¹/₃	16	10	8	8	30
	—New York (A.L.)	5	6	.455	5.37	26	21	0	0	0	120²/₃	126	81	72	51	112
A.L. totals (2 years)		5	6	.455	5.39	33	21	0	0	0	128²/₃	134	87	77	56	123
N.L. totals (1 year)		0	1	.000	7.61	9	3	0	0	0	23²/₃	30	20	20	9	28
Major League totals (3 years)		5	7	.417	5.73	42	24	0	0	0	152¹/₃	164	107	97	65	151

L

PERSONAL: Born September 30, 1972, in Santiago, Dominican Republic. ... 6-2/205. ... Throws right, bats right. ... Full name: Jose D. Lima. ... Name pronounced LEE-mah.
HIGH SCHOOL: Escuela Primaria Las Charcas (Santiago, Dominican Republic).
TRANSACTIONS/CAREER NOTES: Signed as non-drafted free agent by Detroit Tigers organization (July 5, 1989). ... Traded by Tigers with C Brad Ausmus, P C.J. Nitkowski, P Trever Miller and IF Daryle Ward to Houston Astros for OF Brian Hunter, IF Orlando Miller, P Doug Brocail, P Todd Jones and cash (December 10, 1996). ... On suspended list (May 9-15, 2001). ... Traded by Astros to Detroit Tigers for P Dave Mlicki (June 23, 2001).
RECORDS: Shares major league record for most home runs allowed in one inning—4 (April 27, 2000, first inning). ... Holds N.L. single-season record for most home runs allowed—48 (2000). ... Shares N.L. single-inning record for most consecutive home runs allowed—3 (September 17, 1999, fourth inning).
HONORS: Named righthanded pitcher on THE SPORTING NEWS N.L. All-Star team (1999).
STATISTICAL NOTES: Led Florida State League with 14 home runs allowed in 1992. ... Led Eastern League with 13 balks in 1993. ... Pitched 3-0 no-hit victory for Toledo against Pawtucket (August 17, 1994). ... Led N.L. with 48 home runs allowed in 2000.
MISCELLANEOUS: Appeared in one game as third baseman with no chances (1999).

Year	League	W	L	Pct.	ERA	G	GS	CG	ShO	Sv.	IP	H	R	ER	BB	SO
1990—	Bristol (Appl.)	3	8	.273	5.02	14	12	1	0	1	75¹/₃	89	49	42	22	64
1991—	Lakeland (FSL)	0	1	.000	10.38	4	1	0	0	0	8²/₃	16	10	10	2	5
	—Fayetteville (S.Atl.)	1	3	.250	4.97	18	7	0	0	0	58	53	38	32	25	60
1992—	Lakeland (FSL)	5	11	.313	3.16	25	25	5	2	0	151	132	57	53	21	137
1993—	London (East.)	8	•13	.381	4.07	27	27	2	0	0	177	160	96	80	59	138
1994—	Toledo (I.L.)	7	9	.438	3.60	23	22	3	2	0	142¹/₃	124	70	57	48	117
	—Detroit (A.L.)	0	1	.000	13.50	3	1	0	0	0	6²/₃	11	10	10	3	7
1995—	Lakeland (FSL)	3	1	.750	2.57	4	4	0	0	0	21	23	11	6	0	20
	—Toledo (I.L.)	5	3	.625	3.01	11	11	1	0	0	74²/₃	69	26	25	14	40
	—Detroit (A.L.)	3	9	.250	6.11	15	15	0	0	0	73²/₃	85	52	50	18	37
1996—	Toledo (I.L.)	5	4	.556	6.78	12	12	0	0	0	69	93	53	52	12	57
	—Detroit (A.L.)	5	6	.455	5.70	39	4	0	0	3	72²/₃	87	48	46	22	59
1997—	Houston (N.L.)■	1	6	.143	5.28	52	1	0	0	2	75	79	45	44	16	63
1998—	Houston (N.L.)	16	8	.667	3.70	33	33	3	1	0	233¹/₃	229	100	96	32	169
1999—	Houston (N.L.)	21	10	.677	3.58	35	•35	3	0	0	246¹/₃	256	108	98	44	187
2000—	Houston (N.L.)	7	16	.304	6.65	33	33	0	0	0	196¹/₃	251	*152	*145	68	124
2001—	Houston (N.L.)	1	2	.333	7.30	14	9	0	0	0	53	77	48	43	16	41
	—Detroit (A.L.)■	5	10	.333	4.71	18	18	2	0	0	112²/₃	120	66	59	22	43
A.L. totals (4 years)		13	26	.333	5.59	75	38	2	0	3	265²/₃	303	176	165	65	146
N.L. totals (5 years)		46	42	.523	4.77	167	111	6	1	2	804	892	453	426	176	584
Major League totals (8 years)		59	68	.465	4.97	242	149	8	1	5	1069²/₃	1195	629	591	241	730

DIVISION SERIES RECORD

Year	League	W	L	Pct.	ERA	G	GS	CG	ShO	Sv.	IP	H	R	ER	BB	SO
1997—	Houston (N.L.)	0	0	...	0.00	1	0	0	0	0	1	0	0	0	1	1
1998—	Houston (N.L.)							Did not play.								
1999—	Houston (N.L.)	0	1	.000	5.40	1	1	0	0	0	6²/₃	9	4	4	2	4
Division series totals (2 years)		0	1	.000	4.70	2	1	0	0	0	7²/₃	9	4	4	3	5

ALL-STAR GAME RECORD

Year	League	W	L	Pct.	ERA	GS	CG	ShO	Sv.	IP	H	R	ER	BB	SO
1999—	National	0	0	...	0.00	0	0	0	0	1	1	0	0	0	0

LINCOLN, MIKE P PIRATES

PERSONAL: Born April 10, 1975, in Carmichael, Calif. ... 6-2/210. ... Throws right, bats right. ... Full name: Michael George Lincoln.
HIGH SCHOOL: Casa Roble (Orangevale, Calif.).
JUNIOR COLLEGE: American River College (Calif.).
COLLEGE: Tennessee.
TRANSACTIONS/CAREER NOTES: Selected by Minnesota Twins organization in 13th round of free-agent draft (June 4, 1996). ... On Minnesota disabled list (July 23, 2000-remainder of season). ... Released by Twins (January 15, 2001). ... Signed by Pittsburgh Pirates organization (February 17, 2001). ... On Pittsburgh disabled list (August 13-28, 2001).

Year League	W	L	Pct.	ERA	G	GS	CG	ShO	Sv.	IP	H	R	ER	BB	SO
1996— Fort Myers (FSL)	5	2	.714	4.07	12	11	0	0	0	59 2/3	64	31	27	25	24
1997— Fort Myers (FSL)	13	4	.765	2.28	20	20	1	1	0	134	130	41	34	25	75
1998— New Britain (East.)	*15	7	.682	3.22	26	26	1	0	0	173 1/3	180	80	62	35	109
1999— Minnesota (A.L.)	3	10	.231	6.84	18	15	0	0	0	76 1/3	102	59	58	26	27
— Salt Lake (PCL)	5	2	.714	7.78	9	9	0	0	0	59	82	52	51	21	39
2000— Salt Lake (PCL)	4	1	.800	3.87	12	12	2	1	0	74 1/3	72	35	32	16	37
— Minnesota (A.L.)	0	3	.000	10.89	8	4	0	0	0	20 2/3	36	25	25	13	15
2001— Nashville (PCL)■	5	4	.556	3.44	18	13	1	0	0	91 2/3	90	39	35	25	71
— Pittsburgh (N.L.)	2	1	.667	2.68	31	0	0	0	0	40 1/3	34	16	12	11	24
A.L. totals (2 years)	3	13	.188	7.70	26	19	0	0	0	97	138	84	83	39	42
N.L. totals (1 year)	2	1	.667	2.68	31	0	0	0	0	40 1/3	34	16	12	11	24
Major League totals (3 years)	5	14	.263	6.23	57	19	0	0	0	137 1/3	172	100	95	50	66

LINEBRINK, SCOTT P ASTROS

PERSONAL: Born August 4, 1976, in Austin, Texas. ... 6-3/185. ... Throws right, bats right. ... Full name: Scott Cameron Linebrink.
HIGH SCHOOL: McNeil (Austin, Texas).
COLLEGE: Concordia, then Southwest Texas State.
TRANSACTIONS/CAREER NOTES: Selected by San Francisco Giants organization in second round of free-agent draft (June 3, 1997). ... On disabled list (April 8-July 17, 1999). ... Traded by Giants to Houston Astros for P Doug Henry (July 30, 2000).

Year League	W	L	Pct.	ERA	G	GS	CG	ShO	Sv.	IP	H	R	ER	BB	SO
1997— Salem-Kaizer (N'West)	0	0	...	4.50	3	3	0	0	0	10	7	5	5	6	6
— San Jose (Calif.)	2	1	.667	3.18	6	6	0	0	0	28 1/3	29	11	10	10	40
1998— Shreveport (Texas)	10	8	.556	5.22	21	21	0	0	0	113	101	66	63	58	128
1999— Shreveport (Texas)	1	8	.111	6.44	10	10	0	0	0	43 1/3	48	31	31	14	33
2000— Fresno (PCL)	1	4	.200	5.23	28	7	0	0	4	62	54	42	36	12	49
— San Francisco (N.L.)	0	0	...	11.57	3	0	0	0	0	2 1/3	3	3	3	2	0
— Houston (N.L.)■	0	0	...	4.66	8	0	0	0	0	9 2/3	11	5	5	6	6
— New Orleans (PCL)	2	0	1.000	1.80	11	0	0	0	1	15	15	4	3	7	22
2001— Houston (N.L.)	0	0	...	2.61	9	0	0	0	0	10 1/3	6	4	3	6	9
— New Orleans (PCL)	7	6	.538	3.50	50	0	0	0	8	72	52	28	28	24	72
Major League totals (2 years)	0	0	...	4.43	20	0	0	0	0	22 1/3	24	12	11	14	15

LIRA, FELIPE P

PERSONAL: Born April 26, 1972, in Miranda, Venezuela. ... 6-0/170. ... Throws right, bats right. ... Full name: Antonio Felipe Lira.
HIGH SCHOOL: Rafael O. Figueroa (Venezuela).
TRANSACTIONS/CAREER NOTES: Signed as non-drafted free agent by Detroit Tigers organization (February 20, 1990). ... On Lakeland disabled list (April 10-June 10, 1991). ... Traded by Tigers with P Omar Olivares to Seattle Mariners for P Scott Sanders, P Dean Crow and 3B Carlos Villalobos (July 18, 1997). ... Granted free agency (October 15, 1998). ... Re-signed by Tigers organization (November 24, 1998). ... Granted free agency (October 15, 1999). ... Signed by Montreal Expos organization (February 16, 2000). ... Granted free agency (October 10, 2000). ... Re-signed by Expos organization (November 17, 2000). ... Released by Expos (August 16, 2001). ... Signed by Philadelphia Phillies organization (August 25, 2001). ... Granted free agency (October 15, 2001).
STATISTICAL NOTES: Pitched seven-inning, 4-0 no-hit victory against Columbus (May 4, 1994). ... Led International League with 16 wild pitches in 1994.
MISCELLANEOUS: Struck out in only appearance as pinch hitter (2000).

Year League	W	L	Pct.	ERA	G	GS	CG	ShO	Sv.	IP	H	R	ER	BB	SO
1990— Bristol (Appl.)	5	5	.500	2.41	13	10	2	1	1	78 1/3	70	26	21	16	71
— Lakeland (FSL)	0	0	...	5.40	1	0	0	0	0	1 2/3	3	1	1	3	4
1991— Fayetteville (S.Atl.)	5	5	.500	4.66	15	13	0	0	1	73 1/3	79	43	38	19	56
1992— Lakeland (FSL)	11	5	.688	2.39	32	8	2	1	1	109	95	36	29	16	84
1993— London (East.)	10	4	.714	3.38	22	22	2	0	0	152	157	63	57	39	122
— Toledo (I.L.)	1	2	.333	4.60	5	5	0	0	0	31 1/3	32	18	16	11	23
1994— Toledo (I.L.)	7	12	.368	4.70	26	26	1	1	0	151 1/3	171	91	79	45	110
1995— Detroit (A.L.)	9	13	.409	4.31	37	22	0	0	1	146 1/3	151	74	70	56	89
1996— Detroit (A.L.)	6	14	.300	5.22	32	32	3	2	0	194 2/3	204	123	113	66	113
1997— Detroit (A.L.)	5	7	.417	5.77	20	15	1	1	0	92	101	61	59	45	64
— Seattle (A.L.)■	0	4	.000	9.16	8	3	0	0	0	18 2/3	31	21	19	10	9
— Everett (N'West)	1	0	1.000	3.60	1	1	0	0	0	5	6	3	2	2	9
— Tacoma (PCL)	2	0	1.000	3.43	3	3	0	0	0	21	21	8	8	5	17
1998— Tacoma (PCL)	6	8	.429	4.26	20	20	2	1	0	129	142	69	61	42	88
— Seattle (A.L.)	1	0	1.000	4.60	7	0	0	0	0	15 2/3	22	10	8	5	16
1999— Detroit (A.L.)■	0	0	...	10.80	2	0	0	0	0	3 1/3	7	5	4	2	3
— Toledo (I.L.)	2	11	.154	6.71	30	17	0	0	1	114	163	97	85	35	70
2000— Ottawa (I.L.)■	0	3	.000	4.95	4	4	0	0	0	20	24	12	11	3	10
— Montreal (N.L.)	5	8	.385	5.40	53	7	0	0	0	101 2/3	129	71	61	36	51
2001— Ottawa (I.L.)	5	4	.556	2.08	42	0	0	0	6	60 2/3	56	17	14	10	47
— Montreal (N.L.)	0	0	...	12.60	4	0	0	0	0	5	11	7	7	2	3
— Scranton/W.B. (I.L.)■	0	1	.000	5.19	2	2	0	0	0	8 2/3	17	5	5	0	6
A.L. totals (5 years)	21	38	.356	5.22	106	72	4	3	1	470 2/3	516	294	273	184	294
N.L. totals (2 years)	5	8	.385	5.74	57	7	0	0	0	106 2/3	140	78	68	38	54
Major League totals (7 years)	26	46	.361	5.32	163	79	4	3	1	577 1/3	656	372	341	222	348

L

PERSONAL: Born July 11, 1972, in Edwardsville, Ill. ... 6-0/195. ... Bats right, throws right. ... Full name: Mark Travis Little.
HIGH SCHOOL: Edwardsville (Ill.).
COLLEGE: Memphis.
TRANSACTIONS/CAREER NOTES: Selected by Texas Rangers organization in eighth round of free-agent draft (June 2, 1994). ... On disabled list (August 5-September 5, 1996). ... On Oklahoma disabled list (June 23-July 25, 1998). ... Traded by Rangers organization to St. Louis Cardinals organization (August 9, 1998); completing deal in which Cardinals traded P Todd Stottlemyre and SS Royce Clayton to Rangers for P Darren Oliver, 3B Fernando Tatis and a player to be named later (July 31, 1998). ... On Memphis disabled list (April 8-June 9 and June 19-29, 1999). ... On Memphis disabled ist (May 18-June 14, 2000). ... Granted free agency (October 18, 2000). ... Signed by Colorado Rockies organization (November 21, 2000). ... On Colorado disabled list (May 29-August 5 and August 25, 2001-remainder of season); included rehabilitation assignment to Colorado Springs (July 24-August 5).
STATISTICAL NOTES: Led American Association outfielders with 280 putouts and 297 total chances in 1997.

							BATTING								FIELDING		
Year Team (League)	Pos.	G	AB	R	H	2B	3B	HR	RBI	Avg.	BB	SO	SB	PO	A	E	Avg.
1994— Hudson Valley (NY-P.)	OF	54	208	33	61	15	5	3	27	.293	22	38	14	136	3	6	.959
1995— Charlotte (FSL)	OF	115	438	75	112	31	8	9	50	.256	51	108	20	274	8	10	.966
1996— Tulsa (Texas)	OF	101	409	69	119	24	2	13	50	.291	48	88	22	263	9	9	.968
1997— Oklahoma City (A.A.)..	OF-DH-1B	121	415	72	109	23	4	15	45	.263	39	100	21	†282	8	9	.973
1998— Oklahoma (PCL)	OF-DH	69	274	58	81	20	4	8	46	.296	16	60	9	161	6	1	.994
— Memphis (PCL)■	OF	19	63	9	17	3	3	0	6	.270	6	10	0	33	0	1	.971
— St. Louis (N.L.)	OF	7	12	0	1	0	0	0	0	.083	2	5	1	11	0	0	1.000
1999— Memphis (PCL)	OF	51	196	40	58	11	5	3	22	.296	10	48	12	114	6	5	.960
2000— Memphis (PCL)	OF	107	424	70	120	29	7	15	64	.283	51	98	22	253	13	7	.974
2001— Colorado (N.L.)■	OF	51	85	18	29	6	0	3	13	.341	1	20	5	36	3	0	1.000
— Colo. Springs (PCL) ...	OF	9	40	6	15	2	0	0	4	.375	3	9	0	20	2	0	1.000
Major League totals (2 years)		58	97	18	30	6	0	3	13	.309	3	25	6	47	3	0	1.000

PERSONAL: Born April 9, 1967, in Geelong, Victoria, Australia. ... 6-7/225. ... Throws left, bats left. ... Full name: Graeme John Lloyd. ... Name pronounced GRAM.
HIGH SCHOOL: Geelong Technical School (Victoria, Australia).
COLLEGE: Geelong Tech.
TRANSACTIONS/CAREER NOTES: Signed as non-drafted free agent by Toronto Blue Jays organization (January 26, 1988). ... On Myrtle Beach disabled list (June 29-September 1, 1989). ... Selected by Philadelphia Phillies from Blue Jays organization in Rule 5 major league draft (December 7, 1992). ... Traded by Phillies to Milwaukee Brewers for P John Trisler (December 8, 1992). ... On disabled list (August 20-September 4, 1993 and July 25-September 10, 1995). ... On suspended list (September 5-9, 1993). ... Traded by Brewers with OF Pat Listach to New York Yankees for OF Gerald Williams and P Bob Wickman (August 23, 1996). ... On disabled list (April 22-May 8, 1998). ... On suspended list (May 25-27, 1998). ... Traded by Yankees with P David Wells and 2B Homer Bush to Toronto Blue Jays for P Roger Clemens (February 18, 1999). ... Granted free agency (October 29, 1999). ... Signed by Montreal Expos (December 20, 1999). ... On disabled list (March 29, 2000-entire season).

Year League	W	L	Pct.	ERA	G	GS	CG	ShO	Sv.	IP	H	R	ER	BB	SO
1988— Myrtle Beach (S.Atl.)	3	2	.600	3.62	41	0	0	0	2	59 2/3	71	33	24	30	43
1989— Dunedin (FSL)	0	0	...	10.13	2	0	0	0	0	2 2/3	6	3	3	1	0
— Myrtle Beach (S.Atl.)	0	0	...	5.40	1	1	0	0	0	5	5	4	3	0	3
1990— Myrtle Beach (S.Atl.)	5	2	.714	2.72	19	6	0	0	6	49 2/3	51	20	15	16	42
1991— Dunedin (FSL)	2	5	.286	2.24	50	0	0	0	24	60 1/3	54	17	15	25	39
— Knoxville (Sou.)	0	0	...	0.00	2	0	0	0	0	1 2/3	1	0	0	1	2
1992— Knoxville (Sou.)	4	8	.333	1.96	49	7	1	0	14	92	79	30	20	25	65
1993— Milwaukee (A.L.)■	3	4	.429	2.83	55	0	0	0	0	63 2/3	64	24	20	13	31
1994— Milwaukee (A.L.)	2	3	.400	5.17	43	0	0	0	3	47	49	28	27	15	31
1995— Milwaukee (A.L.)	0	5	.000	4.50	33	0	0	0	4	32	28	16	16	8	13
1996— Milwaukee (A.L.)	2	4	.333	2.82	52	0	0	0	0	51	49	19	16	17	24
— New York (A.L.)■	0	2	.000	17.47	13	0	0	0	0	5 2/3	12	11	11	5	6
1997— New York (A.L.)	1	1	.500	3.31	46	0	0	0	1	49	55	24	18	20	26
1998— New York (A.L.)	3	0	1.000	1.67	50	0	0	0	0	37 2/3	26	10	7	6	20
1999— Toronto (A.L.)■	5	3	.625	3.63	74	0	0	0	3	72	68	36	29	23	47
2000— Montreal (N.L.)■							Did not play.								
2001— Montreal (N.L.)	9	5	.643	4.35	84	0	0	0	1	70 1/3	74	38	34	21	44
A.L. totals (7 years)	16	22	.421	3.62	366	0	0	0	11	358	351	168	144	107	198
N.L. totals (1 year)	9	5	.643	4.35	84	0	0	0	1	70 1/3	74	38	34	21	44
Major League totals (8 years)	25	27	.481	3.74	450	0	0	0	12	428 1/3	425	206	178	128	242

DIVISION SERIES RECORD

Year League	W	L	Pct.	ERA	G	GS	CG	ShO	Sv.	IP	H	R	ER	BB	SO
1996— New York (A.L.)	0	0	...	0.00	2	0	0	0	0	1	1	0	0	0	0
1997— New York (A.L.)	0	0	...	0.00	2	0	0	0	0	1 1/3	0	0	0	0	1
1998— New York (A.L.)	0	0	...	0.00	1	0	0	0	0	1/3	0	0	0	0	0
Division series totals (3 years)	0	0	...	0.00	5	0	0	0	0	2 2/3	1	0	0	0	1

CHAMPIONSHIP SERIES RECORD

Year League	W	L	Pct.	ERA	G	GS	CG	ShO	Sv.	IP	H	R	ER	BB	SO
1996— New York (A.L.)	0	0	...	0.00	2	0	0	0	0	1 2/3	0	0	0	0	1
1998— New York (A.L.)	0	0	...	0.00	1	0	0	0	0	2/3	1	0	0	0	0
Champ. series totals (2 years)	0	0	...	0.00	3	0	0	0	0	2 1/3	1	0	0	0	1

WORLD SERIES RECORD

NOTES: Member of World Series championship team (1996 and 1998).

Year League	W	L	Pct.	ERA	G	GS	CG	ShO	Sv.	IP	H	R	ER	BB	SO
1996— New York (A.L.)	1	0	1.000	0.00	4	0	0	0	0	2 2/3	0	0	0	0	4
1998— New York (A.L.)	0	0	...	0.00	1	0	0	0	0	1/3	0	0	0	0	0
World Series totals (2 years)	1	0	1.000	0.00	5	0	0	0	0	3	0	0	0	0	4

Lo DUCA, PAUL   C   DODGERS

PERSONAL: Born April 12, 1972, in Brooklyn, N.Y. ... 5-10/185. ... Bats right, throws right. ... Full name: Paul Anthony Lo Duca.
HIGH SCHOOL: Apollo (Phoenix).
JUNIOR COLLEGE: Glendale (Ariz.) Community College.
COLLEGE: Arizona State.
TRANSACTIONS/CAREER NOTES: Selected by Los Angeles Dodgers organization in 25th round of free-agent draft (June 3, 1993). ... On Albuquerque disabled list (June 4-July 20, 1999). ... On Los Angeles disabled list (April 29-May 21, 2001); included rehabilitation assignment to Las Vegas (May 18-21).
STATISTICAL NOTES: Led Florida State League with .400 on-base percentage in 1996. ... Led Florida State League catchers with 17 errors in 1996. ... Led Texas League catchers with .990 fielding percentage, 84 assists and 667 total chances in 1997. ... Led Pacific Coast League in grounding into double plays with 20 in 1998. ... Collected six hits in one game (May 28, 2001).

| | | | | | | | | | | | | BATTING | | | | FIELDING | | |
Year	Team (League)	Pos.	G	AB	R	H	2B	3B	HR	RBI	Avg.	BB	SO	SB	PO	A	E	Avg.
1993—	Vero Beach (FSL)	C	39	134	17	42	6	0	0	13	.313	13	22	0	209	26	2	.992
1994—	Bakersfield (Calif.)	1B-C	123	455	65	144	32	1	6	68	.316	52	49	16	657	59	5	.993
1995—	San Antonio (Texas)	C-1B-3B	61	199	27	49	8	0	1	8	.246	26	25	5	353	43	11	.973
1996—	Vero Beach (FSL)	C-1B-3B	124	439	54	134	22	0	3	66	.305	70	38	8	747	116	†18	.980
1997—	San Antonio (Texas)	C-1B	105	385	63	126	28	2	7	69	.327	46	27	16	636	†91	7	†.990
1998—	Albuquerque (PCL)	C-1B-3B	126	451	69	144	30	3	8	58	.319	59	40	19	742	92	17	.980
	—Los Angeles (N.L.)	C	6	14	2	4	1	0	0	1	.286	0	1	0	18	2	0	1.000
1999—	Los Angeles (N.L.)	C	36	95	11	22	1	0	3	11	.232	10	9	1	178	21	2	.990
	—Albuquerque (PCL)	C-DH-1B	26	76	17	28	9	0	1	8	.368	10	1	1	162	15	4	.978
2000—	Albuquerque (PCL)	C-0-1-3-2	78	279	47	98	27	3	4	54	.351	33	14	8	364	48	9	.979
	—Los Angeles (N.L.)	C-OF-3B	34	65	6	16	2	0	2	8	.246	6	8	0	122	14	1	.993
2001—	Los Angeles (N.L.)	C-1B-OF-DH	125	460	71	147	28	0	25	90	.320	39	30	2	837	70	9	.990
	—Las Vegas (PCL)	C-1B	3	9	3	3	2	0	0	3	.333	1	0	0	17	2	1	.950
Major League totals (4 years)			201	634	90	189	32	0	30	110	.298	55	48	3	1155	107	12	.991

LOAIZA, ESTEBAN   P   BLUE JAYS

PERSONAL: Born December 31, 1971, in Tijuana, Mexico. ... 6-3/205. ... Throws right, bats right. ... Full name: Esteban Antonio Veyna Loaiza. ... Name pronounced low-EYE-zah.
HIGH SCHOOL: Mar Vista (Imperial Beach, Calif.).
TRANSACTIONS/CAREER NOTES: Signed as non-drafted free agent by Pittsburgh Pirates organization (March 21, 1991). ... Loaned by Pirates organization to Mexico City Red Devils of Mexican League (May 7-28, 1993). ... On disabled list (April 7-28 and July 7-14, 1994). ... Loaned to Red Devils of Mexican League (June 19-August 14, 1996). ... Traded by Pirates to Texas Rangers for P Todd Van Poppel and 2B Warren Morris (July 17, 1998). ... On Texas disabled list (May 12-July 5, 1999); included rehabilitation assignment to Oklahoma City (June 26-July 5). ... Traded by Rangers to Toronto Blue Jays for P Darwin Cubillan and 2B/SS Mike Young (July 19, 2000).
MISCELLANEOUS: Made an out in only appearance as pinch hitter (1995). ... Had a sacrifice hit in only appearance as pinch hitter (1996).

Year	League	W	L	Pct.	ERA	G	GS	CG	ShO	Sv.	IP	H	R	ER	BB	SO
1991—	Gulf Coast Pirates (GCL)	5	1	.833	2.26	11	11	1	•1	0	51 2/3	48	17	13	14	41
1992—	Augusta (S.Atl.)	10	8	.556	3.89	26	25	3	0	0	143 1/3	134	72	62	60	123
1993—	Salem (Caro.)	6	7	.462	3.39	17	17	3	0	0	109	113	53	41	30	61
	—M.C. Red Devils (Mex.)■	1	1	.500	5.18	4	3	0	0	0	24 1/3	32	18	14	4	15
	—Carolina (Sou.)	2	1	.667	3.77	7	7	1	0	0	43	39	18	18	12	40
1994—	Carolina (Sou.)	10	5	.667	3.79	24	24	3	0	0	154 1/3	169	69	65	30	115
1995—	Pittsburgh (N.L.)	8	9	.471	5.16	32	•31	1	0	0	172 2/3	205	*115	*99	55	85
1996—	Calgary (PCL)	3	4	.429	4.02	12	11	1	1	0	69 1/3	61	34	31	25	38
	—M.C. Red Devils (Mex.)■	2	0	1.000	2.43	5	5	0	0	0	33 1/3	28	12	9	14	16
	—Pittsburgh (N.L.)■	2	3	.400	4.96	10	10	1	1	0	52 2/3	65	32	29	19	32
1997—	Pittsburgh (N.L.)	11	11	.500	4.13	33	32	1	0	0	196 1/3	214	99	90	56	122
1998—	Pittsburgh (N.L.)	6	5	.545	4.52	21	14	0	0	0	91 2/3	96	50	46	30	53
	—Texas (A.L.)■	3	6	.333	5.90	14	14	1	0	0	79 1/3	103	57	52	22	55
1999—	Texas (A.L.)	9	5	.643	4.56	30	15	0	0	0	120 1/3	128	65	61	40	77
	—Oklahoma (PCL)	0	0	...	0.00	2	2	0	0	0	4 1/3	3	0	0	3	6
2000—	Texas (A.L.)	5	6	.455	5.37	20	17	0	0	1	107 1/3	133	67	64	31	75
	—Toronto (A.L.)■	5	7	.417	3.62	14	14	1	1	0	92	95	45	37	26	62
2001—	Toronto (A.L.)	11	11	.500	5.02	36	30	1	1	0	190	239	113	106	40	110
A.L. totals (4 years)		33	35	.485	4.89	114	90	3	2	1	589	698	347	320	159	379
N.L. totals (4 years)		27	28	.491	4.63	96	87	3	1	0	513 1/3	580	296	264	160	292
Major League totals (7 years)		60	63	.488	4.77	210	177	6	3	1	1102 1/3	1278	643	584	319	671

DIVISION SERIES RECORD

Year	League	W	L	Pct.	ERA	G	GS	CG	ShO	Sv.	IP	H	R	ER	BB	SO
1998—	Texas (A.L.)					Did not play.										
1999—	Texas (A.L.)	0	1	.000	3.86	1	1	0	0	0	7	5	3	3	1	4

LOCKHART, KEITH   2B   BRAVES

PERSONAL: Born November 10, 1964, in Whittier, Calif. ... 5-10/170. ... Bats left, throws right. ... Full name: Keith Virgil Lockhart.
HIGH SCHOOL: Northview (Covina, Calif.).
JUNIOR COLLEGE: Mount San Antonio College (Calif.).
COLLEGE: Oral Roberts.
TRANSACTIONS/CAREER NOTES: Selected by Cincinnati Reds organization in 11th round of free-agent draft (June 2, 1986). ... Contract sold by Reds organization to Oakland Athletics organization (February 4, 1992). ... Granted free agency (October 15, 1992). ... Signed by St. Louis Cardinals organization (December 12, 1992). ... Granted free agency (October 15, 1993). ... Signed by San Diego Padres organization (January 7, 1994). ... Granted free agency (October 15, 1994). ... Signed by Kansas City Royals organization (November 14, 1994). ...

Traded by Royals with OF Michael Tucker to Atlanta Braves for OF Jermaine Dye and P Jamie Walker (March 27, 1997). ... On disabled list (August 6-22, 1997). ... Granted free agency (November 5, 2001). ... Re-signed by Braves organization (January 8, 2002).

STATISTICAL NOTES: Led Midwest League third basemen with 33 double plays in 1987. ... Led Southern League with 11 sacrifice flies in 1988. ... Led American Association second basemen with 631 total chances in 1989. ... Career major league grand slams: 1.

Year	Team (League)	Pos.	G	AB	R	H	2B	3B	HR	RBI	Avg.	BB	SO	SB	PO	A	E	Avg.
1986—	Billings (Pio.)	2B-3B	53	202	51	70	11	3	7	31	.347	35	22	4	81	150	17	.931
	— Cedar Rapids (Midw.)	2B-3B	13	42	4	8	2	0	0	1	.190	6	6	1	17	15	0	1.000
1987—	Cedar Rapids (Midw.)	3B-2B	*140	511	101	160	37	5	23	84	.313	86	70	20	85	292	28	.931
1988—	Chattanooga (Sou.)....	3B-2B	139	515	74	137	27	3	12	67	.266	61	59	7	102	323	36	.922
1989—	Nashville (A.A.)	2B	131	479	77	128	21	6	14	58	.267	61	41	4	*279	*335	17	.973
1990—	Nashville (A.A.)	2B-3B-OF	126	431	48	112	25	4	9	63	.260	51	74	8	173	248	9	.979
1991—	Nashville (A.A.)	3B-2B-OF	116	411	53	107	25	3	8	36	.260	24	64	3	199	239	11	.976
1992—	Tacoma (PCL)■	3B-2B-SS	107	363	44	101	25	3	5	37	.278	29	21	5	199	239	11	.976
1993—	Louisville (A.A.)■.......	3B-2B-OF-1B	132	467	66	140	24	3	13	68	.300	60	43	3	157	239	12	.971
1994—	San Diego (N.L.)■	3B-2B-SS-OF	27	43	4	9	0	0	2	6	.209	4	10	1	10	21	1	.969
	— Las Vegas (PCL)	O-S-2-3-P-C	89	331	61	106	15	5	7	43	.320	26	37	3	143	113	10	.962
1995—	Omaha (A.A.)■............	3B-DH	44	148	24	56	7	1	5	19	.378	16	10	1	31	72	8	.928
	— Kansas City (A.L.)	2B-3B-DH	94	274	41	88	19	3	6	33	.321	14	21	8	111	178	8	.973
1996—	Kansas City (A.L.)	2B-3B-DH	138	433	49	118	33	3	7	55	.273	30	40	11	137	281	13	.970
1997—	Atlanta (N.L.)■...........	3B-2B-DH	96	147	25	41	5	3	6	32	.279	14	17	0	24	48	3	.960
1998—	Atlanta (N.L.).............	2B-DH-3B	109	366	50	94	21	0	9	37	.257	29	37	2	130	250	6	.984
1999—	Atlanta (N.L.).............	2B-3B-DH	108	161	20	42	3	1	1	21	.261	19	21	3	27	64	1	.989
2000—	Atlanta (N.L.).............	2B-3B	113	275	32	73	12	3	2	32	.265	29	31	4	111	204	8	.975
2001—	Atlanta (N.L.).............	2B-3B	104	178	17	39	6	0	3	12	.219	16	22	1	66	85	0	1.000
American League totals (2 years)			232	707	90	206	52	6	13	88	.291	44	61	19	248	459	21	.971
National League totals (6 years)			557	1170	148	298	47	7	23	140	.255	111	138	11	368	672	19	.982
Major League totals (8 years)			789	1877	238	504	99	13	36	228	.269	155	199	30	616	1131	40	.978

DIVISION SERIES RECORD

Year	Team (League)	Pos.	G	AB	R	H	2B	3B	HR	RBI	Avg.	BB	SO	SB	PO	A	E	Avg.
1997—	Atlanta (N.L.).............	2B	2	6	0	0	0	0	0	0	.000	0	1	0	1	8	1	.900
1998—	Atlanta (N.L.).............	2B	3	12	2	4	0	0	0	0	.333	1	0	0	9	9	0	1.000
1999—	Atlanta (N.L.).............	PH-2B	3	1	0	0	0	0	0	0	.000	0	1	0	0	0	0	...
2000—	Atlanta (N.L.).............	2B	3	8	0	1	0	0	0	0	.125	0	1	0	4	6	0	1.000
2001—	Atlanta (N.L.).............	PH-2B	1	2	1	1	1	0	0	0	.500	0	0	0	0	1	0	1.000
Division series totals (5 years)			12	29	3	6	1	0	0	0	.207	1	3	0	14	24	1	.974

CHAMPIONSHIP SERIES RECORD

Year	Team (League)	Pos.	G	AB	R	H	2B	3B	HR	RBI	Avg.	BB	SO	SB	PO	A	E	Avg.
1997—	Atlanta (N.L.).............	2B-PH	5	16	4	8	1	1	0	3	.500	1	1	0	14	5	0	1.000
1998—	Atlanta (N.L.).............	2B-PH	6	17	2	4	1	1	0	0	.235	0	4	0	5	12	0	1.000
1999—	Atlanta (N.L.).............	PH-2B	3	5	0	2	0	1	0	1	.400	0	2	0	1	3	0	1.000
2001—	Atlanta (N.L.).............	PH	2	1	0	0	0	0	0	0	.000	1	0	0	...	...	...	...
Championship series totals (4 years)			16	39	6	14	2	3	0	4	.359	2	7	0	20	20	0	1.000

WORLD SERIES RECORD

Year	Team (League)	Pos.	G	AB	R	H	2B	3B	HR	RBI	Avg.	BB	SO	SB	PO	A	E	Avg.
1999—	Atlanta (N.L.).............	PH-2B-DH	4	7	1	1	0	0	0	0	.143	2	0	0	1	2	0	1.000

RECORD AS PITCHER

Year	League	W	L	Pct.	ERA	G	GS	CG	ShO	Sv.	IP	H	R	ER	BB	SO
1994—	Las Vegas (PCL)	0	0	...	0.00	1	1	0	0	0	1	0	0	0	0	0

LOEWER, CARLTON   P

PERSONAL: Born September 24, 1973, in Lafayette, La. ... 6-6/211. ... Throws right, bats right. ... Full name: Carlton Edward Loewer.
HIGH SCHOOL: St. Edmund (Eunice, La.).
COLLEGE: Mississippi State.
TRANSACTIONS/CAREER NOTES: Selected by Toronto Blue Jays organization in seventh round of free-agent draft (June 3, 1991); did not sign. ... Selected by Philadelphia Phillies organization in first round (23rd pick overall) of free-agent draft (June 2, 1994). ... On Philadelphia disabled list (June 6-September 6, 1999); included rehabilitation assignments to Gulf Coast League Phillies (August 26-30) and Clearwater (August 31-September 6). ... Traded by Phillies with P Steve Montgomery and P Adam Eaton to San Diego Padres for P Andy Ashby (November 10, 1999). ... On San Diego disabled list (March 28, 2000-remainder of season); included rehabilitation assignments to Las Vegas (May 27-30) and Rancho Cucamonga (May 31-June 12). ... On San Diego disabled list (March 27-May 31, 2001); included rehabilitation assignments to Lake Elsinore (May 4-24) and Portland (May 25-31). ... On Portland disabled list (August 8-29, 2001). ... Granted free agency (October 16, 2001).
STATISTICAL NOTES: Led Eastern League with 24 home runs allowed in 1996.

Year	League	W	L	Pct.	ERA	G	GS	CG	ShO	Sv.	IP	H	R	ER	BB	SO
1995—	Clearwater (FSL)	7	5	.583	3.30	20	20	1	0	0	114 2/3	124	59	42	36	83
	— Reading (East.)	4	1	.800	2.16	8	8	0	0	0	50	42	17	12	31	35
1996—	Reading (East.).................	7	10	.412	5.26	27	27	3	1	0	171	*191	100	57	119	
1997—	Scranton/W.B. (I.L.)	5	13	.278	4.60	29	*29	4	0	0	184	*198	*120	94	50	152
1998—	Scranton/W.B. (I.L.)	7	3	.700	2.87	12	12	*5	*2	0	94	89	34	30	22	69
	— Philadelphia (N.L.)............	7	8	.467	6.09	21	21	1	0	0	122 2/3	154	86	83	39	58
1999—	Philadelphia (N.L.)............	2	6	.250	5.12	20	13	2	1	0	89 2/3	100	54	51	26	48
	— Gulf Coast Phillies (GCL)..	0	0	...	0.00	1	1	0	0	0	2	2	0	0	0	2
	— Clearwater (FSL)	0	2	.000	7.71	3	3	0	0	0	7	10	6	6	1	5

Year	League	W	L	Pct.	ERA	G	GS	CG	ShO	Sv.	IP	H	R	ER	BB	SO
2000— Las Vegas (PCL)■		0	0	...	0.00	1	1	0	0	0	4²/₃	3	0	0	0	4
— Rancho Cuca. (Calif.)		0	0	...	2.57	1	1	0	0	0	7	7	3	2	0	4
2001— Lake Elsinore (Calif.)		0	1	.000	1.59	4	4	0	0	0	11¹/₃	6	7	2	4	14
— Portland (PCL)		5	4	.556	3.87	14	12	0	0	0	81¹/₃	97	42	35	15	64
— San Diego (N.L.)		0	2	.000	24.92	2	2	0	0	0	4¹/₃	13	12	12	3	1
Major League totals (3 years)		**9**	**16**	**.360**	**6.06**	**43**	**36**	**3**	**1**	**0**	**216²/₃**	**267**	**152**	**146**	**68**	**107**

LOFTON, JAMES   SS

PERSONAL: Born March 6, 1974, in Los Angeles. ... 5-10/170. ... Bats both, throws right. ... Full name: James O'Neal Lofton.

HIGH SCHOOL: Fremont (Los Angeles).

JUNIOR COLLEGE: Los Angeles City College.

TRANSACTIONS/CAREER NOTES: Selected by Cincinnati Reds organization in 13th round of free-agent draft (June 3, 1993). ... Released by Reds (October 23, 1997). ... Signed by Tri-City, Western League (1998). ... Signed by Nashua, Atlantic League (2000). ... Signed by Sonoma County, Western League (2001). ... Signed by Boston Red Sox organization (June 1, 2001). ... Granted free agency (October 15, 2001).

STATISTICAL NOTES: Tied for Pioneer League lead in total chances by second basemen with 339 and led with 41 double plays in 1994.

								BATTING							FIELDING		
Year	Team (League)	Pos.	G	AB	R	H	2B	3B	HR	RBI	Avg.	BB	SO	SB	PO	A	E	Avg.
1993— Princeton (Appl.).......		SS	50	174	26	39	4	2	1	13	.224	19	41	11	63	143	23	.900
1994— Billings (Pio.)		2B	66	282	64	91	11	10	4	47	.323	26	46	18	*151	174	14	*.959
1995— Win.-Salem (Caro.)		2B	38	123	15	27	5	1	0	14	.220	8	22	1	74	76	11	.932
— Charl., W.Va. (S.Atl.) ..		2B-OF-3B	65	192	20	40	10	1	0	14	.208	18	43	8	43	67	3	.973
1996— Win.-Salem (Caro.)		2B-3B-OF	82	277	27	62	9	0	3	33	.224	27	55	14	123	145	11	.961
1997— Burlington (Midw.)		2B-3B-OF	129	483	83	128	18	3	4	45	.265	54	89	20	184	286	24	.951
1998— Tri-City (West.)■.......		SS	89	394	69	112	20	3	3	34	.284	22	64	33	...	...	...	...
1999— Tri-City (West.)		SS	87	353	66	105	13	3	2	48	.297	24	40	25	...	...	...	...
2000— Tri-City (West.)		SS	90	389	67	118	20	4	7	52	.303	32	52	*44	...	...	...	...
— Nashua (Atl.)■		SS	22	87	17	21	6	0	3	12	.241	10	19	2	...	...	...	...
2001— Sonoma Cty.(West.)■		SS	12	52	10	11	2	0	0	2	.212	6	11	1	...	5	...	...
— Trenton (East.)■........		SS-3B-2B	29	111	22	35	7	0	5	11	.315	10	23	3	39	59	5	.951
— Pawtucket (I.L.)..........		SS	42	151	19	48	8	0	6	13	.318	10	29	3	49	125	10	.946
— Boston (A.L.)............		SS	8	26	1	5	1	0	0	1	.192	1	4	2	9	14	2	.920
Major League totals (1 year)			**8**	**26**	**1**	**5**	**1**	**0**	**0**	**1**	**.192**	**1**	**4**	**2**	**9**	**14**	**2**	**.920**

LOFTON, KENNY   OF

PERSONAL: Born May 31, 1967, in East Chicago, Ind. ... 6-0/190. ... Bats left, throws left. ... Full name: Kenneth Lofton.

HIGH SCHOOL: Washington (East Chicago, Ind.).

COLLEGE: Arizona.

TRANSACTIONS/CAREER NOTES: Selected by Houston Astros organization in 17th round of free-agent draft (June 1, 1988). ... Traded by Astros with IF Dave Rohde to Cleveland Indians for P Willie Blair and C Eddie Taubensee (December 10, 1991). ... On disabled list (July 17-August 1, 1995). ... Traded by Indians with P Alan Embree to Atlanta Braves for OF Marquis Grissom and OF Dave Justice (March 25, 1997). ... On disabled list (June 18-July 5 and July 6-28, 1997). ... Granted free agency (October 28, 1997). ... Signed by Indians (December 8, 1997). ... On disabled list (July 28-August 14 and August 17-September 1, 1999; April 30-May 12, 2000; and May 16-June 1, 2001). ... Granted free agency (November 5, 2001).

RECORDS: Holds A.L. rookie-season record for most stolen bases—66 (1992). ... Shares A.L. single-season record for fewest errors by outfielder who led league in errors—8 (1998). ... Shares A.L. record for most consecutive games scoring one or more runs—18 (26 runs, August 15-September 3, 2000).

HONORS: Won A.L. Gold Glove as outfielder (1993-96).

STATISTICAL NOTES: Tied for Pacific Coast League lead in caught stealing with 23 in 1991. ... Led Pacific Coast League outfielders with 344 total chances in 1991. ... Led N.L. in caught stealing with 20 in 1997. ... Career major league grand slams: 2.

MISCELLANEOUS: Holds Cleveland Indians all-time record for most stolen bases (450).

								BATTING							FIELDING		
Year	Team (League)	Pos.	G	AB	R	H	2B	3B	HR	RBI	Avg.	BB	SO	SB	PO	A	E	Avg.
1988— Auburn (NY-Penn)......		OF	48	187	23	40	6	1	1	14	.214	19	51	26	94	5	4	.961
1989— Auburn (NY-Penn)......		OF	34	110	21	29	3	1	0	8	.264	14	30	26	37	4	8	.837
— Asheville (S.Atl.)........		OF	22	82	14	27	2	0	1	9	.329	12	10	14	38	1	2	.951
1990— Osceola (FSL)..........		OF	124	481	98	*159	15	5	2	35	.331	61	77	62	246	13	7	.974
1991— Tucson (PCL)		OF	130	*545	93	*168	19	*17	2	50	.308	52	95	40	*308	*27	9	.974
— Houston (N.L.)		OF	20	74	9	15	1	0	0	0	.203	5	19	2	41	1	1	.977
1992— Cleveland (A.L.)■......		OF	148	576	96	164	15	8	5	42	.285	68	54	*66	420	14	8	.982
1993— Cleveland (A.L.).........		OF	148	569	116	185	28	8	1	42	.325	81	83	*70	402	11	•9	.979
1994— Cleveland (A.L.).........		OF	112	459	105	*160	32	9	12	57	.349	52	56	*60	276	•13	2	.993
1995— Cleveland (A.L.).........		OF-DH	118	481	93	149	22	*13	7	53	.310	40	49	*54	248	11	•8	.970
1996— Cleveland (A.L.).........		OF	154	*662	132	210	35	4	14	67	.317	61	82	*75	376	13	10	.975
1997— Atlanta (N.L.)■..........		OF	122	493	90	164	20	6	5	48	.333	64	83	27	290	5	5	.983
1998— Cleveland (A.L.)■.......		OF	154	600	101	169	31	6	12	64	.282	87	80	54	339	*19	•8	.978
1999— Cleveland (A.L.).........		OF-DH	120	465	110	140	28	6	7	39	.301	79	84	25	255	11	3	.989
2000— Cleveland (A.L.).........		OF-DH	137	543	107	151	23	5	15	73	.278	79	72	30	348	4	4	.989
2001— Cleveland (A.L.).........		OF	133	517	91	135	21	4	14	66	.261	47	69	16	310	3	6	.981
American League totals (9 years)			**1224**	**4872**	**951**	**1463**	**235**	**63**	**87**	**503**	**.300**	**594**	**629**	**450**	**2974**	**99**	**58**	**.981**
National League totals (2 years)			**142**	**567**	**99**	**179**	**21**	**6**	**5**	**48**	**.316**	**69**	**102**	**29**	**331**	**6**	**6**	**.983**
Major League totals (11 years)			**1366**	**5439**	**1050**	**1642**	**256**	**69**	**92**	**551**	**.302**	**663**	**731**	**479**	**3305**	**105**	**64**	**.982**

DIVISION SERIES RECORD

Year Team (League)	Pos.	G	AB	R	H	2B	3B	HR	RBI	Avg.	BB	SO	SB	PO	A	E	Avg.
1995—Cleveland (A.L.).........	OF	3	13	1	2	0	0	0	0	.154	1	3	0	9	0	2	.818
1996—Cleveland (A.L.).........	OF	4	18	3	3	0	0	0	1	.167	2	3	5	10	0	0	1.000
1997—Atlanta (N.L.).............	OF	3	13	2	2	1	0	0	0	.154	1	2	0	6	1	0	1.000
1998—Cleveland (A.L.).........	OF	4	16	5	6	1	0	2	4	.375	1	1	2	10	0	0	1.000
1999—Cleveland (A.L.).........	OF	5	16	5	2	1	0	0	1	.125	5	6	2	14	0	1	.933
2001—Cleveland (A.L.).........	OF	5	19	2	2	0	0	1	3	.105	3	5	0	9	0	0	1.000
Division series totals (6 years)		24	95	18	17	3	0	3	9	.179	13	20	9	58	1	3	.952

CHAMPIONSHIP SERIES RECORD

Year Team (League)	Pos.	G	AB	R	H	2B	3B	HR	RBI	Avg.	BB	SO	SB	PO	A	E	Avg.
1995—Cleveland (A.L.).........	OF	6	24	4	11	0	2	0	3	.458	4	6	5	15	0	0	1.000
1997—Atlanta (N.L.).............	OF	6	27	3	5	0	1	0	1	.185	1	7	1	9	1	2	.833
1998—Cleveland (A.L.).........	OF	6	27	2	5	1	0	1	3	.185	1	7	1	8	0	1	.889
Championship series totals (3 years)		18	78	9	21	1	3	1	7	.269	6	20	7	32	1	3	.917

WORLD SERIES RECORD

RECORDS: Shares single-inning record for most stolen bases—2 (October 21, 1995, first inning).

Year Team (League)	Pos.	G	AB	R	H	2B	3B	HR	RBI	Avg.	BB	SO	SB	PO	A	E	Avg.
1995—Cleveland (A.L.).........	OF	6	25	6	5	0	0	0	0	.200	3	1	6	12	0	0	1.000

ALL-STAR GAME RECORD

RECORDS: Shares single-game record for most stolen bases—2 (July 9, 1996).

Year League	Pos.	AB	R	H	2B	3B	HR	RBI	Avg.	BB	SO	SB	PO	A	E	Avg.
1994—American..................	OF	2	0	1	0	0	0	2	.500	0	1	1	1	0	0	1.000
1995—American..................	OF	3	0	0	0	0	0	0	.000	0	1	0	0	0	0	...
1996—American..................	OF	3	0	2	0	0	0	0	.667	0	0	2	0	0	0	...
1997—National...................						Selected, did not play—injured.										
1998—American..................	OF	3	0	1	0	0	0	0	.333	1	0	1	2	0	0	1.000
1999—American..................	OF	3	1	1	0	0	0	0	.333	0	1	1	0	0	0	...
All-Star Game totals (5 years)		14	1	5	0	0	0	2	.357	1	3	5	3	0	0	1.000

LOHSE, KYLE   P   TWINS

PERSONAL: Born October 4, 1978, in Chico, Calif. ... 6-2/190. ... Throws right, bats right. ... Full name: Kyle Matthew Lohse.
HIGH SCHOOL: Hamilton Union (Hamilton City, Calif.).
COLLEGE: Butte (Calif.).
TRANSACTIONS/CAREER NOTES: Selected by Chicago Cubs organization in 29th round of free-agent draft (June 4, 1996). ... Traded with P Jason Ryan by Cubs to Minnesota Twins for P Rick Aguilera and P Scott Downs (May 21, 1999).

Year League	W	L	Pct.	ERA	G	GS	CG	ShO	Sv.	IP	H	R	ER	BB	SO
1997—Arizona Cubs (Ariz.)..........	2	2	.500	3.02	12	11	0	0	0	47²/₃	46	22	16	22	49
1998—Rockford (Midw.)..............	13	8	.619	3.22	28	26	3	1	0	170²/₃	158	76	61	45	121
1999—Daytona (FSL)	5	3	.625	2.89	9	9	1	1	0	53	48	21	17	16	41
—Fort Myers (FSL)■..............	2	3	.400	5.18	7	7	0	0	0	41²/₃	47	28	24	9	33
—New Britain (East.)	3	4	.429	5.89	11	11	1	0	0	70¹/₃	87	49	46	23	41
2000—New Britain (East.)	3	*18	.143	6.04	28	28	0	0	0	167	•196	*123	*112	55	124
2001—New Britain (East.)	3	1	.750	2.37	6	6	0	0	0	38	32	10	10	4	32
—Edmonton (PCL)	4	2	.667	3.12	8	8	1	1	0	49	50	21	17	13	48
—Minnesota (A.L.)	4	7	.364	5.68	19	16	0	0	0	90¹/₃	102	60	57	29	64
Major League totals (1 year)........	4	7	.364	5.68	19	16	0	0	0	90¹/₃	102	60	57	29	64

LOISELLE, RICH   P

PERSONAL: Born January 12, 1972, in Neenah, Wis. ... 6-5/245. ... Throws right, bats right. ... Full name: Richard Frank Loiselle.
HIGH SCHOOL: Lawton (Okla.).
JUNIOR COLLEGE: Odessa (Texas) College.
TRANSACTIONS/CAREER NOTES: Selected by San Diego Padres organization in 38th round of free-agent draft (June 3, 1991). ... Traded by Padres with P Jeff Tabaka to Houston Astros for OF Phil Plantier (July 19, 1995). ... On Tucson disabled list (August 2, 1995-remainder of season). ... Traded by Astros to Pittsburgh Pirates for P Danny Darwin (July 23, 1996). ... On Pittsburgh disabled list (July 20-August 17, 1998); included rehabilitation assignment to Nashville (August 7-16). ... On disabled list (May 8, 1999-remainder of season). ... On Pittsburgh disabled list (April 2-May 22 and June 25-August 3, 2000); included rehabilitation assignments to Altoona (April 26-May 21 and July 22-25), Gulf Coast Pirates (July 18-21) and Nashville (July 25-August 2). ... On Pittsburgh disabled list (March 31-June 12, 2001); included rehabilitation assignment to Nashville (May 11-June 12). ... Granted free agency (October 15, 2001).

Year League	W	L	Pct.	ERA	G	GS	CG	ShO	Sv.	IP	H	R	ER	BB	SO
1991—Arizona Padres (Ariz.)	2	3	.400	3.52	12	12	0	0	0	61¹/₃	72	40	24	26	47
1992—Charleston, S.C. (S.Atl.)	4	8	.333	3.71	19	19	2	2	0	97	93	51	40	42	64
1993—Waterloo (Midw.)	1	5	.167	3.94	14	10	1	1	0	59¹/₃	55	28	26	29	47
—Rancho Cuca. (Calif.)	5	8	.385	5.77	14	14	1	0	0	82²/₃	109	64	53	34	53
1994—Rancho Cuca. (Calif.)	9	10	.474	3.96	27	27	0	0	0	156²/₃	160	83	69	76	120
1995—Memphis (Sou.)	6	3	.667	3.55	13	13	1	0	0	78²/₃	82	46	31	33	48
—Las Vegas (PCL)	2	2	.500	7.24	8	7	1	1	0	27¹/₃	36	27	22	9	16
—Tucson (PCL)■..................	0	0	...	2.61	2	1	0	0	0	10¹/₃	8	4	3	4	4

Year	League	W	L	Pct.	ERA	G	GS	CG	ShO	Sv.	IP	H	R	ER	BB	SO
1996—	Jackson (Texas)	7	4	.636	3.47	16	16	2	0	0	98²/₃	107	46	38	27	65
—	Tucson (PCL)	2	2	.500	2.43	5	5	1	1	0	33¹/₃	28	20	9	11	31
—	Calgary (PCL)■.............	2	2	.500	4.09	8	8	0	0	0	50²/₃	64	28	23	16	41
—	Pittsburgh (N.L.)	1	0	1.000	3.05	5	3	0	0	0	20²/₃	22	8	7	8	9
1997—	Pittsburgh (N.L.)	1	5	.167	3.10	72	0	0	0	29	72²/₃	76	29	25	24	66
1998—	Pittsburgh (N.L.)	2	7	.222	3.44	54	0	0	0	19	55	56	26	21	36	48
—	Nashville (PCL)	0	0	...	0.00	4	0	0	0	2	5	3	0	0	0	6
1999—	Pittsburgh (N.L.)	3	2	.600	5.28	13	0	0	0	0	15¹/₃	16	9	9	9	14
2000—	Altoona (East.)	0	1	.000	5.27	13	0	0	0	0	13²/₃	17	9	8	6	18
—	Pittsburgh (N.L.)	2	3	.400	5.10	40	0	0	0	0	42¹/₃	43	27	24	30	32
—	Gulf Coast Pirates (GCL)....	0	0	...	0.00	1	1	0	0	0	1	0	0	0	0	2
—	Nashville (PCL)	0	0	...	0.00	4	0	0	0	0	4²/₃	2	0	0	2	3
2001—	Nashville (PCL)	0	2	.000	6.15	26	1	0	0	0	33²/₃	33	24	23	23	18
—	Pittsburgh (N.L.)	0	1	.000	11.50	18	0	0	0	1	18	28	24	23	17	9
Major League totals (6 years)		**9**	**18**	**.333**	**4.38**	**202**	**3**	**0**	**0**	**49**	**224**	**241**	**123**	**109**	**124**	**178**

LOMASNEY, STEVE   C   RED SOX

PERSONAL: Born August 29, 1977, in Melrose, Mass. ... 6-0/195. ... Bats right, throws right. ... Full name: Steven James Lomasney.
HIGH SCHOOL: Peabody (Mass.).
TRANSACTIONS/CAREER NOTES: Selected by Boston Red Sox organization in fifth round of free-agent draft (June 1, 1995). ... On Sarasota disabled list (April 8-17 and June 10-21, 1999). ... On Trenton disabled list (April 30-June 7, 2001). ... On Pawtucket disabled list (August 17, 2001-remainder of season). ... Granted free agency (December 21, 2001). ... Re-signed by Red Sox organization (December 21, 2001).
STATISTICAL NOTES: Led New York-Pennsylvania League catchers with 21 passed balls in 1996.

								BATTING						FIELDING		
Year	Team (League)	Pos.	G	AB	R	H	2B	3B	HR	RBI	Avg.	BB	SO	SB	PO	A	E	Avg.
1995—	GC Red Sox (GCL)	C	29	92	10	15	6	0	0	7	.163	8	16	2	146	29	5	.972
1996—	Lowell (NY-Penn)	C	59	173	26	24	10	0	4	21	.139	42	63	2	402	47	9	.980
1997—	Michigan (Midw.)	C	102	324	50	89	27	3	12	51	.275	32	98	3	623	83	12	.983
1998—	Sarasota (FSL)	C-1B	122	443	74	106	22	1	22	63	.239	59	145	13	590	79	13	.981
1999—	Sarasota (FSL)	C-DH-1B	55	189	35	51	10	0	8	28	.270	26	57	5	284	46	9	.973
—	Trenton (East.)	C-DH	47	151	24	37	6	0	12	31	.245	31	44	7	355	33	12	.970
—	Boston (A.L.)	C	1	2	0	0	0	0	0	0	.000	0	2	0	7	2	0	1.000
2000—	Trenton (East.)	C-O-1-3-2	66	233	30	57	16	.1	8	27	.245	24	81	4	418	35	6	.987
—	GC Red Sox (GCL)	C	6	15	2	4	2	0	0	1	.267	4	6	0	37	6	2	.956
2001—	Trenton (East.)	C	58	209	24	52	14	2	10	29	.249	23	76	0	399	48	6	.987
—	Pawtucket (I.L.)..........	C	17	63	10	18	4	0	2	9	.286	4	21	2	121	2	4	.969
Major League totals (1 year)			**1**	**2**	**0**	**0**	**0**	**0**	**0**	**0**	**.000**	**0**	**2**	**0**	**7**	**2**	**0**	**1.000**

LONG, TERRENCE   OF   ATHLETICS

PERSONAL: Born February 29, 1976, in Montgomery, Ala. ... 6-1/190. ... Bats left, throws left. ... Full name: Terrence Deon Long.
HIGH SCHOOL: Stanhope Elmore (Millbrook, Ala.).
TRANSACTIONS/CAREER NOTES: Selected by New York Mets organization in first round (20th pick overall) of free-agent draft (June 2, 1994); pick received as compensation for Baltimore Orioles signing Type A free-agent P Sid Fernandez. ... On disabled list (May 15-27, 1996). ... Traded by Mets with P Leo Vasquez to Oakland Athletics for P Kenny Rogers (July 23, 1999).
STATISTICAL NOTES: Had 17-game hitting streak (June 10-29, 2000). ... Career major league grand slams: 1.

								BATTING						FIELDING		
Year	Team (League)	Pos.	G	AB	R	H	2B	3B	HR	RBI	Avg.	BB	SO	SB	PO	A	E	Avg.
1994—	Kingsport (Appl.)........	OF-1B	60	215	39	50	9	2	12	39	.233	32	52	9	237	5	5	.980
1995—	Capital City (S.Atl.)......	OF	55	178	27	35	1	2	2	13	.197	28	43	8	69	5	5	.937
—	Pittsfield (NY-Penn)....	OF	51	187	24	48	9	4	4	31	.257	18	36	11	111	3	1	*.991
1996—	Columbia (S.Atl.)........	OF-DH	123	473	66	136	26	9	12	78	.288	36	120	32	246	8	5	.981
1997—	St. Lucie (FSL)...........	OF-DH	126	470	52	118	29	7	8	61	.251	40	102	24	235	7	7	.972
1998—	Binghamton (East.)	OF-DH	130	455	69	135	20	*10	16	58	.297	62	105	23	218	9	10	.958
1999—	Norfolk (I.L.).............	OF	78	304	41	99	20	4	7	47	.326	23	41	14	192	8	4	.980
—	New York (N.L.)..........	PH	3	3	0	0	0	0	0	0	.000	0	2	0	0	0	0	...
—	Vancouver (PCL)■.....	OF-DH	40	154	16	38	6	2	2	21	.247	10	29	7	95	3	4	.961
2000—	Sacramento (PCL)......	OF	15	60	11	24	6	0	3	15	.400	4	4	0	28	0	3	.903
—	Oakland (A.L.)	OF	138	584	104	168	34	4	18	80	.288	43	77	5	328	2	•10	.971
2001—	Oakland (A.L.)	OF	162	629	90	178	37	4	12	85	.283	52	103	9	332	5	7	.980
American League totals (2 years)			**300**	**1213**	**194**	**346**	**71**	**8**	**30**	**165**	**.285**	**95**	**180**	**14**	**660**	**7**	**17**	**.975**
National League totals (1 year)			**3**	**3**	**0**	**0**	**0**	**0**	**0**	**0**	**.000**	**0**	**2**	**0**	**0**	**0**	**0**	**...**
Major League totals (3 years)			**303**	**1216**	**194**	**346**	**71**	**8**	**30**	**165**	**.285**	**95**	**182**	**14**	**660**	**7**	**17**	**.975**

DIVISION SERIES RECORD

RECORDS: Shares single-game record for most home runs—2 (October 10, 2001).

								BATTING						FIELDING		
Year	Team (League)	Pos.	G	AB	R	H	2B	3B	HR	RBI	Avg.	BB	SO	SB	PO	A	E	Avg.
2000—	Oakland (A.L.)	OF	5	19	2	3	0	0	1	1	.158	3	2	0	11	1	1	.923
2001—	Oakland (A.L.)	OF	5	18	3	7	3	0	2	3	.389	1	2	0	7	1	0	1.000
Division series totals (2 years)			**10**	**37**	**5**	**10**	**3**	**0**	**3**	**4**	**.270**	**4**	**4**	**0**	**18**	**2**	**1**	**.952**

LOOPER, BRADEN   P   MARLINS

PERSONAL: Born October 28, 1974, in Weatherford, Okla. ... 6-5/225. ... Throws right, bats right. ... Full name: Braden LaVern Looper. ... Name pronounced BRAY-dun.
HIGH SCHOOL: Mangum (Okla.).
COLLEGE: Wichita State.

TRANSACTIONS/CAREER NOTES: Selected by St. Louis Cardinals organization in first round (third pick overall) of free-agent draft (June 2, 1996). ... On Memphis disabled list (May 6-June 21, 1998). ... Traded by Cardinals with P Armando Almanza and SS Pablo Ozuna to Florida Marlins for SS Edgar Renteria (December 14, 1998).

MISCELLANEOUS: Member of 1996 U.S. Olympic baseball team.

Year League	W	L	Pct.	ERA	G	GS	CG	ShO	Sv.	IP	H	R	ER	BB	SO
1997— Prince William (Caro.)	3	6	.333	4.48	12	12	0	0	0	64 1/3	71	38	32	25	58
— Arkansas (Texas)	1	4	.200	5.91	19	0	0	0	5	21 1/3	24	14	14	7	20
1998— St. Louis (N.L.)	0	1	.000	5.40	4	0	0	0	0	3 1/3	5	4	2	1	4
— Memphis (PCL)	2	3	.400	3.10	40	0	0	0	20	40 2/3	43	16	14	13	43
1999— Florida (N.L.)■	3	3	.500	3.80	72	0	0	0	0	83	96	43	35	31	50
2000— Florida (N.L.)	5	1	.833	4.41	73	0	0	0	2	67 1/3	71	41	33	36	29
2001— Florida (N.L.)	3	3	.500	3.55	71	0	0	0	3	71	63	28	28	30	52
Major League totals (4 years)	11	8	.579	3.93	220	0	0	0	5	224 2/3	235	116	98	98	135

LOPEZ, ALBIE   P   BRAVES

PERSONAL: Born August 18, 1971, in Mesa, Ariz. ... 6-2/240. ... Throws right, bats right. ... Full name: Albert Anthony Lopez.
HIGH SCHOOL: Westwood (Mesa, Ariz.).
JUNIOR COLLEGE: Mesa (Ariz.) Community College.
TRANSACTIONS/CAREER NOTES: Selected by San Francisco Giants organization in 46th round of free-agent draft (June 5, 1989); did not sign. ... Selected by Seattle Mariners organization in 19th round of free-agent draft (June 4, 1990); did not sign. ... Selected by Cleveland Indians organization in 20th round of free-agent draft (June 3, 1991). ... On Cleveland disabled list (July 2-28 and August 13-September 1, 1997). ... Selected by Tampa Bay Devil Rays in second round (48th pick overall) of expansion draft (November 18, 1997). ... On Tampa Bay disabled list (August 1-26, 1998); included rehabilitation assignments to Durham (August 15-18) and St. Petersburg (August 25-26). ... On Tampa Bay disabled list (May 12-June 20, 1999); included rehabilitation assignment to St. Petersburg (June 14-20). ... Traded by Devil Rays with C Mike Difelice to Arizona Diamondbacks for OF Jason Conti and P Nick Bierbrodt (July 25, 2001). ... Granted free agency (November 6, 2001). ... Signed by Atlanta Braves (December 20, 2001).
STATISTICAL NOTES: Led American Association with 10 hit batsmen and tied for lead with three balks in 1996.
MISCELLANEOUS: Holds Tampa Bay Devil Rays all-time record for most wins (26). ... Shares Tampa Bay Devil Rays all-time record for most shutouts (2).

Year League	W	L	Pct.	ERA	G	GS	CG	ShO	Sv.	IP	H	R	ER	BB	SO
1991— Burlington (Appl.)	4	5	.444	3.44	13	13	0	0	0	73 1/3	61	33	28	23	81
1992— Columbus (S.Atl.)	7	2	.778	2.88	16	16	1	0	0	97	80	41	31	33	117
— Kinston (Caro.)	5	2	.714	3.52	10	10	1	1	0	64	56	28	25	26	44
1993— Canton/Akron (East.)	9	4	.692	3.11	16	16	2	0	0	110	79	44	38	47	80
— Cleveland (A.L.)	3	1	.750	5.98	9	9	0	0	0	49 2/3	49	34	33	32	25
— Charlotte (I.L.)	1	0	1.000	2.25	3	2	0	0	0	12	8	3	3	2	7
1994— Charlotte (I.L.)	13	3	.813	3.94	22	22	3	0	0	144	136	68	63	42	105
— Cleveland (A.L.)	1	2	.333	4.24	4	4	1	1	0	17	20	11	8	6	18
1995— Buffalo (A.A.)	5	10	.333	4.44	18	18	1	1	0	101 1/3	101	57	50	51	82
— Cleveland (A.L.)	0	0	...	3.13	6	2	0	0	0	23	17	8	8	7	22
1996— Buffalo (A.A.)	10	2	*.833	3.87	17	17	2	0	0	104 2/3	90	54	45	40	89
— Cleveland (A.L.)	5	4	.556	6.39	13	10	0	0	0	62	80	47	44	22	45
1997— Cleveland (A.L.)	3	7	.300	6.93	37	6	0	0	0	76 2/3	101	61	59	40	63
— Buffalo (A.A.)	1	0	1.000	0.00	7	0	0	0	1	11 1/3	6	0	0	2	13
— Akron (East.)	0	0	...	0.00	1	0	0	0	0	1	2	0	0	0	2
1998— Tampa Bay (A.L.)■	7	4	.636	2.60	54	0	0	0	1	79 2/3	73	31	23	32	62
— Durham (I.L.)	0	0	...	0.00	2	0	0	0	0	3	4	0	0	1	2
— St. Petersburg (FSL)	0	1	.000	18.00	1	1	0	0	0	1	2	2	2	0	1
1999— Tampa Bay (A.L.)	3	2	.600	4.64	51	0	0	0	1	64	66	40	33	24	37
— St. Petersburg (FSL)	0	0	...	5.40	2	1	0	0	0	3 1/3	7	5	2	0	3
2000— Tampa Bay (A.L.)	11	13	.458	4.13	45	24	4	1	2	185 1/3	199	95	85	70	96
— Princeton (Appl.)	0	0	...	0.00	1	0	0	0	0	2/3	0	0	0	0	1
2001— Tampa Bay (A.L.)	5	12	.294	5.34	20	20	1	1	0	124 2/3	152	87	74	51	67
— Arizona (N.L.)■	4	7	.364	4.00	13	13	2	2	0	81	74	36	36	24	69
A.L. totals (9 years)	38	45	.458	4.84	239	75	6	3	4	682	757	414	367	284	435
N.L. totals (1 year)	4	7	.364	4.00	13	13	2	2	0	81	74	36	36	24	69
Major League totals (9 years)	42	52	.447	4.75	252	88	8	5	4	763	831	450	403	308	504

DIVISION SERIES RECORD

Year League	W	L	Pct.	ERA	G	GS	CG	ShO	Sv.	IP	H	R	ER	BB	SO
2001— Arizona (N.L.)	0	1	.000	12.00	1	1	0	0	0	3	4	4	4	3	0

CHAMPIONSHIP SERIES RECORD

Year League	W	L	Pct.	ERA	G	GS	CG	ShO	Sv.	IP	H	R	ER	BB	SO
2001— Arizona (N.L.)	0	0	...	6.00	1	1	0	0	0	3	5	2	2	1	1

WORLD SERIES RECORD

NOTES: Member of World Series championship team (2001).

Year League	W	L	Pct.	ERA	G	GS	CG	ShO	Sv.	IP	H	R	ER	BB	SO
2001— Arizona (N.L.)	0	1	.000	27.00	1	0	0	0	0	1/3	2	1	1	0	0

LOPEZ, FELIPE   SS   BLUE JAYS

PERSONAL: Born May 12, 1980, in Bayamon, Puerto Rico. ... 6-0/175. ... Bats both, throws right.
HIGH SCHOOL: Lake Brantley (Altamonte Springs, Fla.).
TRANSACTIONS/CAREER NOTES: Selected by Toronto Blue Jays organization in first round (eighth pick overall) of free-agent draft (June 2, 1998).

Year	Team (League)	Pos.	G	AB	R	H	2B	3B	HR	RBI	Avg.	BB	SO	SB	PO	A	E	Avg.
1998	St. Catharines (NY-P)	SS	19	83	14	31	5	2	1	11	.373	3	14	4	21	56	9	.895
	—Dunedin (FSL)	SS	4	13	3	5	0	1	1	1	.385	0	3	0	2	7	4	.692
1999	—Hagerstown (S.Atl.)	SS	134	537	87	149	27	4	14	80	.277	61	157	21	182	352	22	.960
2000	—Tennessee (Sou.)	SS	127	463	52	119	18	4	9	41	.257	31	110	12	177	351	*44	.923
2001	—Tennessee (Sou.)	SS-2B	19	72	12	16	2	1	2	4	.222	9	23	4	26	49	8	.904
	—Syracuse (I.L.)	SS-2B-3B	89	358	65	100	19	7	16	44	.279	30	94	13	125	238	19	.950
	—Toronto (A.L.)	3B-SS	49	177	21	46	5	4	5	23	.260	12	39	4	32	105	9	.938
Major League totals (1 year)			49	177	21	46	5	4	5	23	.260	12	39	4	32	105	9	.938

LOPEZ, JAVY   C   BRAVES

PERSONAL: Born November 5, 1970, in Ponce, Puerto Rico. ... 6-3/200. ... Bats right, throws right. ... Full name: Javier Torres Lopez.
HIGH SCHOOL: Academia Cristo Rey (Urb la Ramble Ponce, Puerto Rico).
TRANSACTIONS/CAREER NOTES: Signed as non-drafted free agent by Atlanta Braves organization (November 6, 1987). ... On Greenville disabled list (July 18-August 2, 1992). ... On Atlanta disabled list (July 6-22, 1997; and June 21-July 15 and July 25, 1999-remainder of season). ... Granted free agency (November 5, 2001). ... Re-signed by Braves (December 7, 2001).
HONORS: Named Southern League Most Valuable Player (1992).
STATISTICAL NOTES: Led Midwest League catchers with 11 double plays and 31 passed balls in 1990. ... Led Carolina League catchers with 701 total chances and 14 double plays in 1991. ... Led Southern League catchers with 763 total chances and 19 passed balls in 1992. ... Led International League catchers with 15 passed balls in 1993. ... Tied for N.L. lead with 10 passed balls in 1994. ... Career major league grand slams: 4.

Year	Team (League)	Pos.	G	AB	R	H	2B	3B	HR	RBI	Avg.	BB	SO	SB	PO	A	E	Avg.
1988	—GC Braves (GCL)	C	31	94	8	18	4	0	1	9	.191	3	19	1	131	30	7	.958
1989	—Pulaski (Appl.)	C	51	153	27	40	8	1	3	27	.261	5	35	3	264	26	5	.983
1990	—Burlington (Midw.)	C	116	422	48	112	17	3	11	55	.265	14	84	0	724	79	11	.986
1991	—Durham (Caro.)	C	113	384	43	94	14	2	11	51	.245	25	88	10	*610	85	6	.991
1992	—Greenville (Sou.)	C	115	442	63	142	28	3	16	60	.321	24	47	7	*680	75	8	.990
	—Atlanta (N.L.)	C	9	16	3	6	2	0	0	2	.375	0	1	0	28	2	0	1.000
1993	—Richmond (I.L.)	C-DH	100	380	56	116	23	2	17	74	.305	12	53	1	718	70	10	.987
	—Atlanta (N.L.)	C	8	16	1	6	1	1	1	2	.375	0	2	0	37	2	1	.975
1994	—Atlanta (N.L.)	C	80	277	27	68	9	0	13	35	.245	17	61	0	559	35	3	.995
1995	—Atlanta (N.L.)	C	100	333	37	105	11	4	14	51	.315	14	57	0	625	50	8	.988
1996	—Atlanta (N.L.)	C	138	489	56	138	19	1	23	69	.282	28	84	1	993	*81	6	.994
1997	—Atlanta (N.L.)	C	123	414	52	122	28	1	23	68	.295	40	82	1	792	56	6	.993
1998	—Atlanta (N.L.)	C-DH	133	489	73	139	21	1	34	106	.284	30	85	5	978	68	5	*.995
1999	—Atlanta (N.L.)	C-DH	65	246	34	78	18	1	11	45	.317	20	41	0	413	29	4	.991
2000	—Atlanta (N.L.)	C	134	481	60	138	21	1	24	89	.287	35	80	0	817	62	6	.993
2001	—Atlanta (N.L.)	C	128	438	45	117	16	1	17	66	.267	28	82	1	826	50	10	.989
Major League totals (10 years)			918	3199	388	917	146	11	160	533	.287	212	575	8	6068	435	49	.993

DIVISION SERIES RECORD

Year	Team (League)	Pos.	G	AB	R	H	2B	3B	HR	RBI	Avg.	BB	SO	SB	PO	A	E	Avg.
1995	—Atlanta (N.L.)	C	3	9	0	4	0	0	0	3	.444	0	3	0	22	3	0	1.000
1996	—Atlanta (N.L.)	C	2	7	1	2	0	0	1	1	.286	1	0	1	21	2	1	.958
1997	—Atlanta (N.L.)	C	2	7	3	2	2	0	0	1	.286	2	1	0	18	0	0	1.000
1998	—Atlanta (N.L.)	C	2	7	1	2	0	0	1	1	.286	1	1	0	20	3	0	1.000
2000	—Atlanta (N.L.)	PH-C	3	11	0	1	0	0	0	0	.091	0	1	0	15	2	0	1.000
Division series totals (5 years)			12	41	2	11	2	0	2	6	.268	4	6	1	96	10	1	.991

CHAMPIONSHIP SERIES RECORD

RECORDS: Shares career record for most doubles—7; and extra base hits—12. ... Shares single-game record for most runs—4 (October 14, 1996). ... Holds single-series records for most doubles—5 (1996); extra base hits—7 (1996); and hits—13 (1996). ... Shares single-series record for most total bases—24 (1996). ... Shares N.L. single-series records for most runs—8 (1996); and most consecutive hits—5 (1996).
NOTES: Named N.L. Championship Series Most Valuable Player (1996).

Year	Team (League)	Pos.	G	AB	R	H	2B	3B	HR	RBI	Avg.	BB	SO	SB	PO	A	E	Avg.
1992	—Atlanta (N.L.)	C	1	1	0	0	0	0	0	0	.000	0	0	0	2	0	0	1.000
1995	—Atlanta (N.L.)	C	3	14	2	5	1	0	1	3	.357	0	1	0	28	2	0	1.000
1996	—Atlanta (N.L.)	C	7	24	8	13	5	0	2	6	.542	4	1	1	48	3	0	1.000
1997	—Atlanta (N.L.)	C-PH	5	17	0	1	1	0	0	2	.059	1	7	0	40	3	0	1.000
1998	—Atlanta (N.L.)	C-PH	6	20	2	6	0	0	1	1	.300	0	7	0	43	2	1	.978
2001	—Atlanta (N.L.)	PH-C	5	14	1	2	0	0	1	2	.143	1	4	0	22	0	1	.957
Championship series totals (6 years)			27	90	13	27	7	0	5	14	.300	6	20	1	183	10	2	.990

WORLD SERIES RECORD

NOTES: Member of World Series championship team (1995).

Year	Team (League)	Pos.	G	AB	R	H	2B	3B	HR	RBI	Avg.	BB	SO	SB	PO	A	E	Avg.
1992	—Atlanta (N.L.)								Did not play.									
1995	—Atlanta (N.L.)	C-PH	6	17	1	3	2	0	1	3	.176	1	1	0	32	4	0	1.000
1996	—Atlanta (N.L.)	C	6	21	3	4	0	0	0	1	.190	3	4	0	41	4	0	1.000
World Series totals (2 years)			12	38	4	7	2	0	1	4	.184	4	5	0	73	8	0	1.000

ALL-STAR GAME RECORD

RECORDS: Hit home run in first at-bat (July 8, 1997).

Year	League	Pos.	AB	R	H	2B	3B	HR	RBI	Avg.	BB	SO	SB	PO	A	E	Avg.
1997	—National	C	1	1	1	0	0	1	1	1.000	0	0	0	4	1	0	1.000
1998	—National	C	1	0	0	0	0	0	0	.000	0	1	0	3	0	0	1.000
All-Star Game totals (2 years)			2	1	1	0	0	1	1	.500	0	1	0	7	1	0	1.000

L

LOPEZ, LUIS — IF — BREWERS

PERSONAL: Born September 4, 1970, in Cidra, Puerto Rico. ... 5-11/170. ... Bats both, throws right. ... Full name: Luis Manuel Lopez.
HIGH SCHOOL: San Jose (Caguas, Puerto Rico).
TRANSACTIONS/CAREER NOTES: Signed as non-drafted free agent by San Diego Padres organization (September 9, 1987). ... On Las Vegas disabled list (July 3-14, 1994). ... Granted free agency (October 15, 1994). ... Re-signed by Padres (April 20, 1995). ... On disabled list (April 24, 1995-entire season). ... On San Diego disabled list (March 29-April 18 and July 31-September 1, 1996); included rehabilitation assignments to Las Vegas (March 30-April 18 and August 17-September 1). ... Traded by Padres to Houston Astros for P Sean Runyan (March 15, 1997). ... Traded by Astros to New York Mets for IF Tim Bogar (March 31, 1997). ... Traded by Mets to Milwaukee Brewers for P Bill Pulsipher (January 21, 2000).
STATISTICAL NOTES: Led Northwest League shortstops with 382 total chances in 1988. ... Led South Atlantic League shortstops with 703 total chances and 78 double plays in 1989. ... Led Pacific Coast League shortstops with 30 errors in 1992. ... Tied for Pacific Coast League lead with 13 sacrifice hits in 1993. ... Career major league grand slams: 1.

| | | | | | | | BATTING | | | | | | | | FIELDING | | |
Year	Team (League)	Pos.	G	AB	R	H	2B	3B	HR	RBI	Avg.	BB	SO	SB	PO	A	E	Avg.
1988—	Spokane (N'West)	SS	70	312	50	95	13	1	0	35	.304	18	59	14	*118	217	*47	.877
1989—	Charl., S.C. (S.Atl.)	SS	127	460	50	102	15	1	1	29	.222	17	85	12	*256	*373	*74	.895
1990—	Riverside (Calif.)	SS	14	46	5	17	3	1	1	4	.370	3	3	4	18	38	6	.903
1991—	Wichita (Texas)	2B-SS	125	452	43	121	17	1	1	41	.268	18	70	6	274	339	26	.959
1992—	Las Vegas (PCL)	SS-OF	120	395	44	92	8	8	1	31	.233	19	65	6	200	358	†30	.949
1993—	Las Vegas (PCL)	SS-2B-DH	131	491	52	150	36	6	6	58	.305	27	62	8	230	380	29	.955
—	San Diego (N.L.)	2B	17	43	1	5	1	0	0	1	.116	0	8	0	23	34	1	.983
1994—	Las Vegas (PCL)	2B	12	49	2	10	2	2	0	6	.204	1	5	0	28	43	2	.973
—	San Diego (N.L.)	SS-2B-3B	77	235	29	65	16	1	2	20	.277	15	39	3	101	174	14	.952
1995—	San Diego (N.L.)					Did not play.												
1996—	Las Vegas (PCL)	2B-SS	18	68	4	14	3	0	1	12	.206	2	15	0	39	43	2	.976
—	San Diego (N.L.)	SS-2B-3B	63	139	10	25	3	0	0	11	.180	9	35	0	57	100	4	.975
1997—	Norfolk (I.L.)■	SS-2B-DH	48	203	32	67	12	1	4	19	.330	9	29	2	79	123	14	.935
—	New York (N.L.)	2B	78	178	19	48	12	1	1	19	.270	12	42	2	79	156	9	.963
1998—	New York (N.L.)	2-S-3-0	117	266	37	67	13	2	4	22	.252	20	60	2	123	144	11	.960
1999—	New York (N.L.)	SS-2B-3B	68	104	11	22	4	0	2	13	.212	12	33	1	34	68	4	.962
2000—	Milwaukee (N.L.)■	SS-2B-3B	78	201	24	53	14	0	6	27	.264	9	35	1	101	146	8	.969
2001—	Milwaukee (N.L.)	3B-SS-2B	92	222	22	60	8	3	4	18	.270	14	44	0	70	116	8	.959
	Major League totals (8 years)		590	1388	153	345	71	7	19	131	.249	91	296	9	588	938	59	.963

DIVISION SERIES RECORD

| | | | | | | | BATTING | | | | | | | | FIELDING | | |
Year	Team (League)	Pos.	G	AB	R	H	2B	3B	HR	RBI	Avg.	BB	SO	SB	PO	A	E	Avg.
1996—	San Diego (N.L.)	PR	1	0	0	0	0	0	0	0	...	0	0	0	...	...	...	...
1999—	New York (N.L.)					Did not play.												

CHAMPIONSHIP SERIES RECORD

| | | | | | | | BATTING | | | | | | | | FIELDING | | |
Year	Team (League)	Pos.	G	AB	R	H	2B	3B	HR	RBI	Avg.	BB	SO	SB	PO	A	E	Avg.
1999—	New York (N.L.)					Did not play.												

LOPEZ, LUIS — 1B/3B

PERSONAL: Born October 5, 1973, in Brooklyn, N.Y. ... 6-0/205. ... Bats right, throws right. ... Full name: Luis Lopez Jr.
TRANSACTIONS/CAREER NOTES: Signed by Ogden of Pioneer League (July 8, 1995). ... Signed as non-drafted free agent by Toronto Blue Jays organization (June 15, 1996). ... Released by Blue Jays (December 13, 2001).
HONORS: Named South Atlantic League Most Valuable Player (1997).
STATISTICAL NOTES: Led New York-Pennsylvania League first baseman with 50 assists and .995 fielding percentage in 1996. ... Led South Atlantic League in on-base percentage with .430 in 1997. ... Led International League with 22 grounded into double plays in 1999.

| | | | | | | | BATTING | | | | | | | | FIELDING | | |
Year	Team (League)	Pos.	G	AB	R	H	2B	3B	HR	RBI	Avg.	BB	SO	SB	PO	A	E	Avg.
1995—	St. Paul (Nor.)	3B	13	27	4	3	0	0	0	0	.111	7	3	0	10	16	1	.963
—	Ogden (Pio.)■	3B	46	182	36	65	15	0	7	39	.357	16	20	1	33	114	11	.930
1996—	St. Catharines (NY-P)■	1B-3B-OF	74	260	36	74	17	2	7	40	.285	27	31	2	567	*52	3	*.995
1997—	Hagerstown (S.Atl.)	1B-3B	136	503	96	*180	47	4	11	99	*.358	60	45	5	753	64	3	.996
1998—	Knoxville (Sou.)	1B-3B	119	450	70	141	27	1	15	85	.313	58	55	0	548	92	3	.995
—	Syracuse (I.L.)	3B-1B	11	41	6	9	0	0	1	3	.220	6	6	0	6	23	1	.967
1999—	Syracuse (I.L.)	1B-3B	136	531	76	171	35	2	4	69	.322	40	58	1	658	100	6	.992
2000—	Syracuse (I.L.)	3B-1B	130	491	64	161	27	1	7	79	.328	48	33	3	302	101	7	.983
2001—	Syracuse (I.L.)	1B-3B	87	339	57	110	26	2	10	73	.324	39	31	1	731	56	0	1.000
—	Toronto (A.L.)	3B-1B-DH	41	119	10	29	4	0	3	10	.244	8	16	0	27	57	5	.944
	Major League totals (1 year)		41	119	10	29	4	0	3	10	.244	8	16	0	27	57	5	.944

LOPEZ, MENDY — IF

PERSONAL: Born October 15, 1974, in Santo Domingo, Dominican Republic. ... 6-2/190. ... Bats right, throws right. ... Full name: Mendy Aude Lopez.
HIGH SCHOOL: Liceo Los Trinitanos (Santo Domingo, Dominican Republic).
TRANSACTIONS/CAREER NOTES: Signed as non-drafted free agent by Kansas City Royals organization (February 26, 1992). ... On Omaha disabled list (May 28-July 7, 1999). ... Released by Royals (December 13, 1999). ... Signed by Florida Marlins organization (January 12, 2000). ... On Calgary disabled list (April 6-June 23, 2000). ... Granted free agency (October 2, 2000). ... Signed by Houston Astros organization (January 8, 2001). ... Claimed on waivers by Pittsburgh Pirates (August 13, 2001). ... Granted free agency (October 15, 2001).
STATISTICAL NOTES: Led Gulf Coast League shortstops with .971 fielding percentage, 80 putouts, 154 assists, 241 total chances and 39 double plays in 1994. ... Tied for Texas League lead with 28 double plays by third baseman in 1996.

							BATTING								FIELDING			
Year	Team (League)	Pos.	G	AB	R	H	2B	3B	HR	RBI	Avg.	BB	SO	SB	PO	A	E	Avg.
1992— Dom. Royals (DSL)		SS	49	145	22	40	1	0	1	23	.276	22	15	7	81	155	26	.901
1993— Dom. Royals (DSL)		IF	28	98	15	27	5	2	0	20	.276	11	5	2	52	75	15	.894
1994— GC Royals (GCL)		SS-3B-2B	59	*235	56	85	*19	3	5	*50	.362	22	27	10	†84	†195	12	†.959
1995— Wilmington (Caro.).....		3B-SS	130	428	42	116	29	3	2	36	.271	28	73	18	84	335	25	.944
1996— Wichita (Texas)		3B-SS	93	327	47	92	20	5	6	32	.281	26	67	14	80	265	24	.935
1997— Omaha (A.A.)		3B	17	52	6	12	2	0	1	6	.231	8	21	0	15	38	6	.898
— Wichita (Texas)		SS	101	357	56	83	16	3	5	42	.232	36	70	7	193	296	20	.961
1998— Omaha (PCL).............		SS-3B	60	195	18	35	6	1	3	14	.179	18	44	2	71	167	10	.960
— Kansas City (A.L.)		SS-3B	74	206	18	50	10	2	1	15	.243	12	40	5	102	225	15	.956
1999— Omaha (PCL)............SS-2B-3B-DH			61	222	41	69	8	0	12	40	.311	18	41	2	98	171	8	.971
— GC Royals (GCL)		SS-DH	3	5	0	1	1	0	0	2	.200	3	1	0	2	4	0	1.000
— Kansas City (A.L.)		2B-SS	7	20	2	8	0	1	0	3	.400	0	5	0	11	16	0	1.000
2000— Calgary (PCL)■........		SS-2B-3B	56	225	34	73	20	1	7	29	.324	13	38	1	97	155	12	.955
— Florida (N.L.).............		PH	4	3	0	0	0	0	0	0	.000	1	1	0	...	...	...	...
2001— New Orleans (PCL)■......		2-S-1-O-3	63	208	37	58	11	1	14	36	.279	18	49	2	149	148	3	.990
— Houston (N.L.)		2B-3B	10	15	3	4	0	0	1	3	.267	2	4	0	5	3	0	1.000
— Pittsburgh (N.L.)■......		2B-SS-3B	22	43	5	10	3	1	0	4	.233	4	16	0	22	35	1	.983
American League totals (2 years)			81	226	20	58	10	3	1	18	.257	12	45	5	113	241	15	.959
National League totals (2 years)			36	61	8	14	3	1	1	7	.230	7	21	0	27	38	1	.985
Major League totals (4 years)			117	287	28	72	13	4	2	25	.251	19	66	5	140	279	16	.963

LORETTA, MARK — IF — BREWERS

PERSONAL: Born August 14, 1971, in Santa Monica, Calif. ... 6-0/189. ... Bats right, throws right. ... Full name: Mark David Loretta.
HIGH SCHOOL: St. Francis (La Canada, Calif.).
COLLEGE: Northwestern.
TRANSACTIONS/CAREER NOTES: Selected by Milwaukee Brewers organization in seventh round of free-agent draft (June 3, 1993). ... On New Orleans suspended list (May 17-20, 1996). ... On Milwaukee disabled list (June 3-August 16, 2000); included rehabilitation assignment to Indianapolis (August 3-16). ... On Milwaukee disabled list (March 27-May 19, 2001); included rehabilitation assignment to Indianapolis (May 9-17).
STATISTICAL NOTES: Led American Association shortstops with 200 putouts and 591 total chances in 1995. ... Had 16-game hitting streak (May 20-June 9, 2001).

							BATTING								FIELDING			
Year	Team (League)	Pos.	G	AB	R	H	2B	3B	HR	RBI	Avg.	BB	SO	SB	PO	A	E	Avg.
1993— Helena (Pio.)		SS	6	28	5	9	1	0	1	8	.321	1	4	0	11	18	0	1.000
— Stockton (Calif.)		SS-3B	53	201	36	73	4	1	4	31	.363	22	17	8	75	173	15	.943
1994— El Paso (Texas)		SS-P	77	302	50	95	13	6	0	38	.315	27	33	8	125	271	11	.973
— New Orleans (A.A.).....		SS-2B	43	138	16	29	7	0	1	14	.210	12	13	2	68	121	11	.945
1995— New Orleans (A.A.)........		S-3-DH-2	127	479	48	137	22	5	7	79	.286	34	47	8	†204	376	25	.959
— Milwaukee (A.L.)		SS-2B-DH	19	50	13	13	3	0	1	3	.260	4	7	1	18	42	1	.984
1996— New Orleans (A.A.)		SS	19	71	10	18	5	1	0	11	.254	9	8	1	31	60	5	.948
— Milwaukee (A.L.)		2B-3B-SS	73	154	20	43	3	0	1	13	.279	14	15	2	63	116	2	.989
1997— Milwaukee (A.L.) 2-S-1-3-DH			132	418	56	120	17	5	5	47	.287	47	60	5	334	277	15	.976
1998— Milwaukee (N.L.)		1-S-3-2-O	140	434	55	137	29	0	6	54	.316	42	47	9	450	215	6	.991
1999— Milwaukee (N.L.) SS-1B-2B-3B			153	587	93	170	34	5	5	67	.290	52	59	4	625	260	13	.986
2000— Milwaukee (N.L.)........		SS-2B	91	352	49	99	21	1	7	40	.281	37	38	0	122	254	2	.995
— Indianapolis (I.L.).......		SS	10	25	6	6	1	0	0	5	.240	2	4	0	4	14	0	1.000
2001— Indianapolis (I.L.)		SS-2B-3B	8	31	4	3	0	0	1	1	.097	2	4	0	3	14	3	.850
— Milwaukee (N.L.)		2-3-S-D-P	102	384	40	111	14	2	2	29	.289	28	46	1	142	218	8	.978
American League totals (3 years)			224	622	89	176	23	5	7	63	.283	65	82	8	415	435	18	.979
National League totals (4 years)			486	1757	237	517	98	8	20	190	.294	159	190	14	1339	947	29	.987
Major League totals (7 years)			710	2379	326	693	121	13	27	253	.291	224	272	22	1754	1382	47	.985

RECORD AS PITCHER

Year	League	W	L	Pct.	ERA	G	GS	CG	ShO	Sv.	IP	H	R	ER	BB	SO
1994— El Paso (Texas)..................		0	0	...	...	1	0	0	0	0	0	0	1	1	1	0
2001— Milwaukee (N.L.).................		0	1	...	0.00	1	0	0	0	0	1	0	0	0	1	2

LOUX, SHANE — P — TIGERS

PERSONAL: Born August 13, 1979, in Rapid City, S.D. ... 6-2/205. ... Throws right, bats right. ... Full name: Shane A. Loux.
HIGH SCHOOL: Highland (Gilbert, Ariz.).
TRANSACTIONS/CAREER NOTES: Selected by Detroit Tigers organization in second round of free-agent draft (June 3, 1997).
STATISTICAL NOTES: Tied for International League lead with 10 sacrifice flies allowed and 15 hit batsmen in 2001.

Year	League	W	L	Pct.	ERA	G	GS	CG	ShO	Sv.	IP	H	R	ER	BB	SO
1997— Gulf Coast Tigers (GCL)		4	1	.800	0.84	10	9	1	1	0	43	19	7	4	10	33
1998— West Michigan (Midw.)......		7	13	.350	4.64	28	•28	2	1	0	157	184	96	81	52	88
1999— West Michigan (Midw.)		1	3	.250	6.27	8	8	0	0	0	47 1/3	55	39	33	16	43
— Lakeland (FSL)		6	5	.545	4.05	17	17	0	0	0	91	92	48	41	47	52
2000— Lakeland (FSL)		0	1	.000	1.80	1	1	0	0	0	5	2	1	1	3	6
— Jacksonville (Sou.).............		12	9	.571	3.82	26	26	2	0	0	157 2/3	150	78	67	55	130
2001— Toledo (I.L.).......................		10	11	.476	5.78	28	28	2	0	0	151	203	111	*97	73	72

LOWE, DEREK — P — RED SOX

PERSONAL: Born June 1, 1973, in Dearborn, Mich. ... 6-6/200. ... Throws right, bats right. ... Full name: Derek Christopher Lowe.
HIGH SCHOOL: Edsel Ford (Dearborn, Mich.).
TRANSACTIONS/CAREER NOTES: Selected by Seattle Mariners organization in eighth round of free-agent draft (June 3, 1991). ... Traded by Mariners with C Jason Varitek to Boston Red Sox for P Heathcliff Slocumb (July 31, 1997).

STATISTICAL NOTES: Led Southern League with seven balks in 1994.
MISCELLANEOUS: Struck out in only appearance as pinch hitter (2000).

Year League	W	L	Pct.	ERA	G	GS	CG	ShO	Sv.	IP	H	R	ER	BB	SO
1991—Arizona Mariners (Ariz.)	5	3	.625	2.41	12	12	0	0	0	71	58	26	19	21	60
1992—Bellingham (N'West)	7	3	.700	2.42	14	13	2	•1	0	85²/₃	69	34	23	22	66
1993—Riverside (Calif.).............	12	9	.571	5.26	27	26	3	2	0	154	189	104	90	60	80
1994—Jacksonville (Sou.).............	7	10	.412	4.94	26	26	2	0	0	151¹/₃	177	92	83	50	75
1995—Port City (Sou.).................	1	6	.143	6.07	10	10	1	0	0	53¹/₃	70	41	36	22	30
—Arizona Mariners (Ariz.)	1	0	1.000	0.93	2	2	0	0	0	9²/₃	5	1	1	2	11
1996—Port City (Sou.).................	5	3	.625	3.05	10	10	0	0	0	65	56	27	22	17	33
—Tacoma (PCL)	6	9	.400	4.54	17	16	1	1	0	105	118	64	53	37	54
1997—Tacoma (PCL)	3	4	.429	3.45	10	9	1	0	0	57¹/₃	53	26	22	20	49
—Seattle (A.L.)......................	2	4	.333	6.96	12	9	0	0	0	53	59	43	41	20	39
—Pawtucket (I.L.)■...............	4	0	1.000	2.37	6	5	0	0	0	30¹/₃	23	8	8	11	21
—Boston (A.L.)....................	0	2	.000	3.38	8	0	0	0	0	16	15	6	6	3	13
1998—Boston (A.L.)....................	3	9	.250	4.02	63	10	0	0	4	123	126	65	55	42	77
1999—Boston (A.L.)....................	6	3	.667	2.63	74	0	0	0	15	109¹/₃	84	35	32	25	80
2000—Boston (A.L.)....................	4	4	.500	2.56	74	0	0	0	•42	91¹/₃	90	27	26	22	79
2001—Boston (A.L.)....................	5	10	.333	3.53	67	3	0	0	24	91²/₃	103	39	36	29	82
Major League totals (5 years)	20	32	.385	3.64	298	22	0	0	85	484¹/₃	477	215	196	141	370

DIVISION SERIES RECORD

Year League	W	L	Pct.	ERA	G	GS	CG	ShO	Sv.	IP	H	R	ER	BB	SO
1998—Boston (A.L.)....................	0	0	...	2.08	2	0	0	0	0	4¹/₃	3	1	1	2	2
1999—Boston (A.L.)....................	1	1	.500	4.32	3	0	0	0	0	8¹/₃	6	7	4	1	7
Division series totals (2 years)	1	1	.500	3.55	5	0	0	0	0	12²/₃	9	8	5	3	9

CHAMPIONSHIP SERIES RECORD

Year League	W	L	Pct.	ERA	G	GS	CG	ShO	Sv.	IP	H	R	ER	BB	SO
1999—Boston (A.L.)....................	0	0	...	1.42	3	0	0	0	0	6¹/₃	6	3	1	2	7

ALL-STAR GAME RECORD

Year League	W	L	Pct.	ERA	GS	CG	ShO	Sv.	IP	H	R	ER	BB	SO
2000—American..........................	0	0	...	0.00	0	0	0	0	1	0	0	0	0	0

LOWE, SEAN   P   PIRATES

PERSONAL: Born March 29, 1971, in Dallas. ... 6-2/205. ... Throws right, bats right. ... Full name: Jonathan Sean Lowe.
HIGH SCHOOL: Mesquite (Texas).
JUNIOR COLLEGE: McLennan Community College (Texas).
COLLEGE: Arizona State.
TRANSACTIONS/CAREER NOTES: Selected by Cincinnati Reds organization in 43rd round of free-agent draft (June 5, 1989); did not sign. ... Selected by Oakland Athletics organization in 43rd round of free-agent draft (June 4, 1990); did not sign. ... Selected by St. Louis Cardinals organization in first round (15th pick overall) of free-agent draft (June 1, 1992). ... On St. Petersburg disabled list (July 19-August 8, 1994). ... On Arkansas disabled list (May 28-June 4, 1996). ... On Louisville disabled list (April 9-18, 1997). ... Traded by Cardinals to Chicago White Sox for P John Ambrose (February 9, 1999). ... On Chicago disabled list (July 29-August 23, 2000); included rehabilitation assignment to Charlotte (August 8-23). ... Traded by White Sox with P Kip Wells and P Josh Fogg to Pittsburgh Pirates for P Todd Ritchie and C Lee Evans (December 13, 2001).
STATISTICAL NOTES: Tied for American Association lead with 10 hit batsmen in 1997.

Year League	W	L	Pct.	ERA	G	GS	CG	ShO	Sv.	IP	H	R	ER	BB	SO
1992—Hamilton (NY-Penn)	2	0	1.000	1.61	5	5	0	0	0	28	14	8	5	14	22
1993—St. Petersburg (FSL)	6	11	.353	4.27	25	25	0	0	0	132²/₃	152	80	63	62	87
1994—St. Petersburg (FSL)	5	6	.455	3.47	21	21	0	0	0	114	119	51	44	37	92
—Arkansas (Texas)...............	2	1	.667	1.40	3	3	0	0	0	19¹/₃	13	3	3	8	11
1995—Arkansas (Texas)...............	9	8	.529	4.88	24	24	0	0	0	129	143	84	70	64	77
1996—Louisville (A.A.)	8	9	.471	4.70	25	18	0	0	0	115	127	72	60	51	76
—Arkansas (Texas)...............	2	3	.400	6.00	6	6	0	0	0	33	32	24	22	15	25
1997—Louisville (A.A.)	6	10	.375	4.37	26	23	1	0	1	131²/₃	142	74	64	53	117
—St. Louis (N.L.)................	0	2	.000	9.35	6	4	0	0	0	17¹/₃	27	21	18	10	8
1998—Memphis (PCL)	12	8	.600	3.18	25	21	0	0	0	153	147	57	54	61	114
—St. Louis (N.L.)................	0	3	.000	15.19	4	1	0	0	0	5¹/₃	11	9	9	5	2
1999—Chicago (A.L.)■	4	1	.800	3.67	64	0	0	0	0	95²/₃	90	39	39	46	62
2000—Chicago (A.L.)	4	1	.800	5.48	50	5	0	0	0	70²/₃	78	47	43	39	53
—Charlotte (I.L.)................	0	0	...	3.00	2	1	0	0	0	3	5	1	1	1	1
2001—Chicago (A.L.)	9	4	.692	3.61	45	11	0	0	3	127	123	55	51	32	71
—Charlotte (I.L.)................	1	1	.500	4.50	2	2	0	0	0	10	9	6	5	2	8
A.L. totals (3 years)	17	6	.739	4.08	159	16	0	0	3	293¹/₃	291	141	133	117	186
N.L. totals (2 years)	0	5	.000	10.72	10	5	0	0	0	22²/₃	38	30	27	15	10
Major league totals (5 years)	17	11	.607	4.56	169	21	0	0	3	316	329	171	160	132	196

LOWELL, MIKE   3B   MARLINS

PERSONAL: Born February 24, 1974, in San Juan, Puerto Rico. ... 6-4/205. ... Bats right, throws right. ... Full name: Michael Averett Lowell.
HIGH SCHOOL: Coral Gables (Fla.).
COLLEGE: Florida International.
TRANSACTIONS/CAREER NOTES: Selected by New York Yankees organization in 20th round of free-agent draft (June 1, 1995). ... Traded by Yankees to Florida Marlins for P Ed Yarnall, P Mark Johnson and P Todd Noel (February 1, 1999). ... On Florida disabled list (March 26-May 29, 1999); included rehabilitation assignments to Calgary (April 8-13 and May 6-29). ... On disabled list (May 13-29, 2000).
RECORDS: Holds major league single-season record for fewest putouts by third baseman for leader—107 (2001).

STATISTICAL NOTES: Led New York-Pennsylvania League third basemen with 271 total chances in 1995. ... Led South Atlantic League third basemen with .926 fielding percentage, 301 putouts and 421 total chances in 1996. ... Tied for International League lead with 20 errors by third baseman in 1998. ... Had 16-game hitting streak (August 18-September 5, 2000). ... Career major league grand slams: 3.

Year — Team (League)	Pos.	G	AB	R	H	2B	3B	HR	RBI	Avg.	BB	SO	SB	PO	A	E	Avg.
1995— Oneonta (NY-Penn)	3B	72	281	36	73	18	0	1	27	.260	23	34	3	59	188	24	.911
1996— Greensboro (S.Atl.) ...	3B-SS	113	433	58	122	33	0	8	64	.282	46	43	10	91	†302	32	.925
—Tampa (FSL)..............	3B	24	78	8	22	5	0	0	11	.282	3	13	1	22	40	3	.954
1997— Norwich (East.)	3B-SS	78	285	60	98	17	0	15	47	.344	48	30	2	57	133	15	.927
—Columbus (I.L.)..........	3B-SS	57	210	36	58	13	1	15	45	.276	23	34	2	31	73	5	.954
1998— Columbus (I.L.)..........	3B-1B-SS	126	510	79	155	34	3	26	99	.304	37	85	4	114	283	‡21	.950
—New York (A.L.)..........	3B-DH	8	15	1	4	0	0	0	0	.267	0	1	0	2	5	0	1.000
1999— Calgary (PCL)■.........	3B	24	83	11	26	3	0	2	9	.313	8	19	0	11	51	4	.939
—Florida (N.L.).............	3B	97	308	32	78	15	0	12	47	.253	26	69	0	59	143	4	.981
2000— Florida (N.L.).............	3B	140	508	73	137	38	0	22	91	.270	54	75	4	102	260	12	.968
2001— Florida (N.L.).............	3B	146	551	65	156	37	0	18	100	.283	43	79	1	107	261	9	.976
American League totals (1 year)		8	15	1	4	0	0	0	0	.267	0	1	0	2	5	0	1.000
National League totals (3 years)		383	1367	170	371	90	0	52	238	.271	123	223	5	268	664	25	.974
Major League totals (4 years)		391	1382	171	375	90	0	52	238	.271	123	224	5	270	669	25	.974

PERSONAL: Born July 13, 1978, in Sattelite Beach, Fla. ... 6-3/205. ... Bats right, throws left. ... Full name: Ryan Andrew Ludwick.
HIGH SCHOOL: Durango (Las Vegas, Nev.).
COLLEGE: Nevada-Las Vegas.
TRANSACTIONS/CAREER NOTES: Selected by Oakland Athletics organization in second round of free-agent draft (June 2, 1999). ... Traded by A's with 1B Jason Hart, P Mario Ramos and C Gerald Laird to Texas Rangers for 1B Carlos Pena and P Mike Venafro (January 14, 2002).

Year — Team (League)	Pos.	G	AB	R	H	2B	3B	HR	RBI	Avg.	BB	SO	SB	PO	A	E	Avg.
1999— Modesto (Calif.)	OF	43	171	28	47	11	3	4	34	.275	19	45	2	69	2	0	1.000
2000— Modesto (Calif.)	OF	129	493	86	130	26	3	29	102	.264	68	128	10	281	9	5	.983
2001— Midland (Texas)..........	OF	119	443	82	119	23	3	25	96	.269	53	113	9	250	4	6	.977
—Sacramento (PCL)......	OF	17	57	10	13	3	0	1	7	.228	2	16	2	51	1	1	.981

PERSONAL: Born November 16, 1975, in Barahona, Dominican Republic. ... 6-2/165. ... Bats right, throws right. ... Full name: Julio Cesar Lugo.
JUNIOR COLLEGE: Connors State College (Okla.).
TRANSACTIONS/CAREER NOTES: Selected by Houston Astros organization in 43rd round of free-agent draft (June 2, 1994). ... On disabled list (July 21-29, 1999).
STATISTICAL NOTES: Led Florida State League shortstops with 40 errors in 1997. ... Career major league grand slams: 1.

Year — Team (League)	Pos.	G	AB	R	H	2B	3B	HR	RBI	Avg.	BB	SO	SB	PO	A	E	Avg.
1995— Auburn (NY-Penn)......	2B-SS-OF	59	230	36	67	6	3	1	16	.291	26	31	17	85	116	12	.944
1996— Quad City (Midw.)	SS-2B-3B	101	393	60	116	18	2	10	50	.295	32	75	24	122	289	29	.934
1997— Kissimmee (FSL)........	SS-2B-3B	125	505	89	135	22	*14	7	61	.267	46	99	35	186	433	†41	.938
1998— Kissimmee (FSL)........	SS	128	509	81	154	20	*14	7	62	.303	49	72	51	181	308	42	.921
1999— Jackson (Texas)	SS-2B-DH	116	445	77	142	24	5	10	42	.319	44	53	25	185	328	29	.946
2000— Houston (N.L.)	SS-2B-OF	116	420	78	119	22	5	10	40	.283	37	93	22	189	249	17	.963
2001— Houston (N.L.)	SS-OF-2B	140	513	93	135	20	3	10	37	.263	46	116	12	213	373	22	.964
Major League totals (2 years)		256	933	171	254	42	8	20	77	.272	83	209	34	402	622	39	.963

DIVISION SERIES RECORD

Year — Team (League)	Pos.	G	AB	R	H	2B	3B	HR	RBI	Avg.	BB	SO	SB	PO	A	E	Avg.
2001— Houston (N.L.)	SS-PH	3	8	1	0	0	0	0	0	.000	0	2	0	7	4	3	.786

PERSONAL: Born March 8, 1973, in Jersey City, N.J. ... 6-7/240. ... Throws left, bats left. ... Full name: Mark Francis Lukasiewicz.
HIGH SCHOOL: Secaucus (N.J.).
JUNIOR COLLEGE: Brevard.
COLLEGE: Oklahoma State.
TRANSACTIONS/CAREER NOTES: Selected by Toronto Blue Jays organization in supplemental round ("sandwich pick" between first and second round, 41st pick overall) of free-agent draft (June 3, 1993); pick received as partial compensation for New York Yankees signing Type A free agent P Jimmy Key. ... Loaned by Blue Jays organization to Bakersfield, California League (June 19-July 12, 1996). ... Claimed on waivers by Anaheim Angels (October 10, 2000).

Year — League	W	L	Pct.	ERA	G	GS	CG	ShO	Sv.	IP	H	R	ER	BB	SO
1994— Hagerstown (S.Atl.)...........	3	6	.333	4.78	29	17	0	0	0	98	108	70	52	21	84
1995— Dunedin (FSL)...................	3	6	.333	5.73	31	13	0	0	1	86 1/3	80	62	55	42	71
1996— Dunedin (FSL)	2	1	.667	4.60	23	0	0	0	1	31 1/3	28	20	16	22	31
—Bakersfield (Calif.)■............	0	2	.000	9.24	7	0	0	0	0	12 2/3	17	14	13	11	9
—Hagerstown (S.Atl.)■..........	2	0	1.000	2.30	9	1	0	0	0	15 2/3	8	5	4	7	20
1997— Knoxville (Sou.).................	2	0	1.000	3.65	27	0	0	0	7	37	26	17	15	14	43
—Syracuse (I.L.).................	2	3	.400	5.17	30	0	0	0	0	31 1/3	37	22	18	13	31

Year League	W	L	Pct.	ERA	G	GS	CG	ShO	Sv.	IP	H	R	ER	BB	SO
1998— Syracuse (I.L.)	2	2	.500	3.40	22	4	0	0	1	47 2/3	38	18	18	24	30
— Knoxville (Sou.)	0	0	...	1.93	5	0	0	0	1	9 1/3	6	2	2	1	16
— Dunedin (FSL)	1	1	.500	0.84	9	0	0	0	0	10 2/3	7	2	1	4	8
1999— Syracuse (I.L.)	4	4	.500	5.34	37	9	1	0	3	97 2/3	109	59	58	40	77
2000— Syracuse (I.L.)	2	1	.667	3.48	42	0	0	0	0	41 1/3	34	17	16	25	52
— Tennessee (Sou.)	0	0	...	5.79	3	0	0	0	0	4 2/3	4	3	3	4	6
2001— Salt Lake (PCL)■	3	0	1.000	1.48	20	0	0	0	2	30 1/3	12	5	5	2	41
— Anaheim (A.L.)	0	2	.000	6.04	24	0	0	0	0	22 1/3	21	17	15	9	25
Major League totals (1 year)	0	2	.000	6.04	24	0	0	0	0	22 1/3	21	17	15	9	25

LUNAR, FERNANDO   C   ORIOLES

PERSONAL: Born May 25, 1977, in Cantanura, Venezuela. ... 6-1/190. ... Bats right, throws right. ... Full name: Fernando Jose Lunar.
HIGH SCHOOL: Liceo Anaco Venezuela (Anzoategui, El Salvador).
TRANSACTIONS/CAREER NOTES: Signed as non-drafted free agent by Atlanta Braves organization (March 15, 1994). ... On disabled list (April 16-24, 1995). ... Traded by Braves with OF Trenidad Hubbard and P Luis Rivera to Baltimore Orioles for OF B.J. Surhoff and P Gabe Molina (July 31, 2000).
STATISTICAL NOTES: Tied for Gulf Coast League lead in double plays by catcher with three in 1994. ... Led South Atlantic League catchers with 11 double plays in 1996. ... Led South Atlantic League catchers with 1,036 total chances in 1997. ... Led Carolina League catchers with nine double plays in 1998. ... Led Southern League catchers with 12 double plays in 1999.

						BATTING								FIELDING		
Year Team (League)	Pos.	G	AB	R	H	2B	3B	HR	RBI	Avg.	BB	SO	SB	PO	A	E	Avg.
1994— GC Braves (GCL)	C	33	100	9	24	5	0	2	12	.240	1	13	0	203	32	7	.971
1995— Eugene (N'West)	C	39	131	13	32	6	0	2	16	.244	9	28	0	298	41	8	.000
— Macon (S.Atl.)	C	39	134	13	24	2	0	0	9	.179	10	38	1	261	35	10	.967
1996— Macon (S.Atl.)	C	104	343	33	63	9	0	7	33	.184	20	65	3	648	112	12	.984
1997— Macon (S.Atl.)	C	105	380	41	99	26	2	7	37	.261	18	42	0	*888	*135	13	.987
1998— Danville (Caro.)	C	91	286	19	63	9	0	3	28	.220	6	52	1	726	103	8	.990
1999— Greenville (Sou.)	C-DH	105	343	33	77	15	1	3	35	.224	12	64	0	611	*88	10	.986
2000— Greenville (Sou.)	C	31	102	6	17	3	0	0	4	.167	8	15	0	228	37	3	.989
— Atlanta (N.L.)	C	22	54	5	10	1	0	0	5	.185	3	15	0	125	12	1	.993
— Bowie (East.)■	C	22	80	12	23	7	1	0	8	.288	6	8	0	165	22	2	.989
— Baltimore (A.L.)	C	9	16	0	2	0	0	0	1	.125	0	4	0	43	2	0	1.000
2001— Baltimore (A.L.)	C	64	167	8	41	7	0	0	16	.246	7	32	0	267	32	4	.987
American League totals (2 years)		73	183	8	43	7	0	0	17	.235	7	36	0	310	34	4	.989
National League totals (1 year)		22	54	5	10	1	0	0	5	.185	3	15	0	125	12	1	.993
Major League totals (2 years)		95	237	13	53	8	0	0	22	.224	10	51	0	435	46	5	.990

LUNDQUIST, DAVID   P   PADRES

PERSONAL: Born June 4, 1973, in Beverly, Mass. ... 6-2/200. ... Throws right, bats right. ... Full name: David Bruce Lundquist Jr.
HIGH SCHOOL: Carson City (Nev.).
JUNIOR COLLEGE: Cochise County Community College (Ariz.).
COLLEGE: UNLV.
TRANSACTIONS/CAREER NOTES: Selected by Chicago White Sox organization in fifth round of free-agent draft (June 3, 1993). ... On Prince William disabled list (April 5-June 5 and June 19, 1996-remainder of season). ... On Charlotte disabled list (July 1, 1999-remainder of season). ... Claimed on waivers by Kansas City Royals (October 15, 1999). ... Released by Royals (March 29, 2000). ... Played with Aberdeen, Northern League (2000). ... Signed by San Diego Padres organization (February 6, 2001). ... Granted free agency (October 15, 2001). ... Re-signed by Padres organization (December 6, 2001).

Year League	W	L	Pct.	ERA	G	GS	CG	ShO	Sv.	IP	H	R	ER	BB	SO
1993— GC White Sox (GCL)	5	3	.625	3.14	11	10	0	0	0	63	70	26	22	15	40
1994— Hickory (S.Atl.)	13	10	.565	3.48	27	27	3	2	0	178 2/3	170	88	69	43	133
1995— South Bend (Midw.)	8	4	.667	3.58	18	18	5	1	0	118	107	54	47	38	60
1996— GC White Sox (GCL)	1	1	.500	2.63	3	3	0	0	0	13 2/3	8	4	4	2	16
— Prince William (Caro.)	0	2	.000	5.67	5	5	0	0	0	27	31	17	17	14	23
1997— Winston-Salem (Caro.)	3	1	.750	6.75	20	6	0	0	0	48	65	41	36	23	39
— Birmingham (Sou.)	0	0	...	8.77	7	0	0	0	0	13 1/3	26	20	13	5	15
1998— Winston-Salem (Caro.)	1	0	1.000	2.53	6	0	0	0	0	10 2/3	9	4	3	3	9
— Birmingham (Sou.)	1	1	.500	3.29	33	0	0	0	10	41	28	15	15	15	41
— Calgary (PCL)	3	0	1.000	3.60	12	0	0	0	2	15	12	6	6	7	12
1999— Chicago (A.L.)	1	1	.500	8.59	17	0	0	0	0	22	28	21	21	12	18
— Charlotte (I.L.)	0	0	...	0.00	3	0	0	0	0	3 2/3	3	0	0	1	4
2000— Aberdeen (Nor.)■	4	3	.571	9.07	21	0	0	0	0	41 2/3	69	49	42	17	32
2001— Portland (PCL)■	4	7	.364	3.11	50	0	0	0	7	63 2/3	59	25	22	20	67
— San Diego (N.L.)	0	1	.000	5.95	17	0	0	0	0	19 2/3	20	13	13	7	19
A.L. totals (1 year)	1	1	.500	8.59	17	0	0	0	0	22	28	21	21	12	18
N.L. totals (1 year)	0	1	.000	5.95	17	0	0	0	0	19 2/3	20	13	13	7	19
Major League totals (2 years)	1	2	.333	7.34	34	0	0	0	0	41 2/3	48	34	34	19	37

LYON, BRANDON   P   BLUE JAYS

PERSONAL: Born August 10, 1979, in Salt Lake City. ... 6-1/175. ... Throws right, bats right. ... Full name: Brandon J. Lyon.
HIGH SCHOOL: Taylorsville (Salt Lake City).
JUNIOR COLLEGE: Dixie (Utah).
TRANSACTIONS/CAREER NOTES: Selected by Toronto Blue Jays organization in 14th round of free-agent draft (June 2, 1999).

Year	League	W	L	Pct.	ERA	G	GS	CG	ShO	Sv.	IP	H	R	ER	BB	SO
2000—Queens (NY-Penn)		5	3	.625	2.39	15	13	0	0	0	60 $^1/_3$	43	20	16	6	55
2001—Tennessee (Sou.)		5	0	1.000	3.68	9	9	0	0	0	58 $^2/_3$	57	25	24	9	45
—Syracuse (I.L.)		5	3	.625	3.69	11	11	2	1	0	68 $^1/_3$	68	33	28	10	53
—Toronto (A.L.)		5	4	.556	4.29	11	11	0	0	0	63	63	31	30	15	35
Major League totals (1 year)		5	4	.556	4.29	11	11	0	0	0	63	63	31	30	15	35

MABRY, JOHN   OF/3B

PERSONAL: Born October 17, 1970, in Wilmington, Del. ... 6-4/210. ... Bats left, throws right. ... Full name: John Steven Mabry. ... Name pronounced MAY-bree.

HIGH SCHOOL: Bohemia Manor (Chesapeake City, Md.).

COLLEGE: West Chester (Pa.) University.

TRANSACTIONS/CAREER NOTES: Selected by St. Louis Cardinals organization in sixth round of free-agent draft (June 3, 1991). ... On disabled list (April 22-30 and May 6-18, 1992). ... On disabled list (August 20-September 24, 1997). ... Granted free agency (December 21, 1998). ... Signed by Seattle Mariners (December 30, 1998). ... On disabled list (August 14, 1999-remainder of season). ... On Seattle disabled list (April 22-May 12, 2000); included rehabilitation assignment to Tacoma (May 8-12). ... Traded by Mariners with P Tom Davey to San Diego Padres for OF Al Martin (July 31, 2000). ... Granted free agency (October 30, 2000). ... Signed by Cardinals organization (January 5, 2001). ... Traded by Cardinals to Florida Marlins for cash considerations (April 9, 2001). ... On Florida disabled list (April 16-May 20, 2001); included rehabilitation assignment to Brevard County (May 16-20). ... Granted free agency (November 5, 2001).

STATISTICAL NOTES: Led Texas League in grounding into double plays with 17 in 1993. ... Led Texas League outfielders with six double plays in 1993. ... Hit for the cycle (May 18, 1996). ... Had 20-game hitting streak (May 19-June 9, 1997).

							BATTING							FIELDING			
Year	Team (League)	Pos.	G	AB	R	H	2B	3B	HR	RBI	Avg.	BB	SO	SB	PO	A	E	Avg.
1991—Hamilton (NY-Penn) ...	OF	49	187	25	58	11	0	1	31	.310	17	18	9	73	*10	5	.943
—Savannah (S.Atl.)	OF	22	86	10	20	6	1	0	8	.233	7	12	1	36	1	1	.974
1992—Springfield (Midw.)	OF	115	438	63	115	13	6	11	57	.263	24	39	2	171	14	6	.969
1993—Arkansas (Texas)	OF	*136	528	68	153	32	2	16	72	.290	27	68	7	262	15	3	*.989
—Louisville (A.A.)	OF	4	7	0	1	0	0	0	1	.143	0	1	0	3	0	0	1.000
1994—Louisville (A.A.)	OF	122	477	76	125	30	1	15	66	.262	32	67	2	237	4	2	.992
—St. Louis (N.L.)	OF	6	23	2	7	3	0	0	3	.304	2	4	0	16	0	0	1.000
1995—St. Louis (N.L.)	1B-OF	129	388	35	119	21	1	5	41	.307	24	45	0	652	58	4	.994
—Louisville (A.A.)	OF	4	12	0	1	0	0	0	0	.083	0	0	0	8	0	1	.889
1996—St. Louis (N.L.)	1B-OF	151	543	63	161	30	2	13	74	.297	37	84	3	1182	76	8	.994
1997—St. Louis (N.L.)	OF-1B-3B	116	388	40	110	19	0	5	36	.284	39	77	0	455	30	1	.998
1998—St. Louis (N.L.)	OF-3B-1B	142	377	41	94	22	0	9	46	.249	30	76	0	206	64	9	.968
1999—Seattle (A.L.)■	OF-3B-1B-DH	87	262	34	64	14	0	9	33	.244	20	60	2	221	50	10	.964
2000—Seattle (A.L.)	3-O-D-1-P	48	103	18	25	5	0	1	7	.243	10	31	0	37	20	4	.934
—Tacoma (PCL)	1B-3B	4	14	1	3	1	0	0	1	.214	0	4	0	2	2	1	.800
—San Diego (N.L.)■	OF-1B	48	123	17	28	8	0	7	25	.228	5	38	0	57	2	1	.983
2001—St. Louis (N.L.)■	OF	5	7	0	0	0	0	0	0	.000	0	2	0	3	0	0	1.000
—Florida (N.L.)■	OF-1B-DH-P	82	147	14	32	7	0	6	20	.218	13	44	1	51	3	2	.964
—Brevard County (FSL)	OF	4	13	0	2	0	0	0	4	.154	2	1	0	4	0	0	1.000
American League totals (2 years)		135	365	52	89	19	0	10	40	.244	30	91	2	258	70	14	.959
National League totals (7 years)		679	1996	212	551	110	3	45	245	.276	150	370	4	2622	233	25	.991
Major League totals (8 years)		814	2361	264	640	129	3	55	285	.271	180	461	6	2880	303	39	.988

RECORDS: Shares career record for most triples—1.

DIVISION SERIES RECORD

							BATTING							FIELDING			
Year	Team (League)	Pos.	G	AB	R	H	2B	3B	HR	RBI	Avg.	BB	SO	SB	PO	A	E	Avg.
1996—St. Louis (N.L.)	1B	3	10	1	3	0	1	0	1	.300	2	1	0	20	1	0	1.000

CHAMPIONSHIP SERIES RECORD

							BATTING							FIELDING			
Year	Team (League)	Pos.	G	AB	R	H	2B	3B	HR	RBI	Avg.	BB	SO	SB	PO	A	E	Avg.
1996—St. Louis (N.L.)	1B-OF	7	23	1	6	0	0	0	0	.261	0	6	0	45	1	0	1.000

RECORD AS PITCHER

Year	League	W	L	Pct.	ERA	G	GS	CG	ShO	Sv.	IP	H	R	ER	BB	SO
2000—Seattle (N.L.)		0	0	...	27.27	1	0	0	0	0	$^2/_3$	3	2	2	1	0
2001—Florida (N.L.)		0	0	...	135.00	1	0	0	0	0	$^1/_3$	3	5	5	3	0
Major League totals (2 years)		0	0	...	63.00	2	0	0	0	0	1	6	7	7	4	0

MacDOUGAL, MIKE   P   ROYALS

PERSONAL: Born March 5, 1977, in Las Vegas, Nev. ... 6-4/195. ... Throws right, bats both. ... Full name: Robert Meiklejohn MacDougal.

HIGH SCHOOL: Mesa (Ariz.).

COLLEGE: Wake Forest.

TRANSACTIONS/CAREER NOTES: Selected by Baltimore Orioles organization in 22nd round of free-agent draft (June 4, 1996); did not sign. ... Selected by Baltimore Orioles organization in 17th round of free-agent draft (June 2, 1998); did not sign. ... Selected by Kansas City Royals organization in first round (25th pick overall) of free-agent draft (June 2, 1999); pick received from Boston Red Sox as part of compensation for signing Type A free agent 2B Jose Offerman.

Year	League	W	L	Pct.	ERA	G	GS	CG	ShO	Sv.	IP	H	R	ER	BB	SO
1999—Spokane (N'West)		2	2	.500	4.47	11	11	0	0	0	46 $^1/_3$	43	25	23	17	57
2000—Wilmington (Caro.)		9	7	.563	3.92	26	25	0	0	1	144 $^2/_3$	115	79	63	76	129
—Wichita (Texas)		0	1	.000	7.71	2	2	0	0	0	11 $^2/_3$	16	10	10	7	9
2001—Omaha (PCL)		8	8	.500	4.68	28	27	1	0	0	144 $^1/_3$	144	90	75	76	110
—Kansas City (A.L.)		1	1	.500	4.70	3	3	0	0	0	15 $^1/_3$	18	10	8	4	7
Major League totals (1 year)		1	1	.500	4.70	3	3	0	0	0	15 $^1/_3$	18	10	8	4	7

PERSONAL: Born June 3, 1973, in Caracas, Venezuela. ... 6-1/205. ... Bats right, throws right. ... Full name: Robert Alexis Machado.

TRANSACTIONS/CAREER NOTES: Signed as non-drafted free agent by Chicago White Sox organization (August 10, 1989). ... Released by White Sox (May 19, 1999). ... Signed by Montreal Expos organization (May 21, 1999). ... Granted free agency (October 15, 1999). ... Signed by Seattle Mariners organization (November 17, 1999). ... Granted free agency (October 2, 2000). ... Signed by Chicago Cubs organization (December 13, 2000).

STATISTICAL NOTES: Led Gulf Coast League catchers with 349 total chances in 1991. ... Tied for Southern League lead in double plays by catcher with 10 in 1996. ... Tied for American Association lead in passed balls with nine in 1997.

Year Team (League)	Pos.	G	AB	R	H	2B	3B	HR	RBI	Avg.	BB	SO	SB	PO	A	E	Avg.
1990—Dominican (DSL)........		55	191	28	53	9	0	5	20	.277	14	32	2	...	...	...	...
1991—GC White Sox (GCL) ..	C	38	126	11	31	4	1	0	15	.246	6	21	2	*287	*54	8	.977
1992—Utica (NY-Penn)	C	45	161	16	44	13	1	2	20	.273	5	26	1	279	30	12	.963
1993—South Bend (Midw.) ...	C	75	281	34	86	14	3	2	33	.306	19	59	1	490	66	12	.979
1994—Prince William (Caro.)	C	93	312	45	81	17	1	11	47	.260	27	68	0	562	66	*16	.975
1995—Nashville (A.A.)	C	16	49	7	7	3	0	1	5	.143	7	12	0	87	17	3	.972
—Prince William (Caro.)	C	83	272	37	69	14	0	6	31	.254	40	47	0	548	78	5	.992
1996—Birmingham (Sou.).....	C-DH	87	309	35	74	16	0	6	28	.239	20	56	1	502	67	5	.991
—Chicago (A.L.)	C	4	6	1	4	1	0	0	2	.667	0	0	0	6	0	0	1.000
1997—Nashville (A.A.)	C-DH	84	308	43	83	18	0	8	30	.269	12	61	5	461	49	6	.988
—Chicago (A.L.)	C	10	15	1	3	0	1	0	2	.200	1	6	0	34	3	0	1.000
1998—Calgary (PCL).............	C-DH	66	239	31	63	19	0	4	27	.264	20	33	2	409	39	6	.987
—Chicago (A.L.)	C	34	111	14	23	6	0	3	15	.207	7	22	0	189	17	4	.981
1999—Charlotte (I.L.)...........	C	16	54	4	11	3	0	2	7	.204	4	13	0	111	12	3	.976
—Ottawa (I.L.)■..........	C-DH	21	75	6	17	5	0	0	3	.227	0	13	0	141	12	3	.981
—Montreal (N.L.)..........	C	17	22	3	4	1	0	0	0	.182	2	6	0	33	3	0	1.000
2000—Tacoma (PCL)■	C	92	330	41	99	20	0	9	58	.300	28	43	1	491	57	•11	.980
—Seattle (A.L.)............	C	8	14	2	3	0	0	1	1	.214	1	4	0	35	2	0	1.000
2001—Iowa (PCL)■.............	C	53	180	20	51	11	0	8	30	.283	11	36	0	396	27	5	.988
—Chicago (N.L.)...........	C	52	135	13	30	10	0	2	13	.222	7	26	0	317	20	1	.997
American League totals (4 years)		56	146	18	33	7	1	4	20	.226	9	32	0	264	22	4	.986
National League totals (2 years)		69	157	16	34	11	0	2	13	.217	9	32	0	350	23	1	.997
Major League totals (6 years)		125	303	34	67	18	1	6	33	.221	18	64	0	614	45	5	.992

PERSONAL: Born January 25, 1974, in Panama City, Panama. ... 5-10/173. ... Bats both, throws right. ... Full name: Jose Prade Macias.

HIGH SCHOOL: Instituto Technologico (Panama City, Panama).

TRANSACTIONS/CAREER NOTES: Signed as non-drafted free agent by Montreal Expos organization (February 14, 1992). ... Selected by Detroit Tigers organization from Expos organization in Rule 5 minor league draft (December 9, 1996).

STATISTICAL NOTES: Led Florida State League second basemen with 255 putouts, 349 assists, 611 total chances and .989 fielding percentage in 1997. ... Tied for International League lead with 16 errors by second baseman in 1999. ... Career major league grand slams: 1.

Year Team (League)	Pos.	G	AB	R	H	2B	3B	HR	RBI	Avg.	BB	SO	SB	PO	A	E	Avg.
1992—Dom. Expos (DSL)	OF	61	198	58	58	5	1	2	23	.293	60	11	41	73	41	7	.942
1993—Dom. Expos (DSL)	OF	64	211	60	66	12	1	4	26	.313	59	26	38	100	44	7	.954
1994—GC Expos (GCL)	OF-2B-3B	31	104	23	28	8	2	1	6	.269	14	15	4	39	20	4	.937
1995—Vermont (NY-Penn)....	OF-2B-3B	53	176	24	42	4	2	0	9	.239	19	19	11	93	76	9	.949
1996—Delmarva (S.Atl.)........	OF-2B-3B	116	369	64	91	13	4	1	33	.247	56	48	38	179	80	6	.970
1997—Lakeland (FSL)■.......	2B-OF	122	424	54	113	18	2	2	52	.267	52	33	10	†255	†349	7	†.989
1998—Jacksonville (Sou.).....	2B	128	511	82	156	28	10	12	71	.305	52	46	6	246	354	14	*.977
1999—Toledo (I.L.)...............	2B-OF-SS	112	438	44	107	18	8	2	36	.244	36	60	10	218	351	‡18	.969
—Detroit (A.L.)	2B	5	4	2	1	0	0	1	2	.250	0	1	0	1	6	0	1.000
2000—Toledo (I.L.)...............	OF-SS-2B	33	130	19	30	5	0	0	8	.231	17	17	2	64	30	6	.940
—Detroit (A.L.)	2-3-O-DH-S	73	173	25	44	3	5	2	24	.254	18	24	2	53	116	4	.977
2001—Detroit (A.L.)	3B-OF-2B-DH	137	488	62	131	24	6	8	51	.268	32	54	21	165	219	12	.970
Major League totals (3 years)		215	665	89	176	27	11	11	77	.265	50	79	23	219	341	16	.972

RECORD AS PITCHER

Year League	W	L	Pct.	ERA	G	GS	CG	ShO	Sv.	IP	H	R	ER	BB	SO
1994—GC Expos (GCL).................	0	0	...	0.00	1	0	0	0	0	1	0	0	0	0	0

PERSONAL: Born June 20, 1976, in Oak Lawn, Ill. ... 5-10/170. ... Bats left, throws right. ... Full name: Robert William Mackowiak.

HIGH SCHOOL: Oak Lawn (Ill.), then Lake Central (Schererville, Ind.).

JUNIOR COLLEGE: South Suburban (Ill.).

TRANSACTIONS/CAREER NOTES: Selected by Pittsburgh Pirates organization in 53rd round of free-agent draft (June 4, 1996). ... On Pittsburgh disabled list (July 20-August 18, 2001); included rehabilitation assignment to Nashville (August 9-18).

Year Team (League)	Pos.	G	AB	R	H	2B	3B	HR	RBI	Avg.	BB	SO	SB	PO	A	E	Avg.
1996—GC Pirates (GCL)........	OF-SS	27	86	8	23	6	1	0	14	.267	13	11	3	31	8	10	.796
1997—Erie (NY-Penn)	OF-3B-1B-C-P	61	203	26	58	14	2	1	25	.286	21	47	1	74	37	6	.949
1998—Augusta (S.Atl.)...........	OF-1B	25	70	16	17	4	0	1	8	.243	13	19	4	29	3	2	.941
—Lynchburg (Caro.).......	3B-2B-OF	86	292	30	80	24	6	3	31	.274	17	65	6	53	143	18	.916
1999—Lynchburg (Caro.)	2B-OF	74	263	51	80	7	4	7	30	.304	18	57	9	117	158	1	.996
—Altoona (East.)	1B-OF	53	195	21	51	15	3	3	27	.262	8	34	0	114	158	8	.971

Year	Team (League)	Pos.	G	AB	R	H	2B	3B	HR	RBI	Avg.	BB	SO	SB	PO	A	E	Avg.
									BATTING							FIELDING		
2000—	Altoona (East.)	2B-OF-3B-SS	134	526	82	156	33	4	13	87	.297	22	96	18	208	255	17	.965
2001—	Nashville (PCL)	OF-2B-3B	32	118	14	31	5	0	4	14	.263	7	39	1	57	52	7	.940
—	Pittsburgh (N.L.)	OF-2B-3B-1B	83	214	30	57	15	2	4	21	.266	15	52	4	104	60	6	.965
Major League totals (1 year)			83	214	30	57	15	2	4	21	.266	15	52	4	104	60	6	.965

RECORD AS PITCHER

Year	League	W	L	Pct.	ERA	G	GS	CG	ShO	Sv.	IP	H	R	ER	BB	SO
1997—	Erie (NY-Penn)	0	0	...	0.00	1	0	0	0	0	1 1/3	1	0	0	0	1

MacRAE, SCOTT   P   REDS

PERSONAL: Born August 13, 1974, in Dearborn, Mich. ... 6-3/205. ... Throws right, bats right. ... Full name: Scott Patrick MacRae.
HIGH SCHOOL: Walton (Marietta, Ga.).
COLLEGE: Valdosta State.
TRANSACTIONS/CAREER NOTES: Selected by Cincinnati Reds organization in 32nd round of free-agent draft (June 1, 1995). ... Released by Reds (November 16, 2001). ... Re-signed by Reds organization (December 21, 2001).

Year	League	W	L	Pct.	ERA	G	GS	CG	ShO	Sv.	IP	H	R	ER	BB	SO
1995—	Billings (Pio.)	0	1	.000	5.67	18	0	0	0	1	27	32	24	17	20	9
1996—	Charleston, W.Va. (S.Atl.)	8	7	.533	3.35	29	20	1	0	0	123 2/3	118	61	46	53	82
1997—	Burlington (Midw.)	11	4	.733	3.82	27	26	4	1	0	160 1/3	159	76	68	57	89
1998—	Chattanooga (Sou.)	9	4	.692	4.43	49	5	0	0	0	113 2/3	105	70	56	56	67
1999—	Chattanooga (Sou.)	8	7	.533	4.42	39	17	0	0	0	128 1/3	139	76	63	49	81
2000—	Chattanooga (Sou.)	4	1	.800	3.59	55	0	0	0	1	77 2/3	75	32	31	40	61
2001—	Chattanooga (Sou.)	5	2	.714	3.68	19	8	1	0	0	58 2/3	60	29	24	14	42
—	Louisville (I.L.)	2	2	.500	1.23	11	0	0	0	2	22	14	5	3	6	15
—	Cincinnati (N.L.)	0	1	.000	4.02	24	0	0	0	0	31 1/3	33	15	14	8	18
Major League totals (1 year)		0	1	.000	4.02	24	0	0	0	0	31 1/3	33	15	14	8	18

MADDUX, GREG   P   BRAVES

PERSONAL: Born April 14, 1966, in San Angelo, Texas. ... 6-0/185. ... Throws right, bats right. ... Full name: Gregory Alan Maddux. ... Brother of Mike Maddux, pitcher with nine major league teams (1986-2000).
HIGH SCHOOL: Valley (Las Vegas).
TRANSACTIONS/CAREER NOTES: Selected by Chicago Cubs organization in second round of free-agent draft (June 4, 1984). ... Granted free agency (October 26, 1992). ... Signed by Atlanta Braves (December 9, 1992).
RECORDS: Holds major league career records for most years leading league in putouts by pitcher—7; most years leading league in chances accepted by pitcher—12; most putouts by pitcher—422; and most years leading league in assists by pitcher—8. ... Shares major league career records for most years leading league in double plays by pitcher—5; most years leading league in assists by pitcher—7. ... Shares major league single-season record for fewest complete games for leader—8 (1993). ... Shares major league single-game record for most putouts by pitcher—7 (April 29, 1990). ... Holds N.L. single season record for most consecutive innings with no bases on balls—72 1/3 (June 20 through August 12, 2001).
HONORS: Won N.L. Gold Glove at pitcher (1990-2001). ... Named righthanded pitcher on THE SPORTING NEWS N.L. All-Star team (1992-95 and 2000). ... Named N.L. Cy Young Award winner by Baseball Writers' Association of America (1992-95). ... Named N.L. Pitcher of the Year by THE SPORTING NEWS (1993-95).
STATISTICAL NOTES: Led Appalachian League with eight hit batsmen in 1984. ... Led American Association with 12 hit batsmen in 1986. ... Led N.L. with 14 hit batsmen in 1992. ... Pitched 3-1 one-hit, complete-game victory against Houston (May 28, 1995). ... Pitched 2-0 one-hit, complete-game victory against San Diego (April 27, 1997).
MISCELLANEOUS: Appeared in three games as pinch runner (1988). ... Singled and scored and struck out in two appearances as pinch hitter (1991). ... Appeared in one game as pinch hitter (2001).

Year	League	W	L	Pct.	ERA	G	GS	CG	ShO	Sv.	IP	H	R	ER	BB	SO
1984—	Pikeville (Appl.)	6	2	.750	2.63	14	12	2	•2	0	85 2/3	63	35	25	41	62
1985—	Peoria (Midw.)	13	9	.591	3.19	27	27	6	0	0	186	176	86	66	52	125
1986—	Pittsfield (East.)	4	3	.571	2.73	8	8	4	2	0	62 2/3	49	22	19	15	35
—	Iowa (A.A.)	10	1	*.909	3.02	18	18	5	•2	0	128 1/3	127	49	43	30	65
—	Chicago (N.L.)	2	4	.333	5.52	6	5	1	0	0	31	44	20	19	11	20
1987—	Chicago (N.L.)	6	14	.300	5.61	30	27	1	1	0	155 2/3	181	111	97	74	101
—	Iowa (A.A.)	3	0	1.000	0.98	4	4	2	•2	0	27 2/3	17	3	3	12	22
1988—	Chicago (N.L.)	18	8	.692	3.18	34	34	9	3	0	249	230	97	88	81	140
1989—	Chicago (N.L.)	19	12	.613	2.95	35	35	7	1	0	238 1/3	222	90	78	82	135
1990—	Chicago (N.L.)	15	15	.500	3.46	35	•35	8	2	0	237	*242	*116	91	71	144
1991—	Chicago (N.L.)	15	11	.577	3.35	37	*37	7	2	0	*263	232	113	98	66	198
1992—	Chicago (N.L.)	•20	11	.645	2.18	35	•35	9	4	0	*268	201	68	65	70	199
1993—	Atlanta (N.L.)■	20	10	.667	*2.36	36	•36	*8	1	0	*267	228	85	70	52	197
1994—	Atlanta (N.L.)	•16	6	.727	*1.56	25	25	*10	•3	0	*202	150	44	35	31	156
1995—	Atlanta (N.L.)	*19	2	*.905	*1.63	28	28	*10	•3	0	•209 2/3	147	39	38	23	181
1996—	Atlanta (N.L.)	15	11	.577	2.72	35	35	5	1	0	245	225	85	74	28	172
1997—	Atlanta (N.L.)	19	4	*.826	2.20	33	33	5	2	0	232 2/3	200	58	57	20	177
1998—	Atlanta (N.L.)	18	9	.667	*2.22	34	34	9	*5	0	251	201	75	62	45	204
1999—	Atlanta (N.L.)	19	9	.679	3.57	33	33	4	0	0	219 1/3	258	103	87	37	136
2000—	Atlanta (N.L.)	19	9	.679	3.00	35	•35	6	•3	0	249 1/3	225	91	83	42	190
2001—	Atlanta (N.L.)	17	11	.607	3.05	34	34	3	•3	0	233	220	86	79	27	173
Major League totals (16 years)		257	146	.638	2.84	505	501	102	34	0	3551	3206	1281	1121	760	2523

DIVISION SERIES RECORD

RECORDS: Holds N.L. career records for most wins—8; games started—8; innings pitched—54; runs allowed—24; games pitched—9; hits allowed—59; and earned runs allowed—19. ... Shares N.L. career record for strikeouts—36.
NOTES: Appeared in one game as pinch runner (2000).

M

Year League	W	L	Pct.	ERA	G	GS	CG	ShO	Sv.	IP	H	R	ER	BB	SO
1995— Atlanta (N.L.)	1	0	1.000	4.50	2	2	0	0	0	14	19	7	7	2	7
1996— Atlanta (N.L.)	1	0	1.000	0.00	1	1	0	0	0	7	3	2	0	0	7
1997— Atlanta (N.L.)	1	0	1.000	1.00	1	1	1	0	0	9	7	1	1	1	6
1998— Atlanta (N.L.)	1	0	1.000	2.57	1	1	0	0	0	7	7	2	2	0	4
1999— Atlanta (N.L.)	0	1	.000	2.57	2	1	0	0	0	7	10	2	2	5	5
2000— Atlanta (N.L.)	0	1	.000	11.25	1	1	0	0	0	4	9	7	5	3	2
2001— Atlanta (N.L.)	0	0	...	3.00	1	1	0	0	0	6	4	3	2	3	5
Division series totals (7 years)	4	2	.667	3.17	9	8	1	0	0	54	59	24	19	14	36

CHAMPIONSHIP SERIES RECORD

RECORDS: Holds career records for most runs allowed—50; earned runs allowed—36; and sacrifice hits—6. ... Shares career record for hit batsmen—5. ... Shares single-series record for most earned runs allowed—11 (1989). ... Holds N.L. single-series record for most runs allowed—12 (1989).

NOTES: Scored in only appearance as pinch runner (1989).

Year League	W	L	Pct.	ERA	G	GS	CG	ShO	Sv.	IP	H	R	ER	BB	SO
1989— Chicago (N.L.)	0	1	.000	13.50	2	2	0	0	0	7 1/3	13	12	11	4	5
1993— Atlanta (N.L.)	1	1	.500	4.97	2	2	0	0	0	12 2/3	11	8	7	7	11
1995— Atlanta (N.L.)	1	0	1.000	1.13	1	1	0	0	0	8	7	1	1	2	4
1996— Atlanta (N.L.)	1	1	.500	2.51	2	2	0	0	0	14 1/3	15	9	4	2	10
1997— Atlanta (N.L.)	0	2	.000	1.38	2	2	0	0	0	13	9	7	2	4	16
1998— Atlanta (N.L.)	0	1	.000	3.00	2	1	0	0	1	6	5	2	2	3	4
1999— Atlanta (N.L.)	1	0	1.000	1.93	2	2	0	0	0	14	12	3	3	1	7
2001— Atlanta (N.L.)	0	2	.000	5.40	2	2	0	0	0	10	14	8	6	2	7
Champ. series totals (8 years)	4	8	.333	3.80	15	14	0	0	1	85 1/3	86	50	36	25	64

WORLD SERIES RECORD

NOTES: Member of World Series championship team (1995).

Year League	W	L	Pct.	ERA	G	GS	CG	ShO	Sv.	IP	H	R	ER	BB	SO
1995— Atlanta (N.L.)	1	1	.500	2.25	2	2	1	0	0	16	9	6	4	3	8
1996— Atlanta (N.L.)	1	1	.500	1.72	2	2	0	0	0	15 2/3	14	3	3	1	5
1999— Atlanta (N.L.)	0	1	.000	2.57	1	1	0	0	0	7	5	4	2	3	5
World Series totals (3 years)	2	3	.400	2.09	5	5	1	0	0	38 2/3	28	13	9	7	18

ALL-STAR GAME RECORD

Year League	W	L	Pct.	ERA	GS	CG	ShO	Sv.	IP	H	R	ER	BB	SO
1988— National				Did not play.										
1992— National	0	0	...	6.75	0	0	0	0	1 1/3	1	1	1	0	0
1994— National	0	0	...	3.00	1	0	0	0	3	3	1	1	0	2
1995— National				Selected, did not play—injured.										
1996— National				Did not play.										
1997— National	0	0		4.50	1	0	0	0	2	2	1	1	0	0
1998— National	0	0		0.00	1	0	0	0	2	3	0	0	1	1
2000— National				Selected, did not play—injured.										
All-Star Game totals (4 years)	0	0	...	3.24	3	0	0	0	8 1/3	9	3	3	1	3

M

MADURO, CALVIN   P   ORIOLES

PERSONAL: Born September 5, 1974, in Santa Cruz, Aruba. ... 6-0/180. ... Throws right, bats right. ... Full name: Calvin Gregory Maduro.
HIGH SCHOOL: Tourist Economy School (Santa Cruz, Aruba).
COLLEGE: St. Antonius College (Aruba).
TRANSACTIONS/CAREER NOTES: Signed as non-drafted free agent by Baltimore Orioles organization (September 9, 1991). ... Traded by Orioles with P Garrett Stephenson to Philadelphia Phillies (September 4, 1996), completing deal in which Phillies traded 3B Todd Zeile and OF Pete Incaviglia to Orioles for two players to be named later (August 29, 1996). ... Released by Phillies (November 19, 1998). ... Signed by Orioles organization (February 5, 1999). ... On Baltimore disabled list (May 14-June 20 and June 22, 2000-remainder of season); included rehabilitation assignments to Rochester (June 10-16) and Frederick (June 17). ... Granted free agency (December 21, 2000). ... Re-signed by Orioles (February 16, 2001).
STATISTICAL NOTES: Pitched 5-0 no-hit victory for Bowie against Portland (May 28, 1996, first game).
MISCELLANEOUS: Appeared in one game as pinch runner with Philadelphia (1997).

Year League	W	L	Pct.	ERA	G	GS	CG	ShO	Sv.	IP	H	R	ER	BB	SO
1992— Gulf Coast Orioles (GCL)	1	4	.200	2.27	13	•12	1	1	0	71 1/3	56	29	18	26	66
1993— Bluefield (Appl.)	•9	4	.692	3.96	14	•14	*3	0	0	*91	90	46	40	17	*83
1994— Frederick (Caro.)	9	8	.529	4.25	27	26	0	0	0	152 1/3	132	86	72	59	137
1995— Frederick (Caro.)	8	5	.615	2.94	20	20	2	2	0	122 1/3	109	43	40	34	120
— Bowie (East.)	0	6	.000	5.09	7	7	0	0	0	35 1/3	39	28	20	27	26
1996— Bowie (East.)	9	7	.563	3.26	19	19	4	*3	0	124 1/3	116	50	45	36	87
— Rochester (I.L.)	3	5	.375	4.74	8	8	0	0	0	43 2/3	49	25	23	18	40
— Philadelphia (N.L.)■	0	1	.000	3.52	4	2	0	0	0	15 1/3	13	6	6	3	11
1997— Philadelphia (N.L.)	3	7	.300	7.23	15	13	0	0	0	71	83	59	57	41	31
— Scranton/W.B. (I.L.)	6	4	.600	4.99	13	13	2	0	0	79 1/3	71	48	44	57	53
1998— Scranton/W.B. (I.L.)	12	9	.571	5.98	28	27	4	1	0	177 2/3	*211	123	118	68	120
1999— Rochester (I.L.)■■	11	11	.500	3.99	29	•28	2	1	0	169	179	88	75	60	149
2000— Baltimore (A.L.)	0	0	...	9.64	15	2	0	0	0	23 1/3	29	25	25	16	18
— Rochester (I.L.)	1	0	1.000	0.00	4	1	0	0	0	4	1	1	0	4	6
— Frederick (Caro.)	0	0	...	0.00	1	1	0	0	0	2	1	0	0	0	6
2001— Baltimore (A.L.)	5	6	.455	4.23	22	12	0	0	0	93 2/3	83	44	44	36	51
— Rochester (I.L.)	2	7	.222	4.03	12	11	1	1	0	67	61	37	30	22	48
A.L. totals (2 years)	5	6	.455	5.31	37	14	0	0	0	117	112	69	69	52	69
N.L. totals (2 years)	3	8	.273	6.57	19	15	0	0	0	86 1/3	96	65	63	44	42
Major League totals (4 years)	8	14	.364	5.84	56	29	0	0	0	203 1/3	208	134	132	96	111

PERSONAL: Born September 30, 1962, in Tampa. ... 6-4/215. ... Bats left, throws right. ... Full name: David Joseph Magadan. ... Cousin of Lou Piniella, manager, Seattle Mariners, and outfielder/designated hitter with four major league teams (1964 and 1968-84). ... Name pronounced MAG-uh-dun.

HIGH SCHOOL: Jesuit (Tampa).

COLLEGE: Alabama.

TRANSACTIONS/CAREER NOTES: Selected by Boston Red Sox organization in 12th round of free-agent draft (June 3, 1980); did not sign. ... Selected by New York Mets organization in second round of free-agent draft (June 6, 1983). ... On disabled list (August 7-September 10, 1984; March 29-April 17, 1987; May 5-20, 1988; and August 9, 1992-remainder of season). ... Granted free agency (October 27, 1992). ... Signed by Florida Marlins organization (December 8, 1992). ... Traded by Marlins to Seattle Mariners for OF Henry Cotto and P Jeff Darwin (June 27, 1993). ... Traded by Mariners to Marlins for P Jeff Darwin and cash (November 9, 1993). ... On disabled list (March 29-April 13 and July 21, 1994-remainder of season). ... Granted free agency (October 19, 1994). ... Signed by Houston Astros (April 15, 1995). ... Granted free agency (October 30, 1995). ... Signed by Chicago Cubs (December 26, 1995). ... On Chicago disabled list (March 22-April 16 and April 17-May 31, 1996); included rehabilitation assignment to Daytona (May 17-29). ... Granted free agency (November 18, 1996). ... Signed by Oakland Athletics organization (January 23, 1997). ... Granted free agency (October 27, 1997). ... Re-signed by A's (November 12, 1997). ... On disabled list (May 16, 1998-remainder of season). ... Granted free agency (October 29, 1998). ... Signed by San Diego Padres (December 21, 1998). ... On disabled list (April 11-30, 2000). ... Granted free agency (October 27, 2000). ... Re-signed by Padres (January 5, 2001). ... Granted free agency (November 5, 2001).

HONORS: Named Golden Spikes Award winner by USA Baseball (1983). ... Named designated hitter on The Sporting News college All-America team (1983).

STATISTICAL NOTES: Led Carolina League with 10 intentional bases on balls received in 1984. ... Led Texas League third basemen with 87 putouts, 275 assists, 393 total chances and 31 errors in 1985. ... Led International League third basemen with .934 fielding percentage, 283 assists and 31 double plays in 1986. ... Led N.L. first basemen with .998 fielding percentage in 1990.

									BATTING				FIELDING			
Year	Team (League)	Pos.	G	AB	R	H	2B	3B	HR	RBI	Avg.	BB	SO	SB	PO	A	E	Avg.
1983— Columbia (S.Atl.)		1B	64	220	41	74	13	1	3	32	.336	51	29	2	520	37	7	.988
1984— Lynchburg (Caro.)		1B	112	371	78	130	22	4	0	62	*.350	104	43	2	896	64	16	.984
1985— Jackson (Texas)		3B-1B	134	466	84	144	22	0	0	76	.309	*106	57	0	†106	†276	†31	.925
1986— Tidewater (I.L.)		3B-1B	133	473	68	147	33	6	1	64	.311	84	45	2	78	†284	25	†.935
— New York (N.L.)		1B	10	18	3	8	0	0	0	3	.444	3	1	0	48	5	0	1.000
1987— New York (N.L.)		3B-1B	85	192	21	61	13	1	3	24	.318	22	22	0	88	92	4	.978
1988— New York (N.L.)		1B-3B	112	314	39	87	15	0	1	35	.277	60	39	0	459	99	10	.982
1989— New York (N.L.)		1B-3B	127	374	47	107	22	3	4	41	.286	49	37	1	587	89	7	.990
1990— New York (N.L.)		1B-3B	144	451	74	148	28	6	6	72	.328	74	55	2	837	99	3	†.997
1991— New York (N.L.)		1B	124	418	58	108	23	0	4	51	.258	83	50	1	1035	90	5	.996
1992— New York (N.L.)		3B-1B	99	321	33	91	9	1	3	28	.283	56	44	1	54	136	11	.945
1993— Florida (N.L.)■		3B-1B	66	227	22	65	12	0	4	29	.286	44	30	0	55	122	7	.962
— Seattle (A.L.)■	1B-3B-DH	71	228	27	59	11	0	1	21	.259	36	33	2	325	72	5	.988
1994— Florida (N.L.)■		3B-1B	74	211	30	58	7	0	1	17	.275	39	25	0	127	78	4	.981
1995— Houston (N.L.)■		3B-1B	127	348	44	109	24	0	2	51	.313	71	56	2	121	163	18	.940
1996— Daytona (FSL)■		3B-DH	7	20	5	6	1	0	0	3	.300	7	2	0	0	6	1	.857
— Iowa (A.A.)		3B	3	9	0	2	1	0	0	1	.222	1	2	0	3	3	0	1.000
— Chicago (N.L.)		3B-1B	78	169	23	43	10	0	3	17	.254	29	23	0	75	67	3	.979
1997— Oakland (A.L.)■	3B-1B-DH	128	271	38	82	10	1	4	30	.303	50	40	1	148	65	5	.977
1998— Oakland (A.L.)		3B-1B	35	109	12	35	8	0	1	13	.321	13	12	0	48	55	6	.945
1999— San Diego (N.L.)■		3B-1B	116	248	20	68	12	1	2	30	.274	45	36	1	209	85	6	.980
2000— San Diego (N.L.)	3B-1B-DH-SS	95	132	13	36	7	0	2	21	.273	32	23	0	58	41	2	.980
2001— San Diego (N.L.)	3-1-DH-2-S	91	128	12	32	7	0	1	12	.250	12	20	0	39	25	3	.955
American League totals (3 years)			234	608	77	176	29	1	6	64	.289	99	85	3	521	192	16	.978
National League totals (14 years)			1348	3551	439	1021	189	12	36	431	.288	619	461	8	3792	1191	83	.984
Major League totals (16 years)			1582	4159	516	1197	218	13	42	495	.288	718	546	11	4313	1383	99	.983

CHAMPIONSHIP SERIES RECORD

									BATTING				FIELDING			
Year	Team (League)	Pos.	G	AB	R	H	2B	3B	HR	RBI	Avg.	BB	SO	SB	PO	A	E	Avg.
1988— New York (N.L.)		PH	3	3	0	0	0	0	0	0	.000	0	2	0	...	...	...	...

PERSONAL: Born August 3, 1972, in Hattiesburg, Miss. ... 6-0/220. ... Bats right, throws right. ... Full name: Wendell Errol Magee Jr.

HIGH SCHOOL: Hattiesburg (Miss.).

JUNIOR COLLEGE: Pearl River Community College (Miss.).

COLLEGE: Samford.

TRANSACTIONS/CAREER NOTES: Selected by Philadelphia Phillies organization in 12th round of free-agent draft (June 2, 1994). ... Traded by Phillies to Detroit Tigers for P Bobby Sismondo (March 10, 2000). ... On Detroit disabled list (May 7-29, 2000); included rehabilitation assignment to Toledo (May 27-29). ... On Detroit disabled list (April 28-May 22, 2001); included rehabilitation assignment to Toledo (May 20-22).

STATISTICAL NOTES: Led International League outfielders with 320 total chances in 1998. ... Led International League outfielders with 325 total chances in 1999.

									BATTING				FIELDING			
Year	Team (League)	Pos.	G	AB	R	H	2B	3B	HR	RBI	Avg.	BB	SO	SB	PO	A	E	Avg.
1994— Batavia (NY-Penn)		OF	63	229	42	64	12	4	2	35	.279	16	24	10	115	7	6	.953
1995— Clearwater (FSL)		OF	96	388	67	137	24	5	6	46	*.353	33	40	7	166	12	5	.973
— Reading (East.)		OF	39	136	17	40	9	1	3	21	.294	21	17	3	65	4	5	.932
1996— Reading (East.)		OF	71	270	38	79	15	5	6	30	.293	24	40	10	101	8	3	.973
— Scranton/W.B. (I.L.)		OF	44	155	31	44	9	2	10	32	.284	21	31	3	92	2	4	.959
— Philadelphia (N.L.)		OF	38	142	9	29	7	0	2	14	.204	9	33	0	88	2	2	.978
1997— Philadelphia (N.L.)		OF	38	115	7	23	4	0	1	9	.200	9	20	1	95	2	4	.960
— Scranton/W.B. (I.L.)		OF	83	294	39	72	20	1	10	39	.245	30	56	4	167	3	3	.983

M

Year Team (League)	Pos.	G	AB	R	H	2B	3B	HR	RBI	Avg.	BB	SO	SB	PO	A	E	Avg.
						BATTING								FIELDING			
1998— Scranton/W.B. (I.L.) ...	OF	126	507	86	147	30	7	24	72	.290	46	102	7	*302	7	•11	.966
— Philadelphia (N.L.)......	OF	20	75	9	22	6	1	1	11	.293	7	11	0	31	1	2	.941
1999— Scranton/W.B. (I.L.) ...	OF	*142	*566	95	160	34	2	20	79	.283	55	124	10	*310	7	*8	.975
— Philadelphia (N.L.)......	OF	12	14	4	5	1	0	2	5	.357	1	4	0	5	0	0	1.000
2000— Detroit (A.L.)■........	OF-DH	91	186	31	51	4	2	7	31	.274	10	28	1	86	3	0	1.000
— Toledo (I.L.).............	OF	2	7	1	4	1	0	0	1	.571	1	1	0	2	0	0	1.000
2001— Detroit (A.L.)	OF-DH	90	207	26	44	11	4	5	17	.213	23	44	3	123	7	1	.992
— Toledo (I.L.).............	OF	2	9	0	4	0	0	0	1	.444	0	0	0	2	0	0	1.000
American League totals (2 years)		181	393	57	95	15	6	12	48	.242	33	72	4	209	10	1	.995
National League totals (4 years)		108	346	29	79	18	1	6	39	.228	26	68	1	219	5	8	.966
Major League totals (6 years)		289	739	86	174	33	7	18	87	.235	59	140	5	428	15	9	.980

MAGNANTE, MIKE — P — ATHLETICS

PERSONAL: Born June 17, 1965, in Glendale, Calif. ... 6-1/185. ... Throws left, bats left. ... Full name: Michael Anthony Magnante. ... Name pronounced mag-NAN-tee.
HIGH SCHOOL: John Burroughs (Burbank, Calif.).
COLLEGE: UCLA.
TRANSACTIONS/CAREER NOTES: Selected by Kansas City Royals organization in 11th round of free-agent draft (June 1, 1988). ... On disabled list (June 17, 1990-remainder of season; July 2-20, 1992; and July 16-31, 1994). ... On Kansas City disabled list (May 19-June 13, 1996); included rehabilitation assignment to Omaha (June 8-13). ... Released by Royals (October 2, 1996). ... Signed by Houston Astros organization (December 19, 1996). ... On disabled list (May 10-25, 1998). ... Granted free agency (October 23, 1998). ... Signed by Anaheim Angels (January 27, 1999). ... Granted free agency (October 29, 1999). ... Signed by Oakland Athletics (November 19, 1999). ... On Oakland disabled list (May 27-June 27, 2000); included rehabilitation assignments to Sacramento (June 8-14 and June 23-27).
RECORDS: Shares major league record for striking out side on nine pitches (August 22, 1997, ninth inning).

Year League	W	L	Pct.	ERA	G	GS	CG	ShO	Sv.	IP	H	R	ER	BB	SO
1988— Eugene (N'West)...............	1	1	.500	0.56	3	3	0	0	0	16	10	6	1	2	26
— Appleton (Midw.).............	3	2	.600	3.21	9	8	0	0	0	47 2/3	48	20	17	15	40
— Baseball City (FSL)...........	1	1	.500	4.13	4	4	1	0	0	24	19	12	11	8	19
1989— Memphis (Sou.)...............	8	9	.471	3.66	26	26	4	1	0	157 1/3	137	70	64	53	118
1990— Omaha (A.A.).................	2	5	.286	4.11	13	13	2	0	0	76 2/3	72	39	35	25	56
1991— Omaha (A.A.).................	6	1	.857	3.02	10	10	2	0	0	65 2/3	53	23	22	23	50
— Kansas City (A.L.)	0	1	.000	2.45	38	0	0	0	0	55	55	19	15	23	42
1992— Kansas City (A.L.)	4	9	.308	4.94	44	12	0	0	0	89 1/3	115	53	49	35	31
1993— Omaha (A.A.).................	2	6	.250	3.67	33	13	0	0	2	105 1/3	97	46	43	29	74
— Kansas City (A.L.)	1	2	.333	4.08	7	6	0	0	0	35 1/3	37	16	16	11	16
1994— Kansas City (A.L.)	2	3	.400	4.60	36	1	0	0	0	47	55	27	24	16	21
1995— Omaha (A.A.).................	5	1	.833	2.84	15	8	0	0	0	57	55	23	18	13	38
— Kansas City (A.L.)	1	1	.500	4.23	28	0	0	0	0	44 2/3	45	23	21	16	28
1996— Kansas City (A.L.)	2	2	.500	5.67	38	0	0	0	0	54	58	38	34	24	32
— Omaha (A.A.).................	1	0	1.000	0.00	1	0	0	0	0	3	3	1	0	0	6
1997— New Orleans (A.A.)■.........	2	3	.400	4.50	17	0	0	0	1	24	31	14	12	5	23
— Houston (N.L.)...............	3	1	.750	2.27	40	0	0	0	1	47 2/3	39	16	12	11	43
1998— Houston (N.L.)...............	4	7	.364	4.88	48	0	0	0	2	51 2/3	56	28	28	26	39
1999— Anaheim (A.L.)■.............	5	2	.714	3.38	53	0	0	0	0	69 1/3	68	30	26	29	44
2000— Oakland (A.L.)■.............	1	1	.500	4.31	55	0	0	0	0	39 2/3	50	22	19	19	17
— Sacramento (PCL)............	0	0	...	4.05	5	2	0	0	0	6 2/3	6	3	3	1	4
2001— Oakland (A.L.)..............	3	1	.750	2.77	66	0	0	0	0	55 1/3	50	23	17	13	23
A.L. totals (9 years)	19	22	.463	4.06	364	19	0	0	0	489 2/3	533	251	221	186	254
N.L. totals (2 years)	7	8	.467	3.62	88	0	0	0	3	99 1/3	95	44	40	37	82
Major League totals (11 years).....	26	30	.464	3.99	452	19	0	0	3	589	628	295	261	223	336

DIVISION SERIES RECORD

Year League	W	L	Pct.	ERA	G	GS	CG	ShO	Sv.	IP	H	R	ER	BB	SO
1997— Houston (N.L.)	0	0	...	4.50	2	0	0	0	0	2	4	3	1	0	2
1998— Houston (N.L.)							Did not play.								
2000— Oakland (A.L.)	0	0	...	0.00	2	0	0	0	0	3	1	0	0	0	2
2001— Oakland (A.L.)	0	0	...	0.00	1	0	0	0	0	1 1/3	3	0	0	1	1
Division series totals (3 years)	0	0	...	1.42	5	0	0	0	0	6 1/3	8	3	1	1	5

MAGRUDER, CHRIS — OF — RANGERS

PERSONAL: Born April 26, 1977, in Tacoma, Wash. ... 5-11/200. ... Bats both, throws right. ... Full name: Christopher James Magruder.
HIGH SCHOOL: West Valley (Yakima, Wash.).
COLLEGE: Washington.
TRANSACTIONS/CAREER NOTES: Selected by San Francisco Giants in second round of free agent draft (June 2, 1998); choice received from Tampa Bay Devil Rays as part of compensation for signing of Type A free agent P Wilson Alvarez. ... Traded with P Todd Ozias and P Erasmo Ramirez to Texas Rangers for 1B Andres Galarraga (July 24, 2001).

Year Team (League)	Pos.	G	AB	R	H	2B	3B	HR	RBI	Avg.	BB	SO	SB	PO	A	E	Avg.
						BATTING								FIELDING			
1998— Salem-Kaizer (NW).....	OF	47	177	43	59	8	5	3	18	.333	37	21	14	82	1	2	.976
— Bakersfield (Calif.)	OF	22	92	21	28	7	0	1	4	.304	13	16	3	48	2	0	1.000
1999— Shreveport (Texas)	OF	133	476	78	122	21	4	6	60	.256	69	85	17	241	5	3	*.988
2000— Shreveport (Texas)	OF	134	496	85	140	33	3	4	39	.282	67	75	18	277	6	5	.983
2001— Fresno (PCL)	OF	54	214	37	60	7	1	10	30	.280	18	45	3	118	2	1	.992
— Shreveport (Texas)	OF	40	149	22	38	6	3	2	11	.255	15	27	5	93	0	2	.979
— Oklahoma (PCL)■.....	OF	33	127	28	46	14	4	5	21	.362	21	19	1	69	2	1	.986
— Texas (A.L.)	OF	17	29	3	5	0	0	0	1	.172	1	5	0	21	1	0	1.000
Major League totals (1 year)		17	29	3	5	0	0	0	1	.172	1	5	0	21	1	0	1.000

M

PERSONAL: Born June 28, 1971, in Crestwood, Ill. ... 6-2/190. ... Throws left, bats left. ... Full name: Ronald Matthew Mahay.

HIGH SCHOOL: Alan B. Shepard (Palos Heights, Ill.).

JUNIOR COLLEGE: South Suburban College (Ill.).

TRANSACTIONS/CAREER NOTES: Selected by Boston Red Sox organization in 18th round of free-agent draft (June 3, 1991). ... On disabled list (May 5, 1992-remainder of season). ... On Lynchburg disabled list (August 6-September 9, 1993). ... On disabled list (August 23-September 1, 1994). ... On Pawtucket temporarily inactive list (April 19-25, 1995). ... On Sarasota disabled list (April 4-25, 1996). ... Claimed on waivers by Oakland Athletics (March 30, 1999). ... Traded by Athletics to Florida Marlins for cash (May 11, 2000). ... Granted free agency (October 2, 2000). ... Signed by San Diego Padres organization (November 20, 2000). ... On Portland disabled list (April 12-24, 2001). ... Released by Padres (May 15, 2001). ... Signed by Chicago Cubs organization (May 19, 2001).

MISCELLANEOUS: Played outfield (1991-95). ... Appeared in one game as pinch runner with Oakland (2000).

Year League	W	L	Pct.	ERA	G	GS	CG	ShO	Sv.	IP	H	R	ER	BB	SO
1996— Sarasota (FSL)	2	2	.500	3.82	31	4	0	0	2	70²/₃	61	33	30	35	68
— Trenton (East.)	0	1	.000	29.45	1	1	0	0	0	3²/₃	12	13	12	6	0
1997— Trenton (East.)	3	3	.500	3.10	17	4	0	0	5	40²/₃	29	16	14	13	47
— Pawtucket (I.L.)	1	0	1.000	0.00	2	0	0	0	0	4²/₃	3	0	0	1	6
— Boston (A.L.)	3	0	1.000	2.52	28	0	0	0	0	25	19	7	7	11	22
1998— Pawtucket (I.L.)	3	1	.750	4.17	23	1	0	0	3	41	37	20	19	19	41
— Boston (A.L.)	1	1	.500	3.46	29	0	0	0	1	26	26	16	10	15	14
1999— Oakland (A.L.)■	2	0	1.000	1.86	6	1	0	0	1	19¹/₃	8	4	4	3	15
— Vancouver (PCL)	7	2	.778	4.29	32	15	0	0	0	107	116	57	51	45	73
2000— Oakland (A.L.)	0	1	.000	9.00	5	2	0	0	0	16	26	18	16	9	5
— Florida (N.L.)■	1	0	1.000	6.04	18	0	0	0	0	25¹/₃	31	17	17	16	27
— Calgary (PCL)	0	1	.000	4.85	8	0	0	0	0	13	7	7	7	7	15
2001— Portland (PCL)■	1	2	.333	3.78	14	0	0	0	0	16²/₃	13	9	7	5	18
— Iowa (PCL)■	3	1	.750	2.31	36	0	0	0	14	46²/₃	29	12	12	10	52
— Chicago (N.L.)	0	0	...	2.61	17	0	0	0	0	20²/₃	14	6	6	15	24
A.L. totals (5 years)	6	2	.750	3.86	73	3	0	0	2	86¹/₃	79	45	37	38	56
N.L. totals (2 years)	1	0	1.000	4.50	35	0	0	0	0	46	45	23	23	31	51
Major League totals (6 years)	7	2	.778	4.08	108	3	0	0	2	132¹/₃	124	68	60	69	107

RECORD AS POSITION PLAYER

Year Team (League)	Pos.	G	AB	R	H	2B	3B	HR	RBI	Avg.	BB	SO	SB	PO	A	E	Avg.
1991— GC Red Sox (GCL)	OF	54	187	30	51	6	5	1	29	.273	33	40	2	97	2	3	.971
1992— Winter Haven (FSL)	OF	19	63	6	16	2	1	0	4	.254	2	19	0	33	2	1	.972
1993— Lynchburg (Caro.)	OF-C	73	254	28	54	8	1	5	23	.213	11	63	2	174	7	5	.973
— New Britain (East.)	OF	8	25	2	3	0	0	1	2	.120	1	6	1	15	1	2	.889
1994— Sarasota (FSL)	OF	105	367	43	102	18	0	4	46	.278	39	67	3	189	16	4	.981
1995— Pawtucket (I.L.)	OF	11	44	5	14	4	0	0	3	.318	4	9	1	30	2	0	1.000
— Trenton (East.)	OF	93	310	37	73	12	3	5	28	.235	44	90	5	187	9	6	.970
— Boston (A.L.)	OF	5	20	3	4	2	0	1	3	.200	1	6	0	9	0	0	1.000
Major League totals (1 year)		5	20	3	4	2	0	1	3	.200	1	6	0	9	0	0	1.000

PERSONAL: Born August 9, 1970, in Bryan, Texas. ... 6-4/212. ... Throws right, bats right. ... Full name: Patrick Lavon Mahomes. ... Name pronounced muh-HOMES.

HIGH SCHOOL: Lindale (Texas).

TRANSACTIONS/CAREER NOTES: Selected by Minnesota Twins organization in sixth round of free-agent draft (June 1, 1988). ... On disabled list (July 6-23, 1994). ... Traded by Twins to Boston Red Sox for a player to be named later (August 26, 1996); Twins acquired P Brian Looney to complete deal (December 17, 1996). ... Signed by Yokohoma BayStars of Japan Central League (1997). ... Signed by New York Mets (December 21, 1998). ... Granted free agency (December 21, 2000). ... Signed by Texas Rangers organization (January 11, 2001). ... Granted free agency (November 5, 2001).

RECORDS: Shares major league record for most home runs allowed in one inning—4 (August 17, 2001, sixth inning).

MISCELLANEOUS: Appeared in one game as pinch runner (1994). ... Struck out in only appearance as pinch hitter and appeared in one game as pinch runner (1999).

Year League	W	L	Pct.	ERA	G	GS	CG	ShO	Sv.	IP	H	R	ER	BB	SO
1988— Elizabethton (Appl.)	6	3	.667	3.69	13	13	3	0	0	78	66	45	32	51	93
1989— Kenosha (Midw.)	13	7	.650	3.28	25	25	3	1	0	156¹/₃	120	66	57	•100	167
1990— Visalia (Calif.)	11	11	.500	3.30	28	*28	5	1	0	•185¹/₃	136	77	68	*118	178
1991— Orlando (Sou.)	8	5	.615	*1.78	18	17	2	0	0	116	77	30	23	57	136
— Portland (PCL)	3	5	.375	3.44	9	9	2	0	0	55	50	26	21	36	41
1992— Minnesota (A.L.)	3	4	.429	5.04	14	13	0	0	0	69²/₃	73	41	39	37	44
— Portland (PCL)	9	5	.643	3.41	17	16	3	*3	1	111	97	43	42	43	87
1993— Minnesota (A.L.)	1	5	.167	7.71	12	5	0	0	0	37¹/₃	47	34	32	16	23
— Portland (PCL)	11	4	•.733	*3.03	17	16	3	1	0	115²/₃	89	47	39	54	94
1994— Minnesota (A.L.)	9	5	.643	4.72	21	21	0	0	0	120	121	68	63	62	53
1995— Minnesota (A.L.)	4	10	.286	6.37	47	7	0	0	3	94²/₃	100	74	67	47	67
1996— Minnesota (A.L.)	1	4	.200	7.20	20	5	0	0	0	45	63	38	36	27	30
— Salt Lake (PCL)	3	1	.750	3.74	22	2	0	0	7	33²/₃	32	14	14	12	41
— Boston (A.L.)■	2	0	1.000	5.84	11	0	0	0	2	12¹/₃	9	8	8	6	6
1997— Boston (A.L.)	1	0	1.000	8.10	10	0	0	0	0	10	15	10	9	10	5
— Pawtucket (I.L.)	5	1	.833	2.84	18	1	0	0	7	31²/₃	22	11	10	17	40
— Yokohama (Jap. Cen.)■	3	4	.429	4.82	11	9	0	0	0	52¹/₃	54	30	28	25	42
1998— Yokohama (Jap. Cen.)	0	4	.000	5.98	10	8	0	0	0	43²/₃	61	30	29	29	24
1999— Norfolk (I.L.)■	4	1	.800	3.49	6	6	0	0	0	38²/₃	38	17	15	12	24
— New York (N.L.)	8	0	1.000	3.68	39	0	0	0	0	63²/₃	44	26	26	37	51
2000— New York (N.L.)	5	3	.625	5.46	53	5	0	0	0	94	96	63	57	66	76
2001— Texas (A.L.)■	7	6	.538	5.70	56	4	0	0	0	107¹/₃	115	71	68	55	61
A.L. totals (7 years)	28	34	.452	5.84	191	55	0	0	5	496¹/₃	543	344	322	260	289
N.L. totals (2 years)	13	3	.813	4.74	92	5	0	0	0	157²/₃	140	89	83	103	127
Major League totals (9 years)	41	37	.526	5.57	283	60	0	0	5	654	683	433	405	363	416

DIVISION SERIES RECORD

Year League	W	L	Pct.	ERA	G	GS	CG	ShO	Sv.	IP	H	R	ER	BB	SO
1999— New York (N.L.)	0	0	...	5.40	1	0	0	0	0	$1\frac{2}{3}$	3	1	1	0	1
2000— New York (N.L.)							Did not play.								

CHAMPIONSHIP SERIES RECORD

Year League	W	L	Pct.	ERA	G	GS	CG	ShO	Sv.	IP	H	R	ER	BB	SO
1999— New York (N.L.)	0	0	...	1.42	3	0	0	0	0	$6\frac{1}{3}$	4	1	1	3	3
2000— New York (N.L.)							Did not play.								

WORLD SERIES RECORD

Year League	W	L	Pct.	ERA	G	GS	CG	ShO	Sv.	IP	H	R	ER	BB	SO
2000— New York (N.L.)							Did not play.								

MANESS, NICK   P   METS

PERSONAL: Born October 17, 1978, in Pinehurst, N.C. ... 6-4/210. ... Throws right, bats right. ... Full name: Nicholas Maurice Maness.
HIGH SCHOOL: North Moore (Robbins, N.C.).
TRANSACTIONS/CAREER NOTES: Selected by New York Mets organization in 12th round of free-agent draft (June 3, 1997).
STATISTICAL NOTES: Tied for Florida State League lead with five balks in 2000.

Year League	W	L	Pct.	ERA	G	GS	CG	ShO	Sv.	IP	H	R	ER	BB	SO
1997— Gulf Coast Mets (GCL)	3	2	.600	3.02	11	6	0	0	0	$44\frac{2}{3}$	52	25	15	20	54
1998— Kingsport (Appl.)	5	3	.625	4.48	13	13	0	0	0	$64\frac{1}{3}$	68	41	32	30	76
1999— Capital City (S.Atl.)	5	6	.455	4.95	23	22	0	0	0	$107\frac{1}{3}$	92	74	59	57	99
2000— St. Lucie (FSL)	11	7	.611	3.22	26	25	0	0	0	$145\frac{1}{3}$	116	58	52	68	124
— Binghamton (East.)	1	0	1.000	1.93	2	1	0	0	0	$9\frac{1}{3}$	8	2	2	4	3
2001— Binghamton (East.)	6	12	.333	4.97	28	26	1	0	0	143	168	94	79	65	107

MANN, JIM   P   ASTROS

PERSONAL: Born November 17, 1974, in Brockton, Mass. ... 6-3/225. ... Throws right, bats right. ... Full name: James Joseph Mann.
HIGH SCHOOL: Holbrook (Mass.).
JUNIOR COLLEGE: Massasoit Community College (Mass.).
TRANSACTIONS/CAREER NOTES: Selected by Toronto Blue Jays organization in 54th round of free-agent draft (June 3, 1993). ... Selected by New York Mets from Blue Jays organization in Rule 5 major league draft (December 13, 1999); Blue Jays acquired IF Jersen Perez as compensation for Mets keeping Mann (March 22, 2000). ... Granted free agency (October 18, 2000). ... Signed by Houston Astros organization (January 3, 2001).

Year League	W	L	Pct.	ERA	G	GS	CG	ShO	Sv.	IP	H	R	ER	BB	SO
1994— Gulf Coast Blue Jays (GCL)	3	2	.600	3.74	11	9	0	0	0	53	54	28	22	26	41
1995— Medicine Hat (Pio.)	5	4	.556	4.29	14	14	1	•1	0	$77\frac{2}{3}$	78	47	37	37	66
1996— St. Catharines (NY-Penn)	2	1	.667	3.62	26	0	0	0	17	$27\frac{1}{3}$	22	12	11	10	37
1997— Hagerstown (S.Atl.)	0	1	.000	5.06	19	0	0	0	4	$26\frac{2}{3}$	35	18	15	11	30
— Dunedin (FSL)	1	0	1.000	6.00	12	0	0	0	0	18	27	12	12	6	13
1998— Dunedin (FSL)	0	2	.000	3.04	51	0	0	0	25	$50\frac{1}{3}$	31	19	17	24	59
1999— Knoxville (Sou.)	1	2	.333	0.93	6	0	0	0	0	$9\frac{2}{3}$	6	2	1	1	12
— Syracuse (I.L.)	6	5	.545	4.64	47	0	0	0	5	66	53	35	34	39	72
2000— Norfolk (I.L.)■	3	4	.429	2.98	49	0	0	0	3	$81\frac{2}{3}$	61	27	27	33	74
— New York (N.L.)	0	0	...	10.13	2	0	0	0	0	$2\frac{2}{3}$	6	3	3	1	0
2001— New Orleans (PCL)■	6	3	.667	2.51	53	0	0	0	27	68	52	21	19	17	81
— Houston (N.L.)	0	0	...	3.38	4	0	0	0	0	$5\frac{1}{3}$	3	2	2	4	5
Major League totals (2 years)	0	0	...	5.63	6	0	0	0	0	8	9	5	5	5	5

M

MANTEI, MATT   P   DIAMONDBACKS

PERSONAL: Born July 7, 1973, in Tampa. ... 6-1/190. ... Throws right, bats right. ... Full name: Matthew Bruce Mantei. ... Name pronounced MAN-tay.
HIGH SCHOOL: River Valley (Three Oaks, Mich.).
TRANSACTIONS/CAREER NOTES: Selected by Seattle Mariners organization in 25th round of free-agent draft (June 3, 1991). ... Selected by Florida Marlins from Mariners organization in Rule 5 major league draft (December 5, 1994). ... On Florida disabled list (April 20-June 18 and July 29-September 1, 1995); included rehabilitation assignments to Portland and Charlotte (May 13-June 18). ... On Florida disabled list (June 19, 1996-remainder of season). ... Granted free agency (December 21, 1997). ... Re-signed by Marlins organization (December 21, 1997). ... On Florida disabled list (August 19-September 4, 1998). ... Traded by Marlins to Arizona Diamondbacks for P Vladimir Nunez, P Brad Penny and a player to be named later (July 9, 1999); Marlins acquired OF Abraham Nunez to complete deal (December 13, 1999). ... On Arizona disabled list (April 2-21 and May 5-21, 2000); included rehabilitation assignment to Tucson (April 14-21). ... On disabled list (April 25, 2001-remainder of season).
STATISTICAL NOTES: Tied for Arizona League lead with eight balks in 1991.

Year League	W	L	Pct.	ERA	G	GS	CG	ShO	Sv.	IP	H	R	ER	BB	SO
1991— Arizona Mariners (Ariz.)	1	4	.200	6.69	17	5	0	0	0	$40\frac{1}{3}$	54	40	30	28	29
1992— Arizona Mariners (Ariz.)	1	1	.500	5.63	3	3	0	0	0	16	18	10	10	5	19
1993— Bellingham (N'West)	1	1	.500	5.96	26	0	0	0	*12	$25\frac{2}{3}$	26	19	17	15	34
1994— Appleton (Midw.)	5	1	.833	2.06	48	0	0	0	26	48	42	14	11	21	70
1995— Portland (East.)■	1	0	1.000	2.38	8	0	0	0	1	$11\frac{1}{3}$	10	3	3	5	15
— Charlotte (I.L.)	0	1	.000	2.57	6	0	0	0	0	7	1	3	2	5	10
— Florida (N.L.)	0	0	...	4.72	12	0	0	0	0	$13\frac{1}{3}$	12	8	7	13	15
1996— Florida (N.L.)	1	0	1.000	6.38	14	0	0	0	0	$18\frac{1}{3}$	13	13	13	21	25
— Charlotte (I.L.)	0	2	.000	4.70	7	0	0	0	2	$7\frac{2}{3}$	6	4	4	7	8
1997— Brevard County (FSL)	0	0	...	6.00	4	0	0	0	0	6	4	4	4	6	11
— Portland (East.)	1	0	1.000	6.75	5	0	0	0	0	4	1	3	3	8	7
1998— Charlotte (I.L.)	1	2	.333	5.51	16	0	0	0	3	$16\frac{1}{3}$	11	10	10	18	25
— Florida (N.L.)	3	4	.429	2.96	42	0	0	0	9	$54\frac{2}{3}$	38	19	18	23	63

Year League	W	L	Pct.	ERA	G	GS	CG	ShO	Sv.	IP	H	R	ER	BB	SO
1999—Florida (N.L.)	1	2	.333	2.72	35	0	0	0	10	36⅓	24	11	11	25	50
—Arizona (N.L.)■	0	1	.000	2.79	30	0	0	0	22	29	20	10	9	19	49
2000—Tucson (PCL)	0	0	...	2.45	4	2	0	0	0	3⅔	1	1	1	3	2
—Arizona (N.L.)	1	1	.500	4.57	47	0	0	0	17	45⅓	31	24	23	35	53
2001—Arizona (N.L.)	0	0	...	2.57	8	0	0	0	2	7	6	2	2	4	12
Major League totals (6 years)	6	9	.400	3.66	188	0	0	0	60	204	144	87	83	140	267

DIVISION SERIES RECORD

Year League	W	L	Pct.	ERA	G	GS	CG	ShO	Sv.	IP	H	R	ER	BB	SO
1999—Arizona (N.L.)	0	1	.000	4.50	1	0	0	0	0	2	1	1	1	3	1

MANZANILLO, JOSIAS   P

PERSONAL: Born October 16, 1967, in San Pedro de Macoris, Dominican Republic. ... 6-0/205. ... Throws right, bats right. ... Brother of Ravelo Manzanillo, pitcher with Chicago White Sox (1988) and Pittsburgh Pirates (1994-95). ... Name pronounced hose-EYE-ess MAN-zan-EE-oh..

TRANSACTIONS/CAREER NOTES: Signed as non-drafted free agent by Boston Red Sox organization (January 10, 1983). ... On disabled list (June 8, 1987-remainder of season; and April 8, 1988-entire season). ... Granted free agency (March 24, 1992). ... Signed by Kansas City Royals organization (April 3, 1992). ... Granted free agency (October 15, 1992). ... Signed by Milwaukee Brewers (November 20, 1992). ... Traded by Brewers to New York Mets for OF Wayne Housie (June 12, 1993). ... On New York disabled list (July 27, 1994-remainder of season). ... Claimed on waivers by New York Yankees (June 5, 1995). ... On New York disabled list (July 6, 1995-remainder of season). ... Granted free agency (October 16, 1995). ... Played in Taiwan for 1996 season. ... Signed by Seattle Mariners organization (December 21, 1996). ... On Seattle disabled list (April 9-May 6 and May 25-July 1, 1997); included rehabilitation assignments to Memphis (May 1-6) and Tacoma (May 25-July 1). ... Released by Mariners (July 17, 1997). ... Signed by Houston Astros organization (July 27, 1997). ... Granted free agency (October 15, 1997). ... Signed by Tampa Bay Devil Rays organization (December 18, 1997). ... Released by Devil Rays (July 1, 1998). ... Signed by Mets organization (July 3, 1998). ... Granted free agency (October 15, 1998). ... Re-signed by Mets organization (December 18, 1998). ... On Norfolk disabled list (June 21, 1999-remainder of season). ... Granted free agency (October 4, 1999). ... Signed by Pittsburgh Pirates organization (February 9, 2000). ... Granted free agency (November 5, 2001).

MISCELLANEOUS: Appeared in one game as pinch runner (1999).

Year League	W	L	Pct.	ERA	G	GS	CG	ShO	Sv.	IP	H	R	ER	BB	SO
1983—Elmira (NY-Penn)	1	5	.167	7.98	12	4	0	0	0	38⅓	52	44	34	20	19
1984—Elmira (NY-Penn)	2	3	.400	5.26	14	0	0	0	1	25⅔	27	24	15	26	15
1985—Greensboro (S.Atl.)	1	1	.500	9.75	7	0	0	0	0	12	12	13	13	18	10
—Elmira (NY-Penn)	2	4	.333	3.86	19	4	0	0	1	39⅔	36	19	17	36	43
1986—Winter Haven (FSL)	13	5	.722	2.27	23	21	3	2	0	142⅔	110	51	36	81	102
1987—New Britain (East.)	2	0	1.000	4.50	2	2	0	0	0	10	8	5	5	8	12
1988—New Britain (East.)							Did not play.								
1989—New Britain (East.)	9	10	.474	3.66	26	•26	3	1	0	147⅔	129	78	60	85	93
1990—New Britain (East.)	4	4	.500	3.41	12	12	2	1	0	74	66	34	28	37	51
—Pawtucket (I.L.)	4	7	.364	5.55	15	15	5	0	0	82⅔	75	57	51	45	77
1991—Pawtucket (I.L.)	5	5	.500	5.61	20	16	0	0	0	102⅔	109	69	64	53	65
—New Britain (East.)	2	2	.500	2.90	7	7	0	0	0	49⅔	37	25	16	28	35
—Boston (A.L.)■	0	0	...	18.00	1	0	0	0	0	1	2	2	2	3	1
1992—Omaha (A.A.)■	7	10	.412	4.36	26	21	0	0	0	136⅓	138	76	66	71	114
—Memphis (Sou.)	0	2	.000	7.36	2	0	0	0	0	7⅓	6	6	6	6	8
1993—Milwaukee (A.L.)■	1	1	.500	9.53	10	1	0	0	1	17	22	20	18	10	10
—New Orleans (A.A.)	0	1	.000	9.00	1	0	0	0	0	1	1	1	1	0	3
—Norfolk (I.L.)	1	5	.167	3.11	14	12	2	1	0	84	82	40	29	25	79
—New York (N.L.)	0	0	...	3.00	6	0	0	0	0	12	8	7	4	9	11
1994—Norfolk (I.L.)	0	1	.000	4.38	8	0	0	0	3	12⅓	12	6	6	6	10
—New York (N.L.)	3	2	.600	2.66	37	0	0	0	2	47⅓	34	15	14	13	48
1995—New York (N.L.)	1	2	.333	7.88	12	0	0	0	0	16	18	15	14	6	14
—New York (A.L.)■	0	0	...	2.08	11	0	0	0	0	17⅓	19	4	4	9	11
1996—							Statistics unavailable.								
1997—Seattle (A.L.)■	0	1	.000	5.40	16	0	0	0	0	18⅓	19	13	11	17	18
—Memphis (Sou.)	0	0	...	3.00	2	0	0	0	0	3	1	1	1	0	6
—Tacoma (PCL)	0	0	...	6.43	11	0	0	0	0	14	16	10	10	8	15
—New Orleans (A.A.)■	0	0	...	4.40	11	0	0	0	0	14⅓	17	7	7	6	11
1998—Durham (I.L.)	7	6	.538	4.64	19	14	0	0	1	85⅓	93	57	44	30	61
—Norfolk (I.L.)■	4	4	.500	3.24	13	12	1	0	1	77⅔	77	35	28	31	72
1999—New York (N.L.)	0	0	...	5.79	12	0	0	0	0	18⅔	19	12	12	4	25
2000—Nashville (PCL)■	0	2	.000	2.70	15	0	0	0	3	23⅓	19	8	7	6	23
—Pittsburgh (N.L.)	2	2	.500	3.38	43	0	0	0	0	58⅔	50	23	22	32	39
2001—Pittsburgh (N.L.)	3	2	.600	3.39	71	0	0	0	0	79⅔	60	32	30	26	80
A.L. totals (4 years)	1	2	.333	5.87	38	1	0	0	1	53⅔	62	39	35	39	40
N.L. totals (6 years)	9	8	.529	3.72	181	0	0	0	4	232⅓	189	104	96	90	217
Major League totals (8 years)	10	10	.500	4.12	219	1	0	0	5	286	251	143	131	129	257

M

MAROTH, MIKE   P   TIGERS

PERSONAL: Born August 17, 1977, in Orlando, Fla. ... 6-0/180. ... Throws left, bats left. ... Full name: Michael Wayne Maroth.

HIGH SCHOOL: William R. Boone (Orlando, Fla.).

COLLEGE: Central Florida.

TRANSACTIONS/CAREER NOTES: Selected by Boston Red Sox organization in third round of free-agent draft (June 2, 1998). ... Traded by Red Sox to Detroit Tigers for P Bryce Florie (July 31, 1999). ... On disabled list (July 31-August 22, 2001).

Year League	W	L	Pct.	ERA	G	GS	CG	ShO	Sv.	IP	H	R	ER	BB	SO
1998—Gulf Coast Red Sox (GCL)	1	1	.500	0.00	4	2	0	0	0	12⅔	9	3	0	2	14
—Lowell (NY-Penn)	2	3	.400	2.90	6	6	0	0	0	31	22	13	10	13	34
1999—Sarasota (FSL)	11	6	.647	4.04	20	19	0	0	0	111⅓	124	65	50	35	64
—Lakeland (FSL)■	2	1	.667	3.24	3	3	0	0	0	16⅔	18	7	6	7	11
—Jacksonville (Sou.)	1	2	.333	4.79	4	4	0	0	0	20⅔	27	15	11	7	10
2000—Jacksonville (Sou.)	9	14	.391	3.94	27	26	2	1	0	164⅓	176	79	72	58	85
2001—Toledo (I.L.)	7	10	.412	4.65	24	23	0	0	0	131⅔	158	80	68	50	63

MARQUIS, JASON — P — BRAVES

PERSONAL: Born August 21, 1978, in Manhasset, N.Y. ... 6-1/185. ... Throws right, bats left. ... Full name: Jason Scott Marquis.
HIGH SCHOOL: Tottenville (Staten Island, N.Y.).
TRANSACTIONS/CAREER NOTES: Selected by Atlanta Braves organization as "sandwich" pick between first and second round of free-agent draft (June 4, 1996); pick received as supplemental pick for failure to signed 1995 first-round choice. ... On Greenville disabled list (July 5-31, 1999).
MISCELLANEOUS: Appeared in two games as pinch runner (2001).

Year League	W	L	Pct.	ERA	G	GS	CG	ShO	Sv.	IP	H	R	ER	BB	SO
1996— Danville (Appl.)	1	1	.500	4.63	7	4	0	0	0	23 1/3	30	18	12	7	24
1997— Macon (S.Atl.)	•14	10	.583	4.38	28	28	0	0	0	141 2/3	156	78	69	55	121
1998— Danville (Caro.)	2	12	.143	4.87	22	22	1	0	0	114 2/3	120	65	62	41	135
1999— Myrtle Beach (Caro.)	3	0	1.000	0.28	6	6	0	0	0	32	22	2	1	17	41
— Greenville (Sou.)	3	4	.429	4.58	12	12	1	0	0	55	52	33	28	29	35
2000— Greenville (Sou.)	4	2	.667	3.57	11	11	0	0	0	68	68	35	27	23	49
— Atlanta (N.L.)	1	0	1.000	5.01	15	0	0	0	0	23 1/3	23	16	13	12	17
— Richmond (I.L.)	0	3	.000	9.00	6	6	0	0	0	20	26	21	20	13	18
2001— Atlanta (N.L.)	5	6	.455	3.48	38	16	0	0	0	129 1/3	113	62	50	59	98
Major League totals (2 years)	**6**	**6**	**.500**	**3.71**	**53**	**16**	**0**	**0**	**0**	**152 2/3**	**136**	**78**	**63**	**71**	**115**

CHAMPIONSHIP SERIES RECORD

Year League	W	L	Pct.	ERA	G	GS	CG	ShO	Sv.	IP	H	R	ER	BB	SO
2001— Atlanta (N.L.)	0	0	...	0.00	1	0	0	0	0	2	2	4	0	2	3

DIVISION SERIES RECORD

Year League	W	L	Pct.	ERA	G	GS	CG	ShO	Sv.	IP	H	R	ER	BB	SO
2001— Atlanta (N.L.)							Did not play.								

MARRERO, ELI — C — CARDINALS

PERSONAL: Born November 17, 1973, in Havana, Cuba. ... 6-1/180. ... Bats right, throws right. ... Full name: Elieser Marrero.
HIGH SCHOOL: Coral Gables (Fla.).
TRANSACTIONS/CAREER NOTES: Selected by St. Louis Cardinals organization in third round of free-agent draft (June 3, 1993). ... On St. Louis disabled list (March 22-April 13, 1998). ... On St. Louis disabled list (July 2-September 1, 2000); included rehabilitation assignment to Memphis (August 24-September 1).
STATISTICAL NOTES: Led Texas League catchers with 746 total chances in 1996. ... Led American Association catchers with 750 total chances in 1997. ... Career major league grand slams: 1.

							BATTING							FIELDING		
Year Team (League)	Pos.	G	AB	R	H	2B	3B	HR	RBI	Avg.	BB	SO	SB	PO	A	E	Avg.
1993— Johnson City (Appl.)	C	18	61	10	22	8	0	2	14	.361	12	9	2	154	18	1	.994
1994— Savannah (S.Atl.)	C	116	421	71	110	16	3	21	79	.261	39	92	5	821	92	•15	.984
1995— St. Petersburg (FSL)	C	107	383	43	81	16	1	10	55	.211	23	55	9	574	52	10	.984
1996— Arkansas (Texas)	C-DH	116	374	65	101	17	3	19	65	.270	32	55	9	*676	67	3	*.996
1997— Louisville (A.A.)	C-DH	112	395	60	108	21	7	20	68	.273	25	53	4	*675	*68	7	.991
— St. Louis (N.L.)	C	17	45	4	11	2	0	2	7	.244	2	13	4	82	12	3	.969
1998— St. Louis (N.L.)	C-1B	83	254	28	62	18	1	4	20	.244	28	42	6	427	31	4	.991
— Memphis (PCL)	C-DH	32	130	22	31	5	0	7	21	.238	13	23	5	195	17	2	.991
1999— St. Louis (N.L.)	C-1B	114	317	32	61	13	1	6	34	.192	18	56	11	537	47	7	.988
2000— St. Louis (N.L.)	C-1B	53	102	21	23	3	1	5	17	.225	9	16	5	212	14	0	1.000
— Memphis (PCL)	C	6	15	1	1	0	0	0	0	.067	0	2	0	16	1	0	1.000
2001— St. Louis (N.L.)	C-OF-1B	86	203	37	54	11	3	6	23	.266	15	36	6	382	23	7	.983
Major League totals (5 years)		**353**	**921**	**122**	**211**	**47**	**6**	**23**	**101**	**.229**	**72**	**163**	**32**	**1640**	**127**	**21**	**.988**

DIVISION SERIES RECORD

							BATTING							FIELDING		
Year Team (League)	Pos.	G	AB	R	H	2B	3B	HR	RBI	Avg.	BB	SO	SB	PO	A	E	Avg.
2000— St. Louis (N.L.)								Did not play.									
2001— St. Louis (N.L.)	PH-C	3	7	0	0	0	0	0	0	.000	0	0	0	12	0	0	1.000

CHAMPIONSHIP SERIES RECORD

							BATTING							FIELDING		
Year Team (League)	Pos.	G	AB	R	H	2B	3B	HR	RBI	Avg.	BB	SO	SB	PO	A	E	Avg.
2000— St. Louis (N.L.)	PR-C	4	4	0	0	0	0	0	1	.000	0	1	0	11	0	0	1.000

MARTE, DAMASO — P — PIRATES

PERSONAL: Born February 14, 1975, in Santo Domingo, Dominican Republic. ... 6-0/170. ... Throws left, bats left. ... Full name: Damaso Sabinon Marte.
TRANSACTIONS/CAREER NOTES: Signed as non-drafted free agent by Seattle Mariners organization (October 28, 1992). ... On disabled list (April 3-17, 1997). ... On disabled list (April 2-May 3 and September 2, 1998-remainder of season). ... On New Haven disabled list (April 7-August 22, 2000). ... Granted free agency (October 18, 2000). ... Signed by New York Yankees organization (November 16, 2000). ... Traded by Yankees to Pittsburgh Pirates for IF Enrique Wilson (June 13, 2001).

Year League	W	L	Pct.	ERA	G	GS	CG	ShO	Sv.	IP	H	R	ER	BB	SO
1993— Dominican Mariners (DSL)	2	5	.286	6.55	17	15	2	0	0	56 1/3	62	48	41	50	29
1994— Dominican Mariners (DSL)	7	0	1.000	3.86	17	13	0	0	0	65 1/3	53	41	28	48	80
1995— Everett (N'West)	2	2	.500	2.21	11	11	5	0	0	36 2/3	25	11	9	10	39
1996— Wisconsin Rapids (Midw.)	8	6	.571	4.49	26	26	2	•1	0	142 1/3	134	82	71	75	115
1997— Lancaster (Calif.)	8	8	.500	4.13	25	25	2	1	0	139 1/3	144	75	64	62	127
1998— Orlando (Sou.)	7	6	.538	5.27	22	20	0	0	0	121 1/3	136	82	71	47	99

Year League	W	L	Pct.	ERA	G	GS	CG	ShO	Sv.	IP	H	R	ER	BB	SO
1999— Tacoma (PCL)	3	3	.500	5.13	31	11	0	0	0	73 2/3	79	43	42	40	59
— Seattle (A.L.)	0	1	.000	9.35	5	0	0	0	0	8 2/3	16	9	9	6	3
2000— Arizona Mariners (Ariz.)	0	0	...	0.00	2	2	0	0	0	5	1	0	0	0	6
— New Haven (East.).............	0	0	...	1.59	4	0	0	0	0	5 2/3	6	1	1	2	4
2001— Norwich (East.)■	3	1	.750	3.50	23	0	0	0	1	36	29	16	14	7	36
— Nashville (PCL)■	0	0	...	3.38	4	0	0	0	0	5 1/3	3	2	2	0	4
— Pittsburgh (N.L.)	0	1	.000	4.71	23	0	0	0	0	36 1/3	34	21	19	12	39
A.L. totals (1 year).....................	0	1	.000	9.35	5	0	0	0	0	8 2/3	16	9	9	6	3
N.L. totals (1 year).....................	0	1	.000	4.71	23	0	0	0	0	36 1/3	34	21	19	12	39
Major League totals (2 years).......	0	2	.000	5.60	28	0	0	0	0	45	50	30	28	18	42

MARTIN, AL — OF

PERSONAL: Born November 24, 1967, in West Covina, Calif. ... 6-2/214. ... Bats left, throws left. ... Full name: Albert Lee Martin. ... Formerly known as Albert Scales-Martin. ... Nephew of Rod Martin, linebacker with Oakland/Los Angeles Raiders (1977-88).

HIGH SCHOOL: West Covina (Calif.).

COLLEGE: Southern California.

TRANSACTIONS/CAREER NOTES: Selected by Atlanta Braves organization in eighth round of free-agent draft (June 3, 1985). ... Granted free agency (October 15, 1991). ... Signed by Pittsburgh Pirates organization (November 11, 1991). ... On suspended list (September 17-20, 1993). ... On disabled list (July 11, 1994-remainder of season). ... On Pittsburgh disabled list (May 22-June 24, 1997); included rehabilitation assignment to Carolina (June 21-23). ... Traded by Pirates with cash to San Diego Padres for OF John Vander Wal, P Geraldo Padua and P James Sak (February 23, 2000). ... Traded by Padres to Seattle Mariners for OF/3B John Mabry and P Tom Davey (July 31, 2000). ... Granted free agency (November 5, 2001).

RECORDS: Shares major league record for fewest double plays by outfielder (150 or more games)—0 (1996). ... Holds modern N.L. single-season record for fewest putouts by outfielder (150 or more games)—217 (1996). ... Holds N.L. single-season record for fewest chances accepted by outfielder (150 or more games)—222 (1996).

STATISTICAL NOTES: Led Gulf Coast League first basemen with 15 errors in 1985. ... Led American Association with .557 slugging percentage in 1992. ... Led American Association outfielders with six double plays in 1992. ... Had 20-game hitting streak (June 20-July 11, 1999). ... Had 15-game hitting streak (August 25-September 11, 1999). ... Career major league grand slams: 1.

							BATTING								FIELDING		
Year Team (League)	Pos.	G	AB	R	H	2B	3B	HR	RBI	Avg.	BB	SO	SB	PO	A	E	Avg.
1985— GC Braves (GCL)	1B-OF	40	138	16	32	3	0	0	9	.232	19	36	1	246	13	†15	.945
1986— Sumter (S.Atl.)	1B	44	156	23	38	5	0	1	24	.244	23	36	6	299	12	8	.975
— Idaho Falls (Pio.).........	OF-1B	63	242	39	80	17	•6	4	44	.331	20	53	11	272	15	8	.973
1987— Sumter (S.Atl.)	OF-1B	117	375	59	95	18	5	12	64	.253	44	69	27	137	7	9	.941
1988— Burlington (Midw.)	OF	123	480	69	134	21	3	7	42	.279	30	88	40	224	4	8	.966
1989— Durham (Caro.)	OF	128	457	*84	124	26	3	9	48	.271	34	107	27	169	7	7	.962
1990— Greenville (Sou.)	OF	133	455	64	110	17	4	11	50	.242	43	102	20	200	8	7	.967
1991— Greenville (Sou.)	OF-1B	86	301	38	73	13	3	7	38	.243	32	84	19	134	7	6	.959
— Richmond (I.L.)	OF	44	151	20	42	11	1	5	18	.278	7	33	11	73	4	2	.975
1992— Buffalo (A.A.)■	OF	125	420	85	128	16	*15	20	59	.305	35	93	20	222	10	8	.967
— Pittsburgh (N.L.)	OF	12	12	1	2	0	1	0	2	.167	0	5	0	6	0	0	1.000
1993— Pittsburgh (N.L.)	OF	143	480	85	135	26	8	18	64	.281	42	122	16	268	6	7	.975
1994— Pittsburgh (N.L.)	OF	82	276	48	79	12	4	9	33	.286	34	56	15	129	8	3	.979
1995— Pittsburgh (N.L.)	OF	124	439	70	124	25	3	13	41	.282	44	92	20	206	8	5	.977
1996— Pittsburgh (N.L.)	OF	155	630	101	189	40	1	18	72	.300	54	116	38	217	5	8	.965
1997— Pittsburgh (N.L.)	OF	113	423	64	123	24	7	13	59	.291	45	83	23	125	8	6	.957
— Carolina (Sou.)	OF	3	9	0	1	0	0	0	0	.111	0	0	0	2	0	0	1.000
1998— Pittsburgh (N.L.)	OF-DH	125	440	57	105	15	2	12	47	.239	32	91	20	192	6	3	.985
1999— Pittsburgh (N.L.)	OF	143	541	97	150	36	8	24	63	.277	49	119	20	196	3	10	.952
2000— San Diego (N.L.)■	OF	93	346	62	106	13	6	11	27	.306	28	54	6	128	4	7	.950
— Seattle (A.L.)■..............	OF-DH	42	134	19	31	2	4	4	9	.231	8	31	4	76	3	3	.963
2001— Seattle (A.L.)	OF-DH	100	283	41	68	15	2	7	42	.240	37	59	9	132	3	4	.971
American League totals (2 years)		142	417	60	99	17	6	11	51	.237	45	90	13	208	6	7	.968
National League totals (9 years)		990	3587	585	1013	191	40	118	408	.282	328	738	158	1467	48	49	.969
Major League totals (10 years)		1132	4004	645	1112	208	46	129	459	.278	373	828	171	1675	54	56	.969

DIVISION SERIES RECORD

							BATTING								FIELDING		
Year Team (League)	Pos.	G	AB	R	H	2B	3B	HR	RBI	Avg.	BB	SO	SB	PO	A	E	Avg.
2000— Seattle (A.L.)	PH	1	1	0	0	0	0	0	0	.000	0	0	0	...	...	...	...
2001— Seattle (A.L.)	PH-PR	3	2	1	0	0	0	0	0	.000	0	0	0	...	...	...	...
Division series totals (2 years)		4	3	1	0	0	0	0	0	.000	0	0	0	...	...	...	...

CHAMPIONSHIP SERIES RECORD

							BATTING								FIELDING		
Year Team (League)	Pos.	G	AB	R	H	2B	3B	HR	RBI	Avg.	BB	SO	SB	PO	A	E	Avg.
2000— Seattle (A.L.)	OF-PH	4	11	1	2	2	0	0	0	.182	2	3	0	9	0	0	1.000
2001— Seattle (A.L.)	PH-DH	2	2	1	1	0	1	0	0	.500	0	0	0	...	...	...	...
Championship series totals (2 years)		6	13	2	3	2	1	0	0	.231	2	3	0	9	0	0	1.000

MARTIN, TOM — P

PERSONAL: Born May 21, 1970, in Charleston, S.C. ... 6-1/200. ... Throws left, bats left. ... Full name: Thomas Edgar Martin.

HIGH SCHOOL: Bay (Panama City, Fla.).

TRANSACTIONS/CAREER NOTES: Selected by Baltimore Orioles organization in sixth round of free-agent draft (June 1, 1988). ... Traded by Orioles with 3B Craig Worthington to San Diego Padres for P Jim Lewis and OF Steve Martin (February 17, 1992). ... Selected by Atlanta Braves organization from Padres organization in Rule 5 minor league draft (December 13, 1993). ... Loaned by Braves organization to Mexico City

M

Tigres, Mexican League (May 1-7, 1995). ... Released by Braves (January 25, 1996). ... Signed by Houston Astros organization (February 21, 1996). ... On disabled list (May 30-June 15, 1997). ... Selected by Arizona Diamondbacks in second round (29th pick overall) of expansion draft (November 18, 1997). ... Traded by Diamondbacks with 3B Travis Fryman and cash to Cleveland Indians for 3B Matt Williams (December 1, 1997). ... On Cleveland disabled list (April 30-May 18 and August 31-September 19, 1998); included rehabilitation assignments to Buffalo (May 13-18 and September 3-19). ... On Cleveland disabled list (April 4-August 9, 1999); included rehabilitation assignment to Akron (July 27-August 9). ... On Cleveland disabled list (June 13-August 4, 2000); included rehabilitation assignment to Buffalo (July 28-August 4). ... Traded by Indians to New York Mets for C Javier Ochoa (January 11, 2001). ... On New York disabled list (May 13-August 16, 2001); included rehabilitation assignments to Brooklyn (July 27-30) and Norfolk (July 31-August 16). ... Released by Mets (October 11, 2001).

Year League	W	L	Pct.	ERA	G	GS	CG	ShO	Sv.	IP	H	R	ER	BB	SO
1989—Bluefield (Appl.)	3	3	.500	4.62	8	8	0	0	0	39	36	28	20	25	31
— Erie (NY-Penn)	0	5	.000	6.64	7	7	0	0	0	40 2/3	42	39	30	25	44
1990—Wausau (Midw.)	2	3	.400	2.47	9	9	0	0	0	40	31	25	11	27	45
1991—Kane County (Midw.)	4	10	.286	3.64	38	10	0	0	6	99	92	50	40	56	106
1992—High Desert (Calif.)■	0	2	.000	9.37	11	0	0	0	0	16 1/3	23	19	17	16	10
— Waterloo (Midw.)	2	6	.250	4.25	39	2	0	0	3	55	62	38	26	22	57
1993—Rancho Cuca. (Calif.)	1	4	.200	5.61	47	1	0	0	0	59 1/3	72	41	37	39	53
1994—Greenville (Sou.)■	5	6	.455	4.62	36	6	0	0	0	74	82	40	38	27	51
1995—Richmond (I.L.)	0	0	...	9.00	7	0	0	0	0	9	10	9	9	10	3
— M.C. Tigres (Mex.)■	0	1	.000	27.00	1	1	0	0	0	1 1/3	5	5	4	1	0
1996—Tucson (PCL)■	0	0	...	0.00	5	0	0	0	0	6	6	0	0	2	1
— Jackson (Texas)	6	2	.750	3.24	57	0	0	0	3	75	71	35	27	42	58
1997—Houston (N.L.)	5	3	.625	2.09	55	0	0	0	2	56	52	13	13	23	36
1998—Cleveland (A.L.)■	1	1	.500	12.89	14	0	0	0	0	14 2/3	29	21	21	12	9
— Buffalo (I.L.)	3	1	.750	6.00	41	0	0	0	0	36	46	25	24	13	35
1999—Akron (East.)	0	0	...	1.00	3	3	0	0	0	9	4	1	1	3	9
— Cleveland (A.L.)	0	1	.000	8.68	6	0	0	0	0	9 1/3	13	9	9	3	8
— Buffalo (I.L.)	1	0	1.000	3.00	5	0	0	0	0	6	5	2	2	1	6
2000—Cleveland (A.L.)	1	0	1.000	4.05	31	0	0	0	0	33 1/3	32	16	15	15	21
— Buffalo (I.L.)	0	1	.000	3.60	9	3	0	0	0	10	12	4	4	1	4
2001—Norfolk (I.L.)■	2	1	.667	6.26	23	0	0	0	1	23	31	17	16	10	24
— New York (N.L.)	1	0	1.000	10.06	14	0	0	0	0	17	23	22	19	10	12
— Brooklyn (NY-Penn)	0	0	...	0.00	1	1	0	0	0	1	2	0	0	0	0
A.L. totals (3 years)	2	2	.500	7.06	51	0	0	0	0	57 1/3	74	46	45	30	38
N.L. totals (2 years)	6	3	.667	3.95	69	0	0	0	2	73	75	35	32	33	48
Major League totals (5 years)	8	5	.615	5.32	120	0	0	0	2	130 1/3	149	81	77	63	86

DIVISION SERIES RECORD

Year League	W	L	Pct.	ERA	G	GS	CG	ShO	Sv.	IP	H	R	ER	BB	SO
1997—Houston (N.L.)	0	0	...	0.00	2	0	0	0	0	2/3	1	1	0	1	0

MARTINEZ, ANASTACIO   P   RED SOX

PERSONAL: Born November 3, 1980, in Santa Cruz de Villomello, Domincan Republic. ... 6-2/180. ... Throws right, bats right. ... Full name: Anastacio Euclides Martinez.

TRANSACTIONS/CAREER NOTES: Signed as non-drafted free agent by Boston Red Sox organization (January 13, 1998). ... On Augusta disabled list (June 7-July 3, 2000).

Year League	W	L	Pct.	ERA	G	GS	CG	ShO	Sv.	IP	H	R	ER	BB	SO
1998—Dominican Red Sox (DSL)	0	1	.000	12.86	2	2	0	0	0	7	13	11	10	7	8
— Gulf Coast Red Sox (GCL)	2	3	.400	3.18	12	10	0	0	0	51	45	28	18	12	50
1999—Augusta (S.Atl.)	2	4	.333	6.30	10	10	0	0	0	40	44	37	28	18	36
— Lowell (NY-Penn)	0	3	.000	3.68	11	11	0	0	0	51 1/3	61	36	21	18	43
2000—Augusta (S.Atl.)	9	6	.600	4.64	23	23	0	0	0	120 1/3	130	69	62	50	107
— Gulf Coast Red Sox (GCL)	0	1	.000	9.45	2	1	0	0	0	6 2/3	15	9	7	3	1
2001—Sarasota (FSL)	9	12	.429	3.35	25	24	1	0	0	145	130	69	54	39	123

MARTINEZ, DAVE   OF   BRAVES

PERSONAL: Born September 26, 1964, in Brooklyn, N.Y. ... 5-10/190. ... Bats left, throws left. ... Full name: David Martinez.

HIGH SCHOOL: Lake Howell (Casselberry, Fla.).

JUNIOR COLLEGE: Valencia Community College (Fla.).

TRANSACTIONS/CAREER NOTES: Selected by Texas Rangers organization in 40th round of free-agent draft (June 7, 1982); did not sign. ... Selected by Chicago Cubs organization in secondary phase of free-agent draft (January 11, 1983). ... On disabled list (April 27, 1984-remainder of season). ... Traded by Cubs to Montreal Expos for OF Mitch Webster (July 14, 1988). ... On disqualified list (October 4-5, 1991). ... Traded by Expos with P Scott Ruskin and SS Willie Greene to Cincinnati Reds for P John Wetteland and P Bill Risley (December 11, 1991). ... Granted free agency (October 27, 1992). ... Signed by San Francisco Giants (December 9, 1992). ... On San Francisco disabled list (April 30-June 4, 1993); included rehabilitation assignment to Phoenix (June 1-4). ... Granted free agency (October 14, 1994). ... Signed by Chicago White Sox (April 5, 1995). ... Granted free agency (November 3, 1995). ... Re-signed by White Sox (November 14, 1995). ... Granted free agency (October 27, 1997). ... Signed by Tampa Bay Devil Rays (December 4, 1997). ... On disabled list (July 22, 1998-remainder of season). ... Traded by Devil Rays to Cubs for P Mark Guthrie (May 12, 2000). ... Traded by Cubs to Rangers for IF/OF Brant Brown (June 9, 2000). ... Traded by Rangers to Toronto Blue Jays for a player to be named later (August 4, 2000); Rangers acquired P Peter Munro to complete deal (August 8, 2000). ... Granted free agency (October 31, 2000). ... Signed by Atlanta Braves (December 10, 2000).

RECORDS: Shares major league single-game record for most unassisted double plays by first baseman—2 (June 21, 1997). ... Shares major league record for most clubs played for in one season—4 (2000).

STATISTICAL NOTES: Had 21-game hitting streak (August 6-September 1, 2000). ... Career major league grand slams: 2.

							BATTING						FIELDING		
Year Team (League)	Pos.	G	AB	R	H	2B	3B	HR	RBI	Avg.	BB	SO	SB	PO	A	E	Avg.
1983—Quad Cities (Midw.)	OF	44	119	17	29	6	2	0	10	.244	26	30	10	47	8	1	.982
— Geneva (NY-Penn)	OF	64	241	35	63	15	2	5	33	.261	40	52	16	132	6	8	.945
1984—Quad Cities (Midw.)	OF	12	41	6	9	2	2	0	5	.220	9	13	3	13	2	1	.938
1985—Win.-Salem (Caro.)	OF	115	386	52	132	14	4	5	54	*.342	62	35	38	206	11	7	.969

Year Team (League)	Pos.	G	AB	R	H	2B	3B	HR	RBI	Avg.	BB	SO	SB	PO	A	E	Avg.
1986—Iowa (A.A.)	OF	83	318	52	92	11	5	5	32	.289	36	34	42	214	7	2	.991
—Chicago (N.L.)	OF	53	108	13	15	1	1	1	7	.139	6	22	4	77	2	1	.988
1987—Chicago (N.L.)	OF	142	459	70	134	18	8	8	36	.292	57	96	16	283	10	6	.980
1988—Chicago (N.L.)	OF	75	256	27	65	10	1	4	34	.254	21	46	7	162	2	5	.970
—Montreal (N.L.)■	OF	63	191	24	49	3	5	2	12	.257	17	48	16	119	2	1	.992
1989—Montreal (N.L.)	OF	126	361	41	99	16	7	3	27	.274	27	57	23	199	7	7	.967
1990—Montreal (N.L.)	OF-P	118	391	60	109	13	5	11	39	.279	24	48	13	257	6	3	.989
1991—Montreal (N.L.)	OF	124	396	47	117	18	5	7	42	.295	20	54	16	213	10	4	.982
1992—Cincinnati (N.L.)■	OF-1B	135	393	47	100	20	5	3	31	.254	42	54	12	382	18	6	.985
1993—San Fran. (N.L.)■	OF	91	241	28	58	12	1	5	27	.241	27	39	6	131	6	1	.993
—Phoenix (PCL)	OF	3	15	4	7	0	0	0	2	.467	1	1	1	5	1	0	1.000
1994—San Francisco (N.L.)..	OF-1B	97	235	23	58	9	3	4	27	.247	21	22	3	256	18	3	.989
1995—Chicago (A.L.)■ OF-1B-DH-P	119	303	49	93	16	4	5	37	.307	32	41	8	392	25	3	.993
1996—Chicago (A.L.)	OF-1B	146	440	85	140	20	8	10	53	.318	52	52	15	368	16	6	.985
1997—Chicago (A.L.)■	OF-1B-DH	145	504	78	144	16	6	12	55	.286	55	69	12	485	30	7	.987
1998—Tampa Bay (A.L.)	OF-DH-1B	90	309	31	79	11	0	3	20	.256	35	52	8	163	9	1	.994
1999—Tampa Bay (A.L.)	OF	143	514	79	146	25	5	6	66	.284	60	76	13	253	8	4	.985
2000—Tampa Bay (A.L.)	OF	29	104	12	27	4	2	1	12	.260	10	17	1	46	5	0	1.000
—Chicago (N.L.)	OF-1B	18	54	5	10	1	1	0	1	.185	2	8	1	77	5	1	.988
—Texas (A.L.)■	OF-1B	38	119	14	32	4	1	2	12	.269	14	20	2	93	2	0	1.000
—Toronto (A.L.)■	OF	47	180	29	56	10	1	2	22	.311	24	28	4	101	8	2	.982
2001—Atlanta (N.L.)■	OF-1B-DH	120	237	33	68	11	3	2	20	.287	21	44	3	120	8	0	1.000
American League totals (6 years)		757	2473	377	717	106	27	41	277	.290	282	355	63	1901	103	23	.989
National League totals (11 years)		1162	3322	418	882	132	45	50	303	.266	285	538	120	2276	94	38	.984
Major League totals (16 years)		1919	5795	795	1599	238	72	91	580	.276	567	893	183	4177	197	61	.986

DIVISION SERIES RECORD

Year Team (League)	Pos.	G	AB	R	H	2B	3B	HR	RBI	Avg.	BB	SO	SB	PO	A	E	Avg.
2001—Atlanta (N.L.)	PH	1	1	0	0	0	0	0	0	.000	0	0	0	...	...	...	...

CHAMPIONSHIP SERIES RECORD

Year Team (League)	Pos.	G	AB	R	H	2B	3B	HR	RBI	Avg.	BB	SO	SB	PO	A	E	Avg.
2001—Atlanta (N.L.)	PH-OF	4	5	0	1	0	0	0	0	.200	0	1	0	1	0	0	1.000

RECORD AS PITCHER

Year League	W	L	Pct.	ERA	G	GS	CG	ShO	Sv.	IP	H	R	ER	BB	SO
1990—Montreal (N.L.)	0	0	...	54.00	1	0	0	0	0	1/3	2	2	2	2	2
1995—Chicago (A.L.)	0	0	...	0.00	1	0	0	0	0	1	0	0	0	2	0
Major League totals (2 years)	0	0	...	13.50	2	0	0	0	0	1 1/3	2	2	2	4	0

MARTINEZ, EDGAR   DH   MARINERS

M

PERSONAL: Born January 2, 1963, in New York. ... 5-11/210. ... Bats right, throws right. ... Cousin of Carmelo Martinez, first baseman/out-fielder with six major league teams (1983-91).

HIGH SCHOOL: Dorado (Puerto Rico).

COLLEGE: American College (Puerto Rico).

TRANSACTIONS/CAREER NOTES: Signed as non-drafted free agent by Seattle Mariners organization (December 19, 1982). ... On Seattle disabled list (April 4-May 17, June 15-July 21 and August 17, 1993-remainder of season); included rehabilitation assignment to Jacksonville (July 17-21). ... On disabled list (April 16-May 6, 1994; July 21-August 12, 1996; and July 17-August 3, 2001). ... On suspended list (October 3-5, 2001).

RECORDS: Shares A.L. single-game record for most errors by third baseman—4 (May 6, 1990).

HONORS: Named third baseman on THE SPORTING NEWS A.L. All-Star team (1992). ... Named third baseman on THE SPORTING NEWS A.L. Silver Slugger team (1992). ... Named designated hitter on THE SPORTING NEWS A.L. All-Star team (1995, 1997 and 2001). ... Named designated hitter on THE SPORTING NEWS A.L. Silver Slugger team (1995 and 1997). ... Named designated hitter on A.L. Silver Slugger team (2001).

STATISTICAL NOTES: Led Southern League third basemen with 360 total chances and 34 double plays in 1985. ... Led Southern League with 12 sacrifice flies in 1985. ... Led Southern League third basemen with .960 fielding percentage in 1986. ... Led Pacific Coast League third basemen with 389 total chances and 31 double plays in 1987. ... Led A.L. in on-base percentage with .479 in 1995 and .429 in 1998. ... Hit three home runs in one game (July 6, 1996 and May 18, 1999). ... Led A.L. with a .447 on-base percentage in 1999. ... Career major league grand slams: 9.

MISCELLANEOUS: Holds Seattle Mariners franchise all-time records for most hits (1,882), doubles (443) and highest batting average (.319).

Year Team (League)	Pos.	G	AB	R	H	2B	3B	HR	RBI	Avg.	BB	SO	SB	PO	A	E	Avg.
1983—Bellingham (N'West) ..	3B	32	104	14	18	1	1	0	5	.173	18	24	1	22	58	6	.930
1984—Wausau (Midw.)	3B	126	433	72	131	32	2	15	66	.303	84	57	11	85	246	25	.930
1985—Chattanooga (Sou.)	3B	111	357	43	92	15	5	3	47	.258	71	30	1	*94	*247	19	*.947
—Calgary (PCL)	3B-2B	20	68	8	24	7	1	0	14	.353	12	7	1	15	44	4	.937
1986—Chattanooga (Sou.)	3B	132	451	71	119	29	5	6	74	.264	89	35	2	94	263	15	†.960
1987—Calgary (PCL)	3B	129	438	75	144	31	1	10	66	.329	82	47	3	*91	*278	20	.949
—Seattle (A.L.)	3B-DH	13	43	6	16	5	2	0	5	.372	2	5	0	13	19	0	1.000
1988—Calgary (PCL)	3B-2B	95	331	63	120	19	4	8	64	*.363	66	40	9	48	185	20	.921
—Seattle (A.L.)	3B	14	32	0	9	4	0	0	5	.281	4	7	0	5	8	1	.929
1989—Seattle (A.L.)	3B	65	171	20	41	5	0	2	20	.240	17	26	2	40	72	6	.949
—Calgary (PCL)	3B-2B	32	113	30	39	11	0	3	23	.345	22	13	2	22	56	12	.867
1990—Seattle (A.L.)	3B-DH	144	487	71	147	27	2	11	49	.302	74	62	1	89	259	*27	.928
1991—Seattle (A.L.)	3B-DH	150	544	98	167	35	1	14	52	.307	84	72	0	84	299	15	.962
1992—Seattle (A.L.)	3B-DH-1B	135	528	100	181	•46	3	18	73	*.343	54	61	14	88	211	17	.946
1993—Seattle (A.L.)	DH-3B	42	135	20	32	7	0	4	13	.237	28	19	0	5	11	2	.889
—Jacksonville (Sou.)......	DH	4	14	2	5	0	0	1	3	.357	2	0	0	...	...	...	...

Year Team (League)	Pos.	G	AB	R	H	2B	3B	HR	RBI	Avg.	BB	SO	SB	PO	A	E	Avg.
1994—Seattle (A.L.)	3B-DH	89	326	47	93	23	1	13	51	.285	53	42	6	44	128	9	.950
1995—Seattle (A.L.)	DH-3B-1B	•145	511	•121	182	•52	0	29	113	*.356	116	87	4	30	4	2	.944
1996—Seattle (A.L.)	DH-1-3-0	139	499	121	163	52	2	26	103	.327	123	84	3	29	1	1	.968
1997—Seattle (A.L.)	DH-1B-3B	155	542	104	179	35	1	28	108	.330	119	86	2	68	4	1	.986
1998—Seattle (A.L.)	DH-1B	154	556	86	179	46	1	29	102	.322	106	96	1	22	6	0	1.000
1999—Seattle (A.L.)	DH-1B	142	502	86	169	35	1	24	86	.337	97	99	7	29	2	0	1.000
2000—Seattle (A.L.)	DH-1B	153	556	100	180	31	0	37	*145	.324	96	95	3	12	1	0	1.000
2001—Seattle (A.L.)	DH-1B	132	470	80	144	40	1	23	116	.306	93	90	4	8	0	0	1.000
Major League totals (15 years)		1672	5902	1060	1882	443	15	258	1041	.319	1066	931	47	566	1025	81	.952

RECORDS: Holds A.L. career record for highest slugging percentage (50 or more at-bats)—.781. ... Shares single-series record for most hits—12 (1995). ... Shares single-game records for most runs batted in—7; and most home runs—2 (October 7, 1995).
NOTES: Shares postseason single-game record for most RBIs—7 (October 7, 1995).

DIVISION SERIES RECORD

Year Team (League)	Pos.	G	AB	R	H	2B	3B	HR	RBI	Avg.	BB	SO	SB	PO	A	E	Avg.
1995—Seattle (A.L.)	DH	5	21	6	12	3	0	2	10	.571	6	2	0	...	...	...	...
1997—Seattle (A.L.)	DH	4	16	2	3	0	0	2	3	.188	0	3	0	...	...	...	...
2000—Seattle (A.L.)	DH	3	11	2	4	1	0	1	2	.364	2	1	0	...	...	...	...
2001—Seattle (A.L.)	DH	5	16	3	5	1	0	2	5	.313	5	2	1	...	...	...	...
Division series totals (4 years)		17	64	13	24	5	0	7	20	.375	13	8	1	...	...	...	...

CHAMPIONSHIP SERIES RECORD

Year Team (League)	Pos.	G	AB	R	H	2B	3B	HR	RBI	Avg.	BB	SO	SB	PO	A	E	Avg.
1995—Seattle (A.L.)	DH	6	23	0	2	0	0	0	0	.087	2	5	1	...	...	...	...
2000—Seattle (A.L.)	DH	6	21	2	5	1	0	1	4	.238	3	5	0	...	...	...	...
2001—Seattle (A.L.)	DH	5	20	1	3	1	0	0	0	.150	1	6	0	...	...	...	...
Championship series totals (3 years)		17	64	3	10	2	0	1	4	.156	6	16	1	...	...	...	...

ALL-STAR GAME RECORD

Year League	Pos.	AB	R	H	2B	3B	HR	RBI	Avg.	BB	SO	SB	PO	A	E	Avg.
1992—American	PH	1	0	0	0	0	0	0	.000	0	0	0	...	...	...	...
1995—American	DH	3	0	0	0	0	0	0	.000	0	1	0	...	...	...	...
1996—American	PH	1	0	0	0	0	0	0	.000	0	0	0	...	...	...	...
1997—American	DH	2	1	2	0	0	1	1	1.000	0	0	0	...	...	...	...
2000—American	PH	1	0	0	0	0	0	0	.000	0	0	0	...	...	...	...
2001—American	DH	2	0	0	0	0	0	0	.000	0	1	0	...	...	...	...
All-Star Game totals (6 years)		10	1	2	0	0	1	1	.200	0	2	0	...	...	...	...

M

MARTINEZ, FELIX   SS   DEVIL RAYS

PERSONAL: Born May 18, 1974, in Nagua, Dominican Republic. ... 6-0/180. ... Bats both, throws right. ... Full name: Felix Mata Martinez.
HIGH SCHOOL: Solome Urena (Nagua, Dominican Republic).
TRANSACTIONS/CAREER NOTES: Contract purchased by Kansas City Royals organization from Hiroshima Toyo Carp of Japan Central League (March 5, 1993). ... Suspended four games by American League (June 5, 1998) to be served in 1999 season. ... On suspended list (September 1-6, 1999). ... Claimed on waivers by Philadelphia Phillies (October 6, 1999). ... Claimed on waivers by Tampa Bay Devil Rays (April 5, 2000). ... On Tampa Bay disabled list (May 28-June 15, 2001); included rehabilitation assignment to Orlando (June 12-15).
STATISTICAL NOTES: Led Texas League shortstops with 643 total chances in 1995.

Year Team (League)	Pos.	G	AB	R	H	2B	3B	HR	RBI	Avg.	BB	SO	SB	PO	A	E	Avg.
1993—GC Royals (GCL)	SS-2B-3B	57	165	23	42	5	1	0	12	.255	17	26	22	79	136	30	.878
1994—Wilmington (Caro.)	SS	117	400	65	107	16	4	2	43	.268	30	91	19	177	329	30	.944
1995—Wichita (Texas)	SS	127	426	53	112	15	3	3	30	.263	31	71	*44	*222	371	*50	.922
1996—Omaha (A.A.)	SS	118	395	54	93	13	3	5	35	.235	44	79	18	177	374	*42	.929
1997—Omaha (A.A.)	SS	112	410	55	104	19	4	2	36	.254	29	86	21	175	312	*36	.931
—Kansas City (A.L.)	SS-DH	16	31	3	7	1	1	0	3	.226	6	8	0	17	22	1	.975
1998—Kansas City (A.L.)	SS-2B	34	85	7	11	1	1	0	5	.129	5	21	3	49	80	6	.956
—Omaha (PCL)	SS-DH-2B	51	164	27	41	8	3	2	16	.250	15	40	6	74	135	14	.937
1999—Wichita (Texas)	SS-2B-3B-DH	87	327	57	88	22	2	4	37	.269	37	43	19	141	274	23	.947
—Omaha (PCL)	SS	8	23	2	7	5	0	0	2	.304	2	6	0	8	18	1	.963
—Kansas City (A.L.)	SS-2B	6	7	1	1	0	0	0	0	.143	0	0	0	1	2	0	1.000
2000—Durham (I.L.)■	SS	42	149	17	36	7	2	3	17	.242	7	28	3	66	132	6	.971
—Tampa Bay (A.L.)	SS-2B	106	299	42	64	11	4	2	17	.214	32	68	9	191	368	14	.976
2001—Tampa Bay (A.L.)	SS-2B	77	219	24	54	13	1	1	14	.247	10	46	6	118	168	15	.950
—Orlando (Sou.)	SS	3	10	1	1	1	0	0	1	.100	0	2	1	0	4	1	.800
Major League totals (5 years)		239	641	77	137	26	7	3	39	.214	53	143	18	376	640	36	.966

MARTINEZ, PEDRO   P   RED SOX

PERSONAL: Born October 25, 1971, in Manoguayabo, Dominican Republic. ... 5-11/170. ... Throws right, bats right. ... Full name: Pedro Jaime Martinez. ... Brother of Ramon J. Martinez, pitcher with three teams (1988-2001); and brother of Jesus Martinez, pitcher in Los Angeles Dodgers (1991-97) and Cincinnati Reds (1998) organizations.
COLLEGE: Ohio Dominican College (Dominican Republic).
TRANSACTIONS/CAREER NOTES: Signed as non-drafted free agent by Los Angeles Dodgers organization (June 18, 1988). ... On Albuquerque disabled list (June 20-July 2 and July 13-August 25, 1992). ... Traded by Dodgers to Montreal Expos for 2B Delino DeShields (November 19, 1993). ... On suspended list (April 1-9, 1997). ... Traded by Expos to Boston Red Sox for P Carl Pavano and a player to be named later

(November 18, 1997); Expos acquired P Tony Armas Jr. to complete deal (December 18, 1997). ... On disabled list (July 19-August 3, 1999; June 29-July 13, 2000; June 27-August 26 and September 8, 2001-remainder of season).

RECORDS: Shares A.L. record for most strikeouts in two consecutive games—32 (May 6 [17] and 12 [15], 2000, 18 innings).

HONORS: Named Minor League Player of the Year by The Sporting News (1991). ... Named N.L. Pitcher of the Year by The Sporting News (1997). ... Named righthanded pitcher on The Sporting News N.L. All-Star team (1997). ... Named N.L. Cy Young Award winner by Baseball Writers' Association of America (1997). ... Named righthanded pitcher on The Sporting News A.L. All-Star team (1998, 1999 and 2000). ... Named A.L. Pitcher of the Year by The Sporting News (1999 and 2000). ... Named A.L. Cy Young Award winner by Baseball Writers' Association of America (1999 and 2000).

STATISTICAL NOTES: Led N.L. with 11 hit batsmen in 1994. ... Pitched nine perfect innings against San Diego, before being relieved after yielding leadoff double in 10th inning (June 3, 1995). ... Tied for N.L. lead with 16 sacrifice hits in 1996. ... Pitched 2-0 one-hit, complete-game victory against Cincinnati (July 13, 1997). ... Struck out 15 batters in one game (May 7, May 12, August 24 and September 4, 1999; May 12 and July 23, 2000). ... Struck out 16 batters in one game (June 4, 1999; and April 8, 2001). ... Struck out 17 batters in one game (September 10, 1999; and May 6, 2000). ... Pitched 3-1 one-hit, complete-game victory against New York Yankees (September 10, 1999). ... Pitched 8-0 one-hit, complete-game victory against Tampa Bay (August 29, 2000).

Year League	W	L	Pct.	ERA	G	GS	CG	ShO	Sv.	IP	H	R	ER	BB	SO
1988—Dominican Dodgers (DSL) .	5	1	.833	3.10	8	7	1	0	0	49 1/3	45	25	17	16	28
1989—Dominican Dodgers (DSL) .	7	2	.778	2.73	13	7	2	3	1	85 2/3	59	30	26	25	63
1990—Great Falls (Pio.)	8	3	.727	3.62	14	•14	0	0	0	77	74	39	31	40	82
1991—Bakersfield (Calif.)	8	0	1.000	2.05	10	10	0	0	0	61 1/3	41	17	14	19	83
—San Antonio (Texas)	7	5	.583	1.76	12	12	4	•3	0	76 2/3	57	21	15	31	74
—Albuquerque (PCL)	3	3	.500	3.66	6	6	0	0	0	39 1/3	28	17	16	16	35
1992—Albuquerque (PCL)	7	6	.538	3.81	20	20	3	1	0	125 1/3	104	57	53	57	124
—Los Angeles (N.L.)	0	1	.000	2.25	2	1	0	0	0	8	6	2	2	1	8
1993—Albuquerque (PCL)	0	0	...	3.00	1	1	0	0	0	3	1	1	1	1	4
—Los Angeles (N.L.)	10	5	.667	2.61	65	2	0	0	2	107	76	34	31	57	119
1994—Montreal (N.L.)■	11	5	.688	3.42	24	23	1	1	1	144 2/3	115	58	55	45	142
1995—Montreal (N.L.)	14	10	.583	3.51	30	30	2	2	0	194 2/3	158	79	76	66	174
1996—Montreal (N.L.)	13	10	.565	3.70	33	33	4	1	0	216 2/3	189	100	89	70	222
1997—Montreal (N.L.)	17	8	.680	*1.90	31	31	*13	4	0	241 1/3	158	65	51	67	305
1998—Boston (A.L.)■	19	7	.731	2.89	33	33	3	2	0	233 2/3	188	82	75	67	251
1999—Boston (A.L.)	*23	4	*.852	*2.07	31	29	5	1	0	213 1/3	160	56	49	37	*313
2000—Boston (A.L.)	18	6	.750	*1.74	29	29	7	*4	0	217	128	44	42	32	284
2001—Boston (A.L.)	7	3	.700	2.39	18	18	1	0	0	116 2/3	84	33	31	25	163
A.L. totals (4 years)	67	20	.770	2.27	111	109	16	7	0	780 2/3	560	215	197	161	1011
N.L. totals (6 years)	65	39	.625	3.00	185	120	20	8	3	912 1/3	702	338	304	306	970
Major League totals (10 years)	132	59	.691	2.66	296	229	36	15	3	1693	1262	553	501	467	1981

DIVISION SERIES RECORD

Year League	W	L	Pct.	ERA	G	GS	CG	ShO	Sv.	IP	H	R	ER	BB	SO
1998—Boston (A.L.)	1	0	1.000	3.86	1	1	0	0	0	7	6	3	3	0	8
1999—Boston (A.L.)	1	0	1.000	0.00	2	1	0	0	0	10	3	0	0	4	11
Division series totals (2 years)	2	0	1.000	1.59	3	2	0	0	0	17	9	3	3	4	19

CHAMPIONSHIP SERIES RECORD

Year League	W	L	Pct.	ERA	G	GS	CG	ShO	Sv.	IP	H	R	ER	BB	SO
1999—Boston (A.L.)	1	0	1.000	0.00	1	1	0	0	0	7	2	0	0	2	12

ALL-STAR GAME RECORD

RECORDS: Holds record for most consecutive strikeouts from start of game—4 (1999).

NOTES: Named Most Valuable Player (1999).

Year League	W	L	Pct.	ERA		GS	CG	ShO	Sv.	IP	H	R	ER	BB	SO
1996—National	0	0	...	0.00		0	0	0	0	1	2	0	0	0	1
1997—National	0	0	...	0.00		0	0	0	0	1	0	0	0	0	2
1998—American							Did not play.								
1999—American	1	0	1.000	0.00		1	0	0	0	2	0	0	0	0	5
All-Star Game totals (3 years)	1	0	1.000	0.00		1	0	0	0	4	2	0	0	0	8

MARTINEZ, RAMON — P

PERSONAL: Born March 22, 1968, in Santo Domingo, Dominican Republic. ... 6-4/184. ... Throws right, bats right. ... Full name: Ramon Jaime Martinez. ... Brother of Pedro Martinez, pitcher, Boston Red Sox; and brother of Jesus Martinez, pitcher with Los Angeles Dodgers (1991-97) and Cincinnati Reds (1998) organizations.

HIGH SCHOOL: Liceo Secunderia Las Americas (Dominican Republic).

TRANSACTIONS/CAREER NOTES: Signed as non-drafted free agent by Los Angeles Dodgers organization (September 1, 1984). ... On suspended list (July 8-12, 1993). ... Granted free agency (November 1, 1995). ... Re-signed by Dodgers (November 16, 1995). ... On Los Angeles disabled list (April 7-May 14, 1996); included rehabilitation assignments to San Antonio (May 4-9) and Vero Beach (May 9-14). ... On Los Angeles disabled list (June 15-August 20, 1997); included rehabilitation assignment to San Bernardino (July 26-August 20). ... On disabled list (June 19, 1998-remainder of season). ... Granted free agency (November 17, 1998). ... Signed by Boston Red Sox (March 11, 1999). ... On Boston disabled list (April 1-September 2, 1999); included rehabilitation assignments to Lowell (June 21-25), Gulf Coast Red Sox (July 11-August 1), Sarasota (August 2-21) and Pawtucket (August 22-30). ... On Boston disabled list (August 1-September 2, 2000); included rehabilitation assignment to Pawtucket (August 20-September 2). ... Granted free agency (November 1, 2000). ... Signed by Dodgers (January 18, 2001). ... Released by Dogers (March 28, 2001). ... Signed by Pittsburgh Pirates (April 11, 2001). ... Announced retirement (May 2, 2001).

STATISTICAL NOTES: Struck out 18 batters in one game (June 4, 1990). ... Pitched 7-0 no-hit victory against Florida (July 14, 1995).

MISCELLANEOUS: Member of 1984 Dominican Republic Olympic baseball team. ... Appeared in one game as pinch runner (1989). ... Appeared in one game as pinch runner (1992). ... Appeared in one game as pinch hitter and appeared in one game as pinch runner with Los Angeles (1996).

Year League	W	L	Pct.	ERA	G	GS	CG	ShO	Sv.	IP	H	R	ER	BB	SO
1985—Gulf Coast Dodgers (GCL)..	4	1	.800	2.59	23	6	0	0	1	59	57	30	17	23	42
1986—Bakersfield (Calif.)	4	8	.333	4.75	20	20	2	1	0	106	119	73	56	63	78
1987—Vero Beach (FSL)	16	5	.762	2.17	25	25	6	1	0	170 1/3	128	45	41	78	148
1988—San Antonio (Texas)	8	4	.667	2.46	14	14	2	1	0	95	79	29	26	34	89
—Albuquerque (PCL)	5	2	.714	2.76	10	10	1	1	0	58 2/3	43	24	18	32	49
—Los Angeles (N.L.)	1	3	.250	3.79	9	6	0	0	0	35 2/3	27	17	15	22	23

Year	League	W	L	Pct.	ERA	G	GS	CG	ShO	Sv.	IP	H	R	ER	BB	SO
1989—Albuquerque (PCL)		10	2	.833	2.79	18	18	2	1	0	113	92	40	35	50	127
—Los Angeles (N.L.)		6	4	.600	3.19	15	15	2	2	0	98 2/3	79	39	35	41	89
1990—Los Angeles (N.L.)		20	6	.769	2.92	33	33	*12	3	0	234 1/3	191	89	76	67	223
1991—Los Angeles (N.L.)		17	13	.567	3.27	33	33	6	4	0	220 1/3	190	89	80	69	150
1992—Los Angeles (N.L.)		8	11	.421	4.00	25	25	1	1	0	150 2/3	141	82	67	69	101
1993—Los Angeles (N.L.)		10	12	.455	3.44	32	32	4	3	0	211 2/3	202	88	81	*104	127
1994—Los Angeles (N.L.)		12	7	.632	3.97	24	24	4	•3	0	170	160	83	75	56	119
1995—Los Angeles (N.L.)		17	7	.708	3.66	30	30	4	2	0	206 1/3	176	95	84	*81	138
1996—San Antonio (Texas)		0	0	...	0.00	1	1	0	0	0	2 2/3	0	0	0	3	1
—Vero Beach (FSL)		1	0	1.000	0.00	1	1	0	0	0	7	5	1	0	0	10
—Los Angeles (N.L.)		15	6	.714	3.42	29	27	2	2	0	168 2/3	153	76	64	86	133
1997—Los Angeles (N.L.)		10	5	.667	3.64	22	22	1	0	0	133 2/3	123	64	54	68	120
—San Bernardino (Calif.)		0	1	.000	1.15	4	4	0	0	0	15 2/3	10	2	2	4	16
1998—Los Angeles (N.L.)		7	3	.700	2.83	15	15	1	0	0	101 2/3	76	41	32	41	91
1999—Lowell (NY-Penn)■		0	0	...	0.00	1	1	0	0	0	2	0	0	0	0	3
—Gulf Coast Red Sox (GCL)		1	0	1.000	1.38	4	4	0	0	0	13	9	4	2	3	15
—Sarasota (FSL)		1	0	1.000	3.00	3	3	0	0	0	12	11	7	4	7	9
—Pawtucket (I.L.)		0	1	.000	9.00	2	2	0	0	0	9	10	9	9	6	7
—Boston (A.L.)		2	1	.667	3.05	4	4	0	0	0	20 2/3	14	8	7	8	15
2000—Boston (A.L.)		10	8	.556	6.13	27	27	0	0	0	127 2/3	143	94	87	67	89
—Pawtucket (I.L.)		1	0	1.000	2.31	2	2	0	0	0	11 2/3	8	4	3	4	10
2001—Pittsburgh (N.L.)■		0	2	.000	8.62	4	4	0	0	0	15 2/3	16	15	15	16	9
A.L. totals (2 years)		12	9	.571	5.70	31	31	0	0	0	148 1/3	157	102	94	75	104
N.L. totals (12 years)		123	79	.609	3.49	271	266	37	20	0	1747 1/3	1534	778	678	720	1323
Major League totals (14 years)		135	88	.605	3.67	302	297	37	20	0	1895 2/3	1691	880	772	795	1427

DIVISION SERIES RECORD

Year	League	W	L	Pct.	ERA	G	GS	CG	ShO	Sv.	IP	H	R	ER	BB	SO
1995—Los Angeles (N.L.)		0	1	.000	14.54	1	1	0	0	0	4 1/3	10	7	7	2	3
1996—Los Angeles (N.L.)		0	0	...	1.13	1	1	0	0	0	8	3	1	1	3	6
1999—Boston (A.L.)		0	0	...	3.18	1	1	0	0	0	5 2/3	5	2	2	3	6
Division series totals (3 years)		0	1	.000	5.00	3	3	0	0	0	18	18	10	10	8	15

CHAMPIONSHIP SERIES RECORD

Year	League	W	L	Pct.	ERA	G	GS	CG	ShO	Sv.	IP	H	R	ER	BB	SO
1999—Boston (A.L.)		0	1	.000	4.05	1	1	0	0	0	6 2/3	6	3	3	3	5

MARTINEZ, RAMON — 2B/SS — GIANTS

PERSONAL: Born October 10, 1972, in Philadelphia. ... 6-1/187. ... Bats right, throws right. ... Full name: Ramon E. Martinez.
HIGH SCHOOL: Escuela Superior Catholica (Bayamon, Puerto Rico).
JUNIOR COLLEGE: Vernon (Texas) Regional Junior College.
TRANSACTIONS/CAREER NOTES: Signed as non-drafted free agent by Kansas City Royals organization (January 15, 1993). ... Traded by Royals to San Francisco Giants (December 9, 1996), completing deal in which Giants traded P Jamie Brewington to Royals for a player to be named later (November 26, 1996). ... On Fresno disabled list (June 10-23, 1999). ... On San Francisco disabled list (August 21-September 5, 1999).
STATISTICAL NOTES: Led Texas League with 18 sacrifice hits and nine sacrifice flies in 1995. ... Led Texas League second basemen with .984 fielding percentage in 1995. ... Led American Association with 13 sacrifice hits in 1996.

Year	Team (League)	Pos.	G	AB	R	H	2B	3B	HR	RBI	Avg.	BB	SO	SB	PO	A	E	Avg.
1993—GC Royals (GCL)		2B	37	97	16	23	5	0	0	9	.237	8	6	3	71	108	5	.973
—Wilmington (Caro.)		2B-SS	24	75	8	19	4	0	0	6	.253	11	9	1	52	72	6	.954
1994—Wilmington (Caro.)		2B	90	325	40	87	13	2	2	35	.268	35	25	6	176	249	16	.964
—Rockford (Midw.)		2B	6	18	3	5	0	0	0	3	.278	4	2	1	9	12	1	.955
1995—Wichita (Texas)		2B-SS	103	393	58	108	20	2	3	51	.275	42	50	11	186	311	9	†.982
1996—Omaha (A.A.)		2B	85	320	35	81	12	3	6	41	.253	21	34	3	163	207	12	.969
—Wichita (Texas)		2B	26	93	16	32	4	1	1	8	.344	7	8	4	47	84	6	.956
1997—Shreveport (Texas)■		SS	105	404	72	129	32	4	5	54	.319	40	48	4	167	370	18	.968
—Phoenix (PCL)		2B-SS	18	57	6	16	2	0	1	7	.281	5	9	1	26	44	3	.959
1998—Fresno (PCL)		2B-SS	98	364	58	114	21	2	14	59	.313	38	42	0	209	280	10	.980
—San Francisco (N.L.)		2B	19	19	4	6	1	0	0	0	.316	4	2	0	15	20	0	1.000
1999—San Francisco (N.L.)		2B-SS-3B-DH	61	144	21	38	6	0	5	19	.264	14	17	1	66	102	6	.966
—Fresno (PCL)		SS-3B	29	114	13	37	7	1	2	17	.325	10	17	2	26	72	5	.951
2000—San Francisco (N.L.)		SS-2B-1B-3B	88	189	30	57	13	2	6	25	.302	15	22	3	88	108	1	.995
2001—San Francisco (N.L.)		3B-SS	128	391	48	99	18	3	5	37	.253	38	52	11	123	261	8	.980
Major League totals (4 years)			296	743	103	200	38	5	16	81	.269	71	93	5	292	491	15	.981

DIVISION SERIES RECORD

Year	Team (League)	Pos.	G	AB	R	H	2B	3B	HR	RBI	Avg.	BB	SO	SB	PO	A	E	Avg.
2000—San Francisco (N.L.)		2B-SS	2	6	0	2	0	0	0	0	.333	0	2	0	3	7	0	1.000

MARTINEZ, SANDY — C — EXPOS

PERSONAL: Born October 3, 1972, in Villa Mella, Dominican Republic. ... 6-2/215. ... Bats left, throws right. ... Full name: Angel Sandy Martinez.
HIGH SCHOOL: Villa Mella (Dominican Republic).
TRANSACTIONS/CAREER NOTES: Signed as non-drafted free agent by Toronto Blue Jays organization (January 10, 1990). ... On disabled list (May 15-June 8, 1993). ... On Toronto disabled list (August 17-September 1, 1996); included rehabilitation assignment to Knoxville (August

26-September 1). ... On Syracuse disabled list (June 14-24, 1997). ... Traded by Blue Jays to Chicago Cubs for a player to be named later (December 11, 1997); Blue Jays acquired P Trevor Schaffer to complete deal (December 19, 1997). ... On suspended list (July 1-3, 1998). ... On Chicago disabled list (May 13-June 10, 1999); included rehabilitation assignment to Iowa (June 5-10). ... Granted free agency (October 15, 1999). ... Signed by Florida Marlins organization (December 6, 1999). ... Granted free agency (October 11, 2000). ... Signed by Montreal Expos organization (November 17, 2000). ... On disabled list (April 4, 2001-remainder of season).

RECORDS: Shares major league single-game record for most putouts by catcher (nine-inning game)—20 (May 6, 1998); and most chances accepted by catcher (nine-inning game) since 1900—20 (May 6, 1998).

STATISTICAL NOTES: Led Pioneer League with 24 passed balls in 1992. ... Led Florida State League catchers with 14 errors in 1994.

Year	Team (League)	Pos.	G	AB	R	H	2B	3B	HR	RBI	Avg.	BB	SO	SB	PO	A	E	Avg.
1990— Dom. Blue Jays (DSL)	C	44	145	21	35	2	0	0	10	.241	18	15	1	...	...	...	...
1991— Dunedin (FSL)	C	12	38	3	7	1	0	0	3	.184	7	7	0	82	9	2	.978
— Medicine Hat (Pio.)	C	34	98	8	17	1	0	2	16	.173	12	29	0	141	19	3	.982
1992— Dunedin (FSL)	C	4	15	4	3	1	0	2	4	.200	0	3	0	11	2	1	.929
— Medicine Hat (Pio.)	C-1B-SS	57	206	27	52	15	0	4	39	.252	14	62	0	275	58	5	.985
1993— Hagerstown (S.Atl.)	C-DH	94	338	41	89	16	1	9	46	.263	19	71	1	493	68	14	.976
1994— Dunedin (FSL)	C-DH-1B	122	450	50	117	14	6	7	52	.260	22	79	1	615	79	†14	.980
1995— Knoxville (Sou.)	C-DH	41	144	14	33	8	1	2	22	.229	6	34	0	219	30	5	.980
— Toronto (A.L.)	C	62	191	12	46	12	0	2	25	.241	7	45	0	329	28	5	.986
1996— Toronto (A.L.)	C	76	229	17	52	9	3	3	18	.227	16	58	0	413	33	3	.993
— Knoxville (Sou.)	C-DH	4	16	2	3	0	0	0	0	.188	0	5	0	17	2	1	.950
1997— Syracuse (I.L.)	C-DH	96	322	28	72	12	1	4	29	.224	27	76	7	588	50	9	.986
— Toronto (A.L.)	C	3	2	1	0	0	0	0	0	.000	1	1	0	12	2	1	.933
1998— Chicago (N.L.)■	C	45	87	7	23	9	1	0	7	.264	13	21	1	185	7	3	.985
1999— Chicago (N.L.)	C	17	30	1	5	0	0	1	1	.167	0	11	0	45	2	2	.959
— Iowa (PCL)	C	36	125	8	29	6	0	2	18	.232	5	29	1	239	17	1	.996
2000— Florida (N.L.)■	C	10	18	1	4	2	0	0	0	.222	0	8	0	43	2	0	1.000
— Calgary (PCL)	C	86	277	45	83	20	0	15	48	.300	16	57	2	373	38	4	.990
2001— Montreal (N.L.)■	C	1	1	0	0	0	0	0	0	.000	0	0	0	2	0	0	1.000
American League totals (3 years)		141	422	30	98	21	3	5	43	.232	24	104	0	754	63	9	.989
National League totals (4 years)		73	136	9	32	11	1	1	8	.235	13	40	1	275	11	5	.983
Major League totals (7 years)		214	558	39	130	32	4	6	51	.233	37	144	1	1029	74	14	.987

DIVISION SERIES RECORD

Year	Team (League)	Pos.	G	AB	R	H	2B	3B	HR	RBI	Avg.	BB	SO	SB	PO	A	E	Avg.
1998— Chicago (N.L.)	C	1	1	1	1	0	0	0	0	1.000	0	0	0	1	0	0	1.000

MARTINEZ, TINO 1B CARDINALS

PERSONAL: Born December 7, 1967, in Tampa. ... 6-2/210. ... Bats left, throws right. ... Full name: Constantino Martinez.

HIGH SCHOOL: Tampa Catholic.

COLLEGE: Tampa (Fla.).

TRANSACTIONS/CAREER NOTES: Selected by Boston Red Sox organization in third round of free-agent draft (June 3, 1985); did not sign. ... Selected by Seattle Mariners organization in first round (14th pick overall) of free-agent draft (June 1, 1988). ... On disabled list (August 10, 1993-remainder of season). ... Traded by Mariners with P Jeff Nelson and P Jim Mecir to New York Yankees for P Sterling Hitchcock and 3B Russ Davis (December 7, 1995). ... Granted free agency (November 5, 2001). ... Signed by St. Louis Cardinals (December 18, 2001).

RECORDS: Holds A.L. single-season record for fewest putouts by first baseman (150 or more games)—1,154 (2000); and fewest chances accepted by first baseman (150 or more games)—1,242 (2000).

HONORS: Named first baseman on The Sporting News college All-America team (1988). ... Named Pacific Coast League Most Valuable Player (1991). ... Named first baseman on The Sporting News A.L. All-Star team (1997). ... Named first baseman on The Sporting News A.L. Silver Slugger team (1997).

STATISTICAL NOTES: Led Eastern League with 13 intentional bases on balls received in 1989. ... Led Eastern League first basemen with 1,348 total chances and 106 double plays in 1989. ... Tied for Pacific Coast League lead with 11 intentional bases on balls received in 1990. ... Led Pacific Coast League first basemen with .991 fielding percentage, 1,051 putouts, 98 assists, 1,159 total chances and 117 double plays in 1990. ... Led Pacific Coast League first basemen with .992 fielding percentage and 122 double plays in 1991. ... Hit three home runs in one game (April 2, 1997). ... Led A.L. with 13 sacrifice flies in 1997. ... Led A.L. first basemen with 1,410 total chances in 1999. ... Career major league grand slams: 9.

MISCELLANEOUS: Member of 1988 U.S. Olympic baseball team.

Year	Team (League)	Pos.	G	AB	R	H	2B	3B	HR	RBI	Avg.	BB	SO	SB	PO	A	E	Avg.
1989— Williamsport (East.)	1B	*137	*509	51	131	29	2	13	64	.257	59	54	7	*1260	*81	7	*.995
1990— Calgary (PCL)	1B-3B	128	453	83	145	28	1	17	93	.320	74	37	8	†1051	†98	10	†.991
— Seattle (A.L.)	1B	24	68	4	15	4	0	0	5	.221	9	9	0	155	12	0	1.000
1991— Calgary (PCL)	1B-3B	122	442	94	144	34	5	18	86	.326	82	44	3	1078	106	9	†.992
— Seattle (A.L.)	1B-DH	36	112	11	23	2	0	4	9	.205	11	24	0	249	22	2	.993
1992— Seattle (A.L.)	1B-DH	136	460	53	118	19	2	16	66	.257	42	77	2	678	58	4	.995
1993— Seattle (A.L.)	1B-DH	109	408	48	108	25	1	17	60	.265	45	56	0	932	60	3	.997
1994— Seattle (A.L.)	1B-DH	97	329	42	86	21	0	20	61	.261	29	52	1	705	45	2	.997
1995— Seattle (A.L.)	1B-DH	141	519	92	152	35	3	31	111	.293	62	91	0	1048	101	8	.993
1996— New York (A.L.)■	1B-DH	155	595	82	174	28	0	25	117	.292	68	85	2	1238	83	5	*.996
1997— New York (A.L.)	1B-DH	158	594	96	176	31	2	44	141	.296	75	75	3	1302	105	8	.994
1998— New York (A.L.)	1B	142	531	92	149	33	1	28	123	.281	61	83	2	1180	93	10	.992
1999— New York (A.L.)	1B	159	589	95	155	27	2	28	105	.263	69	86	3	1297	*106	7	.995
2000— New York (A.L.)	1B	155	569	69	147	37	4	16	91	.258	52	74	4	1154	88	7	.994
2001— New York (A.L.)	1B-DH	154	589	89	165	24	2	34	113	.280	42	89	1	1144	99	5	.996
Major League totals (12 years)		1466	5363	773	1468	286	17	263	1002	.274	565	801	18	11082	872	61	.995

DIVISION SERIES RECORD

RECORDS: Holds A.L. career record for at-bats—114. ... Shares A.L. career records for most games—30; and hits—32. ... Shares single-game record for most at-bats—7 (October 4, 1995).

Year Team (League)	Pos.	G	AB	R	H	2B	3B	HR	RBI	Avg.	BB	SO	SB	PO	A	E	Avg.
1995— Seattle (A.L.)	1B	5	22	4	9	1	0	1	5	.409	3	4	0	39	5	0	1.000
1996— New York (A.L.).........	1B	4	15	3	4	2	0	0	0	.267	4	1	0	33	3	0	1.000
1997— New York (A.L.).........	1B	5	18	1	4	1	0	1	4	.222	2	4	0	48	6	0	1.000
1998— New York (A.L.).........	1B	3	11	1	3	2	0	0	0	.273	0	2	0	27	1	0	1.000
1999— New York (A.L.).........	1B	3	11	2	2	0	0	0	0	.182	2	2	0	29	1	1	.968
2000— New York (A.L.).........	1B	5	19	2	8	2	0	0	4	.421	1	3	0	45	5	1	.980
2001— New York (A.L.).........	1B	5	18	1	2	0	0	1	2	.111	1	6	0	47	4	0	1.000
Division series totals (7 years)		30	114	14	32	8	0	3	15	.281	13	22	0	268	25	2	.993

CHAMPIONSHIP SERIES RECORD

RECORDS: Shares A.L. career record for most times hit by pitch—3.

Year Team (League)	Pos.	G	AB	R	H	2B	3B	HR	RBI	Avg.	BB	SO	SB	PO	A	E	Avg.
1995— Seattle (A.L.)	1B	6	22	1	3	0	0	0	0	.136	3	7	0	45	5	1	.980
1996— New York (A.L.).........	1B	5	22	3	4	1	0	0	0	.182	0	2	0	49	2	0	1.000
1998— New York (A.L.).........	1B	6	19	1	2	1	0	0	1	.105	6	8	2	47	4	1	.981
1999— New York (A.L.).........	1B	5	19	3	5	1	0	1	3	.263	2	4	0	29	5	0	1.000
2000— New York (A.L.).........	1B	6	25	5	8	2	0	1	1	.320	2	4	0	47	6	0	1.000
2001— New York (A.L.).........	1B	5	20	3	5	1	0	1	3	.250	0	4	0	39	5	0	1.000
Championship series totals (6 years)		33	127	16	27	6	0	3	8	.213	13	29	2	256	27	2	.993

WORLD SERIES RECORD

RECORDS: Shares single-game record for most grand slams—1 (October 17, 1998). ... Shares single-inning record for most runs batted in—4 (October 17, 1998, seventh inning).
NOTES: Member of World Series championship team (1996, 1998, 1999 and 2000).

Year Team (League)	Pos.	G	AB	R	H	2B	3B	HR	RBI	Avg.	BB	SO	SB	PO	A	E	Avg.
1996— New York (A.L.).........	1B-PH	6	11	0	1	0	0	0	0	.091	2	5	0	27	0	0	1.000
1998— New York (A.L.).........	1B	4	13	4	5	0	0	1	4	.385	6	2	0	36	3	0	1.000
1999— New York (A.L.).........	1B	4	15	3	4	0	0	1	5	.267	2	4	0	41	2	0	1.000
2000— New York (A.L.).........	1B	5	22	3	8	1	0	0	2	.364	1	4	0	39	4	0	1.000
2001— New York (A.L.).........	1B	6	21	1	4	0	0	1	3	.190	2	2	0	45	7	0	1.000
World Series totals (5 years)		25	82	11	22	1	0	3	14	.268	13	17	0	188	16	0	1.000

ALL-STAR GAME RECORD

Year League	Pos.	AB	R	H	2B	3B	HR	RBI	Avg.	BB	SO	SB	PO	A	E	Avg.
1995— American	PH	1	0	1	0	0	0	0	1.000	0	0	0	...	...	...	...
1997— American	1B	2	0	0	0	0	0	0	.000	0	0	0	10	0	0	1.000
All-Star Game totals (2 years)		3	0	1	0	0	0	0	.333	0	0	0	10	0	0	1.000

M

MARTINEZ, VICTOR   C   INDIANS

PERSONAL: Born December 23, 1978, in Ciudad Bolivar, Venezuela. ... 6-2/170. ... Bats both, throws right. ... Full name: Victor Jesus Martinez.
TRANSACTIONS/CAREER NOTES: Signed as non-drafted free agent by Cleveland Indians organization (July 15, 1996). ... On Kinston disabled list (May 25-July 19, 2000).
HONORS: Named Carolina League Most Valuable Player (2001).
STATISTICAL NOTES: Led Carolina League with .488 slugging percentage in 2001. ... Led Carolina League catchers with 1,061 total chances in 2001.

Year Team (League)	Pos.	G	AB	R	H	2B	3B	HR	RBI	Avg.	BB	SO	SB	PO	A	E	Avg.
1997— Maracay (VSL)		53	122	21	42	12	0	0	26	.344	32	11	6	...	...	...	...
1998— Guacara 1 (VSL)........		55	160	28	43	13	0	1	27	.269	32	14	8	...	...	...	...
1999— Mahoning Valley (NY-P)	C	64	235	37	65	9	0	4	36	.277	27	31	0	427	*56	8	.984
2000— Kinston (Caro.)..........	C	26	83	9	18	7	0	0	8	.217	11	5	1	232	16	5	.980
—Columbus (S.Atl.).......	C	21	70	11	26	9	1	2	12	.371	11	6	0	154	14	2	.988
2001— Kinston (Caro.)..........	C	114	420	59	138	33	2	10	57	.329	39	60	3	*967	78	*16	.985

MASAOKA, ONAN   P   WHITE SOX

PERSONAL: Born October 27, 1977, in Hilo, Hawaii. ... 6-0/188. ... Throws left, bats right. ... Full name: Onan Kinoa Satoshi Masaoka.
HIGH SCHOOL: Waiakea (Hilo, Hawaii).
TRANSACTIONS/CAREER NOTES: Selected by Los Angeles Dodgers organization in third round of free-agent draft (June 1, 1995). ... Traded by Dodgers with P Gary Majewski and OF Jeff Barry to Chicago White Sox for P James Baldwin (July 26, 2001).

Year League	W	L	Pct.	ERA	G	GS	CG	ShO	Sv.	IP	H	R	ER	BB	SO
1995— Yakima (N'West)	2	4	.333	3.65	15	7	0	0	3	49 1/3	28	25	20	47	75
1996— Savannah (S.Atl.)	2	5	.286	4.29	13	13	0	0	0	65	55	35	31	35	80
1997— Vero Beach (FSL)	6	8	.429	3.87	28	24	2	1	1	148 2/3	113	72	64	55	132
1998— San Antonio (Texas).........	6	6	.500	5.32	27	20	1	•1	1	110	114	79	65	63	94
1999— Los Angeles (N.L.)	2	4	.333	4.32	54	0	0	0	1	66 2/3	55	33	32	47	61
2000— Los Angeles (N.L.)	1	1	.500	4.00	29	0	0	0	0	27	23	12	12	15	27
—Albuquerque (PCL).............	3	1	.750	3.86	18	5	0	0	0	37 1/3	31	17	16	36	22
2001— Las Vegas (PCL)	8	4	.667	5.55	31	5	0	0	1	73	80	87	49	45	28	61
—Charlotte (I.L.)■................	0	1	.000	4.30	14	0	0	0	5	14 2/3	11	8	7	5	22
Major League totals (2 years)	3	5	.375	4.23	83	0	0	0	1	93 2/3	78	45	44	62	88

MATEO, HENRY — 2B — EXPOS

PERSONAL: Born October 14, 1976, in Santo Domingo, Dominican Republic. ... 5-11/170. ... Bats both, throws right. ... Full name: Henry Valera Mateo.
HIGH SCHOOL: Centro Estudios Libres (Santurce, Puerto Rico).
TRANSACTIONS/CAREER NOTES: Selected by Montreal Expos organization in second round of free-agent draft (June 1, 1995).
STATISTICAL NOTES: Tied for Florida State League lead with 17 sacrifice hits in 1999. ... Led International League second basemen with 601 total chances in 2001.

Year Team (League)	Pos.	G	AB	R	H	2B	3B	HR	RBI	Avg.	BB	SO	SB	PO	A	E	Avg.
1995— GC Expos (GCL)	2B-SS	38	122	11	18	0	0	0	6	.148	14	47	2	71	105	9	.951
1996— GC Expos (GCL)	2B	14	44	8	11	3	0	0	3	.250	5	11	5	29	35	7	.901
1997— Vermont (NY-Penn)	2B	67	228	32	56	9	3	1	31	.246	30	44	21	134	173	14	.956
1998— Cape Fear (S.Atl.)	2B	114	416	72	115	20	5	4	41	.276	40	111	22	250	257	15	.971
— Jupiter (FSL)	2B	12	43	11	12	3	1	0	6	.279	2	6	3	23	24	0	1.000
1999— Jupiter (FSL)	2B	118	447	69	116	27	7	4	58	.260	44	112	32	193	235	17	.962
2000— Harrisburg (East.)	2B	140	530	91	152	25	11	5	63	.287	58	97	48	233	374	24	.962
2001— Ottawa (I.L.)	2B	118	500	71	134	14	*12	5	43	.268	33	89	*47	*251	•328	22	.963
— Montreal (N.L.)	2B	5	9	1	3	1	0	0	0	.333	0	1	0	3	6	2	.818
Major League totals (1 year)		5	9	1	3	1	0	0	0	.333	0	1	0	3	6	2	.818

MATEO, RUBEN — OF — REDS

PERSONAL: Born February 10, 1978, in San Cristobal, Dominican Republic. ... 6-0/185. ... Bats right, throws right. ... Full name: Ruben Amaurys Mateo.
HIGH SCHOOL: Liceo Jose Manuel Maria Balance (San Cristobal, Dominican Republic).
TRANSACTIONS/CAREER NOTES: Signed as non-drafted free agent by Texas Rangers organization (October 24, 1994). ... On Tulsa disabled list (April 13-May 13, 1998). ... On Texas disabled list (June 23-July 9 and August 5, 1999-remainder of season); included rehabilitation assignment to Oklahoma (July 6-9). ... On disabled list (June 3, 2000-remainder of season). ... Traded by Rangers with 3B Edwin Encarnacion to Cincinnati Reds for P Rob Bell (June 15, 2001). ... On Louisville disabled list (September 11-13, 2001).

Year Team (League)	Pos.	G	AB	R	H	2B	3B	HR	RBI	Avg.	BB	SO	SB	PO	A	E	Avg.
1995— Dom. Rangers (DSL)	OF	48	176	30	53	9	3	4	42	.301	20	23	1	55	1	1	.982
1996— Charl., S.C. (S.Atl.)	OF-DH	134	496	65	129	30	8	8	58	.260	26	78	30	215	15	7	.970
1997— Charlotte (FSL)	OF-DH	99	385	63	121	23	8	12	67	.314	22	55	20	174	10	8	.958
1998— Tulsa (Texas)	OF	107	433	79	134	32	3	18	75	.309	30	56	18	215	11	7	.970
— Charlotte (FSL)	OF	1	4	0	0	0	0	0	1	.000	0	1	0	2	0	0	1.000
1999— Texas (A.L.)	OF-DH	32	122	16	29	9	1	5	18	.238	4	28	3	62	3	0	1.000
— Oklahoma (PCL)	OF-DH	63	253	53	85	12	0	18	62	.336	14	36	6	128	3	5	.963
2000— Texas (A.L.)	OF	52	206	32	60	11	0	7	19	.291	10	34	6	140	4	3	.980
2001— Texas (A.L.)	OF	40	129	18	32	5	2	1	13	.248	9	28	1	70	0	1	.986
— Oklahoma (PCL)	OF	14	51	3	11	3	0	1	8	.216	2	8	1	22	0	1	.957
— Louisville (I.L.)■	OF	65	251	35	63	16	4	2	25	.251	13	45	2	100	3	5	.954
Major League totals (3 years)		124	457	66	121	25	3	13	50	.265	23	90	10	272	7	4	.986

MATHENY, MIKE — C — CARDINALS

PERSONAL: Born September 22, 1970, in Reynoldsburg, Ohio. ... 6-3/205. ... Bats right, throws right. ... Full name: Michael Scott Matheny.
HIGH SCHOOL: Reynoldsburg (Ohio).
COLLEGE: Michigan.
TRANSACTIONS/CAREER NOTES: Selected by Toronto Blue Jays organization in 31st round of free-agent draft (June 1, 1988); did not sign. ... Selected by Milwaukee Brewers organization in eighth round of free-agent draft (June 3, 1991). ... On Milwaukee suspended list (June 20-23, 1996). ... On Milwaukee disabled list (June 15-July 12, 1998); included rehabilitation assignment to Beloit (July 11-13). ... Granted free agency (December 21, 1998). ... Signed by Blue Jays (December 23, 1998). ... Released by Blue Jays (November 16, 1999). ... Signed by St. Louis Cardinals (December 15, 1999).
HONORS: Won N.L. Gold Glove as catcher (2000).
STATISTICAL NOTES: Led California League catchers with 20 double plays in 1992. ... Led Texas League catchers with 18 double plays in 1993. ... Career major league grand slams: 2.

Year Team (League)	Pos.	G	AB	R	H	2B	3B	HR	RBI	Avg.	BB	SO	SB	PO	A	E	Avg.
1991— Helena (Pio.)	C	64	253	35	72	14	0	2	34	.285	19	52	2	456	68	5	*.991
1992— Stockton (Calif.)	C	106	333	42	73	13	2	6	46	.219	35	81	2	582	114	8	*.989
1993— El Paso (Texas)	C	107	339	39	86	21	2	2	28	.254	17	73	1	524	*100	9	.986
1994— Milwaukee (A.L.)	C	28	53	3	12	3	0	1	2	.226	3	13	0	81	8	1	.989
— New Orleans (A.A.)	C-DH-1B	57	177	20	39	10	1	4	21	.220	16	39	1	345	43	5	.987
1995— New Orleans (A.A.)	C	6	17	3	6	2	0	3	4	.353	0	5	0	30	4	0	1.000
— Milwaukee (A.L.)	C	80	166	13	41	9	1	0	21	.247	12	28	2	261	18	4	.986
1996— Milwaukee (A.L.)	C-DH	106	313	31	64	15	2	8	46	.204	14	80	3	475	40	8	.985
— New Orleans (A.A.)	C-DH	20	66	3	15	4	0	1	6	.227	2	17	1	87	6	0	1.000
1997— Milwaukee (A.L.)	C-1B	123	320	29	78	16	1	4	32	.244	17	68	0	697	58	5	.993
1998— Milwaukee (N.L.)	C	108	320	24	76	13	0	6	27	.238	11	63	1	570	45	8	.987
— Beloit (Midw.)	DH-C	2	8	1	2	1	0	0	2	.250	1	3	0	13	1	0	1.000
1999— Toronto (A.L.)■	C	57	163	16	35	6	0	3	17	.215	12	37	0	346	33	2	.995
2000— St. Louis (N.L.)■	C-1B	128	417	43	109	22	1	6	47	.261	32	96	0	815	76	5	.994
2001— St. Louis (N.L.)	C-1B	121	381	40	83	12	0	7	42	.218	28	76	0	779	69	4	.992
American League totals (5 years)		394	1015	92	230	49	4	16	118	.227	58	226	5	1860	157	20	.990
National League totals (3 years)		357	1118	107	268	47	1	19	116	.240	71	235	1	2164	190	17	.993
Major League totals (8 years)		751	2133	199	498	96	5	35	234	.233	129	461	6	4024	347	37	.992

M

DIVISION SERIES RECORD

Year Team (League)	Pos.	G	AB	R	H	2B	3B	HR	RBI	Avg.	BB	SO	SB	PO	A	E	Avg.
2000— St. Louis (N.L.)								Did not play.									
2001— St. Louis (N.L.)..........	C	4	10	0	2	0	0	0	0	.200	0	3	0	20	1	0	1.000

CHAMPIONSHIP SERIES RECORD

Year Team (League)	Pos.	G	AB	R	H	2B	3B	HR	RBI	Avg.	BB	SO	SB	PO	A	E	Avg.
2000— St. Louis (N.L.)								Did not play.									

MATHEWS, T.J.   P   ASTROS

PERSONAL: Born January 19, 1970, in Belleville, Ill. ... 6-1/214. ... Throws right, bats right. ... Full name: Timothy Jay Mathews. ... Son of Nelson Mathews, outfielder with Chicago Cubs (1960-63) and Kansas City Athletics (1964-65).
HIGH SCHOOL: Columbia (Ill.).
JUNIOR COLLEGE: Meramec Community College (Mo.).
COLLEGE: UNLV.
TRANSACTIONS/CAREER NOTES: Selected by St. Louis Cardinals organization in 36th round of free-agent draft (June 1, 1992). ... On Louisville disabled list (May 30-June 6, 1995). ... On suspended list (April 1-7, 1997). ... Traded by Cardinals with P Eric Ludwick and P Blake Stein to Oakland Athletics for 1B Mark McGwire (July 31, 1997). ... On Oakland disabled list (July 1-24, 1999); included rehabilitation assignment to Vancouver (July 21-24). ... On Oakland disabled list (August 11-September 1, 2000); included rehabilitation assignment to Sacramento (August 27-September 1). ... Released by A's (June 22, 2001). ... Signed by Cardinals organization (August 7, 2001). ... Granted free agency (November 5, 2001). ... Signed by Houston Astros organization (December 21, 2001).
STATISTICAL NOTES: Pitched 4-0 no-hit victory against Burlington (August 13, 1993).

Year League	W	L	Pct.	ERA	G	GS	CG	ShO	Sv.	IP	H	R	ER	BB	SO
1992— Hamilton (NY-Penn)	10	1	*.909	2.18	14	14	1	0	0	86²/₃	70	25	21	30	89
1993— Springfield (Midw.)	12	9	.571	2.71	25	25	5	2	0	159¹/₃	121	59	48	29	144
1994— St. Petersburg (FSL)	5	5	.500	2.44	11	11	1	0	0	66¹/₃	52	22	18	23	62
— Arkansas (Texas)..............	5	5	.500	3.15	16	16	1	0	0	97	83	37	34	24	93
1995— Louisville (A.A.).............	9	4	.692	2.70	32	7	0	0	1	66²/₃	60	35	20	27	50
— St. Louis (N.L.).............	1	1	.500	1.52	23	0	0	0	2	29²/₃	21	7	5	11	28
1996— St. Louis (N.L.).............	2	6	.250	3.01	67	0	0	0	6	83²/₃	62	32	28	32	80
1997— St. Louis (N.L.).............	4	4	.500	2.15	40	0	0	0	0	46	41	14	11	18	46
— Oakland (A.L.)■..............	6	2	.750	4.40	24	0	0	0	3	28²/₃	34	18	14	12	24
1998— Oakland (A.L.).............	7	4	.636	4.58	66	0	0	0	1	72²/₃	71	44	37	29	53
1999— Oakland (A.L.).............	9	5	.643	3.81	50	0	0	0	3	59	46	28	25	20	42
— Vancouver (PCL).............	0	0	...	9.00	1	1	0	0	0	1	1	1	1	0	0
2000— Oakland (A.L.).............	2	3	.400	6.03	50	0	0	0	0	59²/₃	73	40	40	25	42
— Sacramento (PCL)............	0	0	.000	0.00	3	1	0	0	0	3²/₃	2	1	0	1	5
2001— Oakland (A.L.).............	0	1	.000	5.09	30	0	0	0	1	23	28	14	13	11	19
— Memphis (PCL)■.............	1	1	.500	1.80	15	0	0	0	0	15	16	4	3	1	14
— St. Louis (N.L.).............	1	0	1.000	3.07	10	0	0	0	4	14²/₃	11	6	5	1	10
A.L. totals (5 years)	24	15	.615	4.78	210	0	0	0	8	243	252	144	129	97	180
N.L. totals (4 years)	8	11	.421	2.53	140	0	0	0	8	174	135	59	49	62	164
Major League totals (7 years)	32	26	.552	3.84	350	0	0	0	16	417	387	203	178	159	344

DIVISION SERIES RECORD

Year League	W	L	Pct.	ERA	G	GS	CG	ShO	Sv.	IP	H	R	ER	BB	SO
1996— St. Louis (N.L.)..................	1	0	1.000	0.00	1	0	0	0	0	1	1	0	0	0	2

CHAMPIONSHIP SERIES RECORD

Year League	W	L	Pct.	ERA	G	GS	CG	ShO	Sv.	IP	H	R	ER	BB	SO
1996— St. Louis (N.L.)..................	0	0	...	0.00	2	0	0	0	0	²/₃	2	0	0	2	2

MATOS, LUIS   OF   ORIOLES

PERSONAL: Born October 30, 1978, in Bayamon, Puerto Rico. ... 6-0/179. ... Bats right, throws right. ... Full name: Luis D. Matos.
HIGH SCHOOL: Disciple of Christ Academy (Bayamon, Puerto Rico).
TRANSACTIONS/CAREER NOTES: Selected by Baltimore Orioles organization in 10th round of free-agent draft (June 4, 1996). ... On Baltimore disabled list (March 30-August 24, 2001); included rehabilitation assignments to Gulf Coast Orioles (August 7-10), Frederick (August 11-13) and Bowie (August 14-24).

Year Team (League)	Pos.	G	AB	R	H	2B	3B	HR	RBI	Avg.	BB	SO	SB	PO	A	E	Avg.
1996— GC Orioles (GCL).......	OF	43	130	21	38	2	0	0	13	.292	15	18	12	56	3	1	.983
1997— Delmarva (S.Atl.).......	OF	36	119	10	25	1	2	0	13	.210	9	21	8	66	3	2	.972
— Bluefield (Appl.)	OF	61	240	37	66	7	3	2	35	.275	20	36	26	125	4	3	.977
1998— Delmarva (S.Atl.).......	OF	133	503	73	137	26	6	7	32	.272	38	90	42	254	12	10	.964
— Bowie (East.).............	OF	5	19	2	5	0	0	1	3	.263	1	1	1	4	1	1	.833
1999— Frederick (Caro.)	OF-DH	68	273	40	81	15	1	7	41	.297	20	35	27	143	6	2	.987
— Bowie (East.).............	OF	66	283	41	67	11	1	9	36	.237	15	39	14	152	8	3	.982
2000— Bowie (East.).............	OF	50	181	26	49	7	5	2	33	.271	17	23	8	117	4	2	.984
— Baltimore (A.L.).........	OF-DH	72	182	21	41	6	3	1	17	.225	12	30	13	168	3	2	.988
2001— GC Orioles (GCL).......	DH	3	14	1	4	2	0	0	2	.286	0	3	0	...	...	...	...
— Frederick (Caro.)	DH	2	7	3	3	0	0	0	2	.429	1	3	0	...	...	...	...
— Bowie (East.).............	OF	13	46	6	14	5	0	1	8	.304	5	7	0	20	1	1	.955
— Baltimore (A.L.).........	OF	31	98	16	21	7	0	4	12	.214	11	30	7	65	2	1	.985
Major League totals (2 years)		103	280	37	62	13	3	5	29	.221	23	60	20	233	5	3	.988

PERSONAL: Born August 26, 1975, in Champaign, Ill. ... 6-7/185. ... Throws right, bats right. ... Full name: Troy Walter Mattes.
HIGH SCHOOL: Riverview (Sarasota, Fla.).
JUNIOR COLLEGE: Miami-Dade (South) Community College.
TRANSACTIONS/CAREER NOTES: Selected by Montreal Expos organization in 16th round of free-agent draft (June 3, 1993). ... On Ottawa disabled list (May 1-June 3, 2001).

Year League	W	L	Pct.	ERA	G	GS	CG	ShO	Sv.	IP	H	R	ER	BB	SO
1994— Gulf Coast Expos (GCL)	3	2	.600	3.40	12	11	1	1	0	55²/₃	35	25	21	21	51
1995— Albany (S.Atl.)	0	2	.000	5.03	4	4	0	0	0	19²/₃	21	12	11	12	15
— Vermont (NY-Penn)	3	4	.429	3.72	10	10	0	0	0	46	51	34	19	25	23
— Gulf Coast Expos (GCL)	2	0	1.000	0.00	2	2	0	0	0	12	7	0	0	3	8
1996— Delmarva (S.Atl.)	10	9	.526	2.86	27	27	5	3	0	173¹/₃	142	77	55	50	151
1997— West Palm Beach (FSL)	6	9	.400	4.94	20	16	2	•2	1	102	123	61	56	20	61
1998— Jupiter (FSL)	7	6	.538	3.07	17	10	0	0	0	73¹/₃	73	33	25	19	42
1999— Jupiter (FSL)	3	0	1.000	3.70	5	5	0	0	0	24¹/₃	27	11	10	7	12
— Harrisburg (East.)	5	8	.385	5.36	20	19	0	0	0	97¹/₃	114	67	58	38	58
2000— Harrisburg (East.)	11	9	.550	4.18	28	28	4	0	0	174¹/₃	170	91	81	56	109
2001— Ottawa (I.L.)	5	5	.500	3.61	15	15	0	0	0	82¹/₃	75	38	33	33	70
— Montreal (N.L.)	3	3	.500	6.00	8	8	0	0	0	45	51	33	30	21	26
Major League totals (1 year)	3	3	.500	6.00	8	8	0	0	0	45	51	33	30	21	26

PERSONAL: Born August 25, 1974, in San Francisco. ... 6-3/200. ... Bats both, throws right. ... Full name: Gary Nathaniel Matthews Jr. ... Son of Gary Matthews, hitting coach with Toronto Blue Jays (1997-99); and outfielder with five major league teams (1972-87).
HIGH SCHOOL: Granada Hills (Calif.).
JUNIOR COLLEGE: Mission College (Calif.).
TRANSACTIONS/CAREER NOTES: Selected by San Diego Padres organization in 13th round of free-agent draft (June 3, 1993). ... Traded by Padres to Chicago Cubs for P Rodney Myers (March 23, 2000). ... Claimed on waivers by Pittsburgh Pirates (August 10, 2001). ... Traded by Pirates to New York Mets for cash (December 28, 2001).

Year Team (League)	Pos.	G	AB	R	H	2B	3B	HR	RBI	Avg.	BB	SO	SB	PO	A	E	Avg.
1994— Spokane (N'West)	OF-2B	52	191	23	40	6	1	0	18	.209	19	58	3	96	2	4	.961
1995— Clinton (Midw.)	OF	128	421	57	100	18	4	2	40	.238	68	109	28	245	9	9	.966
1996— Rancho Cuca. (Calif.)	OF	123	435	65	118	21	11	7	54	.271	60	102	7	218	7	16	.934
1997— Rancho Cuca. (Calif.)	OF	69	268	66	81	15	4	8	40	.302	49	57	10	110	6	5	.959
— Mobile (Sou.)	OF	28	90	14	22	4	1	2	12	.244	15	29	3	45	3	2	.960
1998— Mobile (Sou.)	OF	72	254	62	78	15	4	7	51	.307	55	50	11	184	8	1	.995
1999— Las Vegas (PCL)	OF	121	422	57	108	22	3	9	52	.256	58	104	17	273	7	7	.976
— San Diego (N.L.)	OF	23	36	4	8	0	0	0	7	.222	9	9	2	22	0	0	1.000
2000— Iowa (PCL)■	OF	60	211	27	51	11	3	5	22	.242	18	41	6	125	5	4	.970
— Chicago (N.L.)	OF	80	158	24	30	1	2	4	14	.190	15	28	3	84	3	2	.978
2001— Chicago (N.L.)	OF	106	258	41	56	9	1	9	30	.217	38	55	5	159	3	4	.976
— Pittsburgh (N.L.)■	OF	46	147	22	36	6	1	5	14	.245	22	45	3	100	1	3	.971
Major League totals (3 years)		255	599	91	130	16	4	18	65	.217	84	137	13	365	7	9	.976

PERSONAL: Born October 24, 1973, in Fredericksburg, Va. ... 6-2/180. ... Throws left, bats left. ... Full name: Michael Scott Matthews.
HIGH SCHOOL: Woodbridge Senior (Va.).
JUNIOR COLLEGE: Montgomery-Rockville College (Md.).
TRANSACTIONS/CAREER NOTES: Selected by Cleveland Indians organization in second round of free-agent draft (June 1, 1992). ... On Watertown disabled list (June 17, 1993-entire season). ... On disabled list (June 7-28, 1995). ... On disabled list (June 8-July 1, 1998). ... Traded by Indians to Boston Red Sox for IF Jose Olmeda (August 4, 1999). ... Traded by Red Sox with C David Menham to St. Louis Cardinals for P Kent Mercker (August 24, 1999). ... On St. Louis disabled list (July 16, 2000-remainder of season).
STATISTICAL NOTES: Tied for Eastern League lead with four balks in 1997.
MISCELLANEOUS: Appeared in one game as pinch runner (2001).

Year League	W	L	Pct.	ERA	G	GS	CG	ShO	Sv.	IP	H	R	ER	BB	SO
1992— Burlington (Appl.)	7	0	•1.000	*1.01	10	10	0	0	0	62¹/₃	33	13	7	27	55
— Watertown (NY-Penn)	1	0	1.000	3.27	2	2	0	0	0	11	10	4	4	8	5
1993—							Did not play.								
1994— Columbus (S.Atl.)	6	8	.429	3.08	23	23	0	0	0	119²/₃	120	53	41	44	99
1995— Canton/Akron (East.)	5	8	.385	5.93	15	15	1	0	0	74¹/₃	82	62	49	43	37
1996— Canton/Akron (East.)	9	11	.450	4.66	27	27	3	0	0	162¹/₃	178	96	84	74	112
1997— Buffalo (A.A.)	0	2	.000	7.71	5	5	0	0	0	21	32	19	18	10	17
— Akron (East.)	6	8	.429	3.82	19	19	3	1	0	113	116	62	48	57	69
1998— Buffalo (I.L.)	9	6	.600	4.63	24	23	0	0	0	130¹/₃	137	79	67	68	86
1999— Buffalo (I.L.)	1	2	.333	7.59	25	0	0	0	0	21¹/₃	23	18	18	18	16
— Akron (East.)	0	5	.000	8.77	6	6	0	0	0	25²/₃	36	30	25	15	10
— Trenton (East.)■	0	0	...	4.63	3	3	0	0	0	11²/₃	11	7	6	9	8
— Arkansas (Texas)■	2	0	1.000	0.00	2	2	1	1	0	12	3	0	0	1	10
2000— Memphis (PCL)	3	1	.750	3.12	9	9	0	0	0	52	33	19	18	32	50
— St. Louis (N.L.)	0	0	...	11.57	14	0	0	0	0	9¹/₃	15	12	12	10	8
2001— St. Louis (N.L.)	3	4	.429	3.24	51	10	0	0	1	89	74	32	32	33	72
Major League totals (2 years)	3	4	.429	4.03	65	10	0	0	1	98¹/₃	89	44	44	43	80

DIVISION SERIES RECORD

Year League	W	L	Pct.	ERA	G	GS	CG	ShO	Sv.	IP	H	R	ER	BB	SO
2001— St. Louis (N.L.)	0	1	.000	40.50	1	0	0	0	0	²/₃	4	3	3	0	0

PERSONAL: Born February 23, 1975, in Minneapolis. ... 6-2/205. ... Throws left, bats right. ... Full name: David Charles Maurer. ... Brother of Mike Maurer, pitcher, Oakland Athletics organization; son of Thomas Maurer, pitcher in Minnesota Twins organization.
HIGH SCHOOL: Apple Valley (Minn.).
COLLEGE: Oklahoma State.
TRANSACTIONS/CAREER NOTES: Selected by San Diego Padres organization in 11th round of free-agent draft (June 3, 1997). ... Selected by San Francisco Giants from Padres organization in Rule 5 major league draft (December 13, 1999). ... Returned to Padres (March 20, 2000). ... Released by Padres (June 1, 2001). ... Signed by Cincinnati Reds organization (June 1, 2001). ... Released by Reds (July 26, 2001). ... Signed by Oakland Athletics organization (July 29, 2001). ... Granted free agency (October 15, 2001). ... Signed by Cleveland Indians organization (December 18, 2001).

Year League	W	L	Pct.	ERA	G	GS	CG	ShO	Sv.	IP	H	R	ER	BB	SO
1997—Clinton (Midw.)	0	4	.000	2.88	25	0	0	0	3	34 1/3	24	15	11	15	43
1998—Rancho Cuca. (Calif.)	5	2	.714	2.70	48	0	0	0	5	83 1/3	56	27	25	46	93
1999—Mobile (Sou.)	4	4	.500	3.63	54	0	0	0	3	72	59	30	29	26	59
2000—Mobile (Sou.)	1	2	.333	2.70	24	0	0	0	0	26 2/3	15	8	8	3	28
—Las Vegas (PCL)	4	1	.800	3.25	35	0	0	0	0	44 1/3	47	19	16	15	44
—San Diego (N.L.)	1	0	1.000	3.68	14	0	0	0	0	14 2/3	15	8	6	5	13
2001—San Diego (N.L.)	0	0	...	10.80	3	0	0	0	0	5	8	6	6	4	4
—Portland (PCL)	0	0	...	4.34	17	0	0	0	1	18 2/3	11	9	9	9	21
—Louisville (I.L.)■	0	1	.000	4.15	18	6	0	0	1	21 2/3	18	11	10	7	23
—Sacramento (PCL)■	0	0	...	5.54	11	0	0	0	0	13	14	9	8	8	21
Major League totals (2 years)	1	0	1.000	5.49	17	0	0	0	0	19 2/3	23	14	12	9	17

PERSONAL: Born March 26, 1972, in Lewisburg, Tenn. ... 6-1/180. ... Bats right, throws right. ... Full name: Jason Ramond Maxwell.
HIGH SCHOOL: Marshall County (Lewisburg, Tenn.).
COLLEGE: Middle Tennessee State.
TRANSACTIONS/CAREER NOTES: Selected by Chicago Cubs organization in 74th round of free-agent draft (June 3, 1993). ... Claimed on waivers by Detroit Tigers (March 24, 1999). ... Granted free agency (October 15, 1999). ... Signed by Minnesota Twins organization (November 15, 1999). ... On disabled list (May 9-26, 2000). ... On Minnesota disabled list (June 7-July 7, 2001); included rehabilitation assignments to Fort Myers (July 2-4) and Gulf Coast Twins (July 5-7). ... Granted free agency (October 10, 2001). ... Signed by Texas Rangers organization (November 16, 2001).
STATISTICAL NOTES: Led Southern League with nine sacrifice flies in 1997.

Year Team (League)	Pos.	G	AB	R	H	2B	3B	HR	RBI	Avg.	BB	SO	SB	PO	A	E	Avg.
1993—Huntington (Appl.)	SS	61	179	50	52	7	2	7	38	.291	35	39	6	60	140	9	.957
1994—Daytona (FSL)	SS	116	368	71	85	18	2	10	31	.231	55	96	7	167	333	*38	.929
1995—Daytona (FSL)	SS	117	388	66	102	13	3	10	58	.263	63	68	12	181	325	16	*.969
1996—Orlando (Sou.)	S-2-3-DH	126	433	64	115	20	1	9	45	.266	56	77	19	188	336	29	.948
1997—Orlando (Sou.)	SS-2B	122	409	87	114	22	6	14	58	.279	82	72	12	176	376	28	.952
1998—Iowa (PCL)	2B-SS-DH	124	483	86	144	40	3	15	60	.298	52	93	8	237	306	16	.971
—Chicago (N.L.)	2B	7	3	2	1	0	0	1	2	.333	0	2	0	0	1	0	1.000
1999—Toledo (I.L.)■	S-2-3-1	119	419	60	99	17	2	15	62	.236	53	87	6	191	328	18	.966
2000—Minnesota (A.L.)■	2-3-DH-S-O	64	111	14	27	6	0	1	11	.243	9	32	2	38	95	6	.957
2001—Minnesota (A.L.)	SS-2B-3B	39	68	4	13	4	0	1	10	.191	9	23	2	20	51	3	.959
—Fort Myers (FSL)	2B-3B	2	9	1	4	1	0	0	2	.444	0	0	0	2	5	0	1.000
—GC Twins (GCL)	SS-3B	3	10	2	5	2	0	0	0	.500	1	2	0	0	7	0	1.000
American League totals (2 years)		103	179	18	40	10	0	2	21	.223	18	55	4	58	146	9	.958
National League totals (1 year)		7	3	2	1	0	0	1	2	.333	0	2	0	0	1	0	1.000
Major League totals (3 years)		110	182	20	41	10	0	3	23	.225	18	57	4	58	147	9	.958

PERSONAL: Born June 13, 1972, in San Bernardino, Calif. ... 6-2/184. ... Throws left, bats left. ... Full name: Darrell Kevin May.
HIGH SCHOOL: Rogue River (Ore.).
JUNIOR COLLEGE: Sacramento City College.
TRANSACTIONS/CAREER NOTES: Selected by Atlanta Braves organization in 46th round of free-agent draft (June 1, 1992). ... Claimed on waivers by Pittsburgh Pirates (April 4, 1996). ... Claimed on waivers by California Angels (September 6, 1996). ... Angels franchise renamed Anaheim Angels for 1997 season. ... Released by Angels (March 27, 1998). ... Played with Hanshin Tigers of Japan Central League (1998-99). ... Played with Yomiuri Giants of Japan Central League (2000-01). ... Signed by Kansas City Royals organization (December 17, 2001).
STATISTICAL NOTES: Pitched 4-0 no-hit victory against Colorado Springs (April 30, 1997, second game).

Year League	W	L	Pct.	ERA	G	GS	CG	ShO	Sv.	IP	H	R	ER	BB	SO
1992—Gulf Coast Braves (GCL)	4	3	.571	1.36	12	7	0	0	1	53	34	13	8	13	61
1993—Macon (S.Atl.)	10	4	.714	2.24	17	17	0	0	0	104 1/3	81	29	26	22	111
—Durham (Caro.)	5	2	.714	2.09	9	9	0	0	0	51 2/3	44	18	12	16	47
1994—Greenville (Sou.)	5	3	.625	3.11	11	11	1	0	0	63 2/3	61	25	22	17	42
—Durham (Caro.)	8	2	*.800	3.01	12	12	1	0	0	74 2/3	74	29	25	17	73
1995—Greenville (Sou.)	2	8	.200	3.55	15	15	0	0	0	91 1/3	81	44	36	20	79
—Richmond (I.L.)	4	2	.667	3.71	9	9	0	0	0	51	53	21	21	16	42
—Atlanta (N.L.)	0	0	...	11.25	2	0	0	0	0	4	10	5	5	0	1
1996—Calgary (PCL)■	7	6	.538	4.10	23	22	1	1	0	131 2/3	146	64	60	36	75
—Pittsburgh (N.L.)	0	1	.000	9.35	5	2	0	0	0	8 2/3	15	10	9	4	5
—California (A.L.)■	0	0	...	10.13	5	0	0	0	0	2 2/3	3	3	3	2	1
1997—Vancouver (PCL)	7	5	.583	3.26	13	12	2	2	0	80	65	31	29	31	62
—Anaheim (A.L.)	2	1	.667	5.23	29	2	0	0	0	51 2/3	56	31	30	25	42

Year League	W	L	Pct.	ERA	G	GS	CG	ShO	Sv.	IP	H	R	ER	BB	SO
1998—Hanshin (Jap. Cen.)■	4	9	.308	3.47	21	21	1	1	0	129 2/3	122	55	50	55	94
1999—Hanshin (Jap. Cen.)............	6	7	.462	4.25	18	18	0	0	0	112 1/3	101	56	53	38	113
2000—Yomiuri (Jap. Cen.)■	12	7	.632	2.95	24	24	3	3	0	155 1/3	123	52	51	40	165
2001—Yomiuri (Jap. Cen.)	10	8	.556	4.13	26	26	1	0	0	159	160	74	73	45	168
A.L. totals (2 years)	2	1	.667	5.47	34	2	0	0	0	54 1/3	59	34	33	27	43
N.L. totals (2 years)	0	1	.000	9.95	7	2	0	0	0	12 2/3	25	15	14	4	6
Major League totals (3 years)	2	2	.500	6.31	41	4	0	0	0	67	84	49	47	31	49

MAYNE, BRENT — C — ROYALS

PERSONAL: Born April 19, 1968, in Loma Linda, Calif. ... 6-1/192. ... Bats left, throws right. ... Full name: Brent Danem Mayne.
HIGH SCHOOL: Costa Mesa (Calif.).
JUNIOR COLLEGE: Orange Coast College (Calif.).
COLLEGE: Cal State Fullerton.
TRANSACTIONS/CAREER NOTES: Selected by Kansas City Royals organization in first round (13th pick overall) of free-agent draft (June 5, 1989). ... On disabled list (July 24, 1989-remainder of season). ... Traded by Royals to New York Mets for OF Al Shirley (December 19, 1995). ... Granted free agency (December 7, 1996). ... Signed by Seattle Mariners organization (January 10, 1997). ... Released by Mariners (March 28, 1997). ... Signed by Oakland Athletics organization (April 8, 1997). ... Granted free agency (October 30, 1997). ... Signed by San Francisco Giants (November 21, 1997). ... Granted free agency (October 28, 1999). ... Signed by Colorado Rockies (December 9, 1999). ... Traded by Rockies to Royals for P Mac Suzuki and C Sal Fasano (June 24, 2001).
STATISTICAL NOTES: Led A.L. catchers with 11 double plays in 1995. ... Career major league grand slams: 2.

Year Team (League)	Pos.	G	AB	R	H	2B	3B	HR	RBI	Avg.	BB	SO	SB	PO	A	E	Avg.
1989—Baseball City (FSL)	C	7	24	5	13	3	1	0	8	.542	0	3	0	31	2	0	1.000
1990—Memphis (Sou.)	C	115	412	48	110	16	3	2	61	.267	52	51	5	591	61	11	.983
—Kansas City (A.L.)	C	5	13	2	3	0	0	0	1	.231	3	3	0	29	3	1	.970
1991—Kansas City (A.L.)	C-DH	85	231	22	58	8	0	3	31	.251	23	42	2	425	38	6	.987
1992—Kansas City (A.L.)	C-3B-DH	82	213	16	48	10	0	0	18	.225	11	26	0	281	33	3	.991
1993—Kansas City (A.L.)	C-DH	71	205	22	52	9	1	2	22	.254	18	31	3	356	27	2	.995
1994—Kansas City (A.L.)	C-DH	46	144	19	37	5	1	2	20	.257	14	27	1	246	14	1	.996
1995—Kansas City (A.L.)	C	110	307	23	77	18	1	1	27	.251	25	41	0	540	40	3	.995
1996—New York (N.L.)■	C	70	99	9	26	6	0	1	6	.263	12	22	0	85	3	0	1.000
1997—Edmonton (PCL)■	C	2	3	0	0	0	0	0	0	.000	0	1	0	5	0	0	1.000
—Oakland (A.L.)	C	85	256	29	74	12	0	6	22	.289	18	33	1	419	36	2	.996
1998—San Fran. (N.L.)■	C	94	275	26	75	15	0	3	32	.273	37	47	2	493	39	5	.991
1999—San Francisco (N.L.) ..	C	117	322	39	97	32	0	2	39	.301	43	65	2	597	47	3	.995
2000—Colorado (N.L.)	C-P	117	335	36	101	21	0	6	64	.301	47	48	1	582	36	6	.990
2001—Colorado (N.L.)	C-1B	49	160	15	53	7	0	0	20	.331	16	24	0	317	19	1	.997
—Kansas City (A.L.)	C	51	166	13	40	4	1	2	20	.241	10	17	1	269	19	2	.993
American League totals (8 years)		535	1535	146	389	66	4	16	161	.253	122	220	8	2565	210	20	.993
National League totals (5 years)		447	1191	125	352	81	0	12	161	.296	155	206	5	2074	144	15	.993
Major League totals (12 years)		982	2726	271	741	147	4	28	322	.272	277	426	13	4639	354	35	.993

RECORD AS PITCHER

Year League	W	L	Pct.	ERA	G	GS	CG	ShO	Sv.	IP	H	R	ER	BB	SO
2000—Colorado (N.L.)	1	0	1.000	0.00	1	0	0	0	0	1	1	0	0	1	0

MAYS, JOE — P — TWINS

PERSONAL: Born December 10, 1975, in Flint, Mich. ... 6-1/185. ... Throws right, bats both. ... Full name: Joseph E. Mays.
HIGH SCHOOL: Southeast (Bradenton, Fla.).
JUNIOR COLLEGE: Manatee.
TRANSACTIONS/CAREER NOTES: Selected by Seattle Mariners organization in sixth round of free-agent draft (June 2, 1994). ... Traded by Mariners to Minnesota Twins (October 8, 1997), completing deal in which Twins traded OF Roberto Kelly to Mariners for P Jeromy Palki and a player to be named later (August 20, 1997).

Year League	W	L	Pct.	ERA	G	GS	CG	ShO	Sv.	IP	H	R	ER	BB	SO
1995—Arizona Mariners (Ariz.)	2	3	.400	3.25	10	10	0	0	0	44 1/3	41	24	16	18	44
1996—Everett (N'West)	4	4	.500	3.08	13	10	0	0	0	64 1/3	55	33	22	22	56
1997—Wisconsin (Midw.)	9	3	.750	2.09	13	13	1	0	0	81 2/3	62	20	19	23	79
—Lancaster (Cal.)	7	4	.636	4.86	15	15	1	0	0	96 1/3	108	55	52	34	82
1998—Fort Myers (FSL)■	7	2	.778	3.04	16	15	0	0	0	94 2/3	101	45	32	23	83
—New Britain (East.)	5	3	.625	4.99	11	10	0	0	0	57 2/3	63	40	32	21	45
1999—Minnesota (A.L.)	6	11	.353	4.37	49	20	2	1	0	171	179	92	83	67	115
2000—Minnesota (A.L.)	7	15	.318	5.56	31	28	2	1	0	160 1/3	193	105	99	67	102
—Salt Lake (PCL)	2	0	1.000	1.72	3	3	0	0	0	15 2/3	16	4	3	2	18
2001—Minnesota (A.L.)	17	13	.567	3.16	34	34	4	2	0	233 2/3	205	87	82	64	123
Major League totals (3 years)	30	39	.435	4.21	114	82	8	4	0	565	577	284	264	198	340

ALL-STAR GAME RECORD

Year League	W	L	Pct.	ERA	GS	CG	ShO	Sv.	IP	H	R	ER	BB	SO
2001—American	0	0	...	0.00	0	0	0	0	1	0	0	0	0	0

McCARTY, DAVE — 1B/OF — ROYALS

PERSONAL: Born November 23, 1969, in Houston. ... 6-5/215. ... Bats right, throws left. ... Full name: David Andrew McCarty.
HIGH SCHOOL: Sharpstown (Houston).
COLLEGE: Stanford.

M

TRANSACTIONS/CAREER NOTES: Selected by Minnesota Twins organization in first round (third pick overall) of free-agent draft (June 3, 1991). ... Traded by Twins to Cincinnati Reds for P John Courtright (June 8, 1995). ... Traded by Reds with OF Deion Sanders, P Ricky Pickett, P Scott Service and P John Roper to San Francisco Giants for OF Darren Lewis, P Mark Portugal and P Dave Burba (July 21, 1995). ... On San Francisco disabled list (June 6-27, 1996); included rehabilitation assignment to Phoenix (June 20-27). ... Traded by Giants to Seattle Mariners for OF Jay Leach and OF Scott Smith (January 30, 1998). ... Granted free agency (September 30, 1998). ... Signed by Detroit Tigers organization (December 18, 1998). ... Granted free agency (October 15, 1999). ... Signed by Oakland Athletics organization (November 23, 1999). ... Traded by A's to Kansas City Royals for cash (March 24, 2000).

STATISTICAL NOTES: Led International League first basemen with 104 assists and .999 fielding percentage in 1999. ... Career major league grand slams: 1.

Year Team (League)	Pos.	G	AB	R	H	2B	3B	HR	RBI	Avg.	BB	SO	SB	PO	A	E	Avg.
1991— Visalia (Calif.)	OF	15	50	16	19	3	0	3	8	.380	13	7	3	23	1	0	1.000
— Orlando (Sou.)	OF	28	88	18	23	4	0	3	11	.261	10	20	0	38	4	1	.977
1992— Orlando (Sou.)	OF-1B	129	456	75	124	16	2	18	79	.272	55	89	6	357	32	9	.977
— Portland (PCL)	OF-1B	7	26	7	13	2	0	1	8	.500	5	3	1	40	3	1	.977
1993— Portland (PCL)	OF-1B	40	143	42	55	11	0	8	31	.385	27	25	5	185	21	2	.990
— Minnesota (A.L.)	OF-1B-DH	98	350	36	75	15	2	2	21	.214	19	80	2	412	38	8	.983
1994— Minnesota (A.L.)	1B-OF	44	131	21	34	8	2	1	12	.260	7	32	2	243	28	5	.982
— Salt Lake (PCL)	OF-1B	55	186	32	47	9	3	3	19	.253	35	34	1	191	16	5	.976
1995— Minnesota (A.L.)	1B-OF	25	55	10	12	3	1	0	4	.218	4	18	0	130	10	1	.993
— Indianapolis (A.A.)■..	1B	37	140	31	47	10	1	8	32	.336	15	30	0	335	14	2	.994
— Phoenix (PCL)■...	1B-OF-DH	37	151	31	53	19	2	4	19	.351	17	27	1	330	32	2	.995
— San Francisco (N.L.) ..	OF-1B	12	20	1	5	1	0	0	2	.250	2	4	1	19	0	1	.950
1996— San Francisco (N.L.) ..	1B-OF	91	175	16	38	3	0	6	24	.217	18	43	2	291	18	3	.990
— Phoenix (PCL)	OF-1B	6	25	4	10	1	1	1	7	.400	2	4	0	29	1	0	1.000
1997— Phoenix (PCL)	1B-DH-OF	121	434	85	153	27	5	22	92	.353	49	75	9	563	53	3	.995
1998— Tacoma (PCL)■	OF-1B-DH	108	398	73	126	30	2	11	52	.317	59	85	9	430	32	2	.996
— Seattle (A.L.)	OF-1B	8	18	1	5	0	0	1	2	.278	5	4	1	21	0	0	1.000
1999— Toledo (I.L.)■	1B-OF-P-DH	132	466	85	125	24	3	31	77	.268	70	110	6	1001	†106	2	†.998
2000— Kansas City (A.L.)■ ..	1B-OF-DH	103	270	34	75	14	2	12	53	.278	22	68	0	482	61	5	.991
2001— Kansas City (A.L.) ...	1B-OF-DH	98	200	26	50	10	0	7	26	.250	24	45	0	447	45	8	.984
American League totals (6 years)		376	1024	128	251	50	7	23	118	.245	81	247	5	1735	182	27	.986
National League totals (2 years)		103	195	17	43	4	0	6	26	.221	20	47	3	310	18	4	.988
Major League totals (7 years)		479	1219	145	294	54	7	29	144	.241	101	294	8	2045	200	31	.986

RECORD AS PITCHER

Year League	W	L	Pct.	ERA	G	GS	CG	ShO	Sv.	IP	H	R	ER	BB	SO
1999— Toledo (I.L.)	0	0	...	4.50	2	0	0	0	0	2	1	1	1	1	0

McCRACKEN, QUINTON — OF

PERSONAL: Born March 16, 1970, in Wilmington, N.C. ... 5-7/173. ... Bats both, throws right. ... Full name: Quinton Antoine McCracken.
HIGH SCHOOL: South Brunswick (Southport, N.C.).
COLLEGE: Duke.
TRANSACTIONS/CAREER NOTES: Selected by Colorado Rockies organization in 25th round of free-agent draft (June 1, 1992). ... Selected by Tampa Bay Devil Rays in first round (fourth pick overall) of expansion draft (November 18, 1997). ... On disabled list (May 25, 1999-remainder of season). ... Released by Devil Rays (November 27, 2000). ... Signed by St. Louis Cardinals (December 22, 2000). ... Released by Cardinals (March 28, 2001). ... Signed by Minnesota Twins organization (April 13, 2001). ... Granted free agency (October 8, 2001).
STATISTICAL NOTES: Tied for Northwest League lead with 17 errors by second basemen in 1992. ... Led California League with 12 sacrifice hits in 1993. ... Led Eastern League in caught stealing with 19 in 1994. ... Had 18-game hitting streak (August 18-September 9, 1998). ... Tied for Pacific Coast League lead in caught stealing with 10 in 2001.

Year Team (League)	Pos.	G	AB	R	H	2B	3B	HR	RBI	Avg.	BB	SO	SB	PO	A	E	Avg.
1992— Bend (N'West)	2B-OF	67	232	37	65	13	2	0	27	.280	25	39	18	98	129	‡17	.930
1993— Central Valley (Calif.)	OF-2B	127	483	94	141	17	7	2	58	.292	78	90	60	153	75	13	.946
1994— New Haven (East.)	OF	136	544	94	151	27	4	5	39	.278	48	72	36	273	6	8	.972
1995— New Haven (East.)	OF-DH	55	221	33	79	11	4	1	26	.357	21	32	26	92	10	3	.971
— Colo. Springs (PCL)	OF-DH	61	244	55	88	14	6	3	28	.361	23	30	17	104	5	1	.991
— Colorado (N.L.)	OF	3	1	0	0	0	0	0	0	.000	0	1	0	0	0	0	....
1996— Colorado (N.L.)	OF	124	283	50	82	13	6	3	40	.290	32	62	17	131	3	6	.957
1997— Colorado (N.L.)	OF	147	325	69	95	11	1	3	36	.292	42	62	28	195	5	4	.980
1998— Tampa Bay (A.L.)■....	OF	155	614	77	179	38	7	7	59	.292	41	107	19	343	18	3	.992
1999— Tampa Bay (A.L.)	OF	40	148	20	37	6	1	1	18	.250	14	23	6	80	1	1	.988
2000— Tampa Bay (A.L.)	OF	15	31	5	4	0	0	0	2	.129	6	4	0	19	0	0	1.000
— Durham (I.L.)	OF	85	334	54	87	18	2	2	28	.260	34	57	13	161	8	4	.977
2001— Edmonton (PCL)■	OF	81	361	53	122	27	4	4	45	.338	21	54	8	164	3	5	.971
— Minnesota (A.L.)	OF-DH	24	64	7	14	2	2	0	3	.219	5	13	0	13	0	0	1.000
American League totals (4 years)		234	857	109	234	46	10	8	82	.273	66	147	25	455	19	4	.992
National League totals (3 years)		274	609	119	177	24	7	6	76	.291	74	125	45	326	8	10	.971
Major League totals (7 years)		508	1466	228	411	70	17	14	158	.280	140	272	70	781	27	14	.983

McDILL, ALLEN — P

PERSONAL: Born August 23, 1971, in Greenville, Miss. ... 6-0/170. ... Throws left, bats left. ... Full name: Allen Gabriel McDill.
HIGH SCHOOL: Lake Hamilton (Ark.).
TRANSACTIONS/CAREER NOTES: Selected by New York Mets organization in 20th round of free-agent draft (June 1, 1992). ... Traded by Mets with P Jason Jacome to Kansas City Royals for P Derek Wallace and a player to be named later (July 21, 1995); Mets acquired P John Carter to complete deal (November 16, 1995). ... Granted free agency (December 21, 1998). ... Re-signed by Royals (January 14, 1999). ... Released by Royals (March 12, 1999). ... Signed by Texas Rangers organization (March 17, 1999). ... Granted free agency (October 15, 1999). ... Signed

by Detroit Tigers organization (December 16, 1999). ... Released by Tigers (June 24, 2000). ... Signed by St. Louis Cardinals organization (June 27, 2000). ... On Memphis disabled list (July 23-30, 2000). ... Granted free agency (October 18, 2000). ... Signed by Boston Red Sox organization (December 18, 2000). ... Granted free agency (December 21, 2001).

Year	League	W	L	Pct.	ERA	G	GS	CG	ShO	Sv.	IP	H	R	ER	BB	SO
1992—	Gulf Coast Mets (GCL)	3	4	.429	2.70	10	9	0	0	0	53 1/3	36	23	16	15	60
—	Kingsport (Appl.)	0	0	...	0.00	1	0	0	0	0	1/3	0	0	0	2	0
1993—	Kingsport (Appl.)	5	2	.714	2.19	9	9	0	0	0	53 1/3	52	19	13	14	42
—	Pittsfield (NY-Penn)	2	3	.400	5.40	5	5	0	0	0	28 1/3	31	22	17	15	24
1994—	Columbia (S.Atl.)	9	6	.600	3.55	19	19	1	0	0	111 2/3	101	52	44	38	102
1995—	Binghamton (East.)	3	5	.375	4.56	12	12	1	0	0	73	69	42	37	38	44
—	St. Lucie (FSL)	4	2	.667	1.64	7	7	1	1	0	49 1/3	36	11	9	13	28
—	Wichita (Texas)■	1	0	1.000	2.11	12	1	1·	0	1	21 1/3	16	7	5	5	20
1996—	Wichita (Texas)	1	5	.167	5.54	54	0	0	0	11	65	79	43	40	21	62
—	Omaha (A.A.)....................	0	1	.000	54.00	2	0	0	0	0	1/3	3	2	2	1	1
1997—	Omaha (A.A.)....................	5	2	.714	5.88	23	6	0	0	2	64 1/3	80	42	42	26	51
—	Kansas City (A.L.)	0	0	...	13.50	3	0	0	0	0	4	3	6	6	8	2
—	Wichita (Texas)	0	1	.000	3.12	16	0	0	0	3	17 1/3	18	7	6	7	14
1998—	Omaha (PCL).....................	6	4	.600	2.39	61	0	0	0	4	60 1/3	54	22	16	24	62
—	Kansas City (A.L.)	0	0	...	10.50	7	0	0	0	0	6	9	7	7	2	3
1999—	Oklahoma (PCL)■.............	1	3	.250	3.72	42	0	0	0	18	48 1/3	45	22	20	17	46
2000—	Toledo (I.L.)■....................	1	0	1.000	0.96	16	0	0	0	0	18 2/3	21	4	2	7	15
—	Detroit (A.L.)	0	0	...	7.20	13	0	0	0	0	10	13	9	8	1	7
—	Memphis (PCL)■................	0	2	.000	4.38	23	0	0	0	0	24 2/3	24	13	12	17	28
2001—	Pawtucket (I.L.)■...............	3	3	.500	3.42	47	0	0	0	2	71	62	27	27	19	72
—	Boston (A.L.).....................	0	0	...	5.52	15	0	0	0	0	14 2/3	13	9	9	7	16
Major League totals (4 years).......		0	0	...	7.79	38	0	0	0	0	34 2/3	38	31	30	18	28

McDONALD, DONZELL   OF

PERSONAL: Born February 20, 1975, in Long Beach, Calif. ... 5-11/180. ... Bats both, throws right. ... Brother of Darnell McDonald, outfielder, Baltimore Orioles organization.
HIGH SCHOOL: Cherry Creek (Colo.).
JUNIOR COLLEGE: Yavapai College (Ariz.).
TRANSACTIONS/CAREER NOTES: Selected by New York Yankees organization in 22nd round of free-agent draft (June 1, 1995). ... On disabled list (July 3-August 6, 1997). ... On Columbus disabled list (May 10-July 21, 2000). ... Granted free agency (October 15, 2001).
STATISTICAL NOTES: Led New York-Pennsylvania League outfielders with 179 total chances in 1996. ... Led Eastern League in caught stealing with 22 in 1998. ... Led Eastern League outfielders with 328 total chances in 1998.

							BATTING								FIELDING		
Year	Team (League)	Pos.	G	AB	R	H	2B	3B	HR	RBI	Avg.	BB	SO	SB	PO	A	E	Avg.
1995—	GC Yankees (GCL)......	OF	28	110	23	26	5	1	0	9	.236	16	24	11	44	0	3	.936
1996—	Oneonta (NY-Penn)	OF	74	282	57	78	8	*10	2	30	.277	43	62	*54	*169	4	6	.966
1997—	Tampa (FSL).............	OF	77	297	69	88	23	8	3	23	.296	48	75	39	173	3	4	.978
1998—	Norwich (East.)	OF	134	495	80	125	20	7	6	36	.253	55	127	35	*312	8	8	.976
—	Tampa (FSL).............	OF	5	18	6	6	1	2	0	2	.333	2	7	2	14	0	0	1.000
1999—	Norwich (East.)	OF-DH	137	533	95	145	19	10	4	33	.272	90	110	54	314	8	9	.973
2000—	Columbus (I.L.)	OF	24	77	17	19	4	4	1	6	.247	23	11	12	51	2	0	1.000
—	Norwich (East.)	OF	44	170	23	41	7	2	2	10	.241	35	36	13	96	1	2	.980
2001—	Columbus (I.L.)	OF	105	374	59	96	11	9	8	36	.257	42	79	20	232	4	5	.979
—	New York (A.L.).........	OF	5	3	0	1	0	0	0	0	.333	0	2	0	2	0	0	1.000
Major League totals (1 year)			5	3	0	1	0	0	0	0	.333	0	2	0	2	0	0	1.000

McDONALD, JOHN   SS/2B   INDIANS

PERSONAL: Born September 24, 1974, in New London, Conn. ... 5-11/175. ... Bats right, throws right. ... Full name: John J. McDonald.
HIGH SCHOOL: East Lyme (Conn.).
JUNIOR COLLEGE: Connecticut-Avery Point.
COLLEGE: Providence.
TRANSACTIONS/CAREER NOTES: Selected by Cleveland Indians organization in 12th round of free-agent draft (June 4, 1996). ... On Buffalo disabled list (April 27-May 9 and May 10-June 22, 2000). ... On Buffalo disabled list (May 10-17, 2001).
STATISTICAL NOTES: Led Carolina League shortstops with 647 total chances and 105 double plays in 1997. ... Led Eastern League shortstops with 672 total chances in 1998.

							BATTING								FIELDING		
Year	Team (League)	Pos.	G	AB	R	H	2B	3B	HR	RBI	Avg.	BB	SO	SB	PO	A	E	Avg.
1996—	Watertown (NY-Penn)	SS	75	278	48	75	11	0	2	26	.270	32	49	11	85	228	18	.946
1997—	Kinston (Caro.)..........	SS	130	541	77	140	27	3	5	53	.259	51	75	6	*209	*413	25	*.961
1998—	Akron (East.)	SS	132	514	68	118	18	2	2	43	.230	43	61	17	*242	407	23	.966
1999—	Akron (East.)	SS-2B	55	226	31	67	12	0	1	26	.296	19	26	7	102	153	8	.970
—	Buffalo (I.L.)	SS-3B-2B	66	237	30	75	12	1	0	25	.316	11	23	6	87	194	13	.956
—	Cleveland (A.L.)..........	2B-SS	18	21	2	7	0	0	0	0	.333	0	3	0	8	21	1	.967
2000—	Buffalo (I.L.)	SS-2B-3B	75	286	37	77	17	2	1	36	.269	21	29	4	112	202	8	.975
—	Mahoning Valley (NY-P)	SS	5	17	0	2	1	0	0	1	.118	2	3	0	2	16	0	1.000
—	Cleveland (A.L.)..........	SS-2B	9	9	0	4	0	0	0	0	.444	0	1	0	4	8	0	1.000
—	Kinston (Caro.)..........	SS	1	3	0	1	0	0	0	0	.333	0	0	0	1	3	0	1.000
2001—	Cleveland (A.L.)..........	SS-2B-3B	17	22	1	2	1	0	0	0	.091	1	7	0	10	17	1	.964
—	Buffalo (I.L.)	SS-2B-3B	116	410	52	100	17	1	2	33	.244	33	72	17	177	336	23	.957
Major League totals (3 years)			44	52	3	13	1	0	0	0	.250	1	11	0	22	46	2	.971

M

McDONALD, KEITH   C   CARDINALS

PERSONAL: Born February 8, 1973, in Yokosuka, Japan. ... 6-2/215. ... Bats right, throws right. ... Full name: William Keith McDonald.
HIGH SCHOOL: Esperanza (Anaheim, Calif.).
COLLEGE: Pepperdine.
TRANSACTIONS/CAREER NOTES: Selected by St. Louis Cardinals organization in 24th round of free-agent draft (June 2, 1994). ... On Memphis disabled list (May 4-11, 2000). ... On Memphis disabled list (July 4-24, 2001).
STATISTICAL NOTES: Hit home run in first major league at-bat (July 4, 2000).

										BATTING					FIELDING		
Year Team (League)	Pos.	G	AB	R	H	2B	3B	HR	RBI	Avg.	BB	SO	SB	PO	A	E	Avg.
1994—Johnson City (Appl.) ..	C	59	199	32	49	12	0	6	31	.246	27	36	3	274	27	5	.984
1995—Peoria (Midw.)...........	C	65	179	22	48	6	0	1	20	.268	22	38	0	411	54	4	.991
1996—St. Petersburg (FSL)..	C	114	410	30	111	25	0	2	52	.271	34	65	1	679	76	11	.986
1997—Arkansas (Texas)........	C	79	233	32	56	16	0	5	30	.240	31	56	0	384	29	5	.988
1998—Memphis (PCL)..........	C-1B	58	170	21	54	8	0	7	22	.318	10	30	1	202	16	1	.995
1999—Arkansas (Texas)........	C	49	163	21	50	10	0	2	14	.307	15	35	1	236	22	6	.977
—Memphis (PCL).........	C-1B	39	113	20	34	7	0	5	27	.301	20	25	1	174	9	0	1.000
2000—Memphis (PCL)..........	C	83	266	34	70	15	0	5	30	.263	28	59	0	466	51	7	.987
—St. Louis (N.L.)..........	C	6	7	3	3	0	0	3	5	.429	2	1	0	13	1	0	1.000
2001—Memphis (PCL)..........	C	94	333	42	87	22	1	11	42	.261	24	60	1	600	53	1	*.998
—St. Louis (N.L.)..........	C	2	2	0	0	0	0	0	0	.000	0	1	0	1	1	0	1.000
Major League totals (2 years)		8	9	3	3	0	0	3	5	.333	2	2	0	14	2	0	1.000

McDOWELL, ARTURO   OF   GIANTS

PERSONAL: Born September 7, 1979, in Jackson, Miss. ... 6-1/175. ... Bats left, throws left. ... Full name: Arturo Jamaal McDowell.
HIGH SCHOOL: Forest Hill (Jackson, Miss.).
TRANSACTIONS/CAREER NOTES: Selected by San Francisco Giants organization in first round (28th pick overall) of free-agent draft (June 1, 1998); pick received from Tampa Bay Devil Rays as part of compensation for signing of Type A free agent P Roberto Hernandez.

										BATTING					FIELDING		
Year Team (League)	Pos.	G	AB	R	H	2B	3B	HR	RBI	Avg.	BB	SO	SB	PO	A	E	Avg.
1998—Salem-Kaizer (NW).....	OF	47	172	32	38	3	2	0	18	.221	29	46	13	79	3	2	.976
1999—Bakersfield (Calif.)......	OF	121	441	66	98	16	10	2	37	.222	49	140	28	260	8	8	.971
2000—Bakersfield (Calif.)......	OF	122	453	77	97	13	4	7	53	.214	77	129	38	281	11	3	.990
2001—San Jose (Calif.)........	OF	118	425	57	103	12	*11	1	31	.242	46	132	25	218	7	10	.957

McELROY, CHUCK   P

PERSONAL: Born October 1, 1967, in Port Arthur, Texas. ... 6-0/205. ... Throws left, bats left. ... Full name: Charles Dwayne McElroy. ... Name pronounced MACK-il-roy.
HIGH SCHOOL: Lincoln (Port Arthur, Texas).
TRANSACTIONS/CAREER NOTES: Selected by Philadelphia Phillies organization in eighth round of free-agent draft (June 2, 1986). ... Traded by Phillies with P Bob Scanlan to Chicago Cubs for P Mitch Williams (April 7, 1991). ... Traded by Cubs to Cincinnati Reds for P Larry Luebbers, P Mike Anderson and C Darron Cox (December 10, 1993). ... On disabled list (June 7-23, 1995). ... On Cincinnati disabled list (March 28-April 28, 1996); included rehabilitation assignment to Indianapolis (April 12-28). ... Traded by Reds to California Angels for P Lee Smith (May 27, 1996). ... On California disabled list (August 11-28, 1996). ... Angels franchise renamed Anaheim Angels for 1997 season. ... Traded by Angels with C Jorge Fabregas to Chicago White Sox for OF Tony Phillips and C Chad Kreuter (May 18, 1997). ... Selected by Arizona Diamondbacks in third round (67th pick overall) of expansion draft (November 18, 1997). ... Traded by Diamondbacks to Colorado Rockies for OF Harvey Pulliam (November 18, 1997). ... Traded by Rockies with OF Darryl Hamilton to New York Mets for OF Brian McRae, P Rigo Beltran and OF Thomas Johnson (July 31, 1999). ... Traded by Mets to Baltimore Orioles for P Jesse Orosco (December 10, 1999). ... Released by Orioles (July 19, 2001). ... Signed by San Diego Padres (July 23, 2001). ... Granted free agency (November 5, 2001).
MISCELLANEOUS: Appeared in one game as pinch runner with Chicago (1997). ... Appeared in one game as outfielder with one putout for Mets (1999).

Year League	W	L	Pct.	ERA	G	GS	CG	ShO	Sv.	IP	H	R	ER	BB	SO
1986—Utica (NY-Penn)	4	6	.400	2.95	14	14	5	1	0	94 2/3	85	40	31	28	91
1987—Spartanburg (S.Atl.)..........	14	4	.778	3.11	24	21	5	2	0	130 1/3	117	51	45	48	115
—Clearwater (FSL)...............	1	0	1.000	0.00	2	2	0	0	0	7 1/3	1	1	0	4	7
1988—Reading (East.)..............	9	12	.429	4.50	28	26	4	2	0	160	•173	89	*80	70	92
1989—Reading (East.)..............	3	1	.750	2.68	32	0	0	0	12	47	39	14	14	14	39
—Scranton/W.B. (I.L.).........	1	2	.333	2.93	14	0	0	0	3	15 1/3	13	6	5	11	12
—Philadelphia (N.L.)............	0	0	...	1.74	11	0	0	0	0	10 1/3	13	2	2	4	8
1990—Scranton/W.B. (I.L.)............	6	8	.429	2.72	57	1	0	0	7	76	62	24	23	34	78
—Philadelphia (N.L.)............	0	1	.000	7.71	16	0	0	0	0	14	24	13	12	10	16
1991—Chicago (N.L.)■.............	6	2	.750	1.95	71	0	0	0	3	101 1/3	73	33	22	57	92
1992—Chicago (N.L.)..............	4	7	.364	3.55	72	0	0	0	0	83 2/3	73	40	33	51	83
1993—Chicago (N.L.)..............	2	2	.500	4.56	49	0	0	0	0	47 1/3	51	30	24	25	31
—Iowa (A.A.)..................	0	1	.000	4.60	9	0	0	0	2	15	19	10	8	9	13
1994—Cincinnati (N.L.)■............	1	2	.333	2.34	52	0	0	0	5	57 2/3	52	15	15	15	38
1995—Cincinnati (N.L.)............	3	4	.429	6.02	44	0	0	0	0	40 1/3	46	29	27	15	27
1996—Indianapolis (A.A.)............	1	1	.500	2.70	5	3	0	0	0	13 1/3	11	4	4		10
—Cincinnati (N.L.)............	2	0	1.000	6.57	12	0	0	0	0	12 1/3	13	10	9	10	13
—California (A.L.)■............	5	1	.833	2.95	40	0	0	0	0	36 2/3	32	12	12	13	32
1997—Anaheim (A.L.).............	0	0	...	3.45	13	0	0	0	0	15 2/3	17	7	6	3	18
—Chicago (A.L.)■............	1	3	.250	3.94	48	0	0	0	1	59 1/3	56	29	26	19	44
1998—Colorado (N.L.)■..........	6	4	.600	2.90	78	0	0	0	2	68 1/3	68	23	22	24	61
1999—Colorado (N.L.)...........	3	1	.750	6.20	41	0	0	0	0	40 2/3	48	29	28	28	37
—New York (N.L.)■...........	0	0	...	3.38	15	0	0	0	0	13 1/3	12	5	5	8	7
2000—Baltimore (A.L.)■..........	3	0	1.000	4.69	43	2	0	0	0	63 1/3	60	36	33	34	50

M

Year League	W	L	Pct.	ERA	G	GS	CG	ShO	Sv.	IP	H	R	ER	BB	SO
2001—Baltimore (A.L.)	1	2	.333	5.36	18	5	0	0	0	45 1/3	49	29	27	28	22
—San Diego (N.L.)■	1	1	.500	5.16	31	0	0	0	0	29 2/3	38	24	17	18	25
A.L. totals (4 years)	10	6	.625	4.25	162	7	0	0	1	220 1/3	214	113	104	97	166
N.L. totals (11 years)	28	24	.538	3.75	492	0	0	0	16	519	510	253	216	265	438
Major League totals (13 years)	38	30	.559	3.90	654	7	0	0	17	739 1/3	724	366	320	362	604

DIVISION SERIES RECORD

Year League	W	L	Pct.	ERA	G	GS	CG	ShO	Sv.	IP	H	R	ER	BB	SO
1999—New York (N.L.)							Did not play.								

CHAMPIONSHIP SERIES RECORD

Year League	W	L	Pct.	ERA	G	GS	CG	ShO	Sv.	IP	H	R	ER	BB	SO
1999—New York (N.L.)							Did not play.								

McEWING, JOE — OF/IF — METS

PERSONAL: Born October 19, 1972, in Bristol, Pa. ... 5-11/170. ... Bats right, throws right. ... Full name: Joseph Earl McEwing.
HIGH SCHOOL: Bishop Egan (Fairless Hills, Pa.).
JUNIOR COLLEGE: County College of Morris (N.J.).
TRANSACTIONS/CAREER NOTES: Selected by St. Louis Cardinals organization in 28th round of free-agent draft (June 1, 1992). ... Traded by Cardinals to New York Mets for P Jesse Orosco (March 18, 2000).
STATISTICAL NOTES: Led Arizona League outfielders with 94 putouts, 11 assists, four double plays, 106 total chances and .991 fielding percentage in 1992. ... Led South Atlantic League with 15 sacrifice hits in 1993. ... Led Texas League outfielders with .993 fielding percentage in 1996. ... Tied for Pacific Coast League lead with three double plays by outfielder in 1998. ... Had 25-game hitting streak (June 8-July 4, 1999).

Year Team (League)	Pos.	G	AB	R	H	2B	3B	HR	RBI	Avg.	BB	SO	SB	PO	A	E	Avg.
1992—Ariz. Cardinals (Ariz.)	OF-SS	55	211	*55	71	4	2	0	13	.336	24	18	23	†94	†12	1	†.991
1993—Savannah (S.Atl.)	OF	138	511	*94	127	35	1	0	43	.249	89	73	22	262	13	5	.982
1994—Madison (Midw.)	OF	90	346	58	112	24	2	4	47	.324	32	53	18	184	6	5	.974
—St. Petersburg (FSL)	OF-2B	50	197	22	49	7	0	1	20	.249	19	32	8	105	23	2	.985
1995—St. Petersburg (FSL)	2B-OF	75	281	33	64	13	0	1	23	.228	25	49	2	139	176	15	.955
—Arkansas (Texas)	OF-2B	42	121	16	30	4	0	2	12	.248	9	13	3	61	12	0	1.000
1996—Arkansas (Texas)	OF-2B	106	216	27	45	7	3	2	14	.208	13	32	2	134	15	2	†.987
1997—Arkansas (Texas)	O-2-1-3-P	103	263	33	68	6	3	4	35	.259	19	39	2	134	24	2	.988
1998—Arkansas (Texas)	OF-SS-P	60	223	45	79	21	4	9	46	.354	21	18	4	130	25	1	.994
—Memphis (PCL)	OF-3B-SS-2B	78	329	52	110	30	7	6	46	.334	21	39	11	143	24	3	.982
—St. Louis (N.L.)	2B-OF	10	20	5	4	1	0	0	1	.200	1	3	0	10	10	0	1.000
1999—St. Louis (N.L.)	2-0-3-1-S	152	513	65	141	28	4	9	44	.275	41	87	7	320	246	11	.981
2000—Norfolk (I.L.)■	OF-2B-3B-SS	43	171	28	44	10	2	5	18	.257	16	34	7	77	67	4	.973
—New York (N.L.)	OF-3B-2B-SS	87	153	20	34	14	1	2	19	.222	5	29	3	67	45	5	.957
2001—New York (N.L.)	O-3-S-2-1-DH	116	283	41	80	17	3	8	30	.283	17	57	8	101	58	3	.981
Major League totals (4 years)		365	969	131	259	60	8	19	94	.267	64	176	18	498	359	19	.978

DIVISION SERIES RECORD

Year Team (League)	Pos.	G	AB	R	H	2B	3B	HR	RBI	Avg.	BB	SO	SB	PO	A	E	Avg.
2000—New York (N.L.)	OF-PR-3B	4	1	0	1	0	0	0	0	1.000	0	0	0	0	0	0	...

CHAMPIONSHIP SERIES RECORD

Year Team (League)	Pos.	G	AB	R	H	2B	3B	HR	RBI	Avg.	BB	SO	SB	PO	A	E	Avg.
2000—New York (N.L.)	PR-OF-3B	4	0	2	0	0	0	0	0	...	0	0	0	1	0	0	1.000

WORLD SERIES RECORD

Year Team (League)	Pos.	G	AB	R	H	2B	3B	HR	RBI	Avg.	BB	SO	SB	PO	A	E	Avg.
2000—New York (N.L.)	OF-PR	3	1	1	0	0	0	0	0	.000	0	0	0	2	0	0	1.000

RECORD AS PITCHER

Year League	W	L	Pct.	ERA	G	GS	CG	ShO	Sv.	IP	H	R	ER	BB	SO
1997—Arkansas (Texas)	0	0	...	27.00	1	0	0	0	0	1/3	1	1	1	0	0
1998—Arkansas (Texas)	0	0	...	27.00	1	0	0	0	0	1	3	3	3	1	1

McGLINCHY, KEVIN — P — DEVIL RAYS

PERSONAL: Born June 28, 1977, in Malden, Mass. ... 6-5/220. ... Throws right, bats right. ... Full name: Kevin Michael McGlinchy.
HIGH SCHOOL: Malden (Mass.).
JUNIOR COLLEGE: Central Florida Community College.
TRANSACTIONS/CAREER NOTES: Selected by Atlanta Braves organization in fifth round of free-agent draft (June 1, 1995). ... On Atlanta disabled list (April 17-May 13 and May 23-September 9, 2000); included rehabilitation assignments to Greenville (April 30-May 13), Richmond (July 6-20 and August 27-September 5) and Gulf Coast Braves (August 14-26). ... On Atlanta disabled list (March 28, 2001-entire season); included rehabilitation assignments to Gulf Coast Braves (August 20-25) and Myrtle Beach (August 26-September 13). ... Selected by Tampa Bay Devil Rays from Braves organization in Rule 5 major league draft (December 13, 2001).

Year League	W	L	Pct.	ERA	G	GS	CG	ShO	Sv.	IP	H	R	ER	BB	SO
1996—Danville (Appl.)	3	2	.600	1.13	13	13	0	0	0	72	52	21	9	11	77
—Eugene (N'West)	0	0	...	5.40	2	2	0	0	0	6 2/3	7	5	4	1	5
1997—Durham (Caro.)	3	7	.300	4.90	26	26	0	0	0	139 2/3	145	78	76	39	113
1998—Danville (Caro.)	9	8	.529	2.91	22	22	1	0	0	142 1/3	122	55	46	29	129
—Greenville (Sou.)	1	1	.500	5.18	6	6	0	0	0	33	35	19	19	15	20
1999—Atlanta (N.L.)	7	3	.700	2.82	64	0	0	0	0	70 1/3	66	25	22	30	67

Year	League	W	L	Pct.	ERA	G	GS	CG	ShO	Sv.	IP	H	R	ER	BB	SO
2000— Atlanta (N.L.)		0	0	...	2.16	10	0	0	0	0	$8\frac{1}{3}$	11	4	2	6	9
— Greenville (Sou.)		0	0	...	0.00	4	0	0	0	0	4	2	1	0	0	7
— Richmond (I.L.)		0	1	.000	3.60	9	0	0	0	1	10	9	4	4	3	7
— Gulf Coast Braves (GCL)		0	0	...	9.00	4	2	0	0	0	5	12	8	5	1	6
2001— Gulf Coast Braves (GCL)		0	0	...	0.00	2	2	0	0	0	2	1	0	0	0	2
Major League totals (2 years)		7	3	.700	2.75	74	0	0	0	0	$78\frac{2}{3}$	77	29	24	36	76

DIVISION SERIES RECORD

Year	League	W	L	Pct.	ERA	G	GS	CG	ShO	Sv.	IP	H	R	ER	BB	SO
1999— Atlanta (N.L.)		0	0	...	0.00	1	0	0	0	0	$\frac{1}{3}$	0	0	0	0	0

CHAMPIONSHIP SERIES RECORD

Year	League	W	L	Pct.	ERA	G	GS	CG	ShO	Sv.	IP	H	R	ER	BB	SO
1999— Atlanta (N.L.)		0	1	.000	18.00	1	0	0	0	0	1	2	2	2	4	1

WORLD SERIES RECORD

Year	League	W	L	Pct.	ERA	G	GS	CG	ShO	Sv.	IP	H	R	ER	BB	SO
1999— Atlanta (N.L.)		0	0	...	0.00	1	0	0	0	0	2	2	0	0	1	2

McGRIFF, FRED — 1B — CUBS

PERSONAL: Born October 31, 1963, in Tampa. ... 6-3/215. ... Bats left, throws left. ... Full name: Frederick Stanley McGriff. ... Cousin of Terry McGriff, catcher with four major league teams (1987-90, 1993 and 1994); and uncle of Charles Johnson, catcher, Florida Marlins.

HIGH SCHOOL: Jefferson (Tampa).

TRANSACTIONS/CAREER NOTES: Selected by New York Yankees organization in ninth round of free-agent draft (June 8, 1981). ... Traded by Yankees with OF Dave Collins, P Mike Morgan and cash to Toronto Blue Jays for OF/C Tom Dodd and P Dale Murray (December 9, 1982). ... On disabled list (June 5-August 14, 1985). ... Traded by Blue Jays with SS Tony Fernandez to San Diego Padres for OF Joe Carter and 2B Roberto Alomar (December 5, 1990). ... On suspended list (June 23-26, 1992). ... Traded by Padres to Atlanta Braves for OF Melvin Nieves, P Donnie Elliott and OF Vince Moore (July 18, 1993). ... Granted free agency (November 6, 1995). ... Re-signed by Braves (December 2, 1995). ... Traded by Braves to Tampa Bay Devil Rays for a player to be named later or cash (November 18, 1997); Braves received an undisclosed amount of cash to complete deal (April 1, 1998). ... Traded by Devil Rays to Chicago Cubs for P Manny Aybar and a player to be named later (July 27, 2001); Devil Rays acquired SS Jason Smith to complete deal (August 5, 2001).

RECORDS: Shares major league career record for most major league ballparks, one or more home runs (since 1900)—39. ... Shares major league record for most grand slams in two consecutive games—2 (August 13 and 14, 1991). ... Shares N.L. single-season record for fewest errors by first baseman who led league in errors—12 (1992).

HONORS: Named first baseman on THE SPORTING NEWS A.L. All-Star team (1989). ... Named first baseman on THE SPORTING NEWS A.L. Silver Slugger team (1989). ... Named first baseman on THE SPORTING NEWS N.L. All-Star team (1992-93). ... Named first baseman on THE SPORTING NEWS N.L. Silver Slugger team (1992-93).

STATISTICAL NOTES: Led International League first basemen with .992 fielding percentage, 1,219 putouts, 85 assists, 1,314 total chances and 108 double plays in 1986. ... Tied for International League lead in intentional bases on balls received with eight and in grounding into double plays with 16 in 1986. ... Led A.L. first basemen with 1,592 total chances and 148 double plays in 1989. ... Led N.L. with 26 intentional base on balls received in 1991. ... Led N.L. first basemen with 1,077 total chances in 1994. ... Led N.L. in grounding into double plays with 22 in 1997. ... Led A.L. first basemen with 140 double plays in 1998. ... Career major league grand slams: 8.

MISCELLANEOUS: Holds Tampa Bay Devil Rays all-time records for most runs (270), hits (590), doubles (99), home runs (97), runs batted in (352) and highest career batting average (.295).

Year Team (League)	Pos.	G	AB	R	H	2B	3B	HR	RBI	Avg.	BB	SO	SB	PO	A	E	Avg.
1981— GC Yankees (GCL)	1B	29	81	6	12	2	0	0	9	.148	11	20	0	176	8	7	.963
1982— GC Yankees (GCL)	1B	62	217	38	59	11	1	•9	•41	.272	•48	63	6	514	*56	8	.986
1983— Florence (S.Atl.)■	1B	33	119	26	37	3	1	7	26	.311	20	35	3	250	14	6	.978
— Kinston (Caro.)	1B	94	350	53	85	14	1	21	57	.243	55	112	3	784	57	10	.988
1984— Knoxville (Sou.)	1B	56	189	29	47	13	2	9	25	.249	29	55	0	481	45	10	.981
— Syracuse (I.L.)	1B	70	238	28	56	10	1	13	28	.235	26	89	0	644	45	3	.996
1985— Syracuse (I.L.)	1B	51	176	19	40	8	2	5	20	.227	23	53	0	433	37	5	.989
1986— Syracuse (I.L.)	1B-OF	133	468	69	121	23	4	19	74	.259	83	119	0	†1219	†85	10	†.992
— Toronto (A.L.)	DH-1B	3	5	1	1	0	0	0	0	.200	0	2	0	3	0	0	1.000
1987— Toronto (A.L.)	DH-1B	107	295	58	73	16	0	20	43	.247	60	104	3	108	7	2	.983
1988— Toronto (A.L.)	1B	154	536	100	151	35	4	34	82	.282	79	149	6	1344	93	5	*.997
1989— Toronto (A.L.)	1B-DH	161	551	98	148	27	3	*36	92	.269	119	131	7	1460	115	*17	.989
1990— Toronto (A.L.)	1B-DH	153	557	91	167	21	1	35	88	.300	94	108	5	1246	126	6	.996
1991— San Diego (N.L.)■	1B	153	528	84	147	19	1	31	106	.278	105	135	4	1370	87	14	.990
1992— San Diego (N.L.)	1B	152	531	79	152	30	4	*35	104	.286	96	108	8	1219	108	•12	.991
1993— San Diego (N.L.)	1B	83	302	52	83	11	1	18	46	.275	42	55	4	640	47	12	.983
— Atlanta (N.L.)■	1B	68	255	59	79	18	1	19	55	.310	34	51	1	563	45	5	.992
1994— Atlanta (N.L.)	1B	113	424	81	135	25	1	34	94	.318	50	76	7	*1004	66	7	.994
1995— Atlanta (N.L.)	1B	•144	528	85	148	27	1	27	93	.280	65	99	3	1285	96	5	.996
1996— Atlanta (N.L.)	1B	159	617	81	182	37	1	28	107	.295	68	116	7	1416	124	12	.992
1997— Atlanta (N.L.)	1B	152	564	77	156	25	1	22	97	.277	68	112	5	1191	96	13	.990
1998— Tampa Bay (A.L.)■	1B-DH	151	564	73	160	33	0	19	81	.284	79	118	7	1150	81	6	.995
1999— Tampa Bay (A.L.)	1B-DH	144	529	75	164	30	1	32	104	.310	86	107	1	1037	88	13	.989
2000— Tampa Bay (A.L.)	1B-DH	158	566	82	157	18	0	27	106	.277	91	120	2	1300	82	10	.993
2001— Tampa Bay (A.L.)	1B-DH	97	343	40	109	18	0	19	61	.318	40	69	1	558	59	9	.986
— Chicago (N.L.)■	1B	49	170	27	48	7	2	12	41	.282	26	37	0	366	23	4	.990
American League totals (9 years)		1128	3946	618	1130	198	9	222	657	.286	648	908	32	8206	651	68	.992
National League totals (8 years)		1073	3919	625	1130	199	13	226	743	.288	554	789	39	9054	692	86	.991
Major League totals (16 years)		2201	7865	1243	2260	397	22	448	1400	.287	1202	1697	71	17260	1343	152	.992

DIVISION SERIES RECORD

RECORDS: Holds N.L. single-game record for most runs batted in—5 (October 7, 1995). ... Shares single-game record for most home runs—2 (October 7, 1995).

					BATTING									FIELDING		
Year Team (League)	Pos.	G	AB	R	H	2B	3B	HR	RBI	Avg.	BB	SO	SB	PO	A	E	Avg.
1995—Atlanta (N.L.).............	1B	4	18	4	6	0	0	2	6	.333	2	3	0	39	2	0	1.000
1996—Atlanta (N.L.).............	1B	3	9	1	3	1	0	1	3	.333	2	1	0	25	3	0	1.000
1997—Atlanta (N.L.).............	1B	3	9	4	2	0	0	0	1	.222	3	2	0	27	3	0	1.000
Division series totals (3 years)		10	36	9	11	1	0	3	10	.306	7	6	0	91	8	0	1.000

CHAMPIONSHIP SERIES RECORD

RECORDS: Holds single-game record for most doubles—3 (October 11, 1995). ... Shares N.L. single-game records for most at-bats—6 (October 14, 1996); and most runs—4 (October 17, 1996). ... Shares career record for most doubles—7.

					BATTING									FIELDING		
Year Team (League)	Pos.	G	AB	R	H	2B	3B	HR	RBI	Avg.	BB	SO	SB	PO	A	E	Avg.
1989—Toronto (A.L.).............	1B	5	21	1	3	0	0	0	3	.143	0	4	0	35	2	1	.974
1993—Atlanta (N.L.).............	1B	6	23	6	10	2	0	1	4	.435	4	7	0	49	4	0	1.000
1995—Atlanta (N.L.).............	1B	4	16	5	7	4	0	0	0	.438	3	0	0	42	4	0	1.000
1996—Atlanta (N.L.).............	1B	7	28	6	7	0	1	2	7	.250	3	5	0	54	2	1	.982
1997—Atlanta (N.L.).............	1B	6	21	0	7	1	0	0	4	.333	2	7	0	41	2	1	.977
Championship series totals (5 years)		28	109	18	34	7	1	3	18	.312	12	23	0	221	14	3	.987

WORLD SERIES RECORD

RECORDS: Holds single game record for chances accepted, nine inning game—20 (October 21, 1995). ... Shares single-game record for most putouts by first baseman—19 (October 21, 1995).
NOTES: Hit home run in first at-bat (October 21, 1995). ... Member of World Series championship team (1995).

					BATTING									FIELDING		
Year Team (League)	Pos.	G	AB	R	H	2B	3B	HR	RBI	Avg.	BB	SO	SB	PO	A	E	Avg.
1995—Atlanta (N.L.).............	1B	6	23	5	6	2	0	2	3	.261	3	7	1	68	2	1	.986
1996—Atlanta (N.L.).............	1B	6	20	4	6	0	0	2	6	.300	5	4	0	62	4	0	1.000
World Series totals (2 years)		12	43	9	12	2	0	4	9	.279	8	11	1	130	6	1	.993

ALL-STAR GAME RECORD

NOTES: Named Most Valuable Player (1994).

				BATTING								FIELDING		
Year League	Pos.	AB	R	H	2B	3B	HR	RBI	Avg.	BB	SO	SB	PO	A	E	Avg.
1992— National....................	1B	3	0	2	0	0	0	1	.667	0	0	0	7	1	0	1.000
1994— National....................	PH-1B	1	1	1	0	0	1	2	1.000	0	0	0	0	0	0	...
1995— National....................	1B	3	0	0	0	0	0	0	.000	0	2	0	5	0	0	1.000
1996— National....................	1B	2	0	0	0	0	0	0	.000	0	2	0	2	1	0	1.000
2000— American..................	1B	2	0	0	0	0	0	0	.000	0	1	0	5	0	0	1.000
All-Star Game totals (5 years)		11	1	3	0	0	1	3	.273	0	5	0	19	2	0	1.000

McGUIRE, RYAN — 1B — ORIOLES

PERSONAL: Born November 23, 1971, in Bellflower, Calif. ... 6-0/215. ... Bats left, throws left. ... Full name: Ryan Byron McGuire.
HIGH SCHOOL: El Camino Real (Woodland Hills, Calif.).
COLLEGE: UCLA.
TRANSACTIONS/CAREER NOTES: Selected by Boston Red Sox organization in third round of free-agent draft (June 3, 1993). ... Traded by Red Sox with P Rheal Cormier and P Shayne Bennett to Montreal Expos for SS Wil Cordero and P Bryan Eversgerd (January 10, 1996). ... Granted free agency (November 19, 1999). ... Signed by New York Mets organization (December 13, 1999). ... Granted free agency (October 3, 2000). ... Signed by Florida Marlins organization (November 3, 2000). ... Granted free agency (October 8, 2001). ... Signed by Baltimore Orioles organization (November 16, 2001).
STATISTICAL NOTES: Led Carolina League first basemen with 1,312 total chances in 1994. ... Tied for Carolina League lead with 19 grounded into double plays in 1994. ... Career major league grand slams: 1.

					BATTING									FIELDING		
Year Team (League)	Pos.	G	AB	R	H	2B	3B	HR	RBI	Avg.	BB	SO	SB	PO	A	E	Avg.
1993—Fort Lauderdale (FSL)	1B	56	213	23	69	12	2	4	38	.324	27	34	2	513	61	5	.991
1994—Lynchburg (Caro.)......	1B	*137	489	70	133	29	0	10	73	.272	79	77	10	*1165	*129	18	.986
1995—Trenton (East.)	1B	109	414	59	138	29	1	7	59	.333	58	51	11	708	55	10	.987
1996—Ottawa (I.L.)■.............	1B-DH-OF	134	451	62	116	21	2	12	60	.257	59	80	11	987	73	8	.993
1997—Ottawa (I.L.)...............	1B	50	184	37	55	11	1	3	15	.299	36	29	5	421	52	2	.996
—Montreal (N.L.)...........	OF-1B-DH	84	199	22	51	15	2	3	17	.256	19	34	1	226	19	3	.988
1998—Montreal (N.L.)...........	1B-OF	130	210	17	39	9	0	1	10	.186	32	55	0	326	26	7	.981
1999—Ottawa (I.L.)...............	1B-OF-DH	53	183	23	46	6	1	4	27	.251	35	37	1	275	15	1	.997
—Montreal (N.L.)...........	1B-OF	88	140	17	31	7	2	2	18	.221	27	33	1	290	38	2	.994
2000—Norfolk (I.L.)■.............	OF-1B	122	392	63	117	23	1	10	62	.298	*87	84	6	394	26	1	.997
—New York (N.L.).........	OF	1	2	0	0	0	0	0	0	.000	1	0	0	3	0	0	1.000
2001—Calgary (PCL)■...........	OF-1B	62	239	45	72	14	2	8	42	.301	26	49	0	289	31	3	.991
—Florida (N.L.).............	OF-1B	48	54	8	10	2	0	1	8	.185	7	15	1	23	0	0	1.000
Major League totals (5 years)		351	605	64	131	33	4	7	53	.217	86	137	3	868	83	12	.988

McGWIRE, MARK — 1B

PERSONAL: Born October 1, 1963, in Pomona, Calif. ... 6-5/250. ... Bats right, throws right. ... Full name: Mark David McGwire. ... Brother of Dan McGwire, quarterback with Seattle Seahawks (1991-94) and Miami Dolphins (1995).
HIGH SCHOOL: Damien (Claremont, Calif.).
COLLEGE: Southern California.
TRANSACTIONS/CAREER NOTES: Selected by Montreal Expos organization in eighth round of free-agent draft (June 8, 1981); did not sign. ... Selected by Oakland Athletics organization in first round (10th pick overall) of free-agent draft (June 4, 1984). ... On disabled list (April 11-26, 1989 and August 22-September 11, 1992). ... Granted free agency (October 26, 1992). ... Re-signed by A's (December 24, 1992). ... On disabled list (May 14-September 3, 1993; April 30-June 18 and July 27, 1994-remainder of season). ... On suspended list (September 4-8, 1993).

M

... On disabled list (July 18-August 2 and August 5-26, 1995; and March 22-April 23, 1996). ... Traded by A's to St. Louis Cardinals for P T.J. Mathews, P Eric Ludwick and P Blake Stein (July 31, 1997). ... On disabled list (July 7-September 8, 2000; and April 16-May 28, 2001). ... Announced retirement (November 12, 2001).

RECORDS: Holds major league career record for most home runs by first baseman—566 (1986-2000). ... Holds major league single-season record for most home runs by first baseman—69 (1998). ... Holds major league records for most home runs in consecutive years—135 (1998-99). ... Holds major league rookie-season records for most home runs—49; and extra bases on long hits—183 (1987). ... Shares major league career record for most major league ballparks, one or more home runs (since 1900)—39; and most consecutive seasons with 50 or more home runs—4 (1996-99). ... Shares major league single-inning record for most home runs—2 (September 22, 1996, fifth inning). ... Shares major league records for most home runs in two consecutive games—5 (June 27 [3] and 28 [2], 1987 and June 10 [2] and 11 [3], 1995); most home runs in one inning—2 (September 22, 1996, fifth inning); most seasons with 50 or more home runs—4; and most home runs in July—16 (1999). ... Shares modern major league record for most runs in two consecutive games—9 (June 27 and 28, 1987). ... Shares major league single-month record for most home runs—16 (July 1999). ... Holds A.L. rookie-season record for highest slugging percentage—.618 (1987).

HONORS: Named College Player of the Year by THE SPORTING NEWS (1984). ... Named first baseman on THE SPORTING NEWS college All-America team (1984). ... Named A.L. Rookie Player of the Year by THE SPORTING NEWS (1987). ... Named A.L. Rookie of the Year by Baseball Writers' Association of America (1987). ... Won A.L. Gold Glove at first base (1990). ... Named first baseman on THE SPORTING NEWS A.L. All-Star team (1992 and 1996). ... Named first baseman on THE SPORTING NEWS A.L. Silver Slugger team (1992 and 1996). ... Named Sportsman of the Year by THE SPORTING NEWS (1997). ... Named first baseman on THE SPORTING NEWS N.L. All-Star team (1998). ... Named first baseman on THE SPORTING NEWS N.L. Silver Slugger team (1998). ... Named co-Sportsman of the Year by THE SPORTING NEWS (1998).

STATISTICAL NOTES: Led California League third basemen with 239 assists and 354 total chances in 1985. ... Hit three home runs in one game (June 27, 1987; June 11, 1995; April 14 and May 19, 2000). ... Led A.L. in slugging percentage with .618 in 1987, .585 in 1992 and .730 in 1996. ... Led A.L. first basemen with 1,429 total chances in 1990. ... Led A.L. with .467 on-base percentage in 1996. ... Led major leagues with 58 home runs in 1997. ... Led N.L. with .752 slugging percentage and .470 on-base percentage in 1998. ... Led N.L. first basemen with 1,435 total chances in 1998. ... Led N.L. with 21 intentional bases on balls received in 1999. ... Career major league grand slams: 14.

MISCELLANEOUS: Holds Oakland Athletics franchise all-time records for most home runs (363) and runs batted in (941). ... Member of 1984 U.S. Olympic baseball team.

M

Year	Team (League)	Pos.	G	AB	R	H	2B	3B	HR	RBI	Avg.	BB	SO	SB	PO	A	E	Avg.
1984—	Modesto (Calif.)	1B	16	55	7	11	3	0	1	1	.200	8	21	0	107	6	1	.991
1985—	Modesto (Calif.)	3B-1B	138	489	95	134	23	3	•24	•106	.274	96	108	1	105	†240	33	.913
1986—	Huntsville (Sou.)	3B	55	195	40	59	15	0	10	53	.303	46	45	3	34	124	16	.908
—Tacoma (PCL)		3B	78	280	42	89	21	5	13	59	.318	42	67	1	53	126	25	.877
—Oakland (A.L.)		3B	18	53	10	10	1	0	3	9	.189	4	18	0	10	20	6	.833
1987—	Oakland (A.L.)	1B-3B-OF	151	557	97	161	28	4	*49	118	.289	71	131	1	1176	101	13	.990
1988—	Oakland (A.L.)	1B-OF	155	550	87	143	22	1	32	99	.260	76	117	0	1228	88	9	.993
1989—	Oakland (A.L.)	1B-DH	143	490	74	113	17	0	33	95	.231	83	94	1	1170	114	6	.995
1990—	Oakland (A.L.)	1B-DH	156	523	87	123	16	0	39	108	.235	*110	116	2	*1329	95	5	.997
1991—	Oakland (A.L.)	1B	154	483	62	97	22	0	22	75	.201	93	116	2	1191	•101	4	.997
1992—	Oakland (A.L.)	1B	139	467	87	125	22	0	42	104	.268	90	105	0	1118	71	6	.995
1993—	Oakland (A.L.)	1B	27	84	16	28	6	0	9	24	.333	21	19	0	197	14	0	1.000
1994—	Oakland (A.L.)	1B-DH	47	135	26	34	3	0	9	25	.252	37	40	0	307	18	4	.988
1995—	Oakland (A.L.)	1B-DH	104	317	75	87	13	0	39	90	.274	88	77	1	775	64	*12	.986
1996—	Oakland (A.L.)	1B-DH	130	423	104	132	21	0	*52	113	.312	116	112	0	913	60	10	.990
1997—	Oakland (A.L.)	1B	105	366	48	104	24	0	34	81	.284	58	98	1	884	60	6	.994
—St. Louis (N.L.)■		1B	51	174	38	44	3	0	§24	42	.253	43	61	2	438	34	1	.998
1998—	St. Louis (N.L.)	1B	155	509	130	152	21	0	*70	147	.299	*162	155	1	1326	97	12	.992
1999—	St. Louis (N.L.)	1B	153	521	118	145	21	1	*65	*147	.278	133	141	0	1180	80	13	.990
2000—	St. Louis (N.L.)	1B	89	236	60	72	8	0	32	73	.305	76	78	1	535	23	1	.998
2001—	St. Louis (N.L.)	1B	97	299	48	56	4	0	29	64	.187	56	118	0	686	33	4	.994
American League totals (12 years)			1329	4448	773	1157	195	5	363	941	.260	847	1043	8	10298	806	81	.993
National League totals (5 years)			545	1739	394	469	57	1	220	473	.270	470	553	4	4165	267	31	.993
Major League totals (16 years)			1874	6187	1167	1626	252	6	583	1414	.263	1317	1596	12	14463	1073	112	.993

DIVISION SERIES RECORD

Year	Team (League)	Pos.	G	AB	R	H	2B	3B	HR	RBI	Avg.	BB	SO	SB	PO	A	E	Avg.
2000—	St. Louis (N.L.)	PH	3	2	1	1	0	0	1	1	.500	1	0	0	...	...	...	...
2001—	St. Louis (N.L.)	1B-PH	4	11	0	1	0	0	0	0	.091	0	6	0	24	2	0	1.000
Division series totals (2 years)			7	13	1	2	0	0	1	1	.154	1	6	0	24	2	0	1.000

CHAMPIONSHIP SERIES RECORD

Year	Team (League)	Pos.	G	AB	R	H	2B	3B	HR	RBI	Avg.	BB	SO	SB	PO	A	E	Avg.
1988—	Oakland (A.L.)	1B	4	15	4	5	0	0	1	3	.333	1	5	0	24	2	0	1.000
1989—	Oakland (A.L.)	1B	5	18	3	7	1	0	1	3	.389	1	4	0	46	1	1	.979
1990—	Oakland (A.L.)	1B	4	13	2	2	0	0	2	2	.154	3	3	0	40	0	0	1.000
1992—	Oakland (A.L.)	1B	6	20	1	3	0	0	1	3	.150	5	4	0	46	2	1	.980
2000—	St. Louis (N.L.)	PH	3	2	0	0	0	0	0	0	.000	1	0	0	...	...	...	...
Championship series totals (5 years)			22	68	10	17	1	0	3	11	.250	11	16	0	156	5	2	.988

WORLD SERIES RECORD

NOTES: Member of World Series championship team (1989).

Year	Team (League)	Pos.	G	AB	R	H	2B	3B	HR	RBI	Avg.	BB	SO	SB	PO	A	E	Avg.
1988—	Oakland (A.L.)	1B	5	17	1	1	0	0	1	1	.059	3	4	0	40	3	0	1.000
1989—	Oakland (A.L.)	1B	4	17	0	5	1	0	0	1	.294	1	3	0	28	2	0	1.000
1990—	Oakland (A.L.)	1B	4	14	1	3	0	0	0	0	.214	2	4	0	42	1	2	.956
World Series totals (3 years)			13	48	2	9	1	0	1	2	.188	6	11	0	110	6	2	.983

ALL-STAR GAME RECORD

NOTES: Named to A.L. All-Star team for 1991 game; replaced by Rafael Palmeiro due to injury.

Year	League	Pos.	AB	R	H	2B	3B	HR	RBI	Avg.	BB	SO	SB	PO	A	E	Avg.
1987—	American	1B	3	0	0	0	0	0	0	.000	0	0	0	7	0	1	.875
1988—	American	1B	2	0	1	0	0	0	0	.500	0	1	0	8	0	0	1.000
1989—	American	1B	3	0	1	0	0	0	0	.333	0	0	0	5	0	0	1.000
1990—	American	1B	2	0	0	0	0	0	0	.000	0	2	0	7	0	0	1.000
1991—	American							Selected, did not play—injured.									
1992—	American	1B	3	1	1	0	0	0	2	.333	0	0	0	4	0	0	1.000
1995—	American							Selected, did not play—injured.									
1996—	American	1B	1	0	1	0	0	0	0	1.000	0	0	0	2	1	0	1.000
1997—	American	1B	2	0	0	0	0	0	0	.000	0	2	0	4	0	0	1.000
1998—	National	1B	2	1	0	0	0	0	0	.000	1	1	0	6	0	0	1.000
1999—	National	1B	2	0	0	0	0	0	0	.000	1	2	0	3	0	0	1.000
2000—	National							Selected, did not play—injured.									
All-Star Game totals (9 years)			20	2	4	0	0	0	2	.200	2	8	0	46	1	1	.979

McKNIGHT, TONY   P   PIRATES

PERSONAL: Born June 29, 1977, in Texarkana, Ark. ... 6-5/205. ... Throws right, bats right. ... Full name: Tony Mark McKnight.

HIGH SCHOOL: Arkansas (Texarkana, Ark.).

TRANSACTIONS/CAREER NOTES: Selected by Houston Astros organization in first round (22nd pick overall) of free-agent draft (June 1, 1995). ... On disabled list (June 19-July 15, 1996). ... On disabled list (July 20-August 2, 1999). ... On New Orleans disabled list (April 6-16, 2000). ... Traded by Astros to Pittsburgh Pirates for P Mike Williams (July 31, 2001).

STATISTICAL NOTES: Led Texas League pitchers with 18 putouts in 1999.

Year	League	W	L	Pct.	ERA	G	GS	CG	ShO	Sv.	IP	H	R	ER	BB	SO
1995—	Gulf Coast Astros (GCL)	1	1	.500	3.86	3	3	0	0	0	11 2/3	14	5	5	2	8
1996—	Gulf Coast Astros (GCL)	2	1	.667	6.23	8	5	0	0	0	21 2/3	28	21	15	7	15
1997—	Quad City (Midw.)	4	9	.308	4.68	20	20	0	0	0	115 1/3	116	71	60	55	92
1998—	Kissimmee (FSL)	11	13	.458	4.67	28	•28	0	0	0	154 1/3	191	101	80	50	104
1999—	Jackson (Texas)	9	9	.500	2.75	24	24	0	0	0	160 1/3	134	60	49	44	118
2000—	Round Rock (Texas)	0	2	.000	4.78	6	6	0	0	0	32	39	19	17	10	24
—	New Orleans (PCL)	4	8	.333	4.56	19	19	0	0	0	118 1/3	129	66	60	36	63
—	Houston (N.L.)	4	1	.800	3.86	6	6	1	0	0	35	35	19	15	9	23
2001—	New Orleans (PCL)	9	5	.643	4.76	18	18	1	0	0	92 2/3	104	56	49	24	61
—	Houston (N.L.)	1	0	1.000	4.00	3	3	0	0	0	18	21	8	8	3	10
—	Pittsburgh (N.L.)■	2	6	.250	5.19	12	12	0	0	0	69 1/3	88	44	40	21	36
Major League totals (2 years)		7	7	.500	4.63	21	21	1	0	0	122 1/3	144	71	63	33	69

McLEMORE, MARK   OF/IF   MARINERS

PERSONAL: Born October 4, 1964, in San Diego. ... 5-11/207. ... Bats both, throws right. ... Full name: Mark Tremell McLemore.

HIGH SCHOOL: Samuel F.B. Morse (San Diego).

TRANSACTIONS/CAREER NOTES: Selected by California Angels organization in ninth round of free-agent draft (June 7, 1982). ... On disabled list (May 15-27, 1985). ... On California disabled list (May 24-August 2, 1988); included rehabilitation assignments to Palm Springs (July 7-21) and Edmonton (July 22-27). ... On California disabled list (May 17-August 17, 1990); included rehabilitation assignments to Edmonton (May 24-June 6) and Palm Springs (August 9-13). ... Traded by Angels to Cleveland Indians (August 17, 1990), completing deal in which Indians traded C Ron Tingley to Angels for a player to be named later (September 6, 1989). ... Released by Indians (December 13, 1990). ... Signed by Houston Astros organization (March 6, 1991). ... On Houston disabled list (May 9-June 25, 1991); included rehabilitation assignments to Tucson (May 24-29) and Jackson (June 14-22). ... Released by Astros (June 25, 1991). ... Signed by Baltimore Orioles organization (July 5, 1991). ... Granted free agency (October 15, 1991). ... Re-signed by Orioles organization (February 5, 1992). ... Granted free agency (December 19, 1992). ... Re-signed by Orioles organization (January 6, 1993). ... Granted free agency (October 18, 1994). ... Signed by Texas Rangers (December 13, 1994). ... Granted free agency (December 7, 1996). ... Re-signed by Rangers (December 13, 1996). ... On Texas disabled list (May 15-June 12 and August 19-September 28, 1997); included rehabilitation assignments to Charlotte (June 7-8) and Oklahoma City (June 9-12). ... On disabled list (June 7-22, 1998). ... Granted free agency (October 29, 1999). ... Signed by Seattle Mariners (December 20, 1999). ... On suspended list (June 20-24, 2000). ... Granted free agency (November 5, 2001). ... Re-signed by Mariners (December 7, 2001).

STATISTICAL NOTES: Led California League second basemen with 400 assists and 84 double plays in 1984. ... Led Pacific Coast League second basemen with 597 total chances and 95 double plays in 1989. ... Led A.L. second basemen with 473 assists and 798 total chances in 1996. ... Led A.L. in caught stealing with 14 in 2000.

Year	Team (League)	Pos.	G	AB	R	H	2B	3B	HR	RBI	Avg.	BB	SO	SB	PO	A	E	Avg.
1982—	Salem (N'West)	2B-SS	55	165	42	49	6	2	0	25	.297	39	38	14	81	125	11	.949
1983—	Peoria (Midw.)	2B-SS	95	329	42	79	7	3	0	18	.240	53	64	15	170	250	24	.946
1984—	Redwood (Calif.)	2B-SS	134	482	102	142	8	3	0	45	.295	106	75	59	274	†429	25	.966
1985—	Midland (Texas)	2B-SS	117	458	80	124	17	6	2	46	.271	66	59	31	301	339	19	.971
1986—	Midland (Texas)	2B	63	237	54	75	9	1	1	29	.316	48	18	38	155	194	13	.964
—	Edmonton (PCL)	2B	73	286	41	79	13	1	0	23	.276	39	30	29	173	215	7	.982
—	California (A.L.)	2B	5	4	0	0	0	0	0	0	.000	1	2	0	3	10	0	1.000
1987—	California (A.L.)	2B-SS-DH	138	433	61	102	13	3	3	41	.236	48	72	25	293	363	17	.975
1988—	California (A.L.)	2B-3B-DH	77	233	38	56	11	2	2	16	.240	25	25	13	108	178	6	.979
—	Palm Springs (Calif.)	2B	11	44	9	15	3	1	0	6	.341	11	7	7	18	24	1	.977
—	Edmonton (PCL)	2B	12	45	7	12	3	0	0	6	.267	4	4	7	35	33	1	.986
1989—	Edmonton (PCL)	2B	114	430	60	105	13	2	4	34	.244	49	67	26	*264	323	10	*.983
—	California (A.L.)	2B-DH	32	103	12	25	3	1	0	14	.243	7	19	6	55	88	5	.966
1990—	California (A.L.)	2B	20	48	4	7	2	0	0	2	.146	4	9	1	14	15	0	1.000
—	Edmonton (PCL)	2B-SS	9	39	4	10	2	0	0	3	.256	6	10	0	24	32	4	.933
—	Palm Springs (Calif.)	2B	6	22	3	6	0	0	0	2	.273	3	7	0	20	22	0	1.000
—	Colo. Springs (PCL)■	2B-3B-SS	14	54	11	15	2	0	1	7	.278	11	8	5	23	40	2	.969
—	Cleveland (A.L.)	SS-3B-2B	8	12	2	2	0	0	0	0	.167	0	6	0	23	24	4	.922

Year	Team (League)	Pos.	G	AB	R	H	2B	3B	HR	RBI	Avg.	BB	SO	SB	PO	A	E	Avg.
1991—	Houston (N.L.)■	2B	21	61	6	9	1	0	0	2	.148	6	13	0	25	54	2	.975
	—Tucson (PCL)	2B	4	14	2	5	1	0	0	0	.357	2	1	0	8	6	0	1.000
	—Jackson (Texas)	2B	7	22	6	5	3	0	1	4	.227	6	3	1	27	24	0	1.000
	—Rochester (I.L.)■	2B	57	228	32	64	11	4	1	28	.281	27	29	12	134	166	5	.984
1992—	Baltimore (A.L.)	2B-DH	101	228	40	56	7	2	0	27	.246	21	26	11	126	186	7	.978
1993—	Baltimore (A.L.)	O-2-3-DH	148	581	81	165	27	5	4	72	.284	64	92	21	335	80	6	.986
1994—	Baltimore (A.L.)	2B-OF-DH	104	343	44	88	11	1	3	29	.257	51	50	20	219	269	9	.982
1995—	Texas (A.L.)■	OF-2B-DH	129	467	73	122	20	5	5	41	.261	59	71	21	248	184	4	.991
1996—	Texas (A.L.)	2B-OF	147	517	84	150	23	4	5	46	.290	87	69	27	313	†473	12	.985
1997—	Texas (A.L.)	2B-OF	89	349	47	91	17	2	1	25	.261	40	54	7	148	254	8	.980
	—Charlotte (FSL)	2B	2	7	1	4	1	0	0	3	.571	2	1	1	3	3	0	1.000
	—Oklahoma City (A.A.)	2B-DH	3	10	0	1	0	0	0	1	.100	1	1	1	2	3	0	1.000
1998—	Texas (A.L.)	2B	126	461	79	114	15	1	5	53	.247	89	64	12	249	332	15	.975
1999—	Texas (A.L.)	2B-OF-DH	144	566	105	155	20	7	6	45	.274	83	79	16	276	433	12	.983
2000—	Seattle (A.L.)■	2B-OF	138	481	72	118	23	1	3	46	.245	81	78	30	286	346	8	.988
2001—	Seattle (A.L.)	O-3-S-2-DH	125	409	78	117	16	9	5	57	.286	69	84	39	165	147	12	.963
American League totals (15 years)			1531	5235	820	1368	208	43	42	514	.261	729	800	249	2861	3382	125	.980
National League totals (1 year)			21	61	6	9	1	0	0	2	.148	6	13	0	25	54	2	.975
Major League totals (16 years)			1552	5296	826	1377	209	43	42	516	.260	735	813	249	2886	3436	127	.980

DIVISION SERIES RECORD

Year	Team (League)	Pos.	G	AB	R	H	2B	3B	HR	RBI	Avg.	BB	SO	SB	PO	A	E	Avg.
1996—	Texas (A.L.)	2B	4	15	1	2	0	0	0	2	.133	0	4	0	10	16	0	1.000
1998—	Texas (A.L.)	2B	3	10	0	1	1	0	0	0	.100	2	3	0	4	12	0	1.000
1999—	Texas (A.L.)	2B	3	10	0	1	0	0	0	0	.100	1	3	0	2	9	0	1.000
2000—	Seattle (A.L.)	2B	3	9	1	1	0	0	0	0	.111	2	1	0	6	9	0	1.000
2001—	Seattle (A.L.)	SS-OF	5	18	0	3	0	0	0	3	.167	1	8	0	10	12	1	.957
Division series totals (5 years)			18	62	2	8	1	0	0	5	.129	6	19	0	32	58	1	.989

CHAMPIONSHIP SERIES RECORD

Year	Team (League)	Pos.	G	AB	R	H	2B	3B	HR	RBI	Avg.	BB	SO	SB	PO	A	E	Avg.
2000—	Seattle (A.L.)	2B	5	16	2	4	3	0	0	2	.250	2	1	0	6	18	2	.923
2001—	Seattle (A.L.)	PH-SS-OF-2B	5	14	1	2	0	1	0	3	.143	2	2	0	5	2	0	1.000
Championship series totals (2 years)			10	30	3	6	3	1	0	5	.200	4	3	0	11	20	2	.939

McMILLON, BILLY   OF

PERSONAL: Born November 17, 1971, in Otero, N.M. ... 5-11/179. ... Bats left, throws left. ... Full name: William Edward McMillon.
HIGH SCHOOL: Bishopville (S.C.).
COLLEGE: Clemson.
TRANSACTIONS/CAREER NOTES: Selected by Florida Marlins organization in eighth round of free-agent draft (June 3, 1993). ... On Charlotte disabled list (April 20-29, 1997). ... Traded by Marlins to Philadelphia Phillies for OF/1B Darren Daulton (July 21, 1997). ... On Scranton/Wilkes-Barre disabled list (May 20-July 13, 1998). ... Granted free agency (December 21, 1998). ... Re-signed by Phillies organization (January 25, 1999). ... Granted free agency (October 15, 1999). ... Signed by Detroit Tigers organization (January 10, 2000). ... Claimed on waivers by Oakland Athletics (June 13, 2001). ... On Oakland disabled list (July 23, 2001-remainder of season). ... Released by A's (November 12, 2001).
STATISTICAL NOTES: Tied for New York-Pennsylvania League lead with four intentional bases on balls received in 1993. ... Tied for Midwest League lead with nine sacrifice flies in 1994. ... Led Eastern League with .423 on-base percentage in 1995. ... Led International League with .418 on-base percentage in 1996. ... Led International League with 10 sacrifice flies in 1999. ... Led International League with .446 on-base percentage in 2000. ... Career major league grand slams: 2.

Year	Team (League)	Pos.	G	AB	R	H	2B	3B	HR	RBI	Avg.	BB	SO	SB	PO	A	E	Avg.
1993—	Elmira (NY-Penn)	OF	57	226	38	69	14	2	6	35	.305	31	43	5	66	1	5	.931
1994—	Kane County (Midw.)	OF	•137	496	88	125	25	3	17	*101	.252	*84	99	7	187	9	7	.966
1995—	Portland (East.)	OF	*141	518	92	*162	29	3	14	93	.313	*96	90	15	207	14	4	.982
1996—	Charlotte (I.L.)	OF-DH	97	347	72	122	32	2	17	70	*.352	36	76	5	135	10	4	.973
	—Florida (N.L.)	OF	28	51	4	11	0	0	0	4	.216	5	14	0	17	0	0	1.000
1997—	Charlotte (I.L.)	OF	57	204	34	57	18	0	8	26	.279	32	51	8	84	5	2	.978
	—Florida (N.L.)	OF	13	18	0	2	1	0	0	1	.111	0	7	0	4	0	0	1.000
	—Scranton/W.B. (I.L.)■	OF	26	92	18	27	8	1	4	21	.293	12	24	2	49	3	0	1.000
	—Philadelphia (N.L.)	OF	24	72	10	21	4	1	2	13	.292	6	17	2	42	2	2	.957
1998—	Scranton/W.B. (I.L.)	OF-DH	77	267	42	69	16	1	13	38	.258	34	59	6	133	9	2	.986
1999—	Scranton/W.B. (I.L.)	OF-DH	132	464	97	141	38	4	16	85	.304	65	79	11	219	11	5	.979
2000—	Toledo (I.L.)■	OF	105	380	61	131	30	1	13	50	.345	71	65	3	208	7	6	.973
	—Detroit (A.L.)	DH-OF	46	123	20	37	7	1	4	24	.301	19	19	1	27	0	1	.964
2001—	Detroit (A.L.)	OF-DH	20	34	1	3	1	0	1	4	.088	2	12	0	10	0	0	1.000
	—Oakland (A.L.)	OF-DH	20	58	6	17	7	1	0	10	.293	5	13	1	18	1	1	.950
American League totals (2 years)			86	215	27	57	15	2	5	38	.265	26	44	2	55	1	2	.966
National League totals (2 years)			65	141	14	34	5	1	2	18	.241	11	38	2	63	2	2	.970
Major League totals (4 years)			151	356	41	91	20	3	7	56	.256	37	82	4	118	3	4	.968

MEACHAM, RUSTY   P

PERSONAL: Born January 27, 1968, in Stuart, Fla. ... 6-2/175. ... Throws right, bats right. ... Full name: Russell Loren Meacham.
JUNIOR COLLEGE: Indian River Community College (Fla.).

TRANSACTIONS/CAREER NOTES: Selected by Detroit Tigers organization in 33rd round of free-agent draft (June 2, 1987). ... Claimed on waivers by Kansas City Royals (October 23, 1991). ... On Kansas City disabled list (May 1-June 4 and June 15, 1993-remainder of season); included rehabilitation assignment to Omaha (May 18-June 4). ... Traded by Royals to Seattle Mariners for IF Jose Amado (June 21, 1996). ... Released by Mariners (March 28, 1997). ... Signed by Boston Red Sox organization (May 8, 1997). ... Granted free agency (October 15, 1997). ... Signed by St. Louis Cardinals organization (December 18, 1997). ... Released by Cardinals (July 14, 1998). ... Signed by Pittsburgh Pirates organization (July 25, 1998). ... Granted free agency (October 15, 1998). ... Signed by Cincinnati Reds organization (February 2, 1999). ... On Indianapolis disabled list (April 8-18, 1999). ... Released by Reds (June 4, 1999). ... Signed by Houston Astros organization (June 26, 1999). ... On New Orleans disabled list (June 22-July 18, 2000). ... Granted free agency (October 14, 2000). ... Signed by Tampa Bay Devil Rays organization (January 31, 2001). ... Granted free agency (October 8, 2001).

Year	League	W	L	Pct.	ERA	G	GS	CG	ShO	Sv.	IP	H	R	ER	BB	SO
1988—	Fayetteville (S.Atl.)	0	3	.000	6.20	6	5	0	0	0	24²/₃	37	19	17	6	16
—	Bristol (Appl.)	•9	1	•.900	*1.43	13	9	2	•2	0	75¹/₃	55	14	12	22	85
1989—	Fayetteville (S.Atl.)	10	3	.769	2.29	16	15	2	0	0	102	103	33	26	23	74
—	Lakeland (FSL)	5	4	.556	1.95	11	9	4	2	0	64²/₃	59	15	14	12	39
1990—	London (East.)	*15	9	.625	3.13	26	26	•9	•3	0	178	161	70	62	36	123
1991—	Toledo (I.L.)	9	7	.563	3.09	26	17	3	1	2	125¹/₃	117	53	43	40	70
—	Detroit (A.L.)	2	1	.667	5.20	10	4	0	0	0	27³/₃	35	17	16	11	14
1992—	Kansas City (A.L.)■	10	4	.714	2.74	64	0	0	0	2	101²/₃	88	39	31	21	64
1993—	Kansas City (A.L.)	2	2	.500	5.57	15	0	0	0	0	21	31	15	13	5	13
—	Omaha (A.A.)	0	0	...	4.82	7	0	0	0	0	9¹/₃	9	5	5	1	10
1994—	Omaha (A.A.)	1	1	.500	7.00	8	0	0	0	0	9	9	7	7	3	16
—	Kansas City (A.L.)	3	3	.500	3.73	36	0	0	0	4	50²/₃	51	23	21	12	36
1995—	Kansas City (A.L.)	4	3	.571	4.98	49	0	0	0	0	59²/₃	72	36	33	19	30
1996—	Omaha (A.A.)	3	3	.500	4.82	23	4	0	0	2	52¹/₃	56	30	28	18	39
—	Seattle (A.L.)■	1	1	.500	5.74	15	5	0	0	1	42¹/₃	57	28	27	13	25
—	Tacoma (PCL)	2	1	.667	2.29	7	2	0	0	2	19²/₃	13	7	5	5	20
1997—	Pawtucket (I.L.)■	3	3	.500	4.78	28	2	0	0	1	43¹/₃	54	23	23	15	42
1998—	Memphis (PCL)■	1	2	.333	5.16	38	0	0	0	2	52¹/₃	68	30	30	15	56
—	Nashville (PCL)■	2	1	.667	3.34	15	2	0	0	3	29²/₃	35	14	11	8	25
1999—	Indianapolis (I.L.)■	1	3	.250	6.98	16	1	0	0	1	29²/₃	38	27	23	15	19
—	New Orleans (PCL)■	3	4	.429	4.94	17	5	0	0	1	47¹/₃	56	26	26	9	47
2000—	New Orleans (PCL)	4	3	.571	2.20	33	4	0	0	0	57¹/₃	43	16	14	14	56
—	Houston (N.L.)	0	0	...	11.57	5	0	0	0	0	4²/₃	8	6	6	2	3
2001—	Durham (I.L.)	2	1	.667	0.87	27	0	0	0	15	31	17	4	3	5	30
—	Tampa Bay (A.L.)	1	3	.250	5.60	24	0	0	0	0	35¹/₃	39	24	22	10	13
A.L. totals (7 years)		23	17	.575	4.34	213	9	0	0	9	338¹/₃	373	182	163	91	195
N.L. totals (1 year)		0	0	...	11.57	5	0	0	0	0	4²/₃	8	6	6	2	3
Major League totals (8 years)		23	17	.575	4.43	218	9	0	0	9	343	381	188	169	93	198

MEADOWS, BRIAN   P   TWINS

M

PERSONAL: Born November 21, 1975, in Montgomery, Ala. ... 6-4/220. ... Throws right, bats right. ... Full name: Matthew Brian Meadows.
HIGH SCHOOL: Charles Henderson (Troy, Ala.).
TRANSACTIONS/CAREER NOTES: Selected by Florida Marlins organization in third round of free-agent draft (June 2, 1994); pick received as compensation for Colorado Rockies signing Type B free-agent SS Walt Weiss. ... On disabled list (July 28-August 13, 1998). ... Traded by Marlins to San Diego Padres for P Dan Miceli (November 15, 1999). ... Traded by Padres to Kansas City Royals for P Jay Witasick (July 31, 2000). ... Granted free agency (October 8, 2001). ... Signed by Minnesota Twins organization (January 15, 2002).
RECORDS: Shares major league single-inning record for most putouts by pitcher—3 (June 2, 1998, second inning).
STATISTICAL NOTES: Tied for Florida State League lead with 13 home runs allowed.

Year	League	W	L	Pct.	ERA	G	GS	CG	ShO	Sv.	IP	H	R	ER	BB	SO
1994—	Gulf Coast Marlins (GCL)	3	0	1.000	1.95	8	7	0	0	0	37	34	9	8	6	33
1995—	Kane County (Midw.)	9	9	.500	4.22	26	26	1	1	0	147	163	90	69	41	103
1996—	Portland (East.)	0	1	.000	4.33	4	4	1	0	0	27	26	15	13	4	13
—	Brevard County (FSL)	8	7	.533	3.58	24	23	3	1	0	146	129	73	58	25	69
1997—	Portland (East.)	9	7	.563	4.61	29	•29	4	0	0	175²/₃	204	99	90	48	115
1998—	Florida (N.L.)	11	13	.458	5.21	31	31	1	0	0	174¹/₃	222	106	101	46	88
1999—	Florida (N.L.)	11	15	.423	5.60	31	31	0	0	0	178¹/₃	214	117	111	57	72
2000—	San Diego (N.L.)■	7	8	.467	5.34	22	22	0	0	0	124²/₃	150	80	74	50	53
—	Kansas City (A.L.)■	6	2	.750	4.77	11	10	2	0	0	71²/₃	84	39	38	14	26
2001—	Kansas City (A.L.)	1	6	.143	6.97	10	10	0	0	0	50¹/₃	73	41	39	12	21
—	Omaha (PCL)	6	5	.545	6.17	18	18	0	0	0	105	143	73	72	20	74
A.L. totals (2 years)		7	8	.467	5.68	21	20	2	0	0	122	157	80	77	26	47
N.L. totals (3 years)		29	36	.446	5.39	84	84	1	0	0	477¹/₃	586	303	286	153	213
Major League totals (4 years)		36	44	.450	5.45	105	104	3	0	0	599¹/₃	743	383	363	179	260

MEARES, PAT   SS   PIRATES

PERSONAL: Born September 6, 1968, in Salina, Kan. ... 6-0/187. ... Bats right, throws right. ... Full name: Patrick James Meares.
HIGH SCHOOL: Sacred Heart (Salina, Kan.).
COLLEGE: Wichita State.
TRANSACTIONS/CAREER NOTES: Selected by Minnesota Twins organization in 15th round of free-agent draft (June 4, 1990). ... On disabled list (June 22-July 7, 1994; and August 11-26, 1997). ... Granted free agency (December 21, 1998). ... Signed by Pittsburgh Pirates (February 20, 1999). ... On Pittsburgh disabled list (April 2-23 and May 12-September 21, 1999); included rehabilitation assignment to Nashville (August 26-September 3). ... On disabled list (June 27-July 23, 2001).
STATISTICAL NOTES: Career major league grand slams: 1.

Year	Team (League)	Pos.	G	AB	R	H	2B	3B	HR	RBI	Avg.	BB	SO	SB	PO	A	E	Avg.
1990—	Kenosha (Midw.)	3B-2B	52	197	26	47	10	2	4	22	.239	25	45	2	35	94	16	.890
1991—	Visalia (Calif.)	2B-3B-OF	89	360	53	109	21	4	6	44	.303	24	63	15	155	224	26	.936
1992—	Orlando (Sou.)	SS	81	300	42	76	19	0	3	23	.253	11	57	5	91	190	35	.889
1993—	Portland (PCL)	SS	18	54	6	16	5	0	0	3	.296	3	11	0	28	48	5	.938
—	Minnesota (A.L.)	SS	111	346	33	87	14	3	0	33	.251	7	52	4	165	304	19	.961
1994—	Minnesota (A.L.)	SS	80	229	29	61	12	1	2	24	.266	14	50	5	133	209	13	.963
1995—	Minnesota (A.L.)	SS-OF	116	390	57	105	19	4	12	49	.269	15	68	10	187	317	•18	.966
1996—	Minnesota (A.L.)	SS-OF	152	517	66	138	26	7	8	67	.267	17	90	9	257	344	22	.965
1997—	Minnesota (A.L.)	SS	134	439	63	121	23	3	10	60	.276	18	86	7	211	415	20	.969
1998—	Minnesota (A.L.)	SS	149	543	56	141	26	3	9	70	.260	24	86	7	263	412	24	.966
1999—	Pittsburgh (N.L.)■	SS	21	91	15	28	4	0	0	7	.308	9	20	0	26	67	6	.939
—	Nashville (PCL)	SS	5	18	3	3	0	0	0	0	.167	1	3	1	2	6	2	.800
2000—	Pittsburgh (N.L.)	SS	132	462	55	111	22	2	13	47	.240	36	91	1	191	401	20	.967
2001—	Pittsburgh (N.L.)	2B	87	270	27	57	11	1	4	25	.211	10	45	0	149	213	10	.973
American League totals (6 years)			742	2464	304	653	120	21	41	303	.265	95	432	42	1216	2001	116	.965
National League totals (3 years)			240	823	97	196	37	3	17	79	.238	55	156	1	366	681	36	.967
Major League totals (9 years)			982	3287	401	849	157	24	58	382	.258	150	588	43	1582	2682	152	.966

MECHE, GIL P MARINERS

PERSONAL: Born September 8, 1978, in Lafayette, La. ... 6-3/200. ... Throws right, bats right. ... Full name: Gilbert Allen Meche.
HIGH SCHOOL: Acadiana (Lafayette, La.).
TRANSACTIONS/CAREER NOTES: Selected by Seattle Mariners organization in first round (22nd pick overall) of free-agent draft (June 4, 1996). ... On Seattle disabled list (May 29-June 13 and July 31, 2000-remainder of season); included rehabilitation assignments to Tacoma (June 7-13), Wisconsin (August 22-27) and Everett (August 27-28). ... On disabled list (March 31, 2001-entire season).
STATISTICAL NOTES: Pitched 7-0 one-hit, complete-game victory against Kansas City (June 13, 2000).

Year	League	W	L	Pct.	ERA	G	GS	CG	ShO	Sv.	IP	H	R	ER	BB	SO
1996—	Arizona Mariners (Ariz.)	0	1	.000	6.00	2	0	0	0	0	3	4	2	2	1	4
1997—	Everett (N'West)	3	4	.429	3.98	12	12	•1	0	0	74 2/3	75	40	33	24	62
—	Wisconsin (Midw.)	0	2	.000	3.00	2	2	0	0	0	12	12	5	4	4	14
1998—	Wisconsin (Midw.)	8	7	.533	3.44	26	0	0	0	0	149	136	77	57	63	168
1999—	New Haven (East.)	3	4	.429	3.05	10	10	0	0	0	59	51	24	20	26	56
—	Tacoma (PCL)	2	2	.500	3.19	6	6	0	0	0	31	31	12	11	13	24
—	Seattle (A.L.)	8	4	.667	4.73	16	15	0	0	0	85 2/3	73	48	45	57	47
2000—	Seattle (A.L.)	4	4	.500	3.78	15	15	1	1	0	85 2/3	75	37	36	40	60
—	Tacoma (PCL)	1	1	.500	3.86	3	3	0	0	0	14	10	7	6	10	15
—	Wisconsin (Midw.)	0	0	...	0.00	1	1	0	0	0	5	1	0	0	2	6
—	Everett (N'West)	0	1	.000	9.00	1	1	0	0	0	1	3	1	1	0	0
2001—	Seattle (A.L.)							Did not play.								
Major League totals (2 years)		12	8	.600	4.25	31	30	1	1	0	171 1/3	148	85	81	97	107

MECIR, JIM P ATHLETICS

PERSONAL: Born May 16, 1970, in Queens, N.Y. ... 6-1/210. ... Throws right, bats both. ... Full name: James Jason Mecir. ... Name pronounced ma-SEER.
HIGH SCHOOL: Smithtown East (St. James, N.Y.).
COLLEGE: Eckerd (Fla.).
TRANSACTIONS/CAREER NOTES: Selected by Seattle Mariners organization in third round of free-agent draft (June 3, 1991). ... On disabled list (June 25-August 25, 1992). ... Traded by Mariners with 1B Tino Martinez and P Jeff Nelson to New York Yankees for P Sterling Hitchcock and 3B Russ Davis (December 7, 1995). ... Traded by Yankees to Boston Red Sox (September 29, 1997), completing deal in which Yankees traded P Tony Armas Jr. and a player to be named later to Red Sox for C Mike Stanley and IF Randy Brown (August 13, 1997). ... Selected by Tampa Bay Devil Rays in second round (36th pick overall) of expansion draft (November 18, 1997). ... On disabled list (May 12, 1999-remainder of season). ... On Tampa Bay disabled list (April 27-May 23, 2000). ... Traded by Devil Rays with P Todd Belitz to Oakland Athletics for P Jesus Colome and a player to be named later (July 28, 2000). ... On Oakland disabled list (August 2-September 5, 2001); included rehabilitation assignment to Sacramento (September 3-5).
STATISTICAL NOTES: Led California League with 15 hit batsmen in 1993.

Year	League	W	L	Pct.	ERA	G	GS	CG	ShO	Sv.	IP	H	R	ER	BB	SO
1991—	San Bernardino (Calif.)	3	5	.375	4.22	14	12	0	0	1	70 1/3	72	40	33	37	48
1992—	San Bernardino (Calif.)	4	5	.444	4.67	14	11	0	0	0	61 2/3	72	40	32	26	53
1993—	Riverside (Calif.)	9	11	.450	4.33	26	26	1	0	0	145 1/3	160	89	70	58	85
1994—	Jacksonville (Sou.)	6	5	.545	2.69	46	0	0	0	13	80 1/3	73	28	24	35	53
1995—	Tacoma (PCL)	1	4	.200	3.10	40	0	0	0	8	69 2/3	63	29	24	28	46
—	Seattle (A.L.)	0	0	...	0.00	2	0	0	0	0	4 2/3	5	1	0	2	3
1996—	Columbus (I.L.)■	3	3	.500	2.27	33	0	0	0	7	47 2/3	37	14	12	15	52
—	New York (A.L.)	1	1	.500	5.13	26	0	0	0	0	40 1/3	42	24	23	23	38
1997—	Columbus (I.L.)	1	1	.500	1.00	24	0	0	0	11	27	14	4	3	6	34
—	New York (A.L.)	0	4	.000	5.88	25	0	0	0	0	33 2/3	36	23	22	10	25
1998—	Tampa Bay (A.L.)■	7	2	.778	3.11	68	0	0	0	0	84	68	30	29	33	77
1999—	Tampa Bay (A.L.)	0	1	.000	2.61	17	0	0	0	0	20 2/3	15	7	6	14	15
2000—	Tampa Bay (A.L.)	7	2	.778	3.08	38	0	0	0	1	49 2/3	35	17	17	22	33
—	Oakland (A.L.)■	3	1	.750	2.80	25	0	0	0	4	35 1/3	35	14	11	14	37
2001—	Oakland (A.L.)	2	8	.200	3.43	54	0	0	0	3	63	54	25	24	26	61
—	Sacramento (PCL)	0	0	...	0.00	1	1	0	0	0	1	1	0	0	0	0
Major League totals (7 years)		20	19	.513	3.59	255	0	0	0	8	331 1/3	290	141	132	144	289

DIVISION SERIES RECORD

Year	League	W	L	Pct.	ERA	G	GS	CG	ShO	Sv.	IP	H	R	ER	BB	SO
2000—	Oakland (A.L.)	0	0	...	0.00	3	0	0	0	0	5 1/3	1	0	0	0	2
2001—	Oakland (A.L.)	0	0	...	5.40	2	0	0	0	0	3 1/3	4	2	2	0	4
Division series totals (2 years)		0	0	...	2.08	5	0	0	0	0	8 2/3	5	2	2	0	6

M

MELHUSE, ADAM — C

PERSONAL: Born March 27, 1972, in Santa Clara, Calif. ... 6-2/185. ... Bats both, throws right. ... Full name: Adam Michael Melhuse.
HIGH SCHOOL: Lincoln (Stockton, Calif.).
COLLEGE: UCLA.
TRANSACTIONS/CAREER NOTES: Selected by Toronto Blue Jays organization in 13th round of free-agent draft (June 3, 1993). ... Released by Blue Jays (April 2, 1999). ... Re-signed by Blue Jays (April 6, 1999). ... Granted free agency (October 15, 1999). ... Signed by Los Angeles Dodgers organization (December 15, 1999). ... Traded by Dodgers to Colorado Rockies for a player to be named later (June 17, 2000). ... Granted free agency (October 18, 2000). ... Re-signed by Rockies (May 29, 2001). ... Granted free agency (October 17, 2001).
STATISTICAL NOTES: Tied for New York-Pennsylvania League lead in double plays by third basemen with 12 in 1993. ... Tied for Florida State League lead in double plays by catcher with eight in 1995. ... Tied for Florida State League lead in passed balls with 18 in 1996. ... Led Southern League in on-base percentage with .454 in 1999.

									BATTING						FIELDING		
Year Team (League)	Pos.	G	AB	R	H	2B	3B	HR	RBI	Avg.	BB	SO	SB	PO	A	E	Avg.
1993— St. Catharines (NY-P).	3B	73	266	40	68	14	2	5	32	.256	45	61	4	37	140	14	.927
1994— Hagerstown (S.Atl.)....	C-1B	118	422	61	109	16	3	11	58	.258	53	77	6	703	59	13	.983
1995— Dunedin (FSL)	C-1B-OF	123	428	43	92	20	0	4	41	.215	61	87	6	592	60	13	.980
1996— Dunedin (FSL) C-1B-3B-OF		97	315	50	78	23	2	13	51	.248	69	68	3	573	84	15	.978
— Knoxville (Sou.)..........	C	32	94	13	20	3	0	1	6	.213	14	29	0	162	15	2	.989
1997— Knoxville (Sou.)..........	C-1B-OF	31	87	14	20	3	0	3	10	.230	19	19	0	172	26	2	.990
— Syracuse (I.L.)............	C-2B-OF	118	118	7	28	5	1	2	9	.237	12	18	1	212	23	2	.992
1998— Knoxville (Sou.)..........	C-1B-OF	76	240	56	72	22	0	15	43	.300	70	39	4	424	51	11	.977
— Syracuse (I.L.)............	C-3B	12	38	4	11	3	0	1	7	.289	7	6	0	43	12	2	.965
1999— Knoxville (Sou.)..........	1B-C-3B	107	374	79	110	25	0	19	69	.294	*108	76	5	244	31	4	.986
— Syracuse (I.L.)............	C	21	71	15	20	5	0	2	16	.282	10	20	1	121	8	0	1.000
2000— San Antonio (Texas)■C-OF-1B-3B		16	58	17	23	7	0	2	9	.397	11	9	3	65	7	2	.973
— Albuquerque (PCL).....C-1B-3B-OF		36	108	21	37	9	0	1	19	.343	22	21	4	185	23	0	1.000
— Los Angeles (N.L.)	PH	1	1	0	0	0	0	0	0	.000	0	1	0	...	...	...	...
— Colorado (N.L.)■.........	1B-C-OF	23	23	3	4	0	1	0	4	.174	3	5	0	11	2	0	1.000
— Colo. Springs (PCL)	OF-C-1B	42	140	23	39	5	1	3	18	.279	21	35	2	145	10	2	.987
2001— Colo. Springs (PCL)	C-1B-OF	54	184	26	49	10	1	7	32	.266	31	42	0	326	28	5	.986
— Colorado (N.L.)	C-1B	40	71	5	13	2	0	1	8	.183	6	18	1	105	4	1	.991
Major League totals (2 years)		64	95	8	17	2	1	1	12	.179	9	24	1	116	6	1	.992

MELIAN, JACKSON — OF — REDS

PERSONAL: Born January 7, 1980, in Barcelona, Venezuela. ... 6-2/190. ... Bats right, throws right.
TRANSACTIONS/CAREER NOTES: Signed as non-drafted free agent by New York Yankees organization (July 2, 1996). ... Traded by Yankees with 3B Drew Henson, P Brian Reith and P Ed Yarnall to Cincinnati Reds for P Denny Neagle and OF Mike Frank (July 12, 2000). ... On disabled list (July 21-28 and August 17-24, 2001).
STATISTICAL NOTES: Led Gulf Coast League outfielders with 120 total chances in 1997.

									BATTING						FIELDING		
Year Team (League)	Pos.	G	AB	R	H	2B	3B	HR	RBI	Avg.	BB	SO	SB	PO	A	E	Avg.
1997— GC Yankees (GCL)......	OF	57	213	32	56	11	2	3	36	.263	20	52	9	*110	7	3	.975
1998— Greensboro (S.Atl.)	OF	135	467	66	119	18	2	8	45	.255	41	120	15	201	13	8	.964
1999— Tampa (FSL)..............	OF	128	467	65	132	17	13	6	61	.283	49	98	11	268	7	10	.965
2000— Norwich (East.)	OF	81	290	34	73	8	4	9	38	.252	18	69	17	181	4	•9	.954
— Chattanooga (Sou.)■.	OF	2	6	0	1	0	0	0	0	.167	0	0	0	2	0	1	.667
2001— Chattanooga (Sou.)....	OF	120	426	64	101	22	0	16	52	.237	36	95	10	184	•15	11	.948

MELUSKEY, MITCH — C — TIGERS

PERSONAL: Born September 18, 1973, in Yakima, Wash. ... 6-0/185. ... Bats both, throws right. ... Full name: Mitchell Wade Meluskey.
HIGH SCHOOL: Eisenhower (Yakima, Wash.).
TRANSACTIONS/CAREER NOTES: Selected by Cleveland Indians organization in 12th round of free-agent draft (June 1, 1992). ... Traded by Indians to Houston Astros for OF Buck McNabb (April 27, 1995). ... On disabled list (April 26, 1999-remainder of season; and July 31-August 18, 2000). ... Traded by Astros with P Chris Holt and OF Roger Cedeno to Detroit Tigers for C Brad Ausmus, P Doug Brocail and P Nelson Cruz (December 11, 2000). ... On disabled list (March 23, 2001-entire season).
STATISTICAL NOTES: Led South Atlantic catchers with nine double plays in 1993. ... Tied for Texas League lead with four intentional bases on balls received in 1997. ... Led Pacific Coast League with 10 intentional bases on balls received in 1998.

									BATTING						FIELDING		
Year Team (League)	Pos.	G	AB	R	H	2B	3B	HR	RBI	Avg.	BB	SO	SB	PO	A	E	Avg.
1992— Burlington (Appl.).......	C	43	126	23	29	7	0	3	16	.230	29	36	3	227	29	4	.985
1993— Columbus (S.Atl.).......	C	101	342	36	84	18	3	3	47	.246	35	69	1	639	87	7	.990
1995— Kinston (Caro.)...........	C	8	29	5	7	5	0	0	2	.241	2	9	0	58	6	1	.985
— Kissimmee (FSL)■.....	C	78	261	23	56	18	1	3	31	.215	27	33	3	443	40	10	.980
1996— Kissimmee (FSL)........	C	74	231	29	77	19	0	1	31	.333	29	26	1	315	27	9	.974
— Jackson (Texas)	C	38	134	18	42	11	0	0	21	.313	18	24	0	207	18	5	.978
1997— Jackson (Texas)	C	73	241	49	82	18	0	14	46	.340	31	39	1	356	43	6	.985
— New Orleans (A.A.).....	C	51	172	22	43	7	0	3	21	.250	25	38	0	323	26	4	.989
1998— New Orleans (PCL)......	C-OF	121	397	76	140	41	0	17	71	.353	85	59	2	702	49	10	.987
— Houston (N.L.)	C	8	8	1	2	1	0	0	0	.250	1	4	0	9	0	0	1.000
1999— Houston (N.L.)	C	10	33	4	7	1	0	1	3	.212	5	6	1	62	6	0	1.000
2000— Houston (N.L.)	C-3B	117	337	47	101	21	0	14	69	.300	55	74	1	623	31	13	.981
2001— Detroit (A.L.)■..........							Did not play.											
Major League totals (3 years)		135	378	52	110	23	0	15	72	.291	61	84	2	694	37	13	.983

MENCH, KEVIN   OF   RANGERS

PERSONAL: Born January 7, 1978, in Wilmington, Del. ... 6-0/215. ... Bats right, throws right.
HIGH SCHOOL: St. Mark's (Wilmington, Del.).
COLLEGE: Delaware.
TRANSACTIONS/CAREER NOTES: Selected by Texas Rangers organization in fourth round of free-agent draft (June 2, 1999); pick received as part of compensation for Arizona Diamondbacks signing Type A free agent P Todd Stottlemyre. ... On disabled list (June 10-30, 2001).
HONORS: Named Florida State League Most Valuable Player (2000).
STATISTICAL NOTES: Led Florida State League with 302 total bases and .615 slugging percentage in 2000. ... Tied outfielders for Texas League lead with three double plays in 2001.

Year Team (League)	Pos.	G	AB	R	H	2B	3B	HR	RBI	Avg.	BB	SO	SB	PO	A	E	Avg.
1999—Pulaski (Appl.)............	OF	65	260	36	94	22	1	*16	60	.362	28	48	12	85	6	1	*.989
— Savannah (S.Atl.)	OF	6	23	4	7	1	1	2	8	.304	2	4	0	17	1	2	.900
2000—Charlotte (FSL).........	OF	132	491	*118	*164	*39	9	27	*121	.334	78	72	19	228	12	1	*.996
2001—Tulsa (Texas)............	OF	120	475	78	126	34	2	26	83	.265	34	76	4	228	10	4	.983

MENDEZ, DONALDO   SS   PADRES

PERSONAL: Born June 7, 1978, in Barquisimeto, Venezuela. ... 6-1/155. ... Bats right, throws right. ... Full name: Donaldo Alfonso Mendez.
TRANSACTIONS/CAREER NOTES: Signed as non-drafted free agent by Houston Astros organization (November 16, 1995). ... On disabled list (June 19, 1998-entire season). ... Selected by San Diego Padres from Astros organization in Rule 5 major league draft (December 11, 2000). ... On disabled list (June 5-September 4, 2001).

Year Team (League)	Pos.	G	AB	R	H	2B	3B	HR	RBI	Avg.	BB	SO	SB	PO	A	E	Avg.
1996—Dom. Astros (DSL).....		38	122	20	32	3	1	0	19	.262	17	17	3	...	...	...	...
1997—Kissimmee (FSL)........	SS	5	16	0	3	0	0	0	0	.188	1	4	1	12	12	1	.960
— GC Astros (GCL)	SS-3B	48	150	16	29	4	0	1	13	.193	13	32	9	62	157	18	.924
1998—								Did not play.									
1999—Auburn (NY-Penn)......	SS-2B	25	86	9	18	1	1	0	10	.209	2	23	10	37	63	14	.877
2000—Michigan (Midw.).......	SS	101	370	65	100	17	0	2	51	.270	33	68	39	166	326	22	.957
2001—San Diego (N.L.)■	SS	46	118	11	18	2	1	1	5	.153	5	37	1	47	91	12	.920
Major League totals (1 year)		46	118	11	18	2	1	1	5	.153	5	37	1	47	91	12	.920

MENDOZA, RAMIRO   P   YANKEES

PERSONAL: Born June 15, 1972, in Los Santos, Panama. ... 6-2/195. ... Throws right, bats right.
TRANSACTIONS/CAREER NOTES: Signed as non-drafted free agent by New York Yankees organization (November 13, 1991). ... On New York disabled list (June 28-July 28 and August 4, 2000-remainder of season); included rehabilitation assignment to Tampa (July 19-27). ... On disabled list (March 26-April 10, 2001).

Year League	W	L	Pct.	ERA	G	GS	CG	ShO	Sv.	IP	H	R	ER	BB	SO
1992—Dominican Yankees (DSL)..	10	2	.833	2.13	15	15	5	0	0	109²/₃	93	37	26	28	79
1993—Gulf Coast Yankees (GCL)..	4	5	.444	2.79	15	9	0	0	1	67²/₃	59	26	21	7	61
— Greensboro (S.Atl.)	0	1	.000	2.45	2	0	0	0	0	3²/₃	3	1	1	5	3
1994—Tampa (FSL)...................	12	6	.667	3.01	22	21	1	0	0	134¹/₃	133	54	45	35	110
1995—Norwich (East.)	5	6	.455	3.21	19	19	2	1	0	89²/₃	87	39	32	33	68
— Columbus (I.L.)	1	0	1.000	2.57	2	2	0	0	0	14	10	4	4	2	13
1996—Columbus (I.L.)	6	2	.750	2.51	15	15	0	0	0	97	96	30	27	19	61
— New York (A.L.)	4	5	.444	6.79	12	11	0	0	0	53	80	43	40	10	34
1997—Columbus (I.L.)	0	0	...	5.68	1	1	0	0	0	6¹/₃	7	6	4	1	4
— New York (A.L.)	8	6	.571	4.24	39	15	0	0	2	133²/₃	157	67	63	28	82
1998—New York (A.L.)	10	2	.833	3.25	41	14	1	1	1	130¹/₃	131	50	47	30	56
1999—New York (A.L.)	9	9	.500	4.29	53	6	0	0	3	123²/₃	141	68	59	27	80
2000—New York (A.L.)	7	4	.636	4.25	14	9	1	1	0	65²/₃	66	32	31	20	30
— Tampa (FSL).....................	0	2	.000	7.20	2	2	0	0	0	5	9	4	4	0	7
2001—New York (A.L.)	8	4	.667	3.75	56	2	0	0	6	100²/₃	89	44	42	23	70
Major League totals (6 years)......	46	30	.605	4.18	215	57	2	2	12	607	664	304	282	138	352

DIVISION SERIES RECORD

Year League	W	L	Pct.	ERA	G	GS	CG	ShO	Sv.	IP	H	R	ER	BB	SO
1997—New York (A.L.)..............	1	1	.500	2.45	2	0	0	0	0	3²/₃	3	1	1	0	2
1998—New York (A.L.)..............							Did not play.								
1999—New York (A.L.)..............							Did not play.								
2001—New York (A.L.)..............	0	0	...	0.00	3	0	0	0	0	4¹/₃	2	0	0	1	5
Division series totals (2 years)	1	1	.500	1.13	5	0	0	0	0	8	5	1	1	1	7

CHAMPIONSHIP SERIES RECORD

Year League	W	L	Pct.	ERA	G	GS	CG	ShO	Sv.	IP	H	R	ER	BB	SO
1998—New York (A.L.).............	0	0	...	0.00	2	0	0	0	0	4¹/₃	4	0	0	0	1
1999—New York (A.L.).............	0	0	...	0.00	2	0	0	0	0	2¹/₃	0	0	0	0	2
2001—New York (A.L.).............	0	0	...	1.69	3	0	0	0	1	5¹/₃	3	1	1	2	4
Champ. series totals (3 years)	0	0	...	0.75	7	0	0	0	1	12	7	1	1	2	7

WORLD SERIES RECORD

NOTES: Member of World Series championship team (1998 and 1999).

Year League	W	L	Pct.	ERA	G	GS	CG	ShO	Sv.	IP	H	R	ER	BB	SO
1998—New York (A.L.)..............	1	0	1.000	9.00	1	0	0	0	0	1	2	1	1	0	1
1999—New York (A.L.)..............	0	0	...	10.80	1	0	0	0	0	1²/₃	3	2	2	1	0
2001—New York (A.L.)..............	0	0	...	0.00	2	0	0	0	0	2²/₃	1	0	0	0	1
World Series totals (3 years)	1	0	1.000	5.06	4	0	0	0	0	5¹/₃	6	3	3	1	2

MENECHINO, FRANK   IF   ATHLETICS

PERSONAL: Born January 7, 1971, in Staten Island, N.Y. ... 5-9/175. ... Bats right, throws right.
HIGH SCHOOL: Susan E. Wagner (Staten Island, N.Y.).
JUNIOR COLLEGE: Gulf Coast Community College (Fla.).
COLLEGE: Alabama.
TRANSACTIONS/CAREER NOTES: Selected by Chicago White Sox organization in 45th round of free-agent draft (June 3, 1993). ... Selected by Oakland Athletics organization from White Sox organization in Rule 5 minor league draft (December 15, 1997).
STATISTICAL NOTES: Led Carolina League second basemen with 603 total chances in 1995. ... Led Pacific Coast League with seven intentional bases on balls received in 1999.

Year	Team (League)	Pos.	G	AB	R	H	2B	3B	HR	RBI	Avg.	BB	SO	SB	PO	A	E	Avg.
1993—	GC White Sox (GCL) ..	2B	17	45	10	11	4	1	1	9	.244	12	4	3	22	25	1	.979
—	Hickory (S.Atl.)..........	2B	50	178	35	50	6	3	4	19	.281	33	28	11	102	148	6	.977
1994—	South Bend (Midw.)...	2B	106	379	77	113	21	5	5	48	.298	78	70	15	213	254	10	*.979
1995—	Prince William (Caro.)	2B	*137	476	65	124	31	3	6	58	.261	96	75	6	*293	295	15	.975
1996—	Birmingham (Sou.)......	2B	125	415	77	121	25	3	12	62	.292	64	84	7	*273	308	13	*.978
1997—	Nashville (A.A.)	2B-3B-OF	37	113	20	26	4	0	4	11	.230	26	31	3	79	86	9	.948
—	Birmingham (Sou.)......	2B-3B	90	318	78	95	28	4	12	60	.299	79	77	7	176	237	11	.974
1998—	Edmonton (PCL)■.....	2B	106	378	72	105	11	7	10	40	.278	70	75	9	133	192	7	.979
1999—	Vancouver (PCL)	3-S-2-DH	130	501	103	155	31	•9	15	88	.309	73	97	4	152	341	10	.980
—	Oakland (A.L.)	SS-DH-3B	9	9	0	2	0	0	0	0	.222	0	4	0	4	7	0	1.000
2000—	Oakland (A.L.) 2-S-DH-3-P		66	145	31	37	9	1	6	26	.255	20	45	1	90	139	6	.974
—	Sacramento (PCL)......	SS-3B	9	38	8	12	2	0	2	2	.316	5	4	1	13	30	0	1.000
2001—	Oakland (A.L.)	2-S-3-DH	139	471	82	114	22	2	12	60	.242	79	97	2	253	407	16	.976
Major League totals (3 years)			214	625	113	153	31	3	18	86	.245	99	146	3	347	553	22	.976

DIVISION SERIES RECORD

Year	Team (League)	Pos.	G	AB	R	H	2B	3B	HR	RBI	Avg.	BB	SO	SB	PO	A	E	Avg.
2000—	Oakland (A.L.)	2B	1	0	0	0	0	0	0	0	...	0	0	0	2	0	0	1.000
2001—	Oakland (A.L.)	2B	4	12	2	1	0	0	0	0	.083	1	4	0	10	12	1	.957
Division series totals (2 years)			5	12	2	1	0	0	0	0	.083	1	4	0	12	12	1	.960

RECORD AS PITCHER

Year	League	W	L	Pct.	ERA	G	GS	CG	ShO	Sv.	IP	H	R	ER	BB	SO
2000—	Oakland (A.L.)	0	0	...	36.00	1	0	0	0	0	1	6	4	4	0	0

MERCADO, HECTOR   P   REDS

PERSONAL: Born April 29, 1974, in Catano, Puerto Rico. ... 6-3/235. ... Throws left, bats left. ... Full name: Hector Luis Mercado.
HIGH SCHOOL: Jose S. Alegria (Dorado, Puerto Rico).
TRANSACTIONS/CAREER NOTES: Selected by Houston Astros organization in 13th round of free-agent draft (June 1, 1992). ... Selected by Florida Marlins organization from Astros organization in Rule 5 minor league draft (December 9, 1996). ... Selected by Philadelphia Phillies from Marlins organization in Rule 5 major league draft (December 15, 1997). ... Traded by Phillies to New York Mets for P Mike Welch (December 15, 1997). ... On disabled list (March 21, 1998-entire season). ... On disabled list (April 8-18 and April 24, 1999-remainder of season). ... Released by Mets (August 4, 1999). ... Signed by Cincinnati Reds organization (December 16, 1999).

M

Year	League	W	L	Pct.	ERA	G	GS	CG	ShO	Sv.	IP	H	R	ER	BB	SO
1992—	Gulf Coast Astros (GCL).....	1	2	.333	4.20	13	3	0	0	0	30	22	17	14	25	36
1993—	Gulf Coast Astros (GCL).....	5	4	.556	2.42	11	11	1	1	0	67	49	26	18	29	59
—	Osceola (FSL)...................	1	1	.500	5.19	2	2	0	0	0	8 2/3	9	7	5	6	5
1994—	Osceola (FSL)...................	6	•13	.316	3.95	25	25	1	1	0	136 2/3	123	75	60	79	88
1995—	Jackson (Texas)	1	4	.200	7.80	8	7	0	0	0	30	36	33	26	32	20
—	Kissimmee (FSL)...............	6	8	.429	3.46	19	17	2	0	0	104	96	50	40	37	75
1996—	Kissimmee (FSL)...............	3	5	.375	4.16	56	0	0	0	3	80	78	43	37	48	68
1997—	Portland (East.)■..............	11	3	.786	3.96	31	17	1	1	0	129 2/3	129	66	57	54	125
—	Charlotte (I.L.)..................	0	1	.000	9.00	1	1	0	0	0	5	5	5	5	5	1
1998—	New York (N.L.)■							Did not play.								
1999—	Norfolk (I.L.)	0	0	...	1.50	2	2	0	0	0	6	3	1	1	1	2
2000—	Cincinnati (N.L.)■.............	0	0	...	4.50	12	0	0	0	0	14	12	7	7	8	13
—	Louisville (I.L.)	1	5	.167	3.04	47	5	0	0	2	77	69	26	26	48	67
2001—	Louisville (I.L.)	1	0	1.000	1.35	12	0	0	0	1	13 1/3	12	2	2	6	13
—	Cincinnati (N.L.)................	3	2	.600	4.08	56	0	0	0	0	53	55	27	24	30	59
Major League totals (2 years).......		3	2	.600	4.16	68	0	0	0	0	67	67	34	31	38	72

MERCED, ORLANDO   OF/1B   ASTROS

PERSONAL: Born November 2, 1966, in San Juan, Puerto Rico. ... 6-1/195. ... Bats left, throws right. ... Full name: Orlando Luis Merced. ... Name pronounced mer-SED.
HIGH SCHOOL: University Garden (San Juan, Puerto Rico).
TRANSACTIONS/CAREER NOTES: Signed as non-drafted free agent by Pittsburgh Pirates organization (February 22, 1985). ... On Macon disabled list (April 18-28, 1987). ... On Watertown disabled list (June 23, 1987-remainder of season). ... On disabled list (May 1-18, August 1-16 and August 22-September 6, 1996). ... Traded by Pirates with IF Carlos Garcia and P Dan Plesac to Toronto Blue Jays for P Jose Silva, P Jose Pett, IF Brandon Cromer and three players to be named later (November 14, 1996); Pirates acquired P Mike Halperin, IF Abraham Nunez and C/OF Craig Wilson to complete deal (December 11, 1996). ... On disabled list (July 29-September 28, 1997). ... Granted free agency (October 27, 1997). ... Signed by Minnesota Twins organization (January 12, 1998). ... Traded by Twins with P Greg Swindell to Boston Red Sox for P Matt Kinney, P Joe Thomas and P John Barnes (July 31, 1998). ... Released by Red Sox (August 31, 1998). ... Signed by Chicago Cubs (September 5, 1998). ... Granted free agency (October 28, 1998). ... Signed by Montreal Expos organization (January 28, 1999). ... On disabled list (July 1-28, 1999). ... Granted free agency (October 15, 1999). ... Played with Orix Blue Wave of Japan Pacific League (2000). ... Signed by Houston Astros organization (August 16, 2000). ... Granted free agency (October 18, 2000). ... Re-signed by Astros organization (January 8, 2001). ... On disabled list (June 23-July 12, 2001). ... Granted free agency (November 5, 2001). ... Re-signed by Astros (December 7, 2001).

STATISTICAL NOTES: Led N.L. outfielders in double plays with five in 1993 and five in 1996. ... Career major league grand slams: 3.
MISCELLANEOUS: Batted as switch hitter (1985-92).

Year Team (League)	Pos.	G	AB	R	H	2B	3B	HR	RBI	Avg.	BB	SO	SB	PO	A	E	Avg.
1985—GC Pirates (GCL)	SS-3B-1B	40	136	16	31	6	0	1	13	.228	9	9	3	46	78	28	.816
1986—Macon (S.Atl.)	OF-3B	65	173	20	34	4	1	2	24	.197	12	38	5	53	15	13	.840
—Watertown (NY-Penn)	3B-1B-OF	27	89	12	16	0	1	3	9	.180	14	21	6	49	28	10	.885
1987—Macon (S.Atl.)	OF	4	4	1	0	0	0	0	0	.000	1	3	0	1	1	0	1.000
—Watertown (NY-Penn)	2B	4	12	4	5	0	1	0	3	.417	1	1	1	11	7	2	.900
1988—Augusta (S.Atl.)	2B-3B-SS	37	136	19	36	6	3	1	17	.265	7	20	2	35	39	7	.914
—Salem (Caro.)	3B-2B-OF-SS	80	298	47	87	12	7	7	42	.292	27	64	13	77	183	31	.893
1989—Harrisburg (East.)	1B-OF-3B	95	341	43	82	16	4	6	48	.240	32	66	13	435	32	10	.979
—Buffalo (A.A.)	1B-OF-3B	35	129	18	44	5	3	1	16	.341	7	26	0	173	15	3	.984
1990—Buffalo (A.A.)	1B-3B-OF	101	378	52	99	12	6	9	55	.262	46	63	14	689	83	20	.975
—Pittsburgh (N.L.)	OF-C	25	24	3	5	1	0	0	0	.208	1	9	0	0	0	0	...
1991—Buffalo (A.A.)	1B	3	12	1	2	0	0	0	0	.167	1	4	1	29	2	0	1.000
—Pittsburgh (N.L.)	1B-OF	120	411	83	113	17	2	10	50	.275	64	81	8	916	60	12	.988
1992—Pittsburgh (N.L.)	1B-OF	134	405	50	100	28	5	6	60	.247	52	63	5	906	75	5	.995
1993—Pittsburgh (N.L.)	OF-1B	137	447	68	140	26	4	8	70	.313	77	64	3	485	31	10	.981
1994—Pittsburgh (N.L.)	OF-1B	108	386	48	105	21	3	9	51	.272	42	58	4	508	29	5	.991
1995—Pittsburgh (N.L.)	OF-1B	132	487	75	146	29	4	15	83	.300	52	74	7	374	23	6	.985
1996—Pittsburgh (N.L.)	OF-1B	120	453	69	130	24	1	17	80	.287	51	74	8	242	15	3	.988
1997—Toronto (A.L.)■	OF-DH-1B	98	368	45	98	23	2	9	40	.266	47	62	7	193	10	3	.985
1998—Minnesota (A.L.)	1B-OF-DH	63	204	22	59	12	0	5	33	.289	17	29	1	324	23	6	.983
—Boston (A.L.)■	DH-OF	9	9	0	0	0	0	0	2	.000	2	3	0	2	0	0	1.000
—Chicago (N.L.)■	OF	12	10	2	3	0	0	1	5	.300	1	2	0	3	0	0	1.000
1999—Montreal (N.L.)■	OF-1B-DH	93	194	25	52	12	1	8	26	.268	26	27	2	95	4	5	.952
2000—Orix (Jap. Pac.)■		23	80	9	18	2	1	2	15	.225	4	14	0	...	...	...	...
—New Orleans (PCL)■	OF-3B-1B	17	67	8	18	4	0	1	14	.269	2	4	0	37	16	1	.981
2001—Houston (N.L.)	3B-1B-OF	94	137	19	36	6	1	6	29	.263	14	32	5	39	1	1	.976
American League totals (2 years)		170	581	67	157	35	2	14	75	.270	66	94	8	519	33	9	.984
National League totals (10 years)		975	2954	442	830	164	21	80	454	.281	380	484	42	3568	238	47	.988
Major League totals (11 years)		1145	3535	509	987	199	23	94	529	.279	446	578	50	4087	271	56	.987

DIVISION SERIES RECORD

Year Team (League)	Pos.	G	AB	R	H	2B	3B	HR	RBI	Avg.	BB	SO	SB	PO	A	E	Avg.
1998—Chicago (N.L.)								Did not play.									
2001—Houston (N.L.)	PH	1	1	0	0	0	0	0	0	.000	0	0	0	...	...	...	...

CHAMPIONSHIP SERIES RECORD

NOTES: Hit home run in first at-bat (October 12, 1991).

Year Team (League)	Pos.	G	AB	R	H	2B	3B	HR	RBI	Avg.	BB	SO	SB	PO	A	E	Avg.
1991—Pittsburgh (N.L.)	1B-PH	3	9	1	2	0	0	1	1	.222	0	1	0	13	0	1	.929
1992—Pittsburgh (N.L.)	1B-PH	4	10	0	1	1	0	0	2	.100	2	4	0	27	2	1	.967
Championship series totals (2 years)		7	19	1	3	1	0	1	3	.158	2	5	0	40	2	2	.955

MERCEDES, JOSE   P

PERSONAL: Born March 5, 1971, in El Seibo, Dominican Republic. ... 6-1/180. ... Throws right, bats right. ... Full name: Jose Miguel Mercedes.
TRANSACTIONS/CAREER NOTES: Signed as non-drafted free agent by Baltimore Orioles organization (August 10, 1989). ... Selected by Milwaukee Brewers from Orioles organization in Rule 5 major league draft (December 13, 1993). ... On Milwaukee disabled list (April 2-May 30, 1994); included rehabilitation assignments to El Paso (April 30-May 14) and New Orleans (May 14-28). ... On disabled list (May 14, 1995-remainder of season). ... On Milwaukee disabled list (May 5, 1998-remainder of season); included rehabilitation assignment to El Paso (June 15-16). ... Released by Brewers (December 16, 1998). ... Signed by San Diego Padres organization (March 19, 1999). ... Released by Padres (June 24, 1999). ... Signed by Florida Marlins organization (June 30, 1999). ... Released by Marlins (July 30, 1999). ... Signed by New York Mets organization (August 6, 1999). ... Granted free agency (October 15, 1999). ... Signed by Orioles organization (January 3, 2000). ... Granted free agency (November 5, 2001).

Year League	W	L	Pct.	ERA	G	GS	CG	ShO	Sv.	IP	H	R	ER	BB	SO
1990—				Dominican Summer League statistics unavailable.											
1991—				Dominican Summer League statistics unavailable.											
1992—Gulf Coast Orioles (GCL)	2	3	.400	1.78	8	5	2	0	0	35 1/3	31	12	7	13	21
—Kane County (Midw.)	3	2	.600	2.66	8	8	2	•2	0	47 1/3	40	26	14	15	45
1993—Bowie (East.)	6	8	.429	4.78	26	23	3	0	0	147	170	86	78	65	75
1994—El Paso (Texas)■	2	0	1.000	4.66	3	0	0	0	0	9 2/3	13	6	5	4	8
—New Orleans (A.A.)	0	0	...	4.91	3	3	0	0	0	18 1/3	19	10	10	8	7
—Milwaukee (A.L.)	2	0	1.000	2.32	19	0	0	0	0	31	22	9	8	16	11
1995—Milwaukee (A.L.)	0	1	.000	9.82	5	0	0	0	0	7 1/3	12	9	8	8	6
1996—New Orleans (A.A.)	3	7	.300	3.56	25	15	0	0	1	101	109	58	40	28	47
—Milwaukee (A.L.)	0	2	.000	9.18	11	0	0	0	0	16 2/3	20	18	17	5	6
1997—Milwaukee (A.L.)	7	10	.412	3.79	29	23	2	1	0	159	146	76	67	53	80
1998—Milwaukee (N.L.)	2	2	.500	6.75	7	5	0	0	0	32	42	25	24	9	11
—El Paso (Texas)	0	0	...	10.80	1	1	0	0	0	3 1/3	9	4	4	0	0
1999—Las Vegas (PCL)■	2	6	.250	4.30	15	14	0	0	0	88	110	57	42	20	57
—Calgary (PCL)■	1	2	.333	3.12	4	4	0	0	0	26	30	13	9	3	13
—Norfolk (I.L.)■	2	1	.667	2.53	6	6	0	0	0	32	36	15	9	11	19
2000—Baltimore (A.L.)■	14	7	.667	4.02	36	20	1	0	0	145 2/3	150	71	65	64	70
2001—Baltimore (A.L.)	8	*17	.320	5.82	33	31	2	0	0	184	219	125	119	63	123
A.L. totals (6 years)	31	37	.456	4.70	133	74	5	1	0	543 2/3	569	308	284	209	296
N.L. totals (1 year)	2	2	.500	6.75	7	5	0	0	0	32	42	25	24	9	11
Major League totals (7 years)	33	39	.458	4.82	140	79	5	1	0	575 2/3	611	333	308	218	307

MERLONI, LOU — IF — RED SOX

PERSONAL: Born April 6, 1971, in Framingham, Mass. ... 5-10/195. ... Bats right, throws right. ... Full name: Louis William Merloni.
HIGH SCHOOL: Framingham (Mass.) South.
COLLEGE: Providence.
TRANSACTIONS/CAREER NOTES: Selected by Boston Red Sox organization in 10th round of free-agent draft (June 3, 1993). ... On Boston disabled list (June 29-September 12, 1998); included rehabilitation assignment to Gulf Coast Red Sox (August 8-20). ... Contract sold by Red Sox to Yokohama BayStars of Japan Central League (November 22, 1999). ... Re-signed by Red Sox organization (July 28, 2000). ... On Boston disabled list (June 6-21, 2001); included rehabilitation assignment to Pawtucket (June 10-21).

Year Team (League)	Pos.	G	AB	R	H	2B	3B	HR	RBI	Avg.	BB	SO	SB	PO	A	E	Avg.
1993— GC Red Sox (GCL)	SS	4	14	4	5	1	0	0	1	.357	1	1	1	7	13	1	.952
— Fort Lauderdale (FSL)	3B-SS	44	156	14	38	1	1	2	21	.244	13	26	1	40	114	8	.951
1994— Sarasota (FSL)	2B-3B-SS	113	419	59	120	16	2	1	63	.286	36	57	5	196	304	18	.965
1995— Trenton (East.)	2B-3B-SS	93	318	42	88	16	1	1	30	.277	39	50	7	166	222	20	.951
1996— GC Red Sox (GCL)	2B	1	4	1	1	0	0	0	1	.250	0	0	0	3	3	0	1.000
— Trenton (East.) 3B-2B-SS-1B		28	95	11	22	6	1	3	16	.232	9	18	0	39	67	8	.930
— Pawtucket (I.L.).........	3B-2B-SS	38	115	19	29	6	0	1	12	.252	10	20	0	39	99	8	.945
1997— Trenton (East.)	3B-2B-SS	69	255	49	79	17	4	5	37	.310	30	43	3	68	130	9	.957
— Pawtucket (I.L.).........	2B-3B-SS	49	165	24	49	10	0	5	24	.297	15	20	0	61	122	4	.979
1998— Pawtucket (I.L.).........	SS-2B-3B	27	88	17	34	3	1	8	22	.386	16	13	2	27	56	2	.976
— Boston (A.L.)............	2B-3B-SS	39	96	10	27	6	0	1	15	.281	7	20	1	52	73	5	.962
— GC Red Sox (GCL)	2B	1	1	0	0	0	0	0	0	.000	0	0	0	0	0	0	...
1999— Boston (A.L.).............S-3-2-DH-1-O		43	126	18	32	7	0	1	13	.254	8	16	0	68	88	10	.940
— Pawtucket (I.L.).........S-3-DH-1-2		66	229	45	64	14	1	7	36	.279	30	38	1	79	127	12	.945
2000— Yokohama (Jp. Cn.)■		42	94	10	20	1	0	1	3	.213	7	15	0	...	...	...	...
— Pawtucket (I.L.)■......SS-1B-2B-3B		11	39	6	16	2	0	1	5	.410	3	3	0	23	12	4	.897
— Boston (A.L.)............	3B	40	128	10	41	11	2	0	18	.320	4	22	1	26	64	7	.928
2001— Pawtucket (I.L.).........SS-2B-3B-1B		52	195	30	51	12	0	4	20	.262	15	37	2	80	127	10	.954
— Boston (A.L.).............	SS-2B-3B	52	146	21	39	10	0	3	13	.267	6	31	2	64	108	3	.983
Major League totals (4 years)		**174**	**496**	**59**	**139**	**34**	**2**	**5**	**59**	**.280**	**25**	**89**	**4**	**210**	**333**	**25**	**.956**

DIVISION SERIES RECORD

Year Team (League)	Pos.	G	AB	R	H	2B	3B	HR	RBI	Avg.	BB	SO	SB	PO	A	E	Avg.
1999— Boston (A.L.).............	SS-PH	3	6	1	2	0	0	0	1	.333	1	1	0	3	2	1	.833

CHAMPIONSHIP SERIES RECORD

Year Team (League)	Pos.	G	AB	R	H	2B	3B	HR	RBI	Avg.	BB	SO	SB	PO	A	E	Avg.
1999— Boston (A.L.).............	PH	1	0	0	0	0	0	0	0	...	1	0	0	...	...	...	...

MESA, JOSE — P — PHILLIES

M

PERSONAL: Born May 22, 1966, in Azua, Dominican Republic. ... 6-3/225. ... Throws right, bats right. ... Full name: Jose Ramon Mesa.
HIGH SCHOOL: Santa School (Azua, Dominican Republic).
TRANSACTIONS/CAREER NOTES: Signed as non-drafted free agent by Toronto Blue Jays organization (October 31, 1981). ... On Kinston disabled list (August 27, 1984-remainder of season). ... Traded by Blue Jays to Baltimore Orioles (September 4, 1987), completing deal in which Orioles traded P Mike Flanagan to Blue Jays for P Oswald Peraza and a player to be named later (August 31, 1987). ... On Rochester disabled list (April 18-May 16 and June 30, 1988-remainder of season; May 27, 1989-remainder of season; and August 21-September 5, 1991). ... Traded by Orioles to Cleveland Indians for OF Kyle Washington (July 14, 1992). ... On suspended list (April 5-8, 1993). ... Traded by Indians with IF Shawon Dunston and P Alvin Morman to San Francisco Giants for P Steve Reed and OF Jacob Cruz (July 23, 1998). ... Granted free agency (October 23, 1998). ... Signed by Seattle Mariners (November 13, 1998). ... Granted free agency (November 6, 2000). ... Signed by Philadelphia Phillies (November 17, 2000). ... On suspended list (August 28-30, 2001).
HONORS: Named A.L. Fireman of the Year by THE SPORTING NEWS (1995).
STATISTICAL NOTES: Tied for Carolina League lead with nine hit batsmen in 1985.
MISCELLANEOUS: Appeared in one game as pinch runner for Baltimore (1991).

Year League	W	L	Pct.	ERA	G	GS	CG	ShO	Sv.	IP	H	R	ER	BB	SO
1982— Gulf Coast Blue Jays (GCL)	6	4	.600	2.70	13	12	6	*3	1	83 1/3	58	34	25	20	40
1983— Florence (S.Atl.)	6	12	.333	5.48	28	27	1	0	0	141 1/3	153	*116	86	93	91
1984— Florence (S.Atl.)	4	3	.571	3.76	7	7	0	0	0	38 1/3	38	24	16	25	35
— Kinston (Caro.)..................	5	2	.714	3.91	10	9	0	0	0	50 2/3	51	23	22	28	24
1985— Kinston (Caro.)..................	5	10	.333	6.16	30	20	0	0	1	106 2/3	110	89	73	79	71
1986— Ventura County (Calif.).......	10	6	.625	3.86	24	24	2	1	0	142 1/3	141	71	61	58	113
— Knoxville (Sou.)..................	2	2	.500	4.35	9	8	2	1	0	41 1/3	40	32	20	23	30
1987— Knoxville (Sou.)..................	10	•13	.435	5.21	35	*35	4	2	0	*193 1/3	*206	*131	*112	104	115
— Baltimore (A.L.)■...............	1	3	.250	6.03	6	5	0	0	0	31 1/3	38	23	21	15	17
1988— Rochester (I.L.)..................	0	3	.000	8.62	11	2	0	0	0	15 2/3	21	20	15	14	15
1989— Rochester (I.L.)..................	0	2	.000	5.40	7	1	0	0	0	10	10	6	6	6	3
— Hagerstown (East.)............	0	0	...	1.38	3	3	0	0	0	13	9	2	2	4	12
1990— Hagerstown (East.)............	5	5	.500	3.42	15	15	3	1	0	79	77	35	30	30	72
— Rochester (I.L.)..................	1	2	.333	2.42	4	4	0	0	0	26	21	11	7	12	23
— Baltimore (A.L.)................	3	2	.600	3.86	7	7	0	0	0	46 2/3	37	20	20	27	24
1991— Baltimore (A.L.)................	6	11	.353	5.97	23	23	2	1	0	123 2/3	151	86	82	62	64
— Rochester (I.L.)..................	3	3	.500	3.86	8	8	1	1	0	51 1/3	37	25	22	30	48
1992— Baltimore (A.L.)■...............	3	8	.273	5.19	13	12	0	0	0	67 2/3	77	41	39	27	22
— Cleveland (A.L.)■...............	4	4	.500	4.16	15	15	1	1	0	93	92	45	43	43	40
1993— Cleveland (A.L.)..................	10	12	.455	4.92	34	33	3	0	0	208 2/3	232	122	114	62	118
1994— Cleveland (A.L.)..................	7	5	.583	3.82	51	0	0	0	2	73	71	33	31	26	63
1995— Cleveland (A.L.)..................	3	0	1.000	1.13	62	0	0	0	*46	64	49	9	8	17	58

Year	League	W	L	Pct.	ERA	G	GS	CG	ShO	Sv.	IP	H	R	ER	BB	SO
1996— Cleveland (A.L.)		2	7	.222	3.73	69	0	0	0	39	72 1/3	69	32	30	28	64
1997— Cleveland (A.L.)		4	4	.500	2.40	66	0	0	0	16	82 1/3	83	28	22	28	69
1998— Cleveland (A.L.)		3	4	.429	5.17	44	0	0	0	1	54	61	36	31	20	35
— San Francisco (N.L.)■		5	3	.625	3.52	32	0	0	0	0	30 2/3	30	14	12	18	28
1999— Seattle (A.L.)■		3	6	.333	4.98	68	0	0	0	33	68 2/3	84	42	38	40	42
2000— Seattle (A.L.)		4	6	.400	5.36	66	0	0	0	1	80 2/3	89	48	48	41	84
2001— Philadelphia (N.L.)■		3	3	.500	2.34	71	0	0	0	42	69 1/3	65	26	18	20	59
A.L. totals (12 years)		53	72	.424	4.45	524	95	6	2	138	1066	1133	565	527	436	700
N.L. totals (2 years)		8	6	.571	2.70	103	0	0	0	42	100	95	40	30	38	87
Major League totals (13 years)		61	78	.439	4.30	627	95	6	2	180	1166	1228	605	557	474	787

DIVISION SERIES RECORD

Year	League	W	L	Pct.	ERA	G	GS	CG	ShO	Sv.	IP	H	R	ER	BB	SO
1995— Cleveland (A.L.)		0	0	...	0.00	2	0	0	0	0	2	0	0	0	2	0
1996— Cleveland (A.L.)		0	1	.000	3.86	2	0	0	0	0	4 2/3	8	2	2	0	7
1997— Cleveland (A.L.)		0	0	...	2.70	2	0	0	0	1	3 1/3	5	1	1	1	2
2000— Seattle (A.L.)		1	0	1.000	0.00	2	0	0	0	0	2	0	0	0	1	2
Division series totals (4 years)		1	1	.500	2.25	8	0	0	0	1	12	13	3	3	4	11

CHAMPIONSHIP SERIES RECORD

Year	League	W	L	Pct.	ERA	G	GS	CG	ShO	Sv.	IP	H	R	ER	BB	SO
1995— Cleveland (A.L.)		0	0	...	2.25	4	0	0	0	1	4	3	1	1	1	1
1997— Cleveland (A.L.)		1	0	1.000	3.38	4	0	0	0	2	5 1/3	5	2	2	3	5
2000— Seattle (A.L.)		0	0	...	12.46	3	0	0	0	0	4 1/3	5	6	6	3	3
Champ. series totals (3 years)		1	0	1.000	5.93	11	0	0	0	3	13 2/3	13	9	9	7	9

WORLD SERIES RECORD

Year	League	W	L	Pct.	ERA	G	GS	CG	ShO	Sv.	IP	H	R	ER	BB	SO
1995— Cleveland (A.L.)		1	0	1.000	4.50	2	0	0	0	1	4	5	2	2	1	4
1997— Cleveland (A.L.)		0	0	...	5.40	5	0	0	0	1	5	10	3	3	1	5
World Series totals (2 years)		1	0	1.000	5.00	7	0	0	0	2	9	15	5	5	2	9

ALL-STAR GAME RECORD

Year	League	W	L	Pct.	ERA	G	GS	CG	ShO	Sv.	IP	H	R	ER	BB	SO
1995— American		0	0	...	0.00	0	0	0	0	0	1	0	0	0	0	1
1996— American								Did not play.								

MEYERS, CHAD   2B/OF   ATHLETICS

PERSONAL: Born August 8, 1975, in Omaha, Neb. ... 6-0/190. ... Bats right, throws right. ... Full name: Chad William Meyers.
HIGH SCHOOL: Daniel J. Gross (Omaha, Neb.).
COLLEGE: Creighton.
TRANSACTIONS/CAREER NOTES: Selected by Chicago Cubs organization in fifth round of free-agent draft (June 4, 1996). ... Released by Cubs (October 12, 2001). ... Signed by Oakland Athletics organization (November 7, 2001).
STATISTICAL NOTES: Led New York-Pennsylvania League second basemen with 33 double plays in 1996. ... Led Pacific Coast League in being hit by pitch with 26 in 2001. ... Led Pacific Coast League second basemen with .965 fielding percentage and 15 errors in 2001.

								BATTING							FIELDING		
Year	Team (League)	Pos.	G	AB	R	H	2B	3B	HR	RBI	Avg.	BB	SO	SB	PO	A	E	Avg.
1996— Williamsport (NY-P)		2B-OF	67	230	46	56	9	2	2	26	.243	33	39	27	123	136	12	.956
1997— Rockford (Midw.)		2-O-3-S	125	439	89	132	28	4	4	58	.301	74	72	54	205	266	26	.948
1998— Daytona (FSL)		2B-OF	48	186	39	60	8	3	3	25	.323	33	29	23	97	109	13	.941
— West Tenn (Sou.)		2B	77	293	63	79	14	0	0	26	.270	58	43	37	154	173	23	.934
1999— West Tenn (Sou.)		2B	64	238	45	69	19	2	3	29	.290	26	40	22	106	148	9	.966
— Iowa (PCL)		2B-OF	44	175	39	62	13	2	0	16	.354	29	20	17	104	99	4	.981
— Chicago (N.L.)		2B-OF	43	142	17	33	9	0	0	4	.232	9	27	4	76	69	2	.986
2000— Chicago (N.L.)		2B-3B	36	52	8	9	2	0	0	5	.173	3	11	1	11	19	2	.938
— Iowa (PCL)		2B-OF-3B-SS	80	301	54	81	10	0	2	26	.269	43	41	34	171	143	19	.943
2001— Iowa (PCL)		2B-OF-3B	132	446	92	134	31	5	9	54	.300	58	72	*27	224	233	†16	†.966
— Chicago (N.L.)		2B-OF-3B	18	17	1	2	0	0	0	0	.118	2	5	0	6	10	0	1.000
Major League totals (3 years)			97	211	26	44	11	0	0	9	.209	14	43	5	93	98	4	.979

MEYERS, MIKE   P   CUBS

PERSONAL: Born October 18, 1977, in London, Ont. ... 6-2/210. ... Throws right, bats right. ... Full name: Michael Gregory Meyers.
HIGH SCHOOL: Annadale (Tillsonburg, Ont.).
JUNIOR COLLEGE: Blackhawk College (Ill.).
TRANSACTIONS/CAREER NOTES: Selected by Chicago Cubs organization in 26th round of free-agent draft (June 3, 1997). ... On Iowa disabled list (June 8-16 and July 22-August 17, 2000; and May 29-June 7, 2001).

Year	League	W	L	Pct.	ERA	G	GS	CG	ShO	Sv.	IP	H	R	ER	BB	SO
1997— Arizona Cubs (Ariz.)		3	1	.750	1.41	12	2	0	0	3	38 1/3	34	15	6	13	45
— Williamsport (NY-Penn)		0	0	...	0.00	1	1	0	0	0	4	3	0	0	1	2
1998— Rockford (Midw.)		7	5	.583	3.36	17	16	0	0	0	85 2/3	75	37	32	32	86
1999— Daytona (FSL)		10	3	.769	1.93	19	17	2	0	0	107 1/3	68	30	23	40	122
— West Tenn (Sou.)		4	0	1.000	1.09	5	5	0	0	0	33	21	5	4	10	51
2000— West Tenn (Sou.)		5	2	.714	2.44	9	9	3	1	0	59	41	18	16	26	51
— Iowa (PCL)		2	6	.250	7.28	13	12	0	0	0	59 1/3	74	51	48	30	44
2001— Iowa (PCL)		7	4	.636	3.23	25	25	0	0	0	147 2/3	129	58	53	64	124

MIADICH, BART P ANGELS

PERSONAL: Born February 3, 1976, in Torrance, Calif. ... 6-4/205. ... Throws right, bats right. ... Full name: John Barton Miadich.
HIGH SCHOOL: Lakeridge (Lake Oswego, Ore.).
COLLEGE: UC San Diego.
TRANSACTIONS/CAREER NOTES: Selected by Colorado Rockies organization in 49th round of free-agent draft (June 2, 1994); did not sign. ... Signed as non-drafted free agent by Boston Red Sox organization (August 31, 1997). ... Traded by Red Sox to Arizona Diamondbacks organization (December 15, 1998), completing deal in which Diamondbacks traded P Bob Wolcott to Red Sox for a player to be named later (November 11, 1998). ... Released by Diamondbacks (March 30, 2000). ... Signed by Anaheim Angels organization (May 23, 2000).

Year League	W	L	Pct.	ERA	G	GS	CG	ShO	Sv.	IP	H	R	ER	BB	SO
1998— Sarasota (FSL)	3	2	.600	3.14	22	0	0	0	7	48²/₃	40	20	17	15	64
—Trenton (East.)	1	6	.143	5.96	22	8	0	0	1	54¹/₃	66	39	36	26	33
1999— El Paso (Texas)■	0	2	.000	8.10	12	0	0	0	1	20	37	22	18	7	16
—High Desert (Calif.)............	3	8	.273	5.42	21	16	0	0	0	98	125	71	59	40	85
2000— Erie (East.)	3	1	.750	3.35	28	0	0	0	2	40¹/₃	27	16	15	21	38
—Edmonton (PCL)	2	1	.667	4.57	10	0	0	0	1	21²/₃	25	14	11	9	20
2001— Salt Lake (PCL)	4	4	.500	2.44	55	0	0	0	*27	59	40	20	16	29	73
—Anaheim (A.L.)	0	0	...	4.50	11	0	0	0	0	10	6	5	5	8	11
Major League totals (1 year)........	0	0	...	4.50	11	0	0	0	0	10	6	5	5	8	11

MICELI, DAN P

PERSONAL: Born September 9, 1970, in Newark, N.J. ... 6-0/225. ... Throws right, bats right. ... Full name: Daniel Miceli.
HIGH SCHOOL: Dr. Phillips (Orlando).
TRANSACTIONS/CAREER NOTES: Signed as non-drafted free agent by Kansas City Royals organization (March 7, 1990). ... Traded by Royals with P Jon Lieber to Pittsburgh Pirates for P Stan Belinda (July 31, 1993). ... Traded by Pirates to Detroit Tigers for P Clint Sodowsky (November 1, 1996). ... Traded by Tigers with P Donne Wall and 3B Ryan Balfe to San Diego Padres for P Tim Worrell and OF Trey Beamon (November 19, 1997). ... Traded by Padres to Florida Marlins for P Brian Meadows (November 15, 1999). ... On Florida disabled list (May 30-July 19, 2000); included rehabilitation assignments to Gulf Coast Marlins (July 4-8) and Brevard County (July 9-19). ... Released by Marlins (June 25, 2001). ... Signed by Colorado Rockies organization (July 2, 2001). ... Granted free agency (November 5, 2001).

Year League	W	L	Pct.	ERA	G	GS	CG	ShO	Sv.	IP	H	R	ER	BB	SO
1990— Gulf Coast Royals (GCL)	3	4	.429	3.91	*27	0	0	0	4	53	45	27	23	29	48
1991— Eugene (N'West)	0	1	.000	2.14	25	0	0	0	10	33²/₃	18	8	8	18	43
1992— Appleton (Midw.)	1	1	.500	1.93	23	0	0	0	9	23¹/₃	12	6	5	4	44
—Memphis (Sou.)	3	0	1.000	1.91	32	0	0	0	4	37²/₃	20	10	8	13	46
1993— Memphis (Sou.)	6	4	.600	4.60	40	0	0	0	7	58²/₃	54	30	30	39	68
—Carolina (Sou.)■	0	2	.000	5.11	13	0	0	0	10	12¹/₃	11	8	7	4	19
—Pittsburgh (N.L.)	0	0	...	5.06	9	0	0	0	0	5¹/₃	6	3	3	3	4
1994— Buffalo (A.A.)	1	1	.500	1.88	19	0	0	0	2	24	15	5	5	6	31
—Pittsburgh (N.L.)	2	1	.667	5.93	28	0	0	0	2	27¹/₃	28	19	18	11	27
1995— Pittsburgh (N.L.)	4	4	.500	4.66	58	0	0	0	21	58	61	30	30	28	56
1996— Pittsburgh (N.L.)	2	10	.167	5.78	44	9	0	0	1	85²/₃	99	65	55	45	66
—Carolina (Sou.)	1	0	1.000	1.00	3	0	0	0	1	9	4	1	1	1	17
1997— Detroit (A.L.)■	3	2	.600	5.01	71	0	0	0	3	82²/₃	77	49	46	38	79
1998— San Diego (N.L.)■	10	5	.667	3.22	67	0	0	0	2	72²/₃	64	28	26	27	70
1999— San Diego (N.L.)	4	5	.444	4.46	66	0	0	0	2	68²/₃	67	39	34	36	59
2000— Florida (N.L.)■	6	4	.600	4.25	45	0	0	0	0	48²/₃	45	23	23	18	40
—Gulf Coast Marlins (GCL) ..	0	0	...	0.00	2	2	0	0	0	3	0	0	0	1	3
—Brevard County (FSL)........	1	0	1.000	3.00	5	4	0	0	0	6	3	2	2	0	7
2001— Florida (N.L.)	0	5	.000	6.93	29	0	0	0	0	24²/₃	29	21	19	11	31
—Colorado Springs (PCL)■..	0	2	.000	6.00	4	0	0	0	0	3	2	2	2	1	4
—Colorado (N.L.)	2	0	1.000	2.21	22	0	0	0	1	20¹/₃	18	8	5	5	17
A.L. totals (1 year)	3	2	.600	5.01	71	0	0	0	3	82²/₃	77	49	46	38	79
N.L. totals (8 years)	30	34	.469	4.66	368	9	0	0	29	411¹/₃	417	236	213	184	370
Major League totals (9 years)	33	36	.478	4.72	439	9	0	0	32	494	494	285	259	222	449

DIVISION SERIES RECORD

Year League	W	L	Pct.	ERA	G	GS	CG	ShO	Sv.	IP	H	R	ER	BB	SO
1998— San Diego (N.L.)	1	1	.500	2.70	3	0	0	0	0	3¹/₃	2	1	1	0	4

CHAMPIONSHIP SERIES RECORD

Year League	W	L	Pct.	ERA	G	GS	CG	ShO	Sv.	IP	H	R	ER	BB	SO
1998— San Diego (N.L.)	0	0	...	13.50	3	0	0	0	0	²/₃	4	1	1	0	1

WORLD SERIES RECORD

Year League	W	L	Pct.	ERA	G	GS	CG	ShO	Sv.	IP	H	R	ER	BB	SO
1998— San Diego (N.L.)	0	0	...	0.00	2	0	0	0	0	1²/₃	2	0	0	2	1

MICHAELS, JASON OF PHILLIES

PERSONAL: Born May 4, 1976, in Tampa, Fla. ... 6-0/205. ... Bats right, throws right. ... Full name: Jason Drew Michaels. ... Grandson of John Michaels, pitcher with Boston Red Sox (1932).
HIGH SCHOOL: Jesuit (Tampa, Fla.).
JUNIOR COLLEGE: Okaloosa-Walton.
COLLEGE: Miami (Fla.).
TRANSACTIONS/CAREER NOTES: Selected by San Diego Padres organization in 49th round of free-agent draft (June 2, 1994); did not sign. ... Selected by Tampa Bay Devil Rays organization in 44th round of free-agent draft (June 4, 1996); did not sign. ... Selected by St. Louis Cardinals organization in 15th round of free-agent draft (June 3, 1997); did not sign. ... Selected by Philadelphia Phillies organization in fourth round of free-agent draft (June 2, 1998). ... On Scranton/Wilkes-Barre disabled list (May 1-10, 2001).

M

Year	Team (League)	Pos.	G	AB	R	H	2B	3B	HR	RBI	Avg.	BB	SO	SB	PO	A	E	Avg.
1998—	Batavia (NY-Penn)	OF	67	235	45	63	14	3	11	49	.268	40	69	4	93	1	5	.949
1999—	Clearwater (FSL)	OF	122	451	91	138	31	6	14	65	.306	68	103	10	247	12	1	.996
2000—	Reading (East.)	OF	113	437	71	129	30	4	10	74	.295	28	87	7	244	8	6	.977
2001—	Scranton/W.B. (I.L.) ...	OF	109	418	58	109	19	3	17	69	.261	37	126	11	168	4	0	1.000
	—Philadelphia (N.L.) ...	OF	6	6	0	1	0	0	0	1	.167	0	2	0	0	0	0	...
Major League totals (1 year)			6	6	0	1	0	0	0	1	.167	0	2	0	0	0	0	...

MICHALAK, CHRIS — P — RANGERS

PERSONAL: Born January 4, 1971, in Joliet, Ill. ... 6-3/195. ... Throws left, bats left. ... Full name: Christian Matthew Michalak.
HIGH SCHOOL: Joliet (Ill.) Catholic.
COLLEGE: Notre Dame.
TRANSACTIONS/CAREER NOTES: Selected by Oakland Athletics organization in 12th round of free-agent draft (June 3, 1993). ... Released by A's (April 1, 1997). ... Signed by Arizona Diamondbacks organization (April 8, 1997). ... Loaned to Tulsa, Texas Rangers organization by Diamondbacks (March 24-May 6, 1998). ... Granted free agency (October 17, 1998). ... Signed by Anaheim Angels organization (January 25, 1999). ... Released by Angels (June 19, 1999). ... Signed by Diamondbacks organization (June 23, 1999). ... Granted free agency (October 15, 1999). ... Signed by Tampa Bay Devil Rays organization (January 9, 2000). ... Released by Devil Rays (April 25, 2000). ... Signed by Los Angeles Dodgers organization (May 6, 2000). ... Granted free agency (October 18, 2000). ... Signed by Toronto Blue Jays organization (December 13, 2000). ... Claimed on waivers by Rangers (August 22, 2001).
STATISTICAL NOTES: Led A.L. with six balks in 2001.

Year	League	W	L	Pct.	ERA	G	GS	CG	ShO	Sv.	IP	H	R	ER	BB	SO
1993—	Southern Oregon (N'West.)	7	3	.700	2.85	16	15	0	0	0	79	77	41	25	36	57
1994—	West Michigan (Midw.)	5	3	.625	3.90	15	10	0	0	0	67	66	32	29	28	38
	—Modesto (Calif.)	5	3	.625	2.91	17	10	1	0	2	77 1/3	67	28	25	20	46
1995—	Huntsville (Sou.)	1	1	.500	11.12	7	0	0	0	1	5 2/3	10	7	7	5	4
	—Modesto (Calif.)	3	2	.600	2.62	44	0	0	0	0	65 1/3	56	26	19	27	49
1996—	Modesto (Calif.)	2	2	.500	3.03	21	0	0	0	4	38 2/3	37	21	13	17	39
	—Huntsville (Sou.)	4	0	1.000	7.71	21	0	0	0	0	23 1/3	32	29	20	26	15
1997—	High Desert (Calif.)■	3	7	.300	2.65	49	0	0	0	4	85	76	36	25	31	74
1998—	Tulsa (Texas)■	1	2	.333	1.83	10	0	0	0	0	19 2/3	10	4	4	2	15
	—Tucson (PCL)■	3	8	.273	5.03	29	9	0	0	0	73 1/3	91	47	41	29	50
	—Arizona (N.L.)	0	0	...	11.81	5	0	0	0	0	5 1/3	9	7	7	4	5
1999—	Edmonton (PCL)■	1	0	1.000	5.72	24	0	0	0	0	28 1/3	28	20	18	14	25
	—Tucson (PCL)■	5	0	1.000	3.66	21	6	0	0	3	64	64	30	26	26	41
2000—	Durham (I.L.)■	0	0	...	5.68	6	0	0	0	0	6 1/3	6	4	4	1	7
	—Albuquerque (PCL)■........	11	3	.786	4.26	23	21	1	0	0	133	166	72	63	55	83
2001—	Toronto (A.L.)■..............	6	7	.462	4.62	24	18	0	0	0	115	133	66	59	49	57
	—Texas (A.L.)■................	2	2	.500	3.32	11	0	0	0	1	21 2/3	24	8	8	6	10
A.L. totals (1 year)		8	9	.471	4.41	35	18	0	0	1	136 2/3	157	74	67	55	67
N.L. totals (1 year)		0	0	...	11.81	5	0	0	0	0	5 1/3	9	7	7	4	5
Major League totals (2 years)		8	9	.471	4.69	40	18	0	0	1	142	166	81	74	59	72

MIDDLEBROOK, JASON — P — PADRES

PERSONAL: Born June 26, 1975, in Jackson, Mich. ... 6-3/215. ... Throws right, bats right. ... Full name: Jason Douglas Middlebrook.
HIGH SCHOOL: Grass Lake (Mich.).
COLLEGE: Stanford.
TRANSACTIONS/CAREER NOTES: Selected by New York Mets organization in 18th round of free-agent draft (June 3, 1993); did not sign. ... Selected by San Diego Padres organization in ninth round of free-agent draft (June 4, 1996). ... On Rancho Cucamonga disabled list (April 8-June 25, 1999). ... On Mobile disabled list (May 8-June 2, 2000). ... Claimed on waivers by Mets (October 5, 2000). ... Claimed on waivers by Padres (November 22, 2000). ... On Mobile disabled list (May 22-June 1, 2001).

Year	League	W	L	Pct.	ERA	G	GS	CG	ShO	Sv.	IP	H	R	ER	BB	SO
1997—	Rancho Cuca. (Calif.)	0	2	.000	4.03	6	6	0	0	0	22 1/3	29	15	10	12	18
	—Clinton (Midw.)	6	4	.600	3.98	14	14	2	1	0	81 1/3	76	46	36	39	86
1998—	Rancho Cuca. (Calif.)	10	12	.455	4.92	28	•28	0	0	0	150	162	99	82	63	132
1999—	Arizona Padres (Ariz.)	1	0	1.000	7.20	1	1	0	0	0	5	9	5	4	1	3
	—Mobile (Sou.)	4	6	.400	8.06	13	13	0	0	0	63 2/3	78	59	57	30	38
2000—	Mobile (Sou.)	5	13	.278	6.15	24	24	0	0	0	120	133	89	82	52	75
	—Las Vegas (PCL)	0	1	.000	216.00	1	1	0	0	0	1/3	8	8	8	0	0
2001—	Mobile (Sou.)	3	0	1.000	1.20	10	9	0	0	0	52 1/3	36	10	7	9	51
	—Portland (PCL)	7	4	.636	3.29	15	15	0	0	0	90 1/3	86	34	33	23	66
	—San Diego (N.L.)	2	1	.667	5.12	4	3	0	0	0	19 1/3	18	11	11	10	10
Major League totals (1 year)		2	1	.667	5.12	4	3	0	0	0	19 1/3	18	11	11	10	10

MIENTKIEWICZ, DOUG — 1B — TWINS

PERSONAL: Born June 19, 1974, in Toledo, Ohio. ... 6-2/200. ... Bats left, throws right. ... Full name: Douglas Andrew Mientkiewicz. ... Name pronounced mint-KAY-vich.
HIGH SCHOOL: Westminster Christian (Miami).
COLLEGE: Florida State.
TRANSACTIONS/CAREER NOTES: Selected by Minnesota Twins organization in fifth round of free-agent draft (June 1, 1995).
HONORS: Won A.L. Gold Glove at first base (2001).
STATISTICAL NOTES: Led Florida State League first basemen with 1,271 total chances and 113 double plays in 1996. ... Led Eastern League first basemen with .995 fielding percentage in 1997. ... Had 15-game hitting streak (April 16-May 2, 2001).
MISCELLANEOUS: Member of 2000 U.S. Olympic baseball team.

Year	Team (League)	Pos.	G	AB	R	H	2B	3B	HR	RBI	Avg.	BB	SO	SB	PO	A	E	Avg.
1995— Fort Myers (FSL)		1B	38	110	9	27	6	1	1	15	.245	18	19	2	160	12	1	.994
1996— Fort Myers (FSL)		1B	133	492	69	143	•36	4	5	79	.291	66	47	12	*1183	85	3	*.998
1997— New Britain (East.)		1B-OF	132	467	87	119	28	2	15	61	.255	*98	67	21	989	63	5	†.995
1998— New Britain (East.)		1B-OF	139	502	*96	162	*45	0	16	88	*.323	96	58	11	1171	92	12	.991
— Minnesota (A.L.)		1B	8	25	1	5	1	0	0	2	.200	4	3	1	61	3	0	1.000
1999— Minnesota (A.L.)		1B	118	327	34	75	21	3	2	32	.229	43	51	1	882	50	3	*.997
2000— Salt Lake (PCL)	1B-3B-2B-OF	130	485	96	162	32	3	18	96	.334	61	68	9	786	154	10	.989
— Minnesota (A.L.)		1B	3	14	0	6	0	0	0	4	.429	0	0	0	22	0	0	1.000
2001— Minnesota (A.L.)		1B-DH	151	543	77	166	39	1	15	74	.306	67	92	2	1263	69	4	.997
Major League totals (4 years)			280	909	112	252	61	4	17	112	.277	114	146	4	2228	122	7	.997

MIESES, JOSE   P   BREWERS

PERSONAL: Born October 14, 1979, in Santo Domingo, Dominican Republic. ... 6-1/165. ... Throws right, bats right. ... Full name: Jose Rincon Mieses.

TRANSACTIONS/CAREER NOTES: Signed as non-drafted free agent by Milwaukee Brewers organization (November 2, 1996). ... On Indianapolis disabled list (May 15-August 15, 2001). ... On Beloit disabled list (August 21-September 6, 2001).

Year	League	W	L	Pct.	ERA	G	GS	CG	ShO	Sv.	IP	H	R	ER	BB	SO
1997— Dominican Brewers (DSL)..		3	2	.600	2.40	20	5	0	0	1	56 1/3	34	22	15	36	49
1998— Dominican Brewers (DSL)..		4	5	.444	3.00	14	13	3	0	0	84	70	39	28	38	77
1999— Helena (Pio.)		*10	2	.833	*2.67	15	15	*3	•1	0	*108	79	36	32	28	87
2000— Beloit (Midw.)		13	6	.684	2.53	21	21	2	2	0	135	107	43	38	37	132
— Mudville (Calif.)		4	1	.800	2.65	6	6	0	0	0	34	25	11	10	18	40
2001— Huntsville (Sou.)		0	0	...	2.22	5	4	0	0	0	24 1/3	21	7	6	3	35
— Indianapolis (I.L.)...............		0	3	.000	6.07	3	3	0	0	0	13 1/3	23	12	9	7	13
— Arizona Brewers (Ariz.)		0	1	.000	0.00	2	2	0	0	0	4 1/3	3	1	0	1	5
— Ogden (Pio.)......................		0	1	.000	27.00	1	1	0	0	0	1	3	3	3	1	2

MILLAR, KEVIN   OF/1B   MARLINS

PERSONAL: Born September 24, 1971, in Los Angeles. ... 6-0/210. ... Bats right, throws right. ... Full name: Kevin Charles Millar. ... Nephew of Wayne Nordhagen, outfielder with four major league teams (1976-83). ... Name pronounced mi-LAR.

HIGH SCHOOL: University (Los Angeles).

JUNIOR COLLEGE: Los Angeles Community College.

COLLEGE: Lamar.

TRANSACTIONS/CAREER NOTES: Contract sold by St. Paul, Northern League to Florida Marlins organization (September 20, 1993). ... Granted free agency (December 21, 1997). ... Re-signed by Marlins (December 21, 1997). ... On Florida disabled list (April 19, 1998-remainder of season); included rehabilitation assignment to Charlotte (June 14-29).

HONORS: Named Eastern League Player of the Year (1997).

STATISTICAL NOTES: Led Midwest League with 240 total bases in 1994. ... Led Florida State League with 10 sacrifice flies in 1995. ... Led Florida State League first basemen with 1,320 total chances and 134 double plays in 1995. ... Led Eastern League with 309 total bases and .423 on-base percentage and tied for league lead with seven sacrifice flies in 1997. ... Led Eastern League first basemen with 93 assists and 116 double plays in 1997. ... Career major league grand slams: 2.

Year	Team (League)	Pos.	G	AB	R	H	2B	3B	HR	RBI	Avg.	BB	SO	SB	PO	A	E	Avg.
1993— St. Paul (Nor.)	3B-2B	63	227	33	59	11	1	5	30	.260	24	27	2	51	133	18	.911
1994— Kane Co. (Midw.)■	1B	135	477	75	144	35	2	19	93	.302	74	48	3	1010	64	11	.990
1995— Brevard County (FSL).	1B	129	459	53	132	32	2	13	68	.288	70	66	4	*1213	95	12	.991
1996— Portland (East.)	1B-3B	130	472	69	150	32	0	18	86	.318	37	53	6	753	134	15	.983
1997— Portland (East.)	1B-3B	135	511	94	*175	*34	2	32	*131	*.342	66	53	2	1146	†121	17	.987
1998— Florida (N.L.).............	3B	2	2	1	1	0	0	0	0	.500	1	0	0	2	3	1	.833
— Charlotte (I.L.)............	3B-1B	14	46	14	15	3	0	4	15	.326	9	7	1	34	19	4	.930
1999— Calgary (PCL)............	OF-3B-1B	36	143	24	43	11	1	7	26	.301	11	19	2	63	9	2	.973
— Florida (N.L.)............	1B-3B-OF	105	351	48	100	17	4	9	67	.285	40	64	1	720	53	4	.995
2000— Florida (N.L.).............1B-OF-3B-DH	123	259	36	67	14	3	14	42	.259	36	47	0	269	52	5	.985
2001— Florida (N.L.)............OF-1B-3B-DH	144	449	62	141	39	5	20	85	.314	39	70	0	268	19	2	.993
Major League totals (4 years)		374	1061	147	309	70	12	43	194	.291	116	181	1	1259	127	12	.991

MILLER, CORKY   C   REDS

PERSONAL: Born March 18, 1976, in Yucaipa, Calif. ... 6-1/225. ... Bats right, throws right. ... Full name: Abraham Philip Miller.

HIGH SCHOOL: Yucaipa (Calif.).

JUNIOR COLLEGE: San Bernardino Valley.

COLLEGE: Nevada-Reno.

TRANSACTIONS/CAREER NOTES: Signed as non-drafted free agent by Cincinnati Reds organization (June 5, 1998).

STATISTICAL NOTES: Led Pioneer League catchers with six double plays in 1998. ... Led Midwest League catchers with six double plays in 1999. ... Tied for Midwest League lead in hit by pitch with 20 in 1999. ... Led Southern League catchers with 851 total chances in 2000. ... Tied for Southern League lead in passed balls with 11 in 2000. ... Led Southern League in being hit by pitch with 30 in 2001.

Year	Team (League)	Pos.	G	AB	R	H	2B	3B	HR	RBI	Avg.	BB	SO	SB	PO	A	E	Avg.
1998— Billings (Pio.)	C	45	129	28	35	8	0	5	24	.271	24	24	1	319	48	*14	.963
1999— Rockford (Midw.).......	C	66	195	43	56	10	1	10	40	.287	33	42	3	497	60	*14	.975
— Chattanooga (Sou.)....	C	33	104	20	23	10	0	4	16	.221	11	30	0	227	35	3	.989
2000— Chattanooga (Sou.)....	C	103	317	40	74	18	0	9	44	.233	41	51	5	*732	103	*16	.981
2001— Chattanooga (Sou.)....	C	59	170	25	47	12	0	9	42	.276	25	32	1	432	39	7	.985
— Louisville (I.L.)	C	44	144	30	50	11	0	7	28	.347	10	19	2	294	35	2	.994
— Cincinnati (N.L.)	C	17	49	5	9	2	0	3	7	.184	4	16	1	104	12	1	.991
Major League totals (1 year)		17	49	5	9	2	0	3	7	.184	4	16	1	104	12	1	.991

PERSONAL: Born October 13, 1969, in La Crosse, Wis. ... 6-2/212. ... Bats right, throws right. ... Full name: Damian Donald Miller.
HIGH SCHOOL: West Salem (Wis.).
COLLEGE: Viterbo (Wis.).
TRANSACTIONS/CAREER NOTES: Selected by Minnesota Twins organization in 20th round of free-agent draft (June 4, 1990). ... Selected by Arizona Diamondbacks in second round (47th pick overall) of expansion draft (November 18, 1997).
RECORDS: Shares major league single-game records for most double plays (nine-inning game)—3 (May 25, 1999); and most double plays started (nine-inning game)—3 (May 25, 1999).
STATISTICAL NOTES: Led Pacific Coast League catchers with .998 fielding percentage in 1995. ... Led Pacific Coast League catchers with 70 assists and 695 total chances in 1996. ... Tied for N.L. lead with 11 passed balls in 1999. ... Career major league grand slams: 3.

							BATTING							FIELDING			
Year	Team (League)	Pos.	G	AB	R	H	2B	3B	HR	RBI	Avg.	BB	SO	SB	PO	A	E	Avg.
1990—Elizabethton (Appl.)....		C	14	45	7	10	1	0	1	6	.222	9	3	1	102	6	2	.982
1991—Kenosha (Midw.)........		C-1B-OF	80	267	28	62	11	1	3	34	.232	24	53	3	357	52	4	.990
1992—Kenosha (Midw.)........		C	115	377	53	110	27	2	5	56	.292	53	66	6	696	89	9	.989
1993—Fort Myers (FSL)........		C	87	325	31	69	12	1	1	26	.212	31	44	6	465	62	8	.985
—Nashville (Sou.)..........		C	4	13	0	3	0	0	0	0	.231	2	4	0	26	3	0	1.000
1994—Nashville (Sou.)........		C	103	328	36	88	10	0	8	35	.268	35	51	4	628	81	8	.989
1995—Salt Lake (PCL)........		C-OF	83	295	39	84	23	1	3	41	.285	15	39	2	395	52	1	†.998
1996—Salt Lake (PCL)........		C-1B	104	385	54	110	27	1	7	55	.286	25	58	1	630	†71	6	.992
1997—Salt Lake (PCL)........		C-DH	85	314	48	106	19	3	11	82	.338	29	62	6	445	35	6	.988
—Minnesota (A.L.)........		C-DH	25	66	5	18	1	0	2	13	.273	2	12	0	85	3	0	1.000
1998—Tucson (PCL)■.........		C	18	63	14	22	7	1	0	11	.349	9	9	0	95	15	3	.973
—Arizona (N.L.).........C-DH-OF-1B			57	168	17	48	14	2	3	14	.286	11	43	1	255	27	4	.986
1999—Arizona (N.L.)............		C	86	296	35	80	19	0	11	47	.270	19	78	0	622	61	6	.991
2000—Arizona (N.L.)............		C-1B	100	324	43	89	24	0	10	44	.275	36	74	2	683	47	7	.991
2001—Arizona (N.L.)............		C	123	380	45	103	19	0	13	47	.271	35	80	0	966	81	7	.993
American League totals (1 year)			25	66	5	18	1	0	2	13	.273	2	12	0	85	3	0	1.000
National League totals (4 years)			366	1168	140	320	76	2	37	152	.274	101	275	3	2526	216	24	.991
Major League totals (5 years)			391	1234	145	338	77	2	39	165	.274	103	287	3	2611	219	24	.992

DIVISION SERIES RECORD

							BATTING							FIELDING			
Year	Team (League)	Pos.	G	AB	R	H	2B	3B	HR	RBI	Avg.	BB	SO	SB	PO	A	E	Avg.
2001—Arizona (N.L.)............		C	5	15	1	4	0	0	0	0	.267	1	3	0	39	3	0	1.000

CHAMPIONSHIP SERIES RECORD

							BATTING							FIELDING			
Year	Team (League)	Pos.	G	AB	R	H	2B	3B	HR	RBI	Avg.	BB	SO	SB	PO	A	E	Avg.
2001—Arizona (N.L.)............		C	5	17	0	3	0	0	0	0	.176	2	5	0	38	1	0	1.000

WORLD SERIES RECORD

RECORDS: Shares record for most consecutive strikeouts in one series—5 (November 3 [2] and 4 [3], 2000).
NOTES: Member of World Series championship team (2001).

							BATTING							FIELDING			
Year	Team (League)	Pos.	G	AB	R	H	2B	3B	HR	RBI	Avg.	BB	SO	SB	PO	A	E	Avg.
2001—Arizona (N.L.)............		C	6	21	3	4	2	0	0	2	.190	1	11	0	54	0	1	.982

M

PERSONAL: Born September 30, 1979, in Aurora, Ill. ... 6-5/215. ... Throws left, bats left. ... Full name: Gregory Thomas Miller.
HIGH SCHOOL: West (Aurora, Ill.).
TRANSACTIONS/CAREER NOTES: Selected by Boston Red Sox organization in fifth round of free-agent draft (June 3, 1997). ... Traded with SS Adam Everett by Red Sox to Houston Astros for OF Carl Everett (December 15, 1999). ... On disabled list (April 5-18 and May 11-July 18, 2001).

Year	League	W	L	Pct.	ERA	G	GS	CG	ShO	Sv.	IP	H	R	ER	BB	SO
1997—Gulf Coast Red Sox (GCL)..		0	2	.000	3.72	4	4	0	0	0	9²/₃	8	6	4	6	6
1998—Gulf Coast Red Sox (GCL)..		6	0	1.000	2.49	11	7	0	0	0	43¹/₃	33	18	12	18	47
1999—Augusta (S.Atl.)............		10	6	.625	3.10	25	25	1	0	0	136²/₃	109	54	47	56	146
2000—Kissimmee (FSL)............		10	8	.556	3.70	24	24	1	0	0	146	131	63	60	46	109
—Round Rock (Texas)..........		0	0	...	0.00	2	0	0	0	0	2¹/₃	0	0	0	1	2
2001—Round Rock (Texas)..........		5	3	.625	3.25	14	14	0	0	0	55¹/₃	38	22	20	35	37

PERSONAL: Born August 27, 1977, in Torrance, Calif. ... 6-2/195. ... Throws right, bats right. ... Full name: Justin M. Miller.
HIGH SCHOOL: Torrance (Calif.).
JUNIOR COLLEGE: Los Angeles Harbor College.
TRANSACTIONS/CAREER NOTES: Selected by San Francisco Giants organization in 34th round of free-agent draft (June 1, 1995); did not sign. ... Selected by Colorado Rockies organization in fifth round of free-agent draft (June 3, 1997). ... On Salem disabled list (May 5-June 18, 1999). ... Traded by Rockies with cash to Oakland Athletics as part of three-way deal in which Brewers received P Jimmy Haynes from A's, Rockies received 3B Jeff Cirillo, P Scott Karl and cash from Brewers and Brewers received P Jamey Wright and C Henry Blanco from Rockies (December 13, 1999). ... On Midland disabled list (June 8-17 and June 22-30, 2000). ... Traded by A's with 3B Eric Hinske to Toronto Blue Jays for P Billy Koch (December 7, 2001).
STATISTICAL NOTES: Led Pacific Coast League with 16 hit batsmen in 2001.

Year League	W	L	Pct.	ERA	G	GS	CG	ShO	Sv.	IP	H	R	ER	BB	SO
1997—Portland (N'West)	4	2	.667	*2.14	14	11	0	0	0	67 1/3	68	26	16	20	54
1998—Asheville (S.Atl.)	13	8	.619	3.69	27	27	3	1	0	163 1/3	177	89	67	40	142
1999—Salem (Caro.)	1	2	.333	4.14	8	8	0	0	0	37	35	18	17	11	35
2000—Midland (Texas)■...............	5	4	.556	4.55	18	18	0	0	0	87	74	49	44	41	82
— Sacramento (PCL)	4	1	.800	2.47	9	9	0	0	0	54 2/3	42	18	15	13	34
2001— Sacramento (PCL)	7	10	.412	4.75	29	28	1	0	0	165	174	94	87	64	134

MILLER, MATT   P

PERSONAL: Born August 2, 1974, in Lubbock, Texas. ... 6-3/175. ... Throws left, bats left. ... Full name: Matthew Lincoln Miller.

HIGH SCHOOL: Monterey (Lubbock, Texas).

COLLEGE: Texas Tech.

TRANSACTIONS/CAREER NOTES: Selected by Detroit Tigers organization in second round of free-agent draft (June 4, 1996). ... On disabled list (April 3, 1997-entire season). ... On disabled list (April 25-June 3, 2000). ... On Toledo disabled list (May 31-June 18, 2001). ... Granted free agency (October 15, 2001).

Year League	W	L	Pct.	ERA	G	GS	CG	ShO	Sv.	IP	H	R	ER	BB	SO
1996—Jamestown (NY-Penn)	1	3	.250	4.62	6	6	0	0	0	25 1/3	33	16	13	13	21
1997—					Did not play.										
1998—West Michigan (Midw.)	7	4	.636	1.52	14	14	3	0	0	95	59	20	16	26	102
— Jacksonville (Sou.).............	3	7	.300	7.04	13	13	0	0	0	61 1/3	70	49	48	50	49
1999—Lakeland (FSL)	4	9	.308	4.15	19	19	1	0	0	108 1/3	108	58	50	45	82
— Jacksonville (Sou.).............	4	1	.800	4.43	7	7	0	0	0	40 2/3	43	23	20	12	25
2000—Jacksonville (Sou.).............	8	5	.615	3.18	20	20	1	0	0	121 2/3	126	50	43	32	99
2001—Toledo (I.L.)	1	2	.333	2.87	50	0	0	0	4	62 2/3	60	26	20	18	49
— Detroit (A.L.)	0	0	...	7.45	13	0	0	0	0	9 2/3	16	8	8	4	6
Major League totals (1 year)........	0	0	...	7.45	13	0	0	0	0	9 2/3	16	8	8	4	6

MILLER, TRAVIS   P   TWINS

PERSONAL: Born November 2, 1972, in Dayton, Ohio. ... 6-3/215. ... Throws left, bats right. ... Full name: Travis Eugene Miller.

HIGH SCHOOL: National Trail (New Paris, Ohio).

COLLEGE: Kent.

TRANSACTIONS/CAREER NOTES: Selected by Minnesota Twins organization in supplemental round ("sandwich pick" between first and second round, 34th pick overall) of free-agent draft (June 2, 1994); pick received as compensation for Twins failing to sign 1993 first-round pick C Jason Varitek. ... On Salt Lake disabled list (April 20-May 3, 1998).

Year League	W	L	Pct.	ERA	G	GS	CG	ShO	Sv.	IP	H	R	ER	BB	SO
1994—Fort Wayne (Midw.)............	4	1	.800	2.60	11	9	1	0	0	55 1/3	52	17	16	12	50
— Nashville (Sou.)..................	0	0	...	2.84	1	1	0	0	0	6 1/3	3	3	2	2	4
1995—New Britain (East.)	7	9	.438	4.37	28	27	1	1	0	162 2/3	*172	93	79	65	151
1996—Minnesota (A.L.)	1	2	.333	9.23	7	7	0	0	0	26 1/3	45	29	27	9	15
— Salt Lake (PCL)	8	10	.444	4.83	27	27	1	0	0	160 1/3	187	97	86	57	*143
1997—Salt Lake (PCL)	10	6	.625	4.73	21	21	0	0	0	125 2/3	140	73	66	57	86
— Minnesota (A.L.)	1	5	.167	7.63	13	7	0	0	0	48 1/3	64	49	41	23	26
1998—Salt Lake (PCL)	3	4	.429	4.84	34	2	0	0	9	57 2/3	60	33	31	31	65
— Minnesota (A.L.)	0	2	.000	3.86	14	0	0	0	0	23 1/3	25	10	10	11	23
1999—Salt Lake (PCL)	1	2	.333	2.50	16	0	0	0	1	18	16	7	5	6	19
— Minnesota (A.L.)	2	2	.500	2.72	52	0	0	0	0	49 2/3	55	19	15	16	40
2000—Minnesota (A.L.)	2	3	.400	3.90	67	0	0	0	1	67	83	35	29	32	62
2001—Minnesota (A.L.)	1	4	.200	4.81	45	0	0	0	0	48 2/3	54	30	26	20	30
Major League totals (6 years).......	7	18	.280	5.06	198	14	0	0	1	263 1/3	326	172	148	111	196

M

MILLER, WADE   P   ASTROS

PERSONAL: Born September 13, 1976, in Reading, Pa. ... 6-2/185. ... Throws right, bats right. ... Full name: Wade T. Miller.

HIGH SCHOOL: Brandywine Heights (Pa.).

COLLEGE: Alvernia (Pa.) College.

TRANSACTIONS/CAREER NOTES: Selected by Houston Astros organization in 20th round of free-agent draft (June 4, 1996). ... On disabled list (June 1, 1998-remainder of season). ... On New Orleans disabled list (May 16-25, 2000).

Year League	W	L	Pct.	ERA	G	GS	CG	ShO	Sv.	IP	H	R	ER	BB	SO
1996—Auburn (NY-Penn)...............	1	1	.500	5.00	2	2	0	0	0	9	8	9	5	4	11
— Gulf Coast Astros (GCL)......	3	4	.429	3.79	11	10	0	0	0	57	49	26	24	12	53
1997—Quad City (Midw.)...............	5	3	.625	3.36	10	8	2	0	0	59	45	27	22	10	50
— Kissimmee (FSL).................	10	2	.833	1.80	14	14	4	1	0	100	79	28	20	14	76
1998—Jackson (Texas)	5	0	1.000	2.32	10	10	0	0	0	62	49	23	16	27	48
1999—New Orleans (PCL)..............	11	9	.550	4.38	26	26	2	0	0	162 1/3	156	85	79	64	135
— Houston (N.L.)	0	1	.000	9.58	5	1	0	0	0	10 1/3	17	11	11	5	8
2000—New Orleans (PCL)..............	4	5	.444	3.67	16	15	0	0	0	105 1/3	95	46	43	38	81
— Houston (N.L.)	6	6	.500	5.14	16	16	2	0	0	105	104	66	60	42	89
2001—Houston (N.L.)	16	8	.667	3.40	32	32	1	0	0	212	183	91	80	76	183
Major League totals (3 years).......	22	15	.595	4.15	53	49	3	0	0	327 1/3	304	168	151	123	280

DIVISION SERIES RECORD

Year League	W	L	Pct.	ERA	G	GS	CG	ShO	Sv.	IP	H	R	ER	BB	SO
2001—Houston (N.L.)	0	0	...	2.57	1	1	0	0	0	7	7	2	2	0	6

PERSONAL: Born October 18, 1966, in Lakeland, Fla. ... 6-1/195. ... Throws right, bats right. ... Full name: Alan Bernard Mills.
HIGH SCHOOL: Kathleen (Fla.).
JUNIOR COLLEGE: Polk Community College (Fla.).
COLLEGE: Tuskegee.
TRANSACTIONS/CAREER NOTES: Selected by Boston Red Sox organization in first round (13th pick overall) of free-agent draft (January 14, 1986); did not sign. ... Selected by California Angels organization in secondary phase of free-agent draft (June 2, 1986). ... Traded by Angels to New York Yankees (June 22, 1987), completing deal in which Angels traded P Ron Romanick and a player to be named later to Yankees for C Butch Wynegar (December 19, 1986). ... Traded by Yankees to Baltimore Orioles for two players to be named later (February 29, 1992); Yankees acquired P Francisco de la Rosa (February 29, 1992) and P Mark Carper (June 8, 1992) to complete deal. ... On suspended list (June 26-30, 1993). ... On Rochester disabled list (July 4-September 16, 1995). ... On disabled list (March 22-May 12, 1996; and April 10-June 15, 1997). ... On suspended list (May 29-30, 1998). ... Granted free agency (October 23, 1998). ... Signed by Los Angeles Dodgers (December 10, 1998). ... Traded by Dodgers with cash considerations to Orioles for P Al Reyes (June 13, 2000). ... On Baltimore disabled list (August 11-30, 2000); included rehabilitation assignment to Frederick (August 28-30). ... On Baltimore disabled list (March 30-July 12, 2001); included rehabilitation asssignments to Frederick (June 8-12 and June 22-28) and Bowie (June 13-22 and June 28-July 6). ... Granted free agency (November 5, 2001).

Year League	W	L	Pct.	ERA	G	GS	CG	ShO	Sv.	IP	H	R	ER	BB	SO
1986— Salem (N'West)	6	6	.500	4.63	14	14	1	0	0	83 2/3	77	58	43	60	50
1987— Prince William (Caro.)■	2	11	.154	6.09	35	8	0	0	1	85 2/3	102	75	58	64	53
1988— Prince William (Caro.)	3	8	.273	4.13	42	5	0	0	4	93 2/3	93	56	43	43	59
1989— Prince William (Caro.)	6	1	.857	0.91	26	0	0	0	7	39 2/3	22	5	4	13	44
— Fort Lauderdale (FSL)	1	4	.200	3.77	22	0	0	0	6	31	40	15	13	9	25
1990— New York (A.L.)	1	5	.167	4.10	36	0	0	0	0	41 2/3	48	21	19	33	24
— Columbus (I.L.)	3	3	.500	3.38	17	0	0	0	6	29 1/3	22	11	11	14	30
1991— Columbus (I.L.)	7	5	.583	4.43	38	15	0	0	8	113 2/3	109	65	56	75	77
— New York (A.L.)	1	1	.500	4.41	6	2	0	0	0	16 1/3	16	9	8	8	11
1992— Rochester (I.L.)■	0	1	.000	5.40	3	0	0	0	1	5	6	3	3	2	8
— Baltimore (A.L.)	10	4	.714	2.61	35	3	0	0	2	103 1/3	78	33	30	54	60
1993— Baltimore (A.L.)	5	4	.556	3.23	45	0	0	0	4	100 1/3	80	39	36	51	68
1994— Baltimore (A.L.)	3	3	.500	5.16	47	0	0	0	2	45 1/3	43	26	26	24	44
1995— Baltimore (A.L.)	3	0	1.000	7.43	21	0	0	0	0	23	30	20	19	18	16
— Rochester (I.L.)	0	1	.000	0.00	1	1	0	0	0	2 2/3	2	6	0	5	2
— Gulf Coast Orioles (GCL)	0	0	...	0.00	1	1	0	0	0	2	3	0	0	2	1
1996— Baltimore (A.L.)	3	2	.600	4.28	49	0	0	0	3	54 2/3	40	26	26	35	50
1997— Baltimore (A.L.)	2	3	.400	4.89	39	0	0	0	0	38 2/3	41	23	21	33	32
1998— Baltimore (A.L.)	3	4	.429	3.74	72	0	0	0	2	77	55	32	32	50	57
1999— Los Angeles (N.L.)■	3	4	.429	3.73	68	0	0	0	0	72 1/3	70	33	30	43	49
2000— Los Angeles (N.L.)	2	1	.667	4.21	18	0	0	0	1	25 2/3	31	12	12	16	18
— Baltimore (A.L.)■	2	0	1.000	6.46	23	0	0	0	1	23 2/3	25	17	17	19	18
— Frederick (Caro.)	0	0	...	4.50	1	1	0	0	0	2	2	1	1	0	1
2001— Frederick (Caro.)	0	0	...	1.80	5	0	0	0	1	5	3	4	1	0	10
— Bowie (East.)	0	0	...	2.25	7	0	0	0	0	8	5	2	2	3	10
— Baltimore (A.L.)	1	1	.500	9.64	15	0	0	0	0	14	20	15	15	11	9
A.L. totals (11 years)	34	27	.557	4.17	388	5	0	0	14	538	476	261	249	336	389
N.L. totals (2 years)	5	5	.500	3.86	86	0	0	0	1	98	101	45	42	59	67
Major League totals (12 years)	39	32	.549	4.12	474	5	0	0	15	636	577	306	291	395	456

DIVISION SERIES RECORD

Year League	W	L	Pct.	ERA	G	GS	CG	ShO	Sv.	IP	H	R	ER	BB	SO
1996— Baltimore (A.L.)							Did not play.								
1997— Baltimore (A.L.)	0	0	...	0.00	1	0	0	0	0	1	1	0	0	0	1

CHAMPIONSHIP SERIES RECORD

Year League	W	L	Pct.	ERA	G	GS	CG	ShO	Sv.	IP	H	R	ER	BB	SO
1996— Baltimore (A.L.)	0	0	...	3.86	3	0	0	0	0	2 1/3	3	1	1	1	3
1997— Baltimore (A.L.)	0	1	.000	2.70	3	0	0	0	0	3 1/3	1	1	1	2	3
Champ. series totals (2 years)	0	1	.000	3.18	6	0	0	0	0	5 2/3	4	2	2	3	6

PERSONAL: Born July 21, 1977, in Peoria, Ill. ... 6-5/205. ... Throws right, bats left. ... Full name: Ryan Adam Mills.
HIGH SCHOOL: Horizon (Scottsdale, Ariz.).
COLLEGE: Arizona State.
TRANSACTIONS/CAREER NOTES: Selected by Minnesota Twins organization in first round (sixth pick overall) of free-agent draft (June 2, 1998). ... On disabled list (May 25, 2001-remainder of season).
STATISTICAL NOTES: Led Florida State League with 20 wild pitches in 1999.

Year League	W	L	Pct.	ERA	G	GS	CG	ShO	Sv.	IP	H	R	ER	BB	SO
1998— Fort Myers (FSL)	0	0	...	1.80	2	2	0	0	0	5	2	3	1	1	3
1999— Fort Myers (FSL)	3	10	.231	8.87	27	21	0	0	0	95 1/3	121	107	•94	87	70
2000— Quad City (Midw.)	3	6	.333	3.53	20	20	0	0	0	119 2/3	101	54	47	64	110
— New Britain (East.)	0	7	.000	9.28	8	8	0	0	0	32	47	49	33	34	21
2001— New Britain (East.)	2	5	.286	6.42	8	8	0	0	0	40 2/3	45	31	29	14	29

PERSONAL: Born December 24, 1974, in Gastonia, N.C. ... 6-4/220. ... Throws right, bats right. ... Full name: Kevin Austin Millwood.
HIGH SCHOOL: Bessemer City (N.C.).
TRANSACTIONS/CAREER NOTES: Selected by Atlanta Braves organization in 11th round of free-agent draft (June 3, 1993). ... On Atlanta disabled list (May 7-July 20, 2001); included rehabilitation assignments to Macon (July 4-9) and Greenville (July 10-20).
STATISTICAL NOTES: Pitched 6-0 one-hit, complete-game victory against Pittsburgh (April 14, 1998).

M

Year League	W	L	Pct.	ERA	G	GS	CG	ShO	Sv.	IP	H	R	ER	BB	SO
1993— Gulf Coast Braves (GCL)	3	3	.500	3.06	12	9	0	0	0	50	36	27	17	28	49
1994— Danville (Appl.)................	3	3	.500	3.72	13	5	0	0	1	46	42	25	19	34	56
— Macon (S.Atl.)	0	5	.000	5.79	12	4	0	0	1	32²/₃	31	31	21	32	24
1995— Macon (S.Atl.)	5	6	.455	4.63	29	12	0	0	0	103	86	65	53	57	89
1996— Durham (Caro.)	6	9	.400	4.28	33	20	1	0	1	149¹/₃	138	77	71	58	139
1997— Greenville (Sou.)	3	5	.375	4.11	11	11	0	0	0	61¹/₃	59	37	28	24	61
— Richmond (I.L.)................	7	0	1.000	1.93	9	9	1	0	0	60²/₃	38	13	13	16	46
— Atlanta (N.L.).................	5	3	.625	4.03	12	8	0	0	0	51¹/₃	55	26	23	21	42
1998— Atlanta (N.L.)	17	8	.680	4.08	31	29	3	1	0	174¹/₃	175	86	79	56	163
1999— Atlanta (N.L.)	18	7	.720	2.68	33	33	2	0	0	228	168	80	68	59	205
2000— Atlanta (N.L.)	10	13	.435	4.66	36	•35	0	0	0	212²/₃	213	115	110	62	168
2001— Atlanta (N.L.)	7	7	.500	4.31	21	21	0	0	0	121	121	66	58	40	84
— Macon (S.Atl.)	0	0	...	0.00	1	1	0	0	0	3	0	0	0	0	5
— Greenville (Sou.)	0	1	.000	4.50	2	2	0	0	0	10	9	6	5	3	10
Major League totals (5 years)	57	38	.600	3.86	133	126	5	1	0	787¹/₃	732	373	338	238	662

DIVISION SERIES RECORD

Year League	W	L	Pct.	ERA	G	GS	CG	ShO	Sv.	IP	H	R	ER	BB	SO
1999— Atlanta (N.L.)	1	0	1.000	0.90	2	1	1	0	1	10	1	1	1	0	9
2000— Atlanta (N.L.)	0	1	.000	7.71	1	1	0	0	0	4²/₃	4	4	4	3	3
2001— Atlanta (N.L.)							Did not play.								
Division series totals (2 years)	1	1	.500	3.07	3	2	1	0	1	14²/₃	5	5	5	3	12

CHAMPIONSHIP SERIES RECORD

Year League	W	L	Pct.	ERA	G	GS	CG	ShO	Sv.	IP	H	R	ER	BB	SO
1999— Atlanta (N.L.)	1	0	1.000	3.55	2	2	0	0	0	12²/₃	13	6	5	1	9
2001— Atlanta (N.L.)	0	0	...	0.00	1	0	0	0	0	1	0	0	0	0	1
Champ. series totals (2 years)	1	0	1.000	3.29	3	2	0	0	0	13²/₃	13	6	5	1	10

WORLD SERIES RECORD

Year League	W	L	Pct.	ERA	G	GS	CG	ShO	Sv.	IP	H	R	ER	BB	SO
1999— Atlanta (N.L.)	0	1	.000	18.00	1	1	0	0	0	2	8	5	4	2	2

ALL-STAR GAME RECORD

Year League	W	L	Pct.	ERA	GS	CG	ShO	Sv.	IP	H	R	ER	BB	SO
1999— National	0	0	...	0.00	0	0	0	0	1	1	0	0	0	1

MILTON, ERIC   P   TWINS

PERSONAL: Born August 4, 1975, in State College, Pa. ... 6-3/220. ... Throws left, bats left. ... Full name: Eric Robert Milton.
HIGH SCHOOL: Bellefonte (Pa.).
COLLEGE: Maryland.
TRANSACTIONS/CAREER NOTES: Selected by New York Yankees organization in first round (20th pick overall) of free-agent draft (June 2, 1996). ... Traded by Yankees with P Danny Mota, OF Brian Buchanan, SS Cristian Guzman and cash to Minnesota Twins for 2B Chuck Knoblauch (February 6, 1998).
STATISTICAL NOTES: Tied for Eastern League lead with four balks in 1997. ... Pitched 7-0 no-hit victory against Anaheim (September 11, 1999).

Year League	W	L	Pct.	ERA	G	GS	CG	ShO	Sv.	IP	H	R	ER	BB	SO
1997— Tampa (FSL).....................	8	3	.727	3.09	14	14	1	0	0	93¹/₃	78	35	32	14	95
— Norwich (East.)	6	3	.667	3.13	14	14	1	0	0	77²/₃	59	29	27	36	67
1998— Minnesota (A.L.)■.............	8	14	.364	5.64	32	32	1	0	0	172¹/₃	195	113	108	70	107
1999— Minnesota (A.L.)	7	11	.389	4.49	34	34	5	2	0	206¹/₃	190	111	103	63	163
2000— Minnesota (A.L.)	13	10	.565	4.86	33	33	0	0	0	200	205	123	108	44	160
2001— Minnesota (A.L.)	15	7	.682	4.32	35	34	2	1	0	220²/₃	222	109	106	61	157
Major League totals (4 years)	43	42	.506	4.79	134	133	8	3	0	799¹/₃	812	456	425	238	587

ALL-STAR GAME RECORD

Year League	W	L	Pct.	ERA	GS	CG	ShO	Sv.	IP	H	R	ER	BB	SO
2001— American					Selected, did not play.									

MINOR, DAMON   1B   GIANTS

PERSONAL: Born January 9, 1975, in Canton, Ohio. ... 6-7/230. ... Bats left, throws left. ... Full name: Damon Reed Minor. ... Brother of Ryan Minor, third baseman, Seattle Mariners.
HIGH SCHOOL: Hammon (Okla.).
COLLEGE: Oklahoma.
TRANSACTIONS/CAREER NOTES: Selected by San Francisco Giants organization in 12th round of free-agent draft (June 4, 1996). ... On San Francisco disabled list (March 23-April 10, 2001).
STATISTICAL NOTES: Tied for Northwest League lead in intentional bases on balls received with four in 1996. ... Led Northwest League first basemen with 693 total chances and 56 double plays in 1996. ... Led California League with eight intentional bases in balls received in 1997. ... Led California League first basemen with 127 double plays and 1,371 total chances in 1997. ... Led Texas League first baseman with 1,273 total chances in 1999. ... Led Pacific Coast League with 1,205 total chances and 115 double plays in 2000.

Year Team (League)	Pos.	G	AB	R	H	2B	3B	HR	RBI	Avg.	BB	SO	SB	PO	A	E	Avg.
							BATTING								FIELDING		
1996— Bellingham (N'West) ..	1B	75	269	44	65	11	1	12	55	.242	47	86	0	*650	38	5	.993
1997— Bakersfield (Calif.)	1B	*140	532	98	154	34	1	31	99	.289	87	143	2	*1261	*88	*22	.984
1998— Shreveport (Texas).....	1B	81	289	39	69	11	1	14	52	.239	30	51	1	641	39	8	.988
— San Jose (Calif.).........	1B	48	176	26	50	10	1	7	36	.284	28	40	0	413	36	6	.987
1999— Shreveport (Texas).....	1B-DH	136	473	76	129	33	4	20	82	.273	80	115	1	*1160	*104	9	*.993
2000— Fresno (PCL)..............	1B	133	482	84	140	27	1	30	106	.290	87	97	0	*1134	60	11	.991
— San Francisco (N.L.) ..	1B-2B	10	9	3	4	0	0	3	6	.444	2	1	0	5	0	0	1.000
2001— San Francisco (N.L.) ..	1B	19	45	3	7	1	0	0	3	.156	3	8	0	86	4	1	.989
— Fresno (PCL)..............	1B-OF	112	406	74	125	22	3	24	71	.308	44	83	1	804	69	11	.988
Major League totals (2 years)		29	54	6	11	1	0	3	9	.204	5	9	0	91	4	1	.990

PERSONAL: Born January 5, 1974, in Canton, Ohio. ... 6-7/245. ... Bats right, throws right. ... Full name: Ryan Dale Minor. ... Brother of Damon Minor, first baseman, San Francisco Giants organization.

HIGH SCHOOL: Hammon (Okla.).

COLLEGE: Oklahoma.

TRANSACTIONS/CAREER NOTES: Selected by Baltimore Orioles organization in 15th round of free-agent draft (June 1, 1992); did not sign. ... Selected by Orioles organization in 33rd round of free-agent draft (June 4, 1996). ... On Baltimore disabled list (July 5-28, 2000); included rehabilitation assignment to Frederick (July 26-28). ... Traded by Orioles to Montreal Expos for P Jorge Julio (December 22, 2000). ... Claimed on waivers by Seattle Mariners (November 16, 2001).

STATISTICAL NOTES: Led Eastern League third basemen with 27 double plays in 1998.

									BATTING							FIELDING			
Year	Team (League)	Pos.	G	AB	R	H	2B	3B	HR	RBI	Avg.	BB	SO	SB	PO	A	E	Avg.
1996—Bluefield (Appl.)		3B-SS	25	87	14	22	6	0	4	9	.253	7	32	1	13	45	5	.921
1997—Delmarva (S.Atl.)		3B-1B-DH	134	488	83	150	42	1	24	97	.307	51	102	7	193	209	34	.922
1998—Bowie (East.)		3B-DH	138	521	73	130	20	3	17	71	.250	34	*152	1	89	245	*26	.928
—Baltimore (A.L.)		3B-1B-DH	9	14	3	6	1	0	0	1	.429	0	3	0	6	5	1	.917
1999—Rochester (I.L.)		3B-1B-DH	101	383	56	98	24	1	21	67	.256	37	119	3	170	148	13	.961
—Baltimore (A.L.)		3B-1B	46	124	13	24	7	0	3	10	.194	8	43	1	36	80	5	.959
2000—Rochester (I.L.)		3B-1B	68	241	33	71	9	1	14	48	.295	32	57	1	97	112	17	.925
—Baltimore (A.L.)		3B-1B	32	84	4	11	1	0	0	3	.131	3	20	0	44	35	4	.952
—Frederick (Caro.)		3B	2	9	3	3	0	0	0	0	.333	0	4	0	1	1	0	1.000
—GC Orioles (GCL)		3B	3	13	2	2	1	0	1	4	.154	1	6	0	2	1	1	.750
2001—Ottawa (I.L.)■		OF-3B-1B	42	143	20	35	6	2	5	19	.245	16	41	0	102	24	0	1.000
—Montreal (N.L.)		3B-DH-OF-1B	55	95	10	15	2	0	2	13	.158	9	31	0	15	20	2	.946
American League totals (3 years)			87	222	20	41	9	0	3	14	.185	11	66	1	86	120	10	.954
National League totals (1 year)			55	95	10	15	2	0	2	13	.158	9	31	0	15	20	2	.946
Major League totals (4 years)			142	317	30	56	11	0	5	27	.177	20	97	1	101	140	12	.953

CBA REGULAR-SEASON RECORD

TRANSACTIONS/CAREER NOTES: Selected by Philadelphia 76ers in second round (32nd pick overall) of 1996 NBA draft. ... Played in Continental Basketball Association with Oklahoma City Calvary (1996-97).

													AVERAGES		
Season Team	G	Min.	FGM	FGA	Pct.	FTM	FTA	Pct.	Reb.	Ast.	Pts.		RPG	APG	PPG
96-97—Oklahoma City	32	892	124	270	.459	38	50	.760	141	62	304		4.4	1.9	9.5

M

PERSONAL: Born October 18, 1970, in Kingman, Ariz. ... 6-1/218. ... Bats right, throws right. ... Full name: Douglas Anthony Mirabelli. ... Name pronounced mirr-uh-BEL-ee.

HIGH SCHOOL: Valley (Las Vegas).

COLLEGE: Wichita State.

TRANSACTIONS/CAREER NOTES: Selected by Detroit Tigers organization in sixth round of free-agent draft (June 5, 1989); did not sign. ... Selected by San Francisco Giants organization in fifth round of free-agent draft (June 1, 1992). ... On Phoenix disabled list (May 16-23, 1995). ... Contract purchased by Texas Rangers from Giants (March 27, 2001). ... Traded by Rangers to Boston Red Sox for P Justin Duchscherer (June 12, 2001).

STATISTICAL NOTES: Led Texas League with .419 on-base percentage in 1996. ... Led Pacific Coast League catchers with 680 total chances in 1997. ... Career major league grand slams: 1.

									BATTING							FIELDING			
Year	Team (League)	Pos.	G	AB	R	H	2B	3B	HR	RBI	Avg.	BB	SO	SB	PO	A	E	Avg.
1992—San Jose (Calif.)		C	53	177	30	41	11	1	0	21	.232	24	18	1	321	38	10	.973
1993—San Jose (Calif.)		C	113	371	58	100	19	2	1	48	.270	72	55	0	737	99	9	.989
1994—Shreveport (Texas)		C-1B	85	255	23	56	8	0	4	24	.220	36	48	3	391	51	3	.993
1995—Shreveport (Texas)		C-1B	40	126	14	38	13	0	0	16	.302	20	14	1	193	21	3	.986
—Phoenix (PCL)		C	23	66	3	11	0	1	0	7	.167	12	10	1	115	17	2	.985
1996—Shreveport (Texas)		C-DH-1B	115	380	60	112	23	0	21	70	.295	76	49	0	548	56	7	.989
—Phoenix (PCL)		C	47	10	14	7	0	0	7	.298	4	7	0	97	10	2	.982
—San Francisco (N.L.)		C	9	18	2	4	1	0	0	1	.222	3	4	0	29	2	0	1.000
1997—Phoenix (PCL)		C-DH	100	332	49	88	23	2	8	48	.265	58	69	1	*629	47	4	.994
—San Francisco (N.L.)		C	6	7	0	1	0	0	0	0	.143	1	3	0	16	0	0	1.000
1998—Fresno (PCL)		C-DH	85	265	45	69	12	2	13	53	.260	52	55	2	605	50	3	*.995
—San Francisco (N.L.)		C	10	17	2	4	2	0	1	4	.235	2	6	0	34	4	1	.974
1999—Fresno (PCL)		C-1B-DH	86	320	63	100	24	1	14	51	.313	48	56	8	619	73	5	.993
—San Francisco (N.L.)		C	33	87	10	22	6	0	1	10	.253	9	25	0	156	11	0	1.000
2000—San Francisco (N.L.)		C	82	230	23	53	10	2	6	28	.230	36	57	1	429	38	7	.985
2001—Texas (A.L.)■		C-DH	23	49	4	5	2	0	2	3	.102	10	21	0	84	16	1	.990
—Boston (A.L.)		C-DH	54	141	16	38	8	0	9	26	.270	17	36	0	329	33	2	.995
American League totals (1 year)			77	190	20	43	10	0	11	29	.226	27	57	0	413	49	3	.994
National League totals (5 years)			140	359	37	84	19	2	8	43	.234	51	95	1	664	55	8	.989
Major League totals (6 years)			217	549	57	127	29	2	19	72	.231	78	152	1	1077	104	11	.991

DIVISION SERIES RECORD

									BATTING							FIELDING			
Year	Team (League)	Pos.	G	AB	R	H	2B	3B	HR	RBI	Avg.	BB	SO	SB	PO	A	E	Avg.
2000—San Francisco (N.L.)		C	2	2	0	0	0	0	0	0	.000	1	1	0	6	1	0	1.000

PERSONAL: Born June 8, 1968, in Cleveland. ... 6-4/205. ... Throws right, bats right. ... Full name: David John Mlicki. ... Brother of Doug Mlicki, minor league pitcher (1992-99). ... Name pronounced muh-LICK-ee.
HIGH SCHOOL: Cheyenne Mountain (Colorado Springs, Colo.).
COLLEGE: Oklahoma State.
TRANSACTIONS/CAREER NOTES: Selected by Seattle Mariners organization in 23rd round of free-agent draft (June 5, 1989); did not sign. ... Selected by Cleveland Indians organization in 17th round of free-agent draft (June 4, 1990). ... On Cleveland disabled list (April 4-August 4, 1993); included rehabilitation assignment to Canton/Akron (July 19-August 4). ... Traded by Indians with P Jerry DiPoto, P Paul Byrd and a player to be named later to New York Mets for OF Jeromy Burnitz and P Joe Roa (November 18, 1994); Mets acquired 2B Jesus Azuaje to complete deal (December 6, 1994). ... Traded by Mets with P Greg McMichael to Los Angeles Dodgers for P Hideo Nomo and P Brad Clontz (June 5, 1998). ... Traded by Dodgers with P Mel Rojas and cash considerations to Detroit Tigers for P Robinson Checo, P Apostol Garcia and P Rick Roberts (April 16, 1999). ... On Detroit disabled list (July 23-September 5, 2000); included rehabilitation assignment to West Michigan (August 25-31) and Toledo (August 31-September 5). ... Traded by Tigers to Houston Astros for P Jose Lima (June 23, 2001).
RECORDS: Shares N.L. single-inning record for most consecutive home runs allowed—3 (September 29, 2001).
STATISTICAL NOTES: Led International League with 26 home runs allowed in 1994.
MISCELLANEOUS: Struck out in only appearance as pinch hitter (1996). ... Appeared in one game as pinch runner (1997).

Year	League	W	L	Pct.	ERA	G	GS	CG	ShO	Sv.	IP	H	R	ER	BB	SO
1990—	Burlington (Appl.)	3	1	.750	3.50	8	1	0	0	0	18	16	11	7	6	17
—	Watertown (NY-Penn)	3	0	1.000	3.38	7	4	0	0	0	32	33	15	12	11	28
1991—	Columbus (S.Atl.)	8	6	.571	4.20	22	19	2	0	0	115 2/3	101	70	54	70	136
1992—	Canton/Akron (East.)	11	9	.550	3.60	27	*27	2	0	0	172 2/3	143	77	69	•80	146
—	Cleveland (A.L.)	0	2	.000	4.98	4	4	0	0	0	21 2/3	23	14	12	16	16
1993—	Canton/Akron (East.)	2	1	.667	0.39	6	6	0	0	0	23	15	2	1	8	21
—	Cleveland (A.L.)	0	0	...	3.38	3	3	0	0	0	13 1/3	11	6	5	6	7
1994—	Charlotte (I.L.)	6	10	.375	4.25	28	28	0	0	0	165 1/3	179	85	78	64	152
1995—	New York (N.L.)■	9	7	.563	4.26	29	25	0	0	0	160 2/3	160	82	76	54	123
1996—	New York (N.L.)	6	7	.462	3.30	51	2	0	0	1	90	95	46	33	33	83
1997—	New York (N.L.)	8	12	.400	4.00	32	32	1	1	0	193 2/3	194	89	86	76	157
1998—	New York (N.L.)	1	4	.200	5.68	10	10	1	0	0	57	68	38	36	25	39
—	Los Angeles (N.L.)■	7	3	.700	4.05	20	20	2	1	0	124 1/3	120	64	56	38	78
1999—	Los Angeles (N.L.)	0	1	.000	4.91	2	0	0	0	0	7 1/3	10	4	4	2	1
—	Detroit (A.L.)■	14	12	.538	4.60	31	31	2	0	0	191 2/3	209	108	98	70	119
2000—	Detroit (A.L.)	6	11	.353	5.58	24	21	0	0	0	119 1/3	143	79	74	44	57
—	West Michigan (Midw.)	1	0	1.000	0.00	1	1	0	0	0	6	1	0	0	1	6
—	Toledo (I.L.)	0	1	.000	7.94	1	1	0	0	0	5 2/3	11	5	5	0	3
2001—	Detroit (A.L.)	4	8	.333	7.33	15	15	0	0	0	81	118	69	66	41	48
—	Houston (N.L.)■	7	3	.700	5.09	19	14	0	0	0	86 2/3	85	53	49	33	49
A.L. totals (5 years)		24	33	.421	5.37	77	74	2	0	0	427	504	276	255	177	247
N.L. totals (6 years)		38	37	.507	4.25	163	103	4	2	1	719 2/3	732	376	340	261	530
Major League totals (9 years)		62	70	.470	4.67	240	177	6	2	1	1146 2/3	1236	652	595	438	777

DIVISION SERIES RECORD

Year	League	W	L	Pct.	ERA	G	GS	CG	ShO	Sv.	IP	H	R	ER	BB	SO
2001—	Houston (N.L.)	0	1	.000	0.00	1	1	0	0	0	5	4	1	0	2	0

PERSONAL: Born December 31, 1971, in Rockingham, N.C. ... 6-3/235. ... Throws right, bats right. ... Full name: Brian Merritt Moehler.
HIGH SCHOOL: Richmond (N.C.) South.
COLLEGE: UNC Greensboro.
TRANSACTIONS/CAREER NOTES: Selected by Detroit Tigers organization in sixth round of free-agent draft (June 3, 1993). ... On disabled list (August 9-22, 1997). ... On suspended list (May 3-13, 1999). ... On Detroit disabled list (April 17-May 19, 2000); included rehabilitation assignment to West Michigan (May 12-19). ... On Detroit disabled list (April 7, 2001-remainder of season); included rehabilitation assignment to Toledo (May 20-June 1).

Year	League	W	L	Pct.	ERA	G	GS	CG	ShO	Sv.	IP	H	R	ER	BB	SO
1993—	Niagara Falls (NY-Penn)	6	5	.545	3.22	12	11	0	0	0	58 2/3	51	33	21	27	38
1994—	Lakeland (FSL)	12	12	.500	3.01	26	25	5	2	0	164 2/3	153	66	55	65	92
1995—	Jacksonville (Sou.)	8	10	.444	4.82	28	27	0	0	0	162 1/3	176	94	87	52	89
1996—	Detroit (A.L.)	0	1	.000	4.35	2	2	0	0	0	10 1/3	11	10	5	8	2
—	Jacksonville (Sou.)	*15	6	.714	3.48	28	28	1	0	0	173 1/3	186	80	67	50	120
1997—	Detroit (A.L.)	11	12	.478	4.67	31	31	2	1	0	175 1/3	198	97	91	61	97
1998—	Detroit (A.L.)	14	13	.519	3.90	33	33	4	3	0	221 1/3	220	103	96	56	123
1999—	Detroit (A.L.)	10	*16	.385	5.04	32	32	2	2	0	196 1/3	229	116	110	59	103
2000—	Detroit (A.L.)	12	9	.571	4.50	29	29	2	0	0	178	222	99	89	40	103
—	West Michigan (Midw.)	0	1	.000	4.26	1	1	0	0	0	6 1/3	5	3	3	1	4
2001—	Detroit (A.L.)	0	0	...	3.38	1	1	0	0	0	8	6	3	3	1	2
—	Toledo (I.L.)	0	2	.000	4.35	2	2	0	0	0	10 1/3	12	6	5	2	6
Major League totals (6 years)		47	51	.480	4.49	128	128	10	6	0	789 1/3	886	428	394	225	433

PERSONAL: Born February 18, 1975, in Upland, Calif. ... 6-3/210. ... Bats right, throws right. ... Full name: Chad Edward Moeller.
HIGH SCHOOL: Upland (Calif.).
COLLEGE: Southern California.
TRANSACTIONS/CAREER NOTES: Selected by New York Yankees organization in 25th round of free-agent draft (June 3, 1993); did not sign. ... Selected by Minnesota Twins organization in seventh round of free-agent draft (June 4, 1996). ... On disabled list (July 12, 1996-remainder of season). ... On Minnesota disabled list (August 12-30, 2000). ... Traded by Twins to Arizona Diamondbacks for SS Hanley Frias (March 28, 2001).

Year Team (League)	Pos.	G	AB	R	H	2B	3B	HR	RBI	Avg.	BB	SO	SB	PO	A	E	Avg.
						BATTING									FIELDING		
1996—Elizabethton (Appl.)....	C	17	59	17	21	4	0	4	13	.356	18	9	1	99	16	1	.991
1997—Fort Wayne (Midw.)....	C	108	384	58	111	18	3	9	39	.289	48	76	11	824	90	*15	.984
1998—Fort Myers (FSL).......	C	66	254	37	83	24	1	6	39	.327	31	37	2	395	36	9	.980
—New Britain (East.).....	C	58	187	21	44	10	0	6	23	.235	24	41	2	414	25	6	.987
1999—New Britain (East.).....	C	89	250	29	62	11	3	4	24	.248	21	44	0	548	59	10	.984
2000—Salt Lake (PCL).......	C	47	167	30	48	13	1	5	20	.287	9	45	0	256	25	2	.993
—Minnesota (A.L.)........	C	48	128	13	27	3	1	1	9	.211	9	33	1	266	13	6	.979
2001—Tucson (PCL)■.........	C	78	274	41	75	20	0	8	36	.274	25	54	1	442	20	5	.989
—Arizona (N.L.)........	C	25	56	8	13	0	1	1	2	.232	6	12	0	111	7	0	1.000
American League totals (1 year)		48	128	13	27	3	1	1	9	.211	9	33	1	266	13	6	.979
National League totals (1 year)		25	56	8	13	0	1	1	2	.232	6	12	0	111	7	0	1.000
Major League totals (2 years)		73	184	21	40	3	2	2	11	.217	15	45	1	377	20	6	.985

MOHLER, MIKE P

PERSONAL: Born July 26, 1968, in Dayton, Ohio. ... 6-2/208. ... Throws left, bats right. ... Full name: Michael Ross Mohler.
HIGH SCHOOL: East Ascension (Gonzales, La.).
COLLEGE: Nicholls State (La.).
TRANSACTIONS/CAREER NOTES: Selected by Oakland Athletics organization in 42nd round of free-agent draft (June 5, 1989). ... On Tacoma disabled list (April 7-May 24, 1994). ... Granted free agency (December 21, 1998). ... Signed by St. Louis Cardinals (January 15, 1999). ... Released by Cardinals (June 5, 2000). ... Signed by Cleveland Indians organization (June 16, 2000). ... Released by Indians (July 1, 2000). ... Signed by A's organization (July 6, 2000). ... Granted free agency (October 18, 2000). ... Signed by Arizona Diamondbacks organization (March 8, 2001). ... Granted free agency (November 5, 2001).
MISCELLANEOUS: Appeared in two games as pinch runner (1997).

Year League	W	L	Pct.	ERA	G	GS	CG	ShO	Sv.	IP	H	R	ER	BB	SO
1990—Madison (Midw.)	1	1	.500	3.41	42	2	0	0	1	63 1/3	56	34	24	32	72
1991—Modesto (Calif.)	9	4	.692	2.86	21	20	1	0	0	122 2/3	106	48	39	45	98
—Huntsville (Sou.)	4	2	.667	3.57	8	8	0	0	0	53	55	22	21	20	27
1992—Huntsville (Sou.)	3	8	.273	3.59	44	6	0	0	3	80 1/3	72	41	32	39	56
1993—Oakland (A.L.)	1	6	.143	5.60	42	9	0	0	0	64 1/3	57	45	40	44	42
1994—Modesto (Calif.)	1	1	.500	2.76	7	5	0	0	1	29 1/3	21	9	9	6	29
—Tacoma (PCL)	1	3	.250	3.53	17	11	0	0	1	63 2/3	66	31	25	21	50
—Oakland (A.L.)	0	1	.000	7.71	1	1	0	0	0	2 1/3	2	3	2	2	4
1995—Edmonton (PCL)	2	1	.667	2.60	29	0	0	0	5	45	40	16	13	20	28
—Oakland (A.L.)	1	1	.500	3.04	28	0	0	0	1	23 2/3	16	8	8	18	15
1996—Oakland (A.L.)	6	3	.667	3.67	72	0	0	0	7	81	79	36	33	41	64
1997—Oakland (A.L.)	1	10	.091	5.13	62	10	0	0	1	101 2/3	116	65	58	54	66
1998—Oakland (A.L.)	3	3	.500	5.16	57	0	0	0	0	61	70	38	35	26	42
1999—St. Louis (N.L.)■	1	1	.500	4.38	48	0	0	0	1	49 1/3	47	26	24	23	31
—Memphis (PCL)	2	1	.667	3.07	10	0	0	0	1	14 2/3	16	5	5	5	17
2000—St. Louis (N.L.)	1	1	.500	9.00	22	0	0	0	0	19	26	20	19	15	8
—Buffalo (I.L.)■	0	0	...	0.00	3	0	0	0	0	6	3	0	0	3	3
—Cleveland (A.L.)	0	1	.000	0.00	2	0	0	0	0	1	1	1	1	0	2
—Sacramento (PCL)■.............	2	0	1.000	6.50	18	0	0	0	1	18	22	13	13	16	14
2001—Tucson (PCL)■	5	0	1.000	3.18	40	0	0	0	3	45 1/3	52	28	16	14	48
—Arizona (N.L.)	0	0	...	7.24	13	0	0	0	0	13 2/3	14	11	11	9	7
A.L. totals (7 years)	12	25	.324	4.76	264	20	0	0	9	335	341	196	177	185	235
N.L. totals (3 years)	2	2	.500	5.93	83	0	0	0	1	82	87	57	54	47	46
Major League totals (9 years)	14	27	.341	4.99	347	20	0	0	10	417	428	253	231	232	281

MOHR, DUSTAN OF TWINS

PERSONAL: Born June 19, 1976, in Hattiesburg, Miss. ... 6-0/210. ... Bats right, throws right. ... Full name: Dustan Kyle Mohr.
HIGH SCHOOL: Oak Grove (Miss.).
COLLEGE: Alabama.
TRANSACTIONS/CAREER NOTES: Selected by California Angels organization in 20th round of free-agent draft (June 2, 1994); did not sign. ... Selected by Cleveland Indians organization in ninth round of free-agent draft (June 3, 1997). ... Released by Indians (March 31, 2000). ... Signed by Minnesota Twins organization (April 1, 2000). ... On disabled list (August 24-31, 2000).
STATISTICAL NOTES: Led New York-Pennsylvania League outfielders with 152 total chances in 1997. ... Tied for New York-Pennsylvania League lead in double plays by outfielder with 11 in 1997. ... Tied for Carolina League lead in double plays by outfielder with four in 1999.

Year Team (League)	Pos.	G	AB	R	H	2B	3B	HR	RBI	Avg.	BB	SO	SB	PO	A	E	Avg.
						BATTING									FIELDING		
1997—Watertown (NY-Penn)	OF	74	275	52	80	20	2	7	53	.291	31	76	3	*140	11	1	*.993
1998—Kinston (Caro.).........	OF	134	491	60	119	23	9	19	65	.242	39	146	8	203	10	7	.968
1999—Akron (East.)............	OF	12	42	3	7	2	1	0	2	.167	5	7	0	28	1	0	1.000
—Kinston (Caro.).........	OF	112	429	46	120	29	3	8	60	.280	26	104	6	207	13	6	.973
2000—Fort Myers (FSL)■......	OF	101	370	58	98	19	2	11	75	.265	35	65	7	170	6	4	.978
2001—New Britain (East.).....	OF	135	518	90	174	41	3	24	91	.336	49	111	9	261	9	6	.978
—Minnesota (A.L.)........	OF-DH	20	51	6	12	2	0	0	4	.235	5	17	1	45	0	0	1.000
Major League totals (1 year)		20	51	6	12	2	0	0	4	.235	5	17	1	45	0	0	1.000

PERSONAL: Born July 20, 1974, in Rio Pedras, Puerto Rico. ... 5-11/207. ... Bats right, throws right. ... Full name: Benjamin Jose Molina. ... Brother of Jose Molina, catcher, Anaheim Angels.
HIGH SCHOOL: Maestra Ladi (Puerto Rico).
JUNIOR COLLEGE: Arizona Western.
TRANSACTIONS/CAREER NOTES: Signed as non-drafted free agent by California Angels organization (May 23, 1993). ... Angels franchise renamed Anaheim Angels for 1997 season. ... On Vancouver disabled list (May 13-22, 1998). ... On Edmonton disabled list (June 4-14, 1999). ... On Anaheim disabled list (May 5-June 27, 2001); included rehabilitation assignments to Rancho Cucamonga (June 9-11, June 17-18 and June 26-27) and Salt Lake (June 19-26).
STATISTICAL NOTES: Led Texas League catchers with nine double plays in 1996. ... Career major league grand slams: 1.

Year Team (League)	Pos.	G	AB	R	H	2B	3B	HR	RBI	Avg.	BB	SO	SB	PO	A	E	Avg.
1993—Arizona Angels (Ariz.).	C	27	80	9	21	6	2	0	10	.263	10	4	0	47	2	0	1.000
1994—Cedar Rapids (Midw.)	C	48	171	14	48	8	0	3	16	.281	8	12	1	349	40	10	.975
1995—Vancouver (PCL)		2	2	0	0	0	0	0	0	.000	0	1	0	4	0	0	1.000
—Cedar Rapids (Midw.)	C	39	133	15	39	9	0	4	17	.293	15	11	1	283	32	7	.978
—Lake Elsinore (Calif.)..	C	27	96	21	37	7	2	2	12	.385	8	7	0	195	16	1	.995
1996—Midland (Texas).........	C	108	365	45	100	21	2	8	54	.274	25	25	0	615	*81	7	.990
1997—Lake Elsinore (Calif.)..	C	36	149	18	42	10	2	4	33	.282	7	9	0	239	36	1	.996
—Midland (Texas).........	C	29	106	18	35	8	0	6	30	.330	10	7	0	74	15	2	.978
1998—Vancouver (PCL)	C	49	184	13	54	9	1	1	22	.293	5	14	1	316	24	5	.986
—Midland (Texas).........	C	41	154	28	55	8	0	9	39	.357	14	7	0	233	21	3	.988
—Anaheim (A.L.)...........	C	2	1	0	0	0	0	0	0	.000	0	0	0	1	0	0	1.000
1999—Edmonton (PCL)	C-DH	65	241	28	69	16	0	7	41	.286	15	17	1	351	47	3	.993
—Anaheim (A.L.)...........	C	31	101	8	26	5	0	1	10	.257	6	6	0	192	19	2	.991
2000—Anaheim (A.L.)...........	C-DH	130	473	59	133	20	2	14	71	.281	23	33	1	683	61	7	.991
2001—Anaheim (A.L.)...........	C-DH	96	325	31	85	11	0	6	40	.262	16	51	0	527	36	5	.991
—Rancho Cuca. (Calif.) .	C	3	11	1	6	1	0	0	2	.545	0	1	0	15	4	0	1.000
—Salt Lake (PCL)	C	5	18	2	5	1	0	0	3	.278	2	3	0	27	2	0	1.000
Major League totals (4 years)		259	900	98	244	36	2	21	121	.271	45	90	1	1403	116	14	.991

PERSONAL: Born June 3, 1975, in Bayamon, Puerto Rico. ... 6-1/215. ... Bats right, throws right. ... Full name: Jose Benjamin Molina Matta. ... Brother of Bengie Molina, catcher, Anaheim Angels.
HIGH SCHOOL: Maestro Ladi (Vega Alta, Puerto Rico).
TRANSACTIONS/CAREER NOTES: Selected by Chicago Cubs organization in 14th round of free-agent draft (June 3, 1993). ... On Iowa disabled list (July 31-August 10, 1999). ... On disabled list (August 4-September 5, 2000). ... Released by Cubs (November 27, 2000). ... Signed by Anaheim Angels organization (May 17, 2001). ... On Anaheim disabled list (May 21-July 1, 2001); included rehabilitation assignment to Salt Lake (June 26-July 1).
STATISTICAL NOTES: Led Southern League catchers with 108 assists and tied for lead with 21 passed balls in 1998. ... Tied for Pacific Coast League lead in errors by catcher with 11 in 2000.

M

Year Team (League)	Pos.	G	AB	R	H	2B	3B	HR	RBI	Avg.	BB	SO	SB	PO	A	E	Avg.
1993—GC Cubs (GCL)..........	C-1B	33	78	5	17	2	0	0	4	.218	12	12	3	143	27	7	.960
—Daytona (FSL)	C	3	7	0	1	0	0	0	1	.143	2	0	0	13	2	0	1.000
1994—Peoria (Midw.)..........	C	78	253	31	58	13	1	1	33	.229	24	61	4	567	79	13	.980
1995—Daytona (FSL)	C	82	233	27	55	9	1	1	19	.236	29	53	1	501	91	8	.987
1996—Rockford (Midw.)	C	96	305	35	69	10	1	2	27	.226	36	71	2	620	98	11	.985
1997—Daytona (FSL)	C	55	179	17	45	9	1	0	23	.251	14	25	4	341	71	8	.981
—Iowa (A.A.)	C	1	3	0	1	0	0	0	0	.333	1	1	0	1	0	0	1.000
—Orlando (Sou.)	C	37	99	10	17	3	0	1	15	.172	12	28	0	237	28	2	.993
1998—West Tenn (Sou.)	C-1B	109	320	33	71	10	1	2	28	.222	32	74	1	740	†108	8	.991
1999—West Tenn (Sou.)	C	14	35	2	6	3	0	0	5	.171	2	14	0	97	13	2	.982
—Iowa (PCL)	C	74	240	24	63	11	1	4	26	.263	20	54	0	488	44	7	.987
—Chicago (N.L.)	C	10	19	3	5	1	0	0	1	.263	2	4	0	44	5	0	1.000
2000—Iowa (PCL)	C-1B	76	248	22	58	9	0	1	17	.234	23	61	1	505	67	‡11	.981
2001—Salt Lake (PCL)■	C	61	213	29	64	11	1	5	31	.300	14	49	1	451	43	2	.996
—Anaheim (A.L.)	C	15	37	8	10	3	0	2	4	.270	3	8	0	78	6	0	1.000
American League totals (1 year)		15	37	8	10	3	0	2	4	.270	3	8	0	78	6	0	1.000
National League totals (1 year)		10	19	3	5	1	0	0	1	.263	2	4	0	44	5	0	1.000
Major League totals (2 years)		25	56	11	15	4	0	2	5	.268	5	12	0	122	11	0	1.000

PERSONAL: Born March 12, 1971, in San Cristobal, Dominican Republic. ... 5-11/230. ... Bats right, throws right. ... Name pronounced MON-de-see.
HIGH SCHOOL: Liceo Manuel Maria Valencia (Dominican Republic).
TRANSACTIONS/CAREER NOTES: Signed as non-drafted free agent by Los Angeles Dodgers organization (June 6, 1988). ... On Bakersfield disabled list (May 8-July 5, 1991). ... On Albuquerque disabled list (May 8-16, 1992). ... On San Antonio disabled list (June 2-16, June 24-August 10 and August 24, 1992-remainder of season). ... Traded by Dodgers with P Pedro Borbon to Toronto Blue Jays for OF Shawn Green and 2B Jorge Nunez (November 8, 1999). ... On disabled list (July 22-September 20, 2000).
RECORDS: Shares major league single-season record for fewest double plays by outfielder, 150 or more games—0 (1997).
HONORS: Named N.L. Rookie Player of the Year by THE SPORTING NEWS (1994). ... Named N.L. Rookie of the Year by Baseball Writers' Association of America (1994). ... Won N.L. Gold Glove as outfielder (1995 and 1997).
STATISTICAL NOTES: Career major league grand slams: 4.

Year Team (League)	Pos.	G	AB	R	H	2B	3B	HR	RBI	Avg.	BB	SO	SB	PO	A	E	Avg.
1988— Dom. Dodgers (DSL) .	OF	36	117	21	26	10	1	2	44	.222	23	36	4	...	...	...	...
1989— Dom. Dodgers (DSL) .	OF	46	156	32	43	15	3	2	27	.276	16	26	8	...	...	...	...
1990— Great Falls (Pio.)	OF	44	175	35	53	10	4	8	31	.303	11	30	30	65	4	1	.986
1991— Bakersfield (Calif.)......	OF	28	106	23	30	7	2	3	13	.283	5	21	9	42	5	3	.940
— San Antonio (Texas)...	OF	53	213	32	58	11	5	5	26	.272	8	47	8	101	6	4	.964
— Albuquerque (PCL).....	OF	2	9	3	3	0	1	0	0	.333	0	1	1	0	0	1	.000
1992— Albuquerque (PCL).....	OF	35	138	23	43	4	7	4	15	.312	9	35	2	89	8	7	.933
— San Antonio (Texas)...	OF	18	68	8	18	2	2	2	14	.265	1	24	3	31	6	1	.974
1993— Albuquerque (PCL).....	OF	110	425	65	119	22	7	12	65	.280	18	85	13	211	10	10	.957
— Los Angeles (N.L.)....	OF	42	86	13	25	3	1	4	10	.291	4	16	4	55	3	3	.951
1994— Los Angeles (N.L.)....	OF	112	434	63	133	27	8	16	56	.306	16	78	11	206	*16	8	.965
1995— Los Angeles (N.L.)....	OF	139	536	91	153	23	6	26	88	.285	33	96	27	282	*16	6	.980
1996— Los Angeles (N.L.)....	OF	157	634	98	188	40	7	24	88	.297	32	122	14	337	11	•12	.967
1997— Los Angeles (N.L.)....	OF	159	616	95	191	42	5	30	87	.310	44	105	32	338	10	4	.989
1998— Los Angeles (N.L.)....	OF	148	580	85	162	26	5	30	90	.279	30	112	16	284	6	6	.980
1999— Los Angeles (N.L.)....	OF	159	601	98	152	29	5	33	99	.253	71	134	36	315	7	6	.982
2000— Toronto (A.L.).■........	OF	96	388	78	105	22	2	24	67	.271	32	73	22	203	5	7	.967
2001— Toronto (A.L.)............	OF	149	572	88	144	26	4	27	84	.252	73	128	30	263	18	8	.972
American League totals (2 years)		245	960	166	249	48	6	51	151	.259	105	201	52	466	23	15	.970
National League totals (7 years)		916	3487	543	1004	190	37	163	518	.288	230	663	140	1817	69	45	.977
Major League totals (9 years)		1161	4447	709	1253	238	43	214	669	.282	335	864	192	2283	92	60	.975

DIVISION SERIES RECORD

Year Team (League)	Pos.	G	AB	R	H	2B	3B	HR	RBI	Avg.	BB	SO	SB	PO	A	E	Avg.
1995— Los Angeles (N.L.)	OF	3	9	0	2	0	0	0	1	.222	0	2	0	8	0	0	1.000
1996— Los Angeles (N.L.)	OF	3	11	0	2	2	0	0	1	.182	0	4	0	2	0	0	1.000
Division series totals (2 years)		6	20	0	4	2	0	0	2	.200	0	6	0	10	0	0	1.000

ALL-STAR GAME RECORD

Year League	Pos.	AB	R	H	2B	3B	HR	RBI	Avg.	BB	SO	SB	PO	A	E	Avg.
1995— National....................	OF	1	0	0	0	0	0	0	.000	0	0	0	2	0	0	1.000

MONROE, CRAIG — OF — RANGERS

PERSONAL: Born February 27, 1977, in Texarkana, Texas. ... 6-1/195. ... Bats right, throws right. ... Full name: Craig Keystone Monroe.
HIGH SCHOOL: Texas (Texarkana, Texas).
TRANSACTIONS/CAREER NOTES: Selected by Texas Rangers organization in eighth round of free-agent draft (June 1, 1995).
STATISTICAL NOTES: Led Florida State League outfielders with 346 total chances in 1999.

Year Team (League)	Pos.	G	AB	R	H	2B	3B	HR	RBI	Avg.	BB	SO	SB	PO	A	E	Avg.
1995— GC Rangers (GCL)......	OF	54	193	22	48	6	2	0	33	.249	18	25	13	94	7	4	.962
1996— Charl., S.C. (S.Atl.)......	OF	49	153	11	23	11	1	0	9	.150	18	48	2	76	7	4	.954
— Hudson Valley (NY-P).	OF	67	268	53	74	16	6	5	29	.276	23	63	21	86	5	6	.938
1997— Charlotte (FSL)..........	OF	92	328	54	77	23	1	7	41	.235	44	80	24	151	13	7	.959
1998— Charlotte (FSL)..........	OF	132	472	73	114	26	7	17	76	.242	66	102	50	198	•17	11	.951
1999— Charlotte (FSL)..........	OF	130	480	77	125	21	1	17	81	.260	42	102	40	*326	13	7	.980
— Oklahoma (PCL)........	OF	6	16	2	4	1	0	0	1	.250	1	4	0	17	0	0	1.000
2000— Tulsa (Texas)	OF	120	464	89	131	34	5	20	89	.282	64	91	12	199	*18	*12	.948
2001— Oklahoma (PCL)	OF	114	410	60	115	25	5	20	75	.280	46	85	10	185	9	5	.975
— Texas (A.L.).............	OF-DH	27	52	8	11	1	0	2	5	.212	6	18	2	42	3	0	1.000
Major League totals (1 year)		27	52	8	11	1	0	2	5	.212	6	18	2	42	3	0	1.000

MOORE, TREY — P

PERSONAL: Born October 2, 1972, in Houston. ... 6-0/190. ... Throws left, bats left. ... Full name: Warren Neal Moore III.
HIGH SCHOOL: Keller (Texas).
COLLEGE: Texas A&M.
TRANSACTIONS/CAREER NOTES: Selected by Seattle Mariners organization in second round of free-agent draft (June 2, 1994). ... Traded by Mariners with C Chris Widger and P Matt Wagner to Montreal Expos for P Alex Pacheco and P Jeff Fassero (October 29, 1996). ... On Montreal disabled list (June 7, 1998-remainder of season); included rehabilitation assignment to Ottawa (July 9-20). ... On disabled list (March 31, 1999-entire season). ... On Ottawa disabled list (April 6-May 11 and June 2-22, 2000). ... Claimed on waivers by Atlanta Braves (December 4, 2000). ... Contract sold by Braves to Hanshin of Japan Central League (December 2, 2001).
MISCELLANEOUS: Struck out in only appearance as pinch hitter with Montreal (1998).

Year League	W	L	Pct.	ERA	G	GS	CG	ShO	Sv.	IP	H	R	ER	BB	SO
1994— Bellingham (N'West) ..	5	2	.714	2.63	11	10	1	0	0	61 2/3	48	18	18	24	73
1995— Riverside (Calif.).............	14	6	.700	3.09	24	24	0	0	0	148 1/3	122	65	51	58	134
1996— Port City (Sou.)	1	6	.143	7.71	11	11	0	0	0	53 2/3	73	54	46	33	42
— Lancaster (Calif.)........	7	5	.583	4.10	15	15	2	0	0	94 1/3	106	57	43	31	77
1997— Harrisburg (East.)■.......	11	6	.647	4.15	27	27	2	•2	0	162 2/3	152	91	75	66	137
1998— Montreal (N.L.)...............	2	5	.286	5.02	13	11	0	0	0	61	78	37	34	17	35
— Ottawa (I.L.)................	1	1	.500	5.54	3	3	0	0	0	13	18	8	8	4	8
1999— Montreal (N.L.)...............							Did not play.								
2000— Ottawa (I.L.)................	3	2	.600	4.17	12	12	1	0	0	58 1/3	56	36	27	18	43
— Montreal (N.L.)...........	1	5	.167	6.62	8	8	0	0	0	35 1/3	55	31	26	21	24
2001— Richmond (I.L.)■............	9	8	.529	3.31	26	25	2	0	0	163	140	64	60	41	122
— Atlanta (N.L.)..............	0	0	...	11.25	2	0	0	0	0	4	7	5	5	2	1
Major League totals (3 years)	3	10	.231	5.83	23	19	0	0	0	100 1/3	140	73	65	40	60

PERSONAL: Born February 2, 1972, in Aqua Negar, Venezuela. ... 5-10/180. ... Bats right, throws right.
HIGH SCHOOL: Libertador (Venezuela).
TRANSACTIONS/CAREER NOTES: Signed as non-drafted free agent by Houston Astros organization (March 30, 1991). ... Granted free agency (October 17, 1997). ... Played in Taiwan (1998). ... Signed by New York Mets organization (July 24, 1998). ... Granted free agency (October 16, 1998). ... Re-signed by Mets organization (February 5, 1999). ... On New York disabled list (May 13-30, 2000); included rehabilitation assignment to Norfolk (May 22-30). ... Traded by Mets with 3B Mike Kinkade, P Leslie Brea and P Pat Gorman to Baltimore Orioles for SS Mike Bordick (July 28, 2000).
STATISTICAL NOTES: Tied for Texas League lead in double plays by outfielder with six in 1995.

									BATTING						FIELDING		
Year	Team (League)	Pos.	G	AB	R	H	2B	3B	HR	RBI	Avg.	BB	SO	SB	PO	A	E	Avg.
1991—Dom. Astros (DSL).....			58	211	38	63	18	1	0	20	.299	19	22	21	...	...	...	...
1992—GC Astros (GCL)	OF-2B-3B		49	144	28	32	3	0	0	8	.222	18	16	16	71	27	4	.961
1993—Asheville (S.Atl.)	2-0-3-S		108	365	66	104	22	2	2	31	.285	36	46	20	135	114	17	.936
1994—Osceola (FSL)	OF-3B		118	425	57	120	29	4	8	46	.282	37	60	24	198	70	15	.947
1995—Jackson (Texas)	OF-3B-2B		123	467	63	139	32	0	3	45	.298	32	57	22	244	16	6	.977
—Tucson (PCL)	OF		2	5	3	3	0	1	0	1	.600	2	0	1	2	0	0	1.000
1996—Jackson (Texas)	OF-2B-SS-3B		70	255	36	73	6	1	5	23	.286	14	23	4	108	56	7	.959
—Tucson (PCL)	3B-OF-2B		62	228	35	64	11	2	3	26	.281	17	27	3	75	70	14	.912
1997—New Orleans (A.A.)	0-3-2-S		119	370	55	95	15	3	2	38	.257	47	52	7	161	80	11	.956
1998—Mercury (Taiwan)■			...	164	34	55	11	2	3	11	.335	...	...	...	...	...	...	...
—St. Lucie (FSL)■	2B-SS-OF		17	55	5	15	0	0	0	8	.273	5	9	1	21	43	1	.985
—Norfolk (I.L.)	3B-OF-2B		11	28	5	5	1	0	0	2	.179	5	7	0	8	6	2	.875
1999—Norfolk (I.L.)	SS-OF-2B-3B		82	304	55	92	17	2	8	36	.303	41	54	18	126	134	16	.942
—New York (N.L.)	OF-2B-3B-SS		66	31	6	5	0	0	0	1	.161	4	7	2	21	7	0	1.000
2000—New York (N.L.)	SS-OF-2B		79	215	35	56	13	2	6	30	.260	18	48	7	89	115	8	.962
—Norfolk (I.L.)	OF-2B-SS		8	27	7	9	2	0	0	7	.333	7	3	2	11	7	0	1.000
—Baltimore (A.L.)■	SS-2B		53	199	25	58	9	3	2	17	.291	17	32	5	80	161	12	.953
2001—Baltimore (A.L.)	OF-SS-2B		128	436	49	109	28	0	7	48	.250	41	91	11	287	130	11	.974
American League totals (2 years)			181	635	74	167	37	3	9	65	.263	58	123	16	367	291	23	.966
National League totals (2 years)			145	246	41	61	13	2	6	31	.248	22	55	9	110	122	8	.967
Major League totals (3 years)			326	881	115	228	50	5	15	96	.259	80	178	25	477	413	31	.966

DIVISION SERIES RECORD

									BATTING						FIELDING		
Year	Team (League)	Pos.	G	AB	R	H	2B	3B	HR	RBI	Avg.	BB	SO	SB	PO	A	E	Avg.
1999—New York (N.L.)	OF		3	1	1	0	0	0	0	0	.000	1	0	0	2	1	0	1.000

CHAMPIONSHIP SERIES RECORD

									BATTING						FIELDING		
Year	Team (League)	Pos.	G	AB	R	H	2B	3B	HR	RBI	Avg.	BB	SO	SB	PO	A	E	Avg.
1999—New York (N.L.)	PH-OF		6	14	3	6	0	0	1	2	.429	2	2	2	7	3	0	1.000

RECORD AS PITCHER

Year	League	W	L	Pct.	ERA	G	GS	CG	ShO	Sv.	IP	H	R	ER	BB	SO
1993—Asheville (SAL)		0	0	...	0.00	1	0	0	0	0	$2/_3$	1	0	0	0	0
1997—New Orleans (A.A.)		0	0	...	0.00	1	0	0	0	0	1	2	1	1	1	0

PERSONAL: Born December 13, 1967, in Birmingham, Ala. ... 5-10/185. ... Bats right, throws right. ... Full name: Michael Howard Mordecai.
HIGH SCHOOL: Hewitt Trussville (Ala.).
COLLEGE: Southern Alabama.
TRANSACTIONS/CAREER NOTES: Selected by Pittsburgh Pirates organization in 33rd round of free-agent draft (June 2, 1986); did not sign. ... Selected by Atlanta Braves organization in sixth round of free-agent draft (June 5, 1989). ... On disabled list (April 8-29, 1993). ... On Atlanta disabled list (April 19-May 11, 1996); included rehabilitation assignment to Richmond (May 8-11). ... Granted free agency (December 21, 1997). ... Signed by Montreal Expos organization (March 27, 1998). ... On Montreal disabled list (June 24-July 24, 1998); included rehabilitation assignments to Jupiter (July 16-19) and Ottawa (July 19-24).

									BATTING						FIELDING		
Year	Team (League)	Pos.	G	AB	R	H	2B	3B	HR	RBI	Avg.	BB	SO	SB	PO	A	E	Avg.
1989—Burlington (Midw.)	SS-3B		65	241	39	61	11	1	1	22	.253	33	43	12	80	163	21	.920
—Greenville (Sou.)	3B-2B		4	8	0	3	0	0	1		.375	1	1	0	4	6	0	1.000
1990—Durham (Caro.)	SS		72	271	42	76	11	7	3	36	.280	42	45	10	111	221	29	.920
1991—Durham (Caro.)	SS		109	397	52	104	15	2	4	42	.262	40	58	30	164	302	27	.945
1992—Greenville (Sou.)	SS		65	222	31	58	13	1	4	31	.261	29	31	9	93	204	11	.964
—Richmond (I.L.)	SS-2B-3B		36	118	12	29	3	0	1	6	.246	5	19	0	48	101	10	.937
1993—Richmond (I.L.)	2-S-3-0-C-1		72	205	29	55	8	1	2	14	.268	14	33	10	98	145	9	.964
1994—Richmond (I.L.)	SS-1B-DH-3B		99	382	67	107	25	1	14	57	.280	35	50	14	117	279	22	.947
—Atlanta (N.L.)	SS		4	4	1	1	0	0	1	3	.250	1	0	0	1	4	0	1.000
1995—Atlanta (N.L.)	2-1-3-S-O		69	75	10	21	6	0	3	11	.280	9	16	0	39	31	0	1.000
1996—Atlanta (N.L.)	2B-3B-SS-1B		66	108	12	26	5	0	2	8	.241	9	24	1	33	52	2	.977
—Richmond (I.L.)	SS		3	11	2	2	0	0	1	2	.182	0	3	0	3	13	0	1.000
1997—Atlanta (N.L.)	3-2-S-1-DH-O		61	81	8	14	2	1	0	3	.173	6	16	0	26	17	0	1.000
—Richmond (I.L.)	2B-3B-DH-SS		31	122	23	38	10	0	3	15	.311	9	17	0	29	61	1	.989
1998—Montreal (N.L.)■	SS-2B-3B-1B		73	119	12	24	4	2	3	10	.202	9	20	1	38	82	5	.960
—Jupiter (FSL)	2B-SS		2	8	0	0	0	0	0	0	.000	1	3	0	4	4	0	1.000
—Ottawa (I.L.)	SS-2B		6	22	2	5	2	0	0	1	.227	3	3	0	9	22	1	.969
1999—Montreal (N.L.)	2-S-3-1		109	226	29	53	10	2	5	25	.235	20	31	2	72	156	7	.970
2000—Montreal (N.L.)	3B-SS-2B-1B		86	169	20	48	16	0	4	16	.284	12	34	2	42	88	8	.942
2001—Montreal (N.L.)	3-2-S-C-1-O-D		96	254	28	71	17	2	3	32	.280	19	53	2	74	117	3	.985
Major League totals (8 years)			564	1036	120	258	60	7	21	108	.249	85	194	8	325	547	25	.972

DIVISION SERIES RECORD

Year Team (League)	Pos.	G	AB	R	H	2B	3B	HR	RBI	Avg.	BB	SO	SB	PO	A	E	Avg.
1995—Atlanta (N.L.).............	PH-SS	2	3	1	2	1	0	0	2	.667	0	0	0	1	0	0	1.000
1996—Atlanta (N.L.)							Did not play.										

CHAMPIONSHIP SERIES RECORD

Year Team (League)	Pos.	G	AB	R	H	2B	3B	HR	RBI	Avg.	BB	SO	SB	PO	A	E	Avg.
1995—Atlanta (N.L.).............	PH-SS	2	2	0	0	0	0	0	0	.000	0	1	0	0	0	0	...
1996—Atlanta (N.L.).............	3B-PH-2B	4	4	1	1	0	0	0	0	.250	0	1	0	1	1	0	1.000
Championship series totals (2 years)		6	6	1	1	0	0	0	0	.167	0	2	0	1	1	0	1.000

NOTES: Member of World Series championship team (1995).

WORLD SERIES RECORD

Year Team (League)	Pos.	G	AB	R	H	2B	3B	HR	RBI	Avg.	BB	SO	SB	PO	A	E	Avg.
1995—Atlanta (N.L.).............	SS-DH	3	3	0	1	0	0	0	0	.333	0	1	0	0	6	0	1.000
1996—Atlanta (N.L.)............	PH	1	1	0	0	0	0	0	0	.000	0	0	0	...	...	...	...
World Series totals (2 years)		4	4	0	1	0	0	0	0	.250	0	1	0	0	6	0	1.000

MORENO, JUAN — P — RANGERS

PERSONAL: Born February 28, 1975, in Maiquetia, Venezuela. ... 6-1/205. ... Throws left, bats left. ... Full name: Juan Carlos Moreno.
HIGH SCHOOL: Josefina Crespo (Venezuela).
TRANSACTIONS/CAREER NOTES: Signed as non-drafted free agent by Oakland Athletics organization (April 14, 1993). ... Released by Athletics (February 4, 1997). ... Missed entire 1997 season due to injury. ... Missed entire 1998 season due to injury. ... Signed by Texas Rangers organization (November 24, 1998). ... On Tulsa disabled list (April 6-May 28 and June 20-September 13, 2000). ... Granted free agency (October 18, 2000). ... Re-signed by Rangers (December 1, 2000).

Year League	W	L	Pct.	ERA	G	GS	CG	ShO	Sv.	IP	H	R	ER	BB	SO
1993—Dominican Athletics (DSL).	3	1	.750	3.33	13	3	0	0	1	48 2/3	47	25	18	35	36
1994—Dominican Athletics (DSL).	3	1	.750	4.23	17	4	0	0	3	38 1/3	26	27	18	44	41
1995—Arizona Athletics (Ariz.)......	6	2	.750	1.21	20	0	0	0	0	44 2/3	36	10	6	20	49
1996—West Michigan (Midw.)......	4	6	.400	4.37	38	11	0	0	0	107	98	60	52	69	97
1997—							Did not play.								
1998—							Did not play.								
1999—Tulsa (Texas)■...............	4	3	.571	2.30	42	0	0	0	3	62 2/3	33	20	16	32	83
2000—Charlotte (FSL).................	0	0	...	0.00	1	1	0	0	0	2	0	0	0	1	0
—Tulsa (Texas)	0	0	...	5.40	5	0	0	0	1	6 2/3	6	4	4	5	12
2001—Texas (A.L.)	3	3	.500	3.92	45	0	0	0	0	41 1/3	22	21	18	28	36
Major League totals (1 year)........	3	3	.500	3.92	45	0	0	0	0	41 1/3	22	21	18	28	36

MORENO, ORBER — P — ROYALS

M

PERSONAL: Born April 27, 1977, in Caracas, Venezuela. ... 6-3/200. ... Throws right, bats right. ... Full name: Orber Aquiles Moreno.
HIGH SCHOOL: Luisa Caceres (Venezuela).
TRANSACTIONS/CAREER NOTES: Signed as non-drafted free agent by Kansas City Royals organization (November 10, 1993). ... On Kansas City disabled list (June 10, 1999-remainder of season); included rehabilitation assignment to Gulf Coast Royals (July 26-27). ... On disabled list (March 24, 2000-entire season). ... On Kansas City disabled list (March 31-May 28, 2001).

Year League	W	L	Pct.	ERA	G	GS	CG	ShO	Sv.	IP	H	R	ER	BB	SO
1994—Dominican Royals (DSL)....	3	3	.500	3.19	16	11	0	0	1	67 2/3	51	33	24	27	44
1995—Gulf Coast Royals (GCL)	1	1	.500	2.45	8	3	0	0	0	22	15	9	6	7	21
1996—Gulf Coast Royals (GCL)	5	1	.833	1.36	12	7	0	0	1	46 1/3	37	15	7	10	50
1997—Lansing (Midw.)	4	8	.333	4.81	27	25	0	0	0	138 1/3	150	83	74	45	128
1998—Wilmington (Caro.)............	3	2	.600	0.82	23	0	0	0	7	33	8	3	3	10	50
—Wichita (Texas)	0	1	.000	2.88	24	0	0	0	7	34 1/3	28	13	11	12	40
1999—Omaha (PCL)...................	3	1	.750	2.10	16	0	0	0	4	25 2/3	17	6	6	4	30
—Kansas City (A.L.)	0	0	...	5.63	7	0	0	0	0	8	4	5	5	6	7
—Gulf Coast Royals (GCL)	0	0	...	0.00	1	1	0	0	0	1	0	0	0	0	1
2000—Kansas City (A.L.)							Did not play.								
2001—Wilmington (Caro.)............	1	1	.500	2.53	8	1	0	0	0	10 2/3	12	5	3	1	16
—Wichita (Texas)	0	0	...	0.00	5	0	0	0	1	8 2/3	3	0	0	2	10
—Omaha (PCL)...................	1	1	.500	4.71	17	0	0	0	3	21	19	11	11	8	25
Major League totals (1 year)........	0	0	...	5.63	7	0	0	0	0	8	4	5	5	6	7

MORGAN, MIKE — P — DIAMONDBACKS

PERSONAL: Born October 8, 1959, in Tulare, Calif. ... 6-2/220. ... Throws right, bats right. ... Full name: Michael Thomas Morgan.
HIGH SCHOOL: Valley (Las Vegas).
TRANSACTIONS/CAREER NOTES: Selected by Oakland Athletics organization in first round (fourth pick overall) of free-agent draft (June 6, 1978). ... On disabled list (May 14-June 27, 1980). ... Traded by A's to New York Yankees for SS Fred Stanley and a player to be named later (November 3, 1980); A's acquired 2B Brian Doyle to complete deal (November 17, 1980). ... On disabled list (April 9-22, 1981). ... Traded by Yankees with OF/1B Dave Collins, 1B Fred McGriff and cash to Toronto Blue Jays for P Dale Murray and OF/C Tom Dodd (December 9, 1982). ... On Toronto disabled list (July 2-August 23, 1983); included rehabilitation assignment to Syracuse (August 1-18). ... Selected by Seattle Mariners from Blue Jays organization in Rule 5 major league draft (December 3, 1984). ... On Seattle disabled list (April 17, 1985-remainder of season); included rehabilitation assignment to Calgary (July 19-22). ... Traded by Mariners to Baltimore Orioles for P Ken Dixon (December 9, 1987). ... On Baltimore disabled list (June 9-July 19, 1988); included rehabilitation assignment to Rochester (June 30-July 17). ... On Baltimore disabled list (August 12, 1988-remainder of season). ... Traded by Orioles to Los Angeles Dodgers for OF Mike Devereaux (March 12, 1989). ...

Granted free agency (October 28, 1991). ... Signed by Chicago Cubs (December 3, 1991). ... On disabled list (June 14-29, 1993; May 9-27, June 2-22 and July 28, 1994-remainder of season). ... On Chicago disabled list (April 24-May 25, 1995); included rehabilitation assignment to Orlando (May 15-25). ... Traded by Cubs with 3B/OF Paul Torres and C Francisco Morales to St. Louis Cardinals for 3B Todd Zeile and cash (June 16, 1995). ... On St. Louis disabled list (July 4-24, 1995). ... Granted free agency (November 6, 1995). ... Re-signed by Cardinals (December 7, 1995). ... On St. Louis disabled list (March 22-May 18, 1996); included rehabilitation assignment to St. Petersburg (April 20-May 15). ... Released by Cardinals (August 28, 1996). ... Signed by Cincinnati Reds (September 4, 1996). ... On disabled list (June 8-24, 1997). ... Granted free agency (October 28, 1997). ... Signed by Minnesota Twins (December 16, 1997). ... On Minnesota disabled list (June 27-July 13 and July 15-August 16, 1998). ... Traded by Twins to Cubs for cash and a player to be named later (August 25, 1998); Twins acquired P Scott Downs to complete deal (November 3, 1998). ... Granted free agency (October 30, 1998). ... Signed by Texas Rangers organization (January 26, 1999). ... On disabled list (May 25-June 9, 1999). ... Granted free agency (November 8, 1999). ... Signed by Arizona Diamondbacks organization (January 14, 2000). ... On Arizona disabled list (April 15-July 23, 2001); included rehabilitation assignment to Tucson (July 16-23). ... Granted free agency (November 19, 2001). ... Re-signed by Diamondbacks (January 3, 2002).

RECORDS: Holds major league record for most clubs played and pitched for in career (since 1900)—12.

Year League	W	L	Pct.	ERA	G	GS	CG	ShO	Sv.	IP	H	R	ER	BB	SO
1978—Oakland (A.L.)	0	3	.000	7.50	3	3	1	0	0	12	19	12	10	8	0
—Vancouver (PCL)	5	6	.455	5.58	14	14	5	1	0	92	109	67	57	54	31
1979—Ogden (PCL)	5	5	.500	3.48	13	13	6	0	0	101	93	48	39	49	42
—Oakland (A.L.)	2	10	.167	5.96	13	13	2	0	0	77	102	57	51	50	17
1980—Ogden (PCL)	6	9	.400	5.40	20	20	3	0	0	115	135	79	69	77	46
1981—Nashville (Sou.)■	8	7	.533	4.42	26	26	7	0	0	169	164	97	83	83	100
1982—New York (A.L.)	7	11	.389	4.37	30	23	2	0	0	150 1/3	167	77	73	67	71
1983—Toronto (A.L.)■	0	3	.000	5.16	16	4	0	0	0	45 1/3	48	26	26	21	22
—Syracuse (I.L.)	0	3	.000	5.59	5	4	0	0	1	19 1/3	20	12	12	13	17
1984—Syracuse (I.L.)	13	11	.542	4.07	34	28	10	•4	1	*185 2/3	167	•101	84	•100	105
1985—Seattle (A.L.)■	1	1	.500	12.00	2	2	0	0	0	6	11	8	8	5	2
—Calgary (PCL)	0	0	...	4.50	1	1	0	0	0	2	3	1	1	0	0
1986—Seattle (A.L.)	11	•17	.393	4.53	37	33	9	1	1	216 1/3	243	122	109	86	116
1987—Seattle (A.L.)	12	17	.414	4.65	34	31	8	2	0	207	245	117	107	53	85
1988—Baltimore (A.L.)■	1	6	.143	5.43	22	10	2	0	1	71 1/3	70	45	43	23	29
—Rochester (I.L.)	0	2	.000	4.76	3	3	0	0	0	17	19	10	9	6	7
1989—Los Angeles (N.L.)■	8	11	.421	2.53	40	19	0	0	0	152 1/3	130	51	43	33	72
1990—Los Angeles (N.L.)	11	15	.423	3.75	33	33	6	•4	0	211	216	100	88	60	106
1991—Los Angeles (N.L.)	14	10	.583	2.78	34	33	5	1	1	236 1/3	197	85	73	61	140
1992—Chicago (N.L.)■	16	8	.667	2.55	34	34	6	1	0	240	203	80	68	79	123
1993—Chicago (N.L.)	10	15	.400	4.03	32	32	1	1	0	207 2/3	206	100	93	74	111
1994—Chicago (N.L.)	2	10	.167	6.69	15	15	1	0	0	80 2/3	111	65	60	35	57
1995—Orlando (Sou.)	0	2	.000	7.59	2	2	0	0	0	10 2/3	13	9	9	7	5
—Chicago (N.L.)	2	1	.667	2.19	4	4	0	0	0	24 2/3	19	8	6	9	15
—St. Louis (N.L.)■	5	6	.455	3.88	17	17	1	0	0	106 2/3	114	48	46	25	46
1996—St. Petersburg (FSL)	1	0	1.000	0.00	1	1	0	0	0	5 2/3	4	0	0	1	4
—Louisville (A.A.)	1	3	.250	7.04	4	4	1	0	0	23	29	18	18	11	10
—St. Louis (N.L.)	4	8	.333	5.24	18	18	0	0	0	103	118	63	60	40	55
—Cincinnati (N.L.)■	2	3	.400	2.30	5	5	0	0	0	27 1/3	28	9	7	7	19
1997—Cincinnati (N.L.)	9	12	.429	4.78	31	30	1	0	0	162	165	91	86	49	103
1998—Minnesota (A.L.)■	4	2	.667	3.49	18	17	0	0	0	98	108	41	38	24	50
—Chicago (N.L.)	0	1	.000	7.15	5	5	0	0	0	22 2/3	30	21	18	15	10
1999—Texas (A.L.)■	13	10	.565	6.24	34	25	1	0	0	140	184	108	97	48	61
2000—Arizona (N.L.)■	5	5	.500	4.87	60	4	0	0	5	101 2/3	123	55	55	40	56
2001—Arizona (N.L.)	1	0	1.000	4.26	31	1	0	0	0	38	45	20	18	17	24
—Tucson (PCL)	0	0	...	3.00	2	2	0	0	0	3	5	1	1	0	4
A.L. totals (10 years)	51	80	.389	4.94	209	161	25	3	2	1023 1/3	1197	613	562	385	453
N.L. totals (12 years)	89	105	.459	3.79	359	250	21	7	6	1714 1/3	1705	796	721	544	937
Major League totals (21 years)	140	185	.431	4.22	568	411	46	10	8	2737 2/3	2902	1409	1283	929	1390

DIVISION SERIES RECORD

Year League	W	L	Pct.	ERA	G	GS	CG	ShO	Sv.	IP	H	R	ER	BB	SO
1998—Chicago (N.L.)	0	0	...	0.00	2	0	0	0	0	1 1/3	0	0	0	0	1
2001—Arizona (N.L.)	0	0	...	4.50	3	0	0	0	0	2	2	1	1	2	1
Division series totals (2 years)	0	0	...	2.70	5	0	0	0	0	3 1/3	2	1	1	2	2

CHAMPIONSHIP SERIES RECORD

Year League	W	L	Pct.	ERA	G	GS	CG	ShO	Sv.	IP	H	R	ER	BB	SO
2001—Arizona (N.L.)	0	0	...	27.00	2	0	0	0	0	1	3	3	3	1	1

WORLD SERIES RECORD

NOTES: Member of World Series championship team (2001).

Year League	W	L	Pct.	ERA	G	GS	CG	ShO	Sv.	IP	H	R	ER	BB	SO
2001—Arizona (N.L.)	0	0	...	0.00	3	0	0	0	0	4 2/3	1	0	0	0	1

ALL-STAR GAME RECORD

Year League	W	L	Pct.	ERA	GS	CG	ShO	Sv.	IP	H	R	ER	BB	SO
1991—National	0	0	...	0.00	0	0	0	0	1	0	0	0	0	1

M

MORRIS, MATT P CARDINALS

PERSONAL: Born August 9, 1974, in Middletown, N.Y. ... 6-5/210. ... Throws right, bats right. ... Full name: Matthew Christian Morris.
HIGH SCHOOL: Valley Central (Montgomery, N.Y.).
COLLEGE: Seton Hall.
TRANSACTIONS/CAREER NOTES: Selected by Milwaukee Brewers organization in 25th round of free-agent draft (June 1, 1992); did not sign. ... Selected by St. Louis Cardinals organization in first round (12th pick overall) of free-agent draft (June 1, 1995). ... On St. Louis disabled list (March 24-April 11 and April 12-July 10, 1998); included rehabilitation assignments to Arkansas (April 6-11) and Memphis (June 21-July 10). ... On disabled list (March 26, 1999-entire season). ... On St. Louis disabled list (April 2-May 28, 2000); included rehabilitation assignments to Arkansas (May 2-11) and Memphis (May 12-May 28).

HONORS: Named N.L. Rookie Pitcher of the Year by THE SPORTING NEWS (1997). ... Named N.L. Comeback Player of the Year by THE SPORTING NEWS (2001).

MISCELLANEOUS: Struck out in only appearance as pinch hitter (1997). ... Appeared in one game as pinch runner (2000).

Year League	W	L	Pct.	ERA	G	GS	CG	ShO	Sv.	IP	H	R	ER	BB	SO
1995— New Jersey (NY-Penn)	2	0	1.000	1.64	2	2	0	0	0	11	12	3	2	3	13
— St. Petersburg (FSL)	3	2	.600	2.38	6	6	1	1	0	34	22	16	9	11	31
1996— Arkansas (Texas)	12	12	.500	3.88	27	27	4	*4	0	167	178	79	72	48	120
— Louisville (A.A.)	0	1	.000	3.38	1	1	0	0	0	8	8	3	3	1	9
1997— St. Louis (N.L.)	12	9	.571	3.19	33	33	3	0	0	217	208	88	77	69	149
1998— Arkansas (Texas)	0	0	...	0.00	1	0	0	0	1	4	4	0	0	0	2
— St. Louis (N.L.)	7	5	.583	2.53	17	17	2	1	0	113²/₃	101	37	32	42	79
— Memphis (PCL)	1	0	1.000	4.50	4	4	0	0	0	14	16	8	7	4	21
1999— St. Louis (N.L.)							Did not play.								
2000— Arkansas (Texas)	0	0	...	6.43	2	2	0	0	0	7	8	5	5	4	7
— Memphis (PCL)	1	2	.333	7.98	3	3	0	0	0	14²/₃	20	13	13	6	8
— St. Louis (N.L.)	3	3	.500	3.57	31	0	0	0	4	53	53	22	21	17	34
2001— St. Louis (N.L.)	•22	8	.733	3.16	34	34	2	1	0	216¹/₃	218	86	76	54	185
Major League totals (4 years)	**44**	**25**	**.638**	**3.09**	**115**	**84**	**7**	**2**	**4**	**600**	**580**	**233**	**206**	**182**	**447**

DIVISION SERIES RECORD

Year League	W	L	Pct.	ERA	G	GS	CG	ShO	Sv.	IP	H	R	ER	BB	SO
2000— St. Louis (N.L.)	0	0	...	0.00	2	0	0	0	0	2	0	0	0	1	0
2001— St. Louis (N.L.)	0	1	.000	1.20	2	2	0	0	0	15	13	2	2	5	12
Division series totals (2 years)	**0**	**1**	**.000**	**1.06**	**4**	**2**	**0**	**0**	**0**	**17**	**13**	**2**	**2**	**6**	**12**

CHAMPIONSHIP SERIES RECORD

Year League	W	L	Pct.	ERA	G	GS	CG	ShO	Sv.	IP	H	R	ER	BB	SO
2000— St. Louis (N.L.)	0	0	...	4.91	2	0	0	0	0	3²/₃	2	2	2	2	2

ALL-STAR GAME RECORD

Year League	W	L	Pct.	ERA	GS	CG	ShO	Sv.	IP	H	R	ER	BB	SO
2001— National	0	0	...	0.00	0	0	0	0	1	1	0	0	0	1

MORRIS, WARREN · 2B · PIRATES

PERSONAL: Born January 11, 1974, in Alexandria, La. ... 5-11/180. ... Bats left, throws right. ... Full name: Warren Randall Morris.
HIGH SCHOOL: Bolton (Alexandria, La.).
COLLEGE: Louisiana State.
TRANSACTIONS/CAREER NOTES: Selected by Texas Rangers organization in fifth round of free-agent draft (June 2, 1996). ... Traded by Rangers with P Todd Van Poppel to Pittsburgh Pirates for P Esteban Loaiza (July 17, 1998). ... On Nashville disabled list (July 1-12, 2001). ... On Pittsburgh disabled list (August 14-September 1, 2001).
MISCELLANEOUS: Member of 1996 U.S. Olympic baseball team.

							BATTING								FIELDING		
Year Team (League)	Pos.	G	AB	R	H	2B	3B	HR	RBI	Avg.	BB	SO	SB	PO	A	E	Avg.
1997— Charlotte (FSL)	2B-3B	128	494	78	151	27	9	12	75	.306	62	100	16	193	247	18	.961
— Oklahoma City (A.A.)	2B	8	32	3	7	1	0	1	3	.219	3	5	0	17	31	0	1.000
1998— Tulsa (Texas)	2B	95	390	59	129	22	5	14	73	.331	43	63	12	179	274	17	.964
— Carolina (Sou.)■	2B	44	151	28	50	8	3	5	30	.331	24	34	5	87	100	7	.964
1999— Pittsburgh (N.L.)	2B	147	511	65	147	20	3	15	73	.288	59	88	3	263	403	14	.979
2000— Pittsburgh (N.L.)	2B	144	528	68	137	31	2	3	43	.259	65	78	7	291	414	15	.979
2001— Nashville (PCL)	2B-3B	57	223	26	68	16	2	5	40	.305	12	21	3	106	149	9	.966
— Pittsburgh (N.L.)	2B-3B	48	103	6	21	6	0	2	11	.204	3	9	2	41	70	4	.965
Major League totals (3 years)		**339**	**1142**	**139**	**305**	**57**	**5**	**20**	**127**	**.267**	**127**	**175**	**12**	**595**	**887**	**33**	**.978**

MOSS, DAMIAN · P · BRAVES

PERSONAL: Born November 24, 1976, in Darlinghurst, Australia. ... 6-0/187. ... Throws left, bats right. ... Full name: Damian Joseph Moss.
HIGH SCHOOL: Liverpool Boys (Australia).
TRANSACTIONS/CAREER NOTES: Signed as non-drafted free agent by Atlanta Braves organization (July 1, 1993). ... On disabled list (March 27, 1998-entire season). ... On Atlanta disabled list (April 3-June 1, 1999). ... On Atlanta disabled list (May 11-June 18, 2001); included rehabilitation assignment to Greenville (June 8-18). ... On Richmond disabled list (August 3-12, 2001).
STATISTICAL NOTES: Pitched 6-0 no-hit victory vs. Bluefield (June 26, 1994; second game). ... Led Appalachian League with 14 hit batsmen in 1994.

Year League	W	L	Pct.	ERA	G	GS	CG	ShO	Sv.	IP	H	R	ER	BB	SO
1994— Danville (Appl.)	2	5	.286	3.58	12	12	1	1	0	60¹/₃	30	28	24	55	77
1995— Macon (S.Atl.)	9	10	.474	3.56	27	27	0	0	0	149¹/₃	134	73	59	70	•177
1996— Durham (Caro.)	9	1	*.900	2.25	14	14	0	0	0	84	52	25	21	40	89
— Greenville (Sou.)	2	5	.286	4.97	11	10	0	0	0	58	57	41	32	35	48
1997— Greenville (Sou.)	6	8	.429	5.35	21	19	1	0	0	112²/₃	111	73	67	58	116
1998— Greenville (Sou.)							Did not play.								
1999— Macon (S.Atl.)	0	3	.000	4.32	12	12	0	0	0	41²/₃	33	20	20	15	49
— Greenville (Sou.)	1	3	.250	8.54	7	7	0	0	0	32²/₃	50	33	31	21	22
2000— Richmond (I.L.)	9	6	.600	3.14	29	•28	0	0	0	160²/₃	130	67	56	*106	123
2001— Richmond (I.L.)	5	4	.556	3.15	17	16	0	0	0	88²/₃	75	34	31	38	94
— Atlanta (N.L.)	0	0	...	3.00	5	1	0	0	0	9	3	3	3	9	8
— Greenville (Sou.)	0	1	.000	3.00	3	2	0	0	0	9	7	3	3	0	10
Major League totals (1 year)	**0**	**0**	**...**	**3.00**	**5**	**1**	**0**	**0**	**0**	**9**	**3**	**3**	**3**	**9**	**8**

MOTA, DANNY   P   DODGERS

PERSONAL: Born October 9, 1975, in Santo Domingo, Dominican Republic. ... 6-0/170. ... Throws right, bats right. ... Full name: Daniel Avila Mota.

TRANSACTIONS/CAREER NOTES: Signed as non-drafted free agent by New York Yankees organization (April 15, 1994). ... Traded by Yankees with P Eric Milton, SS Cristian Guzman, OF Brian Buchanan and cash to Minnesota Twins for 2B Chuck Knoblauch (February 5, 1998). ... On Fort Myers disabled list (April 8-27, 1999). ... On New Britain disabled list (June 26, 1999-remainder of season). ... Claimed on waivers by Los Angeles Dodgers (July 23, 2001). ... On Las Vegas disabled list (July 25-August 1, 2001).

Year League	W	L	Pct.	ERA	G	GS	CG	ShO	Sv.	IP	H	R	ER	BB	SO
1994— Dominican Yankees (DSL)..	2	3	.400	4.53	13	12	0	0	0	57²/₃	50	39	29	24	51
1995— Gulf Coast Yankees (GCL)..	2	3	.400	2.20	14	0	0	0	0	32²/₃	27	9	8	4	35
1996— Oneonta (NY-Penn)	0	1	.000	4.50	10	0	0	0	0	10	10	5	5	2	11
1997— Oneonta (NY-Penn)	1	0	1.000	2.22	27	0	0	0	*17	28¹/₃	21	8	7	16	40
— Greensboro (S.Atl.)	2	0	1.000	1.82	20	0	0	0	1	29²/₃	17	6	6	11	30
1998— Fort Wayne (Midw.)■........	4	3	.571	2.25	25	0	0	0	7	32	24	14	8	8	39
— Fort Myers (FSL)	3	5	.375	2.85	19	4	0	0	0	47¹/₃	45	21	15	22	49
1999— Fort Myers (FSL)	1	1	.500	2.41	11	0	0	0	0	18²/₃	19	5	5	5	22
— New Britain (East.)	0	1	.000	3.55	6	0	0	0	0	12²/₃	11	5	5	5	12
2000— Fort Myers (FSL)	2	2	.500	2.05	29	1	0	0	4	48¹/₃	38	20	11	23	52
— New Britain (East.)	3	1	.750	2.86	24	0	0	0	4	28¹/₃	19	13	9	8	40
— Salt Lake (PCL)	0	0	...	1.59	4	0	0	0	0	5²/₃	5	1	1	1	5
— Minnesota (A.L.)	0	0	...	8.44	4	0	0	0	0	5¹/₃	10	5	5	1	3
2001— Edmonton (PCL)	3	3	.500	5.89	34	0	0	0	2	47¹/₃	52	31	31	23	43
— Las Vegas (PCL)■	1	2	.333	7.71	12	0	0	0	1	11²/₃	16	10	10	8	7
Major League totals (1 year)........	0	0	...	8.44	4	0	0	0	0	5¹/₃	10	5	5	1	3

MOTA, GUILLERMO   P   EXPOS

PERSONAL: Born July 25, 1973, in San Pedro de Macoris, Dominican Republic. ... 6-4/205. ... Throws right, bats right. ... Full name: Guillermo Reynoso Mota.

HIGH SCHOOL: Jose Joaquin Perez (San Pedro de Macoris, Dominican Republic).

TRANSACTIONS/CAREER NOTES: Signed as non-drafted free agent by New York Mets organization (September 7, 1990). ... Selected by Montreal Expos organization from Mets organization in Rule 5 minor league draft (December 9, 1996). ... Re-signed by Expos organization (March 20, 1999). ... On Montreal disabled list (July 13-September 1, 2001); included rehabilitation assignment to Ottawa (August 24-31).

STATISTICAL NOTES: Led Gulf Coast League third basemen with .943 fielding percentage and tied for Gulf Coast League lead with 40 putouts and 11 double plays in 1993. ... Led Appalachian League third basemen with 44 putouts, 157 assists, 214 total chances, 12 double plays and .939 fielding percentage in 1994. ... Led South Atlantic League shortstops with 615 total chances and 66 double plays in 1995. ... Hit home run in first major league at-bat (June 9, 1999).

MISCELLANEOUS: Played infield (1991-96).

Year League	W	L	Pct.	ERA	G	GS	CG	ShO	Sv.	IP	H	R	ER	BB	SO
1997— Cape Fear (S.Atl.)■	5	10	.333	4.36	25	23	0	0	0	126	135	65	61	33	112
1998— Jupiter (FSL)	3	2	.600	0.66	20	0	0	0	2	41	18	6	3	6	27
— Harrisburg (East.)	2	0	1.000	1.06	12	0	0	0	4	17	10	2	2	2	19
1999— Ottawa (I.L.)	2	0	1.000	1.89	14	0	0	0	5	19	16	6	4	5	17
— Montreal (N.L.)	2	4	.333	2.93	51	0	0	0	0	55¹/₃	54	24	18	25	27
2000— Ottawa (I.L.)	4	5	.444	2.29	35	0	0	0	7	63	49	16	16	31	35
— Montreal (N.L.)	1	1	.500	6.00	29	0	0	0	0	30	27	21	20	12	24
2001— Montreal (N.L.)	1	3	.250	5.26	53	0	0	0	0	49²/₃	51	30	29	18	31
— Ottawa (I.L.)	0	0	...	2.25	4	0	0	0	0	4	1	1	1	0	4
Major League totals (3 years).......	4	8	.333	4.47	133	0	0	0	0	135	132	75	67	55	82

RECORD AS POSITION PLAYER

				BATTING										FIELDING		
Year Team (League)	Pos.	G	AB	R	H	2B	3B	HR	RBI	Avg.	BB	SO	SB	PO	A	E	Avg.
1991— Dom. Mets (DSL)		32	90	4	22	2	0	0	12	.244	9	19	0	...	...	...	...
1992— Dom. Mets (DSL)	IF	70	228	49	68	10	3	6	40	.298	28	40	10	133	173	24	.927
1993— GC Mets (GCL)	3B-SS	43	169	23	42	7	2	1	22	.249	7	37	1	‡42	95	8	†.945
1994— St. Lucie (FSL)	3B	1	4	1	0	0	0	0	0	.000	0	0	0	1	5	1	.857
— Kingsport (Appl.)........	3B-SS	65	245	40	60	10	2	9	37	.245	20	78	5	†55	†175	16	†.935
1995— Columbia (S.Atl.)........	SS-1B	123	400	45	97	24	3	4	45	.243	32	127	8	205	373	40	.935
1996— St. Lucie (FSL)	SS-3B	102	304	34	71	10	3	1	21	.234	34	90	8	127	293	21	.952

MOTTOLA, CHAD   OF   BLUE JAYS

PERSONAL: Born October 15, 1971, in Augusta, Ga. ... 6-3/225. ... Bats right, throws right. ... Full name: Charles Edward Mottola.

HIGH SCHOOL: St. Thomas Aquinas (Fort Lauderdale, Fla.).

COLLEGE: Central Florida.

TRANSACTIONS/CAREER NOTES: Selected by Baltimore Orioles organization in 10th round of free-agent draft (June 5, 1989); did not sign. ... Selected by Cincinnati Reds organization in first round (fifth pick overall) of free-agent draft (June 1, 1992). ... On disabled list (May 11-20, 1994). ... Traded by Reds to Texas Rangers for a player to be named later (April 18, 1998). ... On Oklahoma disabled list (May 18-June 30, 1998). ... Granted free agency (October 15, 1998). ... Signed by Chicago White Sox organization (October 15, 1998). ... Granted free agency (October 15, 1999). ... Signed by Toronto Blue Jays organization (December 17, 1998). ... Granted free agency (October 15, 1999). ... Signed by Toronto Blue Jays organization (November 17, 1999). ... Traded by Blue Jays to Florida Marlins for a player to be named later or cash (January 16, 2001); Blue Jays acquired cash to complete deal (March 22, 2001). ... On Calgary disabled list (May 3-15, 2001). ... Granted free agency (October 8, 2001). ... Signed by Blue Jays organization (December 18, 2001).

HONORS: Named International League Most Valuable Player (2000).

STATISTICAL NOTES: Tied for International League lead with four double plays by outfielder in 1999. ... Led International League with .566 slugging percentage in 2000.

Year	Team (League)	Pos.	G	AB	R	H	2B	3B	HR	RBI	Avg.	BB	SO	SB	PO	A	E	Avg.
							BATTING									FIELDING		
1992—Billings (Pio.)		OF	57	213	53	61	8	3	12	37	.286	25	43	12	89	9	3	.970
1993—Win.-Salem (Caro.)		OF	137	493	76	138	25	3	21	91	.280	62	109	13	214	*20	*15	.940
1994—Chattanooga (Sou.)		OF	118	402	44	97	19	1	7	41	.241	30	68	9	230	17	1	.996
1995—Chattanooga (Sou.)		OF	51	181	32	53	13	1	10	39	.293	13	32	1	106	6	3	.974
—Indianapolis (A.A.)		OF	69	239	40	62	11	1	8	37	.259	20	50	8	151	11	4	.976
1996—Indianapolis (A.A.)		OF-DH	103	362	45	95	24	3	9	47	.262	21	93	9	176	8	6	.968
—Cincinnati (N.L.)		OF	35	79	10	17	3	0	3	6	.215	6	16	2	42	2	0	1.000
1997—Indianapolis (A.A.)		OF-DH	83	284	33	82	10	6	7	45	.289	16	43	12	136	8	8	.947
—Chattanooga (Sou.)		OF-DH	46	174	35	63	9	3	5	32	.362	16	23	7	74	5	3	.963
1998—Indianapolis (I.L.)		OF	5	12	2	5	0	0	1	2	.417	4	0	0	7	2	0	1.000
—Tulsa (Texas)		DH-OF	8	26	9	13	1	0	1	7	.500	10	1	3	5	0	0	1.000
—Oklahoma (PCL)		OF-DH	74	257	29	68	13	1	2	22	.265	18	49	8	118	5	6	.953
1999—Charlotte (I.L.)		OF-DH	140	511	95	164	32	4	20	94	.321	60	83	18	288	•17	6	.981
2000—Syracuse (I.L.)		OF	134	505	85	156	25	3	*33	102	.309	37	99	30	259	8	*10	.964
—Toronto (A.L.)		OF	3	9	1	2	0	0	0	2	.222	0	4	0	5	0	0	1.000
2001—Calgary (PCL)		OF	119	457	66	135	23	2	15	66	.295	30	85	11	235	9	8	.968
—Florida (N.L.)		OF	5	7	1	0	0	0	0	1	.000	2	2	0	8	1	0	1.000
American League totals (1 year)			3	9	1	2	0	0	0	2	.222	0	4	0	5	0	0	1.000
National League totals (2 years)			40	86	11	17	3	0	3	7	.198	8	18	2	50	3	0	1.000
Major League totals (3 years)			43	95	12	19	3	0	3	9	.200	8	22	2	55	3	0	1.000

MOUTON, JAMES — OF

PERSONAL: Born December 29, 1968, in Denver. ... 5-9/175. ... Bats right, throws right. ... Full name: James Raleigh Mouton. ... Name pronounced MOO-tawn.

HIGH SCHOOL: Burbank (Calif.).

COLLEGE: St. Mary's (Calif.).

TRANSACTIONS/CAREER NOTES: Selected by New York Yankees organization in 42nd round of free-agent draft (June 2, 1987); did not sign. ... Selected by Minnesota Twins organization in eighth round of free-agent draft (June 4, 1990); did not sign. ... Selected by Houston Astros organization in seventh round of free-agent draft (June 3, 1991). ... On Houston disabled list (June 12-30, 1995); included rehabilitation assignment to Tucson (June 27-30). ... Traded by Astros to San Diego Padres for P Sean Bergman (January 14, 1998). ... On San Diego disabled list (May 16-June 1, 1998); included rehabilitation assignment to Las Vegas (May 27-June 1). ... Granted free agency (December 21, 1998). ... Signed by Montreal Expos organization (April 5, 1999). ... Granted free agency (October 15, 1999). ... Signed by Milwaukee Brewers organization (December 13, 1999). ... Granted free agency (October 30, 2000). ... Re-signed by Brewers organization (December 7, 2000). ... On Milwaukee disabled list (July 3-18, 2001); included rehabilitation assignment to Indianapolis (July 16-18). ... Granted free agency (November 5, 2001).

HONORS: Named Pacific Coast League Most Valuable Player (1993).

STATISTICAL NOTES: Led New York-Pennsylvania League in caught stealing with 18 in 1991. ... Led New York-Pennsylvania League second basemen with 382 total chances in 1991. ... Led Florida State League second basemen with 623 total chances in 1992. ... Led Pacific Coast League with 286 total bases and tied for lead in caught stealing with 18 in 1993. ... Led Pacific Coast League second basemen with 674 total chances and 75 double plays in 1993. ... Career major league grand slams: 1.

Year	Team (League)	Pos.	G	AB	R	H	2B	3B	HR	RBI	Avg.	BB	SO	SB	PO	A	E	Avg.
							BATTING									FIELDING		
1991—Auburn (NY-Penn)		2B	76	288	71	76	15	*10	2	40	.264	55	32	*60	*170	184	*28	.927
1992—Osceola (FSL)		2B	133	507	*110	143	•30	6	11	62	.282	71	78	*51	*288	294	*41	.934
1993—Tucson (PCL)		2B	134	*546	*126	*172	*42	12	16	92	.315	72	82	40	*277	*354	*43	.936
1994—Houston (N.L.)		OF	99	310	43	76	11	0	2	16	.245	27	69	24	163	5	3	.982
—Tucson (PCL)		OF	4	17	2	7	1	0	1	1	.412	2	3	1	7	1	0	1.000
1995—Tucson (PCL)		OF	3	11	1	5	0	0	1	1	.455	0	2	0	1	0	1	.500
—Houston (N.L.)		OF	104	298	42	78	18	2	4	27	.262	25	59	25	136	4	0	1.000
1996—Houston (N.L.)		OF	122	300	40	79	15	1	3	34	.263	38	55	21	158	7	5	.971
—Tucson (PCL)		OF	1	4	1	1	0	0	0	0	.250	1	0	0	2	0	0	1.000
1997—Houston (N.L.)		OF	86	180	24	38	9	1	3	23	.211	18	30	9	86	1	0	1.000
1998—San Diego (N.L.)		OF-DH	55	63	8	12	2	1	0	7	.190	7	11	4	30	1	1	.969
—Las Vegas (PCL)		OF-DH-2B	50	192	38	68	17	3	4	31	.354	17	31	15	57	2	1	.983
1999—Montreal (N.L.)		OF-DH	95	122	18	32	5	1	2	13	.262	18	31	6	50	2	1	.981
2000—Milwaukee (N.L.)		OF	87	159	28	37	7	1	2	17	.233	30	43	13	84	3	1	.989
2001—Milwaukee (N.L.)		OF-DH	75	138	20	34	8	0	2	10	.246	11	40	7	81	2	3	.965
—Indianapolis (I.L.)		OF	2	9	0	4	2	0	0	2	.444	0	2	0	4	0	0	1.000
Major League totals (8 years)			723	1570	223	386	75	7	18	147	.246	174	338	109	788	25	14	.983

MOUTON, LYLE — OF — EXPOS

PERSONAL: Born May 13, 1969, in Lafayette, La. ... 6-4/230. ... Bats right, throws right. ... Full name: Lyle Joseph Mouton. ... Name pronounced MOO-tawn.

HIGH SCHOOL: St. Thomas More (Lafayette, La.).

COLLEGE: Louisiana State.

TRANSACTIONS/CAREER NOTES: Selected by New York Yankees organization in fifth round of free-agent draft (June 3, 1991). ... Traded by Yankees to Chicago White Sox (April 22, 1995), completing deal in which White Sox traded P Jack McDowell to Yankees for P Keith Heberling and a player to be named later (December 14, 1994). ... On Chicago disabled list (May 11-27, 1997); included rehabilitation assignment to Birmingham (May 25-27). ... Contract sold by White Sox to Yakult Swallows of Japan Central League (November 21, 1997). ... Contract purchased by Baltimore Orioles organization (July 2, 1999). ... Traded by Orioles to Milwaukee Brewers for OF Todd Dunn (June 1, 1999). ... On disabled list (June 2-June 16, 2000). ... Released by Brewers (November 27, 2000). ... Signed by Florida Marlins organization (April 2, 2001). ... Released by Marlins (May 23, 2001). ... Signed by Detroit Tigers organization (May 25, 2001). ... Traded by Tigers to Houston Astros for a player to be named later (August 31, 2001). ... Granted free agency (October 15, 2001). ... Signed by Montreal Expos organization (January 11, 2002).

Year	Team (League)	Pos.	G	AB	R	H	2B	3B	HR	RBI	Avg.	BB	SO	SB	PO	A	E	Avg.
1991—	Oneonta (NY-Penn)	OF	70	272	53	84	11	2	7	41	.309	31	38	15	106	5	5	.957
1992—	Prince William (Caro.)	OF	50	189	28	50	14	1	6	34	.265	17	42	4	49	5	4	.931
—	Albany (East.)	OF	64	214	25	46	12	2	2	27	.215	24	55	1	102	1	0	1.000
1993—	Albany (East.)	OF	135	491	74	125	22	3	16	76	.255	50	125	18	189	9	5	.975
1994—	Albany/Colonie (East.)	OF-3B	74	274	42	84	23	1	12	42	.307	27	62	7	118	4	2	.984
—	Columbus (I.L.)	OF	59	204	26	64	14	5	4	32	.314	14	45	5	99	5	1	.990
1995—	Nashville (A.A.)■	OF-DH	71	267	40	79	17	0	8	41	.296	23	58	10	123	8	3	.978
—	Chicago (A.L.)	OF-DH	58	179	23	54	16	0	5	27	.302	19	46	1	93	5	1	.990
1996—	Chicago (A.L.)	OF-DH	87	214	25	63	8	1	7	39	.294	22	50	3	64	1	2	.970
1997—	Chicago (A.L.)	OF-DH	88	242	26	65	9	0	5	23	.269	14	66	4	126	1	4	.969
—	Birmingham (Sou.)	OF	3	11	1	2	0	0	1	1	.182	1	4	0	5	0	0	1.000
1998—	Yakult (Jap. Cen.)■	OF	30	97	7	21	8	0	3	12	.216	9	27	0	...	...	...	...
—	Rochester (I.L.)■	OF-DH	37	137	23	44	9	2	7	32	.321	13	31	1	56	1	1	.983
—	Baltimore (A.L.)	OF-DH	18	39	5	12	2	0	2	7	.308	4	8	0	19	1	0	1.000
1999—	Rochester (I.L.)	OF-DH	44	162	25	36	9	1	4	17	.222	13	31	3	63	1	4	.941
—	Louisville (I.L.)■	OF-DH-1B	83	305	64	109	34	2	19	77	.357	27	67	19	181	7	2	.989
—	Milwaukee (N.L.)	OF	14	17	2	3	1	0	1	3	.176	2	3	0	1	0	0	1.000
2000—	Milwaukee (N.L.)	OF	42	97	14	27	7	1	2	16	.278	10	29	1	41	4	1	.978
—	Indianapolis (I.L.)	OF	52	197	33	60	23	0	12	51	.305	23	41	4	107	2	1	.991
2001—	Florida (N.L.)■	OF	21	17	1	1	0	0	0	1	.059	0	7	0	4	0	0	1.000
—	Toledo (I.L.)■	OF	67	262	59	83	18	2	18	49	.317	29	66	4	113	6	2	.983
—	New Orleans (PCL)■..	OF	2	9	1	3	1	0	1	1	.333	0	3	0	2	0	0	1.000
American League totals (4 years)			251	674	79	194	35	1	19	96	.288	59	170	8	302	8	7	.978
National League totals (3 years)			77	131	17	31	8	1	3	20	.237	12	39	1	46	4	1	.980
Major League totals (7 years)			328	805	96	225	43	2	22	116	.280	71	209	9	348	12	8	.978

MOYER, JAMIE   P   MARINERS

PERSONAL: Born November 18, 1962, in Sellersville, Pa. ... 6-0/175. ... Throws left, bats left. ... Son-in-law of Digger Phelps, ESPN college basketball analyst, and Notre Dame basketball coach (1971-72 through 1990-91).

HIGH SCHOOL: Souderton (Pa.) Area.

COLLEGE: St. Joseph's (Pa.).

TRANSACTIONS/CAREER NOTES: Selected by Chicago Cubs organization in sixth round of free-agent draft (June 4, 1984). ... Traded by Cubs with OF Rafael Palmeiro and P Drew Hall to Texas Rangers for P Mitch Williams, P Paul Kilgus, P Steve Wilson, IF Curtis Wilkerson, IF Luis Benitez and OF Pablo Delgado (December 5, 1988). ... On Texas disabled list (May 31-September 1, 1989); included rehabilitation assignments to Gulf Coast Rangers (August 5-14) and Tulsa (August 15-24). ... Released by Rangers (November 13, 1990). ... Signed by St. Louis Cardinals organization (January 9, 1991). ... Released by Cardinals (October 14, 1991). ... Signed by Cubs organization (January 8, 1992). ... Released by Cubs (March 30, 1992). ... Signed by Detroit Tigers organization (May 24, 1992). ... Granted free agency (December 8, 1992). ... Signed by Baltimore Orioles organization (December 14, 1992). ... Granted free agency (November 1, 1995). ... Signed by Boston Red Sox (January 2, 1996). ... Traded by Red Sox to Seattle Mariners for OF Darren Bragg (July 30, 1996). ... Granted free agency (October 29, 1996). ... Re-signed by Mariners (November 20, 1996). ... On Seattle disabled list (March 23-April 29, 1997); included rehabilitation assignment to Tacoma (April 24-29). ... On disabled list (April 15-June 2, 2000).

HONORS: Named lefthanded pitcher on THE SPORTING NEWS A.L. All-Star team (1999).

STATISTICAL NOTES: Led American Association with 16 home runs allowed in 1991. ... Led A.L. with .813 winning percentage in 1996. ... Led A.L. pitchers with 47 assists and nine double plays in 1999.

Year	League	W	L	Pct.	ERA	G	GS	CG	ShO	Sv.	IP	H	R	ER	BB	SO
1984—	Geneva (NY-Penn)	•9	3	.750	1.89	14	14	5	2	0	*104 2/3	59	27	22	31	*120
1985—	Winston-Salem (Caro.)	8	2	.800	2.30	12	12	6	2	0	94	82	36	24	22	94
—	Pittsfield (East.)	7	6	.538	3.72	15	15	3	0	0	96 2/3	99	49	40	32	51
1986—	Pittsfield (East.)	3	1	.750	0.88	6	6	0	0	0	41	27	10	4	16	42
—	Iowa (A.A.)	3	2	.600	2.55	6	6	2	0	0	42 1/3	25	14	12	11	25
—	Chicago (N.L.)	7	4	.636	5.05	16	16	1	1	0	87 1/3	107	52	49	42	45
1987—	Chicago (N.L.)	12	15	.444	5.10	35	33	1	0	0	201	210	127	*114	97	147
1988—	Chicago (N.L.)	9	15	.375	3.48	34	30	3	1	0	202	212	84	78	55	121
1989—	Texas (A.L.)■	4	9	.308	4.86	15	15	1	0	0	76	84	51	41	33	44
—	Gulf Coast Rangers (GCL)..	1	0	1.000	1.64	3	3	0	0	0	11	8	4	2	1	18
—	Tulsa (Texas)	1	1	.500	5.11	2	2	1	1	0	12 1/3	16	8	7	3	9
1990—	Texas (A.L.)	2	6	.250	4.66	33	10	1	0	0	102 1/3	115	59	53	39	58
1991—	St. Louis (N.L.)■	0	5	.000	5.74	8	7	0	0	0	31 1/3	38	21	20	16	20
—	Louisville (A.A.)	5	10	.333	3.80	20	20	1	0	0	125 2/3	125	64	53	43	69
1992—	Toledo (I.L.)■	10	8	.556	2.86	21	20	5	0	0	138 2/3	128	48	44	37	80
1993—	Rochester (I.L.)■	6	0	1.000	1.67	8	8	1	1	0	54	42	13	10	13	41
—	Baltimore (A.L.)	12	9	.571	3.43	25	25	3	1	0	152	154	63	58	38	90
1994—	Baltimore (A.L.)	5	7	.417	4.77	23	23	0	0	0	149	158	81	79	38	87
1995—	Baltimore (A.L.)	8	6	.571	5.21	27	18	0	0	0	115 2/3	117	70	67	30	65
1996—	Boston (A.L.)■	7	1	.875	4.50	23	10	0	0	0	90	111	50	45	27	50
—	Seattle (A.L.)	6	2	§.750	3.31	11	11	0	0	0	70 2/3	66	36	26	19	29
1997—	Tacoma (PCL)	1	0	1.000	0.00	1	1	0	0	0	5	1	0	0	0	6
—	Seattle (A.L.)	17	5	.773	3.86	30	30	2	0	0	188 2/3	187	82	81	43	113
1998—	Seattle (A.L.)	15	9	.625	3.53	34	34	4	3	0	234 1/3	234	99	92	42	158
1999—	Seattle (A.L.)	14	8	.636	3.87	32	32	4	0	0	228	235	108	98	48	137
2000—	Seattle (A.L.)	13	10	.565	5.49	26	26	0	0	0	154	173	103	94	53	98
2001—	Seattle (A.L.)	20	6	.769	3.43	33	33	1	0	0	209 2/3	187	84	80	44	119
A.L. totals (11 years)		123	78	.612	4.14	312	267	16	4	0	1770 1/3	1821	886	814	454	1048
N.L. totals (4 years)		28	39	.418	4.50	93	86	5	2	0	521 2/3	567	284	261	210	333
Major League totals (15 years)		151	117	.563	4.22	405	353	21	6	0	2292	2388	1170	1075	664	1381

DIVISION SERIES RECORD

Year League	W	L	Pct.	ERA	G	GS	CG	ShO	Sv.	IP	H	R	ER	BB	SO
1997—Seattle (A.L.)	0	1	.000	5.79	1	1	0	0	0	4²/₃	5	3	3	1	2
2001—Seattle (A.L.)	2	0	1.000	1.50	2	2	0	0	0	12	8	2	2	2	10
Division series totals (2 years)	2	1	.667	2.70	3	3	0	0	0	16²/₃	13	5	5	3	12

CHAMPIONSHIP SERIES RECORD

Year League	W	L	Pct.	ERA	G	GS	CG	ShO	Sv.	IP	H	R	ER	BB	SO
2001—Seattle (A.L.)	1	0	1.000	2.57	1	1	0	0	0	7	4	2	2	1	5

MUELLER, BILL   3B   CUBS

PERSONAL: Born March 17, 1971, in Maryland Heights, Mo. ... 5-10/180. ... Bats both, throws right. ... Full name: William Richard Mueller. ... Name pronounced MILL-er.
HIGH SCHOOL: DeSmet (Creve Coeur, Mo.).
COLLEGE: Southwest Missouri State.
TRANSACTIONS/CAREER NOTES: Selected by San Francisco Giants organization in 15th round of free-agent draft (June 3, 1993). ... On disabled list (July 1-16, 1997). ... On San Francisco disabled list (April 6-May 17, 1999); included rehabilitation assignment to Fresno (May 11-17). ... Traded by Giants to Chicago Cubs for P Tim Worrell (November 19, 2000). ... On Chicago disabled list (May 14-August 13, 2001); included rehabilitation assignment to Iowa (August 2-13).
STATISTICAL NOTES: Led California League with .435 on-base percentage in 1994. ... Led Pacific Coast League third basemen with 25 double plays in 1996. ... Had 17-game hitting streak (April 24-May 14, 1998). ... Had 15-game hitting streak (May 1-19, 2000). ... Led N.L. third basemen with .974 fielding percentage in 2000. ... Career major league grand slams: 2.

						BATTING								FIELDING		
Year Team (League)	Pos.	G	AB	R	H	2B	3B	HR	RBI	Avg.	BB	SO	SB	PO	A	E	Avg.
1993—Everett (N'West)	2B	58	200	31	60	8	2	1	24	.300	42	17	13	86	143	8	.966
1994—San Jose (Calif.)	3B-2B-SS	120	431	79	130	20	•9	5	72	.302	*103	47	4	83	276	29	.925
1995—Shreveport (Texas)	3B-2B	88	330	56	102	16	2	1	39	.309	53	36	6	52	169	5	.978
—Phoenix (PCL)	3B-2B	41	172	23	51	13	6	2	19	.297	19	31	0	26	85	7	.941
1996—Phoenix (PCL)	3-S-2-DH	106	440	73	133	14	6	4	36	.302	44	40	2	92	250	11	.969
—San Francisco (N.L.) ..	3B-2B	55	200	31	66	15	1	0	19	.330	24	26	0	51	99	6	.962
1997—San Francisco (N.L.) ..	3B	128	390	51	114	26	3	7	44	.292	48	71	4	85	218	14	.956
1998—San Francisco (N.L.) ..	3B-2B	145	534	93	157	27	0	9	59	.294	79	83	3	99	287	19	.953
1999—San Francisco (N.L.) ..	3B-2B	116	414	61	120	24	0	2	36	.290	65	52	4	83	195	12	.959
—Fresno (PCL)	3B	3	12	3	5	0	1	0	6	.417	0	0	0	2	10	3	.800
2000—San Francisco (N.L.) ..	3B-2B	153	560	97	150	29	4	10	55	.268	52	62	4	100	244	9	†.975
2001—Chicago (N.L.)■	3B-2B	70	210	38	62	12	1	6	23	.295	37	19	1	33	97	8	.942
—Iowa (PCL)	3B	8	26	3	11	3	0	0	4	.423	1	2	0	1	6	0	1.000
Major League totals (6 years)		667	2308	371	669	133	9	34	236	.290	305	313	16	451	1140	68	.959

DIVISION SERIES RECORD

						BATTING								FIELDING		
Year Team (League)	Pos.	G	AB	R	H	2B	3B	HR	RBI	Avg.	BB	SO	SB	PO	A	E	Avg.
1997—San Francisco (N.L.) ..	3B	3	12	1	3	0	0	1	1	.250	0	0	0	2	9	0	1.000
2000—San Francisco (N.L.) ..	3B	4	20	2	5	2	0	0	0	.250	0	4	0	3	5	0	1.000
Division series totals (2 years)		7	32	3	8	2	0	1	1	.250	0	4	0	5	14	0	1.000

M

MULDER, MARK   P   ATHLETICS

PERSONAL: Born August 5, 1977, in South Holland, Ill. ... 6-6/200. ... Throws left, bats left. ... Full name: Mark Alan Mulder.
HIGH SCHOOL: Thornwood (South Holland, Ill.).
COLLEGE: Michigan State.
TRANSACTIONS/CAREER NOTES: Selected by Detroit Tigers organization in 55th round of free-agent draft (June 1, 1995); did not sign. ... Selected by Oakland Athletics organization in first round (second pick overall) of free-agent draft (June 2, 1998).
HONORS: Named lefthanded pitcher on THE SPORTING NEWS A.L. All-Star team (2001).
STATISTICAL NOTES: Pitched 3-0 one-hit, complete-game victory against Arizona (July 6, 2001).

Year League	W	L	Pct.	ERA	G	GS	CG	ShO	Sv.	IP	H	R	ER	BB	SO
1999—Vancouver (PCL)	6	7	.462	4.06	22	22	1	0	0	128²/₃	152	69	58	31	81
2000—Sacramento (PCL)	1	1	.500	5.40	2	2	0	0	0	8¹/₃	15	11	5	4	6
—Oakland (A.L.)	9	10	.474	5.44	27	27	0	0	0	154	191	106	93	69	88
2001—Oakland (A.L.)	*21	8	.724	3.45	34	34	6	*4	0	229¹/₃	214	92	88	51	153
Major League totals (2 years)	30	18	.625	4.25	61	61	6	4	0	383¹/₃	405	198	181	120	241

DIVISION SERIES RECORD

Year League	W	L	Pct.	ERA	G	GS	CG	ShO	Sv.	IP	H	R	ER	BB	SO
2000—Oakland (A.L.)							Did not play.								
2001—Oakland (A.L.)	1	1	.500	2.45	2	2	0	0	0	11	14	5	3	2	7

MULHOLLAND, TERRY   P   DODGERS

PERSONAL: Born March 9, 1963, in Uniontown, Pa. ... 6-3/220. ... Throws left, bats right. ... Full name: Terence John Mulholland.
HIGH SCHOOL: Laurel Highlands (Uniontown, Pa.).
COLLEGE: Marietta College (Ohio).
TRANSACTIONS/CAREER NOTES: Selected by San Francisco Giants organization in first round (24th pick overall) of free-agent draft (June 4, 1984); pick received as compensation for Detroit Tigers signing free-agent IF Darrell Evans. ... On San Francisco disabled list (August 1, 1988-remainder of season). ... Traded by Giants with P Dennis Cook and 3B Charlie Hayes to Philadelphia Phillies for P Steve Bedrosian and a player

to be named later (June 18, 1989); Giants acquired IF Rick Parker to complete deal (August 7, 1989). ... On Philadelphia disabled list (June 12-28, 1990); included rehabilitation assignment to Scranton/Wilkes-Barre (June 23-24). ... Traded by Phillies with a player to be named later to New York Yankees for P Bobby Munoz, 2B Kevin Jordan and P Ryan Karp (February 9, 1994); Yankees acquired P Jeff Patterson to complete deal (November 8, 1994). ... Granted free agency (October 17, 1994). ... Signed by Giants (April 8, 1995). ... On San Francisco disabled list (June 6-July 4, 1995); included rehabilitation assignment to Phoenix (June 23-July 4). ... Granted free agency (November 3, 1995). ... Signed by Phillies organization (February 17, 1996). ... Traded by Phillies to Seattle Mariners for IF Desi Relaford (July 31, 1996). ... Granted free agency (October 28, 1996). ... Signed by Chicago Cubs (December 10, 1996). ... Claimed on waivers by Giants (August 8, 1997). ... Granted free agency (October 27, 1997). ... Signed by Cubs (February 2, 1998). ... Granted free agency (October 28, 1998). ... Re-signed by Cubs (November 6, 1998). ... Traded by Cubs with IF Jose Hernandez to Atlanta Braves for P Micah Bowie, P Ruben Quevado and a player to be named later (July 31, 1999); Cubs acquired P Joey Nation to complete deal (August 24, 1999). ... Granted free agency (October 31, 2000). ... Signed by Pittsburgh Pirates (December 10, 2000). ... On Pittsburgh disabled list (April 6-20 and June 12-August 1, 2001); included rehabilitation assignment to Altoona (July 27-29). ... Traded by Pirates to Los Angeles Dodgers for P Mike Fetters and P Adrian Burnside (July 31, 2001).

STATISTICAL NOTES: Pitched 6-0 no-hit victory for Philadelphia against San Francisco (August 15, 1990).

MISCELLANEOUS: Appeared in one game as pinch runner (1991). ... Appeared in one game as pinch runner with San Francisco (1995).

Year League	W	L	Pct.	ERA	G	GS	CG	ShO	Sv.	IP	H	R	ER	BB	SO
1984— Everett (N'West)	1	0	1.000	0.00	3	3	0	0	0	19	10	2	0	4	15
— Fresno (Calif.)	5	2	.714	2.95	9	9	0	0	0	42²/₃	32	17	14	36	39
1985— Shreveport (Texas)	9	8	.529	2.90	26	26	8	*3	0	176²/₃	166	79	57	87	122
1986— Phoenix (PCL)	8	5	.615	4.46	17	17	3	0	0	111	112	60	55	56	77
— San Francisco (N.L.)	1	7	.125	4.94	15	10	0	0	0	54²/₃	51	33	30	35	27
1987— Phoenix (PCL)	7	12	.368	5.07	37	*29	3	1	1	172¹/₃	200	*124	•97	90	94
1988— Phoenix (PCL)	7	3	.700	3.58	19	14	3	2	0	100²/₃	116	45	40	44	57
— San Francisco (N.L.)	2	1	.667	3.72	9	6	2	1	0	46	50	20	19	7	18
1989— San Francisco (N.L.)	0	0	...	4.09	5	1	0	0	0	11	15	5	5	4	6
— Phoenix (PCL)	4	5	.444	2.99	13	10	3	0	0	78¹/₃	67	30	26	26	61
— Philadelphia (N.L.)■	4	7	.364	5.00	20	17	2	1	0	104¹/₃	122	61	58	32	60
1990— Philadelphia (N.L.)	9	10	.474	3.34	33	26	6	1	0	180²/₃	172	78	67	42	75
— Scranton/W.B. (I.L.)	0	1	.000	3.00	1	1	0	0	0	6	9	4	2	2	2
1991— Philadelphia (N.L.)	16	13	.552	3.61	34	34	8	3	0	232	231	100	93	49	142
1992— Philadelphia (N.L.)	13	11	.542	3.81	32	32	*12	2	0	229	227	101	97	46	125
1993— Philadelphia (N.L.)	12	9	.571	3.25	29	28	7	2	0	191	177	80	69	40	116
1994— New York (A.L.)■	6	7	.462	6.49	24	19	2	0	0	120²/₃	150	94	87	37	72
1995— San Francisco (N.L.)■	5	13	.278	5.80	29	24	2	0	0	149	190	112	96	38	65
— Phoenix (PCL)	0	0	...	2.25	1	1	0	0	0	4	4	3	1	1	4
1996— Philadelphia (N.L.)■	8	7	.533	4.66	21	21	3	0	0	133¹/₃	157	74	69	21	52
— Seattle (A.L.)	5	4	.556	4.67	12	12	0	0	0	69¹/₃	75	38	36	28	34
1997— Chicago (N.L.)■	6	12	.333	4.07	25	25	1	0	0	157	162	79	71	45	74
— San Francisco (N.L.)■	0	1	.000	5.16	15	2	0	0	0	29²/₃	28	21	17	6	25
1998— Chicago (N.L.)■	6	5	.545	2.89	70	6	0	0	3	112	100	49	36	39	72
1999— Chicago (N.L.)	6	6	.500	5.15	26	16	0	0	0	110	137	71	63	32	44
— Atlanta (N.L.)■	4	2	.667	2.98	16	8	0	0	1	60¹/₃	64	24	20	13	39
2000— Atlanta (N.L.)	9	9	.500	5.11	54	20	1	0	1	156²/₃	198	96	89	41	78
2001— Pittsburgh (N.L.)■	0	0	...	3.72	22	1	0	0	0	36¹/₃	38	15	15	10	17
— Altoona (East.)	0	2	.000	3.86	2	2	0	0	0	2¹/₃	5	3	1	1	3
— Los Angeles (N.L.)■	1	1	.500	5.83	19	3	0	0	0	29¹/₃	40	20	19	7	25
A.L. totals (2 years)	11	11	.500	5.83	36	31	2	0	0	190	225	132	123	65	106
N.L. totals (14 years)	102	114	.472	4.15	474	280	44	10	5	2022¹/₃	2159	1039	933	507	1060
Major League totals (15 years)	113	125	.475	4.30	510	311	46	10	5	2212¹/₃	2384	1171	1056	572	1166

DIVISION SERIES RECORD

Year League	W	L	Pct.	ERA	G	GS	CG	ShO	Sv.	IP	H	R	ER	BB	SO
1998— Chicago (N.L.)	0	1	.000	11.57	2	0	0	0	0	2¹/₃	2	3	3	2	2
1999— Atlanta (N.L.)	0	0	...	27.00	2	0	0	0	0	²/₃	3	2	2	0	0
2000— Atlanta (N.L.)	0	0	...	5.40	3	0	0	0	0	3¹/₃	1	2	2	2	1
Division series totals (3 years)	0	1	.000	9.95	7	0	0	0	0	6¹/₃	6	7	7	4	3

CHAMPIONSHIP SERIES RECORD

Year League	W	L	Pct.	ERA	G	GS	CG	ShO	Sv.	IP	H	R	ER	BB	SO
1993— Philadelphia (N.L.)	0	1	.000	7.20	1	1	0	0	0	5	9	5	4	1	2
1999— Atlanta (N.L.)	0	0	...	0.00	2	0	0	0	0	2²/₃	1	0	0	1	2
Champ. series totals (2 years)	0	1	.000	4.70	3	1	0	0	0	7²/₃	10	5	4	2	4

WORLD SERIES RECORD

Year League	W	L	Pct.	ERA	G	GS	CG	ShO	Sv.	IP	H	R	ER	BB	SO
1993— Philadelphia (N.L.)	1	0	1.000	6.75	2	2	0	0	0	10²/₃	14	8	8	3	5
1999— Atlanta (N.L.)	0	0	...	7.36	2	0	0	0	0	3²/₃	5	3	3	1	3
World Series totals (2 years)	1	0	1.000	6.91	4	2	0	0	0	14¹/₃	19	11	11	4	8

ALL-STAR GAME RECORD

Year League	W	L	Pct.	ERA	GS	CG	ShO	Sv.	IP	H	R	ER	BB	SO
1993— National	0	0	...	4.50	1	0	0	0	2	1	1	1	2	0

M

MULLEN, SCOTT   P   ROYALS

PERSONAL: Born January 17, 1975, in San Benito, Texas. ... 6-2/190. ... Throws left, bats right. ... Full name: Kenneth Scott Mullen.
HIGH SCHOOL: Beaufort (S.C.).
COLLEGE: Dallas Baptist.
TRANSACTIONS/CAREER NOTES: Selected by Kansas City Royals organization in seventh round of free-agent draft (June 4, 1996). ... On Kansas City disabled list (March 31-May 4, 2001); included rehabilitation assignment to Omaha (April 5-May 4).

Year League	W	L	Pct.	ERA	G	GS	CG	ShO	Sv.	IP	H	R	ER	BB	SO
1996—Spokane (N'West)	5	6	.455	3.92	15	15	0	0	0	80 1/3	78	45	35	29	78
1997—Lansing (Midw.)	5	2	.714	3.70	16	16	0	0	0	92 1/3	90	46	38	31	78
—Wilmington (Caro.)	4	4	.500	4.55	11	11	0	0	0	59 1/3	64	35	30	26	43
1998—Wilmington (Caro.)	8	4	.667	2.21	14	14	1	1	0	85 2/3	68	28	21	25	56
—Wichita (Texas)	8	2	.800	4.11	12	12	0	0	0	70	66	34	32	26	42
1999—Wichita (Texas)	4	3	.571	4.01	9	9	0	0	0	49 1/3	47	28	22	18	30
—Omaha (PCL)	6	7	.462	6.26	20	20	0	0	0	119 1/3	150	91	83	53	87
2000—Wichita (Texas)	3	2	.600	3.19	33	1	0	0	7	73 1/3	65	27	26	26	61
—Omaha (PCL)	2	1	.667	3.05	16	0	0	0	0	20 2/3	15	10	7	8	21
—Kansas City (A.L.)	0	0	...	4.35	11	0	0	0	0	10 1/3	10	5	5	3	7
2001—Omaha (PCL)	5	4	.556	6.62	48	0	0	0	5	53	66	39	39	22	38
—Kansas City (A.L.)	0	0	...	4.50	17	0	0	0	0	10	13	6	5	9	3
Major League totals (2 years)	0	0	...	4.43	28	0	0	0	0	20 1/3	23	11	10	12	10

MUNOZ, BOBBY P

PERSONAL: Born March 3, 1968, in Rio Piedras, Puerto Rico. ... 6-7/237. ... Throws right, bats right. ... Full name: Roberto Munoz.
HIGH SCHOOL: Hialeah (Fla.) Miami Lakes.
JUNIOR COLLEGE: Palm Beach Junior College (Fla.) and Polk Community College (Fla.).
TRANSACTIONS/CAREER NOTES: Selected by New York Yankees organization in 15th round of free-agent draft (June 1, 1988). ... Traded by Yankees with 2B Kevin Jordan and P Ryan Karp to Philadelphia Phillies for P Terry Mulholland and a player to be named later (February 9, 1994); Yankees acquired P Jeff Patterson to complete deal (November 8, 1994). ... On Philadelphia disabled list (April 18-July 22 and August 3, 1995-remainder of season); included rehabilitation assignments to Reading (June 19-July 10) and Scranton/Wilkes-Barre (July 10-17). ... On Philadelphia disabled list (March 23-June 11, June 17-July 22 and August 8, 1996-remainder of season); included rehabilitation assignments to Clearwater (May 21-June 11), Scranton/Wilkes-Barre (June 22-July 19) and Reading (August 13-September 2). ... Granted free agency (May 19, 1997). ... Signed by San Diego Padres organization (May 29, 1997). ... Released by Padres (July 15, 1997). ... Signed by Los Angeles Dodgers organization (July 21, 1997). ... Granted free agency (October 15, 1997). ... Signed by Baltimore Orioles organization (February 6, 1998). ... Granted free agency (October 15, 1998). ... Signed by Tampa Bay Devil Rays organization (November 19, 1998). ... On Durham disabled list (April 21-June 2 and June 28-July 7, 1999). ... Granted free agency (October 15, 1999). ... Signed by Cincinnati Reds organization (November 16, 1999). ... Released by Reds (July 25, 2000). ... Signed by Montreal Expos organization (December 5, 2000). ... Granted free agency (October 15, 2001).

Year League	W	L	Pct.	ERA	G	GS	CG	ShO	Sv.	IP	H	R	ER	BB	SO
1989—Gulf Coast Yankees (GCL)	1	1	.500	3.48	2	2	0	0	0	10 1/3	5	4	4	4	13
—Fort Lauderdale (FSL)	1	2	.333	4.72	3	3	0	0	0	13 1/3	16	8	7	7	2
1990—Greensboro (S.Atl.)	5	12	.294	3.73	25	24	0	0	0	132 2/3	133	70	55	58	100
1991—Fort Lauderdale (FSL)	5	8	.385	2.33	19	19	4	2	0	108	91	45	28	40	53
—Columbus (I.L.)	0	1	.000	24.00	1	1	0	0	0	3	8	8	8	3	2
1992—Albany/Colonie (East.)	7	5	.583	3.28	22	22	0	0	0	112 1/3	96	55	41	70	66
1993—Columbus (I.L.)	3	1	.750	1.44	22	1	0	0	10	31 1/3	24	6	5	8	16
—New York (A.L.)	3	3	.500	5.32	38	0	0	0	0	45 2/3	48	27	27	26	33
1994—Philadelphia (N.L.)■	7	5	.583	2.67	21	14	1	0	1	104 1/3	101	40	31	35	59
—Scranton/W.B. (I.L.)	2	3	.400	2.12	6	5	0	0	0	34	27	9	8	14	24
1995—Reading (East.)	0	4	.000	10.80	4	4	0	0	0	15	28	19	18	3	8
—Scranton/W.B. (I.L.)	1	0	1.000	0.56	2	2	1	1	0	16	8	2	1	3	10
—Philadelphia (N.L.)	0	2	.000	5.74	3	3	0	0	0	15 2/3	15	13	10	9	6
1996—Clearwater (FSL)	1	1	.500	1.93	2	2	0	0	0	14	15	4	3	2	7
—Philadelphia (N.L.)	0	3	.000	7.82	6	6	0	0	0	25 1/3	42	28	22	7	8
—Scranton/W.B. (I.L.)	4	2	.667	3.91	8	8	0	0	0	50 2/3	50	24	22	7	34
—Reading (East.)	0	1	.000	2.93	4	4	0	0	0	27 2/3	24	13	9	8	29
1997—Philadelphia (N.L.)	1	5	.167	8.91	8	7	0	0	0	33 1/3	47	35	33	15	20
—Las Vegas (PCL)■	0	2	.000	9.93	17	1	0	0	0	22 2/3	30	26	25	11	13
—Albuquerque (PCL)■	0	3	.000	4.35	18	0	0	0	0	31	43	17	15	15	20
1998—Rochester (I.L.)■	3	1	.750	1.06	44	0	0	0	19	59 1/3	40	9	7	13	46
—Baltimore (A.L.)	0	0	...	9.75	9	1	0	0	0	12	18	13	13	6	6
1999—Durham (I.L.)■	3	3	.500	4.39	39	3	0	0	5	55 1/3	55	35	27	31	50
2000—Louisville (I.L.)■	6	8	.429	4.78	21	15	1	0	1	84 2/3	77	55	45	56	64
2001—Ottawa (I.L.)■	4	6	.400	3.44	19	18	1	1	0	110	98	47	42	39	66
—Montreal (N.L.)	0	4	.000	5.14	15	7	0	0	0	42	53	25	24	21	21
A.L. totals (2 years)	3	3	.500	6.24	47	1	0	0	0	57 2/3	66	40	40	32	39
N.L. totals (5 years)	8	19	.296	4.89	53	37	1	0	1	220 2/3	258	141	120	87	114
Major League totals (7 years)	11	22	.333	5.17	100	38	1	0	1	278 1/3	324	181	160	119	153

MUNSON, ERIC 1B TIGERS

PERSONAL: Born October 3, 1977, in San Diego, Calif. ... 6-3/220. ... Bats left, throws right.
HIGH SCHOOL: Mount Carmel (San Diego).
COLLEGE: Southern California.
TRANSACTIONS/CAREER NOTES: Selected by Atlanta Braves organization in second round of free-agent draft (June 4, 1996); did not sign. ... Selected by Detroit Tigers organization in first round (third pick overall) of free-agent draft (June 2, 1999). ... On Jacksonville disabled list (August 28-September 18, 2000).
STATISTICAL NOTES: Led Eastern League first basemen with 94 double plays and 1,141 total chances in 2001.

Year Team (League)	Pos.	G	AB	R	H	2B	3B	HR	RBI	Avg.	BB	SO	SB	PO	A	E	Avg.
1999—Lakeland (FSL)	DH	2	6	0	2	0	0	0	1	.333	1	1	0	...	...	...	...
—W. Michigan (Midw.)	1B-C	67	252	42	67	16	1	14	44	.266	37	47	3	319	29	3	.991
2000—Jacksonville (Sou.)	1B	98	365	52	92	21	4	15	68	.252	39	96	5	640	51	8	.989
—Detroit (A.L.)	1B	3	5	0	0	0	0	0	1	.000	0	1	0	16	0	1	.941
2001—Erie (East.)	1B	*142	519	88	135	35	1	26	*102	.260	*84	141	0	*1031	*93	*17	.985
—Detroit (A.L.)	1B	17	66	4	10	3	1	1	6	.152	3	21	0	142	14	1	.994
Major League totals (2 years)		20	71	4	10	3	1	1	7	.141	3	22	0	158	14	2	.989

M

PERSONAL: Born July 30, 1971, in Dallas. ... 5-11/190. ... Bats right, throws right. ... Full name: Calvin Duane Murray.
HIGH SCHOOL: Warren Travis White (Dallas).
COLLEGE: Texas.
TRANSACTIONS/CAREER NOTES: Selected by San Francisco Giants organization in first round (seventh pick overall) of free-agent draft (June 1, 1992).
HONORS: Named Pacific Coast League Most Valuable Player (1999).
STATISTICAL NOTES: Led Pacific Coast League with 297 total bases in 1999. ... Career major league grand slams: 1.
MISCELLANEOUS: Member of 1992 U.S. Olympic Baseball team.

								BATTING							FIELDING		
Year Team (League)	Pos.	G	AB	R	H	2B	3B	HR	RBI	Avg.	BB	SO	SB	PO	A	E	Avg.
1993— San Jose (Calif.).........	OF	85	345	61	97	24	1	9	42	.281	40	63	42	203	9	2	.991
— Shreveport (Texas).....	OF	37	138	15	26	6	0	0	6	.188	14	29	12	79	2	2	.976
— Phoenix (PCL)	OF	5	19	4	6	1	1	0	0	.316	2	5	1	13	0	2	.867
1994— Shreveport (Texas).....	OF	480	480	67	111	19	5	2	35	.231	47	81	33	268	5	3	.989
1995— Phoenix (PCL)	OF	13	50	8	9	1	0	4	10	.180	4	6	2	19	2	0	1.000
— Shreveport (Texas).....	OF	110	441	77	104	17	3	2	29	.236	59	70	26	286	5	2	.993
1996— Shreveport (Texas).....	OF	50	169	32	44	7	0	7	24	.260	25	33	6	89	4	3	.969
— Phoenix (PCL)	OF	83	311	50	76	16	6	3	28	.244	43	60	12	207	3	2	.991
1997— Shreveport (Texas).....	OF	122	419	83	114	25	3	10	56	.272	66	73	*52	214	9	5	.978
1998— Fresno (PCL)	OF	33	90	16	21	3	1	3	5	.233	12	18	3	27	1	0	1.000
— Shreveport (Texas).....	OF	88	337	63	104	22	5	8	39	.309	58	45	34	198	3	7	.966
1999— Fresno (PCL)	OF-DH	130	*548	*122	*183	31	7	23	73	.334	49	88	*42	284	8	6	.980
— San Francisco (N.L.) ..	OF	15	19	1	5	2	0	0	5	.263	2	4	1	6	0	0	1.000
2000— San Francisco (N.L.) ..	OF	108	194	35	47	12	1	2	22	.242	29	33	9	143	2	3	.980
2001— Fresno (PCL)	OF	35	138	17	36	6	1	4	12	.261	12	33	3	88	2	2	.978
— San Francisco (N.L.) ..	OF	106	326	54	80	14	2	6	25	.245	32	57	8	232	4	5	.979
Major League totals (3 years)		229	539	90	132	28	3	8	52	.245	63	94	18	381	6	8	.980

DIVISION SERIES RECORD

								BATTING							FIELDING		
Year Team (League)	Pos.	G	AB	R	H	2B	3B	HR	RBI	Avg.	BB	SO	SB	PO	A	E	Avg.
2000— San Francisco (N.L.) ..	OF	3	5	0	1	0	0	0	0	.200	0	3	0	3	0	0	1.000

PERSONAL: Born April 19, 1973, in Troy, Ohio. ... 6-4/215. ... Throws left, bats left. ... Full name: Heath Robertson Murray.
HIGH SCHOOL: Troy (Ohio).
COLLEGE: Michigan.
TRANSACTIONS/CAREER NOTES: Selected by San Diego Padres organization in third round of free-agent draft (June 2, 1994). ... On San Diego disabled list (June 23-July 10, 1997). ... On San Diego disabled list (September 19, 1998-remainder of season). ... Claimed on waivers by Cincinnati Reds (October 6, 1999). ... Released by Reds (March 29, 2000). ... Signed by Los Angeles Dodgers organization (April 5, 2000). ... Granted free agency (October 18, 2000). ... Signed by Detroit Tigers organization (January 18, 2001). ... Released by Tigers (November 20, 2001). ... Signed by Cleveland Indians organization (December 18, 2001).
STATISTICAL NOTES: Tied for Pacific Coast League lead with four double plays by pitcher in 1999.

Year League	W	L	Pct.	ERA	G	GS	CG	ShO	Sv.	IP	H	R	ER	BB	SO
1994— Spokane (N'West)	5	6	.455	2.90	15	15	•2	•1	0	*99 1/3	101	46	32	18	78
1995— Rancho Cuca. (Calif.)	9	4	.692	3.12	14	14	4	•2	0	92 1/3	80	37	32	38	81
— Memphis (Sou.)	5	4	.556	3.38	14	14	0	0	0	77 1/3	83	36	29	42	71
1996— Memphis (Sou.)	13	9	.591	3.21	27	27	1	1	0	174	154	83	62	60	156
1997— Las Vegas (PCL)	6	8	.429	5.45	19	19	2	1	0	109	142	72	66	41	99
— San Diego (N.L.)	1	2	.333	6.75	17	3	0	0	0	33 1/3	50	25	25	21	16
1998— Las Vegas (PCL)	9	11	.450	4.99	27	27	3	0	0	162 1/3	191	103	90	62	121
1999— Las Vegas (PCL)	5	4	.556	4.26	15	15	1	1	0	82 1/3	99	45	39	32	65
— San Diego (N.L.)	0	4	.000	5.76	22	8	0	0	0	50	60	33	32	26	25
2000— Albuquerque (PCL)■...........	7	10	.412	4.73	29	24	3	1	0	156	184	96	82	66	110
2001— Toledo (I.L.)■....................	1	1	.500	2.00	11	3	0	0	1	36	22	9	8	2	44
— Detroit (A.L.)......................	1	7	.125	6.54	40	4	0	0	0	63 1/3	82	48	46	40	42
A.L. totals (1 year)	1	7	.125	6.54	40	4	0	0	0	63 1/3	82	48	46	40	42
N.L. totals (2 years)	1	6	.143	6.16	39	11	0	0	0	83 1/3	110	58	57	47	41
Major League totals (3 years)	2	13	.133	6.32	79	15	0	0	0	146 2/3	192	106	103	87	83

PERSONAL: Born December 8, 1968, in Williamsport, Pa. ... 6-2/185. ... Throws right, bats right. ... Full name: Michael Cole Mussina. ... Name pronounced myoo-SEEN-uh.
HIGH SCHOOL: Montoursville (Pa.).
COLLEGE: Stanford.
TRANSACTIONS/CAREER NOTES: Selected by Baltimore Orioles organization in 11th round of free-agent draft (June 2, 1987); did not sign. ... Selected by Orioles organization in first round (20th pick overall) of free-agent draft (June 4, 1990). ... On Rochester disabled list (May 5-12, 1991). ... On Baltimore disabled list (July 22-August 20, 1993); included rehabilitation assignment to Bowie (August 9-20). ... On disabled list (April 17-May 3 and May 15-June 6, 1998). ... Granted free agency (October 27, 2000). ... Signed by New York Yankees (November 30, 2000).
HONORS: Named International League Most Valuable Pitcher (1991). ... Named righthanded pitcher on The Sporting News A.L. All-Star team (1995). ... Won A.L. Gold Glove at pitcher (1996-99) and 2001).
STATISTICAL NOTES: Pitched 8-0 one-hit, complete-game victory against Texas (July 17, 1992). ... Pitched 3-0 one-hit, complete-game victory against Cleveland (May 30, 1997). ... Struck out 15 batters in one game (August 1 and September 24, 2000). ... Pitched 10-0 one-hit, complete-game victory against Minnesota (August 1, 2000). ... Pitched 1-0 one-hit, complete-game victory against Boston (September 2, 2001).

M

Year League	W	L	Pct.	ERA	G	GS	CG	ShO	Sv.	IP	H	R	ER	BB	SO
1990— Hagerstown (East.)............	3	0	1.000	1.49	7	7	2	1	0	42 1/3	34	10	7	7	40
—Rochester (I.L.)..................	0	0	...	1.35	2	2	0	0	0	13 1/3	8	2	2	4	15
1991— Rochester (I.L.)..................	10	4	.714	2.87	19	19	3	1	0	122 1/3	108	42	39	31	107
—Baltimore (A.L.)..............	4	5	.444	2.87	12	12	2	0	0	87 2/3	77	31	28	21	52
1992— Baltimore (A.L.)..............	18	5	*.783	2.54	32	32	8	4	0	241	212	70	68	48	130
1993— Baltimore (A.L.)..............	14	6	.700	4.46	25	25	3	2	0	167 2/3	163	84	83	44	117
—Bowie (East.)..................	1	0	1.000	2.25	2	2	0	0	0	8	5	2	2	1	10
1994— Baltimore (A.L.)..............	16	5	.762	3.06	24	24	3	0	0	176 1/3	163	63	60	42	99
1995— Baltimore (A.L.)..............	*19	9	.679	3.29	32	32	7	*4	0	221 2/3	187	86	81	50	158
1996— Baltimore (A.L.)..............	19	11	.633	4.81	36	*36	4	1	0	243 1/3	264	137	130	69	204
1997— Baltimore (A.L.)..............	15	8	.652	3.20	33	33	4	1	0	224 2/3	197	87	80	54	218
1998— Baltimore (A.L.)..............	13	10	.565	3.49	29	29	4	2	0	206 1/3	189	85	80	41	175
1999— Baltimore (A.L.)..............	18	7	.720	3.50	31	31	4	0	0	203 1/3	207	88	79	52	172
2000— Baltimore (A.L.)..............	11	15	.423	3.79	34	34	6	1	0	*237 2/3	236	105	100	46	210
2001— New York (A.L.)■..........	17	11	.607	3.15	34	34	4	3	0	228 2/3	202	87	80	42	214
Major League totals (11 years)..... 164	164	92	.641	3.49	322	322	49	18	0	2238 1/3	2097	923	869	509	1749

RECORDS: Shares A.L. career record for most wins—3.

DIVISION SERIES RECORD

Year League	W	L	Pct.	ERA	G	GS	CG	ShO	Sv.	IP	H	R	ER	BB	SO
1996— Baltimore (A.L.)................	0	0	...	4.50	1	1	0	0	0	6	7	4	3	2	6
1997— Baltimore (A.L.)................	2	0	1.000	1.93	2	2	0	0	0	14	7	3	3	3	16
2001— New York (A.L.)................	1	0	1.000	0.00	1	1	0	0	0	7	4	0	0	1	4
Division series totals (3 years)	3	0	1.000	2.00	4	4	0	0	0	27	18	7	6	6	26

CHAMPIONSHIP SERIES RECORD

Year League	W	L	Pct.	ERA	G	GS	CG	ShO	Sv.	IP	H	R	ER	BB	SO
1996— Baltimore (A.L.)................	0	1	.000	5.87	1	1	0	0	0	7 2/3	8	5	5	2	6
1997— Baltimore (A.L.)................	0	0	...	0.60	2	2	0	0	0	15	4	1	1	4	25
2001— New York (A.L.)................	1	0	1.000	3.00	1	1	0	0	0	6	4	2	2	1	3
Champ. series totals (3 years)	1	1	.500	2.51	4	4	0	0	0	28 2/3	16	8	8	7	34

WORLD SERIES RECORD

Year League	W	L	Pct.	ERA	G	GS	CG	ShO	Sv.	IP	H	R	ER	BB	SO
2001— New York (A.L.)................	0	1	.000	4.09	2	2	0	0	0	11	11	7	5	4	14

ALL-STAR GAME RECORD

Year League	W	L	Pct.	ERA	GS	CG	ShO	Sv.	IP	H	R	ER	BB	SO
1992— American	0	0	...	0.00	0	0	0	0	1	0	0	0	0	0
1993— American						Did not play.								
1994— American	0	0	...	0.00	0	0	0	0	1	1	0	0	0	1
1997— American						Did not play.								
1999— American	0	0	...	0.00	0	0	0	0	1	1	0	0	1	2
All-Star Game totals (3 years)	0	0	...	0.00	0	0	0	0	3	2	0	0	1	3

M MYERS, GREG   C   ATHLETICS

PERSONAL: Born April 14, 1966, in Riverside, Calif. ... 6-2/225. ... Bats left, throws right. ... Full name: Gregory Richard Myers.

HIGH SCHOOL: Riverside (Calif.) Polytechnical.

TRANSACTIONS/CAREER NOTES: Selected by Toronto Blue Jays organization in third round of free-agent draft (June 4, 1984). ... On disabled list (June 17, 1988-remainder of season). ... On Toronto disabled list (March 26-June 5, 1989); included rehabilitation assignment to Knoxville (May 17-June 5). ... On Toronto disabled list (May 5-25, 1990); included rehabilitation assignment to Syracuse (May 21-24). ... Traded by Blue Jays with OF Rob Ducey to California Angels for P Mark Eichhorn (July 30, 1992). ... On California disabled list (August 27, 1992-remainder of season). ... On California disabled list (April 24-June 21, 1994); included rehabilitation assignments to Lake Elsinore (May 20-June 6 and June 13-21). ... On disabled list (April 21-May 6, June 1-21 and September 30, 1995-remainder of season). ... Granted free agency (November 3, 1995). ... Signed by Minnesota Twins (December 8, 1995). ... On disabled list (July 14-August 2, 1996). ... On Minnesota disabled list (August 9-24, 1997). ... Traded by Twins to Atlanta Braves for a player to be named later (September 5, 1997); Twins acquired 1B Steve Hacker to complete deal (December 18, 1997). ... Granted free agency (October 28, 1997). ... Signed by San Diego Padres (November 25, 1997). ... On San Diego disabled list (June 4-July 24, 1998); included rehabilitation assignments to Rancho Cucamonga (July 17-19) and Las Vegas (July 21-23). ... On San Diego disabled list (June 29-July 26, 1999); included rehabilitation assignment to Rancho Cucamonga (July 20-26). ... Traded by Padres to Braves for P Doug Dent (July 26, 1999). ... Granted free agency (November 1, 1999). ... Signed by Baltimore Orioles (December 17, 1999). ... On disabled list (April 2-17, 2000). ... Released by Orioles (June 14, 2001). ... Signed by Oakland Athletics (June 23, 2001). ... Granted free agency (November 5, 2001). ... Re-signed by A's (November 15, 2001).

STATISTICAL NOTES: Led California League catchers with 967 total chances in 1986. ... Led International League catchers with 698 total chances in 1987.

									BATTING					FIELDING			
Year Team (League)	Pos.	G	AB	R	H	2B	3B	HR	RBI	Avg.	BB	SO	SB	PO	A	E	Avg.
1984— Medicine Hat (Pio.)	C	38	133	20	42	9	0	2	20	.316	16	6	0	216	24	4	.984
1985— Florence (S.Atl.)	C	134	489	52	109	19	2	5	62	.223	39	54	0	551	61	7	*.989
1986— Ventura (Calif.)	C	124	451	65	133	23	4	20	79	.295	43	46	9	*849	99	19	.980
1987— Syracuse (I.L.)..........	C	107	342	35	84	19	1	10	47	.246	22	46	3	*637	50	11	.984
—Toronto (A.L.)............	C	7	9	1	1	0	0	0	0	.111	0	3	0	24	1	0	1.000
1988— Syracuse (I.L.)..........	C	34	120	18	34	7	1	7	21	.283	8	24	1	63	9	1	.986
1989— Knoxville (Sou.).........	C	29	90	11	30	10	0	5	19	.333	3	16	1	130	12	1	.993
—Toronto (A.L.)............	C-DH	17	44	0	5	2	0	0	1	.114	2	9	0	46	6	0	1.000
—Syracuse (I.L.)...........	C	24	89	8	24	6	0	1	11	.270	4	9	0	60	7	1	.985
1990— Toronto (A.L.)............	C	87	250	33	59	7	1	5	22	.236	22	33	0	411	30	3	.993
—Syracuse (I.L.)...........	C	3	11	0	2	1	0	0	2	.182	1	1	0	14	0	1	1.000
1991— Toronto (A.L.)............	C	107	309	25	81	22	0	8	36	.262	21	45	0	484	37	11	.979
1992— Toronto (A.L.)............	C	22	61	4	14	6	0	1	13	.230	5	5	0	92	13	1	.991
—California (A.L.)■......	C-DH	8	17	0	4	1	0	0	0	.235	0	6	0	33	3	0	1.000
1993— California (A.L.).........	C-DH	108	290	27	74	10	0	7	40	.255	17	47	3	369	44	6	.986

Year	Team (League)	Pos.	G	AB	R	H	2B	3B	HR	RBI	Avg.	BB	SO	SB	PO	A	E	Avg.
1994—	California (A.L.).........	C-DH	45	126	10	31	6	0	2	8	.246	10	27	0	194	28	2	.991
	— Lake Elsinore (Calif.)..	C-DH	10	32	4	8	2	0	0	5	.250	2	6	0	31	3	0	1.000
1995—	California (A.L.).........	C-DH	85	273	35	71	12	2	9	38	.260	17	49	0	341	21	4	.989
1996—	Minnesota (A.L.)■......	C	97	329	37	94	22	3	6	47	.286	19	52	0	488	27	8	.985
1997—	Minnesota (A.L.).........	C-DH	62	165	24	44	11	1	5	28	.267	16	29	0	196	11	3	.986
	— Atlanta (N.L.)■..........	C	9	9	0	1	0	0	0	1	.111	1	3	0	11	2	0	1.000
1998—	San Diego (N.L.)■......	C	69	171	19	42	10	0	4	20	.246	17	36	0	276	29	4	.987
	— Rancho Cuca. (Calif.) .	C-DH	3	9	1	0	0	0	0	0	.000	2	1	0	8	0	0	1.000
	— Las Vegas (PCL)	C	3	9	0	5	0	0	0	1	.556	0	0	0	16	1	0	1.000
1999—	San Diego (N.L.)■......	C	50	128	9	37	4	0	3	15	.289	13	14	0	199	14	3	.986
	— Rancho Cuca. (Calif.) .	C-DH	3	3	0	0	0	0	0	0	.000	1	1	0	7	1	0	1.000
	— Atlanta (N.L.)■..........	C	34	72	10	16	2	0	2	9	.222	13	16	0	166	12	1	.994
2000—	Baltimore (A.L.)■......	C-DH	43	125	9	28	6	0	3	12	.224	8	29	0	166	14	0	1.000
2001—	Baltimore (A.L.).........	DH-C	25	74	11	20	2	0	4	18	.270	8	17	0	41	4	0	1.000
	— Sacramento (PCL)■...	C	2	5	0	0	0	0	0	1	.000	3	2	0	5	0	0	1.000
	— Oakland (A.L.)	C-DH	33	87	13	16	1	0	7	13	.184	13	21	0	152	15	0	1.000
American League totals (12 years)			746	2159	229	542	108	7	57	276	.251	158	372	3	3037	254	38	.989
National League totals (3 years)			162	380	38	96	16	0	9	45	.253	44	69	0	652	57	8	.989
Major League totals (14 years)			908	2539	267	638	124	7	66	321	.251	202	441	3	3689	311	46	.989

DIVISION SERIES RECORD

Year	Team (League)	Pos.	G	AB	R	H	2B	3B	HR	RBI	Avg.	BB	SO	SB	PO	A	E	Avg.
1998—	San Diego (N.L.)	C	1	0	0	0	0	0	0	0	...	0	0	0	0	0	0	...
1999—	Atlanta (N.L.)							Did not play.										
2001—	Oakland (A.L.)	PH-C	3	7	0	1	0	0	0	0	.143	0	3	0	9	4	1	.929
Division series totals (2 years)			4	7	0	1	0	0	0	0	.143	0	3	0	9	4	1	.929

CHAMPIONSHIP SERIES RECORD

Year	Team (League)	Pos.	G	AB	R	H	2B	3B	HR	RBI	Avg.	BB	SO	SB	PO	A	E	Avg.
1991—	Toronto (A.L.)							Did not play.										
1998—	San Diego (N.L.)	PH	2	1	1	1	0	0	1	2	1.000	1	0	0	...	...	...	...
1999—	Atlanta (N.L.)	C	2	2	0	0	0	0	0	0	.000	1	1	0	8	0	0	1.000
Championship series totals (2 years)			4	3	1	1	0	0	1	2	.333	2	1	0	8	0	0	1.000

WORLD SERIES RECORD

Year	Team (League)	Pos.	G	AB	R	H	2B	3B	HR	RBI	Avg.	BB	SO	SB	PO	A	E	Avg.
1998—	San Diego (N.L.)	PH-C	2	4	0	0	0	0	0	0	.000	0	2	0	4	1	0	1.000
1999—	Atlanta (N.L.)	PH-C	4	6	0	2	0	0	0	1	.333	1	0	0	9	0	0	1.000
World Series totals (2 years)			6	10	0	2	0	0	0	1	.200	1	2	0	13	1	0	1.000

MYERS, MIKE   P   DIAMONDBACKS   M

PERSONAL: Born June 26, 1969, in Arlington Heights, Ill. ... 6-4/214. ... Throws left, bats left. ... Full name: Michael Stanley Myers.
HIGH SCHOOL: Crystal Lake (Ill.) Central.
COLLEGE: Iowa State.
TRANSACTIONS/CAREER NOTES: Selected by San Francisco Giants organization in fourth round of free-agent draft (June 4, 1990). ... On Clinton disabled list (June 3-September 16, 1991; April 9-June 2 and June 21-July 6, 1992). ... Selected by Florida Marlins from Giants organization in Rule 5 major league draft (December 7, 1992). ... On Edmonton disabled list (April 13-June 7, 1994). ... On Florida disabled list (June 7-August 5, 1994); included rehabilitation assignment to Brevard County (June 23-July 11). ... Traded by Marlins to Detroit Tigers (August 9, 1995), completing deal in which Marlins acquired P Buddy Groom for a player to be named later (August 7, 1995). ... Traded by Tigers with P Rick Greene and SS Santiago Perez to Milwaukee Brewers for P Bryce Florie and a player to be named later (November 20, 1997). ... Traded by Brewers to Colorado Rockies for P Curtis Leskanic (November 17, 1999). ... Traded by Rockies to Arizona Diamondbacks for OF Jack Cust and C J.D. Closser (January 7, 2002).
STATISTICAL NOTES: Led Pacific Coast League with 10 hit batsmen in 1993.

Year	League	W	L	Pct.	ERA	G	GS	CG	ShO	Sv.	IP	H	R	ER	BB	SO
1990—	Everett (N'West)	4	5	.444	3.90	15	14	1	0	0	85 1/3	91	43	37	30	73
1991—	Clinton (Midw.)	5	3	.625	2.62	11	11	1	0	0	65 1/3	61	23	19	18	59
1992—	San Jose (Calif.)	5	1	.833	2.30	8	8	0	0	0	54 2/3	43	20	14	17	40
	— Clinton (Midw.)	1	2	.333	1.19	7	7	0	0	0	37 2/3	28	11	5	8	32
1993—	Edmonton (PCL)■	7	14	.333	5.18	27	27	3	0	0	161 2/3	195	109	93	52	112
1994—	Edmonton (PCL)	1	5	.167	5.55	12	11	0	0	0	60	78	42	37	21	55
	— Brevard County (FSL).......	0	0	...	0.79	3	2	0	0	0	11 1/3	7	1	1	4	15
1995—	Charlotte (I.L.)	0	0	.000	5.65	37	0	0	0	0	36 2/3	41	25	23	15	24
	— Florida (N.L.)	0	0	...	0.00	2	0	0	0	0	2	1	0	0	3	0
	— Toledo (I.L.)■................	0	0	...	4.32	6	0	0	0	0	8 1/3	6	4	4	3	8
	— Detroit (A.L.)	1	0	1.000	9.95	11	0	0	0	0	6 1/3	10	7	7	4	4
1996—	Detroit (A.L.)	1	5	.167	5.01	•83	0	0	0	6	64 2/3	70	41	36	34	69
1997—	Detroit (A.L.)	0	4	.000	5.70	*88	0	0	0	2	53 2/3	58	36	34	25	50
1998—	Milwaukee (N.L.)■	2	2	.500	2.70	70	0	0	0	1	50	44	19	15	22	40
1999—	Milwaukee (N.L.)	2	1	.667	5.23	71	0	0	0	0	41 1/3	46	24	24	13	35
2000—	Colorado (N.L.)■	0	1	.000	1.99	78	0	0	0	1	45 1/3	24	10	10	24	41
2001—	Colorado (N.L.)	2	3	.400	3.60	73	0	0	0	0	40	32	17	16	24	36
A.L. totals (3 years)		2	9	.182	5.56	182	0	0	0	8	124 2/3	138	84	77	63	123
N.L. totals (5 years)		6	7	.462	3.27	294	0	0	0	2	178 2/3	147	70	65	86	152
Major League totals (7 years)		8	16	.333	4.21	476	0	0	0	10	303 1/3	285	154	142	149	275

PERSONAL: Born June 26, 1969, in Rockford, Ill. ... 6-1/215. ... Throws right, bats right. ... Full name: Rodney Luther Myers.
HIGH SCHOOL: Rockford (Ill.) East.
COLLEGE: Wisconsin.
TRANSACTIONS/CAREER NOTES: Selected by Kansas City Royals organization in 12th round of free-agent draft (June 4, 1990). ... On disabled list (May 17-June 3 and June 21-September 15, 1994; and June 30-July 21, 1995). ... Selected by Chicago Cubs from Royals organization in Rule 5 major league draft (December 4, 1995). ... On Iowa disabled list (June 7-15, 1998). ... Traded by Cubs to San Diego Padres for OF Gary Matthews Jr. (March 23, 2000). ... On San Diego disabled list (March 29-May 5 and May 12, 2000-remainder of season); included rehabilitation assignment to Rancho Cucamonga (April 30-May 5). ... On San Diego disabled list (May 20-June 19, 2001); included rehabilitation assignment to Portland (June 14-19). ... Granted free agency (October 8, 2001).
MISCELLANEOUS: Doubled in only appearance as pinch hitter (1999).

Year	League	W	L	Pct.	ERA	G	GS	CG	ShO	Sv.	IP	H	R	ER	BB	SO
1990—	Eugene (N'West)	0	2	.000	1.19	6	4	0	0	0	22 2/3	19	9	3	13	17
1991—	Appleton (Midw.)	1	1	.500	2.60	9	4	0	0	0	27 1/3	22	9	8	26	29
1992—	Lethbridge (Pio.)	5	•8	.385	4.01	15	15	*5	0	0	*103 1/3	93	57	46	61	76
1993—	Rockford (Midw.)	7	3	.700	1.79	12	12	5	2	0	85 1/3	65	22	17	18	65
—	Memphis (Sou.)	3	6	.333	5.62	12	12	1	1	0	65 2/3	73	46	41	32	42
1994—	Wilmington (Caro.)	1	1	.500	4.82	4	0	0	0	1	9 1/3	9	6	5	1	9
—	Memphis (Sou.)	5	1	.833	1.03	42	0	0	0	9	69 2/3	45	20	8	29	53
1995—	Omaha (A.A.)	4	5	.444	4.10	38	0	0	0	2	48 1/3	52	26	22	19	38
1996—	Chicago (N.L.)■	2	1	.667	4.68	45	0	0	0	0	67 1/3	61	38	35	38	50
1997—	Iowa (A.A.)	7	8	.467	4.09	24	23	1	0	0	140 2/3	140	76	64	38	79
—	Chicago (N.L.)	0	0	...	6.00	5	1	0	0	0	9	12	6	6	7	6
1998—	Iowa (PCL)	7	5	.583	3.91	33	13	2	1	11	101 1/3	84	47	44	45	86
—	Chicago (N.L.)	0	0	...	7.00	12	0	0	0	0	18	26	14	14	6	15
1999—	Iowa (PCL)	2	4	.333	4.06	20	1	0	0	2	31	29	18	14	11	24
—	Chicago (N.L.)	3	1	.750	4.38	46	0	0	0	0	63 2/3	71	34	31	25	41
2000—	San Diego (N.L.)■	0	0	...	4.50	3	0	0	0	0	2	2	1	1	0	3
—	Rancho Cuca. (Calif.)	0	0	...	0.00	3	2	0	0	0	4	2	0	0	0	4
2001—	San Diego (N.L.)	1	2	.333	5.32	37	0	0	0	1	47 1/3	53	31	28	20	29
—	Portland (PCL)	1	1	.500	3.00	8	1	0	0	0	15	13	5	5	5	14
Major League totals (6 years)		6	4	.600	4.99	148	1	0	0	1	207 1/3	225	124	115	96	144

PERSONAL: Born September 26, 1977, in New Westminster, B.C. ... 6-4/195. ... Throws right, bats right. ... Full name: Aaron Kenneth Myette. ... Son of Kenneth Myette, pitcher with Cincinnati Reds organization (1969).
HIGH SCHOOL: Johnston Heights Sectional (Surrey, B.C.).
JUNIOR COLLEGE: Central Arizona College.
TRANSACTIONS/CAREER NOTES: Selected by Chicago White Sox organization in supplemental round ("sandwich pick" between first and second round, 43rd pick overall) of free-agent draft (June 3, 1997); pick received as part of compensation for Florida Marlins signing P Alex Fernandez. ... On Hickory disabled list (April 2-May 2, 1998). ... On Birmingham disabled list (July 25-August 2, 1999). ... On Chicago disabled list (March 25-May 9, 2000). ... Traded by White Sox with P Brian Schmack to Texas Rangers for SS Royce Clayton (December 14, 2000).
STATISTICAL NOTES: Led Southern League with 15 hit batsmen in 1999.

Year	League	W	L	Pct.	ERA	G	GS	CG	ShO	Sv.	IP	H	R	ER	BB	SO
1997—	Bristol (Appl.)	4	3	.571	3.61	9	8	1	0	0	47 1/3	39	28	19	20	50
—	Hickory (S.Atl.)	3	1	.750	1.14	5	5	0	0	0	31 2/3	19	6	4	11	27
1998—	Hickory (S.Atl.)	9	4	.692	2.47	17	17	0	0	0	102	84	43	28	30	103
—	Winston-Salem (Caro.)	4	2	.667	2.01	6	6	1	1	0	44 2/3	32	14	10	14	54
1999—	Birmingham (Sou.)	12	7	.632	3.66	28	•28	0	0	0	164 2/3	138	76	67	77	135
—	Chicago (A.L.)	0	2	.000	6.32	4	3	0	0	0	15 2/3	17	11	11	14	11
2000—	Birmingham (Sou.)	2	0	1.000	3.52	3	3	0	0	0	15 1/3	11	7	6	8	21
—	Charlotte (I.L.)	5	5	.500	4.35	19	18	0	0	0	111 2/3	103	58	54	56	85
—	Chicago (A.L.)	0	0	...	0.00	2	0	0	0	0	2 2/3	0	0	0	4	1
2001—	Oklahoma (PCL)■	4	3	.571	3.73	12	12	2	0	0	70	64	32	29	30	76
—	Texas (A.L.)	4	5	.444	7.14	19	15	0	0	0	80 2/3	94	65	64	37	67
—	Tulsa (Texas)	1	0	1.000	0.00	1	1	0	0	0	6	3	0	0	1	2
Major League totals (3 years)		4	7	.364	6.82	25	18	0	0	0	99	111	76	75	55	79

PERSONAL: Born November 14, 1978, in Carmel, Calif. ... 6-2/205. ... Bats right, throws right. ... Full name: Xavier Clifford Nady.
HIGH SCHOOL: Salinas (Calif.).
COLLEGE: California.
TRANSACTIONS/CAREER NOTES: Selected by San Diego Padres organization in second round of free-agent draft (June 5, 2000).
HONORS: Named California League Most Valuable Player (2001).
STATISTICAL NOTES: Led California League with 276 total bases in 2001.

Year	Team (League)	Pos.	G	AB	R	H	2B	3B	HR	RBI	Avg.	BB	SO	SB	PO	A	E	Avg.
2000—	San Diego (N.L.)	PH	1	1	1	1	0	0	0	0	1.000	0	0	0	...	...	...	...
2001—	Lake Elsinore (Calif.)	1B	137	524	96	158	38	1	26	100	.302	62	109	6	852	61	10	*.989
Major League totals (1 year)			1	1	1	1	0	0	0	0	1.000	0	0	0	...	...	...	...

M
N

PERSONAL: Born May 5, 1967, in Fairfield, Conn. ... 6-3/200. ... Throws right, bats left. ... Full name: Charles Harrison Nagy. ... Name pronounced NAG-ee.

HIGH SCHOOL: Roger Ludlowe (Fairfield, Conn.).

COLLEGE: Connecticut.

TRANSACTIONS/CAREER NOTES: Selected by Cleveland Indians organization in first round (17th pick overall) of free-agent draft (June 1, 1988); pick received as part of compensation for San Francisco Giants signing Type A free-agent OF Brett Butler. ... On Cleveland disabled list (May 16-October 1, 1993); included rehabilitation assignment to Canton/Akron (June 10-24). ... On Cleveland disabled list (May 17-September 14 and September 25, 2000-remainder of season); included rehabilitation assignments to Buffalo (June 19-July 12 and September 3-14) and Akron (July 13 and August 28-September 2). ... On Cleveland disabled list (March 31-June 1 and August 24, 2001-remainder of season); included rehabilitation assignment to Buffalo (April 30-May 29).

HONORS: Named Carolina League Pitcher of the Year (1989).

STATISTICAL NOTES: Pitched 6-0 one-hit, complete-game victory against Baltimore (August 8, 1992).

MISCELLANEOUS: Member of 1988 U.S. Olympic baseball team. ... Struck out once in two appearances as designated hitter and appeared in one game as pinch runner (1999).

Year League	W	L	Pct.	ERA	G	GS	CG	ShO	Sv.	IP	H	R	ER	BB	SO
1989— Kinston (Caro.)	8	4	.667	1.51	13	13	6	*4	0	95 1/3	69	22	16	24	99
— Canton/Akron (East.)	4	5	.444	3.35	15	14	2	0	0	94	102	44	35	32	65
1990— Canton/Akron (East.)	13	8	.619	2.52	23	23	•9	0	0	175	132	62	49	39	99
— Cleveland (A.L.)	2	4	.333	5.91	9	8	0	0	0	45 2/3	58	31	30	21	26
1991— Cleveland (A.L.)	10	15	.400	4.13	33	33	6	1	0	211 1/3	228	103	97	66	109
1992— Cleveland (A.L.)	17	10	.630	2.96	33	33	10	3	0	252	245	91	83	57	169
1993— Cleveland (A.L.)	2	6	.250	6.29	9	9	1	0	0	48 2/3	66	38	34	13	30
— Canton/Akron (East.)	0	0	...	1.13	2	2	0	0	0	8	8	1	1	2	4
1994— Cleveland (A.L.)	10	8	.556	3.45	23	23	3	0	0	169 1/3	175	76	65	48	108
1995— Cleveland (A.L.)	16	6	.727	4.55	29	29	2	1	0	178	194	95	90	61	139
1996— Cleveland (A.L.)	17	5	.773	3.41	32	32	5	0	0	222	217	89	84	61	167
1997— Cleveland (A.L.)	15	11	.577	4.28	34	34	1	1	0	227	253	115	108	77	149
1998— Cleveland (A.L.)	15	10	.600	5.22	33	33	2	0	0	210 1/3	250	*139	122	66	120
1999— Cleveland (A.L.)	17	11	.607	4.95	33	32	1	0	0	202	238	120	111	59	126
2000— Cleveland (A.L.)	2	7	.222	8.21	11	11	0	0	0	57	71	53	52	21	41
— Buffalo (I.L.)	1	1	.500	4.30	3	3	0	0	0	14 2/3	12	7	7	4	5
— Akron (East.)	1	0	1.000	1.00	2	2	0	0	0	9	4	1	1	2	10
2001— Buffalo (I.L.)	5	1	.833	2.56	6	6	0	0	0	38 2/3	40	12	11	9	18
— Cleveland (A.L.)	5	6	.455	6.40	15	13	0	0	0	70 1/3	102	53	50	20	29
Major League totals (12 years)	128	99	.564	4.40	294	290	31	6	0	1893 2/3	2097	1003	926	570	1213

DIVISION SERIES RECORD

RECORDS: Holds career record for most earned runs allowed—23; and bases on balls allowed—18. ... Shares A.L. career record for most wins—3.

Year League	W	L	Pct.	ERA	G	GS	CG	ShO	Sv.	IP	H	R	ER	BB	SO
1995— Cleveland (A.L.)	1	0	1.000	1.29	1	1	0	0	0	7	4	1	1	5	6
1996— Cleveland (A.L.)	0	1	.000	7.15	2	2	0	0	0	11 1/3	15	9	9	5	13
1997— Cleveland (A.L.)	0	1	.000	9.82	1	1	0	0	0	3 2/3	2	5	4	6	1
1998— Cleveland (A.L.)	1	0	1.000	1.13	1	1	0	0	0	8	4	1	1	0	3
1999— Cleveland (A.L.)	1	0	1.000	7.20	2	2	0	0	0	10	11	9	8	2	6
Division series totals (5 years)	3	2	.600	5.18	7	7	0	0	0	40	36	25	23	18	29

CHAMPIONSHIP SERIES RECORD

RECORDS: Shares A.L. single-game record for most consecutive strikeouts—4 (October 13, 1995).

Year League	W	L	Pct.	ERA	G	GS	CG	ShO	Sv.	IP	H	R	ER	BB	SO
1995— Cleveland (A.L.)	0	0	...	1.13	1	1	0	0	0	8	5	2	1	0	6
1997— Cleveland (A.L.)	0	0	...	2.77	2	2	0	0	0	13	17	4	4	5	5
1998— Cleveland (A.L.)	0	1	.000	3.72	2	2	0	0	0	9 2/3	13	7	4	1	6
Champ. series totals (3 years)	0	1	.000	2.64	5	5	0	0	0	30 2/3	35	13	9	6	17

WORLD SERIES RECORD

RECORDS: Shares single-inning record for most consecutive bases on balls allowed—3 (October 21, 1997, third inning).

Year League	W	L	Pct.	ERA	G	GS	CG	ShO	Sv.	IP	H	R	ER	BB	SO
1995— Cleveland (A.L.)	0	0	...	6.43	1	1	0	0	0	7	8	5	5	1	4
1997— Cleveland (A.L.)	0	1	.000	6.43	2	1	0	0	0	7	8	6	5	5	5
World Series totals (2 years)	0	1	.000	6.43	3	2	0	0	0	14	16	11	10	6	9

ALL-STAR GAME RECORD

Year League	W	L	Pct.	ERA	GS	CG	ShO	Sv.	IP	H	R	ER	BB	SO
1992— American	0	0	...	0.00	0	0	0	0	1	0	0	0	0	1
1996— American	0	1	.000	13.50	1	0	0	0	2	4	3	3	0	1
1999— American					Selected, did not play.									
All-Star Game totals (2 years)	0	1	.000	9.00	1	0	0	0	3	4	3	3	0	2

PERSONAL: Born November 22, 1974, in Houston. ... 6-4/195. ... Throws right, bats right. ... Full name: Joseph Michael Nathan.

HIGH SCHOOL: Pine Bush (N.Y.).

COLLEGE: New York-Stony Brook.

TRANSACTIONS/CAREER NOTES: Selected by San Francisco Giants organization in sixth round of free-agent draft (June 1, 1995). ... On San Francisco disabled list (May 13-June 6 and July 14-August 19, 2000); included rehabilitation assignments to San Jose (May 26-31), Bakersfield (May 31-June 6) and Fresno (August 2-19).

MISCELLANEOUS: Played shortstop (1995).

N

Year League	W	L	Pct.	ERA	G	GS	CG	ShO	Sv.	IP	H	R	ER	BB	SO
1996—							Did not play-attended New York-Stony Brook.								
1997—Salem-Kaizer (N'West)	2	1	.667	2.47	18	5	0	0	2	62	53	22	17	26	44
1998—San Jose (Calif.)................	8	6	.571	3.32	22	22	0	0	0	122	100	51	45	48	118
— Shreveport (Texas)............	1	3	.250	8.80	4	4	0	0	0	15 1/3	20	15	15	9	10
1999—Shreveport (Texas)............	0	1	.000	3.12	2	2	0	0	0	8 2/3	5	4	3	7	7
— San Francisco (N.L.)..........	7	4	.636	4.18	19	14	0	0	1	90 1/3	84	45	42	46	54
— Fresno (PCL)..................	6	4	.600	4.46	13	13	1	0	0	74 2/3	68	44	37	36	82
2000—San Francisco (N.L.)..........	5	2	.714	5.21	20	15	0	0	0	93 1/3	89	63	54	63	61
— San Jose (Calif.)..............	0	1	.000	3.60	1	1	0	0	0	5	4	2	2	1	2
— Bakersfield (Calif.)...........	1	0	1.000	5.06	1	1	0	0	0	5 1/3	2	3	3	7	6
— Fresno (PCL)..................	0	2	.000	4.40	3	3	0	0	0	14 1/3	15	8	7	7	9
2001—Fresno (PCL)..................	0	5	.000	7.77	10	10	0	0	0	46 1/3	63	47	40	33	21
— Shreveport (Texas)...........	3	6	.333	6.93	21	7	0	0	0	62 1/3	73	49	48	37	33
Major League totals (2 years)......	12	6	.667	4.70	39	29	0	0	1	183 2/3	173	108	96	109	115

RECORD AS POSITION PLAYER

Year Team (League)	Pos.	G	AB	R	H	2B	3B	HR	RBI	Avg.	BB	SO	SB	PO	A	E	Avg.
								BATTING							FIELDING		
1995—Bellingham (N'West) ..	SS	56	177	23	41	7	2	3	20	.232	22	48	3	76	150	26	.897

NEAGLE, DENNY   P   ROCKIES

PERSONAL: Born September 13, 1968, in Gambrills, Md. ... 6-3/225. ... Throws left, bats left. ... Full name: Dennis Edward Neagle Jr. ... Name pronounced NAY-ghul.

HIGH SCHOOL: Arundel (Gambrills, Md.).

COLLEGE: Minnesota.

TRANSACTIONS/CAREER NOTES: Selected by Minnesota Twins organization in third round of free-agent draft (June 5, 1989). ... On Portland disabled list (April 5-23, 1991). ... On Minnesota disabled list (July 28-August 12, 1991). ... Traded by Twins with OF Midre Cummings to Pittsburgh Pirates for P John Smiley (March 17, 1992). ... Traded by Pirates to Atlanta Braves for 1B Ron Wright and a player to be named later (August 28, 1996); Pirates acquired P Jason Schmidt to complete deal (August 30, 1996). ... Traded by Braves with OF Michael Tucker and P Rob Bell to Cincinnati Reds for 2B Bret Boone and P Mike Remlinger (November 10, 1998). ... On Cincinnati disabled list (March 24-April 21 and May 24-July 29, 1999); included rehabilitation assignment to Indianapolis (April 8-21 and July 23-29). ... Traded by Reds with OF Mike Frank to New York Yankees for 3B Drew Henson, OF Jackson Melian, P Brian Reith and P Ed Yarnall (July 12, 2000). ... Granted free agency (October 31, 2000). ... Signed by Colorado Rockies (December 4, 2000). ... On disabled list (June 9-24, 2001).

HONORS: Named lefthanded pitcher on THE SPORTING NEWS N.L. All-Star team (1997).

STATISTICAL NOTES: Tied for N.L. lead with 16 sacrifice hits in 1996. ... Career major league grand slams: 2.

MISCELLANEOUS: Appeared in one game as pinch runner (1992). ... Appeared in one game as pinch runner (1995). ... Doubled and had a sacrifice hit in three appearances as pinch hitter with Pittsburgh (1996). ... Struck out in only appearance as pinch hitter with Cincinnati (2000).

Year League	W	L	Pct.	ERA	G	GS	CG	ShO	Sv.	IP	H	R	ER	BB	SO
1989—Elizabethton (Appl.)............	1	2	.333	4.50	6	3	0	0	1	22	20	11	11	8	32
— Kenosha (Midw.)...............	2	1	.667	1.65	6	6	1	1	0	43 2/3	25	9	8	16	40
1990—Visalia (Calif.)..................	8	0	1.000	1.43	10	10	0	0	0	63	39	13	10	16	92
— Orlando (Sou.)................	12	3	.800	2.45	17	17	4	1	0	121 1/3	94	40	33	31	94
1991—Portland (PCL).................	9	4	.692	3.27	19	17	1	1	0	104 2/3	101	41	38	32	94
— Minnesota (A.L.)..............	0	1	.000	4.05	7	3	0	0	0	20	28	9	9	7	14
1992—Pittsburgh (N.L.)■.............	4	6	.400	4.48	55	6	0	0	2	86 1/3	81	46	43	43	77
1993—Pittsburgh (N.L.)...............	3	5	.375	5.31	50	7	0	0	1	81 1/3	82	49	48	37	73
— Buffalo (A.A.).................	0	0	...	0.00	3	0	0	0	0	3 1/3	3	0	0	2	6
1994—Pittsburgh (N.L.)...............	9	10	.474	5.12	24	24	2	0	0	137	135	80	78	49	122
1995—Pittsburgh (N.L.)...............	13	8	.619	3.43	31	•31	5	1	0	•209 2/3	*221	91	80	45	150
1996—Pittsburgh (N.L.)...............	14	6	.700	3.05	27	27	1	0	0	182 2/3	186	67	62	34	131
— Atlanta (N.L.)■..............	2	3	.400	5.59	6	6	1	0	0	38 2/3	40	26	24	14	18
1997—Atlanta (N.L.)................	*20	5	.800	2.97	34	34	4	4	0	233 1/3	204	87	77	49	172
1998—Atlanta (N.L.)................	16	11	.593	3.55	32	31	5	2	0	210 1/3	196	91	83	60	165
1999—Indianapolis (I.L.)■..........	2	0	1.000	4.67	3	3	0	0	0	17 1/3	11	9	9	2	9
— Cincinnati (N.L.)............	9	5	.643	4.27	20	19	0	0	0	111 2/3	95	54	53	40	76
2000—Cincinnati (N.L.)............	8	2	.800	3.52	18	18	0	0	0	117 2/3	111	48	46	50	88
— New York (A.L.)■...........	7	7	.500	5.81	16	15	1	0	0	91 1/3	99	61	59	31	58
2001—Colorado (N.L.)■.............	9	8	.529	5.38	30	30	0	0	0	170 2/3	192	107	102	60	139
A.L. totals (2 years)	7	8	.467	5.50	23	18	1	0	0	111 1/3	127	70	68	38	72
N.L. totals (10 years)	107	69	.608	3.97	327	233	18	7	3	1579 1/3	1543	746	696	481	1211
Major League totals (11 years)	114	77	.597	4.07	350	251	19	7	3	1690 2/3	1670	816	764	519	1283

DIVISION SERIES RECORD

Year League	W	L	Pct.	ERA	G	GS	CG	ShO	Sv.	IP	H	R	ER	BB	SO
1998—Atlanta (N.L.)..................							Did not play.								
2000—New York (A.L.)................							Did not play.								

CHAMPIONSHIP SERIES RECORD

Year League	W	L	Pct.	ERA	G	GS	CG	ShO	Sv.	IP	H	R	ER	BB	SO
1992—Pittsburgh (N.L.)	0	0	...	27.00	2	0	0	0	0	1 2/3	4	5	5	3	0
1996—Atlanta (N.L.)	0	0	...	2.35	2	1	0	0	0	7 2/3	2	2	2	3	8
1997—Atlanta (N.L.)	1	0	1.000	0.00	2	1	1	1	0	12	5	0	0	1	9
1998—Atlanta (N.L.)	0	0	...	3.52	2	1	0	0	0	7 2/3	8	3	3	2	9
2000—New York (A.L.)	0	2	.000	4.50	2	2	0	0	0	10	6	5	5	7	7
Champ. series totals (5 years)	1	2	.333	3.46	10	5	1	1	0	39	25	15	15	16	33

WORLD SERIES RECORD

NOTES: Member of World Series championship team (2000).

Year League	W	L	Pct.	ERA	G	GS	CG	ShO	Sv.	IP	H	R	ER	BB	SO
1996—Atlanta (N.L.)	0	0	...	3.00	2	1	0	0	0	6	5	3	2	4	3
2000—New York (A.L.)	0	0	...	3.86	1	1	0	0	0	4 2/3	4	2	2	2	3
World Series totals (2 years)	0	0	...	3.38	3	2	0	0	0	10 2/3	9	5	4	6	6

ALL-STAR GAME RECORD

Year League	W	L	Pct.	ERA	GS	CG	ShO	Sv.	IP	H	R	ER	BB	SO
1995—National	0	0	...	0.00	0	0	0	0	1	1	0	0	0	1
1997—National							Did not play.							

NEAL, BLAINE — P — MARLINS

PERSONAL: Born April 6, 1978, in Maurelton, N.J. ... 6-5/205. ... Throws left, bats right.
HIGH SCHOOL: Bishop Eustace Prep (Pennsauken, N.J.).
TRANSACTIONS/CAREER NOTES: Selected by Florida Marlins organization in fourth round of free-agent draft (June 4, 1996).
MISCELLANEOUS: Played first base/outfield (1998).

Year League	W	L	Pct.	ERA	G	GS	CG	ShO	Sv.	IP	H	R	ER	BB	SO
1996— Gulf Coast Marlins (GCL) ...	1	1	.500	4.60	7	5	0	0	1	29 1/3	32	18	15	6	15
1997— Gulf Coast Marlins (GCL) ...	4	1	.800	3.63	10	0	0	0	1	22 1/3	24	11	9	11	19
1999— Kane County (Midw.)	4	2	.667	2.32	26	0	0	0	6	31	21	8	8	10	31
2000— Brevard County (FSL)	2	2	.500	2.15	41	0	0	0	11	54 1/3	40	27	13	24	65
2001— Portland (East.)	2	3	.400	2.36	54	0	0	0	21	53 1/3	43	17	14	21	45
— Florida (N.L.)	0	0	...	6.75	4	0	0	0	0	5 1/3	7	4	4	5	3
Major League totals (1 year)	0	0	...	6.75	4	0	0	0	0	5 1/3	7	4	4	5	3

RECORD AS POSITION PLAYER

Year Team (League)	Pos.	G	AB	R	H	2B	3B	HR	RBI	Avg.	BB	SO	SB	PO	A	E	Avg.
1998— Utica (NY-Penn)	1B-OF	53	121	13	23	4	0	0	13	.190	23	32	2	254	16	5	.982

NELSON, JEFF — P — MARINERS

PERSONAL: Born November 17, 1966, in Baltimore. ... 6-8/235. ... Throws right, bats right. ... Full name: Jeffrey Allan Nelson. ... Nephew of Cole Nelson, who played in the Washington Senators organization.
HIGH SCHOOL: Catonsville (Md.).
JUNIOR COLLEGE: Catonsville (Md.) Community College.
TRANSACTIONS/CAREER NOTES: Selected by Los Angeles Dodgers organization in 22nd round of free-agent draft (June 4, 1984). ... On Great Falls disabled list (April 10-June 4, 1986). ... Selected by Seattle Mariners organization from Dodgers organization in Rule 5 minor league draft (December 9, 1986). ... On disabled list (July 16, 1989-remainder of season). ... Traded by Mariners with 1B Tino Martinez and P Jim Mecir to New York Yankees for P Sterling Hitchcock and 3B Russ Davis (December 7, 1995). ... On suspended list (September 3-5, 1996). ... On suspended list (May 28-29, 1998). ... On New York disabled list (June 26-September 4, 1998); included rehabilitation assignment to Tampa (August 31-September 4). ... On New York disabled list (May 3-20 and June 3-August 11, 1999); included rehabilitation assignments to Gulf Coast Yankees (August 2-4 and August 9-10) and Tampa (August 5-8). ... Granted free agency (October 31, 2000). ... Signed by Mariners (December 4, 2000).
MISCELLANEOUS: Appeared in one game as outfielder with no chances for Seattle (1993).

Year League	W	L	Pct.	ERA	G	GS	CG	ShO	Sv.	IP	H	R	ER	BB	SO
1984— Great Falls (Pio.)	0	0	...	54.00	1	0	0	0	0	2/3	3	4	4	3	1
— Gulf Coast Dodgers (GCL)..	0	0	...	1.35	9	0	0	0	0	13 1/3	6	3	2	6	7
1985— Gulf Coast Dodgers (GCL)..	0	5	.000	5.51	14	7	0	0	0	47 1/3	72	50	29	32	31
1986— Great Falls (Pio.)	0	0	...	13.50	3	0	0	0	0	2	5	3	3	3	1
— Bakersfield (Calif.)	0	7	.000	6.69	24	11	0	0	0	71 1/3	79	83	53	84	37
1987— Salinas (Calif.)■...............	3	7	.300	5.74	17	16	1	0	0	80	80	61	51	71	43
1988— San Bernardino (Calif.).......	8	9	.471	5.54	27	27	1	1	0	149 1/3	163	115	92	91	94
1989— Williamsport (East.)	7	5	.583	3.31	15	15	2	0	0	92 1/3	72	41	34	53	61
1990— Williamsport (East.)	1	4	.200	6.44	10	10	0	0	0	43 1/3	65	35	31	18	14
— Peninsula (Caro.)	2	2	.500	3.15	18	7	1	1	6	60	47	21	21	25	49
1991— Jacksonville (Sou.)	4	0	1.000	1.27	21	0	0	0	12	28 1/3	23	5	4	9	34
— Calgary (PCL)......................	3	4	.429	3.90	28	0	0	0	21	32 1/3	39	19	14	15	26
1992— Calgary (PCL)......................	1	0	1.000	0.00	2	0	0	0	0	3 2/3	0	0	0	1	0
— Seattle (A.L.)......................	1	7	.125	3.44	66	0	0	0	6	81	71	34	31	44	46
1993— Calgary (PCL)......................	1	0	1.000	1.17	5	0	0	0	1	7 2/3	6	1	1	2	6
— Seattle (A.L.)......................	5	3	.625	4.35	71	0	0	0	1	60	57	30	29	34	61
1994— Seattle (A.L.)......................	0	0	...	2.76	28	0	0	0	0	42 1/3	35	18	13	20	44
— Calgary (PCL)......................	1	4	.200	2.84	18	0	0	0	8	25 1/3	21	9	8	7	30
1995— Seattle (A.L.)......................	7	3	.700	2.17	62	0	0	0	2	78 2/3	58	21	19	27	96
1996— New York (A.L.)■...............	4	4	.500	4.36	73	0	0	0	2	74 1/3	75	38	36	36	91
1997— New York (A.L.)..................	3	7	.300	2.86	77	0	0	0	2	78 2/3	53	32	25	37	81
1998— New York (A.L.)..................	5	3	.625	3.79	45	0	0	0	3	40 1/3	44	18	17	22	35
— Tampa (FSL)......................	0	0	...	0.00	2	1	0	0	0	2	1	1	0	1	4
1999— New York (A.L.)..................	2	1	.667	4.15	39	0	0	0	1	30 1/3	27	14	14	22	35
— Gulf Coast Yankees (GCL)..	0	0	...	0.00	2	2	0	0	0	2	1	0	0	1	3
— Tampa (FSL)......................	0	0	...	0.00	3	3	0	0	0	3	1	0	0	2	5
2000— New York (A.L.)..................	8	4	.667	2.45	73	0	0	0	0	69 2/3	44	24	19	45	71
2001— Seattle (A.L.)■..................	4	3	.571	2.76	69	0	0	0	4	65 1/3	30	21	20	44	88
Major League totals (10 years)	39	35	.527	3.23	603	0	0	0	21	620 2/3	494	250	223	331	648

DIVISION SERIES RECORD

RECORDS: Holds A.L. career record for most games pitched—19.

Year League	W	L	Pct.	ERA	G	GS	CG	ShO	Sv.	IP	H	R	ER	BB	SO
1995— Seattle (A.L.)	0	1	.000	3.18	3	0	0	0	0	5 2/3	7	2	2	3	7
1996— New York (A.L.)..................	1	0	1.000	0.00	2	0	0	0	0	3 2/3	2	0	0	3	5
1997— New York (A.L.)..................	0	0	...	0.00	4	0	0	0	0	4	4	0	0	2	0
1998— New York (A.L.)..................	0	0	...	0.00	2	0	0	0	0	2 2/3	2	0	0	1	2
1999— New York (A.L.)..................	0	0	...	0.00	3	0	0	0	0	1 2/3	1	0	0	1	3
2000— New York (A.L.)..................	0	0	...	0.00	2	0	0	0	0	2	0	0	0	0	2
2001— Seattle (A.L.)	0	0	...	0.00	3	0	0	0	0	3	1	0	0	1	5
Division series totals (7 years)	1	1	.500	0.79	19	0	0	0	0	22 2/3	17	2	2	11	24

N

CHAMPIONSHIP SERIES RECORD

Year	League	W	L	Pct.	ERA	G	GS	CG	ShO	Sv.	IP	H	R	ER	BB	SO
1995—	Seattle (A.L.)	0	0	...	0.00	3	0	0	0	0	3	3	0	0	5	3
1996—	New York (A.L.)	0	1	.000	11.57	2	0	0	0	0	2 1/3	5	3	3	0	2
1998—	New York (A.L.)	0	1	.000	20.25	3	0	0	0	0	1 1/3	3	3	3	1	3
1999—	New York (A.L.)	0	0	...	0.00	2	0	0	0	0	2/3	0	0	0	0	0
2000—	New York (A.L.)	0	0	...	9.00	3	0	0	0	0	3	5	3	3	0	6
2001—	Seattle (A.L.)	0	0	...	0.00	2	0	0	0	0	2 1/3	1	0	0	1	3
Champ. series totals (6 years)		**0**	**2**	**.000**	**6.39**	**15**	**0**	**0**	**0**	**0**	**12 2/3**	**17**	**9**	**9**	**7**	**17**

WORLD SERIES RECORD

NOTES: Member of World Series championship team (1996, 1998, 1999 and 2000).

Year	League	W	L	Pct.	ERA	G	GS	CG	ShO	Sv.	IP	H	R	ER	BB	SO
1996—	New York (A.L.)	0	0	...	0.00	3	0	0	0	0	4 1/3	1	0	0	1	5
1998—	New York (A.L.)	0	0	...	0.00	3	0	0	0	0	2 1/3	2	1	0	1	4
1999—	New York (A.L.)	0	0	...	0.00	4	0	0	0	0	2 2/3	2	0	0	1	3
2000—	New York (A.L.)	1	0	1.000	10.13	3	0	0	0	0	2 2/3	5	3	3	1	1
World Series totals (4 years)		**1**	**0**	**1.000**	**2.25**	**13**	**0**	**0**	**0**	**0**	**12**	**10**	**4**	**3**	**4**	**13**

ALL-STAR GAME RECORD

Year	League	W	L	Pct.	ERA	GS	CG	ShO	Sv.	IP	H	R	ER	BB	SO
2001—	American	0	0	...	0.00	0	0	0	0	1	0	0	0	1	1

NELSON, JOE   P   BRAVES

PERSONAL: Born October 25, 1974, in Alameda, Calif. ... 6-2/185. ... Throws right, bats right. ... Full name: Joseph George Nelson.

COLLEGE: San Francisco.

TRANSACTIONS/CAREER NOTES: Selected by Atlanta Braves organization in fourth round of free-agent draft (June 4, 1996). ... On Richmond disabled list (August 19, 1999-remainder of season). ... On Richmond disabled list (April 6-July 28, 2000). ... On Atlanta disabled list (June 19, 2001-remainder of season).

Year	League	W	L	Pct.	ERA	G	GS	CG	ShO	Sv.	IP	H	R	ER	BB	SO
1996—	Eugene (N'West)	5	3	.625	4.37	14	13	0	0	0	70	69	43	34	29	67
1997—	Durham (Caro.)	10	6	.625	4.76	25	24	0	0	0	124 2/3	114	74	66	61	99
1998—	Greenville (Sou.)	6	9	.400	4.98	45	12	1	1	2	108 1/3	124	76	60	69	74
1999—	Greenville (Sou.)	1	1	.500	2.37	25	0	0	0	8	30 1/3	19	15	8	14	37
—	Richmond (I.L.)	2	3	.400	4.54	12	3	0	0	1	33 2/3	33	18	17	15	31
2000—	Gulf Coast Braves (GCL)	1	0	1.000	2.25	4	0	0	0	1	4	3	1	1	3	7
—	Jamestown (NY-Penn)	0	0	...	2.25	3	0	0	0	0	4	3	3	1	1	7
2001—	Richmond (I.L.)	1	2	.333	1.13	29	0	0	0	8	39 2/3	23	5	5	14	40
—	Atlanta (N.L.)	0	0	...	36.00	2	0	0	0	0	2	7	9	8	2	0
Major League totals (1 year)		**0**	**0**	**...**	**36.00**	**2**	**0**	**0**	**0**	**0**	**2**	**7**	**9**	**8**	**2**	**0**

NEN, ROBB   P   GIANTS

PERSONAL: Born November 28, 1969, in San Pedro, Calif. ... 6-5/215. ... Throws right, bats right. ... Full name: Robert Allen Nen. ... Son of Dick Nen, first baseman with three major league teams (1963, 1965-68 and 1970).

HIGH SCHOOL: Los Alamitos (Calif.).

TRANSACTIONS/CAREER NOTES: Selected by Texas Rangers organization in 32nd round of free-agent draft (June 2, 1987). ... On Charlotte disabled list (April 6-26 and May 6-24, 1990). ... On disabled list (April 23-June 10, June 28-July 8 and July 11-September 3, 1991; and May 7-September 9, 1992). ... On Texas disabled list (June 12-July 17, 1993); included rehabilitation assignment to Oklahoma City (June 21-July 17). ... Traded by Rangers with P Kurt Miller to Florida Marlins for P Cris Carpenter (July 17, 1993). ... Traded by Marlins to San Francisco Giants for P Mike Villano, P Joe Fontenot and P Mick Pageler (November 18, 1997).

HONORS: Named N.L. co-Reliever of the Year by THE SPORTING NEWS (2001).

MISCELLANEOUS: Holds Florida Marlins all-time record for most saves (108).

Year	League	W	L	Pct.	ERA	G	GS	CG	ShO	Sv.	IP	H	R	ER	BB	SO
1987—	Gulf Coast Rangers (GCL)	0	0	...	7.71	2	0	0	0	0	2 1/3	4	2	2	3	4
1988—	Gastonia (S.Atl.)	0	5	.000	7.45	14	10	0	0	0	48 1/3	69	57	40	45	36
—	Butte (Pio.)	4	5	.444	8.75	14	13	0	0	0	48 1/3	65	55	47	45	30
1989—	Gastonia (S.Atl.)	7	4	.636	2.41	24	24	1	1	0	138 1/3	96	47	37	76	146
1990—	Charlotte (FSL)	1	4	.200	3.69	11	11	1	0	0	53 2/3	44	28	22	36	38
—	Tulsa (Texas)	0	5	.000	5.06	7	7	0	0	0	26 2/3	23	20	15	21	21
1991—	Tulsa (Texas)	0	2	.000	5.79	6	6	0	0	0	28	24	21	18	20	23
1992—	Tulsa (Texas)	1	1	.500	2.16	4	4	1	0	0	25	21	7	6	2	20
1993—	Texas (A.L.)	1	1	.500	6.35	9	3	0	0	0	22 2/3	28	17	16	26	12
—	Oklahoma City (A.A.)	0	2	.000	6.67	6	5	0	0	0	28 1/3	45	22	21	18	12
—	Florida (N.L.)■	1	0	1.000	7.02	15	1	0	0	0	33 1/3	35	28	26	20	27
1994—	Florida (N.L.)	5	5	.500	2.95	44	0	0	0	15	58	46	20	19	17	60
1995—	Florida (N.L.)	0	7	.000	3.29	62	0	0	0	23	65 2/3	62	26	24	23	68
1996—	Florida (N.L.)	5	1	.833	1.95	75	0	0	0	35	83	67	21	18	21	92
1997—	Florida (N.L.)	9	3	.750	3.89	73	0	0	0	35	74	72	35	32	40	81
1998—	San Francisco (N.L.)■	7	7	.500	1.52	78	0	0	0	40	88 2/3	59	21	15	25	110
1999—	San Francisco (N.L.)	3	8	.273	3.98	72	0	0	0	37	72 1/3	79	36	32	27	77
2000—	San Francisco (N.L.)	4	3	.571	1.50	68	0	0	0	41	66	37	15	11	19	92
2001—	San Francisco (N.L.)	4	5	.444	3.01	79	0	0	0	*45	77 2/3	58	28	26	22	93
A.L. totals (1 year)		**1**	**1**	**.500**	**6.35**	**9**	**3**	**0**	**0**	**0**	**22 2/3**	**28**	**17**	**16**	**26**	**12**
N.L. totals (9 years)		**38**	**39**	**.494**	**2.95**	**566**	**1**	**0**	**0**	**271**	**618 2/3**	**515**	**230**	**203**	**214**	**700**
Major League totals (9 years)		**39**	**40**	**.494**	**3.07**	**575**	**4**	**0**	**0**	**271**	**641 1/3**	**543**	**247**	**219**	**240**	**712**

DIVISION SERIES RECORD

Year League	W	L	Pct.	ERA	G	GS	CG	ShO	Sv.	IP	H	R	ER	BB	SO
1997— Florida (N.L.)	1	0	1.000	0.00	2	0	0	0	0	2	1	1	0	2	2
2000— San Francisco (N.L.)	0	0	...	0.00	2	0	0	0	0	2 1/3	2	0	0	1	3
Division series totals (2 years)	1	0	1.000	0.00	4	0	0	0	0	4 1/3	3	1	0	3	5

CHAMPIONSHIP SERIES RECORD

Year League	W	L	Pct.	ERA	G	GS	CG	ShO	Sv.	IP	H	R	ER	BB	SO
1997— Florida (N.L.)	0	0	...	0.00	2	0	0	0	2	2	0	0	0	0	0

WORLD SERIES RECORD

NOTES: Member of World Series championship team (1997).

Year League	W	L	Pct.	ERA	G	GS	CG	ShO	Sv.	IP	H	R	ER	BB	SO
1997— Florida (N.L.)	0	0	...	7.71	0	0	0	0	2	4 2/3	8	5	4	2	7

ALL-STAR GAME RECORD

Year League	W	L	Pct.	ERA	GS	CG	ShO	Sv.	IP	H	R	ER	BB	SO
1998— National	0	0	...	9.00	0	0	0	0	1	3	3	1	0	0
1999— National					Selected, did not play—injured.									

NEUGEBAUER, NICK   P   BREWERS

PERSONAL: Born July 15, 1980, in Riverside, Calif. ... 6-3/235. ... Throws right, bats right. ... Full name: Nickolas D. Neugebauer.
HIGH SCHOOL: Arlington (Riverside, Calif.).
TRANSACTIONS/CAREER NOTES: Selected by Milwaukee Brewers organization in second round of free-agent draft (June 2, 1998). ... On Milwaukee disabled list (August 25, 2001-remainder of season).

Year League	W	L	Pct.	ERA	G	GS	CG	ShO	Sv.	IP	H	R	ER	BB	SO
1999— Beloit (Midw.)	7	5	.583	3.90	18	18	0	0	0	80 2/3	50	41	35	80	125
2000— Mudville (Calif.)	4	4	.500	4.19	18	18	0	0	0	77 1/3	43	40	36	87	117
— Huntsville (Sou.)	1	3	.250	3.73	10	10	0	0	0	50 2/3	35	28	21	47	57
2001— Huntsville (Sou.)	5	6	.455	3.46	21	21	1	1	0	106 2/3	94	46	41	52	*149
— Indianapolis (I.L.)	2	1	.667	1.50	4	4	0	0	0	24	10	5	4	9	26
— Milwaukee (N.L.)	1	1	.500	7.50	2	2	0	0	0	6	6	5	5	6	11
Major League totals (1 year)	1	1	.500	7.50	2	2	0	0	0	6	6	5	5	6	11

NEVIN, PHIL   3B   PADRES

PERSONAL: Born January 19, 1971, in Fullerton, Calif. ... 6-2/231. ... Bats right, throws right. ... Full name: Phillip Joseph Nevin.
HIGH SCHOOL: El Dorado (Placentia, Calif.).
COLLEGE: Cal State-Fullerton.
TRANSACTIONS/CAREER NOTES: Selected by Los Angeles Dodgers organization in third round of free-agent draft (June 5, 1989); did not sign. ... Selected by Houston Astros organization in first round (first pick overall) of free-agent draft (June 1, 1992). ... On Tucson disabled list (July 12-30, 1995). ... Traded by Astros to Detroit Tigers (August 15, 1995), completing deal in which Tigers traded P Mike Henneman to Astros for a player to be named later (August 10, 1995). ... On Detroit disabled list (March 21-April 16, 1997); included rehabilitation assignment to Lakeland (April 8-16). ... Traded by Tigers with C Matt Walbeck to Anaheim Angels for P Nick Skuse (November 20, 1997). ... On suspended list (June 12-15, 1998). ... Traded by Angels with P Keith Volkman to San Diego Padres for INF Andy Sheets and OF Gus Kennedy (March 29, 1999). ... On San Diego disabled list (April 1-16, 1999); included rehabilitaion assignment to Las Vegas (April 12-15).
HONORS: Named Golden Spikes Award winner by USA Baseball (1992). ... Named third baseman on The Sporting News college All-America team (1992). ... Named Most Outstanding Player of College World Series (1992).
STATISTICAL NOTES: Led Pacific Coast League third basemen with .891 fielding percentage in 1993. ... Led Pacific Coast League in grounding into double plays with 21 in 1994. ... Led Pacific Coast League third basemen with 31 errors and 32 double plays in 1994. ... Led A.L. catchers with 20 passed balls in 1998. ... Hit three home runs in one game (October 6, 2001). ... Career major league grand slams: 5.
MISCELLANEOUS: Member of 1992 U.S. Olympic baseball team.

Year Team (League)	Pos.	G	AB	R	H	2B	3B	HR	RBI	Avg.	BB	SO	SB	PO	A	E	Avg.
1993— Tucson (PCL)	3B-OF	123	448	67	128	21	3	10	93	.286	52	99	8	68	187	29	†.898
1994— Tucson (PCL)	3B-OF	118	445	67	117	20	1	12	79	.263	55	101	3	73	240	†32	.907
1995— Tucson (PCL)	3B-DH	62	223	31	65	16	0	7	41	.291	27	39	2	39	128	14	.923
— Houston (N.L.)	3B	18	60	4	7	1	0	0	1	.117	7	13	1	10	32	3	.933
— Toledo (I.L.)■	OF-DH	7	23	3	7	2	0	1	3	.304	1	5	0	2	0	0	1.000
— Detroit (A.L.)	OF-DH	29	96	9	21	3	1	2	12	.219	11	27	0	50	2	2	.963
1996— Jacksonville (Sou.)	C-DH-3-0-1	98	344	77	101	18	1	24	69	.294	60	83	6	384	76	11	.977
— Detroit (A.L.)	3B-OF-C-DH	38	120	15	35	5	0	8	19	.292	8	39	1	45	51	5	.950
1997— Lakeland (FSL)	DH-1B-3B	3	9	3	5	1	0	1	4	.556	3	2	0	9	4	1	.929
— Toledo (I.L.)	1B-DH-3B	5	19	1	3	0	0	1	3	.158	2	9	0	19	4	0	1.000
— Detroit (A.L.)	O-DH-3-1-C	93	251	32	59	16	1	9	35	.235	25	68	0	94	18	2	.982
1998— Anaheim (A.L.)■	C-DH-1B	75	237	27	54	8	1	8	27	.228	17	67	0	402	32	5	.989
1999— Las Vegas (PCL)■	C-1B-3B	3	10	2	2	0	0	2	2	.200	0	2	0	12	4	0	1.000
— San Diego (N.L.)	3-C-0-1-DH	128	383	52	103	27	0	24	85	.269	51	82	1	276	154	5	.989
2000— San Diego (N.L.)	3B	143	538	87	163	34	1	31	107	.303	59	121	2	96	242	*26	.929
2001— San Diego (N.L.)	3B-DH	149	546	97	167	31	0	41	126	.306	71	147	4	96	265	27	.930
American League totals (4 years)		235	704	83	169	32	3	27	93	.240	61	201	1	591	103	14	.980
National League totals (4 years)		438	1527	240	440	93	1	96	319	.288	188	363	8	478	693	61	.950
Major League totals (7 years)		673	2231	323	609	125	4	123	412	.273	249	564	9	1069	796	75	.961

ALL-STAR GAME RECORD

		BATTING											FIELDING			
Year League	Pos.	AB	R	H	2B	3B	HR	RBI	Avg.	BB	SO	SB	PO	A	E	Avg.
2001— National	PH-3B	1	0	0	0	0	0	0	.000	0	0	0	0	0	0	...

NEWHAN, DAVID — 2B

PERSONAL: Born September 7, 1973, in Fullerton, Calif. ... 5-10/180. ... Bats left, throws right. ... Full name: David Matthew Newhan.
HIGH SCHOOL: Esperanza (Calif.).
COLLEGE: Pepperdine.
TRANSACTIONS/CAREER NOTES: Selected by Oakland Athletics organization in 17th round of free-agent draft (June 1, 1995). ... Traded by A's with P Don Wengert to San Diego Padres for P Doug Bochtler and SS Jorge Velandia (December 15, 1997). ... On Las Vegas disabled list (June 15-July 6, 2000). ... Traded by Padres to Philadelphia Phillies (August 7, 2000), completing deal in which Phillies traded SS Desi Relaford to Padres for a player to be named (August 4, 2000). ... On Philadelphia disabled list (April 15, 2001-remainder of season); included rehabilitation assignments to Scranton/Wilkes-Barre (April 22-May 1 and May 7-9). ... Granted free agency (October 15, 2001).

Year	Team (League)	Pos.	G	AB	R	H	2B	3B	HR	RBI	Avg.	BB	SO	SB	PO	A	E	Avg.
1995—	S. Oregon (N'West)	OF	42	145	25	39	8	1	6	21	.269	29	30	10	50	4	2	.964
—	W. Michigan (Midw.) ..	OF	25	96	9	21	5	0	3	8	.219	13	26	3	37	3	1	.976
1996—	Modesto (Calif.)	OF	117	455	96	137	27	3	25	75	.301	62	106	17	128	5	5	.964
1997—	Visalia (Calif.)	2B	67	241	52	67	15	2	7	48	.278	44	58	9	123	157	10	.966
—	Huntsville (Sou.)	2B	57	212	40	67	13	2	5	35	.316	28	59	5	96	129	16	.934
1998—	Mobile (Sou.)■........	2B-3B-SS	121	491	89	128	26	3	12	45	.261	68	110	27	228	314	14	.975
1999—	Las Vegas (PCL)	2B-SS	98	374	49	107	25	1	14	49	.286	30	84	22	164	235	20	.952
—	San Diego (N.L.)	2B-3B-1B	32	43	7	6	1	0	2	6	.140	1	11	2	28	36	2	.970
2000—	Las Vegas (PCL)	2B-OF	66	244	41	62	5	2	5	35	.254	37	61	9	132	140	7	.975
—	San Diego (N.L.)	OF-2B-3B	14	20	5	3	1	0	1	2	.150	6	7	0	9	4	0	1.000
—	Scranton/W.B. (I.L.)■	2B	25	83	10	21	3	0	3	8	.253	11	15	3	42	71	1	.991
—	Philadelphia (N.L.).....	2B	10	17	3	3	0	0	0	0	.176	2	6	0	9	15	0	1.000
2001—	Philadelphia (N.L.).....	2B	7	6	2	2	1	0	0	1	.333	1	0	0	2	0	0	1.000
—	Scranton/W.B. (I.L.) ...	2B	13	55	4	6	1	0	0	2	.109	4	11	0	15	16	1	.969
Major League totals (3 years)			63	86	17	14	3	0	3	9	.163	10	24	2	48	55	2	.981

NICHTING, CHRIS — P

PERSONAL: Born May 13, 1966, in Cincinnati. ... 6-1/205. ... Throws right, bats right. ... Full name: Christopher Thomas Nichting. ... Name pronounced NICK-ting.
HIGH SCHOOL: Elder (Cincinnati).
COLLEGE: Northwestern.
TRANSACTIONS/CAREER NOTES: Selected by Los Angeles Dodgers organization in third round of free-agent draft (June 2, 1987). ... On disabled list (April 10, 1990-entire season). ... On disabled list (June 17, 1991-entire season). ... On San Antonio disabled list (August 12, 1992-remainder of season). ... On Albuquerque disabled list (April 8-July 2, 1993). ... On Vero Beach disabled list (July 15-26 and July 28, 1993-remainder of season). ... On San Antonio disabled list (April 7-23, 1994). ... Granted free agency (October 15, 1994). ... Signed by Texas Rangers (November 18, 1994). ... On Oklahoma City suspended list (June 8-10, 1995). ... On Texas disabled list (March 22-September 3, 1996); included rehabilitation assignment to Oklahoma City (August 19-September 3). ... Granted free agency (October 15, 1996). ... Signed by Oakland Athletics organization (November 19, 1996). ... Granted free agency (October 15, 1997). ... Signed by Cleveland Indians organization (February 26, 1998). ... Granted free agency (October 15, 1998). ... Signed by New York Yankees organization (December 15, 1998). ... On Columbus disabled list (July 7-15, 1999). ... Granted free agency (October 15, 1999). ... Signed by Indians organization (February 8, 2000). ... Granted free agency (October 18, 2000). ... Signed by Cincinnati Reds organization (June 6, 2001). ... Granted free agency (September 18, 2001). ... Signed by Colorado Rockies organization (September 19, 2001). ... Released by Rockies (October 19, 2001).

Year	League	W	L	Pct.	ERA	G	GS	CG	ShO	Sv.	IP	H	R	ER	BB	SO
1988—	Vero Beach (FSL)	11	4	.733	2.09	21	19	5	1	1	138	90	40	32	51	*151
1989—	San Antonio (Texas)..........	4	*14	.222	5.03	26	26	2	0	0	154	160	96	86	*101	*136
1990—	San Antonio (Texas)..........						Did not play.									
1991—	Yakima (N'West)						Did not play.									
1992—	Albuquerque (PCL)............	1	3	.250	7.93	10	9	0	0	0	42	64	42	37	23	25
—	San Antonio (Texas)..........	4	5	.444	2.52	13	13	0	0	0	78 2/3	58	25	22	37	81
1993—	Vero Beach (FSL)	0	1	.000	4.15	4	4	0	0	0	17 1/3	18	9	8	6	18
—	Albuquerque (PCL)............	3	4	.429	1.64	21	8	0	0	1	65 2/3	47	21	12	34	74
1994—	San Antonio (Texas)..........	2	2	.500	7.40	10	7	0	0	0	41 1/3	61	39	34	28	25
1995—	Oklahoma City (A.A.)■......	5	5	.500	2.13	23	7	3	•2	1	67 2/3	58	19	16	19	72
—	Texas (A.L.)	0	0	...	7.03	13	0	0	0	0	24 1/3	36	19	19	13	6
1996—	Oklahoma City (A.A.)..........	1	0	1.000	1.00	4	1	0	0	0	9	9	1	1	3	7
1997—	Edmonton (PCL)■..............	7	13	.350	7.76	33	24	3	0	1	131	170	120	*113	46	90
1998—	Buffalo (I.L.)■...................	8	6	.571	4.39	43	5	0	0	1	96 1/3	104	54	47	37	97
1999—	Columbus (I.L.)■..............	8	5	.615	5.29	25	21	2	0	0	127 2/3	135	80	75	47	110
2000—	Buffalo (I.L.)■...................	2	3	.400	4.23	47	3	0	0	26	66	65	31	31	16	60
—	Cleveland (A.L.)................	0	0	...	7.00	7	0	0	0	0	9	13	7	7	5	7
2001—	Louisville (I.L.)■..............	2	1	.667	2.97	27	0	0	0	17	33 1/3	24	11	11	10	45
—	Cincinnati (N.L.)................	0	3	.000	4.46	36	0	0	0	1	36 1/3	46	24	18	8	33
—	Colorado (N.L.)■..............	0	0	...	4.50	7	0	0	0	0	6	9	3	3	0	7
A.L. totals (2 years)		0	0	...	7.02	20	0	0	0	0	33 1/3	49	26	26	18	13
N.L. totals (1 year)		0	3	.000	4.46	43	0	0	0	1	42 1/3	55	27	21	8	40
Major League totals (3 years)		0	3	.000	5.59	63	0	0	0	1	75 2/3	104	53	47	26	53

NICKLE, DOUG — P — PHILLIES

PERSONAL: Born October 2, 1974, in Sonoma, Calif. ... 6-4/210. ... Throws right, bats right. ... Full name: Douglas A. Nickle.
HIGH SCHOOL: Sonoma Valley (Sonoma, Calif.).
COLLEGE: California.
TRANSACTIONS/CAREER NOTES: Selected by Anaheim Angels organization in 13th round of free-agent draft (June 3, 1997). ... Traded by Angels to Philadelphia Phillies (September 10, 1998), completing deal in which Phillies traded OF Gregg Jefferies for a player to be named later (August 26, 1998). ... On Reading disabled list (May 3-26, 2000).
STATISTICAL NOTES: Led International League with seven intentional bases on balls issued in 2001.

Year League	W	L	Pct.	ERA	G	GS	CG	ShO	Sv.	IP	H	R	ER	BB	SO
1997— Boise (N'West)	0	1	.000	6.41	17	2	0	0	0	19²/₃	27	17	14	8	22
1998— Cedar Rapids (Midw.)	8	4	.667	3.78	20	7	1	1	0	69	66	30	29	20	59
— Lake Elsinore (Calif.)	3	4	.429	4.48	11	10	1	0	0	66¹/₃	68	40	33	25	69
1999— Clearwater (FSL)■............	2	4	.333	2.29	*60	0	0	0	28	70²/₃	60	25	18	23	70
2000— Reading (East.)................	8	3	.727	2.44	49	0	0	0	16	77¹/₃	55	25	21	22	58
— Philadelphia (N.L.)..............	0	0	...	13.50	4	0	0	0	0	2²/₃	5	4	4	2	0
2001— Scranton/W.B. (I.L.)	9	3	.750	1.68	47	1	0	0	7	85²/₃	62	19	16	37	60
— Philadelphia (N.L.)..............	0	0	...	0.00	2	0	0	0	0	2	1	0	0	0	1
Major League totals (2 years).......	0	0	...	7.71	6	0	0	0	0	4²/₃	6	4	4	2	1

NIEVES, JOSE — SS/2B — ANGELS

PERSONAL: Born June 16, 1975, in Guacara, Venezuela. ... 6-0/180. ... Bats right, throws right. ... Full name: Jose Miguel Nieves Pinto. ... Brother of Juan Nieves, former outfielder with Toronto Blue Jays organization. ... Name pronounced nee-A-vez.

HIGH SCHOOL: Enrique Delgado Palacios (Carabobo, Venezuela).

TRANSACTIONS/CAREER NOTES: Signed as non-drafted free agent by Milwaukee Brewers organization (June 10, 1992). ... Released by Brewers (October 19, 1993). ... Signed by Chicago Cubs organization (June 30, 1994). ... On disabled list (May 29-June 12, 1997). ... On Chicago disabled list (May 31-June 18, 2000); included rehabilitation assignments to Daytona (June 14-16) and West Tenn (June 16-18). ... Traded by Cubs to Anaheim Angels for P Mike Fyhrie and a player to be named later (March 25, 2001). ... On Anaheim disabled list (August 9-28, 2001).

Year Team (League)	Pos.	G	AB	R	H	2B	3B	HR	RBI	Avg.	BB	SO	SB	PO	A	E	Avg.
1992— Dom. Brewers (DSL)..	IF	8	15	2	5	0	0	1	3	.333	4	4	0	9	13	5	.815
1993— Dom. Brewers (DSL)..	IF	54	144	21	29	4	3	2	14	.201	22	25	6	43	78	19	.864
1994— Dom. Cubs (DSL)■....	2B	37	137	21	39	6	1	4	24	.285	13	23	5	50	76	9	.933
1995— Williamsport (NY-P) ...	SS-2B	69	276	46	59	13	1	4	44	.214	21	39	11	85	193	33	.894
1996— Rockford (Midw.)	SS-2B-3B	113	396	55	96	20	4	5	57	.242	33	59	17	156	318	37	.928
1997— Daytona (FSL)	SS-2B	85	331	51	91	20	1	4	42	.275	17	55	16	151	218	27	.932
1998— West Tenn (Sou.)	SS-2B	82	314	42	91	27	5	8	39	.290	18	55	17	130	211	24	.934
— Iowa (PCL).................	SS	19	75	7	19	4	0	0	4	.253	2	11	1	35	61	4	.960
— Chicago (N.L.)............	SS	2	1	0	0	0	0	0	0	.000	0	0	0	0	0	0	...
1999— Iowa (PCL)	SS-2B	104	392	55	105	25	3	11	59	.268	24	65	11	122	315	19	.958
— Chicago (N.L.)............	SS	54	181	16	45	9	1	2	18	.249	8	25	0	67	162	16	.935
2000— Chicago (N.L.)	SS	82	198	17	42	6	3	5	24	.212	11	43	1	46	103	5	.968
— Daytona (FSL)	3B-SS	2	6	2	1	0	0	0	0	.167	1	0	0	2	4	0	1.000
— West Tenn (Sou.)	3B-SS	2	7	2	4	0	0	2	2	.571	0	0	0	4	1	0	1.000
— Iowa (PCL)	3B-SS-2B	7	32	7	9	4	1	1	7	.281	2	5	1	3	15	1	.947
2001— Anaheim (A.L.)■........2-S-DH-3-1		29	53	5	13	3	1	2	3	.245	2	20	0	33	46	1	.988
— Salt Lake (PCL)	2B-SS-3B	61	258	50	85	15	4	11	37	.329	8	36	8	112	161	13	.955
American League totals (1 year)		29	53	5	13	3	1	2	3	.245	2	20	0	33	46	1	.988
National League totals (3 years)		138	380	33	87	15	4	7	42	.229	19	68	1	113	265	21	.947
Major League totals (4 years)		167	433	38	100	18	5	9	45	.231	21	88	1	146	311	22	.954

NINA, ELVIN — P — ANGELS

PERSONAL: Born November 25, 1975, in San Cristobal, Dominican Republic. ... 6-0/185. ... Throws right, bats right. ... Full name: Elvin Alexis Nina.

HIGH SCHOOL: Elizabeth (N.J.).

COLLEGE: Oklahoma State.

TRANSACTIONS/CAREER NOTES: Selected by Oakland Athletics organization in 17th round of free-agent draft (June 3, 1997). ... Traded by A's with OF Jeff DaVanon and OF Nathan Haynes to Anaheim Angels for P Omar Olivares and 2B Randy Velarde (July 29, 1999). ... On Erie disabled list (August 24, 1999-remainder of season). ... On Erie disabled list (April 6-24 and June 26-July 20, 2000). ... On Edmonton disabled list (August 17-September 2, 2000).

Year League	W	L	Pct.	ERA	G	GS	CG	ShO	Sv.	IP	H	R	ER	BB	SO
1997— Southern Oregon (N'West).	1	3	.250	5.23	18	2	0	0	1	31	36	24	18	18	26
1998— Visalia (Calif.)	8	8	.500	4.49	30	21	1	•1	0	130¹/₃	135	77	65	62	131
— Edmonton (PCL)	0	0	...	0.00	1	0	0	0	0	¹/₃	1	0	0	2	0
1999— Modesto (Calif.)	5	2	.714	2.09	17	12	0	0	0	73¹/₃	59	31	17	41	74
— Midland (Texas)................	3	2	.600	4.80	7	4	0	0	0	30	36	21	16	18	18
— Erie (East.)■...................	3	0	1.000	4.07	4	4	0	0	0	24¹/₃	20	12	11	15	19
2000— Erie (East.)	2	4	.333	4.24	12	10	2	0	0	57¹/₃	51	31	27	24	30
— Edmonton (PCL)	0	0	...	2.89	3	2	0	0	0	9¹/₃	11	6	3	6	3
2001— Salt Lake (PCL)	10	11	.476	5.47	29	28	1	0	0	158	195	112	96	79	101

NITKOWSKI, C.J. — P — ASTROS

PERSONAL: Born March 9, 1973, in Suffern, N.Y. ... 6-3/205. ... Throws left, bats left. ... Full name: Christopher John Nitkowski.

HIGH SCHOOL: Don Bosco (N.J.).

COLLEGE: St. John's.

TRANSACTIONS/CAREER NOTES: Selected by Cincinnati Reds organization in first round (ninth pick overall) of free-agent draft (June 2, 1994). ... Traded by Reds with P David Tuttle and a player to be named later to Detroit Tigers for P David Wells (July 31, 1995); Tigers acquired IF Mark Lewis to complete deal (November 16, 1995). ... On Detroit disabled list (August 11-29, 1996). ... Traded by Tigers with C Brad Ausmus, P Jose Lima, P Trever Miller and IF Daryle Ward to Houston Astros for C Brian Hunter, IF Orlando Miller, P Doug Brocail, P Todd Jones and cash (December 10, 1996). ... Traded by Astros with C Brad Ausmus to Tigers for C Paul Bako, P Dean Crow, P Mark Persails, P Brian Powell and 3B Carlos Villalobos (January 14, 1999). ... On suspended list (May 28-30, 1999). ... Traded by Tigers with cash to New York Mets for a player to be named later (September 1, 2001); Tigers acquired P Kyle Kessel to complete deal (December 13, 2001). ... Granted free agency (October 15, 2001). ... Signed by Astros organization (December 21, 2001).

RECORDS: Shares major league record for most hit batsmen in one inning—3 (August 3, 1998, eighth inning).

STATISTICAL NOTES: Tied for A.L. lead with three balks in 1999.

MISCELLANEOUS: Struck out in only appearance as pinch hitter and appeared in one game as pinch runner (1999).

Year League	W	L	Pct.	ERA	G	GS	CG	ShO	Sv.	IP	H	R	ER	BB	SO
1994—Chattanooga (Sou.)	6	3	.667	3.50	14	14	0	0	0	74 2/3	61	30	29	40	60
1995—Chattanooga (Sou.)	4	2	.667	2.50	8	8	0	0	0	50 1/3	39	20	14	20	52
—Indianapolis (A.A.)	0	2	.000	5.20	6	6	0	0	0	27 2/3	28	16	16	10	21
—Cincinnati (N.L.)	1	3	.250	6.12	9	7	0	0	0	32 1/3	41	25	22	15	18
—Detroit (A.L.)■	1	4	.200	7.09	11	11	0	0	0	39 1/3	53	32	31	20	13
1996—Toledo (I.L.)	4	6	.400	4.46	19	19	1	0	0	111	104	60	55	53	103
—Detroit (A.L.)	2	3	.400	8.08	11	8	0	0	0	45 2/3	62	44	41	38	36
1997—New Orleans (A.A.)■	8	10	.444	3.98	28	28	1	0	0	174 1/3	183	82	77	56	*141
1998—Houston (N.L.)	3	3	.500	3.77	43	0	0	0	3	59 2/3	49	27	25	23	44
—New Orleans (PCL)	0	1	.000	6.00	5	3	0	0	1	15	22	12	10	7	18
1999—Detroit (A.L.)■	4	5	.444	4.30	68	7	0	0	0	81 2/3	63	44	39	45	66
2000—Detroit (A.L.)	4	9	.308	5.25	67	11	0	0	0	109 2/3	124	79	64	49	81
2001—Detroit (A.L.)	0	3	.000	5.56	56	0	0	0	0	45 1/3	51	30	28	31	38
—Toledo (I.L.)	0	0	...	0.00	1	0	0	0	0	1	1	0	0	0	1
—New York (N.L.)■	1	0	1.000	0.00	5	0	0	0	0	5 2/3	3	0	0	3	4
A.L. totals (5 years)	11	24	.314	5.68	213	37	0	0	0	321 2/3	353	229	203	183	234
N.L. totals (3 years)	5	6	.455	4.33	57	7	0	0	3	97 2/3	93	52	47	41	66
Major League totals (6 years)	16	30	.348	5.37	270	44	0	0	3	419 1/3	446	281	250	224	300

NIXON, TROT   OF   RED SOX

PERSONAL: Born April 11, 1974, in Durham, N.C. ... 6-2/200. ... Bats left, throws left. ... Full name: Christopher Trotman Nixon.
HIGH SCHOOL: New Hanover (Wilmington, N.C.).
TRANSACTIONS/CAREER NOTES: Selected by Boston Red Sox organization in first round (seventh pick overall) of free-agent draft (June 3, 1993). ... On disabled list (July 12, 1994-remainder of season). ... On Boston disabled list (June 27-July 25, 2000); included rehabilitation assignment to Gulf Coast Red Sox (July 8-9 and July 20-23).
STATISTICAL NOTES: Tied for Eastern League lead with four double plays by outfielders in 1996. ... Tied for International League lead with 11 errors and three double plays by outfielder in 1998. ... Hit three home runs in one game (July 24, 1999). ... Career major league grand slams: 3.

| | | | | | | BATTING | | | | | | | | FIELDING | | |
Year Team (League)	Pos.	G	AB	R	H	2B	3B	HR	RBI	Avg.	BB	SO	SB	PO	A	E	Avg.
1994—Lynchburg (Caro.)	OF	71	264	33	65	12	0	12	43	.246	44	53	10	143	8	4	.974
1995—Sarasota (FSL)	OF	73	264	43	80	11	4	5	39	.303	45	46	7	140	4	2	.986
—Trenton (East.)	OF	25	94	9	15	3	1	2	8	.160	7	20	2	66	2	0	1.000
1996—Trenton (East.)	OF-DH	123	438	55	110	11	4	11	63	.251	50	65	7	224	*14	5	.979
—Boston (A.L.)	OF	2	4	2	2	1	0	0	0	.500	0	1	1	3	0	0	1.000
1997—Pawtucket (I.L.)	OF	130	475	80	116	18	3	20	61	.244	63	86	11	268	10	4	.986
1998—Pawtucket (I.L.)	OF-DH-1B	135	509	97	158	26	4	23	74	.310	76	81	26	231	11	‡11	.957
—Boston (A.L.)	OF-DH	13	27	3	7	1	0	0	0	.259	1	3	0	16	0	0	1.000
1999—Boston (A.L.)	OF	124	381	67	103	22	5	15	52	.270	53	75	3	209	3	7	.968
2000—Boston (A.L.)	OF-DH	123	427	66	118	27	8	12	60	.276	63	85	8	216	8	2	.991
—GC Red Sox (GCL)	OF	3	10	3	4	0	0	1	5	.400	2	0	0	3	0	0	1.000
2001—Boston (A.L.)	OF-DH	148	535	100	150	31	4	27	88	.280	79	113	7	280	7	8	.973
Major League totals (5 years)		410	1374	238	380	82	17	54	200	.277	196	277	19	724	18	17	.978

DIVISION SERIES RECORD

| | | | | | | BATTING | | | | | | | | FIELDING | | |
Year Team (League)	Pos.	G	AB	R	H	2B	3B	HR	RBI	Avg.	BB	SO	SB	PO	A	E	Avg.
1998—Boston (A.L.)	OF	2	3	0	1	0	0	0	0	.333	1	0	0	3	0	0	1.000
1999—Boston (A.L.)	OF	5	14	5	3	3	0	0	6	.214	4	5	0	3	0	0	1.000
Division series totals (2 years)		7	17	5	4	3	0	0	6	.235	5	5	0	6	0	0	1.000

CHAMPIONSHIP SERIES RECORD

| | | | | | | BATTING | | | | | | | | FIELDING | | |
Year Team (League)	Pos.	G	AB	R	H	2B	3B	HR	RBI	Avg.	BB	SO	SB	PO	A	E	Avg.
1999—Boston (A.L.)	OF	4	14	2	4	2	0	0	0	.286	1	5	0	7	0	0	1.000

NOMO, HIDEO   P   DODGERS

PERSONAL: Born August 31, 1968, in Osaka, Japan. ... 6-2/230. ... Throws right, bats right.
HIGH SCHOOL: Seijyo Kogyo (Japan).
TRANSACTIONS/CAREER NOTES: Selected by Kintetsu Buffaloes in first round of 1989 Japanese free-agent draft. ... Signed as free agent by Los Angeles Dodgers organization (February 8, 1995). ... On Albuquerque temporarily inactive list (April 3-27, 1995). ... Traded by Dodgers with P Brad Clontz to New York Mets for P Dave Mlicki and P Greg McMichael (June 4, 1998). ... Released by Mets (March 26, 1999). ... Signed by Chicago Cubs organization (April 2, 1999). ... Released by Cubs (April 23, 1999). ... Signed by Milwaukee Brewers (April 29, 1999). ... Claimed on waivers by Philadelphia Phillies (October 28, 1999). ... Granted free agency (October 29, 1999). ... Signed by Detroit Tigers organization (January 21, 2000). ... On disabled list (July 30-August 18, 2000). ... Released by Tigers (November 2, 2000). ... Signed by Boston Red Sox (December 15, 2000). ... Granted free agency (November 5, 2001). ... Signed by Dodgers (December 20, 2001).
HONORS: Named N.L. Rookie Pitcher of the Year by THE SPORTING NEWS (1995). ... Named N.L. Rookie of the Year by Baseball Writers' Association of America (1995).
STATISTICAL NOTES: Struck out 16 batters in one game (June 14, 1995). ... Pitched 3-0 one-hit, complete-game victory against San Francisco (August 5, 1995). ... Led N.L. with 19 wild pitches and five balks in 1995. ... Led N.L. with five balks in 1995 and four in 1997. ... Struck out 17 batters in one game (April 13, 1996). ... Pitched 9-0 no-hit victory against Colorado (September 17, 1996). ... Pitched 3-0 no-hit victory against Baltimore (April 4, 2001). ... Pitched 4-0 one-hit, complete-game victory against Toronto (May 25, 2001).
MISCELLANEOUS: Member of 1988 Japanese Olympic baseball team. ... Appeared in one game as pinch runner (1999).

Year League	W	L	Pct.	ERA	G	GS	CG	ShO	Sv.	IP	H	R	ER	BB	SO
1990— Kintetsu (Jap. Pac.)	*18	8	.692	*2.91	29	27	21	2	0	235	167	...	76	*109	*287
1991— Kintetsu (Jap. Pac.)	*17	11	.607	3.05	31	29	22	*4	1	242 1/3	183	...	82	*128	*287
1992— Kintetsu (Jap. Pac.)	*18	8	.692	2.66	30	29	17	*5	0	216 2/3	150	...	64	*117	*228
1993— Kintetsu (Jap. Pac.)	*17	12	.586	3.70	32	32	14	2	0	243 1/3	*201	...	100	*148	*276
1994— Kintetsu (Jap. Pac.)	8	7	.533	3.63	17	17	6	0	0	114	...	...	46	86	126
1995— Bakersfield (Calif.)■	0	1	.000	3.38	1	1	0	0	0	5 1/3	6	2	2	1	6
— Los Angeles (N.L.)	13	6	.684	2.54	28	28	4	•3	0	191 1/3	124	63	54	78	*236
1996— Los Angeles (N.L.)	16	11	.593	3.19	33	33	3	2	0	228 1/3	180	93	81	85	234
1997— Los Angeles (N.L.)	14	12	.538	4.25	33	33	1	0	0	207 1/3	193	104	98	92	233
1998— Los Angeles (N.L.)	2	7	.222	5.05	12	12	2	0	0	67 2/3	57	39	38	38	73
— New York (N.L.)■	4	5	.444	4.82	17	16	1	0	0	89 2/3	73	49	48	56	94
1999— Iowa (PCL)■	1	1	.500	3.71	3	3	0	0	0	17	12	7	7	12	18
— Huntsville (Sou.)■	1	0	1.000	0.00	1	1	0	0	0	7	5	0	0	1	7
— Milwaukee (N.L.)	12	8	.600	4.54	28	28	0	0	0	176 1/3	173	96	89	78	161
2000— Detroit (A.L.)■	8	12	.400	4.74	32	31	1	0	0	190	191	102	100	89	181
2001— Boston (A.L.)■	13	10	.565	4.50	33	33	2	2	0	198	171	105	99	*96	*220
A.L. totals (2 years)	21	22	.488	4.62	65	64	3	2	0	388	362	207	199	185	401
N.L. totals (5 years)	61	49	.555	3.82	151	150	11	5	0	960 2/3	800	444	408	427	1031
Major League totals (7 years)	82	71	.536	4.05	216	214	14	7	0	1348 2/3	1162	651	607	612	1432

DIVISION SERIES RECORD

Year League	W	L	Pct.	ERA	G	GS	CG	ShO	Sv.	IP	H	R	ER	BB	SO
1995— Los Angeles (N.L.)	0	1	.000	9.00	1	1	0	0	0	5	7	5	5	2	6
1996— Los Angeles (N.L.)	0	1	.000	12.27	1	1	0	0	0	3 2/3	5	5	5	5	3
Division series totals (2 years)	0	2	.000	10.38	2	2	0	0	0	8 2/3	12	10	10	7	9

ALL-STAR GAME RECORD

Year League	W	L	Pct.	ERA	GS	CG	ShO	Sv.	IP	H	R	ER	BB	SO
1995— National	0	0	...	0.00	1	0	0	0	2	1	0	0	0	3

NORTON, GREG   IF   ROCKIES

PERSONAL: Born July 6, 1972, in San Leandro, Calif. ... 6-1/205. ... Bats both, throws right. ... Full name: Gregory Blakemoor Norton. ... Son of Jerry Norton, outfielder with Pittsburgh Pirates organization.
HIGH SCHOOL: Bishop O'Dowd (Oakland).
COLLEGE: Oklahoma.
TRANSACTIONS/CAREER NOTES: Selected by San Francisco Giants organization in seventh round of free-agent draft (June 4, 1990); did not sign. ... Selected by Chicago White Sox organization in second round of free-agent draft (June 3, 1993). ... Granted free agency (December 21, 2000). ... Signed by Colorado Rockies (January 5, 2001).
STATISTICAL NOTES: Led Midwest League third basemen with 387 total chances in 1994. ... Led American Association with .534 slugging percentage in 1997. ... Led American Association third basemen with 29 errors in 1997. ... Tied for A.L. third baseman lead with 25 errors in 1999.

Year Team (League)	Pos.	G	AB	R	H	2B	3B	HR	RBI	Avg.	BB	SO	SB	PO	A	E	Avg.
1993— GC White Sox (GCL)	3B	3	9	1	2	0	0	0	2	.222	1	1	0	1	7	0	1.000
— Hickory (S.Atl.)	3B-SS	71	254	36	62	12	2	4	36	.244	41	44	0	57	161	17	.928
1994— South Bend (Midw.)	3B	127	477	73	137	22	2	6	64	.287	62	71	5	92	*265	30	.922
1995— Birmingham (Sou.)	3B	133	469	65	117	23	2	6	64	.249	64	90	19	102	277	25	*.938
1996— Birmingham (Sou.)	SS	76	287	40	81	14	3	8	44	.282	33	55	5	104	214	17	.949
— Nashville (A.A.)	SS-DH-3B	43	164	28	47	14	2	7	26	.287	17	42	2	43	95	13	.914
— Chicago (A.L.)	SS-3B-DH	11	23	4	5	0	0	2	3	.217	4	6	0	8	5	2	.867
1997— Nashville (A.A.)	3-S-2-DH	114	414	82	114	27	1	26	76	.275	57	101	3	83	247	†38	.897
— Chicago (A.L.)	3B-DH	18	34	5	9	2	2	0	1	.265	2	8	0	4	15	3	.864
1998— Chicago (A.L.)	1-3-DH-2	105	299	38	71	17	2	9	36	.237	26	77	3	654	42	6	.991
1999— Chicago (A.L.)	3B-1B-DH	132	436	62	111	26	0	16	50	.255	69	93	4	160	204	‡27	.931
2000— Chicago (A.L.)	3B-1B-DH	71	201	25	49	6	1	6	28	.244	26	47	1	126	66	8	.960
— Charlotte (I.L.)	3B-SS-1B	29	97	18	28	4	0	5	17	.289	24	23	1	55	54	1	.991
2001— Colorado (N.L.)■	OF-3B-1B-DH	117	225	30	60	13	2	13	40	.267	19	65	1	90	31	4	.968
American League totals (5 years)		337	993	134	245	51	5	33	118	.247	127	231	8	952	332	46	.965
National League totals (1 year)		117	225	30	60	13	2	13	40	.267	19	65	1	90	31	4	.968
Major League totals (6 years)		454	1218	164	305	64	7	46	158	.250	146	296	9	1042	363	50	.966

NORTON, PHIL   P   CUBS

PERSONAL: Born February 1, 1976, in Texarkana, Texas. ... 6-1/190. ... Throws left, bats right. ... Full name: Phillip Douglas Norton.
HIGH SCHOOL: Pleasant Grove (Texarkana, Texas).
JUNIOR COLLEGE: Texarkana (Texas) College.
TRANSACTIONS/CAREER NOTES: Selected by Chicago Cubs organization in 10th round of free-agent draft (June 4, 1996).
RECORDS: Shares major league record for most home runs allowed in one inning—4 (August 8, 2000, fourth inning).
STATISTICAL NOTES: Led Pacific Coast League with nine sacrifice hits allowed in 2001. ... Tied for Pacific Coast League lead with seven intentional bases on balls allowed in 2001.

Year League	W	L	Pct.	ERA	G	GS	CG	ShO	Sv.	IP	H	R	ER	BB	SO
1996— Gulf Coast Cubs (GCL)	0	0	...	0.00	1	0	0	0	0	3	1	0	0	0	6
— Williamsport (NY-Penn)	7	4	.636	2.54	15	13	2	1	0	85	68	33	24	33	77
1997— Rockford (Midw.)	9	3	.750	3.22	18	18	3	0	0	109	92	51	39	44	114
— Daytona (FSL)	3	2	.600	2.34	7	6	3	0	0	42 1/3	40	11	11	12	44
— Orlando (Sou.)	1	0	1.000	2.57	2	1	0	0	0	7	8	2	2	2	7
1998— Daytona (FSL)	4	3	.571	3.27	10	10	0	0	0	66	57	30	24	26	54
— West Tenn (Sou.)	6	6	.500	3.52	19	19	1	1	0	120 1/3	118	60	47	50	119
1999— West Tenn (Sou.)	7	4	.636	2.39	14	13	0	0	0	86 2/3	72	32	23	42	81
— Iowa (PCL)	5	6	.455	6.67	14	14	0	0	0	79 2/3	98	63	59	33	61
2000— Iowa (PCL)	8	•13	.381	4.96	28	26	2	1	0	159 2/3	166	100	88	*104	126
— Chicago (N.L.)	0	1	.000	9.35	2	2	0	0	0	8 2/3	14	10	9	7	6
2001— Iowa (PCL)	6	3	.667	2.69	46	3	0	0	2	73 2/3	65	27	22	41	75
Major League totals (1 year)	0	1	.000	9.35	2	2	0	0	0	8 2/3	14	10	9	7	6

PERSONAL: Born March 16, 1976, in Santo Domingo, Dominican Republic. ... 5-11/185. ... Bats both, throws right. ... Full name: Abraham Orlando Nunez Adames.
HIGH SCHOOL: Emmanuel (Santo Domingo, Dominican Republic).
TRANSACTIONS/CAREER NOTES: Signed as non-drafted free agent by Toronto Blue Jays organization (May 5, 1994). ... Traded by Blue Jays with P Mike Halperin and C/OF Craig Wilson to Pittsburgh Pirates (December 11, 1996), completing deal in which Blue Jays traded P Jose Silva, P Jose Pett, IF Brandon Cromer and three players to be named later to Pirates for OF/1B Orlando Merced, IF Carlos Garcia, and P Dan Plesac (November 14, 1996).
STATISTICAL NOTES: Tied for New York-Pennsylvania League lead in caught stealing with 14 in 1996. ... Led New York-Pennsylvania League shortstops with .953 fielding percentage in 1996.

Year Team (League)	Pos.	G	AB	R	H	2B	3B	HR	RBI	Avg.	BB	SO	SB	PO	A	E	Avg.
1994— Dom. Blue Jays (DSL)	2B	59	188	31	47	5	0	0	15	.250	42	37	22	155	27	12	.938
1995— Dom. Blue Jays (DSL)	2B	54	186	49	56	10	3	4	25	.301	30	27	24	80	97	7	.962
1996— St. Catharines (NY-P)	SS-2B	75	*297	43	83	6	4	3	26	.279	31	43	37	136	239	15	‡.962
1997— Lynchburg (Caro.)■...	SS	78	304	45	79	9	4	3	32	.260	23	47	29	100	219	15	.955
— Carolina (Sou.)..........	SS	47	198	31	65	6	1	1	14	.328	20	28	10	76	129	11	.949
— Pittsburgh (N.L.)........	SS-2B	19	40	3	9	2	2	0	6	.225	3	10	1	14	37	0	1.000
1998— Nashville (PCL).......	SS	94	366	50	91	12	3	3	32	.249	39	73	16	155	274	21	.953
— Lynchburg (Caro.)......	SS-2B	5	18	2	4	1	0	0	2	.222	3	1	1	6	18	1	.960
— Pittsburgh (N.L.)........	SS	24	52	6	10	2	0	1	2	.192	12	14	4	33	60	7	.930
1999— Pittsburgh (N.L.).....	SS-2B	90	259	25	57	8	0	0	17	.220	28	54	9	113	214	14	.959
— Nashville (PCL).........	SS	15	58	12	18	0	0	0	3	.310	5	8	1	23	43	2	.971
2000— Pittsburgh (N.L.).....	SS-2B	40	91	10	20	1	0	1	8	.220	8	14	0	43	65	2	.982
2001— Pittsburgh (N.L.)........	2B-SS-3B-OF	115	301	30	79	11	4	1	21	.262	28	53	8	144	234	4	.990
Major League totals (5 years)		288	743	74	175	24	6	3	54	.236	79	145	22	347	610	27	.973

NUNEZ, ABRAHAM   OF   MARLINS

PERSONAL: Born February 5, 1980, in Haina, Dominican Republic. ... 6-2/185. ... Bats right, throws right.
TRANSACTIONS/CAREER NOTES: Signed as non-drafted free agent by Arizona Diamondbacks organization (September 17, 1996). ... On disabled list (June 30-July 16, 1998). ... On disabled list (April 13-20, 1999). ... Traded by Diamondbacks to Florida Marlins (December 13, 1999), completing deal in which Diamondbacks traded P Vladamir Nunez, P Brad Penny and a player to be named to Marlins for P Matt Mantei (July 9, 1999). ... On Portland disabled list (April 7-14 and June 24-July 14, 2000).
STATISTICAL NOTES: Led Arizona League outfielders with 103 total chances in 1997.

Year Team (League)	Pos.	G	AB	R	H	2B	3B	HR	RBI	Avg.	BB	SO	SB	PO	A	E	Avg.
1997— Ariz. D'backs (Ariz.)....	OF	54	213	52	65	17	4	0	21	.305	26	40	3	*94	•8	1	*.990
— Lethbridge (Pio.)........	OF	2	6	2	1	0	0	0	1	.167	1	0	0	1	1	0	1.000
1998— South Bend (Midw.)....	OF	110	364	44	93	14	2	9	47	.255	67	81	12	226	8	*14	.944
1999— High Desert (Calif.)......	OF	130	488	106	133	29	6	22	93	.273	86	122	40	254	*20	*14	.951
2000— Portland (East.)■.......	OF	74	221	39	61	17	3	6	42	.276	44	64	8	5	0	0	1.000
— Brevard County (FSL).	OF	31	103	17	20	4	0	1	9	.194	28	34	11	...	...	...	...
2001— Portland (East.)........	OF	136	467	75	112	14	*9	17	53	.240	83	155	26	315	13	8	.976

NUNEZ, FRANKLIN   P   PHILLIES

PERSONAL: Born January 18, 1977, in Nagua, Dominican Republic. ... 6-0/175. ... Throws right, bats right.
HIGH SCHOOL: Escuela Cano Abajo (Dominican Republic).
TRANSACTIONS/CAREER NOTES: Signed as non-drafted free agent by Los Angeles Dodgers organization (September 1, 1994). ... Released by Dodgers (January 12, 1996). ... Signed by Philadelphia Phillies organization (June 20, 1998). ... On disabled list (July 13, 1999-remainder of season).

Year League	W	L	Pct.	ERA	G	GS	CG	ShO	Sv.	IP	H	R	ER	BB	SO
1995— Dominican Dodgers (DSL) .	1	0	1.000	7.36	12	1	0	0	0	22	27	25	18	20	17
1996—						Did not play.									
1997—						Did not play.									
1998— Dominican Phillies (DSL)■	0	2	.000	2.18	5	5	1	0	0	33	23	14	8	14	37
— Martinsville (Appl.).............	2	2	.500	2.49	6	4	0	0	0	25 1/3	23	10	7	8	19
1999— Piedmont (S.Atl.)...............	4	8	.333	3.39	13	13	1	0	0	77	69	39	29	25	88
2000— Clearwater (FSL)	10	4	.714	3.62	23	14	1	0	2	112	112	54	45	57	81

NUNEZ, JORGE   2B/SS   DODGERS

PERSONAL: Born March 1, 1978, in Villa Mella, Dominican Republic. ... 5-10/158. ... Bats right, throws right. ... Full name: Jorge Marte Nunez.
TRANSACTIONS/CAREER NOTES: Signed as non-drafted free agent by Toronto Blue Jays organization (April 17, 1995). ... Traded by Blue Jays with P Shawn Green to Los Angeles Dodgers for OF Raul Mondesi and P Pedro Borbon (November 8, 1999). ... Granted free agency (December 21, 2000). ... Re-signed by Dodgers organization (January 4, 2001).
STATISTICAL NOTES: Led Pioneer League shortstops with 35 errors in 1998. ... Led Florida State League with 22 caught stealing in 2000. ... Led Florida State League shortstops with 656 total chances in 2000.

Year Team (League)	Pos.	G	AB	R	H	2B	3B	HR	RBI	Avg.	BB	SO	SB	PO	A	E	Avg.
1995— Dom. Blue Jays (DSL)	SS	13	15	1	2	0	0	1	4	.133	1	5	0	0	1	0	1.000
1996— Dom. Blue Jays (DSL)	IF	69	258	51	76	10	2	7	40	.295	19	36	19	69	182	38	.869
1997— Dom. Blue Jays (DSL)	1B-2B	71	262	46	66	5	5	4	33	.252	29	48	*44	...	...	...	...
1998— Medicine Hat (Pio.)	SS-2B-3B	•74	*317	74	101	9	•11	6	52	.319	28	45	31	121	215	†38	.898
— Hagerstown (S.Atl.)......	3B	4	16	0	4	0	0	0	1	.250	0	1	1	2	3	1	.833
1999— Hagerstown (S.Atl.).....	2B-SS-3B	133	564	*116	151	28	•11	14	61	.268	40	103	51	247	387	32	.952
2000— Albuquerque (PCL)■...	SS	3	1	0	0	0	0	0	0	.000	0	0	0	0	0	0	...
— Vero Beach (FSL)	SS	128	534	86	154	17	8	4	39	.288	38	104	54	*212	386	*58	.912
2001— Jacksonville (Sou.).....	SS-2B	123	473	63	123	15	2	4	28	.260	33	88	*44	159	301	30	.939

N

NUNEZ, JOSE — P — PADRES

PERSONAL: Born March 14, 1979, in Montecristi, Dominican Republic. ... 6-2/175. ... Throws left, bats left. ... Full name: Jose Antonio Nunez.
HIGH SCHOOL: Liceo Cristo Liberador.
TRANSACTIONS/CAREER NOTES: Signed as non-drafted free agent by New York Mets organization (February 21, 1996). ... Selected by Los Angeles Dodgers from Mets organization in Rule 5 major league draft (December 11, 2000). ... Claimed on waivers by San Diego Padres (May 11, 2001).

Year League	W	L	Pct.	ERA	G	GS	CG	ShO	Sv.	IP	H	R	ER	BB	SO
1996— Dominican Mets (DSL)......	0	1	.000	6.38	11	3	0	0	0	24	33	19	17	9	25
1997— Dominican Mets (DSL)......	2	2	.500	2.93	18	6	0	0	0	46	43	21	15	15	37
1998— Gulf Coast Mets (GCL)......	3	4	.429	2.38	13	11	1	0	0	68	60	26	18	12	69
1999— Kingsport (Appl.)......	3	4	.429	3.75	13	13	0	0	0	69 $^2/_3$	75	36	29	15	63
2000— Columbia (S.Atl.)......	3	4	.429	3.02	34	5	0	0	8	95 $^1/_3$	82	36	32	23	112
2001— Los Angeles (N.L.)■......	0	1	.000	13.50	6	0	0	0	0	7 $^1/_3$	14	15	11	5	11
— San Diego (N.L.)■......	4	1	.800	3.31	56	0	0	0	0	51 $^2/_3$	48	20	19	20	49
Major League totals (1 year)........	**4**	**2**	**.667**	**4.58**	**62**	**0**	**0**	**0**	**0**	**59**	**62**	**35**	**30**	**25**	**60**

NUNEZ, VLADIMIR — P — MARLINS

PERSONAL: Born March 15, 1975, in Havana, Cuba. ... 6-4/224. ... Throws right, bats right. ... Full name: Vladimir Nunez Zarabaza.
TRANSACTIONS/CAREER NOTES: Signed as non-drafted free agent by Arizona Diamondbacks organization (February 1, 1996). ... On Tucson disabled list (April 7-24, 1998). ... Traded by Diamondbacks with P Brad Penny and a player to be named later to Florida Marlins for P Matt Mantei (July 9, 1999); Marlins acquired OF Abraham Nunez to complete deal (December 13, 1999). ... On Florida disabled list (July 19-August 3, 2001); included rehabilitation assignment to Kane County (August 1-2).
STATISTICAL NOTES: Led California League with 36 home runs allowed in 1997.

Year League	W	L	Pct.	ERA	G	GS	CG	ShO	Sv.	IP	H	R	ER	BB	SO
1996— Visalia (Calif.)......	1	6	.143	5.43	12	10	0	0	0	53	64	45	32	17	37
— Lethbridge (Pio.)......	*10	0	*1.000	*2.22	14	13	0	0	0	85	78	25	21	10	*93
1997— High Desert (Calif.)......	8	5	.615	5.17	28	28	1	1	0	158 $^1/_3$	169	102	91	40	142
1998— Tucson (PCL)	4	4	.500	4.91	31	13	1	0	2	95 $^1/_3$	103	58	52	37	78
— Arizona (N.L.)......	0	0	...	10.13	4	0	0	0	0	5 $^1/_3$	7	6	6	2	2
1999— Tucson (PCL)	1	0	1.000	6.75	3	0	0	0	0	2 $^2/_3$	5	2	2	0	3
— Arizona (N.L.)......	3	2	.600	2.91	27	0	0	0	1	34	29	15	11	20	28
— Florida (N.L.)■......	4	8	.333	4.58	17	12	0	0	0	74 $^2/_3$	66	48	38	34	58
2000— Florida (N.L.)......	0	6	.000	7.90	17	12	0	0	0	68 $^1/_3$	88	63	60	34	45
— Calgary (PCL)......	6	7	.462	4.12	15	15	1	0	0	89 $^2/_3$	92	43	41	38	95
2001— Florida (N.L.)......	4	5	.444	2.74	52	3	0	0	0	92	79	33	28	30	64
— Kane County (Midw.)......	0	0	...	9.00	1	1	0	0	0	1	3	1	1	0	0
Major League totals (4 years)......	**11**	**21**	**.344**	**4.69**	**117**	**27**	**0**	**0**	**1**	**274 $^1/_3$**	**269**	**165**	**143**	**120**	**197**

OCHOA, ALEX — OF — BREWERS

PERSONAL: Born March 29, 1972, in Miami Lakes, Fla. ... 6-0/195. ... Bats right, throws right.
HIGH SCHOOL: Hialeah (Fla.) Miami Lakes.
TRANSACTIONS/CAREER NOTES: Selected by Baltimore Orioles organization in third round of free-agent draft (June 3, 1991). ... Traded by Orioles with OF Damon Buford to New York Mets for 3B/OF Bobby Bonilla and a player to be named later (July 28, 1995); Orioles acquired P Jimmy Williams to complete deal (August 17, 1995). ... Traded by Mets to Minnesota Twins for OF Rich Becker (December 12, 1997). ... Traded by Twins to Milwaukee Brewers for a player to be named later (December 14, 1998); Twins acquired OF Darrell Nicholas to complete deal (December 15, 1998). ... Traded by Brewers to Cincinnati Reds for OF/1B Mark Sweeney and a player to be named later (January 14, 2000); Brewers acquired P Gene Altman to complete deal (May 15, 2000). ... On Cincinnati disabled list (May 31-June 16, 2000); included rehabilitation assignment to Chattanooga (June 11-16). ... Traded by Reds to Colorado Rockies for 2B Todd Walker and OF Robin Jennings (July 19, 2001). ... Traded by Rockies to Milwaukee Brewers as part of three-way deal in which New York Mets traded P Glendon Rusch to Brewers, Rockies traded 1B/OF Ross Gload and P Craig House to Mets, Brewers traded P Jeff D'Amico, OF Jeromy Burnitz, IF Lou Collier, OF/1B Mark Sweeney and cash to Mets and Mets traded 1B/3B Todd Zeile, OF, Benny Agbayani, IF/OF Lenny Harris and cash to Rockies (January 21, 2002).
STATISTICAL NOTES: Led Carolina League in grounding into double plays with 15 in 1993. ... Led Eastern League with 12 sacrifice flies in 1994. ... Tied for Eastern League lead in double plays by outfielder with five in 1994. ... Led International League outfielders with 249 putouts and 266 total chances in 1995. ... Hit for the cycle (July 3, 1996). ... Tied for International League lead in double plays by outfielder with three in 1996. ... Career major league grand slams: 1.

						BATTING									FIELDING		
Year Team (League)	Pos.	G	AB	R	H	2B	3B	HR	RBI	Avg.	BB	SO	SB	PO	A	E	Avg.
1991— GC Orioles (GCL)......	OF	53	179	26	55	8	3	1	30	.307	16	14	11	45	3	2	.960
1992— Kane County (Midw.)..	OF	133	499	65	147	22	7	1	59	.295	58	55	31	225	•17	•12	.953
1993— Frederick (Caro.)	OF	137	532	84	147	29	5	13	90	.276	46	67	34	169	13	11	.943
1994— Bowie (East.)......	OF	134	519	77	156	25	2	14	82	.301	49	67	28	237	*22	6	.977
1995— Rochester (I.L.)......	OF	91	336	41	92	18	2	8	46	.274	26	50	17	183	9	5	.975
— Norfolk (I.L.)■......	OF-DH	34	123	17	38	6	2	2	15	.309	14	12	7	§66	1	2	.971
— New York (N.L.)......	OF	11	37	7	11	1	0	0	0	.297	2	10	1	20	1	0	1.000
1996— Norfolk (I.L.)......	OF-DH	67	233	45	79	12	4	8	39	.339	32	22	5	110	9	5	.960
— New York (N.L.)......	OF	82	282	37	83	19	3	4	33	.294	17	30	4	135	8	5	.966
1997— New York (N.L.)......	OF-DH	113	238	31	58	14	1	3	22	.244	18	32	3	104	7	2	.982
1998— Minnesota (A.L.)■......	OF-DH	94	249	35	64	14	2	2	25	.257	10	35	6	117	8	4	.969
1999— Milwaukee (N.L.)■......	OF-DH	119	277	47	83	16	3	8	40	.300	45	43	6	133	5	3	.979
2000— Cincinnati (N.L.)......	OF	118	244	50	77	21	3	13	58	.316	24	27	8	125	4	3	.977
— Chattanooga (Sou.)	OF	4	16	3	3	2	0	1	2	.188	2	1	1	7	0	1	1.000
2001— Cincinnati (N.L.)	OF-DH	90	349	48	101	20	4	7	35	.289	24	53	12	176	6	2	.989
— Colorado (N.L.)......	OF	58	187	25	47	10	3	1	17	.251	21	23	5	90	6	1	.990
American League totals (1 year)		**94**	**249**	**35**	**64**	**14**	**2**	**2**	**25**	**.257**	**10**	**35**	**6**	**117**	**8**	**4**	**.969**
National League totals (6 years)		**591**	**1614**	**245**	**460**	**101**	**17**	**36**	**205**	**.285**	**151**	**218**	**39**	**783**	**37**	**16**	**.981**
Major League totals (7 years)		**685**	**1863**	**280**	**524**	**115**	**19**	**38**	**230**	**.281**	**161**	**253**	**45**	**900**	**45**	**20**	**.979**

N
O

PERSONAL: Born November 8, 1968, in San Pedro de Macoris, Dominican Republic. ... 6-0/190. ... Bats both, throws right. ... Full name: Jose Antonio Dono Offerman.

HIGH SCHOOL: Colegio Biblico Cristiano (Dominican Republic).

TRANSACTIONS/CAREER NOTES: Signed as non-drafted free agent by Los Angeles Dodgers organization (July 24, 1986). ... Traded by Dodgers to Kansas City Royals for P Billy Brewer (December 17, 1995). ... On Kansas City disabled list (April 6-29, July 10-22 and August 14-September 6, 1997). ... Granted free agency (October 23, 1998). ... Signed by Boston Red Sox (November 16, 1998). ... On disabled list (May 27-June 10 and July 30-August 16, 2000).

RECORDS: Holds A.L. single-season record for most consecutive games batted safely by switch hitter—27 (1998).

HONORS: Named Minor League Player of the Year by THE SPORTING NEWS (1990). ... Named Pacific Coast League Player of the Year (1990).

STATISTICAL NOTES: Tied for Pioneer League lead in caught stealing with 10 in 1988. ... Tied for Pacific Coast League lead in caught stealing with 18 in 1990. ... Led Pacific Coast League shortstops with 36 errors in 1990. ... Hit home run in first major league at-bat (August 19, 1990). ... Led N.L. with 25 sacrifice hits in 1993. ... Had 27-game hitting streak (July 11-August 7, 1998). ... Career major league grand slams: 1.

Year Team (League)	Pos.	G	AB	R	H	2B	3B	HR	RBI	Avg.	BB	SO	SB	PO	A	E	Avg.
1987—							Dominican Summer League statistics unavailable.										
1988—Vero Beach (FSL)......	SS	4	14	4	4	2	0	0	2	.286	2	0	0	4	5	5	.643
—Great Falls (Pio.).......	SS	60	251	75	83	11	5	2	28	.331	38	42	*57	82	143	18	*.926
1989—Bakersfield (Calif.)......	SS	62	245	53	75	9	4	2	22	.306	35	48	37	94	179	30	.901
—San Antonio (Texas)....	SS	68	278	47	80	6	3	2	22	.288	40	39	32	106	168	20	.932
1990—Albuquerque (PCL).....	SS-2B	117	454	104	148	16	11	0	56	.326	71	81	*60	174	361	†36	.937
—Los Angeles (N.L.).....	SS	29	58	7	9	0	0	1	7	.155	4	14	1	30	40	4	.946
1991—Albuquerque (PCL).....	SS	79	289	58	86	8	4	0	29	.298	47	58	32	126	241	17	.956
—Los Angeles (N.L.).....	SS	52	113	10	22	2	0	0	3	.195	25	32	3	50	121	10	.945
1992—Los Angeles (N.L.).....	SS	149	534	67	139	20	8	1	30	.260	57	98	23	208	398	*42	.935
1993—Los Angeles (N.L.).....	SS	158	590	77	159	21	6	1	62	.269	71	75	30	250	454	*37	.950
1994—Los Angeles (N.L.).....	SS	72	243	27	51	8	4	1	25	.210	38	38	2	123	195	11	.967
—Albuquerque (PCL).....	SS	56	224	43	74	7	5	1	31	.330	37	48	9	91	196	13	.957
1995—Los Angeles (N.L.).....	SS	119	429	69	123	14	6	4	33	.287	69	67	2	165	312	*35	.932
1996—Kansas City (A.L.)■...1B-2B-SS-OF	151	561	85	170	33	8	5	47	.303	74	98	24	920	234	16	.986
1997—Kansas City (A.L.)......	2B-DH	106	424	59	126	23	6	2	39	.297	41	64	9	201	254	9	.981
1998—Kansas City (A.L.)......	2B-DH	158	607	102	191	28	*13	7	66	.315	89	96	45	277	440	19	.974
1999—Boston (A.L.)■........	2B-DH-1B	149	586	107	172	37	*11	8	69	.294	96	79	18	285	321	14	.977
2000—Boston (A.L.)..........	2B-1B-DH	116	451	73	115	14	3	9	41	.255	70	70	0	403	231	11	.983
2001—Boston (A.L.)............	2B-1B	128	524	76	140	23	3	9	49	.267	61	97	5	458	288	14	.982
American League totals (6 years)		808	3153	502	914	158	44	40	311	.290	431	504	101	2544	1768	83	.981
National League totals (6 years)		579	1967	257	503	65	24	8	160	.256	264	324	61	826	1520	139	.944
Major League totals (12 years)		1387	5120	759	1417	223	68	48	471	.277	695	828	162	3370	3288	222	.968

DIVISION SERIES RECORD

Year Team (League)	Pos.	G	AB	R	H	2B	3B	HR	RBI	Avg.	BB	SO	SB	PO	A	E	Avg.
1995—Los Angeles (N.L.).....	PR	1	0	0	0	0	0	0	0	...	0	0	0	...	...	...	...
1999—Boston (A.L.)............	2B	5	18	4	7	1	0	1	6	.389	7	0	0	11	9	0	1.000
Division series totals (2 years)		6	18	4	7	1	0	1	6	.389	7	0	0	11	9	0	1.000

CHAMPIONSHIP SERIES RECORD

RECORDS: Shares single-game record for most at-bats (nine-inning game)—6 (October 16, 1999).

Year Team (League)	Pos.	G	AB	R	H	2B	3B	HR	RBI	Avg.	BB	SO	SB	PO	A	E	Avg.
1999—Boston (A.L.)............	2B	5	24	4	11	0	1	0	2	.458	1	3	1	16	6	2	.917

ALL-STAR GAME RECORD

Year League	Pos.	AB	R	H	2B	3B	HR	RBI	Avg.	BB	SO	SB	PO	A	E	Avg.
1995—National..................	SS	0	0	0	0	0	0	0	...	0	0	0	0	0	0	...
1999—American..................	2B	1	0	0	0	0	0	0	.000	0	0	0	3	0	1	.750
All-Star Game totals (2 years)		1	0	0	0	0	0	0	.000	0	0	0	3	0	1	.750

PERSONAL: Born March 18, 1976, in Kyoto, Japan. ... 6-1/179. ... Throws right, bats right. ... Full name: Tomokazu Ohka.

HIGH SCHOOL: Kyoto Siesio (Kyoto, Japan).

TRANSACTIONS/CAREER NOTES: Contract purchased by Boston Red Sox from Yokohama BayStars of Japan Central League (November 20, 1998). ... Traded by Red Sox with P Rich Rundles to Montreal Expos for P Ugueth Urbina (July 31, 2001).

STATISTICAL NOTES: Pitched 2-0 no-hit victory for Pawtucket against Charlotte (June 1, 2000).

Year League	W	L	Pct.	ERA	G	GS	CG	ShO	Sv.	IP	H	R	ER	BB	SO
1994—Yokohama (Jap. Cen.)........	1	1	.500	4.18	15	2	0	0	0	28	29	13	13	18	18
1995—Yokohama (Jap. Cen.)........	0	0	...	1.93	3	1	0	0	0	9 1/3	3	2	2	13	6
1996—Yokohama (Jap. Cen.)........	0	1	.000	9.50	14	1	0	0	0	18	27	19	19	14	11
1997—					Japan minor league statistics unavailable.										
1998—Yokohama (Jap. Cen.)........	0	0	...	9.00	2	0	0	0	0	2	2	2	2	2	1
1999—Trenton (East.)■	8	0	1.000	3.00	12	12	0	0	0	72	63	26	24	25	53
—Pawtucket (I.L.)................	7	0	1.000	1.58	12	12	1	1	0	68 1/3	60	17	12	11	63
—Boston (A.L.)................	1	2	.333	6.23	8	2	0	0	0	13	21	12	9	6	8
2000—Pawtucket (I.L.)................	9	6	.600	2.96	19	19	3	•2	0	130 2/3	111	52	43	23	78
—Boston (A.L.)................	3	6	.333	3.12	13	13	0	0	0	69 1/3	70	25	24	26	40
2001—Boston (A.L.)................	2	5	.286	6.19	12	11	0	0	0	51 1/3	69	40	36	19	37
—Pawtucket (I.L.)................	2	5	.286	5.57	8	8	1	0	0	42	55	35	26	9	33
—Montreal (N.L.)■...........	1	4	.200	4.77	10	10	0	0	0	54 2/3	65	30	29	10	31
A.L. totals (3 years)	6	13	.316	4.61	33	25	0	0	0	134 2/3	160	77	69	51	85
N.L. totals (1 year)	1	4	.200	4.77	10	10	0	0	0	54 2/3	65	30	29	10	31
Major League totals (3 years)	7	17	.292	4.66	43	35	0	0	0	189 1/3	225	107	98	61	116

OHMAN, WILL — P — CUBS

PERSONAL: Born August 13, 1977, in Frankfurt, West Germany. ... 6-2/195. ... Throws left, bats left. ... Full name: William McDaniel Ohman.
HIGH SCHOOL: Ponderos (Parker, Colo.).
COLLEGE: Pepperdine.
TRANSACTIONS/CAREER NOTES: Selected by Chicago Cubs organization in eighth round of free-agent draft (June 2, 1998).

Year	League	W	L	Pct.	ERA	G	GS	CG	ShO	Sv.	IP	H	R	ER	BB	SO
1998—	Williamsport (NY-Penn)	4	4	.500	8.77	10	7	0	0	0	39	39	32	38	13	35
	—Rockford (Midw.)	1	1	.500	4.44	4	4	0	0	0	24 1/3	25	13	12	7	21
1999—	Daytona (FSL)	4	7	.364	3.46	31	15	2	•2	5	106 2/3	102	59	41	41	97
2000—	West Tenn (Sou.)	6	4	.600	1.89	59	0	0	0	3	71 1/3	53	20	15	36	85
	—Chicago (N.L.)	1	0	1.000	8.10	6	0	0	0	0	3 1/3	4	3	3	4	2
2001—	Iowa (PCL)	5	2	.714	4.06	40	1	0	0	4	51	51	24	23	18	66
	—Chicago (N.L.)	0	1	.000	7.71	11	0	0	0	0	11 2/3	14	10	10	6	12
Major League totals (2 years)		1	1	.500	7.80	17	0	0	0	0	15	18	13	13	10	14

OJEDA, AUGIE — SS — CUBS

PERSONAL: Born December 20, 1974, in Eldorado Culican, Mexico. ... 5-9/170. ... Bats both, throws right. ... Full name: Octavio Augie Ojeda.
HIGH SCHOOL: Pius X (Downey, Calif.).
JUNIOR COLLEGE: Cypress (Calif.) College.
COLLEGE: Tennessee.
TRANSACTIONS/CAREER NOTES: Selected by Baltimore Orioles organization in 13th round of free-agent draft (June 4, 1996). ... Traded by Orioles to Chicago Cubs for P Richard Negrette (December 13, 1999).
STATISTICAL NOTES: Led Eastern League with 25 sacrifice hits in 1999. ... Led Eastern League shortstops with .969 fielding percentage in 1999. ... Led Pacific Coast League shortstops with .976 fielding percentage in 2000.
MISCELLANEOUS: Member of 1996 U.S. Olympic baseball team.

Year	Team (League)	Pos.	G	AB	R	H	2B	3B	HR	RBI	Avg.	BB	SO	SB	PO	A	E	Avg.
1997—	Bowie (East.)	SS	58	204	33	60	9	1	2	23	.294	31	17	7	84	176	9	.967
	—Frederick (Caro.)	SS	34	128	25	44	11	1	1	20	.344	18	18	2	36	108	5	.966
	—Rochester (I.L.)	SS	15	47	5	11	3	1	0	6	.234	8	4	1	24	35	5	.922
1998—	GC Orioles (GCL)	SS	4	15	6	6	2	0	0	2	.400	3	1	3	9	16	0	1.000
	—Bowie (East.)	SS-3B	73	254	36	65	10	2	1	19	.256	36	30	0	95	199	11	.964
1999—	Rochester (I.L.)	SS	1	1	0	0	0	0	0	0	.000	0	0	0	0	0	0	...
	—Bowie (East.)	SS-3B	134	460	73	123	18	4	10	60	.267	57	47	6	211	379	19	†.969
2000—	Iowa (PCL)■	SS-2B	113	396	56	111	23	2	8	43	.280	33	27	16	161	294	11	†.976
	—Chicago (N.L.)	SS-2B	28	77	10	17	3	1	2	8	.221	10	9	0	30	65	1	.990
2001—	Chicago (N.L.)	3B-SS-2B	78	144	16	29	5	1	1	12	.201	12	20	1	50	103	6	.962
Major League totals (2 years)			106	221	26	46	8	2	3	20	.208	22	29	1	80	168	7	.973

O'LEARY, TROY — OF

PERSONAL: Born August 4, 1969, in Compton, Calif. ... 6-0/200. ... Bats left, throws left. ... Full name: Troy Franklin O'Leary.
HIGH SCHOOL: Cypress (Calif.).
JUNIOR COLLEGE: Chaffey College (Calif.).
TRANSACTIONS/CAREER NOTES: Selected by Milwaukee Brewers organization in 13th round of free-agent draft (June 2, 1987). ... Claimed on waivers by Boston Red Sox (April 14, 1995). ... On Boston disabled list (June 19-July 3, 2000); included rehabilitation assignment to Gulf Coast Red Sox (June 30-July 3). ... Granted free agency (November 5, 2001).
HONORS: Named Texas League Most Valuable Player (1992).
STATISTICAL NOTES: Led Pioneer League with 144 total bases in 1989. ... Led Texas League with 227 total bases and .399 on-base percentage in 1992. ... Led Texas League outfielders with 242 total chances in 1992. ... Had 15-game hitting streak (July 30-August 14, 1999). ... Career major league grand slams: 2.

Year	Team (League)	Pos.	G	AB	R	H	2B	3B	HR	RBI	Avg.	BB	SO	SB	PO	A	E	Avg.
1987—	Helena (Pio.)	OF	3	5	0	2	0	0	0	1	.400	0	0	0	0	0	0	...
1988—	Helena (Pio.)	OF	67	203	40	70	11	1	0	27	.345	30	32	10	64	4	3	.958
1989—	Beloit (Midw.)	OF	42	115	7	21	4	0	0	8	.183	15	20	1	55	1	1	.982
	—Helena (Pio.)	OF	•68	263	54	*89	16	3	11	*56	.338	28	43	9	92	6	3	.970
1990—	Beloit (Midw.)	OF	118	436	73	130	29	1	6	62	.298	41	90	12	184	14	8	.961
	—Stockton (Calif.)	OF	2	6	1	3	1	0	0	0	.500	2	1	0	3	0	1	.750
1991—	Stockton (Calif.)	OF	126	418	63	110	20	4	5	46	.263	73	96	4	163	4	3	.982
1992—	El Paso (Texas)	OF	*135	*506	*92	*169	27	8	5	79	*.334	59	87	28	*220	11	*11	.955
1993—	New Orleans (A.A.)	OF-1B	111	388	65	106	32	1	7	59	.273	43	61	6	189	8	6	.970
	—Milwaukee (A.L.)	OF	19	41	3	12	3	0	0	3	.293	5	9	0	32	1	0	1.000
1994—	New Orleans (A.A.)	OF-DH-1B	63	225	44	74	18	5	8	43	.329	32	37	10	99	10	2	.982
	—Milwaukee (A.L.)	OF-DH	27	66	9	18	1	1	2	7	.273	5	12	1	37	2	0	1.000
1995—	Boston (A.L.)■	OF-DH	112	399	60	123	31	6	10	49	.308	29	64	5	196	6	5	.976
1996—	Boston (A.L.)	OF	149	497	68	129	28	5	15	81	.260	47	80	3	227	8	7	.971
1997—	Boston (A.L.)	OF-DH	146	499	65	154	32	4	15	80	.309	39	70	0	267	8	6	.979
1998—	Boston (A.L.)	OF	156	611	95	165	36	8	23	83	.270	36	108	2	303	9	3	.990
1999—	Boston (A.L.)	OF	157	596	84	167	36	4	28	103	.280	56	91	1	296	9	2	.993
2000—	Boston (A.L.)	OF	138	513	68	134	30	4	13	70	.261	44	76	0	243	9	3	.988
	—GC Red Sox (GCL)	DH	3	8	3	6	1	0	0	1	.750	3	1	0	...	...	...	...
2001—	Boston (A.L.)	OF-DH	104	341	50	82	16	6	13	50	.240	25	73	1	163	3	1	.994
Major League totals (9 years)			1008	3563	502	984	213	38	119	526	.276	286	583	13	1764	55	27	.985

O

DIVISION SERIES RECORD

RECORDS: Shares single-game record for most home runs—2; grand slams—1; and runs batted in—7 (October 11, 1999). ... Shares single-inning record for most runs batted in—4 (October 11, 1999, third inning).

Year	Team (League)	Pos.	G	AB	R	H	2B	3B	HR	RBI	Avg.	BB	SO	SB	PO	A	E	Avg.
1998—Boston (A.L.)............		OF	4	16	0	1	0	0	0	0	.063	1	4	0	8	0	0	1.000
1999—Boston (A.L.)............		OF	5	20	4	4	0	0	2	7	.200	2	3	0	7	0	0	1.000
Division series totals (2 years)			9	36	4	5	0	0	2	7	.139	3	7	0	15	0	0	1.000

CHAMPIONSHIP SERIES RECORD

Year	Team (League)	Pos.	G	AB	R	H	2B	3B	HR	RBI	Avg.	BB	SO	SB	PO	A	E	Avg.
1999—Boston (A.L.)............		OF	5	20	2	7	3	0	0	1	.350	2	5	0	7	0	0	1.000

OLERUD, JOHN — 1B — MARINERS

PERSONAL: Born August 5, 1968, in Seattle. ... 6-5/220. ... Bats left, throws left. ... Full name: John Garrett Olerud. ... Son of John E. Olerud, minor league catcher (1965-70); and cousin of Dale Sveum, infielder with seven major league teams (1986-99). ... Name pronounced OH-luh-rude.
HIGH SCHOOL: Interlake (Bellevue, Wash.).
COLLEGE: Washington State.
TRANSACTIONS/CAREER NOTES: Selected by New York Mets organization in 27th round of free-agent draft (June 2, 1986); did not sign. ... Selected by Toronto Blue Jays organization in third round of free-agent draft (June 5, 1989). ... Traded by Blue Jays with cash to Mets for P Robert Person (December 20, 1996). ... Granted free agency (October 27, 1997). ... Re-signed by Mets (November 24, 1997). ... Granted free agency (October 29, 1999). ... Signed by Seattle Mariners (December 15, 1999).
RECORDS: Holds A.L. single-season records for most intentional bases on balls received—33 (1993); and most intentional bases on balls received by lefthanded hitter—33 (1993). ... Shares N.L. single-season record for most consecutive times reached base safely—15 (September 16 [1], 18 [5], 20 [4], 22 [1], 1998; 6 singles, 1 double, 2 home runs, 6 bases on balls).
HONORS: Won A.L. Gold Glove as first baseman (2000).
STATISTICAL NOTES: Tied for A.L. lead with 10 sacrifice flies in 1991. ... Had 26-game hitting streak (May 26-June 22, 1993). ... Led A.L. with 33 intentional bases on balls received and .473 on-base percentage in 1993. ... Hit for the cycle (September 11, 1997; and June 16, 2001). ... Had 23-game hitting streak (July 19-August 9, 1998). ... Led A.L. in grounding into double plays with 21 in 2001. ... Career major league grand slams: 6.

Year	Team (League)	Pos.	G	AB	R	H	2B	3B	HR	RBI	Avg.	BB	SO	SB	PO	A	E	Avg.
1989—Toronto (A.L.)............		1B-DH	6	8	2	3	0	0	0	0	.375	0	1	0	19	2	0	1.000
1990—Toronto (A.L.)............		DH-1B	111	358	43	95	15	1	14	48	.265	57	75	0	133	10	2	.986
1991—Toronto (A.L.)............		1B-DH	139	454	64	116	30	1	17	68	.256	68	84	0	1120	78	5	.996
1992—Toronto (A.L.)............		1B-DH	138	458	68	130	28	0	16	66	.284	70	61	1	1057	81	7	.994
1993—Toronto (A.L.)............		1B-DH	158	551	109	200	*54	2	24	107	*.363	114	65	0	1160	97	10	.992
1994—Toronto (A.L.)............		1B-DH	108	384	47	114	29	2	12	67	.297	61	53	1	824	68	6	.993
1995—Toronto (A.L.)............		1B	135	492	72	143	32	0	8	54	.291	84	54	0	1099	89	4	.997
1996—Toronto (A.L.)............		1B-DH	125	398	59	109	25	0	18	61	.274	60	37	1	781	56	2	.998
1997—New York (N.L.)■......		1B	154	524	90	154	34	1	22	102	.294	85	67	0	1292	120	7	.995
1998—New York (N.L.)........		1B	160	557	91	197	36	4	22	93	.354	96	73	2	1258	116	5	.996
1999—New York (N.L.)........		1B	•162	581	107	173	39	0	19	96	.298	125	66	3	1344	105	9	.994
2000—Seattle (A.L.)■.........		1B	159	565	84	161	45	0	14	103	.285	102	96	0	1271	*132	5	*.996
2001—Seattle (A.L.)............		1B	159	572	91	173	32	1	21	95	.302	94	70	3	1211	121	9	.993
American League totals (10 years)			1238	4240	639	1244	290	7	144	669	.293	710	596	6	8675	734	50	.995
National League totals (3 years)			476	1662	288	524	109	5	63	291	.315	306	206	5	3894	341	21	.995
Major League totals (13 years)			1714	5902	927	1768	399	12	207	960	.300	1016	802	11	12569	1075	71	.995

DIVISION SERIES RECORD

Year	Team (League)	Pos.	G	AB	R	H	2B	3B	HR	RBI	Avg.	BB	SO	SB	PO	A	E	Avg.
1999—New York (N.L.).........		1B	4	16	3	7	0	0	1	6	.438	3	2	0	31	4	0	1.000
2000—Seattle (A.L.)............		1B	3	10	2	3	0	0	1	2	.300	2	1	0	25	0	0	1.000
2001—Seattle (A.L.)............		1B	5	17	1	3	0	0	0	1	.176	3	5	0	32	4	0	1.000
Division series totals (3 years)			12	43	6	13	0	0	2	9	.302	8	8	0	88	8	0	1.000

CHAMPIONSHIP SERIES RECORD

Year	Team (League)	Pos.	G	AB	R	H	2B	3B	HR	RBI	Avg.	BB	SO	SB	PO	A	E	Avg.
1991—Toronto (A.L.)............		1B	5	19	1	3	0	0	0	3	.158	3	1	0	40	3	0	1.000
1992—Toronto (A.L.)............		1B	6	23	4	8	2	0	1	4	.348	2	5	0	51	1	0	1.000
1993—Toronto (A.L.)............		1B	6	23	5	8	1	0	0	3	.348	4	1	0	48	9	1	.983
1999—New York (N.L.).........		1B	6	27	4	8	0	0	2	6	.296	2	3	0	59	4	2	.969
2000—Seattle (A.L.)............		1B	6	20	3	7	3	0	1	2	.350	2	2	1	45	7	0	1.000
2001—Seattle (A.L.)............		1B	5	19	2	4	0	0	1	3	.211	2	4	0	45	3	0	1.000
Championship series totals (6 years)			34	131	19	38	6	0	5	21	.290	15	16	1	288	27	3	.991

WORLD SERIES RECORD

NOTES: Member of World Series championship team (1992 and 1993).

Year	Team (League)	Pos.	G	AB	R	H	2B	3B	HR	RBI	Avg.	BB	SO	SB	PO	A	E	Avg.
1992—Toronto (A.L.)............		1B	4	13	2	4	0	0	0	0	.308	0	4	0	25	3	0	1.000
1993—Toronto (A.L.)............		1B	5	17	5	4	1	0	1	2	.235	4	1	0	36	0	0	1.000
World Series totals (2 years)			9	30	7	8	1	0	1	2	.267	4	5	0	61	3	0	1.000

ALL-STAR GAME RECORD

Year	League	Pos.	AB	R	H	2B	3B	HR	RBI	Avg.	BB	SO	SB	PO	A	E	Avg.
1993—American...................		1B	2	0	0	0	0	0	0	.000	0	0	0	4	0	0	1.000
2001—American...................		1B	2	0	0	0	0	0	0	.000	0	0	0	4	0	0	1.000
All-Star Game totals (2 years)			4	0	0	0	0	0	0	.000	0	0	0	8	0	0	1.000

O

OLIVARES, OMAR   P

PERSONAL: Born July 6, 1967, in Mayaguez, Puerto Rico. ... 6-1/205. ... Throws right, bats right. ... Full name: Omar Palqu Olivares. ... Son of Ed Olivares, outfielder with St. Louis Cardinals (1960-61).

HIGH SCHOOL: Hostos (Mayaguez, Puerto Rico).

JUNIOR COLLEGE: Miami Dade College (Fla.).

TRANSACTIONS/CAREER NOTES: Signed as non-drafted free agent by San Diego Padres organization (September 15, 1986). ... Traded by Padres to St. Louis Cardinals for OF Alex Cole and P Steve Peters (February 27, 1990). ... On St. Louis disabled list (May 27-June 13, 1992; and June 4-20, 1993). ... Granted free agency (April 7, 1995). ... Signed by Colorado Rockies (April 9, 1995). ... Claimed on waivers by Philadelphia Phillies (July 11, 1995). ... Granted free agency (October 16, 1995). ... Signed by Detroit Tigers (December 20, 1995). ... On Detroit disabled list (April 16-May 30, 1996; included rehabilitation assignment to Toledo (May 24-30). ... Traded by Tigers with P Felipe Lira to Seattle Mariners for P Scott Sanders, P Dean Crow and 3B Carlos Villalobos (July 18, 1997). ... Granted free agency (October 30, 1997). ... Signed by Anaheim Angels (December 11, 1997). ... Traded by Angels with 2B Randy Velarde to Oakland Athletics for P Elvin Nina, OF Jeff DaVanon and OF Nathan Hayes (July 29, 1999). ... Granted free agency (October 29, 1999). ... Re-signed by A's (January 8, 2000). ... On Oakland disabled list (June 17-August 12, 2000); included rehabilitation assignments to Modesto (July 28-August 7) and Sacramento (August 8-12). ... Traded by A's to Pittsburgh Pirates for cash considerations (March 28, 2001). ... Granted free agency (November 6, 2001).

RECORDS: Shares major league single-season record for fewest double plays by pitcher who led league in double plays—4 (1992). ... Shares A.L. single-game record for most hit batsmen (nine innings)—4 (June 13, 1999).

STATISTICAL NOTES: Tied for Texas League lead with 10 hit batsmen in 1989.

MISCELLANEOUS: Appeared in one game as pinch runner and singled and scored in three games as pinch hitter (1992). ... Appeared in one game as pinch runner and made an out in one game as pinch hitter (1993). ... Made an out in only appearance as pinch hitter with St. Louis (1994). ... Appeared in one game as pinch runner with Colorado (1995). ... Hit two-run home run in only appearance as pinch hitter with Philadelphia (1995). ... Appeared in three games as pinch runner with Detroit (1997). ... Struck out in only appearance as pinch hitter and scored one run in two games as pinch runner (1998). ... Appeared in two games as pinch runner (2001).

Year League	W	L	Pct.	ERA	G	GS	CG	ShO	Sv.	IP	H	R	ER	BB	SO
1987—Charleston, S.C. (S.Atl.)	4	14	.222	4.60	31	24	5	0	0	170 1/3	182	107	87	57	86
1988—Charleston, S.C. (S.Atl.)	13	6	.684	2.23	24	24	*10	3	0	185 1/3	166	63	46	43	94
— Riverside (Calif.)	3	0	1.000	1.16	4	3	1	0	0	23 1/3	18	9	3	9	16
1989—Wichita (Texas)	12	11	.522	3.39	26	26	6	1	0	*185 2/3	175	87	70	61	79
1990—Louisville (A.A.)	10	11	.476	2.82	23	23	5	2	0	159 1/3	127	58	50	59	88
— St. Louis (N.L.)	1	1	.500	2.92	9	6	0	0	0	49 1/3	45	17	16	17	20
1991—St. Louis (N.L.)	11	7	.611	3.71	28	24	0	0	1	167 1/3	148	72	69	61	91
— Louisville (A.A.)	1	2	.333	3.47	6	6	0	0	0	36 1/3	39	15	14	16	27
1992—St. Louis (N.L.)	9	9	.500	3.84	32	30	1	0	0	197	189	84	84	63	124
1993—St. Louis (N.L.)	5	3	.625	4.17	58	9	0	0	1	118 2/3	134	60	55	54	63
1994—Louisville (A.A.)	2	1	.667	4.37	9	9	0	0	0	47 1/3	47	24	23	16	38
— St. Louis (N.L.)	3	4	.429	5.74	14	12	1	0	1	73 2/3	84	53	47	37	26
1995—Colorado Springs (PCL)	0	1	.000	5.40	3	2	0	0	0	11 2/3	14	7	7	2	6
— Colorado (N.L.)	1	3	.250	7.39	11	6	0	0	0	31 2/3	44	28	26	21	15
— Philadelphia (N.L.)	0	1	.000	5.40	5	0	0	0	0	10	11	6	6	2	7
— Scranton/W.B. (I.L.)	0	3	.000	4.87	7	7	0	0	0	44 1/3	49	25	24	20	28
1996—Detroit (A.L.)	7	11	.389	4.89	25	25	4	0	0	160	169	90	87	75	81
— Toledo (I.L.)	1	0	1.000	8.44	1	1	0	0	0	5 1/3	4	5	5	3	5
1997—Detroit (A.L.)	5	6	.455	4.70	19	19	3	2	0	115	110	68	60	53	74
— Seattle (A.L.)	1	4	.200	5.49	13	12	0	0	0	62 1/3	81	41	38	28	29
1998—Anaheim (A.L.)	9	9	.500	4.03	37	26	1	0	0	183	189	92	82	91	112
1999—Anaheim (A.L.)	8	9	.471	4.05	20	20	3	0	0	131	135	62	59	49	49
— Oakland (A.L.)	7	2	.778	4.34	12	12	1	0	0	74 2/3	82	43	36	32	36
2000—Oakland (A.L.)	4	8	.333	6.75	21	16	1	0	0	108	134	86	81	60	57
— Modesto (Calif.)	0	0	...	1.50	2	2	0	0	0	6	3	1	1	1	3
— Sacramento (PCL)	0	0	...	0.00	1	1	0	0	0	6	3	1	0	2	3
2001—Pittsburgh (N.L.)	6	9	.400	6.55	45	12	1	0	1	110	123	87	80	42	69
A.L. totals (5 years)	41	49	.456	4.78	147	130	13	2	0	834	900	482	443	388	438
N.L. totals (7 years)	36	37	.493	4.55	202	99	3	0	4	757 2/3	778	407	383	297	415
Major League totals (12 years)	77	86	.472	4.67	349	229	16	2	4	1591 2/3	1678	889	826	685	853

OLIVER, DARREN   P   RED SOX

PERSONAL: Born October 6, 1970, in Kansas City, Mo. ... 6-2/210. ... Throws left, bats right. ... Full name: Darren Christopher Oliver. ... Son of Bob Oliver, first baseman/outfielder with five major league teams (1965 and 1969-1975).

HIGH SCHOOL: Rio Linda (Calif.) Senior.

TRANSACTIONS/CAREER NOTES: Selected by Texas Rangers organization in third round of free-agent draft (June 1, 1988). ... On Gulf Coast Rangers disabled list (April 6-August 9, 1990). ... On disabled list (May 1, 1991-remainder of season). ... On Tulsa disabled list (July 1, 1992-remainder of season). ... On disabled list (June 27, 1995-remainder of season). ... On Texas disabled list (June 11-26, 1998); included rehabilitation assignment to Oklahoma City (June 21-26). ... Traded by Rangers with 3B Fernando Tatis and a player to be named later to St. Louis Cardinals for P Todd Stottlemyre and SS Royce Clayton (July 31, 1998); Cardinals acquired OF Mark Little to complete deal (August 9, 1998). ... Granted free agency (October 29, 1999). ... Signed by Rangers (January 27, 2000). ... On Texas disabled list (June 21-July 20 and August 1-September 1, 2000); included rehabilitation assignments to Oklahoma (July 5-20 and August 12-26) and Tulsa (August 27-31). ... On Texas disabled list (May 8-June 6, 2001); included rehabilitation assignments to Oklahoma (May 27-31) and Tulsa (June 1-6). ... Traded by Rangers to Boston Red Sox for OF Carl Everett (December 13, 2001).

MISCELLANEOUS: Made an out in only appearance as pinch hitter with St. Louis (1998). ... Had one sacrifice hit and struck out once in five appearances as pinch hitter (1999).

Year League	W	L	Pct.	ERA	G	GS	CG	ShO	Sv.	IP	H	R	ER	BB	SO
1988—Gulf Coast Rangers (GCL)	5	1	.833	2.15	12	9	0	0	0	54 1/3	39	16	13	18	59
1989—Gastonia (S.Atl.)	8	7	.533	3.16	24	23	2	1	0	122 1/3	86	54	43	82	108
1990—Gulf Coast Rangers (GCL)	0	0	...	0.00	3	3	0	0	0	6	1	1	0	1	7
— Gastonia (S.Atl.)	0	0	...	13.50	1	1	0	0	0	2	1	3	3	4	2
1991—Charlotte (FSL)	0	1	.000	4.50	2	2	0	0	0	8	6	4	4	3	12
1992—Charlotte (FSL)	1	0	1.000	0.72	8	2	1	1	2	25	11	2	2	10	33
— Tulsa (Texas)	0	1	.000	3.14	3	3	0	0	0	14 1/3	15	9	5	4	14

Year League	W	L	Pct.	ERA	G	GS	CG	ShO	Sv.	IP	H	R	ER	BB	SO
1993— Tulsa (Texas)	7	5	.583	1.96	46	0	0	0	6	73 1/3	51	18	16	41	77
— Texas (A.L.)	0	0	...	2.70	2	0	0	0	0	3 1/3	2	1	1	1	4
1994— Texas (A.L.)	4	0	1.000	3.42	43	0	0	0	2	50	40	24	19	35	50
— Oklahoma City (A.A.)	0	0	...	0.00	6	0	0	0	1	7 1/3	1	0	0	3	6
1995— Texas (A.L.)	4	2	.667	4.22	17	7	0	0	0	49	47	25	23	32	39
1996— Charlotte (FSL)	0	1	.000	3.00	2	1	0	0	0	12	8	4	4	3	9
— Texas (A.L.)	14	6	.700	4.66	30	30	1	1	0	173 2/3	190	97	90	76	112
1997— Texas (A.L.)	13	12	.520	4.20	32	32	3	1	0	201 1/3	213	111	94	82	104
1998— Texas (A.L.)	6	7	.462	6.53	19	19	2	0	0	103 1/3	140	84	75	43	58
— Oklahoma (PCL)	0	0	...	0.00	1	1	0	0	0	5	2	0	0	1	1
— St. Louis (N.L.)■	4	4	.500	4.26	10	10	0	0	0	57	64	31	27	23	29
1999— St. Louis (N.L.)	9	9	.500	4.26	30	30	2	1	0	196 1/3	197	96	93	74	119
2000— Texas (A.L.)■	2	9	.182	7.42	21	21	0	0	0	108	151	95	89	42	49
— Oklahoma (PCL)	2	1	.667	1.97	7	7	1	0	0	32	22	11	7	14	28
— Tulsa (Texas)	0	1	.000	11.57	1	1	0	0	0	4 2/3	10	7	6	2	5
2001— Texas (A.L.)	11	11	.500	6.02	28	28	1	0	0	154	189	109	103	65	104
— Oklahoma (PCL)	0	0	...	0.00	1	1	0	0	0	3	3	0	0	0	3
— Tulsa (Texas)	0	1	.000	5.40	1	1	0	0	0	5	4	3	3	2	5
A.L. totals (8 years)	54	47	.535	5.28	192	137	7	2	2	842 2/3	972	546	494	376	520
N.L. totals (2 years)	13	13	.500	4.26	40	40	2	1	0	253 1/3	261	127	120	97	148
Major League totals (9 years)	67	60	.528	5.04	232	177	9	3	2	1096	1233	673	614	473	668

DIVISION SERIES RECORD

Year League	W	L	Pct.	ERA	G	GS	CG	ShO	Sv.	IP	H	R	ER	BB	SO
1996— Texas (A.L.)	0	1	.000	3.38	1	1	0	0	0	8	6	3	3	2	3

OLIVER, JOE   C

PERSONAL: Born July 24, 1965, in Memphis. ... 6-3/220. ... Bats right, throws right. ... Full name: Joseph Melton Oliver.
HIGH SCHOOL: Boone (Orlando).
TRANSACTIONS/CAREER NOTES: Selected by Cincinnati Reds organization in second round of free-agent draft (June 6, 1983); pick received as compensation for New York Yankees signing Type A free-agent P Bob Shirley. ... On disabled list (April 23-May 6, 1986; and April 12, 1994-remainder of season). ... Released by Reds (November 3, 1994). ... Signed by Milwaukee Brewers organization (March 24, 1995). ... On Milwaukee disabled list (July 14-August 15, 1995); included rehabilitation assignment to New Orleans (August 10-15). ... Granted free agency (October 31, 1995). ... Signed by Reds (February 26, 1996). ... Granted free agency (November 18, 1996). ... Re-signed by Reds organization (February 7, 1997). ... Granted free agency (October 30, 1997). ... Signed by Detroit Tigers organization (December 22, 1997). ... Released by Tigers (July 16, 1998). ... Signed by Seattle Mariners (July 24, 1998). ... Granted free agency (October 27, 1998). ... Signed by Tampa Bay Devil Rays organization (February 3, 1999). ... On Durham disabled list (June 13-24, 1999). ... Traded by Devil Rays with C Humberto Cota to Pittsburgh Pirates for Of Jose Guillen and P Jeff Sparks (July 23, 1999). ... Granted free agency (November 5, 1999). ... Signed by Mariners organization (January 19, 2000). ... Granted free agency (November 4, 2000). ... Signed by New York Yankees (November 21, 2000). ... Released by Yankees (June 20, 2001). ... Signed by Boston Red Sox organization (July 2, 2001). ... On Pawtucket disabled list (July 17-August 22, 2001). ... Granted free agency (November 5, 2001).
STATISTICAL NOTES: Led Pioneer League catchers with .989 fielding percentage, 425 putouts, 38 assists and 468 total chances in 1983. ... Led Midwest League catchers with 855 total chances and 30 passed balls in 1984. ... Led Florida State League catchers with 84 assists and 33 passed balls in 1985. ... Led American Association catchers with 13 errors in 1989. ... Tied for N.L. lead with 16 passed balls in 1990. ... Led N.L. catchers with 925 putouts and 997 total chances in 1992. ... Career major league grand slams: 5.

Year Team (League)	Pos.	G	AB	R	H	2B	3B	HR	RBI	Avg.	BB	SO	SB	PO	A	E	Avg.
1983— Billings (Pio.)	C-1B	56	186	21	40	4	0	4	28	.215	15	47	1	†426	†39	5	†.989
1984— Cedar Rapids (Midw.)	C	102	335	34	73	11	0	3	29	.218	17	83	2	*757	85	13	.985
1985— Tampa (FSL)	C-1B	112	386	38	104	23	2	7	62	.269	32	75	1	615	†94	16	.978
1986— Vermont (East.)	C	84	282	32	78	18	1	6	41	.277	21	47	2	383	62	14	.969
1987— Vermont (East.)	C-1B	66	236	31	72	13	2	10	60	.305	17	30	0	247	35	10	.966
1988— Nashville (A.A.)	C	73	220	19	45	7	2	4	24	.205	18	39	0	413	37	7	.985
— Chattanooga (Sou.)	C	28	105	9	26	6	0	3	12	.248	5	19	0	176	15	0	1.000
1989— Nashville (A.A.)	C-1B	71	233	22	68	13	0	6	31	.292	13	35	0	388	37	†13	.970
— Cincinnati (N.L.)	C	49	151	13	41	8	0	3	23	.272	6	28	0	260	21	4	.986
1990— Cincinnati (N.L.)	C	121	364	34	84	23	0	8	52	.231	37	75	1	686	59	6	*.992
1991— Cincinnati (N.L.)	C	94	269	21	58	11	0	11	41	.216	18	53	0	496	40	11	.980
1992— Cincinnati (N.L.)	C-1B	143	485	42	131	25	1	10	57	.270	35	75	2	†926	64	8	.992
1993— Cincinnati (N.L.)	C-1B-OF	139	482	40	115	28	0	14	75	.239	27	91	0	825	70	7	.992
1994— Cincinnati (N.L.)	C	6	19	1	4	0	0	1	5	.211	2	3	0	48	2	1	.980
1995— Milwaukee (A.L.)■	C-DH-1B	97	337	43	92	20	0	12	51	.273	27	66	2	414	40	8	.983
— New Orleans (A.A.)	C-DH	4	13	0	1	1	0	0	0	.077	0	3	0	14	7	0	1.000
1996— Cincinnati (N.L.)■	C-1B-OF	106	289	31	70	12	1	11	46	.242	28	54	2	583	45	5	.992
1997— Indianapolis (A.A.)	C	2	9	1	3	0	0	1	1	.333	0	1	0	21	4	0	1.000
— Cincinnati (N.L.)	C-1B	111	349	28	90	13	0	14	43	.258	25	58	1	681	55	7	.991
1998— Detroit (A.L.)■	C-1B-DH	50	155	8	35	8	0	4	22	.226	7	33	0	261	17	5	.982
— Seattle (A.L.)■	C	29	85	12	19	3	0	2	10	.224	10	15	1	174	9	3	.984
1999— Durham (I.L.)■	C-DH-3B	57	219	27	66	18	1	7	43	.301	7	50	1	399	27	7	.984
— Pittsburgh (N.L.)■	C	45	134	10	27	8	0	1	13	.201	10	33	2	285	12	2	.993
2000— Seattle (A.L.)■	C-DH-1B	69	200	33	53	13	1	10	35	.265	14	38	2	359	18	2	.995
— Tacoma (PCL)	C	18	61	2	12	2	0	0	8	.197	5	12	0	118	12	1	.992
2001— New York (A.L.)■	C	12	36	3	9	1	0	1	2	.250	1	12	0	101	4	1	.991
— Pawtucket (I.L.)■	C-1B	13	41	3	10	1	0	2	6	.244	0	9	1	66	5	1	.986
— GC Red Sox (GCL)	C	2	5	2	5	0	0	1	1	1.000	0	0	0	6	1	0	1.000
— Boston (A.L.)	C	5	12	1	3	1	0	0	1	.250	1	3	0	33	1	1	.971
American League totals (4 years)		262	825	100	211	46	1	29	121	.256	60	167	5	1342	89	20	.986
National League totals (9 years)		814	2542	220	620	128	2	73	355	.244	188	470	8	4790	368	51	.990
Major League totals (13 years)		1076	3367	320	831	174	3	102	476	.247	248	637	13	6132	457	71	.989

DIVISION SERIES RECORD

Year Team (League)	Pos.	G	AB	R	H	2B	3B	HR	RBI	Avg.	BB	SO	SB	PO	A	E	Avg.
						BATTING									FIELDING		
2000— Seattle (A.L.)	C	3	4	4	4	0	0	1	1	1.000	0	1	0	12	0	0	1.000

CHAMPIONSHIP SERIES RECORD

Year Team (League)	Pos.	G	AB	R	H	2B	3B	HR	RBI	Avg.	BB	SO	SB	PO	A	E	Avg.
						BATTING									FIELDING		
1990— Cincinnati (N.L.)	C	5	14	1	2	0	0	0	0	.143	0	2	0	27	1	0	1.000
2000— Seattle (A.L.)	C	4	6	0	1	0	0	0	0	.167	1	1	0	22	1	0	1.000
Championship series totals (2 years)		9	20	1	3	0	0	0	0	.150	1	3	0	49	2	0	1.000

WORLD SERIES RECORD

NOTES: Member of World Series championship team (1990).

Year Team (League)	Pos.	G	AB	R	H	2B	3B	HR	RBI	Avg.	BB	SO	SB	PO	A	E	Avg.
						BATTING									FIELDING		
1990— Cincinnati (N.L.)	C	4	18	2	6	3	0	0	2	.333	0	1	0	27	1	3	.903

OLIVO, MIGUEL — C — WHITE SOX

PERSONAL: Born July 15, 1978, in Villa Vasquez, Dominican Republic. ... 6-0/180. ... Bats right, throws right. ... Full name: Miguel Eduardo Olivo.

TRANSACTIONS/CAREER NOTES: Signed as non-drafted free agent by Oakland Athletics organization (September 30, 1996). ... On Midland inactive list (July 8-10, 2000). ... On Modesto suspended list (July 13-23, 2000). ... On Modesto disabled list (August 8, 2000-remainder of season). ... Traded by A's to Chicago White Sox (December 12, 2000), completing deal in which White Sox traded P Chad Bradford to A's for player to be named later (December 7, 2000). ... On disabled list (April 22-May 2, 2001).

STATISTICAL NOTES: Led Arizona League catchers with 44 assists and 22 passed balls in 1998. ... Led Southern League catchers with 19 passed balls in 2001.

Year Team (League)	Pos.	G	AB	R	H	2B	3B	HR	RBI	Avg.	BB	SO	SB	PO	A	E	Avg.
						BATTING									FIELDING		
1997— Dom. Athletics (DSL) .		63	221	37	60	11	4	6	57	.271	34	36	6				
1998— Ariz. Athletics (Ariz.) ..	C-OF	46	164	30	51	11	3	2	23	.311	8	43	2	294	†44	8	.977
1999— Modesto (Calif.)	C	73	243	46	74	13	6	9	42	.305	21	60	4	509	50	15	.974
2000— Midland (Texas).........	C	19	59	8	14	2	0	1	9	.237	5	15	0	95	5	2	.980
— Modesto (Calif.)	C	58	227	40	64	11	5	5	35	.282	16	53	5	375	64	*19	.959
2001— Birmingham (Sou.)■ .	C	93	316	45	82	23	1	14	55	.259	37	62	6	633	*78	9	.988

OLSEN, KEVIN — P — MARLINS

PERSONAL: Born July 26, 1976, in Covina, Calif. ... 6-2/200. ... Throws right, bats right. ... Full name: Kevin Gary Olsen.
HIGH SCHOOL: Norco (Calif.).
JUNIOR COLLEGE: Riverside (Calif.).
COLLEGE: Oklahoma.
TRANSACTIONS/CAREER NOTES: Selected by Florida Marlins organization in 26th round of free-agent draft (June 2, 1998).

Year League	W	L	Pct.	ERA	G	GS	CG	ShO	Sv.	IP	H	R	ER	BB	SO
1998— Utica (NY-Penn)	4	3	.571	2.60	21	4	0	0	2	45	37	21	13	10	56
1999— Brevard County (FSL)........	2	5	.286	5.05	11	11	0	0	0	57	70	37	32	13	45
— Kane County (Midw.)........	5	2	.714	3.38	10	9	0	0	0	61 1/3	65	25	23	16	52
2000— Brevard County (FSL)........	4	8	.333	2.86	18	18	1	0	0	110	93	40	35	25	77
— Portland (East.)	3	4	.429	4.83	9	9	0	0	0	54	54	30	29	21	47
2001— Portland (East.)	10	3	.769	2.68	26	26	2	1	0	154 2/3	123	56	46	21	144
— Florida (N.L.).....................	0	0	...	1.20	4	2	0	0	0	15	11	2	2	2	13
Major League totals (1 year)........	0	0	...	1.20	4	2	0	0	0	15	11	2	2	2	13

OLSON, GREGG — P — DODGERS

PERSONAL: Born October 11, 1966, in Scribner, Neb. ... 6-4/208. ... Throws right, bats right. ... Full name: Gregg William Olson.
HIGH SCHOOL: Northwest (Omaha, Neb.).
COLLEGE: Auburn.
TRANSACTIONS/CAREER NOTES: Selected by Baltimore Orioles organization in first round (fourth pick overall) of free-agent draft (June 1, 1988). ... On disabled list (August 9-September 20, 1993). ... Granted free agency (December 20, 1993). ... Signed by Atlanta Braves (February 8, 1994). ... On Atlanta disabled list (March 26-May 30, 1994); included rehabilitation assignment to Richmond (May 14-30). ... Granted free agency (December 23, 1994). ... Signed by Cleveland Indians organization (March 24, 1995). ... On Buffalo disabled list (April 6-14, 1995). ... Contract sold by Buffalo to Kansas City Royals (July 24, 1995). ... Granted free agency (November 1, 1995). ... Signed by St. Louis Cardinals organization (January 23, 1996). ... Released by Cardinals (March 26, 1996). ... Signed by Cincinnati Reds organization (March 26, 1996). ... Traded by Reds to Detroit Tigers for IF Yuri Sanchez (April 26, 1996). ... Traded by Tigers to Houston Astros for two players to be named later (August 26, 1996); Tigers acquired P Kevin Gallaher and IF Pedro Santana to complete deal (August 27, 1996). ... Granted free agency (October 28, 1996). ... Signed by Minnesota Twins organization (December 20, 1996). ... Released by Twins (May 16, 1997). ... Signed by Royals organization (May 25, 1997). ... Granted free agency (October 28, 1997). ... Signed by Arizona Diamondbacks organization (January 31, 1998). ... On disabled list (June 23-July 8, 1999). ... Granted free agency (October 29, 1999). ... Signed by Los Angeles Dodgers (January 10, 2000). ... On Los Angeles disabled list (April 9-July 28, 2000); included rehabilitation assignments to San Bernardino (May 5-6 and June 30-July 13) and Albuquerque (July 13-27). ... Released by Dodgers (June 29, 2001).
HONORS: Named righthanded pitcher on THE SPORTING NEWS college All-America team (1988). ... Named A.L. Rookie of the Year by Baseball Writers' Association of America (1989).
STATISTICAL NOTES: Pitched one inning, combining with starter Bob Milacki (six innings), Mike Flanagan (one inning) and Mark Williamson (one inning) in 2-0 no-hit victory against Oakland (July 13, 1991).
MISCELLANEOUS: Holds Baltimore Orioles all-time record for most saves (160). ... Holds Arizona Diamondbacks all-time records for most saves (44). ... Struck out in only plate appearance (1993).

Year League	W	L	Pct.	ERA	G	GS	CG	ShO	Sv.	IP	H	R	ER	BB	SO
1988— Hagerstown (Caro.)	1	0	1.000	2.00	8	0	0	0	4	9	5	2	2	2	9
— Charlotte (Sou.)	0	1	.000	5.87	8	0	0	0	1	15 1/3	24	13	10	6	22
— Baltimore (A.L.)	1	1	.500	3.27	10	0	0	0	0	11	10	4	4	10	9
1989— Baltimore (A.L.)	5	2	.714	1.69	64	0	0	0	27	85	57	17	16	46	90
1990— Baltimore (A.L.)	6	5	.545	2.42	64	0	0	0	37	74 1/3	57	20	20	31	74
1991— Baltimore (A.L.)	4	6	.400	3.18	72	0	0	0	31	73 2/3	74	28	26	29	72
1992— Baltimore (A.L.)	1	5	.167	2.05	60	0	0	0	36	61 1/3	46	14	14	24	58
1993— Baltimore (A.L.)	0	2	.000	1.60	50	0	0	0	29	45	37	9	8	18	44
1994— Richmond (I.L.)■	0	0	...	1.59	8	2	0	0	2	11 1/3	8	3	2	8	13
— Atlanta (N.L.)	0	2	.000	9.20	16	0	0	0	1	14 2/3	19	15	15	13	10
1995— Buffalo (A.A.)■	1	0	1.000	2.49	18	0	0	0	13	21 2/3	16	6	6	9	25
— Cleveland (A.L.)	0	0	...	13.50	3	0	0	0	0	2 2/3	5	4	4	2	0
— Omaha (A.A.)■	0	0	...	0.00	1	0	0	0	0	1	0	0	0	1	1
— Kansas City (A.L.)	3	3	.500	3.26	20	0	0	0	3	30 1/3	23	11	11	17	21
1996— Indianapolis (A.A.)■	0	0	...	4.26	7	0	0	0	4	6 1/3	6	4	3	6	4
— Detroit (A.L.)■	3	0	1.000	5.02	43	0	0	0	8	43	43	25	24	28	29
— Houston (N.L.)■	1	0	1.000	4.82	9	0	0	0	0	9 1/3	12	5	5	7	8
1997— Minnesota (A.L.)■	0	0	...	18.36	11	0	0	0	0	8 1/3	19	17	17	11	6
— Omaha (A.A.)■	3	1	.750	3.31	9	5	0	0	0	35 1/3	30	13	13	10	20
— Kansas City (A.L.)	4	3	.571	3.02	34	0	0	0	1	41 2/3	39	18	14	17	28
1998— Arizona (N.L.)■	3	4	.429	3.01	64	0	0	0	30	68 2/3	56	25	23	25	55
1999— Arizona (N.L.)	9	4	.692	3.71	61	0	0	0	14	60 2/3	54	28	25	25	45
2000— Los Angeles (N.L.)■	0	1	.000	5.09	13	0	0	0	0	17 2/3	21	11	10	7	15
— San Bernardino (Calif.)	0	0	...	4.05	6	4	0	0	0	6 2/3	8	4	3	4	8
— Albuquerque (PCL)	0	0	...	4.50	4	0	0	0	0	4	3	2	2	2	2
2001— Los Angeles (N.L.)	0	1	.000	8.03	28	0	0	0	0	24 2/3	26	24	22	20	24
A.L. totals (9 years)	27	27	.500	2.99	431	0	0	0	172	476 1/3	410	167	158	233	431
N.L. totals (6 years)	13	12	.520	4.60	191	0	0	0	45	195 2/3	188	108	100	97	157
Major League totals (14 years)	40	39	.506	3.46	622	0	0	0	217	672	598	275	258	330	588

DIVISION SERIES RECORD

Year League	W	L	Pct.	ERA	G	GS	CG	ShO	Sv.	IP	H	R	ER	BB	SO
1999— Arizona (N.L.)	0	0	...	0.00	2	0	0	0	0	1/3	0	1	0	1	0

ALL-STAR GAME RECORD

Year League	W	L	Pct.	ERA	GS	CG	ShO	Sv.	IP	H	R	ER	BB	SO
1990— American						Did not play.								

O'NEILL, PAUL   OF

PERSONAL: Born February 25, 1963, in Columbus, Ohio. ... 6-4/215. ... Bats left, throws left. ... Full name: Paul Andrew O'Neill. ... Son of Charles O'Neill, minor league pitcher (1945-48).
HIGH SCHOOL: Brookhaven (Columbus, Ohio).
COLLEGE: Otterbein College (Ohio).
TRANSACTIONS/CAREER NOTES: Selected by Cincinnati Reds organization in fourth round of free-agent draft (June 8, 1981). ... On Denver disabled list (May 10-July 16, 1986). ... On Cincinnati disabled list (July 21-September 1, 1989); included rehabilitation assignment to Nashville (August 27-September 1). ... Traded by Reds with 1B Joe DeBerry to New York Yankees for OF Roberto Kelly (November 3, 1992). ... On disabled list (May 7-23, 1995). ... On suspended list (September 6-8, 1996). ... Granted free agency (November 10, 2000). ... Re-signed by Yankees (November 16, 2000). ... Granted free agency (November 19, 2001).
STATISTICAL NOTES: Led American Association outfielders with 19 assists and eight double plays in 1985. ... Hit three home runs in one game (August 31, 1995). ... Had 17-game hitting streak (May 24-June 10, 1998). ... Tied for A.L. lead in grounding into double plays with 22 in 1998. ... Led A.L. outfielders with six double plays in 1998. ... Career major league grand slams: 4.

								BATTING						FIELDING		
Year Team (League)	Pos.	G	AB	R	H	2B	3B	HR	RBI	Avg.	BB	SO	SB	PO	A	E	Avg.
1981— Billings (Pio.)	OF	66	241	37	76	7	2	3	29	.315	21	35	6	87	4	5	.948
1982— Cedar Rapids (Midw.)	OF	116	386	50	105	19	2	8	71	.272	21	79	12	137	7	8	.947
1983— Tampa (FSL)	OF-1B	121	413	62	115	23	7	8	51	.278	56	70	20	218	14	10	.959
— Waterbury (East.)	OF	14	43	6	12	0	0	0	6	.279	6	8	2	26	0	0	1.000
1984— Vermont (East.)	OF	134	475	70	126	31	5	16	76	.265	52	72	29	246	5	7	.973
1985— Denver (A.A.)	OF-1B	*137	*509	63	*155	*32	3	7	74	.305	28	73	5	248	†20	7	.975
— Cincinnati (N.L.)	OF	5	12	1	4	1	0	0	1	.333	0	2	0	3	1	0	1.000
1986— Cincinnati (N.L.)	PH	3	2	0	0	0	0	0	0	.000	1	1	0	...	...	...	...
— Denver (A.A.)	OF	55	193	20	49	9	2	5	27	.254	9	28	1	98	7	4	.963
1987— Cincinnati (N.L.)	OF-1B-P	84	160	24	41	14	1	7	28	.256	18	29	2	90	2	4	.958
— Nashville (A.A.)	OF	11	37	12	11	0	0	3	6	.297	5	5	1	19	1	0	1.000
1988— Cincinnati (N.L.)	OF-1B	145	485	58	122	25	3	16	73	.252	38	65	8	410	13	6	.986
1989— Cincinnati (N.L.)	OF	117	428	49	118	24	2	15	74	.276	46	64	20	223	7	4	.983
— Nashville (A.A.)	OF	4	12	1	4	0	0	0	3	.333	3	1	1	7	1	0	1.000
1990— Cincinnati (N.L.)	OF	145	503	59	136	28	0	16	78	.270	53	103	13	271	12	2	.993
1991— Cincinnati (N.L.)	OF	152	532	71	136	36	0	28	91	.256	73	107	12	301	13	2	.994
1992— Cincinnati (N.L.)	OF	148	496	59	122	19	1	14	66	.246	77	85	6	291	12	1	*.997
1993— New York (A.L.)■	OF-DH	141	498	71	155	34	1	20	75	.311	44	69	2	230	7	2	.992
1994— New York (A.L.)	OF-DH	103	368	68	132	25	1	21	83	*.359	72	56	5	203	7	1	.995
1995— New York (A.L.)	OF-DH	127	460	82	138	30	4	22	96	.300	71	76	1	220	3	3	.987
1996— New York (A.L.)	OF-DH-1B	150	546	89	165	35	1	19	91	.302	102	76	0	293	7	0	•1.000
1997— New York (A.L.)	OF-DH-1B	149	553	89	179	42	0	21	117	.324	75	92	10	293	7	5	.984
1998— New York (A.L.)	OF-DH	152	602	95	191	40	2	24	116	.317	57	103	15	293	11	4	.987
1999— New York (A.L.)	OF	153	597	70	170	39	4	19	110	.285	66	89	11	291	10	8	.974
2000— New York (A.L.)	OF-DH	142	566	79	160	26	0	18	100	.283	51	90	14	293	5	2	.993
2001— New York (A.L.)	OF-DH	137	510	77	136	33	1	21	70	.267	48	59	22	210	1	4	.981
American League totals (9 years)		1254	4700	720	1426	304	14	185	858	.303	586	710	80	2326	58	29	.988
National League totals (8 years)		799	2618	321	679	147	7	96	411	.259	306	456	61	1589	60	19	.989
Major League totals (17 years)		2053	7318	1041	2105	451	21	281	1269	.288	892	1166	141	3915	118	48	.988

DIVISION SERIES RECORD

Year	Team (League)	Pos.	G	AB	R	H	2B	3B	HR	RBI	Avg.	BB	SO	SB	PO	A	E	Avg.
1995— New York (A.L.)	OF-PH	5	18	5	6	0	0	3	6	.333	5	5	0	13	0	0	1.000
1996— New York (A.L.)	OF	4	15	0	2	0	0	0	0	.133	0	2	0	13	0	0	1.000
1997— New York (A.L.)	OF	5	19	5	8	2	0	2	7	.421	3	0	0	9	0	0	1.000
1998— New York (A.L.)	OF	3	11	1	4	2	0	1	1	.364	1	1	0	2	0	0	1.000
1999— New York (A.L.)	OF	2	8	2	2	0	0	0	0	.250	1	1	0	4	0	0	1.000
2000— New York (A.L.)	OF	5	19	4	4	1	0	0	0	.211	2	4	0	8	1	0	1.000
2001— New York (A.L.)	DH-OF	3	11	1	1	1	0	0	0	.091	0	0	0	1	0	0	1.000
Division series totals (7 years)		27	101	18	27	6	0	6	14	.267	12	13	0	50	1	0	1.000

CHAMPIONSHIP SERIES RECORD

Year	Team (League)	Pos.	G	AB	R	H	2B	3B	HR	RBI	Avg.	BB	SO	SB	PO	A	E	Avg.
1990— Cincinnati (N.L.)	OF	5	17	1	8	3	0	1	4	.471	1	1	1	9	2	0	1.000
1996— New York (A.L.)	OF	4	11	1	3	0	0	1	2	.273	3	2	0	9	1	0	1.000
1998— New York (A.L.)	OF	6	25	6	7	2	0	1	3	.280	3	4	2	10	0	0	1.000
1999— New York (A.L.)	OF	5	21	2	6	0	0	0	1	.286	1	5	0	18	0	0	1.000
2000— New York (A.L.)	OF	6	20	0	5	0	0	0	5	.250	1	2	0	8	0	0	1.000
2001— New York (A.L.)	OF	5	12	2	5	0	0	2	3	.417	1	0	0	7	0	0	1.000
Championship series totals (6 years)		31	106	12	34	5	0	5	18	.321	10	14	3	61	3	0	1.000

WORLD SERIES RECORD

NOTES: Member of World Series championship team (1990, 1996, 1998, 1999 and 2000).

Year	Team (League)	Pos.	G	AB	R	H	2B	3B	HR	RBI	Avg.	BB	SO	SB	PO	A	E	Avg.
1990— Cincinnati (N.L.)	OF	4	12	2	1	0	0	0	1	.083	5	2	1	11	0	0	1.000
1996— New York (A.L.)	OF-PH	5	12	1	2	2	0	0	0	.167	3	2	0	12	0	0	1.000
1998— New York (A.L.)	OF	4	19	3	4	1	0	0	4	.211	1	2	0	8	0	1	.889
1999— New York (A.L.)	OF	4	15	0	3	0	0	0	4	.200	2	2	0	8	0	0	1.000
2000— New York (A.L.)	OF	5	19	2	9	2	2	0	2	.474	3	4	0	10	0	0	1.000
2001— New York (A.L.)	PH-OF	5	15	1	5	1	0	0	0	.333	2	2	1	4	0	0	1.000
World Series totals (6 years)		27	92	9	24	6	2	0	7	.261	16	14	2	53	0	1	.981

ALL-STAR GAME RECORD

Year	League	Pos.	AB	R	H	2B	3B	HR	RBI	Avg.	BB	SO	SB	PO	A	E	Avg.
1991— National	OF	2	0	0	0	0	0	0	.000	0	1	0	0	0	0	...
1994— American	PH	1	0	0	0	0	0	0	.000	0	0	0	...	...	...	...
1995— American	OF	1	0	0	0	0	0	0	.000	0	0	0	0	0	0	...
1997— American	OF	2	0	0	0	0	0	0	.000	0	1	0	1	0	0	1.000
1998— American	OF	2	0	0	0	0	0	0	.000	0	0	0	0	1	0	1.000
All-Star Game totals (5 years)		8	0	0	0	0	0	0	.000	0	2	0	1	1	0	1.000

RECORD AS PITCHER

Year	League	W	L	Pct.	ERA	G	GS	CG	ShO	Sv.	IP	H	R	ER	BB	SO
1987— Cincinnati (N.L.)	0	0	...	13.50	1	0	0	0	0	2	2	3	3	4	2

ORDAZ, LUIS   SS

PERSONAL: Born August 12, 1975, in Maracaibo, Venezuela. ... 5-11/170. ... Bats right, throws right. ... Full name: Luis Javier Ordaz.
HIGH SCHOOL: Santa Maria Gorette (Maracaibo, Venezuela).
TRANSACTIONS/CAREER NOTES: Signed as non-drafted free agent by Cincinnati Reds organization (January 27, 1993). ... Traded by Reds to St. Louis Cardinals as part of three-team deal in which Reds sent P Mike Remlinger to Kansas City Royals, Cardinals sent OF Andre King to Reds and Royals sent OF Miguel Mejia to Cardinals (December 4, 1995). ... On Memphis disabled list (April 7-16, 1998). ... Traded by Cardinals to Arizona Diamondbacks for OF Dante Powell (December 15, 1999). ... Claimed on waivers by Kansas City Royals (April 5, 2000). ... On Kansas City disabled list (May 18-July 1, 2001); included rehabilitation assignment to Omaha (June 20-July 1). ... Granted free agency (October 15, 2001).
STATISTICAL NOTES: Led Appalachian League shortstops with 277 total chances and 24 errors and tied for lead with 173 assists in 1994. ... Led Texas League in grounding into double plays with 19 in 1997.

Year	Team (League)	Pos.	G	AB	R	H	2B	3B	HR	RBI	Avg.	BB	SO	SB	PO	A	E	Avg.
1993— Princeton (Appl.)	3B-SS-2B	57	217	28	65	9	7	2	39	.300	7	32	3	58	117	13	.931
1994— Charl., W.Va. (S.Atl.)	SS	9	31	3	7	0	0	0	0	.226	1	4	1	16	18	7	.829
— Princeton (Appl.)	SS-2B	60	211	33	52	12	3	0	12	.246	10	27	7	81	‡173	†24	.914
1995— Charl., W.Va. (S.Atl.)	SS	112	359	43	83	14	7	2	42	.231	13	47	12	164	290	22	.954
1996— St. Pete. (FSL)■	SS	126	423	46	115	13	3	3	49	.272	30	53	10	228	317	21	.963
1997— Arkansas (Texas)	SS-DH	115	390	44	112	20	6	4	58	.287	22	39	11	149	327	33	.935
— St. Louis (N.L.)	SS	12	22	3	6	1	0	0	1	.273	1	2	3	9	17	1	.963
1998— Memphis (PCL)	SS-2B	59	214	29	62	9	2	6	35	.290	16	20	3	104	174	14	.952
— St. Louis (N.L.)	SS-3B-2B	57	153	9	31	5	0	0	8	.203	12	18	2	70	157	13	.946
1999— St. Louis (N.L.)	SS-2B-3B	10	9	3	1	0	0	0	2	.111	1	2	1	4	8	3	.800
— Memphis (PCL)	SS	107	362	31	103	25	4	1	45	.285	24	40	3	150	346	23	.956
2000— Kansas City (A.L.)■	SS-2B	65	104	17	23	2	0	0	11	.221	5	10	4	64	65	1	.992
2001— Kansas City (A.L.)	2B-SS-3B-DH	28	56	8	14	3	0	0	4	.250	3	8	0	27	66	3	.969
— Omaha (PCL)	SS-2B-3B	14	52	5	16	1	0	1	4	.308	2	10	3	13	23	2	.947
American League totals (2 years)		93	160	25	37	5	0	0	15	.231	8	18	4	91	131	4	.982
National League totals (3 years)		79	184	15	38	6	0	0	11	.207	14	22	6	83	182	17	.940
Major League totals (5 years)		172	344	40	75	11	0	0	26	.218	22	40	10	174	313	21	.959

ORDONEZ, MAGGLIO — OF — WHITE SOX

PERSONAL: Born January 28, 1974, in Caracas, Venezuela. ... 6-0/200. ... Bats right, throws right.
TRANSACTIONS/CAREER NOTES: Signed as non-drafted free agent by Chicago White Sox organization (May 18, 1991). ... On suspended list (May 1-6, 2000).
RECORDS: Shares major league single-season record for fewest double plays by outfielder (150 or more games)—0 (2001).
HONORS: Named American Association Most Valuable Player (1997). ... Named outfielder on THE SPORTING NEWS A.L. All-Star team (2000). ... Named outfielder on THE SPORTING NEWS A.L. Silver Slugger team (2000).
STATISTICAL NOTES: Led American Association with nine sacrifice flies and tied for league lead with 249 total bases in 1997. ... Led A.L. with 15 sacrifice flies in 2000. ... Career major league grand slams: 4.

Year Team (League)	Pos.	G	AB	R	H	2B	3B	HR	RBI	Avg.	BB	SO	SB	PO	A	E	Avg.
1991— Dominican (DSL)		25	94	17	28	3	1	0	8	.298	6	12	4	...	...	...	...
1992— GC White Sox (GCL)	OF	38	111	17	20	10	2	1	14	.180	13	26	6	26	2	0	1.000
1993— Hickory (S.Atl.)	OF	84	273	32	59	14	4	3	20	.216	26	66	5	131	10	6	.959
1994— Hickory (S.Atl.)	OF	132	490	86	144	24	5	11	69	.294	45	57	16	275	16	6	.980
1995— Prince William (Caro.)	OF	131	487	61	116	24	2	12	65	.238	41	71	11	256	5	6	.978
1996— Birmingham (Sou.)	OF	130	479	66	126	41	0	18	67	.263	39	74	9	231	12	6	.976
1997— Nashville (A.A.)	OF-DH	135	523	65	*172	29	3	14	90	*.329	32	61	14	278	8	5	.983
— Chicago (A.L.)	OF	21	69	12	22	6	0	4	11	.319	2	8	1	43	1	0	1.000
1998— Chicago (A.L.)	OF	145	535	70	151	25	2	14	65	.282	28	53	9	323	10	5	.985
1999— Chicago (A.L.)	OF-DH	157	624	100	188	34	3	30	117	.301	47	64	13	331	12	3	.991
2000— Chicago (A.L.)	OF	153	588	102	185	34	3	32	126	.315	60	64	18	280	12	5	.983
2001— Chicago (A.L.)	OF-DH	160	593	97	181	40	1	31	113	.305	70	70	25	286	11	5	.983
Major League totals (5 years)		636	2409	381	727	139	9	111	432	.302	207	259	66	1263	46	18	.986

DIVISION SERIES RECORD

Year Team (League)	Pos.	G	AB	R	H	2B	3B	HR	RBI	Avg.	BB	SO	SB	PO	A	E	Avg.
2000— Chicago (A.L.)	OF	3	11	0	2	0	1	0	1	.182	2	2	1	8	1	0	1.000

ALL-STAR GAME RECORD

Year League	Pos.	AB	R	H	2B	3B	HR	RBI	Avg.	BB	SO	SB	PO	A	E	Avg.
1999— American	OF	1	0	0	0	0	0	0	.000	0	0	0	0	0	0	
2000— American	OF	1	0	1	1	0	0	1	1.000	0	0	0	1	0	0	1.000
2001— American	OF	3	1	2	0	0	1	1	.667	0	0	0	4	0	0	1.000
All-Star Game totals (3 years)		5	1	3	1	0	1	2	.600	0	0	0	5	0	0	1.000

ORDONEZ, REY — SS — METS

PERSONAL: Born November 11, 1972, in Havana, Cuba. ... 5-9/159. ... Bats right, throws right. ... Full name: Reynaldo Ordonez.
HIGH SCHOOL: Espa (Havana, Cuba).
COLLEGE: Fajardo College (Havana, Cuba).
TRANSACTIONS/CAREER NOTES: Played with St. Paul Saints of Northern League (1993). ... Rights acquired by New York Mets organization in lottery of Cuban defectors (October 29, 1993). ... Signed by Mets organization (February 8, 1994). ... On disabled list (June 2-July 11, 1997; and May 30, 2000-remainder of season).
RECORDS: Holds major league career record for most consecutive errorless games by shortstop—100 (June 14-October 4, 1999). ... Holds N.L. career record for most consecutive chances accepted without an error by shortstop—412 (June 13-October 4, 1999). ... Holds N.L. single-season records for highest fielding average by shortstop (150 or more games)—.994 (1999); fewest errors by shortstop (150 or more games—4 (1999); most consecutive errorless games by shortstop—100 (June 14-October 4, 1999); and most consecutive chances accepted without an error by shortstop—412 (June 13-October 4, 1999).
HONORS: Won N.L. Gold Glove at shortstop (1997-99).
STATISTICAL NOTES: Led International League shortstops in total chances with 645 in 1995. ... Led N.L. shortstops with 705 total chances and 102 double plays in 1996. ... Career major league grand slams: 1.

Year Team (League)	Pos.	G	AB	R	H	2B	3B	HR	RBI	Avg.	BB	SO	SB	PO	A	E	Avg.
1993— St. Paul (Nor.)	SS-2B	15	60	10	17	4	0	0	7	.283	3	9	3	18	48	2	.971
1994— St. Lucie (FSL)■	SS	79	314	47	97	21	2	2	40	.309	14	28	11	141	291	15	.966
— Binghamton (East.)	SS	48	191	22	50	10	2	1	20	.262	4	18	4	57	139	8	.961
1995— Norfolk (I.L.)	SS	125	439	49	94	21	4	2	50	.214	27	50	11	188	*436	21	.967
1996— New York (N.L.)	SS	151	502	51	129	12	4	1	30	.257	22	53	1	228	450	27	.962
1997— New York (N.L.)	SS	120	356	35	77	5	3	1	33	.216	18	36	11	171	355	9	*.983
1998— New York (N.L.)	SS	153	505	46	124	20	2	1	42	.246	23	60	3	265	401	17	.975
1999— New York (N.L.)	SS	154	520	49	134	24	2	1	60	.258	49	59	8	220	416	4	*.994
2000— New York (N.L.)	SS	45	133	10	25	5	0	0	9	.188	17	16	0	58	108	6	.965
2001— New York (N.L.)	SS	149	461	31	114	24	4	3	44	.247	34	43	3	213	383	12	.980
Major League totals (6 years)		772	2477	222	603	90	15	7	218	.243	163	267	26	1155	2113	75	.978

DIVISION SERIES RECORD

Year Team (League)	Pos.	G	AB	R	H	2B	3B	HR	RBI	Avg.	BB	SO	SB	PO	A	E	Avg.
1999— New York (N.L.)	SS	4	14	1	4	1	0	0	2	.286	0	5	1	7	9	0	1.000

CHAMPIONSHIP SERIES RECORD

Year Team (League)	Pos.	G	AB	R	H	2B	3B	HR	RBI	Avg.	BB	SO	SB	PO	A	E	Avg.
1999— New York (N.L.)	SS	6	24	0	1	0	0	0	0	.042	0	2	0	7	24	0	1.000

0

PERSONAL: Born November 23, 1971, in Colon, Cuba. ... 6-3/215. ... Throws left, bats left. ... Full name: Edilberto Oropesa.

COLLEGE: Mantazas (Cuba).

TRANSACTIONS/CAREER NOTES: Signed by St. Paul of Northern League (August, 1993). ... Selected by Los Angeles Dodgers organization in 14th round of free-agent draft (June 2, 1994). ... Selected by San Francisco Giants organization from Dodgers organization in Rule 5 minor league draft (December 9, 1996). ... Loaned by Giants organization to Reynosa, Mexican League (July 8-August 5, 1999). ... Granted free agency (October 15, 2000). ... Signed by Philadelphia Phillies organization (November 15, 2000). ... On Philadelphia disabled list (June 13-July 5, 2001); included rehabilitation assignment to Scranton/Wilkes-Barre (June 29-July 5). ... Granted free agency (October 15, 2001). ... Signed by Arizona Diamondbacks organization (November 20, 2001).

STATISTICAL NOTES: Tied for Texas League lead with 15 wild pitches in 1998. ... Tied for Pacific Coast League lead with four balks in 1999.

Year	League	W	L	Pct.	ERA	G	GS	CG	ShO	Sv.	IP	H	R	ER	BB	SO
1993—	St. Paul (Nor.)	3	1	.750	1.93	6	3	0	0	0	18²/₃	6	4	4	9	19
1994—	Vero Beach (FSL)■	4	3	.571	2.13	19	10	1	1	0	72	54	24	17	25	67
1995—	San Antonio (Texas)	1	1	.500	3.12	16	0	0	0	1	17¹/₃	22	8	6	12	16
	—Vero Beach (FSL)	3	1	.750	3.81	19	1	0	0	1	28¹/₃	25	12	12	10	23
	—San Bernardino (Calif.)	0	0	...	0.00	1	0	0	0	1	1	0	0	0	0	0
1996—	San Bernardino (Calif.)	11	6	.647	3.34	33	19	0	0	0	156¹/₃	133	74	58	77	133
1997—	Shreveport (Texas)■	7	7	.500	3.92	43	9	1	0	0	124	122	58	54	64	65
1998—	Shreveport (Texas)	7	11	.389	3.78	32	20	2	0	0	143	143	71	60	67	104
	—President Lions (Taiwan)■	0	2	.000	6.43	8	0	0	0	1	14	...	...	10	11	6
1999—	Fresno (PCL)■	6	5	.545	4.85	21	18	1	0	0	102	113	69	55	49	61
	—Bakersfield (Calif.)	2	0	1.000	3.60	2	1	0	0	0	10	13	5	4	1	10
	—Reynosa (Mex.)■	0	4	.000	7.06	7	3	0	0	0	21²/₃	32	19	17	16	8
2000—	Shreveport (Texas)■	2	4	.333	3.07	59	2	0	0	4	76¹/₃	70	38	26	40	76
2001—	Philadelphia (N.L.)■	1	0	1.000	4.74	30	0	0	0	0	19	16	10	10	17	15
	—Scranton/W.B. (I.L.)	1	1	.500	2.35	14	1	0	0	0	15¹/₃	14	5	4	4	11
	—Clearwater (FSL)	0	0	...	0.00	2	0	0	0	0	2	2	0	0	1	3
Major League totals (1 year)		1	0	1.000	4.74	30	0	0	0	0	19	16	10	10	17	15

PERSONAL: Born April 21, 1957, in Santa Barbara, Calif. ... 6-2/205. ... Throws left, bats right. ... Full name: Jesse Russell Orosco. ... Name pronounced oh-ROSS-koh.

HIGH SCHOOL: Santa Barbara (Calif.).

JUNIOR COLLEGE: Santa Barbara (Calif.) City College.

TRANSACTIONS/CAREER NOTES: Selected by St. Louis Cardinals organization in seventh round of free-agent draft (January 11, 1977); did not sign. ... Selected by Minnesota Twins organization in second round of free-agent draft (January 10, 1978). ... Traded by Twins to New York Mets (February 7, 1979), completing deal in which Twins traded P Greg Field and a player to be named later to Mets for P Jerry Koosman (December 8, 1978). ... Traded by Mets as part of an eight-player, three-team deal in which Mets sent Orosco to Oakland Athletics (December 11, 1987); A's then traded Orosco, SS Alfredo Griffin and P Jay Howell to Los Angeles Dodgers for P Bob Welch, P Matt Young and P Jack Savage; A's then traded Savage, P Wally Whitehurst and P Kevin Tapani to Mets. ... Granted free agency (November 4, 1988). ... Signed by Cleveland Indians (December 3, 1988). ... Traded by Indians to Milwaukee Brewers for a player to be named later (December 6, 1991); deal settled in cash. ... Granted free agency (November 5, 1992). ... Re-signed by Brewers (December 4, 1992). ... Granted free agency (October 15, 1994). ... Signed by Baltimore Orioles (April 9, 1995). ... Granted free agency (October 27, 1996). ... Re-signed by Orioles (November 15, 1996). ... Traded by Orioles to Mets for P Chuck McElroy (December 10, 1999). ... Traded by Mets to Cardinals for 2B/OF Joe McEwing (March 18, 2000). ... On St. Louis disabled list (April 9-June 9 and June 22, 2000-remainder of season); included rehabilitation assignments to Peoria (May 30-June 5) and Memphis (June 6-9). ... Granted free agency (October 30, 2000). ... Signed by Los Angeles Dodgers organization (February 8, 2001). ... Released by Dodgers (March 30, 2001). ... Re-signed by Dodgers organization (April 24, 2001). ... On Los Angeles disabled list (August 13-September 1, 2001). ... Granted free agency (November 5, 2001). ... Re-signed by Dodgers organization (December 7, 2001).

RECORDS: Holds major league career records for most games pitched—1,131; and most games as relief pitcher—1,127.

MISCELLANEOUS: Appeared in one game as outfielder with one putout (1986). ... Struck out in only plate appearance (1993).

Year	League	W	L	Pct.	ERA	G	GS	CG	ShO	Sv.	IP	H	R	ER	BB	SO
1978—	Elizabethton (Appl.)	4	4	.500	1.13	20	0	0	0	6	40	29	7	5	20	48
1979—	Tidewater (I.L.)■	4	4	.500	3.89	16	15	1	0	0	81	82	45	35	43	55
	—New York (N.L.)	1	2	.333	4.89	18	2	0	0	0	35	33	20	19	22	22
1980—	Jackson (Texas)	4	4	.500	3.68	37	1	0	0	3	71	52	36	29	62	85
1981—	Tidewater (I.L.)	9	5	.643	3.31	46	10	0	0	8	87	80	39	32	32	81
	—New York (N.L.)	0	1	.000	1.59	8	0	0	0	1	17	13	4	3	6	18
1982—	New York (N.L.)	4	10	.286	2.72	54	2	0	0	4	109¹/₃	92	37	33	40	89
1983—	New York (N.L.)	13	7	.650	1.47	62	0	0	0	17	110	76	27	18	38	84
1984—	New York (N.L.)	10	6	.625	2.59	60	0	0	0	31	87	58	29	25	34	85
1985—	New York (N.L.)	8	6	.571	2.73	54	0	0	0	17	79	66	26	24	34	68
1986—	New York (N.L.)	8	6	.571	2.33	58	0	0	0	21	81	64	23	21	35	62
1987—	New York (N.L.)	3	9	.250	4.44	58	0	0	0	16	77	78	41	38	31	78
1988—	Los Angeles (N.L.)■	3	2	.600	2.72	55	0	0	0	9	53	41	18	16	30	43
1989—	Cleveland (A.L.)■	3	4	.429	2.08	69	0	0	0	3	78	54	20	18	26	79
1990—	Cleveland (A.L.)	5	4	.556	3.90	55	0	0	0	2	64²/₃	58	35	28	38	55
1991—	Cleveland (A.L.)	2	0	1.000	3.74	47	0	0	0	0	45²/₃	52	20	19	15	36
1992—	Milwaukee (A.L.)■	3	1	.750	3.23	59	0	0	0	1	39	33	15	14	13	40
1993—	Milwaukee (A.L.)	3	5	.375	3.18	57	0	0	0	8	56²/₃	47	25	20	17	67
1994—	Milwaukee (A.L.)	3	1	.750	5.08	40	0	0	0	0	39	32	26	22	26	36
1995—	Baltimore (A.L.)■	2	4	.333	3.26	*65	0	0	0	3	49²/₃	28	19	18	27	58
1996—	Baltimore (A.L.)	3	1	.750	3.40	66	0	0	0	0	55²/₃	42	22	21	28	52
1997—	Baltimore (A.L.)	6	3	.667	2.32	71	0	0	0	0	50¹/₃	29	13	13	30	46
1998—	Baltimore (A.L.)	4	1	.800	3.18	69	0	0	0	7	56²/₃	46	20	20	28	50
1999—	Baltimore (A.L.)	0	2	.000	5.34	65	0	0	0	1	32	28	21	19	20	35

O

Year	League	W	L	Pct.	ERA	G	GS	CG	ShO	Sv.	IP	H	R	ER	BB	SO
2000—	St. Louis (N.L.)■	0	0	...	3.86	6	0	0	0	0	2 1/3	3	3	1	3	4
—	Peoria (Midw.)..................	0	0	...	0.00	2	2	0	0	0	1 2/3	0	0	0	0	1
—	Memphis (PCL)................	0	1	.000	9.00	2	1	0	0	0	1	1	1	1	0	0
2001—	Las Vegas (PCL)■	1	0	1.000	0.00	10	0	0	0	0	7 1/3	4	0	0	2	11
—	Los Angeles (N.L.)	0	1	.000	3.94	35	0	0	0	0	16	17	7	7	7	21
A.L. totals (11 years)		34	26	.567	3.36	663	0	0	0	25	567 1/3	449	236	212	268	554
N.L. totals (11 years)		50	50	.500	2.77	468	4	0	0	116	666 2/3	541	235	205	280	574
Major League totals (22 years)		84	76	.525	3.04	1131	4	0	0	141	1234	990	471	417	548	1128

DIVISION SERIES RECORD

Year	League	W	L	Pct.	ERA	G	GS	CG	ShO	Sv.	IP	H	R	ER	BB	SO
1996—	Baltimore (A.L.).................	0	1	.000	36.00	4	0	0	0	0	1	2	4	4	3	2
1997—	Baltimore (A.L.).................	0	0	...	0.00	2	0	0	0	0	1 1/3	1	0	0	0	1
Division series totals (2 years)		0	1	.000	15.43	6	0	0	0	0	2 1/3	3	4	4	3	3

CHAMPIONSHIP SERIES RECORD

RECORDS: Holds single-series record for most games won—3 (1986).

Year	League	W	L	Pct.	ERA	G	GS	CG	ShO	Sv.	IP	H	R	ER	BB	SO
1986—	New York (N.L.).................	3	0	1.000	3.38	4	0	0	0	0	8	5	3	3	2	10
1988—	Los Angeles (N.L.)	0	0	...	7.71	4	0	0	0	0	2 1/3	4	2	2	3	0
1996—	Baltimore (A.L.).................	0	0	...	4.50	4	0	0	0	0	2	2	1	1	2	2
1997—	Baltimore (A.L.).................	0	0	...	0.00	2	0	0	0	0	1 1/3	0	0	0	1	1
Champ. series totals (4 years)		3	0	1.000	3.95	14	0	0	0	0	13 2/3	11	6	6	8	13

WORLD SERIES RECORD

NOTES: Member of World Series championship team (1986 and 1988).

Year	League	W	L	Pct.	ERA	G	GS	CG	ShO	Sv.	IP	H	R	ER	BB	SO
1986—	New York (N.L.).................	0	0	...	0.00	4	0	0	0	2	5 2/3	2	0	0	0	6
1988—	Los Angeles (N.L.)				Did not play.											

ALL-STAR GAME RECORD

Year	League	W	L	Pct.	ERA	GS	CG	ShO	Sv.	IP	H	R	ER	BB	SO
1983—	National	0	0	...	0.00	0	0	0	0	1/3	0	0	0	0	1
1984—	National				Did not play.										

ORTEGA, BILL — OF — CARDINALS

PERSONAL: Born July 24, 1975, in Havana, Cuba. ... 6-4/205. ... Bats right, throws right. ... Full name: William Ortega.
TRANSACTIONS/CAREER NOTES: Signed as non-drafted free agent by St. Louis Cardinals organization (March 11, 1997).
STATISTICAL NOTES: Led Carolina League outfielders with 266 total chances in 1999.

							BATTING								FIELDING		
Year	Team (League)	Pos.	G	AB	R	H	2B	3B	HR	RBI	Avg.	BB	SO	SB	PO	A	E	Avg.
1997—	Prince William (Caro.)	OF	73	249	23	57	14	0	0	15	.229	21	42	1	89	5	7	.931
1998—	Peoria (Midw.)............	OF	105	398	57	110	23	2	2	60	.276	39	69	4	74	3	4	.951
1999—	Potomac (Caro.).........	OF	110	421	66	129	27	4	9	74	.306	38	69	7	*252	11	3	*.989
—	Arkansas (Texas).......	OF	20	69	10	26	9	0	2	10	.377	10	9	0	43	0	0	1.000
2000—	Arkansas (Texas).......	OF	86	332	51	108	18	5	12	62	.325	28	42	1	163	8	8	.955
2001—	Memphis (PCL).........	OF	134	495	55	142	26	4	6	62	.287	40	74	6	219	8	7	.970
—	St. Louis (N.L.)..........	PH	5	5	0	1	0	0	0	0	.200	0	1	0	...	...	...	...
Major League totals (1 year)			5	5	0	1	0	0	0	0	.200	0	1	0	...	...	...	...

ORTIZ, DAVID — 1B — TWINS

PERSONAL: Born November 18, 1975, in Santo Domingo, Dominican Republic. ... 6-4/230. ... Bats left, throws left. ... Full name: David Americo Ortiz. ... Formerly known as David Arias.
HIGH SCHOOL: Estudia Espallat (Dominican Republic).
TRANSACTIONS/CAREER NOTES: Signed as non-drafted free agent by Seattle Mariners organization (November 28, 1992). ... Traded by Mariners to Minnesota Twins (September 13, 1996), completing deal in which Twins traded 3B Dave Hollins to Mariners for a player to be named later (August 29, 1996). ... On Minnesota disabled list (May 10-July 9, 1998); included rehabilitation assignment to Salt Lake (June 25-July 9). ... On Minnesota disabled list (May 5-July 21, 2001); included rehabilitation assignments to Gulf Coast Twins (July 5-11), Fort Myers (July 11-12) and New Britain (July 12-21).
STATISTICAL NOTES: Led Arizona League first basemen with 393 total chances in 1994. ... Tied for Arizona League lead with 99 total bases in 1995. ... Career major league grand slams: 1.

							BATTING								FIELDING		
Year	Team (League)	Pos.	G	AB	R	H	2B	3B	HR	RBI	Avg.	BB	SO	SB	PO	A	E	Avg.
1994—	Ariz. Mariners (Ariz.)..	1B	53	167	14	41	10	1	2	20	.246	14	46	1	*372	15	6	.985
1995—	Ariz. Mariners (Ariz.)..	1B	48	184	30	61	*18	4	4	*37	.332	23	52	2	436	*27	5	*.989
1996—	Wisconsin (Midw.).....	1B-3B-DH	129	485	89	156	34	2	18	93	.322	52	108	3	1126	80	13	.989
1997—	Fort Myers (FSL)■.....	1B-DH	61	239	45	79	15	0	13	58	.331	22	53	2	524	44	9	.984
—	New Britain (East.)	DH-1B	69	258	40	83	22	2	14	56	.322	21	78	2	268	16	3	.990
—	Salt Lake (PCL)	1B-DH	10	42	5	9	1	0	4	10	.214	2	11	0	71	2	0	1.000
—	Minnesota (A.L.)	1B-DH	15	49	10	16	3	0	1	6	.327	2	19	0	84	10	1	.989
1998—	Minnesota (A.L.)	1B-DH	86	278	47	77	20	0	9	46	.277	39	72	1	503	46	6	.989
—	Salt Lake (PCL)	1B-DH	11	37	5	9	3	0	2	6	.243	3	9	0	76	10	3	.966
1999—	Salt Lake (PCL)	1B-DH	130	476	85	150	35	3	30	*110	.315	79	105	2	896	77	•20	.980
—	Minnesota (A.L.)	DH-1B	10	20	1	0	0	0	0	0	.000	5	12	0	7	0	0	1.000
2000—	Minnesota (A.L.)	DH-1B	130	415	59	117	36	1	10	63	.282	57	81	1	210	12	1	.996
2001—	Minnesota (A.L.)	DH-1B	89	303	46	71	17	1	18	48	.234	40	68	1	60	2	0	1.000
—	GC Twins (GCL)	DH	4	10	3	4	0	0	0	1	.400	3	1	1	...	...	...	...
—	Fort Myers (FSL)	1B	1	3	0	0	0	0	0	0	.000	1	0	0	10	1	0	1.000
—	New Britain (East.)	1B	9	37	3	9	4	0	0	1	.243	3	9	0	78	4	0	1.000
Major League totals (5 years)			330	1065	163	281	76	2	38	163	.264	143	252	3	864	70	8	.992

ORTIZ, HECTOR C

PERSONAL: Born October 14, 1969, in Rio Piedras, Puerto Rico. ... 6-0/205. ... Bats right, throws right. ... Full name: Hector Ortiz Jr.
HIGH SCHOOL: Luis Hernaiz Verone (Canovanas, Puerto Rico).
JUNIOR COLLEGE: Ranger (Texas) College.
TRANSACTIONS/CAREER NOTES: Selected by Los Angeles Dodgers organization in 35th round of free-agent draft (June 1, 1988). ... Granted free agency (October 17, 1994). ... Signed by Chicago Cubs organization (January 22, 1995). ... Granted free agency (October 15, 1996). ... Signed by Kansas City Royals organization (January 29, 1997). ... On Omaha disabled list (May 19-June 6, 1998). ... Granted free agency (October 15, 1998). ... Signed by Dodgers organization (January 18, 1999). ... Granted free agency (October 15, 1999). ... Signed by Royals organization (November 30, 1999). ... Granted free agency (October 15, 2001).
STATISTICAL NOTES: Led Northwest League catchers with 461 total chances in 1990. ... Tied for Northwest League lead in double plays by catcher with five in 1990.

Year Team (League)	Pos.	G	AB	R	H	2B	3B	HR	RBI	Avg.	BB	SO	SB	PO	A	E	Avg.
1988—Salem (N'West)	C-3B	32	77	5	11	1	0	0	4	.143	5	16	0	157	19	7	.962
1989—Vero Beach (FSL)	C	42	85	5	12	0	1	0	4	.141	6	15	0	174	23	6	.970
—Salem (N'West)	C	44	140	13	32	3	1	0	12	.229	4	24	2	268	24	*12	.961
1990—Yakima (N'West)	C	52	173	16	47	3	1	0	12	.272	5	15	1	*392	*62	7	.985
1991—Vero Beach (FSL)	C	42	123	3	28	2	0	0	8	.228	5	8	0	238	28	7	.974
1992—Bakersfield (Calif.)	C	63	206	19	58	8	1	1	31	.282	21	16	2	428	44	3	.994
—San Antonio (Texas)	C	26	59	1	12	1	0	0	5	.203	11	13	0	140	23	3	.982
1993—San Antonio (Texas)	C-3B	49	131	6	28	5	0	1	6	.214	9	17	0	311	43	8	.978
—Albuquerque (PCL)	C	18	44	0	8	1	1	0	3	.182	0	6	0	78	11	2	.978
1994—Albuquerque (PCL)	C	34	93	7	28	1	1	0	10	.301	3	12	0	144	20	4	.976
—San Antonio (Texas)	C-P	24	75	4	9	0	0	0	4	.120	2	7	0	166	23	2	.990
1995—Orlando (Sou.)■	C	96	299	13	70	12	0	0	18	.234	20	39	0	567	72	6	.991
1996—Orlando (Sou.)	C	78	216	16	47	8	0	0	15	.218	26	23	1	475	32	6	.988
—Iowa (A.A.)	C	27	79	6	19	2	0	0	3	.241	3	16	0	139	9	2	.987
1997—Omaha (A.A.)■	C	21	63	7	12	3	0	0	3	.190	13	15	0	130	6	3	.978
—Wichita (Texas)	C	59	180	20	45	3	0	1	25	.250	21	15	1	340	40	*15	.962
1998—Wichita (Texas)	C	4	13	1	2	0	0	0	0	.154	2	1	0	24	6	1	.968
—Omaha (PCL)	C	63	191	17	43	7	0	0	12	.225	9	26	0	318	30	8	.978
—Kansas City (A.L.)	C-1B	4	4	1	0	0	0	0	0	.000	0	0	0	4	0	0	1.000
1999—San Antonio (Texas)■	C	40	121	10	29	4	0	0	13	.240	10	17	0	238	26	6	.978
—Albuquerque (PCL)	C-1B	55	164	21	50	9	0	6	20	.305	7	27	2	312	32	10	.972
2000—Omaha (PCL)■	C	68	227	30	73	12	0	6	24	.322	22	18	4	291	28	6	.982
—Kansas City (A.L.)	C	26	88	15	34	6	0	0	5	.386	8	8	0	130	18	1	.993
2001—Kansas City (A.L.)	C-DH	56	154	12	38	6	1	0	11	.247	9	24	1	280	28	3	.990
—Omaha (PCL)	C	42	150	19	39	7	0	2	15	.260	15	26	0	198	11	2	.991
Major League totals (3 years)		86	246	28	72	12	1	0	16	.293	17	32	1	414	46	4	.991

RECORD AS PITCHER

Year League	W	L	Pct.	ERA	G	GS	CG	ShO	Sv.	IP	H	R	ER	BB	SO
1994—San Antonio (Texas)	0	0	...	0.00	1	0	0	0	0	1	0	0	0	1	1

ORTIZ, RAMON P ANGELS

PERSONAL: Born March 23, 1976, in Cotui, Dominican Republic. ... 6-0/175. ... Throws right, bats right. ... Full name: Diogenes Ramon Ortiz.
HIGH SCHOOL: 8th Intermedian (Dominican Republic).
TRANSACTIONS/CAREER NOTES: Signed as non-drafted free agent by California Angels organization (June 20, 1995). ... Angels franchise renamed Anaheim Angels for 1997 season. ... On disabled list (May 9, 1998-remainder of season). ... On Anaheim disabled list (March 20-April 11, 2000); included rehabilitation assignment to Lake Elsinore (April 6).
STATISTICAL NOTES: Pitched 12-0 no-hit victory against Quad City (August 7, 1997).

Year League	W	L	Pct.	ERA	G	GS	CG	ShO	Sv.	IP	H	R	ER	BB	SO
1995—Dominican Angels (DSL)	8	6	.571	2.23	16	16	7	0	0	97	79	44	24	54	100
1996—Arizona Angels (Ariz.)	5	4	.556	2.12	16	8	•2	*2	1	68	55	28	16	27	78
—Boise (N'West)	1	1	.500	3.66	3	3	0	0	0	$19\frac{2}{3}$	21	10	8	6	18
1997—Cedar Rapids (Midw.)	11	10	.524	3.58	27	•27	*8	*4	0	181	156	78	72	53	*225
1998—Midland (Texas)	2	1	.667	5.55	7	7	0	0	0	47	50	31	29	16	53
1999—Erie (East.)	9	4	.692	2.82	15	15	2	•2	0	102	88	38	32	40	86
—Edmonton (PCL)	5	3	.625	4.05	9	9	0	0	0	$53\frac{1}{3}$	46	26	24	19	64
—Anaheim (A.L.)	2	3	.400	6.52	9	9	0	0	0	$48\frac{1}{3}$	50	35	35	25	44
2000—Lake Elsinore (Calif.)	1	0	1.000	3.00	1	1	0	0	0	6	8	2	2	2	7
—Anaheim (A.L.)	8	6	.571	5.09	18	18	2	0	0	$111\frac{1}{3}$	96	69	63	55	73
—Edmonton (PCL)	6	6	.500	4.55	15	15	1	0	0	89	74	49	45	37	76
2001—Anaheim (A.L.)	13	11	.542	4.36	32	32	2	0	0	$208\frac{2}{3}$	223	114	101	76	135
Major League totals (3 years)	23	20	.535	4.86	59	59	4	0	0	$368\frac{1}{3}$	369	218	199	156	252

ORTIZ, RUSS P GIANTS

PERSONAL: Born June 5, 1974, in Encino, Calif. ... 6-1/210. ... Throws right, bats right. ... Full name: Russell Reid Ortiz.
HIGH SCHOOL: Montclair Prep (Van Nuys, Calif.).
COLLEGE: Oklahoma.
TRANSACTIONS/CAREER NOTES: Selected by San Francisco Giants organization in fourth round of free-agent draft (June 1, 1995).
RECORDS: Shares N.L. single-inning record for most consecutive home runs allowed—3 (August 10, 1998, fifth inning).

O

Year League	W	L	Pct.	ERA	G	GS	CG	ShO	Sv.	IP	H	R	ER	BB	SO
1995—Bellingham (N'West)	2	0	1.000	0.52	25	0	0	0	11	$34\frac{1}{3}$	19	4	2	13	55
—San Jose (Calif.)	0	1	.000	1.50	5	0	0	0	0	6	4	1	1	2	7
1996—San Jose (Calif.)	0	0	...	0.25	34	0	0	0	23	$36\frac{2}{3}$	16	2	1	20	63
—Shreveport (Texas)	1	2	.333	4.05	26	0	0	0	13	$26\frac{2}{3}$	22	14	12	21	29
1997—Shreveport (Texas)	2	3	.400	4.13	12	12	0	0	0	$56\frac{2}{3}$	52	28	26	37	50
—Phoenix (PCL)	4	3	.571	5.51	14	14	0	0	0	85	96	57	52	34	70
1998—San Francisco (N.L.)	4	4	.500	4.99	22	13	0	0	0	$88\frac{1}{3}$	90	51	49	46	75
—Fresno (PCL)	3	1	.750	1.60	10	10	0	0	0	$50\frac{2}{3}$	35	10	9	22	59
1999—San Francisco (N.L.)	18	9	.667	3.81	33	33	3	0	0	$207\frac{2}{3}$	189	109	88	*125	164
2000—San Francisco (N.L.)	14	12	.538	5.01	33	32	0	0	0	$195\frac{2}{3}$	192	117	109	112	167
2001—San Francisco (N.L.)	17	9	.654	3.29	33	33	1	1	0	$218\frac{2}{3}$	187	90	80	91	169
Major League totals (4 years)	53	34	.609	4.13	121	111	4	1	0	$710\frac{1}{3}$	658	367	326	374	575

DIVISION SERIES RECORD

Year League	W	L	Pct.	ERA	G	GS	CG	ShO	Sv.	IP	H	R	ER	BB	SO
2000—San Francisco (N.L.)	0	0	...	1.69	1	1	0	0	0	$5\frac{1}{3}$	2	1	1	4	4

ORTIZ, JOSE — 2B/SS — ROCKIES

PERSONAL: Born June 13, 1977, in Santo Domingo, Dominican Republic. ... 5-9/177. ... Bats right, throws right. ... Full name: Jose Daniel Ortiz Santos.

TRANSACTIONS/CAREER NOTES: Signed as non-drafted free agent by Oakland Athletics organization (November 8, 1994). ... On disabled list (May 10-June 30, 1998). ... On disabled list (June 15-25, 1999). ... On Oakland disabled list (April 15-May 16, 2001); included rehabilitation assignment to Sacramento (May 8-16). ... Traded by A's with OF Mario Encarnacion and P Todd Belitz to Colorado Rockies for OF Jermaine Dye (July 25, 2001).

HONORS: Named Pacific Coast League Most Valuable Player (2000).

STATISTICAL NOTES: Led Arizona League with .530 slugging percentage in 1996. ... Led Arizona League shortstops with 279 total chances and 42 double plays in 1996. ... Led California League shortstops with 53 errors and 80 double plays in 1997. ... Hit three home runs in one game (August 17, 2001).

Year Team (League)	Pos.	G	AB	R	H	2B	3B	HR	RBI	Avg.	BB	SO	SB	PO	A	E	Avg.
1995—Dom. Athletics (DSL)	SS	61	217	45	65	12	2	9	41	.300	32	22	14	182	38	17	.928
1996—Ariz. Athletics (Ariz.)	SS	52	200	*43	66	12	8	4	25	.330	20	34	16	*93	*165	21	.925
—Modesto (Calif.)	2B	1	4	0	1	0	0	0	0	.250	0	1	0	2	5	0	1.000
1997—Modesto (Calif.)	SS-2B	128	497	92	122	25	7	16	58	.245	60	107	22	186	373	†53	.913
1998—Huntsville (Sou.)	2B-SS-OF	94	354	70	98	24	2	6	55	.277	48	63	22	159	274	27	.941
1999—Vancouver (PCL)	SS-2B	107	377	66	107	29	2	9	45	.284	29	50	13	179	295	28	.944
2000—Sacramento (PCL)	2B-SS-3B	131	*518	107	*182	34	5	24	108	.351	47	64	22	247	347	32	.949
—Oakland (A.L.)	DH-2B	7	11	4	2	0	0	0	3	.182	2	3	0	2	4	1	.857
2001—Oakland (A.L.)	2B-DH	11	42	4	7	0	0	0	3	.167	3	5	1	16	23	2	.951
—Sacramento (PCL)	2B-SS	65	256	41	70	16	4	7	39	.273	25	50	7	116	149	10	.964
—Colorado (N.L.)■	2B	53	204	38	52	8	1	13	35	.255	14	36	3	86	137	8	.965
American League totals (2 years)		18	53	8	9	0	0	0	4	.170	5	8	1	18	27	3	.938
National League totals (1 year)		53	204	38	52	8	1	13	35	.255	14	36	3	86	137	8	.965
Major League totals (2 years)		71	257	46	61	8	1	13	39	.237	19	44	4	104	164	11	.961

OSIK, KEITH — C — PIRATES

PERSONAL: Born October 22, 1968, in Port Jefferson, N.Y. ... 6-0/195. ... Bats right, throws right. ... Full name: Keith Richard Osik. ... Name pronounced OH-sik.

HIGH SCHOOL: Shoreham (N.Y.)-Wading River.

COLLEGE: Louisiana State.

TRANSACTIONS/CAREER NOTES: Selected by Texas Rangers organization in 47th round of free-agent draft (June 2, 1987); did not sign. ... Selected by Pittsburgh Pirates organization in 24th round of free-agent draft (June 4, 1990). ... On Pittsburgh disabled list (July 16-August 13, 1996); included rehabilitation assignment to Erie (August 10-13). ... On Pittsburgh disabled list (July 21-August 13, 1999); included rehabilitation assignment to Nashville (August 9-13). ... On disabled list (April 30-May 15, 2001).

Year Team (League)	Pos.	G	AB	R	H	2B	3B	HR	RBI	Avg.	BB	SO	SB	PO	A	E	Avg.
1990—Welland (NY-Penn)	3-C-1-2-S	29	97	13	27	4	0	1	20	.278	11	12	2	59	29	2	.978
1991—Salem (Caro.)	C-3B-2B	87	300	31	81	12	1	6	35	.270	38	48	2	307	85	12	.970
—Carolina (Sou.)	C-3B	17	43	9	13	3	1	0	5	.302	5	5	0	84	13	2	.980
1992—Carolina (Sou.)	3B-C-2B-P	129	425	41	110	17	1	5	45	.259	52	69	2	222	195	19	.956
1993—Carolina (Sou.)	C-3B-DH	103	371	47	104	21	2	10	47	.280	30	46	0	662	69	6	.992
1994—Buffalo (A.A.)	C-O-1-DH-P-2	83	260	27	55	16	0	5	34	.212	28	41	0	403	50	8	.983
1995—Calgary (PCL)	C-1B-OF-P-3B	90	301	40	101	25	1	10	59	.336	21	42	2	458	35	4	.992
1996—Pittsburgh (N.L.)	C-3B-OF	48	140	18	41	14	1	1	14	.293	14	22	1	237	25	6	.978
—Erie (NY-Penn)	C	3	10	1	3	1	0	0	0	.300	1	2	0	19	2	0	1.000
1997—Pittsburgh (N.L.)	C-2B-1B-3B	49	105	10	27	9	1	0	7	.257	9	21	0	163	14	2	.989
1998—Pittsburgh (N.L.)	C-3B	39	98	8	21	4	0	0	7	.214	13	16	1	152	30	1	.995
1999—Pittsburgh (N.L.)	C-P	66	167	12	31	3	1	2	13	.186	11	30	0	289	22	1	.997
—Nashville (PCL)	C-OF	4	11	0	1	0	0	0	0	.091	0	1	0	24	3	0	1.000
2000—Pittsburgh (N.L.)	C-3B-1B-DH-P	46	123	11	36	6	1	4	22	.293	14	11	3	156	23	2	.989
2001—Pittsburgh (N.L.)	C-1-3-2-O	56	120	9	25	4	0	2	13	.208	13	24	1	213	17	1	.996
Major League totals (6 years)		304	753	68	181	40	4	9	76	.240	74	124	6	1210	131	13	.990

RECORD AS PITCHER

Year League	W	L	Pct.	ERA	G	GS	CG	ShO	Sv.	IP	H	R	ER	BB	SO
1992—Carolina (Sou.)	0	0	...	0.00	1	0	0	0	0	$2\frac{2}{3}$	2	0	0	0	3
1994—Buffalo (A.A.)	0	1	.000	13.50	1	0	0	0	0	$\frac{2}{3}$	2	1	1	1	0
1995—Calgary (PCL)	0	0	...	4.50	2	0	0	0	0	2	1	1	1	1	3
1999—Pittsburgh (N.L.)	0	0	...	36.00	1	0	0	0	0	1	2	4	4	2	1
2000—Pittsburgh (N.L.)	0	0	...	45.00	1	0	0	0	0	1	5	5	5	0	1
Major League totals (2 years)	0	0	...	40.50	2	0	0	0	0	2	7	9	9	2	2

OSTING, JIMMY   P   INDIANS

PERSONAL: Born April 7, 1977, in Louisville, Ky. ... 6-5/180. ... Throws left, bats right. ... Full name: James Michael Osting.
HIGH SCHOOL: Trinity (Louisville, Ky.).
TRANSACTIONS/CAREER NOTES: Selected by Atlanta Braves in fourth round of free-agent draft (June 1, 1995). ... On disabled list (April 2, 1998-entire season). ... Traded by Braves with P Bruce Chen to Philadelphia Phillies for P Andy Ashby (July 12, 2000). ... Claimed on waivers by Colorado Rockies (April 4, 2001). ... Claimed on waivers by San Diego Padres (April 11, 2001). ... Granted free agency (October 15, 2001). ... Signed by Cleveland Indians organization (November 20, 2001).

Year League	W	L	Pct.	ERA	G	GS	CG	ShO	Sv.	IP	H	R	ER	BB	SO
1995—Danville (Appl.)	2	7	.222	7.15	11	10	0	0	0	39	46	34	31	25	43
1996—Eugene (N'West)	2	1	.667	2.59	5	5	0	0	0	24 1/3	14	11	7	13	35
1997—Macon (S.Atl.)	2	3	.400	3.28	15	15	0	0	0	57 2/3	54	28	21	29	62
1998—							Did not play.								
1999—Macon (S.Atl.)	*14	4	.778	2.88	27	22	0	0	2	147	130	52	47	30	131
2000—Myrtle Beach (Caro.)	2	2	.500	3.13	4	4	0	0	0	23	25	8	8	5	17
—Greenville (Sou.)	2	6	.250	2.65	11	11	0	0	0	71 1/3	67	30	21	29	52
—Richmond (I.L.)	0	2	.000	11.57	3	3	0	0	0	9 1/3	15	12	12	11	2
—Reading (East.)■	4	2	.667	2.38	10	9	1	1	0	56 2/3	53	17	15	26	31
2001—Carolina (Sou.)■	1	0	1.000	1.80	1	1	0	0	0	5	3	1	1	3	3
—Mobile (Sou.)■	9	4	.692	3.59	18	18	0	0	0	97 2/3	85	41	39	42	69
—San Diego (N.L.)	0	0	...	0.00	3	0	0	0	0	2	1	0	0	2	3
—Portland (PCL)	1	4	.200	9.59	5	5	0	0	0	25 1/3	41	27	27	10	15
Major League totals (1 year)	0	0	...	0.00	3	0	0	0	0	2	1	0	0	2	3

OSUNA, ANTONIO   P   WHITE SOX

PERSONAL: Born April 12, 1973, in Sinaloa, Mexico. ... 5-11/206. ... Throws right, bats right. ... Full name: Antonio Pedro Osuna.
HIGH SCHOOL: Secondaria Federal (Mexico).
TRANSACTIONS/CAREER NOTES: Signed as non-drafted free agent by Los Angeles Dodgers organization (June 12, 1991). ... On suspended list (April 8-July 17, 1993). ... On San Antonio disabled list (April 8-June 6, 1994). ... On Los Angeles disabled list (May 19-June 16, 1995); included rehabilitation assignment to San Bernardino (June 6-16). ... On disabled list (September 9, 1998-remainder of season). ... On Los Angeles disabled list (March 25-April 16, April 18-May 3 and May 19, 1999-remainder of season); included rehabilitation assignments to San Bernardino (April 10-16, April 25-May 3, July 7-15 and September 1-29). ... On Los Angeles disabled list (March 31-May 5, 2000); included rehabilitation assignment to San Bernardino (April 8-May 5). ... Traded by Dodgers with P Carlos Ortega to Chicago White Sox for P Gary Majewski, P Andre Simpson and P Orlando Rodriguez (March 17, 2001). ... On disabled list (April 12, 2001-remainder of season).

Year League	W	L	Pct.	ERA	G	GS	CG	ShO	Sv.	IP	H	R	ER	BB	SO
1991—Gulf Coast Dodgers (GCL)	0	0	...	0.82	8	0	0	0	4	11	8	5	1	0	13
—Yakima (N'West)	0	0	...	3.20	13	0	0	0	5	25 1/3	18	10	9	8	39
1992—Mexico City Tigres (Mex.)	13	7	.650	4.05	28	26	3	1	0	166 2/3	181	80	75	74	129
1993—Bakersfield (Calif.)	0	2	.000	4.91	14	2	0	0	2	18 1/3	19	10	10	5	20
1994—San Antonio (Texas)	1	2	.333	0.98	35	0	0	0	19	46	19	6	5	18	53
—Albuquerque (PCL)	0	0	...	0.00	6	0	0	0	4	6	5	1	0	1	8
1995—Los Angeles (N.L.)	2	4	.333	4.43	39	0	0	0	0	44 2/3	39	22	22	20	46
—San Bernardino (Calif.)	0	0	...	1.29	5	0	0	0	0	7	3	1	1	5	11
—Albuquerque (PCL)	0	1	.000	4.42	19	0	0	0	11	18 1/3	15	9	9	9	19
1996—Albuquerque (PCL)	0	0	...	0.00	1	0	0	0	0	1	2	0	0	0	1
—Los Angeles (N.L.)	9	6	.600	3.00	73	0	0	0	4	84	65	33	28	32	85
1997—Albuquerque (PCL)	1	1	.500	1.93	13	0	0	0	6	14	9	3	3	4	26
—Los Angeles (N.L.)	3	4	.429	2.19	48	0	0	0	0	61 2/3	46	15	15	19	68
1998—Los Angeles (N.L.)	7	1	.875	3.06	54	0	0	0	6	64 2/3	50	26	22	32	72
1999—San Bernardino (Calif.)	0	0	...	2.33	13	4	0	0	0	19 1/3	19	6	5	6	27
—Los Angeles (N.L.)	0	0	...	7.71	5	0	0	0	0	4 2/3	4	5	4	3	5
2000—San Bernardino (Calif.)	0	2	.000	4.91	3	3	0	0	0	7 1/3	4	4	4	3	11
—Los Angeles (N.L.)	3	6	.333	3.74	46	0	0	0	0	67 1/3	57	30	28	35	70
—Albuquerque (PCL)	0	0	...	0.00	3	1	0	0	0	5 2/3	2	2	0	5	7
2001—Chicago (A.L.)■	0	0	...	20.77	4	0	0	0	0	4 1/3	8	10	10	2	6
A.L. totals (1 year)	0	0	...	20.77	4	0	0	0	0	4 1/3	8	10	10	2	6
N.L. totals (6 years)	24	21	.533	3.28	265	0	0	0	10	327	261	131	119	141	346
Major League totals (7 years)	24	21	.533	3.50	269	0	0	0	10	331 1/3	269	141	129	143	352

DIVISION SERIES RECORD

Year League	W	L	Pct.	ERA	G	GS	CG	ShO	Sv.	IP	H	R	ER	BB	SO
1995—Los Angeles (N.L.)	0	1	.000	2.70	3	0	0	0	0	3 1/3	3	1	1	1	3
1996—Los Angeles (N.L.)	0	1	.000	4.50	2	0	0	0	0	2	3	1	1	1	4
Division series totals (2 years)	0	2	.000	3.38	5	0	0	0	0	5 1/3	6	2	2	2	7

O

OSWALT, ROY   P   ASTROS

PERSONAL: Born August 29, 1977, in Kosciusko, Miss. ... 6-0/170. ... Throws right, bats right. ... Full name: Roy Edward Oswalt. ... Name pronounced OZE-walt.
HIGH SCHOOL: Weir (Miss.).
JUNIOR COLLEGE: Holmes Community College (Miss.).
TRANSACTIONS/CAREER NOTES: Selected by Houston Astros organization in 23rd round of free-agent draft (June 4, 1996).
HONORS: Named N.L. Rookie Pitcher of the Year by THE SPORTING NEWS (2001).
MISCELLANEOUS: Member of 2000 U.S. Olympic baseball team.

Year League	W	L	Pct.	ERA	G	GS	CG	ShO	Sv.	IP	H	R	ER	BB	SO
1997— Gulf Coast Astros (GCL).....	1	1	.500	0.64	5	5	0	0	0	28 1/3	25	7	2	7	28
— Auburn (NY-Penn)..............	2	4	.333	4.53	9	9	1	1	0	51 2/3	50	29	26	15	44
1998— Gulf Coast Astros (GCL).....	1	1	.500	2.25	4	4	0	0	0	16	10	6	4	1	27
— Auburn (NY-Penn)..............	4	5	.444	2.18	11	11	0	0	0	70 1/3	49	24	17	31	67
1999— Michigan (Midw.)..............	13	4	.765	4.46	22	22	2	0	0	151 1/3	144	78	75	54	143
2000— Kissimmee (FSL)..............	4	3	.571	2.98	8	8	0	0	0	45 1/3	52	15	15	11	47
— Round Rock (Texas)..........	11	4	.733	1.94	19	18	2	2	0	129 2/3	106	37	28	22	141
2001— New Orleans (PCL)............	2	3	.400	4.35	5	5	0	0	0	31	32	16	15	6	34
— Houston (N.L.)..............	14	3	.824	2.73	28	20	3	1	0	141 2/3	126	48	43	24	144
Major League totals (1 year)........	14	3	.824	2.73	28	20	3	1	0	141 2/3	126	48	43	24	144

OVERBAY, LYLE　　　　1B　　　　DIAMONDBACKS

PERSONAL: Born January 28, 1977, in Centralia, Wash. ... 6-2/215. ... Bats left, throws left. ... Full name: Lyle Stefan Overbay.
COLLEGE: Nevada.
TRANSACTIONS/CAREER NOTES: Selected by Arizona Diamondbacks organization in 18th round of free-agent draft (June 2, 1999).
HONORS: Named Pioneer League Most Valuable Player (1999).
STATISTICAL NOTES: Led Pioneer League with 180 total bases and grounding into double plays with 14 in 1999. ... Led Pioneer League first baseman with 697 total chances, 641 putouts and .986 fielding percentage in 1999. ... Led Texas League with .423 on-base percentage in 2001. ... Tied for Texas League lead with eight sacrifice flies and 11 intentional bases on balls received in 2001.

							BATTING							FIELDING		
Year Team (League)	Pos.	G	AB	R	H	2B	3B	HR	RBI	Avg.	BB	SO	SB	PO	A	E	Avg.
1999— Missoula (Pio.)..........	1B-OF	75	*306	66	*105	25	7	12	*101	.343	40	53	10	†647	46	10	†.986
2000— South Bend (Midw.) ...	1B	71	259	47	86	19	3	6	47	.332	27	36	9	587	45	11	.983
— El Paso (Texas)..........	1B	62	244	43	86	16	2	8	49	.352	28	39	3	536	37	12	.979
2001— El Paso (Texas)..........	1B-OF	*138	*532	82	*187	*49	3	13	100	.352	67	92	5	899	76	13	.987
— Arizona (N.L.).............	PH	2	2	0	1	0	0	0	0	.500	0	1	0	...	...	...	...
Major League totals (1 year)		2	2	0	1	0	0	0	0	.500	0	1	0	...	...	...	...

OWENS, ERIC　　　　OF　　　　MARLINS

PERSONAL: Born February 3, 1971, in Danville, Va. ... 6-0/198. ... Bats right, throws right. ... Full name: Eric Blake Owens.
HIGH SCHOOL: Tunstall (Dry Fork, Va.).
COLLEGE: Ferrum (Va.).
TRANSACTIONS/CAREER NOTES: Selected by Cincinnati Reds organization in fourth round of free-agent draft (June 1, 1992). ... On Indianapolis disabled list (August 20-September 11, 1995). ... Traded by Reds to Florida Marlins for a player to be named later (March 21, 1998); Reds acquired P Jesus Martinez to complete deal (March 26, 1998). ... Contract sold by Marlins to Milwaukee Brewers (March 25, 1998). ... Granted free agency (October 15, 1998). ... Signed by San Diego Padres organization (December 10, 1998). ... Traded by Padres with P Matt Clement and P Omar Ortiz to Marlins for OF Mark Kotsay and OF Cesar Crespo (March 28, 2001). ... On Florida disabled list (August 2-22, 2001); included rehabilitation assignment to Calgary (August 19-22).
HONORS: Named American Association Most Valuable Player (1995).
STATISTICAL NOTES: Tied for Pioneer League lead in errors by shortstops with 28 in 1992. ... Tied for American Association lead in errors by second baseman with 17 in 1997. ... Had 18-game hitting streak (June 17-July 6, 1999). ... Led N.L. outfielders with 1.000 fielding percentage in 2000.

							BATTING							FIELDING		
Year Team (League)	Pos.	G	AB	R	H	2B	3B	HR	RBI	Avg.	BB	SO	SB	PO	A	E	Avg.
1992— Billings (Pio.).)	SS-3B	67	239	41	72	10	3	3	26	.301	23	22	15	82	164	‡29	.895
1993— Win.-Salem (Caro.)....	SS	122	487	74	132	25	4	10	63	.271	53	69	21	*215	347	34	.943
1994— Chattanooga (Sou.)....	3B-2B	134	523	73	133	17	3	3	36	.254	54	86	38	151	266	40	.912
1995— Indianapolis (A.A.)......	2B	108	427	*86	134	24	•8	12	63	.314	52	61	*33	219	274	*17	.967
— Cincinnati (N.L.).......	3B	2	2	0	2	0	0	0	1	1.000	0	0	0	0	0	0	...
1996— Indianapolis (A.A.)......SS-3B-2B-OF		33	128	24	41	8	2	4	14	.320	11	16	6	44	64	6	.947
— Cincinnati (N.L.).......	OF-2B-3B	88	205	26	41	6	0	0	9	.200	23	38	16	76	14	2	.978
1997— Cincinnati (N.L.).......	OF-2B	27	57	8	15	0	0	0	3	.263	4	11	3	15	0	1	.938
— Indianapolis (A.A.).......	2-S-O-3	104	391	56	112	15	4	11	44	.286	42	55	23	184	241	‡27	.940
1998— Milwaukee (N.L.)■....	OF-2B	40	5	5	2	0	1	4	.125	2	6	0	14	2	1	.941
— Louisville (I.L.)...........	OF-3B-DH	77	254	48	85	11	4	5	40	.335	34	30	21	85	57	8	.947
1999— San Diego (N.L.)■ OF-1B-3B-2B		149	440	55	117	22	3	9	61	.266	38	50	33	278	12	4	.986
2000— San Diego (N.L.).......	OF-2B	145	583	87	171	19	7	6	51	.293	45	63	29	315	6	0	†1.000
2001— Florida (N.L.)■..........	OF-DH	119	400	51	101	16	1	5	28	.253	29	59	8	180	6	3	.984
— Calgary (PCL)............	OF	3	15	2	4	2	0	0	2	.267	0	2	1	2	0	1	.667
Major League totals (7 years)		564	1727	232	452	65	11	21	157	.262	141	227	89	878	40	11	.988

OWENS, JEREMY　　　　OF　　　　PADRES

PERSONAL: Born December 9, 1976, in Johnson City, Tenn. ... 6-1/200. ... Bats right, throws right. ... Full name: Jeremy Scott Owens.
HIGH SCHOOL: Science Hill (Johnson City, Tenn.).
COLLEGE: Middle Tennessee.
TRANSACTIONS/CAREER NOTES: Selected by San Diego Padres organization in eighth round of free-agent draft (June 2, 1998).
STATISTICAL NOTES: Led Midwest League outfielders with 344 total chances in 1999. ... Tied outfielders for Southern League lead with five double plays in 2001.

							BATTING							FIELDING		
Year Team (League)	Pos.	G	AB	R	H	2B	3B	HR	RBI	Avg.	BB	SO	SB	PO	A	E	Avg.
1998— Idaho Falls (Pio.)........	OF-3B	69	284	61	79	16	4	8	52	.278	36	81	30	114	11	4	.969
1999— Fort Wayne (Midw.).....	OF	129	513	*111	144	26	12	9	66	.281	63	*153	65	*309	*18	*17	.951
— Rancho Cuca. (Calif.) .	OF	9	38	2	6	1	0	0	1	.158	1	13	2	20	2	1	.957
2000— Rancho Cuca. (Calif.) .	OF	138	570	99	146	29	10	16	63	.256	63	183	54	344	16	5	.986
2001— Mobile (Sou.)	OF	107	395	46	85	20	6	7	26	.215	55	149	33	251	•15	4	.985
— Lake Elsinore (Calif.) ..	OF	24	91	8	18	1	1	3	9	.198	7	39	4	44	2	0	1.000

OZUNA, PABLO — SS — MARLINS

PERSONAL: Born August 25, 1978, in Santo Domingo, Dominican Republic. ... 6-0/160. ... Bats right, throws right. ... Full name: Pablo Jose Ozuna.

TRANSACTIONS/CAREER NOTES: Signed as non-drafted free agent by St. Louis Cardinals orgnaization (April 8, 1996). ... Traded by Cardinals with P Braden Looper and P Armando Almanza to Florida Marlins for SS Edgar Renteria (December 14, 1998). ... On disabled list (March 23, 2001-entire season).

HONORS: Named Midwest League Most Valuable Player (1998).

STATISTICAL NOTES: Tied for Appalachian League lead in sacrifice hits with six in 1997. ... Led Midwest League with 26 caught stealing and tied for lead in double plays by a shortstop with 80 in 1998. ... Tied for Midwest League lead with 80 double plays by shortstop in 1998. ... Led Eastern League with 24 caught stealing in 2000.

Year	Team (League)	Pos.	G	AB	R	H	2B	3B	HR	RBI	Avg.	BB	SO	SB	PO	A	E	Avg.
1996—	Dom. Cardinals (DSL)	SS	74	295	57	107	12	4	6	60	.363	23	19	19	126	219	32	.915
1997—	Johnson City (Appl.) ..	SS	56	232	40	75	13	1	5	24	.323	10	24	23	80	139	25	.898
1998—	Peoria (Midw.)............	SS	133	538	*122	*192	27	10	9	62	*.357	29	56	62	195	*395	45	.929
1999—	Portland (East.)■......	SS	117	502	62	141	25	7	7	46	.281	13	50	31	179	309	28	.946
2000—	Portland (East.)...........	2B	118	464	74	143	25	6	7	59	.308	40	55	35	*242	302	*25	.956
—	Florida (N.L.)..............	2B	14	24	2	8	1	0	0	0	.333	0	2	1	12	17	1	.967
2001—	Florida (N.L.)..............							Did not play.										
Major League totals (1 year)			14	24	2	8	1	0	0	0	.333	0	2	1	12	17	1	.967

PADILLA, VICENTE — P — PHILLIES

PERSONAL: Born September 27, 1977, in Chinandoga, Nicaragua. ... 6-2/200. ... Throws right, bats right. ... Full name: Vicente D. Padilla.

HIGH SCHOOL: Ruben Dario (Nicaragua).

TRANSACTIONS/CAREER NOTES: Signed as non-drafted free agent by Arizona Diamondbacks organization (August 31, 1998). ... Traded by Diamondbacks with OF Travis Lee, P Omar Daal and P Nelson Figueroa to Philadelphia Phillies for P Curt Schilling (July 26, 2000). ... On Philadelphia disabled list (May 4-30, 2001); included rehabilitation assignment to Scranton/Wilkes-Barre (May 22-30).

Year	League	W	L	Pct.	ERA	G	GS	CG	ShO	Sv.	IP	H	R	ER	BB	SO
1999—	High Desert (Calif.).............	4	1	.800	3.73	9	9	0	0	0	50²/₃	50	27	21	17	55
—	Tucson (PCL)	7	4	.636	3.75	18	14	0	0	0	93²/₃	107	47	39	24	58
—	Arizona (N.L.)...................	0	1	.000	16.88	5	0	0	0	0	2²/₃	7	5	5	3	0
2000—	Tucson (PCL)	0	1	.000	4.42	12	3	0	0	1	18¹/₃	22	9	9	8	22
—	Arizona (N.L.)...................	2	1	.667	2.31	27	0	0	0	0	35	32	10	9	10	30
—	Philadelphia (N.L.)■	2	6	.250	5.34	28	0	0	0	2	30¹/₃	40	23	18	18	21
2001—	Philadelphia (N.L.)...........	3	1	.750	4.24	23	0	0	0	0	34	36	18	16	12	29
—	Scranton/W.B. (I.L.)	7	0	1.000	2.42	16	16	0	0	0	81²/₃	64	24	22	11	75
Major League totals (3 years)......		7	9	.438	4.24	83	0	0	0	2	102	115	56	48	43	80

PAINTER, LANCE — P

PERSONAL: Born July 21, 1967, in Bedford, England. ... 6-1/200. ... Throws left, bats left. ... Full name: Lance Telford Painter.

HIGH SCHOOL: Nicolet (Glendale, Wis.).

COLLEGE: Wisconsin.

TRANSACTIONS/CAREER NOTES: Selected by San Diego Padres organization in 25th round of free-agent draft (June 4, 1990). ... Selected by Colorado Rockies in second round (34th pick overall) of expansion draft (November 17, 1992). ... On disabled list (April 17-May 6, 1995). ... On disabled list (August 6, 1996-remainder of season). ... Claimed on waivers by St. Louis Cardinals (December 2, 1996). ... On St. Louis disabled list (April 5-May 12 and May 20-June 20, 1997); included rehabilitation assignment to Louisville (May 1-12). ... On St. Louis disabled list (June 13-29, 1999); included rehabilitation assignment to Arkansas (June 28-29). ... Traded by Cardinals with C Alberto Castillo and P Matt DeWitt to Toronto Blue Jays for P Pat Hentgen and P Paul Spoljaric (November 11, 1999). ... On Toronto disabled list (May 17-June 6, 2000); included rehabilitation assignment to Dunedin (June 4). ... On Toronto disabled list (April 9-May 10, 2001); included rehabilitation assignment to Dunedin (April 26-May 7). ... Released by Blue Jays (June 29, 2001). ... Signed by Milwaukee Brewers organization (July 3, 2001). ... On Milwaukee disabled list (August 22, 2001-remainder of season). ... Granted free agency (November 9, 2001).

STATISTICAL NOTES: Led Texas League with 10 hit batsmen in 1992.

MISCELLANEOUS: Received base on balls in only appearance as pinch hitter with Colorado (1995). ... Struck out twice in two appearances as pinch hitter (1996).

Year	League	W	L	Pct.	ERA	G	GS	CG	ShO	Sv.	IP	H	R	ER	BB	SO
1990—	Spokane (N'West)	7	3	.700	1.51	23	1	0	0	3	71²/₃	45	18	12	15	104
1991—	Waterloo (Midw.)	14	8	.636	2.30	28	28	7	*4	0	200	162	64	51	57	201
1992—	Wichita (Texas)	10	5	*.667	3.53	27	•27	1	1	0	163¹/₃	138	74	64	55	137
1993—	Colorado Springs (PCL)■..	9	7	.563	4.30	23	22	•4	1	0	138	165	90	66	44	91
—	Colorado (N.L.)	2	2	.500	6.00	10	6	1	0	0	39	52	26	26	9	16
1994—	Colorado Springs (PCL)	4	3	.571	4.79	13	13	1	0	0	71¹/₃	82	38	38	28	59
—	Colorado (N.L.)	4	6	.400	6.11	15	14	0	0	0	73²/₃	91	51	50	26	41
1995—	Colorado (N.L.)	3	0	1.000	4.37	33	1	0	0	1	45¹/₃	55	23	22	10	36
—	Colorado Springs (PCL)	0	3	.000	5.96	11	4	0	0	0	25²/₃	32	20	17	11	12
1996—	Colorado (N.L.)	4	2	.667	5.86	34	1	0	0	0	50²/₃	56	37	33	25	48
1997—	St. Louis (N.L.)■...............	1	1	.500	4.76	14	0	0	0	0	17	13	9	9	8	11
—	Louisville (A.A.)................	1	0	1.000	5.23	18	2	0	0	0	20²/₃	18	14	12	4	22
1998—	St. Louis (N.L.)	4	0	1.000	3.99	65	0	0	0	1	47¹/₃	42	24	21	28	39
1999—	St. Louis (N.L.)	4	5	.444	4.83	56	4	0	0	1	63¹/₃	63	37	34	25	56
—	Arkansas (Texas)	0	0	...	0.00	1	1	0	0	0	2	1	0	0	0	4
2000—	Toronto (A.L.)■...............	2	0	1.000	4.72	42	2	0	0	0	66²/₃	69	37	35	22	53
—	Dunedin (FSL)	0	0	...	0.00	1	1	0	0	0	1	0	0	0	0	0
2001—	Toronto (A.L.)	0	1	.000	7.85	10	0	0	0	0	18¹/₃	27	17	16	11	14
—	Dunedin (FSL)	1	1	.500	0.96	5	1	0	0	0	9¹/₃	10	1	1	1	10
—	Indianapolis (I.L.)■...........	0	0	...	5.00	8	0	0	0	0	9	10	5	5	6	7
—	Milwaukee (N.L.)...............	1	0	1.000	4.22	13	0	0	0	0	10²/₃	11	5	5	7	6
A.L. totals (2 years)		2	1	.667	5.40	52	2	0	0	0	85	96	54	51	33	67
N.L. totals (8 years)		23	16	.590	5.19	240	26	1	0	3	347	383	212	200	138	253
Major League totals (9 years).......		25	17	.595	5.23	292	28	1	0	3	432	479	266	251	171	320

O
P

NOTES: Struck out in only appearance as pinch hitter (1995).

Year	League	W	L	Pct.	ERA	G	GS	CG	ShO	Sv.	IP	H	R	ER	BB	SO
1995—Colorado (N.L.)		0	0	...	5.40	1	1	0	0	0	5	5	3	3	2	4

PALMEIRO, ORLANDO — OF — ANGELS

PERSONAL: Born January 19, 1969, in Hoboken, N.J. ... 5-11/175. ... Bats left, throws left. ... Cousin of Rafael Palmeiro, first baseman, Texas Rangers. ... Name pronounced pal-MAIR-oh.

HIGH SCHOOL: Southridge (Miami).

JUNIOR COLLEGE: Miami-Dade (South) Community College.

COLLEGE: Miami (Fla.).

TRANSACTIONS/CAREER NOTES: Selected by California Angels organization in 33rd round of free-agent draft (June 3, 1991). ... On disabled list (September 1-26, 1994). ... Angels franchise renamed Anaheim Angels for 1997 season. ... On disabled list (August 23-September 7, 1997).

STATISTICAL NOTES: Led Texas League with 18 sacrifice hits in 1993. ... Led Texas League outfielders with 328 total chances in 1993. ... Led Pacific Coast League in caught stealing with 16 in 1994. ... Led Pacific Coast League with 11 sacrifice hits in 1995.

Year	Team (League)	Pos.	G	AB	R	H	2B	3B	HR	RBI	Avg.	BB	SO	SB	PO	A	E	Avg.
1991—Boise (N'West)		OF	70	277	56	77	11	2	1	24	.278	33	22	8	130	8	2	*.986
1992—Quad City (Midw.)		OF	127	451	83	143	22	4	0	41	*.317	56	41	31	211	9	6	.973
1993—Midland (Texas)		OF	131	*535	85	163	19	5	0	64	.305	42	35	18	*307	12	9	.973
1994—Vancouver (PCL)		OF	117	458	79	150	28	4	1	47	.328	58	46	21	254	6	1	.996
1995—Vancouver (PCL)		OF-DH	107	398	66	122	21	4	0	47	.307	41	34	16	192	4	1	*.995
—California (A.L.)		OF-DH	15	20	3	7	0	0	0	1	.350	1	1	0	7	0	0	1.000
1996—Vancouver (PCL)		OF	62	245	40	75	13	4	0	33	.306	30	19	7	113	4	5	.959
—California (A.L.)		OF-DH	50	87	6	25	6	1	0	6	.287	8	13	0	33	0	0	1.000
1997—Anaheim (A.L.)		OF-DH	74	134	19	29	2	2	0	8	.216	17	11	2	78	1	2	.975
1998—Vancouver (PCL)		OF	43	140	21	42	13	3	1	29	.300	16	10	3	70	4	0	1.000
—Anaheim (A.L.)		OF-DH	75	165	28	53	7	2	0	21	.321	20	11	5	92	0	0	1.000
1999—Anaheim (A.L.)		OF-DH	109	317	46	88	12	1	1	23	.278	39	30	5	154	6	1	.994
2000—Anaheim (A.L.)		OF-DH	108	243	38	73	20	2	0	25	.300	38	20	4	117	6	2	.984
2001—Anaheim (A.L.)		OF-DH	104	230	29	56	10	1	2	23	.243	25	24	6	87	2	1	.989
Major League totals (7 years)			535	1196	169	331	57	9	3	107	.277	148	110	22	568	15	6	.990

PALMEIRO, RAFAEL — 1B — RANGERS

PERSONAL: Born September 24, 1964, in Havana, Cuba. ... 6-0/190. ... Bats left, throws left. ... Full name: Rafael Corrales Palmeiro. ... Cousin of Orlando Palmeiro, outfielder, Anaheim Angels. ... Name pronounced pal-MAIR-oh.

HIGH SCHOOL: Jackson (Miami).

COLLEGE: Mississippi State.

TRANSACTIONS/CAREER NOTES: Selected by New York Mets organization in eighth round of free-agent draft (June 7, 1982); did not sign. ... Selected by Chicago Cubs organization in first round (22nd pick overall) of free-agent draft (June 3, 1985); pick received as compensation for San Diego Padres signing Type A free-agent P Tim Stoddard. ... Traded by Cubs with P Jamie Moyer and P Drew Hall to Texas Rangers for P Mitch Williams, P Paul Kilgus, P Steve Wilson, IF Curtis Wilkerson, IF Luis Benitez and OF Pablo Delgado (December 5, 1988). ... Granted free agency (October 25, 1993). ... Signed by Baltimore Orioles (December 12, 1993). ... Granted free agency (October 23, 1998). ... Signed by Rangers (December 4, 1998).

RECORDS: Holds A.L. career record for most major league ballparks, one or more home runs (since 1900)—30. ... Shares A.L. record for most seasons leading league in assists by first baseman—6.

HONORS: Named outfielder on THE SPORTING NEWS college All-America team (1985). ... Named Eastern League Most Valuable Player (1986). ... Won A.L. Gold Glove at first base (1997-99). ... Named first baseman on THE SPORTING NEWS A.L. All-Star team (1998 and 1999). ... Named first baseman on THE SPORTING NEWS A.L. Silver Slugger team (1998). ... Named Major League Player of the Year by THE SPORTING NEWS (1999). ... Named designated hitter on THE SPORTING NEWS A.L. Silver Slugger team (1999).

STATISTICAL NOTES: Led Eastern League with 225 total bases, 13 sacrifice flies and 13 intentional bases on balls received in 1986. ... Had 20-game hitting streak (July 18-August 11, 1988). ... Led A.L. first basemen in total chances with 1,540 in 1993 and 1,510 in 1996. ... Led A.L. first basemen in double plays with 133 in 1993 and 157 in 1996. ... Led A.L. first basemen with 1,568 total chances in 1998. ... Had 24-game hitting streak (April 23-May 22, 1994). ... Career major league grand slams: 9.

Year	Team (League)	Pos.	G	AB	R	H	2B	3B	HR	RBI	Avg.	BB	SO	SB	PO	A	E	Avg.
1985—Peoria (Midw.)............		OF	73	279	34	83	22	4	5	51	.297	31	34	9	113	7	1	.992
1986—Pittsfield (East.)..........		OF	•140	509	66	*156	29	2	12	*95	.306	54	32	15	248	9	3	*.988
—Chicago (N.L.)		OF	22	73	9	18	4	0	3	12	.247	4	6	1	34	2	4	.900
1987—Iowa (A.A.)		OF-1B	57	214	36	64	14	3	11	41	.299	22	22	4	150	13	2	.988
—Chicago (N.L.)		OF-1B	84	221	32	61	15	1	14	30	.276	20	26	2	176	9	1	.995
1988—Chicago (N.L.)		OF-1B	152	580	75	178	41	5	8	53	.307	38	34	12	322	11	5	.985
1989—Texas (A.L.)■............		1B-DH	156	559	76	154	23	4	8	64	.275	63	48	4	1167	*119	12	.991
1990—Texas (A.L.).............		1B-DH	154	598	72	*191	35	6	14	89	.319	40	59	3	1215	91	7	.995
1991—Texas (A.L.).............		1B-DH	159	631	115	203	*49	3	26	88	.322	68	72	4	1305	96	*12	.992
1992—Texas (A.L.).............		1B-DH	159	608	84	163	27	4	22	85	.268	72	83	2	1251	*143	7	.995
1993—Texas (A.L.).............		1B	160	597	*124	176	40	2	37	105	.295	73	85	22	*1388	*147	5	.997
1994—Baltimore (A.L.)■......		1B	111	436	82	139	32	0	23	76	.319	54	63	7	959	66	4	.996
1995—Baltimore (A.L.).........		1B	143	554	89	172	30	2	39	104	.310	62	65	3	1181	*119	4	.997
1996—Baltimore (A.L.).........		1B-DH	162	626	110	181	40	2	39	142	.289	95	96	8	*1383	*119	8	.995
1997—Baltimore (A.L.).........		1B-DH	158	614	95	156	24	2	38	110	.254	67	109	5	1305	112	10	.993
1998—Baltimore (A.L.).........		1B-DH	162	619	98	183	36	1	43	121	.296	79	91	11	*1435	*124	9	.994
1999—Texas (A.L.)■...........		DH-1B	158	565	96	183	30	1	47	148	.324	97	69	2	261	13	1	.996
2000—Texas (A.L.)..............		1B-DH	158	565	102	163	29	3	39	120	.288	103	77	2	820	56	4	.995
2001—Texas (A.L.)..............		1B-DH	160	600	98	164	33	0	47	123	.273	101	90	1	906	83	8	.992
American League totals (13 years)			2000	7572	1241	2228	428	30	422	1375	.294	974	1007	74	14576	1288	91	.994
National League totals (3 years)			258	874	116	257	60	6	25	95	.294	62	66	15	532	22	10	.982
Major League totals (16 years)			2258	8446	1357	2485	488	36	447	1470	.294	1036	1073	89	15108	1310	101	.994

P

DIVISION SERIES RECORD

					BATTING									FIELDING		
Year	Team (League)	Pos.	G	AB	R	H	2B	3B	HR	RBI	Avg.	BB	SO	SB	PO	A	E	Avg.
1996—	Baltimore (A.L.)..........	1B	4	17	4	3	1	0	1	2	.176	1	6	0	35	1	1	.973
1997—	Baltimore (A.L.)..........	1B	4	12	2	3	2	0	0	0	.250	0	2	0	27	2	0	1.000
1999—	Texas (A.L.)	DH	3	11	0	3	0	0	0	0	.273	1	1	0	...	...	...	...
Division series totals (3 years)			11	40	6	9	3	0	1	2	.225	2	9	0	62	3	1	.985

CHAMPIONSHIP SERIES RECORD

NOTES: Hit home run in first at-bat (October 9, 1996).

					BATTING									FIELDING		
Year	Team (League)	Pos.	G	AB	R	H	2B	3B	HR	RBI	Avg.	BB	SO	SB	PO	A	E	Avg.
1996—	Baltimore (A.L.).........	1B	5	17	4	4	0	0	2	4	.235	4	4	0	44	3	0	1.000
1997—	Baltimore (A.L.)..........	1B	6	25	3	7	2	0	1	2	.280	0	10	0	55	2	0	1.000
Championship series totals (2 years)			11	42	7	11	2	0	3	6	.262	4	14	0	99	5	0	1.000

ALL-STAR GAME RECORD

			BATTING										FIELDING		
Year	League	Pos.	AB	R	H	2B	3B	HR	RBI	Avg.	BB	SO	SB	PO	A	E	Avg.
1988—	National	PH-OF	0	0	0	0	0	0	0	...	1	0	0	1	0	0	1.000
1991—	American	1B	0	0	0	0	0	0	0	...	1	0	0	2	0	0	1.000
1998—	American	1B	2	1	2	0	0	0	1	1.000	0	0	0	2	0	0	1.000
1999—	American	DH	2	0	1	0	0	0	0	.500	0	0	0	...	...	...	...
All-Star Game totals (4 years)			4	1	3	0	0	0	2	.750	2	0	0	5	0	0	1.000

PALMER, DEAN   DH/3B   TIGERS

PERSONAL: Born December 27, 1968, in Tallahassee, Fla. ... 6-1/210. ... Bats right, throws right. ... Full name: Dean William Palmer.

HIGH SCHOOL: Florida (Tallahassee, Fla.).

TRANSACTIONS/CAREER NOTES: Selected by Texas Rangers organization in third round of free-agent draft (June 2, 1986). ... On disabled list (July 19, 1988-remainder of season; April 28-May 13, 1994; and June 4-September 22, 1995). ... Traded by Rangers to Kansas City Royals for OF Tom Goodwin (July 25, 1997). ... Granted free agency (October 27, 1997). ... Re-signed by Royals (December 15, 1997). ... Granted free agency (October 23, 1998). ... Signed by Detroit Tigers (November 13, 1998). ... On suspended list (April 28-May 5 and June 15-18, 2000). ... On Detroit disabled list (March 23-April 7, April 13-29 and July 3, 2001-remainder of season); included rehabilitation assignment to Toledo (April 28-29). ... On suspended list (June 15-18, 2001).

RECORDS: Shares major league single-season record for fewest assists by third baseman (150 or more games)—221 (1996). ... Holds A.L. single-season record for fewest chances accepted by third baseman (150 or more games)—326 (1996). ... Shares A.L. single-season record for fewest double plays by third baseman (150 or more games)—17 (1996).

HONORS: Named third baseman on THE SPORTING NEWS A.L. Silver Slugger team (1998 and 1999). ... Named third baseman on THE SPORTING NEWS A.L. All-Star team (1999).

STATISTICAL NOTES: Led Texas League third basemen with 30 errors in 1989. ... Led A.L. third basemen with 29 errors in 1993. ... Career major league grand slams: 8.

					BATTING									FIELDING		
Year	Team (League)	Pos.	G	AB	R	H	2B	3B	HR	RBI	Avg.	BB	SO	SB	PO	A	E	Avg.
1986—	GC Rangers (GCL)......	3B	50	163	19	34	7	1	0	12	.209	22	34	6	25	75	13	.885
1987—	Gastonia (S.Atl.).........	3B	128	484	51	104	16	0	9	54	.215	36	126	5	58	209	*59	.819
1988—	Charlotte (FSL)..........	3B	74	305	38	81	12	1	4	35	.266	15	69	0	49	144	28	.873
1989—	Tulsa (Texas)	3B-SS	133	498	82	125	32	5	*25	90	.251	41	*152	15	85	213	†31	.906
	— Texas (A.L.) 3B-DH-SS-OF	16	19	0	2	2	0	0	1	.105	0	12	0	3	4	2	.778
1990—	Tulsa (Texas)	3B	7	24	4	7	0	1	3	9	.292	4	10	0	9	6	3	.833
	— Oklahoma City (A.A.)..	3B-1B	88	316	33	69	17	4	12	39	.218	20	106	1	206	110	21	.938
1991—	Oklahoma City (A.A.)..	3B-OF	60	234	45	70	11	2	*22	59	.299	20	61	4	49	105	11	.933
	— Texas (A.L.) 3B-OF-DH	81	268	38	50	9	2	15	37	.187	32	98	0	69	75	9	.941
1992—	Texas (A.L.)	3B	152	541	74	124	25	0	26	72	.229	62	*154	10	124	254	22	.945
1993—	Texas (A.L.)	3B-SS	148	519	88	127	31	2	33	96	.245	53	154	11	86	258	†29	.922
1994—	Texas (A.L.)	3B	93	342	50	84	14	2	19	59	.246	26	89	3	50	179	*22	.912
1995—	Texas (A.L.)	3B	36	119	30	40	6	0	9	24	.336	21	21	1	19	72	5	.948
1996—	Texas (A.L.)	3B-DH	154	582	98	163	26	2	38	107	.280	59	145	2	105	221	16	.953
1997—	Texas (A.L.)	3B	94	355	47	87	21	0	14	55	.245	26	84	1	72	162	10	.959
	— Kansas City (A.L.)■..	3B-DH	49	187	23	52	10	1	9	31	.278	15	50	1	27	82	9	.924
1998—	Kansas City (A.L.)	3B-DH	152	572	84	159	27	2	34	119	.278	48	134	8	69	187	22	.921
1999—	Detroit (A.L.)■.........	3B-DH	150	560	92	147	25	2	38	100	.263	57	153	3	89	240	19	.945
2000—	Detroit (A.L.)	3B-1B-DH	145	524	73	134	22	2	29	102	.256	66	146	4	188	185	25	.937
2001—	Toledo (I.L.)...............	DH	1	2	0	1	0	0	0	0	.500	2	0	0	...	...	...	...
	— Detroit (A.L.)	DH	57	216	34	48	11	0	11	40	.222	27	59	4	...	...	...	...
Major League totals (12 years)			1327	4804	731	1217	229	15	275	843	.253	492	1299	48	901	1919	190	.937

DIVISION SERIES RECORD

					BATTING									FIELDING		
Year	Team (League)	Pos.	G	AB	R	H	2B	3B	HR	RBI	Avg.	BB	SO	SB	PO	A	E	Avg.
1996—	Texas (A.L.)	3B	4	19	3	4	1	0	1	2	.211	0	5	0	3	10	1	.929

ALL-STAR GAME RECORD

			BATTING										FIELDING		
Year	League	Pos.	AB	R	H	2B	3B	HR	RBI	Avg.	BB	SO	SB	PO	A	E	Avg.
1998—	American	PH	1	0	0	0	0	0	0	.000	0	0	0	...	...	...	...

P

PERSONAL: Born August 20, 1973, in San Jose de Ocoa, Dominican Republic. ... 6-2/190. ... Throws right, bats right. ... Full name: Jose Luis Sanchez Paniagua.

HIGH SCHOOL: Liceo Nuestra Senora del Altagracia (Santo Domingo, Dominican Republic).

TRANSACTIONS/CAREER NOTES: Signed as non-drafted free agent by Montreal Expos organization (September 17, 1990). ... On Montreal disabled list (May 25-June 11, 1996). ... On Ottawa disabled list (July 16-August 2, 1996). ... Selected by Tampa Bay Devil Rays in second round (50th pick overall) of expansion draft (November 18, 1997). ... Claimed on waivers by Seattle Mariners (March 26, 1998). ... On suspended list (August 10-16, 1999; and August 22-24, 2001). ... Traded by Mariners with P Dennis Stark and P Brian Fuentes to Colorado Rockies for 3B Jeff Cirillo (December 15, 2001).

Year League	W	L	Pct.	ERA	G	GS	CG	ShO	Sv.	IP	H	R	ER	BB	SO
1991— Dominican Expos (DSL)	2	2	.500	2.18	13	2	0	0	0	33	24	16	8	17	19
1992— Dominican Expos (DSL)	3	7	.300	4.15	13	13	3	1	0	73²/₃	69	50	34	46	60
1993— Gulf Coast Expos (GCL)	3	0	1.000	0.67	4	4	1	0	0	27	13	2	2	5	25
1994— West Palm Beach (FSL)	9	9	.500	3.64	26	26	1	0	0	141	131	82	57	54	110
1995— Harrisburg (East.)	7	•12	.368	5.34	25	25	2	1	0	126¹/₃	140	84	75	62	89
1996— Ottawa (I.L.)	9	5	.643	3.18	15	14	2	1	0	85	72	39	30	23	61
— Montreal (N.L.)	2	4	.333	3.53	13	11	0	0	0	51	55	24	20	23	27
— Harrisburg (East.)	3	0	1.000	0.00	3	3	0	0	0	18	12	1	0	2	16
1997— West Palm Beach (FSL)	1	0	1.000	0.00	2	2	0	0	0	10	5	0	0	2	11
— Ottawa (I.L.)	8	10	.444	4.64	22	22	1	0	0	137²/₃	164	79	71	44	87
— Montreal (N.L.)	1	2	.333	12.00	9	3	0	0	0	18	29	24	24	16	8
1998— Tacoma (PCL)■	3	1	.750	2.77	44	0	0	0	5	68¹/₃	66	25	21	22	61
— Seattle (A.L.)	2	0	1.000	2.05	18	0	0	0	1	22	15	5	5	5	16
1999— Seattle (A.L.)	6	11	.353	4.06	59	0	0	0	3	77²/₃	75	37	35	52	74
2000— Seattle (A.L.)	3	0	1.000	3.47	69	0	0	0	5	80¹/₃	68	31	31	38	71
2001— Seattle (A.L.)	4	3	.571	4.36	60	0	0	0	3	66	59	35	32	38	46
A.L. totals (4 years)	15	14	.517	3.77	206	0	0	0	12	246	217	108	103	133	207
N.L. totals (2 years)	3	6	.333	5.74	22	14	0	0	0	69	84	48	44	39	35
Major League totals (6 years)	18	20	.474	4.20	228	14	0	0	12	315	301	156	147	172	242

DIVISION SERIES RECORD

Year League	W	L	Pct.	ERA	G	GS	CG	ShO	Sv.	IP	H	R	ER	BB	SO
2000— Seattle (A.L.)	1	0	1.000	0.00	2	0	0	0	0	2¹/₃	1	0	0	2	3
2001— Seattle (A.L.)	0	0	...	27.00	2	0	0	0	0	2	4	6	6	2	1
Division series totals (2 years)	1	0	1.000	12.46	4	0	0	0	0	4¹/₃	5	6	6	4	4

CHAMPIONSHIP SERIES RECORD

Year League	W	L	Pct.	ERA	G	GS	CG	ShO	Sv.	IP	H	R	ER	BB	SO
2000— Seattle (A.L.)	0	1	.000	4.15	5	0	0	0	0	4¹/₃	4	2	2	1	4
2001— Seattle (A.L.)	0	0	...	12.27	3	0	0	0	0	3²/₃	7	5	5	1	1
Champ. series totals (2 years)	0	1	.000	7.88	8	0	0	0	0	8	11	7	7	2	5

PERSONAL: Born March 28, 1969, in Long Beach, Calif. ... 6-0/190. ... Bats right, throws right. ... Full name: Craig Howard Paquette.

HIGH SCHOOL: Ranchos Alamitos (Garden Grove, Calif.).

JUNIOR COLLEGE: Golden West College (Calif.).

TRANSACTIONS/CAREER NOTES: Selected by Minnesota Twins organization in 36th round of free-agent draft (June 2, 1987); did not sign. ... Selected by Oakland Athletics organization in eighth round of free-agent draft (June 5, 1989). ... On Modesto disabled list (April 10-May 5, 1991). ... On Huntsville disabled list (June 1-11, 1991). ... On Tacoma disabled list (July 18, 1994-remainder of season). ... Released by A's (March 26, 1996). ... Signed by Kansas City Royals organization (April 3, 1996). ... Granted free agency (October 15, 1997). ... Signed by New York Mets organization (December 23, 1997). ... On New York disabled list (May 7, 1998-remainder of season). ... Granted free agency (October 15, 1998). ... Re-signed by Mets organization (December 18, 1998). ... On Norfolk disabled list (April 22-May 1, 1999). ... Traded by Mets to St. Louis Cardinals for IF/OF Shawon Dunston (July 31, 1999). ... Granted free agency (November 5, 2001). ... Signed by Detroit Tigers (December 13, 2001).

STATISTICAL NOTES: Tied for Northwest League lead with 163 total bases in 1989. ... Led Northwest League third basemen with .936 fielding percentage and 12 double plays in 1989. ... Led Southern League third basemen with 349 total chances in 1992. ... Career major league grand slams: 2.

Year Team (League)	Pos.	G	AB	R	H	2B	3B	HR	RBI	Avg.	BB	SO	SB	PO	A	E	Avg.
1989— S. Oregon (N'West)	3B-SS-2B	71	277	53	93	*22	3	14	56	.336	30	46	9	61	155	15	†.935
1990— Modesto (Calif.)	3B	130	495	65	118	23	4	15	59	.238	47	123	8	*88	218	26	*.922
1991— Huntsville (Sou.)	3B-1B	102	378	50	99	18	1	8	60	.262	28	87	0	51	132	16	.920
1992— Huntsville (Sou.)	3B	115	450	59	116	25	4	17	71	.258	29	118	13	69	*248	*32	.908
— Tacoma (PCL)	3B	17	66	10	18	7	0	2	11	.273	2	16	3	14	33	3	.940
1993— Tacoma (PCL)	3B	50	183	29	49	8	0	8	29	.268	14	54	3	32	116	15	.908
— Oakland (A.L.)	3B-DH-OF	105	393	35	86	20	4	12	46	.219	14	108	4	82	165	13	.950
1994— Tacoma (PCL)	3B	65	245	39	70	12	3	17	48	.286	14	48	3	40	166	14	.936
— Oakland (A.L.)	3B	14	49	0	7	2	0	0	0	.143	0	14	1	14	22	0	1.000
1995— Oakland (A.L.)	3-0-S-1	105	283	42	64	13	1	13	49	.226	12	88	5	72	92	8	.953
1996— Omaha (A.A.)■	DH-3B-1B-OF	18	63	9	21	3	0	4	13	.333	8	14	1	24	9	3	.917
— Kansas City (A.L.)	3-O-1-S-DH	118	429	61	111	15	1	22	67	.259	23	101	5	261	102	14	.963
1997— Kansas City (A.L.)	3B-OF	77	252	26	58	15	1	8	33	.230	10	57	2	51	130	12	.938
— Omaha (A.A.)	3B-DH	23	91	9	28	6	0	3	20	.308	6	26	0	12	29	2	.953
1998— Norfolk (I.L.)■	3B-SS-OF	15	61	11	17	1	1	3	14	.279	1	13	2	9	39	4	.923
— New York (N.L.)	3B-1B-OF	7	19	3	5	2	0	0	0	.263	0	6	1	5	2	0	1.000
1999— Norfolk (I.L.)	3B-OF-1B-SS	70	283	40	77	20	3	15	54	.272	10	47	3	168	82	8	.969
— St. Louis (N.L.)■	OF-3B-2B-1B	48	157	21	45	6	0	10	37	.287	6	38	1	75	42	3	.975
2000— St. Louis (N.L.)	3B-OF-1B-2B	134	384	47	94	24	2	15	61	.245	27	83	4	216	123	15	.958
2001— St. Louis (N.L.)	3B-OF-1B-2B	123	340	47	96	17	0	15	64	.282	18	67	3	218	52	5	.982
American League totals (5 years)		419	1406	164	326	65	7	55	195	.232	59	368	17	480	511	47	.955
National League totals (4 years)		312	900	118	240	49	2	40	162	.267	51	194	9	514	219	23	.970
Major League totals (9 years)		731	2306	282	566	114	9	95	357	.245	110	562	26	994	730	70	.961

DIVISION SERIES RECORD

							BATTING								FIELDING		
Year	Team (League)	Pos.	G	AB	R	H	2B	3B	HR	RBI	Avg.	BB	SO	SB	PO	A	E	Avg.
2000— St. Louis (N.L.)..........		OF-3B	2	2	0	0	0	0	0	0	.000	0	0	0	2	0	0	1.000
2001— St. Louis (N.L.)..........		OF-3B	2	7	0	1	0	0	0	0	.143	0	5	0	2	1	0	1.000
Division series totals (2 years)			4	9	0	1	0	0	0	0	.111	0	5	0	4	1	0	1.000

CHAMPIONSHIP SERIES RECORD

							BATTING								FIELDING		
Year	Team (League)	Pos.	G	AB	R	H	2B	3B	HR	RBI	Avg.	BB	SO	SB	PO	A	E	Avg.
2000— St. Louis (N.L.)..........		3B-OF-PH	4	6	0	1	0	0	0	0	.167	0	2	0	2	1	0	1.000

PARADIS, MIKE P ORIOLES

PERSONAL: Born May 3, 1978, in Worcester, Mass. ... 6-3/190. ... Throws right, bats right. ... Full name: Michael Paul Paradis.
HIGH SCHOOL: Auburn (Mass.).
COLLEGE: Clemson.
TRANSACTIONS/CAREER NOTES: Selected by Oakland Athletics organization in seventh round of free-agent draft (June 4, 1996); did not sign. ... Selected by Baltimore Orioles organization in first round (13th pick overall) of free-agent draft (June 2, 1999).

Year	League	W	L	Pct.	ERA	G	GS	CG	ShO	Sv.	IP	H	R	ER	BB	SO
1999— Delmarva (S.Atl.)................		0	1	.000	15.00	2	2	0	0	0	3	3	5	5	4	6
2000— Delmarva (S.Atl.)................		6	5	.545	3.99	18	18	0	0	0	97	95	53	43	49	81
—Frederick (Caro.)		2	5	.286	4.17	8	8	1	0	0	45 1/3	55	24	21	24	32
2001— Bowie (East.)		8	13	.381	4.71	27	26	1	0	0	137 2/3	157	•98	72	62	108

PARK, CHAN HO P RANGERS

PERSONAL: Born June 30, 1973, in Kong Ju City, Korea. ... 6-2/204. ... Throws right, bats right.
HIGH SCHOOL: Kong Ju (Kong Ju City, Korea).
COLLEGE: Hanyang University (Seoul, Korea).
TRANSACTIONS/CAREER NOTES: Signed as non-drafted free agent by Los Angeles Dodgers organization (January 14, 1994). ... On Albuquerque disabled list (July 16-29, 1995). ... On suspended list (June 8-17, 1999). ... Granted free agency (November 5, 2001). ... Signed by Texas Rangers (December 23, 2001).
RECORDS: Shares major league single-season record for most grand slams allowed—4 (1999).
STATISTICAL NOTES: Tied for N.L. lead with 20 hit batsmen and with three balks in 2001.

Year	League	W	L	Pct.	ERA	G	GS	CG	ShO	Sv.	IP	H	R	ER	BB	SO
1994— Los Angeles (N.L.)		0	0	...	11.25	2	0	0	0	0	4	5	5	5	5	6
—San Antonio (Texas)..........		5	7	.417	3.55	20	20	0	0	0	101 1/3	91	52	40	57	100
1995— Albuquerque (PCL)............		6	7	.462	4.91	23	22	0	0	0	110	93	64	60	76	101
—Los Angeles (N.L.)		0	0	...	4.50	2	1	0	0	0	4	2	2	2	2	7
1996— Los Angeles (N.L.)		5	5	.500	3.64	48	10	0	0	0	108 2/3	82	48	44	71	119
1997— Los Angeles (N.L.)		14	8	.636	3.38	32	29	2	0	0	192	149	80	72	70	166
1998— Los Angeles (N.L.)		15	9	.625	3.71	34	34	2	0	0	220 2/3	199	101	91	97	191
1999— Los Angeles (N.L.)		13	11	.542	5.23	33	33	0	0	0	194 1/3	208	120	113	100	174
2000— Los Angeles (N.L.)		18	10	.643	3.27	34	34	3	1	0	226	173	92	82	124	217
2001— Los Angeles (N.L.)		15	11	.577	3.50	36	•35	2	1	0	234	183	98	91	91	218
Major League totals (8 years).......		80	54	.597	3.80	221	176	9	2	0	1183 2/3	1001	546	500	560	1098

ALL-STAR GAME RECORD

Year	League	W	L	Pct.	ERA	GS	CG	ShO	Sv.	IP	H	R	ER	BB	SO
2001— National		0	1	.000	9.00	0	0	0	0	1	1	1	1	0	1

PARKER, CHRISTIAN P YANKEES

PERSONAL: Born July 3, 1975, in Albuquerque, N.M. ... 6-1/200. ... Throws right, bats right. ... Full name: Christian Michael Parker.
HIGH SCHOOL: Eldorado (Albuquerque, N.M.).
COLLEGE: Notre Dame.
TRANSACTIONS/CAREER NOTES: Selected by Montreal Expos organization in fourth round of free-agent draft (June 4, 1996). ... Traded by Expos to New York Yankees (March 22, 2000), completing deal in which Yankees traded P Hideki Irabu to Expos for P Jake Westbrook and two players to be named later (December 22, 1999). ... On disabled list (April 10, 2001-remainder of season).

Year	League	W	L	Pct.	ERA	G	GS	CG	ShO	Sv.	IP	H	R	ER	BB	SO
1996— Vermont (NY-Penn)...........		7	1	.875	2.47	14	14	2	1	0	80	63	26	22	22	61
1997— Cape Fear (S.Atl.)		11	10	.524	3.12	25	25	0	0	0	153	146	72	53	49	106
—West Palm Beach (FSL)		0	1	.000	3.32	3	3	0	0	0	19	22	7	7	5	10
1998— Harrisburg (East.)..............		6	6	.500	3.48	36	16	0	0	5	126 2/3	124	66	49	47	73
1999— Ottawa (I.L.)		0	1	.000	7.59	7	0	0	0	0	10 2/3	10	9	9	7	5
—Harrisburg (East.)		8	5	.615	3.65	36	6	0	0	3	88 2/3	86	39	36	37	45
2000— Norwich (East.)■...............		14	6	.700	3.13	28	28	4	0	0	204	196	86	71	58	147
2001— New York (A.L.)		0	1	.000	21.00	1	1	0	0	0	3	8	7	7	1	1
Major League totals (1 year)........		0	1	.000	21.00	1	1	0	0	0	3	8	7	7	1	1

PARONTO, CHAD P INDIANS

PERSONAL: Born July 28, 1975, in Woodsville, N.H. ... 6-5/225. ... Throws right, bats right. ... Full name: Chad Michael Paronto. ... Nephew of Dennis Paronto, pitcher with Atlanta Braves organization.
HIGH SCHOOL: Woodsville (N.H.).
COLLEGE: Massachusetts.
TRANSACTIONS/CAREER NOTES: Selected by Baltimore Orioles organization in eighth round of free-agent draft (June 4, 1996). ... On Bowie disabled list (April 7-June 2, 2000). ... Claimed on waivers by Cleveland Indians (November 19, 2001).

P

Year	League	W	L	Pct.	ERA	G	GS	CG	ShO	Sv.	IP	H	R	ER	BB	SO
1996—Bluefield (Appl.)		1	1	.500	1.69	9	2	0	0	1	21 1/3	16	4	4	5	24
—Frederick (Caro.)		0	1	.000	4.80	8	1	0	0	0	15	11	9	8	8	6
1997—Delmarva (S.Atl.)		6	9	.400	4.74	28	23	0	0	0	127 1/3	133	95	67	56	93
1998—Frederick (Caro.)		7	6	.538	3.13	18	18	0	0	0	103 2/3	116	44	36	39	87
—Bowie (East.)		1	3	.250	5.80	8	7	0	0	1	35 2/3	38	30	23	23	28
1999—Bowie (East.)		0	4	.000	8.12	15	9	0	0	0	41	59	39	37	32	27
—Frederick (Caro.)		3	5	.375	4.73	13	13	1	0	0	72 1/3	81	46	38	26	55
2000—Rochester (I.L.)		1	1	.500	5.75	12	6	0	0	0	36	40	26	23	15	18
—Bowie (East.)		4	2	.667	2.87	8	8	1	0	0	47	29	19	15	16	31
2001—Rochester (I.L.)		3	3	.500	4.57	33	0	0	0	1	43 1/3	44	28	22	24	39
—Baltimore (A.L.)		1	3	.250	5.00	24	0	0	0	0	27	33	24	15	11	16
Major League totals (1 year)		1	3	.250	5.00	24	0	0	0	0	27	33	24	15	11	16

PARQUE, JIM   P   WHITE SOX

PERSONAL: Born February 8, 1976, in Norwalk, Calif. ... 5-11/165. ... Throws left, bats left. ... Full name: James Vo Parque.
HIGH SCHOOL: Crescenta Valley (Calif.).
COLLEGE: UCLA.
TRANSACTIONS/CAREER NOTES: Selected by Chicago White Sox organization in second round of free-agent draft (June 3, 1997). ... On suspended list (May 7-9, 2000). ... On disabled list (April 27, 2001-remainder of season).
STATISTICAL NOTES: Tied for A.L. lead with three balks in 1998. ... Led A.L. with five balks in 2000.
MISCELLANEOUS: Member of 1996 U.S. Olympic baseball team.

Year	League	W	L	Pct.	ERA	G	GS	CG	ShO	Sv.	IP	H	R	ER	BB	SO
1997—Winston-Salem (Caro.)		7	2	.778	2.77	11	11	0	0	0	61 2/3	29	19	19	23	76
—Nashville (PCL)		1	0	1.000	4.22	2	2	0	0	0	10 2/3	9	5	5	9	5
1998—Calgary (PCL)		2	3	.400	3.94	8	8	0	0	0	48	49	26	21	25	31
—Chicago (A.L.)		7	5	.583	5.10	21	21	0	0	0	113	135	72	64	49	77
1999—Chicago (A.L.)		9	15	.375	5.13	31	30	1	0	0	173 2/3	210	111	99	79	111
2000—Chicago (A.L.)		13	6	.684	4.28	33	32	0	0	0	187	208	105	89	71	111
2001—Chicago (A.L.)		0	3	.000	8.04	5	5	1	0	0	28	36	26	25	10	15
Major League totals (4 years)		29	29	.500	4.97	90	88	2	0	0	501 2/3	589	314	277	209	314

DIVISION SERIES RECORD

Year	League	W	L	Pct.	ERA	G	GS	CG	ShO	Sv.	IP	H	R	ER	BB	SO
2000—Chicago (A.L.)		0	0	...	4.50	1	1	0	0	0	6	6	3	3	1	2

PARRIS, STEVE   P   BLUE JAYS

PERSONAL: Born December 17, 1967, in Joliet, Ill. ... 6-0/195. ... Throws right, bats right. ... Full name: Steven Michael Parris.
HIGH SCHOOL: Joliet (Ill.) West.
COLLEGE: College of St. Francis (Ill.).
TRANSACTIONS/CAREER NOTES: Selected by Philadelphia Phillies organization in fifth round of free-agent draft (June 5, 1989). ... Claimed on waivers by Los Angeles Dodgers (April 19, 1993). ... Claimed on waivers by Seattle Mariners (April 26, 1993). ... On Jacksonville disabled list (May 12-June 23 and July 17-31, 1993). ... Released by Mariners (July 31, 1993). ... Signed by Pittsburgh Pirates organization (June 24, 1994). ... On Pittsburgh disabled list (March 6-July 11 and August 18-September 10, 1996); included rehabilitation assignments to Augusta (June 12-13) and Carolina (June 13-July 11). ... Released by Pirates (March 13, 1997). ... Signed by Cincinnati Reds organization (May 6, 1997). ... Granted free agency (October 15, 1997). ... Re-signed by Reds organization (October 27, 1997). ... On Cincinnati disabled list (July 31-September 1, 1999); included rehabilitation assignment to Indianapolis (August 22-30). ... Traded by Reds to Toronto Blue Jays for P Clayton Andrews and P Leo Estrella (November 22, 2000). ... On Toronto disabled list (July 24, 2001-remainder of season); included rehabilitation assignments to Tennessee (August 24-29) and Syracuse (August 30-September 4).
MISCELLANEOUS: Scored one run in two appearances as pinch runner (2000).

Year	League	W	L	Pct.	ERA	G	GS	CG	ShO	Sv.	IP	H	R	ER	BB	SO
1989—Batavia (NY-Penn)		3	5	.375	3.91	13	10	1	0	0	66 2/3	69	38	29	20	46
1990—Batavia (NY-Penn)		7	1	*.875	2.64	14	14	0	0	0	81 2/3	70	34	24	22	50
1991—Clearwater (FSL)		7	5	.583	3.39	43	6	0	0	1	93	101	43	35	25	59
1992—Reading (East.)		5	7	.417	4.64	18	14	0	0	0	85 1/3	94	55	44	21	60
—Scranton/W.B. (I.L.)		3	3	.500	4.03	11	6	0	0	1	51 1/3	57	25	23	17	29
1993—Scranton/W.B. (I.L.)		0	0	...	12.71	3	0	0	0	0	5 2/3	9	9	8	3	4
—Jacksonville (Sou.)■		0	1	.000	5.93	7	1	0	0	0	13 2/3	15	9	9	6	5
1994—Salem (Caro.)■		3	3	.500	3.63	17	7	0	0	0	57	58	24	23	21	48
1995—Carolina (Sou.)		9	1	.900	2.51	14	14	2	2	0	89 2/3	61	25	25	16	86
—Pittsburgh (N.L.)		6	6	.500	5.38	15	15	1	1	0	82	89	49	49	33	61
1996—Augusta (S.Atl.)		0	0	...	0.00	1	1	0	0	0	5	1	0	0	1	6
—Carolina (Sou.)		2	0	1.000	3.04	5	5	0	0	0	26 2/3	24	11	9	6	22
—Pittsburgh (N.L.)		0	3	.000	7.18	8	4	0	0	0	26 1/3	35	22	21	11	27
1997—Chattanooga (Sou.)■		6	2	.750	4.13	14	14	0	0	0	80 2/3	78	44	37	29	68
—Indianapolis (A.A.)		2	3	.400	3.57	5	5	1	1	0	35 1/3	26	15	14	11	27
1998—Indianapolis (I.L.)		6	1	.857	3.84	13	13	1	1	0	84 1/3	74	38	36	26	102
—Cincinnati (N.L.)		6	5	.545	3.73	18	16	1	1	0	99	89	44	41	32	77
1999—Indianapolis (I.L.)		0	2	.000	4.04	6	6	0	0	0	35 2/3	39	16	16	9	31
—Cincinnati (N.L.)		11	4	.733	3.50	22	21	2	1	0	128 2/3	124	59	50	52	86
2000—Cincinnati (N.L.)		12	17	.414	4.81	33	33	0	0	0	192 2/3	227	109	103	71	117
2001—Toronto (A.L.)■		4	6	.400	4.60	19	19	1	0	0	105 2/3	126	60	54	41	49
—Tennessee (Sou.)		0	0	...	0.00	1	1	0	0	0	3	2	0	0	1	2
—Syracuse (I.L.)		0	0	...	4.70	2	2	0	0	0	7 2/3	6	4	4	2	8
A.L. totals (1 year)		4	6	.400	4.60	19	19	1	0	0	105 2/3	126	60	54	41	49
N.L. totals (5 years)		35	35	.500	4.49	96	89	4	3	0	528 2/3	564	283	264	199	368
Major League totals (6 years)		39	41	.488	4.51	115	108	5	3	0	634 1/3	690	343	318	240	417

P

PARRISH, JOHN   P   ORIOLES

PERSONAL: Born November 26, 1977, in Lancaster, Pa. ... 5-11/180. ... Throws left, bats left. ... Full name: John Henry Parrish Jr.
HIGH SCHOOL: J.P. McCaskey (Lancaster, Pa.).
TRANSACTIONS/CAREER NOTES: Selected by Baltimore Orioles organization in 25th round of free-agent draft (June 4, 1996).

Year League	W	L	Pct.	ERA	G	GS	CG	ShO	Sv.	IP	H	R	ER	BB	SO
1996— Gulf Coast Orioles (GCL)....	2	0	1.000	1.86	11	0	0	0	2	19 1/3	13	5	4	11	33
— Bluefield (Appl.)	2	1	.667	2.70	8	0	0	0	1	13 1/3	11	6	4	9	18
1997— Delmarva (S.Atl.)................	3	3	.500	3.84	23	10	0	0	1	72 2/3	69	39	31	32	76
— Bowie (East.).....................	1	0	1.000	1.80	1	1	0	0	0	5	3	1	1	2	3
— Frederick (Caro.)	1	3	.250	6.04	5	5	0	0	0	22 1/3	23	18	15	16	17
1998— Frederick (Caro.)	4	4	.500	3.27	16	16	1	0	0	82 2/3	77	39	30	27	81
1999— Delmarva (S.Atl.)................	0	1	.000	7.20	4	0	0	0	0	10	9	8	8	6	10
— Frederick (Caro.)	2	2	.500	4.17	6	6	0	0	0	36 2/3	34	17	17	12	44
— Bowie (East.).....................	0	2	.000	4.04	12	10	0	0	0	55 2/3	49	28	25	43	42
2000— Bowie (East.).....................	2	0	1.000	1.69	3	3	0	0	0	16	12	3	3	7	16
— Rochester (I.L.)................	6	7	.462	4.24	18	18	0	0	0	104	85	54	49	56	87
— Baltimore (A.L.)................	2	4	.333	7.18	8	8	0	0	0	36 1/3	40	32	29	35	28
2001— Rochester (I.L.)................	7	7	.500	3.52	26	19	1	0	0	133	115	68	52	51	126
— Baltimore (A.L.)................	1	2	.333	6.14	16	1	0	0	0	22	22	17	15	17	20
Major League totals (2 years)	3	6	.333	6.79	24	9	0	0	0	58 1/3	62	49	44	52	48

PATTERSON, COREY   OF   CUBS

PERSONAL: Born August 13, 1979, in Atlanta. ... 5-10/180. ... Bats left, throws right. ... Full name: Donald Corey Patterson. ... Son of Don Patterson, defensive back with Detroit Lions (1979) and New York Giants (1980).
HIGH SCHOOL: Harrison (Kennesaw, Ga.).
TRANSACTIONS/CAREER NOTES: Selected by Chicago Cubs organization in first round (third pick overall) of free-agent draft (June 2, 1998). ... On disabled list (May 27-June 11, 1999).
STATISTICAL NOTES: Led Midwest League in slugging percentage with .592 in 1999.

Year Team (League)	Pos.	G	AB	R	H	2B	3B	HR	RBI	Avg.	BB	SO	SB	PO	A	E	Avg.
1999— Lansing (Midw.)	OF	112	475	94	152	35	*17	20	79	.320	25	85	33	244	7	9	.965
2000— West Tenn (Sou.)	OF	118	444	73	116	26	5	22	82	.261	45	115	27	296	7	3	.990
— Chicago (N.L.)..............	OF	11	42	9	7	1	0	2	2	.167	3	14	1	26	0	1	.963
2001— Iowa (PCL)	OF	89	367	63	93	22	3	7	32	.253	29	65	19	180	3	6	.968
— Chicago (N.L.)............	OF	59	131	26	29	3	0	4	14	.221	6	33	4	82	0	2	.976
Major League totals (2 years)		70	173	35	36	4	0	6	16	.208	9	47	5	108	0	3	.973

PATTERSON, DANNY   P   TIGERS

PERSONAL: Born February 17, 1971, in San Gabriel, Calif. ... 6-0/185. ... Throws right, bats right. ... Full name: Danny Shane Patterson.
HIGH SCHOOL: San Gabriel (Calif.).
JUNIOR COLLEGE: Cerritos College (Calif.).
TRANSACTIONS/CAREER NOTES: Selected by Texas Rangers organization in 47th round of free-agent draft (June 5, 1989). ... On Texas disabled list (May 22-June 14, 1997); included rehabilitation assignment to Tulsa (June 9-14). ... On Texas disabled list (March 22-April 17, 1998); included rehabilitation assignments to Tulsa (April 7-12) and Oklahoma (April 13-17). ... Traded by Rangers with OF Juan Gonzalez and C Gregg Zaun to Detroit Tigers for P Justin Thompson, P Francisco Cordero, OF Gabe Kapler, C Bill Haselman, 2B Frank Catalanotto and P Alan Webb (November 2, 1999). ... On disabled list (July 22-August 7, 2000).

Year League	W	L	Pct.	ERA	G	GS	CG	ShO	Sv.	IP	H	R	ER	BB	SO
1990— Butte (Pio.)......................	0	3	.000	6.35	13	3	0	0	1	28 1/3	36	23	20	14	18
1991— Gulf Coast Rangers (GCL)..	5	3	.625	3.24	11	9	0	0	0	50	43	21	18	12	46
1992— Gastonia (S.Atl.)	4	6	.400	3.59	23	21	3	1	0	105 1/3	106	47	42	33	84
1993— Charlotte (FSL)...................	5	6	.455	2.51	47	0	0	0	7	68	55	22	19	28	41
1994— Tulsa (Texas)	1	4	.200	1.64	30	1	0	0	6	44	35	13	8	17	33
— Charlotte (FSL)...................	1	0	1.000	4.61	7	0	0	0	0	13 2/3	13	7	7	5	9
1995— Tulsa (Texas)	2	2	.500	6.19	26	0	0	0	5	36 1/3	45	27	25	13	24
— Oklahoma City (A.A.)	1	0	1.000	1.65	14	0	0	0	2	27 1/3	23	8	5	9	9
1996— Oklahoma City (A.A.)..........	6	2	.750	1.68	44	0	0	0	10	80 1/3	79	22	15	15	53
— Texas (A.L.)	0	0	...	0.00	7	0	0	0	0	8 2/3	10	4	0	3	5
1997— Texas (A.L.)	10	6	.625	3.42	54	0	0	0	1	71	70	29	27	23	69
— Tulsa (Texas)	0	0	...	4.50	2	2	0	0	0	2	5	4	1	0	4
1998— Texas (A.L.)	0	0	...	4.50	2	1	0	0	0	4	3	2	2	0	4
— Oklahoma (PCL)	0	0	...	4.50	1	0	0	0	0	2	4	1	1	1	2
— Texas (A.L.)	2	5	.286	4.45	56	0	0	0	2	60 2/3	64	31	30	19	33
1999— Texas (A.L.)	2	0	1.000	5.67	53	0	0	0	0	60 1/3	77	38	38	19	43
— Oklahoma (PCL)	1	0	1.000	0.00	2	0	0	0	0	3	1	0	0	1	4
2000— Detroit (A.L.)■	5	1	.833	3.97	58	0	0	0	0	56 2/3	69	26	25	14	29
2001— Detroit (A.L.)	5	4	.556	3.06	60	0	0	0	1	64 2/3	64	24	22	12	27
Major League totals (6 years)	24	16	.600	3.97	288	0	0	0	4	322	354	152	142	90	206

DIVISION SERIES RECORD

Year League	W	L	Pct.	ERA	G	GS	CG	ShO	Sv.	IP	H	R	ER	BB	SO
1996— Texas (A.L.)	0	0	...	0.00	1	0	0	0	0	1/3	1	0	0	0	0
1999— Texas (A.L.)	0	0	...	0.00	1	0	0	0	0	1	1	0	0	0	0
Division series totals (2 years)	0	0	...	0.00	2	0	0	0	0	1 1/3	2	0	0	0	0

P

PATTERSON, JARROD   3B   TIGERS

PERSONAL: Born September 7, 1973, in Montgomery, Ala. ... 6-1/195. ... Bats left, throws right. ... Full name: Jarrod Lane Patterson.
HIGH SCHOOL: Chilton County (Chilton, Ala.).
JUNIOR COLLEGE: Jefferson Davis (Ala.).
TRANSACTIONS/CAREER NOTES: Selected by New York Mets organization in 20th round of free-agent draft (June 3, 1993). ... Released by Mets (March 25, 1997). ... Signed by Regina, Prairie League (June 1997). ... Signed by Arizona Diamondbacks organization (June 24, 1998). ... Granted free agency (Ocotober 15, 1999). ... Signed by Pittsburgh Pirates organization (November 4, 1999). ... Released by Pirates (February 13, 1999). ... Re-signed by Pirates organization (February 14, 1999). ... Traded by Pirates to Montreal Expos for P Matt Skrmetta (August 12, 2000). ... Granted free agency (October 15, 2000). ... Signed by Detroit Tigers organization (November 21, 2000).
HONORS: Named Appalachian League Most Valuable Player (1995).
STATISTICAL NOTES: Led California League with .551 slugging percentage in 1998.

Year	Team (League)	Pos.	G	AB	R	H	2B	3B	HR	RBI	Avg.	BB	SO	SB	PO	A	E	Avg.
1993—GC Mets (GCL)		1B	46	166	27	40	9	1	2	25	.241	24	28	1	328	26	2	.994
1994—Kingsport (Appl.)		1B	36	112	12	29	5	2	5	18	.259	12	39	2	225	11	6	.975
—Pittsfield (NY-Penn)		1B	29	106	8	19	6	1	1	15	.179	10	34	0	262	29	5	.983
1995—Kingsport (Appl.)		1B	64	240	45	67	17	3	13	*57	.279	28	50	3	463	35	4	*.992
1996—St. Lucie (FSL)		1B	17	61	6	11	2	0	1	6	.180	3	19	1	137	12	5	.968
—Capital City (S.Atl.)		1B	70	213	26	49	9	1	3	37	.230	33	65	1	201	14	1	.995
1997—Regina (PRA)■			65	240	52	87	•24	2	7	50	.363	38	47	7	...	...	...	...
1998—High Desert (Calif.)■	3B-1B-2B		131	492	89	165	34	9	18	102	.335	66	97	9	392	168	24	.959
1999—El Paso (Texas)	3B-1B-OF		67	249	63	95	27	3	8	51	.382	51	45	3	58	126	12	.939
—Tucson (PCL)	3B-C		75	274	46	92	25	3	11	47	.336	36	37	4	47	101	13	.919
2000—Nashville (PCL)■	3B-1B-C		70	198	25	55	10	0	5	30	.278	13	40	0	40	105	9	.942
—Altoona (NAL)	3B		11	36	1	5	1	0	0	4	.139	3	11	0	6	22	6	.824
—Ottawa (I.L.)■	3B		25	92	9	25	6	1	0	16	.272	4	13	1	19	44	4	.940
2001—Toledo (I.L.)■	3B-1B-2B-OF		69	213	41	63	15	2	7	25	.296	30	47	2	64	94	7	.958
—Erie (East.)	3B		20	70	17	28	5	1	7	18	.400	11	11	0	14	32	4	.920
—Detroit (A.L.)	3B		13	41	6	11	1	1	2	4	.268	0	4	0	9	15	2	.923
Major League totals (1 year)			13	41	6	11	1	1	2	4	.268	0	4	0	9	15	2	.923

PATTERSON, JOHN   P   DIAMONDBACKS

PERSONAL: Born January 30, 1978, in Orange, Texas. ... 6-5/183. ... Throws right, bats right. ... Full name: John Hollis Patterson.
HIGH SCHOOL: West Orange-Stark (Orange, Texas).
TRANSACTIONS/CAREER NOTES: Signed as non-drafted free agent by Arizona Diamondbacks organization (November 7, 1996). ... On disabled list (April 6-24 and May 6-September 8, 2000). ... On El Paso disabled list (April 5-19 and April 25-May 13, 2001).

Year	League	W	L	Pct.	ERA	G	GS	CG	ShO	Sv.	IP	H	R	ER	BB	SO
1997—South Bend (Midw.)		1	9	.100	3.23	18	18	0	0	0	78	63	32	28	34	95
1998—High Desert (Calif.)		8	7	.533	*2.83	25	25	0	0	0	127	102	54	40	42	148
1999—El Paso (Texas)		8	6	.571	4.77	18	18	2	0	0	100	98	61	53	42	117
—Tucson (PCL)		1	5	.167	7.04	7	6	0	0	0	30⅔	43	26	24	18	29
2000—Tucson (PCL)		0	2	.000	7.80	3	2	0	0	0	15	21	14	13	9	10
2001—El Paso (Texas)		1	2	.333	4.26	5	5	0	0	0	25⅓	30	15	12	9	19
—Lancaster (Calif.)		0	0	...	5.79	2	2	0	0	0	9⅓	9	6	6	3	9
—Tucson (PCL)		2	7	.222	5.85	13	12	0	0	0	67⅔	82	50	44	31	40

PAUL, JOSH   C   WHITE SOX

PERSONAL: Born May 19, 1975, in Evanston, Ill. ... 6-1/185. ... Bats right, throws right. ... Full name: Joshua William Paul.
HIGH SCHOOL: Buffalo Grove (Ill.).
COLLEGE: Vanderbilt.
TRANSACTIONS/CAREER NOTES: Selected by Chicago White Sox organization in second round of free-agent draft (June 4, 1996). ... On Birmingham disabled list (April 13-July 13, 1997; and July 9-27, 1999). ... On Charlotte disabled list (July 5-August 3, 2000; and July 25-August 9, 2001).
STATISTICAL NOTES: Led Carolina League catchers with 939 total chances in 1998.

Year	Team (League)	Pos.	G	AB	R	H	2B	3B	HR	RBI	Avg.	BB	SO	SB	PO	A	E	Avg.
1996—Hickory (S.Atl.)		C	59	226	41	74	16	0	8	37	.327	21	53	13	197	29	2	.991
1997—Birmingham (Sou.)		C	34	115	18	34	5	0	1	16	.296	12	25	6	221	17	3	.988
—GC White Sox (GCL)		C	5	14	3	6	0	1	0	0	.429	1	3	1	21	6	3	.900
1998—Win.-Salem (Caro.)		C	123	444	66	113	20	7	11	63	.255	38	91	20	*818	*118	3	*.997
1999—Birmingham (Sou.)		C-DH	93	319	47	89	19	3	4	42	.279	29	68	6	526	66	5	.992
—Chicago (A.L.)		C	6	18	2	4	1	0	0	1	.222	0	4	0	40	2	0	1.000
2000—Chicago (A.L.)		C-OF	36	71	15	20	3	2	1	8	.282	5	17	1	130	17	4	.974
—Charlotte (I.L.)		C-OF	51	168	28	40	5	1	4	19	.238	13	38	6	291	25	2	.994
2001—Chicago (A.L.)		C	57	139	20	37	11	0	3	18	.266	13	25	6	266	24	6	.980
—Charlotte (I.L.)		C	22	75	11	21	4	0	4	14	.280	7	18	0	125	7	0	1.000
Major League totals (3 years)			99	228	37	61	15	2	4	27	.268	18	46	7	436	43	10	.980

DIVISION SERIES RECORD

Year	Team (League)	Pos.	G	AB	R	H	2B	3B	HR	RBI	Avg.	BB	SO	SB	PO	A	E	Avg.
2000—Chicago (A.L.)		PR-C	1	0	0	0	0	0	0	0	...	0	0	0	1	0	0	1.000

P

PERSONAL: Born January 8, 1976, in New Britain, Conn. ... 6-5/230. ... Throws right, bats right. ... Full name: Carl Anthony Pavano.
HIGH SCHOOL: Southington (Conn.).
TRANSACTIONS/CAREER NOTES: Selected by Boston Red Sox organization in 13th round of free-agent draft (June 2, 1994). ... Traded by Red Sox with a player to be named later to Montreal Expos for P Pedro Martinez (November 18, 1997); Expos acquired P Tony Armas Jr. to complete deal (December 18, 1997). ... On Montreal disabled list (July 12-September 11, 1999); included rehabilitation assignments to Ottawa (July 29-30 and September 6-7). ... On disabled list (June 25, 2000-remainder of season). ... On Montreal disabled list (March 23-August 15, 2001); included rehabilitation assignments to Jupiter (July 14-29) and Ottawa (July 30-August 9).
HONORS: Named Eastern League Pitcher of the Year (1996).

Year League	W	L	Pct.	ERA	G	GS	CG	ShO	Sv.	IP	H	R	ER	BB	SO
1994— Gulf Coast Red Sox (GCL)..	4	3	.571	1.84	9	7	0	0	0	44	31	14	9	7	47
1995— Michigan (Midw.)	6	6	.500	3.45	22	22	1	0	0	141	118	63	54	52	138
1996— Trenton (East.)	*16	5	.762	2.63	27	26	•6	2	0	185	154	66	54	47	146
1997— Pawtucket (I.L.)	11	6	.647	3.12	23	23	3	0	0	161 2/3	148	62	56	34	147
1998— Jupiter (FSL)■................	0	0	...	6.60	4	4	0	0	0	15	20	11	11	3	14
—Ottawa (I.L.)	1	0	1.000	2.41	3	3	0	0	0	18 2/3	12	5	5	7	14
—Montreal (N.L.)..................	6	9	.400	4.21	24	23	0	0	0	134 2/3	130	70	63	43	83
1999— Montreal (N.L.)..................	6	8	.429	5.63	19	18	1	1	0	104	117	66	65	35	70
—Ottawa (I.L.)	0	1	.000	9.00	2	2	0	0	0	5	7	5	5	0	3
2000— Montreal (N.L.)..................	8	4	.667	3.06	15	15	0	0	0	97	89	40	33	34	64
2001— Jupiter (FSL)	1	1	.500	2.19	3	3	0	0	0	12 1/3	10	7	3	2	11
—Ottawa (I.L.)	2	1	.667	3.58	4	4	0	0	0	27 2/3	27	13	11	5	19
—Montreal (N.L.)..................	1	6	.143	6.33	8	8	0	0	0	42 2/3	59	33	30	16	36
Major League totals (4 years)	21	27	.438	4.54	66	64	1	1	0	378 1/3	395	209	191	128	253

PERSONAL: Born November 22, 1972, in Zanesville, Ohio. ... 5-10/185. ... Bats right, throws right. ... Full name: Jayson Lee Payton.
HIGH SCHOOL: Zanesville (Ohio).
COLLEGE: Georgia Tech.
TRANSACTIONS/CAREER NOTES: Selected by New York Mets organization in supplemental round ("sandwich pick" between first and second round, 29th pick overall) of free-agent draft (June 2, 1994); pick received as part of compensation for Baltimore Orioles signing Type A free-agent P Sid Fernandez. ... On Norfolk disabled list (April 29-July 3, 1996). ... On disabled list (April 3, 1997-entire season). ... On Norfolk disabled list (May 27-June 15 and June 24-July 20, 1998). ... On New York disabled list (March 21-June 8, 1999); included rehabilitation assignment to St. Lucie (May 30-June 8). ... On Norfolk disabled list (July 10-August 19, 1999); included rehabilitation assignment to St. Lucie (June 22-26). ... On New York disabled list (May 8-June 26, 2001); included rehabilitation assignment to St. Lucie (June 22-26).
STATISTICAL NOTES: Career major league grand slams: 1.

						BATTING								FIELDING		
Year Team (League)	Pos.	G	AB	R	H	2B	3B	HR	RBI	Avg.	BB	SO	SB	PO	A	E	Avg.
1994— Pittsfield (NY-Penn)....	OF	58	219	47	80	16	2	3	37	.365	23	18	10	124	8	5	.964
—Binghamton (East.)	OF	8	25	3	7	1	0	0	1	.280	2	3	1	11	0	1	.917
1995— Binghamton (East.)	OF	85	357	59	123	20	3	14	54	.345	29	32	16	230	7	3	.988
—Norfolk (I.L.)	OF	50	196	33	47	11	4	4	30	.240	11	22	11	106	3	2	.982
1996— Norfolk (I.L.)	DH-OF	55	153	30	47	6	3	6	26	.307	11	26	10	7	1	0	1.000
—GC Mets (GCL)	DH	3	13	3	5	1	0	1	2	.385	0	1	1	...	...	...	...
—St. Lucie (FSL)	DH	9	26	4	8	2	0	0	1	.308	4	5	2	...	...	...	...
—Binghamton (East.)	DH	4	10	0	2	0	0	0	2	.200	2	2	0	...	...	...	...
1997—						Did not play.										
1998— Norfolk (I.L.)	OF-1B-DH	82	322	45	84	14	4	8	30	.261	26	50	12	315	20	7	.980
—St. Lucie (FSL)	OF	3	7	0	1	0	0	0	0	.143	3	1	0	8	0	0	1.000
—New York (N.L.)..........	OF	15	22	2	7	1	0	0	0	.318	1	4	0	6	1	0	1.000
1999— St. Lucie (FSL)	OF	7	26	3	9	1	1	0	3	.346	4	5	0	20	1	1	.955
—Norfolk (I.L.)	OF-DH	38	144	27	56	13	2	8	35	.389	12	13	2	59	3	1	.984
—New York (N.L.)..........	OF	13	8	1	2	1	0	0	1	.250	0	2	1	3	0	0	1.000
2000— New York (N.L.)..........	OF	149	488	63	142	23	1	17	62	.291	30	60	5	311	7	6	.981
2001— New York (N.L.)..........	OF	104	361	44	92	16	1	8	34	.255	18	52	4	237	6	4	.984
—St. Lucie (FSL)	OF	4	16	7	6	3	0	0	0	.375	4	1	0	5	1	0	1.000
Major League totals (4 years)		281	879	110	243	41	2	25	97	.276	49	118	10	557	14	10	.983

DIVISION SERIES RECORD

						BATTING								FIELDING		
Year Team (League)	Pos.	G	AB	R	H	2B	3B	HR	RBI	Avg.	BB	SO	SB	PO	A	E	Avg.
2000— New York (N.L.)..........	OF	4	17	1	3	0	0	0	2	.176	0	4	1	10	0	0	1.000

CHAMPIONSHIP SERIES RECORD

						BATTING								FIELDING		
Year Team (League)	Pos.	G	AB	R	H	2B	3B	HR	RBI	Avg.	BB	SO	SB	PO	A	E	Avg.
2000— New York (N.L.)..........	OF	5	19	1	3	0	0	1	3	.158	2	5	0	10	0	0	1.000

WORLD SERIES RECORD

						BATTING								FIELDING		
Year Team (League)	Pos.	G	AB	R	H	2B	3B	HR	RBI	Avg.	BB	SO	SB	PO	A	E	Avg.
2000— New York (N.L.)..........	OF	5	21	3	7	0	0	1	3	.333	0	5	0	17	0	2	.895

PERSONAL: Born February 16, 1975, in San Pedro de Macoris, Dominican Republic. ... 5-10/228. ... Bats right, throws right. ... Full name: Angel Maria Pena.
HIGH SCHOOL: Escuela Puerto Rico (San Pedro de Macoris, Dominican Republic).

P

TRANSACTIONS/CAREER NOTES: Signed as non-drafted free agent by Los Angeles Dodgers organization (July 24, 1992). ... Missed entire 1994 season due to injury. ... On disabled list (July 26-September 17, 1997). ... On Albuquerque disabled list (August 24, 1999-remainder of season). ... On disabled list (April 30-May 19 and May 30-June 9, 2000). ... On Las Vegas disabled list (July 7-22, 2001). ... Granted free agency (October 15, 2001).
STATISTICAL NOTES: Led California League catchers with 31 passed balls in 1997. ... Led Texas League catchers with 781 putouts, 81 assists, 14 errors and 876 total chances in 1998.

						BATTING								FIELDING			
Year Team (League)	Pos.	G	AB	R	H	2B	3B	HR	RBI	Avg.	BB	SO	SB	PO	A	E	Avg.
1993—Dom. Dodgers (DSL) .	C	50	168	27	47	3	2	1	24	.280	10	41	6	197	57	15	.944
1994—							Did not play.										
1995—Great Falls (Pio.)	C	49	138	24	40	11	1	4	15	.290	21	32	2	297	42	7	.980
1996—Savannah (S.Atl.)	C	36	127	13	26	4	0	6	16	.205	7	37	1	238	39	6	.979
—Dom. Dodgers (DSL) .	C	23	78	30	37	9	1	8	40	.474	24	12	1	86	11	1	.990
1997—San Bern. (Calif.)	C	86	322	53	89	22	4	16	64	.276	32	84	3	661	83	10	.987
1998—San Antonio (Texas) ...	C-OF	126	483	81	162	32	2	22	105	.335	48	80	9	†781	†81	†14	.984
—Los Angeles (N.L.)	C	6	13	1	3	0	0	0	0	.231	0	6	0	26	2	0	1.000
1999—Albuquerque (PCL)	C-DH	34	127	15	37	10	1	1	24	.291	10	24	3	200	28	3	.987
—Los Angeles (N.L.)	C	43	120	14	25	6	0	4	21	.208	12	24	0	233	26	3	.989
2000—Albuquerque (PCL).....	C-1B-3B	87	315	52	97	12	3	17	61	.308	28	75	3	531	60	7	.988
2001—Los Angeles (N.L.)	C	22	54	3	11	1	0	1	2	.204	1	17	0	125	11	0	1.000
—Las Vegas (PCL)	C-1B	53	198	39	62	8	2	16	41	.313	18	52	1	340	19	6	.984
Major League totals (3 years)		71	187	18	39	7	0	5	23	.209	13	47	0	384	39	3	.993

PENA, CARLOS — 1B — ATHLETICS

PERSONAL: Born May 17, 1978, in Santo Domingo, Dominican Republic. ... 6-2/210. ... Bats left, throws left.
HIGH SCHOOL: Haverhill (Mass.).
COLLEGE: Wright State, Northeastern.
TRANSACTIONS/CAREER NOTES: Selected by Texas Rangers organization in first round (10th pick overall) of free-agent draft (June 2, 1998). ... Traded by Rangers with P Mike Venafro to Oakland Athletics for 1B Jason Hart, P Mario Ramos, C Gerald Laird and OF Ryan Ludwick (January 14, 2002).
STATISTICAL NOTES: Led Florida State League first basemen with 121 double plays in 1999.

						BATTING								FIELDING			
Year Team (League)	Pos.	G	AB	R	H	2B	3B	HR	RBI	Avg.	BB	SO	SB	PO	A	E	Avg.
1998—GC Rangers (GCL)......	1B	2	5	1	2	0	0	0	0	.400	3	1	1	10	1	0	1.000
—Savannah (S.Atl.)	1B-OF	30	117	22	38	14	0	6	20	.325	8	26	3	197	16	3	.986
—Charlotte (FSL)..........	1B	7	22	1	6	1	0	0	3	.273	2	8	0	41	2	1	.977
1999—Charlotte (FSL).........	1B	136	501	85	128	31	8	18	103	.255	74	135	2	1056	83	16	.986
2000—Tulsa (Texas)	1B	138	529	117	158	36	2	28	105	.299	101	108	12	1101	79	22	.982
2001—Oklahoma (PCL).........	1B	119	431	71	124	38	3	23	74	.288	80	127	11	925	89	11	.989
—Texas (A.L.)	1B-DH	22	62	6	16	4	1	3	12	.258	10	17	0	138	*15	2	.987
Major League totals (1 year)		22	62	6	16	4	1	3	12	.258	10	17	0	138	15	2	.987

PENA, ELVIS — 2B/SS — BREWERS

PERSONAL: Born September 15, 1976, in Santo Domingo, Dominican Republic. ... 5-11/155. ... Bats both, throws right.
TRANSACTIONS/CAREER NOTES: Signed as non-drafted free agent by Colorado Rockies organization (June 22, 1993). ... Traded by Rockies with P Mark Leiter and P Mike DeJean to Milwaukee Brewers for P Juan Acevedo, P Kane Davis and IF Jose Flores (April 4, 2001).
STATISTICAL NOTES: Led Carolina League with 14 sacrifice hits in 1997.

						BATTING								FIELDING			
Year Team (League)	Pos.	G	AB	R	H	2B	3B	HR	RBI	Avg.	BB	SO	SB	PO	A	E	Avg.
1994—Ariz. Rockies (Ariz.)...	2B-SS	49	171	31	39	5	2	0	9	.228	35	47	20	86	143	21	.916
1995—Asheville (S.Atl.).........	2B	48	145	27	33	2	0	0	4	.228	28	32	23	86	140	11	.954
—Portland (N'West)	2B	58	215	29	54	6	3	0	18	.251	26	45	28	92	137	11	.954
1996—Salem (Caro.)	2B	102	341	48	76	9	4	0	28	.223	61	70	30	211	245	19	.960
1997—Salem (Caro.)	2B-SS-3B	93	279	41	62	9	2	1	30	.222	37	53	16	127	199	20	.942
1998—Asheville (S.Atl.).........	2B	115	428	93	123	24	4	6	48	.287	70	85	41	197	306	29	.945
1999—Carolina (Sou.)	2B-SS	110	356	57	107	24	6	2	31	.301	48	64	21	206	267	13	.973
—Colo. Springs (PCL) ...	SS-2B	13	43	5	7	1	0	0	1	.163	3	7	4	23	33	7	.889
2000—Carolina (Sou.)	SS-2B	126	477	92	143	16	7	3	37	.300	69	76	*48	205	321	33	.941
—Colorado (N.L.)	SS-2B	10	9	1	3	1	0	0	1	.333	1	1	1	2	2	0	1.000
2001—Indianapolis (I.L.)■....	SS-2B-3B	127	437	56	105	15	3	1	28	.240	30	76	12	192	313	31	.942
—Milwaukee (N.L.)	2B	15	40	5	9	2	0	0	6	.225	6	6	2	14	36	1	.980
Major League totals (2 years)		25	49	6	12	3	0	0	7	.245	7	7	3	15	38	1	.981

PENA, JUAN — P — RED SOX

PERSONAL: Born June 27, 1977, in Santo Domingo, Dominican Republic. ... 6-5/215. ... Throws right, bats right. ... Full name: Juan Francisco Pena.
HIGH SCHOOL: Miami High.
JUNIOR COLLEGE: Miami-Dade (Wolfson) Community College.
TRANSACTIONS/CAREER NOTES: Selected by Boston Red Sox organization in 27th round of free-agent draft (June 1, 1995). ... On disabled list (April 9-24 and June 17-27, 1998). ... On Boston disabled list (May 20-June 6 and June 11-July 22, 1999); included rehabilitation assignments to Pawtucket (May 30-June 6), Gulf Coast Red Sox (July 8-11) and Sarasota (July 12-22). ... On Pawtucket disabled list (July 31-August 9 and August 12, 1999-remainder of season). ... On disabled list (March 29, 2000-entire season). ... On Boston disabled list (March 22-May 28, 2001); included rehabilitation assignment to Sarasota (May 8-28).
STATISTICAL NOTES: Pitched 5-0 no-hit victory for Pawtucket against Durham (July 22, 1998).

Year	League	W	L	Pct.	ERA	G	GS	CG	ShO	Sv.	IP	H	R	ER	BB	SO
1995—	Gulf Coast Red Sox (GCL)..	3	2	.600	1.95	13	4	2	1	1	55 1/3	41	17	12	6	47
—	Sarasota (FSL)	1	1	.500	4.91	2	2	0	0	0	7 1/3	8	4	4	3	5
1996—	Michigan (Midw.)	12	10	.545	2.97	26	26	4	0	0	*187 2/3	149	70	62	34	156
1997—	Sarasota (FSL)	4	6	.400	2.96	13	13	3	0	0	91 1/3	67	39	30	23	88
—	Trenton (East.)	5	6	.455	4.73	16	14	0	0	0	97	98	56	51	31	79
1998—	Pawtucket (I.L.)	8	10	.444	4.38	24	23	1	1	0	139 2/3	141	73	68	51	*146
1999—	Pawtucket (I.L.)	4	2	.667	4.13	10	10	0	0	0	48	44	28	22	13	61
—	Boston (A.L.)	2	0	1.000	0.69	2	2	0	0	0	13	9	1	1	3	15
—	Gulf Coast Red Sox (GCL)..	0	0	...	0.00	1	1	0	0	0	2	0	0	0	0	4
—	Sarasota (FSL)	0	1	.000	7.11	2	2	0	0	0	6 1/3	12	6	5	0	5
2000—	Boston (A.L.)							Did not play.								
2001—	Sarasota (FSL)	0	3	.000	5.19	8	8	0	0	0	26	29	15	15	11	31
Major League totals (1 year).........		2	0	1.000	0.69	2	2	0	0	0	13	9	1	1	3	15

PENA, JUAN   P   ATHLETICS

PERSONAL: Born June 4, 1979, in Santo Domingo, Dominican Republic. ... 6-3/165. ... Throws left, bats left. ... Full name: Juan Antonio Pena.
TRANSACTIONS/CAREER NOTES: Signed as non-drafted free agent by Oakland Athletics organization (November 1, 1995).

Year	League	W	L	Pct.	ERA	G	GS	CG	ShO	Sv.	IP	H	R	ER	BB	SO
1996—	Dominican Athletics (DSL).	8	2	.800	3.21	12	12	0	0	0	70	75	34	25	15	59
1997—	Dominican Athletics (DSL).	6	2	.750	2.91	14	13	0	0	0	65	54	38	21	33	67
1998—	Southern Oregon (N'West).	1	2	.333	2.15	8	8	0	0	0	46	46	21	11	10	38
—	Modesto (Calif.)	3	2	.600	5.18	6	6	0	0	0	33	50	25	19	7	32
1999—	Visalia (Calif.)	9	5	.643	5.76	33	18	0	0	1	131 1/3	168	106	84	61	107
2000—	Modesto (Calif.)	6	9	.400	3.86	29	27	0	0	0	154	132	85	66	75	177
2001—	Midland (Texas).................	11	9	.550	4.07	27	27	0	0	0	148 1/3	164	88	67	46	106

PENA, WILY   OF   REDS

PERSONAL: Born January 23, 1982, in Lagunda Salada, Dominican Republic. ... 6-3/215. ... Bats right, throws right. ... Full name: Wily Modesto Pena.
TRANSACTIONS/CAREER NOTES: Signed by New York Mets organization (1998); contract nullified by Baseball Commissioner's Office. ... Declared a free agent (March 7, 1999). ... Signed by New York Yankees organization (April 1, 1999). ... On New York disabled list (July 13, 2000-remainder of season). ... Traded by Yankees to Cincinnati Reds for 3B Drew Henson and OF Michael Coleman (March 21, 2001).
STATISTICAL NOTES: Led Midwest League outfielders with three double plays in 2001.

Year	Team (League)	Pos.	G	AB	R	H	2B	3B	HR	RBI	Avg.	BB	SO	SB	PO	A	E	Avg.
								BATTING								FIELDING		
1999—	GC Yankees (GCL)......	OF	45	166	21	41	10	1	7	26	.247	12	54	3	35	1	2	.947
2000—	Greensboro (S.Atl.)	OF	67	249	41	51	7	1	10	28	.205	18	91	6	102	6	4	.964
—	Staten Island (NY-P) ..	OF	20	73	7	22	1	2	0	10	.301	2	23	2	37	0	0	1.000
2001—	Dayton (Midw.)■	OF	*135	511	87	135	25	5	26	*113	.264	33	*177	26	300	13	9	.972

PENNY, BRAD   P   MARLINS

PERSONAL: Born May 24, 1978, in Broken Arrow, Okla. ... 6-4/200. ... Throws right, bats right. ... Full name: Bradley Wayne Penny.
HIGH SCHOOL: Broken Arrow (Okla.).
TRANSACTIONS/CAREER NOTES: Selected by Arizona Diamondbacks organization in fifth round of free-agent draft (June 4, 1996). ... On El Paso disabled list (April 20-30, 1999). ... Traded by Diamondbacks with P Vladimir Nunez and a player to be named later to Florida Marlins for P Matt Mantei (July 9, 1999); Marlins acquired OF Abraham Nunez to complete deal (December 13, 1999). ... On Florida disabled list (July 20-September 2, 2000); included rehabilitation assignments to Brevard County (August 5-15) and Calgary (August 16-September 2).
HONORS: Named California League Most Valuable Player and Pitcher of the Year (1998).
MISCELLANEOUS: Flied out in only appearance as pinch hitter (2000).

Year	League	W	L	Pct.	ERA	G	GS	CG	ShO	Sv.	IP	H	R	ER	BB	SO
1996—	Ariz. Diamondbacks (Ariz.).	2	2	.500	2.36	11	8	0	0	0	49 2/3	36	18	13	14	52
1997—	South Bend (Midw.)..........	10	5	.667	2.73	25	25	0	0	0	118 2/3	91	44	36	43	116
1998—	High Desert (Calif.)...........	*14	5	.737	2.96	28	•28	1	0	0	164	138	65	54	35	*207
1999—	El Paso (Texas).................	2	7	.222	4.80	17	17	0	0	0	90	109	56	48	25	100
—	Portland (East.)■............	1	0	1.000	3.90	6	6	0	0	0	32 1/3	28	15	14	14	35
2000—	Florida (N.L.)	8	7	.533	4.81	23	22	0	0	0	119 2/3	120	70	64	60	80
—	Brevard County (FSL).........	0	1	.000	1.13	2	2	0	0	0	8	5	2	1	4	11
—	Calgary (PCL)...................	2	0	1.000	3.90	3	3	0	0	0	15	8	8	3	10	16
2001—	Florida (N.L.)	10	10	.500	3.69	31	31	1	1	0	205	183	92	84	54	154
Major League totals (2 years).......		18	17	.514	4.10	54	53	1	1	0	324 2/3	303	162	148	114	234

PEOPLES, DANNY   OF   METS

PERSONAL: Born January 20, 1975, in Round Rock, Texas. ... 6-1/207. ... Bats right, throws right. ... Full name: Daniel Laurence Peoples.
HIGH SCHOOL: Round Rock (Texas).
COLLEGE: Texas.
TRANSACTIONS/CAREER NOTES: Selected by Cleveland Indians organization in first round (28th pick overall) of free-agent draft (June 4, 1996). ... On disabled list (July 31, 1996-remainder of season). ... On disabled list (April 10-24, June 3-10, June 15-July 31 and August 21, 1998-remainder of season). ... On disabled list (April 8-21, 2000). ... On Buffalo disabled list (August 14-31, 2001). ... On Cleveland disabled list (August 31, 2001-remainder of season). ... Traded by Indians with 2B Roberto Alomar and P Mike Bacsik to New York Mets for OF Matt Lawton, OF Alex Escobar, P Jerrod Riggan and two players to be named later (December 11, 2001); Indians acquired P Billy Traber and 1B Earl Snyder to complete deal (December 13, 2001).

P

Year	Team (League)	Pos.	G	AB	R	H	2B	3B	HR	RBI	Avg.	BB	SO	SB	PO	A	E	Avg.
1996—Watertown (NY-Penn)	DH	35	117	20	28	7	0	3	26	.239	28	36	3	...	...	...	...
1997—Kinston (Caro.)	OF	121	409	82	102	21	1	*34	84	.249	84	145	8	86	2	4	.957
1998—Akron (East.)	OF	60	222	30	62	19	0	8	32	.279	29	61	1	71	2	2	.973
1999—Akron (East.)	1B-DH	127	494	75	124	23	3	21	78	.251	55	142	2	775	81	14	.984
2000—Buffalo (I.L.)	1B	124	420	68	109	19	2	21	74	.260	63	122	2	945	60	7	.993
2001—Buffalo (I.L.)	1B-OF	106	370	62	82	20	1	17	48	.222	56	133	0	727	51	9	.989

PERCIVAL, TROY   P   ANGELS

PERSONAL: Born August 9, 1969, in Fontana, Calif. ... 6-3/236. ... Throws right, bats right. ... Full name: Troy Eugene Percival. ... Name pronounced PER-sih-vol.
HIGH SCHOOL: Moreno Valley (Calif.).
COLLEGE: UC Riverside.
TRANSACTIONS/CAREER NOTES: Selected by California Angels organization in sixth round of free-agent draft (June 5, 1990). ... On Palm Springs disabled list (June 3-July 2, 1992). ... On disabled list (May 28, 1993-remainder of season). ... Angels franchise renamed Anaheim Angels for 1997 season. ... On disabled list (April 7-May 16, 1997); included rehabilitation assignment to Lake Elsinore (May 13-16). ... On Anaheim disabled list (August 5-26, 2000); included rehabilitation assignment to Lake Elsinore (August 22-26).
MISCELLANEOUS: Played catcher (1990). ... Struck out in only appearance as pinch hitter (1996). ... Holds Anaheim Angels franchise all-time record for most saves (210).

Year	League	W	L	Pct.	ERA	G	GS	CG	ShO	Sv.	IP	H	R	ER	BB	SO
1991—Boise (N'West)	2	0	1.000	1.41	28	0	0	0	*12	38 1/3	23	7	6	18	63
1992—Palm Springs (Calif.)	1	1	.500	5.06	11	0	0	0	2	10 2/3	6	7	6	8	16
—Midland (Texas)	3	0	1.000	2.37	20	0	0	0	5	19	18	5	5	11	21
1993—Vancouver (PCL)	0	1	.000	6.27	18	0	0	0	4	18 2/3	24	14	13	13	19
1994—Vancouver (PCL)	2	6	.250	4.13	49	0	0	0	15	61	63	31	28	29	73
1995—California (A.L.)	3	2	.600	1.95	62	0	0	0	3	74	37	19	16	26	94
1996—California (A.L.)	0	2	.000	2.31	62	0	0	0	36	74	38	20	19	31	100
1997—Anaheim (A.L.)	5	5	.500	3.46	55	0	0	0	27	52	40	20	20	22	72
—Lake Elsinore (Calif.)	0	0	...	0.00	2	1	0	0	0	2	1	0	0	0	3
1998—Anaheim (A.L.)	2	7	.222	3.64	67	0	0	0	42	66 2/3	45	31	27	37	87
1999—Anaheim (A.L.)	4	6	.400	3.79	60	0	0	0	31	57	38	24	24	22	58
2000—Anaheim (A.L.)	5	5	.500	4.50	54	0	0	0	32	50	42	27	25	30	49
—Lake Elsinore (Calif.)	0	0	...	4.50	2	2	0	0	0	2	1	1	1	1	1
2001—Anaheim (A.L.)	4	2	.667	2.65	57	0	0	0	39	57 2/3	39	19	17	18	71
Major League totals (7 years)	23	29	.442	3.09	417	0	0	0	210	431 1/3	279	160	148	186	531

ALL-STAR GAME RECORD

Year	League	W	L	Pct.	ERA	GS	CG	ShO	Sv.	IP	H	R	ER	BB	SO
1996—American	0	0	...	0.00	0	0	0	0	1	1	0	0	0	1
1998—American	0	0	...	0.00	0	0	0	0	1	1	0	0	0	2
1999—American					Selected, did not play.										
2001—American	0	0	...	0.00	0	0	0	0	1	0	0	0	1	1
All-Star Game totals (3 years)	0	0	...	0.00	0	0	0	0	3	2	0	0	1	4

RECORD AS POSITION PLAYER

Year	Team (League)	Pos.	G	AB	R	H	2B	3B	HR	RBI	Avg.	BB	SO	SB	PO	A	E	Avg.
1990—Boise (N'West)	C	29	79	12	16	0	0	0	5	.203	19	25	0	215	25	5	.980

PEREZ, ANTONIO   SS   MARINERS

PERSONAL: Born July 28, 1981, in Bani, Dominican Republic. ... 5-11/175. ... Bats right, throws right. ... Full name: Antonio Miguel Perez.
TRANSACTIONS/CAREER NOTES: Signed as non-drafted free agent by Cincinnati Reds organization (March 21, 1998). ... Traded by Reds with OF Mike Cameron, P Brett Tomko and P Jake Meyer to Seattle Mariners for OF Ken Griffey Jr. (February 10, 2000). ... On disabled list (May 2-June 5, 2000). ... On disabled list (April 5-June 1 and June 6, 2001-remainder of season).
STATISTICAL NOTES: Tied for Midwest League lead in caught stealing with 24 in 1999. ... Led California League with .527 slugging percentage in 2000.

Year	Team (League)	Pos.	G	AB	R	H	2B	3B	HR	RBI	Avg.	BB	SO	SB	PO	A	E	Avg.
1998—Dom. Reds (DSL)		63	212	57	54	11	0	2	24	.255	53	33	58	...	...	...	...
1999—Rockford (Midw.)	SS-2B	119	385	69	111	20	3	7	41	.288	43	80	35	175	299	36	.929
2000—Lancaster (Calif.)■	SS	98	395	90	109	36	6	17	63	.276	58	99	28	144	271	27	.939
2001—San Antonio (Texas)	SS	5	21	3	3	0	0	0	0	.143	0	7	0	9	18	6	.818

PEREZ, EDDIE   C   BRAVES

PERSONAL: Born May 4, 1968, in Cuidad Ojeda, Venezuela. ... 6-1/185. ... Bats right, throws right. ... Full name: Eduardo Rafael Perez.
HIGH SCHOOL: Doctor Raul Cuenca (Cuidad Ojeda, Venezuela).
TRANSACTIONS/CAREER NOTES: Signed as non-drafted free agent by Atlanta Braves organization (September 27, 1986). ... On disabled list (August 30-September 14, 1996; and May 5, 2000-remainder of season). ... On Atlanta disabled list (March 28-September 1, 2001); included rehabilitation assignment to Greenville (August 21-September 1). ... Granted free agency (November 14, 2001). ... Re-signed by Braves organization (December 17, 2001).
STATISTICAL NOTES: Led South Atlantic League catchers with 13 errors in 1989. ... Tied for International League lead in errors by catcher with 11 in 1994. ... Led International League catchers with 539 putouts, 69 assists and 615 total chances in 1995. ... Tied for International League lead with seven double plays in 1995. ... Career major league grand slams: 1.

P

Year	Team (League)	Pos.	G	AB	R	H	2B	3B	HR	RBI	Avg.	BB	SO	SB	PO	A	E	Avg.
1987—	GC Braves (GCL).......	C	31	89	8	18	1	0	1	5	.202	8	14	0	161	31	4	.980
1988—	Burlington (Midw.).....	C-1B	64	186	14	43	8	0	4	19	.231	10	33	1	245	42	11	.963
1989—	Sumter (S.Atl.).........	C-1B	114	401	39	93	21	0	5	44	.232	44	68	2	760	96	†13	.985
1990—	Sumter (S.Atl.).........	C-1B	41	123	11	22	7	1	3	17	.179	14	18	0	315	32	3	.991
	— Durham (Caro.)..........	C-1B	31	93	9	22	1	0	3	10	.237	1	12	0	197	17	3	.986
1991—	Durham (Caro.)	C-1B	92	277	38	75	10	1	9	41	.271	17	33	0	497	55	8	.986
	— Greenville (Sou.)	1B	1	4	0	1	0	0	0	0	.250	0	1	0	9	0	0	1.000
1992—	Greenville (Sou.).......	C-1B	91	275	28	63	16	0	6	41	.229	24	41	3	631	64	14	.980
1993—	Greenville (Sou.).......	1B-C	28	84	15	28	6	0	6	17	.333	2	8	1	146	19	3	.982
1994—	Richmond (I.L.).........	C-1B	113	388	37	101	16	2	9	49	.260	18	47	1	718	80	‡12	.985
1995—	Richmond (I.L.).........	C-DH-1B	92	324	31	86	19	0	5	40	.265	12	58	1	†540	†69	7	.989
	— Atlanta (N.L.).............	C-1B	7	13	1	4	1	0	1	4	.308	0	2	0	34	2	0	1.000
1996—	Atlanta (N.L.).............	C-1B	68	156	19	40	9	1	4	17	.256	8	19	0	281	22	3	.990
1997—	Atlanta (N.L.).............	C-1B	73	191	20	41	5	0	6	18	.215	10	35	0	417	24	5	.989
1998—	Atlanta (N.L.).............	C-1B-DH	61	149	18	50	12	0	6	32	.336	15	28	1	290	29	2	.994
1999—	Atlanta (N.L.).............	C-1B	104	309	30	77	17	0	7	30	.249	17	40	0	620	48	5	.993
2000—	Atlanta (N.L.).............	C	7	22	0	4	1	0	0	3	.182	0	2	0	39	2	1	.976
2001—	Greenville (Sou.).......	C-1B	10	38	7	13	2	0	4	5	.342	0	9	0	56	4	1	.984
	— Atlanta (N.L.).............	C	5	10	0	3	0	0	0	0	.300	0	2	0	10	1	0	1.000
Major League totals (7 years)			325	850	88	219	45	1	24	104	.258	50	128	1	1691	128	16	.991

DIVISION SERIES RECORD

RECORDS: Shares career record for most grand slams—1 (October 3, 1998). ... Shares single-inning record for most runs batted in—4 (October 3, 1998, eighth inning).

Year	Team (League)	Pos.	G	AB	R	H	2B	3B	HR	RBI	Avg.	BB	SO	SB	PO	A	E	Avg.
1995—	Atlanta (N.L.)..............								Did not play.									
1996—	Atlanta (N.L.)..............	C	1	3	0	1	0	0	0	0	.333	0	0	0	10	0	0	1.000
1997—	Atlanta (N.L.)..............	C	1	3	0	0	0	0	0	0	.000	0	1	0	6	0	0	1.000
1998—	Atlanta (N.L.)..............	C	1	5	1	1	0	0	1	4	.200	0	2	0	6	0	0	1.000
1999—	Atlanta (N.L.)..............	C	4	16	1	4	0	0	0	3	.250	0	3	0	35	1	0	1.000
Division series totals (4 years)			7	27	2	6	0	0	1	7	.222	0	6	0	57	1	0	1.000

CHAMPIONSHIP SERIES RECORD

NOTES: Named Most Valuable Player (1999).

Year	Team (League)	Pos.	G	AB	R	H	2B	3B	HR	RBI	Avg.	BB	SO	SB	PO	A	E	Avg.
1995—	Atlanta (N.L.)								Did not play.									
1996—	Atlanta (N.L.)..............	C-1B	4	1	0	0	0	0	0	0	.000	1	0	0	7	0	0	1.000
1997—	Atlanta (N.L.)..............	C	2	3	0	0	0	0	0	0	.000	0	0	0	14	0	0	1.000
1998—	Atlanta (N.L.)..............	C	3	4	0	3	0	0	0	0	.750	0	0	0	6	0	0	1.000
1999—	Atlanta (N.L.)..............	C	6	20	2	10	2	0	2	5	.500	1	3	0	42	2	0	1.000
Championship series totals (4 years)			15	28	2	13	2	0	2	5	.464	2	3	0	69	2	0	1.000

WORLD SERIES RECORD

NOTES: Member of World Series championship team (1995).

Year	Team (League)	Pos.	G	AB	R	H	2B	3B	HR	RBI	Avg.	BB	SO	SB	PO	A	E	Avg.
1995—	Atlanta (N.L.)..............								Did not play.									
1996—	Atlanta (N.L.)..............	C	2	1	0	0	0	0	0	0	.000	0	0	0	2	0	0	1.000
1999—	Atlanta (N.L.)..............	C	3	8	0	1	0	0	0	0	.125	1	3	0	23	1	0	1.000
World Series totals (2 years)			5	9	0	1	0	0	0	0	.111	1	3	0	25	1	0	1.000

PEREZ, GEORGE   P   BREWERS

PERSONAL: Born March 20, 1979, in San Pedro de Macoris, Dominican Republic. ... 6-4/220. ... Throws right, bats right. ... Full name: George Alonso Perez.

TRANSACTIONS/CAREER NOTES: Signed as non-drafted free agent by Toronto Blue Jays organization (February 5, 1997). ... Claimed on waivers by Milwaukee Brewers (January 4, 2002).

Year	League	W	L	Pct.	ERA	G	GS	CG	ShO	Sv.	IP	H	R	ER	BB	SO
1997—	Dom. Blue Jays (DSL)........	1	3	.250	3.94	20	4	0	0	1	48	35	24	21	29	34
1998—	Dom. Blue Jays (DSL)........	0	0	...	7.31	12	2	0	0	2	16	17	17	13	17	12
1999—	Medicine Hat (Pio.).........	2	2	.500	5.79	15	8	0	0	1	56	65	46	36	26	41
2000—	Queens (NY-Penn)............	5	1	.833	0.78	29	0	0	0	12	34 2/3	21	3	3	15	35
2001—	Dunedin (FSL)...................	4	3	.571	3.12	41	0	0	0	8	86 2/3	81	39	30	42	48

PEREZ, NEIFI   SS   ROYALS

PERSONAL: Born June 2, 1975, in Villa Mella, Dominican Republic. ... 6-0/175. ... Bats both, throws right. ... Full name: Neifi Neftali Perez Diaz.

TRANSACTIONS/CAREER NOTES: Signed as non-drafted free agent by Colorado Rockies organization (November 9, 1992). ... On Colorado disabled list (April 8-23, 2001). ... Traded by Rockies to Kansas City Royals for OF Jermaine Dye (July 25, 2001).

RECORDS: Holds N.L. single-season record for most at-bats with no intentional bases on balls—690 (1999).

HONORS: Won N.L. Gold Glove as shortstop (2000).

STATISTICAL NOTES: Led California League shortstops with 650 total chances and 86 double plays in 1994. ... Tied for Eastern League lead in double plays by shortstop with 80 in 1995. ... Led Pacific Coast League shortstops with 678 total chances and 91 double plays in 1996. ... Hit for the cycle (July 25, 1998). ... Had 15-game hitting streak (July 27-August 11, 1998). ... Led N.L. with 22 sacrifice hits in 1998. ... Led N.L. shortstops with 272 putouts, 516 assists, 808 total chances and 127 double plays in 1998. ... Led N.L. shortstops with 755 total chances and 124 double plays in 1999. ... Led N.L. shortstops with 829 total chances and 120 double plays in 2000. ... Had 17-game hitting streak (June 1-19, 2001). ... Career major league grand slams: 1.

MISCELLANEOUS: Holds Colorado Rockies all-time record for most triples (49).

P

Year	Team (League)	Pos.	G	AB	R	H	2B	3B	HR	RBI	Avg.	BB	SO	SB	PO	A	E	Avg.
1993—	Bend (N'West)............	SS-2B	75	296	35	77	11	4	3	32	.260	19	43	19	127	244	25	.937
1994—	Central Valley (Calif.)...	SS	•134	506	64	121	16	7	1	35	.239	32	79	9	*223	388	*39	.940
1995—	Colo. Springs (PCL)...	SS	11	36	4	10	4	0	0	2	.278	0	5	1	16	28	3	.936
	—New Haven (East.)......	SS	116	427	59	108	28	3	5	43	.253	24	52	5	175	358	18	*.967
1996—	Colo. Springs (PCL)...	SS	133	*570	77	180	28	12	7	72	.316	21	48	16	*244	*409	*25	.963
	—Colorado (N.L.)........	SS-2B	17	45	4	7	2	0	0	3	.156	0	8	2	21	28	2	.961
1997—	Colo. Springs (PCL)...	SS	68	303	68	110	24	3	8	46	.363	17	27	8	119	198	8	.975
	—Colorado (N.L.).........	SS-2B-3B	83	313	46	91	13	10	5	31	.291	21	43	4	185	287	9	.981
1998—	Colorado (N.L.)........	SS-C	•162	647	80	177	25	9	9	59	.274	38	70	5	†272	†516	20	.975
1999—	Colorado (N.L.).........	SS	157	*690	108	193	27	•11	12	70	.280	28	54	13	*260	*481	14	.980
2000—	Colorado (N.L.).........	SS	•162	651	92	187	39	11	10	71	.287	30	63	3	*288	*523	18	.978
2001—	Colorado (N.L.)........	SS	87	382	65	114	19	8	7	47	.298	16	49	6	145	264	10	.976
	—Kansas City (A.L.)■...	SS-2B	49	199	18	48	7	1	1	12	.241	10	19	3	105	144	5	.980
American League totals (1 year)			49	199	18	48	7	1	1	12	.241	10	19	3	105	144	5	.980
National League totals (6 years)			668	2728	395	769	125	49	43	281	.282	133	287	33	1171	2099	73	.978
Major League totals (6 years)			717	2927	413	817	132	50	44	293	.279	143	306	36	1276	2243	78	.978

PEREZ, ODALIS — P — DODGERS

PERSONAL: Born June 7, 1978, in Las Matas de Farfan, Dominican Republic. ... 6-0/150. ... Throws left, bats left. ... Full name: Odalis Amadol Perez.

HIGH SCHOOL: Damian Davis Ortiz (Las Matas de Farfan, Dominican Republic).

TRANSACTIONS/CAREER NOTES: Signed as non-drafted free agent by Atlanta Braves organization (July 2, 1994). ... On disabled list (July 23, 1999-remainder of season; and April 2, 2000-entire season). ... On Atlanta disabled list (July 22-September 1, 2001); included rehabilitation assignment to Richmond (August 9-September 1). ... Traded by Braves with OF Brian Jordan and P Andy Brown to Los Angeles Dodgers for OF Gary Sheffield (January 15, 2002).

STATISTICAL NOTES: Tied for N.L. lead with three balks in 2001.

Year	League	W	L	Pct.	ERA	G	GS	CG	ShO	Sv.	IP	H	R	ER	BB	SO
1995—	Gulf Coast Braves (GCL)....	3	5	.375	2.22	12	12	1	1	0	65	48	22	16	18	62
1996—	Eugene (N'West)	2	1	.667	3.80	10	6	0	0	0	$23\frac{2}{3}$	26	16	10	11	38
1997—	Macon (S.Atl.)	4	5	.444	1.65	36	0	0	0	5	$87\frac{1}{3}$	67	31	16	27	100
1998—	Greenville (Sou.)	6	5	.545	4.02	23	21	0	0	0	132	127	67	59	53	143
	—Richmond (I.L.)	1	2	.333	2.96	13	0	0	0	3	$24\frac{1}{3}$	26	10	8	7	22
	—Atlanta (N.L.)	0	1	.000	4.22	10	0	0	0	0	$10\frac{2}{3}$	10	5	5	4	5
1999—	Atlanta (N.L.)	4	6	.400	6.00	18	17	0	0	0	93	100	65	62	53	82
2000—	Atlanta (N.L.)							Did not play.								
2001—	Atlanta (N.L.)	7	8	.467	4.91	24	16	0	0	0	$95\frac{1}{3}$	108	55	52	39	71
	—Richmond (I.L.)	1	0	1.000	2.74	5	5	0	0	0	23	23	7	7	2	22
Major League totals (3 years)		11	15	.423	5.38	52	33	0	0	0	199	218	125	119	96	158

DIVISION SERIES RECORD

Year	League	W	L	Pct.	ERA	G	GS	CG	ShO	Sv.	IP	H	R	ER	BB	SO
1998—	Atlanta (N.L.)	1	0	1.000	0.00	1	0	0	0	0	$\frac{2}{3}$	0	0	0	0	1

CHAMPIONSHIP SERIES RECORD

Year	League	W	L	Pct.	ERA	G	GS	CG	ShO	Sv.	IP	H	R	ER	BB	SO
1998—	Atlanta (N.L.)	0	0	...	54.00	2	0	0	0	0	$\frac{1}{3}$	5	2	2	3	0

PEREZ, ROBERT — OF — INDIANS

PERSONAL: Born June 4, 1969, in Bolivar, Venezuela. ... 6-3/230. ... Bats right, throws right. ... Full name: Robert Alexander Jimenez Perez.

HIGH SCHOOL: Raul Leoni Otero (Bolivar, Venezuela).

TRANSACTIONS/CAREER NOTES: Signed as non-drafted free agent by Toronto Blue Jays organization (May 1, 1989). ... Claimed on waivers by Seattle Mariners (March 30, 1998). ... Traded by Mariners to Montreal Expos for C Raul Chavez (May 8, 1998). ... On Montreal disabled list (June 22-July 14, 1998). ... Granted free agency (September 29, 1998). ... Signed by Orix Blue Wave of Japan Pacific League (1999). ... Signed by Toronto Blue Jays organization (March 14, 2000). ... Granted free agency (October 18, 2000). ... Signed by New York Yankees organization (November 16, 2000). ... Granted free agency (June 15, 2001). ... Signed by Milwaukee Brewers organization (June 18, 2001).

STATISTICAL NOTES: Led International League outfielders with 303 total chances in 1993. ... Tied for International League lead in grounding into double plays with 19 in 1993. ... Led International League in grounding into double plays with 21 in 1994. ... Tied for International League lead with eight sacrifice flies in 1994. ... Led International League with 249 total bases in 1995.

Year	Team (League)	Pos.	G	AB	R	H	2B	3B	HR	RBI	Avg.	BB	SO	SB	PO	A	E	Avg.
1989—	Dom. Dodgers (DSL) .	OF	52	219	34	*79	*20	3	5	40	.361	21	23	5	...	...	...	...
1990—	St. Catharines (NY-P) .	OF	52	207	21	54	10	2	5	25	.261	8	34	7	80	5	1	.988
	—Myrtle Beach (S.Atl.)..	OF	21	72	8	21	2	0	1	10	.292	3	9	2	40	1	1	.976
1991—	Dunedin (FSL)	OF	127	480	50	*145	28	6	4	50	*.302	22	72	8	160	10	5	.971
	—Syracuse (I.L.)	OF	4	20	2	4	1	0	0	1	.200	0	2	0	5	0	1	.833
1992—	Knoxville (Sou.)	OF	*139	•526	59	137	25	5	9	59	.260	13	87	11	241	13	7	.973
1993—	Syracuse (I.L.)	OF	138	524	72	154	26	10	12	64	.294	24	65	13	278	•13	*12	.960
1994—	Syracuse (I.L.)	OF-DH	128	510	63	155	28	3	10	65	.304	27	76	4	231	8	9	.964
	—Toronto (A.L.)	OF	4	8	0	1	0	0	0	0	.125	0	1	0	3	1	0	1.000
1995—	Syracuse (I.L.)	OF-DH	122	502	70	*172	*38	6	9	67	*.343	13	60	7	208	7	8	.964
	—Toronto (A.L.)	OF	17	48	2	9	2	0	1	3	.188	0	5	0	30	0	0	1.000
1996—	Toronto (A.L.)	OF-DH	86	202	30	66	10	0	2	21	.327	8	17	3	114	3	2	.983
1997—	Toronto (A.L.)	OF-DH	37	78	4	15	4	1	2	6	.192	0	16	0	35	0	0	1.000
1998—	Seattle (A.L.)■	OF	17	35	3	6	1	0	2	6	.171	0	5	0	20	1	0	1.000
	—Montreal (N.L.)■...	OF	52	106	9	25	1	0	1	8	.236	2	23	0	20	3	4	.852

P

Year	Team (League)	Pos.	G	AB	R	H	2B	3B	HR	RBI	Avg.	BB	SO	SB	PO	A	E	Avg.
1999—	Orix (Jap. Pac.)■		50	166	16	42	10	2	2	23	.253	12	33	0	...	...	...	...
—	Orix (Jp. West.)		46	170	24	61	7	3	10	28	.359	3	21	2	...	...	...	...
2000—	Tennessee (Sou.)	OF	136	*547	66	157	33	1	19	92	.287	26	82	8	222	13	4	.983
2001—	Columbus (I.L.)■	OF	36	146	20	47	7	3	7	27	.322	4	23	6	68	2	0	1.000
—	New York (A.L.)	OF-DH	6	15	1	4	1	0	0	0	.267	1	7	0	7	0	0	1.000
—	Indianapolis (I.L.)■....	OF	20	84	13	28	9	0	3	16	.333	4	11	0	47	0	2	.959
—	Milwaukee (N.L.)	OF	2	5	0	0	0	0	0	0	.000	0	0	0	3	0	0	1.000
American League totals (6 years)			167	386	40	101	18	1	7	36	.262	9	51	3	209	5	2	.991
National League totals (2 years)			54	111	9	25	1	0	1	8	.225	2	23	0	23	3	4	.867
Major League totals (6 years)			221	497	49	126	19	1	8	44	.254	11	74	3	232	8	6	.976

PEREZ, SANTIAGO — SS — RANGERS

PERSONAL: Born December 30, 1975, in Santo Domingo, Dominican Republic. ... 6-2/150. ... Bats both, throws right. ... Full name: Santiago Alberto Perez.

HIGH SCHOOL: Liceo Victor Estrella Luz (Santo Domingo, Dominican Republic).

TRANSACTIONS/CAREER NOTES: Signed as non-drafted free agent by Detroit Tigers organization (March 10, 1993). ... Traded by Tigers with P Mike Myers and P Rick Greene to Milwaukee Brewers for P Bryce Florie and a player to be named later (November 20, 1997). ... On Louisville disabled list (August 1-14 and August 19-31, 1999). ... Traded by Brewers with a player to be named later or cash to San Deigo Padres for P Brandon Kolb (December 1, 2000); Padres traded P Wil Cunnane to Brewers for OF Chad Green to complete deal (December 20, 2000). ... On San Diego disabled list (May 18-June 5, 2001). ... Granted free agency (October 15, 2001). ... Signed by Texas Rangers organization (November 27, 2001).

STATISTICAL NOTES: Led International League shortstops with 29 errors in 1999. ... Led International League shortstops with 27 errors in 2000.

Year	Team (League)	Pos.	G	AB	R	H	2B	3B	HR	RBI	Avg.	BB	SO	SB	PO	A	E	Avg.
1993—	Dom. Tigers (DSL)	IF-OF	58	171	28	45	6	2	0	17	.263	20	22	17	59	47	16	.869
1994—	Dom. Tigers (DSL)	SS	60	227	54	78	7	9	2	47	.344	32	43	20	106	183	39	.881
1995—	Fayetteville (S.Atl.)	SS	130	425	54	101	15	1	4	44	.238	30	98	10	176	327	46	.916
1996—	Lakeland (FSL)	SS	122	418	33	105	18	2	1	27	.251	16	88	6	192	310	41	.924
1997—	Lakeland (FSL)	SS	111	445	66	122	20	12	4	46	.274	20	98	21	148	322	34	.933
1998—	El Paso (Texas)■	SS	107	454	73	139	20	*13	11	64	.306	28	70	21	186	310	*36	.932
—	Louisville (I.L.)	SS-2B	36	133	18	36	4	3	3	14	.271	6	31	6	67	91	6	.963
1999—	Louisville (I.L.)	SS-2B-DH	108	407	57	107	23	8	7	38	.263	31	94	21	150	281	†30	.935
2000—	Indianapolis (I.L.)■....	SS-2B	106	408	74	112	26	7	5	34	.275	44	96	31	156	274	†27	.941
—	Milwaukee (N.L.)	SS	24	52	8	9	2	0	0	2	.173	8	9	4	21	45	6	.917
2001—	San Diego (N.L.)■	OF-SS-2B	43	81	13	16	1	0	0	4	.198	15	29	5	47	13	4	.938
—	Portland (PCL)	OF-2B-SS	46	184	31	50	12	0	5	10	.272	15	59	18	88	29	3	.975
Major League totals (2 years)			67	133	21	25	3	0	0	6	.188	23	38	9	68	58	10	.926

PEREZ, TIMO — OF — METS

PERSONAL: Born April 8, 1977, in Bani, Dominican Republic. ... 5-9/165. ... Bats left, throws left. ... Full name: Timoniel Perez.

TRANSACTIONS/CAREER NOTES: Played with Hiroshima Toyo Carp of Japan Central League (1996-99). ... Signed as non-drafted free agent by New York Mets organization (March 17, 2000). ... On New York disabled list (April 9-27, 2001); included rehabilitation assignment to Norfolk (April 20-27).

Year	Team (League)	Pos.	G	AB	R	H	2B	3B	HR	RBI	Avg.	BB	SO	SB	PO	A	E	Avg.
1996—	Hiroshima (Jap. Cen.)		31	54	8	15	1	0	1	7	.278	2	7	3	...	...	...	...
1997—	Hiroshima (Jap. Cen.)		86	139	17	34	4	2	3	15	.245	10	16	4	...	...	...	...
1998—	Hiroshima (Jap. Cen.)		98	230	22	68	8	1	5	35	.296	20	21	2	...	...	...	...
1999—	Hiroshima (Jap. Cen.)		12	23	2	4	0	0	0	2	.174	3	3	0	...	...	...	...
2000—	St. Lucie (FSL)■	OF	8	31	3	11	4	0	1	8	.355	2	1	3	11	2	0	1.000
—	Norfolk (I.L.)	OF	72	291	45	104	17	5	6	37	.357	16	25	13	198	7	5	.976
—	New York (N.L.)■	OF	24	49	11	14	4	1	1	3	.286	3	5	1	30	2	1	.970
2001—	New York (N.L.)	OF	85	239	26	59	9	1	5	22	.247	12	25	1	128	5	0	1.000
—	Norfolk (I.L.)	OF	48	192	37	69	10	2	6	19	.359	12	18	15	90	8	5	.951
Major League totals (2 years)			109	288	37	73	13	2	6	25	.253	15	30	2	158	7	1	.994

DIVISION SERIES RECORD

Year	Team (League)	Pos.	G	AB	R	H	2B	3B	HR	RBI	Avg.	BB	SO	SB	PO	A	E	Avg.
2000—	New York (N.L.)	PH-RF	4	17	2	5	1	0	0	3	.294	0	2	1	10	0	0	1.000

CHAMPIONSHIP SERIES RECORD

Year	Team (League)	Pos.	G	AB	R	H	2B	3B	HR	RBI	Avg.	BB	SO	SB	PO	A	E	Avg.
2000—	New York (N.L.)	OF	5	23	8	7	2	0	0	0	.304	1	3	2	16	2	1	.947

WORLD SERIES RECORD

Year	Team (League)	Pos.	G	AB	R	H	2B	3B	HR	RBI	Avg.	BB	SO	SB	PO	A	E	Avg.
2000—	New York (N.L.)	OF	5	16	1	2	0	0	0	0	.125	1	4	0	8	1	1	.900

P

PERSONAL: Born December 29, 1973, in Barquisimeto, Venezuela. ... 5-11/177. ... Bats both, throws right. ... Full name: Tomas Orlando Perez.

TRANSACTIONS/CAREER NOTES: Signed as non-drafted free agent by Montreal Expos organization (July 11, 1991). ... Selected by California Angels from Expos organization in Rule 5 major league draft (December 5, 1994). ... Contract sold by Angels to Toronto Blue Jays (December 5, 1994). ... On Toronto disabled list (June 25-July 25, 1997); included rehabilitation assignment to Syracuse (July 12-24). ... Traded by Blue Jays to Angels for IF Dave Hollins and cash (March 30, 1999). ... On Edmonton disabled list (April 21-June 10, 1999). ... Granted free agency (October 15, 1999). ... Signed by Philadelphia Phillies organization (December 15, 1999).

STATISTICAL NOTES: Led Gulf Coast League shortstops with 338 total chances and 39 double plays in 1993. ... Led Midwest League shortstops with 217 putouts and 65 double plays in 1994. ... Led International League with 14 sacrifice hits in 1997. ... Led International League shortstops with .977 fielding percentage in 1998. ... Switch-hit home runs in one game (July 24, 2001).

							BATTING								FIELDING		
Year Team (League)	Pos.	G	AB	R	H	2B	3B	HR	RBI	Avg.	BB	SO	SB	PO	A	E	Avg.
1992—Dom. Expos (DSL)	IF	44	151	35	46	7	0	1	19	.305	27	20	12	112	138	12	.954
1993—GC Expos (GCL)	SS	52	189	27	46	3	1	2	21	.243	23	25	8	*121	*205	12	*.964
1994—Burlington (Midw.)	SS-2B	119	465	76	122	22	1	8	47	.262	48	78	8	†221	347	34	.944
1995—Toronto (A.L.).............	SS-2B-3B	41	98	12	24	3	1	1	8	.245	7	18	0	48	77	5	.962
1996—Syracuse (I.L.)...........	SS-2B	40	123	15	34	10	1	1	13	.276	7	19	8	80	97	7	.962
—Toronto (A.L.).............	2B-3B-SS	91	295	24	74	13	4	1	19	.251	25	29	1	151	250	15	.964
1997—Syracuse (I.L.)...........	SS	89	303	32	68	13	0	1	20	.224	37	67	3	158	274	12	.973
—Toronto (A.L.).............	SS-2B	40	123	9	24	3	2	0	9	.195	11	28	1	58	124	3	.984
1998—Syracuse (I.L.)...........	SS-2B	116	404	40	102	15	4	3	37	.252	18	67	4	205	437	15	†.977
—Toronto (A.L.).............	SS-2B	6	9	1	1	0	0	0	0	.111	1	3	0	6	6	0	1.000
1999—Edmonton (PCL)■......	SS-2B	83	296	31	77	17	1	4	40	.260	19	43	2	149	243	11	.973
2000—Reading (East.)■	PR	0	0	0	0	0	0	0	0	...	0	0	0	...	...	...	...
—Philadelphia (N.L.)......	SS	45	140	17	31	7	1	1	13	.221	11	30	1	76	89	4	.976
—Scranton/W.B. (I.L.) ...	3B-SS-2B	77	279	44	82	16	2	10	56	.294	16	48	4	72	158	9	.962
2001—Philadelphia (N.L.)......	2B-3B-SS-OF	62	135	11	41	7	1	3	19	.304	7	22	0	57	87	1	.993
American League totals (4 years)		178	525	46	123	19	7	2	36	.234	44	78	2	263	457	23	.969
National League totals (2 years)		107	275	28	72	14	2	4	32	.262	18	52	1	133	176	5	.984
Major League totals (6 years)		285	800	74	195	33	9	6	68	.244	62	130	3	396	633	28	.974

PERSONAL: Born June 8, 1975, in Burlington, Iowa. ... 6-0/205. ... Throws left, bats left. ... Full name: Matthew Alan Perisho.

HIGH SCHOOL: McClintock (Tempe, Ariz.).

TRANSACTIONS/CAREER NOTES: Selected by California Angels organization in third round of free-agent draft (June 3, 1993). ... Angels franchise renamed Anaheim Angels for 1997 season. ... Traded by Angels to Texas Rangers for IF Mike Bell (October 31, 1997). ... On Oklahoma disabled list (June 29-July 25, 1998). ... Traded by Rangers to Detroit Tigers for P Kevin Mobley and P Brandon Villafuerte (December 15, 2000). ... On Detroit disabled list (May 5-25, 2001); included rehabilitation assignment to Toledo (May 16-25).

Year League	W	L	Pct.	ERA	G	GS	CG	ShO	Sv.	IP	H	R	ER	BB	SO
1993—Arizona Angels (Ariz.)........	7	3	.700	3.66	11	11	1	1	0	64	58	32	26	23	65
1994—Cedar Rapids (Midw.)	12	9	.571	4.33	27	27	0	0	0	147 2/3	165	90	71	88	107
1995—Lake Elsinore (Calif.)	8	9	.471	6.32	24	22	0	0	0	115 1/3	137	91	81	60	68
1996—Lake Elsinore (Calif.)	7	5	.583	4.20	21	18	1	1	0	128 2/3	131	72	60	58	97
—Midland (Texas).................	3	2	.600	3.21	8	8	0	0	0	53 1/3	48	22	19	20	50
1997—Midland (Texas)................	5	2	.714	2.96	10	10	3	•1	0	73	60	26	24	26	62
—Anaheim (A.L.).................	0	2	.000	6.00	11	8	0	0	0	45	50	34	30	28	35
—Vancouver (PCL)	4	4	.500	5.33	9	9	1	0	0	52 1/3	68	42	31	29	47
1998—Tulsa (Texas)■.................	0	0	...	6.00	1	1	0	0	0	3	3	2	2	3	1
—Oklahoma (PCL)	8	5	.615	3.89	15	15	1	0	0	90 1/3	91	41	39	42	60
—Texas (A.L.)...................	0	2	.000	27.00	2	2	0	0	0	5	15	17	15	8	2
1999—Oklahoma (PCL)...............	*15	7	.682	4.61	27	27	2	0	0	156 1/3	160	86	80	*78	150
—Texas (A.L.)...................	0	0	...	2.61	4	1	0	0	0	10 1/3	8	3	3	2	17
2000—Texas (A.L.)■.................	2	7	.222	7.37	34	13	0	0	0	105	136	99	86	67	74
2001—Detroit (A.L.)■...............	2	3	.400	5.72	30	4	0	0	0	39 1/3	54	29	25	14	19
—Toledo (I.L.)......................	2	2	.400	1.71	25	2	0	0	9	42	42	10	8	11	28
Major League totals (5 years)	4	14	.222	6.99	81	28	0	0	0	204 2/3	272	182	159	119	147

PERSONAL: Born September 15, 1969, in Mayo, Fla. ... 6-2/220. ... Bats right, throws right. ... Full name: Herbert Edward Perry Jr. ... Brother of Chan Perry, outfielder/first baseman, Atlanta Braves organization.

HIGH SCHOOL: Lafayette (Mayo, Fla.).

COLLEGE: Florida.

TRANSACTIONS/CAREER NOTES: Selected by Cleveland Indians organization in second round of free-agent draft (June 3, 1991). ... On disabled list (June 18-July 13, 1991; and July 23, 1993-remainder of season). ... On Buffalo disabled list (June 7-27, 1996). ... On Cleveland disabled list (September 11, 1996-remainder of season; and March 26, 1997-entire season). ... Selected by Tampa Bay Devil Rays in third round (68th pick overall) of expansion draft (November 18, 1997). ... On Tampa Bay disabled list (March 25, 1998-entire season); included rehabilitation assignments to Durham (June 1-7), Gulf Coast Devil Rays (August 17-25) and St. Petersburg (August 27-28). ... On Tampa Bay disabled list (July 22-September 1, 1999); included rehabilitation assignment to Durham (August 25-31). ... Claimed on waivers by Chicago White Sox (April 21, 2000). ... On disabled list (June 8-22, 2001). ... Traded by White Sox to Texas Rangers for a player to be named later (November 27, 2001); White Sox acquired P Corey Lee to complete deal (December 17, 2001).

STATISTICAL NOTES: Led Eastern League in being hit by pitch with 15 in 1993.

Year Team (League)	Pos.	G	AB	R	H	2B	3B	HR	RBI	Avg.	BB	SO	SB	PO	A	E	Avg.
1991— Watertown (NY-Penn)	DH	14	52	3	11	2	0	0	5	.212	8	7	0	...	...	...	...
1992— Kinston (Caro.)..........	1B-OF-3B	121	449	74	125	16	1	19	77	.278	46	89	12	297	39	5	.985
1993— Canton/Akron (East.)..1B-3B-DH-OF		89	327	52	88	21	1	9	55	.269	37	47	7	378	86	10	.979
1994— Charlotte (I.L.)...........	1-3-DH-O	102	376	67	123	20	4	13	70	.327	41	55	9	747	55	6	.993
— Cleveland (A.L.)........	1B-3B	4	9	1	1	0	0	0	1	.111	3	1	0	25	5	1	.968
1995— Buffalo (A.A.)............	1B-DH	49	180	27	57	14	1	2	17	.317	15	18	1	419	44	3	.994
— Cleveland (A.L.)........	1B-DH-3B	52	162	23	51	13	1	3	23	.315	13	28	1	391	30	0	1.000
1996— Buffalo (A.A.)............1B-3B-DH-OF		40	151	21	51	7	1	5	30	.338	7	19	4	217	24	4	.984
— Cleveland (A.L.)........	1B-3B	7	12	1	1	1	0	0	0	.083	1	2	1	29	2	0	1.000
1997— Cleveland (A.L.)								Did not play.									
1998— Durham (I.L.)■	1B-DH	5	17	1	5	4	0	0	1	.294	0	2	0	19	2	0	1.000
— GC Devil Rays (GCL) ..	DH-3B	8	26	1	3	0	0	0	1	.115	3	5	0	1	8	1	.900
— St. Petersburg (FSL) ..	3B	2	8	1	1	0	0	0	0	.125	2	2	0	2	5	1	.875
1999— Durham (I.L.)..........	3B	27	103	21	32	8	0	5	20	.311	6	21	0	56	12	2	.971
— Tampa Bay (A.L.).......3B-1B-OF-DH		66	209	29	53	10	1	6	32	.254	16	42	0	113	79	5	.975
2000— Tampa Bay (A.L.)........	3B-1B	7	28	2	6	1	0	0	1	.214	2	7	0	7	10	1	.944
— Chicago (A.L.)■........	3B-DH-1B	109	383	69	118	29	1	12	61	.308	22	68	4	92	200	9	.970
2001— Chicago (A.L.)	3B-1B-DH	92	285	38	73	21	1	7	32	.256	23	55	2	105	115	10	.957
Major League totals (6 years)		337	1088	163	303	75	4	28	150	.278	80	203	8	762	441	26	.979

DIVISION SERIES RECORD

Year Team (League)	Pos.	G	AB	R	H	2B	3B	HR	RBI	Avg.	BB	SO	SB	PO	A	E	Avg.
1995— Cleveland (A.L.).........	PH	1	1	0	0	0	0	0	0	.000	0	0	0	...	...	...	...
2000— Chicago (A.L.)	3B	3	9	0	4	1	0	0	1	.444	2	2	0	5	7	0	1.000
Division series totals (2 years)		4	10	0	4	1	0	0	1	.400	2	2	0	5	7	0	1.000

CHAMPIONSHIP SERIES RECORD

Year Team (League)	Pos.	G	AB	R	H	2B	3B	HR	RBI	Avg.	BB	SO	SB	PO	A	E	Avg.
1995— Cleveland (A.L.)..........	1B	3	8	0	0	0	0	0	0	.000	1	3	0	30	0	0	1.000

WORLD SERIES RECORD

Year Team (League)	Pos.	G	AB	R	H	2B	3B	HR	RBI	Avg.	BB	SO	SB	PO	A	E	Avg.
1995— Cleveland (A.L.)..........	1B	3	5	0	0	0	0	0	0	.000	0	2	0	13	2	0	1.000

PERSON, ROBERT P PHILLIES

PERSONAL: Born October 6, 1969, in St. Louis. ... 6-0/194. ... Throws right, bats right. ... Full name: Robert Alan Person.

HIGH SCHOOL: University City (Mo.).

JUNIOR COLLEGE: Seminole (Okla.) Junior College.

TRANSACTIONS/CAREER NOTES: Selected by Cleveland Indians organization in 25th round of free-agent draft (June 5, 1989). ... Loaned by Indians organization to Bend, independent (June 12-25, 1991). ... Traded by Indians to Chicago White Sox for P Grady Hall (June 27, 1991). ... On disabled list (April 10-May 13, 1992). ... Selected by Florida Marlins in second round (47th pick overall) of expansion draft (November 17, 1992). ... Granted free agency (December 19, 1992). ... Re-signed by Marlins organization (January 8, 1993). ... Traded by Marlins to New York Mets for P Steve Long (March 30, 1994). ... Traded by Mets to Toronto Blue Jays for 1B John Olerud and cash (December 20, 1996). ... On Toronto disabled list (May 8-26 and September 9-28, 1997). ... On Syracuse disabled list (April 19-27, 1998). ... On Toronto disabled list (March 25-April 12, 1999); included rehabilitation assignment to Dunedin (April 9-10). ... Traded by Blue Jays to Philadelphia Phillies for P Paul Spoljaric (May 5, 1999). ... On Philadelphia disabled list (June 19-July 22, 2000); included rehabilitation assignments to Clearwater (July 12-16) and Reading (July 17-22). ... On suspended list (June 22-28, 2001).

MISCELLANEOUS: Appeared in two games as pinch runner with New York (1996).

Year League	W	L	Pct.	ERA	G	GS	CG	ShO	Sv.	IP	H	R	ER	BB	SO
1989— Burlington (Appl.)................	0	1	.000	3.18	10	5	0	0	1	34	23	13	12	17	19
1990— Watertown (NY-Penn)	1	0	1.000	1.10	5	2	0	0	0	16 1/3	8	2	2	7	19
— Kinston (Caro.).................	1	0	1.000	2.70	4	3	0	0	0	16 2/3	17	6	5	9	7
— Gulf Coast Indians (GCL) ...	0	2	.000	7.36	24	0	0	0	2	7 1/3	10	7	6	4	8
1991— Kinston (Caro.).................	3	5	.375	4.67	11	11	0	0	0	52	56	37	27	42	45
— Bend (N'West)■..............	1	1	.500	3.60	2	2	0	0	0	10	6	6	4	5	6
— South Bend (Midw.)■.......	4	3	.571	3.30	13	13	0	0	0	76 1/3	50	35	28	56	66
1992— Sarasota (FSL)	5	7	.417	3.59	19	18	1	0	0	105 1/3	90	48	42	62	85
1993— High Desert (Calif.)■........	12	10	.545	4.69	28	26	4	0	0	169	184	*115	88	48	107
1994— Binghamton (East.)■.........	9	6	.600	3.45	31	23	3	2	0	159	124	68	61	68	130
1995— Binghamton (East.)............	5	4	.556	3.11	26	7	1	0	7	66 2/3	46	27	23	25	65
— Norfolk (I.L.)...................	2	1	.667	4.50	5	4	0	0	0	32	30	17	16	13	33
— New York (N.L.).............	1	0	1.000	0.75	3	1	0	0	0	12	5	1	1	2	10
1996— New York (N.L.).............	4	5	.444	4.52	27	13	0	0	0	89 2/3	86	50	45	35	76
— Norfolk (I.L.)...................	5	0	1.000	3.35	8	8	0	0	0	43	30	16	16	21	32
1997— Toronto (A.L.)■..............	5	10	.333	5.61	23	22	0	0	0	128 1/3	125	86	80	60	99
— Syracuse (I.L.).................	1	0	1.000	0.00	1	1	0	0	0	7	4	1	0	2	5
1998— Toronto (A.L.)................	3	1	.750	7.04	27	0	0	0	6	38 1/3	45	31	30	22	31
— Syracuse (I.L.).................	3	3	.500	2.29	20	6	1	0	6	59	38	17	15	29	55
1999— Dunedin (FSL)...............	0	0	...	3.00	1	1	0	0	0	3	4	1	1	1	3
— Toronto (A.L.).................	0	2	.000	9.82	11	0	0	0	2	11	9	12	12	15	12
— Philadelphia (N.L.)■.........	10	5	.667	4.27	31	22	0	0	0	137	130	72	65	70	127
2000— Philadelphia (N.L.)...........	9	7	.563	3.63	28	28	1	1	0	173 1/3	144	73	70	95	164
— Clearwater (FSL)	0	0	...	6.75	1	1	0	0	0	2 2/3	3	2	2	1	2
— Reading (East.)...............	1	0	1.000	5.79	1	0	0	0	0	4 2/3	3	3	3	3	7
2001— Philadelphia (N.L.)...........	15	7	.682	4.19	33	33	3	1	0	208 1/3	179	103	97	80	183
A.L. totals (3 years)	8	13	.381	6.18	61	22	0	0	8	177 2/3	179	129	122	97	142
N.L. totals (5 years)	39	24	.619	4.03	122	97	4	2	0	620 1/3	544	299	278	282	560
Major League totals (7 years).......	47	37	.560	4.51	183	119	4	2	8	798	723	428	400	379	702

RECORD AS POSITION PLAYER

Year Team (League)	Pos.	G	AB	R	H	2B	3B	HR	RBI	Avg.	BB	SO	SB	PO	A	E	Avg.
1990— GC Indians (GCL)	OF	24	46	6	4	0	0	0	3	.087	10	12	1	10	2	0	1.000

P

PERSONAL: Born January 28, 1972, in Fort Thomas, Ky. ... 6-1/170. ... Throws left, bats left. ... Full name: Christopher Michael Peters.
HIGH SCHOOL: Peters Township (McMurray, Pa.).
COLLEGE: Indiana.
TRANSACTIONS/CAREER NOTES: Selected by Pittsburgh Pirates organization in 37th round of free-agent draft (June 3, 1993). ... On Pittsburgh disabled list (May 24-August 21, 1999); included rehabilitation assignments to Nashville (June 8-18, June 28-July 16 and July 30-August 21). ... On Pittsburgh disabled list (August 11, 2000-remainder of season); included rehabilitation assignment to Nashville (August 28-September 3). ... Granted free agency (December 21, 2000). ... Signed by Montreal Expos organization (January 10, 2001). ... Released by Expos (May 30, 2001). ... Signed by Cincinnati Reds organization (June 6, 2001). ... Released by Reds (July 17, 2001). ... Signed by New York Yankees organization (July 18, 2001). ... Granted free agency (October 15, 2001). ... Signed by Toronto Blue Jays organization (December 18, 2001).

Year League	W	L	Pct.	ERA	G	GS	CG	ShO	Sv.	IP	H	R	ER	BB	SO
1993— Welland (NY-Penn)	1	0	1.000	4.55	16	0	0	0	0	27 2/3	33	16	14	20	25
1994— Augusta (S.Atl.)	4	5	.444	4.30	54	0	0	0	4	60 2/3	51	34	29	33	83
— Salem (Caro.)	1	0	1.000	13.50	3	0	0	0	0	3 1/3	5	5	5	1	2
1995— Lynchburg (Caro.)	11	5	.688	2.43	24	24	3	*3	0	144 2/3	126	57	39	35	132
— Carolina (Sou.)	2	0	1.000	1.29	2	2	0	0	0	14	9	2	2	2	7
1996— Carolina (Sou.)	7	3	.700	2.64	14	14	0	0	0	92	73	37	27	34	69
— Calgary (PCL)	1	1	.500	0.98	4	4	0	0	0	27 2/3	18	3	3	8	16
— Pittsburgh (N.L.)	2	4	.333	5.63	16	10	0	0	0	64	72	43	40	25	28
1997— Calgary (PCL)	2	4	.333	4.38	14	9	0	0	1	51 1/3	52	32	25	30	55
— Pittsburgh (N.L.)	2	2	.500	4.58	31	1	0	0	0	37 1/3	38	23	19	21	17
1998— Pittsburgh (N.L.)	8	10	.444	3.47	39	21	1	0	1	148	142	63	57	55	103
1999— Pittsburgh (N.L.)	5	4	.556	6.59	19	11	0	0	0	71	98	59	52	27	46
— Nashville (PCL)	3	1	.750	2.19	11	9	0	0	1	49 1/3	54	18	12	15	34
2000— Pittsburgh (N.L.)	0	1	.000	2.86	18	0	0	0	1	28 1/3	23	9	9	14	16
— Nashville (PCL)	2	4	.333	5.47	11	11	0	0	0	52 2/3	71	38	32	26	32
2001— Montreal (N.L.)■	2	4	.333	7.55	13	6	0	0	0	31	47	26	26	15	14
— Louisville (I.L.)■	3	1	.750	6.89	8	6	0	0	0	31 1/3	46	26	24	18	16
— Columbus (I.L.)■	2	4	.333	4.27	9	8	0	0	0	52 2/3	56	36	25	25	29
Major League totals (6 years)	**19**	**25**	**.432**	**4.81**	**136**	**49**	**1**	**0**	**2**	**379 2/3**	**420**	**223**	**203**	**157**	**224**

PERSONAL: Born April 9, 1976, in Elkhorn, Neb. ... 6-3/220. ... Throws right, bats left. ... Full name: Kyle J. Peterson.
HIGH SCHOOL: Creighton Prep (Omaha, Neb.).
COLLEGE: Stanford.
TRANSACTIONS/CAREER NOTES: Selected by Milwaukee Brewers organization in first round (13th pick overall) of free-agent draft (June 3, 1997). ... On Milwaukee disabled list (March 28, 2000-entire season); included rehabilitation assignments to Beloit (August 1-12) and Huntsville (August 13-18). ... On Indianapolis disabled list (August 3-21, 2001).

Year League	W	L	Pct.	ERA	G	GS	CG	ShO	Sv.	IP	H	R	ER	BB	SO
1997— Ogden (Pio.)	0	0	...	0.87	3	3	0	0	0	10 1/3	5	2	1	4	11
1998— Stockton (Calif.)	4	7	.364	3.55	17	17	0	0	0	96 1/3	99	54	38	33	109
— El Paso (Texas)	3	2	.600	4.40	7	7	1	0	0	43	41	24	21	16	33
— Louisville (I.L.)	1	0	1.000	7.94	1	1	0	0	0	5 2/3	8	5	5	2	4
1999— Louisville (I.L.)	7	6	.538	3.55	18	18	1	1	0	109	90	52	43	42	95
— Milwaukee (N.L.)	4	7	.364	4.56	17	12	0	0	0	77	87	46	39	25	34
2000— Beloit (Midw.)	1	1	.500	1.80	3	3	0	0	0	15	10	4	3	4	17
— Huntsville (Sou.)	0	1	.000	7.71	1	1	0	0	0	4 2/3	6	7	4	4	1
2001— Indianapolis (I.L.)	2	10	.167	5.71	21	20	0	0	0	115	143	81	73	26	73
— Milwaukee (N.L.)	1	2	.333	5.52	3	2	0	0	0	14 2/3	19	10	9	4	12
Major League totals (2 years)	**5**	**9**	**.357**	**4.71**	**20**	**14**	**0**	**0**	**0**	**91 2/3**	**106**	**56**	**48**	**29**	**46**

PERSONAL: Born November 18, 1965, in Beaumont, Texas. ... 6-0/198. ... Throws right, bats right. ... Full name: Mark Joseph Petkovsek. ... Name pronounced PET-kie-zeck.
HIGH SCHOOL: Kelly (Beaumont, Texas).
COLLEGE: Texas.
TRANSACTIONS/CAREER NOTES: Selected by Texas Rangers organization in supplemental round ("sandwich pick" between first and second round, 29th pick overall) of free-agent draft (June 2, 1987); pick received as compensation for New York Yankees signing Type A free-agent OF Gary Ward. ... Granted free agency (October 16, 1991). ... Signed by Pittsburgh Pirates organization (January 22, 1992). ... Granted free agency (October 15, 1992). ... Re-signed by Pirates organization (November 9, 1992). ... On Buffalo disabled list (July 4-23, 1993). ... Granted free agency (October 12, 1993). ... Signed by Houston Astros organization (March 4, 1994). ... On disabled list (July 20-August 12, 1994). ... Granted free agency (October 15, 1994). ... Signed by St. Louis Cardinals organization (November 18, 1994). ... On Louisville suspended list (May 12-17, 1995). ... On St. Louis disabled list (March 22-April 19, 1996); included rehabilitation assignments to St. Petersburg (April 5-12) and Louisville (April 12-19). ... On suspended list (September 9-12, 1997). ... Traded by Cardinals to Anaheim Angels for a player to be named later or cash (December 14, 1998); Cardinals acquired C Matt Garrick to complete deal (December 14, 1998). ... On Anaheim disabled list (May 17-June 12, 2000); included rehabilitation assignment to Lake Elsinore (June 7-12). ... Granted free agency (November 1, 2000). ... Signed by Texas Rangers (December 10, 2000).
STATISTICAL NOTES: Pitched 5-0 no-hit victory against Colorado Springs (May 16, 1994).

Year League	W	L	Pct.	ERA	G	GS	CG	ShO	Sv.	IP	H	R	ER	BB	SO
1987— Gulf Coast Rangers (GCL)	0	0	...	3.18	3	1	0	0	0	5 2/3	4	2	2	2	7
— Charlotte (FSL)	3	4	.429	4.02	11	10	0	0	0	56	67	36	25	17	23
1988— Charlotte (FSL)	10	11	.476	2.97	28	28	7	•5	0	175 2/3	156	71	58	42	95
1989— Tulsa (Texas)	8	5	.615	3.47	21	21	1	0	0	140	144	63	54	35	66
— Oklahoma City (A.A.)	0	4	.000	7.34	6	6	0	0	0	30 2/3	39	27	25	18	8
1990— Oklahoma City (A.A.)	7	*14	.333	5.25	28	28	2	1	0	151	*187	*103	88	42	81

P

Year League	W	L	Pct.	ERA	G	GS	CG	ShO	Sv.	IP	H	R	ER	BB	SO
1991— Oklahoma City (A.A.).........	9	8	.529	4.93	25	24	3	1	0	149²/₃	162	89	82	38	67
— Texas (A.L.)....................	0	1	.000	14.46	4	1	0	0	0	9¹/₃	21	16	15	4	6
1992— Buffalo (A.A.)■	8	8	.500	3.53	32	22	1	0	1	150¹/₃	150	76	59	44	49
1993— Buffalo (A.A.)................	3	4	.429	4.33	14	11	1	0	0	70²/₃	74	38	34	16	27
— Pittsburgh (N.L.).............	3	0	1.000	6.96	26	0	0	0	0	32¹/₃	43	25	25	9	14
1994— Tucson (PCL)■................	10	7	.588	4.62	25	23	1	1	0	138¹/₃	176	87	71	40	69
1995— Louisville (A.A.)■............	4	1	.800	2.32	8	8	2	1	0	54¹/₃	38	16	14	8	30
— St. Louis (N.L.)................	6	6	.500	4.00	26	21	1	1	0	137¹/₃	136	71	61	35	71
1996— St. Petersburg (FSL)	0	0	...	4.50	3	0	0	0	0	6	6	3	3	0	5
— Louisville (A.A.)...............	0	1	.000	9.00	2	1	0	0	0	3	5	4	3	1	4
— St. Louis (N.L.)................	11	2	.846	3.55	48	6	0	0	0	88²/₃	83	37	35	35	45
1997— St. Louis (N.L.)................	4	7	.364	5.06	55	2	0	0	2	96	109	61	54	31	51
1998— St. Louis (N.L.)................	7	4	.636	4.77	48	10	0	0	0	105²/₃	131	63	56	36	55
1999— Anaheim (A.L.)■..............	10	4	.714	3.47	64	0	0	0	1	83	85	37	32	21	43
2000— Anaheim (A.L.)..............	4	2	.667	4.22	64	1	0	0	2	81	86	39	38	23	31
— Lake Elsinore (Calif.)..........	0	0	...	3.38	2	0	0	0	0	2²/₃	3	1	1	3	3
2001— Texas (A.L.)■................	1	2	.333	6.69	55	0	0	0	0	76²/₃	103	61	57	28	42
A.L. totals (4 years)	15	9	.625	5.11	187	2	0	0	3	250	295	153	142	76	122
N.L. totals (5 years)	31	19	.620	4.52	203	39	1	1	2	460	502	257	231	146	236
Major League totals (9 years).......	46	28	.622	4.73	390	41	1	1	5	710	797	410	373	222	358

DIVISION SERIES RECORD

Year League	W	L	Pct.	ERA	G	GS	CG	ShO	Sv.	IP	H	R	ER	BB	SO
1996— St. Louis (N.L.)..................	0	0	...	0.00	1	0	0	0	0	2	0	0	0	0	1

CHAMPIONSHIP SERIES RECORD

RECORDS: Shares single-series record for most games pitched—6 (1996).

Year League	W	L	Pct.	ERA	G	GS	CG	ShO	Sv.	IP	H	R	ER	BB	SO
1996— St. Louis (N.L.).................	0	1	.000	7.36	6	0	0	0	0	7¹/₃	11	6	6	4	7

PETRICK, BEN — C — ROCKIES

PERSONAL: Born April 7, 1977, in Hillsboro, Ore. ... 6-0/205. ... Bats right, throws right. ... Full name: Benjamin Wayne Petrick.
HIGH SCHOOL: Glencoe (Hillsboro, Ore.).
TRANSACTIONS/CAREER NOTES: Selected by Colorado Rockies organization in second round of free-agent draft (June 3, 1995). ... On Carolina disabled list (April 26-May 6, 1999). ... On Colorado disabled list (August 2-September 1, 2001); included rehabilitation assignment to Colorado Springs (August 9-29).
STATISTICAL NOTES: Led Pacific Coast League catchers with 14 passed balls in 1999.

Year Team (League)	Pos.	G	AB	R	H	2B	3B	HR	RBI	Avg.	BB	SO	SB	PO	A	E	Avg.
1996— Asheville (S.Atl.)............	C-DH	122	446	74	105	24	2	14	52	.235	75	98	19	766	95	12	.986
1997— Salem (Caro.)............	C-DH	121	412	68	102	23	4	15	56	.248	62	100	30	754	91	10	.988
1998— New Haven (East.)......	C-DH-OF	106	349	52	83	21	3	18	50	.238	56	89	7	536	43	5	.991
1999— Carolina (Sou.)..........	C-DH	20	68	18	21	5	1	4	22	.309	9	15	3	113	10	1	.992
— Colo. Springs (PCL) ...	C-DH-OF	84	282	56	88	16	5	19	64	.312	44	58	9	411	32	9	.980
— Colorado (N.L.)	C	19	62	13	20	3	0	4	12	.323	10	13	1	100	7	2	.982
2000— Colo. Springs (PCL) ...	C	63	248	38	78	22	3	9	47	.315	32	40	7	375	39	6	.986
— Colorado (N.L.)	C	52	146	32	47	10	1	3	20	.322	20	33	1	248	19	4	.985
2001— Colorado (N.L.)	C-1B	85	244	41	58	15	3	11	39	.238	31	67	3	459	29	8	.984
— Colo. Springs (PCL) ...	OF-C-1B	18	64	11	16	2	0	1	9	.250	13	21	1	81	8	4	.957
Major League totals (3 years)		156	452	86	125	28	4	18	71	.277	61	113	5	807	55	14	.984

PETTITTE, ANDY — P — YANKEES

PERSONAL: Born June 15, 1972, in Baton Rouge, La. ... 6-5/225. ... Throws left, bats left. ... Full name: Andrew Eugene Pettitte.
HIGH SCHOOL: Deer Park (Texas).
JUNIOR COLLEGE: San Jacinto (North) College (Texas).
TRANSACTIONS/CAREER NOTES: Selected by New York Yankees organization in 22nd round of free-agent draft (June 4, 1990); did not sign. ... Signed as non-drafted free agent by Yankees organization (May 25, 1991). ... On Albany temporarily inactive list (June 5-10, 1994). ... On New York disabled list (March 26-April 17, 1999); included rehabilitation assignment to Tampa (April 12). ... On disabled list (April 13-26, 2000; and June 15-July 1, 2001).
HONORS: Named lefthanded pitcher on THE SPORTING NEWS A.L. All-Star team (1996).

Year League	W	L	Pct.	ERA	G	GS	CG	ShO	Sv.	IP	H	R	ER	BB	SO
1991— Gulf Coast Yankees (GCL)..	4	1	.800	0.98	6	6	0	0	0	36²/₃	16	6	4	8	51
— Oneonta (NY-Penn)	2	2	.500	2.18	6	6	1	0	0	33	33	18	8	16	32
1992— Greensboro (S.Atl.)............	10	4	.714	2.20	27	27	2	1	0	168	141	53	41	55	130
1993— Prince William (Caro.)........	11	9	.550	3.04	26	26	2	1	0	159²/₃	146	68	54	47	129
— Albany (East.)..................	1	0	1.000	3.60	1	1	0	0	0	5	5	4	2	2	6
1994— Albany/Colonie (East.)........	7	2	.778	2.71	11	11	0	0	0	73	60	32	22	18	50
— Columbus (I.L.)..............	7	2	.778	2.98	16	16	3	0	0	96²/₃	101	40	32	21	61
1995— Columbus (I.L.)	0	0	...	0.00	2	2	0	0	0	11²/₃	7	0	0	0	8
— New York (A.L.).............	12	9	.571	4.17	31	26	3	0	0	175	183	86	81	63	114
1996— New York (A.L.)..............	*21	8	.724	3.87	35	34	2	0	0	221	229	105	95	72	162
1997— New York (A.L.)..............	18	7	.720	2.88	35	•35	4	1	0	240¹/₃	233	86	77	65	166
1998— New York (A.L.)..............	16	11	.593	4.24	33	32	5	0	0	216¹/₃	226	110	102	87	146
1999— Tampa (FSL).....................	1	0	1.000	0.00	1	1	0	0	0	5	4	0	0	2	8
— New York (A.L.)..............	14	11	.560	4.70	31	31	0	0	0	191²/₃	216	105	100	89	121
2000— New York (A.L.)..............	19	9	.679	4.35	32	32	3	1	0	204²/₃	219	111	99	80	125
2001— New York (A.L.)..............	15	10	.600	3.99	31	31	2	0	0	200²/₃	224	103	89	41	164
Major League totals (7 years).......	115	65	.639	3.99	228	221	19	2	0	1449²/₃	1530	706	643	497	998

P

RECORDS: Holds A.L. career records for most games started—9; innings pitched 57; hits allowed—60; runs allowed—27; and earned runs allowed—27. ... Shares A.L. career record for most wins—3; and losses—3.

Year League	W	L	Pct.	ERA	G	GS	CG	ShO	Sv.	IP	H	R	ER	BB	SO
1995— New York (A.L.)	0	0	...	5.14	1	1	0	0	0	7	9	4	4	3	0
1996— New York (A.L.)	0	0	...	5.68	1	1	0	0	0	6 1/3	4	4	4	6	3
1997— New York (A.L.)	0	2	.000	8.49	2	2	0	0	0	11 2/3	15	11	11	1	5
1998— New York (A.L.)	1	0	1.000	1.29	1	1	0	0	0	7	3	1	1	0	8
1999— New York (A.L.)	1	0	1.000	1.23	1	1	0	0	0	7 1/3	7	1	1	0	5
2000— New York (A.L.)	1	0	1.000	3.97	2	2	0	0	0	11 1/3	15	5	5	3	7
2001— New York (A.L.)	0	1	.000	1.42	1	1	0	0	0	6 1/3	7	1	1	2	4
Division series totals (7 years)	3	3	.500	4.26	9	9	0	0	0	57	60	27	27	15	32

NOTES: Named Most Valuable Player (2001).

CHAMPIONSHIP SERIES RECORD

Year League	W	L	Pct.	ERA	G	GS	CG	ShO	Sv.	IP	H	R	ER	BB	SO
1996— New York (A.L.)	1	0	1.000	3.60	2	2	0	0	0	15	10	6	6	5	7
1998— New York (A.L.)	0	1	.000	11.57	1	1	0	0	0	4 2/3	8	6	6	3	1
1999— New York (A.L.)	1	0	1.000	2.45	1	1	0	0	0	7 1/3	8	2	2	1	5
2000— New York (A.L.)	1	0	1.000	2.70	1	1	0	0	0	6 2/3	9	2	2	1	2
2001— New York (A.L.)	2	0	1.000	2.51	2	2	0	0	0	14 1/3	11	4	4	2	8
Champ. series totals (5 years)	5	1	.833	3.75	7	7	0	0	0	48	46	20	20	12	23

NOTES: Member of World Series championship team (1996, 1998, 1999 and 2000).

WORLD SERIES RECORD

Year League	W	L	Pct.	ERA	G	GS	CG	ShO	Sv.	IP	H	R	ER	BB	SO
1996— New York (A.L.)	1	1	.500	5.91	2	2	0	0	0	10 2/3	11	7	7	4	5
1998— New York (A.L.)	1	0	1.000	0.00	1	1	0	0	0	7 1/3	5	0	0	3	4
1999— New York (A.L.)	0	0	...	12.27	1	1	0	0	0	3 2/3	10	5	5	1	1
2000— New York (A.L.)	0	0	...	1.98	2	2	0	0	0	13 2/3	16	5	3	4	9
2001— New York (A.L.)	0	2	.000	10.00	2	2	0	0	0	9	12	10	10	2	9
World Series totals (5 years)	2	3	.400	5.08	8	8	0	0	0	44 1/3	54	27	25	14	28

ALL-STAR GAME RECORD

Year League	W	L	Pct.	ERA	GS	CG	ShO	Sv.	IP	H	R	ER	BB	SO
1996— American						Did not play.								
2001— American	0	0	...	0.00	0	0	0	0	1	1	0	0	0	1

PETTYJOHN, ADAM P TIGERS

PERSONAL: Born June 11, 1977, in Phoenix, Ariz. ... 6-3/190. ... Throws right, bats left. ... Full name: Adam Christopher Pettyjohn.
HIGH SCHOOL: Exeter Union (Exeter, Calif.).
COLLEGE: Fresno State.
TRANSACTIONS/CAREER NOTES: Selected by Detroit Tigers organization in second round of free agent draft (June 2, 1998); choice received as part of compensation for Arizona Diamondbacks signing Type A free agent P Willie Blair. ... On Jacksonville disabled list (April 10-June 10, 2000).

Year League	W	L	Pct.	ERA	G	GS	CG	ShO	Sv.	IP	H	R	ER	BB	SO
1998— Jamestown (NY-Penn)	2	2	.500	2.86	4	4	0	0	0	22	21	10	7	4	24
— West Michigan (Midw.)	4	2	.667	1.97	8	8	1	1	0	50 1/3	46	15	11	9	64
1999— Lakeland (FSL)	3	4	.429	3.77	9	9	2	0	0	59 2/3	62	35	25	11	51
— Jacksonville (Sou.)	9	5	.643	4.69	20	20	0	0	0	126 2/3	134	75	66	35	92
2000— Jacksonville (Sou.)	2	2	.500	3.40	8	8	0	0	0	50 1/3	43	20	19	12	45
— Toledo (I.L.)	0	4	.000	6.69	7	7	0	0	0	39	45	34	29	22	23
2001— Toledo (I.L.)	5	8	.385	3.44	17	17	0	0	0	107 1/3	107	51	41	26	78
— Detroit (A.L.)	1	6	.143	5.82	16	9	0	0	0	65	81	48	42	21	40
Major League totals (1 year)	1	6	.143	5.82	16	9	0	0	0	65	81	48	42	21	40

PHELPS, JOSH C BLUE JAYS

PERSONAL: Born May 12, 1978, in Anchorage, Alaska. ... 6-3/220. ... Bats right, throws right. ... Full name: Joshua Lee Phelps.
HIGH SCHOOL: Lakeland (Rathdrum, Idaho).
TRANSACTIONS/CAREER NOTES: Selected by Toronto Blue Jays organization in 10th round of free-agent draft (June 4, 1996). ... On Tennessee disabled list (April 6-May 1, 2000).
HONORS: Named Southern League Most Valuable Player (2001).
STATISTICAL NOTES: Led South Atlantic League catchers with 19 errors in 1998. ... Led Florida State League with a .562 slugging percentage in 1999. ... Led Southern League with 273 total bases in 2001.

Year Team (League)	Pos.	G	AB	R	H	2B	3B	HR	RBI	Avg.	BB	SO	SB	PO	A	E	Avg.
1996— Medicine Hat (Pio.)	C-OF	59	191	26	46	3	0	5	29	.241	27	65	5	214	24	9	.964
1997— Hagerstown (S.Atl.)	C	68	233	26	49	9	1	7	24	.210	15	72	3	519	56	21	.965
1998— Hagerstown (S.Atl.)	C-3B-OF	117	385	48	102	24	1	8	44	.265	40	80	2	688	62	†19	.975
1999— Dunedin (FSL)	DH-C	110	406	72	133	27	4	20	88	.328	28	104	6	161	13	1	.994
2000— Tennessee (Sou.)	C	56	184	23	42	9	1	9	28	.228	15	66	1	274	15	5	.983
— Toronto (A.L.)	C	1	1	0	0	0	0	0	0	.000	0	1	0	1	0	0	1.000
— Dunedin (FSL)	C	30	113	26	36	7	0	12	34	.319	12	34	0	98	19	1	.992
2001— Tennessee (Sou.)	C	•136	486	95	142	*36	1	*31	97	.292	80	127	3	447	29	2	.996
— Toronto (A.L.)	C	8	12	3	0	0	0	0	1	.000	2	5	1	28	2	0	1.000
Major League totals (2 years)		9	13	3	0	0	0	0	1	.000	2	6	1	29	2	0	1.000

PHELPS, TRAVIS   P   DEVIL RAYS

PERSONAL: Born July 25, 1977, in Rocky Comfort, Mo. ... 6-2/195. ... Throws right, bats right.
HIGH SCHOOL: Wheaton (Mo.).
JUNIOR COLLEGE: Crowder College (Mo.).
TRANSACTIONS/CAREER NOTES: Selected by Tampa Bay Devil Rays organization in 89th round of free-agent draft (June 4, 1996).

Year League	W	L	Pct.	ERA	G	GS	CG	ShO	Sv.	IP	H	R	ER	BB	SO
1997—Princeton (Appl.)	4	3	.571	4.88	14	13	1	0	0	62²/₃	73	42	34	23	60
1998—Charleston, S.C. (S.Atl.)	5	8	.385	4.85	18	18	0	0	0	91	100	54	49	35	96
1999—St. Petersburg (FSL)	10	8	.556	4.24	24	23	1	1	0	133²/₃	148	70	63	39	101
2000—Orlando (Sou.)	7	8	.467	3.00	21	21	2	0	0	108	85	44	36	46	106
—Durham (I.L.)	3	1	.750	4.85	6	6	0	0	0	29²/₃	29	17	16	16	21
2001—Durham (I.L.)	2	0	1.000	0.00	9	0	0	0	0	15²/₃	11	0	0	1	12
—Tampa Bay (A.L.)	2	2	.500	3.48	49	0	0	0	5	62	53	30	24	24	54
Major League totals (1 year)	**2**	**2**	**.500**	**3.48**	**49**	**0**	**0**	**0**	**5**	**62**	**53**	**30**	**24**	**24**	**54**

PHILLIPS, JASON   P   BREWERS

PERSONAL: Born March 22, 1974, in Williamsport, Pa. ... 6-6/225. ... Throws right, bats right. ... Full name: Jason Charles Phillips.
HIGH SCHOOL: Hughesville (Pa.).
TRANSACTIONS/CAREER NOTES: Selected by Pittsburgh Pirates organization in 14th round of free-agent draft (June 1, 1992). ... On Nashville disabled list (May 26, 1999-remainder of season). ... Granted free agency (October 15, 1999). ... Re-signed by Pirates organization (January 6, 1999). ... On Nashville disabled list (May 9-September 6, 2000). ... Granted free agency (October 18, 2000). ... Re-signed by Pirates organization (January 9, 2001). ... On Lynchburg disabled list (April 5-May 10, 2001). ... Released by Pirates (June 4, 2001). ... Signed by Cleveland Indians organization (June 7, 2001). ... On Buffalo disabled list (July 27-August 3, 2001). ... Granted free agency (October 15, 2001). ... Signed by Milwaukee Brewers organization (October 26, 2001).

Year League	W	L	Pct.	ERA	G	GS	CG	ShO	Sv.	IP	H	R	ER	BB	SO
1992—Gulf Coast Pirates (GCL)	1	2	.333	8.47	4	4	0	0	0	17	21	21	16	13	10
1993—Welland (NY-Penn)	4	6	.400	3.53	14	14	0	0	0	71¹/₃	60	44	28	36	66
1994—Augusta (S.Atl.)	6	12	.333	6.73	23	23	1	0	0	108¹/₃	118	97	81	88	108
1995—Augusta (S.Atl.)	4	3	.571	3.60	30	6	0	0	0	80	76	46	32	53	65
1996—Augusta (S.Atl.)	5	4	.556	2.41	14	14	1	1	0	89²/₃	79	35	24	29	75
—Lynchburg (Caro.)	5	6	.455	4.52	13	13	1	1	0	73²/₃	82	47	37	35	63
1997—Lynchburg (Caro.)	11	6	.647	3.76	23	23	2	1	0	138²/₃	129	66	58	35	140
—Carolina (Sou.)	1	2	.333	2.32	4	4	2	1	0	31	21	8	8	9	22
1998—Carolina (Sou.)	7	•13	.350	4.71	25	25	1	1	0	151	161	89	79	52	114
—Nashville (PCL)	2	0	1.000	2.59	5	5	0	0	0	31¹/₃	38	10	9	12	21
1999—Nashville (PCL)	0	0	...	15.00	1	1	0	0	0	3	6	6	5	5	5
—Pittsburgh (N.L.)	0	0	...	11.57	6	0	0	0	0	7	11	9	9	6	7
2000—Nashville (PCL)	2	4	.333	4.70	6	6	0	0	0	30²/₃	30	20	16	18	18
2001—Altoona (East.)	0	1	.000	10.00	6	1	0	0	0	9	18	11	10	4	4
—Akron (East.)■	2	1	.667	4.13	10	3	0	0	0	24	18	11	11	15	20
—Buffalo (I.L.)	2	2	.500	3.34	8	6	1	0	0	35	27	15	13	8	25
Major League totals (1 year)	**0**	**0**	**...**	**11.57**	**6**	**0**	**0**	**0**	**0**	**7**	**11**	**9**	**9**	**6**	**7**

PHILLIPS, JASON   C   METS

PERSONAL: Born September 27, 1976, in La Mesa, Calif. ... 6-1/180. ... Bats right, throws right. ... Full name: Jason Lloyd Phillips.
HIGH SCHOOL: El Capitan (Lakeside, Calif.).
COLLEGE: San Diego State.
TRANSACTIONS/CAREER NOTES: Selected by New York Mets organization in 24th round of free-agent draft (June 3, 1997).

Year Team (League)	Pos.	G	AB	R	H	2B	3B	HR	RBI	Avg.	BB	SO	SB	PO	A	E	Avg.
1997—Pittsfield (NY-Penn)	C	48	155	15	32	9	0	2	17	.206	13	24	4	353	43	4	.990
1998—Capital City (S.Atl.)	C	69	251	36	68	15	1	5	37	.271	23	35	5	575	52	4	.994
—St. Lucie (FSL)	C	8	28	4	13	2	0	0	2	.464	2	1	0	48	3	0	1.000
1999—St. Lucie (FSL)	C	81	283	36	73	12	1	9	46	.258	43	28	0	457	64	4	.992
—Binghamton (East.)	C	39	141	13	32	5	0	7	23	.227	13	20	0	271	28	5	.984
2000—St. Lucie (FSL)	C	80	297	53	82	21	0	6	41	.276	23	19	1	478	52	6	.989
—Binghamton (East.)	C	27	98	16	38	4	0	0	13	.388	7	9	0	164	14	3	.983
2001—Binghamton (East.)	C	93	317	42	93	21	0	11	55	.293	31	25	0	561	54	3	*.995
—New York (N.L.)	C	6	7	2	1	1	0	0	0	.143	0	1	0	15	0	0	1.000
—Norfolk (I.L.)	C	19	66	8	20	2	0	2	14	.303	7	8	0	103	5	0	1.000
Major League totals (1 year)		**6**	**7**	**2**	**1**	**1**	**0**	**0**	**0**	**.143**	**0**	**1**	**0**	**15**	**0**	**0**	**1.000**

PIATT, ADAM   OF/DH   ATHLETICS

PERSONAL: Born February 8, 1976, in Chicago. ... 6-2/195. ... Bats right, throws right. ... Full name: Adam David Piatt.
HIGH SCHOOL: Bishop Verot (Fort Myers, Fla.).
COLLEGE: Mississippi State.
TRANSACTIONS/CAREER NOTES: Selected by Oakland Athletics organization in eighth round of free-agent draft (June 3, 1997). ... On Oakland disabled list (June 6-September 1, 2001); included rehabilitation assignments to Sacramento (July 12-28 and August 17-27) and Modesto (August 27-September 1).
HONORS: Named Texas League Most Valuable Player (1999).
STATISTICAL NOTES: Led California League third basemen with 32 errors in 1998. ... Led Texas League with 335 total bases, .451 on-base percentage, .704 slugging percentage and 10 intentional bases on balls received in 1999.

Year	Team (League)	Pos.	G	AB	R	H	2B	3B	HR	RBI	Avg.	BB	SO	SB	PO	A	E	Avg.
							BATTING									FIELDING		
1997—S. Oregon (N'West)....	3B-1B	57	216	63	63	9	1	13	35	.292	35	58	19	26	107	21	.864
1998—Modesto (Calif.)	3B-2B	133	500	91	144	•40	3	20	*107	.288	80	99	20	64	200	†32	.892
1999—Midland (Texas)	3B-SS-DH	129	476	*128	164	48	3	*39	*135	*.345	•93	101	7	91	253	31	.917
—Vancouver (PCL)	3B-SS	6	18	1	4	1	0	0	3	.222	6	2	0	6	16	2	.917
2000—Sacramento (PCL)	OF-3B-1B	65	254	36	72	15	0	8	42	.283	26	57	3	160	49	9	.959
—Oakland (A.L.)	OF-DH-3B-1B	60	157	24	47	5	5	5	23	.299	23	44	0	46	12	2	.967
2001—Oakland (A.L.)	OF-DH	36	95	9	20	5	1	0	6	.211	13	26	0	48	3	2	.962
—Sacramento (PCL)	OF	35	109	14	28	9	0	1	15	.257	11	27	2	40	2	3	.933
—Modesto (Calif.)	OF	4	15	4	7	2	0	1	2	.467	1	5	0	7	0	0	1.000
Major League totals (2 years)		96	252	33	67	10	6	5	29	.266	36	70	0	94	15	4	.965

DIVISION SERIES RECORD

Year	Team (League)	Pos.	G	AB	R	H	2B	3B	HR	RBI	Avg.	BB	SO	SB	PO	A	E	Avg.
							BATTING									FIELDING		
2000—Oakland (A.L.)	OF-PR-DH	3	6	2	1	0	0	0	0	.167	0	1	0	5	0	0	1.000

PIAZZA, MIKE   C   METS

PERSONAL: Born September 4, 1968, in Norristown, Pa. ... 6-3/215. ... Bats right, throws right. ... Full name: Michael Joseph Piazza. ... Name pronounced pee-AH-za.

HIGH SCHOOL: Phoenixville (Pa.) Area.

JUNIOR COLLEGE: Miami-Dade (North) Community College.

TRANSACTIONS/CAREER NOTES: Selected by Los Angeles Dodgers organization in 62nd round of free-agent draft (June 1, 1988). ... On disabled list (May 11-June 4, 1995). ... Traded by Dodgers with 3B Todd Zeile to Florida Marlins for OF Gary Sheffield, 3B Bobby Bonilla, C Charles Johnson, OF Jim Eisenreich and P Manuel Barrios (May 15, 1998). ... Traded by Marlins to New York Mets for OF Preston Wilson, P Ed Yarnall and P Geoff Goetz (May 22, 1998). ... On disabled list (April 10-25, 1999).

RECORDS: Shares major league single-season record for most major league ballparks, one or more home runs—18 (2000). ... Shares major league record for most grand slams in two consecutive games—2 (April 9 and 10, 1998). ... Shares major league single-month record for most grand slams—3 (April 1998). ... Holds single-season record for highest batting average by a catcher (100 or more games)—.362 (1997). ... Shares N.L. career record for most major league ballparks, one or more home runs (since 1900)—29.

HONORS: Named N.L. Rookie Player of the Year by THE SPORTING NEWS (1993). ... Named catcher on THE SPORTING NEWS N.L. All-Star team (1993-2001). ... Named catcher on THE SPORTING NEWS N.L. Silver Slugger team (1993-2000). ... Named N.L. Rookie of the Year by Baseball Writers' Association of America (1993). ... Named catcher on N.L. Silver Slugger team (2001).

STATISTICAL NOTES: Led California League with .540 slugging percentage and in grounding into double plays with 19 in 1991. ... Led N.L. catchers with 98 assists and tied for lead with 11 errors in 1993. ... Led N.L. catchers in total chances with 866 in 1995 and 1,055 in 1996. ... Led N.L. catchers in passed balls with 12 in 1995 and 12 in 1996. ... Hit three home runs in one game (June 29, 1996). ... Led N.L. catchers in total chances with 1,135 in 1997. ... Led N.L. catchers with 83 assists in 1998. ... Had 24-game hitting streak (May 25-June 22, 1999). ... Led N.L. in grounding into double plays with 27 in 1999. ... Led N.L. catchers in total chances with 1,011 in 1999. ... Had 21-game hitting streak (June 7-July 3, 2000). ... Career major league grand slams: 12.

MISCELLANEOUS: Holds New York Mets all-time record for highest career batting average (.317).

Year	Team (League)	Pos.	G	AB	R	H	2B	3B	HR	RBI	Avg.	BB	SO	SB	PO	A	E	Avg.
							BATTING									FIELDING		
1989—Salem (N'West)	C	57	198	22	53	11	0	8	25	.268	13	51	0	230	21	6	.977
1990—Vero Beach (FSL)	C-1B	88	272	27	68	20	0	6	45	.250	11	68	0	428	38	16	.967
1991—Bakersfield (Calif.)	C-1B	117	448	71	124	27	2	29	80	.277	47	83	0	723	69	15	.981
1992—San Antonio (Texas)	C	31	114	18	43	11	0	7	21	.377	13	18	0	189	22	4	.981
—Albuquerque (PCL)	C-1B	94	358	54	122	22	5	16	69	.341	37	57	1	550	50	9	.985
—Los Angeles (N.L.)	C	21	69	5	16	3	0	1	7	.232	4	12	0	94	7	1	.990
1993—Los Angeles (N.L.)	C-1B	149	547	81	174	24	2	35	112	.318	46	86	3	901	†98	‡11	.989
1994—Los Angeles (N.L.)	C	107	405	64	129	18	0	24	92	.319	33	65	1	640	38	*10	.985
1995—Los Angeles (N.L.)	C	112	434	82	150	17	0	32	93	.346	39	80	1	*805	52	9	.990
1996—Los Angeles (N.L.)	C	148	547	87	184	16	0	36	105	.336	81	93	0	*1055	70	9	.992
1997—Los Angeles (N.L.)	C-DH	152	556	104	201	32	1	40	124	.362	69	77	5	*1045	74	*16	.986
1998—Los Angeles (N.L.)	C	37	149	20	42	5	0	9	30	.282	11	27	0	277	25	2	.993
—Florida (N.L.)■	C	5	18	1	5	0	1	0	5	.278	0	0	0	27	3	1	.968
—New York (N.L.)■	C-DH	109	394	67	137	33	0	23	76	.348	47	53	1	680	§57	8	.989
1999—New York (N.L.)	C-DH	141	534	100	162	25	0	40	124	.303	51	70	2	*953	47	11	.989
2000—New York (N.L.)	C-DH	136	482	90	156	26	0	38	113	.324	58	69	4	862	38	3	*.997
2001—New York (N.L.)	C-DH	141	503	81	151	29	0	36	94	.300	67	87	0	919	58	9	.991
Major League totals (10 years)		1258	4638	782	1507	228	4	314	975	.325	506	719	17	8258	567	90	.990

DIVISION SERIES RECORD

Year	Team (League)	Pos.	G	AB	R	H	2B	3B	HR	RBI	Avg.	BB	SO	SB	PO	A	E	Avg.
							BATTING									FIELDING		
1995—Los Angeles (N.L.)	C	3	14	1	3	1	0	1	1	.214	0	2	0	31	0	0	1.000
1996—Los Angeles (N.L.)	C	3	10	1	3	0	0	2	2	.300	1	2	0	25	4	0	1.000
1999—New York (N.L.)	C	2	9	0	2	0	0	0	0	.222	0	4	0	13	0	0	1.000
2000—New York (N.L.)	C	4	14	1	3	1	0	0	0	.214	4	3	0	32	2	0	1.000
Division series totals (4 years)		12	47	3	11	2	0	1	3	.234	5	11	0	101	6	0	1.000

CHAMPIONSHIP SERIES RECORD

Year	Team (League)	Pos.	G	AB	R	H	2B	3B	HR	RBI	Avg.	BB	SO	SB	PO	A	E	Avg.
							BATTING									FIELDING		
1999—New York (N.L.)	C	6	24	1	4	0	0	1	4	.167	1	6	0	44	3	3	.940
2000—New York (N.L.)	C	5	17	7	7	3	0	2	4	.412	5	0	0	40	1	0	1.000
Championship series totals (2 years)		11	41	8	11	3	0	3	8	.268	6	6	0	84	4	3	.967

WORLD SERIES RECORD

Year	Team (League)	Pos.	G	AB	R	H	2B	3B	HR	RBI	Avg.	BB	SO	SB	PO	A	E	Avg.
							BATTING									FIELDING		
2000—New York (N.L.)	DH-C	5	22	3	6	2	0	2	4	.273	0	4	0	34	1	0	1.000

P

ALL-STAR GAME RECORD

NOTES: Named Most Valuable Player (1996).

Year	League	Pos.	AB	R	H	2B	3B	HR	RBI	Avg.	BB	SO	SB	PO	A	E	Avg.
1993— National		C	1	0	0	0	0	0	0	.000	0	1	0	3	0	0	1.000
1994— National		C	4	0	1	0	0	0	1	.250	0	0	0	6	0	0	1.000
1995— National		C	3	1	1	0	0	1	1	.333	0	0	0	6	1	0	1.000
1996— National		C	3	1	2	1	0	1	2	.667	0	1	0	4	0	0	1.000
1997— National		C	1	0	0	0	0	0	0	.000	1	0	0	2	0	0	1.000
1998— National		C	3	0	1	0	0	0	0	.333	0	0	0	2	0	0	1.000
1999— National		C	2	0	1	0	0	0	0	.500	0	1	0	6	0	0	1.000
2000— National								Selected, did not play—injured.									
2001— National		C	2	0	0	0	0	0	0	.000	0	0	0	5	0	0	1.000
All-Star Game totals (8 years)			**19**	**2**	**6**	**1**	**0**	**2**	**4**	**.316**	**1**	**3**	**0**	**34**	**1**	**0**	**1.000**

PICHARDO, HIPOLITO — P

PERSONAL: Born August 22, 1969, in Esperanza, Dominican Republic. ... 6-1/195. ... Throws right, bats right. ... Full name: Hipolito Antonio Pichardo. ... Name pronounced ee-POL-uh-toe puh-CHAR-doh.
HIGH SCHOOL: Liceo Enriguillo (Jicome Esperanza, Dominican Republic).
TRANSACTIONS/CAREER NOTES: Signed as non-drafted free agent by Kansas City Royals organization (December 16, 1987). ... On disabled list (August 14-September 1, 1993; and August 15-September 1, 1995). ... On Kansas City disabled list (July 5-August 25, 1997); included rehabilitation assignment to Omaha (July 25-August 25). ... Granted free agency (October 31, 1997). ... Re-signed by Royals (December 4, 1997). ... On Kansas City disabled list (May 6-23 and August 21, 1998-remainder of season); included rehabilitation assignment to Lansing (August 21). ... On disabled list (March 28, 1999-entire season). ... Granted free agency (November 11, 1999). ... Signed by Boston Red Sox organization (February 16, 2000). ... On Pawtucket disabled list (April 6-20, 2000). ... On Boston disabled list (March 21-May 14 and August 3-18, 2001); included rehabilitation assignments to Sarasota (April 18-May 6) and Pawtucket (May 7-14). ... Announced retirement (August 20, 2001).
STATISTICAL NOTES: Pitched 8-0 one-hit, complete-game victory for Kansas City against Boston (July 21, 1992).
MISCELLANEOUS: Struck out in only appearance as pinch hitter (2000).

Year	League	W	L	Pct.	ERA	G	GS	CG	ShO	Sv.	IP	H	R	ER	BB	SO
1988— Gulf Coast Royals (GCL)		0	0	...	13.50	1	0	0	0	0	1 1/3	3	2	2	1	3
1989— Appleton (Midw.)		5	4	.556	2.97	12	12	2	0	0	75 2/3	58	29	25	18	50
1990— Baseball City (FSL)		1	6	.143	3.80	11	10	0	0	0	45	47	28	19	25	40
1991— Memphis (Sou.)		3	11	.214	4.27	34	11	0	0	0	99	116	56	47	38	75
1992— Memphis (Sou.)		0	0	...	0.64	2	2	0	0	0	14	13	2	1	1	10
— Kansas City (A.L.)		9	6	.600	3.95	31	24	1	1	0	143 2/3	148	71	63	49	59
1993— Kansas City (A.L.)		7	8	.467	4.04	30	25	2	0	0	165	183	85	74	53	70
1994— Kansas City (A.L.)		5	3	.625	4.92	45	0	0	0	3	67 2/3	82	42	37	24	36
1995— Kansas City (A.L.)		8	4	.667	4.36	44	0	0	0	1	64	66	34	31	30	43
1996— Kansas City (A.L.)		3	5	.375	5.43	57	0	0	0	3	68	74	41	41	26	43
1997— Kansas City (A.L.)		3	5	.375	4.22	47	0	0	0	11	49	51	24	23	24	34
— Omaha (A.A.)		0	0	...	5.79	5	1	0	0	1	4 2/3	5	3	3	3	3
1998— Kansas City (A.L.)		7	8	.467	5.13	27	18	0	0	1	112 1/3	126	73	64	43	55
— Lansing (Midw.)		0	0	...	0.00	1	0	0	0	0	1	0	0	0	0	0
1999— Kansas City (A.L.)								Did not play.								
2000— Pawtucket (I.L.)■		0	0	...	0.00	3	0	0	0	0	4 2/3	2	0	0	0	4
— Sarasota (FSL)		1	1	.500	1.38	7	2	0	0	0	13	9	3	2	0	12
— Boston (A.L.)		6	3	.667	3.46	38	1	0	0	1	65	63	29	25	26	37
2001— Sarasota (FSL)		0	0	...	4.50	3	3	0	0	0	6	8	3	3	2	8
— Pawtucket (I.L.)		0	0	...	5.40	3	3	0	0	0	5	3	3	3	4	2
— Boston (A.L.)■		2	1	.667	4.93	30	0	0	0	0	34 2/3	42	23	19	10	17
Major League totals (9 years)		**50**	**43**	**.538**	**4.41**	**349**	**68**	**3**	**1**	**20**	**769 1/3**	**835**	**422**	**377**	**285**	**394**

PICKERING, CALVIN — 1B — RED SOX

PERSONAL: Born September 29, 1976, in St. Thomas, Virgin Islands. ... 6-5/278. ... Bats left, throws left. ... Full name: Calvin E. Pickering.
HIGH SCHOOL: King (Tampa).
TRANSACTIONS/CAREER NOTES: Selected by Baltimore Orioles organization in 35th round of free-agent draft (June 3, 1995). ... On disabled list (June 24-August 6, 2000). ... Traded by Orioles to Cincinnati Reds for future considerations (August 30, 2001). ... Claimed on waivers by Boston Red Sox (September 6, 2001).
HONORS: Named Eastern League Most Valuable Player (1998).
STATISTICAL NOTES: Led Appalachian League with 135 totals bases, .675 slugging pecentage and four intentional bases on balls received in 1996. ... Led Eastern League with 276 total bases, .434 on-base percentage, .566 slugging percentage, 16 intentional bases on balls received and grounding into double plays with 20 in 1998. ... Led Eastern League first basemen with 20 errors in 1998. ... Led International League with 99 RBI and 151 strikeouts in 2001.

Year	Team (League)	Pos.	G	AB	R	H	2B	3B	HR	RBI	Avg.	BB	SO	SB	PO	A	E	Avg.
1995— GC Orioles (GCL)		1B-DH	15	60	8	30	10	0	1	22	.500	2	6	0	86	6	3	.968
1996— Bluefield (Appl.)		1B-DH	60	200	45	65	14	1	*18	*66	.325	28	64	8	396	26	9	.979
1997— Delmarva (S.Atl.)		1B-DH	122	444	88	138	31	1	25	79	.311	53	139	6	940	70	*27	.974
1998— Bowie (East.)		1B-OF-DH	139	488	93	151	28	2	*31	*114	.309	*98	119	4	1068	60	†22	.981
— Baltimore (A.L.)		1B-DH	9	21	4	5	0	0	2	3	.238	3	4	1	31	0	1	.969
1999— Rochester (I.L.)		1B-DH-OF	103	372	63	106	20	0	16	63	.285	60	99	1	822	45	13	.985
— Baltimore (A.L.)		1B-DH	23	40	4	5	1	0	1	5	.125	11	16	0	46	2	2	.960
2000— Rochester (I.L.)		1B	60	197	20	43	10	0	6	30	.218	36	70	2	497	30	12	.978
2001— Rochester (I.L.)		1B	131	461	62	130	25	0	21	98	.282	64	149	0	516	31	8	.986
— Louisville (I.L.)■		1B	1	4	1	1	0	0	1	§1	.250	1	§2	0	4	0	0	1.000
— Cincinnati (N.L.)		DH	4	4	0	1	0	0	0	1	.250	0	2	0	...	...	...	...
— Boston (A.L.)■		1B-DH	17	50	4	14	1	0	3	7	.280	8	13	0	90	6	0	1.000
American League totals (3 years)			**49**	**111**	**12**	**24**	**2**	**0**	**6**	**15**	**.216**	**22**	**33**	**1**	**167**	**8**	**3**	**.983**
National League totals (1 year)			**4**	**4**	**0**	**1**	**0**	**0**	**0**	**1**	**.250**	**0**	**2**	**0**	**0**	**0**	**0**	**...**
Major League totals (3 years)			**53**	**115**	**12**	**25**	**2**	**0**	**6**	**16**	**.217**	**22**	**35**	**1**	**167**	**8**	**3**	**.983**

PIERRE, JUAN — OF — ROCKIES

PERSONAL: Born August 14, 1977, in Mobile, Ala. ... 6-0/170. ... Bats left, throws left. ... Full name: Juan D'Vaughn Pierre.
HIGH SCHOOL: Alexandria (La.).
COLLEGE: South Alabama.
TRANSACTIONS/CAREER NOTES: Selected by Colorado Rockies organization in 13th round of free-agent draft (June 2, 1998).
STATISTICAL NOTES: Tied for South Atlantic League lead in double plays by outfielder with four in 1999. ... Had 16-game hitting streak (August 8-23, 2000). ... Had 15-game hitting streak (September 6-22, 2000). ... Led N.L. in caught stealing with 17 in 2001.

								BATTING							FIELDING		
Year	Team (League)	Pos.	G	AB	R	H	2B	3B	HR	RBI	Avg.	BB	SO	SB	PO	A	E	Avg.
1998— Portland (N'West)		OF	64	264	55	93	9	2	0	30	*.352	19	11	*38	100	5	5	.955
1999— Asheville (S.Atl.)		OF	*140	*585	93	*187	28	5	1	55	.320	38	37	66	193	13	4	.981
2000— Carolina (Sou.)		OF	107	439	63	143	16	4	0	32	.326	33	26	46	261	2	2	.992
— Colo. Springs (PCL)		OF	4	17	3	8	0	1	0	1	.471	0	0	1	11	0	0	1.000
— Colorado (N.L.)		OF	51	200	26	62	2	0	0	20	.310	13	15	7	115	1	3	.975
2001— Colorado (N.L.)		OF	156	617	108	202	26	11	2	55	.327	41	29	•46	362	3	8	.979
Major League totals (2 years)			207	817	134	264	28	11	2	75	.323	54	44	53	477	4	11	.978

PIERSOLL, CHRIS — P — REDS

PERSONAL: Born September 25, 1977, in Van Nuys, Calif. ... 6-4/195. ... Throws right, bats right. ... Full name: Christopher Earl Piersoll.
HIGH SCHOOL: Carlsbad (Calif.).
JUNIOR COLLEGE: Fullerton.
TRANSACTIONS/CAREER NOTES: Selected by Chicago Cubs organization in 19th round of free-agent draft (June 3, 1997). ... Selected by Cincinnati Reds organization from Cubs organization in Rule 5 minor league draft (December 11, 2000).

Year	League	W	L	Pct.	ERA	G	GS	CG	ShO	Sv.	IP	H	R	ER	BB	SO
1997— Arizona Cubs (Ariz.)		4	0	1.000	2.08	15	0	0	0	2	34 2/3	26	12	8	9	41
1998— Rockford (Midw.)		2	0	1.000	3.92	27	4	1	0	2	59 2/3	52	28	26	20	55
1999— Daytona (FSL)		7	3	.700	3.72	33	0	0	0	5	67 2/3	68	30	28	24	74
— West Tenn (Sou.)		0	0	...	0.63	8	1	0	0	1	14 1/3	12	1	1	3	14
2000— West Tenn (Sou.)		3	3	.500	1.56	47	0	0	0	2	80 2/3	51	17	14	28	54
2001— Chattanooga (Sou.)■		1	4	.200	3.38	50	0	0	0	19	56	48	24	21	30	78
— Cincinnati (N.L.)		0	0	...	2.38	11	0	0	0	0	11 1/3	12	4	3	6	7
Major League totals (1 year)		0	0	...	2.38	11	0	0	0	0	11 1/3	12	4	3	6	7

PIERZYNSKI, A.J. — C — TWINS

PERSONAL: Born December 30, 1976, in Bridgehampton, N.Y. ... 6-3/220. ... Bats left, throws right. ... Full name: Anthony John Pierzynski.
HIGH SCHOOL: Dr. Phillips (Orlando).
TRANSACTIONS/CAREER NOTES: Selected by Minnesota Twins organization in third round of free-agent draft (June 2, 1994). ... On Salt Lake disabled list (August 24, 1999-remainder of season).
STATISTICAL NOTES: Tied for Appalachian League lead in errors by catcher with 12 in 1995. ... Led Appalachian League catchers with 71 assists in 1995. ... Led Midwest League catchers with 22 passed balls and tied for lead with 20 errors by catcher in 1996.

								BATTING							FIELDING		
Year	Team (League)	Pos.	G	AB	R	H	2B	3B	HR	RBI	Avg.	BB	SO	SB	PO	A	E	Avg.
1994— GC Twins (GCL)		C-DH	43	152	21	44	8	1	1	19	.289	12	19	0	198	28	8	.966
1995— Fort Wayne (Midw.)		C	22	84	10	26	5	1	2	14	.310	2	10	0	119	34	10	.939
— Elizabethton (Appl.)		C-1B	56	205	29	68	13	1	7	45	.332	14	23	0	376	†72	‡12	.974
1996— Fort Wayne (Midw.)		C-DH-OF	114	431	48	118	30	3	7	70	.274	22	53	0	658	80	†21	.972
1997— Fort Myers (FSL)		C-DH-1B	118	412	49	115	23	1	9	64	.279	16	59	2	677	78	10	.987
1998— New Britain (East.)		C-DH	59	212	30	63	11	0	3	17	.297	10	25	0	409	37	2	.996
— Salt Lake (PCL)		C	59	208	29	53	7	2	7	30	.255	9	24	3	366	30	7	.983
— Minnesota (A.L.)		C	7	10	1	3	0	0	0	1	.300	1	2	0	33	2	0	1.000
1999— Salt Lake (PCL)		C-DH	67	228	29	59	10	0	1	25	.259	16	29	0	376	45	7	.984
— Minnesota (A.L.)		C	9	22	3	6	2	0	0	3	.273	1	4	0	35	2	0	1.000
2000— New Britain (East.)		C	62	228	36	68	17	2	4	34	.298	8	22	0	304	31	6	.982
— Salt Lake (PCL)		C	41	155	22	52	14	1	4	25	.335	5	22	1	263	20	3	.990
— Minnesota (A.L.)		C	33	88	12	27	5	1	2	11	.307	5	14	1	160	10	0	1.000
2001— Minnesota (A.L.)		C-DH	114	381	51	110	33	2	7	55	.289	16	57	1	611	44	10	.985
Major League totals (4 years)			163	501	67	146	40	3	9	70	.291	23	77	2	839	58	10	.989

PINEDA, LUIS — P — REDS

PERSONAL: Born June 10, 1978, in San Cristobal, Dominican Republic. ... 6-1/160. ... Throws right, bats right. ... Full name: Luis A. Pineda.
TRANSACTIONS/CAREER NOTES: Signed as non-drafted free agent by Texas Rangers organization (June 14, 1995). ... Released by Rangers (May 22, 1997). ... Signed by Arizona Diamondbacks organization (June 25, 1998). ... Released by Diamondbacks (July 4, 1998). ... Signed by Detroit Tigers organization (July 30, 1998). ... Granted free agency (October 16, 1998). ... Signed by Tigers organization (December 29, 1998). ... On Lakeland disabled list (June 8-September 18, 2000). ... On Erie disabled list (June 14-July 13, 2001). ... Traded by Tigers with OF Juan Encarnacion to Cincinnati Reds for OF Dmitri Young (December 11, 2001).

Year	League	W	L	Pct.	ERA	G	GS	CG	ShO	Sv.	IP	H	R	ER	BB	SO
1995— Dominican Rangers (DSL)		6	1	.857	3.00	12	5	0	0	0	39	36	17	13	31	19
1996— Gulf Coast Rangers (GCL)		6	3	.667	3.52	11	11	1	0	0	71 2/3	67	31	28	25	66
1997—								Did not play.								
1998— Dominican Tigers (DSL)■		2	0	1.000	0.89	12	0	0	0	5	20 1/3	7	3	2	14	43
1999— West Michigan (Midw.)		0	2	.000	7.45	24	3	0	0	7	19 1/3	30	18	16	26	55
— Lakeland (FSL)		1	0	1.000	1.04	8	0	0	0	0	8 2/3	6	2	1	7	8
2000— Lakeland (FSL)		1	3	.250	3.38	18	0	0	0	4	26 2/3	23	13	10	19	42
2001— Erie (East.)		6	2	.750	3.05	16	12	2	1	0	85 2/3	68	33	29	28	92
— Toledo (I.L.)		1	0	1.000	0.00	2	0	0	0	0	8	3	0	0	0	6
— Detroit (A.L.)		0	1	.000	4.91	16	0	0	0	0	18 1/3	16	10	10	14	13
Major League totals (1 year)		0	1	.000	4.91	16	0	0	0	0	18 1/3	16	10	10	14	13

P

PINEIRO, JOEL — P — MARINERS

PERSONAL: Born September 25, 1978, in Rio Pedres, Puerto Rico. ... 6-1/180. ... Throws right, bats right. ... Full name: Joel Alberto Pineiro.
HIGH SCHOOL: Colonial (Orlando).
JUNIOR COLLEGE: Edison Community College (Fla.).
TRANSACTIONS/CAREER NOTES: Selected by Seattle Mariners organization in 12th round of free-agent draft (June 3, 1997). ... On suspended list (October 3-6, 2001).

Year League	W	L	Pct.	ERA	G	GS	CG	ShO	Sv.	IP	H	R	ER	BB	SO
1997— Arizona Mariners (Ariz.)	1	0	1.000	0.00	1	0	0	0	0	3	1	0	0	0	4
— Everett (N'West)	4	2	.667	5.33	18	6	0	0	2	49	54	33	29	18	59
1998— Wisconsin (Midw.)	8	4	.667	3.19	16	16	1	0	0	96	92	40	34	28	84
— Lancaster (Calif.)	2	0	1.000	7.80	9	9	1	•1	0	45	58	40	39	22	48
— Orlando (Sou.)	1	0	1.000	5.40	1	1	0	0	0	5	7	4	3	2	2
1999— New Haven (East.)	10	*15	.400	4.72	28	25	4	0	0	166	190	105	87	52	116
2000— New Haven (East.)	2	1	.667	4.13	9	9	0	0	0	52 1/3	42	25	24	12	43
— Tacoma (PCL)	7	1	.875	2.80	10	9	2	2	0	61	53	20	19	22	41
— Seattle (A.L.)	1	0	1.000	5.59	8	1	0	0	0	19 1/3	25	13	12	13	10
2001— Tacoma (PCL)	6	3	.667	3.62	18	10	0	0	0	77	68	31	31	33	64
— Seattle (A.L.)	6	2	.750	2.03	17	11	0	0	0	75 1/3	50	24	17	21	56
Major League totals (2 years)	7	2	.778	2.76	25	12	0	0	0	94 2/3	75	37	29	34	66

DIVISION SERIES RECORD

Year League	W	L	Pct.	ERA	G	GS	CG	ShO	Sv.	IP	H	R	ER	BB	SO
2001— Seattle (A.L.)							Did not play.								

CHAMPIONSHIP SERIES RECORD

Year League	W	L	Pct.	ERA	G	GS	CG	ShO	Sv.	IP	H	R	ER	BB	SO
2001— Seattle (A.L.)	0	0	...	4.50	1	0	0	0	0	2	4	1	1	2	5

PLESAC, DAN — P — BLUE JAYS

PERSONAL: Born February 4, 1962, in Gary, Ind. ... 6-5/217. ... Throws left, bats left. ... Full name: Daniel Thomas Plesac. ... Name pronounced PLEE-sack.
HIGH SCHOOL: Crown Point (Ind.).
COLLEGE: North Carolina State.
TRANSACTIONS/CAREER NOTES: Selected by St. Louis Cardinals organization in second round of free-agent draft (June 3, 1980); did not sign. ... Selected by Milwaukee Brewers organization in first round (26th pick overall) of free-agent draft (June 6, 1983). ... Granted free agency (October 27, 1992). ... Signed by Chicago Cubs (December 8, 1992). ... Granted free agency (October 25, 1994). ... Signed by Pittsburgh Pirates (November 9, 1994). ... Traded by Pirates with OF Orlando Merced and IF Carlos Garcia to Toronto Blue Jays for P Jose Silva, P Jose Pett, IF Brandon Cromer and three players to be named later (November 14, 1996); Pirates acquired P Mike Halperin, IF Abraham Nunez and C/OF Craig Wilson to complete deal (December 11, 1996). ... Traded by Blue Jays to Arizona Diamondbacks for SS Tony Batista and P John Frascatore (June 12, 1999). ... Granted free agency (October 30, 2000). ... Signed by Blue Jays (December 8, 2000).
STATISTICAL NOTES: Led Appalachian League pitchers with three balks in 1983.
MISCELLANEOUS: Holds Milwaukee Brewers all-time records for lowest earned run average (3.21), most games pitched (365) and most saves (133).

Year League	W	L	Pct.	ERA	G	GS	CG	ShO	Sv.	IP	H	R	ER	BB	SO
1983— Paintsville (Appl.)	*9	1	*.900	3.50	14	•14	2	0	0	82 1/3	76	44	32	57	*85
1984— Stockton (Calif.)	6	6	.500	3.32	16	16	2	0	0	108 1/3	106	51	40	50	101
— El Paso (Texas)	2	2	.500	3.46	7	7	0	0	0	39	43	19	15	16	24
1985— El Paso (Texas)	12	5	.706	4.97	25	24	2	0	0	150 1/3	171	91	83	68	128
1986— Milwaukee (A.L.)	10	7	.588	2.97	51	0	0	0	14	91	81	34	30	29	75
1987— Milwaukee (A.L.)	5	6	.455	2.61	57	0	0	0	23	79 1/3	63	30	23	23	89
1988— Milwaukee (A.L.)	1	2	.333	2.41	50	0	0	0	30	52 1/3	46	14	14	12	52
1989— Milwaukee (A.L.)	3	4	.429	2.35	52	0	0	0	33	61 1/3	47	16	16	17	52
1990— Milwaukee (A.L.)	3	7	.300	4.43	66	0	0	0	24	69	67	36	34	31	65
1991— Milwaukee (A.L.)	2	7	.222	4.29	45	10	0	0	8	92 1/3	92	49	44	39	61
1992— Milwaukee (A.L.)	5	4	.556	2.96	44	4	0	0	1	79	64	28	26	35	54
1993— Chicago (N.L.)■	2	1	.667	4.74	57	0	0	0	0	62 2/3	74	37	33	21	47
1994— Chicago (N.L.)	2	3	.400	4.61	54	0	0	0	1	54 2/3	61	30	28	13	53
1995— Pittsburgh (N.L.)■	4	4	.500	3.58	58	0	0	0	3	60 1/3	53	26	24	27	57
1996— Pittsburgh (N.L.)	6	5	.545	4.09	73	0	0	0	11	70 1/3	67	35	32	24	76
1997— Toronto (A.L.)■	2	4	.333	3.58	73	0	0	0	1	50 1/3	47	22	20	19	61
1998— Toronto (A.L.)	4	3	.571	3.78	78	0	0	0	4	50	41	23	21	16	55
1999— Toronto (A.L.)	0	3	.000	8.34	30	0	0	0	0	22 2/3	28	21	21	9	26
— Arizona (N.L.)■	2	1	.667	3.32	34	0	0	0	1	21 2/3	22	9	8	8	27
2000— Arizona (N.L.)	5	1	.833	3.15	62	0	0	0	0	40	34	21	14	26	45
2001— Toronto (A.L.)■	4	5	.444	3.57	62	0	0	0	1	45 1/3	34	18	18	24	68
A.L. totals (11 years)	39	52	.429	3.47	608	14	0	0	139	692 2/3	610	291	267	254	658
N.L. totals (6 years)	21	15	.583	4.04	338	0	0	0	16	309 2/3	311	158	139	119	305
Major League totals (16 years)	60	67	.472	3.65	946	14	0	0	155	1002 1/3	921	449	406	373	963

DIVISION SERIES RECORD

Year League	W	L	Pct.	ERA	G	GS	CG	ShO	Sv.	IP	H	R	ER	BB	SO
1999— Arizona (N.L.)	0	0	...	54.00	1	0	0	0	0	1/3	3	2	2	0	0

ALL-STAR GAME RECORD

Year League	W	L	Pct.	ERA	GS	CG	ShO	Sv.	IP	H	R	ER	BB	SO
1987— American	0	0	...	0.00	0	0	0	0	1	0	0	0	0	1
1988— American	0	0	...	0.00	0	0	0	0	1/3	0	0	0	0	1
1989— American	0	0	...	...	0	0	0	0	1	0	0	0	0	0
All-Star Game totals (3 years)	0	0	...	0.00	0	0	0	0	1 1/3	1	0	0	0	2

P

PERSONAL: Born March 18, 1976, in West, Texas. ... 6-0/170. ... Bats left, throws left. ... Full name: Scott Eric Podsednik.
HIGH SCHOOL: West (Texas).
TRANSACTIONS/CAREER NOTES: Selected by Texas Rangers organization in third round of free-agent draft (June 2, 1994). ... Traded by Rangers to Florida Marlins (October 8, 1995), completing deal in which Marlins traded P Bobby Witt to Texas Rangers for two players to be named (August 8, 1995); Rangers also sent P Wilson Heredia to Marlins (August 11, 1995). ... Selected by Rangers from Marlins organization in Rule 5 minor league draft (December 15, 1997). ... On Charlotte disabled list (April 6-May 22, 2000). ... Granted free agency (October 15, 2000). ... Signed by Seattle Mariners organization (November 1, 2000). ... On Tacoma disabled list (May 4-June 12 and August 14-26, 2001).
STATISTICAL NOTES: Led Gulf Coast League outfielders with 118 total chances in 1994. ... Tied for Florida State League lead in double plays by outfielder with four in 1996.

							BATTING								FIELDING		
Year Team (League)	Pos.	G	AB	R	H	2B	3B	HR	RBI	Avg.	BB	SO	SB	PO	A	E	Avg.
1994— GC Rangers (GCL)......	OF	60	211	34	48	7	1	1	17	.227	•41	34	18	*112	6	0	*1.000
1995— Hudson Valley (NY-P).	OF	65	252	42	67	3	0	0	20	.266	35	31	20	125	6	3	.978
1996— Brevard Co. (FSL)■ ...	OF	108	383	39	100	9	2	0	30	.261	45	65	20	231	10	4	.984
1997— Kane County (Midw.)..	OF	*135	*531	80	147	23	4	3	49	.277	60	72	28	202	10	5	.977
1998— Charlotte (FSL)■........	OF	81	302	55	86	12	4	4	39	.285	44	32	26	143	3	2	.986
—Tulsa (Texas)	OF	17	75	9	18	4	1	0	4	.240	6	11	5	33	1	0	1.000
1999— GC Rangers (GCL)......	OF	5	17	6	7	2	0	0	5	.412	2	3	1	1	0	0	1.000
—Tulsa (Texas)	OF	37	116	10	18	4	0	0	1	.155	5	13	6	72	3	1	.987
2000— Tulsa (Texas)	OF	49	169	20	42	7	2	2	13	.249	30	33	19	90	1	3	.968
2001— Tacoma (PCL)■	OF	66	269	46	78	15	4	3	30	.290	13	46	12	147	0	5	.967
—Seattle (A.L.)	OF	5	6	1	1	0	1	0	3	.167	0	1	0	3	0	0	1.000
Major League totals (1 year)		5	6	1	1	0	1	0	3	.167	0	1	0	3	0	0	1.000

PERSONAL: Born October 10, 1975, in Santo Domingo, Dominican Republic. ... 5-10/168. ... Bats right, throws right. ... Full name: Placido Enrique Polanco. ... Name pronounced Plah-SEE-doh Poh-LAHN-co.
HIGH SCHOOL: Santo Clara (Santo Domingo, Dominican Republic).
JUNIOR COLLEGE: Miami-Dade (Wolfson) Community College.
TRANSACTIONS/CAREER NOTES: Selected by St. Louis Cardinals in 19th round of free-agent draft (June 3, 1994). ... On Memphis suspended list (August 28-29, 1999). ... On disabled list (July 1-16, 2000).
STATISTICAL NOTES: Led Florida State League in grounding into double plays with 31 in 1996. ... Tied for Texas League lead in double plays by second baseman with 110 in 1997. ... Had 20-game hitting streak (July 21-August 11, 2001). ... Career major league grand slams: 1.

							BATTING								FIELDING		
Year Team (League)	Pos.	G	AB	R	H	2B	3B	HR	RBI	Avg.	BB	SO	SB	PO	A	E	Avg.
1994— Ariz. Cardinals (Ariz.) .	SS-2B	32	127	17	27	4	0	1	10	.213	7	15	4	47	89	10	.932
1995— Peoria (Midw.)...........	SS-2B	103	361	43	96	7	4	2	41	.266	18	30	7	114	285	21	.950
1996— St. Petersburg (FSL) ..	2B	*137	*540	65	*157	29	5	0	51	.291	24	34	4	198	*383	4	*.993
1997— Arkansas (Texas).......	2B	129	508	71	148	16	3	2	51	.291	29	51	19	240	*425	14	*.979
1998— Memphis (PCL)	2B-SS	70	246	36	69	19	1	1	21	.280	16	15	6	113	193	5	.984
—St. Louis (N.L.)...........	2B	45	114	10	29	3	2	1	11	.254	5	9	2	72	102	7	.961
1999— St. Louis (N.L.)..........	2B-3B-SS	88	220	24	61	9	3	1	19	.277	15	24	1	123	150	8	.972
—Memphis (PCL)	2B-SS-3B	29	120	18	33	4	1	0	10	.275	3	11	2	43	84	2	.984
2000— St. Louis (N.L.).........	2B-3B-SS-1B	118	323	50	102	12	3	5	39	.316	16	26	4	131	202	3	.991
2001— St. Louis (N.L.).........	3B-SS-2B-DH	144	564	87	173	26	4	3	38	.307	25	43	12	133	344	4	.992
Major League totals (4 years)		395	1221	171	365	50	12	10	107	.299	61	102	19	459	798	22	.983

DIVISION SERIES RECORD

							BATTING								FIELDING		
Year Team (League)	Pos.	G	AB	R	H	2B	3B	HR	RBI	Avg.	BB	SO	SB	PO	A	E	Avg.
2000— St. Louis (N.L.)..........	3B	3	10	1	3	0	0	0	3	.300	1	0	1	1	5	0	1.000
2001— St. Louis (N.L.)..........	3B	5	15	1	4	0	0	0	1	.267	1	1	1	1	15	1	.941
Division series totals (2 years)		8	25	2	7	0	0	0	4	.280	2	1	2	2	20	1	.957

CHAMPIONSHIP SERIES RECORD

							BATTING								FIELDING		
Year Team (League)	Pos.	G	AB	R	H	2B	3B	HR	RBI	Avg.	BB	SO	SB	PO	A	E	Avg.
2000— St. Louis (N.L.)..........	3B-PH	4	5	0	1	0	0	0	0	.200	2	1	0	2	4	0	1.000

PERSONAL: Born February 27, 1974, in St. Louis. ... 5-11/185. ... Throws right, bats right. ... Full name: Cliff Anthony Politte. ... Son of Clifford Politte, pitcher in St. Louis Cardinals organization (1959-65). ... Name pronounced po-LEET.
HIGH SCHOOL: Vianney (Kirkwood, Mo.).
JUNIOR COLLEGE: Jefferson College (Mo.).
TRANSACTIONS/CAREER NOTES: Selected by St. Louis Cardinals organization in 54th round of free agent draft (June 1, 1995). ... Traded by Cardinals with OF Ron Gant and P Jeff Brantley to Philadelphia Phillies for P Ricky Bottalico and P Garrett Stephenson (November 19, 1998). ... On Scranton/Wilkes-Barre disabled list (April 30-May 9, 2000). ... On Philadelphia disabled list (March 31-July 6, 2001); included rehabilitation assignment to Clearwater (June 18-July 6).
HONORS: Named Carolina League Pitcher of the Year (1997).

P

Year	League	W	L	Pct.	ERA	G	GS	CG	ShO	Sv.	IP	H	R	ER	BB	SO
1996—	Peoria (Midw.)...................	14	6	.700	2.59	25	25	0	0	0	149²/₃	108	50	43	47	151
1997—	Prince William (Caro.).......	11	1	*.917	*2.24	19	19	0	0	0	120¹/₃	89	37	30	31	118
—	Arkansas (Texas)...............	4	1	.800	2.15	6	6	0	0	0	37²/₃	35	15	9	9	26
1998—	St. Louis (N.L.).................	2	3	.400	6.32	8	8	0	0	0	37	45	32	26	18	22
—	Memphis (PCL).................	1	4	.200	7.64	10	10	0	0	0	50²/₃	71	46	43	24	42
—	Arkansas (Texas)...............	5	3	.625	2.96	10	10	1	•1	0	67	56	25	22	16	61
1999—	Reading (East.)■	9	8	.529	3.63	37	13	1	0	5	109	112	45	44	33	97
—	Philadelphia (N.L.).............	1	0	1.000	7.13	13	0	0	0	0	17²/₃	19	14	14	15	15
2000—	Scranton/W.B. (I.L.)...........	8	4	.667	3.12	21	20	1	0	0	112²/₃	94	45	39	41	106
—	Philadelphia (N.L.).............	4	3	.571	3.66	12	8	0	0	0	59	55	24	24	27	50
2001—	Clearwater (FSL)	0	1	.000	2.45	7	7	0	0	0	11	8	4	3	3	15
—	Philadelphia (N.L.).............	2	3	.400	2.42	23	0	0	0	0	26	24	8	7	8	23
Major League totals (4 years).......		9	9	.500	4.58	56	16	0	0	0	139²/₃	143	78	71	68	110

PONSON, SIDNEY   P   ORIOLES

PERSONAL: Born November 2, 1976, in Noord, Aruba. ... 6-1/225. ... Throws right, bats right. ... Full name: Sidney Alton Ponson.
COLLEGE: Maria (Aruba).
TRANSACTIONS/CAREER NOTES: Signed as non-drafted free agent by Baltimore Orioles organization (August 17, 1993). ... On Bowie disabled list (June 13-July 15, 1997). ... On Baltimore disabled list (April 16-May 9, 2001); included rehabilitation assignment to Bowie (May 4-9).

Year	League	W	L	Pct.	ERA	G	GS	CG	ShO	Sv.	IP	H	R	ER	BB	SO
1994—	Gulf Coast Orioles (GCL)....	4	3	.571	2.96	12	10	1	0	0	•73	68	30	24	17	53
1995—	Bluefield (Appl.)	6	3	.667	4.17	13	13	0	0	0	77²/₃	79	44	36	16	56
1996—	Frederick (Caro.)	7	6	.538	3.45	18	16	3	0	0	107	98	56	41	28	110
1997—	Bowie (East.)....................	2	7	.222	5.42	13	13	1	1	0	74²/₃	77	51	45	32	56
—	Gulf Coast Orioles (GCL)....	1	0	1.000	0.00	1	0	0	0	0	2	0	0	0	0	1
1998—	Rochester (I.L.).................	1	0	1.000	0.00	1	1	0	0	0	5	4	0	0	1	3
—	Baltimore (A.L.).................	8	9	.471	5.27	31	20	0	0	1	135	157	82	79	42	85
1999—	Baltimore (A.L.).................	12	12	.500	4.71	32	32	6	0	0	210	227	118	110	80	112
2000—	Baltimore (A.L.).................	9	13	.409	4.82	32	32	6	1	0	222	223	125	119	83	152
2001—	Baltimore (A.L.).................	5	10	.333	4.94	23	23	3	1	0	138¹/₃	161	83	76	37	84
—	Bowie (East.)....................	0	0	...	0.00	1	1	0	0	0	4	3	0	0	1	2
Major League totals (4 years).......		34	44	.436	4.90	118	107	15	2	1	705¹/₃	768	408	384	242	433

PORTER, BO   OF

PERSONAL: Born July 5, 1972, in Newark, N.J. ... 6-2/195. ... Bats right, throws right. ... Full name: Marquis Donnell Porter.
HIGH SCHOOL: Weequahic (Newark, N.J.).
COLLEGE: Iowa.
TRANSACTIONS/CAREER NOTES: Selected by Chicago Cubs organization in 40th round of free-agent draft (June 3, 1993). ... Selected by Oakland Athleticss from Cubs organization in Rule 5 major league draft (December 13, 1999). ... Claimed on waivers by Texas Rangers (October 11, 2000). ... Granted free agency (October 17, 2001).
STATISTICAL NOTES: Led Midwest League outfielders with seven double plays in 1996. ... Tied for Pacific Coast League lead in caught stealing with 17 in 1999.

							BATTING							FIELDING			
Year	Team (League)	Pos.	G	AB	R	H	2B	3B	HR	RBI	Avg.	BB	SO	SB	PO	A	E	Avg.
1994—	Peoria (Midw.)............	OF	66	221	40	60	11	2	6	29	.271	27	59	6	128	3	3	.978
1995—	Daytona (FSL)	OF	113	336	54	73	12	2	3	19	.217	32	104	22	183	10	4	.980
1996—	Daytona (FSL)	OF	20	63	9	11	4	1	0	6	.175	6	24	5	44	3	4	.922
—	Rockford (Midw.)	OF	105	378	83	91	22	3	7	44	.241	72	107	30	172	8	3	.984
1997—	Daytona (FSL)	OF-2B	122	440	87	135	20	6	17	65	.307	61	115	23	237	10	4	.984
—	Orlando (Sou.)	OF	8	31	4	8	1	0	1	3	.258	0	11	0	13	2	1	.938
1998—	West Tenn (Sou.)	OF	125	464	91	134	26	*11	10	68	.289	82	117	*50	258	10	3	.989
—	Iowa (PCL)	OF	4	11	2	4	1	0	0	3	.364	4	4	1	6	0	0	1.000
1999—	Iowa (PCL)	OF-DH	111	414	86	121	24	2	27	64	.292	65	121	15	223	5	0	*1.000
—	Chicago (N.L.)	OF	24	26	2	5	1	0	0	0	.192	2	13	0	16	0	1	.941
2000—	Sacramento (PCL)■...	OF	129	481	94	131	21	3	14	64	.272	88	117	39	299	6	3	.990
—	Oakland (A.L.)	OF	17	13	3	2	0	0	1	2	.154	2	5	0	13	0	0	1.000
2001—	Texas (A.L.)■............	OF-DH	48	87	18	20	4	2	1	6	.230	9	34	3	61	1	2	.969
—	Oklahoma (PCL).........	OF	58	224	40	55	9	2	13	40	.246	26	60	10	110	3	0	1.000
American League totals (2 years)			65	100	21	22	4	2	2	8	.220	11	39	3	74	1	2	.974
National League totals (1 year)			24	26	2	5	1	0	0	0	.192	2	13	0	16	0	1	.941
Major League totals (3 years)			89	126	23	27	5	2	2	8	.214	13	52	3	90	1	3	.968

DIVISION SERIES RECORD

							BATTING							FIELDING			
Year	Team (League)	Pos.	G	AB	R	H	2B	3B	HR	RBI	Avg.	BB	SO	SB	PO	A	E	Avg.
2000—	Oakland (A.L.)	OF-PR	2	1	0	1	0	0	0	1	1.000	0	0	0	1	0	0	1.000

POSADA, JORGE   C   YANKEES

P

PERSONAL: Born August 17, 1971, in Santurce, Puerto Rico. ... 6-2/200. ... Bats both, throws right. ... Full name: Jorge Rafael Posada Jr. ... Name pronounced HOR-hay po-SOD-a.
HIGH SCHOOL: Colegio Alejandrino (Puerto Rico).
JUNIOR COLLEGE: Calhoon Community College (Ala.).

TRANSACTIONS/CAREER NOTES: Selected by New York Yankees organization in 24th round of free-agent draft (June 4, 1990). ... On disabled list (July 26-September 4, 1994). ... On Columbus disabled list (May 3-12, 1995). ... On suspended list (July 17-18, 2000; and September 26-October 2, 2001).

RECORDS: Shares major league single-season record for most unassisted double plays by catcher—2 (2000).

HONORS: Named catcher on THE SPORTING NEWS A.L. All-Star team (2000-01). ... Named catcher on THE SPORTING NEWS A.L. Silver Slugger team (2000). ... Named catcher on A.L. Silver Slugger team (2001).

STATISTICAL NOTES: Led New York-Pennsylvania League second basemen with 42 double plays in 1991. ... Led Carolina League with 38 passed balls in 1993. ... Tied for Carolina League lead in intentional bases on balls received with four in 1993. ... Tied for International League lead in errors by catcher with 11 in 1994. ... Tied for International League lead in double plays by catcher with seven in 1995. ... Led International League with 14 passed balls in 1995. ... Switch-hit home runs in one game three times (August 23, 1998; July 10, 1999; and April 23, 2000). ... Career major league grand slams: 3.

							BATTING								FIELDING			
Year Team (League)	Pos.	G	AB	R	H	2B	3B	HR	RBI	Avg.	BB	SO	SB	PO	A	E	Avg.
1991—Oneonta (NY-Penn)	2B-C	71	217	34	51	5	5	4	33	.235	51	51	6	172	205	21	.947
1992—Greensboro (S.Atl.)	C-3B	101	339	60	94	22	4	12	58	.277	58	87	11	263	84	11	.965
1993—Prince William (Caro.)	C-3B	118	410	71	106	27	2	17	61	.259	67	90	17	677	98	15	.981
—Albany (East.)............	C	7	25	3	7	0	0	0	0	.280	2	7	0	39	7	2	.958
1994—Columbus (I.L.).........	C-OF	92	313	46	75	13	3	11	48	.240	32	81	5	425	39	‡11	.977
1995—Columbus (I.L.).........	C-DH	108	368	60	94	32	5	8	51	.255	54	101	4	500	58	4	*.993
—New York (A.L.).........	C	1	0	0	0	0	0	0	0	...	0	0	0	1	0	0	1.000
1996—Columbus (I.L.).........	C-DH-OF	106	354	76	96	22	6	11	62	.271	*79	86	3	598	51	10	.985
—New York (A.L.).........	C-DH	8	14	1	1	0	0	0	0	.071	1	6	0	17	2	0	1.000
1997—New York (A.L.).........	C	60	188	29	47	12	0	6	25	.250	30	33	1	367	23	3	.992
1998—New York (A.L.).........	C-DH-1B	111	358	56	96	23	0	17	63	.268	47	92	0	594	47	4	.994
1999—New York (A.L.).........	C-DH-1B	112	379	50	93	19	2	12	57	.245	53	91	1	709	47	5	.993
2000—New York (A.L.).........	C-1B-DH	151	505	92	145	35	1	28	86	.287	107	151	2	955	64	8	.992
2001—New York (A.L.).........	C-DH-1B	138	484	59	134	28	1	22	95	.277	62	132	2	1003	52	11	.990
Major League totals (7 years)		581	1928	287	516	117	4	85	326	.268	300	505	6	3646	235	31	.992

DIVISION SERIES RECORD

							BATTING								FIELDING			
Year Team (League)	Pos.	G	AB	R	H	2B	3B	HR	RBI	Avg.	BB	SO	SB	PO	A	E	Avg.
1995—New York (A.L.).........	PR	1	0	1	0	0	0	0	0	...	0	0	0	...	...	...	...
1997—New York (A.L.).........	C-PH	2	2	0	0	0	0	0	0	.000	0	1	0	1	1	0	1.000
1998—New York (A.L.).........	C	1	2	1	0	0	0	0	0	.000	1	2	0	11	1	0	1.000
1999—New York (A.L.).........	C	1	4	0	1	1	0	0	0	.250	0	0	0	5	0	0	1.000
2000—New York (A.L.).........	C	5	17	2	4	2	0	0	1	.235	3	5	0	34	1	0	1.000
2001—New York (A.L.).........	C	5	18	3	8	1	0	1	2	.444	2	2	1	33	0	0	1.000
Division series totals (6 years)		15	43	7	13	4	0	1	3	.302	6	10	1	84	3	0	1.000

CHAMPIONSHIP SERIES RECORD

							BATTING								FIELDING			
Year Team (League)	Pos.	G	AB	R	H	2B	3B	HR	RBI	Avg.	BB	SO	SB	PO	A	E	Avg.
1998—New York (A.L.).........	C-PH	5	11	1	2	0	0	1	2	.182	4	2	0	35	1	0	1.000
1999—New York (A.L.).........	C	3	10	1	1	0	0	1	2	.100	1	2	0	20	1	1	.955
2000—New York (A.L.).........	C	6	19	2	3	1	0	0	3	.158	5	5	0	51	3	0	1.000
2001—New York (A.L.).........	C	5	14	4	3	1	0	0	0	.214	6	7	0	34	3	0	1.000
Championship series totals (4 years)		19	54	8	9	2	0	2	7	.167	16	16	0	140	8	1	.993

WORLD SERIES RECORD

NOTES: Member of World Series championship team (1998, 1999 and 2000).

							BATTING								FIELDING			
Year Team (League)	Pos.	G	AB	R	H	2B	3B	HR	RBI	Avg.	BB	SO	SB	PO	A	E	Avg.
1998—New York (A.L.).........	C-PH	4	9	2	3	0	0	1	2	.333	2	2	0	20	0	0	1.000
1999—New York (A.L.).........	C	2	8	0	2	1	0	0	1	.250	0	3	0	17	1	0	1.000
2000—New York (A.L.).........	C	5	18	2	4	1	0	0	1	.222	5	4	0	52	1	0	1.000
2001—New York (A.L.).........	C	7	23	2	4	1	0	1	1	.174	3	8	0	69	4	1	.986
World Series totals (4 years)		18	58	6	13	3	0	2	5	.224	10	17	0	158	6	1	.994

ALL-STAR GAME RECORD

					BATTING							FIELDING			
Year League	Pos.	AB	R	H	2B	3B	HR	RBI	Avg.	BB	SO	SB	PO	A	E	Avg.
2000—American..................	C	2	0	0	0	0	0	0	.000	0	1	0	2	0	0	1.000
2001—American..................	C	1	0	1	1	0	0	0	1.000	0	0	0	3	0	0	1.000
All-Star Game totals (2 years)		3	0	1	1	0	0	0	.333	0	1	0	5	0	0	1.000

POTE, LOU   P   ANGELS

PERSONAL: Born August 27, 1971, in Evergreen Park, Ill. ... 6-3/208. ... Throws right, bats right. ... Full name: Louis William Pote.

HIGH SCHOOL: De La Salle Institute (Chicago).

JUNIOR COLLEGE: Kishwaukee (Illinois).

TRANSACTIONS/CAREER NOTES: Selected by San Francisco Giants organization in 29th round of free-agent draft (June 4, 1990). ... On Shreveport disabled list (April 8-July 31, 1994). ... Traded by Giants to Montreal Expos for P Luis Aquino (July 24, 1995). ... Released by Expos (March 28, 1997). ... Signed by St. Louis Cardinals organization (August 7, 1997). ... Granted free agency (October 17, 1997). ... Signed by Anaheim Angels organization (December 15, 1997).

Year League	W	L	Pct.	ERA	G	GS	CG	ShO	Sv.	IP	H	R	ER	BB	SO
1991—Arizona Giants (Ariz.)........	2	3	.400	2.55	8	8	0	0	0	42 1/3	38	23	12	19	41
—Everett (N'West)................	2	0	1.000	2.51	5	4	0	0	0	28 2/3	24	8	8	7	26
1992—Shreveport (Texas).............	4	2	.667	0.96	20	3	0	0	0	37 2/3	20	7	4	15	26
—San Jose (Calif.)...............	0	1	.000	4.66	4	3	0	0	0	9 2/3	11	5	5	7	8
1993—Shreveport (Texas).............	8	7	.533	4.07	19	19	0	0	0	108 1/3	111	53	49	45	81

Year League	W	L	Pct.	ERA	G	GS	CG	ShO	Sv.	IP	H	R	ER	BB	SO
1994—Arizona Giants (Ariz.)	1	0	1.000	0.00	4	4	0	0	0	19 2/3	9	0	0	6	30
—Shreveport (Texas)	2	2	.500	2.83	5	5	0	0	0	28 2/3	31	11	9	7	15
1995—Shreveport (Texas)	2	2	.500	5.33	28	0	0	0	3	50 2/3	63	41	30	26	30
—Harrisburg (East.)■	0	1	.000	5.40	9	4	0	0	0	28 1/3	32	17	17	7	24
1996—Harrisburg (East.)	1	7	.125	5.07	25	18	0	0	1	104 2/3	114	66	59	48	61
1997—Arkansas (Texas)■	0	0	...	1.54	7	3	0	0	0	23 1/3	15	10	4	8	21
1998—Midland (Texas)■	8	10	.444	5.31	32	19	*6	•1	0	154 1/3	194	110	91	54	117
1999—Edmonton (PCL)	7	9	.438	4.50	24	23	3	0	0	150	171	80	75	41	118
—Anaheim (A.L.)	1	1	.500	2.15	20	0	0	0	3	29 1/3	23	9	7	12	20
2000—Anaheim (A.L.)	1	1	.500	3.40	32	1	0	0	1	50 1/3	52	23	19	17	44
—Edmonton (PCL)	2	1	.667	3.52	24	0	0	0	12	30 2/3	27	14	12	14	28
2001—Anaheim (A.L.)	2	0	1.000	4.15	44	1	0	0	2	86 2/3	88	41	40	32	66
Major League totals (3 years)	4	2	.667	3.57	96	2	0	0	6	166 1/3	163	73	66	61	130

POWELL, BRIAN — P — TIGERS

PERSONAL: Born October 10, 1973, in Bainbridge, Ga. ... 6-2/205. ... Throws right, bats right. ... Full name: William Brian Powell.
HIGH SCHOOL: Bainbridge (Ga.).
COLLEGE: Georgia.
TRANSACTIONS/CAREER NOTES: Selected by Detroit Tigers organization in second round of free-agent draft (June 1, 1995). ... Traded by Tigers with C Paul Bako, P Dean Crow, P Mark Persails and 3B Carlos Villalobos to Houston Astros for C Brad Ausmus and P C.J. Nitkowski (January 14, 1999). ... On disabled list (May 25, 1999-remainder of season). ... On New Orleans disabled list (April 6-22, 2000). ... Granted free agency (October 8, 2001). ... Signed by Tigers organization (December 19, 2001).

Year League	W	L	Pct.	ERA	G	GS	CG	ShO	Sv.	IP	H	R	ER	BB	SO
1995—Jamestown (NY-Penn)	2	1	.667	3.08	5	5	0	0	0	26 1/3	19	12	9	8	15
—Fayetteville (S.Atl.)	4	0	1.000	1.61	5	5	0	0	0	28	15	5	5	11	37
1996—Lakeland (FSL)	8	13	.381	4.90	29	27	*5	0	0	•174 1/3	*195	106	*95	47	84
1997—Lakeland (FSL)	13	9	.591	2.50	27	27	*8	•2	0	*183 1/3	153	70	51	35	122
1998—Jacksonville (Sou.)	10	2	*.833	3.07	14	14	2	1	0	93 2/3	84	37	32	24	51
—Toledo (I.L.)	0	0	...	0.00	1	1	0	0	0	7	5	0	0	0	7
—Detroit (A.L.)	3	8	.273	6.35	18	16	0	0	0	83 2/3	101	67	59	36	46
1999—New Orleans (PCL)■	4	4	.500	6.19	9	9	0	0	0	48	54	39	33	21	36
2000—New Orleans (PCL)	9	4	.692	4.95	18	18	1	0	0	103 2/3	103	63	57	41	57
—Houston (N.L.)	2	1	.667	5.74	9	5	0	0	0	31 1/3	34	21	20	13	14
2001—New Orleans (PCL)	9	8	.529	3.17	24	23	0	•2	0	144 2/3	142	65	51	39	96
—Houston (N.L.)	0	1	.000	18.00	1	1	0	0	0	3	5	6	6	3	3
A.L. totals (1 year)	3	8	.273	6.35	18	16	0	0	0	83 2/3	101	67	59	36	46
N.L. totals (2 years)	2	2	.500	6.82	10	6	0	0	0	34 1/3	39	27	26	16	17
Major League totals (3 years)	5	10	.333	6.48	28	22	0	0	0	118	140	94	85	52	63

POWELL, DANTE — OF

PERSONAL: Born August 25, 1973, in Long Beach, Calif. ... 6-2/185. ... Bats right, throws right. ... Full name: LeJon Dante Powell.
HIGH SCHOOL: Millikan (Long Beach, Calif.).
COLLEGE: Cal State-Fullerton.
TRANSACTIONS/CAREER NOTES: Selected by Toronto Blue Jays in supplemental round ("sandwich pick" between first and second round, 42nd pick overall) of free-agent draft (June 3, 1991); did not sign. ... Selected by San Francisco Giants organization in first round (22nd pick overall) of free-agent draft (June 2, 1994). ... Traded by Giants to Arizona Diamondbacks for P Alan Embree (November 10, 1998). ... On Tucson disabled list (May 25-June 26, 1999). ... Traded by Diamondbacks to St. Louis Cardinals for SS Luis Ordaz (December 15, 1999). ... Granted free agency (October 18, 2000). ... Signed by Giants organization (February 7, 2001). ... On Fresno disabled list (April 9-19, 2001). ... Released by Giants (November 28, 2001).
STATISTICAL NOTES: Led California League outfielders with 337 total chances in 1995. ... Led Texas League with 23 caught stealing in 1996. ... Led Texas League outfielders with 347 total chances in 1996. ... Led Pacific Coast League outfielders with 293 total chances in 1998.

Year Team (League)	Pos.	G	AB	R	H	2B	3B	HR	RBI	Avg.	BB	SO	SB	PO	A	E	Avg.
						BATTING								FIELDING			
1994—Everett (N'West)	OF	41	165	31	51	15	1	5	25	.309	19	47	27	88	3	2	.978
—San Jose (Calif.)	OF	1	4	0	2	0	0	0	0	.500	0	1	0	1	0	0	1.000
1995—San Jose (Calif.)	OF	135	505	74	125	23	8	10	70	.248	46	131	43	*308	*18	11	.967
1996—Shreveport (Texas)	OF-DH	135	508	*92	142	27	2	21	78	.280	72	92	*43	*331	8	8	.977
—Phoenix (PCL)	OF	2	8	0	2	0	1	0	0	.250	2	3	0	4	0	0	1.000
1997—Phoenix (PCL)	OF	108	452	91	109	24	4	11	42	.241	52	105	34	*266	4	4	.986
—San Francisco (N.L.)	OF	27	39	8	12	1	0	1	3	.308	4	11	1	27	0	0	1.000
1998—Fresno (PCL)	OF	134	448	83	103	17	3	14	52	.230	71	138	41	*284	2	7	.976
—San Francisco (N.L.)	OF	8	4	2	2	0	0	1	1	.500	3	0	0	2	0	0	1.000
1999—Arizona (N.L.)■	OF	22	25	4	4	3	0	0	1	.160	2	6	2	13	0	1	.929
—Tucson (PCL)	OF-DH	51	187	29	62	14	2	7	30	.332	14	38	22	94	5	5	.952
2000—San Antonio (Texas)■	OF	17	64	12	17	4	0	1	6	.266	12	16	10	44	2	1	.979
—Albuquerque (PCL)	OF	65	181	36	40	7	1	6	21	.221	21	51	13	84	3	3	.967
2001—Fresno (PCL)■	OF	114	426	74	120	23	3	22	62	.282	34	122	25	189	7	7	.966
—San Francisco (N.L.)	OF	13	6	5	2	0	0	0	0	.333	0	0	0	8	0	0	1.000
Major League totals (4 years)		70	74	19	20	4	0	2	5	.270	9	17	3	50	0	1	.980

DIVISION SERIES RECORD

Year Team (League)	Pos.	G	AB	R	H	2B	3B	HR	RBI	Avg.	BB	SO	SB	PO	A	E	Avg.
						BATTING								FIELDING			
1997—San Francisco (N.L.)	OF	1	0	0	0	0	0	0	0	...	0	0	0	0	0	0	...

P

PERSONAL: Born January 9, 1972, in Meridian, Miss. ... 6-4/225. ... Throws right, bats right. ... Full name: James Willard Powell Jr. ... Brother-in-law of Bud Brown, defensive back with Miami Dolphins (1984-88).

HIGH SCHOOL: West Lauderdale (Collinsville, Miss.).

COLLEGE: Mississippi State.

TRANSACTIONS/CAREER NOTES: Selected by San Diego Padres organization in 11th round of free-agent draft (June 4, 1990); did not sign. ... Selected by Baltimore Orioles organization in first round (19th pick overall) of free-agent draft (June 3, 1993). ... On disabled list (April 7-26, 1994). ... Traded by Orioles to Florida Marlins for IF Bret Barberie (December 6, 1994). ... On Florida disabled list (April 20-May 10, 1996); included rehabilitation assignment to Brevard County (May 8-10). ... Traded by Marlins with C Scott Makarewicz to Houston Astros for C Ramon Castro (July 6, 1998). ... On Houston disabled list (May 17-June 3, June 19-August 6 and August 18, 2000-remainder of season); included rehabilitation assignments to New Orleans (May 30-June 3) and Round Rock (August 3). ... Traded by Astros to Colorado Rockies for P Ron Villone (June 27, 2001). ... Granted free agency (November 5, 2001). ... Signed by Texas Rangers (December 13, 2001).

MISCELLANEOUS: Struck out in only appearance as pinch hitter with Florida (1996). ... Struck out in only appearance as pinch hitter (2000).

Year League	W	L	Pct.	ERA	G	GS	CG	ShO	Sv.	IP	H	R	ER	BB	SO
1993— Albany (S.Atl.)	0	2	.000	4.55	6	6	0	0	0	27²/₃	29	19	14	13	29
1994— Frederick (Caro.)	7	7	.500	4.96	26	20	0	0	1	123¹/₃	132	79	68	54	87
1995— Portland (East.)■	5	4	.556	1.87	50	0	0	0	*24	53	42	12	11	15	53
— Florida (N.L.)	0	0	...	1.08	9	0	0	0	0	8¹/₃	7	2	1	6	4
1996— Florida (N.L.)	4	3	.571	4.54	67	0	0	0	2	71¹/₃	71	41	36	36	52
— Brevard County (FSL)	0	0	...	0.00	1	1	0	0	0	2	0	0	0	0	4
1997— Florida (N.L.)	7	2	.778	3.28	74	0	0	0	2	79²/₃	71	35	29	30	65
1998— Florida (N.L.)	4	4	.500	4.21	33	0	0	0	3	36¹/₃	36	19	17	22	24
— Houston (N.L.)■	3	3	.500	2.38	29	0	0	0	4	34	22	9	9	15	38
1999— Houston (N.L.)	5	4	.556	4.32	67	0	0	0	4	75	82	38	36	40	77
2000— Houston (N.L.)	1	1	.500	5.67	29	0	0	0	0	27	29	18	17	19	16
— New Orleans (PCL)	0	0	...	4.50	2	1	0	0	0	2	2	1	1	2	2
— Round Rock (Texas)	0	0	...	0.00	1	1	0	0	0	2	0	0	0	1	1
2001— Houston (N.L.)	2	2	.500	3.72	35	0	0	0	0	36¹/₃	41	18	15	19	28
— Colorado (N.L.)■	3	1	.750	2.79	39	0	0	0	7	38²/₃	34	18	12	12	26
Major League totals (7 years)	29	20	.592	3.81	382	0	0	0	22	406²/₃	393	198	172	199	330

DIVISION SERIES RECORD

Year League	W	L	Pct.	ERA	G	GS	CG	ShO	Sv.	IP	H	R	ER	BB	SO
1997— Florida (N.L.)							Did not play.								
1998— Houston (N.L.)	0	0	...	11.57	3	0	0	0	0	2¹/₃	2	3	3	3	3
1999— Houston (N.L.)	0	1	.000	6.00	3	0	0	0	0	3	3	2	2	1	3
Division series totals (2 years)	0	1	.000	8.44	6	0	0	0	0	5¹/₃	5	5	5	4	6

CHAMPIONSHIP SERIES RECORD

Year League	W	L	Pct.	ERA	G	GS	CG	ShO	Sv.	IP	H	R	ER	BB	SO
1997— Florida (N.L.)	0	0	...	0.00	1	0	0	0	0	²/₃	0	0	0	0	1

WORLD SERIES RECORD

NOTES: Member of World Series championship team (1997).

Year League	W	L	Pct.	ERA	G	GS	CG	ShO	Sv.	IP	H	R	ER	BB	SO
1997— Florida (N.L.)	1	0	1.000	7.36	4	0	0	0	0	3²/₃	5	3	3	4	2

PERSONAL: Born August 27, 1979, in Mesa, Ariz. ... 5-11/160. ... Throws left, bats left. ... Full name: Andrew Elias Pratt.

HIGH SCHOOL: Chino Valley (Ariz.).

TRANSACTIONS/CAREER NOTES: Selected by Texas Rangers organization in ninth round of free-agent draft (June 2, 1998).

Year League	W	L	Pct.	ERA	G	GS	CG	ShO	Sv.	IP	H	R	ER	BB	SO
1998— Gulf Coast Rangers (GCL)	4	3	.571	3.86	12	8	0	0	0	56	49	25	24	14	49
1999— Savannah (S.Atl.)	4	4	.500	2.89	13	13	1	1	0	71²/₃	66	30	23	16	100
2000— Charlotte (FSL)	7	4	.636	2.72	16	16	2	1	0	92¹/₃	68	37	28	26	95
— Tulsa (Texas)	1	6	.143	7.22	11	11	0	0	0	52¹/₃	66	48	42	33	42
2001— Tulsa (Texas)	8	10	.444	4.61	27	26	3	1	0	168	175	99	86	57	132

PERSONAL: Born February 9, 1967, in Bellevue, Neb. ... 6-3/230. ... Bats right, throws right. ... Full name: Todd Alan Pratt.

HIGH SCHOOL: Hilltop (Chula Vista, Calif.).

TRANSACTIONS/CAREER NOTES: Selected by Boston Red Sox organization in sixth round of free-agent draft (June 3, 1985). ... Selected by Cleveland Indians organization from Red Sox organization in Rule 5 minor league draft (December 7, 1987). ... Returned to Red Sox organization (March 28, 1988). ... Granted free agency (October 15, 1991). ... Signed by Baltimore Orioles organization (November 13, 1991). ... Selected by Philadelphia Phillies from Orioles organization in Rule 5 major league draft (December 9, 1991). ... On Philadelphia disabled list (April 28-May 27, 1993); included rehabilitation assignment to Scranton/Wilkes-Barre (May 23-27). ... Granted free agency (December 23, 1994). ... Signed by Chicago Cubs organization (April 8, 1995). ... Granted free agency (October 16, 1995). ... Signed by Seattle Mariners organization (January 25, 1996). ... Released by Mariners (March 27, 1996). ... Signed by New York Mets organization (December 23, 1996). ... On New York disabled list (May 7-June 23, 1998); included rehabilitation assignments to St. Lucie (June 14-18), Gulf Coast Mets (June 19-21) and Norfolk (June 22-23). ... Traded by Mets to Phillies for C Gary Bennett (July 23, 2001). ... Granted free agency (November 5, 2001).

STATISTICAL NOTES: Led South Atlantic League catchers with 660 putouts and nine double plays and tied for lead with 13 errors in 1986. ... Led Eastern League catchers with 11 errors in 1989. ... Career major league grand slams: 1.

P

Year Team (League)	Pos.	G	AB	R	H	2B	3B	HR	RBI	Avg.	BB	SO	SB	PO	A	E	Avg.
1985—Elmira (NY-Penn)	C	39	119	7	16	1	1	0	5	.134	10	27	0	254	29	6	.979
1986—Greensboro (S.Atl.)	C-1B	107	348	63	84	16	0	12	56	.241	75	114	0	†826	55	‡15	.983
1987—Winter Haven (FSL)	C-1B-OF	118	407	57	105	22	0	12	65	.258	70	94	0	672	64	15	.980
1988—New Britain (East.)	C-1B	124	395	41	89	15	2	8	49	.225	41	110	1	540	46	15	.975
1989—New Britain (East.)	C-1B	109	338	30	77	17	1	2	35	.228	44	66	1	435	42	†11	.977
1990—New Britain (East.)	C-1B	70	195	15	45	14	1	2	22	.231	18	56	0	166	15	4	.978
1991—Pawtucket (I.L.)	C-1B	68	219	68	64	16	0	11	41	.292	23	42	0	236	21	4	.985
1992—Reading (East.)■	C	41	132	20	44	6	1	6	26	.333	24	28	2	90	6	3	.970
— Scranton/W.B. (I.L.)	C-1B	41	125	20	40	9	1	7	28	.320	30	14	1	152	16	4	.977
— Philadelphia (N.L.)	C	16	46	6	13	1	0	2	10	.283	4	12	0	65	4	2	.972
1993—Philadelphia (N.L.)	C	33	87	8	25	6	0	5	13	.287	5	19	0	169	7	2	.989
— Scranton/W.B. (I.L.)	C	3	9	1	2	1	0	0	1	.222	3	1	0	11	0	0	1.000
1994—Philadelphia (N.L.)	C	28	102	10	20	6	1	2	9	.196	12	29	0	172	8	0	1.000
1995—Iowa (A.A.)■	C-1B-DH	23	58	3	19	1	0	0	5	.328	4	17	0	82	8	2	.978
— Chicago (N.L.)	C	25	60	3	8	2	0	0	4	.133	6	21	0	149	9	3	.981
1996—								Out of organized baseball.									
1997—Norfolk (I.L.)■	C-DH	59	206	42	62	8	3	9	34	.301	26	48	1	317	24	4	.988
— New York (N.L.)	C	39	106	12	30	6	0	2	19	.283	13	32	0	186	22	2	.990
1998—Norfolk (I.L.)	DH-C-OF-1B	35	118	16	42	6	0	7	30	.356	15	19	2	115	8	2	.984
— New York (N.L.)	C-1B	41	69	9	19	9	1	2	18	.275	2	20	0	78	4	2	.976
— St. Lucie (FSL)	C-1B-OF	5	20	2	9	1	0	1	3	.450	1	5	1	40	6	0	1.000
— GC Mets (GCL)	C-OF	2	4	1	1	0	0	0	0	.250	4	1	0	7	2	0	1.000
1999—New York (N.L.)	C-1B-OF	71	140	18	41	4	0	3	21	.293	15	32	2	263	13	1	.996
2000—New York (N.L.)	C-DH	80	160	33	44	6	0	8	25	.275	22	31	0	314	24	1	.997
2001—New York (N.L.)	C	45	80	6	13	5	0	2	4	.163	15	36	1	152	4	1	.994
— Philadelphia (N.L.)■	C-1B	35	93	12	19	3	0	2	7	.204	19	25	0	196	8	3	.986
Major League totals (9 years)		413	943	117	232	48	2	28	130	.246	113	257	3	1744	103	17	.991

DIVISION SERIES RECORD

Year Team (League)	Pos.	G	AB	R	H	2B	3B	HR	RBI	Avg.	BB	SO	SB	PO	A	E	Avg.
1999—New York (N.L.)	PH-C	3	8	2	1	0	0	1	1	.125	2	1	0	11	1	0	1.000
2000—New York (N.L.)	PH-C	1	1	0	0	0	0	0	0	.000	0	0	0	4	0	0	1.000
Division series totals (2 years)		4	9	2	1	0	0	1	1	.111	2	1	0	15	1	0	1.000

CHAMPIONSHIP SERIES RECORD

Year Team (League)	Pos.	G	AB	R	H	2B	3B	HR	RBI	Avg.	BB	SO	SB	PO	A	E	Avg.
1993—Philadelphia (N.L.)	C	1	1	0	0	0	0	0	0	.000	0	1	0	1	0	0	1.000
1999—New York (N.L.)	PH-C	4	2	0	1	0	0	0	3	.500	1	1	0	6	0	0	1.000
Championship series totals (2 years)		5	3	0	1	0	0	0	3	.333	1	2	0	7	0	0	1.000

WORLD SERIES RECORD

Year Team (League)	Pos.	G	AB	R	H	2B	3B	HR	RBI	Avg.	BB	SO	SB	PO	A	E	Avg.
1993—Philadelphia (N.L.)								Did not play.										
2000—New York (N.L.)	C	1	2	1	0	0	0	0	0	.000	1	2	0	10	0	0	1.000

PRIDE, CURTIS OF

PERSONAL: Born December 17, 1968, in Washington, D.C. ... 5-11/195. ... Bats left, throws right. ... Full name: Curtis John Pride.
HIGH SCHOOL: John F. Kennedy (Silver Spring, Md.).
COLLEGE: William & Mary.
TRANSACTIONS/CAREER NOTES: Selected by New York Mets organization in 10th round of free-agent draft (June 2, 1986). ... Granted free agency (October 15, 1992). ... Signed by Montreal Expos organization (December 8, 1992). ... On Ottawa disabled list (April 7-May 13, July 6-15 and August 7-14, 1994). ... Granted free agency (October 16, 1995). ... Signed by Detroit Tigers (March 31, 1996). ... On Detroit disabled list (April 13-May 10, 1996); included rehabilitation assignment to Toledo (April 30-May 10). ... Granted free agency (August 21, 1997). ... Signed by Boston Red Sox organization (August 30, 1997). ... Granted free agency (October 15, 1997). ... Signed by Atlanta Braves organization (February 6, 1998). ... On suspended list (May 27-28, 1998). ... On Atlanta disabled list (June 28-July 14, 1998); included rehabilitation assignment to Richmond (July 13-14). ... Released by Braves (December 1, 1998). ... Signed by Kansas City Royals organization (February 24, 1999). ... Released by Royals (March 4, 1999). ... Signed by Mets organization (January 20, 2000). ... Traded by Mets to Red Sox for a player to be named later (April 26, 2000); Mets acquired SS Gavin Jackson to complete deal (July 9, 2000). ... Released by Red Sox (July 8, 2000). ... Signed by Los Angeles Dodgers organization (July 18, 2000). ... Granted free agency (October 18, 2000). ... Signed by Expos organization (December 21, 2000). ... On Ottawa disabled list (April 14-24, 2001). ... On Montreal disabled list (June 18-August 21, 2001); included rehabilitation assignments to Jupiter (August 6-13) and Ottawa (August 14-21). ... Granted free agency (October 11, 2001).

Year Team (League)	Pos.	G	AB	R	H	2B	3B	HR	RBI	Avg.	BB	SO	SB	PO	A	E	Avg.
1986—Kingsport (Appl.)	OF	27	46	5	5	0	0	1	4	.109	6	24	5	17	1	0	1.000
1987—Kingsport (Appl.)	OF	31	104	22	25	4	0	1	9	.240	16	34	14	39	3	5	.894
1988—Kingsport (Appl.)	OF	70	268	*59	76	13	1	8	27	.284	50	48	23	118	6	5	.961
1989—Pittsfield (NY-Penn)	OF	55	212	35	55	7	3	6	23	.259	25	47	9	105	3	4	.964
1990—Columbia (S.Atl.)	OF	53	191	38	51	4	4	6	25	.267	21	45	11	72	4	11	.874
1991—St. Lucie (FSL)	OF	116	392	57	102	21	4	9	37	.260	43	94	24	199	5	4	.981
1992—Binghamton (East.)	OF	118	388	54	88	15	3	10	42	.227	47	110	14	214	3	8	.964
1993—Harrisburg (East.)■	OF	50	180	51	64	6	3	15	39	.356	12	36	21	69	0	2	.972
— Ottawa (I.L.)	OF	69	262	55	79	11	4	6	22	.302	34	61	29	136	3	2	.986
— Montreal (N.L.)	OF	10	9	3	4	1	1	1	5	.444	0	3	1	2	0	0	1.000
1994—W.P. Beach (FSL)	OF	3	8	5	6	1	0	1	3	.750	4	2	2	11	0	0	1.000
— Ottawa (I.L.)	OF-DH	82	300	56	77	16	4	9	32	.257	39	81	22	164	1	3	.982

P

Year	Team (League)	Pos.	G	AB	R	H	2B	3B	HR	RBI	Avg.	BB	SO	SB	PO	A	E	Avg.
									BATTING							FIELDING		
1995— Ottawa (I.L.)		OF-DH	42	154	25	43	8	3	4	24	.279	12	35	8	69	5	2	.974
— Montreal (N.L.)		OF	48	63	10	11	1	0	0	2	.175	5	16	3	23	0	2	.920
1996— Detroit (A.L.)		OF-DH	95	267	52	80	17	5	10	31	.300	31	63	11	89	0	3	.967
— Toledo (I.L.)		DH-OF	9	26	4	6	1	0	1	2	.231	9	7	4	3	0	0	1.000
1997— Detroit (A.L.)		OF-DH	79	162	21	34	4	4	2	19	.210	24	45	6	49	0	1	.980
— Pawtucket (I.L.)■.......		OF	1	3	0	0	0	0	0	0	.000	0	2	0	2	0	0	1.000
— Boston (A.L.)		PH	2	2	1	1	0	0	1	1	.500	0	1	0	...	...	...	...
1998— Atlanta (N.L.)■.........		OF-DH	70	107	19	27	6	1	3	9	.252	9	29	4	41	0	0	1.000
— Richmond (I.L.)		OF-DH	21	78	11	19	2	1	2	6	.244	15	17	8	28	1	0	1.000
1999— Nashua (Atl.)■.........		DH	14	32	0	2	0	0	0	2	.063	7	11	0	...	...	...	...
2000— Norfolk (I.L.)		OF	15	31	9	9	2	2	1	4	.290	11	7	3	13	0	1	.929
— Pawtucket (I.L.)■.......		OF	48	154	44	47	10	2	9	31	.305	38	31	12	102	0	1	.990
— Boston (A.L.)		OF-DH	9	20	4	5	1	0	0	0	.250	1	7	0	15	0	0	1.000
— Albuquerque (PCL)■..		OF	38	133	30	39	7	3	6	17	.293	20	37	7	68	2	3	.959
2001— Ottawa (I.L.)■.........		OF	22	81	14	27	4	1	5	15	.333	12	26	6	26	0	1	.963
— Montreal (N.L.)		OF-DH	36	76	8	19	3	1	1	9	.250	9	22	3	32	1	0	1.000
— Jupiter (FSL)		OF	6	21	3	4	1	0	0	0	.190	3	3	0	12	1	0	1.000
American League totals (3 years)			185	451	78	120	22	9	13	51	.266	56	116	17	153	0	4	.975
National League totals (4 years)			164	255	40	61	11	3	5	25	.239	23	70	11	98	1	2	.980
Major League totals (7 years)			349	706	118	181	33	12	18	76	.256	79	186	28	251	1	6	.977

PRIETO, ARIEL   P

PERSONAL: Born October 22, 1969, in Havana, Cuba. ... 6-2/247. ... Throws right, bats right.
COLLEGE: Fajardo University (Isle of Pines, Cuba).
TRANSACTIONS/CAREER NOTES: Signed by Palm Springs, Western League (May 1995). ... Selected by Oakland Athletics organization in first round (fifth pick overall) of free-agent draft (June 1, 1995). ... On disabled list (August 19-September 3, 1995). ... On Oakland disabled list (May 19-July 28, 1996); included rehabilitation assignments to Modesto (July 1-11) and Edmonton (July 11-28). ... On Oakland disabled list (July 13-August 8 and August 23, 1997-remainder of season); included rehabilitation assignment to Edmonton (August 8-17). ... On Edmonton disabled list (July 29-September 10, 1998). ... On disabled list (March 26, 1999-entire season). ... On Sacramento disabled list (August 16-24, 2000). ... Released by A's (January 19, 2001). ... Signed by Cleveland Indians organization (February 10, 2001). ... Released by Indians (March 27, 2001). ... Signed by Tampa Bay Devil Rays (March 28, 2001). ... On Durham disabled list (April 23-May 4, 2001). ... On Tampa Bay disabled list (May 11, 2001-remainder of season). ... Released by Devil Rays (October 30, 2001).
STATISTICAL NOTES: Led Pacific Coast League pitchers with five double plays in 2000.

Year	League	W	L	Pct.	ERA	G	GS	CG	ShO	Sv.	IP	H	R	ER	BB	SO
1995— Palm Springs (West.)........		4	0	1.000	0.97	6	6	1	...	0	37	23	6	4	7	48
— Oakland (A.L.)■..........		2	6	.250	4.97	14	9	1	0	0	58	57	35	32	32	37
1996— Oakland (A.L.)		6	7	.462	4.15	21	21	2	0	0	125²/₃	130	66	58	54	75
— Modesto (Calif.)		0	0	...	3.00	2	1	0	0	1	9	9	4	3	2	8
— Edmonton (PCL)		3	0	1.000	0.57	3	3	0	0	0	15²/₃	11	1	1	6	18
1997— Oakland (A.L.)		6	8	.429	5.04	22	22	0	0	0	125	155	84	70	70	90
— Edmonton (PCL)		0	0	...	1.50	2	2	0	0	0	6	4	1	1	1	7
1998— Edmonton (PCL)		5	1	.833	2.56	10	10	1	0	0	52²/₃	47	20	15	12	50
— Oakland (A.L.)		0	1	.000	11.88	2	2	0	0	0	8¹/₃	17	11	11	5	8
1999— Oakland (A.L.)								Did not play.								
2000— Sacramento (PCL).............		8	4	.667	3.27	20	18	0	0	0	113	110	51	41	31	79
— Oakland (A.L.)		1	2	.333	5.12	8	6	0	0	0	31²/₃	42	21	18	13	19
2001— Tampa Bay (A.L.)■..........		0	0	...	2.45	3	0	0	0	0	3²/₃	6	1	1	2	2
— Durham (I.L.)		0	0	...	1.35	3	0	0	0	0	6²/₃	3	2	1	2	10
Major League totals (6 years)........		15	24	.385	4.85	70	60	3	0	0	352¹/₃	407	218	190	176	231

PRINCE, TOM   C   TWINS

PERSONAL: Born August 13, 1964, in Kankakee, Ill. ... 5-11/206. ... Bats right, throws right. ... Full name: Thomas Albert Prince.
HIGH SCHOOL: Bradley-Bourbonnais (Bradley, Ill.).
JUNIOR COLLEGE: Kankakee (Ill.) Community College.
TRANSACTIONS/CAREER NOTES: Selected by Atlanta Braves organization in eighth round of free-agent draft (January 11, 1983); did not sign. ... Selected by Braves organization in secondary phase of free-agent draft (June 6, 1983); did not sign. ... Selected by Pittsburgh Pirates organization in secondary phase of free-agent draft (January 17, 1984). ... On Pittsburgh disabled list (August 13-September 1, 1991); included rehabilitation assignment to Buffalo (August 28-September 1). ... Granted free agency (October 15, 1993). ... Signed by Los Angeles Dodgers organization (November 12, 1993). ... On Albuquerque disabled list (April 30-May 7, 1994). ... Released by Dodgers (December 5, 1994). ... Re-signed by Dodgers organization (January 5, 1995). ... On Los Angeles disabled list (June 4-July 10, 1995); included rehabilitation assignment to Albuquerque (June 26-July 10). ... Granted free agency (October 15, 1995). ... Re-signed by Dodgers organization (November 1, 1995). ... Granted free agency (October 22, 1998). ... Signed by Philadelphia Phillies (December 18, 1998). ... On Philadelphia disabled list (March 23-September 3, 1999); included rehabilitation assignments to Gulf Coast Phillies (July 21-28), Clearwater (July 29-August 9) and Scranton (August 10-29). ... Granted free agency (October 31, 2000). ... Signed by Minnesota Twins organization (December 19, 2000).
STATISTICAL NOTES: Led South Atlantic League catchers with 930 total chances, 10 double plays and 27 passed balls in 1985. ... Led Carolina League catchers with 954 total chances and 15 passed balls in 1986. ... Led Eastern League catchers with 721 total chances and nine double plays in 1987. ... Led American Association catchers with 12 double plays in 1992. ... Led Pacific Coast League catchers with 677 total chances and nine double plays in 1994.

Year	Team (League)	Pos.	G	AB	R	H	2B	3B	HR	RBI	Avg.	BB	SO	SB	PO	A	E	Avg.
									BATTING							FIELDING		
1984— Watertown (NY-Penn)		C-3B	23	69	6	14	3	0	2	13	.203	9	13	0	155	26	2	.989
— GC Pirates (GCL)........		C-1B	18	48	4	11	0	0	1	6	.229	8	10	1	75	16	4	.958
1985— Macon (S.Atl.)		C	124	360	60	75	20	1	10	42	.208	96	92	13	*810	*101	*19	.980
1986— Prince William (Caro.)		C	121	395	59	100	34	1	10	47	.253	50	74	4	*821	•113	20	.979
1987— Harrisburg (East.).......		C	113	365	41	112	23	2	6	54	.307	51	46	6	*622	*88	•11	.985
— Pittsburgh (N.L.)		C	4	9	1	2	1	0	1	2	.222	0	2	0	14	3	0	1.000

P

| | | | | | | BATTING | | | | | | | | FIELDING | | |
Year Team (League)	Pos.	G	AB	R	H	2B	3B	HR	RBI	Avg.	BB	SO	SB	PO	A	E	Avg.
1988— Buffalo (A.A.).............	C	86	304	35	79	16	0	14	42	.260	23	53	3	456	51	*12	.977
— Pittsburgh (N.L.).......	C	29	74	3	13	2	0	0	6	.176	4	15	0	108	8	2	.983
1989— Buffalo (A.A.).............	C	65	183	21	37	8	1	6	33	.202	22	30	2	312	22	5	.985
— Pittsburgh (N.L.).......	C	21	52	1	7	4	0	0	5	.135	6	12	1	85	11	4	.960
1990— Pittsburgh (N.L.).......	C	4	10	1	1	0	0	0	0	.100	1	2	0	16	1	0	1.000
— Buffalo (A.A.).............	C-1B	94	284	38	64	13	0	7	37	.225	39	46	4	461	62	8	.985
1991— Pittsburgh (N.L.).......	C-1B	26	34	4	9	3	0	1	2	.265	7	3	0	53	9	1	.984
— Buffalo (A.A.).............	C	80	221	29	46	8	3	6	32	.208	37	31	3	379	61	5	.989
1992— Pittsburgh (N.L.).......	C-3B	27	44	1	4	2	0	0	5	.091	6	9	1	76	8	2	.977
— Buffalo (A.A.).............	C-OF	75	244	34	64	17	0	9	35	.262	20	35	3	307	50	8	.978
1993— Pittsburgh (N.L.).......	C	66	179	14	35	14	0	2	24	.196	13	38	1	271	31	5	.984
1994— Albuquerque (PCL)■..	C-DH	103	330	61	94	31	2	20	54	.285	51	67	2	593	*75	9	.987
— Los Angeles (N.L.)	C	3	6	2	2	0	0	0	1	.333	1	3	0	11	1	0	1.000
1995— Los Angeles (N.L.)	C	18	40	3	8	2	1	1	4	.200	4	10	0	71	8	1	.988
— Albuquerque (PCL).....	C-DH	61	192	30	61	15	0	7	36	.318	27	41	0	310	34	4	.989
1996— Albuquerque (PCL).....C-DH-3B-OF		32	95	24	39	5	1	7	22	.411	15	14	0	88	20	1	.991
— Los Angeles (N.L.)	C	40	64	6	19	6	0	1	11	.297	6	15	0	161	11	1	.994
1997— Los Angeles (N.L.)	C	47	100	17	22	5	0	3	14	.220	5	15	0	221	25	1	.996
1998— Los Angeles (N.L.)	C	37	81	7	15	5	1	0	5	.185	7	24	0	175	16	0	1.000
1999— GC Phillies (GCL)■ ..	C-DH	7	21	3	5	3	0	0	3	.238	4	0	0	19	6	0	1.000
— Clearwater (FSL)	C	9	33	5	12	0	0	2	9	.364	3	3	1	47	4	1	.981
— Scranton/W.B. (I.L.) ...	C-DH	7	22	2	2	0	0	1	1	.091	3	5	1	31	2	0	1.000
— Philadelphia (N.L.)......	C	4	6	1	1	0	0	0	0	.167	1	1	0	13	1	0	1.000
2000— Philadelphia (N.L.)......	C	46	122	14	29	9	0	2	16	.238	13	31	1	250	20	1	.996
2001— Minnesota (A.L.)■	C	64	196	19	43	4	1	7	23	.219	12	39	3	380	41	0	1.000
American League totals (1 year)		64	196	19	43	4	1	7	23	.219	12	39	3	380	41	0	1.000
National League totals (14 years)		372	821	75	167	53	2	11	95	.203	74	180	4	1525	153	18	.989
Major League totals (15 years)		436	1017	94	210	57	3	18	118	.206	86	219	7	1905	194	18	.991

PRINZ, BRET P DIAMONDBACKS

PERSONAL: Born June 15, 1977, in Chicago Heights, Ill. ... 6-3/185. ... Throws right, bats right. ... Full name: Bret Randolph Prinz.
HIGH SCHOOL: Centennial (Peoria, Ariz.).
JUNIOR COLLEGE: Phoenix College.
TRANSACTIONS/CAREER NOTES: Selected by Arizona Diamondbacks organization in 18th round of 1998 free-agent draft (June 3, 1998).

Year League	W	L	Pct.	ERA	G	GS	CG	ShO	Sv.	IP	H	R	ER	BB	SO
1998— Ariz. Diamondbacks (Ariz.).	0	0	...	3.38	4	0	0	0	0	5 1/3	7	3	2	0	3
— Lethbridge (Pio.)..........	4	2	.667	3.09	11	0	0	0	0	46 2/3	49	26	16	13	30
1999— South Bend (Midw.)...........	6	10	.375	4.48	30	23	0	0	0	138 2/3	129	82	69	52	98
2000— South Bend (Midw.)..........	1	0	1.000	0.00	6	0	0	0	1	7 1/3	2	2	0	1	10
— El Paso (Texas)..................	9	1	.900	3.56	53	0	0	0	26	60 2/3	71	24	24	16	69
2001— Tucson (PCL)..................	0	0	...	0.00	5	0	0	0	3	5 2/3	1	0	0	0	6
— Arizona (N.L.)..................	4	1	.800	2.63	46	0	0	0	9	41	33	13	12	19	27
Major League totals (1 year)........	4	1	.800	2.63	46	0	0	0	9	41	33	13	12	19	27

PROKOPEC, LUKE P BLUE JAYS

PERSONAL: Born February 23, 1978, in Blackwood, South Australia. ... 5-11/166. ... Throws right, bats left. ... Full name: Kenneth Luke Prokopec.
HIGH SCHOOL: Renmark (South Australia).
TRANSACTIONS/CAREER NOTES: Signed as non-drafted free agent by Los Angeles Dodgers organization (August 28, 1994). ... On San Antonio disabled list (April 29-May 12 and July 8-21, 2000). ... On Los Angeles disabled list (August 9-25, 2001). ... Traded by Dodgers with P Chad Ricketts to Toronto Blue Jays for P Paul Quantrill and 2B/SS Cesar Izturis (December 13, 2001).
MISCELLANEOUS: Played outfield (1995-97). ... Appeared in one game as pinch runner (2000). ... Appeared in one game as pinch runner (2001).

Year League	W	L	Pct.	ERA	G	GS	CG	ShO	Sv.	IP	H	R	ER	BB	SO
1997— Savannah (S.Atl.)	3	1	.750	4.07	13	6	0	0	0	42	37	21	19	12	45
1998— San Bernardino (Calif.).......	8	5	.615	2.69	13	20	0	0	0	110 1/3	99	43	33	33	148
— San Antonio (Texas)...........	3	0	1.000	1.38	5	5	0	0	0	26	16	5	4	13	25
1999— San Antonio (Texas)...........	8	12	.400	5.42	27	27	0	0	0	157 2/3	172	*113	*95	46	128
2000— San Antonio (Texas)...........	7	3	.700	2.45	22	22	1	0	0	128 2/3	118	40	35	23	124
— Los Angeles (N.L.).............	1	1	.500	3.00	5	3	0	0	0	21	19	10	7	9	12
2001— Los Angeles (N.L.).............	8	7	.533	4.88	29	22	0	0	0	138 1/3	146	80	75	40	91
— Las Vegas (PCL)	1	0	1.000	3.00	1	1	0	0	0	6	3	2	2	2	8
Major League totals (2 years)	9	8	.529	4.63	34	25	0	0	0	159 1/3	165	90	82	49	103

RECORD AS POSITION PLAYER

| | | | | | | BATTING | | | | | | | | FIELDING | | |
Year Team (League)	Pos.	G	AB	R	H	2B	3B	HR	RBI	Avg.	BB	SO	SB	PO	A	E	Avg.
1995— Great Falls (Pio.)	OF	43	119	16	29	6	2	2	24	.244	8	37	5	30	4	0	1.000
1996— Savannah (S.Atl.)	OF	82	245	34	53	12	1	4	29	.216	27	78	0	59	5	8	.889
1997— Savannah (S.Atl.)	OF-P	61	164	11	38	7	3	2	20	.232	12	49	3	79	11	2	.978

PUFFER, BRANDON P ASTROS

P

PERSONAL: Born October 5, 1975, in Downey, Calif. ... 6-3/190. ... Throws right, bats right. ... Full name: Brandon Duane Puffer.
HIGH SCHOOL: Capistrano Valley (Mission Viejo, Calif.).

TRANSACTIONS/CAREER NOTES: Selected by Minnesota Twins organization in 27th round of free-agent draft (June 2, 1994). ... Released by Twins (May 6, 1996). ... Signed by California Angels organization (May 28, 1996). ... Released by Angels (December 15, 1997). ... Signed by Cincinnati Reds organization (January 14, 1998). ... Granted free agency (October 16, 1998). ... Re-signed by Reds organization (November 17, 1998). ... Granted free agency (October 15, 1999). ... Signed by Colorado Rockies organization (November 18, 1999). ... Released by Rockies (May 18, 2000). ... Signed by Somerset, Atlantic League (May 2000). ... Contract sold by Somerset to Houston Astros organization (July 17, 2000).

STATISTICAL NOTES: Led Midwest League pitchers with 55 games finished in 1999.

Year	League	W	L	Pct.	ERA	G	GS	CG	ShO	Sv.	IP	H	R	ER	BB	SO
1994—	Gulf Coast Twins (GCL)......	2	2	.500	3.06	18	0	0	0	2	35 1/3	33	18	12	19	40
1995—	Gulf Coast Twins (GCL)......	0	3	.000	2.88	14	5	0	0	1	40 2/3	29	21	13	21	35
1996—	Arizona Angels (Ariz.)■	0	1	.000	3.60	1	1	0	0	0	5	7	2	2	1	3
	— Boise (N'West)	2	0	1.000	4.45	16	0	0	0	1	30 1/3	27	19	15	11	22
1997—	Boise (N'West)	0	0	...	2.35	6	0	0	0	1	15 1/3	10	5	4	2	15
	— Cedar Rapids (Midw.)	0	0	...	2.60	10	0	0	0	0	17 1/3	8	6	5	10	11
1998—	Charleston, W.Va. (S.Atl.)■	2	7	.222	6.93	29	0	0	0	1	50 2/3	68	45	39	23	36
	— Chattanooga (Sou.)	0	0	...	3.12	7	0	0	0	0	8 2/3	2	3	3	3	6
1999—	Clinton (Midw.)	1	2	.333	1.99	59	0	0	0	*34	63 1/3	53	20	14	24	60
2000—	Asheville (S.Atl.)■.............	0	0	...	8.16	14	0	0	0	5	14 1/3	19	16	13	11	15
	— Somerset (Atl.)■.............	2	2	.500	3.52	15	0	0	0	1	23	25	12	9	9	21
	— Kissimmee (FSL)■.............	2	3	.400	1.27	18	0	0	0	9	21 1/3	18	6	3	11	26
2001—	Round Rock (Texas)..........	6	1	.857	2.07	56	0	0	0	8	82 2/3	52	19	19	35	91

PUJOLS, ALBERT   3B   CARDINALS

PERSONAL: Born January 16, 1980, in Santo Domingo, Dominican Republic. ... 6-3/210. ... Bats right, throws right. ... Full name: Jose Albert Pujols.

HIGH SCHOOL: Fort Osage (Independence, Mo.).

JUNIOR COLLEGE: Maple Woods.

TRANSACTIONS/CAREER NOTES: Selected by St. Louis Cardinals organization in 13th round of free-agent draft (June 2, 1999).

RECORDS: Holds N.L. single-season rookie record for most total bases—360 (2001); and most runs batted in—130 (2001).

HONORS: Named Midwest League Most Valuable Player (2000). ... Named third baseman on N.L. Silver Slugger team (2001). ... Named N.L. Rookie of the Year by THE SPORTING NEWS (2001). ... Named N.L. Rookie of the Year by Baseball Writers' Association of America (2001).

STATISTICAL NOTES: Had 17-game hitting streak (July 31-August 16, 2001). ... Career major league grand slams: 1.

								BATTING								FIELDING			
Year	Team (League)	Pos.	G	AB	R	H	2B	3B	HR	RBI	Avg.	BB	SO	SB	PO	A	E	Avg.
2000—	Peoria (Midw.)............	3B	109	395	62	128	32	6	17	84	.324	38	37	2	92	254	19	.948
	— Potomac (Caro.)........	3B	21	81	11	23	8	1	2	10	.284	7	8	1	12	54	3	.957
	— Memphis (PCL).........	3B-OF	3	14	1	3	1	0	0	2	.214	1	2	1	7	2	0	1.000
2001—	St. Louis (N.L.)..........OF-3B-1B-DH	161	590	112	194	47	4	37	130	.329	69	93	1	451	136	20	.967
Major League totals (1 year)			161	590	112	194	47	4	37	130	.329	69	93	1	451	136	20	.967

DIVISION SERIES RECORD

								BATTING								FIELDING			
Year	Team (League)	Pos.	G	AB	R	H	2B	3B	HR	RBI	Avg.	BB	SO	SB	PO	A	E	Avg.
2001—	St. Louis (N.L.)...........	OF-1B	5	18	1	2	0	0	1	2	.111	2	2	0	25	2	1	.964

ALL-STAR GAME RECORD

						BATTING						FIELDING			
Year	League	Pos.	AB	R	H	2B	3B	HR	RBI	Avg.	BB	SO	SB	PO	A	E	Avg.
2001—	National	3B-2B	0	0	0	0	0	0	0	...	1	0	0	0	1	0	1.000

PULSIPHER, BILL   P   RANGERS

PERSONAL: Born October 9, 1973, in Fort Benning, Ga. ... 6-3/200. ... Throws left, bats left. ... Full name: William Thomas Pulsipher.

HIGH SCHOOL: Fairfax (Va.).

TRANSACTIONS/CAREER NOTES: Selected by New York Mets organization in second round of free-agent draft (June 3, 1991). ... On disabled list (March 22, 1996-entire season). ... On New York disabled list (March 24-May 3, 1997); included rehabilitation assignment to Norfolk (April 4-May 3). ... On Norfolk disabled list (June 30-July 30, 1997). ... Traded by Mets to Milwaukee Brewers for 3B Mike Kinkade (July 31, 1998). ... On Milwaukee disabled list (April 19-July 3, 1999); included rehabilitation assignment to Louisville (June 1-30). ... Traded by Brewers to Mets for IF Luis Lopez (January 21, 2000). ... On Norfolk disabled list (April 6-14, 2000). ... Traded by Mets to Arizona Diamondbacks for IF/OF Lenny Harris (June 2, 2000). ... On Tucson disabled list (June 22-July 17, 2000). ... Granted free agency (October 14, 2000). ... Signed by Tampa Bay Devil Rays organization (November 2, 2000). ... Released by Devil Rays (March 23, 2001). ... Signed by Boston Red Sox organization (April 18, 2001). ... Claimed on waivers by Chicago White Sox (August 23, 2001). ... Granted free agency (October 16, 2001). ... Signed by Texas Rangers organization (December 27, 2001).

STATISTICAL NOTES: Tied for Eastern League lead with five balks in 1994.

MISCELLANEOUS: Appeared in one game as pinch runner with Mets (1998).

Year	League	W	L	Pct.	ERA	G	GS	CG	ShO	Sv.	IP	H	R	ER	BB	SO
1992—	Pittsfield (NY-Penn)............	6	3	.667	2.84	14	14	0	0	0	95	88	40	30	56	83
1993—	Capital City (S.Atl.)............	2	3	.400	2.08	6	6	1	0	0	43 1/3	34	17	10	12	29
	— St. Lucie (FSL)	7	3	.700	2.24	13	13	3	1	0	96 1/3	63	27	24	39	102
1994—	Binghamton (East.)	14	9	.609	3.22	28	28	5	1	0	*201	179	90	72	89	171
1995—	Norfolk (I.L.)..................	6	4	.600	3.14	13	13	•4	2	0	91 2/3	84	36	32	33	63
	— New York (N.L.)..................	5	7	.417	3.98	17	17	2	0	0	126 2/3	122	58	56	45	81
1996—	New York (N.L.)..................							Did not play.								
1997—	Norfolk (I.L.)	0	5	.000	7.81	8	5	0	0	0	27 2/3	23	29	24	38	18
	— St. Lucie (FSL)	1	4	.200	5.89	12	7	0	0	0	36 2/3	29	27	24	35	35
	— Binghamton (East.)	0	0	...	1.42	10	0	0	0	0	12 2/3	11	3	2	7	12
	— Gulf Coast Mets (GCL)	0	0	...	1.80	2	2	0	0	0	5	3	1	1	1	4

P

Year League	W	L	Pct.	ERA	G	GS	CG	ShO	Sv.	IP	H	R	ER	BB	SO
1998—Norfolk (I.L.)	7	5	.583	3.96	14	14	1	0	0	86⅓	91	50	38	41	58
—New York (N.L.).................	0	0	...	6.91	15	1	0	0	0	14⅓	23	11	11	5	13
—Milwaukee (N.L.)■...........	3	4	.429	4.66	11	10	0	0	0	58	63	30	30	26	38
1999—Milwaukee (N.L.)	5	6	.455	5.98	19	16	0	0	0	87⅓	100	65	58	36	42
—Louisville (I.L.)	0	2	.000	4.28	6	6	0	0	0	27⅓	22	14	13	19	21
2000—Norfolk (I.L.)■	2	3	.400	6.55	7	5	0	0	0	33	41	28	24	15	25
—New York (N.L.)...............	0	2	.000	12.15	2	2	0	0	0	6⅔	12	9	9	6	7
—Tucson (PCL)■..................	3	8	.273	3.95	13	13	0	0	0	70⅔	73	39	31	37	51
—Ariz. Diamondbacks (Ariz.).	0	0	...	4.50	3	3	0	0	0	6	8	3	3	0	4
2001—Pawtucket (I.L.)■............	1	1	.500	2.87	24	0	0	0	10	31⅓	27	12	10	10	23
—Boston (A.L.)....................	0	0	...	5.32	23	0	0	0	0	22	25	15	13	14	16
—Chicago (A.L.)■...............	0	0	...	7.88	14	0	0	0	0	8	11	8	7	7	4
A.L. totals (1 year)	0	0	...	6.00	37	0	0	0	0	30	36	23	20	21	20
N.L. totals (4 years)	13	19	.406	5.04	64	46	2	0	0	293	320	173	164	118	181
Major League totals (5 years).......	13	19	.406	5.13	101	46	2	0	0	323	356	196	184	139	201

PUNTO, NICK   SS   PHILLIES

PERSONAL: Born November 8, 1977, in San Diego. ... 5-9/170. ... Bats right, throws right. ... Full name: Nicholas Paul Punto.
HIGH SCHOOL: Trabuco Hills (Mission Vieh Vijo, Calif.).
JUNIOR COLLEGE: Saddleback.
TRANSACTIONS/CAREER NOTES: Selected by Minnesota Twins organization in 33rd round of free-agent draft (June 3, 1997); did not sign. ... Selected by Philadelphia Phillies organization in 21st round of free-agent draft (June 2, 1998). ... On Scranton/Wilkes-Barre disabled list (June 8-16, 2001).
STATISTICAL NOTES: Led New York-Pennsylvania League shortstops with 45 double plays in 1998.

									BATTING					FIELDING		
Year Team (League)	Pos.	G	AB	R	H	2B	3B	HR	RBI	Avg.	BB	SO	SB	PO	A	E	Avg.
1998—Batavia (NY-Penn)	SS-2B	72	279	51	69	9	4	1	20	.247	42	48	19	107	222	27	.924
1999—Clearwater (FSL)	SS	106	400	65	122	18	6	1	48	.305	67	53	16	168	380	24	.958
2000—Reading (East.)..........	SS	121	456	77	116	15	4	5	47	.254	69	71	33	186	331	20	.963
2001—Scranton/W.B. (I.L.) ...	SS	123	463	57	106	19	5	1	39	.229	68	114	33	158	*398	21	.964
—Philadelphia (N.L.)......	SS	4	5	0	2	0	0	0	0	.400	0	0	0	1	2	0	1.000
Major League totals (1 year)		4	5	0	2	0	0	0	0	.400	0	0	0	1	2	0	1.000

PUTZ, J.J.   P   MARINERS

PERSONAL: Born February 22, 1977, in Trenton, Mich. ... 6-5/220. ... Throws right, bats right. ... Full name: Joseph Jason Putz.
HIGH SCHOOL: Trenton (Mich.).
COLLEGE: Michigan.
TRANSACTIONS/CAREER NOTES: Selected by Seattle Mariners organization in sixth round of free-agent draft (June 2, 1999).
STATISTICAL NOTES: Pitched 6-1 no-hit victory for Wisconsin against Kane County (April 29, 2000, first game). ... Led Texas League with 10 sacrifice hits allowed in 2001.

Year League	W	L	Pct.	ERA	G	GS	CG	ShO	Sv.	IP	H	R	ER	BB	SO
1999—Everett (N'West)	0	0	...	4.84	10	0	0	0	2	22⅓	23	13	12	11	17
2000—Wisconsin (Midw.)	12	6	.667	3.15	26	25	3	2	0	142⅔	130	71	50	63	105
2001—San Antonio (Texas)	7	9	.438	3.83	27	26	0	0	0	148	145	80	63	59	135

QUANTRILL, PAUL   P   DODGERS

PERSONAL: Born November 3, 1968, in London, Ont. ... 6-1/195. ... Throws right, bats left. ... Full name: Paul John Quantrill. ... Name pronounced KWON-trill.
HIGH SCHOOL: Okemos (Mich.).
COLLEGE: Wisconsin.
TRANSACTIONS/CAREER NOTES: Selected by Los Angeles Dodgers organization in 26th round of free-agent draft (June 2, 1986); did not sign. ... Selected by Boston Red Sox organization in sixth round of free-agent draft (June 5, 1989). ... Traded by Red Sox with OF Billy Hatcher to Philadelphia Phillies for OF Wes Chamberlain and P Mike Sullivan (May 31, 1994). ... Traded by Phillies to Toronto Blue Jays for 3B Howard Battle and P Ricardo Jordan (December 6, 1995). ... On Toronto disabled list (March 27-June 15, 1999); included rehabilitation assignments to Dunedin (June 4-10) and Syracuse (June 11-13). ... Traded by Blue Jays with 2B/SS Cesar Izturis to Los Angeles Dodgers for P Luke Prokopec and P Chad Ricketts (December 13, 2001).

Year League	W	L	Pct.	ERA	G	GS	CG	ShO	Sv.	IP	H	R	ER	BB	SO
1989—Gulf Coast Red Sox (GCL)..	0	0	...	0.00	2	0	0	0	2	5	2	0	0	0	5
—Elmira (NY-Penn)	5	4	.556	3.43	20	7	•5	0	2	76	90	37	29	12	57
1990—Winter Haven (FSL)	2	5	.286	4.14	7	7	1	0	0	45⅔	46	24	21	6	14
—New Britain (East.)	7	11	.389	3.53	22	22	1	1	0	132⅔	148	65	52	23	53
1991—New Britain (East.)	2	1	.667	2.06	5	5	1	0	0	35	32	14	8	8	18
—Pawtucket (I.L.)	10	7	.588	4.45	25	23	•6	2	0	155⅔	169	81	77	30	75
1992—Pawtucket (I.L.)	6	8	.429	4.46	19	18	4	1	0	119	143	63	59	20	56
—Boston (A.L.).....................	2	3	.400	2.19	27	0	0	0	1	49⅓	55	18	12	15	24
1993—Boston (A.L.)....................	6	12	.333	3.91	49	14	1	1	1	138	151	73	60	44	66
1994—Boston (A.L.)....................	1	1	.500	3.52	17	0	0	0	1	23	25	10	9	5	15
—Philadelphia (N.L.)■	2	2	.500	6.00	18	1	0	0	1	30	39	21	20	10	13
—Scranton/W.B. (I.L.) ...	3	3	.500	3.47	8	8	1	1	0	57	55	25	22	6	36
1995—Philadelphia (N.L.)..............	11	12	.478	4.67	33	29	0	0	0	179⅓	212	102	93	44	103
1996—Toronto (A.L.)■...............	5	14	.263	5.43	38	20	0	0	0	134⅓	172	90	81	51	86
1997—Toronto (A.L.)....................	6	7	.462	1.94	77	0	0	0	5	88	103	25	19	17	56
1998—Toronto (A.L.)....................	3	4	.429	2.59	82	0	0	0	7	80	88	26	23	22	59

Year League	W	L	Pct.	ERA	G	GS	CG	ShO	Sv.	IP	H	R	ER	BB	SO
1999—Dunedin (FSL)..................	0	1	.000	4.50	5	4	0	0	0	6	5	3	3	1	2
— Syracuse (I.L.)..................	0	0	...	0.00	2	0	0	0	0	2	1	0	0	0	1
—Toronto (A.L.)..................	3	2	.600	3.33	41	0	0	0	0	48²/₃	53	19	18	17	28
2000—Toronto (A.L.)..................	2	5	.286	4.52	68	0	0	0	1	83²/₃	100	45	42	25	47
2001—Toronto (A.L.)..................	11	2	.846	3.04	*80	0	0	0	2	83	86	29	28	12	58
A.L. totals (9 years)	39	50	.438	3.61	479	34	1	1	17	728	833	335	292	208	439
N.L. totals (2 years)	13	14	.481	4.86	51	30	0	0	1	209¹/₃	251	123	113	54	116
Major League totals (10 years).....	52	64	.448	3.89	530	64	1	1	18	937¹/₃	1084	458	405	262	555

ALL-STAR GAME RECORD

Year League	W	L	Pct.	ERA	GS	CG	ShO	Sv.	IP	H	R	ER	BB	SO
2001— American..........................	0	0	...	27.00	0	0	0	0	¹/₃	2	1	1	0	0

Q R

QUEVEDO, RUBEN   P   BREWERS

PERSONAL: Born January 5, 1979, in Valencia, Venezuela. ... 6-1/230. ... Throws right, bats right. ... Full name: Ruben Eduardo Quevedo Yetez. ... Name pronounced keh-VAY-doh.

HIGH SCHOOL: Don Bosco (Valencia, Venezuela).

TRANSACTIONS/CAREER NOTES: Signed as non-drafted free agent by Atlanta Braves organization (September 6, 1995). ... Traded by Braves with P Micah Bowie and a player to be named later to Chicago Cubs for P Terry Mulholland and SS Jose Hernandez (July 31, 1999); Cubs acquired P Joey Nation to complete deal (August 24, 1999). ... Traded by Cubs with OF Peter Zoccolillo to Milwaukee Brewers for P David Weathers and P Roberto Miniel (July 30, 2001).

Year League	W	L	Pct.	ERA	G	GS	CG	ShO	Sv.	IP	H	R	ER	BB	SO
1996— Gulf Coast Braves (GCL)	2	6	.250	2.29	10	10	0	0	0	55	50	19	14	9	49
1997—Danville (Appl.)..................	1	5	.167	3.56	13	11	0	0	0	68¹/₃	46	37	27	27	78
1998—Macon (S.Atl.)..................	11	3	.786	3.13	25	15	1	0	0	112	114	50	39	31	117
—Danville (Caro.)..................	0	2	.000	3.58	6	6	0	0	0	32²/₃	28	22	13	13	35
1999—Richmond (I.L.)..................	6	5	.545	5.37	21	21	0	0	0	105²/₃	112	65	63	34	98
— Iowa (PCL)■..........................	3	1	.750	3.45	7	7	1	1	0	44¹/₃	34	18	17	21	50
2000— Iowa (PCL)..........................	7	2	.778	4.22	13	13	0	0	0	74²/₃	68	37	35	31	77
—Chicago (N.L.)..................	3	10	.231	7.47	21	15	1	0	0	88	96	81	73	54	65
2001— Iowa (PCL)..........................	9	5	.643	2.99	22	22	1	1	0	141²/₃	124	54	47	48	150
—Milwaukee (N.L.)■.............	4	5	.444	4.61	10	10	0	0	0	56²/₃	56	30	29	30	60
Major League totals (2 years).......	7	15	.318	6.35	31	25	1	0	0	144²/₃	152	111	102	84	125

QUINN, MARK   OF   ROYALS

PERSONAL: Born May 21, 1974, in La Miranda, Calif. ... 6-1/195. ... Bats right, throws right. ... Full name: Mark David Quinn.

HIGH SCHOOL: Clements (Sugar Land, Texas).

COLLEGE: Rice.

TRANSACTIONS/CAREER NOTES: Selected by Kansas City Royals organization in 11th round of free-agent draft (June 1, 1995). ... On Kansas City disabled list (June 9-July 6, 2001); included rehabilitation assignment to Omaha (June 25-July 6).

RECORDS: Shares major league record for most home runs, first game in major leagues—2 (September 14, 1999, second game).

HONORS: Named A.L. Rookie Player of the Year by THE SPORTING NEWS (2000).

STATISTICAL NOTES: Career major league grand slams: 1.

Year Team (League)	Pos.	G	AB	R	H	2B	3B	HR	RBI	Avg.	BB	SO	SB	PO	A	E	Avg.
														BATTING		FIELDING	
1995—Spokane (N'West)	3B	44	162	28	46	12	2	6	36	.284	15	28	0	8	33	8	.837
1996—Lansing (Midw.)	OF	113	437	63	132	23	3	9	71	.302	43	54	14	143	15	7	.958
1997—Wilmington (Caro.)......	OF	87	299	51	92	22	3	16	71	.308	42	47	3	75	7	6	.932
— Wichita (Texas)	OF	26	96	26	36	13	0	2	19	.375	15	19	1	35	0	1	.972
1998— Wichita (Texas)	OF	100	372	82	130	26	6	16	84	*.349	43	54	4	157	11	8	.955
1999—Omaha (PCL)..............	OF-DH	107	428	67	154	27	0	25	84	*.360	28	69	7	216	13	4	.983
—Kansas City (A.L.)	OF-DH	17	60	11	20	4	1	6	18	.333	4	11	1	25	2	1	.964
2000—Kansas City (A.L.)	OF-DH	135	500	76	147	33	4	20	78	.294	35	91	6	158	9	2	.988
—Omaha (PCL)..............	OF	13	61	8	23	5	0	3	13	.377	0	8	0	23	1	0	1.000
2001—Kansas City (A.L.)	OF-DH	118	453	57	122	31	2	17	60	.269	12	69	9	197	8	5	.976
—Omaha (PCL)..............	OF	11	43	4	8	1	0	2	3	.186	0	9	0	12	1	0	1.000
Major League totals (3 years)		270	1013	144	289	68	5	43	156	.285	51	171	15	380	19	8	.980

RADINSKY, SCOTT   P   INDIANS

PERSONAL: Born March 3, 1968, in Glendale, Calif. ... 6-3/215. ... Throws left, bats left. ... Full name: Scott David Radinsky.

HIGH SCHOOL: Simi Valley (Calif.).

TRANSACTIONS/CAREER NOTES: Selected by Chicago White Sox organization in third round of free-agent draft (June 2, 1986). ... On disabled list (March 2, 1994-entire season). ... On Chicago disabled list (July 17-August 15, 1995); included rehabilitation assignment to South Bend (August 1-15). ... Granted free agency (December 21, 1995). ... Signed by Los Angeles Dodgers organization (January 16, 1996). ... On Los Angeles disabled list (March 28-April 12, 1996); included rehabilitation assignment to San Bernardino (April 4-12). ... Granted free agency (October 23, 1998). ... Signed by St. Louis Cardinals (November 23, 1998). ... On disabled list (July 27, 1999-remainder of season; and April 2-May 27 and June 2, 2000-remainder of season). ... Granted free agency (October 31, 2000). ... Signed by Cleveland Indians organization (January 20, 2001). ... On Buffalo disabled list (April 5-June 4, 2001).

STATISTICAL NOTES: Led Eastern League with six balks in 2001.

Year	League	W	L	Pct.	ERA	G	GS	CG	ShO	Sv.	IP	H	R	ER	BB	SO
1986—	GC White Sox (GCL)	1	0	1.000	3.38	7	7	0	0	0	26 2/3	24	20	10	17	18
1987—	Peninsula (Caro.)	1	7	.125	5.77	12	8	0	0	0	39	43	30	25	32	37
—	GC White Sox (GCL)	3	3	.500	2.31	11	10	0	0	0	58 1/3	43	23	15	39	41
1988—	GC White Sox (GCL)	0	0	...	5.40	5	0	0	0	0	3 1/3	2	2	2	4	7
1989—	South Bend (Midw.)	7	5	.583	1.75	53	0	0	0	31	61 2/3	39	21	12	19	83
1990—	Chicago (A.L.)	6	1	.857	4.82	62	0	0	0	4	52 1/3	47	29	28	36	46
1991—	Chicago (A.L.)	5	5	.500	2.02	67	0	0	0	8	71 1/3	53	18	16	23	49
1992—	Chicago (A.L.)	3	7	.300	2.73	68	0	0	0	15	59 1/3	54	21	18	34	48
1993—	Chicago (A.L.)	8	2	.800	4.28	73	0	0	0	4	54 2/3	61	33	26	19	44
1994—	Chicago (A.L.)							Did not play.								
1995—	Chicago (A.L.)	2	1	.667	5.45	46	0	0	0	1	38	46	23	23	17	14
—	South Bend (Midw.)	0	0	...	0.00	6	0	0	0	2	9 2/3	5	0	0	0	11
1996—	San Bernardino (Calif.)■...	0	0	...	2.08	3	0	0	0	0	4 1/3	2	1	1	2	4
—	Los Angeles (N.L.)	5	1	.833	2.41	56	0	0	0	1	52 1/3	52	19	14	17	48
1997—	Los Angeles (N.L.)	5	1	.833	2.89	75	0	0	0	3	62 1/3	54	22	20	21	44
1998—	Los Angeles (N.L.)	6	6	.500	2.63	62	0	0	0	13	61 2/3	63	21	18	20	45
1999—	St. Louis (N.L.)■...............	2	1	.667	4.88	43	0	0	0	3	27 2/3	27	16	15	18	17
2000—	St. Louis (N.L.)	0	0	...	...	1	0	0	0	0	0	0	0	0	1	0
2001—	Akron (East.)■..................	2	2	.500	3.47	23	0	0	0	3	23 1/3	30	10	9	3	19
—	Cleveland (A.L.)	0	0	...	27.00	2	0	0	0	0	2	4	6	6	3	3
—	Buffalo (I.L.)	0	1	.000	4.11	16	0	0	0	1	15 1/3	13	7	7	1	7
A.L. totals (6 years)		24	16	.600	3.79	318	0	0	0	32	277 2/3	265	130	117	132	204
N.L. totals (5 years)		18	9	.667	2.96	237	0	0	0	20	204	196	78	67	77	154
Major League totals (11 years)....		42	25	.627	3.44	555	0	0	0	52	481 2/3	461	208	184	209	358

DIVISION SERIES RECORD

Year	League	W	L	Pct.	ERA	G	GS	CG	ShO	Sv.	IP	H	R	ER	BB	SO
1996—	Los Angeles (N.L.)	0	0	...	0.00	2	0	0	0	0	1 1/3	0	0	0	1	2

CHAMPIONSHIP SERIES RECORD

Year	League	W	L	Pct.	ERA	G	GS	CG	ShO	Sv.	IP	H	R	ER	BB	SO
1993—	Chicago (A.L.)	0	0	...	10.80	4	0	0	0	0	1 2/3	3	4	2	1	1

RADKE, BRAD   P   TWINS

PERSONAL: Born October 27, 1972, in Eau Claire, Wis. ... 6-2/188. ... Throws right, bats right. ... Full name: Brad William Radke.
HIGH SCHOOL: Jesuit (Tampa).
TRANSACTIONS/CAREER NOTES: Selected by Minnesota Twins organization in eighth round of free-agent draft (June 3, 1991). ... On disabled list (August 4-21, 2001).
STATISTICAL NOTES: Led A.L. in home runs allowed with 32 in 1995. ... Tied for A.L. lead in home runs allowed with 40 in 1996.

Year	League	W	L	Pct.	ERA	G	GS	CG	ShO	Sv.	IP	H	R	ER	BB	SO
1991—	Gulf Coast Twins (GCL)......	3	4	.429	3.08	10	9	1	0	1	49 2/3	41	21	17	14	46
1992—	Kenosha (Midw.)	10	10	.500	2.93	26	25	4	1	0	165 2/3	149	70	54	47	127
1993—	Fort Myers (FSL)	3	5	.375	3.82	14	14	0	0	0	92	85	42	39	21	69
—	Nashville (Sou.).................	2	6	.250	4.62	13	13	1	0	0	76	81	42	39	16	76
1994—	Nashville (Sou.)	12	9	.571	2.66	29	*28	5	1	0	186 1/3	167	66	55	34	123
1995—	Minnesota (A.L.)	11	14	.440	5.32	29	28	2	1	0	181	195	112	107	47	75
1996—	Minnesota (A.L.)	11	16	.407	4.46	35	35	3	0	0	232	231	125	115	57	148
1997—	Minnesota (A.L.)	20	10	.667	3.87	35	•35	4	1	0	239 2/3	238	114	103	48	174
1998—	Minnesota (A.L.)	12	14	.462	4.30	32	32	5	1	0	213 2/3	238	109	102	43	146
1999—	Minnesota (A.L.)	12	14	.462	3.75	33	33	4	0	0	218 2/3	239	97	91	44	121
2000—	Minnesota (A.L.)	12	*16	.429	4.45	34	34	4	1	0	226 2/3	261	119	112	51	141
2001—	Minnesota (A.L.)	15	11	.577	3.94	33	33	6	2	0	226	235	105	99	26	137
Major League totals (7 years).......		93	95	.495	4.27	231	230	28	6	0	1537 2/3	1637	781	729	316	942

ALL-STAR GAME RECORD

Year	League	W	L	Pct.	ERA	GS	CG	ShO	Sv.	IP	H	R	ER	BB	SO
1998—	American	0	0	...	9.00	0	0	0	0	1	2	1	1	1	1

RAINES, TIM   OF

PERSONAL: Born September 16, 1959, in Sanford, Fla. ... 5-8/186. ... Bats both, throws right. ... Full name: Timothy Raines. ... Father of Tim Raines Jr., outfielder, Baltimore Orioles; and brother of Ned Raines, minor league outfielder (1978-80).
HIGH SCHOOL: Seminole (Sanford, Fla.).
TRANSACTIONS/CAREER NOTES: Selected by Montreal Expos organization in fifth round of free-agent draft (June 7, 1977). ... On disabled list (May 23-June 5, 1978). ... Granted free agency (November 12, 1986). ... Re-signed by Expos (May 2, 1987). ... On disabled list (June 24-July 9, 1988 and June 25-July 10, 1990). ... Traded by Expos with P Jeff Carter and a player to be named later to Chicago White Sox for OF Ivan Calderon and P Barry Jones (December 23, 1990); White Sox acquired P Mario Brito to complete deal (February 15, 1991). ... On Chicago disabled list (April 10-May 22, 1993); included rehabilitation assignment to Nashville (May 19-22). ... Granted free agency (November 1, 1993). ... Re-signed by White Sox (December 22, 1993). ... Traded by White Sox to New York Yankees for a player to be named later (December 28, 1995); White Sox acquired 3B Blaise Kozeniewski to complete deal (February 6, 1996). ... On New York disabled list (March 21-April 16 and May 22-August 11, 1996); included rehabilitation assignments to Tampa (April 12-13 and July 25-August 2), Columbus (April 13-16 and June 23-24), Gulf Coast Yankees (June 22-23) and Norwich (August 2-10). ... On New York disabled list (March 27-April 11 and July 2-August 12, 1997); included rehabilitation assignment to Tampa (April 7-10, July 24-27, and August 5-7), Gulf Coast Yankees (July 24), Norwich (July 26-27) and Columbus (August 8-11). ... Granted free agency (October 29, 1997). ... Re-signed by Yankees (December 19, 1997). ... Granted free agency (October 26, 1998). ... Signed by Oakland Athletics (January 25, 1999). ... On disabled list (July 19, 1999-remainder of season). ... Granted free agency (November 5, 1999). ... Signed by Yankees organization (February 1, 2000). ... Announced retirement (March 23, 2000). ... Signed by Somerset, Atlantic League (July 8, 2000). ... Signed by Expos organization (December 21, 2000). ... On Montreal disabled list (May 4-August 22, 2001); included rehabilitation assignments to Jupiter (August 9-20) and Ottawa (August 21-22). ... Traded by Expos to Baltimore Orioles for a player to be named later (October 3, 2001). ... Granted free agency (November 6, 2001).

RECORDS: Holds major league single-season record for most intentional bases on balls received by switch hitter—26 (1987). ... Holds A.L. career record for most consecutive stolen bases without being caught stealing—40 (July 23, 1993 through August 4, 1995). ... Holds N.L. career record for highest stolen-base percentage (300 or more attempts)—.857. ... Shares A.L. single-game record for most consecutive times reached base safely—7 (April 20, 1994, 12 innings).

HONORS: Named Minor League Player of the Year by THE SPORTING NEWS (1980). ... Named N.L. Rookie Player of the Year by THE SPORTING NEWS (1981). ... Named outfielder on THE SPORTING NEWS N.L. All-Star team (1983 and 1986). ... Won THE SPORTING NEWS Gold Shoe Award (1984). ... Named outfielder on THE SPORTING NEWS N.L. Silver Slugger team (1986).

STATISTICAL NOTES: Led Southern League second basemen with 777 total chances in 1979. ... Led N.L. outfielders with 21 assists in 1983. ... Led N.L. with .413 on-base percentage in 1986. ... Hit for the cycle (August 16, 1987). ... Switch-hit home runs in one game (July 16, 1988 and August 31, 1993). ... Hit three home runs in one game (April 18, 1994). ... Career major league grand slams: 6.

MISCELLANEOUS: Holds Montreal Expos all-time records for most runs (947), triples (82) and stolen bases (634).

Year	Team (League)	Pos.	G	AB	R	H	2B	3B	HR	RBI	Avg.	BB	SO	SB	PO	A	E	Avg.
1977—	GC Expos (GCL)	2B-3B-OF	49	161	28	45	6	2	0	21	.280	27	16	29	79	72	13	.921
1978—	W.P. Beach (FSL)	2B-SS	100	359	67	103	10	0	0	23	.287	64	44	57	219	273	24	.953
1979—	Memphis (Sou.)	2B	•145	552	*104	160	25	10	5	50	.290	90	51	59	*341	*413	*23	.970
	— Montreal (N.L.)	PR	6	0	3	0	0	0	0	0	...	0	0	2	...	...	...	...
1980—	Denver (A.A.)	2B	108	429	105	152	23	•11	6	64	*.354	61	42	*77	226	338	16	.972
	— Montreal (N.L.)	2B-OF	15	20	5	1	0	0	0	0	.050	6	3	5	15	16	0	1.000
1981—	Montreal (N.L.)	OF-2B	88	313	61	95	13	7	5	37	.304	45	31	*71	162	8	4	.977
1982—	Montreal (N.L.)	OF-2B	156	647	90	179	32	8	4	43	.277	75	83	*78	293	126	8	.981
1983—	Montreal (N.L.)	OF-2B	156	615	*133	183	32	8	11	71	.298	97	70	*90	314	†23	4	.988
1984—	Montreal (N.L.)	OF-2B	160	622	106	192	•38	9	8	60	.309	87	69	*75	420	8	6	.986
1985—	Montreal (N.L.)	OF	150	575	115	184	30	13	11	41	.320	81	60	70	284	8	2	.993
1986—	Montreal (N.L.)	OF	151	580	91	194	35	10	9	62	*.334	78	60	70	270	13	6	.979
1987—	Montreal (N.L.)	OF	139	530	*123	175	34	8	18	68	.330	90	52	50	297	9	4	.987
1988—	Montreal (N.L.)	OF	109	429	66	116	19	7	12	48	.270	53	44	33	235	5	3	.988
1989—	Montreal (N.L.)	OF	145	517	76	148	29	6	9	60	.286	93	48	41	253	7	1	.996
1990—	Montreal (N.L.)	OF	130	457	65	131	11	5	9	62	.287	70	43	49	239	3	6	.976
1991—	Chicago (A.L.)■	OF-DH	155	609	102	163	20	6	5	50	.268	83	68	51	273	12	3	.990
1992—	Chicago (A.L.)	OF-DH	144	551	102	162	22	9	7	54	.294	81	48	45	312	12	2	.994
1993—	Chicago (A.L.)	OF	115	415	75	127	16	4	16	54	.306	64	35	21	200	5	0	*1.000
	— Nashville (A.A.)	OF	3	11	3	5	1	0	0	2	.455	2	0	2	3	0	0	1.000
1994—	Chicago (A.L.)	OF	101	384	80	102	15	5	10	52	.266	61	43	13	204	3	4	.981
1995—	Chicago (A.L.)	OF-DH	133	502	81	143	25	4	12	67	.285	70	52	13	193	7	4	.980
1996—	Tampa (FSL)■	OF-DH	9	36	9	13	2	0	2	11	.361	8	3	0	10	2	0	1.000
	— Columbus (I.L.)	DH-OF	4	12	3	3	1	0	0	0	.250	1	3	1	2	0	0	1.000
	— New York (A.L.)	OF-DH	59	201	45	57	10	0	9	33	.284	34	29	10	79	3	1	.988
	— GC Yankees (GCL)	DH	1	5	2	3	2	0	0	3	.600	1	0	0	...	...	...	...
	— Norwich (East.)	OF-DH	8	27	8	5	1	0	1	1	.185	9	2	2	4	0	0	1.000
1997—	Tampa (FSL)	OF-DH	11	35	8	12	0	0	2	5	.343	11	1	1	13	1	0	1.000
	— New York (A.L.)	OF-DH	74	271	56	87	20	2	4	38	.321	41	34	8	79	1	1	.988
	— GC Yankees (GCL)	OF	1	4	0	1	0	0	0	2	.250	1	1	0	2	0	0	1.000
	— Norwich (East.)	OF	2	7	0	2	1	0	0	0	.286	1	0	2	2	0	0	1.000
	— Columbus (I.L.)	OF	4	13	1	2	0	0	0	0	.154	3	2	0	4	0	0	1.000
1998—	New York (A.L.)	DH-OF	109	321	53	93	13	1	5	47	.290	55	49	8	61	3	1	.985
1999—	Oakland (A.L.)■	OF-DH	58	135	20	29	5	0	4	17	.215	26	17	4	61	0	0	1.000
2000—	Somerset (Atl.)■		7	26	5	9	3	0	0	2	.346	5	2	0	...	...	...	...
2001—	Montreal (N.L.)■	OF	47	78	13	24	8	1	0	4	.308	18	6	1	23	0	0	1.000
	— Jupiter (FSL)	OF	8	23	7	8	1	1	1	5	.348	5	4	1	2	0	0	1.000
	— Ottawa (I.L.)	DH	2	7	1	1	1	0	0	0	.143	1	1	0	...	...	...	...
	— Baltimore (A.L.)	OF-DH	4	11	1	3	0	0	1	5	.273	0	3	0	7	0	0	1.000
American League totals (10 years)			952	3400	615	966	146	31	73	417	.284	515	378	173	1469	46	16	.990
National League totals (13 years)			1452	5383	947	1622	281	82	96	556	.301	793	569	635	2805	226	44	.986
Major League totals (22 years)			2404	8783	1562	2588	427	113	169	973	.295	1308	947	808	4274	272	60	.987

DIVISION SERIES RECORD

Year	Team (League)	Pos.	G	AB	R	H	2B	3B	HR	RBI	Avg.	BB	SO	SB	PO	A	E	Avg.
1996—	New York (A.L.)	OF	4	16	3	4	0	0	0	0	.250	3	1	0	5	0	0	1.000
1997—	New York (A.L.)	DH-OF	5	19	4	4	0	0	1	3	.211	3	1	2	7	0	0	1.000
1998—	New York (A.L.)	PH-DH	2	4	1	1	1	0	0	0	.250	1	1	0	...	...	...	...
Division series totals (3 years)			11	39	8	9	1	0	1	3	.231	7	3	2	12	0	0	1.000

CHAMPIONSHIP SERIES RECORD

RECORDS: Holds single-series record for most singles—10 (1993). ... Shares A.L. single-series record for most hits—12 (1993).

Year	Team (League)	Pos.	G	AB	R	H	2B	3B	HR	RBI	Avg.	BB	SO	SB	PO	A	E	Avg.
1981—	Montreal (N.L.)	OF	5	21	1	5	2	0	0	1	.238	0	3	0	9	0	0	1.000
1993—	Chicago (A.L.)	OF	6	27	5	12	2	0	0	1	.444	2	2	1	12	2	0	1.000
1996—	New York (A.L.)	OF	5	15	2	4	1	0	0	0	.267	1	1	0	5	0	0	1.000
1998—	New York (A.L.)	DH-OF	3	10	0	1	0	0	0	1	.100	2	5	0	1	0	0	1.000
Championship series totals (4 years)			19	73	8	22	5	0	0	3	.301	5	11	1	27	2	0	1.000

WORLD SERIES RECORD

NOTES: Member of World Series championship team (1996 and 1998).

Year	Team (League)	Pos.	G	AB	R	H	2B	3B	HR	RBI	Avg.	BB	SO	SB	PO	A	E	Avg.
1996—	New York (A.L.)	OF	4	14	2	3	0	0	0	0	.214	2	1	0	5	0	1	.833
1998—	New York (A.L.)								Did not play.									

NOTES: Named Most Valuable Player (1987).

Year	League	Pos.	AB	R	H	2B	3B	HR	RBI	Avg.	BB	SO	SB	PO	A	E	Avg.
1981—National		PR-OF	0	0	0	0	0	0	0	...	0	0	0	1	0	0	1.000
1982—National		OF	1	0	0	0	0	0	0	.000	1	1	1	0	0	0	...
1983—National		OF	3	0	0	0	0	0	0	.000	0	1	1	2	0	0	1.000
1984—National		OF	1	0	0	0	0	0	0	.000	0	1	0	4	0	0	1.000
1985—National		PH-OF	0	1	0	0	0	0	0	...	1	0	0	0	0	0	...
1986—National		PH-OF	2	0	0	0	0	0	0	.000	0	1	0	1	0	0	1.000
1987—National		OF	3	0	3	0	1	0	2	1.000	0	0	1	1	0	0	1.000
All-Star Game totals (7 years)			10	1	3	0	1	0	2	.300	2	4	3	9	0	0	1.000

RAINES JR., TIM — OF — ORIOLES — R

PERSONAL: Born August 31, 1979, in Memphis, Tenn. ... 5-10/185. ... Bats right, throws right. ... Full name: Timothy Raines Jr. ... Son of Tim Raines, outfielder with five major league teams (1979-99 and 2001).
HIGH SCHOOL: Seminole (Sanford, Fla.).
TRANSACTIONS/CAREER NOTES: Selected by Baltimore Orioles organization in sixth round of free-agent draft (June 2, 1998).
STATISTICAL NOTES: Led Gulf Coast League outfielders with 134 total chances in 1998.

Year	Team (League)	Pos.	G	AB	R	H	2B	3B	HR	RBI	Avg.	BB	SO	SB	PO	A	E	Avg.
1998—GC Orioles (GCL)		OF	56	197	40	48	7	4	1	13	.244	30	53	37	*125	6	3	.978
1999—Delmarva (S.Atl.)		OF	117	415	80	103	24	8	2	49	.248	71	130	49	237	8	10	.961
2000—Frederick (Caro.)		OF	127	457	89	108	21	3	2	36	.236	67	106	81	302	8	9	.972
2001—Frederick (Caro.)		OF	23	84	15	21	3	1	3	13	.250	13	23	14	40	1	1	.976
—Bowie (East.)		OF	65	254	46	74	14	1	4	30	.291	34	60	29	159	6	4	.976
—Rochester (I.L.)		OF	40	133	19	34	5	1	2	12	.256	11	30	11	70	1	1	.986
—Baltimore (A.L.)		OF	7	23	6	4	2	0	0	0	.174	3	8	3	12	0	0	1.000
Major League totals (1 year)			7	23	6	4	2	0	0	0	.174	3	8	3	12	0	0	1.000

RAMIREZ, ARAMIS — 3B — PIRATES

PERSONAL: Born June 25, 1978, in Santo Domingo, Dominican Republic. ... 6-1/219. ... Bats right, throws right. ... Full name: Aramis Nin Ramirez.
TRANSACTIONS/CAREER NOTES: Signed as non-drafted free agent by Pittsburgh Pirates organization (November 7, 1994). ... On suspended list (July 24-29, 1998). ... On Pittsburgh disabled list (August 10-September 4, 1998); included rehabilitation assignment to Nashville (August 27). ... On Pittsburgh disabled list (August 29, 2000-remainder of season).
HONORS: Named Carolina League Most Valuable Player (1997).
STATISTICAL NOTES: Led Carolina League third basemen with 379 total chances in 1997. ... Hit three home runs in one game (April 8, 2001). ... Career major league grand slams: 3.

Year	Team (League)	Pos.	G	AB	R	H	2B	3B	HR	RBI	Avg.	BB	SO	SB	PO	A	E	Avg.
1995—Dom. Pirates (DSL)		3B	64	214	41	63	13	0	11	54	.294	42	26	2	65	82	19	.886
1996—Erie (NY-Penn)		3B	61	223	37	68	14	4	9	42	.305	31	41	0	39	107	17	.896
—Augusta (S.Atl.)		3B	6	20	3	4	1	0	1	2	.200	1	7	0	3	7	2	.833
1997—Lynchburg (Caro.)		3B-DH	137	482	85	134	24	2	29	*114	.278	80	103	5	75	*265	*39	.897
1998—Nashville (PCL)		3B-DH-SS	47	168	19	46	10	0	5	18	.274	24	28	0	33	77	8	.932
—Pittsburgh (N.L.)		3B	72	251	23	59	9	1	6	24	.235	18	72	0	29	114	9	.941
1999—Nashville (PCL)		3B-DH	131	460	92	151	35	1	21	74	.328	73	56	5	70	250	*42	.884
—Pittsburgh (N.L.)		3B	18	56	2	10	2	1	0	7	.179	6	9	0	11	29	3	.930
2000—Pittsburgh (N.L.)		3B	73	254	19	65	15	2	6	35	.256	10	36	0	26	128	14	.917
—Nashville (PCL)		3B	44	167	28	59	12	2	4	26	.353	11	26	2	34	85	9	.930
2001—Pittsburgh (N.L.)		3B	158	603	83	181	40	0	34	112	.300	40	100	5	92	335	25	.945
Major League totals (4 years)			321	1164	127	315	66	4	46	178	.271	74	217	5	158	606	51	.937

RAMIREZ, HORACIO — P — BRAVES

PERSONAL: Born November 24, 1979, in Carlson, Calif. ... 6-1/170. ... Throws left, bats left.
HIGH SCHOOL: Inglewood (Calif.).
TRANSACTIONS/CAREER NOTES: Selected by Atlanta Braves organization in fifth round of free-agent draft (June 3, 1997). ... On disabled list (May 7, 2001-remainder of season).

Year	League	W	L	Pct.	ERA	G	GS	CG	ShO	Sv.	IP	H	R	ER	BB	SO
1997—Gulf Coast Braves (GCL)		3	3	.500	2.25	11	8	0	0	0	44	30	13	11	18	61
1998—Macon (S.Atl.)		1	7	.125	5.86	12	12	0	0	0	55 1/3	70	50	36	16	38
—Eugene (N'West)		2	7	.222	6.31	16	8	0	0	0	55 2/3	84	51	39	17	39
1999—Macon (S.Atl.)		6	3	.667	2.67	17	14	1	1	0	77 2/3	70	30	23	25	43
2000—Myrtle Beach (Caro.)		15	8	.652	3.22	27	26	3	2	0	148 1/3	136	57	53	42	125
2001—Greenville (Sou.)		1	1	.500	4.91	3	3	0	0	0	14 2/3	17	8	8	8	17

RAMIREZ, JULIO — OF — WHITE SOX

PERSONAL: Born August 10, 1977, in San Juan de la Maguana, Dominican Republic. ... 5-11/170. ... Bats right, throws right. ... Full name: Julio Caesar Ramirez.
HIGH SCHOOL: Escuela Otilia Pelaez (Santo Domingo, Dominican Republic).
TRANSACTIONS/CAREER NOTES: Signed as non-drafted free agent by Florida Marlins organization (December 6, 1993). ... On Calgary disabled list (April 15-May 2 and July 18-August 14, 2000). ... Traded by Marlins to Chicago White Sox for OF Jeff Abbott (December 10, 2000). ... On Charlotte disabled list (August 13-20, 2001).
STATISTICAL NOTES: Led Florida State League outfielders with 390 total chances in 1998. ... Led Eastern League outfielders with 351 total chances in 1999.

Year Team (League)	Pos.	G	AB	R	H	2B	3B	HR	RBI	Avg.	BB	SO	SB	PO	A	E	Avg.
1994—Dom. Marlins (DSL)...	OF	67	274	54	75	18	0	7	32	.274	28	41	29	136	11	10	.936
1995—GC Marlins (GCL).......	OF	48	204	35	58	9	4	2	13	.284	13	42	17	109	7	2	.983
1996—Brevard County (FSL).	OF	17	61	11	15	0	1	0	2	.246	4	18	2	12	2	1	.933
—GC Marlins (GCL).......	OF	43	174	35	50	5	4	0	16	.287	15	34	26	95	2	2	.980
1997—Kane County (Midw.)..	OF	99	376	70	96	18	7	14	53	.255	37	122	41	179	8	4	.979
1998—Brevard County (FSL).	OF	135	*559	90	156	20	12	13	58	.279	45	147	71	*365	•17	8	.979
1999—Portland (East.).........	OF	138	*568	87	148	30	10	13	64	.261	39	150	*64	*326	14	•11	.969
—Florida (N.L.)............	OF	15	21	3	3	1	0	0	2	.143	1	6	0	19	0	1	.950
2000—Calgary (PCL)..........	OF	94	350	45	93	18	3	7	52	.266	21	86	20	220	9	*11	.954
2001—Chicago (A.L.)■........	OF	22	37	2	3	0	0	0	1	.081	2	15	2	43	2	1	.978
—Charlotte (I.L.)..........	OF	88	319	36	69	11	1	8	25	.216	20	80	15	191	9	8	.962
American League totals (1 year)		22	37	2	3	0	0	0	1	.081	2	15	2	43	2	1	.978
National League totals (1 year)		15	21	3	3	1	0	0	2	.143	1	6	0	19	0	1	.950
Major League totals (2 years)		37	58	5	6	1	0	0	3	.103	3	21	2	62	2	2	.970

RAMIREZ, MANNY   OF   RED SOX

PERSONAL: Born May 30, 1972, in Santo Domingo, Dominican Republic. ... 6-0/205. ... Bats right, throws right. ... Full name: Manuel Aristides Ramirez.

HIGH SCHOOL: George Washington (New York).

TRANSACTIONS/CAREER NOTES: Selected by Cleveland Indians organization in first round (13th pick overall) of free-agent draft (June 3, 1991). ... On disabled list (July 10, 1992-remainder of season). ... On suspended list (June 8-11, 1999). ... On Cleveland disabled list (May 30-July 13, 2000); included rehabilitation assignments to Akron (June 16-23) and Buffalo (July 6-13). ... Granted free agency (October 27, 2000). ... Signed by Boston Red Sox (December 13, 2000).

RECORDS: Shares major league record for most consecutive home runs—4 (September 15 [3], 16 [1], 1998; most home runs in two consecutive games—5 (September 15 [3], 16 [2], 1998); and most home runs in three consecutive games—6 (September 15 [3], 16 [2], 17 [1], 1998).

HONORS: Named Appalachian League Most Valuable Player (1991). ... Named outfielder on The Sporting News A.L. All-Star team (1995, 1999 and 2001). ... Named outfielder on The Sporting News A.L. Silver Slugger team (1995, 1999 and 2000). ... Named outfielder on A.L. Silver Slugger team (2001).

STATISTICAL NOTES: Led Appalachian League with 146 total bases and .679 slugging percentage and tied for lead with five intentional bases on balls received in 1991. ... Hit three home runs in one game (September 15, 1998 and August 25, 1999). ... Led A.L. with a .663 slugging percentage in 1999 and .697 slugging percentage in 2000. ... Had 20-game hitting streak (August 15-September 5, 2000). ... Led A.L. with 25 intentional bases on balls received in 2001. ... Career major league grand slams: 14.

Year Team (League)	Pos.	G	AB	R	H	2B	3B	HR	RBI	Avg.	BB	SO	SB	PO	A	E	Avg.
1991—Burlington (Appl.).......	OF	59	215	44	70	11	4	*19	*63	.326	34	41	7	83	2	3	.966
1992—Kinston (Caro.)..........	OF	81	291	52	81	18	4	13	63	.278	45	74	1	128	3	6	.956
1993—Canton/Akron (East.)..	OF	89	344	67	117	32	0	17	79	*.340	45	68	2	142	4	5	.967
—Charlotte (I.L.)..........	OF	40	145	38	46	12	0	14	36	.317	27	35	1	70	3	3	.961
—Cleveland (A.L.)..........	DH-OF	22	53	5	9	1	0	2	5	.170	2	8	0	3	0	0	1.000
1994—Cleveland (A.L.)..........	OF-DH	91	290	51	78	22	0	17	60	.269	42	72	4	150	7	1	.994
1995—Cleveland (A.L.)..........	OF-DH	137	484	85	149	26	1	31	107	.308	75	112	6	220	3	5	.978
1996—Cleveland (A.L.)..........	OF-DH	152	550	94	170	45	3	33	112	.309	85	104	8	272	*19	9	.970
1997—Cleveland (A.L.)..........	OF-DH	150	561	99	184	40	0	26	88	.328	79	115	2	259	10	7	.975
1998—Cleveland (A.L.)..........	OF-DH	150	571	108	168	35	2	45	145	.294	76	121	5	291	10	7	.977
1999—Cleveland (A.L.)..........	OF-DH	147	522	131	174	34	3	44	*165	.333	96	131	2	267	7	7	.975
2000—Cleveland (A.L.)..........	OF-DH	118	439	92	154	34	2	38	122	.351	86	117	1	134	7	2	.986
—Akron (East.)..........	DH	1	2	1	1	0	0	1	2	.500	2	1	0	...	...	...	...
—Buffalo (I.L.)...............	DH	5	11	5	5	1	0	3	7	.455	6	1	0	...	...	...	...
2001—Boston (A.L.)■..........	DH-OF	142	529	93	162	33	2	41	125	.306	81	147	0	98	1	0	1.000
Major League totals (9 years)		1109	3999	758	1248	270	13	277	929	.312	622	927	28	1694	64	38	.979

DIVISION SERIES RECORD

RECORDS: Shares career record for most extra-base hits—10. ... Shares single-game record for most home runs—2 (October 2, 1998).

Year Team (League)	Pos.	G	AB	R	H	2B	3B	HR	RBI	Avg.	BB	SO	SB	PO	A	E	Avg.
1995—Cleveland (A.L.)..........	OF	3	12	1	0	0	0	0	0	.000	1	2	0	3	0	0	1.000
1996—Cleveland (A.L.)..........	OF	4	16	4	6	2	0	2	2	.375	1	4	0	8	2	0	1.000
1997—Cleveland (A.L.)..........	OF	5	21	2	3	1	0	0	3	.143	0	3	0	3	0	1	.750
1998—Cleveland (A.L.)..........	OF	4	14	2	5	2	0	2	3	.357	1	4	0	4	0	0	1.000
1999—Cleveland (A.L.)..........	OF	5	18	5	1	1	0	0	1	.056	4	8	0	8	1	0	1.000
Division series totals (5 years)		21	81	14	15	6	0	4	9	.185	7	21	0	26	3	1	.967

CHAMPIONSHIP SERIES RECORD

Year Team (League)	Pos.	G	AB	R	H	2B	3B	HR	RBI	Avg.	BB	SO	SB	PO	A	E	Avg.
1995—Cleveland (A.L.)..........	OF	6	21	2	6	0	0	2	2	.286	2	5	0	9	0	0	1.000
1997—Cleveland (A.L.)..........	OF	6	21	3	6	1	0	2	3	.286	5	5	0	14	0	1	.933
1998—Cleveland (A.L.)..........	OF	6	21	2	7	1	0	2	4	.333	4	9	0	12	0	0	1.000
Championship series totals (3 years)		18	63	7	19	2	0	6	9	.302	11	19	0	35	0	1	.972

WORLD SERIES RECORD

Year Team (League)	Pos.	G	AB	R	H	2B	3B	HR	RBI	Avg.	BB	SO	SB	PO	A	E	Avg.
1995—Cleveland (A.L.)..........	OF	6	18	2	4	0	0	1	2	.222	4	5	1	8	0	0	1.000
1997—Cleveland (A.L.)..........	OF	7	26	3	4	0	0	2	6	.154	6	5	0	16	1	1	.944
World Series totals (2 years)		13	44	5	8	0	0	3	8	.182	10	10	1	24	1	1	.962

Year	League	Pos.	AB	R	H	2B	3B	HR	RBI	Avg.	BB	SO	SB	PO	A	E	Avg.
1995—American		PH-OF	0	0	0	0	0	0	0	...	2	0	0	2	0	0	1.000
1998—American		OF	1	0	0	0	0	0	1	.000	0	0	0	0	0	0	...
1999—American		OF	1	1	0	0	0	0	0	.000	1	1	0	0	0	0	...
2000—American							Selected, did not play—injured.										
2001—American		OF	1	0	0	0	0	0	0	.000	0	1	0	3	0	0	1.000
All-Star Game totals (4 years)			3	1	0	0	0	0	1	.000	3	2	0	5	0	0	1.000

RAMSAY, ROBERT   P   PADRES

R

PERSONAL: Born December 3, 1973, in Vancouver, Wash. ... 6-5/215. ... Throws left, bats left. ... Full name: Robert Arthur Ramsay.

HIGH SCHOOL: Mountain View (Vancouver, Wash.).

COLLEGE: Washington State.

TRANSACTIONS/CAREER NOTES: Selected by Boston Red Sox organization in seventh round of free-agent draft (June 2, 1996). ... Traded by Red Sox to Seattle Mariners for OF Butch Huskey (July 26, 1999). ... On Seattle disabled list (August 14-29, 2000); included rehabilitation assignment to Everett (August 26-29). ... On disabled list (September 10, 2001-remainder of season). ... Claimed on waivers by San Diego Padres (November 20, 2001).

STATISTICAL NOTES: Led Pacific Coast League with 10 sacrifice flies allowed in 2001.

Year	League	W	L	Pct.	ERA	G	GS	CG	ShO	Sv.	IP	H	R	ER	BB	SO
1996—Gulf Coast Red Sox (GCL)..		0	1	.000	4.91	2	0	0	0	0	3 2/3	5	2	2	3	5
—Sarasota (FSL)		2	2	.500	6.09	12	7	0	0	0	34	42	23	23	27	32
1997—Sarasota (FSL)		9	9	.500	4.78	23	22	1	0	0	135 2/3	134	90	72	63	115
1998—Trenton (East.)		12	6	.667	3.49	27	27	1	1	0	162 2/3	137	67	63	50	166
1999—Pawtucket (I.L.)		6	6	.500	5.35	20	20	0	0	0	114 1/3	114	81	68	36	79
—Seattle (A.L.)■		0	2	.000	6.38	6	3	0	0	0	18 1/3	23	13	13	9	11
—Tacoma (PCL)		4	1	.800	1.08	5	5	0	0	0	33 1/3	20	6	4	14	37
2000—Tacoma (PCL)		0	1	.000	4.50	3	3	0	0	0	16	16	8	8	6	6
—Seattle (A.L.)		1	1	.500	3.40	37	1	0	0	0	50 1/3	43	22	19	40	32
—Everett (N'West)		0	0	...	0.00	1	1	0	0	0	2	2	0	0	0	4
2001—Tacoma (PCL)		10	11	.476	4.82	26	26	0	0	0	149 1/3	160	98	80	60	113
Major League totals (2 years)		1	3	.250	4.19	43	4	0	0	0	68 2/3	66	35	32	49	43

CHAMPIONSHIP SERIES RECORD

Year	League	W	L	Pct.	ERA	G	GS	CG	ShO	Sv.	IP	H	R	ER	BB	SO
2000—Seattle (A.L.)		0	0	...	0.00	2	0	0	0	0	1 2/3	2	0	0	0	1

RANDA, JOE   3B   ROYALS

PERSONAL: Born December 18, 1969, in Milwaukee. ... 5-11/190. ... Bats right, throws right. ... Full name: Joseph Gregory Randa.

HIGH SCHOOL: Kettle-Moraine (Wales, Wis.).

JUNIOR COLLEGE: Indian River Community College (Fla.).

COLLEGE: Tennessee.

TRANSACTIONS/CAREER NOTES: Selected by California Angels organization in 30th round of free-agent draft (June 5, 1989); did not sign. ... Selected by Kansas City Royals organization in 11th round of free-agent draft (June 3, 1991). ... On Kansas City disabled list (May 5-27, 1996); included rehabilitation assignment to Omaha (May 23-27). ... Traded by Royals with P Jeff Granger, P Jeff Martin and P Jeff Wallace to Pittsburgh Pirates for SS Jay Bell and 1B Jeff King (December 13, 1996). ... On Pittsburgh disabled list (June 28-July 27, 1997); included rehabilitation assignment to Calgary (July 25-27). ... Selected by Arizona Diamondbacks in third round (57th pick overall) of expansion draft (November 18, 1997). ... Traded by Diamondbacks with P Matt Drews and 3B Gabe Alvarez to Detroit Tigers for 3B Travis Fryman (November 18, 1997). ... Traded by Tigers to New York Mets for P Willie Blair (December 4, 1998). ... Traded by Mets to Royals for OF Juan LeBron (December 10, 1998).

RECORDS: Holds A.L. single-season record for fewest putouts by third baseman for leader—111 (2001).

HONORS: Named Northwest League Most Valuable Player (1991).

STATISTICAL NOTES: Led Northwest League with 150 total bases and .438 on-base percentage in 1991. ... Led Northwest League third basemen with 182 total chances and 12 double plays in 1991. ... Led Southern League with 10 sacrifice flies in 1993. ... Led American Association third basemen with 433 total chances and 28 double plays in 1994. ... Had 18-game hitting streak (July 1-21, 1999). ... Led A.L. third baseman with 455 total chances and 28 double plays in 1999. ... Career major league grand slams: 1.

Year	Team (League)	Pos.	G	AB	R	H	2B	3B	HR	RBI	Avg.	BB	SO	SB	PO	A	E	Avg.
1991—Eugene (N'West)		3B	72	275	53	*93	20	2	11	59	.338	46	29	6	*57	*111	14	*.923
1992—Appleton (Midw.)		3B	72	266	55	80	13	0	5	43	.301	34	37	6	53	137	12	.941
—Baseball City (FSL)		3B-SS	51	189	22	52	7	0	1	12	.275	12	21	4	43	105	6	.961
1993—Memphis (Sou.)		3B	131	505	74	149	31	5	11	72	.295	39	64	8	*97	309	25	.942
1994—Omaha (A.A.)		3B	127	455	65	125	27	2	10	51	.275	30	49	5	*85	*324	*24	.945
1995—Omaha (A.A.)		3B	64	233	33	64	10	2	8	33	.275	23	33	2	42	96	6	.958
—Kansas City (A.L.)		3B-2B-DH	34	70	6	12	2	0	1	5	.171	6	17	0	15	44	3	.952
1996—Kansas City (A.L.)		3-2-1-DH	110	337	36	102	24	1	6	47	.303	26	47	13	80	160	10	.960
—Omaha (A.A.)		3B	9	9	1	1	0	1	0	0	.111	1	1	0	1	10	0	1.000
1997—Pittsburgh (N.L.)■		3B-2B	126	443	58	134	27	9	7	60	.302	41	64	4	91	288	21	.948
—Calgary (PCL)		3B	3	11	4	4	1	0	1	4	.364	3	4	0	2	7	1	.900
1998—Detroit (A.L.)■		3-2-DH-1	138	460	56	117	21	2	9	50	.254	41	70	8	102	252	7	.981
1999—Kansas City (A.L.)■		3B	156	628	92	197	36	8	16	84	.314	50	80	5	*119	*314	22	.952
2000—Kansas City (A.L.)		3B-DH	158	612	88	186	29	4	15	106	.304	36	66	6	*132	293	19	.957
2001—Kansas City (A.L.)		3B-DH-2B	151	581	59	147	34	2	13	83	.253	42	80	3	†114	256	13	.966
American League totals (6 years)			747	2688	337	761	146	17	60	375	.283	201	360	35	562	1319	74	.962
National League totals (1 year)			126	443	58	134	27	9	7	60	.302	41	64	4	91	288	21	.948
Major League totals (7 years)			873	3131	395	895	173	26	67	435	.286	242	424	39	653	1607	95	.960

RANSOM, CODY   SS   GIANTS

PERSONAL: Born February 17, 1976, in Mesa, Ariz. ... 6-2/190. ... Bats right, throws right. ... Full name: Bryan Cody Ransom.
HIGH SCHOOL: Chandler (Ariz.).
JUNIOR COLLEGE: South Mountain (Ariz.).
COLLEGE: Grand Canyon.
TRANSACTIONS/CAREER NOTES: Selected by San Francisco Giants organization in ninth round of free-agent draft (June 2, 1998).
STATISTICAL NOTES: Tied for Northwest League lead in double plays by shortstop with 37 in 1998.

| | | | | | | | BATTING | | | | | | | | FIELDING | | |
Year Team (League)	Pos.	G	AB	R	H	2B	3B	HR	RBI	Avg.	BB	SO	SB	PO	A	E	Avg.
1998— Salem-Kaizer (NW).....	SS	71	236	52	55	12	7	6	27	.233	43	56	19	92	216	*24	.928
1999— Bakersfield (Calif.)......	SS	99	356	69	98	12	6	11	47	.275	54	108	15	133	318	30	.938
— Shreveport (Texas).....	SS	14	41	6	5	0	0	2	4	.122	4	22	0	13	48	3	.953
2000— Shreveport (Texas).....	SS	130	459	58	92	21	3	7	47	.200	40	141	9	210	366	25	.958
2001— Fresno (PCL)	SS	134	469	77	113	21	6	23	78	.241	44	137	17	202	374	12	*.980
— San Francisco (N.L.) ..	SS	9	7	1	0	0	0	0	0	.000	0	5	0	0	4	0	1.000
Major League totals (1 year)		9	7	1	0	0	0	0	0	.000	0	5	0	0	4	0	1.000

RAPP, PAT   P

PERSONAL: Born July 13, 1967, in Jennings, La. ... 6-3/215. ... Throws right, bats right. ... Full name: Patrick Leland Rapp.
HIGH SCHOOL: Sulphur (La.).
JUNIOR COLLEGE: Hinds Community College (Miss.).
COLLEGE: Southern Mississippi.
TRANSACTIONS/CAREER NOTES: Selected by San Francisco Giants organization in 15th round of free-agent draft (June 5, 1989). ... Selected by Florida Marlins in first round (10th pick overall) of expansion draft (November 17, 1992). ... Traded by Marlins to Giants for P Brandon Leese and P Bobby Rector (July 18, 1997). ... On San Francisco disabled list (July 20-August 5, 1997). ... Granted free agency (December 21, 1997). ... Signed by Kansas City Royals organization (January 22, 1998). ... Granted free agency (December 21, 1998). ... Signed by Boston Red Sox (January 11, 1999). ... Granted free agency (November 2, 1999). ... Signed by Baltimore Orioles (January 28, 2000). ... Granted free agency (October 31, 2000). ... Signed by Anaheim Angels (December 11, 2000). ... Granted free agency (November 5, 2001).
STATISTICAL NOTES: Pitched 17-0 one-hit, complete-game victory against Colorado (September 17, 1995).
MISCELLANEOUS: Appeared in one game as pinch runner (1994). ... Holds Florida Marlins all-time record for most innings pitched (665²/₃). ... Shares Florida Marlins all-time record for most wins (37).

Year League	W	L	Pct.	ERA	G	GS	CG	ShO	Sv.	IP	H	R	ER	BB	SO
1989— Pocatello (Pio.)..................	4	6	.400	5.30	16	12	1	0	0	73	90	54	43	29	40
1990— Clinton (Midw.)	14	10	.583	2.64	27	26	4	0	0	167¹/₃	132	60	49	79	132
1991— San Jose (Calif.)	7	5	.583	2.50	16	15	1	0	0	90	88	41	25	37	73
— Shreveport (Texas)...........	6	2	.750	2.69	10	10	1	1	0	60¹/₃	52	23	18	22	46
1992— Phoenix (PCL)	7	8	.467	3.05	39	12	2	1	3	121	115	54	41	40	79
— San Francisco (N.L.)	0	2	.000	7.20	3	2	0	0	0	10	8	8	8	6	3
1993— Edmonton (PCL)■	8	3	.727	3.43	17	17	•4	1	0	107²/₃	89	45	41	34	93
— Florida (N.L.)	4	6	.400	4.02	16	16	1	0	0	94	101	49	42	39	57
1994— Florida (N.L.)	7	8	.467	3.85	24	23	2	1	0	133¹/₃	132	67	57	69	75
1995— Charlotte (I.L.)	0	1	.000	6.00	1	1	0	0	0	6	6	4	4	1	5
— Florida (N.L.)	14	7	.667	3.44	28	28	3	2	0	167¹/₃	158	72	64	76	102
1996— Florida (N.L.)	8	•16	.333	5.10	30	29	0	0	0	162¹/₃	184	95	92	91	86
— Charlotte (I.L.)...........	1	1	.500	8.18	2	2	0	0	0	11	18	12	10	4	9
1997— Florida (N.L.)	4	6	.400	4.47	19	19	1	1	0	108²/₃	121	59	54	51	64
— San Francisco (N.L.)■	1	2	.333	6.00	8	6	0	0	0	33	37	24	22	21	28
— Phoenix (PCL)	2	0	1.000	3.60	3	3	0	0	0	15	16	6	6	9	6
1998— Kansas City (A.L.)■	12	13	.480	5.30	32	32	1	1	0	188¹/₃	208	117	111	107	132
1999— Boston (A.L.)■...............	6	7	.462	4.12	37	26	0	0	0	146¹/₃	147	78	67	69	90
2000— Baltimore (A.L.)■..............	9	12	.429	5.90	31	30	0	0	0	174	203	125	114	83	106
2001— Anaheim (A.L.)■...............	5	12	.294	4.76	31	28	1	0	0	170	169	96	90	71	82
A.L. totals (4 years)	32	44	.421	5.07	131	116	2	1	0	678²/₃	727	416	382	330	410
N.L. totals (6 years)	38	47	.447	4.31	128	123	7	4	0	708²/₃	741	374	339	353	415
Major League totals (10 years)	70	91	.435	4.68	259	239	9	5	0	1387¹/₃	1468	790	721	683	825

DIVISION SERIES RECORD

Year League	W	L	Pct.	ERA	G	GS	CG	ShO	Sv.	IP	H	R	ER	BB	SO
1999— Boston (A.L.)...................						Did not play.									

CHAMPIONSHIP SERIES RECORD

Year League	W	L	Pct.	ERA	G	GS	CG	ShO	Sv.	IP	H	R	ER	BB	SO
1999— Boston (A.L.)...................	0	0	...	0.00	1	0	0	0	0	1	0	0	0	1	0

RAUCH, JON   P   WHITE SOX

PERSONAL: Born November 27, 1978, in Louisville, Ky. ... 6-11/230. ... Throws right, bats right. ... Full name: Jon Erich Rauch.
HIGH SCHOOL: Oldham County (Buckner, Ky.).
COLLEGE: Morehead State (Ky.).
TRANSACTIONS/CAREER NOTES: Selected by Chicago White Sox organization in third round of free-agent draft (June 2, 1999). ... On disabled list (April 9-22 and May 14, 2001-remainder of season).
HONORS: Named Minor League Player of the Year by THE SPORTING NEWS (2000).
MISCELLANEOUS: Member of 2000 Olympic baseball team.

Year League	W	L	Pct.	ERA	G	GS	CG	ShO	Sv.	IP	H	R	ER	BB	SO
1999— Bristol (Appl.)...................	4	4	.500	4.45	14	9	0	0	2	56²/₃	65	44	28	16	66
— Winston-Salem (Caro.)........	0	0	...	3.00	1	1	0	0	0	6	4	3	2	3	7
2000— Winston-Salem (Caro.).......	11	3	.786	2.86	18	18	1	0	0	110	102	49	35	33	124
— Birmingham (Sou.).............	5	1	.833	2.25	8	8	2	2	0	56	36	18	14	16	63
2001— Charlotte (I.L.)..................	1	3	.250	5.79	6	6	0	0	0	28	28	20	18	7	27

PERSONAL: Born August 19, 1973, in Seneca, S.C. ... 5-11/170. ... Throws right, bats right. ... Full name: William Britt Reames.
HIGH SCHOOL: Seneca (S.C.).
COLLEGE: The Citadel.
TRANSACTIONS/CAREER NOTES: Selected by St. Louis Cardinals organization in 17th round of free-agent draft (June 1, 1995). ... On disabled list (April 4, 1997-entire season; and April 10, 1998-entire season). ... On Potomac disabled list (April 23-June 10 and June 14-August 10, 1999). ... On Memphis disabled list (July 7-14 and July 20-August 3, 2000). ... Traded by Cardinals with 3B Fernando Tatis to Montreal Expos for P Dustin Hermanson and P Steve Kline (December 14, 2000).
MISCELLANEOUS: Appeared in two games as pinch runner (2000).

Year League	W	L	Pct.	ERA	G	GS	CG	ShO	Sv.	IP	H	R	ER	BB	SO
1995—New Jersey (NY-Penn)	2	1	.667	1.52	5	5	0	0	0	29²/₃	19	7	5	12	42
—Savannah (S.Atl.)	3	5	.375	3.46	10	10	1	0	0	54²/₃	41	23	21	15	63
1996—Peoria (Midw.)	15	7	.682	*1.90	25	25	2	•1	0	161	97	43	34	41	*167
1997—							Did not play.								
1998—							Did not play.								
1999—Potomac (Caro.)	3	2	.600	3.19	10	8	0	0	0	36²/₃	34	21	13	21	22
2000—Arkansas (Texas)	2	3	.400	6.13	8	8	0	0	0	39²/₃	46	28	27	18	39
—Memphis (PCL)	6	2	.750	2.28	13	13	2	1	0	75	55	20	19	20	77
—St. Louis (N.L.)	2	1	.667	2.88	8	7	0	0	0	40²/₃	30	17	13	23	31
2001—Montreal (N.L.)■	4	8	.333	5.59	41	13	0	0	0	95	101	68	59	48	86
—Ottawa (I.L.)	4	3	.571	3.50	8	8	1	0	0	54	47	24	21	13	38
Major League totals (2 years)	**6**	**9**	**.400**	**4.78**	**49**	**20**	**0**	**0**	**0**	**135²/₃**	**131**	**85**	**72**	**71**	**117**

DIVISION SERIES RECORD

Year League	W	L	Pct.	ERA	G	GS	CG	ShO	Sv.	IP	H	R	ER	BB	SO
2000—St. Louis (N.L.)	1	0	1.000	0.00	2	0	0	0	0	3¹/₃	0	0	0	3	2

CHAMPIONSHIP SERIES RECORD

Year League	W	L	Pct.	ERA	G	GS	CG	ShO	Sv.	IP	H	R	ER	BB	SO
2000—St. Louis (N.L.)	0	0	...	1.42	2	0	0	0	0	6¹/₃	5	1	1	4	6

R

PERSONAL: Born April 30, 1964, in Dayton, Ohio. ... 6-0/175. ... Bats right, throws right. ... Full name: Jeffrey Allen Reboulet. ... Brother of Jim Reboulet, second baseman in St. Louis Cardinals and Pittsburgh Pirates organizations. ... Name pronounced REB-uh-lay.
HIGH SCHOOL: Alter (Kettering, Ohio).
JUNIOR COLLEGE: Triton Junior College (Ill.).
COLLEGE: Louisiana State.
TRANSACTIONS/CAREER NOTES: Selected by Houston Astros organization in 26th round of free-agent draft (June 3, 1985); did not sign. ... Selected by Minnesota Twins organization in 10th round of free-agent draft (June 2, 1986). ... Granted free agency (October 4, 1996). ... Signed by Baltimore Orioles organization (January 30, 1997). ... Traded by Orioles to Kansas City Royals for a player to be named later (December 12, 1999). ... Granted free agency (October 31, 2000). ... Signed by Los Angeles Dodgers organization (February 20, 2001).
STATISTICAL NOTES: Led Southern League shortstops with 602 total chances in 1988. ... Led Pacific Coast League with 17 sacrifice hits in 1991. ... Led Pacific Coast League shortstops with 649 total chances in 1991.

														BATTING				FIELDING		
Year Team (League)	Pos.	G	AB	R	H	2B	3B	HR	RBI	Avg.	BB	SO	SB	PO	A	E	Avg.			
1986—Visalia (Calif.)	SS	72	254	54	73	13	1	0	29	.287	54	33	14	118	188	20	.939			
1987—Orlando (Sou.)	SS-2B-3B	129	422	52	108	15	1	1	35	.256	58	56	9	220	370	26	.958			
1988—Orlando (Sou.)	SS	125	439	57	112	24	2	4	41	.255	53	55	18	*225	347	30	.950			
—Portland (PCL)	2B-SS	4	12	0	1	0	0	0	1	.083	3	2	0	8	13	1	.955			
1989—Portland (PCL)	SS-2B-3B-OF	26	65	9	16	1	0	0	3	.246	12	11	2	38	62	7	.935			
—Orlando (Sou.)	SS-2B-OF	81	291	43	63	5	1	0	26	.216	49	33	11	129	228	22	.942			
1990—Orlando (Sou.)	2-3-S-O-1	97	287	43	66	12	2	2	28	.230	57	37	10	131	230	12	.968			
1991—Portland (PCL)	SS	134	391	50	97	27	3	3	46	.248	57	52	5	*202	415	*32	.951			
1992—Portland (PCL)	SS	48	161	21	46	11	1	2	21	.286	35	18	3	72	141	7	.968			
—Minnesota (A.L.)	S-3-2-O-DH	73	137	15	26	7	1	1	16	.190	23	26	3	71	163	5	.979			
1993—Minnesota (A.L.)	S-3-2-O-DH	109	240	33	62	8	0	1	15	.258	35	37	5	122	215	6	.983			
1994—Minnesota (A.L.)	S-2-1-3-O-DH	74	189	28	49	11	1	3	23	.259	18	23	0	150	131	7	.976			
1995—Minnesota (A.L.)	S-3-1-2-C	87	216	39	63	11	0	4	23	.292	27	34	1	164	160	4	.988			
1996—Minnesota (A.L.)	IF-OF-DH	107	234	20	52	9	0	0	23	.222	25	34	4	138	114	2	.992			
1997—Baltimore (A.L.)■	2B-SS-3B-OF	99	228	26	54	9	0	4	27	.237	23	44	3	106	163	7	.975			
1998—Baltimore (A.L.)	2B-SS-3B	79	126	20	31	6	0	1	8	.246	19	34	0	51	120	6	.966			
1999—Baltimore (A.L.)	3B-2B-SS	99	154	25	25	4	0	0	4	.162	33	29	1	79	152	2	.991			
2000—Kansas City (A.L.)■	2B-3B-SS-DH	66	182	29	44	7	0	0	14	.242	23	32	3	84	167	9	.965			
2001—Los Angeles (N.L.)■	SS-2B-3B-OF	94	214	35	57	15	2	3	22	.266	33	48	0	103	135	10	.960			
American League totals (9 years)		793	1706	235	406	72	2	14	153	.238	226	293	20	965	1385	48	.980			
National League totals (1 year)		94	214	35	57	15	2	3	22	.266	33	48	0	103	135	10	.960			
Major League totals (10 years)		887	1920	270	463	87	4	17	175	.241	259	341	20	1068	1520	58	.978			

DIVISION SERIES RECORD

						BATTING								FIELDING		
Year Team (League)	Pos.	G	AB	R	H	2B	3B	HR	RBI	Avg.	BB	SO	SB	PO	A	E	Avg.
1997—Baltimore (A.L.)	2B	2	5	1	1	0	0	1	1	.200	0	2	0	2	3	0	1.000

CHAMPIONSHIP SERIES RECORD

						BATTING								FIELDING		
Year Team (League)	Pos.	G	AB	R	H	2B	3B	HR	RBI	Avg.	BB	SO	SB	PO	A	E	Avg.
1997—Baltimore (A.L.)	SS-PR	1	2	1	0	0	0	0	0	.000	0	1	0	0	0	0	...

REDDING, TIM   P   ASTROS

PERSONAL: Born February 12, 1978, in Rochester, N.Y. ... 6-0/180. ... Throws right, bats right. ... Full name: Timothy J. Redding.
JUNIOR COLLEGE: Monroe (Rochester, N.Y.).
TRANSACTIONS/CAREER NOTES: Selected by Houston Astros organization in 20th round of free-agent draft (June 3, 1997).
HONORS: Named Florida State League Most Valuable Pitcher (2000). ... Named Texas League Pitcher of the Year (2001).

Year League	W	L	Pct.	ERA	G	GS	CG	ShO	Sv.	IP	H	R	ER	BB	SO
1998— Auburn (NY-Penn)	7	3	.700	4.52	16	15	0	0	1	73²/₃	49	44	37	*50	98
1999— Michigan (Midw.)	8	6	.571	4.97	43	11	0	0	14	105	84	69	58	76	144
2000— Kissimmee (FSL)	12	5	.706	2.68	24	24	0	0	0	154²/₃	125	62	46	57	*170
— Round Rock (Texas)	2	0	1.000	3.46	5	5	0	0	0	26	14	12	10	22	22
2001— Round Rock (Texas)	10	2	.833	2.18	14	14	1	1	0	90²/₃	64	26	22	25	113
— New Orleans (PCL)	4	1	.800	4.54	6	6	0	0	0	37²/₃	22	21	19	19	42
— Houston (N.L.)	3	1	.750	5.50	13	9	0	0	0	55²/₃	62	38	34	24	55
Major League totals (1 year)	3	1	.750	5.50	13	9	0	0	0	55²/₃	62	38	34	24	55

REDMAN, MARK   P   TIGERS

PERSONAL: Born January 5, 1974, in San Diego. ... 6-5/220. ... Throws left, bats left. ... Full name: Mark Allen Redman.
HIGH SCHOOL: Escondido (Calif.).
COLLEGE: The Master's College (Calif.), then Oklahoma.
TRANSACTIONS/CAREER NOTES: Selected by Detroit Tigers organization in 41st round of free-agent draft (June 1, 1992); did not sign. ... Selected by Minnesota Twins organization in first round (13th pick overall) of free-agent draft (June 1, 1995). ... On Salt Lake disabled list (August 1-8, 1998). ... On Minnesota disabled list (July 25-August 10, 1999). ... On Minnesota disabled list (May 21-July 28, 2001); included rehabilitation assignment to Edmonton (June 15-27). ... Traded by Twins to Tigers for P Todd Jones (July 28, 2001). ... On Detroit disabled list (July 28-August 22, 2001); included rehabilitation assignment to Toledo (August 6-22).

Year League	W	L	Pct.	ERA	G	GS	CG	ShO	Sv.	IP	H	R	ER	BB	SO
1995— Fort Myers (FSL)	2	1	.667	2.76	8	5	0	0	0	32²/₃	28	13	10	13	26
1996— Fort Myers (FSL)	3	4	.429	1.85	13	13	0	0	0	82²/₃	63	24	17	34	75
— New Britain (East.)	7	7	.500	3.81	16	16	3	0	0	106¹/₃	101	51	45	50	96
— Salt Lake (PCL)	0	0	...	9.00	1	1	0	0	0	4	7	4	4	2	4
1997— Salt Lake (PCL)	8	*15	.348	6.31	29	28	0	0	1	158¹/₃	204	*123	111	80	125
1998— New Britain (East.)	4	2	.667	1.52	8	8	0	0	0	47¹/₃	40	11	8	17	51
— Salt Lake (PCL)	6	7	.462	5.53	19	18	0	0	0	99¹/₃	111	75	61	41	88
1999— Salt Lake (PCL)	9	9	.500	5.05	24	24	1	0	0	133²/₃	141	87	75	51	114
— Minnesota (A.L.)	1	0	1.000	8.53	5	1	0	0	0	12²/₃	17	13	12	7	11
2000— Minnesota (A.L.)	12	9	.571	4.76	32	24	0	0	0	151¹/₃	168	81	80	45	117
2001— Minnesota (A.L.)	2	4	.333	4.22	9	9	0	0	0	49	57	26	23	19	29
— Edmonton (PCL)	0	0	...	13.50	1	1	0	0	0	1¹/₃	3	2	2	1	0
— Toledo (I.L.)■	0	1	.000	5.27	3	3	0	0	0	13²/₃	14	10	8	1	12
— Detroit (A.L.)	0	2	.000	6.00	2	2	0	0	0	9	11	6	6	4	4
Major League totals (3 years)	15	15	.500	4.91	48	36	0	0	0	222	253	126	121	75	161

REDMAN, TIKE   OF   PIRATES

PERSONAL: Born March 10, 1977, in Tuscaloosa, Ala. ... 5-11/166. ... Bats left, throws left. ... Full name: Julian Jawann Redman.
HIGH SCHOOL: Tuscaloosa (Ala.) Academy.
TRANSACTIONS/CAREER NOTES: Selected by Pittsburgh Pirates organization in fifth round of free-agent draft (June 4, 1996).
STATISTICAL NOTES: Tied Pacific Coast League lead with 18 caught stealing in 2000.

Year Team (League)	Pos.	G	AB	R	H	2B	3B	HR	RBI	Avg.	BB	SO	SB	PO	A	E	Avg.
1996— GC Pirates (GCL)	OF	26	104	20	31	4	1	1	16	.298	12	12	15	43	2	1	.978
— Erie (NY-Penn)	OF	43	170	31	50	4	6	2	21	.294	17	30	7	79	1	7	.920
1997— Lynchburg (Caro.)	OF-1B	125	415	55	104	18	5	4	45	.251	45	82	21	227	8	6	.975
1998— Lynchburg (Caro.)	OF	131	525	70	135	26	10	6	46	.257	32	73	36	263	7	8	.971
1999— Altoona (East.)	OF	136	532	84	143	20	*12	3	60	.269	52	52	29	301	12	9	.972
2000— Nashville (PCL)	OF	121	506	62	132	24	11	4	51	.261	32	73	24	251	5	5	.981
— Pittsburgh (N.L.)	OF	9	18	2	6	1	0	1	1	.333	1	7	1	12	1	0	1.000
2001— Nashville (PCL)	OF	95	398	53	121	18	10	3	42	.304	24	37	21	216	12	7	.970
— Pittsburgh (N.L.)	OF	37	125	8	28	4	1	1	4	.224	4	25	3	92	5	2	.980
Major League totals (2 years)		46	143	10	34	5	1	2	5	.238	5	32	4	104	6	2	.982

REDMOND, MIKE   C   MARLINS

PERSONAL: Born May 5, 1971, in Seattle. ... 6-1/185. ... Bats right, throws right. ... Full name: Michael Patrick Redmond.
HIGH SCHOOL: Gonzaga Prep (Spokane, Wash.).
COLLEGE: Gonzaga.
TRANSACTIONS/CAREER NOTES: Signed as a non-drafted free agent by Florida Marlins organization (August 18, 1992). ... On Florida disabled list (August 24-September 8, 1998).
STATISTICAL NOTES: Led Eastern League catchers with 95 assists in 1995. ... Led Eastern League catchers with 906 total chances in 1996.

Year Team (League)	Pos.	G	AB	R	H	2B	3B	HR	RBI	Avg.	BB	SO	SB	PO	A	E	Avg.
1993— Kane County (Midw.)	C	43	100	10	20	2	0	0	10	.200	6	17	2	213	26	1	.996
1994— Kane County (Midw.)	C	92	306	39	83	10	0	1	24	.271	26	31	3	638	78	6	.992
— Brevard County (FSL)	C	12	42	4	11	4	0	0	2	.262	3	4	0	60	10	0	1.000
1995— Portland (East.)	C-3B	105	333	37	85	11	1	3	39	.255	22	27	2	657	†95	6	.992

Year	Team (League)	Pos.	G	AB	R	H	2B	3B	HR	RBI	Avg.	BB	SO	SB	PO	A	E	Avg.
1996—Portland (East.)		C	120	394	43	113	22	0	4	44	.287	26	45	3	*814	88	4	*.996
1997—Charlotte (I.L.)		C	22	61	8	13	5	1	1	2	.213	1	10	0	119	13	2	.985
—GC Marlins (GCL)		DH	16	55	7	19	3	0	0	5	.345	9	5	2	...	...	...	...
—Brevard County (FSL).		1B	5	17	2	0	0	0	0	0	.000	2	2	0	8	0	0	1.000
1998—Portland (East.)		C	8	28	7	9	4	0	1	7	.321	2	2	0	53	6	1	.983
—Charlotte (I.L.)		C	18	58	4	14	2	0	2	7	.241	0	3	0	101	20	0	1.000
—Florida (N.L.)		C	37	118	10	39	9	0	2	12	.331	5	16	0	216	25	2	.992
1999—Florida (N.L.)		C	84	242	22	73	9	0	1	27	.302	26	34	0	444	45	4	.992
2000—Florida (N.L.)		C	87	210	17	53	8	1	0	15	.252	13	19	0	446	40	2	.996
2001—Florida (N.L.)		C	48	141	19	44	4	0	4	14	.312	13	13	0	291	23	2	.994
Major League totals (4 years)			256	711	68	209	30	1	7	68	.294	57	82	0	1397	133	10	.994

REED, RICK — P — TWINS

R

PERSONAL: Born August 16, 1965, in Huntington, W.Va. ... 6-1/195. ... Throws right, bats right. ... Full name: Richard Allen Reed.
HIGH SCHOOL: Huntington (W.Va.).
COLLEGE: Marshall.
TRANSACTIONS/CAREER NOTES: Selected by Pittsburgh Pirates organization in 26th round of free-agent draft (June 2, 1986). ... On Buffalo disabled list (May 2-13, 1991). ... Granted free agency (April 3, 1992). ... Signed by Kansas City Royals organization (April 4, 1992). ... Granted free agency (August 5, 1993). ... Signed by Texas Rangers organization (August 11, 1993). ... Claimed on waivers by Cincinnati Reds (May 13, 1994). ... On Indianapolis disabled list (May 29-June 9, 1995). ... Granted free agency (October 16, 1995). ... Signed by New York Mets organization (November 7, 1995). ... On New York disabled list (April 12-May 3 and August 9-September 4, 1999); included rehabilitation assignments to Norfolk (August 27-31) and Binghamton (September 1-4). ... On disabled list (June 30-July 17, 2000). ... Granted free agency (November 8, 2000). ... Re-signed by Mets (December 6, 2000). ... Traded by Mets to Minnesota Twins for OF Matt Lawton (July 30, 2001).
HONORS: Named American Association Most Valuable Pitcher (1991).
MISCELLANEOUS: Appeared in one game as outfielder with no chances (1999).

Year	League	W	L	Pct.	ERA	G	GS	CG	ShO	Sv.	IP	H	R	ER	BB	SO
1986—Gulf Coast Pirates (GCL)		0	0	.000	3.75	8	3	0	0	0	24	20	12	10	6	15
—Macon (S.Atl.)		0	0	...	2.84	1	1	0	0	0	6 1/3	5	3	2	2	1
1987—Macon (S.Atl.)		8	4	.667	2.50	46	0	0	0	7	93 2/3	80	38	26	29	92
1988—Salem (Caro.)		6	2	.750	2.74	15	8	4	1	0	72 1/3	56	28	22	17	73
—Harrisburg (East.)		1	0	1.000	1.13	2	2	0	0	0	16	11	2	2	2	17
—Buffalo (A.A.)		5	2	.714	1.64	10	9	3	2	0	77	62	15	14	12	50
—Pittsburgh (N.L.)		1	0	1.000	3.00	2	2	0	0	0	12	10	4	4	2	6
1989—Buffalo (A.A.)		9	8	.529	3.72	20	20	3	0	0	125 2/3	130	58	52	28	75
—Pittsburgh (N.L.)		1	4	.200	5.60	15	7	0	0	0	54 2/3	62	35	34	11	34
1990—Buffalo (A.A.)		7	4	.636	3.46	15	15	2	2	0	91	82	37	35	21	63
—Pittsburgh (N.L.)		2	3	.400	4.36	13	8	1	1	1	53 2/3	62	32	26	12	27
1991—Buffalo (A.A.)		*14	4	*.778	*2.15	25	25	•5	2	0	167 2/3	151	45	40	26	102
—Pittsburgh (N.L.)		0	0	...	10.38	1	1	0	0	0	4 1/3	8	6	5	1	2
1992—Omaha (A.A.)■		5	4	.556	4.35	11	10	3	0	1	62	67	33	30	12	35
—Kansas City (A.L.)		3	7	.300	3.68	19	18	1	1	0	100 1/3	105	47	41	20	49
1993—Omaha (A.A.)		11	4	.733	3.09	19	19	3	*2	0	128 1/3	116	48	44	14	58
—Kansas City (A.L.)		0	0	...	9.82	1	0	0	0	0	3 2/3	6	4	4	1	3
—Oklahoma City (A.A.)■		1	3	.250	4.19	5	5	1	0	0	34 1/3	43	20	16	2	21
—Texas (A.L.)		1	0	1.000	2.25	2	0	0	0	0	4	6	1	1	1	2
1994—Oklahoma City (A.A.)		1	1	.500	3.86	2	2	0	0	0	11 2/3	10	5	5	0	8
—Texas (A.L.)		1	1	.500	5.94	4	3	0	0	0	16 2/3	17	13	11	7	12
—Indianapolis (A.A.)■		9	5	.643	4.68	21	21	3	1	0	140 1/3	162	80	73	19	79
1995—Indianapolis (A.A.)		11	4	.733	3.33	22	21	3	1	0	135	127	60	50	26	92
—Cincinnati (N.L.)		0	0	...	5.82	4	3	0	0	0	17	18	12	11	3	10
1996—Norfolk (I.L.)■		8	10	.444	3.16	28	28	1	0	0	182	164	72	64	33	128
1997—New York (N.L.)		13	9	.591	2.89	33	31	2	0	0	208 1/3	186	76	67	31	113
1998—New York (N.L.)		16	11	.593	3.48	31	31	2	1	0	212 1/3	208	84	82	29	153
1999—New York (N.L.)		11	5	.688	4.58	26	26	1	1	0	149 1/3	163	77	76	47	104
—Norfolk (I.L.)		0	1	.000	27.00	1	1	0	0	0	3	10	9	9	2	2
—Binghamton (East.)		0	0	...	1.80	1	1	0	0	0	5	1	1	1	1	5
2000—New York (N.L.)		11	5	.688	4.11	30	30	0	0	0	184	192	90	84	34	121
2001—New York (N.L.)		8	6	.571	3.48	20	20	3	1	0	134 2/3	119	53	52	17	99
—Minnesota (A.L.)■		4	6	.400	5.19	12	12	0	0	0	67 2/3	92	45	39	14	43
A.L. totals (4 years)		9	14	.391	4.49	38	33	1	1	0	192 1/3	226	110	96	43	109
N.L. totals (10 years)		63	43	.594	3.85	175	159	9	4	1	1030 1/3	1028	469	441	187	669
Major League totals (13 years)		72	57	.558	3.95	213	192	10	5	1	1222 2/3	1254	579	537	230	778

DIVISION SERIES RECORD

Year	League	W	L	Pct.	ERA	G	GS	CG	ShO	Sv.	IP	H	R	ER	BB	SO
1999—New York (N.L.)		1	0	1.000	3.00	1	1	0	0	0	6	4	2	2	3	2
2000—New York (N.L.)		0	0	...	3.00	1	1	0	0	0	6	7	2	2	2	6
Division series totals (2 years)		1	0	1.000	3.00	2	2	0	0	0	12	11	4	4	5	8

CHAMPIONSHIP SERIES RECORD

Year	League	W	L	Pct.	ERA	G	GS	CG	ShO	Sv.	IP	H	R	ER	BB	SO
1999—New York (N.L.)		0	0	...	2.57	1	1	0	0	0	7	3	2	2	0	5
2000—New York (N.L.)		0	1	.000	10.80	1	1	0	0	0	3 1/3	8	5	4	1	4
Champ. series totals (2 years)		0	1	.000	5.23	2	2	0	0	0	10 1/3	11	7	6	1	9

WORLD SERIES RECORD

Year	League	W	L	Pct.	ERA	G	GS	CG	ShO	Sv.	IP	H	R	ER	BB	SO
2000—New York (N.L.)		0	0	...	3.00	1	0	0	0	0	6	6	2	2	1	8

ALL-STAR GAME RECORD

Year	League	W	L	Pct.	ERA	GS	CG	ShO	Sv.	IP	H	R	ER	BB	SO
1998—National						Did not play.									
2001—National						Selected, did not play.									

REED, STEVE — P — PADRES

PERSONAL: Born March 11, 1966, in Los Angeles. ... 6-2/212. ... Throws right, bats right. ... Full name: Steven Vincent Reed.
HIGH SCHOOL: Chatsworth (Calif.).
COLLEGE: Lewis-Clark State College (Idaho).
TRANSACTIONS/CAREER NOTES: Signed as non-drafted free agent by San Francisco Giants organization (June 24, 1988). ... On disabled list (July 17-August 13, 1990). ... Selected by Colorado Rockies in third round (60th pick overall) of expansion draft (November 17, 1992). ... Granted free agency (December 21, 1997). ... Signed by Giants (December 24, 1997). ... Traded by Giants with OF Jacob Cruz to Cleveland Indians for P Jose Mesa, IF Shawon Dunston and P Alvin Morman (July 23, 1998). ... Traded by Indians with P Steve Karsay to Atlanta Braves for P John Rocker and 3B Troy Cameron (June 22, 2001). ... Granted free agency (November 5, 2001). ... Signed by San Diego Padres organization (January 23, 2002).
MISCELLANEOUS: Holds Colorado Rockies all-time record for lowest earned-run average (3.68).

Year	League	W	L	Pct.	ERA	G	GS	CG	ShO	Sv.	IP	H	R	ER	BB	SO
1988—	Pocatello (Pio.)	4	1	.800	2.54	31	0	0	0	*13	46	42	20	13	8	49
1989—	Clinton (Midw.)	5	3	.625	1.05	60	0	0	0	26	94 2/3	54	16	11	38	104
—	San Jose (Calif.)	0	0	...	0.00	2	0	0	0	0	2	0	0	0	1	3
1990—	Shreveport (Texas)	3	1	.750	1.64	45	1	0	0	8	60 1/3	53	20	11	20	59
1991—	Shreveport (Texas)	2	0	1.000	0.83	15	0	0	0	7	21 2/3	17	2	2	3	26
—	Phoenix (PCL)	2	3	.400	4.31	41	0	0	0	6	56 1/3	62	33	27	12	46
1992—	Shreveport (Texas)	1	0	1.000	0.62	27	0	0	0	23	29	18	3	2	0	33
—	Phoenix (PCL)	0	1	.000	3.48	29	0	0	0	20	31	27	13	12	10	30
—	San Francisco (N.L.)	1	0	1.000	2.30	18	0	0	0	0	15 2/3	13	5	4	3	11
1993—	Colorado (N.L.)■	9	5	.643	4.48	64	0	0	0	3	84 1/3	80	47	42	30	51
—	Colorado Springs (PCL)	0	0	...	0.00	11	0	0	0	7	12 1/3	8	1	0	3	10
1994—	Colorado (N.L.)	3	2	.600	3.94	*61	0	0	0	3	64	79	33	28	26	51
1995—	Colorado (N.L.)	5	2	.714	2.14	71	0	0	0	3	84	61	24	20	21	79
1996—	Colorado (N.L.)	4	3	.571	3.96	70	0	0	0	0	75	66	38	33	19	51
1997—	Colorado (N.L.)	4	6	.400	4.04	63	0	0	0	6	62 1/3	49	28	28	27	43
1998—	San Francisco (N.L.)■	2	1	.667	1.48	50	0	0	0	1	54 2/3	30	10	9	19	50
—	Cleveland (A.L.)■	2	2	.500	6.66	20	0	0	0	0	25 2/3	26	19	19	8	23
1999—	Cleveland (A.L.)	3	2	.600	4.23	63	0	0	0	0	61 2/3	69	33	29	20	44
2000—	Cleveland (A.L.)	2	0	1.000	4.34	57	0	0	0	0	56	58	30	27	21	39
2001—	Cleveland (A.L.)	1	1	.500	3.62	31	0	0	0	0	27 1/3	22	11	11	10	21
—	Atlanta (N.L.)■	2	2	.500	3.48	39	0	0	0	1	31	30	14	12	13	25
A.L. totals (4 years)		8	5	.615	4.54	171	0	0	0	0	170 2/3	175	93	86	59	127
N.L. totals (8 years)		30	21	.588	3.36	436	0	0	0	17	471	408	199	176	158	361
Major League totals (10 years)		38	26	.594	3.67	607	0	0	0	17	641 2/3	583	292	262	217	488

DIVISION SERIES RECORD

Year	League	W	L	Pct.	ERA	G	GS	CG	ShO	Sv.	IP	H	R	ER	BB	SO
1995—	Colorado (N.L.)	0	0	...	0.00	3	0	0	0	0	2 2/3	2	0	0	1	3
1998—	Cleveland (A.L.)	1	0	1.000	40.50	2	0	0	0	0	2/3	1	3	3	1	1
1999—	Cleveland (A.L.)	0	0	...	30.86	2	0	0	0	0	2 1/3	9	8	8	1	1
2001—	Atlanta (N.L.)	0	0	...	0.00	1	0	0	0	0	1/3	0	0	0	0	0
Division series totals (4 years)		1	0	1.000	16.50	8	0	0	0	0	6	12	11	11	3	5

CHAMPIONSHIP SERIES RECORD

Year	League	W	L	Pct.	ERA	G	GS	CG	ShO	Sv.	IP	H	R	ER	BB	SO
1998—	Cleveland (A.L.)	0	0	...	0.00	3	0	0	0	0	1 2/3	0	0	0	1	0

REESE, POKEY — 2B

PERSONAL: Born June 10, 1973, in Columbia, S.C. ... 5-11/180. ... Bats right, throws right. ... Full name: Calvin Reese Jr.
HIGH SCHOOL: Lower Richland (Hopkins, S.C.).
TRANSACTIONS/CAREER NOTES: Selected by Cincinnati Reds organization in first round (20th pick overall) of free-agent draft (June 3, 1991). ... On disabled list (June 23-July 25, 1995; September 17, 1996-remainder of season; and July 31, 1998-remainder of season). ... Traded by Reds with P Dennys Reyes to Colorado Rockies for P Gabe White and P Luke Hudson (December 18, 2001). ... Traded by Rockies to Boston Red Sox for C Scott Hatteberg (December 19, 2001). ... Granted free agency (December 21, 2001).
RECORDS: Shares N.L. record for most errors by shortstop in opening game of season (nine-inning game) since 1900—4 (March 31, 1998).
HONORS: Won N.L. Gold Glove at second base (1999 and 2000).

Year	Team (League)	Pos.	G	AB	R	H	2B	3B	HR	RBI	Avg.	BB	SO	SB	PO	A	E	Avg.
1991—	Princeton (Appl.)	SS	62	231	30	55	8	3	3	27	.238	23	44	10	93	146	*31	.885
1992—	Charl., W.Va. (S.Atl.)	SS	106	380	50	102	19	3	6	53	.268	24	75	19	181	287	34	.932
1993—	Chattanooga (Sou.)	SS	102	345	35	73	17	4	3	37	.212	23	77	8	181	300	25	.951
1994—	Chattanooga (Sou.)	SS	134	484	77	130	23	4	12	49	.269	43	75	21	*221	362	38	.939
1995—	Indianapolis (A.A.)	SS	89	343	51	82	21	1	10	46	.239	36	81	8	131	258	27	.935
1996—	Indianapolis (A.A.)	SS-3B	79	280	26	65	16	0	1	23	.232	21	46	5	131	239	22	.944
1997—	Cincinnati (N.L.)	SS-2B-3B	128	397	48	87	15	0	4	26	.219	31	82	25	182	284	15	.969
—	Indianapolis (A.A.)	SS-2B	17	72	12	17	2	0	4	11	.236	9	12	4	43	42	3	.966
1998—	Cincinnati (N.L.)	3B-SS-2B	59	133	20	34	2	2	1	16	.256	14	28	3	50	78	8	.941
1999—	Cincinnati (N.L.)	2B-SS	149	585	85	167	37	5	10	52	.285	35	81	38	340	425	7	.991
2000—	Cincinnati (N.L.)	2B	135	518	76	132	20	6	12	46	.255	45	86	29	289	393	14	.980
2001—	Cincinnati (N.L.)	SS-2B	133	428	50	96	20	2	9	40	.224	34	82	25	217	366	15	.975
Major League totals (5 years)			604	2061	279	516	94	15	36	180	.250	159	359	120	1078	1546	59	.978

REICHERT, DAN — P — ROYALS

PERSONAL: Born July 12, 1976, in Monterey, Calif. ... 6-3/175. ... Throws right, bats right. ... Full name: Daniel Robert Reichert.
HIGH SCHOOL: Turlock (Calif.).
COLLEGE: Pacific.

TRANSACTIONS/CAREER NOTES: Selected by Kansas City Royals organization in first round (seventh pick overall) of free-agent draft (June 3, 1997). ... On Kansas City disabled list (August 25, 1999-remainder of season).
STATISTICAL NOTES: Led A.L. in wild pitches with 18 in 2000.

Year League	W	L	Pct.	ERA	G	GS	CG	ShO	Sv.	IP	H	R	ER	BB	SO
1997— Spokane (N'West)	3	4	.429	2.84	9	9	0	0	0	38	40	25	12	16	39
1998— Wichita (Texas)	1	4	.200	9.75	8	8	0	0	0	36	52	40	39	29	24
— Lansing (Midw.)	1	1	.500	3.28	13	6	0	0	0	$35^2/_3$	25	16	13	20	35
— Wilmington (Caro.)....................	2	0	1.000	3.21	2	2	0	0	0	14	13	5	5	4	10
— Omaha (PCL)....................	1	1	.500	4.67	3	3	0	0	0	$17^1/_3$	14	10	9	2	11
1999— Omaha (PCL)..................	9	2	.818	3.71	17	17	1	0	0	$111^2/_3$	92	51	46	50	123
— Kansas City (A.L.)	2	2	.500	9.08	8	8	0	0	0	$36^2/_3$	48	38	37	32	20
2000— Kansas City (A.L.)	8	10	.444	4.70	44	18	1	1	2	$153^1/_3$	157	92	80	91	94
2001— Kansas City (A.L.)	8	8	.500	5.63	27	19	0	0	0	123	131	83	77	67	77
— Omaha (PCL)....................	1	5	.167	8.27	10	5	1	0	0	$32^2/_3$	45	30	30	16	30
Major League totals (3 years)	**18**	**20**	**.474**	**5.58**	**79**	**45**	**1**	**1**	**2**	**313**	**336**	**213**	**194**	**190**	**191**

REITH, BRIAN — P — REDS

PERSONAL: Born February 28, 1978, in Fort Wayne, Ind. ... 6-5/190. ... Throws right, bats right. ... Full name: Brian Eric Reith.
HIGH SCHOOL: Concordia Lutheran (Fort Wayne, Ind.).
TRANSACTIONS/CAREER NOTES: Selected by New York Yankees organization in sixth round of free-agent draft (June 4, 1996). ... Traded by Yankees with 3B Drew Henson, OF Jackson Melian and P Ed Yarnall to Cincinnati Reds for P Denny Neagle and OF Mike Frank (July 12, 2000). ... On Louisville disabled list (June 8-16, 2001).

Year League	W	L	Pct.	ERA	G	GS	CG	ShO	Sv.	IP	H	R	ER	BB	SO
1996— Gulf Coast Yankees (GCL)..	2	3	.400	4.13	10	4	0	0	0	$32^2/_3$	31	16	15	16	21
1997— Gulf Coast Yankees (GCL)..	4	2	.667	2.86	12	11	1	0	0	63	70	28	20	14	40
1998— Greensboro (S.Atl.)	6	7	.462	2.28	20	20	3	1	0	$118^1/_3$	86	42	30	32	116
1999— Tampa (FSL)	9	9	.500	4.70	26	23	0	0	0	$139^2/_3$	174	87	73	35	101
2000— Tampa (FSL)	9	4	.692	2.18	18	18	1	1	0	$119^2/_3$	101	39	29	33	100
— Dayton (Midw.)■	2	1	.667	2.88	5	5	0	0	0	$34^1/_3$	33	12	11	8	30
— Chattanooga (Sou.)	1	3	.250	3.90	5	5	0	0	0	30	31	14	13	11	29
2001— Chattanooga (Sou.)	6	4	.600	3.97	18	18	1	1	0	$104^1/_3$	103	63	46	42	89
— Cincinnati (N.L.)	0	7	.000	7.81	9	8	0	0	0	$40^1/_3$	56	37	35	16	22
— Louisville (I.L.)	0	0	...	3.60	1	1	0	0	0	5	7	2	2	1	6
Major League totals (1 year)	**0**	**7**	**.000**	**7.81**	**9**	**8**	**0**	**0**	**0**	**$40^1/_3$**	**56**	**37**	**35**	**16**	**22**

REITSMA, CHRIS — P — REDS

PERSONAL: Born December 31, 1977, in Minneapolis. ... 6-5/214. ... Throws right, bats right. ... Full name: Christopher Michael Reitsma.
HIGH SCHOOL: Calgary (Alta.) Christian.
TRANSACTIONS/CAREER NOTES: Selected by Boston Red Sox organization as "sandwich pick" between first and second round of free-agent draft (June 4, 1996); pick received as compensation for Toronto Blue Jays signing P Erik Hanson. ... On disabled list (June 5-September 8, 1997). ... On disabled list (April 8-May 3, 1999). ... Selected by Tampa Bay Devil Rays from Red Sox organization in Rule 5 major league draft (December 13, 1999). ... Returned to Red Sox (March 28, 2000). ... On Trenton disabled list (July 14-22, 2000). ... Traded by Red Sox with P John Curtice to Cincinnati Reds for OF Dante Bichette (August 31, 2000).
MISCELLANEOUS: Appeared in two games as pinch runner (2001).

Year League	W	L	Pct.	ERA	G	GS	CG	ShO	Sv.	IP	H	R	ER	BB	SO
1996— Gulf Coast Red Sox (GCL)..	3	1	.750	1.35	7	6	0	0	0	$26^2/_3$	24	7	4	1	32
1997— Michigan (Midw.)	4	1	.800	2.90	9	9	0	0	0	$49^2/_3$	57	23	16	13	41
1998— Sarasota (FSL)	0	0	...	2.84	8	8	0	0	0	$12^2/_3$	12	6	4	5	9
1999— Sarasota (FSL)	4	10	.286	5.61	19	19	0	0	0	$96^1/_3$	116	71	60	31	79
2000— Sarasota (FSL)	3	4	.429	3.66	11	11	0	0	0	64	57	29	26	17	47
— Trenton (East.)	7	2	.778	2.58	14	14	1	0	0	$90^1/_3$	78	28	26	21	58
2001— Cincinnati (N.L.)■	7	15	.318	5.29	36	29	0	0	0	182	209	121	107	49	96
Major League totals (1 year)	**7**	**15**	**.318**	**5.29**	**36**	**29**	**0**	**0**	**0**	**182**	**209**	**121**	**107**	**49**	**96**

REKAR, BRYAN — P

PERSONAL: Born June 3, 1972, in Oak Lawn, Ill. ... 6-3/220. ... Throws right, bats right. ... Full name: Bryan Robert Rekar. ... Cousin of Pete Bercich, linebacker with Minnesota Vikings (1994-2000); and nephew of Bob Bercich, defensive back with Dallas Cowboys (1960 and 1961).
HIGH SCHOOL: Providence Catholic (New Lenox, Ill.).
COLLEGE: Bradley.
TRANSACTIONS/CAREER NOTES: Selected by Colorado Rockies organization in second round of free-agent draft (June 3, 1993). ... Selected by Tampa Bay Devil Rays in second round (38th pick overall) of expansion draft (November 18, 1997). ... On Tampa Bay disabled list (March 19-July 6, 1998); included rehabilitation assignments to St. Petersburg (May 16-25 and June 25-July 4) and Durham (May 26-June 1 and July 4-6). ... On Tampa Bay disabled list (March 31-April 30, 2000); included rehabilitation assignment to Durham (April 9-30). ... On Tampa Bay disabled list (July 20-August 26, 2001); included rehabilitation assignment to Orlando (August 9-26). ... Released by Devil Rays (December 13, 2001).
MISCELLANEOUS: Holds Tampa Bay Devil Rays all-time record for most innings pitched ($495^1/_3$).

Year League	W	L	Pct.	ERA	G	GS	CG	ShO	Sv.	IP	H	R	ER	BB	SO
1993— Bend (N'West)....................	3	5	.375	4.08	13	13	1	0	0	75	81	36	34	18	59
1994— Central Valley (Calif.)..........	6	6	.500	3.48	22	19	0	0	0	$111^1/_3$	120	52	43	31	91
1995— New Haven (East.).............	6	3	.667	2.13	12	12	1	1	0	$80^1/_3$	65	28	19	16	80
— Colorado Springs (PCL)	4	2	.667	1.49	7	7	2	1	0	$48^1/_3$	29	10	8	13	39
— Colorado (N.L.)	4	6	.400	4.98	15	14	1	0	0	85	95	51	47	24	60
1996— Colorado Springs (PCL)	8	8	.500	4.46	19	19	0	0	0	123	138	68	61	36	75
— Colorado (N.L.)	2	4	.333	8.95	14	11	0	0	0	$58^1/_3$	87	61	58	26	25
1997— Colorado Springs (PCL)	10	9	.526	5.46	28	25	0	0	0	145	169	96	88	39	116
— Colorado (N.L.)	1	0	1.000	5.79	2	2	0	0	0	$9^1/_3$	11	7	6	6	4

Year	League	W	L	Pct.	ERA	G	GS	CG	ShO	Sv.	IP	H	R	ER	BB	SO
1998—St. Petersburg (FSL)■		0	0	...	0.69	4	4	0	0	0	13	6	2	1	2	15
—Durham (I.L.)		0	1	.000	3.27	3	3	0	0	0	11	10	4	4	2	9
—Tampa Bay (A.L.)...............		2	8	.200	4.98	16	15	1	0	0	86²/₃	95	56	48	21	55
1999—Durham (I.L.)...............		4	1	.800	3.86	6	5	0	0	0	35	29	15	15	8	26
—Tampa Bay (A.L.)...............		6	6	.500	5.80	27	12	0	0	0	94²/₃	121	68	61	41	55
2000—Durham (I.L.)		3	0	1.000	2.05	4	4	0	0	0	22	16	5	5	4	18
—Tampa Bay (A.L.)...............		7	10	.412	4.41	30	27	2	0	0	173¹/₃	200	92	85	39	95
2001—Tampa Bay (A.L.)...........		3	13	.188	5.89	25	25	0	0	0	140²/₃	167	104	92	45	87
—Orlando (Sou.)		1	0	1.000	2.25	3	3	0	0	0	12	8	3	3	1	11
A.L. totals (4 years)		18	37	.327	5.20	98	79	3	0	0	495¹/₃	583	320	286	146	292
N.L. totals (3 years)		7	10	.412	6.54	31	27	1	0	0	152²/₃	193	119	111	56	89
Major League totals (7 years).......		25	47	.347	5.51	129	106	4	0	0	648	776	439	397	202	381

R — RELAFORD, DESI — SS — GIANTS

PERSONAL: Born September 16, 1973, in Valdosta, Ga. ... 5-9/174. ... Bats both, throws right. ... Full name: Desmond Lamont Relaford.

HIGH SCHOOL: Sandalwood (Jacksonville).

TRANSACTIONS/CAREER NOTES: Selected by Seattle Mariners organization in fourth round of free-agent draft (June 3, 1991). ... Traded by Mariners to Philadelphia Phillies for P Terry Mulholland (July 31, 1996). ... On Philadelphia disabled list (June 17-September 13, 1999); included rehabilitation assignment to Clearwater (September 4-13). ... Traded by Phillies to San Diego Padres for a player to be named later (August 4, 2000); Phillies acquired IF David Newhan to complete deal (August 7, 2000). ... Claimed on waivers by New York Mets (October 12, 2000). ... Traded by Mets with OF Tsuyoshi Shinjo to San Francisco Giants for P Shawn Estes (December 16, 2001).

STATISTICAL NOTES: Tied for Southern League lead in errors by shortstops with 35 in 1993. ... Led International League shortstops with 587 total chances and 81 double plays in 1997. ... Led N.L. shortstops with 31 errors in 2000.

							BATTING								FIELDING		
Year	Team (League)	Pos.	G	AB	R	H	2B	3B	HR	RBI	Avg.	BB	SO	SB	PO	A	E	Avg.
1991—Ariz. Mariners (Ariz.)..		SS-2B	46	163	36	44	7	3	0	18	.270	22	24	17	58	126	24	.885
1992—Peninsula (Caro.)		SS	130	445	53	96	18	1	3	34	.216	39	88	27	167	*382	*52	.913
1993—Jacksonville (Sou.)......		SS-2B-3B	133	472	49	115	16	4	8	47	.244	50	103	16	157	386	‡38	.935
1994—Jacksonville (Sou.)......		SS	37	143	24	29	7	3	3	11	.203	22	28	10	71	119	4	.979
—Riverside (Calif.)........		SS	99	374	95	116	27	5	5	59	.310	78	78	27	125	296	36	.921
1995—Port City (Sou.).........		SS-2B-DH	90	352	51	101	11	2	7	27	.287	41	58	25	134	276	31	.930
—Tacoma (PCL)		2B-SS	30	113	20	27	5	1	2	7	.239	13	24	6	52	93	6	.960
1996—Tacoma (PCL)		2B-SS-DH	93	317	27	65	12	0	4	32	.205	23	58	10	174	306	20	.960
—Scranton/W.B. (I.L.)■		SS	21	85	12	20	4	1	1	11	.235	8	19	7	25	65	6	.938
—Philadelphia (N.L.)......		SS-2B	15	40	2	7	2	0	0	1	.175	3	9	1	21	26	2	.959
1997—Scranton/W.B. (I.L.) ...		SS	131	517	82	138	34	4	9	53	.267	43	77	29	180	*373	34	.942
—Philadelphia (N.L.)......		SS	15	38	3	7	1	2	0	6	.184	5	6	3	12	31	1	.977
1998—Philadelphia (N.L.)......		SS	142	494	45	121	25	3	5	41	.245	33	87	9	189	380	24	.960
1999—Philadelphia (N.L.)......		SS	65	211	31	51	11	2	1	26	.242	19	34	4	97	182	14	.952
—Clearwater (FSL)........		SS	2	7	1	2	0	0	0	1	.286	1	1	0	3	1	1	.800
2000—Philadelphia (N.L.)......		SS	83	253	29	56	12	3	3	30	.221	48	45	5	116	202	24	.930
—San Diego (N.L.)■......		SS	45	157	26	32	2	0	2	16	.204	27	26	8	73	120	§7	.965
2001—New York (N.L.)■ 2B-SS-3B-P			120	301	43	91	27	0	8	36	.302	27	65	13	115	174	11	.963
Major League totals (6 years)			485	1494	179	365	80	10	19	156	.244	162	272	43	623	1115	83	.954

RECORD AS PITCHER

Year	League	W	L	Pct.	ERA	G	GS	CG	ShO	Sv.	IP	H	R	ER	BB	SO
2001—New York (N.L.)................		0	0	...	0.00	1	0	0	0	0	1	0	0	0	0	1

REMLINGER, MIKE — P — BRAVES

PERSONAL: Born March 23, 1966, in Middletown, N.Y. ... 6-1/210. ... Throws left, bats left. ... Full name: Michael John Remlinger. ... Name pronounced REM-lynn-jer.

HIGH SCHOOL: Carver (Plymouth, Mass.).

COLLEGE: Dartmouth.

TRANSACTIONS/CAREER NOTES: Selected by San Francisco Giants organization in first round (16th pick overall) of free-agent draft (June 2, 1987). ... Traded by Giants with OF Kevin Mitchell to Seattle Mariners for P Bill Swift, P Mike Jackson and P Dave Burba (December 11, 1991). ... On Jacksonville disabled list (July 30, 1992-remainder of season). ... Granted free agency (October 15, 1993). ... Signed by New York Mets organization (November 22, 1993). ... Traded by Mets to Cincinnati Reds for OF Cobi Cradle (May 11, 1995). ... Granted free agency (October 6, 1995). ... Re-signed by Reds (October 22, 1995). ... Traded by Reds to Kansas City Royals as part of a three-team deal in which Reds sent SS Luis Ordaz to St. Louis Cardinals for OF Andre King. Royals then sent OF Miguel Mejia to Cardinals to complete deal (December 4, 1995). ... Claimed on waivers by Reds (April 4, 1996). ... Traded by Reds with 2B Bret Boone to Atlanta Braves for P Denny Neagle, OF Michael Tucker and P Rob Bell (November 10, 1998). ... On disabled list (April 3-18, 1999; and June 23-July 13, 2000).

RECORDS: Shares major league record for pitching shutout in first major league game (June 15, 1991).

STATISTICAL NOTES: Led American Association with 18 wild pitches in 1996. ... Led N.L. with 12 wild pitches in 1997.

MISCELLANEOUS: Appeared in two games as pinch runner (1997).

Year	League	W	L	Pct.	ERA	G	GS	CG	ShO	Sv.	IP	H	R	ER	BB	SO
1987—Everett (N'West)................		0	0	...	3.60	2	1	0	0	0	5	1	2	2	5	11
—Clinton (Midw.)		2	1	.667	3.30	6	5	0	0	0	30	21	12	11	14	43
—Shreveport (Texas)...........		4	2	.667	2.36	6	6	0	0	0	34¹/₃	14	11	9	22	51
1988—Shreveport (Texas)...........		1	0	1.000	0.69	3	3	0	0	0	13	7	4	1	4	18
1989—Shreveport (Texas)...........		4	6	.400	2.98	16	16	0	0	0	90²/₃	68	43	30	73	92
—Phoenix (PCL)..................		1	6	.143	9.21	11	10	0	0	0	43	51	47	44	52	28
1990—Shreveport (Texas)...........		9	11	.450	3.90	25	25	2	1	0	147²/₃	149	82	64	72	75
1991—Phoenix (PCL).................		5	5	.500	6.38	19	19	1	1	0	108²/₃	134	86	77	59	68
—San Francisco (N.L.)		2	1	.667	4.37	8	6	1	1	0	35	36	17	17	20	19

Year League	W	L	Pct.	ERA	G	GS	CG	ShO	Sv.	IP	H	R	ER	BB	SO
1992—Calgary (PCL)■	1	7	.125	6.65	21	11	0	0	0	70 1/3	97	65	52	48	24
—Jacksonville (Sou.)	1	1	.500	3.46	5	5	0	0	0	26	25	15	10	11	21
1993—Calgary (PCL)	4	3	.571	5.53	19	18	0	0	0	84 2/3	100	57	52	52	51
—Jacksonville (Sou.)	1	3	.250	6.58	7	7	0	0	0	39 2/3	40	30	29	19	23
1994—Norfolk (I.L.)■	2	4	.333	3.14	12	9	0	0	0	63	57	29	22	25	45
—New York (N.L.)	1	5	.167	4.61	10	9	0	0	0	54 2/3	55	30	28	35	33
1995—New York (N.L.)	0	1	.000	6.35	5	0	0	0	0	5 2/3	7	5	4	2	6
—Cincinnati (N.L.)■	0	0	...	9.00	2	0	0	0	0	1	2	1	1	3	1
—Indianapolis (A.A.)	5	3	.625	4.05	41	1	0	0	0	46 2/3	40	24	21	32	58
1996—Indianapolis (A.A.)	4	3	.571	2.52	28	13	0	0	0	89 1/3	64	29	25	44	97
—Cincinnati (N.L.)	0	1	.000	5.60	19	4	0	0	0	27 1/3	24	17	17	19	19
1997—Cincinnati (N.L.)	8	8	.500	4.14	69	12	2	0	2	124	100	61	57	60	145
1998—Cincinnati (N.L.)	8	15	.348	4.82	35	28	1	1	0	164 1/3	164	96	88	87	144
1999—Atlanta (N.L.)■	10	1	.909	2.37	73	0	0	0	1	83 2/3	66	24	22	35	81
2000—Atlanta (N.L.)	5	3	.625	3.47	71	0	0	0	12	72 2/3	55	29	28	37	72
2001—Atlanta (N.L.)	3	3	.500	2.76	74	0	0	0	1	75	67	25	23	23	93
Major League totals (9 years)	37	38	.493	3.99	366	59	4	2	16	643 1/3	576	305	285	321	613

DIVISION SERIES RECORD

Year League	W	L	Pct.	ERA	G	GS	CG	ShO	Sv.	IP	H	R	ER	BB	SO
1999—Atlanta (N.L.)	0	0	...	9.82	2	0	0	0	0	3 2/3	4	4	4	3	4
2000—Atlanta (N.L.)	0	0	...	2.70	3	0	0	0	0	3 1/3	6	1	1	0	3
2001—Atlanta (N.L.)	0	0	...	0.00	1	0	0	0	0	1/3	0	0	0	0	0
Division series totals (3 years)	0	0	...	6.14	6	0	0	0	0	7 1/3	10	5	5	3	7

CHAMPIONSHIP SERIES RECORD

Year League	W	L	Pct.	ERA	G	GS	CG	ShO	Sv.	IP	H	R	ER	BB	SO
1999—Atlanta (N.L.)	0	1	.000	3.18	5	0	0	0	0	5 2/3	3	2	2	3	4
2001—Atlanta (N.L.)	0	0	...	0.00	3	0	0	0	0	2 1/3	3	0	0	2	2
Champ. series totals (2 years)	0	1	.000	2.25	8	0	0	0	0	8	6	2	2	5	6

WORLD SERIES RECORD

Year League	W	L	Pct.	ERA	G	GS	CG	ShO	Sv.	IP	H	R	ER	BB	SO
1999—Atlanta (N.L.)	0	1	.000	9.00	2	0	0	0	0	1	1	1	1	1	0

RENTERIA, EDGAR — SS — CARDINALS

PERSONAL: Born August 7, 1975, in Barranquilla, Colombia. ... 6-1/180. ... Bats right, throws right. ... Full name: Edgar Enrique Renteria. ... Brother of Edinson Renteria, infielder in Houston Astros and Florida Marlins organizations (1985-94).

HIGH SCHOOL: Instituto Los Alpes (Barranquilla, Colombia).

TRANSACTIONS/CAREER NOTES: Signed as non-drafted free agent by Florida Marlins organization (February 14, 1992). ... On Florida disabled list (June 24-July 11, 1996); included rehabilitation assignment to Charlotte (July 3-11). ... On disabled list (August 25-September 9, 1998). ... Traded by Marlins to St. Louis Cardinals for P Braden Looper, P Armando Almanza and SS Pablo Ozuna (December 14, 1998).

HONORS: Named shortstop on THE SPORTING NEWS N.L. All-Star team (2000). ... Named shortstop on THE SPORTING NEWS N.L. Silver Slugger team (2000).

STATISTICAL NOTES: Had 22-game hitting streak (July 25-August 16, 1996). ... Led N.L. with 19 sacrifice hits in 1997. ... Led N.L. in caught stealing with 22 in 1998.

						BATTING							FIELDING		
Year Team (League)	Pos.	G	AB	R	H	2B	3B	HR	RBI	Avg.	BB	SO	SB	PO	A	E	Avg.
1992—GC Marlins (GCL)	SS	43	163	25	47	8	1	0	9	.288	8	29	10	56	152	*24	.897
1993—Kane County (Midw.)	SS	116	384	40	78	8	0	1	35	.203	35	94	7	•173	306	34	.934
1994—Brevard County (FSL)	SS	128	439	46	111	15	1	0	36	.253	35	56	6	167	372	23	.959
1995—Portland (East.)	SS	135	508	70	147	15	7	7	68	.289	32	85	30	179	379	33	.944
1996—Charlotte (I.L.)	SS	35	132	17	37	8	0	2	16	.280	9	17	10	48	114	7	.959
—Florida (N.L.)	SS	106	431	68	133	18	3	5	31	.309	33	68	16	163	344	11	.979
1997—Florida (N.L.)	SS	154	617	90	171	21	3	4	52	.277	45	108	32	*242	415	17	.975
1998—Florida (N.L.)	SS	133	517	79	146	18	2	3	31	.282	48	78	41	194	372	20	.966
1999—St. Louis (N.L.)■	SS	154	585	92	161	36	2	11	63	.275	53	82	37	219	393	26	.959
2000—St. Louis (N.L.)	SS	150	562	94	156	32	1	16	76	.278	63	77	21	231	379	27	.958
2001—St. Louis (N.L.)	SS-1B-DH	141	493	54	128	19	3	10	57	.260	39	73	17	209	390	24	.961
Major League totals (6 years)		838	3205	477	895	144	14	49	310	.279	281	486	164	1258	2293	125	.966

DIVISION SERIES RECORD

						BATTING							FIELDING		
Year Team (League)	Pos.	G	AB	R	H	2B	3B	HR	RBI	Avg.	BB	SO	SB	PO	A	E	Avg.
1997—Florida (N.L.)	SS	3	13	1	2	0	0	0	1	.154	2	4	0	9	11	2	.909
2000—St. Louis (N.L.)	SS	3	10	5	2	0	0	0	0	.200	4	1	2	6	4	1	.909
2001—St. Louis (N.L.)	SS	5	17	2	4	1	0	1	1	.235	2	4	0	7	14	1	.955
Division series totals (3 years)		11	40	8	8	1	0	1	2	.200	8	9	2	22	29	4	.927

CHAMPIONSHIP SERIES RECORD

RECORDS: Shares N.L. single-game record for most stolen bases—3 (October 12, 2000).

						BATTING							FIELDING		
Year Team (League)	Pos.	G	AB	R	H	2B	3B	HR	RBI	Avg.	BB	SO	SB	PO	A	E	Avg.
1997—Florida (N.L.)	SS	6	22	4	5	1	0	0	0	.227	3	6	1	14	15	0	1.000
2000—St. Louis (N.L.)	SS	5	20	4	6	1	0	0	4	.300	0	2	3	5	12	0	1.000
Championship series totals (2 years)		11	42	8	11	2	0	0	4	.262	3	8	4	19	27	0	1.000

RECORDS: Holds record for most strikeouts in one inning—2 (October 23, 1997, sixth inning).
NOTES: Member of World Series championship team (1997).

Year Team (League)	Pos.	G	AB	R	H	2B	3B	HR	RBI	Avg.	BB	SO	SB	PO	A	E	Avg.
						BATTING									FIELDING		
1997—Florida (N.L.)	SS	7	31	3	9	2	0	0	3	.290	3	5	0	12	26	1	.974

ALL-STAR GAME RECORD

Year League	Pos.	AB	R	H	2B	3B	HR	RBI	Avg.	BB	SO	SB	PO	A	E	Avg.
					BATTING									FIELDING		
1998—National	SS	1	1	0	0	0	0	0	.000	0	0	0	0	3	0	1.000
2000—National	SS	2	0	0	0	0	0	0	.000	0	0	0	0	2	0	1.000
All-Star Game totals (2 years)		3	1	0	0	0	0	0	.000	0	0	0	0	5	0	1.000

R

RESTOVICH, MICHAEL   OF   TWINS

PERSONAL: Born January 3, 1979, in Rochester, Minn. ... 6-4/235. ... Bats right, throws right. ... Full name: Michael Jerome Restovich.
HIGH SCHOOL: Mayo (Rochester, Minn.).
TRANSACTIONS/CAREER NOTES: Selected by Minnesota Twins organization in second round of free-agent draft (June 3, 1997).
HONORS: Named Appalachian League Player of the Year (1998).
STATISTICAL NOTES: Led Appalachian League with .489 on-base percentage and tied for lead in hit by pitch with nine in 1998. ... Tied for Eastern League lead with eight intentional bases on balls received in 2001.

Year Team (League)	Pos.	G	AB	R	H	2B	3B	HR	RBI	Avg.	BB	SO	SB	PO	A	E	Avg.
						BATTING									FIELDING		
1998—Elizabethton (Appl.)....	OF	65	242	*68	86	20	1	13	*64	.355	*54	58	5	86	7	9	.912
—Fort Wayne (Midw.)....	OF	11	45	9	20	5	2	0	6	.444	4	12	0	13	1	0	1.000
1999—Quad City (Midw.)....	OF-3B	131	493	91	154	30	6	19	107	.312	74	100	7	200	6	9	.958
2000—Fort Myers (FSL)........	OF	135	475	73	125	27	9	8	64	.263	61	100	19	229	6	6	.975
2001—New Britain (East.)	OF-1B	140	501	69	135	33	4	23	84	.269	54	125	15	258	9	3	.989

REYES, AL   P

PERSONAL: Born April 10, 1971, in San Cristobal, Dominican Republic. ... 6-1/206. ... Throws right, bats right. ... Full name: Rafael Alberto Reyes.
HIGH SCHOOL: Francisco del Rosario Sanche (Santo Domingo, Dominican Republic).
TRANSACTIONS/CAREER NOTES: Signed as non-drafted free agent by Montreal Expos organization (February 17, 1988). ... On disabled list (May 23, 1991-remainder of season). ... Selected by Milwaukee Brewers from Expos organization in Rule 5 major league draft (December 5, 1994). ... On disabled list (July 19, 1995-remainder of season). ... On New Orleans disabled list (April 4-August 2, 1996). ... On Milwaukee disabled list (July 25-September 8, 1998; included rehabilitation assignment to Louisville (September 1-8). ... Traded by Brewers to Baltimore Orioles (July 21, 1999), completing deal in which Orioles traded P Rocky Coppinger to Brewers for a player to be named later (July 16, 1999). ... Traded by Orioles to Los Angeles Dodgers for P Alan Mills and cash considerations (June 13, 2000). ... On Las Vegas disabled list (April 5-May 8, 2001). ... Granted free agency (October 17, 2001).

Year League	W	L	Pct.	ERA	G	GS	CG	ShO	Sv.	IP	H	R	ER	BB	SO
1989—Dominican Expos (DSL).....	3	4	.429	2.79	12	10	1	0	0	71	68	36	22	33	49
1990—West Palm Beach (FSL).....	5	4	.556	4.74	16	10	0	0	1	57	58	32	30	32	47
1991—Rockford (Midw.)................	0	1	.000	5.56	3	3	0	0	0	11 1/3	14	8	7	2	10
1992—Albany (S.Atl.)...................	0	2	.000	3.95	27	0	0	0	4	27 1/3	24	14	12	13	29
1993—Burlington (Midw.).............	7	6	.538	2.68	53	0	0	0	11	74	52	33	22	26	80
1994—Harrisburg (East.).............	2	2	.500	3.25	60	0	0	0	*35	69 1/3	68	26	25	13	60
1995—Milwaukee (A.L.)■............	1	1	.500	2.43	27	0	0	0	1	33 1/3	19	9	9	18	29
1996—Beloit (Midw.)....................	1	0	1.000	1.83	13	0	0	0	0	19 2/3	17	7	4	6	22
—Milwaukee (A.L.)	1	0	1.000	7.94	5	0	0	0	0	5 2/3	8	5	5	2	2
1997—Tucson (PCL)	2	4	.333	5.02	38	0	0	0	7	57 1/3	52	39	32	34	70
—Milwaukee (A.L.)	1	2	.333	5.46	19	0	0	0	1	29 2/3	32	19	18	9	28
1998—Milwaukee (N.L.)...............	5	1	.833	3.95	50	0	0	0	0	57	55	26	25	31	58
—Louisville (I.L.).........................	0	1	.000	8.31	3	2	0	0	0	4 1/3	5	5	4	2	5
1999—Louisville (I.L.)..................	0	2	.000	8.38	6	0	0	0	0	9 2/3	12	9	9	7	8
—Milwaukee (N.L.)	2	0	1.000	4.25	26	0	0	0	0	36	27	17	17	25	39
—Baltimore (A.L.)■......................	2	3	.400	4.85	27	0	0	0	0	29 2/3	23	16	16	16	28
2000—Rochester (I.L.)................	0	1	.000	7.71	9	0	0	0	2	11 2/3	13	11	10	9	17
—Baltimore (A.L.)........................	1	0	1.000	6.92	13	0	0	0	0	13	13	10	10	11	10
—Albuquerque (PCL)■.................	3	2	.600	3.72	30	0	0	0	8	38 2/3	33	20	16	21	39
—Los Angeles (N.L.)	0	0	....	0.00	6	0	0	0	0	6 2/3	2	0	0	1	9
2001—Las Vegas (PCL)	0	1	.000	3.38	19	0	0	0	0	29 1/3	24	11	11	10	37
—Los Angeles (N.L.)	2	1	.667	3.86	19	0	0	0	1	25 2/3	28	13	11	13	23
A.L. totals (5 years)	6	6	.500	4.69	91	0	0	0	2	111 1/3	95	59	58	56	97
N.L. totals (4 years)	9	2	.818	3.81	101	0	0	0	1	125 1/3	112	56	53	70	128
Major League totals (7 years)	15	8	.652	4.22	192	0	0	0	3	236 2/3	207	115	111	126	225

REYES, DENNYS   P   ROCKIES

PERSONAL: Born April 19, 1977, in Higuera de Zaragoza, Mexico. ... 6-3/246. ... Throws left, bats right.
HIGH SCHOOL: Ignacio Zaragoza (Higuera de Zaragoza, Mexico).
TRANSACTIONS/CAREER NOTES: Signed as non-drafted free agent by Los Angeles Dodgers organization (July 5, 1993). ... Loaned by Dodgers organization to Mexico City Red Devils, Mexican League (March 28-August 22, 1995). ... Traded by Dodgers with 1B/3B Paul Konerko to Cincinnati Reds for P Jeff Shaw (July 4, 1998). ... On Cincinnati disabled list (May 30-July 2, 2001). ... Traded by Reds with 2B Pokey Reese to Colorado Rockies for P Gabe White and P Luke Hudson (December 18, 2001).
MISCELLANEOUS: Appeared in one game as pinch hitter (2001).

Year	League	W	L	Pct.	ERA	G	GS	CG	ShO	Sv.	IP	H	R	ER	BB	SO
1994—	Vero Beach (FSL)	2	4	.333	6.70	9	9	0	0	0	41 2/3	58	37	31	18	25
—	Great Falls (Pio.)	7	1	.875	3.78	14	9	0	0	0	66 2/3	71	37	28	25	70
1995—	Vero Beach (FSL)	1	0	1.000	1.80	3	2	0	0	0	10	8	2	2	6	9
—	M.C. Red Devils (Mex.)■...	5	5	.500	6.60	17	15	1	0	0	58 2/3	76	49	43	41	44
1996—	San Bernardino (Calif.)■....	11	12	.478	4.17	29	•28	0	0	0	166	166	106	77	77	176
1997—	San Antonio (Texas)..........	8	1	.889	3.02	12	12	1	0	0	80 1/3	79	33	27	28	66
—	Albuquerque (PCL).............	6	3	.667	5.65	10	10	1	0	0	57 1/3	70	40	36	33	45
—	Los Angeles (N.L.)	2	3	.400	3.83	14	5	0	0	0	47	51	21	20	18	36
1998—	Albuquerque (PCL).............	1	4	.200	1.44	7	7	1	1	0	43 2/3	31	13	7	18	58
—	Los Angeles (N.L.)	0	4	.000	4.71	11	3	0	0	0	28 2/3	27	17	15	20	33
—	Indianapolis (I.L.)■.............	2	0	1.000	3.00	4	4	0	0	0	24	20	10	8	14	27
—	Cincinnati (N.L.)	3	1	.750	4.42	8	7	0	0	0	38 2/3	35	19	19	27	44
1999—	Cincinnati (N.L.)	2	2	.500	3.79	65	1	0	0	2	61 2/3	53	30	26	39	72
2000—	Cincinnati (N.L.)	2	1	.667	4.53	62	0	0	0	0	43 2/3	43	31	22	29	36
2001—	Cincinnati (N.L.)	2	6	.250	4.92	35	6	0	0	0	53	51	35	29	35	52
—	Louisville (I.L.)	4	2	.667	3.67	7	6	0	0	0	34 1/3	34	15	14	16	34
Major League totals (5 years)		11	17	.393	4.32	195	22	0	0	2	272 2/3	260	153	131	168	273

REYES, RENE — OF/1B — ROCKIES

PERSONAL: Born February 21, 1978, in Margarita, Venezuela. ... 5-11/215. ... Bats both, throws right.
HIGH SCHOOL: Nueva Esparata (Margarita, Venezuela).
TRANSACTIONS/CAREER NOTES: Signed as non-drafted free agent by Colorado Rockies organization (August 29, 1996). ... On Asheville disabled list (April 8-June 23, 1999). ... On disabled list (April 6, 2000-entire season). ... On disabled list (August 30, 2001-remainder of season).
HONORS: Named Arizona League Most Valuable Player (1998). ... Named South Atlantic League Most Valuable Player (2001).
STATISTICAL NOTES: Led Arizona League with 108 total bases, .493 on-base percentage and 15 times being hit by pitch in 1998. ... Tied for Arizona League lead in errors by first baseman with nine in 1998.

Year	Team (League)	Pos.	G	AB	R	H	2B	3B	HR	RBI	Avg.	BB	SO	SB	PO	A	E	Avg.
1997—	Guacara 1 (VSL)........		38	82	8	18	2	2	1	9	.220	7	14	1	...	...	...	...
1998—	Ariz. Rockies (Ariz.)■	1B-C	49	177	40	*76	9	4	5	•39	*.429	8	15	16	388	26	†17	.961
1999—	Asheville (S.Atl.)........	1B	40	160	26	56	6	1	3	19	.350	6	22	1	20	1	0	1.000
—	Ariz. Rockies (Ariz.)....	1B	22	97	21	35	4	4	1	20	.361	4	14	6	163	10	2	.989
2000—	Carolina (Sou.)								Did not play.									
2001—	Asheville (S.Atl.).........	OF-1B	128	484	71	156	27	2	11	61	.322	28	80	53	587	45	11	.983

REYNOLDS, SHANE — P — ASTROS

PERSONAL: Born March 26, 1968, in Bastrop, La. ... 6-3/210. ... Throws right, bats right. ... Full name: Richard Shane Reynolds.
HIGH SCHOOL: Ouachita Christian (Monroe, La.).
JUNIOR COLLEGE: Faulkner State Junior College (Ala.).
COLLEGE: Texas.
TRANSACTIONS/CAREER NOTES: Selected by Houston Astros organization in third round of free-agent draft (June 5, 1989). ... On Houston disabled list (June 10-July 14, 1997); included rehabilitation assignment to New Orleans (July 10-14). ... On disabled list (August 2, 2000-remainder of season). ... On Houston disabled list (March 31-April 18 and August 14-September 1, 2001); included rehabilitation assignments to Round Rock (April 3-5) and New Orleans (April 5-18).
STATISTICAL NOTES: Led N.L. with 17 sacrifice hits in 1999.
MISCELLANEOUS: Appeared in one game as pinch runner (1995).

Year	League	W	L	Pct.	ERA	G	GS	CG	ShO	Sv.	IP	H	R	ER	BB	SO
1989—	Auburn (NY-Penn).............	3	2	.600	2.31	6	6	1	0	0	35	36	16	9	14	23
—	Asheville (S.Atl.)................	5	3	.625	3.68	8	8	2	1	0	51 1/3	53	25	21	21	33
1990—	Columbus (Sou.)	9	10	.474	4.81	29	27	2	1	0	155 1/3	•181	104	83	70	92
1991—	Jackson (Texas)	8	9	.471	4.47	27	•27	2	0	0	151	165	93	75	62	116
1992—	Tucson (PCL)	9	8	.529	3.68	25	22	2	0	1	142	156	73	58	34	106
—	Houston (N.L.)	1	3	.250	7.11	8	5	0	0	0	25 1/3	42	22	20	6	10
1993—	Tucson (PCL)	10	6	.625	3.62	25	20	2	0	1	139 1/3	147	74	56	21	106
—	Houston (N.L.)	0	0	...	0.82	5	1	0	0	0	11	11	4	1	6	10
1994—	Houston (N.L.)	8	5	.615	3.05	33	14	1	1	0	124	128	46	42	21	110
1995—	Houston (N.L.)	10	11	.476	3.47	30	30	3	2	0	189 1/3	196	87	73	37	175
1996—	Houston (N.L.)	16	10	.615	3.65	35	35	4	1	0	239	227	103	97	44	204
1997—	Houston (N.L.)	9	10	.474	4.23	30	30	2	0	0	181	189	92	85	47	152
—	New Orleans (A.A.)............	1	0	1.000	0.00	1	1	0	0	0	5	3	0	0	1	6
1998—	Houston (N.L.)	19	8	.704	3.51	35	•35	3	1	0	233 1/3	257	99	91	53	209
1999—	Houston (N.L.)	16	14	.533	3.85	35	•35	4	2	0	231 2/3	250	108	99	37	197
2000—	Houston (N.L.)	7	8	.467	5.22	22	22	0	0	0	131	150	86	76	45	93
2001—	Round Rock (Texas)..........	1	0	1.000	1.29	1	1	0	0	0	7	5	1	1	2	5
—	New Orleans (PCL)............	1	0	1.000	0.00	1	1	0	0	0	7	8	0	0	0	7
—	Houston (N.L.)	14	11	.560	4.34	28	28	3	0	0	182 2/3	208	95	88	36	102
Major League totals (10 years)		100	80	.556	3.91	261	235	20	7	0	1548 1/3	1658	742	672	332	1262

DIVISION SERIES RECORD

Year	League	W	L	Pct.	ERA	G	GS	CG	ShO	Sv.	IP	H	R	ER	BB	SO
1997—	Houston (N.L.)	0	1	.000	3.00	1	1	0	0	0	6	5	2	2	1	5
1998—	Houston (N.L.)	0	0	...	2.57	1	1	0	0	0	7	4	2	2	1	5
1999—	Houston (N.L.)	1	1	.500	4.09	2	2	0	0	0	11	16	5	5	3	5
2001—	Houston (N.L.)	0	1	.000	9.00	1	1	0	0	0	4	6	4	4	1	1
Division series totals (4 years)		1	3	.250	4.18	5	5	0	0	0	28	31	13	13	6	16

ALL-STAR GAME RECORD

Year	League	W	L	Pct.	ERA	GS	CG	ShO	Sv.	IP	H	R	ER	BB	SO
2000—	National						Did not play.								

PERSONAL: Born May 1, 1966, in San Luis Potosi, Mexico. ... 6-0/204. ... Throws right, bats right. ... Full name: Martin Armando Gutierrez Reynoso. ... Name pronounced ray-NO-so.

HIGH SCHOOL: Escuela Secandaria Mita del Estado (Jalisco, Mexico).

TRANSACTIONS/CAREER NOTES: Signed as free agent by Saltillo of Mexican League (1988). ... Contract sold by Saltillo to Atlanta Braves organization (August 15, 1990). ... Selected by Colorado Rockies in third round (58th pick overall) of expansion draft (November 17, 1992). ... On disabled list (May 21, 1994-remainder of season). ... On Colorado disabled list (April 17-June 18, 1995); included rehabilitation assignments to Colorado Springs (May 9-20 and June 8-14). ... Traded by Rockies to New York Mets for P Jerry Dipoto (November 27, 1996). ... On New York disabled list (March 24-April 15 and July 17, 1997-remainder of season); included rehabilitation assignment to St. Lucie (April 5-15). ... On New York disabled list (March 24-July 24, 1998); included rehabilitation assignments to St. Lucie (June 18-July 3) and Norfolk (July 12-17). ... Granted free agency (October 26, 1998). ... Signed by Arizona Diamondbacks (December 2, 1998). ... Granted free agency (November 1, 2000). ... Re-signed by Diamondbacks (December 6, 2000). ... On Arizona disabled list (May 5-29 and June 10, 2001-remainder of season); included rehabilitation assignment to Tucson (May 24-29).

STATISTICAL NOTES: Led International League with six balks in 1991 and five in 1992. ... Tied for International League lead with 10 hit batsmen in 1991.

MISCELLANEOUS: Appeared in one game as pinch runner with Colorado (1993).

Year	League	W	L	Pct.	ERA	G	GS	CG	ShO	Sv.	IP	H	R	ER	BB	SO
1988—	Saltillo (Mex.)	11	11	.500	4.30	32	29	10	2	2	180	176	98	86	85	92
1989—	Saltillo (Mex.)	13	9	.591	3.48	27	25	7	2	0	160 1/3	155	78	62	64	107
1990—	Saltillo (Mex.)	*20	3	.870	2.60	27	•27	12	5	0	200 2/3	174	61	58	73	*170
—	Richmond (I.L.)■	3	1	.750	2.25	4	3	0	0	0	24	26	7	6	7	15
1991—	Richmond (I.L.)	10	6	.625	*2.61	22	19	3	•3	0	131	117	44	38	39	97
—	Atlanta (N.L.)	2	1	.667	6.17	6	5	0	0	0	23 1/3	26	18	16	10	10
1992—	Richmond (I.L.)	12	9	.571	2.66	28	27	4	1	0	169 1/3	156	65	50	52	108
—	Atlanta (N.L.)	1	0	1.000	4.70	3	1	0	0	1	7 2/3	11	4	4	2	2
1993—	Colorado Springs (PCL)■	2	1	.667	3.22	4	4	0	0	0	22 1/3	19	10	8	8	22
—	Colorado (N.L.)	12	11	.522	4.00	30	30	4	0	0	189	206	101	84	63	117
1994—	Colorado (N.L.)	3	4	.429	4.82	9	9	1	0	0	52 1/3	54	30	28	22	25
1995—	Colorado Springs (PCL)	2	1	.667	1.57	5	5	0	0	0	23	14	4	4	6	17
—	Colorado (N.L.)	7	7	.500	5.32	20	18	0	0	0	93	116	61	55	36	40
1996—	Colorado (N.L.)	8	9	.471	4.96	30	30	0	0	0	168 2/3	195	97	93	49	88
1997—	St. Lucie (FSL)■	1	1	.500	2.70	2	2	0	0	0	10	9	3	3	1	6
—	New York (N.L.)	6	3	.667	4.53	16	16	1	1	0	91 1/3	95	47	46	29	47
1998—	St. Lucie (FSL)	0	1	.000	3.75	4	4	0	0	0	12	14	6	5	1	6
—	Norfolk (I.L.)	0	2	.000	10.61	2	2	0	0	0	9 1/3	14	11	11	4	8
—	New York (N.L.)	7	3	.700	3.82	11	11	0	0	0	68 1/3	64	31	29	32	40
1999—	Arizona (N.L.)■	10	6	.625	4.37	31	27	0	0	0	167	178	90	81	67	79
2000—	Arizona (N.L.)	11	12	.478	5.27	31	30	2	0	0	170 2/3	179	102	100	52	89
2001—	Arizona (N.L.)	1	6	.143	5.98	9	9	0	0	0	46 2/3	58	32	31	13	15
—	Tucson (PCL)	0	0	...	0.00	1	1	0	0	0	3 2/3	3	0	0	2	5
Major League totals (11 years)		68	62	.523	4.73	196	186	8	1	1	1078	1182	613	567	375	552

DIVISION SERIES RECORD

Year	League	W	L	Pct.	ERA	G	GS	CG	ShO	Sv.	IP	H	R	ER	BB	SO
1995—	Colorado (N.L.)	0	0	...	0.00	1	0	0	0	0	1	2	0	0	0	0
1999—	Arizona (N.L.)							Did not play.								

PERSONAL: Born October 24, 1969, in Waco, Texas. ... 6-2/205. ... Throws left, bats left. ... Full name: Arthur Lee Rhodes Jr. ... Brother of Ricky Rhodes, pitcher in New York Yankees organization (1988-92).

HIGH SCHOOL: LaVega (Waco, Texas).

TRANSACTIONS/CAREER NOTES: Selected by Baltimore Orioles organization in second round of free-agent draft (June 1, 1988). ... On Hagerstown disabled list (May 13-June 5, 1991). ... On Baltimore disabled list (May 16-August 2, 1993); included rehabilitation assignment to Rochester (July 4-August 2). ... On Baltimore disabled list (May 2-20, 1994); included rehabilitation assignment to Frederick (May 16-20). ... On Baltimore disabled list (August 25, 1995-remainder of season). ... On disabled list (July 14-August 2 and August 6-September 27, 1996). ... On Baltimore disabled list (July 5-August 17, 1998); included rehabilitation assignment to Rochester (August 15-17). ... Granted free agency (November 1, 1999). ... Signed by Seattle Mariners (December 21, 1999).

HONORS: Named Eastern League Pitcher of the Year (1991).

MISCELLANEOUS: Appeared in one game as pinch runner (1997).

Year	League	W	L	Pct.	ERA	G	GS	CG	ShO	Sv.	IP	H	R	ER	BB	SO
1988—	Bluefield (Appl.)	3	4	.429	3.31	11	7	0	0	0	35 1/3	29	17	13	15	44
1989—	Erie (NY-Penn)	2	0	1.000	1.16	5	5	1	0	0	31	13	7	4	10	45
—	Frederick (Caro.)	2	2	.500	5.18	7	6	0	0	0	24 1/3	19	16	14	19	28
1990—	Frederick (Caro.)	4	6	.400	2.12	13	13	3	0	0	80 2/3	62	25	19	21	103
—	Hagerstown (East.)	3	4	.429	3.73	12	12	0	0	0	72 1/3	62	32	30	39	60
1991—	Hagerstown (East.)	7	4	.636	2.70	19	19	2	2	0	106 2/3	73	37	32	47	115
—	Baltimore (A.L.)	0	3	.000	8.00	8	8	0	0	0	36	47	35	32	23	23
1992—	Rochester (I.L.)	6	6	.500	3.72	17	17	1	0	0	101 2/3	84	48	42	46	115
—	Baltimore (A.L.)	7	5	.583	3.63	15	15	2	1	0	94 1/3	87	39	38	38	77
1993—	Baltimore (A.L.)	5	6	.455	6.51	17	17	0	0	0	85 2/3	91	62	62	49	49
—	Rochester (I.L.)	1	1	.500	4.05	6	6	0	0	0	26 2/3	26	12	12	15	33
1994—	Baltimore (A.L.)	3	5	.375	5.81	10	10	3	2	0	52 2/3	51	34	34	30	47
—	Frederick (Caro.)	0	0	...	0.00	1	1	0	0	0	5	3	0	0	0	7
—	Rochester (I.L.)	7	5	.583	2.79	15	15	3	0	0	90 1/3	70	41	28	34	86
1995—	Rochester (I.L.)	2	1	.667	2.70	4	4	1	0	0	30	27	12	9	8	33
—	Baltimore (A.L.)	2	5	.286	6.21	19	9	0	0	0	75 1/3	68	53	52	48	77
1996—	Baltimore (A.L.)	9	1	.900	4.08	28	2	0	0	1	53	48	28	24	23	62
1997—	Baltimore (A.L.)	10	3	.769	3.02	53	0	0	0	1	95 1/3	75	32	32	26	102

Year League	W	L	Pct.	ERA	G	GS	CG	ShO	Sv.	IP	H	R	ER	BB	SO
1998—Baltimore (A.L.)	4	4	.500	3.51	45	0	0	0	4	77	65	30	30	34	83
—Rochester (I.L.)	0	0	...	4.50	1	1	0	0	0	2	3	1	1	1	1
1999—Baltimore (A.L.)	3	4	.429	5.43	43	0	0	0	3	53	43	37	32	45	59
2000—Seattle (A.L.)■	5	8	.385	4.28	72	0	0	0	0	69 1/3	51	34	33	29	77
2001—Seattle (A.L.)	8	0	1.000	1.72	71	0	0	0	3	68	46	14	13	12	83
Major League totals (11 years)	56	44	.560	4.53	381	61	5	3	12	759 2/3	672	398	382	357	739

DIVISION SERIES RECORD

Year League	W	L	Pct.	ERA	G	GS	CG	ShO	Sv.	IP	H	R	ER	BB	SO
1996—Baltimore (A.L.)	0	0	...	9.00	2	0	0	0	0	1	1	1	1	1	1
1997—Baltimore (A.L.)	0	0	...	0.00	1	0	0	0	0	2 1/3	0	0	0	0	4
2000—Seattle (A.L.)	0	0	...	0.00	3	0	0	0	0	2 2/3	0	0	0	2	2
2001—Seattle (A.L.)	0	0	...	0.00	3	0	0	0	0	2 2/3	1	0	0	0	1
Division series totals (4 years)	0	0	...	1.04	9	0	0	0	0	8 2/3	2	1	1	3	8

CHAMPIONSHIP SERIES RECORD

Year League	W	L	Pct.	ERA	G	GS	CG	ShO	Sv.	IP	H	R	ER	BB	SO
1996—Baltimore (A.L.)	0	0	...	0.00	3	0	0	0	0	2	2	0	0	0	2
1997—Baltimore (A.L.)	0	0	...	0.00	2	0	0	0	0	2 1/3	2	0	0	3	2
2000—Seattle (A.L.)	0	1	.000	31.50	4	0	0	0	0	2	8	7	7	4	5
2001—Seattle (A.L.)	0	0	...	4.50	2	0	0	0	0	2	2	1	1	0	2
Champ. series totals (4 years)	0	1	.000	8.64	11	0	0	0	0	8 1/3	14	8	8	7	11

RICHARD, CHRIS — OF/1B — ORIOLES

PERSONAL: Born June 7, 1974, in San Diego. ... 6-2/185. ... Bats left, throws left. ... Full name: Christopher Robert Richard.

HIGH SCHOOL: University City (San Diego).

JUNIOR COLLEGE: San Diego City College, then San Diego Mesa College.

COLLEGE: Oklahoma State.

TRANSACTIONS/CAREER NOTES: Selected by St. Louis Cardinals organization in 19th round of free-agent draft (June 1, 1995). ... On Arkansas disabled list (April 2-June 16, 1998 and July 31-August 11, 1998). ... On Prince William disabled list (June 28-July 16, 1998). ... Traded by Cardinals with P Mark Nussbeck to Baltimore Orioles for P Mike Timlin and cash (July 29, 2000). ... On disabled list (June 20-July 5, 2001).

STATISTICAL NOTES: Led Texas League first baseman with 119 double plays in 1999. ... Hit home run in first major league at-bat (July 17, 2000).

Year Team (League)	Pos.	G	AB	R	H	2B	3B	HR	RBI	Avg.	BB	SO	SB	PO	A	E	Avg.
1995—New Jersey (NY-P)	1B	75	284	36	80	14	3	3	43	.282	47	31	6	620	43	11	.984
1996—St. Petersburg (FSL)	1B-OF	129	460	65	130	28	6	14	82	.283	57	50	7	1138	58	7	.994
1997—Arkansas (Texas)	1B-OF	113	390	62	105	24	3	11	58	.269	60	59	6	924	68	10	.990
1998—Prince William (Caro.)	DH	8	30	5	8	2	0	0	1	.267	1	5	1	...	...	...	...
—Arkansas (Texas)	1B	28	89	7	18	5	1	2	17	.202	9	10	0	202	8	3	.986
1999—Arkansas (Texas)	1B-OF	133	442	78	130	26	3	29	94	.294	43	75	7	1079	68	13	.989
—Memphis (PCL)	1B	4	17	3	7	2	0	1	4	.412	1	2	0	34	5	0	1.000
2000—Memphis (PCL)	OF-1B	95	375	64	104	24	0	16	75	.277	50	70	9	274	15	2	.993
—St. Louis (N.L.)	OF-1B	6	16	1	2	0	0	1	1	.125	2	2	0	10	0	0	1.000
—Baltimore (A.L.)■	1B-DH-OF	56	199	38	55	14	2	13	36	.276	15	38	1	443	18	5	.989
2001—Baltimore (A.L.)	OF-DH-1B	136	483	74	128	31	3	15	61	.265	45	100	11	355	15	0	1.000
American League totals (2 years)		192	682	112	183	45	5	28	97	.268	60	138	18	798	33	5	.994
National League totals (1 year)		6	16	1	2	0	0	1	1	.125	2	2	0	10	0	0	1.000
Major League totals (2 years)		198	698	113	185	45	5	29	98	.265	62	140	18	808	33	5	.994

RICKETTS, CHAD — P — BLUE JAYS

PERSONAL: Born February 12, 1975, in Waterloo, Ont. ... 6-5/225. ... Throws right, bats right. ... Full name: Robert Chad Ricketts.

HIGH SCHOOL: East Lake (Tarpon Springs, Fla.).

JUNIOR COLLEGE: Polk Community College (Fla.).

TRANSACTIONS/CAREER NOTES: Selected by Chicago Cubs organization in ninth round of free-agent draft (June 1, 1995). ... Traded by Cubs with P Terry Adams and a player to be named later to Los Angeles Dodgers for P Ismael Valdes and 2B Eric Young (December 12, 1999); Dodgers acquired P Brian Stephenson to complete deal (December 16, 1999). ... On disabled list (May 27-June 24, 2001). ... Traded by Dodgers with P Luke Prokopec to Toronto Blue Jays for P Paul Quantrill and 2B/SS Cesar Izturis (December 13, 2001).

Year League	W	L	Pct.	ERA	G	GS	CG	ShO	Sv.	IP	H	R	ER	BB	SO
1995—Gulf Coast Cubs (GCL)	1	0	1.000	0.00	2	2	0	0	0	9	1	1	0	1	5
—Williamsport (NY-Penn)	4	5	.444	4.19	12	12	0	0	0	68 2/3	89	46	32	16	37
1996—Rockford (Midw.)	3	8	.273	5.03	37	9	0	0	4	87 2/3	89	60	49	29	70
1997—Rockford (Midw.)	4	0	1.000	2.48	16	0	0	0	3	29	19	9	8	11	32
—Daytona (FSL)	3	1	.750	0.44	20	0	0	0	8	20 1/3	13	4	1	6	18
—Orlando (Sou.)	0	0	...	18.00	2	0	0	0	0	2	7	4	4	2	3
1998—Daytona (FSL)	2	1	.667	1.84	47	0	0	0	19	49	41	15	10	11	59
—West Tenn (Sou.)	0	2	.000	3.52	13	0	0	0	6	15 1/3	19	7	6	4	13
1999—West Tenn (Sou.)	6	4	.600	3.09	57	0	0	0	8	67	55	25	23	21	80
2000—Albuquerque (PCL)■	6	2	.750	3.46	54	0	0	0	7	67 2/3	59	35	26	36	75
2001—Las Vegas (PCL)	1	3	.250	2.91	48	0	0	0	3	58 2/3	49	24	19	25	70

RIEDLING, JOHN P REDS

PERSONAL: Born August 29, 1975, in Fort Lauderdale, Fla. ... 5-11/190. ... Throws right, bats right. ... Full name: John Richard Riedling Jr.
HIGH SCHOOL: Ely (Pompano Beach, Fla.).
TRANSACTIONS/CAREER NOTES: Selected by Cincinnati Reds organization in 22nd round of free-agent draft (June 2, 1994). ... Released by Reds (December 14, 1998). ... Re-signed by Reds organization (January 5, 1999). ... On Cincinnati disabled list (May 27-August 12 and August 31, 2001-remainder of season); included rehabilitation assignment to Louisville (August 10-12).

Year League	W	L	Pct.	ERA	G	GS	CG	ShO	Sv.	IP	H	R	ER	BB	SO
1994— Billings (Pio.)	4	1	.800	5.48	15	15	0	0	0	44 1/3	62	36	27	28	27
1995— Billings (Pio.)	2	2	.500	7.04	13	7	0	0	1	38 1/3	51	38	30	21	28
1996— Charleston, W.Va. (S.Atl.)	6	10	.375	3.99	26	26	0	0	0	140	135	85	62	66	90
1997— Burlington (Midw.)	4	6	.400	5.26	35	16	0	0	0	102 2/3	101	70	60	47	104
1998— Chattanooga (Sou.)	3	10	.231	5.00	24	20	0	0	0	102 2/3	112	70	57	60	86
1999— Chattanooga (Sou.)	9	5	.643	3.43	40	0	0	0	5	42	41	23	16	20	38
— Indianapolis (I.L.)	1	0	1.000	1.54	24	0	0	0	1	35	19	9	6	18	26
2000— Louisville (I.L.)	6	3	.667	2.52	53	0	0	0	5	75	63	24	21	30	75
— Cincinnati (N.L.)	3	1	.750	2.35	13	0	0	0	1	15 1/3	11	7	4	8	18
2001— Cincinnati (N.L.)	1	1	.500	2.41	29	0	0	0	1	33 2/3	22	9	9	14	23
— Louisville (I.L.)	0	0	...	0.00	1	0	0	0	0	1	0	0	0	1	1
Major League totals (2 years)	4	2	.667	2.39	42	0	0	0	2	49	33	16	13	22	41

RIGDON, PAUL P BREWERS

PERSONAL: Born November 2, 1975, in Jacksonville, Fla. ... 6-5/242. ... Throws right, bats right. ... Full name: Paul David Rigdon.
HIGH SCHOOL: Trinity Christian Academy (Jacksonville, Fla.).
COLLEGE: Florida.
TRANSACTIONS/CAREER NOTES: Selected by Cleveland Indians organization in sixth-round of free-agent draft (June 4, 1996). ... On disabled list (June 17, 1997-entire season). ... Traded by Indians with 1B/OF Richie Sexson, P Kane Davis and a player to be named later to Milwaukee Brewers for P Bob Wickman, P Steve Woodard and P Jason Bere (July 28, 2000); Brewers acquired 2B Marcos Scutaro to complete deal (August 30). ... On Milwaukee disabled list (May 22-June 7, 2000). ... On disabled list (June 9-24 and July 2, 2001-remainder of season).

Year League	W	L	Pct.	ERA	G	GS	CG	ShO	Sv.	IP	H	R	ER	BB	SO
1996— Watertown (NY-Penn)	2	2	.500	4.08	22	0	0	0	6	39 2/3	41	24	18	10	46
1997—							Did not play.								
1998— Kinston (Caro.)	11	7	.611	4.03	24	24	0	0	0	127 1/3	126	65	57	35	97
1999— Akron (East.)	7	0	1.000	0.90	8	7	0	0	0	50	20	5	5	10	25
— Buffalo (I.L.)	7	4	.636	4.53	19	19	0	0	0	103 1/3	114	60	52	28	60
2000— Buffalo (I.L.)	6	1	.857	3.30	12	12	1	0	0	71	72	27	26	18	41
— Cleveland (A.L.)	1	1	.500	7.64	5	4	0	0	0	17 2/3	21	15	15	9	15
— Milwaukee (N.L.)■	4	4	.500	4.52	12	12	0	0	0	69 2/3	68	37	35	26	48
2001— Milwaukee (N.L.)	3	5	.375	5.79	15	15	0	0	0	79 1/3	86	52	51	46	49
A.L. totals (1 year)	1	1	.500	7.64	5	4	0	0	0	17 2/3	21	15	15	9	15
N.L. totals (2 years)	7	9	.438	5.19	27	27	0	0	0	149	154	89	86	72	97
Major League totals (2 years)	8	10	.444	5.45	32	31	0	0	0	166 2/3	175	104	101	81	112

RIGGAN, JERROD P INDIANS

PERSONAL: Born May 16, 1974, in Brewster, Wash. ... 6-3/200. ... Throws right, bats right. ... Full name: Jerrod Ashley Riggan.
HIGH SCHOOL: Brewster (Wash.).
COLLEGE: San Diego State.
TRANSACTIONS/CAREER NOTES: Selected by California Angels organization in eighth round of free-agent draft (June 4, 1996). ... Angels franchise renamed Anaheim Angels for 1997 season. ... Released by Angels (April 17, 1998). ... Signed by New York Mets organization (July 9, 1998). ... Traded by Mets with OF Matt Lawton, OF Alex Escobar and two players to be named later to Cleveland Indians for 2B Roberto Alomar, P Mike Bacsik and OF Danny Peoples (December 11, 2001); Indians acquired P Billy Traber and 1B Earl Snyder to complete deal (December 13, 2001).

Year League	W	L	Pct.	ERA	G	GS	CG	ShO	Sv.	IP	H	R	ER	BB	SO
1996— Boise (N'West)	3	5	.375	4.63	15	15	•1	0	0	89 1/3	90	62	46	38	80
1997— Cedar Rapids (Midw.)	9	8	.529	4.89	19	19	3	1	0	116	132	70	63	36	65
— Lake Elsinore (Calif.)	2	5	.286	6.07	8	8	0	0	0	43	60	36	29	16	31
1998— Capital City (S.Atl.)■	4	1	.800	3.70	14	0	0	0	1	41 1/3	38	21	17	14	40
1999— St. Lucie (FSL)	5	5	.500	3.33	44	0	0	0	12	73	69	33	27	24	66
2000— Binghamton (East.)	2	0	1.000	1.11	52	0	0	0	•28	65	43	9	8	18	79
— New York (N.L.)	0	0	...	0.00	1	0	0	0	0	2	3	2	0	0	1
2001— Norfolk (I.L.)	2	0	1.000	1.95	28	0	0	0	13	32 1/3	26	7	7	4	37
— New York (N.L.)	3	3	.500	3.40	35	0	0	0	0	47 2/3	42	19	18	24	41
Major League totals (2 years)	3	3	.500	3.26	36	0	0	0	0	49 2/3	45	21	18	24	42

RIGGS, ADAM 2B TIGERS

PERSONAL: Born October 4, 1972, in Steubenville, Ohio. ... 6-0/190. ... Bats right, throws right. ... Full name: Adam David Riggs.
HIGH SCHOOL: Lenape Valley (Stanhope, N.J.).
COLLEGE: South Carolina-Aiken.
TRANSACTIONS/CAREER NOTES: Selected by Los Angeles Dodgers organization in 22nd round of free-agent draft (June 2, 1994). ... On Albuquerque disabled list (April 4-June 9, 1997; and May 28-June 5, 1998). ... On Los Angeles disabled list (June 5, 1998-remainder of season). ... Granted free agency (October 18, 2000). ... Signed by San Diego Padres organization (December 15, 2000). ... Granted free agency (October 8, 2001). ... Signed by Detroit Tigers organization (December 19, 2001).
HONORS: Named California League Most Valuable Player (1995).

STATISTICAL NOTES: Led California League with 317 total bases and .431 on-base percentage in 1995. ... Led Texas League second basemen with 717 total chances and 91 double plays in 1996. ... Tied for Pacific Coast League lead in caught stealing with 17 in 1999. ... Led Pacific Coast League second baseman with 21 errors in 1999.

Year Team (League)	Pos.	G	AB	R	H	2B	3B	HR	RBI	Avg.	BB	SO	SB	PO	A	E	Avg.
1994— Yakima (N'West)	2B	4	7	1	2	1	0	0	0	.286	0	1	0	...	...	...	...
— Great Falls (Pio.)	2B	62	234	55	73	20	3	5	44	.312	31	38	19	93	133	23	.908
1995— San Bern. (Calif.)	2B	134	*542	*111	*196	*39	5	24	106	*.362	59	93	31	223	303	*41	.928
1996— San Antonio (Texas)	2B	134	506	68	143	31	6	14	66	.283	37	82	16	*295	*395	27	.962
1997— Albuquerque (PCL)	2B-3B-OF	57	227	59	69	8	3	13	28	.304	29	39	12	131	162	8	.973
— Los Angeles (N.L.)	2B	9	20	3	4	1	0	0	1	.200	4	3	1	6	19	0	1.000
1998— Albuquerque (PCL)	2B	44	170	30	63	13	3	4	25	.371	21	29	12	82	125	10	.954
1999— Albuquerque (PCL)	2B-3B-DH	133	513	87	150	29	7	13	81	.292	54	114	25	264	329	†23	.963
2000— Albuquerque (PCL)	3B-2B-OF	124	348	71	109	24	4	12	57	.313	35	67	11	94	199	19	.939
2001— Portland (PCL)■	2B-OF	110	394	42	103	18	2	21	65	.261	12	78	8	158	238	16	.961
— San Diego (N.L.)	2B-3B	12	36	2	7	1	0	0	1	.194	2	8	1	13	24	0	1.000
Major League totals (2 years)		21	56	5	11	2	0	0	2	.196	6	11	2	19	43	0	1.000

RIJO, JOSE — P — REDS

PERSONAL: Born May 13, 1965, in San Cristobal, Dominican Republic. ... 6-3/200. ... Throws right, bats right. ... Full name: Jose Antonio Abreau Rijo. ... Name pronounced REE-ho.

TRANSACTIONS/CAREER NOTES: Signed as non-drafted free agent by New York Yankees organization (August 1, 1980). ... Traded by Yankees organization with OF Stan Javier, P Jay Howell, P Eric Plunk and P Tim Birtsas to Oakland Athletics for OF Rickey Henderson, P Bert Bradley and cash (December 5, 1984). ... Traded by A's organization with P Tim Birtsas to Cincinnati Reds for OF Dave Parker (December 8, 1987). ... On disabled list (August 18-September 8, 1988 and July 17-September 1, 1989). ... On Cincinnati disabled list (June 29-July 21, 1990); included rehabilitation assignment to Nashville (July 16-20). ... On disabled list (June 21-July 25, 1991; April 18-May 3, 1992; June 2-17, 1995; July 19, 1995-remainder of season; March 23, 1996-entire season; and February 17, 1997-entire season). ... Granted free agency (October 29, 1997). ... Re-signed by Cincinnati Reds organization (January 8, 1998). ... On disabled list (April 9, 1998-entire season). ... Granted free agency (October 15, 1998). ... Signed by Reds organization (July 1, 2001). ... Granted free agency (November 5, 2001). ... Re-signed by Reds organization (January 7, 2002).

HONORS: Named Florida State League Most Valuable Player (1983). ... Named righthanded pitcher on THE SPORTING NEWS N.L. All-Star team (1991).

STATISTICAL NOTES: Led Pacific Coast League with 11 balks in 1985. ... Struck out 16 batters in one game (April 19, 1986). ... Tied for N.L. lead with five balks in 1990. ... Pitched 6-0 one-hit, complete-game victory against Colorado (September 25, 1993).

MISCELLANEOUS: Struck out in only appearance as pinch hitter (1991).

Year League	W	L	Pct.	ERA	G	GS	CG	ShO	Sv.	IP	H	R	ER	BB	SO
1981— Gulf Coast Yankees (GCL)	3	3	.500	4.50	11	1	0	0	1	22	37	16	11	7	22
1982— Paintsville (Appl.)	8	4	.667	2.50	13	12	6	•3	0	79 1/3	76	33	22	22	66
1983— Fort Lauderdale (FSL)	*15	5	.750	*1.68	21	21	*15	•4	0	160 1/3	129	38	30	43	152
— Nashville (Sou.)	3	2	.600	2.68	5	5	3	0	0	40 1/3	31	12	12	22	32
1984— New York (A.L.)	2	8	.200	4.76	24	5	0	0	2	62 1/3	74	40	33	33	47
— Columbus (I.L.)	3	3	.500	4.41	11	11	0	0	0	65 1/3	67	35	32	40	47
1985— Tacoma (PCL)■	7	10	.412	2.90	24	24	3	1	0	149	116	64	48	*108	*179
— Oakland (A.L.)	6	4	.600	3.53	12	9	0	0	0	63 2/3	57	26	25	28	65
1986— Oakland (A.L.)	9	11	.450	4.65	39	26	4	0	1	193 2/3	172	116	100	108	176
1987— Oakland (A.L.)	2	7	.222	5.90	21	14	1	0	0	82 1/3	106	67	54	41	67
— Tacoma (PCL)	2	4	.333	3.95	9	8	0	0	0	54 2/3	44	27	24	28	67
1988— Cincinnati (N.L.)■	13	8	.619	2.39	49	19	0	0	0	162	120	47	43	63	160
1989— Cincinnati (N.L.)	7	6	.538	2.84	19	19	1	1	0	111	101	39	35	48	86
1990— Cincinnati (N.L.)	14	8	.636	2.70	29	29	7	1	0	197	151	65	59	78	152
— Nashville (A.A.)	0	0	...	8.31	1	1	0	0	0	4 1/3	5	4	4	2	2
1991— Cincinnati (N.L.)	15	6	.714	2.51	30	30	3	1	0	204 1/3	165	69	57	55	172
1992— Cincinnati (N.L.)	15	10	.600	2.56	33	33	2	0	0	211	185	67	60	44	171
1993— Cincinnati (N.L.)	14	9	.609	2.48	36	•36	2	1	0	257 1/3	218	76	71	62	*227
1994— Cincinnati (N.L.)	9	6	.600	3.08	26	*26	2	0	0	172 1/3	177	73	59	52	171
1995— Cincinnati (N.L.)	5	4	.556	4.17	14	14	0	0	0	69	76	33	32	22	62
1996— Cincinnati (N.L.)							Did not play.								
1997— Cincinnati (N.L.)							Did not play.								
1998— Indianapolis (I.L.)							Did not play.								
1999—							Did not play.								
2000—							Did not play.								
2001— Dayton (Midw.)	0	0	...	3.00	1	1	0	0	0	3	3	1	1	0	1
— Chattanooga (Sou.)	0	0	...	0.00	1	1	0	0	0	3	1	0	0	1	3
— Louisville (I.L.)	0	0	...	5.14	6	4	0	0	0	14	16	9	8	5	7
— Cincinnati (N.L.)	0	0	...	2.12	13	0	0	0	0	17	19	6	4	9	12
A.L. totals (4 years)	19	30	.388	4.75	96	54	5	0	3	402	409	249	212	210	355
N.L. totals (9 years)	92	57	.617	2.70	249	206	17	4	0	1401	1212	475	420	433	1213
Major League totals (13 years)	111	87	.561	3.15	345	260	22	4	3	1803	1621	724	632	643	1568

CHAMPIONSHIP SERIES RECORD

Year League	W	L	Pct.	ERA	G	GS	CG	ShO	Sv.	IP	H	R	ER	BB	SO
1990— Cincinnati (N.L.)	1	0	1.000	4.38	2	2	0	0	0	12 1/3	10	6	6	7	15

WORLD SERIES RECORD

NOTES: Named Most Valuable Player (1990). ... Member of World Series championship team (1990).

Year League	W	L	Pct.	ERA	G	GS	CG	ShO	Sv.	IP	H	R	ER	BB	SO
1990— Cincinnati (N.L.)	2	0	1.000	0.59	2	2	0	0	0	15 1/3	9	1	1	5	14

ALL-STAR GAME RECORD

Year League	W	L	Pct.	ERA	GS	CG	ShO	Sv.	IP	H	R	ER	BB	SO
1994— National						Selected, did not play—injured.								

RILEY, MATT   P   ORIOLES

PERSONAL: Born August 2, 1979, in Antioch, Calif. ... 6-1/201. ... Throws left, bats left. ... Full name: Matthew P. Riley.
HIGH SCHOOL: Liberty Union (Oakley, Calif.).
JUNIOR COLLEGE: Sacramento City College.
TRANSACTIONS/CAREER NOTES: Selected by Baltimore Orioles organization in third round of free-agent draft (June 3, 1997). ... On Bowie disabled list (June 30-July 8, 1999). ... On Rochester disabled list (April 16-May 28, 2000). ... On Baltimore disabled list (September 29, 2000-remainder of season). ... On disabled list (April 1, 2001-entire season).

Year League	W	L	Pct.	ERA	G	GS	CG	ShO	Sv.	IP	H	R	ER	BB	SO
1998— Delmarva (S.Atl.)	5	4	.556	1.19	16	14	0	0	0	83	42	19	11	44	136
1999— Frederick (Caro.)	3	2	.600	2.61	8	8	0	0	0	51²/₃	34	19	15	14	58
— Bowie (East.)	10	6	.625	3.22	20	20	3	0	0	125²/₃	113	53	45	42	131
— Baltimore (A.L.)	0	0	...	7.36	3	3	0	0	0	11	17	9	9	13	6
2000— Rochester (I.L.)	0	2	.000	14.14	2	2	0	0	0	7	15	12	11	4	8
— Bowie (East.)	5	7	.417	6.08	19	14	2	0	1	74	74	56	50	49	66
2001— Baltimore (A.L.)							Did not play.								
Major League totals (1 year)	0	0	...	7.36	3	3	0	0	0	11	17	9	9	13	6

RINCON, JUAN   P   TWINS

PERSONAL: Born January 23, 1979, in Maracaibo, Venezuela. ... 5-11/190. ... Throws right, bats right. ... Full name: Juan Manuel Rincon.
HIGH SCHOOL: Instituto Cervantes (Maracaibo, Venezuela).
TRANSACTIONS/CAREER NOTES: Signed as non-drafted free agent by Minnesota Twins organization (November 15, 1996).

Year League	W	L	Pct.	ERA	G	GS	CG	ShO	Sv.	IP	H	R	ER	BB	SO
1997— Gulf Coast Twins (GCL)	3	3	.500	2.95	11	10	1	0	0	58	55	21	19	24	46
— Elizabethton (Appl.)	0	1	.000	3.86	2	1	0	0	0	9¹/₃	11	4	4	3	7
1998— Fort Wayne (Midw.)	6	4	.600	3.83	37	13	0	0	6	96¹/₃	84	51	41	54	74
1999— Quad City (Midw.)	14	8	.636	2.92	28	•28	0	0	0	163¹/₃	146	67	53	66	*153
2000— Fort Myers (FSL)	5	3	.625	2.13	13	13	0	0	0	76	67	26	18	23	55
— New Britain (East.)	3	9	.250	4.65	15	15	2	0	0	89	96	55	46	39	79
2001— New Britain (East.)	14	6	.700	2.88	29	23	2	1	0	153¹/₃	130	60	49	57	133
— Minnesota (A.L.)	0	0	...	6.35	4	0	0	0	0	5²/₃	7	5	4	5	4
Major League totals (1 year)	0	0	...	6.35	4	0	0	0	0	5²/₃	7	5	4	5	4

RINCON, RICKY   P   INDIANS

PERSONAL: Born April 13, 1970, in Veracruz, Mexico. ... 5-10/187. ... Throws left, bats left. ... Full name: Ricardo Rincon Espinoza.
TRANSACTIONS/CAREER NOTES: Signed as non-drafted free agent by Pittsburgh Pirates organization (March 30, 1997). ... On Pittsburgh disabled list (March 22-April 14, 1998); included rehabilitation assignments to Carolina (April 6) and Nashville (April 11-April 14). ... Traded by Pirates to Cleveland Indians for OF Brian Giles (November 18, 1998). ... On Cleveland disabled list (April 12-May 14, 1999); included rehabilitation assignment to Akron (May 11-14). ... On Cleveland disabled list (May 17-August 23, 2000); included rehabilitation assignment to Buffalo (August 20-23).
STATISTICAL NOTES: Pitched one inning, combining with Francisco Cordova (eight innings) in 3-0 no-hit victory against Houston (July 12, 1997).

Year League	W	L	Pct.	ERA	G	GS	CG	ShO	Sv.	IP	H	R	ER	BB	SO
1990— Union Laguna (Mex.)	3	0	1.000	3.78	19	4	0	0	0	47²/₃	53	22	20	32	29
1991— Union Laguna (Mex.)	2	8	.200	6.54	32	9	0	0	1	74¹/₃	99	60	54	48	66
1992— Union Laguna (Mex.)	6	5	.545	3.91	49	9	0	0	4	89²/₃	87	45	39	46	91
1993— Torreon (Mex.)■	7	3	.700	3.17	57	4	0	0	8	82¹/₃	80	33	29	36	81
1994— M.C. Red Devils (Mex.)■	2	4	.333	3.21	20	9	0	0	1	53¹/₃	57	23	19	20	38
1995— M.C. Red Devils (Mex.)	6	6	.500	5.16	27	11	0	0	3	75	86	45	43	41	41
1996— M.C. Red Devils (Mex.)	5	3	.625	2.97	50	0	0	0	10	78²/₃	58	28	26	27	60
1997— Pittsburgh (N.L.)■	4	8	.333	3.45	62	0	0	0	4	60	51	26	23	24	71
1998— Carolina (Sou.)	0	0	...	6.00	2	0	0	0	0	3	5	2	2	2	1
— Nashville (PCL)	0	0	...	0.00	1	0	0	0	0	1	0	0	0	0	1
— Pittsburgh (N.L.)	0	2	.000	2.91	60	0	0	0	14	65	50	31	21	29	64
1999— Cleveland (A.L.)■	2	3	.400	4.43	59	0	0	0	0	44²/₃	41	22	22	24	30
— Akron (East.)	0	0	...	5.40	2	2	0	0	0	1²/₃	2	1	1	0	2
2000— Cleveland (A.L.)	2	0	1.000	2.70	35	0	0	0	0	20	17	7	6	13	20
— Buffalo (I.L.)	0	0	...	0.00	2	0	0	0	0	2	1	1	0	0	2
2001— Cleveland (A.L.)	2	1	.667	2.83	67	0	0	0	2	54	44	18	17	21	50
A.L. totals (3 years)	6	4	.600	3.41	161	0	0	0	2	118²/₃	102	47	45	58	100
N.L. totals (2 years)	4	10	.286	3.17	122	0	0	0	18	125	101	57	44	53	135
Major League totals (5 years)	10	14	.417	3.29	283	0	0	0	20	243²/₃	203	104	89	111	235

DIVISION SERIES RECORD

Year League	W	L	Pct.	ERA	G	GS	CG	ShO	Sv.	IP	H	R	ER	BB	SO
1999— Cleveland (A.L.)	0	0	...	40.50	1	0	0	0	0	²/₃	2	3	3	1	1
2001— Cleveland (A.L.)	0	0	...	9.00	3	0	0	0	0	2	2	2	2	0	3
Division series totals (2 years)	0	0	...	16.88	4	0	0	0	0	2²/₃	4	5	5	1	4

RIOS, ARMANDO   OF   PIRATES

PERSONAL: Born September 13, 1971, in Santurce, Puerto Rico. ... 5-9/185. ... Bats left, throws left.
HIGH SCHOOL: Villa Fontana (Carolina, Puerto Rico).
COLLEGE: UNC Charlotte, then Louisiana State.

TRANSACTIONS/CAREER NOTES: Signed as non-drafted free agent by San Francisco Giants organization (January 6, 1994). ... On disabled list (May 15-29, 1996). ... On San Francisco disabled list (June 22-September 2, 1999); included rehabilitation assignment to Fresno (July 23-30 and August 12-31). ... Traded by Giants with P Ryan Vogelsong to Pittsburgh Pirates for P Jason Schmidt and OF John Vander Wal (July 30, 2001). ... On Pittsburgh disabled list (August 2, 2001-remainder of season).

STATISTICAL NOTES: Career major league grand slams: 2.

								BATTING							FIELDING		
Year Team (League)	Pos.	G	AB	R	H	2B	3B	HR	RBI	Avg.	BB	SO	SB	PO	A	E	Avg.
1994— Clinton (Midw.)	OF	119	407	67	120	23	4	8	60	.295	59	69	16	216	17	12	.951
1995— San Jose (Calif.)	OF	128	488	76	143	34	3	8	75	.293	74	75	51	220	16	9	.963
1996— Shreveport (Texas)	OF	92	329	62	93	22	2	12	49	.283	44	42	9	165	*15	7	.963
1997— Shreveport (Texas)	OF-DH	127	461	86	133	30	6	14	79	.289	63	85	17	191	*17	6	.972
1998— Fresno (PCL)	OF-DH-1B	125	445	85	134	23	1	26	103	.301	55	73	17	226	14	7	.972
— San Francisco (N.L.) ..	OF	12	7	3	4	0	0	2	3	.571	3	2	0	5	0	0	1.000
1999— Fresno (PCL)	OF-DH-1B	31	109	24	30	3	0	4	21	.275	11	22	3	28	1	0	1.000
— San Francisco (N.L.) ..	OF	72	150	32	49	9	0	7	29	.327	24	35	7	84	5	2	.978
2000— San Francisco (N.L.) ..	OF-1B	115	233	38	62	15	5	10	50	.266	31	43	3	133	6	6	.959
2001— San Francisco (N.L.) ..	OF	93	316	38	82	17	3	14	49	.259	34	73	3	196	7	6	.971
— Pittsburgh (N.L.)■.....	OF	2	3	0	1	0	0	0	1	.333	2	1	0	0	0	0	...
Major League totals (4 years)		294	709	111	198	41	8	33	132	.279	94	154	13	418	18	14	.969

DIVISION SERIES RECORD

								BATTING							FIELDING		
Year Team (League)	Pos.	G	AB	R	H	2B	3B	HR	RBI	Avg.	BB	SO	SB	PO	A	E	Avg.
2000— San Francisco (N.L.) ..	PH	2	2	1	1	0	0	0	0	.500	0	0	0	...	...	...	...

RIPKEN, CAL   3B

PERSONAL: Born August 24, 1960, in Havre de Grace, Md. ... 6-4/220. ... Bats right, throws right. ... Full name: Calvin Edwin Ripken Jr. ... Son of Cal Ripken Sr., minor league catcher (1957-62 and 1964), manager with Baltimore Orioles (1987-88) and coach, Orioles (1976-86 and 1989-92); and brother of Bill Ripken, infielder with four major league teams (1987-98).

HIGH SCHOOL: Aberdeen (Md.).

TRANSACTIONS/CAREER NOTES: Selected by Baltimore Orioles organization in second round of free-agent draft (June 6, 1978). ... On disabled list (April 18-May 13 and August 1-September 1, 1999; and June 28-September 1, 2000). ... Granted free agency (November 16, 2001).

RECORDS: Holds major league career records for most consecutive games played—2,632 (May 30, 1982-September 19, 1998); most years leading league in games played—9; most consecutive years played all club's games—15 (1983-97); most years played all club's games—15 (1983-97); most home runs by shortstop—345; most years leading league in games by shortstop—12; most consecutive games by short-stop—2,216; and most years leading league in double plays by shortstop—8. ... Holds major league single-season records for most at-bats without a triple—646 (1989) and highest fielding percentage by shortstop (150 or more games)—.996 (1990). ... Shares major league single-season record for fewest errors by shortstop (150 or more games)—3 (1990). ... Holds A.L. career records for most double plays by short-stop—1,565; most years leading league in putouts by shortstop—6; most consecutive years played 150 or more games—12 (1982-93); most years played 150 or more games— 15 (1982-93 and 1996-98); and most years with 600 or more at-bats—13. ... Holds A.L. single-season record for most assists by shortstop—583 (1984). ... Shares A.L. career records for most years leading league in assists by shortstop—7. ... Shares A.L. single-season record for most consecutive errorless games by shortstop—95 (April 14-July 27, 1990).

HONORS: Named A.L. Rookie Player of the Year by THE SPORTING NEWS (1982). ... Named A.L. Rookie of the Year by THE SPORTING NEWS (1983 and 1991). ... Named A.L. Player of the Year by THE SPORTING NEWS (1983 and 1991). ... Named shortstop on THE SPORTING NEWS A.L. All-Star team (1983-85, 1989, 1991 and 1993-95). ... Named shortstop on THE SPORTING NEWS A.L. Silver Slugger team (1983-86, 1989, 1991 and 1993-94). ... Named A.L. Most Valuable Player by Baseball Writers' Association of America (1983 and 1991). ... Won A.L. Gold Glove at shortstop (1991-92). ... Named Sportsman of the Year by THE SPORTING NEWS (1995).

STATISTICAL NOTES: Tied for Appalachian League lead in total chances by shortstop with 329 and double plays by shortstop with 31 in 1978. ... Led Southern League third basemen with .933 fielding percentage, 119 putouts, 268 assists, 415 total chances and 34 double plays in 1980. ... Tied for Southern League lead with nine sacrifice flies in 1980. ... Led A.L. shortstops with 831 total chances in 1983, 906 in 1984, 815 in 1989, 806 in 1991 and 738 in 1993. ... Led A.L. shortstops with 113 double plays in 1983, 122 in 1984, 123 in 1985, 119 in 1989, 114 in 1991, 119 in 1992, 72 in 1994 and 100 in 1995. ... Hit for the cycle (May 6, 1984). ... Tied for A.L. lead with 25 game-winning RBIs in 1986. ... Tied for A.L. lead with 10 sacrifice flies in 1988. ... Led A.L. with 368 total bases in 1991. ... Hit three home runs in one game (May 28, 1996). ... Led A.L. in grounding into double plays with 28 in 1996. ... Collected six hits in one game (June 13, 1999). ... Had 16-game hitting streak (July 21-August 8, 2001). ... Had 15-game hitting streak (June 20-July 14, 2001). ... Career major league grand slams: 8.

MISCELLANEOUS: Holds Baltimore Orioles all-time records for most hits (3,184), runs (1,647), doubles (603), home runs (431) and runs batted in (1,695).

								BATTING							FIELDING		
Year Team (League)	Pos.	G	AB	R	H	2B	3B	HR	RBI	Avg.	BB	SO	SB	PO	A	E	Avg.
1978— Bluefield (Appl.)	SS	63	239	27	63	7	1	0	24	.264	24	46	1	*92	204	*33	.900
1979— Miami (FSL)	3B-SS-2B	105	393	51	119	*28	1	5	54	.303	31	64	4	149	260	30	.932
— Charlotte (Sou.).........	3B	17	61	6	11	0	1	3	8	.180	3	13	1	13	26	3	.929
1980— Charlotte (Sou.).........	3B-SS	•144	522	91	144	28	5	25	78	.276	77	81	4	†151	†341	35	†.934
1981— Rochester (I.L.).........	3B-SS	114	437	74	126	31	4	23	75	.288	66	85	0	128	320	21	.955
— Baltimore (A.L.).........	SS-3B	23	39	1	5	0	0	0	0	.128	1	8	0	13	30	3	.935
1982— Baltimore (A.L.).........	SS-3B	160	598	90	158	32	5	28	93	.264	46	95	3	221	440	19	.972
1983— Baltimore (A.L.).........	SS	•162	*663	*121	*211	*47	2	27	102	.318	58	97	0	272	*534	25	.970
1984— Baltimore (A.L.).........	SS	•162	641	103	195	37	7	27	86	.304	71	89	2	*297	*583	26	.971
1985— Baltimore (A.L.).........	SS	161	642	116	181	32	5	26	110	.282	67	68	2	*286	474	26	.967
1986— Baltimore (A.L.).........	SS	162	627	98	177	35	1	25	81	.282	70	60	4	240	*482	13	.982
1987— Baltimore (A.L.).........	SS	*162	624	97	157	28	3	27	98	.252	81	77	3	240	*480	20	.973
1988— Baltimore (A.L.).........	SS	161	575	87	152	25	1	23	81	.264	102	69	2	*284	480	21	.973
1989— Baltimore (A.L.).........	SS	•162	646	80	166	30	0	21	93	.257	57	72	3	*276	*531	8	.990
1990— Baltimore (A.L.).........	SS	161	600	78	150	28	4	21	84	.250	82	66	3	242	435	3	*.996
1991— Baltimore (A.L.).........	SS	•162	650	99	210	46	5	34	114	.323	53	46	6	*267	*528	11	*.986
1992— Baltimore (A.L.).........	SS	*162	637	73	160	29	1	14	72	.251	64	50	4	*287	445	12	.984
1993— Baltimore (A.L.).........	SS	*162	*641	87	165	26	3	24	90	.257	65	58	1	226	*495	17	.977
1994— Baltimore (A.L.).........	SS	112	444	71	140	19	3	13	75	.315	32	41	1	132	321	7	*.985
1995— Baltimore (A.L.).........	SS	144	550	71	144	33	2	17	88	.262	52	59	0	206	409	7	*.989

Year Team (League)	Pos.	G	AB	R	H	2B	3B	HR	RBI	Avg.	BB	SO	SB	PO	A	E	Avg.
1996—Baltimore (A.L.).........	SS-3B	*163	640	94	178	40	1	26	102	.278	59	78	1	233	483	14	.981
1997—Baltimore (A.L.).........	3B-SS	•162	615	79	166	30	0	17	84	.270	56	73	1	100	313	22	.949
1998—Baltimore (A.L.).........	3B	161	601	65	163	27	1	14	61	.271	51	68	0	101	265	8	*.979
1999—Baltimore (A.L.).........	3B	86	332	51	113	27	0	18	57	.340	13	31	0	36	142	13	.932
2000—Baltimore (A.L.).........	3B-DH	83	309	43	79	16	0	15	56	.256	23	37	0	56	134	5	.974
2001—Baltimore (A.L.).........	3B-DH	128	477	43	114	16	0	14	68	.239	26	63	0	97	209	14	.956
Major League totals (21 years)		3001	11551	1647	3184	603	44	431	1695	.276	1129	1305	36	4112	8213	294	.977

DIVISION SERIES RECORD

Year Team (League)	Pos.	G	AB	R	H	2B	3B	HR	RBI	Avg.	BB	SO	SB	PO	A	E	Avg.
1996—Baltimore (A.L.).........	SS	4	18	2	8	3	0	0	2	.444	0	3	0	7	15	0	1.000
1997—Baltimore (A.L.).........	3B	4	16	1	7	2	0	0	1	.438	2	2	0	4	4	0	1.000
Division series totals (2 years)		8	34	3	15	5	0	0	3	.441	2	5	0	11	19	0	1.000

CHAMPIONSHIP SERIES RECORD

Year Team (League)	Pos.	G	AB	R	H	2B	3B	HR	RBI	Avg.	BB	SO	SB	PO	A	E	Avg.
1983—Baltimore (A.L.).........	SS	4	15	5	6	2	0	0	1	.400	2	3	0	7	11	0	1.000
1996—Baltimore (A.L.).........	SS	5	20	1	5	1	0	0	0	.250	1	4	0	4	14	1	.947
1997—Baltimore (A.L.).........	3B	6	23	3	8	2	0	1	3	.348	4	6	0	1	14	0	1.000
Championship series totals (3 years)		15	58	9	19	5	0	1	4	.328	7	13	0	12	39	1	.981

NOTES: Member of World Series championship team (1983).

WORLD SERIES RECORD

Year Team (League)	Pos.	G	AB	R	H	2B	3B	HR	RBI	Avg.	BB	SO	SB	PO	A	E	Avg.
1983—Baltimore (A.L.).........	SS	5	18	2	3	0	0	0	1	.167	3	4	0	6	14	0	1.000

ALL-STAR GAME RECORD

RECORDS: Holds major league record for most consecutive games started—16. ... Shares single-game record for most at-bats (nine-inning game)—5 (July 12, 1994).
NOTES: Named Most Valuable Player (1991 and 2001).

Year League	Pos.	AB	R	H	2B	3B	HR	RBI	Avg.	BB	SO	SB	PO	A	E	Avg.
1983—American..................	SS	0	0	0	0	0	0	0	...	1	0	0	1	0	0	1.000
1984—American..................	SS	3	0	0	0	0	0	0	.000	0	0	0	0	0	0	...
1985—American..................	SS	3	0	1	0	0	0	0	.333	0	0	0	2	1	0	1.000
1986—American..................	SS	4	0	0	0	0	0	0	.000	0	0	0	0	1	0	1.000
1987—American..................	SS	2	0	1	0	0	0	0	.500	0	0	0	0	5	0	1.000
1988—American..................	SS	3	0	0	0	0	0	0	.000	1	0	0	1	4	0	1.000
1989—American..................	SS	3	0	1	1	0	0	0	.333	0	0	0	0	0	0	...
1990—American..................	SS	2	0	0	0	0	0	0	.000	0	0	0	1	1	0	1.000
1991—American..................	SS	3	1	2	0	0	1	3	.667	0	0	0	2	1	0	1.000
1992—American..................	SS	3	0	1	0	0	0	1	.333	0	0	0	1	1	0	1.000
1993—American..................	SS	3	0	0	0	0	0	0	.000	0	1	0	1	2	0	1.000
1994—American..................	SS	5	0	1	1	0	0	0	.200	0	2	0	1	2	0	1.000
1995—American..................	SS	3	0	2	0	0	0	0	.667	0	0	0	2	1	0	1.000
1996—American..................	SS	3	0	0	0	0	0	0	.000	0	0	0	1	1	0	1.000
1997—American..................	3B	2	0	1	0	0	0	0	.500	0	0	0	0	4	0	1.000
1998—American..................	3B	4	1	1	1	0	0	2	.250	0	0	0	1	1	0	1.000
1999—American..................	3B	1	1	1	0	0	0	1	1.000	0	0	0	0	0	0	...
2000—American..................							Selected, did not play—injured.										
2001—American..................	3B-SS	2	1	1	0	0	1	1	.500	0	0	0	1	2	0	1.000
All-Star Game totals (18 years)		49	4	13	3	0	2	8	.265	2	3	0	15	27	0	1.000

RISKE, DAVE — P — INDIANS

PERSONAL: Born October 23, 1976, in Renton, Wash. ... 6-2/180. ... Throws right, bats right. ... Full name: David R. Riske.
HIGH SCHOOL: Lindbergh (Renton, Wash.).
JUNIOR COLLEGE: Green River (Wash.) Community College.
TRANSACTIONS/CAREER NOTES: Selected by Cleveland Indians organization in 56th round of free-agent draft (June 4, 1996). ... On Cleveland disabled list (March 25-April 28 and May 29-September 4 and September 14, 2000-remainder of season); included rehabilitation assignment to Akron (April 22-26 and August 28-September 4).

Year League	W	L	Pct.	ERA	G	GS	CG	ShO	Sv.	IP	H	R	ER	BB	SO
1997—Kinston (Caro.).................	4	4	.500	2.25	39	0	0	0	2	72	58	22	18	33	90
1998—Kinston (Caro.).................	1	1	.500	2.33	53	0	0	0	*33	54	48	15	14	15	67
—Akron (East.).....................	0	0	...	0.00	2	0	0	0	1	3	1	0	0	1	5
1999—Akron (East.).....................	0	0	...	1.90	23	0	0	0	12	23 2/3	5	6	5	13	33
—Buffalo (I.L.).....................	3	0	1.000	0.65	23	0	0	0	6	27 2/3	14	3	2	7	22
—Cleveland (A.L.).....................	1	1	.500	8.36	12	0	0	0	0	14	20	15	13	6	16
2000—Akron (East.).....................	0	0	...	0.00	3	1	0	0	1	4	2	0	0	0	4
—Buffalo (I.L.).....................	0	0	...	3.00	2	0	0	0	0	3	2	1	1	2	2
2001—Buffalo (I.L.).....................	1	2	.333	2.36	38	0	0	0	15	53 1/3	45	16	14	17	72
—Cleveland (A.L.).....................	2	0	1.000	1.98	26	0	0	0	1	27 1/3	20	7	6	18	29
Major League totals (2 years).......	3	1	.750	4.14	38	0	0	0	1	41 1/3	40	22	19	24	45

DIVISION SERIES RECORD

Year League	W	L	Pct.	ERA	G	GS	CG	ShO	Sv.	IP	H	R	ER	BB	SO
2001—Cleveland (A.L.).................	0	0	...	0.00	3	0	0	0	0	3 1/3	2	0	0	1	5

PERSONAL: Born November 7, 1971, in Portsmouth, Va. ... 6-3/220. ... Throws right, bats right. ... Full name: Todd Everett Ritchie.
HIGH SCHOOL: Duncanville (Texas).
TRANSACTIONS/CAREER NOTES: Selected by Minnesota Twins organization in first round (12th pick overall) of free-agent draft (June 4, 1990). ... On disabled list (August 19, 1991-remainder of season; June 24-July 9, 1993; and April 28, 1994-remainder of season). ... Released by Twins (October 3, 1998). ... Signed by Pittsburgh Pirates organization (December 22, 1998). ... On Pittsburgh disabled list (August 21-September 6, 1999). ... On disabled list (July 24-August 11, 2000). ... Traded by Pirates with C Lee Evans to Chicago White Sox for P Kip Wells, P Sean Lowe and P Josh Fogg (December 13, 2001).
STATISTICAL NOTES: Pitched 1-0 one-hit, complete-game victory against Kansas City (July 13, 2001).
MISCELLANEOUS: Grounded out in only appearance as pinch hitter (1999).

Year	League	W	L	Pct.	ERA	G	GS	CG	ShO	Sv.	IP	H	R	ER	BB	SO
1990—	Elizabethton (Appl.)	5	2	.714	1.94	11	11	1	0	0	65	45	22	14	24	49
1991—	Kenosha (Midw.)	7	6	.538	3.55	21	21	0	0	0	116²/₃	113	53	46	50	101
1992—	Visalia (Calif.)	11	9	.550	5.06	28	•28	3	1	0	172²/₃	193	113	97	65	129
1993—	Nashville (Sou.)	3	2	.600	3.66	12	10	0	0	0	46²/₃	46	21	19	15	41
1994—	Nashville (Sou.)	0	2	.000	4.24	4	4	0	0	0	17	24	10	8	7	9
1995—	New Britain (East.)	4	9	.308	5.73	24	21	0	0	0	113	135	78	72	54	60
1996—	New Britain (East.)	3	7	.300	5.44	29	10	0	0	4	82²/₃	101	55	50	30	53
—	Salt Lake (PCL)	0	4	.000	5.47	16	0	0	0	0	24²/₃	27	15	15	11	19
1997—	Minnesota (A.L.)	2	3	.400	4.58	42	0	0	0	0	74²/₃	87	41	38	28	44
1998—	Minnesota (A.L.)	0	0	...	5.63	15	0	0	0	0	24	30	17	15	9	21
—	Salt Lake (PCL)	1	3	.250	4.15	36	0	0	0	4	60²/₃	55	38	28	31	62
1999—	Nashville (PCL)■	0	0	...	1.80	1	1	0	0	0	5	6	1	1	1	2
—	Pittsburgh (N.L.)	15	9	.625	3.49	28	26	2	0	0	172²/₃	169	79	67	54	107
2000—	Pittsburgh (N.L.)	9	8	.529	4.81	31	31	1	1	0	187	208	111	100	51	124
2001—	Pittsburgh (N.L.)	11	15	.423	4.47	33	33	4	2	0	207¹/₃	211	118	103	52	124
A.L. totals (2 years)		2	3	.400	4.83	57	0	0	0	0	98²/₃	117	58	53	37	65
N.L. totals (3 years)		35	32	.522	4.29	92	90	7	3	0	567	588	308	270	157	355
Major League totals (5 years)		37	35	.514	4.37	149	90	7	3	0	665²/₃	705	366	323	194	420

PERSONAL: Born August 30, 1979, in La Guaria, Venezuela. ... 5-11/175. ... Bats right, throws right. ... Full name: Luis Wilfredo Rivas.
HIGH SCHOOL: Riceniado Le Guaria (La Guaria, Venezuela).
TRANSACTIONS/CAREER NOTES: Signed as non-drafted free agent by Minnesota Twins organization (October 9, 1995). ... On New Britain disabled list (July 7-21, 2000).
RECORDS: Shares A.L. single-season record for fewest putouts by second baseman (150 or more games)—230 (2001). ... Shares major league single-season record for fewest double plays by second baseman (150 or more games)—65 (2001).
STATISTICAL NOTES: Led Gulf Coast League shortstops with 40 double plays in 1996. ... Led Midwest League shortstops with 621 total chances and 92 double plays in 1997. ... Led Florida State League shortstops with 78 double plays in 1998. ... Led Eastern League shortstops with 37 errors in 1999.

Year	Team (League)	Pos.	G	AB	R	H	2B	3B	HR	RBI	Avg.	BB	SO	SB	PO	A	E	Avg.
1996—	GC Twins (GCL)	SS	53	201	29	52	12	1	1	13	.259	18	37	•35	68	181	21	.922
1997—	Fort Wayne (Midw.)	SS	121	419	61	100	20	6	1	30	.239	33	90	28	169	*394	*58	.907
1998—	Fort Myers (FSL)	SS	126	463	58	130	21	5	4	51	.281	14	75	34	162	*415	55	.913
1999—	New Britain (East.)	SS-2B	132	527	78	134	30	7	7	49	.254	41	92	31	164	392	†39	.934
2000—	New Britain (East.)	2B-SS	82	328	56	82	23	6	3	40	.250	36	41	11	141	226	11	.971
—	Salt Lake (PCL)	2B-SS	41	157	33	50	14	1	3	25	.318	13	21	7	70	107	2	.989
—	Minnesota (A.L.)	2B-SS	16	58	8	18	4	1	0	6	.310	2	4	2	31	29	1	.984
2001—	Minnesota (A.L.)	2B	153	563	70	150	21	6	7	47	.266	40	99	31	230	335	15	.974
Major League totals (2 years)			169	621	78	168	25	7	7	53	.271	42	103	33	261	364	16	.975

PERSONAL: Born July 3, 1978, in Guarenas, Venezuela. ... 6-2/170. ... Bats right, throws right. ... Full name: Juan Luis Rivera.
TRANSACTIONS/CAREER NOTES: Signed as non-drafted free agent by New York Yankees organization (April 12, 1996).
STATISTICAL NOTES: Led Gulf Coast League with 117 total bases in 1998. ... Led Gulf Coast League outfielders with four double plays in 1998.

Year	Team (League)	Pos.	G	AB	R	H	2B	3B	HR	RBI	Avg.	BB	SO	SB	PO	A	E	Avg.
1996—	Dom. Yankees (DSL)	OF	10	18	0	3	0	0	0	2	.167	0	1	0	4	0	0	1.000
1997—	Maracay 2 (VSL)		52	142	25	40	9	0	0	14	.282	12	16	12	...	...	...	...
1998—	GC Yankees (GCL)	OF	57	210	43	70	9	1	*12	*45	.333	26	27	8	86	•8	2	.979
—	Oneonta (NY-Penn)	OF	6	18	2	5	0	0	1	3	.278	1	4	1	3	1	0	1.000
1999—	Tampa (FSL)	OF	109	426	50	112	20	2	14	77	.263	26	67	5	181	8	4	.979
—	GC Yankees (GCL)	OF	5	18	7	6	0	0	1	4	.333	4	1	0	1	0	0	1.000
2000—	Norwich (East.)	OF	17	62	9	14	5	0	2	12	.226	6	15	0	20	1	1	.955
—	Tampa (FSL)	OF-1B	115	409	62	113	26	1	14	69	.276	33	56	11	206	17	5	.978
2001—	Norwich (East.)	OF	77	316	50	101	18	3	14	58	.320	15	50	5	141	16	6	.963
—	Columbus (I.L.)	OF	55	199	39	65	11	1	14	40	.327	15	31	4	124	5	4	.970
—	New York (A.L.)	OF	3	4	0	0	0	0	0	0	.000	0	0	0	1	0	0	1.000
Major League totals (1 year)			3	4	0	0	0	0	0	0	.000	0	0	0	1	0	0	1.000

R

PERSONAL: Born June 21, 1978, in Chihuahua, Mexico. ... 6-3/163. ... Throws right, bats right. ... Full name: Luis Gutierrez Rivera.
HIGH SCHOOL: Sistema Preparatoria Abierta (Telucha, Mexico).
TRANSACTIONS/CAREER NOTES: Signed as non-drafted free agent by Atlanta Braves organization (February 18, 1995). ... Loaned by Braves organization to Mexico City Tigres, Mexican League (May 4-October 18, 1995); did not play. ... On Myrtle Beach disabled list (April 18-May 14, 1999) ... On Richmond disabled list (May 5-June 29, 2000). ... Traded by Braves with OF Trenidad Hubbard and C Fernando Lunar to Baltimore Orioles for OF B.J. Surhoff and P Gabe Molina (July 31, 2000). ... On disabled list (March 30, 2001-entire season).
STATISTICAL NOTES: Tied for International League lead with four balks in 2000.

Year	League	W	L	Pct.	ERA	G	GS	CG	ShO	Sv.	IP	H	R	ER	BB	SO
1996—	Gulf Coast Braves (GCL)	1	1	.500	2.59	8	6	0	0	0	24 1/3	18	9	7	7	26
1997—	Danville (Appl.)	3	1	.750	2.41	9	9	0	0	0	41	28	15	11	17	57
—	Macon (S.Atl.)	2	0	1.000	1.29	4	4	0	0	0	21	13	4	3	7	27
1998—	Macon (S.Atl.)	5	5	.500	3.98	20	20	0	0	0	92 2/3	78	53	41	41	118
1999—	Myrtle Beach (Caro.)	0	2	.000	3.11	25	13	0	0	0	66 2/3	45	25	23	23	81
2000—	Atlanta (N.L.)	1	0	1.000	1.35	5	0	0	0	0	6 2/3	4	1	1	5	5
—	Richmond (I.L.)	0	2	.000	8.06	8	7	0	0	0	22 1/3	29	20	20	18	12
—	Gulf Coast Braves (GCL)	0	0	...	0.00	3	3	0	0	0	4	2	0	0	1	2
—	Rochester (I.L.)■	0	1	.000	3.38	3	3	0	0	0	8	11	5	3	5	4
—	Baltimore (A.L.)	0	0	...	0.00	1	0	0	0	0	2/3	1	0	0	1	0
2001—	Baltimore (A.L.)							Did not play.								
A.L. totals (1 year)		0	0	...	0.00	1	0	0	0	0	2/3	1	0	0	1	0
N.L. totals (1 year)		1	0	1.000	1.35	5	0	0	0	0	6 2/3	4	1	1	5	5
Major League totals (1 year)		1	0	1.000	1.23	6	0	0	0	0	7 1/3	5	1	1	6	5

PERSONAL: Born November 29, 1969, in Panama City, Panama. ... 6-2/185. ... Throws right, bats right. ... Cousin of Ruben Rivera, outfielder with New York Yankees (1995-96), San Diego Padres (1997-2000) and Cincinnati Reds (2001).
TRANSACTIONS/CAREER NOTES: Signed as non-drafted free agent by New York Yankees organization (February 17, 1990). ... On disabled list (April 10-May 19, July 11-28 and August 12-September 8, 1992). ... On Albany/Colonie disabled list (April 9-June 28, 1993). ... On Greensboro disabled list (September 6, 1993-remainder of season). ... On Tampa disabled list (April 23-May 9, 1994). ... On Columbus disabled list (August 4-14, 1994). ... On disabled list (April 6-24, 1998).
HONORS: Named A.L. Fireman of the Year by THE SPORTING NEWS (1997 and 1999). ... Named A.L. Reliever of the Year by THE SPORTING NEWS (2001).
STATISTICAL NOTES: Pitched seven-inning, 3-0 no-hit victory against Gulf Coast Pirates (August 31, 1990). ... Pitched five-inning, 3-0 no-hit victory for Columbus against Rochester (June 26, 1995).

Year	League	W	L	Pct.	ERA	G	GS	CG	ShO	Sv.	IP	H	R	ER	BB	SO
1990—	Gulf Coast Yankees (GCL)	5	1	.833	*0.17	22	1	1	1	1	52	17	3	1	7	58
1991—	Greensboro (S.Atl.)	4	9	.308	2.75	29	15	1	0	0	114 2/3	103	48	35	36	123
1992—	Fort Lauderdale (FSL)	5	3	.625	2.28	10	10	3	1	0	59 1/3	40	17	15	5	42
1993—	Greensboro (S.Atl.)	1	0	1.000	2.06	10	10	0	0	0	39 1/3	31	12	9	15	32
—	Gulf Coast Yankees (GCL)	0	1	.000	2.25	2	2	0	0	0	4	2	1	1	1	6
1994—	Tampa (FSL)	3	0	1.000	2.21	7	7	0	0	0	36 2/3	34	12	9	12	27
—	Albany/Colonie (East.)	3	0	1.000	2.27	9	9	0	0	0	63 1/3	58	20	16	8	39
—	Columbus (I.L.)	4	2	.667	5.81	6	6	1	0	0	31	34	22	20	10	23
1995—	Columbus (I.L.)	2	2	.500	2.10	7	7	1	1	0	30	25	10	7	3	30
—	New York (A.L.)	5	3	.625	5.51	19	10	0	0	0	67	71	43	41	30	51
1996—	New York (A.L.)	8	3	.727	2.09	61	0	0	0	5	107 2/3	73	25	25	34	130
1997—	New York (A.L.)	6	4	.600	1.88	66	0	0	0	43	71 2/3	65	17	15	20	68
1998—	New York (A.L.)	3	0	1.000	1.91	54	0	0	0	36	61 1/3	48	13	13	17	36
1999—	New York (A.L.)	4	3	.571	1.83	66	0	0	0	*45	69	43	15	14	18	52
2000—	New York (A.L.)	7	4	.636	2.85	66	0	0	0	36	75 2/3	58	26	24	25	58
2001—	New York (A.L.)	4	6	.400	2.34	71	0	0	0	*50	80 2/3	61	24	21	12	83
Major League totals (7 years)		37	23	.617	2.58	403	10	0	0	215	533	419	163	153	156	478

DIVISION SERIES RECORD

RECORDS: Holds major league career record for most saves—10.

Year	League	W	L	Pct.	ERA	G	GS	CG	ShO	Sv.	IP	H	R	ER	BB	SO
1995—	New York (A.L.)	1	0	1.000	0.00	3	0	0	0	0	5 1/3	3	0	0	1	8
1996—	New York (A.L.)	0	0	...	0.00	2	0	0	0	0	4 2/3	0	0	0	1	1
1997—	New York (A.L.)	0	0	...	4.50	2	0	0	0	1	2	2	1	1	0	1
1998—	New York (A.L.)	0	0	...	0.00	3	0	0	0	2	3 1/3	1	0	0	1	2
1999—	New York (A.L.)	0	0	...	0.00	2	0	0	0	2	3	1	0	0	0	3
2000—	New York (A.L.)	0	0	...	0.00	3	0	0	0	3	5	2	0	0	0	2
2001—	New York (A.L.)	0	0	...	0.00	3	0	0	0	2	5	4	1	0	0	4
Division series totals (7 years)		1	0	1.000	0.32	18	0	0	0	10	28 1/3	13	2	1	3	21

CHAMPIONSHIP SERIES RECORD

Year	League	W	L	Pct.	ERA	G	GS	CG	ShO	Sv.	IP	H	R	ER	BB	SO
1996—	New York (A.L.)	1	0	1.000	0.00	2	0	0	0	0	4	6	0	0	1	5
1998—	New York (A.L.)	0	0	...	0.00	4	0	0	0	1	5 2/3	0	0	0	1	5
1999—	New York (A.L.)	1	0	1.000	0.00	3	0	0	0	2	4 2/3	5	0	0	0	3
2000—	New York (A.L.)	0	0	...	1.93	3	0	0	0	1	4 2/3	4	1	1	0	1
2001—	New York (A.L.)	1	0	1.000	1.93	4	0	0	0	2	4 2/3	2	1	1	1	3
Champ. series totals (5 years)		3	0	1.000	0.76	16	0	0	0	6	23 2/3	17	2	2	3	17

WORLD SERIES RECORD

RECORDS: Holds career record for most saves—8.
NOTES: Named Most Valuable Player (1999). ... Member of World Series championship team (1996, 1998, 1999 and 2000).

Year League	W	L	Pct.	ERA	G	GS	CG	ShO	Sv.	IP	H	R	ER	BB	SO
1996— New York (A.L.)	0	0	...	1.59	4	0	0	0	0	5²/₃	4	1	1	3	4
1998— New York (A.L.)	0	0	...	0.00	3	0	0	0	3	4¹/₃	5	0	0	0	4
1999— New York (A.L.)	1	0	1.000	0.00	3	0	0	0	2	4²/₃	3	0	0	1	3
2000— New York (A.L.)	0	0	...	3.00	4	0	0	0	2	6	4	2	2	1	7
2001— New York (A.L.)	1	1	.500	1.42	4	0	0	0	1	6¹/₃	6	2	1	1	7
World Series totals (5 years)	2	1	.667	1.33	18	0	0	0	8	27	22	5	4	6	25

ALL-STAR GAME RECORD

Year League	W	L	Pct.	ERA	GS	CG	ShO	Sv.	IP	H	R	ER	BB	SO
1997— American	0	0	...	0.00	0	0	0	1	1	0	0	0	0	1
1999— American					Selected, did not play—injured.									
2000— American	0	0	...	0.00	0	0	0	0	1	2	1	0	0	0
All-Star Game totals (2 years)	0	0	...	0.00	0	0	0	1	2	2	1	0	0	1

RIVERA, MIKE — C — TIGERS

PERSONAL: Born September 8, 1976, in Rio Piedras, Puerto Rico. ... 6-0/190. ... Bats right, throws right. ... Full name: Michael R. Rivera.
HIGH SCHOOL: Dr. Augustin Stahl (Bayamon, Puerto Rico).
TRANSACTIONS/CAREER NOTES: Signed as non-drafted free agent by Detroit Tigers organization (January 20, 1997).
STATISTICAL NOTES: Tied for Gulf Coast League lead in intentional bases on balls received with two in 1997. ... Led Midwest League catchers with 1,007 total chances in 1998. ... Led Eastern League catchers with 886 total chances in 2001.

							BATTING								FIELDING			
Year Team (League)	Pos.	G	AB	R	H	2B	3B	HR	RBI	Avg.	BB	SO	SB	PO	A	E	Avg.
1997— GC Tigers (GCL)	C-1B	47	154	34	44	9	2	*10	36	.286	18	25	0	210	23	1	.996
1998— W. Michigan (Midw.)	C	108	403	40	111	34	3	9	67	.275	15	68	0	*889	108	10	.990
1999— Lakeland (FSL)	C	104	370	44	103	20	2	14	72	.278	20	59	1	588	*104	8	.989
— Jacksonville (Sou.)	C	7	23	3	4	1	0	2	6	.174	2	5	0	46	4	0	1.000
2000— Lakeland (FSL)	C	64	243	30	71	19	4	11	53	.292	16	45	2	374	43	5	.988
— Toledo (I.L.)	C	4	13	0	3	3	0	0	1	.231	0	2	0	26	4	1	.968
— Jacksonville (Sou.)	C	39	150	10	29	8	1	2	9	.193	7	30	0	231	17	8	.969
2001— Erie (East.)	C	112	415	76	120	19	1	*33	101	.289	44	96	2	*793	*83	10	.989
— Detroit (A.L.)	C	4	12	2	4	2	0	0	1	.333	0	2	2	24	2	2	.929
Major League totals (1 year)		4	12	2	4	2	0	0	1	.333	0	2	2	24	2	2	.929

RIVERA, RUBEN — OF

PERSONAL: Born November 14, 1973, in La Chorrera, Panama. ... 6-3/208. ... Bats right, throws right. ... Full name: Ruben Moreno Rivera. ... Cousin of Mariano Rivera, pitcher, New York Yankees.
TRANSACTIONS/CAREER NOTES: Signed as non-drafted free agent by New York Yankees organization (November 21, 1990). ... On New York disabled list (March 27-May 30, 1997). ... Traded by Yankees with P Rafael Medina and $3 million to San Diego Padres for the rights to P Hideki Irabu, 2B Homer Bush, OF Gordon Amerson and a player to be named later (April 22, 1997); Yankees acquired OF Vernon Maxwell to complete deal (June 9, 1997). ... On San Diego disabled list (May 30-August 13, 1997); included rehabilitation assignments to Rancho Cucamonga (May 30-July 22) and Las Vegas (July 23-August 4). ... On San Diego disabled list (April 12-May 5, 2000); included rehabilitation assignment to Las Vegas (May 3-5). ... Released by Padres (March 14, 2001). ... Signed by Cincinnati Reds (March 21, 2001). ... Claimed on waivers by San Francisco Giants (November 16, 2001). ... Granted free agency (December 21, 2001).
HONORS: Named New York-Pennsylvania League Most Valuable Player (1993). ... Named South Atlantic League Most Valuable Player (1994).
STATISTICAL NOTES: Tied for New York-Pennsylvania League lead in double plays by outfielders with three in 1993. ... Led South Atlantic League with .573 slugging percentage in 1994. ... Career major league grand slams: 2.

							BATTING								FIELDING			
Year Team (League)	Pos.	G	AB	R	H	2B	3B	HR	RBI	Avg.	BB	SO	SB	PO	A	E	Avg.
1991— Dom. Yankees (DSL)		51	170	27	34	3	2	2	16	.200	23	37	14	...	...	...	...
1992— GC Yankees (GCL)	OF	53	194	37	53	10	3	1	20	.273	42	49	21	67	10	4	.951
1993— Oneonta (NY-Penn)	OF	55	199	45	55	7	6	13	47	.276	32	66	12	111	9	3	.976
1994— Greensboro (S.Atl.)	OF	105	400	83	115	24	3	*28	81	.288	47	125	36	217	14	5	.979
— Tampa (FSL)	OF	34	134	18	35	4	3	5	20	.261	8	38	12	76	6	2	.976
1995— Norwich (East.)	OF	71	256	49	75	16	8	9	39	.293	37	77	16	176	7	3	.984
— Columbus (I.L.)	OF	48	174	37	47	8	2	15	35	.270	26	62	8	113	6	3	.975
— New York (A.L.)	OF	5	1	0	0	0	0	0	0	.000	0	1	0	2	0	0	1.000
1996— Columbus (I.L.)	OF	101	362	59	85	20	4	10	46	.235	40	96	15	239	6	7	.972
— New York (A.L.)	OF	46	88	17	25	6	1	2	16	.284	13	26	6	77	2	0	1.000
1997— Rancho Cuca. (Calif.)■	DH	6	23	6	4	1	0	1	3	.174	3	9	1	...	...	...	...
— Las Vegas (PCL)	DH-1B	12	48	6	12	5	1	1	6	.250	1	20	1	1	0	0	1.000
— San Diego (N.L.)	OF	17	20	2	5	1	0	0	1	.250	2	9	2	13	0	0	1.000
1998— Las Vegas (PCL)	OF	30	104	9	15	3	0	3	11	.144	11	42	4	53	2	0	1.000
— San Diego (N.L.)	OF	95	172	31	36	7	2	6	29	.209	28	52	5	104	3	3	.973
1999— San Diego (N.L.)	OF	147	411	65	80	16	1	23	48	.195	55	143	18	312	8	8	.976
2000— San Diego (N.L.)	OF	135	423	62	88	18	6	17	57	.208	44	137	8	303	10	5	.984
— Las Vegas (PCL)	OF	2	10	1	2	0	0	0	1	.200	0	3	0	1	0	0	1.000
2001— Cincinnati (N.L.)■	OF	117	263	37	67	13	1	10	34	.255	21	83	6	171	4	3	.983
American League totals (2 years)		51	89	17	25	6	1	2	16	.281	13	27	6	79	2	0	1.000
National League totals (5 years)		511	1289	197	276	55	10	56	169	.214	150	424	39	903	25	19	.980
Major League totals (7 years)		562	1378	214	301	61	11	58	185	.218	163	451	45	982	27	19	.982

DIVISION SERIES RECORD

							BATTING								FIELDING			
Year Team (League)	Pos.	G	AB	R	H	2B	3B	HR	RBI	Avg.	BB	SO	SB	PO	A	E	Avg.
1996— New York (A.L.)	OF-PH	2	1	0	0	0	0	0	0	.000	0	1	0	0	0	0	...
1998— San Diego (N.L.)	OF	3	6	0	0	0	0	0	0	.000	0	3	0	3	0	0	1.000
Division series totals (2 years)		5	7	0	0	0	0	0	0	.000	0	4	0	3	0	0	1.000

CHAMPIONSHIP SERIES RECORD

Year	Team (League)	Pos.	G	AB	R	H	2B	3B	HR	RBI	Avg.	BB	SO	SB	PO	A	E	Avg.
1996— New York (A.L.)										Did not play.								
1998—San Diego (N.L.)		OF-PH	6	13	1	3	2	0	0	0	.231	0	7	1	8	1	0	1.000

WORLD SERIES RECORD

NOTES: Member of World Series championship team (1996); inactive due to injury.

Year	Team (League)	Pos.	G	AB	R	H	2B	3B	HR	RBI	Avg.	BB	SO	SB	PO	A	E	Avg.
1996— New York (A.L.)										Did not play.								
1998—San Diego (N.L.)		PH-OF-PR	3	5	1	4	2	0	0	1	.800	0	0	0	3	0	0	1.000

R ROBERTS, BRIAN   SS   ORIOLES

PERSONAL: Born October 9, 1977, in Durham, N.C. ... 5-9/170. ... Bats both, throws right. ... Full name: Brian Michael Roberts.
HIGH SCHOOL: Chapel Hill (N.C.).
COLLEGE: North Carolina, then South Carolina.
TRANSACTIONS/CAREER NOTES: Selected by Baltimore Orioles organization in supplemental round ("sandwich pick" between first and second round, 50th pick overall) of free-agent draft (June 2, 1999); pick received as part of compensation for Texas Rangers signing Type A free agent 1B Rafael Palmeiro. ... On Frederick disabled list (April 19-July 13, 2000); included rehabilitation assignment to Gulf Coast Orioles (July 2-13).
STATISTICAL NOTES: Had 15-game hitting streak (June 22-July 12, 2001).

Year	Team (League)	Pos.	G	AB	R	H	2B	3B	HR	RBI	Avg.	BB	SO	SB	PO	A	E	Avg.
1999—Delmarva (S.Atl.)........	SS	47	167	22	40	12	1	0	21	.240	27	42	17	76	138	8	.964
2000—Frederick (Caro.)	SS	48	163	27	49	6	3	0	16	.301	27	24	13	60	97	8	.952
— GC Orioles (GCL)........	SS	9	29	8	9	1	2	1	3	.310	7	4	7	8	11	2	.905
2001—Bowie (East.)..............	2B-SS	22	81	12	24	7	0	1	7	.296	9	12	10	31	59	3	.968
— Rochester (I.L.)..........	SS	44	161	16	43	4	1	1	12	.267	28	22	23	62	104	13	.927
— Baltimore (A.L.)..........	SS-2B-DH	75	273	42	69	12	3	2	17	.253	13	36	12	97	156	16	.941
Major League totals (1 year)		75	273	42	69	12	3	2	17	.253	13	36	12	97	156	16	.941

ROBERTS, DAVE   OF   DODGERS

PERSONAL: Born May 31, 1972, in Okinawa, Japan. ... 5-10/175. ... Bats left, throws left. ... Full name: David Ray Roberts.
HIGH SCHOOL: Rancho Buena Vista (Oceanside, Calif.).
COLLEGE: UCLA.
TRANSACTIONS/CAREER NOTES: Selected by Detroit Tigers organization in 28th round of free-agent draft (June 2, 1994). ... Loaned by Tigers to Visalia, Oakland Athletics organization (March 30-August 30, 1996). ... Traded by Tigers with P Tim Worrell to Cleveland Indians for OF Geronimo Berroa (June 24, 1998). ... On Akron disabled list (August 10-18, 1998). ... On Cleveland disabled list (March 31-June 24, 2001); included rehabilitation assignment to Akron (June 4-24). ... Traded by Indians to Los Angeles Dodgers for P Christian Bridenbaugh and P Nial Hughes (December 21, 2001).
STATISTICAL NOTES: Career major league grand slams: 1.

Year	Team (League)	Pos.	G	AB	R	H	2B	3B	HR	RBI	Avg.	BB	SO	SB	PO	A	E	Avg.
1994—Jamestown (NY-P)	OF	54	178	33	52	7	2	0	12	.292	29	27	12	2	0	0	1.000
1995—Lakeland (FSL)	OF	92	357	67	108	10	5	3	30	.303	39	43	30	61	3	1	.985
1996—Visalia (Calif.)■..........	OF	126	482	*112	131	24	7	5	37	.272	98	105	*65	201	8	5	.977
— Jacksonville (Sou.)■..	OF	3	9	0	2	0	0	0	0	.222	1	0	0	5	0	0	1.000
1997—Jacksonville (Sou.).....	OF	105	415	76	123	24	2	4	41	.296	45	62	23	82	1	4	.954
1998—Jacksonville (Sou.).....	OF	69	279	71	91	14	5	5	42	.326	53	59	21	105	1	0	1.000
— Akron (East.)■...........	OF	56	227	49	82	10	5	7	33	.361	35	30	28	124	4	1	.992
— Buffalo (I.L.)..............	OF	5	15	2	2	0	0	0	2	.133	0	3	2	12	1	0	1.000
1999—Buffalo (I.L.)..............	OF-DH	89	350	65	95	17	*10	0	38	.271	43	52	39	247	4	1	.996
— Cleveland (A.L.).........	OF	41	143	26	34	4	0	2	12	.238	9	16	11	87	0	0	1.000
2000—Buffalo (I.L.)..............	OF	120	462	93	135	16	3	13	55	.292	59	68	39	284	8	1	*.997
— Cleveland (A.L.).........	OF	19	10	1	2	0	0	0	0	.200	2	2	1	10	0	0	1.000
2001—Akron (East.)	OF	17	64	9	13	5	0	0	2	.203	9	8	4	31	0	1	.969
— Buffalo (I.L.)..............	OF	62	241	34	73	12	4	0	22	.303	18	44	17	132	1	3	.978
— Cleveland (A.L.)..........	OF-DH	15	12	3	4	1	0	0	2	.333	1	2	0	8	0	0	1.000
Major League totals (3 years)		75	165	30	40	5	0	2	14	.242	12	20	12	105	0	0	1.000

DIVISION SERIES RECORD

Year	Team (League)	Pos.	G	AB	R	H	2B	3B	HR	RBI	Avg.	BB	SO	SB	PO	A	E	Avg.
1999—Cleveland (A.L.).........	PH-OF	2	3	0	0	0	0	0	0	.000	0	2	0	3	0	0	1.000

ROBERTS, GRANT   P   METS

PERSONAL: Born September 13, 1977, in El Cajon, Calif. ... 6-3/205. ... Throws right, bats right. ... Full name: Grant William Roberts.
HIGH SCHOOL: Grossmont (La Mesa, Calif.).
TRANSACTIONS/CAREER NOTES: Selected by New York Mets organization in 11th round of free-agent draft (June 1, 1995).
STATISTICAL NOTES: Tied for International League lead with 12 wild pitches in 2000.

Year	League	W	L	Pct.	ERA	G	GS	CG	ShO	Sv.	IP	H	R	ER	BB	SO
1995— Gulf Coast Mets (GCL)	2	1	.667	2.15	11	3	0	0	0	29 1/3	19	13	7	14	24
1996— Kingsport (Appl.)	*9	1	*.900	2.10	13	13	2	*2	0	68 2/3	43	18	16	37	*92
1997— Capital City (S.Atl.)	11	3	*.786	2.36	22	22	2	1	0	129 2/3	98	37	34	44	122
1998— St. Lucie (FSL)	4	5	.444	4.23	17	17	0	0	0	72 1/3	72	37	34	37	70
1999— Binghamton (East.)	7	6	.538	4.87	23	23	0	0	0	131 1/3	135	81	71	49	94
— Norfolk (I.L.)	2	1	.667	4.50	5	5	0	0	0	28	32	15	14	11	30
2000— Norfolk (I.L.)	7	8	.467	3.38	25	25	5	0	0	157 1/3	154	67	59	63	115
— New York (N.L.)	0	0	...	11.57	4	1	0	0	0	7	11	10	9	4	6
2001— Norfolk (I.L.)	3	5	.375	4.52	30	6	0	0	2	67 2/3	80	38	34	19	54
— New York (N.L.)	1	0	1.000	3.81	16	0	0	0	0	26	24	11	11	8	29
Major League totals (2 years)	1	0	1.000	5.45	20	1	0	0	0	33	35	21	20	12	35

ROBERTS, WILLIS — P — ORIOLES

R

PERSONAL: Born June 19, 1975, in San Cristobal, Dominican Republic. ... 6-3/175. ... Throws right, bats right. ... Full name: Willis Augusto Roberts.

TRANSACTIONS/CAREER NOTES: Signed as non-drafted free agent by Detroit Tigers organization (February 18, 1992). ... On disabled list (July 14-August 1 and August 1-September 13, 1994). ... On Toledo disabled list (May 3-20, 1999). ... Released by Tigers (February 1, 2000). ... Signed by Cincinnati Reds organization (February 1, 2000). ... Granted free agency (October 18, 2000). ... Signed by Baltimore Orioles organization (November 16, 2000).

Year	League	W	L	Pct.	ERA	G	GS	CG	ShO	Sv.	IP	H	R	ER	BB	SO
1992— Dominican Tigers (DSL)	0	6	.000	8.23	12	7	1	0	0	35	43	49	32	46	17
1993— Bristol (Appl.)	2	3	.400	1.38	10	2	0	0	1	26	24	16	4	11	23
1994— Bristol (Appl.)	1	2	.333	3.92	4	4	0	0	0	20 2/3	9	9	9	8	17
1995— Fayetteville (S.Atl.)	6	3	.667	2.70	17	15	0	0	0	80	72	33	24	40	52
1996— Lakeland (FSL)	9	7	.563	2.89	23	22	2	0	0	149 1/3	133	60	48	69	105
1997— Jacksonville (Sou.)	6	*15	.286	6.28	26	26	2	0	0	149	181	*120	*104	64	86
1998— Jacksonville (Sou.)	3	1	.750	2.19	12	2	0	0	0	24 2/3	21	10	6	10	15
— Toledo (I.L.)	3	3	.500	4.61	39	0	0	0	2	54 2/3	63	33	28	28	40
1999— Toledo (I.L.)	5	8	.385	6.26	31	12	2	0	0	92	112	68	64	59	52
— Detroit (A.L.)	0	0	...	13.50	1	0	0	0	0	1 1/3	3	4	2	0	0
2000— Chattanooga (Sou.)■	4	0	1.000	3.06	5	5	0	0	0	32 1/3	33	12	11	13	28
— Louisville (I.L.)	7	8	.467	5.66	25	20	2	1	0	124	138	80	78	55	66
2001— Baltimore (A.L.)■	9	10	.474	4.91	46	18	1	0	6	132	142	75	72	55	95
Major League totals (2 years)	9	10	.474	4.99	47	18	1	0	6	133 1/3	145	79	74	55	95

ROBINSON, KERRY — OF — CARDINALS

PERSONAL: Born October 3, 1973, in St. Louis. ... 6-0/175. ... Bats left, throws left. ... Full name: Kerry Keith Robinson. ... Son of Rogers Robinson, outfielder in St. Louis Cardinals organization (1957-69).

HIGH SCHOOL: Hazelwood East (St. Louis).

COLLEGE: Southeast Missouri State.

TRANSACTIONS/CAREER NOTES: Selected by St. Louis Cardinals organization in 34th round of free-agent draft (June 1, 1995). ... Selected by Tampa Bay Devil Rays in second round (44th pick overall) of expansion draft (November 18, 1997). ... Claimed on waivers by Seattle Mariners (November 19, 1998). ... Traded by Mariners to Cincinnati Reds for P Todd Williams (July 22, 1999). ... Granted free agency (October 18, 2000). ... Signed by Cardinals organization (May 17, 2001).

STATISTICAL NOTES: Led Midwest League in caught stealing with 27 in 1996. ... Led Texas League in caught stealing with 23 in 1997.

Year	Team (League)	Pos.	G	AB	R	H	2B	3B	HR	RBI	Avg.	BB	SO	SB	PO	A	E	Avg.
							BATTING								FIELDING			
1995— Johnson City (Appl.) ..	OF	60	250	44	74	12	8	1	26	.296	16	30	14	86	5	6	.938
1996— Peoria (Midw.)	OF	123	440	98	158	17	4	2	47	*.359	51	51	•50	168	7	7	.962
1997— Arkansas (Texas)	OF	135	*523	80	168	16	3	2	62	.321	54	64	40	193	6	7	.966
— Louisville (A.A.)	OF	2	9	0	1	0	0	0	0	.111	0	1	0	3	0	0	1.000
1998— Orlando (Sou.)■	OF	72	309	45	83	7	5	2	26	.269	27	28	28	135	5	0	1.000
— Durham (I.L.)	OF	58	242	28	73	7	4	1	28	.302	23	30	18	146	3	2	.987
— Tampa Bay (A.L.)	OF	2	3	0	0	0	0	0	0	.000	0	1	0	4	0	0	1.000
1999— Tacoma (PCL)■	OF-DH	79	335	53	108	16	•9	0	34	.322	14	44	30	141	6	4	.974
— Indianapolis (I.L.)■...	OF	34	129	24	34	3	2	1	14	.264	4	12	14	83	3	2	.977
— Cincinnati (N.L.)	OF	9	1	4	0	0	0	0	0	.000	0	1	0	0	0	0	...
2000— Columbus (I.L.)■.......	OF	119	437	71	139	17	9	0	32	.318	41	40	37	237	4	3	.988
2001— St. Louis (N.L.)■	OF	114	186	34	53	6	1	1	15	.285	12	20	11	101	2	2	.981
— Memphis (PCL)	OF	10	40	4	13	1	0	0	3	.325	4	10	4	15	0	0	1.000
American League totals (1 year)		2	3	0	0	0	0	0	0	.000	0	1	0	4	0	0	1.000
National League totals (2 years)		123	187	38	53	6	1	1	15	.283	12	21	11	101	2	2	.981
Major League totals (3 years)		125	190	38	53	6	1	1	15	.279	12	22	11	105	2	2	.982

DIVISION SERIES RECORD

Year	Team (League)	Pos.	G	AB	R	H	2B	3B	HR	RBI	Avg.	BB	SO	SB	PO	A	E	Avg.
							BATTING								FIELDING			
2001— St. Louis (N.L.)..........	PH-OF	4	2	0	1	0	0	0	1	.500	0	0	0	0	0	0	...

ROCKER, JOHN — P — RANGERS

PERSONAL: Born October 17, 1974, in Statesboro, Ga. ... 6-4/225. ... Throws left, bats right. ... Full name: John Loy Rocker.

HIGH SCHOOL: First Presbyterian Day School (Macon, Ga.).

COLLEGE: Mercer (Ga.).

TRANSACTIONS/CAREER NOTES: Selected by Atlanta Braves organization in 18th round of free-agent draft (June 3, 1993). ... On suspended list (April 3-18, 2000). ... Traded by Braves with 3B Troy Cameron to Cleveland Indians for P Steve Karsay and P Steve Reed (June 22, 2001). ... Traded by Indians to Texas Rangers for P David Elder (December 18, 2001).
STATISTICAL NOTES: Pitched 2-0 no-hit victory against Charleston, S.C. (June 9, 1996). ... Led Southern League in wild pitches with 17 in 1997.

Year League	W	L	Pct.	ERA	G	GS	CG	ShO	Sv.	IP	H	R	ER	BB	SO
1994—Danville (Appl.)...................	1	5	.167	3.53	12	12	1	0	0	63 2/3	50	36	25	38	72
1995—Eugene (N'West)	1	5	.167	5.16	12	12	0	0	0	59 1/3	45	40	34	36	74
—Macon (S.Atl.).............	4	4	.500	4.50	16	16	0	0	0	86	86	50	43	52	61
1996—Macon (S.Atl.).............	5	3	.625	3.89	20	19	2	2	0	106 1/3	85	60	46	63	107
—Durham (Caro.).............	4	3	.571	3.39	9	9	0	0	0	58 1/3	63	24	22	25	43
1997—Durham (Caro.).............	1	1	.500	4.33	11	1	0	0	0	35 1/3	33	21	17	22	39
—Greenville (Sou.).............	5	6	.455	4.86	22	18	0	0	0	113	119	69	61	61	96
1998—Richmond (I.L.).............	1	1	.500	1.42	9	0	0	0	1	19	13	4	3	10	22
—Atlanta (N.L.).............	1	3	.250	2.13	47	0	0	0	2	38	22	10	9	22	42
1999—Atlanta (N.L.).............	4	5	.444	2.49	74	0	0	0	38	72 1/3	47	24	20	37	104
2000—Atlanta (N.L.).............	1	2	.333	2.89	59	0	0	0	24	53	42	25	17	48	77
—Richmond (I.L.).............	0	0	...	3.00	3	0	0	0	1	3	3	1	1	1	6
2001—Atlanta (N.L.).............	2	2	.500	3.09	30	0	0	0	19	32	25	13	11	16	36
—Cleveland (A.L.)■.............	3	7	.300	5.45	38	0	0	0	4	34 2/3	33	23	21	25	43
A.L. totals (1 year)	3	7	.300	5.45	38	0	0	0	4	34 2/3	33	23	21	25	43
N.L. totals (4 years)	8	12	.400	2.63	210	0	0	0	83	195 1/3	136	72	57	123	259
Major League totals (4 years)	11	19	.367	3.05	248	0	0	0	87	230	169	95	78	148	302

DIVISION SERIES RECORD

Year League	W	L	Pct.	ERA	G	GS	CG	ShO	Sv.	IP	H	R	ER	BB	SO
1998—Atlanta (N.L.).....................	0	0	...	0.00	2	0	0	0	0	1 1/3	1	0	0	0	2
1999—Atlanta (N.L.).....................	1	0	1.000	0.00	2	0	0	0	1	3 1/3	0	0	0	2	5
2000—Atlanta (N.L.).....................	0	0	...	0.00	1	0	0	0	0	2/3	0	0	0	1	0
2001—Cleveland (A.L.).................	0	0	...	0.00	1	0	0	0	0	1	1	0	0	0	1
Division series totals (4 years)	1	0	1.000	0.00	6	0	0	0	1	6 1/3	2	0	0	3	8

CHAMPIONSHIP SERIES RECORD

RECORDS: Shares single-series record for most games pitched—6 (1998 and 1999).

Year League	W	L	Pct.	ERA	G	GS	CG	ShO	Sv.	IP	H	R	ER	BB	SO
1998—Atlanta (N.L.).....................	1	0	1.000	0.00	6	0	0	0	0	4 2/3	3	0	0	1	5
1999—Atlanta (N.L.).....................	0	0	...	0.00	6	0	0	0	2	6 2/3	3	2	0	2	9
Champ. series totals (2 years)	1	0	1.000	0.00	12	0	0	0	2	11 1/3	6	2	0	3	14

WORLD SERIES RECORD

Year League	W	L	Pct.	ERA	G	GS	CG	ShO	Sv.	IP	H	R	ER	BB	SO
1999—Atlanta (N.L.).....................	0	0	...	0.00	2	0	0	0	0	3	2	0	0	2	4

RODNEY, FERNANDO P TIGERS

PERSONAL: Born March 17, 1981, in Samana, Dominican Republic. ... 5-11/170. ... Throws right, bats right.
TRANSACTIONS/CAREER NOTES: Signed as non-drafted free agent by Detroit Tigers organization (November 1, 1997). ... On disabled list (August 14, 2000-remainder of season). ... On Lakeland disabled list (May 22-June 30 and July 13-18, 2001).

Year League	W	L	Pct.	ERA	G	GS	CG	ShO	Sv.	IP	H	R	ER	BB	SO
1998—Dominican Tigers (DSL).....	1	3	.250	3.38	11	5	0	0	1	32	25	16	12	19	37
1999—Gulf Coast Tigers (GCL)	3	3	.500	2.40	22	0	0	0	9	30	20	8	8	21	39
—Lakeland (FSL).................	1	0	1.000	1.42	4	0	0	0	2	6 1/3	7	1	1	1	5
2000—West Michigan (Midw.).....	6	4	.600	2.94	22	10	0	0	0	82 2/3	74	34	27	35	56
2001—Lakeland (FSL)	4	2	.667	3.42	16	9	0	0	0	55 1/3	53	26	21	19	44
—Erie (East.)	0	0	...	4.26	4	0	0	0	1	6 1/3	7	3	3	3	8
—Gulf Coast Tigers (GCL)	0	0	...	0.00	1	1	0	0	0	1	0	0	0	1	1

RODRIGUEZ, ALEX SS RANGERS

PERSONAL: Born July 27, 1975, in New York. ... 6-3/210. ... Bats right, throws right. ... Full name: Alexander Emmanuel Rodriguez.
HIGH SCHOOL: Westminster Christian (Miami).
TRANSACTIONS/CAREER NOTES: Selected by Seattle Mariners organization in first round (first pick overall) of free-agent draft (June 3, 1993). ... On Seattle disabled list (April 22-May 7, 1996); included rehabilitation assignment to Tacoma (May 5-7). ... On disabled list (June 12-27, 1997; April 7-May 14, 1999; and July 8-24, 2000). ... Granted free agency (October 30, 2000). ... Signed by Texas Rangers (December 11, 2000).
RECORDS: Hold A.L. single-season record for most home runs by shortstop—52 (2001).
HONORS: Named Major League Player of the Year by THE SPORTING NEWS (1996). ... Named shortstop on THE SPORTING NEWS A.L. All-Star team (1996, 1998 and 2000-01). ... Named shortstop on THE SPORTING NEWS A.L. Silver Slugger team (1996, 1998-99 and 2000). ... Named shortstop on A.L. Silver Slugger team (2001).
STATISTICAL NOTES: Had 20-game hitting streak (August 16-September 4, 1996). ... Led A.L. with 379 total bases in 1996 and 393 in 2001. ... Hit for the cycle (June 5, 1997). ... Led A.L. shortstops with 731 total chances in 1998. ... Hit three home runs in one game (April 16, 2000). ... Had 17-game hitting streak (May 5-23, 2000). ... Led A.L. shortstops with 123 double plays in 2000. ... Career major league grand slams: 8.

Year Team (League)	Pos.	G	AB	R	H	2B	3B	HR	RBI	Avg.	BB	SO	SB	PO	A	E	Avg.
1994—Appleton (Midw.)........	SS-DH	65	248	49	79	17	6	14	55	.319	24	44	16	86	185	19	.934
—Jacksonville (Sou.)....	SS	17	59	7	17	4	1	1	8	.288	10	13	2	17	63	3	.964
—Seattle (A.L.).............	SS	17	54	4	11	0	0	0	2	.204	3	20	3	20	45	6	.915
—Calgary (PCL)............	SS	32	119	22	37	7	4	6	21	.311	8	25	2	45	104	3	.980
1995—Tacoma (PCL).............	SS-DH	54	214	37	77	12	3	15	45	.360	18	44	2	90	157	10	.961
—Seattle (A.L.).............	SS-DH	48	142	15	33	6	2	5	19	.232	6	42	4	56	106	8	.953

Year	Team (League)	Pos.	G	AB	R	H	2B	3B	HR	RBI	Avg.	BB	SO	SB	PO	A	E	Avg.
							BATTING									FIELDING		
1996—	Seattle (A.L.)	SS	146	601	*141	215	*54	1	36	123	*.358	59	104	15	238	404	15	.977
	—Tacoma (PCL)	SS	2	5	0	1	0	0	0	0	.200	2	1	0	1	4	1	.833
1997—	Seattle (A.L.)	SS-DH	141	587	100	176	40	3	23	84	.300	41	99	29	209	394	*24	.962
1998—	Seattle (A.L.)	SS-DH	161	*686	123	*213	35	5	42	124	.310	45	121	46	268	445	18	.975
1999—	Seattle (A.L.)	SS	129	502	110	143	25	0	42	111	.285	56	109	21	213	382	14	.977
2000—	Seattle (A.L.)	SS	148	554	134	175	34	2	41	132	.316	100	121	15	243	438	10	.986
2001—	Texas (A.L.)■	SS-DH	•162	632	*133	201	34	1	*52	135	.318	75	131	18	280	452	18	.976
Major League totals (8 years)			952	3758	760	1167	228	14	241	730	.311	385	747	151	1527	2666	113	.974

DIVISION SERIES RECORD

Year	Team (League)	Pos.	G	AB	R	H	2B	3B	HR	RBI	Avg.	BB	SO	SB	PO	A	E	Avg.
							BATTING									FIELDING		
1995—	Seattle (A.L.)	SS-PR	1	1	0	0	0	0	0	0	.000	0	0	0	0	0	0	...
1997—	Seattle (A.L.)	SS	4	16	1	5	1	0	1	1	.313	0	5	0	5	10	0	1.000
2000—	Seattle (A.L.)	SS	3	13	0	4	0	0	0	2	.308	0	2	0	8	9	0	1.000
Division series totals (3 years)			8	30	2	9	1	0	1	3	.300	0	7	0	13	19	0	1.000

CHAMPIONSHIP SERIES RECORD

RECORDS: Shares A.L. single-game record for most long hits—3 (October 17, 2000).

Year	Team (League)	Pos.	G	AB	R	H	2B	3B	HR	RBI	Avg.	BB	SO	SB	PO	A	E	Avg.
							BATTING									FIELDING		
1995—	Seattle (A.L.)	PH	1	1	0	0	0	0	0	0	.000	0	1	0	...	...	...	...
2000—	Seattle (A.L.)	SS	6	22	4	9	2	0	2	5	.409	3	8	1	9	11	0	1.000
Championship series totals (2 years)			7	23	4	9	2	0	2	5	.391	3	9	1	9	11	0	1.000

ALL-STAR GAME RECORD

Year	League	Pos.	AB	R	H	2B	3B	HR	RBI	Avg.	BB	SO	SB	PO	A	E	Avg.
						BATTING									FIELDING		
1996—	American	SS	1	0	0	0	0	0	0	.000	0	0	0	0	0	0	...
1997—	American	SS	3	0	1	0	0	0	0	.333	0	2	0	0	1	0	1.000
1998—	American	SS	3	2	2	0	0	1	1	.667	0	1	0	1	2	0	1.000
2000—	American						Selected, did not play—injured.											
2001—	American	SS-3B	2	0	0	0	0	0	0	.000	0	2	0	1	2	0	1.000
All-Star Game totals (4 years)			9	2	3	0	0	1	1	.333	0	5	0	2	5	0	1.000

RODRIGUEZ, FELIX   P   GIANTS

PERSONAL: Born December 5, 1972, in Monte Cristi, Dominican Republic. ... 6-1/190. ... Throws right, bats right. ... Full name: Felix Antonio Rodriguez.

HIGH SCHOOL: Liceo Bijiador (Monte Cristi, Dominican Republic).

TRANSACTIONS/CAREER NOTES: Signed as non-drafted free agent by Los Angeles Dodgers organization (October 17, 1989). ... On disabled list (August 11, 1992-remainder of season). ... On Albuquerque disabled list (July 5-18, 1995). ... On disabled list (April 20-May 2 and May 12-27, 1996). ... Claimed on waivers by Cincinnati Reds (December 18, 1996). ... Traded by Reds to Arizona Diamondbacks for a player to be named later (November 11, 1997); Reds acquired P Scott Winchester to complete deal (November 18, 1997). ... On Arizona disabled list (June 21-July 30, 1998); included rehabilitation assignments to Arizona League Diamondbacks (July 20-27) and Tucson (July 28-30). ... Traded by Diamondbacks to San Francisco Giants for future considerations (December 8, 1998); Diamondbacks acquired P Troy Brohawn and OF Chris Van Rossum to complete deal (December 21, 1998).

STATISTICAL NOTES: Pitched 11-0 no-hit victory against Sarasota (August 28, 1993).

MISCELLANEOUS: Played catcher (1990-92).

Year	League	W	L	Pct.	ERA	G	GS	CG	ShO	Sv.	IP	H	R	ER	BB	SO
1993—	Vero Beach (FSL)	8	8	.500	3.75	32	20	2	1	0	132	109	71	55	71	80
1994—	San Antonio (Texas)	6	8	.429	4.03	26	26	0	0	0	136 1/3	106	70	61	*88	126
1995—	Albuquerque (PCL)	3	2	.600	4.24	14	11	0	0	0	51	52	29	24	26	46
	—Los Angeles (N.L.)	1	1	.500	2.53	11	0	0	0	0	10 2/3	11	3	3	5	5
1996—	Albuquerque (PCL)	3	9	.250	5.53	27	19	0	0	0	107 1/3	111	70	66	60	65
1997—	Indianapolis (A.A.)■	3	3	.500	1.01	23	0	0	0	1	26 2/3	22	10	3	16	26
	—Cincinnati (N.L.)	0	0	...	4.30	26	1	0	0	0	46	48	23	22	28	34
1998—	Arizona (N.L.)■	0	2	.000	6.14	43	0	0	0	5	44	44	31	30	29	36
	—Ariz. Diamondbacks (Ariz.).	0	0	...	4.15	3	2	0	0	0	4 1/3	3	4	2	2	5
	—Tucson (PCL)	0	0	...	9.00	1	0	0	0	0	1	1	1	1	2	0
1999—	San Francisco (N.L.)■	2	3	.400	3.80	47	0	0	0	0	66 1/3	67	32	28	29	55
2000—	San Francisco (N.L.)	4	2	.667	2.64	76	0	0	0	3	81 2/3	65	29	24	42	95
2001—	San Francisco (N.L.)	9	1	.900	1.68	80	0	0	0	0	80 1/3	53	16	15	27	91
Major League totals (6 years)		16	9	.640	3.34	283	1	0	0	8	329	288	134	122	160	316

DIVISION SERIES RECORD

Year	League	W	L	Pct.	ERA	G	GS	CG	ShO	Sv.	IP	H	R	ER	BB	SO
2000—	San Francisco (N.L.)	0	1	.000	6.23	3	0	0	0	0	4 1/3	6	3	3	1	6

RECORD AS POSITION PLAYER

Year	Team (League)	Pos.	G	AB	R	H	2B	3B	HR	RBI	Avg.	BB	SO	SB	PO	A	E	Avg.
							BATTING									FIELDING		
1990—	Dom. Dodgers (DSL) .		63	241	23	55	10	0	2	33	.228	15	52	4	...	...	...	...
1991—	GC Dodgers (GCL)	C	45	139	15	37	8	1	2	21	.266	6	32	1	161	18	5	.973
1992—	Great Falls (Pio.)	C-OF	32	110	20	32	8	0	2	20	.291	1	16	2	221	33	2	.992

RODRIGUEZ, FRANKIE   P

PERSONAL: Born December 11, 1972, in Brooklyn, N.Y. ... 6-0/210. ... Throws right, bats right. ... Full name: Francisco Rodriguez.
HIGH SCHOOL: Eastern District (Brooklyn, N.Y.).
JUNIOR COLLEGE: Howard College (Texas).
TRANSACTIONS/CAREER NOTES: Selected by Boston Red Sox in second round of free-agent draft (June 4, 1990); pick received as compensation for Atlanta Braves signing of Type B free-agent 1B Nick Esasky. ... Traded by Red Sox with a player to be named later to Minnesota Twins for P Rick Aguilera (July 6, 1995); Twins acquired OF J.J. Johnson to complete deal (October 11, 1995). ... Claimed on waivers by Seattle Mariners (May 26, 1999). ... On suspended list (August 17-25, 1999). ... On Seattle disabled list (July 7-September 1, 2000); included rehabilitation assignment to Tacoma (July 24-September 1). ... Released by Mariners (December 20, 2000). ... Signed by Cincinnati Reds organization (January 16, 2001). ... Granted free agency (October 15, 2001).
RECORDS: Shares major league single-inning record for most strikeouts—4 (July 22, 2001, seventh inning).
STATISTICAL NOTES: Pitched 2-1 no-hit victory for Salt Lake against Iowa (May 8, 1999; first game).
MISCELLANEOUS: Played shortstop (1991). ... Scored one run in two appearances as pinch hitter (1999).

Year	League	W	L	Pct.	ERA	G	GS	CG	ShO	Sv.	IP	H	R	ER	BB	SO
1992—	Lynchburg (Caro.)	12	7	.632	3.09	25	25	1	0	0	148 2/3	125	56	51	65	129
1993—	New Britain (East.)	7	11	.389	3.74	28	26	•4	1	0	170 2/3	147	79	71	78	151
1994—	Pawtucket (I.L.)	8	13	.381	3.92	28	28	*8	1	0	*186	182	95	81	60	*160
1995—	Boston (A.L.)	0	2	.000	10.57	9	2	0	0	0	15 1/3	21	19	18	10	14
—	Pawtucket (I.L.)	1	1	.500	4.00	13	2	0	0	2	27	19	12	12	8	18
—	Minnesota (A.L.)■	5	6	.455	5.38	16	16	0	0	0	90 1/3	93	64	54	47	45
1996—	Minnesota (A.L.)	13	14	.481	5.05	38	33	3	0	2	206 2/3	218	129	116	78	110
1997—	Minnesota (A.L.)	3	6	.333	4.62	43	15	0	0	0	142 1/3	147	82	73	60	65
1998—	Minnesota (A.L.)	4	6	.400	6.56	20	11	0	0	0	70	88	58	51	30	62
—	Salt Lake (PCL)	5	7	.417	4.67	16	16	2	1	0	96 1/3	97	53	50	35	79
1999—	Salt Lake (PCL)	3	4	.429	6.70	9	9	1	0	0	43	40	34	32	14	33
—	Seattle (A.L.)■	2	4	.333	5.65	28	5	0	0	3	73 1/3	94	47	46	30	47
2000—	Seattle (A.L.)	2	1	.667	6.27	23	0	0	0	0	47 1/3	60	33	33	22	19
—	Tacoma (PCL)	2	1	.667	4.84	9	6	0	0	0	35 1/3	30	20	19	11	26
2001—	Louisville (I.L.)■	8	6	.571	2.46	43	0	0	0	5	80 1/3	67	25	22	24	56
—	Cincinnati (N.L.)	0	0	...	11.42	7	0	0	0	0	8 2/3	16	12	11	5	9
A.L. totals (6 years)		29	39	.426	5.45	177	82	3	0	5	645 1/3	721	432	391	277	362
N.L. totals (1 year)		0	0	...	11.42	7	0	0	0	0	8 2/3	16	12	11	5	9
Major League totals (7 years)		29	39	.426	5.53	184	82	3	0	5	654	737	444	402	282	371

RECORD AS POSITION PLAYER

Year	Team (League)	Pos.	G	AB	R	H	2B	3B	HR	RBI	Avg.	BB	SO	SB	PO	A	E	Avg.
1991—	GC Red Sox (GCL)	SS	3	14	3	7	0	1	0	3	.500	0	1	0	9	10	1	.950
—	Elmira (NY-Penn)	SS	67	255	36	69	5	3	6	31	.271	13	38	3	95	209	24	.927

RODRIGUEZ, HENRY   OF

PERSONAL: Born November 8, 1967, in Santo Domingo, Dominican Republic. ... 6-2/225. ... Bats left, throws left. ... Full name: Henry Anderson Lorenzo Rodriguez Garcia.
HIGH SCHOOL: Liceo Republica de Paraguay. (Santo Domingo).
TRANSACTIONS/CAREER NOTES: Signed as non-drafted free agent by Los Angeles Dodgers organization (July 14, 1985). ... Traded by Dodgers with IF Jeff Treadway to Montreal Expos for OF Roberto Kelly and P Joey Eischen (May 23, 1995). ... On Montreal disabled list (June 2-September 1, 1995); included rehabilitation assignment to Ottawa (August 7-16). ... On suspended list (August 16-19, 1996). ... Traded by Expos to Chicago Cubs for P Miguel Batista (December 12, 1997). ... On disabled list (August 24-September 8, 1998). ... Granted free agency (October 23, 1998). ... Re-signed by Cubs (December 2, 1998). ... Traded by Cubs to Florida Marlins for 1B/OF Ross Gload and P Dave Noyce (July 31, 2000). ... Granted free agency (November 1, 2000). ... Signed by New York Yankees (February 15, 2001). ... On New York disabled list (March 31-May 23, 2001); included rehabilitation assignment to Columbus (May 1-20). ... Released by Yankees (June 19, 2001).
HONORS: Named Texas League Most Valuable Player (1990).
STATISTICAL NOTES: Tied for Gulf Coast League lead with seven intentional bases on balls received in 1987. ... Led Texas League with 14 sacrifice flies in 1990. ... Tied for Pacific Coast League lead with 10 sacrifice flies in 1992. ... Had 15-game hitting streak (July 31-August 14, 1999). ... Career major league grand slams: 5.

Year	Team (League)	Pos.	G	AB	R	H	2B	3B	HR	RBI	Avg.	BB	SO	SB	PO	A	E	Avg.
1987—	GC Dodgers (GCL)	1B-SS	49	148	23	49	7	3	0	15	*.331	16	15	3	309	23	6	.982
1988—	Dom. Dodgers (DSL)		19	21	9	8	2	0	0	10	.381	10	6	4	...	...	...	...
—	Salem (N'West)	1B	72	291	47	84	14	4	2	39	.289	21	42	14	585	•38	7	.989
1989—	Vero Beach (FSL)	1B-OF	126	433	53	123	*33	1	10	73	.284	48	58	7	1072	66	12	.990
—	Bakersfield (Calif.)	1B	3	9	2	2	0	0	1	2	.222	0	3	0	8	0	0	1.000
1990—	San Antonio (Texas)	OF	129	495	82	144	22	9	*28	*109	.291	61	66	5	223	5	10	.958
1991—	Albuquerque (PCL)	OF-1B	121	446	61	121	22	5	10	67	.271	25	62	4	234	12	5	.980
1992—	Albuquerque (PCL)	OF-1B	94	365	59	111	21	5	14	72	.304	31	57	1	484	41	10	.981
—	Los Angeles (N.L.)	OF-1B	53	146	11	32	7	0	3	14	.219	8	30	0	68	8	3	.962
1993—	Albuquerque (PCL)	1B-OF	46	179	26	53	13	5	4	30	.296	14	37	1	277	18	5	.983
—	Los Angeles (N.L.)	OF-1B	76	176	20	39	10	0	8	23	.222	11	39	1	127	9	1	.993
1994—	Los Angeles (N.L.)	OF-1B	104	306	33	82	14	2	8	49	.268	17	58	0	198	9	2	.990
1995—	Los Angeles (N.L.)	OF-1B	21	80	6	21	4	1	1	10	.263	5	17	0	37	0	0	1.000
—	Montreal (N.L.)■	1B-OF	24	58	7	12	0	0	1	5	.207	6	11	0	88	7	1	.990
—	Ottawa (I.L.)	DH	4	15	0	3	1	0	0	2	.200	1	4	0	...	...	...	...
1996—	Montreal (N.L.)	OF-1B	145	532	81	147	42	4	36	103	.276	37	*160	2	528	33	11	.981
1997—	Montreal (N.L.)	OF-1B	132	476	55	116	28	3	26	83	.244	42	149	3	220	6	3	.987
1998—	Chicago (N.L.)■	OF-DH	128	415	56	104	21	4	31	85	.251	54	113	1	215	7	1	.996
1999—	Chicago (N.L.)	OF-DH	130	447	72	136	29	0	26	87	.304	56	113	2	222	7	6	.974

Year	Team (League)	Pos.	G	AB	R	H	2B	3B	HR	RBI	Avg.	BB	SO	SB	PO	A	E	Avg.
							BATTING									FIELDING		
2000—Chicago (N.L.)............	OF	76	259	37	65	15	1	18	51	.251	22	76	1	110	5	2	.983	
—Florida (N.L.)■........	OF	36	108	10	29	6	0	2	10	.269	14	23	0	40	1	0	1.000	
2001—Columbus (I.L.)■.......	OF	18	63	9	15	2	0	5	13	.238	7	21	0	3	0	0	1.000	
—New York (A.L.)..........	DH	5	8	0	0	0	0	0	0	.000	0	6	0	...	...	...	...	
American League totals (1 year)		5	8	0	0	0	0	0	0	.000	0	6	0	...	...	...	...	
National League totals (9 years)		925	3003	388	783	176	9	160	520	.261	272	789	10	1853	92	30	.985	
Major League totals (10 years)		930	3011	388	783	176	9	160	520	.260	272	795	10	1853	92	30	.985	

DIVISION SERIES RECORD

Year	Team (League)	Pos.	G	AB	R	H	2B	3B	HR	RBI	Avg.	BB	SO	SB	PO	A	E	Avg.
							BATTING									FIELDING		
1998—Chicago (N.L.)............	OF-PH	3	7	0	1	1	0	0	0	.143	1	2	0	5	1	0	1.000	

ALL-STAR GAME RECORD

Year	League	Pos.	AB	R	H	2B	3B	HR	RBI	Avg.	BB	SO	SB	PO	A	E	Avg.
						BATTING									FIELDING		
1996—National......................	PH	1	0	1	0	0	0	1	1.000	0	0	0	...	...	...	...

RODRIGUEZ, IVAN   C   RANGERS

PERSONAL: Born November 30, 1971, in Vega Baja, Puerto Rico. ... 5-9/205. ... Bats right, throws right. ... Nickname: Pudge.

HIGH SCHOOL: Lina Padron Rivera (Vega Baja, Puerto Rico).

TRANSACTIONS/CAREER NOTES: Signed as non-drafted free agent by Texas Rangers organization (July 27, 1988). ... On disabled list (June 6-27, 1992; July 25, 2000-remainder of season; May 2-17 and August 31, 2001-remainder of season).

RECORDS: Shares major league single-inning record for most doubles—2 (June 14, 2000, fourth inning). ... Holds A.L. single-season record for most home runs by catcher—35 (1999).

HONORS: Won A.L. Gold Glove at catcher (1992-2001). ... Named catcher on THE SPORTING NEWS A.L. All-Star team (1994-99). ... Named catcher on THE SPORTING NEWS A.L. Silver Slugger team (1994-99). ... Named A.L. Most Valuable Player by Baseball Writers' Association of America (1999).

STATISTICAL NOTES: Led South Atlantic League catchers with 34 double plays in 1989. ... Led Florida State League catchers with 842 total chances in 1990. ... Led A.L. catchers with 941 total chances and 11 double plays in 1996. ... Hit three home runs in one game (September 11, 1997). ... Led A.L. catchers with 942 total chances in 1998. ... Had 20-game hitting streak (May 8-June 1, 1999). ... Led A.L. in grounding into double plays with 31 in 1999. ... Led A.L. catchers with 10 double plays in 2000. ... Career major league grand slams: 4.

MISCELLANEOUS: Holds Texas Rangers all-time record for hits (1,595) and doubles (312).

Year	Team (League)	Pos.	G	AB	R	H	2B	3B	HR	RBI	Avg.	BB	SO	SB	PO	A	E	Avg.
							BATTING									FIELDING		
1989—Gastonia (S.Atl.).........	C	112	386	38	92	22	1	7	42	.238	21	58	2	691	*96	11	.986	
1990—Charlotte (FSL)..........	C	109	408	48	117	17	7	2	55	.287	12	50	1	*727	101	14	.983	
1991—Tulsa (Texas).............	C	50	175	16	48	7	2	3	28	.274	6	27	1	210	33	3	.988	
—Texas (A.L.)............	C	88	280	24	74	16	0	3	27	.264	5	42	0	517	62	10	.983	
1992—Texas (A.L.).............	C-DH	123	420	39	109	16	1	8	37	.260	24	73	0	763	85	*15	.983	
1993—Texas (A.L.).............	C-DH	137	473	56	129	28	4	10	66	.273	29	70	8	801	76	8	.991	
1994—Texas (A.L.).............	C	99	363	56	108	19	1	16	57	.298	31	42	6	600	44	5	.992	
1995—Texas (A.L.).............	C-DH	130	492	56	149	32	2	12	67	.303	16	48	0	707	*67	8	.990	
1996—Texas (A.L.).............	C-DH	153	639	116	192	47	3	19	86	.300	38	55	5	*850	*81	•10	.989	
1997—Texas (A.L.).............	C-DH	150	597	98	187	34	4	20	77	.313	38	89	7	821	*75	7	.992	
1998—Texas (A.L.).............	C-DH	145	579	88	186	40	4	21	91	.321	32	88	9	*864	*72	6	.994	
1999—Texas (A.L.).............	C-DH	144	600	116	199	29	1	35	113	.332	24	64	25	850	83	7	.993	
2000—Texas (A.L.).............	C-DH	91	363	66	126	27	4	27	83	.347	19	48	5	507	34	2	*.996	
2001—Texas (A.L.).............	C-DH	111	442	70	136	24	2	25	65	.308	23	73	10	631	52	7	.990	
Major League totals (11 years)		1371	5248	785	1595	312	26	196	769	.304	279	692	75	7911	731	85	.990	

DIVISION SERIES RECORD

Year	Team (League)	Pos.	G	AB	R	H	2B	3B	HR	RBI	Avg.	BB	SO	SB	PO	A	E	Avg.
							BATTING									FIELDING		
1996—Texas (A.L.)...............	C	4	16	1	6	1	0	0	2	.375	2	3	0	21	3	0	1.000	
1998—Texas (A.L.)...............	C	3	10	0	1	0	0	0	1	.100	0	5	0	27	3	0	1.000	
1999—Texas (A.L.)...............	C	3	12	0	3	1	0	0	0	.250	0	2	1	21	0	0	1.000	
Division series totals (3 years)		10	38	1	10	2	0	0	3	.263	2	10	1	69	6	0	1.000	

ALL-STAR GAME RECORD

RECORDS: Shares single-game record for most at-bats (nine-inning game)—5 (July 12, 1994). ... Shares single-game records for most putouts by catcher—10; and most chances accepted by catcher—11 (1999).

Year	League	Pos.	AB	R	H	2B	3B	HR	RBI	Avg.	BB	SO	SB	PO	A	E	Avg.
						BATTING									FIELDING		
1992—American....................	C	2	0	0	0	0	0	0	.000	0	1	0	4	0	0	1.000
1993—American....................	C	2	1	1	1	0	0	0	.500	0	0	0	3	0	0	1.000
1994—American....................	C	5	1	2	0	0	0	0	.400	0	1	0	5	0	0	1.000
1995—American....................	C	3	0	0	0	0	0	0	.000	0	1	0	6	1	0	1.000
1996—American....................	C	2	0	0	0	0	0	0	.000	0	1	0	6	2	0	1.000
1997—American....................	C	2	0	0	0	0	0	0	.000	0	0	0	3	1	0	1.000
1998—American....................	C	4	1	3	0	0	0	1	.750	0	0	1	5	0	0	1.000
1999—American....................	C	2	0	0	0	0	0	0	.000	0	1	0	10	1	0	1.000
2000—American....................	C	3	0	1	0	0	0	0	.333	0	0	0	3	0	0	1.000
2001—American....................	C	2	0	1	0	0	0	1	.500	0	0	0	2	0	0	1.000
All-Star Game totals (10 years)		27	3	8	1	0	0	2	.296	0	5	1	47	5	0	1.000

RODRIGUEZ, RICARDO   P   DODGERS

PERSONAL: Born May 21, 1979, in Guayubin, Dominican Republic. ... 6-3/165. ... Throws right, bats right. ... Full name: Ricardo Antonio Rodriguez.
TRANSACTIONS/CAREER NOTES: Signed as non-drafted free agent by Los Angeles Dodgers organization (September 2, 1996).
HONORS: Named Florida State League Most Valuable Pitcher (2001).
STATISTICAL NOTES: Led Florida State League with 18 wild pitches in 2001.

Year	League	W	L	Pct.	ERA	G	GS	CG	ShO	Sv.	IP	H	R	ER	BB	SO
1997—	Dom. Dodgers (DSL)	1	2	.333	6.40	12	10	0	0	0	32 1/3	42	39	23	26	20
1998—	Dom. Dodgers (DSL)	1	1	.500	3.55	13	9	1	1	0	33	28	19	13	34	36
1999—	Dom. Dodgers (DSL)	3	2	.600	3.43	9	9	0	0	0	42	34	22	16	18	51
2000—	Great Falls (Pio.)	*10	3	.769	1.88	15	15	*2	0	0	*95 2/3	66	32	20	23	*129
2001—	Vero Beach (FSL)	*14	6	.700	3.21	26	26	2	0	0	154 1/3	133	67	55	60	*154

RODRIGUEZ, RICH   P

PERSONAL: Born March 1, 1963, in Downey, Calif. ... 6-0/205. ... Throws left, bats left. ... Full name: Richard Anthony Rodriguez.
HIGH SCHOOL: Mountain View (El Monte, Calif.).
COLLEGE: Tennessee.
TRANSACTIONS/CAREER NOTES: Selected by Kansas City Royals organization in 17th round of free-agent draft (June 8, 1981); did not sign. ... Selected by New York Mets organization in ninth round of free-agent draft (June 4, 1984). ... Traded by Mets to San Diego Padres for 1B Brad Pounders and 1B Bill Stevenson (January 13, 1989). ... Traded by Padres with 3B Gary Sheffield to Florida Marlins for P Trevor Hoffman, P Jose Martinez and P Andres Berumen (June 24, 1993). ... Released by Marlins (March 29, 1994). ... Signed by St. Louis Cardinals (April 1, 1994). ... On disabled list (April 27, 1995-remainder of season). ... Released by Cardinals (November 20, 1995). ... Signed by Cincinnati Reds organization (January 2, 1996). ... Released by Reds (March 24, 1996). ... Signed by Kansas City Royals organization (April 9, 1996). ... On disabled list (May 18-29, 1996). ... Granted free agency (October 15, 1996). ... Signed by San Francisco Giants organization (November 25, 1996). ... Granted free agency (October 30, 1997). ... Re-signed by Giants (December 7, 1997). ... Granted free agency (October 28, 1999). ... Signed by Mets (February 8, 2000). ... Released by Mets (March 29, 2001). ... Signed by Cleveland Indians organization (April 8, 2001). ... Granted free agency (November 6, 2001).
MISCELLANEOUS: Appeared in one game as pinch runner (1991). ... Had sacrifice hit in only appearance as pinch hitter (1992).

Year	League	W	L	Pct.	ERA	G	GS	CG	ShO	Sv.	IP	H	R	ER	BB	SO
1984—	Little Falls (NY-Penn)	2	1	.667	2.80	25	1	0	0	0	35 1/3	28	21	11	36	27
1985—	Columbia (S.Atl.)	6	3	.667	4.03	49	3	0	0	6	80 1/3	89	41	36	36	71
1986—	Lynchburg (Caro.)	2	1	.667	3.57	36	0	0	0	3	45 1/3	37	20	18	19	38
—	Jackson (Texas)	3	4	.429	9.00	13	5	1	0	0	33	51	35	33	15	15
1987—	Lynchburg (Caro.)	3	1	.750	2.78	*69	0	0	0	5	68	69	23	21	26	59
1988—	Jackson (Texas)	2	7	.222	2.87	47	1	0	0	6	78 1/3	66	35	25	42	68
1989—	Wichita (Texas)■	8	3	.727	3.63	54	0	0	0	8	74 1/3	74	30	30	37	40
1990—	Las Vegas (PCL)	3	4	.429	3.51	27	2	0	0	8	59	50	24	23	22	46
—	San Diego (N.L.)	1	1	.500	2.83	32	0	0	0	1	47 2/3	52	17	15	16	22
1991—	San Diego (N.L.)	3	1	.750	3.26	64	1	0	0	0	80	66	31	29	44	40
1992—	San Diego (N.L.)	6	3	.667	2.37	61	1	0	0	0	91	77	28	24	29	64
1993—	San Diego (N.L.)	2	3	.400	3.30	34	0	0	0	2	30	34	15	11	9	22
—	Florida (N.L.)■	0	1	.000	4.11	36	0	0	0	1	46	39	23	21	24	21
1994—	St. Louis (N.L.)■	3	5	.375	4.03	56	0	0	0	0	60 1/3	62	30	27	26	43
1995—	St. Louis (N.L.)	0	0	...	0.00	1	0	0	0	0	1 2/3	0	0	0	0	0
1996—	Omaha (A.A.)■	2	3	.400	3.99	47	0	0	0	3	70	75	40	31	20	68
1997—	San Francisco (N.L.)■	4	3	.571	3.17	71	0	0	0	1	65 1/3	65	24	23	21	32
1998—	San Francisco (N.L.)	4	0	1.000	3.70	68	0	0	0	2	65 2/3	69	28	27	20	44
1999—	San Francisco (N.L.)	3	0	1.000	5.24	62	0	0	0	0	56 2/3	60	33	33	28	44
2000—	New York (N.L.)■	0	1	.000	7.78	32	0	0	0	0	37	59	40	32	15	18
—	Norfolk (I.L.)	0	1	.000	3.05	14	3	0	0	1	20 2/3	17	7	7	6	16
2001—	Cleveland (A.L.)■	2	2	.500	4.15	53	0	0	0	0	39	41	24	18	17	31
—	Akron (East.)	0	0	...	0.00	4	0	0	0	1	5	2	0	0	0	4
A.L. totals (1 year)		2	2	.500	4.15	53	0	0	0	0	39	41	24	18	17	31
N.L. totals (10 years)		26	18	.591	3.75	517	2	0	0	7	581 1/3	583	269	242	232	350
Major League totals (11 years)		28	20	.583	3.77	570	2	0	0	7	620 1/3	624	293	260	249	381

DIVISION SERIES RECORD

Year	League	W	L	Pct.	ERA	G	GS	CG	ShO	Sv.	IP	H	R	ER	BB	SO
1997—	San Francisco (N.L.)	0	0	...	0.00	2	0	0	0	0	1	1	0	0	0	0

RODRIGUEZ, WILFREDO   P   ASTROS

PERSONAL: Born March 20, 1979, in Ciudad Bolivar, Venezuela. ... 6-3/180. ... Throws left, bats left. ... Full name: Wilfredo Jose Rodriguez.
TRANSACTIONS/CAREER NOTES: Signed as non-drafted free agent by Houston Astros organization (July 25, 1995). ... On Round Rock disabled list (April 6-May 10, 2000).
STATISTICAL NOTES: Led Midwest League with nine balks in 1998.

Year	League	W	L	Pct.	ERA	G	GS	CG	ShO	Sv.	IP	H	R	ER	BB	SO
1996—	Dominican Astros (DSL)	1	2	.333	2.97	18	0	0	0	0	33 1/3	28	17	11	21	29
1997—	Gulf Coast Astros (GCL)	•8	2	.800	3.04	12	12	1	1	0	*68	54	30	23	32	71
1998—	Quad City (Midw.)	11	5	.688	3.05	28	27	1	0	0	165	122	70	56	62	170
1999—	Kissimmee (FSL)	*15	7	.682	2.88	25	24	0	0	0	153 1/3	108	55	49	62	*148
2000—	Round Rock (Texas)	2	4	.333	5.77	11	11	0	0	0	57 2/3	54	42	37	52	55
—	Kissimmee (FSL)	3	5	.375	4.75	9	9	1	0	0	53	43	29	28	30	52
2001—	Round Rock (Texas)	5	9	.357	4.78	42	10	0	0	0	92 1/3	94	61	49	56	94
—	Houston (N.L.)	0	0	...	15.00	2	0	0	0	0	3	6	5	5	1	3
Major League totals (1 year)		0	0	...	15.00	2	0	0	0	0	3	6	5	5	1	3

ROGERS, BRIAN   P   YANKEES

PERSONAL: Born February 13, 1977, in Pinehurst, N.C. ... 6-6/200. ... Throws right, bats right. ... Full name: Brian Christopher Rogers.
HIGH SCHOOL: Carthage (N.C.).
COLLEGE: The Citadel.
TRANSACTIONS/CAREER NOTES: Selected by New York Yankees organization in fifth round of free-agent draft (June 2, 1998).

Year League	W	L	Pct.	ERA	G	GS	CG	ShO	Sv.	IP	H	R	ER	BB	SO
1998—Oneonta (NY-Penn)	2	2	.500	2.31	6	6	0	0	0	35	23	9	9	10	34
—Tampa (FSL)......................	0	0	...	4.20	3	3	0	0	0	15	12	7	7	14	13
—Greensboro (S.Atl.)	2	1	.667	7.88	3	3	0	0	0	16	18	15	14	6	19
1999—Tampa (FSL)......................	8	10	.444	3.83	25	23	1	1	0	134	141	62	57	43	129
2000—Norwich (East.)	11	6	.647	3.94	27	27	1	0	0	164 1/3	155	90	72	70	132
2001—Norwich (East.)	10	9	.526	3.96	29	*29	1	0	0	177 1/3	187	97	78	63	150

ROGERS, EDDIE   SS/2B   ORIOLES

PERSONAL: Born August 10, 1981, in San Pedro de Macoris, Dominican Republic. ... 6-1/150. ... Bats right, throws right. ... Full name: Edward Antonio Rogers. ... Brother of Omar Rogers, second baseman, Baltimore Orioles organization.
TRANSACTIONS/CAREER NOTES: Signed as non-drafted free agent by Baltimore Orioles organization (November 1, 1997). ... On Delmarva disabled list (April 6-22, 2000). ... On Bowie disabled list (August 8, 2000-remainder of season).

								BATTING							FIELDING		
Year Team (League)	Pos.	G	AB	R	H	2B	3B	HR	RBI	Avg.	BB	SO	SB	PO	A	E	Avg.
1998—Dominican (DSL)........		58	194	33	56	9	2	2	27	.289	26	29	8	...	...	...	...
1999—GC Orioles (GCL).......	SS-3B-2B	53	177	34	51	5	1	1	19	.288	23	22	20	61	119	10	.947
2000—Delmarva (S.Atl.)........	SS-2B	80	332	46	91	14	5	5	42	.274	22	63	27	118	222	19	.947
—Bowie (East.)..............	SS	13	49	4	14	3	0	1	8	.286	3	15	1	22	20	0	1.000
2001—Bowie (East.)	SS	53	191	11	38	10	1	0	13	.199	6	40	10	90	147	10	.960
—Frederick (Caro.)	SS	73	292	39	76	20	3	8	41	.260	14	47	18	109	193	14	.956

ROGERS, KENNY   P   RANGERS

PERSONAL: Born November 10, 1964, in Savannah, Ga. ... 6-1/217. ... Throws left, bats left. ... Full name: Kenneth Scott Rogers.
HIGH SCHOOL: Plant City (Fla.).
TRANSACTIONS/CAREER NOTES: Selected by Texas Rangers organization in 39th round of free-agent draft (June 7, 1982). ... On Tulsa disabled list (April 12-30, 1986). ... Granted free agency (October 31, 1995). ... Signed by New York Yankees (December 30, 1995). ... Traded by Yankees with IF Mariano Duncan and P Kevin Henthorne to San Diego Padres for OF Greg Vaughn, P Kerry Taylor and P Chris Clark (July 4, 1997); trade later voided because Vaughn failed physical (July 6). ... Traded by Yankees with cash to Oakland Athletics for a player to be named later (November 7, 1997); Yankees acquired 3B Scott Brosius to complete deal (November 18, 1997). ... Traded by A's to New York Mets for OF Terrance Long and P Leo Vasquez (July 23, 1999). ... Granted free agency (October 29, 1999). ... Signed by Rangers (December 29, 1999). ... On disabled list (July 24, 2001-remainder of season).
HONORS: Won A.L. Gold Glove as pitcher (2000).
STATISTICAL NOTES: Tied for A.L. lead with five balks in 1993. ... Pitched 4-0 perfect game against California (July 28, 1994).

Year League	W	L	Pct.	ERA	G	GS	CG	ShO	Sv.	IP	H	R	ER	BB	SO
1982—Gulf Coast Rangers (GCL)..	0	0	...	0.00	2	0	0	0	0	3	0	0	0	0	4
1983—Gulf Coast Rangers (GCL)..	4	1	.800	2.36	15	6	0	0	1	53 1/3	40	21	14	20	36
1984—Burlington (Midw.)...........	4	7	.364	3.98	39	4	1	0	3	92 2/3	87	52	41	33	93
1985—Daytona Beach (FSL).........	0	1	.000	7.20	6	0	0	0	0	10	12	9	8	11	9
—Burlington (Midw.)...........	2	5	.286	2.84	33	4	2	1	4	95	67	34	30	62	96
1986—Tulsa (Texas).................	0	3	.000	9.91	10	4	0	0	0	26 1/3	39	30	29	18	23
—Salem (Caro.)	2	7	.222	6.27	12	12	0	0	0	66	75	54	46	26	46
1987—Tulsa (Texas).................	0	3	.000	4.76	5	3	0	0	0	17	17	13	9	8	14
—Charlotte (FSL).............	1	5	.167	5.35	28	6	0	0	2	69	80	51	41	35	59
1988—Tulsa (Texas).................	4	6	.400	4.00	13	13	2	0	0	83 1/3	73	43	37	34	76
—Charlotte (FSL).............	2	0	1.000	1.27	8	6	0	0	1	35 1/3	22	8	5	11	26
1989—Texas (A.L.)	3	4	.429	2.93	73	0	0	0	2	73 2/3	60	28	24	42	63
1990—Texas (A.L.)	10	6	.625	3.13	69	3	0	0	15	97 2/3	93	40	34	42	74
1991—Texas (A.L.)	10	10	.500	5.42	63	9	0	0	5	109 2/3	121	80	66	61	73
1992—Texas (A.L.)	3	6	.333	3.09	*81	0	0	0	6	78 2/3	80	32	27	26	70
1993—Texas (A.L.)	16	10	.615	4.10	35	33	5	0	0	208 1/3	210	108	95	71	140
1994—Texas (A.L.)	11	8	.579	4.46	24	24	6	2	0	167 1/3	169	93	83	52	120
1995—Texas (A.L.)	17	7	.708	3.38	31	31	3	1	0	208	192	87	78	76	140
1996—New York (A.L.)■........	12	8	.600	4.68	30	30	2	1	0	179	179	97	93	83	92
1997—New York (A.L.)	6	7	.462	5.65	31	22	1	0	0	145	161	100	91	62	78
1998—Oakland (A.L.)■..........	16	8	.667	3.17	34	34	7	1	0	238 2/3	215	96	84	67	138
1999—Oakland (A.L.)	5	3	.625	4.30	19	19	3	0	0	119 1/3	135	66	57	41	68
—New York (N.L.)■	5	1	.833	4.03	12	12	2	1	0	76	71	37	34	28	58
2000—Texas (A.L.)■............	13	13	.500	4.55	34	34	2	0	0	227 1/3	257	126	115	78	127
2001—Texas (A.L.)	5	7	.417	6.19	20	20	0	0	0	120 2/3	150	88	83	49	74
A.L. totals (13 years)	127	97	.567	4.24	544	259	29	5	28	1973 1/3	2022	1041	930	750	1257
N.L. totals (1 year)	5	1	.833	4.03	12	12	2	1	0	76	71	35	34	28	58
Major League totals (13 years)	132	98	.574	4.23	556	271	31	6	28	2049 1/3	2093	1076	964	778	1315

DIVISION SERIES RECORD

Year League	W	L	Pct.	ERA	G	GS	CG	ShO	Sv.	IP	H	R	ER	BB	SO
1996—New York (A.L.).................	0	0	...	9.00	2	1	0	0	0	2	5	2	2	2	1
1999—New York (N.L.).................	0	1	.000	8.31	1	1	0	0	0	4 1/3	5	4	4	2	6
Division series totals (2 years)	0	1	.000	8.53	3	2	0	0	0	6 1/3	10	6	6	4	7

R

CHAMPIONSHIP SERIES RECORD

Year League	W	L	Pct.	ERA	G	GS	CG	ShO	Sv.	IP	H	R	ER	BB	SO
1996— New York (A.L.)	0	0	...	12.00	1	1	0	0	0	3	5	4	4	2	3
1999— New York (N.L.)	0	2	.000	5.87	3	1	0	0	0	7²/₃	11	5	5	7	2
Champ. series totals (2 years)	0	2	.000	7.59	4	2	0	0	0	10²/₃	16	9	9	9	5

NOTES: Member of World Series championship team (1996).

WORLD SERIES RECORD

Year League	W	L	Pct.	ERA	G	GS	CG	ShO	Sv.	IP	H	R	ER	BB	SO
1996— New York (A.L.)	0	0	...	22.50	1	1	0	0	0	2	5	5	5	2	0

ALL-STAR GAME RECORD

Year League	W	L	Pct.	ERA	GS	CG	ShO	Sv.	IP	H	R	ER	BB	SO
1995— American	0	0	...	9.00	0	0	0	0	1	1	1	1	0	2

R

ROLEN, SCOTT — 3B — PHILLIES

PERSONAL: Born April 4, 1975, in Jasper, Ind. ... 6-4/226. ... Bats right, throws right. ... Full name: Scott Bruce Rolen.
HIGH SCHOOL: Jasper (Ind.).
TRANSACTIONS/CAREER NOTES: Selected by Philadelphia Phillies organization in second round of free-agent draft (June 3, 1993). ... On disabled list (May 24-June 8, 2000).
RECORDS: Shares major league single-game record for most strikeouts (nine-inning game)—5 (August 23, 1999).
HONORS: Named N.L. Rookie Player of the Year by THE SPORTING NEWS (1997). ... Named N.L. Rookie of the Year by Baseball Writers' Association of America (1997). ... Won N.L. Gold Glove at third base (1998 and 2000-01).
STATISTICAL NOTES: Led South Atlantic League third basemen with 457 total chances and 36 double plays in 1994. ... Led N.L. third basemen in total chances with 459 in 1997 and 468 in 1998. ... Career major league grand slams: 2.

							BATTING							FIELDING		
Year Team (League)	Pos.	G	AB	R	H	2B	3B	HR	RBI	Avg.	BB	SO	SB	PO	A	E	Avg.
1993— Martinsville (Appl.)	3B	25	80	8	25	5	0	0	12	.313	10	15	3	23	57	10	.889
1994— Spartanburg (S.Atl.)	3B	138	513	83	151	34	5	14	72	.294	55	90	6	•96	*323	38	.917
1995— Clearwater (FSL)	3B	66	238	45	69	13	2	10	39	.290	37	46	4	43	135	20	.899
— Reading (East.)	3B	20	76	16	22	3	0	3	15	.289	7	14	1	10	47	4	.934
1996— Reading (East.)	3B	61	230	44	83	22	2	9	42	.361	34	32	8	41	125	9	.949
— Scranton/W.B. (I.L.)	3B	45	168	23	46	17	0	2	19	.274	28	28	4	32	88	6	.952
— Philadelphia (N.L.)	3B	37	130	10	33	7	0	4	18	.254	13	27	0	29	54	4	.954
1997— Philadelphia (N.L.)	3B	156	561	93	159	35	3	21	92	.283	76	138	16	*144	291	24	.948
1998— Philadelphia (N.L.)	3B	160	601	120	174	45	4	31	110	.290	93	141	14	*135	319	14	.970
1999— Philadelphia (N.L.)	3B	112	421	74	113	28	1	26	77	.268	67	114	12	111	227	14	.960
2000— Philadelphia (N.L.)	3B	128	483	88	144	32	6	26	89	.298	51	99	8	89	245	10	.971
2001— Philadelphia (N.L.)	3B	151	554	96	160	39	1	25	107	.289	74	127	16	104	325	12	.973
Major League totals (6 years)		744	2750	481	783	186	15	133	493	.285	374	646	66	612	1461	78	.964

ROLISON, NATE — 1B — MARLINS

PERSONAL: Born March 27, 1977, in Hattiesburg, Miss. ... 6-6/240. ... Bats left, throws right. ... Full name: Nathan Mardis Rolison.
HIGH SCHOOL: Petal (Miss.).
TRANSACTIONS/CAREER NOTES: Selected by Florida Marlins organization in second round of free-agent draft (June 1, 1995). ... On Calgary disabled list (April 19-May 2, 2000). ... On Florida disabled list (March 23, 2001-entire season); included rehabilitation assignments to Gulf Coast Marlins (July 17-20), Brevard County (July 21-25 and August 20-September 8), Portland (July 26-30) and Calgary (July 31-August 4).
STATISTICAL NOTES: Led Midwest League first basemen with 1,254 total chances and 114 double plays in 1996. ... Led Florida State first basemen with 89 double plays in 1997.

							BATTING							FIELDING		
Year Team (League)	Pos.	G	AB	R	H	2B	3B	HR	RBI	Avg.	BB	SO	SB	PO	A	E	Avg.
1995— GC Marlins (GCL)	1B	37	134	22	37	10	2	1	19	.276	15	34	0	283	20	5	.984
1996— Kane County (Midw.)	1B	131	474	63	115	28	1	14	75	.243	66	170	3	*1161	•80	13	.990
1997— Brevard County (FSL)	1B	122	473	59	121	22	0	16	65	.256	38	*143	3	1036	69	17	.985
1998— Portland (East.)	1B	131	484	80	134	35	2	16	83	.277	64	150	5	1081	85	13	.989
1999— Portland (East.)	1B-DH	124	438	71	131	20	1	17	69	.299	68	112	0	920	69	13	.987
2000— Calgary (PCL)	1B	123	443	88	146	37	3	23	88	.330	70	117	3	945	76	•12	.988
— Florida (N.L.)	1B	8	13	0	1	0	0	0	2	.077	1	4	0	21	2	0	1.000
2001— GC Marlins (GCL)	1B	2	4	1	2	0	0	0	1	.500	3	1	0	15	0	1	.938
— Brevard County (FSL)	1B	14	45	7	17	3	0	1	6	.378	10	7	0	114	12	1	.992
— Portland (East.)	1B	5	19	1	4	1	0	0	2	.211	1	7	0	28	2	0	1.000
— Calgary (PCL)	1B	3	12	1	2	0	0	0	1	.167	1	3	0	19	2	0	1.000
Major League totals (1 year)		8	13	0	1	0	0	0	2	.077	1	4	0	21	2	0	1.000

ROLLINS, JIMMY — SS — PHILLIES

PERSONAL: Born November 27, 1978, in Oakland. ... 5-8/165. ... Bats both, throws right. ... Full name: James Calvin Rollins. ... Cousin of Tony Tarasco, outfielder with six major league teams (1988-99).
HIGH SCHOOL: Encinal (Alameda, Calif.).
TRANSACTIONS/CAREER NOTES: Selected by Philadelphia Phillies organization in second round of free-agent draft (June 4, 1996).
STATISTICAL NOTES: Led South Atlantic League shortstops wth 648 total chances in 1997.

Year Team (League)	Pos.	G	AB	R	H	2B	3B	HR	RBI	Avg.	BB	SO	SB	PO	A	E	Avg.
1996—Martinsville (Appl.).....	SS	49	172	22	41	3	1	1	16	.238	28	20	11	66	126	20	.906
1997—Piedmont (S.Atl.)........	SS	139	560	94	151	22	8	6	59	.270	52	80	46	*201	*421	26	*.960
1998—Clearwater (FSL)........	SS	119	495	72	121	18	9	6	35	.244	41	62	23	192	380	29	*.952
1999—Reading (East.)..........	SS	133	532	81	145	21	8	11	56	.273	51	47	24	211	*392	22	.965
—Scranton/W.B. (I.L.) ...	SS	4	13	0	1	1	0	0	0	.077	1	1	1	9	15	1	.960
2000—Scranton/W.B. (I.L.) ...	SS	133	470	67	129	28	•11	12	69	.274	49	55	24	183	*411	26	.958
—Philadelphia (N.L.).....	SS	14	53	5	17	1	1	0	5	.321	2	7	3	23	22	1	.978
2001—Philadelphia (N.L.)......	SS	158	656	97	180	29	12	14	54	.274	48	108	•46	216	426	14	.979
Major League totals (2 years)		172	709	102	197	30	13	14	59	.278	50	115	49	239	448	15	.979

ALL-STAR GAME RECORD

Year League	Pos.	AB	R	H	2B	3B	HR	RBI	Avg.	BB	SO	SB	PO	A	E	Avg.
2001—National	SS	0	0	0	0	0	0	0	...	1	0	1	0	1	0	1.000

R

ROLLS, DAMIAN   3B   DEVIL RAYS

PERSONAL: Born September 15, 1977, in Manhattan, Kan. ... 6-2/205. ... Bats right, throws right. ... Full name: Damian Michael Rolls.
HIGH SCHOOL: F.L. Schlagle (Kansas City, Kan.).
TRANSACTIONS/CAREER NOTES: Selected by Los Angeles Dodgers organization in first round (23rd pick overall) of free-agent draft (June 4, 1996). ... Selected by Kansas City Royals from Dodgers organization in Rule 5 major league draft (December 13, 1999). ... Traded by Royals to Tampa Bay Devil Rays for a player to be named later and cash (December 13, 1999). ... On Tampa Bay disabled list (March 25-September 1, 2000); included rehabilitation assignments to St. Petersburg (August 12-18) and Orlando (August 19-September 1).
STATISTICAL NOTES: Led Northwest League third basemen with 215 total chances in 1996. ... Led South Atlantic League third basemen with 388 total chances in 1997.

Year Team (League)	Pos.	G	AB	R	H	2B	3B	HR	RBI	Avg.	BB	SO	SB	PO	A	E	Avg.
1996—Yakima (N'West)	3B	66	257	31	68	11	1	4	27	.265	7	46	8	*58	*134	•23	.893
1997—Savannah (S.Atl.)	3B	130	475	57	100	17	5	5	47	.211	38	83	11	*111	*246	31	.920
1998—Vero Beach (FSL)	3B	73	266	28	65	9	0	0	30	.244	23	43	13	65	187	13	.951
—San Antonio (Texas)...	3B	50	160	18	35	6	0	1	9	.219	6	28	2	38	124	9	.947
1999—Vero Beach (FSL)	3B-2B	127	474	68	141	26	2	9	54	.297	36	66	24	91	213	25	.924
2000—St. Pete. (FSL)■........	3B	5	16	2	3	2	0	0	0	.188	2	3	1	2	9	0	1.000
—Orlando (Sou.).........	3B	14	51	6	13	5	0	0	3	.255	7	6	1	7	22	3	.906
—Tampa Bay (A.L.).....	DH-3B	4	3	0	1	0	0	0	0	.333	0	1	0	0	0	0	...
2001—Tampa Bay (A.L.)........	2B-OF-DH-3B	81	237	33	62	11	1	2	12	.262	10	47	12	110	118	6	.974
Major League totals (2 years)		85	240	33	63	11	1	2	12	.263	10	48	12	110	118	6	.974

ROMANO, JASON   2B   RANGERS

PERSONAL: Born June 24, 1979, in Tampa, Fla. ... 6-0/185. ... Bats right, throws right. ... Full name: Jason Anthony Romano. ... Brother of Jimmie Romano, catcher, Texas Rangers organization.
HIGH SCHOOL: Hillsborough (Tampa, Fla.).
TRANSACTIONS/CAREER NOTES: Selected by Texas Rangers organization in supplemental round ("sandwich pick" between first and second round, 39th pick overall) of free-agent draft (June 3, 1997); pick received as part of compensation of New York Yankees signed Type-A free agent P Mike Stanton. ... On Oklahoma disabled list (June 17-August 9, 2001).
STATISTICAL NOTES: Led Texas League with 16 sacrifice hits in 2000.

Year Team (League)	Pos.	G	AB	R	H	2B	3B	HR	RBI	Avg.	BB	SO	SB	PO	A	E	Avg.
1997—GC Rangers (GCL)......	3B	34	109	27	28	5	3	2	11	.257	13	19	13	14	50	15	.810
1998—Savannah (S.Atl.)	2B	134	524	72	142	19	4	7	52	.271	46	94	40	*305	326	•32	.952
—Charlotte (FSL)..........	2B	7	24	3	5	1	0	0	1	.208	2	2	1	20	25	1	.978
1999—Charlotte (FSL)..........	2B	120	459	84	143	27	*14	13	71	.312	39	72	34	232	282	23	.957
2000—Tulsa (Texas)	2B	131	535	87	145	35	2	8	70	.271	56	84	25	292	336	24	.963
2001—Tulsa (Texas)	2B	46	186	19	45	9	1	1	19	.242	16	31	8	105	97	8	.962
—Oklahoma (PCL)........	2B-OF	41	149	32	47	6	1	4	13	.315	20	28	3	52	52	2	.981
—GC Rangers (GCL)......	2B-OF	5	21	2	3	0	0	0	0	.143	4	1	1	13	8	5	.808
—Charlotte (FSL)..........	OF	3	10	3	4	2	0	0	1	.400	4	1	1	10	0	0	1.000

ROMERO, J.C.   P   TWINS

PERSONAL: Born June 4, 1976, in Rio Piedras, Puerto Rico. ... 5-11/195. ... Throws left, bats both. ... Full name: Juan C. Romero.
HIGH SCHOOL: Berwing (San Juan, Puerto Rico).
COLLEGE: Mobile.
TRANSACTIONS/CAREER NOTES: Selected by Minnesota Twins organization in 21st round of free-agent draft (June 3, 1997). ... On Minnesota disabled list (March 25-May 10, 2000); included rehabilitation assignment to Fort Myers (May 3-10).

Year League	W	L	Pct.	ERA	G	GS	CG	ShO	Sv.	IP	H	R	ER	BB	SO
1997—Elizabethton (Appl.)............	3	2	.600	4.88	18	0	0	0	3	24	27	16	13	7	29
—Fort Myers (FSL)................	1	1	.500	4.38	7	1	0	0	0	12 1/3	11	6	6	4	9
1998—New Britain (East.)	6	3	.667	2.19	51	1	0	0	2	78	48	28	19	43	79
1999—New Britain (East.)	4	4	.500	3.40	36	1	0	0	7	53	51	25	20	34	53
—Salt Lake (PCL)	4	1	.800	3.20	15	0	0	0	1	19 2/3	18	11	7	14	20
—Minnesota (A.L.)	0	0	...	3.72	5	0	0	0	0	9 2/3	13	4	4	0	4
2000—Fort Myers (FSL)	0	0	...	1.93	2	0	0	0	0	4 2/3	4	1	1	1	3
—Minnesota (A.L.)	2	7	.222	7.02	12	11	0	0	0	57 2/3	72	51	45	30	50
—Salt Lake (PCL)	4	2	.667	3.44	17	11	1	0	4	65 1/3	60	40	25	25	38
2001—Minnesota (A.L.)	1	4	.200	6.23	14	11	0	0	0	65	71	48	45	24	39
—Edmonton (PCL)	3	3	.500	3.68	12	10	0	0	0	63 2/3	67	33	26	24	55
Major League totals (3 years)	3	11	.214	6.39	31	22	0	0	0	132 1/3	156	103	94	54	93

ROSADO, JOSE P ROYALS

PERSONAL: Born November 9, 1974, in Jersey City, N.J. ... 6-0/185. ... Throws left, bats left. ... Full name: Jose Antonio Rosado.
HIGH SCHOOL: Jose S. Alegria (Dorado, Puerto Rico).
JUNIOR COLLEGE: Galveston College (Texas).
TRANSACTIONS/CAREER NOTES: Selected by Kansas City Royals organization in 12th round of free-agent draft (June 2, 1994). ... On disabled list (May 1, 2000-remainder of season; and March 31, 2001-entire season).
MISCELLANEOUS: Appeared in one game as pinch runner (1997).

Year League	W	L	Pct.	ERA	G	GS	CG	ShO	Sv.	IP	H	R	ER	BB	SO
1994— Gulf Coast Royals (GCL)	6	2	.750	*1.25	14	12	0	0	0	64²/₃	45	14	9	7	56
1995— Wilmington (Caro.)............	10	7	.588	3.13	25	25	0	0	0	138	128	53	48	30	117
1996— Wichita (Texas)	2	0	1.000	0.00	2	2	0	0	0	13	10	0	0	1	12
— Omaha (A.A.).................	8	3	.727	3.17	15	15	1	0	0	96²/₃	80	38	34	38	82
— Kansas City (A.L.)	8	6	.571	3.21	16	16	2	1	0	106²/₃	101	39	38	26	64
1997— Kansas City (A.L.)	9	12	.429	4.69	33	33	2	0	0	203¹/₃	208	117	106	73	129
1998— Kansas City (A.L.)	8	11	.421	4.69	38	25	2	1	1	174²/₃	180	106	91	57	135
1999— Kansas City (A.L.)	10	14	.417	3.85	33	33	5	0	0	208	197	103	89	72	141
2000— Kansas City (A.L.)	2	2	.500	5.86	5	5	0	0	0	27²/₃	29	18	18	9	15
2001— Kansas City (A.L.)							Did not play.								
Major League totals (5 years)	37	45	.451	4.27	125	112	11	2	1	720¹/₃	715	383	342	237	484

ALL-STAR GAME RECORD

Year League	W	L	Pct.	ERA	GS	CG	ShO	Sv.	IP	H	R	ER	BB	SO
1997— American	1	0	1.000	9.00	0	0	0	0	1	2	1	1	1	1
1999— American	0	0	...	0.00	0	0	0	0	1	1	0	0	0	1
All-Star Game totals (2 years)	1	0	1.000	4.50	0	0	0	0	2	3	1	1	1	2

ROSARIO, RODRIGO P ASTROS

PERSONAL: Born December 14, 1979, in La Romana, Dominican Republic. ... 6-2/165. ... Throws right, bats right.
TRANSACTIONS/CAREER NOTES: Signed as non-drafted free agent by Houston Astros organization (July 6, 1996).

Year League	W	L	Pct.	ERA	G	GS	CG	ShO	Sv.	IP	H	R	ER	BB	SO
1997— Dominican Astros (DSL)	6	4	.600	2.46	15	14	0	0	0	91¹/₃	63	30	25	24	81
1998— Gulf Coast Astros (GCL).....	2	2	.500	4.12	13	•12	0	0	0	67²/₃	61	36	31	30	65
— Auburn (NY-Penn)........	0	0	...	0.00	2	2	0	0	0	2	0	0	0	3	2
1999— Martinsville (Appl.)............	5	5	.500	4.69	14	•14	0	0	0	78²/₃	78	46	41	32	86
2000— Auburn (NY-Penn)............	5	6	.455	3.45	14	14	0	0	0	75²/₃	67	36	29	32	67
2001— Lexington (S.Atl.)	13	4	.765	2.14	30	21	1	0	2	147	105	46	35	36	131

ROSE, BRIAN P

PERSONAL: Born February 13, 1976, in New Bedford, Mass. ... 6-3/215. ... Throws right, bats right. ... Full name: Brian Leonard Rose.
HIGH SCHOOL: Dartmouth (North Dartmouth, Mass.).
TRANSACTIONS/CAREER NOTES: Selected by Boston Red Sox organization in third round of free-agent draft (June 2, 1994). ... On Boston disabled list (May 13, 1998-remainder of season); included rehabilitation assignment to Pawtucket (June 13-July 10). ... Traded by Red Sox with P John Wasdin, P Jeff Taglienti and 2B Jeff Frye to Colorado Rockies for P Rolando Arrojo, P Rick Croushore, 2B Mike Lansing and cash (July 27, 2000). ... Traded by Rockies to New York Mets for P Mark Leiter (March 26, 2001). ... Claimed on waivers by Tampa Bay Devil Rays (April 24, 2001). ... On Durham disabled list (September 2-9, 2001). ... Granted free agency (October 15, 2001).
HONORS: Named International League Most Valuable Pitcher (1997).

Year League	W	L	Pct.	ERA	G	GS	CG	ShO	Sv.	IP	H	R	ER	BB	SO
1995— Michigan (Midw.)	8	5	.615	3.44	21	20	2	0	0	136	127	63	52	31	105
1996— Trenton (East.)	12	7	.632	4.01	27	27	4	2	0	163²/₃	157	82	73	45	115
1997— Pawtucket (I.L.).................	*17	5	.773	*3.02	27	26	3	0	0	*190²/₃	188	74	64	46	116
— Boston (A.L.)................	0	0	...	12.00	1	1	0	0	0	3	5	4	4	2	3
1998— Boston (A.L.)................	1	4	.200	6.93	8	8	0	0	0	37¹/₃	43	32	29	14	18
— Pawtucket (I.L.)...........	0	3	.000	7.64	6	6	0	0	0	17²/₃	24	19	15	4	17
1999— Pawtucket (I.L.)...........	2	1	.667	2.89	7	7	0	0	0	28	28	10	9	8	30
— Boston (A.L.)................	7	6	.538	4.87	22	18	0	0	0	98	112	59	53	29	51
2000— Boston (A.L.)................	3	5	.375	6.11	15	12	0	0	0	53	58	37	36	21	24
— Pawtucket (I.L.)...........	4	1	.800	3.19	5	5	1	0	0	31	28	13	11	13	20
— Colorado (N.L.)■..........	4	5	.444	5.51	12	12	0	0	0	63²/₃	72	41	39	30	40
2001— New York (N.L.)■...........	0	1	.000	4.15	3	0	0	0	0	8²/₃	10	4	4	2	4
— Tampa Bay (A.L.)■.......	0	2	.000	8.85	7	3	0	0	0	20¹/₃	31	20	20	12	11
— Durham (I.L.)	9	2	.818	3.10	19	15	0	0	1	98²/₃	88	35	34	19	88
A.L. totals (5 years)	11	17	.393	6.03	53	42	0	0	0	212	249	152	142	78	107
N.L. totals (2 years)	4	6	.400	5.35	15	12	0	0	0	72¹/₃	82	45	43	32	44
Major League totals (5 years)	15	23	.395	5.86	68	54	0	0	0	284¹/₃	331	197	185	110	151

DIVISION SERIES RECORD

Year League	W	L	Pct.	ERA	G	GS	CG	ShO	Sv.	IP	H	R	ER	BB	SO
1999— Boston (A.L.)......................							Did not play.								

CHAMPIONSHIP SERIES RECORD

Year League	W	L	Pct.	ERA	G	GS	CG	ShO	Sv.	IP	H	R	ER	BB	SO
1999— Boston (A.L.)......................							Did not play.								

ROWAND, AARON — OF — WHITE SOX

PERSONAL: Born August 29, 1977, in Portland, Ore. ... 6-1/200. ... Bats right, throws right. ... Full name: Aaron Ryan Rowand.
HIGH SCHOOL: Glendora (Calif.).
COLLEGE: Cal State-Fullerton.
TRANSACTIONS/CAREER NOTES: Selected by New York Mets organization in 40th round of free-agent draft (June 1, 1995); did not sign. ... Selected by Chicago White Sox organization in supplemental round ("sandwich pick" between first and second round, 35th pick overall) of free-agent draft (June 2, 1998); pick received as part of compensation for Tampa Bay Devil Rays signing Type A free agent OF Dave Martinez.
STATISTICAL NOTES: Led Carolina League with 258 total bases in 1999.

Year Team (League)	Pos.	G	AB	R	H	2B	3B	HR	RBI	Avg.	BB	SO	SB	PO	A	E	Avg.
1998—Hickory (S.Atl.)..........	OF	61	222	42	76	13	3	5	32	.342	21	36	7	79	7	3	.966
1999—Win.-Salem (Caro.)	OF	133	512	•96	143	37	3	24	88	.279	33	94	15	172	9	5	.973
2000—Birmingham (Sou.)......	OF	139	532	80	137	26	5	20	98	.258	38	117	22	299	18	8	.975
2001—Charlotte (I.L.)...........	OF	82	329	54	97	28	0	16	48	.295	21	47	8	170	1	6	.966
—Chicago (A.L.)	OF	63	123	21	36	5	0	4	20	.293	15	28	5	103	3	1	.991
Major League totals (1 year)		63	123	21	36	5	0	4	20	.293	15	28	5	103	3	1	.991

RUAN, WILKEN — OF — EXPOS

PERSONAL: Born November 18, 1979, in Ramon Santana, Dominican Republic. ... 6-0/170. ... Bats right, throws right.
TRANSACTIONS/CAREER NOTES: Signed as non-drafted free agent by Montreal Expos organization (November 15, 1996). ... On Harrisburg disabled list (July 12-August 11, 2001).
STATISTICAL NOTES: Led South Atlantic League outfielders with 285 total chances and tied for the lead in double plays with four in 1999.

Year Team (League)	Pos.	G	AB	R	H	2B	3B	HR	RBI	Avg.	BB	SO	SB	PO	A	E	Avg.
1997—Dom. Expos (DSL)	OF	69	293	53	102	16	5	4	46	.348	31	34	33	...	...	...	...
1998—Jupiter (FSL)	OF	5	18	2	3	0	0	0	0	.167	1	3	2	8	0	0	1.000
—GC Expos (GCL)		54	201	22	48	9	3	1	19	.239	5	43	13	...	...	...	...
1999—Cape Fear (S.Atl.)	OF	112	397	43	89	16	4	1	47	.224	18	79	29	263	18	4	.986
2000—Cape Fear (S.Atl.)	OF	134	574	95	165	29	10	0	51	.287	24	75	64	292	18	3	.990
2001—Jupiter (FSL)	OF	72	293	41	83	8	2	2	26	.283	10	35	25	179	8	7	.964
—Harrisburg (East.).......	OF	30	117	14	29	7	0	0	6	.248	3	18	6	81	2	2	.976

RUETER, KIRK — P — GIANTS

PERSONAL: Born December 1, 1970, in Centralia, Ill. ... 6-3/205. ... Throws left, bats left. ... Full name: Kirk Wesley Rueter. ... Name pronounced REE-ter.
HIGH SCHOOL: Nashville (Ill.) Community.
COLLEGE: Murray State.
TRANSACTIONS/CAREER NOTES: Selected by Montreal Expos organization in 19th round of free-agent draft (June 3, 1991). ... On Montreal disabled list (May 10-26, 1996); included rehabilitation assignment to Ottawa (May 20-24). ... Traded by Expos with P Tim Scott to San Francisco Giants for P Mark Leiter (July 30, 1996).
HONORS: Named N.L. Rookie Pitcher of the Year by THE SPORTING NEWS (1993).
STATISTICAL NOTES: Pitched 1-0 one-hit, complete-game victory for Montreal against San Francisco (August 27, 1995).
MISCELLANEOUS: Caught stealing in only appearance as pinch runner (1998). ... Scored one run in two appearances as pinch runner (2000). ... Appeared in one game as pinch runner (2001). ... Appeared in one game as pinch hitter (2001).

Year League	W	L	Pct.	ERA	G	GS	CG	ShO	Sv.	IP	H	R	ER	BB	SO
1991—Gulf Coast Expos (GCL)	1	1	.500	0.95	5	4	0	0	0	19	16	5	2	4	19
—Sumter (S.Atl.)	3	1	.750	1.33	8	5	0	0	0	40 2/3	32	8	6	10	27
1992—Rockford (Midw.)	11	9	.550	2.58	26	26	6	•2	0	174 1/3	150	68	50	36	153
1993—Harrisburg (East.)...............	5	0	1.000	1.36	9	8	1	1	0	59 2/3	47	10	9	7	56
—Ottawa (I.L.)	4	2	.667	2.70	7	7	1	0	0	43 1/3	46	20	13	3	27
—Montreal (N.L.)..................	8	0	1.000	2.73	14	14	1	0	0	85 2/3	85	33	26	18	31
1994—Montreal (N.L.)..................	7	3	.700	5.17	20	20	0	0	0	92 1/3	106	60	53	23	50
—Ottawa (I.L.)	0	0	...	4.50	1	1	0	0	0	2	1	1	1	0	1
1995—Montreal (N.L.)..................	5	3	.625	3.23	9	9	1	1	0	47 1/3	38	17	17	9	28
—Ottawa (I.L.)	9	7	.563	3.06	20	20	3	1	0	120 2/3	120	50	41	25	67
1996—Ottawa (I.L.)	1	2	.333	4.20	3	3	1	0	0	15	21	7	7	3	3
—Montreal (N.L.)..................	5	6	.455	4.58	16	16	0	0	0	78 2/3	91	44	40	22	30
—San Francisco (N.L.)■	1	2	.333	1.93	4	3	0	0	0	23 1/3	18	6	5	5	16
—Phoenix (PCL)	1	2	.333	3.51	5	5	0	0	0	25 2/3	25	12	10	12	15
1997—San Francisco (N.L.)	13	6	.684	3.45	32	32	0	0	0	190 2/3	194	83	73	51	115
1998—San Francisco (N.L.)	16	9	.640	4.36	33	33	1	0	0	187 2/3	193	100	91	57	102
1999—San Francisco (N.L.)	15	10	.600	5.41	33	33	1	0	0	184 2/3	219	118	111	55	94
2000—San Francisco (N.L.)	11	9	.550	3.96	32	31	0	0	0	184	205	92	81	62	71
2001—San Francisco (N.L.)	14	12	.538	4.42	34	34	0	0	0	195 1/3	213	105	96	66	83
Major League totals (9 years).......	95	60	.613	4.20	227	225	4	1	0	1269 2/3	1362	658	593	368	620

DIVISION SERIES RECORD

Year League	W	L	Pct.	ERA	G	GS	CG	ShO	Sv.	IP	H	R	ER	BB	SO
1997—San Francisco (N.L.)	0	0	...	1.29	1	1	0	0	0	7	4	1	1	3	5
2000—San Francisco (N.L.)	0	0	...	0.00	1	0	0	0	0	4 1/3	3	0	0	1	1
Division series totals (2 years)	0	0	...	0.79	2	1	0	0	0	11 1/3	7	1	1	4	6

RUFFIN, JOHNNY   P

PERSONAL: Born July 29, 1971, in Butler, Ala. ... 6-3/170. ... Throws right, bats right. ... Full name: Johnny Renando Ruffin.
HIGH SCHOOL: Choctaw County (Butler, Ala.).
TRANSACTIONS/CAREER NOTES: Selected by Chicago White Sox organization in fourth round of free-agent draft (June 1, 1988). ... Traded by White Sox with P Jeff Pierce to Cincinnati Reds for P Tim Belcher (July 31, 1993). ... On Cincinnati disabled list (September 1, 1995-remainder of season). ... Granted free agency (December 20, 1996). ... Signed by Boston Red Sox organization (December 27, 1996). ... Contract sold by Red Sox to Kintetsu Buffaloes of Japan Pacific League (May 1, 1997). ... Signed by Milwaukee Brewers organization (November 17, 1997). ... Traded by Brewers to New York Mets for P Ryan Henderson (July 9, 1998). ... Granted free agency (October 15, 1998). ... Signed by Kansas City Royals organization (March 1, 1999). ... Released by Royals (March 27, 1999). ... Signed by Oaxaca, Mexican League (1999). ... Contract purchased by Los Angeles Dodgers from Oaxaca (April 30, 1999). ... Granted free agency (October 15, 1999). ... Signed by Cincinnati Reds organization (January 20, 2000). ... Released by Reds (March 5, 2000). ... Signed by Arizona Diamondbacks organization (April 10, 2000). ... On disabled list (August 14, 2000-remainder of season). ... Released by Diamondbacks (November 15, 2000). ... Signed by Marlins organization (July 25, 2001). ... Released by Marlins (August 3, 2001). ... Signed by Reds organization (August 13, 2001). ... Granted free agency (October 15, 2001).
STATISTICAL NOTES: Pitched 6-1 no-hit victory against Charlotte (June 14, 1991, second game).

Year League	W	L	Pct.	ERA	G	GS	CG	ShO	Sv.	IP	H	R	ER	BB	SO
1988—GC White Sox (GCL)	4	2	.667	2.30	13	11	1	0	0	58 2/3	43	27	15	22	31
1989—Utica (NY-Penn)	4	8	.333	3.36	15	15	0	0	0	88 1/3	67	43	33	46	92
1990—South Bend (Midw.)	7	6	.538	4.17	24	24	0	0	0	123	117	86	57	82	92
1991—Sarasota (FSL)	11	4	.733	3.23	26	26	6	2	0	158 2/3	126	68	57	62	117
1992—Birmingham (Sou.)	0	7	.000	6.04	10	10	0	0	0	47 2/3	51	48	32	34	44
—Sarasota (FSL)	3	7	.300	5.89	23	8	0	0	0	62 2/3	56	46	41	41	61
1993—Birmingham (Sou.)	0	4	.000	2.82	11	0	0	0	2	22 1/3	16	9	7	9	23
—Nashville (A.A.)	3	4	.429	3.30	29	0	0	0	1	60	48	24	22	16	69
—Indianapolis (A.A.)■	1	1	.500	1.35	3	0	0	0	1	6 2/3	3	1	1	2	6
—Cincinnati (N.L.)	2	1	.667	3.58	21	0	0	0	2	37 2/3	36	16	15	11	30
1994—Cincinnati (N.L.)	7	2	.778	3.09	51	0	0	0	1	70	57	26	24	27	44
1995—Cincinnati (N.L.)	0	0	...	1.35	10	0	0	0	0	13 1/3	4	3	2	11	11
—Indianapolis (A.A.)	3	1	.750	2.90	36	1	0	0	0	49 2/3	27	19	16	37	58
1996—Cincinnati (N.L.)	1	3	.250	5.49	49	0	0	0	0	62 1/3	71	42	38	37	69
1997—Pawtucket (I.L.)■	0	1	.000	4.50	6	1	0	0	0	14	5	7	7	16	16
—Kintetsu (Jap. Pac.)■	0	0	...	5.40	1	1	0	0	0	5	3	3	3	...	...
1998—Louisville (I.L.)■	5	3	.625	3.00	35	2	0	0	0	60	40	27	20	48	57
—Norfolk (I.L.)■	1	0	1.000	2.77	17	3	0	0	0	39	31	15	12	20	40
—Oaxaca (Mex.)■	0	1	.000	5.68	5	0	0	0	1	6 1/3	5	6	4	5	5
—Albuquerque (PCL)■	1	1	.500	3.17	46	0	0	0	10	54	41	21	19	26	66
Tucson (PCL)■	5	3	.625	2.98	45	0	0	0	20	57 1/3	48	21	19	25	66
Arizona (N.L.)	0	0	...	9.00	5	0	0	0	0	9	14	9	9	3	5
Calgary (PCL)■	2	3	.400	4.36	37	0	0	0	22	33	37	17	16	10	47
Florida (N.L.)	0	0	...	4.91	3	0	0	0	0	3 2/3	5	4	2	4	4
Louisville (I.L.)■	0	0	...	0.00	9	0	0	0	5	8 1/3	6	1	0	3	11
League totals (6 years)	10	6	.625	4.13	139	0	0	0	3	196	187	100	90	93	163

RUPE, RYAN   P   DEVIL RAYS

PERSONAL: Born March 31, 1975, in Houston. ... 6-5/230. ... Throws right, bats right. ... Full name: Ryan Kittman Rupe.
HIGH SCHOOL: Northbrook (Houston).
COLLEGE: Texas A&M.
TRANSACTIONS/CAREER NOTES: Selected by New York Mets organization in 19th round of free-agent draft (June 3, 1993); did not sign. ... Selected by Kansas City Royals organization in 36th round of free-agent draft (June 4, 1996); did not sign. ... Selected by Tampa Bay Devil Rays organization in sixth round of free-agent draft (June 2, 1998). ... On Durham disabled list (May 9-June 16, 2000). ... On disabled list (September 11, 2000-remainder of season).

Year League	W	L	Pct.	ERA	G	GS	CG	ShO	Sv.	IP	H	R	ER	BB	SO
1998—Hudson Valley (NY-Penn)	1	0	1.000	0.68	3	3	0	0	0	13 1/3	8	1	1	2	18
—Charleston, S.C. (S.Atl.)	6	1	.857	2.40	10	10	0	0	0	56 1/3	33	18	15	9	62
1999—Orlando (Sou.)	2	2	.500	2.73	5	5	0	0	0	26 1/3	18	13	8	6	22
—Tampa Bay (A.L.)	8	9	.471	4.55	24	24	0	0	0	142 1/3	136	81	72	57	97
2000—Tampa Bay (A.L.)	5	6	.455	6.92	18	18	0	0	0	91	121	75	70	31	61
—Durham (I.L.)	0	1	.000	6.52	5	5	0	0	0	19 1/3	24	16	14	7	18
2001—Tampa Bay (A.L.)	5	12	.294	6.59	28	26	0	0	0	143 1/3	161	111	105	48	123
—Durham (I.L.)	0	1	.000	0.82	2	2	0	0	0	11	3	1	1	1	17
Major League totals (3 years)	18	27	.400	5.90	70	68	0	0	0	376 2/3	418	267	247	136	281

RUSCH, GLENDON   P   BREWERS

PERSONAL: Born November 7, 1974, in Seattle. ... 6-1/200. ... Throws left, bats left. ... Full name: Glendon James Rusch.
HIGH SCHOOL: Shorecrest (Seattle).
TRANSACTIONS/CAREER NOTES: Selected by Kansas City Royals organization in 17th round of free-agent draft (June 3, 1993). ... On Kansas City disabled list (June 16-July 1, 1997); included rehabilitation assignment to Omaha (June 26-July 1). ... On Kansas City disabled list (August 9-September 4, 1998); included rehabilitation assignment to Omaha (August 24-September 4). ... On Omaha disabled list (May 31-July 1, 1999). ... Traded by Royals to New York Mets for P Dan Murray (September 14, 1999). ... Traded by Mets to Milwaukee Brewers as part of three-way deal in which Mets traded 1B/3B Todd Zeile, IF/OF Lenny Harris, OF Benny Agbayani and cash to Colorado Rockies, Rockies sent OF Alex Ochoa to Brewers, Brewers sent OF Jeromy Burnitz, P Jeff D'Amico, IF Lou Collier, OF/1B Mark Sweeney and cash to Mets and Mets acquired 1B/OF Russ Gload and P Craig House from Rockies (January 21, 2002).

STATISTICAL NOTES: Pitched 9-0 no-hit victory against Kane County (August 7, 1994).

Year	League	W	L	Pct.	ERA	G	GS	CG	ShO	Sv.	IP	H	R	ER	BB	SO
1993—	Gulf Coast Royals (GCL)	4	2	.667	1.60	11	10	0	0	0	62	43	14	11	11	48
—	Rockford (Midw.)	0	1	.000	3.38	2	2	0	0	0	8	10	6	3	7	8
1994—	Rockford (Midw.)	8	5	.615	4.66	28	17	1	1	1	114	111	61	59	34	122
1995—	Wilmington (Caro.)............	*14	6	.700	*1.74	26	26	1	1	0	165²/₃	110	41	32	34	147
1996—	Omaha (A.A.)	11	9	.550	3.98	28	28	1	0	0	169²/₃	177	88	75	40	117
1997—	Kansas City (A.L.)	6	9	.400	5.50	30	27	1	0	0	170¹/₃	206	111	104	52	116
—	Omaha (A.A.)	0	1	.000	4.50	1	1	0	0	0	6	7	3	3	1	2
1998—	Kansas City (A.L.)	6	15	.286	5.88	29	24	1	1	1	154²/₃	191	104	101	50	94
—	Omaha (PCL)....................	1	1	.500	7.98	3	3	0	0	0	14²/₃	20	18	13	6	14
1999—	Omaha (PCL)....................	4	7	.364	4.42	20	20	1	0	0	114	143	68	56	33	102
—	Gulf Coast Royals (GCL)	0	0	...	1.50	2	2	0	0	0	6	3	1	1	3	9
—	Kansas City (A.L.)	0	1	.000	15.75	3	0	0	0	0	4	7	7	7	3	4
—	New York (N.L.)■	0	0	...	0.00	1	0	0	0	0	1	1	0	0	0	0
2000—	New York (N.L.)	11	11	.500	4.01	31	30	2	0	0	190²/₃	196	91	85	44	157
2001—	New York (N.L.)	8	12	.400	4.63	33	33	1	0	0	179	216	101	92	43	156
A.L. totals (3 years)		**12**	**25**	**.324**	**5.80**	**62**	**51**	**2**	**1**	**1**	**329**	**404**	**222**	**212**	**105**	**214**
N.L. totals (3 years)		**19**	**23**	**.452**	**4.30**	**65**	**63**	**3**	**0**	**0**	**370²/₃**	**413**	**192**	**177**	**87**	**313**
Major League totals (5 years)		**31**	**48**	**.392**	**5.00**	**127**	**114**	**5**	**1**	**1**	**699²/₃**	**817**	**414**	**389**	**192**	**527**

DIVISION SERIES RECORD

Year	League	W	L	Pct.	ERA	G	GS	CG	ShO	Sv.	IP	H	R	ER	BB	SO
2000—	New York (N.L.).................	0	0	...	0.00	1	0	0	0	0	²/₃	0	0	0	0	2

CHAMPIONSHIP SERIES RECORD

Year	League	W	L	Pct.	ERA	G	GS	CG	ShO	Sv.	IP	H	R	ER	BB	SO
2000—	New York (N.L.).................	1	0	1.000	0.00	2	0	0	0	0	3²/₃	3	0	0	0	3

WORLD SERIES RECORD

Year	League	W	L	Pct.	ERA	G	GS	CG	ShO	Sv.	IP	H	R	ER	BB	SO
2000—	New York (N.L.).................	0	0	...	2.25	3	0	0	0	0	4	6	1	1	2	2

RYAN, B.J.   P   ORIOLES

PERSONAL: Born December 28, 1975, in Bossier City, La. ... 6-6/230. ... Throws left, bats left. ... Full name: Robert Victor Ryan Jr.
HIGH SCHOOL: Airline (Bossier City, La.).
COLLEGE: Southwestern Louisiana.
TRANSACTIONS/CAREER NOTES: Selected by Cincinnati Reds organization in 17th round of free-agent draft (June 2, 1998). ... Traded by Reds with P Jacobo Sequea to Baltimore Orioles for P Juan Guzman (July 31, 1999).

Year	League	W	L	Pct.	ERA	G	GS	CG	ShO	Sv.	IP	H	R	ER	BB	SO
1998—	Billings (Pio.)	2	1	.667	1.93	14	0	0	0	4	18²/₃	15	4	4	5	25
—	Charleston, W.Va. (S.Atl.)...	0	0	...	2.08	3	0	0	0	2	4¹/₃	1	1	1	1	5
—	Chattanooga (Sou.)	1	0	1.000	2.20	16	0	0	0	4	16¹/₃	13	4	4	6	21
1999—	Chattanooga (Sou.)	2	1	.667	2.59	35	0	0	0	6	41²/₃	33	13	12	17	46
—	Indianapolis (I.L.)..............	1	0	1.000	4.00	11	0	0	0	0	9	9	4	4	3	12
—	Cincinnati (N.L.)	0	0	...	4.50	1	0	0	0	0	2	4	1	1	1	1
—	Rochester (I.L.)■...............	0	0	...	2.51	11	0	0	0	1	14¹/₃	8	4	4	4	20
—	Baltimore (A.L.)	1	0	1.000	2.95	13	0	0	0	0	18¹/₃	9	6	6	12	28
2000—	Baltimore (A.L.)	2	3	.400	5.91	42	0	0	0	0	42²/₃	36	29	28	31	41
—	Rochester (I.L.)	0	1	.000	4.74	14	4	0	0	0	24²/₃	23	13	13	9	28
2001—	Baltimore (A.L.)	2	4	.333	4.25	61	0	0	0	2	53	47	31	25	30	54
A.L. totals (3 years)		**5**	**7**	**.417**	**4.66**	**116**	**0**	**0**	**0**	**2**	**114**	**92**	**66**	**59**	**73**	**123**
N.L. totals (1 year)		**0**	**0**	**...**	**4.50**	**1**	**0**	**0**	**0**	**0**	**2**	**4**	**1**	**1**	**1**	**1**
Major League totals (3 years)		**5**	**7**	**.417**	**4.66**	**117**	**0**	**0**	**0**	**2**	**116**	**96**	**67**	**60**	**74**	**124**

RYAN, ROB   OF   ATHLETICS

PERSONAL: Born June 24, 1973, in Havre, Mont. ... 5-11/190. ... Bats left, throws left. ... Full name: Robert James Ryan.
HIGH SCHOOL: Shadle Park (Spokane, Wash.).
COLLEGE: Washington State.
TRANSACTIONS/CAREER NOTES: Selected by Arizona Diamondbacks organization in 36th round of free-agent draft (June 4, 1996). ... On Tucson disabled list (June 15-July 3, 2000). ... Traded by Diamondbacks to Oakland Athletics for OF Ryan Christenson (June 19, 2001).
STATISTICAL NOTES: Led Pacific Coast League with nine intentional bases on balls received in 2001.

Year	Team (League)	Pos.	G	AB	R	H	2B	3B	HR	RBI	Avg.	BB	SO	SB	PO	A	E	Avg.
											BATTING						**FIELDING**	
1996—	Lethbridge (Pio.)	OF	59	211	55	64	8	1	4	37	.303	43	33	23	107	3	4	.965
1997—	South Bend (Midw.) ...	OF	121	421	71	132	35	5	8	73	.314	89	58	12	188	11	7	.966
1998—	Tucson (PCL)	OF	116	394	71	125	18	2	17	66	.317	63	61	9	224	3	4	.983
1999—	Tucson (PCL)	OF-DH	117	414	72	120	30	5	19	88	.290	56	70	4	182	8	6	.969
—	Arizona (N.L.)............	OF	20	29	4	7	1	0	2	5	.241	1	8	0	7	0	0	1.000
2000—	Tucson (PCL)	OF	92	332	56	102	19	1	8	55	.307	45	35	1	156	7	1	.994
—	Arizona (N.L.)............	OF-DH	27	27	4	8	1	1	0	2	.296	4	7	0	1	0	0	1.000
2001—	Tucson (PCL)	OF	63	216	45	71	17	5	12	50	.329	29	34	1	77	2	1	.988
—	Arizona (N.L.)............	PH	1	1	0	0	0	0	0	0	.000	0	1	0	...	...	...	...
—	Sacramento (PCL)■...	OF	62	218	35	49	8	3	7	32	.225	39	51	1	98	2	2	.980
—	Oakland (A.L.)	OF-DH	7	7	0	0	0	0	0	0	.000	0	5	0	2	0	0	1.000
American League totals (1 year)			**7**	**7**	**0**	**0**	**0**	**0**	**0**	**0**	**.000**	**0**	**5**	**0**	**2**	**0**	**0**	**1.000**
National League totals (3 years)			**48**	**57**	**8**	**15**	**2**	**1**	**2**	**7**	**.263**	**5**	**16**	**0**	**8**	**0**	**0**	**1.000**
Major League totals (3 years)			**55**	**64**	**8**	**15**	**2**	**1**	**2**	**7**	**.234**	**5**	**21**	**0**	**10**	**0**	**0**	**1.000**

SABATHIA, C.C.　　　　　　　P　　　　　　　INDIANS

PERSONAL: Born July 21, 1980, in Vallejo, Calif. ... 6-7/235. ... Throws left, bats left. ... Full name: Carsten Charles Sabathia.
HIGH SCHOOL: Vallejo (Calif.).
TRANSACTIONS/CAREER NOTES: Selected by Cleveland Indians organization in first round (20th pick overall) of free-agent draft (June 2, 1998).
HONORS: Named A.L. Rookie Pitcher of the Year by THE SPORTING NEWS (2001).

Year League	W	L	Pct.	ERA	G	GS	CG	ShO	Sv.	IP	H	R	ER	BB	SO
1998—Burlington (Appl.)	1	0	1.000	4.50	5	5	0	0	0	18	20	14	9	8	35
1999—Mahoning Valley (NY-P)	0	0	...	1.83	6	6	0	0	0	19²/₃	9	5	4	12	57
—Columbus (S.Atl.)	2	0	1.000	1.08	3	3	0	0	0	16²/₃	8	2	2	5	20
—Kinston (Caro.)	3	3	.500	5.34	7	7	0	0	0	32	30	22	19	19	29
2000—Kinston (Caro.)	3	2	.600	3.54	10	10	2	2	0	56	48	23	22	24	69
—Akron (East.)	3	7	.300	3.59	17	17	0	0	0	90¹/₃	75	41	36	48	90
2001—Cleveland (A.L.)	17	5	.773	4.39	33	33	0	0	0	180¹/₃	149	93	88	95	171
Major League totals (1 year)	17	5	.773	4.39	33	33	0	0	0	180¹/₃	149	93	88	95	171

DIVISION SERIES RECORD

Year League	W	L	Pct.	ERA	G	GS	CG	ShO	Sv.	IP	H	R	ER	BB	SO
2001—Cleveland (A.L.)	1	0	1.000	3.00	1	1	0	0	0	6	6	2	2	5	5

SABEL, ERIK　　　　　　　P　　　　　　　DIAMONDBACKS

PERSONAL: Born October 14, 1974, in West Lafayette, Ind. ... 6-2/185. ... Throws right, bats right. ... Full name: Erik Douglas Sabel.
HIGH SCHOOL: Harrison (West Lafayette, Ind.).
COLLEGE: Tennessee Tech.
TRANSACTIONS/CAREER NOTES: Selected by Arizona Diamondbacks organization in 42nd round of free-agent draft (June 4, 1996). ... Loaned by Diamondbacks to Tulsa, Texas Rangers organization (June 3-September 14, 1998). ... On Tucson disabled list (May 26-June 15, 1999; and August 7-September 8, 2000).

Year League	W	L	Pct.	ERA	G	GS	CG	ShO	Sv.	IP	H	R	ER	BB	SO
1996—Lethbridge (Pio.)	1	4	.200	2.79	20	3	0	0	1	42	43	23	13	7	41
1997—High Desert (Calif.)	11	11	.500	5.32	31	22	0	0	1	143²/₃	174	101	85	40	86
1998—High Desert (Calif.)	0	1	.000	3.18	14	0	0	0	4	22²/₃	25	8	8	4	18
—Tucson (PCL)	1	0	1.000	8.71	7	0	0	0	0	10¹/₃	17	10	10	5	7
—Tulsa (Texas)■	7	0	1.000	3.20	24	2	0	0	2	56¹/₃	46	24	20	13	33
1999—El Paso (Texas)■	0	1	.000	6.30	8	1	0	0	1	10	16	9	7	4	7
—Tucson (PCL)	5	2	.714	3.34	22	9	0	0	2	72²/₃	79	36	27	24	38
—Arizona (N.L.)	0	0	...	6.52	7	0	0	0	0	9²/₃	12	7	7	6	6
2000—Tucson (PCL)	4	11	.267	7.23	29	15	0	0	1	98¹/₃	149	90	79	31	61
2001—Tucson (PCL)	2	2	.500	2.95	18	2	0	0	2	39²/₃	35	14	13	7	32
—Arizona (N.L.)	3	2	.600	4.38	42	0	0	0	0	51¹/₃	57	26	25	12	25
Major League totals (2 years)	3	2	.600	4.72	49	0	0	0	0	61	69	33	32	18	31

SABERHAGEN, BRET　　　　　　　P

PERSONAL: Born April 11, 1964, in Chicago Heights, Ill. ... 6-1/200. ... Throws right, bats right. ... Full name: Bret William Saberhagen. ... Name pronounced SAY-ber-HAY-gun.
HIGH SCHOOL: Cleveland (Reseda, Calif.).
TRANSACTIONS/CAREER NOTES: Selected by Kansas City Royals organization in 19th round of free-agent draft (June 7, 1982). ... On disabled list (August 10-September 1, 1986; July 16-September 10, 1990; and June 15-July 13, 1991). ... Traded by Royals with IF Bill Pecota to New York Mets for OF Kevin McReynolds, IF Gregg Jefferies and 2B Keith Miller (December 11, 1991). ... On disabled list (May 16-July 18 and August 2-September 7, 1992; and August 3, 1993-remainder of season). ... On suspended list (April 3-8, 1994). ... Traded by Mets with a player to be named later to Colorado Rockies for P Juan Acevedo and P Arnold Gooch (July 31, 1995); Rockies acquired P David Swanson to complete deal (August 4, 1995). ... On disabled list (March 22, 1996-entire season). ... Granted free agency (October 29, 1996). ... Signed by Boston Red Sox organization (December 9, 1996). ... On Boston disabled list (March 31-Augut 22, 1997); included rehabilitation assignments to Lowell (July 27-August 1), Trenton (August 1-12) and Pawtucket (August 12-22). ... Granted free agency (October 31, 1997). ... Re-signed by Red Sox (November 17, 1997). ... On Boston disabled list (May 7-June 1, June 8-23 and August 18-September 10, 1999); included rehabilitation assignment to Trenton (May 27-June 1). ... On Boston disabled list (March 19, 2000-entire season); included rehabilitation assignments to Sarasota (May 15-16), Lowell (July 18-24), Pawtucket (July 25-August 6 and August 19-September 1) and Trenton (August 14-18). ... On Boston disabled list (March 30-July 27 and August 8, 2001-remainder of season); included rehabilitation assignments to Sarasota (April 8-11), Gulf Coast Red Sox (July 3-15), Trenton (July 16-20) and Pawtucket (July 21-25). ... Granted free agency (November 5, 2001).
HONORS: Named A.L. Pitcher of the Year by THE SPORTING NEWS (1985 and 1989). ... Named righthanded pitcher on THE SPORTING NEWS A.L. All-Star team (1985 and 1989). ... Named A.L. Cy Young Award winner by Baseball Writers' Association of America (1985 and 1989). ... Named A.L. Comeback Player of the Year by THE SPORTING NEWS (1987 and 1998). ... Won A.L. Gold Glove at pitcher (1989).
STATISTICAL NOTES: Pitched 7-0 no-hit victory against Chicago (August 26, 1991).
MISCELLANEOUS: Appeared in one game as pinch runner (1984). ... Appeared in three games as pinch runner (1989).

Year League	W	L	Pct.	ERA	G	GS	CG	ShO	Sv.	IP	H	R	ER	BB	SO
1983—Fort Myers (FSL)	10	5	.667	2.30	16	16	3	1	0	109²/₃	98	34	28	19	82
—Jacksonville (Sou.)	6	2	.750	2.91	11	11	2	1	0	77¹/₃	66	31	25	29	48
1984—Kansas City (A.L.)	10	11	.476	3.48	38	18	2	1	1	157²/₃	138	71	61	36	73
1985—Kansas City (A.L.)	20	6	.769	2.87	32	32	10	1	0	235¹/₃	211	79	75	38	158
1986—Kansas City (A.L.)	7	12	.368	4.15	30	25	4	2	0	156	165	77	72	29	112
1987—Kansas City (A.L.)	18	10	.643	3.36	33	33	15	4	0	257	246	99	96	53	163
1988—Kansas City (A.L.)	14	16	.467	3.80	35	35	*9	0	0	260²/₃	*271	122	110	59	171
1989—Kansas City (A.L.)	*23	6	.793	*2.16	36	35	*12	4	0	*262¹/₃	209	74	63	43	193
1990—Kansas City (A.L.)	5	9	.357	3.27	20	20	5	0	0	135	146	52	49	28	87
1991—Kansas City (A.L.)	13	8	.619	3.07	28	28	7	2	0	196¹/₃	165	76	67	45	136

Year League	W	L	Pct.	ERA	G	GS	CG	ShO	Sv.	IP	H	R	ER	BB	SO
1992— New York (N.L.)■	3	5	.375	3.50	17	15	1	1	0	97 2/3	84	39	38	27	81
1993— New York (N.L.).................	7	7	.500	3.29	19	19	4	1	0	139 1/3	131	55	51	17	93
1994— New York (N.L.).................	14	4	.778	2.74	24	24	4	0	0	177 1/3	169	58	54	13	143
1995— New York (N.L.).................	5	5	.500	3.35	16	16	3	0	0	110	105	45	41	20	71
— Colorado (N.L.)■	2	1	.667	6.28	9	9	0	0	0	43	60	33	30	13	29
1996— Colorado (N.L.)							Did not play.								
1997— Lowell (NY-Penn)■	0	0	...	0.00	1	1	0	0	0	3	1	0	0	0	2
— Trenton (East.)	0	0	...	0.00	2	2	0	0	0	8	2	0	0	1	9
— Pawtucket (I.L.)	0	1	.000	3.27	2	2	0	0	0	11	11	4	4	1	9
— Boston (A.L.)	0	1	.000	6.58	6	6	0	0	0	26	30	20	19	10	14
1998— Boston (A.L.)	15	8	.652	3.96	31	31	0	0	0	175	181	82	77	29	100
1999— Boston (A.L.)	10	6	.625	2.95	22	22	0	0	0	119	122	43	39	11	81
— Trenton (East.)	1	0	1.000	0.00	1	1	0	0	0	6	2	0	0	0	5
2000— Sarasota (FSL)	0	1	.000	27.00	1	1	0	0	0	1	5	3	3	0	2
— Lowell (NY-Penn)	0	0	...	0.00	1	1	0	0	0	3	1	0	0	0	5
— Pawtucket (I.L.).................	0	0	...	5.54	4	4	0	0	0	13	14	8	8	4	9
— Trenton (East.)	0	0	...	6.00	1	1	0	0	0	3	1	2	2	1	3
2001— Sarasota (FSL)	0	0	...	6.75	1	1	0	0	0	4	5	3	3	0	3
— Gulf Coast Red Sox (GCL)..	0	1	.000	1.59	2	2	0	0	0	5 2/3	3	1	1	0	2
— Trenton (East.)	0	0	...	2.45	1	1	0	0	0	3 2/3	5	1	1	1	4
— Pawtucket (I.L.).................	0	0	...	3.00	1	1	0	0	0	6	3	2	2	1	4
— Boston (A.L.)	1	2	.333	6.00	3	3	0	0	0	15	19	11	10	0	10
A.L. totals (12 years)	136	95	.589	3.33	314	288	64	14	1	1995 1/3	1903	806	738	381	1298
N.L. totals (4 years)	31	22	.585	3.39	85	83	12	2	0	567 1/3	549	230	214	90	417
Major League totals (16 years)	167	117	.588	3.34	399	371	76	16	1	2562 2/3	2452	1036	952	471	1715

DIVISION SERIES RECORD

Year League	W	L	Pct.	ERA	G	GS	CG	ShO	Sv.	IP	H	R	ER	BB	SO
1995— Colorado (N.L.)	0	1	.000	11.25	1	1	0	0	0	4	7	6	5	1	3
1998— Boston (A.L.)	0	1	.000	3.86	1	1	0	0	0	7	4	3	3	1	7
1999— Boston (A.L.)	0	1	.000	27.00	2	2	0	0	0	3 2/3	9	11	11	4	2
Division series totals (3 years)	0	3	.000	11.66	4	4	0	0	0	14 2/3	20	20	19	6	12

CHAMPIONSHIP SERIES RECORD

Year League	W	L	Pct.	ERA	G	GS	CG	ShO	Sv.	IP	H	R	ER	BB	SO
1984— Kansas City (A.L.)	0	0	...	2.25	1	1	0	0	0	8	6	3	2	1	5
1985— Kansas City (A.L.)	0	0	...	6.14	2	2	0	0	0	7 1/3	12	5	5	2	6
1999— Boston (A.L.)	0	1	.000	1.50	1	1	0	0	0	6	5	3	1	1	5
Champ. series totals (3 years)	0	1	.000	3.38	4	4	0	0	0	21 1/3	23	11	8	4	16

WORLD SERIES RECORD

NOTES: Named Most Valuable Player (1985). ... Member of World Series championship team (1985).

Year League	W	L	Pct.	ERA	G	GS	CG	ShO	Sv.	IP	H	R	ER	BB	SO
1985— Kansas City (A.L.)	2	0	1.000	0.50	2	2	2	1	0	18	11	1	1	1	10

ALL-STAR GAME RECORD

Year League	W	L	Pct.	ERA	GS	CG	ShO	Sv.	IP	H	R	ER	BB	SO
1987— American	0	0	...	0.00	1	0	0	0	3	1	0	0	0	0
1990— American	1	0	1.000	0.00	0	0	0	0	2	0	0	0	0	1
1994— National							Did not play.							
All-Star Game totals (2 years)	1	0	1.000	0.00	1	0	0	0	5	1	0	0	0	1

SADLER, DONNIE   IF

PERSONAL: Born June 17, 1975, in Gohlson, Texas. ... 5-6/175. ... Bats right, throws right. ... Full name: Donnie Lamont Sadler.
HIGH SCHOOL: Valley Mills (Texas).
TRANSACTIONS/CAREER NOTES: Selected by Boston Red Sox organization in 10th round of free-agent draft (June 2, 1994). ... On Pawtucket disabled list (May 4-June 4 and June 23-30, 1998; and June 25-July 18, 1999). ... Traded by Red Sox with OF Michael Coleman to Cincinnati Reds for IF Chris Stynes (November 16, 2000). ... Traded by Reds to Kansas City Royals for P Cary Ammons (June 20, 2001). ... Granted free agency (December 21, 2001).
STATISTICAL NOTES: Tied for International League lead in errors by second baseman with 12 in 1997. ... Tied for International League lead in caught stealing with 14 in 1997.

Year Team (League)	Pos.	G	AB	R	H	2B	3B	HR	RBI	Avg.	BB	SO	SB	PO	A	E	Avg.
1994— GC Red Sox (GCL)	SS-3B-2B	53	206	52	56	8	6	1	16	.272	23	27	32	80	151	18	.928
1995— Michigan (Midw.)	SS	118	438	*103	124	25	8	9	55	.283	79	85	41	168	307	28	.944
1996— Trenton (East.)	SS-OF	115	454	68	121	20	8	6	44	.267	38	75	34	185	237	27	.940
1997— Pawtucket (I.L.)	2B-SS-OF	125	481	74	102	18	2	11	36	.212	57	121	20	252	354	‡15	.976
1998— Boston (A.L.)	2B-DH-SS	58	124	21	28	4	4	3	15	.226	6	28	4	81	101	5	.973
— Pawtucket (I.L.)........	2B-SS	36	131	25	29	5	1	2	10	.221	26	23	11	73	104	4	.978
1999— Boston (A.L.) S-2-3-0-DH		49	107	18	30	5	1	0	4	.280	5	20	2	46	52	9	.916
— Pawtucket (I.L.)........	SS-DH	43	172	23	50	12	4	1	17	.291	16	36	4	73	96	10	.944
— GC Red Sox (GCL)	SS	4	13	2	5	2	0	0	1	.385	2	1	0	7	12	1	.950
2000— Boston (A.L.)	OF-SS-2B	91	313	45	63	6	5	5	23	.201	45	60	10	211	108	7	.979
— Boston (A.L.)...........S-O-2-3-DH		49	99	14	22	5	0	1	10	.222	5	18	3	49	71	3	.976
2001— Cincinnati (N.L.)■ 2B-SS-OF-DH		39	84	9	17	3	0	1	3	.202	9	20	3	30	53	3	.965
— Kansas City (A.L.)■ ...0-3-2-S-DH		54	101	19	13	3	0	0	2	.129	9	17	4	71	84	2	.987
American League totals (4 years)		210	431	72	93	17	5	4	31	.216	25	83	13	247	308	19	.967
National League totals (1 year)		39	84	9	17	3	0	1	3	.202	9	20	3	30	53	3	.965
Major League totals (4 years)		249	515	81	110	20	5	5	34	.214	34	103	16	277	361	22	.967

DIVISION SERIES RECORD

Year Team (League)	Pos.	G	AB	R	H	2B	3B	HR	RBI	Avg.	BB	SO	SB	PO	A	E	Avg.
1998— Boston (A.L.)..............	2B-PR	3	0	0	0	0	0	0	0	...	0	0	0	1	1	0	1.000
1999— Boston (A.L.)..............PH-3B-PR-DH		2	2	1	1	1	0	0	0	.500	0	1	0	1	1	0	1.000
Division series totals (2 years)		5	2	1	1	1	0	0	0	.500	0	1	0	2	2	0	1.000

CHAMPIONSHIP SERIES RECORD

Year Team (League)	Pos.	G	AB	R	H	2B	3B	HR	RBI	Avg.	BB	SO	SB	PO	A	E	Avg.
1999— Boston (A.L.)..............	PR-OF-DH	2	0	0	0	0	0	0	0	...	0	0	0	0	0	0	...

SAENZ, OLMEDO　　3B/1B　　ATHLETICS

PERSONAL: Born October 8, 1970, in Chitre Herrera, Panama. ... 6-0/185. ... Bats right, throws right. ... Full name: Olmedo Sanchez Saenz. ... Name pronounced SIGNS.

TRANSACTIONS/CAREER NOTES: Signed as non-drafted free agent by Chicago White Sox organization (May 11, 1990). ... Granted free agency (October 15, 1997). ... Re-signed by White Sox organization (January 25, 1998). ... Granted free agency (October 15, 1998). ... Signed by Oakland Athletics (November 13, 1998). ... On Oakland disabled list (July 26-August 16, 1999); included rehabilitation assignment to Vancouver (August 13-16). ... On Oakland disabled list (August 1-September 19, 2000); included rehabilitation assignment to Sacramento (August 29-30).

STATISTICAL NOTES: Led American Association third basemen with 395 total chances in 1995. ... Tied for American Association lead in being hit by pitch with 13 in 1996. ... Led American Association third basemen with 363 total chances and 24 double plays in 1996. ... Led Pacific Coast League in being hit by pitch with 22 in 1998.

Year Team (League)	Pos.	G	AB	R	H	2B	3B	HR	RBI	Avg.	BB	SO	SB	PO	A	E	Avg.
1991— South Bend (Midw.) ...	3B	56	192	23	47	10	1	2	22	.245	21	48	5	29	68	12	.890
—Sarasota (FSL)	3B	5	19	1	2	0	1	0	2	.105	2	0	0	5	11	3	.842
1992— South Bend (Midw.) ...	3B-1B	132	493	66	121	26	4	7	59	.245	36	52	16	113	294	48	.895
1993— South Bend (Midw.) ...	3B	13	50	3	18	4	1	0	7	.360	7	7	1	11	31	4	.913
—Sarasota (FSL)	3B	33	121	13	31	9	4	0	27	.256	9	18	3	15	55	5	.933
—Birmingham (Sou.)......	3B	49	173	30	60	17	2	6	29	.347	20	21	2	38	87	14	.899
1994— Nashville (A.A.)	3B-DH	107	383	48	100	27	2	12	59	.261	30	57	3	76	167	22	.917
—Chicago (A.L.)	3B	5	14	2	2	0	1	0	0	.143	0	5	0	3	5	0	1.000
1995— Nashville (A.A.)	3B	111	415	60	126	26	1	13	74	.304	45	60	0	*82	*289	*24	*.939
1996— Nashville (A.A.)	3B-DH	134	476	86	124	29	1	18	63	.261	53	80	4	*97	244	22	.939
1997— GC White Sox (GCL) ..	DH	2	1	0	1	1	0	0	0	1.000	0	0	0	...	...	...	...
1998— Calgary (PCL)..........	3B-DH	124	466	89	146	29	0	29	102	.313	45	49	3	75	235	21	.937
1999— Oakland (A.L.)■........	3B-1B-DH	97	255	41	70	18	0	11	41	.275	22	47	1	180	91	8	.971
—Vancouver (PCL)........	3B	2	5	1	3	1	0	0	2	.600	0	0	0	1	0	0	1.000
2000— Oakland (A.L.)	DH-3B-1B	76	214	40	67	12	2	9	33	.313	25	40	1	137	33	4	.977
—Sacramento (PCL)......	DH	1	4	1	2	0	0	0	1	.500	0	0	0	...	...	...	...
2001— Oakland (A.L.)	DH-1B-3B	106	305	33	67	21	1	9	32	.220	19	64	0	201	35	5	.979
Major League totals (4 years)		284	788	116	206	51	4	29	106	.261	66	156	2	521	164	17	.976

DIVISION SERIES RECORD

RECORDS: Holds A.L. career record for most games by pinch-hitter—4.

Year Team (League)	Pos.	G	AB	R	H	2B	3B	HR	RBI	Avg.	BB	SO	SB	PO	A	E	Avg.
2000— Oakland (A.L.)	PH-DH	4	13	1	3	0	0	1	4	.231	0	2	0	...	...	...	...
2001— Oakland (A.L.)	PH-DH	3	4	0	0	0	0	0	0	.000	0	1	0	...	...	...	...
Division series totals (2 years)		7	17	1	3	0	0	1	4	.176	0	3	0	...	...	...	...

SALAZAR, OSCAR　　IF　　TIGERS

PERSONAL: Born June 27, 1978, in Maracay, Venezuela. ... 6-0/155. ... Bats right, throws right. ... Full name: Oscar Enrique Salazar.
TRANSACTIONS/CAREER NOTES: Signed as non-drafted free agent by Oakland Athletics organization (July 2, 1994). ... Claimed on waivers by Detroit Tigers (January 24, 2002).

Year Team (League)	Pos.	G	AB	R	H	2B	3B	HR	RBI	Avg.	BB	SO	SB	PO	A	E	Avg.
1995— Dom. Athletics (DSL) .	SS	53	166	29	45	10	1	0	23	.271	22	23	5	94	159	32	.888
1996— Dom. Athletics (DSL) .	2B	69	219	49	56	9	4	3	29	.256	47	37	9	138	178	11	.966
1997— Dom. Athletics (DSL) .		66	268	65	80	20	4	12	48	.299	34	39	3	...	...	...	...
1998— Ariz. Athletics (Ariz.) ..	3B-SS-2B	26	102	29	33	7	5	2	18	.324	12	15	4	29	60	9	.908
—S. Oregon (N'West)....	3B-2B-SS	28	101	19	32	4	1	5	28	.317	16	22	5	39	59	13	.883
1999— Modesto (Calif.) 2B-3B-SS-1B		130	525	100	155	26	18	18	105	.295	39	106	14	100	182	22	.928
2000— Sacramento (PCL)......	SS	4	13	0	2	1	0	0	1	.154	1	1	1	5	8	0	1.000
—Midland (Texas)........	SS-OF-3B	111	427	70	128	27	1	13	57	.300	39	71	4	172	303	34	.933
2001— Midland (Texas).........SS-3B-2B-OF		130	521	75	139	31	4	18	95	.267	49	100	10	176	376	37	.937
—Sacramento (PCL)......	2B-3B	5	16	0	1	0	0	0	1	.063	1	5	0	7	8	0	1.000

SALMON, TIM　　OF　　ANGELS

PERSONAL: Born August 24, 1968, in Long Beach, Calif. ... 6-3/231. ... Bats right, throws right. ... Full name: Timothy James Salmon. ... Brother of Mike Salmon, safety with San Francisco 49ers (1997). ... Name pronounced SA-mon.
HIGH SCHOOL: Greenway (Phoenix).
COLLEGE: Grand Canyon (Ariz.).

TRANSACTIONS/CAREER NOTES: Selected by Atlanta Braves organization in 18th round of free-agent draft (June 2, 1986); did not sign. ... Selected by California Angels organization in third round of free-agent draft (June 5, 1989). ... On disabled list (May 12-23 and May 27-August 7, 1990; and July 18-August 3, 1994). ... Angels franchise renamed Anaheim Angels for 1997 season. ... On disabled list (April 23-May 9, 1998). ... On Anaheim disabled list (May 4-July 17, 1999); included rehabilitation assignment to Lake Elsinore (July 16-17). ... On Anaheim disabled list (July 1-19, 2001); included rehabilitation assignment to Rancho Cucamonga (July 17-19).

RECORDS: Shares major league record for fewest double plays by outfielder (150 or more games)—0 (1996). ... Shares major league single-inning record for most doubles—2 (September 23, 2000, second inning). ... Shares A.L. record for most hits in three consecutive games— 13 (May 10 [4], 11 [4] and 13 [5], 1994).

HONORS: Named Minor League Player of the Year by THE SPORTING NEWS (1992). ... Named Pacific Coast League Most Valuable Player (1992). ... Named A.L. Rookie Player of the Year by THE SPORTING NEWS (1993). ... Named A.L. Rookie of the Year by Baseball Writers' Association of America (1993). ... Named outfielder on THE SPORTING NEWS A.L. All-Star team (1995 and 1997). ... Named outfielder on THE SPORTING NEWS Silver Slugger team (1995).

STATISTICAL NOTES: Led Pacific Coast League with 275 total bases, .672 slugging percentage and .469 on-base percentage in 1992. ... Led A.L. outfielders with four double plays in 1994. ... Tied for A.L. lead in double plays by outfielder with five in 1997. ... Had 17-game hitting streak (July 23-August 9, 2000). ... Career major league grand slams: 5.

MISCELLANEOUS: Holds Anaheim Angels franchise all-time record for home runs (247).

							BATTING							FIELDING		
Year	Team (League)	Pos.	G	AB	R	H	2B	3B	HR	RBI	Avg.	BB	SO	SB	PO	A	E	Avg.
1989— Bend (N'West)	OF	55	196	37	48	6	5	6	31	.245	33	60	2	84	7	4	.958
1990— Palm Springs (Calif.)	OF	36	118	19	34	6	0	2	21	.288	21	44	11	63	3	1	.985
— Midland (Texas)	OF	27	97	17	26	3	1	3	16	.268	18	38	1	51	6	3	.950
1991— Midland (Texas)	OF	131	465	100	114	26	4	23	94	.245	*89	*166	12	265	16	10	.966
1992— Edmonton (PCL)	OF	118	409	•101	142	38	4	*29	*105	.347	91	103	9	231	14	3	.988
— California (A.L.)	OF	23	79	8	14	1	0	2	6	.177	11	23	1	40	1	2	.953
1993— California (A.L.)	OF-DH	142	515	93	146	35	1	31	95	.283	82	135	5	335	12	7	.980
1994— California (A.L.)	OF	100	373	67	107	18	2	23	70	.287	54	102	1	219	9	8	.966
1995— California (A.L.)	OF-DH	143	537	111	177	34	3	34	105	.330	91	111	5	320	7	4	.988
1996— California (A.L.)	OF-DH	156	581	90	166	27	4	30	98	.286	93	125	4	299	13	8	.975
1997— Anaheim (A.L.)	OF-DH	157	582	95	172	28	1	33	129	.296	95	142	9	352	15	11	.971
1998— Anaheim (A.L.)	DH-OF	136	463	84	139	28	1	26	88	.300	90	100	0	46	1	2	.959
1999— Anaheim (A.L.)	OF-DH	98	353	60	94	24	2	17	69	.266	63	82	4	204	7	4	.981
— Lake Elsinore (Calif.)	DH	1	5	0	3	2	0	0	2	.600	0	1	0	...	...	...	...
2000— Anaheim (A.L.)	OF-DH	158	568	108	165	36	2	34	97	.290	104	139	0	274	12	6	.979
2001— Anaheim (A.L.)	OF-DH	137	475	63	108	21	1	17	49	.227	96	121	9	254	13	3	.989
— Rancho Cuca. (Calif.)	OF	2	7	1	1	1	0	0	0	.143	1	4	0	2	0	1	.667
Major League totals (10 years)		1250	4526	779	1288	252	17	247	806	.285	779	1080	38	2343	90	55	.978

SANCHEZ, ALEX   OF   BREWERS

PERSONAL: Born August 26, 1976, in Havana, Cuba. ... 5-10/180. ... Bats left, throws left. ... Full name: Alexis Sanchez.
JUNIOR COLLEGE: Miami-Dade (Wolfson) Community College.
TRANSACTIONS/CAREER NOTES: Selected by Tampa Bay Devil Rays organization in fifth round of free-agent draft (June 4, 1996). ... Claimed on waivers by Milwaukee Brewers (April 6, 2001). ... On Milwaukee disabled list (July 16-31, 2001).
STATISTICAL NOTES: Led Gulf Coast League with 12 caught stealing in 1996. ... Led South Atlantic League outfielders with 296 total chances in 1997. ... Led South Atlantic League in caught stealing with 40 in 1997. ... Led Florida State League in caught stealing with 33 and sacrifice flies with 12 in 1998. ... Led Southern League in caught stealing with 27 and sacrifice hits with 10 in 1999. ... Led International League in caught stealing with 20 in 2000.

							BATTING							FIELDING		
Year	Team (League)	Pos.	G	AB	R	H	2B	3B	HR	RBI	Avg.	BB	SO	SB	PO	A	E	Avg.
1995— Oneonta (NY-Penn)		59	223	25	73	16	7	1	28	.327	20	28	9	...	...	...	...
1996— GC Devil Rays (GCL)	OF	56	227	36	64	7	6	1	22	.282	10	35	20	91	1	3	.968
1997— Charl., S.C. (S.Atl.)	OF	131	537	73	155	15	6	0	34	.289	37	72	*92	279	6	11	.963
1998— St. Petersburg (FSL)	OF	128	545	77	*180	17	9	1	50	.330	31	70	66	330	5	•12	.965
1999— Orlando (Sou.)	OF	121	500	68	127	12	4	2	29	.254	26	88	48	314	8	*14	.958
— Durham (I.L.)	OF	3	10	2	2	1	0	0	0	.200	1	0	0	8	0	0	1.000
2000— Durham (I.L.)	OF	107	446	76	130	18	3	2	33	.291	30	66	*52	243	11	6	.977
— Orlando (Sou.)	OF	20	86	12	25	2	1	0	4	.291	1	13	2	34	1	1	.972
2001— Indianapolis (I.L.)■	OF	83	335	52	105	14	5	1	26	.313	22	44	27	178	2	6	.968
— Milwaukee (N.L.)	OF	30	68	7	14	3	2	0	4	.206	5	13	6	24	2	1	.963
Major League totals (1 year)		30	68	7	14	3	2	0	4	.206	5	13	6	24	2	1	.963

SANCHEZ, DUANER   P   DIAMONDBACKS

PERSONAL: Born November 14, 1979, in Cotui, Dominican Republic. ... 6-0/160. ... Throws right, bats right.
HIGH SCHOOL: Francisco H. Carvajal (Cotui, Dominican Repblic).
TRANSACTIONS/CAREER NOTES: Signed as non-drafted free agent by Arizona Diamondbacks organization (October 16, 1996). ... On El Paso disabled list (June 12-July 16, 2001).

Year	League	W	L	Pct.	ERA	G	GS	CG	ShO	Sv.	IP	H	R	ER	BB	SO
1997— Dom. D'backs (DSL)	4	4	.500	5.13	21	6	0	0	1	59²/₃	57	50	34	48	44
1998— Dom. D'backs (DSL)	2	3	.400	1.79	14	8	1	0	1	50¹/₃	36	19	10	24	44
1999— High Desert (Calif.)	0	0	...	7.53	3	3	0	0	0	14¹/₃	15	13	12	9	9
— Missoula (Pio.)	5	3	.625	3.13	13	11	0	0	0	63¹/₃	54	34	22	23	51
2000— South Bend (Midw.)	8	9	.471	3.65	28	28	4	0	0	165¹/₃	152	80	67	54	121
2001— El Paso (Texas)	3	7	.300	6.78	13	13	0	0	0	70¹/₃	92	56	53	25	41
— Lancaster (Calif.)	2	4	.333	4.58	10	10	1	0	0	59	65	44	30	18	49

SANCHEZ, JESUS   P   CUBS

PERSONAL: Born October 11, 1974, in Nizao Bani, Dominican Republic. ... 5-10/155. ... Throws left, bats left. ... Full name: Jesus Paulino Sanchez.

TRANSACTIONS/CAREER NOTES: Signed as non-drafted free agent by New York Mets organization (June 7, 1992). ... On disabled list (April 4-May 28, 1996). ... Traded by Mets with P A.J. Burnett and OF Robert Stratton to Florida Marlins for P Al Leiter and 2B Ralph Milliard (February 6, 1998). ... Traded by Marlins to Chicago Cubs for P Nate Teut (December 11, 2001).

STATISTICAL NOTES: Led Dominican Summer League in home runs allowed with 14 in 1992.

MISCELLANEOUS: Appeared in two games as pinch runner (1998). ... Appeared in one game as pinch runner (1999). ... Scored two runs in 13 appearances as pinch runner (2000). ... Appeared in one game as pinch runner (2001).

Year League	W	L	Pct.	ERA	G	GS	CG	ShO	Sv.	IP	H	R	ER	BB	SO
1992—Dominican Mets (DSL)	5	5	.500	4.19	15	15	1	0	0	81 2/3	86	52	38	38	72
1993—Dominican Mets (DSL)	7	3	.700	2.40	16	13	2	•2	0	82 1/3	63	30	22	36	94
1994—Kingsport (Appl.)	7	4	.636	1.96	13	12	•3	0	0	87 1/3	61	27	19	27	71
1995—Capital City (S.Atl.)	9	7	.563	3.13	27	27	4	0	0	169 2/3	154	76	59	58	•177
1996—St. Lucie (FSL)	9	3	.750	1.96	16	16	2	1	0	92	53	22	20	24	81
1997—Binghamton (East.)	*13	10	.565	4.30	26	26	3	0	0	165 1/3	146	87	79	61	*176
1998—Florida (N.L.)■	7	9	.438	4.47	35	29	0	0	0	173	178	98	86	91	137
1999—Florida (N.L.)	5	7	.417	6.01	59	10	0	0	0	76 1/3	84	53	51	60	62
—Calgary (PCL)	0	0	...	5.79	4	1	0	0	1	9 1/3	8	6	6	5	14
2000—Florida (N.L.)	9	12	.429	5.34	32	32	2	2	0	182	197	118	108	76	123
2001—Calgary (PCL)	6	1	.857	3.21	16	11	0	0	0	75 2/3	61	32	27	33	58
—Florida (N.L.)	2	4	.333	4.74	16	9	0	0	0	62 2/3	61	33	33	23	46
Major League totals (4 years)	23	32	.418	5.06	142	80	2	2	0	494	520	302	278	258	368

SANCHEZ, REY   SS

PERSONAL: Born October 5, 1967, in Rio Piedras, Puerto Rico. ... 5-9/175. ... Bats right, throws right. ... Full name: Rey Francisco Guadalupe Sanchez.

HIGH SCHOOL: Live Oak (Morgan Hill, Calif.).

TRANSACTIONS/CAREER NOTES: Selected by Texas Rangers organization in 13th round of free-agent draft (June 2, 1986). ... Traded by Rangers to Chicago Cubs for IF Bryan House (January 3, 1990). ... On disabled list (April 6, 1990-entire season). ... On Chicago disabled list (May 6-21, 1992); included rehabilitation assignment to Iowa (May 13-21). ... On disabled list (July 24-August 9, 1995). ... On Chicago disabled list (June 5-July 20 and August 11-September 1, 1996); included rehabilitation assignment to Iowa (July 16-20). ... Traded by Cubs to New York Yankees for P Frisco Parotte (August 16, 1997). ... Granted free agency (November 3, 1997). ... Signed by San Francisco Giants (January 22, 1998). ... Granted free agency (November 5, 1998). ... Signed by Kansas City Royals (December 11, 1998). ... Granted free agency (October 29, 1999). ... Re-signed by Royals (December 7, 1999). ... Traded by Royals to Atlanta Braves for P Brad Voyles and IF Alejandro Machado (July 31, 2001). ... Granted free agency (November 5, 2001).

STATISTICAL NOTES: Led Gulf Coast League shortstops with .932 fielding percentage in 1986. ... Led American Association shortstops with 684 total chances and 104 double plays in 1989. ... Led American Association shortstops with 596 total chances and 81 double plays in 1991. ... Had 21-game hitting streak (May 11-June 3, 2001).

Year Team (League)	Pos.	G	AB	R	H	2B	3B	HR	RBI	Avg.	BB	SO	SB	PO	A	E	Avg.
1986—GC Rangers (GCL)	SS-2B	52	169	27	49	3	1	0	23	.290	41	18	10	69	158	15	†.938
1987—Gastonia (S.Atl.)	SS	50	160	19	35	1	2	1	10	.219	22	17	6	88	162	18	.933
—Butte (Pio.)	SS	49	189	36	69	10	6	0	25	.365	21	12	22	84	162	12	.953
1988—Charlotte (FSL)	SS	128	418	60	128	6	5	0	38	.306	35	24	29	226	*415	35	.948
1989—Oklahoma City (A.A.)	SS	134	464	38	104	10	4	1	39	.224	21	50	4	*237	*418	29	*.958
1990—Iowa (A.A.)■							Did not play.										
1991—Iowa (A.A.)	SS	126	417	60	121	16	5	2	46	.290	37	27	13	204	*375	17	*.971
—Chicago (N.L.)	SS-2B	13	23	1	6	0	0	0	2	.261	4	3	0	11	25	0	1.000
1992—Chicago (N.L.)	SS-2B	74	255	24	64	14	3	1	19	.251	10	17	2	148	202	9	.975
—Iowa (A.A.)	SS-2B	20	76	12	26	3	0	0	3	.342	4	1	6	31	77	5	.956
1993—Chicago (N.L.)	SS	105	344	35	97	11	2	0	28	.282	15	22	1	158	316	15	.969
1994—Chicago (N.L.)	2B-SS-3B	96	291	26	83	13	1	0	24	.285	20	29	2	152	278	9	.979
1995—Chicago (N.L.)	2B-SS	114	428	57	119	22	2	3	27	.278	14	48	6	195	351	7	.987
1996—Chicago (N.L.)	SS	95	289	28	61	9	0	1	12	.211	22	42	7	151	307	11	.977
—Iowa (A.A.)	SS	3	12	2	2	0	0	0	1	.167	1	2	2	4	10	1	.933
1997—Chicago (N.L.)	SS-2B-3B	97	205	14	51	9	0	1	12	.249	11	26	4	100	157	6	.977
—New York (A.L.)■	2B-SS	38	138	21	43	12	0	1	15	.312	5	21	0	66	110	4	.978
1998—San Fran. (N.L.)■	SS-2B	109	316	44	90	14	2	2	30	.285	16	47	0	142	261	8	.981
1999—Kansas City (A.L.)■	SS	134	479	66	141	18	6	2	56	.294	22	48	11	242	452	13	.982
2000—Kansas City (A.L.)	SS	143	509	68	139	18	2	1	38	.273	28	55	7	224	446	4	.994
2001—Kansas City (A.L.)	SS	100	390	46	118	14	5	0	28	.303	11	34	9	155	333	3	.994
—Atlanta (N.L.)	SS	49	154	10	35	4	1	0	9	.227	4	15	2	62	146	3	.986
American League totals (4 years)		415	1516	201	441	62	13	4	137	.291	66	158	27	687	1341	24	.988
National League totals (9 years)		752	2305	239	606	96	11	8	163	.263	116	249	24	1119	2043	68	.979
Major League totals (11 years)		1167	3821	440	1047	158	24	12	300	.274	182	407	51	1806	3384	92	.983

DIVISION SERIES RECORD

Year Team (League)	Pos.	G	AB	R	H	2B	3B	HR	RBI	Avg.	BB	SO	SB	PO	A	E	Avg.
1997—New York (A.L.)	2B	5	15	1	3	1	0	0	1	.200	0	2	0	15	14	0	1.000
2001—Atlanta (N.L.)	SS	3	9	1	2	1	0	0	0	.222	0	2	0	8	9	1	.944
Division series totals (2 years)		8	24	2	5	2	0	0	1	.208	0	4	0	23	23	1	.979

CHAMPIONSHIP SERIES RECORD

Year Team (League)	Pos.	G	AB	R	H	2B	3B	HR	RBI	Avg.	BB	SO	SB	PO	A	E	Avg.
2001—Atlanta (N.L.)	SS	5	17	1	5	1	0	0	1	.294	0	4	0	6	12	2	.900

SANDBERG, JARED 3B DEVIL RAYS

PERSONAL: Born March 2, 1978, in Olympia, Wash. ... 6-3/212. ... Bats right, throws right. ... Full name: Jared Lawrence Sandberg. ... Nephew of Ryne Sandberg, second baseman with Philadelphia Phillies (1981) and Chicago Cubs (1982-94 and 1996-97).
HIGH SCHOOL: Capital (Olympia, Wash.).
TRANSACTIONS/CAREER NOTES: Selected by Tampa Bay Devil Rays organization in 16th round of free-agent draft (June 4, 1996). ... On Orlando disabled list (April 13-25 and May 9-June 30, 2000).
HONORS: Named Appalachian League Player of the Year (1997).
STATISTICAL NOTES: Led Appalachian League with 157 total bases amd five intentional bases on balls received in 1997. ... Led New York-Pennsylvania League with 133 total bases in 1998. ... Led New York-Pennsylvania League third basemen with 234 total chances and 15 double plays in 1998. ... Led Florida State League third basemen with 423 total chances in 1999. ... Tied for Florida State League lead with 25 double plays by third basemen in 1999.

Year Team (League)	Pos.	G	AB	R	H	2B	3B	HR	RBI	Avg.	BB	SO	SB	PO	A	E	Avg.
1996— GC Devil Rays (GCL)..	2B	22	77	6	13	2	1	0	7	.169	9	26	1	30	63	3	.969
1997— St. Petersburg (FSL)..	2B	2	3	1	1	0	0	0	2	.333	2	2	0	4	5	0	1.000
— Princeton (Appl.)..	2B-3B	•67	*268	61	81	15	5	17	*68	.302	42	*94	12	84	158	13	.949
1998— Charl.n, S.C. (S.Atl.)—	3B	56	191	31	35	11	0	3	15	.183	27	76	4	43	94	22	.862
— Hudson Valley (NY-P)..	3B	73	271	49	78	15	2	•12	54	.288	42	76	13	*55	•159	20	.915
1999— St. Petersburg (FSL)..	3B	136	504	73	139	24	1	22	96	.276	51	133	8	*102	*284	*37	.913
2000— Orlando (Sou.)	3B	67	244	30	63	15	1	5	35	.258	33	55	5	45	131	10	.946
— Durham (I.L.)	3B	3	15	2	6	3	0	2	7	.400	0	6	0	1	13	1	.933
2001— Orlando (Sou.)	3B-1B	8	28	4	8	2	0	1	4	.286	6	10	0	10	20	0	1.000
— Durham (I.L.)	3B	93	322	39	77	16	0	16	50	.239	38	81	0	56	181	13	.948
— Tampa Bay (A.L.).......	3B-1B	39	136	13	28	7	0	1	15	.206	10	45	1	33	68	6	.944
Major League totals (1 year)		39	136	13	28	7	0	1	15	.206	10	45	1	33	68	6	.944

SANDERS, ANTHONY OF REDS

PERSONAL: Born March 2, 1974, in Tucson, Ariz. ... 6-2/200. ... Bats right, throws right. ... Full name: Anthony Marcus Sanders.
HIGH SCHOOL: Santa Rita (Tucson, Ariz.).
TRANSACTIONS/CAREER NOTES: Selected by Toronto Blue Jays organization in seventh round of free-agent draft (June 1, 1992). ... On Syracuse disabled list (July 22, 1998-remainder of season). ... Claimed on waivers by Seattle Mariners (March 31, 2000). ... On Tacoma disabled list (July 17-28, 2000). ... Released by Mariners (April 30, 2001). ... Signed by Cincinnati Reds organization (December 21, 2001).
MISCELLANEOUS: Member of 2000 U.S. Olympic baseball team.

Year Team (League)	Pos.	G	AB	R	H	2B	3B	HR	RBI	Avg.	BB	SO	SB	PO	A	E	Avg.
1993— Medicine Hat (Pio.)	OF	63	225	44	59	9	3	4	33	.262	20	49	6	88	8	2	.980
1994— St. Catharines (NY-P)..	OF	74	258	36	66	17	3	6	45	.256	27	53	8	120	9	3	.977
1995— Hagerstown (S.Atl.)....	OF	133	512	72	119	28	1	8	48	.232	52	103	26	274	15	3	.990
1996— Dunedin (FSL)	OF	102	417	75	108	25	0	17	50	.259	34	93	16	209	8	4	.982
— Knoxville (Sou.)..........	OF	38	133	16	36	8	0	1	18	.271	7	33	1	66	1	3	.957
1997— Dunedin (FSL)	OF	1	5	0	1	1	0	0	1	.200	1	1	0	1	0	0	1.000
— Knoxville (Sou.)..........	OF-DH	111	429	68	114	20	4	26	69	.266	44	121	20	224	7	4	.983
1998— Syracuse (I.L.)...........	OF	60	209	23	40	9	2	4	19	.191	20	65	5	145	6	1	.993
— Knoxville (Sou.)..........	OF	6	25	9	10	2	0	4	9	.400	2	6	0	15	3	0	1.000
1999— Syracuse (I.L.)...........	OF-DH	124	496	71	121	22	5	18	59	.244	46	111	18	279	•17	6	.980
— Toronto (A.L.)............	DH-OF	3	7	1	2	1	0	0	2	.286	0	2	0	1	0	0	1.000
2000— Tacoma (PCL)▬........	OF	114	428	72	131	21	3	20	80	.306	33	109	9	177	11	3	.984
— Seattle (A.L.)	OF	1	1	1	1	0	0	0	0	1.000	0	0	0	1	0	0	1.000
2001— Seattle (A.L.)	OF	9	17	1	3	2	0	0	2	.176	2	3	0	13	0	0	1.000
Major League totals (3 years)		13	25	3	6	3	0	0	4	.240	2	5	0	15	0	0	1.000

SANDERS, DEION OF

PERSONAL: Born August 9, 1967, in Fort Myers, Fla. ... 6-1/195. ... Bats left, throws left. ... Full name: Deion Luwynn Sanders.
HIGH SCHOOL: North Fort Myers (Fla.).
COLLEGE: Florida State.
TRANSACTIONS/CAREER NOTES: Selected by Kansas City Royals organization in sixth round of free-agent draft (June 3, 1985); did not sign. ... Selected by New York Yankees organization in 30th round of free-agent draft (June 1, 1988). ... On disqualified list (August 1-September 24, 1990). ... Released by Yankees organization (September 24, 1990). ... Signed by Atlanta Braves (January 29, 1991). ... Placed on Richmond temporarily inactive list (August 1, 1991). ... On disqualified list (April 29-May 21, 1993). ... On disabled list (August 22-September 6, 1993). ... Traded by Braves to Cincinnati Reds for OF Roberto Kelly and P Roger Etheridge (May 29, 1994). ... On Cincinnati disabled list (June 1-July 16, 1995); included rehabilitation assignment to Chattanooga (July 12-14). ... Traded by Reds with P John Roper, P Ricky Pickett, P Scott Service and IF Dave McCarty to San Francisco Giants for OF Darren Lewis, P Mark Portugal and P Dave Burba (July 21, 1995). ... Granted free agency (December 21, 1995). ... Did not play baseball during 1996 season. ... Re-signed by Reds (February 17, 1997). ... Granted free agency (November 5, 1997). ... Re-signed by Reds organization (January 8, 1998). ... Granted free agency (December 21, 1999). ... Re-signed by Reds organization (January 20, 2000). ... On Cincinnati disabled list (March 29-June 2, 2000); included rehabilitation assignment to Louisville (April 12-May 11). ... On restricted list (June 22, 2000-remainder of season). ... Granted free agency (November 10, 2000). ... Re-signed by Reds organization (January 24, 2001). ... Contract voided by Commissioner's Office (January 26, 2001). ... Re-signed by Reds organization (February 19, 2001). ... Released by Reds (June 22, 2001). ... Signed by Toronto Blue Jays organization (June 27, 2001). ... Released by Blue Jays (July 27, 2001).
STATISTICAL NOTES: Led N.L. in caught stealing with 16 in 1994.
MISCELLANEOUS: Only person in history to play in both the World Series (1992) and Super Bowl (1994 and 1995 seasons).

Year Team (League)	Pos.	G	AB	R	H	2B	3B	HR	RBI	Avg.	BB	SO	SB	PO	A	E	Avg.
1988— GC Yankees (GCL)	OF	17	75	7	21	4	2	0	6	.280	2	10	11	33	1	2	.944
—Fort Lauderdale (FSL)	OF	6	21	5	9	2	0	0	2	.429	1	3	2	22	2	0	1.000
—Columbus (I.L.)	OF	5	20	3	3	1	0	0	0	.150	1	4	1	13	0	0	1.000
1989—Albany/Colonie (East.)	OF	33	119	28	34	2	2	1	6	.286	11	20	17	79	3	0	1.000
—New York (A.L.)	OF	14	47	7	11	2	0	2	7	.234	3	8	1	30	1	1	.969
—Columbus (I.L.)	OF	70	259	38	72	12	7	5	30	.278	22	46	16	165	0	4	.976
1990—New York (A.L.)	OF-DH	57	133	24	21	2	2	3	9	.158	13	27	8	69	2	2	.973
—Columbus (I.L.)	OF	22	84	21	27	7	1	2	10	.321	17	15	9	49	1	0	1.000
1991— Atlanta (N.L.)■	OF	54	110	16	21	1	2	4	13	.191	12	23	11	57	3	3	.952
—Richmond (I.L.)	OF	29	130	20	34	6	3	5	16	.262	10	28	12	73	1	1	.987
1992—Atlanta (N.L.)	OF	97	303	54	92	6	*14	8	28	.304	18	52	26	174	4	3	.980
1993—Atlanta (N.L.)	OF	95	272	42	75	18	6	6	28	.276	16	42	19	137	1	4	.986
1994—Atlanta (N.L.)	OF	46	191	32	55	10	0	4	21	.288	16	28	19	99	0	2	.980
—Cincinnati (N.L.)■	OF	46	184	26	51	7	4	0	7	.277	16	35	19	110	2	0	1.000
1995—Cincinnati (N.L.)	OF	33	129	19	31	2	3	1	10	.240	9	18	16	88	2	3	.968
—Chattanooga (Sou.)	DH-OF	2	7	1	4	0	0	1	2	.571	0	1	1	3	1	0	1.000
—San Fran. (N.L.)■	OF	52	214	29	61	9	5	5	18	.285	18	42	8	127	0	2	.984
1996—									Did not play.								
1997—Cincinnati (N.L.)■	OF	115	465	53	127	13	7	5	23	.273	34	67	56	236	3	4	.984
1998—Cincinnati (N.L.)									Did not play.								
1999—Cincinnati (N.L.)									Did not play.								
2000—Louisville (I.L.)	OF	25	105	13	21	1	1	3	7	.200	14	9	10	49	3	1	.981
2001—Louisville (I.L.)	OF	19	74	12	34	4	5	1	9	.459	2	4	6	36	0	1	.973
—Cincinnati (N.L.)	OF-DH	32	75	6	13	2	0	1	4	.173	4	10	3	34	4	0	1.000
—Syracuse (I.L.)■	OF	25	107	15	27	7	1	1	6	.252	7	12	5	17	1	0	1.000
American League totals (2 years)		71	180	31	32	4	2	5	16	.178	16	35	9	99	3	3	.971
National League totals (7 years)		570	1943	277	526	68	41	34	152	.271	143	317	177	1062	19	19	.983
Major League totals (9 years)		641	2123	308	558	72	43	39	168	.263	159	352	186	1161	22	22	.982

CHAMPIONSHIP SERIES RECORD

Year Team (League)	Pos.	G	AB	R	H	2B	3B	HR	RBI	Avg.	BB	SO	SB	PO	A	E	Avg.
1992—Atlanta (N.L.)	OF-PH	4	5	0	0	0	0	0	0	.000	0	3	0	1	0	0	1.000
1993—Atlanta (N.L.)	PH-OF-PR	5	3	0	0	0	0	0	0	.000	0	1	0	0	0	0	...
Championship series totals (2 years)		9	8	0	0	0	0	0	0	.000	0	4	0	1	0	0	1.000

WORLD SERIES RECORD

Year Team (League)	Pos.	G	AB	R	H	2B	3B	HR	RBI	Avg.	BB	SO	SB	PO	A	E	Avg.
1992—Atlanta (N.L.)	OF	4	15	4	8	2	0	0	1	.533	2	1	5	5	1	0	1.000

RECORD AS FOOTBALL PLAYER

TRANSACTIONS/CAREER NOTES: Selected by Atlanta Falcons in first round (fifth pick overall) of 1989 NFL draft. ... Signed by Falcons (September 7, 1989). ... On reserve/did not report list (July 27-August 13, 1990). ... Granted roster exemption for one game (September 1992). ... On reserve/did not report list (July 23-October 14, 1993). ... Designated by Falcons as transition player (February 15, 1994). ... Free agency status changed by Falcons from transitional to unconditional (April 28, 1994). ... Signed by San Francisco 49ers (September 15, 1994). ... Granted unconditional free agency (February 17, 1995). ... Signed by Dallas Cowboys (September 9, 1995).

CHAMPIONSHIP GAME EXPERIENCE: Played in NFC championship game (1994 and 1995 seasons). ... Member of Super Bowl championship team (1994 and 1995 seasons).

HONORS: Named defensive back on The Sporting News college All-America first team (1986-1988). ... Jim Thorpe Award winner (1988). ... Named cornerback on The Sporting News NFL All-Pro team (1991-1997). ... Played in Pro Bowl (1991-1994 and 1997 seasons). ... Named kick returner on The Sporting News NFL All-Pro team (1992). ... Named to play in Pro Bowl (1996 season); replaced by Darrell Green due to injury.

PRO STATISTICS: 1989—Fumbled twice and recovered one fumble. 1990—Fumbled four times and recovered two fumbles. 1991—Credited with a sack, fumbled once and recovered one fumble. 1992—Rushed once for minus four yards, fumbled three times and recovered two fumbles. 1993—Attempted one pass without a completion. 1994—Recovered one fumble. 1995—Rushed once for nine yards. 1996—Rushed three times for two yards, fumbled twice and recovered three fumbles for 15 yards and a touchdown. 1997—Rushed once for minus 11 yards.

			INTERCEPTIONS				RECEIVING				PUNT RETURNS				KICKOFF RETURNS				TOTALS		
Year Team	G	GS	No.	Yds.	Avg.	TD	No.	Yds.	Avg.	TD	No.	Yds.	Avg.	TD	No.	Yds.	Avg.	TD	TD	2pt.	Pts.
1989—Atlanta NFL	15	10	5	52	10.4	0	1	-8	-8.0	0	28	307	11.0	†1	35	725	20.7	0	1	...	6
1990—Atlanta NFL	16	16	∞3	153	51.0	2	0	0	...	0	29	250	8.6	†1	39	851	21.8	0	3	...	18
1991—Atlanta NFL	15	15	6	119	19.8	∞1	1	17	17.0	0	21	170	8.1	0	26	576	22.2	†1	2	...	12
1992—Atlanta NFL	13	12	3	105	35.0	0	3	45	15.0	1	13	41	3.2	0	40	*1067	‡26.7	*2	3	...	18
1993—Atlanta NFL	11	10	‡7	91	13.0	0	6	106	17.7	1	2	21	10.5	0	7	169	24.1	0	1	...	6
1994—San Fran. NFL	14	12	6	*303	50.5	†3	0	0	...	0	0	0	...	0	0	0	...	0	3	0	18
1995—Dallas NFL	9	9	2	34	17.0	0	2	25	12.5	0	1	54	54.0	0	1	15	15.0	0	0	0	0
1996—Dallas NFL	16	15	2	3	1.5	0	36	475	13.2	1	1	4	4.0	0	0	0	...	0	2	0	12
1997—Dallas NFL	12	12	2	81	40.5	1	0	0	...	0	33	407	12.3	1	1	18	18.0	0	2	0	12
Pro totals (9 years)	121	111	36	941	26.1	7	49	660	13.5	3	128	1254	9.8	3	149	3421	23.0	3	17	0	102

SANDERS, REGGIE   OF   GIANTS

PERSONAL: Born December 1, 1967, in Florence, S.C. ... 6-1/185. ... Bats right, throws right. ... Full name: Reginald Laverne Sanders.

HIGH SCHOOL: Wilson (Florence, S.C.).

COLLEGE: Spartanburg (S.C.) Methodist.

TRANSACTIONS/CAREER NOTES: Selected by Cincinnati Reds organization in seventh round of free-agent draft (June 2, 1987). ... On disabled list (July 11-September 15, 1988; and July 15-September 5, 1989). ... On Chattanooga disabled list (June 30-July 26, 1991). ... On Cincinnati disabled list (August 24-September 20, 1991; May 13-29 and July 17-August 2, 1992). ... On suspended list (June 3-9, 1994). ... On Cincinnati disabled list (April 20-May 22, May 31-June 15 and September 17, 1996-remainder of season); included rehabilitation assignment to Indianapolis (May 17-22). ... On Cincinnati disabled list (April 19-May 6 and May 24-July 23, 1997); included rehabilitation assignments to Chattanooga (May 3-5) and Indianapolis (July 15-22). ... Traded by Reds with SS Damian Jackson and P Josh Harris to San Diego Padres for OF Greg Vaughn and OF/1B Mark Sweeney (February 2, 1999). ... On disabled list (June 3-18, 1999). ... Traded by Padres with 2B Quilvio Veras and 1B Wally Joyner to Atlanta Braves for OF/1B Ryan Klesko, 2B Bret Boone and P Jason Shiell (December 22, 1999). ... On disabled list (April 30-May 23 and July 28-August 15, 2000). ... Granted free agency (October 31, 2000). ... Signed by Arizona Diamondbacks (January 5, 2001). ... On Arizona disabled list (March 23-April 8, 2001); included rehabilitation assignment to Tuscon (April 5-8). ... Granted free agency (November 6, 2001). ... Signed by San Francisco Giants (January 5, 2002).

HONORS: Named Midwest League Most Valuable Player (1990). ... Named outfielder on THE SPORTING NEWS N.L. All-Star team (1995).

STATISTICAL NOTES: Hit three home runs in one game (August 15, 1995). ... Career major league grand slams: 1.

Year Team (League)	Pos.	G	AB	R	H	2B	3B	HR	RBI	Avg.	BB	SO	SB	PO	A	E	Avg.
1988— Billings (Pio.)	SS	17	64	11	15	1	1	0	3	.234	6	4	10	18	33	3	.944
1989— Greensboro (S.Atl.)	SS	81	315	53	91	18	5	9	53	.289	29	63	21	125	169	42	.875
1990— Cedar Rapids (Midw.) ..	OF	127	466	89	133	21	4	17	63	.285	59	97	40	241	10	10	.962
1991— Chattanooga (Sou.)	OF	86	302	50	95	15	•8	8	49	.315	41	67	15	158	2	3	.982
— Cincinnati (N.L.)	OF	9	40	6	8	0	0	1	3	.200	0	9	1	22	0	0	1.000
1992— Cincinnati (N.L.)	OF	116	385	62	104	26	6	12	36	.270	48	98	16	262	11	6	.978
1993— Cincinnati (N.L.)	OF	138	496	90	136	16	4	20	83	.274	51	118	27	312	3	8	.975
1994— Cincinnati (N.L.)	OF	107	400	66	105	20	8	17	62	.263	41	*114	21	218	12	6	.975
1995— Cincinnati (N.L.)	OF	133	484	91	148	36	6	28	99	.306	69	122	36	268	12	5	.982
1996— Cincinnati (N.L.)	OF	81	287	49	72	17	1	14	33	.251	44	86	24	160	7	2	.988
— Indianapolis (A.A.)......	OF-DH	4	12	3	5	2	0	0	1	.417	1	4	0	4	1	0	1.000
1997— Cincinnati (N.L.)	OF	86	312	52	79	19	2	19	56	.253	42	93	13	183	4	5	.974
— Chattanooga (Sou.)	OF	3	11	3	6	1	1	1	3	.545	1	2	0	11	0	0	1.000
— Indianapolis (A.A.)......	OF	5	19	1	4	0	0	0	1	.211	1	6	0	6	0	2	.750
1998— Cincinnati (N.L.)	OF	135	481	83	129	18	6	14	59	.268	51	137	20	263	4	6	.978
1999— San Diego (N.L.)	OF-DH	133	478	92	136	24	7	26	72	.285	65	108	36	233	4	6	.975
2000— Atlanta (N.L.)■..........	OF	103	340	43	79	23	1	11	37	.232	32	78	21	155	7	6	.964
2001— Tucson (PCL)■	OF	2	6	0	2	1	0	0	1	.333	2	0	1	2	0	0	1.000
— Arizona (N.L.)	OF	126	441	84	116	21	3	33	90	.263	46	126	14	231	5	1	.996
Major League totals (11 years)		1167	4144	718	1112	220	44	195	630	.268	489	1089	229	2307	69	51	.979

DIVISION SERIES RECORD

Year Team (League)	Pos.	G	AB	R	H	2B	3B	HR	RBI	Avg.	BB	SO	SB	PO	A	E	Avg.
1995— Cincinnati (N.L.)	OF	3	13	3	2	1	0	1	2	.154	1	9	2	7	0	1	.875
2000— Atlanta (N.L.)	OF	3	9	0	0	0	0	0	0	.000	2	5	0	4	0	0	...
2001— Arizona (N.L.)	OF	5	14	2	5	1	0	1	1	.357	3	3	1	12	0	0	1.000
Division series totals (3 years)		11	36	5	7	2	0	2	3	.194	6	17	3	23	0	1	.958

CHAMPIONSHIP SERIES RECORD

Year Team (League)	Pos.	G	AB	R	H	2B	3B	HR	RBI	Avg.	BB	SO	SB	PO	A	E	Avg.
1995— Cincinnati (N.L.)	OF	4	16	0	2	0	0	0	0	.125	2	10	0	7	0	1	.875
2001— Arizona (N.L.)	OF	5	17	2	2	0	0	0	1	.118	5	5	1	14	0	0	1.000
Championship series totals (2 years)		9	33	2	4	0	0	0	1	.121	7	15	1	21	0	1	.955

WORLD SERIES RECORD

RECORDS: Shares single-inning record for most at-bats—2 (November 3, 2001, third inning).
NOTES: Member of World Series championship team (2001).

Year Team (League)	Pos.	G	AB	R	H	2B	3B	HR	RBI	Avg.	BB	SO	SB	PO	A	E	Avg.
2001— Arizona (N.L.)	OF	6	23	6	7	1	0	0	1	.304	1	7	1	9	0	0	1.000

ALL-STAR GAME RECORD

Year League	Pos.	AB	R	H	2B	3B	HR	RBI	Avg.	BB	SO	SB	PO	A	E	Avg.
1995— National	OF	1	0	0	0	0	0	0	.000	0	1	0	0	0	0	...

SANTANA, JOHAN   P   TWINS

PERSONAL: Born March 13, 1979, in Tovar, Venezuela. ... 6-0/195. ... Throws left, bats left. ... Full name: Johan Alexander Santana.
HIGH SCHOOL: Liceo Nucete Sardi (Venezuela).
TRANSACTIONS/CAREER NOTES: Signed as non-drafted free agent by Houston Astros organization (July 2, 1995). ... Selected by Florida Marlins from Astros organization in Rule 5 major league draft (December 13, 1999). ... Traded by Marlins with cash to Minnesota Twins for P Jared Camp (December 13, 1999). ... On disabled list (July 7-September 21, 2001).
STATISTICAL NOTES: Led New York-Pennsylvania League with 10 hit batsmen in 1998.

Year League	W	L	Pct.	ERA	G	GS	CG	ShO	Sv.	IP	H	R	ER	BB	SO
1996— Dominican Astros (DSL)	4	3	.571	2.70	23	1	0	0	3	40	26	16	12	22	51
1997— Gulf Coast Astros (GCL).....	0	4	.000	7.93	9	5	1	0	0	36 1/3	49	36	32	18	25
— Auburn (NY-Penn)..........	0	0	...	2.25	1	1	0	0	0	4	1	1	1	6	5
1998— Quad City (Midw.)	0	1	.000	9.45	2	1	0	0	0	6 2/3	14	7	7	3	6
— Auburn (NY-Penn).............	7	5	.583	4.36	15	15	1	•1	0	86 2/3	81	52	42	21	88
1999— Michigan (Midw.)...............	8	8	.500	4.66	27	26	1	0	0	160 1/3	162	94	83	55	150
2000— Minnesota (A.L.)■	2	3	.400	6.49	30	5	0	0	0	86	102	64	62	54	64
2001— Minnesota (A.L.)	1	0	1.000	4.74	15	4	0	0	0	43 2/3	50	25	23	16	28
Major League totals (2 years)	3	3	.500	5.90	45	9	0	0	0	129 2/3	152	89	85	70	92

SANTANA, PEDRO   2B   TIGERS

PERSONAL: Born September 21, 1976, in San Pedro de Macoris, Dominican Republic. ... 5-11/160. ... Bats right, throws right. ... Full name: Pedro C. Santana.

HIGH SCHOOL: Gaston F. Delinge (San Pedro de Macoris, Dominican Republic).

TRANSACTIONS/CAREER NOTES: Signed as non-drafted free agent by Houston Astros organization (July 2, 1994). ... Traded by Astros with P Kevin Gallaher to Detroit Tigers (August 27, 1996), completing deal in which Tigers traded P Gregg Olson to Astros for two players to be named later (August 26, 1996). ... On disabled list (July 12-19, 2000). ... Granted free agency (October 15, 2001). ... Re-signed by Tigers organization (December 19, 2001).

						BATTING									FIELDING		
Year Team (League)	Pos.	G	AB	R	H	2B	3B	HR	RBI	Avg.	BB	SO	SB	PO	A	E	Avg.
1995— Dom. Astros (DSL).....	2B	52	184	39	53	6	1	2	14	.288	31	29	34	110	126	17	.933
1996— GC Astros (GCL)	SS-2B-3B-OF	56	207	40	56	6	5	1	20	.271	21	44	33	84	142	14	.942
1997— W. Mich. (Midw.)■.....	2B-SS	74	287	36	75	10	6	3	28	.261	14	55	20	120	205	32	.910
1998— W. Michigan (Midw.)..	2B	118	438	79	115	21	7	4	45	.263	28	93	64	205	309	22	.959
1999— Jacksonville (Sou.).....	2B	120	512	89	143	35	6	5	49	.279	34	98	34	277	338	*20	.969
2000— Jacksonville (Sou.).....	2B	112	448	61	126	20	4	6	53	.281	38	83	40	230	292	19	.965
2001— Toledo (I.L.).............	2B	115	432	45	98	10	3	5	30	.227	27	97	36	234	328	*31	.948
— Detroit (A.L.).............	2B	1	0	0	0	0	0	0	0	...	0	0	0	1	0	0	1.000
Major League totals (1 year)		1	0	0	0	0	0	0	0	...	0	0	0	1	0	0	1.000

SANTANGELO, F.P.   OF/IF   YANKEES

S

PERSONAL: Born October 24, 1967, in Livonia, Mich. ... 5-10/190. ... Bats both, throws right. ... Full name: Frank Paul Santangelo.
HIGH SCHOOL: Valley (Sacramento).
JUNIOR COLLEGE: Sacramento City College.
COLLEGE: Miami (Fla.).
TRANSACTIONS/CAREER NOTES: Selected by Montreal Expos organization in 20th round of free-agent draft (June 5, 1989). ... On disabled list (April 21-May 2, 1994). ... On Montreal disabled list (July 16-31, 1998); included rehabilitation assignment to Ottawa (July 28-31). ... Granted free agency (December 21, 1998). ... Signed by San Francisco Giants (December 23, 1998). ... Granted free agency (December 21, 1999). ... Signed by Los Angeles Dodgers (January 11, 2000). ... On Los Angeles disabled list (July 17-August 2 and August 23-September 22, 2000); included rehabilitation assignment to San Bernardino (July 24-August 2). ... On suspended list (August 2-8, 2000). ... Released by Dodgers (March 29, 2001). ... Signed by Oakland Athletics organization (April 5, 2001). ... Released by A's (November 6, 2001). ... Signed by New York Yankees organization (December 21, 2001).
STATISTICAL NOTES: Led Eastern League with 13 sacrifice hits in 1991. ... Switch-hit home runs in one game (June 7, 1997).

						BATTING									FIELDING		
Year Team (League)	Pos.	G	AB	R	H	2B	3B	HR	RBI	Avg.	BB	SO	SB	PO	A	E	Avg.
1989— Jamestown (NY-P)	2B	2	6	0	3	1	0	0	0	.500	1	0	1	5	5	2	.833
— W.P. Beach (FSL)........	SS-2B-OF	57	173	18	37	4	0	0	14	.214	23	12	3	32	67	8	.925
1990— W.P. Beach (FSL).....	S-O-2-3	116	394	63	109	19	2	0	38	.277	51	49	22	151	202	22	.941
1991— Harrisburg (East.).......	2-O-S-3	132	462	78	113	12	7	5	42	.245	74	45	21	234	253	16	.968
1992— Indianapolis (A.A.)......	O-2-S-3	137	462	83	123	25	0	5	34	.266	62	58	12	291	119	4	.990
1993— Ottawa (I.L.)..............	O-S-3-2	131	453	86	124	21	2	4	45	.274	59	52	18	246	186	14	.969
1994— Ottawa (I.L.)..............	O-2-S-3	119	413	62	104	28	1	5	41	.252	59	64	7	235	140	12	.969
1995— Ottawa (I.L.)..............	3-2-O-S-C	95	267	37	68	15	3	2	25	.255	32	22	7	89	185	10	.965
— Montreal (N.L.)..........	OF-2B	35	98	11	29	5	1	1	9	.296	12	9	1	47	0	1	.979
1996— Montreal (N.L.)..........	O-3-2-S	152	393	54	109	20	5	7	56	.277	49	61	5	251	45	6	.980
1997— Montreal (N.L.)..........	O-3-2-S	130	350	56	87	19	5	5	31	.249	50	73	8	175	56	3	.987
1998— Montreal (N.L.)..........	OF-2B-3B	122	383	53	82	18	0	4	23	.214	44	72	7	211	77	5	.983
— Ottawa (I.L.)..............	DH-OF	2	8	1	2	0	0	0	1	.250	0	3	0	2	0	0	1.000
1999— San Fran. (N.L.)■......	O-2-3-S	113	254	49	66	17	3	3	26	.260	53	54	12	144	25	1	.994
2000— Los Angeles (N.L.)■...	OF-2B	81	142	19	28	4	0	1	9	.197	21	33	3	76	15	2	.978
— San Bern. (Calif.)........	OF-2B	7	19	2	9	2	1	0	1	.474	2	2	1	10	1	0	1.000
2001— Oakland (A.L.)........2B-3B-OF-DH		32	71	16	14	4	0	0	8	.197	11	17	1	43	40	0	1.000
— Sacramento (PCL).....OF-2B-3B-SS		71	188	32	38	7	1	5	17	.202	30	49	5	125	70	1	.995
American League totals (1 year)		32	71	16	14	4	0	0	8	.197	11	17	1	43	40	0	1.000
National League totals (6 years)		633	1620	242	401	83	14	21	154	.248	229	302	36	904	218	18	.984
Major League totals (7 years)		665	1691	258	415	87	14	21	162	.245	240	319	37	947	258	18	.985

DIVISION SERIES RECORD

						BATTING									FIELDING		
Year Team (League)	Pos.	G	AB	R	H	2B	3B	HR	RBI	Avg.	BB	SO	SB	PO	A	E	Avg.
2001— Oakland (A.L.)	2B	2	3	0	1	1	0	0	0	.333	0	0	0	5	4	1	.900

SANTIAGO, BENITO   C   GIANTS

PERSONAL: Born March 9, 1965, in Ponce, Puerto Rico. ... 6-1/195. ... Bats right, throws right. ... Full name: Benito Rivera Santiago.
HIGH SCHOOL: John F. Kennedy (Ponce, Puerto Rico).
TRANSACTIONS/CAREER NOTES: Signed as non-drafted free agent by San Diego Padres organization (September 1, 1982). ... On disabled list (June 21-July 2, 1985). ... On San Diego disabled list (June 15-August 10, 1990); included rehabilitation assignment to Las Vegas (August 2-9). ... On San Diego disabled list (May 31-July 11, 1992); included rehabilitation assignment to Las Vegas (July 7-11). ... Granted free agency (October 26, 1992). ... Signed by Florida Marlins (December 16, 1992). ... On suspended list (May 5-9, 1994). ... Granted free agency (October 20, 1994). ... Signed by Cincinnati Reds (April 17, 1995). ... On disabled list (May 8-July 4, 1995). ... Granted free agency (October 31, 1995). ... Signed by Philadelphia Phillies (January 30, 1996). ... Granted free agency (November 18, 1996). ... Signed by Toronto Blue Jays (December 9, 1996). ... On disabled list (April 14-29, 1997). ... On Toronto disabled list (March 18-September 3, 1998); included rehabilitation assignments to Dunedin (August 15-26) and Syracuse (August 28-September 3). ... Granted free agency (October 23, 1998). ... Signed by Chicago Cubs (December 10, 1998). ... Granted free agency (October 29, 1999). ... Signed by Reds organization (February 24, 2000). ... Granted free

agency (November 3, 2000). ... Signed by San Francisco Giants organization (March 17, 2001). ... Granted free agency (November 7, 2001). ... Re-signed by Giants (December 7, 2001).

RECORDS: Holds major league rookie-season record for most consecutive games batted safely—34 (August 25-October 2, 1987). ... Shares major league single-season record for fewest passed balls (100 or more games)—0 (1992). ... Shares major league record for most consecutive home runs—4 (September 14 [1] and 15 [3], 1996).

HONORS: Named N.L. Rookie Player of the Year by THE SPORTING NEWS (1987). ... Named catcher on THE SPORTING NEWS N.L. All-Star team (1987, 1989 and 1991). ... Named catcher on THE SPORTING NEWS N.L. Silver Slugger team (1987-88 and 1990-91). ... Named N.L. Rookie of the Year by Baseball Writers' Association of America (1987). ... Won N.L. Gold Glove at catcher (1988-90).

STATISTICAL NOTES: Led Florida State League catchers with 26 passed balls and 12 double plays in 1983. ... Led Texas League catchers with 78 assists and 16 passed balls in 1985. ... Led Pacific Coast League catchers with 655 total chances in 1986. ... Had 34-game hitting streak (August 25-October 2, 1987). ... Led N.L. with 22 passed balls in 1987, 14 in 1989 and 23 in 1993. ... Led N.L. in grounding into double plays with 21 in 1991. ... Tied for N.L. lead in double plays by catcher with 11 in 1988 and 14 in 1991. ... Led N.L. catchers with 100 assists and 14 errors in 1991. ... Tied for N.L. lead in errors by catcher with 11 in 1993. ... Led N.L. catchers with .996 fielding percentage in 1995. ... Hit three home runs in one game (September 15, 1996). ... Career major league grand slams: 7.

Year	Team (League)	Pos.	G	AB	R	H	2B	3B	HR	RBI	Avg.	BB	SO	SB	PO	A	E	Avg.
1983—Miami (FSL)		C	122	429	34	106	25	3	5	56	.247	11	79	3	471	*69	*21	.963
1984—Reno (Calif.)		C	114	416	64	116	20	6	16	83	.279	36	75	5	692	96	25	.969
1985—Beaumont (Texas)		C-1B-3B	101	372	55	111	16	6	5	52	.298	16	59	12	525	†78	15	.976
1986—Las Vegas (PCL)		C	117	437	55	125	26	3	17	71	.286	17	81	19	*563	71	*21	.968
—San Diego (N.L.)		C	17	62	10	18	2	0	3	6	.290	2	12	0	80	7	5	.946
1987—San Diego (N.L.)		C	146	546	64	164	33	2	18	79	.300	16	112	21	817	80	*22	.976
1988—San Diego (N.L.)		C	139	492	49	122	22	2	10	46	.248	24	82	15	725	*75	*12	.985
1989—San Diego (N.L.)		C	129	462	50	109	16	3	16	62	.236	26	89	11	685	81	*20	.975
1990—San Diego (N.L.)		C	100	344	42	93	8	5	11	53	.270	27	55	5	538	51	12	.980
—Las Vegas (PCL)		C	6	20	5	6	2	0	1	8	.300	3	1	0	25	5	0	1.000
1991—San Diego (N.L.)		C-OF	152	580	60	155	22	3	17	87	.267	23	114	8	830	†100	†14	.985
1992—San Diego (N.L.)		C	106	386	37	97	21	0	10	42	.251	21	52	2	584	53	*12	.982
—Las Vegas (PCL)		C	4	13	3	4	0	0	1	2	.308	1	1	0	13	2	0	1.000
1993—Florida (N.L.)■		C-OF	139	469	49	108	19	6	13	50	.230	37	88	10	740	64	•11	.987
1994—Florida (N.L.)		C	101	337	35	92	14	2	11	41	.273	25	57	1	511	*66	5	.991
1995—Cincinnati (N.L.)■		C-1B	81	266	40	76	20	0	11	44	.286	24	48	2	480	35	2	†.996
1996—Philadelphia (N.L.)■ ■		C-1B	136	481	71	127	21	2	30	85	.264	49	104	2	834	67	11	.988
1997—Toronto (A.L.)■		C-DH	97	341	31	83	10	0	13	42	.243	17	80	1	621	40	2	.997
1998—Dunedin (FSL)		DH-C	11	37	4	6	1	0	1	5	.162	3	9	3	19	6	0	1.000
—Syracuse (I.L.)		C-DH	5	22	0	5	2	0	0	2	.227	1	3	0	19	1	0	1.000
—Toronto (A.L.)		C	15	29	3	9	5	0	0	4	.310	1	6	0	45	2	0	1.000
1999—Chicago (N.L.)■		C-1B	109	350	28	87	18	3	7	36	.249	32	71	1	562	43	6	.990
2000—Cincinnati (N.L.)■		C	89	252	22	66	11	1	8	45	.262	19	45	2	428	36	3	.994
2001—San Fran. (N.L.)■		C-1B	133	477	39	125	25	4	6	45	.262	23	78	5	837	62	5	.994
American League totals (2 years)			112	370	34	92	15	0	13	46	.249	18	86	1	666	42	2	.997
National League totals (14 years)			1577	5504	596	1439	252	33	171	721	.261	348	1007	85	8651	820	140	.985
Major League totals (16 years)			1689	5874	630	1531	267	33	184	767	.261	366	1093	86	9317	862	142	.986

DIVISION SERIES RECORD

NOTES: Hit home run in first at-bat (October 3, 1995).

Year	Team (League)	Pos.	G	AB	R	H	2B	3B	HR	RBI	Avg.	BB	SO	SB	PO	A	E	Avg.
1995—Cincinnati (N.L.)		C	3	9	2	3	0	0	1	3	.333	3	3	0	20	0	0	1.000

CHAMPIONSHIP SERIES RECORD

Year	Team (League)	Pos.	G	AB	R	H	2B	3B	HR	RBI	Avg.	BB	SO	SB	PO	A	E	Avg.
1995—Cincinnati (N.L.)		C	4	13	0	3	0	0	0	0	.231	2	3	0	23	1	0	1.000

ALL-STAR GAME RECORD

Year	League	Pos.	AB	R	H	2B	3B	HR	RBI	Avg.	BB	SO	SB	PO	A	E	Avg.
1989—National		C	1	0	0	0	0	0	0	.000	0	1	0	0	0	1	.000
1990—National							Selected, did not play—injured.										
1991—National		C	3	0	0	0	0	0	0	.000	0	1	0	4	0	0	1.000
1992—National		C	1	0	0	0	0	0	0	.000	0	1	0	3	0	0	1.000
All-Star Game totals (3 years)			5	0	0	0	0	0	0	.000	0	3	0	7	0	1	.875

SANTIAGO, JOSE   P   PHILLIES

PERSONAL: Born November 5, 1974, in Fajardo, Puerto Rico. ... 6-3/215. ... Throws right, bats right. ... Full name: Jose Rafael Santiago.

HIGH SCHOOL: Carlos Escobar Lopez (Loiza, Puerto Rico).

TRANSACTIONS/CAREER NOTES: Selected by Kansas City Royals organization in 70th round of free agent draft (June 3, 1994). ... On Kansas City disabled list (June 26-July 9, 1997). ... On Kansas City disabled list (June 20-September 13, 1999); included rehabilitation assignments to Gulf Coast Royals (July 3-9), Wichita (July 10-11 and August 30-September 5) and Omaha (July 18-19 and September 6-12). ... Traded by Royals to Philadelphia Phillies for P Paul Byrd (June 5, 2001).

Year	League	W	L	Pct.	ERA	G	GS	CG	ShO	Sv.	IP	H	R	ER	BB	SO
1994—Gulf Coast Royals (GCL)		1	0	1.000	2.37	10	1	0	0	2	19	17	7	5	7	10
1995—Spokane (N'West)		2	4	.333	3.14	22	0	0	0	1	48²/₃	60	26	17	20	32
1996—Lansing (Midw.)		7	6	.538	3.74	54	0	0	0	19	77	78	34	32	21	55
1997—Wilmington (Caro.)		1	1	.500	4.91	4	0	0	0	2	3²/₃	3	3	2	1	1
—Lansing (Midw.)		1	0	1.000	2.08	9	0	0	0	1	13	10	6	3	6	8
—Kansas City (A.L.)		0	0	...	1.93	4	0	0	0	0	4²/₃	7	2	1	2	1
—Wichita (Texas)		2	1	.667	4.00	22	0	0	0	3	27	32	13	12	8	12

Year League	W	L	Pct.	ERA	G	GS	CG	ShO	Sv.	IP	H	R	ER	BB	SO
1998— Wichita (Texas)	3	4	.429	3.61	52	0	0	0	22	72⅓	79	36	29	27	31
— Kansas City (A.L.)	0	0	...	9.00	2	0	0	0	0	2	4	2	2	0	2
— Omaha (PCL)	0	0	...	7.04	4	0	0	0	1	7⅔	10	9	6	5	4
1999— Kansas City (A.L.)	3	4	.429	3.42	34	0	0	0	2	47⅓	46	23	18	14	15
— Gulf Coast Royals (GCL)	0	0	...	1.80	3	3	0	0	0	5	1	1	1	0	4
— Wichita (Texas)	0	1	.000	2.00	4	2	0	0	0	9	8	2	2	0	0
— Omaha (PCL)	0	0	...	0.00	1	0	0	0	0	1⅔	3	0	0	0	0
2000— Kansas City (A.L.)	8	6	.571	3.91	45	0	0	0	2	69	70	33	30	26	44
— Omaha (PCL)	0	1	.000	3.18	11	0	0	0	4	17	19	7	6	3	14
2001— Kansas City (A.L.)	2	2	.500	6.75	20	0	0	0	0	29⅓	40	22	22	9	15
— Philadelphia (N.L.)■	2	4	.333	3.61	53	0	0	0	0	62⅓	66	25	25	13	28
A.L. totals (5 years)	13	12	.520	4.31	105	0	0	0	4	152⅓	167	82	73	51	77
N.L. totals (1 year)	2	4	.333	3.61	53	0	0	0	0	62⅓	66	25	25	13	28
Major League totals (5 years)	15	16	.484	4.11	158	0	0	0	4	214⅔	233	107	98	64	105

SANTOS, ANGEL   2B   RED SOX

PERSONAL: Born August 14, 1979, in Rio Piedras, Puerto Rico. ... 5-11/180. ... Bats both, throws right. ... Full name: Angel Ramon Santos.
HIGH SCHOOL: Miguel Melendez Munoz (Cayey, Puerto Rico).
TRANSACTIONS/CAREER NOTES: Selected by Boston Red Sox organization in fourth round of free-agent draft (June 3, 1997). ... On disabled list (July 19, 2000-remainder of season).
STATISTICAL NOTES: Led Eastern League second basemen with 566 total chances and 81 double plays in 2001.

Year Team (League)	Pos.	G	AB	R	H	2B	3B	HR	RBI	Avg.	BB	SO	SB	PO	A	E	Avg.
1997— GC Red Sox (GCL)	SS	17	60	8	11	1	0	0	7	.183	7	11	8	10	17	1	.964
1998— GC Red Sox (GCL)	SS-2B-3B	23	77	14	27	5	1	0	13	.351	13	10	7	27	54	9	.900
— Lowell (NY-Penn)	SS-2B-3B	28	102	19	25	4	1	1	12	.245	9	12	2	40	72	12	.903
1999— Augusta (S.Atl.)........	2B-SS-3B	130	466	83	126	30	2	15	55	.270	62	88	25	163	310	34	.933
2000— Trenton (East.)	2B	80	275	32	71	17	2	3	32	.258	32	60	18	144	224	12	.968
2001— Pawtucket (I.L.).........	2B	4	15	1	3	1	0	0	2	.200	1	4	1	8	7	0	1.000
— Trenton (East.)	2B	129	510	75	138	32	0	14	52	.271	54	106	26	*274	273	•19	.966
— Boston (A.L.)............	2B	9	16	2	2	1	0	0	1	.125	2	7	0	7	12	2	.905
Major League totals (1 year)		9	16	2	2	1	0	0	1	.125	2	7	0	7	12	2	.905

SANTOS, DEIVIS   1B   GIANTS

PERSONAL: Born February 9, 1980, in Santo Domingo, Dominican Republic. ... 6-1/175. ... Bats left, throws left. ... Full name: Deivis Alejandro Santos.
TRANSACTIONS/CAREER NOTES: Signed as non-drafted free agent by San Francisco Giants organization (May 30, 1997). ... On Arizona Giants disabled list (July 10-August 27, 2000).
STATISTICAL NOTES: Led South Atlantic League first basemen with 1,145 total chances and 97 double plays in 2001.

Year Team (League)	Pos.	G	AB	R	H	2B	3B	HR	RBI	Avg.	BB	SO	SB	PO	A	E	Avg.
1997— Dom. Giants (DSL).....		70	258	29	70	13	2	4	24	.271	23	40	5	...	...	...	...
1998— Dom. Giants (DSL).....		60	221	26	62	17	0	1	22	.281	24	22	5	...	...	...	...
1999— Dom. Giants (DSL).....		67	237	27	56	10	2	3	40	.236	44	31	7	...	...	...	...
2000— Arizona Giants (Ariz.) .	1B	12	43	13	16	2	1	2	10	.372	7	6	4	103	8	0	1.000
— Salem-Kaizer (NW).....	1B	2	7	0	0	0	0	0	0	.000	0	0	0	14	2	0	1.000
2001— Hagerstown (S.Atl.)....	1B-OF	131	520	64	151	27	3	12	80	.290	25	91	16	1049	83	14	.988

SANTOS, VICTOR   P   TIGERS

PERSONAL: Born October 2, 1976, in San Pedro de Macoris, Dominican Republic. ... 6-3/175. ... Throws right, bats right. ... Full name: Victor Irving Santos.
HIGH SCHOOL: Passaic (N.J.).
TRANSACTIONS/CAREER NOTES: Signed as non-drafted free agent by Detroit Tigers organization (June 11, 1995). ... On Toledo disabled list (April 6-July 1, July 7-14 and July 19-September 18, 2000).
STATISTICAL NOTES: Led Southern League pitchers with seven errors in 1999.

Year League	W	L	Pct.	ERA	G	GS	CG	ShO	Sv.	IP	H	R	ER	BB	SO
1995— Dominican Tigers (DSL).....	7	5	.583	3.72	15	12	3	2	0	77⅓	88	46	32	18	75
1996— Lakeland (FSL)	2	2	.500	2.22	5	4	0	0	0	28⅓	19	11	7	9	25
— Gulf Coast Tigers (GCL)	3	2	.600	1.98	9	9	0	0	0	50	44	12	11	13	39
1997— Lakeland (FSL)	10	5	.667	3.23	26	26	4	•2	0	145	136	74	52	59	108
1998— Lakeland (FSL)	5	2	.714	2.51	16	15	0	0	1	100⅓	88	38	28	24	74
— Toledo (I.L.)	1	2	.333	11.05	5	3	0	0	0	14⅔	24	18	18	10	12
— Jacksonville (Sou.)...........	4	2	.667	4.17	6	6	0	0	0	36⅔	40	20	17	15	37
1999— Jacksonville (Sou.)...........	12	6	.667	3.49	28	•28	2	1	0	173	150	86	67	58	*146
2000— Toledo (I.L.)	0	1	.000	11.37	2	2	0	0	0	6⅓	7	8	8	6	2
— Lakeland (FSL)	1	0	1.000	0.00	1	1	0	0	0	5	5	0	0	1	4
— Gulf Coast Tigers (GCL)	0	0	...	0.00	1	1	0	0	0	3	2	1	0	2	5
2001— Toledo (I.L.)	2	1	.667	6.37	6	6	0	0	0	35⅓	50	27	25	12	22
— Detroit (A.L.)	2	2	.500	3.30	33	7	0	0	0	76⅓	62	33	28	49	52
Major League totals (1 year).........	2	2	.500	3.30	33	7	0	0	0	76⅓	62	33	28	49	52

SARDINHA, DANE   C   REDS

PERSONAL: Born April 8, 1979, in Kahuku, Hawaii. ... 5-11/205. ... Bats right, throws right.
COLLEGE: Pepperdine.
TRANSACTIONS/CAREER NOTES: Selected by Cincinnati Reds organization in second round of free-agent draft (June 5, 2000).

							BATTING								FIELDING		
Year Team (League)	Pos.	G	AB	R	H	2B	3B	HR	RBI	Avg.	BB	SO	SB	PO	A	E	Avg.
2001— Mudville (Calif.)	C	109	422	45	99	24	2	9	55	.235	12	97	0	962	*89	10	.991

SASAKI, KAZUHIRO   P   MARINERS

PERSONAL: Born February 22, 1968, in Sendai City, Japan. ... 6-4/209. ... Throws right, bats right.
COLLEGE: Tohoku Fukushi University (Sendai City, Japan).
TRANSACTIONS/CAREER NOTES: Signed as non-drafted free agent by Seattle Mariners (December 18, 1999).
RECORDS: Holds major league rookie-season record for most saves—37 (2000).
HONORS: Named A.L. Rookie Pitcher of the Year by THE SPORTING NEWS (2000). ... Named A.L. Rookie of the Year by Baseball Writers' Association of America (2000).

Year League	W	L	Pct.	ERA	G	GS	CG	ShO	Sv.	IP	H	R	ER	BB	SO
1990— Yokohama (Jap. Cen.)	2	4	.333	5.85	16	...	...	...	2	47²/₃	49	31	31	30	44
1991— Yokohama (Jap. Cen.)	6	9	.400	2.00	58	...	...	...	17	117	72	33	26	55	137
1992— Yokohama (Jap. Cen.)	12	6	.667	2.46	53	...	...	...	21	87²/₃	47	32	24	40	135
1993— Yokohama (Jap. Cen.)	3	6	.333	3.27	38	...	...	...	20	55	35	24	20	23	84
1994— Yokohama (Jap. Cen.)	3	1	.750	2.15	31	...	...	...	10	46	27	11	11	15	59
1995— Yokohama (Jap. Cen.)	7	2	.778	1.75	47	...	...	...	32	56²/₃	30	12	11	17	78
1996— Yokohama (Jap. Cen.)	4	3	.571	2.90	39	...	...	...	25	49²/₃	37	17	16	17	80
1997— Yokohama (Jap. Cen.)	3	0	1.000	0.90	49	...	...	...	38	60	25	6	6	18	99
1998— Yokohama (Jap. Cen.)	1	1	.500	0.64	51	...	...	...	45	56	32	7	4	14	78
1999— Yokohama (Jap. Cen.)	1	1	.500	1.93	23	...	...	...	19	23¹/₃	19	5	5	16	34
2000— Seattle (A.L.)■	2	5	.286	3.16	63	0	0	0	37	62²/₃	42	25	22	31	78
2001— Seattle (A.L.)	0	4	.000	3.24	69	0	0	0	45	66²/₃	48	24	24	11	62
Major League totals (2 years)	2	9	.182	3.20	132	0	0	0	82	129¹/₃	90	49	46	42	140

DIVISION SERIES RECORD

Year League	W	L	Pct.	ERA	G	GS	CG	ShO	Sv.	IP	H	R	ER	BB	SO
2000— Seattle (A.L.)	0	0	...	0.00	2	0	0	0	2	2	1	0	0	0	5
2001— Seattle (A.L.)	0	0	...	0.00	3	0	0	0	1	3	1	0	0	0	5
Division series totals (2 years)	0	0	...	0.00	5	0	0	0	3	5	2	0	0	0	10

CHAMPIONSHIP SERIES RECORD

Year League	W	L	Pct.	ERA	G	GS	CG	ShO	Sv.	IP	H	R	ER	BB	SO
2000— Seattle (A.L.)	0	0	...	0.00	2	0	0	0	1	2²/₃	3	0	0	1	3
2001— Seattle (A.L.)	0	1	.000	54.00	1	0	0	0	0	¹/₃	2	2	2	0	0
Champ. series totals (2 years)	0	1	.000	6.00	3	0	0	0	1	3	5	2	2	1	3

ALL-STAR GAME RECORD

Year League	W	L	Pct.	ERA	GS	CG	ShO	Sv.	IP	H	R	ER	BB	SO
2001— American	0	0	...	0.00	0	0	0	1	1	0	0	0	0	1

SATURRIA, LUIS   OF

PERSONAL: Born July 21, 1976, in San Pedro de Macoris, Dominican Republic. ... 6-2/165. ... Bats right, throws right. ... Full name: Luis Arturo Saturria. ... Name pronounced sah-TUR-E-ah.
TRANSACTIONS/CAREER NOTES: Signed as non-drafted free agent by St. Louis Cardinals organization (March 5, 1994). ... Selected by Toronto Blue Jays from Cardinals organization in Rule 5 major league draft (December 15, 1997). ... Returned to Cardinals (March 20, 1998). ... Granted free agency (December 21, 2001).
STATISTICAL NOTES: Tied for Carolina League lead with three double plays by outfielder in 1998. ... Led Texas League outfielders with 350 total chances in 2000. ... Tied for Texas League outfielders lead with three double plays in 2000. ... Led Pacific Coast League outfielders with 361 total chances in 2001.

							BATTING								FIELDING		
Year Team (League)	Pos.	G	AB	R	H	2B	3B	HR	RBI	Avg.	BB	SO	SB	PO	A	E	Avg.
1994— Dom. Cardinals (DSL)	OF	61	227	29	63	2	6	1	23	.278	25	49	16	118	13	8	.942
1995— Dom. Cardinals (DSL)	OF	66	245	48	78	16	7	2	33	.318	34	26	12	126	14	22	.864
1996— Johnson City (Appl.) ..	OF	57	227	43	58	7	1	5	40	.256	24	61	12	68	5	3	.961
1997— Peoria (Midw.)............	OF	122	445	81	122	19	5	11	51	.274	44	95	23	196	*24	9	.961
1998— Prince William (Caro.)	OF	129	462	70	136	25	9	12	73	.294	28	104	26	235	11	*15	.943
1999— Arkansas (Texas)........	OF	•139	484	66	118	30	4	16	61	.244	35	134	16	255	13	9	.968
2000— Arkansas (Texas)........	OF	129	478	78	131	25	10	20	76	.274	45	124	18	*338	9	3	.991
— St. Louis (N.L.)..........	OF	12	5	1	0	0	0	0	0	.000	1	3	1	3	0	0	1.000
2001— Memphis (PCL)..........	OF	119	413	63	93	16	5	13	49	.225	31	115	6	*344	7	10	.972
— St. Louis (N.L.)..........	OF	13	5	0	1	1	0	0	1	.200	0	1	1	2	0	0	1.000
— New Haven (East.)......	OF	8	29	5	8	3	0	0	4	.276	3	7	0	11	0	2	.846
Major League totals (2 years)		25	10	1	1	1	0	0	1	.100	1	4	1	5	0	0	1.000

SAUERBECK, SCOTT   P   PIRATES

PERSONAL: Born November 9, 1971, in Cincinnati. ... 6-3/197. ... Throws left, bats right. ... Full name: Scott William Sauerbeck.
HIGH SCHOOL: Northwest (Cincinnati).
COLLEGE: Miami of Ohio.

TRANSACTIONS/CAREER NOTES: Selected by New York Mets organization in 23rd round of free-agent draft (June 2, 1994). ... Selected by Pittsburgh Pirates from Mets organization in Rule 5 major league draft (December 14, 1998). ... On Pittsburgh disabled list (June 14-July 3, 2000); included rehabilitation assignment to Nashville (June 29-July 3).

Year League	W	L	Pct.	ERA	G	GS	CG	ShO	Sv.	IP	H	R	ER	BB	SO
1994—Pittsfield (NY-Penn)	3	1	.750	2.05	21	0	0	0	1	48 1/3	39	16	11	19	39
1995—St. Lucie (FSL)	0	1	.000	2.03	20	1	0	0	0	26 2/3	26	10	6	14	25
—Capital City (S.Atl.)	5	4	.556	3.27	19	0	0	0	2	33	28	14	12	14	33
1996—St. Lucie (FSL)	6	6	.500	2.27	17	16	2	•2	0	99 1/3	101	37	25	27	62
—Binghamton (East.)	3	3	.500	3.47	8	8	2	0	0	46 2/3	48	24	18	12	30
1997—Binghamton (East.)	8	9	.471	4.93	27	20	2	0	0	131 1/3	144	89	72	50	88
—Norfolk (I.L.)	1	0	1.000	3.60	1	1	0	0	0	5	3	2	2	4	4
1998—Norfolk (I.L.)	7	13	.350	3.93	27	27	2	0	0	160 1/3	178	82	70	69	119
1999—Pittsburgh (N.L.)■	4	1	.800	2.00	65	0	0	0	2	67 2/3	53	19	15	38	55
2000—Pittsburgh (N.L.)	5	4	.556	4.04	75	0	0	0	1	75 2/3	76	36	34	61	83
—Nashville (PCL)	0	0	...	0.00	2	0	0	0	0	2	1	0	0	0	0
2001—Pittsburgh (N.L.)	2	2	.500	5.60	70	0	0	0	2	62 2/3	61	41	39	40	79
Major League totals (3 years)	**11**	**7**	**.611**	**3.84**	**210**	**0**	**0**	**0**	**5**	**206**	**190**	**96**	**88**	**139**	**217**

SCANLAN, BOB   P

S

PERSONAL: Born August 9, 1966, in Beverly Hills, Calif. ... 6-8/215. ... Throws right, bats right. ... Full name: Robert Guy Scanlan Jr.
HIGH SCHOOL: Harvard (North Hollywood, Calif.).
TRANSACTIONS/CAREER NOTES: Selected by Philadelphia Phillies organization in 25th round of free-agent draft (June 4, 1984). ... Traded by Phillies with P Chuck McElroy to Chicago Cubs organization for P Mitch Williams (April 7, 1991). ... On suspended list (September 30-October 4, 1992; and September 17-20, 1993). ... Traded by Cubs to Milwaukee Brewers for P Rafael Novoa and OF Mike Carter (December 19, 1993). ... On Milwaukee disabled list (June 12-August 21, 1995); included rehabilitation assignment to New Orleans (August 4-21). ... Released by Brewers (December 18, 1995). ... Signed by Detroit Tigers organization (January 15, 1996). ... Claimed on waivers by Kansas City Royals organization (August 8, 1996). ... Released by Royals (March 26, 1997). ... Signed by San Diego Padres organization (May 29, 1997). ... Granted free agency (October 15, 1997). ... Signed by Houston Astros organization (December 22, 1997). ... Granted free agency (October 15, 1998). ... Re-signed by Astros organization (January 21, 1999). ... Granted free agency (October 15, 1999). ... Signed by Milwaukee Brewers organization (January 14, 2000). ... Granted free agency (October 13, 2000). ... Signed by Montreal Expos organization (December 21, 2000). ... Granted free agency (November 5, 2001).
STATISTICAL NOTES: Led International League with 17 wild pitches in 1988. ... Tied for Pacific Coast League lead with 12 hit batsmen in 1999.

Year League	W	L	Pct.	ERA	G	GS	CG	ShO	Sv.	IP	H	R	ER	BB	SO
1984—Gulf Coast Phillies (GCL)	0	2	.000	6.48	13	6	0	0	0	33 1/3	43	31	24	30	17
1985—Spartanburg (S.Atl.)	8	12	.400	4.14	26	25	4	0	0	152 1/3	160	95	70	53	108
1986—Clearwater (FSL)	8	12	.400	4.15	24	22	5	0	0	125 2/3	146	73	58	45	51
1987—Reading (East.)	*15	5	.750	5.10	27	26	3	1	0	164	187	98	93	55	91
1988—Maine (I.L.)	5	*18	.217	5.59	28	27	4	1	0	161	181	*110	*100	50	79
1989—Reading (East.)	6	10	.375	5.78	31	17	4	1	0	118 1/3	124	88	•76	58	63
1990—Scranton/W.B. (I.L.)	8	1	.889	4.85	23	23	1	0	0	130	128	79	70	59	74
1991—Iowa (A.A.)■	2	0	1.000	2.95	4	3	0	0	0	18 1/3	14	8	6	10	15
—Chicago (N.L.)	7	8	.467	3.89	40	13	0	0	1	111	114	60	48	40	44
1992—Chicago (N.L.)	3	6	.333	2.89	69	0	0	0	14	87 1/3	76	32	28	30	42
1993—Chicago (N.L.)	4	5	.444	4.54	70	0	0	0	0	75 1/3	79	41	38	28	44
1994—Milwaukee (A.L.)■	2	6	.250	4.11	30	12	0	0	2	103	117	53	47	28	65
1995—Milwaukee (A.L.)	4	7	.364	6.59	17	14	0	0	0	83 1/3	101	66	61	44	29
—New Orleans (A.A.)	0	1	.000	5.40	3	3	0	0	0	11 2/3	17	7	7	3	5
1996—Lakeland (FSL)■	0	1	.000	5.00	2	2	0	0	0	9	9	6	5	3	4
—Toledo (I.L.)	1	3	.250	7.50	14	5	0	0	0	36	46	35	30	15	18
—Detroit (A.L.)	0	0	...	10.64	8	0	0	0	0	11	16	15	13	9	3
—Omaha (A.A.)■	0	0	...	0.73	12	0	0	0	5	12 1/3	10	2	1	3	9
—Kansas City (A.L.)	0	1	.000	3.18	9	0	0	0	0	11 1/3	13	4	4	3	3
1997—Las Vegas (PCL)■	3	1	.750	3.53	36	1	0	0	1	51	51	24	20	17	20
1998—Houston (N.L.)■	0	1	.000	3.08	27	0	0	0	0	26 1/3	24	12	9	13	9
—New Orleans (PCL)	5	4	.556	6.46	14	12	1	0	0	61 1/3	90	50	44	24	35
1999—New Orleans (PCL)	8	*15	.348	5.61	28	•28	2	0	0	163 2/3	*208	116	•102	55	78
2000—Indianapolis (I.L.)■	2	2	.500	1.79	57	0	0	0	*35	60 1/3	42	16	12	18	23
—Milwaukee (N.L.)	0	0	...	27.00	2	0	0	0	0	1 2/3	6	6	5	0	1
2001—Ottawa (I.L.)■	0	5	.000	3.90	32	0	0	0	23	32 1/3	41	20	14	10	21
—Montreal (N.L.)	0	0	...	7.86	18	0	0	0	0	26 1/3	37	23	23	14	5
A.L. totals (3 years)	**6**	**14**	**.300**	**5.39**	**64**	**26**	**0**	**0**	**2**	**208 2/3**	**247**	**138**	**125**	**84**	**100**
N.L. totals (6 years)	**14**	**20**	**.412**	**4.14**	**226**	**13**	**0**	**0**	**15**	**328**	**336**	**174**	**151**	**125**	**145**
Major League totals (9 years)	**20**	**34**	**.370**	**4.63**	**290**	**39**	**0**	**0**	**17**	**536 2/3**	**583**	**312**	**276**	**209**	**245**

SCHILLING, CURT   P   DIAMONDBACKS

PERSONAL: Born November 14, 1966, in Anchorage, Alaska. ... 6-4/231. ... Throws right, bats right. ... Full name: Curtis Montague Schilling.
HIGH SCHOOL: Shadow Mountain (Phoenix).
JUNIOR COLLEGE: Yavapai College (Ariz.).
TRANSACTIONS/CAREER NOTES: Selected by Boston Red Sox organization in second round of free-agent draft (January 14, 1986). ... Traded by Red Sox with OF Brady Anderson to Baltimore Orioles for P Mike Boddicker (July 29, 1988). ... Traded by Orioles with P Pete Harnisch and OF Steve Finley to Houston Astros for 1B Glenn Davis (January 10, 1991). ... Traded by Astros to Philadelphia Phillies for P Jason Grimsley (April 2, 1992). ... On Philadelphia disabled list (May 17-July 25, 1994); included rehabilitation assignments to Scranton/Wilkes-Barre (July 10-15) and Reading (July 15-20). ... On disabled list (July 19, 1995-remainder of season). ... On Philadelphia disabled list (March 23-May 14, 1996); included rehabilitation assignments to Clearwater (April 23-May 3) and Scranton/Wilkes-Barre (May 3-14). ... On disabled list (August 8-September 3, 1999). ... On Philadelphia disabled list (March 25-April 30, 2000); included rehabilitation assignments to Clearwater (April 6-29) and Scranton/Wilkes-Barre (April 30). ... Traded by Phillies to Arizona Diamondbacks for OF Travis Lee, P Omar Daal, P Vicente Padilla and P Nelson Figueroa (July 26, 2000).

RECORDS: Holds N.L. single-season record for fewest complete games for leader—6 (2001). ... Holds N.L. single-season record for most strikeouts by righthander—319 (1997).
HONORS: Named N.L. Pitcher of the Year by THE SPORTING NEWS (2001). ... Named righthanded pitcher on THE SPORTING NEWS N.L. All-Star team (2001). ... Named Sportsman of the Year by THE SPORTING NEWS (2001).
STATISTICAL NOTES: Tied for International League lead with six balks in 1989. ... Pitched 2-1 one-hit, complete-game victory against New York (September 9, 1992). ... Struck out 15 batters in one game (July 21, 1997; and April 5, 1998). ... Struck out 16 batters in one game (September 1, 1997). ... Tied for N.L. lead with 37 home runs allowed in 2001.
MISCELLANEOUS: Struck out once in two appearances as pinch hitter with Philadelphia (1996).

Year	League	W	L	Pct.	ERA	G	GS	CG	ShO	Sv.	IP	H	R	ER	BB	SO
1986—	Elmira (NY-Penn)	7	3	.700	2.59	16	15	2	1	0	93²/₃	92	34	27	30	75
1987—	Greensboro (S.Atl.)	8	*15	.348	3.82	29	28	7	3	0	184	179	96	78	65	*189
1988—	New Britain (East.)	8	5	.615	2.97	21	17	4	1	0	106	91	44	35	40	62
	— Charlotte (Sou.)■	5	2	.714	3.18	7	7	2	1	0	45¹/₃	36	19	16	23	32
	— Baltimore (A.L.)	0	3	.000	9.82	4	4	0	0	0	14²/₃	22	19	16	10	4
1989—	Rochester (I.L.)	•13	11	.542	3.21	27	•27	•9	•3	0	*185¹/₃	176	76	66	59	109
	— Baltimore (A.L.)	0	1	.000	6.23	5	1	0	0	0	8²/₃	10	6	6	3	6
1990—	Rochester (I.L.)	4	4	.500	3.92	15	14	1	0	0	87¹/₃	95	46	38	25	83
	— Baltimore (A.L.)	1	2	.333	2.54	35	0	0	0	3	46	38	13	13	19	32
1991—	Houston (N.L.)■	3	5	.375	3.81	56	0	0	0	8	75²/₃	79	35	32	39	71
	— Tucson (PCL)	0	1	.000	3.42	13	0	0	0	3	23²/₃	16	9	9	12	21
1992—	Philadelphia (N.L.)■	14	11	.560	2.35	42	26	10	4	2	226¹/₃	165	67	59	59	147
1993—	Philadelphia (N.L.)	16	7	.696	4.02	34	34	7	2	0	235¹/₃	234	114	105	57	186
1994—	Philadelphia (N.L.)	2	8	.200	4.48	13	13	1	0	0	82¹/₃	87	42	41	28	58
	— Scranton/W.B. (I.L.)	0	0	...	1.80	2	2	0	0	0	10	6	2	2	5	6
	— Reading (East.)	0	0	...	0.00	1	1	0	0	0	4	6	0	0	1	4
1995—	Philadelphia (N.L.)	7	5	.583	3.57	17	17	1	0	0	116	96	52	46	26	114
1996—	Clearwater (FSL)	2	0	1.000	1.29	2	2	0	0	0	14	9	2	2	1	17
	— Scranton/W.B. (I.L.)	1	0	1.000	1.38	2	2	0	0	0	13	9	2	2	5	10
	— Philadelphia (N.L.)	9	10	.474	3.19	26	26	•8	2	0	183¹/₃	149	69	65	50	182
1997—	Philadelphia (N.L.)	17	11	.607	2.97	35	•35	7	2	0	254¹/₃	208	96	84	58	*319
1998—	Philadelphia (N.L.)	15	14	.517	3.25	35	•35	*15	2	0	*268²/₃	236	101	97	61	*300
1999—	Philadelphia (N.L.)	15	6	.714	3.54	24	24	8	1	0	180¹/₃	159	74	71	44	152
2000—	Clearwater (FSL)	1	0	1.000	1.31	4	4	0	0	0	20²/₃	10	3	3	2	23
	— Scranton/W.B. (I.L.)	0	0	...	3.60	1	1	0	0	0	5	9	2	2	1	7
	— Philadelphia (N.L.)	6	6	.500	3.91	16	16	4	1	0	112²/₃	110	49	49	32	96
	— Arizona (N.L.)■	5	6	.455	3.69	13	13	§4	1	0	97²/₃	94	41	40	13	72
2001—	Arizona (N.L.)	•22	6	.786	2.98	35	•35	*6	1	0	*256²/₃	237	86	85	39	293
A.L. totals (3 years)		1	6	.143	4.54	44	5	0	0	3	69¹/₃	70	38	35	32	42
N.L. totals (11 years)		131	95	.580	3.33	346	274	71	16	10	2089¹/₃	1854	826	774	506	1990
Major League totals (14 years)		132	101	.567	3.37	390	279	71	16	13	2158²/₃	1924	864	809	538	2032

DIVISION SERIES RECORD

RECORDS: Holds N.L. career record for most complete games—2. ... Shares career record for most shutouts—1.

Year	League	W	L	Pct.	ERA	G	GS	CG	ShO	Sv.	IP	H	R	ER	BB	SO
2001—	Arizona (N.L.)	2	0	1.000	0.50	2	2	2	1	0	18	9	1	1	2	18

CHAMPIONSHIP SERIES RECORD

RECORDS: Holds single-game records for most consecutive strikeouts—5; and most consecutive strikeouts from start of the game—5 (October 6, 1993).
NOTES: Named N.L. Championship Series Most Valuable Player (1993).

Year	League	W	L	Pct.	ERA	G	GS	CG	ShO	Sv.	IP	H	R	ER	BB	SO
1993—	Philadelphia (N.L.)	0	0	...	1.69	2	2	0	0	0	16	11	4	3	5	19
2001—	Arizona (N.L.)	1	0	1.000	1.00	1	1	1	0	0	9	4	1	1	2	12
Champ. series totals (2 years)		1	0	1.000	1.44	3	3	1	0	0	25	15	5	4	7	31

WORLD SERIES RECORD

NOTES: Named co-Most Valuable Player (2001). ... Member of World Series championship team (2001).

Year	League	W	L	Pct.	ERA	G	GS	CG	ShO	Sv.	IP	H	R	ER	BB	SO
1993—	Philadelphia (N.L.)	1	1	.500	3.52	2	2	1	1	0	15¹/₃	13	7	6	5	9
2001—	Arizona (N.L.)	1	0	1.000	1.69	3	3	0	0	0	21¹/₃	12	4	4	2	26
World Series totals (2 years)		2	1	.667	2.45	5	5	1	1	0	36²/₃	25	11	10	7	35

ALL-STAR GAME RECORD

Year	League	W	L	Pct.	ERA		GS	CG	ShO	Sv.	IP	H	R	ER	BB	SO
1997—	National	0	0	...	0.00		0	0	0	0	2	2	0	0	0	3
1998—	National						Did not play.									
1999—	National	0	1	.000	9.00		1	0	0	0	2	3	2	2	1	3
2001—	National						Selected, did not play.									
All-Star Game totals (2 years)		0	1	.000	4.50		1	0	0	0	4	5	2	2	1	6

SCHMIDT, JASON   P   GIANTS

PERSONAL: Born January 29, 1973, in Lewiston, Idaho. ... 6-5/220. ... Throws right, bats right. ... Full name: Jason David Schmidt.
HIGH SCHOOL: Kelso (Wash.).
TRANSACTIONS/CAREER NOTES: Selected by Atlanta Braves organization in eighth round of free-agent draft (June 3, 1991). ... On Atlanta disabled list (July 15-August 30, 1996); included rehabilitation assignment to Greenville (August 11-30). ... Traded by Braves to Pittsburgh Pirates (August 30, 1996), completing deal in which Pirates traded P Denny Neagle to Braves for a player to be named later (August 28, 1996). ... On Pittsburgh disabled list (April 15-May 1 and June 10, 2000-remainder of season); included rehabilitation assignment to Gulf Coast Pirates (July 29-August 23). ... On Pittsburgh disabled list (March 31-May 10, 2001); included rehabilitation assignments to Altoona (April 13-May 5) and Nashville (May 5-7). ... Traded by Pirates with OF John Vander Wal to San Francisco Giants for OF Armando Rios and P Ryan Vogelsong (July 30, 2001). ... Granted free agency (November 5, 2001). ... Re-signed by Giants (December 14, 2001).
RECORDS: Shares N.L. single-inning record for most consecutive home runs allowed—3 (August 22, 1999, first inning).
STATISTICAL NOTES: Led N.L. with 15 wild pitches in 1998. ... Tied for N.L. lead with four balks in 1999.
MISCELLANEOUS: Received base on balls in only appearance as pinch hitter with Atlanta (1995).

Year	League	W	L	Pct.	ERA	G	GS	CG	ShO	Sv.	IP	H	R	ER	BB	SO
1991— Gulf Coast Braves (GCL)		3	4	.429	2.38	11	11	0	0	0	45 1/3	32	21	12	23	44
1992— Pulaski (Appl.).................		3	4	.429	4.01	11	11	0	0	0	58 1/3	38	36	26	31	56
— Macon (S.Atl.)....................		0	3	.000	4.01	7	7	0	0	0	24 2/3	31	18	11	19	33
1993— Durham (Caro.)................		7	11	.389	4.94	22	22	0	0	0	116 2/3	128	69	64	47	110
1994— Greenville (Sou.)		8	7	.533	3.65	24	24	1	0	0	140 2/3	135	64	57	54	131
1995— Atlanta (N.L.)...................		2	2	.500	5.76	9	2	0	0	0	25	27	17	16	18	19
— Richmond (I.L.).................		8	6	.571	*2.25	19	19	0	0	0	116	97	40	29	48	95
1996— Atlanta (N.L.)...................		3	4	.429	6.75	13	11	0	0	0	58 2/3	69	48	44	32	48
— Richmond (I.L.).................		3	0	1.000	2.56	7	7	0	0	0	45 2/3	36	17	13	19	41
— Greenville (Sou.)		0	0	...	9.00	1	1	0	0	0	2	4	2	2	0	2
— Pittsburgh (N.L.)■..............		2	2	.500	4.06	6	6	1	0	0	37 2/3	39	19	17	21	26
1997— Pittsburgh (N.L.)..............		10	9	.526	4.60	32	32	2	0	0	187 2/3	193	106	96	76	136
1998— Pittsburgh (N.L.)..............		11	14	.440	4.07	33	33	0	0	0	214 1/3	228	106	97	71	158
1999— Pittsburgh (N.L.)..............		13	11	.542	4.19	33	33	2	0	0	212 2/3	219	110	99	85	148
2000— Pittsburgh (N.L.)		2	5	.286	5.40	11	11	0	0	0	63 1/3	71	43	38	41	51
— Gulf Coast Pirates (GCL)....		0	0	...	2.25	1	1	0	0	0	4	4	2	1	1	1
2001— Altoona (East.)		0	1	.000	0.96	3	3	0	0	0	9 1/3	7	1	1	1	17
— Nashville (PCL)		1	0	1.000	0.00	1	1	0	0	0	7	4	0	0	0	6
— Pittsburgh (N.L.)...............		6	6	.500	4.61	14	14	1	0	0	84	81	46	43	28	77
— San Francisco (N.L.)■.......		7	1	.875	3.39	11	11	0	0	0	66 1/3	57	29	25	33	65
Major League totals (7 years)		**56**	**54**	**.509**	**4.50**	**162**	**153**	**6**	**0**	**0**	**949 2/3**	**984**	**524**	**475**	**405**	**728**

S — SCHNEIDER, BRIAN — C — EXPOS

PERSONAL: Born November 26, 1976, in Jacksonville. ... 6-1/180. ... Bats left, throws right. ... Full name: Brian Duncan Schneider.
HIGH SCHOOL: Northampton (Pa.).
TRANSACTIONS/CAREER NOTES: Selected by Montreal Expos organization in fifth round of free-agent draft (June 1, 1995).
STATISTICAL NOTES: Led Eastern League catchers with 91 assists and .992 fielding percentage and tied for league lead with seven double plays by catcher in 1999. ... Tied for International League lead with nine sacrifice flies in 2000. ... Led International League catchers with 712 total chances in 2001.

Year	Team (League)	Pos.	G	AB	R	H	2B	3B	HR	RBI	Avg.	BB	SO	SB	PO	A	E	Avg.
1995— GC Expos (GCL)		C	30	97	7	22	3	0	0	4	.227	14	23	2	138	26	3	.982
1996— GC Expos (GCL)		C	52	144	26	44	5	2	0	23	.306	24	15	2	214	26	3	.988
— Delmarva (S.Atl.).......		C	5	9	0	3	0	0	0	1	.333	1	1	0	20	3	0	1.000
1997— Cape Fear (S.Atl.).......		C	113	381	46	96	20	1	4	49	.252	53	45	3	724	99	10	.988
1998— Cape Fear (S.Atl.)		C	38	134	33	40	7	2	7	30	.299	16	9	6	261	32	6	.980
— Jupiter (FSL)...........		C	82	302	32	82	12	1	3	30	.272	22	38	4	483	81	11	.981
1999— Harrisburg (East.).......		C-DH-1B	121	421	48	111	19	1	17	66	.264	32	56	2	622	†92	6	*.992
2000— Ottawa (I.L.)		C-1B	67	238	22	59	22	3	4	31	.248	16	42	1	391	52	8	.982
— Montreal (N.L.)...........		C	45	115	6	27	6	0	0	11	.235	7	24	0	205	19	6	.974
2001— Ottawa (I.L.)		C	97	338	33	93	27	1	6	43	.275	27	55	2	*629	*79	4	.994
— Montreal (N.L.)...........		C	27	41	4	13	3	0	1	6	.317	6	3	0	77	7	0	1.000
Major League totals (2 years)			**72**	**156**	**10**	**40**	**9**	**0**	**1**	**17**	**.256**	**13**	**27**	**0**	**282**	**26**	**6**	**.981**

SCHOENEWEIS, SCOTT — P — ANGELS

PERSONAL: Born October 2, 1973, in Long Branch, N.J. ... 6-0/186. ... Throws left, bats left. ... Full name: Scott David Schoeneweis.
HIGH SCHOOL: Lenape (Medford, N.J.).
COLLEGE: Duke.
TRANSACTIONS/CAREER NOTES: Selected by California Angels organization in third round of free-agent draft (June 4, 1996). ... Angels franchise renamed Anaheim Angels for 1997 season. ... On Anaheim disabled list (June 17-July 26, 2000); included rehabilitation assignments to Lake Elsinore (July 14-17) and Edmonton (July 18-24).

Year	League	W	L	Pct.	ERA	G	GS	CG	ShO	Sv.	IP	H	R	ER	BB	SO
1996— Lake Elsinore (Calif.)		8	3	.727	3.94	14	12	0	0	0	93 2/3	86	47	41	27	83
1997— Midland (Texas)................		7	5	.583	5.96	20	20	3	0	0	113 1/3	145	84	75	39	84
1998— Vancouver (PCL)		11	8	.579	4.50	27	27	2	0	0	180	188	102	90	59	133
1999— Anaheim (A.L.)		1	1	.500	5.49	31	0	0	0	0	39 1/3	47	27	24	14	22
— Edmonton (PCL)		2	4	.333	7.64	9	7	0	0	0	35 1/3	58	35	30	12	29
2000— Anaheim (A.L.)		7	10	.412	5.45	27	27	1	1	0	170	183	112	103	67	78
— Lake Elsinore (Calif.)		0	0	...	1.93	1	1	0	0	0	4 2/3	3	1	1	3	3
— Edmonton (PCL)		0	0	...	0.00	1	1	0	0	0	7	2	1	0	1	6
2001— Anaheim (A.L.)		10	11	.476	5.08	32	32	1	0	0	205 1/3	227	122	116	77	104
Major League totals (3 years)		**18**	**22**	**.450**	**5.27**	**90**	**59**	**2**	**1**	**0**	**414 2/3**	**457**	**261**	**243**	**158**	**204**

SCHOUREK, PETE — P — PHILLIES

PERSONAL: Born May 10, 1969, in Austin, Texas. ... 6-5/220. ... Throws left, bats left. ... Full name: Peter Alan Schourek. ... Name pronounced SHUR-ek.
HIGH SCHOOL: George C. Marshall (Falls Church, Va.).
TRANSACTIONS/CAREER NOTES: Selected by New York Mets organization in second round of free-agent draft (June 2, 1987). ... On disabled list (June 17, 1988-entire season). ... Claimed on waivers by Cincinnati Reds (April 7, 1994). ... On disabled list (June 1-22 and July 2, 1996-remainder of season). ... On disabled list (June 14-July 18 and July 31-September 2, 1997). ... Released by Reds (October 10, 1997). ... Signed by Houston Astros organization (January 9, 1998). ... On New Orleans disabled list (April 7-24, 1998). ... Traded by Astros to Boston Red Sox for cash (August 6, 1998). ... Granted free agency (October 23, 1998). ... Signed by Pittsburgh Pirates (December 18, 1998). ... On disabled list (August 17-September 1, 1999). ... Released by Pirates (March 29, 2000). ... Signed by Red Sox (April 2, 2000). ... On Boston disabled list (July 21-September 2 and September 20, 2000-remainder of season); included rehabilitation assignments to Pawtucket (August 22-28)

and Sarasota (August 28-September 2). ... Granted free agency (November 1, 2000). ... Re-signed by Red Sox organization (December 7, 2000). ... On disabled list (July 4-22, 2001). ... Released by Red Sox (August 3, 2001). ... Signed by Philadelphia Phillies organization (January 14, 2002).

HONORS: Named lefthanded pitcher on THE SPORTING NEWS N.L. All-Star team (1995).

STATISTICAL NOTES: Pitched 9-0 one-hit, complete-game victory for New York against Montreal (September 10, 1991).

MISCELLANEOUS: Appeared in one game as pinch runner with New York (1992). ... Struck out in only appearance as pinch hitter (1996). ... Appeared in one game as pinch runner (1997). ... Singled in only appearance as pinch hitter (2000).

Year — League	W	L	Pct.	ERA	G	GS	CG	ShO	Sv.	IP	H	R	ER	BB	SO
1987— Kingsport (Appl.)	4	5	.444	3.68	12	12	2	0	0	78 1/3	70	37	32	34	57
1988— Little Falls (NY-Penn)							Did not play.								
1989— Columbia (S.Atl.)	5	9	.357	2.85	27	19	5	1	1	136	120	66	43	66	131
— St. Lucie (FSL)	0	0	...	2.25	2	1	0	0	0	4	3	1	1	2	4
1990— St. Lucie (FSL)	4	1	.800	0.97	5	5	2	2	0	37	29	4	4	8	28
— Tidewater (I.L.)	1	0	1.000	2.57	2	2	1	1	0	14	9	4	4	5	14
— Jackson (Texas)	11	4	.733	3.04	19	19	1	0	0	124 1/3	109	53	42	39	94
1991— Tidewater (I.L.)	1	1	.500	2.52	4	4	0	0	0	25	18	7	7	10	17
— New York (N.L.)	5	4	.556	4.27	35	8	1	1	2	86 1/3	82	49	41	43	67
1992— Tidewater (I.L.)	2	5	.286	2.73	8	8	2	1	0	52 2/3	46	20	16	23	42
— New York (N.L.)	6	8	.429	3.64	22	21	0	0	0	136	137	60	55	44	60
1993— New York (N.L.)	5	12	.294	5.96	41	18	0	0	0	128 1/3	168	90	85	45	72
1994— Cincinnati (N.L.)■	7	2	.778	4.09	22	10	0	0	0	81 1/3	90	39	37	29	69
1995— Cincinnati (N.L.)	18	7	.720	3.22	29	29	2	0	0	190 1/3	158	72	68	45	160
1996— Cincinnati (N.L.)	4	5	.444	6.01	12	12	0	0	0	67 1/3	79	48	45	24	54
1997— Cincinnati (N.L.)	5	8	.385	5.42	18	17	0	0	0	84 2/3	78	59	51	38	59
1998— Kissimmee (FSL)■	0	0	...	1.08	2	1	0	0	0	8 1/3	8	1	1	4	9
— Houston (N.L.)	7	6	.538	4.50	15	15	0	0	0	80	82	43	40	36	59
— Boston (A.L.)■	1	3	.250	4.30	10	8	0	0	0	44	45	21	21	14	36
1999— Pittsburgh (N.L.)■	4	7	.364	5.34	30	17	0	0	0	113	128	75	67	49	94
2000— Boston (A.L.)■	3	10	.231	5.11	21	21	0	0	0	107 1/3	116	67	61	38	63
— Pawtucket (I.L.)	0	0	...	0.00	1	1	0	0	0	3	1	0	0	1	1
— Sarasota (FSL)	0	0	...	2.08	1	1	0	0	0	4 1/3	2	1	1	0	5
2001— Boston (A.L.)	1	5	.167	4.45	33	0	0	0	0	30 1/3	35	19	15	15	20
A.L. totals (3 years)	5	18	.217	4.81	64	29	0	0	0	181 2/3	196	107	97	67	119
N.L. totals (9 years)	61	59	.508	4.55	224	147	3	1	2	967 1/3	1002	535	489	353	694
Major League totals (11 years)	66	77	.462	4.59	288	176	3	1	2	1149	1198	642	586	420	813

DIVISION SERIES RECORD

Year — League	W	L	Pct.	ERA	G	GS	CG	ShO	Sv.	IP	H	R	ER	BB	SO
1995— Cincinnati (N.L.)	1	0	1.000	2.57	1	1	0	0	0	7	5	2	2	3	5
1998— Boston (A.L.)	0	0	...	0.00	1	1	0	0	0	5 1/3	2	0	0	4	1
Division series totals (2 years)	1	0	1.000	1.46	2	2	0	0	0	12 1/3	7	2	2	7	6

CHAMPIONSHIP SERIES RECORD

Year — League	W	L	Pct.	ERA	G	GS	CG	ShO	Sv.	IP	H	R	ER	BB	SO
1995— Cincinnati (N.L.)	0	1	.000	1.26	2	2	0	0	0	14 1/3	14	2	2	3	13

SEABOL, SCOTT — 3B — YANKEES

PERSONAL: Born May 17, 1975, in McKeesport, Pa. ... 6-4/200. ... Bats right, throws right. ... Full name: Scott Anthony Seabol.

HIGH SCHOOL: South Allegheny (Pa.).

COLLEGE: West Virginia.

TRANSACTIONS/CAREER NOTES: Selected by New York Yankees organization in 88th round of free-agent draft (June 4, 1996). ... On disabled list (August 27, 2000-remainder of season).

HONORS: Named South Atlantic League Most Valuable Player (1999).

STATISTICAL NOTES: Led South Atlantic League with 283 total bases and 11 sacrifice flies in 1999. ... Led South Atlantic League third basemen with 377 total chances in 1999.

							BATTING							FIELDING		
Year — Team (League)	Pos.	G	AB	R	H	2B	3B	HR	RBI	Avg.	BB	SO	SB	PO	A	E	Avg.
1996— Oneonta (NY-Penn)	1B-2B-SS-3B	43	142	16	30	9	1	3	10	.211	15	30	2	195	50	11	.957
1997— Greensboro (S.Atl.)	OF-3B-SS	48	136	11	36	12	2	2	15	.265	9	26	3	33	14	6	.887
1998— Greensboro (S.Atl.)	OF-3B-1B-C-P	71	210	24	60	11	0	7	33	.286	13	40	2	73	22	4	.960
1999— Greensboro (S.Atl.)	3B	138	543	86	171	*55	6	15	89	.315	45	91	6	79	*274	24	.936
2000— Norwich (East.)	3B-OF-1B-2B	132	493	82	146	*45	2	20	78	.296	42	108	2	164	146	22	.934
2001— New York (A.L.)	DH	1	1	0	0	0	0	0	0	.000	0	0	0	...	...	...	...
— Columbus (I.L.)	3B-OF-1B-SS	78	282	32	75	19	1	10	42	.266	14	56	3	125	98	13	.945
— Norwich (East.)	3B-1B-OF	31	128	16	32	7	0	4	19	.250	5	30	1	36	41	11	.875
Major League totals (1 year)		1	1	0	0	0	0	0	0	.000	0	0	0	...	...	...	...

RECORD AS PITCHER

Year — League	W	L	Pct.	ERA	G	GS	CG	ShO	Sv.	IP	H	R	ER	BB	SO
1988— Greensboro (S.Atl.)	0	0	...	4.50	1	0	0	0	0	2	3	1	1	0	1

SEANEZ, RUDY — P

PERSONAL: Born October 20, 1968, in Brawley, Calif. ... 5-11/205. ... Throws right, bats right. ... Full name: Rudy Caballero Seanez. ... Name pronounced see-AHN-yez.

HIGH SCHOOL: Brawley (Calif.) Union.

TRANSACTIONS/CAREER NOTES: Selected by Cleveland Indians organization in fourth round of free-agent draft (June 10, 1986). ... On disabled list (May 4-July 11 and August 9-29, 1987). ... On Cleveland disabled list (April 1-16 and July 30-September 2, 1991); included rehabilitation assignment to Colorado Springs (August 14-September 2). ... Traded by Indians to Los Angeles Dodgers for P Dennis Cook and P

Mike Christopher (December 10, 1991). ... On disabled list (March 29, 1992-entire season). ... Traded by Dodgers to Colorado Rockies for 2B Jody Reed (November 17, 1992). ... On Colorado disabled list (April 4-July 16, 1993); included rehabilitation assignments to Central Valley (June 16-July 4) and Colorado Springs (July 4-15). ... Granted free agency (July 16, 1993). ... Signed by San Diego Padres organization (July 22, 1993). ... Released by Padres (November 18, 1993). ... Signed by Dodgers organization (January 12, 1994). ... On Los Angeles disabled list (May 28-June 16, 1995); included rehabilitation assignment to San Bernardino (June 9-16). ... Granted free agency (October 15, 1996). ... Signed by New York Mets organization (January 15, 1997). ... Traded by Mets to Kansas City Royals for future considerations (May 30, 1997). ... Granted free agency (October 15, 1997). ... Signed by Atlanta Braves organization (December 9, 1997). ... On disabled list (August 21, 1999-remainder of season). ... Granted free agency (November 2, 1999). ... Re-signed by Braves (December 12, 1999). ... On Atlanta disabled list (March 23-April 27, 2000 and June 14-remainder of season); included rehabilitation assignment to Greenville (April 22-27). ... Granted free agency (October 30, 2000). ... Signed by Padres organization (February 14, 2001). ... On Portland disabled list (April 5-May 6, 2001). ... On San Diego disabled list (June 6-21, 2001). ... Traded by Padres to Braves for a player to be named later (August 31, 2001); Padres acquired P Winston Abreu to complete deal (September 6, 2001). ... Granted free agency (November 5, 2001).

STATISTICAL NOTES: Pitched 4-0 no-hit victory against Pulaski (August 2, 1986).

Year	League	W	L	Pct.	ERA	G	GS	CG	ShO	Sv.	IP	H	R	ER	BB	SO
1986—	Burlington (Appl.)	5	2	.714	3.20	13	12	1	1	0	76	59	37	27	32	56
1987—	Waterloo (Midw.)	0	4	.000	6.75	10	10	0	0	0	34²/₃	35	29	26	23	23
1988—	Waterloo (Midw.)	6	6	.500	4.69	22	22	1	1	0	113¹/₃	98	69	59	68	93
1989—	Kinston (Caro.)	8	10	.444	4.14	25	25	1	0	0	113	94	66	52	*111	149
	—Colorado Springs (PCL)	0	0	...	0.00	1	0	0	0	0	1	1	0	0	0	0
	—Cleveland (A.L.)	0	0	...	3.60	5	0	0	0	0	5	1	2	2	4	7
1990—	Canton/Akron (East.)	1	0	1.000	2.16	15	0	0	0	5	16²/₃	9	4	4	12	27
	—Cleveland (A.L.)	2	1	.667	5.60	24	0	0	0	0	27¹/₃	22	17	17	25	24
	—Colorado Springs (PCL)	1	4	.200	6.75	12	0	0	0	1	12	15	10	9	10	7
1991—	Colorado Springs (PCL)	0	0	...	7.27	16	0	0	0	0	17¹/₃	17	14	14	22	19
	—Canton/Akron (East.)	4	2	.667	2.58	25	0	0	0	7	38¹/₃	17	12	11	30	73
	—Cleveland (A.L.)	0	0	...	16.20	5	0	0	0	0	5	10	12	9	7	7
1992—	Los Angeles (N.L.)■							Did not play.								
1993—	Central Valley (Calif.)■	0	2	.000	9.72	5	1	0	0	0	8¹/₃	9	9	9	11	7
	—Colorado Springs (PCL)	0	0	...	9.00	3	0	0	0	0	3	3	3	3	1	5
	—Las Vegas (PCL)■	0	1	.000	6.41	14	0	0	0	0	19²/₃	24	15	14	11	14
	—San Diego (N.L.)	0	0	...	13.50	3	0	0	0	0	3¹/₃	8	6	5	2	1
1994—	Albuquerque (PCL)■	2	1	.667	5.32	20	0	0	0	9	22	28	14	13	13	26
	—Los Angeles (N.L.)	1	1	.500	2.66	17	0	0	0	0	23²/₃	24	7	7	9	18
1995—	Los Angeles (N.L.)	1	3	.250	6.75	37	0	0	0	3	34²/₃	39	27	26	18	29
	—San Bernardino (Calif.)	2	0	1.000	0.00	4	0	0	0	1	6	2	0	0	3	5
1996—	Albuquerque (PCL)	0	2	.000	6.52	21	0	0	0	6	19¹/₃	27	18	14	11	20
1997—	Norfolk (I.L.)■	1	0	1.000	4.05	9	0	0	0	0	13¹/₃	12	8	6	11	17
	—Omaha (A.A.)■	2	5	.286	6.51	28	3	0	0	0	47	53	42	34	25	46
1998—	Richmond (I.L.)■	2	0	1.000	1.29	16	0	0	0	7	21	13	9	3	7	33
	—Atlanta (N.L.)	4	1	.800	2.75	34	0	0	0	2	36	25	13	11	16	50
1999—	Atlanta (N.L.)	6	1	.857	3.35	56	0	0	0	3	53²/₃	47	21	20	21	41
2000—	Greenville (Sou.)	0	0	...	0.00	2	1	0	0	0	2	2	0	0	0	3
	—Atlanta (N.L.)	2	4	.333	4.29	23	0	0	0	2	21	15	11	10	9	20
2001—	Lake Elsinore (Calif.)■	2	0	1.000	2.08	7	0	0	0	0	8²/₃	7	3	2	2	8
	—San Diego (N.L.)	0	2	.000	2.63	26	0	0	0	1	24	15	8	7	15	24
	—Atlanta (N.L.)■	0	0	...	3.00	12	0	0	0	0	12	8	4	4	4	17
A.L. totals (3 years)		2	1	.667	6.75	34	0	0	0	0	37¹/₃	33	31	28	36	38
N.L. totals (7 years)		14	12	.538	3.89	208	0	0	0	11	208¹/₃	181	97	90	94	200
Major League totals (10 years)		16	13	.552	4.32	242	0	0	0	11	245²/₃	214	128	118	130	238

DIVISION SERIES RECORD

Year	League	W	L	Pct.	ERA	G	GS	CG	ShO	Sv.	IP	H	R	ER	BB	SO
1998—	Atlanta (N.L.)	0	0	...	0.00	1	0	0	0	0	1	0	0	0	0	0
2001—	Atlanta (N.L.)	1	0	1.000	0.00	1	0	0	0	0	1	0	0	0	1	0
Division series totals (2 years)		1	0	1.000	0.00	2	0	0	0	0	2	0	0	0	1	0

CHAMPIONSHIP SERIES RECORD

Year	League	W	L	Pct.	ERA	G	GS	CG	ShO	Sv.	IP	H	R	ER	BB	SO
1998—	Atlanta (N.L.)	0	0	...	6.00	4	0	0	0	0	3	2	2	2	1	4
2001—	Atlanta (N.L.)	0	0	...	0.00	2	0	0	0	0	2	1	0	0	3	3
Champ. series totals (2 years)		0	0	...	3.60	6	0	0	0	0	5	3	2	2	4	7

SEARS, TODD   1B   TWINS

PERSONAL: Born October 23, 1975, in Des Moines, Iowa. ... 6-1/185. ... Bats right, throws right. ... Full name: Todd A. Sears.
HIGH SCHOOL: Ankeny (Iowa).
COLLEGE: Nebraska.
TRANSACTIONS/CAREER NOTES: Selected by California Angels organization in 19th round of free-agent draft (June 2, 1994); did not sign. ... Selected by Colorado Rockies organization in third round of free-agent draft (June 3, 1997). ... Traded by Rockies with cash to Minnesota Twins for 2B Todd Walker and OF Butch Huskey (July 16, 2000).
STATISTICAL NOTES: Led Pacific Coast League first basemen with .993 fielding percentage in 2001.

							BATTING								FIELDING		
Year	Team (League)	Pos.	G	AB	R	H	2B	3B	HR	RBI	Avg.	BB	SO	SB	PO	A	E	Avg.
1997—	Portland (N'West)	1B	55	200	37	54	13	1	2	29	.270	41	49	2	509	23	6	.989
1998—	Asheville (S.Atl.)	3B	130	459	71	133	26	2	11	82	.290	72	89	10	49	197	•31	.888
1999—	Salem (Caro.)	1B-3B	109	385	58	108	21	0	14	59	.281	58	99	11	422	69	26	.950
2000—	Carolina (Sou.)	1B	86	299	54	90	21	0	12	72	.301	72	76	12	634	30	12	.982
	—New Britain (East.)■	1B	40	140	15	44	8	1	3	15	.314	18	40	1	275	18	2	.993
	—Salt Lake (PCL)	1B	3	11	2	4	1	0	1	4	.364	1	2	0	32	1	0	1.000
2001—	Edmonton (PCL)	1B-3B	118	408	61	127	25	2	13	50	.311	41	71	2	842	69	6	†.993

SEAY, BOBBY — P — DEVIL RAYS

PERSONAL: Born June 20, 1978, in Sarasota, Fla. ... 6-2/221. ... Throws left, bats left. ... Full name: Robery Michael Seay.
HIGH SCHOOL: Sarasota (Fla.).
TRANSACTIONS/CAREER NOTES: Selected by Chicago White Sox organization in first round (12th pick overall) of free-agent draft (June 4, 1996). ... Rights relinquished by White Sox (August 15, 1996). ... Signed by Tampa Bay Devil Rays organization (November 8, 1996). ... On disabled list (June 9, 1997-remainder of season). ... On Orlando disabled list (May 8-June 30, 2001).
MISCELLANEOUS: Member of 2000 U.S. Olympic baseball team.

Year League	W	L	Pct.	ERA	G	GS	CG	ShO	Sv.	IP	H	R	ER	BB	SO
1997—Charleston, S.C. (S.Atl.)	3	4	.429	4.55	13	13	0	0	0	61 1/3	56	35	31	37	64
1998—Charleston, S.C. (S.Atl.)	1	7	.125	4.30	15	15	0	0	0	69	59	40	33	29	74
1999—St. Petersburg (FSL)	2	6	.250	3.00	12	11	0	0	0	57	56	25	19	23	45
—Orlando (Sou.)	1	2	.333	7.94	6	6	0	0	0	17	22	15	15	15	16
2000—Orlando (Sou.)	8	7	.533	3.88	24	24	0	0	0	132 1/3	132	64	57	53	106
2001—Orlando (Sou.)	2	5	.286	5.98	15	13	0	0	0	64 2/3	81	48	43	26	49
—Tampa Bay (A.L.)	1	1	.500	6.23	12	0	0	0	0	13	13	11	9	5	12
Major League totals (1 year)	1	1	.500	6.23	12	0	0	0	0	13	13	11	9	5	12

SEELBACH, CHRIS — P — BRAVES

PERSONAL: Born December 18, 1972, in Lufkin, Texas. ... 6-4/180. ... Throws right, bats right. ... Full name: Christopher Don Seelbach.
HIGH SCHOOL: Lufkin (Texas).
TRANSACTIONS/CAREER NOTES: Selected by Atlanta Braves organization in fourth round of free-agent draft (June 3, 1991). ... Traded by Braves to Florida Marlins (September 15, 1995), completing deal in which Braves acquired P Alejandro Pena for a player to be named later (August 31, 1995). ... Granted free agency (October 17, 1997). ... Signed by Seattle Mariners (January 20, 1998). ... Granted free agency (October 15, 1998). ... Signed by Braves organization (November 19, 1998). ... On Richmond disabled list (April 8-May 18, 1999). ... Granted free agency (October 15, 1999). ... Re-signed by Braves organization (October 28, 1999). ... On Richmond disabled list (August 15-31, 2000). ... Granted free agency (October 8, 2001).
STATISTICAL NOTES: Led International League with 26 home runs allowed in 1996.

Year League	W	L	Pct.	ERA	G	GS	CG	ShO	Sv.	IP	H	R	ER	BB	SO
1991—Gulf Coast Braves (GCL)	0	1	.000	4.20	4	4	0	0	0	15	13	7	7	6	19
1992—Macon (S.Atl.)	9	11	.450	3.20	27	27	1	0	0	157 1/3	134	65	56	68	144
1993—Durham (Caro.)	9	9	.500	4.93	25	25	0	0	0	131 1/3	133	85	72	74	112
1994—Greenville (Sou.)	4	6	.400	2.33	15	15	2	0	0	92 2/3	64	26	24	38	79
—Richmond (I.L.)	3	5	.375	4.84	12	11	0	0	0	61 1/3	68	37	33	36	35
1995—Richmond (I.L.)	4	6	.400	4.66	14	14	1	0	0	73 1/3	64	39	38	39	65
—Greenville (Sou.)	6	0	1.000	1.64	9	9	1	1	0	60 1/3	38	15	11	30	65
1996—Charlotte (I.L.)■	6	*13	.316	7.35	25	25	1	0	0	138 1/3	167	*123	*113	76	98
1997—Charlotte (I.L.)	5	0	1.000	6.26	16	6	0	0	0	50 1/3	58	36	35	34	50
1998—Orlando (Sou.)■	8	3	.727	4.03	23	21	0	0	0	116	103	63	52	52	106
—Tacoma (PCL)	1	0	1.000	6.17	6	0	0	0	0	11 2/3	13	9	8	2	10
1999—Richmond (I.L.)■	6	1	.857	5.15	13	8	1	0	0	57 2/3	51	34	33	34	48
—Greenville (Sou.)	3	2	.600	3.89	8	6	1	0	0	39 1/3	31	18	17	19	47
2000—Richmond (I.L.)	5	9	.357	4.78	29	22	1	1	2	118 2/3	118	71	63	55	96
—Atlanta (N.L.)	0	1	.000	10.80	2	0	0	0	0	1 2/3	3	2	2	0	1
2001—Atlanta (N.L.)	0	0	...	7.88	5	0	0	0	0	8	9	7	7	5	8
—Richmond (I.L.)	7	7	.500	5.09	22	14	0	0	1	88 1/3	85	50	50	36	82
Major League totals (2 years)	0	1	.000	8.38	7	0	0	0	0	9 2/3	12	9	9	5	9

SEFCIK, KEVIN — OF — DEVIL RAYS

PERSONAL: Born February 10, 1971, in Oak Lawn, Ill. ... 5-10/182. ... Bats right, throws right. ... Full name: Kevin John Sefcik.
HIGH SCHOOL: Victor Andrews (Tinley Park, Ill.).
COLLEGE: St. Xavier (Ill.).
TRANSACTIONS/CAREER NOTES: Selected by Philadelphia Phillies organization in 33rd round of free-agent draft (June 3, 1993). ... Granted free agency (November 20, 2000). ... Signed by Colorado Rockies organization (January 11, 2001). ... Released by Rockies (June 6, 2001). ... Signed by Cleveland Indians organization (June 9, 2001). ... Granted free agency (October 15, 2001). ... Signed by Tampa Bay Devil Rays organization (January 24, 2002).
STATISTICAL NOTES: Led New York-Pennsylvania League second basemen with 212 assists and 359 total chances in 1993.

						BATTING									FIELDING		
Year Team (League)	Pos.	G	AB	R	H	2B	3B	HR	RBI	Avg.	BB	SO	SB	PO	A	E	Avg.
1993—Batavia (NY-Penn)	2B-3B	74	281	49	84	24	4	2	28	.299	27	22	20	136	†216	16	.957
1994—Clearwater (FSL)	3B-2B	130	516	83	147	29	8	2	46	.285	49	43	30	91	293	21	.948
1995—Scranton/W.B. (I.L.)	2B	7	26	5	9	6	1	0	6	.346	3	1	0	13	16	0	1.000
—Reading (East.)	SS-3B-DH	128	508	68	138	18	4	4	46	.272	38	48	14	166	349	18	.966
—Philadelphia (N.L.)	3B	5	4	1	0	0	0	0	0	.000	0	2	0	0	1	0	1.000
1996—Philadelphia (N.L.)	SS-3B-2B	44	116	10	33	5	3	0	9	.284	9	16	3	30	83	7	.942
—Scranton/W.B. (I.L.)	SS-2B-3B	45	180	34	60	7	5	0	19	.333	15	20	11	63	143	10	.954
1997—Philadelphia (N.L.)	2B-SS-3B	61	119	11	32	3	0	2	6	.269	4	9	1	39	62	4	.962
—Scranton/W.B. (I.L.)	2B-3B-OF	29	123	19	41	11	2	1	7	.333	9	11	5	51	56	6	.947
1998—Philadelphia (N.L.)	O-3-DH-2	104	169	27	53	7	2	3	20	.314	25	32	4	89	1	2	.978
1999—Philadelphia (N.L.)	OF-2B	111	209	28	58	15	3	1	11	.278	29	24	9	93	18	2	.982
2000—Philadelphia (N.L.)	OF-DH	99	153	15	36	6	2	0	10	.235	13	19	4	74	0	0	1.000
2001—Colo. Springs (PCL)■	OF-2B-3B	49	199	37	62	14	0	2	22	.312	24	26	5	86	31	7	.944
—Colorado (N.L.)	PH	1	1	0	0	0	0	0	0	.000	0	0	0	...	...	...	...
—Buffalo (I.L.)■	2B-OF-3B	70	233	30	46	10	2	5	24	.197	18	20	4	108	135	5	.980
Major League totals (7 years)		425	771	92	212	36	10	6	56	.275	80	102	21	325	165	15	.970

PERSONAL: Born July 19, 1966, in Kansas City, Kan. ... 6-1/202. ... Bats both, throws left. ... Full name: David Vincent Segui. ... Son of Diego Segui, pitcher with five major league teams (1962-75 and 1977); and brother of Dan Segui, minor league infielder (1987-90). ... Name pronounced seh-GHEE.

HIGH SCHOOL: Bishop Ward (Kansas City, Kan.).

JUNIOR COLLEGE: Kansas City Kansas Community College.

COLLEGE: Louisiana Tech.

TRANSACTIONS/CAREER NOTES: Selected by Baltimore Orioles organization in 18th round of free-agent draft (June 2, 1987). ... On Rochester disabled list (April 19-26, 1991). ... On suspended list (August 16-19, 1993). ... Traded by Orioles to New York Mets for SS Kevin Baez and P Tom Wegmann (March 27, 1994). ... On disabled list (June 20-July 5, 1994). ... Traded by Mets to Montreal Expos for P Reid Cornelius (June 8, 1995). ... On disabled list (July 4-August 16, 1996). ... On disabled list (June 4-21, 1997). ... On suspended list (July 26, 1997). ... Granted free agency (October 28, 1997). ... Signed by Seattle Mariners (December 12, 1997). ... Traded by Mariners to Toronto Blue Jays for P Tom Davey and P Steve Sinclair (July 28, 1999). ... On suspended list (July 30-31, 1999). ... On Toronto disabled list (August 8-September 2, 1999). ... Granted free agency (October 29, 1999). ... Re-signed by Blue Jays (January 18, 2000). ... Traded by Blue Jays with cash to Texas Rangers as part of three-way deal in which Rangers sent 1B Lee Stevens to Montreal Expos and Expos sent 1B Brad Fullmer to Blue Jays (March 16, 2000). ... Traded by Rangers to Cleveland Indians for OF Ricky Ledee (July 28, 2000). ... Granted free agency (October 30, 2000). ... Signed by Orioles (December 21, 2000). ... On disabled list (April 28-May 15 and July 16-August 4, 2001).

STATISTICAL NOTES: Led N.L. first basemen with .996 fielding percentage in 1994. ... Switch-hit home runs in one game (April 1, 1998). ... Led A.L. first basemen with .999 fielding percentage in 1998. ... Had 15-game hitting streak (May 10-29, 1999). ... Career major league grand slams: 6.

Year	Team (League)	Pos.	G	AB	R	H	2B	3B	HR	RBI	Avg.	BB	SO	SB	PO	A	E	Avg.
1988—	Hagerstown (Caro.)....	1B-OF	60	190	35	51	12	4	3	31	.268	22	23	0	342	25	9	.976
1989—	Frederick (Caro.)........	1B	83	284	43	90	19	0	10	50	.317	41	32	2	707	47	4	.995
	—Hagerstown (East.)......	1B	44	173	22	56	14	1	1	27	.324	16	16	0	381	30	1	.998
1990—	Rochester (I.L.).........	1B-OF	86	307	55	103	28	0	2	51	.336	45	28	5	704	62	3	.996
	—Baltimore (A.L.)......	1B-DH	40	123	14	30	7	0	2	15	.244	11	15	0	283	26	3	.990
1991—	Rochester (I.L.).........	1B-OF	28	96	9	26	2	0	1	10	.271	15	6	1	165	15	0	1.000
	—Baltimore (A.L.)......	OF-1B-DH	86	212	15	59	7	0	2	22	.278	12	19	1	264	23	3	.990
1992—	Baltimore (A.L.).........	1B-OF	115	189	21	44	9	0	1	17	.233	20	23	1	406	35	1	.998
1993—	Baltimore (A.L.).........	1B-DH	146	450	54	123	27	0	10	60	.273	58	53	2	1152	98	5	.996
1994—	New York (N.L.).■....	1B-OF	92	336	46	81	17	1	10	43	.241	33	43	0	695	52	5	†.993
1995—	New York (N.L.).........	OF-1B	33	73	9	24	3	1	2	11	.329	12	9	1	56	5	0	1.000
	—Montreal (N.L.)■........	1B-OF	97	383	59	117	22	3	10	57	.305	28	38	1	840	70	3	.997
1996—	Montreal (N.L.).........	1B	115	416	69	119	30	1	11	58	.286	60	54	4	944	90	7	.993
1997—	Montreal (N.L.).........	1B	125	459	75	141	22	3	21	68	.307	57	66	1	1035	88	6	.995
1998—	Seattle (A.L.)■.........	1B-OF	143	522	79	159	36	1	19	84	.305	49	80	3	1045	116	1	†.999
1999—	Seattle (A.L.).........	1B	90	345	43	101	22	3	9	39	.293	32	43	1	700	61	3	.996
	—Toronto (A.L.)■........	DH-1B	31	95	14	30	5	0	5	13	.316	8	17	0	19	2	1	.955
2000—	Texas (A.L.)■....	DH-1B	93	351	52	118	29	1	11	57	.336	34	51	0	295	28	0	1.000
	—Cleveland (A.L.)■.......	1B-DH-OF	57	223	41	74	13	0	8	46	.332	19	33	0	267	33	0	1.000
2001—	Baltimore (A.L.)■........	1B-DH	82	292	48	88	18	1	10	46	.301	49	61	1	487	33	9	.983
American League totals (8 years)			883	2802	381	826	173	6	77	399	.295	292	395	9	4918	455	26	.995
National League totals (4 years)			462	1667	258	482	94	9	54	237	.289	190	210	7	3570	305	21	.995
Major League totals (12 years)			1345	4469	639	1308	267	15	131	636	.293	482	605	16	8488	760	47	.995

PERSONAL: Born January 19, 1975, in Bocas del Toro, Panama. ... 6-5/230. ... Bats both, throws right. ... Full name: Fernando Alfredo Seguignol.

HIGH SCHOOL: Almirante de Bocas del Toro (Bocas del Toro, Panama).

TRANSACTIONS/CAREER NOTES: Signed as non-drafted free agent by New York Yankees organization (January 29, 1993). ... Traded by Yankees with and cash to Montreal Expos for P John Wetteland (April 5, 1995). ... On Harrisburg disabled list (June 24-July 17, 1998). ... On Montreal disabled list (July 11-September 7, 1999); included rehabilitation assignment to Ottawa (August 9-September 7). ... On Ottawa disabled list (May 1-12, 2000). ... Granted free agency (October 8, 2001).

STATISTICAL NOTES: Led Florida State League with 14 sacrifice flies in 1997. ... Tied for Florida State League lead in assists by first basemen with 91 in 1997.

Year	Team (League)	Pos.	G	AB	R	H	2B	3B	HR	RBI	Avg.	BB	SO	SB	PO	A	E	Avg.
1993—	GC Yankees (GCL)......	OF-1B	45	161	16	35	3	3	2	20	.217	9	37	2	86	8	2	.979
1994—	Oneonta (NY-Penn)	OF	73	266	36	77	14	*9	2	32	.289	16	61	4	77	3	4	.952
1995—	Albany (S.Atl.)■........	OF	121	457	59	95	22	2	12	66	.208	28	141	12	205	7	8	.964
1996—	Delmarva (S.Atl.)........	OF	118	410	59	98	14	5	8	55	.239	48	126	12	173	4	4	.978
1997—	W.P. Beach (FSL)........	1B-OF	124	456	70	116	27	5	18	83	.254	30	129	5	967	‡91	15	.986
1998—	Harrisburg (East.)........	1B-OF	80	281	54	81	13	0	25	69	.288	29	77	6	503	50	9	.984
	—Ottawa (I.L.)...........	OF-1B	32	109	16	28	8	0	6	16	.257	12	43	0	44	2	1	.979
	—Montreal (N.L.)..........	OF-1B	16	42	6	11	4	0	2	3	.262	3	15	0	65	5	0	1.000
1999—	Ottawa (I.L.)...........	1B-DH-OF	87	312	54	89	17	3	23	74	.285	40	96	3	397	40	10	.978
	—Montreal (N.L.)..........	1B-OF	35	105	14	27	9	0	5	10	.257	5	33	0	183	11	2	.990
2000—	Ottawa (I.L.)...........	1B-OF	41	141	20	39	16	0	8	31	.277	13	26	1	213	23	5	.979
	—Montreal (N.L.)..........	OF-1B-DH	76	162	22	45	8	0	10	22	.278	9	46	0	161	12	5	.972
2001—	Montreal (N.L.)..........	OF-1B	46	50	0	7	2	0	0	5	.140	2	17	0	28	4	2	.941
	—Ottawa (I.L.)...........	1B-OF	60	242	36	75	12	0	14	45	.310	15	49	0	457	37	4	.992
Major League totals (4 years)			173	359	42	90	23	0	17	40	.251	19	111	0	437	32	9	.981

PERSONAL: Born June 11, 1970, in Monroeville, Ala. ... 5-9/190. ... Bats left, throws right. ... Full name: William Frank Selby.
HIGH SCHOOL: Horn Lake (Mich.).
JUNIOR COLLEGE: Northwest Mississippi Community College.
COLLEGE: Southern Mississippi.
TRANSACTIONS/CAREER NOTES: Selected by Boston Red Sox organization in 13th round of free-agent draft (June 1, 1992). ... Granted free agency (October 16, 1998). ... Signed by Cleveland Indians organization (February 3, 1999). ... Granted free agency (October 15, 1999). ... Re-signed by Indians organization (December 23, 1999). ... Released by Indians (October 20, 2000). ... Signed by Cincinnati Reds organization (May 29, 2001). ... On Louisville disabled list (August 28, 2001-remainder of season). ... Granted free agency (October 15, 2001). ... Signed by Indians organization (December 18, 2001).
STATISTICAL NOTES: Led New York-Pennsylvania League with six intentional bases on balls received in 1992.

| | | | | | | | | — BATTING — | | | | — FIELDING — | | | |
Year	Team (League)	Pos.	G	AB	R	H	2B	3B	HR	RBI	Avg.	BB	SO	SB	PO	A	E	Avg.
1992—	Elmira (NY-Penn)	3B-2B	73	275	38	72	16	1	10	41	.262	31	53	4	75	138	16	.930
1993—	Lynchburg (Caro.)	3B-1B	113	394	57	99	22	1	7	38	.251	24	66	1	66	99	8	.954
1994—	Lynchburg (Caro.)	3B-2B-1B	97	352	58	109	20	2	19	69	.310	28	62	3	96	185	23	.924
	— New Britain (East.)	3B	35	107	15	28	5	0	1	18	.262	15	16	0	23	57	6	.930
1995—	Trenton (East.)	3B-2B-DH	117	451	64	129	29	2	13	68	.286	46	52	4	119	206	29	.918
1996—	Pawtucket (I.L.)	2B-3B-OF	71	260	39	66	14	5	11	47	.254	22	39	—	95	140	16	.936
	— Boston (A.L.)	2B-3B-OF	40	95	12	26	4	0	3	6	.274	9	11	1	30	43	4	.948
1997—	Yokohama (Jap. Cen.)		...	171	19	39	4	1	5	17	.228	...	...	3	...	...	...	...
1998—	Buffalo (I.L.)■	3B-OF-2B	97	334	45	85	23	0	14	52	.254	38	50	3	45	74	4	.967
	— Akron (East.)	OF-3B-2B	20	77	15	30	7	1	3	10	.390	3	11	—	32	10	1	.977
1999—	Buffalo (I.L.)	3B-OF-2B	122	447	75	132	32	5	20	85	.295	57	63	4	65	80	5	.967
2000—	Buffalo (I.L.)	3B-OF-2B	100	384	69	106	21	6	21	86	.276	48	61	1	108	172	15	.949
	— Cleveland (A.L.)	OF-DH-2B-3B	30	46	8	11	1	0	0	4	.239	1	9	0	19	3	0	1.000
2001—	Louisville (I.L.)■	2B-1B-3B-OF	88	330	47	85	19	1	14	56	.258	25	47	1	250	144	10	.975
	— Cincinnati (N.L.)	2B-3B-1B	36	92	7	21	7	1	2	12	.228	5	13	0	46	57	2	.981
American League totals (2 years)			70	141	20	37	5	0	3	10	.262	10	20	1	49	46	4	.960
National League totals (1 year)			36	92	7	21	7	1	2	12	.228	5	13	0	46	57	2	.981
Major League totals (3 years)			106	233	27	58	12	1	5	22	.249	15	33	1	95	103	6	.971

S

PERSONAL: Born June 25, 1970, in Golden Valley, Minn. ... 6-5/215. ... Throws right, bats right. ... Full name: Aaron Helmer Sele. ... Name pronounced SEE-lee.
HIGH SCHOOL: North Kitsap (Poulsbo, Wash.).
COLLEGE: Washington State.
TRANSACTIONS/CAREER NOTES: Selected by Minnesota Twins organization in 37th round of free-agent draft (June 1, 1988); did not sign. ... Selected by Boston Red Sox organization in first round (23rd pick overall) of free-agent draft (June 3, 1991). ... On Boston disabled list (May 24, 1995-remainder of season); included rehabilitation assignments to Trenton (June 19-22), Sarasota (July 10-21 and August 7-16) and Pawtucket (August 16-23). ... On Boston disabled list (August 14-September 1, 1996); included rehabilitation assignment to Pawtucket (August 26-27). ... Traded by Red Sox with P Mark Brandenburg and C Bill Haselman to Texas Rangers for C Jim Leyritz and OF Damon Buford (November 6, 1997). ... Granted free agency (November 5, 1999). ... Signed by Seattle Mariners (January 10, 2000). ... Granted free agency (November 5, 2001). ... Signed by Anaheim Angels (December 26, 2001).
HONORS: Named A.L. Rookie Pitcher of the Year by THE SPORTING NEWS (1993). ... Named International League Most Valuable Pitcher (1993).
STATISTICAL NOTES: Led Carolina League with 14 hit batsmen in 1992. ... Tied for A.L. lead with nine hit batsmen in 1994.

Year	League	W	L	Pct.	ERA	G	GS	CG	ShO	Sv.	IP	H	R	ER	BB	SO
1991—	Winter Haven (FSL)	3	6	.333	4.96	13	11	4	0	1	69	65	42	38	32	51
1992—	Lynchburg (Caro.)	13	5	.722	2.91	20	19	2	1	0	127	104	51	41	46	112
	— New Britain (East.)	2	1	.667	6.27	7	6	1	0	0	33	43	29	23	15	29
1993—	Pawtucket (I.L.)	8	2	.800	2.19	14	14	2	1	0	94 1/3	74	30	23	23	87
	— Boston (A.L.)	7	2	.778	2.74	18	18	0	0	0	111 2/3	100	42	34	48	93
1994—	Boston (A.L.)	8	7	.533	3.83	22	22	2	0	0	143 1/3	140	68	61	60	105
1995—	Boston (A.L.)	3	1	.750	3.06	6	6	0	0	0	32 1/3	32	14	11	14	21
	— Trenton (East.)	0	1	.000	3.38	2	2	0	0	0	8	8	3	3	2	9
	— Sarasota (FSL)	0	0	...	0.00	2	2	0	0	0	7	6	0	0	1	8
	— Pawtucket (I.L.)	0	0	...	9.00	2	2	0	0	0	5	9	5	5	2	1
1996—	Boston (A.L.)	7	11	.389	5.32	29	29	1	0	0	157 1/3	192	110	93	67	137
	— Pawtucket (I.L.)	0	0	...	6.00	1	1	0	0	0	3	3	2	2	1	4
1997—	Boston (A.L.)	13	12	.520	5.38	33	33	1	0	0	177 1/3	196	115	106	80	122
1998—	Texas (A.L.)■	19	11	.633	4.23	33	33	3	2	0	212 2/3	239	116	100	84	167
1999—	Texas (A.L.)	18	9	.667	4.79	33	33	2	2	0	205	244	115	109	70	186
2000—	Seattle (A.L.)■	17	10	.630	4.51	34	34	2	2	0	211 2/3	221	110	106	74	137
2001—	Seattle (A.L.)	15	5	.750	3.60	34	33	2	1	0	215	216	93	86	51	114
Major League totals (9 years)		107	68	.611	4.33	242	241	13	7	0	1466 1/3	1580	783	706	548	1082

DIVISION SERIES RECORD

RECORDS: Shares A.L. career record for most losses—3.

Year	League	W	L	Pct.	ERA	G	GS	CG	ShO	Sv.	IP	H	R	ER	BB	SO
1998—	Texas (A.L.)	0	1	.000	6.00	1	1	0	0	0	6	8	4	4	1	4
1999—	Texas (A.L.)	0	1	.000	5.40	1	1	0	0	0	5	6	4	3	5	3
2000—	Seattle (A.L.)	0	0	...	1.23	1	1	0	0	0	7 1/3	3	1	1	3	1
2001—	Seattle (A.L.)	0	1	.000	9.00	1	1	0	0	0	2	5	4	2	0	0
Division series totals (4 years)		0	3	.000	4.43	4	4	0	0	0	20 1/3	22	13	10	9	8

CHAMPIONSHIP SERIES RECORD

Year	League	W	L	Pct.	ERA	G	GS	CG	ShO	Sv.	IP	H	R	ER	BB	SO
2000—	Seattle (A.L.)	0	1	.000	6.00	1	1	0	0	0	6	9	4	4	0	4
2001—	Seattle (A.L.)	0	2	.000	3.60	2	2	0	0	0	10	11	8	4	4	5
Champ. series totals (2 years)		0	3	.000	4.50	3	3	0	0	0	16	20	12	8	4	9

ALL-STAR GAME RECORD

Year	League	W	L	Pct.	ERA	GS	CG	ShO	Sv.	IP	H	R	ER	BB	SO
1998—	American				Did not play.										
2000—	American	0	0	...	0.00	0	0	0	0	1	1	0	0	0	0

PERSONAL: Born May 24, 1977, in Kwanju, South Korea. ... 6-1/215. ... Throws right, bats right. ... Full name: Jae Weong Seo.
HIGH SCHOOL: First (Kwanju, South Korea).
COLLEGE: Inha University (South Korea).
TRANSACTIONS/CAREER NOTES: Signed as non-drafted free agent by New York Mets organization (December 17, 1997). ... On Binghamton disabled list (May 4, 1999-remainder of season). ... On disabled list (April 6, 2000-entire season).

Year	League	W	L	Pct.	ERA	G	GS	CG	ShO	Sv.	IP	H	R	ER	BB	SO
1998—	St. Lucie (FSL)	3	1	.750	2.27	8	7	0	0	0	35 2/3	26	13	9	10	37
—	Gulf Coast Mets (GCL)	0	0	...	0.00	2	0	0	0	0	5	4	0	0	0	0
1999—	St. Lucie (FSL)	2	0	1.000	1.84	3	3	0	0	0	14 2/3	8	3	3	2	14
2000—	St. Lucie (FSL)							Did not play.								
2001—	Binghamton (East.)	5	1	.833	1.94	12	10	0	0	0	60 1/3	44	14	13	11	47
—	St. Lucie (FSL)	2	3	.400	3.55	6	5	0	0	0	25 1/3	21	11	10	6	19
—	Norfolk (I.L.)	2	2	.500	3.42	9	9	0	0	0	47 1/3	53	18	18	6	25

PERSONAL: Born June 2, 1978, in Santo Domingo, Dominican Republic. ... 6-2/178. ... Throws right, bats right. ... Full name: Wascar Radames Serrano.
HIGH SCHOOL: Las Carreres (Dominican Republic).
TRANSACTIONS/CAREER NOTES: Signed as non-drafted free agent by San Diego Padres organization (May 31, 1995). ... On Mobile disabled list (July 30-August 28, 2000). ... Traded by Padres for with C Ben Davis and SS Alex Arias to Seattle Mariners for P Brett Tomko, C Tom Lampkin and SS Ramon Vazquez (December 11, 2001).
STATISTICAL NOTES: Tied for California League lead with five balks in 1999.

Year	League	W	L	Pct.	ERA	G	GS	CG	ShO	Sv.	IP	H	R	ER	BB	SO
1995—	Dominican Padres (DSL)	3	3	.500	3.11	12	7	0	0	0	46 1/3	63	24	16	15	23
1996—	Dominican Padres (DSL)	3	7	.300	7.88	22	2	0	0	1	53 2/3	77	58	47	24	44
1997—	Idaho Falls (Pio.)	0	1	.000	11.88	2	2	0	0	0	8 1/3	13	12	11	4	13
—	Arizona Padres (Ariz.)	•6	3	.667	3.18	12	11	0	0	1	70 2/3	60	43	25	22	75
—	Clinton (Midw.)	0	1	.000	6.00	1	1	1	0	0	6	6	5	4	2	2
1998—	Clinton (Midw.)	9	7	.563	3.22	26	26	0	0	0	156 2/3	150	74	56	54	143
1999—	Rancho Cuca. (Calif.)	9	8	.529	3.33	21	21	1	1	0	132 1/3	110	58	49	43	129
—	Mobile (Sou.)	2	3	.400	5.53	7	7	0	0	0	42 1/3	48	27	26	17	29
2000—	Mobile (Sou.)	9	4	.692	2.80	20	20	1	0	0	112 1/3	93	42	35	42	112
—	Las Vegas (PCL)	0	1	.000	14.18	4	4	0	0	0	13 1/3	24	23	21	10	19
2001—	Portland (PCL)	6	5	.545	4.53	27	13	0	0	0	93 1/3	98	50	47	35	73
—	San Diego (N.L.)	3	3	.500	6.56	20	5	0	0	0	46 2/3	60	37	34	21	39
Major League totals (1 year)		3	3	.500	6.56	20	5	0	0	0	46 2/3	60	37	34	21	39

PERSONAL: Born June 4, 1967, in La Crosse, Wis. ... 6-2/210. ... Bats right, throws right. ... Full name: Scott Daniel Servais. ... Name pronounced SER-viss.
HIGH SCHOOL: Westby (Wis.).
COLLEGE: Creighton.
TRANSACTIONS/CAREER NOTES: Selected by New York Mets organization in second round of free-agent draft (June 3, 1985); did not sign. ... Selected by Houston Astros organization in third round of free-agent draft (June 1, 1988). ... On Tucson disabled list (June 29-July 1, 1991). ... On Houston disabled list (August 4-September 7, 1991). ... Traded by Astros with OF Luis Gonzalez to Chicago Cubs for C Rick Wilkins (June 28, 1995). ... On Chicago disabled list (July 10-August 3, 1995). ... Granted free agency (October 23, 1998). ... Signed by San Francisco Giants (January 17, 1999). ... On San Francisco disabled list (June 17-July 9, 1999); included rehabilitation assignment to Fresno (July 4-9). ... Granted free agency (October 29, 1999). ... Signed by Colorado Rockies organization (December 17, 1999). ... On Colorado disabled list (April 18-May 3 and July 9-August 22, 2000); included rehabilitation assignments to Colorado Springs (April 28-May 3 and July 26-August 16). ... Claimed on waivers by Giants (August 31, 2000). ... Granted free agency (October 31, 2000). ... Signed by Detroit Tigers organization (January 16, 2001). ... Released by Tigers (March 23, 2001). ... Signed by Astros organization (March 28, 2001). ... On Houston disabled list (August 17-September 1, 2001). ... Granted free agency (November 5, 2001). ... Signed by Giants (January 16, 2002).
STATISTICAL NOTES: Tied for Pacific Coast League lead in double plays by catcher with nine in 1990. ... Led N.L. catchers with 12 errors in 1995.
MISCELLANEOUS: Member of 1988 U.S. Olympic baseball team.

Year	Team (League)	Pos.	G	AB	R	H	2B	3B	HR	RBI	Avg.	BB	SO	SB	PO	A	E	Avg.
							BATTING									FIELDING		
1989—	Osceola (FSL)	C-1B	46	153	16	41	9	0	2	23	.268	16	35	0	168	24	4	.980
—	Columbus (Sou.)	C	63	199	20	47	5	0	1	24	.236	19	42	0	330	45	3	.992
1990—	Tucson (PCL)	C	89	303	37	66	11	3	5	37	.218	18	61	0	453	63	9	.983
1991—	Tucson (PCL)	C	60	219	34	71	12	0	2	27	.324	13	19	0	350	33	6	.985
—	Houston (N.L.)	C	16	37	0	6	3	0	0	6	.162	4	8	0	77	4	1	.988
1992—	Houston (N.L.)	C	77	205	12	49	9	0	0	15	.239	11	25	0	386	27	2	.995
1993—	Houston (N.L.)	C	85	258	24	63	11	0	11	32	.244	22	45	0	493	40	2	.996
1994—	Houston (N.L.)	C	78	251	27	49	15	1	9	41	.195	10	44	0	481	29	2	.996
1995—	Houston (N.L.)	C	28	89	7	20	10	0	1	12	.225	9	15	0	198	17	5	.977
—	Chicago (N.L.)■	C	52	175	31	50	12	0	12	35	.286	23	37	2	328	33	§7	.981
1996—	Chicago (N.L.)	C-1B	129	445	42	118	20	0	11	63	.265	30	75	0	798	73	11	.988
1997—	Chicago (N.L.)	C-DH-1B	122	385	36	100	21	0	6	45	.260	24	56	0	736	73	8	.990
1998—	Chicago (N.L.)	C-1B	113	325	35	72	15	1	7	36	.222	26	51	1	654	48	4	.994
1999—	San Fran. (N.L.)■	C-1B	69	198	21	54	10	0	5	21	.273	13	31	0	363	23	3	.992
—	Fresno (PCL)	C	3	11	3	3	1	1	0	2	.273	0	1	0	23	1	0	1.000
2000—	Colo. (N.L.)■	C	33	101	6	22	4	0	1	13	.218	7	16	0	204	17	3	.987
—	Colo. Springs (PCL)	C	20	65	7	19	2	1	3	12	.292	4	8	0	80	8	1	.989
—	San Fran. (N.L.)■	C	7	8	1	2	0	0	0	0	.250	2	1	0	18	0	0	1.000
2001—	New Orleans (PCL)■	C	44	148	22	50	10	1	6	31	.338	12	21	0	288	34	1	.997
—	Houston (N.L.)	C	11	16	1	6	0	0	0	0	.375	2	3	0	38	1	0	1.000
Major League totals (11 years)			820	2493	243	611	130	2	63	319	.245	183	407	3	4774	385	48	.991

DIVISION SERIES RECORD

					BATTING								FIELDING			
Year	Team (League)	Pos.	G	AB	R	H	2B	3B	HR	RBI	Avg.	BB	SO	SB	PO	A	E	Avg.
1998— Chicago (N.L.)...........	C	1	3	0	2	0	0	0	0	.667	0	0	0	6	1	0	1.000
2000— San Francisco (N.L.)..						Did not play.										

SEXSON, RICHIE   1B   BREWERS

PERSONAL: Born December 29, 1974, in Portland. ... 6-8/215. ... Bats right, throws right. ... Full name: Richmond Lockwood Sexson.

HIGH SCHOOL: Prairie (Brush Prairie, Wash.).

TRANSACTIONS/CAREER NOTES: Selected by Cleveland Indians organization in 24th round of free-agent draft (June 2, 1993). ... Traded by Indians with P Paul Rigdon, P Kane Davis and a player to be named later to Milwaukee Brewers for P Bob Wickman, P Steve Woodard and P Jason Bere (July 28, 2000); Brewers acquired 2B Marcos Scutaro to complete deal (August 30).

RECORDS: Shares major league single-month record for most home runs—5 (October 2001). ... Shares major league single-game record for most strikeouts (nine-inning game)—5 (May 29, 2001).

STATISTICAL NOTES: Led Carolina League with 251 total bases in 1995. ... Led Carolina League first basemen with 1,226 total chances and 109 double plays in 1995. ... Led American Association first basemen with 1,003 total chances and 105 double plays in 1997. ... Hit three home runs in one game (September 25, 2001). ... Career major league grand slams: 4.

					BATTING								FIELDING			
Year	Team (League)	Pos.	G	AB	R	H	2B	3B	HR	RBI	Avg.	BB	SO	SB	PO	A	E	Avg.
1993— Burlington (Appl.).......	1B	40	97	11	18	3	0	1	5	.186	18	21	1	309	15	4	.988
1994— Columbus (S.Atl.).......	1B	130	488	88	133	25	2	14	77	.273	37	87	7	933	*63	10	*.990
1995— Kinston (Caro.)...........	1B	131	494	80	*151	*34	0	22	*85	.306	43	115	4	*1135	*79	12	.990
1996— Canton/Akron (East.)..	1B	133	518	85	143	33	3	16	76	.276	39	118	2	892	76	11	.989
1997— Buffalo (A.A.).............	1B-DH	115	434	57	113	20	2	*31	88	.260	27	87	5	*922	*77	4	*.996
— Cleveland (A.L.)......	1B-DH	5	11	1	3	0	0	0	0	.273	0	2	0	11	1	0	1.000
1998— Buffalo (I.L.)..............	OF-1B-DH	89	344	58	102	20	1	21	74	.297	50	68	1	270	29	3	.990
— Cleveland (A.L.)........	1B-OF-DH	49	174	28	54	14	1	11	35	.310	6	42	1	325	38	6	.984
1999— Cleveland (A.L.)........	1B-OF-DH	134	479	72	122	17	7	31	116	.255	34	117	3	583	54	7	.989
2000— Cleveland (A.L.)........	OF-1B-DH	91	324	45	83	16	1	16	44	.256	25	96	1	277	28	1	.997
— Milwaukee (N.L.)■......	1B	57	213	44	63	14	0	14	47	.296	34	63	1	470	66	5	.991
2001— Milwaukee (N.L.).......	1B	158	598	94	162	24	3	45	125	.271	60	178	2	1356	129	8	.995
American League totals (4 years)		279	988	146	262	47	9	58	195	.265	65	257	5	1196	121	14	.989
National League totals (2 years)		215	811	138	225	38	3	59	172	.277	94	241	3	1826	195	13	.994
Major League totals (5 years)		494	1799	284	487	85	12	117	367	.271	159	498	8	3022	316	27	.992

DIVISION SERIES RECORD

					BATTING								FIELDING			
Year	Team (League)	Pos.	G	AB	R	H	2B	3B	HR	RBI	Avg.	BB	SO	SB	PO	A	E	Avg.
1998— Cleveland (A.L.)..........	1B	3	2	0	0	0	0	0	0	.000	2	1	0	12	1	0	1.000
1999— Cleveland (A.L.)..........	PH-1B-OF	3	6	1	1	0	0	0	1	.167	1	3	0	1	0	0	1.000
Division series totals (2 years)		6	8	1	1	0	0	0	1	.125	3	4	0	13	1	0	1.000

CHAMPIONSHIP SERIES RECORD

					BATTING								FIELDING			
Year	Team (League)	Pos.	G	AB	R	H	2B	3B	HR	RBI	Avg.	BB	SO	SB	PO	A	E	Avg.
1998— Cleveland (A.L.)..........	1B	3	6	0	0	0	0	0	0	.000	0	3	0	20	3	0	1.000

SHAW, JEFF   P

PERSONAL: Born July 7, 1966, in Washington Court House, Ohio. ... 6-2/200. ... Throws right, bats right. ... Full name: Jeffrey Lee Shaw.

HIGH SCHOOL: Washington (Washington Court House, Ohio).

JUNIOR COLLEGE: Cuyahoga Community College-Western Campus (Ohio).

COLLEGE: Rio Grande (Ohio) College.

TRANSACTIONS/CAREER NOTES: Selected by Cleveland Indians organization in first round (first pick overall) of free-agent draft (January 14, 1986). ... Granted free agency (October 16, 1992). ... Signed by Kansas City Royals organization (November 9, 1992). ... Traded by Royals with C Tim Spehr to Montreal Expos for P Mark Gardner and P Doug Piatt (December 9, 1992). ... Granted free agency (February 17, 1995). ... Re-signed by Expos organization (April 9, 1995). ... Traded by Expos to Chicago White Sox for P Jose DeLeon (August 28, 1995). ... Granted free agency (December 21, 1995). ... Signed by Cincinnati Reds (January 2, 1996). ... Traded by Reds to Los Angeles Dodgers for 1B/3B Paul Konerko and P Dennis Reyes (July 4, 1998). ... On disabled list (June 27-July 13, 2000). ... Granted free agency (November 9, 2001).

HONORS: Named N.L. Fireman of the Year by THE SPORTING NEWS (1997).

STATISTICAL NOTES: Led Eastern League with 14 hit batsmen in 1989. ... Tied for Pacific Coast League lead with 10 hit batsmen in 1992.

MISCELLANEOUS: Holds Los Angeles Dodgers all-time record for most saves (129).

Year	League	W	L	Pct.	ERA	G	GS	CG	ShO	Sv.	IP	H	R	ER	BB	SO
1986— Batavia (NY-Penn).............	8	4	.667	2.44	14	12	3	1	0	88²/₃	79	32	24	35	71
1987— Waterloo (Midw.)	11	11	.500	3.52	28	*28	6	*4	0	184¹/₃	192	89	72	56	117
1988— Williamsport (East.)	5	*19	.208	3.63	27	•27	6	1	0	163²/₃	•173	*94	66	75	61
1989— Canton/Akron (East.).........	7	10	.412	3.62	30	22	6	3	0	154¹/₃	134	84	62	67	95
1990— Colorado Springs (PCL)	10	3	.769	4.29	17	16	4	0	0	98²/₃	98	54	47	52	55
— Cleveland (A.L.).................	3	4	.429	6.66	12	9	0	0	0	48²/₃	73	38	36	20	25
1991— Colorado Springs (PCL)	6	3	.667	4.64	12	12	1	0	0	75²/₃	77	47	39	25	55
— Cleveland (A.L.).................	0	5	.000	3.36	29	1	0	0	1	72¹/₃	72	34	27	27	31
1992— Colorado Springs (PCL)	10	5	.667	4.76	25	24	1	0	0	155	174	88	82	45	84
— Cleveland (A.L.).................	0	1	.000	8.22	2	1	0	0	0	7²/₃	7	7	7	4	3
1993— Ottawa (I.L.)■..................	0	0	...	0.00	2	1	0	0	0	4	5	0	0	2	1
— Montreal (N.L.).................	2	7	.222	4.14	55	8	0	0	0	95²/₃	91	47	44	32	50
1994— Montreal (N.L.).................	5	2	.714	3.88	46	0	0	0	1	67¹/₃	67	32	29	15	47
1995— Montreal (N.L.).................	1	6	.143	4.62	50	0	0	0	3	62¹/₃	58	35	32	26	45
— Chicago (A.L.)■.................	0	0	...	6.52	9	0	0	0	0	9²/₃	12	7	7	1	6

Year League	W	L	Pct.	ERA	G	GS	CG	ShO	Sv.	IP	H	R	ER	BB	SO
1996— Cincinnati (N.L.)■■	8	6	.571	2.49	78	0	0	0	4	104 2/3	99	34	29	29	69
1997— Cincinnati (N.L.)	4	2	.667	2.38	78	0	0	0	*42	94 2/3	79	26	25	12	74
1998— Cincinnati (N.L.)	2	4	.333	1.81	39	0	0	0	23	49 2/3	40	11	10	12	29
— Los Angeles (N.L.)■	1	4	.200	2.55	34	0	0	0	25	35 1/3	35	11	10	7	26
1999— Los Angeles (N.L.)	2	4	.333	2.78	64	0	0	0	34	68	64	25	21	15	43
2000— Los Angeles (N.L.)	3	4	.429	4.24	60	0	0	0	27	57 1/3	61	29	27	16	39
2001— Los Angeles (N.L.)	3	5	.375	3.62	77	0	0	0	43	74 2/3	63	32	30	18	58
A.L. totals (4 years)	3	10	.231	5.01	52	11	0	0	1	138 1/3	164	86	77	52	65
N.L. totals (9 years)	31	44	.413	3.26	581	8	0	0	202	709 2/3	657	282	257	182	480
Major League totals (12 years)	34	54	.386	3.54	633	19	0	0	203	848	821	368	334	234	545

ALL-STAR GAME RECORD

Year League	W	L	Pct.	ERA	GS	CG	ShO	Sv.	IP	H	R	ER	BB	SO
1998— National	0	0	...	9.00	0	0	0	0	1	3	1	1	0	0
2001— National	0	0	...	0.00	0	0	0	0	1/3	1	0	0	0	0
All-Star Game totals (2 years)	0	0	...	6.75	0	0	0	0	1 1/3	4	1	1	0	0

SHEARN, TOM   P   ASTROS

PERSONAL: Born August 28, 1977, in Columbus, Ohio. ... 6-4/200. ... Throws right, bats right. ... Full name: Thomas Aaron Shearn.
HIGH SCHOOL: Briggs (Columbus, Ohio).
TRANSACTIONS/CAREER NOTES: Selected by Houston Astros organization in 29th round of free-agent draft (June 4, 1996).

Year League	W	L	Pct.	ERA	G	GS	CG	ShO	Sv.	IP	H	R	ER	BB	SO
1996— Gulf Coast Astros (GCL)	5	2	.714	1.73	17	3	0	0	0	41 2/3	34	13	8	10	43
1997— Auburn (NY-Penn)	4	6	.400	3.50	14	14	2	•2	0	82 1/3	79	42	32	26	59
1998— Quad City (Midw.)	7	7	.500	2.25	21	21	2	1	0	120	88	38	30	52	93
1999— Kissimmee (FSL)	10	6	.625	3.90	24	24	0	0	0	145 1/3	144	75	63	53	107
2000— Round Rock (Texas)	9	6	.600	4.69	25	23	0	0	0	136 1/3	134	79	71	67	102
2001— Round Rock (Texas)	5	6	.455	3.85	43	8	0	0	1	110	94	54	47	51	136

SHEETS, ANDY   2B/SS

PERSONAL: Born November 19, 1971, in Baton Rouge, La. ... 6-2/180. ... Bats right, throws right. ... Full name: Andrew Mark Sheets.
HIGH SCHOOL: St. Amant (La.).
COLLEGE: Tulane, then Louisiana State.
TRANSACTIONS/CAREER NOTES: Selected by Seattle Mariners organization in fourth round of free-agent draft (June 1, 1992). ... Selected by Tampa Bay Devil Rays in first round (24th pick overall) of expansion draft (November 18, 1997). ... Traded by Devil Rays with P Brian Boehringer to San Diego Padres for C John Flaherty (November 18, 1997). ... Traded by Padres with OF Gus Kennedy to Anaheim Angels for C Phil Nevin and P Keith Volkman (March 29, 1999). ... Granted free agency (December 21, 1999). ... Signed by Red Sox organization (January 23, 2000). ... Granted free agency (October 13, 2000). ... Signed by Devil Rays organization (November 15, 2000). ... Granted free agency (October 9, 2001).
STATISTICAL NOTES: Led Pacific Coast League shortstops with .973 fielding percentage in 1997. ... Career major league grand slams: 1.

							BATTING							FIELDING		
Year Team (League)	Pos.	G	AB	R	H	2B	3B	HR	RBI	Avg.	BB	SO	SB	PO	A	E	Avg.
1993— Riverside (Calif.)	SS	52	176	23	34	9	1	1	12	.193	17	51	2	80	159	17	.934
— Appleton (Midw.)	SS-2B-OF	69	259	32	68	10	4	1	25	.263	20	59	7	98	194	11	.964
1994— Riverside (Calif.)	SS	31	100	17	27	5	1	2	10	.270	16	22	6	39	95	14	.905
— Jacksonville (Sou.)	SS	70	232	26	51	12	0	0	17	.220	20	54	3	105	205	17	.948
— Calgary (PCL)	SS	26	93	22	32	8	1	2	16	.344	11	20	1	32	80	2	.982
1995— Tacoma (PCL)	SS	132	437	57	128	29	9	2	47	.293	32	83	8	157	382	27	.952
1996— Tacoma (PCL)	SS-2B-3B	62	232	44	83	16	5	5	33	.358	25	56	6	95	176	14	.951
— Seattle (A.L.)	3B-2B-SS	47	110	18	21	8	0	0	9	.191	10	41	2	40	77	5	.959
1997— Tacoma (PCL)	SS	113	401	57	104	23	0	14	53	.259	46	97	7	174	314	13	†.974
— Seattle (A.L.)	3B-SS-2B	32	89	18	22	3	0	4	9	.247	7	34	2	14	62	8	.905
1998— San Diego (N.L.)■	SS-3B-2B-1B	88	194	31	47	5	3	7	29	.242	21	62	7	96	145	9	.964
1999— Anaheim (A.L.)■	SS-2B-3B	113	244	22	48	10	0	3	29	.197	14	59	1	113	182	12	.961
— Edmonton (PCL)	SS-2B	12	45	6	13	1	1	0	4	.289	2	11	0	13	34	1	.979
2000— Pawtucket (I.L.)■	SS-3B-2B-1B	83	281	38	64	9	3	8	36	.228	38	48	4	125	159	9	.969
— Boston (A.L.)	SS-DH-1B	12	21	1	2	0	0	1	1	.095	0	3	0	7	18	0	1.000
2001— Durham (I.L.)■	S-3-O-1-2	66	225	28	63	14	2	4	22	.280	25	45	8	114	153	11	.960
— Tampa Bay (A.L.)	SS	49	153	10	30	8	0	1	14	.196	12	35	2	80	121	2	.990
American League totals (5 years)		227	617	69	123	29	0	8	62	.199	43	172	7	254	460	27	.964
National League totals (1 year)		88	194	31	47	5	3	7	29	.242	21	62	7	96	145	9	.964
Major League totals (6 years)		315	811	100	170	34	3	15	91	.210	64	234	14	350	605	36	.964

DIVISION SERIES RECORD

							BATTING							FIELDING		
Year Team (League)	Pos.	G	AB	R	H	2B	3B	HR	RBI	Avg.	BB	SO	SB	PO	A	E	Avg.
1997— Seattle (A.L.)	3B	2	3	0	1	0	0	0	0	.333	0	2	0	0	0	0	...
1998— San Diego (N.L.)	PR-2B	2	0	0	0	0	0	0	0	...	0	0	0	0	0	0	...
Division series totals (2 years)		4	3	0	1	0	0	0	0	.333	0	2	0	0	0	0	...

CHAMPIONSHIP SERIES RECORD

							BATTING							FIELDING		
Year Team (League)	Pos.	G	AB	R	H	2B	3B	HR	RBI	Avg.	BB	SO	SB	PO	A	E	Avg.
1998— San Diego (N.L.)	SS-PH	3	3	0	0	0	0	0	0	.000	0	1	0	0	2	0	1.000

WORLD SERIES RECORD

							BATTING							FIELDING		
Year Team (League)	Pos.	G	AB	R	H	2B	3B	HR	RBI	Avg.	BB	SO	SB	PO	A	E	Avg.
1998— San Diego (N.L.)	SS	2	2	0	0	0	0	0	0	.000	0	1	0	0	2	0	1.000

SHEETS, BEN — P — BREWERS

PERSONAL: Born July 18, 1978, in Baton Rouge, La. ... 6-1/195. ... Throws right, bats right. ... Full name: Ben M. Sheets.
HIGH SCHOOL: St. Amant (La.).
COLLEGE: Northeast Louisiana.
TRANSACTIONS/CAREER NOTES: Selected by Milwaukee Brewers organization in first round (10th pick overall) of free-agent draft (June 2, 1999). ... On Milwaukee disabled list (August 6-September 21, 2001).
MISCELLANEOUS: Member of 2000 U.S. Olympic baseball team.

Year League	W	L	Pct.	ERA	G	GS	CG	ShO	Sv.	IP	H	R	ER	BB	SO
1999— Ogden (Pio.)	0	1	.000	5.63	2	2	0	0	0	8	8	5	5	2	12
— Stockton (Calif.)	1	0	1.000	3.58	5	5	0	0	0	27²/₃	23	11	11	14	28
2000— Huntsville (Sou.)	5	3	.625	1.88	13	13	0	0	0	72	55	17	15	25	60
— Indianapolis (I.L.)	3	5	.375	2.87	14	13	1	0	0	81²/₃	77	31	26	31	59
2001— Indianapolis (I.L.)	1	1	.500	3.38	2	2	0	0	0	10²/₃	14	5	4	3	6
— Milwaukee (N.L.)	11	10	.524	4.76	25	25	1	1	0	151¹/₃	166	89	80	48	94
Major League totals (1 year)	11	10	.524	4.76	25	25	1	1	0	151¹/₃	166	89	80	48	94

ALL-STAR GAME RECORD

Year League	W	L	Pct.	ERA	GS	CG	ShO	Sv.	IP	H	R	ER	BB	SO
2001— National	0	0	...	0.00	0	0	0	0	¹/₃	0	0	0	0	0

SHEFFIELD, GARY — OF — BRAVES

S

PERSONAL: Born November 18, 1968, in Tampa. ... 5-11/205. ... Bats right, throws right. ... Full name: Gary Antonian Sheffield. ... Nephew of Dwight Gooden, pitcher with five major league teams (1984-2000).
HIGH SCHOOL: Hillsborough (Tampa).
TRANSACTIONS/CAREER NOTES: Selected by Milwaukee Brewers organization in first round (sixth pick overall) of free-agent draft (June 2, 1986). ... On Milwaukee disabled list (July 14-September 9, 1989). ... On suspended list (August 31-September 3, 1990). ... On disabled list (June 15-July 3 and July 25, 1991-remainder of season). ... Traded by Brewers with P Geoff Kellogg to San Diego Padres for P Ricky Bones, SS Jose Valentin and OF Matt Mieske (March 27, 1992). ... Traded by Padres with P Rich Rodriguez to Florida Marlins for P Trevor Hoffman, P Jose Martinez and P Andres Berumen (June 24, 1993). ... On Florida suspended list (July 9-12, 1993). ... On Florida disabled list (May 10-25 and May 28-June 12, 1994; included rehabilitation assignment to Portland (June 10-12). ... On disabled list (June 11-September 1, 1995; and May 14-29, 1997). ... Traded by Marlins with 3B Bobby Bonilla, C Charles Johnson, OF Jim Eisenreich and 3B Manuel Barrios to Los Angeles Dodgers for C Mike Piazza and 3B Todd Zeile (May 15, 1998). ... On suspended list (August 4-6, 1998). ... On suspended list (August 23-27, 2000). ... On disabled list (May 24-June 8, 2001). ... Traded by Dodgers to Atlanta Braves for OF Brian Jordan, P Odalis Perez and P Andy Brown (January 15, 2002).
RECORDS: Shares major league record for fewest double plays by outfielder (150 or more games)—0 (1996). ... Shares major league single-inning record for most home runs—2 (July 13, 1997, fourth inning).
HONORS: Named Minor League co-Player of the Year by THE SPORTING NEWS (1988). ... Named Major League Player of the Year by THE SPORTING NEWS (1992). ... Named N.L. Comeback Player of the Year by THE SPORTING NEWS (1992). ... Named third baseman on THE SPORTING NEWS N.L. All-Star team (1992). ... Named third baseman on THE SPORTING NEWS N.L. Silver Slugger team (1992). ... Named outfielder on THE SPORTING NEWS N.L. All-Star team (1996). ... Named outfielder on THE SPORTING NEWS N.L. Silver Slugger team (1996).
STATISTICAL NOTES: Led Pioneer League shortstops with 34 double plays in 1986. ... Led California League shortstops with 77 double plays in 1987. ... Led N.L. with 323 total bases in 1992. ... Led N.L. with .465 on-base percentage in 1996. ... Career major league grand slams: 7.
MISCELLANEOUS: Holds Florida Marlins all-time records for most home runs (122) and runs (365).

							BATTING						FIELDING		
Year Team (League)	Pos.	G	AB	R	H	2B	3B	HR	RBI	Avg.	BB	SO	SB	PO	A	E	Avg.
1986— Helena (Pio.)	SS	57	222	53	81	12	2	15	*71	.365	20	14	14	97	149	24	.911
1987— Stockton (Calif.)	SS	129	469	84	130	23	3	17	*103	.277	81	49	25	235	345	39	.937
1988— El Paso (Texas)	SS-3B-OF	77	296	70	93	19	3	19	65	.314	35	41	5	130	206	23	.936
— Denver (A.A.)	3B-SS	57	212	42	73	9	5	9	54	.344	21	22	8	54	97	8	.950
— Milwaukee (A.L.)	SS	24	80	12	19	1	0	4	12	.238	7	7	3	39	48	3	.967
1989— Milwaukee (A.L.)	SS-3B-DH	95	368	34	91	18	0	5	32	.247	27	33	10	100	238	16	.955
— Denver (A.A.)	SS	7	29	3	4	1	1	0	0	.138	2	0	0	2	6	0	1.000
1990— Milwaukee (A.L.)	3B	125	487	67	143	30	1	10	67	.294	44	41	25	98	254	25	.934
1991— Milwaukee (A.L.)	3B-DH	50	175	25	34	12	2	2	22	.194	19	15	5	29	65	8	.922
1992— San Diego (N.L.)■	3B	146	557	87	184	34	3	33	100	*.330	48	40	5	99	299	16	.961
1993— San Diego (N.L.)	3B	68	258	34	76	12	2	10	36	.295	18	30	5	41	102	15	.905
— Florida (N.L.)■	3B	72	236	33	69	8	3	10	37	.292	29	34	12	38	123	19	.894
1994— Florida (N.L.)	OF	87	322	61	89	16	1	27	78	.276	51	50	12	154	7	5	.970
— Portland (East.)	OF	2	7	1	2	1	0	0	0	.286	1	3	0	3	0	0	1.000
1995— Florida (N.L.)	OF	63	213	46	69	8	0	16	46	.324	55	45	19	109	5	7	.942
1996— Florida (N.L.)	OF	161	519	118	163	33	1	42	120	.314	142	66	16	238	8	6	.976
1997— Florida (N.L.)	OF-DH	135	444	86	111	22	1	21	71	.250	121	79	11	226	14	5	.980
1998— Florida (N.L.)	OF	40	136	21	37	11	1	6	28	.272	26	16	4	68	3	1	.986
— Los Angeles (N.L.)■	OF	90	301	52	95	16	1	16	57	.316	69	30	18	149	6	1	.994
1999— Los Angeles (N.L.)	OF-DH	152	549	103	165	20	0	34	101	.301	101	64	11	235	7	7	.972
2000— Los Angeles (N.L.)	OF-DH	141	501	105	163	24	3	43	109	.325	101	71	4	203	5	•10	.954
2001— Los Angeles (N.L.)	OF-DH	143	515	98	160	28	2	36	100	.311	94	67	10	195	17	6	.972
American League totals (4 years)		294	1110	138	287	61	3	21	133	.259	97	96	43	266	605	52	.944
National League totals (10 years)		1298	4551	844	1381	232	18	294	883	.303	855	592	127	1755	596	98	.960
Major League totals (14 years)		1592	5661	982	1668	293	21	315	1016	.295	952	688	170	2021	1201	150	.956

DIVISION SERIES RECORD

							BATTING						FIELDING		
Year Team (League)	Pos.	G	AB	R	H	2B	3B	HR	RBI	Avg.	BB	SO	SB	PO	A	E	Avg.
1997— Florida (N.L.)	OF	3	9	3	5	1	0	1	1	.556	5	0	1	6	0	0	1.000

CHAMPIONSHIP SERIES RECORD

							BATTING						FIELDING		
Year Team (League)	Pos.	G	AB	R	H	2B	3B	HR	RBI	Avg.	BB	SO	SB	PO	A	E	Avg.
1997— Florida (N.L.)	OF	6	17	6	4	0	0	1	1	.235	7	3	0	5	2	0	1.000

NOTES: Member of World Series championship team (1997).

Year Team (League)	Pos.	G	AB	R	H	2B	3B	HR	RBI	Avg.	BB	SO	SB	PO	A	E	Avg.
							BATTING								FIELDING		
1997— Florida (N.L.)	OF	7	24	4	7	1	0	1	5	.292	8	5	0	16	0	1	.941

ALL-STAR GAME RECORD

Year League	Pos.	AB	R	H	2B	3B	HR	RBI	Avg.	BB	SO	SB	PO	A	E	Avg.
					BATTING									FIELDING		
1992— National	3B	2	0	0	0	0	0	0	.000	0	0	0	0	0	0	...
1993— National	3B	3	1	2	0	0	1	2	.667	0	0	0	0	2	0	1.000
1996— National	OF	1	0	0	0	0	0	0	.000	0	0	0	2	0	0	1.000
1998— National	PH	1	0	0	0	0	0	0	.000	0	0	0	...	...	...	...
1999— National	PH-DH	1	0	0	0	0	0	0	.000	0	0	0	...	...	...	...
2000— National	OF	1	1	0	0	0	0	0	.000	1	0	0	1	0	0	1.000
All-Star Game totals (6 years)		9	2	2	0	0	1	2	.222	1	0	0	3	2	0	1.000

SHELDON, SCOTT   IF

PERSONAL: Born November 20, 1968, in Hammond, Ind. ... 6-3/215. ... Bats right, throws right. ... Full name: Scott Patrick Sheldon.
HIGH SCHOOL: Clear Lake (Houston).
COLLEGE: Houston.
TRANSACTIONS/CAREER NOTES: Selected by Oakland Athletics organization in eighth round of free-agent draft (June 3, 1991). ... Granted free agency (October 17, 1997). ... Signed by Texas Rangers organization (November 20, 1997). ... Granted free agency (December 21, 2001).

Year Team (League)	Pos.	G	AB	R	H	2B	3B	HR	RBI	Avg.	BB	SO	SB	PO	A	E	Avg.
						BATTING									FIELDING		
1991— S. Oregon (N'West) 2B-3B-SS-1B	65	229	34	58	10	3	0	24	.253	23	44	9	122	124	14	.946
1992— Madison (Midw.)	SS-1B	74	275	41	76	16	0	6	24	.276	32	78	5	107	217	25	.928
1993— Madison (Midw.)	3B-SS	131	428	67	91	22	1	8	67	.213	49	121	8	90	275	26	.934
1994— Huntsville (Sou.)	3-0-S-2-1	91	268	31	62	10	1	0	28	.231	28	69	7	69	185	11	.958
1995— Huntsville (Sou.) 2B-SS-1B-3B	66	235	25	51	10	2	4	15	.217	23	60	5	203	188	12	.970
— Edmonton (PCL) 3B-SS-1B-2B	45	128	21	33	7	1	4	12	.258	15	15	4	44	89	5	.964
1996— Edmonton (PCL)	S-1-2-3-0	98	350	61	105	27	3	10	60	.300	43	83	5	259	230	14	.972
1997— Edmonton (PCL)	SS-2B	118	422	89	133	39	6	19	77	.315	59	104	5	139	313	11	.976
— Oakland (A.L.)	SS-2B-3B	13	24	2	6	0	0	1	2	.250	1	6	0	16	18	2	.944
1998— Oklahoma (PCL)■.......	SS-OF	131	493	74	126	31	4	29	96	.256	62	143	2	163	397	24	.959
— Texas (A.L.) 3B-SS-DH-1B	7	16	0	2	0	0	0	1	.125	1	6	0	8	11	1	.950
1999— Oklahoma (PCL)........2-S-1-3-C-0	122	453	94	141	35	3	28	97	.311	56	112	12	254	325	9	.985
— Texas (A.L.)	3B	2	2	0	0	0	0	0	0	.000	0	0	0	2	3	0	1.000
2000— Texas (A.L.) ....IF-C-OF-DH-P	58	124	21	35	11	0	4	19	.282	10	37	0	93	85	5	.973
2001— Texas (A.L.) 3B-SS-OF-C	61	120	11	24	5	0	3	11	.200	3	35	1	51	77	6	.955
Major League totals (5 years)		141	286	34	67	16	0	8	33	.234	15	84	1	170	194	14	.963

RECORD AS PITCHER

Year League	W	L	Pct.	ERA	G	GS	CG	ShO	Sv.	IP	H	R	ER	BB	SO
2000— Texas (A.L.)	0	0	...	0.00	1	0	0	0	0	$\frac{1}{3}$	0	0	0	0	1

SHIBILO, ANDY   P   PADRES

PERSONAL: Born September 16, 1976, in Massapequa Park, N.Y. ... 6-7/220. ... Throws right, bats right. ... Full name: Andrew Joseph Shibilo.
HIGH SCHOOL: Massapequa (N.Y.).
COLLEGE: Pepperdine.
TRANSACTIONS/CAREER NOTES: Selected by St. Louis Cardinals organization in 23rd round of free-agent draft (June 2, 1998). ... Released by Cardinals (March 2000). ... Signed by Lehigh Valley, Atlantic League (2000). ... Signed by San Diego Padres organization (March 2001).

Year League	W	L	Pct.	ERA	G	GS	CG	ShO	Sv.	IP	H	R	ER	BB	SO
1998— New Jersey (NY-Penn)	4	4	.500	3.45	9	9	0	0	0	47	51	21	18	8	54
— Peoria (Midw.)...................	1	3	.250	8.51	7	7	0	0	0	30 $\frac{2}{3}$	42	30	29	11	22
1999— Peoria (Midw.)...................	4	*13	.235	5.11	27	24	2	0	0	135 $\frac{2}{3}$	157	*105	77	41	96
2000— Lehigh Valley (Atl.)■...........	11	*13	.458	4.02	27	26	*11	...	0	179	173	99	80	61	128
2001— Lake Elsinore (Calif.)■.......	10	2	.833	1.96	*60	0	0	0	15	82 $\frac{2}{3}$	66	24	18	27	105

SHIELDS, SCOT   P   ANGELS

PERSONAL: Born July 22, 1975, in Fort Lauderdale, Fla. ... 6-1/175. ... Throws right, bats right. ... Full name: Robert Scot Shields.
HIGH SCHOOL: Fort Lauderdale (Fla.).
COLLEGE: Lincoln Memorial University (Tenn.).
TRANSACTIONS/CAREER NOTES: Selected by Anaheim Angels organization in 38th round of free-agent draft (June 3, 1997).
STATISTICAL NOTES: Led Pacific Coast League with 14 hit batsmen in 2000.

Year League	W	L	Pct.	ERA	G	GS	CG	ShO	Sv.	IP	H	R	ER	BB	SO
1997— Boise (N'West)	7	2	.778	2.94	30	0	0	0	2	52	45	20	17	24	61
1998— Cedar Rapids (Midw.)	6	5	.545	3.65	58	0	0	0	7	74	62	33	30	29	81
1999— Lake Elsinore (Calif.)	10	3	.769	2.52	24	9	2	1	1	107 $\frac{1}{3}$	91	37	30	39	113
— Erie (East.)	4	4	.500	2.89	10	10	1	1	0	74 $\frac{2}{3}$	57	26	24	26	81
2000— Edmonton (PCL)	7	13	.350	5.41	27	27	4	1	0	163	158	114	98	82	*156
2001— Salt Lake (PCL)	6	11	.393	4.97	21	21	4	0	0	137 $\frac{2}{3}$	141	84	76	31	104
— Anaheim (A.L.)	0	0	...	0.00	8	0	0	0	0	11	8	1	0	7	7
Major League totals (1 year)........	0	0	...	0.00	8	0	0	0	0	11	8	1	0	7	7

PERSONAL: Born January 28, 1972, in Fukuoka, Japan. ... 6-1/185. ... Bats right, throws right.
HIGH SCHOOL: Nishinihon Tandai Fuzoku (Fukuoka, Japan).
TRANSACTIONS/CAREER NOTES: Signed by Hanshin Tigers of Japan Central League (1991). ... Signed as non-drafted free agent by New York Mets (December 11, 2000). ... On New York disabled list (June 18-July 16, 2001); included rehabilitation assignment to Brooklyn (July 14-16). ... Traded by Mets with SS Desi Relaford to San Francisco Giants for P Shawn Estes (December 16, 2001).

						BATTING								FIELDING			
Year	Team (League)	Pos.	G	AB	R	H	2B	3B	HR	RBI	Avg.	BB	SO	SB	PO	A	E	Avg.
1991— Hanshin (Jap. Cen.)....			13	17	...	2	...	...	0	1	.118	...	...	0	...	...	...	...
1992— Hanshin (Jap. Cen.)....			95	353	...	98	...	...	11	46	.278	...	...	5	...	...	...	...
1993— Hanshin (Jap. Cen.)....			102	408	50	105	13	1	23	62	.257	...	...	13	...	...	...	...
1994— Hanshin (Jap. Cen.)....			122	466	...	117	...	...	17	68	.251	...	...	7	...	...	...	...
1995— Hanshin (Jap. Cen.)....			87	311	...	70	...	...	7	37	.225	...	...	6	...	...	...	...
1996— Hanshin (Jap. Cen.)....			113	408	97	97	...	...	19	66	.238	...	...	2	...	...	...	...
1997— Hanshin (Jap. Cen.)....			136	482	...	112	...	...	20	68	.232	...	...	8	...	...	...	...
1998— Hanshin (Jap. Cen.)....			132	414	...	92	...	...	6	27	.222	...	...	1	...	...	...	...
1999— Hanshin (Jap. Cen.)....			123	471	53	120	21	7	14	58	.255	...	...	8	...	...	...	...
2000— Hanshin (Jap. Cen.)....			131	511	71	142	23	1	28	85	.278	32	93	15	...	...	...	...
2001— New York (N.L.)■	OF		123	400	46	107	23	1	10	56	.268	25	70	4	256	12	3	.989
— Brooklyn (NY-Penn) ...	OF		2	7	0	2	0	0	0	1	.286	1	2	0	2	0	0	1.000
Major League totals (1 year)			123	400	46	107	23	1	10	56	.268	25	70	4	256	12	3	.989

PERSONAL: Born September 16, 1970, in Lima, Ohio. ... 6-3/215. ... Throws right, bats right. ... Full name: Paul Kenneth Shuey. ... Name pronounced SHOO-ee.
HIGH SCHOOL: Millbrook (Raleigh, N.C.).
COLLEGE: North Carolina.
TRANSACTIONS/CAREER NOTES: Selected by Cleveland Indians organization in first round (second pick overall) of free-agent draft (June 1, 1992). ... On Cleveland disabled list (June 27-July 21, 1994); included rehabilitation assignment to Charlotte (July 5-21). ... On Cleveland disabled list (May 4-22, 1995). ... On Buffalo disabled list (June 2-July 10, 1995). ... On Cleveland disabled list (April 25-May 18, June 19-July 4 and July 11-August 1, 1997); included rehabilitation assignments to Buffalo (May 5-10) and Akron (May 1-18). ... On Cleveland disabled list (April 11-June 15, 1998); included rehabilitation assignments to Akron (April 24) and Buffalo (May 23-June 14). ... On Cleveland disabled list (April 26-May 11, 1999); included rehabilitation assignment to Buffalo (May 9-11). ... On Cleveland disabled list (May 21-June 27, 2000); included rehabilitation assignment to Akron (June 24-27). ... On Cleveland disabled list (June 13-29 and July 22-September 18, 2001); included rehabilitation assignment to Akron (June 27).
RECORDS: Shares major single-inning league record for most strikeouts—4 (May 14, 1994, ninth inning).

Year	League	W	L	Pct.	ERA	G	GS	CG	ShO	Sv.	IP	H	R	ER	BB	SO
1992— Columbus (S.Atl.)................	5	5	.500	3.35	14	14	0	0	0	78	62	35	29	47	73
1993— Canton/Akron (East.).........	4	8	.333	7.30	27	7	0	0	0	61 2/3	76	50	50	36	41
— Kinston (Caro.)..................	1	0	1.000	4.84	15	0	0	0	0	22 1/3	29	12	12	8	27
1994— Kinston (Caro.)..................	1	0	1.000	3.75	13	0	0	0	8	12	10	5	5	3	16
— Cleveland (A.L.).................	0	1	.000	8.49	14	0	0	0	5	11 2/3	14	11	11	12	16
— Charlotte (I.L.).................	2	1	.667	1.93	20	0	0	0	10	23 1/3	15	9	5	10	25
1995— Cleveland (A.L.).................	0	2	.000	4.26	7	0	0	0	0	6 1/3	5	4	3	5	5
— Buffalo (A.A.)...................	1	2	.333	2.63	25	0	0	0	11	27 1/3	21	9	8	7	27
1996— Buffalo (A.A.)...................	3	2	.600	0.81	19	0	0	0	4	33 1/3	14	4	3	9	57
— Cleveland (A.L.).................	5	2	.714	2.85	42	0	0	0	4	53 2/3	45	19	17	26	44
1997— Cleveland (A.L.).................	4	2	.667	6.20	40	0	0	0	2	45	52	31	31	28	46
— Buffalo (A.A.)...................	0	0	...	3.60	2	0	0	0	0	5	4	2	2	4	6
— Akron (East.)	0	0	...	3.38	3	0	0	0	0	8	10	3	3	0	9
1998— Cleveland (A.L.).................	5	4	.556	3.00	43	0	0	0	2	51	44	19	17	25	58
— Akron (East.)	0	0	...	54.00	1	0	0	0	0	1/3	3	2	2	1	0
— Buffalo (I.L.)...................	0	0	...	2.51	11	0	0	0	2	14 1/3	11	4	4	6	22
1999— Cleveland (A.L.).................	8	5	.615	3.53	72	0	0	0	6	81 2/3	68	37	32	40	103
— Buffalo (I.L.)...................	0	0	...	0.00	1	0	0	0	1	1	0	0	0	1	1
2000— Cleveland (A.L.).................	4	2	.667	3.39	57	0	0	0	0	63 2/3	51	25	24	30	69
— Akron (East.)	0	0	...	4.50	2	1	0	0	0	2	1	1	1	1	1
2001— Cleveland (A.L.).................	5	3	.625	2.82	47	0	0	0	2	54 1/3	53	25	17	26	70
— Akron (East.)	0	0	...	0.00	1	1	0	0	0	1	0	0	0	1	2
Major League totals (8 years).......	31	21	.596	3.72	322	0	0	0	21	367 1/3	332	171	152	192	411

DIVISION SERIES RECORD

Year	League	W	L	Pct.	ERA	G	GS	CG	ShO	Sv.	IP	H	R	ER	BB	SO
1996— Cleveland (A.L.).................	0	0	...	9.00	3	0	0	0	0	2	5	2	2	2	2
1998— Cleveland (A.L.).................	0	0	...	0.00	3	0	0	0	0	3	3	0	0	1	4
1999— Cleveland (A.L.).................	1	1	.500	11.25	3	0	0	0	0	4	4	5	5	4	5
2001— Cleveland (A.L.).................	0	0	...	4.50	2	0	0	0	0	2	3	1	1	0	2
Division series totals (4 years)	1	1	.500	6.55	11	0	0	0	0	11	15	8	8	7	13

CHAMPIONSHIP SERIES RECORD

Year	League	W	L	Pct.	ERA	G	GS	CG	ShO	Sv.	IP	H	R	ER	BB	SO
1998— Cleveland (A.L.).................	0	0	...	0.00	5	0	0	0	0	6 1/3	4	0	0	9	7

PERSONAL: Born August 16, 1966, in Paducah, Ky. ... 6-0/200. ... Bats right, throws right. ... Full name: Terrance Darnell Shumpert.
HIGH SCHOOL: Paducah (Ky.) Tilghman.
COLLEGE: Kentucky.

TRANSACTIONS/CAREER NOTES: Selected by Kansas City Royals organization in second round of free-agent draft (June 2, 1987). ... On disabled list (July 19-August 13, 1989). ... On Kansas City disabled list (June 3-September 10, 1990); included rehabilitation assignment to Omaha (August 7-25). ... On Kansas City disabled list (August 7-September 7, 1992). ... Traded by Royals to Boston Red Sox for a player to be named later (December 13, 1994). ... Granted free agency (October 6, 1995). ... Signed by Chicago Cubs organization (March 12, 1996). ... On Chicago disabled list (August 19-September 3, 1996). ... Granted free agency (October 15, 1996). ... Signed by San Diego Padres (November 4, 1996). ... On San Diego disabled list (May 27-August 5, 1997). ... Released by Padres (August 5, 1997). ... Signed by Colorado Rockies organization (August 13, 1997). ... Granted free agency (October 15, 1998). ... Re-signed by Rockies organization (December 18, 1998). ... On Colorado Springs disabled list (May 13-23, 1999). ... Granted free agency (October 29, 1999). ... Re-signed by Rockies (January 1, 1999).

STATISTICAL NOTES: Led American Association with 21 sacrifice hits in 1993. ... Career major league grand slams: 1.

								BATTING								FIELDING		
Year	Team (League)	Pos.	G	AB	R	H	2B	3B	HR	RBI	Avg.	BB	SO	SB	PO	A	E	Avg.
1987—	Eugene (N'West)........	2B	48	186	38	54	16	1	4	22	.290	27	41	16	81	107	11	.945
1988—	Appleton (Midw.)......	2B-OF	114	422	64	102	*37	2	7	38	.242	56	90	36	235	266	20	.962
1989—	Omaha (A.A.).............	2B	113	355	54	88	29	2	4	22	.248	25	63	23	218	295	*22	.959
1990—	Omaha (A.A.)..............	2B	39	153	24	39	6	4	2	12	.255	14	28	18	72	95	7	.960
	— Kansas City (A.L.)	2B-DH	32	91	7	25	6	1	0	8	.275	2	17	3	56	74	3	.977
1991—	Kansas City (A.L.)	2B	144	369	45	80	16	4	5	34	.217	30	75	17	249	368	16	.975
1992—	Kansas City (A.L.)	2B-DH-SS	36	94	6	14	5	1	1	11	.149	3	17	2	50	77	4	.969
	— Omaha (A.A.)..............	2B-SS	56	210	23	42	12	0	1	14	.200	13	33	3	113	154	9	.967
1993—	Omaha (A.A.).............	2B	111	413	70	124	29	1	14	59	.300	41	62	*36	190	303	14	.972
	— Kansas City (A.L.)	2B	8	10	0	1	0	0	0	0	.100	2	2	1	11	11	0	1.000
1994—	Kansas City (A.L.) ...2B-3B-DH-SS		64	183	28	44	6	2	8	24	.240	13	39	18	70	129	8	.961
1995—	Boston (A.L.)■.........2B-3B-SS-DH		21	47	6	11	3	0	0	3	.234	4	13	3	21	35	2	.966
	— Pawtucket (I.L.)........3B-2B-SS-OF		37	133	17	36	7	0	2	11	.271	14	27	10	29	69	11	.899
1996—	Iowa (A.A.)■.........2-3-DH-1-S		72	246	45	68	13	4	5	32	.276	24	44	13	119	165	7	.976
	— Chicago (N.L.)...........	3B-2B-SS	27	31	5	7	1	0	2	6	.226	2	11	0	11	9	1	.952
1997—	Las Vegas (PCL)■...3B-2B-SS-OF		32	109	18	31	8	1	1	16	.284	9	20	3	37	58	4	.960
	— San Diego (N.L.)	2B-OF-3B	13	33	4	9	3	0	1	6	.273	3	4	0	23	17	2	.952
	— New Haven (East.)■...	2B	5	17	2	4	0	0	1	1	.235	0	2	0	8	17	0	1.000
	— Colo. Springs (PCL) ...SS-2B-3B-OF		10	37	8	11	3	0	1	2	.297	2	7	0	8	20	5	.848
1998—	Colo. Springs (PCL) ...2-O-3-DH-S		97	376	66	115	29	8	12	50	.306	35	59	11	141	133	4	.986
	— Colorado (N.L.)	2B	23	26	3	6	1	0	1	2	.231	2	8	0	2	14	0	1.000
1999—	Colo. Springs (PCL) ...2B-OF-3B-SS		29	79	15	30	8	1	6	17	.380	4	9	3	23	36	5	.922
	— Colorado (N.L.)........2B-OF-3B-SS		92	262	58	91	26	3	10	37	.347	31	41	14	129	165	5	.983
2000—	Colorado (N.L.) .... OF-IF-DH		115	263	52	68	11	7	9	40	.259	28	40	8	109	58	4	.977
2001—	Colorado (N.L.) ...2B-OF-3B-SS		114	242	37	70	14	5	4	24	.289	15	44	14	96	92	8	.959
American League totals (6 years)			305	794	92	175	36	8	14	80	.220	54	163	44	457	694	33	.972
National League totals (6 years)			384	857	159	251	56	15	27	115	.293	81	148	36	370	355	20	.973
Major League totals (12 years)			689	1651	251	426	92	23	41	195	.258	135	311	80	827	1049	53	.973

SIERRA, RUBEN — OF — MARINERS

PERSONAL: Born October 6, 1965, in Rio Piedras, Puerto Rico. ... 6-1/200. ... Bats both, throws right. ... Full name: Ruben Angel Garcia Sierra.
HIGH SCHOOL: Dr. Secario Rosario (Rio Piedras, Puerto Rico).
TRANSACTIONS/CAREER NOTES: Signed as non-drafted free agent by Texas Rangers organization (November 21, 1982). ... Traded by Rangers with P Jeff Russell, P Bobby Witt and cash to Oakland Athletics for OF Jose Canseco (August 31, 1992). ... Granted free agency (October 26, 1992). ... Re-signed by A's (December 21, 1992). ... On Oakland disabled list (July 7-22, 1995). ... Traded by A's with P Jason Beverlin to New York Yankees for OF/DH Danny Tartabull (July 28, 1995). ... Traded by Yankees with P Matt Drews to Detroit Tigers for 1B/DH Cecil Fielder (July 31, 1996). ... Traded by Tigers to Cincinnati Reds for OF Decomba Conner and P Ben Bailey (November 28, 1996). ... Released by Reds (May 9, 1997). ... Signed by Toronto Blue Jays organization (May 11, 1997). ... Released by Blue Jays (June 16, 1997). ... Signed by Chicago White Sox organization (January 9, 1998). ... Released by White Sox (May 29, 1998). ... Signed by New York Mets organization (June 20, 1998). ... Granted free agency (October 16, 1998). ... Signed by Atlantic City, Atlantic League (May 1, 1999). ... Signed by Cleveland Indians organization (December 23, 1999). ... Released by Indians (March 20, 2000). ... Signed by Rangers organization (May 1, 2000). ... Granted free agency (October 30, 2000). ... Re-signed by Rangers organization (December 13, 2000). ... On Texas disabled list (July 27-August 11, 2001). ... Granted free agency (November 5, 2001). ... Signed by Seattle Mariners (December 26, 2001).
HONORS: Named A.L. Player of the Year by THE SPORTING NEWS (1989). ... Named outfielder on THE SPORTING NEWS A.L. All-Star team (1989). ... Named outfielder on THE SPORTING NEWS A.L. Silver Slugger team (1989). ... Named A.L. Comeback Player of the Year by THE SPORTING NEWS (2001).
STATISTICAL NOTES: Switch-hit home runs in one game six times (September 13, 1986; August 27, 1988; June 8, 1989; June 7, 1994; June 22, 1996; and June 13, 2001). ... Led A.L. with 12 sacrifice flies in 1987. ... Led A.L. outfielders with six double plays in 1987. ... Led A.L. with 344 total bases and .543 slugging percentage in 1989. ... Led Pacific Coast League in grounding into double plays with 24 in 2000. ... Career major league grand slams: 4.
MISCELLANEOUS: Holds Texas Rangers all-time record for most triples (44). ... Batted righthanded only (1983).

								BATTING								FIELDING		
Year	Team (League)	Pos.	G	AB	R	H	2B	3B	HR	RBI	Avg.	BB	SO	SB	PO	A	E	Avg.
1983—	GC Rangers (GCL)......	OF	48	182	26	44	7	3	1	26	.242	16	38	3	67	6	4	.948
1984—	Burlington (Midw.)......	OF	•138	482	55	127	33	5	6	75	.263	49	97	13	239	18	*20	.928
1985—	Tulsa (Texas).............	OF	*137	*545	63	138	34	*8	13	74	.253	35	111	22	234	12	*15	.943
1986—	Oklahoma City (A.A.)..	OF	46	189	31	56	11	2	9	41	.296	15	27	8	114	4	2	.983
	— Texas (A.L.)...............	OF-DH	113	382	50	101	13	10	16	55	.264	22	65	7	200	7	6	.972
1987—	Texas (A.L.)	OF	158	*643	97	169	35	4	30	109	.263	39	114	16	272	•17	11	.963
1988—	Texas (A.L.)	OF-DH	156	615	77	156	32	2	23	91	.254	44	91	18	310	11	7	.979
1989—	Texas (A.L.)	OF	•162	634	101	194	35	*14	29	*119	.306	43	82	8	313	13	9	.973
1990—	Texas (A.L.)	OF-DH	159	608	70	170	37	2	16	96	.280	49	86	9	283	7	10	.967
1991—	Texas (A.L.)	OF	161	661	110	203	44	5	25	116	.307	56	91	16	305	15	7	.979
1992—	Texas (A.L.)	OF-DH	124	500	66	139	30	6	14	70	.278	31	59	12	224	6	7	.970
	— Oakland (A.L.)■■........	OF-DH	27	101	17	28	4	1	3	17	.277	14	9	2	59	0	0	1.000
1993—	Oakland (A.L.)	OF-DH	158	630	77	147	23	5	22	101	.233	52	97	25	291	9	7	.977
1994—	Oakland (A.L.)	OF-DH	110	426	71	114	21	1	23	92	.268	23	64	8	155	8	*9	.948

Year	Team (League)	Pos.	G	AB	R	H	2B	3B	HR	RBI	Avg.	BB	SO	SB	PO	A	E	Avg.
1995—	Oakland (A.L.)	OF-DH	70	264	40	70	17	0	12	42	.265	24	42	4	89	1	4	.957
—	New York (A.L.)■.......	DH-OF	56	215	33	56	15	0	7	44	.260	22	34	1	18	1	1	.950
1996—	Campeche (Mex.)■....		1	1	1	0	0	0	0	0	.000	0	0	0	0	0	0	...
—	New York (A.L.)■.......	DH-OF	96	360	39	93	17	1	11	52	.258	40	58	1	56	5	1	.984
—	Detroit (A.L.)■..........	OF-DH	46	158	22	35	9	1	1	20	.222	20	25	3	52	1	5	.914
1997—	Cincinnati (N.L.)■	OF	25	90	6	22	5	1	2	7	.244	6	21	0	34	3	0	1.000
—	Syracuse (I.L.)■	OF	8	32	5	7	2	0	1	5	.219	2	6	0	10	2	1	.923
—	Toronto (A.L.)	OF-DH	14	48	4	10	0	2	1	5	.208	3	13	0	13	0	1	.929
1998—	Chicago (A.L.)■	OF-DH	27	74	7	16	4	1	4	11	.216	3	11	2	19	1	0	1.000
—	Norfolk (I.L.)■	OF-DH	28	108	16	28	5	0	3	19	.259	13	18	3	50	1	0	1.000
1999—	Atlantic City (Atl.)■....	DH-OF	112	422	76	124	22	2	28	82	.294	59	63	3	71	1	3	.960
2000—	Cancun (Mex.)■........	DH	16	62	8	22	2	1	3	12	.355	10	10	0	...	...	...	...
—	Texas (A.L.)■..........	DH	20	60	5	14	0	0	1	7	.233	4	9	1	...	...	...	...
—	Oklahoma (PCL)........	OF	112	439	70	143	26	3	18	82	.326	55	63	5	141	9	6	.962
2001—	Oklahoma (PCL)........	OF	24	94	14	25	2	1	3	12	.266	10	14	2	2	0	0	1.000
—	Texas (A.L.)	DH-OF	94	344	55	100	22	1	23	67	.291	19	52	2	59	0	4	.937
American League totals (15 years)			1751	6723	941	1815	358	56	261	1114	.270	508	1002	135	2718	102	89	.969
National League totals (1 year)			25	90	6	22	5	1	2	7	.244	6	21	0	34	3	0	1.000
Major League totals (15 years)			1776	6813	947	1837	363	57	263	1121	.270	514	1023	135	2752	105	89	.970

DIVISION SERIES RECORD

RECORDS: Shares single-game record for most at-bats—7 (October 4, 1995).

Year	Team (League)	Pos.	G	AB	R	H	2B	3B	HR	RBI	Avg.	BB	SO	SB	PO	A	E	Avg.
1995—	New York (A.L.)..........	DH	5	23	2	4	2	0	2	5	.174	2	7	0	...	...	...	...

CHAMPIONSHIP SERIES RECORD

Year	Team (League)	Pos.	G	AB	R	H	2B	3B	HR	RBI	Avg.	BB	SO	SB	PO	A	E	Avg.
1992—	Oakland (A.L.)	OF	6	24	4	8	2	1	1	7	.333	2	1	1	12	0	0	1.000

ALL-STAR GAME RECORD

Year	League	Pos.	AB	R	H	2B	3B	HR	RBI	Avg.	BB	SO	SB	PO	A	E	Avg.
1989—	American	OF	3	1	2	0	0	0	1	.667	0	0	0	1	0	0	1.000
1991—	American	OF	2	0	0	0	0	0	0	.000	0	2	0	0	0	0	...
1992—	American	OF	2	2	1	0	0	1	2	.500	0	0	0	1	0	0	1.000
1994—	American	OF	2	0	1	0	0	0	0	.500	0	0	0	1	0	0	1.000
All-Star Game totals (4 years)			9	3	4	0	0	1	3	.444	0	2	0	3	0	0	1.000

S

SILVA, CARLOS   P   PHILLIES

PERSONAL: Born April 23, 1979, in Bolivar, Venezuela. ... 6-4/225. ... Throws right, bats right.
HIGH SCHOOL: U.E. General Ezequiel Zamora Bolivar.
TRANSACTIONS/CAREER NOTES: Signed as non-drafted free agent by Philadelphia Phillies organization (March 22, 1996).

Year	League	W	L	Pct.	ERA	G	GS	CG	ShO	Sv.	IP	H	R	ER	BB	SO
1996—	Martinsville (Appl.)............	0	0	...	4.00	7	1	0	0	0	18	20	11	8	5	16
1997—	Martinsville (Appl.)............	2	2	.500	5.15	11	11	0	0	0	57 2/3	66	46	33	14	31
1998—	Martinsville (Appl.)............	1	4	.200	5.05	7	7	1	0	0	41	48	24	23	4	21
—	Batavia (NY-Penn)........	2	3	.400	6.35	9	7	0	0	0	45 1/3	61	37	32	9	27
1999—	Piedmont (S.Atl.)...............	11	8	.579	3.12	26	26	3	1	0	164 1/3	176	79	57	41	99
2000—	Clearwater (FSL)	8	*13	.381	3.57	26	24	*4	0	0	176 1/3	*229	99	70	26	82
2001—	Reading (East.).................	15	8	.652	3.90	28	28	4	1	0	180	*197	85	78	27	100

SILVA, JOSE   P   REDS

PERSONAL: Born December 19, 1973, in Tijuana, Mexico. ... 6-5/235. ... Throws right, bats right. ... Full name: Jose Leonel Silva.
HIGH SCHOOL: Hilltop (Chula Vista, Calif.).
TRANSACTIONS/CAREER NOTES: Selected by Toronto Blue Jays organization in sixth round of free-agent draft (June 3, 1991). ... On disabled list (April 6-August 17, 1995). ... On Knoxville disabled list (April 4-June 5, 1996). ... Traded by Blue Jays with IF Jose Pett, IF Brandon Cromer and three players to be named later to Pittsburgh Pirates for OF Orlando Merced, IF Carlos Garcia and P Dan Plesac (November 14, 1996); Pirates acquired P Mike Halperin, IF Abraham Nunez and C/OF Craig Wilson to complete deal (December 11, 1996). ... On Calgary disabled list (April 29-June 2, 1997). ... On Pittsburgh disabled list (June 17-September 10, 1998); included rehabilitation assignment to Nashville (August 25-September 6). ... On Pittsburgh disabled list (March 26-April 23, 1999); included rehabilitation assignment to Nashville (April 14-23). ... On Pittsburgh disabled list (June 5, 2001-remainder of season); included rehabilitation assignments to Altoona (August 27-September 2) and Williamsport (September 2-13). ... Traded to Cincinnati Reds for P Ben Shaffar (December 20, 2001).

Year	League	W	L	Pct.	ERA	G	GS	CG	ShO	Sv.	IP	H	R	ER	BB	SO
1992—	Gulf Coast Blue Jays (GCL)	6	4	.600	2.28	12	•12	0	0	0	59 1/3	42	23	15	18	78
1993—	Hagerstown (S.Atl.)..........	12	5	.706	2.52	24	24	0	0	0	142 2/3	103	50	40	62	161
1994—	Dunedin (FSL)	0	2	.000	3.77	8	7	0	0	0	43	41	32	18	24	41
—	Knoxville (Sou.).................	4	8	.333	4.14	16	16	1	1	0	91 1/3	89	47	42	31	71
1995—	Knoxville (Sou.).................	0	0	...	9.00	3	0	0	0	0	2	3	2	2	6	2
1996—	Knoxville (Sou.).................	2	3	.400	4.91	22	6	0	0	0	44	45	27	24	22	26
—	Toronto (A.L.).................	0	0	...	13.50	2	0	0	0	0	2	5	3	3	0	0
1997—	Calgary (PCL)■.................	5	1	.833	3.41	17	11	0	0	0	66	74	27	25	22	54
—	Pittsburgh (N.L.)............	2	1	.667	5.94	11	4	0	0	0	36 1/3	52	26	24	16	30
1998—	Pittsburgh (N.L.)	6	7	.462	4.40	18	18	1	0	0	100 1/3	104	55	49	30	54
—	Nashville (PCL)	0	0	...	4.82	3	3	0	0	0	9 1/3	10	5	5	4	6

Year League	W	L	Pct.	ERA	G	GS	CG	ShO	Sv.	IP	H	R	ER	BB	SO
1999—Nashville (PCL)	2	0	1.000	1.50	2	2	0	0	0	12	14	4	2	4	10
—Pittsburgh (N.L.)	2	8	.200	5.73	34	12	0	0	4	97 1/3	108	70	62	39	77
2000—Pittsburgh (N.L.)	11	9	.550	5.56	51	19	1	0	0	136	178	96	84	50	98
2001—Pittsburgh (N.L.)	3	3	.500	6.75	26	0	0	0	0	32	35	24	24	9	23
—Altoona (East.)	0	0	...	0.00	2	0	0	0	0	1 1/3	2	0	0	1	2
—Williamsport (NY-Penn)	0	0	...	0.00	2	2	0	0	0	2	2	0	0	0	2
A.L. totals (1 year)	0	0	...	13.50	2	0	0	0	0	2	5	3	3	0	0
N.L. totals (5 years)	24	28	.462	5.44	140	53	2	0	4	402	477	271	243	144	292
Major League totals (6 years)	24	28	.462	5.48	142	53	2	0	4	404	482	274	246	144	292

SIMMONS, BRIAN — OF — WHITE SOX

PERSONAL: Born September 4, 1973, in Lebanon, Pa. ... 6-2/190. ... Bats both, throws right. ... Full name: Brian Lee Simmons.
HIGH SCHOOL: Peters Township (McMurray, Pa.).
COLLEGE: Michigan.
TRANSACTIONS/CAREER NOTES: Selected by Baltimore Orioles organization in 35th round of free-agent draft (June 1, 1992); did not sign. ... Selected by Chicago White Sox organization in second round of free-agent draft (June 1, 1995). ... On South Bend disabled list (April 5-17, 1996). ... On Calgary disabled list (June 22-August 10, 1998); included rehabilitation assignment to Arizona White Sox (August 1-8). ... On Chicago disabled list (March 31-April 29, 1999); included rehabilitation assignment to Charlotte (April 8-27). ... On disabled list (March 30, 2000-entire season). ... Traded by White Sox with P Mike Sirotka, P Kevin Beirne and P Mike Williams to Toronto Blue Jays for P David Wells and P Matt DeWitt (January 14, 2001). ... Claimed on waivers by White Sox (November 20, 2001).
STATISTICAL NOTES: Led Southern League outfielders with 334 total chances in 1997. ... Switch-hit home runs in one game (September 26, 1998).

Year Team (League)	Pos.	G	AB	R	H	2B	3B	HR	RBI	Avg.	BB	SO	SB	PO	A	E	Avg.
1995—Sarasota (GCL)	OF	5	17	5	3	1	0	1	5	.176	6	1	0	13	1	0	1.000
—Hickory (S.Atl.)	OF	41	163	13	31	6	1	2	11	.190	19	44	4	77	2	1	.988
1996—South Bend (Midw.)	OF-DH	92	356	73	106	29	6	17	58	.298	48	69	14	204	10	7	.968
—Prince William (Caro.)	OF	33	131	17	26	4	3	4	14	.198	9	39	2	70	2	2	.973
1997—Birmingham (Sou.)	OF	138	546	108	143	28	*12	15	72	.262	*88	124	15	*322	7	5	.985
1998—Calgary (PCL)	OF-DH	94	355	72	103	21	4	13	51	.290	41	82	10	197	6	7	.967
—Ariz. White Sox (Ariz.)	OF-DH	5	12	1	2	0	0	0	0	.167	1	1	0	3	0	0	1.000
—Chicago (A.L.)	OF	5	19	4	7	0	0	2	6	.368	0	2	0	13	0	0	1.000
1999—Chicago (A.L.)	OF-DH	54	126	14	29	3	3	4	17	.230	9	30	4	79	2	2	.976
—Charlotte (I.L.)	OF	78	285	53	77	14	0	10	44	.270	37	60	8	171	6	5	.973
2000—Chicago (A.L.)							Did not play.										
2001—Toronto (A.L.)■	OF-DH	60	107	8	19	5	0	2	8	.178	8	26	1	59	1	0	1.000
—Syracuse (I.L.)	OF	52	201	24	53	10	1	2	20	.264	19	36	4	91	5	3	.970
Major League totals (3 years)		119	252	26	55	8	3	8	31	.218	17	58	5	151	3	2	.987

SIMON, RANDALL — 1B — TIGERS

PERSONAL: Born May 26, 1975, in Willemstad, Curacao. ... 6-0/180. ... Bats left, throws left. ... Full name: Randall Carlito Simon.
HIGH SCHOOL: Juan Pablo Duarte Tech (Willemstad, Curacao).
TRANSACTIONS/CAREER NOTES: Signed as non-drafted free agent by Atlanta Braves organization (July 17, 1992). ... Released by Braves (March 31, 2000). ... Signed by Florida Marlins organization (April 5, 2000). ... Released by Marlins (May 8, 2000). ... Signed by New York Yankees organization (May 14, 2000). ... On Columbus disabled list (July 6-13, 2000). ... Granted free agency (October 18, 2000). ... Signed by Detroit Tigers organization (January 18, 2001).
STATISTICAL NOTES: Led Carolina League with 14 intentional bases on balls received in 1995. ... Led International League first basemen with 1,149 total chances in 1997. ... Tied for International League lead in grounding into double plays with 18 in 1997. ... Led International League in grounding into double plays with 22 in 1998. ... Career major league grand slams: 1.

Year Team (League)	Pos.	G	AB	R	H	2B	3B	HR	RBI	Avg.	BB	SO	SB	PO	A	E	Avg.
1992—Dom. Braves (DSL)	C	11	43	7	12	4	2	0	7	.279	5	6	1	146	40	4	.979
1993—Danville (Appl.)	1B	61	232	28	59	17	1	3	31	.254	10	34	1	463	37	10	.980
1994—Macon (S.Atl.)	1B	106	358	48	105	23	1	10	54	.293	6	56	7	582	49	9	.986
1995—Durham (Caro.)	1B	122	420	56	111	18	1	18	79	.264	36	63	6	864	51	10	.989
1996—Greenville (Sou.)	1B-OF	134	498	74	139	26	2	18	77	.279	37	61	4	723	55	16	.980
1997—Richmond (I.L.)	1B-DH	133	519	62	160	*45	1	14	*102	.308	17	76	1	*1063	72	•14	.988
—Atlanta (N.L.)	1B	13	14	2	6	1	0	0	1	.429	1	2	0	16	2	0	1.000
1998—Richmond (I.L.)	1B-DH	126	484	52	124	20	1	13	70	.256	24	62	4	981	51	*11	.989
—Atlanta (N.L.)	1B	7	16	2	3	0	0	0	4	.188	0	1	0	36	1	0	1.000
1999—Atlanta (N.L.)	1B	90	218	26	69	16	0	5	25	.317	17	25	2	462	27	3	.994
—Richmond (I.L.)	1B-DH	15	59	7	16	4	0	1	8	.271	3	10	0	115	14	0	1.000
2000—Calgary (PCL)■	1B	22	68	5	20	3	0	1	11	.294	0	3	0	104	9	4	.966
—Columbus (I.L.)■	1B-OF	94	364	52	97	20	4	17	74	.266	35	42	6	627	34	9	.987
2001—Toledo (I.L.)■	1B	59	222	27	75	13	0	10	31	.338	21	21	0	462	23	7	.986
—Detroit (A.L.)	1B-DH	81	256	28	78	14	2	6	37	.305	15	28	0	353	26	3	.992
American League totals (1 year)		81	256	28	78	14	2	6	37	.305	15	28	0	353	26	3	.992
National League totals (3 years)		110	248	30	78	17	0	5	30	.315	18	28	2	514	30	3	.995
Major League totals (4 years)		191	504	58	156	31	2	11	67	.310	33	56	2	867	56	6	.994

DIVISION SERIES RECORD

Year Team (League)	Pos.	G	AB	R	H	2B	3B	HR	RBI	Avg.	BB	SO	SB	PO	A	E	Avg.
1999—Atlanta (N.L.)							Did not play.										

CHAMPIONSHIP SERIES RECORD

						BATTING								FIELDING		
Year	Team (League)	Pos.	G	AB	R	H	2B	3B	HR	RBI	Avg.	BB	SO	SB	PO	A	E	Avg.
1999— Atlanta (N.L.)							Did not play.										

WORLD SERIES RECORD

						BATTING								FIELDING		
Year	Team (League)	Pos.	G	AB	R	H	2B	3B	HR	RBI	Avg.	BB	SO	SB	PO	A	E	Avg.
1999— Atlanta (N.L.)							Did not play.										

SIMPSON, ALLAN　　　　P　　　　MARINERS

PERSONAL: Born August 26, 1977, in Springfield, Ill. ... 6-4/185. ... Throws right, bats right. ... Full name: Larry Allan Simpson.
HIGH SCHOOL: Cheyenne (North Las Vegas, Nev.).
JUNIOR COLLEGE: Taft (Calif.).
TRANSACTIONS/CAREER NOTES: Selected by Seattle Mariners organization in eighth round of free-agent draft (June 3, 1997). ... On San Antonio disabled list (April 5-May 2, 2001).

Year	League	W	L	Pct.	ERA	G	GS	CG	ShO	Sv.	IP	H	R	ER	BB	SO
1997— Everett (N'West)	0	3	.000	6.84	16	0	0	0	0	26 1/3	26	23	20	24	26
1998— Wisconsin (Midw.)	3	5	.375	4.44	19	19	0	0	0	93 1/3	89	52	46	61	86
— Arizona Mariners (Ariz.)	1	0	1.000	0.96	3	0	0	0	1	9 1/3	8	2	1	3	12
1999— Wisconsin (Midw.)	2	9	.182	4.38	24	13	1	0	0	90 1/3	83	56	44	48	88
— Lancaster (Calif.)	0	0	...	6.33	9	0	0	0	0	21 1/3	17	16	15	14	25
2000— Lancaster (Calif.)	3	2	.600	2.08	46	0	0	0	6	52	34	17	12	27	67
2001— San Antonio (Texas)	2	1	.667	1.86	22	0	0	0	3	38 2/3	25	8	8	15	37
— San Bernardino (Calif.)	1	0	1.000	1.80	16	0	0	0	1	30	19	7	6	12	40

SINGLETON, CHRIS　　　　OF　　　　WHITE SOX

PERSONAL: Born August 15, 1972, in Mesa, Ariz. ... 6-2/195. ... Bats left, throws left. ... Full name: Christopher Verdell Singleton.
HIGH SCHOOL: Pinole (Calif.) Valley.
COLLEGE: Nevada.
TRANSACTIONS/CAREER NOTES: Selected by San Francisco Giants organization in second round of free-agent draft (June 3, 1993). ... Traded by Giants with P Alberto Castillo to New York Yankees for 3B Charlie Hayes and cash (November 11, 1997). ... Traded by Yankees to Chicago White Sox for a player to be named later (December 8, 1998); Yankees acquired P Rich Pratt to complete deal (January 10, 1999).
STATISTICAL NOTES: Led Texas League with nine sacrifice flies in 1997. ... Led Texas League outfielders with 271 total chances and tied for league lead with four double plays in 1997. ... Tied for Texas League lead with four intentional bases on balls received in 1997. ... Hit for the cycle (July 6, 1999).

						BATTING								FIELDING		
Year	Team (League)	Pos.	G	AB	R	H	2B	3B	HR	RBI	Avg.	BB	SO	SB	PO	A	E	Avg.
1993— Everett (N'West)	OF	58	219	39	58	14	4	3	18	.265	18	46	14	106	6	3	.974
1994— San Jose (Calif.)	OF	113	425	51	106	17	5	2	49	.249	27	62	19	248	10	13	.952
1995— San Jose (Calif.)	OF	94	405	55	112	13	5	2	31	.277	17	49	33	142	6	7	.955
1996— Shreveport (Texas)	OF	129	500	68	149	31	9	5	72	.298	24	58	27	262	10	4	.986
— Phoenix (PCL)	OF	9	32	3	4	0	0	0	0	.125	1	2	0	18	1	0	1.000
1997— Shreveport (Texas)	OF	126	464	85	147	26	10	9	61	.317	22	50	27	*253	11	7	.974
1998— Columbus (I.L.)■........	OF	121	413	55	105	17	10	6	45	.254	27	78	9	251	10	7	.974
1999— Chicago (A.L.)■...........	OF-DH	133	496	72	149	31	6	17	72	.300	22	45	20	376	9	4	.990
2000— Chicago (A.L.)	OF-DH	147	511	83	130	22	5	11	62	.254	35	85	22	373	9	3	.992
2001— Chicago (A.L.)	OF-DH	140	392	57	117	21	5	7	45	.298	20	61	12	310	8	3	.991
Major League totals (3 years)		420	1399	212	396	74	16	35	179	.283	77	191	54	1059	26	10	.991

DIVISION SERIES RECORD

						BATTING								FIELDING		
Year	Team (League)	Pos.	G	AB	R	H	2B	3B	HR	RBI	Avg.	BB	SO	SB	PO	A	E	Avg.
2000— Chicago (A.L.)	OF	3	9	1	1	0	1	0	1	.111	0	2	0	3	0	0	1.000

SIROTKA, MIKE　　　　P　　　　BLUE JAYS

PERSONAL: Born May 13, 1971, in Chicago. ... 6-1/200. ... Throws left, bats left. ... Full name: Michael Robert Sirotka.
HIGH SCHOOL: Westfield (Houston).
COLLEGE: Louisiana State.
TRANSACTIONS/CAREER NOTES: Selected by Chicago White Sox organization in 15th round of free-agent draft (June 3, 1993). ... On Hickory disabled list (July 1-28, 1993). ... On South Bend temporarily inactive list (August 27-October 4, 1993). ... Traded by White Sox with P Kevin Beirne, OF Brian Simmons and P Mike Williams to Toronto Blue Jays P David Wells and P Matt DeWitt (January 14, 2001). ... On disabled list (March 23, 2001-entire season).
RECORDS: Shares major league single-inning record for most errors by pitcher—3 (April 9, 1999, fifth inning).

Year	League	W	L	Pct.	ERA	G	GS	CG	ShO	Sv.	IP	H	R	ER	BB	SO
1993— GC White Sox (GCL)	0	0	...	0.00	3	0	0	0	0	5	4	1	0	2	8
— South Bend (Midw.)	0	1	.000	6.10	7	1	0	0	0	10 1/3	12	8	7	6	12
1994— South Bend (Midw.)	12	9	.571	3.07	27	27	8	2	0	196 2/3	183	99	67	56	173
1995— Birmingham (Sou.).............	7	6	.538	3.20	16	16	1	0	0	101 1/3	95	42	36	22	79
— Chicago (A.L.)	1	2	.333	4.19	6	6	0	0	0	34 1/3	39	16	16	17	19
— Nashville (A.A.)	1	5	.167	2.83	8	8	0	0	0	54	51	21	17	13	34
1996— Nashville (A.A.)	7	5	.583	3.60	15	15	1	1	0	90	90	44	36	24	58
— Chicago (A.L.)	1	2	.333	7.18	15	4	0	0	0	26 1/3	34	27	21	12	11
1997— Nashville (A.A.)	7	5	.583	3.28	19	19	1	0	0	112 1/3	115	49	41	22	92
— Chicago (A.L.)	3	0	1.000	2.25	7	4	0	0	0	32	36	9	8	5	24

Year League	W	L	Pct.	ERA	G	GS	CG	ShO	Sv.	IP	H	R	ER	BB	SO
1998—Chicago (A.L.)	14	15	.483	5.06	33	33	5	0	0	211²/₃	255	137	119	47	128
1999—Chicago (A.L.)	11	13	.458	4.00	32	32	3	1	0	209	236	108	93	57	125
2000—Chicago (A.L.)	15	10	.600	3.79	32	32	1	0	0	197	203	101	83	69	128
2001—Toronto (A.L.)■								Did not play.							
Major League totals (6 years)	45	42	.517	4.31	125	111	9	1	0	710¹/₃	803	398	340	207	435

DIVISION SERIES RECORD

Year League	W	L	Pct.	ERA	G	GS	CG	ShO	Sv.	IP	H	R	ER	BB	SO
2000—Chicago (A.L.)	0	1	.000	4.76	1	1	0	0	0	5²/₃	7	4	3	2	0

SLUSARSKI, JOE   P

PERSONAL: Born December 19, 1966, in Indianapolis. ... 6-4/195. ... Throws right, bats right. ... Full name: Joseph Andrew Slusarski.
HIGH SCHOOL: Griffin (Springfield, Ill.).
JUNIOR COLLEGE: Lincoln Land Community College (Ill.).
COLLEGE: New Orleans.
TRANSACTIONS/CAREER NOTES: Selected by Seattle Mariners organization in sixth round of free-agent draft (June 2, 1987); did not sign. ... Selected by Oakland Athletics organization in second round of free-agent draft (June 1, 1988). ... On Huntsville disabled list (May 18-25, 1990). ... On Tacoma disabled list (August 2-11, 1992 and July 22-August 11, 1993). ... Released by A's (May 11, 1994). ... Signed by Philadelphia Phillies organization (June 3, 1994). ... Granted free agency (October 15, 1994). ... Signed by Cleveland Indians organization (January 20, 1995). ... Released by Indians (April 24, 1995). ... Signed by Milwaukee Brewers organization (May 19, 1995). ... Granted free agency (October 16, 1995). ... Signed by California Angels organization (February 26, 1996). ... Released by Angels (April 4, 1996). ... Signed by Brewers organization (May 12, 1996). ... Granted free agency (October 15, 1996). ... Signed by Sinon, Taiwan (1997). ... Signed by Houston Astros organization (May 4, 1998). ... Granted free agency (October 16, 1998). ... Re-signed by Astros organization (December 17, 1998). ... On Houston disabled list (July 9-24, 1999). ... Granted free agency (October 20, 1999). ... Re-signed by Astros organization (January 3, 2000). ... Granted free agency (December 21, 2000). ... Signed by Atlanta Braves organization (Apri 1, 2001). ... On Atlanta disabled list (April 10-May 8, 2001); included rehabilitation assignment to Richmond (April 23-May 8). ... Released by Braves (May 11, 2001). ... Signed by Astros organization (May 12, 2001). ... Granted free agency (October 10, 2001).
STATISTICAL NOTES: Led California League with 15 home runs allowed in 1989.
MISCELLANEOUS: Member of 1988 U.S. Olympic baseball team.

Year League	W	L	Pct.	ERA	G	GS	CG	ShO	Sv.	IP	H	R	ER	BB	SO
1989—Modesto (Calif.)	•13	10	.565	3.18	27	27	4	1	0	184	155	78	65	50	160
1990—Huntsville (Sou.)	6	8	.429	4.47	17	17	2	0	0	108²/₃	114	65	54	35	75
—Tacoma (PCL)	4	2	.667	3.40	9	9	0	0	0	55²/₃	54	24	21	22	37
1991—Oakland (A.L.)	5	7	.417	5.27	20	19	1	0	0	109¹/₃	121	69	64	52	60
—Tacoma (PCL)	4	2	.667	2.72	7	7	0	0	0	46¹/₃	42	20	14	10	25
1992—Oakland (A.L.)	5	5	.500	5.45	15	14	0	0	0	76	85	52	46	27	38
—Tacoma (PCL)	2	4	.333	3.77	11	10	0	0	0	57¹/₃	67	30	24	18	26
1993—Tacoma (PCL)	7	5	.583	4.76	24	21	1	1	0	113¹/₃	133	67	60	40	61
—Oakland (A.L.)	0	0		5.19	2	1	0	0	0	8²/₃	9	5	5	11	1
1994—Tacoma (PCL)	2	3	.400	6.03	7	7	0	0	0	37¹/₃	45	28	25	11	24
—Reading (East.)■	1	2	.333	4.63	5	4	0	0	0	23¹/₃	25	15	12	5	17
—Scranton/W.B. (I.L.)	2	3	.400	7.82	10	4	0	0	0	38	50	36	33	10	29
1995—Buffalo (A.A.)■	1	1	.500	6.32	4	2	0	0	0	15²/₃	18	12	11	4	9
—New Orleans (A.A.)■	1	1	.500	1.12	33	0	0	0	11	48¹/₃	37	10	6	11	30
—Milwaukee (A.L.)	1	1	.500	5.40	12	0	0	0	0	15	21	11	9	6	6
1996—New Orleans (A.A.)	2	4	.333	4.95	40	0	0	0	1	60	70	38	33	24	36
1997—Sinon (Taiwan)■	2	4	.333	4.18	25	...	...	0	2	71	76	...	...	24	31
1998—Jackson (Texas)■	2	2	.500	6.33	9	2	0	0	0	21¹/₃	22	17	15	2	13
—New Orleans (PCL)	1	4	.200	5.11	31	0	0	0	2	49¹/₃	53	31	28	9	32
1999—New Orleans (PCL)	1	4	.200	3.64	40	2	0	0	1	64¹/₃	71	31	26	13	40
—Houston (N.L.)	0	0		0.00	3	0	0	0	0	3²/₃	1	0	0	3	3
2000—New Orleans (PCL)	2	1	.667	2.25	13	0	0	0	0	20	14	9	5	7	21
—Houston (N.L.)	2	7	.222	4.21	54	0	0	0	3	77	80	36	36	22	54
2001—Richmond (I.L.)■	0	0		2.25	6	0	0	0	0	8	9	2	2	2	5
—Atlanta (N.L.)	0	0		9.00	4	0	0	0	0	6	9	6	6	1	5
—New Orleans (PCL)■	5	2	.714	2.47	31	0	0	0	1	40	37	17	11	8	24
—Houston (N.L.)	0	1	.000	9.00	8	0	0	0	0	10	16	10	10	3	6
A.L. totals (4 years)	11	13	.458	5.34	49	34	1	0	0	209	236	137	124	96	105
N.L. totals (3 years)	2	8	.200	4.84	69	0	0	0	3	96²/₃	106	52	52	29	68
Major League totals (7 years)	13	21	.382	5.18	118	34	1	0	3	305²/₃	342	189	176	125	173

SMART, J.D.   P

PERSONAL: Born November 12, 1973, in San Saba, Texas. ... 6-2/180. ... Throws right, bats right. ... Full name: Jon David Smart.
HIGH SCHOOL: Westlake (Austin, Texas).
COLLEGE: Texas.
TRANSACTIONS/CAREER NOTES: Selected by Montreal Expos organization in fourth round of free-agent draft (June 1, 1995). ... On Ottawa disabled list (August 16, 1999-remainder of season). ... On disabled list (April 23-May 30, 2000). ... On Montreal disabled list (May 31, 2000-remainder of season). ... Released by Expos (November 15, 2000). ... Signed by Texas Rangers organization (February 7, 2001). ... On Texas disabled list (July 1, 2001-remainder of season). ... Granted free agency (October 11, 2001).

Year League	W	L	Pct.	ERA	G	GS	CG	ShO	Sv.	IP	H	R	ER	BB	SO
1995—Gulf Coast Expos (GCL)	2	0	1.000	1.69	2	2	0	0	0	10²/₃	10	2	2	1	6
—Vermont (NY-Penn)	0	1	.000	2.28	5	5	0	0	0	27¹/₃	29	9	7	7	21
1996—Delmarva (S.Atl.)	9	8	.529	3.39	25	25	3	2	0	156²/₃	155	75	59	31	109
1997—West Palm Beach (FSL)	5	4	.556	3.26	17	13	1	0	1	102	105	45	37	21	65
—Harrisburg (East.)	6	3	.667	3.69	12	12	0	0	0	70²/₃	75	34	29	24	43
1998—Cape Fear (S.Atl.)	3	0	1.000	2.45	3	1	0	0	0	11	7	3	3	0	12
—Harrisburg (East.)	3	5	.375	2.45	14	11	0	0	1	77	67	23	21	18	47
—Ottawa (I.L.)	2	3	.400	4.89	6	6	0	0	0	35	34	22	19	11	16

Year	League	W	L	Pct.	ERA	G	GS	CG	ShO	Sv.	IP	H	R	ER	BB	SO
1999— Montreal (N.L.)		0	1	.000	5.02	29	0	0	0	0	52	56	30	29	17	21
— Ottawa (I.L.)		0	1	.000	2.61	6	4	0	0	0	20²/₃	22	7	6	6	9
2000— Ottawa (I.L.)		0	1	.000	10.80	4	0	0	0	1	6²/₃	15	8	8	1	3
2001— Oklahoma (PCL)■		2	2	.500	2.74	16	0	0	0	3	23	22	9	7	6	13
— Texas (A.L.)		1	2	.333	6.46	15	0	0	0	0	15¹/₃	19	11	11	4	10
A.L. totals (1 year)		1	2	.333	6.46	15	0	0	0	0	15¹/₃	19	11	11	4	10
N.L. totals (1 year)		0	1	.000	5.02	29	0	0	0	0	52	56	30	29	17	21
Major League totals (2 years)		1	3	.250	5.35	44	0	0	0	0	67¹/₃	75	41	40	21	31

SMITH, BOBBY — IF — DEVIL RAYS

PERSONAL: Born May 10, 1974, in Oakland. ... 6-3/190. ... Bats right, throws right. ... Full name: Robert Eugene Smith.
HIGH SCHOOL: Fremont (Oakland).
TRANSACTIONS/CAREER NOTES: Selected by Atlanta Braves organization in 11th round of free-agent draft (June 1, 1992). ... Selected by Tampa Bay Devil Rays in first round (12th pick overall) of expansion draft (November 18, 1997). ... On disabled list (May 13-28, 1998). ... On Tampa Bay disabled list (July 6-August 19, 2000); included rehabilitation assignment to Durham (August 14-19). ... On suspended list (September 8-9, 2000). ... On Durham disabled list (April 30-May 14, 2001).
STATISTICAL NOTES: Tied for Carolina League lead in grounding into double plays with 19 in 1994. ... Led Carolina League third basemen with 388 total chances and 27 double plays in 1994.

							BATTING									FIELDING		
Year	Team (League)	Pos.	G	AB	R	H	2B	3B	HR	RBI	Avg.	BB	SO	SB	PO	A	E	Avg.
1992— GC Braves (GCL)		3B	57	217	31	51	9	1	3	28	.235	17	55	5	37	115	15	.910
1993— Macon (S.Atl.)		3B	108	384	53	94	16	7	4	38	.245	23	81	12	65	167	30	.885
1994— Durham (Caro.)		3B	127	478	49	127	27	2	12	71	.266	41	112	18	*104	253	31	*.920
1995— Greenville (Sou.)		3B	127	444	75	116	27	3	14	58	.261	40	109	12	*120	265	26	.937
1996— Richmond (I.L.)		3B-SS-DH	124	445	49	114	27	0	8	58	.256	32	114	15	116	228	24	.935
1997— Richmond (I.L.)		SS-DH	100	357	47	88	10	2	12	47	.246	44	109	6	161	297	23	.952
1998— Tampa Bay (A.L.)■		3-DH-S-2	117	370	44	102	15	3	11	55	.276	34	110	5	89	203	13	.957
1999— Tampa Bay (A.L.)		3B-2B	68	199	18	36	4	1	3	19	.181	16	64	4	48	132	11	.942
— Durham (I.L.)		3B-SS	57	225	52	75	15	3	14	47	.333	27	61	13	46	126	10	.945
2000— Durham (I.L.)		2B-SS-3B	66	261	48	76	20	2	17	58	.291	23	61	15	120	184	9	.971
— Tampa Bay (A.L.)		2B-3B	49	175	21	41	8	0	6	26	.234	14	59	2	84	151	8	.967
2001— Durham (I.L.)		O-2-S-3-1	107	396	67	119	25	2	22	70	.301	46	91	10	209	92	7	.977
— Tampa Bay (A.L.)		2B	6	19	1	2	0	0	1	1	.105	3	10	1	12	11	1	.958
Major League totals (4 years)			240	763	84	181	27	4	20	101	.237	67	243	11	233	497	33	.957

SMITH, BUD — P — CARDINALS

PERSONAL: Born October 23, 1979, in Torrance, Calif. ... 6-0/170. ... Throws left, bats left. ... Full name: Robert Allan Smith.
HIGH SCHOOL: St. John Bosco (Bellflower, Calif.).
JUNIOR COLLEGE: Los Angeles Harbor.
TRANSACTIONS/CAREER NOTES: Selected by St. Louis Cardinals organization in fourth round of free-agent draft (June 2, 1998).
HONORS: Named Texas League Pitcher of the Year (2000).
STATISTICAL NOTES: Pitched 5-0 no-hit victory for Arkansas against Midland (May 6, 2000, second game). ... Pitched 1-0 no-hit victory for Arkansas against San Antonio (June 11, 2000, second game). ... Pitched 3-0 no-hit victory against San Diego (September 3, 2001).

Year	League	W	L	Pct.	ERA	G	GS	CG	ShO	Sv.	IP	H	R	ER	BB	SO
1998— Johnson City (Appl.)		3	3	.500	5.18	14	•14	0	0	0	64¹/₃	85	47	37	34	65
1999— Peoria (Midw.)		4	1	.800	2.83	9	9	0	0	0	54	53	20	17	16	59
— Potomac (Caro.)		4	9	.308	2.96	18	18	0	0	0	103¹/₃	91	47	34	32	93
2000— Arkansas (Texas)		12	1	.923	2.32	18	18	•3	*3	0	108²/₃	93	32	28	27	102
— Memphis (PCL)		5	1	.833	2.15	9	8	0	0	0	54¹/₃	40	24	13	15	34
2001— St. Louis (N.L.)		6	3	.667	3.83	16	14	1	1	0	84²/₃	79	40	36	24	59
— Memphis (PCL)		8	5	.615	2.75	17	17	0	0	0	108	114	38	33	28	78
Major League totals (1 year)		6	3	.667	3.83	16	14	1	1	0	84²/₃	79	40	36	24	59

DIVISION SERIES RECORD

Year	League	W	L	Pct.	ERA	G	GS	CG	ShO	Sv.	IP	H	R	ER	BB	SO
2001— St. Louis (N.L.)		1	0	1.000	1.80	1	1	0	0	0	5	4	1	1	4	2

SMITH, CHUCK — P — MARLINS

PERSONAL: Born October 21, 1969, in Memphis, Tenn. ... 6-1/185. ... Throws right, bats right. ... Full name: Charles Edward Smith.
HIGH SCHOOL: John Adams (Cleveland).
JUNIOR COLLEGE: Central Arizona College.
COLLEGE: Indiana State.
TRANSACTIONS/CAREER NOTES: Signed as non-drafted free agent by Houston Astros organization (June 17, 1991). ... Selected by Chicago White Sox organization from Astros organization in Rule 5 minor league draft (December 6, 1994). ... Granted free agency (October 17, 1997). ... Signed by President, Taiwan League (1998). ... Signed by Sioux Falls, Northern League (May 1998). ... Contract purchased by Colorado Rockies organization from Sioux Falls (December 15, 1998). ... Released by Rockies (April 2, 1999). ... Signed by Texas Rangers organization (April 9, 1999). ... On Oklahoma disabled list (July 22-August 5, 1999). ... Traded by Rangers to Florida Marlins for IF/OF Brant Brown (June 9, 2000). ... On Florida disabled list (March 25-May 6 and July 25, 2001-remainder of season); included rehabilitation assignments to Brevard County (April 14-24) and Calgary (April 25-May 1).
STATISTICAL NOTES: Led Midwest League with 11 balks in 1995.
MISCELLANEOUS: Appeared in two games as pinch runner (2000).

Year League	W	L	Pct.	ERA	G	GS	CG	ShO	Sv.	IP	H	R	ER	BB	SO
1991—Gulf Coast Astros (GCL).....	4	3	.571	3.49	15	7	2	0	0	59 1/3	56	36	23	37	64
1992—Asheville (S.Atl.).............	9	9	.500	5.18	28	20	1	0	1	132	120	93	76	78	117
1993—Quad City (Midw.)	7	5	.583	4.64	22	17	2	0	0	110 2/3	109	73	57	52	103
1994—Jackson (Texas)	0	0	...	4.50	2	0	0	0	0	6	6	6	3	5	7
—Osceola (FSL).................	4	4	.500	3.72	35	2	0	0	0	84 2/3	73	41	35	49	60
1995—South Bend (Midw.)■	10	10	.500	2.69	26	25	4	•2	0	167	128	70	50	61	*145
1996—Prince William (Caro.)........	6	6	.500	4.01	20	20	2	1	0	123 1/3	125	65	55	49	99
—Birmingham (Sou.)............	2	1	.667	2.64	7	3	0	0	1	30 2/3	25	11	9	15	30
—Nashville (A.A.)...............	0	0	...	27.00	1	0	0	0	0	2/3	2	2	2	1	1
1997—Birmingham (Sou.)............	2	2	.500	3.16	25	0	0	0	0	62 2/3	63	35	22	27	57
—Nashville (A.A.)...............	0	3	.000	8.81	20	1	0	0	0	31 2/3	39	33	31	23	29
1998—President (Taiwan)■	0	0	...	54.00	2	0	0	0	0	1/3	...	...	2	4	0
—Sioux Falls (Nor.)■	5	3	.625	2.62	8	8	2	•1	0	55	44	18	16	21	70
1999—Oklahoma (PCL)■.............	5	4	.556	2.96	32	4	2	0	4	85	73	31	28	28	76
2000—Oklahoma (PCL).............	5	3	.625	3.78	11	11	1	0	0	66 2/3	73	31	28	38	73
—Florida (N.L.)■.................	6	6	.500	3.23	19	19	1	0	0	122 2/3	111	53	44	54	118
2001—Brevard County (FSL)........	0	0	...	3.38	2	2	0	0	0	8	7	3	3	1	6
—Calgary (PCL)	2	0	1.000	2.84	2	2	0	0	0	12 2/3	12	4	4	2	9
—Florida (N.L.)	5	5	.500	4.70	15	15	0	0	0	88	89	47	46	35	71
Major League totals (2 years)	11	11	.500	3.84	34	34	1	0	0	210 2/3	200	100	90	89	189

SMITH, JASON   SS   DEVIL RAYS

PERSONAL: Born July 24, 1977, in Meridian, Miss. ... 6-3/190. ... Bats left, throws right. ... Full name: Jason William Smith.
HIGH SCHOOL: Demopolis (Ala.).
JUNIOR COLLEGE: Meridian (Miss.) Community College.
TRANSACTIONS/CAREER NOTES: Selected by Chicago Cubs organization in 23rd round free-agent draft (June 4, 1996). ... On Iowa disabled list (July 9-August 2, 2001). ... Traded by Cubs to Tampa Bay Devil Rays (August 5, 2001), completing deal in which Devil Rays traded 1B Fred McGriff to Cubs for P Manny Aybar and a player to be named later (July 27, 2001).

							BATTING							FIELDING		
Year Team (League)	Pos.	G	AB	R	H	2B	3B	HR	RBI	Avg.	BB	SO	SB	PO	A	E	Avg.
1997—Williamsport (NY-P) ...	SS	51	205	25	59	5	2	0	11	.288	10	44	9	95	158	19	.930
—Rockford (Midw.)	SS	9	33	4	6	0	1	0	3	.182	2	11	1	14	24	5	.884
1998—Rockford (Midw.)	SS	126	464	67	111	15	9	7	60	.239	31	122	23	203	379	38	.939
1999—Daytona (FSL)	SS	39	142	22	37	5	2	5	26	.261	12	29	9	66	75	7	.953
2000—West Tenn (Sou.)	SS	119	481	55	114	22	7	12	61	.237	22	130	16	190	281	37	.927
2001—Iowa (PCL)	SS	70	240	31	56	8	6	4	15	.233	12	71	6	108	199	19	.942
—Chicago (N.L.)	SS	2	1	0	0	0	0	0	0	.000	0	1	0	2	0	0	1.000
—Durham (I.L.)■	SS	8	31	2	6	1	0	0	3	.194	0	11	0	9	24	3	.917
Major League totals (1 year)		2	1	0	0	0	0	0	0	.000	0	1	0	2	0	0	1.000

SMITH, MARK   OF   EXPOS

PERSONAL: Born May 7, 1970, in Pasadena, Calif. ... 6-3/225. ... Bats right, throws right. ... Full name: Mark Edward Smith.
HIGH SCHOOL: Arcadia (Calif.).
COLLEGE: Southern California.
TRANSACTIONS/CAREER NOTES: Selected by Baltimore Orioles organization in first round (ninth pick overall) of free-agent draft (June 3, 1991). ... On Baltimore disabled list (July 23, 1996-remainder of season); included rehabilitation assignments to Frederick (August 12-13), Bowie (August 21-23) and Rochester (September 3-13). ... Traded by Orioles to San Diego Padres for C Leroy McKinnis (January 9, 1997). ... Traded by Padres with P Hal Garrett to Pittsburgh Pirates for OF Trey Beamon and OF Angelo Encarnacion (March 29, 1997). ... On Pittsburgh disabled list (May 23-June 14, 1997); included rehabilitation assignment to Carolina (June 12-14). ... On Pittsburgh disabled list (May 4-19, 1998); included rehabilitation assignment to Nashville (May 9-19). ... Granted free agency (September 29, 1998). ... Signed by Florida Marlins organization (December 22, 1999). ... On disabled list (May 11-June 5, 2000). ... Granted free agency (October 5, 2000). ... Signed by Montreal Expos organization (November 17, 2000). ... Granted free agency (October 12, 2001). ... Re-signed by Expos organization (December 21, 2001).

							BATTING							FIELDING		
Year Team (League)	Pos.	G	AB	R	H	2B	3B	HR	RBI	Avg.	BB	SO	SB	PO	A	E	Avg.
1991—Frederick (Caro.)	OF	38	148	20	37	5	1	4	29	.250	9	24	1	49	1	1	.980
1992—Hagerstown (East.).....	OF	128	472	51	136	*32	6	4	62	.288	45	55	15	226	9	4	.983
1993—Rochester (I.L.)..........	OF-DH	129	485	69	136	27	1	12	68	.280	37	90	4	261	9	7	.975
1994—Rochester (I.L.)..........	OF-DH	114	437	69	108	27	1	19	66	.247	35	88	4	207	9	5	.977
—Baltimore (A.L.)..........	OF	3	7	0	1	0	0	0	2	.143	0	2	0	8	0	0	1.000
1995—Rochester (I.L.)..........	OF-DH	96	364	55	101	25	3	12	66	.277	24	69	7	167	4	7	.961
—Baltimore (A.L.)..........	OF-DH	37	104	11	24	5	0	3	15	.231	12	22	3	60	2	0	1.000
1996—Rochester (I.L.)..........	OF-DH	39	132	24	46	14	1	8	32	.348	14	22	10	55	1	2	.966
—Baltimore (A.L.)..........	OF-DH	27	78	9	19	2	0	4	10	.244	3	20	0	50	0	1	.980
—Frederick (Caro.)	DH	1	1	0	0	0	0	0	0	.000	0	0	0	...	...	...	...
—Bowie (East.)..............	DH	6	22	1	2	0	0	1	2	.091	1	6	0	...	...	...	...
1997—Calgary (PCL)■..........	OF-DH	39	137	37	51	14	1	14	42	.372	21	15	2	55	1	1	.982
—Pittsburgh (N.L.)........	OF-1B-DH	71	193	29	55	13	1	9	35	.285	28	36	3	111	9	0	1.000
—Carolina (Sou.)..........	OF	3	12	5	5	1	0	3	4	.417	0	1	0	4	0	1	.800
1998—Pittsburgh (N.L.)........	OF-1B-DH	59	128	18	25	6	0	2	13	.195	10	26	7	72	4	1	.987
—Nashville (PCL)........	OF-1B-3B-DH	24	93	18	33	10	1	8	30	.355	11	20	3	83	17	2	.980
2000—Florida (N.L.)■..........	OF-DH	104	192	22	47	8	1	5	27	.245	17	54	2	65	4	0	1.000
2001—Ottawa (I.L.)■............	OF	40	145	20	30	8	0	6	17	.207	15	38	4	72	4	2	.974
—Montreal (N.L.)............	OF-1B	80	194	28	47	13	1	6	18	.242	23	38	0	100	2	0	1.000
American League totals (3 years)		67	189	20	44	7	0	7	27	.233	15	44	3	118	2	1	.992
National League totals (4 years)		314	707	97	174	40	3	22	93	.246	78	154	12	348	19	1	.997
Major League totals (7 years)		381	896	117	218	47	3	29	120	.243	93	198	15	466	21	2	.996

PERSONAL: Born May 18, 1976, in St. Petersburg, Fla. ... 6-6/235. ... Throws right, bats right. ... Full name: Walter Roy Smith.
HIGH SCHOOL: Dixie Hollins (St. Petersburg, Fla.).
JUNIOR COLLEGE: St. Petersburg.
TRANSACTIONS/CAREER NOTES: Selected by Seattle Mariners organization in 13th round of free-agent draft (June 2, 1994). ... Released by Mariners (March 24, 1998). ... Signed by St. Paul, Northern League (May, 1998). ... Signed by Cleveland Indians organization (January 17, 2000). ... Granted free agency (October 15, 2000). ... Re-signed by Indians organization (December 20, 2000).

Year	League	W	L	Pct.	ERA	G	GS	CG	ShO	Sv.	IP	H	R	ER	BB	SO
1994—	Arizona Mariners (Ariz.)	3	1	.750	1.60	15	5	0	0	0	45	30	9	8	4	35
1995—	Wisconsin (Midw.)	7	14	.333	5.38	27	•27	1	0	0	149	*179	*100	*89	54	109
1996—	Wisconsin (Midw.)	6	13	.316	5.12	27	27	0	0	0	146	164	113	83	73	99
1997—	Wisconsin (Midw.)	3	4	.429	5.59	18	11	0	0	0	66	81	50	41	31	38
	—Memphis (Sou.)	0	0	...	10.38	4	0	0	0	0	4 1/3	6	5	5	1	6
1998—	St. Paul (Nor.)■	6	7	.462	5.03	18	18	1	•1	0	105 2/3	119	75	59	36	74
1999—	St. Paul (Nor.)	4	2	.667	3.21	8	7	1	1	0	42	38	18	15	23	43
2000—	Kinston (Caro.)■	2	2	.500	2.80	21	0	0	0	2	45	35	15	14	21	45
	—Akron (East.)	5	1	.833	1.96	28	0	0	0	6	55	36	14	12	22	50
2001—	Buffalo (I.L.)	0	5	.000	2.19	48	0	0	0	18	74	59	25	18	29	86
	—Cleveland (A.L.)	0	0	...	6.06	9	0	0	0	0	16 1/3	16	14	11	13	17
Major League totals (1 year)		0	0	...	6.06	9	0	0	0	0	16 1/3	16	14	11	13	17

PERSONAL: Born May 15, 1967, in Warren, Mich. ... 6-3/220. ... Throws right, bats right. ... Full name: John Andrew Smoltz.
HIGH SCHOOL: Waverly (Lansing, Mich.).
TRANSACTIONS/CAREER NOTES: Selected by Detroit Tigers organization in 22nd round of free-agent draft (June 3, 1985). ... Traded by Tigers to Atlanta Braves for P Doyle Alexander (August 12, 1987). ... On suspended list (June 20-29, 1994). ... Granted free agency (October 31, 1996). ... Re-signed by Braves (November 20, 1996). ... On Atlanta disabled list (March 29-April 15, and May 24-June 20, 1998); included rehabilitation assignments to Greenville (April 2-10 and June 10-14) and Macon (April 10-14 and June 14-16). ... On Atlanta disabled list (May 17-June 1 and July 5-24, 1999); included rehabilitation assignment to Greenville (July 15-18). ... On disabled list (April 2, 2000-entire season). ... On Atlanta disabled list (March 23-May 17 and June 10-July 22, 2001); included rehabilitation assignments to Macon (May 9-17) and Greenville (May 5-8 and July 17-22). ... Granted free agency (November 5, 2001). ... Re-signed by Braves (December 4, 2001).
RECORDS: Shares major league record for most home runs allowed in one inning—4 (June 19, 1994, first inning).
HONORS: Named N.L. Pitcher of the Year by THE SPORTING NEWS (1996). ... Named righthanded pitcher on THE SPORTING NEWS N.L. All-Star team (1996). ... Named N.L. Cy Young Award winner by Baseball Writers' Association of America (1996). ... Named pitcher on THE SPORTING NEWS N.L. Silver Slugger team (1997).
STATISTICAL NOTES: Tied for Florida State League lead with six balks in 1986. ... Led N.L. with 14 wild pitches in 1990, 20 in 1991 and 17 in 1992. ... Struck out 15 batters in one game (May 24, 1992). ... Pitched 3-0 one-hit, complete-game victory against Cincinnati (May 28, 1995).
MISCELLANEOUS: Appeared in three games as pinch runner and struck out in only appearance in pinch hitter (1989). ... Appeared in four games as pinch runner (1990). ... Appeared in two games as pinch runner (1991). ... Struck out in only appearance as pinch hitter (1992). ... Appeared in one game as pinch runner (1997).

Year	League	W	L	Pct.	ERA	G	GS	CG	ShO	Sv.	IP	H	R	ER	BB	SO
1986—	Lakeland (FSL)	7	8	.467	3.56	17	14	2	1	0	96	86	44	38	31	47
1987—	Glens Falls (East.)	4	10	.286	5.68	21	21	0	0	0	130	131	89	82	81	86
	—Richmond (I.L.)■	0	1	.000	6.19	3	3	0	0	0	16	17	11	11	11	5
1988—	Richmond (I.L.)	10	5	.667	2.79	20	20	3	0	0	135 1/3	118	49	42	37	115
	—Atlanta (N.L.)	2	7	.222	5.48	12	12	0	0	0	64	74	40	39	33	37
1989—	Atlanta (N.L.)	12	11	.522	2.94	29	29	5	0	0	208	160	79	68	72	168
1990—	Atlanta (N.L.)	14	11	.560	3.85	34	34	6	2	0	231 1/3	206	109	99	*90	170
1991—	Atlanta (N.L.)	14	13	.519	3.80	36	36	5	0	0	229 2/3	206	101	97	77	148
1992—	Atlanta (N.L.)	15	12	.556	2.85	35	•35	9	3	0	246 2/3	206	90	78	80	*215
1993—	Atlanta (N.L.)	15	11	.577	3.62	35	35	3	1	0	243 2/3	208	104	98	100	208
1994—	Atlanta (N.L.)	6	10	.375	4.14	21	21	1	0	0	134 2/3	120	69	62	48	113
1995—	Atlanta (N.L.)	12	7	.632	3.18	29	29	2	1	0	192 2/3	166	76	68	72	193
1996—	Atlanta (N.L.)	*24	8	*.750	2.94	35	35	6	2	0	*253 2/3	199	93	83	55	*276
1997—	Atlanta (N.L.)	15	12	.556	3.02	35	•35	7	2	0	*256	*234	97	86	63	241
1998—	Greenville (Sou.)	0	1	.000	2.57	3	3	0	0	0	14	11	4	4	3	16
	—Macon (S.Atl.)	0	0	...	3.60	2	2	0	0	0	10	7	4	4	1	14
	—Atlanta (N.L.)	17	3	*.850	2.90	26	26	2	2	0	167 2/3	145	58	54	44	173
1999—	Atlanta (N.L.)	11	8	.579	3.19	29	29	1	1	0	186 1/3	168	70	66	40	156
	—Greenville (Sou.)	0	0	...	4.50	2	1	0	0	0	4	5	2	2	1	7
2000—	Atlanta (N.L.)						Did not play.									
2001—	Greenville (Sou.)	0	0	...	0.00	3	1	0	0	0	6	3	0	0	0	6
	—Macon (S.Atl.)	0	0	...	1.80	1	1	0	0	0	5	4	1	1	0	5
	—Atlanta (N.L.)	3	3	.500	3.36	36	5	0	0	10	59	53	24	22	10	57
Major League totals (13 years)		160	116	.580	3.35	392	361	47	14	10	2473 1/3	2145	1010	920	784	2155

DIVISION SERIES RECORD

RECORDS: Shares N.L. career record for most wins—4; and strikeouts—36. ... Holds N.L. single-game record for most strikeouts—11 (October 3, 1997).

Year	League	W	L	Pct.	ERA	G	GS	CG	ShO	Sv.	IP	H	R	ER	BB	SO
1995—	Atlanta (N.L.)	0	0	...	7.94	1	1	0	0	0	5 2/3	5	5	5	1	6
1996—	Atlanta (N.L.)	1	0	1.000	1.00	1	1	0	0	0	9	4	1	1	2	7
1997—	Atlanta (N.L.)	1	0	1.000	1.00	1	1	1	0	0	9	3	1	1	1	11
1998—	Atlanta (N.L.)	1	0	1.000	1.17	1	1	0	0	0	7 2/3	5	1	1	0	6
1999—	Atlanta (N.L.)	1	0	1.000	5.14	1	1	0	0	0	7	6	4	4	3	3
2001—	Atlanta (N.L.)	0	0	...	2.25	3	0	0	0	2	4	3	1	1	0	3
Division series totals (6 years)		4	0	1.000	2.76	8	5	1	0	2	42 1/3	26	13	13	7	36

RECORDS: Holds career records for most innings pitched—95$^{1}/_{3}$; and most strikeouts—89. ... Shares N.L. career records for most wins—6; and home runs allowed—8.

NOTES: Named Most Valuable Player (1992).

Year League	W	L	Pct.	ERA	G	GS	CG	ShO	Sv.	IP	H	R	ER	BB	SO
1991— Atlanta (N.L.)	2	0	1.000	1.76	2	2	1	1	0	15$^{1}/_{3}$	14	3	3	3	15
1992— Atlanta (N.L.)	2	0	1.000	2.66	3	3	0	0	0	20$^{1}/_{3}$	14	7	6	10	19
1993— Atlanta (N.L.)	0	1	.000	0.00	1	1	0	0	0	6$^{1}/_{3}$	8	2	0	5	10
1995— Atlanta (N.L.)	0	0	...	2.57	1	1	0	0	0	7	7	2	2	2	2
1996— Atlanta (N.L.)	2	0	1.000	1.20	2	2	0	0	0	15	12	2	2	3	12
1997— Atlanta (N.L.)	0	1	.000	7.50	1	1	0	0	0	6	5	5	5	5	9
1998— Atlanta (N.L.)	0	0	...	3.95	2	2	0	0	0	13$^{2}/_{3}$	13	6	6	6	13
1999— Atlanta (N.L.)	0	0	...	6.23	3	1	0	0	1	8$^{2}/_{3}$	8	6	6	0	8
2001— Atlanta (N.L.)	0	0	...	0.00	2	0	0	0	0	3	0	0	0	0	1
Champ. series totals (9 years)	**6**	**2**	**.750**	**2.83**	**17**	**13**	**1**	**1**	**1**	**95$^{1}/_{3}$**	**81**	**33**	**30**	**34**	**89**

NOTES: Appeared in one game as pinch runner (1992). ... Member of World Series championship team (1995).

Year League	W	L	Pct.	ERA	G	GS	CG	ShO	Sv.	IP	H	R	ER	BB	SO
1991— Atlanta (N.L.)	0	0	...	1.26	2	2	0	0	0	14$^{1}/_{3}$	13	2	2	1	11
1992— Atlanta (N.L.)	1	0	1.000	2.70	2	2	0	0	0	13$^{1}/_{3}$	13	5	4	7	12
1995— Atlanta (N.L.)	0	0	...	15.43	1	1	0	0	0	2$^{1}/_{3}$	6	4	4	2	4
1996— Atlanta (N.L.)	1	1	.500	0.64	2	2	0	0	0	14	6	2	1	8	14
1999— Atlanta (N.L.)	0	1	.000	3.86	1	1	0	0	0	7	6	3	3	3	11
World Series totals (5 years)	**2**	**2**	**.500**	**2.47**	**8**	**8**	**0**	**0**	**0**	**51**	**44**	**16**	**14**	**21**	**52**

RECORDS: Shares single-game record for most wild pitches—2 (July 13, 1993). ... Shares single-inning record for most wild pitches—2 (July 13, 1993, sixth inning).

Year League	W	L	Pct.	ERA	GS	CG	ShO	Sv.	IP	H	R	ER	BB	SO
1989— National	0	1	.000	9.00	0	0	0	0	1	2	1	1	0	0
1992— National	0	0	...	0.00	0	0	0	0	$^{1}/_{3}$	1	0	0	0	0
1993— National	0	0	...	0.00	0	0	0	0	$^{1}/_{3}$	0	0	0	1	0
1996— National	1	0	1.000	0.00	1	0	0	0	2	2	0	0	0	1
All-Star Game totals (4 years)	**1**	**1**	**.500**	**2.45**	**1**	**0**	**0**	**0**	**3$^{2}/_{3}$**	**5**	**1**	**1**	**1**	**1**

SMYTH, STEVE   P   CUBS

PERSONAL: Born June 3, 1978, in Brawley, Calif. ... 6-1/220. ... Throws left, bats left. ... Full name: Steven Selton Smyth.
HIGH SCHOOL: Temecula Valley (Temecula, Calif.).
JUNIOR COLLEGE: Cypress.
COLLEGE: Southern California.
TRANSACTIONS/CAREER NOTES: Selected by Chicago Cubs organization in fourth round of free-agent draft (June 2, 1999). ... On disabled list (July 16, 2001-remainder of season).

Year League	W	L	Pct.	ERA	G	GS	CG	ShO	Sv.	IP	H	R	ER	BB	SO
1999— Eugene (N'West)	1	1	.500	4.38	5	5	0	0	0	24$^{2}/_{3}$	29	17	12	7	14
— Lansing (Midw.)	5	3	.625	6.93	10	10	0	0	0	50$^{2}/_{3}$	68	40	39	30	46
2000— Daytona (FSL)	8	8	.500	3.25	24	23	1	0	0	138$^{1}/_{3}$	134	62	50	57	100
2001— West Tenn (Sou.)	9	3	.750	2.54	18	18	3	1	0	120$^{1}/_{3}$	110	38	34	40	93

SNEAD, ESIX   OF   METS

PERSONAL: Born June 7, 1976, in Fort Myers, Fla. ... 5-10/175. ... Bats both, throws right.
HIGH SCHOOL: Williston (Fla.).
COLLEGE: Central Florida.
TRANSACTIONS/CAREER NOTES: Selected by St. Louis Cardinals organization in 18th round of free-agent draft (June 2, 1998). ... On disabled list (August 20-September 5, 2001). ... Claimed on waivers by New York Mets (November 20, 2001).
STATISTICAL NOTES: Led Carolina League in caught stealing with 35 in 2000. ... Led Eastern League in caught stealing with 23 in 2001. ... Led Eastern League outfielders with 363 total chances in 2001.

Year Team (League)	Pos.	G	AB	R	H	2B	3B	HR	RBI	Avg.	BB	SO	SB	PO	A	E	Avg.
1998— New Jersey (NY-P)	OF	58	193	38	45	4	4	1	16	.233	33	54	*42	123	1	3	.976
1999— Potomac (Caro.)	OF	67	249	37	45	8	5	0	14	.181	32	57	45	179	4	2	.989
— Peoria (Midw.)	OF	59	181	35	35	7	1	2	18	.193	35	42	29	153	4	4	.975
2000— Potomac (Caro.)	OF	132	493	82	116	14	3	1	34	.235	72	98	109	313	10	7	.979
2001— New Haven (East.)	OF	133	520	71	121	21	6	1	33	.233	44	115	64	*347	10	6	.983

SNOW, BERT   P   ATHLETICS

PERSONAL: Born March 23, 1977, in Brooksville, Fla. ... 6-1/190. ... Throws right, bats right. ... Full name: Robert Bruce Snow.
HIGH SCHOOL: Hernando (Brooksville, Fla.).
COLLEGE: Vanderbilt.
TRANSACTIONS/CAREER NOTES: Selected by Oakland Athletics organization in 10th round of free-agent draft (June 2, 1998). ... On disabled list (April 5, 2001-entire season).

Year	League	W	L	Pct.	ERA	G	GS	CG	ShO	Sv.	IP	H	R	ER	BB	SO
1998—	Southern Oregon (N'West).	1	3	.250	5.64	11	8	0	0	0	44²/₃	52	38	28	28	18
—	Modesto (Calif.)	1	1	.500	3.12	2	2	0	0	0	8²/₃	12	8	3	6	12
1999—	Visalia (Calif.)	3	2	.600	5.15	31	3	0	0	5	64²/₃	55	43	37	40	90
—	Midland (Texas)	1	1	.500	1.71	21	0	0	0	13	21	14	4	4	9	32
—	Vancouver (PCL)	1	0	1.000	3.86	2	0	0	0	0	2¹/₃	3	1	1	1	3
2000—	Sacramento (PCL)	0	0	...	4.50	3	0	0	0	0	2	1	1	1	3	3
—	Midland (Texas)	1	7	.125	3.59	59	0	0	0	27	67²/₃	58	33	27	36	98
2001—	Sacramento (PCL)								Did not play.							

SNOW, J.T.   1B   GIANTS

PERSONAL: Born February 26, 1968, in Long Beach, Calif. ... 6-2/205. ... Bats left, throws left. ... Full name: Jack Thomas Snow Jr. ... Son of Jack Snow, wide receiver with Los Angeles Rams (1965-75).

HIGH SCHOOL: Los Alamitos (Calif.).

COLLEGE: Arizona.

TRANSACTIONS/CAREER NOTES: Selected by New York Yankees organization in fifth round of free-agent draft (June 5, 1989). ... Traded by Yankees with P Jerry Nielsen and P Russ Springer to California Angels for P Jim Abbott (December 6, 1992). ... Traded by Angels to San Francisco Giants for P Allen Watson and P Fausto Macey (November 27, 1996). ... On San Francisco disabled list (May 27-June 14, June 24-July 15 and July 27-August 7, 2001); included rehabilitation assignments to Fresno (June 12-14 and July 12-15).

RECORDS: Shares major league career record for highest fielding percentage for first baseman—.996.

HONORS: Named International League Most Valuable Player (1992). ... Won A.L. Gold Glove at first base (1995-96). ... Won N.L. Gold Glove at first base (1997-2000).

STATISTICAL NOTES: Led New York-Pennsylvania League first basemen with 649 total chances in 1989. ... Led Carolina League in grounding into double plays with 20 in 1990. ... Led Carolina League first basemen with 1,298 total chances and 120 double plays in 1990. ... Tied for Eastern League lead with 10 sacrifice flies in 1991. ... Led Eastern League first basemen with 1,200 total chances in 1991. ... Led International League with 11 intentional bases on balls received in 1992. ... Led International League first basemen with .995 fielding percentage, 1,097 putouts, 93 assists, 1,196 total chances and 107 double plays in 1992. ... Switch-hit home runs in one game (June 9, 1996). ... Led N.L. in sacrifice flies with 14 in 2000. ... Career major league grand slams: 7.

MISCELLANEOUS: Batted as switch-hitter (1989-98).

							BATTING								FIELDING		
Year	Team (League)	Pos.	G	AB	R	H	2B	3B	HR	RBI	Avg.	BB	SO	SB	PO	A	E	Avg.
1989—	Oneonta (NY-Penn)	1B	73	274	41	80	18	2	8	51	.292	29	35	4	*590	53	6	*.991
1990—	Prince William (Caro.)	1B	*138	520	57	133	25	1	8	72	.256	46	65	2	*1208	*78	12	.991
1991—	Albany/Colonie (East.)	1B	132	477	78	133	33	3	13	76	.279	67	78	5	*1102	90	8	*.993
1992—	Columbus (I.L.)	1B-OF	135	492	81	154	26	4	15	78	•.313	70	65	3	†1103	†93	8	†.993
—	New York (A.L.)	1B-DH	7	14	1	2	1	0	0	2	.143	5	5	0	43	2	0	1.000
1993—	California (A.L.)■.......	1B	129	419	60	101	18	2	16	57	.241	55	88	3	1010	81	6	.995
—	Vancouver (PCL)	1B	23	94	19	32	9	1	5	24	.340	10	13	0	200	13	2	.991
1994—	Vancouver (PCL)	1B-DH	53	189	35	56	13	2	8	43	.296	22	32	1	413	42	1	.998
—	California (A.L.)	1B	61	223	22	49	4	0	8	30	.220	19	48	0	489	37	2	.996
1995—	California (A.L.)	1B	143	544	80	157	22	1	24	102	.289	52	91	2	1161	57	4	.997
1996—	California (A.L.)	1B	155	575	69	148	20	1	17	67	.257	56	96	1	1274	103	10	.993
1997—	San Fran. (N.L.)■.......	1B	157	531	81	149	36	1	28	104	.281	96	124	6	1308	108	7	.995
1998—	San Francisco (N.L.) ..	1B	138	435	65	108	29	1	15	79	.248	58	84	1	1040	94	1	*.999
1999—	San Francisco (N.L.) ..	1B	161	570	93	156	25	2	24	98	.274	86	121	0	1221	122	6	.996
2000—	San Francisco (N.L.) ..	1B	155	536	82	152	33	2	19	96	.284	66	129	1	1197	91	6	.995
2001—	San Francisco (N.L.) ..	1B	101	285	43	70	12	1	8	34	.246	55	81	0	658	47	1	.999
—	Fresno (PCL)	1B	4	12	1	0	0	0	0	0	.000	2	7	0	26	0	0	1.000
American League totals (5 years)			495	1775	232	457	65	4	65	258	.257	187	328	6	3977	280	22	.995
National League totals (5 years)			712	2357	364	635	135	7	94	411	.269	361	539	8	5424	462	21	.996
Major League totals (10 years)			1207	4132	596	1092	200	11	159	669	.264	548	867	14	9401	742	43	.996

DIVISION SERIES RECORD

							BATTING								FIELDING		
Year	Team (League)	Pos.	G	AB	R	H	2B	3B	HR	RBI	Avg.	BB	SO	SB	PO	A	E	Avg.
1997—	San Francisco (N.L.) ..	1B	3	6	0	1	0	0	0	0	.167	1	1	0	12	0	0	1.000
2000—	San Francisco (N.L.) ..	1B-PH	4	10	1	4	0	0	1	3	.400	4	1	0	23	0	0	1.000
Division series totals (2 years)			7	16	1	5	0	0	1	3	.313	5	2	0	35	0	0	1.000

SOBKOWIAK, SCOTT   P   BRAVES

PERSONAL: Born October 26, 1977, in Woodstock, Ill. ... 6-5/230. ... Throws right, bats right.

HIGH SCHOOL: Montini Catholic (Lombard, Ill.).

COLLEGE: Northern Iowa.

TRANSACTIONS/CAREER NOTES: Selected by Atlanta Braves organization in seventh round of free-agent draft (June 2, 1998). ... On Greenville disabled list (April 26-September 12, 2000). ... On Atlanta disabled list (March 28-July 16, 2001); included rehabilitation assignments to Gulf Coast Braves (June 21-30) and Greenville (July 1-16).

Year	League	W	L	Pct.	ERA	G	GS	CG	ShO	Sv.	IP	H	R	ER	BB	SO
1998—	Eugene (N'West)	3	2	.600	1.55	8	8	0	0	0	40²/₃	25	12	7	13	55
1999—	Myrtle Beach (S.Atl.)	9	4	.692	2.84	27	26	0	0	0	139¹/₃	100	50	44	63	161
2000—	Greenville (Sou.)	2	1	.667	4.63	4	4	0	0	0	23¹/₃	26	16	12	15	27
2001—	Gulf Coast Braves (GCL)	0	0	...	1.29	2	2	0	0	0	7	4	2	1	1	11
—	Greenville (Sou.)	2	5	.286	5.54	12	12	0	0	0	65	71	45	40	40	48
—	Atlanta (N.L.)	0	0	...	9.00	1	0	0	0	0	1	2	1	1	0	0
Major League totals (1 year)		0	0	...	9.00	1	0	0	0	0	1	2	1	1	0	0

PERSONAL: Born January 3, 1966, in Barquisimeto, Venezuela. ... 5-11/185. ... Bats right, throws right. ... Name pronounced SO-ho.

TRANSACTIONS/CAREER NOTES: Signed as non-drafted free agent by Toronto Blue Jays organization (January 3, 1986). ... Traded by Blue Jays with OF Junior Felix and a player to be named later to California Angels for OF Devon White, P Willie Fraser and a player to be named later (December 2, 1990); Blue Jays acquired P Marcus Moore and Angels acquired C Ken Rivers to complete deal (December 4, 1990). ... Traded by Angels to Blue Jays for 3B Kelly Gruber and cash (December 8, 1992). ... On Toronto disabled list (May 10-30, 1993). ... Granted free agency (October 15, 1993). ... Signed by Seattle Mariners organization (January 10, 1994). ... On Seattle disabled list (June 7-23, 1995); included rehabilitation assignment to Tacoma (June 19-23). ... Claimed on waivers by New York Yankees (August 22, 1996). ... Granted free agency (December 20, 1996). ... Re-signed by Yankees (January 9, 1997). ... On disabled list (August 15, 1997-remainder of season). ... Granted free agency (October 31, 1997). ... Re-signed by Yankees (November 12, 1997). ... On New York disabled list (March 22-April 27, 1998); included rehabilitation assignments to Tampa (April 17-20) and Columbus (April 20-27). ... Granted free agency (November 10, 1999). ... Signed by Pittsburgh Pirates organization (January 19, 2000). ... On Pittsburgh disabled list (July 6-24, 2000). ... Traded by Pirates to Yankees for P Chris Spurling (August 7, 2000). ... Granted free agency (November 7, 2000). ... Re-signed by Yankees (December 7, 2000). ... Granted free agency (November 6, 2001). ... Re-signed by Yankees organization (January 8, 2002).

STATISTICAL NOTES: Led International League shortstops with .957 fielding percentage in 1989. ... Led International League with nine sacrifice flies in 1990. ... Led A.L. with 19 sacrifice hits in 1991. ... Career major league grand slams: 1.

Year Team (League)	Pos.	G	AB	R	H	2B	3B	HR	RBI	Avg.	BB	SO	SB	PO	A	E	Avg.
1986—																	
							Dominican Summer League statistics unavailable.										
1987—Myrtle Beach (S.Atl.)	SS-2B-3B-OF	72	223	23	47	5	4	2	15	.211	17	18	5	104	123	14	.942
1988—Myrtle Beach (S.Atl.)	SS	135	*536	83	*155	22	5	5	56	.289	35	35	14	191	407	28	.955
1989—Syracuse (I.L.)	SS-2B	121	482	54	133	20	5	3	54	.276	21	42	9	170	348	23	†.957
1990—Syracuse (I.L.)	2B-SS	75	297	39	88	12	3	6	25	.296	14	23	10	138	212	10	.972
—Toronto (A.L.)	2-S-O-3-DH	33	80	14	18	3	0	1	9	.225	5	5	1	34	31	5	.929
1991—California (A.L.)■	2-S-3-O-DH	113	364	38	94	14	1	3	20	.258	14	26	4	233	335	11	.981
1992—Edmonton (PCL)	3B-2B-SS	37	145	22	43	9	1	1	24	.297	9	17	4	32	106	4	.972
—California (A.L.)	2B-3B-SS	106	368	37	100	12	3	7	43	.272	14	24	7	196	293	9	.982
1993—Toronto (A.L.)■	SS-2B-3B	19	47	5	8	2	0	0	6	.170	4	2	0	24	35	2	.967
—Syracuse (I.L.)	2-O-DH-3-S-1	43	142	17	31	7	2	1	12	.218	8	12	2	46	60	4	.964
1994—Calgary (PCL)■	SS-2B-DH	24	102	19	33	9	3	1	18	.324	10	7	5	36	81	2	.983
—Seattle (A.L.)	2B-SS-DH-3B	63	213	32	59	9	2	6	22	.277	8	25	2	97	186	7	.976
1995—Seattle (A.L.)	SS-2B-OF	102	339	50	98	18	2	7	39	.289	23	19	4	141	221	7	.976
—Tacoma (PCL)	2B-DH-SS	4	17	1	3	0	0	1	1	.176	0	2	0	4	9	0	1.000
1996—Seattle (A.L.)	3B-2B-SS	77	247	20	52	8	1	1	16	.211	10	13	2	97	158	8	.970
—New York (A.L.)■	2B-SS-3B	18	40	3	11	2	0	0	5	.275	1	4	0	16	37	0	1.000
1997—New York (A.L.)	2B-SS-3B-1B	77	215	27	66	6	1	2	25	.307	16	14	3	131	153	5	.983
1998—Tampa (FSL)	SS	3	9	1	2	0	0	0	0	.222	2	0	0	4	8	1	.923
—Columbus (I.L.)	SS-DH-2B	6	23	1	5	2	0	0	2	.217	1	1	1	9	16	1	.962
—New York (A.L.)	S-1-2-3-DH	54	147	16	34	3	1	0	14	.231	4	15	1	146	74	3	.987
1999—New York (A.L.)	3-2-S-1-DH	49	127	20	32	6	0	2	16	.252	4	17	1	65	72	2	.986
2000—Pittsburgh (N.L.)■	3B-2B	61	176	14	50	11	0	5	20	.284	11	16	1	24	97	5	.960
—later (A.L.)■	2B-3B-1B-SS	34	125	19	36	7	1	2	17	.288	6	6	1	64	75	2	.986
2001—New York (A.L.)	3-1-2-S-D	39	79	5	13	2	0	0	9	.165	4	12	1	51	42	2	.979
American League totals (12 years)		784	2391	286	621	92	12	31	241	.260	113	182	27	1295	1712	65	.979
National League totals (1 year)		61	176	14	50	11	0	5	20	.284	11	16	1	24	97	5	.960
Major League totals (12 years)		845	2567	300	671	103	12	36	261	.261	124	198	28	1319	1809	70	.978

DIVISION SERIES RECORD

RECORDS: Shares single-game record for most at-bats—7 (October 4, 1995).

Year Team (League)	Pos.	G	AB	R	H	2B	3B	HR	RBI	Avg.	BB	SO	SB	PO	A	E	Avg.
1995—Seattle (A.L.)	SS	5	20	0	5	0	0	0	3	.250	0	3	0	9	15	1	.960
1996—New York (A.L.)	2B	2	0	0	0	0	0	0	0	...	0	0	0	1	1	0	1.000
1998—New York (A.L.)								Did not play.									
1999—New York (A.L.)								Did not play.									
2000—New York (A.L.)	2B	5	16	2	3	2	0	0	5	.188	2	1	0	9	22	1	.969
2001—New York (A.L.)								Did not play.									
Division series totals (3 years)		12	36	2	8	2	0	0	8	.222	2	4	0	19	38	2	.966

CHAMPIONSHIP SERIES RECORD

Year Team (League)	Pos.	G	AB	R	H	2B	3B	HR	RBI	Avg.	BB	SO	SB	PO	A	E	Avg.
1995—Seattle (A.L.)	SS	6	20	0	5	2	0	0	1	.250	0	2	0	9	18	1	.964
1996—New York (A.L.)	2B	3	5	0	1	0	0	0	0	.200	0	1	0	4	4	0	1.000
1998—New York (A.L.)	1B	1	0	0	0	0	0	0	0	...	0	0	0	1	1	0	1.000
1999—New York (A.L.)	PH-2B	2	1	0	0	0	0	0	0	.000	0	0	0	1	1	0	1.000
2000—New York (A.L.)	2B-3B	6	23	1	6	1	0	0	2	.261	2	3	0	10	15	0	1.000
2001—New York (A.L.)	1B	1	1	0	0	0	0	0	0	.000	0	0	0	4	0	0	1.000
Championship series totals (6 years)		19	50	1	12	3	0	0	3	.240	2	6	0	29	39	1	.986

WORLD SERIES RECORD

NOTES: Member of World Series championship team (1996, 1998, 1999 and 2000).

Year Team (League)	Pos.	G	AB	R	H	2B	3B	HR	RBI	Avg.	BB	SO	SB	PO	A	E	Avg.
1996—New York (A.L.)	PH-2B	5	5	0	3	1	0	0	1	.600	0	0	0	5	2	0	1.000
1998—New York (A.L.)								Did not play.									
1999—New York (A.L.)	2B	1	0	0	0	0	0	0	0	...	0	0	0	1	1	0	1.000
2000—New York (A.L.)	3B-2B	4	7	0	2	0	0	0	2	.286	1	0	1	4	1	0	1.000
2001—New York (A.L.)	PH-1B	2	3	0	1	0	0	0	1	.333	0	0	0	3	0	0	1.000
World Series totals (4 years)		12	15	0	6	1	0	0	4	.400	1	0	1	13	4	0	1.000

SOLER, RAMON   SS   DEVIL RAYS

PERSONAL: Born July 6, 1981, in Las Caobas, Dominican Republic. ... 6-0/175. ... Bats both, throws right.
TRANSACTIONS/CAREER NOTES: Signed as non-drafted free agent by Tampa Bay Devil Rays organization (July 23, 1997). ... On disabled list (April 6, 2000-entire season). ... On disabled list (April 5-20 and August 22, 2001-remainder of season).
STATISTICAL NOTES: Led Gulf Coast League shortstops with 301 total chances and 36 double plays in 1998.

Year	Team (League)	Pos.	G	AB	R	H	2B	3B	HR	RBI	Avg.	BB	SO	SB	PO	A	E	Avg.
1998—	GC Devil Rays (GCL)..	SS	58	•226	*47	57	7	*7	1	19	.252	27	48	23	75	*209	17	.944
1999—	Charl., S.C. (S.Atl.).....	SS	108	389	74	92	17	2	1	28	.237	56	93	46	116	279	*40	.908
2000—	Charl., S.C. (S.Atl.)							Did not play.										
2001—	Bakersfield (Calif.)......	2B	103	418	72	110	14	4	2	27	.263	46	75	25	120	206	14	.959

SONNIER, SHAWN   P   ROYALS

PERSONAL: Born July 5, 1976, in Rayne, La. ... 6-5/210. ... Throws right, bats right. ... Full name: Shawn Matthew Sonnier.
HIGH SCHOOL: North Vermilion (Monroe, La.).
JUNIOR COLLEGE: Chipola, then Panola.
COLLEGE: Louisiana Tech.
TRANSACTIONS/CAREER NOTES: Signed as non-drafted free agent by Kansas City Royals organization (September 21, 1998).

Year	League	W	L	Pct.	ERA	G	GS	CG	ShO	Sv.	IP	H	R	ER	BB	SO
1998—	Spokane (N'West)	0	0	...	1.35	7	0	0	0	1	6⅔	7	1	1	1	10
1999—	Wilmington (Caro.).............	1	2	.333	2.88	44	0	0	0	13	59⅓	46	20	19	19	73
2000—	Wichita (Texas)	0	3	.000	2.25	48	0	0	0	21	64	41	22	16	26	90
2001—	Omaha (PCL)......................	5	5	.500	4.82	47	2	0	0	6	71	69	41	38	33	63

SORIANO, ALFONSO   2B   YANKEES

PERSONAL: Born January 7, 1978, in San Pedro de Macoris, Dominican Republic. ... 6-1/160. ... Bats right, throws right.
HIGH SCHOOL: Eugenio Maria de Osto (Dominican Republic).
TRANSACTIONS/CAREER NOTES: Signed by Hiroshima Toyo Carp of Japan Central League (November 1994). ... Played in Toyo Carp organization (1995-97). ... Retired from Japan Central League and declared free agent by Major League Baseball (1998). ... Signed by New York Yankees (September 29, 1998). ... On Norwich disabled list (July 15-August 15, 1999).

Year	Team (League)	Pos.	G	AB	R	H	2B	3B	HR	RBI	Avg.	BB	SO	SB	PO	A	E	Avg.
1995—	Hiroshima (DSL)		63	227	52	83	12	3	4	55	.366	30	19	8	...	...	...	...
1996—	Hiroshima (Jap.West.)■		57	131	11	28	...	...	0	13	.214	...	...	...	...	...	...	...
1997—	Hiroshima (Jap. Cen.)	OF	9	17	2	2	0	0	0	0	.118	2	4	0	...	...	...	...
	Hiroshima (Jap.West.)		68	242	28	61	13	2	8	34	.252	13	35	14	...	...	...	...
1998—	....							Out of organized baseball.										
1999—	Norwich (East.)■	SS-DH	89	361	57	110	20	3	15	68	.305	32	67	24	160	243	27	.937
	GC Yankees (GCL)......	SS-DH	5	19	7	5	2	0	1	5	.263	1	3	0	2	11	1	.929
	Columbus (I.L.)	SS-3B-2B	20	82	8	15	5	1	2	11	.183	5	18	1	19	44	3	.955
	New York (A.L.)	DH-SS	9	8	2	1	0	0	1	1	.125	0	3	0	0	1	1	.500
2000—	Columbus (I.L.)	SS-2B	111	459	90	133	32	6	12	66	.290	25	85	14	175	245	21	.952
	New York (A.L.) 3B-SS-DH-2B		22	50	5	9	3	0	2	3	.180	1	15	2	18	18	7	.837
2001—	New York (A.L.)	2B-DH	158	574	77	154	34	3	18	73	.268	29	125	43	318	366	19	.973
	Major League totals (3 years)		189	632	84	164	37	3	21	77	.259	30	143	45	336	385	27	.964

DIVISION SERIES RECORD

Year	Team (League)	Pos.	G	AB	R	H	2B	3B	HR	RBI	Avg.	BB	SO	SB	PO	A	E	Avg.
2001—	New York (A.L.).........	2B	5	18	2	4	3	0	0	3	.222	1	5	2	7	9	0	1.000

CHAMPIONSHIP SERIES RECORD

Year	Team (League)	Pos.	G	AB	R	H	2B	3B	HR	RBI	Avg.	BB	SO	SB	PO	A	E	Avg.
2001—	New York (A.L.).........	2B	5	15	5	6	0	0	1	2	.400	3	3	2	8	13	1	.955

WORLD SERIES RECORD

Year	Team (League)	Pos.	G	AB	R	H	2B	3B	HR	RBI	Avg.	BB	SO	SB	PO	A	E	Avg.
2001—	New York (A.L.).........	2B	7	25	1	6	0	0	1	2	.240	0	7	0	18	20	3	.927

SORIANO, RAFAEL   P   MARINERS

PERSONAL: Born December 19, 1979, in San Jose, Dominican Republic. ... 6-1/175. ... Throws right, bats right.
TRANSACTIONS/CAREER NOTES: Signed as non-drafted free agent by Seattle Mariners organization (August 30, 1996). ... On Wisconsin disabled list (April 6-May 5, 2000). ... On San Bernardino disabled list (April 26-May 6, 2001). ... On San Antonio disabled list (July 4-12 and August 31, 2001-remainder of season).

RECORD AS PITCHER

Year	League	W	L	Pct.	ERA	G	GS	CG	ShO	Sv.	IP	H	R	ER	BB	SO
1999—	Everett (N'WWest)..............	5	4	.556	3.11	14	14	0	0	0	75⅓	56	34	26	49	83
2000—	Wisconsin (Midw.).............	8	4	.667	2.87	21	21	1	0	0	122⅓	97	41	39	50	90
2001—	San Bernardino (Calif.).....	6	3	.667	2.53	15	15	*2	1	0	89	49	28	25	39	98
	San Antonio (Texas)	2	2	.500	3.35	8	8	0	0	0	48⅓	34	18	18	14	53

Year	Team (League)	Pos.	G	AB	R	H	2B	3B	HR	RBI	Avg.	BB	SO	SB	PO	A	E	Avg.
1997—	Ariz. Mariners (Ariz.) ..	1B-OF	38	119	19	32	3	2	0	12	.269	14	31	7	187	10	6	.970
1998—	Ariz. Mariners (Ariz.) ..	1B-OF	32	108	17	18	4	0	0	6	.167	11	34	5	173	21	5	.975

S

SOSA, JORGE — P — BREWERS

PERSONAL: Born April 28, 1978, in Santo Domingo, Dominican Republic. ... 6-2/180. ... Throws right, bats both. ... Full name: Jorge Bolivar Sosa.

TRANSACTIONS/CAREER NOTES: Signed as non-drafted free agent by Colorado Rockies organization (June 23, 1995).... Selected by Seattle Mariners from Rockies organization in Rule 5 minor league draft (December 11, 2000).... Selected by Milwaukee Brewers from Mariners organization in Rule 5 major league draft (December 13, 2001).

Year League	W	L	Pct.	ERA	G	GS	CG	ShO	Sv.	IP	H	R	ER	BB	SO
2001— Everett (N'West)■	3	1	.750	1.69	21	7	0	0	7	58 2/3	45	22	11	19	57
— Wisconsin (Midw.)	0	0	...	9.00	2	0	0	0	0	2	3	2	2	0	4

RECORD AS POSITION PLAYER

						BATTING								FIELDING		
Year Team (League)	Pos.	G	AB	R	H	2B	3B	HR	RBI	Avg.	BB	SO	SB	PO	A	E	Avg.
1995— Dom. Rockies (DSL) ..	SS	32	91	10	23	3	0	0	1	.253	8	26	1	13	46	15	.797
1996— Dom. Rockies (DSL) ..		51	162	29	39	13	2	3	25	.241	25	54	2	...	...	...	...
1997— Ariz. Rockies (Ariz.)....	OF	29	93	13	13	1	2	0	6	.140	13	36	6	31	2	4	.892
1998— Ariz. Rockies (Ariz.)..	OF	45	152	23	36	6	1	2	11	.237	12	57	4	60	4	5	.928
1999— Portland (N'West)	OF	35	113	15	23	3	0	2	8	.204	13	57	2	45	2	3	.940
2000— Portland (N'West)	OF	62	200	24	46	7	5	4	26	.230	37	102	4	61	4	7	.903

SOSA, JUAN — SS — TIGERS

PERSONAL: Born August 19, 1975, in San Francisco de Macoris, Dominican Republic. ... 6-1/175. ... Bats right, throws right. ... Full name: Juan Luis Encarnacion Sosa.

HIGH SCHOOL: Renacimiento (Dominican Republic).

TRANSACTIONS/CAREER NOTES: Signed as non-drafted free agent by Los Angeles Dodgers organization (July 24, 1992). ... Selected by Colorado Rockies organization from Dodgers organization in Rule 5 minor league draft (December 15, 1997). ... On disabled list (April 6-21, 2000). ... Traded by Rockies to Arizona Diamondbacks for 3B Ryan Owens (April 23, 2001). ... Granted free agency (October 15, 2001). ... Signed by Detroit Tigers organization (December 19, 2001).

STATISTICAL NOTES: Led Carolina League shortstops with 555 total chances in 1998. ... Led Southern League shortstops with 191 putouts and .958 fielding percentage in 1999. ... Tied for Pacific Coast League with nine sacrifice hits in 2000.

						BATTING								FIELDING		
Year Team (League)	Pos.	G	AB	R	H	2B	3B	HR	RBI	Avg.	BB	SO	SB	PO	A	E	Avg.
1993— Dom. Dodgers (DSL) .	IF	63	237	51	66	7	4	0	39	.278	45	52	8	209	28	16	.937
1994— Dom. Dodgers (DSL) .	2B	59	224	55	65	11	3	6	60	.290	44	27	13	141	168	17	.948
1995— Vero Beach (FSL) ...	2B-SS	8	27	2	6	1	1	1	6	.222	0	4	0	10	21	1	.969
— Yakima (N'West) ...	2B-3B-SS	61	217	26	51	10	4	3	16	.235	15	39	8	93	174	16	.943
1996— Savannah (S.Atl.) ...2B-SS-3B-OF	112	370	58	94	21	2	7	38	.254	30	64	14	139	261	22	.948	
1997— Vero Beach (FSL) ...	SS-2B-3B	92	250	32	55	5	2	5	29	.220	14	39	20	130	193	19	.944
1998— Salem (Caro.)■	SS	133	529	88	147	20	*12	8	47	.278	43	83	*64	*196	328	31	.944
1999— Carolina (Sou.)	SS-OF	125	490	70	135	22	5	7	42	.276	31	65	38	†202	361	24	†.959
— Colo. Springs (PCL) ...	OF-SS	6	28	3	11	1	1	1	5	.393	0	1	1	15	8	1	.958
— Colorado (N.L.) ...	OF-SS	11	9	3	2	0	0	0	0	.222	2	2	0	6	3	1	.900
2000— Colo. Springs (PCL) ...	SS-OF	118	449	67	123	25	9	9	69	.274	31	54	23	177	334	25	.953
2001— Colo. Springs (PCL) ...	3B-SS	14	40	2	9	1	0	0	2	.225	5	7	1	7	32	5	.886
— Tucson (PCL)■ 2B-SS-3B-OF	64	182	17	35	6	1	0	12	.192	9	22	5	88	121	9	.959	
— Arizona (N.L.)	3B	2	1	0	0	0	0	0	0	.000	0	1	0	0	1	0	1.000
— El Paso (Texas)	SS	29	113	14	29	5	1	0	8	.257	7	20	5	48	78	7	.947
Major League totals (2 years)		13	10	3	2	0	0	0	0	.200	2	3	0	6	4	1	.909

SOSA, SAMMY — OF — CUBS

PERSONAL: Born November 12, 1968, in San Pedro de Macoris, Dominican Republic. ... 6-0/220. ... Bats right, throws right. ... Full name: Samuel Sosa Peralta.

TRANSACTIONS/CAREER NOTES: Signed as non-drafted free agent by Texas Rangers organization (July 30, 1985). ... Traded by Rangers with SS Scott Fletcher and P Wilson Alvarez to Chicago White Sox for OF Harold Baines and IF Fred Manrique (July 29, 1989). ... Traded by White Sox with P Ken Patterson to Chicago Cubs for OF George Bell (March 30, 1992). ... On Chicago disabled list (June 13-July 27, and August 7-September 16, 1992); included rehabilitation assignment to Iowa (July 21-27). ... On disabled list (August 21, 1996-remainder of season).

RECORDS: Holds major league single-season record for most at-bats without a triple—643 (1998). ... Holds major league single-month record for most home runs—20 (June 1998). ... Shares major league single-season record for most major league ballparks, one or more home runs—18 (1998); and most times hitting three or more home runs in a game—2 (2001). ... Shares major league record for most grand slams in two consecutive games—2 (July 27 and 28, 1998); and most consecutive seasons with 50 or more home runs—4 (1998-2001). ... Shares major league single-season record for most times hitting two or more home runs in a game—11 (1998). ... Shares major league single-inning record for most home runs—2 (May 16, 1996, seventh inning). ... Shares N.L. single-month record for most home runs—17 (August 2001); and career record for most times hitting three or more home runs in a game—5. ... Shares major league single-month record for most home runs—5 (October 2001).

HONORS: Named outfielder on THE SPORTING NEWS N.L. All-Star team (1995, 1998, 1999, 2000 and 2001). ... Named outfielder on THE SPORTING NEWS N.L. Silver Slugger team (1995, 1998, 1999 and 2000). ... Named co-Sportsman of the Year by THE SPORTING NEWS (1998). ... Named Major League Player of the Year by THE SPORTING NEWS (1998). ... Named N.L. Most Valuable Player by Baseball Writers' Association of America (1998). ... Named outfielder on N.L. Silver Slugger team (2001).

STATISTICAL NOTES: Led Gulf Coast League with 96 total bases in 1986. ... Tied for South Atlantic League lead in double plays by outfielder with four in 1987. ... Collected six hits in one game (July 2, 1993). ... Tied for N.L. lead in double plays by outfielder with four in 1995. ... Hit three home runs in one game (June 5, 1996; June 15, 1998; August 9, 2001; August 22, 2001; and September 23, 2001). ... Led N.L. with 416 total bases in 1998. ... Had 18-game hitting streak (May 26-June 15, 1999). ... Led N.L. with 397 total bases in 1999. ... Had 15-game hitting streak (July 4-22, 2000). ... Led N.L. with 425 total bases and with 37 intentional bases on balls received in 2001. ... Career major league grand slams: 6.

Year	Team (League)	Pos.	G	AB	R	H	2B	3B	HR	RBI	Avg.	BB	SO	SB	PO	A	E	Avg.
1986—	GC Rangers (GCL)......	OF	61	229	38	63	*19	1	4	28	.275	22	51	11	92	9	•6	.944
1987—	Gastonia (S.Atl.)........	OF	129	519	73	145	27	4	11	59	.279	21	123	22	183	12	17	.920
1988—	Charlotte (FSL)........	OF	131	507	70	116	13	*12	9	51	.229	35	106	42	227	11	7	.971
1989—	Tulsa (Texas)..............	OF	66	273	45	81	15	4	7	31	.297	15	52	16	110	7	4	.967
—Texas (A.L.).............	OF-DH	25	84	8	20	3	0	1	3	.238	0	20	0	33	1	2	.944
—Oklahoma City (A.A.)..	OF	10	39	2	4	2	0	0	1	.103	2	8	4	22	0	2	.917
—Vancouver (PCL).......	OF	13	49	7	18	3	0	1	5	.367	0	20	0	43	1	0	1.000
—Chicago (A.L.)■......	OF	33	99	19	27	5	0	3	10	.273	11	27	7	61	1	2	.969
1990—	Chicago (A.L.)...........	OF	153	532	72	124	26	10	15	70	.233	33	150	32	315	14	*13	.962
1991—	Chicago (A.L.)...........	OF-DH	116	316	39	64	10	1	10	33	.203	14	98	13	214	6	6	.973
—Vancouver (PCL).......	OF	32	116	19	31	7	2	3	19	.267	17	32	9	95	2	3	.970
1992—	Chicago (A.L.)■.......	OF	67	262	41	68	7	2	8	25	.260	19	63	15	145	4	6	.961
—Iowa (A.A.).............	OF	5	19	3	6	2	0	0	1	.316	1	2	5	14	0	0	1.000
1993—	Chicago (N.L.)...........	OF	159	598	92	156	25	5	33	93	.261	38	135	36	344	17	9	.976
1994—	Chicago (N.L.)...........	OF	105	426	59	128	17	6	25	70	.300	25	92	22	248	5	7	.973
1995—	Chicago (N.L.)...........	OF	•144	564	89	151	17	3	36	119	.268	58	134	34	320	13	*13	.962
1996—	Chicago (N.L.)...........	OF	124	498	84	136	21	2	40	100	.273	34	134	18	253	15	10	.964
1997—	Chicago (N.L.)...........	OF	•162	642	90	161	31	4	36	119	.251	45	*174	22	325	16	8	.977
1998—	Chicago (N.L.)...........	OF	159	643	*134	198	20	0	66	*158	.308	73	*171	18	334	14	9	.975
1999—	Chicago (N.L.)...........	OF	•162	625	114	180	24	2	63	141	.288	78	*171	7	399	8	9	.978
2000—	Chicago (N.L.)...........	OF	156	604	106	193	38	1	*50	138	.320	91	168	7	318	3	•10	.970
2001—	Chicago (N.L.)...........	OF	160	577	*146	189	34	5	64	*160	.328	116	153	0	326	8	6	.982
American League totals (3 years)			327	1031	138	235	44	11	29	116	.228	58	295	52	623	22	23	.966
National League totals (10 years)			1398	5439	955	1560	234	30	421	1123	.287	577	1395	179	3012	103	87	.973
Major League totals (13 years)			1725	6470	1093	1795	278	41	450	1239	.277	635	1690	231	3635	125	110	.972

DIVISION SERIES RECORD

Year	Team (League)	Pos.	G	AB	R	H	2B	3B	HR	RBI	Avg.	BB	SO	SB	PO	A	E	Avg.
1998—	Chicago (N.L.)...........	OF	3	11	0	2	1	0	0	0	.182	1	4	0	5	0	0	1.000

ALL-STAR GAME RECORD

NOTES: Named to All-Star team for 1998 game; replaced by Bret Boone due to injury.

Year	League	Pos.	AB	R	H	2B	3B	HR	RBI	Avg.	BB	SO	SB	PO	A	E	Avg.
1995—	National......................	OF	1	0	0	0	0	0	0	.000	0	0	0	2	0	0	1.000
1998—	National......................		Selected, did not play—injured.														
1999—	National......................	OF	3	0	0	0	0	0	0	.000	0	2	0	1	0	0	1.000
2000—	National......................	OF	3	0	0	0	0	0	0	.000	0	1	0	1	0	0	1.000
2001—	National......................	OF	2	0	0	0	0	0	0	.000	0	0	0	1	0	0	1.000
All-Star Game totals (4 years)			9	0	0	0	0	0	0	.000	0	3	0	5	0	0	1.000

SPARKS, STEVE   P   TIGERS

PERSONAL: Born July 2, 1965, in Tulsa, Okla. ... 6-0/180. ... Throws right, bats right. ... Full name: Steven William Sparks.

HIGH SCHOOL: Holland Hall (Tulsa, Okla.).

COLLEGE: Sam Houston State.

TRANSACTIONS/CAREER NOTES: Selected by Milwaukee Brewers organization in fifth round of free-agent draft (June 2, 1987). ... On disabled list (March 24, 1997-entire season). ... Granted free agency (October 15, 1997). ... Signed by Anaheim Angels (February 23, 1998). ... On Cedar Rapids disabled list (April 9-19, 1998). ... Granted free agency (October 15, 1999). ... Signed by Philadelphia Phillies organization (February 1, 2000). ... Released by Phillies (February 28, 2000). ... Signed by Detroit Tigers organization (March 2, 2000).

RECORDS: Shares major league single-inning record for most hit batsmen—3 (May 22, 1999, third inning). ... Shares A.L. single-game record for most hit batsmen (nine innings)—4 (May 22, 1999).

MISCELLANEOUS: Appeared in one game as pinch runner (1999). ... Appeared in one game as pinch runner (2001).

Year	League	W	L	Pct.	ERA	G	GS	CG	ShO	Sv.	IP	H	R	ER	BB	SO
1987—	Helena (Pio.)	6	3	.667	4.68	10	9	2	0	0	57 2/3	68	44	30	20	47
1988—	Beloit (Midw.).....................	9	13	.409	3.79	25	24	5	1	0	164	162	80	69	51	96
1989—	Stockton (Calif.)	•13	5	.722	2.41	23	22	3	2	0	164	125	55	44	53	126
1990—	Stockton (Calif.)	10	7	.588	3.69	19	19	5	1	0	129 1/3	136	63	53	31	77
—El Paso (Texas)...................	1	2	.333	6.53	7	6	1	0	0	30 1/3	43	24	22	15	17
1991—	Stockton (Calif.)	9	10	.474	3.06	24	24	•8	2	0	179 2/3	160	70	61	98	139
—El Paso (Texas)...................	1	2	.333	9.53	4	4	0	0	0	17	30	22	18	9	10
1992—	El Paso (Texas)....................	9	8	.529	5.37	28	22	3	0	1	140 2/3	159	99	84	50	79
1993—	New Orleans (A.A.)..............	9	13	.409	3.84	29	•28	*7	1	0	*180 1/3	174	89	77	*80	104
1994—	New Orleans (A.A.)..............	10	12	.455	4.46	28	27	5	1	0	*183 2/3	183	101	91	68	105
1995—	Milwaukee (A.L.).................	9	11	.450	4.63	33	27	3	0	0	202	210	111	104	86	96
1996—	Milwaukee (A.L.).................	4	7	.364	6.60	20	13	1	0	0	88 2/3	103	66	65	52	21
—New Orleans (A.A.)..............	2	6	.250	4.99	11	10	3	0	0	57 2/3	64	43	32	35	27
1997—					Did not play.											
1998—	Midland (Texas)■................	0	4	.000	7.08	7	7	0	0	0	40 2/3	49	38	32	15	34
—Vancouver (PCL)	0	4	.000	2.89	4	4	2	0	0	28	23	11	9	6	19
—Anaheim (A.L.)...................	9	4	.692	4.34	22	20	0	0	0	128 2/3	130	66	62	58	90
1999—	Anaheim (A.L.)...................	5	11	.313	5.42	28	26	0	0	0	147 1/3	165	101	89	82	73
2000—	Toledo (I.L.)■....................	5	7	.417	3.77	16	14	1	0	0	90 2/3	86	53	38	41	44
—Detroit (A.L.)....................	7	5	.583	4.07	20	15	1	1	1	104	108	55	47	29	53
2001—	Detroit (A.L.)....................	14	9	.609	3.65	35	33	*8	1	0	232	244	110	94	64	116
Major League totals (6 years)	48	47	.505	4.59	158	134	13	2	1	903	960	509	461	371	449

PERSONAL: Born November 6, 1973, in Walnut Creek, Calif. ... 6-4/205. ... Throws right, bats right. ... Full name: Justin James Speier. ... Son of Chris Speier, infielder with five major league teams (1971-89).
HIGH SCHOOL: Brophy College Prep (Phoenix).
COLLEGE: San Francisco, then Nicholls State.
TRANSACTIONS/CAREER NOTES: Selected by Chicago Cubs organization in 55th round of free-agent draft (June 1, 1995). ... Traded by Cubs with 3B Kevin Orie and P Todd Noel to Florida Marlins for P Felix Heredia and P Steve Hoff (July 31, 1998). ... Traded by Marlins to Atlanta Braves for a player to be named (April 1, 1999); Marlins acquired P Matthew Targac to complete deal (June 11, 1999). ... Claimed on waivers by Cleveland Indians (November 23, 1999). ... Traded by Indians to New York Mets for OF Brian Jenkins (May 19, 2001). ... Claimed on waivers by Colorado Rockies (May 29, 2001).

Year	League	W	L	Pct.	ERA	G	GS	CG	ShO	Sv.	IP	H	R	ER	BB	SO
1995—	Williamsport (NY-Penn)	2	1	.667	1.49	30	0	0	0	12	36 1/3	27	6	6	4	39
1996—	Daytona (FSL)	2	4	.333	3.76	33	0	0	0	13	38 1/3	32	19	16	19	34
—	Orlando (Sou.)	4	1	.800	2.05	24	0	0	0	6	26 1/3	23	7	6	5	14
1997—	Orlando (Sou.)	6	5	.545	4.48	50	0	0	0	6	78 1/3	77	46	39	23	63
—	Iowa (A.A.)	2	0	1.000	0.00	8	0	0	0	1	12 1/3	5	0	0	1	9
1998—	Iowa (PCL)	3	3	.500	5.05	45	0	0	0	12	51 2/3	52	31	29	19	49
—	Chicago (N.L.)	0	0	...	13.50	1	0	0	0	0	1 1/3	2	2	2	1	2
—	Florida (N.L.)■	0	3	.000	8.38	18	0	0	0	0	19 1/3	25	18	18	12	15
1999—	Richmond (I.L.)■	2	4	.333	5.62	27	0	0	0	3	41 2/3	51	28	26	22	39
—	Atlanta (N.L.)	0	0	...	5.65	19	0	0	0	0	28 2/3	28	18	18	13	22
2000—	Buffalo (I.L.)■	0	0	...	4.15	13	0	0	0	9	13	13	6	6	3	12
—	Cleveland (A.L.)	5	2	.714	3.29	47	0	0	0	0	68 1/3	57	27	25	28	69
2001—	Cleveland (A.L.)	2	0	1.000	6.97	12	0	0	0	0	20 2/3	24	16	16	8	15
—	Colorado (N.L.)■	4	3	.571	3.70	42	0	0	0	0	56	47	24	23	12	42
—	Colorado Springs (PCL)	1	0	1.000	1.46	11	0	0	0	2	12 1/3	10	2	2	7	16
A.L. totals (2 years)		7	2	.778	4.15	59	0	0	0	0	89	81	43	41	36	84
N.L. totals (3 years)		4	6	.400	5.21	80	0	0	0	0	105 1/3	102	62	61	38	86
Major League totals (4 years)		11	8	.579	4.72	139	0	0	0	0	194 1/3	183	105	102	74	170

PERSONAL: Born February 20, 1972, in Key West, Fla. ... 5-11/225. ... Bats right, throws right. ... Full name: Michael Shane Spencer.
HIGH SCHOOL: Granite Hills (El Cajon, Calif.).
TRANSACTIONS/CAREER NOTES: Selected by New York Yankees organization in 28th round of free-agent draft (June 4, 1990). ... On disabled list (April 10-May 9, 1994). ... On New York disabled list (July 3-27, 1999); included rehabilitation assignment to Columbus (July 21-27). ... On disabled list (July 12, 2000-remainder of season). ... On New York disabled list (March 31-April 29, 2001); included rehabilitation assignment to Columbus (April 14-29).
RECORDS: Shares major league single-month record for most grand slams—3 (September 1998).
HONORS: Named Florida State League Most Valuable Player (1995).
STATISTICAL NOTES: Led Florida State League with 235 total bases in 1995. ... Career major league grand slams: 3.

Year	Team (League)	Pos.	G	AB	R	H	2B	3B	HR	RBI	Avg.	BB	SO	SB	PO	A	E	Avg.
1990—	GC Yankees (GCL)......	OF	42	147	20	27	4	0	0	7	.184	20	23	11	79	3	3	.965
1991—	GC Yankees (GCL)......	OF	44	160	25	49	7	0	0	30	.306	14	19	9	64	6	3	.959
—	Oneonta (NY-Penn)	OF	18	53	10	13	2	1	0	3	.245	10	9	2	11	0	1	.917
1992—	Greensboro (S.Atl.)	OF-P	83	258	43	74	10	2	3	27	.287	33	37	8	135	6	0	1.000
1993—	Greensboro (S.Atl.)	OF-P	122	431	89	116	35	2	12	80	.269	52	62	14	138	10	5	.967
1994—	Tampa (FSL)..............	OF	90	334	44	97	22	3	8	53	.290	30	53	5	90	10	4	.962
1995—	Tampa (FSL)..............	OF	•134	500	87	*150	31	3	16	*88	.300	61	60	14	166	6	6	.966
1996—	Norwich (East.)	OF-1B-3B	126	450	70	114	19	0	29	89	.253	68	99	4	218	24	3	.988
—	Columbus (I.L.)..........	OF	9	31	7	11	4	0	3	6	.355	5	5	0	25	1	1	.963
1997—	Columbus (I.L.)..........	OF-DH-3B	125	452	78	109	34	4	30	86	.241	71	105	0	189	7	4	.980
1998—	New York (A.L.).........	OF-DH-1B	27	67	18	25	6	0	10	27	.373	5	12	0	29	2	0	1.000
—	Columbus (I.L.)..........	OF-DH-1B	87	342	66	110	29	1	18	67	.322	41	59	1	225	11	5	.979
1999—	New York (A.L.).........	OF-DH	71	205	25	48	8	0	8	20	.234	18	51	0	108	5	0	1.000
—	Columbus (I.L.)..........	OF-DH	14	50	17	18	2	0	2	10	.360	9	8	0	23	0	1	.958
2000—	New York (A.L.).........	OF-DH	73	248	33	70	11	3	9	40	.282	19	45	1	83	3	1	.989
2001—	Columbus (I.L.)..........	OF	49	173	17	40	10	1	3	14	.231	23	21	4	64	2	1	.985
—	New York (A.L.).........	OF-DH	80	283	40	73	14	2	10	46	.258	21	58	4	139	7	1	.993
Major League totals (4 years)			251	803	116	216	39	5	37	133	.269	63	166	5	359	17	2	.995

DIVISION SERIES RECORD

Year	Team (League)	Pos.	G	AB	R	H	2B	3B	HR	RBI	Avg.	BB	SO	SB	PO	A	E	Avg.
1998—	New York (A.L.)..........	OF	2	6	3	3	0	0	2	4	.500	0	1	0	1	0	0	1.000
1999—	New York (A.L.)							Did not play.										
2001—	New York (A.L.)..........	OF-PH	3	8	1	2	1	0	0	0	.250	1	4	0	4	1	0	1.000
Division series totals (2 years)			5	14	4	5	1	0	2	4	.357	1	5	0	5	1	0	1.000

CHAMPIONSHIP SERIES RECORD

Year	Team (League)	Pos.	G	AB	R	H	2B	3B	HR	RBI	Avg.	BB	SO	SB	PO	A	E	Avg.
1998—	New York (A.L.)..........	OF	3	10	1	1	0	0	0	0	.100	1	3	0	7	1	0	1.000
1999—	New York (A.L.)..........	OF	3	9	1	1	0	0	0	0	.111	1	6	0	5	0	0	1.000
2001—	New York (A.L.)..........	PH-OF-PR	5	7	1	2	1	0	0	0	.286	1	1	1	2	0	0	1.000
Championship series totals (3 years)			11	26	3	4	1	0	0	0	.154	3	10	1	14	1	0	1.000

WORLD SERIES RECORD

NOTES: Member of World Series championship team (1998 and 1999).

							BATTING								FIELDING		
Year Team (League)	Pos.	G	AB	R	H	2B	3B	HR	RBI	Avg.	BB	SO	SB	PO	A	E	Avg.
1998— New York (A.L.)..........	OF	1	3	1	1	1	0	0	0	.333	0	2	0	2	1	0	1.000
1999— New York (A.L.)						Did not play.											
2001— New York (A.L.)..........	PH-OF	7	20	1	4	0	0	1	2	.200	2	6	0	6	1	0	1.000
World Series totals (2 years)		8	23	2	5	1	0	1	2	.217	2	8	0	8	2	0	1.000

RECORD AS PITCHER

Year League	W	L	Pct.	ERA	G	GS	CG	ShO	Sv.	IP	H	R	ER	BB	SO
1992— Greensboro (S.Atl.)	0	0	...	0.00	1	0	0	0	0	1	2	0	0	1	1
1993— Greensboro (S.Atl.)	0	0	...	4.50	2	0	0	0	0	4	5	2	2	2	5

SPIERS, BILL   IF   S

PERSONAL: Born June 5, 1966, in Orangeburg, S.C. ... 6-2/190. ... Bats left, throws right. ... Full name: William James Spiers III. ... Name pronounced SPY-ers.
HIGH SCHOOL: Wade Hampton Academy (Orangeburg, S.C.).
COLLEGE: Clemson.
TRANSACTIONS/CAREER NOTES: Selected by Milwaukee Brewers organization in first round (13th pick overall) of free-agent draft (June 2, 1987). ... On Milwaukee disabled list (April 6-May 15, 1990); included rehabilitation assignment to Denver (April 27-May 14). ... On Milwaukee disabled list (April 5-September 2, 1992); included rehabilitation assignments to Beloit (May 6-15 and August 20-September 2). ... Granted free agency (December 20, 1993). ... Re-signed by Brewers (December 21, 1993). ... Claimed on waivers by New York Mets (October 25, 1994). ... On New York disabled list (May 15-June 5 and June 26-July 16, 1995); included rehabilitation assignment to Norfolk (May 22-June 5). ... Granted free agency (November 3, 1995). ... Signed by Houston Astros organization (January 10, 1996). ... Granted free agency (November 14, 1996). ... Re-signed by Astros (December 2, 1996). ... Granted free agency (November 3, 1997). ... Re-signed by Astros (November 25, 1997). ... On disabled list (April 16, 2001-remainder of season). ... Announced retirement (October 24, 2001).
HONORS: Named shortstop on THE SPORTING NEWS college All-America team (1987).
STATISTICAL NOTES: Career major league grand slams: 3.

							BATTING								FIELDING		
Year Team (League)	Pos.	G	AB	R	H	2B	3B	HR	RBI	Avg.	BB	SO	SB	PO	A	E	Avg.
1987— Helena (Pio.)	SS	6	22	4	9	1	0	0	3	.409	3	3	2	8	6	6	.700
— Beloit (Midw.).............	SS	64	258	43	77	10	1	3	26	.298	15	38	11	111	160	20	.931
1988— Stockton (Calif.)	SS	84	353	68	95	17	3	5	52	.269	42	41	27	140	240	19	.952
— El Paso (Texas)...........	SS	47	168	22	47	5	2	3	21	.280	15	20	4	73	141	13	.943
1989— Milwaukee (A.L.) S-3-2-DH-1		114	345	44	88	9	3	4	33	.255	21	63	10	164	295	21	.956
— Denver (A.A.)...............	SS	14	47	9	17	2	1	2	8	.362	5	6	1	32	33	2	.970
1990— Denver (A.A.)...............	SS	11	38	6	12	0	0	1	7	.316	10	8	1	22	23	2	.957
— Milwaukee (A.L.)	SS	112	363	44	88	15	3	2	36	.242	16	46	11	159	326	12	.976
1991— Milwaukee (A.L.)..........	SS-DH-OF	133	414	71	117	13	6	8	54	.283	34	55	14	201	345	17	.970
1992— Beloit (Midw.).............	SS	16	55	9	13	3	0	0	7	.236	7	7	4	12	28	3	.930
— Milwaukee (A.L.) SS-2B-DH-3B		12	16	2	5	2	0	0	2	.313	1	4	1	6	6	0	1.000
1993— Milwaukee (A.L.)..........	2-O-DH	113	340	43	81	8	4	2	36	.238	29	51	9	213	231	13	.972
1994— Milwaukee (A.L.)..........	3-S-DH-O-1	73	214	27	54	10	1	0	17	.252	19	42	7	70	129	8	.961
1995— New York (N.L.)■........	3B-2B	63	72	5	15	2	1	0	11	.208	12	15	0	13	30	7	.860
— Norfolk (I.L.)................	2B-3B	12	41	4	9	2	0	0	4	.220	8	6	0	23	29	4	.929
1996— Houston (N.L.)■.........	3-2-S-1-O	122	218	27	55	10	1	6	26	.252	20	34	7	44	108	5	.968
1997— Houston (N.L.)...........	3-S-1-2	132	291	51	93	27	4	4	48	.320	61	42	10	104	200	18	.944
1998— Houston (N.L.)...........	3-2-1-S	123	384	66	105	27	4	4	43	.273	45	62	11	101	184	9	.969
1999— Houston (N.L.)..........	3-0-S-2-1	127	393	56	113	18	5	4	39	.288	47	45	10	110	176	9	.969
2000— Houston (N.L.)..........	3-S-2-0	124	355	41	107	17	3	3	43	.301	49	38	7	118	196	8	.975
2001— Houston (N.L.)...........	PH	4	3	0	1	0	0	0	0	.333	1	0	0	...	...	...	...
American League totals (6 years)		557	1692	231	433	57	17	16	178	.256	120	261	52	813	1332	71	.968
National League totals (7 years)		695	1716	246	489	101	18	21	210	.285	235	236	45	490	894	56	.961
Major League totals (13 years)		1252	3408	477	922	158	35	37	388	.271	355	497	97	1303	2226	127	.965

DIVISION SERIES RECORD

							BATTING								FIELDING		
Year Team (League)	Pos.	G	AB	R	H	2B	3B	HR	RBI	Avg.	BB	SO	SB	PO	A	E	Avg.
1997— Houston (N.L.)	3B	3	11	1	0	0	0	0	0	.000	1	2	0	1	3	0	1.000
1998— Houston (N.L.)	3B-PH	4	14	2	4	3	0	0	1	.286	1	3	0	1	5	0	1.000
1999— Houston (N.L.)	OF-PH	4	11	0	3	0	0	0	1	.273	0	1	1	3	0	1	.750
Division series totals (3 years)		11	36	3	7	3	0	0	2	.194	2	6	1	5	8	1	.929

SPIEZIO, SCOTT   1B/DH   ANGELS

PERSONAL: Born September 21, 1972, in Joliet, Ill. ... 6-2/225. ... Bats both, throws right. ... Full name: Scott Edward Spiezio. ... Son of Ed Spiezio, third baseman with St. Louis Cardinals (1964-68), San Diego Padres (1969-72) and Chicago White Sox (1972).
HIGH SCHOOL: Morris (Ill.).
COLLEGE: Illinois.
TRANSACTIONS/CAREER NOTES: Selected by Oakland Athletics organization in sixth round of free-agent draft (June 3, 1993). ... On Oakland disabled list (June 8-25, 1997); included rehabilitation assignment to Southern Oregon (June 23-25). ... On Oakland disabled list (June 15-July 31, 1998); included rehabilitation assignment to Edmonton (July 26-31). ... Granted free agency (December 21, 1999). ... Signed by Anaheim Angels (January 11, 2000).
RECORDS: Shares A.L. single-season record for highest fielding percentage for first baseman (100 or more games)—.999.
STATISTICAL NOTES: Led California League third basemen with .948 fielding percentage in 1994. ... Led Southern League with 14 sacrifice flies in 1995. ... Led Southern League third basemen with 291 assists, 29 errors, 424 total chances and 34 double plays in 1995. ... Led Pacific Coast League third basemen with 91 putouts, 302 assists, 405 total chances and .970 fielding percentage in 1996. ... Led A.L. second basemen with .990 fielding percentage in 1997. ... Had 18-game hitting streak (May 21-June 9, 1998). ... Career major league grand slams: 3.

Year	Team (League)	Pos.	G	AB	R	H	2B	3B	HR	RBI	Avg.	BB	SO	SB	PO	A	E	Avg.
1993—S. Oregon (N'West)....	3B-1B	31	125	32	41	10	2	3	19	.328	16	18	0	76	40	9	.928
—Modesto (Calif.)........	3B-1B	32	110	12	28	9	1	1	13	.255	23	19	1	42	51	5	.949
1994—Modesto (Calif.)........	3B-1B-SS	127	453	84	127	32	5	14	68	.280	88	72	5	66	281	18	†.951
1995—Huntsville (Sou.)........	3B-1B-2B	141	528	78	149	33	8	13	86	.282	67	78	10	122	†295	†29	.935
1996—Edmonton (PCL)........	3B-1B-DH	*140	523	87	137	30	4	20	91	.262	56	66	6	†174	†304	15	†.970
—Oakland (A.L.)........	3B-DH	9	29	6	9	2	0	2	8	.310	4	4	0	6	5	2	.846
1997—Oakland (A.L.)........	2B-3B	147	538	58	131	28	4	14	65	.243	44	75	9	280	415	7	†.990
—S. Oregon (N'West)....	DH-2B	2	9	1	5	0	0	0	2	.556	2	1	0	3	4	1	.875
1998—Oakland (A.L.)........	2B-DH	114	406	54	105	19	1	9	50	.259	44	56	1	198	316	13	.975
—Edmonton (PCL)........	2B-DH	5	13	3	3	1	0	1	4	.231	3	2	0	5	3	1	.889
1999—Oakland	2B-3B-1B-DH	89	247	31	60	24	0	8	33	.243	29	36	0	124	163	7	.976
—Vancouver (PCL)........	2B-DH-3B	28	105	27	41	7	1	6	27	.390	15	16	0	50	73	4	.969
2000—Anaheim (A.L.)■......	DH-1-3-O-2	123	297	47	72	11	2	17	49	.242	40	56	1	164	21	3	.984
2001—Anaheim (A.L.)........	1B-DH-OF-3B	139	457	57	124	29	4	13	54	.271	34	65	5	840	83	2	.998
Major League totals (6 years)		621	1974	253	501	113	11	63	259	.254	195	292	16	1612	1003	34	.987

SPIVEY, JUNIOR — 2B/SS — DIAMONDBACKS

PERSONAL: Born January 28, 1975, in Oklahoma City. ... 6-0/185. ... Bats right, throws right. ... Full name: Ernest Lee Spivey Jr.
HIGH SCHOOL: Douglass (Oklahoma City).
JUNIOR COLLEGE: Cowley County Community College (Kan.).
TRANSACTIONS/CAREER NOTES: Selected by Arizona Diamondbacks organization in 26th round of free-agent draft (June 4, 1996). ... Loaned by Diamondbacks to Tulsa, Texas Rangers organization (July 18-August 29, 1998). ... On El Paso disabled list (April 8-May 15 and July 4-August 19, 1999). ... On Arizona disabled list (August 19, 1999-remainder of season). ... On Tucson disabled list (May 8-June 14, 2000). ... On El Paso disabled list (June 25-August 17, 2000). ... On Arizona disabled list (August 31, 2000-remainder of season).
STATISTICAL NOTES: Led California League second basemen with 653 total chances in 1997. ... Tied for California League lead with 20 errors by second baseman in 1998.

Year	Team (League)	Pos.	G	AB	R	H	2B	3B	HR	RBI	Avg.	BB	SO	SB	PO	A	E	Avg.
1996—Ariz. D'backs (Ariz.)....	2B-SS-3B	20	69	13	23	0	0	0	3	.333	12	16	11	35	61	3	.970
—Lethbridge (Pio.)........	2B-SS	31	107	30	36	3	4	2	25	.336	23	24	8	63	70	10	.930
1997—High Desert (Calif.)........	2B	136	491	88	134	24	6	6	53	.273	69	115	14	226	*394	*33	.949
1998—High Desert (Calif.)........	2B-3B-SS	79	285	64	80	14	5	5	35	.281	64	61	34	147	224	‡20	.949
—Tulsa (Texas)■..........	2B	34	119	26	37	10	1	3	16	.311	28	25	8	62	84	3	.980
1999—El Paso (Texas)■......	2B-SS	44	164	40	48	10	4	3	19	.293	36	27	14	115	119	9	.963
2000—Tucson (PCL)........	2B-SS-3B	28	117	21	33	8	4	3	16	.282	11	17	3	63	74	6	.958
—El Paso (Texas)........	2B	6	19	5	8	5	0	1	2	.421	0	5	0	12	11	0	1.000
2001—Tucson (PCL)........	2B-SS	54	194	25	45	6	0	6	27	.232	27	32	9	135	163	3	.990
—Arizona (N.L.)........	2B-SS	72	163	33	42	6	3	5	21	.258	23	47	3	96	104	3	.985
Major League totals (1 year)		72	163	33	42	6	3	5	21	.258	23	47	3	96	104	3	.985

SPOONEYBARGER, TIM — P — BRAVES

PERSONAL: Born October 21, 1979, in San Diego, Calif. ... 6-3/190. ... Throws right, bats right. ... Full name: Timothy F. Spooneybarger.
HIGH SCHOOL: Pine Forest (Pensacola, Fla.).
JUNIOR COLLEGE: Okaloosa-Walton.
TRANSACTIONS/CAREER NOTES: Selected by Atlanta Braves organization in 29th round of free-agent draft (June 2, 1998). ... On disabled list (May 21-July 22, 2000).

Year	League	W	L	Pct.	ERA	G	GS	CG	ShO	Sv.	IP	H	R	ER	BB	SO
1999—Danville (Appl.)..................	3	0	1.000	2.22	12	0	0	0	0	24 1/3	15	11	6	14	36
—Macon (S.Atl.)................	0	1	.000	3.60	7	0	0	0	0	10	7	4	4	10	17
2000—Myrtle Beach (Caro.).............	3	0	1.000	0.91	19	6	0	0	0	49 2/3	18	7	5	19	57
2001—Richmond (I.L.)..............	3	0	1.000	0.71	42	0	0	0	5	50 2/3	33	5	4	21	58
—Greenville (Sou.)	1	1	.500	5.14	15	0	0	0	0	21	20	12	12	4	24
—Atlanta (N.L.)	0	1	.000	2.25	4	0	0	0	0	4	5	1	1	2	3
Major League totals (1 year)........	0	1	.000	2.25	4	0	0	0	0	4	5	1	1	2	3

SPRAGUE, ED — 3B

PERSONAL: Born July 25, 1967, in Castro Valley, Calif. ... 6-2/205. ... Bats right, throws right. ... Full name: Edward Nelson Sprague Jr. ... Son of Ed Sprague, major league pitcher with four teams (1968-69 and 1971-76); and husband of Kristen Babb, Olympic gold-medal synchronized swimmer (1992).
HIGH SCHOOL: St. Mary's (Stockton, Calif.).
COLLEGE: Stanford.
TRANSACTIONS/CAREER NOTES: Selected by Boston Red Sox organization in 26th round of free-agent draft (June 3, 1985); did not sign. ... Selected by Toronto Blue Jays organization in first round (25th pick overall) of free-agent draft (June 1, 1988). ... On suspended list (August 8-10, 1993). ... On disabled list (September 4-28, 1997). ... Traded by Blue Jays to Oakland Athletics for P Scott Rivette (July 31, 1998). ... Granted free agency (October 27, 1998). ... Signed by Pittsburgh Pirates (December 16, 1998). ... On disabled list (September 20, 1999-remainder of season). ... Granted free agency (October 29, 1999). ... Signed by San Diego Padres organization (February 3, 2000). ... Traded by Padres to Red Sox for P Dennis Tankersley and IF Cesar Saba (June 30, 2000). ... Released by Red Sox (August 23, 2000). ... Re-signed by Padres organization (August 31, 2000). ... Granted free agency (October 31, 2000). ... Re-signed by Padres organization (December 7, 2000). ... Released by Padres (March 28, 2001). ... Signed by Seattle Mariners organization (May 3, 2001). ... On Seattle disabled list (August 8-September 1, 2001). ... Granted free agency (November 6, 2001).

STATISTICAL NOTES: Led International League third basemen with 31 errors and 364 total chances and tied for lead with 240 assists in 1990. ... Led A.L. in grounding into double plays with 23 in 1993. ... Led A.L. third basemen with 98 putouts in 1994 and 133 in 1995. ... Led A.L. in being hit by pitch with 15 in 1995. ... Led N.L in being hit by pitch with 17 in 1999. ... Career major league grand slams: 4.

MISCELLANEOUS: Member of 1988 U.S. Olympic baseball team.

											BATTING					FIELDING			
Year	Team (League)	Pos.	G	AB	R	H	2B	3B	HR	RBI	Avg.	BB	SO	SB	PO	A	E	Avg.
1989—Dunedin (FSL)	3B	52	192	21	42	9	2	7	23	.219	16	40	1	33	86	14	.895
—Syracuse (I.L.)	3B	86	288	23	60	14	1	5	33	.208	18	73	0	51	149	*25	.889
1990—Syracuse (I.L.)	3B-1B-C	142	*519	60	124	23	5	20	75	.239	31	100	4	171	‡246	†35	.923
1991—Syracuse (I.L.)	C-3B	23	88	24	32	8	0	5	25	.364	10	21	2	111	17	6	.955
—Toronto (A.L.)	3B-1B-C-DH	61	160	17	44	7	0	4	20	.275	19	43	0	167	72	14	.945
1992—Syracuse (I.L.)	C-1B-3B	100	369	49	102	18	2	16	50	.276	44	73	0	438	44	12	.976
—Toronto (A.L.)	C-1B-DH-3B	22	47	6	11	2	0	1	7	.234	3	7	0	82	5	1	.989
1993—Toronto (A.L.)	3B	150	546	50	142	31	1	12	73	.260	32	85	1	*127	232	17	.955
1994—Toronto (A.L.)	3B-1B	109	405	38	97	19	1	11	44	.240	23	95	1	†117	147	14	.950
1995—Toronto (A.L.)	3B-1B-DH	144	521	77	127	27	2	18	74	.244	58	96	0	†167	234	17	.959
1996—Toronto (A.L.)	3B-DH	159	591	88	146	35	2	36	101	.247	60	146	0	108	218	15	.956
1997—Toronto (A.L.)	3B-DH	138	504	63	115	29	4	14	48	.228	51	102	0	106	202	18	.945
1998—Toronto (A.L.)	3B	105	382	49	91	20	0	17	51	.238	24	73	0	87	157	20	.924
—Oakland (A.L.)■	3B-1B	27	87	8	13	5	0	3	7	.149	2	17	1	24	37	6	.910
1999—Pittsburgh (N.L.)■	3B	137	490	71	131	27	2	22	81	.267	50	93	3	79	254	•29	.920
2000—San Diego (N.L.)■	1B-3B-OF-2B	73	157	19	41	12	0	10	27	.261	13	40	0	194	21	7	.968
—Rancho Cuca. (Calif.)	2B	2	7	1	2	0	0	1	2	.286	1	0	0	0	6	0	1.000
—Boston (A.L.)■	3B-1B-DH	33	111	11	24	4	0	2	9	.216	12	18	0	36	54	2	.978
2001—Tacoma (PCL)■	OF-3B	5	19	6	6	2	0	2	4	.316	1	5	0	6	0	0	1.000
—Seattle (A.L.)■	1-O-DH-3-C	45	94	9	28	7	0	2	16	.298	11	18	0	68	13	2	.976
American League totals (10 years)		993	3448	416	838	186	10	120	450	.243	295	700	3	1089	1371	126	.951
National League totals (2 years)		210	647	90	172	39	2	32	108	.266	63	133	3	273	275	36	.938
Major League totals (11 years)		1203	4095	506	1010	225	12	152	558	.247	358	833	6	1362	1646	162	.949

DIVISION SERIES RECORD

											BATTING					FIELDING			
Year	Team (League)	Pos.	G	AB	R	H	2B	3B	HR	RBI	Avg.	BB	SO	SB	PO	A	E	Avg.
2001—Seattle (A.L.)	PH	1	1	0	0	0	0	0	0	.000	0	0	0	...	...	...	...

CHAMPIONSHIP SERIES RECORD

											BATTING					FIELDING			
Year	Team (League)	Pos.	G	AB	R	H	2B	3B	HR	RBI	Avg.	BB	SO	SB	PO	A	E	Avg.
1991—Toronto (A.L.)							Did not play.										
1992—Toronto (A.L.)	PH	2	2	0	1	0	0	0	0	.500	0	1	0	...	...	...	...
1993—Toronto (A.L.)	3B	6	21	0	6	0	1	0	4	.286	2	4	0	5	9	0	1.000
2001—Seattle (A.L.)							Did not play.										
Championship series totals (2 years)		8	23	0	7	0	1	0	4	.304	2	5	0	5	9	0	1.000

WORLD SERIES RECORD

NOTES: Hit home run in first at-bat (October 18, 1992). ... Member of World Series championship team (1992 and 1993).

											BATTING					FIELDING			
Year	Team (League)	Pos.	G	AB	R	H	2B	3B	HR	RBI	Avg.	BB	SO	SB	PO	A	E	Avg.
1992—Toronto (A.L.)	PH-1B	3	2	1	1	0	0	1	2	.500	1	0	0	0	0	0	...
1993—Toronto (A.L.)	3B-PH-1B	5	15	0	1	0	0	0	2	.067	1	6	0	4	9	2	.867
World Series totals (2 years)		8	17	1	2	0	0	1	4	.118	2	6	0	4	9	2	.867

ALL-STAR GAME RECORD

							BATTING						FIELDING			
Year	League	Pos.	AB	R	H	2B	3B	HR	RBI	Avg.	BB	SO	SB	PO	A	E	Avg.
1999—National	3B	1	0	0	0	0	0	0	.000	0	0	0	0	0	0	...

SPRINGER, DENNIS — P

PERSONAL: Born February 12, 1965, in Fresno, Calif. ... 5-10/185. ... Throws right, bats both. ... Full name: Dennis LeRoy Springer.

HIGH SCHOOL: Washington (Fresno, Calif.).

JUNIOR COLLEGE: Kings River Community College (Calif.).

COLLEGE: Fresno State.

TRANSACTIONS/CAREER NOTES: Selected by Los Angeles Dodgers organization in 21st round of free-agent draft (June 2, 1987). ... On San Antonio disabled list (April 19-27, 1992). ... On disabled list (August 24-September 6, 1993). ... Granted free agency (October 15, 1993). ... Signed by Philadelphia Phillies organization (May 19, 1994). ... Granted free agency (December 21, 1995). ... Signed by California Angels organization (January 5, 1996). ... Angels franchise renamed Anaheim Angels for 1997 season. ... Selected by Tampa Bay Devil Rays in first round (26th pick overall) of expansion draft (November 18, 1997). ... Released by Devil Rays (November 3, 1998). ... Signed by Florida Marlins organization (January 29, 1999). ... Granted free agency (October 6, 1999). ... Signed by New York Mets organization (February 4, 2000). ... Granted free agency (October 18, 2000). ... Signed by Los Angeles Dodgers organization (May 11, 2001). ... Granted free agency (October 15, 2001).

Year	League	W	L	Pct.	ERA	G	GS	CG	ShO	Sv.	IP	H	R	ER	BB	SO
1987—Great Falls (Pio.)	4	3	.571	2.88	23	5	1	0	6	65²/₃	70	38	21	16	54
1988—Bakersfield (Calif.)	13	7	.650	3.27	32	20	6	•4	2	154	135	75	56	62	108
1989—San Antonio (Texas)	6	8	.429	3.15	19	19	4	1	0	140	128	58	49	46	89
—Albuquerque (PCL)	4	1	.800	4.83	8	7	0	0	0	41	58	28	22	14	18
1990—San Antonio (Texas)	8	6	.571	3.31	24	24	3	0	0	*163¹/₃	147	76	60	73	77
1991—San Antonio (Texas)	10	10	.500	4.43	30	24	2	0	0	164²/₃	153	96	81	91	*138
1992—San Antonio (Texas)	6	7	.462	4.35	18	18	4	0	0	122	114	61	59	49	73
—Albuquerque (PCL)	2	7	.222	5.66	11	11	1	0	0	62	70	45	39	22	36
1993—Albuquerque (PCL)	3	8	.273	5.99	35	18	0	0	0	130²/₃	173	104	87	39	69

Year League	W	L	Pct.	ERA	G	GS	CG	ShO	Sv.	IP	H	R	ER	BB	SO
1994— Reading (East.)■	5	8	.385	3.40	24	19	2	0	2	135	125	74	51	44	118
1995— Scranton/W.B. (I.L.)	10	11	.476	4.68	30	23	•4	0	0	171	163	*101	89	47	115
— Philadelphia (N.L.)	0	3	.000	4.84	4	4	0	0	0	22 1/3	21	15	12	9	15
1996— California (A.L.)■	5	6	.455	5.51	20	15	2	1	0	94 2/3	91	65	58	43	64
— Vancouver (PCL)	10	3	.769	2.72	16	12	6	0	0	109 1/3	89	35	33	36	78
1997— Anaheim (A.L.)	9	9	.500	5.18	32	28	3	1	0	194 2/3	199	118	112	73	75
— Vancouver (PCL)	1	1	.500	3.00	2	2	2	0	0	15	12	6	5	6	7
1998— Tampa Bay (A.L.)■	3	11	.214	5.45	29	17	1	0	0	115 2/3	120	77	70	60	46
— Durham (I.L.)	2	3	.400	2.87	5	5	0	0	0	37 2/3	34	13	12	15	23
1999— Florida (N.L.)■	6	16	.273	4.86	38	29	3	2	1	196 1/3	231	121	106	64	83
2000— Norfolk (I.L.)■	5	5	.500	4.38	25	17	1	1	0	117	120	65	57	35	35
— New York (N.L.)	0	1	.000	8.74	2	2	0	0	0	11 1/3	20	11	11	5	5
2001— Las Vegas (PCL)■	7	7	.500	5.27	19	18	2	1	0	114 1/3	142	74	67	28	51
— Los Angeles (N.L.)	1	1	.500	3.32	4	3	0	0	0	19	19	7	7	2	7
A.L. totals (3 years)	17	26	.395	5.33	81	60	6	2	0	405	410	260	240	176	185
N.L. totals (4 years)	7	21	.250	4.92	48	38	3	2	1	249	291	154	136	80	110
Major League totals (7 years)	24	47	.338	5.17	129	98	9	4	1	654	701	414	376	256	295

SPRINGER, RUSS   P

PERSONAL: Born November 7, 1968, in Alexandria, La. ... 6-4/205. ... Throws right, bats right. ... Full name: Russell Paul Springer.
HIGH SCHOOL: Grant (Dry Prong, La.).
COLLEGE: Louisiana State.
TRANSACTIONS/CAREER NOTES: Selected by New York Yankees organization in seventh round of free-agent draft (June 5, 1989). ... Traded by Yankees with 1B J.T. Snow and P Jerry Nielsen to California Angels for P Jim Abbott (December 6, 1992). ... On California disabled list (August 2, 1993-remainder of season). ... Traded by Angels to Philadelphia Phillies (August 15, 1995), completing deal in which Phillies traded OF Dave Gallagher to Angels for 2B Kevin Flora and a player to be named later (August 9, 1995). ... Released by Phillies (December 20, 1996). ... Signed by Houston Astros organization (December 30, 1996). ... On Houston disabled list (June 17-July 10, 1997); included rehabilitation assignment to Jackson (July 8-10). ... Selected by Arizona Diamondbacks in third round (61st pick overall) of expansion draft (November 18, 1997). ... Traded by Diamondbacks to Atlanta Braves for P Alan Embree (June 23, 1998). ... On Atlanta disabled list (August 6-21, 1998). ... On Atlanta disabled list (April 3-May 17, 1999); included rehabilitation assignment to Richmond (April 20-May 16). ... Granted free agency (November 2, 1999). ... Signed by Diamondbacks (December 3, 1999). ... On Arizona disabled list (May 23, 2001-remainder of season); included rehabilitation assignment to Tucson (July 16-31). ... Granted free agency (November 7, 2001).

Year League	W	L	Pct.	ERA	G	GS	CG	ShO	Sv.	IP	H	R	ER	BB	SO
1989— Gulf Coast Yankees (GCL)	3	0	1.000	1.50	6	6	0	0	0	24	14	8	4	10	34
1990— Gulf Coast Yankees (GCL)	0	2	.000	1.20	4	4	0	0	0	15	10	6	2	4	17
— Greensboro (S.Atl.)	2	3	.400	3.67	10	10	0	0	0	56 1/3	51	33	23	31	51
1991— Fort Lauderdale (FSL)	5	9	.357	3.49	25	25	2	0	0	152 1/3	118	68	59	62	139
— Albany/Colonie (East.)	1	0	1.000	1.80	2	2	0	0	0	15	9	4	3	6	16
1992— Columbus (I.L.)	8	5	.615	2.69	20	20	1	0	0	123 2/3	89	46	37	54	95
— New York (A.L.)	0	0	...	6.19	14	0	0	0	0	16	18	11	11	10	12
1993— Vancouver (PCL)■	5	4	.556	4.27	11	9	1	0	0	59	58	37	28	33	40
— California (A.L.)	1	6	.143	7.20	14	9	1	0	0	60	73	48	48	32	31
1994— Vancouver (PCL)	7	4	.636	3.04	12	12	•4	0	0	83	77	35	28	19	58
— California (A.L.)	2	2	.500	5.52	18	5	0	0	2	45 2/3	53	28	28	14	28
1995— Vancouver (PCL)	2	0	1.000	3.44	6	6	0	0	0	34	24	16	13	23	23
— California (A.L.)	1	2	.333	6.10	19	6	0	0	1	51 2/3	60	37	35	25	38
— Philadelphia (N.L.)■	0	0	...	3.71	14	0	0	0	0	26 2/3	22	11	11	10	32
1996— Philadelphia (N.L.)	3	10	.231	4.66	51	7	0	0	0	96 2/3	106	60	50	38	94
1997— Houston (N.L.)■	3	3	.500	4.23	54	0	0	0	3	55 1/3	48	28	26	27	74
— Jackson (Texas)	0	0	...	9.00	1	0	0	0	0	1	2	1	1	0	2
1998— Arizona (N.L.)■	4	3	.571	4.13	26	0	0	0	0	32 2/3	29	16	15	14	37
— Atlanta (N.L.)■	1	1	.500	4.05	22	0	0	0	0	20	22	10	9	16	19
1999— Richmond (I.L.)	1	0	1.000	1.17	11	0	0	0	2	15 1/3	9	2	2	1	13
— Atlanta (N.L.)	2	1	.667	3.42	49	0	0	0	1	47 1/3	31	20	18	22	49
2000— Arizona (N.L.)■	2	4	.333	5.08	52	0	0	0	0	62	63	36	35	34	59
2001— Arizona (N.L.)	0	0	...	7.13	18	0	0	0	1	17 2/3	20	16	14	4	12
— Tucson (PCL)	0	0	...	4.91	7	3	0	0	0	7 1/3	7	4	4	3	6
A.L. totals (4 years)	4	10	.286	6.33	65	20	1	0	3	173 1/3	204	124	122	81	109
N.L. totals (7 years)	15	22	.405	4.47	286	7	0	0	5	358 1/3	341	197	178	165	376
Major League totals (10 years)	19	32	.373	5.08	351	27	1	0	8	531 2/3	545	321	300	246	485

DIVISION SERIES RECORD

Year League	W	L	Pct.	ERA	G	GS	CG	ShO	Sv.	IP	H	R	ER	BB	SO
1997— Houston (N.L.)	0	0	...	5.40	2	0	0	0	0	1 2/3	2	1	1	1	3
1998— Atlanta (N.L.)							Did not play.								
1999— Atlanta (N.L.)	0	0	...	0.00	1	0	0	0	0	1	2	0	0	1	1
Division series totals (2 years)	0	0	...	3.38	3	0	0	0	0	2 2/3	4	1	1	2	4

CHAMPIONSHIP SERIES RECORD

Year League	W	L	Pct.	ERA	G	GS	CG	ShO	Sv.	IP	H	R	ER	BB	SO
1998— Atlanta (N.L.)							Did not play.								
1999— Atlanta (N.L.)	1	0	1.000	0.00	2	0	0	0	0	2	0	0	0	1	1

WORLD SERIES RECORD

NOTES: Member of World Series championship team (2001).

Year League	W	L	Pct.	ERA	G	GS	CG	ShO	Sv.	IP	H	R	ER	BB	SO
1999— Atlanta (N.L.)	0	0	...	0.00	2	0	0	0	0	2 1/3	1	0	0	0	1

PERSONAL: Born February 27, 1968, in Saint John, N.B. ... 5-9/217. ... Bats left, throws right. ... Full name: Matthew Wade Stairs.
HIGH SCHOOL: Fredericton (N.B.).
TRANSACTIONS/CAREER NOTES: Signed as non-drafted free agent by Montreal Expos organization (January 17, 1989). ... On disabled list (May 16-23, 1991). ... On Ottawa disabled list (May 7-18, 1993). ... Contract sold by Expos to Chunichi Dragons of Japan Central League (June 8, 1993). ... Signed by Expos organization (December 15, 1993). ... Traded by Expos with P Pete Young to Boston Red Sox for cash (February 18, 1994). ... Granted free agency (October 14, 1995). ... Signed by Oakland Athletics organization (December 1, 1995). ... Traded by A's to Chicago Cubs for P Eric Ireland (November 20, 2000). ... Granted free agency (November 5, 2001). ... Signed by Milwaukee Brewers (January 25, 2002).
RECORDS: Shares A.L. single-inning record for most runs batted in—6 (July 5, 1996, first inning).
HONORS: Named Eastern League Most Valuable Player (1991).
STATISTICAL NOTES: Led Eastern League with .509 slugging percentage, 257 total bases and tied for lead with eight intentional bases on balls received in 1991. ... Career major league grand slams: 7.
MISCELLANEOUS: Member of 1988 Canadian Olympic baseball team.

								BATTING							FIELDING			
Year	Team (League)	Pos.	G	AB	R	H	2B	3B	HR	RBI	Avg.	BB	SO	SB	PO	A	E	Avg.
1989—W.P. Beach (FSL)	3B-SS-2B	36	111	12	21	3	1	1	9	.189	9	18	0	21	66	4	.956
—Jamestown (NY-P)	2B-3B	14	43	8	11	1	0	1	5	.256	3	5	1	15	35	6	.893
—Rockford (Midw.)	3B	44	141	20	40	9	2	2	14	.284	15	29	5	30	62	7	.929
1990—W.P. Beach (FSL)	3B-2B	55	183	30	62	9	3	3	30	.339	41	19	15	40	112	17	.899
—Jacksonville (Sou.)	3B-OF-2B-SS	79	280	26	71	17	0	3	34	.254	22	43	5	76	107	22	.893
1991—Harrisburg (East.)	2B-3B-OF	129	505	87	*168	30	•10	13	78	*.333	66	47	23	193	314	22	.958
1992—Indianapolis (A.A.)	OF	110	401	57	107	23	4	11	56	.267	49	61	11	188	11	3	.985
—Montreal (N.L.)	OF	13	30	2	5	2	0	0	5	.167	7	7	0	14	0	1	.933
1993—Ottawa (I.L.)	OF	34	125	18	35	4	2	3	20	.280	11	15	4	49	4	0	1.000
—Montreal (N.L.)	OF	6	8	1	3	1	0	0	2	.375	0	1	0	1	0	0	1.000
—Chunichi (Jap. Cen.)■		60	132	10	33	6	0	6	23	.250	7	34	1	...	...	...	...
1994—New Britain (East.)■	OF-DH-1B	93	317	44	98	25	2	9	61	.309	53	38	10	106	12	3	.975
1995—Pawtucket (I.L.)	OF-DH	75	271	40	77	17	0	13	56	.284	29	41	3	79	13	0	1.000
—Boston (A.L.)	OF-DH	39	88	8	23	7	1	1	17	.261	4	14	0	19	2	2	.913
1996—Oakland (A.L.)■	OF-DH-1B	61	137	21	38	5	1	10	23	.277	19	23	1	65	11	1	.987
—Edmonton (PCL)	DH-OF-1B	51	180	35	62	16	1	8	41	.344	21	34	0	49	2	3	.944
1997—Oakland (A.L.)	OF-DH-1B	133	352	62	105	19	0	27	73	.298	50	60	3	142	9	4	.974
1998—Oakland (A.L.)	DH-OF-1B	149	523	88	154	33	1	26	106	.294	59	93	8	67	11	0	1.000
1999—Oakland (A.L.)	OF-DH-1B	146	531	94	137	26	3	38	102	.258	89	124	2	247	13	5	.981
2000—Oakland (A.L.)	OF-DH-1B	143	476	74	108	26	0	21	81	.227	78	122	5	187	5	4	.980
2001—Chicago (N.L.)■	1B-OF-DH-2B	128	340	48	85	21	0	17	61	.250	52	76	2	547	52	4	.993
American League totals (6 years)		671	2107	347	565	116	6	123	402	.268	299	436	19	727	51	16	.980
National League totals (3 years)		147	378	51	93	24	0	17	68	.246	59	84	2	562	52	5	.992
Major League totals (9 years)		818	2485	398	658	140	6	140	470	.265	358	520	21	1289	103	21	.985

DIVISION SERIES RECORD

								BATTING							FIELDING			
Year	Team (League)	Pos.	G	AB	R	H	2B	3B	HR	RBI	Avg.	BB	SO	SB	PO	A	E	Avg.
1995—Boston (A.L.)	PH	1	1	0	0	0	0	0	0	.000	0	1	0	...	...	...	...
2000—Oakland (A.L.)	OF-PH	3	9	0	1	1	0	0	0	.111	0	1	0	6	0	0	1.000
Division series totals (2 years)		4	10	0	1	1	0	0	0	.100	0	2	0	6	0	0	1.000

PERSONAL: Born November 9, 1978, in Birmingham, Ala. ... 6-4/217. ... Throws right, bats right. ... Full name: Jason Wayne Standridge.
HIGH SCHOOL: Hewitt-Trussville (Ala.).
TRANSACTIONS/CAREER NOTES: Selected by Tampa Bay Devil Rays organization in first round (31st pick overall) of free-agent draft (June 3, 1997).
HONORS: Named South Atlantic League Most Valuable Pitcher (1999).

Year	League	W	L	Pct.	ERA	G	GS	CG	ShO	Sv.	IP	H	R	ER	BB	SO
1997—GC Devil Rays (GCL)		0	6	.000	3.59	13	13	0	0	0	57²/₃	56	30	23	13	55
1998—Princeton (Appal.)		4	4	.500	7.00	12	12	0	0	0	63	82	61	49	28	47
1999—Charleston, S.C. (S.Atl.)		9	1	.900	*2.02	18	18	3	*3	0	116	80	35	26	31	84
—St. Petersburg (FSL)		4	4	.500	3.91	8	8	0	0	0	48¹/₃	49	21	21	20	26
2000—St. Petersburg (FSL)		2	4	.333	3.38	10	10	1	0	0	56	45	28	21	31	41
—Orlando (Sou.)		6	8	.429	3.62	17	17	2	0	0	97	85	46	39	43	55
2001—Durham (I.L.)		5	10	.333	5.28	20	20	0	0	0	102¹/₃	130	73	60	50	48
—Tampa Bay (A.L.)		0	0	...	4.66	9	1	0	0	0	19¹/₃	19	10	10	14	9
—Orlando (Sou.)		0	2	.000	5.59	2	2	0	0	0	9²/₃	12	6	6	4	7
Major League totals (1 year)		0	0	...	4.66	9	1	0	0	0	19¹/₃	19	10	10	14	9

PERSONAL: Born June 2, 1967, in Houston. ... 6-1/215. ... Throws left, bats left. ... Full name: William Michael Stanton.
HIGH SCHOOL: Midland (Texas).
JUNIOR COLLEGE: Alvin (Texas) Community College.
TRANSACTIONS/CAREER NOTES: Selected by Atlanta Braves organization in 13th round of free-agent draft (June 2, 1987). ... On Atlanta disabled list (April 27, 1990-remainder of season); included rehabilitation assignments to Greenville (May 31-June 5 and August 21-29). ... Granted free agency (December 23, 1994). ... Re-signed by Braves (April 12, 1995). ... Traded by Braves with a player to be named later to Boston Red Sox for two players to be named later (July 31, 1995); Red Sox acquired P Matt Murray and Braves acquired OF Marc Lewis and P Mike Jacobs to complete deal (August 31, 1995). ... Traded by Red Sox to Texas Rangers for P Mark Brandenburg and P Kerry Lacy (July 31, 1996). ... Granted free agency (October 27, 1996). ... Signed by New York Yankees (December 11, 1996). ... On suspended list (July 3-10, 1998). ... Granted free agency (November 5, 1999). ... Re-signed by Yankees (November 29, 1999).

Year League	W	L	Pct.	ERA	G	GS	CG	ShO	Sv.	IP	H	R	ER	BB	SO
1987—Pulaski (Appl.)	4	8	.333	3.24	15	13	3	2	0	83 1/3	64	37	30	42	82
1988—Burlington (Midw.)	11	5	.688	3.62	30	23	1	1	0	154	154	86	62	69	160
—Durham (Caro.)	1	0	1.000	1.46	2	2	1	1	0	12 1/3	14	3	2	5	14
1989—Greenville (Sou.)	4	1	.800	1.58	47	0	0	0	19	51 1/3	32	10	9	31	58
—Richmond (I.L.)	2	0	1.000	0.00	13	0	0	0	8	20	6	0	0	13	20
—Atlanta (N.L.)	0	1	.000	1.50	20	0	0	0	7	24	17	4	4	8	27
1990—Atlanta (N.L.)	0	3	.000	18.00	7	0	0	0	2	7	16	16	14	4	7
—Greenville (Sou.)	0	1	.000	1.59	4	4	0	0	0	5 2/3	7	1	1	3	4
1991—Atlanta (N.L.)	5	5	.500	2.88	74	0	0	0	7	78	62	27	25	21	54
1992—Atlanta (N.L.)	5	4	.556	4.10	65	0	0	0	8	63 2/3	59	32	29	20	44
1993—Atlanta (N.L.)	4	6	.400	4.67	63	0	0	0	27	52	51	35	27	29	43
1994—Atlanta (N.L.)	3	1	.750	3.55	49	0	0	0	3	45 2/3	41	18	18	26	35
1995—Atlanta (N.L.)	1	1	.500	5.59	26	0	0	0	1	19 1/3	31	14	12	6	13
—Boston (A.L.)■	1	0	1.000	3.00	22	0	0	0	0	21	17	9	7	8	10
1996—Boston (A.L.)	4	3	.571	3.83	59	0	0	0	1	56 1/3	58	24	24	23	46
—Texas (A.L.)■	0	1	.000	3.22	22	0	0	0	0	22 1/3	20	8	8	4	14
1997—New York (A.L.)■	6	1	.857	2.57	64	0	0	0	3	66 2/3	50	19	19	34	70
1998—New York (A.L.)	4	1	.800	5.47	67	0	0	0	6	79	71	51	48	26	69
1999—New York (A.L.)	2	2	.500	4.33	73	1	0	0	0	62 1/3	71	30	30	18	59
2000—New York (A.L.)	2	3	.400	4.10	69	0	0	0	0	68	68	32	31	24	75
2001—New York (A.L.)	9	4	.692	2.58	76	0	0	0	0	80 1/3	80	25	23	29	78
A.L. totals (7 years)	28	15	.651	3.75	452	1	0	0	10	456	435	198	190	166	421
N.L. totals (7 years)	18	21	.462	4.01	304	0	0	0	55	289 2/3	277	146	129	114	223
Major League totals (13 years)	46	36	.561	3.85	756	1	0	0	65	745 2/3	712	344	319	280	644

DIVISION SERIES RECORD

Year League	W	L	Pct.	ERA	G	GS	CG	ShO	Sv.	IP	H	R	ER	BB	SO
1995—Boston (A.L.)	0	0	...	0.00	1	0	0	0	0	2 1/3	1	0	0	0	4
1996—Texas (A.L.)	0	1	.000	2.70	3	0	0	0	0	3 1/3	2	2	1	3	3
1997—New York (A.L.)	0	0	...	0.00	3	0	0	0	0	1	1	0	0	1	3
1998—New York (A.L.)										Did not play.					
1999—New York (A.L.)										Did not play.					
2000—New York (A.L.)	1	0	1.000	2.08	3	0	0	0	0	4 1/3	5	1	1	1	3
2001—New York (A.L.)	1	0	1.000	0.00	3	0	0	0	0	4 2/3	3	0	0	0	1
Division series totals (5 years)	2	1	.667	1.15	13	0	0	0	0	15 2/3	12	3	2	5	14

CHAMPIONSHIP SERIES RECORD

Year League	W	L	Pct.	ERA	G	GS	CG	ShO	Sv.	IP	H	R	ER	BB	SO
1991—Atlanta (N.L.)	0	0	...	2.45	3	0	0	0	0	3 2/3	4	1	1	3	3
1992—Atlanta (N.L.)	0	0	...	0.00	5	0	0	0	0	4 1/3	2	1	0	2	5
1993—Atlanta (N.L.)	0	0	...	0.00	1	0	0	0	0	1	1	0	0	1	0
1998—New York (A.L.)	0	0	...	0.00	3	0	0	0	0	3 2/3	2	0	0	2	4
1999—New York (A.L.)	0	0	...	0.00	3	0	0	0	0	1/3	1	0	0	1	0
2000—New York (A.L.)										Did not play.					
2001—New York (A.L.)	0	0	...	27.00	2	0	0	0	0	1	1	3	3	2	0
Champ. series totals (6 years)	0	0	...	2.57	17	0	0	0	0	14	11	5	4	11	12

WORLD SERIES RECORD

RECORDS: Holds record for most games as relief pitcher—20.

NOTES: Member of World Series championship team (1998, 1999 and 2000).

Year League	W	L	Pct.	ERA	G	GS	CG	ShO	Sv.	IP	H	R	ER	BB	SO
1991—Atlanta (N.L.)	1	0	1.000	0.00	5	0	0	0	0	7 1/3	5	0	0	2	7
1992—Atlanta (N.L.)	0	0	...	0.00	4	0	0	0	1	5	3	0	0	2	1
1998—New York (A.L.)	0	0	...	27.00	1	0	0	0	0	2/3	3	2	2	0	1
1999—New York (A.L.)	0	0	...	0.00	1	0	0	0	0	1	0	0	0	0	1
2000—New York (A.L.)	2	0	1.000	0.00	4	0	0	0	0	4 1/3	0	0	0	0	7
2001—New York (A.L.)	0	0	...	3.18	5	0	0	0	0	5 2/3	3	2	2	1	3
World Series totals (6 years)	3	0	1.000	1.54	20	0	0	0	1	23 1/3	14	4	4	5	20

ALL-STAR GAME RECORD

Year League	W	L	Pct.	ERA	GS	CG	ShO	Sv.	IP	H	R	ER	BB	SO
2001—American	0	0	...	0.00	0	0	0	0	2/3	0	0	0	0	0

STARK, DENNIS　　　　　P　　　　　ROCKIES

PERSONAL: Born October 27, 1974, in Hicksville, Ohio. ... 6-2/210. ... Throws right, bats right.

HIGH SCHOOL: Edgerton (Ohio).

COLLEGE: Toledo.

TRANSACTIONS/CAREER NOTES: Selected by Seattle Mariners organization in fourth round of free-agent draft (June 4, 1996). ... On Lancaster disabled list (April 26, 1998-remainder of season); included rehabilitation assignment to Arizona League Mariners (July 30-August 11). ... On New Haven disabled list (May 20-August 30, 2000). ... On Seattle disabled list (August 31, 2000-remainder of season). ... Traded by Mariners with P Jose Paniagua and P Brian Fuentes to Colorado Rockies for 3B Jeff Cirillo (December 15, 2001).

HONORS: Named Pacific Coast League Pitcher of the Year (2001).

STATISTICAL NOTES: Tied for Eastern League lead with four double plays in 2000.

Year League	W	L	Pct.	ERA	G	GS	CG	ShO	Sv.	IP	H	R	ER	BB	SO
1996—Everett (N'West)	1	3	.250	4.45	12	4	0	0	0	30 1/3	25	19	15	17	49
1997—Wisconsin (Midw.)	6	3	.667	1.97	16	15	1	0	0	91 1/3	52	27	20	33	105
—Lancaster (Calif.)	1	1	.500	3.24	3	3	0	0	0	16 2/3	13	7	6	10	17
1998—Lancaster (Calif.)	1	2	.333	4.29	5	5	0	0	0	21	18	12	10	17	21
—Arizona Mariners (Ariz.)	0	0	...	2.16	3	1	0	0	0	8 1/3	9	2	2	2	13

Year	League	W	L	Pct.	ERA	G	GS	CG	ShO	Sv.	IP	H	R	ER	BB	SO
1999—	New Haven (East.)	9	11	.450	4.40	26	26	2	1	0	147 1/3	151	82	72	62	103
—	Seattle (A.L.)	0	0	...	9.95	5	0	0	0	0	6 1/3	10	8	7	4	4
2000—	New Haven (East.)	4	3	.571	2.19	8	8	1	0	0	49 1/3	31	13	12	17	42
2001—	Tacoma (PCL)	*14	2	*.875	2.37	24	24	0	0	0	151 2/3	124	52	40	41	130
—	Seattle (A.L.)	1	1	.500	9.20	4	3	0	0	0	14 2/3	21	15	15	4	12
—	San Antonio (Texas)	1	0	1.000	0.00	1	1	0	0	0	6	2	0	0	3	7
Major League totals (2 years)		1	1	.500	9.43	9	3	0	0	0	21	31	23	22	8	16

STECHSCHULTE, GENE — P — CARDINALS

PERSONAL: Born August 12, 1973, in Lima, Ohio. ... 6-5/210. ... Throws right, bats right. ... Full name: Gene Urban Stechschulte.
HIGH SCHOOL: Kalida (Ohio).
COLLEGE: Ashland (Ohio).
TRANSACTIONS/CAREER NOTES: Signed as non-drafted free agent by St. Louis Cardinals organization (June 13, 1996). ... On Arkansas disabled list (July 31-September 1, 1999).
STATISTICAL NOTES: Hit home run in first major league at-bat (April 17, 2001).
MISCELLANEOUS: Appeared in two games as pinch hitter (2001).

Year	League	W	L	Pct.	ERA	G	GS	CG	ShO	Sv.	IP	H	R	ER	BB	SO
1996—	New Jersey (NY-Penn)	1	2	.333	3.27	20	1	0	0	0	33	41	17	12	16	27
1997—	New Jersey (NY-Penn)	1	1	.500	3.22	30	0	0	0	1	36 1/3	45	16	13	16	28
1998—	Peoria (Midw.)	4	8	.333	2.59	57	0	0	0	*33	66	58	26	19	21	70
1999—	Arkansas (Texas)	2	6	.250	3.40	39	0	0	0	19	42 1/3	41	26	16	20	41
—	Memphis (PCL)	0	0	...	7.71	2	0	0	0	0	2 1/3	2	2	2	5	2
2000—	Memphis (PCL)	4	1	.800	2.45	41	0	0	0	26	47 2/3	38	13	13	18	37
—	St. Louis (N.L.)	1	0	1.000	6.31	20	0	0	0	0	25 2/3	24	22	18	17	12
—	Arkansas (Texas)	0	0	...	0.00	2	0	0	0	0	2	0	0	0	0	3
2001—	St. Louis (N.L.)	1	5	.167	3.86	67	0	0	0	6	70	71	35	30	30	51
Major League totals (2 years)		2	5	.286	4.52	87	0	0	0	6	95 2/3	95	57	48	47	63

DIVISION SERIES RECORD

Year	League	W	L	Pct.	ERA	G	GS	CG	ShO	Sv.	IP	H	R	ER	BB	SO
2001—	St. Louis (N.L.)	0	0	...	0.00	2	0	0	0	0	1/3	3	0	0	0	0

STEIN, BLAKE — P — ROYALS

PERSONAL: Born August 3, 1973, in McComb, Miss. ... 6-7/240. ... Throws right, bats right. ... Full name: William Blake Stein.
HIGH SCHOOL: Covington (La.).
COLLEGE: Spring Hill College (Ala.).
TRANSACTIONS/CAREER NOTES: Selected by St. Louis Cardinals organization in sixth round of free-agent draft (June 2, 1994). ... Traded by Cardinals with P T.J. Mathews and P Eric Ludwick to Oakland Athletics for 1B Mark McGwire (July 31, 1997). ... Traded by A's with P Jeff D'Amico and P Brad Rigby to Kansas City Royals for P Kevin Appier (July 31, 1999). ... On Kansas City disabled list (March 24-July 5, 2000); included rehabilitation assignments to Wilmington (June 7-18), Wichita (June 21-22) and Omaha (June 23-July 5).
RECORDS: Shares major league single-inning record for most strikeouts—4 (July 27, 1998, fourth inning).

Year	League	W	L	Pct.	ERA	G	GS	CG	ShO	Sv.	IP	H	R	ER	BB	SO
1994—	Johnson City (Appl.)	4	1	.800	2.87	13	13	1	0	0	59 2/3	44	21	19	24	69
1995—	Peoria (Midw.)	10	6	.625	3.80	27	•27	1	0	0	139 1/3	122	69	59	61	133
1996—	St. Petersburg (FSL)	•16	5	.762	*2.15	28	27	2	1	1	172	122	48	41	54	*159
1997—	Arkansas (Texas)	8	7	.533	4.24	22	22	1	0	0	133 2/3	128	67	63	49	114
—	Huntsville (Sou.)■	3	2	.600	5.71	7	7	0	0	0	34 2/3	36	24	22	20	25
1998—	Edmonton (PCL)	3	1	.750	3.47	5	4	0	0	0	23 1/3	22	13	9	11	31
—	Oakland (A.L.)	5	9	.357	6.37	24	20	1	1	0	117 1/3	117	92	83	71	89
1999—	Vancouver (PCL)	4	2	.667	4.10	19	19	0	0	0	109 2/3	94	54	50	43	111
—	Oakland (A.L.)	0	0	...	16.88	1	1	0	0	0	2 2/3	6	5	5	6	4
—	Kansas City (A.L.)■	1	2	.333	4.09	12	11	0	0	0	70 1/3	59	33	32	41	43
2000—	Wilmington (Caro.)	0	0	...	6.75	2	2	0	0	0	5 1/3	6	4	4	2	12
—	Wichita (Texas)	1	0	1.000	6.23	2	2	0	0	0	8 2/3	10	6	6	1	12
—	Omaha (PCL)	2	0	1.000	0.73	2	2	0	0	0	12 1/3	9	1	1	2	14
—	Kansas City (A.L.)	8	5	.615	4.68	17	17	1	0	0	107 2/3	98	57	56	57	78
2001—	Kansas City (A.L.)	7	8	.467	4.74	36	15	0	0	1	131	112	73	69	79	113
Major League totals (4 years)		21	24	.467	5.14	90	64	2	1	1	429	392	260	245	254	327

STENSON, DERNELL — 1B/OF — RED SOX

PERSONAL: Born June 17, 1978, in La Grange, Ga. ... 6-1/230. ... Bats left, throws left. ... Full name: Dernell Renauld Stenson.
HIGH SCHOOL: La Grange (Ga.).
TRANSACTIONS/CAREER NOTES: Selected by Boston Red Sox organization in third round of free-agent draft (June 2, 1996). ... On Pawtucket disabled list (June 24-July 15, 1999). ... On disabled list (April 17-May 10 and June 1-18, 2000; and May 8-17, 2001).

							BATTING							FIELDING		
Year	Team (League)	Pos.	G	AB	R	H	2B	3B	HR	RBI	Avg.	BB	SO	SB	PO	A	E	Avg.
1996—	GC Red Sox (GCL)	OF	32	97	16	21	3	1	2	15	.216	16	26	4	30	2	0	1.000
1997—	Michigan (Midw.)	OF	131	471	79	137	35	2	15	80	.291	72	105	6	145	11	14	.918
1998—	Trenton (East.)	OF	138	505	90	130	21	1	24	71	.257	84	135	5	218	*15	6	.975
1999—	Pawtucket (I.L.)	1B-DH	121	440	64	119	28	2	18	82	.270	55	119	2	919	56	*34	.966
—	GC Red Sox (GCL)	DH-1B	6	23	2	5	0	0	2	7	.217	3	5	0	16	2	1	.947
2000—	Pawtucket (I.L.)	1B-OF	98	380	59	102	14	0	23	71	.268	45	99	0	559	41	12	.980
2001—	Pawtucket (I.L.)	OF	122	464	53	110	18	1	16	69	.237	43	116	0	204	9	8	.964

STEPHENS, JOHN   P   ORIOLES

PERSONAL: Born November 15, 1979, in Sydney, Australia. ... 6-1/200. ... Throws right, bats right. ... Full name: John M. Stephens.
HIGH SCHOOL: Parramatta Marist (Westmead, Australia).
TRANSACTIONS/CAREER NOTES: Signed as non-drafted free agent by Baltimore Orioles organization (July 3, 1996). ... On disabled list (May 11, 1998-remainder of season).
HONORS: Named Eastern League Pitcher of the Year (2001).

Year	League	W	L	Pct.	ERA	G	GS	CG	ShO	Sv.	IP	H	R	ER	BB	SO
1997—	Gulf Coast Orioles (GCL)....	3	0	1.000	0.82	9	3	0	0	1	33	15	3	3	9	43
—	Bluefield (Appl.)	2	0	1.000	2.25	4	4	0	0	0	24	17	6	6	5	34
1998—	Delmarva (S.Atl.).................	1	2	.333	2.60	6	6	1	1	0	34 2/3	25	11	10	13	40
1999—	Delmarva (S.Atl.).................	10	8	.556	3.22	28	27	•4	2	0	170 1/3	148	75	61	36	*217
2000—	Frederick (Caro.)	7	6	.538	3.05	20	20	0	0	0	118	119	45	40	22	121
2001—	Bowie (East.)......................	11	4	.733	1.84	18	17	3	•3	0	132	95	32	27	21	130
—	Rochester (I.L.)...................	2	5	.286	4.03	9	9	0	0	0	58	52	31	26	19	61

STEPHENSON, GARRETT   P   CARDINALS

PERSONAL: Born January 2, 1972, in Takoma Park, Md. ... 6-5/208. ... Throws right, bats right. ... Full name: Garrett Charles Stephenson.
HIGH SCHOOL: Boonsboro (Md.).
JUNIOR COLLEGE: Ricks College (Idaho).
COLLEGE: Idaho State.
TRANSACTIONS/CAREER NOTES: Selected by Baltimore Orioles organization in 18th round of free-agent draft (June 1, 1992). ... Traded by Orioles with P Calvin Maduro to Philadelphia Phillies (September 4, 1996), completing deal in which Phillies traded 3B Todd Zeile and OF Pete Incaviglia to Orioles for two players to be named later (August 29, 1996). ... On Philadelphia disabled list (June 5-22 and August 18-September 2, 1997). ... On Scranton/Wilkes-Barre disabled list (July 8-August 3, 1998). ... Traded by Phillies with P Ricky Bottalico to St. Louis Cardinals for OF Ron Gant, P Jeff Brantley and P Cliff Politte (November 19, 1998). ... On Memphis disabled list (April 8-June 13, 1999). ... On St. Louis disabled list (March 28, 2001-entire season); included rehabilitation assignment to Memphis (April 5-9).
STATISTICAL NOTES: Led Eastern League with 23 home runs allowed and 18 hit batsmen in 1995.

Year	League	W	L	Pct.	ERA	G	GS	CG	ShO	Sv.	IP	H	R	ER	BB	SO
1992—	Bluefield (Appl.)	3	1	.750	4.73	12	3	0	0	0	32 1/3	35	22	17	7	30
1993—	Albany (S.Atl.)...................	16	7	.696	2.84	30	24	3	•2	1	171 1/3	142	65	54	44	147
1994—	Frederick (Caro.)	7	5	.583	4.02	18	17	1	0	0	107 1/3	91	62	48	36	133
—	Bowie (East.)......................	3	2	.600	5.15	7	7	1	1	0	36 2/3	47	22	21	11	32
1995—	Bowie (East.)......................	7	10	.412	3.64	29	*29	1	0	0	175 1/3	154	87	71	47	139
1996—	Rochester (I.L.)	7	6	.538	4.81	23	21	3	1	0	121 2/3	123	66	65	44	86
—	Baltimore (A.L.)..................	0	1	.000	12.79	3	0	0	0	0	6 1/3	13	9	9	3	3
1997—	Scranton/W.B. (I.L.)■........	3	1	.750	5.90	7	3	0	0	0	29	27	19	19	12	27
—	Philadelphia (N.L.).............	8	6	.571	3.15	20	18	2	0	0	117	104	45	41	38	81
1998—	Philadelphia (N.L.).............	0	2	.000	9.00	6	6	0	0	0	23	31	24	23	19	17
—	Scranton/W.B. (I.L.)	1	8	.111	5.25	13	11	2	0	0	73 2/3	81	49	43	16	48
1999—	Memphis (PCL)■...............	1	1	.500	3.16	4	4	0	0	0	25 2/3	22	9	9	7	19
—	Arkansas (Texas)...............	0	0	...	3.38	1	1	0	0	0	5 1/3	8	3	2	1	2
—	St. Louis (N.L.)...................	6	3	.667	4.22	18	12	0	0	0	85 1/3	90	43	40	29	59
2000—	St. Louis (N.L.)...................	16	9	.640	4.49	32	31	3	2	0	200 1/3	209	105	100	63	123
2001—	Memphis (PCL)	0	0	...	0.00	1	1	0	0	0	2	2	0	0	0	2
A.L. totals (1 year)		0	1	.000	12.79	3	0	0	0	0	6 1/3	13	9	9	3	3
N.L. totals (4 years)		30	20	.600	4.31	76	67	5	2	0	425 2/3	434	217	204	149	280
Major League totals (5 years)		30	21	.588	4.44	79	67	5	2	0	432	447	226	213	152	283

DIVISION SERIES RECORD

Year	League	W	L	Pct.	ERA	G	GS	CG	ShO	Sv.	IP	H	R	ER	BB	SO
2000—	St. Louis (N.L.)...................	0	0	...	2.45	1	1	0	0	0	3 2/3	3	1	1	2	2

STEVENS, LEE   1B   EXPOS

PERSONAL: Born July 10, 1967, in Kansas City, Mo. ... 6-4/219. ... Bats left, throws left. ... Full name: DeWain Lee Stevens.
HIGH SCHOOL: Lawrence (Kan.).
TRANSACTIONS/CAREER NOTES: Selected by California Angels organization in first round (22nd pick overall) of free-agent draft (June 2, 1986). ... Traded by Angels to Montreal Expos for P Jeff Tuss (January 15, 1993); Tuss announced his retirement and Angels acquired P Keith Morrison to complete deal (January 21, 1993). ... Released by Expos (March 30, 1993). ... Signed by Toronto Blue Jays organization (April 8, 1993). ... Granted free agency (October 15, 1993). ... Signed by Angels organization (October 25, 1993). ... Contract sold by Angels to Kintetsu Buffaloes of Japan Pacific League (November 16, 1993). ... Signed by Texas Rangers organization (April 3, 1996). ... On Texas disabled list (August 4-September 1, 1996); included rehabilitation assignment to Oklahoma City (August 13-September 1, 1996). ... On Texas disabled list (August 8-September 1, 1998); included rehabilitation assignment to Oklahoma (August 25-September 1). ... Traded by Rangers to Expos as part of three-way deal in which Expos sent 1B Brad Fullmer to Toronto Blue Jays and Blue Jays sent 1B/DH David Segui and cash to Rangers (March 16, 2000).
HONORS: Named American Association Most Valuable Player (1996).
STATISTICAL NOTES: Led California League first basemen with .986 fielding percentage, 1,028 putouts and 66 assists in 1987. ... Led Texas League outfielders with 12 errors in 1988. ... Tied for Pacific Coast League lead with 11 intentional bases on balls received in 1990. ... Led American Association with 277 total bases, .643 slugging percentage and .404 on-base percentage in 1996. ... Tied for American Association lead with eight intentional bases on balls received in 1996. ... Hit three home runs in one game (April 13, 1998). ... Career major league grand slams: 2.

Year	Team (League)	Pos.	G	AB	R	H	2B	3B	HR	RBI	Avg.	BB	SO	SB	PO	A	E	Avg.
1986—	Salem (N'West)	OF-1B	72	267	45	75	18	2	6	47	.281	45	49	13	231	18	5	.980
1987—	Palm Springs (Calif.)..	1B-OF	140	532	82	130	29	2	19	97	.244	61	117	1	††1031	†68	18	†.984
1988—	Midland (Texas)..........	OF-1B	116	414	79	123	26	2	23	76	.297	58	108	0	217	16	†14	.943
1989—	Edmonton (PCL)	1B-OF	127	446	72	110	29	9	14	74	.247	61	115	5	635	40	7	.990
1990—	Edmonton (PCL)	OF-1B	90	338	57	99	31	2	16	66	.293	55	83	1	284	10	6	.980
	— California (A.L.)	1B	67	248	28	53	10	0	7	32	.214	22	75	1	597	36	4	.994
1991—	Edmonton (PCL) ■.......	OF-1B	123	481	75	151	29	3	19	66	.314	37	79	3	519	33	7	.987
	— California (A.L.)	OF-1B	18	58	8	17	7	0	0	9	.293	6	12	1	100	6	1	.991
1992—	California (A.L.)	1B-DH	106	312	25	69	19	0	7	37	.221	29	64	1	764	49	4	.995
1993—	Syracuse (I.L.)■.........	OF-1B	116	401	61	106	30	1	14	66	.264	39	85	2	201	12	3	.986
1994—	Kintetsu (Jap. Pac.)■.	OF	93	302	44	87	21	0	20	66	.288	28	100	3	...	...	...	...
1995—	Kintetsu (Jap. Pac.).....	OF	129	476	54	117	29	1	23	70	.246	46	129	0	...	...	...	...
1996—	Okla. City (A.A.)■■......	DH-1B-OF	117	431	84	140	*37	2	*32	94	.325	58	90	3	348	24	3	.992
	— Texas (A.L.)	1B-OF	27	78	6	18	2	3	3	12	.231	6	22	0	157	14	1	.994
1997—	Texas (A.L.)	1B-DH-OF	137	426	58	128	24	2	21	74	.300	23	83	1	486	33	3	.994
1998—	Texas (A.L.)	DH-1B-OF	120	348	52	91	17	4	20	59	.265	31	93	0	220	15	1	.996
	— Oklahoma (PCL)	DH-1B	3	12	2	4	0	0	1	1	.333	0	2	0	12	1	0	1.000
1999—	Texas (A.L.)	1B-DH	146	517	76	146	31	1	24	81	.282	52	132	2	1228	60	8	.994
2000—	Montreal (N.L.)■........	1B	123	449	60	119	27	2	22	75	.265	48	105	0	1072	85	11	.991
2001—	Montreal (N.L.)............	1B	152	542	77	133	35	1	25	95	.245	74	157	2	1287	92	19	.986
American League totals (7 years)			621	1983	253	522	110	10	82	304	.263	169	481	6	3552	213	22	.994
National League totals (2 years)			275	991	137	252	62	3	47	170	.254	122	262	2	2359	177	30	.988
Major League totals (9 years)			896	2974	390	774	172	13	129	474	.260	291	743	8	5911	390	52	.992

DIVISION SERIES RECORD

Year	Team (League)	Pos.	G	AB	R	H	2B	3B	HR	RBI	Avg.	BB	SO	SB	PO	A	E	Avg.
1998—	Texas (A.L.)	DH	1	3	0	0	0	0	0	0	.000	0	1	0	...	...	...	...
1999—	Texas (A.L.)	1B	3	9	0	1	1	0	0	0	.111	1	2	0	25	2	0	1.000
Division series totals (2 years)			4	12	0	1	1	0	0	0	.083	1	3	0	25	2	0	1.000

S

STEWART, SCOTT — P — EXPOS

PERSONAL: Born August 14, 1975, in Stoughton, Mass. ... 6-2/225. ... Throws left, bats right. ... Full name: Scott Edward Stewart.

HIGH SCHOOL: East Gaston (Mount Holly, N.C.).

TRANSACTIONS/CAREER NOTES: Selected by Texas Rangers organization in 20th round of free-agent draft (June 2, 1994). ... Released by Rangers (May 30, 1995). ... Signed by Minnesota Twins organization (June 13, 1995). ... Released by Twins (July 13, 1995). ... Signed by St. Paul, Northern League (June, 1996). ... Sold by St. Paul to New York Mets organization (February 25, 1997). ... Granted free agency (October 15, 2000). ... Signed by Montreal Expos organization (November 17, 2000). ... On Montreal disabled list (May 11-June 2, 2001); included rehabilitation assignment to Ottawa (May 19-June 2).

STATISTICAL NOTES: Led Gulf Coast League with nine balks in 1994. ... Tied for Florida State League lead in balks with seven in 1997. ... Led Eastern League with four balks in 1998.

Year	League	W	L	Pct.	ERA	G	GS	CG	ShO	Sv.	IP	H	R	ER	BB	SO
1994—	Gulf Coast Rangers (GCL)..	4	1	.800	2.82	14	8	0	0	1	$54\frac{1}{3}$	47	22	17	12	62
1995—	Charleston, S.C. (S.Atl.)	1	7	.125	3.69	11	11	1	0	0	$75\frac{2}{3}$	76	38	31	14	47
	— Gulf Coast Twins (GCL)■...	0	0	...	6.35	3	1	0	0	0	$5\frac{2}{3}$	7	4	4	4	9
1996—	St. Paul (Nor.)■	6	8	.429	5.84	19	18	0	0	0	$86\frac{1}{3}$	121	70	56	42	54
1997—	St. Lucie (FSL)■	5	10	.333	4.01	22	18	4	0	0	$123\frac{1}{3}$	114	62	55	18	64
1998—	Binghamton (East.)	8	5	.615	3.70	24	13	0	0	2	90	91	44	37	29	65
	— Norfolk (I.L.)	0	6	.000	6.66	9	9	0	0	0	$51\frac{1}{3}$	60	43	38	22	32
1999—	Norfolk (I.L.)	6	4	.600	4.42	35	14	0	0	0	$99\frac{2}{3}$	109	55	49	36	85
	— Binghamton (East.)	1	0	1.000	0.00	1	1	0	0	0	5	3	0	0	0	5
2000—	Norfolk (I.L.)	3	5	.375	3.50	53	1	0	0	5	72	80	32	28	18	57
2001—	Montreal (N.L.)■	3	1	.750	3.78	62	0	0	0	3	$47\frac{2}{3}$	43	20	20	13	39
	— Ottawa (I.L.)	0	0	...	1.80	4	0	0	0	0	5	5	1	1	1	4
Major League totals (1 year)		3	1	.750	3.78	62	0	0	0	3	$47\frac{2}{3}$	43	20	20	13	39

STEWART, SHANNON — OF — BLUE JAYS

PERSONAL: Born February 25, 1974, in Cincinnati. ... 6-1/205. ... Bats right, throws right. ... Full name: Shannon Harold Stewart.

HIGH SCHOOL: Southridge Senior (Miami).

TRANSACTIONS/CAREER NOTES: Selected by Toronto Blue Jays organization in first round (19th pick overall) of free-agent draft (June 1, 1992); pick received as part of compensation for Los Angeles Dodgers signing Type A free-agent P Tom Candiotti. ... On disabled list (June 13, 1994-remainder of season). ... On Syracuse disabled list (May 13-31, 1996). ... On Toronto disabled list (May 1-14, 2000); included rehabilitation assignment to Dunedin (May 12-14).

RECORDS: Shares major league single-game record for most doubles—4 (July 18, 2000).

STATISTICAL NOTES: Led International League outfielders with 286 total chances in 1996. ... Had 16-game hitting streak (June 15-30, 1999). ... Had 26-game hitting streak (August 1-29, 1999). ... Tied for A.L. lead in caught stealing with 14 in 1999. ... Had 16-game hitting streak (May 9-26, 2001).

Year	Team (League)	Pos.	G	AB	R	H	2B	3B	HR	RBI	Avg.	BB	SO	SB	PO	A	E	Avg.
1992—	GC Blue Jays (GCL)....	OF	50	172	44	40	1	0	1	11	.233	24	27	*32	81	1	1	.988
1993—	St. Catharines (NY-P)..	OF	75	*301	•53	84	15	2	3	29	.279	33	43	25	81	0	0	1.000
1994—	Hagerstown (S.Atl.)....	OF	56	225	39	73	10	5	4	25	.324	23	39	15	92	4	1	.990
1995—	Knoxville (Sou.)..........	OF-DH	138	498	89	143	24	6	5	55	.287	*89	61	42	283	6	6	.980
	— Toronto (A.L.)............	OF	12	38	2	8	0	0	0	1	.211	5	5	2	20	1	1	.955

Year	Team (League)	Pos.	G	AB	R	H	2B	3B	HR	RBI	Avg.	BB	SO	SB	PO	A	E	Avg.
1996—Syracuse (I.L.)............	OF	112	420	77	125	26	8	6	42	.298	54	61	*35	*274	7	5	.983
—Toronto (A.L.)...............	OF	7	17	2	3	1	0	0	2	.176	1	4	1	4	0	1	.800
1997—Toronto (A.L.).............	OF-DH	44	168	25	48	13	7	0	22	.286	19	24	10	97	1	2	.980
—Syracuse (I.L.)...............	OF	58	208	41	72	13	1	5	24	.346	36	26	9	115	1	2	.983
1998—Toronto (A.L.).............	OF	144	516	90	144	29	3	12	55	.279	67	77	51	295	4	6	.980
1999—Toronto (A.L.).............	OF-DH	145	608	102	185	28	2	11	67	.304	59	83	37	257	4	5	.981
2000—Toronto (A.L.).............	OF	136	583	107	186	43	5	21	69	.319	37	79	20	298	5	2	.993
—Dunedin (FSL)	OF	1	3	2	3	1	0	0	1	1.000	2	0	0	0	0	0	...
2001—Toronto (A.L.).............	OF-DH	155	640	103	202	44	7	12	60	.316	46	72	27	257	7	5	.981
Major League totals (7 years)		643	2570	431	776	158	24	56	276	.302	234	344	148	1228	22	22	.983

STINNETT, KELLY — C — REDS

PERSONAL: Born February 4, 1970, in Lawton, Okla. ... 5-11/225. ... Bats right, throws right. ... Full name: Kelly Lee Stinnett. ... Name pronounced stih-NET.

HIGH SCHOOL: Lawton (Okla.).

JUNIOR COLLEGE: Seminole (Okla.) Junior College.

TRANSACTIONS/CAREER NOTES: Selected by Cleveland Indians organization in 11th round of free-agent draft (June 5, 1989). ... Selected by New York Mets from Indians organization in Rule 5 major league draft (December 13, 1993). ... Traded by Mets to Milwaukee Brewers for P Cory Lidle (January 17, 1996). ... On Milwaukee disabled list (July 27-September 2, 1997). ... Selected by Arizona Diamondbacks in third round (65th pick overall) of expansion draft (November 18, 1997). ... Granted free agency (December 21, 2000). ... Signed by Cincinnati Reds (January 9, 2001). ... On disabled list (September 4, 2001-remainder of season).

STATISTICAL NOTES: Led New York-Pennsylvania League catchers with 18 errors in 1990. ... Led South Atlantic League catchers with 27 errors in 1991. ... Tied for American Association lead in being hit by pitch with 13 in 1996. ... Led American Association catchers with 10 errors and tied for lead with nine double plays in 1996.

Year	Team (League)	Pos.	G	AB	R	H	2B	3B	HR	RBI	Avg.	BB	SO	SB	PO	A	E	Avg.
1990—Watertown (NY-Penn)	C-1B	60	192	29	46	10	2	2	21	.240	40	43	3	348	48	†18	.957
1991—Columbus (S.Atl.).......	C-1B	102	384	49	101	15	1	14	74	.263	26	70	4	685	100	†28	.966
1992—Canton/Akron (East.)..	C	91	296	37	84	10	0	6	32	.284	16	43	7	560	57	*13	.979
1993—Charlotte (I.L.)...........	C	98	288	42	79	10	3	6	33	.274	17	52	0	495	48	8	.985
1994—New York (N.L.)■	C	47	150	20	38	6	2	2	14	.253	11	28	2	211	20	5	.979
1995—New York (N.L.).........	C	77	196	23	43	8	1	4	18	.219	29	65	2	380	22	7	.983
1996—Milwaukee (A.L.)■.....	C-DH	14	26	1	2	0	0	0	0	.077	2	11	0	46	2	2	.960
—New Orleans (A.A.)	C-DH-3B	95	334	63	96	21	1	27	70	.287	31	83	3	485	52	†11	.980
1997—Tucson (PCL)	C-DH-1B	64	209	50	67	15	3	10	43	.321	42	46	1	256	34	2	.993
—Milwaukee (A.L.).......	C-DH	30	36	2	9	4	0	0	3	.250	3	9	0	81	5	1	.989
1998—Arizona (N.L.)■.........	C-DH	92	274	35	71	14	1	11	34	.259	35	74	0	458	37	8	.984
1999—Arizona (N.L.)...........	C	88	284	36	66	13	0	14	38	.232	24	83	2	549	37	6	.990
2000—Arizona (N.L.)...........	C	76	240	22	52	7	0	8	33	.217	19	56	0	539	40	6	.990
2001—Cincinnati (N.L.)■.....	C-DH	63	187	27	48	11	0	9	25	.257	17	61	2	322	21	12	.966
American League totals (2 years)		44	62	3	11	4	0	0	3	.177	5	20	0	127	7	3	.978
National League totals (6 years)		443	1331	163	318	59	4	48	162	.239	135	367	8	2459	177	44	.984
Major League totals (8 years)		487	1393	166	329	63	4	48	165	.236	140	387	8	2586	184	47	.983

DIVISION SERIES RECORD

Year	Team (League)	Pos.	G	AB	R	H	2B	3B	HR	RBI	Avg.	BB	SO	SB	PO	A	E	Avg.
1999—Arizona (N.L.)............	C	4	14	1	2	1	0	0	0	.143	1	4	0	29	2	0	1.000

STONE, RICKY — P — ASTROS

PERSONAL: Born February 28, 1975, in Hamilton, Ohio. ... 6-1/168. ... Throws right, bats right. ... Full name: Ricky L. Stone.

HIGH SCHOOL: Hamilton (Ohio).

TRANSACTIONS/CAREER NOTES: Selected by Los Angeles Dodgers organization in fourth round of free-agent draft (June 2, 1994). ... Granted free agency (October 18, 2000). ... Signed by Houston Astros organization (January 8, 2001).

Year	League	W	L	Pct.	ERA	G	GS	CG	ShO	Sv.	IP	H	R	ER	BB	SO
1994—Great Falls (Pio.)	2	2	.500	4.44	13	7	0	0	2	50²/₃	55	40	25	24	48
1995—San Bernardino (Calif.).......	3	5	.375	6.52	12	12	0	0	0	58	79	50	42	25	31
—Yakima (N'West)	4	4	.500	5.25	16	6	0	0	2	48	54	31	28	20	28
1996—Savannah (S.Atl.)	2	1	.667	3.98	5	5	0	0	0	31²/₃	34	15	14	9	31
—Vero Beach (FSL)	8	6	.571	3.83	21	21	1	0	0	112²/₃	115	58	48	46	74
1997—San Bernardino (Calif.).......	3	3	.500	3.35	8	8	0	0	0	53²/₃	40	22	20	10	40
—San Antonio (Texas)..........	0	3	.000	5.47	25	5	0	0	3	52²/₃	63	33	32	30	46
1998—San Antonio (Texas)...........	7	2	.778	3.84	13	13	1	1	0	82	76	40	35	26	69
—Albuquerque (PCL)...........	5	5	.500	5.38	18	16	0	0	0	105¹/₃	120	69	63	41	85
1999—Albuquerque (PCL)...........	6	10	.375	5.50	27	27	2	0	0	167	205	*123	•102	71	132
2000—Albuquerque (PCL)...........	9	5	.643	4.94	48	7	0	0	5	120¹/₃	146	79	66	42	75
2001—Houston (N.L.)■.............	0	0	...	2.35	6	0	0	0	0	7²/₃	8	3	2	2	4
—New Orleans (PCL)............	6	3	.667	3.59	51	8	0	0	2	95¹/₃	98	42	38	27	78
Major League totals (1 year)........	0	0	...	2.35	6	0	0	0	0	7²/₃	8	3	2	2	4

PERSONAL: Born May 20, 1965, in Yakima, Wash. ... 6-3/215. ... Throws right, bats left. ... Full name: Todd Vernon Stottlemyre. ... Son of Mel Stottlemyre Sr., pitching coach, New York Yankees; pitcher with New York Yankees (1964-74) and pitching coach for New York Mets (1984-93); and brother of Mel Stottlemyre Jr., pitcher with Kansas City Royals (1990).

HIGH SCHOOL: A.C. Davis (Yakima, Wash.).

JUNIOR COLLEGE: Yakima (Wash.) Valley College.

COLLEGE: UNLV.

TRANSACTIONS/CAREER NOTES: Selected by New York Yankees organization in fifth round of free-agent draft (June 6, 1983); did not sign. ... Selected by St. Louis Cardinals organization in secondary phase of free-agent draft (January 9, 1985); did not sign. ... Selected by Toronto Blue Jays organization in secondary phase of free-agent draft (June 3, 1985). ... On disabled list (June 20-July 13, 1992). ... On suspended list (September 23-28, 1992). ... On disabled list (May 23-June 13, 1993). ... Granted free agency (October 18, 1994). ... Signed by Oakland Athletics (April 11, 1995). ... Traded by A's to St. Louis Cardinals for P Bret Wagner, P Jay Witasick and P Carl Dale (January 9, 1996). ... Traded by Cardinals with SS Royce Clayton to Texas Rangers for P Darren Oliver, 3B Fernando Tatis and a player to be named later (July 31, 1998); Cardinals acquired OF Mark Little to complete deal (August 9, 1998). ... Granted free agency (October 22, 1998). ... Signed by Arizona Diamondbacks (December 2, 1998). ... On Arizona disabled list (May 18-August 19, 1999); included rehabilitation assignment to Arizona League Diamondbacks (August 3-15). ... On Arizona disabled list (May 30-June 15 and June 26-September 1, 2000); included rehabilitation assignment to Arizona League Diamondbacks (August 23-September 1). ... On disabled list (March 23, 2001-entire season).

STATISTICAL NOTES: Pitched 9-0 one-hit, complete-game victory against Chicago (August 26, 1992). ... Struck out 15 batters in one game (June 16, 1995).

MISCELLANEOUS: Struck out in only appearance as pinch hitter (1997).

Year	League	W	L	Pct.	ERA	G	GS	CG	ShO	Sv.	IP	H	R	ER	BB	SO
1986—	Ventura County (Calif.)	9	4	.692	2.43	17	17	2	0	0	103²/₃	76	39	28	36	104
	Knoxville (Sou.)	8	7	.533	4.18	18	18	1	0	0	99	93	56	46	49	81
1987—	Syracuse (I.L.)	11	•13	.458	4.44	34	*34	1	0	0	186²/₃	189	•103	*92	*87	143
1988—	Toronto (A.L.)	4	8	.333	5.69	28	16	0	0	0	98	109	70	62	46	67
	Syracuse (I.L.)	5	0	1.000	2.05	7	7	1	0	0	48¹/₃	36	12	11	8	51
1989—	Toronto (A.L.)	7	7	.500	3.88	27	18	0	0	0	127²/₃	137	56	55	44	63
	Syracuse (I.L.)	3	2	.600	3.23	10	9	2	0	0	55²/₃	46	23	20	15	45
1990—	Toronto (A.L.)	13	17	.433	4.34	33	33	4	0	0	203	214	101	98	69	115
1991—	Toronto (A.L.)	15	8	.652	3.78	34	34	1	0	0	219	194	97	92	75	116
1992—	Toronto (A.L.)	12	11	.522	4.50	28	27	6	2	0	174	175	99	87	63	98
1993—	Toronto (A.L.)	11	12	.478	4.84	30	28	1	1	0	176²/₃	204	107	95	69	98
1994—	Toronto (A.L.)	7	7	.500	4.22	26	19	3	1	1	140²/₃	149	67	66	48	105
1995—	Oakland (A.L.)■	14	7	.667	4.55	31	31	2	0	0	209²/₃	228	117	106	80	205
1996—	St. Louis (N.L.)■	14	11	.560	3.87	34	33	5	2	0	223¹/₃	191	100	96	93	194
1997—	St. Louis (N.L.)	12	9	.571	3.88	28	28	0	0	0	181	155	86	78	65	160
1998—	St. Louis (N.L.)	9	9	.500	3.51	23	23	3	0	0	161¹/₃	146	74	63	51	147
	Texas (A.L.)■	5	4	.556	4.33	10	10	0	0	0	60¹/₃	68	33	29	30	57
1999—	Arizona (N.L.)■	6	3	.667	4.09	17	17	0	0	0	101¹/₃	106	51	46	40	74
	Ariz. Diamondbacks (Ariz.)	2	0	1.000	0.53	3	3	1	0	0	17	11	1	1	1	25
2000—	Arizona (N.L.)	9	6	.600	4.91	18	18	0	0	0	95¹/₃	98	55	52	36	76
	Ariz. Diamondbacks (Ariz.)	1	1	.500	3.60	2	2	0	0	0	10	10	4	4	1	10
2001—	Arizona (N.L.)						Did not play.									
A.L. totals (9 years)		88	81	.521	4.41	247	216	17	4	1	1409	1478	747	690	524	924
N.L. totals (5 years)		50	38	.568	3.95	120	119	8	2	0	762¹/₃	696	366	335	285	651
Major League totals (13 years)		138	119	.537	4.25	367	335	25	6	1	2171¹/₃	2174	1113	1025	809	1575

DIVISION SERIES RECORD

Year	League	W	L	Pct.	ERA	G	GS	CG	ShO	Sv.	IP	H	R	ER	BB	SO
1996—	St. Louis (N.L.)	1	0	1.000	1.35	1	1	0	0	0	6²/₃	5	1	1	2	7
1998—	Texas (A.L.)	0	1	.000	2.25	1	1	0	0	0	8	6	2	2	4	8
1999—	Arizona (N.L.)	1	0	1.000	1.35	1	1	0	0	0	6²/₃	4	1	1	5	6
Division series totals (3 years)		2	1	.667	1.69	3	3	1	0	0	21¹/₃	15	4	4	11	21

CHAMPIONSHIP SERIES RECORD

RECORDS: Shares single-series record for most earned runs allowed—11 (1996). ... Shares single-game record for most earned runs allowed—7 (October 14, 1996). ... Shares record for most hits allowed in one inning—6 (October 14, 1996, first inning).

Year	League	W	L	Pct.	ERA	G	GS	CG	ShO	Sv.	IP	H	R	ER	BB	SO
1989—	Toronto (A.L.)	0	1	.000	7.20	1	1	0	0	0	5	7	4	4	2	3
1991—	Toronto (A.L.)	0	1	.000	9.82	1	1	0	0	0	3²/₃	7	4	4	1	3
1992—	Toronto (A.L.)	0	0	...	2.45	1	0	0	0	0	3²/₃	3	1	1	0	1
1993—	Toronto (A.L.)	0	1	.000	7.50	1	1	0	0	0	6	6	5	5	4	4
1996—	St. Louis (N.L.)	1	1	.500	12.38	3	2	0	0	0	8	15	11	11	3	11
Champ. series totals (5 years)		1	4	.200	8.54	7	5	0	0	0	26¹/₃	38	25	25	10	22

WORLD SERIES RECORD

RECORDS: Shares records for most bases on balls allowed in one inning—4 (October 20, 1993, first inning); and most consecutive bases on balls allowed in one inning—3 (October 20, 1993, first inning).

NOTES: Member of World Series championship team (1992, 1993 and 2001).

Year	League	W	L	Pct.	ERA	G	GS	CG	ShO	Sv.	IP	H	R	ER	BB	SO
1992—	Toronto (A.L.)	0	0	...	0.00	4	0	0	0	0	3²/₃	4	0	0	0	4
1993—	Toronto (A.L.)	0	0	...	27.00	1	1	0	0	0	2	3	6	6	4	1
World Series totals (2 years)		0	0	...	9.53	5	1	0	0	0	5²/₃	7	6	6	4	5

PERSONAL: Born April 26, 1976, in Houston. ... 5-11/180. ... Throws right, bats right. ... Full name: Scott Michael Strickland.

HIGH SCHOOL: Klein Oak (Spring, Texas).

COLLEGE: New Mexico.

TRANSACTIONS/CAREER NOTES: Selected by Montreal Expos organization in 10th round of free-agent draft (June 3, 1997). ... On Montreal disabled list (May 3-July 3, 2000); included rehabilitation assignment to Ottawa (June 25-July 1).

Year	League	W	L	Pct.	ERA	G	GS	CG	ShO	Sv.	IP	H	R	ER	BB	SO
1997—Cape Fear (S.Atl.)		0	1	.000	6.35	3	1	0	0	1	5 2/3	8	7	4	1	8
—Vermont (NY-Penn)		5	2	.714	3.82	15	9	1	0	0	61 1/3	56	27	26	20	69
1998—Cape Fear (S.Atl.)		0	3	.000	4.46	15	2	0	0	4	36 1/3	36	19	18	12	53
—Jupiter (FSL)		4	3	.571	3.39	22	11	0	0	2	69	64	28	26	20	51
1999—Jupiter (FSL)		1	1	.500	3.51	12	1	0	0	2	25 2/3	21	11	10	4	33
—Harrisburg (East.)		1	1	.500	2.48	14	1	0	0	3	29	25	8	8	10	36
—Ottawa (I.L.)		3	0	1.000	1.63	19	0	0	0	5	27 2/3	23	5	5	11	34
—Montreal (N.L.)		0	1	.000	4.50	17	0	0	0	0	18	15	10	9	11	23
2000—Montreal (N.L.)		4	3	.571	3.00	49	0	0	0	9	48	38	18	16	16	48
—Ottawa (I.L.)		0	0	...	0.00	3	0	0	0	0	4	1	0	0	0	4
2001—Montreal (N.L.)		2	6	.250	3.21	77	0	0	0	9	81 1/3	67	36	29	41	85
Major League totals (3 years)		6	10	.375	3.30	143	0	0	0	18	147 1/3	120	64	54	68	156

STRONG, JOE — P

PERSONAL: Born September 9, 1962, in Fairfield, Calif. ... 6-0/200. ... Throws right, bats right. ... Full name: Joseph Benjamin Strong.
HIGH SCHOOL: St. Patrick's (Vallejo, Calif.).
JUNIOR COLLEGE: Contra Costa College (Calif.).
COLLEGE: UC Riverside.
TRANSACTIONS/CAREER NOTES: Selected by Oakland Athletics organization in 15th round of free-agent draft (June 4, 1984). ... Released by A's (January 7, 1987). ... Signed by Reno, California League (April 7, 1988). ... Released by Reno (January 1, 1990). ... Pitched in Taiwan (1990-92). ... Signed by San Diego Padres organization (February 12, 1993). ... Released by Padres (September 2, 1993). ... Signed by San Bernardino, California League (April 6, 1994). ... Granted free agency (October 17, 1994). ... Signed by Chicago Cubs organization (January 24, 1995). ... Released by Cubs (April 2, 1995). ... Signed by Surrey, Western League (May 1995). ... Signed by Hyundai, Korean League (1998). ... Signed by Tampa Bay Devil Rays organization (February 23, 1999). ... On Durham disabled list (April 27-May 7, 1999). ... Loaned by Devil Rays to Mexico City Tigres, Mexican League (July 5-September 20, 1999). ... Granted free agency (October 15, 1999). ... Signed by Florida Marlins organization (February 1, 2000). ... On Calgary disabled list (April 12-24, 2000). ... Granted free agency (October 18, 2000). ... Re-signed by Marlins organization (November 3, 2000). ... Granted free agency (October 9, 2001).

Year	League	W	L	Pct.	ERA	G	GS	CG	ShO	Sv.	IP	H	R	ER	BB	SO
1984—Medford (N'West)		5	6	.455	3.88	20	9	3	0	2	72	64	33	31	36	66
1985—Modesto (Calif.)		7	7	.500	5.06	42	11	2	0	6	110 1/3	103	79	62	60	82
1986—Modesto (Calif.)		2	2	.500	3.42	36	0	0	0	11	52 2/3	43	23	20	28	39
—Huntsville (Sou.)		1	1	.500	5.40	6	0	0	0	0	8	8	5	5	7	5
1987—						Did not play.										
1988—Reno (Calif.)■		4	13	.235	4.79	31	24	2	0	0	161 2/3	168	114	86	96	107
1989—Reno (Calif.)		8	1	.889	3.58	53	0	0	0	18	73	62	35	29	22	79
1990—Taipei (Taiwan)■		18	7	.720	1.79	...	...	...	...	...	...	...	...	...	...	...
1991—Taipei (Taiwan)		15	7	.682	2.10	...	...	...	...	...	...	...	...	...	...	...
1992—Taipei (Taiwan)		12	10	.545	2.60	...	...	...	...	...	...	...	...	...	...	...
1993—Las Vegas (PCL)■		1	3	.250	5.67	21	0	0	0	0	27	37	23	17	10	18
—Rancho Cuca. (Calif.)		1	0	1.000	2.70	7	0	0	0	1	10	10	3	3	2	13
—Wichita (Texas)		1	0	1.000	6.75	4	3	0	0	0	14 2/3	13	13	11	11	13
1994—San Bernardino (Calif.)■		2	3	.400	6.71	12	11	0	0	0	53 2/3	60	46	40	27	43
1995—Surrey (West.)■		8	9	.471	2.75	20	19	9	...	0	131	120	55	40	48	129
1996—						Did not play.										
1997—						Did not play.										
1998—Hyundai (Korean)■		6	5	.545	6.21	53	0	0	...	27	58	64	...	...	29	54
1999—Durham (I.L.)■		0	1	.000	7.98	6	1	0	0	1	14 2/3	20	13	13	8	12
—Orlando (Sou.)		1	4	.200	5.68	11	7	2	0	0	38	40	24	24	18	34
—M.C. Tigres (Mex.)■		1	1	.500	4.72	11	0	0	0	2	13 1/3	17	9	7	10	10
2000—Calgary (PCL)■		2	1	.667	4.03	29	1	0	0	9	44 2/3	44	21	20	20	33
—Florida (N.L.)		1	1	.500	7.32	18	0	0	0	1	19 2/3	26	16	16	12	18
2001—Calgary (PCL)■		6	3	.667	6.25	46	0	0	0	1	59	80	45	41	18	48
—Florida (N.L.)		0	0	...	1.35	5	0	0	0	0	6 2/3	3	1	1	3	4
Major League totals (2 years)		1	1	.500	5.81	23	0	0	0	1	26 1/3	29	17	17	15	22

STURTZE, TANYON — P — DEVIL RAYS

PERSONAL: Born October 12, 1970, in Worcester, Mass. ... 6-5/205. ... Throws right, bats right. ... Full name: Tanyon James Sturtze. ... Name pronounced STURTS.
HIGH SCHOOL: St. Peter-Marian (Worcester, Mass.).
JUNIOR COLLEGE: Quinsigamond Community College (Mass.).
TRANSACTIONS/CAREER NOTES: Selected by Oakland Athletics organization in 23rd round of free-agent draft (June 4, 1990). ... On Huntsville disabled list (April 7-16, 1994). ... Selected by Chicago Cubs from A's organization in Rule 5 major league draft (December 5, 1994). ... Granted free agency (October 15, 1996). ... Signed by Texas Rangers (November 20, 1996). ... Released by Rangers (March 6, 1998). ... Re-signed by Rangers organization (March 11, 1998). ... Granted free agency (October 15, 1998). ... Signed by Florida Marlins organization (November 23, 1998). ... Signed by Chicago White Sox organization (November 23, 1998). ... On suspended list (May 1-3, 2000). ... Traded by White Sox to Tampa Bay Devil Rays for 2B/SS Tony Graffanino (May 31, 2000). ... On Tampa Bay disabled list (August 27, 2000-remainder of season).
STATISTICAL NOTES: Pitched 5-0 no-hit victory against Chattanooga (June 13, 1993).

Year	League	W	L	Pct.	ERA	G	GS	CG	ShO	Sv.	IP	H	R	ER	BB	SO
1990—Arizona Athletics (Ariz.)		2	5	.286	5.44	12	10	0	0	0	48	55	41	29	27	30
1991—Madison (Midw.)		10	5	.667	3.09	27	27	0	0	0	163	136	77	56	58	88
1992—Modesto (Calif.)		7	11	.389	3.75	25	25	1	0	0	151	143	72	63	78	126
1993—Huntsville (Sou.)		5	12	.294	4.78	28	•28	1	1	0	165 2/3	169	102	*88	85	112
1994—Huntsville (Sou.)		6	3	.667	3.22	17	17	1	0	0	103 1/3	100	40	37	39	63
—Tacoma (PCL)		4	5	.444	4.04	11	9	0	0	0	64 2/3	73	36	29	34	28
1995—Chicago (N.L.)■		0	0	...	9.00	2	0	0	0	0	2	2	2	2	1	0
—Iowa (A.A.)		4	7	.364	6.80	23	17	1	1	0	86	108	66	65	42	48

Year League	W	L	Pct.	ERA	G	GS	CG	ShO	Sv.	IP	H	R	ER	BB	SO
1996— Iowa (A.A.)	6	4	.600	4.85	51	1	0	0	4	72 1/3	80	42	39	33	51
— Chicago (N.L.)	1	0	1.000	9.00	6	0	0	0	0	11	16	11	11	5	7
1997— Oklahoma City (A.A.)■	8	6	.571	5.10	25	19	1	0	0	114 2/3	133	76	65	47	79
— Texas (A.L.)	1	1	.500	8.27	9	5	0	0	0	32 2/3	45	30	30	18	18
1998— Gulf Coast Rangers (GCL)..	0	1	.000	7.71	3	3	0	0	0	7	12	7	6	4	10
— Charlotte (FSL)	0	1	.000	6.00	1	0	0	0	0	3	2	3	2	1	3
— Tulsa (Texas)	1	0	1.000	5.40	1	0	0	0	0	1 2/3	2	1	1	2	3
— Oklahoma (PCL)	3	1	.750	3.34	13	3	0	0	0	35	33	13	13	18	31
1999— Charlotte (I.L.)■	9	4	.692	4.05	33	14	2	1	3	104 1/3	83	53	47	41	107
— Chicago (A.L.)	0	0	...	0.00	1	1	0	0	0	6	4	0	0	2	2
2000— Chicago (A.L.)	1	2	.333	12.06	10	1	0	0	0	15 2/3	25	23	21	15	6
— Tampa Bay (A.L.)■	4	0	1.000	2.56	19	5	0	0	0	52 2/3	47	16	15	14	38
2001— Tampa Bay (A.L.)	11	12	.478	4.42	39	27	0	0	1	195 1/3	200	98	96	79	110
A.L. totals (4 years)	17	15	.531	4.82	78	39	0	0	1	302 1/3	321	167	162	128	174
N.L. totals (2 years)	1	0	1.000	9.00	8	0	0	0	0	13	18	13	13	6	7
Major League totals (6 years)	18	15	.545	4.99	86	39	0	0	1	315 1/3	339	180	175	134	181

STYNES, CHRIS — IF — CUBS

PERSONAL: Born January 19, 1973, in Queens, N.Y. ... 5-10/185. ... Bats right, throws right. ... Full name: Christopher Desmond Stynes.
HIGH SCHOOL: Boca Raton (Fla.).
TRANSACTIONS/CAREER NOTES: Selected by Toronto Blue Jays in third round of free-agent draft (June 3, 1991). ... Traded by Blue Jays with P David Sinnes and IF Tony Medrano to Kansas City Royals for P David Cone (April 6, 1995). ... Traded by Royals with OF Jon Nunnally to Cincinnati Reds for P Hector Carrasco and P Scott Service (July 15, 1997). ... Traded by Reds to Boston Red Sox for OF Michael Coleman and IF Donnie Sadler (November 16, 2000). ... On Boston disabled list (April 6-24 and May 10-June 7, 2001); included rehabilitation assignment to Pawtucket (June 3-7). ... Granted free agency (December 21, 2001). ... Signed by Chicago Cubs (January 2, 2002).
STATISTICAL NOTES: Tied for Florida State League lead in double plays by third basemen with 22 in 1993. ... Led Southern League with 237 total bases in 1994.

Year Team (League)	Pos.	G	AB	R	H	2B	3B	HR	RBI	Avg.	BB	SO	SB	PO	A	E	Avg.
1991— GC Blue Jays (GCL)	3B	57	219	29	67	15	1	4	39	.306	9	39	10	42	*138	8	*.957
1992— Myrtle Beach (S.Atl.)	3B	127	489	67	139	36	0	7	46	.284	16	43	28	86	208	26	.919
1993— Dunedin (FSL)	3B	123	496	72	151	28	5	7	48	.304	25	40	19	83	234	21	*.938
1994— Knoxville (Sou.)	2B	136	*545	79	*173	32	4	8	79	.317	23	36	28	247	*366	20	.968
1995— Omaha (A.A.)■	2B-3B	83	306	51	84	12	5	9	42	.275	27	24	4	144	204	13	.964
— Kansas City (A.L.)	2B-DH	22	35	7	6	1	0	0	2	.171	4	3	0	21	35	1	.982
1996— Omaha (A.A.)	OF-3B-2B-DH	72	284	50	101	22	2	10	40	.356	18	17	7	98	77	9	.951
— Kansas City (A.L.)	OF-2B-DH-3B	36	92	8	27	6	0	0	6	.293	2	5	5	38	8	3	.939
1997— Omaha (A.A.)	2B-OF-DH-3B	82	332	53	88	18	1	8	44	.265	19	25	3	101	80	10	.948
— Indianapolis (A.A.)■	2B	21	86	14	31	8	0	1	17	.360	2	5	4	47	61	2	.982
— Cincinnati (N.L.)	OF-2B-3B	49	198	31	69	7	1	6	28	.348	11	13	11	87	33	2	.984
1998— Cincinnati (N.L.)	O-3-2-S	123	347	52	88	10	1	6	27	.254	32	36	15	148	54	2	.990
1999— Cincinnati (N.L.)	2B-3B-OF	73	113	18	27	1	0	2	14	.239	12	13	5	50	71	6	.953
2000— Cincinnati (N.L.)	2B-3B-OF	119	380	71	127	24	1	12	40	.334	32	54	5	83	145	7	.970
2001— Boston (A.L.)■	3B-2B-OF	96	361	52	101	19	2	8	33	.280	20	56	4	109	179	6	.980
— Pawtucket (I.L.)	2B-3B	4	15	1	5	1	0	0	1	.333	1	2	0	3	3	0	1.000
American League totals (3 years)		154	488	67	134	26	2	8	41	.275	26	64	9	168	222	10	.975
National League totals (4 years)		364	1038	172	311	42	3	26	109	.300	87	116	36	368	303	17	.975
Major League totals (7 years)		518	1526	239	445	68	5	34	150	.292	113	180	45	536	525	27	.975

SULLIVAN, SCOTT — P — REDS

PERSONAL: Born March 13, 1971, in Carrollton, Ala. ... 6-3/210. ... Throws right, bats right. ... Full name: William Scott Sullivan.
HIGH SCHOOL: Pickens Academy (Carrollton, Ala.).
COLLEGE: Auburn.
TRANSACTIONS/CAREER NOTES: Selected by Cincinnati Reds organization in second round of free-agent draft (June 3, 1993). ... On Indianapolis disabled list (August 21, 1995-remainder of season).
MISCELLANEOUS: Appeared in one game as pinch runner (2000).

Year League	W	L	Pct.	ERA	G	GS	CG	ShO	Sv.	IP	H	R	ER	BB	SO
1993— Billings (Pio.)	5	0	1.000	1.67	18	7	2	2	3	54	33	13	10	25	79
1994— Chattanooga (Sou.)	11	7	.611	3.41	34	13	2	0	7	121 1/3	101	60	46	40	111
1995— Indianapolis (A.A.)	4	3	.571	3.53	44	0	0	0	1	58 2/3	51	31	23	24	54
— Cincinnati (N.L.)	0	0	...	4.91	3	0	0	0	0	3 2/3	4	2	2	2	2
1996— Indianapolis (A.A.)	5	2	.714	2.73	53	3	0	0	1	108 2/3	95	38	33	37	77
— Cincinnati (N.L.)	0	0	...	2.25	7	0	0	0	0	8	7	2	2	5	3
1997— Cincinnati (N.L.)	5	3	.625	3.24	59	0	0	0	1	97 1/3	79	36	35	30	96
— Indianapolis (A.A.)	3	1	.750	1.30	19	0	0	0	2	27 2/3	16	4	4	4	23
1998— Cincinnati (N.L.)	5	5	.500	5.21	67	0	0	0	1	102	98	62	59	36	86
1999— Cincinnati (N.L.)	5	4	.556	3.01	79	0	0	0	3	113 2/3	88	41	38	47	78
2000— Cincinnati (N.L.)	3	6	.333	3.47	79	0	0	0	3	106 1/3	87	44	41	38	96
2001— Cincinnati (N.L.)	7	1	.875	3.31	79	0	0	0	8	103 1/3	94	44	38	36	82
Major League totals (7 years)	25	19	.568	3.62	373	0	0	0	8	534 1/3	457	231	215	194	443

SUPPAN, JEFF — P — ROYALS

PERSONAL: Born January 2, 1975, in Oklahoma City. ... 6-2/210. ... Throws right, bats right. ... Full name: Jeffrey Scot Suppan.
HIGH SCHOOL: Crespi (Encino, Calif.).

TRANSACTIONS/CAREER NOTES: Selected by Boston Red Sox organization in second round of free-agent draft (June 3, 1993). ... On Trenton disabled list (April 9-29, 1995). ... On Boston disabled list (August 25, 1996-remainder of season). ... Selected by Arizona Diamondbacks in first round (third pick overall) of expansion draft (November 18, 1997). ... Contract purchased by Kansas City Royals from Diamondbacks (September 3, 1998).

STATISTICAL NOTES: Led A.L. with 36 home runs allowed in 2000.

Year League	W	L	Pct.	ERA	G	GS	CG	ShO	Sv.	IP	H	R	ER	BB	SO
1993—Gulf Coast Red Sox (GCL)..	4	3	.571	2.18	10	9	2	1	0	57 2/3	52	20	14	16	64
1994—Sarasota (FSL)	•13	7	.650	3.26	27	27	4	2	0	174	153	74	63	50	*173
1995—Trenton (East.)	6	2	.750	2.36	15	15	1	1	0	99	86	35	26	26	88
—Boston (A.L.)...................	1	2	.333	5.96	8	3	0	0	0	22 2/3	29	15	15	5	19
—Pawtucket (I.L.)...............	2	3	.400	5.32	7	7	0	0	0	45 2/3	50	29	27	9	32
1996—Boston (A.L.)...................	1	1	.500	7.54	8	4	0	0	0	22 2/3	29	19	19	13	13
—Pawtucket (I.L.)...............	10	6	.625	3.22	22	22	7	1	0	145 1/3	130	66	52	25	142
1997—Pawtucket (I.L.)...............	5	1	.833	3.71	9	9	2	1	0	60 2/3	51	26	25	15	40
—Boston (A.L.)...................	7	3	.700	5.69	23	22	0	0	0	112 1/3	140	75	71	36	67
1998—Arizona (N.L.)■..............	1	7	.125	6.68	13	13	1	0	0	66	82	55	49	21	39
—Tucson (PCL)	4	3	.571	3.63	13	12	0	0	0	67	75	29	27	17	62
—Kansas City (A.L.)■.........	0	0	...	0.71	4	1	0	0	0	12 2/3	9	1	1	1	12
1999—Kansas City (A.L.)	10	12	.455	4.53	32	32	4	1	0	208 2/3	222	113	105	62	103
2000—Kansas City (A.L.)	10	9	.526	4.94	35	33	3	1	0	217	240	121	119	84	128
2001—Kansas City (A.L.)	10	14	.417	4.37	34	34	1	0	0	218 1/3	227	120	106	74	120
A.L. totals (7 years)	39	41	.488	4.82	144	129	8	2	0	814 1/3	896	464	436	275	462
N.L. totals (1 year)	1	7	.125	6.68	13	13	1	0	0	66	82	55	49	21	39
Major League totals (7 years)	40	48	.455	4.96	157	142	9	2	0	880 1/3	978	519	485	296	501

S

SURHOFF, B.J.   OF   BRAVES

PERSONAL: Born August 4, 1964, in Bronx, N.Y. ... 6-1/200. ... Bats left, throws right. ... Full name: William James Surhoff. ... Son of Dick Surhoff, forward with New York Knicks and Milwaukee Hawks of National Basketball Association (1952-53 and 1953-54); and brother of Rich Surhoff, pitcher with Philadelphia Phillies and Texas Rangers (1985).

HIGH SCHOOL: Rye (N.Y.).

COLLEGE: North Carolina.

TRANSACTIONS/CAREER NOTES: Selected by New York Yankees organization in fifth round of free-agent draft (June 7, 1982); did not sign. ... Selected by Milwaukee Brewers organization in first round (first pick overall) of free-agent draft (June 3, 1985). ... On suspended list (August 23-25, 1990). ... On Milwaukee disabled list (March 25-April 16, April 20-May 23 and July 7, 1994-remainder of season); included rehabilitation assignments to El Paso (April 12-16) and New Orleans (May 17-23). ... Granted free agency (October 20, 1994). ... Re-signed by Brewers organization (April 7, 1995). ... Granted free agency (November 6, 1995). ... Signed by Baltimore Orioles (December 20, 1995). ... On disabled list (May 18-June 2, 1996). ... Granted free agency (October 26, 1998). ... Re-signed by Orioles (December 7, 1998). ... Traded by Orioles with P Gabe Molina to Atlanta Braves for OF Trenidad Hubbard, C Fernando Lunar and P Luis Rivera (July 31, 2000).

RECORDS: Shares major league single-inning record for most doubles—2 (September 14, 1999, fifth inning).

HONORS: Named College Player of the Year by THE SPORTING NEWS (1985). ... Named catcher on THE SPORTING NEWS college All-America team (1985).

STATISTICAL NOTES: Tied for Pacific Coast League lead in double plays by catcher with 10 in 1986. ... Led A.L. catchers with 68 assists in 1991. ... Had 15-game hitting streak (May 9-25, 1999). ... Had 21-game hitting streak (May 29-June 20, 1999). ... Led A.L. outfielders with 1.000 fielding percentage in 1999. ... Had 21-game hitting streak (June 5-28, 2000). ... Career major league grand slams: 5.

MISCELLANEOUS: Member of 1984 U.S. Olympic baseball team.

Year Team (League)	Pos.	G	AB	R	H	2B	3B	HR	RBI	Avg.	BB	SO	SB	PO	A	E	Avg.
										BATTING					FIELDING		
1985—Beloit (Midw.)............	C	76	289	39	96	13	4	7	58	.332	22	35	10	475	44	3	.994
1986—Vancouver (PCL)	C	116	458	71	141	19	3	5	59	.308	29	30	21	539	70	7	*.989
1987—Milwaukee (A.L.)	C-3-DH-1	115	395	50	118	22	3	7	68	.299	36	30	11	648	56	11	.985
1988—Milwaukee (A.L.)........	C-3-1-S-O	139	493	47	121	21	0	5	38	.245	31	49	21	550	94	8	.988
1989—Milwaukee (A.L.)........	C-DH-3B	126	436	42	108	17	4	5	55	.248	25	29	14	530	58	10	.983
1990—Milwaukee (A.L.)........	C-3B	135	474	55	131	21	4	6	59	.276	41	37	18	619	62	12	.983
1991—Milwaukee (A.L.).......C-DH-3-O-2		143	505	57	146	19	4	5	68	.289	26	33	5	665	†71	4	.995
1992—Milwaukee (A.L.).....C-1-DH-O-3		139	480	63	121	19	1	4	62	.252	46	41	14	699	74	6	.992
1993—Milwaukee (A.L.) 3-O-1-C-DH		148	552	66	151	38	3	7	79	.274	36	47	12	175	220	18	.956
1994—El Paso (Texas)..........	OF	3	12	2	3	1	0	0	0	.250	0	2	0	3	0	0	1.000
—Milwaukee (A.L.)........3-C-1-O-DH		40	134	20	35	11	2	5	22	.261	16	14	0	121	29	4	.974
—New Orleans (A.A.).......3B-OF-C-1B		5	19	3	6	2	0	0	1	.316	1	2	0	21	3	0	1.000
1995—Milwaukee (A.L.)	O-1-C-DH	117	415	72	133	26	3	13	73	.320	37	43	7	530	44	5	.991
1996—Baltimore (A.L.)■......	3-O-DH-1	143	537	74	157	27	6	21	82	.292	47	79	0	137	178	15	.955
1997—Baltimore (A.L.).........	O-DH-1-3	147	528	80	150	30	4	18	88	.284	49	60	1	268	16	2	.993
1998—Baltimore (A.L.).........	OF-1B	162	573	79	160	34	1	22	92	.279	49	81	9	256	12	3	.989
1999—Baltimore (A.L.)........	OF-DH-3B	*162	*673	104	207	38	1	28	107	.308	43	78	5	283	21	0	†1.000
2000—Baltimore (A.L.).........	OF-DH	103	411	56	120	27	0	13	57	.292	29	46	7	226	5	3	.987
—Atlanta (N.L.)■..............	OF	44	128	13	37	9	2	1	11	.289	12	13	3	50	1	0	1.000
2001—Atlanta (N.L.)............	OF-DH	141	484	68	131	33	1	10	58	.271	38	48	9	200	8	3	.986
American League totals (14 years)		1819	6606	865	1858	350	36	159	950	.281	511	667	124	5707	940	101	.985
National League totals (2 years)		185	612	81	168	42	3	11	69	.275	50	60	12	250	9	3	.989
Major League totals (15 years)		2004	7218	946	2026	392	39	170	1019	.281	561	727	136	5957	949	104	.985

DIVISION SERIES RECORD

RECORDS: Shares single-game record for most home runs—2 (October 1, 1996).

Year Team (League)	Pos.	G	AB	R	H	2B	3B	HR	RBI	Avg.	BB	SO	SB	PO	A	E	Avg.
										BATTING					FIELDING		
1996—Baltimore (A.L.)..........	OF-PH	4	13	3	5	0	0	3	5	.385	0	1	0	6	0	0	1.000
1997—Baltimore (A.L.)..........	OF-PH	3	11	0	3	1	0	0	2	.273	0	2	0	1	1	0	1.000
2000—Atlanta (N.L.)............	PH	2	2	0	1	0	0	0	0	.500	0	0	0	...	...	...	...
2001—Atlanta (N.L.)............	OF	3	11	1	3	1	0	0	0	.273	0	0	1	7	0	0	1.000
Division series totals (4 years)		12	37	4	12	2	0	3	7	.324	0	3	1	14	1	0	1.000

CHAMPIONSHIP SERIES RECORD

						BATTING									FIELDING		
Year	Team (League)	Pos.	G	AB	R	H	2B	3B	HR	RBI	Avg.	BB	SO	SB	PO	A	E	Avg.
1996—Baltimore (A.L.)..........		OF-PH	5	15	0	4	0	0	0	2	.267	1	2	0	11	1	0	1.000
1997—Baltimore (A.L.)..........		OF-1B	6	25	1	5	2	0	0	1	.200	2	2	0	13	0	0	1.000
2001—Atlanta (N.L.)..............		OF-PH	4	13	1	3	0	0	1	2	.231	0	1	0	3	1	0	1.000
Championship series totals (3 years)			15	53	2	12	2	0	1	5	.226	3	5	0	27	2	0	1.000

ALL-STAR GAME RECORD

					BATTING							FIELDING		
Year	League	Pos.	AB	R	H	2B	3B	HR	RBI	Avg.	BB	SO	SB	PO	A	E	Avg.
1999—American		OF	2	0	0	0	0	0	0	.000	0	0	0	0	0	0	...

SUTTON, LARRY — 1B/OF

S

PERSONAL: Born May 14, 1970, in West Covina, Calif. ... 6-0/185. ... Bats left, throws left. ... Full name: Larry James Sutton.
HIGH SCHOOL: Mater Dei (Santa Ana, Calif.).
COLLEGE: Illinois.
TRANSACTIONS/CAREER NOTES: Selected by Kansas City organization in 21st round of free-agent draft (June 1, 1992). ... On Kansas City disabled list (June 6-July 27, 1999); included rehabilitation assignments to Gulf Coast Royals (July 5-15) and Omaha (July 16-25). ... Granted free agency (October 18, 1999). ... Signed by St. Louis Cardinals organization (December 8, 1999). ... Traded by Cardinals to Minnesota Twins for SS Hanley Frias (July 2, 2001). ... Granted free agency (October 15, 2001).
HONORS: Named Northwest League Most Valuable Player (1992). ... Named Carolina League Most Valuable Player (1994).
STATISTICAL NOTES: Led Northwest League with 142 total bases in 1992. ... Led Midwest League first basemen with 92 double plays in 1993. ... Led Carolina League with .542 slugging percentage, 10 intentional bases on balls received and nine sacrifice flies in 1994. ... Led Texas League first basemen with .989 fielding percentage in 1996. ... Career major league grand slams: 1.

						BATTING									FIELDING		
Year	Team (League)	Pos.	G	AB	R	H	2B	3B	HR	RBI	Avg.	BB	SO	SB	PO	A	E	Avg.
1992—Eugene (N'West)	1B	70	238	45	74	17	3	*15	*58	.311	48	33	3	517	29	14	.975
—Appleton (Midw.)........	DH	1	2	1	0	0	0	0	0	.000	2	1	0	...	...	...	...
1993—Rockford (Midw.)........	1B	113	361	67	97	24	1	7	50	.269	*95	65	3	911	76	11	.989
1994—Wilmington (Caro.).....	1B	129	480	91	147	33	1	26	94	.306	*81	71	2	1086	71	12	*.990
1995—Wichita (Texas)	1B	53	197	31	53	11	1	5	32	.269	26	33	1	452	25	7	.986
1996—Wichita (Texas)	1B-OF-DH	125	463	84	137	22	2	22	84	.296	77	66	4	1105	76	13	*.989
1997—Omaha (A.A.)..............	1B-DH	106	380	61	114	27	1	19	72	.300	61	57	0	839	54	5	.994
—Kansas City (A.L.).......	1B-DH-OF	27	69	9	20	2	0	2	8	.290	5	12	0	92	8	0	1.000
1998—Kansas City (A.L.)	OF-1B-DH	111	310	29	76	14	2	5	42	.245	29	46	3	179	7	2	.989
1999—Kansas City (A.L.)	1B-DH-OF	43	102	14	23	6	0	2	15	.225	13	17	1	215	13	3	.987
—GC Royals (GCL)........	1B-DH-OF	9	31	7	8	2	0	1	6	.258	7	6	0	43	0	1	.977
—Omaha (PCL)..............	1B-OF	39	148	28	41	8	1	3	12	.277	27	24	4	247	21	4	.985
2000—Memphis (PCL)■.......	1B	95	347	61	89	21	2	12	70	.256	67	56	4	771	84	8	.991
—St. Louis (N.L.)...........	1B-OF	23	25	5	8	0	0	1	6	.320	5	7	0	31	2	0	1.000
2001—St. Louis (N.L.).........	1B-OF	33	42	3	5	1	0	1	3	.119	1	10	0	39	5	0	1.000
—Memphis (PCL)	1B	29	99	12	26	5	0	2	13	.263	21	16	1	202	14	1	.995
—Edmonton (PCL)■	OF-1B	45	147	23	37	7	3	3	24	.252	23	32	0	116	6	2	.984
American League totals (3 years)		181	481	52	119	22	2	9	65	.247	47	75	4	486	28	5	.990
National League totals (2 years)		56	67	8	13	1	0	2	9	.194	6	17	0	70	7	0	1.000
Major League totals (5 years)		237	548	60	132	23	2	11	74	.241	53	92	4	556	35	5	.992

SUZUKI, ICHIRO — OF — MARINERS

PERSONAL: Born October 22, 1973, in Kasugai, Japan. ... 5-9/156. ... Bats left, throws right.
HIGH SCHOOL: Aikoudai Meiden (Kasugai, Japan).
TRANSACTIONS/CAREER NOTES: Signed as non-drafted free agent by Seattle Mariners organization (November 18, 2000).
RECORDS: Holds major league rookie-season record for most hits—242 (2001). ... Shares major league single-season record for most games with at least one hit—135 (1999). ... Holds A.L. rookie-season record for highest batting average (100 or more games)—.350; most at-bats—692; and most singles—192 (2001). ... Holds A.L. single-season record for most at-bats by lefthander—692; and most singles—192 (2001).
HONORS: Named outfielder on A.L. Silver Slugger team (2001). ... Named A.L. Rookie of the Year by The Sporting News (2001). ... Named outfielder on The Sporting News A.L. All-Star team (2001). ... Named A.L. Rookie of the Year by Baseball Writers' Association of America (2001). ... Named A.L. Most Valuable Player by Baseball Writers' Association of America (2001). ... Won A.L. Gold Glove as outfielder (2001).
STATISTICAL NOTES: Had 23-game hitting streak (April 22-May 18, 2001). ... Had 21-game hitting streak (August 3-24, 2001). ... Had 15-game hitting streak (April 4-20, 2001).

						BATTING									FIELDING		
Year	Team (League)	Pos.	G	AB	R	H	2B	3B	HR	RBI	Avg.	BB	SO	SB	PO	A	E	Avg.
1992—Orix (Jap. Pac.)		40	95	9	24	5	0	0	5	.253	3	11	3	...	...	...	...
1993—Orix (Jap. Pac.)		43	64	4	12	2	0	1	3	.188	2	7	0	...	...	...	...
1994—Orix (Jap. Pac.)		130	546	111	210	41	5	13	54	.385	51	53	29	...	...	...	...
1995—Orix (Jap. Pac.)		130	524	104	179	23	4	25	80	.342	68	52	49	...	...	...	...
1996—Orix (Jap. Pac.)		130	542	104	193	24	4	16	84	.356	56	52	35	...	...	...	...
1997—Orix (Jap. Pac.)		135	536	94	185	31	4	17	91	.345	62	36	39	...	...	...	...
1998—Orix (Jap. Pac.)		135	506	79	181	36	3	13	71	.358	43	35	11	...	...	...	...
1999—Orix (Jap. Pac.)		103	411	80	141	27	2	21	68	.343	45	46	12	...	...	...	...
2000—Orix (Jap. Pac.)		105	395	73	153	22	1	12	74	.387	54	36	21	...	...	...	...
2001—Seattle (A.L.)■...........	OF-DH	157	*692	127	*242	34	8	8	69	.350	30	53	*56	335	8	1	.997
Major League totals (1 year)		157	692	127	242	34	8	8	69	.350	30	53	56	335	8	1	.997

DIVISION SERIES RECORD

RECORDS: Shares single-series record for most hits—12 (2001).

Year	Team (League)	Pos.	G	AB	R	H	2B	3B	HR	RBI	Avg.	BB	SO	SB	PO	A	E	Avg.
							BATTING									FIELDING		
2001— Seattle (A.L.)		OF	5	20	4	12	1	0	0	2	.600	1	0	1	9	0	1	.900

CHAMPIONSHIP SERIES RECORD

Year	Team (League)	Pos.	G	AB	R	H	2B	3B	HR	RBI	Avg.	BB	SO	SB	PO	A	E	Avg.
							BATTING									FIELDING		
2001— Seattle (A.L.)		OF	5	18	3	4	1	0	0	1	.222	4	4	2	7	0	0	1.000

ALL-STAR GAME RECORD

Year	League	Pos.	AB	R	H	2B	3B	HR	RBI	Avg.	BB	SO	SB	PO	A	E	Avg.
						BATTING									FIELDING		
2001— American		OF	3	0	1	0	0	0	0	.333	0	0	1	0	0	0	...

SUZUKI, MAC   P

PERSONAL: Born May 31, 1975, in Kobe, Japan. ... 6-3/205. ... Throws right, bats right. ... Full name: Makoto Suzuki.
HIGH SCHOOL: Takigawa Daini (Kobe, Japan).
TRANSACTIONS/CAREER NOTES: Played with Salinas, independent (August 30, 1992). ... Signed by San Bernardino, independent (April 9, 1993). ... Contract purchased by Seattle Mariners organization from San Bernardino (September 5, 1993). ... On disabled list (April 19-June 15 and July 10, 1994-remainder of season). ... On Riverside temporarily inactive list (April 22-August 3, 1995). ... On Riverside disabled list (August 3-18, 1995). ... On Port City disabled list (May 8-17, 1996). ... Traded by Mariners with a player to be named later to New York Mets for P Allen Watson and cash (June 18, 1999); Mets acquired P Justin Dunning to complete deal (September 14, 1999). ... Claimed on waivers by Kansas City Royals (June 22, 1999). ... Traded by Royals with C Sal Fasano to Colorado Rockies for C Brent Mayne (June 24, 2001). ... Claimed on waivers by Milwaukee Brewers (July 12, 2001). ... Released by Brewers (October 12, 2001).

Year	League	W	L	Pct.	ERA	G	GS	CG	ShO	Sv.	IP	H	R	ER	BB	SO
1992— Salinas (Calif.)		0	0	...	0.00	1	0	0	0	0	1	0	0	0	0	1
1993— San Bernardino (Calif.)■.......		4	4	.500	3.68	48	1	0	0	12	80²/₃	59	37	33	56	87
1994— Jacksonville (Sou.)■............		1	0	1.000	2.84	8	0	0	0	1	12⅔	15	4	4	6	10
1995— Riverside (Calif.)		0	1	.000	4.70	6	0	0	0	0	7²/₃	10	4	4	6	6
— Arizona Mariners (Ariz.)		1	0	1.000	6.75	4	3	0	0	0	4	5	4	3	0	3
1996— Tacoma (PCL)		0	3	.000	7.25	13	2	0	0	0	22¹/₃	31	19	18	12	14
— Port City (Sou.)		3	6	.333	4.72	16	16	0	0	0	74¹/₃	69	41	39	32	66
— Seattle (A.L.)		0	0	...	20.25	1	0	0	0	0	1¹/₃	2	3	3	2	1
1997— Tacoma (PCL)		4	9	.308	5.94	32	10	0	0	0	83¹/₃	79	60	55	64	63
1998— Tacoma (PCL)		9	10	.474	4.37	28	21	2	1	0	131²/₃	130	70	64	70	117
— Seattle (A.L.)		1	2	.333	7.18	6	5	0	0	0	26¹/₃	34	23	21	15	19
1999— Seattle (A.L.)		0	2	.000	9.43	16	4	0	0	0	42	47	47	44	34	32
— Kansas City (A.L.)■............		2	3	.400	5.16	22	9	0	0	0	68	77	45	39	30	36
2000— Kansas City (A.L.)		8	10	.444	4.34	32	29	1	1	0	188²/₃	195	100	91	94	135
2001— Kansas City (A.L.)		2	5	.286	5.30	15	9	0	0	0	56	61	38	33	25	37
— Colorado (N.L.)■...............		0	2	.000	15.63	3	1	0	0	0	6¹/₃	9	12	11	11	5
— Milwaukee (N.L.)■............		3	5	.375	5.30	15	9	0	0	0	56	52	37	33	37	47
A.L. totals (5 years)		13	22	.371	5.44	92	56	1	1	0	382¹/₃	416	256	231	200	260
N.L. totals (1 year)		3	7	.300	6.35	18	10	0	0	0	62¹/₃	61	49	44	48	52
Major league totals (5 years)		16	29	.356	5.57	110	66	1	1	0	444²/₃	477	305	275	248	312

SWEENEY, MARK   OF/1B   METS

PERSONAL: Born October 26, 1969, in Framingham, Mass. ... 6-1/215. ... Bats left, throws left. ... Full name: Mark Patrick Sweeney.
HIGH SCHOOL: Holliston (Mass.).
COLLEGE: Maine.
TRANSACTIONS/CAREER NOTES: Selected by Los Angeles Dodgers organization in 39th round of free-agent draft (June 4, 1990); did not sign. ... Selected by California Angels organization in ninth round of free-agent draft (June 3, 1991). ... Traded by Angels with a player to be named later to St. Louis Cardinals for P John Habyan (July 8, 1995); Cardinals acquired IF Rod Correia to complete deal (January 31, 1996). ... Traded by Cardinals with P Danny Jackson and P Rich Batchelor to San Diego Padres for P Fernando Valenzuela, 3B Scott Livingstone and OF Phil Plantier (June 13, 1997). ... Traded by Padres with OF Greg Vaughn to Cincinnati Reds for OF Reggie Sanders, SS Damian Jackson and P Josh Harris (February 2, 1999). ... Traded by Reds with a player to be named later to Milwaukee Brewers for OF Alex Ochoa (January 14, 2000); Brewers acquired P Gene Altman to complete deal (May 15, 2000). ... On Milwaukee disabled list (March 31-May 7 and July 18-August 14, 2000); included rehabilitation assignments to Indianapolis (July 21-26 and August 3-14). ... Granted free agency (October 5, 2000). ... Re-signed by Brewers organization (January 3, 2001). ... Traded by Brewers to New York Mets as part of three-way deal in which Brewers sent P Jeff D'Amico, OF Jeromy Burnitz, IF Lou Collier and cash to Mets, Mets sent 1B/3B Todd Zeile, OF Benny Agbayani, IF/OF Lenny Harris and cash to Colorado Rockies, Rockies traded 1B/OF Ross Gload and P Craig House to Mets and Brewers received OF Alex Ochoa from Rockies (January 21, 2002).

Year	Team (League)	Pos.	G	AB	R	H	2B	3B	HR	RBI	Avg.	BB	SO	SB	PO	A	E	Avg.
							BATTING									FIELDING		
1991— Boise (N'West)		OF	70	234	45	66	10	3	4	34	.282	*51	42	9	81	2	4	.954
1992— Quad City (Midw.)		OF	120	424	65	115	20	5	14	76	.271	47	85	15	205	5	4	.981
1993— Palm Springs (Calif.)..		OF-1B-DH	66	245	41	87	18	3	3	47	.355	42	29	9	145	2	7	.955
— Midland (Texas)		OF	51	188	41	67	13	2	9	32	.356	27	22	1	85	3	1	.989
1994— Vancouver (PCL)		DH-1B-OF	103	344	59	98	12	3	8	49	.285	59	50	3	330	12	2	.994
— Midland (Texas)		OF-1B-DH	14	50	13	15	3	0	3	18	.300	10	10	1	66	5	2	.973
1995— Vancouver (PCL)		OF-DH-1B	69	226	48	78	14	2	7	59	.345	43	33	3	102	2	2	.981
— Louisville (A.A.)■.......		1B	22	76	15	28	8	0	2	22	.368	14	8	2	176	19	2	.990
— St. Louis (N.L.)		1B-OF	37	77	5	21	2	0	2	13	.273	10	15	1	153	11	2	.988
1996— St. Louis (N.L.)		OF-1B	98	170	32	45	9	0	3	22	.265	33	29	3	126	3	3	.977
1997— St. Louis (N.L.)		OF-1B	44	61	5	13	3	0	4	13	.213	9	14	0	31	1	0	1.000
— San Diego (N.L.)■.......		OF-1B	71	103	11	33	4	0	2	19	.320	11	18	2	41	3	2	.957
1998— San Diego (N.L.)		OF-1B-DH	122	192	17	45	8	3	2	15	.234	26	37	1	165	5	1	.994
1999— Cincinnati (N.L.)■......		1B-OF	37	31	6	11	3	0	2	7	.355	4	9	0	3	0	0	1.000
— Indianapolis (I.L.)■......		OF-DH-1B	86	311	66	100	17	1	12	51	.322	59	40	3	257	9	5	.982
2000— Indianapolis (I.L.)■....		1B-OF	18	55	13	28	8	0	2	14	.509	10	8	0	18	3	0	1.000
— Milwaukee (N.L.)		DH-1B-OF	71	73	9	16	6	0	1	6	.219	12	18	0	11	0	0	1.000
2001— Indianapolis (I.L.)		OF-1B	109	404	65	116	34	1	6	69	.287	56	71	3	164	7	1	.994
— Milwaukee (N.L.)		OF-1B	48	89	9	23	3	1	3	11	.258	12	23	2	33	0	1	.971
Major League totals (7 years)			528	796	94	207	38	4	15	97	.260	117	163	9	563	23	9	.985

DIVISION SERIES RECORD

						BATTING								FIELDING		
Year Team (League)	Pos.	G	AB	R	H	2B	3B	HR	RBI	Avg.	BB	SO	SB	PO	A	E	Avg.
1996—St. Louis (N.L.).........	PH	1	1	0	1	0	0	0	0	1.000	0	0	0	...	...	...	...
1998—San Diego (N.L.)	PH	2	1	0	0	0	0	0	0	.000	1	0	0	...	...	...	...
Division series totals (2 years)		3	2	0	1	0	0	0	0	.500	1	0	0	...	...	...	...

CHAMPIONSHIP SERIES RECORD

						BATTING								FIELDING		
Year Team (League)	Pos.	G	AB	R	H	2B	3B	HR	RBI	Avg.	BB	SO	SB	PO	A	E	Avg.
1996—St. Louis (N.L.)..........	PH-OF	5	4	1	0	0	0	0	0	.000	0	2	0	2	0	0	1.000
1998—San Diego (N.L.)	PH	3	2	1	0	0	0	0	0	.000	1	1	0	...	...	...	...
Championship series totals (2 years)		8	6	2	0	0	0	0	0	.000	1	3	0	2	0	0	1.000

WORLD SERIES RECORD

						BATTING								FIELDING		
Year Team (League)	Pos.	G	AB	R	H	2B	3B	HR	RBI	Avg.	BB	SO	SB	PO	A	E	Avg.
1998—San Diego (N.L.)	PH	3	3	0	2	0	0	0	1	.667	0	0	0	...	...	...	...

SWEENEY, MIKE   1B   ROYALS

PERSONAL: Born July 22, 1973, in Orange, Calif. ... 6-3/225. ... Bats right, throws right. ... Full name: Michael John Sweeney.
HIGH SCHOOL: Ontario (Calif.).
TRANSACTIONS/CAREER NOTES: Selected by Kansas City Royals organization in 10th round of free-agent draft (June 3, 1991). ... On disabled list (May 24-July 5, 1994). ... On suspended list (August 17-27, 2001).
RECORDS: Shares A.L. single-season record for most consecutive games with one or more runs batted in—13 (June 23-July 4, 1999).
STATISTICAL NOTES: Led Carolina League with .548 slugging percentage in 1995. ... Tied for A.L. lead in double plays by catcher with 13 in 1997. ... Had 16-game hitting streak (June 22-July 7, 1999). ... Had 25-game hitting streak (July 18-August 13, 1999). ... Had 16-game hitting streak (August 13-30, 2000). ... Tied for A.L. lead in being hit by pitch with 15 in 2000. ... Career major league grand slams: 1.

						BATTING								FIELDING		
Year Team (League)	Pos.	G	AB	R	H	2B	3B	HR	RBI	Avg.	BB	SO	SB	PO	A	E	Avg.
1991—GC Royals (GCL)	C-1B	38	102	8	22	3	0	1	11	.216	11	9	1	124	16	4	.972
1992—Eugene (N'West)	C	59	199	17	44	12	1	4	28	.221	13	54	3	367	42	14	.967
1993—Eugene (N'West)	C	53	175	32	42	10	2	6	29	.240	30	41	1	364	46	7	.983
1994—Rockford (Midw.)	C	86	276	47	83	20	3	10	52	.301	55	43	0	453	54	6	.988
1995—Wilmington (Caro.)......	C-DH-3B	99	332	61	103	23	1	18	53	*.310	60	39	6	575	45	7	.989
—Kansas City (A.L.)	C	4	4	1	1	0	0	0	0	.250	0	0	0	7	0	1	.875
1996—Wichita (Texas)	DH-C	66	235	45	75	18	1	14	51	.319	32	29	3	201	13	1	.995
—Omaha (A.A.)..............	C-DH	25	101	14	26	9	0	3	16	.257	6	13	0	167	8	0	1.000
—Kansas City (A.L.)	C-DH	50	165	23	46	10	0	4	24	.279	18	21	1	158	7	1	.994
1997—Kansas City (A.L.)	C-DH	84	240	30	58	8	0	7	31	.242	17	33	3	425	31	3	.993
—Omaha (A.A.)..............	C-DH	40	144	22	34	8	1	10	29	.236	18	20	0	229	15	1	.996
1998—Kansas City (A.L.)	C	92	282	32	73	18	0	8	35	.259	24	38	2	517	33	•9	.984
1999—Kansas City (A.L.)	1B-DH-C	150	575	101	185	44	2	22	102	.322	54	48	6	588	43	12	.981
2000—Kansas City (A.L.)	1B-DH	159	618	105	206	30	0	29	144	.333	71	67	8	960	88	9	.991
2001—Kansas City (A.L.)	1B-DH	147	559	97	170	46	0	29	99	.304	64	64	10	945	88	12	.989
Major League totals (7 years)		686	2443	389	739	156	2	99	435	.302	248	271	30	3600	290	47	.988

ALL-STAR GAME RECORD

					BATTING								FIELDING		
Year League	Pos.	AB	R	H	2B	3B	HR	RBI	Avg.	BB	SO	SB	PO	A	E	Avg.
2000—American	PH	1	0	0	0	0	0	0	.000	0	0	0	...	...	...	...
2001—American	1B	1	0	0	0	0	0	0	.000	0	0	0	2	1	0	1.000
All-Star Game totals (2 years)		2	0	0	0	0	0	0	.000	0	0	0	2	1	0	1.000

SWINDELL, GREG   P   DIAMONDBACKS

PERSONAL: Born January 2, 1965, in Fort Worth, Texas. ... 6-3/230. ... Throws left, bats left. ... Full name: Forest Gregory Swindell.
HIGH SCHOOL: Sharpstown (Houston).
COLLEGE: Texas.
TRANSACTIONS/CAREER NOTES: Selected by Cleveland Indians organization in first round (second pick overall) of free-agent draft (June 2, 1986). ... On disabled list (June 30, 1987-remainder of season; and July 26-August 30, 1989). ... Traded by Indians to Cincinnati Reds for P Jack Armstrong, P Scott Scudder and P Joe Turek (November 15, 1991). ... On disabled list (August 23-September 7, 1992). ... Granted free agency (October 26, 1992). ... Signed by Houston Astros (December 4, 1992). ... On disabled list (July 6-26, 1993). ... On Houston disabled list (April 20-May 22, 1996). ... Released by Astros (June 3, 1996). ... Signed by Indians (June 15, 1996). ... On Cleveland disabled list (July 4-21, 1996). ... Granted free agency (October 3, 1996). ... Signed by Minnesota Twins organization (December 18, 1996). ... Traded by Twins with 1B Orlando Merced to Boston Red Sox for P Matt Kinney, P Joe Thomas and P John Barnes (July 31, 1998). ... Granted free agency (October 27, 1998). ... Signed by Arizona Diamondbacks (November 13, 1998). ... On disabled list (June 13-28, 1999).
HONORS: Named lefthanded pitcher on THE SPORTING NEWS college All-America team (1985-86).
STATISTICAL NOTES: Struck out 15 batters in one game (May 10, 1987).
MISCELLANEOUS: Holds Arizona Diamondbacks all-time records for most games pitched (191). ... Struck out in only appearance as pinch hitter (1995).

Year League	W	L	Pct.	ERA	G	GS	CG	ShO	Sv.	IP	H	R	ER	BB	SO
1986—Waterloo (Midw.)	2	1	.667	1.00	3	3	0	0	0	18	12	2	2	3	25
—Cleveland (A.L.)..................	5	2	.714	4.23	9	9	1	0	0	61²/₃	57	35	29	15	46
1987—Cleveland (A.L.)................	3	8	.273	5.10	16	15	4	1	0	102¹/₃	112	62	58	37	97
1988—Cleveland (A.L.)................	18	14	.563	3.20	33	33	12	4	0	242	234	97	86	45	180
1989—Cleveland (A.L.)................	13	6	.684	3.37	28	28	5	2	0	184¹/₃	170	71	69	51	129
1990—Cleveland (A.L.)................	12	9	.571	4.40	34	34	3	0	0	214²/₃	245	110	105	47	135

Year League	W	L	Pct.	ERA	G	GS	CG	ShO	Sv.	IP	H	R	ER	BB	SO
1991— Cleveland (A.L.)	9	16	.360	3.48	33	33	7	0	0	238	241	112	92	31	169
1992— Cincinnati (N.L.)■	12	8	.600	2.70	31	30	5	3	0	213 2/3	210	72	64	41	138
1993— Houston (N.L.)■	12	13	.480	4.16	31	30	1	1	0	190 1/3	215	98	88	40	124
1994— Houston (N.L.)	8	9	.471	4.37	24	24	1	0	0	148 1/3	175	80	72	26	74
1995— Houston (N.L.)	10	9	.526	4.47	33	26	1	1	0	153	180	86	76	39	96
1996— Houston (N.L.)	0	3	.000	7.83	8	4	0	0	0	23	35	25	20	11	15
— Cleveland (A.L.)■	1	1	.500	6.59	13	2	0	0	0	28 2/3	31	21	21	8	21
1997— Minnesota (A.L.)■	7	4	.636	3.58	65	1	0	0	1	115 2/3	102	46	46	25	75
1998— Boston (A.L.)■	2	3	.400	3.38	29	0	0	0	0	24	25	13	9	13	18
1999— Arizona (N.L.)■	4	0	1.000	2.51	63	0	0	0	1	64 2/3	54	19	18	21	51
2000— Arizona (N.L.)	2	6	.250	3.20	64	0	0	0	1	76	71	29	27	20	64
2001— Arizona (N.L.)	2	6	.250	4.53	64	0	0	0	2	53 2/3	51	27	27	8	42
A.L. totals (9 years)	70	63	.526	3.83	260	155	32	7	1	1211 1/3	1217	567	515	272	870
N.L. totals (8 years)	50	54	.481	3.82	318	114	8	5	4	922 2/3	991	436	392	206	604
Major League totals (16 years)	120	117	.506	3.83	578	269	40	12	5	2134	2208	1003	907	478	1474

DIVISION SERIES RECORD

Year League	W	L	Pct.	ERA	G	GS	CG	ShO	Sv.	IP	H	R	ER	BB	SO
1998— Boston (A.L.)	0	0	...	0.00	1	0	0	0	0	1 1/3	0	0	0	1	1
1999— Arizona (N.L.)	0	0	...	0.00	3	0	0	0	0	3 1/3	1	0	0	3	1
2001— Arizona (N.L.)	0	0	...	0.00	2	0	0	0	0	1 2/3	1	0	0	0	2
Division series totals (3 years)	0	0	...	0.00	6	0	0	0	0	6 1/3	2	0	0	4	4

CHAMPIONSHIP SERIES RECORD

Year League	W	L	Pct.	ERA	G	GS	CG	ShO	Sv.	IP	H	R	ER	BB	SO
2001— Arizona (N.L.)	0	0	...	27.00	2	0	0	0	0	1/3	1	1	1	0	1

WORLD SERIES RECORD

NOTES: Member of World Series championship team (2001).

Year League	W	L	Pct.	ERA	G	GS	CG	ShO	Sv.	IP	H	R	ER	BB	SO
2001— Arizona (N.L.)	0	0	...	0.00	3	0	0	0	0	2 2/3	1	0	0	1	2

ALL-STAR GAME RECORD

Year League	W	L	Pct.	ERA	G	GS	CG	ShO	Sv.	IP	H	R	ER	BB	SO
1989— American	0	0	...	0.00	0	0	0	0	0	1 2/3	2	0	0	0	3

SYLVESTER, BILLY — P — BRAVES

PERSONAL: Born October 1, 1976, in Darlington, S.C. ... 6-5/220. ... Throws right, bats right. ... Full name: William Eugene Sylvester.
JUNIOR COLLEGE: Spartanburg (S.C.) Methodist.
TRANSACTIONS/CAREER NOTES: Signed as non-drafted free agent by Atlanta Braves organization (June 18, 1997). ... On disabled list (July 17-September 11, 2000).

Year League	W	L	Pct.	ERA	G	GS	CG	ShO	Sv.	IP	H	R	ER	BB	SO
1997— Gulf Coast Braves (GCL)	3	4	.429	3.91	12	9	0	0	0	53	45	25	23	28	58
1998— Eugene (N'West)	0	*11	.000	6.51	16	•16	0	0	0	55 1/3	73	61	40	24	42
1999— Macon (S.Atl.)	5	4	.556	3.12	44	1	0	0	2	83 2/3	78	37	29	37	75
2000— Myrtle Beach (Caro.)	3	0	1.000	0.79	32	0	0	0	16	45 2/3	16	8	4	15	48
2001— Greenville (Sou.)	1	0	1.000	2.37	26	0	0	0	12	30 1/3	18	8	8	24	41
— Richmond (I.L.)	0	4	.000	5.11	36	0	0	0	11	37	28	21	21	27	41

TABAKA, JEFF — P

PERSONAL: Born January 17, 1964, in Barberton, Ohio. ... 6-2/201. ... Throws left, bats right. ... Full name: Jeffrey Jon Tabaka. ... Name pronounced tuh-BAW-kuh.
HIGH SCHOOL: Copley (Ohio).
COLLEGE: Kent.
TRANSACTIONS/CAREER NOTES: Selected by Montreal Expos organization in free-agent draft (June 2, 1986). ... On West Palm Beach disabled list (May 2-June 23, 1988). ... Selected by Philadelphia Phillies from Expos organization in Rule 5 major league draft (December 5, 1988); Expos waived right to reclaim him as part of deal in which Expos traded P Floyd Youmans and P Jeff Parrett to Phillies for P Kevin Gross (December 6, 1988). ... Released by Phillies organization (July 26, 1991). ... Signed by Milwaukee Brewers organization (August 8, 1991). ... On disabled list (June 18-July 4, 1992). ... Granted free agency (October 15, 1992). ... Re-signed by Brewers (October 30, 1992). ... Selected by Florida Marlins in third round (71st pick overall) of expansion draft (November 17, 1992). ... Granted free agency (March 21, 1993). ... Signed by Brewers organization (March 26, 1993). ... Granted free agency (October 15, 1993). ... Re-signed by Brewers organization (January 6, 1994). ... Released by Brewers (April 2, 1994). ... Signed by Pittsburgh Pirates organization (April 3, 1994). ... Claimed on waivers by San Diego Padres (May 12, 1994). ... Traded by Padres with P Rich Loiselle to Houston Astros for OF Phil Plantier (July 19, 1995). ... Granted free agency (December 20, 1996). ... Signed by Cincinnati Reds organization (January 10, 1997). ... Granted free agency (October 15, 1997). ... Signed by Pirates (December 10, 1997). ... On Pittsburgh disabled list (May 25-July 3, 1998); included rehabilitation assignment to Nashville (June 24-30). ... On disabled list (March 25, 1999-entire season). ... Granted free agency (October 20, 1999). ... Signed by Colorado Rockies organization (January 26, 2000). ... On Colorado Springs disabled list (April 6-May 7 and July 24, 2000-remainder of season). ... Granted free agency (October 18, 2000). ... Signed by St. Louis Cardinals organization (February 6, 2001). ... On St. Louis disabled list (April 3-June 20, 2001); included rehabilitation assignment to Memphis (June 11-20). ... Released by Cardinals (November 16, 2001).
MISCELLANEOUS: Made two outs in one game as designated hitter with New Orleans (1993).

Year League	W	L	Pct.	ERA	G	GS	CG	ShO	Sv.	IP	H	R	ER	BB	SO
1986— Jamestown (NY-Penn)	2	4	.333	4.30	13	9	0	0	0	52 1/3	51	31	25	34	57
1987— West Palm Beach (FSL)	8	6	.571	4.17	28	15	0	0	5	95	90	46	44	58	71
1988— West Palm Beach (FSL)	7	5	.583	1.71	16	16	2	2	0	95	71	38	18	34	52
— Jacksonville (Sou.)	1	0	1.000	6.55	2	2	0	0	0	11	14	8	8	5	7
1989— Reading (East.)■	8	7	.533	4.65	21	17	6	1	0	100 2/3	109	59	52	54	80
— Scranton/W.B. (I.L.)	0	4	.000	6.32	6	6	0	0	0	31 1/3	32	26	22	23	15

Year League	W	L	Pct.	ERA	G	GS	CG	ShO	Sv.	IP	H	R	ER	BB	SO
1990—Clearwater (FSL)	5	2	.714	3.03	8	5	0	0	0	35²/₃	39	17	12	18	23
1991—Reading (East.)	4	8	.333	5.07	21	20	1	1	0	108¹/₃	117	65	61	78	68
—Stockton (Calif.)■	0	2	.000	5.19	4	4	0	0	0	17¹/₃	19	11	10	16	19
1992—El Paso (Texas)■	9	5	.643	2.52	50	0	0	0	10	82	67	23	23	38	75
1993—New Orleans (A.A.)	6	6	.500	3.24	53	0	0	0	1	58¹/₃	50	26	21	30	63
1994—Buffalo (A.A.)■	1	0	1.000	3.38	9	0	0	0	1	5¹/₃	3	2	2	4	4
—Pittsburgh (N.L.)■	0	0	...	18.00	5	0	0	0	0	4	4	8	8	8	2
—San Diego (N.L.)■	3	1	.750	3.89	34	0	0	0	1	37	28	21	16	19	30
1995—Las Vegas (PCL)	0	1	.000	1.99	19	0	0	0	6	22²/₃	16	6	5	14	27
—San Diego (N.L.)	0	0	...	7.11	10	0	0	0	0	6¹/₃	10	5	5	5	6
—Houston (N.L.)■	1	0	1.000	2.22	24	0	0	0	0	24¹/₃	17	6	6	12	19
1996—Houston (N.L.)■	0	2	.000	6.64	18	0	0	0	1	20¹/₃	28	18	15	14	18
—Tucson (PCL)	6	2	.750	2.93	41	0	0	0	4	43	40	16	14	21	51
1997—Indianapolis (A.A.)■	3	2	.600	2.65	58	0	0	0	3	57²/₃	44	19	17	19	68
—Cincinnati (N.L.)	0	0	...	4.50	3	0	0	0	0	2	1	1	1	1	1
1998—Pittsburgh (N.L.)■	2	2	.500	3.02	37	0	0	0	0	50²/₃	37	19	17	22	40
—Nashville (PCL)	0	1	.000	7.71	4	0	0	0	0	4²/₃	9	4	4	0	4
1999—Pittsburgh (N.L.)							Did not play.								
2000—Colorado Springs (PCL)■..	0	2	.000	7.66	22	0	0	0	0	22¹/₃	30	19	19	9	26
—Carolina (Sou.)	0	0	...	1.93	9	0	0	0	0	9¹/₃	7	2	2	1	7
2001—St. Louis (N.L.)■	0	0	...	7.36	8	0	0	0	0	3²/₃	6	3	3	1	3
—Memphis (PCL)	0	2	.000	2.60	32	0	0	0	2	27²/₃	24	10	8	10	23
Major League totals (6 years)	6	5	.545	4.31	139	0	0	0	2	148¹/₃	131	81	71	82	119

TAGUCHI, SO   OF   CARDINALS

PERSONAL: Born July 2, 1969, in Japan. ... 5-10/163. ... Bats right, throws right.
TRANSACTIONS/CAREER NOTES: Signed as non-drafted free agent by St. Louis Cardinals (January 10, 2002).

Year Team (League)	Pos.	G	AB	R	H	2B	3B	HR	RBI	Avg.	BB	SO	SB	PO	A	E	Avg.
1992—Orix (Jap. Pac.)	OF	47	123	...	33	...	...	1	7	.268	...	...	5	...	...	...	...
1993—Orix (Jap. Pac.)	OF	31	83	...	23	...	...	0	5	.277	...	...	3	...	...	...	...
1994—Orix (Jap. Pac.)	OF	108	329	...	101	...	...	6	43	.307	...	...	10	...	...	...	...
1995—Orix (Jap. Pac.)	OF	130	495	...	122	...	...	9	61	.246	...	...	14	...	...	...	...
1996—Orix (Jap. Pac.)	OF	128	509	...	142	...	...	7	44	.279	...	...	10	...	...	...	...
1997—Orix (Jap. Pac.)	OF	135	572	...	168	...	...	10	56	.294	...	...	7	...	...	...	...
1998—Orix (Jap. Pac.)	OF	132	497	...	135	...	...	9	41	.272	...	...	8	...	...	...	...
1999—Orix (Jap. Pac.)	OF	133	524	...	141	...	...	9	56	.269	...	...	11	...	...	...	...
2000—Orix (Jap. Pac.)	OF	129	509	...	142	...	...	8	49	.279	...	...	9	...	...	...	...
2001—Orix (Jap. Pac.)	OF	134	453	...	127	...	...	8	42	.280	...	...	6	...	...	...	...

TAM, JEFF   P   ATHLETICS

PERSONAL: Born August 19, 1970, in Fullerton, Calif. ... 6-1/202. ... Throws right, bats right. ... Full name: Jeffery Eugene Tam.
HIGH SCHOOL: Eau Gaille (Melbourne, Fla.).
COLLEGE: Florida State.
TRANSACTIONS/CAREER NOTES: Signed as a non-drafted free agent by New York Mets organization (June 27, 1993). ... On New York disabled list (March 21-May 16, 1999); included rehabilitation assignment to St. Lucie (May 2-16). ... Claimed on waivers by Cleveland Indians (June 18, 1999). ... On Buffalo disabled list (July 23-August 1, 1999). ... Claimed on waivers by Mets (August 11, 1999). ... Granted free agency (October 15, 1999). ... Signed by Oakland Athletics organization (November 23, 1999).

Year League	W	L	Pct.	ERA	G	GS	CG	ShO	Sv.	IP	H	R	ER	BB	SO
1993—Pittsfield (NY-Penn)	3	3	.500	3.35	21	1	0	0	0	40¹/₃	50	21	15	7	31
1994—Columbia (S.Atl.)	1	1	.500	1.29	26	0	0	0	18	28	23	14	4	6	22
—St. Lucie (FSL)	0	0	...	0.00	24	0	0	0	16	26²/₃	13	0	0	6	15
—Binghamton (East.)	0	0	...	8.10	4	0	0	0	0	6²/₃	9	6	6	5	7
1995—Binghamton (East.)	0	2	.000	4.50	14	0	0	0	3	18	20	11	9	4	9
—Gulf Coast Mets (GCL)	0	0	...	3.00	2	1	0	0	0	3	2	1	1	1	2
1996—Binghamton (East.)	6	2	.750	2.44	49	0	0	0	2	62²/₃	51	19	17	16	48
1997—Norfolk (I.L.)	7	5	.583	4.67	40	11	0	0	6	111²/₃	137	72	58	14	67
1998—Norfolk (I.L.)	3	3	.500	1.83	45	0	0	0	11	64	42	14	13	6	54
—New York (N.L.)	1	1	.500	6.28	15	0	0	0	0	14¹/₃	13	10	10	4	8
1999—St. Lucie (FSL)	0	0	...	3.38	2	0	0	0	0	2²/₃	4	1	1	0	3
—Norfolk (I.L.)	0	1	.000	3.10	16	0	0	0	3	20¹/₃	24	7	7	3	10
—Buffalo (I.L.)■	2	2	.500	2.08	16	0	0	0	0	26	23	9	6	8	13
—Cleveland (A.L.)	0	0	...	81.00	1	0	0	0	0	¹/₃	2	3	3	1	0
—New York (N.L.)	0	0	...	3.18	9	0	0	0	0	11¹/₃	6	4	4	3	8
2000—Oakland (A.L.)■	3	3	.500	2.63	72	0	0	0	3	85²/₃	86	30	25	23	46
2001—Oakland (A.L.)	2	4	.333	3.01	70	0	0	0	3	74²/₃	68	27	25	29	44
A.L. totals (3 years)	5	7	.417	2.97	143	0	0	0	6	160²/₃	156	60	53	53	90
N.L. totals (2 years)	1	1	.500	4.91	24	0	0	0	0	25²/₃	19	14	14	7	16
Major League totals (4 years)	6	8	.429	3.24	167	0	0	0	6	186¹/₃	175	74	67	60	106

DIVISION SERIES RECORD

Year League	W	L	Pct.	ERA	G	GS	CG	ShO	Sv.	IP	H	R	ER	BB	SO
2000—Oakland (A.L.)	0	0	...	0.00	3	0	0	0	0	2	3	1	0	1	1
2001—Oakland (A.L.)	0	0	...	18.00	1	0	0	0	0	1	3	2	2	0	0
Division series totals (2 years)	0	0	...	6.00	4	0	0	0	0	3	6	3	2	1	1

PERSONAL: Born February 24, 1979, in Troy, Mo. ... 6-2/185. ... Throws right, bats right. ... Full name: Dennis Lee Tankersley Jr.
HIGH SCHOOL: St. Charles (Mo.).
JUNIOR COLLEGE: Meramec (Mo.).
TRANSACTIONS/CAREER NOTES: Selected by Boston Red Sox organization in 38th round of free-agent draft (June 2, 1998). ... Traded by Red Sox with IF Cesar Saba to San Diego Padres for 3B Ed Sprague (June 30, 2000).

Year League	W	L	Pct.	ERA	G	GS	CG	ShO	Sv.	IP	H	R	ER	BB	SO
1999— Gulf Coast Red Sox (GCL)..	1	0	1.000	0.76	11	6	0	0	1	35²/₃	14	7	3	9	57
2000— Augusta (S.Atl.)................	5	3	.625	4.06	15	15	1	1	0	75¹/₃	73	41	34	32	74
— Fort Wayne (Midw.)■........	5	2	.714	2.85	12	12	0	0	0	66¹/₃	48	25	21	25	87
2001— Lake Elsinore (Calif.)	5	1	.833	0.52	9	8	0	0	0	52¹/₃	29	5	3	12	68
— Mobile (Sou.).................	4	1	.800	2.07	13	13	0	0	0	69²/₃	44	23	16	24	89
— Portland (PCL)	1	2	.333	6.91	3	3	0	0	0	14¹/₃	16	13	11	8	16

PERSONAL: Born February 18, 1964, in Des Moines, Iowa. ... 6-1/190. ... Throws right, bats right. ... Full name: Kevin Ray Tapani. ... Name pronounced TAP-ah-nee.
HIGH SCHOOL: Escanaba (Mich.).
COLLEGE: Central Michigan.
TRANSACTIONS/CAREER NOTES: Selected by Chicago Cubs organization in ninth round of free-agent draft (June 3, 1985); did not sign. ... Selected by Oakland Athletics organization in second round of free-agent draft (June 2, 1986). ... Traded by A's as part of an eight-player, three-team deal in which New York Mets traded P Jesse Orosco to A's (December 11, 1987); A's traded Orosco, SS Alfredo Griffin and P Jay Howell to Los Angeles Dodgers for P Bob Welch, P Matt Young and P Jack Savage. A's then traded Savage, P Wally Whitehurst and Tapani to Mets. ... Traded by Mets with P Tim Drummond to Minnesota (August 1, 1989), as partial completion of deal in which Twins traded P Frank Viola to Mets for P Rick Aguilera, P David West and three players to be named later (July 31, 1989); Twins acquired P Jack Savage to complete deal (October 16, 1989). ... On disabled list (August 17-September 10, 1990). ... Traded by Twins with P Mark Guthrie to Los Angeles Dodgers for 1B/3B Ron Coomer, P Greg Hansell, P Jose Parra and a player to be named later (July 31, 1995); Twins acquired OF Chris Latham to complete deal (October 30, 1995). ... Granted free agency (December 21, 1995). ... Signed by Chicago White Sox (February 3, 1996). ... Granted free agency (October 29, 1996). ... Signed by Cubs (December 16, 1996). ... On Chicago disabled list (March 27-July 23, 1997); included rehabilitation assignments to Rockford (June 25-26 and July 12-13), Orlando (July 1-7), Daytona (July 7-8) and Iowa (July 18-19). ... On disabled list (April 13-May 1 and August 26-September 25, 1999; and September 18, 2000-remainder of season). ... Granted free agency (November 7, 2001).
STATISTICAL NOTES: Pitched 5-0 one-hit, complete-game victory for Chicago against Cincinnati (September 16, 1997). ... Career major league grand slams: 1.

Year League	W	L	Pct.	ERA	G	GS	CG	ShO	Sv.	IP	H	R	ER	BB	SO
1986— Medford (N'West)	1	0	1.000	0.00	2	2	0	0	0	8¹/₃	6	3	0	3	9
— Modesto (Calif.)	6	1	.857	2.48	11	11	1	0	0	69	74	26	19	22	44
— Huntsville (Sou.)	1	0	1.000	6.00	1	1	0	0	0	6	8	4	4	1	2
— Tacoma (PCL)	0	1	.000	15.43	1	1	0	0	0	2¹/₃	5	6	4	1	1
1987— Modesto (Calif.)	10	7	.588	3.76	24	24	6	1	0	148¹/₃	122	74	62	60	121
1988— St. Lucie (FSL)■...............	1	0	1.000	1.42	3	3	0	0	0	19	17	5	3	4	11
— Jackson (Texas)	5	1	.833	2.74	24	5	0	0	3	62¹/₃	46	23	19	19	35
1989— Tidewater (I.L.)..................	7	5	.583	3.47	17	17	2	1	0	109	113	49	42	25	63
— New York (N.L.)	0	0	...	3.68	3	0	0	0	0	7¹/₃	5	3	3	4	2
— Portland (PCL)■...............	4	2	.667	2.20	6	6	1	0	0	41	38	15	10	12	30
— Minnesota (A.L.)	2	2	.500	3.86	5	5	0	0	0	32²/₃	34	15	14	8	21
1990— Minnesota (A.L.)	12	8	.600	4.07	28	28	1	1	0	159¹/₃	164	75	72	29	101
1991— Minnesota (A.L.)	16	9	.640	2.99	34	34	4	1	0	244	225	84	81	40	135
1992— Minnesota (A.L.)	16	11	.593	3.97	34	34	4	1	0	220	226	103	97	48	138
1993— Minnesota (A.L.)	12	15	.444	4.43	36	35	3	1	0	225²/₃	243	123	111	57	150
1994— Minnesota (A.L.)	11	7	.611	4.62	24	24	4	1	0	156	181	86	80	39	91
1995— Minnesota (A.L.)	6	11	.353	4.92	20	20	3	1	0	133²/₃	155	79	73	34	88
— Los Angeles (N.L.)■........	4	2	.667	5.05	13	11	0	0	0	57	72	37	32	14	43
1996— Chicago (A.L.)■..............	13	10	.565	4.59	34	34	1	0	0	225¹/₃	236	123	115	76	150
1997— Rockford (Midw.)	1	0	1.000	0.82	2	2	0	0	0	11	5	1	1	0	7
— Orlando (Sou.)	0	0	...	4.50	1	1	0	0	0	4	3	2	2	2	2
— Daytona (FSL)	0	0	...	3.86	1	1	0	0	0	4²/₃	5	2	2	4	2
— Iowa (A.A.)	0	1	.000	4.00	1	1	0	0	0	9	5	4	4	1	4
— Chicago (N.L.)	9	3	.750	3.39	13	13	1	1	0	85	77	33	32	23	55
1998— Chicago (N.L.)	19	9	.679	4.85	35	34	2	2	0	219	244	120	118	62	136
1999— Chicago (N.L.)	6	12	.333	4.83	23	23	1	0	0	136	151	81	73	33	73
2000— Chicago (N.L.)	8	12	.400	5.01	30	30	0	0	0	195²/₃	208	113	109	47	150
2001— Chicago (N.L.)	9	14	.391	4.49	29	29	0	0	0	168¹/₃	186	93	84	40	149
A.L. totals (8 years)	88	73	.547	4.14	215	214	20	6	0	1396²/₃	1464	688	643	331	874
N.L. totals (7 years)	55	52	.514	4.67	146	140	6	3	0	868¹/₃	943	480	451	223	608
Major League totals (13 years).....	143	125	.534	4.35	361	354	26	9	0	2265	2407	1168	1094	554	1482

DIVISION SERIES RECORD

Year League	W	L	Pct.	ERA	G	GS	CG	ShO	Sv.	IP	H	R	ER	BB	SO
1995— Los Angeles (N.L.)	0	0	...	81.00	2	0	0	0	0	¹/₃	0	3	3	4	1
1998— Chicago (N.L.)	0	1	.000	1.00	1	1	0	0	0	9	5	1	1	3	6
Division series totals (2 years)	0	0	...	3.86	3	1	0	0	0	9¹/₃	5	4	4	7	7

CHAMPIONSHIP SERIES RECORD

Year League	W	L	Pct.	ERA	G	GS	CG	ShO	Sv.	IP	H	R	ER	BB	SO
1991— Minnesota (A.L.)	0	1	.000	7.84	2	2	0	0	0	10¹/₃	16	9	9	3	9

WORLD SERIES RECORD

NOTES: Member of World Series championship team (1991).

Year League	W	L	Pct.	ERA	G	GS	CG	ShO	Sv.	IP	H	R	ER	BB	SO
1991— Minnesota (A.L.)	1	1	.500	4.50	2	2	0	0	0	12	13	6	6	2	7

PERSONAL: Born January 1, 1975, in San Pedro de Macoris, Dominican Republic. ... 5-10/180. ... Bats right, throws right. ... Full name: Fernando Tatis Jr. ... Name pronounced ta-TEES.

TRANSACTIONS/CAREER NOTES: Signed as non-drafted free agent by Texas Rangers organization (August 25, 1992). ... Traded by Rangers with P Darren Oliver and a player to be named later to St. Louis Cardinals for P Todd Stottlemyre and SS Royce Clayton (July 31, 1998); Cardinals acquired OF Mark Little to complete deal (August 9, 1998). ... On St. Louis disabled list (April 30-June 30, 2000); included rehabilitation assignment to Memphis (June 26-30). ... Traded by Cardinals with P Britt Reames to Montreal Expos for P Dustin Hermanson and P Steve Kline (December 14, 2000). ... On disabled list (May 11-26 and June 3, 2001-remainder of season). ... On suspended list (July 8-9, 2001).

RECORDS: Holds major league single-inning records for most grand slams—2; and most runs batted in—8 (April 23, 1999, third inning). ... Shares major league single-game record for most grand slams—2 (April 23, 1999). ... Shares major league single-inning record for most home runs—2 (April 23, 1999, third inning).

STATISTICAL NOTES: Led Gulf Coast League with four intentional bases on balls received in 1994. ... Led Gulf Coast League third basemen with 165 assists, 227 total chances and .925 fielding percentage in 1994. ... Tied for Texas League lead with four intentional bases on balls received in 1997. ... Career major league grand slams: 5.

							BATTING								FIELDING		
Year Team (League)	Pos.	G	AB	R	H	2B	3B	HR	RBI	Avg.	BB	SO	SB	PO	A	E	Avg.
1993—Dom. Rangers (DSL)..	IF	59	198	22	54	5	1	4	34	.273	27	12	7	135	37	11	.940
1994—GC Rangers (GCL)......	3B-2B	•60	212	34	70	10	2	6	32	.330	25	33	21	47	†168	17	†.927
1995—Charl., S.C. (SAL).......		131	499	74	•151	*43	4	15	84	.303	45	94	22	98	235	37	.900
1996—Charlotte (FSL).........	3B	85	325	46	93	25	0	12	53	.286	30	48	9	53	148	24	.893
—Oklahoma City (A.A.)..	3B	2	4	0	2	1	0	0	0	.500	0	1	0	0	1	0	1.000
1997—Tulsa (Texas)	3B-DH	102	382	73	120	26	1	24	64	.314	46	72	17	53	193	21	.921
—Texas (A.L.)	3B	60	223	29	57	9	0	8	29	.256	14	42	3	45	90	7	.951
1998—Texas (A.L.)	3B	95	330	41	89	17	2	3	32	.270	12	66	6	74	184	15	.945
—St. Louis (N.L.)■.......	3B-SS	55	202	28	58	16	2	8	26	.287	24	57	7	36	123	12	.930
1999—St. Louis (N.L.)...........	3B	149	537	104	160	31	2	34	107	.298	82	128	21	101	267	16	.958
2000—St. Louis (N.L.)...........	3B-DH-1B	96	324	59	82	21	1	18	64	.253	57	94	2	42	129	8	.955
—Memphis (PCL)..........	3B	3	9	0	0	0	0	0	0	.000	1	3	0	3	2	0	1.000
2001—Montreal (N.L.)■.........	3B	41	145	20	37	9	0	2	11	.255	16	43	0	18	54	9	.889
American League totals (2 years)		155	553	70	146	26	2	11	61	.264	26	108	9	119	274	22	.947
National League totals (4 years)		341	1208	211	337	77	5	62	208	.279	179	322	30	197	573	45	.945
Major League totals (5 years)		496	1761	281	483	103	7	73	269	.274	205	430	39	316	847	67	.946

DIVISION SERIES RECORD

						BATTING								FIELDING		
Year Team (League)	Pos.	G	AB	R	H	2B	3B	HR	RBI	Avg.	BB	SO	SB	PO	A	E	Avg.
2000—St. Louis (N.L.)							Did not play.										

CHAMPIONSHIP SERIES RECORD

						BATTING								FIELDING		
Year Team (League)	Pos.	G	AB	R	H	2B	3B	HR	RBI	Avg.	BB	SO	SB	PO	A	E	Avg.
2000—St. Louis (N.L.)..........	PH-3B	5	13	1	3	2	0	0	2	.231	1	5	0	3	5	2	.800

PERSONAL: Born October 31, 1968, in Beeville, Texas. ... 6-3/230. ... Bats left, throws right. ... Full name: Edward Kenneth Taubensee. ... Name pronounced TAW-ben-see.

HIGH SCHOOL: Lake Howell (Casselberry, Fla.).

TRANSACTIONS/CAREER NOTES: Selected by Cincinnati Reds organization in sixth round of free-agent draft (June 2, 1986). ... Selected by Oakland Athletics from Reds organization in Rule 5 major league draft (December 3, 1990). ... Claimed on waivers by Cleveland Indians (April 4, 1991). ... Traded by Indians with P Willie Blair to Houston Astros for OF Kenny Lofton and IF Dave Rohde (December 10, 1991). ... Traded by Astros to Reds for P Ross Powell and P Marty Lister (April 19, 1994). ... On disabled list (August 1, 2000-remainder of season). ... Traded by Reds to Indians for P Jim Brower and P Robert Pugmire (November 16, 2000). ... On Cleveland disabled list (June 17-July 27, 2001); included rehabilitation assignments to Buffalo (July 16-24) and Akron (July 25-26).

STATISTICAL NOTES: Led Pioneer League with 19 passed balls in 1987. ... Tied for South Atlantic League lead in double plays by catcher with seven in 1988. ... Had 16-game hitting streak (May 22-June 13, 1999). ... Career major league grand slams: 1.

							BATTING								FIELDING		
Year Team (League)	Pos.	G	AB	R	H	2B	3B	HR	RBI	Avg.	BB	SO	SB	PO	A	E	Avg.
1986—GC Reds (GCL)..........	C-1B	35	107	8	21	3	0	1	11	.196	11	33	0	208	27	8	.967
1987—Billings (Pio.)...........	C	55	162	24	43	7	0	5	28	.265	25	47	2	344	29	6	.984
1988—Greensboro (S.Atl.)	C	103	330	36	85	16	1	10	41	.258	44	93	8	640	70	15	.979
—Chattanooga (Sou.).....	C	5	12	2	2	0	0	1	1	.167	3	4	0	17	5	1	.957
1989—Cedar Rapids (Midw.)..	C	59	196	25	39	5	0	8	22	.199	25	55	4	400	9	1	.998
—Chattanooga (Sou.).....	C	45	127	11	24	2	0	3	13	.189	11	28	0	213	31	6	.976
1990—Cedar Rapids (Midw.)..	C	122	417	57	108	21	1	16	62	.259	51	98	11	795	94	16	.982
1991—Cleveland (A.L.)■........	C	26	66	5	16	2	1	0	8	.242	5	16	0	89	6	2	.979
—Colo. Springs (PCL) ...	C	91	287	53	89	23	3	13	39	.310	31	61	0	412	47	12	.975
1992—Houston (N.L.)■........	C	104	297	23	66	15	0	5	28	.222	31	78	2	557	66	5	.992
—Tucson (PCL)	C	20	74	13	25	8	1	1	10	.338	8	17	0	127	10	4	.972
1993—Houston (N.L.)	C	94	288	26	72	11	1	9	42	.250	21	44	1	551	41	5	.992
1994—Houston (N.L.)	C	5	10	0	1	0	0	0	0	.100	0	3	0	19	2	0	1.000
—Cincinnati (N.L.)■......	C	61	177	29	52	8	2	8	21	.294	15	28	2	362	17	4	.990
1995—Cincinnati (N.L.)	C-1B	80	218	32	62	14	2	9	44	.284	22	52	2	338	22	6	.984
1996—Cincinnati (N.L.)	C	108	327	46	95	20	0	12	48	.291	26	64	3	538	42	11	.981
1997—Cincinnati (N.L.)	C-OF-1B-DH	108	254	26	68	18	0	10	34	.268	22	66	0	408	26	5	.989
1998—Cincinnati (N.L.)	C	130	431	61	120	27	0	11	72	.278	52	93	1	776	44	10	.988
1999—Cincinnati (N.L.)	C	126	424	58	132	22	2	21	87	.311	30	67	0	733	48	9	.989
2000—Cincinnati (N.L.)	C	81	266	29	71	12	0	6	24	.267	21	44	0	420	26	5	.989

Year Team (League)	Pos.	G	AB	R	H	2B	3B	HR	RBI	Avg.	BB	SO	SB	PO	A	E	Avg.
2001— Cleveland (A.L.)■.......	C-DH	52	116	16	29	2	1	3	11	.250	10	19	0	212	3	3	.986
— Buffalo (I.L.)..............	C	7	26	5	7	1	0	2	7	.269	2	6	0	23	1	1	.960
— Akron (East.).............	C	2	7	1	1	0	0	0	1	.143	1	1	0	9	0	0	1.000
American League totals (2 years)		78	182	21	45	4	2	3	19	.247	15	35	0	301	9	5	.984
National League totals (9 years)		897	2692	330	739	147	7	91	400	.275	240	539	11	4702	334	60	.988
Major League totals (11 years)		975	2874	351	784	151	9	94	419	.273	255	574	11	5003	343	65	.988

CHAMPIONSHIP SERIES RECORD

Year Team (League)	Pos.	G	AB	R	H	2B	3B	HR	RBI	Avg.	BB	SO	SB	PO	A	E	Avg.
1995— Cincinnati (N.L.)	PH-C	2	2	0	1	0	0	0	0	.500	0	0	0	0	0	0	...

TAVAREZ, JULIAN   P   CUBS

PERSONAL: Born May 22, 1973, in Santiago, Dominican Republic. ... 6-2/190. ... Throws right, bats left.

HIGH SCHOOL: Santiago (Dominican Republic) Public School.

TRANSACTIONS/CAREER NOTES: Signed as non-drafted free agent by Cleveland Indians organization (March 16, 1990). ... On Cleveland suspended list (June 18-21, 1996). ... Traded by Indians with IF Jeff Kent, IF Jose Vizcaino and a player to be named later to San Francisco Giants for 3B Matt Williams and a player to be named later (November 13, 1996); Indians traded P Joe Roa to Giants for OF Trenidad Hubbard to complete deal (December 16, 1996). ... On San Francisco disabled list (July 13-August 7, 1998); included rehabilitation assignment to Fresno (August 5-7). ... On suspended list (September 14-16, 1998). ... On San Francisco disabled list (May 1-June 1, 1999); included rehabilitation assignment to Fresno (May 25-June 1). ... Claimed on waivers by Colorado Rockies (November 21, 1999). ... Granted free agency (October 31, 2000). ... Signed by Chicago Cubs (November 16, 2000). ... On suspended list (April 29-May 5, 2001).

HONORS: Named A.L. Rookie Pitcher of the Year by THE SPORTING NEWS (1995).

STATISTICAL NOTES: Led Appalachian League with 10 hit batsmen in 1992.

Year League	W	L	Pct.	ERA	G	GS	CG	ShO	Sv.	IP	H	R	ER	BB	SO
1990— Dominican Indians (DSL)...	5	5	.500	3.29	14	12	3	0	0	82	85	53	30	48	33
1991— Dominican Indians (DSL)...	8	2	.800	2.67	19	18	1	0	0	121 1/3	95	41	36	28	75
1992— Burlington (Appl.)..........	6	3	.667	2.68	14	*14	2	•2	0	87 1/3	86	41	26	12	69
1993— Kinston (Caro.)..............	11	5	.688	2.42	18	18	2	0	0	119	102	48	32	28	107
— Canton/Akron (East.).........	2	1	.667	0.95	3	2	1	1	0	19	14	2	2	1	11
— Cleveland (A.L.)..............	2	2	.500	6.57	8	7	0	0	0	37	53	29	27	13	19
1994— Charlotte (I.L.)..............	•15	6	.714	3.48	26	26	2	2	0	176	167	79	68	43	102
— Cleveland (A.L.)..............	0	1	.000	21.60	1	1	0	0	0	1 2/3	6	8	4	1	0
1995— Cleveland (A.L.)..............	10	2	.833	2.44	57	0	0	0	0	85	76	36	23	21	68
1996— Cleveland (A.L.)..............	4	7	.364	5.36	51	4	0	0	0	80 2/3	101	49	48	22	46
— Buffalo (A.A.)...............	1	0	1.000	1.29	2	2	0	0	0	14	10	2	2	3	10
1997— San Francisco (N.L.)■	6	4	.600	3.87	*89	0	0	0	0	88 1/3	91	43	38	34	38
1998— San Francisco (N.L.)	5	3	.625	3.80	60	0	0	0	1	85 1/3	96	41	36	36	52
— Fresno (PCL)	0	0	...	19.29	1	0	0	0	0	2 1/3	6	5	5	0	1
1999— San Francisco (N.L.)	2	0	1.000	5.93	47	0	0	0	0	54 2/3	65	38	36	25	33
— Fresno (PCL)	0	0	...	2.25	4	1	0	0	0	8	3	2	2	3	9
— San Jose (Calif.)...........	0	0	...	0.00	1	1	0	0	0	4	1	0	0	1	3
2000— Colorado (N.L.)..............	11	5	.688	4.43	51	12	1	0	1	120	124	68	59	53	62
2001— Chicago (N.L.)■..............	10	9	.526	4.52	34	28	0	0	0	161 1/3	172	98	81	69	107
A.L. totals (4 years)	16	12	.571	4.49	117	12	0	0	0	204 1/3	236	122	102	57	133
N.L. totals (5 years)	34	21	.618	4.41	281	40	1	0	2	509 2/3	548	288	250	217	292
Major League totals (9 years).......	50	33	.602	4.44	398	52	1	0	2	714	784	410	352	274	425

DIVISION SERIES RECORD

Year League	W	L	Pct.	ERA	G	GS	CG	ShO	Sv.	IP	H	R	ER	BB	SO
1995— Cleveland (A.L.)................	0	0	...	6.75	3	0	0	0	0	2 2/3	5	2	2	0	3
1996— Cleveland (A.L.)................	0	0	...	0.00	2	0	0	0	0	1 1/3	1	0	0	2	1
1997— San Francisco (N.L.)	0	1	.000	4.50	3	0	0	0	0	4	4	2	2	2	0
Division series totals (3 years)	0	1	.000	4.50	8	0	0	0	0	8	10	4	4	4	4

CHAMPIONSHIP SERIES RECORD

Year League	W	L	Pct.	ERA	G	GS	CG	ShO	Sv.	IP	H	R	ER	BB	SO
1995— Cleveland (A.L.)................	0	1	.000	2.70	4	0	0	0	0	3 1/3	3	1	1	1	2

WORLD SERIES RECORD

Year League	W	L	Pct.	ERA	G	GS	CG	ShO	Sv.	IP	H	R	ER	BB	SO
1995— Cleveland (A.L.)................	0	0	...	0.00	5	0	0	0	0	4 1/3	3	0	0	2	1

TAYLOR, AARON   P   MARINERS

PERSONAL: Born August 20, 1977, in Valdosta, Ga. ... 6-3/205. ... Throws right, bats right. ... Full name: Aaron Wade Taylor.

HIGH SCHOOL: Lowndes (Valdosta, Ga.).

TRANSACTIONS/CAREER NOTES: Selected by Atlanta Braves organization in 11th round of free-agent draft (June 4, 1996). ... Selected by Seattle Mariners organization from Braves organization in Rule 5 minor league draft (December 13, 1999).

STATISTICAL NOTES: Led Gulf Coast League in wild pitches with 14 in 1996.

Year League	W	L	Pct.	ERA	G	GS	CG	ShO	Sv.	IP	H	R	ER	BB	SO
1996— Gulf Coast Braves (GCL)	0	*9	.000	7.74	13	9	0	0	0	52 1/3	68	*54	45	28	33
1997— Danville (Appl.)..................	1	•8	.111	5.53	15	7	0	0	0	55 1/3	65	49	34	31	38
1998— Danville (Appl.)..................	3	6	.333	6.25	14	•14	1	0	0	72	87	60	*50	36	55
1999— Macon (S.Atl.)...................	6	7	.462	4.88	27	8	0	0	1	79 1/3	86	56	43	27	78
2000— Everett (N'West)■...............	1	4	.200	7.43	15	14	0	0	0	63	76	54	52	37	57
2001— Wisconsin (Midw.).............	3	1	.750	2.45	28	0	0	0	9	29 1/3	19	9	8	11	50

PERSONAL: Born October 16, 1961, in Monticello, Fla. ... 6-8/235. ... Throws right, bats right. ... Full name: William Howell Taylor.
HIGH SCHOOL: Central (Thomasville, Ga.).
COLLEGE: Abraham Baldwin Agricultural College (Ga.).
TRANSACTIONS/CAREER NOTES: Selected by Texas Rangers organization in second round of free-agent draft (January 8, 1980). ... Loaned by Rangers organization to Wausau, Seattle Mariners organization (April 5-June 23, 1982). ... Granted free agency (October 22, 1988). ... Signed by San Diego Padres organization (March 30, 1989). ... Granted free agency (October 22, 1989). ... Signed by Atlanta Braves organization (August 16, 1990). ... Selected by Toronto Blue Jays from Braves organization in Rule 5 major league draft (December 7, 1992). ... Returned to Braves organization (April 3, 1993). ... Granted free agency (October 15, 1993). ... Signed by Oakland Athletics organization (December 13, 1993). ... On disabled list (July 27, 1994-remainder of season; April 12, 1995-entire season; and August 15-September 13, 1996). ... Traded by A's to New York Mets for P Jason Isringhausen and P Greg McMichael (July 31, 1999). ... Granted free agency (December 21, 1999). ... Signed by Colorado Rockies (February 4, 2000). ... Released by Rockies (March 23, 2000). ... Signed by Tampa Bay Devil Rays organization (March 31, 2000). ... Granted free agency (October 10, 2000). ... Signed by Pittsburgh Pirates organization (May 1, 2001). ... On Nashville disabled list (June 25-September 4, 2001). ... Granted free agency (October 8, 2001).

Year	League	W	L	Pct.	ERA	G	GS	CG	ShO	Sv.	IP	H	R	ER	BB	SO
1980—	Asheville (S.Atl.)	0	2	.000	10.93	6	2	0	0	0	14	24	24	17	9	12
	—Gulf Coast Rangers (GCL)..	0	0	...	2.31	14	2	0	0	0	35	36	14	9	16	22
1981—	Asheville (S.Atl.)	1	7	.125	4.64	14	12	1	0	0	64	76	43	33	35	44
	—Gulf Coast Rangers (GCL)..	4	2	.667	2.72	12	11	0	0	0	53	42	23	16	29	35
1982—	Wausau (Midw.)■	2	5	.286	5.03	19	1	0	0	2	39 1/3	36	27	22	27	34
	—Burlington (Midw.)■	5	4	.556	3.72	18	8	2	0	1	72 2/3	64	37	30	36	61
1983—	Salem (Caro.)	1	1	.500	6.26	7	7	1	0	0	41 2/3	30	34	29	42	42
	—Tulsa (Texas)	5	8	.385	6.87	21	12	0	0	0	76	86	65	58	51	75
1984—	Tulsa (Texas)	5	3	.625	3.83	42	2	0	0	7	80	65	38	34	51	80
1985—	Tulsa (Texas)	3	9	.250	3.47	20	17	2	0	0	103 2/3	84	55	40	48	87
1986—	Tulsa (Texas)	3	7	.300	3.95	11	11	2	1	0	68 1/3	65	40	30	37	64
	—Oklahoma City (A.A.)	5	5	.500	4.60	16	16	1	0	0	101 2/3	94	56	52	57	68
1987—	Oklahoma City (A.A.)	*12	9	.571	5.61	28	•28	0	0	0	168 1/3	198	122	105	91	100
1988—	Oklahoma City (A.A.)	4	8	.333	5.49	20	12	1	1	1	82	98	55	50	35	42
1989—	Las Vegas (PCL)■	7	4	.636	5.13	47	0	0	0	1	79	93	48	45	27	71
1990—	Durham (Caro.)■	0	0	...	3.24	5	0	0	0	0	8 1/3	8	3	3	1	10
	—Richmond (I.L.)	0	0	...	0.00	2	0	0	0	0	2 1/3	4	0	0	0	0
1991—	Greenville (Sou.)	6	2	.750	1.51	•59	0	0	0	22	77 1/3	49	16	13	15	65
1992—	Richmond (I.L.)	2	3	.400	2.28	47	0	0	0	12	79	72	27	20	27	82
1993—	Richmond (I.L.)	2	4	.333	1.98	59	0	0	0	*26	68 1/3	56	19	15	26	81
1994—	Oakland (A.L.)■	1	3	.250	3.50	41	0	0	0	1	46 1/3	38	24	18	18	48
1995—	Oakland (A.L.)							Did not play.								
1996—	Edmonton (PCL)	0	0	...	0.79	7	0	0	0	4	11 1/3	10	1	1	3	13
	—Oakland (A.L.)	6	3	.667	4.33	55	0	0	0	17	60 1/3	52	30	29	25	67
1997—	Oakland (A.L.)	3	4	.429	3.82	72	0	0	0	23	73	70	32	31	36	66
1998—	Oakland (A.L.)	4	9	.308	3.58	70	0	0	0	33	73	71	37	29	22	58
1999—	Oakland (A.L.)	1	5	.167	3.98	43	0	0	0	26	43	48	23	19	14	38
	—New York (N.L.)■	0	1	.000	8.10	18	0	0	0	0	13 1/3	20	12	12	9	14
2000—	Durham (I.L.)■	4	0	1.000	4.17	42	0	0	0	26	45 1/3	47	22	21	17	47
	—Tampa Bay (A.L.)	1	3	.250	8.56	17	0	0	0	0	13 2/3	13	13	13	9	13
2001—	Nashville (PCL)■	0	3	.000	7.20	20	0	0	0	8	20	29	17	16	3	16
	—Pittsburgh (N.L.)	0	0	...	4.50	1	0	0	0	0	2	2	1	1	0	3
A.L. totals (6 years)		16	27	.372	4.04	298	0	0	0	100	309 1/3	292	159	139	124	290
N.L. totals (2 years)		0	1	.000	7.63	19	0	0	0	0	15 1/3	22	13	13	9	17
Major League totals (7 years)		16	28	.364	4.21	317	0	0	0	100	324 2/3	314	172	152	133	307

DIVISION SERIES RECORD

Year	League	W	L	Pct.	ERA	G	GS	CG	ShO	Sv.	IP	H	R	ER	BB	SO
1999—	New York (N.L.)							Did not play.								

CHAMPIONSHIP SERIES RECORD

Year	League	W	L	Pct.	ERA	G	GS	CG	ShO	Sv.	IP	H	R	ER	BB	SO
1999—	New York (N.L.)							Did not play.								

PERSONAL: Born January 12, 1977, in Newberry, S.C. ... 6-1/178. ... Bats left, throws right. ... Full name: Reginald Tremain Taylor.
HIGH SCHOOL: Newberry (S.C.).
TRANSACTIONS/CAREER NOTES: Selected by Philadelphia Phillies organization in first round (14th pick overall) of free-agent draft (June 1, 1995). ... On disabled list (July 23, 1998-remainder of season). ... On Scranton/Wilkes-Barre disabled list (April 6-May 26, 2000; and April 6-May 1, 2001).
STATISTICAL NOTES: Led Appalachian League outfielders with three double plays in 1995. ... Led Florida State League outfielders with 354 total chances in 1997. ... Led Eastern League in caught stealing with 22 in 1999. ... Led International League in caught stealing with 15 in 2001.

							BATTING							FIELDING		
Year	Team (League)	Pos.	G	AB	R	H	2B	3B	HR	RBI	Avg.	BB	SO	SB	PO	A	E	Avg.
1995—	Martinsville (Appl.)	OF	64	239	36	53	4	6	2	32	.222	23	58	18	116	9	8	.940
1996—	Piedmont (S.Atl.)	OF	128	499	68	131	20	6	0	31	.263	29	136	36	287	9	•12	.961
1997—	Clearwater (FSL)	OF	134	545	73	133	18	6	12	47	.244	30	130	40	324	*19	11	.969
1998—	Reading (East.)	OF	79	337	49	92	14	6	5	22	.273	12	73	22	164	6	10	.944
1999—	Reading (East.)	OF	127	526	75	140	17	10	15	61	.266	18	79	38	295	9	9	.971
2000—	Scranton/W.B. (I.L.)	OF	98	422	60	116	10	8	15	43	.275	21	87	23	241	9	5	.980
	—Philadelphia (N.L.)	OF	9	11	1	1	0	0	0	0	.091	0	8	1	3	0	1	.750
2001—	Scranton/W.B. (I.L.)	OF	111	464	56	122	20	9	7	50	.263	24	94	31	243	6	5	.980
	—Philadelphia (N.L.)	OF	5	7	1	0	0	0	0	0	.000	1	1	0	4	0	0	1.000
Major League totals (2 years)			14	18	2	1	0	0	0	0	.056	1	9	1	7	0	1	.875

PERSONAL: Born May 25, 1976, in Bani, Dominican Republic. ... 5-9/188. ... Bats right, throws right. ... Full name: Miguel Odalis Tejada.

TRANSACTIONS/CAREER NOTES: Signed as non-drafted free agent by Oakland Athletics organization (July 17, 1993). ... On suspended list (July 4-7, 1996). ... On disabled list (July 20-August 10, 1996). ... On Oakland disabled list (March 22-May 20, 1998); included rehabilitation assignments to Edmonton (May 11-12) and Huntsville (May 12-20).

STATISTICAL NOTES: Led Northwest League shortstops with 369 total chances in 1995. ... Led California League shortstops with 44 errors in 1996. ... Led Southern League shortstops with 688 total chances and 97 double plays in 1997. ... Hit three home runs in one game (June 11, 1999 and June 30, 2001). ... Led A.L. shortstops with 755 total chances in 2000. ... Hit for the cycle (September 29, 2001). ... Career major league grand slams: 5.

						BATTING								FIELDING			
Year Team (League)	Pos.	G	AB	R	H	2B	3B	HR	RBI	Avg.	BB	SO	SB	PO	A	E	Avg.
1993—					Dominican Summer League statistics unavailable.												
1994—Dom. Athletics (DSL) .	2B	74	218	51	64	9	1	18	62	.294	37	36	13	76	126	16	.927
1995—S. Oregon (NW)	SS	74	269	45	66	15	5	8	44	.245	41	54	19	*129	*214	26	.930
1996—Modesto (Calif.)	SS-DH-3B	114	458	97	128	12	5	20	72	.279	51	93	27	194	358	†45	.925
1997—Huntsville (Sou.)	SS	128	502	85	138	20	3	22	97	.275	50	99	15	*229	*423	*36	.948
—Oakland (A.L.)	SS	26	99	10	20	3	2	2	10	.202	2	22	2	54	69	4	.969
1998—Edmonton (PCL)	SS	1	3	0	0	0	0	0	0	.000	1	1	0	0	5	0	1.000
—Huntsville (Sou.)	SS-DH	15	52	9	17	6	0	2	7	.327	4	8	1	18	41	5	.922
—Oakland (A.L.)	SS	105	365	53	85	20	1	11	45	.233	28	86	5	173	327	26	.951
1999—Oakland (A.L.)	SS	159	593	93	149	33	4	21	84	.251	57	94	8	*292	471	21	.973
2000—Oakland (A.L.)	SS	160	607	105	167	32	1	30	115	.275	66	102	6	233	*501	21	.972
2001—Oakland (A.L.)	SS	•162	622	107	166	31	3	31	113	.267	43	89	11	256	473	20	.973
Major League totals (5 years)		612	2286	368	587	119	11	95	367	.257	196	393	32	1008	1841	92	.969

DIVISION SERIES RECORD

						BATTING								FIELDING			
Year Team (League)	Pos.	G	AB	R	H	2B	3B	HR	RBI	Avg.	BB	SO	SB	PO	A	E	Avg.
2000—Oakland (A.L.)	SS	5	20	5	7	2	0	0	1	.350	2	2	1	8	14	0	1.000
2001—Oakland (A.L.)	SS	5	21	1	6	3	0	0	1	.286	0	3	0	8	15	1	.958
Division series totals (2 years)		10	41	6	13	5	0	0	2	.317	2	5	1	16	29	1	.978

PERSONAL: Born October 18, 1976, in Havana, Cuba. ... 5-9/175. ... Throws left, bats left.

HIGH SCHOOL: Southwest (Miami).

TRANSACTIONS/CAREER NOTES: Selected by Florida Marlins organization in sixth round of free-agent draft (June 1, 1995). ... On disabled list (April 2, 2000-entire season).

HONORS: Named Eastern League Pitcher of the Year (1999).

Year League	W	L	Pct.	ERA	G	GS	CG	ShO	Sv.	IP	H	R	ER	BB	SO
1995—Gulf Coast Marlins (GCL) ...	3	1	.750	2.65	11	3	0	0	2	34	28	13	10	16	28
1996—Gulf Coast Marlins (GCL) ...	1	0	1.000	3.60	2	0	0	0	0	5	6	2	2	0	2
1997—Utica (NY-Penn)	3	3	.500	3.76	12	12	0	0	0	69 1/3	65	36	29	11	67
1998—Kane County (Midw.).........	6	1	.857	2.77	10	10	0	0	0	55 1/3	44	20	17	13	47
—Portland (East.)	9	5	.643	4.11	18	18	2	2	0	107 1/3	113	55	49	36	47
1999—Portland (East.)	13	4	.765	2.62	25	25	0	0	0	154 2/3	137	55	45	45	152
—Calgary (PCL)	0	2	.000	12.00	2	2	0	0	0	9	19	14	12	4	5
—Florida (N.L.)	0	0	...	11.37	3	1	0	0	0	6 1/3	10	8	8	5	7
2000—Florida (N.L.)							Did not play.								
2001—Portland (East.)	9	8	.529	3.57	25	25	0	0	0	141	143	61	56	41	131
Major League totals (1 year)........	0	0	...	11.37	3	1	0	0	0	6 1/3	10	8	8	5	7

PERSONAL: Born January 19, 1974, in Higuey, Dominican Republic. ... 6-3/222. ... Throws right, bats right. ... Full name: Amaury Regalado Telemaco. ... Name pronounced AH-mer-ee tel-ah-MAH-ko.

HIGH SCHOOL: Cristo Rey (La Romana, Dominican Republic).

TRANSACTIONS/CAREER NOTES: Signed as non-drafted free agent by Chicago Cubs organization (May 23, 1991). ... On temporarily inactive list (August 17, 1993-remainder of season). ... On Orlando disabled list (August 23-September 8, 1994). ... On Chicago disabled list (August 20-September 4, 1996); included rehabilitation assignment to Iowa (September 2-4). ... Claimed on waivers by Arizona Diamondbacks (May 15, 1998). ... On Arizona disabled list (March 26-May 8, 1999); included rehabilitation assignment to Tucson (April 8-May 7). ... Claimed on waivers by Philadelphia Phillies (June 8, 1999). ... On Scranton/Wilkes-Barre disabled list (July 19-August 5, 2000; and August 22, 2001-remainder of season). ... Granted free agency (October 8, 2001).

Year League	W	L	Pct.	ERA	G	GS	CG	ShO	Sv.	IP	H	R	ER	BB	SO
1991—Puerta Plata (DSL)	3	3	.500	3.55	15	13	0	0	0	66	81	43	26	32	43
1992—Huntington (Appl.)	3	5	.375	4.01	12	12	2	0	0	76 1/3	71	45	34	17	*93
—Peoria (Midw.)	0	1	.000	7.94	2	1	0	0	0	5 2/3	9	5	5	5	5
1993—Peoria (Midw.)..................	8	11	.421	3.45	23	23	3	0	0	143 2/3	129	69	55	54	133
1994—Daytona (FSL)	7	3	.700	3.40	11	11	2	0	0	76 1/3	62	35	29	23	59
—Orlando (Sou.)	3	5	.375	3.45	12	12	2	0	0	62 2/3	56	29	24	20	49
1995—Orlando (Sou.)	8	8	.500	3.29	22	22	3	1	0	147 2/3	112	60	54	42	151
1996—Iowa (A.A.)	3	1	.750	3.06	8	8	1	0	0	50	38	19	17	18	42
—Chicago (N.L.)	5	7	.417	5.46	25	17	0	0	0	97 1/3	108	67	59	31	64
1997—Iowa (A.A.)	5	9	.357	4.51	18	18	3	•2	0	113 2/3	121	70	57	38	75
—Chicago (N.L.)	0	3	.000	6.16	10	5	0	0	0	38	47	26	26	11	29
—Orlando (Sou.)	1	0	1.000	2.25	1	1	0	0	0	8	9	2	2	2	6

Year	League	W	L	Pct.	ERA	G	GS	CG	ShO	Sv.	IP	H	R	ER	BB	SO
1998—	Chicago (N.L.)	1	1	.500	3.90	14	0	0	0	0	27 2/3	23	12	12	13	18
	— Arizona (N.L.)■...............	6	9	.400	3.94	27	18	0	0	0	121	127	63	53	33	60
1999—	Tucson (PCL)	0	3	.000	5.09	13	12	0	0	0	17 2/3	21	11	10	6	17
	— Arizona (N.L.)	1	0	1.000	7.50	5	0	0	0	0	6	7	5	5	6	2
	— Philadelphia (N.L.)■	3	0	1.000	5.55	44	0	0	0	0	47	45	29	29	20	41
2000—	Philadelphia (N.L.)............	1	3	.250	6.66	13	2	0	0	0	24 1/3	25	22	18	14	22
	— Scranton/W.B. (I.L.)	8	3	.727	3.87	21	21	0	0	0	123 1/3	115	60	53	42	88
2001—	Philadelphia (N.L.)............	5	5	.500	5.54	24	14	1	0	0	89 1/3	93	59	55	32	59
	— Scranton/W.B. (I.L.)	1	2	.333	4.01	4	4	0	0	0	24 2/3	31	11	11	6	25
Major League totals (6 years)		22	28	.440	5.13	162	56	1	0	0	450 2/3	475	283	257	160	295

TELFORD, ANTHONY — P — RANGERS

PERSONAL: Born March 6, 1966, in San Jose, Calif. ... 6-0/195. ... Throws right, bats right. ... Full name: Anthony Charles Telford.
HIGH SCHOOL: Silver Creek (Calif.).
COLLEGE: San Jose State.
TRANSACTIONS/CAREER NOTES: Selected by Baltimore Orioles organization in third round of free-agent draft (June 2, 1987). ... On disabled list (April 20, 1988-remainder of season). ... On Frederick disabled list (April 7-18, 1989). ... On Erie disabled list (June 16-30, 1989). ... Granted free agency (October 15, 1993). ... Signed by Atlanta Braves organization (November 23, 1993). ... Granted free agency (October 15, 1994). ... Signed by Oakland Athletics organization (January 20, 1995). ... Released by A's (May 16, 1995). ... Signed by Cleveland Indians organization (June 15, 1995). ... Granted free agency (October 16, 1995). ... Signed by Montreal Expos organization (February 22, 1996). ... Granted free agency (October 15, 1996). ... Re-signed by Expos organization (December 18, 1996). ... On disabled list (May 19-June 3, 2000). ... On Montreal disabled list (March 23-April 25, 2001); included rehabilitation assignments to Jupiter (April 8-9 and April 24-25). ... Granted free agency (October 15, 2001). ... Signed by Texas Rangers organization (November 20, 2001).

Year	League	W	L	Pct.	ERA	G	GS	CG	ShO	Sv.	IP	H	R	ER	BB	SO
1987—	Newark (NY-Penn)............	1	0	1.000	1.02	6	2	0	0	0	17 2/3	16	2	2	3	27
	— Hagerstown (Caro.)............	1	0	1.000	1.59	2	2	0	0	0	11 1/3	9	2	2	5	10
	— Rochester (I.L.)................	0	0	...	0.00	1	0	0	0	0	2	0	0	0	3	3
1988—	Hagerstown (Caro.)	1	0	1.000	0.00	1	1	0	0	0	7	3	0	0	0	10
1989—	Frederick (Caro.)	2	1	.667	4.21	9	5	0	0	1	25 2/3	25	15	12	12	19
1990—	Frederick (Caro.)	4	2	.667	1.68	8	8	1	0	0	53 2/3	35	15	10	11	49
	— Hagerstown (East.)............	10	2	.833	1.97	14	13	3	1	0	96	80	26	21	25	73
	— Baltimore (A.L.)................	3	3	.500	4.95	8	8	0	0	0	36 1/3	43	22	20	19	20
1991—	Rochester (I.L.)	•12	9	.571	3.95	27	25	3	0	0	157 1/3	166	82	69	48	115
	— Baltimore (A.L.)................	0	0	...	4.05	9	1	0	0	0	26 2/3	27	12	12	6	24
1992—	Rochester (I.L.)................	12	7	.632	4.18	27	26	3	0	0	*181	*183	89	84	64	129
1993—	Rochester (I.L.)................	7	7	.500	4.27	38	6	0	0	2	90 2/3	98	51	43	33	66
	— Baltimore (A.L.)................	0	0	...	9.82	3	0	0	0	0	7 1/3	11	8	8	1	6
1994—	Richmond (I.L.)■..............	10	6	.625	4.23	38	20	3	1	0	142 2/3	148	82	67	41	111
1995—	Edmonton (PCL)■	3	2	.600	7.18	8	6	0	0	0	36 1/3	47	32	29	16	17
	— Canton/Akron (East.)■......	2	0	1.000	0.82	2	2	0	0	0	11	6	2	1	4	4
	— Buffalo (A.A.)..................	4	1	.800	3.46	16	2	0	0	0	39	35	15	15	10	24
1996—	Ottawa (I.L.)■	7	2	.778	4.11	30	15	1	1	0	118 1/3	128	62	54	34	69
1997—	Montreal (N.L.)	4	6	.400	3.24	65	0	0	0	1	89	77	34	32	33	61
1998—	Montreal (N.L.)	3	6	.333	3.86	77	0	0	0	1	91	85	45	39	36	59
1999—	Montreal (N.L.)	5	4	.556	3.94	79	0	0	0	2	96	112	52	42	38	69
2000—	Montreal (N.L.)	5	4	.556	3.79	64	0	0	0	3	78 1/3	76	38	33	23	68
2001—	Jupiter (FSL)	0	1	.000	7.20	4	2	0	0	0	5	9	5	4	1	5
	— Montreal (N.L.)	0	1	.000	10.29	8	0	0	0	0	7	14	12	8	5	5
	— Ottawa (I.L.)	3	5	.375	4.50	28	8	0	0	1	76	79	42	38	17	62
A.L. totals (3 years)		3	3	.500	5.12	20	9	0	0	0	70 1/3	81	42	40	26	50
N.L. totals (5 years)		17	21	.447	3.84	293	0	0	0	7	361 1/3	364	181	154	135	262
Major League totals (8 years)		20	24	.455	4.04	313	9	0	0	7	431 2/3	445	223	194	161	312

TEUT, NATHAN — P — MARLINS

PERSONAL: Born March 11, 1976, in Newton, Iowa. ... 6-7/215. ... Throws left, bats right. ... Full name: Nathan Mark Teut. ... Name pronounced TOIT.
HIGH SCHOOL: Paton-Churdan (Churdan, Iowa).
COLLEGE: Iowa State.
TRANSACTIONS/CAREER NOTES: Selected by Chicago Cubs organization in fourth round of free-agent draft (June 3, 1997). ... Traded by Cubs to Florida Marlins for P Jesus Sanchez (December 11, 2001).

Year	League	W	L	Pct.	ERA	G	GS	CG	ShO	Sv.	IP	H	R	ER	BB	SO
1997—	Williamsport (NY-Penn)	3	4	.429	2.57	9	9	0	0	0	49	55	23	14	6	37
	— Rockford (Midw.)	0	1	.000	10.13	2	2	0	0	0	10 2/3	18	12	12	2	6
1998—	Rockford (Midw.)	8	5	.615	3.31	16	16	1	0	0	103 1/3	99	49	38	23	67
	— Daytona (FSL)	5	3	.625	5.48	11	11	1	0	0	65 2/3	88	48	40	19	54
1999—	Daytona (FSL)	5	12	.294	6.38	26	26	1	0	0	132 2/3	180	*113	•94	41	91
2000—	West Tenn (Sou.)	11	6	.647	3.06	27	21	1	1	0	138 1/3	133	53	47	44	106
2001—	Iowa (PCL)	13	8	.619	5.12	29	•29	0	0	0	167	184	109	95	69	125

THAMES, MARCUS — OF — YANKEES

PERSONAL: Born March 6, 1977, in Louisville, Miss. ... 6-2/205. ... Bats right, throws right. ... Full name: Marcus Markey Thames.
JUNIOR COLLEGE: East Central (Miss.).
TRANSACTIONS/CAREER NOTES: Selected by New York Yankees organization in 30th round of free-agent draft (June 4, 1996).

STATISTICAL NOTES: Led Gulf Coast League with 113 total bases and .579 slugging percentage in 1997. ... Led Eastern League with .410 on-base percentage, .598 slugging percentage and 311 total bases in 2001. ... Tied for Eastern League lead with eight intentional bases on balls received in 2001.

Year	Team (League)	Pos.	G	AB	R	H	2B	3B	HR	RBI	Avg.	BB	SO	SB	PO	A	E	Avg.
1997—GC Yankees (GCL)......		OF	57	195	*51	67	*17	4	7	36	.344	16	26	6	86	4	2	.978
—Greensboro (S.Atl.)....		OF	4	16	2	5	1	0	0	2	.313	0	3	1	6	0	0	1.000
1998—Tampa (FSL)...............		OF	122	457	62	130	18	3	11	59	.284	24	78	13	282	7	9	.970
1999—Norwich (East.).........		OF	51	182	25	41	6	2	4	26	.225	22	40	0	84	8	7	.929
—Tampa (FSL)...............		OF	69	266	47	65	12	4	11	38	.244	33	58	3	104	8	3	.974
2000—Norwich (East.).........		OF	131	474	72	114	30	2	15	79	.241	50	89	1	197	11	•9	.959
2001—Norwich (East.).........		OF	139	520	*114	167	*43	4	31	97	.321	73	101	10	277	7	8	.973

THOMAS, BRAD   P   TWINS

PERSONAL: Born October 22, 1977, in Sydney, Australia. ... 6-3/205. ... Throws left, bats left. ... Full name: Bradley Richard Thomas.
HIGH SCHOOL: Mitchell (Australia).
TRANSACTIONS/CAREER NOTES: Signed as non-drafted free agent by Los Angeles Dodgers organization (July 2, 1995). ... Released by Dodgers (May 9, 1997). ... Signed by Minnesota Twins organization (May 12, 1997). ... On New Britain disabled list (August 20-September 2, 2001).
STATISTICAL NOTES: Pitched 9-0 no-hit victory for Fort Myers against Charlotte (July 12, 1999).

Year	League	W	L	Pct.	ERA	G	GS	CG	ShO	Sv.	IP	H	R	ER	BB	SO
1996—Great Falls (Pio.)...............		3	2	.600	6.31	11	5	0	0	0	35²/₃	48	27	25	11	28
1997—Elizabethton (Appl.)■........		3	4	.429	4.48	14	13	0	0	0	70¹/₃	78	43	35	21	53
1998—Fort Wayne (Midw.).........		11	8	.579	2.95	27	26	1	0	0	152¹/₃	146	68	50	45	126
1999—Fort Myers (FSL)...............		8	11	.421	4.78	27	*27	1	1	0	152²/₃	182	99	81	46	108
2000—Fort Myers (FSL)...............		6	2	.750	1.66	12	12	0	0	0	65	62	33	12	16	57
—New Britain (East.)...............		6	6	.500	4.06	14	13	1	1	0	75¹/₃	80	47	34	46	66
2001—New Britain (East.)...............		10	3	.769	1.96	19	19	1	0	0	119¹/₃	91	37	26	26	97
—Minnesota (A.L.)...............		0	2	.000	9.37	5	5	0	0	0	16¹/₃	20	17	17	14	6
Major League totals (1 year)........		0	2	.000	9.37	5	5	0	0	0	16¹/₃	20	17	17	14	6

THOMAS, FRANK   DH/1B   WHITE SOX

PERSONAL: Born May 27, 1968, in Columbus, Ga. ... 6-5/270. ... Bats right, throws right. ... Full name: Frank Edward Thomas.
HIGH SCHOOL: Columbus (Ga.).
COLLEGE: Auburn.
TRANSACTIONS/CAREER NOTES: Selected by Chicago White Sox organization in first round (seventh pick overall) of free-agent draft (June 5, 1989). ... On disabled list (July 11-30, 1996; June 7-22, 1997; and May 10, 2001-remainder of season).
RECORDS: Shares major league single-inning record for most doubles—2 (September 3, 2000, first inning). ... Shares A.L. single-season record for most intentional bases on balls received by righthanded batter—29 (1995).
HONORS: Named first baseman on The Sporting News college All-America team (1989). ... Named designated hitter on The Sporting News A.L. All-Star team (1991). ... Named designated hitter on The Sporting News A.L. Silver Slugger team (1991 and 2000). ... Named Major League Player of the Year by The Sporting News (1993). ... Named first baseman on The Sporting News A.L. All-Star team (1993-94). ... Named first baseman on The Sporting News A.L. Silver Slugger team (1993-94). ... Named A.L. Most Valuable Player by Baseball Writers' Association of America (1993-94). ... Named A.L. Comeback Player of the Year by The Sporting News (2000).
STATISTICAL NOTES: Led Southern League with .581 slugging percentage and .487 on-base percentage in 1990. ... Led A.L. with .453 on-base percentage in 1991, .439 in 1992, .487 in 1994 and .456 in 1997. ... Led A.L. first basemen with 1,533 total chances in 1992. ... Led A.L. with .729 slugging percentage in 1994. ... Led A.L. with 12 sacrifice flies in 1995. ... Led A.L. with 29 intentional bases on balls received in 1995 and 26 in 1996. ... Hit three home runs in one game (September 15, 1996) ... Had 21-game hitting streak (May 24-June 15, 1999). ... Career major league grand slams: 7.
MISCELLANEOUS: Holds Chicago White Sox all-time record for most home runs (348) and runs batted in (1,193).

Year	Team (League)	Pos.	G	AB	R	H	2B	3B	HR	RBI	Avg.	BB	SO	SB	PO	A	E	Avg.
1989—GC White Sox (GCL) ..		1B	17	52	8	19	5	0	1	11	.365	10	24	4	130	8	2	.986
—Sarasota (FSL)...............		1B	55	188	27	52	9	1	4	30	.277	31	33	0	420	31	7	.985
1990—Birmingham (Sou.)......		1B	109	353	85	114	27	5	18	71	.323	*112	74	7	954	77	14	.987
—Chicago (A.L.)...............		1B-DH	60	191	39	63	11	3	7	31	.330	44	54	0	428	26	5	.989
1991—Chicago (A.L.)...............		DH-1B	158	559	104	178	31	2	32	109	.318	*138	112	1	459	27	2	.996
1992—Chicago (A.L.)...............		1B-DH	160	573	108	185	•46	2	24	115	.323	•122	88	6	*1428	92	13	.992
1993—Chicago (A.L.)...............		1B-DH	153	549	106	174	36	0	41	128	.317	112	54	4	1222	83	15	.989
1994—Chicago (A.L.)...............		1B-DH	113	399	*106	141	34	1	38	101	.353	109	61	2	735	45	7	.991
1995—Chicago (A.L.)...............		1B-DH	•145	493	102	152	27	0	40	111	.308	*136	74	3	738	34	7	.991
1996—Chicago (A.L.)...............		1B	141	527	110	184	26	0	40	134	.349	109	70	1	1098	85	9	.992
1997—Chicago (A.L.)...............		1B-DH	146	530	110	184	35	0	35	125	*.347	109	69	1	739	49	11	.986
1998—Chicago (A.L.)...............		DH-1B	160	585	109	155	35	2	29	109	.265	110	93	7	116	6	2	.984
1999—Chicago (A.L.)...............		DH-1B	135	486	74	148	36	0	15	77	.305	87	66	3	385	18	4	.990
2000—Chicago (A.L.)...............		DH-1B	159	582	115	191	44	0	43	143	.328	112	94	1	267	15	1	.996
2001—Chicago (A.L.)...............		DH-1B	20	68	8	15	3	0	4	10	.221	10	12	0	20	1	1	.955
Major League totals (12 years)			1550	5542	1091	1770	364	10	348	1193	.319	1198	847	29	7635	481	77	.991

DIVISION SERIES RECORD

Year	Team (League)	Pos.	G	AB	R	H	2B	3B	HR	RBI	Avg.	BB	SO	SB	PO	A	E	Avg.
2000—Chicago (A.L.)............		DH-1B	3	9	0	0	0	0	0	0	.000	4	0	0	8	0	0	1.000

CHAMPIONSHIP SERIES RECORD

RECORDS: Holds single-series record for most bases on balls received—10 (1993). ... Shares single-game record for most bases on balls received—4 (October 5, 1993).

						BATTING								FIELDING		
Year Team (League)	Pos.	G	AB	R	H	2B	3B	HR	RBI	Avg.	BB	SO	SB	PO	A	E	Avg.
1993— Chicago (A.L.)	1B-DH	6	17	2	6	0	0	1	3	.353	10	5	0	24	3	0	1.000

ALL-STAR GAME RECORD

					BATTING								FIELDING		
Year League	Pos.	AB	R	H	2B	3B	HR	RBI	Avg.	BB	SO	SB	PO	A	E	Avg.
1993— American	PH-DH	1	0	1	0	0	0	0	1.000	0	0	0	...	...	...	
1994— American	1B	2	1	2	0	0	0	1	1.000	1	0	0	6	0	0	1.000
1995— American	1B	2	1	1	0	0	1	2	.500	0	0	0	5	1	0	1.000
1996— American						Selected, did not play—injured.											
1997— American						Selected, did not play—injured.											
All-Star Game totals (3 years)		5	2	4	0	0	1	3	.800	1	0	0	11	1	0	1.000

THOME, JIM   1B   INDIANS

PERSONAL: Born August 27, 1970, in Peoria, Ill. ... 6-4/240. ... Bats left, throws right. ... Full name: James Howard Thome. ... Name pronounced TOE-me.

HIGH SCHOOL: Limestone (Bartonville, Ill.).

JUNIOR COLLEGE: Illinois Central College.

TRANSACTIONS/CAREER NOTES: Selected by Cleveland Indians organization in 13th round of free-agent draft (June 5, 1989). ... On Cleveland disabled list (March 28-May 18, 1992); included rehabilitation assignment to Canton/Akron (May 9-18). ... On Cleveland disabled list (May 20-June 15, 1992); included rehabilitation assignment to Canton/Akron (June 1-15). ... On disabled list (August 8-September 16, 1998).

RECORDS: Shares major league single-game record for most strikeouts (nine-inning game)—5 (April 9, 2000).

HONORS: Named International League Most Valuable Player (1993). ... Named third baseman on THE SPORTING NEWS A.L. All-Star team (1995 and 1996). ... Named third baseman on THE SPORTING NEWS A.L. Silver Slugger team (1996). ... Named first baseman on THE SPORTING NEWS A.L. All-Star team (2001).

STATISTICAL NOTES: Led International League with .441 on-base percentage in 1993. ... Hit three home runs in one game (July 22, 1994 and July 6, 2001). ... Had 16-game hitting streak (May 25-June 10, 1998). ... Career major league grand slams: 5.

MISCELLANEOUS: Holds Cleveland Indians all-time record for most home runs (282).

						BATTING								FIELDING		
Year Team (League)	Pos.	G	AB	R	H	2B	3B	HR	RBI	Avg.	BB	SO	SB	PO	A	E	Avg.
1989— GC Indians (GCL)	SS-3B	55	186	22	44	5	3	0	22	.237	21	33	6	65	144	21	.909
1990— Burlington (Appl.).......	3B	34	118	31	44	7	1	12	34	.373	27	18	6	28	79	11	.907
— Kinston (Caro.)........	3B	33	117	19	36	4	1	4	16	.308	24	26	4	10	66	8	.905
1991— Canton/Akron (East.)..	3B	84	294	47	99	20	2	5	45	.337	44	58	8	41	167	17	.924
— Colo. Springs (PCL) ..	3B	41	151	20	43	7	3	2	28	.285	12	29	0	28	84	6	.949
— Cleveland (A.L.)........	3B	27	98	7	25	4	2	1	9	.255	5	16	1	12	60	8	.900
1992— Colo. Springs (PCL) ...	3B	12	48	11	15	4	1	2	14	.313	6	16	0	9	20	8	.784
— Cleveland (A.L.)........	3B	40	117	8	24	3	1	2	12	.205	10	34	2	21	61	11	.882
— Canton/Akron (East.)..	3B	30	107	16	36	9	2	1	14	.336	24	30	0	11	35	4	.920
1993— Charlotte (I.L.)...........	3B-DH	115	410	85	136	21	4	25	*102	*.332	76	94	1	67	226	15	.951
— Cleveland (A.L.)........	3B	47	154	28	41	11	0	7	22	.266	29	36	2	29	86	6	.950
1994— Cleveland (A.L.).........	3B	98	321	58	86	20	1	20	52	.268	46	84	3	62	173	15	.940
1995— Cleveland (A.L.).........	3B-DH	137	452	92	142	29	3	25	73	.314	97	113	4	75	214	16	.948
1996— Cleveland (A.L.).........	3B-DH	151	505	122	157	28	5	38	116	.311	123	141	2	86	262	17	.953
1997— Cleveland (A.L.).........	1B	147	496	104	142	25	0	40	102	.286	*120	146	1	1233	95	10	.993
1998— Cleveland (A.L.).........	1B-DH	123	440	89	129	34	2	30	85	.293	89	141	1	998	85	10	.991
1999— Cleveland (A.L.).........	1B-DH	146	494	101	137	27	2	33	108	.277	*127	*171	0	930	83	6	.994
2000— Cleveland (A.L.).........	1B-DH	158	557	106	150	33	1	37	106	.269	118	171	1	834	91	5	.995
2001— Cleveland (A.L.).........	1B-DH	156	526	101	153	26	1	49	124	.291	111	*185	0	1177	78	10	.992
Major League totals (11 years)		1230	4160	816	1186	240	18	282	809	.285	875	1238	17	5457	1288	114	.983

DIVISION SERIES RECORD

RECORDS: Holds major league career record for most strikeouts—34. ... Shares A.L. career record for most home runs—8. ... Shares single-game records for most home runs—2 (October 11, 1999); and most grand slams—1 (October 7, 1999). ... Shares single-inning record for most runs batted in—4 (October 7, 1999, fourth inning). ... Shares single-game record for most at-bats (nine-inning game)—6 (October 13, 2001).

						BATTING								FIELDING		
Year Team (League)	Pos.	G	AB	R	H	2B	3B	HR	RBI	Avg.	BB	SO	SB	PO	A	E	Avg.
1995— Cleveland (A.L.)..........	3B	3	13	1	2	0	0	1	3	.154	1	6	0	6	6	0	1.000
1996— Cleveland (A.L.)..........	3B	4	10	1	3	0	0	0	0	.300	1	5	0	1	1	0	1.000
1997— Cleveland (A.L.)..........	1B	4	15	1	3	0	0	0	1	.200	0	5	0	45	3	0	1.000
1998— Cleveland (A.L.)..........	1B-DH	4	15	2	2	0	0	2	2	.133	3	5	0	26	1	0	1.000
1999— Cleveland (A.L.)..........	1B	5	17	7	6	0	0	4	10	.353	4	5	0	29	7	0	1.000
2001— Cleveland (A.L.)..........	1B	5	19	2	3	0	0	1	1	.158	2	8	0	40	5	0	1.000
Division series totals (6 years)		25	89	14	19	0	0	8	17	.213	11	34	0	147	23	0	1.000

CHAMPIONSHIP SERIES RECORD

RECORDS: Shares single-game record for most grand slams—1 (October 13, 1998). ... Shares single-inning record for most runs batted in—4 (October 13, 1998, fifth inning). ... Shares A.L. single series record for most home runs—4 (1998).

						BATTING								FIELDING		
Year Team (League)	Pos.	G	AB	R	H	2B	3B	HR	RBI	Avg.	BB	SO	SB	PO	A	E	Avg.
1995— Cleveland (A.L.)..........	3B	5	15	2	4	0	0	2	5	.267	2	3	0	1	5	1	.857
1997— Cleveland (A.L.)..........	1B-PH	6	14	3	1	0	0	0	0	.071	5	4	0	35	2	0	1.000
1998— Cleveland (A.L.)..........	DH-1B	6	23	4	7	0	0	4	8	.304	1	8	0	45	4	0	1.000
Championship series totals (3 years)		17	52	9	12	0	0	6	13	.231	8	15	0	81	11	1	.989

WORLD SERIES RECORD

Year Team (League)	Pos.	G	AB	R	H	2B	3B	HR	RBI	Avg.	BB	SO	SB	PO	A	E	Avg.
1995—Cleveland (A.L.).........	3B-PH	6	19	1	4	1	0	1	2	.211	2	5	0	3	5	1	.889
1997—Cleveland (A.L.).........	1B	7	28	8	8	0	1	2	4	.286	5	7	0	57	5	1	.984
World Series totals (2 years)		13	47	9	12	1	1	3	6	.255	7	12	0	60	10	2	.972

ALL-STAR GAME RECORD

Year League	Pos.	AB	R	H	2B	3B	HR	RBI	Avg.	BB	SO	SB	PO	A	E	Avg.
1997—American..................	PH-DH	1	0	0	0	0	0	0	.000	0	0	0	...	...	...	...
1998—American..................	1B	2	1	0	0	0	0	0	.000	2	1	0	4	0	0	1.000
1999—American..................	1B	2	1	1	0	0	0	1	.500	1	0	0	4	0	0	1.000
All-Star Game totals (3 years)		5	2	1	0	0	0	1	.200	3	1	0	8	0	0	1.000

THOMPSON, RYAN   OF   BREWERS

PERSONAL: Born November 4, 1967, in Chestertown, Md. ... 6-3/215. ... Bats right, throws right. ... Full name: Ryan Orlando Thompson.
HIGH SCHOOL: Kent County (Rock Hall, Md.).
TRANSACTIONS/CAREER NOTES: Selected by Toronto Blue Jays organization in 13th round of free-agent draft (June 2, 1987). ... On disabled list (May 29-June 7, 1991). ... On Syracuse disabled list (May 4-11 and July 20-27, 1992). ... Traded by Blue Jays to New York Mets (September 1, 1992), completing deal in which Mets traded P David Cone to Blue Jays for IF Jeff Kent and a player to be named later (August 27, 1992). ... On New York disabled list (April 18-May 30 and July 18-August 18, 1995); included rehabilitation assignments to Norfolk (May 13-30) and Binghamton (August 16-18). ... Traded by Mets with P Reid Cornelius to Cleveland Indians for P Mark Clark (March 30, 1996). ... Granted free agency (December 20, 1996). ... Signed by Kansas City Royals organization (January 16, 1997). ... Released by Royals (March 26, 1997). ... Signed by Indians organization (April 21, 1997). ... Traded by Indians to Toronto Blue Jays for IF Jeff Manto (June 6, 1997). ... Granted free agency (October 15, 1997). ... Signed to play for Fukuoka Dalei Hawks of Japan Pacific League (1998). ... Signed by Houston Astros organization (January 21, 1999). ... On New Orleans disabled list (August 5-13, 1999). ... Granted free agency (October 20, 1999). ... Signed by New York Yankees organization (December 15, 1999). ... Released by Yankees (April 2, 2000). ... Re-signed by Yankees organization (May 1, 2000). ... Released by Yankees (November 15, 2000). ... Signed by Blue Jays organization (December 13, 2000). ... Released by Blue Jays (April 2, 2001). ... Signed by Florida Marlins organization (April 6, 2001). ... Released by Marlins (August 1, 2001). ... Signed by Montreal Expos organization (August 3, 2001). ... Granted free agency (October 15, 2001). ... Signed by Milwaukee Brewers organization (December 20, 2001).
STATISTICAL NOTES: Led American Association outfielders with 334 total chances in 1996. ... Career major league grand slams: 1.

Year Team (League)	Pos.	G	AB	R	H	2B	3B	HR	RBI	Avg.	BB	SO	SB	PO	A	E	Avg.
1987—Medicine Hat (Pio.)....	OF	40	110	13	27	3	1	1	9	.245	6	34	1	56	2	4	.935
1988—St. Catharines (NY-P).	OF	23	57	13	10	4	0	0	2	.175	24	21	2	29	1	4	.882
—Dunedin (FSL)...........	OF	17	29	2	4	0	0	1	2	.138	2	12	0	11	0	0	1.000
1989—St. Catharines (NY-P).	OF	74	278	39	76	14	1	6	36	.273	16	60	9	111	•11	5	.961
1990—Dunedin (FSL)...........	OF	117	438	56	101	15	5	6	37	.231	20	100	18	237	7	7	.972
1991—Knoxville (Sou.)..........	OF	114	403	48	97	14	3	8	40	.241	26	88	17	222	5	4	.983
1992—Syracuse (I.L.)..........	OF	112	429	74	121	20	7	14	46	.282	43	114	12	270	5	4	.986
—New York (N.L.)■......	OF	30	108	15	24	7	1	3	10	.222	8	24	2	77	2	1	.988
1993—New York (N.L.).........	OF	80	288	34	72	19	2	11	26	.250	19	81	2	228	4	3	.987
—Norfolk (I.L.)...........	OF	60	224	39	58	11	2	12	34	.259	24	81	6	138	4	3	.973
1994—New York (N.L.).........	OF	98	334	29	75	14	1	18	59	.225	28	94	1	274	5	3	.989
1995—Norfolk (I.L.)...........	OF-DH	15	53	7	18	3	0	2	11	.340	4	15	4	15	2	0	1.000
—New York (N.L.).........	OF	75	267	39	67	13	0	7	31	.251	19	77	3	193	4	3	.985
—Binghamton (East.)....	OF	8	2	2	4	0	0	1	4	.500	1	2	0	2	0	0	1.000
1996—Buffalo (A.A.)■.........	OF-DH	•138	*540	79	140	26	4	21	83	.259	21	119	12	*317	8	*9	.973
—Cleveland (A.L.).........	OF	8	22	2	7	0	0	1	5	.318	1	6	0	5	0	0	1.000
1997—Buffalo (A.A.).........	OF-DH	24	66	10	16	0	0	1	6	.242	5	16	2	20	1	1	.955
—Syracuse (I.L.)■.........	OF-DH	83	330	37	95	23	1	16	58	.288	21	59	4	117	4	1	.992
1998—Fukuoka (Jap. Pac.)■.		26	107	10	29	7	0	2	16	.271	12	32	1	...	...	...	...
1999—New Orleans (PCL)■.	OF-DH	112	404	60	125	23	2	16	58	.309	37	78	4	209	12	8	.965
—Houston (N.L.)...........	OF	12	20	2	4	1	0	1	5	.200	2	7	0	3	1	1	.800
2000—Columbus (I.L.)■......	OF	86	326	45	93	23	3	23	75	.285	27	72	10	155	10	2	.988
—New York (A.L.).........	OF	33	50	12	13	3	0	3	14	.260	5	12	0	33	0	0	1.000
2001—Calgary (PCL)■.........	OF	78	300	53	93	26	0	19	69	.310	14	65	4	159	6	9	.948
—Florida (N.L.).............	OF	18	31	6	9	5	0	0	2	.290	1	8	0	11	1	1	.923
—Ottawa (I.L.)■.........	OF-1B	21	85	6	14	4	0	2	9	.165	3	22	0	56	3	1	.983
American League totals (2 years)		41	72	14	20	3	0	4	19	.278	6	18	0	38	0	0	1.000
National League totals (6 years)		313	1048	125	251	59	4	40	133	.240	77	291	8	786	17	12	.985
Major League totals (8 years)		354	1120	139	271	62	4	44	152	.242	83	309	8	824	17	12	.986

THOMSON, JOHN   P   ROCKIES

PERSONAL: Born October 1, 1973, in Vicksburg, Miss. ... 6-3/187. ... Throws right, bats right. ... Full name: John Carl Thomson.
HIGH SCHOOL: Sulphur (La.).
JUNIOR COLLEGE: Blinn College (Texas).
COLLEGE: McNeese State.
TRANSACTIONS/CAREER NOTES: Selected by Colorado Rockies organization in seventh round of free-agent draft (June 3, 1993). ... On Colorado disabled list (June 16-July 26, 1998); included rehabilitation assignment to Asheville (July 16-22). ... On Colorado Springs disabled list (May 19-July 19, 1999); included rehabilitation assignment to Salem (July 17-19). ... On Colorado disabled list (March 23, 2000-remainder of season); included rehabilitation assignments to Arizona League Rockies (August 16-September 1) and Portland (September 2-4). ... On Colorado disabled list (March 23-May 12 and May 26-August 2, 2001); included rehabilitation assignments to Colorado Springs (April 1-6, April 17-May 12 and June 24-July 23).
STATISTICAL NOTES: Tied for Arizona League lead with 14 wild pitches in 1993.
MISCELLANEOUS: Shares Colorado Rockies all-time record for most shutouts (2).

Year	League	W	L	Pct.	ERA	G	GS	CG	ShO	Sv.	IP	H	R	ER	BB	SO
1993— Arizona Rockies (Ariz.)		3	5	.375	4.62	11	11	0	0	0	50 2/3	43	40	26	31	36
1994— Asheville (S.Atl.)		6	6	.500	2.85	19	15	1	1	0	88 1/3	70	34	28	33	79
— Central Valley (Calif.)		3	1	.750	3.28	9	8	0	0	0	49 1/3	43	20	18	18	41
1995— New Haven (East.)		7	8	.467	4.18	26	24	0	0	0	131 1/3	132	69	61	56	82
1996— New Haven (East.)		9	4	.692	2.86	16	16	1	0	0	97 2/3	82	35	31	27	86
— Colorado Springs (PCL)		4	7	.364	5.04	11	11	0	0	0	69 2/3	76	45	39	26	62
1997— Colorado Springs (PCL)		4	2	.667	3.43	7	7	0	0	0	42	36	18	16	14	49
— Colorado (N.L.)		7	9	.438	4.71	27	27	2	1	0	166 1/3	193	94	87	51	106
1998— Colorado (N.L.)		8	11	.421	4.81	26	26	2	0	0	161	174	86	86	49	106
— Asheville (S.Atl.)		1	0	1.000	0.00	2	2	0	0	0	9	5	1	0	1	12
1999— Colorado (N.L.)		1	10	.091	8.04	14	13	1	0	0	62 2/3	85	62	56	36	34
— Colorado Springs (PCL)		0	2	.000	9.45	5	5	1	0	0	20	36	25	21	8	19
— Salem (Caro.)		0	1	.000	9.00	1	1	0	0	0	2	4	2	2	0	2
2000— Arizona Rockies (Ariz.)		0	1	.000	13.50	3	3	0	0	0	5 1/3	8	8	8	4	7
— Portland (N'West)		0	0	...	2.25	1	1	0	0	0	4	4	1	1	1	3
2001— Colorado Springs (PCL)		5	3	.625	3.31	12	12	0	0	0	68	74	29	25	13	52
— Colorado (N.L.)		4	5	.444	4.04	14	14	1	1	0	93 2/3	84	46	42	25	68
Major League totals (4 years)		**20**	**35**	**.364**	**5.04**	**81**	**80**	**6**	**2**	**0**	**483 2/3**	**536**	**288**	**271**	**161**	**314**

THURMAN, MIKE · P

PERSONAL: Born July 22, 1973, in Corvallis, Ore. ... 6-5/210. ... Throws right, bats right. ... Full name: Michael Richard Thurman.
HIGH SCHOOL: Philomath (Ore.).
COLLEGE: Oregon State.
TRANSACTIONS/CAREER NOTES: Selected by Montreal Expos organization in supplemental round ("sandwich pick" between first and second round, 31st pick overall) of free-agent draft (June 2, 1994); pick received as compensation for Cleveland Indians signing Type A free-agent P Dennis Martinez. ... On Harrisburg disabled list (June 17-July 5, 1997). ... On Montreal disabled list (March 23-May 12 and May 25-July 21, 2000); included rehabilitation assignments to Jupiter (April 21-May 7) and Ottawa (May 8-9, June 29-July 10 and July 17-19) and Harrisburg (July 11-16). ... On Montreal disabled list (May 24-June 26, 2001); included rehabilitation assignment to Jupiter (June 21-26). ... Granted free agency (December 21, 2001).

Year	League	W	L	Pct.	ERA	G	GS	CG	ShO	Sv.	IP	H	R	ER	BB	SO
1994— Vermont (NY-Penn)		0	1	.000	5.40	2	2	0	0	0	6 2/3	6	4	4	2	3
1995— Albany (S.Atl.)		3	8	.273	5.47	22	22	2	0	0	110 1/3	133	79	67	32	77
1996— West Palm Beach (FSL)		6	8	.429	3.33	19	19	0	0	0	113 2/3	122	53	42	23	68
— Harrisburg (East.)		3	1	.750	5.11	4	4	1	0	0	24 2/3	25	14	14	5	14
1997— Harrisburg (East.)		9	6	.600	3.81	20	20	1	0	0	115 2/3	102	54	49	30	85
— Ottawa (I.L.)		1	3	.250	5.49	4	4	0	0	0	19 2/3	17	13	12	9	15
— Montreal (N.L.)		1	0	1.000	5.40	5	2	0	0	0	11 2/3	8	9	7	4	8
1998— Ottawa (I.L.)		7	7	.500	3.41	19	19	0	0	0	105 2/3	107	50	40	49	76
— Montreal (N.L.)		4	5	.444	4.70	14	13	0	0	0	67	60	38	35	26	32
1999— Montreal (N.L.)		7	11	.389	4.05	29	27	0	0	0	146 2/3	140	84	66	52	85
2000— Jupiter (FSL)		1	1	.500	2.08	3	3	0	0	0	13	14	3	3	0	6
— Ottawa (I.L.)		0	3	.000	7.71	4	4	0	0	0	16 1/3	23	14	14	9	8
— Montreal (N.L.)		4	9	.308	6.42	17	17	0	0	0	88 1/3	112	69	63	46	52
— Harrisburg (East.)		0	0	...	4.15	1	0	0	0	0	4 1/3	4	2	2	3	1
2001— Montreal (N.L.)		9	11	.450	5.33	28	26	0	0	0	147	172	90	87	50	96
— Jupiter (FSL)		1	0	1.000	0.00	1	1	1	1	0	5	2	0	0	0	3
Major League totals (5 years)		**25**	**36**	**.410**	**5.04**	**93**	**85**	**0**	**0**	**0**	**460 2/3**	**492**	**290**	**258**	**178**	**273**

TIMLIN, MIKE · P · CARDINALS

PERSONAL: Born March 10, 1966, in Midland, Texas. ... 6-4/210. ... Throws right, bats right. ... Full name: Michael August Timlin.
HIGH SCHOOL: Midland (Texas).
COLLEGE: Southwestern University (Texas).
TRANSACTIONS/CAREER NOTES: Selected by Toronto Blue Jays organization in fifth round of free-agent draft (June 2, 1987). ... On disabled list (April 4-May 2, 1989 and August 2-17, 1991). ... On Toronto disabled list (March 27-June 12, 1992); included rehabilitation assignments to Dunedin (April 11-15 and May 24-June 5) and Syracuse (June 5-12). ... On disabled list (May 25-June 9, 1994). ... On Toronto disabled list (June 22-August 18, 1995); included rehabilitation assignment to Syracuse (July 31-August 18). ... Traded by Blue Jays with P Paul Spoljaric to Seattle Mariners for OF Jose Cruz Jr. (July 31, 1997). ... Granted free agency (October 22, 1998). ... Signed by Baltimore Orioles (November 16, 1998). ... On Baltimore disabled list (April 2-17, 2000). ... Traded by Orioles with cash to St. Louis Cardinals for 1B Chris Richard and P Mark Nussbeck (July 29, 2000). ... On disabled list (July 26-August 17, 2001).
STATISTICAL NOTES: Led South Atlantic League with 19 hit batsmen in 1988.

Year	League	W	L	Pct.	ERA	G	GS	CG	ShO	Sv.	IP	H	R	ER	BB	SO
1987— Medicine Hat (Pio.)		4	8	.333	5.14	13	12	2	0	0	75 1/3	79	50	43	26	66
1988— Myrtle Beach (S.Atl.)		10	6	.625	2.86	35	22	0	0	0	151	119	68	48	77	106
1989— Dunedin (FSL)		5	8	.385	3.25	33	7	1	0	7	88 2/3	90	44	32	36	64
1990— Dunedin (FSL)		7	2	.778	1.43	42	0	0	0	22	50 1/3	36	11	8	16	46
— Knoxville (Sou.)		1	2	.333	1.73	17	0	0	0	8	26	20	6	5	7	21
1991— Toronto (A.L.)		11	6	.647	3.16	63	3	0	0	3	108 1/3	94	43	38	50	85
1992— Dunedin (FSL)		0	0	...	0.90	6	1	0	0	1	10	9	2	1	2	7
— Syracuse (I.L.)		0	1	.000	8.74	7	1	0	0	3	11 1/3	15	11	11	5	7
— Toronto (A.L.)		0	2	.000	4.12	26	0	0	0	1	43 2/3	45	23	20	20	35
1993— Toronto (A.L.)		4	2	.667	4.69	54	0	0	0	1	55 2/3	63	32	29	27	49
— Dunedin (FSL)		0	0	...	1.00	4	0	0	0	1	9	4	1	1	0	8
1994— Toronto (A.L.)		0	1	.000	5.18	34	0	0	0	2	40	41	25	23	20	38
1995— Toronto (A.L.)		4	3	.571	2.14	31	0	0	0	5	42	38	13	10	17	36
— Syracuse (I.L.)		1	1	.500	1.04	8	0	0	0	0	17 1/3	13	6	2	4	13
1996— Toronto (A.L.)		1	6	.143	3.65	59	0	0	0	31	56 2/3	47	25	23	18	52
1997— Toronto (A.L.)		3	2	.600	2.87	38	0	0	0	9	47	41	17	15	15	36
— Seattle (A.L.)■		3	3	.600	3.86	26	0	0	0	1	25 2/3	28	13	11	5	9
1998— Seattle (A.L.)		3	3	.500	2.95	70	0	0	0	19	79 1/3	78	26	26	16	60

Year	League	W	L	Pct.	ERA	G	GS	CG	ShO	Sv.	IP	H	R	ER	BB	SO
1999— Baltimore (A.L.)■		3	9	.250	3.57	62	0	0	0	27	63	51	30	25	23	50
2000— Baltimore (A.L.)		2	3	.400	4.89	37	0	0	0	11	35	37	22	19	15	26
— St. Louis (N.L.)■		3	1	.750	3.34	25	0	0	0	1	$29^2/_3$	30	11	11	20	26
2001— St. Louis (N.L.)		4	5	.444	4.09	67	0	0	0	3	$72^2/_3$	78	35	33	19	47
A.L. totals (10 years)		34	39	.466	3.61	500	3	0	0	110	$596^1/_3$	563	269	239	226	476
N.L. totals (2 years)		7	6	.538	3.87	92	0	0	0	4	$102^1/_3$	108	46	44	39	73
Major League totals (11 years)		41	45	.477	3.65	592	3	0	0	114	$698^2/_3$	671	315	283	265	549

DIVISION SERIES RECORD

Year	League	W	L	Pct.	ERA	G	GS	CG	ShO	Sv.	IP	H	R	ER	BB	SO
1997— Seattle (A.L.)		0	0	...	54.00	1	0	0	0	0	$^2/_3$	3	4	4	1	1
2000— St. Louis (N.L.)		0	0	...	10.80	2	0	0	0	0	$1^2/_3$	5	2	2	1	2
2001— St. Louis (N.L.)		0	0	...	0.00	1	0	0	0	0	$1^1/_3$	1	0	0	0	0
Division series totals (3 years)		0	0	...	14.73	4	0	0	0	0	$3^2/_3$	9	6	6	2	3

CHAMPIONSHIP SERIES RECORD

Year	League	W	L	Pct.	ERA	G	GS	CG	ShO	Sv.	IP	H	R	ER	BB	SO
1991— Toronto (A.L.)		0	1	.000	3.18	4	0	0	0	0	$5^2/_3$	5	4	2	2	5
1992— Toronto (A.L.)		0	0	...	6.75	2	0	0	0	0	$1^1/_3$	4	1	1	0	1
1993— Toronto (A.L.)		0	0	...	3.86	1	0	0	0	0	$2^1/_3$	3	1	1	0	2
2000— St. Louis (N.L.)		0	1	.000	0.00	3	0	0	0	0	$3^1/_3$	1	3	0	2	0
Champ. series totals (4 years)		0	2	.000	2.84	10	0	0	0	0	$12^2/_3$	13	9	4	4	8

WORLD SERIES RECORD

NOTES: Member of World Series championship team (1992 and 1993).

Year	League	W	L	Pct.	ERA	G	GS	CG	ShO	Sv.	IP	H	R	ER	BB	SO
1992— Toronto (A.L.)		0	0	...	0.00	2	0	0	0	1	$1^1/_3$	0	0	0	0	0
1993— Toronto (A.L.)		0	0	...	0.00	2	0	0	0	0	$2^1/_3$	2	0	0	0	4
World Series totals (2 years)		0	0	...	0.00	4	0	0	0	1	$3^2/_3$	2	0	0	0	4

TOCA, JORGE — 1B — METS

PERSONAL: Born January 7, 1975, in Villaclara, Cuba. ... 6-3/220. ... Bats right, throws right. ... Full name: Jorge Luis Toca.
TRANSACTIONS/CAREER NOTES: Signed as non-drafted free agent by New York Mets organization (September 7, 1998).
MISCELLANEOUS: Member of Cuban National Team (1994-95).

Year	Team (League)	Pos.	G	AB	R	H	2B	3B	HR	RBI	Avg.	BB	SO	SB	PO	A	E	Avg.
1999— Binghamton (East.)	OF-1B-DH-3B	75	279	60	86	15	1	20	67	.308	32	43	5	251	22	5	.982
— Norfolk (I.L.)	1B-DH-OF	49	176	25	59	12	1	5	29	.335	6	23	0	351	42	5	.987
— New York (N.L.)	1B	4	3	0	1	0	0	0	0	.333	0	2	0	2	0	0	1.000
2000— Norfolk (I.L.)	1B	120	453	58	123	25	3	11	70	.272	17	72	9	665	46	12	.983
— Binghamton (East.)	1B-OF	3	11	1	1	1	0	0	0	.091	0	0	0	13	3	0	1.000
— New York (N.L.)	1B-OF	8	7	1	3	1	0	0	4	.429	0	1	0	9	0	0	1.000
2001— Norfolk (I.L.)	1B-OF	111	407	53	109	13	1	11	51	.268	23	63	12	574	49	10	.984
— New York (N.L.)	1B-OF	13	17	3	3	0	0	0	1	.176	0	8	0	16	1	0	1.000
Major League totals (3 years)		25	27	4	7	1	0	0	5	.259	0	11	0	27	1	0	1.000

TOLAR, KEVIN — P — PIRATES

PERSONAL: Born January 28, 1971, in Panama City, Fla. ... 6-3/225. ... Throws left, bats right. ... Full name: Kevin Anthony Tolar.
HIGH SCHOOL: A. Crawford Mosley (Panama City, Fla.).
TRANSACTIONS/CAREER NOTES: Selected by Chicago White Sox organization in ninth round of free-agent draft (June 5, 1989). ... Loaned by White Sox organization to Salinas, California League (April 19-June 9, 1992). ... Released by White Sox (April 4, 1994). ... Signed by Pittsburgh Pirates organization (March 28, 1995). ... Granted free agency (October 16, 1995). ... Signed by Cleveland Indians organization (November 17, 1995). ... Granted free agency (October 15, 1996). ... Signed by Chicago Cubs organization (November 30, 1996). ... Released by Cubs (March 28, 1997). ... Signed by New York Mets organization (April 18, 1997). ... Granted free agency (October 17, 1997). ... Signed by Pirates organization (December 27, 1997). ... Traded by Pirates to Cincinnati Reds for future considerations (July 31, 1998). ... Granted free agency (October 15, 1999). ... Signed by Detroit Tigers organization (December 17, 1999). ... On Toledo disabled list (June 20-July 3, 2000). ... Granted free agency (October 15, 2001). ... Signed by Pirates organization (January 8, 2002).

Year	League	W	L	Pct.	ERA	G	GS	CG	ShO	Sv.	IP	H	R	ER	BB	SO
1989— GC White Sox (GCL)		6	2	.750	1.65	13	12	1	0	0	60	29	16	11	*54	58
1990— Utica (NY-Penn)		4	6	.400	3.29	15	15	1	0	0	$90^1/_3$	80	44	33	61	69
1991— South Bend (Midw.)		8	5	.615	2.83	30	19	0	0	1	$114^2/_3$	87	54	36	85	87
1992— Salinas (Calif.)		1	8	.111	6.07	14	8	3	0	0	$53^1/_3$	55	43	36	46	24
— South Bend (Midw.)■		6	5	.545	2.88	18	10	0	0	0	$81^1/_3$	59	34	26	41	81
1993— Sarasota (FSL)		2	6	.250	5.35	23	11	0	0	1	$77^1/_3$	75	55	46	51	60
1994—								Did not play.								
1995— Lynchburg (Caro.)■		2	0	1.000	2.79	18	0	0	0	0	$19^1/_3$	13	7	6	6	19
— Carolina (Sou.)		1	0	1.000	3.65	12	0	0	0	0	$12^1/_3$	16	5	5	7	9
1996— Canton/Akron (East.)■		1	3	.250	2.62	50	0	0	0	1	$44^2/_3$	42	19	13	26	39
1997— Binghamton (East.)■		1	1	.500	5.12	22	0	0	0	1	$31^2/_3$	38	20	18	22	26
— St. Lucie (FSL)		0	0	...	2.03	9	0	0	0	0	$13^1/_3$	9	3	3	6	8
1998— Carolina (Sou.)■		1	2	.333	2.22	42	0	0	0	1	$48^2/_3$	35	12	12	33	48
— Nashville (PCL)		0	0	...	6.00	1	0	0	0	0	3	2	2	2	4	1
— Indianapolis (I.L.)■		0	1	.000	10.43	19	0	0	0	0	$14^2/_3$	21	18	17	17	19
1999— Chattanooga (Sou.)		4	4	.500	4.97	47	1	0	0	1	$54^1/_3$	61	32	30	45	60
— Indianapolis (I.L.)		1	0	1.000	2.08	8	1	0	0	0	13	8	4	3	7	18
2000— Jacksonville (Sou.)■		2	0	1.000	0.52	9	0	0	0	0	$17^1/_3$	7	3	1	8	19
— Toledo (I.L.)		4	2	.667	3.30	33	0	0	0	2	$46^1/_3$	37	23	17	26	42
— Detroit (A.L.)		0	0	...	3.00	5	0	0	0	0	3	1	1	1	1	3
2001— Toledo (I.L.)		3	4	.429	2.73	44	0	0	0	7	56	49	18	17	21	73
— Detroit (A.L.)		0	0	...	6.75	9	0	0	0	0	$10^2/_3$	7	8	8	13	11
Major League totals (2 years)		0	0	...	5.93	14	0	0	0	0	$13^2/_3$	8	9	9	14	14

TOLLBERG, BRIAN — P — PADRES

PERSONAL: Born September 16, 1972, in Tampa. ... 6-3/195. ... Throws right, bats right. ... Full name: Brian Patrick Tollberg.
HIGH SCHOOL: Manatee (Bradenton, Fla.).
COLLEGE: North Florida.
TRANSACTIONS/CAREER NOTES: Signed by Chillicothe, Frontier League (1994). ... Signed as non-drafted free agent by Milwaukee Brewers organization (January 31, 1995). ... Traded by Brewers to San Diego Padres for 3B Antonio Fernandez (March 13, 1997). ... On Las Vegas disabled list (May 6, 1999-remainder of season). ... On San Diego disabled list (May 7-July 16, 2001); included rehabilitation assignments to Lake Elsinore (July 2-6 and July 11-16) and Portland (June 27-July 1 and July 7-10).

Year	League	W	L	Pct.	ERA	G	GS	CG	ShO	Sv.	IP	H	R	ER	BB	SO
1994—	Chillicothe (Fron.)	7	4	.636	2.85	13	13	4	0	0	94 2/3	90	34	30	27	69
1995—	Beloit (Midw.)■	13	4	.765	3.41	22	22	1	1	0	132	119	59	50	27	110
1996—	El Paso (Texas)	7	5	.583	4.90	26	26	0	0	0	154 1/3	183	90	84	23	109
1997—	Mobile (Sou.)■	6	3	.667	3.72	31	13	1	0	0	123 1/3	123	60	51	24	108
1998—	Mobile (Sou.)	3	2	.600	2.41	6	6	1	0	0	41	31	11	11	4	45
—	Las Vegas (PCL)	6	6	.500	6.38	33	15	1	0	3	110	138	85	78	27	109
1999—	Las Vegas (PCL)	1	2	.333	4.85	5	5	0	0	0	29 2/3	34	17	16	6	23
—	Arizona Padres (Ariz.)	0	0	...	4.50	2	2	0	0	0	4	4	2	2	0	6
2000—	Las Vegas (PCL)	6	0	1.000	2.83	13	13	0	0	0	76 1/3	72	28	24	11	60
—	San Diego (N.L.)	4	5	.444	3.58	19	19	1	0	0	118	126	58	47	35	76
2001—	San Diego (N.L.)	10	4	.714	4.30	19	19	0	0	0	117 1/3	133	58	56	25	71
—	Portland (PCL)	1	0	1.000	4.50	4	4	0	0	0	20	24	11	10	4	10
—	Lake Elsinore (Calif.)	0	2	.000	6.30	2	2	0	0	0	10	18	11	7	1	9
Major League totals (2 years)		14	9	.609	3.94	38	38	1	0	0	235 1/3	259	116	103	60	147

TOMKO, BRETT — P — PADRES

PERSONAL: Born April 7, 1973, in San Diego. ... 6-4/215. ... Throws right, bats right. ... Full name: Brett Daniel Tomko.
HIGH SCHOOL: El Dorado (Placentia, Calif.).
JUNIOR COLLEGE: Mount San Antonio College (Calif.).
COLLEGE: Florida Southern.
TRANSACTIONS/CAREER NOTES: Selected by Cincinnati Reds organization in second round of free-agent draft (June 1, 1995). ... Traded by Reds with OF Mike Cameron, IF Antonio Perez and P Jake Meyer to Seattle Mariners for OF Ken Griffey Jr. (February 10, 2000). ... On disabled list (June 7-24, 2000). ... Traded by Mariners with C Tom Lampkin and SS Ramon Vazquez to San Diego Padres for C Ben Davis, P Wascar Serrano and SS Alex Arias (December 11, 2001).
RECORDS: Shares N.L. single-inning record for most consecutive home runs allowed—3 (April 28, 1999, first inning).
MISCELLANEOUS: Appeared in two games as pinch runner (1997). ... Appeared in one game as pinch runner and struck out in only appearance as pinch hitter (1998).

Year	League	W	L	Pct.	ERA	G	GS	CG	ShO	Sv.	IP	H	R	ER	BB	SO
1995—	Charleston, W.Va. (S.Atl.)	4	2	.667	1.84	9	7	0	0	0	49	41	12	10	9	46
1996—	Chattanooga (Sou.)	11	7	.611	3.88	27	27	0	0	0	157 2/3	131	73	68	54	164
1997—	Indianapolis (A.A.)	6	3	.667	2.95	10	10	0	0	0	61	53	21	20	9	60
—	Cincinnati (N.L.)	11	7	.611	3.43	22	19	0	0	0	126	106	50	48	47	95
1998—	Cincinnati (N.L.)	13	12	.520	4.44	34	34	1	0	0	210 2/3	198	111	104	64	162
1999—	Cincinnati (N.L.)	5	7	.417	4.92	33	26	1	0	0	172	175	103	94	60	132
—	Indianapolis (I.L.)	2	0	1.000	4.97	2	2	0	0	0	12 2/3	15	7	7	1	9
2000—	Tacoma (PCL)■	1	0	1.000	2.84	2	2	0	0	0	12 2/3	13	4	4	5	8
—	Seattle (A.L.)	7	5	.583	4.68	32	8	0	0	1	92 1/3	92	53	48	40	59
2001—	Seattle (A.L.)	3	1	.750	5.19	11	4	0	0	0	34 2/3	42	24	20	15	22
—	Tacoma (PCL)	10	6	.625	4.04	19	18	3	•2	0	127	124	64	57	25	117
A.L. totals (2 years)		10	6	.625	4.82	43	12	0	0	1	127	134	77	68	55	81
N.L. totals (3 years)		29	26	.527	4.35	89	79	2	0	0	508 2/3	479	264	246	171	389
Major League totals (5 years)		39	32	.549	4.45	132	91	2	0	1	635 2/3	613	341	314	226	470

DIVISION SERIES RECORD

Year	League	W	L	Pct.	ERA	G	GS	CG	ShO	Sv.	IP	H	R	ER	BB	SO
2000—	Seattle (A.L.)	0	0	...	0.00	1	0	0	0	0	2 2/3	1	0	0	1	0

CHAMPIONSHIP SERIES RECORD

Year	League	W	L	Pct.	ERA	G	GS	CG	ShO	Sv.	IP	H	R	ER	BB	SO
2000—	Seattle (A.L.)	0	0	...	7.20	2	0	0	0	0	5	3	4	4	4	4

TORCATO, TONY — OF/3B — GIANTS

PERSONAL: Born October 25, 1979, in Woodland, Calif. ... 6-1/195. ... Bats left, throws right. ... Full name: Anthony Dale Torcato.
HIGH SCHOOL: Woodland (Calif.).
TRANSACTIONS/CAREER NOTES: Selected by San Francisco Giants organization in first round (19th pick overall) of free-agent draft (June 2, 1998); pick received from Houston Astros as part of compensation for signing Type B free agent P Doug Henry.
STATISTICAL NOTES: Led California League with eight intentional bases on balls received in 2000. ... Led California League third basemen with 24 double plays in 2000.

						BATTING								FIELDING		
Year	Team (League)	Pos.	G	AB	R	H	2B	3B	HR	RBI	Avg.	BB	SO	SB	PO	A	E	Avg.
1998—	Salem-Kaizer (NW)	3B	59	220	31	64	15	2	3	43	.291	14	38	4	20	112	17	.886
1999—	Bakersfield (Calif.)	3B	110	422	50	123	25	0	4	58	.291	30	67	2	54	164	28	.886
2000—	San Jose (Calif.)	3B	119	490	77	159	37	2	7	88	.324	41	62	19	77	222	40	.882
—	Shreveport (Texas)	3B	2	8	1	4	0	0	0	2	.500	0	1	0	0	1	0	1.000
2001—	San Jose (Calif.)	OF	67	258	38	88	21	2	2	47	.341	17	40	9	20	0	1	.952
—	Shreveport (Texas)	OF	36	147	13	43	9	1	1	23	.293	9	15	0	76	3	2	.975
—	Fresno (PCL)	OF	35	150	20	48	8	1	2	8	.320	2	20	0	64	3	1	.985

TORREALBA, STEVE — C — BRAVES

PERSONAL: Born February 24, 1978, in Barquisimeto, Venezuela. ... 6-0/175. ... Bats right, throws right. ... Full name: Steve Alexander Torrealba.
HIGH SCHOOL: Mario Bricamo Iragorri (Barquisimeto, Venezuela).
TRANSACTIONS/CAREER NOTES: Signed as non-drafted free agent by Atlanta Braves organization (March 1, 1995). ... On Greenville disabled list (April 13-May 10, 2001).
STATISTICAL NOTES: Led Appalachian League catchers with 457 total chances in 1997. ... Led Carolina League catchers with 815 total chances in 2000.

Year Team (League)	Pos.	G	AB	R	H	2B	3B	HR	RBI	Avg.	BB	SO	SB	PO	A	E	Avg.
1995—GC Braves (GCL)	C	30	92	3	19	4	0	0	10	.207	11	20	0	185	33	4	.982
1996—GC Braves (GCL)	C-1B-OF	52	146	9	25	2	0	0	7	.171	16	19	1	42	260	4	.987
—Danville (Appl.)	C	2	5	1	1	0	0	0	0	.200	0	2	0	10	1	1	.917
1997—Danville (Appl.)	C	44	150	17	34	9	0	2	18	.227	15	27	0	*398	41	*18	.961
1998—Macon (S.Atl.)	C-3B	67	209	28	57	10	0	10	37	.273	20	31	3	500	58	7	.988
1999—Myrtle Beach (Caro.)	C	52	175	23	37	9	0	6	23	.211	13	47	1	378	57	10	.978
2000—Myrtle Beach (Caro.)	C	99	334	43	90	16	0	7	35	.269	31	79	5	*723	82	10	.988
2001—Greenville (Sou.)	C	90	295	37	80	21	0	8	34	.271	33	54	0	596	64	*14	.979
—Atlanta (N.L.)	C	2	2	0	1	0	0	0	0	.500	0	0	0	2	0	0	1.000
Major League totals (1 year)		2	2	0	1	0	0	0	0	.500	0	0	0	2	0	0	1.000

DIVISION SERIES RECORD

Year Team (League)	Pos.	G	AB	R	H	2B	3B	HR	RBI	Avg.	BB	SO	SB	PO	A	E	Avg.
2001—Atlanta (N.L.)	C	1	1	0	1	1	0	0	0	1.000	0	0	0	1	0	0	1.000

CHAMPIONSHIP SERIES RECORD

Year Team (League)	Pos.	G	AB	R	H	2B	3B	HR	RBI	Avg.	BB	SO	SB	PO	A	E	Avg.
2001—Atlanta (N.L.)							Did not play.										

TORREALBA, YORVIT — C — GIANTS

PERSONAL: Born July 19, 1978, in Caracas, Venezuela. ... 5-11/190. ... Bats right, throws right. ... Full name: Yorvit Adolfo Torrealba.
HIGH SCHOOL: Vincente Emilio Sojo (Venezuela).
COLLEGE: Alberto Sequin Vera (Venezuela).
TRANSACTIONS/CAREER NOTES: Signed as non-drafted free agent by San Francisco Giants organization (September 14, 1994).
STATISTICAL NOTES: Led California League catchers with 10 double plays in 1997. ... Led Pacific Coast League catchers with 850 total chances in 2001.

Year Team (League)	Pos.	G	AB	R	H	2B	3B	HR	RBI	Avg.	BB	SO	SB	PO	A	E	Avg.
1995—Bellingham (N'West)	C	26	71	2	11	3	0	0	8	.155	2	14	0	152	26	5	.973
1996—San Jose (Calif.)	C	2	5	0	0	0	0	0	0	.000	1	1	0	16	1	0	1.000
—Burlington (Midw.)	C	1	4	0	0	0	0	0	0	.000	0	1	0	7	1	0	1.000
—Bellingham (N'West)	C	48	150	23	40	4	0	1	10	.267	9	27	4	290	33	2	.994
1997—Bakersfield (Calif.)	C	119	446	52	122	15	3	4	40	.274	31	58	4	779	*119	6	.993
1998—Shreveport (Texas)	C	59	196	18	46	7	0	0	13	.235	18	30	0	397	70	2	.996
—San Jose (Calif.)	C	21	70	10	20	2	0	0	10	.286	1	6	2	171	16	2	.989
—Fresno (PCL)	C	4	11	1	2	1	0	0	1	.182	1	4	0	22	0	0	1.000
1999—Shreveport (Texas)	C-DH	65	217	25	53	10	1	4	19	.244	9	34	0	299	43	2	.994
—Fresno (PCL)	C	17	63	9	16	2	0	2	10	.254	4	11	0	155	12	2	.988
—San Jose (Calif.)	C	19	73	10	23	3	0	2	14	.315	6	15	0	176	16	5	.975
2000—Shreveport (Texas)	C	108	398	50	114	21	1	4	32	.286	34	55	2	719	86	8	.990
2001—Fresno (PCL)	C	115	394	56	108	23	3	8	36	.274	19	65	2	*779	•62	9	.989
—San Francisco (N.L.)	C	3	4	0	2	0	1	0	2	.500	0	0	0	8	0	0	1.000
Major League totals (1 year)		3	4	0	2	0	1	0	2	.500	0	0	0	8	0	0	1.000

TORRES, ANDRES — OF — TIGERS

PERSONAL: Born January 26, 1978, in Aguada, Puerto Rico. ... 5-10/175. ... Bats both, throws right.
JUNIOR COLLEGE: Miami-Dade North.
TRANSACTIONS/CAREER NOTES: Selected by Florida Marlins organization in 23rd round of free-agent draft (June 3, 1997); did not sign. Selected by Detroit Tigers organization in fourth round of free-agent draft (June 2, 1998). ... On disabled list (July 2, 2001-remainder of season).

Year Team (League)	Pos.	G	AB	R	H	2B	3B	HR	RBI	Avg.	BB	SO	SB	PO	A	E	Avg.
1998—Jamestown (NY-P)	OF	48	192	28	45	2	6	1	21	.234	25	50	13	80	5	5	.944
1999—W. Michigan (Midw.)	OF	117	407	72	96	20	5	2	34	.236	92	116	39	233	9	7	.972
2000—Lakeland (FSL)	OF	108	398	82	118	11	11	3	33	.296	63	82	65	267	*18	6	.979
—Jacksonville (Sou.)	OF	14	54	3	8	0	0	0	0	.148	5	14	2	32	1	1	.971
2001—Erie (East.)	OF	64	252	54	74	16	3	1	23	.294	36	50	19	136	3	1	.993

TOWERS, JOSH — P — ORIOLES

PERSONAL: Born February 26, 1977, in Port Hueneme, Calif. ... 6-1/165. ... Throws right, bats right. ... Full name: Joshua Eric Towers. ... Nephew of Roger Frash, infielder/outfielder with New York Mets organization (1980-82).
HIGH SCHOOL: Hueneme (Oxnard, Calif.).
JUNIOR COLLEGE: Oxnard (Calif.) College.

TRANSACTIONS/CAREER NOTES: Selected by Baltimore Orioles organization in 15th round of free-agent draft (June 4, 1996). ... On Rochester disabled list (May 30-June 13 and August 5-24, 2000). ... On disabled list (October 1, 2001-remainder of season).
STATISTICAL NOTES: Led Carolina League pitchers with 786 batters faced and 26 home runs allowed in 1996. ... Tied Carolina League lead in sacrifice hits allowed with 12 in 1996.

Year	League	W	L	Pct.	ERA	G	GS	CG	ShO	Sv.	IP	H	R	ER	BB	SO
1996—	Bluefield (Appl.)	4	1	.800	5.24	14	9	0	0	0	55	63	35	32	5	61
1997—	Delmarva (S.Atl.)	0	0	...	3.44	9	1	0	0	1	18 1/3	18	8	7	2	16
	— Frederick (Caro.)	6	2	.750	4.86	25	3	0	0	1	53 2/3	74	36	29	18	64
1998—	Frederick (Caro.)	8	7	.533	3.34	25	20	3	0	1	145 1/3	137	58	54	9	122
	— Bowie (East.)	2	1	.667	3.50	5	2	0	0	0	18	20	9	7	4	7
1999—	Bowie (East.)	12	7	.632	3.76	29	•28	5	•2	0	*189	*204	86	79	26	106
2000—	Rochester (I.L.)	8	6	.571	3.47	24	24	5	1	0	148	157	63	57	21	102
2001—	Rochester (I.L.)	3	1	.750	3.51	6	6	1	1	0	41	40	18	16	8	27
	— Baltimore (A.L.)	8	10	.444	4.49	24	20	1	1	0	140 1/3	165	74	70	16	58
Major League totals (1 year)		8	10	.444	4.49	24	20	1	1	0	140 1/3	165	74	70	16	58

TRACHSEL, STEVE — P — METS

PERSONAL: Born October 31, 1970, in Oxnard, Calif. ... 6-4/205. ... Throws right, bats right. ... Full name: Stephen Christopher Trachsel. ... Name pronounced TRACK-sul.
HIGH SCHOOL: Troy (Fullerton, Calif.).
JUNIOR COLLEGE: Fullerton (Calif.) College.
COLLEGE: Long Beach State.
TRANSACTIONS/CAREER NOTES: Selected by Chicago Cubs organization in eighth round of free-agent draft (June 3, 1991). ... On Chicago disabled list (July 20-August 4, 1994). ... Granted free agency (October 28, 1999). ... Signed by Tampa Bay Devil Rays (January 28, 2000). ... Traded by Devil Rays with P Mark Guthrie to Toronto Blue Jays for 2B Brent Abernathy and a player to be named later (July 31, 2000). ... Granted free agency (October 31, 2000). ... Signed by New York Mets (December 11, 2000).
RECORDS: Shares major league record for most home runs allowed in one inning—4 (May 17, 2001, third inning).
HONORS: Named N.L. Rookie Pitcher of the Year by THE SPORTING NEWS (1994).
STATISTICAL NOTES: Pitched 4-2 no-hit victory for Winston-Salem against Peninsula (July 12, 1991, second game). ... Pitched 6-0 one-hit, complete-game victory against Houston (May 13, 1996). ... Led N.L. with 32 home runs allowed in 1997.

Year	League	W	L	Pct.	ERA	G	GS	CG	ShO	Sv.	IP	H	R	ER	BB	SO
1991—	Geneva (NY-Penn)	1	0	1.000	1.26	2	2	0	0	0	14 1/3	10	2	2	6	7
	— Winston-Salem (Caro.)	4	4	.500	3.67	12	12	1	0	0	73 2/3	70	38	30	19	69
1992—	Charlotte (Sou.)	•13	8	.619	3.06	29	•29	5	2	0	*191	180	76	65	35	135
1993—	Iowa (A.A.)	13	6	.684	3.96	27	26	1	1	0	170 2/3	170	78	75	45	135
	— Chicago (N.L.)	0	2	.000	4.58	3	3	0	0	0	19 2/3	16	10	10	3	14
1994—	Chicago (N.L.)	9	7	.563	3.21	22	22	1	0	0	146	133	57	52	54	108
	— Iowa (A.A.)	0	2	.000	10.00	2	2	0	0	0	9	11	10	10	7	8
1995—	Chicago (N.L.)	7	13	.350	5.15	30	29	2	0	0	160 2/3	174	104	92	76	117
1996—	Orlando (Sou.)	0	1	.000	2.77	2	2	0	0	0	13	11	6	4	0	12
	— Chicago (N.L.)	13	9	.591	3.03	31	31	3	2	0	205	181	82	69	62	132
1997—	Chicago (N.L.)	8	12	.400	4.51	34	34	0	0	0	201 1/3	225	110	101	69	160
1998—	Chicago (N.L.)	15	8	.652	4.46	33	33	1	0	0	208	204	107	103	84	149
1999—	Chicago (N.L.)	8	*18	.308	5.56	34	34	4	0	0	205 2/3	226	133	127	64	149
2000—	Tampa Bay (A.L.)■	6	10	.375	4.58	23	23	3	1	0	137 2/3	160	76	70	49	78
	— Toronto (A.L.)■	2	5	.286	5.29	11	11	0	0	0	63	72	40	37	25	32
2001—	New York (N.L.)■	11	13	.458	4.46	28	28	1	1	0	173 2/3	168	90	86	47	144
	— Norfolk (I.L.)	2	0	1.000	2.79	3	3	1	1	0	19 1/3	13	6	6	6	12
A.L. totals (1 year)		8	15	.348	4.80	34	34	3	1	0	200 2/3	232	116	107	74	110
N.L. totals (8 years)		71	82	.464	4.36	215	214	12	3	0	1320	1327	693	640	459	973
Major League totals (9 years)		79	97	.449	4.42	249	248	15	4	0	1520 2/3	1559	809	747	533	1083

ALL-STAR GAME RECORD

Year	League	W	L	Pct.	ERA	GS	CG	ShO	Sv.	IP	H	R	ER	BB	SO
1996—	National	0	0	...	0.00	0	0	0	0	1	0	0	0	0	3

TRACY, ANDY — 3B/1B — EXPOS

PERSONAL: Born December 11, 1973, in Bowling Green, Ohio. ... 6-3/220. ... Bats left, throws left. ... Full name: Andrew Michael Tracy.
HIGH SCHOOL: Bowling Green (Ohio).
COLLEGE: Bowling Green State.
TRANSACTIONS/CAREER NOTES: Selected by Montreal Expos organization in 16th round of free-agent draft (June 4, 1996). ... On disabled list (July 31-August 7, 1999). ... On Ottawa disabled list (August 4-September 6, 2001).
HONORS: Named Eastern League Most Valuable Player (1999).
STATISTICAL NOTES: Led Eastern League with 276 total bases in 1999. ... Career major league grand slams: 1.

Year	Team (League)	Pos.	G	AB	R	H	2B	3B	HR	RBI	Avg.	BB	SO	SB	PO	A	E	Avg.
1996—	Vermont (NY-Penn)	1B-3B	57	175	26	47	11	1	4	24	.269	32	37	1	426	33	6	.987
1997—	Cape Fear (S.Atl.)	1B	59	210	31	63	9	2	8	43	.300	21	47	6	483	37	8	.985
1998—	Jupiter (FSL)	1B-3B	71	251	37	67	16	1	11	53	.267	39	69	6	638	51	5	.993
	— Harrisburg (East.)	1B-OF	62	211	33	48	12	3	10	33	.227	24	62	1	481	36	6	.989
1999—	Harrisburg (East.)	3B-1B-OF	134	493	96	135	26	2	37	*128	.274	70	139	6	227	200	25	.945
2000—	Ottawa (I.L.)	1B-3B	55	195	28	60	18	0	10	36	.308	34	63	2	367	56	6	.986
	— Montreal (N.L.)	3B-1B	83	192	29	50	8	1	11	32	.260	22	61	1	187	46	6	.975
2001—	Montreal (N.L.)	3B-1B-DH	38	55	4	6	1	0	2	8	.109	6	26	0	16	12	0	1.000
	— Ottawa (I.L.)	3B-1B	53	190	17	39	11	1	4	19	.205	24	72	4	98	89	8	.959
Major League totals (2 years)			121	247	33	56	9	1	13	40	.227	28	87	1	203	58	6	.978

PERSONAL: Born November 6, 1971, in Knoxville, Tenn. ... 6-2/220. ... Bats right, throws right. ... Full name: Thomas Bubba Trammell.
HIGH SCHOOL: Knoxville (Tenn.) Central.
JUNIOR COLLEGE: Cleveland (Tenn.) State Community College.
COLLEGE: Tennessee.
TRANSACTIONS/CAREER NOTES: Selected by Detroit Tigers organization in 11th round of free-agent draft (June 2, 1994). ... Selected by Tampa Bay Devil Rays in first round (22nd pick overall) of expansion draft (November 18, 1997). ... On Durham disabled list (May 17-25, 1999). ... Traded by Devil Rays with P Rick White to New York Mets for OF Jason Tyner and P Paul Wilson (July 28, 2000). ... Traded by Mets to San Diego Padres for P Donne Wall (December 11, 2001).
STATISTICAL NOTES: Career major league grand slams: 2.

Year Team (League)	Pos.	G	AB	R	H	2B	3B	HR	RBI	Avg.	BB	SO	SB	PO	A	E	Avg.
1994— Jamestown (NY-P)	OF	65	235	37	70	18	6	5	41	.298	23	32	9	77	3	5	.941
1995— Lakeland (FSL)	OF	122	454	61	129	32	6	16	72	.284	48	80	13	176	7	5	.973
1996— Jacksonville (Sou.)	OF	83	311	63	102	23	2	27	75	.328	32	61	3	100	6	5	.955
— Toledo (I.L.)	OF	51	180	32	53	14	1	6	24	.294	22	44	5	72	5	1	.987
1997— Detroit (A.L.)	OF-DH	44	123	14	28	5	0	4	13	.228	15	35	3	52	1	0	1.000
— Toledo (I.L.)	OF-DH	90	319	56	80	15	1	28	75	.251	38	91	2	103	3	3	.972
1998— Tampa Bay (A.L.)■	OF-DH	59	199	28	57	18	1	12	35	.286	16	45	0	50	3	0	1.000
— Durham (I.L.)	OF	57	217	46	63	12	0	16	48	.290	38	42	6	110	5	2	.983
1999— Durham (I.L.)	OF-DH-3B	47	186	25	50	12	0	7	31	.269	15	36	0	65	8	3	.961
— Tampa Bay (A.L.)	OF-DH	82	283	49	82	19	0	14	39	.290	43	37	0	142	2	1	.993
2000— Tampa Bay (A.L.)	OF-DH	66	189	19	52	11	2	7	33	.275	21	30	3	66	2	0	1.000
— New York (N.L.)	OF	36	56	9	13	2	0	3	12	.232	8	19	1	25	1	1	.963
2001— San Diego (N.L.)■	OF-DH	142	490	66	128	20	3	25	92	.261	48	78	2	261	5	4	.985
American League totals (4 years)		251	794	110	219	53	3	37	120	.276	95	147	6	310	8	1	.997
National League totals (2 years)		178	546	75	141	22	3	28	104	.258	56	97	3	286	6	5	.983
Major League totals (5 years)		429	1340	185	360	75	6	65	224	.269	151	244	9	596	14	6	.990

DIVISION SERIES RECORD

Year Team (League)	Pos.	G	AB	R	H	2B	3B	HR	RBI	Avg.	BB	SO	SB	PO	A	E	Avg.
2000— New York (N.L.)						Did not play.											

CHAMPIONSHIP SERIES RECORD

Year Team (League)	Pos.	G	AB	R	H	2B	3B	HR	RBI	Avg.	BB	SO	SB	PO	A	E	Avg.
2000— New York (N.L.)	PH	3	3	0	0	0	0	0	0	.000	0	2	0	...	...	...	...

WORLD SERIES RECORD

Year Team (League)	Pos.	G	AB	R	H	2B	3B	HR	RBI	Avg.	BB	SO	SB	PO	A	E	Avg.
2000— New York (N.L.)	PH-OF	4	5	1	2	0	0	0	3	.400	1	1	0	3	0	1	.750

PERSONAL: Born April 14, 1967, in Springfield, Mass. ... 6-2/204. ... Throws right, bats right. ... Full name: Michael Scott Trombley.
HIGH SCHOOL: Minnechaug Regional (Wilbraham, Mass.).
COLLEGE: Duke.
TRANSACTIONS/CAREER NOTES: Selected by Minnesota Twins organization in 14th round of free-agent draft (June 5, 1989). ... Granted free agency (October 29, 1999). ... Signed by Baltimore Orioles (November 18, 1999). ... Traded by Orioles to Los Angeles Dodgers for P Kris Foster and C Geronimo Gil (July 31, 2001).
STATISTICAL NOTES: Pitched 3-0 no-hit victory against Knoxville (August 8, 1991). ... Led Pacific Coast League with 18 home runs allowed in 1992.

Year League	W	L	Pct.	ERA	G	GS	CG	ShO	Sv.	IP	H	R	ER	BB	SO
1989— Kenosha (Midw.)	5	1	.833	3.12	12	3	0	0	2	49	45	23	17	13	41
— Visalia (Calif.)	2	2	.500	2.14	6	6	2	1	0	42	31	12	10	11	36
1990— Visalia (Calif.)	14	6	.700	3.43	27	25	3	1	0	176	163	79	67	50	164
1991— Orlando (Sou.)	12	7	.632	2.54	27	27	7	2	0	*191	153	65	54	57	*175
1992— Portland (PCL)	10	8	.556	3.65	25	25	2	0	0	165	149	70	67	58	*138
— Minnesota (A.L.)	3	2	.600	3.30	10	7	0	0	0	46 1/3	43	20	17	17	38
1993— Minnesota (A.L.)	6	6	.500	4.88	44	10	0	0	2	114 1/3	131	72	62	41	85
1994— Minnesota (A.L.)	2	0	1.000	6.33	24	0	0	0	0	48 1/3	56	36	34	18	32
— Salt Lake (PCL)	4	4	.500	5.04	11	10	0	0	0	60 2/3	75	37	34	20	63
1995— Salt Lake (PCL)	5	3	.625	3.62	12	12	0	0	0	69 2/3	71	32	28	26	59
— Minnesota (A.L.)	4	8	.333	5.62	20	18	0	0	0	97 2/3	107	68	61	42	68
1996— Salt Lake (PCL)	2	2	.500	2.45	24	0	0	0	10	36 2/3	24	12	10	10	38
— Minnesota (A.L.)	5	1	.833	3.01	43	0	0	0	6	68 2/3	61	24	23	25	57
1997— Minnesota (A.L.)	2	3	.400	4.37	67	0	0	0	1	82 1/3	77	43	40	31	74
1998— Minnesota (A.L.)	6	5	.545	3.63	77	1	0	0	1	96 2/3	90	41	39	41	89
1999— Minnesota (A.L.)	2	8	.200	4.33	75	0	0	0	24	87 1/3	93	42	42	28	82
2000— Baltimore (A.L.)■	4	5	.444	4.13	75	0	0	0	4	72	67	34	33	38	72
2001— Baltimore (A.L.)	3	4	.429	3.46	50	0	0	0	6	54 2/3	38	23	21	27	45
— Los Angeles (N.L.)■	0	4	.000	6.56	19	0	0	0	0	23 1/3	27	17	17	10	27
A.L. totals (10 years)	37	42	.468	4.36	485	36	0	0	44	768 1/3	763	403	372	308	642
N.L. totals (1 year)	0	4	.000	6.56	19	0	0	0	0	23 1/3	27	17	17	10	27
Major League totals (10 years)	37	46	.446	4.42	504	36	0	0	44	791 2/3	790	420	389	318	669

PERSONAL: Born December 9, 1973, in Palm Springs, Calif. ... 6-2/190. ... Bats right, throws right. ... Full name: Christopher John Truby.
HIGH SCHOOL: Damien (Hawaii).
TRANSACTIONS/CAREER NOTES: Signed as non-drafted free agent by Houston Astros organization (August 25, 1992). ... On disabled list (April 26-May 11, 1999).
STATISTICAL NOTES: Tied for Gulf Coast League lead with 21 errors by third basemen in 1993. ... Led New York-Pennsylvania League with 141 total bases and eight sacrifice flies in 1994. ... Led Midwest League third basemen with 279 assists and 26 double plays in 1995. ... Led Texas League with 12 sacrifice flies in 1999. ... Led Texas League third baseman with 93 putouts, 35 double plays and a .950 fielding percentage in 1999. ... Career major league grand slams: 1.

							BATTING								FIELDING		
Year	Team (League)	Pos.	G	AB	R	H	2B	3B	HR	RBI	Avg.	BB	SO	SB	PO	A	E	Avg.
1993—	GC Astros (GCL)	3B-SS	57	215	30	49	10	2	1	24	.228	22	30	16	42	158	‡26	.885
	— Osceola (FSL)........	3B	3	13	0	0	0	0	0	0	.000	0	2	0	3	9	2	.857
1994—	Quad City (Midw.)	3B-1B	36	111	12	24	4	1	2	19	.216	3	29	1	54	29	6	.933
	— Auburn (NY-Penn).....	3B	73	282	*56	*91	17	6	7	*61	.323	23	48	20	48	153	•27	.882
1995—	Quad City (Midw.)	3B-OF	118	400	68	93	23	4	9	64	.233	41	66	27	73	†279	38	.903
1996—	Quad City (Midw.)	1B-3B	109	362	45	91	15	3	8	37	.251	28	74	6	545	128	17	.975
1997—	Quad City (Midw.)	3B	68	268	34	75	14	1	7	46	.280	22	32	13	39	149	15	.926
	— Kissimmee (FSL)........	3B-1B-SS-2B	57	199	23	49	11	0	2	29	.246	8	40	8	52	122	16	.916
1998—	Kissimmee (FSL)......	3B	52	212	36	66	16	1	14	48	.311	19	30	6	45	130	9	.951
	— Jackson (Texas)......	3B-1B	80	308	46	89	20	5	16	63	.289	20	50	8	94	161	15	.944
	— New Orleans (PCL).....	3B	5	17	6	7	1	1	1	1	.412	1	3	1	4	7	1	.917
1999—	Jackson (Texas)......	3B-SS	124	465	78	131	21	3	28	87	.282	36	88	20	†95	275	20	†.949
2000—	Houston (N.L.)	3B	78	268	28	67	15	4	11	59	.260	10	56	2	51	125	14	.926
	— New Orleans (PCL).....	3B	64	268	31	76	11	3	2	30	.284	17	32	6	46	151	12	.943
2001—	Houston (N.L.)	3B-1B	48	136	11	28	6	1	8	23	.206	13	38	1	18	55	6	.924
	— New Orleans (PCL).....	3B-1B	81	321	53	100	25	6	12	71	.312	24	66	10	279	120	11	.973
Major League totals (2 years)			**126**	**394**	**39**	**95**	**21**	**5**	**19**	**82**	**.241**	**23**	**94**	**3**	**69**	**180**	**20**	**.926**

DIVISION SERIES RECORD

							BATTING								FIELDING		
Year	Team (League)	Pos.	G	AB	R	H	2B	3B	HR	RBI	Avg.	BB	SO	SB	PO	A	E	Avg.
2001—	Houston (N.L.)	PH	1	1	0	0	0	0	0	0	.000	0	1	0	...	...	...	...

PERSONAL: Born June 25, 1971, in South Boston, Va. ... 6-2/185. ... Bats left, throws right. ... Full name: Michael Anthony Tucker.
HIGH SCHOOL: Bluestone (Skipwith, Va.).
COLLEGE: Longwood (Va.).
TRANSACTIONS/CAREER NOTES: Selected by Kansas City Royals organization in first round (10th pick overall) of free-agent draft (June 1, 1992). ... On Kansas City disabled list (June 4-21 and August 28, 1996-remainder of season); included rehabilitation assignment to Wichita (June 15-21). ... Traded by Royals with IF Keith Lockhart to Atlanta Braves for OF Jermaine Dye and P Jamie Walker (March 27, 1997). ... Traded by Braves with P Denny Neagle and P Rob Bell to Cincinnati Reds for 2B Bret Boone and P Mike Remlinger (November 10, 1998). ... Traded by Reds to Chicago Cubs for P Chris Booker and P Ben Shaffar (July 20, 2001). ... Traded by Cubs to Royals for a player to be named later (December 19, 2001).
STATISTICAL NOTES: Tied for Carolina League lead with four intentional bases on balls received in 1994.

							BATTING								FIELDING		
Year	Team (League)	Pos.	G	AB	R	H	2B	3B	HR	RBI	Avg.	BB	SO	SB	PO	A	E	Avg.
1993—	Wilmington (Caro.).....	2B	61	239	42	73	14	2	6	44	.305	34	49	12	120	157	10	.965
	— Memphis (Sou.)	2B	72	244	38	68	7	4	9	35	.279	42	51	12	153	176	13	.962
1994—	Omaha (A.A.).............	OF	132	485	75	134	16	7	21	77	.276	69	111	11	196	11	•7	.967
1995—	Kansas City (A.L.)	OF-DH	62	177	23	46	10	0	4	17	.260	18	51	2	67	3	1	.986
	— Omaha (A.A.).............	OF	71	275	37	84	18	4	4	28	.305	24	39	11	133	11	2	.986
1996—	Kansas City (A.L.)	OF-1B-DH	108	339	55	88	18	4	12	53	.260	40	69	10	235	8	2	.992
	— Wichita (Texas)	OF-1B	6	20	4	9	1	3	0	7	.450	5	4	0	17	1	0	1.000
1997—	Atlanta (N.L.)■..........	OF	138	499	80	141	25	7	14	56	.283	44	116	12	237	6	5	.980
1998—	Atlanta (N.L.).............	OF	130	414	54	101	27	3	13	46	.244	49	112	8	194	5	1	.995
1999—	Cincinnati (N.L.)■.....	OF	133	296	55	75	8	5	11	44	.253	37	81	11	182	8	2	.990
2000—	Cincinnati (N.L.)	OF-2B	148	270	55	72	13	4	15	36	.267	44	64	13	153	5	5	.969
2001—	Cincinnati (N.L.)	OF	86	231	31	56	10	1	7	30	.242	23	55	12	126	7	3	.978
	— Chicago (N.L.)■........	OF-1B	63	205	31	54	9	7	5	31	.263	23	47	4	125	8	3	.978
American League totals (2 years)			**170**	**516**	**78**	**134**	**28**	**4**	**16**	**70**	**.260**	**58**	**120**	**12**	**302**	**11**	**3**	**.991**
National League totals (5 years)			**698**	**1915**	**306**	**499**	**92**	**27**	**65**	**243**	**.261**	**220**	**475**	**60**	**1017**	**39**	**19**	**.982**
Major League totals (7 years)			**868**	**2431**	**384**	**633**	**120**	**31**	**81**	**313**	**.260**	**278**	**595**	**72**	**1319**	**50**	**22**	**.984**

DIVISION SERIES RECORD

							BATTING								FIELDING		
Year	Team (League)	Pos.	G	AB	R	H	2B	3B	HR	RBI	Avg.	BB	SO	SB	PO	A	E	Avg.
1997—	Atlanta (N.L.)..............	OF	2	6	0	1	0	0	1	1	.167	0	1	0	3	0	0	1.000
1998—	Atlanta (N.L.)..............	OF	3	8	1	2	0	0	1	2	.250	2	0	1	6	0	0	1.000
Division series totals (2 years)			**5**	**14**	**1**	**3**	**0**	**0**	**1**	**3**	**.214**	**2**	**1**	**1**	**9**	**0**	**0**	**1.000**

CHAMPIONSHIP SERIES RECORD

							BATTING								FIELDING		
Year	Team (League)	Pos.	G	AB	R	H	2B	3B	HR	RBI	Avg.	BB	SO	SB	PO	A	E	Avg.
1997—	Atlanta (N.L.)..............	OF-PH	5	10	1	1	0	0	1	1	.100	3	4	0	5	1	0	1.000
1998—	Atlanta (N.L.)..............	OF-PH	6	13	1	5	1	0	1	5	.385	2	5	0	7	0	0	1.000
Championship series totals (2 years)			**11**	**23**	**2**	**6**	**1**	**0**	**2**	**6**	**.261**	**5**	**9**	**0**	**12**	**1**	**0**	**1.000**

TUCKER, T.J.   P   EXPOS

PERSONAL: Born August 20, 1978, in Clearwater, Fla. ... 6-3/245. ... Throws right, bats right. ... Full name: Thomas John Tucker.
HIGH SCHOOL: River Ridge (New Port Richey, Fla.).
TRANSACTIONS/CAREER NOTES: Selected by Montreal Expos organization in supplemental round ("sandwich pick" between first and second round, 47th pick overall) of free-agent draft (June 3, 1997); pick received as compensation for Chicago Cubs signing P Mel Rojas. ... On Harrisburg disabled list (April 6-23, 2000). ... On Montreal disabled list (June 10, 2000-remainder of season). ... On Harrisburg disabled list (May 25-June 6, 2001).

Year League	W	L	Pct.	ERA	G	GS	CG	ShO	Sv.	IP	H	R	ER	BB	SO
1997—Gulf Coast Expos (GCL)	1	0	1.000	1.93	3	2	0	0	0	4 2/3	5	1	1	1	11
1998—Gulf Coast Expos (GCL)	1	0	1.000	0.75	7	7	0	0	0	36	23	5	3	5	40
— Vermont (NY-Penn)	3	1	.750	2.18	6	6	0	0	0	33	24	9	8	15	34
— Jupiter (FSL)	1	1	.500	1.00	2	1	0	0	0	9	5	1	1	0	10
1999—Jupiter (FSL)	5	1	.833	1.23	7	7	0	0	0	44	24	7	6	16	35
— Harrisburg (East.)	8	5	.615	4.10	19	19	1	1	0	116 1/3	110	55	53	38	85
2000—Harrisburg (East.)	2	1	.667	3.60	8	8	0	0	0	45	33	19	18	17	24
— Montreal (N.L.)	0	1	.000	11.57	2	2	0	0	0	7	11	9	9	3	2
2001—Harrisburg (East.)	5	5	.500	3.73	13	13	0	0	0	82	77	38	34	37	57
— Ottawa (I.L.)	3	5	.375	3.11	14	14	1	0	0	84	68	42	29	33	63
Major League totals (1 year)	0	1	.000	11.57	2	2	0	0	0	7	11	9	9	3	2

TURNBOW, DERRICK   P   ANGELS

PERSONAL: Born January 25, 1978, in Union City, Tenn. ... 6-3/180. ... Throws right, bats right. ... Full name: Thomas Derrick Turnbow.
HIGH SCHOOL: Franklin (Tenn.).
TRANSACTIONS/CAREER NOTES: Selected by Philadelphia Phillies organization in fifth round of free-agent draft (June 3, 1997). ... Selected by Anaheim Angels from Phillies organization in Rule 5 major league draft (December 13, 1999). ... On disabled list (April 20, 2001-remainder of season).

Year League	W	L	Pct.	ERA	G	GS	CG	ShO	Sv.	IP	H	R	ER	BB	SO
1997—Martinsville (Appl.)	1	3	.250	7.40	7	7	0	0	0	24 1/3	34	29	20	16	7
1998—Martinsville (Appl.)	2	6	.250	5.01	13	13	1	0	0	70	66	44	39	26	45
1999—Piedmont (S.Atl.)	12	8	.600	3.35	26	26	•4	1	0	161	130	67	60	53	149
2000—Anaheim (A.L.)■	0	0	...	4.74	24	1	0	0	0	38	36	21	20	36	25
2001—Arkansas (Texas)	0	0	...	2.57	3	3	0	0	0	14	12	4	4	5	11
Major League totals (1 year)	0	0	...	4.74	24	1	0	0	0	38	36	21	20	36	25

TYNER, JASON   OF   DEVIL RAYS

PERSONAL: Born April 23, 1977, in Beaumont, Texas. ... 6-1/170. ... Bats left, throws left. ... Full name: Jason Renyt Tyner.
HIGH SCHOOL: Westbrook (Beaumont, Texas).
COLLEGE: Texas A&M.
TRANSACTIONS/CAREER NOTES: Selected by New York Mets organization in first round (21st pick overall) of free-agent draft (June 2, 1998). ... Traded by Mets with P Paul Wilson to Tampa Bay Devil Rays for P Rick White and OF Bubba Trammell (July 28, 2000).

Year Team (League)	Pos.	G	AB	R	H	2B	3B	HR	RBI	Avg.	BB	SO	SB	PO	A	E	Avg.
1998—St. Lucie (FSL)	OF	50	201	30	61	2	3	0	16	.303	17	20	15	80	0	2	.976
1999—Binghamton (East.)	OF	129	518	91	162	19	5	0	33	.313	62	46	49	255	11	2	.993
— Norfolk (I.L.)	OF	3	8	0	0	0	0	0	0	.000	0	5	0	4	0	0	1.000
2000—Norfolk (I.L.)	OF	84	327	54	105	5	2	0	28	.321	30	32	33	188	5	1	.995
— New York (N.L.)	OF	13	41	3	8	2	0	0	5	.195	1	4	1	22	1	2	.920
— Tampa Bay (A.L.)■	OF-DH	37	83	6	20	2	0	0	8	.241	4	12	6	51	4	0	1.000
2001—Durham (I.L.)	OF	39	157	25	49	2	1	0	12	.312	15	10	11	88	2	0	1.000
— Tampa Bay (A.L.)	OF	105	396	51	111	8	5	0	21	.280	15	42	31	219	8	5	.978
American League totals (2 years)		142	479	57	131	10	5	0	29	.273	19	54	37	270	12	5	.983
National League totals (1 year)		13	41	3	8	2	0	0	5	.195	1	4	1	22	1	2	.920
Major League totals (2 years)		155	520	60	139	12	5	0	34	.267	20	58	38	292	13	7	.978

URBAN, JEFF   P   GIANTS

PERSONAL: Born January 25, 1977, in Anderson, Ind. ... 6-8/215. ... Throws right, bats left. ... Full name: Jeffrey Thomas Urban.
HIGH SCHOOL: Alexandria (Ind.).
COLLEGE: Ball State.
TRANSACTIONS/CAREER NOTES: Selected by San Francisco Giants organization in supplemental round ("sandwich pick" between first and second round, 41st pick overall) of free-agent draft (June 2, 1998); pick received as part of compensation for Tampa Bay Devil Rays signing Type A free-agent P Wilson Alvarez. ... On disabled list (April 6, 2000-entire season).

Year League	W	L	Pct.	ERA	G	GS	CG	ShO	Sv.	IP	H	R	ER	BB	SO
1998—Salem-Kaizer (N'West)	1	2	.333	4.98	5	3	0	0	0	21 2/3	21	14	12	8	22
— San Jose (Calif.)	4	0	1.000	3.52	4	4	0	0	0	23	27	13	9	5	23
1999—Shreveport (Texas)	2	7	.222	5.81	14	14	0	0	0	69 2/3	100	54	45	19	54
— San Jose (Calif.)	8	5	.615	3.76	15	13	0	0	0	81 1/3	78	41	34	18	89
2000—Shreveport (Texas)							Did not play.								
2001—Shreveport (Texas)	7	11	.389	3.91	27	27	0	0	0	156 2/3	178	85	68	32	117

URBINA, UGUETH   P   RED SOX

PERSONAL: Born February 15, 1974, in Caracas, Venezuela. ... 6-0/205. ... Throws right, bats right. ... Full name: Ugueth Urtain Urbina. ... Name pronounced OOO-get.

HIGH SCHOOL: Liceo Peres Bonalde de Miranda (Miranda, Venezuela).

TRANSACTIONS/CAREER NOTES: Signed as non-drafted free agent by Montreal Expos organization (July 2, 1990). ... On disabled list (April 8-17, 1994). ... On temporarily inactive list (May 9-June 6, 1994). ... On Ottawa disabled list (August 10-September 14, 1995). ... On disabled list (May 9, 2000-remainder of season). ... Traded by Expos to Boston Red Sox for P Tomo Ohka and P Rich Rundles (July 31, 2001).

HONORS: Named N.L. Fireman of the Year by THE SPORTING NEWS (1999).

Year League	W	L	Pct.	ERA	G	GS	CG	ShO	Sv.	IP	H	R	ER	BB	SO
1991—Gulf Coast Expos (GCL)	3	3	.500	2.29	10	10	3	•1	0	63	58	24	16	10	51
1992—Albany (S.Atl.)	7	•13	.350	3.22	24	24	5	2	0	142 1/3	111	68	51	54	100
1993—Burlington (Midw.)	2	3	.400	4.50	10	8	0	0	0	46	41	31	23	22	30
—Harrisburg (East.)	4	5	.444	3.99	11	11	3	1	0	70	66	32	31	32	45
1994—Harrisburg (East.)	9	3	.750	3.28	21	21	0	0	0	120 2/3	95	49	44	43	86
1995—West Palm Beach (FSL)	1	0	1.000	0.00	2	2	0	0	0	9	4	0	0	1	11
—Ottawa (I.L.)	6	2	.750	3.04	13	11	2	1	0	68	46	26	23	26	55
—Montreal (N.L.)	2	2	.500	6.17	7	4	0	0	0	23 1/3	26	17	16	14	15
1996—West Palm Beach (FSL)	1	1	.500	1.29	3	3	0	0	0	14	13	3	2	3	21
—Ottawa (I.L.)	2	0	1.000	2.66	5	5	0	0	0	23 2/3	17	9	7	6	28
—Montreal (N.L.)	10	5	.667	3.71	33	17	0	0	0	114	102	54	47	44	108
1997—Montreal (N.L.)	5	8	.385	3.78	63	0	0	0	27	64 1/3	52	29	27	29	84
1998—Montreal (N.L.)	6	3	.667	1.30	64	0	0	0	34	69 1/3	37	11	10	33	94
1999—Montreal (N.L.)	6	6	.500	3.69	71	0	0	0	*41	75 2/3	59	35	31	36	100
2000—Montreal (N.L.)	0	1	.000	4.05	13	0	0	0	8	13 1/3	11	6	6	5	22
2001—Montreal (N.L.)	2	1	.667	4.24	45	0	0	0	15	46 2/3	42	24	22	21	57
—Boston (A.L.)■	0	1	.000	2.25	19	0	0	0	9	20	16	5	5	3	32
A.L. totals (1 year)	0	1	.000	2.25	19	0	0	0	9	20	16	5	5	3	32
N.L. totals (7 years)	31	26	.544	3.52	296	21	0	0	125	406 2/3	329	176	159	182	480
Major League totals (7 years)	31	27	.534	3.46	315	21	0	0	134	426 2/3	345	181	164	185	512

ALL-STAR GAME RECORD

Year League	W	L	Pct.	ERA	GS	CG	ShO	Sv.	IP	H	R	ER	BB	SO
1998—National	0	1	.000	27.00	0	0	0	0	1	3	3	3	1	2

URIBE, JUAN   SS   ROCKIES

PERSONAL: Born July 22, 1980, in Bani, Dominican Republic. ... 5-11/175. ... Bats right, throws right. ... Full name: Juan C. Uribe.

HIGH SCHOOL: Abel Uribe (Dominican Republic).

TRANSACTIONS/CAREER NOTES: Signed as non-drafted free agent by Colorado Rockies organization (January 15, 1997).

STATISTICAL NOTES: Led South Atlantic League shortstops with 615 total chances and 72 double plays in 1999.

						BATTING								FIELDING			
Year Team (League)	Pos.	G	AB	R	H	2B	3B	HR	RBI	Avg.	BB	SO	SB	PO	A	E	Avg.
1997—DSL Rockies (DSL)		65	234	32	63	12	6	0	29	.269	31	22	7	...	...	...	...
1998—Ariz. Rockies (Ariz.)	SS	40	148	25	41	5	3	0	17	.277	12	25	8	55	122	14	.927
1999—Asheville (S.Atl.)	SS	125	430	57	115	28	3	9	46	.267	20	79	11	187	*390	38	.938
2000—Salem (Caro.)	SS	134	485	64	124	22	7	13	65	.256	38	100	22	213	428	26	.961
2001—Carolina (Sou.)	SS	3	13	1	3	1	0	0	1	.231	0	4	1	4	6	2	.833
—Colorado (N.L.)	SS	72	273	32	82	15	11	8	53	.300	8	55	3	108	184	5	.983
—Colo. Springs (PCL)	SS	74	281	40	87	27	7	7	48	.310	12	43	11	156	230	16	.960
Major League totals (1 year)		72	273	32	82	15	11	8	53	.300	8	55	3	108	184	5	.983

VALDERRAMA, CARLOS   OF   GIANTS

PERSONAL: Born November 30, 1977, in Bachaquero, Venezuela. ... 6-3/186. ... Bats right, throws right. ... Full name: Carlos Alberto Valderrama.

TRANSACTIONS/CAREER NOTES: Signed as non-drafted free agent by San Francisco Giants organization (February 23, 1995). ... On disabled list (May 23-September 3, 2001).

						BATTING								FIELDING			
Year Team (League)	Pos.	G	AB	R	H	2B	3B	HR	RBI	Avg.	BB	SO	SB	PO	A	E	Avg.
1995—Dom. Giants (DSL)	OF	22	57	7	13	1	0	0	4	.228	6	10	1	32	0	0	1.000
1996—Dom. Giants (DSL)	OF	46	166	29	37	4	1	0	11	.223	29	24	6	...	...	...	...
1997—Salem-Kaizer (NW)	OF	41	138	21	44	7	3	3	28	.319	12	29	22	25	1	1	.963
1998—Salem-Kaizer (NW)	OF	7	29	5	10	1	0	0	4	.345	1	7	4	3	0	0	1.000
1999—San Jose (Calif.)	OF	26	90	12	23	2	0	0	12	.256	4	19	8	32	4	0	1.000
—Salem-Kaizer (NW)	OF	40	134	27	39	3	1	2	18	.291	12	34	17	66	7	2	.973
2000—Bakersfield (Calif.)	OF	121	435	78	137	21	5	13	81	.315	39	96	54	199	8	6	.972
2001—Shreveport (Texas)	OF	41	159	29	49	12	2	1	8	.308	18	29	11	85	3	0	1.000

VALDES, ISMAEL   P

PERSONAL: Born August 21, 1973, in Victoria, Mexico. ... 6-4/225. ... Throws right, bats right.

HIGH SCHOOL: Mexico (Ciudad Victoria).

TRANSACTIONS/CAREER NOTES: Signed as non-drafted free agent by Los Angeles Dodgers (June 14, 1991). ... Loaned by Dodgers organization to Mexico City Tigers of Mexican League (April 21-June 26, 1992; and March 17-August 19, 1993). ... On disabled list (July 6-28, 1997). ... On Los Angeles disabled list (July 26-September 1, 1998); included rehabilitation assignments to Vero Beach (August 22) and San Bernardino (August 27). ... Traded by Dodgers with 2B Eric Young to Chicago Cubs for P Terry Adams, P Chad Ricketts and a player to be named later (December 12, 1999); Dodgers acquired P Brian Stephenson to complete deal (December 16, 1999). ... On Chicago disabled list (March 20-May 4, 2000); included rehabilitation assignment to Daytona (April 29-May 1). ... Traded by Cubs to Dodgers for P Jamie Arnold, OF Jorge Piedra and cash (July 26, 2000). ... On suspended list (September 12-18, 2000). ... Granted free agency (October 30, 2000). ... Signed by Anaheim Angels (January 4, 2001). ... On disabled list (March 29-April 14 and June 15-July 4, 2001). ... Granted free agency (November 5, 2001).

STATISTICAL NOTES: Led N.L. with five balks in 1996. ... Pitched 2-0 one-hit, complete-game victory against Pittsburgh (June 27, 1998).
MISCELLANEOUS: Had sacrifice hit in only appearance as pinch hitter (2000).

Year League	W	L	Pct.	ERA	G	GS	CG	ShO	Sv.	IP	H	R	ER	BB	SO
1991—Gulf Coast Dodgers (GCL)..	2	2	.500	2.32	10	10	0	0	0	50 1/3	44	15	13	13	44
1992—M.C. Tigres (Mex.)■	0	0	...	19.64	5	0	0	0	0	3 2/3	15	9	8	1	2
—La Vega (DSL)■	3	0	1.000	1.42	6	0	0	0	0	38	27	9	6	17	34
1993—M.C. Tigres (Mex.)■	16	7	.696	3.94	26	25	11	1	0	173 2/3	192	87	76	55	113
—San Antonio (Texas)■	1	0	1.000	1.38	3	2	0	0	0	13	12	2	2	0	11
1994—San Antonio (Texas)	2	3	.400	3.38	8	8	0	0	0	53 1/3	54	22	20	9	55
—Albuquerque (PCL)	4	1	.800	3.40	8	8	0	0	0	45	44	21	17	13	39
—Los Angeles (N.L.)	3	1	.750	3.18	21	1	0	0	0	28 1/3	21	10	10	10	28
1995—Los Angeles (N.L.)	13	11	.542	3.05	33	27	6	2	1	197 2/3	168	76	67	51	150
1996—Los Angeles (N.L.)	15	7	.682	3.32	33	33	0	0	0	225	219	94	83	54	173
1997—Los Angeles (N.L.)	10	11	.476	2.65	30	30	0	0	0	196 2/3	171	68	58	47	140
1998—Los Angeles (N.L.)	11	10	.524	3.98	27	27	2	2	0	174	171	82	77	66	122
—Vero Beach (FSL)	0	0	...	0.00	1	1	0	0	0	3	2	0	0	1	3
—San Bernardino (Calif.)	1	0	1.000	2.84	1	1	0	0	0	6 1/3	7	2	2	1	4
1999—Los Angeles (N.L.)	9	14	.391	3.98	32	32	2	1	0	203 1/3	213	97	90	58	143
2000—Daytona (FSL)■	1	0	1.000	1.80	1	1	0	0	0	5	3	2	1	3	5
—Chicago (N.L.)	2	4	.333	5.37	12	12	0	0	0	67	71	40	40	27	45
—Los Angeles (N.L.)■	0	3	.000	6.07	9	8	0	0	0	40	53	29	27	13	29
2001—Anaheim (A.L.)■	9	13	.409	4.45	27	27	1	0	0	163 2/3	177	82	81	50	100
A.L. totals (1 year)	9	13	.409	4.45	27	27	1	0	0	163 2/3	177	82	81	50	100
N.L. totals (7 years)	63	61	.508	3.59	197	170	10	5	1	1132	1087	496	452	326	830
Major League totals (8 years)	72	74	.493	3.70	224	197	11	5	1	1295 2/3	1264	578	533	376	930

DIVISION SERIES RECORD

Year League	W	L	Pct.	ERA	G	GS	CG	ShO	Sv.	IP	H	R	ER	BB	SO
1995—Los Angeles (N.L.)	0	0	...	0.00	1	1	0	0	0	7	3	2	0	1	6
1996—Los Angeles (N.L.)	0	1	.000	4.26	1	1	0	0	0	6 1/3	5	3	3	0	5
Division series totals (2 years)	0	1	.000	2.03	2	2	0	0	0	13 1/3	8	5	3	1	11

VALDES, MARC   P

PERSONAL: Born December 20, 1971, in Dayton, Ohio. ... 6-0/185. ... Throws right, bats right. ... Full name: Marc Christopher Valdes.
HIGH SCHOOL: Jesuit (Tampa).
COLLEGE: Florida.
TRANSACTIONS/CAREER NOTES: Selected by Cincinnati Reds organization in 20th round of free-agent draft (June 4, 1990); did not sign. ... Selected by Florida Marlins organization in first round (27th pick overall) of free-agent draft (June 3, 1993). ... Claimed on waivers by Montreal Expos (December 12, 1996). ... On disabled list (May 27-June 11 and June 23, 1998-remainder of season). ... Granted free agency (December 21, 1998). ... Signed by Tampa Bay Devil Rays organization (January 20, 1999). ... On Durham disabled list (April 8-June 18, 1999). ... Granted free agency (October 15, 1999). ... Re-signed by Devil Rays organization (January 14, 2000). ... Traded by Devil Rays to Houston Astros for 3B Russ Johnson (May 27, 2000). ... Granted free agency (December 21, 2000). ... Signed by Atlanta Braves organization (January 12, 2001). ... Granted free agency (December 21, 2001).

Year League	W	L	Pct.	ERA	G	GS	CG	ShO	Sv.	IP	H	R	ER	BB	SO
1993—Elmira (NY-Penn)	0	2	.000	5.59	3	3	0	0	0	9 2/3	8	9	6	7	15
1994—Kane County (Midw.)	7	4	.636	2.95	11	11	2	0	0	76 1/3	62	30	25	21	68
—Portland (East.)	8	4	.667	2.55	15	15	0	0	0	99	77	31	28	39	70
1995—Charlotte (I.L.)	9	•13	.409	4.86	27	27	3	2	0	170 1/3	189	98	•92	59	104
—Florida (N.L.)	0	0	...	14.14	3	3	0	0	0	7	17	13	11	9	2
1996—Charlotte (I.L.)	2	4	.333	5.12	8	8	1	0	0	51	66	32	29	15	24
—Portland (East.)	6	2	.750	2.66	10	10	1	0	0	64 1/3	60	25	19	12	49
—Florida (N.L.)	1	3	.250	4.81	11	8	0	0	0	48 2/3	63	32	26	23	13
1997—Montreal (N.L.)■	4	4	.500	3.13	48	7	0	0	2	95	84	36	33	39	54
1998—Montreal (N.L.)	1	3	.250	7.43	20	4	0	0	0	36 1/3	41	34	30	21	28
1999—Durham (I.L.)■	1	2	.333	5.18	9	9	0	0	0	40	39	25	23	12	23
—Orlando (Sou.)	0	1	1.000	5.87	2	2	0	0	0	7 2/3	7	5	5	2	5
2000—Durham (I.L.)	5	2	.714	4.15	9	9	0	0	0	47 2/3	52	25	22	17	25
—Houston (N.L.)■	5	5	.500	5.08	53	0	0	0	2	56 2/3	69	41	32	25	35
2001—Atlanta (N.L.)■	1	0	1.000	7.71	9	0	0	0	0	7	7	6	6	1	3
—Richmond (I.L.)	9	11	.450	4.51	29	21	0	0	2	123 2/3	133	67	62	41	97
Major League totals (6 years)	12	15	.444	4.95	144	22	0	0	4	250 2/3	281	162	138	118	135

VALDEZ, MARIO   1B/OF   ATHLETICS

PERSONAL: Born November 19, 1974, in Obregon, Mexico. ... 6-1/210. ... Bats left, throws right. ... Full name: Mario A. Valdez.
HIGH SCHOOL: Miami Senior.
JUNIOR COLLEGE: Miami-Dade (North) Community College.
TRANSACTIONS/CAREER NOTES: Selected by Chicago White Sox organization in 48th round of free-agent draft (June 3, 1993). ... On Charlotte disabled list (June 18-26 and July 25-August 1, 1999). ... Claimed on waivers by Minnesota Twins (September 29, 1999). ... Traded by Twins to Oakland Athletics for C Danny Ardoin (July 31, 2000). ... On Sacramento disabled list (July 31-August 7, 2000). ... On Oakland disabled list (September 8, 2000-remainder of season). ... On Oakland disabled list (May 14-June 8 and June 23, 2001-remainder of season); included rehabilitation assignment to Modesto (June 2-8).
STATISTICAL NOTES: Led Pacific Coast League first basemen with 14 errors in 1998.

Year	Team (League)	Pos.	G	AB	R	H	2B	3B	HR	RBI	Avg.	BB	SO	SB	PO	A	E	Avg.
								BATTING								FIELDING		
1994— GC White Sox (GCL) ..	1B-OF	53	157	20	37	11	2	2	25	.236	30	28	0	351	28	8	.979
1995— Hickory (S.Atl.)..........	1B	130	441	65	120	30	5	11	56	.272	67	107	9	1040	67	12	.989
1996— South Bend (Midw.) ...	1B	61	202	46	76	19	0	10	43	.376	36	42	2	438	41	8	.984
— Birmingham (Sou.).....	1B-OF	50	168	22	46	10	2	3	28	.274	32	34	0	284	26	2	.994
1997— Nashville (A.A.)	1B-DH	81	282	44	79	20	1	15	61	.280	43	77	1	616	44	6	.991
— Chicago (A.L.)	1B-DH-3B	54	115	11	28	7	0	1	13	.243	17	39	1	256	12	0	1.000
1998— Calgary (PCL).............	1B-DH-OF	123	448	86	148	32	0	20	81	.330	60	102	1	1003	75	†15	.986
1999— Charlotte (I.L.)	1B-OF-DH	121	402	78	110	17	2	26	76	.274	76	91	1	762	54	7	.991
2000— Salt Lake (PCL)■	1B	88	317	76	116	24	1	18	85	.366	57	46	1	353	34	5	.987
— Sacramento (PCL)■...	1B	17	61	11	14	3	0	2	11	.230	9	13	0	122	6	0	1.000
— Visalia (Calif.)	1B-OF-3B	1	2	0	1	0	0	0	0	.500	1	1	0	5	1	0	1.000
— Oakland (A.L.)	1B	5	12	0	0	0	0	0	0	.000	0	3	0	26	0	0	1.000
2001— Oakland (A.L.)	DH-1B	32	54	7	15	1	0	1	8	.278	12	18	0	25	1	0	1.000
— Modesto (Calif.)	OF	6	19	3	8	1	0	2	5	.421	2	1	0	2	0	0	1.000
Major League totals (3 years)		91	181	18	43	8	0	2	21	.238	29	60	1	307	15	0	1.000

VALENT, ERIC — OF — PHILLIES

PERSONAL: Born April 4, 1977, in La Mirada, Calif. ... 6-0/190. ... Bats left, throws left. ... Full name: Eric Christian Valent.
HIGH SCHOOL: Canyon (Anaheim, Calif.).
COLLEGE: UCLA.
TRANSACTIONS/CAREER NOTES: Selected by Detroit Tigers organization in 26th round of free-agent draft (June 1, 1995); did not sign. ... Selected by Philadelphia Phillies organization in supplemental round ('sandwich pick" between first and second round, 42nd pick overall) of free-agent draft (June 2, 1998); pick received for failure to sign 1997 first-round pick J.D. Drew.

Year	Team (League)	Pos.	G	AB	R	H	2B	3B	HR	RBI	Avg.	BB	SO	SB	PO	A	E	Avg.
								BATTING								FIELDING		
1998— Piedmont (S.Atl.)........	OF	22	89	24	38	12	0	8	28	.427	14	19	0	38	2	2	.952
— Clearwater (FSL)	OF	34	125	24	33	8	1	5	25	.264	16	29	1	57	6	0	1.000
1999— Clearwater (FSL)	OF	134	520	91	150	31	9	20	*106	.288	58	110	5	265	17	9	.969
2000— Reading (East.)	OF	128	469	81	121	22	5	22	90	.258	70	89	2	233	16	4	.984
2001— Scranton/W.B. (I.L.) ...	OF-1B	117	448	65	122	30	2	21	78	.272	49	105	0	364	27	3	.992
— Philadelphia (N.L.)......	OF-DH	22	41	3	4	2	0	0	1	.098	4	11	0	20	2	0	1.000
Major League totals (1 year)		22	41	3	4	2	0	0	1	.098	4	11	0	20	2	0	1.000

VALENTIN, JAVIER — C — TWINS

PERSONAL: Born September 19, 1975, in Manati, Puerto Rico. ... 5-10/192. ... Bats both, throws right. ... Full name: Jose Javier Valentin. ... Brother of Jose Valentin, shortstop, Chicago White Sox. ... Name pronounced VAL-un-TEEN.
HIGH SCHOOL: Fernando Callejo (Manati, Puerto Rico).
TRANSACTIONS/CAREER NOTES: Selected by Minnesota Twins organization in third round of free-agent draft (June 3, 1993). ... On disabled list (May 25-July 5 and September 4-20, 2000).
STATISTICAL NOTES: Led Appalachian League catchers with 48 assists and 348 total chances in 1993. ... Led Midwest League catchers with 730 putouts, 108 assists, 861 total chances, 23 errors and 11 double plays in 1995.

Year	Team (League)	Pos.	G	AB	R	H	2B	3B	HR	RBI	Avg.	BB	SO	SB	PO	A	E	Avg.
								BATTING								FIELDING		
1993— GC Twins (GCL).........	C-DH-3B	32	103	18	27	6	1	1	19	.262	14	19	0	120	23	5	.966
— Elizabethton (Appl.)...	C	9	24	3	5	1	0	0	3	.208	4	2	0	81	3	2	.977
1994— Elizabethton (Appl.)...	C-3B	54	210	23	44	5	0	9	27	.210	15	44	0	288	†50	12	.966
1995— Fort Wayne (Midw.)....	C-3B	112	383	59	124	26	5	19	65	.324	47	75	0	†736	†122	†23	.974
1996— Fort Myers (FSL)	C-DH-3B	87	338	34	89	26	1	7	54	.263	32	65	1	360	71	4	.991
— New Britain (East.)	C-3B-DH	48	165	22	39	8	0	3	14	.236	16	35	0	188	36	5	.978
1997— New Britain (East.)	C-DH-3B	102	370	41	90	17	0	8	50	.243	30	61	2	516	65	6	.990
— Minnesota (A.L.)	C	4	7	1	2	0	0	0	0	.286	1	3	0	11	2	0	1.000
1998— Minnesota (A.L.)	C-DH	55	162	11	32	7	1	3	18	.198	11	30	0	281	17	5	.983
1999— Minnesota (A.L.)	C	78	218	22	54	12	1	5	28	.248	22	39	0	387	27	1	.998
2000— Salt Lake (PCL)	C	39	140	25	50	16	2	7	35	.357	9	27	1	155	11	1	.994
2001— Edmonton (PCL)	C-3B-1B	121	431	53	121	29	2	17	71	.281	47	108	0	499	95	14	.977
Major League totals (3 years)		137	387	34	88	19	2	8	46	.227	33	72	0	679	46	6	.992

VALENTIN, JOHN — 3B

PERSONAL: Born February 18, 1967, in Mineola, N.Y. ... 6-0/185. ... Bats right, throws right. ... Full name: John William Valentin.
HIGH SCHOOL: St. Anthony (Jersey City, N.J.).
COLLEGE: Seton Hall.
TRANSACTIONS/CAREER NOTES: Selected by Boston Red Sox organization in fifth round of free-agent draft (June 1, 1988). ... On Boston disabled list (April 1-20, 1993); included rehabilitation assignment to Pawtucket (April 16-20). ... On Boston disabled list (May 4-June 6, 1994); included rehabilitation assignment to Pawtucket (May 31-June 6). ... On disabled list (August 3-18, 1996; and August 31-September 23, 1999; April 16-May 19 and May 31, 2000-remainder of season). ... On disabled list (April 6-May 19 and May 31, 2000-remainder of season). ... On Boston disabled list (March 21-May 9 and June 7, 2001-remainder of season); included rehabilitation assignments to Pawtucket (April 24-28, May 4-9 and June 26-28) and Trenton (April 29-May 3). ... Granted free agency (November 5, 2001).
HONORS: Named shortstop on THE SPORTING NEWS A.L. Silver Slugger team (1995).
STATISTICAL NOTES: Led New York-Pennsylvania League shortstops with .949 fielding percentage in 1988. ... Hit three home runs in one game (June 2, 1995). ... Led A.L. shortstops with 659 total chances in 1995. ... Hit for the cycle (June 6, 1996). ... Led A.L. third basemen with 121 putouts in 1998. ... Career major league grand slams: 4.
MISCELLANEOUS: Turned unassisted triple play while playing shortstop (July 8, 1994, sixth inning); 10th player ever to accomplish feat.

Year	Team (League)	Pos.	G	AB	R	H	2B	3B	HR	RBI	Avg.	BB	SO	SB	PO	A	E	Avg.
											BATTING					FIELDING		
1988—	Elmira (NY-Penn)	SS-3B	60	207	18	45	5	1	2	16	.217	36	35	5	96	175	14	†.951
1989—	Winter Haven (FSL)....	SS-3B	55	215	27	58	13	1	3	18	.270	13	29	4	99	177	12	.958
	—Lynchburg (Caro.)	SS	75	264	47	65	7	2	8	34	.246	41	40	5	105	220	16	.953
1990—	New Britain (East.)	SS	94	312	20	68	18	1	2	31	.218	25	46	1	139	266	21	.951
1991—	New Britain (East.)	SS	23	81	8	16	3	0	0	5	.198	9	14	1	50	65	3	.975
	—Pawtucket (I.L.)	SS	100	329	52	87	22	4	9	49	.264	60	42	0	184	300	25	.951
1992—	Pawtucket (I.L.)	SS	97	331	47	86	18	1	9	29	.260	48	50	1	148	*358	20	.962
	—Boston (A.L.).............	SS	58	185	21	51	13	0	5	25	.276	20	17	1	79	182	10	.963
1993—	Pawtucket (I.L.)	SS	2	9	3	3	0	0	1	1	.333	0	1	0	8	9	0	1.000
	—Boston (A.L.).............	SS	144	468	50	130	40	3	11	66	.278	49	77	3	238	432	20	.971
1994—	Boston (A.L.).............	SS-DH	84	301	53	95	26	2	9	49	.316	42	38	3	134	242	8	.979
	—Pawtucket (I.L.)	SS	5	18	2	6	0	0	1	2	.333	3	4	0	7	16	3	.885
1995—	Boston (A.L.).............	SS	135	520	108	155	37	2	27	102	.298	81	67	20	227	*414	•18	.973
1996—	Boston (A.L.).............	SS-3B-DH	131	527	84	156	29	3	13	59	.296	63	59	9	202	357	17	.970
1997—	Boston (A.L.).............	2B-3B	143	575	95	176	*47	5	18	77	.306	58	66	7	239	380	22	.966
1998—	Boston (A.L.).............	3B-2B	153	588	113	145	44	1	23	73	.247	77	82	4	†121	292	15	.965
1999—	Boston (A.L.).............	3B-DH	113	449	58	114	27	1	12	70	.254	40	68	0	84	208	14	.954
2000—	Boston (A.L.).............	3B	10	35	6	9	1	0	2	2	.257	2	5	0	6	9	0	1.000
2001—	Boston (A.L.).............	SS-3B	20	60	8	12	2	0	1	5	.200	9	8	0	23	43	2	.971
	—Pawtucket (I.L.)	3B	10	36	7	9	1	0	2	4	.250	8	4	0	5	12	3	.850
	—Trenton (East.)	SS	3	13	1	2	1	0	0	0	.154	1	3	0	3	8	1	.917
Major League totals (10 years)			991	3708	596	1043	266	17	121	528	.281	441	487	47	1353	2559	126	.969

DIVISION SERIES RECORD

RECORDS: Shares single-game records for most home runs—2; and most runs batted in—7 (October 10, 1999).

Year	Team (League)	Pos.	G	AB	R	H	2B	3B	HR	RBI	Avg.	BB	SO	SB	PO	A	E	Avg.
											BATTING					FIELDING		
1995—	Boston (A.L.)	SS	3	12	1	3	1	0	1	2	.250	3	1	0	5	5	1	.909
1998—	Boston (A.L.)	3B	4	15	5	7	1	0	0	0	.467	3	1	0	5	10	0	1.000
1999—	Boston (A.L.)	3B	5	22	6	7	2	0	3	12	.318	0	4	0	5	11	2	.889
Division series totals (3 years)			12	49	12	17	4	0	4	14	.347	6	6	0	15	26	3	.932

CHAMPIONSHIP SERIES RECORD

RECORDS: Shares single-game record for most at-bats (nine-inning game)—6 (October 16, 1999). ... Shares A.L. single-game record for most runs batted in—5 (October 16, 1999).

Year	Team (League)	Pos.	G	AB	R	H	2B	3B	HR	RBI	Avg.	BB	SO	SB	PO	A	E	Avg.
											BATTING					FIELDING		
1999—	Boston (A.L.)	3B	5	23	3	8	2	0	1	5	.348	2	4	0	4	7	0	1.000

VALENTIN, JOSE   SS   WHITE SOX

PERSONAL: Born October 12, 1969, in Manati, Puerto Rico. ... 5-10/190. ... Bats left, throws right. ... Full name: Jose Antonio Valentin. ... Brother of Javier Valentin, catcher, Minnesota Twins organization.
HIGH SCHOOL: Fernando Callejo (Manati, Puerto Rico).
TRANSACTIONS/CAREER NOTES: Signed as non-drafted free agent by San Diego Padres organization (October 12, 1986). ... On disabled list (April 16-May 1 and May 18-July 11, 1990). ... Traded by Padres with P Ricky Bones and OF Matt Mieske to Milwaukee Brewers for 3B Gary Sheffield and P Geoff Kellogg (March 27, 1992). ... On Milwaukee disabled list (April 14-May 5, 1997); included rehabilitation assignment to Beloit (May 3-5). ... On Milwaukee disabled list (April 13-June 16, 1999); included rehabilitation assignment to Louisville (June 9-16). ... Traded by Brewers with P Cal Eldred to Chicago White Sox for P Jaime Navarro and P John Snyder (January 12, 2000). ... Granted free agency (October 30, 2000). ... Re-signed by White Sox (November 22, 2000). ... On disabled list (June 8-24, 2001).
STATISTICAL NOTES: Led Texas League shortstops with 658 total chances in 1991. ... Led American Association shortstops with 639 total chances and 70 double plays in 1992. ... Led American Association shortstops with 211 putouts and 80 double plays in 1993. ... Led A.L. shortstops with 20 errors in 1994. ... Hit three home runs in one game (April 3, 1998). ... Hit for the cycle (April 27, 2000). ... Switch-hit home runs in one game (September 30, 2000). ... Led A.L. shortstops with 36 errors in 2000. ... Career major league grand slams: 5.

Year	Team (League)	Pos.	G	AB	R	H	2B	3B	HR	RBI	Avg.	BB	SO	SB	PO	A	E	Avg.
											BATTING					FIELDING		
1987—	Spokane (N'West)	SS	70	244	52	61	8	2	2	24	.250	35	38	8	101	175	26	.914
1988—	Charl., S.C. (S.Atl.)	SS	133	444	56	103	20	1	6	44	.232	45	83	11	204	412	60	.911
1989—	Riverside (Calif.)	SS	114	381	40	74	10	5	10	41	.194	37	93	8	*227	333	*46	.924
	—Wichita (Texas)	SS-3B	18	49	8	12	1	0	2	5	.245	5	12	1	26	45	8	.899
1990—	Wichita (Texas)	SS	11	36	4	10	2	0	0	2	.278	5	7	2	14	33	2	.959
1991—	Wichita (Texas)	SS	129	447	73	112	22	5	17	68	.251	55	115	8	176	*442	40	.939
1992—	Denver (A.A.)■	SS	*139	492	78	118	19	11	3	45	.240	53	99	9	*187	*414	*38	.941
	—Milwaukee (A.L.)	SS-2B	4	3	1	0	0	0	0	1	.000	0	0	0	1	1	1	.667
1993—	New Orleans (A.A.)	SS-1B	122	389	56	96	22	5	9	53	.247	47	87	9	†212	351	29	.951
	—Milwaukee (A.L.)	SS	19	53	10	13	1	2	1	7	.245	7	16	1	20	51	6	.922
1994—	Milwaukee (A.L.)	SS-2B-DH-3B	97	285	47	68	19	0	11	46	.239	38	75	12	151	336	†20	.961
1995—	Milwaukee (A.L.)	SS-DH-3B	112	338	62	74	23	3	11	49	.219	37	83	16	164	335	15	.971
1996—	Milwaukee (A.L.)	SS	154	552	90	143	33	7	24	95	.259	66	145	17	243	*460	*37	.950
1997—	Milwaukee (A.L.)	SS-DH	136	494	58	125	23	1	17	58	.253	39	109	19	208	383	20	.967
	—Beloit (Midw.)	SS	2	6	3	3	1	0	0	1	.500	2	1	0	1	8	0	1.000
1998—	Milwaukee (N.L.)	SS-DH	151	428	65	96	24	0	16	49	.224	63	105	10	173	370	21	.963
1999—	Milwaukee (N.L.)	SS	89	256	45	58	9	5	10	38	.227	48	52	3	113	214	22	.937
	—Louisville (I.L.)	SS	6	20	6	5	0	0	3	3	.250	4	3	0	7	17	0	1.000
2000—	Chicago (A.L.)■	SS-OF	144	568	107	155	37	6	25	92	.273	59	106	19	233	456	†36	.950
2001—	Chicago (A.L.)	3B-SS-OF	124	438	74	113	22	2	28	68	.258	50	114	9	159	234	22	.947
American League totals (8 years)			790	2731	449	691	158	21	117	416	.253	296	648	93	1179	2256	157	.956
National League totals (2 years)			240	684	110	154	33	5	26	87	.225	111	157	13	286	584	43	.953
Major League totals (10 years)			1030	3415	559	845	191	26	143	503	.247	407	805	106	1465	2840	200	.956

DIVISION SERIES RECORD

Year	Team (League)	Pos.	G	AB	R	H	2B	3B	HR	RBI	Avg.	BB	SO	SB	PO	A	E	Avg.
											BATTING					FIELDING		
2000—	Chicago (A.L.)	SS	3	10	2	3	2	0	0	1	.300	2	2	3	10	17	1	.964

PERSONAL: Born July 31, 1979, in Holland, Mich. ... 6-3/175. ... Throws left, bats right. ... Full name: Andrew William Van Hekken.
HIGH SCHOOL: Holland (Mich.).
TRANSACTIONS/CAREER NOTES: Selected by Seattle Mariners organization in third round of free-agent draft (June 2, 1998). ... Traded by Mariners to Detroit Tigers (June 26, 1999); part of trade in which Tigers traded OF Brian Hunter to Mariners for two players to be named later (April 21, 1999); Mariners traded OF Jerry Amador to Tigers to complete deal (August 26, 1999).

Year	League	W	L	Pct.	ERA	G	GS	CG	ShO	Sv.	IP	H	R	ER	BB	SO
1998—	Arizona Mariners (Ariz.)	6	3	.667	4.43	11	8	0	0	0	40 2/3	34	23	20	18	55
1999—	Oneonta (NY-Penn)■	4	2	.667	2.15	11	10	0	0	0	50 1/3	44	17	12	16	50
2000—	West Michigan (Midw.)	•16	6	.727	2.45	26	25	3	1	1	158	139	48	43	37	126
2001—	Lakeland (FSL)	10	4	.714	3.17	19	19	2	0	0	110 2/3	105	43	39	33	82
—	Erie (East.)	5	0	1.000	4.69	8	8	0	0	0	48	63	29	25	8	29

PERSONAL: Born December 9, 1971, in Hinsdale, Ill. ... 6-5/235. ... Throws right, bats right. ... Full name: Todd Matthew Van Poppel.
HIGH SCHOOL: St. Martin (Arlington, Texas).
TRANSACTIONS/CAREER NOTES: Selected by Oakland Athletics organization in first round (14th pick overall) of free-agent draft (June 4, 1990); pick received as part of compensation for Milwaukee Brewers signing Type A free-agent DH Dave Parker. ... On disabled list (May 28-September 11, 1992). ... Claimed on waivers by Detroit Tigers (August 6, 1996). ... Claimed on waivers by California Angels (November 12, 1996). ... Released by Angels (March 26, 1997). ... Signed by Kansas City Royals organization (April 17, 1997). ... Released by Royals (June 6, 1997). ... Signed by Texas Rangers organization (June 20, 1997). ... Traded by Rangers with 2B Warren Morris to Pittsburgh Pirates for P Esteban Loaiza (July 17, 1998). ... Granted free agency (October 15, 1998). ... Re-signed by Pirates (January 18, 1999). ... Granted free agency (October 15, 1999). ... Signed by Chicago Cubs organization (November 22, 1999). ... Granted free agency (November 5, 2001). ... Signed by Texas Rangers (November 26, 2001).

Year	League	W	L	Pct.	ERA	G	GS	CG	ShO	Sv.	IP	H	R	ER	BB	SO
1990—	Southern Oregon (N'West)	1	1	.500	1.13	5	5	0	0	0	24	10	5	3	9	32
—	Madison (Midw.)	2	1	.667	3.95	3	3	0	0	0	13 2/3	8	11	6	10	17
1991—	Huntsville (Sou.)	6	*13	.316	3.47	24	24	1	1	0	132 1/3	118	69	51	90	115
—	Oakland (A.L.)	0	0	...	9.64	1	1	0	0	0	4 2/3	7	5	5	2	6
1992—	Tacoma (PCL)	4	2	.667	3.97	9	9	0	0	0	45 1/3	44	22	20	35	29
1993—	Tacoma (PCL)	4	8	.333	5.83	16	16	0	0	0	78 2/3	67	53	51	54	71
—	Oakland (A.L.)	6	6	.500	5.04	16	16	0	0	0	84	76	50	47	62	47
1994—	Oakland (A.L.)	7	10	.412	6.09	23	23	0	0	0	116 2/3	108	80	79	•89	83
1995—	Oakland (A.L.)	4	8	.333	4.88	36	14	1	0	0	138 1/3	125	77	75	56	122
1996—	Oakland (A.L.)	1	5	.167	7.71	28	6	0	0	1	63	86	56	54	33	37
—	Detroit (A.L.)■	2	4	.333	11.39	9	9	1	1	0	36 1/3	53	51	46	29	16
1997—	Omaha (A.A.)■	1	5	.167	8.03	11	6	0	0	0	37	50	36	33	24	27
—	Charlotte (FSL)■	0	4	.000	4.04	6	6	2	0	0	35 2/3	36	19	16	10	33
—	Tulsa (Texas)	3	3	.500	5.06	7	7	0	0	0	42 2/3	53	27	24	15	26
1998—	Tulsa (Texas)■	0	0	...	4.50	1	1	0	0	0	4	2	2	2	4	2
—	Oklahoma (PCL)	5	5	.500	3.72	15	13	2	0	0	87	88	44	36	25	69
—	Texas (A.L.)	1	2	.333	8.84	4	4	0	0	0	19 1/3	26	20	19	10	10
—	Pittsburgh (N.L.)■	1	2	.333	5.36	18	7	0	0	0	47	53	32	28	18	32
1999—	Nashville (PCL)	10	6	.625	4.95	27	27	2	0	0	163 2/3	173	95	90	62	*157
2000—	Iowa (PCL)■	3	4	.429	3.10	10	6	0	0	0	40 2/3	37	18	14	10	52
—	Chicago (N.L.)	4	5	.444	3.75	51	2	0	0	2	86 1/3	80	38	36	48	77
2001—	Chicago (N.L.)	4	1	.800	2.52	59	0	0	0	0	75	63	22	21	38	90
A.L. totals (6 years)		21	35	.375	6.33	117	73	2	1	1	462 1/3	481	339	325	281	321
N.L. totals (3 years)		9	8	.529	3.67	128	9	0	0	2	208 1/3	196	92	85	104	199
Major League totals (8 years)		30	43	.411	5.50	245	82	2	1	3	670 2/3	677	431	410	385	520

PERSONAL: Born April 29, 1966, in Grand Rapids, Mich. ... 6-1/197. ... Bats left, throws left. ... Full name: John Henry Vander Wal.
HIGH SCHOOL: Hudsonville (Mich.).
COLLEGE: Western Michigan.
TRANSACTIONS/CAREER NOTES: Selected by Houston Astros organization in eighth round of free-agent draft (June 4, 1984); did not sign. ... Selected by Montreal Expos organization in third round of free-agent draft (June 2, 1987). ... Contract purchased by Rockies with OF Ronnie Hall from Expos (March 31, 1994). ... Traded by Rockies to San Diego Padres for a player to be named later (August 31, 1998). ... Granted free agency (October 26, 1998). ... Re-signed by Padres (November 13, 1998). ... Traded by Padres with P Geraldo Padua and P James Sak to Pittsburgh Pirates for OF Al Martin and cash (February 23, 2000). ... Traded by Pirates with P Jason Schmidt to San Francisco Giants for OF Armando Rios and P Ryan Vogelsong (July 30, 2001). ... Traded by Giants to New York Yankees for P Jay Witasick (December 13, 2001).
RECORDS: Holds major league single-season record for most hits by pinch hitter—28 (1995).
STATISTICAL NOTES: Had 16-game hitting streak (August 29-September 16, 2000). ... Career major league grand slams: 2.

							BATTING							FIELDING		
Year	Team (League)	Pos.	G	AB	R	H	2B	3B	HR	RBI	Avg.	BB	SO	SB	PO	A	E	Avg.
1987—	Jamestown (NY-P)	OF	18	69	24	33	12	3	3	15	.478	3	14	3	20	0	0	1.000
—	W. Palm Beach (FSL)	OF	50	189	29	54	11	2	2	22	.286	30	25	8	103	1	3	.972
1988—	W. Palm Beach (FSL)	OF	62	231	50	64	15	2	10	33	.277	32	40	11	109	3	1	.991
—	Jacksonville (Sou.)	OF	58	208	22	54	14	0	3	14	.260	17	49	3	99	0	0	1.000
1989—	Jacksonville (Sou.)	OF	71	217	30	55	9	2	6	24	.253	22	51	2	72	3	1	.987
1990—	Indianapolis (A.A.)	OF	51	135	16	40	6	0	2	14	.296	13	28	0	48	4	2	.963
—	Jacksonville (Sou.)	OF	77	277	45	84	25	3	8	40	.303	39	46	6	106	4	1	.991
1991—	Indianapolis (A.A.)	OF	133	478	84	140	36	8	15	71	.293	79	118	8	197	7	1	*.995
—	Montreal (N.L.)	OF	21	61	4	13	4	1	1	8	.213	1	18	0	29	0	0	1.000
1992—	Montreal (N.L.)	OF-1B	105	213	21	51	8	2	4	20	.239	24	36	3	122	6	2	.985

Year	Team (League)	Pos.	G	AB	R	H	2B	3B	HR	RBI	Avg.	BB	SO	SB	PO	A	E	Avg.
1993—	Montreal (N.L.)	1B-OF	106	215	34	50	7	4	5	30	.233	27	30	6	271	14	4	.986
1994—	Colorado (N.L.)■	1B-OF	91	110	12	27	3	1	5	15	.245	16	31	2	106	3	0	1.000
1995—	Colorado (N.L.)	1B-OF	105	101	15	35	8	1	5	21	.347	16	23	1	51	4	2	.965
1996—	Colorado (N.L.)	OF-1B	104	151	20	38	6	2	5	31	.252	19	38	2	72	2	1	.987
1997—	Colorado (N.L.)	1B-OF	76	92	7	16	2	0	1	11	.174	10	33	1	38	0	1	.974
—Colo. Springs (PCL) ...	1B-OF-DH	25	103	29	42	12	1	3	19	.408	11	28	1	158	10	4	.977
1998—	Colorado (N.L.)	OF-DH-1B	89	104	18	30	10	1	5	20	.288	16	29	0	29	3	0	1.000
—San Diego (N.L.)■ ...	OF-1B	20	25	3	6	3	0	0	0	.240	6	5	0	21	2	0	1.000
1999—	San Diego (N.L.)	OF-1B-DH	132	246	26	67	18	0	6	41	.272	37	59	2	227	10	1	.996
2000—	Pittsburgh (N.L.)■	OF-1B-DH	134	384	74	115	29	0	24	94	.299	72	92	11	385	12	6	.985
2001—	Pittsburgh (N.L.)	OF-1B-DH	97	313	39	87	22	3	11	50	.278	42	84	7	217	6	4	.982
—San Fran. (N.L.)■ ...	OF-1B	49	139	19	35	6	1	3	20	.252	26	38	1	84	1	0	1.000
Major League totals (11 years)			1129	2154	292	570	126	16	75	361	.265	312	516	36	1652	63	21	.988

DIVISION SERIES RECORD

RECORDS: Holds N.L. career record for most games by pinch-hitter—7. ... Shares career record for most triples—1.

Year	Team (League)	Pos.	G	AB	R	H	2B	3B	HR	RBI	Avg.	BB	SO	SB	PO	A	E	Avg.
1995—	Colorado (N.L.)	PH	4	4	0	0	0	0	0	0	.000	0	2	0	...	...	...	...
1998—	San Diego (N.L.)	PH	3	3	1	1	0	1	0	2	.333	0	1	0	...	...	...	...
Division series totals (2 years)			7	7	1	1	0	1	0	2	.143	0	3	0	...	...	...	...

CHAMPIONSHIP SERIES RECORD

Year	Team (League)	Pos.	G	AB	R	H	2B	3B	HR	RBI	Avg.	BB	SO	SB	PO	A	E	Avg.
1998—	San Diego (N.L.)	OF-PH	3	7	1	3	0	0	1	2	.429	0	2	0	5	1	0	1.000

WORLD SERIES RECORD

Year	Team (League)	Pos.	G	AB	R	H	2B	3B	HR	RBI	Avg.	BB	SO	SB	PO	A	E	Avg.
1998—	San Diego (N.L.)	OF-PH	4	5	0	2	1	0	0	0	.400	0	2	0	1	0	0	1.000

VARGAS, CLAUDIO   P   MARLINS

PERSONAL: Born May 19, 1979, in Valverde Mao, Dominican Republic. ... 6-3/210. ... Throws right, bats right. ... Full name: Claudio Almonte Vargas.

TRANSACTIONS/CAREER NOTES: Signed as non-drafted free agent by Florida Marlins organization (August 25, 1995). ... On Kane County disabled list (July 22-August 13, 1999). ... Granted free agency (December 21, 1999). ... Re-signed by Marlins organization (December 21, 1999).

STATISTICAL NOTES: Tied for Eastern League lead in home runs allowed with 25 and sacrifice hits allowed with eight in 2001.

Year	League	W	L	Pct.	ERA	G	GS	CG	ShO	Sv.	IP	H	R	ER	BB	SO
1996—	Dominican Marlins (DSL)...	2	3	.400	3.09	15	4	0	0	0	46²/₃	41	25	16	26	37
1997—	Dominican Marlins (DSL)...	6	2	.750	2.50	13	10	3	1	0	72	62	32	20	31	81
1998—	Brevard County (FSL).........	0	1	.000	4.66	2	2	0	0	0	9²/₃	15	5	5	4	9
—Gulf Coast Marlins (GCL) ...	0	4	.000	4.08	5	4	0	0	0	28²/₃	24	13	13	7	27
1999—	Kane County (Midw.).........	5	5	.500	3.88	19	19	1	0	0	99²/₃	97	47	43	41	88
2000—	Brevard County (FSL).........	10	5	.667	3.28	24	23	0	0	0	145¹/₃	126	64	53	44	143
—Portland (East.)	1	1	.500	3.60	3	2	0	0	0	15	16	9	6	6	13
2001—	Portland (East.)	8	9	.471	4.19	27	27	0	0	0	159	122	77	74	47	151

VARGAS, MARTIN   P   INDIANS

PERSONAL: Born February 22, 1978, in San Pedro de Macoris, Dominican Republic. ... 6-0/155. ... Throws right, bats right.

TRANSACTIONS/CAREER NOTES: Signed as non-drafted free agent by Cleveland Indians organization (July 5, 1995).

Year	League	W	L	Pct.	ERA	G	GS	CG	ShO	Sv.	IP	H	R	ER	BB	SO
1997—	Dominican Indians (DSL)...	3	5	.375	2.45	14	14	0	0	0	69²/₃	52	33	19	39	43
1998—	Burlington (Appl.)..............	3	7	.300	4.76	13	13	1	0	0	73²/₃	78	49	39	35	64
—Columbus (S.Atl.)..............	1	4	.200	10.01	7	7	0	0	0	29²/₃	42	36	33	24	25
1999—	Columbus (S.Atl.)..............	6	3	.667	4.95	15	12	0	0	0	67¹/₃	80	46	37	20	51
—Kinston (Caro.).................	6	1	.857	2.76	20	0	0	0	2	42¹/₃	31	16	13	20	44
2000—	Akron (East.)	10	8	.556	5.42	53	0	0	0	7	81¹/₃	96	52	49	30	58
2001—	Akron (East.)	1	5	.167	5.63	32	0	0	0	9	40	52	29	25	23	35
—Buffalo (I.L.).....................	0	3	.000	2.93	22	0	0	0	4	27²/₃	20	11	9	17	22

RECORD AS POSITION PLAYER

Year	Team (League)	Pos.	G	AB	R	H	2B	3B	HR	RBI	Avg.	BB	SO	SB	PO	A	E	Avg.
1996—	Dom. Indians (DSL) ...		39	103	7	23	6	1	0	12	.223	12	25	1	...	...	...	...

VARITEK, JASON   C   RED SOX

PERSONAL: Born April 11, 1972, in Rochester, Minn. ... 6-2/220. ... Bats both, throws right. ... Full name: Jason A. Varitek.

HIGH SCHOOL: Lake Brantley (Longwood, Fla.).

COLLEGE: Georgia Tech.

TRANSACTIONS/CAREER NOTES: Selected by Minnesota Twins organization first round (21st pick overall) of free-agent draft (June 3, 1993); did not sign. ... Selected by Seattle Mariners organization in first round (14th pick overall) of free-agent draft (June 2, 1994). ... Traded by Mariners with P Derek Lowe to Boston Red Sox for P Heathcliff Slocumb (July 31, 1997). ... On disabled list (June 8, 2001-remainder of season).

STATISTICAL NOTES: Led Southern league catchers with .993 fielding percentage and 21 passed balls and tied for lead in double plays by catcher with 10 in 1996. ... Led A.L. catchers with 1,049 total chances and 25 passed balls in 1999. ... Led A.L. catchers with 14 passed balls in 2000. ... Hit three home runs in one game (May 20, 2001).

Year Team (League)	Pos.	G	AB	R	H	2B	3B	HR	RBI	Avg.	BB	SO	SB	PO	A	E	Avg.
1995— Port City (Sou.)	C	104	352	42	79	14	3	10	44	.224	61	126	0	589	59	8	.988
1996— Port City (Sou.)	C-DH-3B-OF	134	503	63	132	34	1	12	67	.262	66	93	7	663	79	5	*.993
1997— Tacoma (PCL)	C-DH	87	307	54	78	13	0	15	48	.254	34	71	0	613	49	3	*.995
— Pawtucket (I.L.)■	C	20	66	6	13	5	0	1	5	.197	8	12	0	123	10	1	.993
— Boston (A.L.)	C	1	1	0	1	0	0	0	0	1.000	0	0	0	1	0	0	1.000
1998— Boston (A.L.)	C-DH	86	221	31	56	13	0	7	33	.253	17	45	2	367	32	5	.988
1999— Boston (A.L.)	C-DH	144	483	70	130	39	2	20	76	.269	46	85	1	*972	66	*11	.990
2000— Boston (A.L.)	C-DH	139	448	55	111	31	1	10	65	.248	60	84	1	867	46	7	.992
2001— Boston (A.L.)	C	51	174	19	51	11	1	7	25	.293	21	35	0	425	32	2	.996
Major League totals (5 years)		421	1327	175	349	94	4	44	199	.263	144	249	4	2632	176	25	.991

DIVISION SERIES RECORD

RECORDS: Holds single-game record for most runs scored—5 (October 10, 1999). ... Shares career and single-series record for most consecutive hits—5 (October 9-10, 1999).

Year Team (League)	Pos.	G	AB	R	H	2B	3B	HR	RBI	Avg.	BB	SO	SB	PO	A	E	Avg.
1998— Boston (A.L.)	C	1	4	0	1	0	0	0	1	.250	0	1	0	5	0	0	1.000
1999— Boston (A.L.)	C	5	21	7	5	3	0	1	3	.238	0	4	0	40	0	0	1.000
Division series totals (2 years)		6	25	7	6	3	0	1	4	.240	0	5	0	45	0	0	1.000

CHAMPIONSHIP SERIES RECORD

Year Team (League)	Pos.	G	AB	R	H	2B	3B	HR	RBI	Avg.	BB	SO	SB	PO	A	E	Avg.
1999— Boston (A.L.)	C	5	20	1	4	1	1	1	1	.200	1	4	0	44	1	1	.978

VAUGHN, GREG   OF/DH   DEVIL RAYS

PERSONAL: Born July 3, 1965, in Sacramento. ... 6-0/202. ... Bats right, throws right. ... Full name: Gregory Lamont Vaughn. ... Cousin of Mo Vaughn, first baseman, New York Mets; and cousin of Jerry Royster, infielder with five major league teams (1973-88).
HIGH SCHOOL: John F. Kennedy (Sacramento).
JUNIOR COLLEGE: Sacramento City College.
COLLEGE: Miami (Fla.).
TRANSACTIONS/CAREER NOTES: Selected by St. Louis Cardinals organization in fifth round of free-agent draft (January 17, 1984); did not sign. ... Selected by Milwaukee Brewers organization in secondary phase of free-agent draft (June 4, 1984); did not sign. ... Selected by Pittsburgh Pirates organization in secondary phase of free-agent draft (January 9, 1985); did not sign. ... Selected by California Angels organization in secondary phase of free-agent draft (June 3, 1985); did not sign. ... Selected by Brewers organization in secondary phase of free-agent draft (June 2, 1986). ... On disabled list (May 26-June 10, 1990). ... On Milwaukee disabled list (April 8-27, 1994); included rehabilitation assignment to Beloit (April 25-27). ... Traded by Brewers with a player to be named later to San Diego Padres for P Bryce Florie, P Ron Villone and OF Marc Newfield (July 31, 1996); Padres acquired OF Gerald Parent to complete deal (September 16, 1996). ... Granted free agency (October 28, 1996). ... Re-signed by Padres (December 19, 1996). ... Traded by Padres with P Kerry Taylor and P Chris Clark to New York Yankees for P Kenny Rogers, IF Mariano Duncan and P Kevin Henthorne (July 4, 1997); trade later voided because Vaughn failed physical (July 6, 1997). ... Traded by Padres with OF/1B Mark Sweeney to Cincinnati Reds for OF Reggie Sanders, SS Damian Jackson and P Josh Harris (February 2, 1999). ... Granted free agency (October 28, 1999). ... Signed by Tampa Bay Devil Rays (December 13, 1999). ... On disabled list (June 18-July 7, 2000).
HONORS: Named Midwest League co-Most Valuable Player (1987). ... Named American Association Most Valuable Player (1989). ... Named N.L. Comeback Player of the Year by THE SPORTING NEWS (1998). ... Named outfielder on THE SPORTING NEWS N.L. All-Star team (1998). ... Named outfielder on THE SPORTING NEWS N.L. Silver Slugger team (1998).
STATISTICAL NOTES: Led Midwest League with 292 total bases in 1987. ... Led Texas League with 279 total bases in 1988. ... Led American Association with .548 slugging percentage in 1989. ... Hit three home runs in one game (September 7, 1999). ... Career major league grand slams: 6.

Year Team (League)	Pos.	G	AB	R	H	2B	3B	HR	RBI	Avg.	BB	SO	SB	PO	A	E	Avg.
1986— Helena (Pio.)	OF	66	258	64	75	13	2	16	54	.291	30	69	23	99	5	3	.972
1987— Beloit (Midw.)	OF	139	492	*120	150	31	6	*33	105	.305	102	115	36	247	11	10	.963
1988— El Paso (Texas)	OF	131	505	*104	152	*39	2	*28	*105	.301	63	120	22	216	12	7	.970
1989— Denver (A.A.)	OF	110	387	74	107	17	5	*26	*92	.276	62	94	20	140	4	3	.980
— Milwaukee (A.L.)	OF-DH	38	113	18	30	3	0	5	23	.265	13	23	4	32	1	2	.943
1990— Milwaukee (A.L.)	OF-DH	120	382	51	84	26	2	17	61	.220	33	91	7	195	8	7	.967
1991— Milwaukee (A.L.)	OF-DH	145	542	81	132	24	5	27	98	.244	62	125	2	315	5	2	.994
1992— Milwaukee (A.L.)	OF-DH	141	501	77	114	18	2	23	78	.228	60	123	15	288	6	3	.990
1993— Milwaukee (A.L.)	OF-DH	154	569	97	152	28	2	30	97	.267	89	118	10	214	1	3	.986
1994— Milwaukee (A.L.)	OF-DH	95	370	59	94	24	1	19	55	.254	51	93	9	162	5	3	.982
— Beloit (Midw.)	DH	2	6	1	1	0	0	0	0	.167	4	1	0	...	...	...	...
1995— Milwaukee (A.L.)	DH	108	392	67	88	19	1	17	59	.224	55	89	10	...	...	...	...
1996— Milwaukee (A.L.)	OF-DH	102	375	78	105	16	0	31	95	.280	58	99	5	192	5	4	.980
— San Diego (N.L.)■	OF	43	141	20	29	3	1	10	22	.206	24	31	4	74	2	2	.974
1997— San Diego (N.L.)	OF-DH	120	361	60	78	10	0	18	57	.216	56	110	7	153	7	1	.994
1998— San Diego (N.L.)	OF-DH	158	573	112	156	28	4	50	119	.272	79	121	11	270	5	2	.993
1999— Cincinnati (N.L.)■	OF-DH	153	550	104	135	20	2	45	118	.245	85	137	15	264	8	4	.986
2000— Tampa Bay (A.L.)■	OF-DH	127	461	83	117	27	1	28	74	.254	80	128	8	145	6	1	.993
2001— Tampa Bay (A.L.)	DH-OF	136	485	74	113	25	0	24	82	.233	71	130	11	127	4	3	.978
American League totals (10 years)		1166	4190	685	1029	210	14	221	722	.246	572	1019	81	1670	41	28	.984
National League totals (4 years)		474	1625	296	398	61	7	123	316	.245	244	399	37	761	22	9	.989
Major League totals (13 years)		1640	5815	981	1427	271	21	344	1038	.245	816	1418	118	2431	63	37	.985

DIVISION SERIES RECORD

Year Team (League)	Pos.	G	AB	R	H	2B	3B	HR	RBI	Avg.	BB	SO	SB	PO	A	E	Avg.
1996— San Diego (N.L.)	PH	3	3	0	0	0	0	0	0	.000	0	1	0	...	...	...	...
1998— San Diego (N.L.)	OF	4	15	2	5	1	0	1	1	.333	0	4	0	2	0	0	1.000
Division series totals (2 years)		7	18	2	5	1	0	1	1	.278	0	5	0	2	0	0	1.000

CHAMPIONSHIP SERIES RECORD

Year	Team (League)	Pos.	G	AB	R	H	2B	3B	HR	RBI	Avg.	BB	SO	SB	PO	A	E	Avg.
								BATTING								FIELDING		
1998—San Diego (N.L.)	OF-PH	3	8	1	2	0	0	0	0	.250	1	1	0	2	0	0	1.000

WORLD SERIES RECORD

Year	Team (League)	Pos.	G	AB	R	H	2B	3B	HR	RBI	Avg.	BB	SO	SB	PO	A	E	Avg.
								BATTING								FIELDING		
1998—San Diego (N.L.)	OF-DH	4	15	3	2	0	0	2	4	.133	1	2	0	4	0	1	.800

ALL-STAR GAME RECORD

Year	League	Pos.	AB	R	H	2B	3B	HR	RBI	Avg.	BB	SO	SB	PO	A	E	Avg.
						BATTING									FIELDING		
1993— American	OF	1	1	1	0	0	0	0	1.000	0	0	0	0	0	0	...
1996— American....................						Selected, did not play.										
1998— National....................	OF	1	0	1	0	0	0	2	1.000	0	0	0	0	0	0	...
2001— American....................						Selected, did not play.										
All-Star Game totals (2 years)		2	1	2	0	0	0	2	1.000	0	0	0	0	0	0	...

VAUGHN, MO   1B   METS

PERSONAL: Born December 15, 1967, in Norwalk, Conn. ... 6-1/268. ... Bats left, throws right. ... Full name: Maurice Samuel Vaughn. ... Cousin of Greg Vaughn, outfielder/designated hitter, Tampa Bay Devil Rays.
HIGH SCHOOL: Trinity Pawling Prep (Pawling, N.Y.).
COLLEGE: Seton Hall.
TRANSACTIONS/CAREER NOTES: Selected by Boston Red Sox organization in first round (23rd pick overall) of free-agent draft (June 9, 1989). ... On disabled list (June 17-July 10, 1997). ... Granted free agency (October 23, 1998). ... Signed by Anaheim Angels (December 11, 1998). ... On disabled list (April 7-22, 1999; and March 23, 2001-entire season). ... Traded by Angels to New York Mets for P Kevin Appier (December 27, 2001).
RECORDS: Holds major league single-season record for most strikeouts by lefthander—181 (2000). ... Holds major league record for most seasons leading league in errors by first baseman—6.
HONORS: Named first baseman on The Sporting News A.L. All-Star team (1995). ... Named first baseman on The Sporting News A.L. Silver Slugger team (1995). ... Named A.L. Most Valuable Player by Baseball Writers' Association of America (1995).
STATISTICAL NOTES: Led A.L. with 20 intentional bases on balls received in 1994. ... Led A.L. first basemen with 103 double plays in 1994. ... Led A.L. first basemen with 1,368 total chances and 128 double plays in 1995. ... Hit three home runs in one game (September 24, 1996 and May 30, 1997). ... Had 16-game hitting streak (September 13-27, 1998). ... Led A.L. first basemen with 14 errors in 2000. ... Career major league grand slams: 10.

Year	Team (League)	Pos.	G	AB	R	H	2B	3B	HR	RBI	Avg.	BB	SO	SB	PO	A	E	Avg.
								BATTING								FIELDING		
1989— New Britain (East.)	1B	73	245	28	68	15	0	8	38	.278	25	47	1	541	45	•10	.983
1990— Pawtucket (I.L.)..........	1B	108	386	62	114	26	1	22	72	.295	44	87	3	828	60	11	.988
1991— Pawtucket (I.L.)..........	1B	69	234	35	64	10	0	14	50	.274	60	44	2	432	24	3	.993
— Boston (A.L.)................	1B-DH	74	219	21	57	12	0	4	32	.260	26	43	2	378	26	6	.985
1992— Boston (A.L.).............	1B-DH	113	355	42	83	16	2	13	57	.234	47	67	3	741	57	*15	.982
— Pawtucket (I.L.)............	1B	39	149	15	42	6	0	6	28	.282	18	35	1	368	15	8	.980
1993— Boston (A.L.).............	1B-DH	152	539	86	160	34	1	29	101	.297	79	130	4	1110	70	*16	.987
1994— Boston (A.L.).............	1B-DH	111	394	65	122	25	1	26	82	.310	57	112	4	880	57	•10	.989
1995— Boston (A.L.).............	1B-DH	140	550	98	165	28	3	39	•126	.300	68	*150	11	*1262	95	11	.992
1996— Boston (A.L.).............	1B-DH	161	635	118	207	29	1	44	143	.326	95	154	2	1207	74	*15	.988
1997— Boston (A.L.).............	1B-DH	141	527	91	166	24	0	35	96	.315	86	154	2	1088	75	*14	.988
1998— Boston (A.L.).............	1B-DH	154	609	107	205	31	2	40	115	.337	61	144	0	1176	90	12	.991
1999— Anaheim (A.L.)■.........	1B-DH	139	524	63	147	20	0	33	108	.281	54	127	0	584	35	3	.995
2000— Anaheim (A.L.)..........	1B-DH-OF	161	614	93	167	31	0	36	117	.272	79	*181	2	1257	69	†14	.990
2001— Anaheim (A.L.)..........						Did not play.											
Major League totals (10 years)		1346	4966	784	1479	250	10	299	977	.298	652	1262	30	9683	648	116	.989

DIVISION SERIES RECORD

RECORDS: Shares single-game records for most home runs—2 (September 29, 1998); and most runs batted in—7 (September 29, 1998).
NOTES: Shares postseason single-game record for most runs batted in—7 (September 29, 1998).

Year	Team (League)	Pos.	G	AB	R	H	2B	3B	HR	RBI	Avg.	BB	SO	SB	PO	A	E	Avg.
								BATTING								FIELDING		
1995— Boston (A.L.).............	1B	3	14	0	0	0	0	0	0	.000	1	7	0	27	2	0	1.000
1998— Boston (A.L.).............	1B	4	17	3	7	2	0	2	7	.412	1	5	0	30	4	0	1.000
Division series totals (2 years)		7	31	3	7	2	0	2	7	.226	2	12	0	57	6	0	1.000

ALL-STAR GAME RECORD

NOTES: Named to A.L. All-Star team for 1998 game; replaced by Rafael Palmeiro due to injury.

Year	League	Pos.	AB	R	H	2B	3B	HR	RBI	Avg.	BB	SO	SB	PO	A	E	Avg.
						BATTING									FIELDING		
1995— American....................	1B	2	0	0	0	0	0	0	.000	0	2	0	4	0	0	1.000
1998— American....................						Selected, did not play—injured.										

VAZQUEZ, JAVIER   P   EXPOS

PERSONAL: Born July 25, 1976, in Ponce, Puerto Rico. ... 6-2/195. ... Throws right, bats right. ... Full name: Javier Carlos Vazquez.
HIGH SCHOOL: Colegio de Ponce (Ponce, Puerto Rico).
TRANSACTIONS/CAREER NOTES: Selected by Montreal Expos organization in fifth round of free-agent draft (June 2, 1994). ... On suspended list (July 23-27, 1998).
STATISTICAL NOTES: Pitched 3-0 one-hit, complete-game victory against Los Angeles (September 14, 1999).

V

Year League	W	L	Pct.	ERA	G	GS	CG	ShO	Sv.	IP	H	R	ER	BB	SO
1994— Gulf Coast Expos (GCL)	5	2	.714	2.53	15	11	1	1	0	67²/₃	37	25	19	15	56
1995— Albany (S.Atl.)	6	6	.500	5.08	21	21	1	0	0	102²/₃	109	67	58	47	87
1996— Delmarva (S.Atl.)	14	3	*.824	2.68	27	27	1	0	0	164¹/₃	138	64	49	57	173
1997— Harrisburg (East.).............	4	0	1.000	1.07	6	6	1	0	0	42	15	5	5	12	47
— West Palm Beach (FSL)	6	3	.667	2.16	19	19	1	0	0	112²/₃	98	40	27	28	100
1998— Montreal (N.L.)...................	5	15	.250	6.06	33	32	0	0	0	172¹/₃	196	121	116	68	139
1999— Montreal (N.L.)...................	9	8	.529	5.00	26	26	3	1	0	154²/₃	154	98	86	52	113
— Ottawa (I.L.)	4	2	.667	4.85	7	7	0	0	0	42²/₃	45	24	23	16	46
2000— Montreal (N.L.)...................	11	9	.550	4.05	33	33	2	1	0	217²/₃	247	104	98	61	196
2001— Montreal (N.L.)...................	16	11	.593	3.42	32	32	5	•3	0	223²/₃	197	92	85	44	208
Major League totals (4 years)......	41	43	.488	4.51	124	123	10	5	0	768¹/₃	794	415	385	225	656

VAZQUEZ, RAMON   SS   PADRES

PERSONAL: Born August 21, 1976, in Aibonito, Puerto Rico. ... 5-11/170. ... Bats left, throws right. ... Full name: Ramon Luis Vazquez.
JUNIOR COLLEGE: Indian Hills.
TRANSACTIONS/CAREER NOTES: Selected by Seattle Mariners organization in 27th round of free-agent draft (June 1, 1995). ... On disabled list (June 29-July 11, 2000). ... On Tacoma disabled list (June 20-29, 2001). ... Traded by Mariners with P Brett Tomko and C Tom Lampkin to San Diego Padres for C Ben Davis, P Wascar Serrano and SS Alex Arias (December 11, 2001).
STATISTICAL NOTES: Led Eastern League shortstops with 75 double plays in 2000.

Year Team (League)	Pos.	G	AB	R	H	2B	3B	HR	RBI	Avg.	BB	SO	SB	PO	A	E	Avg.
							BATTING								FIELDING		
1995— Ariz. Mariners (Ariz.)..	SS-3B-2B	39	141	20	29	3	1	0	11	.206	19	27	4	60	114	11	.941
1996— Everett (N'West)..........	SS	33	126	25	35	5	2	1	18	.278	26	26	7	38	100	20	.873
— Tacoma (PCL)	2B-SS	18	49	7	11	2	1	0	4	.224	4	12	0	21	45	1	.985
— Wisconsin (Midw.)	3B	3	10	1	3	1	0	0	1	.300	2	2	0	4	5	2	.818
1997— Wisconsin (Midw.)	SS	131	479	79	129	25	5	8	49	.269	78	93	16	170	333	35	.935
1998— Lancaster (Calif.).........	SS	121	468	77	129	26	4	2	72	.276	81	66	15	150	368	31	.944
1999— New Haven (East.).......	SS-3B-2B	127	438	58	113	27	3	5	45	.258	62	77	8	157	343	31	.942
2000— New Haven (East.).......	SS	124	405	58	116	25	4	8	59	.286	52	76	1	194	*350	22	.961
2001— Tacoma (PCL)	SS	127	466	85	140	28	1	10	79	.300	76	84	9	190	381	12	.979
— Seattle (A.L.)...........SS-2B-3B-DH	17	35	5	8	0	0	0	4	.229	0	3	0	14	17	1	.969
Major League totals (1 year)		17	35	5	8	0	0	0	4	.229	0	3	0	14	17	1	.969

DIVISION SERIES RECORD

Year Team (League)	Pos.	G	AB	R	H	2B	3B	HR	RBI	Avg.	BB	SO	SB	PO	A	E	Avg.
							BATTING								FIELDING		
2001— Seattle (A.L.)	SS	1	0	0	0	0	0	0	0	...	0	0	0	0	1	0	1.000

CHAMPIONSHIP SERIES RECORD

Year Team (League)	Pos.	G	AB	R	H	2B	3B	HR	RBI	Avg.	BB	SO	SB	PO	A	E	Avg.
							BATTING								FIELDING		
2001— Seattle (A.L.)								Did not play.									

VELANDIA, JORGE   SS

PERSONAL: Born January 12, 1975, in Caracas, Venezuela. ... 5-9/185. ... Bats right, throws right. ... Full name: Jorge Macias Velandia.
TRANSACTIONS/CAREER NOTES: Signed as non-drafted free agent by Detroit Tigers organization (January 15, 1992). ... Traded by Tigers with 3B Scott Livingstone to San Diego Padres for P Gene Harris (May 11, 1994). ... Traded by Padres with P Doug Bochtler to Oakland Athletics for P Don Wengert and IF David Newhan (November 26, 1997). ... On disabled list (August 7, 1999-remainder of season). ... Traded by A's to New York Mets for OF Nelson Cruz (August 30, 2000). ... Granted free agency (December 21, 2000). ... Re-signed by Mets (January 5, 2001). ... On New York disabled list (June 29-September 8, 2001); included rehabilitation assignment to Norfolk (August 27-September 8). ... Granted free agency (October 15, 2001).
STATISTICAL NOTES: Led Pacific Coast League shortstop with 648 total chances and 93 double plays in 1998.

V

Year Team (League)	Pos.	G	AB	R	H	2B	3B	HR	RBI	Avg.	BB	SO	SB	PO	A	E	Avg.
							BATTING								FIELDING		
1992— Bristol (Appl.).............	SS-2B	45	119	20	24	6	1	0	9	.202	15	16	3	54	88	12	.922
1993— Niagara Falls (NY-P)...	SS	72	212	30	41	11	0	1	22	.193	19	48	22	82	186	24	.918
— Fayetteville (S.Atl.)	SS-2B-3B	37	106	15	17	4	0	0	11	.160	13	21	5	47	94	9	.940
1994— Lakeland (FSL)	SS-2B-3B	22	60	8	14	4	0	0	3	.233	6	14	0	40	56	4	.960
— Springfield (Midw.)■..	SS-2B	98	290	42	71	14	0	4	36	.245	21	46	5	118	303	26	.942
1995— Memphis (Sou.)	SS	63	186	23	38	10	2	4	17	.204	14	37	0	88	152	12	.952
— Las Vegas (PCL)	SS	66	206	25	54	12	3	0	25	.262	13	37	0	97	190	*31	.903
1996— Memphis (Sou.)	SS	122	392	42	94	19	0	9	48	.240	31	65	3	173	368	33	.943
1997— Las Vegas (PCL)	SS	114	405	46	110	15	2	3	35	.272	29	62	13	170	*347	21	.961
— San Diego (N.L.)	SS-2B-3B	14	29	0	3	2	0	0	0	.103	1	7	0	11	23	3	.919
1998— Oakland (A.L.)■.........	SS-2B	8	4	0	1	0	0	0	0	.250	0	1	0	4	10	1	.933
— Edmonton (PCL)	SS-DH	128	488	64	140	35	1	6	57	.287	37	52	8	203	*428	17	.974
1999— Oakland (A.L.) 2B-SS-3B-DH	63	48	4	9	1	0	0	2	.188	2	13	2	46	79	3	.977
2000— Oakland (A.L.)	2B-SS	18	24	1	3	1	0	0	2	.125	0	6	0	17	24	0	1.000
— Sacramento (PCL)......	SS	83	302	56	84	20	1	9	57	.278	34	52	4	127	262	11	.973
— Norfolk (I.L.)■..........	SS	4	10	0	1	0	0	0	0	.100	1	1	1	7	10	0	1.000
— New York (N.L.)..........	2B-SS-3B	15	7	1	0	0	0	0	0	.000	2	2	0	8	5	1	.929
2001— Norfolk (I.L.)■..........	SS	67	260	25	65	21	0	5	37	.250	16	47	9	97	215	7	.978
— New York (N.L.)..........	SS-3B	9	9	1	0	0	0	0	0	.000	2	1	0	2	8	0	1.000
American League totals (3 years)		89	76	5	13	2	0	0	4	.171	2	20	2	67	113	4	.978
National League totals (3 years)		38	45	2	3	2	0	0	4	.067	5	10	0	21	36	4	.934
Major League totals (5 years)		127	121	7	16	4	0	0	4	.132	7	30	2	88	149	8	.967

PERSONAL: Born November 24, 1962, in Midland, Texas. ... 6-0/200. ... Bats right, throws right. ... Full name: Randy Lee Velarde. ... Name pronounced vel-ARE-dee.

HIGH SCHOOL: Robert E. Lee (Midland, Texas).

COLLEGE: Lubbock (Texas) Christian College.

TRANSACTIONS/CAREER NOTES: Selected by Chicago White Sox organization in 19th round of free-agent draft (June 3, 1985). ... Traded by White Sox with P Pete Filson to New York Yankees for P Scott Nielsen and IF Mike Soper (January 5, 1987). ... On New York disabled list (August 9-29, 1989). ... On New York disabled list (June 6-July 30, 1993); included rehabilitation assignment to Albany/Colonie (July 24-30). ... Granted free agency (December 23, 1994). ... Re-signed by Yankees organization (April 12, 1995). ... Granted free agency (November 2, 1995). ... Signed by California Angels (November 21, 1995). ... Angels franchise renamed Anaheim Angels for 1997 season. ... On disabled list (March 23-September 1 and September 2, 1997-remainder of season). ... On Anaheim disabled list (March 19-May 13 and May 16-August 3, 1998); included rehabilitation assignments to Lake Elsinore (May 7-13) and Vancouver (July 29-August 3). ... Granted free agency (October 23, 1998). ... Re-signed by Angels (December 7, 1998). ... Traded by Angels with P Omar Olivares to Oakland Athletics for P Elvin Nina, OF Jeff DaVanon and OF Nathan Haynes (July 29, 1999). ... On Oakland disabled list (April 2-May 8, 2000); included rehabilitation assignments to Midland (April 28-May 2) and Sacramento (May 3-8). ... Traded by A's to Texas Rangers for P Ryan Cullen and P Aaron Harang (November 17, 2000). ... On Texas disabled list (May 25-July 12, 2001); included rehabilitation assignment to Tulsa (July 4-12). ... Traded by Rangers to Yankees for two players to be named later (August 31, 2001); Rangers acquired P Randy Flores and P Rosman Garcia to complete deal (October 12, 2001). ... Granted free agency (November 5, 2001). ... Signed by A's (January 11, 2002).

STATISTICAL NOTES: Led Midwest League shortstops with 52 errors in 1986. ... Had 21-game hitting streak (June 9-July 4, 1996). ... Led A.L. second baseman with 805 total chances in 1999. ... Career major league grand slams: 1.

								BATTING								FIELDING		
Year	Team (League)	Pos.	G	AB	R	H	2B	3B	HR	RBI	Avg.	BB	SO	SB	PO	A	E	Avg.
1985—Niagara Falls (NY-P)	OF-SS-2B-3B		67	218	28	48	7	3	1	16	.220	35	72	8	124	117	15	.941
1986—Appleton (Midw.)	SS-3B-OF		124	417	55	105	31	4	11	50	.252	58	96	13	205	300	†54	.903
—Buffalo (A.A.)	SS		9	20	2	4	1	0	0	2	.200	2	4	1	9	28	3	.925
1987—Alb./Colonie (East.)■	SS-OF		71	263	40	83	20	2	7	32	.316	25	47	8	128	254	17	.957
—Columbus (I.L.)	SS		49	185	21	59	10	6	5	33	.319	15	36	8	100	164	16	.943
—New York (A.L.)	SS		8	22	1	4	0	0	0	1	.182	0	6	0	8	20	2	.933
1988—Columbus (I.L.)	SS-2B-3B		78	293	39	79	23	4	5	37	.270	25	71	7	123	271	25	.940
—New York (A.L.)	2B-SS-3B		48	115	18	20	6	0	5	12	.174	8	24	1	72	98	8	.955
1989—Columbus (I.L.)	SS-3B		103	387	59	103	26	3	11	53	.266	38	105	3	150	295	22	.953
—New York (A.L.)	3B-SS		33	100	12	34	4	2	2	11	.340	7	14	0	26	61	4	.956
1990—New York (A.L.)	3-S-O-2-B		95	229	21	48	6	2	5	19	.210	20	53	0	70	159	12	.950
1991—New York (A.L.)	3B-SS-OF		80	184	19	45	11	1	1	15	.245	18	43	3	64	148	15	.934
1992—New York (A.L.)	S-3-O-2		121	412	57	112	24	1	7	46	.272	38	78	7	179	257	15	.967
1993—New York (A.L.)	OF-SS-3B-DH		85	226	28	68	13	2	7	24	.301	18	39	2	102	92	9	.956
—Alb./Colonie (East.)	SS-OF-DH		5	17	2	4	0	0	1	2	.235	2	2	0	6	12	2	.900
1994—New York (A.L.)	SS-3B-OF-2B		77	280	47	78	16	1	9	34	.279	22	61	4	92	188	19	.936
1995—New York (A.L.)	2-S-O-3		111	367	60	102	19	1	7	46	.278	55	64	5	168	258	10	.977
1996—California (A.L.)■	2B-3B-SS		136	530	82	151	27	3	14	54	.285	70	118	7	255	306	16	.972
1997—Anaheim (A.L.)	PR		1	0	0	0	0	0	0	0	...	0	0	0	...	...	...	...
1998—Lake Elsinore (Calif.)	2B		5	20	6	11	2	1	1	7	.550	2	0	1	10	18	1	.966
—Anaheim (A.L.)	2B		51	188	29	49	13	1	4	26	.261	34	42	7	88	132	4	.982
—Vancouver (PCL)	2B-DH		4	16	0	4	2	0	0	2	.250	1	4	1	3	7	0	1.000
1999—Anaheim (A.L.)	2B		95	376	57	115	15	4	9	48	.306	43	56	13	191	§307	7	.986
—Oakland (A.L.)■	2B		61	255	48	85	10	3	7	28	.333	27	42	11	107	§186	5	.977
2000—Midland (Texas)	2B		5	16	4	2	0	0	1	1	.125	4	4	0	7	9	1	.941
—Sacramento (PCL)	2B		3	11	3	5	0	0	0	2	.455	4	2	2	6	11	0	1.000
—Oakland (A.L.)	2B		122	485	82	135	23	0	12	41	.278	54	95	9	243	399	12	.982
2001—Texas (A.L.)■	2-1-3-D-O		78	296	46	88	16	2	9	31	.297	29	73	4	187	146	4	.988
—Tulsa (Texas)	2B		6	21	5	8	2	0	0	5	.381	1	5	0	5	12	0	1.000
—New York (A.L.)■	3B-DH-OF-1B		15	46	4	7	3	0	0	1	.152	5	13	2	18	18	1	.973
Major League totals (15 years)			1217	4111	611	1141	206	23	98	437	.278	448	821	75	1870	2775	145	.970

DIVISION SERIES RECORD

								BATTING								FIELDING		
Year	Team (League)	Pos.	G	AB	R	H	2B	3B	HR	RBI	Avg.	BB	SO	SB	PO	A	E	Avg.
1995—New York (A.L.)	2B-3B-OF		5	17	3	3	0	0	1	.176	6	4	0	15	11	1	.963
2000—Oakland (A.L.)	2B		5	20	2	5	1	0	0	3	.250	2	3	1	9	14	2	.920
2001—New York (A.L.)	DH		2	5	0	1	0	0	0	0	.200	0	1	0	...	...	...	...
Division series totals (3 years)			12	42	5	9	1	0	0	4	.214	8	8	1	24	25	3	.942

CHAMPIONSHIP SERIES RECORD

								BATTING								FIELDING		
Year	Team (League)	Pos.	G	AB	R	H	2B	3B	HR	RBI	Avg.	BB	SO	SB	PO	A	E	Avg.
2001—New York (A.L.)	PH-3B		1	1	0	0	0	0	0	0	.000	0	0	0	0	2	0	1.000

WORLD SERIES RECORD

								BATTING								FIELDING		
Year	Team (League)	Pos.	G	AB	R	H	2B	3B	HR	RBI	Avg.	BB	SO	SB	PO	A	E	Avg.
2001—New York (A.L.)	1B		1	3	0	0	0	0	0	0	.000	1	1	0	10	0	0	1.000

PERSONAL: Born August 2, 1973, in Takoma Park, Md. ... 5-10/180. ... Throws left, bats left. ... Full name: Michael Robert Venafro.

HIGH SCHOOL: Paul VI (Fairfax, Va.).

COLLEGE: James Madison.

TRANSACTIONS/CAREER NOTES: Selected by Texas Rangers organization in 29th round of free-agent draft (June 1, 1995). ... Traded by Rangers with 1B Carlos Pena to Oakland Athletics for 1B Jason Hart, P Mario Ramos, C Gerald Laird and OF Ryan Ludwick (January 14, 2002).

V

Year League	W	L	Pct.	ERA	G	GS	CG	ShO	Sv.	IP	H	R	ER	BB	SO
1995— Hudson Valley (NY-Penn)...	9	1	.900	2.13	32	0	0	0	2	50²/₃	37	13	12	21	32
1996— Charleston, S.C. (S.Atl.)	1	3	.250	3.51	50	0	0	0	19	59	57	27	23	21	62
1997— Charlotte (FSL)..................	4	2	.667	3.43	35	0	0	0	10	44²/₃	51	17	17	21	35
— Tulsa (Texas)	0	1	.000	3.45	11	0	0	0	1	15²/₃	13	12	6	12	13
1998— Tulsa (Texas)	3	4	.429	3.10	46	0	0	0	14	52¹/₃	42	21	18	26	45
— Oklahoma City (PCL).......	0	0	...	6.35	13	0	0	0	0	17	19	12	12	10	15
1999— Oklahoma (PCL).....................	0	0	...	5.40	6	0	0	0	1	11²/₃	16	7	7	0	7
— Texas (A.L.)	3	2	.600	3.29	65	0	0	0	0	68¹/₃	63	29	25	22	37
2000— Texas (A.L.)	3	1	.750	3.83	77	0	0	0	1	56¹/₃	64	27	24	21	32
2001— Texas (A.L.)	5	5	.500	4.80	70	0	0	0	4	60	54	35	32	28	29
Major League totals (3 years)	11	8	.579	3.95	212	0	0	0	5	184²/₃	181	91	81	71	98

DIVISION SERIES RECORD

Year League	W	L	Pct.	ERA	G	GS	CG	ShO	Sv.	IP	H	R	ER	BB	SO
1999— Texas (A.L.)	0	0	...	0.00	2	0	0	0	0	1	2	2	0	1	0

VENTURA, ROBIN   3B   YANKEES

PERSONAL: Born July 14, 1967, in Santa Maria, Calif. ... 6-1/198. ... Bats left, throws right. ... Full name: Robin Mark Ventura.

HIGH SCHOOL: Righetti (Santa Maria, Calif.).

COLLEGE: Oklahoma State.

TRANSACTIONS/CAREER NOTES: Selected by Chicago White Sox organization in first round (10th pick overall) of free-agent draft (June 1, 1988). ... On suspended list (August 23-25, 1993). ... On disabled list (March 31-July 24, 1997); included rehabilitation assignments to Nashville (July 13-17) and Birmingham (July 18-22). ... Granted free agency (October 23, 1998). ... Signed by New York Mets (December 1, 1998). ... On disabled list (July 14-29, 2000). ... Traded by Mets to New York Yankees for OF David Justice (December 7, 2001).

RECORDS: Holds A.L. single-season record for fewest chances accepted by third baseman for leader—372 (1996). ... Shares N.L. single-season record for highest fielding average by third baseman (150 or more games)—.980 (1999). ... Shares major league single-game record for most grand slams—2 (September 4, 1995).

HONORS: Named College Player of the Year by THE SPORTING NEWS (1987-88). ... Named third baseman on THE SPORTING NEWS college All-America team (1987-88). ... Named Golden Spikes Award winner by USA Baseball (1988). ... Won A.L. Gold Glove at third base (1991-93, 1996 and 1998). ... Won N.L. Gold Glove at third base (1999).

STATISTICAL NOTES: Led Southern League with 12 intentional bases on balls received in 1989. ... Led Southern League third basemen with .930 fielding percentage and tied for lead with 21 double plays in 1989. ... Led A.L. third basemen with 18 errors in 1991. ... Led A.L. third basemen in putouts with 134 in 1991, 141 in 1992 and 133 in 1996. ... Led A.L. third basemen in total chances with 536 in 1992, 404 in 1993 and 382 in 1996. ... Led A.L. third basemen with 372 assists and tied for lead in double plays with 29 in 1992. ... Led A.L. third basemen in double plays with 22 in 1994 and 34 in 1996 and tied for lead with 29 in 1992. ... Led A.L. with 15 intentional bases on balls received in 1998. ... Led A.L. third basemen with 447 total chances and 38 double plays in 1998. ... Led N.L. third basemen with 320 assists, 452 total chances and .980 fielding percentage in 1999. ... Career major league grand slams: 15.

MISCELLANEOUS: Member of 1988 U.S. Olympic baseball team.

Year— Team (League)	Pos.	G	AB	R	H	2B	3B	HR	RBI	Avg.	BB	SO	SB	PO	A	E	Avg.
1989— Birmingham (Sou.).....	3B-1B-2B	129	454	75	126	25	2	3	67	.278	93	51	9	108	249	27	†.930
— Chicago (A.L.)	3B	16	45	5	8	3	0	0	7	.178	8	6	0	17	33	2	.962
1990— Chicago (A.L.)	3B-1B	150	493	48	123	17	1	5	54	.249	55	53	1	116	268	25	.939
1991— Chicago (A.L.)	3B-1B	157	606	92	172	25	1	23	100	.284	80	67	2	†225	291	†18	.966
1992— Chicago (A.L.)	3B-1B	157	592	85	167	38	1	16	93	.282	93	71	2	†141	†375	23	.957
1993— Chicago (A.L.)	3B-1B	157	554	85	145	27	1	22	94	.262	105	82	1	119	278	14	.966
1994— Chicago (A.L.)	3B-1B-SS	109	401	57	113	15	1	18	78	.282	61	69	3	89	180	20	.931
1995— Chicago (A.L.)	3B-1B-DH	135	492	79	145	22	0	26	93	.295	75	98	4	201	216	19	.956
1996— Chicago (A.L.)	3B-1B	158	586	96	168	31	2	34	105	.287	78	81	1	†189	247	11	.975
1997— Nashville (A.A.)	3B-DH	5	15	3	6	1	0	2	5	.400	2	1	0	1	12	0	1.000
— Birmingham (Sou.).....	3B	4	17	3	5	1	0	1	2	.294	1	1	0	2	3	2	.714
— Chicago (A.L.)	3B	54	183	27	48	10	1	6	26	.262	34	21	0	53	99	7	.956
1998— Chicago (A.L.)	3B	161	590	84	155	31	4	21	91	.263	79	111	1	102	*330	15	.966
1999— New York (N.L.)■	3B-1B	161	588	88	177	38	0	32	120	.301	74	109	1	124	†320	9	†.980
2000— New York (N.L.).........	3B-1B	141	469	61	109	23	0	24	84	.232	75	91	3	96	261	17	.955
2001— New York (N.L.).........	3B	142	456	70	108	20	0	21	61	.237	88	101	2	91	264	16	.957
American League totals (10 years)		1254	4542	658	1244	219	12	171	741	.274	668	659	15	1252	2317	154	.959
National League totals (3 years)		444	1513	219	394	81	1	77	265	.260	237	301	6	311	845	42	.965
Major League totals (13 years)		1698	6055	877	1638	300	13	248	1006	.271	905	960	21	1563	3162	196	.960

DIVISION SERIES RECORD

Year Team (League)	Pos.	G	AB	R	H	2B	3B	HR	RBI	Avg.	BB	SO	SB	PO	A	E	Avg.
1999— New York (N.L.).........	3B	4	14	1	3	2	0	0	1	.214	4	2	0	3	8	0	1.000
2000— New York (N.L.).........	3B-1B	4	14	1	2	0	0	1	2	.143	4	1	0	7	6	0	1.000
Division series totals (2 years)		8	28	2	5	2	0	1	3	.179	8	3	0	10	14	0	1.000

CHAMPIONSHIP SERIES RECORD

Year Team (League)	Pos.	G	AB	R	H	2B	3B	HR	RBI	Avg.	BB	SO	SB	PO	A	E	Avg.
1993— Chicago (A.L.)...........	3B-1B	6	20	2	4	0	0	0	5	.200	6	6	0	9	6	1	.938
1999— New York (N.L.).........	3B	6	25	2	3	1	0	0	1	.120	2	5	0	5	16	0	1.000
2000— New York (N.L.).........	3B	5	14	4	3	1	0	0	5	.214	6	0	0	2	13	1	.938
Championship series totals (3 years)		17	59	8	10	2	0	1	11	.169	14	11	0	16	35	2	.962

WORLD SERIES RECORD

Year Team (League)	Pos.	G	AB	R	H	2B	3B	HR	RBI	Avg.	BB	SO	SB	PO	A	E	Avg.
2000— New York (N.L.)..........	3B	5	20	1	3	1	0	1	1	.150	1	5	0	1	8	0	1.000

ALL-STAR GAME RECORD

Year League	Pos.	AB	R	H	2B	3B	HR	RBI	Avg.	BB	SO	SB	PO	A	E	Avg.
1992— American	3B	2	1	2	1	0	0	1	1.000	0	0	0	1	1	0	1.000

V

PERSONAL: Born July 9, 1981, in Santo Domingo, Dominican Republic. ... 6-5/230. ... Throws right, bats right.
TRANSACTIONS/CAREER NOTES: Signed as non-drafted free agent by Tampa Devil Rays organization (January 19, 1998).

Year League	W	L	Pct.	ERA	G	GS	CG	ShO	Sv.	IP	H	R	ER	BB	SO
1998— GC Devil Rays (GCL)	1	1	.500	6.75	5	4	0	0	0	16	19	14	12	12	19
1999— Princeton (Appl.)	3	5	.375	7.12	14	•14	0	0	0	60 2/3	74	57	48	*50	48
2000— Charleston, S.C. (S.Atl.)	8	8	.500	4.81	20	20	1	0	0	106 2/3	125	74	57	41	102
2001— Bakersfield (Calif.)	9	8	.529	4.53	27	27	0	0	0	153	163	104	77	55	138

PERSONAL: Born April 3, 1971, in Santo Domingo, Dominican Republic. ... 5-10/183. ... Bats both, throws right. ... Full name: Quilvio Alberto Perez Veras.
HIGH SCHOOL: Victor E. Liz (Santo Domingo, Dominican Republic).
TRANSACTIONS/CAREER NOTES: Signed as non-drafted free agent by New York Mets organization (November 22, 1989). ... On suspended list (July 31-August 2, 1994). ... On disabled list (August 7-15, 1994). ... Traded by Mets to Florida Marlins for OF Carl Everett (November 29, 1994). ... On Florida disabled list (May 10-June 21, 1996); included rehabilitation assignment to Charlotte (June 13-21). ... Traded by Marlins to San Diego Padres for P Dustin Hermanson (November 21, 1996). ... On disabled list (August 8-23, 1999). ... Traded by Padres with 1B Wally Joyner and OF Reggie Sanders to Atlanta Braves for OF/1B Ryan Klesko, 2B Bret Boone and P Jason Shiell (December 22, 1999). ... On disabled list (July 16, 2000-remainder of season). ... On Atlanta disabled list (July 14-31, 2001). ... Released by Braves (August 7, 2001). ... Signed by Boston Red Sox organization (August 19, 2001). ... On Pawtucket disabled list (August 30, 2001-remainder of season). ... Granted free agency (October 15, 2001).
STATISTICAL NOTES: Tied for Appalachian League lead in double plays by second baseman with 30 in 1991. ... Led Appalachian League second basemen with 282 total chances in 1991. ... Led South Atlantic League in on-base percentage with .441 and in caught stealing with 35 in 1992. ... Led Eastern League in on-base percentage with .430 and in caught stealing with 19 in 1993. ... Led Eastern League second basemen with 669 total chances in 1993. ... Led International League in caught stealing with 18 in 1994. ... Led International League second basemen with 589 total chances and 84 double plays in 1994. ... Led N.L. in caught stealing with 21 in 1995. ... Career major league grand slams: 1.

Year Team (League)	Pos.	G	AB	R	H	2B	3B	HR	RBI	Avg.	BB	SO	SB	PO	A	E	Avg.
1990— GC Mets (GCL)	2B	30	98	26	29	3	3	1	5	.296	19	16	16	45	76	3	.976
— Kingsport (Appl.)	2B	24	94	21	36	6	0	1	14	.383	13	14	9	55	79	8	.944
1991— Kingsport (Appl.)	2B	64	226	*54	76	11	4	1	16	.336	36	28	38	*113	*161	8	.972
— Pittsfield (NY-Penn)....	2B-SS	5	15	3	4	0	1	0	2	.267	5	1	2	16	16	1	.970
1992— Columbia (S.Atl.)	2B	117	414	97	132	24	10	2	40	*.319	84	52	*66	208	313	20	.963
1993— Binghamton (East.)	2B	128	444	87	136	19	7	2	51	.306	*91	62	52	*274	*372	23	.966
1994— Norfolk (I.L.)	2B-DH	123	457	71	114	22	4	0	43	.249	59	56	40	*267	*308	*14	.976
1995— Florida (N.L.)■.........	2B-OF	124	440	86	115	20	7	5	32	.261	80	68	*56	299	315	9	.986
1996— Florida (N.L.)	2B	73	253	40	64	8	1	4	14	.253	51	42	8	174	191	5	.986
— Charlotte (I.L.)	2B-DH	28	104	22	34	5	2	2	8	.327	13	14	8	44	66	3	.973
1997— San Diego (N.L.)■.......	2B	145	539	74	143	23	1	3	45	.265	72	84	33	276	407	11	.984
1998— San Diego (N.L.)	2B	138	517	79	138	24	2	6	45	.267	84	78	24	258	405	9	.987
1999— San Diego (N.L.)	2B	132	475	95	133	25	2	6	41	.280	65	88	30	271	334	12	.981
2000— Atlanta (N.L.)■............	2B	84	298	56	92	15	0	5	37	.309	51	50	25	146	223	6	.984
2001— Atlanta (N.L.)..............	2B	71	258	39	65	14	2	3	25	.252	24	52	7	132	181	3	.991
— Pawtucket (I.L.)■.......	2B	3	10	1	3	1	0	0	0	.300	0	3	0	2	5	0	1.000
Major League totals (7 years)		767	2780	469	750	129	15	32	239	.270	427	462	183	1556	2056	55	.985

DIVISION SERIES RECORD

Year Team (League)	Pos.	G	AB	R	H	2B	3B	HR	RBI	Avg.	BB	SO	SB	PO	A	E	Avg.
1998— San Diego (N.L.)	2B	4	15	1	2	0	0	0	0	.133	1	6	0	8	12	0	1.000

CHAMPIONSHIP SERIES RECORD

Year Team (League)	Pos.	G	AB	R	H	2B	3B	HR	RBI	Avg.	BB	SO	SB	PO	A	E	Avg.
1998— San Diego (N.L.)	2B	6	24	2	6	1	0	0	2	.250	5	7	0	7	13	0	1.000

WORLD SERIES RECORD

Year Team (League)	Pos.	G	AB	R	H	2B	3B	HR	RBI	Avg.	BB	SO	SB	PO	A	E	Avg.
1998— San Diego (N.L.)	2B	4	15	3	3	2	0	0	1	.200	3	4	0	9	16	0	1.000

PERSONAL: Born January 19, 1978, in Monte Cristi, Dominican Republic. ... 6-2/198. ... Bats right, throws right. ... Full name: Wilton Andres Veras.
HIGH SCHOOL: Monte Cristi (Dominican Republic).
TRANSACTIONS/CAREER NOTES: Signed as non-drafted free agent by Boston Red Sox organization (February 9, 1995).
STATISTICAL NOTES: Led New York-Pennsylvania League in grounding into double plays with nine in 1996. ... Led Midwest League third basemen with 29 double plays in 1997. ... Led Midwest League in grounding into double plays with 19 in 1997. ... Led Eastern League third basemen with 377 total chances in 1998. ... Led Eastern League in grounding into double plays with 23 in 1999. ... Led Eastern League third basemen with 27 double plays in 1999. ... Led International League in grounding into double plays with 24 in 2001. ... Led International League third basemen with 388 total chances in 2001.

Year Team (League)	Pos.	G	AB	R	H	2B	3B	HR	RBI	Avg.	BB	SO	SB	PO	A	E	Avg.
1995—GC Red Sox (GCL)	1B-3B	31	91	7	24	1	0	0	5	.264	7	9	1	80	2	1	.988
1996—Lowell (NY-Penn)	3B	67	250	22	60	15	0	0	19	.240	13	29	2	*57	106	12	.931
1997—Michigan (Midw.)	3B	131	489	51	141	21	3	8	68	.288	31	51	3	99	220	19	*.944
1998—Trenton (East.)	3B	126	470	70	137	27	4	16	67	.291	15	66	5	*100	*259	18	*.952
1999—Trenton (East.)	3B-DH	116	474	65	133	23	2	11	75	.281	23	55	7	83	*245	19	*.945
— Boston (A.L.)	3B	36	119	14	34	5	1	2	13	.286	5	14	0	23	56	6	.929
2000—Pawtucket (I.L.).........	3B	60	218	18	46	9	0	3	25	.211	12	18	0	45	98	4	.973
— Boston (A.L.)	3B	49	164	21	40	7	1	0	14	.244	7	20	0	33	94	13	.907
2001—Pawtucket (I.L.).........	3B	136	521	44	120	16	2	8	52	.230	14	63	5	128	234	*26	.933
Major League totals (2 years)		85	283	35	74	12	2	2	27	.261	12	34	0	56	150	19	.916

DIVISION SERIES RECORD

Year Team (League)	Pos.	G	AB	R	H	2B	3B	HR	RBI	Avg.	BB	SO	SB	PO	A	E	Avg.
1999—Boston (A.L.)							Did not play.										

CHAMPIONSHIP SERIES RECORD

Year Team (League)	Pos.	G	AB	R	H	2B	3B	HR	RBI	Avg.	BB	SO	SB	PO	A	E	Avg.
1999—Boston (A.L.)							Did not play.										

VERES, DAVE — P — CARDINALS

PERSONAL: Born October 19, 1966, in Montgomery, Ala. ... 6-2/220. ... Throws right, bats right. ... Full name: David Scott Veres. ... Name pronounced VEERZ.

HIGH SCHOOL: Gresham (Ore.).

JUNIOR COLLEGE: Mount Hood Community College (Ore.).

TRANSACTIONS/CAREER NOTES: Selected by Oakland Athletics organization in fourth round of free-agent draft (January 14, 1986). ... Traded by A's to Los Angeles Dodgers for P Kevin Campbell (January 15, 1991). ... Loaned by Dodgers organization to Mexico City Tigers, Mexican League (April 3-May 15, 1992). ... Released by Dodgers (May 15, 1992). ... Signed by Houston Astros organization (May 28, 1992). ... Traded by Astros with C Raul Chavez to Montreal Expos for 3B Sean Berry (December 20, 1995). ... On disabled list (August 21-September 17, 1997). ... Traded by Expos with a player to be named later to Colorado Rockies for OF Terry Jones and a player to be named later (December 10, 1997). ... Traded by Rockies with P Darryl Kile and P Luther Hackman to St. Louis Cardinals for P Jose Jimenez, P Manny Aybar, P Rick Croushore and SS Brent Butler (November 16, 1999).

STATISTICAL NOTES: Tied for California League lead with 29 wild pitches in 1987. ... Led Southern League with 16 wild pitches in 1989.

MISCELLANEOUS: Made an out in only appearance as pinch hitter (1998).

Year League	W	L	Pct.	ERA	G	GS	CG	ShO	Sv.	IP	H	R	ER	BB	SO
1986—Medford (N'West)	5	2	.714	3.26	15	•15	0	0	0	77 1/3	58	38	28	57	60
1987—Modesto (Calif.)	8	9	.471	4.79	26	26	2	0	0	148 1/3	124	90	79	108	124
1988—Modesto (Calif.)	4	11	.267	3.31	19	19	3	0	0	125	100	61	46	78	91
— Huntsville (Sou.)	3	4	.429	4.15	8	8	0	0	0	39	50	20	18	15	17
1989—Huntsville (Sou.)	8	11	.421	4.86	29	28	2	1	0	159 1/3	160	93	86	83	105
1990—Tacoma (PCL)	11	8	.579	4.69	32	23	2	0	1	151 2/3	136	90	79	88	88
1991—Albuquerque (PCL)■	7	6	.538	4.47	57	3	0	0	5	100 2/3	89	52	50	52	81
1992—M.C. Tigres (Mex.)■	1	5	.167	8.10	14	1	0	0	1	23 1/3	29	21	21	12	12
— Tucson (PCL)■	2	3	.400	5.30	29	1	0	0	0	52 2/3	60	36	31	17	46
1993—Tucson (PCL)	6	10	.375	4.90	43	15	1	0	5	130 1/3	156	88	71	32	122
1994—Tucson (PCL)	1	1	.500	1.88	16	0	0	0	1	24	17	8	5	10	19
— Houston (N.L.)	3	3	.500	2.41	32	0	0	0	1	41	39	13	11	7	28
1995—Houston (N.L.)	5	1	.833	2.26	72	0	0	0	1	103 1/3	89	29	26	30	94
1996—Montreal (N.L.)■	6	3	.667	4.17	68	0	0	0	4	77 2/3	85	39	36	32	81
1997—Montreal (N.L.)	2	3	.400	3.48	53	0	0	0	1	62	68	28	24	27	47
1998—Colorado (N.L.)■	3	1	.750	2.83	63	0	0	0	8	76 1/3	67	26	24	27	74
1999—Colorado (N.L.)	4	8	.333	5.14	73	0	0	0	31	77	88	46	44	37	71
2000—St. Louis (N.L.)■	3	5	.375	2.85	71	0	0	0	29	75 2/3	65	26	24	25	67
2001—St. Louis (N.L.)	3	2	.600	3.70	71	0	0	0	15	65 2/3	57	29	27	28	61
Major League totals (8 years)	29	26	.527	3.36	503	0	0	0	90	578 2/3	558	236	216	213	523

DIVISION SERIES RECORD

Year League	W	L	Pct.	ERA	G	GS	CG	ShO	Sv.	IP	H	R	ER	BB	SO
2000—St. Louis (N.L.)...................	0	0	...	0.00	2	0	0	0	1	2	1	1	0	0	4
2001—St. Louis (N.L.)...................	0	0	...	0.00	2	0	0	0	0	1	1	0	0	1	1
Division series totals (2 years)	0	0	...	0.00	4	0	0	0	1	3	2	1	0	1	5

CHAMPIONSHIP SERIES RECORD

Year League	W	L	Pct.	ERA	G	GS	CG	ShO	Sv.	IP	H	R	ER	BB	SO
2000—St. Louis (N.L.)...................	0	0	...	0.00	3	0	0	0	0	2 1/3	2	0	0	0	3

V

VIDRO, JOSE — 2B — EXPOS

PERSONAL: Born August 27, 1974, in Mayaguez, Puerto Rico. ... 5-11/190. ... Bats both, throws right. ... Full name: Jose Angel Cetty Vidro.

HIGH SCHOOL: Blanco Morales (Sabana Grande, Puerto Rico).

TRANSACTIONS/CAREER NOTES: Selected by Montreal Expos organization in sixth round of free agent draft (June 1, 1992). ... On disabled list (June 1-15 and July 26, 1993-remainder of season). ... On disabled list (May 20-June 12, 2001).

RECORDS: Shares major league single-season record for fewest putouts by second baseman (150 or more games)—260 (2000).

STATISTICAL NOTES: Switch-hit home runs in one game (July 3, 2000). ... Career major league grand slams: 1.

Year	Team (League)	Pos.	G	AB	R	H	2B	3B	HR	RBI	Avg.	BB	SO	SB	PO	A	E	Avg.
1992—	GC Expos (GCL)	2B	54	200	29	66	6	2	4	31	.330	16	31	10	114	107	4	*.982
1993—	Burlington (Midw.)	2B	76	287	39	69	19	0	2	34	.240	28	54	3	107	153	7	.974
1994—	W. Palm Beach (FSL) .	2B	125	465	57	124	30	2	4	49	.267	51	56	8	204	328	20	.964
1995—	W. Palm Beach (FSL) .	IF	44	163	20	53	15	2	3	24	.325	8	21	0	101	110	4	.981
—	Harrisburg (East.).......	IF	64	246	33	64	16	2	4	38	.260	20	37	7	97	162	9	.966
1996—	Harrisburg (East.)	IF	126	452	57	117	25	3	18	82	.259	29	71	3	135	271	15	.964
1997—	Ottawa (I.L.)	3B-2B-DH	73	279	40	90	17	0	13	47	.323	22	40	2	70	161	8	.967
—	Montreal (N.L.)..........	3B-DH-2B	67	169	19	42	12	1	2	17	.249	11	20	1	25	59	4	.955
1998—	Montreal (N.L.)..........	2B-3B	83	205	24	45	12	0	0	18	.220	27	33	2	81	126	6	.972
—	Ottawa (I.L.)	2B-3B-DH	63	235	35	68	14	2	2	32	.289	24	25	5	91	124	6	.973
1999—	Montreal (N.L.)..........	2-1-0-3	140	494	67	150	45	2	12	59	.304	29	51	0	270	296	11	.981
2000—	Montreal (N.L.)..........	2B	153	606	101	200	51	2	24	97	.330	49	69	5	260	*442	10	.986
2001—	Montreal (N.L.)..........	2B-DH	124	486	82	155	34	1	15	59	.319	31	49	4	204	315	9	.983
Major League totals (5 years)			567	1960	293	592	154	6	53	250	.302	147	222	12	840	1238	40	.981

ALL-STAR GAME RECORD

Year	League	Pos.	AB	R	H	2B	3B	HR	RBI	Avg.	BB	SO	SB	PO	A	E	Avg.
2000—	National	PH-2B	1	0	0	0	0	0	0	.000	0	0	0	0	0	1	.000

VILLAFUERTE, BRANDON   P   PADRES

PERSONAL: Born December 17, 1975, in Hilo, Hawaii. ... 5-11/165. ... Throws right, bats right. ... Full name: Brandon Paul Villafuerte.

HIGH SCHOOL: Live Oak (Morgan Hill, Calif.).

JUNIOR COLLEGE: West Valley College (Calif.).

TRANSACTIONS/CAREER NOTES: Selected by New York Mets organization 66th round of free-agent draft (June 2, 1994). ... Traded by Mets with a player to be named later to Florida Marlins for OF Robert Stratton (March 20,1998); Marlins acquired 2B Cesar Crespo to complete deal (September 14, 1998). ... Traded by Marlins to Detroit Tigers for P Mike Drumright (July 31, 1999). ... Traded by Tigers with P Kevin Mobley to Texas Rangers for P Matt Perisho (December 15, 2000). ... Granted free agency (October 11, 2001). ... Signed by San Diego Padres organization (December 6, 2001).

STATISTICAL NOTES: Tied for International League lead with 12 wild pitches in 2000.

Year	League	W	L	Pct.	ERA	G	GS	CG	ShO	Sv.	IP	H	R	ER	BB	SO
1995—	Little Falls (NY-Penn) ...	5	1	.833	5.63	20	0	0	0	0	32	28	21	20	26	42
1996—	Pittsfield (NY-Penn)..........	8	3	.727	3.02	18	7	1	0	1	62²/₃	53	21	21	27	59
1997—	Capital City (S.Atl.)............	3	1	.750	2.38	47	3	0	0	7	75²/₃	58	23	20	33	88
1998—	Brevard County (FSL)■......	1	0	1.000	0.93	3	0	0	0	0	9²/₃	7	3	1	1	6
—	Portland (East.)............	0	2	.000	4.97	30	0	0	0	1	54¹/₃	68	35	30	33	52
—	Charlotte (I.L.).............	1	0	1.000	6.35	10	0	0	0	0	11¹/₃	15	8	8	8	9
1999—	Portland (East.)............	6	8	.429	3.50	22	12	0	0	0	100¹/₃	97	45	39	40	85
—	Jacksonville (Sou.)■......	0	2	.000	1.88	15	0	0	0	5	24	17	6	5	12	20
2000—	Toledo (I.L.)....................	4	9	.308	6.67	46	6	0	0	4	87²/₃	112	70	65	49	85
—	Detroit (A.L.)................	0	0	...	10.38	3	0	0	0	0	4¹/₃	4	5	5	4	1
2001—	Oklahoma (PCL)■.............	5	5	.500	2.83	38	0	0	0	10	63²/₃	63	21	20	26	65
—	Texas (A.L.)	0	0	...	14.29	6	0	0	0	0	5²/₃	12	9	9	4	4
Major League totals (2 years)		0	0	...	12.60	9	0	0	0	0	10	16	14	14	8	5

VILLONE, RON   P

PERSONAL: Born January 16, 1970, in Englewood, N.J. ... 6-3/237. ... Throws left, bats left. ... Full name: Ronald Thomas Villone Jr.

HIGH SCHOOL: South Bergenfield (Bergenfield, N.J.).

COLLEGE: Massachusetts.

TRANSACTIONS/CAREER NOTES: Selected by Seattle Mariners in first round (14th pick overall) of free-agent draft (June 1, 1992). ... On disabled list (April 19-26, 1994). ... Traded by Mariners with OF Marc Newfield to San Diego Padres for P Andy Benes and a player to be named later (July 31, 1995); Mariners acquired P Greg Keagle to complete deal (September 16, 1995). ... Traded by Padres with P Bryce Florie and OF Marc Newfield to Milwaukee Brewers for OF Greg Vaughn and a player to be named later (July 31, 1996); Padres acquired OF Gerald Parent to complete deal (September 16, 1996). ... Traded by Brewers with P Ben McDonald and P Mike Fetters to Cleveland Indians for OF Marquis Grissom and P Jeff Juden (December 8, 1997). ... On Cleveland disabled list (August 15-September 1, 1998); included rehabilitation assignment to Buffalo (August 22-September 1). ... Released by Indians (April 2, 1999). ... Signed by Cincinnati Reds organization (April 5, 1999). ... Traded by Reds to Colorado Rockies for two players to be named later (November 8, 2000); Reds acquired P Jeff Taglienti and P Justin Carter to complete deal (December 20, 2000). ... Traded by Rockies to Houston Astros for P Jay Powell (June 27, 2001). ... Granted free agency (November 9, 2001).

STATISTICAL NOTES: Struck out 16 batters in one game (September 29, 2000).

MISCELLANEOUS: Member of 1992 U.S. Olympic baseball team.

Year	League	W	L	Pct.	ERA	G	GS	CG	ShO	Sv.	IP	H	R	ER	BB	SO
1993—	Riverside (Calif.)	7	4	.636	4.21	16	16	0	0	0	83¹/₃	74	47	39	62	82
—	Jacksonville (Sou.)............	3	4	.429	4.38	11	11	0	0	0	63²/₃	49	34	31	41	66
1994—	Jacksonville (Sou.)............	6	7	.462	3.86	41	5	0	0	8	79¹/₃	56	37	34	68	94
1995—	Seattle (A.L.)	0	2	.000	7.91	19	0	0	0	0	19¹/₃	20	19	17	23	26
—	Tacoma (PCL)	1	0	1.000	0.61	22	0	0	0	13	29²/₃	9	6	2	19	43
—	San Diego (N.L.)■...........	2	1	.667	4.21	19	0	0	0	1	25²/₃	24	12	12	11	37
1996—	Las Vegas (PCL)	2	1	.667	1.64	23	0	0	0	3	22	13	5	4	9	29
—	San Diego (N.L.)	1	1	.500	2.95	21	0	0	0	0	18¹/₃	17	6	6	7	19
—	Milwaukee (A.L.)■..........	0	0	...	3.28	23	0	0	0	2	24²/₃	14	9	9	18	19
1997—	Milwaukee (A.L.)	1	0	1.000	3.42	50	0	0	0	0	52²/₃	54	23	20	36	40
1998—	Buffalo (I.L.)■.................	2	2	.500	2.01	23	0	0	0	7	22¹/₃	20	11	5	11	28
—	Cleveland (A.L.)	0	0	...	6.00	25	0	0	0	0	27	30	18	18	22	15
1999—	Indianapolis (I.L.)■..........	2	0	1.000	1.42	18	0	0	0	1	19	9	3	3	13	23
—	Cincinnati (N.L.).............	9	7	.563	4.23	29	22	0	0	2	142²/₃	114	70	67	73	97

Year	League	W	L	Pct.	ERA	G	GS	CG	ShO	Sv.	IP	H	R	ER	BB	SO
2000—Cincinnati (N.L.)		10	10	.500	5.43	35	23	2	0	0	141	154	95	85	78	77
2001—Colorado (N.L.)■		1	3	.250	6.36	22	6	0	0	0	46²/₃	56	35	33	29	48
—Houston (N.L.)■		5	7	.417	5.56	31	6	0	0	0	68	77	46	42	24	65
A.L. totals (4 years)		1	2	.333	4.66	117	0	0	0	2	123²/₃	118	69	64	99	100
N.L. totals (5 years)		28	29	.491	4.98	157	57	2	0	3	442¹/₃	442	264	245	222	343
Major League totals (7 years)		29	31	.483	4.91	274	57	2	0	5	566	560	333	309	321	443

DIVISION SERIES RECORD

Year	League	W	L	Pct.	ERA	G	GS	CG	ShO	Sv.	IP	H	R	ER	BB	SO
2001—Houston (N.L.)		0	0	...	0.00	1	0	0	0	0	²/₃	0	0	0	0	0

VINA, FERNANDO 2B CARDINALS

PERSONAL: Born April 16, 1969, in Sacramento. ... 5-9/174. ... Bats left, throws right. ... Name pronounced VEEN-ya.
HIGH SCHOOL: Valley (Sacramento).
JUNIOR COLLEGE: Cosumnes River College (Calif.), then Sacramento City College.
COLLEGE: Arizona State.
TRANSACTIONS/CAREER NOTES: Selected by New York Yankees organization in 51st round of free-agent draft (June 1, 1988); did not sign. ... Selected by New York Mets organization in ninth round of free-agent draft (June 4, 1990). ... Selected by Seattle Mariners from Mets organization in Rule 5 major league draft (December 7, 1992). ... Returned to Mets organization (June 15, 1993). ... On New York disabled list (May 22-June 6, 1994). ... On Norfolk disabled list (August 30-September 6, 1994). ... Traded by Mets to Milwaukee Brewers (December 22, 1994), completing deal in which Brewers traded P Doug Henry for two players to be named later (November 30, 1994); Brewers acquired C Javier Gonzalez as partial completion of deal (December 6, 1994). ... On Milwaukee disabled list (April 20-July 17, 1997); included rehabilitation assignments to Stockton (July 9-11) and Tucson (July 12-17). ... On suspended list (May 11-13 and May 25-27, 1999). ... On Milwaukee disabled list (May 10-25 and June 4, 1999-remainder of season); included rehabilitation assignment to Beloit (August 6-8). ... Traded by Brewers to St. Louis Cardinals for P Juan Acevedo and two players to be named later (December 20, 1999); Brewers acquired P Matt Parker and C Eliezer Alfonzo to complete deal (June 13, 2000). ... On disabled list (June 20-July 4, 2000).
HONORS: Won N.L. Gold Glove at second base (2001).
STATISTICAL NOTES: Tied for South Atlantic League lead in caught stealing with 22 in 1991. ... Led South Atlantic League second basemen with 600 total chances and 61 double plays in 1991. ... Led Florida State League second basemen with 85 double plays in 1992. ... Led N.L. in being hit by pitch with 12 in 1994. ... Led A.L. second basemen with 116 double plays in 1996. ... Led N.L. second basemen with 884 total chances and 135 double plays in 1998. ... Had 17-game hitting streak (August 8-25, 2000). ... Led N.L. in being hit by pitch with 28 in 2000. ... Career major league grand slams: 1.

Year	Team (League)	Pos.	G	AB	R	H	2B	3B	HR	RBI	Avg.	BB	SO	SB	PO	A	E	Avg.
1991—Columbia (S.Atl.)		2B	129	498	77	135	23	6	6	50	.271	46	27	42	194	*385	21	*.965
1992—St. Lucie (FSL)		2B	111	421	61	124	15	5	1	42	.295	32	26	36	219	*360	17	.971
—Tidewater (I.L.)		2B	11	30	3	6	0	0	0	2	.200	0	2	0	16	28	1	.978
1993—Seattle (A.L.)■		2B-SS-DH	24	45	5	10	2	0	0	2	.222	4	3	6	28	40	0	1.000
—Norfolk (I.L.)■		SS-2B-DH-OF	73	287	24	66	6	4	4	27	.230	7	17	16	146	232	14	.964
1994—New York (N.L.)		2B-3B-SS-OF	79	124	20	31	6	0	0	6	.250	12	11	3	46	59	4	.963
—Norfolk (I.L.)		SS-2B	6	17	2	3	0	0	0	1	.176	1	1	1	9	11	1	.952
1995—Milwaukee (A.L.)■		2B-SS-3B	113	288	46	74	7	7	3	29	.257	22	28	6	194	245	8	.982
1996—Milwaukee (A.L.)		2B	140	554	94	157	19	10	7	46	.283	38	35	16	*333	412	*16	.979
1997—Milwaukee (A.L.)		2B-DH	79	324	37	89	12	2	4	28	.275	12	23	8	149	227	7	.982
—Stockton (Calif.)		2B	3	9	2	4	0	1	0	3	.444	0	0	0	2	7	0	1.000
—Tucson (PCL)		2B	6	19	3	9	3	0	1	5	.474	3	1	0	8	16	2	.923
1998—Milwaukee (N.L.)		2B	159	637	101	198	39	7	7	45	.311	54	46	22	*404	*468	12	.986
1999—Milwaukee (N.L.)		2B	37	154	17	41	7	0	1	16	.266	14	6	5	84	104	1	.995
—Beloit (Midw.)		DH-2B	2	10	1	2	1	0	0	0	.200	0	2	0	0	2	2	.500
2000—St. Louis (N.L.)■		2B	123	487	81	146	24	6	4	31	.300	36	36	10	261	325	7	*.988
2001—St. Louis (N.L.)		2B	154	631	95	191	30	8	9	56	.303	33	35	17	313	383	9	.987
American League totals (4 years)			356	1211	182	330	40	19	14	105	.273	76	89	36	704	924	31	.981
National League totals (5 years)			552	2033	314	607	106	21	21	154	.299	148	134	57	1108	1339	33	.987
Major League totals (9 years)			908	3244	496	937	146	40	35	259	.289	224	223	93	1812	2263	64	.985

DIVISION SERIES RECORD

Year	Team (League)	Pos.	G	AB	R	H	2B	3B	HR	RBI	Avg.	BB	SO	SB	PO	A	E	Avg.
2000—St. Louis (N.L.)		2B	3	13	3	4	0	0	1	3	.308	1	1	0	7	13	0	1.000
2001—St. Louis (N.L.)		2B	5	19	2	6	0	0	1	2	.316	0	1	1	14	8	0	1.000
Division series totals (2 years)			8	32	5	10	0	0	2	5	.313	1	2	1	21	21	0	1.000

CHAMPIONSHIP SERIES RECORD

Year	Team (League)	Pos.	G	AB	R	H	2B	3B	HR	RBI	Avg.	BB	SO	SB	PO	A	E	Avg.
2000—St. Louis (N.L.)		2B	5	23	3	6	1	0	0	1	.261	1	4	0	14	10	1	.960

ALL-STAR GAME RECORD

Year	League	Pos.	AB	R	H	2B	3B	HR	RBI	Avg.	BB	SO	SB	PO	A	E	Avg.
1998—National		2B	1	0	1	0	0	0	0	1.000	1	0	0	1	1	1	.667

V

VINING, KEN P WHITE SOX

PERSONAL: Born December 5, 1974, in Decatur, Ga. ... 6-0/180. ... Throws left, bats left. ... Full name: Kenneth Edward Vining.
HIGH SCHOOL: Cardinal Newman (Decatur, Ga.).
COLLEGE: Clemson.

TRANSACTIONS/CAREER NOTES: Selected by San Francisco Giants organization in fourth round of free-agent draft (June 4, 1996). ... Traded by Giants with P Keith Foulke, SS Mike Caruso, OF Brian Manning, Lorenzo Barcelo and P Bobby Howry to Chicago White Sox for P Wilson Alvarez, P Danny Darwin and P Roberto Hernandez (July 31, 1997). ... On Birmingham disabled list (May 19-June 14, 2000).

STATISTICAL NOTES: Led Southern League pitchers in batters faced with 793 in 1998.

Year	League	W	L	Pct.	ERA	G	GS	CG	ShO	Sv.	IP	H	R	ER	BB	SO
1996—	Bellingham (N'West)	4	2	.667	2.09	12	11	0	0	0	60 1/3	45	16	14	23	69
1997—	Winston-Salem (Caro.)■ ...	2	2	.500	2.86	5	5	0	0	0	34 2/3	36	17	11	11	38
	—San Jose (Calif.)................	9	6	.600	4.21	23	23	1	1	0	136 2/3	140	77	64	60	142
1998—	Birmingham (Sou.)............	10	12	.455	4.07	29	28	1	0	0	172 2/3	187	103	78	91	133
1999—	Birmingham (Sou.)............	0	2	.000	9.26	3	3	0	0	0	11 2/3	20	16	12	9	8
2000—	Birmingham (Sou.)............	1	5	.167	4.08	43	0	0	0	1	46 1/3	36	26	21	18	41
2001—	Charlotte (I.L.)....................	2	3	.400	1.96	41	0	0	0	4	46	35	10	10	19	47
	—Chicago (A.L.)...................	0	0	...	17.55	8	0	0	0	0	6 2/3	15	14	13	7	3
Major League totals (1 year)........		0	0	...	17.55	8	0	0	0	0	6 2/3	15	14	13	7	3

VIZCAINO, JOSE — IF — ASTROS

PERSONAL: Born March 26, 1968, in San Cristobal, Dominican Republic. ... 6-1/180. ... Bats both, throws right. ... Full name: Jose Luis Pimental Vizcaino. ... Name pronounced VIS-ky-EE-no.

HIGH SCHOOL: Americo Tolentino (Palenque de San Cristobal, Dominican Republic).

TRANSACTIONS/CAREER NOTES: Signed as non-drafted free agent by Los Angeles Dodgers organization (February 18, 1986). ... Traded by Dodgers to Chicago Cubs for IF Greg Smith (December 14, 1990). ... On disabled list (April 20-May 6 and August 26-September 16, 1992). ... Traded by Cubs to New York Mets for P Anthony Young and P Ottis Smith (March 30, 1994). ... Traded by Mets with IF Jeff Kent to Cleveland Indians for 2B Carlos Baerga and IF Alvaro Espinoza (July 29, 1996). ... Traded by Indians with IF Jeff Kent, P Julian Tavarez and a player to be named later to San Francisco Giants for 3B Matt Williams and a player to be named later (November 13, 1996); Indians traded P Joe Roa to Giants for OF Trenidad Hubbard to complete deal (December 16, 1996). ... Granted free agency (October 29, 1997). ... Signed by Dodgers (December 8, 1997). ... On disabled list (June 22-September 9, 1998; and May 19-June 4, 1999). ... Traded by Dodgers to New York Yankees for IF/DH Jim Leyritz (June 20, 2000). ... Granted free agency (November 1, 2000). ... Signed by Houston Astros (November 20, 2000). ... Granted free agency (November 5, 2001). ... Re-signed by Astros (December 3, 2001).

STATISTICAL NOTES: Led Gulf Coast League shortstops with 23 double plays in 1987. ... Led Pacific Coast League shortstops with 611 total chances and 82 double plays in 1989. ... Led N.L. shortstops in fielding percentage with .984 and tied for lead in assists by shortstop with 411 in 1995.

								BATTING								FIELDING			
Year	Team (League)	Pos.	G	AB	R	H	2B	3B	HR	RBI	Avg.	BB	SO	SB	PO	A	E	Avg.
1987—	GC Dodgers (GCL)	SS-1B	49	150	26	38	5	1	0	12	.253	22	24	8	73	107	13	.933
1988—	Bakersfield (Calif.)......	SS	122	433	77	126	11	4	0	38	.291	50	54	13	185	340	30	.946
1989—	Albuquerque (PCL).....	SS	129	434	60	123	10	4	1	44	.283	33	41	16	*191	*390	*30	.951
	—Los Angeles (N.L.).....	SS	7	10	2	2	0	0	0	0	.200	0	1	0	6	9	2	.882
1990—	Albuquerque (PCL).....	2B-SS	81	276	46	77	10	2	2	38	.279	30	33	13	141	229	14	.964
	—Los Angeles (N.L.).....	SS-2B	37	51	3	14	1	1	0	2	.275	4	8	1	23	27	2	.962
1991—	Chicago (N.L.)■	3B-SS-2B	93	145	7	38	5	0	0	10	.262	5	18	2	49	118	7	.960
1992—	Chicago (N.L.)............	SS-3B-2B	86	285	25	64	10	4	1	17	.225	14	35	3	93	195	9	.970
1993—	Chicago (N.L.)	SS-3B-2B	151	551	74	158	19	4	4	54	.287	46	71	12	217	410	17	.974
1994—	New York (N.L.)■	SS	103	410	47	105	13	3	3	33	.256	33	62	1	136	291	13	.970
1995—	New York (N.L.)...........	SS-2B	135	509	66	146	21	5	3	56	.287	35	76	8	189	‡411	10	†.984
1996—	New York (N.L.)...........	2B	96	363	47	110	12	6	1	32	.303	28	58	9	179	259	6	.986
	—Cleveland (A.L.)■......	2B-SS-DH	48	179	23	51	5	2	0	13	.285	7	24	6	82	135	4	.982
1997—	San Fran. (N.L.)■.......	2B-SS	151	568	77	151	19	7	5	50	.266	48	87	8	206	450	16	.976
1998—	Los Angeles (N.L.)■..	SS	67	237	30	62	9	0	3	29	.262	17	35	7	89	172	4	.985
1999—	Los Angeles (N.L.) SS-2B-3B-OF		94	266	27	67	9	0	1	29	.252	20	23	2	98	192	7	.976
2000—	Los Angeles (N.L.).....S-3-2-DH-1		40	93	9	19	2	1	0	4	.204	10	15	1	24	63	2	.978
	—New York (A.L.)■......2B-3B-DH-SS		73	174	23	48	8	1	0	10	.276	12	28	5	88	127	2	.991
2001—	Houston (N.L.)■ SS-2B-3B		107	256	38	71	8	3	1	14	.277	15	33	3	72	142	14	.939
American League totals (2 years)			121	353	46	99	13	3	0	23	.280	19	52	11	170	262	6	.986
National League totals (13 years)			1167	3744	452	1007	128	34	22	330	.269	275	522	57	1381	2739	109	.974
Major League totals (13 years)			1288	4097	498	1106	141	37	22	353	.270	294	574	68	1551	3001	115	.975

DIVISION SERIES RECORD

								BATTING								FIELDING			
Year	Team (League)	Pos.	G	AB	R	H	2B	3B	HR	RBI	Avg.	BB	SO	SB	PO	A	E	Avg.
1996—	Cleveland (A.L.)..........	2B	3	12	1	4	2	0	0	1	.333	1	1	0	4	3	1	.875
1997—	San Francisco (N.L.) ..	SS	3	11	1	2	1	0	0	0	.182	0	5	0	3	10	0	1.000
2000—	New York (A.L.)..........	PR-2B	1	0	1	0	0	0	0	0	...	0	0	0	0	1	0	1.000
2001—	Houston (N.L.)	PH-SS	3	6	0	1	0	0	0	0	.167	0	1	0	3	3	0	1.000
Division series totals (4 years)			10	29	3	7	3	0	0	1	.241	1	7	0	10	17	1	.964

CHAMPIONSHIP SERIES RECORD

								BATTING								FIELDING			
Year	Team (League)	Pos.	G	AB	R	H	2B	3B	HR	RBI	Avg.	BB	SO	SB	PO	A	E	Avg.
2000—	New York (A.L.)..........	PR-2B	4	2	3	2	1	0	0	2	1.000	0	0	2	0	2	0	1.000

WORLD SERIES RECORD

NOTES: Member of World Series championship team (2000).

								BATTING								FIELDING			
Year	Team (League)	Pos.	G	AB	R	H	2B	3B	HR	RBI	Avg.	BB	SO	SB	PO	A	E	Avg.
2000—	New York (A.L.)..........	2B	4	17	0	4	0	0	0	1	.235	0	5	0	9	6	0	1.000

VIZCAINO, LUIS   P   ATHLETICS

PERSONAL: Born June 1, 1977, in Bani, Dominican Republic. ... 5-11/169. ... Throws right, bats right. ... Full name: Luis Arias Vizcaino.

TRANSACTIONS/CAREER NOTES: Signed as non-drafted free agent by Oakland Athletics organization (December 9, 1994).

STATISTICAL NOTES: Tied for Arizona League lead with three balks in 1996.

Year League	W	L	Pct.	ERA	G	GS	CG	ShO	Sv.	IP	H	R	ER	BB	SO
1995— Dominican Athletics (DSL).	10	2	.833	2.27	16	15	5	1	0	*115	93	41	29	29	89
1996— Arizona Athletics (Ariz.)......	6	3	.667	4.07	15	10	0	0	1	59 2/3	58	36	27	24	52
1997— Southern Oregon (N'West).	1	6	.143	7.93	22	5	0	0	0	47 2/3	62	51	42	27	42
— Modesto (Calif.)	0	3	.000	13.19	7	0	0	0	0	14 1/3	24	24	21	13	15
1998— Modesto (Calif.)	6	3	.667	2.74	23	16	0	0	0	102	72	39	31	43	108
— Huntsville (Sou.)	3	2	.600	4.66	7	7	0	0	0	38 2/3	43	27	20	22	26
1999— Midland (Texas)................	8	7	.533	5.85	25	19	0	0	0	104 2/3	120	74	68	48	88
— Vancouver (PCL)	0	1	.000	1.38	7	0	0	0	0	13	13	4	2	6	7
— Oakland (A.L.)	0	0	...	5.40	1	0	0	0	0	3 1/3	3	2	2	3	2
2000— Oakland (A.L.)	0	1	.000	7.45	12	0	0	0	0	19 1/3	25	17	16	11	18
— Sacramento (PCL).............	6	2	.750	5.03	33	2	0	0	5	48 1/3	48	27	27	21	41
2001— Oakland (A.L.)	2	1	.667	4.66	36	0	0	0	1	36 2/3	38	19	19	12	31
Major League totals (3 years).......	2	2	.500	5.61	49	0	0	0	2	59 1/3	66	38	37	26	51

VIZQUEL, OMAR   SS   INDIANS

PERSONAL: Born April 24, 1967, in Caracas, Venezuela. ... 5-9/185. ... Bats both, throws right. ... Full name: Omar Enrique Vizquel. ... Name pronounced vis-KEL.

HIGH SCHOOL: Francisco Espejo (Caracas, Venezuela).

TRANSACTIONS/CAREER NOTES: Signed as non-drafted free agent by Seattle Mariners organization (April 1, 1984). ... On Seattle disabled list (April 7-May 13, 1990); included rehabilitation assignments to Calgary (May 3-7) and San Bernardino (May 8-12). ... On Seattle disabled list (April 13-May 11, 1992); included rehabilitation assignment to Calgary (May 5-11). ... Traded by Mariners to Cleveland Indians for SS Felix Fermin, 1B Reggie Jefferson and cash (December 20, 1993). ... On Cleveland disabled list (April 23-June 13, 1994); included rehabilitation assignment to Charlotte (June 6-13). ... On suspended list (September 17-18, 1998).

RECORDS: Shares major league career record for highest fielding percentage by shortstop (1,000 or more games)—.983; fewest errors by shortstop (150 or more games)—3 (2000); and most consecutive errorless games by shortstop—95 (September 26, 1999 through July 21, 2000).

HONORS: Won A.L. Gold Glove at shortstop (1993-2001).

STATISTICAL NOTES: Led Midwest League shortstops with .969 fielding percentage in 1986. ... Tied for A.L. lead in double plays by shortstop with 108 in 1993. ... Led A.L. with 16 sacrifice hits in 1997 and with 17 in 1999. ... Career major league grand slams: 4.

MISCELLANEOUS: Batted righthanded only (1984-88).

Year Team (League)	Pos.	G	AB	R	H	2B	3B	HR	RBI	Avg.	BB	SO	SB	PO	A	E	Avg.
1984— Butte (Pio.).................	SS-2B	15	45	7	14	2	0	0	4	.311	3	8	2	13	29	5	.894
1985— Bellingham (N'West) ..	SS-2B	50	187	24	42	9	0	5	17	.225	12	27	4	85	175	19	.932
1986— Wausau (Midw.).........	SS-2B	105	352	60	75	13	2	4	28	.213	64	56	19	153	328	16	†.968
1987— Salinas (Calif.)..........	SS-2B	114	407	61	107	12	8	0	38	.263	57	55	25	81	295	25	.938
1988— Vermont (East.).........	SS	103	374	54	95	18	2	2	35	.254	42	44	30	173	268	19	*.959
— Calgary (PCL).............	SS	33	107	10	24	2	3	1	12	.224	5	14	2	43	92	6	.957
1989— Calgary (PCL).............	SS	7	28	3	6	2	0	0	3	.214	3	4	0	15	14	0	1.000
— Seattle (A.L.)	SS	143	387	45	85	7	3	1	20	.220	28	40	1	208	388	18	.971
1990— Calgary (PCL).............	SS	48	150	18	35	6	2	0	8	.233	13	10	4	70	142	6	.972
— San Bern. (Calif.)........	SS	6	28	5	7	0	0	0	3	.250	3	1	1	11	21	3	.914
— Seattle (A.L.)	SS	81	255	19	63	3	2	2	18	.247	18	22	4	103	239	7	.980
1991— Seattle (A.L.)	SS-2B	142	426	42	98	16	4	1	41	.230	45	37	7	224	422	13	.980
1992— Seattle (A.L.)	SS	136	483	49	142	20	4	0	21	.294	32	38	15	223	403	7	*.989
— Calgary (PCL).............	SS	6	22	0	6	1	0	0	2	.269	1	3	0	14	21	1	.972
1993— Seattle (A.L.)	SS-DH	158	560	68	143	14	2	2	31	.255	50	71	12	245	475	15	.980
1994— Cleveland (A.L.)■......	SS	69	286	39	78	10	1	1	33	.273	23	23	13	113	204	6	.981
— Charlotte (I.L.).............	SS	7	26	3	7	1	0	0	1	.269	2	1	1	11	18	1	.967
1995— Cleveland (A.L.).........	SS	136	542	87	144	28	0	6	56	.266	59	59	29	210	405	9	.986
1996— Cleveland (A.L.).........	SS	151	542	98	161	36	1	9	64	.297	56	42	35	226	447	20	.971
1997— Cleveland (A.L.).........	SS	153	565	89	158	23	6	5	49	.280	57	58	43	245	428	10	.985
1998— Cleveland (A.L.).........	SS	151	576	86	166	30	6	2	50	.288	62	64	37	*273	442	5	*.993
1999— Cleveland (A.L.).........	SS-OF	144	574	112	191	36	4	5	66	.333	65	50	42	221	396	15	.976
2000— Cleveland (A.L.).........	SS	156	613	101	176	27	3	7	66	.287	87	72	22	231	414	3	*.995
2001— Cleveland (A.L.).........	SS	155	611	84	156	26	8	2	50	.255	61	72	13	219	414	7	.989
Major League totals (13 years)		1775	6420	919	1761	276	44	43	565	.274	643	648	273	2741	5077	135	.983

DIVISION SERIES RECORD

RECORDS: Holds A.L. career record for triples—2. ... Shares A.L. career records for most stolen bases—10; and hits—32. ... Shares single-game record for most at-bats (nine-inning game)—6 (October 13, 2001).

Year Team (League)	Pos.	G	AB	R	H	2B	3B	HR	RBI	Avg.	BB	SO	SB	PO	A	E	Avg.
1995— Cleveland (A.L.).........	SS	3	12	2	2	1	0	0	4	.167	2	2	1	4	11	0	1.000
1996— Cleveland (A.L.).........	SS	4	14	4	6	1	0	0	2	.429	3	4	4	6	10	0	1.000
1997— Cleveland (A.L.).........	SS	5	18	3	9	0	0	0	1	.500	2	1	4	12	14	0	1.000
1998— Cleveland (A.L.).........	SS	4	15	1	1	0	0	0	0	.067	1	0	0	4	16	0	1.000
1999— Cleveland (A.L.).........	SS	5	21	3	5	1	1	0	3	.238	2	3	0	7	9	0	1.000
2001— Cleveland (A.L.).........	SS	5	22	2	9	1	1	0	6	.409	1	1	1	6	21	1	.964
Division series totals (6 years)		26	102	15	32	4	2	0	16	.314	11	11	10	39	81	1	.992

CHAMPIONSHIP SERIES RECORD

					BATTING									FIELDING			
Year	Team (League)	Pos.	G	AB	R	H	2B	3B	HR	RBI	Avg.	BB	SO	SB	PO	A	E	Avg.
1995—Cleveland (A.L.).........	SS	6	23	2	2	1	0	0	2	.087	5	2	3	9	21	0	1.000
1997—Cleveland (A.L.).........	SS	6	25	1	1	0	0	0	0	.040	2	10	0	16	15	0	1.000
1998—Cleveland (A.L.).........	SS	6	25	2	11	0	1	0	0	.440	1	3	4	11	26	1	.974
Championship series totals (3 years)		18	73	5	14	1	1	0	2	.192	8	15	7	36	62	1	.990

WORLD SERIES RECORD

RECORDS: Shares single-inning record for most stolen bases—2 (October 26, 1997).

					BATTING									FIELDING			
Year	Team (League)	Pos.	G	AB	R	H	2B	3B	HR	RBI	Avg.	BB	SO	SB	PO	A	E	Avg.
1995—Cleveland (A.L.).........	SS	6	23	3	4	0	1	0	1	.174	3	5	1	12	22	0	1.000
1997—Cleveland (A.L.).........	SS	7	30	5	7	2	0	0	1	.233	3	5	5	12	17	0	1.000
World Series totals (2 years)		13	53	8	11	2	1	0	2	.208	6	10	6	24	39	0	1.000

ALL-STAR GAME RECORD

				BATTING								FIELDING			
Year	League	Pos.	AB	R	H	2B	3B	HR	RBI	Avg.	BB	SO	SB	PO	A	E	Avg.
1998—American..................	SS	2	0	1	0	0	0	0	.500	0	0	0	1	1	0	1.000
1999—American..................	SS	1	0	0	0	0	0	0	.000	0	0	0	1	4	0	1.000
All-Star Game totals (2 years)		3	0	1	0	0	0	0	.333	0	0	0	2	5	0	1.000

VOGELSONG, RYAN　　　　　P　　　　　PIRATES

PERSONAL: Born July 22, 1977, in Charlotte. ... 6-3/195. ... Throws right, bats right. ... Full name: Ryan Andrew Vogelsong.
HIGH SCHOOL: Octorara Area (Atglen, Pa.).
COLLEGE: Kutztown (Pa.).
TRANSACTIONS/CAREER NOTES: Selected by San Francisco Giants organization in fifth round of free agent draft (June 2, 1998). ... Traded by Giants with OF Armando Rios to Pittsburgh Pirates for P Jason Schmidt and P Ryan Vogelsong (July 30, 2001).
STATISTICAL NOTES: Led Texas League with 13 hit batsmen and four balks in 2000.

Year	League	W	L	Pct.	ERA	G	GS	CG	ShO	Sv.	IP	H	R	ER	BB	SO
1998—Salem-Kaizer (N'West)	6	1	.857	1.77	10	10	0	0	0	56	37	15	11	16	66
—San Jose (Calif.)................	0	0	...	7.58	4	4	0	0	0	19	23	16	16	4	23
1999—San Jose (Calif.)................	4	4	.500	2.45	13	13	0	0	0	69²/₃	37	26	19	27	86
—Shreveport (Texas)............	0	2	.000	7.31	6	6	0	0	0	28¹/₃	40	25	23	15	23
2000—Shreveport (Texas)............	6	10	.375	4.23	27	27	1	0	0	155¹/₃	153	82	73	69	*147
—San Francisco (N.L.)	0	0	...	0.00	4	0	0	0	0	6	4	0	0	2	6
2001—Fresno (PCL).................	3	3	.500	2.79	10	10	0	0	0	58	35	18	18	18	53
—San Francisco (N.L.)	0	3	.000	5.65	13	0	0	0	0	28²/₃	29	21	18	14	17
—Nashville (PCL)■..............	2	3	.400	3.98	6	6	0	0	0	31²/₃	26	15	14	15	33
—Pittsburgh (N.L.)	0	2	.000	12.00	2	2	0	0	0	6	10	10	8	6	7
Major League totals (2 years)	0	5	.000	5.75	19	2	0	0	0	40²/₃	43	31	26	22	30

VOSBERG, ED　　　　　P

PERSONAL: Born September 28, 1961, in Tucson, Ariz. ... 6-1/210. ... Throws left, bats left. ... Full name: Edward John Vosberg. ... Nephew of Don Vosberg, defensive end with New York Giants (1941).
HIGH SCHOOL: Salpointe (Tucson, Ariz.).
COLLEGE: Arizona.
TRANSACTIONS/CAREER NOTES: Selected by St. Louis Cardinals organization in third round of free-agent draft (June 5, 1979); did not sign. ... Selected by Toronto Blue Jays organization in 11th round of free-agent draft (June 7, 1982); did not sign. ... Selected by San Diego Padres organization in third round of free-agent draft (June 6, 1983). ... Traded by Padres to Houston Astros for C Dan Walters (December 13, 1988). ... Traded by Astros to Los Angeles Dodgers (August 1, 1989), completing deal in which Dodgers traded OF Javier Ortiz to Astros for a player to be named later (July 22, 1989). ... Granted free agency (October 15, 1989). ... Signed by San Francisco Giants organization (March 13, 1990). ... Granted free agency (October 15, 1990). ... Signed by California Angels organization (December 4, 1990). ... Released by Angels (May 11, 1991). ... Signed by Seattle Mariners organization (May 20, 1991). ... Released by Mariners (July 10, 1991). ... Pitched in Italy (1992). ... Signed by Chicago Cubs organization (March 17, 1993). ... Granted free agency (October 15, 1993). ... Signed by Oakland Athletics organization (December 3, 1993). ... Granted free agency (October 15, 1994). ... Re-signed by A's organization (November 11, 1994). ... Selected by Los Angeles Dodgers from A's organization in Rule 5 major league draft (December 5, 1994). ... Granted free agency (April 24, 1995). ... Signed by Texas Rangers organization (April 26, 1995). ... Traded by Rangers to Florida Marlins for P Rick Helling (August 12, 1997). ... Traded by Marlins to Padres for P Chris Clark (November 20, 1997). ... On disabled list (March 25, 1998-entire season). ... On San Diego disabled list (March 30-April 24, 1999); included rehabilitation assignment to Las Vegas (April 8-24). ... Released by Padres (June 5, 1999). ... Signed by Arizona Diamondbacks organization (June 10, 1999). ... Granted free agency (October 15, 1999). ... Signed by Colorado Rockies organization (November 17, 1999). ... Traded by Rockies to Philadelphia Phillies for a player to be named later (June 28, 2000); Rockies acquired P Sean Fesh to complete deal (July 25, 2000). ... Granted free agency (October 12, 2000). ... Re-signed by Phillies organization (December 20, 2000). ... Granted free agency (October 8, 2001).
STATISTICAL NOTES: Led Pacific Coast League with 11 balks in 1987.

Year	League	W	L	Pct.	ERA	G	GS	CG	ShO	Sv.	IP	H	R	ER	BB	SO
1983—Reno (Calif.).....................	6	6	.500	3.87	15	15	3	0	0	97²/₃	111	61	42	39	70
—Beaumont (Texas)	1	0	1.000	0.00	1	1	1	1	0	7	2	0	0	2	1
1984—Beaumont (Texas)	13	•11	.542	3.43	27	•27	5	2	0	183²/₃	196	87	70	74	100
1985—Beaumont (Texas)	9	11	.450	3.91	27	•27	2	1	0	175	178	92	76	69	124
1986—Las Vegas (PCL)	7	8	.467	4.72	25	24	2	1	0	129²/₃	136	80	68	64	93
—San Diego (N.L.)	0	1	.000	6.59	5	3	0	0	0	13²/₃	17	11	10	9	8
1987—Las Vegas (PCL)	9	8	.529	3.92	34	24	3	0	0	167²/₃	154	88	73	97	98
1988—Las Vegas (PCL)	11	7	.611	4.15	45	11	1	0	2	128	137	67	59	56	75
1989—Tucson (PCL)■................	4	7	.364	6.78	23	14	0	0	1	87²/₃	122	70	66	49	68
—Albuquerque (PCL)■........	2	1	.667	2.70	12	0	0	0	0	20	17	8	6	5	18

Year	League	W	L	Pct.	ERA	G	GS	CG	ShO	Sv.	IP	H	R	ER	BB	SO
1990—	Phoenix (PCL)■	1	3	.250	2.65	24	0	0	0	3	34	36	14	10	16	28
—	San Francisco (N.L.)	1	1	.500	5.55	18	0	0	0	0	24 1/3	21	16	15	12	12
1991—	Edmonton (PCL)■	0	1	.000	6.28	12	0	0	0	0	14 1/3	19	10	10	5	14
—	Calgary (PCL)■	0	2	.000	7.23	16	0	0	0	2	23 2/3	38	26	19	12	15
1992—							Italian statistics unavailable.									
1993—	Iowa (A.A.)■	5	1	.833	3.57	52	0	0	0	3	63	67	32	25	22	64
1994—	Tacoma (PCL)■	4	2	.667	3.35	26	1	0	0	3	53 2/3	39	21	20	19	54
—	Oakland (A.L.)	0	2	.000	3.95	16	0	0	0	0	13 2/3	16	7	6	5	12
1995—	Oklahoma City (A.A.)■	1	0	1.000	0.00	1	0	0	0	0	1 2/3	1	0	0	1	2
—	Texas (A.L.)	5	5	.500	3.00	44	0	0	0	4	36	32	15	12	16	36
1996—	Texas (A.L.)	1	1	.500	3.27	52	0	0	0	8	44	51	17	16	21	32
1997—	Texas (A.L.)	2	4	.333	4.61	42	0	0	0	0	41	44	23	21	15	29
—	Florida (N.L.)■	1	1	.500	3.75	17	0	0	0	1	12	15	7	5	6	8
1998—	San Diego (N.L.)■							Did not play.								
1999—	Las Vegas (PCL)	0	0	...	1.08	8	0	0	0	1	8 1/3	3	1	1	4	12
—	San Diego (N.L.)	0	0	...	9.72	15	0	0	0	0	8 1/3	16	11	9	3	6
—	Tucson (PCL)■	1	0	1.000	0.78	26	0	0	0	7	34 2/3	26	5	3	8	30
—	Arizona (N.L.)	0	1	.000	3.38	4	0	0	0	0	2 2/3	6	1	1	0	2
2000—	Colorado Springs (PCL)■	1	2	.333	6.86	29	3	0	0	2	42	59	41	32	20	37
—	Scranton/W.B. (I.L.)■	0	0	...	0.00	1	0	0	0	0	2	0	0	0	0	2
—	Philadelphia (N.L.)	1	1	.500	4.13	31	0	0	0	0	24	21	11	11	18	23
2001—	Scranton/W.B. (I.L.)	1	0	1.000	3.00	27	0	0	0	5	27	24	9	9	13	22
—	Philadelphia (N.L.)	0	0	...	2.84	18	0	0	0	0	12 2/3	8	4	4	3	11
A.L. totals (4 years)		7	10	.412	3.68	154	0	0	0	12	134 2/3	143	62	55	57	109
N.L. totals (6 years)		3	5	.375	5.07	108	3	0	0	1	97 2/3	104	61	55	51	70
Major League totals (9 years)		10	15	.400	4.26	262	3	0	0	13	232 1/3	247	123	110	108	179

DIVISION SERIES RECORD

Year	League	W	L	Pct.	ERA	G	GS	CG	ShO	Sv.	IP	H	R	ER	BB	SO
1996—	Texas (A.L.)	0	0	...	...	1	0	0	0	0	1	1	0	0	0	0

CHAMPIONSHIP SERIES RECORD

Year	League	W	L	Pct.	ERA	G	GS	CG	ShO	Sv.	IP	H	R	ER	BB	SO
1997—	Florida (N.L.)	0	0	...	0.00	2	0	0	0	0	2 2/3	2	0	0	1	3

WORLD SERIES RECORD

NOTES: Member of World Series championship team (1997).

Year	League	W	L	Pct.	ERA	G	GS	CG	ShO	Sv.	IP	H	R	ER	BB	SO
1997—	Florida (N.L.)	0	0	...	6.00	2	0	0	0	0	3	3	2	2	3	2

VOYLES, BRAD   P   ROYALS

PERSONAL: Born December 30, 1976, in Green Bay, Wis. ... 6-0/195. ... Throws right, bats right. ... Full name: Bradley Roy Voyles.
HIGH SCHOOL: Luxemburg-Casco (Luxemburg, Wis.).
JUNIOR COLLEGE: Kishwaukee (Ill.).
COLLEGE: Lincoln Memorial.
TRANSACTIONS/CAREER NOTES: Selected by Atlanta Braves organization in 45th round of free-agent draft (June 2, 1998). ... On Atlanta disabled list (March 28-June 8, 2001); included rehabilitation assignment to Myrtle Beach (June 3-8). ... Traded by Braves with IF Alejandro Machado to Kansas City Royals for SS Rey Sanchez (July 31, 2001).

Year	League	W	L	Pct.	ERA	G	GS	CG	ShO	Sv.	IP	H	R	ER	BB	SO
1998—	Eugene (N'West)	0	0	...	3.09	7	0	0	0	0	11 2/3	9	5	4	10	22
1999—	Macon (S.Atl.)	3	3	.500	2.98	38	0	0	0	14	51 1/3	27	21	17	39	65
—	Myrtle Beach (Caro.)	1	1	.500	2.25	5	0	0	0	0	12	7	3	3	9	13
2000—	Myrtle Beach (Caro.)	5	2	.714	1.11	39	0	0	0	19	56 2/3	21	8	7	25	70
2001—	Myrtle Beach (Caro.)	0	0	...	0.00	2	0	0	0	1	1 2/3	0	0	0	1	3
—	Greenville (Sou.)	0	0	...	1.08	15	0	0	0	6	16 2/3	11	3	2	10	25
—	Wichita (Texas)■	1	0	1.000	0.00	11	0	0	0	4	15 1/3	8	0	0	10	19
—	Kansas City (A.L.)	0	0	...	3.86	7	0	0	0	0	9 1/3	5	4	4	8	6
Major League totals (1 year)		0	0	...	3.86	7	0	0	0	0	9 1/3	5	4	4	8	6

WAGNER, BILLY   P   ASTROS

PERSONAL: Born July 25, 1971, in Tannersville, Va. ... 5-11/180. ... Throws left, bats left. ... Full name: William Edward Wagner.
HIGH SCHOOL: Tazewell (Va.).
COLLEGE: Ferrum (Va.).
TRANSACTIONS/CAREER NOTES: Selected by Houston Astros organization in first round (12th pick overall) of free-agent draft (June 3, 1993). ... On Houston disabled list (August 23-September 7, 1996). ... On Houston disabled list (July 16-August 7, 1998); included rehabilitation assignment to Jackson (August 1-7). ... On disabled list (June 21, 2000-remainder of season). ... On Houston disabled list (June 5-June 19, 2001); included rehabilitation assignment to Round Rock (June 16-17).

Year	League	W	L	Pct.	ERA	G	GS	CG	ShO	Sv.	IP	H	R	ER	BB	SO
1993—	Auburn (NY-Penn)	1	3	.250	4.08	7	7	0	0	0	28 2/3	25	19	13	25	31
1994—	Quad City (Midw.)	8	9	.471	3.29	26	26	2	0	0	153	99	71	56	*91	*204
1995—	Jackson (Texas)	2	2	.500	2.57	12	12	0	0	0	70	49	25	20	36	77
—	Tucson (PCL)	5	3	.625	3.18	13	13	0	0	0	76 1/3	70	28	27	32	80
—	Houston (N.L.)	0	0	...	0.00	1	0	0	0	0	1/3	0	0	0	0	0
1996—	Tucson (PCL)	6	2	.750	3.28	12	12	1	1	0	74	62	32	27	33	86
—	Houston (N.L.)	2	2	.500	2.44	37	0	0	0	9	51 2/3	28	16	14	30	67
1997—	Houston (N.L.)	7	8	.467	2.85	62	0	0	0	23	66 1/3	49	23	21	30	106
1998—	Houston (N.L.)	4	3	.571	2.70	58	0	0	0	30	60	46	19	18	25	97
—	Jackson (Texas)	0	0	...	0.00	3	1	0	0	0	3	1	0	0	0	7

Year League	W	L	Pct.	ERA	G	GS	CG	ShO	Sv.	IP	H	R	ER	BB	SO
1999— Houston (N.L.)	4	1	.800	1.57	66	0	0	0	39	74 2/3	35	14	13	23	124
2000— Houston (N.L.)	2	4	.333	6.18	28	0	0	0	6	27 2/3	28	19	19	18	28
2001— Houston (N.L.)	2	5	.286	2.73	64	0	0	0	39	62 2/3	44	19	19	20	79
— Round Rock (Texas)	0	0	...	0.00	1	1	0	0	0	1	0	0	0	0	2
Major League totals (7 years)	21	23	.477	2.73	316	0	0	0	146	343 1/3	230	110	104	146	501

DIVISION SERIES RECORD

Year League	W	L	Pct.	ERA	G	GS	CG	ShO	Sv.	IP	H	R	ER	BB	SO
1997— Houston (N.L.)	0	0	...	18.00	1	0	0	0	0	1	3	2	2	0	2
1998— Houston (N.L.)	1	0	1.000	18.00	1	0	0	0	0	1	4	2	2	0	1
1999— Houston (N.L.)	0	0	...	0.00	1	0	0	0	0	1	0	0	0	0	1
2001— Houston (N.L.)	0	0	...	5.40	2	0	0	0	0	1 2/3	1	1	1	0	3
Division series totals (4 years)	1	0	1.000	9.64	5	0	0	0	0	4 2/3	8	5	5	0	7

ALL-STAR GAME RECORD

Year League	W	L	Pct.	ERA	GS	CG	ShO	Sv.	IP	H	R	ER	BB	SO
1999— National	0	0	...	0.00	0	0	0	0	2/3	0	0	0	0	2
2001— National	0	0	...	0.00	0	0	0	0	1/3	0	0	0	0	0
All-Star Game totals (2 years)	0	0	...	0.00	0	0	0	0	1	0	0	0	0	2

WAKEFIELD, TIM   P   RED SOX

PERSONAL: Born August 2, 1966, in Melbourne, Fla. ... 6-2/210. ... Throws right, bats right. ... Full name: Timothy Stephen Wakefield.

HIGH SCHOOL: Eau Gallie (Melbourne, Fla.).

COLLEGE: Florida Tech.

TRANSACTIONS/CAREER NOTES: Selected by Pittsburgh Pirates organization in eighth round of free-agent draft (June 1, 1988). ... Released by Pirates (April 20, 1995). ... Signed by Boston Red Sox organization (April 26, 1995). ... On disabled list (April 15-May 6, 1997). ... Granted free agency (November 1, 2000). ... Re-signed by Red Sox (December 7, 2000).

RECORDS: Shares major league single-inning record for most strikeouts—4 (August 10, 1999, ninth inning).

HONORS: Named N.L. Rookie Pitcher of the Year by THE SPORTING NEWS (1992). ... Named A.L. Comeback Player of the Year by THE SPORTING NEWS (1995).

STATISTICAL NOTES: Led Carolina League with 24 home runs allowed in 1990. ... Led American Association with 27 home runs allowed and 23 hit batsmen in 1994. ... Led A.L. with 16 hit batsmen in 1997 and 18 in 2001.

MISCELLANEOUS: Appeared in one game as pinch runner with Pittsburgh (1992). ... Had a sacrifice hit in only appearance as pinch hitter (1998). ... Had a sacrifice hit in only appearance as pinch hitter (2000).

Year League	W	L	Pct.	ERA	G	GS	CG	ShO	Sv.	IP	H	R	ER	BB	SO
1989— Welland (NY-Penn)	1	1	.500	3.40	18	1	0	0	2	39 2/3	30	17	15	21	42
1990— Salem (Caro.)	10	•14	.417	4.73	28	•28	2	0	0	*190 1/3	*187	109	*100	*85	127
1991— Carolina (Sou.)	15	8	.652	2.90	26	25	•8	1	0	183	155	68	59	51	120
— Buffalo (A.A.)	0	1	.000	11.57	1	1	0	0	0	4 2/3	8	6	6	1	4
1992— Buffalo (A.A.)	10	3	.769	3.06	20	20	*6	1	0	135 1/3	122	52	46	51	71
— Pittsburgh (N.L.)	8	1	.889	2.15	13	13	4	1	0	92	76	26	22	35	51
1993— Pittsburgh (N.L.)	6	11	.353	5.61	24	20	3	2	0	128 1/3	145	83	80	75	59
— Carolina (Sou.)	3	5	.375	6.99	9	9	1	0	0	56 2/3	68	48	44	22	36
1994— Buffalo (A.A.)	5	*15	.250	5.84	30	•29	4	1	0	175 2/3	*197	*127	*114	*98	83
1995— Pawtucket (I.L.)■	2	1	.667	2.52	4	4	0	0	0	25	23	10	7	9	14
— Boston (A.L.)	16	8	.667	2.95	27	27	6	1	0	195 1/3	163	76	64	68	119
1996— Boston (A.L.)	14	13	.519	5.14	32	32	6	0	0	211 2/3	238	*151	121	90	140
1997— Boston (A.L.)	12	•15	.444	4.25	35	29	4	2	0	201 1/3	193	109	95	87	151
1998— Boston (A.L.)	17	8	.680	4.58	36	33	2	0	0	216	211	123	110	79	146
1999— Boston (A.L.)	6	11	.353	5.08	49	17	0	0	15	140	146	93	79	72	104
2000— Boston (A.L.)	6	10	.375	5.48	51	17	0	0	0	159 1/3	170	107	97	65	102
2001— Boston (A.L.)	9	12	.429	3.90	45	17	0	0	3	168 2/3	156	84	73	73	148
A.L. totals (7 years)	80	77	.510	4.45	275	172	18	3	18	1292 1/3	1277	743	639	534	910
N.L. totals (2 years)	14	12	.538	4.17	37	33	7	3	0	220 1/3	221	109	102	110	110
Major League totals (9 years)	94	89	.514	4.41	312	205	25	6	18	1512 2/3	1498	852	741	644	1020

DIVISION SERIES RECORD

Year League	W	L	Pct.	ERA	G	GS	CG	ShO	Sv.	IP	H	R	ER	BB	SO
1995— Boston (A.L.)	0	1	.000	11.81	1	1	0	0	0	5 1/3	5	7	7	5	4
1998— Boston (A.L.)	0	1	.000	33.75	1	1	0	0	0	1 1/3	3	5	5	2	1
1999— Boston (A.L.)	0	0	...	13.50	2	0	0	0	0	2	3	3	3	4	4
Division series totals (3 years)	0	2	.000	15.58	4	2	0	0	0	8 2/3	11	15	15	11	9

CHAMPIONSHIP SERIES RECORD

RECORDS: Shares single-series record for most complete games—2 (1992). ... Shares N.L. career record for most complete games—2.

Year League	W	L	Pct.	ERA	G	GS	CG	ShO	Sv.	IP	H	R	ER	BB	SO
1992— Pittsburgh (N.L.)	2	0	1.000	3.00	2	2	2	0	0	18	14	6	6	5	7
1999— Boston (A.L.)							Did not play.								

RECORD AS POSITION PLAYER

Year Team (League)	Pos.	G	AB	R	H	2B	3B	HR	RBI	Avg.	BB	SO	SB	PO	A	E	Avg.
1988— Watertown (NY-Penn)	1B	54	159	24	30	6	2	3	20	.189	25	57	3	377	25	8	.980
1989— Augusta (S.Atl.)	3B-1B	11	34	5	8	2	1	0	5	.235	1	14	1	27	6	3	.917
— Welland (NY-Penn)	3B-2B-1B	36	63	7	13	4	0	1	3	.206	3	21	1	26	31	8	.877

WAKELAND, CHRIS   OF   TIGERS

PERSONAL: Born June 15, 1974, in Huntington Beach, Calif. ... 6-0/185. ... Bats left, throws left. ... Full name: Christopher Robert Wakeland.
HIGH SCHOOL: St. Helens (Ore.).
COLLEGE: Oregon State.
TRANSACTIONS/CAREER NOTES: Selected by Detroit Tigers organization in 15th round of free-agent draft (June 4, 1996). ... On Jacksonville disabled list (June 6-August 26, 1999).
STATISTICAL NOTES: Led New York-Pennsylvania League with .555 slugging percentage and .426 on-base percentage in 1996.

| | | | | | | | | BATTING | | | | | | | FIELDING | | |
Year Team (League)	Pos.	G	AB	R	H	2B	3B	HR	RBI	Avg.	BB	SO	SB	PO	A	E	Avg.
1996— Jamestown (NY-P)	OF	70	220	38	68	14	5	10	49	.309	43	83	8	79	9	2	.978
1997— W. Michigan (Midw.)..	OF	111	414	64	118	38	2	7	75	.285	43	120	20	169	7	5	.972
1998— Lakeland (FSL)	OF	131	487	82	147	26	5	18	89	.302	66	111	19	194	•17	9	.959
1999— Jacksonville (Sou.).....	OF	55	212	42	68	16	3	13	36	.321	35	53	6	97	4	6	.944
— GC Tigers (GCL)........	OF	4	14	2	1	0	0	0	1	.071	0	4	0	6	0	0	1.000
— Lakeland (FSL)	OF	4	17	3	7	1	0	0	7	.412	0	1	0	4	0	0	1.000
2000— Toledo (I.L.).............	OF	141	492	65	133	25	2	28	76	.270	60	*148	4	217	10	8	.966
2001— Toledo (I.L.).............	OF	140	547	85	155	33	3	23	84	.283	39	126	7	213	•13	8	.966
— Detroit (A.L.)	OF	10	36	5	9	2	0	2	6	.250	0	13	0	32	0	2	.941
Major League totals (1 year)		10	36	5	9	2	0	2	6	.250	0	13	0	32	0	2	.941

WALBECK, MATT   C   PADRES

PERSONAL: Born October 2, 1969, in Sacramento. ... 5-11/188. ... Bats both, throws right. ... Full name: Matthew Lovick Walbeck.
HIGH SCHOOL: Sacramento High.
TRANSACTIONS/CAREER NOTES: Selected by Chicago Cubs organization in eighth round of free-agent draft (June 2, 1987). ... On Winston-Salem disabled list (April 12-July 11, 1990). ... On Charleston, W.Va. disabled list (September 5, 1992-remainder of season). ... Traded by Cubs with P Dave Stevens to Minnesota Twins for P Willie Banks (November 24, 1993). ... On Minnesota disabled list (March 31-June 17, 1996); included rehabilitation assignments to Fort Myers (May 31-June 11) and New Britain (June 12-17). ... Traded by Twins to Detroit Tigers for P Brent Stentz (December 11, 1996). ... On Detroit disabled list (April 19-July 9, 1997); included rehabilitation assignments to Lakeland (June 12-15) and Toledo (June 16-July 9). ... Traded by Tigers with 3B Phil Nevin to Anaheim Angels for P Nick Skuse (November 20, 1997). ... On disabled list (August 17-September 1, 2000). ... Granted free agency (November 1, 2000). ... Signed by Cincinnati Reds organization (February 9, 2001). ... Contract purchased Philadelphia Phillies organization from Reds (July 11, 2001). ... Granted free agency (October 8, 2001). ... Signed by San Diego Padres organization (January 2, 2002).
STATISTICAL NOTES: Tied for Carolina League lead with 10 sacrifice flies in 1991. ... Led American Association catchers with 561 total chances and tied for lead with nine double plays in 1993. ... Led International League catchers with 1.000 fielding percentage in 2001. ... Career major league grand slams: 2.
MISCELLANEOUS: Batted righthanded only (1987-89).

| | | | | | | | | BATTING | | | | | | | FIELDING | | |
Year Team (League)	Pos.	G	AB	R	H	2B	3B	HR	RBI	Avg.	BB	SO	SB	PO	A	E	Avg.
1987— Wytheville (Appl.).......	C	51	169	24	53	9	3	1	28	.314	22	39	0	293	22	1	*.997
1988— Charl., W.Va. (S.Atl.) ..	C	104	312	28	68	9	0	2	24	.218	30	44	7	549	68	14	.978
1989— Peoria (Midw.)...........	C	94	341	38	86	19	0	4	47	.252	20	47	5	605	72	11	.984
1990— Peoria (Midw.)...........	C	25	66	2	15	1	0	0	5	.227	5	7	1	137	16	2	.987
1991— Win.-Salem (Caro.)	C	91	260	25	70	11	0	3	41	.269	20	23	3	473	64	12	.978
1992— Charlotte (Sou.).........	C-1B	105	385	48	116	22	1	7	42	.301	33	56	0	552	80	10	.984
1993— Chicago (N.L.)...........	C	11	30	2	6	2	0	1	6	.200	1	6	0	49	2	0	1.000
— Iowa (A.A.).................	C	87	331	31	93	18	2	6	43	.281	18	47	1	496	*64	1	*.998
1994— Minnesota (A.L.)■......	C-DH	97	338	31	69	12	0	5	35	.204	17	37	1	496	45	4	.993
1995— Minnesota (A.L.)........	C	115	393	40	101	18	1	1	44	.257	25	71	3	604	35	6	.991
1996— Fort Myers (FSL)	DH-C	9	33	4	9	1	1	0	9	.273	4	2	0	46	6	0	1.000
— New Britain (East.)......	DH-C	7	24	1	5	0	0	0	0	.208	1	1	0	11	2	0	1.000
— Minnesota (A.L.)	C	63	215	25	48	10	0	2	24	.223	9	34	3	326	19	2	.994
1997— Detroit (A.L.)■..........	C	47	137	18	38	3	0	3	10	.277	12	19	3	240	15	3	.988
— Lakeland (FSL)	C-DH	4	10	4	5	1	0	0	3	.500	4	1	0	14	0	1	.933
— Toledo (I.L.)...............	C-DH	17	59	6	18	2	1	1	8	.305	4	15	0	55	9	3	.955
1998— Anaheim (A.L.)■........	C-DH	108	338	41	87	15	2	6	46	.257	30	68	1	682	46	7	.990
1999— Anaheim (A.L.)...........	C-DH	107	288	26	69	8	1	3	22	.240	26	46	2	407	46	5	.989
2000— Anaheim (A.L.)..........	C-1B-DH	47	146	17	29	5	0	6	12	.199	7	22	0	201	16	2	.991
2001— Louisville (I.L.)■........	C	67	197	20	45	7	0	3	25	.228	23	26	1	300	34	0	1.000
— Scranton/W.B. (I.L.)■	C-1B	40	141	18	42	11	0	2	21	.298	11	20	0	298	20	0	§1.000
— Philadelphia (N.L.)......	PH	1	1	0	1	0	0	0	0	1.000	0	0	0	...	...	...	...
American League totals (7 years)		584	1855	198	441	71	4	26	193	.238	126	297	13	2956	222	29	.991
National League totals (2 years)		12	31	2	7	2	0	1	6	.226	1	6	0	49	2	0	1.000
Major League totals (9 years)		596	1886	200	448	73	4	27	199	.238	127	303	13	3005	224	29	.991

WALKER, KEVIN   P   PADRES

PERSONAL: Born September 20, 1976, in Irvin, Texas. ... 6-4/190. ... Throws left, bats left. ... Full name: Kevin Michael Walker.
HIGH SCHOOL: Grand Prairie (Texas).
TRANSACTIONS/CAREER NOTES: Selected by San Diego Padres organization in sixth round of free-agent draft (June 1, 1995). ... On Mobile disabled list (April 8-24, 1999). ... On Rancho Cucamonga disabled list (June 19-July 30, 1999). ... On disabled list (April 20-May 8 and May 23, 2001-remainder of season).

Year League	W	L	Pct.	ERA	G	GS	CG	ShO	Sv.	IP	H	R	ER	BB	SO
1995— Arizona Padres (Ariz.)	5	5	.500	3.01	13	12	0	0	0	71²/₃	74	34	24	12	69
1996— Idaho Falls (Pio.)...............	1	0	1.000	3.00	1	1	0	0	0	6	4	3	2	2	4
— Clinton (Midw.)	4	6	.400	4.74	13	13	0	0	0	76	80	46	40	33	43

W

Year	League	W	L	Pct.	ERA	G	GS	CG	ShO	Sv.	IP	H	R	ER	BB	SO
1997—Clinton (Midw.)		6	10	.375	4.88	19	19	3	1	0	110 2/3	133	80	60	37	80
1998—Clinton (Midw.)		2	0	1.000	1.23	2	2	0	0	0	14 2/3	11	2	2	7	10
—Rancho Cuca. (Calif.)		11	7	.611	4.15	22	22	0	0	0	121 1/3	122	62	56	48	94
1999—Rancho Cuca. (Calif.)		1	1	.500	3.46	27	1	0	0	4	39	35	19	15	19	35
2000—Mobile (Sou.)		0	1	.000	2.25	4	0	0	0	0	4	1	1	1	1	6
—San Diego (N.L.)		7	1	.875	4.18	70	0	0	0	0	66 2/3	49	35	31	38	56
2001—San Diego (N.L.)		0	0	...	3.00	16	0	0	0	0	12	5	4	4	8	17
Major League totals (2 years)		7	1	.875	4.00	86	0	0	0	0	78 2/3	54	39	35	46	73

WALKER, LARRY   OF   ROCKIES

PERSONAL: Born December 1, 1966, in Maple Ridge, B.C. ... 6-3/237. ... Bats left, throws right. ... Full name: Larry Kenneth Robert Walker.
HIGH SCHOOL: Maple Ridge (B.C.) Senior Secondary School.
TRANSACTIONS/CAREER NOTES: Signed as non-drafted free agent by Montreal Expos organization (November 14, 1984). ... On disabled list (April 4, 1988-entire season; June 28-July 13, 1991; and May 26-June 10, 1993). ... On suspended list (June 24-28, 1994). ... Granted free agency (October 24, 1994). ... Signed by Colorado Rockies (April 8, 1995). ... On Colorado disabled list (June 10-August 15, 1996); included rehabilitation assignments to Salem (August 6-9) and Colorado Springs (August 9-15). ... On disabled list (June 18-July 3, 1998; March 29-April 14, 1999; May 11-June 9 and August 20, 2000-remainder of season).
RECORDS: Shares major league record for most extra-base hits in two consecutive games (May 21-22, 1996; 2 doubles, 3 triples and 1 home run). ... Holds N.L. single-season records for most consecutive long hits—6 (May 21-22, 1996; 2 doubles, 3 triples and 1 home run); and highest slugging average by a lefthander (100 or more games)—.720 (1997).
HONORS: Named outfielder on THE SPORTING NEWS N.L. All-Star team (1992, 1997 and 1999). ... Won N.L. Gold Glove as outfielder (1992-93, 1997-99 and 2001). ... Named outfielder on THE SPORTING NEWS N.L. Silver Slugger team (1992, 1997 and 1999). ... Named N.L. Most Valuable Player by Baseball Writers' Association of America (1997).
STATISTICAL NOTES: Hit three home runs in one game (April 5, 1997 and April 28, 1999). ... Led N.L. with 409 total bases in 1997. ... Led N.L. with .452 on-base percentage in 1997. ... Led N.L. in slugging percentage with .720 in 1997. ... Led N.L. outfielders in double plays with four in 1997 and tied for lead with four in 2000. ... Had 20-game hitting streak (May 4-25, 1998). ... Had 21-game hitting streak (April 25-May 21, 1999). ... Had 18-game hitting streak (June 14-July 3, 1999). ... Led N.L. with a .710 slugging percentage and a .458 on-base percentage in 1999. ... Career major league grand slams: 4.
MISCELLANEOUS: Holds Colorado Rockies all-time record for most runs (689), home runs (210) and highest career batting average (.341).

							BATTING								FIELDING		
Year	Team (League)	Pos.	G	AB	R	H	2B	3B	HR	RBI	Avg.	BB	SO	SB	PO	A	E	Avg.
1985—Utica (NY-Penn)		1B-3B	62	215	24	48	8	2	2	26	.223	18	57	12	354	62	8	.981
1986—Burlington (Midw.)		OF-3B	95	332	67	96	12	6	29	74	.289	46	112	16	106	51	10	.940
—W. Palm Beach (FSL)		OF	38	113	20	32	7	5	4	16	.283	26	32	2	44	5	0	1.000
1987—Jacksonville (Sou.)		OF	128	474	91	136	25	7	26	83	.287	67	120	24	263	9	9	.968
1988—Montreal (N.L.)							Did not play.										
1989—Indianapolis (A.A.)		OF	114	385	68	104	18	2	12	59	.270	50	87	36	241	*18	*11	.959
—Montreal (N.L.)		OF	20	47	4	8	0	0	0	4	.170	5	13	1	19	2	0	1.000
1990—Montreal (N.L.)		OF	133	419	59	101	18	3	19	51	.241	49	112	21	249	12	4	.985
1991—Montreal (N.L.)		OF-1B	137	487	59	141	30	2	16	64	.290	42	102	14	536	36	6	.990
1992—Montreal (N.L.)		OF	143	528	85	159	31	4	23	93	.301	41	97	18	269	16	2	.993
1993—Montreal (N.L.)		OF-1B	138	490	85	130	24	5	22	86	.265	80	76	29	316	16	6	.982
1994—Montreal (N.L.)		OF-1B	103	395	76	127	44	2	19	86	.322	47	74	15	423	29	9	.980
1995—Colorado (N.L.)■		OF	131	494	96	151	31	5	36	101	.306	49	72	16	225	13	3	.988
1996—Colorado (N.L.)		OF	83	272	58	75	18	4	18	58	.276	20	58	18	153	4	1	.994
—Salem (Caro.)		DH	2	8	3	4	3	0	1	1	.500	0	1	0	...	...	...	...
—Colo. Springs (PCL)		OF	3	11	2	4	0	0	2	8	.364	1	4	0	6	2	0	1.000
1997—Colorado (N.L.)		OF-1B-DH	153	568	143	208	46	4	*49	130	.366	78	90	33	254	14	2	.993
1998—Colorado (N.L.)		O-DH-2-3	130	454	113	165	46	3	23	67	*.363	64	61	14	236	8	4	.984
1999—Colorado (N.L.)		OF-DH	127	438	108	166	26	4	37	115	*.379	57	52	11	204	13	4	.982
2000—Colorado (N.L.)		OF-DH	87	314	64	97	21	7	9	51	.309	46	40	5	161	11	1	.994
2001—Colorado (N.L.)		OF-DH	142	497	107	174	35	3	38	123	.350	82	103	14	243	8	4	.984
Major League totals (13 years)			1527	5403	1057	1702	370	46	309	1029	.315	660	950	209	3288	182	46	.987

DIVISION SERIES RECORD

						BATTING								FIELDING		
Year	Team (League)	Pos.	G	AB	R	H	2B	3B	HR	RBI	Avg.	BB	SO	SB	PO	A	E	Avg.
1995—Colorado (N.L.)		OF	4	14	3	3	0		1	3	.214	3	4	1	3	0	0	1.000

ALL-STAR GAME RECORD

					BATTING								FIELDING		
Year	League	Pos.	AB	R	H	2B	3B	HR	RBI	Avg.	BB	SO	SB	PO	A	E	Avg.
1992—National		PH	1	0	1	0	0	0	0	1.000	0	0	0	...	...	...	...
1997—National		OF	1	0	0	0	0	0	0	.000	0	0	0	0	0	...	...
1998—National		OF	1	1	0	0	0	0	0	.000	1	0	0	2	0	0	1.000
1999—National		OF	2	0	0	0	0	0	0	.000	0	1	0	1	0	0	1.000
2001—National		DH	2	0	0	0	0	0	0	.000	0	0	0	...	...	...	...
All-Star Game totals (5 years)			7	1	1	0	0	0	0	.143	2	1	0	3	0	0	1.000

W

WALKER, PETE   P   METS

PERSONAL: Born April 8, 1969, in Beverly, Mass. ... 6-2/195. ... Throws right, bats right. ... Full name: Peter Brian Walker.
HIGH SCHOOL: East Lyme (Conn.).
COLLEGE: Connecticut.
TRANSACTIONS/CAREER NOTES: Selected by New York Mets organization in seventh round of free-agent draft (June 4, 1990). ... On disabled list (June 6-18, 1992; and April 25-May 9, 1993). ... On Norfolk disabled list (April 7-May 16, 1994). ... On Norfolk suspended list (August 5-6, 1994). ... Traded by Mets with P Luis Arroyo to San Diego Padres for 1B Roberto Petagine and P Scott Adair (March 17, 1996).

... On Las Vegas disabled list (May 4-July 11, 1996). ... Granted free agency (October 15, 1996). ... Signed by Boston Red Sox organization (June 30, 1997). ... Granted free agency (October 17, 1997). ... Re-signed by Red Sox organization (January 14, 1998). ... On Pawtucket disabled list (June 11-22 and June 26-September 8, 1998). ... Granted free agency (October 16, 1998). ... Signed by Colorado Rockies organization (February 8, 1999). ... On Colorado Springs disabled list (July 16-August 6, 1999). ... Granted free agency (October 15, 1999). ... Re-signed by Rockies organization (November 17, 1999). ... Released by Rockies (November 13, 2000). ... Signed by Mets organization (December 26, 2000). ... Granted free agency (October 15, 2001). ... Re-signed by Mets organization (December 10, 2001).

Year	League	W	L	Pct.	ERA	G	GS	CG	ShO	Sv.	IP	H	R	ER	BB	SO
1990—	Pittsfield (NY-Penn)...........	5	7	.417	4.16	16	13	1	0	0	80	74	43	37	46	73
1991—	St. Lucie (FSL)	10	12	.455	3.21	26	25	1	0	0	151 1/3	145	77	54	52	95
1992—	Binghamton (East.)	7	12	.368	4.12	24	23	4	0	0	139 2/3	159	77	64	46	72
1993—	Binghamton (East.)	4	9	.308	3.44	45	10	0	0	19	99 1/3	89	45	38	46	89
1994—	St. Lucie (FSL)	0	0	...	2.25	3	0	0	0	0	4	3	2	1	1	5
—	Norfolk (I.L.)	2	4	.333	3.97	37	0	0	0	3	47 2/3	48	22	21	24	42
1995—	Norfolk (I.L.)	5	2	.714	3.91	34	1	0	0	8	48 1/3	51	24	21	16	39
—	New York (N.L.)..................	1	0	1.000	4.58	13	0	0	0	0	17 2/3	24	9	9	5	5
1996—	Las Vegas (PCL)■	5	1	.833	6.83	26	0	0	0	0	27 2/3	37	22	21	14	23
—	Arizona Padres (Ariz.)	0	1	.000	2.25	2	2	0	0	0	4	4	1	1	0	5
—	San Diego (N.L.)	0	0	...	0.00	1	0	0	0	0	2/3	0	0	0	3	1
1997—	Pawtucket (I.L.)■	0	0	...	5.40	7	0	0	0	0	11 2/3	14	8	7	7	8
—	Gulf Coast Red Sox (GCL)..	0	0	...	0.96	4	3	0	0	0	9 1/3	5	1	1	1	14
—	Trenton (East.)	0	0	...	4.05	8	0	0	0	3	13 1/3	14	6	6	7	13
1998—	Pawtucket (I.L.)..................	1	4	.200	5.94	22	0	0	0	0	33 1/3	34	26	22	17	19
1999—	Colorado Springs (PCL)■..	8	4	.667	4.48	48	0	0	0	5	62 1/3	64	37	31	28	57
2000—	Colorado Springs (PCL)	7	3	.700	3.07	58	0	0	0	5	73 1/3	64	29	25	30	61
—	Colorado (N.L.)..................	0	0	...	17.36	3	0	0	0	0	4 2/3	10	9	9	4	2
2001—	Norfolk (I.L.)■..................	13	4	.765	2.99	26	26	0	0	0	168 1/3	145	64	56	46	106
—	New York (N.L.)..................	0	0	...	2.70	2	0	0	0	0	6 2/3	6	2	2	0	4
Major League totals (4 years)		1	0	1.000	6.07	19	0	0	0	0	29 2/3	40	20	20	12	12

WALKER, TODD   2B   REDS

PERSONAL: Born May 25, 1973, in Bakersfield, Calif. ... 6-0/181. ... Bats left, throws right. ... Full name: Todd Arthur Walker.
HIGH SCHOOL: Airline (Bossier City, La.).
COLLEGE: Louisiana State.
TRANSACTIONS/CAREER NOTES: Selected by Texas Rangers organization in 51st round of free-agent draft (June 3, 1991); did not sign. ... Selected by Minnesota Twins organization in first round (eighth pick overall) of free-agent draft (June 2, 1994). ... Traded by Twins with OF/1B Butch Huskey to Colorado Rockies for 2B Todd Sears and cash considerations (July 16, 2000). ... Traded by Rockies with OF Robin Jennings to Cincinnati Reds for OF Alex Ochoa (July 19, 2001).
HONORS: Named Most Outstanding Player of College World Series (1993).
STATISTICAL NOTES: Led Pacific Coast League with 330 total bases and .599 slugging percentage and tied for lead in intentional bases on balls received with 11 in 1996.

							BATTING							FIELDING		
Year	Team (League)	Pos.	G	AB	R	H	2B	3B	HR	RBI	Avg.	BB	SO	SB	PO	A	E	Avg.
1994—	Fort Myers (FSL)	2B	46	171	29	52	5	2	10	34	.304	32	15	6	98	112	9	.959
1995—	New Britain (East.)	2B-3B	137	513	83	149	27	3	21	85	.290	63	101	23	215	355	27	.955
1996—	Salt Lake (PCL)	3B-2B-DH	135	551	94	*187	*41	9	*28	*111	.339	57	91	13	129	276	19	.955
—	Minnesota (A.L.)	3B-2B-DH	25	82	8	21	6	0	0	6	.256	4	13	2	16	39	2	.965
1997—	Minnesota (A.L.)	3B-2B-DH	52	156	15	37	7	1	3	16	.237	11	30	7	35	86	4	.968
—	Salt Lake (PCL)	3B-DH	83	322	69	111	20	1	11	53	.345	46	49	5	44	174	*24	.901
1998—	Minnesota (A.L.)	2B-DH	143	528	85	167	41	3	12	62	.316	47	65	19	219	363	13	.978
1999—	Minnesota (A.L.)	2B-DH	143	531	62	148	37	4	6	46	.279	52	83	18	168	270	7	.984
2000—	Minnesota (A.L.)	2B-DH	23	77	14	18	1	0	2	8	.234	7	10	3	34	36	4	.946
—	Salt Lake (PCL)	2B	63	249	51	81	14	1	2	37	.325	32	32	8	114	180	11	.964
—	Colorado (N.L.)■.......	2B	57	171	28	54	10	4	7	36	.316	20	19	4	81	118	5	.975
2001—	Colorado (N.L.)	2B	85	290	52	86	18	2	12	43	.297	25	40	1	155	198	7	.981
—	Cincinnati (N.L.)■......	2B-SS	66	261	41	77	17	0	5	32	.295	26	42	0	138	169	4	.987
American League totals (5 years)			386	1374	184	391	92	8	23	138	.285	121	201	49	472	794	30	.977
National League totals (2 years)			208	722	121	217	45	6	24	111	.301	71	101	5	374	485	16	.982
Major League totals (6 years)			594	2096	305	608	137	14	47	249	.290	192	302	54	846	1279	46	.979

WALKER, TYLER   P   METS

W

PERSONAL: Born May 15, 1976, in San Francisco. ... 6-3/255. ... Throws right, bats right. ... Full name: Tyler Lanier Walker.
HIGH SCHOOL: University (San Francisco).
COLLEGE: California.
TRANSACTIONS/CAREER NOTES: Selected by New York Mets organization in second round of free-agent draft (June 3, 1997). ... On Norfolk disabled list (August 11-20 and August 21-28, 2000).

Year	League	W	L	Pct.	ERA	G	GS	CG	ShO	Sv.	IP	H	R	ER	BB	SO
1997—	Gulf Coast Mets (GCL)	0	0	...	1.00	5	0	0	0	3	9	8	1	1	2	9
—	Pittsfield (NY-Penn)...........	0	0	...	13.50	1	0	0	0	0	2/3	2	2	1	1	1
1998—	Capital City (S.Atl.)...........	5	5	.500	4.12	34	13	0	0	1	115 2/3	122	63	53	38	110
1999—	St. Lucie (FSL)	6	5	.545	2.94	13	13	2	0	0	79 2/3	64	31	26	29	64
—	Binghamton (East.)	6	4	.600	6.22	13	13	0	0	0	68	78	49	47	32	59
2000—	Binghamton (East.)	7	6	.538	2.75	22	22	0	0	0	121	82	43	37	55	111
—	Norfolk (I.L.)	1	3	.250	2.39	5	5	0	0	0	26 1/3	29	7	7	9	17
2001—	Norfolk (I.L.)	3	2	.600	4.02	8	8	0	0	0	40 1/3	34	19	18	8	35
—	St. Lucie (FSL)	0	2	.000	8.04	4	4	0	0	0	15 2/3	19	14	14	3	11
—	Binghamton (East.)	1	0	1.000	0.40	4	3	0	0	0	22 1/3	9	2	1	13	13

PERSONAL: Born July 11, 1967, in Potosi, Mo. ... 6-1/205. ... Throws right, bats right. ... Full name: Donnell Lee Wall. ... Name pronounced DON-ee.

HIGH SCHOOL: Festus (Mo.).

JUNIOR COLLEGE: Jefferson College (Mo.), then St. Louis Community College at Meramec.

COLLEGE: Southwestern Louisiana.

TRANSACTIONS/CAREER NOTES: Selected by Houston Astros organization in 18th round of free-agent draft (June 5, 1989). ... On disabled list (May 27-June 16, 1994). ... Claimed on waivers by Cincinnati Reds (October 7, 1997). ... Traded by Reds with C Paul Bako to Detroit Tigers for OF Melvin Nieves (November 11, 1997). ... Traded by Tigers with P Dan Miceli and 3B Ryan Balfe to San Diego Padres for P Tim Worrell and OF Trey Beamon (November 19, 1997). ... On San Diego disabled list (June 1-July 1, 2000); included rehabilitation assignment to Las Vegas (June 28-July 1). ... Traded by Padres to New York Mets for OF Bubba Trammell (December 11, 2000). ... On New York disabled list (May 27-July 4, 2001); included rehabilitation assignment to Binghamton (June 25-July 4). ... Granted free agency (October 15, 2001).

HONORS: Named Pacific Coast League Most Valuable Player (1995).

STATISTICAL NOTES: Led South Atlantic League with 18 home runs allowed in 1990.

MISCELLANEOUS: Appeared in one game pinch runner (2001).

Year League	W	L	Pct.	ERA	G	GS	CG	ShO	Sv.	IP	H	R	ER	BB	SO
1989— Auburn (NY-Penn)	7	0	*1.000	1.79	12	8	3	1	1	65 1/3	45	17	13	12	69
1990— Asheville (S.Atl.)	6	8	.429	5.18	28	22	1	0	1	132	149	87	76	47	111
1991— Burlington (Midw.)	7	5	.583	2.03	16	16	3	1	0	106 2/3	73	30	24	21	102
— Osceola (FSL)	6	3	.667	2.09	12	12	4	2	0	77 1/3	55	22	18	11	62
1992— Osceola (FSL)	3	1	.750	2.63	7	7	0	0	0	41	37	13	12	8	30
— Jackson (Texas)	9	6	.600	3.54	18	18	2	0	0	114 1/3	114	51	45	26	99
1993— Tucson (PCL)	6	4	.600	3.83	25	22	0	0	0	131 2/3	147	73	56	25	89
1994— Tucson (PCL)	11	8	.579	4.43	26	24	2	2	0	148 1/3	171	87	73	35	84
1995— Tucson (PCL)	*17	6	.739	*3.30	28	•28	0	0	0	*177 1/3	190	72	65	32	*119
— Houston (N.L.)	3	1	.750	5.55	6	5	0	0	0	24 1/3	33	19	15	5	16
1996— Tucson (PCL)	3	3	.500	4.13	8	8	0	0	0	52 1/3	67	30	24	6	36
— Houston (N.L.)	9	8	.529	4.56	26	23	2	1	0	150	170	84	76	34	99
1997— New Orleans (A.A.)	8	7	.533	3.85	17	17	1	0	0	110	109	49	47	24	84
— Houston (N.L.)	2	5	.286	6.26	8	8	0	0	0	41 2/3	53	31	29	16	25
1998— Las Vegas (PCL)■	2	0	1.000	4.80	3	3	0	0	0	15	11	8	8	8	12
— San Diego (N.L.)	5	4	.556	2.43	46	1	0	0	1	70 1/3	50	20	19	32	56
1999— San Diego (N.L.)	7	4	.636	3.07	55	0	0	0	0	70 1/3	58	31	24	23	53
2000— San Diego (N.L.)	5	2	.714	3.35	44	0	0	0	1	53 2/3	36	20	20	21	29
— Las Vegas (PCL)	0	0	...	0.00	2	0	0	0	0	2	3	0	0	2	1
2001— New York (N.L.)■	0	4	.000	4.85	32	0	0	0	0	42 2/3	51	24	23	17	31
— Binghamton (East.)	0	0	...	0.00	4	4	0	0	0	5	1	0	0	1	5
— Norfolk (I.L.)	0	0	...	10.38	4	0	0	0	1	4 1/3	8	6	5	5	1
Major League totals (7 years)	31	28	.525	4.09	217	37	2	1	2	453	451	229	206	148	309

DIVISION SERIES RECORD

Year League	W	L	Pct.	ERA	G	GS	CG	ShO	Sv.	IP	H	R	ER	BB	SO
1998— San Diego (N.L.)	0	0	...	9.00	1	0	0	0	0	1	2	1	1	0	2

CHAMPIONSHIP SERIES RECORD

Year League	W	L	Pct.	ERA	G	GS	CG	ShO	Sv.	IP	H	R	ER	BB	SO
1998— San Diego (N.L.)	0	0	...	3.00	3	0	0	0	1	3	3	2	1	4	4

WORLD SERIES RECORD

Year League	W	L	Pct.	ERA	G	GS	CG	ShO	Sv.	IP	H	R	ER	BB	SO
1998— San Diego (N.L.)	0	1	.000	6.75	2	0	0	0	0	2 2/3	3	2	2	3	1

PERSONAL: Born April 12, 1976, in Wheeling, W.Va. ... 6-2/238. ... Throws left, bats left. ... Full name: Jeffrey Allen Wallace.

HIGH SCHOOL: Minerva (Ohio).

TRANSACTIONS/CAREER NOTES: Selected by Kansas City Royals organization in 25th round of free-agent draft (June 1, 1995). ... Traded by Royals with P Jeff Granger, P Jeff Martin and 3B Joe Randa to Pittsburgh Pirates for SS Jay Bell and 1B Jeff King (December 13, 1996). ... On disabled list (March 22, 1998-entire season). ... On Pittsburgh disabled list (July 3-August 19, 1999); included rehabilitation assignment to Nashville (July 20-August 18). ... Claimed on waivers by Cincinnati Reds (December 1, 2000). ... Granted free agency (December 21, 2000). ... Signed by Tampa Bay Devil Rays organization (January 10, 2001). ... On Tampa Bay disabled list (August 12-September 1, 2001); included rehabilitation assignment to Orlando (August 31-September 1). ... Claimed on waivers by Boston Red Sox (December 4, 2001).

W

Year League	W	L	Pct.	ERA	G	GS	CG	ShO	Sv.	IP	H	R	ER	BB	SO
1995— Sarasota Royals (GCL)	5	3	.625	1.22	12	7	0	0	1	44 1/3	28	20	6	15	51
1996— Lansing (Midw.)	4	9	.308	5.30	30	21	0	0	0	122 1/3	140	79	72	66	84
1997— Lynchburg (Caro.)■	5	0	1.000	1.65	9	0	0	0	1	16 1/3	9	3	3	10	13
— Carolina (Sou.)	4	8	.333	5.40	38	0	0	0	3	43 1/3	43	37	26	36	39
— Pittsburgh (N.L.)	0	0	...	0.75	11	0	0	0	0	12	8	2	1	8	14
1998— Pittsburgh (N.L.)							Did not play.								
1999— Nashville (PCL)	2	2	.500	8.79	15	0	0	0	3	14 1/3	18	15	14	8	14
— Pittsburgh (N.L.)	1	0	1.000	3.69	41	0	0	0	0	39	26	17	16	38	41
2000— Nashville (PCL)	0	0	...	0.64	13	0	0	0	1	14	11	1	1	6	12
— Pittsburgh (N.L.)	2	0	1.000	7.07	38	0	0	0	0	35 2/3	42	32	28	34	27
2001— Durham (I.L.)■	0	0	...	3.86	7	0	0	0	0	9 1/3	6	4	4	7	11
— Tampa Bay (A.L.)	0	3	.000	3.40	29	1	0	0	0	50 1/3	43	26	19	37	38
— Orlando (Sou.)	0	0	...	0.00	1	0	0	0	0	1	1	0	0	1	3
A.L. totals (1 year)	0	3	.000	3.40	29	1	0	0	0	50 1/3	43	26	19	37	38
N.L. totals (3 years)	3	0	1.000	4.67	90	0	0	0	0	86 2/3	76	51	45	80	82
Major League totals (4 years)	3	3	.500	4.20	119	1	0	0	0	137	119	77	64	117	120

WALROND, LES — P — CARDINALS

PERSONAL: Born November 7, 1976, in Muskogee, Okla. ... 6-0/195. ... Throws left, bats left. ... Full name: Leslie Dale Walrond.
HIGH SCHOOL: Union (Tulsa, Okla.).
COLLEGE: Kansas.
TRANSACTIONS/CAREER NOTES: Selected by St. Louis Cardinals organization in 13th round of free-agent draft (June 2, 1998). ... On disabled list (May 12-July 20, 2001).

Year League	W	L	Pct.	ERA	G	GS	CG	ShO	Sv.	IP	H	R	ER	BB	SO
1998— New Jersey (NY-Penn)	2	4	.333	4.01	13	10	0	0	0	51 2/3	52	31	23	24	52
1999— Peoria (Midw.)..............	7	10	.412	5.70	21	20	0	0	0	109	115	77	69	59	78
2000— Potomac (Caro.).............	10	5	.667	3.34	27	27	0	0	0	151	134	66	56	54	153
2001— New Haven (East.)..........	2	8	.200	3.87	16	16	1	0	0	81 1/3	68	41	35	46	67

WARD, DARYLE — OF/1B — ASTROS

PERSONAL: Born June 27, 1975, in Lynwood, Calif. ... 6-2/230. ... Bats left, throws left. ... Full name: Daryle Lamar Ward. ... Son of Gary Ward, outfielder with four major league teams (1979-90); and hitting coach, Charlotte Knights of International League.
HIGH SCHOOL: Brethren Christian (Riverside, Calif.).
JUNIOR COLLEGE: Rancho Santiago College (Calif.).
TRANSACTIONS/CAREER NOTES: Selected by Detroit Tigers organization in 15th round of free-agent draft (June 2, 1994). ... Traded by Tigers with C Brad Ausmus, P Jose Lima, P C.J. Nitkowski and P Trever Miller to Houston Astros for OF Brian Hunter, IF Orlando Miller, P Doug Brocail, P Todd Jones and cash (December 10, 1996).
STATISTICAL NOTES: Tied for Texas League lead with four intentional bases on balls in 1997. ... Career major league grand slams: 1.

							BATTING							FIELDING		
Year Team (League)	Pos.	G	AB	R	H	2B	3B	HR	RBI	Avg.	BB	SO	SB	PO	A	E	Avg.
1994— Bristol (Appl.)............	1B	48	161	17	43	6	0	5	30	.267	19	33	5	308	23	11	.968
1995— Fayetteville (S.Atl.)	1B	137	524	75	149	32	0	14	106	.284	46	111	1	1009	77	14	.987
1996— Lakeland (FSL).......	1B-DH	128	464	65	135	29	4	10	68	.291	57	77	1	1058	103	8	.993
— Toledo (I.L.)...............	1B	6	23	1	4	0	0	0	1	.174	0	3	0	42	5	1	.979
1997— Jackson (Texas)■.....	1B-DH	114	422	72	139	25	0	19	90	.329	46	68	4	951	76	12	.988
— New Orleans (A.A.).....	1B-DH	14	48	4	18	1	0	2	8	.375	7	7	0	75	6	2	.976
1998— New Orleans (PCL)...	OF-1B-DH	116	463	78	141	31	1	23	96	.305	41	78	2	482	48	13	.976
— Houston (N.L.)...........	PH	4	3	1	1	0	0	0	0	.333	1	2	0	...	...	...	...
1999— New Orleans (PCL)...	1B-OF	61	241	56	85	15	1	28	65	.353	23	43	1	528	35	5	.991
— Houston (N.L.)..........	OF-1B-DH	64	150	11	41	6	0	8	30	.273	9	31	0	69	3	2	.973
2000— Houston (N.L.).........	OF-1B-DH	119	264	36	68	10	2	20	47	.258	15	61	0	125	4	1	.992
2001— Houston (N.L.).........	OF-1B-DH	95	213	21	56	15	0	9	39	.263	19	48	0	81	2	1	.988
Major League totals (4 years)		282	630	69	166	31	2	37	116	.263	44	142	0	275	9	4	.986

DIVISION SERIES RECORD

							BATTING							FIELDING		
Year Team (League)	Pos.	G	AB	R	H	2B	3B	HR	RBI	Avg.	BB	SO	SB	PO	A	E	Avg.
1999— Houston (N.L.)..........	OF-PH	3	7	1	1	0	0	1	1	.143	0	2	0	3	0	1	.750
2001— Houston (N.L.)..........	PH	2	2	1	1	0	0	1	2	.500	0	0	0	...	...	...	...
Division series totals (2 years)		5	9	2	2	0	0	2	3	.222	0	2	0	3	0	1	.750

WARD, TURNER — OF

PERSONAL: Born April 11, 1965, in Orlando. ... 6-2/204. ... Bats both, throws right. ... Full name: Turner Max Ward.
HIGH SCHOOL: Satsuma (Ala.).
JUNIOR COLLEGE: Faulkner State Community College (Ala.).
COLLEGE: South Alabama.
TRANSACTIONS/CAREER NOTES: Selected by New York Yankees organization in 18th round of free-agent draft (June 2, 1986). ... Traded by Yankees with C Joel Skinner to Cleveland Indians for OF Mel Hall (March 19, 1989). ... On Gulf Coast Indians disabled list (April 7-July 24, 1989). ... Traded by Indians with P Tom Candiotti to Toronto Blue Jays for P Denis Boucher, OF Glenallen Hill, OF Mark Whiten and a player to be named later (June 27, 1991); Indians acquired cash to complete deal (October 15, 1991). ... On Toronto disabled list (August 2-September 1, 1993); included rehabilitation assignment to Knoxville (August 21-September 1). ... Claimed on waivers by Milwaukee Brewers (November 24, 1993). ... On Milwaukee disabled list (June 7-22, July 2-19 and July 24, 1995-remainder of season); included rehabilitation assignments to Beloit (July 17-19) and New Orleans (August 10-17 and August 31-September 5). ... On Milwaukee disabled list (May 25-September 1, 1996). ... Released by Brewers (November 1, 1996). ... Signed by Pittsburgh Pirates organization (April 22, 1997). ... On disabled list (August 5-20, 1998). ... On Pittsburgh disabled list (June 9-August 11, 1999); included rehabilitation assignments to Altoona (June 23-24) and Nashville (June 25-August 1 and August 2-9). ... Released by Pirates (August 11, 1999). ... Signed by Arizona Diamondbacks organization (August 18, 1999). ... On Arizona disabled list (August 31-September 15, 1999). ... Granted free agency (November 1, 1999). ... Resigned by Diamondbacks organization (February 19, 2000). ... On Tucson disabled list (June 21-September 1, 2000). ... Released by Diamondbacks (October 5, 2000). ... Signed by Philadelphia Phillies organization (December 20, 2000). ... On Scranton/Wilkes-Barre disabled list (April 5-20, 2001). ... Granted free agency (October 8, 2001).
STATISTICAL NOTES: Led Pacific Coast League outfielders with 292 putouts and 308 total chances in 1990.

							BATTING							FIELDING		
Year Team (League)	Pos.	G	AB	R	H	2B	3B	HR	RBI	Avg.	BB	SO	SB	PO	A	E	Avg.
1986— Oneonta (NY-Penn)	OF-1B-3B	63	221	42	62	4	1	1	19	.281	31	39	6	97	6	5	.954
1987— Fort Lauderdale (FSL)	OF-3B	130	493	83	145	15	2	7	55	.294	64	83	25	332	11	8	.977
1988— Columbus (I.L.).........	OF	134	490	55	123	24	1	7	50	.251	48	100	28	223	5	1	*.996
1989— GC Indians (GCL)■...	DH	4	15	2	3	0	0	0	1	.200	2	2	1	...	...	...	...
— Canton/Akron (East.)..	OF	30	93	19	28	5	1	0	3	.301	15	16	1	2	0	0	1.000
1990— Colo. Springs (PCL) ...	OF-2B	133	495	89	148	24	9	6	65	.299	72	70	22	†292	7	9	.971
— Cleveland (A.L.)..........	OF-DH	14	46	10	16	2	1	1	10	.348	3	8	3	20	2	1	.957

W

Year	Team (League)	Pos.	G	AB	R	H	2B	3B	HR	RBI	Avg.	BB	SO	SB	PO	A	E	Avg.
1991—	Cleveland (A.L.)	OF	40	100	11	23	7	0	0	5	.230	10	16	0	65	1	0	1.000
—	Colo. Springs (PCL)	OF	14	51	5	10	1	1	1	3	.196	6	9	2	30	0	1	.968
—	Toronto (A.L.)■	OF	8	13	1	4	0	0	0	2	.308	1	2	0	5	0	0	1.000
—	Syracuse (I.L.)	OF	59	218	40	72	11	3	7	32	.330	47	22	9	136	5	0	1.000
1992—	Toronto (A.L.)	OF	18	29	7	10	3	0	1	3	.345	4	4	0	18	1	0	1.000
—	Syracuse (I.L.)	OF	81	280	41	67	10	2	10	29	.239	44	43	7	143	3	5	.967
1993—	Toronto (A.L.)	OF-1B	72	167	20	32	4	2	4	28	.192	23	26	3	97	2	1	.990
—	Knoxville (Sou.)	OF	7	23	6	6	2	0	0	2	.261	7	3	3	20	0	0	1.000
1994—	Milwaukee (A.L.)■	OF-3B	102	367	55	85	15	2	9	45	.232	52	68	6	260	9	4	.985
1995—	Milwaukee (A.L.)	OF-DH	44	129	19	34	3	1	4	16	.264	14	21	6	81	5	1	.989
—	Beloit (Midw.)	OF	2	5	0	0	0	0	0	0	.000	3	1	0	1	0	0	1.000
—	New Orleans (A.A.)	OF-DH	11	33	3	8	1	1	1	3	.242	4	10	0	9	0	1	.900
1996—	Milwaukee (A.L.)	OF-DH	43	67	7	12	2	1	2	10	.179	13	17	3	54	1	0	1.000
—	New Orleans (A.A.)	DH	9	23	4	8	1	0	1	1	.348	7	4	0	...	...	...	...
1997—	Calgary (PCL)	OF-DH-1B	59	209	44	71	18	3	9	44	.340	24	26	7	87	6	3	.969
—	Pittsburgh (N.L.)	OF	71	167	33	59	16	1	7	33	.353	18	17	4	71	2	0	1.000
1998—	Pittsburgh (N.L.)	OF-DH	123	282	33	74	13	3	9	46	.262	27	40	5	163	7	3	.983
1999—	Pittsburgh (N.L.)	OF	49	91	2	19	2	0	0	8	.209	13	9	2	41	1	2	.955
—	Altoona (East.)	DH	1	3	1	0	0	0	0	0	.000	2	2	0	0	0	0	...
—	Nashville (PCL)	OF-DH	35	89	15	26	3	1	2	17	.292	16	14	3	17	1	2	.900
—	Tucson (PCL)■	OF	12	40	9	15	2	0	2	8	.375	7	4	4	18	1	2	.905
—	Arizona (N.L.)	OF	10	23	6	8	1	0	2	7	.348	2	6	0	11	0	0	1.000
2000—	Tucson (PCL)	OF	32	82	24	31	10	1	4	16	.378	17	7	0	30	1	0	1.000
—	Arizona (N.L.)	OF	15	52	5	9	4	0	0	4	.173	5	7	1	35	0	0	1.000
2001—	Scranton/W.B. (I.L.)■	OF-1B	70	222	28	61	22	4	4	27	.275	30	31	9	35	1	2	.947
—	Philadelphia (N.L.)	PH	17	15	1	4	1	0	0	2	.267	1	6	0	...	...	...	...
American League totals (7 years)			341	918	130	216	36	7	21	119	.235	120	162	21	600	21	7	.989
National League totals (5 years)			285	630	80	173	37	4	18	100	.275	66	85	12	321	10	5	.985
Major League totals (12 years)			626	1548	210	389	73	11	39	219	.251	186	247	33	921	31	12	.988

DIVISION SERIES RECORD

Year	Team (League)	Pos.	G	AB	R	H	2B	3B	HR	RBI	Avg.	BB	SO	SB	PO	A	E	Avg.
1999—	Arizona (N.L.)	PH	3	2	2	1	0	0	1	3	.500	1	0	0	...	...	...	...

WASDIN, JOHN — P

PERSONAL: Born August 5, 1972, in Fort Belvoir, Va. ... 6-2/195. ... Throws right, bats right. ... Full name: John Truman Wasdin.

HIGH SCHOOL: Amos P. Godby (Tallahassee, Fla.).

COLLEGE: Florida State.

TRANSACTIONS/CAREER NOTES: Selected by New York Yankees organization in 41st round of free-agent draft (June 4, 1990); did not sign. ... Selected by Oakland Athletics organization in first round (25th pick overall) of free-agent draft (June 3, 1993). ... Traded by A's with cash to Boston Red Sox for OF Jose Canseco (January 27, 1997). ... On Boston disabled list (July 18-August 5, 1999); included rehabilitation assignment to Gulf Coast Red Sox (July 30-31). ... Traded by Red Sox with P Brian Rose, P Jeff Taglienti and 2B Jeff Frye to Colorado Rockies for P Rolando Arrojo, P Rick Croushore, 2B Mike Lansing and cash (July 27, 2000). ... On suspended list (September 8-10, 2000). ... Released by Rockies (June 7, 2001). ... Signed by Baltimore Orioles organization (July 18, 2001). ... Traded by Orioles to Philadelphia Phillies for P Chris Brock (December 13, 2001). ... Granted free agency (December 21, 2001). ... Signed by Yomiuri Giants of Japan Central League (January 9, 2002).

STATISTICAL NOTES: Led Pacific Coast League with 26 home runs allowed in 1995.

Year	League	W	L	Pct.	ERA	G	GS	CG	ShO	Sv.	IP	H	R	ER	BB	SO
1993—	Arizona Athletics (Ariz.)	0	0	...	3.00	1	1	0	0	0	3	3	1	1	0	1
—	Madison (Midw.)	2	3	.400	1.86	9	9	0	0	0	48 1/3	32	11	10	9	40
—	Modesto (Calif.)	0	3	.000	3.86	3	3	0	0	0	16 1/3	17	9	7	4	11
1994—	Modesto (Calif.)	3	1	.750	1.69	6	4	0	0	0	26 2/3	17	6	5	5	30
—	Huntsville (Sou.)	12	3	.800	3.43	21	21	0	0	0	141 2/3	126	61	54	29	108
1995—	Edmonton (PCL)	12	8	.600	5.52	29	•28	2	1	0	174 1/3	193	117	107	38	111
—	Oakland (A.L.)	1	1	.500	4.67	5	2	0	0	0	17 1/3	14	9	9	3	6
1996—	Edmonton (PCL)	2	1	.667	4.14	9	9	0	0	0	50	52	23	23	17	30
—	Oakland (A.L.)	8	7	.533	5.96	25	21	1	0	0	131 1/3	145	96	87	50	75
1997—	Boston (A.L.)■	4	6	.400	4.40	53	7	0	0	0	124 2/3	121	68	61	38	84
1998—	Boston (A.L.)	6	4	.600	5.25	47	8	0	0	0	96	111	57	56	27	59
—	Pawtucket (I.L.)	1	0	1.000	3.00	4	2	0	0	0	12	11	6	4	5	10
1999—	Pawtucket (I.L.)	1	1	.500	2.12	5	5	0	0	0	29 2/3	19	9	7	7	28
—	Boston (A.L.)	8	3	.727	4.12	45	0	0	0	2	74 1/3	66	38	34	18	57
—	Gulf Coast Red Sox (GCL)	0	0	...	0.00	1	1	0	0	0	2	1	0	0	0	4
2000—	Boston (A.L.)	1	3	.250	5.04	25	1	0	0	1	44 2/3	48	25	25	15	36
—	Pawtucket (I.L.)	1	0	1.000	2.25	5	3	0	0	1	16	7	4	4	2	11
—	Colorado (N.L.)■	0	3	.000	5.80	14	3	1	0	0	35 2/3	42	23	23	9	35
2001—	Colorado (N.L.)	2	1	.667	7.03	18	0	0	0	0	24 1/3	32	19	19	8	17
—	Rochester (I.L.)■	2	1	.667	3.98	5	3	0	0	0	20 1/3	27	9	9	5	20
—	Baltimore (A.L.)	1	1	.500	4.17	26	0	0	0	0	49 2/3	54	25	23	16	47
A.L. totals (7 years)		29	25	.537	4.93	226	39	1	0	3	538	559	318	295	167	364
N.L. totals (2 years)		2	4	.333	6.30	32	3	1	0	0	60	74	42	42	17	52
Major League totals (7 years)		31	29	.517	5.07	258	42	2	0	3	598	633	360	337	184	416

DIVISION SERIES RECORD

Year	League	W	L	Pct.	ERA	G	GS	CG	ShO	Sv.	IP	H	R	ER	BB	SO
1998—	Boston (A.L.)	0	0	...	10.80	1	0	0	0	0	1 2/3	2	2	2	1	2
1999—	Boston (A.L.)	0	0	...	27.00	2	0	0	0	0	1 2/3	2	5	5	4	1
Division series totals (2 years)		0	0	...	18.90	3	0	0	0	0	3 1/3	4	7	7	5	3

CHAMPIONSHIP SERIES RECORD

Year	League	W	L	Pct.	ERA	G	GS	CG	ShO	Sv.	IP	H	R	ER	BB	SO
1999—	Boston (A.L.)							Did not play.								

W

PERSONAL: Born August 13, 1974, in La Crosse, Wis. ... 6-1/198. ... Throws left, bats left. ... Full name: Jarrod Michael Washburn.
HIGH SCHOOL: Webster (Wis.).
COLLEGE: Wisconsin-Oshkosh.
TRANSACTIONS/CAREER NOTES: Selected by California Angels organizaiton in second round of free-agent draft (June 1, 1995). ... Angels franchise renamed Anaheim Angels for 1997 season. ... On Edmonton disabled list (April 26-June 17, 1999). ... On Anaheim disabled list (March 25-April 9, July 22-August 7 and August 8, 2000-remainder of season); included rehabilitation assignment to Lake Elsinore (April 7). ... On Anaheim disabled list (March 23-April 16, 2001); included rehabilitation assignment to Salt Lake (April 8-16).
STATISTICAL NOTES: Led Texas League with 23 home runs allowed in 1997.

Year League	W	L	Pct.	ERA	G	GS	CG	ShO	Sv.	IP	H	R	ER	BB	SO
1995— Cedar Rapids (Midw.)	0	1	.000	3.44	3	3	0	0	0	18 1/3	17	7	7	7	20
— Boise (N'West)	3	2	.600	3.33	8	8	0	0	0	46	35	17	17	14	54
1996— Lake Elsinore (Calif.)	6	3	.667	3.30	14	14	3	0	0	92 2/3	79	38	34	33	93
— Midland (Texas)	5	6	.455	4.40	13	13	1	0	0	88	77	44	43	25	58
— Vancouver (PCL)	0	2	.000	10.80	2	2	0	0	0	8 1/3	12	16	10	12	5
1997— Midland (Texas)	15	•12	.556	4.80	29	*29	5	•1	0	*189 1/3	*211	*115	*101	65	*146
— Vancouver (PCL)	0	0	...	3.60	1	1	0	0	0	5	4	2	2	2	6
1998— Vancouver (PCL)	4	5	.444	4.32	14	14	2	0	0	91 2/3	91	44	44	43	66
— Anaheim (A.L.)	6	3	.667	4.62	15	11	0	0	0	74	70	40	38	27	48
— Midland (Texas)	0	1	.000	6.23	1	1	0	0	0	8 2/3	13	8	6	2	8
1999— Edmonton (PCL)	1	5	.167	4.73	11	11	1	0	0	59	50	31	31	17	55
— Anaheim (A.L.)	4	5	.444	5.25	16	10	0	0	0	61 2/3	61	36	36	26	39
2000— Lake Elsinore (Calif.)	0	0	...	6.00	1	1	0	0	0	3	3	2	2	2	7
— Edmonton (PCL)	3	0	1.000	3.52	5	5	0	0	0	30 2/3	35	13	12	13	20
— Anaheim (A.L.)	7	2	.778	3.74	14	14	0	0	0	84 1/3	64	38	35	37	49
2001— Salt Lake (PCL)	0	1	.000	5.87	1	1	0	0	0	7 2/3	9	5	5	1	5
— Anaheim (A.L.)	11	10	.524	3.77	30	30	1	0	0	193 1/3	196	89	81	54	126
Major League totals (4 years)	**28**	**20**	**.583**	**4.14**	**75**	**65**	**1**	**0**	**0**	**413 1/3**	**391**	**203**	**190**	**144**	**262**

PERSONAL: Born November 18, 1970, in New York. ... 6-1/224. ... Throws left, bats left. ... Full name: Allen Kenneth Watson.
HIGH SCHOOL: Christ the King (Queens, N.Y.).
COLLEGE: New York State Institute of Technology.
TRANSACTIONS/CAREER NOTES: Selected by St. Louis Cardinals organization in first round (21st pick overall) of free-agent draft (June 3, 1991); pick received as part of compensation for Toronto Blue Jays signing Type A free-agent P Ken Dayley. ... On Savannah disabled list (August 19, 1991-remainder of season). ... On suspended list (June 25-July 3, 1994). ... On St. Louis disabled list (June 7-July 8, 1995); included rehabilitation assignments to Arkansas (June 21-26) and Louisville (June 26-July 8). ... Traded by Cardinals with P Rich DeLucia and P Doug Creek to San Francisco Giants for SS Royce Clayton and a player to be named later (December 14, 1995); Cardinals acquired 2B Chris Wimmer to complete deal (January 16, 1996). ... On San Francisco disabled list (July 2-25, 1996); included rehabilitation assignment to San Jose (July 15-25). ... Traded by Giants with P Fausto Macey to Anaheim Angels for 1B J.T. Snow (November 27, 1996). ... On Anaheim disabled list (May 24-July 13, 1998); included rehabilitation assignments to Midland (June 16), Lake Elsinore (June 21) and Vancouver (June 26). ... Granted free agency (December 21, 1998). ... Signed by New York Mets (January 19, 1999). ... Traded by Mets with cash to Seattle Mariners for P Mac Suzuki and a player to be named later (June 18, 1999); Mets acquired P Justin Dunning to complete deal (September 14, 1999). ... Released by Mariners (June 28, 1999). ... Signed by New York Yankees organization (July 3, 1999). ... Granted free agency (November 5, 1999). ... Re-signed by Yankees (December 7, 1999). ... On New York disabled list (April 24-May 26, June 29-August 4 and August 11, 2000-remainder of season); included rehabilitation assignments to Columbus (May 14-25), Tampa (July 31-August 2) and Gulf Coast Yankees (August 3). ... On disabled list (April 2, 2001-entire season). ... Granted free agency (November 16, 2001).
STATISTICAL NOTES: Led A.L. with 37 home runs allowed in 1997.
MISCELLANEOUS: Singled in three games as pinch hitter with San Francisco (1996).

Year League	W	L	Pct.	ERA	G	GS	CG	ShO	Sv.	IP	H	R	ER	BB	SO
1991— Hamilton (NY-Penn)	1	1	.500	2.52	8	8	0	0	0	39 1/3	22	15	11	17	46
— Savannah (S.Atl.)	1	1	.500	3.95	3	3	0	0	0	13 2/3	16	7	6	8	12
1992— St. Petersburg (FSL)	5	4	.556	1.91	14	14	2	0	0	89 2/3	81	31	19	18	80
— Arkansas (Texas)	8	5	.615	2.15	14	14	3	1	0	96 1/3	77	24	23	23	93
— Louisville (A.A.)	1	0	1.000	1.46	2	2	0	0	0	12 1/3	8	4	2	5	9
1993— Louisville (A.A.)	5	4	.556	2.91	17	17	2	0	0	120 2/3	101	46	39	31	86
— St. Louis (N.L.)	6	7	.462	4.60	16	15	0	0	0	86	90	53	44	28	49
1994— St. Louis (N.L.)	6	5	.545	5.52	22	22	0	0	0	115 2/3	130	73	71	53	74
1995— St. Louis (N.L.)	7	9	.438	4.96	21	19	0	0	0	114 1/3	126	68	63	41	49
— Louisville (A.A.)	2	2	.500	2.63	4	4	1	1	0	24	20	10	7	6	19
— Arkansas (Texas)	1	0	1.000	0.00	1	1	0	0	0	5	4	1	0	0	7
1996— San Francisco (N.L.)■	8	12	.400	4.61	29	29	2	0	0	185 2/3	189	105	95	69	128
— San Jose (Calif.)	0	0	...	1.42	2	2	0	0	0	6 1/3	7	1	1	0	12
1997— Anaheim (A.L.)■	12	12	.500	4.93	35	34	0	0	0	199	220	121	109	73	141
1998— Anaheim (A.L.)	6	7	.462	6.04	28	14	1	0	0	92 1/3	122	67	62	34	64
— Midland (Texas)	0	0	...	2.25	1	1	0	0	0	4	6	2	1	1	3
— Lake Elsinore (Calif.)	1	0	1.000	0.00	1	1	0	0	0	5	3	0	0	1	6
— Vancouver (PCL)	0	1	.000	4.50	1	1	0	0	0	6	6	3	3	2	8
1999— New York (N.L.)■	2	2	.500	4.08	14	4	0	0	1	39 2/3	36	18	18	22	32
— Seattle (A.L.)■	0	1	.000	12.00	3	0	0	0	0	3	6	9	4	3	2
— Columbus (I.L.)■	0	0	...	6.14	2	2	0	0	0	7 1/3	7	5	5	2	5
— New York (A.L.)	4	0	1.000	2.10	21	0	0	0	0	34 1/3	30	8	8	10	30
2000— New York (A.L.)	0	0	...	10.23	17	0	0	0	0	22	30	25	25	18	20
— Columbus (I.L.)	0	1	.000	1.35	5	1	0	0	0	6 2/3	3	2	1	2	4
— Tampa (FSL)	0	0	...	0.00	1	1	0	0	0	2	0	0	0	1	1
— Gulf Coast Yankees (GCL)	0	0	...	0.00	1	1	0	0	0	1	1	0	0	0	2
2001— New York (A.L.)							Did not play.								
A.L. totals (4 years)	**22**	**20**	**.524**	**5.34**	**104**	**48**	**1**	**0**	**0**	**350 2/3**	**408**	**230**	**208**	**138**	**257**
N.L. totals (5 years)	**29**	**35**	**.453**	**4.84**	**102**	**89**	**2**	**0**	**1**	**541 1/3**	**571**	**317**	**291**	**213**	**332**
Major League totals (8 years)	**51**	**55**	**.481**	**5.03**	**206**	**137**	**3**	**0**	**1**	**892**	**979**	**547**	**499**	**351**	**589**

W

DIVISION SERIES RECORD

Year League	W	L	Pct.	ERA	G	GS	CG	ShO	Sv.	IP	H	R	ER	BB	SO
1999— New York (A.L.)..................							Did not play.								

CHAMPIONSHIP SERIES RECORD

Year League	W	L	Pct.	ERA	G	GS	CG	ShO	Sv.	IP	H	R	ER	BB	SO
1999— New York (A.L.)..................	0	0	...	0.00	3	0	0	0	0	1	2	0	0	2	1

WORLD SERIES RECORD

NOTES: Member of World Series championship team (1999).

Year League	W	L	Pct.	ERA	G	GS	CG	ShO	Sv.	IP	H	R	ER	BB	SO
1999— New York (A.L.)..................							Did not play.								

WEATHERS, DAVE   P   METS

PERSONAL: Born September 25, 1969, in Lawrenceburg, Tenn. ... 6-3/233. ... Throws right, bats right. ... Full name: John David Weathers.
HIGH SCHOOL: Loretto (Tenn.).
JUNIOR COLLEGE: Motlow State Community College (Tenn.).
TRANSACTIONS/CAREER NOTES: Selected by Toronto Blue Jays organization in third round of free-agent draft (June 1, 1988). ... On Syracuse disabled list (May 11-July 31, 1992). ... Selected by Florida Marlins in second round (29th pick overall) of expansion draft (November 17, 1992). ... On Florida disabled list (June 26-July 13, 1995); included rehabilitation assignments to Brevard County (July 4-10) and Charlotte (July 11-13). ... Traded by Marlins to New York Yankees for P Mark Hutton (July 31, 1996). ... Traded by Yankees to Cleveland Indians for OF Chad Curtis (June 9, 1997). ... Claimed on waivers by Cincinnati Reds (December 20, 1997). ... Claimed on waivers by Milwaukee Brewers (June 24, 1998). ... Granted free agency (October 29, 1999). ... Re-signed by Brewers (December 2, 1999). ... On disabled list (August 2-22, 2000). ... Traded by Brewers with P Roberto Miniel to Chicago Cubs for P Ruben Quevedo and OF Peter Zoccolillo (July 30, 2001). ... Granted free agency (November 5, 2001). ... Signed by New York Mets (December 13, 2001).
MISCELLANEOUS: Appeared in two games as pinch runner (1994). ... Appeared in one game as pinch runner with Florida (1996). ... Struck out in only appearance as pinch hitter (1999).

Year League	W	L	Pct.	ERA	G	GS	CG	ShO	Sv.	IP	H	R	ER	BB	SO
1988—St. Catharines (NY-Penn) ...	4	4	.500	3.02	15	12	0	0	0	62²/₃	58	30	21	26	36
1989—Myrtle Beach (S.Atl.)...........	11	•13	.458	3.86	31	*31	2	0	0	172²/₃	163	99	74	86	111
1990—Dunedin (FSL)....................	10	7	.588	3.70	27	•27	2	0	0	158	158	82	65	59	96
1991—Knoxville (Sou.)...................	10	7	.588	2.45	24	22	5	2	0	139¹/₃	121	51	38	49	114
—Toronto (A.L.)....................	1	0	1.000	4.91	15	0	0	0	0	14²/₃	15	9	8	17	13
1992—Syracuse (I.L.)..................	1	4	.200	4.66	12	10	0	0	0	48¹/₃	48	29	25	21	30
—Toronto (A.L.)....................	0	0	...	8.10	2	0	0	0	0	3¹/₃	5	3	3	2	3
1993—Edmonton (PCL)■..............	11	4	•.733	3.83	22	22	3	1	0	141	150	77	60	47	117
—Florida (N.L.).....................	2	3	.400	5.12	14	6	0	0	0	45²/₃	57	26	26	13	34
1994—Florida (N.L.).....................	8	12	.400	5.27	24	24	0	0	0	135	166	87	79	59	72
1995—Florida (N.L.).....................	4	5	.444	5.98	28	15	0	0	0	90¹/₃	104	68	60	52	60
—Brevard County (FSL)........	0	0	...	0.00	1	1	0	0	0	4	4	0	0	1	3
—Charlotte (I.L.)...................	0	1	.000	9.00	1	1	0	0	0	5	10	5	5	5	0
1996—Florida (N.L.).....................	2	2	.500	4.54	31	8	0	0	0	71¹/₃	85	41	36	28	40
—Charlotte (I.L.)...................	0	0	...	7.71	1	1	0	0	0	2¹/₃	5	2	2	3	0
—New York (A.L.)■..............	0	2	.000	9.35	11	4	0	0	0	17¹/₃	23	19	18	14	13
—Columbus (I.L.).................	0	2	.000	5.40	3	3	0	0	0	16²/₃	20	13	10	5	7
1997—New York (A.L.).................	0	1	.000	10.00	10	0	0	0	0	9	15	10	10	7	4
—Columbus (I.L.).................	2	2	.500	3.19	5	5	1	0	0	36²/₃	35	18	13	7	35
—Buffalo (A.A.)■..................	4	3	.571	3.15	11	11	2	1	0	68²/₃	71	37	24	17	51
—Cleveland (A.L.)...............	1	2	.333	7.56	9	1	0	0	0	16²/₃	23	14	14	8	14
1998—Cincinnati (N.L.)■.............	2	4	.333	6.21	16	9	0	0	0	62¹/₃	86	47	43	27	51
—Milwaukee (N.L.)■.............	4	1	.800	3.21	28	0	0	0	0	47²/₃	44	22	17	14	43
1999—Milwaukee (N.L.)...............	7	4	.636	4.65	63	0	0	0	2	93	102	49	48	38	74
2000—Milwaukee (N.L.)...............	3	5	.375	3.07	69	0	0	0	1	76¹/₃	73	29	26	32	50
2001—Milwaukee (N.L.)...............	3	4	.429	2.03	52	0	0	0	4	57²/₃	37	14	13	25	46
—Chicago (N.L.)■.................	1	1	.500	3.18	28	0	0	0	0	28¹/₃	28	10	10	9	20
A.L. totals (4 years)	2	5	.286	7.82	47	5	0	0	0	61	81	55	53	48	47
N.L. totals (8 years)	36	41	.468	4.55	353	62	0	0	7	707²/₃	782	393	358	297	490
Major League totals (11 years)	38	46	.452	4.81	400	67	0	0	7	768²/₃	863	448	411	345	537

DIVISION SERIES RECORD

Year League	W	L	Pct.	ERA	G	GS	CG	ShO	Sv.	IP	H	R	ER	BB	SO
1996— New York (A.L.)..................	1	0	1.000	0.00	2	0	0	0	0	5	1	0	0	0	5

CHAMPIONSHIP SERIES RECORD

Year League	W	L	Pct.	ERA	G	GS	CG	ShO	Sv.	IP	H	R	ER	BB	SO
1996— New York (A.L.)..................	1	0	1.000	0.00	2	0	0	0	0	3	3	0	0	0	0

WORLD SERIES RECORD

NOTES: Member of World Series championship team (1996).

Year League	W	L	Pct.	ERA	G	GS	CG	ShO	Sv.	IP	H	R	ER	BB	SO
1996— New York (A.L.)..................	0	0	...	3.00	3	0	0	0	0	3	2	1	1	4	3

W

WEAVER, JEFF   P   TIGERS

PERSONAL: Born August 22, 1976, in Northridge, Calif. ... 6-5/210. ... Throws right, bats right. ... Full name: Jeffery Charles Weaver. ... Cousin of Jed Weaver, tight end, Miami Dolphins.
HIGH SCHOOL: Simi Valley (Calif.).
COLLEGE: Fresno State.
TRANSACTIONS/CAREER NOTES: Selected by Chicago White Sox organziation in second-round of free-agent draft (June 3, 1997); did not sign. ... Selected by Detroit Tigers organization in first round (14th pick overall) of free-agent draft (June 2, 1998).

STATISTICAL NOTES: Led A.L. pitchers with 17 hit batsmen in 1999 and 15 in 2000.
MISCELLANEOUS: Member of 1996 U.S. Olympic baseball team. ... Appeared in one game as pinch runner (1999).

Year League	W	L	Pct.	ERA	G	GS	CG	ShO	Sv.	IP	H	R	ER	BB	SO
1998— Jamestown (NY-Penn)	1	0	1.000	1.50	3	3	0	0	0	12	6	4	2	1	12
— West Michigan (Midw.)	1	0	1.000	1.38	2	2	0	0	0	13	8	3	2	0	21
1999— Jacksonville (Sou.)	0	0	...	3.00	1	1	0	0	0	6	5	2	2	0	6
— Detroit (A.L.)	9	12	.429	5.55	30	29	0	0	0	163 2/3	176	104	101	56	114
2000— Toledo (I.L.)	0	1	.000	3.38	1	1	0	0	0	5 1/3	5	2	2	1	10
— Detroit (A.L.)	11	15	.423	4.32	31	30	2	0	0	200	205	102	96	52	136
2001— Detroit (A.L.)	13	16	.448	4.08	33	33	5	0	0	229 1/3	235	116	104	68	152
Major League totals (3 years)	33	43	.434	4.57	94	92	7	0	0	593	616	322	301	176	402

WEBER, BEN   P   ANGELS

PERSONAL: Born November 17, 1969, in Port Arthur, Texas. ... 6-4/180. ... Throws right, bats right. ... Full name: Benjamin Edward Weber.
HIGH SCHOOL: Port Neches-Groves (Port Neches, Texas).
COLLEGE: Houston.
TRANSACTIONS/CAREER NOTES: Selected by Toronto Blue Jays organization in 20th round of free-agent draft (June 3, 1991). ... Released by Blue Jays (March 24, 1996). ... Signed by Salinas, Western League (May 1996). ... Signed by Taipei, Taiwan League (1997). ... Signed by San Francisco Giants organization (October 30, 2000). ... Claimed on waivers by Anaheim Angels (August 30, 2000).

Year League	W	L	Pct.	ERA	G	GS	CG	ShO	Sv.	IP	H	R	ER	BB	SO
1991— St. Catharines (NY-Penn) ...	6	3	.667	3.24	16	14	1	0	0	97 1/3	•105	43	35	24	60
1992— Myrtle Beach (S.Atl.)	4	7	.364	1.64	41	1	0	0	6	98 2/3	83	27	18	29	65
1993— Dunedin (FSL)	8	3	.727	2.92	55	0	0	0	12	83 1/3	87	36	27	25	45
1994— Dunedin (FSL)	3	2	.600	2.73	18	0	0	0	3	26 1/3	25	8	8	5	19
— Knoxville (Sou.).................	4	3	.571	3.76	25	10	0	0	0	95 2/3	103	49	40	16	55
1995— Syracuse (I.L.)	4	5	.444	5.40	25	15	0	0	1	91 2/3	111	62	55	27	38
— Knoxville (Sou.).................	4	1	.800	3.91	12	1	0	0	0	25 1/3	26	12	11	6	16
1996— Salinas (West.)■	•12	6	.667	3.47	22	22	2	...	0	148	138	68	57	42	102
1997— Taipei (Taiwan)■	7	3	.700	5.18	40	...	...	...	5	99	85	...	...	33	78
1998— Taipei (Taiwan)	12	7	.632	3.56	56	...	...	...	7	144	150	...	...	52	122
1999— Fresno (PCL)■	2	4	.333	3.34	51	0	0	0	8	86 1/3	78	34	32	28	67
2000— San Francisco (N.L.)	0	1	.000	14.63	9	0	0	0	0	8	16	13	13	4	6
— Fresno (PCL)	4	8	.333	2.42	38	3	0	0	7	78	72	31	21	20	66
— Erie (East.)■	0	1	.000	16.20	2	0	0	0	0	1 2/3	3	5	3	2	2
— Anaheim (A.L.)	1	0	1.000	1.84	10	0	0	0	0	14 2/3	12	6	3	2	8
2001— Anaheim (A.L.)	6	2	.750	3.42	56	0	0	0	0	68 1/3	66	28	26	31	40
A.L. totals (2 years)	7	2	.778	3.14	66	0	0	0	0	83	78	34	29	33	48
N.L. totals (1 year).......................	0	1	.000	14.63	9	0	0	0	0	8	16	13	13	4	6
Major League totals (2 years)	7	3	.700	4.15	75	0	0	0	0	91	94	47	42	37	54

WEHNER, JOHN   IF/OF

PERSONAL: Born June 29, 1967, in Pittsburgh. ... 6-3/206. ... Bats right, throws right. ... Full name: John Paul Wehner. ... Name pronounced WAY-ner.
HIGH SCHOOL: Carrick (Pittsburgh).
COLLEGE: Indiana.
TRANSACTIONS/CAREER NOTES: Selected by Pittsburgh Pirates organization in seventh round of free-agent draft (June 1, 1988). ... On Pittsburgh disabled list (August 29-October 7, 1991; and July 20, 1994-remainder of season). ... Claimed on waivers by Los Angeles Dodgers (October 15, 1996). ... Released by Dodgers (March 17, 1997). ... Signed by Florida Marlins organization (March 21, 1997). ... On Florida disabled list (June 26-September 1, 1997). ... Released by Marlins (November 20, 1997). ... Re-signed by Marlins organization (March 4, 1998). ... Granted free agency (September 29, 1998). ... Signed by Pittsburgh Pirates organization (June 9, 1999). ... Granted free agency (October 12, 1999). ... Re-signed by Pirates organization (January 18, 2000). ... On Nashville disabled list (April 6-13, 2000). ... Granted free agency (October 11, 2000). ... Re-signed by Pirates organization (January 9, 2001). ... On Pittsburgh disabled list (June 6-July 3, 2001). ... Released by Pirates (July 28, 2001). ... Re-signed by Pirates organization (August 6, 2001). ... Granted free agency (October 15, 2001).
STATISTICAL NOTES: Led New York-Pennsylvania League third basemen with 219 total chances and 14 double plays in 1988. ... Led Carolina League third basemen with 403 total chances and tied for lead with 24 double plays in 1989. ... Led Eastern League third basemen with 476 total chances and 40 double plays in 1990. ... Led Pacific Coast League second basemen with .984 fielding percentage in 1995.

Year	Team (League)	Pos.	G	AB	R	H	2B	3B	HR	RBI	Avg.	BB	SO	SB	PO	A	E	Avg.
1988— Watertown (NY-Penn)	3B	70	265	41	73	6	0	3	31	.275	21	39	18	*65	137	17	.922	
1989— Salem (Caro.)	3B	*137	*515	69	*155	32	6	14	73	.301	42	81	21	*89	*278	36	.911	
1990— Harrisburg (East.)	3B	•138	*511	71	147	27	1	4	62	.288	40	51	24	*109	*317	*50	.895	
1991— Carolina (Sou.)	3B-1B	61	234	30	62	5	1	3	21	.265	24	32	17	182	134	10	.969	
— Buffalo (A.A.)	3B	31	112	18	34	9	2	1	15	.304	14	12	6	30	69	8	.925	
— Pittsburgh (N.L.)	3B	37	106	15	36	7	0	0	7	.340	7	17	3	23	65	6	.936	
1992— Buffalo (A.A.)	2B-1B-3B	60	223	37	60	13	2	7	27	.269	29	30	10	226	122	7	.980	
— Pittsburgh (N.L.)	3B-1B-2B	55	123	11	22	6	0	0	4	.179	12	22	3	96	64	4	.976	
1993— Pittsburgh (N.L.)	OF-3B-2B	29	35	3	5	0	0	0	0	.143	6	10	0	17	8	0	1.000	
— Buffalo (A.A.)	3B-2B-OF	89	330	61	83	22	2	7	34	.252	40	53	17	133	256	17	.958	
1994— Buffalo (A.A.)	OF-3B-2B	88	330	52	100	19	3	7	44	.303	32	36	21	181	113	11	.957	
— Pittsburgh (N.L.)	3B	2	4	1	1	1	0	0	3	.250	0	1	0	0	2	0	1.000	
1995— Calgary (PCL)	3B-2B-OF	40	158	30	52	12	2	4	24	.329	12	16	8	36	98	12	.918	
— Pittsburgh (N.L.)	OF-3B-C-SS	52	107	13	33	0	3	0	5	.308	10	17	3	35	29	0	1.000	
1996— Pittsburgh (N.L.)	OF-3B-2B-C	86	139	19	36	9	1	2	13	.259	8	22	1	60	43	2	.981	
1997— Charlotte (I.L.)■	3B-OF-1B-2B	31	93	16	26	5	0	3	11	.280	6	18	3	32	33	2	.970	
— Florida (N.L.)	OF-3B	44	36	8	10	2	0	0	2	.278	2	5	1	14	3	0	1.000	
1998— Charlotte (I.L.)	OF-DH-P	30	83	12	27	1	0	3	15	.325	4	16	5	29	3	2	.941	
— Florida (N.L.)	OF-3B	53	88	10	20	2	0	0	5	.227	7	12	1	27	12	0	1.000	

W

Year	Team (League)	Pos.	G	AB	R	H	2B	3B	HR	RBI	Avg.	BB	SO	SB	PO	A	E	Avg.
1999—Altoona (East.)■	3B-OF	4	12	2	2	0	0	0	2	.167	0	0	1	2	5	1	.875
—Nashville (PCL)	SS-OF-2B	17	58	14	25	3	0	8	15	.431	3	6	0	22	37	3	.952
—Pittsburgh (N.L.)	OF-3B-SS-2B	39	65	6	12	2	0	1	4	.185	7	12	1	28	4	1	.970
2000—Nashville (PCL)	2B-3B-1B-OF	121	427	57	109	23	0	16	63	.255	56	65	14	264	303	12	†.979
—Pittsburgh (N.L.)	3B-OF	21	50	10	15	3	0	1	9	.300	4	6	0	14	22	1	.973
2001—Pittsburgh (N.L.)	1-O-3-C-2	43	51	3	10	1	0	0	2	.196	10	12	2	62	8	1	.986
—Altoona (East.)	SS-OF-2B-3B	25	92	10	21	3	0	0	8	.228	3	11	4	40	55	3	.969
Major League totals (11 years)		461	804	99	200	33	4	4	54	.249	73	136	15	376	260	15	.977

DIVISION SERIES RECORD

Year	Team (League)	Pos.	G	AB	R	H	2B	3B	HR	RBI	Avg.	BB	SO	SB	PO	A	E	Avg.
1997—Florida (N.L.)	PR-OF	1	0	0	0	0	0	0	0	...	0	0	0	0	0	0	...

CHAMPIONSHIP SERIES RECORD

Year	Team (League)	Pos.	G	AB	R	H	2B	3B	HR	RBI	Avg.	BB	SO	SB	PO	A	E	Avg.
1992—Pittsburgh (N.L.)	PH	2	2	0	0	0	0	0	0	.000	0	2	0	...	...	...	...

RECORD AS PITCHER

Year	League	W	L	Pct.	ERA	G	GS	CG	ShO	Sv.	IP	H	R	ER	BB	SO
1998—Charlotte (I.L.)...................	0	0	...	0.00	1	0	0	0	0	1	0	0	0	1	0

WELLS, BOB   P   TWINS

PERSONAL: Born November 1, 1966, in Yakima, Wash. ... 6-0/200. ... Throws right, bats right. ... Full name: Robert Lee Wells.
HIGH SCHOOL: Eisenhower (Yakima, Wash.).
JUNIOR COLLEGE: Spokane Falls Community College (Wash.).
TRANSACTIONS/CAREER NOTES: Signed as non-drafted free agent by Philadelphia Phillies organization (August 18, 1988). ... On Reading disabled list (July 21, 1991-remainder of season). ... On Scranton/Wilkes-Barre disabled list (April 9-28, 1992). ... On Reading disabled list (June 9, 1992-remainder of season; and April 8-June 13, 1993). ... Claimed on waivers by Seattle Mariners (June 30, 1994). ... On Seattle disabled list (April 16-May 19, 1998); included rehabilitation assignment to Wisconsin (May 12-19). ... Released by Mariners (November 19, 1998). ... Signed by Minnesota Twins organization (January 27, 1999).

Year	League	W	L	Pct.	ERA	G	GS	CG	ShO	Sv.	IP	H	R	ER	BB	SO
1989—Martinsville (Appl.)...........	0	0	...	4.50	4	0	0	0	0	6	8	5	3	2	3
1990—Spartanburg (S.Atl.).........	5	8	.385	2.87	20	19	2	0	0	113	94	47	36	40	73
—Clearwater (FSL)	0	2	.000	4.91	6	1	0	0	1	14 2/3	17	9	8	6	11
1991—Clearwater (FSL)	7	2	.778	3.11	24	9	1	0	0	75 1/3	63	27	26	19	66
—Reading (East.)...............	1	0	1.000	3.60	1	1	0	0	0	5	4	2	2	1	3
1992—Clearwater (FSL)	1	0	1.000	3.86	9	0	0	0	5	9 1/3	10	4	4	3	9
—Reading (East.)...............	0	1	.000	1.17	3	0	0	0	0	15 1/3	12	2	2	5	11
1993—Clearwater (FSL)	1	0	1.000	0.98	12	1	0	0	2	27 2/3	23	5	3	6	24
—Scranton/W.B. (I.L.)	1	1	.500	2.79	11	0	0	0	0	19 1/3	19	7	6	5	8
1994—Clearwater (FSL)	1	3	.250	2.79	14	0	0	0	4	19 1/3	18	6	6	3	19
—Philadelphia (N.L.)...........	1	0	1.000	1.80	6	0	0	0	0	5	4	1	1	3	3
—Scranton/W.B. (I.L.)	0	2	.000	2.45	11	0	0	0	0	14 2/3	18	6	4	6	13
—Calgary (PCL)■...............	3	2	.600	6.54	6	6	0	0	0	31 2/3	43	27	23	9	17
—Seattle (A.L.)	1	0	1.000	2.25	1	0	0	0	0	4	4	1	1	1	3
1995—Seattle (A.L.)	4	3	.571	5.75	30	4	0	0	0	76 2/3	88	51	49	39	38
1996—Seattle (A.L.)	12	7	.632	5.30	36	16	1	1	0	130 2/3	141	78	77	46	94
1997—Seattle (A.L.)	2	0	1.000	5.75	46	1	0	0	2	67 1/3	88	49	43	18	51
1998—Seattle (A.L.)	2	2	.500	6.10	30	0	0	0	0	51 2/3	54	38	35	16	29
—Wisconsin (Midw.)	0	1	.000	3.00	1	1	0	0	0	3	4	2	1	0	2
1999—Minnesota (A.L.)■............	8	3	.727	3.81	•76	0	0	0	1	87 1/3	79	41	37	28	44
2000—Minnesota (A.L.)............	0	7	.000	3.65	76	0	0	0	10	86 1/3	80	39	35	15	76
2001—Minnesota (A.L.)............	8	5	.615	5.11	65	0	0	0	2	68 2/3	72	39	39	18	49
A.L. totals (8 years)	37	27	.578	4.97	360	21	1	1	15	572 2/3	606	336	316	181	384
N.L. totals (1 year)	1	0	1.000	1.80	6	0	0	0	0	5	4	1	1	3	3
Major League totals (8 years)	38	27	.585	4.94	366	21	1	1	15	577 2/3	610	337	317	184	387

DIVISION SERIES RECORD

Year	League	W	L	Pct.	ERA	G	GS	CG	ShO	Sv.	IP	H	R	ER	BB	SO
1995—Seattle (A.L.)	0	0	...	9.00	1	0	0	0	0	1	2	1	1	1	0
1997—Seattle (A.L.)	0	0	...	0.00	1	0	0	0	0	1 1/3	1	0	0	0	1
Division series totals (2 years)	0	0	...	3.86	2	0	0	0	0	2 1/3	3	1	1	1	1

CHAMPIONSHIP SERIES RECORD

Year	League	W	L	Pct.	ERA	G	GS	CG	ShO	Sv.	IP	H	R	ER	BB	SO
1995—Seattle (A.L.)	0	0	...	3.00	1	0	0	0	0	3	2	1	1	2	2

W

WELLS, DAVID   P   YANKEES

PERSONAL: Born May 20, 1963, in Torrance, Calif. ... 6-4/235. ... Throws left, bats left. ... Full name: David Lee Wells.
HIGH SCHOOL: Point Loma (San Diego).
TRANSACTIONS/CAREER NOTES: Selected by Toronto Blue Jays organization in second round of free-agent draft (June 7, 1982). ... On Knoxville disabled list (June 28, 1984-remainder of season). ... On disabled list (April 10, 1985-entire season). ... On Knoxville disabled list (July 7-August 20, 1986). ... Released by Blue Jays (March 30, 1993). ... Signed by Detroit Tigers (April 3, 1993). ... On disabled list (August 1-20, 1993). ... Granted free agency (October 28, 1993). ... Re-signed by Tigers (December 13, 1993). ... On Detroit disabled list (April 19-June 6, 1994); included rehabilitation assignment to Lakeland (May 27-June 6). ... Traded by Tigers to Cincinnati Reds for P C.J. Nitkowski,

P David Tuttle and a player to be named later (July 31, 1995); Tigers acquired IF Mark Lewis to complete deal (November 16, 1995). ... Traded by Reds to Baltimore Orioles for OF Curtis Goodwin and OF Trovin Valdez (December 26, 1995). ... Granted free agency (October 29, 1996). ... Signed by New York Yankees (December 24, 1996). ... Traded by Yankees with P Graeme Lloyd and 2B Homer Bush to Blue Jays for P Roger Clemens (February 18, 1999). ... Traded by Blue Jays with P Matt DeWitt to Chicago White Sox for P Mike Sirotka, P Kevin Beirne, OF Brian Simmons and P Mike Williams (January 14, 2001). ... On disabled list (July 2, 2001-remainder of season). ... Granted free agency (November 5, 2001). ... Signed by Yankees (January 10, 2002).

RECORDS: Holds major league single-season records for fewest innings pitched by leader—231 2/3 (1999); and fewest complete games for leader—7 (1999). ... Holds A.L. single-season record for most consecutive batsmen retired—38 (May 12 [last 10], 17 [all 27] and 23 [first], 1998).

HONORS: Named lefthanded pitcher on The Sporting News A.L. All-Star team (1998 and 2000).

STATISTICAL NOTES: Struck out 16 batters in one game (July 30, 1997). ... Pitched 4-0 perfect game against Minnesota (May 17, 1998).

Year League	W	L	Pct.	ERA	G	GS	CG	ShO	Sv.	IP	H	R	ER	BB	SO
1982— Medicine Hat (Pio.)	4	3	.571	5.18	12	12	1	0	0	64 1/3	71	42	37	32	53
1983— Kinston (Caro.)	6	5	.545	3.73	25	25	5	0	0	157	141	81	65	71	115
1984— Kinston (Caro.)	1	6	.143	4.71	7	7	0	0	0	42	51	29	22	19	44
— Knoxville (Sou.)	3	2	.600	2.59	8	8	3	1	0	59	58	22	17	17	34
1985— Syracuse (I.L.)							Did not play.								
1986— Florence (S.Atl.)	0	0	...	3.55	4	1	0	0	0	12 2/3	7	6	5	9	14
— Ventura (Calif.)	2	1	.667	1.89	5	2	0	0	0	19	13	5	4	4	26
— Knoxville (Sou.)	1	3	.250	4.05	10	7	1	0	0	40	42	24	18	18	32
— Syracuse (I.L.)	0	1	.000	9.82	3	0	0	0	0	3 2/3	6	4	4	1	2
1987— Syracuse (I.L.)	4	6	.400	3.87	43	12	0	0	6	109 1/3	102	49	47	32	106
— Toronto (A.L.)	4	3	.571	3.99	18	2	0	0	1	29 1/3	37	14	13	12	32
1988— Toronto (A.L.)	3	5	.375	4.62	41	0	0	0	4	64 1/3	65	36	33	31	56
— Syracuse (I.L.)	0	0	...	0.00	6	0	0	0	3	5 2/3	7	1	0	2	8
1989— Toronto (A.L.)	7	4	.636	2.40	54	0	0	0	2	86 1/3	66	25	23	28	78
1990— Toronto (A.L.)	11	6	.647	3.14	43	25	0	0	3	189	165	72	66	45	115
1991— Toronto (A.L.)	15	10	.600	3.72	40	28	2	0	1	198 1/3	188	88	82	49	106
1992— Toronto (A.L.)	7	9	.438	5.40	41	14	0	0	2	120	138	84	72	36	62
1993— Detroit (A.L.)■	11	9	.550	4.19	32	30	0	0	0	187	183	93	87	42	139
1994— Lakeland (FSL)	0	0	...	0.00	2	2	0	0	0	6	5	1	0	0	3
— Detroit (A.L.)	5	7	.417	3.96	16	16	5	1	0	111 1/3	113	54	49	24	71
1995— Detroit (A.L.)	10	3	.769	3.04	18	18	3	0	0	130 1/3	120	54	44	37	83
— Cincinnati (N.L.)■■	6	5	.545	3.59	11	11	3	0	0	72 2/3	74	34	29	16	50
1996— Baltimore (A.L.)■	11	14	.440	5.14	34	34	3	0	0	224 1/3	247	132	128	51	130
1997— New York (A.L.)■	16	10	.615	4.21	32	32	5	2	0	218	239	109	102	45	156
1998— New York (A.L.)	18	4	*.818	3.49	30	30	8	*5	0	214 1/3	195	86	83	29	163
1999— Toronto (A.L.)■	17	10	.630	4.82	34	34	*7	1	0	*231 2/3	*246	132	124	62	169
2000— Toronto (A.L.)	•20	8	.714	4.11	35	•35	*9	1	0	229 2/3	*266	115	105	31	166
2001— Chicago (A.L.)■	5	7	.417	4.47	16	16	1	0	0	100 2/3	120	55	50	21	59
A.L. totals (15 years)	160	109	.595	4.09	484	314	43	10	13	2334 2/3	2388	1149	1061	543	1585
N.L. totals (1 year)	6	5	.545	3.59	11	11	3	0	0	72 2/3	74	34	29	16	50
Major League totals (15 years)	166	114	.593	4.08	495	325	46	10	13	2407 1/3	2462	1183	1090	559	1635

DIVISION SERIES RECORD

RECORDS: Shares career record for most wins—4. ... Shares A.L. career record for most wins—3.

Year League	W	L	Pct.	ERA	G	GS	CG	ShO	Sv.	IP	H	R	ER	BB	SO
1995— Cincinnati (N.L.)	1	0	1.000	0.00	1	1	0	0	0	6 1/3	6	1	0	1	8
1996— Baltimore (A.L.)	1	0	1.000	4.61	2	2	0	0	0	13 2/3	15	7	7	5	6
1997— New York (A.L.)	1	0	1.000	1.00	1	1	1	0	0	9	5	1	1	0	1
1998— New York (A.L.)	1	0	1.000	0.00	1	1	0	0	0	8	5	0	0	1	9
Division series totals (4 years)	4	0	1.000	1.95	5	5	1	0	0	37	31	9	8	7	24

CHAMPIONSHIP SERIES RECORD

NOTES: Named A.L. Championship Series Most Valuable Player (1998).

Year League	W	L	Pct.	ERA	G	GS	CG	ShO	Sv.	IP	H	R	ER	BB	SO
1989— Toronto (A.L.)	0	0	...	0.00	1	0	0	0	0	1	0	1	0	2	1
1991— Toronto (A.L.)	0	0	...	2.35	4	0	0	0	0	7 2/3	6	2	2	2	9
1992— Toronto (A.L.)							Did not play.								
1995— Cincinnati (N.L.)	0	1	.000	4.50	1	1	0	0	0	6	8	3	3	2	3
1996— Baltimore (A.L.)	1	0	1.000	4.05	1	1	0	0	0	6 2/3	8	3	3	3	6
1998— New York (A.L.)	2	0	1.000	2.87	2	2	0	0	0	15 2/3	12	5	5	2	18
Champ. series totals (5 years)	3	1	.750	3.16	9	4	0	0	0	37	34	14	13	11	37

WORLD SERIES RECORD

NOTES: Member of World Series championship team (1992 and 1998).

Year League	W	L	Pct.	ERA	G	GS	CG	ShO	Sv.	IP	H	R	ER	BB	SO
1992— Toronto (A.L.)	0	0	...	0.00	4	0	0	0	0	4 1/3	1	0	0	2	3
1998— New York (A.L.)	1	0	1.000	6.43	1	1	0	0	0	7	7	5	5	2	4
World Series totals (2 years)	1	0	1.000	3.97	5	1	0	0	0	11 1/3	8	5	5	4	7

ALL-STAR GAME RECORD

Year League	W	L	Pct.	ERA	GS	CG	ShO	Sv.	IP	H	R	ER	BB	SO
1995— American	0	0	...	0.00	0	0	0	0	1/3	0	0	0	0	1
1998— American	0	0	...	0.00	1	0	0	0	2	0	0	0	1	1
2000— American	0	0	...	0.00	1	0	0	0	2	0	0	0	0	2
All-Star Game totals (3 years)	0	0	...	0.00	2	0	0	0	4 1/3	0	0	0	1	4

WELLS, KIP P PIRATES

PERSONAL: Born April 21, 1977, in Houston. ... 6-3/196. ... Throws right, bats right. ... Full name: Robert Kip Wells.
HIGH SCHOOL: Elkins (Fort Bend, Texas).
COLLEGE: Baylor.

TRANSACTIONS/CAREER NOTES: Selected by Milwaukee Brewers organization in 58th round of free-agent draft (June 1, 1995); did not sign. ... Selected by Chicago White Sox organization in first round (16th pick overall) of free-agent draft (June 2, 1998). ... Traded by White Sox with P Sean Lowe and P Josh Fogg to Pittsburgh Pirates for P Todd Ritchie and C Lee Evans (December 13, 2001).
STATISTICAL NOTES: Tied for A.L. lead with 14 wild pitches in 2001.

Year League	W	L	Pct.	ERA	G	GS	CG	ShO	Sv.	IP	H	R	ER	BB	SO
1999—Winston-Salem (Caro.)	5	6	.455	3.57	14	14	0	0	0	85²/₃	78	39	34	34	95
—Birmingham (Sou.)	8	2	.800	2.94	11	11	0	0	0	70¹/₃	49	24	23	31	44
—Chicago (A.L.)	4	1	.800	4.04	7	7	0	0	0	35²/₃	33	17	16	15	29
2000—Chicago (A.L.)	6	9	.400	6.02	20	20	0	0	0	98²/₃	126	76	66	58	71
—Charlotte (I.L.)	5	3	.625	5.37	12	12	2	1	0	62	67	38	37	27	38
2001—Charlotte (I.L.)	2	1	.667	3.55	4	4	0	0	0	25¹/₃	26	11	10	8	24
—Chicago (A.L.)	10	11	.476	4.79	40	20	0	0	0	133¹/₃	145	80	71	61	99
Major League totals (3 years)	20	21	.488	5.14	67	47	0	0	0	267²/₃	304	173	153	134	199

WELLS, VERNON — OF — BLUE JAYS

PERSONAL: Born December 8, 1978, in Shreveport, La. ... 6-1/215. ... Bats right, throws right. ... Full name: Vernon Wells III.
HIGH SCHOOL: Bowie (Arlington, Texas).
TRANSACTIONS/CAREER NOTES: Selected by Toronto Blue Jays organization in first round (fifth pick overall) of free-agent draft (June 3, 1997). ... On Syracuse disabled list (April 14-24, 2001).
HONORS: Named Florida State League Most Valuable Player (1999).

					BATTING									FIELDING		
Year Team (League)	Pos.	G	AB	R	H	2B	3B	HR	RBI	Avg.	BB	SO	SB	PO	A	E	Avg.
1997—St. Catharines (NY-P)	OF	66	264	52	81	20	1	10	31	.307	30	44	8	135	6	7	.953
1998—Hagerstown (S.Atl.)	OF	134	509	86	145	35	2	11	65	.285	49	84	13	243	6	5	.980
1999—Dunedin (FSL)	OF-DH	70	265	43	91	16	2	11	43	.343	26	34	13	130	3	1	.993
—Knoxville (Sou.)	OF	26	106	18	36	6	2	3	17	.340	12	15	6	56	4	0	1.000
—Syracuse (I.L.)	OF	33	129	20	40	8	1	4	21	.310	10	22	5	79	2	2	.976
—Toronto (A.L.)	OF	25	88	8	23	5	0	1	8	.261	4	18	1	50	4	0	1.000
2000—Syracuse (I.L.)	OF	127	493	76	120	31	7	16	66	.243	48	88	23	293	8	3	.990
—Toronto (A.L.)	OF	3	2	0	0	0	0	0	0	.000	0	0	0	2	0	0	1.000
2001—Syracuse (I.L.)	OF	107	413	57	116	27	4	12	52	.281	29	68	15	216	7	5	.978
—Toronto (A.L.)	OF	30	96	14	30	8	0	1	6	.313	5	15	5	61	2	2	.969
Major League totals (3 years)		58	186	22	53	13	0	2	14	.285	9	33	6	113	6	2	.983

WENDELL, TURK — P — PHILLIES

PERSONAL: Born May 19, 1967, in Pittsfield, Mass. ... 6-2/205. ... Throws right, bats left. ... Full name: Steven John Wendell.
HIGH SCHOOL: Wahconah Regional (Dalton, Mass.).
COLLEGE: Quinnipiac College (Conn.).
TRANSACTIONS/CAREER NOTES: Selected by Atlanta Braves organization in fifth round of free-agent draft (June 1, 1988). ... Traded by Braves with P Yorkis Perez to Chicago Cubs for P Mike Bielecki and C Damon Berryhill (September 29, 1991). ... On disabled list (May 4, 1992-remainder of season). ... On Chicago disabled list (April 16-May 27, 1995); included rehabilitation assignments to Daytona (May 5-15) and Orlando (May 15-27). ... Traded by Cubs with OF Brian McRae and P Mel Rojas to New York Mets for OF Lance Johnson and two players to be named later (August 8, 1997; Cubs acquired P Mark Clark (August 11, 1997) and IF Manny Alexander (August 14, 1997) to complete deal. ... Granted free agency (November 3, 2000). ... Re-signed by Mets (December 1, 2000). ... Traded by Mets with P Dennis Cook to Philadelphia Phillies for P Bruce Chen and P Adam Walker (July 27, 2001).

Year League	W	L	Pct.	ERA	G	GS	CG	ShO	Sv.	IP	H	R	ER	BB	SO
1988—Pulaski (Appl.)	3	•8	.273	3.83	14	14	•6	1	0	*101	85	50	43	30	87
1989—Burlington (Midw.)	9	11	.450	2.21	22	22	•9	*5	0	159	127	63	39	41	153
—Greenville (Sou.)	0	0	...	9.82	1	1	0	0	0	3²/₃	7	5	4	1	3
—Durham (Caro.)	2	0	1.000	1.13	3	3	1	0	0	24	13	4	3	6	27
1990—Durham (Caro.)	1	3	.250	1.86	6	5	1	0	0	38²/₃	24	10	8	15	26
—Greenville (Sou.)	4	9	.308	5.74	36	13	1	1	2	91	105	70	58	48	85
1991—Greenville (Sou.)	11	3	*.786	2.56	25	20	1	1	0	147²/₃	130	47	42	51	122
—Richmond (I.L.)	0	2	.000	3.43	3	3	1	0	0	21	20	9	8	16	18
1992—Iowa (A.A.)■	2	0	1.000	1.44	4	4	0	0	0	25	17	7	4	15	12
1993—Iowa (A.A.)	10	8	.556	4.60	25	25	3	0	0	148²/₃	148	88	76	47	110
—Chicago (N.L.)	1	2	.333	4.37	7	4	0	0	0	22²/₃	24	13	11	8	15
1994—Iowa (A.A.)	11	6	.647	2.95	23	23	6	•3	0	168	141	58	55	28	118
—Chicago (N.L.)	0	1	.000	11.93	6	2	0	0	0	14¹/₃	22	20	19	10	9
1995—Daytona (FSL)	0	0	...	1.17	4	2	0	0	0	7²/₃	5	2	1	1	8
—Orlando (Sou.)	1	0	1.000	3.86	5	0	0	0	1	7	6	3	3	4	7
—Chicago (N.L.)	3	1	.750	4.92	43	0	0	0	0	60¹/₃	71	35	33	24	50
1996—Chicago (N.L.)	4	5	.444	2.84	70	0	0	0	18	79¹/₃	58	26	25	44	75
1997—Chicago (N.L.)	3	5	.375	4.20	52	0	0	0	4	60	53	32	28	39	54
—New York (N.L.)■	0	0	...	4.96	13	0	0	0	1	16¹/₃	15	10	9	14	10
1998—New York (N.L.)	5	1	.833	2.93	66	0	0	0	4	76²/₃	62	25	25	33	58
1999—New York (N.L.)	5	4	.556	3.05	80	0	0	0	3	85²/₃	80	31	29	37	77
2000—New York (N.L.)	8	6	.571	3.59	77	0	0	0	1	82²/₃	60	36	33	41	73
2001—New York (N.L.)	4	3	.571	3.51	49	0	0	0	1	51¹/₃	42	23	20	22	41
—Philadelphia (N.L.)■	0	2	.000	7.47	21	0	0	0	0	15²/₃	21	13	13	12	15
Major League totals (9 years)	33	30	.524	3.90	484	6	0	0	32	565	508	264	245	284	477

DIVISION SERIES RECORD

Year League	W	L	Pct.	ERA	G	GS	CG	ShO	Sv.	IP	H	R	ER	BB	SO
1999—New York (N.L.)	1	0	1.000	0.00	2	0	0	0	0	2	0	0	0	2	0
2000—New York (N.L.)	0	0	...	0.00	2	0	0	0	0	2	0	0	0	1	5
Division series totals (2 years)	1	0	1.000	0.00	4	0	0	0	0	4	0	0	0	3	5

Year League	W	L	Pct.	ERA	G	GS	CG	ShO	Sv.	IP	H	R	ER	BB	SO
1999— New York (N.L.)	1	0	1.000	4.76	5	0	0	0	0	5 $2/3$	2	3	3	4	5
2000— New York (N.L.)	1	0	1.000	0.00	2	0	0	0	0	1 $1/3$	1	0	0	1	2
Champ. series totals (2 years)	2	0	1.000	3.86	7	0	0	0	0	7	3	3	3	5	7

WORLD SERIES RECORD

Year League	W	L	Pct.	ERA	G	GS	CG	ShO	Sv.	IP	H	R	ER	BB	SO
2000— New York (N.L.)	0	1	.000	5.40	2	0	0	0	0	1 $2/3$	3	1	1	2	2

WENGERT, DON — P

PERSONAL: Born November 6, 1969, in Sioux City, Iowa. ... 6-3/205. ... Throws right, bats right. ... Full name: Donald Paul Wengert. ... Brother of Bill Wengert, pitcher with Los Angeles Dodgers, San Diego Padres and Boston Red Sox organizations (1988-95).
HIGH SCHOOL: Heelan Catholic (Sioux City, Iowa).
COLLEGE: Iowa State.
TRANSACTIONS/CAREER NOTES: Selected by Cincinnati Reds organization in 60th round of free-agent draft (June 1, 1988); did not sign. ... Selected by Oakland Athletics organization in fourth round of free-agent draft (June 1, 1992). ... On Oakland disabled list (July 30-August 18, 1995); included rehabilitation assignment to Edmonton (August 7-18). ... On disabled list (July 24-August 8, 1996). ... Traded by A's with IF David Newhan to San Diego Padres for P Doug Bochtler and IF Jorge Velandia (November 26, 1997). ... Traded by Padres to Chicago Cubs for P Ben VanRyn (May 5, 1998). ... Granted free agency (November 25, 1998). ... Signed by Kansas City Royals organization (December 21, 1998). ... Released by Royals (July 15, 1999). ... Signed by New York Yankees organization (July 27, 1999). ... Released by Yankees (August 27, 1999). ... Signed by Atlanta Braves organization (August 30, 1999). ... Granted free agency (October 15, 1999). ... Signed by Houston Astros organization (January 5, 2000). ... Released by Astros (March 14, 2000). ... Signed by Braves organization (March 30, 2000). ... Granted free agency (October 2, 2000). ... Signed by Pittsburgh Pirates organization (May 17, 2001). ... On Nashville disabled list (August 11-September 4, 2001). ... Granted free agency (October 8, 2001).
MISCELLANEOUS: Appeared in two games as pinch runner and had a sacrifice hit in only appearance as pinch hitter with Chicago (1998).

Year League	W	L	Pct.	ERA	G	GS	CG	ShO	Sv.	IP	H	R	ER	BB	SO
1992— Southern Oregon (N'West)	2	0	1.000	1.46	6	5	1	0	0	37	32	6	6	7	29
— Madison (Midw.)	3	4	.429	3.38	7	7	0	0	0	40	42	20	15	17	29
1993— Madison (Midw.)	6	5	.545	3.32	13	13	2	0	0	78 $2/3$	79	30	29	18	46
— Modesto (Calif.)	3	6	.333	4.73	12	12	0	0	0	70 $1/3$	75	42	37	29	43
1994— Modesto (Calif.)	4	1	.800	2.95	10	7	0	0	2	42 $2/3$	40	15	14	11	52
— Huntsville (Sou.)	6	4	.600	3.26	17	17	1	0	0	99 $1/3$	86	43	36	33	92
1995— Oakland (A.L.)	1	1	.500	3.34	19	0	0	0	0	29 $2/3$	30	14	11	12	16
— Edmonton (PCL)	1	1	.500	7.38	16	6	0	0	1	39	55	32	32	16	20
1996— Oakland (A.L.)	7	11	.389	5.58	36	25	1	1	0	161 $1/3$	200	102	100	60	75
1997— Oakland (A.L.)	5	11	.313	6.04	49	12	1	0	2	134	177	96	90	41	68
1998— San Diego (N.L.)■	0	0	...	5.93	10	0	0	0	1	13 $2/3$	21	9	9	5	5
— Chicago (N.L.)■	1	5	.167	5.07	21	6	0	0	0	49 $2/3$	55	29	28	23	41
— Iowa (PCL)	3	1	.750	4.58	9	9	1	0	0	53	58	30	27	14	48
1999— Kansas City (A.L.)■	0	1	.000	9.25	11	1	0	0	0	24 $1/3$	41	26	25	5	10
— Omaha (PCL)	4	0	1.000	4.17	16	2	0	0	1	41	41	20	19	9	24
— Columbus (I.L.)■	0	1	.000	7.63	6	2	0	0	0	15 $1/3$	25	13	13	3	5
— Richmond (I.L.)■	0	0	...	4.50	1	1	0	0	0	6	7	3	3	0	3
2000— Richmond (I.L.)	4	7	.364	4.23	29	12	1	0	0	110 $2/3$	117	55	52	22	83
— Atlanta (N.L.)	0	1	.000	7.20	10	0	0	0	0	10	12	9	8	5	7
2001— Nashville (PCL)■	7	7	.500	4.10	18	18	0	0	0	112	135	60	51	20	67
— Pittsburgh (N.L.)	0	2	.000	12.38	4	4	0	0	0	16	33	22	22	6	4
A.L. totals (4 years)	13	24	.351	5.82	115	38	2	1	2	349 $1/3$	448	238	226	118	169
N.L. totals (3 years)	1	8	.111	6.75	45	10	0	0	1	89 $1/3$	121	69	67	39	57
Major League totals (7 years)	14	32	.304	6.01	160	48	2	1	3	438 $2/3$	569	307	293	157	226

WERTH, JAYSON — C — BLUE JAYS

PERSONAL: Born May 20, 1979, in Springfield, Ill. ... 6-5/190. ... Bats right, throws right. ... Full name: Jayson Richard Werth. ... Grandson of Dick Schofield, infielder/outfielder with six major league teams (1953-71); nephew of Dick Schofield, infielder with four major league teams (1983-96); stepson of Dennis Werth, outfielder/first baseman with New York Yankees (1979) and Kansas City Royals (1980-82).
HIGH SCHOOL: Chatham Glenwood (Chatham, Ill.).
TRANSACTIONS/CAREER NOTES: Selected by Baltimore Orioles organization in first round (22nd pick overall) of free-agent draft (June 3, 1997). ... Traded by Orioles to Toronto Blue Jays for P John Bale (December 11, 2000). ... On Tennessee disabled list (April 5-14, 2001).
STATISTICAL NOTES: Tied for Gulf Coast League lead in double plays by catcher with four in 1997.

						BATTING								FIELDING		
Year Team (League)	Pos.	G	AB	R	H	2B	3B	HR	RBI	Avg.	BB	SO	SB	PO	A	E	Avg.
1997— GC Orioles (GCL)	C-1B	32	88	16	26	6	0	1	8	.295	22	22	7	186	20	9	.958
1998— Delmarva (S.Atl.)	C	120	408	71	108	20	3	8	53	.265	50	92	21	863	*131	9	.991
— Bowie (East.)	C	5	19	2	3	2	0	0	1	.158	2	6	1	49	4	0	1.000
1999— Frederick (Caro.)	C	66	236	41	72	10	1	3	30	.305	37	37	16	453	56	10	.981
— Bowie (East.)	C-OF	35	121	18	33	5	1	1	11	.273	17	26	7	204	22	1	.996
2000— Bowie (East.)	C-OF	85	276	47	63	16	2	5	26	.228	54	50	9	502	51	7	.988
— Frederick (Caro.)	C	24	83	16	23	3	0	2	18	.277	10	15	5	116	12	2	.985
2001— Tennessee (Sou.)■	C-1B	104	369	51	105	23	1	18	69	.285	63	93	12	521	50	7	.988
— Dunedin (FSL)	C	21	70	9	14	3	0	2	14	.200	17	19	1	66	7	0	1.000

WESTBROOK, JAKE — P — INDIANS

PERSONAL: Born September 29, 1977, in Athens, Ga. ... 6-3/185. ... Throws right, bats right. ... Full name: Jacob Cauthen Westbrook.
HIGH SCHOOL: Madison County (Danielsville, Ga.).

TRANSACTIONS/CAREER NOTES: Selected by Colorado Rockies organization in first round (21st pick overall) of free-agent draft (June 4, 1996). ... Traded by Rockies with P John Nicholson and OF Mark Hamlin to Montreal Expos for 2B Mike Lansing (December 16, 1997). ... Traded by Expos with two players to be named later to New York Yankees for P Hideki Irabu (December 22, 1999); Yankees acquired P Ted Lilly (March 17, 2000) and P Christian Parker (March 22, 2000) to complete deal. ... On Columbus disabled list (July 5-23, 2000). ... Traded by Yankees with P Zach Day to Cleveland Indians (July 25, 2000), completing deal in which Indians traded OF Dave Justice to Yankees for OF Ricky Ledee and two players to be named later (June 29, 2000). ... On Buffalo disabled list (July 25-September 1, 2000). ... On Cleveland disabled list (September 1, 2000-remainder of season).

Year	League	W	L	Pct.	ERA	G	GS	CG	ShO	Sv.	IP	H	R	ER	BB	SO
1996—	Arizona Rockies (Ariz.).......	4	2	.667	2.87	11	11	0	0	0	62 2/3	66	33	20	14	57
	— Portland (N'West)	1	1	.500	2.55	4	4	0	0	0	24 2/3	22	8	7	5	19
1997—	Asheville (S.Atl.)................	*14	11	.560	4.82	28	27	3	2	0	170	176	93	91	55	92
1998—	Jupiter (FSL)■..................	11	6	.647	3.26	27	27	2	0	0	171	169	70	62	60	79
1999—	Harrisburg (East.)..............	11	5	.688	3.92	27	27	2	•2	0	174 2/3	180	88	76	63	90
2000—	Columbus (I.L.)■..............	5	7	.417	4.65	16	15	2	0	0	89	94	53	46	38	61
	— New York (A.L.)................	0	2	.000	13.50	3	2	0	0	0	6 2/3	15	10	10	4	1
2001—	Buffalo (I.L.)■..................	8	1	.889	3.20	12	12	0	0	0	64 2/3	60	27	23	23	45
	— Cleveland (A.L.)................	4	4	.500	5.85	23	6	0	0	0	64 2/3	79	43	42	22	48
Major League totals (2 years)		4	6	.400	6.56	26	8	0	0	0	71 1/3	94	53	52	26	49

WHEELER, DAN   P   BRAVES

PERSONAL: Born December 10, 1977, in Providence, R.I. ... 6-3/222. ... Throws right, bats right. ... Full name: Daniel Michael Wheeler.
HIGH SCHOOL: Pilgrim (Warwick, R.I.).
JUNIOR COLLEGE: Central Arizona College.
TRANSACTIONS/CAREER NOTES: Selected by Tampa Bay Devil Rays organization in 34th round of free-agent draft (June 4, 1996). ... On Durham disabled list (July 7-16, 2001). ... Released by Devil Rays (December 13, 2001). ... Signed by Atlanta Braves organization (January 10, 2002).
STATISTICAL NOTES: Led International League with 35 home runs allowed in 2000.

Year	League	W	L	Pct.	ERA	G	GS	CG	ShO	Sv.	IP	H	R	ER	BB	SO
1997—	Hudson Valley (NY-Penn)...	6	7	.462	3.00	15	15	0	0	0	84	75	38	28	17	81
1998—	Charleston, S.C. (S.Atl.)	12	14	.462	4.43	29	•29	3	1	0	181	206	96	•89	29	136
1999—	Orlando (Sou.)	3	0	1.000	3.26	9	•9	0	0	0	58	56	27	21	8	53
	— Durham (I.L.)	7	5	.583	4.92	14	14	2	1	0	82 1/3	103	59	45	25	58
	— Tampa Bay (A.L.)	0	4	.000	5.87	6	6	0	0	0	30 2/3	35	20	20	13	32
2000—	Tampa Bay (A.L.)	1	1	.500	5.48	11	2	0	0	0	23	29	14	14	11	17
	— Durham (I.L.)	5	11	.313	5.63	26	26	0	0	0	150 1/3	183	*109	94	42	91
2001—	Durham (I.L.)	3	5	.375	5.23	18	10	0	0	0	65 1/3	72	51	38	11	39
	— Tampa Bay (A.L.)	1	0	1.000	8.66	13	0	0	0	0	17 2/3	30	17	17	5	12
	— Orlando (Sou.)	0	2	.000	2.81	3	3	0	0	0	16	15	5	5	6	12
Major League totals (3 years)		2	5	.286	6.43	30	8	0	0	0	71 1/3	94	51	51	29	61

WHITE, DEVON   OF

PERSONAL: Born December 29, 1962, in Kingston, Jamaica. ... 6-2/190. ... Bats both, throws right. ... Full name: Devon Markes White.
HIGH SCHOOL: Park West (New York).
TRANSACTIONS/CAREER NOTES: Selected by California Angels organization in sixth round of free-agent draft (June 8, 1981). ... On suspended list (June 11-12 and July 19, 1982-remainder of season). ... On Edmonton disabled list (May 12-22, 1986). ... On disabled list (May 7-June 10, 1988). ... Traded by Angels with P Willie Fraser and a player to be named later to Toronto Blue Jays for OF Junior Felix, IF Luis Sojo and a player to be named later (December 2, 1990); Blue Jays acquired P Marcus Moore and Angels acquired C Ken Rivers to complete deal (December 4, 1990). ... Granted free agency (November 1, 1995). ... Signed by Florida Marlins (November 21, 1995). ... On disabled list (April 25-May 30 and June 8-July 28, 1997). ... Traded by Marlins to Arizona Diamondbacks for P Jesus Martinez (November 18, 1997). ... Granted free agency (October 23, 1998). ... Signed by Los Angeles Dodgers (November 9, 1998). ... On Los Angeles disabled list (May 3-July 23, 2000); included rehabilitation assignment to San Bernardino (July 20-22). ... Traded by Dodgers to Milwaukee Brewers for OF Marquis Grissom and a player to be named later (February 25, 2001); Dodgers acquired P Rudy Lugo to complete deal (June 1, 2001). ... Granted free agency (November 6, 2001).
RECORDS: Shares major league record for most stolen bases in one inning—3 (September 9, 1989, sixth inning). ... Shares major league single-month record for most grand slams—3 (May 2001).
HONORS: Won A.L. Gold Glove as outfielder (1988-89 and 1991-95).
STATISTICAL NOTES: Led Midwest League outfielders with 286 total chances in 1983. ... Led California League outfielders with 351 total chances in 1984. ... Led Pacific Coast League outfielders with 339 total chances in 1986. ... Switch-hit home runs in one game three times (June 23, 1987; June 29, 1990; and June 1, 1992). ... Led A.L. outfielders with 449 total chances in 1987, 448 in 1991 and 458 in 1992. ... Career major league grand slams: 11.

Year	Team (League)	Pos.	G	AB	R	H	2B	3B	HR	RBI	Avg.	BB	SO	SB	PO	A	E	Avg.
1981—	Idaho Falls (Pio.)........	OF-3B-1B	30	106	10	19	2	0	0	10	.179	12	34	4	33	10	3	.935
1982—	Danville (Midw.)	OF	57	186	21	40	6	1	1	11	.215	11	41	11	89	3	8	.920
1983—	Peoria (Midw.)............	OF	117	430	69	109	17	6	13	66	.253	36	124	32	267	8	11	.962
	— Nashua (East.)...........	OF	17	70	11	18	7	2	0	2	.257	7	22	5	37	0	3	.925
1984—	Redwood (Calif.)	OF	138	520	101	147	25	5	7	55	.283	56	118	36	*322	16	13	.963
1985—	Midland (Texas)..........	OF	70	260	52	77	10	4	4	35	.296	35	46	38	176	10	4	.979
	— Edmonton (PCL)	OF	66	277	53	70	16	5	4	39	.253	24	77	21	205	6	2	.991
	— California (A.L.).........	OF	21	7	7	1	0	0	0	0	.143	1	3	3	10	1	0	1.000
1986—	Edmonton (PCL)	OF	112	461	84	134	25	10	14	60	.291	31	90	*42	317	•16	6	.982
	— California (A.L.).........	OF	29	51	8	12	1	1	1	3	.235	6	8	6	49	0	2	.961
1987—	California (A.L.).........	OF	159	639	103	168	33	5	24	87	.263	39	135	32	*424	16	9	.980
1988—	California (A.L.).........	OF	122	455	76	118	22	2	11	51	.259	23	84	17	364	7	9	.976
1989—	California (A.L.).........	OF-DH	156	636	86	156	18	13	12	56	.245	31	129	44	430	10	5	.989
1990—	California (A.L.).........	OF	125	443	57	96	17	3	11	44	.217	44	116	21	302	11	9	.972
	— Edmonton (PCL)	OF	14	55	9	20	4	4	0	6	.364	7	12	4	31	1	3	.914

W

Year	Team (League)	Pos.	G	AB	R	H	2B	3B	HR	RBI	Avg.	BB	SO	SB	PO	A	E	Avg.
1991—	Toronto (A.L.)■	OF	156	642	110	181	40	10	17	60	.282	55	135	33	*439	8	1	*.998
1992—	Toronto (A.L.)	OF-DH	153	641	98	159	26	7	17	60	.248	47	133	37	*443	8	7	.985
1993—	Toronto (A.L.)	OF	146	598	116	163	42	6	15	52	.273	57	127	34	399	6	3	.993
1994—	Toronto (A.L.)	OF	100	403	67	109	24	6	13	49	.270	21	80	11	268	3	6	.978
1995—	Toronto (A.L.)	OF	101	427	61	121	23	5	10	53	.283	29	97	11	261	7	3	.989
1996—	Florida (N.L.)■	OF	146	552	77	151	37	6	17	84	.274	38	99	22	296	5	4	.987
1997—	Florida (N.L.)	OF	74	265	37	65	13	1	6	34	.245	32	65	13	152	4	2	.987
1998—	Arizona (N.L.)■	OF	146	563	84	157	32	1	22	85	.279	42	102	22	371	3	5	.987
1999—	Los Angeles (N.L.)■ ..	OF-DH	134	474	60	127	20	2	14	68	.268	39	88	19	273	3	4	.986
2000—	Los Angeles (N.L.)	OF	47	158	26	42	5	1	4	13	.266	9	30	3	68	2	2	.972
—	San Bern. (Calif.)	OF	2	5	2	2	1	0	0	1	.400	1	1	0	3	0	0	1.000
2001—	Milwaukee (N.L.)■	OF	126	390	52	108	25	2	14	47	.277	28	95	18	190	3	0	1.000
American League totals (11 years)			1268	4942	789	1284	246	58	131	515	.260	353	1047	249	3389	77	54	.985
National League totals (6 years)			673	2402	336	650	132	13	77	331	.271	188	479	97	1350	20	17	.988
Major League totals (17 years)			1941	7344	1125	1934	378	71	208	846	.263	541	1526	346	4739	97	71	.986

DIVISION SERIES RECORD

Year	Team (League)	Pos.	G	AB	R	H	2B	3B	HR	RBI	Avg.	BB	SO	SB	PO	A	E	Avg.
1997—	Florida (N.L.)	OF	3	11	1	2	0	0	1	4	.182	2	3	0	3	0	0	1.000

CHAMPIONSHIP SERIES RECORD

RECORDS: Holds A.L. career record for highest batting average (50 or more at-bats)—.392. ... Holds single-series record for most times caught stealing—4 (1992). ... Shares A.L. single-series record for most hits—12 (1993). ... Shares A.L. single-game record for most at-bats—6 (October 11, 1992, 11 innings).

Year	Team (League)	Pos.	G	AB	R	H	2B	3B	HR	RBI	Avg.	BB	SO	SB	PO	A	E	Avg.
1986—	California (A.L.)	OF-PR	4	2	2	1	0	0	0	0	.500	0	1	0	3	0	0	1.000
1991—	Toronto (A.L.)	OF	5	22	5	8	1	0	0	0	.364	2	3	3	16	0	1	1.000
1992—	Toronto (A.L.)	OF	6	23	2	8	2	0	0	2	.348	5	6	0	16	0	1	.941
1993—	Toronto (A.L.)	OF	6	27	3	12	1	1	1	2	.444	1	5	0	15	0	0	1.000
1997—	Florida (N.L.)	OF	6	21	4	4	1	0	0	1	.190	2	7	1	16	0	0	1.000
Championship series totals (5 years)			27	95	16	33	5	1	1	5	.347	10	22	4	66	0	1	.985

WORLD SERIES RECORD

RECORDS: Shares record for most consecutive strikeouts in one series—5 (October 21 [1] and 22 [4], 1997).
NOTES: Member of World Series championship team (1992, 1993 and 1997).

Year	Team (League)	Pos.	G	AB	R	H	2B	3B	HR	RBI	Avg.	BB	SO	SB	PO	A	E	Avg.
1992—	Toronto (A.L.)	OF	6	26	2	6	1	0	0	2	.231	0	6	1	22	0	0	1.000
1993—	Toronto (A.L.)	OF	6	24	8	7	3	2	1	7	.292	4	7	1	16	0	0	1.000
1997—	Florida (N.L.)	OF	7	33	0	8	3	1	0	2	.242	3	10	1	16	0	0	1.000
World Series totals (3 years)			19	83	10	21	7	3	1	11	.253	7	23	3	54	0	0	1.000

ALL-STAR GAME RECORD

Year	League	Pos.	AB	R	H	2B	3B	HR	RBI	Avg.	BB	SO	SB	PO	A	E	Avg.
1989—	American	OF	1	0	0	0	0	0	0	.000	0	0	0	0	0	0	...
1993—	American	OF	2	1	1	1	0	0	1	.500	0	0	1	1	0	0	1.000
1998—	National	OF	3	1	3	0	1	0	0	1.000	0	0	0	0	0	0	...
All-Star Game totals (3 years)			6	2	4	1	1	0	1	.667	0	0	1	1	0	0	1.000

WHITE, GABE — P — REDS

PERSONAL: Born November 20, 1971, in Sebring, Fla. ... 6-2/200. ... Throws left, bats left. ... Full name: Gabriel Allen White.
HIGH SCHOOL: Sebring (Fla.).
TRANSACTIONS/CAREER NOTES: Selected by Montreal Expos organization in supplemental round ("sandwich pick" between first and second round, 28th pick overall) of free-agent draft (June 4, 1990); pick received as part of compensation for California Angels signing Type A free-agent P Mark Langston. ... On Harrisburg disabled list (July 2-27, 1993). ... On Ottawa disabled list (April 7-May 6, 1994). ... Traded by Expos to Cincinnati Reds for 2B Jhonny Carvajal (December 15, 1995). ... On disabled list (September 17, 1996-remainder of season). ... Traded by Reds to Colorado Rockies for P Manny Aybar (April 7, 2000). ... Traded by Rockies with P Luke Hudson to Reds for 2B Pokey Reese and P Dennys Reyes (December 18, 2001).
RECORDS: Shares N.L. record for most consecutive home runs allowed in one inning—3 (July 7, 1995, second inning).

Year	League	W	L	Pct.	ERA	G	GS	CG	ShO	Sv.	IP	H	R	ER	BB	SO
1990—	Gulf Coast Expos (GCL)	4	2	.667	3.14	11	11	1	0	0	57 1/3	50	21	20	12	41
1991—	Sumter (S.Atl.)	6	9	.400	3.26	24	24	5	0	0	149	127	73	54	53	140
1992—	Rockford (Midw.)	14	8	.636	2.84	27	27	7	0	0	187	148	73	59	61	*176
1993—	Harrisburg (East.)	7	2	.778	2.16	16	16	2	1	0	100	80	30	24	28	80
—	Ottawa (I.L.)	2	1	.667	3.12	6	6	1	1	0	40 1/3	38	15	14	6	28
1994—	West Palm Beach (FSL)	1	0	1.000	1.50	1	1	0	0	0	6	2	2	1	1	4
—	Ottawa (I.L.)	8	3	.727	5.05	14	14	0	0	0	73	77	49	41	28	63
—	Montreal (N.L.)	1	1	.500	6.08	7	5	0	0	0	23 2/3	24	16	16	11	17
1995—	Ottawa (I.L.)	2	3	.400	3.90	12	12	0	0	0	62 1/3	58	31	27	17	37
—	Montreal (N.L.)	1	2	.333	7.01	19	1	0	0	0	25 2/3	26	21	20	9	25
1996—	Indianapolis (A.A.)■	6	3	.667	2.77	11	11	0	0	0	68 1/3	69	25	21	9	51
1997—	Indianapolis (A.A.)	7	4	.636	2.82	20	19	0	0	0	118	119	46	37	18	62
—	Cincinnati (N.L.)	2	2	.500	4.39	12	6	0	0	0	41	39	20	20	8	25
1998—	Cincinnati (N.L.)	5	5	.500	4.01	69	3	0	0	9	98 2/3	86	46	44	27	83
1999—	Cincinnati (N.L.)	1	2	.333	4.43	50	0	0	0	0	61	68	31	30	14	61
2000—	Cincinnati (N.L.)	0	0	...	18.00	1	0	0	0	0	1	2	2	2	1	2
—	Colorado (N.L.)■	11	2	.846	2.17	67	0	0	0	5	83	62	21	20	14	82
2001—	Colorado (N.L.)	1	7	.125	6.25	69	0	0	0	0	67 2/3	70	47	47	26	47
Major League totals (7 years)		22	21	.512	4.46	294	15	0	0	16	401 2/3	377	204	199	110	342

W

WHITE, MATT — P — DEVIL RAYS

PERSONAL: Born August 13, 1978, in Waynesboro, Pa. ... 6-5/230. ... Throws right, bats right. ... Full name: Matthew Edward White.
HIGH SCHOOL: Waynesboro Area (Waynesboro, Pa.).
TRANSACTIONS/CAREER NOTES: Selected by San Francisco Giants orgaination in first round (seventh pick overall) of free-agent draft (June 4, 1996). ... Granted free agency under draft rule which requires drafting team to make a formal contract offer within 15 days of draft (September 24, 1996). ... Signed by Tampa Bay Devil Rays organization (November 25, 1996). ... On disabled list (May 10-September 4, 2001).

Year — League	W	L	Pct.	ERA	G	GS	CG	ShO	Sv.	IP	H	R	ER	BB	SO
1997— Hudson Valley (NY-Penn)...	4	6	.400	4.07	15	15	0	0	0	84	78	44	38	29	82
1998— Charleston, S.C. (S.Atl.)	4	3	.571	3.82	12	12	0	0	0	75 1/3	72	41	32	21	59
— St. Petersburg (FSL)	4	8	.333	5.55	17	17	1	0	0	95 2/3	107	70	59	41	64
1999— St. Petersburg (FSL)	9	7	.563	5.18	21	20	2	0	0	113	125	75	65	33	92
2000— Orlando (Sou.)	7	6	.538	3.75	20	20	2	0	0	120	94	56	50	58	98
— Durham (I.L.)	3	2	.600	2.83	6	6	0	0	0	35	36	14	11	16	28
2001— Durham (I.L.)	0	5	.000	7.80	7	7	0	0	0	30	33	28	26	25	16

WHITE, RICK — P — ROCKIES

PERSONAL: Born December 23, 1968, in Springfield, Ohio. ... 6-4/230. ... Throws right, bats right. ... Full name: Richard Allen White.
HIGH SCHOOL: Kenton Ridge (Springfield, Ohio).
JUNIOR COLLEGE: Paducah (Ky.) Community College.
TRANSACTIONS/CAREER NOTES: Selected by Pittsburgh Pirates organization in 15th round of free-agent draft (June 4, 1990). ... On Carolina disabled list (May 15-July 6, 1993). ... On Buffalo disabled list (August 28-September 4, 1993). ... On Pittsburgh disabled list (April 14-May 17, 1995); included rehabilitation assignment to Gulf Coast Pirates (April 26-May 17). ... Granted free agency (December 21, 1995). ... Re-signed by Pirates organization (December 21, 1995). ... On Calgary disabled list (April 4-August 7, 1996). ... On Carolina disabled list (August 7-23, 1996). ... Granted free agency (October 15, 1996). ... Signed by Tampa Bay Devil Rays organization (February 4, 1997). ... Loaned by Devil Rays to Orlando, Chicago Cubs organization (April 3-September 11, 1997). ... Traded by Devil Rays with OF Bubba Trammell to New York Mets for OF Jason Tyner and P Paul Wilson (July 28, 2000). ... On disabled list (March 31-April 21, 2001 and May 1-17, 2001). ... Granted free agency (December 21, 2001). ... Signed by Colorado Rockies (January 10, 2002).
MISCELLANEOUS: Struck out and grounded out in two appearances as pinch hitter with New York (2000).

Year — League	W	L	Pct.	ERA	G	GS	CG	ShO	Sv.	IP	H	R	ER	BB	SO
1990— Gulf Coast Pirates (GCL)	3	1	.750	0.76	7	6	0	0	0	35 2/3	26	11	3	4	27
— Welland (NY-Penn)	1	4	.200	3.26	9	5	1	0	0	38 2/3	39	19	14	14	43
1991— Augusta (S.Atl.)	4	4	.500	3.00	34	0	0	0	6	63	68	26	21	18	52
— Salem (Caro.)	2	3	.400	4.66	13	5	1	0	1	46 1/3	41	27	24	9	36
1992— Salem (Caro.)	7	9	.438	3.80	18	18	•5	0	0	120 2/3	116	58	51	24	70
— Carolina (Sou.)	1	7	.125	4.21	10	10	1	0	0	57 2/3	59	32	27	18	45
1993— Carolina (Sou.)	4	3	.571	3.50	12	12	1	0	0	69 1/3	59	29	27	12	52
— Buffalo (A.A.)	0	3	.000	3.54	7	3	0	0	0	28	25	13	11	8	16
1994— Pittsburgh (N.L.)	4	5	.444	3.82	43	5	0	0	6	75 1/3	79	35	32	17	38
1995— Pittsburgh (N.L.)	2	3	.400	4.75	15	9	0	0	0	55	66	33	29	18	29
— Calgary (PCL)	6	4	.600	4.20	14	11	1	0	0	79 1/3	97	40	37	10	56
1996— Carolina (Sou.)	0	1	.000	11.37	2	1	0	0	0	6 1/3	9	8	8	1	7
— Gulf Coast Pirates (GCL)	0	0	...	2.25	3	3	0	0	0	12	8	4	3	3	8
1997— Orlando (Sou.)■	5	7	.417	4.71	39	8	0	0	12	86	93	55	45	22	65
1998— Durham (I.L.)	4	2	.667	4.22	9	9	1	0	0	53 1/3	63	29	25	11	31
— Tampa Bay (A.L.)	2	6	.250	3.80	38	3	0	0	0	68 2/3	66	32	29	23	39
1999— Tampa Bay (A.L.)	5	3	.625	4.08	63	1	0	0	0	108	132	56	49	38	81
2000— Tampa Bay (A.L.)	3	6	.333	3.41	44	0	0	0	2	71 1/3	57	30	27	26	47
— New York (N.L.)■	2	3	.400	3.81	22	0	0	0	1	28 1/3	26	14	12	12	20
2001— New York (N.L.)	4	5	.444	3.88	55	0	0	0	2	69 2/3	71	38	30	17	51
A.L. totals (3 years)	10	15	.400	3.81	145	4	0	0	2	248	255	118	105	87	167
N.L. totals (4 years)	12	16	.429	4.06	135	14	0	0	9	228 1/3	242	120	103	64	138
Major League totals (6 years)	22	31	.415	3.93	280	18	0	0	11	476 1/3	497	238	208	151	305

DIVISION SERIES RECORD

Year — League	W	L	Pct.	ERA	G	GS	CG	ShO	Sv.	IP	H	R	ER	BB	SO
2000— New York (N.L.)	1	0	1.000	0.00	2	0	0	0	0	2 2/3	6	0	0	2	4

CHAMPIONSHIP SERIES RECORD

Year — League	W	L	Pct.	ERA	G	GS	CG	ShO	Sv.	IP	H	R	ER	BB	SO
2000— New York (N.L.)................	0	0	...	9.00	1	0	0	0	0	3	5	3	3	1	1

WORLD SERIES RECORD

Year — League	W	L	Pct.	ERA	G	GS	CG	ShO	Sv.	IP	H	R	ER	BB	SO
2000— New York (N.L.)................	0	0	...	6.75	1	0	0	0	0	1 1/3	1	1	1	1	1

W

WHITE, RONDELL — OF — YANKEES

PERSONAL: Born February 23, 1972, in Milledgeville, Ga. ... 6-1/210. ... Bats right, throws right. ... Full name: Rondell Bernard White.
HIGH SCHOOL: Jones County (Gray, Ga.).
TRANSACTIONS/CAREER NOTES: Selected by Montreal Expos organization in first round (24th pick overall) of free-agent draft (June 4, 1990); pick received as part of compensation for California Angels signing Type A free-agent P Mark Langston. ... On Montreal disabled list (April 28-July 16, 1996); included rehabilitation assignments to West Palm Beach (July 5-10), Gulf Coast Expos (July 5-10) and Harrisburg (July 10-16). ... On disabled list (July 21, 1998-remainder of season; June 14-29 and July 2-17, 1999). ... On Montreal disabled list (July 8-August 31, 2000). ... Traded by Expos to Chicago Cubs for P Scott Downs (July 31, 2000). ... On Chicago disabled list (August 1-6 and August 27, 2000-remainder of season). ... On Chicago disabled list (June 26-July 12 and July 14-September 1, 2001); included rehabilitation assignment to West Tenn (August 15-September 1). ... Granted free agency (November 5, 2001). ... Signed by New York Yankees (December 17, 2001).

STATISTICAL NOTES: Led Gulf Coast League with 96 total bases in 1990. ... Hit for the cycle (June 11, 1995, 13 innings). ... Collected six hits in one game (June 11, 1995). ... Led N.L. outfielders in total chances with 385 in 1997. ... Had 17-game hitting streak (May 23-June 13, 2001). ... Career major league grand slams: 2.

Year	Team (League)	Pos.	G	AB	R	H	2B	3B	HR	RBI	Avg.	BB	SO	SB	PO	A	E	Avg.
1990—	GC Expos (GCL)	OF	57	221	33	66	7	4	5	34	.299	17	33	10	71	1	2	.973
1991—	Sumter (S.Atl.)	OF	123	465	80	122	23	6	13	68	.262	57	109	50	215	6	3	*.987
1992—	W. Palm Beach (FSL)	OF	111	450	80	142	10	*12	4	41	.316	46	78	42	187	2	3	.984
	— Harrisburg (East.)	OF	21	89	22	27	7	1	2	7	.303	6	14	6	29	1	2	.938
1993—	Harrisburg (East.)	OF	90	372	72	122	16	10	12	52	.328	22	72	21	179	4	1	.995
	— Ottawa (I.L.)	OF-DH	37	150	28	57	8	2	7	32	.380	12	20	10	79	0	1	.988
	— Montreal (N.L.)	OF	23	73	9	19	3	1	2	15	.260	7	16	1	33	0	0	1.000
1994—	Montreal (N.L.)	OF	40	97	16	27	10	1	2	13	.278	9	18	1	34	1	2	.946
	— Ottawa (I.L.)	OF	42	169	23	46	7	0	7	18	.272	15	17	9	91	4	2	.979
1995—	Montreal (N.L.)	OF	130	474	87	140	33	4	13	50	.295	41	87	25	270	5	4	.986
1996—	Montreal (N.L.)	OF	88	334	35	98	19	4	6	41	.293	22	53	14	185	5	2	.990
	— W. Palm Beach (FSL)	DH-OF	3	10	0	2	1	0	0	2	.200	0	4	0	2	0	0	1.000
	— GC Expos (GCL)	OF	3	12	3	3	0	0	2	4	.250	0	1	1	4	0	0	1.000
	— Harrisburg (East.)	OF	5	20	5	7	1	0	3	6	.350	1	1	1	12	0	0	1.000
1997—	Montreal (N.L.)	OF	151	592	84	160	29	5	28	82	.270	31	111	16	*376	6	3	*.992
1998—	Montreal (N.L.)	OF-DH	97	357	54	107	21	2	17	58	.300	30	57	16	261	7	1	.996
1999—	Montreal (N.L.)	OF	138	539	83	168	26	6	22	64	.312	32	85	10	286	7	11	.964
2000—	Montreal (N.L.)	OF	75	290	52	89	24	0	11	54	.307	28	67	5	158	4	1	.994
	— Chicago (N.L.)■	OF	19	67	7	22	2	0	2	7	.328	5	12	0	41	0	0	1.000
2001—	Chicago (N.L.)	OF	95	323	43	99	19	1	17	50	.307	26	56	1	133	4	3	.979
	— West Tenn (Sou.)	OF	9	28	2	4	1	0	2	4	.143	1	7	0	2	0	0	1.000
Major League totals (9 years)			856	3146	470	929	186	24	120	441	.295	231	562	89	1777	39	27	.985

WHITESIDE, MATT   P   BRAVES

PERSONAL: Born August 8, 1967, in Charleston, Mo. ... 6-0/200. ... Throws right, bats right. ... Full name: Matthew Christopher Whiteside.
HIGH SCHOOL: Charleston (Mo.).
COLLEGE: Arkansas State.
TRANSACTIONS/CAREER NOTES: Selected by Texas Rangers organization in 25th round of free-agent draft (June 4, 1990). ... On disabled list (May 9-25, 1995). ... Granted free agency (October 30, 1996). ... Re-signed by Rangers (November 22, 1996). ... Released by Rangers (March 23, 1998). ... Signed by Philadelphia Phillies (March 27, 1998). ... Granted free agency (October 15, 1998). ... Signed by San Diego Padres organization (November 23, 1998). ... Granted free agency (October 8, 1999). ... Re-signed by Padres (October 25, 1999). ... On Las Vegas disabled list (April 21-28, 2000). ... Granted free agency (October 2, 2000). ... Signed by Atlanta Braves organization (January 18, 2001). ... On Atlanta disabled list (July 4-5, 2001). ... Released by Braves (July 5, 2001).
STATISTICAL NOTES: Tied for American Association lead with three balks in 1996.

Year	League	W	L	Pct.	ERA	G	GS	CG	ShO	Sv.	IP	H	R	ER	BB	SO
1990—	Butte (Pio.)	4	4	.500	3.45	18	5	0	0	2	57 1/3	57	33	22	25	45
1991—	Gastonia (S.Atl.)	3	1	.750	2.15	48	0	0	0	29	62 2/3	44	19	15	21	71
1992—	Tulsa (Texas)	0	1	.000	2.41	33	0	0	0	21	33 2/3	31	9	9	3	30
	— Oklahoma City (A.A.)	1	0	1.000	0.79	12	0	0	0	8	11 1/3	7	1	1	3	13
	— Texas (A.L.)	1	1	.500	1.93	20	0	0	0	4	28	26	8	6	11	13
1993—	Texas (A.L.)	2	1	.667	4.32	60	0	0	0	1	73	78	37	35	23	39
	— Oklahoma City (A.A.)	2	1	.667	5.56	8	0	0	0	1	11 1/3	17	7	7	8	10
1994—	Texas (A.L.)	2	2	.500	5.02	47	0	0	0	1	61	68	40	34	28	37
1995—	Texas (A.L.)	5	4	.556	4.08	40	0	0	0	3	53	48	24	24	19	46
1996—	Texas (A.L.)	0	1	.000	6.68	14	0	0	0	0	32 1/3	43	24	24	11	15
	— Oklahoma City (A.A.)	9	6	.600	3.45	36	7	0	0	0	94	95	41	36	24	52
1997—	Oklahoma City (A.A.)	1	1	.500	3.54	10	1	0	0	1	28	30	14	11	13	11
	— Texas (A.L.)	4	1	.800	5.08	42	1	0	0	0	72 2/3	85	45	41	26	44
1998—	Philadelphia (N.L.)■	1	1	.500	8.50	10	0	0	0	0	18	27	18	17	5	14
	— Scranton/W.B. (I.L.)	1	4	.200	6.48	30	1	0	0	5	33 1/3	47	24	24	7	21
1999—	Las Vegas (PCL)■	9	5	.643	5.12	47	3	1	1	7	89 2/3	99	59	51	29	88
	— San Diego (N.L.)	1	0	1.000	13.91	10	0	0	0	0	11	19	17	17	5	9
2000—	San Diego (N.L.)	2	3	.400	4.14	28	0	0	0	0	37	32	21	17	17	27
	— Las Vegas (PCL)	2	5	.286	5.28	23	1	0	0	0	30 2/3	34	21	18	15	31
2001—	Richmond (I.L.)■	0	0	...	0.00	9	0	0	0	4	10	4	0	0	1	9
	— Atlanta (N.L.)	0	1	.000	7.16	13	0	0	0	0	16 1/3	23	14	13	7	10
A.L. totals (6 years)		14	10	.583	4.61	223	1	0	0	9	320	348	178	164	118	194
N.L. totals (4 years)		4	5	.444	7.00	61	0	0	0	0	82 1/3	101	70	64	34	60
Major League totals (10 years)		18	15	.545	5.10	284	1	0	0	9	402 1/3	449	248	228	152	254

WICKMAN, BOB   P   INDIANS

PERSONAL: Born February 6, 1969, in Green Bay, Wis. ... 6-1/234. ... Throws right, bats right. ... Full name: Robert Joe Wickman.
HIGH SCHOOL: Oconto Falls (Wis.).
COLLEGE: Wisconsin-Whitewater.
TRANSACTIONS/CAREER NOTES: Selected by Chicago White Sox organization in second round of free-agent draft (June 4, 1990). ... Traded by White Sox with P Melido Perez and P Domingo Jean to New York Yankees for 2B Steve Sax and cash (January 10, 1992). ... Traded by Yankees with OF Gerald Williams to Milwaukee Brewers for P Graeme Lloyd and OF Pat Listach (August 23, 1996). ... Traded by Brewers with P Steve Woodard and P Jason Bere to Cleveland Indians for 1B/OF Richie Sexson, P Paul Rigdon, P Kane Davis and a player to be named later (July 28, 2000); Brewers acquired 2B Marcos Scutaro to complete deal (August 30).

W

Year	League	W	L	Pct.	ERA	G	GS	CG	ShO	Sv.	IP	H	R	ER	BB	SO
1990—	GC White Sox (GCL)	2	0	1.000	2.45	2	2	0	0	0	11	7	4	3	1	15
—	Sarasota (FSL)	0	1	.000	1.98	2	2	0	0	0	13²/₃	17	7	3	4	8
—	South Bend (Midw.)	7	2	.778	1.38	9	9	3	0	0	65¹/₃	50	16	10	16	50
1991—	Sarasota (FSL)	5	1	.833	2.05	7	7	1	1	0	44	43	16	10	11	32
—	Birmingham (Sou.)	6	10	.375	3.56	20	20	4	1	0	131¹/₃	127	68	52	50	81
1992—	Columbus (I.L.)■	12	5	.706	2.92	23	23	2	1	0	157	131	61	51	51	108
—	New York (A.L.)	6	1	.857	4.11	8	8	0	0	0	50¹/₃	51	25	23	20	21
1993—	New York (A.L.)	14	4	.778	4.63	41	19	1	1	4	140	156	82	72	69	70
1994—	New York (A.L.)	5	4	.556	3.09	*53	0	0	0	6	70	54	26	24	27	56
1995—	New York (A.L.)	2	4	.333	4.05	63	1	0	0	1	80	77	38	36	33	51
1996—	New York (A.L.)	4	1	.800	4.67	58	0	0	0	0	79	94	41	41	34	61
—	Milwaukee (A.L.)■	3	0	1.000	3.24	12	0	0	0	0	16²/₃	12	9	6	10	14
1997—	Milwaukee (A.L.)	7	6	.538	2.73	74	0	0	0	1	95²/₃	89	32	29	41	78
1998—	Milwaukee (N.L.)	6	9	.400	3.72	72	0	0	0	25	82¹/₃	79	38	34	39	71
1999—	Milwaukee (N.L.)	3	8	.273	3.39	71	0	0	0	37	74¹/₃	75	31	28	38	60
2000—	Milwaukee (N.L.)	2	2	.500	2.93	43	0	0	0	16	46	37	18	15	20	44
—	Cleveland (A.L.)■	1	3	.250	3.38	26	0	0	0	14	26²/₃	27	12	10	12	11
2001—	Cleveland (A.L.)	5	0	1.000	2.39	70	0	0	0	32	67²/₃	61	18	18	14	66
A.L. totals (8 years)		47	23	.671	3.72	405	28	1	1	58	626	621	283	259	260	428
N.L. totals (3 years)		11	19	.367	3.42	186	0	0	0	78	202²/₃	191	87	77	97	175
Major League totals (10 years)		58	42	.580	3.65	591	28	1	1	136	828²/₃	812	370	336	357	603

DIVISION SERIES RECORD

Year	League	W	L	Pct.	ERA	G	GS	CG	ShO	Sv.	IP	H	R	ER	BB	SO
1995—	New York (A.L.)	0	0	…	0.00	3	0	0	0	0	3	5	0	0	0	3
2001—	Cleveland (A.L.)	0	0	…	0.00	1	0	0	0	0	1	0	0	0	0	2
Division series totals (2 years)		0	0	…	0.00	4	0	0	0	0	4	5	0	0	0	5

ALL-STAR GAME RECORD

Year	League	W	L	Pct.	ERA	GS	CG	ShO	Sv.	IP	H	R	ER	BB	SO
2000—	National	0	0	…	0.00	0	0	0	0	1	0	0	0	0	1

WILKERSON, BRAD — OF — EXPOS

PERSONAL: Born June 1, 1977, in Daviess County, Ky. ... 6-0/200. ... Bats left, throws left. ... Full name: Stephen Bradley Wilkerson.
HIGH SCHOOL: Apollo (Owensboro, Ky.).
COLLEGE: Florida.
TRANSACTIONS/CAREER NOTES: Selected by Montreal Expos organization in supplemental round ("sandwich pick" between first and second round, 33rd pick overall) of free-agent draft (June 2, 1998); pick received as part of compensation for Toronto Blue Jays signing Type A free agent C Darrin Fletcher. ... On Ottawa disabled list (April 5-May 5, 2001).

Year	Team (League)	Pos.	G	AB	R	H	2B	3B	HR	RBI	Avg.	BB	SO	SB	PO	A	E	Avg.
1999—	Harrisburg (East.)	OF-1B	138	422	66	99	21	3	8	49	.235	88	100	3	234	11	7	.972
2000—	Harrisburg (East.)	OF-1B	66	229	53	77	36	2	6	44	.336	42	38	8	168	8	3	.983
—	Ottawa (I.L.)	OF	63	212	40	53	11	1	12	35	.250	45	60	5	123	6	6	.956
2001—	Montreal (N.L.)	OF	47	117	11	24	7	2	1	5	.205	17	41	2	62	2	2	.970
—	Ottawa (I.L.)	OF	69	233	43	63	10	0	12	48	.270	60	68	12	101	6	3	.973
—	Jupiter (FSL)		6	26	3	6	3	0	0	1	.231	3	10	0	0	0	0	…
Major League totals (1 year)			47	117	11	24	7	2	1	5	.205	17	41	2	62	2	2	.970

WILKINS, MARC — P — PIRATES

PERSONAL: Born October 21, 1970, in Mansfield, Ohio. ... 5-11/212. ... Throws right, bats right. ... Full name: Marc Allen Wilkins.
HIGH SCHOOL: Ontario (Ohio).
COLLEGE: Toledo.
TRANSACTIONS/CAREER NOTES: Selected by Pittsburgh Pirates organization in 47th round of free-agent draft (June 1, 1992). ... On Pittsburgh disabled list (April 26-May 11 and May 23, 1998-remainder of season); included rehabilitation assignments to Carolina (May 8-10) and Nashville (August 7-September 6). ... On Pittsburgh disabled list (March 26-May 1, 1999); included rehabilitation assignments to Altoona (April 16-25) and Nashville (April 26-May 1). ... Claimed on waivers by Oakland Athletics (October 13, 2000). ... Released by A's (December 13, 2000). ... Signed by Pirates organization (January 12, 2001). ... Granted free agency (October 12, 2001).
STATISTICAL NOTES: Led Carolina League with 22 hit batsmen in 1994.

Year	League	W	L	Pct.	ERA	G	GS	CG	ShO	Sv.	IP	H	R	ER	BB	SO
1992—	Welland (NY-Penn)	4	2	.667	7.29	28	1	0	0	1	42	49	36	34	24	42
1993—	Augusta (S.Atl.)	5	6	.455	4.21	48	5	0	0	1	77	83	52	36	31	73
1994—	Salem (Caro.)	8	5	.615	3.70	28	•28	0	0	0	151	155	84	62	45	90
1995—	Carolina (Sou.)	5	3	.625	3.99	37	12	0	0	0	99¹/₃	91	47	44	44	80
1996—	Carolina (Sou.)	2	3	.400	4.01	11	3	0	0	0	24²/₃	19	12	11	11	19
—	Pittsburgh (N.L.)	4	3	.571	3.84	47	2	0	0	1	75	75	36	32	36	62
1997—	Pittsburgh (N.L.)	9	5	.643	3.69	70	0	0	0	2	75²/₃	65	33	31	33	47
1998—	Pittsburgh (N.L.)	0	0	…	3.52	16	0	0	0	0	15¹/₃	13	6	6	9	17
—	Carolina (Sou.)	0	0	…	4.50	2	0	0	0	0	2	1	1	1	0	4
—	Nashville (PCL)	1	0	1.000	10.38	5	0	0	0	0	4¹/₃	3	5	5	3	4
1999—	Altoona (East.)	0	1	.000	1.50	5	0	0	0	0	6	4	2	1	4	5
—	Nashville (PCL)	1	1	.500	0.79	8	0	0	0	3	11¹/₃	9	3	1	3	8
—	Pittsburgh (N.L.)■	2	3	.400	4.24	46	0	0	0	0	51	49	28	24	26	44
2000—	Pittsburgh (N.L.)	4	2	.667	5.07	52	0	0	0	0	60¹/₃	54	34	34	43	37
—	Nashville (PCL)	2	3	.400	4.97	17	4	0	0	3	38	34	23	21	24	33
2001—	Pittsburgh (N.L.)	0	1	.000	6.75	14	0	0	0	0	17¹/₃	22	13	13	8	11
—	Nashville (PCL)	4	1	.800	4.75	32	0	0	0	1	36	38	21	19	13	24
Major League totals (6 years)		19	14	.576	4.28	245	2	0	0	3	294²/₃	278	150	140	155	218

W

WILKINS, RICK C

PERSONAL: Born June 4, 1967, in Jacksonville. ... 6-2/215. ... Bats left, throws right. ... Full name: Richard David Wilkins.
HIGH SCHOOL: The Bolles School (Jacksonville).
JUNIOR COLLEGE: Florida Community College-Jacksonville.
COLLEGE: Furman.
TRANSACTIONS/CAREER NOTES: Selected by Chicago Cubs organization in 23rd round of free-agent draft (June 2, 1986). ... On Chicago disabled list (June 2-28, 1995). ... Traded by Cubs to Houston Astros for OF Luis Gonzalez and C Scott Servais (June 28, 1995). ... On Houston disabled list (July 2-September 5, 1995); included rehabilitation assignments to Jackson (August 28-September 1) and Tucson (September 1-5). ... Traded by Astros with cash to San Francisco Giants for C Kirt Manwaring (July 27, 1996). ... Released by Giants (August 1, 1997). ... Signed by Seattle Mariners organization (August 15, 1997). ... On Seattle disabled list (August 15-September 1, 1997); included rehabilitation assignment to Tacoma (August 15-September 1). ... Granted free agency (October 16, 1997). ... Re-signed by Mariners (December 15, 1997). ... Traded by Mariners to New York Mets for P Lindsay Gulin (May 12, 1998). ... On Norfolk disabled list (July 20-August 30, 1998). ... Granted free agency (October 15, 1998). ... Signed by Los Angeles Dodgers organization (March 6, 1999). ... Granted free agency (October 4, 1999). ... Signed by St. Louis Cardinals organization (February 3, 2000). ... Granted free agency (October 31, 2000). ... Signed by San Diego Padres organization (January 29, 2001). ... Released by Padres (October 11, 2001).
STATISTICAL NOTES: Led New York-Pennsylvania League with eight intentional bases on balls received in 1987. ... Led New York-Pennsylvania League catchers with .989 fielding percentage, 483 putouts and 540 total chances and tied for lead with six double plays in 1987. ... Led Midwest League catchers with 984 total chances in 1988. ... Led Carolina League catchers with 860 total chances and tied for lead with eight double plays in 1989. ... Led Southern League catchers with 857 total chances, 11 double plays and 15 passed balls in 1990. ... Tied for N.L. lead with 10 sacrifice flies in 1996. ... Career major league grand slams: 2.

Year	Team (League)	Pos.	G	AB	R	H	2B	3B	HR	RBI	Avg.	BB	SO	SB	PO	A	E	Avg.
1987—	Geneva (NY-Penn)......	C-1B	75	243	35	61	8	2	8	43	.251	58	40	7	†503	51	7	†.988
1988—	Peoria (Midw.)..........	C	137	490	54	119	30	1	8	63	.243	67	110	4	*864	*101	*19	.981
1989—	Win.-Salem (Caro.)....	C	132	445	61	111	24	1	12	54	.249	50	87	6	*764	*78	*18	.979
1990—	Charlotte (Sou.).........	C	127	449	48	102	18	1	17	71	.227	43	95	4	*740	*103	14	.984
1991—	Iowa (A.A.)................	C-OF	38	107	12	29	3	1	5	14	.271	11	17	1	204	24	3	.987
	—Chicago (N.L.)...........	C	86	203	21	45	9	0	6	22	.222	19	56	3	373	42	3	.993
1992—	Chicago (N.L.)...........	C	83	244	20	66	9	1	8	22	.270	28	53	0	408	47	3	.993
	—Iowa (A.A.)................	C	47	155	20	43	11	2	5	28	.277	19	42	0	177	18	2	.990
1993—	Chicago (N.L.)...........	C	136	446	78	135	23	1	30	73	.303	50	99	2	717	89	3	.996
1994—	Chicago (N.L.)...........	C-1B	100	313	44	71	25	2	7	39	.227	40	86	4	550	51	4	.993
1995—	Chicago (N.L.)...........	C-1B	50	162	24	31	2	0	6	14	.191	36	51	0	294	31	4	.988
	—Houston (N.L.)■.......	C	15	40	6	10	1	0	1	5	.250	10	10	0	87	4	0	1.000
	—Jackson (Texas).........	C	4	11	0	0	0	0	0	0	.000	3	2	0	23	1	0	1.000
	—Tucson (PCL)............	C	4	12	0	4	0	0	0	4	.333	2	0	0	27	4	0	1.000
1996—	Houston (N.L.).........	C	84	254	34	54	8	2	6	23	.213	46	81	0	550	39	6	.990
	—San Fran. (N.L.)■....	C-1B	52	157	19	46	10	0	8	36	.293	21	40	0	240	34	2	.993
1997—	San Francisco (N.L.) ..	C	66	190	18	37	5	0	6	23	.195	17	65	0	326	37	5	.986
	—Tacoma (PCL)■.......	C-DH-1B	17	68	16	23	8	0	1	14	.338	8	12	0	82	4	1	.989
	—Seattle (A.L.).............	C-DH	5	12	2	3	1	0	1	4	.250	1	2	0	9	1	0	1.000
1998—	Seattle (A.L.).............	C-1B-DH	19	41	5	8	1	1	1	4	.195	4	14	0	70	4	0	1.000
	—New York (N.L.)■......	C	5	15	3	2	0	0	0	1	.133	2	2	0	21	1	1	.957
	—Norfolk (I.L.).............	C-DH-1B	45	158	17	41	13	1	1	20	.259	14	37	1	231	15	3	.988
1999—	Los Angeles (N.L.)■...	C	3	4	0	0	0	0	0	0	.000	0	2	0	1	0	0	1.000
	—Albuquerque (PCL).....	C-1B-DH	92	300	39	76	8	1	8	33	.253	29	87	1	546	49	9	.985
2000—	Memphis (PCL)■........	C-1B	63	187	23	43	6	1	4	25	.230	27	57	0	344	42	4	.990
	—St. Louis (N.L.).........	C	4	11	3	3	0	0	0	1	.273	2	2	0	28	3	0	1.000
2001—	Portland (PCL)■........	C-1B	68	222	18	47	15	2	6	33	.212	15	77	0	441	32	5	.990
	—San Diego (N.L.).......	C-1B	12	22	3	4	1	0	1	8	.182	2	8	0	39	0	0	1.000
American League totals (2 years)			24	53	7	11	2	1	2	8	.208	5	16	0	79	5	0	1.000
National League totals (11 years)			696	2061	273	504	93	6	79	267	.245	273	555	9	3634	378	31	.992
Major League totals (11 years)			720	2114	280	515	95	7	81	275	.244	278	571	9	3713	383	31	.992

DIVISION SERIES RECORD

Year	Team (League)	Pos.	G	AB	R	H	2B	3B	HR	RBI	Avg.	BB	SO	SB	PO	A	E	Avg.
1997—	Seattle (A.L.)	C-PH	1	1	0	0	0	0	0	0	.000	1	0	0	2	0	0	1.000
2000—	St. Louis (N.L.)							Did not play.										

CHAMPIONSHIP SERIES RECORD

Year	Team (League)	Pos.	G	AB	R	H	2B	3B	HR	RBI	Avg.	BB	SO	SB	PO	A	E	Avg.
2000—	St. Louis (N.L.)..........	PH	2	2	0	0	0	0	0	0	.000	0	0	0	...	...	...	...

WILLIAMS, BERNIE OF YANKEES

PERSONAL: Born September 13, 1968, in San Juan, Puerto Rico. ... 6-2/205. ... Bats both, throws right. ... Full name: Bernabe Figueroa Williams.
HIGH SCHOOL: Escuela Libre de Musica (San Juan, Puerto Rico).
COLLEGE: Puerto Rico.
TRANSACTIONS/CAREER NOTES: Signed as non-drafted free agent by New York Yankees organization (September 13, 1985). ... On disabled list (July 15, 1988-remainder of seasonl; and May 13-June 7, 1993). ... On disabled list (May 11-May 26, 1996; June 16-July 2 and July 15-August 1, 1997). ... On New York disabled list (June 11-July 18, 1998); included rehabilitation assignments to Tampa (July 6-7) and Norwich (July 14-16). ... Granted free agency (October 26, 1998). ... Re-signed by Yankees (November 25, 1998).
RECORDS: Shares major league single-game record for most strikeouts (nine-inning game)—5 (August 21, 1991). ... Shares major league single-inning record for most doubles—2 (June 22, 1994, seventh inning). ... Shares modern major league record for most long hits in one inning—2 (June 22, 1994, seventh inning).
HONORS: Won A.L. Gold Glove as outfielder (1997-2000). ... Named outfielder on THE SPORTING NEWS A.L. All-Star team (2000).

STATISTICAL NOTES: Led Gulf Coast League outfielders with 123 total chances in 1986. ... Tied for Gulf Coast League lead in caught stealing with 12 in 1986. ... Led Eastern League in caught stealing with 18 in 1990. ... Led Eastern League outfielders with 307 total chances and tied for lead with four double plays in 1990. ... Had 21-game hitting streak (August 1-23, 1993). ... Switch-hit home runs in one game seven times (June 6, 1994; September 12, 1996; September 4, 1998; May 4, 1999; April 23 and May 17, 2000; June 30, 2001). ... Led A.L. outfielders with 441 total chances in 1995. ... Had 16-game hitting streak (July 31-August 14, 1998). ... Had 17-game hitting streak (June 8-July 6, 1999). ... Tied for A.L. lead with 17 intentional bases on balls received in 1999. ... Had 17-game hitting streak (June 19-July 7, 2000). ... Had 16-game hitting streak (August 16-September 1, 2001). ... Career major league grand slams: 9.

MISCELLANEOUS: Batted righthanded only (1986-88).

| | | | | | | | BATTING | | | | | | | | FIELDING | | |
Year	Team (League)	Pos.	G	AB	R	H	2B	3B	HR	RBI	Avg.	BB	SO	SB	PO	A	E	Avg.
1986—	GC Yankees (GCL)......	OF	61	230	*45	62	5	3	2	25	.270	39	40	33	*117	3	3	.976
1987—	Fort Lauderdale (FSL)	OF	25	71	11	11	3	0	0	4	.155	18	22	9	49	1	0	1.000
—	Oneonta (NY-Penn)	OF	25	93	13	32	4	0	0	15	.344	10	14	9	40	0	2	.952
1988—	Prince William (Caro.)	OF	92	337	72	113	16	7	7	45	*.335	65	65	29	186	8	5	.975
1989—	Columbus (I.L.)	OF	50	162	21	35	8	1	2	16	.216	25	38	11	112	2	1	.991
—	Albany/Colonie (East.)	OF	91	314	63	79	11	8	11	42	.252	60	72	26	180	5	5	.974
1990—	Albany/Colonie (East.)	OF	134	466	*91	131	28	5	8	54	.281	*98	97	*39	*288	15	4	.987
1991—	Columbus (I.L.)	OF	78	306	52	90	14	6	8	37	.294	38	43	9	164	2	1	.994
—	New York (A.L.).........	OF	85	320	43	76	19	4	3	34	.238	48	57	10	230	3	5	.979
1992—	New York (A.L.).........	OF	62	261	39	73	14	2	5	26	.280	29	36	7	187	5	1	.995
—	Columbus (I.L.)	OF	95	363	68	111	23	•9	8	50	.306	52	61	20	205	2	2	.990
1993—	New York (A.L.)	OF	139	567	67	152	31	4	12	68	.268	53	106	9	366	5	4	.989
1994—	New York (A.L.)	OF	108	408	80	118	29	1	12	57	.289	61	54	16	277	7	3	.990
1995—	New York (A.L.)	OF	144	563	93	173	29	9	18	82	.307	75	98	8	*432	1	•8	.982
1996—	New York (A.L.)	OF-DH	143	551	108	168	26	7	29	102	.305	82	72	17	334	10	5	.986
1997—	New York (A.L.)	OF	129	509	107	167	35	6	21	100	.328	73	80	15	270	2	2	.993
1998—	New York (A.L.)	OF-DH	128	499	101	169	30	5	26	97	*.339	74	81	15	298	4	3	.990
—	Tampa (FSL)............	OF	1	2	0	1	1	0	0	0	.500	1	0	0	2	0	0	1.000
—	Norwich (East.)	OF	3	11	6	6	2	0	2	5	.545	2	1	0	5	0	0	1.000
1999—	New York (A.L.)	OF-DH	158	591	116	202	28	6	25	115	.342	100	95	9	381	9	5	.987
2000—	New York (A.L.)	OF-DH	141	537	108	165	37	6	30	121	.307	71	84	13	353	2	0	*1.000
2001—	New York (A.L.)	OF-DH	146	540	102	166	38	0	26	94	.307	78	67	11	348	3	2	.994
Major League totals (11 years)			1383	5346	964	1629	316	50	207	896	.305	744	830	130	3476	51	38	.989

DIVISION SERIES RECORD

RECORDS: Holds A.L. career records for most runs batted in—23; runs—25; doubles—10; total bases—59; bases on balls—19; and extra-base hits—16. ... Shares career record for most games—30. ... Shares single-game record for most home runs—2 (October 6, 1995 and October 5, 1996).

| | | | | | | | BATTING | | | | | | | | FIELDING | | |
Year	Team (League)	Pos.	G	AB	R	H	2B	3B	HR	RBI	Avg.	BB	SO	SB	PO	A	E	Avg.
1995—	New York (A.L.).........	OF	5	21	8	9	2	0	2	5	.429	7	3	1	13	0	0	1.000
1996—	New York (A.L.).........	OF	4	15	5	7	0	0	3	5	.467	2	1	1	10	0	0	1.000
1997—	New York (A.L.).........	OF	5	17	3	2	1	0	0	1	.118	4	3	0	7	0	0	1.000
1998—	New York (A.L.).........	OF	3	11	0	0	0	0	0	0	.000	1	4	0	8	0	0	1.000
1999—	New York (A.L.).........	OF	3	11	2	4	1	0	1	6	.364	1	2	0	15	0	0	1.000
2000—	New York (A.L.).........	OF	5	20	3	5	3	0	0	1	.250	1	4	0	10	0	0	1.000
2001—	New York (A.L.).........	OF	5	18	4	4	3	0	0	5	.222	3	3	0	13	0	0	1.000
Division series totals (7 years)			30	113	25	31	10	0	6	23	.274	19	20	2	76	0	0	1.000

CHAMPIONSHIP SERIES RECORD

RECORDS: Holds A.L. career record for runs batted in—21; and bases on balls received—22. ... Shares A.L. career record for most runs—22.

NOTES: Named Most Valuable Player (1996).

| | | | | | | | BATTING | | | | | | | | FIELDING | | |
Year	Team (League)	Pos.	G	AB	R	H	2B	3B	HR	RBI	Avg.	BB	SO	SB	PO	A	E	Avg.
1996—	New York (A.L.).........	OF	5	19	6	9	3	0	2	6	.474	6	4	1	20	0	0	1.000
1998—	New York (A.L.).........	OF	6	21	4	8	1	0	0	5	.381	7	4	1	14	0	0	1.000
1999—	New York (A.L.).........	OF	5	20	3	5	1	0	1	2	.250	2	5	1	13	1	0	1.000
2000—	New York (A.L.).........	CF	6	23	5	10	1	0	1	3	.435	2	3	1	14	0	0	1.000
2001—	New York (A.L.).........	OF	5	17	4	4	0	0	3	5	.235	5	4	0	9	0	1	.900
Championship series totals (5 years)			27	100	22	36	6	0	7	21	.360	22	20	4	70	1	1	.986

WORLD SERIES RECORD

NOTES: Member of World Series championship team (1996, 1998, 1999 and 2000).

| | | | | | | | BATTING | | | | | | | | FIELDING | | |
Year	Team (League)	Pos.	G	AB	R	H	2B	3B	HR	RBI	Avg.	BB	SO	SB	PO	A	E	Avg.
1996—	New York (A.L.).........	OF	6	24	3	4	0	0	1	4	.167	4	6	1	15	0	0	1.000
1998—	New York (A.L.).........	OF	4	16	2	1	0	0	1	3	.063	3	5	0	6	0	0	1.000
1999—	New York (A.L.).........	OF	4	13	2	3	0	0	0	0	.231	4	2	1	2	0	0	1.000
2000—	New York (A.L.).........	OF	5	18	2	2	0	0	1	1	.111	5	5	0	10	0	0	1.000
2001—	New York (A.L.).........	OF	7	24	2	5	1	0	0	1	.208	4	6	0	12	1	0	1.000
World Series totals (5 years)			26	95	11	15	1	0	3	9	.158	20	24	2	45	1	0	1.000

ALL-STAR GAME RECORD

NOTES: Named to All-Star team for 1998 game; replaced by Manny Ramirez due to injury.

| | | | | | | BATTING | | | | | | | | FIELDING | | |
Year	League	Pos.	AB	R	H	2B	3B	HR	RBI	Avg.	BB	SO	SB	PO	A	E	Avg.
1997—	American	OF	0	1	0	0	0	0	0	...	1	0	1	1	0	0	1.000
1998—	American..................						Selected, did not play—injured.										
1999—	American..................	OF	1	0	0	0	0	0	0	.000	0	1	0	0	0	0	...
2000—	American..................	OF	3	0	0	0	0	0	0	.000	0	0	0	0	0	0	...
2001—	American..................	OF	1	0	0	0	0	0	0	.000	0	0	0	2	0	0	1.000
All-Star Game totals (4 years)			5	1	0	0	0	0	0	.000	1	1	1	3	0	0	1.000

W

PERSONAL: Born March 12, 1979, in Anchorage, Alaska. ... 6-2/205. ... Throws left, bats left. ... Full name: David Aaron Williams.
JUNIOR COLLEGE: Delaware Tech (Georgetown, Del.).
TRANSACTIONS/CAREER NOTES: Selected by Pittsburgh Pirates organization in 17th round of free-agent draft (June 2, 1998).

Year League	W	L	Pct.	ERA	G	GS	CG	ShO	Sv.	IP	H	R	ER	BB	SO
1998— Erie (NY-Penn)	2	2	.500	3.23	22	2	0	0	0	47 1/3	45	21	17	14	38
1999— Williamsport (NY-Penn)	4	2	.667	2.56	7	7	1	1	0	45 2/3	33	17	13	11	47
— Hickory (S.Atl.)..................	3	1	.750	3.20	9	9	1	1	0	59	42	22	21	11	46
2000— Hickory (S.Atl.)..................	11	9	.550	2.96	24	24	1	1	0	170	145	66	56	39	193
— Lynchburg (Caro.)	1	0	1.000	6.55	2	2	0	0	0	11	18	8	8	3	8
2001— Pittsburgh (N.L.)	3	7	.300	3.71	22	18	0	0	0	114	100	53	47	45	57
— Nashville (PCL)	1	1	.500	3.38	2	2	0	0	0	10 2/3	9	5	4	5	6
— Altoona (East.)	5	2	.714	2.61	9	8	1	0	0	58 2/3	45	17	17	12	39
Major League totals (1 year)........	3	7	.300	3.71	22	18	0	0	0	114	100	53	47	45	57

PERSONAL: Born August 10, 1966, in New Orleans. ... 6-2/187. ... Bats right, throws right. ... Full name: Gerald Floyd Williams.
HIGH SCHOOL: East St. John (Reserve, La.).
COLLEGE: Grambling State.
TRANSACTIONS/CAREER NOTES: Selected by New York Yankees organization in 14th round of free-agent draft (June 2, 1987). ... Traded by Yankees with P Bob Wickman to Milwaukee Brewers for P Graeme Lloyd and OF Pat Listach (August 23, 1996). ... Traded by Brewers to Atlanta Braves for P Chad Fox (December 11, 1997). ... Granted free agency (November 3, 1999). ... Signed by Tampa Bay Devil Rays (December 19, 1999). ... On suspended list (September 22-25, 2000). ... Released by Devil Rays (June 24, 2001). ... Signed by New York Yankees (June 28, 2001).
STATISTICAL NOTES: Led Carolina League outfielders with 307 total chances in 1989. ... Led International League outfielders with 354 total chances in 1992. ... Tied for International League lead in double plays by outfielder with five in 1992. ... Collected six hits in one game (May 1, 1996). ... Had 15-game hitting streak (July 23-August 13, 1999). ... Career major league grand slams: 3.

						BATTING								FIELDING		
Year Team (League)	Pos.	G	AB	R	H	2B	3B	HR	RBI	Avg.	BB	SO	SB	PO	A	E	Avg.
1987— Oneonta (NY-Penn)	OF	29	115	26	42	6	2	2	29	.365	16	18	6	68	3	3	.959
1988— Prince William (Caro.)	OF	54	159	20	29	3	0	2	18	.182	15	47	6	71	2	3	.961
— Fort Lauderdale (FSL)	OF	63	212	21	40	7	2	2	17	.189	16	56	4	163	2	6	.965
1989— Prince William (Caro.)	OF	134	454	63	104	19	6	13	69	.229	51	120	15	*292	7	8	.974
1990— Fort Lauderdale (FSL)	OF	50	204	25	59	4	5	7	43	.289	16	52	19	115	1	3	.975
— Albany/Colonie (East.)	OF	96	324	54	81	17	2	13	58	.250	35	74	18	210	6	7	.969
1991— Albany/Colonie (East.)	OF	45	175	28	50	15	0	5	32	.286	18	26	18	109	4	3	.974
— Columbus (I.L.).........	OF	61	198	20	51	8	3	2	27	.258	16	39	9	124	1	3	.977
1992— Columbus (I.L.).........	OF	*142	547	92	*156	31	6	16	86	.285	38	98	36	*332	*14	8	.977
— New York (A.L.).........	OF	15	27	7	8	2	0	3	6	.296	0	3	2	20	1	2	.913
1993— Columbus (I.L.).........	OF	87	336	53	95	19	6	8	38	.283	20	66	29	191	6	3	.985
— New York (A.L.).........	OF-DH	42	67	11	10	2	3	0	6	.149	1	14	2	41	2	2	.956
1994— New York (A.L.).........	OF-DH	57	86	19	25	8	0	4	13	.291	4	17	1	43	2	2	.957
1995— New York (A.L.).........	OF-DH	100	182	33	45	18	2	6	28	.247	22	34	4	138	6	1	.993
1996— New York (A.L.).........	OF-DH	99	233	37	63	15	4	5	30	.270	15	39	7	132	1	3	.978
— Milwaukee (A.L.)■..	OF	26	92	6	19	4	0	0	4	.207	4	18	3	75	3	1	.987
1997— Milwaukee (A.L.).........	OF-DH	155	566	73	143	32	2	10	41	.253	19	90	23	357	11	3	.992
1998— Atlanta (N.L.)■..........	OF	129	266	46	81	19	2	10	44	.305	17	48	11	158	2	5	.970
1999— Atlanta (N.L.)..........	OF	143	422	76	116	24	1	17	68	.275	33	67	19	188	9	3	.985
2000— Tampa Bay (A.L.)■....	OF-DH	146	632	87	173	30	2	21	89	.274	34	103	12	349	6	6	.983
2001— Tampa Bay (A.L.)......	OF	62	232	30	48	17	0	4	17	.207	13	42	10	179	5	2	.989
— New York (A.L.)■.....	OF-DH	38	47	12	8	1	0	0	2	.170	5	13	3	29	0	1	.967
American League totals (8 years)		740	2164	315	542	129	13	53	236	.250	117	373	67	1363	37	23	.984
National League totals (2 years)		272	688	122	197	43	3	27	112	.286	50	115	30	346	11	8	.978
Major League totals (10 years)		1012	2852	437	739	172	16	80	348	.259	167	488	97	1709	48	31	.983

DIVISION SERIES RECORD

						BATTING								FIELDING		
Year Team (League)	Pos.	G	AB	R	H	2B	3B	HR	RBI	Avg.	BB	SO	SB	PO	A	E	Avg.
1995— New York (A.L.).........	OF-PR	5	5	1	0	0	0	0	0	.000	2	3	0	7	1	0	1.000
1998— Atlanta (N.L.).............	OF	2	2	1	1	0	0	0	1	.500	0	1	0	2	0	0	1.000
1999— Atlanta (N.L.).............	OF	4	18	2	7	1	0	0	3	.389	0	3	1	4	0	0	1.000
Division series totals (3 years)		11	25	4	8	1	0	0	4	.320	2	7	1	13	1	0	1.000

CHAMPIONSHIP SERIES RECORD

RECORDS: Shares single-game record for most strikeouts—4 (October 10, 1998).

						BATTING								FIELDING		
Year Team (League)	Pos.	G	AB	R	H	2B	3B	HR	RBI	Avg.	BB	SO	SB	PO	A	E	Avg.
1998— Atlanta (N.L.)	PH-OF	5	13	0	2	0	0	0	0	.154	1	6	1	3	0	0	1.000
1999— Atlanta (N.L.)	OF	6	28	4	5	2	0	0	1	.179	2	2	3	12	0	1	.923
Championship series totals (2 years)		11	41	4	7	2	0	0	1	.171	3	8	4	15	0	1	.938

WORLD SERIES RECORD

						BATTING								FIELDING		
Year Team (League)	Pos.	G	AB	R	H	2B	3B	HR	RBI	Avg.	BB	SO	SB	PO	A	E	Avg.
1999— Atlanta (N.L.).............	OF	4	17	2	3	0	1	0	0	.176	0	4	0	6	0	0	1.000

W

WILLIAMS, JEFF   P   DODGERS

PERSONAL: Born June 6, 1972, in Canberra, Australia. ... 6-0/185. ... Throws left, bats right. ... Full name: Jeffrey F. Williams.
COLLEGE: Hawker (Canberra, Australia), then Southeastern Louisiana.
TRANSACTIONS/CAREER NOTES: Signed as non-drafted free agent by Los Angeles Dodgers organization (July 3, 1996). ... On Los Angeles disabled list (April 20-June 27, 2000). ... On Las Vegas disabled list (April 25-May 6, 2001).

Year League	W	L	Pct.	ERA	G	GS	CG	ShO	Sv.	IP	H	R	ER	BB	SO
1997—San Bernardino (Calif.)	10	4	.714	3.10	18	18	0	0	0	116	101	52	40	34	72
—San Antonio (Texas)	2	1	.667	5.81	5	5	0	0	0	26⅓	30	17	17	7	14
1998—San Antonio (Texas)	3	0	1.000	2.59	7	7	0	0	0	41⅔	43	19	12	13	35
—Albuquerque (PCL)	8	8	.500	4.98	21	21	0	0	0	121	160	87	67	49	93
1999—Albuquerque (PCL)	9	7	.563	5.01	42	14	1	1	4	125⅔	151	77	70	47	86
—Los Angeles (N.L.)	2	0	1.000	4.08	5	3	0	0	0	17⅔	12	10	8	9	7
2000—Albuquerque (PCL)	4	3	.571	4.26	12	12	0	0	0	63⅓	64	33	30	28	38
—Los Angeles (N.L.)	0	0	...	15.88	7	0	0	0	0	5⅔	12	11	10	8	3
2001—Las Vegas (PCL)	7	5	.583	3.97	16	16	1	1	0	90⅔	102	49	40	24	61
—Los Angeles (N.L.)	2	1	.667	6.29	15	1	0	0	0	24⅓	26	18	17	17	9
Major League totals (3 years)	4	1	.800	6.61	27	4	0	0	0	47⅔	50	39	35	34	19

WILLIAMS, MATT   3B   DIAMONDBACKS

PERSONAL: Born November 28, 1965, in Bishop, Calif. ... 6-2/214. ... Bats right, throws right. ... Full name: Matthew Derrick Williams. ... Grandson of Bartholomew (Bart) Griffith, outfielder/first baseman with Brooklyn Dodgers and Washington Senators (1922-24).
HIGH SCHOOL: Carson (Nev.).
COLLEGE: UNLV.
TRANSACTIONS/CAREER NOTES: Selected by New York Mets organization in 27th round of free-agent draft (June 6, 1983); did not sign. ... Selected by San Francisco Giants organization in first round (third pick overall) of free-agent draft (June 2, 1986). ... On disabled list (June 28-July 14, 1993). ... On San Francisco disabled list (June 4-August 19, 1995); included rehabilitation assignments to San Jose (July 24-25 and August 13-19). ... On disabled list (August 5, 1996-remainder of season). ... Traded by Giants with a player to be named later to Cleveland Indians for IF Jeff Kent, IF Jose Vizcaino, P Julian Tavarez and a player to be named later (November 13, 1996); Giants traded OF Trenidad Hubbard to Indians for P Joe Roa to complete deal (December 16, 1996). ... Traded by Indians to Arizona Diamondbacks for 3B Travis Fryman, P Tom Martin and cash (December 1, 1997). ... On Arizona disabled list (July 18-August 3, 1998); included rehabilitation assignment to Tucson (July 31-August 3). ... On Arizona disabled list (March 29-May 23 and June 25-July 13, 2000); included rehabilitation assignments to El Paso (May 16-23) and High Desert (July 8-10). ... On Arizona disabled list (May 18-July 12, 2001); included rehabilitation assignment to Tucson (July 4-12).
RECORDS: Shares major league record for most home runs in two consecutive games—5 (April 25 [3] and 26 [2], 1997).
HONORS: Named shortstop on The Sporting News college All-America team (1986). ... Named third baseman on The Sporting News N.L. All-Star team (1990 and 1993-94). ... Named third baseman on The Sporting News N.L. Silver Slugger team (1990 and 1993-94). ... Won N.L. Gold Glove at third base (1991 and 1993-94). ... Named third baseman on The Sporting News A.L. All-Star team (1997). ... Won A.L. Gold Glove at third base (1997). ... Named third baseman on The Sporting News A.L. Silver Slugger team (1997).
STATISTICAL NOTES: Led N.L. third basemen with 33 double plays in 1990 and 1992 and 34 in 1993. ... Tied for N.L. lead in total chances by third baseman with 465 in 1990. ... Led N.L. third basemen with 131 putouts in 1991. ... Led N.L. third basemen with 326 total chances in 1994. ... Hit three home runs in one game (April 25, 1997). ... Had 24-game hitting streak (August 13-September 8, 1997). ... Had 19-game hitting streak (May 26-June 18, 1999). ... Career major league grand slams: 11.

Year Team (League)	Pos.	G	AB	R	H	2B	3B	HR	RBI	Avg.	BB	SO	SB	PO	A	E	Avg.
1986—Everett (N'West)	SS	4	17	3	4	0	1	1	10	.235	1	4	0	5	10	2	.882
—Clinton (Midw.)	SS	68	250	32	60	14	3	7	29	.240	23	62	3	89	150	10	.960
1987—Phoenix (PCL)	3B-2B-SS	56	211	36	61	15	2	6	37	.289	19	53	6	53	136	14	.931
—San Francisco (N.L.)	SS-3B	84	245	28	46	9	2	8	21	.188	16	68	4	110	234	9	.975
1988—Phoenix (PCL)	3B-SS-2B-OF	82	306	45	83	19	1	12	51	.271	13	56	6	56	173	13	.946
—San Francisco (N.L.)	3B-SS	52	156	17	32	6	1	8	19	.205	8	41	0	48	108	7	.957
1989—San Francisco (N.L.)	3B-SS	84	292	31	59	18	1	18	50	.202	14	72	1	90	168	10	.963
—Phoenix (PCL)	3B-SS-OF	76	284	61	91	20	2	26	61	.320	32	51	9	57	197	11	.958
1990—San Francisco (N.L.)	3B	159	617	87	171	27	2	33	*122	.277	33	138	7	*140	306	19	.959
1991—San Francisco (N.L.)	3B-SS	157	589	72	158	24	5	34	98	.268	33	128	5	†134	295	16	.964
1992—San Francisco (N.L.)	3B	146	529	58	120	13	5	20	66	.227	39	109	7	105	289	*23	.945
1993—San Francisco (N.L.)	3B	145	579	105	170	33	4	38	110	.294	27	80	1	117	266	12	.970
1994—San Francisco (N.L.)	3B	112	445	74	119	16	3	*43	96	.267	33	87	1	79	*235	12	.963
1995—San Francisco (N.L.)	3B	76	283	53	95	17	1	23	65	.336	30	58	2	49	178	10	.958
—San Jose (Calif.)	3B	4	11	2	2	0	0	1	2	.182	0	3	0	4	0	1	1.000
1996—San Francisco (N.L.)	3B-1B-SS	105	404	69	122	16	1	22	85	.302	39	91	1	164	501	14	.962
1997—Cleveland (A.L.)■	3B	151	596	86	157	32	3	32	105	.263	34	108	12	89	301	12	.970
1998—Arizona (N.L.)■	3B	135	510	72	136	26	1	20	71	.267	43	102	5	99	282	11	.972
—Tucson (PCL)	3B	2	5	0	1	0	0	0	0	.200	0	0	0	1	0	0	1.000
1999—Arizona (N.L.)	3B	154	627	98	190	37	2	35	142	.303	41	93	2	123	299	0	.977
2000—El Paso (Texas)	3B	5	13	3	6	2	0	0	1	.462	2	1	0	2	4	0	1.000
—Arizona (N.L.)	3B-DH	96	371	43	102	18	2	12	47	.275	20	51	1	68	172	9	.964
—High Desert (Calif.)	3B	2	8	1	3	0	0	1	1	.375	0	1	0	1	1	0	1.000
2001—Arizona (N.L.)	3B-SS	106	408	58	112	30	0	16	65	.275	22	70	1	60	182	9	.964
—Tucson (PCL)	3B	5	17	4	6	2	0	2	5	.353	2	2	1	1	4	1	.833
American League totals (1 year)		151	596	86	157	32	3	32	105	.263	34	108	12	89	301	12	.970
National League totals (14 years)		1611	6055	865	1632	290	30	330	1057	.270	398	1188	38	1386	3205	171	.964
Major League totals (15 years)		1762	6651	951	1789	322	33	362	1162	.269	432	1296	50	1475	3506	183	.965

DIVISION SERIES RECORD

Year Team (League)	Pos.	G	AB	R	H	2B	3B	HR	RBI	Avg.	BB	SO	SB	PO	A	E	Avg.
1997—Cleveland (A.L.)	3B	5	17	4	4	1	0	1	3	.235	3	3	0	2	10	0	1.000
1999—Arizona (N.L.)	3B	4	16	3	6	1	0	0	0	.375	0	1	0	3	9	0	1.000
2001—Arizona (N.L.)	3B	5	16	0	1	1	0	0	0	.063	4	4	0	2	15	1	.944
Division series totals (3 years)		14	49	7	11	3	0	1	3	.224	7	8	0	7	34	1	.976

W

CHAMPIONSHIP SERIES RECORD

RECORDS: Holds N.L. single-series record for most runs batted in—9 (1989).

Year	Team (League)	Pos.	G	AB	R	H	2B	3B	HR	RBI	Avg.	BB	SO	SB	PO	A	E	Avg.
1987— San Francisco (N.L.)..									Did not play.									
1989— San Francisco (N.L.)..		3B-SS	5	20	2	6	1	0	2	9	.300	0	2	0	5	12	0	1.000
1997— Cleveland (A.L.).........		3B	6	23	1	5	1	0	0	2	.217	3	7	1	6	18	2	.923
2001— Arizona (N.L.)............		3B	5	18	1	5	1	0	0	2	.278	2	3	0	3	11	3	.824
Championship series totals (3 years)			16	61	4	16	3	0	2	13	.262	5	12	1	14	41	5	.917

WORLD SERIES RECORD

RECORDS: Shares single-inning record for most at-bats—2 (November 3, 2001, third inning). ... Shares single-inning record for most hits—2 (November 3, 2001, third inning). ... Holds single-inning record for most doubles—2 (November 3, 2001, third inning).
NOTES: Member of World Series championship team (2001).

Year	Team (League)	Pos.	G	AB	R	H	2B	3B	HR	RBI	Avg.	BB	SO	SB	PO	A	E	Avg.
1989— San Francisco (N.L.)..		SS-3B	4	16	1	2	0	0	1	1	.125	0	6	0	4	12	0	1.000
1997— Cleveland (A.L.).........		3B	7	26	8	10	1	0	1	3	.385	7	6	0	5	9	0	1.000
2001— Arizona (N.L.)............		3B	7	26	3	7	2	0	1	7	.269	0	6	0	2	13	0	1.000
World Series totals (3 years)			18	68	12	19	3	0	3	11	.279	7	18	0	11	34	0	1.000

ALL-STAR GAME RECORD

NOTES: Named to N.L. All-Star team for 1996 game; replaced by Ken Caminiti due to injury.

Year	League	Pos.	AB	R	H	2B	3B	HR	RBI	Avg.	BB	SO	SB	PO	A	E	Avg.
1990— National......................	PH	1	0	0	0	0	0	0	.000	0	1	0	...	...	...	...
1994— National......................	3B	3	0	0	0	0	0	0	.000	0	2	0	0	1	1	.500
1995— National......................						Selected, did not play—injured.										
1996— National......................						Selected, did not play—injured.										
1999— National......................	3B	3	0	1	0	0	0	0	.333	0	1	0	1	0	1	.500
All-Star Game totals (3 years)		7	0	1	0	0	0	0	.143	0	4	0	1	1	2	.500

WILLIAMS, MIKE   P   PIRATES

PERSONAL: Born July 29, 1968, in Radford, Va. ... 6-2/200. ... Throws right, bats right. ... Full name: Michael Darren Williams.
HIGH SCHOOL: Giles (Pearisburg, Va.).
COLLEGE: Virginia Tech.
TRANSACTIONS/CAREER NOTES: Selected by Philadelphia Phillies organization in 14th round of free-agent draft (June 4, 1990). ... On suspended list (September 26, 1996-remainder of season). ... Granted free agency (December 20, 1996). ... Signed by Boston Red Sox organization (February 15, 1997). ... Released by Red Sox (March 14, 1997). ... Signed by Kansas City Royals organization (April 30, 1997). ... On suspended list (May 16-18, 1997). ... Granted free agency (October 15, 1997). ... Signed by Pittsburgh Pirates organization (December 18, 1997). ... On disabled list (June 24-July 9, 1999). ... Traded by Pirates to Houston Astros for P Tony McKnight (July 31, 2001). ... Granted free agency (November 5, 2001). ... Signed by Pirates (January 2, 2002).
STATISTICAL NOTES: Led N.L. with 16 wild pitches in 1996.
MISCELLANEOUS: Appeared in one game as pinch runner (1996).

Year	League	W	L	Pct.	ERA	G	GS	CG	ShO	Sv.	IP	H	R	ER	BB	SO
1990— Batavia (NY-Penn)	2	3	.400	2.30	27	0	0	0	11	47	39	17	12	13	42
1991— Clearwater (FSL)	7	3	.700	1.74	14	14	2	1	0	93 1/3	65	23	18	14	76
— Reading (East.)..................	7	5	.583	3.69	16	15	2	1	0	102 1/3	93	44	42	36	51
1992— Reading (East.).................	1	2	.333	5.17	3	3	0	0	0	15 2/3	17	10	9	7	12
— Scranton/W.B. (I.L.)	9	1	*.900	2.43	16	16	3	1	0	92 1/3	84	26	25	30	59
— Philadelphia (N.L.)............	1	1	.500	5.34	5	5	1	0	0	28 2/3	29	20	17	7	5
1993— Scranton/W.B. (I.L.)	9	2	*.818	2.87	14	13	1	1	0	97 1/3	93	34	31	16	53
— Philadelphia (N.L.)............	1	3	.250	5.29	17	4	0	0	0	51	50	32	30	22	33
1994— Philadelphia (N.L.)............	2	4	.333	5.01	12	8	0	0	0	50 1/3	61	31	28	20	29
— Scranton/W.B. (I.L.)	2	7	.222	5.79	14	14	1	0	0	84	91	55	54	36	53
1995— Philadelphia (N.L.)............	3	3	.500	3.29	33	8	0	0	0	87 2/3	78	37	32	29	57
— Scranton/W.B. (I.L.)	0	1	.000	4.66	3	3	1	0	0	9 2/3	8	5	5	2	8
1996— Philadelphia (N.L.)............	6	14	.300	5.44	32	29	0	0	0	167	188	107	101	67	103
1997— Omaha (A.A.)■................	3	6	.333	4.22	20	11	1	0	5	79	71	41	37	38	68
— Kansas City (A.L.)	0	2	.000	6.43	10	0	0	0	1	14	20	11	10	8	10
1998— Pittsburgh (N.L.)■..........	4	2	.667	1.94	37	1	0	0	0	51	39	12	11	16	59
— Nashville (PCL)	0	2	.000	5.59	16	4	0	0	0	37	36	25	23	14	34
1999— Pittsburgh (N.L.).............	3	4	.429	5.09	58	0	0	0	23	58 1/3	63	36	33	37	76
2000— Pittsburgh (N.L.).............	3	4	.429	3.50	72	0	0	0	24	72	56	34	28	40	71
2001— Pittsburgh (N.L.).............	2	4	.333	3.67	40	0	0	0	22	41 2/3	39	18	17	21	43
— Houston (N.L.)■..............	4	0	1.000	4.03	25	0	0	0	0	22 1/3	21	10	10	14	16
A.L. totals (1 year)	0	2	.000	6.43	10	0	0	0	1	14	20	11	10	8	10
N.L. totals (9 years)	29	39	.426	4.39	331	55	1	0	69	630	624	337	307	273	492
Major League totals (10 years)	29	41	.414	4.43	341	55	1	0	70	644	644	348	317	281	502

DIVISION SERIES RECORD

Year	League	W	L	Pct.	ERA	G	GS	CG	ShO	Sv.	IP	H	R	ER	BB	SO
2001— Houston (N.L.)	0	0	...	9.00	1	0	0	0	0	1	3	1	1	0	1

WILLIAMS, TODD   P

PERSONAL: Born February 13, 1971, in Syracuse, N.Y. ... 6-3/210. ... Throws right, bats right. ... Full name: Todd Michael Williams.
HIGH SCHOOL: Minoa (East Syracuse, N.Y.).
JUNIOR COLLEGE: Onondaga Community College (N.Y.).
TRANSACTIONS/CAREER NOTES: Selected by Los Angeles Dodgers organization in 54th round of free-agent draft (June 4, 1990). ... On disabled list (April 7-16, 1994). ... Traded by Dodgers to Oakland Athletics for P Matt McDonald (September 8, 1995). ... Released by A's (January 16, 1997).

W

... Signed by Cincinnati Reds organization (February 3, 1997). ... Traded by Reds to Seattle Mariners for OF Kerry Robinson (July 22, 1999). ... On Tacoma disabled list (May 30-June 7, 2000). ... Released by Mariners (November 16, 2000). ... Signed by New York Yankees organization (January 25, 2001). ... On New York disabled list (May 27-July 18, 2000); included rehabilitation assignment to Gulf Coast Yankees (June 25-July 17). ... Granted free agency (October 12, 2001).

MISCELLANEOUS: Member of 2000 U.S. Olympic baseball team.

Year	League	W	L	Pct.	ERA	G	GS	CG	ShO	Sv.	IP	H	R	ER	BB	SO
1991—	Great Falls (Pio.)	5	2	.714	2.72	28	0	0	0	8	53	50	26	16	24	59
1992—	Bakersfield (Calif.)	0	0	...	2.30	13	0	0	0	9	15 2/3	11	4	4	7	11
	—San Antonio (Texas)	7	4	.636	3.27	39	0	0	0	13	44	47	17	16	23	35
1993—	Albuquerque (PCL)	5	5	.500	4.99	*65	0	0	0	*21	70 1/3	87	44	39	31	56
1994—	Albuquerque (PCL)	4	2	.667	3.11	59	0	0	0	13	72 1/3	78	29	25	17	30
1995—	Los Angeles (N.L.)	2	2	.500	5.12	16	0	0	0	0	19 1/3	19	11	11	7	8
	—Albuquerque (PCL)	4	1	.800	3.38	25	0	0	0	0	45 1/3	59	21	17	15	23
1996—	Edmonton (PCL)■	5	3	.625	5.50	35	10	0	0	0	91 2/3	125	71	56	37	33
1997—	Chattanooga (Sou.)■	3	3	.500	2.10	48	0	0	0	*31	55 2/3	38	16	13	25	45
	—Indianapolis (A.A.)	2	0	1.000	2.13	12	0	0	0	2	12 2/3	11	4	3	6	11
1998—	Indianapolis (I.L.)	0	3	.000	2.31	53	0	0	0	*26	58 1/3	54	19	15	24	35
	—Cincinnati (N.L.)	0	1	.000	7.71	6	0	0	0	0	9 1/3	15	8	8	6	4
1999—	Indianapolis (I.L.)	1	3	.250	5.10	38	0	0	0	24	42 1/3	38	24	24	13	35
	—Tacoma (PCL)	0	0	...	0.00	1	0	0	0	1	1 2/3	1	0	0	0	0
	—Seattle (A.L.)	0	0	...	4.66	13	0	0	0	0	9 2/3	11	5	5	7	7
2000—	Tacoma (PCL)	2	3	.400	2.98	50	0	0	0	*32	51 1/3	51	20	17	18	26
2001—	New York (A.L.)■	1	0	1.000	4.70	15	0	0	0	0	15 1/3	22	9	8	9	13
	—GC Yankees (GCL)	0	0	...	0.00	1	1	0	0	0	2	1	0	0	0	5
	—Columbus (Int.)	0	1	.000	7.11	17	0	0	0	2	19	31	19	15	9	14
	—Norwich (East.)	1	0	1.000	0.00	6	0	0	0	1	8	4	0	0	0	5
A.L. totals (2 years)		1	0	1.000	4.68	28	0	0	0	0	25	33	14	13	16	20
N.L. totals (2 years)		2	3	.400	5.97	22	0	0	0	0	28 2/3	34	19	19	13	12
Major League totals (4 years)		3	3	.500	5.37	50	0	0	0	0	53 2/3	67	33	32	29	32

WILLIAMS, WOODY   P   CARDINALS

PERSONAL: Born August 19, 1966, in Houston. ... 6-0/195. ... Throws right, bats right. ... Full name: Gregory Scott Williams.

HIGH SCHOOL: Cypress-Fairbanks (Houston).

COLLEGE: Houston.

TRANSACTIONS/CAREER NOTES: Selected by Toronto Blue Jays organization in 28th round of free-agent draft (June 1, 1988). ... On disabled list (April 9-May 17, 1992). ... On Toronto disabled list (July 17, 1995-remainder of season); included rehabilitation assignment to Syracuse (August 15-25). ... On Toronto disabled list (March 22-May 31 and June 11-July 26, 1996); included rehabilitation assignments to Dunedin (May 2-10), Syracuse (May 10-28 and July 13-20) and St. Catharines (July 20-26). ... Traded by Blue Jays with P Carlos Almanzar and OF Peter Tucci to San Diego Padres for P Joey Hamilton (December 13, 1998). ... On San Diego disabled list (May 2-July 2, 2000); included rehabilitation assignments to Rancho Cucamonga (June 22-27) and Las Vegas (June 28). ... Traded by Padres to St. Louis Cardinals for OF Ray Lankford and cash (August 2, 2001).

MISCELLANEOUS: Appeared in one game as pinch runner (1999). ... Scored three runs in four appearances as pinch runner (2000). ... Struck out twice in two appearances as pinch hitter (2000). ... Appeared in two games as pinch runner (2001). ... Appeared in one game as pinch hitter (2001).

Year	League	W	L	Pct.	ERA	G	GS	CG	ShO	Sv.	IP	H	R	ER	BB	SO
1988—	St. Catharines (NY-Penn)	8	2	.800	1.54	12	12	2	0	0	76	48	22	13	21	58
	—Knoxville (Sou.)	2	2	.500	3.81	6	4	0	0	0	28 1/3	27	13	12	12	25
1989—	Dunedin (FSL)	3	5	.375	2.32	20	9	0	0	3	81 1/3	63	26	21	27	60
	—Knoxville (Sou.)	3	5	.375	3.55	14	12	2	•2	1	71	61	32	28	33	51
1990—	Knoxville (Sou.)	7	9	.438	3.14	42	12	0	0	5	126	111	55	44	39	74
	—Syracuse (I.L.)	0	1	.000	10.00	3	0	0	0	0	9	15	10	10	4	8
1991—	Knoxville (Sou.)	3	2	.600	3.59	18	1	0	0	3	42 2/3	42	18	17	14	37
	—Syracuse (I.L.)	3	4	.429	4.12	31	0	0	0	6	54 2/3	52	27	25	27	37
1992—	Syracuse (I.L.)	6	8	.429	3.13	25	16	1	0	1	120 2/3	115	46	42	41	81
1993—	Syracuse (I.L.)	1	1	.500	2.20	12	0	0	0	3	16 1/3	15	5	4	5	16
	—Toronto (A.L.)	3	1	.750	4.38	30	0	0	0	0	37	40	18	18	22	24
	—Dunedin (FSL)	0	0	...	0.00	2	0	0	0	0	4	0	0	0	2	2
1994—	Toronto (A.L.)	1	3	.250	3.64	38	0	0	0	0	59 1/3	44	24	24	33	56
	—Syracuse (I.L.)	0	0	...	0.00	1	0	0	0	1	1 2/3	0	0	0	0	1
1995—	Toronto (A.L.)	1	2	.333	3.69	23	3	0	0	0	53 2/3	44	23	22	28	41
	—Syracuse (I.L.)	0	0	...	3.52	5	1	0	0	1	7 2/3	5	3	3	5	13
1996—	Dunedin (FSL)	0	2	.000	8.22	2	2	0	0	0	7 2/3	9	7	7	2	11
	—Syracuse (I.L.)	3	1	.750	1.41	7	7	1	1	0	32	22	5	5	7	33
	—Toronto (A.L.)	4	5	.444	4.73	12	10	1	0	0	59	64	33	31	21	43
	—St. Catharines (NY-Penn)	0	0	...	3.68	2	2	0	0	0	7 1/3	7	3	3	4	12
1997—	Toronto (A.L.)	9	14	.391	4.35	31	31	0	0	0	194 2/3	201	98	94	66	124
1998—	Toronto (A.L.)	10	9	.526	4.46	32	32	1	1	0	209 2/3	196	112	104	81	151
1999—	San Diego (N.L.)■	12	12	.500	4.41	33	33	0	0	0	208 1/3	213	106	102	73	137
2000—	San Diego (N.L.)	10	8	.556	3.75	23	23	4	0	0	168	152	74	70	54	111
	—Rancho Cuca. (Calif.)	0	0	...	0.00	1	1	0	0	0	5	3	0	0	1	10
	—Las Vegas (PCL)	0	0	...	1.50	1	1	0	0	0	6	7	2	1	0	5
2001—	San Diego (N.L.)	8	8	.500	4.97	23	23	0	0	0	145	170	88	80	37	102
	—St. Louis (N.L.)■	7	1	.875	2.28	11	11	3	1	0	75	54	22	19	19	52
A.L. totals (6 years)		28	34	.452	4.30	166	76	2	1	0	613 1/3	589	308	293	251	439
N.L. totals (3 years)		37	29	.561	4.09	90	90	7	1	0	596 1/3	589	290	271	183	402
Major League totals (9 years)		65	63	.508	4.20	256	166	9	2	0	1209 2/3	1178	598	564	434	841

DIVISION SERIES RECORD

Year	League	W	L	Pct.	ERA	G	GS	CG	ShO	Sv.	IP	H	R	ER	BB	SO
2001—	St. Louis (N.L.)	1	0	1.000	1.29	1	1	0	0	0	7	4	1	1	1	9

WILLIAMSON, SCOTT　　　　　P　　　　　REDS

PERSONAL: Born February 17, 1976, in Fort Polk, La. ... 6-0/185. ... Throws right, bats right. ... Full name: Scott Ryan Williamson.
HIGH SCHOOL: Friendswood (Texas).
COLLEGE: Tulane, then Oklahoma State.
TRANSACTIONS/CAREER NOTES: Selected by Cincinnati Reds organization in ninth round of free-agent draft (June 3, 1997). ... On disabled list (August 24-September 8, 2000; and April 4, 2001-remainder of season).
RECORDS: Shares N.L. single-game record for most consecutive strikeouts by relief pitcher—6 (May 27, 1999).
HONORS: Named N.L. Rookie Pitcher of the Year by THE SPORTING NEWS (1999). ... Named N.L. Rookie of the Year by Baseball Writers' Association of America (1999).
STATISTICAL NOTES: Tied for Pioneer League lead with 12 wild pitches in 1997.

Year	League	W	L	Pct.	ERA	G	GS	CG	ShO	Sv.	IP	H	R	ER	BB	SO
1997—	Billings (Pio.)	•8	2	.800	1.78	13	13	2	•1	0	86	66	25	17	23	*101
1998—	Chattanooga (Sou.)	4	5	.444	3.78	18	18	0	0	0	100	85	49	42	46	105
—	Indianapolis (I.L.)	0	0	...	3.48	5	5	0	0	0	20 2/3	20	9	8	9	17
1999—	Cincinnati (N.L.)	12	7	.632	2.41	62	0	0	0	19	93 1/3	54	29	25	43	107
2000—	Cincinnati (N.L.)	5	8	.385	3.29	48	10	0	0	6	112	92	45	41	75	136
2001—	Cincinnati (N.L.)	0	0	...	0.00	2	0	0	0	0	2/3	1	0	0	2	0
Major League totals (3 years)		17	15	.531	2.88	112	10	0	0	25	206	147	74	66	120	243

ALL-STAR GAME RECORD

Year	League	W	L	Pct.	ERA	GS	CG	ShO	Sv.	IP	H	R	ER	BB	SO
1999—	National					Selected—did not play.									

WILSON, CRAIG　　　　　1B/C　　　　　PIRATES

PERSONAL: Born November 30, 1976, in Fountain Valley, Calif. ... 6-2/217. ... Bats right, throws right. ... Full name: Craig Alan Wilson.
HIGH SCHOOL: Marina (Huntington Beach, Calif.).
TRANSACTIONS/CAREER NOTES: Selected by Toronto Blue Jays organization in second round of free-agent draft (June 1, 1995). ... Traded by Blue Jays to Pittsburgh Pirates (December 11, 1996), completing deal in which Pirates traded 2B Carlos Garcia, 1B Orlando Merced and P Dan Plesac to Blue Jays for P Mike Halperin, SS Abraham Nunez, P Jose Pett, P Jose Silva, SS Brandon Cromer and a player to be named later (November 14, 1996).
RECORDS: Shares major league single-season record for most home runs by pinch-hitter—7 (2001).
STATISTICAL NOTES: Led Carolina League catchers with 21 double plays in 1997.

Year	Team (League)	Pos.	G	AB	R	H	2B	3B	HR	RBI	Avg.	BB	SO	SB	PO	A	E	Avg.
1995—	Medicine Hat (Pio.)	C	49	184	33	52	14	1	7	35	.283	24	44	8	237	29	5	.982
1996—	Hagerstown (S.Atl.)	C-OF	131	495	66	129	27	5	11	70	.261	32	120	17	552	78	9	.986
1997—	Lynchburg (Caro.)■	C	117	401	54	106	26	1	19	69	.264	39	98	6	714	76	12	.985
1998—	Lynchburg (Caro.)	C-1B	61	219	26	59	12	2	12	45	.269	22	53	2	374	37	6	.986
—	Carolina (Sou.)	C	45	148	20	49	11	0	5	21	.331	14	32	4	185	13	1	.995
1999—	Altoona (East.)	C-OF-1B	111	362	57	97	21	3	20	69	.268	40	104	1	350	41	9	.978
2000—	Nashville (PCL)	C-1B	124	396	83	112	24	1	33	86	.283	44	121	1	638	59	13	.982
2001—	Nashville (PCL)	1B-C	11	45	4	13	2	1	1	3	.289	2	14	0	77	5	2	.976
—	Pittsburgh (N.L.)	1B-OF-C-DH	88	158	27	49	3	1	13	32	.310	15	53	3	205	15	3	.987
Major League totals (1 year)			88	158	27	49	3	1	13	32	.310	15	53	3	205	15	3	.987

WILSON, DAN　　　　　C　　　　　MARINERS

PERSONAL: Born March 25, 1969, in Arlington Heights, Ill. ... 6-3/202. ... Bats right, throws right. ... Full name: Daniel Allen Wilson.
HIGH SCHOOL: Barrington (Ill.).
COLLEGE: Minnesota.
TRANSACTIONS/CAREER NOTES: Selected by New York Mets organization in 26th round of free-agent draft (June 2, 1987); did not sign. ... Selected by Cincinnati Reds organization in first round (seventh pick overall) of free-agent draft (June 4, 1990). ... Traded by Reds with P Bobby Ayala to Seattle Mariners for P Erik Hanson and 2B Bret Boone (November 2, 1993). ... On disabled list (July 21-September 1, 1998). ... On Seattle disabled list (June 15-July 14, 2000); included rehabilitation assignments to Everett (July 12-13) and Tacoma (July 14).
RECORDS: Holds A.L. single-season record for most putouts by catcher—1,051 (1997). ... Shares major league single-game record for most putouts by catcher (nine-inning game)—20 (August 8, 1997); most putouts by catcher (extra-inning game)—21 (March 31, 1996, 12 innings); and most chances accepted by catcher (nine-inning game) since 1900—20 (August 8, 1997). ... Shares A.L. single-game record for most putouts by catcher (extra-inning game)—21 (March 31, 1996, 12 innings).
STATISTICAL NOTES: Led American Association catchers with 810 total chances in 1992. ... Led A.L. catchers with 952 total chances in 1995 and 1,129 in 1997. ... Hit three home runs in one game (April 11, 1996). ... Tied for A.L. lead in double plays by catcher with 13 in 1997. ... Career major league grand slams: 2.

Year	Team (League)	Pos.	G	AB	R	H	2B	3B	HR	RBI	Avg.	BB	SO	SB	PO	A	E	Avg.
1990—	Charl., W.Va. (S.Atl.)	C	32	113	16	28	9	1	2	17	.248	13	17	0	190	24	1	.995
1991—	Charl., W.Va. (S.Atl.)	C	52	197	25	62	11	1	3	29	.315	25	21	1	355	41	3	.992
—	Chattanooga (Sou.)	C	81	292	32	75	19	2	2	38	.257	21	39	2	486	49	4	.993
1992—	Nashville (A.A.)	C	106	366	27	92	16	1	4	34	.251	31	58	1	*733	*69	*8	.990
—	Cincinnati (N.L.)	C	12	25	2	9	1	0	0	3	.360	3	8	0	42	4	0	1.000
1993—	Cincinnati (N.L.)	C	36	76	6	17	3	0	0	8	.224	9	16	0	146	9	1	.994
—	Indianapolis (A.A.)	C	51	191	18	50	11	1	1	17	.262	19	31	1	314	24	2	.994
1994—	Seattle (A.L.)■	C	91	282	24	61	14	2	3	27	.216	10	57	1	602	45	*9	.986
1995—	Seattle (A.L.)	C	119	399	40	111	22	3	9	51	.278	33	63	2	*895	52	5	.995
1996—	Seattle (A.L.)	C	138	491	51	140	24	0	18	83	.285	32	88	1	834	58	4	.996
1997—	Seattle (A.L.)	C	146	508	66	137	31	1	15	74	.270	39	72	7	*1051	72	6	.995
1998—	Seattle (A.L.)	C	96	325	39	82	17	1	9	44	.252	24	56	2	677	35	4	.994
1999—	Seattle (A.L.)	C-1B	123	414	46	110	23	2	7	38	.266	29	83	5	753	48	4	.995

W

Year	Team (League)	Pos.	G	AB	R	H	2B	3B	HR	RBI	Avg.	BB	SO	SB	PO	A	E	Avg.
2000—	Seattle (A.L.)	C-1B-3B	90	268	31	63	12	0	5	27	.235	22	51	1	485	30	5	.990
—Everett (N'West)		C	1	2	2	1	0	0	1	1	.500	1	0	0	3	1	0	1.000
—Tacoma (PCL)		DH	1	4	0	1	1	0	0	0	.250	0	1	0	...	...	...	...
2001—	Seattle (A.L.)	C-1B	123	377	44	100	20	1	10	42	.265	20	69	3	714	32	1	.999
American League totals (8 years)			926	3064	341	804	163	10	76	386	.262	209	539	22	6011	372	38	.994
National League totals (2 years)			48	101	8	26	4	0	0	11	.257	12	24	0	188	13	1	.995
Major League totals (10 years)			974	3165	349	830	167	10	76	397	.262	221	563	22	6199	385	39	.994

DIVISION SERIES RECORD

Year	Team (League)	Pos.	G	AB	R	H	2B	3B	HR	RBI	Avg.	BB	SO	SB	PO	A	E	Avg.
1995—	Seattle (A.L.)	C	5	17	0	2	0	0	0	1	.118	2	6	0	34	1	0	1.000
1997—	Seattle (A.L.)	C	4	13	0	0	0	0	0	0	.000	0	9	0	29	1	0	1.000
2000—	Seattle (A.L.)	C	2	3	0	0	0	0	0	0	.000	1	2	0	5	0	1	.833
2001—	Seattle (A.L.)	C	5	15	0	3	1	0	0	0	.200	0	5	0	40	1	0	1.000
Division series totals (4 years)			16	48	0	5	1	0	0	2	.104	3	22	0	108	3	1	.991

CHAMPIONSHIP SERIES RECORD

Year	Team (League)	Pos.	G	AB	R	H	2B	3B	HR	RBI	Avg.	BB	SO	SB	PO	A	E	Avg.
1995—	Seattle (A.L.)	C	6	16	0	0	0	0	0	0	.000	0	4	0	35	3	1	.974
2000—	Seattle (A.L.)	C	4	11	0	1	0	0	0	0	.091	1	5	0	20	4	1	.960
2001—	Seattle (A.L.)	C-PH	4	13	2	2	0	0	0	0	.154	0	1	0	22	2	0	1.000
Championship series totals (3 years)			14	40	2	3	0	0	0	0	.075	1	10	0	77	9	2	.977

ALL-STAR GAME RECORD

Year	League	Pos.	AB	R	H	2B	3B	HR	RBI	Avg.	BB	SO	SB	PO	A	E	Avg.
1996—	American	PH	1	0	0	0	0	0	0	.000	0	0	0	...	...	...	...

WILSON, ENRIQUE — IF — YANKEES

PERSONAL: Born July 27, 1975, in Santo Domingo, Dominican Republic. ... 5-11/195. ... Bats both, throws right. ... Full name: Enrique Martes Wilson.

HIGH SCHOOL: Liceo Ramon Amelio Jiminez (Santo Domingo, Dominican Republic).

TRANSACTIONS/CAREER NOTES: Signed as non-drafted free agent by Minnesota Twins organization (April 15, 1992). ... Traded by Twins to Cleveland Indians (February 21, 1994), completing deal in which Twins acquired P Shawn Bryant for a player to be named later (February 21, 1994). ... On Cleveland disabled list (April 4-June 15, 1998); included rehabilitation assignment to Buffalo (June 2-15). ... On Cleveland disabled list (July 14-July 28, 2000). ... Traded by Indians with OF Alex Ramirez to Pittsburgh Pirates for 1B/OF Wil Cordero (July 28, 2000). ... On Pittsburgh disabled list (July 29-August 1, 2000); included rehabilitation assignment to Nashville (July 31-August 1). ... Traded by Pirates to New York Yankees for P Damaso Marte (June 13, 2001).

STATISTICAL NOTES: Led South Atlantic League shortstops with 625 total chances and 66 double plays in 1994. ... Led Carolina League with 10 sacrifice flies in 1995. ... Led Eastern League shortstops with 74 double plays in 1996. ... Career major league grand slams: 1.

Year	Team (League)	Pos.	G	AB	R	H	2B	3B	HR	RBI	Avg.	BB	SO	SB	PO	A	E	Avg.
1992—	GC Twins (GCL)	SS	13	44	12	15	1	0	0	8	.341	4	4	3	9	26	4	.897
1993—	Elizabethton (Appl.)	SS-3B	58	197	42	57	8	4	13	50	.289	14	18	5	50	139	19	.909
1994—	Columbus (S.Atl.)■	SS	133	512	82	143	28	12	10	72	.279	44	34	21	*185	*407	33	.947
1995—	Kinston (Caro.)	SS-2B	117	464	55	124	24	•7	6	52	.267	25	38	18	181	375	21	.964
1996—	Canton/Akron (East.)	SS-2B	117	484	70	147	17	5	5	50	.304	31	46	23	179	344	28	.949
—Buffalo (A.A.)		3B-SS	3	8	1	4	1	0	0	0	.500	1	1	0	1	2	1	.750
1997—	Buffalo (A.A.)	SS-2B-3B	118	451	78	138	20	3	11	39	.306	42	41	9	218	332	20	.965
—Cleveland (A.L.)		SS-2B	5	15	2	5	0	0	0	1	.333	0	2	0	7	13	1	.952
1998—	Cleveland (A.L.)	2B-SS-3B	32	90	13	29	6	0	2	12	.322	4	8	2	43	76	2	.983
—Buffalo (I.L.)		2B-SS	56	221	40	62	13	0	4	23	.281	19	21	8	108	141	6	.976
1999—	Cleveland (A.L.)	3-S-2-DH	113	332	41	87	22	1	2	24	.262	25	41	5	77	163	8	.968
2000—	Cleveland (A.L.)	3B-DH-2B-SS	40	117	16	38	9	0	2	12	.325	7	11	2	20	44	1	.985
—Nashville (PCL)■		2B-SS	2	7	0	2	0	0	0	1	.286	0	0	0	4	4	1	.889
—Pittsburgh (N.L.)		3B-2B-SS	40	122	11	32	6	1	3	15	.262	11	13	0	24	73	6	.942
2001—	Pittsburgh (N.L.)	SS-2B-3B	46	129	7	24	3	0	1	8	.186	3	23	0	56	92	4	.974
—New York (A.L.)■		SS-3B-2B-DH	48	99	10	24	5	1	1	12	.242	6	14	0	29	73	2	.981
American League totals (5 years)			238	653	82	183	42	2	7	61	.280	42	76	9	176	369	14	.975
National League totals (2 years)			86	251	18	56	9	1	4	23	.223	14	36	0	80	165	10	.961
Major League totals (5 years)			324	904	100	239	51	3	11	84	.264	56	112	9	256	534	24	.971

DIVISION SERIES RECORD

Year	Team (League)	Pos.	G	AB	R	H	2B	3B	HR	RBI	Avg.	BB	SO	SB	PO	A	E	Avg.
1998—	Cleveland (A.L.)	2B	1	2	0	0	0	0	0	0	.000	0	0	0	2	2	0	1.000
1999—	Cleveland (A.L.)	2B-PH	3	2	0	0	0	0	0	0	.000	0	0	0	3	0	0	1.000
Division series totals (2 years)			4	4	0	0	0	0	0	0	.000	0	0	0	5	2	0	1.000

CHAMPIONSHIP SERIES RECORD

Year	Team (League)	Pos.	G	AB	R	H	2B	3B	HR	RBI	Avg.	BB	SO	SB	PO	A	E	Avg.
1998—	Cleveland (A.L.)	PR-2B	5	14	2	3	0	0	0	1	.214	1	3	0	5	19	1	.960
2001—	New York (A.L.)	SS	1	1	0	1	0	0	0	0	1.000	0	0	0	0	0	0	...
Championship series totals (2 years)			6	15	2	4	0	0	0	1	.267	1	3	0	5	19	1	.960

WORLD SERIES RECORD

Year	Team (League)	Pos.	G	AB	R	H	2B	3B	HR	RBI	Avg.	BB	SO	SB	PO	A	E	Avg.
2001—	New York (A.L.)	PH-SS	2	3	0	0	0	0	0	0	.000	0	0	0	0	1	0	1.000

WILSON, JACK   SS   PIRATES

PERSONAL: Born December 29, 1977, in Westlake, Calif. ... 6-0/175. ... Bats right, throws right. ... Full name: Jack Eugene Wilson.
HIGH SCHOOL: Thousand Oaks (Calif.).
JUNIOR COLLEGE: Oxnard.
TRANSACTIONS/CAREER NOTES: Selected by St. Louis Cardinals organization in ninth round of free-agent draft (June 2, 1998). ... Traded by Cardinals to Pittsburgh Pirates for P Jason Christiansen (July 30, 2000).
STATISTICAL NOTES: Tied for N.L. lead with 17 sacrifice hits in 2001.

							BATTING							FIELDING		
Year	Team (League)	Pos.	G	AB	R	H	2B	3B	HR	RBI	Avg.	BB	SO	SB	PO	A	E	Avg.
1998—	Johnson City (Appl.) ..	SS	61	241	50	90	18	4	4	29	*.373	18	30	22	85	164	16	.940
1999—	Peoria (Midw.)............	SS	64	251	47	86	22	4	3	28	.343	15	23	11	84	182	16	.943
	— Potomac (Caro.)........	SS	64	257	44	76	10	1	2	18	.296	19	31	7	98	187	18	.941
2000—	Potomac (Caro.)........	SS	13	47	7	13	0	1	2	7	.277	5	10	2	20	39	2	.967
	— Arkansas (Texas).......	SS	88	343	65	101	20	8	6	34	.294	36	59	2	140	262	12	.971
	— Altoona (East.)■	SS	33	139	17	35	7	2	1	16	.252	14	17	1	47	93	5	.966
2001—	Pittsburgh (N.L.)......	SS	108	390	44	87	17	1	3	25	.223	16	70	1	136	342	16	.968
	— Nashville (PCL)	SS	27	103	20	38	6	1	1	6	.369	9	13	2	30	81	3	.974
Major League totals (1 year)			108	390	44	87	17	1	3	25	.223	16	70	1	136	342	16	.968

WILSON, KRIS   P   ROYALS

PERSONAL: Born August 6, 1976, in Washington, D.C. ... 6-3/225. ... Throws right, bats right. ... Full name: Kristopher Kyle Wilson.
HIGH SCHOOL: Tarpon Springs (Fla.).
COLLEGE: Georgia Tech.
TRANSACTIONS/CAREER NOTES: Selected by Kansas City Royals organization in ninth round of free-agent draft (June 3, 1997).

Year	League	W	L	Pct.	ERA	G	GS	CG	ShO	Sv.	IP	H	R	ER	BB	SO
1997—	Spokane (N'West)	5	3	.625	4.52	15	15	0	0	0	73²/₃	101	50	37	21	72
1998—	Wilmington (Caro.)............	0	3	.000	3.75	10	2	0	0	1	24	19	10	10	6	20
	— Lansing (Midw.)	10	5	.667	3.53	18	18	1	0	0	117¹/₃	119	50	46	15	74
1999—	Wilmington (Caro.)............	8	1	.889	1.13	14	4	0	0	0	48	25	7	6	11	45
	— Omaha (PCL)......................	0	1	.000	8.44	1	1	0	0	0	5¹/₃	8	5	5	0	3
	— Wichita (Texas)	5	7	.417	5.45	23	10	0	0	0	74¹/₃	91	51	45	14	45
2000—	Kansas City (A.L.)	0	1	.000	4.19	20	0	0	0	0	34¹/₃	38	16	16	11	17
	— Wichita (Texas)	7	3	.700	3.51	21	15	0	0	0	102²/₃	99	52	40	21	69
2001—	Kansas City (A.L.)	6	5	.545	5.19	29	15	0	0	1	109¹/₃	132	78	63	32	67
	— Omaha (PCL)......................	2	2	.500	2.79	6	5	0	0	0	29	31	9	9	6	18
Major League totals (2 years)		6	6	.500	4.95	49	15	0	0	1	143²/₃	170	94	79	43	84

WILSON, PAUL   P   DEVIL RAYS

PERSONAL: Born March 28, 1973, in Orlando. ... 6-5/235. ... Throws right, bats right. ... Full name: Paul Anthony Wilson.
HIGH SCHOOL: William R. Boone (Orlando).
COLLEGE: Florida State.
TRANSACTIONS/CAREER NOTES: Selected by New York Mets organization in first round (first pick overall) of free-agent draft (June 2, 1994). ... On New York disabled list (June 5-July 15, 1996); included rehabilitation assignments to St. Lucie (June 28-July 10) and Binghamton (July 10-15). ... On New York disabled list (March 27, 1997-entire season); included rehabilitation assignments to Gulf Coast Mets (August 2-23) and St. Lucie (August 28-September 8). ... On New York disabled list (March 13-August 4, 1998); included rehabilitation assignment to St. Lucie (July 9-August 1). ... On disabled list (April 8, 1999-entire season). ... Traded by Mets with OF Jason Tyner to Tampa Bay Devil Rays for OF Bubba Trammell and P Rick White (July 28, 2000).
STATISTICAL NOTES: Named Eastern League Pitcher of the Year (1995).

Year	League	W	L	Pct.	ERA	G	GS	CG	ShO	Sv.	IP	H	R	ER	BB	SO
1994—	Gulf Coast Mets (GCL)	0	2	.000	3.00	3	3	0	0	0	12	8	4	4	4	13
	— St. Lucie (FSL)	0	5	.000	5.06	8	8	0	0	0	37¹/₃	32	23	21	17	37
1995—	Binghamton (East.)	6	3	.667	*2.17	16	16	4	1	0	120¹/₃	89	34	29	24	127
	— Norfolk (I.L.)	5	3	.625	2.85	10	10	•4	2	0	66¹/₃	59	25	21	20	67
1996—	New York (N.L.)..................	5	12	.294	5.38	26	26	1	0	0	149	157	102	89	71	109
	— St. Lucie (FSL)	0	1	.000	3.38	2	2	0	0	0	8	6	5	3	4	5
	— Binghamton (East.)	0	1	.000	7.20	1	1	0	0	0	5	6	4	4	5	5
1997—	Gulf Coast Mets (GCL)	1	0	1.000	1.45	4	3	0	0	1	18²/₃	14	7	3	4	18
	— St. Lucie (FSL)	0	0	...	2.57	1	1	0	0	0	7	6	2	2	0	6
1998—	St. Lucie (FSL)	0	1	.000	6.38	5	5	0	0	0	18¹/₃	23	13	13	4	16
	— Norfolk (I.L.)	4	1	.800	4.42	7	7	0	0	0	38²/₃	42	19	19	9	30
1999—	Norfolk (I.L.)							Did not play.								
2000—	St. Lucie (FSL)	2	0	1.000	1.40	5	5	0	0	0	25²/₃	22	9	4	4	19
	— Norfolk (I.L.)	5	5	.500	4.23	15	13	0	0	0	83	85	40	39	25	56
	— Tampa Bay (A.L.)■............	1	4	.200	3.35	11	7	0	0	0	51	38	20	19	16	40
2001—	Tampa Bay (A.L.)................	8	9	.471	4.88	37	24	0	0	0	151¹/₃	165	94	82	52	119
A.L. totals (2 years)		9	13	.409	4.49	48	31	0	0	0	202¹/₃	203	114	101	68	159
N.L. totals (1 year)......................		5	12	.294	5.38	26	26	1	0	0	149	157	102	89	71	109
Major League totals (3 years)		14	25	.359	4.87	74	57	1	0	0	351¹/₃	360	216	190	139	268

WILSON, PRESTON   OF   MARLINS

PERSONAL: Born July 19, 1974, in Bamberg, S.C. ... 6-2/208. ... Bats right, throws right. ... Full name: Preston James Richard Wilson. ... Stepson of Mookie Wilson, first base/outfield coach, New York Mets; and outfielder with Mets (1980-89) and Toronto Blue Jays (1989-91).
HIGH SCHOOL: Bamberg Erhardt (Bamberg, S.C.).

W

TRANSACTIONS/CAREER NOTES: Selected by New York Mets organization in first round (ninth pick overall) of free-agent draft (June 1, 1992). ... On disabled list (April 4-29, May 21-July 13 and July 29-September 8, 1996). ... On Norfolk disabled list (April 20-May 2, 1998). ... Traded by Mets with P Ed Yarnall and P Geoff Goetz to Florida Marlins for C Mike Piazza (May 22, 1998). ... On Florida disabled list (July 2-August 10, 2001); included rehabilitation assignment to Calgary (August 7-10).

HONORS: Named N.L. Rookie Player of the Year by THE SPORTING NEWS (1999).

STATISTICAL NOTES: Led Appalachian League third basemen with 197 total chances in 1993. ... Career major league grand slams: 2.

Year Team (League)	Pos.	G	AB	R	H	2B	3B	HR	RBI	Avg.	BB	SO	SB	PO	A	E	Avg.
1993— Kingsport (Appl.)........	3B	66	259	44	60	10	0	*16	48	.232	24	75	6	*45	*127	*25	.873
— Pittsfield (NY-Penn)....	3B	8	29	6	16	5	1	1	12	.552	2	7	1	5	9	6	.700
1994— Capital City (S.Atl.).....	3B	131	474	55	108	17	4	14	58	.228	20	135	10	78	281	47	.884
1995— Capital City (S.Atl.).....	OF	111	442	70	119	26	5	20	61	.269	19	114	20	189	10	8	.961
1996— St. Lucie (FSL)	OF	23	85	6	15	3	0	1	7	.176	8	21	1	39	4	2	.956
1997— St. Lucie (FSL)	OF-DH	63	245	32	60	12	1	11	48	.245	8	66	3	104	5	3	.973
— Binghamton (East.)	OF-DH-3B	70	259	37	74	12	1	19	47	.286	21	71	7	116	3	6	.952
1998— Norfolk (I.L.)	OF	18	73	9	18	5	1	1	9	.247	2	22	1	44	2	2	.958
— New York (N.L.)..........	OF	8	20	3	6	2	0	0	2	.300	2	8	1	10	0	1	.909
— Charlotte (I.L.)■........	OF-DH	94	356	71	99	25	3	25	77	.278	34	121	14	180	8	4	.979
— Florida (N.L.)	OF	14	31	4	2	0	0	1	1	.065	4	13	0	13	0	0	1.000
1999— Florida (N.L.)	OF	149	482	67	135	21	4	26	71	.280	46	156	11	320	10	9	.973
2000— Florida (N.L.)	OF	161	605	94	160	35	3	31	121	.264	55	*187	36	387	9	5	.988
2001— Florida (N.L.)	OF	123	468	70	128	30	2	23	71	.274	36	107	20	287	12	2	.993
— Calgary (PCL)..........	OF	4	10	3	5	2	0	0	1	.500	5	1	2	9	0	0	1.000
Major League totals (4 years)		455	1606	238	431	88	9	81	266	.268	143	471	68	1017	31	17	.984

WILSON, TOM   C   BLUE JAYS

PERSONAL: Born December 19, 1970, in Fullerton, Calif. ... 6-3/220. ... Bats right, throws right. ... Full name: Thomas Leroy Wilson.
HIGH SCHOOL: Troy (Fullerton, Calif.).
JUNIOR COLLEGE: Fullerton.
TRANSACTIONS/CAREER NOTES: Selected by New York Yankees organization in 23rd round of free-agent draft (June 4, 1990). ... Traded by Yankees to Cleveland Indians for C Ryan Martindale and OF Marc Marini (April 6, 1996). ... Released by Indians (October 15, 1996). ... Signed by Yankees organization (February 1, 1997). ... Granted free agency (October 17, 1997). ... Signed by Arizona Diamondbacks organization (December 15, 1997). ... Granted free agency (October 16, 1998). ... Signed by Tampa Bay Devil Rays organization (November 23, 1998). ... Granted free agency (October 15, 1999). ... Signed by Yankees organization (November 9, 1999). ... Granted free agency (October 15, 2000). ... Signed by Oakland Athletics organization (November 7, 2000). ... Traded by A's to Toronto Blue Jays for C Mike Kremblas (January 2, 2002).
STATISTICAL NOTES: Led New York-Pennsylvania League catchers with 25 passes balls in 1991. ... Led South Atlantic League catchers with 23 passed balls in 1992. ... Led Eastern League catchers with 744 putouts and 822 total chances in 1994. ... Led Eastern League catchers with 694 putouts and 781 total chances in 1997. ... Tied for Pacific Coast League lead in errors by catcher with 12 in 1998.

Year Team (League)	Pos.	G	AB	R	H	2B	3B	HR	RBI	Avg.	BB	SO	SB	PO	A	E	Avg.
1991— Oneonta (NY-Penn)	C-OF	70	243	38	59	12	2	4	42	.243	34	72	4	295	29	17	.950
1992— Greensboro (S.Atl.)	C-OF	117	395	50	83	22	0	6	48	.210	68	128	2	547	76	10	.984
1993— Greensboro (S.Atl.)	C	120	394	55	98	20	1	10	63	.249	•91	112	2	*850	92	13	.986
1994— Albany (East.)............	C-3B	123	408	54	100	20	1	7	42	.245	58	100	4	†746	75	8	.990
1995— Columbus (I.L.)	C	22	62	11	16	3	1	0	9	.258	9	10	0	109	16	5	.962
— Norwich (East.)	C-3B	28	84	6	12	4	0	0	4	.143	17	22	0	135	26	6	.964
— Tampa (FSL).............	C	17	48	3	8	0	0	0	2	.167	11	13	1	85	7	0	1.000
1996— Columbus (I.L.)	DH	1	1	0	0	0	0	0	0	.000	1	0	0	...	...	...	...
— Buffalo (A.A.)■	C-SS	72	208	28	56	14	2	9	30	.269	35	66	0	386	26	5	.988
1997— Norwich (East.)■........	C-1B-3B	124	419	88	124	21	4	21	80	.296	86	126	1	707	84	8	.990
— Columbus (I.L.)	C	1	3	0	0	0	0	0	0	.000	1	0	0	8	0	0	1.000
1998— Tucson (PCL)■........C-1B-OF-3B		111	370	59	112	17	3	12	54	.303	41	81	3	655	56	‡16	.978
1999— Durham (I.L.)■........	C-OF-1B	67	215	41	60	19	0	16	44	.279	49	59	0	400	46	6	.987
— Orlando (Sou.)	C	30	104	12	30	2	0	7	23	.288	18	34	0	121	15	4	.971
2000— Columbus (I.L.)■.......	C-OF-3B	104	330	63	91	20	0	20	71	.276	73	114	2	565	34	8	.987
2001— Sacramento (PCL)■...C-3B-OF-1B		77	259	43	73	15	1	8	48	.282	49	62	0	367	36	5	.988
— Oakland (A.L.)	C	9	21	4	4	0	0	2	4	.190	1	5	0	35	3	1	.974
Major League totals (1 year)		9	21	4	4	0	0	2	4	.190	1	5	0	35	3	1	.974

WILSON, TRAVIS   2B   BRAVES

W

PERSONAL: Born July 10, 1977, in Christ Church, New Zealand. ... 6-2/185. ... Bats right, throws right. ... Full name: Travis David Wilson.
HIGH SCHOOL: St. Bede's (Christ Church, New Zealand).
COLLEGE: Cantebury (Christ Church, New Zealand).
TRANSACTIONS/CAREER NOTES: Signed as non-drafted free agent by Atlanta Braves organization (August 31, 1996). ... On Richmond disabled list (July 27-August 5, 2001).
STATISTICAL NOTES: Led Appalachian League third basemen with 219 total chances and 13 double plays in 1998.

Year Team (League)	Pos.	G	AB	R	H	2B	3B	HR	RBI	Avg.	BB	SO	SB	PO	A	E	Avg.
1997— Danville (Appl.)...........	3B-OF	61	233	29	50	14	6	0	27	.215	14	60	4	33	88	26	.823
1998— Danville (Appl.)..........	3B	65	269	48	87	25	5	9	48	.323	17	54	16	*55	*150	14	.936
— Macon (S.Atl.)..........	3B	3	13	2	6	0	0	1	4	.462	0	3	0	1	0	0	1.000
1999— Macon (S.Atl.)..........	2B-1B	90	363	65	112	20	4	11	63	.309	9	66	14	182	162	9	.975
2000— Myrtle Beach (Caro.)..	2B-OF	125	484	62	133	33	5	12	63	.275	16	111	7	214	287	17	.967
2001— Greenville (Sou.)	2B-OF-1B	31	123	13	40	8	1	2	21	.325	3	24	2	67	59	3	.977
— Richmond (I.L.)..........OF-2B-3B-1B	103	383	34	93	22	3	3	38	.243	7	81	4	184	107	13	.957

WILSON, VANCE   C   METS

PERSONAL: Born March 17, 1973, in Mesa, Ariz. ... 5-11/190. ... Bats right, throws right. ... Full name: Vance Allen Wilson.
HIGH SCHOOL: Red Mountain (Mesa, Ariz.).
JUNIOR COLLEGE: Mesa (Ariz.) Community College.
TRANSACTIONS/CAREER NOTES: Selected by New York Mets organization in 44th round of free-agent draft (June 3, 1993). ... On Norfolk disabled list (May 2-July 18, 1998). ... On New York disabled list (September 8, 1998-remainder of season). ... On Norfolk disabled list (May 13-August 28, 1999). ... On New York disabled list (August 28, 1999-remainder of season).
STATISTICAL NOTES: Led International League with 706 total chances, 10 double plays and 14 passed balls in 2000.

Year Team (League)	Pos.	G	AB	R	H	2B	3B	HR	RBI	Avg.	BB	SO	SB	PO	A	E	Avg.
1994—Pittsfield (NY-Penn)....	C	44	166	22	51	12	0	2	20	.307	5	27	4	190	25	5	.977
1995—Columbia (S.Atl.)........	C	91	324	34	81	11	0	6	32	.250	19	45	4	605	99	*14	.981
1996—St. Lucie (FSL)..........	C	93	311	29	76	14	2	6	44	.244	31	41	2	502	87	8	.987
1997—Binghamton (East.)	C	92	322	46	89	17	0	15	40	.276	20	46	2	604	69	11	.984
1998—Norfolk (I.L.)..........	C	46	154	18	40	3	0	4	16	.260	9	29	0	348	29	4	.990
—GC Mets (GCL).........	C	10	28	5	10	5	0	2	9	.357	0	0	0	35	9	2	.957
—St. Lucie (FSL).........	C	4	16	0	1	0	0	0	0	.063	0	5	0	19	3	0	1.000
1999—Norfolk (I.L.)..........	C	15	53	10	14	3	0	3	5	.264	4	8	1	95	11	1	.991
—New York (N.L.)........	C	1	0	0	0	0	0	0	0	...	0	0	0	0	0	0	...
2000—Norfolk (I.L.)..........	C	111	400	47	104	23	1	16	62	.260	24	65	11	*637	*66	3	.996
—New York (N.L.)........	C	4	4	0	0	0	0	0	0	.000	0	2	0	14	0	0	1.000
2001—Norfolk (I.L.)..........	C	65	228	24	56	14	0	6	31	.246	12	34	0	436	47	8	.984
—New York (N.L.)........	C	32	57	3	17	3	0	0	6	.298	2	16	0	130	9	1	.993
Major League totals (3 years)		37	61	3	17	3	0	0	6	.279	2	18	0	144	9	1	.994

WINCHESTER, SCOTT   P

PERSONAL: Born April 20, 1973, in Midland, Mich. ... 6-2/210. ... Throws right, bats right. ... Full name: Scott Joseph Winchester.
HIGH SCHOOL: H.H. Dow (Midland, Mich.).
COLLEGE: Clemson.
TRANSACTIONS/CAREER NOTES: Selected by Cleveland Indians organization in 14th round of free-agent draft (June 1, 1995). ... Traded by Indians with P Jim Crowell, P Danny Graves and IF Damian Jackson to Cincinnati Reds for P John Smiley and IF Jeff Branson (July 31, 1997). ... Selected by Arizona Diamondbacks in second round (33rd pick overall) of expansion draft (November 18, 1997). ... Traded by Diamondbacks to Reds (November 18, 1997), completing deal in which Reds traded P Felix Rodriguez to Diamondbacks for a player to be named later (November 11, 1997). ... On Indianapolis disabled list (August 18-September 8, 1998). ... On Cincinnati disabled list (March 24, 1999-entire season); included rehabilitation assignment to Rockford (August 8-September 6). ... On Cincinnati disabled list (April 15-May 14, 2001); included rehabilitation assignment to Louisville (May 7-14). ... Granted free agency (October 8, 2001).

Year League	W	L	Pct.	ERA	G	GS	CG	ShO	Sv.	IP	H	R	ER	BB	SO
1995—Watertown (NY-Penn)	3	1	.750	2.83	23	0	0	0	11	$28^{2}/_{3}$	24	10	9	6	27
1996—Columbus (S.Atl.)...............	7	3	.700	3.23	52	0	0	0	26	$61^{1}/_{3}$	50	27	22	16	60
—Columbus (S.Atl.)...............	7	3	.700	3.23	52	0	0	0	26	$61^{1}/_{3}$	50	27	22	16	60
1997—Kinston (Caro.)..................	2	1	.667	1.47	34	0	0	0	29	$36^{2}/_{3}$	21	6	6	11	45
—Akron (East.).....................	0	0	...	3.86	6	0	0	0	1	7	8	3	3	2	8
—Chattanooga (Sou.)■.............	2	1	.667	1.69	9	0	0	0	3	$10^{2}/_{3}$	9	4	2	3	3
—Indianapolis (A.A.)...............	0	0	...	0.00	4	0	0	0	0	$5^{2}/_{3}$	2	0	0	2	2
—Cincinnati (N.L.)	0	0	...	6.00	5	0	0	0	0	6	9	5	4	2	3
1998—Indianapolis (I.L.).............	3	2	.600	6.67	6	5	0	0	0	$29^{2}/_{3}$	39	23	22	8	12
—Cincinnati (N.L.)	3	6	.333	5.81	16	16	1	0	0	79	101	56	51	27	40
1999—Rockford (Midw.)..............	1	1	.500	2.79	6	6	0	0	0	$19^{1}/_{3}$	19	7	6	3	11
2000—Louisville (I.L.).................	1	2	.333	4.08	43	0	0	0	3	$57^{1}/_{3}$	67	29	26	15	33
—Cincinnati (N.L.)	0	0	...	3.68	5	0	0	0	0	$7^{1}/_{3}$	10	4	3	2	3
2001—Louisville (I.L.).................	6	3	.667	3.54	23	6	0	0	0	$53^{1}/_{3}$	50	26	21	10	37
—Cincinnati (N.L.)	0	2	.000	4.50	12	1	0	0	0	24	29	19	12	4	9
Major League totals (4 years).......	3	8	.273	5.42	38	17	1	0	0	$116^{1}/_{3}$	149	84	70	35	55

WINN, RANDY   OF   DEVIL RAYS

PERSONAL: Born June 9, 1974, in Los Angeles. ... 6-2/193. ... Bats both, throws right. ... Full name: Dwight Randolph Winn.
HIGH SCHOOL: San Ramon Valley (Danville, Calif.).
COLLEGE: Santa Clara.
TRANSACTIONS/CAREER NOTES: Selected by Florida Marlins organization in third round of free-agent draft (June 1, 1995). ... On disabled list (August 22-September 11, 1995). ... Selected by Tampa Bay Devil Rays in third round (58th pick overall) of expansion draft (November 18, 1997).
STATISTICAL NOTES: Led Eastern League in caught stealing with 20 in 1997. ... Career major league grand slams: 1.
MISCELLANEOUS: Holds Tampa Bay Devil Rays record for most triples (19).

Year Team (League)	Pos.	G	AB	R	H	2B	3B	HR	RBI	Avg.	BB	SO	SB	PO	A	E	Avg.
1995—Elmira (NY-Penn)	OF	51	213	38	67	7	4	0	22	.315	15	31	19	103	1	5	.954
1996—Kane County (Midw.)..	OF	130	514	90	139	16	3	0	35	.270	47	115	30	260	2	8	.970
1997—Brevard County (FSL).	OF	36	143	26	45	8	2	0	15	.315	16	28	16	95	0	0	1.000
—Portland (East.)..........	OF	96	384	66	112	15	6	8	36	.292	42	92	35	182	6	4	.979
1998—Durham (I.L.)■........	OF	29	123	25	35	5	2	1	16	.285	15	24	10	55	1	2	.966
—Tampa Bay (A.L.)........	OF-DH	109	338	51	94	9	9	1	17	.278	29	69	26	192	7	4	.980
1999—Tampa Bay (A.L.)........	OF	79	303	44	81	16	4	2	24	.267	17	63	9	180	4	1	.995
—Durham (I.L.)	OF	46	207	38	73	20	3	3	30	.353	16	27	9	113	2	4	.966
2000—Durham (I.L.)	OF	79	303	67	100	24	5	7	40	.330	48	53	18	158	10	7	.960
—Tampa Bay (A.L.)........	OF-DH	51	159	28	40	5	0	1	16	.252	26	25	6	92	4	1	.990
2001—Tampa Bay (A.L.)........	OF-DH	128	429	54	117	25	6	6	50	.273	38	81	12	245	12	5	.981
Major League totals (4 years)		367	1229	177	332	55	19	10	107	.270	110	238	53	709	27	11	.985

PERSONAL: Born November 18, 1975, in Montclair, Calif. ... 6-4/190. ... Throws right, bats right. ... Full name: Matthew John Wise.
HIGH SCHOOL: Bonita (Calif.).
COLLEGE: Pepperdine, then Cal State-Fullerton.
TRANSACTIONS/CAREER NOTES: Selected by Anaheim Angels organization in sixth round of free-agent draft (June 3, 1997). ... On disabled list (July 9, 1999-remainder of season).

Year League	W	L	Pct.	ERA	G	GS	CG	ShO	Sv.	IP	H	R	ER	BB	SO
1997— Boise (N'West)	•9	1	*.900	3.25	15	15	0	0	0	83	82	37	30	34	86
1998— Midland (Texas)	9	10	.474	5.42	27	27	3	•1	0	167 2/3	195	111	101	48	131
1999— Erie (East.)	8	5	.615	3.77	16	16	3	0	0	98	102	48	41	24	72
2000— Edmonton (PCL)	9	6	.600	3.69	19	19	2	1	0	124 1/3	122	54	51	26	82
— Anaheim (A.L.)	3	3	.500	5.54	8	6	0	0	0	37 1/3	40	23	23	13	20
2001— Anaheim (A.L.)	1	4	.200	4.38	11	9	0	0	0	49 1/3	47	27	24	18	50
— Salt Lake (PCL)	9	9	.500	5.04	21	21	0	0	0	123 1/3	134	79	69	17	111
Major League totals (2 years)	4	7	.364	4.88	19	15	0	0	0	86 2/3	87	50	47	31	70

PERSONAL: Born August 28, 1972, in Baltimore. ... 6-4/235. ... Throws right, bats right. ... Full name: Gerald Alphonse Witasick Jr.
HIGH SCHOOL: C. Milton Wright (Bel Air, Md.).
JUNIOR COLLEGE: Brevard Community College (Fla.).
COLLEGE: Maryland-Baltimore County.
TRANSACTIONS/CAREER NOTES: Selected by St. Louis Cardinals organization in second round of free-agent draft (June 3, 1993). ... On disabled list (July 17, 1995-remainder of season). ... Traded by Cardinals with OF Allen Battle, P Bret Wagner and P Carl Dale to Oakland Athletics for P Todd Stottlemyre (January 9, 1996). ... On Oakland disabled list (March 31-June 14, 1997); included rehabilitation assignment to Modesto (June 11-14). ... Traded by A's to Kansas City Royals for a player to be named later and cash (March 30, 1999); A's acquired P Scott Chiasson to complete deal (June 10, 1999). ... Traded by Royals to San Diego Padres for P Brian Meadows (July 31, 2000). ... Traded by Padres to New York Yankees for IF D'Angelo Jimenez (June 23, 2001). ... Traded by Yankees to San Francisco Giants for OF John Vander Wal (December 13, 2001).

Year League	W	L	Pct.	ERA	G	GS	CG	ShO	Sv.	IP	H	R	ER	BB	SO
1993— Johnson City (Appl.)	4	3	.571	4.12	12	12	0	0	0	67 2/3	65	42	31	19	74
— Savannah (S.Atl.)	1	0	1.000	4.50	1	1	0	0	0	6	7	3	3	2	8
1994— Madison (Midw.)	10	4	.714	2.32	18	18	2	0	0	112 1/3	74	36	29	42	141
1995— St. Petersburg (FSL)	7	7	.500	2.74	18	18	1	1	0	105	80	39	32	36	109
— Arkansas (Texas)	2	4	.333	6.88	7	7	0	0	0	34	46	29	26	16	26
1996— Huntsville (Sou.)■	0	3	.000	2.30	25	6	0	0	4	66 2/3	47	21	17	26	63
— Oakland (A.L.)	1	1	.500	6.23	12	0	0	0	0	13	12	9	9	5	12
— Edmonton (PCL)	0	0	...	4.15	6	0	0	0	2	8 2/3	9	4	4	6	9
1997— Modesto (Calif.)	0	1	.000	4.15	9	2	0	0	0	17 1/3	16	9	8	5	29
— Edmonton (PCL)	3	2	.600	4.28	13	1	0	0	0	27 1/3	25	13	13	15	17
— Oakland (A.L.)	0	0	...	5.73	8	0	0	0	0	11	14	7	7	6	8
1998— Edmonton (PCL)	11	7	.611	3.87	27	26	2	1	0	149	126	74	64	49	155
— Oakland (A.L.)	1	3	.250	6.33	7	3	0	0	0	27	36	24	19	15	29
1999— Kansas City (A.L.)■	9	12	.429	5.57	32	28	1	1	0	158 1/3	191	108	98	83	102
2000— Kansas City (A.L.)	3	8	.273	5.94	22	14	0	0	0	89 1/3	109	65	59	38	67
— San Diego (N.L.)■	3	2	.600	5.64	11	11	0	0	0	60 2/3	69	42	38	35	54
2001— San Diego (N.L.)	5	2	.714	1.86	31	0	0	0	1	38 2/3	31	14	8	15	53
— New York (A.L.)■	3	0	1.000	4.69	32	0	0	0	0	40 1/3	47	27	21	18	53
A.L. totals (6 years)	17	24	.415	5.65	113	45	3	1	0	339	409	240	213	165	271
N.L. totals (2 years)	8	4	.667	4.17	42	11	0	0	1	99 1/3	100	56	46	50	107
Major League totals (6 years)	25	28	.472	5.32	155	56	3	1	1	438 1/3	509	296	259	215	378

DIVISION SERIES RECORD

Year League	W	L	Pct.	ERA	G	GS	CG	ShO	Sv.	IP	H	R	ER	BB	SO
2001— New York (A.L.)	0	0	...	13.50	1	0	0	0	0	2/3	1	1	1	1	0

CHAMPIONSHIP SERIES RECORD

Year League	W	L	Pct.	ERA	G	GS	CG	ShO	Sv.	IP	H	R	ER	BB	SO
2001— New York (A.L.)	0	0	...	9.00	1	0	0	0	0	3	6	3	3	0	2

WORLD SERIES RECORD

RECORDS: Holds single-game record for most earned runs allowed—8 (November 3, 2001). ... Holds record for most hits allowed in one inning—8 (November 3, 2001, third inning). ... Shares record for most earned runs allowed in one inning—6 (November 3, 2001, third inning).

Year League	W	L	Pct.	ERA	G	GS	CG	ShO	Sv.	IP	H	R	ER	BB	SO
2001— New York (A.L.)	0	0	...	54.00	1	0	0	0	0	1 1/3	10	9	8	0	4

W

PERSONAL: Born May 11, 1964, in Arlington, Va. ... 6-2/215. ... Throws right, bats right. ... Full name: Robert Andrew Witt.
HIGH SCHOOL: Canton (Mass.).
COLLEGE: Oklahoma.
TRANSACTIONS/CAREER NOTES: Selected by Cincinnati Reds organization in seventh round of free-agent draft (June 7, 1982); did not sign. ... Selected by Texas Rangers organization in first round (third pick overall) of free-agent draft (June 3, 1985). ... On Texas disabled list (May 21-June 20, 1987); included rehabilitation assignments to Oklahoma City (June 7-12) and Tulsa (June 13). ... On Texas disabled list (May 27-July 31, 1991); included rehabilitation assignment to Oklahoma City (July 22-29). ... Traded by Rangers with OF Ruben Sierra, P Jeff Russell and cash to Oakland Athletics for OF Jose Canseco (August 31, 1992). ... Granted free agency (October 26, 1994). ... Signed by Florida Marlins (April 9, 1995). ... Traded by Marlins to Rangers for two players to be named later (August 8, 1995); Marlins acquired P Wilson Heredia (August 11, 1995) and OF Scott Podsednik (October 2, 1995) to complete deal. ... Granted free agency (November 3, 1995). ... Re-signed by

Rangers (December 24, 1995). ... Granted free agency (October 27, 1997). ... Re-signed by Rangers (January 19, 1998). ... Traded by Rangers to St. Louis Cardinals for a player to be named later or cash (June 23, 1998). ... Granted free agency (October 29, 1998). ... Signed by Tampa Bay Devil Rays organization (January 20, 1999). ... Granted free agency (November 5, 1999). ... Signed by Cleveland Indians organization (January 19, 2000). ... Released by Indians (May 18, 2000). ... Signed by Arizona Diamondbacks organization (April 4, 2001). ... On Arizona disabled list (April 8-August 6, 2001); included rehabilitation assignments to Tucson (June 21-24 and July 16-August 6). ... Granted free agency (November 5, 2001).

RECORDS: Shares major league record for most strikeouts in one inning—4 (August 2, 1987, second inning).

HONORS: Named righthanded pitcher on THE SPORTING NEWS college All-America team (1985).

STATISTICAL NOTES: Led A.L. with 22 wild pitches in 1986 and tied for lead with 16 in 1988. ... Pitched 4-0 one-hit, complete-game victory against Kansas City (June 23, 1994).

MISCELLANEOUS: Member of 1984 U.S. Olympic baseball team. ... Struck out in only appearance as pinch hitter with Texas (1987). ... Appeared in two games as pinch runner (1990). ... Appeared in one game as pinch runner (1994). ... Appeared in two games as pinch runner with Florida (1995). ... Made an out in only appearance as pinch hitter with Texas (1998). ... Shares Tampa Bay Devil Rays all-time record for most shutouts (2).

Year	League	W	L	Pct.	ERA	G	GS	CG	ShO	Sv.	IP	H	R	ER	BB	SO
1985—	Tulsa (Texas)	0	6	.000	6.43	11	8	0	0	0	35	26	26	25	44	39
1986—	Texas (A.L.)	11	9	.550	5.48	31	31	0	0	0	157 2/3	130	104	96	*143	174
1987—	Texas (A.L.)	8	10	.444	4.91	26	25	1	0	0	143	114	82	78	*140	160
—	Oklahoma City (A.A.)	1	0	1.000	9.00	1	1	0	0	0	5	5	5	5	3	2
—	Tulsa (Texas)	0	1	.000	5.40	1	1	0	0	0	5	5	9	3	6	2
1988—	Texas (A.L.)	8	10	.444	3.92	22	22	13	2	0	174 1/3	134	83	76	101	148
—	Oklahoma City (A.A.)	4	6	.400	4.34	11	11	3	0	0	76 2/3	69	42	37	47	70
1989—	Texas (A.L.)	12	13	.480	5.14	31	31	5	1	0	194 1/3	182	123	•111	*114	166
1990—	Texas (A.L.)	17	10	.630	3.36	33	32	7	1	0	222	197	98	83	110	221
1991—	Texas (A.L.)	3	7	.300	6.09	17	16	1	1	0	88 2/3	84	66	60	74	82
—	Oklahoma City (A.A.)	1	1	.500	1.13	2	2	0	0	0	8	3	1	1	8	12
1992—	Texas (A.L.)■	9	13	.409	4.46	25	25	0	0	0	161 1/3	152	87	80	95	100
—	Oakland (A.L.)	1	1	.500	3.41	6	6	0	0	0	31 2/3	31	12	12	19	25
1993—	Oakland (A.L.)	14	13	.519	4.21	35	33	5	1	0	220	226	112	103	91	131
1994—	Oakland (A.L.)	8	10	.444	5.04	24	24	5	3	0	135 2/3	151	88	76	70	111
1995—	Florida (N.L.)■	2	7	.222	3.90	19	19	1	0	0	110 2/3	104	52	48	47	95
—	Oakland (A.L.)■	3	4	.429	4.55	10	10	1	0	0	61 1/3	81	35	31	21	46
1996—	Texas (A.L.)	16	12	.571	5.41	33	32	2	0	0	199 2/3	235	129	120	96	157
1997—	Texas (A.L.)	12	12	.500	4.82	34	32	3	0	0	209	245	118	112	74	121
1998—	Texas (A.L.)	5	4	.556	7.66	14	13	0	0	0	69 1/3	95	62	59	33	30
—	St. Louis (N.L.)■	2	5	.286	4.94	17	5	0	0	0	47 1/3	55	32	26	20	28
1999—	Tampa Bay (A.L.)■	7	15	.318	5.84	32	32	3	2	0	180 1/3	213	130	117	96	123
2000—	Cleveland (A.L.)■	0	1	.000	7.63	7	2	0	0	0	15 1/3	28	13	13	6	6
2001—	Arizona (N.L.)■	4	1	.800	4.78	14	7	0	0	0	43 1/3	36	23	23	25	31
—	Tucson (PCL)	0	3	.000	3.63	5	5	0	0	0	22 1/3	18	11	9	8	18
A.L. totals (15 years)		134	144	.482	4.88	380	366	46	11	0	2263 2/3	2298	1342	1227	1283	1801
N.L. totals (3 years)		8	13	.381	4.34	50	31	1	0	0	201 1/3	195	107	97	92	154
Major League totals (16 years)		142	157	.475	4.83	430	397	47	11	0	2465	2493	1449	1324	1375	1955

DIVISION SERIES RECORD

Year	League	W	L	Pct.	ERA	G	GS	CG	ShO	Sv.	IP	H	R	ER	BB	SO
1996—	Texas (A.L.)	0	0	...	8.10	1	1	0	0	0	3 1/3	4	3	3	2	3

CHAMPIONSHIP SERIES RECORD

Year	League	W	L	Pct.	ERA	G	GS	CG	ShO	Sv.	IP	H	R	ER	BB	SO
1992—	Oakland (A.L.)	0	0	...	18.00	1	0	0	0	0	1	2	2	2	1	1
2001—	Arizona (N.L.)	0	0	...	27.00	1	0	0	0	0	1/3	3	1	1	0	0
Champ. series totals (2 years)		0	0	...	20.25	2	0	0	0	0	1 1/3	5	3	3	1	1

WORLD SERIES RECORD

NOTES: Member of World Series championship team (2001).

Year	League	W	L	Pct.	ERA	G	GS	CG	ShO	Sv.	IP	H	R	ER	BB	SO
2001—	Arizona (N.L.)	0	0	...	0.00	1	0	0	0	0	1	0	0	0	1	1

WITT, KEVIN   1B/OF   REDS

PERSONAL: Born January 5, 1976, in High Point, N.C. ... 6-4/210. ... Bats left, throws right. ... Full name: Kevin Joseph Witt.

HIGH SCHOOL: Bishop Kenny (Jacksonville, Fla.).

TRANSACTIONS/CAREER NOTES: Selected by Toronto Blue Jays organization in first round (28th pick overall) of free-agent draft (June 2, 1994). ... Granted free agency (October 18, 2000). ... Signed by San Diego Padres organization (December 15, 2000). ... Granted free agency (October 15, 2001). ... Signed by Cincinnati Reds organization (December 21, 2001).

STATISTICAL NOTES: Tied for Southern League lead with seven intentional bases on balls received in 1997. ... Led International League first basemen with .996 fielding percentage and 105 double plays in 1998. ... Led International League first basemen with 14 errors in 2000.

							BATTING						FIELDING			
Year	Team (League)	Pos.	G	AB	R	H	2B	3B	HR	RBI	Avg.	BB	SO	SB	PO	A	E	Avg.
1994—	Medicine Hat (Pio.)	SS	60	243	37	62	10	4	7	36	.255	15	52	4	*99	167	25	.914
1995—	Hagerstown (S.Atl.)	SS	119	479	58	111	35	1	14	50	.232	28	148	1	203	338	48	.919
1996—	Dunedin (FSL)	SS	124	446	63	121	18	6	13	70	.271	39	96	9	161	369	48	.917
1997—	Knoxville (Sou.)	1-3-DH-O-S	127	501	76	145	27	4	•30	91	.289	44	109	1	553	118	15	.978
1998—	Syracuse (I.L.)	1B-OF-DH	126	455	71	124	20	3	23	67	.273	53	124	3	973	68	4	†.996
—	Toronto (A.L.)	1B	5	7	0	1	0	0	0	0	.143	0	3	0	5	1	0	1.000
1999—	Syracuse (I.L.)	1B-OF-DH	114	421	72	117	24	3	24	71	.278	64	109	0	579	55	4	.994
—	Toronto (A.L.)	DH	15	34	3	7	1	0	1	5	.206	2	9	0	0	0	0	...
2000—	Syracuse (I.L.)	1B-OF	135	489	58	121	24	5	26	72	.247	45	132	1	944	54	†14	.986
2001—	Portland (PCL)■	1B-OF-3B	129	456	66	132	28	5	27	87	.289	22	127	1	702	45	12	.984
—	San Diego (N.L.)	1B	14	27	5	5	0	0	2	5	.185	2	7	0	69	3	0	1.000
American League totals (2 years)			20	41	3	8	1	0	1	5	.195	2	12	0	5	1	0	1.000
National League totals (1 year)			14	27	5	5	0	0	2	5	.185	2	7	0	69	3	0	1.000
Major League totals (3 years)			34	68	8	13	1	0	3	10	.191	4	19	0	74	4	0	1.000

W

PERSONAL: Born January 23, 1970, in Holyoke, Mass. ... 6-4/207. ... Throws right, bats right. ... Full name: Mark Edward Wohlers.

HIGH SCHOOL: Holyoke (Mass.).

TRANSACTIONS/CAREER NOTES: Selected by Atlanta Braves organization in eighth round of free-agent draft (June 1, 1988). ... On Atlanta disabled list (May 3-24 and August 21, 1998-remainder of season); included rehabilitation assignments to Greenville (May 23) and Richmond (August 25-September 8). ... Traded by Braves with cash to Cincinnati Reds for P John Hudek (April 16, 1999). ... On Cincinnati disabled list (April 17, 1999-remainder of season); included rehabilitation assignments to Indianapolis (May 2-3), Rockford (June 17-21) and Chattanooga (June 22-July 1). ... Granted free agency (November 5, 1999). ... Re-signed by Reds organization (January 28, 2000). ... On Louisville disabled list (April 6-May 29, 2000). ... Granted free agency (October 31, 2000). ... Re-signed by Reds (December 15, 2000). ... Traded by Reds to New York Yankees for P Ricardo Aromboles (June 30, 2001). ... Granted free agency (November 5, 2001). ... Signed by Cleveland Indians (January 9, 2002).

RECORDS: Shares major league single-inning record for most strikeouts—4 (June 7, 1995, ninth inning).

HONORS: Named Southern League Outstanding Pitcher (1991).

STATISTICAL NOTES: Pitched two innings, combining with starter Kent Mercker (six innings) and Alejandro Pena (one inning) in 1-0 no-hit victory for Atlanta against San Diego (September 11, 1991). ... Led International League with 17 wild pitches in 1998.

Year League	W	L	Pct.	ERA	G	GS	CG	ShO	Sv.	IP	H	R	ER	BB	SO
1988—Pulaski (Appl.)	5	3	.625	3.32	13	9	1	0	0	59²/₃	47	37	22	50	49
1989—Sumter (S.Atl.)	2	7	.222	6.49	14	14	0	0	0	68	74	55	49	59	51
—Pulaski (Appl.)	1	1	.500	5.48	14	8	0	0	0	46	48	36	28	28	50
1990—Greenville (Sou.)	0	1	.000	4.02	14	0	0	0	6	15²/₃	14	7	7	14	20
—Sumter (S.Atl.)	5	4	.556	1.88	37	2	0	0	5	52²/₃	27	13	11	20	85
1991—Greenville (Sou.)	0	0	...	0.57	28	0	0	0	21	31¹/₃	9	4	2	13	44
—Richmond (I.L.)	1	0	1.000	1.03	23	0	0	0	11	26¹/₃	23	4	3	12	22
—Atlanta (N.L.)	3	1	.750	3.20	17	0	0	0	2	19²/₃	17	7	7	13	13
1992—Richmond (I.L.)	0	2	.000	3.93	27	2	0	0	9	34¹/₃	32	16	15	17	33
—Atlanta (N.L.)	1	2	.333	2.55	32	0	0	0	4	35¹/₃	28	11	10	14	17
1993—Richmond (I.L.)	1	3	.250	1.84	25	0	0	0	4	29¹/₃	21	7	6	11	39
—Atlanta (N.L.)	6	2	.750	4.50	46	0	0	0	0	48	37	25	24	22	45
1994—Atlanta (N.L.)	7	2	.778	4.59	51	0	0	0	1	51	51	35	26	33	58
1995—Atlanta (N.L.)	7	3	.700	2.09	65	0	0	0	25	64²/₃	51	16	15	24	90
1996—Atlanta (N.L.)	2	4	.333	3.03	77	0	0	0	39	77¹/₃	71	30	26	21	100
1997—Atlanta (N.L.)	5	7	.417	3.50	71	0	0	0	33	69¹/₃	57	29	27	38	92
1998—Atlanta (N.L.)	0	1	.000	10.18	27	0	0	0	8	20¹/₃	18	23	23	33	22
—Greenville (Sou.)	0	0	...	0.00	1	1	0	0	0	1	1	1	0	1	1
—Richmond (I.L.)	0	3	.000	20.43	16	0	0	0	0	12¹/₃	21	28	28	36	16
1999—Atlanta (N.L.)	0	0	...	27.00	2	0	0	0	0	²/₃	1	2	2	6	0
—Indianapolis (I.L.)■	0	0	...	108.00	1	0	0	0	0	¹/₃	1	4	4	5	1
—Rockford (Midw.)	0	0	...	4.50	2	0	0	0	0	2	1	1	1	2	4
—Chattanooga (Sou.)	0	0	...	16.20	2	0	0	0	0	1²/₃	1	3	3	3	3
2000—Dayton (Midw.)	0	0	...	3.00	3	3	0	0	0	3	1	1	1	1	7
—Louisville (I.L.)	1	2	.333	6.10	17	2	0	0	0	20²/₃	30	21	14	9	16
—Cincinnati (N.L.)	1	2	.333	4.50	20	0	0	0	0	28	19	14	14	17	20
2001—Cincinnati (N.L.)	3	1	.750	3.94	30	0	0	0	0	32	36	20	14	7	21
—New York (A.L.)■	1	0	1.000	4.54	31	0	0	0	0	35²/₃	33	20	18	18	33
A.L. totals (1 year)	1	0	1.000	4.54	31	0	0	0	0	35²/₃	33	20	18	18	33
N.L. totals (11 years)	35	25	.583	3.79	438	0	0	0	112	446¹/₃	386	212	188	228	478
Major League totals (11 years)	36	25	.590	3.85	469	0	0	0	112	482	419	232	206	246	511

DIVISION SERIES RECORD

RECORDS: Holds N.L. career record for most saves—5.

Year League	W	L	Pct.	ERA	G	GS	CG	ShO	Sv.	IP	H	R	ER	BB	SO
1995—Atlanta (N.L.)	0	1	.000	6.75	3	0	0	0	2	2²/₃	6	2	2	2	4
1996—Atlanta (N.L.)	0	0	...	0.00	3	0	0	0	3	3¹/₃	1	0	0	0	4
1997—Atlanta (N.L.)	0	0	...	0.00	1	0	0	0	0	1	1	0	0	0	1
2001—New York (A.L.)								Did not play.							
Division series totals (3 years)	0	1	.000	2.57	7	0	0	0	5	7	8	2	2	2	9

CHAMPIONSHIP SERIES RECORD

RECORDS: Holds N.L. career records for most games pitched—18; and most games as relief pitcher—18.

Year League	W	L	Pct.	ERA	G	GS	CG	ShO	Sv.	IP	H	R	ER	BB	SO
1991—Atlanta (N.L.)	0	0	...	0.00	3	0	0	0	0	1²/₃	3	0	0	1	1
1992—Atlanta (N.L.)	0	0	...	0.00	3	0	0	0	0	3	2	0	0	1	2
1993—Atlanta (N.L.)	0	1	.000	3.38	4	0	0	0	0	5¹/₃	2	2	2	3	10
1995—Atlanta (N.L.)	1	0	1.000	1.80	4	0	0	0	0	5	2	1	1	0	8
1996—Atlanta (N.L.)	0	0	...	0.00	3	0	0	0	2	3	0	0	0	0	4
1997—Atlanta (N.L.)	0	0	...	0.00	1	0	0	0	0	1	0	0	0	1	1
2001—New York (A.L.)	0	0	...	13.50	1	0	0	0	0	²/₃	3	3	1	1	1
Champ. series totals (7 years)	1	1	.500	1.83	19	0	0	0	2	19²/₃	12	6	4	7	27

WORLD SERIES RECORD

NOTES: Member of World Series championship team (1995).

Year League	W	L	Pct.	ERA	G	GS	CG	ShO	Sv.	IP	H	R	ER	BB	SO
1991—Atlanta (N.L.)	0	0	...	0.00	3	0	0	0	0	1²/₃	2	0	0	2	1
1992—Atlanta (N.L.)	0	0	...	0.00	2	0	0	0	0	²/₃	0	0	0	1	0
1995—Atlanta (N.L.)	0	0	...	1.80	4	0	0	0	2	5	4	1	1	3	3
1996—Atlanta (N.L.)	0	0	...	6.23	4	0	0	0	0	4¹/₃	7	3	3	2	4
2001—New York (A.L.)								Did not play.							
World Series totals (4 years)	0	0	...	3.09	13	0	0	0	2	11²/₃	13	4	4	8	8

ALL-STAR GAME RECORD

Year League	W	L	Pct.	ERA		GS	CG	ShO	Sv.	IP	H	R	ER	BB	SO
1996—National	0	0	...	0.00		0	0	0	0	²/₃	1	0	0	0	0

PERSONAL: Born August 22, 1976, in Canoga Park, Calif. ... 6-0/194. ... Throws left, bats left. ... Full name: Randall C. Wolf.
HIGH SCHOOL: El Camino Real (Los Angeles).
COLLEGE: Pepperdine.
TRANSACTIONS/CAREER NOTES: Selected by Los Angeles Dodgers organization in 25th round of free-agent draft (June 2, 1994); did not sign. ... Selected by Philadelphia Phillies organization in second round of free-agent draft (June 3, 1997). ... On Philadelphia disabled list (August 2-September 1, 2001); included rehabilitation assignments to Scranton/Wilkes-Barre (August 17-28) and Reading (August 29-September 1).
STATISTICAL NOTES: Pitched 8-0 one-hit, complete-game victory against Cincinnati (September 26, 2001).

Year	League	W	L	Pct.	ERA	G	GS	CG	ShO	Sv.	IP	H	R	ER	BB	SO
1997—	Batavia (NY-Penn)	4	0	1.000	1.58	7	7	0	0	0	40	29	8	7	8	53
1998—	Reading (East.)	2	0	1.000	1.44	4	4	0	0	0	25	15	4	4	4	33
—	Scranton/W.B. (I.L.)	9	7	.563	4.62	24	23	1	0	0	148	167	88	76	48	118
1999—	Scranton/W.B. (I.L.)	4	5	.444	3.61	12	12	0	0	0	77 1/3	73	36	31	29	72
—	Philadelphia (N.L.)	6	9	.400	5.55	22	21	0	0	0	121 2/3	126	78	75	67	116
2000—	Philadelphia (N.L.)	11	9	.550	4.36	32	32	1	0	0	206 1/3	210	107	100	83	160
2001—	Philadelphia (N.L.)	10	11	.476	3.70	28	25	4	2	0	163	150	74	67	51	152
—	Scranton/W.B. (I.L.)	0	1	.000	5.00	2	2	0	0	0	9	10	6	5	5	7
—	Reading (East.)	0	0	...	4.50	1	1	0	0	0	6	5	3	3	2	7
Major League totals (3 years)		27	29	.482	4.44	82	78	5	2	0	491	486	259	242	201	428

PERSONAL: Born September 25, 1969, in Danville, Va. ... 5-9/159. ... Bats left, throws right. ... Full name: Anthony Darrell Womack.
HIGH SCHOOL: Gretna (Va.).
COLLEGE: Guilford (N.C.); then UNC Greensboro (did not play).
TRANSACTIONS/CAREER NOTES: Selected by Pittsburgh Pirates organization in seventh round of free-agent draft (June 3, 1991). ... On disabled list (April 17-26 and August 28, 1992-remainder of season). ... Traded by Pirates to Arizona Diamondbacks for OF Paul Weichard and a player to be named later (February 26, 1999); Pirates acquired P Jason Boyd to complete deal (August 25, 1999). ... On Arizona disabled list (March 26-April 12, 1999); included rehabilitation assignment to Tucson (April 8-12). ... On Arizona disabled list (July 23-August 6, 2001); included rehabilitation assignment to Tucson (August 2-6).
RECORDS: Holds major league career record for highest stolen-base percentage (300 or more attempts)—.853.
STATISTICAL NOTES: Tied for American Association lead with 12 sacrifice hits in 1994. ... Led Pacific Coast League with 14 sacrifice hits in 1996. ... Led N.L. second basemen with 20 errors in 1997. ... Had 16-game hitting streak (July 3-22, 1998). ... Had 24-game hitting streak (May 2-29, 2000). ... Career major league grand slams: 2.
MISCELLANEOUS: Holds Arizona Diamondbacks all-time record for most stolen bases (145) and triples (29).

Year	Team (League)	Pos.	G	AB	R	H	2B	3B	HR	RBI	Avg.	BB	SO	SB	PO	A	E	Avg.
1991—	Welland (NY-Penn)	SS-2B	45	166	30	46	3	0	1	8	.277	17	39	26	78	109	16	.921
1992—	Augusta (S.Atl.)	SS-2B	102	380	62	93	8	3	0	18	.245	41	59	50	186	291	40	.923
1993—	Salem (Caro.)	SS	72	304	41	91	11	3	2	18	.299	13	34	28	130	223	28	.927
—	Carolina (Sou.)	SS	60	247	41	75	7	2	0	23	.304	17	34	21	102	169	11	.961
—	Pittsburgh (N.L.)	SS	15	24	5	2	0	0	0	0	.083	3	3	2	11	22	1	.971
1994—	Buffalo (A.A.)	SS-2B	106	421	40	93	9	2	0	18	.221	19	76	41	211	283	22	.957
—	Pittsburgh (N.L.)	2B-SS	5	12	4	4	0	0	0	1	.333	2	3	0	3	6	2	.818
1995—	Calgary (PCL)	2B-SS	30	107	12	30	3	1	0	6	.280	12	11	7	37	94	5	.963
—	Carolina (Sou.)	SS-2B	82	332	52	85	9	4	1	19	.256	19	36	27	126	241	18	.953
1996—	Calgary (PCL)	S-2-O-DH	131	506	75	151	19	11	1	47	.298	31	79	37	258	335	24	.961
—	Pittsburgh (N.L.)	OF-2B	17	30	11	10	3	1	0	7	.333	6	1	2	11	8	2	.905
1997—	Pittsburgh (N.L.)	2B-SS	155	641	85	178	26	9	6	50	.278	43	109	*60	335	430	†20	.975
1998—	Pittsburgh (N.L.)	2B-OF-SS	159	655	85	185	26	7	3	45	.282	38	94	*58	309	451	17	.978
1999—	Tucson (PCL)■	OF	4	16	1	4	1	0	1	3	.250	2	3	0	8	1	0	1.000
—	Arizona (N.L.)	OF-2B-SS	144	614	111	170	25	10	4	41	.277	52	68	*72	293	85	5	.987
2000—	Arizona (N.L.)	SS-OF	146	617	95	167	21	*14	7	57	.271	30	74	45	218	365	18	.970
2001—	Arizona (N.L.)	SS-OF	125	481	66	128	19	5	3	30	.266	23	54	28	152	311	22	.955
—	Tucson (PCL)	SS	4	13	1	5	0	1	0	2	.385	0	1	0	3	8	2	.846
Major League totals (8 years)			766	3074	462	844	120	46	23	231	.275	197	406	267	1332	1678	87	.972

DIVISION SERIES RECORD

Year	Team (League)	Pos.	G	AB	R	H	2B	3B	HR	RBI	Avg.	BB	SO	SB	PO	A	E	Avg.
1999—	Arizona (N.L.)	OF-SS	4	18	2	2	0	1	0	0	.111	0	6	0	5	5	2	.833
2001—	Arizona (N.L.)	SS	5	17	1	5	1	0	0	1	.294	3	2	0	8	11	2	.905
Division series totals (2 years)			9	35	3	7	1	1	0	1	.200	3	8	0	13	16	4	.879

CHAMPIONSHIP SERIES RECORD

RECORDS: Shares N.L. single-game record for most at-bats—6 (October 20, 2001).

Year	Team (League)	Pos.	G	AB	R	H	2B	3B	HR	RBI	Avg.	BB	SO	SB	PO	A	E	Avg.
2001—	Arizona (N.L.)	SS	4	20	4	4	1	0	0	0	.200	0	2	0	2	9	0	1.000

WORLD SERIES RECORD

RECORDS: Shares single-game record for most at-bats—6 (November 3, 2001).
NOTES: Member of World Series championship team (2001).

Year	Team (League)	Pos.	G	AB	R	H	2B	3B	HR	RBI	Avg.	BB	SO	SB	PO	A	E	Avg.
2001—	Arizona (N.L.)	SS	7	32	3	8	3	0	0	3	.250	1	7	1	7	23	1	.968

ALL-STAR GAME RECORD

Year	League	Pos.	AB	R	H	2B	3B	HR	RBI	Avg.	BB	SO	SB	PO	A	E	Avg.
1997—	National	2B	1	0	0	0	0	0	0	.000	0	0	0	1	0	0	1.000

W

PERSONAL: Born June 16, 1977, in Irving, Texas. ... 6-5/230. ... Throws right, bats right. ... Full name: Kerry Lee Wood.
HIGH SCHOOL: Grand Prairie (Texas).
TRANSACTIONS/CAREER NOTES: Selected by Chicago Cubs organization in first round (fourth pick overall) of free-agent draft (June 1, 1995). ... On disabled list (May 24-June 19, 1996). ... On disabled list (March 31, 1999-entire season). ... On Chicago disabled list (March 25-May 2 and July 30-August 22, 2000); included rehabilitation assignments to Daytona (April 13-23) and Iowa (April 23-April 28). ... On suspended list (September 8-11, 2000). ... On disabled list (August 4-September 7, 2001).
RECORDS: Shares major league single-game record for most strikeouts (nine-inning game)—20 (May 6, 1998). ... Holds N.L. record for most strikeouts in consecutive games—33 (May 6 [20] and 11 [13], 1998).
HONORS: Named N.L. Rookie Pitcher of the Year by The Sporting News (1998). ... Named N.L. Rookie of the Year by Baseball Writers' Association of America (1998).
STATISTICAL NOTES: Led Florida State League with 14 hit batsmen and seven balks in 1996. ... Pitched 2-0 one-hit, complete-game victory against Houston (May 6, 1998). ... Struck out 20 batters in one game (May 6, 1998). ... Struck out 16 batters in one game (August 26, 1998). ... Pitched 1-0 one-hit, complete-game victory against Milwaukee (May 25, 2001).
MISCELLANEOUS: Struck out and had sacrifice hit in two appearances as pinch hitter (2000). ... Appeared in one game as pinch runner (2001).

Year League	W	L	Pct.	ERA	G	GS	CG	ShO	Sv.	IP	H	R	ER	BB	SO
1995—Fort Myers (FSL)	0	0	...	0.00	1	1	0	0	0	3	0	0	0	1	2
—Williamsport (NY-Penn)	0	0	...	10.38	2	2	0	0	0	4 1/3	5	8	5	5	5
1996—Daytona (FSL)	10	2	•.833	2.91	22	22	0	0	0	114 1/3	72	51	37	70	136
1997—Orlando (Sou.)	6	7	.462	4.50	19	19	0	0	0	94	58	49	47	79	106
—Iowa (A.A.)	4	2	.667	4.68	10	10	0	0	0	57 2/3	35	35	30	52	80
1998—Iowa (PCL)	1	0	1.000	0.00	1	1	0	0	0	5	1	0	0	2	11
—Chicago (N.L.)	13	6	.684	3.40	26	26	1	1	0	166 2/3	117	69	63	85	233
1999—Chicago (N.L.)							Did not play.								
2000—Daytona (FSL)	2	0	1.000	1.50	2	2	0	0	0	12	3	2	2	5	17
—Iowa (PCL)	0	0	...	2.57	1	1	0	0	0	7	4	2	2	4	7
—Chicago (N.L.)	8	7	.533	4.80	23	23	1	0	0	137	112	77	73	87	132
2001—Chicago (N.L.)	12	6	.667	3.36	28	28	1	1	0	174 1/3	127	70	65	92	217
Major League totals (3 years)	33	19	.635	3.78	77	77	3	2	0	478	356	216	201	264	582

DIVISION SERIES RECORD

Year League	W	L	Pct.	ERA	G	GS	CG	ShO	Sv.	IP	H	R	ER	BB	SO
1998—Chicago (N.L.)	0	1	.000	1.80	1	1	0	0	0	5	3	1	1	4	5

PERSONAL: Born May 15, 1975, in Hartselle, Ala. ... 6-4/217. ... Throws right, bats left. ... Full name: Steve Larry Woodard Jr.
HIGH SCHOOL: Hartselle (Ala.).
TRANSACTIONS/CAREER NOTES: Selected by Milwaukee Brewers organization in fifth round of free-agent draft (June 2, 1994). ... On disabled list (August 14-September 11, 1999). ... Traded by Brewers with P Bob Wickman and P Jason Bere to Cleveland Indians for 1B/OF Richie Sexson, P Paul Rigdon, P Kane Davis and a player to be named later (July 28, 2000); Brewers acquired 2B Marcos Scutaro to complete deal (August 30). ... On Cleveland disabled list (April 10-30, 2001); included rehabilitation assignment to Akron (April 30). ... Released by Indians (December 12, 2001). ... Signed by Texas Rangers organization (January 14, 2002).
RECORDS: Shares A.L. record for most strikeouts in first major league game—12 (July 28, 1997).
HONORS: Named Texas League Pitcher of the Year (1997).

Year League	W	L	Pct.	ERA	G	GS	CG	ShO	Sv.	IP	H	R	ER	BB	SO
1994—Arizona Brewers (Ariz.)	•8	0	*1.000	2.40	15	12	2	0	0	82 2/3	68	29	22	13	85
1995—Beloit (Midw.)	7	4	.636	4.54	21	21	0	0	0	115	113	68	58	31	94
1996—Stockton (Calif.)	12	9	.571	4.02	28	•28	0	0	0	*181 1/3	201	89	81	33	142
1997—El Paso (Texas)	14	3	.824	3.17	19	19	*6	•1	0	136 1/3	136	56	48	25	97
—Tucson (PCL)	1	0	1.000	0.00	1	1	0	0	0	7	3	0	0	1	6
—Milwaukee (A.L.)	3	3	.500	5.15	7	7	0	0	0	36 2/3	39	25	21	6	32
1998—Milwaukee (N.L.)	10	12	.455	4.18	34	26	0	0	0	165 2/3	170	83	77	33	135
1999—Milwaukee (N.L.)	11	8	.579	4.52	31	29	2	0	0	185	219	101	93	36	119
2000—Milwaukee (N.L.)	1	7	.125	5.96	27	11	1	0	0	93 2/3	125	70	62	33	65
—Cleveland (A.L.)■	3	3	.500	5.67	13	11	0	0	0	54	57	35	34	11	35
2001—Cleveland (A.L.)	3	3	.500	5.20	29	10	0	0	0	97	129	60	56	17	52
—Akron (East.)	0	0	...	3.00	1	1	0	0	0	3	3	1	1	1	2
—Buffalo (I.L.)	4	2	.667	2.39	6	6	1	0	0	37 2/3	36	11	10	1	32
A.L. totals (3 years)	9	9	.500	5.32	49	28	0	0	0	187 2/3	225	120	111	34	119
N.L. totals (3 years)	22	27	.449	4.70	92	66	3	0	0	444 1/3	514	254	232	102	319
Major League totals (5 years)	31	36	.463	4.88	141	94	3	0	0	632	739	374	343	136	438

PERSONAL: Born June 27, 1976, in Covina, Calif. ... 6-0/185. ... Bats right, throws right. ... Full name: Christopher Michael Woodward.
HIGH SCHOOL: Northview (Covina, Calif.).
JUNIOR COLLEGE: Mount Sacramento (Walnut, Calif.).
TRANSACTIONS/CAREER NOTES: Selected by Toronto Blue Jays organization in 54th round of free-agent draft (June 2, 1994). ... On Syracuse disabled list (May 2-17 and May 21-June 6, 1999). ... On Toronto disabled list (July 1-26, 2001); included rehabilitation assignment to Syracuse (July 20-26).
STATISTICAL NOTES: Led Pioneer League shortstops with 338 total chances in 1995.

W

Year	Team (League)	Pos.	G	AB	R	H	2B	3B	HR	RBI	Avg.	BB	SO	SB	PO	A	E	Avg.
1995—Medicine Hat (Pio.)	SS	•72	241	44	56	8	0	3	21	.232	33	41	9	*106	*202	30	.911	
1996—Hagerstown (S.Atl.)....	SS	123	424	41	95	24	2	1	48	.224	43	70	11	*214	366	30	.951	
1997—Dunedin (FSL)..........	SS	91	314	38	92	13	4	1	38	.293	52	52	4	145	267	12	.972	
1998—Knoxville (Sou.).......	SS	73	253	36	62	12	0	3	27	.245	26	47	3	145	220	11	.971	
—Syracuse (I.L.)..........	SS	25	85	9	17	6	0	2	6	.200	7	20	1	29	69	4	.961	
1999—Syracuse (I.L.)........	SS-2B	75	281	46	82	20	3	1	20	.292	38	49	4	114	200	11	.966	
—Toronto (A.L.)...........	SS-3B	14	26	1	6	1	0	0	2	.231	2	6	0	8	26	2	.944	
2000—Toronto (A.L.).........SS-3B-1B-2B		37	104	16	19	7	0	3	14	.183	10	28	1	42	88	5	.963	
—Syracuse (I.L.)..........	3B-SS	37	143	23	46	13	2	5	25	.322	11	30	2	48	110	2	.988	
2001—Toronto (A.L.).........	2-3-S-1-D	37	63	9	12	3	2	2	5	.190	1	14	0	34	77	8	.933	
—Syracuse (I.L.)..........3B-SS-1B-2B		51	193	29	59	14	3	11	31	.306	16	40	0	72	98	9	.950	
Major League totals (3 years)		88	193	26	37	11	2	5	21	.192	13	48	1	84	191	15	.948	

WOOTEN, GREG — P — MARINERS

PERSONAL: Born March 30, 1974, in Eugene, Ore. ... 6-7/210. ... Throws right, bats right. ... Full name: Gregory J. Wooten.

HIGH SCHOOL: Sheldon (Eugene, Ore.).

COLLEGE: Portland State.

TRANSACTIONS/CAREER NOTES: Selected by Seattle Mariners organization in third round of free-agent draft (June 1, 1995). ... On disabled list (April 2-June 4 and July 11, 1998-remainder of season).

HONORS: Named Eastern League Pitcher of the Year (2000).

Year	League	W	L	Pct.	ERA	G	GS	CG	ShO	Sv.	IP	H	R	ER	BB	SO
1996—Wisconsin (Midw.)...........	7	1	.875	2.47	13	13	3	•1	0	$83^2/_3$	58	27	23	29	68
—Lancaster (Calif.)...............	8	4	.667	3.80	14	14	1	0	0	97	101	47	41	25	71
1997—Memphis (Sou.)	11	10	.524	4.47	26	26	0	0	0	155	166	91	77	59	98
1998—Lancaster (Calif.).............	2	2	.500	7.18	6	6	0	0	0	$31^1/_3$	43	26	25	12	22
1999—Lancaster (Calif.).............	10	4	.714	4.33	17	17	3	0	0	$114^1/_3$	123	62	55	30	72
2000—New Haven (East.)..............	17	3	.850	2.31	26	26	•6	4	0	$179^1/_3$	166	50	46	15	115
2001—Tacoma (PCL)	11	8	.579	3.99	27	26	*5	1	0	$169^1/_3$	201	91	75	32	116

WOOTEN, SHAWN — C — ANGELS

PERSONAL: Born July 24, 1972, in Glendora, Calif. ... 5-10/205. ... Bats right, throws right. ... Full name: William Shawn Wooten.

HIGH SCHOOL: South Hills (Covina, Calif.).

JUNIOR COLLEGE: Mount San Antonio College (Calif.).

TRANSACTIONS/CAREER NOTES: Selected by Detroit Tigers organization in 18th round of free-agent draft (June 3, 1993). ... Released by Tigers (June 19, 1995). ... Signed by Moose Jaw, Prairie League (1995). ... Signed by California Angels organization (February 26, 1997). ... Angels franchise renamed Anaheim Angels for 1997 season.

STATISTICAL NOTES: Led South Atlantic League third basemen with .938 fielding percentage in 1994. ... Led Eastern League third basemen with 91 putouts and 356 total chances in 1999.

Year	Team (League)	Pos.	G	AB	R	H	2B	3B	HR	RBI	Avg.	BB	SO	SB	PO	A	E	Avg.
1993—Bristol (Appl.)............	1B-3B-OF	52	177	26	62	12	2	8	39	*.350	24	20	1	173	43	10	.956
—Fayetteville (S.Atl.)	1B-3B	5	16	2	4	0	0	1	5	.250	3	3	0	13	2	0	1.000
1994—Fayetteville (S.Atl.)	3B-1B	121	439	45	118	25	4	3	61	.269	27	84	1	88	277	24	†.938
1995—Jacksonville (Sou.).....	3B	20	70	4	9	1	0	2	7	.129	1	17	0	8	50	5	.921
—Lakeland (FSL)...........	3B	38	135	11	31	10	1	2	11	.230	10	28	0	23	90	7	.942
—Moose Jaw (PRA)■.....		52	201	38	75	12	2	11	55	.373	18	26	3	...	...	...	...
1996—Moose Jaw (PRA)		77	292	44	89	17	0	12	57	.305	18	46	2	...	...	...	...
1997—Cedar Rapids (Mid.)■	C-1B	80	353	43	102	23	1	15	75	.289	49	71	0	166	19	0	1.000
1998—Lake Elsinore (Calif.) ..	1B-3B-2B	105	395	56	116	31	0	16	74	.294	38	82	0	729	58	1	.999
—Midland (Texas).........	1B	8	28	3	9	4	0	1	6	.321	3	4	0	24	5	1	.967
1999—Erie (East.)	3B-C-1B	137	518	70	151	27	1	19	88	.292	50	102	3	†101	246	22	.940
2000—Erie (East.)	C-3B-1B	51	191	32	56	12	2	9	35	.293	17	30	4	232	57	9	.970
—Edmonton (PCL)	C-3B	66	252	43	89	21	3	11	42	.353	18	38	0	341	51	7	.982
—Anaheim (A.L.)	C-1B	7	9	2	5	1	0	0	1	.556	0	0	0	15	1	0	1.000
2001—Anaheim (A.L.)..........DH-C-1B-3B		79	221	24	69	8	1	8	32	.312	5	42	2	231	22	2	.992
Major League totals (2 years)		86	230	26	74	9	1	8	33	.322	5	42	2	246	23	2	.993

WORRELL, TIM — P — GIANTS

W

PERSONAL: Born July 5, 1967, in Pasadena, Calif. ... 6-4/231. ... Throws right, bats right. ... Full name: Timothy Howard Worrell. ... Brother of Todd Worrell, pitcher with St. Louis Cardinals (1985-92) and Los Angeles Dodgers (1993-97).

HIGH SCHOOL: Maranatha (Sierra Madre, Calif.).

COLLEGE: Biola (Calif.).

TRANSACTIONS/CAREER NOTES: Selected by San Diego Padres organization in 20th round of free-agent draft (June 5, 1989). ... On disabled list (April 19, 1994-remainder of season). ... On San Diego disabled list (April 24-September 1, 1995); included rehabilitation assignments to Rancho Cucamonga (May 3-17 and August 1-10) and Las Vegas (May 17-June 1 and August 10-30). ... Traded by Padres with OF Trey Beamon to Detroit Tigers for P Dan Miceli, P Donne Wall and 3B Ryan Balfe (November 19, 1997). ... Traded by Tigers with OF David Roberts to Cleveland Indians for OF Geronimo Berroa (June 24, 1998). ... Traded by Indians to Oakland Athletics for a player to be named later (July 12, 1998); Indians acquired SS Adam Robinson to complete deal (July 27, 1998). ... On Oakland disabled list (July 20-August 8, 1999); included rehabilitation assignment to Modesto (August 5-8). ... Granted free agency (October 29, 1999). ... Signed by Baltimore Orioles organization (February 4, 2000). ... Released by Orioles (May 1, 2000). ... Signed by Chicago Cubs organization (May 8, 2000). ... Traded by Cubs to San Francisco Giants for 3B Bill Mueller (November 19, 2000). ... On San Francisco disabled list (July 9-26, 2001); included rehabilitation assignment to Arizona League Giants (July 22-26).

STATISTICAL NOTES: Pitched 2-0 no-hit victory for Las Vegas against Phoenix (September 5, 1992).

Year	League	W	L	Pct.	ERA	G	GS	CG	ShO	Sv.	IP	H	R	ER	BB	SO
1990— Charleston, S.C. (S.Atl.)		5	8	.385	4.64	20	19	3	0	0	110 2/3	120	65	57	28	68
1991— Waterloo (Midw.)		8	4	.667	3.34	14	14	3	2	0	86 1/3	70	36	32	33	83
— High Desert (Calif.)............		5	2	.714	4.24	11	11	2	0	0	63 2/3	65	32	30	33	70
1992— Wichita (Texas)		8	6	.571	2.86	19	19	1	1	0	125 2/3	115	46	40	32	109
— Las Vegas (PCL)		4	2	.667	4.26	10	10	1	1	0	63 1/3	61	32	30	19	32
1993— Las Vegas (PCL)		5	6	.455	5.48	15	14	2	0	0	87	102	61	53	26	89
— San Diego (N.L.)		2	7	.222	4.92	21	16	0	0	0	100 2/3	104	63	55	43	52
1994— San Diego (N.L.)		0	1	.000	3.68	3	3	0	0	0	14 2/3	9	7	6	5	14
1995— Rancho Cuca. (Calif.)		0	2	.000	5.16	9	3	0	0	1	22 2/3	25	17	13	6	17
— Las Vegas (PCL)		0	2	.000	6.00	10	3	0	0	0	24	27	21	16	17	18
— San Diego (N.L.)		1	0	1.000	4.72	9	0	0	0	0	13 1/3	16	7	7	6	13
1996— San Diego (N.L.)		9	7	.563	3.05	50	11	0	0	1	121	109	45	41	39	99
1997— San Diego (N.L.)		4	8	.333	5.16	60	10	0	0	3	106 1/3	116	67	61	50	81
1998— Detroit (A.L.)■...................		2	6	.250	5.98	15	9	0	0	0	61 2/3	66	42	41	19	47
— Cleveland (A.L.)■...............		0	0	...	5.06	3	0	0	0	0	5 1/3	6	3	3	2	2
— Oakland (A.L.)■.................		0	1	.000	4.00	25	0	0	0	0	36	34	17	16	8	33
1999— Oakland (A.L.)		2	2	.500	4.15	53	0	0	0	0	69 1/3	69	38	32	34	62
— Modesto (Calif.)................		0	0	...	0.00	1	1	0	0	0	2	0	0	0	0	5
2000— Baltimore (A.L.)■.............		2	2	.500	7.36	5	0	0	0	0	7 1/3	12	6	6	5	5
— Iowa (PCL)■.....................		2	0	1.000	5.06	6	0	0	0	0	10 2/3	9	6	6	5	7
— Chicago (N.L.)		3	4	.429	2.47	54	0	0	0	3	62	60	20	17	24	52
2001— San Francisco (N.L.)■		2	5	.286	3.45	73	0	0	0	0	78 1/3	71	33	30	33	63
— Arizona Giants (Ariz.)		0	0	...	0.00	1	1	0	0	0	3	1	0	0	1	2
A.L. totals (3 years)		6	11	.353	4.91	101	9	0	0	0	179 2/3	187	106	98	68	149
N.L. totals (7 years)		21	32	.396	3.93	270	40	0	0	7	496 1/3	485	242	217	200	374
Major League totals (9 years)		27	43	.386	4.19	371	49	0	0	7	676	672	348	315	268	523

DIVISION SERIES RECORD

Year	League	W	L	Pct.	ERA	G	GS	CG	ShO	Sv.	IP	H	R	ER	BB	SO
1996— San Diego (N.L.)		0	0	...	2.45	2	0	0	0	0	3 2/3	4	1	1	1	2

WRIGHT, DAN   P   WHITE SOX

PERSONAL: Born December 14, 1977, in Longview, Texas. ... 6-5/225. ... Throws right, bats right. ... Full name: Jonathan Daniel Wright.
HIGH SCHOOL: Sullivan South (Kingsport, Tenn.).
COLLEGE: Arkansas.
TRANSACTIONS/CAREER NOTES: Selected by Cleveland Indians organization in 19th round of free-agent draft (June 4, 1996); did not sign. ... Selected by Chicago White Sox organization in second round of free-agent draft (June 2, 1999); choice received from Baltimore Orioles as part of compensation for signing of Type A free-agent OF Albert Belle.

Year	League	W	L	Pct.	ERA	G	GS	CG	ShO	Sv.	IP	H	R	ER	BB	SO
1999— Bristol (Appl.)...................		2	0	1.000	1.00	10	0	0	0	1	18	14	8	2	9	18
— Burlington (Midw.).............		0	0	...	6.00	2	0	0	0	0	6	5	4	4	3	3
2000— Winston-Salem (Caro.).......		9	8	.529	3.74	21	21	1	0	0	132 1/3	135	64	55	50	106
— Birmingham (Sou.)............		2	4	.333	2.49	7	7	0	0	0	43 1/3	28	15	12	24	31
2001— Birmingham (Sou.)............		7	7	.500	2.82	20	20	0	0	0	134	112	54	42	41	128
— Chicago (A.L.)...................		5	3	.625	5.70	13	12	0	0	0	66 1/3	78	45	42	39	36
Major League totals (1 year)........		5	3	.625	5.70	13	12	0	0	0	66 1/3	78	45	42	39	36

WRIGHT, JAMEY   P   BREWERS

PERSONAL: Born December 24, 1974, in Oklahoma City. ... 6-5/236. ... Throws right, bats right. ... Full name: Jamey Alan Wright.
HIGH SCHOOL: Westmoore (Moore, Okla.).
TRANSACTIONS/CAREER NOTES: Selected by Colorado Rockies organization in first round (28th pick overall) of free-agent draft (June 3, 1993). ... On Colorado disabled list (May 15-June 8, 1997); included rehabilitation assignment to Salem (June 1-8). ... Traded by Rockies with C Henry Blanco to Milwaukee Brewers as part of three-way deal in which Rockies received 3B Jeff Cirillo, P Scott Karl and cash from Brewers, Oakland Athletics received P Justin Miller and cash from Rockies and Brewers received P Jimmy Haynes to A's (December 13, 1999). ... On Milwaukee disabled list (March 28-May 23, 2000); included rehabilitation assignments to Huntsville (May 6-13) and Indianapolis (May 14-20). ... On disabled list (May 25-June 10, 2001).
STATISTICAL NOTES: Led N.L. pitchers with 18 hit batsmen in 2000. ... Tied for N.L. lead with 20 hit batsmen in 2001.
MISCELLANEOUS: Appeared in one game as pinch hitter (2001).

Year	League	W	L	Pct.	ERA	G	GS	CG	ShO	Sv.	IP	H	R	ER	BB	SO
1993— Arizona Rockies (Ariz.).......		1	3	.250	4.00	8	8	0	0	0	36	35	19	16	9	26
1994— Asheville (S.Atl.)..............		7	•14	.333	5.97	28	27	2	0	0	143 1/3	*188	107	*95	59	103
1995— Salem (Caro.)..................		10	8	.556	2.47	26	26	2	1	0	•171	160	74	47	72	95
— New Haven (East.)..............		0	1	.000	9.00	1	1	0	0	0	3	6	6	3	3	0
1996— New Haven (East.)............		5	1	.833	0.81	7	7	1	1	0	44 2/3	27	7	4	12	54
— Colorado Springs (PCL)....		4	2	.667	2.72	9	9	0	0	0	59 2/3	53	20	18	22	40
— Colorado (N.L.)		4	4	.500	4.93	16	15	0	0	0	91 1/3	105	60	50	41	45
1997— Colorado (N.L.)		8	12	.400	6.25	26	26	1	0	0	149 2/3	198	113	104	71	59
— Salem (Caro.)..................		0	1	.000	9.00	1	1	0	0	0	1	1	1	1	1	1
— Colorado Springs (PCL).....		1	0	1.000	1.64	2	2	0	0	0	11	9	3	2	5	11
1998— Colorado (N.L.)		9	14	.391	5.67	34	34	1	0	0	206 1/3	235	143	130	95	86
1999— Colorado (N.L.)		4	3	.571	4.87	16	16	0	0	0	94 1/3	110	52	51	54	49
— Colorado Springs (PCL).....		5	7	.417	6.46	17	16	2	0	0	100 1/3	133	87	72	38	75
2000— Huntsville (Sou.)■...........		2	0	1.000	0.00	2	2	0	0	0	12 1/3	7	0	0	6	10
— Indianapolis (I.L.)..............		0	0	...	1.80	1	1	0	0	0	5	8	5	1	3	7
— Milwaukee (N.L.)...............		7	9	.438	4.10	26	25	0	0	0	164 2/3	157	81	75	88	96
2001— Milwaukee (N.L.)...............		11	12	.478	4.90	33	33	1	1	0	194 2/3	201	115	106	98	129
Major League totals (6 years)		43	54	.443	5.15	151	149	3	1	0	901	1006	564	516	447	464

W

PERSONAL: Born December 29, 1975, in Anaheim, Calif. ... 6-2/230. ... Throws right, bats right. ... Full name: Jaret Samuel Wright. ... Son of Clyde Wright, pitcher with California Angels (1966-73), Milwaukee Brewers (1974) and Texas Rangers (1975).

HIGH SCHOOL: Katella (Anaheim, Calif.).

TRANSACTIONS/CAREER NOTES: Selected by Cleveland Indians organization in first round (10th pick overall) of free-agent draft (June 2, 1994). ... On disabled list (June 19-September 23, 1996). ... On suspended list (May 10-16, 1999). ... On disabled list (July 19-August 3 and August 9-September 10, 1999); included rehabilitation assignments to Buffalo (September 2) and Akron (September 6). ... On Cleveland disabled list (May 12-27 and June 3, 2000-remainder of season); included rehabilitation assignments to Buffalo (July 29-August 2) and Akron (August 3-10). ... On Cleveland disabled list (March 31-May 19 and September 1, 2001-remainder of season); included rehabilitation assignments to Buffalo (April 30-May 12) and Akron (May 13-19). ... On Buffalo disabled list (July 4-August 9 and August 19-Septmeber 1, 2001)

Year League	W	L	Pct.	ERA	G	GS	CG	ShO	Sv.	IP	H	R	ER	BB	SO
1994— Burlington (Appl.)	0	1	.000	5.40	4	4	0	0	0	13 1/3	13	10	8	9	16
1995— Columbus (S.Atl.)	5	6	.455	3.00	24	24	0	0	0	129	93	55	43	79	113
1996— Kinston (Caro.)	7	4	.636	2.50	19	19	0	0	0	101	65	32	28	55	109
1997— Cleveland (A.L.)	8	3	.727	4.38	16	16	0	0	0	90 1/3	81	45	44	35	63
— Buffalo (A.A.)	4	1	.800	1.80	7	7	1	1	0	45	30	16	9	19	47
— Akron (East.)	3	3	.500	3.67	8	8	1	0	0	54	43	26	22	23	59
1998— Cleveland (A.L.)	12	10	.545	4.72	32	32	1	1	0	192 2/3	207	109	101	87	140
1999— Cleveland (A.L.)	8	10	.444	6.06	26	26	0	0	0	133 2/3	144	99	90	77	91
— Buffalo (I.L.)	0	0	...	0.00	1	1	0	0	0	3	0	0	0	0	4
— Akron (East.)	1	0	1.000	0.00	1	1	0	0	0	5	3	0	0	1	6
2000— Cleveland (A.L.)	3	4	.429	4.70	9	9	1	1	0	51 2/3	44	27	27	28	36
— Buffalo (I.L.)	0	0	...	0.00	1	1	0	0	0	2	0	0	0	1	1
— Akron (East.)	0	0	...	3.38	2	2	0	0	0	8	4	3	3	3	5
2001— Buffalo (I.L.)	3	1	.750	4.71	7	7	0	0	0	28 2/3	25	18	15	13	28
— Akron (East.)	0	0	...	1.29	1	1	0	0	0	7	2	1	1	0	4
— Cleveland (A.L.)	2	2	.500	6.52	7	7	0	0	0	29	36	22	21	22	18
Major League totals (5 years)	33	29	.532	5.12	90	90	2	2	0	497 1/3	512	302	283	249	348

DIVISION SERIES RECORD

Year League	W	L	Pct.	ERA	G	GS	CG	ShO	Sv.	IP	H	R	ER	BB	SO
1997— Cleveland (A.L.)	2	0	1.000	3.97	2	2	0	0	0	11 1/3	11	6	5	7	10
1998— Cleveland (A.L.)	0	1	.000	12.46	1	1	0	0	0	4 1/3	7	6	6	2	6
1999— Cleveland (A.L.)	0	1	.000	22.50	1	0	0	0	0	2	4	5	5	1	1
Division series totals (3 years)	2	2	.500	8.15	4	3	0	0	0	17 2/3	22	17	16	10	17

CHAMPIONSHIP SERIES RECORD

RECORDS: Shares single-inning record for most home runs allowed—3 (October 12, 1997, third inning).

Year League	W	L	Pct.	ERA	G	GS	CG	ShO	Sv.	IP	H	R	ER	BB	SO
1997— Cleveland (A.L.)	0	0	...	15.00	1	1	0	0	0	3	6	5	5	2	3
1998— Cleveland (A.L.)	0	1	.000	8.10	2	1	0	0	0	6 2/3	7	6	6	8	4
Champ. series totals (2 years)	0	1	.000	10.24	3	2	0	0	0	9 2/3	13	11	11	10	7

WORLD SERIES RECORD

Year League	W	L	Pct.	ERA	G	GS	CG	ShO	Sv.	IP	H	R	ER	BB	SO
1997— Cleveland (A.L.)	1	0	1.000	2.92	2	2	0	0	0	12 1/3	7	4	4	10	12

PERSONAL: Born July 12, 1972, in Houston. ... 6-5/220. ... Throws left, bats left. ... Full name: Kelly Douglas Wunsch.

HIGH SCHOOL: Bellaire (Texas).

COLLEGE: Texas A&M.

TRANSACTIONS/CAREER NOTES: Selected by Atlanta Braves organization in 54th round of free-agent draft (June 4, 1990); did not sign. ... Selected by Milwaukee Brewers organization in first round (26th pick overall) of free-agent draft (June 3, 1993); pick received as compensation for Toronto Blue Jays signing Type-A free agent Paul Molitor. ... On El Paso disabled list (April 4-May 13, 1996; and April 8-May 7, 1998). ... On Stockton disabled list (June 19-September 10, 1996). ... On Louisville disabled list (July 10-17, 1999). ... Granted free agency (October 15, 1999). ... Signed by Chicago White Sox organization (November 15, 1999). ... On disabled list (June 18, 2001-remainder of season).

Year League	W	L	Pct.	ERA	G	GS	CG	ShO	Sv.	IP	H	R	ER	BB	SO
1993— Beloit (Midw.)	1	5	.167	4.83	12	12	0	0	0	63 1/3	58	39	34	39	61
1994— Beloit (Midw.)	3	10	.231	6.16	17	17	0	0	0	83 1/3	88	69	57	47	77
— Helena (Pio.)	4	2	.667	5.12	9	9	1	0	0	51	52	39	29	30	57
1995— Beloit (Midw.)	4	7	.364	4.20	14	14	3	1	0	85 2/3	90	47	40	37	66
— Stockton (Calif.)	5	6	.455	5.33	14	13	1	1	0	74 1/3	89	51	44	39	62
1996—							Did not play.								
1997— Stockton (Calif.)	7	9	.438	3.46	24	22	2	2	0	143	141	65	55	62	98
1998— El Paso (Texas)	5	6	.455	5.95	17	17	1	1	0	101 1/3	127	81	67	31	70
— Louisville (I.L.)	3	1	.750	3.83	9	8	0	0	0	51 2/3	53	23	22	15	36
1999— Huntsville (Sou.)	4	1	.800	1.95	22	3	0	0	1	50 2/3	40	13	11	23	35
— Louisville (I.L.)	2	1	.667	4.75	16	2	0	0	0	41 2/3	52	23	22	14	20
2000— Chicago (A.L.)■	6	3	.667	2.93	*83	0	0	0	1	61 1/3	50	22	20	29	51
2001— Chicago (A.L.)	2	1	.667	7.66	33	0	0	0	0	22 1/3	21	19	19	9	16
Major League totals (2 years)	8	4	.667	4.20	116	0	0	0	1	83 2/3	71	41	39	38	67

DIVISION SERIES RECORD

Year League	W	L	Pct.	ERA	G	GS	CG	ShO	Sv.	IP	H	R	ER	BB	SO
2000— Chicago (A.L.)	0	1	.000	0.00	3	0	0	0	0	2/3	2	1	0	0	0

W

WYLIE, MITCH   P   WHITE SOX

PERSONAL: Born January 14, 1977, in Davenport, Iowa. ... 6-3/190. ... Throws right, bats right. ... Full name: Mitchell Andrew Wylie.
COLLEGE: St. Ambrose.
TRANSACTIONS/CAREER NOTES: Selected by Chicago White Sox organization in eighth round of free-agent draft (June 2, 1998).

Year	League	W	L	Pct.	ERA	G	GS	CG	ShO	Sv.	IP	H	R	ER	BB	SO
1998—	Bristol (Appl.)	0	2	.000	3.30	20	0	0	0	6	30	34	12	11	11	32
1999—	Burlington (Midw.)	1	0	1.000	1.97	6	6	0	0	0	32	28	11	7	11	27
2000—	Winston-Salem (Caro.)	3	7	.300	4.34	17	17	0	0	0	95 1/3	112	59	46	34	57
2001—	Winston-Salem (Caro.)	0	1	.000	3.60	1	1	0	0	0	5	7	2	2	1	4
—	Birmingham (Sou.)	•15	4	.789	4.21	24	24	0	0	0	141	138	70	66	46	123

YAN, ESTEBAN   P   DEVIL RAYS

PERSONAL: Born June 22, 1974, in Campina Del Seibo, Dominican Republic. ... 6-4/230. ... Throws right, bats right. ... Full name: Esteban Luis Yan.
HIGH SCHOOL: Escuela Hicayagua (Dominican Republic).
TRANSACTIONS/CAREER NOTES: Signed as non-drafted free agent by Atlanta Braves organization (November 21, 1990). ... Traded by Braves with OF Roberto Kelly and OF Tony Tarasco to Montreal Expos for OF Marquis Grissom (April 6, 1995). ... Contract sold by Expos to Baltimore Orioles organization (April 6, 1996). ... Selected by Tampa Bay Devil Rays in first round (18th pick overall) of expansion draft (November 18, 1997). ... On Tampa Bay disabled list (June 17-July 15, 1999); included rehabilitation assignment to St. Petersburg (July 10-15). ... On Tampa Bay disabled list (June 22-July 12, 2001); included rehabilitation assignment to Orlando (July 5-12).
STATISTICAL NOTES: Led South Atlantic League with six balks in 1994. ... Hit home run in first major league at-bat (June 4, 2000).
MISCELLANEOUS: Holds Tampa Bay Devil Rays all-time record for most strikeouts (298) and games (211).

Year	League	W	L	Pct.	ERA	G	GS	CG	ShO	Sv.	IP	H	R	ER	BB	SO
1991—	San Pedro (DSL)	4	1	.800	3.63	18	11	0	0	0	72	61	36	29	26	34
1992—	San Pedro (DSL)	12	3	.800	1.32	16	16	7	4	0	115 2/3	85	37	17	23	86
1993—	Danville (Appl.)	4	7	.364	3.03	14	•14	0	0	0	71 1/3	73	46	24	24	50
1994—	Macon (S.Atl.)	11	12	.478	3.27	28	•28	4	•3	0	170 2/3	155	85	62	34	121
1995—	West Palm Beach (FSL)■..	6	8	.429	3.07	24	21	1	0	1	137 2/3	139	63	47	33	89
1996—	Bowie (East.)■	0	2	.000	5.63	9	1	0	0	0	16	18	12	10	8	15
—	Rochester (I.L.)	5	4	.556	4.27	22	10	0	0	1	71 2/3	75	37	34	18	61
—	Baltimore (A.L.)	0	0	...	5.79	4	0	0	0	0	9 1/3	13	7	6	3	7
1997—	Rochester (I.L.)	11	5	.688	3.10	34	12	0	0	2	119	107	54	41	37	131
—	Baltimore (A.L.)	0	1	.000	15.83	3	2	0	0	0	9 2/3	20	18	17	7	4
1998—	Tampa Bay (A.L.)■	5	4	.556	3.86	64	0	0	0	1	88 2/3	78	41	38	41	77
1999—	Tampa Bay (A.L.)	3	4	.429	5.90	50	1	0	0	0	61	77	41	40	32	46
—	St. Petersburg (FSL)	0	0	...	0.00	2	2	0	0	0	4	3	1	0	1	0
2000—	Tampa Bay (A.L.)	7	8	.467	6.21	43	20	0	0	0	137 2/3	158	98	95	42	111
2001—	Tampa Bay (A.L.)	4	6	.400	3.90	54	0	0	0	22	62 1/3	64	34	27	11	64
—	Orlando (Sou.)	0	0	...	3.00	2	2	0	0	0	3	3	1	1	0	4
Major League totals (6 years)		**19**	**23**	**.452**	**5.44**	**218**	**23**	**0**	**0**	**23**	**368 2/3**	**410**	**239**	**223**	**136**	**309**

YATES, TYLER   P   METS

PERSONAL: Born August 7, 1977, in Lihue, Hawaii. ... 6-4/220. ... Throws right, bats right. ... Full name: Tyler Kali Yates.
HIGH SCHOOL: Kauai (Lihue Kauai, Hawaii).
COLLEGE: Hawaii-Hilo.
TRANSACTIONS/CAREER NOTES: Selected by Oakland Athletics organization in 23rd round of free-agent draft (June 2, 1998). ... Traded by Athletics with P Mark Guthrie to New York Mets for OF David Justice (December 14, 2001).
STATISTICAL NOTES: Led Texas League with eight intentional bases on balls allowed in 2001.

Year	League	W	L	Pct.	ERA	G	GS	CG	ShO	Sv.	IP	H	R	ER	BB	SO
1998—	Arizona Athletics (Ariz.)	0	0	...	3.91	15	0	0	0	2	23	28	12	10	14	20
—	Southern Oregon (N'West)	0	0	...	0.00	2	0	0	0	1	2 1/3	2	0	0	0	1
1999—	Visalia (Calif.)	2	5	.286	5.47	47	1	0	0	4	82 1/3	98	64	50	35	74
2000—	Modesto (Calif.)	4	2	.667	2.86	30	0	0	0	1	56 2/3	50	23	18	23	61
—	Midland (Texas)	1	1	.500	6.15	22	0	0	0	0	26 1/3	28	20	18	15	24
2001—	Midland (Texas)	4	6	.400	4.31	56	0	0	0	17	62 2/3	66	39	30	27	61
—	Sacramento (PCL)	1	0	1.000	0.00	4	0	0	0	1	5 1/3	3	0	0	1	3

YOSHII, MASATO   P   EXPOS

PERSONAL: Born April 20, 1965, in Osaka, Japan. ... 6-2/210. ... Throws right, bats right.
HIGH SCHOOL: Minoshima (Japan).
TRANSACTIONS/CAREER NOTES: Played for Kintetsu Buffaloes of Japan Pacific League (1985-94). ... Played for Yakult Swallows of Japan Central League (1995-97). ... Signed as non-drafted free agent by New York Mets (January 13, 1998). ... Traded by Mets to Colorado Rockies for P Bobby M. Jones and P Lariel Gonzalez (January 14, 2000). ... Released by Rockies (March 28, 2001). ... Signed by Montreal Expos (April 13, 2001).

Year	League	W	L	Pct.	ERA	G	GS	CG	ShO	Sv.	IP	H	R	ER	BB	SO
1985—	Kintetsu (Jap. Pac.)	0	1	.000	21.00	2	...	...	...	0	3	...	...	7	3	1
1986—	Kintetsu (Jap. Pac.)	0	0	...	23.14	2	...	...	...	0	2 1/3	...	...	6	2	2
1987—	Kintetsu (Jap. Pac.)	2	1	.667	4.75	13	...	...	...	0	36	...	...	19	12	23
1988—	Kintetsu (Jap. Pac.)	10	2	.833	2.69	50	...	...	...	24	80 1/3	...	...	24	44	44
1989—	Kintetsu (Jap. Pac.)	5	5	.500	2.99	47	...	...	...	20	84 1/3	...	...	28	37	44
1990—	Kintetsu (Jap. Pac.)	8	9	.471	3.39	45	...	...	...	15	74 1/3	...	...	28	30	55
1991—	Kintetsu (Jap. Pac.)	2	1	.667	3.42	21	...	...	...	2	26 1/3	...	...	10	6	13
1992—	Kintetsu (Jap. Pac.)	1	0	1.000	2.31	9	...	...	...	0	11 2/3	...	...	3	2	4

W
Y

Year League	W	L	Pct.	ERA	G	GS	CG	ShO	Sv.	IP	H	R	ER	BB	SO
1993—Kinetsu (Jap. Pac.)	5	5	.500	2.67	22	...	...	...	0	104 2/3	...	...	31	25	66
1994—Kinetsu (Jap. Pac.)	7	7	.500	5.47	21	...	...	...	0	97	...	...	59	37	42
1995—Yakult (Jap. Cen.)■........	10	7	.588	3.12	25	...	...	...	0	147 1/3	...	...	51	39	91
1996—Yakult (Jap. Cen.)	10	7	.588	3.24	25	9	...	...	0	180 1/3	...	...	65	47	145
1997—Yakult (Jap. Cen.)	13	6	.684	2.99	28	26	6	2	0	174 1/3	149	61	58	48	104
1998—New York (N.L.)■	6	8	.429	3.93	29	29	1	0	0	171 2/3	166	79	75	53	117
1999—New York (N.L.)	12	8	.600	4.40	31	29	1	0	0	174	168	86	85	58	105
2000—Colorado (N.L.)■............	6	15	.286	5.86	29	29	0	0	0	167 1/3	201	112	109	53	88
2001—Montreal (N.L.)■............	4	7	.364	4.78	42	11	0	0	0	113	127	65	60	26	63
Major League totals (4 years)	28	38	.424	4.73	131	98	2	0	0	626	662	342	329	190	373

DIVISION SERIES RECORD

Year League	W	L	Pct.	ERA	G	GS	CG	ShO	Sv.	IP	H	R	ER	BB	SO
1999—New York (N.L.)	0	0	...	6.75	1	1	0	0	0	5 1/3	6	4	4	0	3

CHAMPIONSHIP SERIES RECORD

Year League	W	L	Pct.	ERA	G	GS	CG	ShO	Sv.	IP	H	R	ER	BB	SO
1999—New York (N.L.)	0	1	.000	4.70	2	2	0	0	0	7 2/3	9	4	4	3	4

YOUNG, COLIN — P — ROCKIES

PERSONAL: Born August 1, 1977, in Melrose, Mass. ... 6-0/185. ... Throws left, bats left. ... Full name: Colin Michael Young.
HIGH SCHOOL: Pentucket (West Newbury, Mass.), then Milford Academy (Milford, Conn.).
COLLEGE: Fordham.
TRANSACTIONS/CAREER NOTES: Selected by Colorado Rockies organization in ninth round of free-agent draft (June 2, 1999).

Year League	W	L	Pct.	ERA	G	GS	CG	ShO	Sv.	IP	H	R	ER	BB	SO
1999—Portland (N'West)	2	5	.286	4.88	15	13	0	0	0	59	59	39	32	28	74
2000—Asheville (S.Atl.)	3	1	.750	1.41	36	0	0	0	2	64	37	10	10	22	91
2001—Salem (Caro.)	4	3	.571	1.42	47	0	0	0	21	57	35	11	9	12	72

YOUNG, DMITRI — OF/1B — TIGERS

PERSONAL: Born October 11, 1973, in Vicksburg, Miss. ... 6-2/235. ... Bats both, throws right. ... Full name: Dmitri Dell Young.
HIGH SCHOOL: Rio Mesa (Oxnard, Calif.).
TRANSACTIONS/CAREER NOTES: Selected by St. Louis Cardinals organization in first round (fourth pick overall) of free-agent draft (June 3, 1991). ... On disabled list (June 2-9, 1994). ... On Arkansas suspended list (August 1-11 and August 17-27, 1995). ... On Louisville disabled list (July 14-24, 1996). ... On St. Louis disabled list (May 11-29, 1997); included rehabilitation assignment to Louisville (May 25-29). ... Traded by Cardinals to Cincinnati Reds for P Jeff Brantley (November 10, 1997). ... Selected by Tampa Bay Devil Rays in first round (16th pick overall) of expansion draft (November 18, 1997). ... Traded by Devil Rays to Reds (November 11, 1997), completing deal in which Reds traded OF Mike Kelly to Devil Rays for a player to be named later (November 11, 1997). ... Traded by Reds to Detroit Tigers for OF Juan Encarnacion and P Luis Pineda (December 11, 2001).
STATISTICAL NOTES: Led Texas League with 14 intentional bases on balls received in 1994. ... Led Texas League first basemen with 15 errors in 1994. ... Tied for American Association lead with eight bases on balls received in 1996. ... Led American Association first basemen with 1,182 total chances and 102 double plays in 1996. ... Had 18-game hitting streak (April 20-May 13, 2000). ... Career major league grand slams: 2.

							BATTING							FIELDING		
Year Team (League)	Pos.	G	AB	R	H	2B	3B	HR	RBI	Avg.	BB	SO	SB	PO	A	E	Avg.
1991—Johnson City (Appl.) ..	3B	37	129	22	33	10	0	2	22	.256	21	28	2	19	49	5	.932
1992—Springfield (Midw.)	3B	135	493	74	153	*36	6	14	72	.310	51	94	14	66	239	42	.879
1993—St. Petersburg (FSL) ..	3B-1B	69	270	31	85	13	3	5	43	.315	24	28	3	260	90	10	.972
—Arkansas (Texas)	1B-3B	45	166	13	41	11	2	3	21	.247	9	29	4	348	29	7	.982
1994—Arkansas (Texas)	OF-1B	125	453	53	123	33	2	8	54	.272	36	60	0	485	44	†16	.971
1995—Arkansas (Texas)	OF-DH	97	367	54	107	18	6	10	62	.292	30	46	2	116	5	9	.931
—Louisville (A.A.)	OF	2	7	3	2	0	0	0	0	.286	1	1	0	3	0	1	.750
1996—Louisville (A.A.)	1B	122	459	*90	153	31	8	15	64	*.333	34	67	16	*1091	83	8	.993
—St. Louis (N.L.)	1B	16	29	3	7	0	0	0	2	.241	4	5	0	39	1	1	.976
1997—St. Louis (N.L.)	1B-OF-DH	110	333	38	86	14	3	5	34	.258	38	63	6	641	47	13	.981
—Louisville (A.A.)	OF-1B	24	84	10	23	7	0	4	14	.274	13	15	1	64	2	1	.985
1998—Cincinnati (N.L.)■.....	OF-1B	144	536	81	166	48	1	14	83	.310	47	94	2	458	25	12	.976
1999—Cincinnati (N.L.)	OF-1B-DH	127	373	63	112	30	2	14	56	.300	30	71	3	216	5	4	.982
2000—Cincinnati (N.L.)	OF-1B-DH	152	548	68	166	37	6	18	88	.303	36	80	0	401	20	8	.981
2001—Cincinnati (N.L.)	OF-1B-3B	142	540	68	163	28	3	21	69	.302	37	77	8	381	84	16	.967
Major League totals (6 years)		691	2359	321	700	157	15	72	332	.297	192	390	19	2136	182	54	.977

DIVISION SERIES RECORD

							BATTING							FIELDING		
Year Team (League)	Pos.	G	AB	R	H	2B	3B	HR	RBI	Avg.	BB	SO	SB	PO	A	E	Avg.
1996—St. Louis (N.L.)						Did not play.											

CHAMPIONSHIP SERIES RECORD

							BATTING							FIELDING		
Year Team (League)	Pos.	G	AB	R	H	2B	3B	HR	RBI	Avg.	BB	SO	SB	PO	A	E	Avg.
1996—St. Louis (N.L.)	PH-1B	4	7	1	2	0	1	0	2	.286	0	2	0	11	1	0	1.000

YOUNG, ERIC — 2B — BREWERS

PERSONAL: Born May 18, 1967, in New Brunswick, N.J. ... 5-8/175. ... Bats right, throws right. ... Full name: Eric Orlando Young.
HIGH SCHOOL: New Brunswick (N.J.).
COLLEGE: Rutgers.

Y

TRANSACTIONS/CAREER NOTES: Selected by Los Angeles Dodgers organization in 43rd round of free-agent draft (June 5, 1989). ... Selected by Colorado Rockies organization in first round (11th pick overall) of expansion draft (November 17, 1992). ... On Colorado disabled list (March 22-April 22, 1996); included rehabilitation assignments to New Haven (April 5-10), Salem (April 10-13) and Colorado Springs (April 13-22). ... Traded by Rockies to Dodgers for P Pedro Astacio (August 19, 1997). ... On disabled list (July 13-31, 1998). ... On Los Angeles disabled list (July 24-August 13, 1999); included rehabilitation assignment to San Bernardino (August 8-13). ... Traded by Dodgers with P Ismael Valdes to Chicago Cubs for P Terry Adams, P Chad Ricketts and a player to be named later (December 12, 1999); Dodgers acquired P Brian Stephenson to complete deal (December 16, 1999). ... Granted free agency (November 7, 2001). ... Signed by Milwaukee Brewers (January 16, 2002).

RECORDS: Shares modern major league record for most stolen bases in one game—6 (June 30, 1996). ... Shares major league record for most stolen bases in one inning—3 (June 30, 1996, third inning).

HONORS: Named second baseman on THE SPORTING NEWS N.L. All-Star team (1996). ... Named second baseman on THE SPORTING NEWS N.L. Silver Slugger team (1996).

STATISTICAL NOTES: Led Florida State League second basemen with 24 errors in 1990. ... Led Texas League in caught stealing with 26 in 1991. ... Led Texas League second basemen with .974 fielding percentage in 1991. ... Tied for N.L. lead in errors by second baseman with 11 in 1995. ... Led N.L. in caught stealing with 19 in 1996. ... Led N.L. second basemen with 109 double plays in 1996 and 111 in 1997. ... Led N.L. in caught stealing with 22 in 1999.

MISCELLANEOUS: Holds Colorado Rockies all-time record for most stolen bases (180).

Year	Team (League)	Pos.	G	AB	R	H	2B	3B	HR	RBI	Avg.	BB	SO	SB	PO	A	E	Avg.
											BATTING					FIELDING		
1989—	GC Dodgers (GCL)	2B	56	197	53	65	11	5	2	22	.330	33	16	*41	104	128	*15	.939
1990—	Vero Beach (FSL)	2B-OF	127	460	*101	132	23	7	2	50	.287	69	35	*76	156	218	†25	.937
1991—	San Antonio (Texas)...	2B-OF	127	461	82	129	17	4	3	35	.280	67	36	*70	206	282	13	†.974
	— Albuquerque (PCL)...	2B	1	5	0	2	0	0	0	0	.400	0	0	1	2	0	1.000	
1992—	Albuquerque (PCL).....	2B	94	350	61	118	16	5	3	49	.337	33	18	28	210	287	•20	.961
	— Los Angeles (N.L.)	2B	49	132	9	34	1	0	1	11	.258	8	9	6	85	114	9	.957
1993—	Colorado (N.L.)■	2B-OF	144	490	82	132	16	8	3	42	.269	63	41	42	254	230	18	.964
1994—	Colorado (N.L.)	OF-2B	90	228	37	62	13	1	7	30	.272	38	17	18	97	4	2	.981
1995—	Colorado (N.L.)	2B-OF	120	366	68	116	21	•9	6	36	.317	49	29	35	180	230	‡11	.974
1996—	New Haven (East.)......	2B	3	15	0	1	0	0	0	0	.067	0	3	0	9	5	0	1.000
	— Salem (Caro.)	2B	3	10	2	3	3	0	0	0	.300	3	1	2	8	6	2	.875
	— Colo. Springs (PCL) ...	2B	7	23	4	6	1	1	0	3	.261	5	1	0	15	18	3	.917
	— Colorado (N.L.)	2B	141	568	113	184	23	4	8	74	.324	47	31	*53	340	431	12	.985
1997—	Colorado (N.L.)	2B	118	468	78	132	29	6	6	45	.282	57	37	32	258	414	15	.978
	— Los Angeles (N.L.)■ ..	2B	37	154	28	42	4	2	2	16	.273	14	17	13	60	79	3	.979
1998—	Los Angeles (N.L.)	2B-DH	117	452	78	129	24	1	8	43	.285	45	32	42	225	304	13	.976
1999—	Los Angeles (N.L.)	2B	119	456	73	128	24	2	2	41	.281	63	26	51	216	321	9	.984
	— San Bern. (Calif.)........	2B	3	12	0	3	0	0	0	0	.250	0	2	0	3	7	2	.833
2000—	Chicago (N.L.)■	2B	153	607	98	180	40	2	6	47	.297	63	39	54	313	400	15	.979
2001—	Chicago (N.L.)	2B	149	603	98	168	43	4	6	42	.279	42	45	31	263	366	12	.981
	Major League totals (10 years)		1237	4524	762	1307	238	39	55	427	.289	489	323	377	2291	2893	119	.978

DIVISION SERIES RECORD

Year	Team (League)	Pos.	G	AB	R	H	2B	3B	HR	RBI	Avg.	BB	SO	SB	PO	A	E	Avg.
								BATTING								FIELDING		
1995—	Colorado (N.L.)	2B	4	16	3	7	1	0	1	2	.438	2	2	1	8	13	3	.875

ALL-STAR GAME RECORD

Year	League	Pos.	AB	R	H	2B	3B	HR	RBI	Avg.	BB	SO	SB	PO	A	E	Avg.
						BATTING									FIELDING		
1996—	National	PR-2B	1	0	0	0	0	0	0	.000	0	0	0	2	1	0	1.000

YOUNG, KEVIN   1B   PIRATES

PERSONAL: Born June 16, 1969, in Alpena, Mich. ... 6-3/225. ... Bats right, throws right. ... Full name: Kevin Stacey Young.

HIGH SCHOOL: Washington (Kansas City, Kan.).

JUNIOR COLLEGE: Kansas City Kansas Community College.

COLLEGE: Southern Mississippi.

TRANSACTIONS/CAREER NOTES: Selected by Pittsburgh Pirates organization in seventh round of free-agent draft (June 4, 1990). ... On Pittsburgh disabled list (July 24-August 8, 1995). ... Released by Pirates (March 26, 1996). ... Signed by Kansas City Royals organization (April 1, 1996). ... Released by Royals (December 5, 1996). ... Signed by Pirates (March 31, 1997). ... On suspended list (September 28-30, 2000).

STATISTICAL NOTES: Tied for Southern League lead in errors by third baseman with 26 in 1991. ... Tied for American Association lead in being hit by pitch with 11 in 1992. ... Led American Association third basemen with 300 assists, 32 errors, 436 total chances and 41 double plays in 1992. ... Led N.L. first basemen with .998 fielding percentage in 1993. ... Had 15-game hitting streak (April 23-May 8, 1999). ... Led N.L. first basemen with 1,533 total chances in 1999. ... Career major league grand slams: 3.

Year	Team (League)	Pos.	G	AB	R	H	2B	3B	HR	RBI	Avg.	BB	SO	SB	PO	A	E	Avg.
								BATTING								FIELDING		
1990—	Welland (NY-Penn).....	SS	72	238	46	58	16	2	5	30	.244	31	36	10	*79	118	26	.883
1991—	Salem (Caro.).............	3B	56	201	38	63	12	4	6	28	.313	20	34	3	54	93	12	.925
	— Carolina (Sou.)...........	3B-1B	75	263	36	90	19	6	3	33	.342	15	38	9	157	116	‡28	.907
	— Buffalo (A.A.).............	3B-1B	4	9	1	2	1	0	0	2	.222	0	0	1	6	6	2	.857
1992—	Buffalo (A.A.).............	3B-1B	137	490	*91	154	29	6	8	65	.314	67	67	18	129	†313	†32	.932
	— Pittsburgh (N.L.).........	3B-1B	10	7	2	4	0	0	0	4	.571	2	0	1	3	1	1	.800
1993—	Pittsburgh (N.L.)	1B-3B	141	449	38	106	24	3	6	47	.236	36	82	2	1122	112	3	†.998
1994—	Pittsburgh (N.L.)	1B-3B-OF	59	122	15	25	7	2	1	11	.205	8	34	0	179	45	3	.987
	— Buffalo (A.A.).............	3B-1B	60	228	26	63	14	5	5	27	.276	15	45	6	59	162	4	.982
1995—	Calgary (PCL).............	3B-1B-DH	45	163	24	58	23	1	8	34	.356	15	21	6	144	85	12	.950
	— Pittsburgh (N.L.)	3B-1B	56	181	13	42	9	0	6	22	.232	8	53	1	58	110	12	.933
1996—	Omaha (A.A.)■	1B-3B-DH	50	186	29	57	11	1	13	46	.306	12	41	3	280	45	5	.985
	— Kansas City (A.L.)....	1B-OF-3B-DH	55	132	20	32	6	0	8	23	.242	11	32	3	199	19	1	.995
1997—	Pittsburgh (N.L.)■	1B-3B-OF	97	333	59	100	18	3	18	74	.300	16	89	11	644	66	5	.993
1998—	Pittsburgh (N.L.)	1B	159	592	88	160	40	2	27	108	.270	44	127	15	*1334	80	8	.994

Y

Year Team (League)	Pos.	G	AB	R	H	2B	3B	HR	RBI	Avg.	BB	SO	SB	PO	A	E	Avg.
1999— Pittsburgh (N.L.)	1B	156	584	103	174	41	6	26	106	.298	75	124	22	*1413	97	*23	.985
2000— Pittsburgh (N.L.)	1B-DH	132	496	77	128	27	0	20	88	.258	32	96	8	1109	59	*17	.986
2001— Pittsburgh (N.L.)	1B	142	449	53	104	33	0	14	65	.232	42	119	15	1154	70	7	.994
American League totals (1 year)		55	132	20	32	6	0	8	23	.242	11	32	3	199	19	1	.995
National League totals (9 years)		952	3213	448	843	199	16	118	525	.262	263	724	75	7016	640	79	.990
Major League totals (10 years)		1007	3345	468	875	205	16	126	548	.262	274	756	78	7215	659	80	.990

YOUNG, MIKE — 2B — RANGERS

PERSONAL: Born October 19, 1976, in Covina, Calif. ... 6-0/185. ... Bats right, throws right. ... Full name: Michael B. Young.
HIGH SCHOOL: Bishop Amat (La Puente, Calif.).
COLLEGE: UC Santa Barbara.
TRANSACTIONS/CAREER NOTES: Selected by Toronto Blue Jays organization in fifth round of free-agent draft (June 3, 1997). ... Traded by Blue Jays with P Darwin Cubillan to Texas Rangers for P Esteban Loaiza (July 19, 2000).
STATISTICAL NOTES: Led South Atlantic League second basemen with .978 fielding percentage in 1998.

Year Team (League)	Pos.	G	AB	R	H	2B	3B	HR	RBI	Avg.	BB	SO	SB	PO	A	E	Avg.
1997— St. Catharines (NY-P) .	SS-2B	74	276	49	85	18	3	9	48	.308	33	59	9	115	199	18	.946
1998— Hagerstown (S.Atl.)....	2B-SS-OF	*140	522	86	147	33	5	16	87	.282	55	96	16	216	341	13	†.977
1999— Dunedin (FSL)	2B-SS	129	495	86	155	•36	3	5	83	.313	61	78	30	163	375	22	.961
2000— Tennessee (Sou.)	2B-SS	91	345	51	95	24	5	6	47	.275	36	72	16	187	250	16	.965
— Tulsa (Texas)■........	SS	43	188	30	60	13	5	1	32	.319	17	28	9	67	125	7	.965
— Texas (A.L.)	2B	2	2	0	0	0	0	0	0	.000	0	1	0	0	0	0	...
2001— Oklahoma (PCL)........	2B-SS	47	189	28	55	8	0	8	28	.291	20	34	3	62	122	6	.968
— Texas (A.L.)	2B	106	386	57	96	18	4	11	49	.249	26	91	3	211	284	8	.984
Major League totals (2 years)		108	388	57	96	18	4	11	49	.247	26	92	3	211	284	8	.984

ZAMBRANO, CARLOS — P — CUBS

PERSONAL: Born June 1, 1981, in Carabobo, Venezuela. ... 6-4/250. ... Throws right, bats both. ... Full name: Carlos Alberto Zambrano.
TRANSACTIONS/CAREER NOTES: Signed as non-drafted free agent by Chicago Cubs organization (July 12, 1997).

Year League	W	L	Pct.	ERA	G	GS	CG	ShO	Sv.	IP	H	R	ER	BB	SO
1998— Arizona Cubs (Ariz.)	0	1	.000	3.15	14	2	0	0	1	40	39	17	14	25	36
1999— Lansing (Midw.)	13	7	.650	4.17	27	24	2	1	0	153 1/3	150	81	71	62	98
2000— West Tenn (Sou.)	3	1	.750	1.34	9	9	0	0	0	60 1/3	39	14	9	21	43
— Iowa (PCL)	2	5	.286	3.97	34	0	0	0	6	56 2/3	54	30	25	40	46
2001— Iowa (PCL).......................	10	5	.667	3.88	26	25	1	0	0	150 2/3	124	73	65	68	155
— Chicago (N.L.)	1	2	.333	15.26	6	1	0	0	0	7 2/3	11	13	13	8	4
Major League totals (1 year).........	1	2	.333	15.26	6	1	0	0	0	7 2/3	11	13	13	8	4

ZAMBRANO, VICTOR — P — DEVIL RAYS

PERSONAL: Born August 6, 1975, in Los Teques, Venezuela. ... 6-0/190. ... Throws right, bats right. ... Full name: Victor Manuel Zambrano.
HIGH SCHOOL: Manve Maria Billolobo (Los Teques, Venezuela).
TRANSACTIONS/CAREER NOTES: Signed as non-drafted free agent by New York Yankees organization (August 19, 1993). ... Released by Yankees organization (February 7, 1996). ... Signed by Tampa Bay Devil Rays organization (March 14, 1996).
MISCELLANEOUS: Played infield (1994-95).

Year League	W	L	Pct.	ERA	G	GS	CG	ShO	Sv.	IP	H	R	ER	BB	SO
1996— GC Devil Rays (GCL)■.......	0	0	...	8.10	1	0	0	0	0	3 1/3	4	4	3	0	6
1997— GC Devil Rays (GCL)	0	0	...	0.00	2	0	0	0	0	3	1	0	0	0	2
— Princeton (Appl.)..........	0	2	.000	1.82	20	0	0	0	0	29 2/3	18	13	6	9	36
1998— Charleston, S.C. (S.Atl.)	6	4	.600	3.38	48	2	0	0	0	77 1/3	72	32	29	20	89
1999— St. Petersburg (FSL)	0	2	.000	4.00	7	0	0	0	0	9	10	6	4	5	15
— Orlando (Sou.)	7	2	.778	4.59	40	4	0	0	1	82 1/3	92	55	42	38	81
2000— Durham (I.L.)	0	6	.000	5.03	53	0	0	0	8	62 2/3	72	38	35	29	55
2001— Durham (I.L.)	1	2	.333	2.08	29	0	0	0	12	30 1/3	26	10	7	12	29
— Tampa Bay (A.L.)...............	6	2	.750	3.16	36	0	0	0	2	51 1/3	38	21	18	18	58
Major League totals (1 year).........	6	2	.750	3.16	36	0	0	0	2	51 1/3	38	21	18	18	58

RECORD AS POSITION PLAYER

Year Team (League)	Pos.	G	AB	R	H	2B	3B	HR	RBI	Avg.	BB	SO	SB	PO	A	E	Avg.
1994— GC Yankees (GCL)......	SS-2B	50	175	23	63	5	1	0	16	.360	13	43	6	78	138	21	.911
1995— GC Yankees (GCL)......	2B-SS	27	78	10	16	3	1	0	5	.205	5	15	2	37	56	4	.959

ZAMORA, PETE — P — PHILLIES

PERSONAL: Born August 13, 1975, in Carmichael, Calif. ... 6-3/185. ... Throws left, bats left. ... Full name: Peter Andrew Zamora.
HIGH SCHOOL: Capistrano Valley (Mission Viejo, Calif.).
COLLEGE: UCLA.
TRANSACTIONS/CAREER NOTES: Selected by Los Angeles Dodgers organization in 20th round of free-agent draft (June 3, 1997). ... Selected by Philadelphia Phillies organization from Dodgers organization in Rule 5 minor league draft (December 13, 1999).
STATISTICAL NOTES: Pitched 6-0 no-hit victory for Reading against Harrisburg (June 7, 2000; second game).

Year	League	W	L	Pct.	ERA	G	GS	CG	ShO	Sv.	IP	H	R	ER	BB	SO
1997— Great Falls (Pio.)		2	5	.286	2.58	13	10	1	0	2	69 2/3	59	27	20	30	73
1998— San Bernardino (Calif.).......		4	1	.800	2.09	25	5	0	0	6	81 1/3	43	21	19	33	37
— San Antonio (Texas)		3	8	.273	4.45	12	12	0	0	0	66 2/3	71	52	33	27	47
1999— San Antonio (Texas)		2	1	.667	6.08	35	0	0	0	3	63 2/3	79	48	43	30	41
2000— Reading (East.)■.............		2	3	.400	4.09	43	7	1	1	6	101 1/3	105	50	46	45	94
2001— Scranton/W.B. (I.L.)		8	4	.667	2.93	45	6	0	0	3	89	64	29	29	41	79

ZAUN, GREGG — C — ASTROS

PERSONAL: Born April 14, 1971, in Glendale, Calif. ... 5-10/190. ... Bats both, throws right. ... Full name: Gregory Owen Zaun. ... Nephew of Rick Dempsey, catcher with six major league teams (1969-92).

HIGH SCHOOL: St. Francis (La Canada, Calif.).

TRANSACTIONS/CAREER NOTES: Selected by Baltimore Orioles organization in 17th round of free-agent draft (June 5, 1989). ... On Bowie disabled list (June 17-July 15, 1993). ... Traded by Orioles to Florida Marlins (August 23, 1996), completing deal in which Marlins traded P Terry Mathews to Orioles for a player to be named later (August 21, 1996). ... Traded by Marlins to Texas Rangers for a player to be named later or cash (November 23, 1998); Marlins received cash to complete deal (April 15, 1999). ... Traded by Rangers with OF Juan Gonzalez and P Danny Patterson to Detroit Tigers for P Justin Thompson, P Francisco Cordero, OF Gabe Kapler, C Bill Haselman, 2B Frank Catalanotto and P Alan Webb (November 2, 1999). ... Traded by Tigers to Kansas City Royals for a player to be named later or cash (March 7, 2000). ... On Kansas City disabled list (April 15-May 29, 2000); included rehabilitation assignment to Omaha (May 16-29). ... On Kansas City disabled list (March 31-July 23, 2001); included rehabilitation assignments to Gulf Coast Royals (July 3-12) and Omaha (July 13-23). ... Granted free agency (November 5, 2001). ... Signed by Houston Astros (December 11, 2001).

STATISTICAL NOTES: Led Appalachian League catchers with 460 putouts and 501 total chances in 1990. ... Led Midwest League catchers with 796 total chances in 1991. ... Led Carolina League catchers with 746 putouts, 91 assists, 18 errors, 855 total chances and 10 double plays in 1992. ... Led International League catchers with 841 total chances and 11 double plays in 1994. ... Tied for N.L. lead with 12 double plays by catcher in 1998.

Year	Team (League)	Pos.	G	AB	R	H	2B	3B	HR	RBI	Avg.	BB	SO	SB	PO	A	E	Avg.
1990— Wausau (Midw.)		C	37	100	3	13	0	1	1	7	.130	7	17	0	270	26	3	.990
— Bluefield (Appl.)	C-3B-SS-P		61	184	29	55	5	2	2	21	.299	23	15	5	†462	34	10	.980
1991— Kane County (Midw.)..		C	113	409	67	112	17	5	4	51	.274	50	41	4	*697	83	16	.980
1992— Frederick (Caro.)		C-2B	108	383	54	96	18	6	6	52	.251	42	45	3	†746	†91	†18	.979
1993— Bowie (East.)..............	C-DH-2-3-P		79	258	25	79	10	0	3	38	.306	27	26	4	423	51	10	.979
— Rochester (I.L.)		C	21	78	10	20	4	2	1	11	.256	6	11	0	141	18	4	.975
1994— Rochester (I.L.)		C	123	388	61	92	16	4	7	43	.237	56	72	4	*750	82	9	*.989
1995— Rochester (I.L.)	C-DH		42	140	26	41	13	1	6	18	.293	14	21	0	243	18	3	.989
— Baltimore (A.L.)		C	40	104	18	27	5	0	3	14	.260	16	14	1	216	13	3	.987
1996— Baltimore (A.L.)		C	50	108	16	25	8	1	1	13	.231	11	15	0	215	10	3	.987
— Rochester (I.L.)	C-DH		14	47	11	15	2	0	4	4	.319	11	6	0	52	3	2	.965
— Florida (N.L.)■............		C	10	31	4	9	1	0	1	2	.290	3	5	1	60	6	0	1.000
1997— Florida (N.L.)		C-1B	58	143	21	43	10	2	2	20	.301	26	18	1	329	25	8	.978
1998— Florida (N.L.)		C-2B	106	298	19	56	12	2	5	29	.188	35	52	5	531	49	8	.986
1999— Texas (A.L.)■............		C-DH	43	93	12	23	2	1	1	12	.247	10	7	1	165	15	3	.984
2000— Kansas City (A.L.)■...	C-1B-2B		83	234	36	64	11	0	7	33	.274	43	34	7	377	31	5	.988
— Omaha (PCL).............		C	9	25	7	7	3	0	0	3	.280	4	3	1	44	3	0	1.000
2001— GC Royals (GCL)		C	6	18	3	1	0	0	0	1	.056	7	5	0	16	1	0	1.000
— Omaha (PCL).............		C	11	43	5	12	4	0	1	8	.279	3	3	0	63	3	1	.985
— Kansas City (A.L.)	C-DH		39	125	15	40	9	0	6	18	.320	12	16	1	181	11	5	.975
American League totals (5 years)			255	664	97	179	35	2	18	90	.270	92	86	10	1154	80	19	.985
National League totals (3 years)			174	472	44	108	23	4	8	51	.229	64	75	7	920	80	16	.984
Major League totals (7 years)			429	1136	141	287	58	6	26	141	.253	156	161	17	2074	160	35	.985

DIVISION SERIES RECORD

Year	Team (League)	Pos.	G	AB	R	H	2B	3B	HR	RBI	Avg.	BB	SO	SB	PO	A	E	Avg.
1997— Florida (N.L.).............									Did not play.									

CHAMPIONSHIP SERIES RECORD

Year	Team (League)	Pos.	G	AB	R	H	2B	3B	HR	RBI	Avg.	BB	SO	SB	PO	A	E	Avg.
1997— Florida (N.L.)		C	1	0	0	0	0	0	0	0	...	0	0	0	2	0	0	1.000

WORLD SERIES RECORD

NOTES: Member of World Series championship team (1997).

Year	Team (League)	Pos.	G	AB	R	H	2B	3B	HR	RBI	Avg.	BB	SO	SB	PO	A	E	Avg.
1997— Florida (N.L.)	PH-C-PR		2	2	0	0	0	0	0	0	.000	0	0	0	3	0	0	1.000

RECORD AS PITCHER

Year	League	W	L	Pct.	ERA	G	GS	CG	ShO	Sv.	IP	H	R	ER	BB	SO
1990— Bluefield (Appl.)		0	0	...	0.00	1	0	0	0	0	1	1	0	0	1	1
1993— Bowie (East.).....................		0	0	...	0.00	1	0	0	0	0	2 1/3	1	0	0	0	0

ZEILE, TODD — 1B — ROCKIES

PERSONAL: Born September 9, 1965, in Van Nuys, Calif. ... 6-1/200. ... Bats right, throws right. ... Full name: Todd Edward Zeile. ... Husband of Julianne McNamara, Olympic gold-medal gymnast (1984). ... Name pronounced ZEEL.

HIGH SCHOOL: Hart (Newhall, Calif.).

COLLEGE: UCLA.

TRANSACTIONS/CAREER NOTES: Selected by Kansas City Royals organization in 30th round of free-agent draft (June 6, 1983); did not sign. ... Selected by St. Louis Cardinals organization in supplemental round ("sandwich pick" between second and third round 55th pick overall) of free-agent draft (June 2, 1986); pick received as compensation for New York Yankees signing Type C free-agent IF Ivan DeJesus. ... On St. Louis disabled list (April 23-May 9, 1995); included rehabilitation assignment to Louisville (May 6-9). ... Traded by Cardinals with cash to Chicago Cubs for P Mike Morgan, 3B/OF Paul Torres and C Francisco Morales (June 16, 1995). ... Granted free agency (December 21, 1995). ... Signed by Philadelphia Phillies (December 22, 1995). ... Traded by Phillies with OF Pete Incaviglia to Baltimore Orioles for two players to be named later (August 29, 1996); Phillies acquired P Calvin Maduro and P Garrett Stephenson to complete deal (September 4, 1996). ... Granted free agency (October 27, 1996). ... Signed by Los Angeles Dodgers (December 8, 1996). ... Traded by Dodgers with C Mike Piazza to Florida Marlins for OF Gary Sheffield, 3B Bobby Bonilla, C Charles Johnson, OF Jim Eisenreich and P Manuel Barrios (May 15, 1998). ... Traded by Marlins to Texas Rangers for 3B Jose Santo and P Dan DeYoung (July 31, 1998). ... Granted free agency (October 28, 1999). ... Signed by New York Mets (December 11, 1999). ... Traded by Mets to Colorado Rockies as part of three-way deal in which Rockies traded 1B/OF Ross Gload and P Craig House to Mets, Milwaukee Brewers traded P Jeff D'Amico, OF Jeromy Burnitz, IF Lou Collier, OF/1B Mark Sweeney and cash to Mets, Mets traded OF Benny Agbayani, OF/OF Lenny Harris and cash to Rockies, Rockies traded OF Alex Ochoa to Brewers and Mets traded P Glendon Rusch to Brewers (January 21, 2002).

RECORDS: Holds N.L. single-season record for fewest putouts by third baseman (150 or more games)—83 (1993). ... Shares modern N.L. single-game record for most errors by first baseman—4 (August 7, 1996).

HONORS: Named Midwest League co-Most Valuable Player (1987).

STATISTICAL NOTES: Led New York-Pennsylvania League with six sacrifice flies in 1986. ... Tied for New York-Pennsylvania League lead in double plays by catcher with seven in 1986. ... Led Texas League catchers with 687 putouts and 761 total chances in 1988. ... Led American Association catchers with .992 fielding percentage and 17 passed balls in 1989. ... Had 17-game hitting streak (June 21-July 10, 1999). ... Tied for A.L. third baseman lead with 25 errors in 1999. ... Career major league grand slams: 9.

								BATTING							FIELDING			
Year	Team (League)	Pos.	G	AB	R	H	2B	3B	HR	RBI	Avg.	BB	SO	SB	PO	A	E	Avg.
1986—Erie (NY-Penn)		C	70	248	40	64	14	1	14	*63	.258	37	52	5	407	*66	8	.983
1987—Springfield (Midw.)		C-3B	130	487	94	142	24	4	25	*106	.292	70	85	1	867	79	14	.985
1988—Arkansas (Texas)		C-OF-1B	129	430	95	117	33	2	19	75	.272	83	64	6	†697	66	10	.987
1989—Louisville (A.A.)		C-3B-1B	118	453	71	131	26	3	19	85	.289	45	78	0	583	71	6	†.991
—St. Louis (N.L.)		C	28	82	7	21	3	1	1	8	.256	9	14	0	125	10	4	.971
1990—St. Louis (N.L.)	C-3B-1B-OF	144	495	62	121	25	3	15	57	.244	67	77	2	648	106	15	.980
1991—St. Louis (N.L.)		3B	155	565	76	158	36	3	11	81	.280	62	94	17	124	290	*25	.943
1992—St. Louis (N.L.)		3B	126	439	51	113	18	4	7	48	.257	68	70	7	81	235	13	.960
—Louisville (A.A.)		3B	21	74	11	23	4	1	5	13	.311	9	13	0	15	41	5	.918
1993—St. Louis (N.L.)		3B	157	571	82	158	36	1	17	103	.277	70	76	5	83	310	33	.923
1994—St. Louis (N.L.)		3B	113	415	62	111	25	1	19	75	.267	52	56	1	66	224	12	.960
1995—Louisville (A.A.)		1B	2	8	0	1	0	0	0	0	.125	0	2	0	11	1	1	.923
—St. Louis (N.L.)		1B	34	127	16	37	6	0	5	22	.291	18	23	1	310	30	7	.980
—Chicago (N.L.)■	3B-1B	79	299	34	68	16	0	9	30	.227	16	53	0	52	134	12	.939
1996—Philadelphia (N.L.)■ ..	3B-1B	134	500	61	134	24	0	20	80	.268	67	88	1	295	195	14	.972
—Baltimore (A.L.)■		3B	29	117	17	28	8	0	5	19	.239	15	16	0	24	56	3	.964
1997—Los Angeles (N.L.)■ ..		3B	160	575	89	154	17	0	31	90	.268	85	112	8	105	248	*26	.931
1998—Los Angeles (N.L.)	3B-1B	40	158	22	40	6	1	7	27	.253	10	24	1	27	53	6	.930
—Florida (N.L.)■		3B	66	234	37	68	12	1	6	39	.291	31	34	2	43	122	5	.971
—Texas (A.L.)■		3B	52	180	26	47	14	1	6	28	.261	28	32	1	38	91	12	.915
1999—Texas (A.L.)	3B-DH-1B	156	587	80	172	41	1	24	98	.293	56	94	1	105	294	‡25	.941
2000—New York (N.L.)■		1B	153	544	67	146	36	3	22	79	.268	74	85	3	1205	95	10	.992
2001—New York (N.L.)		1B	151	531	66	141	25	1	10	62	.266	73	102	1	1184	112	11	.992
American League totals (3 years)			237	884	123	247	63	2	35	145	.279	99	142	2	167	441	40	.938
National League totals (12 years)			1540	5535	732	1470	285	19	180	801	.266	702	908	49	4348	2164	193	.971
Major League totals (13 years)			1777	6419	855	1717	348	21	215	946	.267	801	1050	51	4515	2605	233	.968

DIVISION SERIES RECORD

								BATTING							FIELDING			
Year	Team (League)	Pos.	G	AB	R	H	2B	3B	HR	RBI	Avg.	BB	SO	SB	PO	A	E	Avg.
1996—Baltimore (A.L.)		3B	4	19	2	5	1	0	0	0	.263	2	5	0	4	9	2	.867
1998—Texas (A.L.)		3B	3	9	0	3	0	0	0	0	.333	0	2	0	0	4	0	1.000
1999—Texas (A.L.)		3B	3	10	0	1	0	0	0	0	.100	2	1	0	1	4	2	.714
2000—New York (N.L.)		1B	4	14	0	1	1	0	0	0	.071	4	3	0	30	4	0	1.000
Division series totals (4 years)			14	52	2	10	2	0	0	0	.192	8	11	0	35	21	4	.933

CHAMPIONSHIP SERIES RECORD

RECORDS: Shares A.L. single-series record for most home runs—3 (1996).

								BATTING							FIELDING			
Year	Team (League)	Pos.	G	AB	R	H	2B	3B	HR	RBI	Avg.	BB	SO	SB	PO	A	E	Avg.
1996—Baltimore (A.L.)		3B	5	22	3	8	0	0	3	5	.364	2	1	0	3	7	1	.909
2000—New York (N.L.)		1B	5	19	1	7	3	0	1	8	.368	2	4	0	38	1	0	1.000
Championship series totals (2 years)			10	41	4	15	3	0	4	13	.366	4	5	0	41	8	1	.980

WORLD SERIES RECORD

								BATTING							FIELDING			
Year	Team (League)	Pos.	G	AB	R	H	2B	3B	HR	RBI	Avg.	BB	SO	SB	PO	A	E	Avg.
2000—New York (N.L.)		1B	5	20	1	8	2	0	0	1	.400	1	5	0	39	2	0	1.000

ZERBE, CHAD — P — GIANTS

PERSONAL: Born April 27, 1972, in Findlay, Ohio. ... 6-0/190. ... Throws left, bats left. ... Full name: William Chad Zerbe.

HIGH SCHOOL: Vivian Gaither (Tampa).

JUNIOR COLLEGE: Hillsborough Community College (Fla.).

TRANSACTIONS/CAREER NOTES: Selected by Los Angeles Dodgers organization in 17th round of free-agent draft (June 3, 1991). ... Released by Dodgers (December 10, 1996). ... Signed by Arizona Diamondbacks organization (January 28, 1997). ... Released by Diamondbacks (May 20, 1997). ... Signed by Sonoma County, Western League (1997). ... Signed by San Francisco Giants organization (November 26, 1997). ... Granted free agency (October 16, 1998). ... Re-signed by Giants organization (March 4, 1999). ... Granted free agency (October 15, 1999). ... Re-signed by Giants organization (October 22, 1999). ... On Shreveport disabled list (May 9-June 7, 2000).

Z

Year	League	W	L	Pct.	ERA	G	GS	CG	ShO	Sv.	IP	H	R	ER	BB	SO
1991— Gulf Coast Dodgers (GCL)..		0	2	.000	2.20	16	1	0	0	0	32 2/3	31	19	8	15	23
1992— Great Falls (Pio.)		8	3	.727	2.14	15	15	1	1	0	92 1/3	75	27	22	26	70
1993— Bakersfield (Calif.)..............		0	10	.000	5.91	14	12	1	0	0	67	83	60	44	47	41
— Vero Beach (FSL)........		1	0	1.000	6.57	10	0	0	0	0	12 1/3	12	10	9	13	11
1994— Vero Beach (FSL)		5	5	.500	3.39	18	18	1	0	0	98 1/3	88	50	37	32	68
1995— San Bernardino (Calif.).......		11	7	.611	4.57	28	27	1	0	0	163 1/3	168	103	83	64	94
1996— San Antonio (Texas)..........		4	6	.400	4.50	17	11	1	0	1	86	98	52	43	37	38
1997— High Desert (Calif.)■........		1	6	.143	7.43	9	8	0	0	0	36 1/3	61	49	30	15	26
— Sonoma County (West.)■..		4	5	.444	5.40	14	13	2	0	0	90	117	70	54	36	52
1998— San Jose (Calif.)■.............		2	0	1.000	3.35	23	0	0	0	1	37 2/3	37	16	14	12	28
1999— Bakersfield (Calif.).............		7	7	.500	3.64	21	21	0	0	0	126	124	66	51	33	81
— Shreveport (Texas)		1	3	.250	1.96	7	6	0	0	0	41 1/3	32	13	9	10	16
2000— Shreveport (Texas)		2	1	.667	2.33	9	9	0	0	0	38 2/3	37	11	10	9	34
— Fresno (PCL)...................		7	3	.700	4.32	17	11	0	0	0	81 1/3	94	46	39	17	41
— San Francisco (N.L.)		0	0	...	4.50	4	0	0	0	0	6	6	3	3	1	5
2001— Fresno (PCL)...................		3	4	.429	3.55	17	0	0	0	5	25 1/3	28	13	10	9	17
— San Francisco (N.L.)		3	0	1.000	3.92	27	1	0	0	0	39	41	21	17	10	22
Major League totals (2 years).......		3	0	1.000	4.00	31	1	0	0	0	45	47	24	20	11	27

ZIMMERMAN, JEFF — P — RANGERS

PERSONAL: Born August 9, 1972, in Kelowna, B.C. ... 6-1/200. ... Throws right, bats right. ... Full name: Jeffery Ross Zimmerman.
HIGH SCHOOL: John G. Diefenbaker (Vancouver).
COLLEGE: Texas Christian, then Simon Fraser (B.C.).
TRANSACTIONS/CAREER NOTES: Signed by Winnipeg, Northern League (May 1997). ... Signed as non-drafted free agent by Texas Rangers organization (January 6, 1998).

Year	League	W	L	Pct.	ERA	G	GS	CG	ShO	Sv.	IP	H	R	ER	BB	SO
1997— Winnipeg (Nor.).................		9	2	.818	2.82	18	16	3	0	0	118	94	49	37	35	140
1998— Charlotte (FSL)■..............		2	1	.667	1.26	10	0	0	0	0	14 1/3	10	2	2	1	14
— Tulsa (Texas)		3	1	.750	1.29	41	0	0	0	9	63	38	16	9	20	67
1999— Oklahoma (PCL)................		1	0	1.000	0.00	2	0	0	0	1	3 2/3	0	0	0	0	2
— Texas (A.L.)		9	3	.750	2.36	65	0	0	0	3	87 2/3	50	24	23	23	67
2000— Texas (A.L.)		4	5	.444	5.30	65	0	0	0	1	69 2/3	80	45	41	34	74
2001— Texas (A.L.)		4	4	.500	2.40	66	0	0	0	28	71 1/3	48	19	19	16	72
Major League totals (3 years).......		17	12	.586	3.27	196	0	0	0	32	228 2/3	178	88	83	73	213

DIVISION SERIES RECORD

Year	League	W	L	Pct.	ERA	G	GS	CG	ShO	Sv.	IP	H	R	ER	BB	SO
1999— Texas (A.L.)		0	0	...	0.00	1	0	0	0	0	1	1	0	0	0	1

ALL-STAR GAME RECORD

Year	League	W	L	Pct.	ERA	GS	CG	ShO	Sv.	IP	H	R	ER	BB	SO
1999— American..........................		0	0	...	0.00	0	0	0	0	1	0	0	0	2	0

ZITO, BARRY — P — ATHLETICS

PERSONAL: Born May 13, 1978, in Las Vegas, Nev. ... 6-4/205. ... Throws left, bats left. ... Full name: Barry William Zito.
HIGH SCHOOL: University (San Diego).
JUNIOR COLLEGE: Pierce Junior College (Calif.).
COLLEGE: UC Santa Barbara, then Southern California.
TRANSACTIONS/CAREER NOTES: Selected by Texas Rangers organization in third round of free-agent draft (June 2, 1998); did not sign. ... Selected by Oakland Athletics organization in first round (ninth pick overall) of free-agent draft (June 2, 1999).

Year	League	W	L	Pct.	ERA	G	GS	CG	ShO	Sv.	IP	H	R	ER	BB	SO
1999— Visalia (Calif.)		3	0	1.000	2.45	8	8	0	0	0	40 1/3	21	13	11	22	62
— Midland (Texas).................		2	1	.667	4.91	4	4	0	0	0	22	22	15	12	11	29
— Vancouver (PCL)		1	0	1.000	1.50	1	1	0	0	0	6	5	1	1	2	6
2000— Sacramento (PCL)............		8	5	.615	3.19	18	18	0	0	0	101 2/3	88	44	36	45	91
— Oakland (A.L.)		7	4	.636	2.72	14	14	1	1	0	92 2/3	64	30	28	45	78
2001— Oakland (A.L.)		17	8	.680	3.49	35	•35	3	2	0	214 1/3	184	92	83	80	205
Major League totals (2 years).......		24	12	.667	3.25	49	49	4	3	0	307	248	122	111	125	283

DIVISION SERIES RECORD

Year	League	W	L	Pct.	ERA	G	GS	CG	ShO	Sv.	IP	H	R	ER	BB	SO
2000— Oakland (A.L.)		1	0	1.000	1.59	1	1	0	0	0	5 2/3	7	1	1	2	5
2001— Oakland (A.L.)		0	1	.000	1.00	1	1	0	0	0	9	2	1	1	1	6
Division series totals (2 years)		1	1	.500	1.23	2	2	0	0	0	14 2/3	9	2	2	3	11

ZULETA, JULIO — 1B — CUBS

PERSONAL: Born March 28, 1975, in Panama City, Panama. ... 6-5/235. ... Bats right, throws right. ... Full name: Julio Ernesto Zuleta.
HIGH SCHOOL: Don Bosco Institute (Panama City, Panama).
COLLEGE: Panama Technological University.
TRANSACTIONS/CAREER NOTES: Signed as non-drafted free agent by Chicago Cubs organization (September 15, 1992). ... On Iowa disabled list (August 16, 2001-remainder of season).
STATISTICAL NOTES: Led Southern League in being hit by pitch with 20 in 1999. ... Tied Pacific Coast League lead first basemen with 12 errors in 2000. ... Career major league grand slams: 1.

Year	Team (League)	Pos.	G	AB	R	H	2B	3B	HR	RBI	Avg.	BB	SO	SB	PO	A	E	Avg.
									BATTING							FIELDING		
1993—	GC Cubs (GCL)..........	C-OF	17	53	3	13	0	1	0	6	.245	3	12	0	20	2	3	.880
1994—	Huntington (Appl.)	C	6	15	0	1	0	0	0	2	.067	4	4	0	22	7	2	.935
	— GC Cubs (GCL)..........	C	30	100	11	31	1	0	0	8	.310	8	18	5	176	19	2	.990
1995—	Williamsport (NY-P) ...	C	30	75	9	13	3	1	0	6	.173	11	12	0	131	12	5	.966
1996—	Williamsport (NY-P) ...	1B	62	221	35	57	12	2	1	29	.258	19	36	7	338	25	4	.989
1997—	Rockford (Midw.)	1B	119	430	59	124	30	5	6	77	.288	35	88	5	828	62	14	.985
1998—	Daytona (FSL)	1B	94	366	69	126	25	1	16	86	.344	35	59	6	643	58	13	.982
	— West Tenn (Sou.)	1B	40	139	18	41	9	0	2	20	.295	10	30	0	203	18	2	.991
1999—	West Tenn (Sou.)	1B	133	482	75	142	37	4	21	97	.295	35	122	4	897	63	9	.991
2000—	Chicago (N.L.)	1B-OF	30	68	13	20	8	0	3	12	.294	2	19	0	83	8	3	.968
	— Iowa (PCL)	1B-OF-3B	107	392	76	122	25	1	26	94	.311	31	77	5	680	51	†13	.983
2001—	Chicago (N.L.)	1B	49	106	11	23	3	0	6	24	.217	8	32	0	213	7	2	.991
	— Iowa (PCL)	1B-3B-OF	37	146	18	45	13	0	7	29	.308	7	33	3	165	19	7	.963
Major League totals (2 years)			79	174	24	43	11	0	9	36	.247	10	51	0	296	15	5	.984

Z

MAJOR LEAGUE MANAGERS

PERSONAL: Born June 15, 1949, in Riverside, Calif. ... 6-2/200. ... Batted right, threw right. ... Full name: Johnnie B. Baker Jr.

HIGH SCHOOL: Del Campo (Fair Oaks, Calif.).

COLLEGE: American River College (Calif.).

TRANSACTIONS/CAREER NOTES: Selected by Atlanta Braves organization in 26th round of free-agent draft (June 6, 1967). ... On West Palm Beach restricted list (April 5-June 13, 1968). ... On Atlanta military list (January 24-April 3, 1969 and June 17-July 3, 1972). ... Traded by Braves with 1B/3B Ed Goodson to Los Angeles Dodgers for OF Jimmy Wynn, 2B Lee Lacy, 1B/OF Tom Paciorek and IF Jerry Royster (November 17, 1975). ... Released on waivers by Dodgers (February 10, 1984); San Francisco Giants claim rejected (February 16, 1984). ... Granted free agency (February 21, 1984). ... Signed by Giants (April 1, 1984). ... On restricted list (April 2-11, 1984). ... Traded by Giants to Oakland Athletics for P Ed Puikunas and C Dan Winters (March 24, 1985). ... Granted free agency (November 10, 1986).

RECORDS: Shares major league records for most plate appearances, most at-bats and most times faced pitcher as batsman in one inning— 3 (September 20, 1972, second inning); and most stolen bases in one inning—3 (June 27, 1984, third inning).

HONORS: Named outfielder on THE SPORTING NEWS N.L. All-Star team (1980). ... Named outfielder on THE SPORTING NEWS N.L. Silver Slugger team (1980-81). ... Won N.L. Gold Glove as outfielder (1981).

STATISTICAL NOTES: Led N.L. outfielders with 407 total chances in 1973. ... Career major league grand slams: 4.

							BATTING							FIELDING		
Year Team (League)	Pos.	G	AB	R	H	2B	3B	HR	RBI	Avg.	BB	SO	SB	PO	A	E	Avg.
1967—Austin (Texas)	OF	9	39	6	9	1	0	0	1	.231	2	7	0	17	0	1	.944
1968—W.Palm Beach (FSL) ...	OF	6	21	2	4	0	0	0	2	.190	1	4	0	6	2	0	1.000
—Greenwood (W. Car.)..	OF	52	199	45	68	11	3	6	39	.342	23	39	6	82	1	3	.965
—Atlanta (N.L.)............	OF	6	5	0	2	0	0	0	0	.400	0	1	0	0	0	0	
1969—Shreveport (Texas)	OF	73	265	40	68	5	1	9	31	.257	36	41	2	135	10	3	.980
—Richmond (Int'l)	OF-3B	25	89	7	22	4	0	0	8	.247	11	22	3	40	9	4	.925
—Atlanta (N.L.)............	OF	3	7	0	0	0	0	0	0	.000	0	3	0	2	0	0	1.000
1970—Richmond (I.L.)..........	OF	118	461	97	150	29	3	11	51	.325	53	45	10	236	10	7	.972
—Atlanta (N.L.)............	OF	13	24	3	7	0	0	0	4	.292	2	4	0	11	1	3	.800
1971—Richmond (I.L.)..........	OF-3B	80	341	62	106	23	2	11	41	.311	25	37	10	136	13	4	.974
—Atlanta (N.L.)............	OF	29	62	2	14	2	0	0	4	.226	1	14	0	29	1	0	1.000
1972—Atlanta (N.L.)............	OF	127	446	62	143	27	2	17	76	.321	45	68	4	344	8	4	.989
1973—Atlanta (N.L.)............	OF	159	604	101	174	29	4	21	99	.288	67	72	24	*390	10	7	.983
1974—Atlanta (N.L.)............	OF	149	574	80	147	35	0	20	69	.256	71	87	18	359	10	7	.981
1975—Atlanta (N.L.)............	OF	142	494	63	129	18	2	19	72	.261	67	57	12	287	10	3	.990
1976—Los Angeles (N.L.)■..	OF	112	384	36	93	13	0	4	39	.242	31	54	2	254	3	1	.996
1977—Los Angeles (N.L.)	OF	153	533	86	155	26	1	30	86	.291	58	89	2	227	8	3	.987
1978—Los Angeles (N.L.)	OF	149	522	62	137	24	1	11	66	.262	47	66	12	250	13	4	.985
1979—Los Angeles (N.L.)	OF	151	554	86	152	29	1	23	88	.274	56	70	11	289	14	3	.990
1980—Los Angeles (N.L.)	OF	153	579	80	170	26	4	29	97	.294	43	66	12	308	5	3	.991
1981—Los Angeles (N.L.)	OF	103	400	48	128	17	3	9	49	.320	29	43	10	181	8	2	.990
1982—Los Angeles (N.L.)	OF	147	570	80	171	19	1	23	88	.300	56	62	17	226	7	6	.975
1983—Los Angeles (N.L.)	OF	149	531	71	138	25	1	15	73	.260	72	59	7	249	4	5	.981
1984—San Fran. (N.L.)■......	OF	100	243	31	71	7	2	3	32	.292	40	27	4	112	1	3	.974
1985—Oakland (A.L.)■........	1B-OF-DH	111	343	48	92	15	1	14	52	.268	50	47	2	465	29	5	.990
1986—Oakland (A.L.)..........	OF-DH-1B	83	242	25	58	8	0	4	19	.240	27	37	0	90	4	0	1.000
American League totals (2 years)		194	585	73	150	23	1	18	71	.256	77	84	2	555	33	5	.992
National League totals (17 years)		1845	6532	891	1831	297	22	224	942	.280	685	842	135	3518	103	54	.985
Major league totals (19 years)		2039	7117	964	1981	320	23	242	1013	.278	762	926	137	4073	136	59	.986

DIVISION SERIES RECORD

							BATTING							FIELDING		
Year Team (League)	Pos.	G	AB	R	H	2B	3B	HR	RBI	Avg.	BB	SO	SB	PO	A	E	Avg.
1981—Los Angeles (N.L.)	OF	5	18	2	3	1	0	0	1	.167	2	0	0	12	0	0	1.000

CHAMPIONSHIP SERIES RECORD

RECORDS: Shares single-game record for most grand slams—1 (October 5, 1977). ... Shares single-inning record for most runs batted in— 4 (October 5, 1977, fourth inning). ... Shares N.L. single-game record for most hits—4 (October 7, 1978).

NOTES: Named N.L. Championship Series Most Valuable Player (1977).

							BATTING							FIELDING		
Year Team (League)	Pos.	G	AB	R	H	2B	3B	HR	RBI	Avg.	BB	SO	SB	PO	A	E	Avg.
1977—Los Angeles (N.L.)	OF	4	14	4	5	1	0	2	8	.357	2	3	0	3	0	0	1.000
1978—Los Angeles (N.L.)	OF	4	15	1	7	2	0	0	1	.467	3	0	0	5	0	0	1.000
1981—Los Angeles (N.L.)	OF	5	19	3	6	1	0	0	3	.316	1	0	0	10	0	1	.909
1983—Los Angeles (N.L.)	OF	4	14	4	5	1	0	1	1	.357	2	0	0	9	0	0	1.000
Championship series totals (4 years)		17	62	12	23	5	0	3	13	.371	8	3	0	27	0	1	.964

WORLD SERIES RECORD

NOTES: Member of World Series championship team (1981).

							BATTING							FIELDING		
Year Team (League)	Pos.	G	AB	R	H	2B	3B	HR	RBI	Avg.	BB	SO	SB	PO	A	E	Avg.
1977—Los Angeles (N.L.)	OF	6	24	4	7	0	0	1	5	.292	0	2	0	11	0	1	.917
1978—Los Angeles (N.L.)	OF	6	21	2	5	0	0	1	1	.238	1	3	0	12	0	0	1.000
1981—Los Angeles (N.L.)	OF	6	24	3	4	0	0	0	1	.167	1	6	0	13	0	0	1.000
World Series totals (3 years)		18	69	9	16	0	0	2	7	.232	2	11	0	36	0	1	.973

ALL-STAR GAME RECORD

			BATTING											FIELDING			
Year League	Pos.	AB	R	H	2B	3B	HR	RBI	Avg.	BB	SO	SB	PO	A	E	Avg.
1981— National	OF	2	0	1	0	0	0	0	.500	0	0	0	2	0	0	1.000
1982— National	OF	2	0	0	0	0	0	0	.000	0	0	0	0	0	0	...
All-Star Game totals (2 years)		4	0	1	0	0	0	0	.250	0	0	0	2	0	0	1.000

RECORD AS MANAGER

BACKGROUND: Coach, San Francisco Giants (1988-92). ... Manager, Scottsdale Scorpions, Arizona Fall League (1992, record: 20-22, second place/Northern Division).

HONORS: Named N.L. Manager of the Year by Baseball Writers' Association of America (1993 and 2000). ... Coach, N.L. All-Star team (1994 and 1997). ... Named N.L. Manager of the Year by THE SPORTING NEWS (1997 and 2000).

	REGULAR SEASON				POSTSEASON							
							Champ.		World		All-Star	
					Playoff		Series		Series		Game	
Year Team (League)	W	L	Pct.	Pos.	W	L	W	L	W	L	W	L
1993— San Francisco (N.L.)...............................	103	59	.636	2nd (W)	—	—	—	—	—	—	—	—
1994— San Francisco (N.L.)...............................	55	60	.478		—	—	—	—	—	—	—	—
1995— San Francisco (N.L.)...............................	67	77	.465	4th (W)	—	—	—	—	—	—	—	—
1996— San Francisco (N.L.)...............................	68	94	.420	4th (W)	—	—	—	—	—	—	—	—
1997— San Francisco (N.L.)...............................	90	72	.556	1st (W)	0	3	—	—	—	—	—	—
1998— San Francisco (N.L.)...............................	89	74	.546	2nd (W)	—	—	—	—	—	—	—	—
1999— San Francisco (N.L.)...............................	86	76	.531	2nd (W)	—	—	—	—	—	—	—	—
2000— San Francisco (N.L.)...............................	97	65	.599	1st (W)	1	3	—	—	—	—	—	—
2001— San Francisco (N.L.)...............................	90	72	.556	2nd (W)	—	—	—	—	—	—	—	—
Major league totals (9 years)..........................	745	649	.534		1	6	—	—	—	—	—	—

NOTES:

1994—San Francisco was in second place in N.L. West at time of season-ending strike (August 12).

1997—Lost to Florida in N.L. divisional playoff.

2000—Lost to New York Mets in N.L. divisional playoff.

BAYLOR, DON — CUBS

PERSONAL: Born June 28, 1949, in Austin, Texas. ... 6-1/220. ... Batted right, threw right. ... Full name: Donald Edward Baylor. ... Cousin of Pat Ballage, safety with Indianapolis Colts (1986-87).

HIGH SCHOOL: Stephen F. Austin (Austin, Texas).

JUNIOR COLLEGE: Miami-Dade Junior College and Blinn College (Texas).

TRANSACTIONS/CAREER NOTES: Selected by Baltimore Orioles organization in second round of free-agent draft (June 6, 1967). ... Traded by Orioles with P Mike Torrez and P Paul Mitchell to Oakland Athletics for OF Reggie Jackson, P Ken Holtzman and P Bill Van Bommel (April 2, 1976). ... Granted free agency (November 1, 1976). ... Signed by California Angels (November 16, 1976). ... On disabled list (May 11-June 26, 1980). ... Granted free agency (November 10, 1982). ... Signed by New York Yankees (December 1, 1982). ... Traded by Yankees to Boston Red Sox for DH Mike Easler (March 28, 1986). ... Traded by Red Sox to Minnesota Twins for a player to be named later (August 31, 1987). ... Red Sox acquired P Enrique Rios to complete deal (December 18, 1987). ... Released by Twins (December 21, 1987). ... Signed by A's (February 9, 1988). ... Granted free agency (November 4, 1988).

RECORDS: Holds major league career record for most times hit by pitch—267. ... Shares major league records for most consecutive home runs in two consecutive games—4 (July 1 [1] and 2 [3], 1975, bases on balls included); and most long hits in opening game of season—4 (2 doubles, 1 triple, 1 home run, April 6, 1973). ... Shares major league record for most times caught stealing in one inning—2 (June 15, 1974, ninth inning). ... Shares modern major league single-game record for most at-bats (nine-inning game)—7 (August 25, 1979). ... Holds A.L. single-season record for most times hit by pitch—35 (1986).

HONORS: Named Appalachian League Player of the Year (1967). ... Named Minor League Player of the Year by THE SPORTING NEWS (1970). ... Named A.L. Player of the Year by THE SPORTING NEWS (1979). ... Named A.L. Most Valuable Player by Baseball Writers' Association of America (1979). ... Named designated hitter on THE SPORTING NEWS A.L. All-Star team (1979, 1985-86). ... Named designated hitter on THE SPORTING NEWS A.L. Silver Slugger team (1983 and 1985-86).

STATISTICAL NOTES: Led Appalachian League with 135 total bases and tied for lead in caught stealing with 6 in 1967. ... Led Texas League in being hit by pitch with 13 in 1969. ... Led International League with 296 total bases in 1970. ... Led International League in being hit by pitch with 19 in 1970 and 16 in 1971. ... Led A.L. in being hit by pitch with 13 in 1973, 20 in 1976, 18 in 1978, 23 in 1984, 24 in 1985, 35 in 1986, 28 in 1987 and tied for lead with 13 in 1975. ... Hit three home runs in one game (July 2, 1975). ... Led A.L. with 12 sacrifice flies in 1978. ... Led A.L. with 21 game-winning RBIs in 1982. ... Career major league grand slams: 12.

						BATTING								FIELDING			
Year Team (League)	Pos.	G	AB	R	H	2B	3B	HR	RBI	Avg.	BB	SO	SB	PO	A	E	Avg.
1967— Bluefield (Appal.)........	OF	•67	246	50	*85	10	*8	8	47	*.346	35	52	*26	106	5	5	.957
1968— Stockton (California) ..	OF	68	244	52	90	6	3	7	40	.369	35	65	14	135	3	7	.952
— Elmira (East.)	OF	6	24	4	8	1	1	1	3	.333	3	4	1	10	1	0	1.000
— Rochester (I.L.).........	OF	15	46	4	10	2	0	0	4	.217	3	17	1	29	1	4	.882
1969— Miami (FSL)	OF	17	56	13	21	5	4	3	24	.375	7	8	3	30	2	3	.914
— Dall./Ft. Worth (Tex.)..	OF	109	406	71	122	17	•10	11	57	.300	48	77	19	241	7	*13	.950
1970— Rochester (I.L.).........	OF	•140	508	*127	166	*34	*15	22	107	.327	76	99	26	286	5	7	.977
— Baltimore (A.L.).........	OF	8	17	4	4	0	0	0	4	.235	2	3	1	15	0	0	1.000
1971— Rochester (I.L.).........	OF	136	492	104	154	•31	10	20	95	.313	79	73	25	210	4	9	.960
— Baltimore (A.L.).........	OF	1	2	0	0	0	0	0	1	.000	2	1	0	4	0	0	1.000
1972— Baltimore (A.L.).........	OF-1B	102	320	33	81	13	3	11	38	.253	29	50	24	206	4	5	.977
1973— Baltimore (A.L.).........	OF-1B-DH	118	405	64	116	20	4	11	51	.286	35	48	32	228	10	6	.975
1974— Baltimore (A.L.).........	OF-1B	137	489	66	133	22	1	10	59	.272	43	56	29	260	2	5	.981
1975— Baltimore (A.L.).........	OF-DH-1B	145	524	79	148	21	6	25	76	.282	53	64	32	286	8	5	.983

Year Team (League)	Pos.	G	AB	R	H	2B	3B	HR	RBI	Avg.	BB	SO	SB	PO	A	E	Avg.
1976— Oakland (A.L.)■	OF-1B-DH	157	595	85	147	25	1	15	68	.247	58	72	52	781	45	12	.986
1977— California (A.L.)■......	OF-DH-1B	154	561	87	141	27	0	25	75	.251	62	76	26	280	16	7	.977
1978— California (A.L.)..........	DH-OF-1B	158	591	103	151	26	0	34	99	.255	56	71	22	194	9	6	.971
1979— California (A.L.)..........	OF-DH-1B	•162	628	*120	186	33	3	36	*139	.296	71	51	22	203	3	5	.976
1980— California (A.L.)..........	OF-DH	90	340	39	85	12	2	5	51	.250	24	32	6	119	4	4	.969
1981— California (A.L.)..........	DH-1B-OF	103	377	52	90	18	1	17	66	.239	42	51	3	38	3	0	1.000
1982— California (A.L.)..........	DH	157	608	80	160	24	1	24	93	.263	57	69	10	...	...	...	...
1983— New York (A.L.)■......	DH-OF-1B	144	534	82	162	33	3	21	85	.303	40	53	17	23	2	1	.962
1984— New York (A.L.)..........	DH-OF	134	493	84	129	29	1	27	89	.262	38	68	1	8	0	1	.889
1985— New York (A.L.)..........	DH	142	477	70	110	24	1	23	91	.231	52	90	0	...	...	...	...
1986— Boston (A.L.)■..........	DH-1B-OF	160	585	93	139	23	1	31	94	.238	62	111	3	71	4	1	.987
1987— Boston (A.L.)..............	DH	108	339	64	81	8	0	16	57	.239	40	47	5	...	...	...	...
—Minnesota (A.L.)■.....	DH	20	49	3	14	1	0	0	6	.286	5	12	0	...	...	...	...
1988— Oakland (A.L.)■..........	DH	92	264	28	58	7	0	7	34	.220	34	44	0	...	...	...	...
Major league totals (19 years)		2292	8198	1236	2135	366	28	338	1276	.260	805	1069	285	2716	110	58	.980

CHAMPIONSHIP SERIES RECORD

RECORDS: Holds career record for most clubs played with—5. ... Holds single-series record for most runs batted in—10 (1982). ... Shares single-game records for most times reached base safely—5 (October 8, 1986); and most grand slams—1 (October 9, 1982). ... Shares record for most runs batted in in one inning—4 (October 9, 1982, eighth inning). ... Holds A.L. record for most consecutive games with one or more hits—12 (1982 [last three games], 1986-87). ... Shares A.L. single-game record for most runs batted in—5 (October 5, 1982).

Year Team (League)	Pos.	G	AB	R	H	2B	3B	HR	RBI	Avg.	BB	SO	SB	PO	A	E	Avg.
1973— Baltimore (A.L.)..........	OF-PH	4	11	3	3	0	0	0	1	.273	3	5	0	7	0	0	1.000
1974— Baltimore (A.L.)..........	OF-DH	4	15	0	4	0	0	0	0	.267	0	2	0	9	0	0	1.000
1979— California (A.L.)..........	DH-OF	4	16	2	3	0	0	1	2	.188	1	2	0	4	0	0	1.000
1982— California (A.L.)..........	DH	5	17	2	5	1	1	1	10	.294	2	0	0	...	...	...	...
1986— Boston (A.L.)..............	DH	7	26	6	9	3	0	1	2	.346	4	5	0	...	...	...	...
1987— Minnesota (A.L.)	PH-DH	2	5	0	2	0	0	0	1	.400	0	0	0	...	...	...	...
1988— Oakland (A.L.)	DH	2	6	0	0	0	0	0	1	.000	1	2	0	...	...	...	...
Championship series totals (7 years)		28	96	13	26	4	1	3	17	.271	11	16	0	20	0	0	1.000

WORLD SERIES RECORD

RECORDS: Shares record for most at-bats in one inning—2 (October 17, 1987, fourth inning).
NOTES: Member of World Series championship team (1987).

Year Team (League)	Pos.	G	AB	R	H	2B	3B	HR	RBI	Avg.	BB	SO	SB	PO	A	E	Avg.
1986— Boston (A.L.)..............	DH-PH	4	11	1	2	1	0	0	1	.182	1	3	0	...	...	...	...
1987— Minnesota (A.L.)	DH-PH	5	13	3	5	0	0	1	3	.385	1	1	0	...	...	...	...
1988— Oakland (A.L.)	PH	1	1	0	0	0	0	0	0	.000	0	1	0	...	...	...	...
World Series totals (3 years)		10	25	4	7	1	0	1	4	.280	2	5	0	...	...	...	...

ALL-STAR GAME RECORD

Year League	Pos.	AB	R	H	2B	3B	HR	RBI	Avg.	BB	SO	SB	PO	A	E	Avg.
1979— American	OF	4	2	2	1	0	0	1	.500	0	0	0	1	0	0	1.000

RECORD AS MANAGER

BACKGROUND: Special assistant to general manager, Milwaukee Brewers (September 5-December 4, 1989). ... Coach, Brewers (December 4, 1989-91). ... Coach, St. Louis Cardinals (1992) ... Coach, Atlanta Braves (1999).
HONORS: Coach, N.L. All-Star team (1994). ... Named N.L. Manager of the Year by THE SPORTING NEWS (1995). ... Named N.L. Manager of the Year by Baseball Writers' Association of America (1995).

	REGULAR SEASON				POSTSEASON						
					Playoff		Champ. Series		World Series		All-Star Game
Year Team (League)	W	L	Pct.	Pos.	W	L	W	L	W	L	W	L
1993— Colorado (N.L.)	67	95	.414	6th (W)	—	—	—	—	—	—	—	—
1994— Colorado (N.L.)	53	64	.453		—	—	—	—	—	—	—	—
1995— Colorado (N.L.)	77	67	.535	2nd (W)	1	3	—	—	—	—	—	—
1996— Colorado (N.L.)	83	79	.512	3rd (W)	—	—	—	—	—	—	—	—
1997— Colorado (N.L.)	83	79	.512	3rd (W)	—	—	—	—	—	—	—	—
1998— Colorado (N.L.)	77	85	.475	4th (W)	—	—	—	—	—	—	—	—
2000— Chicago (N.L.)	65	97	.401	6th (C)	—	—	—	—	—	—	—	—
2001— Chicago (N.L.)	88	74	.543	3rd (C)	—	—	—	—	—	—	—	—
Major league totals (8 years)	593	640	.481		1	3	—	—	—	—	—	—

NOTES:
1994—Colorado was in third place in N.L. West at time of season-ending strike (August 12).
1995—Lost to Atlanta in N.L. divisional playoff.

BELL, BUDDY   ROCKIES

PERSONAL: Born August 27, 1951, in Pittsburgh. ... 6-3/200. ... Batted right, threw right. ... Full name: David Gus Bell. ... Father of David Bell, third baseman, Seattle Mariners; father of Mike Bell, minor league infielder (1993-2001); and son of Gus Bell, major league outfielder with four teams (1950-64).
HIGH SCHOOL: Moeller (Cincinnati).
COLLEGE: Xavier, then Miami of Ohio.

TRANSACTIONS/CAREER NOTES: Selected by Cleveland Indians organization in 16th round of free-agent draft (June 5, 1969). ... On disabled list (May 27-June 17 and August 8-September 1, 1974). ... Traded by Indians to Texas Rangers for 3B Toby Harrah (December 8, 1978). ... On disabled list (June 9-24, 1980). ... Traded by Rangers to Cincinnati Reds for OF Duane Walker and a player to be named later (July 19, 1985); Rangers acquired P Jeff Russell to complete deal (July 23, 1985). ... On Cincinnati disabled list (March 26-April 10 and April 14-May 11, 1988). ... Traded by Reds to Houston Astros for a player to be named later (June 19, 1988); Reds acquired P Carl Grovom to complete deal (October 20, 1988). ... On Houston disabled list (August 4-19, 1988). ... Released by Astros (December 21, 1988). ... Signed by Rangers (January 9, 1989). ... On disabled list (April 8-28, 1989). ... Announced retirement (June 24, 1989).

HONORS: Won A.L. Gold Glove at third base (1979-84). ... Named third baseman on THE SPORTING NEWS A.L. All-Star team (1981 and 1984). ... Named third baseman on THE SPORTING NEWS A.L. Silver Slugger team (1984).

STATISTICAL NOTES: Led Gulf Coast League second basemen with 26 double plays in 1969. ... Led A.L. third basemen with 144 putouts and 44 double plays in 1973. ... Led A.L. third basemen with 495 total chances in 1978, 361 in 1981, 540 in 1982 and 523 in 1983. ... Tied for A.L. lead in double plays by third basemen with 30 in 1978. ... Had 21-game hitting streak (June 24-July 17, 1980). ... Led A.L. third basemen with 364 assists in 1979 and 281 in 1981. ... Led A.L. third basemen with .981 fielding percentage in 1980 and .976 in 1982. ... Led A.L. with 10 sacrifice flies in 1981. ... Career major league grand slams: 8.

							BATTING									FIELDING		
Year	Team (League)	Pos.	G	AB	R	H	2B	3B	HR	RBI	Avg.	BB	SO	SB	PO	A	E	Avg.
1969—Sarasota (GCL)..........		2B	51	170	18	39	4	•3	3	24	.229	17	15	3	119	108	7	*.970
1970—Sumter (SAL).............		3B-2B-SS	121	442	81	117	19	3	12	75	.265	44	43	9	116	189	27	.919
1971—Wichita (A.A.).............		3-2-S-O	129	470	65	136	23	1	11	59	.289	42	51	7	*139	203	16	.955
1972—Cleveland (A.L.).........		OF-3B	132	466	49	119	21	1	9	36	.255	34	29	5	284	23	3	.990
1973—Cleveland (A.L.).........		3B-OF	156	631	86	169	23	7	14	59	.268	49	47	7	†146	363	22	.959
1974—Cleveland (A.L.).........		3B	116	423	51	111	15	1	7	46	.262	35	29	1	112	274	15	.963
1975—Cleveland (A.L.).........		3B	153	553	66	150	20	4	10	59	.271	51	72	6	*146	330	25	.950
1976—Cleveland (A.L.).........		3B-1B	159	604	75	170	26	2	7	60	.281	44	49	3	109	331	20	.957
1977—Cleveland (A.L.).........		3B-OF	129	479	64	140	23	4	11	64	.292	45	63	1	134	253	16	.960
1978—Cleveland (A.L.).........		3B	142	556	71	157	27	8	6	62	.282	39	43	1	125	*355	15	.970
1979—Texas (A.L.)■..........		3B-SS	•162	*670	89	200	42	3	18	101	.299	30	45	5	147	†429	17	.971
1980—Texas (A.L.)...............		3B-SS	129	490	76	161	24	4	17	83	.329	40	39	3	125	282	8	†.981
1981—Texas (A.L.)...............		3B-SS	97	360	44	106	16	1	10	64	.294	42	30	3	67	†284	14	.962
1982—Texas (A.L.)...............		3B-SS	148	537	62	159	27	2	13	67	.296	70	50	5	*131	397	13	†.976
1983—Texas (A.L.)...............		3B	156	618	75	171	35	3	14	66	.277	50	48	3	123	*383	17	.967
1984—Texas (A.L.)...............		3B	148	553	88	174	36	5	11	83	.315	63	54	2	129	323	•20	.958
1985—Texas (A.L.)...............		3B	84	313	33	74	13	3	4	32	.236	33	21	3	70	192	16	.942
—Cincinnati (N.L.)■......		3B	67	247	28	54	15	2	6	36	.219	34	27	0	54	105	9	.946
1986—Cincinnati (N.L.).........		3B-2B	155	568	89	158	29	3	20	75	.278	73	49	2	105	291	10	.975
1987—Cincinnati (N.L.).........		3B	143	522	74	148	19	2	17	70	.284	71	39	4	93	241	7	*.979
1988—Cincinnati (N.L.).........		3B-1B	21	54	3	10	0	0	0	3	.185	7	3	0	14	26	2	.952
—Houston (N.L.)■......		3B-1B	74	269	24	68	10	1	7	37	.253	19	29	1	74	114	13	.935
1989—Texas (A.L.)■..........		3B-1B	34	82	4	15	4	0	0	3	.183	7	10	0	10	13	0	1.000
American League totals (15 years)			1945	7335	933	2076	352	48	151	885	.283	632	629	48	1858	4232	221	.965
National League totals (4 years)			460	1660	218	438	73	8	50	221	.264	204	147	7	340	777	41	.965
Major league totals (18 years)			2405	8995	1151	2514	425	56	201	1106	.279	836	776	55	2198	5009	262	.965

ALL-STAR GAME RECORD

						BATTING								FIELDING		
Year	League	Pos.	AB	R	H	2B	3B	HR	RBI	Avg.	BB	SO	SB	PO	A	E	Avg.
1973—American	PH	1	0	1	0	1	0	0	1.000	0	0	0	...	...	...	...
1980—American	3B	2	0	0	0	0	0	0	.000	0	1	0	0	2	0	1.000
1981—American	3B	1	0	0	0	0	0	1	.000	0	0	0	1	2	0	1.000
1982—American	PH-3B	3	0	0	0	0	0	0	.000	0	2	0	0	1	1	.500
1984—American	3B	1	0	0	0	0	0	0	.000	0	0	0	0	1	0	1.000
All-Star Game totals (5 years)		8	0	1	0	1	0	1	.125	0	3	0	1	6	1	.875

RECORD AS MANAGER

BACKGROUND: Minor league hitting instructor, Cleveland Indians organization (1990). ... Director of minor league instruction, Chicago White Sox organization (1991-93). ... Coach, Indians (1994-95). ... Minor league field coordinator, Cincinnati Reds (September 23, 1998-August 4, 1999). ... Director of player development, Reds (August 5, 1999-remainder of season).

	REGULAR SEASON				POSTSEASON						
					Playoff		Champ. Series		World Series		All-Star Game
Year	Team (League)	W	L	Pct.	Pos.	W	L	W	L	W	L	W	L
1996—Detroit (A.L.).............................	53	109	.327	5th (E)	—	—	—	—	—	—	—	—
1997—Detroit (A.L.).............................	79	83	.488	3rd (E)	—	—	—	—	—	—	—	—
1998—Detroit (A.L.).............................	52	85	.379	—	—	—	—	—	—	—	—	—
2000—Colorado (N.L.)..........................	82	80	.506	4th (W)	—	—	—	—	—	—	—	—
2001—Colorado (N.L.)..........................	73	89	.451	5th (W)	—	—	—	—	—	—	—	—
Major league totals (5 years)..........................	339	446	.432		—	—	—	—	—	—	—	—

NOTES:
1998—Replaced as Detroit manager on interim basis by Larry Parrish with club in fifth place (September 1).

BOCHY, BRUCE   PADRES

PERSONAL: Born April 16, 1955, in Landes de Boussac, France. ... 6-4/225. ... Batted right, threw right. ... Full name: Bruce Douglas Bochy. ... Brother of Joe Bochy, catcher in Minnesota Twins organization (1969-72). ... Name pronounced BO-chee.

HIGH SCHOOL: Melbourne (Fla.).

JUNIOR COLLEGE: Brevard Community College (Fla.).

COLLEGE: Florida State.

TRANSACTIONS/CAREER NOTES: Selected by Chicago White Sox organization in eighth round of free-agent draft (January 9, 1975); did not sign. ... Selected by Houston Astros organization in secondary phase of free-agent draft (June 4, 1975). ... Traded by Astros to New York

Mets for two players to be named later (February 11, 1981); Astros acquired IF Randy Rodgers and C Stan Hough to complete deal (April 3, 1981). ... Released by Mets (January 21, 1983). ... Signed by San Diego Padres organization (February 23, 1983). ... On disabled list (April 13-May 6, 1987). ... Granted free agency (November 9, 1987).

STATISTICAL NOTES: Tied for Florida State League lead with 12 passed balls in 1977.

Year	Team (League)	Pos.	G	AB	R	H	2B	3B	HR	RBI	Avg.	BB	SO	SB	PO	A	E	Avg.
1975—	Covington (Appal.)	C	37	145	31	49	9	0	4	34	.338	11	18	0	231	36	4	.985
1976—	Columbus (Sou.)........	C	69	230	9	53	6	0	0	16	.230	14	30	0	266	45	6	.981
	—Dubuque (Midwest)....	C-1B	30	103	9	25	4	0	1	8	.243	12	11	1	165	25	5	.974
1977—	Cocoa (FSL)	C	128	430	40	109	18	2	3	35	.253	35	50	1	*492	67	12	.979
1978—	Columbus (Sou.)........	C	79	261	25	70	10	2	7	34	.268	13	30	0	419	49	7	.985
	—Houston (N.L.)	C	54	154	8	41	8	0	3	15	.266	11	35	0	268	35	8	.974
1979—	Houston (N.L.)	C	56	129	11	28	4	0	1	6	.217	17	25	0	198	29	7	.970
1980—	Houston (N.L.)	C-1B	22	22	0	4	1	0	0	0	.182	0	0	0	19	1	0	1.000
1981—	Tidewater (I.L.)■.....	C	85	269	23	61	11	2	8	38	.227	22	47	0	253	35	3	.990
1982—	Tidewater (I.L.)	C	81	251	32	57	11	0	15	52	.227	19	47	2	427	57	5	.990
	—New York (N.L.)........	C-1B	17	49	4	15	4	0	2	8	.306	4	6	0	92	8	4	.962
1983—	Las Vegas (PCL)■	C	42	145	28	44	8	1	11	33	.303	15	25	3	157	21	3	.983
	—San Diego (N.L.)	C	23	42	2	9	1	1	0	3	.214	0	9	0	51	5	0	1.000
1984—	Las Vegas (PCL)	C	34	121	18	32	7	0	7	22	.264	17	13	0	189	17	2	.990
	—San Diego (N.L.)	C	37	92	10	21	5	1	4	15	.228	3	21	0	147	12	2	.988
1985—	San Diego (N.L.)	C	48	112	16	30	2	0	6	13	.268	6	30	0	148	11	2	.988
1986—	San Diego (N.L.)	C	63	127	16	32	9	0	8	22	.252	14	23	1	202	22	2	.991
1987—	San Diego (N.L.)	C	38	75	8	12	3	0	2	11	.160	11	21	0	95	7	4	.962
1988—	Las Vegas (PCL)	C	53	147	17	34	5	0	5	13	.231	17	28	0	207	19	3	.987
Major league totals (9 years)			358	802	75	192	37	2	26	93	.239	66	170	1	1220	130	29	.979

CHAMPIONSHIP SERIES RECORD

Year	Team (League)	Pos.	G	AB	R	H	2B	3B	HR	RBI	Avg.	BB	SO	SB	PO	A	E	Avg.
1980—	Houston (N.L.)	C	1	1	0	0	0	0	0	0	.000	0	0	0	5	1	0	1.000

WORLD SERIES RECORD

Year	Team (League)	Pos.	G	AB	R	H	2B	3B	HR	RBI	Avg.	BB	SO	SB	PO	A	E	Avg.
1984—	San Diego (N.L.)	PH	1	1	0	1	0	0	0	0	1.000	0	0	0	...	...	...	...

RECORD AS MANAGER

BACKGROUND: Player/coach, Las Vegas, San Diego Padres organization (1988). ... Coach, Padres (1993-94).

HONORS: Named N.L. Manager of the Year by THE SPORTING NEWS (1996 and 1998). ... Named N.L. Manager of the Year by Baseball Writers' Association of America (1996).

Year	Team (League)	W	L	Pct.	Pos.	Playoff W	Playoff L	Champ. Series W	Champ. Series L	World Series W	World Series L	All-Star Game W	All-Star Game L
1989—	Spokane (Northwest)...............	41	34	.547	1st (N)	2	1	—	—	—	—	—	—
1990—	Riverside (California)	35	36	.493	4th (S)	—	—	—	—	—	—	—	—
	—(Second half)	29	42	.408	5th (S)	—	—	—	—	—	—	—	—
1991—	High Desert (California)	31	37	.456	3rd (S)	—	—	—	—	—	—	—	—
	—(Second half)	42	26	.618	1st (S)	6	2	—	—	—	—	—	—
1992—	Wichita (Texas)	39	29	.574	1st (W)	—	—	—	—	—	—	—	—
	—(Second half)	31	37	.456	4th (W)	6	1	—	—	—	—	—	—
1995—	San Diego (N.L.)	70	74	.486	3rd (W)	—	—	—	—	—	—	—	—
1996—	San Diego (N.L.)	91	71	.562	1st (W)	0	3	—	—	—	—	—	—
1997—	San Diego (N.L.)	76	86	.469	4th (W)	—	—	—	—	—	—	—	—
1998—	San Diego (N.L.)	98	64	.605	1st (W)	3	1	4	2	0	4	—	—
1999—	San Diego (N.L.)	74	88	.457	4th (W)	—	—	—	—	—	—	0	1
2000—	San Diego (N.L.)	76	86	.469	5th (W)	—	—	—	—	—	—	—	—
2001—	San Diego (N.L.)	79	83	.488	4th (W)	—	—	—	—	—	—	—	—
Major league totals (7 years)		564	552	.505		3	4	4	2	0	4	0	1

NOTES:

1989—Defeated Southern Oregon in league championship.

1991—Defeated Bakersfield, three games to none, in semifinals; defeated Stockton, three games to two, in league championship.

1992—Defeated El Paso, two games to one, in semifinals; defeated Shreveport, four games to none, in league championship.

1996—Lost to St. Louis in N.L. divisional playoff.

1998—Defeated Houston in N.L. divisional playoff; defeated Atlanta in N.L. Championship Series; lost to New York Yankees in World Series.

BOONE, BOB   REDS

PERSONAL: Born November 19, 1947, in San Diego. ... 6-2/207. ... Batted right, threw right. ... Full name: Robert Raymond Boone. ... Son of Ray Boone, major league infielder with six teams (1948-60); brother of Rodney Boone, minor league catcher/outfielder (1972-75); father of Bret Boone, second baseman, Seattle Mariners; and father of Aaron Boone, third baseman, Cincinnati Reds.

HIGH SCHOOL: Crawford (San Diego).

COLLEGE: Stanford.

TRANSACTIONS/CAREER NOTES: Selected by Philadelphia Phillies organization in 20th round of free-agent draft (June 5, 1969). ... On military list (May 26, 1970-remainder of season). ... On disabled list (April 10-June 4, 1971). ... Contract sold by Phillies to California Angels (December 6, 1981). ... Granted free agency (November 12, 1986). ... Re-signed by Angels (May 1, 1987). ... Granted free agency (October 24, 1988). ... Signed by Kansas City Royals (November 30, 1988). ... On disabled list (May 17-July 20, 1990). ... Granted free agency (November 5, 1990). ... Signed by Oakland Athletics organization (May 31, 1993). ... Released by A's (June 1, 1993).

RECORDS: Holds major league career record for most years by catcher (100 or more games)—15.

HONORS: Named catcher on THE SPORTING NEWS N.L. All-Star team (1976). ... Won N.L. Gold Glove at catcher (1978-79). ... Won A.L. Gold Glove at catcher (1982 and 1986-1989).

STATISTICAL NOTES: Tied for Carolina League lead in double plays by third baseman with 18 in 1969. ... Led Northwest League catchers with 18 passed balls and 13 double plays in 1972. ... Led N.L. catchers with 924 total chances in 1974. ... Led N.L. catchers with .991 fielding percentage in 1978. ... Led A.L. catchers with 745 total chances in 1982 and 823 in 1989. ... Led A.L. catchers with 12 double plays in 1983, 15 in 1985 and 16 in 1986. ... Career major league grand slams: 2.

Year	Team (League)	Pos.	G	AB	R	H	2B	3B	HR	RBI	Avg.	BB	SO	SB	PO	A	E	Avg.
1969— Ral./Dur. (Caro.)		3B	80	300	45	90	13	1	5	46	.300	19	24	0	71	160	20	.920
1970— Reading (East.)...........		3B	20	80	12	23	2	0	2	10	.288	7	9	0	28	38	7	.904
1971— Reading (East.)...........		3B-C-SS	92	328	41	87	14	3	4	37	.265	28	28	1	206	138	17	.953
1972— Eugene (N'West)		C	138	513	77	158	32	4	17	67	.308	45	35	2	*699	*77	*24	.970
—Philadelphia (N.L.)......		C	16	51	4	14	1	0	1	4	.275	5	7	1	66	7	5	.936
1973— Philadelphia (N.L.).......		C	145	521	42	136	20	2	10	61	.261	41	36	3	868	*89	10	.990
1974— Philadelphia (N.L.).......		C	146	488	41	118	24	3	3	52	.242	35	29	3	*825	77	*22	.976
1975— Philadelphia (N.L.).......		C-3B	97	289	28	71	14	2	2	20	.246	32	14	1	459	48	5	.990
1976— Philadelphia (N.L.).......		C-1B	121	361	40	98	18	2	4	54	.271	45	44	2	587	39	6	.991
1977— Philadelphia (N.L.).......		C-3B	132	440	55	125	26	4	11	66	.284	42	54	5	654	83	8	.989
1978— Philadelphia (N.L.).......		C-1B-OF	132	435	48	123	18	4	12	62	.283	46	37	2	650	55	8	†.989
1979— Philadelphia (N.L.).......		C-3B	119	398	38	114	21	3	9	58	.286	49	33	1	527	66	8	.987
1980— Philadelphia (N.L.).......		C	141	480	34	110	23	1	9	55	.229	48	41	3	741	88	*18	.979
1981— Philadelphia (N.L.).......		C	76	227	19	48	7	0	4	24	.211	22	16	2	365	32	6	.985
1982— California (A.L.)■..		C	143	472	42	121	17	0	7	58	.256	39	34	0	*650	*87	8	.989
1983— California (A.L.)		C	142	468	46	120	18	0	9	52	.256	25	42	4	606	*83	*14	.980
1984— California (A.L.)		C	139	450	33	91	16	1	3	32	.202	25	45	3	660	*71	12	.984
1985— California (A.L.)		C	150	460	37	114	17	0	5	55	.248	37	35	1	670	71	10	.987
1986— California (A.L.)		C	144	442	48	98	12	2	7	49	.222	43	30	1	812	*84	11	.988
1987— Palm Springs (Calif.)..		C	3	9	0	1	1	0	0	0	.111	1	0	0	17	4	1	.955
—California (A.L.)		C-DH	128	389	42	94	18	0	3	33	.242	35	36	0	684	56	*13	.983
1988— California (A.L.)		C	122	352	38	104	17	0	5	39	.295	29	26	2	506	*66	8	.986
1989— Kansas City (A.L.)■		C	131	405	33	111	13	2	1	43	.274	49	37	3	*752	64	7	.991
1990— Kansas City (A.L.)		C	40	117	11	28	3	0	0	9	.239	17	12	1	243	19	4	.985
American League totals (9 years)			1139	3555	330	881	131	5	40	370	.248	298	297	15	5583	601	87	.986
National League totals (10 years)			1125	3690	349	957	172	21	65	456	.259	365	311	23	5742	584	96	.985
Major League totals (19 years)			2264	7245	679	1838	303	26	105	826	.254	663	608	38	11325	1185	183	.986

DIVISION SERIES RECORD

Year	Team (League)	Pos.	G	AB	R	H	2B	3B	HR	RBI	Avg.	BB	SO	SB	PO	A	E	Avg.
1981— Philadelphia (N.L.)......		C	3	5	0	0	0	0	0	0	.000	0	0	0	10	2	0	1.000

RECORDS: Holds career record for most sacrifice hits—5. ... Shares single-series records for most consecutive hits—5; most singles—9 (1986); and most sacrifice hits—2 (1982). ... Shares A.L. career record for most consecutive hits—5.

CHAMPIONSHIP SERIES RECORD

Year	Team (League)	Pos.	G	AB	R	H	2B	3B	HR	RBI	Avg.	BB	SO	SB	PO	A	E	Avg.
1976— Philadelphia (N.L.)......		C	3	7	0	2	0	0	0	1	.286	1	0	0	8	2	0	1.000
1977— Philadelphia (N.L.)......		C	4	10	1	4	0	0	0	0	.400	0	0	0	18	2	0	1.000
1978— Philadelphia (N.L.)......		C	3	11	0	2	0	0	0	0	.182	0	1	0	16	2	1	.947
1980— Philadelphia (N.L.)......		C	5	18	1	4	0	0	0	2	.222	1	2	0	22	3	0	1.000
1982— California (A.L.)		C	5	16	3	4	0	0	1	4	.250	0	2	0	30	3	0	1.000
1986— California (A.L.)		C	7	22	4	10	0	0	1	2	.455	1	3	0	33	3	0	1.000
Championship series totals (6 years)			27	84	9	26	0	0	2	9	.310	3	8	0	127	15	1	.993

WORLD SERIES RECORD

NOTES: Member of World Series championship team (1980).

Year	Team (League)	Pos.	G	AB	R	H	2B	3B	HR	RBI	Avg.	BB	SO	SB	PO	A	E	Avg.
1980— Philadelphia (N.L.)......		C	6	17	3	7	2	0	0	4	.412	4	0	0	49	3	0	1.000

ALL-STAR GAME RECORD

Year	League	Pos.	AB	R	H	2B	3B	HR	RBI	Avg.	BB	SO	SB	PO	A	E	Avg.
1976— National		C	2	0	0	0	0	0	0	.000	0	0	0	5	0	0	1.000
1978— National		C	1	1	1	0	0	0	2	1.000	0	0	0	3	1	0	1.000
1979— National		C	2	1	1	0	0	0	0	.500	0	0	0	0	0	0	...
1983— American		C	0	0	0	0	0	0	0	...	0	0	0	1	0	0	1.000
All-Star Game totals (4 years)			5	2	2	0	0	0	2	.400	0	0	0	9	1	0	1.000

RECORD AS MANAGER

BACKGROUND: Coach, Cincinnati Reds (1994). ... Special assistant to general manager, Reds (1998-2000).

		REGULAR SEASON				POSTSEASON							
						Playoff		Champ. Series		World Series		All-Star Game	
Year	Team (League)	W	L	Pct.	Pos.	W	L	W	L	W	L	W	L
1992— Tacoma (PCL)		26	45	.366	5th (N)	—	—	—	—	—	—	—	—
—(Second half)		30	42	.417	5th (N)	—	—	—	—	—	—	—	—
1993— Tacoma (PCL)		30	42	.417	5th (N)	—	—	—	—	—	—	—	—
—(Second half)		37	35	.514	3rd (N)	—	—	—	—	—	—	—	—
1995— Kansas City (A.L.)		70	74	.486	2nd (C)	—	—	—	—	—	—	—	—
1996— Kansas City (A.L.)		75	86	.466	5th (C)	—	—	—	—	—	—	—	—
1997— Kansas City (A.L.)		36	46	.439	—	—	—	—	—	—	—	—	—
2001— Cincinnati (N.L.)		66	96	.407	5th (C)	—	—	—	—	—	—	—	—
Major League Totals (4 years)		247	302	.450		—	—	—	—	—	—	—	—

NOTES:
1997—Replaced as Kansas City manager by Tony Muser, with club in fourth place (July 9).

MAJOR LEAGUE MANAGERS

PERSONAL: Born December 6, 1945, in Sacramento. ... 5-10/155. ... Batted both, threw right. ... Full name: Lawrence Robert Bowa.
HIGH SCHOOL: McClathy (Sacramento).
JUNIOR COLLEGE: Sacramento City College.
TRANSACTIONS/CAREER NOTES: Signed as non-drafted free agent by Philadelphia Phillies organization (October 12, 1965). ... On military list (March 7-July 18, 1967). ... On disabled list (July 26-September 1, 1973). ... On disabled list (May 27-June 23, 1975). ... On disabled list (May 25-June 9, 1979). ... Traded with 2B Ryne Sandberg to Chicago Cubs for SS Ivan DeJesus (January 27, 1982). ... Released by Cubs (August 13, 1985). ... Signed by New York Mets (August 20, 1985). ... Granted free agency (November 12, 1985).
HONORS: Named shortstop on THE SPORTING NEWS National League All-Star fielding team (1972 and 1978).
STATISTICAL NOTES: Led N.L. in sacrifice hits with 18 in 1972. ... Led N.L. shortstops in total chances with 843 in 1971. ... Tied for N.L. lead in double plays by shortstops with 97 in 1971. ... Led Pacific Coast League shortstops with 468 assists and .974 fielding percentage in 1969. ... Led Eastern League shortstops in double plays with 77 in 1968. ... Named shortstop on THE SPORTING NEWS National League All-Star Team (1975 and 1978).

MAJOR LEAGUE MANAGERS

								BATTING									FIELDING		
Year Team (League)	Pos.	G	AB	R	H	2B	3B	HR	RBI	Avg.	BB	SO	SB	PO	A	E	Avg.
1966—Spartanburg (W.Car.) .	SS	97	429	70	134	14	4	2	36	.312	18	44	24	138	284	12	*.972
—San Diego (PCL)	SS	5	19	0	6	0	1	0	1	.316	1	3	0	13	20	2	.943
1967—Bakersfield (Calif.)......	SS-2B	7	32	4	6	2	0	0	3	.188	1	6	2	15	12	1	.964
—Reading (East.)..........	SS	22	89	11	25	4	0	0	9	.281	3	17	0	35	79	9	.927
1968—Reading (East.)..........	SS	133	480	47	116	14	2	3	36	.242	24	27	14	192	•395	24	.961
1969—Eugene (PCL)............	SS-2B	135	568	80	163	11	6	1	26	.287	31	56	*48	*215	†469	18	†.974
1970—Philadelphia (N.L.)......	SS-2B	145	547	50	137	17	6	0	34	.250	21	48	24	202	418	13	.979
1971—Philadelphia (N.L.)......	SS	159	650	74	162	18	5	0	25	.249	36	61	28	272	*560	11	*.987
1972—Philadelphia (N.L.)......	SS	152	579	67	145	11	*13	1	31	.250	31	32	17	212	494	9	*.987
1973—Philadelphia (N.L.)......	SS	122	446	42	94	11	3	0	23	.211	24	31	10	191	361	12	.979
1974—Philadelphia (N.L.)......	SS	162	669	97	184	19	10	1	36	.275	23	52	39	256	462	12	*.984
1975—Philadelphia (N.L.)......	SS	156	624	71	155	15	9	0	49	.248	32	31	30	227	403	25	.962
1976—Philadelphia (N.L.)......	SS	156	624	17	155	15	9	0	49	.248	32	31	30	180	492	17	.975
1977—Philadelphia (N.L.)......	SS	154	624	93	175	19	3	4	41	.280	32	32	32	222	518	13	.983
1978—Philadelphia (N.L.)......	SS	156	654	78	192	31	5	3	43	.294	24	40	27	224	502	10	*.986
1979—Philadelphia (N.L.)......	SS	147	539	74	130	17	11	0	31	.241	61	32	20	229	448	6	*.991
1980—Philadelphia (N.L.)......	SS	147	540	57	144	16	4	2	39	.267	24	28	21	225	449	17	.975
1981—Philadelphia (N.L.)......	SS	103	360	34	102	14	3	0	31	.283	26	17	16	117	309	11	.975
1982—Chicago (N.L.)■...........	SS	142	499	50	123	15	7	0	29	.246	39	38	8	210	396	17	.973
1983—Chicago (N.L.)..........	SS	147	499	73	133	20	5	2	43	.267	35	30	7	230	464	11	*.984
1984—Chicago (N.L.)..........	SS	133	391	33	87	14	2	0	17	.223	28	24	10	217	378	16	.974
1985—Chicago (N.L.)..........	SS-2B	72	195	13	48	6	4	0	13	.246	11	20	5	91	197	9	.970
—New York (N.L.)■....	SS-2B	14	19	2	2	1	0	0	2	.105	2	2	0	9	6	2	.882
Major League totals (16 years)		2267	8459	925	2168	259	99	13	536	.256	481	549	324	3314	6857	211	.980

DIVISION SERIES RECORD

								BATTING									FIELDING		
Year Team (League)	Pos.	G	AB	R	H	2B	3B	HR	RBI	Avg.	BB	SO	SB	PO	A	E	Avg.
1981—Philadelphia (N.L.)......	SS	5	17	0	3	1	0	0	1	.176	...	...	...	12	9	1	.955

CHAMPIONSHIP SERIES RECORD

								BATTING									FIELDING		
Year Team (League)	Pos.	G	AB	R	H	2B	3B	HR	RBI	Avg.	BB	SO	SB	PO	A	E	Avg.
1976—Philadelphia (N.L.)......	SS	3	8	1	1	1	0	0	1	.125	3	0	0	2	11	0	1.000
1977—Philadelphia (N.L.)......	SS	4	17	2	2	0	0	0	1	.118	0	1	0	0	17	0	1.000
1978—Philadelphia (N.L.)......	SS	4	18	2	6	0	0	0	0	.333	1	2	0	5	16	0	1.000
1980—Philadelphia (N.L.)......	SS	5	19	2	6	0	0	0	0	.316	3	3	1	4	11	1	.938
1984—Chicago (N.L.)...........	SS	5	15	1	3	1	0	0	1	.200	1	0	0	8	15	0	1.000
Championship series totals (5 years)		21	77	8	18	2	0	0	3	.234	8	6	1	19	70	1	.989

WORLD SERIES RECORD

								BATTING									FIELDING		
Year Team (League)	Pos.	G	AB	R	H	2B	3B	HR	RBI	Avg.	BB	SO	SB	PO	A	E	Avg.
1980—Philadelphia (N.L.)......	SS	6	24	3	9	1	0	0	2	.375	0	0	3	5	18	0	1.000

ALL-STAR GAME RECORD

						BATTING								FIELDING		
Year League	Pos.	AB	R	H	2B	3B	HR	RBI	Avg.	BB	SO	SB	PO	A	E	Avg.
1974—National	SS	2	0	0	0	0	0	0	.000	0	0	0	2	0	0	1.000
1975—National	SS	0	1	0	0	0	0	0		0	0	0	2	0	0	1.000
1976—National	SS	1	0	0	0	0	0	0	.000	0	0	0	2	1	0	1.000
1978—National	SS	3	1	2	0	0	0	0	.667	0	0	1	2	4	0	1.000
1979—National	SS	2	0	0	0	0	0	0	.000	0	0	0	1	3	0	1.000
All-Star Game totals (5 years)		8	2	2	0	0	0	0	.250	0	0	1	9	8	0	1.000

RECORD AS MANAGER

BACKGROUND: Coach, Phillies (May 11, 1989-96). ... Coach, Anaheim Angels (1997-99). ... Coach, Seattle Mariners (2000).
HONORS: Named N.L. Manager of the Year by THE SPORTING NEWS (2001). ... Named N.L. Manager of the Year by Baseball Writers' Association of America (2001).

		REGULAR SEASON			POSTSEASON						
							Champ.		World		All-Star
					Playoff		Series		Series		Game
Year Team (League)	W	L	Pct.	Pos.	W	L	W	L	W	L	W	L
1986—Las Vegas (PCL)	36	44	.450	3rd (S)	—	—	—	—	—	—	—	—
—(Second half)	44	28	.611	1st (S)	6	4	—	—	—	—	—	—
1987—San Diego (N.L.)	65	97	.401	6th (W)	—	—	—	—	—	—	—	—
1988—San Diego (N.L.)	16	30	.348	—	—	—	—	—	—	—	—	—
2001—Philadelphia (N.L.)	86	76	.531	2nd (E)	—	—	—	—	—	—	—	—
Major League Totals (3 years)	167	203	.451		0	0	0	0	0	0	0	0

NOTES:
1986—Defeated Phoenix, three games to two, in league semifinals; defeated Vancouver, three games to two, to win league championship.
1988—Replaced as Padres manager by Jack McKeon, with club in fifth place (May 28).

PERSONAL: Born February 25, 1954, in Coshocton, Ohio. ... 6-2/205. ... Batted right, threw right. ... Full name: Robert Earl Brenly.
COLLEGE: Ohio University.
TRANSACTIONS/CAREER NOTES: Signed as non-drafted free agent by San Francisco Giants organization (June 21, 1976). ... On disabled list (March 25-May 13, 1982). ... Released by Giants (December 21, 1988). ... Signed by Toronto Blue Jays (January 18, 1989). ... Released by Blue Jays (July 14, 1989). ... Signed by Giants organization (August 2, 1989). ... Granted free agency (November 13, 1989).
STATISTICAL NOTES: Led N.L. catchers in assists with 83 in 1987. ... Led N.L. catchers in fielding percentage with .995 in 1986. ... Led California League third baseman in double plays with 30 in 1978. ... Led Midwest League third baseman with 263 assists, 383 total chances and in double plays with 21 in 1977.

Year Team (League)	Pos.	G	AB	R	H	2B	3B	HR	RBI	Avg.	BB	SO	SB	PO	A	E	Avg.
1976— Great Falls (Pio.)	3B	25	86	16	27	5	1	1	17	.314	12	9	1	10	16	2	.929
—Fresno (Calif.).............	3B	17	60	16	22	3	1	1	9	.367	12	17	1	2	6	1	.889
1977— Cedar Rapids (Midw.)	3B-OF	136	499	85	135	16	1	22	73	.271	90	108	6	90	†263	‡31	.919
1978— Fresno (Calif.).............	3B	135	489	102	139	34	5	17	89	.284	81	90	12	*118	247	27	.931
1979— Fresno (Calif.).............	3B	56	212	49	65	11	2	9	37	.307	28	31	6	39	133	17	.910
—Shreveport (Texas).....C-3B-OF-1B		64	193	33	57	8	1	9	30	.295	19	38	0	199	55	7	.973
1980— Shreveport (Texas).........	3B	2	10	2	3	0	0	1	3	.300	0	3	1	1	2	0	1.000
—Phoenix (PCL)...........3B-C-SS-OF		84	287	34	74	9	6	7	45	.258	24	51	2	183	110	20	.936
1981— Phoenix (PCL)	C-OF-3B	76	257	42	75	11	3	7	41	.292	29	37	2	177	41	9	.960
—San Francisco (N.L.) ..	C-3B-OF	19	45	5	15	2	1	1	4	.333	6	4	0	52	6	4	.935
1982— San Francisco (N.L.) ..	C-3B	65	180	26	51	4	1	4	15	.283	18	26	6	265	32	12	.961
1983— San Francisco (N.L.) ..	C-1B-OF	104	281	36	63	12	2	7	34	.224	37	48	10	465	73	9	.984
1984— San Francisco (N.L.) ..	C-1B-OF	145	506	74	147	28	0	20	80	.291	48	52	6	807	76	13	.985
1985— San Francisco (N.L.) ..	C-3B-1B	133	440	41	97	16	1	19	56	.220	57	62	1	719	85	17	.979
1986— San Francisco (N.L.) ..	C-3B-1B	149	472	60	116	26	0	16	62	.246	74	97	10	688	118	16	†.981
1987— San Francisco (N.L.) ..	C-1B-3B	123	375	50	100	19	1	18	51	.267	47	85	10	685	†86	9	.984
1988— San Francisco (N.L.) ..	C	73	206	13	39	7	0	5	22	.189	20	40	1	334	27	6	.984
1989— Toronto (A.L.)■........	C-1B	48	88	9	15	3	1	1	6	.170	10	17	0	61	5	1	.985
—Phoenix (PCL)■........	C-3B-1B	27	98	11	25	3	0	2	11	.255	8	12	3	78	16	4	.959
—San Francisco (N.L.) ..	C	12	22	2	4	2	0	0	3	.182	1	7	1	31	5	0	1.000
American League totals (1 year)		48	88	9	15	3	1	1	6	.170	10	17	0	61	5	1	.985
National League totals (9 years)		823	2527	312	632	116	6	90	327	.250	308	421	45	4046	508	86	.981
Major League totals (9 years)		871	2615	321	647	119	7	91	333	.247	318	438	45	4107	513	87	.982

CHAMPIONSHIP SERIES RECORD

Year Team (League)	Pos.	G	AB	R	H	2B	3B	HR	RBI	Avg.	BB	SO	SB	PO	A	E	Avg.
1987— San Francisco (N.L.) ..	C-PH	6	17	3	4	1	0	1	2	.235	3	7	0	28	2	0	1.000

ALL-STAR GAME RECORD

Year League	Pos.	AB	R	H	2B	3B	HR	RBI	Avg.	BB	SO	SB	PO	A	E	Avg.
1984— National	PH	1	0	0	0	0	0	0	.000	0	1	0	...	...	...	...

BACKGROUND: Broadcaster (1989-2000).

RECORD AS MANAGER

	REGULAR SEASON				POSTSEASON					
					Playoff		Champ. Series		World Series		All-Star Game
Year Team (League)	W	L	Pct.	Pos.	W	L	W	L	W	L	W	L
2001— Arizona (N.L.)...	92	70	.568	1st (W)	3	2	4	1	4	3		

NOTES:
2001—Defeated St. Louis in N.L. divisional playoff; defeated Atlanta in N.L. Championship Series; defeated New York Yankees in World Series.

COX, BOBBY   BRAVES

PERSONAL: Born May 21, 1941, in Tulsa, Okla. ... 6-0/185. ... Batted right, threw right. ... Full name: Robert Joe Cox.
HIGH SCHOOL: Selma (Calif.).
JUNIOR COLLEGE: Reedley Junior College (Calif.).
TRANSACTIONS/CAREER NOTES: Signed by Los Angeles Dodgers organization (1959). ... Selected by Chicago Cubs organization from Dodgers organization in Rule 5 minor league draft (November 30, 1964). ... Acquired by Atlanta Braves organization (1966). ... On Austin disabled list (May 8-18 and May 30-June 9, 1966). ... On disabled list (May 1-June 12, 1967). ... Traded by Braves to New York Yankees for C Bob Tillman and P Dale Roberts (December 7, 1967); Roberts later was transferred to Richmond. ... On disabled list (May 28-June 18, 1970). ... Released by Yankees (September 22, 1970). ... Signed by Yankees organization (July 17, 1971). ... Released as player by Fort Lauderdale (August 28, 1971).
STATISTICAL NOTES: Led Alabama-Florida League shortstops with 71 double plays in 1961. ... Led Pacific Coast League third basemen with .954 fielding percentage in 1965.

Year Team (League)	Pos.	G	AB	R	H	2B	3B	HR	RBI	Avg.	BB	SO	SB	PO	A	E	Avg.
1960— Reno (California)	2B	125	440	99	112	20	5	13	75	.255	95	129	28	282	*385	*39	.945
1961— Salem (Northwest)	2B	14	44	3	9	2	0	0	2	.205	0	14	0	25	25	2	.962
—Panama City (Al.-Fla.)	2B	92	335	66	102	27	4	17	73	.304	48	72	17	220	247	8	*.983
1962— Salem (Northwest)	3B-2B	*141	514	83	143	26	7	16	82	.278	63	119	7	174	296	28	.944
1963— Albuquerque (Texas) ..	3B	17	53	5	15	2	0	2	5	.283	3	12	1	8	27	1	.972

Year Team (League)	Pos.	G	AB	R	H	2B	3B	HR	RBI	Avg.	BB	SO	SB	PO	A	E	Avg.
— Great Falls (Pio.)	3B	109	407	103	137	*31	4	19	85	.337	73	84	7	82	211	21	*.933
1964— Albuquerque (Texas) ..	2B	138	523	98	152	29	13	16	91	.291	52	84	8	*322	*415	*28	.963
1965— Salt Lake (PCL)■	3B-2B	136	473	58	125	32	1	12	55	.264	35	96	1	133	337	22	†.955
1966— Tacoma (PCL)	3B-2B	10	34	2	4	1	0	0	4	.118	6	9	0	23	15	0	1.000
— Austin (Texas)■	2B-3B	92	339	35	77	11	1	7	30	.227	25	55	7	140	216	12	.967
1967— Richmond (I.L.)........	3B-1B	99	350	52	104	17	4	14	51	.297	34	73	3	84	136	8	.965
1968— New York (A.L.)■......	3B	135	437	33	100	15	1	7	41	.229	41	85	3	98	279	17	.957
1969— New York (A.L.)■	3B-2B	85	191	17	41	7	1	2	17	.215	34	41	0	50	147	11	.947
1970— Syracuse (I.L.)...........	3B-SS-2B	90	251	34	55	15	0	9	30	.219	49	40	0	86	163	13	.950
1971— Fort Laud. (FSL)........	2B-P	4	9	1	1	0	0	0	0	.111	1	0	0	4	5	0	1.000
Major league totals (2 years)		220	628	50	141	22	2	9	58	.225	75	126	3	148	426	28	.953

RECORD AS PITCHER

Year Team (League)	W	L	Pct.	ERA	G	GS	CG	ShO	Sv.	IP	H	R	ER	BB	SO
1971— Fort Lauderdale (FSL)	0	1	.000	5.40	3	0	0	0	0	10	15	9	6	5	4

RECORD AS MANAGER

BACKGROUND: Minor league instructor, New York Yankees (October 28, 1970-March 24, 1971). ... Player/manager, Fort Lauderdale, Yankees organization (1971). ... Coach, Yankees (1977).

HONORS: Named Major League Manager of the Year by THE SPORTING NEWS (1985). ... Named A.L. Manager of the Year by Baseball Writers' Association of America (1985). ... Named N.L. Manager of the Year by THE SPORTING NEWS (1991, 1993 and 1999). ... Named N.L. Manager of the Year by the Baseball Writers' Association of America (1991).

	REGULAR SEASON				POSTSEASON						
							Champ.		World		All-Star
					Playoff		Series		Series		Game
Year Team (League)	W	L	Pct.	Pos.	W	L	W	L	W	L	W	L
1971— Fort Lauderdale (Florida State)	71	70	.504	4th (E)	—	—	—	—	—	—	—	—
1972— West Haven (East.)	84	56	.600	1st (A)	3	0	—	—	—	—	—	—
1973— Syracuse (International)...........................	76	70	.521	3rd (A)	—	—	—	—	—	—	—	—
1974— Syracuse (International)...........................	74	70	.514	2nd (N)	—	—	—	—	—	—	—	—
1975— Syracuse (International)...........................	72	64	.529	3rd	—	—	—	—	—	—	—	—
1976— Syracuse (International)...........................	82	57	.590	2nd	6	1	—	—	—	—	—	—
1978— Atlanta (N.L.)	69	93	.426	6th (W)	—	—	—	—	—	—	—	—
1979— Atlanta (N.L.)	66	94	.413	6th (W)	—	—	—	—	—	—	—	—
1980— Atlanta (N.L.)	81	80	.503	4th (W)	—	—	—	—	—	—	—	—
1981— Atlanta (N.L.)	25	29	.463	4th (W)	—	—	—	—	—	—	—	—
— (Second half)	25	27	.481	5th (W)	—	—	—	—	—	—	—	—
1982— Toronto (A.L.)	78	84	.481	T6th (E)	—	—	—	—	—	—	—	—
1983— Toronto (A.L.)	89	73	.549	4th (E)	—	—	—	—	—	—	—	—
1984— Toronto (A.L.)	89	73	.549	2nd (E)	—	—	—	—	—	—	—	—
1985— Toronto (A.L.)	99	62	.615	1st (E)	—	—	3	4	—	—	—	—
1990— Atlanta (N.L.)	40	57	.412	6th (W)	—	—	—	—	—	—	—	—
1991— Atlanta (N.L.)	94	68	.580	1st (W)	—	—	4	3	3	4	—	—
1992— Atlanta (N.L.)	98	64	.605	1st (W)	—	—	4	3	2	4	0	1
1993— Atlanta (N.L.)	104	58	.642	1st (W)	—	—	2	4	—	—	0	1
1994— Atlanta (N.L.)	68	46	.596		—	—	—	—	—	—	—	—
1995— Atlanta (N.L.)	90	54	.625	1st (E)	3	1	4	0	4	2	—	—
1996— Atlanta (N.L.)	96	66	.593	1st (E)	3	0	4	3	2	4	1	0
1997— Atlanta (N.L.)	101	61	.623	1st (E)	3	0	2	4	—	—	0	1
1998— Atlanta (N.L.)	106	56	.654	1st (E)	3	0	2	4	—	—	—	—
1999— Atlanta (N.L.)	103	59	.636	1st (E)	3	0	4	2	0	4	—	—
2000— Atlanta (N.L.)	95	67	.586	1st (E)	0	3	—	—	—	—	0	1
2001— Atlanta (N.L.)	88	74	.543	1st (E)	3	0	1	4	—	—	—	—
American League totals (4 years)	355	292	.549		—	—	3	4	—	—	—	—
National League totals (16 years)	1349	1053	.562		18	4	27	27	11	18	1	4
Major league totals (20 years)	1704	1345	.559		18	4	30	31	11	18	1	4

NOTES:

1972—Defeated Three Rivers in playoff.

1976—Defeated Memphis, three games to none, in playoffs; defeated Richmond, three games to one, in league championship.

1985—Lost to Kansas City in A.L. Championship Series.

1990—Replaced Atlanta manager Russ Nixon with club in sixth place and record of 25-40 (June 22).

1991—Defeated Pittsburgh in N.L. Championship Series; lost to Minnesota in World Series.

1992—Defeated Pittsburgh in N.L. Championship Series; lost to Toronto in World Series.

1993—Lost to Philadelphia in N.L. Championship Series.

1994—Atlanta was in second place in N.L. East at time of season-ending strike (August 12).

1995—Defeated Colorado in N.L. divisional playoff; defeated Cincinnati in N.L. Championship Series; defeated Cleveland in World Series.

1996—Defeated Los Angeles in N.L. divisional playoff; defeated St. Louis in N.L. Championship Series; lost to New York Yankees in World Series.

1997—Defeated Houston in N.L. divisional playoff; lost to Florida in N.L. Championship Series.

1998—Defeated Chicago Cubs in N.L. divisional playoff; lost to San Diego in N.L. Championship Series.

1999—Defeated Houston in N.L. divisional playoff; defeated New York Mets in N.L. Championship Series; lost to New York Yankees in World Series.

2000—Lost to St. Louis in N.L. divisional playoff.

2001—Defeated Houston in N.L. divisional playoff; lost to Arizona in N.L. Championship Series.

GARDENHIRE, RON   TWINS

PERSONAL: Born October 24, 1957, in Butzbach, West Germany. ... 6-0/180. ... Bats right, throws right. ... Full name: Ronald Clyde Gardenhire.

HIGH SCHOOL: Okmulgee (Okla.) High School.

JUNIOR COLLEGE: Paris (Texas).

COLLEGE: Texas.

TRANSACTIONS/CAREER NOTES: Selected by New York Mets organization in sixth round of free-agent draft (June 5, 1979). ... On Tidewater disabled list (July 21-31, 1983). ... On disabled list (July 20-August 9 and August 20-September 10, 1984). ... On disabled list (May 2-17, May 25-July 19 and August 16-September 1, 1985); included rehabilitation assignment to Tidewater (June 24-July 13). ... Traded by Mets to Minnesota Twins for P Don Iasparro (November 12, 1986).

										BATTING					FIELDING		
Year Team (League)	Pos.	G	AB	R	H	2B	3B	HR	RBI	Avg.	BB	SO	SB	PO	A	E	Avg.
1979— Lynchburg (Caro.)	SS	70	277	36	82	13	3	4	27	.296	21	45	9	120	252	21	.947
1980— Jackson (Texas)	SS-2B	127	458	58	118	16	6	6	64	.258	45	68	13	168	411	41	.934
1981— Tidewater (I.L.)	SS-2B-3B	125	414	52	105	17	8	2	40	.254	28	61	28	206	373	33	.946
— New York (N.L.)	SS-2B-3B	27	48	2	13	1	0	0	3	.271	5	9	2	28	50	2	.975
1982— New York (N.L.)	SS-2B-3B	141	384	29	92	17	1	3	33	.240	23	55	5	235	399	29	.956
1983— New York (N.L.)	SS	17	32	1	2	0	0	0	1	.063	1	4	0	13	30	0	1.000
— Tidewater (I.L.)	SS	102	387	63	111	20	6	4	39	.287	34	54	9	202	321	27	.951
1984— New York (N.L.)	SS-2B-3B	74	207	20	51	7	1	1	10	.246	9	43	6	98	154	12	.955
1985— New York (N.L.)	SS-2B-3B	26	39	5	7	2	1	0	2	.179	8	11	0	21	32	4	.930
— Tidewater (I.L.)	3B-SS-2B	22	71	3	15	2	0	1	10	.211	6	13	0	20	36	5	.918
1986— Tidewater (I.L.)	2B-SS	96	323	41	89	10	4	4	33	.276	44	48	11	161	288	19	.959
1987— Portland (PCL)■	1B-3B-2B-SS	117	389	49	106	16	4	6	50	.272	45	70	1	384	126	5	.990
Major League totals (5 years)		285	710	57	165	27	3	4	49	.232	46	122	13	395	665	47	.958

RECORD AS MANAGER

BACKGROUND: Coach, Minnesota Twins (1991-2000).
NOTES: Tied one game (1989, first half).

		REGULAR SEASON				POSTSEASON							
								Champ. Series		World Series		All-Star Game	
						Playoff							
Year Team (League)	W	L	Pct.	Pos.		W	L	W	L	W	L	W	L
1988— Kenosha (Midw.)	41	27	.603	1st		3	3	—	—	—	—	—	—
— (Second half)	40	32	.556	2nd		—	—	—	—	—	—	—	—
1989— Orlando (Sou.)	40	31	.563	1st		1	3	—	—	—	—	—	—
— (Second half)	39	34	.534	4th		—	—	—	—	—	—	—	—
1990— Orlando (Sou.)	42	30	.583	1st		5	4	—	—	—	—	—	—
— (Second half)	43	29	.597	2nd		—	—	—	—	—	—	—	—

NOTES:
1988—Defeated Rockford in playoffs; lost to Cedar Rapids in league championship.
1989—Lost to Greenville in playoffs.
1990—Defeated Jacksonville in playoffs; lost to Memphis in league championship.

GARNER, PHIL   TIGERS

PERSONAL: Born April 30, 1949, in Jefferson City, Tenn. ... 5-10/177. ... Batted right, threw right. ... Full name: Philip Mason Garner.
HIGH SCHOOL: Beardon (Knoxville, Tenn.).
COLLEGE: Tennessee (degree in general business, 1973).
TRANSACTIONS/CAREER NOTES: Selected by Montreal Expos organization in eighth round of free-agent draft (June 4, 1970); did not sign. ... Selected by Oakland Athletics organization in secondary phase of free-agent draft (January 13, 1971). ... Traded by A's with IF Tommy Helms and P Chris Batton to Pittsburgh Pirates for P Doc Medich, P Dave Giusti, P Rick Langford, P Doug Bair, OF Mitchell Page and OF Tony Armas (March 15, 1977). ... On Pittsburgh disabled list (April 2-23, 1981). ... Traded by Pirates to Houston Astros for 2B Johnny Ray and two players to be named later (August 31, 1981); Pirates organization acquired OF Kevin Houston and P Randy Niemann to complete deal (September 9, 1981). ... Granted free agency (November 12, 1986). ... Re-signed by Astros (January 6, 1987). ... Traded by Astros to Los Angeles Dodgers for a player to be named later (June 19, 1987); Astros organization acquired P Jeff Edwards to complete deal (June 26, 1987). ... Granted free agency (November 9, 1987). ... Signed by San Francisco Giants (January 28, 1988). ... On San Francisco disabled list (April 13-September 2, 1988); included rehabilitation assignment to Phoenix (August 5-24). ... Granted free agency (November 3, 1988).
RECORDS: Shares major league record for most grand slams in two consecutive games—2 (September 14-15, 1978).
STATISTICAL NOTES: Led Pacific Coast League third basemen with 104 putouts, 261 assists, 35 errors, 400 total chances and 23 double plays in 1973. ... Led A.L. second basemen with 26 errors in 1975. ... Led A.L. second basemen with 865 total chances in 1976. ... Led N.L. second basemen with 499 assists, 21 errors, 869 total chances and 116 double plays in 1980. ... Career major league grand slams: 3.

										BATTING					FIELDING		
Year Team (League)	Pos.	G	AB	R	H	2B	3B	HR	RBI	Avg.	BB	SO	SB	PO	A	E	Avg.
1971— Burlington (Midw.)	3B	116	439	73	122	22	4	11	70	.278	49	73	8	*122	203	29	.918
1972— Birmingham (Sou.)	3B	71	264	45	74	10	6	12	40	.280	27	43	3	74	116	13	.936
— Iowa (A.A.)	3B	70	247	33	60	18	4	9	22	.243	30	73	7	50	140	10	.950
1973— Tucson (PCL)	3B-2B	138	516	87	149	23	12	14	73	.289	72	90	3	†107	*270	†35	.915
— Oakland (A.L.)	3B	9	5	0	0	0	0	0	0	.000	0	3	0	2	3	0	1.000
1974— Tucson (PCL)	3B-SS	96	388	78	128	29	10	11	51	.330	53	58	8	92	182	15	.948
— Oakland (A.L.)	3B-SS-2B	30	28	4	5	1	0	0	1	.179	1	5	1	11	24	1	.972
1975— Oakland (A.L.)	2B-3B	*160	488	46	120	21	5	6	54	.246	30	65	4	355	427	†26	.968
1976— Oakland (A.L.)	2B	159	555	54	145	29	12	8	74	.261	36	71	35	378	*465	22	.975
1977— Pittsburgh (N.L.)■▪	3B-2B-SS	153	585	99	152	35	10	17	77	.260	55	65	32	223	351	17	.971
1978— Pittsburgh (N.L.)	3B-2B-SS	154	528	66	138	25	9	10	66	.261	66	71	27	258	389	28	.959
1979— Pittsburgh (N.L.)	3B-2B-SS	150	549	76	161	32	8	11	59	.293	55	74	17	234	396	22	.966
1980— Pittsburgh (N.L.)	2B-SS	151	548	62	142	27	6	5	58	.259	46	53	32	349	†500	†21	.976
1981— Pittsburgh (N.L.)	2B	56	181	22	46	6	2	1	20	.254	21	21	4	121	148	9	.968
— Houston (N.L.)■	2B	31	113	13	27	3	1	0	6	.239	15	11	6	62	102	3	.982
1982— Houston (N.L.)	2B-3B	155	588	65	161	33	8	13	83	.274	40	92	24	285	464	17	.978
1983— Houston (N.L.)	3B	154	567	76	135	24	2	14	79	.238	63	84	18	100	311	24	.945
1984— Houston (N.L.)	3B-2B	128	374	60	104	17	6	4	45	.278	43	63	3	136	251	12	.970
1985— Houston (N.L.)	3B-2B	135	463	65	124	23	10	6	51	.268	34	72	4	101	229	21	.940
1986— Houston (N.L.)	3B-2B	107	313	43	83	14	3	9	41	.265	30	45	12	66	152	23	.905

Year Team (League)	Pos.	G	AB	R	H	2B	3B	HR	RBI	Avg.	BB	SO	SB	PO	A	E	Avg.
1987— Houston (N.L.)	SS-2B	43	112	15	25	5	0	3	15	.223	8	20	1	28	55	2	.976
—Los Angeles (N.L.)■ ..	3B-2B-SS	70	126	14	24	4	0	2	8	.190	20	24	5	37	89	11	.920
1988— San Fran. (N.L.)■.......	3B	15	13	0	2	0	0	0	1	.154	1	3	0	0	0	0	...
—Phoenix (PCL)	2B-3B	17	45	5	12	2	1	1	5	.267	4	4	0	12	22	0	1.000
American League totals (4 years)		358	1076	104	270	51	17	14	129	.251	67	144	40	746	919	49	.971
National League totals (12 years)		1502	5060	676	1324	248	65	95	609	.262	497	698	185	2000	3437	210	.963
Major league totals (16 years)		1860	6136	780	1594	299	82	109	738	.260	564	842	225	2746	4356	259	.965

DIVISION SERIES RECORD

Year Team (League)	Pos.	G	AB	R	H	2B	3B	HR	RBI	Avg.	BB	SO	SB	PO	A	E	Avg.
1981— Houston (N.L.)	2B	5	18	1	2	0	0	0	0	.111	3	3	0	6	8	1	.933

CHAMPIONSHIP SERIES RECORD

Year Team (League)	Pos.	G	AB	R	H	2B	3B	HR	RBI	Avg.	BB	SO	SB	PO	A	E	Avg.
1975— Oakland (A.L.)	2B	3	5	0	0	0	0	0	0	.000	0	1	0	7	4	1	.917
1979— Pittsburgh (N.L.)	2B-SS	3	12	4	5	0	1	1	1	.417	1	0	0	8	9	0	1.000
1986— Houston (N.L.)	3B	3	9	1	2	1	0	0	2	.222	1	2	0	1	9	0	1.000
Championship series totals (3 years)		9	26	5	7	1	1	1	3	.269	2	3	0	16	22	1	.974

WORLD SERIES RECORD

RECORDS: Shares single-series record for collecting one or more hits in each game (1979).
NOTES: Member of World Series championship team (1979).

Year Team (League)	Pos.	G	AB	R	H	2B	3B	HR	RBI	Avg.	BB	SO	SB	PO	A	E	Avg.
1979— Pittsburgh (N.L.)	2B	7	24	4	12	4	0	0	5	.500	3	1	0	21	23	2	.957

ALL-STAR GAME RECORD

Year League	Pos.	AB	R	H	2B	3B	HR	RBI	Avg.	BB	SO	SB	PO	A	E	Avg.
1976— American	2B	1	0	0	0	0	0	0	.000	0	1	0	1	1	0	1.000
1980— National	2B	2	1	1	0	0	0	0	.500	1	1	1	1	3	0	1.000
1981— National	2B	0	0	0	0	0	0	0	...	0	0	0	0	0	0	...
All-Star Game totals (3 years)		3	1	1	0	0	0	0	.333	1	2	1	2	4	0	1.000

RECORD AS MANAGER

BACKGROUND: Coach, Houston Astros (1989-91).

	REGULAR SEASON				POSTSEASON							
							Champ. Series		World Series		All-Star Game	
					Playoff							
Year Team (League)	W	L	Pct.	Pos.	W	L	W	L	W	L	W	L
1992— Milwaukee (A.L.)	92	70	.568	2nd (E)	—	—	—	—	—	—	—	—
1993— Milwaukee (A.L.)	69	93	.426	7th (E)	—	—	—	—	—	—	—	—
1994— Milwaukee (A.L.)	53	62	.461		—	—	—	—	—	—	—	—
1995— Milwaukee (A.L.)	65	79	.451	4th (C)	—	—	—	—	—	—	—	—
1996— Milwaukee (A.L.)	80	82	.494	3rd (C)	—	—	—	—	—	—	—	—
1997— Milwaukee (A.L.)	78	83	.484	3rd (C)	—	—	—	—	—	—	—	—
1998— Milwaukee (N.L.)	74	88	.457	5th (C)	—	—	—	—	—	—	—	—
1999— Milwaukee (N.L.)	52	60	.464		—	—	—	—	—	—	—	—
2000— Detroit (A.L.)	79	83	.488	3rd (C)	—	—	—	—	—	—	—	—
2001— Detroit (A.L.)	66	96	.407	4th (C)	—	—	—	—	—	—	—	—
American League totals (8 years)	582	648	.473		—	—	—	—	—	—	—	—
National League totals (2 year)	126	148	.460		—	—	—	—	—	—	—	—
Major league totals (10 years)	708	796	.471		—	—	—	—	—	—	—	—

NOTES:
1993—On suspended list (September 24-27).
1994—Milwaukee was in fifth place in A.L. Central at time of season-ending strike (August 12).
1995—On suspended list (July 27-31).
1999—Replaced as manager on interim basis by Joe Lefebvre, with team in fifth place (August 11).

HARGROVE, MIKE — ORIOLES

PERSONAL: Born October 26, 1949, in Perryton, Texas. ... 6-0/195. ... Batted left, threw left. ... Full name: Dudley Michael Hargrove.
HIGH SCHOOL: Perryton (Texas).
COLLEGE: Northwestern State, Okla. (degree in physical education and social sciences).
TRANSACTIONS/CAREER NOTES: Selected by Texas Rangers organization in 25th round of free-agent draft (June 6, 1972). ... Traded by Rangers with 3B Kurt Bevacqua and C Bill Fahey to San Diego Padres for OF Oscar Gamble, C Dave Roberts and cash (October 25, 1978). ... Traded by Padres to Cleveland Indians for OF Paul Dade (June 14, 1979). ... Granted free agency (November 12, 1985).
HONORS: Named Western Carolinas League Player of the Year (1973). ... Named A.L. Rookie Player of the Year by THE SPORTING NEWS (1974). ... Named A.L. Rookie of the Year by Baseball Writers' Association of America (1974).
STATISTICAL NOTES: Led New York-Pennsylvania League first basemen with 58 double plays in 1972. ... Led Western Carolinas League with 247 total bases in 1973. ... Led Western Carolinas League first basemen with 118 double plays in 1973. ... Had 23-game hitting streak (April 16-May 15, 1980). ... Led A.L. first basemen with 1,489 total chances in 1980. ... Led A.L. with .432 on-base percentage in 1981. ... Career major league grand slams: 1.

Year Team (League)	Pos.	G	AB	R	H	2B	3B	HR	RBI	Avg.	BB	SO	SB	PO	A	E	Avg.
1972— Geneva (NY-Penn)	1B	•70	243	38	65	8	0	4	37	.267	52	44	3	*537	•40	10	*.983
1973— Gastonia (W. Car.)	1B	•130	456	88	*160	*35	8	12	82	*.351	68	47	10	*1121	•77	14	*.988
1974— Texas (A.L.)	1B-DH-OF	131	415	57	134	18	6	4	66	.323	49	42	0	638	72	9	.987
1975— Texas (A.L.)	OF-1B-DH	145	519	82	157	22	2	11	62	.303	79	66	4	513	45	13	.977
1976— Texas (A.L.)	1B	151	541	80	155	30	1	7	58	.287	*97	64	2	1222	110	*21	.984
1977— Texas (A.L.)	1B	153	525	98	160	28	4	18	69	.305	103	59	2	1393	100	11	.993
1978— Texas (A.L.)	1B-DH	146	494	63	124	24	1	7	40	.251	*107	47	2	1221	*116	*17	.987
1979— San Diego (N.L.)■	1B	52	125	15	24	5	0	0	8	.192	25	15	0	323	17	5	.986
— Cleveland (A.L.)■	OF-1B-DH	100	338	60	110	21	4	10	56	.325	63	40	2	356	16	2	.995
1980— Cleveland (A.L.)	1B	160	589	86	179	22	2	11	85	.304	111	36	4	*1391	88	10	.993
1981— Cleveland (A.L.)	1B-DH	94	322	43	102	21	0	2	49	.317	60	16	5	766	76	•9	.989
1982— Cleveland (A.L.)	1B-DH	160	591	67	160	26	1	4	65	.271	101	58	2	1293	*123	5	.996
1983— Cleveland (A.L.)	1B-DH	134	469	57	134	21	4	3	57	.286	78	40	0	1098	115	7	.994
1984— Cleveland (A.L.)	1B	133	352	44	94	14	2	4	44	.267	53	38	0	790	83	8	.991
1985— Cleveland (A.L.)	1B-DH-OF	107	284	31	81	14	1	1	27	.285	39	29	1	599	66	6	.991
American League totals (12 years)		1614	5439	768	1590	261	28	80	678	.292	940	535	24	11280	1010	118	.990
National League totals (1 year)		52	125	15	24	5	0	0	8	.192	25	15	0	323	17	5	.986
Major league totals (12 years)		1666	5564	783	1614	266	28	80	686	.290	965	550	24	11603	1027	123	.990

ALL-STAR GAME RECORD

Year League	Pos.	AB	R	H	2B	3B	HR	RBI	Avg.	BB	SO	SB	PO	A	E	Avg.
1975— American	PH	1	0	0	0	0	0	0	.000	0	0	0	...	...	...	...

RECORD AS MANAGER

BACKGROUND: Minor league coach, Cleveland Indians organization (1986). ... Coach, Indians (1990-July 6, 1991).

HONORS: Named Carolina League Manager of the Year (1987). ... Named Pacific Coast League Manager of the Year (1989). ... Named A.L. Manager of the Year by The Sporting News (1995).

					Playoff		Champ. Series		World Series		All-Star Game	
Year Team (League)	W	L	Pct.	Pos.	W	L	W	L	W	L	W	L
1987— Kinston (Carolina)	33	37	.471	T3rd (S)	—	—	—	—	—	—	—	—
— (Second half)	42	28	.600	1st (S)	3	3	—	—	—	—	—	—
1988— Williamsport (East.)	66	73	.475	6th	—	—	—	—	—	—	—	—
1989— Colorado Springs (Pacific Coast)	44	26	.629	1st (S)	—	—	—	—	—	—	—	—
— (Second half)	34	38	.472	3rd (S)	2	3	—	—	—	—	—	—
1991— Cleveland (A.L.)	32	53	.376	7th (E)	—	—	—	—	—	—	—	—
1992— Cleveland (A.L.)	76	86	.469	T4th (E)	—	—	—	—	—	—	—	—
1993— Cleveland (A.L.)	76	86	.469	6th (E)	—	—	—	—	—	—	—	—
1994— Cleveland (A.L.)	66	47	.584		—	—	—	—	—	—	—	—
1995— Cleveland (A.L.)	100	44	.694	1st (C)	3	0	4	2	2	4	—	—
1996— Cleveland (A.L.)	99	62	.615	1st (C)	1	3	—	—	—	—	0	1
1997— Cleveland (A.L.)	86	75	.534	1st (C)	3	2	4	2	3	4	—	—
1998— Cleveland (A.L.)	89	73	.549	1st (C)	3	1	2	4	—	—	1	0
1999— Cleveland (A.L.)	97	65	.599	1st (C)	2	3	—	—	—	—	—	—
2000— Baltimore (A.L.)	74	88	.457	4th (E)	—	—	—	—	—	—	—	—
2001— Baltimore (A.L.)	63	98	.389	4th (E)	—	—	—	—	—	—	—	—
Major league totals (11 years)	858	777	.525		11	9	10	8	5	8	1	1

NOTES:

1987—Defeated Winston-Salem, two games to none, in playoffs; lost to Salem, three games to one, in league championship.

1989—Lost to Albuquerque in playoffs.

1991—Replaced Cleveland manager John McNamara with club in seventh place and record of 25-52 (July 6).

1994—Cleveland was in second place in A.L. Central at time of season-ending strike (August 12).

1995—Defeated Boston in A.L. divisional playoff; defeated Seattle in A.L. Championship Series; lost to Atlanta in World Series.

1996—Lost to Baltimore in A.L. divisional playoff.

1997—Defeated New York in A.L. divisional playoff; defeated Baltimore in A.L. Championship Series; lost to Florida in World Series.

1998—Defeated Boston in A.L. divisional playoff; lost to New York Yankees in A.L. Championship Series.

1999—Lost to Boston in A.L. divisional playoff.

HOWE, ART — ATHLETICS

PERSONAL: Born December 15, 1946, in Pittsburgh. ... 6-1/185. ... Batted right, threw right. ... Full name: Arthur Henry Howe Jr.

HIGH SCHOOL: Shaler (Glenshaw, Pa.).

COLLEGE: Wyoming (bachelor of science degree in business administration, 1969).

TRANSACTIONS/CAREER NOTES: Signed as free agent by Pittsburgh Pirates organization (June, 1971). ... On disabled list (August 17-September 2, 1972 and April 13-May 6, 1973). ... Traded by Pirates to Houston Astros (January 6, 1976), completing deal in which Astros traded 2B Tommy Helms to Pirates for a player to be named later (December 12, 1975). ... On disabled list (May 12-June 19, 1982 and March 27, 1983-entire season). ... Granted free agency (November 7, 1983). ... Signed by St. Louis Cardinals (March 21, 1984). ... Released by Cardinals (April 22, 1985).

STATISTICAL NOTES: Tied for Carolina League lead in putouts by third baseman with 95 in 1971. ... Led International League third basemen with 22 errors and 24 double plays in 1972. ... Had 23-game hitting streak (May 1-24, 1981). ... Career major league grand slams: 1.

Year Team (League)	Pos.	G	AB	R	H	2B	3B	HR	RBI	Avg.	BB	SO	SB	PO	A	E	Avg.
1971—Salem (Carolina)	3B-SS	114	382	77	133	27	7	12	79	*.348	82	74	11	‡110	221	21	.940
1972—Char., W.Va. (I.L.)	3B-2B-SS	109	365	68	99	21	3	14	53	.271	63	69	8	105	248	†24	.936
1973—Char., W.Va. (I.L.)	3B-2B-SS	119	372	50	85	20	1	8	44	.228	54	70	6	141	229	21	.946
1974—Char., W.Va. (I.L.)	3B	60	207	26	70	17	4	8	36	.338	31	27	4	35	90	9	.933
—Pittsburgh (N.L.)	3B-SS	29	74	10	18	4	1	1	5	.243	9	13	0	11	49	4	.938
1975—Char., W.Va. (I.L.)	3B-2B	11	42	4	15	1	3	0	3	.357	2	4	0	15	23	1	.974
—Pittsburgh (N.L.)	3B-SS	63	146	13	25	9	0	1	10	.171	15	15	1	19	89	7	.939
1976—Memphis (I.L.)■	3B-1B	74	259	50	92	21	3	12	59	.355	34	31	1	93	120	14	.938
—Houston (N.L.)	3B-2B	21	29	0	4	1	0	0	0	.138	6	6	0	17	16	1	.971
1977—Houston (N.L.)	2B-3B-SS	125	413	44	109	23	7	8	58	.264	41	60	0	213	333	8	.986
1978—Houston (N.L.)	2B-3B-1B	119	420	46	123	33	3	7	55	.293	34	41	2	240	302	13	.977
1979—Houston (N.L.)	2B-3B-1B	118	355	32	88	15	2	6	33	.248	36	37	3	188	261	7	.985
1980—Houston (N.L.)	1-3-2-S	110	321	34	91	12	5	10	46	.283	34	29	1	598	86	10	.986
1981—Houston (N.L.)	3B-1B	103	361	43	107	22	4	3	36	.296	41	23	1	67	206	9	.968
1982—Houston (N.L.)	3B-1B	110	365	29	87	15	1	5	38	.238	41	45	2	344	174	7	.987
1983—								Did not play.									
1984—St. Louis (N.L.)■	3-1-2-S	89	139	17	30	5	0	2	12	.216	18	18	0	71	80	3	.981
1985—St. Louis (N.L.)..........	1B-3B	4	3	0	0	0	0	0	0	.000	0	0	0	5	1	0	1.000
Major league totals (11 years)		891	2626	268	682	139	23	43	293	.260	275	287	10	1773	1597	69	.980

DIVISION SERIES RECORD

Year Team (League)	Pos.	G	AB	R	H	2B	3B	HR	RBI	Avg.	BB	SO	SB	PO	A	E	Avg.
1981—Houston (N.L.)	3B	5	17	1	4	0	0	1	1	.235	2	1	0	6	9	0	1.000

CHAMPIONSHIP SERIES RECORD

Year Team (League)	Pos.	G	AB	R	H	2B	3B	HR	RBI	Avg.	BB	SO	SB	PO	A	E	Avg.
1974—Pittsburgh (N.L.)	PH	1	1	0	0	0	0	0	0	.000	0	0	0	...	...	...	...
1980—Houston (N.L.)	1B-PH	5	15	0	3	1	1	0	2	.200	2	2	0	29	3	0	1.000
Championship series totals (2 years)		6	16	0	3	1	1	0	2	.188	2	2	0	29	3	0	1.000

RECORD AS MANAGER

BACKGROUND: Coach, Texas Rangers (May 21, 1985-88). ... Scout, Los Angeles Dodgers organization (1994). ... Coach, Colorado Rockies (1995).

		REGULAR SEASON			POSTSEASON							
Year Team (League)	W	L	Pct.	Pos.	Playoff W	L	Champ. Series W	L	World Series W	L	All-Star Game W	L
1989—Houston (N.L.)	86	76	.531	3rd (W)	—	—	—	—	—	—	—	—
1990—Houston (N.L.)	75	87	.463	T4th (W)	—	—	—	—	—	—	—	—
1991—Houston (N.L.)	65	97	.401	6th (W)	—	—	—	—	—	—	—	—
1992—Houston (N.L.)	81	81	.500	4th (W)	—	—	—	—	—	—	—	—
1993—Houston (N.L.)	85	77	.525	3rd (W)	—	—	—	—	—	—	—	—
1996—Oakland (A.L.)	78	84	.481	3rd (W)	—	—	—	—	—	—	—	—
1997—Oakland (A.L.)	65	97	.401	4th (W)	—	—	—	—	—	—	—	—
1998—Oakland (A.L.)	74	88	.457	4th (W)	—	—	—	—	—	—	—	—
1999—Oakland (A.L.)	87	75	.537	2nd (W)	—	—	—	—	—	—	—	—
2000—Oakland (A.L.)	91	70	.565	1st (W)	2	3	—	—	—	—	—	—
2001—Oakland (A.L.)	102	60	.630	2nd (W)	2	3	—	—	—	—	—	—
National League totals (5 years)	392	418	.484		—	—	—	—	—	—	—	—
American League totals (6 years)	497	474	.512		4	6	—	—	—	—	—	—
Major league totals (11 years)	889	892	.499		4	6	—	—	—	—	—	—

NOTES:
2000—Lost to New York Yankees in A.L. divisional playoff.
2001—Lost to New York Yankees in A.L. divisional playoff.

KERRIGAN, JOE
RED SOX

PERSONAL: Born January 30, 1954, in Philadelphia. ... 6-5/210. ... Throws right, bats right. ... Full name: Joseph Thomas Kerrigan. ... Brother of Tim Kerrigan, catcher with Philadelphia Phillies organization (1963-64); father of Joe Kerrigan, third baseman, Boston Red Sox organization.

COLLEGE: Temple.

TRANSACTIONS/CAREER NOTES: Selected by Montreal Expos organization in first round (10th pick overall) of free-agent draft (January 9, 1974). ... Traded by Expos with P Don Stanhouse and OF Gary Roenicke to Baltimore Orioles for P Rudy May, P Bryn Smith and P Randy Miller (December 7, 1977). ... Traded by Orioles with C John Buffamoyer to Cincinnati Reds for OF John Hale and IF Mike Grace (January 22, 1981).

Year League	W	L	Pct.	ERA	G	GS	CG	ShO	Sv.	IP	H	R	ER	BB	SO
1974—Kinston (Caro.)	4	10	.286	4.64	36	14	0	0	4	128	166	97	66	52	83
1975—West Palm Beach (FSL)	0	2	.000	2.74	22	0	0	0	3	23	24	7	7	11	24
—Quebec City (East.)	6	2	.750	0.68	27	0	0	0	4	53	38	11	4	15	28
1976—Denver (A.A.)	2	0	1.000	3.38	22	0	0	0	1	32	26	13	12	12	13
—Montreal (N.L.)	2	6	.250	3.81	38	0	0	0	1	56 2/3	63	27	24	23	22
1977—Montreal (N.L.)	3	5	.375	3.22	66	0	0	0	11	89 1/3	80	37	32	33	43

Year	League	W	L	Pct.	ERA	G	GS	CG	ShO	Sv.	IP	H	R	ER	BB	SO
1978—	Baltimore (A.L.)■..............	3	1	.750	4.77	26	2	0	0	3	71 2/3	75	44	38	36	41
1979—	Rochester (I.L.)..................	10	6	.625	3.51	*64	0	0	0	11	95	88	41	37	49	55
1980—	Rochester (I.L.)..................	3	3	.500	2.78	39	0	0	0	12	55	46	19	17	23	23
—	Baltimore (A.L.)............	0	0	...	3.86	1	0	0	0	0	2 1/3	3	1	1	0	1
1981—	Indianapolis (A.A.)■..........	4	8	.333	2.97	54	0	0	0	12	88	76	34	29	39	57
1982—	Okla. City-Denver (A.A.)■ ..	1	5	.167	5.38	48	1	0	0	2	97	117	61	58	39	52
A.L. totals (2 years)		3	1	.750	4.74	27	2	0	0	3	74	78	45	39	36	42
N.L. totals (2 years)		5	11	.313	3.45	104	0	0	0	12	146	143	64	56	56	65
Major League totals (4 years)		8	12	.400	3.89	131	2	0	0	15	220	221	109	95	92	107

RECORD AS MANAGER

BACKGROUND: Bullpen coach, Montreal Expos (1983-86). ... Minor league coach, Expos organization (1987-91). ... Pitching coach, Expos (1992-96). ... Pitching coach, Boston Red Sox (1996-August 16, 2001).

						REGULAR SEASON			POSTSEASON						
								Playoff		Champ. Series		World Series		All-Star Game	
Year	Team (League)		W	L	Pct.	Pos.		W	L	W	L	W	L	W	L
2001—	Boston (A.L.).........................		17	26	.395	2nd (E)		—	—	—	—	—	—	—	—

NOTES:
2001—Replaced Boston manager Jimy Williams with club in second place and record of 65-53 (August 16).

La RUSSA, TONY   CARDINALS

PERSONAL: Born October 4, 1944, in Tampa. ... 6-0/185. ... Batted right, threw right. ... Full name: Anthony La Russa Jr.
HIGH SCHOOL: Jefferson (Tampa).
COLLEGE: University of Tampa, then South Florida (degree in industrial management), then Florida State (law degree, 1980).
TRANSACTIONS/CAREER NOTES: Signed by Kansas City Athletics organization (June 6, 1962). ... On disabled list (May 9-September 8, 1964; June 3-July 15, 1965; and April 12-May 6 and July 3-September 5, 1967). ... A's franchise moved from Kansas City to Oakland (October 1967). ... Contract sold by A's to Atlanta Braves (August 14, 1971). ... Traded by Braves to Chicago Cubs for P Tom Phoebus (October 20, 1972). ... Contract sold by Cubs to Pittsburgh Pirates organization (March 23, 1974). ... Released by Pirates (April 4, 1975). ... Signed by Chicago White Sox organization (April 7, 1975). ... On disabled list (August 8-18, 1976). ... Contract sold by White Sox to St. Louis Cardinals organization (December 13, 1976). ... Released by Cardinals (September 29, 1977).
STATISTICAL NOTES: Led International League in being hit by pitch with 11 in 1972.

							BATTING								FIELDING			
Year	Team (League)	Pos.	G	AB	R	H	2B	3B	HR	RBI	Avg.	BB	SO	SB	PO	A	E	Avg.
1962—	Daytona Beach (FSL)..	SS	64	225	37	58	7	0	1	32	.258	42	47	11	135	173	38	.890
—	Binghamton (East.)	SS-2B	12	43	3	8	0	0	0	4	.186	5	9	2	20	27	8	.855
1963—	Kansas City (A.L.)	SS-2B	34	44	4	11	1	1	0	1	.250	7	12	0	29	25	2	.964
1964—	Lewiston (N'west)	2B-SS	90	329	50	77	22	1	1	25	.234	53	56	10	188	218	18	.958
1965—	Birmingham (Sou.)......	2B	75	259	24	50	11	2	1	18	.193	26	37	5	202	161	21	.945
1966—	Modesto (California) ..	2B	81	316	67	92	20	1	7	44	.291	44	37	18	201	212	20	.954
—	Mobile (Southern)......	2B	51	170	20	50	9	4	4	26	.294	23	24	4	117	133	10	.962
1967—	Birmingham (Sou.)......	2B	41	139	12	32	6	1	5	22	.230	10	11	3	88	120	5	.977
1968—	Oakland (A.L.)	PH	5	3	0	1	0	0	0	0	.333	0	0	0	...	...	...	...
—	Vancouver (PCL)........	2B	122	455	55	109	16	8	5	29	.240	52	58	4	249	321	14	*.976
1969—	Iowa (A.A.)	2B	67	235	37	72	11	1	4	27	.306	0	1	5	177	222	15	.964
—	Oakland (A.L.)	PH	8	8	0	0	0	0	0	0	.000	42	30	0	...	...	...	...
1970—	Iowa (A.A.)	2B	22	88	13	22	5	0	2	5	.250	9	14	0	52	59	3	.974
—	Oakland (A.L.)	2B	52	106	6	21	4	1	0	6	.198	15	19	0	67	89	5	.969
1971—	Iowa (A.A.)	2-3-S-O	28	107	21	31	5	1	2	11	.290	10	11	0	70	85	2	.987
—	Oakland (A.L.)	2B-SS-3B	23	8	3	0	0	0	0	0	.000	0	4	0	8	7	2	.882
—	Atlanta (N.L.)■..........	2B	9	7	1	2	0	0	0	0	.286	1	1	0	8	6	1	.933
1972—	Richmond (I.L.)	2B	122	389	68	120	13	2	10	42	.308	72	41	0	305	289	20	.967
1973—	Wichita (A.A.)■.........	2B-1B-3B	106	392	82	123	16	0	5	75	.314	60	46	10	423	213	26	.961
—	Chicago (N.L.)...........	PR	1	0	1	0	0	0	0	...	...	0	0	0	...	...	...	...
1974—	Char., W.Va. (I.L.)■....	2B	139	457	50	119	17	1	8	35	.260	51	50	4	262	*378	17	.974
1975—	Denver (A.A.)■...........	3-0-S-2	118	354	87	99	23	2	7	46	.280	70	46	13	95	91	10	.949
1976—	Iowa (A.A.)	3-2-S-1-0-P	107	332	53	86	11	0	4	34	.259	40	43	10	132	160	22	.930
1977—	New Orleans (A.A.)■..	2B-3B	50	128	17	24	2	2	3	6	.188	20	21	0	66	87	7	.956
American League totals (5 years)			122	169	13	33	5	2	0	7	.195	64	65	0	104	121	9	.962
National League totals (2 years)			10	7	2	2	0	0	0	0	.286	1	1	0	8	6	1	.933
Major league totals (6 years)			132	176	15	35	5	2	0	7	.199	65	66	0	112	127	10	.960

RECORD AS PITCHER

Year	Team (League)	W	L	Pct.	ERA	G	GS	CG	ShO	Sv.	IP	H	R	ER	BB	SO
1976—	Iowa (A.A.)	0	0	...	3.00	3	0	0	0	0	3	3	1	1	0	0

RECORD AS MANAGER

BACKGROUND: Coach, St. Louis Cardinals organization (June 20-September 29, 1977). ... Coach, Chicago White Sox (July 3, 1978-remainder of season).
RECORDS: Shares major league single-season record for most clubs managed—2 (1986).
HONORS: Named Major League Manager of the Year by THE SPORTING NEWS (1983). ... Named A.L. Manager of the Year by Baseball Writers' Association of America (1983, 1988 and 1992). ... Named A.L. Manager of the Year by THE SPORTING NEWS (1988 and 1992).

		REGULAR SEASON			POSTSEASON								
						Playoff		Champ. Series		World Series		All-Star Game	
Year Team (League)	W	L	Pct.	Pos.		W	L	W	L	W	L	W	L
1978— Knoxville (Southern)	49	21	.700	1st (W)		—	—	—	—	—	—	—	—
—(Second half)	4	4	.500			—	—	—	—	—	—	—	—
1979— Iowa (American Association)	54	52	.509			—	—	—	—	—	—	—	—
—Chicago (A.L.)	27	27	.500	5th (W)		—	—	—	—	—	—	—	—
1980— Chicago (A.L.)	70	90	.438	5th (W)		—	—	—	—	—	—	—	—
1981— Chicago (A.L.)	31	22	.585	3rd (W)		—	—	—	—	—	—	—	—
—(Second half)	23	30	.434	6th (W)		—	—	—	—	—	—	—	—
1982— Chicago (A.L.)	87	75	.537	3rd (W)		—	—	—	—	—	—	—	—
1983— Chicago (A.L.)	99	63	.611	1st (W)		—	—	1	3	—	—	—	—
1984— Chicago (A.L.)	74	88	.457	T5th (W)		—	—	—	—	—	—	—	—
1985— Chicago (A.L.)	85	77	.525	3rd (W)		—	—	—	—	—	—	—	—
1986— Chicago (A.L.)	26	38	.406			—	—	—	—	—	—	—	—
—Oakland (A.L.)	45	34	.570	T3rd (W)		—	—	—	—	—	—	—	—
1987— Oakland (A.L.)	81	81	.500	3rd (W)		—	—	—	—	—	—	—	—
1988— Oakland (A.L.)	104	58	.642	1st (W)		—	—	4	0	1	4	—	—
1989— Oakland (A.L.)	99	63	.611	1st (W)		—	—	4	1	4	0	1	0
1990— Oakland (A.L.)	103	59	.636	1st (W)		—	—	4	0	0	4	1	0
1991— Oakland (A.L.)	84	78	.519	4th (W)		—	—	—	—	—	—	1	0
1992— Oakland (A.L.)	96	66	.593	1st (W)		—	—	2	4	—	—	—	—
1993— Oakland (A.L.)	68	94	.420	7th (W)		—	—	—	—	—	—	—	—
1994— Oakland (A.L.)	51	63	.447			—	—	—	—	—	—	—	—
1995— Oakland (A.L.)	67	77	.465	4th (W)		—	—	—	—	—	—	—	—
1996— St. Louis (N.L.)	88	74	.543	1st (C)		3	0	3	4	—	—	—	—
1997— St. Louis (N.L.)	73	89	.451	4th (C)		—	—	—	—	—	—	—	—
1998— St. Louis (N.L.)	83	79	.512	3rd (C)		—	—	—	—	—	—	—	—
1999— St. Louis (N.L.)	75	86	.466	4th (C)		—	—	—	—	—	—	—	—
2000— St. Louis (N.L.)	95	67	.586	1st (C)		3	0	1	4	—	—	—	—
2001— St. Louis (N.L.)	93	69	.574	2nd (C)		2	3	—	—	—	—	—	—
American League totals (17 years)	1320	1183	.527			—	—	15	8	5	8	3	0
National League totals (6 years)	507	464	.522			8	3	4	8	—	—	—	—
Major League totals (23 years)	1827	1647	.536			8	3	19	16	5	8	3	0

NOTES:

1978—Became Chicago White Sox coach and replaced as Knoxville manager by Joe Jones, with club in third place (July 3).

1979—Replaced as Iowa manager by Joe Sparks, with club in second place (August 3); replaced Chicago manager Don Kessinger with club in fifth place and record of 46-60 (August 3).

1983—Lost to Baltimore in A.L. Championship Series.

1986—Replaced as White Sox manager by interim manager Doug Rader, with club in sixth place (June 20); replaced Oakland manager Jackie Moore (record of 29-44) and interim manager Jeff Newman (record of 2-8) with club in seventh place and record of 31-52 (July 7).

1988—Defeated Boston in A.L. Championship Series; lost to Los Angeles in World Series.

1989—Defeated Toronto in A.L. Championship Series; defeated San Francisco in World Series.

1990—Defeated Boston in A.L. Championship Series; lost to Cincinnati in World Series.

1992—Lost to Toronto in A.L. Championship Series.

1993—On suspended list (October 1-remainder of season).

1994—Oakland was in second place in A.L. West at time of season-ending strike (August 12).

1996—Defeated San Diego in N.L. divisional playoff; lost to Atlanta in N.L. Championship Series.

2000—Defeated Atlanta in N.L. divisional playoff; lost to New York Mets in N.L. Championship Series.

2001—Lost to Arizona in N.L. divisional playoff.

LOPES, DAVEY BREWERS

PERSONAL: Born May 3, 1945, in East Providence, R.I. ... 5-9/170. ... Batted right, threw right. ... Full name: David Earl Lopes.

HIGH SCHOOL: LaSalle Academy (Providence, R.I.).

COLLEGE: Iowa Weslyan, then Washburn (Kan.), degree in education, 1969.

TRANSACTIONS/CAREER NOTES: Selected by San Francisco Giants organization in 28th round of free agent draft (June 6, 1967); did not sign. ... Selected by Los Angeles Dodgers organization in secondary phase of free-agent draft (January 27, 1968). ... On restricted list (April 11-June 13, 1968). ... On temporary inactive list (April 11-27, 1969). ... On military list (July 22, 1969-April 8, 1970). ... On temporary inactive list (June 9-30, 1970). ... On temporary inactive list (April 26-29 and June 8-July 2, 1971). ... On temporary inactive list (June 16-30 and August 28-September 1, 1972). ... On disabled list (March 31-May 8, 1976). ... On disabled list (August 18-September 2, 1981). ... Traded by Dodgers to Oakland Athletics for 2B Lance Hudson (February 8, 1982). ... On disabled list (July 7-August 8, 1984). ... Traded by Athletics to Chicago Cubs (August 31, 1984) as partial completion of deal in which Cubs traded P Chuck Rainey and a player to be named later to Athletics for a player to be named later (July 15, 1984); Athletics acquired OF Damon Farmar to complete deal (March 18, 1985). ... Traded by Cubs to Houston Astros for P Frank DiPino (July 21, 1986). ... Granted free agency (November 12, 1986). ... Re-signed by Astros (December 19, 1986). ... On disabled list (April 12-June 19, 1987); included rehabilitation assignment to Tucson (June 9-13, 1987). ... Released by Astros (November 12, 1987).

RECORDS: Shares major league single-inning record for most errors by a second baseman—3 (June 2, 1973, first inning). ... Shares N.L. single-game record for most double plays by a second baseman—5 (May 18, 1975).

HONORS: Named second baseman on The Sporting News National League All-Star Team (1978 and 1979). ... Named second baseman on The Sporting News National League All-Star fielding team (1978).

STATISTICAL NOTES: Led Pacific Coast League second basemen in errors with 18 in 1972. ... Tied for Pacific Coast League lead in errors by outfielders with 10 in 1970. ... Hit three home runs in one game (August 20, 1974).

Year Team (League)	Pos.	G	AB	R	H	2B	3B	HR	RBI	Avg.	BB	SO	SB	PO	A	E	Avg.
1968— Daytona Beach (FSL)..	OF	82	271	39	67	6	6	5	33	.247	24	74	26	109	7	4	.967
1969— Daytona Beach (FSL)....	OF	72	264	53	74	7	4	9	33	.280	49	42	32	138	16	7	.957
1970— Spokane (PCL)..........	OF-2B	100	343	48	90	15	4	6	35	.262	37	65	11	202	19	‡12	.948
1971— Spokane (PCL)........	OF-2B	94	353	78	108	9	9	6	36	.306	44	65	37	157	103	11	.959
1972— Albuquerque (PCL).....	2B-OF-SS	104	397	94	126	18	6	11	53	.317	59	64	*48	213	270	†21	.958
— Los Angeles (N.L.)	2B	11	42	6	9	4	0	0	1	.214	7	6	4	27	27	2	.964
1973— Los Angeles (N.L.)	2-O-S-3	142	535	77	147	13	5	6	37	.275	62	77	36	323	380	11	.985
1974— Los Angeles (N.L.)	2B	145	530	95	141	26	3	10	35	.266	66	71	59	309	360	*24	.965
1975— Los Angeles (N.L.)	2B-OF-SS	155	618	108	162	24	6	8	41	.262	91	93	*77	360	386	16	.979
1976— Los Angeles (N.L.)	2B-OF	117	427	72	103	17	7	4	20	.241	56	49	*63	254	268	19	.965
1977— Los Angeles (N.L.)	2B	134	502	85	142	19	5	11	53	.283	73	69	47	287	380	14	.979
1978— Los Angeles (N.L.)	2B-OF	151	587	93	163	25	4	17	58	.278	71	70	45	340	424	*20	.974
1979— Los Angeles (N.L.)	2B	153	582	109	154	20	6	28	73	.265	97	88	44	341	*384	14	.981
1980— Los Angeles (N.L.)	2B	141	553	79	139	15	3	10	49	.251	58	71	23	304	416	15	.980
1981— Los Angeles (N.L.)	2B	58	214	35	44	2	0	5	17	.206	22	35	20	129	161	2	.993
1982— Oakland (A.L.)■........	2B-OF	138	450	58	109	19	3	11	42	.242	40	51	28	295	338	15	.977
1983— Oakland (A.L.)	2B-OF-3B	147	494	64	137	13	4	17	67	.277	51	61	22	267	287	9	.984
1984— Oakland (A.L.)	OF-2B-3B	72	230	32	59	11	1	9	36	.257	31	36	12	99	47	6	.961
— Chicago (N.L.)■.............	OF-3B	16	17	5	4	1	0	0	0	.235	6	5	3	6	2	0	1.000
1985— Chicago (N.L.)	OF-3B-2B	99	275	52	78	11	0	11	44	.284	46	37	47	115	6	1	.992
1986— Chicago (N.L.)	3B-OF	59	157	38	47	8	2	6	22	.299	31	16	17	51	54	8	.929
— Houston (N.L.)■........	OF-3B	37	98	11	23	2	1	1	13	.235	12	9	8	45	11	0	1.000
1987— Houston (N.L.)	OF	47	43	4	10	2	0	1	6	.233	13	8	2	6	0	1	.857
— Tucson (PCL)	DH	4	14	2	9	3	0	0	3	.643	6	2	1	...	...	...	.000
National League totals (14 years)		1465	5180	869	1366	189	42	118	469	.264	711	704	495	2897	3259	147	.977
American League totals (3 years)		347	1174	154	305	43	8	37	145	.260	122	148	62	661	672	30	.978
Major league totals (16 years)		1812	6354	1023	1671	232	50	155	614	.263	833	852	557	3358	3931	177	.977

DIVISION SERIES RECORD

Year Team (League)	Pos.	G	AB	R	H	2B	3B	HR	RBI	Avg.	BB	SO	SB	PO	A	E	Avg.
1981— Los Angeles (N.L.)	2B	5	20	1	4	1	0	0	0	.200	3	7	1	7	12	0	1.000

CHAMPIONSHIP SERIES RECORD

RECORDS: Holds N.L. career record for most stolen bases—9. ... Shares career record for most consecutive games, one or more runs batted in—4. ... Shares N.L. career record for most clubs total Series—3.

Year Team (League)	Pos.	G	AB	R	H	2B	3B	HR	RBI	Avg.	BB	SO	SB	PO	A	E	Avg.
1974— Los Angeles (N.L.)	2B	4	15	4	4	0	1	0	3	.267	3	5	1	9	18	1	.964
1977— Los Angeles (N.L.)	2B	4	17	2	4	0	0	0	3	.235	2	0	0	9	10	1	.950
1978— Los Angeles (N.L.)	2B	4	18	3	7	1	1	2	5	.389	0	1	1	10	10	2	.909
1981— Los Angeles (N.L.)	2B	5	18	0	5	0	0	0	0	.278	1	3	5	13	13	0	1.000
1984— Chicago (N.L.)	OF-PH	2	1	0	0	0	0	0	0	.000	0	0	0	0	0	0	...
1986— Houston (N.L.)	PH	3	2	1	0	0	0	0	0	.000	0	0	0	...	...	...	...
Championship series totals (6 years)		22	71	10	20	1	2	2	11	.282	9	5	9	41	51	4	.958

WORLD SERIES RECORD

RECORDS: Shares World Series records for most stolen bases, inning—2 (October 15, 1974, first inning); most putouts by second baseman, game—8 (October 16, 1974); most chances accepted by second baseman, game—13 (October 16, 1974); most putouts by second baseman, inning—3 (October 16, 1974, sixth inning and October 21, 1981, fourth inning); most times home run as leadoff batter, start of game—1 (October 17, 1978); most errors by second baseman, game—3 (October 25, 1981); most errors by second baseman, inning—2 (October 25, 1981, fourth inning).

Year Team (League)	Pos.	G	AB	R	H	2B	3B	HR	RBI	Avg.	BB	SO	SB	PO	A	E	Avg.
1974— Los Angeles (N.L.)	2B	5	18	2	2	0	0	0	0	.111	3	4	2	19	9	0	1.000
1977— Los Angeles (N.L.)	2B	6	24	3	4	0	1	1	2	.167	4	3	2	12	22	0	1.000
1978— Los Angeles (N.L.)	2B	6	26	7	8	0	0	3	7	.308	2	1	3	10	19	1	.967
1981— Los Angeles (N.L.)	2B	6	22	6	5	1	0	0	2	.227	4	3	4	26	14	6	.870
World Series totals (4 years)		23	90	18	19	1	1	3	11	.211	13	11	11	67	64	7	.949

ALL.STAR GAME RECORD

Year Team (League)	Pos.	AB	R	H	2B	3B	HR	RBI	Avg.	BB	SO	SB	PO	A	E	Avg.
1978— National	PH-2B	1	0	1	0	0	0	1	1.000	0	0	0	0	1	0	1.000
1979— National	2B	3	0	1	0	0	0	0	.333	0	1	0	4	1	0	1.000
1980— National	2B	1	0	0	0	0	0	0	.000	0	0	0	0	2	0	1.000
1981— National	2B	0	0	0	0	0	0	0	.000	1	0	0	1	0	0	1.000
All-Star Game totals (4 years)		5	0	2	0	0	0	1	.400	1	1	0	5	7	0	1.000

BACKGROUND: Coach, Texas Rangers (1988-91). ... Coach, Baltimore Orioles (1992-94). ... Coach, San Diego Padres (1995-99).

RECORD AS MANAGER

		REGULAR SEASON			Playoff		Champ. Series		World Series		All-Star Game	
Year Team (League)	W	L	Pct.	Pos.	W	L	W	L	W	L	W	L
2000—Milwaukee (N.L.)	73	89	.451	3rd (C)	—	—	—	—	—	—	—	—
2001—Milwaukee (N.L.)	68	94	.420	4th (C)	—	—	—	—	—	—	—	—
Major League totals (2 years)..........................	141	183	.435		—	—	—	—	—	—	—	—

PERSONAL: Born January 4, 1944, in North Fork, W.Va. ... 6-3/200. ... Batted left, threw right. ... Full name: Charles Fuqua Manuel.
HIGH SCHOOL: Parry McCluer (Buena Vista, Va.).
HONORS: Named Most Valuable Player of Japan Pacific League (1979).
STATISTICAL NOTES: Led Midwest League in total bases with 205 in 1967. ... Led Southern League in total bases with 230, in sacrifice hits with 10 and in sacrifice flies with nine in 1968.

							BATTING								FIELDING		
Year Team (League)	Pos.	G	AB	R	H	2B	3B	HR	RBI	Avg.	BB	SO	SB	PO	A	E	Avg.
1963—Wytheville (Appal.).....	OF	58	173	32	62	9	2	7	45	.358	25	21	7	58	6	3	.955
1964—Orlando (FSL).........	OF	114	373	43	99	21	7	4	37	.265	43	47	3	155	*15	5	.966
1965—Wilson (Carolina)......	OF	61	167	16	34	6	1	0	19	.204	19	27	2	68	5	0	1.000
—Orlando (FSL)......	OF	61	187	14	42	6	1	1	21	.225	21	26	4	121	8	0	1.000
1966—Wilson (Carolina)......	OF	118	347	39	80	13	5	6	47	.231	43	53	7	140	13	5	.968
1967—Wisconsin (Midw.).....	OF	111	399	*76	125	29	3	15	•70	*.313	56	74	4	178	18	4	.980
1968—Charlotte (Sou.).........	OF	138	505	59	143	26	11	13	79	.283	43	89	6	202	8	5	.977
1969—Minnesota (A.L.)......	OF	83	164	14	34	6	0	2	24	.207	28	33	1	57	2	2	.967
1970—Evansville (A.A.)........	OF-1B	21	70	13	23	5	0	6	26	.329	6	5	0	43	6	4	.925
—Minnesota (A.L.).......	OF	56	64	4	12	0	0	1	7	.188	6	17	1	7	0	0	1.000
1971—Portland (PCL).........	OF-1B	63	191	47	71	8	5	19	46	.372	31	29	0	112	2	7	.942
—Minnesota (A.L.).......	OF	18	16	1	2	1	0	0	1	.125	1	8	0	0	0	0	.000
1972—Minnesota (A.L.).......	OF	63	122	6	25	5	0	1	8	.205	4	16	0	39	4	1	.977
1973—Tacoma (PCL)	OF	105	343	47	94	18	3	16	68	.274	42	58	0	57	6	2	.969
1974—Albuquerque (PCL)■..	OF	129	432	82	142	23	2	30	102	.329	80	68	3	59	4	3	.955
—Los Angeles (N.L.).....	PH	4	3	0	1	0	0	0	1	.333	1	0	0	...	...	...	...
1975—Albuquerque (PCL).....	DH-OF	81	243	40	79	17	1	16	64	.325	39	32	0	1	0	0	1.000
—Los Angeles (N.L.).....	PH	15	15	0	2	0	0	0	2	.133	0	3	0	...	...	...	...
1976—Yakult (Jap. Cen.)■....	OF	84	263	...	64	...	...	11	32	.243	...	...	0	...	...	...	...
1977—Yakult (Jap. Cen.)......	OF	114	358	70	113	8	0	42	97	.316	...	...	3	...	...	...	...
1978—Yakult (Jap. Cen.)......	OF	127	468	85	146	12	2	39	103	.312	...	...	1	...	...	...	...
1979—Kintetsu (Jp. Pac.)■....	OF	97	333	69	108	18	0	*37	94	.324	...	...	0	...	...	...	...
1980—Kintetsu (Jap. Pac.)....	OF	118	459	88	149	16	0	*48	*129	.325	...	...	0	...	...	...	...
1981—Kintetsu (Jap. Cen.)■...	OF	81	246	...	64	...	...	12	36	.260	...	...	0	...	...	...	...
American League totals (4 years)		220	366	25	73	12	0	4	40	.199	39	74	1	...	...	...	...
National League totals (2 years)		19	18	0	3	0	0	0	3	.167	1	3	0	...	...	...	...
Major league totals (6 years)		239	384	25	76	12	0	4	43	.198	40	77	1	...	...	...	...

CHAMPIONSHIP SERIES RECORD

							BATTING								FIELDING		
Year Team (League)	Pos.	G	AB	R	H	2B	3B	HR	RBI	Avg.	BB	SO	SB	PO	A	E	Avg.
1969—Minnesota (A.L.)	PH	1	0	0	0	0	0	0	0	.000	0	0	0	...	...	...	...
1970—Minnesota (A.L.)	PH	1	1	0	0	0	0	0	0	.000	0	0	0	...	...	...	...
Championship series totals (2 years)		2	1	0	0	0	0	0	0	.000	0	0	0	...	...	...	...

RECORD AS MANAGER

BACKGROUND: Scout, Minnesota Twins (1982). ... Hitting instructor, Cleveland Indians (1988-89 and 1994-99).
HONORS: Named International League Manager of the Year (1993).

		REGULAR SEASON			POSTSEASON						
						Playoff		Champ. Series		World Series		All-Star Game	
Year Team (League)	W	L	Pct.	Pos.	W	L	W	L	W	L	W	L
1983—Wisconsin (Midwest)	71	67	.518	2nd (N)	—	—	—	—	—	—	—	—
1984—Orlando (Southern)	34	35	.493	3rd (E)	—	—	—	—	—	—	—	—
—(Second half)	45	30	.600	2nd (E)	0	1	—	—	—	—	—	—
1985—Orlando (Southern)	29	35	.453	5th (E)	—	—	—	—	—	—	—	—
—(Second half)	43	36	.544	2nd (E)	—	—	—	—	—	—	—	—
1986—Toledo (International)	62	77	.446	6th	—	—	—	—	—	—	—	—
1987—Portland (PCL)	20	49	.290	5th (N)	—	—	—	—	—	—	—	—
—(Second half)	25	47	.347	5th (N)	—	—	—	—	—	—	—	—
1990—Colorado Springs (PCL)	37	34	.521	2nd (S)	—	—	—	—	—	—	—	—
—(Second half)	39	33	.541	3rd (S)	—	—	—	—	—	—	—	—
1991—Colorado Springs (PCL)	30	41	.422	5th (S)	—	—	—	—	—	—	—	—
—(Second half)	42	26	.617	1st (S)	1	3	—	—	—	—	—	—
1992—Colorado Springs (PCL)	36	33	.521	2nd (S)	—	—	—	—	—	—	—	—
—(Second half)	48	24	.666	1st (S)	6	2	—	—	—	—	—	—
1993—Charlotte (International)	86	55	.610	1st (W)	6	4	—	—	—	—	—	—
2000—Cleveland (A.L.)	90	72	.556	2nd (C)	—	—	—	—	—	—	—	—
2001—Cleveland (A.L.)	91	71	.562	1st (C)	2	3	—	—	—	—	—	—
Major league totals (2 years)	181	143	.559		2	3	—	—	—	—	—	—

NOTES:
1984—Lost to Charlotte in one game playoff.
1991—Lost to Tucson in playoffs.
1992—Defeated Las Vegas, three games to two, in playoff; defeated Vancouver, three games to none, in championship playoff.
1993—Defeated Richmond, three games to one, in playoff; defeated Rochester, three games to two, in championship playoff.
2001—Lost to Seattle in A.L. divisional playoff.

MANUEL, JERRY

WHITE SOX

PERSONAL: Born December 23, 1953, in Hahira, Ga. ... 5-11/180. ... Batted right, threw right.
HIGH SCHOOL: Cordova (Rancho Cordova, Calif.).
TRANSACTIONS/CAREER NOTES: Selected by Detroit Tigers organization in first round (20th pick overall) of free-agent draft (June 6, 1972).

... On disabled list (August 18-September 1, 1978). ... Traded by Tigers to Montreal Expos for C Duffy Dyer (March 14, 1980). ... On disabled list (May 2-July 31, and August 15-September 1, 1981). ... Traded by Expos to San Diego Padres for P Kim Seaman (May 22, 1982). ... Traded by Padres to Expos for a player to be named later (June 8, 1982); Padres acquired P Mike Griffin to complete deal (August 30, 1982). ... Traded by Expos to Chicago Cubs for C Butch Benton (February 4, 1983). ... Granted free agency following 1983 season. ... Signed by Chicago White Sox organization (April 8, 1984). ... Granted free agency following 1985 season. ... Signed by Expos organization for 1986 season. ... On disabled list (June 23-July 17 and July 25-August 4, 1986).

STATISTICAL NOTES: Led Appalachian League shortstops with 303 total chances in 1972. ... Led American Association second basemen with 688 total chances in 1974. ... Led American Association second basemen with 758 total chances and 108 double plays in 1975. ... Led American Association second basemen with 363 assists and 611 total chances in 1979. ... Led American Association shortstops with 612 total chances in 1980.

							BATTING								FIELDING		
Year Team (League)	Pos.	G	AB	R	H	2B	3B	HR	RBI	Avg.	BB	SO	SB	PO	A	E	Avg.
1972— Bristol (Appal.)	SS	67	233	31	56	8	8	4	29	.240	19	61	11	*112	*176	15	*.950
1973— Lakeland (FSL)	SS	117	433	66	109	17	4	2	28	.252	52	98	20	167	349	29	.947
— Toledo (I.L.)	SS	27	72	8	20	0	0	0	2	.278	3	16	2	44	90	4	.971
1974— Evansville (A.A.)	2B	127	384	44	81	5	5	1	24	.211	35	74	3	*315	356	17	.979
1975— Evansville (A.A.)	2B	*137	501	63	115	10	4	4	43	.230	44	101	5	*348	*394	16	.979
— Detroit (A.L.)	2B	6	18	0	1	0	0	0	0	.056	0	4	0	11	23	2	.944
1976— Detroit (A.L.)	2B-SS	54	43	4	6	1	0	0	2	.140	3	9	1	40	64	8	.929
— Evansville (A.A.)	2B	11	44	6	8	1	0	1	3	.182	2	9	0	25	29	1	.982
1977— Evansville (A.A.)	2B-SS	110	375	52	102	19	7	1	38	.272	45	55	12	198	304	17	.967
1978— Evansville (A.A.)	2B-SS	114	430	65	113	18	5	7	50	.263	50	83	8	264	321	20	.967
1979— Evansville (A.A.)	2B-SS	130	460	71	116	26	3	9	75	.252	67	67	8	265	†434	22	.969
1980— Denver (A.A.)■	SS	128	491	105	136	23	2	3	61	.277	81	62	11	*233	*357	22	.964
— Montreal (N.L.)..........	SS	7	6	0	0	0	0	0	0	.000	0	2	0	5	11	1	.941
1981— Montreal (N.L.)..........	2B-SS	27	55	10	11	5	0	3	10	.200	6	11	0	37	41	1	.987
1982— Wichita (A.A.)■.........	S-3-2-O	71	263	31	67	22	0	3	37	.255	15	34	2	99	152	11	.958
— San Diego (N.L.)	2B-3B-SS	2	5	0	1	0	1	0	1	.200	1	0	0	1	1	0	1.000
— Hawaii (PCL)	SS	26	92	8	18	3	1	0	7	.196	11	12	2	41	73	1	.991
1983— Iowa (A.A.)■.............	2-O-S-3	85	279	37	74	14	3	3	33	.265	22	46	6	129	143	9	.968
1984— Denver (A.A.)■	SS-2B-OF	109	335	43	98	14	3	4	40	.293	37	32	7	184	262	18	.961
1985—							Did not play.										
1986— Indianapolis (A.A.)■ ..	3B-2B	22	41	4	16	2	0	1	9	.390	2	5	0	5	7	1	.923
American League totals (2 years)		60	61	4	7	1	0	0	2	.115	3	13	1	51	87	10	.932
National League totals (3 years)		36	66	10	12	5	1	3	11	.182	7	13	0	43	53	2	.980
Major league totals (5 years)		96	127	14	19	6	1	3	13	.150	10	26	1	94	140	12	.951

DIVISION SERIES RECORD

							BATTING								FIELDING		
Year Team (League)	Pos.	G	AB	R	H	2B	3B	HR	RBI	Avg.	BB	SO	SB	PO	A	E	Avg.
1981— Montreal (N.L.)..........	2B	5	14	0	1	0	0	0	0	.071	2	5	0	13	19	3	.914

CHAMPIONSHIP SERIES RECORD

							BATTING								FIELDING		
Year Team (League)	Pos.	G	AB	R	H	2B	3B	HR	RBI	Avg.	BB	SO	SB	PO	A	E	Avg.
1981— Montreal (N.L.)..........	PR	1	1	0	0	0	0	0	0	.000	0	0	0	...	...	...	...

RECORD AS MANAGER

BACKGROUND: Scout, Chicago White Sox (1985). ... Player/coach, Indianapolis, American Association (1986). ... Roving infield instructor, Montreal Expos organization (1987). ... Minor league field coordinator, Expos (1988-89). ... Coach, Expos (June 3, 1991-1996). ... Coach, Florida Marlins (1997).

HONORS: Named Southern League co-Manager of the Year (1990). ... Named A.L. Manager of the Year by THE SPORTING NEWS (2000). ... Named A.L. Manager of the Year by Baseball Writers' Association of America (2000).

	REGULAR SEASON					POSTSEASON					
						Playoff		Champ. Series		World Series		All-Star Game
Year Team (League)	W	L	Pct.	Pos.		W	L	W	L	W	L	W	L
1990— Jacksonville (Southern)	38	33	.535	2nd (E)		—	—	—	—	—	—	—	—
— (Second half)	46	27	.630	1st (E)		1	3	—	—	—	—	—	—
1991— Indianapolis (A.A.)	28	22	.560	—		—	—	—	—	—	—	—	—
1998— Chicago (A.L.)	80	82	.494	2nd (C)		—	—	—	—	—	—	—	—
1999— Chicago (A.L.)	75	86	.466	2nd (C)		—	—	—	—	—	—	—	—
2000— Chicago (A.L.)	95	67	.586	1st (C)		0	3	—	—	—	—	—	—
2001— Chicago (A.L.)	83	79	.512	3rd (C)		—	—	—	—	—	—	—	—
Major league totals (4 years)	333	314	.515			0	3						

NOTES:
1990—Lost to Orlando in playoffs.
1991—Replaced as Indianapolis manager by Pat Kelly (June 2).
2000—Lost to Seattle in A.L. divisional playoff.

MARTINEZ, BUCK   BLUE JAYS

PERSONAL: Born November 7, 1948, in Redding, Calif. ... 5-11/200. ... Batted right, threw right. ... Full name: John Albert Martinez.
JUNIOR COLLEGE: Sacramento City College.
COLLEGE: Sacramento State.
TRANSACTIONS/CAREER NOTES: Selected by Philadelphia Phillies organization in seventh round of free-agent draft (January 28, 1967); did not sign. ... Drafted by Houston Astros organization (December 2, 1968). ... Traded by Astros with IF Mickey Sinnerud and C Tommie Smith

to Kansas City Royals for C John Jones (December 16, 1968). ... On restricted list (April 7-June 17, 1969). ... On military list (April 2-August 10, 1970). ... On disabled list (July 9-August 25, 1972). ... On disabled list (May 20-June 5, 1976). ... Traded by Royals with P Mark Littell to St. Louis Cardinals for P Al Hrabosky (December 8, 1977). ... Traded by Cardinals to Milwaukee Brewers for P George Frazier (December 8, 1977). ... Traded by Brewers to Toronto Blue Jays for OF Gil Kubski (May 10, 1981). ... Granted free agency (November 13, 1981). ... Re-signed by Blue Jays (December 6, 1981). ... On disabled list (July 10, 1985-remainder of season). ... Granted free agency (November 12, 1986).

STATISTICAL NOTES: Tied for Northwest League lead with 40 assists by catcher in 1967. ... Led American Association catchers with .994 fielding percentage in 1973.

Year	Team (League)	Pos.	G	AB	R	H	2B	3B	HR	RBI	Avg.	BB	SO	SB	PO	A	E	Avg.
1967—	Eugene (N'West)	C-OF-3B	77	269	53	96	16	4	2	46	.357	25	33	4	294	‡48	8	.977
1968—	Spartanburg (W.Car.)	C	8	28	6	11	4	0	0	11	.393	4	1	0	51	2	0	1.000
—Tidewater (Caro.)		C	36	110	10	31	12	1	1	14	.282	7	12	0	272	16	1	.997
1969—	Kansas City (A.L.)	C-OF	72	205	14	47	6	1	4	23	.229	8	25	0	292	26	9	.972
1970—	Kansas City (A.L.)	C	6	9	1	1	0	0	0	0	.111	2	1	0	20	3	1	.958
1971—	Omaha (A.A.)	C	75	269	34	77	23	1	5	39	.286	35	40	0	502	37	8	.985
—Kansas City (A.L.)		C	22	46	3	7	2	0	0	1	.152	5	9	0	84	6	3	.968
1972—	Omaha (A.A.)	C	67	195	23	34	9	0	4	12	.174	35	34	0	493	47	6	.989
1973—	Omaha (A.A.)	C-1B	82	254	24	69	13	0	5	38	.272	29	22	0	522	47	3	†.995
—Kansas City (A.L.)		C	14	32	2	8	1	0	1	6	.250	4	5	0	52	4	2	.966
1974—	Kansas City (A.L.)	C	107	107	10	23	3	1	1	8	.215	14	19	0	151	16	4	.977
1975—	Kansas City (A.L.)	C	80	226	15	51	9	2	3	23	.226	21	28	1	361	39	8	.980
1976—	Kansas City (A.L.)	C	95	267	24	61	13	3	5	34	.228	16	45	0	420	40	4	.991
1977—	Kansas City (A.L.)	C	29	80	3	18	4	0	1	9	.225	3	12	0	133	8	1	.993
1978—	Milwaukee (A.L.)■	C	89	256	26	56	10	1	1	20	.219	14	42	1	327	32	8	.978
1979—	Milwaukee (A.L.)	C-P	69	196	17	53	8	0	4	26	.270	8	25	0	198	39	8	.967
1980—	Milwaukee (A.L.)	C	76	219	16	49	9	0	3	17	.224	12	33	1	293	33	5	.985
1981—	Toronto (A.L.)■	C	45	128	13	29	8	1	4	21	.227	11	16	1	192	22	2	.991
1982—	Toronto (A.L.)	C	96	260	26	63	17	0	10	37	.242	24	34	1	382	35	5	.988
1983—	Toronto (A.L.)	C	88	221	27	56	14	0	10	33	.253	29	39	0	331	25	4	.989
1984—	Toronto (A.L.)	C	102	232	24	51	13	1	5	37	.220	29	49	0	360	34	2	.995
1985—	Toronto (A.L.)	C	42	99	11	16	3	0	4	14	.162	10	12	0	155	16	2	.988
1986—	Toronto (A.L.)	C	81	160	13	29	8	0	2	12	.181	20	25	0	289	19	2	.994
Major League totals (17 years)			1113	2743	245	618	128	10	58	321	.225	230	419	5	4040	397	70	.984

CHAMPIONSHIP SERIES RECORD

Year	Team (League)	Pos.	G	AB	R	H	2B	3B	HR	RBI	Avg.	BB	SO	SB	PO	A	E	Avg.
1976—	Kansas City (A.L.)	C	5	15	0	5	0	0	0	4	.333	1	3	0	15	4	0	1.000

RECORD AS PITCHER

Year	Team (League)	W	L	Pct.	ERA	G	GS	CG	ShO	Sv.	IP	H	R	ER	BB	SO
1979—	Milwaukee (A.L.)	0	0	.000	9.00	1	0	0	0	0	1	1	1	1	1	0

RECORD AS MANAGER

		REGULAR SEASON				POSTSEASON					
						Playoff		Champ. Series		World Series		All-Star Game
Year	Team (League)	W	L	Pct.	Pos.	W	L	W	L	W	L	W	L
2001—	Toronto (A.L.)	80	82	.494	3rd (E)	—	—	—	—	—	—	—	—

BACKGROUND: Broadcaster (1987-2000).

McCLENDON, LLOYD   PIRATES

PERSONAL: Born January 11, 1959, in Gary, Ind. ... 6-0/208. ... Batted right, threw right. ... Full name: Lloyd Glenn McClendon.
HIGH SCHOOL: Roosevelt (Gary, Ind.).
COLLEGE: Valparaiso.
TRANSACTIONS/CAREER NOTES: Selected by New York Mets organization in eighth round of free-agent draft (June 3, 1980). ... On disabled list (April 4-27, 1982). ... Traded by Mets with P Charlie Puleo and OF Jason Felice to Cincinnati Reds for P Tom Seaver (December 16, 1982). ... Traded by Reds to Chicago Cubs for OF Rolando Roomes (December 9, 1988). ... Traded by Cubs to Pittsburgh Pirates for a player to be named later (September 7, 1990). ... Cubs acquired P Mike Pomeranz to complete deal (September 28, 1990). ... Granted free agency (October 25, 1994). ... Signed by Cleveland Indians organization (May 5, 1995). ... Granted free agency (October 16, 1995).
STATISTICAL NOTES: Career major league grand slams: 2.

Year	Team (League)	Pos.	G	AB	R	H	2B	3B	HR	RBI	Avg.	BB	SO	SB	PO	A	E	Avg.
1980—	Kingsport (Appl.)	C	14	46	7	15	2	0	1	9	.326	5	7	0	19	5	3	.889
—Little Falls (NY-Penn)		C	40	117	25	32	9	1	3	20	.274	32	20	2	203	20	7	.970
1981—	Lynchburg (Caro.)	C-3B	103	363	55	91	12	6	7	57	.251	60	68	3	437	74	17	.968
1982—	Lynchburg (Caro.)	C-3B	108	384	61	105	25	1	18	78	.273	55	65	4	492	87	15	.975
1983—	Waterbury (East.)■	C-3B-1B	123	434	58	114	19	2	15	57	.263	42	64	1	466	99	8	.986
1984—	Vermont (East.)	C-1B-3B-OF	60	202	36	56	16	0	7	27	.277	28	28	2	174	24	3	.985
—Wichita (A.A.)		3B-1B-C	48	152	28	45	13	1	6	28	.296	21	33	2	143	45	4	.979
1985—	Denver (A.A.)	1B-3B-C-OF	114	379	57	105	18	5	16	79	.277	51	56	4	470	104	17	.971
1986—	Denver (A.A.)	1B-OF-C-3B	132	433	75	112	30	1	*24	88	.259	70	75	2	656	45	11	.985
1987—	Cincinnati (N.L.)	C-1B-3B-OF	45	72	8	15	5	0	2	13	.208	4	15	1	80	5	2	.977
—Nashville (A.A.)		1B-C	26	84	11	24	6	0	3	14	.286	17	15	1	72	3	1	.987
1988—	Cincinnati (N.L.)	C-OF-1B-3B	72	137	9	30	4	0	3	14	.219	15	22	4	197	13	4	.981
—Nashville (A.A.)		OF-C	2	7	0	1	0	0	0	0	.143	1	1	0	12	2	0	1.000
1989—	Iowa (A.A.)■	1B-OF-C	34	109	18	35	10	0	4	13	.321	21	19	4	115	6	6	.953
—Chicago (N.L.)		OF-1B-3B-C	92	259	47	74	12	1	12	40	.286	37	31	6	310	18	6	.982

Year Team (League)	Pos.	G	AB	R	H	2B	3B	HR	RBI	Avg.	BB	SO	SB	PO	A	E	Avg.
1990—Chicago (N.L.)............	OF-1B-C	49	107	5	17	3	0	1	10	.159	14	21	1	120	9	1	.992
—Iowa (A.A.)................1B-3B-OF-C		25	91	14	26	2	0	2	10	.286	8	19	3	125	12	2	.986
—Pittsburgh (N.L.)■....	OF	4	3	1	1	0	0	1	2	.333	0	1	0	0	0	0	...
1992—Pittsburgh (N.L.).......	OF-1B	84	190	26	48	8	1	3	20	.253	28	24	1	136	9	3	.980
1993—Pittsburgh (N.L.).......	OF-1B	88	181	21	40	11	1	2	19	.221	23	17	0	98	5	3	.972
1994—Pittsburgh (N.L.).......	OF-1B	51	92	9	22	4	0	4	12	.239	4	11	0	46	2	1	.980
1995—Buffalo (A.A.)■	OF-DH-3B	37	108	19	30	6	0	5	19	.278	20	20	0	32	1	2	.943
Major League totals (7 years)		485	1041	126	247	47	3	28	130	.237	125	142	13	987	61	20	.981

CHAMPIONSHIP SERIES RECORD

RECORDS: Shares records for most hits in one inning—2 (October 13, 1992, second inning); and most singles in one inning—2 (October 13, 1992, second inning).

Year Team (League)	Pos.	G	AB	R	H	2B	3B	HR	RBI	Avg.	BB	SO	SB	PO	A	E	Avg.
1989—Chicago (N.L.)............	PH-C-OF	3	3	0	2	0	0	0	0	.667	1	0	0	3	0	0	1.000
1991—Pittsburgh (N.L.).......	PH-1B	3	2	0	0	0	0	0	0	.000	1	0	0	0	0	0	...
1992—Pittsburgh (N.L.).......	OF-PH	5	11	4	8	2	0	1	4	.727	4	1	0	10	0	0	1.000
Championship series totals (3 years)		11	16	4	10	2	0	1	4	.625	6	1	0	13	0	0	1.000

RECORD AS MANAGER

BACKGROUND: Coach, Pittsburgh Pirates (1996-2000).

Year Team (League)		REGULAR SEASON				POSTSEASON							
								Champ.		World		All-Star	
						Playoff		Series		Series		Game	
	W	L	Pct.	Pos.	W	L	W	L	W	L	W	L
2001—Pittsburgh (N.L.)..................................	62	100	.383	6th (C)								

McRAE, HAL   DEVIL RAYS

PERSONAL: Born July 10, 1945, in Avon Park, Fla. ... 5-11/185. ... Bats right, throws right. ... Full name: Harold Abraham McRae. ... Father of Brian McRae, outfielder with five major league teams (1990-1999).
HIGH SCHOOL: Douglas (Sebring, Fla.).
COLLEGE: Florida A&M.
TRANSACTIONS/CAREER NOTES: Selected by Cincinnati Reds organization in sixth round of free-agent draft (June, 1965). ... On disabled list (June 23-July 6, 1966; April 26-May 7, 1967; April 18-May 28 and July 4-August 5, 1969). ... Traded with P Wayne Simpson to Kansas City Royals for P Roger Nelson and OF Richie Scheinblum (November 30, 1972). ... On disabled list (June 11-August 2, 1979 and May 13-June 2, 1980). ... Granted free agency (November 10, 1982). ... Re-signed by Royals (November 15, 1982). ... Granted free agency (November 12, 1985). ... Re-signed by Royals (December 8, 1985). ... Released by Royals (December 19,1986). ... Re-signed by Royals as player/coach (January 12, 1987). ... Released as player (July 21, 1987).
RECORDS: Shares major league doubleheader record for most long hits—6 (August 27, 1974, five doubles, one home run).
HONORS: Named designated hitter on THE SPORTING NEWS A.L. All-Star team (1976-77 and 1982). ... Named designated hitter on THE SPORTING NEWS A.L. Silver Slugger team (1982).
STATISTICAL NOTES: Led A.L. with .406 on-base percentage in 1976. ... Led A.L. in being hit by pitch with 13 in 1977.

Year Team (League)	Pos.	G	AB	R	H	2B	3B	HR	RBI	Avg.	BB	SO	SB	PO	A	E	Avg.
1965—Tampa (FSL)..............	OF	22	65	3	10	3	0	0	4	.154	4	15	1	19	0	0	1.000
1966—Peninsula (Caro.)	2B	109	394	65	113	19	4	11	56	.287	29	59	10	252	226	*28	.945
1967—Buffalo (I.L.).............	2B	73	259	30	65	14	3	10	34	.251	7	43	7	133	208	23	.937
—Knoxville (Sou.)..........	2B	51	186	26	54	10	3	6	25	.290	11	20	2	140	136	12	.958
1968—Indianapolis (PCL).....	2B-OF	119	444	64	131	31	11	16	65	.295	23	65	15	222	307	14	.974
—Cincinnati (N.L.).........	2B	17	51	1	10	1	0	0	2	.196	4	14	1	33	30	5	.926
1969—Indianapolis (A.A.).....	OF	17	41	2	9	1	0	0	4	.220	4	7	0	0	0	0	...
1970—Cincinnati (N.L.)	OF-3B-2B	70	165	18	41	6	1	8	23	.248	15	23	0	53	7	1	.984
1971—Cincinnati (N.L.)	OF	99	337	39	89	24	2	9	36	.264	11	35	3	167	6	6	.966
1972—Cincinnati (N.L.)	OF-3B	61	97	9	27	4	0	5	26	.278	2	10	0	16	14	6	.833
1973—Kansas City (A.L.)■...	OF-DH-3B	106	338	36	79	18	3	9	50	.234	34	38	2	101	6	5	.955
1974—Kansas City (A.L.)	DH-OF-3B	148	539	71	167	36	4	15	88	.310	54	58	11	132	3	7	.951
1975—Kansas City (A.L.)	OF-DH-3B	126	480	57	147	38	6	5	71	.306	47	47	11	207	7	3	.986
1976—Kansas City (A.L.)	DH-OF	149	527	75	175	34	5	8	73	.332	64	43	22	63	2	2	.970
1977—Kansas City (A.L.)	DH-OF	•162	641	104	191	*54	11	21	92	.298	59	43	18	81	8	4	.957
1978—Kansas City (A.L.)	OF	156	623	90	170	39	5	16	72	.273	51	62	17	3	1	0	1.000
1979—Kansas City (A.L.)	DH	101	393	55	113	32	4	10	74	.288	38	46	5	...	...	...	...
1980—Kansas City (A.L.)	DH-OF	124	489	73	145	39	5	14	83	.297	29	56	10	17	0	0	1.000
1981—Kansas City (A.L.)	DH-OF	101	389	38	106	23	2	7	36	.272	34	33	3	10	0	1	.909
1982—Kansas City (A.L.)	DH-OF	159	613	91	189	•46	8	27	*133	.308	55	61	4	1	0	1	.500
1983—Kansas City (A.L.)	DH	157	589	84	183	41	6	12	82	.311	50	68	2	...	...	...	...
1984—Kansas City (A.L.)	DH	106	317	30	96	13	4	3	42	.303	34	47	0	...	...	...	...
1985—Kansas City (A.L.)	DH	112	320	41	83	19	0	14	70	.259	44	45	0	...	...	...	...
1986—Kansas City (A.L.)	DH	112	278	22	70	14	0	7	37	.252	18	39	0	...	...	...	...
1987—Kansas City (A.L.)	DH	18	32	5	10	3	0	1	9	.313	5	1	0	...	...	...	...
American League totals (15 years)		1837	6568	872	1924	449	63	169	1012	.293	616	697	105	615	27	23	.965
National League totals (4 years)		247	650	67	167	35	3	22	85	.257	32	82	4	269	57	18	.948
Major League totals (19 years)		2084	7218	939	2091	484	66	191	1097	.290	648	779	109	884	84	41	.959

MAJOR LEAGUE MANAGERS

DIVISION SERIES RECORD

Year Team (League)	Pos.	G	AB	R	H	2B	3B	HR	RBI	Avg.	BB	SO	SB	PO	A	E	Avg.
1981—Kansas City (A.L.)	DH	3	11	0	1	1	0	0	0	.091	1	1	0	...	...	...	...

CHAMPIONSHIP SERIES RECORD

RECORDS: Holds career record for most times caught stealing—6. ... Shares career record for most doubles—7.

Year Team (League)	Pos.	G	AB	R	H	2B	3B	HR	RBI	Avg.	BB	SO	SB	PO	A	E	Avg.
1970—Cincinnati (N.L.)	OF	2	4	0	0	0	0	0	0	.000	0	2	0	2	0	0	1.000
1972—Cincinnati (N.L.)	PH	1	0	0	0	0	0	0	0	...	0	0	0	...	...	...	...
1976—Kansas City (A.L.)	OF	5	17	2	2	1	1	0	1	.118	1	4	0	5	1	0	1.000
1977—Kansas City (A.L.)	OF	5	18	6	8	3	0	1	2	.444	3	1	0	2	1	0	1.000
1978—Kansas City (A.L.)	DH	4	14	0	3	0	0	0	2	.214	2	2	1	...	...	...	...
1980—Kansas City (A.L.)	DH	3	10	0	2	0	0	0	0	.200	1	3	0	...	...	...	...
1984—Kansas City (A.L.)	PH	2	2	0	2	1	0	0	1	1.000	0	0	0	...	...	...	...
1985—Kansas City (A.L.)	DH	6	23	1	6	2	0	0	3	.261	1	6	0	...	...	...	...
Championship series totals (8 years)		28	88	9	23	7	1	1	9	.261	8	18	1	9	2	0	1.000

WORLD SERIES RECORD

NOTES: Member of World Series championship team (1985).

Year Team (League)	Pos.	G	AB	R	H	2B	3B	HR	RBI	Avg.	BB	SO	SB	PO	A	E	Avg.
1970—Cincinnati (N.L.)	OF	3	11	1	5	2	0	0	3	.455	0	1	0	2	1	0	1.000
1972—Cincinnati (N.L.)	OF	5	9	1	4	1	0	0	2	.444	0	1	0	4	0	0	1.000
1980—Kansas City (A.L.)	DH	6	24	3	9	3	0	0	1	.375	2	2	0	...	...	...	...
1985—Kansas City (A.L.)	PH	3	1	0	0	0	0	0	0	.000	1	0	0	...	...	...	...
World Series totals (4 years)		17	45	5	18	6	0	0	6	.400	3	4	0	6	1	0	1.000

ALL-STAR GAME RECORD

Year League	Pos.	AB	R	H	2B	3B	HR	RBI	Avg.	BB	SO	SB	PO	A	E	Avg.
1975—American	PH	1	0	0	0	0	0	0	.000	0	0	0	...	...	...	...
1976—American	PH	1	0	0	0	0	0	0	.000	0	0	0	...	...	...	...
1982—American	PH	0	0	0	0	0	0	0	...	1	0	0	...	...	...	...
All-Star Game totals (3 years)		2	0	0	0	0	0	0	.000	1	0	0	...	...	...	...

RECORD AS MANAGER

BACKGROUND: Player/hitting coach, Royals (1987-July 21, 1987). ... Minor league coach, Pittsburgh Pirates organization (1988 and 1989). ... Hitting coach, Montreal Expos (1990-May 24, 1991). ... Hitting coach, Cincinnati Reds (1995 and 1996). ... Hitting coach, Philadelphia Phillies (1997-2000). ... Coach, Tampa Bay Devil Rays (2001-April 18, 2001).

	REGULAR SEASON				POSTSEASON							
					Playoff		Champ. Series		World Series		All-Star Game	
Year Team (League)	W	L	Pct.	Pos.	W	L	W	L	W	L	W	L
1991—Kansas City (A.L.)	66	58	.532	6th (W)	—	—	—	—	—	—	—	—
1992—Kansas City (A.L.)	72	90	.444	T5th (W)	—	—	—	—	—	—	—	—
1993—Kansas City (A.L.)	84	78	.519	3rd (W)	—	—	—	—	—	—	—	—
1994—Kansas City (A.L.)	64	51	.557		—	—	—	—	—	—	—	—
2001—Tampa Bay (A.L.)	58	90	.426	5th (E)	—	—	—	—	—	—	—	—
Major league totals (5 years)	344	367	.484		—	—	—	—	—	—	—	—

NOTES:

1991—Replaced Kansas City manager John Wathan (15-22) and interim manager Bob Schaefer (1-0) with club in seventh place and record of 16-22 (May 24). On suspended list (August 13-14).

1994—Kansas City was in third place of A.L. Central at time of season-ending strike.

2001—Replaced Tampa Bay manager Larry Rothschild with club in fifth place and record of 4-10 (April 18).

MUSER, TONY   ROYALS

PERSONAL: Born August 1, 1947, in Los Angeles. ... 6-2/190. ... Batted left, threw left. ... Full name: Anthony Joseph Muser.

HIGH SCHOOL: Lakewood (Calif.).

JUNIOR COLLEGE: San Diego Mesa.

TRANSACTIONS/CAREER NOTES: Signed as non-drafted free agent by Boston Red Sox organization (1967). ... On military list (beginning of 1968 season-July 15, 1968). ... Traded by Red Sox with P Vicente Romo to Chicago White Sox for P Danny Murphy and C Duane Josephson (March 30, 1971). ... Traded by White Sox to Baltimore Orioles for P Jesse Jefferson (June 15, 1975). ... Released by Orioles (February 21, 1978). ... Signed by Milwaukee Brewers organization (March 20, 1978). ... Released by Brewers (February 12, 1979). ... Played in Japan (1979).

Year Team (League)	Pos.	G	AB	R	H	2B	3B	HR	RBI	Avg.	BB	SO	SB	PO	A	E	Avg.
1967—Waterloo (Midw.)	1B	68	251	40	71	15	1	6	42	.283	38	42	3	674	28	11	.985
1968—Greenv. (W. Car.)	1B-OF	33	114	13	31	7	0	2	12	.272	18	17	1	223	23	2	.992
—Win.-Salem (Car.)	OF-1B	7	21	1	8	0	0	0	2	.381	1	3	1	13	1	0	1.000
1969—Louisville (I.L.)	1B	120	457	57	129	14	4	7	62	.282	43	53	7	1029	63	15	.986
—Boston (A.L.)	1B	2	9	0	1	0	0	0	1	.111	1	1	0	17	3	0	1.000
1970—Louisville (I.L.)	1B	114	462	66	130	25	7	5	45	.281	38	49	1	1013	45	9	*.992

Year	Team (League)	Pos.	G	AB	R	H	2B	3B	HR	RBI	Avg.	BB	SO	SB	PO	A	E	Avg.
1971— Indianapolis (A.A.)■ ..		1B	85	310	36	91	10	3	3	31	.294	35	27	0	720	42	6	.992
—Chicago (A.L.)		1B	11	16	2	5	0	1	0	0	.313	1	1	0	23	3	1	.963
1972— Tucson (PCL)		1B	83	318	41	86	17	0	3	40	.270	29	28	3	680	49	12	.984
—Chicago (A.L.)		1B-OF	44	61	6	17	2	2	1	9	.279	2	6	1	135	7	2	.986
1973— Chicago (A.L.)		1B-OF	109	309	38	88	14	3	4	30	.285	33	36	8	681	38	6	.992
1974— Chicago (A.L.)		1B	103	206	16	60	5	1	1	18	.291	6	22	1	419	13	1	.998
1975— Chicago (A.L.)		1B	43	111	11	27	3	0	0	6	.243	7	8	2	263	22	2	.993
—Baltimore (A.L.)■......		1B	80	82	11	26	3	0	0	11	.317	8	9	0	213	15	1	.996
1976— Baltimore (A.L.).........		1B-OF	136	326	25	74	7	1	1	30	.227	21	34	1	693	63	7	.991
1977— Baltimore (A.L.).........		1B-OF	120	118	14	27	6	0	0	7	.229	13	16	1	232	20	3	.988
1978— Spokane (PCL)■........		1B-OF	78	283	48	83	13	0	6	38	.293	33	25	2	572	50	4	.994
—Milwaukee (A.L.)		1B	15	30	0	4	1	1	0	5	.133	3	5	0	79	5	1	.988
1979— Seibu (Jp. Pac.)■		...	65	168	...	33	...	...	2	10	.196	...	...	...	...	...	...	...
Major league totals (9 years)			663	1268	123	329	41	9	7	117	.259	95	138	14	2755	189	24	.992

RECORD AS MANAGER

BACKGROUND: Coach, Milwaukee Brewers (1985-89). ... Scout, Brewers (1990). ... Coach, Chicago Cubs (1993-July 8, 1997).

			REGULAR SEASON				POSTSEASON					
						Playoff		Champ. Series		World Series		All-Star Game
Year	Team (League)	W	L	Pct.	Pos.	W	L	W	L	W	L	W	L
1980— Stockton (California)................................	49	21	.700	1st (N)	—	—	—	—	—	—	—	—	—
—(Second half)	41	30	.577	1st (N)	3	0	—	—	—	—	—	—	—
1981— El Paso (Texas)	37	31	.544	2nd (W)	—	—	—	—	—	—	—	—	—
—(Second half)	28	38	.424	4th (W)	—	—	—	—	—	—	—	—	—
1982— El Paso (Texas)	42	23	.646	1st (W)	—	—	—	—	—	—	—	—	—
—(Second half)	34	37	.479	2nd (W)	2	3	—	—	—	—	—	—	—
1983— El Paso (Texas)	35	33	.515	2nd (W)	—	—	—	—	—	—	—	—	—
—Vancouver (Pacific Coast)	29	41	.414	4th (N)	—	—	—	—	—	—	—	—	—
1984— Vancouver (Pacific Coast)	32	40	.444	3rd (N)	—	—	—	—	—	—	—	—	—
—(Second half)	39	31	.557	3rd (N)	—	—	—	—	—	—	—	—	—
1991— Denver (American Association)	79	65	.549	1st (W)	7	3	—	—	—	—	—	—	—
1992— Denver (American Association)	73	71	.507	2nd (W)	—	—	—	—	—	—	—	—	—
1997— Kansas City (A.L.)	31	48	.392	4th (C)	—	—	—	—	—	—	—	—	—
1998— Kansas City (A.L.)	72	89	.447	3rd (C)	—	—	—	—	—	—	—	—	—
1999— Kansas City (A.L.)	64	97	.398	4th (C)	—	—	—	—	—	—	—	—	—
2000— Kansas City (A.L.)	77	85	.475	4th (C)	—	—	—	—	—	—	—	—	—
2001— Kansas City (A.L.)	65	97	.401	5th (C)	—	—	—	—	—	—	—	—	—
Major league totals (5 years)	309	416	.426		—	—	—	—	—	—	—	—	—

NOTES:
1980—Defeated Visalia in league championship.
1982—Defeated Midland, two games to one, in playoffs; lost to Tulsa, three games to none, in league championship.
1983—Replaced Vancouver manager Dick Phillips (June 22).
1991—Defeated Buffalo, three games to two, in league championship; defeated Columbus (International League), four games to one, in Class AAA Alliance championship.
1997—Replaced Kansas City manager Bob Boone with club in fourth place and record of 36-46 (July 9).
1998—On suspended list (June 9-17).

NARRON, JERRY   RANGERS

PERSONAL: Born January 15, 1956, in Goldsboro, N.C. ... 6-3/205. ... Bats left, throws right. ... Full name: Jerry Austin Narron. ... Brother of John Narron Jr., first baseman with New York Yankees organization and Chicago White Sox organization (1974 and 1975); and nephew of Sam Narron, catcher with St. Louis Cardinals (1935, 1942-43), Pittsburgh Pirates organization (1951-64) and scout with Pirates (1982-85).
HIGH SCHOOL: Goldsboro (N.C.).
COLLEGE: East Carolina.
TRANSACTIONS/CAREER NOTES: Selected by New York Yankees organization in sixth round of 1974 free-agent draft. ... Traded by Yankees OF Juan Beniquez, P Jim Beattie and P Rick Anderson to Seattle Mariners for OF Ruppert Jones and P Jim Lewis (November 1, 1979). ... Released by Mariners (March 30, 1982). ... Signed by California Angels organization (April 1, 1982). ... Released by Angels (April 6, 1987). ... Signed by Mariners organization (April 17, 1987). ... Released by Mariners (November 20, 1987). ... Signed by Baltimore Orioles organization (January 28, 1988).
STATISTICAL NOTES: Tied for Florida State League lead in being hit by pitch with 10 in 1975. ... Led Florida State League catchers in fielding percentage with .986 and double plays with seven in 1976. ... Tied for Pacific Coast League lead in double plays by catchers with 11 in 1978. ... Led Pacific Coast League with intentional bases on balls received with 15 in 1983. ... Led International League catchers with .995 fielding percentage in 1988.

Year	Team (League)	Pos.	G	AB	R	H	2B	3B	HR	RBI	Avg.	BB	SO	SB	PO	A	E	Avg.
1974— Johnson City (Appl.) ..		C-OF	66	226	43	68	15	3	7	49	.301	44	29	3	249	19	8	.971
1975— Fort Lauderdale (FSL)		1B-C-OF	113	360	39	76	12	0	2	34	.211	30	38	6	425	33	2	.996
1976— Fort Lauderdale (FSL)		C-1B	119	412	35	101	17	0	6	56	.245	42	37	0	563	56	8	†.987
1977— West Haven (East.).....		C-1B	121	438	80	131	16	0	28	93	.299	48	53	0	625	40	7	.990
1978— New York (A.L.)........		C	61	123	17	21	3	1	4	18	.171	9	26	0	167	15	5	.973
1980— Spokane (PCL)■........		C-1B	67	233	40	66	14	2	9	39	.283	20	35	1	223	19	6	.976
—Seattle (A.L.).............		C	48	107	7	21	3	0	4	18	.196	13	18	0	115	11	1	.992
1981— Seattle (A.L.)		C	76	203	13	45	5	0	3	17	.222	16	35	0	248	11	1	.996

Year—Team (League)	Pos.	G	AB	R	H	2B	3B	HR	RBI	Avg.	BB	SO	SB	PO	A	E	Avg.
1982— Spokane (PCL)	C	110	408	60	127	24	2	12	61	.311	47	45	0	446	46	12	.976
1983— Edmonton (PCL)■	1B-C	139	532	93	160	30	5	27	102	.301	66	50	1	1298	70	13	.991
— California (A.L.)	C	10	22	1	3	0	0	1	4	.136	1	3	0	14	3	2	.895
1984— California (A.L.)	C-1B	69	150	9	37	5	0	3	17	.247	8	12	0	184	12	1	.995
1985— California (A.L.)	C-1B	67	132	12	29	4	0	5	14	.220	11	17	0	146	14	0	1.000
1986— California (A.L.)	C	57	95	5	21	3	1	1	8	.221	9	14	0	155	14	2	.988
1987— Calgary (PCL)	C-1B	110	370	56	93	23	4	15	58	.251	42	29	2	563	41	11	.982
— Seattle (A.L.)	C	4	8	0	0	0	0	0	0	.000	0	2	0	9	0	0	1.000
1988— Rochester (I.L.)■	C-1B	95	248	31	62	17	0	8	33	.250	31	40	1	406	30	2	†.995
Major League totals (8 years)		392	840	64	177	23	2	21	96	.211	67	127	0	1038	80	12	.989

CHAMPIONSHIP SERIES RECORD

Year—Team (League)	Pos.	G	AB	R	H	2B	3B	HR	RBI	Avg.	BB	SO	SB	PO	A	E	Avg.
1986— California (A.L.)	C-PH	4	2	1	1	0	0	0	0	.500	1	1	0	1	0	0	1.000

RECORD AS MANAGER

BACKGROUND: Third base coach, Texas Rangers (1993-May 4, 2001).

	REGULAR SEASON				POSTSEASON								
						Playoff		Champ. Series		World Series		All-Star Game	
Year—Team (League)	W	L	Pct.	Pos.	W	L	W	L	W	L	W	L	
1989— Frederick (Carolina)	34	36	.486	2nd (N)	—	—	—	—	—	—	—	—	
— (Second half)	39	29	.574	2nd (N)	—	—	—	—	—	—	—	—	
1990— Hagerstown (Eastern)	67	71	.486	6th	—	—	—	—	—	—	—	—	
1991— Hagerstown (Eastern)	81	59	.579	2nd	0	3	—	—	—	—	—	—	
1992— Rochester (International)	70	74	.486	3rd (E)	—	—	—	—	—	—	—	—	
2001— Texas (A.L.)	62	72	.463	4th (W)	—	—	—	—	—	—	—	—	

NOTES:
1991—Lost to Albany, three games to none, in league semifinals.
2001—Replaced Texas manager Johnny Oates with club in third place and record of 11-17 (May 4).

PINIELLA, LOU — MARINERS

PERSONAL: Born August 28, 1943, in Tampa. ... 6-2/199. ... Batted right, threw right. ... Full name: Louis Victor Piniella. ... Cousin of Dave Magadan, third baseman/first baseman, San Diego Padres. ... Name pronounced pin-ELL-uh.
HIGH SCHOOL: Jesuit (Tampa).
COLLEGE: Tampa.
TRANSACTIONS/CAREER NOTES: Signed as free agent by Cleveland Indians organization (June 9, 1962). ... Selected by Washington Senators organization from Jacksonville, Indians organization, in Rule 5 major league draft (November 26, 1962). ... On military list (March 9-July 20, 1964). ... Traded by Senators to Baltimore Orioles (August 4, 1964), completing deal in which Orioles traded P Lester (Buster) Narum to Senators for cash and a player to be named later (March 31, 1964). ... On suspended list (June 27-29, 1965). ... Traded by Orioles to Indians for C Camilo Carreon (March 10, 1966). ... On temporarily inactive list (May 19-22, 1967). ... On temporarily inactive list (June 6-25, 1968). ... Selected by Seattle Pilots in expansion draft (October 15, 1968). ... Traded by Pilots to Kansas City Royals for OF Steve Whitaker and P John Gelnar (April 1, 1969). ... On military list (August 7-22, 1969). ... On disabled list (May 5-June 8, 1971). ... Traded by Royals with P Ken Wright to New York Yankees for P Lindy McDaniel (December 7, 1973). ... On disabled list (June 17-July 6, 1975; August 23-September 7, 1981; and March 30-April 22, 1983). ... Placed on voluntarily retired list (June 17, 1984).
RECORDS: Shares major league record for most assists by outfielder in one inning—2 (May 27, 1974, third inning).
HONORS: Named A.L. Rookie of the Year by Baseball Writers' Association of America (1969).
STATISTICAL NOTES: Led A.L. in grounding into double plays with 25 in 1972. ... Career major league grand slams: 1.

Year—Team (League)	Pos.	G	AB	R	H	2B	3B	HR	RBI	Avg.	BB	SO	SB	PO	A	E	Avg.
1962— Selma (Ala.-Fla.)	OF	70	278	40	75	10	5	8	44	.270	10	57	4	94	6	9	.917
1963— Peninsula (Caro.)■	OF	143	548	71	170	29	4	16	77	.310	34	70	8	271	*23	8	.974
1964— Aberdeen (North.)	OF	20	74	8	20	8	3	0	12	.270	6	9	1	37	1	1	.974
— Baltimore (A.L.)■........	PH	4	1	0	0	0	0	0	0	.000	0	0	0	...	...	...	...
1965— Elmira (East.)	OF	126	490	64	122	29	6	11	64	.249	22	57	5	176	5	7	.963
1966— Portland (PCL)■	OF	133	457	47	132	22	3	7	52	.289	20	52	6	177	11	11	.945
1967— Portland (PCL)	OF	113	396	46	122	20	1	8	56	.308	23	47	2	199	7	6	.972
1968— Portland (PCL)	OF	88	331	49	105	15	3	13	62	.317	19	31	0	167	6	7	.961
— Cleveland (A.L.)	OF	6	5	1	0	0	0	0	1	.000	0	0	1	1	0	0	1.000
1969— Kansas City (A.L.)■	OF	135	493	43	139	21	6	11	68	.282	33	56	2	278	13	7	.977
1970— Kansas City (A.L.)	OF-1B	144	542	54	163	24	5	11	88	.301	35	42	3	250	6	4	.985
1971— Kansas City (A.L.)	OF	126	448	43	125	21	5	3	51	.279	21	43	5	201	6	3	.986
1972— Kansas City (A.L.)	OF	151	574	65	179	*33	4	11	72	.312	34	59	7	275	8	7	.976
1973— Kansas City (A.L.)	OF-DH	144	513	53	128	28	1	9	69	.250	30	65	5	196	9	3	.986
1974— New York (A.L.)■.......	OF-DH-1B	140	518	71	158	26	0	9	70	.305	32	58	1	270	16	3	.990
1975— New York (A.L.)	OF-DH	74	199	7	39	4	1	0	22	.196	16	22	0	65	5	1	.986
1976— New York (A.L.)	OF-DH	100	327	36	92	16	6	3	38	.281	18	34	0	199	10	4	.981
1977— New York (A.L.)	OF-DH-1B	103	339	47	112	19	3	12	45	.330	20	31	2	86	3	2	.978
1978— New York (A.L.)	OF-DH	130	472	67	148	34	5	6	69	.314	34	36	3	213	4	7	.969
1979— New York (A.L.)	OF-DH	130	461	49	137	22	2	11	69	.297	17	31	3	204	13	4	.982
1980— New York (A.L.)	OF-DH	116	321	39	92	18	0	2	27	.287	29	20	0	157	8	5	.971
1981— New York (A.L.)	OF-DH	60	159	16	44	9	0	5	18	.277	13	9	0	69	2	1	.986
1982— New York (A.L.)	DH-OF	102	261	33	80	17	1	6	37	.307	18	18	0	68	2	0	1.000
1983— New York (A.L.)	OF-DH	53	148	19	43	9	1	2	16	.291	11	12	1	67	4	3	.959
1984— New York (A.L.)	OF-DH	29	86	8	26	4	1	1	6	.302	7	5	0	40	3	0	1.000
Major league totals (18 years)		1747	5867	651	1705	305	41	102	766	.291	368	541	33	2639	112	54	.981

DIVISION SERIES RECORD

							BATTING									FIELDING		
Year	Team (League)	Pos.	G	AB	R	H	2B	3B	HR	RBI	Avg.	BB	SO	SB	PO	A	E	Avg.
1981— New York (A.L.)..........		DH-PH	4	10	1	2	1	0	1	3	.200	0	0	0	...	...	...	...

CHAMPIONSHIP SERIES RECORD

							BATTING									FIELDING		
Year	Team (League)	Pos.	G	AB	R	H	2B	3B	HR	RBI	Avg.	BB	SO	SB	PO	A	E	Avg.
1976— New York (A.L.)..........		DH-PH	4	11	1	3	1	0	0	0	.273	0	1	0	...	...	...	...
1977— New York (A.L.)..........		OF-DH	5	21	1	7	3	0	0	2	.333	0	1	0	9	1	0	1.000
1978— New York (A.L.)..........		OF	4	17	2	4	0	0	0	0	.235	0	3	0	13	0	0	1.000
1980— New York (A.L.)..........		OF	2	5	1	1	0	0	1	1	.200	2	1	0	5	0	0	1.000
1981— New York (A.L.)..........		PH-DH-OF	3	5	2	3	0	0	1	3	.600	0	0	0	0	0	0	...
Championship series totals (5 years)			18	59	7	18	4	0	2	6	.305	2	6	0	27	1	0	1.000

WORLD SERIES RECORD

RECORDS: Shares single-series record for collecting one or more hits in each game (1978).

NOTES: Member of World Series championship team (1977 and 1978).

							BATTING									FIELDING		
Year	Team (League)	Pos.	G	AB	R	H	2B	3B	HR	RBI	Avg.	BB	SO	SB	PO	A	E	Avg.
1976— New York (A.L.)..........		DH-OF-PH	4	9	1	3	1	0	0	0	.333	0	0	0	1	0	0	1.000
1977— New York (A.L.)..........		OF	6	22	1	6	0	0	0	3	.273	0	3	0	16	1	1	.944
1978— New York (A.L.)..........		OF	6	25	3	7	0	0	0	4	.280	0	0	1	14	1	0	1.000
1981— New York (A.L.)..........		OF-PH	6	16	2	7	1	0	0	3	.438	0	1	1	7	0	0	1.000
World Series totals (4 years)			22	72	7	23	2	0	0	10	.319	0	4	2	38	2	1	.976

ALL-STAR GAME RECORD

						BATTING									FIELDING		
Year	League	Pos.	AB	R	H	2B	3B	HR	RBI	Avg.	BB	SO	SB	PO	A	E	Avg.
1972— American		PH	1	0	0	0	0	0	0	.000	0	0	0	...	...	...	...

RECORD AS MANAGER

BACKGROUND: Coach, New York Yankees (June 25, 1984-85). ... Vice-president/general manager, Yankees (beginning of 1988 season-June 22, 1988). ... Special adviser, Yankees (1989).

HONORS: Named A.L. Manager of the Year by Baseball Writers' Association of America (1995 and 2001). ... Named A.L. Manager of the Year by THE SPORTING NEWS (2001).

		REGULAR SEASON				POSTSEASON							
						Playoff		Champ. Series		World Series		All-Star Game	
Year	Team (League)	W	L	Pct.	Pos.	W	L	W	L	W	L	W	L
1986— New York (A.L.)		90	72	.556	2nd (E)	—	—	—	—	—	—	—	—
1987— New York (A.L.)		89	73	.549	4th (E)	—	—	—	—	—	—	—	—
1988— New York (A.L.)		45	48	.484	5th (E)	—	—	—	—	—	—	—	—
1990— Cincinnati (N.L.)		91	71	.562	1st (W)	—	—	4	2	4	0	—	—
1991— Cincinnati (N.L.)		74	88	.457	5th (W)	—	—	—	—	—	—	0	1
1992— Cincinnati (N.L.)		90	72	.556	2nd (W)	—	—	—	—	—	—	—	—
1993— Seattle (A.L.)		82	80	.506	4th (W)	—	—	—	—	—	—	—	—
1994— Seattle (A.L.)		49	63	.438		—	—	—	—	—	—	—	—
1995— Seattle (A.L.)		79	66	.545	1st (W)	3	2	2	4	—	—	—	—
1996— Seattle (A.L.)		85	76	.528	2nd (W)	—	—	—	—	—	—	—	—
1997— Seattle (A.L.)		90	72	.556	1st (W)	1	3	—	—	—	—	—	—
1998— Seattle (A.L.)		76	85	.472	3rd (W)	—	—	—	—	—	—	—	—
1999— Seattle (A.L.)		79	83	.488	3rd (W)	—	—	—	—	—	—	—	—
2000— Seattle (A.L.)		91	71	.562	2nd (W)	3	0	2	4	—	—	—	—
2001— Seattle (A.L.)		116	46	.716	1st (W)	3	2	1	4	—	—	—	—
American League totals (12 years)		971	835	.538		10	7	5	12	—	—	—	—
National League totals (3 years)		255	231	.525		—	—	4	2	4	0	0	1
Major league totals (15 years)		1226	1066	.535		10	7	9	14	4	0	0	1

NOTES:

1988—Replaced New York manager Billy Martin, with club in second place and record of 40-28 (June 23).

1990—Defeated Pittsburgh in N.L. Championship Series; defeated Oakland in World Series.

1994—Seattle was in third place in A.L. West at time of season-ending strike (August 12).

1995—Defeated New York in A.L. divisional playoff; lost to Cleveland in A.L. Championship Series.

1997—Lost to Baltimore in A.L. divisional playoff.

2000—Defeated Chicago White Sox in A.L. divisional playoff; lost to New York Yankees in A.L. Championship Series.

2001—Defeated Cleveland in A.L. divisional playoff; lost to New York Yankees in A.L. Championship Series.

SCIOSCIA, MIKE — ANGELS

PERSONAL: Born November 27, 1958, in Upper Darby, Pa. ... 6-2/220. ... Batted left, threw right. ... Full name: Michael Lorri Scioscia. ... Name pronounced SO-sha.

HIGH SCHOOL: Springfield (Pa.).

COLLEGE: Penn State.

TRANSACTIONS/CAREER NOTES: Selected by Los Angeles Dodgers organization in first round (19th pick overall) of free-agent draft (June 8, 1976). ... On disabled list (May 19-August 4, 1978; April 10-20, 1980; May 15, 1983-remainder of season; May 6-21, 1984; June 10-July 15, 1986; June 1-16, 1987; and July 5-20, 1991). ... Granted free agency (November 4, 1992). ... Signed by San Diego Padres (February 11, 1993). ... On San Diego disabled list (March 29, 1993-entire season). ... Released by Padres (October 15, 1993). ... Signed by Texas Rangers organization (December 14, 1993). ... Placed on voluntary retired list (August 2, 1994).

HONORS: Named catcher on THE SPORTING NEWS N.L. All-Star team (1990).

STATISTICAL NOTES: Led Midwest League catchers with 20 errors and 12 double plays in 1977. ... Led Pacific Coast League catchers with 791 total chances, 19 double plays and 22 passed balls in 1979. ... Tied for Pacific Coast League lead in being hit by pitch with seven in 1979. ... Led N.L. with 11 passed balls in 1981 and 14 in 1992. ... Led N.L. catchers with 1,016 total chances in 1987, 915 in 1989 and 910 in 1990.

Year Team (League)	Pos.	G	AB	R	H	2B	3B	HR	RBI	Avg.	BB	SO	SB	PO	A	E	Avg.
1976— Bellingham (N.W.)	C	46	151	25	42	6	0	7	26	.278	36	22	2	202	35	14	.944
1977— Clinton (Midw.)	C-1B	121	364	58	92	20	1	7	44	.253	79	25	9	764	95	†22	.975
1978— San Antonio (Texas)	C	58	204	29	61	16	0	2	34	.299	31	20	3	214	17	4	.983
1979— Albuquerque (PCL)	C	143	461	80	155	34	0	3	68	.336	73	33	5	*690	*86	*15	.981
1980— Albuquerque (PCL)	C	52	160	33	53	11	1	3	33	.331	36	13	3	207	19	5	.978
—Los Angeles (N.L.)	C	54	134	8	34	5	1	1	8	.254	12	9	1	226	26	2	.992
1981— Los Angeles (N.L.)	C	93	290	27	80	10	0	2	29	.276	36	18	0	493	48	7	.987
1982— Los Angeles (N.L.)	C	129	365	31	80	11	1	5	38	.219	44	31	2	631	57	10	.986
1983— Los Angeles (N.L.)	C	12	35	3	11	3	0	1	7	.314	5	2	0	55	4	0	1.000
1984— Los Angeles (N.L.)	C	114	341	29	93	18	0	5	38	.273	52	26	2	701	64	12	.985
1985— Los Angeles (N.L.)	C	141	429	47	127	26	3	7	53	.296	77	21	3	818	66	•13	.986
1986— Los Angeles (N.L.)	C	122	374	36	94	18	1	5	26	.251	62	23	3	756	64	15	.982
1987— Los Angeles (N.L.)	C	142	461	44	122	26	1	6	38	.265	55	23	7	*925	80	11	.989
1988— Los Angeles (N.L.)	C	130	408	29	105	18	0	3	35	.257	38	31	0	748	63	7	.991
1989— Los Angeles (N.L.)	C	133	408	40	102	16	0	10	44	.250	52	29	0	*822	*82	11	.988
1990— Los Angeles (N.L.)	C	135	435	46	115	25	0	12	66	.264	55	31	4	*842	58	10	.989
1991— Los Angeles (N.L.)	C	119	345	39	91	16	2	8	40	.264	47	32	4	677	51	7	.990
1992— Los Angeles (N.L.)	C	117	348	19	77	6	3	3	24	.221	32	31	3	641	*74	9	.988
1993— San Diego (N.L.)■							Did not play.										
1994— Charlotte (FSL)■	C	1	2	0	1	0	0	0	0	.500	0	0	0	3	1	0	1.000
Major League totals (13 years)		1441	4373	398	1131	198	12	68	446	.259	567	307	29	8335	737	114	.988

DIVISION SERIES RECORD

Year Team (League)	Pos.	G	AB	R	H	2B	3B	HR	RBI	Avg.	BB	SO	SB	PO	A	E	Avg.
1981— Los Angeles (N.L.)	C	4	13	0	2	0	0	0	1	.154	1	2	0	21	3	0	1.000

CHAMPIONSHIP SERIES RECORD

Year Team (League)	Pos.	G	AB	R	H	2B	3B	HR	RBI	Avg.	BB	SO	SB	PO	A	E	Avg.
1981— Los Angeles (N.L.)	C	5	15	1	2	0	0	1	1	.133	2	1	0	27	1	0	1.000
1985— Los Angeles (N.L.)	C	6	16	2	4	0	0	0	1	.250	4	0	0	31	4	1	.972
1988— Los Angeles (N.L.)	C	7	22	3	8	1	0	1	2	.364	1	2	0	37	4	0	1.000
Championship series totals (3 years)		18	53	6	14	1	0	2	4	.264	7	3	0	95	9	1	.990

WORLD SERIES RECORD

NOTES: Member of World Series championship teams (1981 and 1988).

Year Team (League)	Pos.	G	AB	R	H	2B	3B	HR	RBI	Avg.	BB	SO	SB	PO	A	E	Avg.
1981— Los Angeles (N.L.)	C-PH	3	4	1	1	0	0	0	0	.250	1	0	0	7	1	0	1.000
1988— Los Angeles (N.L.)	C	4	14	0	3	0	0	0	1	.214	0	2	0	28	0	1	.966
World Series totals (2 years)		7	18	1	4	0	0	0	1	.222	1	2	0	35	1	1	.973

ALL-STAR GAME RECORD

Year League	Pos.	AB	R	H	2B	3B	HR	RBI	Avg.	BB	SO	SB	PO	A	E	Avg.
1989— National	C	1	0	0	0	0	0	0	.000	0	0	0	3	0	0	1.000
1990— National	C	2	0	0	0	0	0	0	.000	0	1	0	6	0	0	1.000
All-Star Game totals (2 years)		3	0	0	0	0	0	0	.000	0	1	0	9	0	0	1.000

RECORD AS MANAGER

BACKGROUND: Minor league catching coordinator, Dodgers organization (1995-96). ... Bench coach, Dodgers (1997-98). ... Manager, Peoria Javelinas, Dodgers organization (1997).

	REGULAR SEASON					POSTSEASON							
						Playoff		Champ. Series		World Series		All-Star Game	
Year Team (League)	W	L	Pct.	Pos.		W	L	W	L	W	L	W	L
1999— Albuquerque (PCL)	65	74	.468	3rd		—	—	—	—	—	—	—	—
2000— Anaheim (A.L.)	82	80	.506	3rd (W)		—	—	—	—	—	—	—	—
2001— Anaheim (A.L.)	75	87	.463	3rd (W)		—	—	—	—	—	—	—	—
Major league totals (2 years)	157	167	.485			—	—	—	—	—	—	—	—

TORBORG, JEFF   EXPOS

PERSONAL: Born November 26, 1941, in Montclair, N.J. ... 6-0/195. ... Bats right, throws right. ... Full name: Jeffrey Allen Torborg. ... Father of Doug Torborg, minor league pitcher (1987-88).

HIGH SCHOOL: Westfield (N.J.).

COLLEGE: Rutgers, then Montclair State.

TRANSACTIONS/CAREER NOTES: Signed as non-drafted free agent by Los Angeles Dodgers organization (May 22, 1963). ... Contract sold by Dodgers to California Angels (March 13, 1971). ... On disabled list (June 25-July 27, 1971; May 12-June 13, 1972; and July 13-August 10, 1973). ... Traded by Angels to St. Louis Cardinals for P John Andrews (December 6, 1973). ... Released by Cardinals (March 25, 1974).

Year Team (League)	Pos.	G	AB	R	H	2B	3B	HR	RBI	Avg.	BB	SO	SB	PO	A	E	Avg.
1963— Albuquerque (Texas) ..	C	64	184	19	41	10	3	1	18	.223	15	37	0	349	27	6	.984
1964— Los Angeles (N.L.)	C	28	43	4	10	1	1	0	4	.233	3	8	0	80	4	2	.977
1965— Los Angeles (N.L.)	C	56	150	8	36	5	1	3	13	.240	10	26	0	300	19	3	.991
1966— Los Angeles (N.L.)	C	46	120	4	27	3	0	1	13	.225	10	23	0	269	17	4	.986
1967— Los Angeles (N.L.)	C	76	196	11	42	4	1	2	12	.214	13	31	1	413	30	5	.989
1968— Los Angeles (N.L.)	C	37	93	2	15	2	0	0	4	.161	6	10	0	206	20	2	.991
1969— Los Angeles (N.L.)	C	51	124	7	23	4	0	0	7	.185	9	17	1	251	26	1	.996
1970— Los Angeles (N.L.)	C	64	134	11	31	8	0	1	17	.231	14	15	1	275	16	5	.983
1971— California (A.L.)■	C	55	123	6	25	5	0	0	5	.203	3	6	0	208	17	3	.987
1972— California (A.L.).........	C	59	153	5	32	3	0	0	8	.209	14	21	0	383	28	1	.998
1973— California (A.L.)..........	C	102	255	20	56	7	0	1	18	.220	21	32	0	611	37	6	.991
American League totals (3 years)		216	531	31	113	15	0	1	31	.213	38	59	0	1202	82	10	.992
National League totals (7 years)		358	860	47	184	27	3	7	70	.214	65	130	3	1794	132	22	.989
Major League totals (10 years)		574	1391	78	297	42	3	8	101	.214	103	189	3	2996	214	32	.990

RECORD AS MANAGER

BACKGROUND: Coach, Cleveland Indians (1975-June 19, 1977). ... Coach, New York Yankees (July 26, 1979-88).

HONORS: Named A.L. Manager of the Year by THE SPORTING NEWS (1990). ... Named A.L. Manager of the Year by Baseball Writers' Association of America (1990).

	REGULAR SEASON				Playoff		Champ. Series		World Series		All-Star Game	
Year Team (League)	W	L	Pct.	Pos.	W	L	W	L	W	L	W	L
1977— Cleveland (A.L.)	45	59	.433	5th (E)	—	—	—	—	—	—	—	—
1978— Cleveland (A.L.)	69	90	.434	6th (E)	—	—	—	—	—	—	—	—
1979— Cleveland (A.L.)	43	52	.453		—	—	—	—	—	—	—	—
1989— Chicago (A.L.)	69	92	.429	7th (W)	—	—	—	—	—	—	—	—
1990— Chicago (A.L.)	94	68	.580	2nd (W)	—	—	—	—	—	—	—	—
1991— Chicago (A.L.)	87	75	.537	2nd (W)	—	—	—	—	—	—	—	—
1992— New York (N.L.)	72	90	.444	5th (E)	—	—	—	—	—	—	—	—
1993— New York (N.L.)	13	25	.342		—	—	—	—	—	—	—	—
2001— Montreal (N.L.)	47	62	.431	5th (E)	—	—	—	—	—	—	—	—
American League totals (6 years)	407	436	.483		—	—	—	—	—	—	—	—
National League totals (3 years)	132	177	.427		—	—	—	—	—	—	—	—
Major league totals (9 years)	539	613	.468		17	8	20	10	19	7	4	0

NOTES:
1977—Replaced Cleveland manager Frank Robinson with club in sixth place and record of 26-31 (June 19).
1979—Replaced as Cleveland manager by Dave Garcia with club in sixth place (July 23).
1993—Replaced as New York manager by Dallas Green with club in seventh place (May 19).
2001—Replaced Montreal manager Felipe Alou with club in fifth place and record of 21-32 (May 31).

TORRE, JOE — YANKEES

PERSONAL: Born July 18, 1940, in Brooklyn, N.Y. ... 6-1/210. ... Batted right, threw right. ... Full name: Joseph Paul Torre. ... Brother of Frank Torre, first baseman with Milwaukee Braves (1956-60) and Philadelphia Phillies (1962-63). ... Name pronounced TORE-ee.

HIGH SCHOOL: St. Francis Prep (Brooklyn, N.Y.).

TRANSACTIONS/CAREER NOTES: Signed by Milwaukee Braves organization (August 24, 1959). ... On military list (September 30, 1962-March 26, 1963). ... Braves franchise moved from Milwaukee to Atlanta (1966). ... On disabled list (April 18-May 9, 1968). ... Traded by Braves to St. Louis Cardinals for 1B Orlando Cepeda (March 17, 1969). ... Traded by Cardinals to New York Mets for P Tommy Moore and P Ray Sadecki (October 13, 1974). ... Released as player by Mets (June 18, 1977).

RECORDS: Shares major league single-game record for most times grounded into double play—4 (July 21, 1975).

HONORS: Named catcher on THE SPORTING NEWS N.L. All-Star team (1964-66). ... Named Major League Player of the Year by THE SPORTING NEWS (1971). ... Won N.L. Gold Glove at catcher (1965). ... Named third baseman on THE SPORTING NEWS N.L. All-Star team (1971). ... Named N.L. Most Valuable Player by Baseball Writers' Association of America (1971).

STATISTICAL NOTES: Led N.L. catchers with .995 fielding percentage in 1964 and .996 in 1968. ... Led N.L. in grounding into double plays with 26 in 1964, 22 in 1965, 22 in 1967 and 21 in 1968. ... Led N.L. catchers with 12 double plays in 1967. ... Led N.L. with 352 total bases in 1971. ... Hit for the cycle (June 27, 1973). ... Led N.L. first basemen with 102 assists and 144 double plays in 1974. ... Career major league grand slams: 3.

Year Team (League)	Pos.	G	AB	R	H	2B	3B	HR	RBI	Avg.	BB	SO	SB	PO	A	E	Avg.
1960— Eau Claire (North.)	C	117	369	63	127	23	3	16	74	*.344	70	45	7	636	64	9	.987
— Milwaukee (N.L.)........	PH	2	2	0	1	0	0	0	0	.500	0	1	0	...	...	...	...
1961— Louisville (A.A.)	C	27	111	18	38	8	2	3	24	.342	6	9	0	185	14	2	.990
— Milwaukee (N.L.)........	C	113	406	40	113	21	4	10	42	.278	28	60	3	494	50	10	.982
1962— Milwaukee (N.L.)..........	C	80	220	23	62	8	1	5	26	.282	24	24	1	325	39	5	.986
1963— Milwaukee (N.L.)..........	C-1B-OF	142	501	57	147	19	4	14	71	.293	42	79	1	919	76	6	.994
1964— Milwaukee (N.L.)..........	C-1B	154	601	87	193	36	5	20	109	.321	36	67	4	1081	94	7	†.994
1965— Milwaukee (N.L.)..........	C-1B	148	523	68	152	21	1	27	80	.291	61	79	0	1022	73	8	.993
1966— Atlanta (N.L.)■..........	C-1B	148	546	83	172	20	3	36	101	.315	60	61	0	874	87	12	.988
1967— Atlanta (N.L.)..........	C-1B	135	477	67	132	18	1	20	68	.277	75	49	2	785	81	8	.991
1968— Atlanta (N.L.)..........	C-1B	115	424	45	115	11	2	10	55	.271	34	72	1	733	48	2	†.997
1969— St. Louis (N.L.)■..........	1B-C	159	602	72	174	29	6	18	101	.289	66	85	0	1360	91	7	.995
1970— St. Louis (N.L.)..........	C-3B-1B	•161	624	89	203	27	9	21	100	.325	70	91	2	651	162	13	.984
1971— St. Louis (N.L.)..........	3B	161	634	97	*230	34	8	24	*137	*.363	63	70	4	*136	271	•21	.951
1972— St. Louis (N.L.)..........	3B-1B	149	544	71	157	26	6	11	81	.289	54	74	3	336	198	15	.973
1973— St. Louis (N.L.)..........	1B-3B	141	519	67	149	17	2	13	69	.287	65	78	2	881	128	12	.988
1974— St. Louis (N.L.)..........	1B-3B	147	529	59	149	28	1	11	70	.282	69	68	1	1173	†121	14	.989
1975— New York (N.L.)■..........	3B-1B	114	361	33	89	16	3	6	35	.247	35	55	0	172	157	15	.956
1976— New York (N.L.)..........	1B-3B	114	310	36	95	10	3	5	31	.306	21	35	1	593	52	7	.989
1977— New York (N.L.)..........	1B-3B	26	51	2	9	3	0	1	9	.176	2	10	0	83	3	1	.989
Major league totals (18 years)		2209	7874	996	2342	344	59	252	1185	.297	805	1058	25	11618	1731	163	.988

ALL-STAR GAME RECORD

Year League	Pos.	AB	R	H	2B	3B	HR	RBI	Avg.	BB	SO	SB	PO	A	E	Avg.
							BATTING							FIELDING		
1963— National....................							Did not play.									
1964— National....................	C	2	0	0	0	0	0	0	.000	0	0	0	5	0	0	1.000
1965— National....................	C	4	1	1	0	0	1	2	.250	0	0	0	5	1	0	1.000
1966— National....................	C	3	0	0	0	0	0	0	.000	0	1	0	5	0	0	1.000
1967— National....................	C	2	0	0	0	0	0	0	.000	0	0	0	4	1	0	1.000
1970— National....................	PH	1	0	0	0	0	0	0	.000	0	0	0	...	...	...	...
1971— National....................	3B	3	0	0	0	0	0	0	.000	0	1	0	1	0	0	1.000
1972— National....................	3B	3	0	0	0	0	0	0	.000	0	1	0	1	2	0	1.000
1973— National....................	1B-3B	3	0	0	0	0	0	0	.000	0	0	0	5	0	0	1.000
All-Star Game totals (8 years)		21	1	1	0	0	1	2	.048	0	3	0	26	4	0	1.000

RECORD AS MANAGER

BACKGROUND: Player/manager, New York Mets (May 31-June 18, 1977).

HONORS: Named Sportsman of the Year by THE SPORTING NEWS (1996). ... Named co-A.L. Manager of the Year by Baseball Writers' Association of America (1996). ... Named A.L. Manager of the Year by The Sporting News (1998). ... Named A.L. Manager of the Year by Baseball Writers' Association of America (1998).

		REGULAR SEASON				POSTSEASON							
								Champ.		World		All-Star	
						Playoff		Series		Series		Game	
Year Team (League)	W	L	Pct.	Pos.		W	L	W	L	W	L	W	L
1977— New York (N.L.)	49	68	.419	6th (E)		—	—	—	—	—	—	—	—
1978— New York (N.L.)	66	96	.407	6th (E)		—	—	—	—	—	—	—	—
1979— New York (N.L.)	63	99	.389	6th (E)		—	—	—	—	—	—	—	—
1980— New York (N.L.)	67	95	.414	5th (E)		—	—	—	—	—	—	—	—
1981— New York (N.L.)	17	34	.333	5th (E)		—	—	—	—	—	—	—	—
—(Second half)	24	28	.462	4th (E)		—	—	—	—	—	—	—	—
1982— Atlanta (N.L.)	89	73	.549	1st (W)		—	—	0	3	—	—	—	—
1983— Atlanta (N.L.)	88	74	.543	2nd (W)		—	—	—	—	—	—	—	—
1984— Atlanta (N.L.)	80	82	.494	T2nd (W)		—	—	—	—	—	—	—	—
1990— St. Louis (N.L.)	24	34	.414	6th (E)		—	—	—	—	—	—	—	—
1991— St. Louis (N.L.)	84	78	.519	2nd (E)		—	—	—	—	—	—	—	—
1992— St. Louis (N.L.)	83	79	.512	3rd (E)		—	—	—	—	—	—	—	—
1993— St. Louis (N.L.)	87	75	.537	3rd (E)		—	—	—	—	—	—	—	—
1994— St. Louis (N.L.)	53	61	.465			—	—	—	—	—	—	—	—
1995— St. Louis (N.L.)	20	27	.426	4th (C)		—	—	—	—	—	—	—	—
1996— New York (A.L.)	92	70	.568	1st (E)		3	1	4	1	4	2	—	—
1997— New York (A.L.)	96	66	.593	2nd (E)		2	3	—	—	—	—	1	0
1998— New York (A.L.)	114	48	.704	1st (E)		3	0	4	2	4	0	—	—
1999— New York (A.L.)	98	64	.605	1st (E)		3	0	4	1	4	0	1	0
2000— New York (A.L.)	87	74	.540	1st (E)		3	2	4	2	4	1	1	0
2001— New York (A.L.)	95	65	.594	1st (E)		3	2	4	1	3	4	1	0
American League totals (6 years)	582	387	.601			17	8	20	7	19	7	4	0
National League totals (14 years)	894	1003	.471			—	—	0	3	—	—	—	—
Major league totals (20 years)	1476	1390	.515			17	8	20	10	19	7	4	0

NOTES:

1977—Replaced New York manager Joe Frazier with club in sixth place and record of 15-30 (May 31); served as player/manager (May 31-June 18, when released as player).

1982—Lost to St. Louis in N.L. Championship Series.

1990—Replaced St. Louis manager Whitey Herzog (33-47) and interim manager Red Schoendienst (13-11) with club in sixth place and record of 46-58 (August 1).

1994—St. Louis was tied for third place in N.L. Central at time of season-ending strike (August 12).

1995—Replaced as Cardinals manager by interim manager Mike Jorgensen, with club in fourth place (June 16).

1996—Defeated Texas in A.L. divisional playoff; defeated Baltimore in A.L. Championship Series; defeated Atlanta in World Series.

1997—Lost to Cleveland in A.L. divisional playoff.

1998—Defeated Texas in A.L. divisional playoff; defeated Cleveland in A.L. Championship Series; defeated San Diego in World Series.

1999—Defeated Texas in A.L. divisional playoff; defeated Boston in A.L. Championship Series; defeated Atlanta in World Series.

2000—Defeated Oakland in A.L. divisional playoff; defeated Seattle in A.L. Championship Series; defeated New York Mets in World Series.

2001—Defeated Oakland in A.L. divisional playoff; defeated Seattle in A.L. Championship Series; lost to Arizona in World Series.

TRACY, JIM — DODGERS

PERSONAL: Born December 31, 1955, in Hamilton, Ohio. ... 6-3/205. ... Batted left, threw right. ... Full name: James Edwin Tracy.

HIGH SCHOOL: Badin (Hamilton, Ohio).

COLLEGE: Marietta College (Ohio).

TRANSACTIONS/CAREER NOTES: Selected by Chicago Cubs organization in fourth round of free-agent draft (January 11, 1977). ... Traded by Cubs to Houston Astros for OF Gary Woods (December 9, 1981).

Year Team (League)	Pos.	G	AB	R	H	2B	3B	HR	RBI	Avg.	BB	SO	SB	PO	A	E	Avg.
								BATTING							FIELDING		
1977— Pom. Beach (FSL)	1B-OF	93	261	27	59	13	2	4	34	.226	41	66	1	147	6	4	.975
1978— Pom. Beach (FSL)	1B-OF	78	225	42	55	7	5	6	43	.244	58	34	2	329	27	4	.989
—Midland (Texas).........	OF-1B	54	189	34	49	9	2	8	29	.259	20	50	2	174	10	2	.989
1979— Midland (Texas).........	1B	86	301	75	107	16	1	15	67	*.355	63	41	7	799	31	6	.993
—Wichita (A.A.)............	1B-OF	44	150	26	41	9	1	4	18	.273	21	36	0	364	20	11	.972
1980— Wichita (A.A.)............	OF-1B-3B	112	406	66	130	17	6	16	63	.320	67	68	4	428	33	5	.989
—Chicago (N.L.)...........	OF-1B	42	122	12	31	3	3	3	9	.254	13	37	2	44	0	2	.957
1981— Midland (Texas).........	OF-1B	22	73	8	20	3	0	2	7	.274	13	22	0	73	2	0	1.000
—Chicago (N.L.)...........	OF	45	63	6	15	2	1	0	5	.238	12	14	1	16	0	0	1.000

Year Team (League)	Pos.	G	AB	R	H	2B	3B	HR	RBI	Avg.	BB	SO	SB	PO	A	E	Avg.
										BATTING					FIELDING		
1982— Tucson (PCL)	OF-1B	133	481	85	153	35	3	12	100	.318	81	83	5	294	14	4	.987
1983— Taiyo (Jap. Cen.)		125	469	61	142	29	2	19	66	.303	32	74	3	...	...	...	...
1984— Taiyo (Jap. Cen.)		3	9	1	2	0	0	1	5	.222	2	1	0	...	...	...	...
— Tucson (PCL)	OF-1B	52	156	22	38	12	3	1	21	.244	31	39	2	67	0	2	.971
Major League totals (2 years)		87	185	18	46	5	4	3	14	.249	25	51	3	60	0	2	.968

RECORD AS MANAGER

BACKGROUND: Coach, Montreal Expos (1995-98). ... Coach, Los Angeles Dodgers (1999 and 2000).

HONORS: Named Minor League Manager of the Year by THE SPORTING NEWS (1993).

Year Team (League)	W	L	Pct.	Pos.	Playoff W	L	Champ. Series W	L	World Series W	L	All-Star Game W	L
		REGULAR SEASON					POSTSEASON						
1987— Peoria (Midw.)	71	69	.507	2nd (S)	—	—	—	—	—	—	—	—
1988— Peoria (Midw.)	29	40	.420	6th (S)	—	—	—	—	—	—	—	—
—(Second half)	41	30	.577	3rd (S)	—	—	—	—	—	—	—	—
1989— Chattanooga (Sou.)	33	38	.465	4th (S)	—	—	—	—	—	—	—	—
—(Second half)	25	43	.368	5th (S)	—	—	—	—	—	—	—	—
1990— Chattanooga (Sou.)	35	36	.493	4th (S)	—	—	—	—	—	—	—	—
—(Second half)	31	42	.425	4th (S)	—	—	—	—	—	—	—	—
1991— Chattanooga (Sou.)	35	32	.522	2nd (S)	—	—	—	—	—	—	—	—
—(Second half)	38	39	.494	3rd (S)	—	—	—	—	—	—	—	—
1993— Harrisburg (East.)	94	44	.681	1st	—	—	—	—	—	—	—	—
1994— Ottawa (I.L.)	70	72	.493	3rd (E)	—	—	—	—	—	—	—	—
2001— Los Angeles (N.L.)	86	76	.531	3rd (W)	—	—	—	—	—	—	—	—

NOTES:
1993—Defeated Albany, three games to one, in playoff; defeated Canton-Akron, three games to two, in championship playoff.

VALENTINE, BOBBY — METS

PERSONAL: Born May 13, 1950, in Stamford, Conn. ... 5-10/185. ... Batted right, threw right. ... Full name: Robert John Valentine. ... Son-in-law of Ralph Branca, pitcher with Brooklyn Dodgers (1944-53 and 1956), Detroit Tigers (1953-54), New York Yankees (1955).

HIGH SCHOOL: Rippowan (Stamford, Conn.).

COLLEGE: Arizona State, then Southern California.

TRANSACTIONS/CAREER NOTES: Selected by Los Angeles Dodgers organization in first round (fifth pick overall) of free-agent draft (June 7, 1968). ... Traded by Dodgers with IF Billy Grabarkewitz, OF Frank Robinson, P Bill Singer and P Mike Strahler to California Angels for P Andy Messersmith and 3B Ken McMullen (November 28, 1972). ... On disabled list (May 17, 1973-remainder of season and May 29-June 13, 1974). ... Loaned by Angels to Charleston, Pittsburgh Pirates organization (April 4-June 20, 1975). ... Traded by Angels with a player to be named later to San Diego Padres for P Gary Ross (September 17, 1975); Padres acquired IF Rudy Meoli to complete deal (November 4, 1975). ... Traded by Padres with P Paul Siebert to New York Mets for IF/OF Dave Kingman (June 15, 1977). ... Released by Mets (March 26, 1979). ... Signed by Seattle Mariners (April 10, 1979). ... Granted free agency (November 1, 1979).

HONORS: Named Pacific Coast League Player of the Year (1970).

STATISTICAL NOTES: Led Pioneer League outfielders with 107 putouts and tied for lead with eight assists in 1968. ... Led Pacific Coast League shortstops with 38 errors in 1969. ... Led Pacific Coast League with 324 total bases, with 10 sacrifice flies and in being hit by pitch with nine in 1970. ... Led Pacific Coast League shortstops with 217 putouts, 54 errors, 745 total chances and in double plays by shortstop with 106 in 1970.

Year Team (League)	Pos.	G	AB	R	H	2B	3B	HR	RBI	Avg.	BB	SO	SB	PO	A	E	Avg.
										BATTING					FIELDING		
1968— Ogden (Pioneer)	OF-SS	62	224	*62	63	14	4	6	26	.281	39	27	*20	†111	‡10	6	.953
1969— Spokane (PCL)	SS-OF	111	402	61	104	19	5	3	35	.259	32	57	34	166	254	†38	.917
— Los Angeles (N.L.)	PR	5	0	3	0	0	0	0	0	...	0	0	0	...	...	...	...
1970— Spokane (PCL)	SS-2B	•146	*621	*122	*211	*39	*16	14	80	*.340	47	51	29	†217	474	†54	.928
1971— Spokane (PCL)	SS	7	30	7	10	2	0	1	2	.333	3	6	3	13	18	3	.912
— Los Angeles (N.L.)	S-3-2-O	101	281	32	70	10	2	1	25	.249	15	20	5	123	176	16	.949
1972— Los Angeles (N.L.)	2-3-O-S	119	391	42	107	11	2	3	32	.274	27	33	5	178	245	23	.948
1973— California (A.L.)■	SS-OF	32	126	12	38	5	2	1	13	.302	5	9	6	63	75	6	.958
1974— California (A.L.)	O-S-3-DH	117	371	39	97	10	3	3	39	.261	25	25	8	160	116	17	.942
1975— Char., W.Va. (I.L.)■ ...	3B	56	175	27	41	4	0	1	17	.234	30	16	8	44	74	6	.952
— Salt Lake (PCL)■	1-O-3-2	46	147	29	45	6	1	0	17	.306	31	15	13	92	14	3	.972
— California (A.L.)	DH-1-3-O	26	57	5	16	2	0	0	5	.281	4	3	0	27	1	2	.933
— San Diego (N.L.)■	OF	7	15	1	2	0	0	1	1	.133	4	0	1	4	0	0	1.000
1976— Hawaii (PCL)	1-O-3-S	120	395	67	120	23	2	13	89	.304	47	32	9	578	47	4	.994
— San Diego (N.L.)■	OF-1B	15	49	3	18	4	0	0	4	.367	6	2	0	55	6	0	1.000
1977— San Diego (N.L.)	...	44	67	5	12	3	0	1	10	.179	7	10	0	...	...	...	...
— New York (N.L.)■	...	42	83	8	11	1	0	1	3	.133	6	9	0	...	...	...	...
1978— New York (N.L.)	2B-3B	69	160	17	43	7	0	1	18	.269	19	18	1	78	109	6	.969
1979— Seattle (A.L.)■	S-O-2-3-C-DH	62	98	9	27	6	0	0	7	.276	22	5	1	32	38	2	.972
American League totals (4 years)		237	652	65	178	23	5	4	64	.273	56	42	15	282	230	27	.950
National League totals (7 years)		488	1196	124	286	40	4	10	106	.239	97	111	12	...	...	...	...
Major league totals (10 years)		725	1848	189	464	63	9	14	170	.251	153	153	27	...	...	...	...

RECORD AS MANAGER

BACKGROUND: Scout and minor league instructor, San Diego Padres (1981). ... Minor league instructor, New York Mets (1982). ... Coach, Mets (1983-May 15, 1985). ... Coach, Cincinnati Reds (1993).

| | | REGULAR SEASON | | | | POSTSEASON | | | | | | All-Star | |
| | | | | | | Playoff | | Champ. Series | | World Series | | Game | |
Year	Team (League)	W	L	Pct.	Pos.	W	L	W	L	W	L	W	L
1985—	Texas (A.L.)	53	76	.411	7th (W)	—	—	—	—	—	—	—	—
1986—	Texas (A.L.)	87	75	.537	2nd (W)	—	—	—	—	—	—	—	—
1987—	Texas (A.L.)	75	87	.463	T6th (W)	—	—	—	—	—	—	—	—
1988—	Texas (A.L.)	70	91	.435	6th (W)	—	—	—	—	—	—	—	—
1989—	Texas (A.L.)	83	79	.512	4th (W)	—	—	—	—	—	—	—	—
1990—	Texas (A.L.)	83	79	.512	3rd (W)	—	—	—	—	—	—	—	—
1991—	Texas (A.L.)	85	77	.525	3rd (W)	—	—	—	—	—	—	—	—
1992—	Texas (A.L.)	45	41	.523		—	—	—	—	—	—	—	—
1994—	Norfolk (I.L.)	67	75	.472	4th (W)	—	—	—	—	—	—	—	—
1995—	Chiba Lotte (Jp. Pac.)	69	58	.543	2nd (P)	—	—	—	—	—	—	—	—
1996—	Norfolk (I.L.)	76	57	.571		—	—	—	—	—	—	—	—
	New York (N.L.)	12	19	.387	4th (E)	—	—	—	—	—	—	—	—
1997—	New York (N.L.)	88	74	.543	3rd (E)	—	—	—	—	—	—	—	—
1998—	New York (N.L.)	88	74	.543	2nd (E)	—	—	—	—	—	—	—	—
1999—	New York (N.L.)	97	66	.595	2nd (E)	3	1	2	4	—	—	—	—
2000—	New York (N.L.)	94	68	.580	2nd (E)	3	1	4	1	1	4	—	—
2001—	New York (N.L.)	82	80	.506	3rd (E)	—	—	—	—	—	—	0	1
American League totals (8 years)		581	605	.490		—	—	—	—	—	—	—	—
National League totals (6 years)		461	381	.548		6	2	6	5	1	4	0	1
Major league totals (14 years)		1042	986	.514		6	2	6	5	1	4	0	1

NOTES:
1985—Replaced Texas manager Doug Rader with club in seventh place and record of 9-23 (May 16).
1992—Replaced as Texas manager by Toby Harrah with club in third place (July 9).
1995—Chiba Lotte tied three games.
1996—Replaced New York manager Dallas Green with club in fourth place and record of 59-72 (August 26).
1999—Defeated Arizona in N.L. divisional playoff; lost to Atlanta in N.L. Championship Series.
2000—Defeated San Francisco in N.L. divisional playoff; defeated St. Louis N.L. Championship Series; lost to New York Yankees in World Series.

WILLIAMS, JIMY   ASTROS

PERSONAL: Born October 4, 1943, in Santa Maria, Calif. ... 5-11/170. ... Batted right, threw right. ... Full name: James Francis Williams.
COLLEGE: Fresno State College (bachelor of science degree in agribusiness).
TRANSACTIONS/CAREER NOTES: Selected by St. Louis Cardinals organization from Toronto, Boston Red Sox organization (November 29, 1965). ... In military service (July 24, 1966-remainder of season). ... Traded by Cardinals with C Pat Corrales to Cincinnati Reds for C John Edwards (February 8, 1968). ... Selected by Montreal Expos in expansion draft (October 14, 1968). ... On disabled list (May 13-30 and June 24-September 2, 1969). ... On suspended list (June 7-16, 1971). ... Sold to New York Mets organization (June 16, 1971). ... On temporary inactive list (August 12-16, 1971). ... On disabled list (May 15-July 17 and July 29-August 20, 1975).

| | | | | | | | BATTING | | | | | | | FIELDING | | |
Year	Team (League)	Pos.	G	AB	R	H	2B	3B	HR	RBI	Avg.	BB	SO	SB	PO	A	E	Avg.
1965—Waterloo (Midw.)		SS	115	435	64	125	19	3	2	31	.287	41	74	10	173	*312	26	*.949
1966—St. Louis (N.L.)		SS-2B	13	11	1	3	0	0	0	1	.273	1	5	0	2	5	0	1.000
1967—Arkansas (Texas)		SS	28	101	8	21	1	1	0	8	.208	9	14	0	49	80	2	.985
—Tulsa (PCL)		SS	61	164	18	37	2	0	1	21	.226	18	33	4	87	156	26	.903
—St. Louis (N.L.)		SS	1	2	0	0	0	0	0	0	.000	0	1	0	6	1	0	1.000
1968—Indianapolis (PCL)■..		SS-2B	120	403	38	91	19	5	2	34	.226	20	59	5	198	323	27	.951
1969—Vancouver (PCL)■..		3B-OF-SS	35	66	7	17	1	1	0	9	.258	4	8	1	17	23	2	.952
1970—Buff.-Winnipeg (I.L.)..		SS-2B-3B	109	361	49	83	15	0	3	18	.230	34	48	5	178	244	30	.934
1971—Winn.-Tide. (I.L.)■..		SS-3B-2B	105	327	40	84	7	4	5	31	.257	38	46	7	120	219	22	.939
1972—								Did not play.										
1973—								Did not play.										
1974—								Did not play.										
1975—El Paso (Texas)		DH	6	17	3	2	0	0	0	2	.118	2	2	0	...	...	...	...
Major league totals (2 years)			14	13	1	3	0	0	0	1	.231	0	0	0	8	6	0	1.000

BACKGROUND: Coach, Toronto Blue Jays (1980-85). ... Minor league instructor, Atlanta Braves (October 4, 1989-June 25, 1990). ... Coach, Braves (1990-96).
HONORS: Named Pacific Coast League Manager of the Year (1976 and 1979). ... Named A.L. Manager of the Year by THE SPORTING NEWS (1999). ... Named A.L. Manager of the Year by Baseball Writers' Association of America (1999).

RECORD AS MANAGER

| | | REGULAR SEASON | | | | POSTSEASON | | | | | | All-Star | |
| | | | | | | Playoff | | Champ. Series | | World Series | | Game | |
Year	Team (League)	W	L	Pct.	Pos.	W	L	W	L	W	L	W	L
1974—Quad Cities (Midwest)		33	26	.559	1st (S)	—	—	—	—	—	—	—	—
—(Second half)		32	32	.500	3rd (S)	1	2	—	—	—	—	—	—
1975—El Paso (Texas)		62	71	.466	3rd (W)	—	—	—	—	—	—	—	—
1976—Salt Lake City (Pacific Coast)		90	54	.625	1st (E)	2	3	—	—	—	—	—	—
1977—Salt Lake City (Pacific Coast)		74	65	.532	2nd (E)	—	—	—	—	—	—	—	—
1978—Springfield (American Association)		70	66	.515	3rd (E)	—	—	—	—	—	—	—	—
1979—Salt Lake City (Pacific Coast)		34	40	.447	4th (E)	—	—	—	—	—	—	—	—
—(Second half)		46	28	.622	1st (S)	5	0	—	—	—	—	—	—
1986—Toronto (A.L.)		86	76	.531	4th (E)	—	—	—	—	—	—	—	—
1987—Toronto (A.L.)		96	66	.593	2nd (E)	—	—	—	—	—	—	—	—
1988—Toronto (A.L.)		87	75	.537	T3rd (E)	—	—	—	—	—	—	—	—
1989—Toronto (A.L.)		12	24	.333		—	—	—	—	—	—	—	—

Year	Team (League)	REGULAR SEASON				POSTSEASON							
		W	L	Pct.	Pos.	Playoff		Champ. Series		World Series		All-Star Game	
						W	L	W	L	W	L	W	L
1997—	Boston (A.L.)	78	84	.481	4th (E)	—	—	—	—	—	—	—	—
1998—	Boston (A.L.)	92	70	.568	2nd (E)	1	3	—	—	—	—	—	—
1999—	Boston (A.L.)	94	68	.580	2nd (E)	3	2	1	4	—	—	—	—
2000—	Boston (A.L.)	85	77	.525	2nd (E)	—	—	—	—	—	—	—	—
2001—	Boston (A.L.)	66	53	.555		—	—	—	—	—	—	—	—
	Major league totals (8 years)............................	696	590	.541		4	5	1	4	—	—	—	—

NOTES:
1974—Lost to Danville in playoffs.
1976—Lost to Hawaii in championship playoff.
1979—Defeated Albuquerque, two games to none, in playoff; defeated Hawaii, three games to none, in championship playoff.
1989—Replaced as Toronto manager by Cito Gaston, with club tied for sixth place (May 15).
1998—Lost to Cleveland in A.L. divisional playoff.
1999—Defeated Cleveland in A.L. divisional playoff; lost to New York Yankees in A.L. Championship Series.
2001—Replaced as manager by Joe Kerrigan with club in second place (August 16).

MAJOR LEAGUE MANAGERS

THE CLASS OF 2002

SMITH, OZZIE — SS

PERSONAL: Born December 26, 1954, in Mobile, Ala. ... 5-10/180. ... Bats both, throws right. ... Full name: Osborne Earl Smith.
HIGH SCHOOL: Locke (Los Angeles).
COLLEGE: Cal Poly San Luis Obispo.
TRANSACTIONS/CAREER NOTES: Selected by Detroit Tigers organization in seventh round of free-agent draft (June 8, 1976); did not sign. ... Selected by San Diego Padres organization in fourth round of free-agent draft (June 7, 1977). ... Traded by Padres to St. Louis Cardinals for SS Garry Templeton (February 11, 1982). ... On disabled list (July 14-August 19, 1984; March 31-April 15, 1989; and June 16-July 1, 1992). ... Granted free agency (November 2, 1992). ... Re-signed by Cardinals (December 6, 1992). ... On suspended list (June 14-16, 1994). ... On disabled list (May 18-August 18, 1995 and April 9-29, 1996). ... Retired after 1996 season.
RECORDS: Holds major league records for most assists by shortstop—8,375; most double plays by shortstop—1,590; most total chances by shortstop—12,624; most years with 500 or more assists by shortstop—8; and most years leading league in assists and chances accepted by shortstop—8. ... Holds major league single-season records for most assists by shortstop—621 (1980); and fewest double plays by shortstop who led league in double plays—79 (1991). ... Shares major league record for most double plays by shortstop in extra-inning game—6 (August 25, 1979, 19 innings). ... Holds N.L. career records for most games by shortstop—2,511. ... Holds N.L. record for most years leading league in fielding percentage by shortstop (100 or more games)—7. ... Shares N.L. records for most consecutive years leading league in assists by shortstop—4 (1979-82); and most years leading league in double plays by shortstop—5. ... Shares modern N.L. record for most consecutive years leading league in fielding percentage by shortstop (100 or more games)—4 (1984-87). ... Shares modern N.L. record for most years by shortstop—19 (San Diego, St. Louis, 1978 through 1996).
HONORS: Elected to Baseball Hall of Fame (2002). ... Won N.L. Gold Glove at shortstop (1980-92). ... Named shortstop on The Sporting News N.L. All-Star team (1982, 1984-87). ... Named shortstop on The Sporting News N.L. Silver Slugger team (1987).
STATISTICAL NOTES: Led Northwest League shortstops with 40 double plays in 1977. ... Led N.L. with 28 sacrifice hits in 1978 and 23 in 1980. ... Led N.L. shortstops with 933 total chances in 1980, 658 in 1981, 844 in 1983, 827 in 1985, 771 in 1987, 775 in 1988 and 709 in 1989. ... Led N.L. shortstops with 113 double plays in 1980, 111 in 1987, 79 in 1991 and tied for lead with 94 in 1984 and 96 in 1986.

Year Team (League)	Pos.	G	AB	R	H	2B	3B	HR	RBI	Avg.	BB	SO	SB	PO	A	E	Avg.
1977—Walla Walla (N'West)..	SS	•68	*287	*69	87	10	2	1	35	.303	40	12	*30	130	*254	23	*.943
1978—San Diego (N.L.)	SS	159	590	69	152	17	6	1	46	.258	47	43	40	264	548	25	.970
1979—San Diego (N.L.)	SS	156	587	77	124	18	6	0	27	.211	37	37	28	256	*555	20	.976
1980—San Diego (N.L.)	SS	158	609	67	140	18	5	0	35	.230	71	49	57	*288	*621	24	.974
1981—San Diego (N.L.)	SS	•110	*450	53	100	11	2	0	21	.222	41	37	22	220	*422	16	*.976
1982—St. Louis (N.L.)■	SS	140	488	58	121	24	1	2	43	.248	68	32	25	279	*535	13	*.984
1983—St. Louis (N.L.)	SS	159	552	69	134	30	6	3	50	.243	64	36	34	*304	519	21	.975
1984—St. Louis (N.L.)	SS	124	412	53	106	20	5	1	44	.257	56	17	35	233	437	12	*.982
1985—St. Louis (N.L.)	SS	158	537	70	148	22	3	6	54	.276	65	27	31	264	*549	14	*.983
1986—St. Louis (N.L.)	SS	153	514	67	144	19	4	0	54	.280	79	27	31	229	453	15	*.978
1987—St. Louis (N.L.)	SS	158	600	104	182	40	4	0	75	.303	89	36	43	245	*516	10	*.987
1988—St. Louis (N.L.)	SS	153	575	80	155	27	1	3	51	.270	74	43	57	234	*519	22	.972
1989—St. Louis (N.L.)	SS	155	593	82	162	30	8	2	50	.273	55	37	29	209	*483	17	.976
1990—St. Louis (N.L.)	SS	143	512	61	130	21	1	1	50	.254	61	33	32	212	378	12	.980
1991—St. Louis (N.L.)	SS	150	550	96	157	30	3	3	50	.285	83	36	35	244	387	8	*.987
1992—St. Louis (N.L.)	SS	132	518	73	153	20	2	0	31	.295	59	34	43	232	420	10	.985
1993—St. Louis (N.L.)	SS	141	545	75	157	22	6	1	53	.288	43	18	21	251	451	19	.974
1994—St. Louis (N.L.)	SS	98	381	51	100	18	3	3	30	.262	38	26	6	135	291	8	*.982
1995—St. Louis (N.L.)	SS	44	156	16	31	5	1	0	11	.199	17	12	4	60	129	7	.964
1996—St. Louis (N.L.)	SS	82	227	36	64	10	2	2	18	.282	25	9	7	90	162	8	.969
Major League totals (19 years)		2573	9396	1257	2460	402	69	28	793	.262	1072	589	580	4249	8375	281	.978

DIVISION SERIES RECORD

Year Team (League)	Pos.	G	AB	R	H	2B	3B	HR	RBI	Avg.	BB	SO	SB	PO	A	E	Avg.
1996—St. Louis (N.L.)	SS-PH	2	3	1	1	0	0	0	0	.333	2	0	0	2	1	0	1.000

CHAMPIONSHIP SERIES RECORD

NOTES: Named N.L. Championship Series Most Valuable Player (1985).

Year Team (League)	Pos.	G	AB	R	H	2B	3B	HR	RBI	Avg.	BB	SO	SB	PO	A	E	Avg.
1982—St. Louis (N.L.)	SS	3	9	0	5	0	0	0	3	.556	3	0	1	4	11	0	1.000
1985—St. Louis (N.L.)	SS	6	23	4	10	1	1	1	3	.435	3	1	1	6	16	0	1.000
1987—St. Louis (N.L.)	SS	7	25	2	5	0	1	0	1	.200	3	4	0	10	19	1	.967
1996—St. Louis (N.L.)	SS-PH	3	9	0	0	0	0	0	0	.000	0	1	0	7	2	0	1.000
Championship series totals (4 years)		19	66	6	20	1	2	1	7	.303	9	6	2	27	48	1	.987

WORLD SERIES RECORD

NOTES: Member of World Series championship team (1982).

Year Team (League)	Pos.	G	AB	R	H	2B	3B	HR	RBI	Avg.	BB	SO	SB	PO	A	E	Avg.
1982—St. Louis (N.L.)	SS	7	24	3	5	0	0	0	1	.208	3	0	1	22	17	0	1.000
1985—St. Louis (N.L.)	SS	7	23	1	2	0	0	0	0	.087	4	0	1	10	16	1	.963
1987—St. Louis (N.L.)	SS	7	28	3	6	0	0	0	2	.214	2	3	2	7	19	0	1.000
World Series totals (3 years)		21	75	7	13	0	0	0	3	.173	9	3	4	39	52	1	.989

ALL-STAR GAME RECORD

Year League	Pos.	AB	R	H	2B	3B	HR	RBI	Avg.	BB	SO	SB	PO	A	E	Avg.
1981—National	SS	0	0	0	0	0	0	0	...	2	0	0	1	0	0	1.000
1982—National	PR-SS	0	0	0	0	0	0	0	...	0	0	0	1	0	0	1.000
1983—National	SS	2	1	1	0	0	0	0	.500	0	0	0	0	0	0	...

Year	League	Pos.	AB	R	H	2B	3B	HR	RBI	Avg.	BB	SO	SB	PO	A	E	Avg.
								BATTING							**FIELDING**		
1984— National		SS	3	0	0	0	0	0	0	.000	0	0	1	3	0	0	1.000
1985— National		SS	4	0	0	0	0	0	0	.000	0	0	0	1	3	0	1.000
1986— National		SS	1	0	0	0	0	0	0	.000	0	0	0	3	2	0	1.000
1987— National		SS	2	0	0	0	0	0	0	.000	0	0	0	3	2	1	.833
1988— National		SS	2	0	0	0	0	0	0	.000	0	1	0	1	4	0	1.000
1989— National		SS	4	0	1	0	0	0	0	.250	0	0	0	1	3	0	1.000
1990— National		SS	1	0	0	0	0	0	0	.000	0	0	0	1	1	0	1.000
1991— National		SS	1	0	0	0	0	0	0	.000	1	0	0	0	1	0	1.000
1992— National		SS	3	0	1	1	0	0	0	.333	0	1	0	1	1	0	1.000
1994— National		SS	3	0	1	0	0	0	0	.333	0	0	0	1	2	0	1.000
1995— National							Selected, did not play—injured.										
1996— National		SS	1	0	0	0	0	0	0	.000	0	0	0	0	3	0	1.000
All-Star Game totals (14 years)			27	1	4	1	0	0	0	.148	3	2	1	16	23	1	.975

2001 STATISTICAL LEADERS

STATISTICAL LEADERS (side margin)

AMERICAN LEAGUE

BATTING

Batting average
- .350 Ichiro Suzuki, Sea.
- .342 Jason Giambi, Oak.
- .336 Roberto Alomar, Cle.
- .331 Bret Boone, Sea.
- .330 Frank Catalanotto, Tex.

Runs
- 133 Alex Rodriguez, Tex.
- 127 Ichiro Suzuki, Sea.
- 118 Bret Boone, Sea.
- 113 Roberto Alomar, Cle.
- 110 Derek Jeter, N.Y.

Hits
- 242 Ichiro Suzuki, Sea.
- 206 Bret Boone, Sea.
- 202 Shannon Stewart, Tor.
- 201 Alex Rodriguez, Tex.
- 194 Garret Anderson, Ana.

RBIs
- 141 Bret Boone, Sea.
- 140 Juan Gonzalez, Cle.
- 135 Alex Rodriguez, Tex.
- 125 Manny Ramirez, Bos.
- 124 Jim Thome, Cle.

Doubles
- 47 Jason Giambi, Oak.
- 46 Mike Sweeney, K.C.
- 44 Shannon Stewart, Tor.
- 43 Eric Chavez, Oak.
- 42 Ray Durham, Chi.

Triples
- 14 Cristian Guzman, Min.
- 12 Roberto Alomar, Cle.
- 12 Carlos Beltran, K.C.
- 11 Roger Cedeno, Det.
- 10 Ray Durham, Chi.

Home runs
- 52 Alex Rodriguez, Tex.
- 49 Jim Thome, Cle.
- 47 Rafael Palmeiro, Tex.
- 41 Troy Glaus, Ana.
- 41 Manny Ramirez, Bos.

Walks
- 129 Jason Giambi, Oak.
- 111 Carlos Delgado, Tor.
- 111 Jim Thome, Cle.
- 107 Troy Glaus, Ana.
- 101 Rafael Palmeiro, Tex.

Strikeouts
- 185 Jim Thome, Cle.
- 159 Ben Grieve, T.B.
- 158 Troy Glaus, Ana.
- 155 Mike Cameron, Sea.
- 149 Alex Gonzalez, Tor.

On-base percentage
- .477 Jason Giambi, Oak.
- .423 Edgar Martinez, Sea.
- .416 Jim Thome, Cle.
- .415 Roberto Alomar, Cle.
- .408 Carlos Delgado, Tor.

Slugging percentage
- .660 Jason Giambi, Oak.
- .624 Jim Thome, Cle.
- .622 Alex Rodriguez, Tex.
- .609 Manny Ramirez, Bos.
- .590 Juan Gonzalez, Cle.

Stolen bases
- 56 Ichiro Suzuki, Sea.
- 55 Roger Cedeno, Det.
- 43 Alfonso Soriano, N.Y.
- 39 Mark McLemore, Sea.
- 38 Chuck Knoblauch, N.Y.

PITCHING

Earned-run average
- 3.05 Freddy Garcia, Sea.
- 3.15 Mike Mussina, N.Y.
- 3.16 Joe Mays, Min.
- 3.29 Mark Buehrle, Chi.
- 3.37 Tim Hudson, Oak.

Wins
- 21 Mark Mulder, Oak.
- 20 Roger Clemens, N.Y.
- 20 Jamie Moyer, Sea.
- 18 Freddy Garcia, Sea.
- 18 Tim Hudson, Oak.

Saves
- 50 Mariano Rivera, N.Y.
- 45 Kazuhiro Sasaki, Sea.
- 42 Keith Foulke, Chi.
- 39 Troy Percival, Ana.
- 36 Billy Koch, Tor.

Innings pitched
- 238.2 Freddy Garcia, Sea.
- 235.0 Tim Hudson, Oak.
- 233.2 Joe Mays, Min.
- 232.0 Steve W. Sparks, Det.
- 229.1 Mark Mulder, Oak.

Hits allowed
- 256 Rick Helling, Tex.
- 244 Steve W. Sparks, Det.
- 239 Esteban Loaiza, Tor.
- 235 Brad Radke, Min.
- 235 Jeff Weaver, Det.

Walks
- 96 Hideo Nomo, Bos.
- 95 C.C. Sabathia, Cle.
- 90 Bartolo Colon, Cle.
- 87 Paul Abbott, Sea.
- 80 Barry Zito, Oak.

Strikeouts
- 220 Hideo Nomo, Bos.
- 214 Mike Mussina, N.Y.
- 213 Roger Clemens, N.Y.
- 205 Barry Zito, Oak.
- 201 Bartolo Colon, Cle.

NATIONAL LEAGUE

BATTING

Batting average
- .350 Larry Walker, Col.
- .336 Todd Helton, Col.
- .331 Moises Alou, Hou.
- .331 Lance Berkman, Hou.
- .330 Chipper Jones, Atl.

Runs
- 146 Sammy Sosa, Chi.
- 132 Todd Helton, Col.
- 129 Barry Bonds, S.F.
- 128 Luis Gonzalez, Ari.
- 126 Jeff Bagwell, Hou.

Hits
- 206 Rich Aurilia, S.F.
- 202 Juan Pierre, Col.
- 198 Luis Gonzalez, Ari.
- 197 Todd Helton, Col.
- 194 Albert Pujols, St.L.

RBIs
- 160 Sammy Sosa, Chi.
- 146 Todd Helton, Col.
- 142 Luis Gonzalez, Ari.
- 137 Barry Bonds, S.F.
- 130 Jeff Bagwell, Hou.
- 130 Albert Pujols, St.L.

Doubles
- 55 Lance Berkman, Hou.
- 54 Todd Helton, Col.
- 49 Jeff Kent, S.F.
- 48 Bobby Abreu, Phi.
- 47 Albert Pujols, St.L.

Triples
- 12 Jimmy Rollins, Phi.
- 11 Juan Pierre, Col.
- 11 Juan Uribe, Col.
- 10 Luis Castillo, Fla.
- 8 Neifi Perez, Col.
- 8 Michael Tucker, Cin.-Chi.
- 8 Fernando Vina, St.L.

Home runs
- 73 Barry Bonds, S.F.
- 64 Sammy Sosa, Chi.
- 57 Luis Gonzalez, Ari.
- 49 Shawn Green, L.A.
- 49 Todd Helton, Col.

Walks
- 177 Barry Bonds, S.F.
- 116 Sammy Sosa, Chi.
- 106 Bobby Abreu, Phi.
- 106 Jeff Bagwell, Hou.
- 100 Luis Gonzalez, Ari.

Strikeouts
- 185 Jose Hernandez, Mil.
- 178 Richie Sexson, Mil.
- 162 Pat Burrell, Phi.
- 157 Lee Stevens, Mon.
- 153 Sammy Sosa, Chi.

On-base percentage
- .515 Barry Bonds, S.F.
- .449 Larry Walker, Col.
- .437 Sammy Sosa, Chi.
- .432 Todd Helton, Col.
- .430 Lance Berkman, Hou.

Slugging percentage
- .863 Barry Bonds, S.F.
- .737 Sammy Sosa, Chi.
- .688 Luis Gonzalez, Ari.
- .685 Todd Helton, Col.
- .662 Larry Walker, Col.

Stolen bases
- 46 Juan Pierre, Col.
- 46 Jimmy Rollins, Phi.
- 37 Vladimir Guerrero, Mon.
- 36 Bobby Abreu, Phi.
- 33 Luis Castillo, Fla.

PITCHING

Earned-run average
- 2.49 Randy Johnson, Ari.
- 2.98 Curt Schilling, Ari.
- 3.04 John Burkett, Atl.
- 3.05 Greg Maddux, Atl.
- 3.09 Darryl Kile, St.L.

Wins
- 22 Curt Schilling, Ari.
- 22 Matt Morris, St.L.
- 21 Randy Johnson, Ari.
- 20 Jon Lieber, Chi.
- 17 Russ Ortiz, S.F.
- 17 Greg Maddux, Atl.

Saves
- 45 Robb Nen, S.F.
- 43 Armando Benitez, N.Y.
- 43 Trevor Hoffman, S.D.
- 43 Jeff Shaw, L.A.
- 42 Jose Mesa, Phi.

Innings pitched
- 256.2 Curt Schilling, Ari.
- 249.2 Randy Johnson, Ari.
- 234.0 Chan Ho Park, L.A.
- 233.0 Greg Maddux, Atl.
- 232.1 Jon Lieber, Chi.

Hits allowed
- 266 Livan Hernandez, S.F.
- 250 Bobby J. Jones, S.D.
- 237 Curt Schilling, Ari.
- 236 Mike Hampton, Col.
- 232 Jimmy Anderson, Pit.

Walks
- 112 Ryan Dempster, Fla.
- 98 Jamey Wright, Mil.
- 97 Tom Glavine, Atl.
- 92 Kerry Wood, Chi.
- 91 Tony Armas Jr., Mon.
- 91 Russ Ortiz, S.F.
- 91 Chan Ho Park, L.A.

Strikeouts
- 372 Randy Johnson, Ari.
- 293 Curt Schilling, Ari.
- 218 Chan Ho Park, L.A.
- 217 Kerry Wood, Chi.
- 208 Javier Vazquez, Mon.